D1033933

Conversations in American Literature
Language • Rhetoric • Culture

Robin Dissin Aufses
Lycée Français de New York

Renée H. Shea
Bowie State University, Maryland

Lawrence Scanlon
Brewster High School, New York

Kate Aufses

Bedford/St. Martin's
Boston • New York

bfw high school
BEDFORD, FREEMAN, & WORTH

For Bedford/St. Martin's
Executive Editor: Daniel McDonough
Senior Editor: Nathan Odell
Senior Production Editor: Peter Jacoby
Production Supervisor: Samuel Jones
Senior Marketing Manager: Lisa Erdely
Editorial Assistant: Kathleen Wisneski
Copy Editor: Mary Lou Wilshaw-Watts
Indexer: Kirsten Kite
Photo Researcher: Susan Doheny
Senior Art Director: Lucy Krikorian
Text Design: Linda M. Robertson
Cover Design: Donna Lee Dennison
Cover Art: Gavin W. Sewell, *Old Glory,* a collage history of America. Mixed media on canvas. 2010.
Composition: Westchester Publishing Services
Printing and Binding: Quad/Graphics

Copyright © 2015 by Bedford/St. Martin's
All rights reserved. No part of this book may be reproduced, stored in a retrieval system, or transmitted in any form or by any means, electronic, mechanical, photocopying, recording, or otherwise, except as may be expressly permitted by the applicable copyright statutes or in writing by the Publisher.

Manufactured in the United States of America.

5 6   18 17

For information, write: Bedford/St. Martin's, 75 Arlington Street, Boston, MA 02116
(617-399-4000)

ISBN 978-1-4576-4676-8

Acknowledgments
Acknowledgments and copyrights are included at the back of the book on pages 1591–1602, which constitute an extension of the copyright page.

It is a violation of the law to reproduce these selections by any means whatsoever without the written permission of the copyright holder.

To our friend and mentor Nancy Perry

About the Authors

 **Robin Dissin Aufses** is director of English Studies at Lycée Français de New York, where she teaches AP English Language. Robin was formerly the English department chair and a teacher at John F. Kennedy High School in Bellmore, New York, for ten years, and prior to that she taught English at Paul D. Schreiber High School in Port Washington, New York, for twenty years. She is co-author of *The Language of Composition* and *Literature & Composition*. Robin also has published articles for the College Board on the novelist Chang Rae Lee and the novel *All the King's Men*.

 **Renée H. Shea** was professor of English and Modern Languages and Director of Freshman Composition at Bowie State University in Maryland. She is co-author of *The Language of Composition* and *Literature & Composition* and two volumes in the NCTE High School Literature series (Amy Tan and Zora Neale Hurston). A faculty consultant for more than thirty years in both AP Language and Literature, she was also a reader and question leader for both exams. Renée recently served as a member of the Development Committee for AP Language and Composition. She is currently a member of the English Academic Advisory Committee for the College Board and the SAT Critical Reading Committee.

 **Lawrence Scanlon** taught at Brewster High School for more than thirty years, and now teaches at Iona College in New York. Over the past twenty years he has been a reader and question leader for the AP Language exam. As a College Board consultant in the United States and abroad, he has conducted AP workshops in both Language and Literature, as well as serving on the AP English Language Test Development Committee. Larry is co-author of *The Language of Composition* and *Literature & Composition* and has published articles for the College Board and elsewhere on composition and curriculum.

 **Kate Aufses** studied English at Kenyon College and holds MPhil degrees in American Literature and Art History from Cambridge University. Kate is currently studying law at the University of Michigan.

Preface

For most of us, American literature is a familiar and beloved subject. We know our history and ourselves through the work of classic writers such as Nathaniel Hawthorne, Walt Whitman, Edith Wharton, Zora Neale Hurston, and Robert Frost. We come to understand our nation and its culture by reading Emily Dickinson, Sherman Alexie, Tim O'Brien, and Edwidge Danticat. Most of these are authors of fiction and poetry, yet today nonfiction has taken its rightful place as part of our American literary tradition. In *Conversations in American Literature: Language · Rhetoric · Culture*, our goal is to bring all of these elements together: poems, short stories, memoir, speeches, essays, visual texts, history, ideas, and culture. You'll find many of the classic examples of fiction and poetry that define American literature set in the context of the cultural conversations, historical debates, and literary legacies that have shaped — and continue to shape — our national identity.

Conversations in American Literature **is designed to help teachers and students explore American literature while balancing the current emphases on nonfiction, rhetoric, argument, and synthesis** required by both the AP English Language and Composition course and the Common Core State Standards. As such, we hope that the book you have in your hands strikes you as a bit different, even innovative: a literature anthology that puts nonfiction on equal footing with fiction and poetry; a literature anthology that is both chronological and thematic; a literature anthology that emphasizes close reading, critical thinking, rhetoric, argument, and synthesis.

How the Opening Chapters Work

Featuring accessible texts for effective scaffolding and an engaging activity-driven approach, the four opening chapters of *Conversations in American Literature* provide an approachable introduction to the fundamentals of rhetoric, close reading, argument, and synthesis.

- **Chapter 1, "An Introduction to Rhetoric,"** provides explanations and examples of rhetorical concepts including the rhetorical triangle; ethos, pathos, and

v

logos; and concession and refutation. Students apply these concepts to both written and visual texts.

- **Chapter 2, "Close Reading,"** guides students through the analysis of diction and syntax with an emphasis on their rhetorical and literary effects.

- **Chapter 3, "Analyzing Argument,"** introduces the essential language of argument — such as claims, evidence, fallacies, and arrangement. The Essay in Progress feature walks students through the process of constructing an argument — from exploring ideas to crafting an arguable claim to developing evidence and structuring the essay itself.

- **Chapter 4, "Synthesizing Sources,"** introduces students to the effective use of sources in developing an informed argument. We ask them first to analyze how skillful writers use sources, then we walk them through the process of using sources to support their own viewpoints.

Working with Literature

Those of you who know *The Language of Composition* will find the structure of these introductory chapters somewhat familiar, but you will also notice that we have added instructional sections on working with literary texts, as well as numerous literary

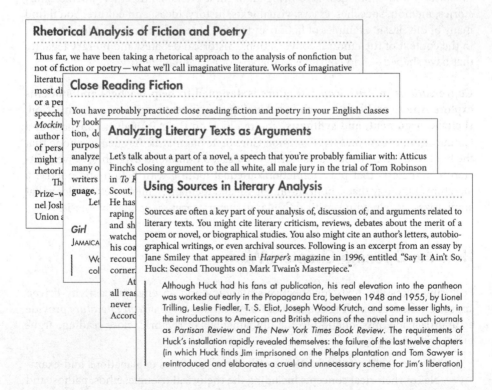

Rhetorical Analysis of Fiction and Poetry

Thus far, we have been taking a rhetorical approach to the analysis of nonfiction but not of fiction or poetry — what we'll call imaginative literature. Works of imaginative literatu...

Close Reading Fiction

You have probably practiced close reading fiction and poetry in your English classes by look...

Analyzing Literary Texts as Arguments

Let's talk about a part of a novel, a speech that you're probably familiar with: Atticus Finch's closing argument to the all white, all male jury in the trial of Tom Robinson in *To K...

Using Sources in Literary Analysis

Sources are often a key part of your analysis of, discussion of, and arguments related to literary texts. You might cite literary criticism, reviews, debates about the merit of a poem or novel, or biographical studies. You also might cite an author's letters, autobiographical writings, or even archival sources. Following is an excerpt from an essay by Jane Smiley that appeared in *Harper's* magazine in 1996, entitled "Say It Ain't So, Huck: Second Thoughts on Mark Twain's Masterpiece."

> Although Huck had his fans at publication, his real elevation into the pantheon was worked out early in the Propaganda Era, between 1948 and 1955, by Lionel Trilling, Leslie Fiedler, T. S. Eliot, Joseph Wood Krutch, and some lesser lights, in the introductions to American and British editions of the novel and in such journals as *Partisan Review* and *The New York Times Book Review*. The requirements of Huck's installation rapidly revealed themselves: the failure of the last twelve chapters (in which Huck finds Jim imprisoned on the Phelps plantation and Tom Sawyer is reintroduced and elaborates a cruel and unnecessary scheme for Jim's liberation)

examples throughout the chapters. While we approach these literary texts aesthetically, we also ask students to consider how literary texts can be read rhetorically, analyzed as arguments, and used as evidence in their own writing. The glossary includes literary and rhetorical terms and examples that are helpful in the analysis of fiction, poetry, and nonfiction.

Working with Visual Texts

We know our students live in a visual world, which makes it vital that they develop the critical tools and habits of mind to be able to analyze how visual texts work — how they persuade a viewer, how they reflect the culture, how they challenge beliefs and ideas. Throughout these introductory chapters, we incorporate instruction in the rhetorical and stylistic analysis of visual texts.

Just as a writer uses verbal humor to make a point, a political cartoonist might use visual humor. Just as a writer uses evocative language to engage her audience, so might a photographer use evocative images. Especially in this information-rich age, facts and figures, statistics, and numerical data are just as likely to be presented in visual form — in charts, tables, graphs — as in prose. For these reasons, we have interspersed visual texts of all kinds throughout the opening chapters rather than focusing on them in a single chapter on visuals.

Analyzing Visual Texts as Arguments

In this section, we'll focus on how to analyze visual texts that present arguments. A visual argument can be an advertisement, a political cartoon, a photograph, a bumper sticker, a T-shirt, a hat, a Web page, or even a piece of fine art. Yet the tools to analyze argu thinking criti tured, consid visual and wr Althougl strategies, su cess of analys make connec any written te sible, who the

How the Readings Chapters Work

In keeping with the tradition of the American literature course, the readings chapters of *Conversations in American Literature* are organized chronologically; however, since we see our American tradition less as a linear progression than an ongoing dialogue, we have introduced thematic TalkBacks and Conversations. We have found in our own classrooms that such connections encourage engagement and stimulate lively discussion of how the past continues to influence the present.

Illustrated historical introductions provide essential context.   To support the historical exploration of American literature, each chapter of readings begins with an introduction to the major events and social forces that define the time period. We have made these introductions brief yet thorough, and whenever possible we have tied the events of the period directly to the pieces within the chapter to provide students with both a sense of the historical importance of each work as well as its context.

TalkBacks pair classic pieces with more recent responses.   We recognize that for students older literature can sometimes seem a bit dusty. The aim of the TalkBacks is to show the enduring relevance of these classic pieces, either as topics of debate in society or as sources of inspiration for more recent writers.

THOMAS JEFFERSON, *The Declaration of Independence* (1776)   389
> TALKBACK   ELIZABETH CADY STANTON, *Declaration of Sentiments* (1848)   393
> TALKBACK   HO CHI MINH, *Proclamation of Independence of the Democratic Republic of Vietnam* (1945)   396

RALPH WALDO EMERSON, from *Self-Reliance* (1841)   590
> TALKBACK   BENJAMIN ANASTAS, *The Foul Reign of Emerson's "Self-Reliance"* (2011)   602

WINSLOW HOMER, *The Veteran in a New Field* (painting, 1865)   831
> TALKBACK   NATASHA TRETHEWEY, *Again, the Fields: After Winslow Homer* (2006)   832

WALLACE STEVENS, *Thirteen Ways of Looking at a Blackbird* (1917)   1084
> TALKBACK   AARON A. ABEYTA, *Thirteen Ways of Looking at a Tortilla* (2001)   1087

Sometimes the TalkBack is a direct response, as is the case with Native American writer Louise Erdrich's twentieth-century poetic response to the seventeenth-century captivity narrative of Mary Rowlandson. At other times, the TalkBacks are indirect responses. For example, Martin Luther King Jr.'s classic "Letter from Birmingham Jail" is paired with "Small Change: Why the Revolution Will Not Be Tweeted," Malcolm Gladwell's comparison of the strategies that made the civil rights movement a success with those of more recent revolutions organized through social media. Another pairs a section of Upton Sinclair's *The Jungle* that describes conditions in a turn-of-the-century slaughterhouse with a startlingly similar passage from Eric Schlosser's *Fast Food Nation*.

Whether direct or indirect, the instructional purpose of the TalkBack pairing remains the same: to inspire students and draw connections between texts and across the ages. In a way, these pairings re-create the old-fashioned filing cabinet in which teachers stored clippings and connections as they developed lessons around central texts of nonfiction, fiction, and poetry.

Conversations explore cultural issues and literary legacies. The heart of *Conversations in American Literature* is the Conversations sections, which make up nearly half of each chronological chapter. These eighteen Conversations are thematic clusters that explore a cultural issue, historical figure, or literary legacy from its historical roots to the present. So, while the Conversations are indeed synthesis practice, they are also much more. They are opportunities to enter long-standing cultural conversations and debates in an informed way and with a true historical understanding of the issues. They are an opportunity for students to investigate how the past continues to shape the present. For instance, the Conversation on the Columbus Day Controversy in Chapter 6 begins with primary-source documents from Columbus and King Ferdinand of Spain before moving forward into argumentative pieces regarding Columbus's legacy and the suitability of a national holiday in his honor.

CONVERSATION   THE INFLUENCE OF PHILLIS WHEATLEY

CONVERSATION   POCAHONTAS: A WOMAN, A MOVIE, A MYTH?

CONVERSATION   JOHN BROWN: PATRIOT OR TERRORIST?

CONVERSATION   THE AMERICAN COWBOY

CONVERSATION   THE INFLUENCE OF JAZZ

CONVERSATION   AMERICA'S ROMANCE WITH THE AUTOMOBILE

Other Conversations ask students to tackle today's controversial issues — such as immigration or income inequality — by studying the history of the issue as expressed in fiction, poetry, and nonfiction of the day along with contemporary op-ed pieces. Other Conversations have literary angles, such as exploring the legacy of Henry David Thoreau, considering the influence of Phillis Wheatley on later African American writers, and asking the larger question about what defines American literature.

Within each Conversation, a set of questions guides students through the individual piece's issues and style. Making Connections questions help students compare and contrast the various arguments in the texts, a key intermediary step in moving from analysis to synthesis. And finally, we ask students to "Enter the Conversation" through writing prompts that require synthesis of the materials and ideas as students develop their own voices and viewpoints.

Guided questions target key skills.   In *Conversations in American Literature*, we have included support for every piece in the book to help your students hone the key AP and Common Core skills of close reading, literary and rhetorical analysis, and synthesis. We want students to read with a writer's eye — to see how the techniques of professional and published writers might be used in their own writing.

EXPLORING THE TEXT questions are approachable yet rigorous prompts for discussion, writing, and even group work that promote close reading and critical thinking. The questions take students from an understanding of the piece and its ideas to an investigation of how authors and artists shape meaning.

MAKING CONNECTIONS questions accompanying the TalkBacks and Conversations move students from analysis to comparison and contrast — a key step on the path to synthesis.

ENTERING THE CONVERSATION questions after each Conversation are synthesis and research prompts that give students an opportunity to bring multiple sources to bear in supporting an argument or illustrating an issue.

SUGGESTIONS FOR WRITING at the end of each chapter guide students toward written responses that connect multiple pieces within and beyond the chapter and even beyond the book. Each set includes — but is not limited to — essay prompts that simulate the rhetorical analysis, argument, and synthesis questions that appear on the AP English Language exam.

Grammar as Rhetoric and Style sections give grammar purpose.   These sections reinforce students' understanding of grammar while showing how grammar can serve a rhetorical and stylistic purpose. In each chapter, we focus on one element — such as appositives, parallel structures, or modifiers — and draw examples from the readings so that students can see, for instance, how Martin Luther King Jr. uses parallel structure and to what effect, or how John Steinbeck uses precise, active verbs.

Resources for You and Your Students

Conversations in American Literature Teacher's Manual (ISBN: 978-1-4576-7300-9)
Comprehensive and user-friendly, this teacher's manual is an indispensable guide for
teaching both AP English Language and Common Core American Literature courses,
offering a wealth of resources for teachers of all levels:

- Robust COURSE PLANNING TOOLS provide an introduction to using the text,
  sample course outlines, and teaching strategies for each pedagogical feature in
  the book. A unique "Bird's-Eye View" feature uncovers thematic connections
  throughout the book, suggests connections to commonly taught novels and
  plays, and aligns the book to AP U.S. History for those who are team teaching.

- Insightful SUGGESTED RESPONSES for the Exploring the Text questions and
  TalkBacks.

- SUGGESTED APPROACHES to teaching key readings provide fresh ideas for
  classroom discussion, collaboration, and exploration.

- A TEST PREP SECTION includes multiple-choice questions, essay prompts, synthesis clusters, and annotated examples of student writing to prepare students
  for the AP Language exam and the work they will do in college.

Conversations in American Literature e-Book   *Conversations in American
Literature* is available electronically in a number of different formats.

- Our ONLINE INTERACTIVE E-BOOK allows students to annotate, take notes,
  share notes, watch videos, submit homework to a grade book, and more. It's
  fully customizable: teachers can add material, remove sections, and rearrange
  the book to suit their needs. ISBN 978-1-4576-5459-6 To package the print
  text with 6-years of e-book access, use ISBN 978-1-4576-9578-0.

- Our DOWNLOADABLE E-BOOKS are perfect for iPads, tablets, and other mobile
  devices and are available on a range of platforms, some of which provide a rich
  interactive experience when connected to the Internet. Ask your sales representative for more information.

ExamView Quizzing Resource for AP English Language   Finally, the AP English
Language exam preparation your students need comes to the ExamView platform
you love. With more than 1600 AP-style multiple-choice questions, this testbank is
our biggest exam preparation tool ever! ISBN 978-1-4576-5762-7

Conversations in American Literature Media Page   Here you will find reading
comprehension quizzes, a links library to audio/video for every piece, and other great
Bedford/St. Martin's resources, like Re:Writing for Literature, a free collection of
tutorials, quizzes, and videos. **bedfordstmartins.com/cialit**

Acknowledgments

We want to extend our heartfelt appreciation to the team at Bedford/St. Martin's. We've enjoyed the support, guidance, and encouragement of many talented professionals, starting with the leadership of founder Joan Feinberg, vice president of editorial for the humanities Denise Wydra, editor in chief Karen Henry, and former director of development Erica Appel, who have been committed to this project from the start. Our decision to dedicate *Conversations in American Literature* to Nancy Perry, former editor in chief and editorial director of custom publishing, was an easy one. She has encouraged us through three books, and it is no exaggeration to call her role in this project, as well as in the others, visionary; none of our books would exist without her initial ideas and continuing belief in them. Our gifted editor, Nathan Odell, just gets better and better. We would be nowhere without his ability to see the big picture; his appreciation for language and literature; his energy, enthusiasm, and patience; and his friendship. Many thanks to senior marketing manager Lisa Erdely for her support, expertise, humor, and perspective. We thank Dan McDonough, executive editor, for his creativity and faith. He brought us together at Bedford/St. Martin's and has supported every project since. We also want to thank our many dedicated and innovative colleagues in the Advanced Placement Program at the College Board, the Educational Testing Service, and classrooms across the country for sharing their knowledge of their subject matter and their passion for preparing students for success in college. We would like to thank our reviewers, whose expertise guided us at every turn: John Brassil, Sandra Coker, Carol Jago, Denise Hayden, Jennifer Barbknecht, Allison Casper, Timothy Cook, Beth Dibler, Frances Fok, Susanne Harrison, M. Kamel Igoudjil, Christine Kervina, Bill Kirby, Sylvia Kranish, Fernanda Kray, Shaylene Krupinski, Linda Mayfield, Linda Mirro, Lisa Moore, Valerie Morehouse, Sherry Neaves, Rebecca Swanigan, Gwendolyn Todd.

As always, we thank our partners, Arthur Aufses, Michael Shea, and Mary-Grace Gannon, for their support and encouragement. This time our list of co-authors does include Kate Aufses, whose study of American literature at Kenyon College and Cambridge University helped jump-start this book. But we know that all our children — Michael Aufses, Meredith Barnes, Christopher Shea, Alison Scanlon, Lindsay Prezzano, Maura Liguori, and Kaitlin Scanlon — are our co-authors of the heart. Finally, we are grateful to our students — the ones in our classrooms and the colleagues in our workshops — for teaching us well.

ROBIN DISSIN AUFSES
RENÉE H. SHEA
LAWRENCE F. SCANLON

Contents

8   RECONSTRUCTING AMERICA: 1865–1913   823

10   REDEFINING AMERICA: 1945 to the Present   1279

An Introduction to Rhetoric
Using the "Available Means"

To many people, the word *rhetoric* automatically signals that trickery or deception is afoot. They assume that an advertiser is trying to manipulate a consumer, a politician wants to obscure a point, or a spin doctor is spinning. "Empty rhetoric!" is a common criticism—and at times an indictment. Yet the Greek philosopher Aristotle (384–322 B.C.E.) defined **rhetoric** as "the faculty of observing in any given case the available means of persuasion."

At its best, rhetoric is a thoughtful, reflective activity leading to effective communication, including the rational exchange of opposing viewpoints. In Aristotle's day and in ours, those who understand and can use the available means to appeal to an **audience** of one or many find themselves in a position of strength. They have the tools to resolve conflicts without confrontation, to persuade readers or listeners to support their position, or to move others to take action.

Rhetoric is not just for Roman senators in togas. You might use rhetoric to convince a friend that John Coltrane is worth listening to, explain to readers of your blog why *Night of the Living Dead* is the most influential horror movie of all time, or persuade your parents that they should buy you a car. Rhetoric is also not just about speeches. Every essay, political cartoon, photograph, and advertisement is designed to convince you of something. To simplify, we will call all of these things **texts** because they are cultural products that can be "read," meaning not just consumed and comprehended, but investigated. We need to be able to "read" between the lines, regardless of whether we're reading a political ad, a political cartoon, or a political speech. Consider documentary films: every decision—such as what lighting to use for an interview, what music to play, what to show and what to leave out—constitutes a rhetorical choice based on what the filmmaker thinks will be most persuasive.

It is part of our job as informed citizens and consumers to understand how rhetoric works so that we can be wary of manipulation or deceit, while appreciating effective and civil communication. And it is essential that each of us communicates as effectively and honestly as possible.

• ACTIVITY •

Identify an article, a speech, a video, or an advertisement that you think is manipulative or deceptive and one that is civil and effective. Use these two examples to explain what you see as the difference.

The Rhetorical Situation

Let's start out by looking at a speech that nearly everyone has read or heard: the speech that baseball player Lou Gehrig gave at an appreciation day held in his honor on July 4, 1939. Gehrig had recently learned that he was suffering from amyotrophic lateral sclerosis (ALS), a neurological disorder that has no cure (today it is known as Lou Gehrig's disease). Although Gehrig was a reluctant speaker, the fans' chant of "We want Lou!" brought him to the podium to deliver one of the most powerful and heartfelt speeches of all time.

Farewell Speech
LOU GEHRIG

Fans, for the past two weeks you have been reading about a bad break I got. Yet today I consider myself the luckiest man on the face of the earth. I have been in ballparks for seventeen years and have never received anything but kindness and encouragement from you fans. Look at these grand men. Which of you wouldn't consider it the highlight of his career just to associate with them for even one day?

Sure, I'm lucky. Who wouldn't consider it an honor to have known Jacob Ruppert; also the builder of baseball's greatest empire, Ed Barrow; to have spent six years with that wonderful little fellow, Miller Huggins; then to have spent the next nine years with that outstanding leader, that smart student of psychology — the best manager in baseball today, Joe McCarthy? Who wouldn't feel honored to have roomed with such a grand guy as Bill Dickey?

Sure, I'm lucky. When the New York Giants, a team you would give your right arm to beat, and vice versa, sends you a gift — that's something! When everybody down to the groundskeepers and those boys in white coats remember you with trophies — that's something!

When you have a wonderful mother-in-law who takes sides with you in squabbles against her own daughter — that's something! When you have a father and mother who work all their lives so that you can have an education and build your body — it's a blessing! When you have a wife who has been a tower of strength and shown more courage than you dreamed existed — that's the finest I know!

So I close in saying that I might have been given a bad break, but I have an awful lot to live for! Thank you. 5

(1939)

While in our time the word *rhetoric* may suggest deception, this speech reminds us that rhetoric can serve sincerity as well. No wonder one commentator wrote, "Lou Gehrig's speech almost rocked Yankee Stadium off its feet."

Occasion, Context, and Purpose

Why is this an effective speech? First of all, rhetoric is always situational. It has an **occasion** — the time and place the text was written or spoken. That occasion exists within a specific **context** — the circumstances, atmosphere, attitudes, and events surrounding the text. And rhetoric always has a **purpose**—the goal the speaker wants to achieve. In the case of Gehrig's speech, the occasion is Lou Gehrig Appreciation Day. More specifically, his moment comes at home plate between games of a doubleheader. The context is first and foremost Gehrig's recent announcement of his illness and his subsequent retirement, but as is often the case, the context goes well beyond that. Gehrig, known as the Iron Horse, held the record for consecutive games played (2,130) and was one of the greatest sluggers of all time. For such a durable and powerful athlete to fall victim to a disease that strips away strength and coordination seemed an especially cruel fate. Just a couple of weeks earlier, Gehrig was still playing ball; but by the time he gave this speech, he was so weak that his manager had to help him walk out to the mound for the ceremony.

One of Gehrig's chief purposes in delivering this speech is to thank his fans and his teammates, but he also wants to demonstrate that he remains positive: he emphasizes his past luck and present optimism and downplays his illness. He makes a single reference to the diagnosis and does so in the strong, straightforward language of an athlete: he got a "bad break." There is no blame, no self-pity, no plea for sympathy. Throughout, he maintains his focus: to thank his fans and teammates for their support and get on with watching the ballgame. Gehrig responds as a true Yankee, not just a member of the team but also with the can-do Yankee spirit of America, by acknowledging his illness and accepting his fate with dignity, honor, humility, and even a touch of humor.

The Rhetorical Triangle

Another important aspect of the rhetorical situation is the relationship among the speaker, audience, and subject. One way to conceptualize the relationship among these elements is through the **rhetorical triangle**. Some refer to it as the **Aristotelian triangle** because Aristotle used a triangle to illustrate how these three elements are interrelated. How a speaker perceives the relationships among these elements will go a long way toward determining what he or she says and how he or she says it. Let's use the rhetorical triangle (see p. 4) to analyze Gehrig's speech.

The **speaker** is the person or group who creates a text. This might be a politician who delivers a speech, a commentator who writes an article, an artist who draws a political cartoon, or even a company that commissions an advertisement. Don't think of the speaker solely as a name, but consider a description of who the speaker is in the context of the text. The speaker of the speech we just read is not just Lou Gehrig

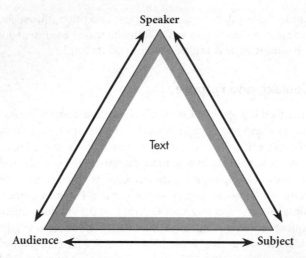

Speaker

Text

Audience ⟷ Subject

Aristotle's rhetorical triangle

but baseball hero and ALS sufferer Lou Gehrig. Sometimes, there is a slight difference between who the speaker is in real life and the role the speaker plays when delivering the speech. This is called a **persona**. *Persona* comes from the Greek word for "mask"; it means the face or character that a speaker shows to his or her audience. Lou Gehrig is a famous baseball hero, but in his speech he presents himself as a common man who is modest and thankful for the opportunities he's had.

The **audience** is the listener, viewer, or reader of a text or performance, but it is important to note that there may be multiple audiences. When making rhetorical decisions, speakers ask what values their audiences hold, particularly whether the audience is hostile, friendly, or neutral, and how informed it is on the topic at hand. Sure, Gehrig's audience was his teammates and the fans in the stadium that day, but it was also the teams he played against, the fans listening on the radio, and posterity — us.

The **subject** is the topic. And the subject should not be confused with the purpose, which is the goal the speaker wants to achieve. Gehrig's subject is his illness, but it is also a catalog of all the lucky breaks that preceded his diagnosis.

• ACTIVITY •

Construct and analyze a rhetorical situation for writing a review of a movie, video game, or concert. Be very specific in your analysis: What is your subject? What is your purpose? Who is your audience? What is your relationship to the audience? Remember, you need not write a full essay; just analyze the rhetorical situation.

SOAPS

In discussing the rhetorical situation surrounding a text, we've talked about some of the background that you should consider (such as the occasion, context, and purpose) and relationships that are more directly related to the text (such as those among the speaker, audience, and subject). One way to remember all of these things is to use the acronym **SOAPS**, which stands for Subject, Occasion, Audience, Purpose, and Speaker. It's a mnemonic device that offers a practical way to approach the concept of the rhetorical situation. Think of it as a kind of checklist that helps you organize your ideas rhetorically. Let's use SOAPS to look at the rhetorical situation in a letter written by Albert Einstein.

Widely considered the greatest scientist of the twentieth century, Einstein (1879–1955) is responsible for the theory of relativity, quantum mechanics, and other foundational scientific concepts. He won the Nobel Prize in Physics in 1921. In 1936, he wrote the following letter to a sixth grade student, Phyllis Wright, in response to her questions: Do scientists pray? And if so, what do they pray for?

January 24, 1936

Dear Phyllis,

I have tried to respond to your question as simply as I could. Here is my answer.

Scientific research is based on the idea that everything that takes place is determined by laws of nature, and therefore this holds for the actions of people. For this reason, a research scientist will hardly be inclined to believe that events could be influenced by a prayer, i.e., by a wish addressed to a supernatural being.

However, it must be admitted that our actual knowledge of these laws is only imperfect and fragmentary, so that, actually, the belief in the existence of basic all-embracing laws in Nature also rests on a sort of faith. All the same this faith has been largely justified so far by the success of scientific research.

But, on the other hand, every one who is seriously involved in the pursuit of science becomes convinced that a spirit is manifest in the laws of the Universe — a spirit vastly superior to that of man, and one in the face of which we with our modest powers must feel humble. In this way the pursuit of science leads to a religious feeling of a special sort, which is indeed quite different from the religiosity of someone more naive.

I hope this answers your question.

Best wishes
Yours,
Albert Einstein

5

Subject	The explicit subject here is whether scientists pray and, if so, what they pray for. Implicitly, the subject is the nature of faith.
Occasion	The occasion is Einstein's receipt of a letter from sixth grader Phyllis Wright asking questions about science and religion.
Audience	The primary audience for the letter is Phyllis herself, though the formality of his response suggests that Einstein realized that his letters would have a larger audience. (Note that he won the Nobel Prize in Physics in 1921, so by 1936 he was a world-renowned scientist.)
Purpose	Einstein's purpose is probably the most complex element here. At its most straightforward, his purpose is to respond to a sincere schoolgirl's question about science and religion. Beyond that, it seems that Einstein's purpose is to expand Phyllis's horizons a bit, to help her understand that science and religion do not necessarily represent two antagonistic ways of thinking.
Speaker	The speaker, a scientist approaching age sixty, is responding to a girl who is likely twelve, so his purpose is intertwined with that speaker-audience relationship: the wise elder in dialogue with the younger generation.

Ultimately, Einstein does not "answer" Phyllis directly at all; rather, he returns the question to her by offering different ways to think about the nature of science and religion and the way spiritual and scientific perspectives interact. Viewed in this light, Einstein's purpose can be seen as engaging a younger person — who might become a scientist — in thinking more deeply about her own question.

• ACTIVITY •

Using SOAPS, analyze the rhetorical situation in the following speech.

9/11 Speech
GEORGE W. BUSH

Good evening.

Today, our fellow citizens, our way of life, our very freedom came under attack in a series of deliberate and deadly terrorist acts.

The victims were in airplanes or in their offices — secretaries, businessmen and -women, military and federal workers. Moms and dads. Friends and neighbors.

Thousands of lives were suddenly ended by evil, despicable acts of terror.

The pictures of airplanes flying into buildings, fires burning, huge structures collapsing, have filled us with disbelief, terrible sadness, and a quiet, unyielding anger.

These acts of mass murder were intended to frighten our nation into chaos and retreat. But they have failed. Our country is strong. A great people has been moved to defend a great nation.

Terrorist attacks can shake the foundations of our biggest buildings, but they cannot touch the foundation of America. These acts shatter steel, but they cannot dent the steel of American resolve.

America was targeted for attack because we're the brightest beacon for freedom and opportunity in the world. And no one will keep that light from shining.

Today, our nation saw evil, the very worst of human nature, and we responded with the best of America, with the daring of our rescue workers, with the caring for strangers and neighbors who came to give blood and help in any way they could.

Immediately following the first attack, I implemented our government's emergency response plans. Our military is powerful, and it's prepared. Our emergency teams are working in New York City and Washington, D.C., to help with local rescue efforts.

Our first priority is to get help to those who have been injured and to take every precaution to protect our citizens at home and around the world from further attacks. The functions of our government continue without interruption. Federal agencies in Washington which had to be evacuated today are reopening for essential personnel tonight and will be open for business tomorrow.

Our financial institutions remain strong, and the American economy will be open for business as well.

The search is under way for those who are behind these evil acts. I've directed the full resources of our intelligence and law enforcement communities to find those responsible and bring them to justice. We will make no distinction between the terrorists who committed these acts and those who harbor them.

I appreciate so very much the members of Congress who have joined me in strongly condemning these attacks. And on behalf of the American people, I thank the many world leaders who have called to offer their condolences and assistance.

America and our friends and allies join with all those who want peace and security in the world, and we stand together to win the war against terrorism. Tonight, I ask for your prayers for all those who grieve, for the children whose worlds have been shattered, for all whose sense of safety and security has been threatened. And I pray they will be comforted by a power greater than any of us, spoken through the ages in Psalm 23: "Even though I walk through the valley of the shadow of death, I fear no evil, for You are with me."

This is a day when all Americans from every walk of life unite in our resolve for justice and peace. America has stood down enemies before, and we will do so this time. None of us will ever forget this day. Yet, we go forward to defend freedom and all that is good and just in our world.

Thank you. Good night, and God bless America.

(2001)

Rhetorical Appeals

Rhetorical appeals are attempts by a speaker to persuade an audience — or to put it another way, attempts to say things that an audience would find *appealing.* After more than two thousand years, we still refer to the classical rhetorical appeals identified by Aristotle — ethos, logos, and pathos — which appeal to the audience's trust, reason, and emotions, respectively.

Ethos

Speakers appeal to **ethos** (Greek for "character") to demonstrate that they are credible and trustworthy people who should be listened to when they discuss a given topic. The first component of ethos is the speaker's qualifications, or authority. Whether it is an explicit title or credential or a less formal sort of expertise or experience, what we as an audience want to know is if the person is qualified to speak on the matter. If a speaker is giving a lecture on raising children, we would likely heed her advice if she had formal qualifications — such as a PhD in child psychology — but we also would be willing to listen to a person with less formal qualifications, such as a father who successfully raised three children. This sort of appeal to ethos is often found outside of the text. For instance, when Lou Gehrig gave his speech, he did not introduce himself as "Lou Gehrig, baseball legend." The audience was well aware of his accomplishments. And Gehrig's purpose was not to reinforce his legendary status; it was to reinforce his humanity, which brings us to the next aspect of ethos.

Relying on authority and reputation can be an effective strategy, but it will only take you so far because speakers are primarily judged not on who they are but on what they say. There are a couple of ways that a speaker can build ethos while speaking on a subject. One is by sounding logical and reasonable. The second way is by demonstrating shared values with the audience. Think, once again, about Lou Gehrig and his speech reprinted at the beginning of the chapter. He brings the ethos of a legendary athlete to his speech, yet in the speech itself he enhances his ethos by remaining calm, reasonable, and dignified in the face of a debilitating disease and by expressing his shared values with the fans. He emphasizes that he's just a regular guy and a good sport who shares the audience's love of baseball and family. And like them, he has known good luck and bad breaks. Remaining reasonable and emphasizing shared values is a great way to win over a hostile crowd, but in Gehrig's case, it was the perfect way to win the heart not only of every baseball fan but also of every American.

Let's look at an example of how a speaker can use these various methods to bring ethos to the rhetorical situation. On March 15, 1965, President Lyndon Baines Johnson gave a nationally televised speech before a joint session of Congress. The occasion was violence that had erupted the week prior in Selma, Alabama, when African Americans preparing to march to Montgomery to protest voting-rights discrimination were attacked by police. The selection below is the beginning of the speech.

Speech to Congress, March 15, 1965
PRESIDENT LYNDON BAINES JOHNSON

Mr. Speaker, Mr. Vice President, Members of the Congress:

I speak tonight for the dignity of man and the destiny of Democracy. I urge every member of both parties, Americans of all religions and of all colors, from every section of this country, to join me in that cause.

At times, history and fate meet at a single time in a single place to shape a turning point in man's unending search for freedom. So it was at Lexington and Concord. So it was a century ago at Appomattox. So it was last week in Selma, Alabama. There, long-suffering men and women peacefully protested the denial of their rights as Americans. Many of them were brutally assaulted. One good man — a man of God — was killed.

There is no cause for pride in what has happened in Selma. There is no cause for self-satisfaction in the long denial of equal rights of millions of Americans. But there is cause for hope and for faith in our Democracy in what is happening here tonight. For the cries of pain and the hymns and protests of oppressed people have summoned into convocation all the majesty of this great government — the government of the greatest nation on earth. Our mission is at once the oldest and the most basic of this country — to right wrong, to do justice, to serve man. In our time we have come to live with the moments of great crisis. Our lives have been marked with debate about great issues, issues of war and peace, issues of prosperity and depression.

But rarely in any time does an issue lay bare the secret heart of America itself. Rarely are we met with a challenge, not to our growth or abundance, or our welfare or our security, but rather to the values and the purposes and the meaning of our beloved nation. The issue of equal rights for American Negroes is such an issue. And should we defeat every enemy, and should we double our wealth and conquer the stars, and still be unequal to this issue, then we will have failed as a people and as a nation. For, with a country as with a person, "What is a man profited if he shall gain the whole world, and lose his own soul?"

There is no Negro problem. There is no Southern problem. There is no Northern   5
problem. There is only an American problem.

And we are met here tonight as Americans — not as Democrats or Republicans; we're met here as Americans to solve that problem. This was the first nation in the history of the world to be founded with a purpose.

The great phrases of that purpose still sound in every American heart, North and South: "All men are created equal." "Government by consent of the governed." "Give me liberty or give me death." And those are not just clever words, and those are not just empty theories. In their name Americans have fought and died for two centuries and tonight around the world they stand there as guardians of our liberty risking their lives. Those words are promised to every citizen that he shall share in the dignity of man. This dignity cannot be found in a man's possessions. It cannot be found in his power or in his position. It really rests on his right to be treated as a man equal in opportunity to all others. It says that he shall share in freedom. He shall choose his leaders, educate his children, provide for his family according to his ability and his merits as a human being.

To apply any other test, to deny a man his hopes because of his color or race or his religion or the place of his birth is not only to do injustice, it is to deny Americans and to dishonor the dead who gave their lives for American freedom. Our fathers believed that if this noble view of the rights of man was to flourish, it must be rooted in democracy. The most basic right of all was the right to choose your own leaders. The history of this country in large measure is the history of expansion of that right to all of our people.

(1965)

The very fact that he is the president of the United States gives Johnson the authority and ethos to speak on the subject of civil rights, yet he also addresses the nation in a reasonable manner, while emphasizing the shared values that unite us as Americans. He uses "our" and "we" to include himself as one of the people while at the same time delivering a commanding challenge. He enjoins his audience to transcend concerns for "growth," "abundance," "welfare," and "security" (par. 4) that democracy gives us and instead to focus on the "values and the purposes and the meaning" (par. 4) on which democracy depends. He bolsters his ethos through appeals to religious faith and to patriotism by quoting the Bible, Thomas Jefferson, and Patrick Henry, while continuing his use of the first-person plural "we." President Johnson brings ethos to his speech by the nature of the office that he holds, but in stating that "*we* are met here tonight as Americans" (par. 6) for "all of *our* people" (par. 8), he constructs ethos through appeals to shared American values that "[o]*ur* fathers believed" (par. 8) (emphasis added): patriotism, freedom, equality, gratitude, responsibility, justice, and ultimately, sacrifice.

• ACTIVITY •

Think of a situation in which you are presenting your view on the same subject to two different audiences. For instance, you might be presenting your ideas on ways to stop bullying (1) to the school board or a group of parents and (2) to a group of middle schoolers. Discuss how you would establish ethos in each situation.

Logos

Speakers appeal to **logos**, or reason, by offering clear, rational ideas. Appealing to logos (Greek for "embodied thought") means thinking logically — having a clear main idea and using specific details, examples, facts, statistics, or expert testimony to support it. Creating a logical argument often involves defining the terms of the argument and identifying connections such as causality. It can also require considerable research. Evidence from expert sources and authorities, facts, and quantitative data can be very persuasive if selected carefully and presented accurately. Sometimes, writers and speakers add charts and graphs as a way to present such information, but often they weave this information into their written argument.

Although at first, Lou Gehrig's speech may seem largely emotional, it is actually based on irrefutable logic. He starts with the thesis that he is "the luckiest man on the face of the earth" and supports it with two points: (1) the love and kindness he's received in his seventeen years of playing baseball and (2) a list of great people who have been his friends, family, and teammates in that time.

Conceding and Refuting

One way to appeal to logos is to acknowledge a **counterargument** — that is, to antici-pate objections or opposing views. While you might worry that raising an opposing view could poke a hole in your argument, you'll be vulnerable if you ignore ideas that run counter to your own. In acknowledging a counterargument, you agree (concede) that an opposing argument may be true or reasonable, but then you deny (refute) the validity of all or part of the argument. This combination of **concession** and **refutation** actually strengthens your own argument; it appeals to logos by demonstrating that you understand a viewpoint other than your own, you've thought through other evidence, and you stand by your position.

In longer, more complex texts, the writer may address the counterargument in greater depth, but Lou Gehrig simply concedes what some of his listeners may think — that his bad break could be a cause for discouragement or despair. Gehrig refutes this response, however, by saying that he has "an awful lot to live for!" Granted, he implies his concession rather than stating it outright; but in addressing it at all, he acknowledges a contrasting way of viewing his situation — that is, a counterargument.

Let's look at an example by Alice Waters, a famous chef, food activist, and author. Writing in the *Nation*, she argues for acknowledgment of the full consequences of what she calls "our national diet":

from *Slow Food Nation*
ALICE WATERS

It's no wonder our national attention span is so short: We get hammered with the message that everything in our lives should be fast, cheap and easy — especially food. So conditioned are we to believe that food should be almost free that even the rich, who pay a tinier fraction of their incomes for food than has ever been paid in human history, grumble at the price of an organic peach — a peach grown for flavor and picked, perfectly ripe, by a local farmer who is taking care of the land and paying his workers a fair wage. And yet, as the writer and farmer David Mas Masumoto recently pointed out, pound for pound, peaches that good still cost less than Twinkies. When we claim that eating well is an elitist preoccupation, we create a smokescreen that obscures the fundamental role our food decisions have in shaping the world. The reason that eating well in this country costs more than eating poorly is that we have a set of agricultural policies that subsidize fast food and make fresh, wholesome foods, which receive no government support, seem expensive. Organic foods seem elitist only because industrial food is artificially cheap, with its real costs being charged to the public purse, the public health, and the environment.

(2006)

To develop a logical argument for better, healthier food for everyone, Waters refutes the counterargument that any food that is not "fast, cheap and easy" is "elitist." She does that by redefining terms such as "cheap," "[eating] well," "expensive," and "cost." She explains in a step-by-step fashion the "smokescreen" of price that many people use to argue that mass-produced fast food is the best alternative for all but the very wealthy. She points out that "[o]rganic foods *seem* elitist only because industrial food is *artificially* cheap" (emphasis added). Waters asks her readers to think more deeply about the relationships among availability, production, and distribution of food: she appeals to reason.

• ACTIVITY •

Following is an excerpt from an article by George Will, a columnist for the *Washington Post* and *Newsweek*, entitled "King Coal: Reigning in China." Discuss how he appeals to logos in this article on "China's appetite for coal."

from *King Coal: Reigning in China*
GEORGE WILL

Half of the 6 billion tons of coal burned globally each year is burned in China. A spokesman for the Sierra Club, which in recent years has helped to block construction of 139 proposed coal-fired plants in America, says, "This is undermining everything we've accomplished." America, say environmentalists, is exporting global warming.

Can something really be exported if it supposedly affects the entire planet? Never mind. America has partners in this crime against nature, if such it is. One Australian company proposes to build the Cowlitz facility; another has signed a $60 billion contract to supply Chinese power plants with Australian coal.

The *Times* says ships — all burning hydrocarbons — hauled about 690 million tons of thermal coal this year, up from 385 million in 2001. China, which imported about 150 million tons this year, was a net exporter of coal until 2009, sending abroad its low-grade coal and importing higher-grade, low-sulfur coal from, for example, the Powder River Basin of Wyoming and Montana. Because much of China's enormous coal reserves is inland, far from coastal factories, it is sometimes more economical to import American and Australian coal.

Writing in the *Atlantic* on China's appetite for coal and possible aptitude for using the old fuel in new, cleaner ways, James Fallows quotes a Chinese official saying that the country's transportation system is the only serious limit on how fast power companies increase their use of coal. One reason China is building light-rail systems is to get passenger traffic out of the way of coal trains.

Fallows reports that 15 years from now China expects that 350 million people will be living in cities that do not exist yet. This will require adding to China's electrical system a capacity almost as large as America's current capacity. The United States, China, Russia and India have 40 percent of the world's population and 60 percent of its coal.

(2010)

Pathos

Pathos is an appeal to emotions, values, desires, and hopes, on the one hand, or fears and prejudices, on the other. Although an argument that appeals exclusively to the emotions is by definition weak — it's generally **propagandistic** in purpose and more **polemical** than persuasive — an effective speaker or writer understands the power of evoking an audience's emotions by using such tools as figurative language, personal anecdotes, and vivid images.

Lou Gehrig uses the informal first person (*I*) quite naturally, which reinforces the friendly sense that this is a guy who is speaking on no one's behalf but his own. He also chooses words with strong positive **connotations**: *grand, greatest, wonderful, honored, blessing.* He uses one image — *tower of strength* — that may not seem very original but strikes the right note. It is a well-known description that his audience understands — in fact, they probably have used it themselves. But, of course, the most striking appeal to pathos is the poignant contrast between Gehrig's horrible diagnosis and his public display of courage.

Let's look at a more direct example of pathos. As a vice-presidential candidate, Richard Nixon gave a speech in 1952 defending himself against allegations of inappropriate use of campaign funds. In it, he related this anecdote, which is the reason that the speech will forever be known as "the Checkers speech":

from *The Checkers Speech*
RICHARD NIXON

> One other thing I probably should tell you, because if I don't they'll probably be saying this about me, too. We did get something, a gift, after the election. A man down in Texas heard Pat [Nixon's wife] on the radio mention the fact that our two youngsters would like to have a dog. And believe it or not, the day before we left on this campaign trip we got a message from Union Station in Baltimore, saying they had a package for us. We went down to get it. You know what it was? It was a little cocker spaniel dog in a crate that he'd sent all the way from Texas, black and white, spotted. And our little girl Tricia, the six-year-old, named it "Checkers." And you know, the kids, like all kids, love the dog, and I just want to say this, right now, that regardless of what they say about it, we're gonna keep it.
>
> *(1952)*

This example of pathos tugs at every possible heartstring: puppies, children, warm paternal feelings, the excitement of getting a surprise package. All of these images fill us with empathetic feelings toward Nixon: our emotions are engaged far more than our reason. Despite never truly addressing the campaign funds issue, Nixon's speech was a profound success with voters, who sent enough dog food to feed Checkers for a year! And yet, history has come to view this part of the speech as baldly manipulative.

Images and Pathos

You can appeal to pathos by using striking imagery in your writing, so it's no surprise that visual images often serve the same purpose. A dramatic photograph, for example, may lend an emotional component that strengthens an argument. Advertisements often lure customers with provocative images. Most political cartoons also rely on visual images to carry the impact of an argument. For example, in "The Thanksgiving Table," a cartoon that appeared in the Scranton (Pennsylvania) *Times-Tribune* after Thanksgiving in 2013, artist John Cole juxtaposes two contrasting images of "then" and "now" to make his point.

The first image is chock full of emotional associations. It depicts a family around the Thanksgiving table with the turkey ready to be carved, calling upon warm nostalgic feelings of togetherness, love, stability, and even home cooking. We see a mother and father, with younger people we assume are their children, the youngest still in a booster seat. They all sit quietly with heads bowed and hands folded, suggesting they are saying a prayer before their meal. Dressed modestly, they have eyes closed, to indicate a looking inward as they give thanks — for the meal, one another, or what they might consider blessings in their lives. No conversation seems necessary at this moment because they are gathered together in harmony. Even the yellow glow (a halo?) surrounding the scene suggests peace, warmth, and safety.

In stark contrast is "now," with an image that screams chaos and conflict even before we notice the specific details. The yellow glow around the table in the first image gives way to a bright yellow sign with "JUNK" in all caps in a garish burgundy

John Cole/Cagle Cartoons, Inc.

(See color insert, Image 1.)

color. The expressions on the shoppers' faces range from fear to anger to greed, all with eyes wide and crazed — a stark contrast to the peaceful closed eyes of the family in the top panel. There is frantic movement, such as the man pushing a cart with his baby in it, others clutching big boxes of would-be purchases, and two people fighting over an LED television set. The symbols above the characters heads — "!★" and "?@" — are familiar from cartoons as signs of harsh language. The "Open Thanksgi-" sign reminds us that this is what the people depicted are doing instead of sitting with family and friends around a traditional Thanksgiving table.

Is the first image a true depiction of Thanksgiving dinner when, we all know, various conflicts may surface and all is not necessarily perfect? Perhaps not, but it is the ideal of how many of us would like to think life was "then." And, regardless of whether it reflects everyone's reality, the cartoonist makes his case that the peace and togetherness of the first image is preferable to the frantic materialism of the second. He engages our emotions by setting two very different scenes, juxtaposing them, and using color and font to make the argument that desperate material strivings threaten traditional family values.

Humor and Pathos

Another way to appeal to pathos is through humor. Since we like to hear things that we already believe are true, our first reaction to anything that challenges our beliefs is often negative: we think "that's all wrong!" and become defensive or outright offended. Humor works rhetorically by wrapping a challenge to our beliefs in something that makes us feel good — a joke — and thus makes us more receptive to the new idea.

This goes not just for new ideas but for the people who are presenting those ideas. Whether it is gentle tongue-in-cheek teasing or bitter irony, humor may help a writer make a point without seeming to preach to the audience or take himself or herself too seriously. Political commentator Ruth Marcus employs gentle humor in the following essay from 2010 in which she addresses the speaker of the House of Representatives and objects to the members of Congress using electronic devices during hearings and other deliberations. Even the title, a play on words, signals the humorous tone: "Crackberry Congress." Let's look at a few passages:

from *Crackberry Congress*
RUTH MARCUS

> Mr. Speaker, please don't.
>
> Go ahead, if you must, and cut taxes. Slash spending. Repeal health care. I understand. Elections have consequences. But BlackBerrys and iPads and laptops on the House floor? Reconsider, before it's too late.
>
> The current rules bar the use of a "wireless telephone or personal computer on the floor of the House." The new rules, unveiled last week, add three dangerous words. They prohibit any device "that impairs decorum."
>
> In other words, as long as you've turned down your cellphone ringer and you're not strolling around the floor chatting with your broker or helping the kids with their homework, feel free to tap away.
>
> If the Senate is the world's greatest deliberative body, the House is poised to   5 be the world's greatest tweeting one.
>
> A few upfront acknowledgements. First, I'm not one to throw stones. I have been known to sneak a peek, or 10, at my BlackBerry during meetings. For a time my daughter had my ringtone set to sound like a squawking chicken; when I invariably forgot to switch to vibrate, the phone would cluck during meetings. In short, I have done my share of decorum impairing.
>
> Second, let's not get too dreamy about the House floor. John Boehner, the incoming speaker, once passed out campaign checks from tobacco companies there. One of his former colleagues once came to the chamber with a paper bag on his head to dramatize his supposed embarrassment at fellow lawmakers' overdrafts at the House bank. Worse things have happened on the House floor than a game of Angry Birds — check it out! — on the iPad.
>
> Nonetheless, lines have to be drawn, and the House floor is not a bad place to draw them. Somehow, it has become acceptable to e-mail away in the midst of meetings. Even Emily Post[1] has blessed what once would have been obvious rude-

---

[1]Emily Post (1872–1960), author of the bestselling *Etiquette in Society, in Business, in Politics, and at Home.* — Eds.

ness, ruling that "tapping on a handheld device is okay if it's related to what's being discussed."

The larger war may be lost, but not the battle to keep some remaining space in life free of gadgetry and its distractions. I'm not talking Walden Pond — just a few minutes of living the unplugged life. There are places — dinner table, church, school and, yes, the House floor — where multitasking is inappropriate, even disrespectful.

(2010)

First of all, Marcus structures her criticism as a letter, which obviously is a fiction and sets a humorous note right away. Who, after all, would begin a letter to the Speaker of the House by saying, "please don't"? Marcus teases about "decorum," yet she makes a serious point about "connectivity" as she exaggerates her fear that "the House is poised to be the world's greatest tweeting [body] (par. 5)." Humor is also one of her strategies for establishing ethos in this case, as she says, "I'm not one to throw stones" (par. 6) and admits to checking her own BlackBerry during meetings. Overall, by taking a more lighthearted approach and not sounding prudish, Marcus makes her point about the inappropriateness of elected officials interacting with their electronic devices while colleagues and others are debating important issues.

Marcus could have marshaled all manner of examples that illustrate the decline in civility and courtesy in modern life, but then readers would likely have dismissed her as old-fashioned or shrill. By taking a humorous approach, she appeals to readers' sense of humor as well as their community values: don't we want our elected officials to forego "instantaneous communication" for more thoughtful deliberations when they are making decisions about the laws of the land?

• ACTIVITY •

General Dwight D. Eisenhower, Supreme Commander of the Allied Expeditionary Force in Europe, distributed the following Order of the Day to the military troops right before the 1944 D-Day invasion of Normandy. Discuss how General Eisenhower appeals to pathos.

Supreme Headquarters *Allied Expeditionary Force*

Soldiers, Sailors and Airmen of the Allied Expeditionary Force!

You are about to embark upon the Great Crusade, toward which we have striven these many months. The eyes of the world are upon you. The hopes and prayers of liberty-loving people everywhere march with you. In company with our brave Allies and brothers-in-arms on other Fronts, you will bring about the destruction of the German war machine, the elimination of Nazi tyranny over the oppressed peoples of Europe, and security for ourselves in a free world.

Your task will not be an easy one. Your enemy is well trained, well equipped, and battle-hardened. He will fight savagely.

But this is the year 1944! Much has happened since the Nazi triumphs of 1940–41. The United Nations have inflicted upon the Germans great defeats, in open battle, man-to-man. Our air offensive has seriously reduced their strength in the air and their capacity to wage war on the ground. Our Home Fronts have given us an overwhelming superiority in weapons and munitions of war and placed at our disposal great reserves of trained fighting men. The tide has turned! The free men of the world are marching together to Victory!

I have full confidence in your courage, devotion to duty, and skill in battle. We will accept nothing less than full Victory!

Good Luck! And let us all beseech the blessing of Almighty God upon this   5
great and noble undertaking.

Dwight D. Eisenhower

(1944)

Combining Ethos, Logos, and Pathos

Most authors don't rely on just a single type of appeal to persuade their audience; they combine these appeals to create an effective argument. And the appeals themselves are inextricably bound together: if you lay out your argument logically, that will help build your ethos. It is only logical to listen to an expert on a subject, so having ethos can help build a foundation for an appeal to logos. It's also possible to build your ethos based on pathos — for example, who better to speak about the pain of losing a loved one than someone who has gone through it? The best political satirists can say things that are both perfectly logical and completely hilarious, thus appealing to both logos and pathos at the same time.

Let's examine a letter that Toni Morrison, the only African American woman to win the Nobel Prize for Literature, wrote to the then senator Barack Obama endorsing him as the Democratic candidate for president in 2008. The letter was published in the *New York Times*.

Dear Senator Obama,

This letter represents a first for me — a public endorsement of a Presidential candidate. I feel driven to let you know why I am writing it. One reason is it may help gather other supporters; another is that this is one of those singular moments that nations ignore at their peril. I will not rehearse the multiple crises facing us, but of one thing I am certain: this opportunity for a national evolution (even revolution) will not come again soon, and I am convinced you are the person to capture it.

May I describe to you my thoughts?

I have admired Senator [Hillary] Clinton for years. Her knowledge always seemed to me exhaustive; her negotiation of politics expert. However I am more compelled by the quality of mind (as far as I can measure it) of a candidate. I cared little for her gender as a source of my admiration, and the little I did care was based on the fact that no liberal woman has ever ruled in America. Only conservative or "new-centrist" ones are allowed into that realm. Nor do I care very much for your race[s]. I would not support you if that was all you had to offer or because it might make me "proud."

In thinking carefully about the strengths of the candidates, I stunned myself when I came to the following conclusion: that in addition to keen intelligence, integrity, and a rare authenticity, you exhibit something that has nothing to do with age, experience, race, or gender and something I don't see in other candidates. That something is a creative imagination which coupled with brilliance equals wisdom. It is too bad if we associate it only with gray hair and old age. Or if we call searing vision naivete. Or if we believe cunning is insight. Or if we settle for finessing cures tailored for each ravaged tree in the forest while ignoring the poisonous landscape that feeds and surrounds it. Wisdom is a gift; you can't train for it, inherit it, learn it in a class, or earn it in the workplace — that access can foster the acquisition of knowledge, but not wisdom.

When, I wondered, was the last time this country was guided by such a leader?   5
Someone whose moral center was un-embargoed? Someone with courage instead of mere ambition? Someone who truly thinks of his country's citizens as "we," not "they"? Someone who understands what it will take to help America realize the virtues it fancies about itself, what it desperately needs to become in the world?

Our future is ripe, outrageously rich in its possibilities. Yet unleashing the glory of that future will require a difficult labor, and some may be so frightened of its birth they will refuse to abandon their nostalgia for the womb.

There have been a few prescient leaders in our past, but you are the man for this time.

Good luck to you and to us.

Toni Morrison

(2008)

Let's take a step back. Who is Morrison's audience for this letter? Of course, she claims Senator Obama is, yet it is an open letter printed in a newspaper. Thus, we have a sense that while she does intend that he read the letter, she also understands that her public endorsement of his candidacy, and not Senator Hillary Clinton's, will have an impact on a much larger audience than Obama himself: her audience is the large national and international readership of the *Times*, readers who value the viewpoint of a Nobel Prize winner.

Given that audience, Morrison need not establish her ethos as a credible person whose opinion should carry some weight. After all, both Obama and the readers of the *New York Times* — in fact, readers in general — know her as an award-winning author, someone who has written many novels, a professor at Princeton University, and the winner of a Nobel Prize. She is not, however, a person accustomed to weighing in publicly on political campaigns, so she opens with her announcement that this endorsement is "a first" for her. She does not assume that she has the authority or position to make Senator Obama (or others) listen to her; instead, she asks, deferentially, "May I describe to you my thoughts?" (par. 2). As a woman in her seventies with a proven record as a respected author and thinker, she could demand that Obama listen to her, but she does not; by asking a question rather than launching into her viewpoint, she presents herself as courteous and reasonable. The ethos she establishes is as a person who cares deeply for the future of America and is moved to speak out because she believes that the country is at a crossroads ("this is one of those singular moments that nations ignore at their peril" [par. 1]).

Although she does not offer facts and figures or cite expert sources, Morrison develops a logical argument. She addresses two counterarguments: (1) Senator Clinton is the better candidate, and (2) her support of Obama is driven primarily by race. In paragraph 3, she concedes and refutes both. She points out that she has "admired" Senator Clinton over the years and offers reasons; gender is not, however, among them. She effectively makes that argument also serve as evidence that she would not support Obama purely because of race, saying, "I would not support you if that was all you had to offer or because it might make me 'proud'" (par. 3). In paragraph 4, Morrison provides reasons for her support of Obama. She acknowledges that he is a person of "keen intelligence, integrity, and a rare authenticity," yet those qualities are neither her only nor her chief reasons for supporting his candidacy. She claims that she sees in him "a creative imagination which coupled with brilliance equals wisdom." Once Morrison makes this point, she addresses another counterargument: that Obama is too young. She refutes that belief by claiming that wisdom is not necessarily a matter of age.

Morrison continues to develop her reasons for supporting Obama as she adds appeals to pathos. By asking a series of rhetorical questions in paragraph 5, she calls up the shared values of the country; for instance, she asks when last the country was actually guided by "[s]omeone whose moral center was un-embargoed?" She chooses language likely to evoke emotions, such as her distinction between "courage instead of mere ambition." By the end of the letter, she uses images of birth ("the glory of that future will require a difficult labor, and some may be so frightened of its birth they will refuse to abandon their nostalgia for the womb" [par. 6]) and language that pulls at our heartstrings, such as "[o]ur future is ripe, outrageously rich."

She draws the conclusion, again appealing to logos, that given all the evidence presented in the letter — Senator Obama is "the man for this time." Morrison closes with a final appeal to ethos as she emphasizes that she is an integral part of the community of the country: "Good luck to you and to us." The "us" is decidedly not just African Americans but all Americans.

• ACTIVITY •

Select one of the following rhetorical situations, and discuss how you would establish your ethos and appeal to logos and pathos.

- You are trying to persuade your skeptical parents that a "gap year" — taking a year off between high school graduation and college — will be beneficial.

- You have been asked to make a presentation to your school's principal and food-service staff to propose healthier food choices in the cafeteria at a time when the overall school budget is constrained.

- You are making the case for the purchase of a specific model and make of car that will best fit your family's needs and resources.

- You are the student representative chosen to go before a group of local businesspeople to ask them to provide financial support for a proposed school trip.

Rhetorical Analysis of Fiction and Poetry

Thus far, we have been taking a rhetorical approach to the analysis of nonfiction but not of fiction or poetry — what we'll call imaginative literature. Works of imaginative literature often have a rhetorical purpose, even if it's not immediately obvious. The most direct use of rhetoric in imaginative literature is through a speech by a character or a persuasive bit of dialogue between characters. Think, for instance, of the famous speeches in Shakespeare's plays or Atticus Finch's closing argument in *To Kill a Mockingbird*. These examples of literary rhetoric usually have two speakers — the author and the character giving the speech. It's important to keep in mind the concept of persona and remember that these two speakers are not necessarily the same and might not have the same purpose. Let's look at an example of this sort of literary rhetoric.

The following speech is from Michael Shaara's *The Killer Angels* (1974), a Pulitzer Prize–winning historical novel about the Civil War. The passage below presents Colonel Joshua Lawrence Chamberlain addressing a group of 120 deserters captured by the Union army. Colonel Chamberlain has to decide what to do with them as his regiment marches to battle at Gettysburg. The episode is fiction but based on actual events. Combining research and imagination, Shaara has created what he thinks Chamberlain might have said.

from *The Killer Angels*
MICHAEL SHAARA

They were silent, watching him. Chamberlain began to relax. He had made many speeches and he had a gift for it. He did not know what it was, but when he spoke most men stopped to listen. Fanny said it was something in his voice. He hoped it was there now.

"I've been ordered to take you men with me. I've been told that if you don't come I can shoot you. Well, you know I won't do that. Not Maine men. I won't shoot any man who doesn't want this fight. Maybe someone else will, but I won't. So that's that."

He paused again. There was nothing on their faces to lead him.

"Here's the situation. I've been ordered to take you along, and that's what I'm going to do. Under guard if necessary. But you can have your rifles if you want them. The whole Reb army is up the road a ways waiting for us and this is no time for an argument like this. I tell you this: we sure can use you. We're down below half strength and we need you, no doubt of that. But whether you fight or not is up to you. Whether you come along, well, you're coming."

Tom had come up with Chamberlain's horse. Over the heads of the prisoners   5
Chamberlain could see the Regiment falling into line out in the flaming road. He took a deep breath.

"Well, I don't want to preach to you. You know who we are and what we're doing here. But if you're going to fight alongside us there's a few things I want you to know."

He bowed his head, not looking at eyes. He folded his hands together.

"This Regiment was formed last fall, back in Maine. There were a thousand of us then. There's not three hundred of us now." He glanced up briefly. "But what is left is choice."

He was embarrassed. He spoke very slowly, staring at the ground.

"Some of us volunteered to fight for Union. Some came in mainly because we   10
were bored at home and this looked like it might be fun. Some came because we were ashamed not to. Many of us came . . . because it was the right thing to do. All of us have seen men die. Most of us never saw a black man back home. We think on that, too. But freedom . . . is not just a word."

He looked up in to the sky, over silent faces.

"This is a different kind of army. If you look at history you'll see men fight for pay, or women, or some other kind of loot. They fight for land, or because a king makes them, or just because they like killing. But we're here for something new. I don't . . . this hasn't happened much in the history of the world. We're an army going out to set other men free."

He bent down, scratched the black dirt into his fingers. He was beginning to warm to it; the words were beginning to flow. No one in front of him was moving. He said, "This is free ground. All the way from here to the Pacific Ocean. No man has to bow. No man born to royalty. Here we judge you by what *you* do, not by what your father was. Here you can be *something*. Here's a place to build a home. It isn't the land — there's always more land. It's the idea that we all have value, you and me, we're worth something more than the dirt. I never saw dirt I'd die for, but I'm not asking you to come join us and fight for dirt. What we're all fighting for, in the end, is each other."

(1974)

Let's apply SOAPS to this episode, bearing in mind the difference between character and author as we do so.

	COLONEL CHAMBERLAIN	MICHAEL SHAARA
Subject	the purpose for fighting, the reason for the war	leadership and heroism, as demonstrated by Colonel Chamberlain
Occasion	the capture of Union deserters and the dilemma of what to do with them as the rest of the regiment marches into battle	the author's characterization of Colonel Chamberlain within the context of the story he is writing
Audience	the group of deserters	the readers, particularly those with an interest in history, especially of the Civil War
Purpose	to argue his case against desertion, to motivate the soldiers to continue fighting, and to convince them of the nobility of their duty	to entertain and to inform; to bring to life a heroic figure in a dramatic setting; to inspire
Speaker	Colonel Chamberlain, the character, is an authoritative and compassionate leader, a gifted rhetorician, and a man of high ideals and purpose.	Michael Shaara is an expert on the history of the period and a skilled writer who esteems heroism and duty.

Now let's analyze Colonel Chamberlain's speech. We hear his smooth and relaxed tone as he tells the men what he has been "ordered" to do. Right away, he establishes his ethos; he is a colonel, a leader to be obeyed, but he is at the same time a man to be trusted — trusted not to shoot the men. It is not long before he appeals to pathos. "I tell you this: we sure can use you," he says (par. 4). His language is colloquial as he asks them to serve and persuades them to sacrifice for a noble cause. He reviews the common reasons that men fight: to escape boredom or shame; to gain property or "loot." But then he says, "This is a different kind of army. . . . We're an army going out to set other men free" (par. 12). In what is at once a highly impassioned but low-key speech, Chamberlain appeals to the common values of freedom, democracy, allegiance, and community. The rhetorical purpose of the character of Colonel Chamberlain is to convince the deserters to join him in battle; Michael Shaara's — the author's — rhetorical purpose is to create a heroic character to exemplify the virtues he esteems.

Following the speech in the story, Shaara writes, "After a moment, Tom [Chamberlain's younger brother] came riding up. His face was delighted. Chamberlain said, 'How many are going to join us?' Tom grinned hugely. "'Would you believe it? All but six.'" Clearly, Colonel Chamberlain's rhetorical strategies were successful. And so were Shaara's, as he created a scene to show not only what heroism is but also what it can do.

Not all imaginative literature is so straightforwardly rhetorical. Sometimes its rhetorical purpose must be inferred by a close, careful reading of the text. Let's look at "When I heard the learn'd astronomer," a nineteenth-century poem by Walt Whitman.

When I heard the learn'd astronomer
WALT WHITMAN

When I heard the learn'd astronomer,
When the proofs, the figures, were ranged in columns before me,
When I was shown the charts and diagrams, to add, divide, and measure them,
When I sitting heard the astronomer where he lectured with much applause
    in the lecture-room,
How soon unaccountable I became tired and sick,   5
Till rising and gliding out I wander'd off by myself,
In the mystical moist night-air, and from time to time,
Look'd up in perfect silence at the stars.

(1865)

This brief poem seems simple enough. But who is the speaker? Is it Whitman? That's hard to say. Written in the first person, the poem's single **periodic sentence** presents the thoughts of a person who attends a lecture, becomes bored, and goes outside to soak in the majesty of nature. What is the rhetorical purpose of this poem? Whitman, or his speaker, is creating a contrast between the scientific study and the mystical experience of nature in order to argue that such a systematic and mathematical approach robs nature of its beauty and wonder. The means of creating that argument are poetic: the speaker characterizes the lecture room with the geometry of "proofs," "figures," "columns," and "charts and diagrams" where the "astronomer" lectures about celestial science; "tired and sick," the speaker walks outside to experience the "mystical moist night-air." The din of the lecture hall (the astronomer's words and the "applause") contrasts with the "perfect silence" of the night sky. It is clear which the poet prefers, and this poem is Whitman's attempt not only to express his view, but also to convince us to share it.

• ACTIVITY •

In 1920, the African American poet Alice Dunbar-Nelson wrote "I Sit and Sew," a dramatic monologue protesting the limitations of her assigned role during a time of war. Analyze the poem rhetorically, paying close attention to the argument the speaker develops.

I sit and sew
ALICE DUNBAR-NELSON

I sit and sew — a useless task it seems,
My hands grown tired, my head weighed down with dreams —
The panoply of war, the martial tread of men,
Grim faced, stern eyed, gazing beyond the ken
Of lesser souls, whose eyes have not seen Death,   5

Nor learned to hold their lives but as a breath —
But — I must sit and sew.

I sit and sew — my heart aches with desire —
That pageant terrible, that fiercely pouring fire
On wasted fields, and writhing grotesque things   10
Once men. My soul in pity flings
Appealing cries, yearning only to go
There in that holocaust of hell, those fields of woe —
But — I must sit and sew

The little useless seam, the idle patch;   15
Why dream I here beneath my homely thatch,
When there they lie in sodden mud and rain,
Pitifully calling me, the quick ones and the slain?
You need me, Christ. It is no roseate dream
That beckons me — this pretty futile seam   20
It stifles me — God, *must* I sit and sew?

(1920)

Rhetorical Analysis of Visual Texts

Many visual texts are full-fledged arguments. Although they may not be written in paragraphs or have a traditional thesis, they are occasioned by specific circumstances, they have a purpose (whether it is to comment on a current event or simply to urge you to buy something), and they make a claim and support it with appeals to authority, emotion, and reason. Consider the cartoon on page 26, which cartoonist Tom Toles drew after the death of civil-rights icon Rosa Parks in 2005. Parks was the woman who in 1955 refused to give up her seat on the bus in Montgomery, Alabama; that act came to symbolize the struggle for racial equality in the United States.

We can discuss the cartoon rhetorically, just as we've been examining texts that are exclusively verbal: The occasion is the death of Rosa Parks. The speaker is Tom Toles, a respected and award-winning political cartoonist. The audience is made up of readers of the *Washington Post* and other newspapers — that is, it's a very broad audience. The speaker can assume that his audience shares his admiration and respect for Parks and that they view her passing as the loss of a public figure as well as a private woman. Finally, the context is a memorial for a well-loved civil-rights activist, and Toles's purpose is to remember Parks as an ordinary citizen whose courage and determination brought extraordinary results. The subject is the legacy of Rosa Parks, a well-known person loved by many.

Readers' familiarity with Toles — along with his obvious respect for his subject — establishes his ethos. The image in the cartoon appeals primarily to pathos. Toles shows Rosa Parks, who was a devout Christian, as she is about to enter heaven through the

TOLES © 2005 The Washington Post. Reprinted with permission of UNIVERSAL UCLICK. All rights reserved.

pearly gates; they are attended by an angel, probably Saint Peter, who is reading a ledger. Toles depicts Parks wearing a simple coat and carrying her pocketbook, as she did while sitting on the bus so many years ago. Her features are somewhat detailed and realistic, making her stand out despite her modest posture and demeanor.

The commentary at the bottom right reads, "We've been holding it [the front row in heaven] open since 1955," a reminder that more than fifty years have elapsed since Parks resolutely sat where she pleased. The caption can be seen as an appeal to both pathos and logos. Its emotional appeal is its acknowledgment that, of course, heaven would have been waiting for this good woman; but the mention of "the front row" appeals to logic because Parks made her mark in history for refusing to sit in the back of the bus. Some readers might even interpret the caption as a criticism of how slow the country was both to integrate and to pay tribute to Parks.

• ACTIVITY •

The following visuals, from the U.S. Army and from the U.S. Navy, depict recruitment posters from World War II.

What rhetorical strategies does each of the posters use to achieve its purpose: the recruitment of women to serve in the U.S. armed forces? Pay particular attention to the interaction of the written text with the visual elements. How does the arrangement on the page affect your response? How do the army and the navy appeal to ethos, logos, and pathos? How effective do you think the posters were in reaching their intended audience? Which of them was likely to have been more effective? Explain.

National Archives Still Picture Branch

(See color insert, Image 2.)

IT'S A WOMAN'S WAR TOO!

JOIN THE
WAVES
YOUR COUNTRY NEEDS YOU NOW

JOHN FALTER USNR

Apply to your nearest
NAVY RECRUITING STATION OR OFFICE OF NAVAL OFFICER PROCUREMENT

John Philip Falter. 1942. Artists Posters, Prints and Photographs Division.

(See color insert, Image 3.)

Determining Effective and Ineffective Rhetoric

What makes rhetoric successful or unsuccessful? Throughout this book, you'll find many examples of exemplary rhetoric, but here we'd like you to make some judgment calls.

Let's start with an ad from PETA, an animal-rights group.

Feeding Kids Meat Is

CHILD ABUSE

Fight the Fat: Go Vegan   **P⋶TA**

Ad courtesy of People for the Ethical Treatment of Animals, www.peta.org. Image courtesy of istock.

(See color insert, Image 4.)

A positive reading would see the image of an overweight child about to bite into a burger as an effective attention getter. The headline, with "meat" the only word in red, makes the bold assertion that parents who allow children to eat meat are guilty of child abuse. Since most people would not have thought of this connection, its boldness might have the shock value to make them stop and think. By choosing a particularly unappetizing burger and plump-looking kid, PETA presents an image of childhood obesity that might want to make the viewer grab the burger from the child before she gets it in her mouth! The smaller print calls for a "vegan" diet to combat obesity, asserting that replacing burgers with vegetables is a healthier alternative — a claim few people would find questionable.

But that's not the only way to interpret this ad. Claiming that allowing a child to eat a hamburger is the same as committing child abuse is a serious allegation, and it could be seen as hyperbole. If you read the large print as an unfounded exaggeration, then the ad's purpose is lost. It's unlikely that anyone would argue with the exhortation to "fight the fat," but to link consumption of any kind of meat with a heinous act of child abuse might not seem logical to every viewer, which could undermine the ad's effectiveness.

Let's turn to an essay, an op-ed piece that appeared in the *Washington Post* in 2011 after Japan was hit by a massive earthquake and tsunami that severely damaged nuclear reactors. Columnist Anne Applebaum uses this devastating situation to argue against further use of nuclear power. As you read the article, analyze it rhetorically and ask yourself if she is likely to achieve her purpose or if her strategies miss the mark.

If the Japanese Can't Build a Safe Reactor, Who Can?
ANNE APPLEBAUM

In the aftermath of a disaster, the strengths of any society become immediately visible. The cohesiveness, resilience, technological brilliance and extraordinary competence of the Japanese are on full display. One report from Rikuzentakata — a town of 25,000, annihilated by the tsunami that followed Friday's massive earthquake — describes volunteer firefighters working to clear rubble and search for survivors; troops and police efficiently directing traffic and supplies; survivors are not only "calm and pragmatic" but also coping "with politeness and sometimes amazingly good cheer."

Thanks to these strengths, Japan will eventually recover. But at least one Japanese nuclear power complex will not. As I write, three reactors at the Fukushima Daiichi nuclear power station appear to have lost their cooling capacity. Engineers are flooding the plant with seawater — effectively destroying it — and then letting off radioactive steam. There have been two explosions. The situation may worsen in the coming hours.

Yet Japan's nuclear power stations were designed with the same care and precision as everything else in the country. More to the point, as the only country in the world to have experienced true nuclear catastrophe, Japan had an incentive to build well, as well as the capability, laws and regulations to do so. Which leads to an unavoidable question: If the competent and technologically brilliant Japanese can't build a completely safe reactor, who can?

It can — and will — be argued that the Japanese situation is extraordinary. Few countries are as vulnerable to natural catastrophe as Japan, and the scale of this earthquake is unprecedented. But there are other kinds of extraordinary situations and unprecedented circumstances. In an attempt to counter the latest worst-possible scenarios, a Franco-German company began constructing a super-safe, "next-generation" nuclear reactor in Finland several years ago. The plant was designed to withstand the impact of an airplane — a post–Sept. 11 concern — and includes a chamber allegedly able to contain a core meltdown. But it was also meant to cost $4 billion and to be completed in 2009. Instead, after numerous setbacks, it is still unfinished — and may now cost $6 billion or more.

Ironically, the Finnish plant was meant to launch the renaissance of the   5
nuclear power industry in Europe — an industry that has, of late, enjoyed a renaissance around the world, thanks almost entirely to fears of climate change. Nuclear plants emit no carbon. As a result, nuclear plants, after a long, post-Chernobyl lull, have became fashionable again. Some 62 nuclear reactors are under construction at the moment, a further 158 are being planned and 324 others have been proposed.

Increasingly, nuclear power is also promoted because it is safe. Which it is — except, of course, when it is not. Chances of a major disaster are tiny, one in a hundred million. But in the event of a statistically improbable major disaster, the damage could include, say, the destruction of a city or the poisoning of a country. The cost of such a potential catastrophe is partly reflected in the price of plant construction, and it partly explains the cost overruns in Finland: Nobody can risk the tiniest flaw in the concrete or the most minimal reduction in the quality of the steel.

But as we are about to learn in Japan, the true costs of nuclear power are never reflected even in the very high price of plant construction. Inevitably, the enormous costs of nuclear waste disposal fall to taxpayers, not the nuclear industry. The costs of cleanup, even in the wake of a relatively small accident, are eventually borne by government, too. Health-care costs will also be paid by society at large, one way or another. If there is true nuclear catastrophe in Japan, the entire world will pay the price.

I hope that this will never, ever happen. I feel nothing but admiration for the Japanese nuclear engineers who have been battling catastrophe for several days. If anyone can prevent a disaster, the Japanese can do it. But I also hope that a near-miss prompts people around the world to think twice about the true "price" of nuclear energy, and that it stops the nuclear renaissance dead in its tracks.

(2011)

Does Applebaum miss her mark? Does she use a worst-case scenario to make her case? Do her references to September 11 and World War II make nuclear power seem alarming, or do they just make Applebaum sound alarmist? Are her fears fully justified, or is this an instance of fear mongering? Consider that she does acknowledge that Japan's situation is unusual because the country is so "vulnerable to natural catastrophe" and the earthquake that struck was unusually strong. She cites facts and figures about the efforts in Finland to build a nuclear plant that is meant to be "super-safe" and withstand every imaginable contingency. She explains that other European nations are following the Finnish lead ("158 are being planned and 324 others have been proposed") because nuclear power, which does not emit carbon dioxide, is not thought to contribute to climate change. There is quite a bit to consider, even in this relatively brief piece.

• ACTIVITY •

Following is a rhetorical analysis of the effectiveness of Anne Applebaum's argument written by an Advanced Placement student, Tamar Demby. How does she develop her position? Do you agree or disagree? Explain. How might she improve her essay?

Alarmist or Alarming Rhetoric?
TAMAR DEMBY

In an age when threats to life as we know it seem to grow too enormous to face, it becomes tempting to regard any danger as an apocalypse waiting to happen. But however huge and urgent an incident appears, it is important to look at the big picture and calmly analyze the true risks of all responses. Within the context of Japan's struggle to avert a nuclear meltdown in Fukushima Prefecture, Anne Applebaum, writing for the *Washington Post*, argues against any further expansion of nuclear power. However, she undermines her own purpose by basing her argument on unsupported claims, relying on highly emotional language, and failing to establish her ethos as a credible authority on the issue.

As a journalist rather than a nuclear physicist or someone with credentials earned by education and training, she has to present a clear viewpoint supported by solid evidence. If she has a history of reporting on nuclear power issues, then she should have explained that expertise. Instead, she relies on hot-button issues such as Chernobyl to alarm her readers, who are likely an educated and well-informed audience. Even though she is writing in the midst of the crisis in Japan when no one knew what would happen to the reactors, she needs to establish a fair-minded ethos and build a more fact-based case. Unless she moves her audience to share her concern and alarm, she fails to achieve her purpose of making them see the true "cost" of nuclear power and oppose further expansion.

Applebaum's central point is spelled out in the title of her piece: "If the Japanese Can't Build a Safe Reactor, Who Can?" In order to ask and then answer this question, she must establish the supremacy of the Japanese to build a safe nuclear reactor. In her first paragraph, she highlights the strengths of the Japanese: "cohesiveness, resilience, technological brilliance and extraordinary competence" and cites examples of all these traits *except* technological brilliance — leaving the reader with no reason to agree with her assessment of Japanese technological prowess. This pattern continues in the second paragraph, as Applebaum attempts to explain that the Japanese can be expected to have built the safest possible nuclear reactors because they were "designed with the same care and precision as everything else in the country" — a statement she fails to support. Verified details seem to be reserved for viscerally effective descriptions of the situation in the Fukushima Daiichi plant. Applebaum states that the plant will not "eventually recover," as three reactors are "letting off radioactive steam . . . (and) there have been two explosions." These facts serve only to appeal to the reader's emotions, focusing on the horrifying results of the catastrophe but not addressing — or supporting — Applebaum's claims. Ultimately, Applebaum's position seems to be based more on personal alarm than analysis of facts.

• ACTIVITY •

Examine the following advertisement sponsored by the Federal Highway Administration. Analyze the rhetorical situation and appeals used in the advertisement, and determine whether you think this advertisement is effective or ineffective.

• CULMINATING ACTIVITY •

By this point, you have analyzed what we mean by the rhetorical situation, and you have learned a number of key concepts and terms. It's time to put all the ideas together to examine a series of texts on a single subject. Following are five texts related to the 1969 *Apollo 11* mission that landed the first humans on the moon. The first is a news article from the *Times* of London reporting the event; it is followed by a poem by Archibald MacLeish; next is a speech by William Safire that President Nixon would have given had the mission not been successful; the fourth is a commentary by novelist Ayn Rand; last is a political cartoon that appeared around the time. Discuss the purpose of each text and how the interaction among speaker, audience, and subject affects the text. How does each text appeal to ethos, pathos, and logos? Finally, how effective is each text in achieving its purpose?

Man Takes First Steps on the Moon
THE TIMES

The following article appeared in a special 5 A.M. edition of the Times *of London on July 21, 1969.*

Neil Armstrong became the first man to take a walk on the moon's surface early today. The spectacular moment came after he had inched his way down the ladder of the fragile lunar bug Eagle while colleague Edwin Aldrin watched his movements from inside the craft. The landing, in the Sea of Tranquillity, was near perfect and the two astronauts on board Eagle reported that it had not tilted too far to prevent a take-off. The first word from man on the moon came from Aldrin: "Tranquillity base. The Eagle has landed." Of the first view of the lunar surface, he said: "There are quite a few rocks and boulders in the near area which are going to have some interesting colours in them." Armstrong said both of them were in good shape and there was no need to worry about them. They had experienced no difficulty in manoeuvring the module in the moon's gravity. There were tense moments in the mission control centre at Houston while they awaited news of the safe landing. When it was confirmed, one ground controller was heard to say: "We got a bunch of guys on the ground about to turn blue. We're breathing again." Ten minutes after landing, Aldrin radioed: "We'll get to the details of what's around here. But it looks like a collection of every variety, shape, angularity, granularity; a collection of just about every kind of rock." He added: "The colour depends on what angle you're looking at . . . rocks and boulders look as though they're going to have some interesting colours."

Armstrong says: one giant leap for mankind
From the News Team in Houston and London
It was 3.56 A.M. (British Standard Time) when Armstrong stepped off the ladder from Eagle and on to the moon's surface. The module's hatch had opened at 3.39 A.M.

"That's one small step for man but one giant leap for mankind," he said as he stepped on the lunar surface.

The two astronauts opened the hatch of their lunar module at 3.39 A.M. in preparation for Neil Armstrong's walk. They were obviously being ultra careful over the operation for there was a considerable time lapse before Armstrong moved backwards out of the hatch to start his descent down the ladder.

Aldrin had to direct Armstrong out of the hatch because he was walking backwards and could not see the ladder.

Armstrong moved on to the porch outside Eagle and prepared to switch the television cameras which showed the world his dramatic descent as he began to inch his way down the ladder.

By this time the two astronauts had spent 25 minutes of their breathing time but their oxygen packs on their backs last four hours.

When the television cameras switched on there was a spectacular shot of Armstrong as he moved down the ladder. Viewers had a clear view as they saw him stepping foot by foot down the ladder, which has nine rungs.

He reported that the lunar surface was a "very fine-grained powder."

Clutching the ladder Armstrong put his left foot on the lunar surface and reported it was like powdered charcoal and he could see his footprints on the surface. He said the L.E.M.'s engine had left a crater about a foot deep but they were "on a very level place here."

Standing directly in the shadow of the lunar module Armstrong said he could see very clearly. The light was sufficiently bright for everything to be clearly visible.

The next step was for Aldrin to lower a hand camera down to Armstrong. This was the camera which Armstrong was to use to film Aldrin when he descends from Eagle.

Armstrong then spent the next few minutes taking photographs of the area in which he was standing and then prepared to take the "contingency" sample of lunar soil.

This was one of the first steps in case the astronauts had to make an emergency take-off before they could complete the whole of their activities on the moon.

Armstrong said: "It is very pretty out here."

Using the scoop to pick up the sample Armstrong said he had pushed six to eight inches into the surface. He then reported to the mission control centre that he placed the sample lunar soil in his pocket.

The first sample was in his pocket at 4.08 A.M. He said the moon "has soft beauty all its own," like some desert of the United States. . . .

Greatest moment of time

President Nixon, watching the events on television, described it as "one of the greatest moments of our time." He told Mr. Ron Ziegler, the White House press secretary, that the last 22 seconds of the descent were the longest he had ever lived through.

Mr. Harold Wilson, in a television statement, expressed "our deep wish for a safe return at the end of what has been a most historic scientific achievement in the history of man." The Prime Minister, speaking from 10 Downing Street, said: "The first feeling of all in Britain is that this very dangerous part of the mission has been safely accomplished."

Moscow Radio announced the news solemnly as the main item in its 11.30 news broadcast. There was no immediate news of Luna 15.   20

At Castelgandolfo the Pope greeted news of the lunar landing by exclaiming: "Glory to God in the highest and peace on earth to men of good will!"

In an unscheduled speech from his summer residence the Pope, who followed the flight on colour television, said: "We, humble representatives of that Christ, who, coming among us from the abyss of divinity, has made to resound in the heavens this blessed voice, today we make an echo, repeating it in a celebration on the part of the whole terrestrial globe, with no more unsurpassable bounds of human existence, but openness to the expanse of endless space and a new destiny."

"Glory to God!" President Saragat of Italy said in a statement: "May this victory be a good omen for an even greater victory: the definite conquest of peace, of justice, of liberty, for all peoples of the World."

President Charles Helou of Lebanon followed the flight and landing with special dispatches from the Information Ministry. A spokesman said he would send an official message later.

In Jordan King Husain sent a congratulatory message to the astronauts and   25
President Nixon.

In Stockholm Mr. Tage Erlander, the Swedish Prime Minister, said he planned to cable President Nixon his congratulations as soon as the astronauts returned to Earth. King Gustav Adolf was watching television at touchdown time and told friends he was "thrilled" by the Apollo performance.

In Cuba the national radio announced the moon landing 12 minutes after it was accomplished.

Sir Bernard Lovell, Director of the Jodrell Bank observatory, said: "The moment of touchdown was one of the moments of greatest drama in the history of man. The success in this part of the enterprize opens the most enormous opportunities for the future exploration of the universe."

(1969)

Voyage to the Moon
Archibald MacLeish

The following poem by Archibald MacLeish, who had been Librarian of Congress during World War II, appeared in the New York Times *on July 21, 1969, the morning after the moon landing.*

Presence among us,

       wanderer in our skies,

dazzle of silver in our leaves and on our
waters silver.

      O   5

silver evasion in our farthest thought —
"the visiting moon" . . . "the glimpses of the moon" . . .

and we have touched you!

         From the first of time,
before the first of time, before the   10
first men tasted time, we thought of you.
You were a wonder to us, unattainable,
a longing past the reach of longing,
a light beyond our light, our lives — perhaps
a meaning to us . . .   15

      Now
our hands have touched you in your depth of night.

Three days and three nights we journeyed,
steered by farthest stars, climbed outward,
crossed the invisible tide-rip where the floating dust   20
falls one way or the other in the void between,
followed that other down, encountered
cold, faced death — unfathomable emptiness . . .

Then, the fourth day evening, we descended,
made fast, set foot at dawn upon your beaches,   25
sifted between our fingers your cold sand.

We stand here in the dusk, the cold, the silence . . .

and here, as at the first of time, we lift our heads.
Over us, more beautiful than the moon, a
moon, a wonder to us, unattainable,   30
a longing past the reach of longing,
a light beyond our light, our lives — perhaps
a meaning to us . . .

      O, a meaning!

over us on these silent beaches the bright   35
earth,
    presence among us

                      (1969)

In Event of Moon Disaster
WILLIAM SAFIRE

The following speech, revealed in 1999, was prepared by President Nixon's speechwriter, William Safire, to be used in the event of a disaster that would maroon the astronauts on the moon.

Fate has ordained that the men who went to the moon to explore in peace will stay on the moon to rest in peace.

These brave men, Neil Armstrong and Edwin Aldrin, know that there is no hope for their recovery. But they also know that there is hope for mankind in their sacrifice. These two men are laying down their lives in mankind's most noble goal: the search for truth and understanding.

They will be mourned by their families and friends; they will be mourned by their nation; they will be mourned by the people of the world; they will be mourned by a Mother Earth that dared send two of her sons into the unknown.

In their exploration, they stirred the people of the world to feel as one; in their sacrifice, they bind more tightly the brotherhood of man.

In ancient days, men looked at stars and saw their heroes in the constellations. In modern times, we do much the same, but our heroes are epic men of flesh and blood.

Others will follow, and surely find their way home. Man's search will not be denied. But these men were the first, and they will remain the foremost in our hearts. For every human being who looks up at the moon in the nights to come will know that there is some corner of another world that is forever mankind.

(1969)

The July 16, 1969, Launch: A Symbol of Man's Greatness
AYN RAND

The following commentary by novelist Ayn Rand first appeared in the Objectivist, *a publication created by Rand and others to put forward their philosophy of objectivism, which values individualism, freedom, and reason.*

"No matter what discomforts and expenses you had to bear to come here," said a NASA guide to a group of guests, at the conclusion of a tour of the Space Center on Cape Kennedy, on July 15, 1969, "there will be seven minutes tomorrow morning that will make you feel it was worth it."

It was.

[The launch] began with a large patch of bright, yellow-orange flame shooting sideways from under the base of the rocket. It looked like a normal kind of flame and I felt an instant's shock of anxiety, as if this were a building on fire. In the next instant the flame and the rocket were hidden by such a sweep of dark red fire that the anxiety vanished: this was not part of any normal experience and could not be integrated with anything. The dark red fire parted into two gigantic wings, as if a hydrant were shooting streams of fire outward and up, toward the zenith — and between the two wings, against a pitch-black sky, the rocket rose slowly, so slowly that it seemed to hang still in the air, a pale cylinder with a blinding oval of white light at the bottom, like an upturned candle with its flame directed at the earth. Then I became aware that this was happening in total silence, because I heard the cries of birds winging frantically away from the flames. The rocket was rising faster, slanting a little, its tense white flame leaving a long, thin spiral of bluish smoke behind it. It had risen into the open blue sky, and the dark red fire had turned into enormous billows of brown smoke, when the sound reached us: it was a long, violent crack, not a rolling sound, but specifically a cracking, grinding sound, as if space were breaking apart, but it seemed irrelevant and unimportant, because it was a sound from the past and the rocket was long since speeding safely out of its reach — though it was strange to realize that only a few seconds had passed. I found myself waving to the rocket involuntarily, I heard people applauding and joined them, grasping our common motive; it was impossible to watch passively, one had to express, by some physical action, a feeling that was not triumph, but more: the feeling that that white object's unobstructed streak of motion was the only thing that mattered in the universe.

What we had seen, in naked essentials — but in reality, not in a work of art — was the concretized abstraction of man's greatness.

The fundamental significance of *Apollo 11*'s triumph is not political; it is philosophical; specifically, moral-epistemological.[1]   5

The meaning of the sight lay in the fact that when those dark red wings of fire flared open, one knew that one was not looking at a normal occurrence, but at a cataclysm which, if unleashed by nature, would have wiped man out of existence — and one knew also that this cataclysm was planned, unleashed, and controlled by man, that this unimaginable power was ruled by his power and, obediently serving his purpose, was making way for a slender, rising craft. One knew that this spectacle was not the product of inanimate nature, like some aurora borealis, or of chance, or of luck, that it was unmistakably human — with "human," for once, meaning grandeur — that a purpose and a long, sustained, disciplined effort had gone to achieve this series of moments, and that man was succeeding, succeeding, succeeding! For once, if only for seven minutes, the worst among those who saw it had to feel — not "How small is man by the side of the Grand Canyon!" — but "How great is man and how safe is nature when he conquers it!"

That we had seen a demonstration of man at his best, no one could doubt — this was the cause of the event's attraction and of the stunned numbed state in which it left us. And no one could doubt that we had seen an achievement of man in his capacity as a rational being — an achievement of reason, of logic, of mathematics, of total dedication to the absolutism of reality.

---

[1]The philosophical study of how humans comprehend moral concepts such as good, evil, glory, magesty, tragedy, etc. — Eds.

Frustration is the leitmotif in the lives of most men, particularly today — the frustration of inarticulate desires, with no knowledge of the means to achieve them. In the sight and hearing of a crumbling world, *Apollo 11* enacted the story of an audacious purpose, its execution, its triumph, and the means that achieved it — the story and the demonstration of man's highest potential.

(1969)

Transported

HERBLOCK

The following editorial cartoon by the famous cartoonist Herb Block, or Herblock, appeared in the Washington Post *on July 18, 1969.*

A 1969 Herblock Cartoon, © The Herb Block Foundation

Close Reading
The Art and Craft of Analysis

Do you ever wonder how your teachers can teach the same books year after year and not be bored by them? One reason is that the works we study in school have many layers of meaning, revealing something new each time we read them. That quality is what distinguishes them from "literary potato chips" — works that are satisfying, even delicious, but that offer little nutritional value. A mystery, romance, gossip blog, or sports rant may absorb us completely, but usually we do not read it a second time.

How do you find the "nutritional value" in the essays, speeches, stories, and poems you study in school? Your teacher may lead you through a work, putting it in context, focusing your attention on themes and techniques, asking for a response. Or you might do these things yourself through a process called close reading. When you read closely, you develop an understanding of a text that is based first on the words themselves and then on the larger ideas those words suggest. That is, you start with the small details, and as you think about them, you discover how they affect the text's larger meaning. When you *write* a close analysis, you start with the larger meaning you've discovered and use the small details — the language itself — to support your interpretation.

Of course, as you read the speeches, essays, letters, editorials, stories, poems, and even blog posts in this book and in your class, you will find that many different factors dictate the stylistic choices a writer makes. Sometimes, it's the genre: a blog post will likely be less formal than, say, an acceptance speech; an editorial will be less personal than an exchange of letters between two friends. Sometimes, it's the context or rhetorical situation — considering subject matter, occasion, audience, purpose, and the persona of the speaker. Often, however, the choices writers make are related to the rhetorical strategies of the text: what words in what arrangement are most likely to create the desired effect in the audience?

Analyzing Style

As with any skill, close reading becomes easier with practice, but it's important to remember that we use it unconsciously — and instantaneously — every day as we respond to people and situations. Just as we notice body language, gestures, facial expressions, and volume in our conversations, we can understand a text better by examining its sentence structure, vocabulary, imagery, and figurative language. These elements make up the style of the written piece and help us discover layers of meaning. Style contributes to the meaning, purpose, and effect of a text, whether it is written, oral, or visual.

Let's begin by taking a look at a piece written by John Muir and published in 1920. Working with older pieces such as this one sometimes seems more difficult than working with texts from the late twentieth or early twenty-first century, yet you may find that you read the older ones more carefully and that their riches reveal themselves more quickly than you might expect.

It may help you begin by knowing a bit more about the author and the context of "Save the Redwoods." John Muir (1838–1914) was a nineteenth-century environmentalist and the founder of the conservation organization the Sierra Club. He was particularly active in preserving the wilderness of the forests of the western United States and is today sometimes called the Father of the National Parks. This piece was discovered in Muir's papers after his death and was published in the *Sierra Club Bulletin* in January 1920.

Save the Redwoods
JOHN MUIR

> We are often told that the world is going from bad to worse, sacrificing everything to mammon.[1] But this righteous uprising in defense of God's trees in the midst of exciting politics and wars is telling a different story, and every Sequoia, I fancy, has heard the good news and is waving its branches for joy. The wrongs done to trees, wrongs of every sort, are done in the darkness of ignorance and unbelief, for when light comes the heart of the people is always right. Forty-seven years ago one of these Calaveras King Sequoias was laboriously cut down, that the stump might be had for a dancing-floor. Another, one of the finest in the grove, more than three hundred feet high, was skinned alive to a height of one hundred and sixteen feet from the ground and the bark sent to London to show how fine and big that Calaveras tree was — as sensible a scheme as skinning our great men would be to prove their greatness. This grand tree is of course dead, a ghastly disfigured ruin, but it still stands erect and holds forth its majestic arms as if alive and saying, "Forgive them; they know not what they do." Now some millmen want to cut all the Calaveras trees into lumber and money. But we have found a better use for them. No doubt these trees would make good lumber after passing through a sawmill, as George Washington after passing through the hands of a French cook would have made good food. But both for Washington and the tree that bears his name higher uses have been found.
>
> Could one of these Sequoia kings come to town in all its godlike majesty so as to be strikingly seen and allowed to plead its own cause, there would never again be any lack of defenders. And the same may be said of all the other Sequoia

---

[1]Money, riches. In the New Testament of the Bible, Mammon is often personified as a false god of greed. See Matthew 6:24 and Luke 16:13. — Eds.

groves and forests of the Sierra with their companions and the noble *Sequoia sampervirens,* or redwood, of the coast mountains.

In a general view we find that the *Sequoia gigantea,* or Big Tree, is distributed in a widely interrupted belt along the west flank of the Sierra, from a small grove on the middle fork of the American River to the head of Deer Creek, a distance of about two hundred and sixty miles, at an elevation of about five thousand to a little over eight thousand feet above the sea. From the American River grove to the forest on Kings River the species occurs only in comparatively small isolated patches or groves so sparsely distributed along the belt that three of the gaps in it are from forty to sixty miles wide. From Kings River southward the Sequoia is not restricted to mere groves, but extends across the broad rugged basins of the Kaweah and Tule rivers in majestic forests a distance of nearly seventy miles, the continuity of this portion of the belt being but slightly broken save by the deep cañons.

In these noble groves and forests to the southward of the Calaveras Grove the axe and saw have long been busy, and thousands of the finest Sequoias have been felled, blasted into manageable dimensions, and sawed into lumber by methods destructive almost beyond belief, while fires have spread still wider and more lamentable ruin. In the course of my explorations twenty-five years ago, I found five sawmills located on or near the lower margin of the Sequoia belt, all of which were cutting more or less Big Tree lumber, which looks like the redwood of the coast, and was sold as redwood. One of the smallest of these mills in the season of 1874 sawed two million feet of Sequoia lumber. Since that time other mills have been built among the Sequoias, notably the large ones on Kings River and the head of the Fresno. The destruction of these grand trees is still going on.

On the other hand, the Calaveras Grove for forty years has been faithfully protected by Mr. Sperry, and with the exception of the two trees mentioned above is still in primeval beauty. The Tuolumne and Merced groves near Yosemite, the Dinky Creek grove, those of the General Grant National Park and the Sequoia National Park, with several outstanding groves that are nameless on the Kings, Kaweah, and Tule river basins, and included in the Sierra forest reservation, have of late years been partially protected by the Federal Government; while the well-known Mariposa Grove has long been guarded by the State. 5

For the thousands of acres of Sequoia forest outside of the reservation and national parks, and in the hands of lumbermen, no help is in sight. Probably more than three times as many Sequoias as are contained in the whole Calaveras Grove have been cut into lumber every year for the last twenty-six years without let or hindrance, and with scarce a word of protest on the part of the public, while at the first whisper of the bonding of the Calaveras Grove to lumbermen most everybody rose in alarm. This righteous and lively indignation on the part of Californians after the long period of deathlike apathy, in which they have witnessed the destruction of other groves unmoved, seems strange until the rapid growth that right public opinion has made during the last few years is considered and the peculiar interest that attaches to the Calaveras giants. They were the first discovered and are best known. Thousands of travelers from every country have come to pay them tribute of admiration and praise, their reputation is world-wide, and the names of great men have long been associated with them — Washington, Humboldt, Torrey and Gray, Sir Joseph Hooker, and others. These kings of the forest, the noblest of a noble race, rightly belong to the world, but as they are in California we cannot escape responsibility as their guardians. Fortunately the American people are equal to this trust, or any other that may arise, as soon as they see it and understand it.

Any fool can destroy trees. They cannot defend themselves or run away. And few destroyers of trees ever plant any; nor can planting avail much toward restoring our grand aboriginal giants. It took more than three thousand years to make some of the oldest of the Sequoias, trees that are still standing in perfect strength and beauty, waving and singing in the mighty forests of the Sierra. Through all the eventful centuries since Christ's time, and long before that, God has cared for these trees, saved them from drought, disease, avalanches, and a thousand storms; but he cannot save them from sawmills and fools; this is left to the American people. The news from Washington is encouraging. On March third [1905?] the House passed a bill providing for the Government acquisition of the Calaveras giants. The danger these Sequoias have been in will do good far beyond the boundaries of the Calaveras Grove, in saving other groves and forests, and quickening interest in forest affairs in general. While the iron of public sentiment is hot let us strike hard. In particular, a reservation or national park of the only other species of Sequoia, the *sempervirens*, or redwood, hardly less wonderful than the *gigantea*, should be quickly secured. It will have to be acquired by gift or purchase, for the Government has sold every section of the entire redwood belt from the Oregon boundary to below Santa Cruz.

(1920)

Establishing the Rhetorical Situation

Using what you learned in Chapter 1, you can begin by identifying the passage's rhetorical situation. The speaker is naturalist and environmentalist John Muir speaking posthumously: the piece was published after his death. We don't know who was meant to be the original audience or what the occasion. But we can consider the audience and occasion for the version published here. In an editorial in that issue of the *Sierra Club Bulletin*, the president of the club notes that Muir's plea for the conservation of the redwoods (written years before) was "almost providentially preserved among his papers for the supreme occasion which has now arisen." That occasion was a renewed effort to preserve the redwood forests in the early days of the Save the Redwoods League, whose efforts helped protect almost 190,000 acres of forests. The audience was comprised of the readers of the *Sierra Club Bulletin*, conservationists from all over the nation who supported the Sierra Club and read their publications. Muir's purpose, to make the case for saving the redwoods, is served by his focus on the nearly mythical beauty of the trees, their spiritual qualities, and his belief in the innate goodness of man.

You can also consider the ways Muir appeals to ethos, logos, and pathos. As founder of the organization, Muir was certainly known to the readers of the magazine, so his name and reputation quickly establish ethos for this audience. Nevertheless, when it was published, Muir's piece was preceded by a note from John Campbell Merriam, founder, chairman, and chief executive of the Save the Redwoods League, in which he describes Muir as a "friend who fought so hard, so faithfully, and so long in this good cause." Muir appeals to pathos by personifying the trees and making emotional pleas for their preservation. He appeals to logos, especially in paragraphs 3–5, by quantifying the magnitude of the redwood forests and the threat to them.

A Model Analysis

Now that you understand the rhetorical situation, let's look a little more closely at the resources of language that Muir uses to achieve his purpose, which is to persuade his audience that they must commit to the cause of saving the redwoods. We're looking specifically for how that purpose is achieved through the speaker's choice of words (also called **diction**) and how those words are arranged (called **syntax**).

You probably noticed that Muir opens his remarks with the word "We." He creates common ground with the assumption that we all believe that the world is going from bad to worse and that greed (as suggested by "mammon") is the cause. He counters that argument, however, noting that the "righteous uprising in defense of God's trees" tells a "different story." His use of the term "righteous," with its religious connotation, and his labeling of the trees as "God's," set the tone for the rest of the piece, in which Muir ennobles both the trees and the humans who he hopes will protect them.

Muir establishes an emotional connection between the reader and the trees by personifying the trees and imagining them feeling both joy and pain. He creates an image of every Sequoia "waving its branches for joy" (par. 1), having heard the good news of the growing conservation movement, and then uses the term "skinned alive" (par. 1) to describe the desecration of a three-hundred-foot tree. In the short second paragraph, Muir asks the reader to imagine the effect if one of these majestic trees could come to town "to plead its own cause," extending the personification of the tree to an entity that not only feels but also thinks. In these examples, we see the full range of the tree's humanity—joy, pain, thought—and come to think of those who cut down the redwoods as murderers.

Muir builds on that emotional appeal by presenting the trees as not just human but divine. He describes the trees as having a "godlike majesty" (par. 2). And after being skinned alive, the tree responds in Christlike fashion by saying, "Forgive them; they know not what they do" (par. 1). Muir's use of a biblical reference to deliver that message increases the emotional impact. Now, those who destroy redwoods are not just murderers; they are killing "God's trees" and possibly even a manifestation of God himself. The emotional stakes can't get much higher than that.

Muir employs a few other resources of diction and syntax that help him connect with his audience at the same time that he keeps his purpose in the forefront. For example, he uses **metonymy** (a figure of speech in which something is represented by another thing that is related to it or emblematic of it), substituting the "axe and saw" (par. 4) for the humans who destroy the trees. He thus separates most of mankind from those who benefit from the destruction. He begins the sixth paragraph with a bit of unconventional syntax, opening with a prepositional phrase — "For the thousands of acres of Sequoia forest outside of the reservation and national parks" — before revealing the subject and predicate: "no help is in sight." The syntax highlights the vulnerability of the redwoods by putting these trees that are dependent on us in a phrase that is grammatically dependent. The vulnerability is further reinforced by Muir menacingly putting these trees "in the hands of lumbermen." This structure delays the subject and predicate, so that when it does come, it carries the grim finality of a death sentence: "no help is in sight."

But Muir's argument is not just emotional. His piece is anchored by facts and figures that both bring to life the majesty of the redwood forests and reveal the rate at which they are being destroyed. He provides examples of how "thousands of the finest Sequoias have been felled, blasted into manageable dimensions, and sawed into lumber by methods destructive almost beyond belief" (par. 4), including specific numbers of sawmills and trees. He names the forests and the men whose names are associated with them. He invokes the "[t]housands of travelers" (par. 6) from around the world who visit them every year.

In his closing, Muir returns to the spiritual tone of the beginning, but he is more direct about his purpose: to remind us both that "[a]ny fool can destroy trees" and that he has faith that his fellow man will prevent that from happening. He acknowledges God's role in creating the beauty of the trees and protecting them from natural disasters such as "drought, disease, avalanches, and a thousand storms," but he puts the responsibility on the American people to save them from "sawmills and fools," and his phrase takes the form of a structure you may recognize as a **zeugma** — the use of two incongruous words in a grammatically parallel way. Muir's metaphor in this paragraph — striking the iron of public sentiment while it is hot — is a bit of a cliché, but in Muir's time it likely had more punch. It is in this paragraph that Muir's call for action is strong and precise. It is essential for the mighty redwoods to come under protection and be permitted to stand in "perfect strength and beauty."

Determining Tone

One of the biggest challenges in analyzing style is understanding and identifying the tone of a piece. True, Muir writes about the importance of saving the redwoods, but how does he get you to feel it's important too? We often consider tone and mood together: **tone** is the speaker's attitude toward the subject as revealed by his or her choice of language, and **mood** is the feeling created by the work. Make sure you take the time to consider both. As always, it's important to be able to support your description of tone and mood with evidence from the text.

We've been looking closely at how Muir's language supports his purpose. Now let's pull back a bit and try to see the big picture. Overall, what is his language like? Does it stay consistent, or does it shift? The piece begins with passionate pleas developed through personification and even spiritualization of the trees. Then Muir shifts to a more measured and logical approach, before concluding with an emotional plea. Because it shifts a few times in this piece, we can't accurately use one word to describe the tone. *Passionate* would be close, but it would not capture the logical middle portion of the essay. This is why you are generally better off using a couple (or even a few) words when describing tone in a piece as complex as this one. For instance, we might describe the tone of this piece as passionate and spiritual yet realistic and even optimistic. Using *yet* in a description of tone is a simple way to signal that it shifts occasionally in the piece. A common way of describing tone that is consistent throughout a piece, yet still complex, is with an adverb and an adjective pairing, such as "warmly didactic" or "begrudgingly generous."

• ACTIVITY •

Read the following excerpt from the beginning of abolitionist Angelina Grimké Weld's 1838 speech, which she gave in Pennsylvania Hall in Philadelphia. The audience consisted of abolitionists, but an angry stone-throwing crowd waited outside. Describe the tone of the speech by using two to three adjectives or an adverb and an adjective; then explain why you chose those words, making specific reference to the text.

Speech at Pennsylvania Hall
ANGELINA GRIMKÉ WELD

Men, brethren and fathers — mothers, daughters and sisters, what came ye out for to see? A reed shaken with the wind? Is it curiosity merely, or a deep sympathy with the perishing slave, that has brought this large audience together? [A yell from the mob without the building.] Those voices without ought to awaken and call out our warmest sympathies. Deluded beings! "they know not what they do." They know not that they are undermining their own rights and their own happiness, temporal and eternal. Do you ask, "what has the North to do with slavery?" Hear it — hear it. Those voices without tell us that the spirit of slavery is *here*, and has been roused to wrath by our abolition speeches and conventions: for surely liberty would not foam and tear herself with rage, because her friends are multiplied daily, and meetings are held in quick succession to set forth her virtues and extend her peaceful kingdom. This opposition shows that slavery has done its deadliest work in the hearts of our citizens. Do you ask, then, "what has the North to do?" I answer, cast out first the spirit of slavery from your own hearts, and then lend your aid to convert the South. Each one present has a work to do, be his or her situation what it may, however limited their means, or insignificant their supposed influence. The great men of this country will not do this work; the church will never do it. A desire to please the world, to keep the favor of all parties and of all conditions, makes them dumb on this and every other unpopular subject. They have become worldly-wise, and therefore God, in his wisdom, employs them not to carry on his plans of reformation and salvation. He hath chosen the foolish things of the world to confound the wise, and the weak to overcome the mighty.

As a Southerner I feel that it is my duty to stand up here to-night and bear testimony against slavery. I have seen it — I have seen it. I know it has horrors that can never be described. I was brought up under its wing: I witnessed for many years its demoralizing influences, and its destructiveness to human happiness. It is admitted by some that the slave is not happy under the *worst* forms of slavery. But I have *never* seen a happy slave. I have seen him dance in his chains, it is true; but he was not happy. There is a wide difference between happiness and mirth. Man cannot enjoy the former while his manhood is destroyed, and that part of the being which is necessary to the making, and to the enjoyment of happiness, is completely blotted out. The slaves, however, may be, and sometimes are, mirthful. When hope is extinguished, they say, "let us eat and drink, for to-morrow we die." [Just then stones were thrown at the windows, — a great noise without, and commotion within.] What is a mob? What would the breaking of every window be? What would the levelling of this Hall be? Any evidence that we are wrong, or that slavery is a good and wholesome institution? What if the mob should now burst in upon us, break up our meeting and commit violence upon our persons — would this be any thing compared with what the slaves endure? No, no: and we do not remember them "as bound with them," if we shrink in the time of peril, or feel unwilling to sacrifice ourselves, if need be, for their sake. [Great noise.] I thank the Lord that there is yet life left enough to feel the truth, even though it rages at it — that conscience is not so completely seared as to be unmoved by the truth of the living God.

(1838)

Talking with the Text

Effective analysis requires active reading, an exchange between the reader and the text that eventually reveals layers of meaning. The first step is to read and reread. That's a good start, but at some point you will have to talk back, ask questions, make comments — in other words, have a conversation with the text. Let's look at some close reading techniques that will help you talk with the text.

Asking Questions

One of the simplest ways to talk with the text is to interrogate it — to ask questions. Remember that we're always trying to consider the choices writers make, so as you read, ask yourself why they chose the words or sentence patterns they did. You don't always need to know the answers to your questions; sometimes just asking them will give you insights into a writer's choices.

Let's take a look at this excerpt from Ralph Ellison's "On Bird, Bird-Watching and Jazz," an essay in which the writer considers the legend — and style — of jazz saxophonist and composer Charlie Parker, nicknamed Yardbird. In the essay, which was published in the *Saturday Review* in 1962, Ellison refers to both Robert Reisner's *Bird: The Legend of Charlie Parker* (a collection of interviews of Parker's friends, family, and colleagues) and Roger Tory Peterson's *A Field Guide to the Birds* (the bird-watcher's bible) as he comments on jazz as art and examines the myths surrounding Parker's nickname.

from *On Bird, Bird-Watching and Jazz*
RALPH ELLISON

Oddly enough, while several explanations are advanced as to how Charles Parker, Jr., became known as "Bird" ("Yardbird," in an earlier metamorphosis), none is conclusive. There is, however, overpowering internal evidence that whatever the true circumstance of his ornithological designation, it had little to do with the chicken yard. Randy roosters and operatic hens are familiars to fans of the animated cartoons, but for all the pathetic comedy of his living — and despite the crabbed and constricted character of his style — Parker was a most inventive melodist, in bird-watcher's terminology, a true songster.

This failure in the exposition of Bird's legend is intriguing, for nicknames are indicative of a change from a given to an achieved identity, whether by rise or fall, and they tell us something of the nicknamed individual's interaction with his fellows. Thus, since we suspect that more of legend is involved in his renaming than Mr. Reisner's title indicates, let us at least consult Roger Tory Peterson's *Field Guide to the Birds* for a hint as to why, during a period when most jazzmen were labeled "cats," someone hung the bird on Charlie. Let us note too that "legend" originally meant "the story of a saint," and that saints were often identified with symbolic animals.

Two species won our immediate attention, the goldfinch and the mocking-bird — the goldfinch because the beatnik phrase "Bird lives," which, following Parker's death, has been chalked endlessly on Village[1] buildings and subway walls, reminds us that during the thirteenth and fourteenth centuries a symbolic goldfinch frequently appeared in European devotional paintings. An apocryphal story has it that upon being given a clay bird for a toy, the infant Jesus brought it miraculously to life as a goldfinch. Thus the small, tawny-brown bird with a bright red patch about the base of its bill and a broad yellow band across its wings became a representative of the soul, the Passion and the Sacrifice. In more worldly late-Renaissance art, the little bird became the ambiguous symbol of death and the soul's immortality. For our own purposes, however, its song poses a major problem: it is like that of a canary — which soul or no soul, rules the goldfinch out.

The mockingbird, *Mimus polyglottos*, is more promising. Peterson informs us that its song consists of "long successions of notes and phrases of great variety, with each phrase repeated a half dozen times before going on to the next," that

---

[1] New York's Greenwich Village neighborhood in lower Manhattan. — Eds.

mockingbirds are "excellent mimics" who "adeptly imitate a score or more species found in the neighborhood," and that they frequently sing at night — a description which not only comes close to Parker's way with a saxophone but even hints at a trait of his character. For although he *usually* sang at night, his playing was characterized by velocity, by long-continued successions of notes and phrases, by swoops, bleats, echoes, rapidly repeated bebops — I mean rebopped bebops — by mocking mimicry of other jazzmen's styles, and by interpolations of motifs from extraneous melodies, all of which added up to a dazzling display of wit, satire, burlesque and pathos. Further, he was as expert at issuing his improvisations from the dense brush as from the extreme treetops of the harmonic landscape, and there was, without doubt, as irrepressible a mockery in his personal conduct as his music.

(1962)

Reread the excerpt, and see what you notice on a second reading. Jot down questions as you go, asking why Ellison might have used the language he did.

Here are some questions about Ellison's style that might come to mind, based on first and second impressions of the passage:

1. Why do the first two sentences contain qualifiers ("Oddly enough," "however")?
2. Why does Ellison suggest that his audience might be "fans of the animated cartoons" (par. 1)?
3. Why does Ellison think a book about bird-watching might be more edifying than a biography of Parker?
4. Why does Ellison say "hung the bird on Charlie" (par. 2) instead of "nicknamed him"?
5. What is the effect of Ellison's references to the story about the infant Jesus (par. 3)?
6. Why does Ellison provide the mockingbird's scientific name (*Mimus polyglottos*) (par. 4)?
7. How does Ellison manage to make this description of jazz sound so jazzy: "by long-continued successions of notes and phrases, by swoops, bleats, echoes, rapidly repeated bebops — I mean rebopped bebops — . . ." (par. 4)?
8. What is the effect of the dashes in the phrase above?

You may notice that these questions fall into the two categories we talked about in relation to the John Muir selection: the choice of words (diction) and the way the words are arranged (syntax). When we talk about diction, we might look for interesting or powerful vocabulary, but we also consider figures of speech like **metaphors, similes, personification**, and **hyperbole**. When we consider syntax, we want to notice interesting constructions like **parallelism, juxtaposition**, and **antithesis**, along with sentence types such as **compound, complex, periodic, inverted, cumulative**, and **imperative**, among others. We also might look at the pacing of a piece of work: Does the writer reveal details quickly or slowly? How does he or she build suspense?

Here are some questions to ask when you analyze diction:

1. What type of words draw your attention? Do they tend to be a particular part of speech, such as verbs, nouns, adjectives, or adverbs? Is the language general and abstract or specific and concrete?
2. Is the language formal, informal, colloquial, or slang?
3. Are some words nonliteral or figurative, creating **figures of speech** such as metaphors?
4. Are there words with strong connotations? Words with a particular emotional punch?

When you analyze syntax, you might ask:

1. What is the order of the parts of the sentence? Is it the usual order (subject-verb-object), or is it inverted (object-subject-verb, or any other pattern that is out of the ordinary)?
2. What are the sentences like? Are they periodic (moving toward something important at the end) or cumulative (beginning with an important idea and then adding details)?
3. Are many of the sentences simple? Complex? Compound? Are the sentences on the long side, or are they short? How are they related to one another?
4. Does the writer ask questions?
5. How does the writer connect words, phrases, and clauses?

These questions do not have simple yes or no answers. They lend themselves to discussion, but as you discuss them, be sure you can support your ideas with evidence from the text. Coming up with answers to questions like these will put you well on your way toward analyzing an author's style and how that style helps the author make his or her point.

• ACTIVITY •

Read the next paragraph from Ellison's essay, then generate two or three questions each about diction and syntax.

from *On Bird, Bird-Watching and Jazz*
RALPH ELLISON

Mimic thrushes, which include the catbird and brown thrasher, along with the mockingbird, are not only great virtuosi, they are the tricksters and con men of the bird world. Like Parker, who is described as a confidence man and a practical joker by several of the commentators, they take off on the songs of other birds, inflating, inverting and turning them wrong side out, and are capable of driving a prowling ("square") cat wild. Utterly irreverent and romantic, they are not beyond bugging human beings. Indeed, on summer nights in the South, when the moon hangs low, mockingbirds sing as though determined to heat every drop of romance in the sleeping adolescent's heart to fever pitch. Their song thrills and swings the entire moon-struck night to arouse one's sense of the mystery, promise and frustration of being human, alive and hot in the blood. They are as delightful to the eye as to the ear, but sometimes a similarity of voice and appearance makes for a confusion with the shrike, a species given to impaling insects and smaller songbirds on the points of thorns, and they are destroyed. They are fond of fruit, especially mulberries, and if there is a tree in your yard, there will be, along with the wonderful music, much chalky, blue-tinted evidence of their presence. Under such conditions, be careful and heed Parker's warning to his friends — who sometimes were subjected to a shrikelike treatment — "you must pay your dues to Bird."

(1962)

Annotating

Another close reading technique you can use is annotation. Annotating a text requires reading with a pencil in hand. If you are not allowed to write in your book, then write on sticky notes. As you read, circle words you don't know, or write them on the sticky notes. Identify main ideas — thesis statements, topic sentences — and also words, phrases, or sentences that appeal to you, that seem important, or that you don't understand. Look for figures of speech such as metaphors, similes, and personification — as well as **imagery** and striking detail. If you don't know the technical term for something, just describe it. For example, if you come across an adjective-and-noun combination that seems contradictory, such as "meager abundance," and you don't know that the term for it is **oxymoron**, you might still note the juxtaposition of two words that have opposite meanings. Ask questions or comment on what you have read. In short, as you read, listen to the voice in your head, and write down what that voice is saying.

Let's try out this approach using a passage by Joan Didion about California's Santa Ana winds from her 1965 essay "Los Angeles Notebook." Read the passage first, and see if you can come up with some ideas about Didion's purpose. Then we will look closely at the choices she makes and the effects of those choices.

The Santa Ana Winds
JOAN DIDION

There is something uneasy in the Los Angeles air this afternoon, some unnatural stillness, some tension. What it means is that tonight a Santa Ana will begin to blow, a hot wind from the northeast whining down through the Cajon and San

Gorgonio Passes, blowing up sand storms out along Route 66, drying the hills and the nerves to flash point. For a few days now we will see smoke back in the canyons, and hear sirens in the night. I have neither heard nor read that a Santa Ana is due, but I know it, and almost everyone I have seen today knows it too. We know it because we feel it. The baby frets. The maid sulks. I rekindle a waning argument with the telephone company, then cut my losses and lie down, given over to whatever it is in the air. To live with the Santa Ana is to accept, consciously or unconsciously, a deeply mechanistic view of human behavior.

I recall being told, when I first moved to Los Angeles and was living on an isolated beach, that the Indians would throw themselves into the sea when the bad wind blew. I could see why. The Pacific turned ominously glossy during a Santa Ana period, and one woke in the night troubled not only by the peacocks screaming in the olive trees but by the eerie absence of surf. The heat was surreal. The sky had a yellow cast, the kind of light sometimes called "earthquake weather." My only neighbor would not come out of her house for days, and there were no lights at night, and her husband roamed the place with a machete. One day he would tell me that he had heard a trespasser, the next a rattlesnake.

"On nights like that," Raymond Chandler once wrote about the Santa Ana, "every booze party ends in a fight. Meek little wives feel the edge of the carving knife and study their husbands' necks. Anything can happen." That was the kind of wind it was. I did not know then that there was any basis for the effect it had on all of us, but it turns out to be another of those cases in which science bears out folk wisdom. The Santa Ana, which is named for one of the canyons it rushes through, is a *foehn* wind, like the *foehn* of Austria and Switzerland and the *hamsin* of Israel. There are a number of persistent malevolent winds, perhaps the best known of which are the *mistral* of France and the Mediterranean *sirocco*, but a *foehn* wind has distinct characteristics: it occurs on the leeward slope of a mountain range and, although the air begins as a cold mass, it is warmed as it comes down the mountain and appears finally as a hot dry wind. Whenever and wherever *foehn* blows, doctors hear about headaches and nausea and allergies, about "nervousness," about "depression." In Los Angeles some teachers do not attempt to conduct formal classes during a Santa Ana, because the children become unmanageable. In Switzerland the suicide rate goes up during the *foehn*, and in the courts of some Swiss cantons the wind is considered a mitigating circumstance for crime. Surgeons are said to watch the wind, because blood does not clot normally during a *foehn*. A few years ago an Israeli physicist discovered that not only during such winds, but for the ten or twelve hours which precede them, the air carries an unusually high ratio of positive to negative ions. No one seems to know exactly why that should be; some talk about friction and others suggest solar disturbances. In any case the positive ions are there, and what an excess of positive ions does, in the simplest terms, is make people unhappy. One cannot get much more mechanistic than that.

(1965)

You probably noticed that while Didion seems to be writing about a natural phenomenon — the Santa Ana winds — she is also commenting on human nature and the way nature affects human behavior. Her purpose, then, is social commentary as much as the observation of an event in nature. In addition, you may notice on a second or third reading that her tone gives you another message: the way Didion sees human nature.

Following is an annotated version of the Didion passage:

Long sentence

There is something (uneasy) in the Los Angeles air this afternoon, some (unnatural) stillness, some tension. What it means is that tonight a Santa Ana will begin to blow, a hot wind from the north-east (whining) down through the Cajon and San Gorgonio Passes, blowing up sand storms out along Route 66, drying the hills and the nerves to (flash point.) For a few days now we will (see) smoke back in the canyons, and (hear) sirens in the night. I have neither heard nor read that a Santa Ana is due, but I know it, and almost (everyone) I have seen today knows it too. We know it because we (feel) it. (The baby frets.) (The maid sulks.) I rekindle a waning argument with the telephone company, then cut my losses and lie down, given over to whatever it is in the air. To live with the Santa Ana is to accept, consciously or unconsciously, a deeply

Look up word (mechanistic) view of human behavior.

Related words. Anxiety, foreboding

Appeal to senses

Short sentences

I recall being told, when I first moved to Los Angeles and was living on an isolated beach, that the Indians would throw themselves into the sea when the bad wind blew. I could see why. The Pacific turned (ominously) glossy during a Santa Ana period, and one woke in the night troubled not only by the (peacocks screaming) in the olive trees but by the eerie (absence of surf.) The heat was surreal. The sky had a (yellow cast,) the kind of light sometimes called "earthquake weather." My only neighbor would not come

More anxiety words

out of her house for days, and there were no lights at night, and her husband roamed the place with a (machete.) One day he would tell me that he had heard a (trespasser,) the next a (rattlesnake.)

Folktale?

Echo of foreboding in opening

Vivid images

Personal anecdote

"On nights like that," (Raymond Chandler) once wrote about the Santa Ana, "every booze party ends in a fight. Meek little wives feel the edge of the carving knife and study their husbands' necks. Anything can happen." That was the kind of wind it was. I did not know then that there was any basis for the effect it had on all of us, but it turns out to be another of those cases in which science bears out folk wisdom. The Santa Ana, which is named for one of the canyons it rushes through, is a *foehn* wind, like the *foehn* of Austria and Switzerland and the *hamsin* of Israel. There

Good description are a number of persistent malevolent winds, perhaps the best

Look up name

Seemingly contradictory sources of information

known of which are the *mistral* of France and the Mediterranean *sirocco*, but a *foehn* wind has distinct characteristics: it occurs on the leeward slope of a mountain range and, although the air begins as a cold mass, it is warmed as it comes down the mountain and appears finally as a hot dry wind. Whenever and wherever *foehn* blows, doctors hear about headaches and nausea and allergies, about "nervousness," about "depression." In Los Angeles some teachers do not attempt to conduct formal classes during a Santa Ana, because the children become unmanageable. In Switzerland the suicide rate goes up during the *foehn*, and in the courts of some Swiss cantons the wind is considered a mitigating circumstance for crime. Surgeons are said to watch the wind, because blood does not clot normally during a *foehn*. A few years ago an Israeli physicist discovered that not only during such winds, but for the ten or twelve hours which precede them, the air carries an unusually high ratio of positive to negative ions. No one seems to know exactly why that should be; some talk about friction and others suggest solar disturbances. In any case the positive ions are there, and what an excess of positive ions does, in the simplest terms, is make people unhappy. One cannot get much more mechanistic than that.

Why in quotes?

At least 7 scientific facts

Strange — should be positive

Using a Graphic Organizer

Another way to organize your thoughts about a specific text is to use a graphic organizer. A graphic organizer lets you look systematically at short passages from a longer text. Your teacher may divide the text for you, or you may divide it yourself; you might use the paragraph divisions as natural breaking points, or you might consider smaller sections that seem interesting stylistically. Although a graphic organizer takes time to complete, it lets you gather a great deal of information that you can use as you prepare to write an essay.

The accompanying graphic organizer asks you to take something the writer has said, restate it in your own words, identify some of the devices that the writer has used, and then analyze how the writer uses those devices to make his or her point. Note that you become increasingly analytical as you move from left to right. The graphic organizer on pages 56–58 has been filled in for you using a portion of the Joan Didion passage that we read above.

Breaking the text into small sections, looking at them closely, and writing down your ideas about them helps you notice the stylistic details in Didion's writing. For example, in paragraph 1, she connects two seemingly different things in the same grammatical construction ("drying the hills and the nerves"; the technical name for this figure of speech is **zeugma**). Later in the essay she alludes to crime writer

QUOTATION	PARAPHRASE OR SUMMARIZE
There is something uneasy in the Los Angeles air this afternoon, some unnatural stillness, some tension. What it means is that tonight a Santa Ana will begin to blow, a hot wind from the northeast whining down through the Cajon and San Gorgonio Passes, blowing up sand storms out along Route 66, drying the hills and the nerves to flash point. For a few days now we will see smoke back in the canyons, and hear sirens in the night. I have neither heard nor read that a Santa Ana is due, but I know it, and almost everyone I have seen today knows it too. We know it because we feel it. The baby frets. The maid sulks. I rekindle a waning argument with the telephone company, then cut my losses and lie down, given over to whatever it is in the air. To live with the Santa Ana is to accept, consciously or unconsciously, a deeply mechanistic view of human behavior.	The winds are creepy. They bring sand storms and cause fires. People know they're coming without being told because babies and maids act strange. The speaker picks a fight and then gives up. The Santa Ana winds make us aware that human behavior can be explained in terms of physical causes and processes.
I recall being told, when I first moved to Los Angeles and was living on an isolated beach, that the Indians would throw themselves into the sea when the bad wind blew. I could see why. The Pacific turned ominously glossy during a Santa Ana period, and one woke in the night troubled not only by the peacocks screaming in the olive trees but by the eerie absence of surf. The heat was surreal. The sky had a yellow cast, the kind of light sometimes called "earthquake weather." My only neighbor would not come out of her house for days, and there were no lights at night, and her husband roamed the place with a machete. One day he would tell me that he had heard a trespasser, the next a rattlesnake.	Didion talks about her early experiences with the winds, plus the folklore about them. She mentions things that seem weird — peacocks screeching and a very quiet ocean. She says her neighbors are strange too; one stays indoors, and the other walks around with a big knife.

RHETORICAL STRATEGY OR STYLE ELEMENT	EFFECT OR FUNCTION
Personification: the wind whines	Giving the wind a human quality makes it even more threatening.
Cumulative sentence	She makes her point by accumulating details about what it means that the Santa Ana is beginning to blow.
Two short sentences: "The baby frets. The maid sulks."	Those simple sentences reduce human behavior to irrefutable evidence. We can't argue with what we see so clearly.
"rekindle"	Though she's talking about restarting an argument with the phone company, the word makes us think of starting a fire, like the wind does up in the hills.
Subordinate clause in the middle of that first sentence: "when I first moved to Los Angeles and was living on an isolated beach."	The clause accentuates Didion's isolation and because it's so long almost makes her experience more important than that of the Indians who threw themselves into the ocean.
"peacocks screaming in the olive trees"	Kind of an upside-down image. Peacocks are usually regal and elegant; these are screaming. Also olive trees are associated with peace (the olive branch). Supports the idea that the Santa Ana turns everything upside down.
Compound sentence: My only neighbor would not come out of her house for days, and there were no lights at night, and her husband roamed the place with a machete.	"And" as the coordinating conjunction makes the wife hiding and the husband with the machete equally important.
"machete"	"Machete" is associated with revolutions in banana republics, vigilantes. Suggests danger.

QUOTATION	PARAPHRASE OR SUMMARIZE
"On nights like that," Raymond Chandler once wrote about the Santa Ana, "every booze party ends in a fight. Meek little wives feel the edge of the carving knife and study their husbands' necks. Anything can happen." That was the kind of wind it was. I did not know then that there was any basis for the effect it had on all of us, but it turns out to be another of those cases in which science bears out folk wisdom.	Didion quotes a writer who describes the effects of the wind as causing women to want to kill their husbands. She says that folklore sometimes has a basis in science.
The Santa Ana, which is named for one of the canyons it rushes through, is a *foehn* wind, like the *foehn* of Austria and Switzerland and the *hamsin* of Israel. . . . A few years ago an Israeli physicist discovered that not only during such winds, but for the ten or twelve hours which precede them, the air carries an unusually high ratio of positive to negative ions.	This section gives scientific facts about the Santa Ana wind, including its generic name, *foehn*. Didion names other winds like it in other parts of the world, but says the *foehn* has its own characteristics. She names some of the effects the *foehn* has on people in various places.

Raymond Chandler, to facts, even to some scientific data. Collecting these bits of information from the text and considering their impression on you prepares you to answer the following questions about Didion's style.

- What effect is she striving for?
- How does she create that effect?
- How does the effect serve the purpose of her writing?

From Close Reading to Analysis

No matter which technique you choose, as you interact with the text you should keep in mind that you're not only identifying techniques and strategies, but also analyzing their effect — you're moving from close reading to analysis. As you read the Didion passage, you probably got a feel for its mood. But how is that mood created? You probably noticed the anxiety-related words in the first paragraph: "uneasy," "unnatural," "tension," "flash point." There is an echo in the second paragraph: the ocean is "ominously glossy." That sense of foreboding imbues even the personal anecdote: a neighbor with a "machete," fear of a "trespasser," hints of a "rattlesnake." Didion uses the word "rekindle" to describe her effort to restart an ongoing argument with the phone company; it serves to remind us of the brush fires that so often threaten

RHETORICAL STRATEGY OR STYLE ELEMENT	EFFECT OR FUNCTION
Allusion to Raymond Chandler	Chandler, who wrote crime fiction, was known for his hard-boiled style and cynical views. The allusion to Chandler helps create the ominous tone.
Complex sentence: "There are a number of persistent malevolent winds, perhaps the best known of which are the *mistral* of France and the Mediterranean *sirocco*, but a *foehn* wind has distinct characteristics: it occurs on the leeward slope of a mountain range and, although the air begins as a cold mass, it is warmed as it comes down the mountain and appears finally as a hot dry wind."	The details accumulate, ending in "hot dry wind," to create a picture of the "persistent malevolent winds."

Southern California. Of course, if you've read other work by Joan Didion you may recognize that foreboding as a hallmark of her style. In either case, you can begin to see how Didion creates an unsettled mood through her word choice, especially in the first two paragraphs.

The passage's syntax also has a role. The second sentence in the first paragraph is long, a cumulative sentence that gathers details (and steam) as it describes the path of the Santa Ana wind and its destination in "flash point." Again, those Southern California brush fires come to mind. The sentence stands, too, in contrast to the short sentences later in the paragraph, simple declarative sentences that observe without comment the behavior that precedes the Santa Ana winds. Didion notes that she has "neither heard nor read that a Santa Ana is due"; nevertheless, the evidence is irrefutable: "The baby frets. The maid sulks."

The third paragraph is different even though it begins in the anxiety-laden mood of the first two, with its quotation from crime fiction writer Raymond Chandler. Though he is a fiction writer, Chandler is nevertheless an authority on both crime and Los Angeles. The quotation helps Didion transition to showing that sometimes "science bears out folk wisdom." What follows are at least seven examples of data — including the names and characteristics of various winds; the effects of the winds on schoolchildren, personal health, and criminals; and the changes in the atmosphere described in terms of positive and negative ions. This scientific language contrasts with the moodiness of the previous paragraphs. Notice the complex sentence that begins by noting a "number of persistent malevolent winds." Didion provides a couple of examples, foregrounding the *foehn*. The second independent clause provides the details of that wind, ending with its impact at the bottom of the mountain as a "hot dry wind."

So let's go back to those three key questions:

- What effect is Didion striving for?
- How does she create that effect?
- How does the effect serve the purpose of her writing?

For the first question, we might say that she is trying to both re-create the effect of the Santa Ana winds and explain the effect scientifically. For the second, we might say that she does this by simulating the feeling of anxiety that precedes the Santa Ana winds at the same time that she offers scientific facts and figures. The mood of foreboding, the tone of barely subdued fear and anger, and the language of violence and natural disaster are juxtaposed with the essay's pseudo-scientific information. For the third question, we could agree that her purpose is to show that some human behavior is mechanistic, meaning it is less a matter of choice than a direct result of outside forces. We might go even further to say that Didion wants to scare us a bit: we sometimes can't help the way we behave. But it's not our fault. Maybe it's a full moon. Maybe a storm is brewing. Or maybe it's the Santa Ana winds.

• ACTIVITY •

Read this speech in which Tecumseh, a Shawnee leader, exhorts the Osages to come together with other tribes to fight the white colonists' encroachment on their lands in the Midwest. Try one of the techniques you have learned for talking with the text. Then answer these questions: What effect is Tecumseh striving for? How does he create that effect? How does the effect serve the purpose of his speech? Develop a thesis statement and an outline for an essay in which you analyze the way Tecumseh's style helps him achieve his purpose.

Address to the Osages
TECUMSEH

Brothers — We all belong to one family, we are all children of the Great Spirit; we walk in the same path; slake our thirst at the same spring; and now affairs of the greatest concern lead us to smoke the pipe around the same council fire!

Brothers — We are friends; we must assist each other to bear our burdens. The blood of many of our fathers and brothers has run like water on the ground, to satisfy the avarice of the white men. We, ourselves, are threatened with a great evil; nothing will pacify them but the destruction of all the red men.

Brothers — When the white men first set foot on our grounds, they were hungry; they had no place on which to spread their blankets, or to kindle their fires. They were feeble, they could do nothing for themselves. Our fathers commiserated their distress, and shared with them whatever the Great Spirit had given his red children. They gave them food when hungry, medicine when sick, spread skins for them to sleep on, and gave them grounds, that they might hunt and raise corn. Brothers, the white people are like poisonous serpents; when chilled, they are feeble and harmless, but invigorate them with warmth, and they sting their benefactors to death.

The white people came among us feeble: and now we have made them strong, they wish to kill us, or drive us back, as they would wolves and panthers.

Brothers — The white men are not friends to the Indians; at first they only asked for land sufficient for a wigwam, now, nothing will satisfy them but the whole of our hunting grounds, from the rising to the setting sun.

Brothers — The white men want more than our hunting grounds — they wish to kill our warriors; they would even kill our old men, women, and little ones.

Brothers — Many winters ago, there was no land — the sun did not rise and set: all was darkness. The Great Spirit made all things. He gave the white people a home beyond the great waters. He supplied these grounds with game, and gave them to his red children, and he gave them strength and courage to defend them.

Brothers — My people wish for peace, the red men all wish for peace: but where the white people are, there is no peace for them, except it be in the bosom of our mother.

Brothers — The white men despise and cheat the Indians; they abuse and insult them; they do not think the red men sufficiently good to live.

The red men have borne many and great injuries; they ought to suffer them no longer. My people will not; they are determined on vengeance; they have taken up the tomahawk; they will make it fat with blood — they will drink the blood of the white people.

Brothers — My people are brave and numerous, but the white people are too strong for them alone. I wish you to take up the tomahawk with them. If we all unite, we will cause the rivers to stain the great waters with their blood.

Brothers — If you do not unite with us, they will first destroy us, and then you will fall an easy prey to them. They have destroyed many nations of red men, because they were not united, because they were not friends to each other.

Brothers — The white people send runners amongst us; they wish to make us enemies, that they may sweep over, and desolate our hunting grounds, like devastating winds, or rushing waters.

Brothers — Our Great Father, over the great waters, is angry with the white people, our enemies. He will send his brave warriors against them; he will send us rifles, and whatever else we want — he is our friend, and we are his children.

Brothers — Who are the white people that we should fear them? They cannot run fast, and are good marks to shoot at; they are only men; our fathers have killed many of them; we are not squaws, and we will stain the earth red with their blood.

Brothers — The Great Spirit is angry with our enemies — he speaks in thunder, and the earth swallows up villages, and drinks up the Mississippi. The great waters will cover their low-lands, their corn cannot grow, and the Great Spirit will sweep those who escape to the hills, from the earth with his terrible breath.

Brothers — We must be united; we must smoke the same pipe; we must fight each other's battles; an[d] more than all, we must love the Great Spirit; he is for us; he will destroy our enemies, and make all his red children happy.

(1811)

Writing a Close-Analysis Essay

We're going to look now at steps you can take to write a close-analysis essay. Good writing comes from careful reading, so the first steps will always be to read, reread, ask questions, and either annotate or create a graphic organizer. We will work here with a 1947 letter from comedian and film star Groucho Marx. Marx performed with his brothers Zeppo, Chico, and Harpo — they were known as the Marx Brothers. The letter is a part of his correspondence with the film production company Warner Bros., which had concerns about an upcoming Marx Brothers film entitled *A Night in Casablanca*; the company worried that the title was too similar to the title of its 1942 film *Casablanca*. Read the letter carefully, and then read it again. Ask some questions, and either annotate the letter or make a graphic organizer. Pay close attention to the diction and syntax choices Marx makes and how they help him achieve his purpose.

Dear Warner Brothers,

Apparently there is more than one way of conquering a city and holding it as your own. For example, up to the time that we contemplated making a picture, I had no idea that the city of Casablanca[1] belonged exclusively to Warner Brothers. However, it was only a few days after our announcement appeared that

---

[1] *Casablanca* is the title of a romantic — and perennially popular — film released by Warner Bros. in 1942 that won the Academy Award for Best Picture. It starred Humphrey Bogart and Ingrid Bergman. — Eds.

we received a long, ominous legal document warning us not to use the name "Casablanca."

It seems that in 1471, Ferdinand Balboa Warner, your great-great-grandfather, while looking for a shortcut to the city of Burbank, had stumbled on the shores of Africa and, raising his alpenstock,[2] which he later turned in for a hundred shares of common,[3] named it Casablanca.

I just can't understand your attitude. Even if you plan on releasing your picture, I am sure that the average movie fan could learn in time to distinguish between Ingrid Bergman[4] and Harpo.[5] I don't know whether I could, but I certainly would like to try.

You claim you own Casablanca and that no one else can use that name without your permission. What about "Warner Brothers"? Do you own that too? You probably have the right to use the name Warner, but what about the name Brothers? Professionally, we were brothers long before you were. We were touring the sticks as the Marx Brothers when Vitaphone[6] was still a gleam in the inventor's eye, and even before us there had been other brothers — the Smith Brothers; the Brothers Karamazov; Dan Brouthers, an outfielder with Detroit; and "Brother, Can You Spare a Dime?" (This was originally "Brothers, Can You Spare a Dime?" but this was spreading a dime pretty thin, so they threw out one brother, gave all the money to the other one, and whittled it down to "Brother, Can You Spare a Dime?")

Now Jack, how about you? Do you maintain that yours is an original name?   5
Well it's not. It was used long before you were born. Offhand, I can think of two Jacks — there was Jack of "Jack and the Beanstalk," and Jack the Ripper, who cut quite a figure in his day.

As for you, Harry, you probably sign your checks sure in the belief that you are the first Harry of all time and that all other Harrys are impostors. Offhand I can think of two Harrys that preceded you. There was Lighthorse Harry of Revolutionary fame and a Harry Appelbaum who lived on the corner of 93rd Street and Lexington Avenue. Unfortunately, Appelbaum wasn't too well-known. The last I heard of him, he was selling neckties at Weber and Heilbroner; but I'll never forget his mother, she made the best apple strudel in Yorkville.

Now about the Burbank studio.[7] I believe this is what you brothers call your place. Old man Burbank is gone. Perhaps you remember him. He was a great man

---

[2]Walking stick. — Eds.
[3]Common stock in a company. — Eds.
[4]The beautiful female star of *Casablanca*. — Eds.
[5]Harpo was Groucho's brother and part of the Marx Brothers; he wore a red, curly-haired wig and did not speak, communicating instead by blowing a horn or whistling. — Eds.
[6]Vitaphone was the process developed by Warner Bros. for adding sound to film. — Eds.
[7]Movie production studios located in Burbank, California, a city close to Los Angeles where many movie production companies have their headquarters. Although there is a Luther Burbank Middle School in Burbank, the city is not named after the botanist Luther Burbank — who invented the Idaho potato — but after a dentist named David Burbank, who was originally from Maine. *Casablanca* was filmed at the Burbank studio. — Eds.

in a garden. He was the wizard who crossed all those fruits and vegetables until he had the poor plants in such confused and jittery condition that they could never decide whether to enter the dining room on the meat platter or the dessert dish.

This is pure conjecture, of course, but who knows — perhaps Burbank's survivors aren't too happy with the fact that a plant that grinds out pictures on a quota settled in their town, appropriated Burbank's name and uses it as a front for their films. It is even possible that the Burbank family is prouder of the potato produced by the old man than they are of the fact that your studio emerged "Casablanca" or even "Gold Diggers of 1931."

This all seems to add up to a pretty bitter tirade, but I assure you it's not meant to. I love Warners. Some of my best friends are Warner Brothers. It is even possible that I am doing you an injustice and that you, yourselves, know nothing about this dog-in-the-Wanger[8] attitude. It wouldn't surprise me at all to discover that the heads of your legal department are unaware of this absurd dispute, for I am acquainted with many of them and they are fine fellows with curly black hair, double-breasted suits and a love of their fellow man that out-Saroyans Saroyan.[9]

I have a hunch that this attempt to prevent us from using the title is the brain-   10
child of some ferret-faced shyster, serving a brief apprenticeship in your legal department. I know the type well — hot out of law school, hungry for success and too ambitious to follow the natural laws of promotion. This bar sinister probably needled your attorneys, most of whom are fine fellows with curly black hair, double-breasted suits, etc., into attempting to enjoin us. Well, he won't get away with it! We'll fight him to the highest court! No pasty-faced legal adventurer is going to cause bad blood between the Warners and the Marxes. We are all brothers under the skin, and we'll remain friends till the last reel of *A Night in Casablanca* goes tumbling over the spool.

Sincerely,

Groucho Marx

(1947)

There is some doubt about whether Warner Bros. had actually objected to the title of the Marx Brothers film; but there's little doubt that this letter was primarily a publicity stunt by Groucho. In any case, it is a great example of the persuasive powers of humor. Groucho's style was instantly recognizable to fans of popular culture in the first half of the twentieth century. Now let's ask some questions to help determine the purpose of Marx's letter, what makes his style so distinctive, and how this style helps him achieve his purpose.

---

[8]A double play on words. Dog-in-the-Manger is one of Aesop's fables, about a dog that didn't eat the grain in the manger but wouldn't let the other animals eat it either. Walter Wanger was a film producer who produced the first Marx Brothers talkie. — Eds.
[9]A reference to William Saroyan, a writer and dramatist whose work was known for its optimism in the face of hardship. — Eds.

1. Why does Marx begin with "Apparently"?
2. Why does he say he had no idea that the city of Casablanca belonged to Warner Bros. (par. 1)?
3. What is the effect of Groucho's short history of Casablanca (par. 2)?
4. Would it really be difficult to distinguish between Ingrid Bergman and Harpo Marx (par. 3)?
5. Why does Marx offer so many examples of "Brothers" (par. 4)?
6. What is the effect of the parenthetical story about "Brother, Can You Spare a Dime" (par. 4)?
7. Why does Marx bring up Luther Burbank's experiments with fruits and vegetables (par. 7)?
8. Why does Marx qualify his statement that he loves Warners with "Some of my best friends are Warner Brothers" (par. 9)?
9. Why does Marx suggest that the source of Warner Bros.' concerns about his film is an ambitious young lawyer, referring to him as a "pasty-faced legal adventurer" (par. 10)?

Developing a Thesis Statement

Answering these questions or others like them may help you get some ideas for a thesis statement, the first step in writing a close-analysis essay. You may change it as you go along, but having an idea about the argument you want to make will help you stay focused. As we mentioned, Groucho Marx uses humor to create his argument; we might even call this letter a kind of **satire** — the use of sarcasm or irony to criticize — so let's think first about Marx's purpose in writing the letter and why he might have chosen to use humor. Even if this letter was a publicity stunt, we can imagine that Marx wanted to highlight the differences between his film and the romantic adventure *Casablanca* to show Warner Bros. that it had little to fear from the Marx Brothers film *A Night in Casablanca*. It's also likely that Marx wanted to comment on the hot air that sometimes emerges from big corporations and their lawyers — especially, in this case, the enormous and powerful movie studio Warner Bros. But he chooses not to take these goals on directly.

As you think about a thesis statement, you will want to be careful that your thesis isn't too broad or just a summary:

Groucho Marx uses humor to defend his movie.

And you will also want to make sure that it's not too narrow or just your personal opinion:

Groucho Marx's letter to Warner Bros. is rude and disrespectful.

Most important, a close-analysis essay must focus on the choices writers make to help them achieve their purpose. Here's a thesis statement that might work:

Rather than take on Warner Bros. directly, Groucho Marx jabs and feints until the studio couldn't possibly take its own claim seriously.

A Sample Close-Analysis Essay

Once you have a working thesis statement (remember, you may change it as you plan and write), think about the ways you will support it. Your essay may look closely at different style elements; it may focus on the way the writer organizes the paragraphs and develops his or her argument; it may be a combination of both. It is important to cite the text, weaving quotes into your essay and explaining each example with at least two sentences of analysis or commentary. Take a look at this sample essay:

Like a boxer who weighs less than his opponent, Groucho Marx circles the great movie moguls — the Warner Bros. — baiting them, drawing them out, blinding them with his fancy footwork in his response to a letter from the studio forbidding the Marx Brothers from using the word "Casablanca" in the title of their upcoming film, *A Night in Casablanca*. Rather than take Warner Bros. on directly, Groucho Marx jabs and feints — humorously, of course — until Warner Bros. couldn't possibly take its own claim seriously.

Marx opens the letter with an intentional misunderstanding, the first way he highlights the absurdity of Warner Bros.' threat of legal action. He claims not to have understood that Warner Bros. had conquered the city of Casablanca until he received their "long, ominous legal document." It's not a big leap from there for Marx to imagine Ferdinand Balboa Warner, conveniently named after a real explorer, claiming the city of Casablanca by "raising his alpenstock." The image conjures up scenes from the lavish epics of early Hollywood, casting Warner as Moses in Cecil B. DeMille's *The Ten Commandments*. Marx extends his misunderstanding by imagining that the studio's main worry might be the trouble that the "average movie fan" will have in distinguishing Ingrid Bergman from Harpo Marx. Humbly, Marx says he "certainly would like to try." This slightly salacious offer reinforces the silliness of Warner Bros.' worries: Bergman was beautiful, blonde and dignified; Harpo Marx was a short, bewigged, mute clown.

Marx creates a sense of familiarity, which serves his purpose by reminding his audience — Warner Bros. and their legal team — that they're all in the same boat, moviemakers with similar cultural knowledge, even shared heritage. Using classic Marx Brothers absurdist humor Groucho claims that he and his brothers — the Marx Brothers — have been around longer than Harry and Jack have and that they might have more right to use the word "Brothers" in their name. He piles on a list of other sets of brothers: "the Smith Brothers" (of cough drop fame), "the Brothers Karamazov" (title of a nineteenth-century Russian novel), a baseball player with the last name of "Brouthers." He even riffs a bit on the song "Brother, Can You Spare a Dime?" He gets even more personal, addressing each Warner brother by name: "Now

Jack, how about you?", "As for you, Harry," and throws in some well-known examples of Harrys and Jacks, just for good measure. Unwilling to stop, Marx even questions the right of Warner Bros. to name its workplace "Burbank studio," suggesting — "pure conjecture, of course" — that Luther Burbank's survivors might not be happy to be associated with the Warner Bros.' body of work. One can imagine the effect of Marx's onslaught of examples on the movie studio's large and serious legal team, who also come under fire.

Content to let the logic of his defense rest, Marx gives Warner Bros.' legal team a break, suggesting that the letter was the brainchild of a young lawyer "hot out of law school, hungry for success and too ambitious to follow the natural laws of promotion." He claims sympathy and admiration for the heads of the legal department, "fine fellows with curly black hair, double-breasted suits and a love of their fellow man," a formulation he uses twice — the second time slightly truncated and ending in "etc." Effortlessly, Marx calls up a vision of mindless automatons, led astray by the "pasty-faced legal adventurer" whom Marx calls responsible for the possible "bad blood between the Warners and the Marxes." Here he reinforces that bond between moviemaking families — "brothers under the skin" — and highlights once more the absurdity of imagining that the reputation or box office receipts of *Casablanca*, the 1942 Academy Award winner for Best Picture, will be sullied by a film made by the likes of Groucho and his brothers.

In this hilarious letter — and in the two letters that followed — Groucho Marx underscored the ridiculousness of comparing the classic *Casablanca* with the silliness of a Marx Brothers film in very much the style of his own films. Fast, clever, not especially logical, but certainly tireless, Marx wore out his bigger opponent. It took two more letters from Marx to get Warner Bros. off his back: each one outlined plots that were so far-fetched as to be nearly incomprehensible, and Warner Bros. finally gave up.

• ACTIVITY •

Read the following essay written by Christopher Morley in 1920. Annotate it or create a graphic organizer. Generate some questions about its style. Develop a thesis statement, and write an essay in which you analyze the ways that the style of the essay helps Morley achieve his purpose.

On Laziness
CHRISTOPHER MORLEY

Today we rather intended to write an essay on Laziness, but were too indolent to do so.

The sort of thing we had in mind to write would have been exceedingly persuasive. We intended to discourse a little in favour of a greater appreciation of Indolence as a benign factor in human affairs.

It is our observation that every time we get into trouble it is due to not having been lazy enough. Unhappily, we were born with a certain fund of energy. We have been hustling about for a number of years now, and it doesn't seem to get us anything but tribulation. Henceforward we are going to make a determined effort to be more languid and demure. It is the bustling man who always gets put on committees, who is asked to solve the problems of other people and neglect his own.

The man who is really, thoroughly, and philosophically slothful is the only thoroughly happy man. It is the happy man who benefits the world. The conclusion is inescapable.

We remember a saying about the meek inheriting the earth. The truly meek man is the lazy man. He is too modest to believe that any ferment and hubbub of his can ameliorate the earth or assuage the perplexities of humanity.

O. Henry said once that one should be careful to distinguish laziness from dignified repose. Alas, that was a mere quibble. Laziness is always dignified, it is always reposeful. Philosophical laziness, we mean. The kind of laziness that is based upon a carefully reasoned analysis of experience. Acquired laziness. We have no respect for those who were born lazy; it is like being born a millionaire: they cannot appreciate their bliss. It is the man who has hammered his laziness out of the stubborn material of life for whom we chant praise and allelulia.

The laziest man we know — we do not like to mention his name, as the brutal world does not yet recognize sloth at its community value — is one of the greatest poets in this country; one of the keenest satirists; one of the most rectilinear thinkers. He began life in the customary hustling way. He was always too busy to enjoy himself. He became surrounded by eager people who came to him to solve their problems. "It's a queer thing," he said sadly; "no one ever comes to me asking for help in solving my problems." Finally the light broke upon him. He stopped answering letters, buying lunches for casual friends and visitors from out of town, he stopped lending money to old college pals and frittering his time away on all the useless minor matters that pester the good-natured. He sat down in a secluded cafe with his cheek against a seidel of dark beer and began to caress the universe with his intellect.

The most damning argument against the Germans is that they were not lazy enough. In the middle of Europe, a thoroughly disillusioned, indolent, and delightful old continent, the Germans were a dangerous mass of energy and bumptious push. If the Germans had been as lazy, as indifferent, and as righteously laissez-fairish as their neighbours the world would have been spared a great deal.

People respect laziness. If you once get a reputation for complete, immovable, and reckless indolence the world will leave you to your own thoughts, which are generally rather interesting.

Doctor Johnson, who was one of the world's great philosophers, was lazy. [10] Only yesterday our friend the Caliph showed us an extraordinarily interesting thing. It was a little leather-bound notebook in which Boswell jotted down memoranda of his talks with the old doctor.[1] These notes he afterward worked up into the immortal Biography. And lo and behold, what was the very first entry in this treasured little relic?

> Doctor Johnson told me in going to Ilam from Ashbourne, 22 September, 1777, that the way the plan of his Dictionary came to be addressed to Lord Chesterfield was this: he had neglected to write it by the time appointed. Dodsley suggested a desire to have it addressed to Lord C. Mr. J. laid hold of this as an excuse for delay, that it might be better done perhaps, and let Dodsley have his desire. Mr. Johnson said to his friend, Doctor Bathurst: "Now if any good comes of my addressing to Lord Chesterfield it will be ascribed to deep policy and address, when, in fact, it was only a casual excuse for laziness."

Thus we see that it was sheer laziness that led to the greatest triumph of Doctor Johnson's life, the noble and memorable letter to Chesterfield in 1775.

Mind your business is a good counsel; but mind your idleness also. It's a tragic thing to make a business of your mind. Save your mind to amuse yourself with.

The lazy man does not stand in the way of progress. When he sees progress roaring down upon him he steps nimbly out of the way. The lazy man doesn't (in the vulgar phrase) pass the buck. He lets the buck pass him. We have always secretly envied our lazy friends. Now we are going to join them. We have burned our boats or our bridges or whatever it is that one burns on the eve of a momentous decision.

Writing on this congenial topic has roused us up to quite a pitch of enthusiasm and energy.

(1920)

Close Reading Fiction

You have probably practiced close reading fiction and poetry in your English classes by looking at how the details in poems, short stories, and novels help convey emotion, develop an idea, or make a statement. The choices writers make serve their purpose, and your close observation of those choices helps you understand and analyze that purpose. Writers of fiction and nonfiction — and even poetry — make many of the same stylistic choices: those about diction and syntax, certainly. Fiction

---

[1]Samuel Johnson (1709–1784) was the British scholar who wrote *A Dictionary of the English Language.* James Boswell wrote his famous biography. — Eds.

writers and poets may be more precise, or more imaginative, using **figurative language, imagery,** tone, and mood to serve their purpose.

Let's take a look at the very short story "Girl," by Jamaica Kincaid.

Girl

JAMAICA KINCAID

Wash the white clothes on Monday and put them on the stone heap; wash the color clothes on Tuesday and put them on the clothesline to dry; don't walk barehead in the hot sun; cook pumpkin fritters in very hot sweet oil; soak your little cloths right after you take them off; when buying cotton to make yourself a nice blouse, be sure that it doesn't have gum on it, because that way it won't hold up well after a wash; soak salt fish overnight before you cook it; is it true that you sing benna in Sunday school?; always eat your food in such a way that it won't turn someone else's stomach; on Sundays try to walk like a lady and not like the slut you are so bent on becoming; don't sing benna in Sunday school; you mustn't speak to wharf-rat boys, not even to give directions; don't eat fruits on the street — flies will follow you; *but I don't sing benna on Sundays at all and never in Sunday school*; this is how to sew on a button; this is how to make a buttonhole for the button you have just sewed on; this is how to hem a dress when you see the hem coming down and so to prevent yourself from looking like the slut I know you are so bent on becoming; this is how you iron your father's khaki shirt so that it doesn't have a crease; this is how you iron your father's khaki pants so that they don't have a crease; this is how you grow okra — far from the house, because okra tree harbors red ants; when you are growing dasheen, make sure it gets plenty of water or else it makes your throat itch when you are eating it; this is how you sweep a corner; this is how you sweep a whole house; this is how you sweep a yard; this is how you smile to someone you don't like too much; this is how you smile to someone you don't like at all; this is how you smile to someone you like completely; this is how you set a table for tea; this is how you set a table for dinner; this is how you set a table for dinner with an important guest; this is how you set a table for lunch; this is how you set a table for breakfast; this is how to behave in the presence of men who don't know you very well, and this way they won't recognize immediately the slut I have warned you against becoming; be sure to wash every day, even if it is with your own spit; don't squat down to play marbles — you are not a boy, you know; don't pick people's flowers — you might catch something; don't throw stones at blackbirds, because it might not be a blackbird at all; this is how to make a bread pudding; this is how to make doukona; this is how to make pepper pot; this is how to make a good medicine for a cold; this is how to make a good medicine to throw away a child before it even becomes a child; this is how to catch a fish; this is how to throw back a fish you don't like, and that way something bad won't fall on you; this is how to bully a man; this is how a man bullies you; this is how to love a man, and if this doesn't work there are other ways, and if they don't work don't feel too bad about giving up; this is how to spit up in the air if you feel like it, and this is how to move quick so that it doesn't fall on you; this is how to make ends meet; always squeeze bread to make sure it's fresh; *but what if the baker won't let me feel the bread?*; you mean to say that after all you are really going to be the kind of woman who the baker won't let near the bread?

(1983)

You probably noticed many of the choices Jamaica Kincaid made in crafting this story and can make some connections between those choices and the purpose of the text. The diction communicates the mother's mixed messages. Many of her rules are crystal clear; the diction is precise and the images of food and clothing are vivid and concrete: ironed khakis, pumpkin fritters fried in very hot sweet oil, bread pudding, the right kind of buttonhole. Some, however, are less clear: how to behave in the presence of men you don't know, how to love a man, how to squeeze the bread to make sure it is fresh. That juxtaposition of the very concrete examples of food, clothing, and etiquette to the less clear examples of morality and behavior are part of the meaning of the story. Can knowing the right ways to behave ensure that you have the respect of the community? That seems to be the mother's hope.

The syntax sends a message as well. The story is one long periodic sentence, its clauses connected almost entirely with semicolons. The only breaks come with the occasional italicized phrase or question from the daughter. The speaker — the mother — barely takes a breath. Does a mother really speak this way or is the story really from the daughter's point of view — the way she hears her mother's hectoring? That ambiguity is part of the meaning of the story: the way the daughter hears her mother, her tough love, her contradictory instructions, her suspicions, tells us a great deal about what it means to be both a mother and a daughter in a small community with traditional values. The vivid diction and breathless syntax create a mood and tone in "Girl" that highlight the love-laced anxiety that is at the heart of mother-daughter relationships the world over.

• ACTIVITY •

Look at this passage from the novel *All the King's Men*, a description of a college football game in which the star quarterback, Tom, happens to be the son of the novel's protagonist, politician Willie Stark. What choices does author Robert Penn Warren make that render this passage more than just a description of a football game? How does it help develop the character of Willie Stark as well as the character of the narrator?

from *All the King's Men*
ROBERT PENN WARREN

Which was:
An oblong field where white lines mathematically gridded the turf which was arsenical green under the light from the great batteries of floodlamps fixed

high on the parapet of the massive arena. Above the field the swollen palpitating tangle of light frayed and thinned out into hot darkness, but the thirty thousand pairs of eyes hanging on the inner slopes of the arena did not look up into the dark but stared down into the pit of light, where men in red silky-glittering shorts and gold helmets hurled themselves against men in blue silky-glittering shorts and gold helmets and spilled and tumbled on the bright arsenical-green turf like spilled dolls, and a whistle sliced chillingly through the thick air like that scimitar through a sofa cushion.

Which was:

The band blaring, the roaring like the sea, the screams like agony, the silence, then one woman-scream, silver and soprano, spangling the silence like the cry of a lost soul, and the roar again so that the hot air seemed to heave. For out of the shock and tangle and glitter on the green a red fragment had exploded outward, flung off from the mass tangentially to spin across the green, turn and wheel and race, yet slow in the out-of-timeness of the moment, under the awful responsibility of the roar.

Which was:

A man pounding me on the back and screaming — a man with a heavy face and coarse dark hair hanging over his forehead — screaming, "That's my boy! That's Tom — Tom — Tom! That's him — and he's won — they won't have a time for a touchdown now — he's won — his first varsity game and it's Tom won — it's my boy!" And the man pounded me on the back and grappled me to him with both arms, powerful arms, and hugged me like his brother, his true love, his son, while tears came into his eyes and tears and sweat ran down the heavy cheeks, and he screamed, "He's my boy — and there's not any like him — he'll be All American — and Lucy wants me to stop him playing — my wife wants him to stop — says it's ruining him — ruining him, hell — he'll be All American — boy, did you see him — fast — fast — he's a fast son-of-a-bitch! Ain't he, ain't he?"

(1946)

5

Close Reading Poetry

Poetry compresses ideas and emotions, so poets generally use more literary techniques than novelists do. In addition to choices in diction, detail, figurative language, and imagery, poets use **rhyme, meter, form, sound**, and special **poetic syntax** to serve their purpose. Consider the choices Paulette Jiles makes in her poem "Paper Matches."

Paper Matches
PAULETTE JILES

My aunts washed dishes while the uncles
squirted each other on the lawn with

garden hoses. Why are we in here,
I said, and they are out there?
    That's the way it is,   5
    said Aunt Hetty, the shriveled-up one.

    I have the rages that small animals have,
being small, being animal.
    Written on me was a message,
"At Your Service,"   10
like a book of paper matches.
One by one we were taken out
and struck.
    We come bearing supper,
our heads on fire.   15

(1988)

Jiles sets the scene with a description of the aunts washing dishes and the uncles fooling around outdoors. In the first line, Jiles uses **enjambment**, a form of poetic syntax in which a line ends without a pause and must continue to the next line to complete its meaning. The speaker's aunts and uncles appear in the indented first line, but the uncles break free in line 2, pushing out toward the left margin. Jiles omits quotation marks or a question mark in the short conversation between the speaker and her aunt in lines 3–6, even burying the "I said" in the middle of the speaker's question in lines 3–4. Aunt Hetty's reply, also without quotation marks, is as brief and as defeated as the description of Aunt Hetty herself — "the shriveled-up one" (l. 6). The omitted punctuation reinforces the mousey subservience and threadbare quality of the speaker and her aunts; their conversation is in undertones, afraid to be noticed. The speaker has a small burst of anger and rebellion, but her rage is the rage of "small animals" — futile. The poem has a shift in line 9, as the speaker subsides into passivity, signaled by the use of the passive voice: the message is "written on" her. The simile in line 11 compares the women to a book of paper matches — used up one by one. The passive voice continues as the women, now "paper matches," are "taken out / and struck" (ll. 12–13). There is a suggestion of physical abuse in the word "struck" as well. The last two lines of the poem paint a vivid and provocative image: women "bearing supper," their "heads on fire." In spite of their lowly stature, there is something fierce and angry about the women in that image. You can see the way Jiles's diction and syntax choices extend the poem's feminist theme and agenda.

• ACTIVITY •

Look at this well-known poem by Langston Hughes and consider the diction and syntax choices he makes. How does he use line length, punctuation, and word choice to achieve maximum effect in eleven lines?

Harlem
LANGSTON HUGHES

What happens to a dream deferred?

Does it dry up
like a raisin in the sun?
Or fester like a sore —
And then run?   5
Does it stink like rotten meat?
Or crust and sugar over —
like a syrupy sweet?

Maybe it just sags
like a heavy load.   10

Or does it explode?

(1951)

Close Reading Visual Texts

Many of the same tools of rhetorical analysis and close reading that we have practiced on written texts are also useful for detecting how visual texts convey their messages. These tools work whether the visual texts are advertisements, photos, fine art, or political cartoons. Let's start by looking at an ad for the Dodge Durango.

The rhetorical triangle still applies: what are the relationships among the text's subject (a powerful sport utility vehicle), its audience (the potential SUV buyer), and the speaker (in this case, Dodge and the advertising agency it hired to create the ad)? The advertisement appeals to ethos in the text at the top left: it banks on associations to Dodge cars and trucks — power, dependability, toughness. Its appeals to pathos play on preconceptions about food: a cheeseburger is real food, tofu is somehow fake; by way of analogy, cheeseburgers are what you want to eat, tofu is what you're supposed to eat; a big powerful truck is what you really want, a small fuel-efficient car is what you are supposed to have. As for logos, the Durango is affordable; it makes sense to own one. Why not enjoy life, drive an affordable SUV, and eat big juicy cheeseburgers?

When we analyze a visual text, we still look at the words, both individually and in the way they are placed on the page. Look at the text at the top left part of the ad.

DODGE DURANGO. This is the most affordable SUV with a V-8. Dodge Durango. With nearly four tons of towing, this baby carries around chunks of those wimpy wanna-bes in its tail pipe.

DODGE DURANGO. This is the most affordable SUV with a V-8. Dodge Durango. With nearly four tons of towing,* this baby carries around chunks of those wimpy wanna-bes in its tail pipe. For more info, call 800-4ADODGE or visit dodge.com

GRAB LIFE BY THE HORNS

DODGE

IT'S A BIG FAT JUICY CHEESEBURGER IN A LAND OF TOFU.
*Depending on model and when properly equipped.

Dodge and Durango are registered trademarks of Chrysler Group LLC.

(See color insert, Image 5.)

Note the aggressive tone. How is that aggressiveness created? It may be the repetition of "Dodge Durango" with its hard consonant sounds; it may be the prepositional phrase announcing that the vehicle can tow four tons. It's a "baby" that carries "chunks" of its competitors in its tail pipe. The use of the colloquialism "baby" contrasts nicely with the image of the car as a predator eating the competition. The owner of a Dodge Durango will be the kind of person whose car is his or her "baby" and who is the leader of the pack, not one "of those wimpy wanna-bes." The Dodge logo — a ram's head — and slogan "Grab life by the horns" appear at the top right of the ad. Both the image and the words play with the connotations of horns: strength, masculinity, and noise. The imperative sentence is a call to action that can be paraphrased as "Don't be a wimp! Enjoy life now!" Finally, the text at the bottom of the ad has yet another message. The large white letters on the dark road are boldly designed, but the message is gentle and even funny. "Big fat juicy cheeseburger" acknowledges our natural desire for pleasures that are not always healthy. But who can resist when the alternative is tofu? The antecedent of *It's* is, of course, the SUV; but the pronoun suggests an understanding, an insider's wink.

We study the images in the text the same way: individually and in terms of composition, or arrangement on the page. For instance, notice that even though the Dodge logo is very aggressive, the photo is less so. In fact, the photo shows a man and a woman in the car, pulling a vintage Airstream motor home, thus suggesting not only a family atmosphere but also good taste, as Airstreams are collectibles. Perhaps it is a pitch to the rising number of women car buyers or to the use of an SUV as a less stodgy replacement for a minivan. Though the front of the Dodge Durango is outsized, a reminder of the power under the hood, the ocean and sky in the background temper the aggressiveness of the looming SUV; it looks like a beautiful day for a cool couple with great taste to be out for a ride.

So what is the advertisement's message? Or are there a few different messages? If you were to write an essay analyzing the "language" of the visual text, you might consider a thesis that argues for the ad's multiple messages. Here's one example:

> The Dodge Durango ad balances aggressiveness with humor; it appeals to men and women with its reminder that life is too short not to enjoy its guilty pleasures.

• ACTIVITY •

Use the following ad, or find one on your own that either appeals to you or provokes you, and analyze it as we have done with the Durango ad.

On Don't Fry Day (and Every Day)

Slip, Slop, Slap & Wrap!

A turtle has a built-in shirt. A hippo's skin secretes oil that acts as a sunscreen. The bumps over a camel's eyes act as a hat. The black rings around a meerkat's eyes are sunglasses.

Slip on a shirt, Slop on sunscreen, Slap on a hat, Wrap on sunglasses, and seek shade between 10 and 4.

Don't Fry Day

EPA United States Environmental Protection Agency

SunWise

US EPA's SunWise Program, American Cancer Society

(See color insert, Image 6.)

• CULMINATING ACTIVITY •

Look carefully at the three documents below. The first is John F. Kennedy's 1961 inaugural address. The second is an article that appeared in January 2011, first on the Web site Daily Beast and then in *Newsweek*. In "Inside Kennedy's Inauguration, 50 Years On," writer Eleanor Clift reports on what intimates of JFK remember from that cold January day. The last document is a photograph of the swearing-in ceremony.

Begin by reading the Kennedy speech and the analysis that follows. As you read the speech, take the time to generate some questions on style. Annotate the speech, or create a graphic organizer, noting passages that stand out, interest you, or even confuse you. Then do the same with the Clift article; read it closely, and generate questions, annotate the article, or create a graphic organizer. Finally, study the photo, and consider the arrangement of the figures in it.

Once you have analyzed all three pieces, develop a thesis statement for an essay that compares and contrasts the styles of the three documents, focusing on how each conveys the legacy of John Fitzgerald Kennedy.

Inaugural Address, January 20, 1961
JOHN F. KENNEDY

Given on a cold January afternoon in 1961, John F. Kennedy's inaugural address was hailed as a return to the tradition of political eloquence.

Vice President Johnson, Mr. Speaker, Mr. Chief Justice, President Eisenhower, Vice President Nixon, President Truman, Reverend Clergy, fellow citizens:

We observe today not a victory of party but a celebration of freedom — symbolizing an end as well as a beginning — signifying renewal as well as change. For I have sworn before you and Almighty God the same solemn oath our forebears prescribed nearly a century and three-quarters ago.

The world is very different now. For man holds in his mortal hands the power to abolish all forms of human poverty and all forms of human life. And yet the same revolutionary beliefs for which our forebears fought are still at issue around the globe — the belief that the rights of man come not from the generosity of the state but from the hand of God.

We dare not forget today that we are the heirs of that first revolution. Let the word go forth from this time and place, to friend and foe alike, that the torch has been passed to a new generation of Americans — born in this century, tempered by war, disciplined by a hard and bitter peace, proud of our ancient heritage — and unwilling to witness or permit the slow undoing of those human rights to which this nation has always been committed, and to which we are committed today at home and around the world.

Let every nation know, whether it wishes us well or ill, that we shall pay any price, bear any burden, meet any hardship, support any friend, oppose any foe to assure the survival and the success of liberty.

This much we pledge — and more.   5

To those old allies whose cultural and spiritual origins we share, we pledge the loyalty of faithful friends. United there is little we cannot do in a host of cooperative ventures. Divided there is little we can do — for we dare not meet a powerful challenge at odds and split asunder.

To those new states whom we welcome to the ranks of the free, we pledge our word that one form of colonial control shall not have passed away merely to be replaced by a far more iron tyranny. We shall not always expect to find them supporting our view. But we shall always hope to find them strongly supporting their own freedom — and to remember that, in the past, those who foolishly sought power by riding the back of the tiger ended up inside.

To those people in the huts and villages of half the globe struggling to break the bonds of mass misery, we pledge our best efforts to help them help themselves, for whatever period is required — not because the communists may be doing it, not because we seek their votes, but because it is right. If a free society cannot help the many who are poor, it cannot save the few who are rich.

To our sister republics south of our border, we offer a special pledge — to convert our good words into good deeds — in a new alliance for progress — to assist free men and free governments in casting off the chains of poverty. But this peaceful revolution of hope cannot become the prey of hostile powers. Let all our neighbors know that we shall join with them to oppose aggression or subversion anywhere in the Americas. And let every other power know that this Hemisphere intends to remain the master of its own house.

To that world assembly of sovereign states, the United Nations, our last best hope in an age where the instruments of war have far outpaced the instruments of peace, we renew our pledge of support — to prevent it from becoming merely a forum for invective — to strengthen its shield of the new and the weak — and to enlarge the area in which its writ may run.

10

Finally, to those nations who would make themselves our adversary, we offer not a pledge but a request: that both sides begin anew the quest for peace, before the dark powers of destruction unleashed by science engulf all humanity in planned or accidental self-destruction.

We dare not tempt them with weakness. For only when our arms are sufficient beyond doubt can we be certain beyond doubt that they will never be employed.

But neither can two great and powerful groups of nations take comfort from our present course — both sides overburdened by the cost of modern weapons, both rightly alarmed by the steady spread of the deadly atom, yet both racing to alter that uncertain balance of terror that stays the hand of mankind's final war.

So let us begin anew — remembering on both sides that civility is not a sign of weakness, and sincerity is always subject to proof. Let us never negotiate out of fear. But let us never fear to negotiate.

Let both sides explore what problems unite us instead of belaboring those problems which divide us.

15

Let both sides, for the first time, formulate serious and precise proposals for the inspection and control of arms — and bring the absolute power to destroy other nations under the absolute control of all nations.

Let both sides seek to invoke the wonders of science instead of its terrors. Together let us explore the stars, conquer the deserts, eradicate disease, tap the ocean depths and encourage the arts and commerce.

Let both sides unite to heed in all corners of the earth the command of Isaiah — to "undo the heavy burdens . . . [and] let the oppressed go free."

And if a beachhead of cooperation may push back the jungle of suspicion, let both sides join in creating a new endeavor, not a new balance of power, but a new world of law, where the strong are just and the weak secure and the peace preserved.

All this will not be finished in the first one hundred days. Nor will it be finished in the first one thousand days, nor in the life of this Administration, nor even perhaps in our lifetime on this planet. But let us begin.

20

In your hands, my fellow citizens, more than mine, will rest the final success or failure of our course. Since this country was founded, each generation of Americans has been summoned to give testimony to its national loyalty. The graves of young Americans who answered the call to service surround the globe.

Now the trumpet summons us again — not as a call to bear arms, though arms we need — not as a call to battle, though embattled we are — but a call to bear the burden of a long twilight struggle, year in and year out, "rejoicing in hope, patient in tribulation" — a struggle against the common enemies of man: tyranny, poverty, disease and war itself.

Can we forge against these enemies a grand and global alliance, North and South, East and West, that can assure a more fruitful life for all mankind? Will you join in that historic effort?

In the long history of the world, only a few generations have been granted the role of defending freedom in its hour of maximum danger. I do not shrink from this responsibility — I welcome it. I do not believe that any of us would exchange places with any other people or any other generation. The energy, the faith, the devotion which we bring to this endeavor will light our country and all who serve it — and the glow from that fire can truly light the world.

And so, my fellow Americans: ask not what your country can do for you — ask what you can do for your country.   25

My fellow citizens of the world: ask not what America will do for you, but what together we can do for the freedom of man.

Finally, whether you are citizens of America or citizens of the world, ask of us here the same high standards of strength and sacrifice which we ask of you. With a good conscience our only sure reward, with history the final judge of our deeds, let us go forth to lead the land we love, asking His blessing and His help, but knowing that here on earth God's work must truly be our own.

(1961)

Inside Kennedy's Inauguration, 50 Years On
ELEANOR CLIFT

This article, in which friends and family of JFK share their memories of the inauguration with reporter Eleanor Clift, originally appeared in January 2011 on the Web site Daily Beast and was then reprinted in Newsweek.

Weather forecasters had predicted light snow turning to rain on the eve of President Kennedy's inauguration, but the snow fell heavily and steadily, covering Pennsylvania Avenue with an eight-inch white blanket and forcing the Army Corps of Engineers' snow-removal force to work through the night to clear the parade route. Jan. 20, 1961, dawned sunny and cold, with gusty winds that made the 22 degrees registered at noon for the swearing-in feel like 7 degrees.

It had just begun to snow when press aide Sue Vogelsinger made her way to the Mayflower Hotel to give Harry Truman an advance copy of the inaugural speech.

She found one Secret Service agent standing guard, told him why she was there, and he said, "Sure, just knock on the door." The former president came to the door in his bedroom slippers. "Have you met Bess?" he asked, inviting the young aide in and introducing her to Mrs. Truman, who sat there knitting away.

It was a day, 50 years ago, frozen in our memories, at least those of us old enough to remember it. But the haze of history masks the random collection of personal experiences and inconveniences for those who were there.

The Mayflower was the favored gathering place for politicians and Democratic activists coming to Washington to celebrate their return to power. Journalist John Seigenthaler was having drinks at the Mayflower with two veteran New York congressmen. "What's the best inaugural you've been to?" he asked. "The one we're going to tomorrow," said Rep. Charles Buckley of New York.

"What about FDR?" exclaimed Seigenthaler. "What Charlie means is tomorrow night an Irish Catholic sleeps in the White House," explained Brooklyn Rep. Eugene Keogh. "We forget, looking back on it, how powerful the anti-Catholic effort was," Seigenthaler says now. "There were frozen tears of joy on the cheeks of Irish Catholics that day," says the journalist, who would go to the Justice Department as a top assistant to Robert Kennedy. "It sounds a bit clichéd now to talk about the New Frontier and what it meant, and sure it was political sloganeering, but for those of us in the campaign and planning to stay on in the administration, it was a meaningful mantra — a passing of the torch and changing of the guard."

Dignitaries assembled on the inaugural platform with seating marked for the various political tribes: the Eisenhower and Nixon contingents, the Kennedy–Johnson family and friends. Philip Bobbitt, age 12, a nephew of Lyndon Johnson, sat next to Gov. Pat Brown of California (father of current governor Jerry). As Cardinal Cushing, a traditionalist with a heavy Boston accent, went on at some length with his prayer, Governor Brown leaned over to the young boy and said, "If he doesn't stop now, I'm quitting the church."

The glare from the sun made it impossible for Robert Frost to read the poem he had written for Kennedy, titled "Dedication." Bobbitt, now a law professor at Columbia University and lecturer at the University of Texas, remembers his Uncle Lyndon gallantly using his hat to try to shield the sun, but it didn't work, and Frost fell back on an earlier poem he knew well, "The Gift Outright," reciting it from memory. "We were all very excited," Bobbitt says, "but my memory is mostly about being cold."

Kathleen, the oldest of the Kennedy grandchildren, watched the swearing-in from the camera platform facing the ceremony. She was with her four younger siblings — Joe, Bobby, David, and Courtney — and to a 9-year-old, standing and cold, the whole thing felt kind of remote. "I knew I was supposed to think this was very historic, but all the adults were taller and we couldn't see

5

well. I remember scooting up to see what I could on a small TV." She does remember how Frank Sinatra stuck his head into her bedroom to say hello: "I thought that was cool." Sinatra had recorded a Kennedy campaign song to the tune of "High Hopes," which Kathleen sings unprompted. Another memorable moment was actress Kim Novak "tobogganing with us in the snow." Joan Kennedy had campaigned in West Virginia for her brother-in-law, going down into a coal mine with him, and sitting there that day she thought how remarkable it was that "you could be in a coal mine and two months later be inaugurated president. The contrast says a lot about democratic politics that's good." She had campaigned for Jack all over the country, but West Virginia stood out. "Jack said we had to win in West Virginia to prove that a Catholic could win because there were so few Catholics there, only 1 or 2 percent." She remembered how cold and dark and dank the mine was, and how the coal miners were so eager to meet them.

As family and friends descended on the White House, cold and hungry,   10
Jackie Kennedy's newly appointed social secretary, Letitia Baldridge, bustled about, worrying whether there was enough heat in the corner bedrooms and whether the food passed muster with Rose Kennedy, the family matriarch. "She wanted proper little sandwiches, the kind they had at tea time, and little cream desserts — she was very thrifty, wanted to make sure we used up everything, and also that we had enough. She whispered in our ears, and when Mama Rose whispered, you jumped. . . . She was the bountiful grandmother orchestrating everybody's stomach."

What Ambassador Jean Kennedy Smith, the last surviving Kennedy sibling, remembers most from the inauguration is an impromptu family lunch of hot soup and sandwiches in the White House. "It was just us," she says, "my brother and sisters and their husbands, and Bobby and Teddy. We just talked about the campaign and how we won everything and that's why he was president, just jokes. And then he signed a picture for us, and it said, 'To Jean, Don't deny you did it,' and I thought how wonderful, and of course he put the same thing to Pat. He meant that we made him president. . . . He always had a terrific sense of humor. And you know he didn't seem young to us because of course he was older than all of us."

After the swearing-in, speechwriter and new special assistant to the president Richard Goodwin, hatless and coatless, walked the two miles from the Capitol to the White House. Freezing, he retreated to the White House to look for his new office, when who should he encounter walking down the hallway but "the guy I had been traveling the country with for the last year and a half — Kennedy. And he said, 'Dick, did you see the Coast Guard contingent in the parade? There was not a single black face in that delegation, and I want you to do something about it right away.'

"So I ran upstairs to my office in the West Wing and I said, 'Who's in charge of the Coast Guard?' I learned they're not under the Defense

Department; they're under the Treasury Department. So I called Douglas Dillon, the new Treasury secretary. And it struck me as I went up the stairs that we'll no longer just make speeches, we actually can do something about this. I told Dillon and within a few months the Coast Guard Academy was integrated."

NBC correspondent Sander Vanocur covered the inauguration from inside the rotunda of the Capitol, watching it on TV. Print still ruled, but the networks were beginning to gain a greater foothold, and the Kennedy campaign wasn't suspicious of the press as the Nixon campaign had been, which made for a freer and easier exchange. Vanocur remembers the new president stopping by a Democratic National Committee meeting at the Mayflower [hotel], and when a reporter asked what Truman thought of the changes in the White House he'd left eight years earlier, Kennedy responded that all Truman would say about Eisenhower is "the sonofabitch moved my piano to the basement."

Sue Vogelsinger, the young press aide, ended up checking herself in to the hospital that evening, suffering from exhaustion after months on the campaign trail. She didn't get to the White House until the following day, and the next night she ran into the new president, who was walking around by himself checking out the West Wing and fretting about the state of disrepair. "This is really bad," he said, looking at the chipped floors. "You think that's bad, come see the press office," Vogelsinger told him, which he pronounced "worse than the Senate office." The press office was around the corner from the Oval Office (it still is), and the three wire machines (AP, UP and Agence France-Presse) were kept in the press secretary's private bathroom. Kennedy could hear the bells go off signaling urgent news and he'd be there.

Kennedy paid close attention to what journalists wrote about him. He would say, "I'd rather be Krocked than Fleesonized," a reference to liberal Democratic columnist Doris Fleeson versus the more conservative *New York Times*'s Arthur Krock. Fleeson was a Kennedy favorite, and in early May 1961, she had a medical problem and needed someone to ghostwrite her column. She was a good friend of Kennedy special assistant Fred Dutton, and he agreed to take on the task, two columns a week for three weeks. "And Fred uses this as a way to goad the president for not being liberal enough, that he's selling out on taxes," recalls Dutton's widow, Nancy. "So the president walks in with the *Washington Star* one afternoon, throws it on Dutton's desk, and says, 'Can't you control that friend of yours?'"

Fifty years after Kennedy's inauguration, the memories that linger remind us of a time when all seemed possible, when a politician could capture the imagination of a country. Those who were there knew it was special, and while Kennedy's presidency was brief, his impact endures.

(2011)

Inauguration of John F. Kennedy
UNITED STATES ARMY SIGNAL CORPS

This photo, credited to the United States Army Signal Corps, shows Chief Justice Earl Warren administering the Oath of Office to John F. Kennedy during the ceremony at the Capitol on January 20, 1961. Among the notables are poet Robert Frost; former presidents Eisenhower and Truman with their wives, Mamie and Bess; former vice president Richard Nixon; Vice President Lyndon B. Johnson and his wife, Lady Bird; as well as the new first lady, Jacqueline, seen at the lower left in her signature pillbox hat.

United States Army Signal Corps/John F. Kennedy Presidential Library and Museum

Analyzing Arguments
From Reading to Writing

Have you ever changed your mind about something? What caused you to re-examine a belief or an idea? Most likely, you read or heard someone else's perspective that challenged you to think about an issue in a different way. It might have been a clear, thoughtful presentation of information, a personal story that tugged at your conscience, a startling statistic, or even a bit of humor or satire that presented a familiar issue in a new and enlightening way. It's less likely that you were bullied into reconsidering your opinion by a loud voice that belittled your ideas.

By carefully and respectfully reading the viewpoints of others and considering a range of ideas on an issue, we develop a clearer understanding of our own beliefs — a necessary foundation to writing effective arguments. In this chapter, we're going to analyze elements of argument as a means of critical thinking and an essential step toward crafting argumentative essays.

What Is Argument?

Although we have been discussing argument in previous chapters, the focus has been primarily on rhetorical appeals and style. We'll continue examining those elements, but here we take a closer look at an argument's claim, evidence, and organization.

Let's start with some definitions. What is argument? Is it a conflict? A contest between opposing forces to prove the other side wrong? A battle with words? Or is it, rather, a process of reasoned inquiry and rational discourse seeking common ground? If it is the last one, then we engage in argument whenever we explore ideas rationally and think clearly about the world. Yet these days argument is often no more than raised voices interrupting one another, exaggerated assertions without adequate support, and scanty evidence from sources that lack credibility. We might call this "crazed rhetoric," as political commentator Tom Toles does in the cartoon on the following page.

This cartoon appeared on January 16, 2011, a few days after Arizona congresswoman Gabrielle Giffords became the victim of a shooting; six people were killed and another thirteen injured. Many people saw this tragedy as stemming from vitriolic political discourse that included violent language. Toles argues that Uncle Sam, and

TOLES © 2011 The Washington Post. Reprinted with permission of UNIVERSAL UCLICK. All rights reserved.

(See color insert, Image 7.)

thus the country, is in danger of being devoured by "crazed rhetoric." There may not be a "next trick" or a "taming," he suggests, if the rhetorical lion continues to roar.

Is Toles's view exaggerated? Whether you answer yes or no to that question, it seems quite clear that partisanship and polarization often hold sway over dialogue and civility when people think of argument. In our discussions, however, we define **argument** as a persuasive discourse, a coherent and considered movement from a claim to a conclusion. The goal of this chapter is to avoid thinking of argument as a zero-sum game of winners and losers but, instead, to see it as a means of better understanding other people's ideas as well as your own.

In Chapter 1, we discussed concession and refutation as a way to acknowledge a counterargument, and we want to re-emphasize the usefulness of that approach. Viewing anyone who disagrees with you as an adversary makes it very likely that the conversation will escalate into an emotional clash, and treating opposing ideas disrespectfully rarely results in mutual understanding. Twentieth-century psychologist Carl Rogers stressed the importance of replacing confrontational argument tactics with ones that promote negotiation, compromise, and cooperation. **Rogerian arguments** are based on the assumption that having a full understanding of an opposing position is essential to responding to it persuasively and refuting it in a way that is accommodating rather than alienating. Ultimately, the goal of a Rogerian argument is not to destroy your opponents or dismantle their viewpoints but rather to reach a satisfactory compromise.

So what does a civil argument look like? Let's examine a short article that appeared in *Ode* magazine in 2009 entitled "Why Investing in Fast Food May Be a Good Thing." In this piece, Amy Domini, a financial advisor and leading voice for socially responsible investing, argues the counterintuitive position that investing in the fast-food industry can be an ethically responsible choice.

Why Investing in Fast Food May Be a Good Thing
AMY DOMINI

My friends and colleagues know I've been an advocate of the Slow Food movement for many years. Founded in Italy 20 years ago, Slow Food celebrates harvests from small-scale family farms, prepared slowly and lovingly with regard for the health and environment of diners. Slow Food seeks to preserve crop diversity, so the unique taste of "heirloom" apples, tomatoes and other foods don't perish from the Earth. I wish everyone would choose to eat this way. The positive effects on the health of our bodies, our local economies and our planet would be incalculable. Why then do I find myself investing in fast-food companies?

The reason is social investing isn't about investing in perfect companies. (Perfect companies, it turns out, don't exist.) We seek to invest in companies that are moving in the right direction and listening to their critics. We offer a road map to bring those companies to the next level, step by step. No social standard causes us to reject restaurants, even fast-food ones, out of hand. Although we favor local, organic food, we recognize it isn't available in every community, and is often priced above the means of the average household. Many of us live more than 100 miles from a working farm.

Fast food is a way of life. In America, the average person eats it more than 150 times a year. In 2007, sales for the 400 largest U.S.-based fast-food chains totaled $277 billion, up 7 percent from 2006.

Fast food is a global phenomenon. Major chains and their local competitors open restaurants in nearly every country. For instance, in Greece, burgers and pizza are supplanting the traditional healthy Mediterranean diet of fish, olive oil and vegetables. Doctors are treating Greek children for diabetes, high cholesterol and high blood pressure — ailments rarely seen in the past.

The fast-food industry won't go away anytime soon. But in the meantime, it   5
can be changed. And because it's so enormous, even seemingly modest changes can have a big impact. In 2006, New York City banned the use of trans-fats (a staple of fast food) in restaurants, and in 2008, California became the first state to do so. When McDonald's moved to non-trans-fats for making French fries, the

health benefits were widespread. Another area of concern is fast-food packaging, which causes forest destruction and creates a lot of waste. In the U.S. alone, 1.8 million tons of packaging is generated each year. Fast-food containers make up about 20 percent of litter, and packaging for drinks and snacks adds another 20 percent.

A North Carolina–based organization called the Dogwood Alliance has launched an effort to make fast-food companies reduce waste and source paper responsibly. Through a campaign called No Free Refills, the group is pressing fast-food companies to reduce their impact on the forests of the southern United States, the world's largest paper-producing region. They're pushing companies to:

- Reduce the overuse of packaging.
- Maximize use of 100 percent post-consumer recycled boxboard.
- Eliminate paper packaging from the most biologically important endangered forests.
- Eliminate paper packaging from suppliers that convert natural forests into industrial pine plantations.
- Encourage packaging suppliers to source fiber from responsibly managed forests certified by the Forest Stewardship Council.
- Recycle waste in restaurants to divert paper and other material from landfills.

Will the fast-food companies adopt all these measures overnight? No. But along with similar efforts worldwide, this movement signals that consumers and investors are becoming more conscious of steps they can take toward a better world — beginning with the way they eat.

While my heart will always be with Slow Food, I recognize the fast-food industry can improve and that some companies are ahead of others on that path.

(2009)

Domini begins by reminding her readers of her ethos as "an advocate of the Slow Food movement for many years." By describing some of the goals and tenets of that movement, including the "positive effects" it can have, she establishes common ground before she discusses her position — one that the Slow Food advocates are not likely to embrace, at least not initially. In fact, instead of asserting her position in a strong declarative sentence, Domini asks a question that invites her audience to hear her explanation: "Why then do I find myself investing in fast-food companies?" (par. 1). She provides evidence that supports her choice to take that action: she uses statistics to show that slow food is not available in all communities, while fast food is an expanding industry. She uses the example of Greece to show that fast food is becoming a global phenomenon. She gives numerous examples of how fast-food companies are improving ingredients and reducing waste to illustrate how working to change fast-food practices can have a significant impact on public health and the environment.

After presenting her viewpoint, Domini ends by acknowledging that her "heart will always be with Slow Food"; but that fact should not preclude her supporting those in the fast-food industry who are making socially and environmentally responsible decisions.

• ACTIVITY •

Identify at least two points in Domini's article where she might have given way to accusation or blame or where she might have dismissed the Slow Food movement as being shortsighted or elitist. Discuss how, instead, she finds common ground and promotes dialogue with her audience through civil discourse.

• ESSAY IN PROGRESS: Selecting a Topic •

What are two controversial topics that interest you? Brainstorm how you might develop an argument about each from two different viewpoints. Consider the potential for volatile or highly emotional responses to each. What could you do to encourage a civil tone and approach? Make sure to choose ideas that you could develop into a full essay. You will have an opportunity to return to them throughout the chapter.

Staking a Claim

Every argument has a **claim** — also called an assertion or a proposition — that states the argument's main idea or position. A claim differs from a topic or a subject in that a claim has to be arguable. It can't just be a simple statement of fact; it has to state a position that some people might disagree with and others might agree with. Going from a simple topic to a claim means stating your informed opinion about a topic. In the essay you just read, the general topic is social investing — specifically, social investing in the fast-food industry. The arguable claim, however, is that investing in fast-food companies can be socially responsible. Notice that the topic may be a single word or a phrase, but the arguable claim is stated as a complete sentence.

It's important to note that neither a published author nor a student writer is likely to develop a strong claim without exploring a topic through reading about it, discussing it with others, brainstorming, taking notes, and rethinking. After looking into a topic thoroughly, then you are ready to develop a position on an issue. For example, let's use the topic of single-sex classrooms. You will notice, first of all, that a simple statement of the topic does not indicate whether you support the notion or challenge it. Let's consider several directions to take with this topic.

- Many schools have single-sex classrooms.
- Single-sex classrooms have been around for years, especially in private schools.
- Single-sex classrooms are ineffective because they do not prepare students for the realities of the workplace.

The first statement may be true, but it is easily verified and not arguable; thus, it is simply a topic and not a claim. The second statement has more detail, but it's easy to verify whether it is true or not. Since it is not arguable, it is not a claim. The third statement is a claim because it is arguable. It argues that single-sex classrooms are ineffective and that preparation for the workplace is an important way to measure the effectiveness of an education. There are those who would disagree with both statements and those who would agree with both. Thus, it presents an arguable position and is a viable claim.

• ACTIVITY •

For each of the following statements, evaluate whether it is arguable or too easily verifiable to develop into an effective argument. Try revising the ones you consider too easily verifiable to make them into arguable claims.

1. SUV owners should be required to pay an energy surcharge.
2. Charter schools are an alternative to public schools.
3. Ronald Reagan was the most charismatic president of the twentieth century.
4. Requiring students to wear uniforms improves school spirit.
5. The terms *global warming* and *climate change* describe different perspectives on this complex issue.
6. Students graduating from college today can expect to have more debt than any previous generation.
7. People who read novels are more likely to attend sports events and movies than those who do not.
8. Print newspapers will not survive another decade.
9. The competition among countries to become a site for the Olympic Games is fierce.
10. Plagiarism is a serious problem in today's schools.

Types of Claims

Typically, we speak of three types of claims: claims of fact, claims of value, and claims of policy. Each type can be used to guide entire arguments, which we would call arguments of fact, arguments of value, and arguments of policy. While it is helpful to separate the three for analysis, in practice it is not always that simple. Indeed, it is quite common for an argument to include more than one type of claim, as you will see in the following examples.

Claims of Fact

Claims of fact assert that something is true or not true. You can't argue whether Zimbabwe is in Africa or whether restaurants on Main Street serve more customers at breakfast than at lunch. These issues can be resolved and verified — in the first case by checking a map, in the second through observation or by checking sales figures. You can, however, argue that Zimbabwe has an unstable government or that restaurants on Main Street are more popular with older patrons than with younger ones. Those statements are arguable: What does "unstable" mean? What does "popular" mean? Who is "older" and who is "younger"?

Arguments of fact often pivot on what exactly is "factual." Facts become arguable when they are questioned, when they raise controversy, when they challenge people's beliefs. "It's a fact that the Social Security program will go bankrupt by 2025" is a claim that could be developed in an argument of fact. Very often, so-called facts are a matter of interpretation. At other times, new "facts" call into question older ones. The claim that cell phones increase the incidence of brain tumors, for instance, requires sifting through new "facts" from medical research and scrutinizing who is carrying out the research, who is supporting it financially, and so on. Whenever you are evaluating or writing an argument of fact, it's important to approach your subject with a healthy skepticism.

In "Why Investing in Fast Food May Be a Good Thing," Domini makes two claims of fact. The argument in paragraph 3 is guided by the claim of fact that "fast food is a way of life." Is it? She supports this claim with sales statistics and information on the growth of this industry. Paragraph 4 is guided by the claim of fact that "fast food is a global phenomenon." She supports this claim with an explanation of fast-food restaurants opening "in nearly every country" and a specific example discussing the changing diet in Greece.

We commonly see arguments of fact that challenge stereotypes or social beliefs. For instance, scientist Matthias Mehl and his colleagues published a study about whether women are more talkative than men. They recorded conversations and concluded that the differences are, in fact, very minor. Their findings call into question the stereotype that women are excessively chatty and more talkative than their male counterparts. Mehl's argument of fact re-evaluates earlier "facts" and challenges a social myth.

Claims of Value

Perhaps the most common type of claim is a **claim of value**, which argues that something is good or bad, right or wrong, desirable or undesirable. Of course, just like any other claim, a claim of value must be arguable. Claims of value may be personal judgments based on taste, or they may be more objective evaluations based on external criteria. For instance, if you argue that Ryan Gosling is the best leading man in Hollywood, that is simply a matter of taste. The criteria for what is "best" and what defines a "leading man" are strictly personal. Another person could argue that while Gosling might be the best-looking actor in Hollywood, Robert Downey Jr. is more highly paid and his movies tend to make more money. That is an evaluation based on external criteria — dollars and cents.

To develop an argument from a claim of value, you must establish specific criteria or standards and then show to what extent the subject meets your criteria. Amy Domini's argument is largely one of value as she supports her claim that investing in fast-food companies can be a positive thing. The very title of Domini's essay suggests a claim of value: "Why Investing in Fast Food May Be a Good Thing." She develops her argument by explaining the impact that such investing can have on what food choices are available and what the impact of those choices is.

Entertainment reviews — of movies, television shows, concerts, books — are good examples of arguments developed from claims of value. Take a look at this one, movie critic Roger Ebert's 1977 review of the first *Star Wars* movie. He raved. Notice how he states his four-star claim — it's a great movie! — in several ways throughout the argument and sets up his criteria at each juncture.

Star Wars
ROGER EBERT

Every once in a while I have what I think of as an out-of-the-body experience at a movie. When the ESP people use a phrase like that, they're referring to the sensation of the mind actually leaving the body and spiriting itself off to China or Peoria or a galaxy far, far away. When I use the phrase, I simply mean that my imagination has forgotten it is actually present in a movie theater and thinks it's up there on the screen. In a curious sense, the events in the movie seem real, and I seem to be a part of them.

Ebert's first criterion is whether a film transports him.

Ebert's claim of value. Stated more formally, it might read: "Star Wars is so good that it will completely draw you in."

Star Wars works like that. My list of other out-of-the-body films is a short and odd one, ranging from the artistry of *Bonnie and Clyde* or *Cries and Whispers* to the slick commercialism of *Jaws* and the brutal strength of *Taxi Driver*. On whatever level (sometimes I'm not at all sure) they engage me so immediately and powerfully that I lose my detachment, my analytical reserve. The movie's happening, and it's happening to me.

What makes the *Star Wars* experience unique, though, is that it happens on such an innocent and often funny level. It's usually violence that draws me so deeply into a movie — violence ranging from the psychological torment of a Bergman character to the mindless crunch of a shark's jaws. Maybe movies that scare us find the most direct route to our imaginations. But there's hardly

Ebert asserts that Star Wars is not just different from the other films he has cited; it is "unique."

any violence at all in *Star Wars* (and even then it's presented as essentially bloodless swashbuckling). Instead, there's entertainment so direct and simple that all of the complications of the modern movie seem to vaporize.

Ebert elaborates on why it is "unique" — pointing out that its power lies in directness and simplicity rather than violence and brutality.

Star Wars is a fairy tale, a fantasy, a legend, finding its roots in some of our most popular fictions. The golden robot, lion-faced space pilot, and insecure little computer on wheels must have been suggested by the Tin Man, the Cowardly Lion, and the Scarecrow in *The Wizard of Oz*. The journey from one end of the galaxy to another is out of countless thousands of space operas. The hardware is from *Flash Gordon* out of *2001: A Space Odyssey*, the chivalry is from Robin Hood, the heroes are from Westerns, and the villains are a cross between Nazis and sorcerers. *Star Wars* taps the pulp fantasies buried in our memories, and because it's done so brilliantly, it reactivates old thrills, fears, and exhilarations we thought we'd abandoned when we read our last copy of *Amazing Stories*.

Another criterion is the effectiveness of the storytelling. Here it is literally the stuff of legends, managing somehow to be both new and nostalgic.

The movie works so well for several reasons, and they don't all have to do with the spectacular special effects. The effects are good, yes, but great effects have been used in such movies as *Silent Running* and *Logan's Run* without setting all-time box-office records. No, I think the key to *Star Wars* is more basic than that.

Ebert addresses a counterargument. He knows that many people will praise the special effects in the film. He acknowledges that they are "good" — but that is not one of his chief criteria.

5

The movie relies on the strength of pure narrative, in the most basic storytelling form known to man, the Journey. All of the best tales we remember from our childhoods had to do with heroes setting out to travel down roads filled with danger, and hoping to find treasure or heroism at the journey's end. In *Star Wars*, George Lucas takes this simple and powerful framework into outer space, and that is an inspired thing to do, because we no longer have maps on Earth that warn, "Here there be dragons." We can't fall off the edge of the map, as Columbus could, and we can't hope to find new continents of prehistoric monsters or lost tribes ruled by immortal goddesses. Not on Earth, anyway, but anything is possible in space, and Lucas goes right ahead and shows us very nearly everything. We get involved quickly, because the characters in *Star Wars* are so strongly and simply drawn and have so many small foibles and large, futile hopes for us to identify with. And then Lucas does an interesting thing. As he sends his heroes off to cross the universe and do battle with the Forces of Darth Vader, the evil Empire, and the awesome Death Star, he gives us lots of special effects, yes — ships passing into hyperspace, alien planets, an infinity of stars — but we also get a

Ebert moves into his principal criterion: the value of the classic hero's journey that *Star Wars* embodies.

Another criterion: The movie is good because the characters are both familiar . . .

...and unfamiliar. [wealth of strange living creatures, and Lucas correctly guesses that they'll be more interesting for us than all the intergalactic hardware.

The most fascinating single scene, for me, was the one set in the bizarre saloon on the planet Tatooine. As that incredible collection of extraterrestrial alcoholics and bug-eyed martini drinkers lined up at the bar, and as Lucas so slyly let them exhibit characteristics that were universally human, I found myself feeling a combination of admiration and delight. *Star Wars* had placed me in the presence of really magical movie invention: Here, all mixed together, were whimsy and fantasy, simple wonderment and quietly sophisticated storytelling.

Ebert applies his criteria to one specific scene.

When Stanley Kubrick was making *2001* in the late 1960s, he threw everything he had into the special effects depicting outer space, but he finally decided not to show any aliens at all — because they were impossible to visualize, he thought. But they weren't at all, as *Star Wars* demonstrates, and the movie's delight in the possibilities of alien life forms is at least as much *He reiterates his claim by emphasizing that it is not the technology of special effects but the humanity of the characters that makes the film great.* fun as its conflicts between the space cruisers of the Empire and the Rebels.

And perhaps that helps to explain the movie's one weakness, which is that the final assault on the Death Star is allowed to go on too long. Maybe, having invested so much money and sweat in his special effects, Lucas couldn't bear to see them trimmed. But the magic of *Star Wars* is only dramatized by the special effects; the movie's heart is in its endearingly human (and non-human) people.

Ebert concedes that the film does have a flaw.

(1977)

• ACTIVITY •

Find a review of a movie, a television show, a concert, an album or a song, or another form of popular culture. Identify the claim in the review. What criteria does the reviewer use to justify a thumbs-up or a thumbs-down?

Claims of Policy

Any time you propose a change, you're making a **claim of policy**. It might be local: a group at your school proposes to raise money to contribute to a school in Haiti. You want your parents to let you spend more time with friends on weeknights. Or it might be a bigger issue such as a proposal for transitioning to alternative energy sources, a change in copyright laws for digital music, a shift in foreign policy, a change in legislation to allow former felons to vote.

An argument of policy generally begins with a definition of the problem (claim of fact), explains why it is a problem (claim of value), and then explains the change that needs to happen (claim of policy). Also, keep in mind that while an argument of policy usually calls for some direct action to take place, it may be a recommendation for a change in attitude or viewpoint.

Let's take a look at the opening paragraphs of an argument of policy. In this piece, published in 1999 in *Newsweek*, Anna Quindlen argues for a change in attitude toward the treatment of mental illness. Notice how she combines claims of fact and value to ground her claim of policy — that is, that attitudes toward mental illness must change so that treatment options become more available.

from *The C Word in the Hallways*
ANNA QUINDLEN

The saddest phrase I've read in a long time is this one: psychological autopsy. That's what the doctors call it when a kid kills himself and they go back over the plowed ground of his short life, and discover all the hidden markers that led to the rope, the blade, the gun.

There's a plague on all our houses, and since it doesn't announce itself with lumps or spots or protest marches, it has gone unremarked in the quiet suburbs and busy cities where it has been laying waste. [*Claim of value*] The number of suicides and homicides committed by teenagers, most often young men, has exploded in the last three decades, until it has become commonplace to have black-bordered photographs in yearbooks and murder suspects with acne problems. [*Claim of fact*] And everyone searches for reasons, and scapegoats, and solutions, most often punitive. Yet one solution continues to elude us, and that is ending the ignorance about mental health, and moving it from the margins of care and into the mainstream where it belongs. [*Claim of policy*] As surely as any vaccine, this would save lives.

So many have already been lost. This month Kip Kinkel was sentenced to life in prison in Oregon for the murders of his parents and a shooting rampage at his high school that killed two students. A psychiatrist who specializes in the care of adolescents testified that Kinkel, now 17, had been hearing voices since he was 12. Sam Manzie is also 17. He is serving a 70-year sentence for luring an 11-year-old boy named Eddie Werner into his New Jersey home and strangling him with the cord of an alarm clock because his Sega Genesis was out of reach. Manzie had his first psychological evaluation in the first grade.

(1999)

Quindlen calls for "ending the ignorance" about mental health and its care. As she develops her argument, she supports this claim of policy by considering both personal examples and general facts about mental health in America. To arrive at this claim of policy, however, she first makes a claim of value — "There's a plague on all our houses": that is, this is a problem deserving of our attention. She then offers a claim of fact that demonstrates the scope of the problem: teenage suicide and homicide in the last decades have "exploded." Granted, all three of these claims need to be explained with appropriate evidence, and Quindlen does that in subsequent paragraphs; but at the outset, she establishes claims of value and fact that lay the foundation for the claim of policy that is the main idea of her argument.

• ACTIVITY •

Read the following argument of policy that appeared as an editorial in the *New York Times* in 2004. Annotate it to identify claims of fact, value, and policy; then describe how these interact throughout the argument.

Felons and the Right to Vote
NEW YORK TIMES EDITORIAL BOARD

About 4.7 million Americans, more than 2 percent of the adult population, are barred from voting because of a felony conviction. Denying the vote to ex-offenders is antidemocratic, and undermines the nation's commitment to rehabilitating people who have paid their debt to society. Felon disenfranchisement laws also have a sizable racial impact: 13 percent of black men have had their votes taken away, seven times the national average. But even if it were acceptable as policy, denying felons the vote has been a disaster because of the chaotic and partisan way it has been carried out.

Thirty-five states prohibit at least some people from voting after they have been released from prison. The rules about which felonies are covered and when the right to vote is restored vary widely from state to state, and often defy logic. In four states, including New York, felons on parole cannot vote, but felons on probation can. In some states, felons must formally apply for restoration of their voting rights, which state officials can grant or deny on the most arbitrary of grounds.

Florida may have changed the outcome of the 2000 presidential election when Secretary of State Katherine Harris oversaw a purge of suspected felons that removed an untold number of eligible voters from the rolls. This year, state officials are conducting a new purge that may be just as flawed. They have developed a list of 47,000 voters who may be felons, and have asked local officials to consider purging them. But the *Miami Herald* found that more than 2,100 of them may have been listed in error, because their voting rights were restored by the state's clemency process. Last week, the state acknowledged that 1,600 of those on the list should be allowed to vote.

Election officials are also far too secretive about felon voting issues, which should be a matter of public record. When Ms. Harris used inaccurate standards for purging voters, the public did not find out until it was too late. This year, the state tried to keep the 47,000 names on its list of possible felons secret, but fortunately a state court ruled this month that they should be open to scrutiny.

There is a stunning lack of information and transparency surrounding felon disenfranchisement across the country. The rules are often highly technical, and little effort is made to explain them to election officials or to the people affected. In New York, the Brennan Center for Justice at New York University Law School found that local elections offices often did not understand the law, and some demanded that felons produce documents that do not exist.

Too often, felon voting is seen as a partisan issue. In state legislatures, it is usually Democrats who try to restore voting rights, and Republicans who resist. Recently, Republicans and election officials in Missouri and South Dakota have raised questions about voter registration groups' employment of ex-felons, although they have every right to be involved in political activity. In Florida, the decision about whether a felon's right to vote will be restored lies with a panel made up of the governor and members of his cabinet. Some voting rights activists believe that Gov. Jeb Bush has moved slowly, and reinstated voting rights for few of the state's ex-felons, to help President Bush's re-election prospects.

The treatment of former felons in the electoral system cries out for reform. The cleanest and fairest approach would be simply to remove the prohibitions on felon voting. In his State of the Union address in January, President Bush announced a new national commitment to helping prisoners re-enter society. Denying them the right to vote belies this commitment.

Restoring the vote to felons is difficult, because it must be done state by state, and because ex-convicts do not have much of a political lobby. There have been legislative successes in recent years in some places, including Alabama and Nevada. But other states have been moving in the opposite direction. The best hope of reform may lie in the courts. The Atlanta-based United States Court of Appeals for the 11th Circuit and the San Francisco–based Court of Appeals for the Ninth Circuit have ruled recently that disenfranchising felons may violate equal protection or the Voting Rights Act.

Until the whole idea of permanently depriving felons of their right to vote is wiped away, the current rules should be applied more fairly. The quality of voting roll purges must be improved. Florida should discontinue its current felon purge until it can prove that the list it is using is accurate.

Mechanisms for restoring voting rights to felons must be improved. Even in states where felons have the right to vote, they are rarely notified of this when they exit prison. Released prisoners should be given that information during the discharge process, and helped with the paperwork.

The process for felons to regain their voting rights should be streamlined. In Nevada, early reports are that the restoration of felon voting rights has had minimal effect, because the paperwork requirements are too burdensome. Ex-felons who apply to vote should have the same presumption of eligibility as other voters.

> Voting rights should not be a political football. There should be bipartisan support for efforts to help ex-felons get their voting rights back, by legislators and by state and local election officials. American democracy is diminished when officeholders and political parties, for their own political gain, try to keep people from voting.
>
> *(2004)*

• ESSAY IN PROGRESS: Staking a Claim •

Choosing one of the topics you explored initially (p. 89), write three different claims that could focus an essay. Be sure each is arguable. Comment on whether your overall argument will likely include more than one type of claim.

From Claim to Thesis

To develop a claim into a thesis statement, you have to be more specific about what you intend to argue. In her essay "The C Word in the Hallways," Anna Quindlen states her main idea explicitly:

> Yet one solution continues to elude us, and that is ending the ignorance about mental health, and moving it from the margins of care and into the mainstream where it belongs. As surely as any vaccine, this would save lives.

The "policy" that Quindlen advocates changing is removing the stigma from mental illness so it can be properly treated. Her second sentence emphasizes her thesis by drawing an analogy: just as vaccines save lives by preventing disease, a shift in policy toward mental illness would save lives by preventing violence.

Sometimes in professional essays the claim may be implicit, but in the formal essays that you will write for your classes, the claim is traditionally stated explicitly as a one-sentence thesis statement that appears in the introduction of your argument. To be effective, a thesis statement must preview the essay by encapsulating in clear, unambiguous language the main point or points the writer intends to make. Let's consider several different types of thesis statements: a closed thesis, an open thesis, and a thesis that includes the counterargument.

Closed Thesis Statements

A **closed thesis** is a statement of the main idea of the argument that also previews the major points the writer intends to make. It is "closed" because it limits the number of points the writer will make. For instance, here is a closed thesis on the appeal of the Harry Potter book series:

> The three-dimensional characters, exciting plot, and complex themes of the Harry Potter series make them not only legendary children's books but enduring literary classics.

This thesis asserts that the series constitutes a "literary classic" and specifies three reasons — characters, plot, and theme — each of which would be discussed in the argument. A closed thesis often includes (or implies) the word *because*. This one might have been written as follows:

> The Harry Potter series have become legendary children's books and enduring literary classics <u>because</u> of their three-dimensional characters, exciting plots, and complex themes.

Indeed, that statement might be a good working thesis.

A closed thesis is a reliable way to focus a short essay, particularly one written under time constraints. Explicitly stating the points you'll make can help you organize your thoughts when you are working against the clock, and it can be a way to address specific points that are required by the prompt or argument.

Open Thesis Statements

If, however, you are writing a longer essay with five, six, or even more main points, then an open thesis is probably more effective. An **open thesis** is one that does not list all the points the writer intends to cover in an essay. If you have six or seven points in an essay, for instance, stringing them all out in the thesis will be awkward; plus, while a reader can remember two or three main points, it's confusing to keep track of a whole string of points made way back in an opening paragraph. For instance, you might argue that the Harry Potter series are far from enduring classics because you think the main characters are either all good or all bad rather than a bit of both, the minor characters devolve into caricatures, the plot is repetitious and formulaic, the magic does not follow a logical system of rules, and so on. Imagine trying to line up all those ideas in a sentence or two with any clarity or grace. By making the overall point without actually stating every subpoint, an open thesis can guide an essay without being cumbersome:

> The popularity of the Harry Potter series demonstrates that simplicity trumps complexity when it comes to the taste of readers, both young and old.

Counterargument Thesis Statements

A variant of the open and closed thesis is the **counterargument thesis,** in which a summary of a counterargument usually qualified by *although* or *but* precedes the writer's opinion. This type of thesis has the advantage of immediately addressing the counterargument. Doing so may make an argument seem both stronger and more reasonable. It may also create a seamless transition to a more thorough concession and refutation of the counterargument later in the argument. Using the Harry Potter example again, let's look at a counterargument thesis:

> Although the Harry Potter series may have some literary merit, its popularity has less to do with storytelling than with merchandising.

This thesis concedes a counterargument that the series "may have some literary merit" before refuting that claim by saying that the storytelling itself is less powerful than the movies, toys, and other merchandise that the books inspired. The thesis promises some discussion of literary merit and a critique of its storytelling (concession and refutation) but will ultimately focus on the role of the merchandising machine in making Harry Potter a household name.

Note that the thesis that considers a counterargument can also lead to a position that is a modification or qualification rather than an absolute statement of support or rejection. If, for instance, you were asked to discuss whether the success of the Harry Potter series has resulted in a reading renaissance, this thesis would let you respond not with a firm "yes" or "no," but with a qualification of "in some respects." It would allow you to ease into a critique by first recognizing its strengths before leveling your criticism that the popularity was the result of media hype rather than quality and thus will not result in a reading renaissance.

• ACTIVITY •

Develop a thesis statement that could focus an argument in response to each of the following prompts. Discuss why you think that the structure (open, closed, counterargument) you chose would be appropriate or effective.

1. Same-sex classrooms have gone in and out of favor in public education. Write an essay explaining why you would support or oppose same-sex classrooms for public schools in grades 10 through 12.

2. Write an essay supporting, challenging, or qualifying English author E. M. Forster's position in the following statement: "I hate the idea of causes, and if I had to choose between betraying my country and betraying my friend, I hope I should have the guts to betray my country."

3. Today's world is full of conflicts and controversies. Choose a local or global issue, and write an essay that considers multiple viewpoints and proposes a solution or compromise.

4. Write an essay explaining why you agree or disagree with the assertion that advertising degrades the people it appeals to and deprives them of their will to choose.

5. Plagiarism is rampant in public high schools and colleges. In fact, some people argue that the definition of *plagiarism* has changed with the proliferation of the Internet. Write an essay explaining what you believe the appropriate response of a teacher should be to a student who turns in a plagiarized essay or exam.

> • **ESSAY IN PROGRESS: Developing a Thesis** •
>
> Now that you understand the different types of claims and how to develop
> them into thesis statements, you can begin drafting an argument. Select one
> of the claims you worked with in the activity on page 98. Draft two different
> thesis statements that might guide an essay on the subject. Which one do you
> think is more promising for a full argumentative essay? Why?

Presenting Evidence

Once a writer has established a claim and developed a thesis statement, the next step
is to support it with effective evidence. What evidence to present, how much is necessary, and how to present it are all rhetorical choices guided by an understanding of
the audience. A person speaking to a group of scientists will more likely need facts
and figures to persuade her audience, while one writing an essay for a local newspaper might want to use an anecdote to grab the reader's attention. Amy Domini,
knowing that her audience — the generally affluent and liberal readers of *Ode* magazine — will include many who are hostile to fast food, presents evidence regarding the
positive changes that fast-food companies are making, as well as numerical evidence
showing that fast food is a growing phenomenon that could have either a positive or
a negative impact on health and the environment. You should keep audience in mind
throughout this discussion of evidence, particularly in terms of whether your audience would be persuaded more by formal or informal sources.

Relevant, Accurate, and Sufficient Evidence

Regardless of the type of evidence a writer chooses to use, it should always be relevant,
accurate, and sufficient. Relevant evidence is evidence that specifically applies to the
argument being made. To argue that a particular car is superior from a dependability
standpoint, bringing in evidence about its maintenance record would be relevant, but
talking about its hand-tooled leather seats would not. Generally, good writers do not
leave the relevance of a piece of evidence to the reader's imagination; they explicitly
spell out what the relationship is between an example and the argument at hand.

Presenting accurate information means taking care to quote sources correctly
without misrepresenting what the sources are saying or taking the information out of
context. One way to ensure that you have accurate evidence is to get it from a credible
source. Think carefully about the bias any source might have. Is it partisan or backed
financially by a company or an industry group? Even statistical data can be inaccurate
if it is from a source that has gathered the data in a way that fits its own agenda.
Accuracy can also be a matter of the audience's perception. You should choose sources
that they will find credible. If you want accurate dependability information about a

car, some reliable sources might be a reputable mechanic, a magazine reviewer who has compared the car's performance to other similar cars, or simply someone who has owned the car for a long time.

Finally, you should include a sufficient amount of evidence to support your thesis. If you based your entire argument about the car's dependability on an interview with a single mechanic, that would not be persuasive. A mechanic only sees the cars that break down, so perhaps his viewpoint is overly negative.

Logical Fallacies

Before we turn to specific types of evidence, let's consider **logical fallacies**: potential vulnerabilities or weaknesses in an argument. Practically speaking, the logical breakdown in most weak arguments occurs in the use of evidence, since evidence is what we use to prove arguments. So a more practical definition of a fallacy might be a failure to make a logical connection between the claim and the evidence used to support that claim. Fallacies may be accidental, but they can also be used deliberately to manipulate or deceive.

Regardless of whether they are intentional or unintentional, logical fallacies work against the clear, civil discourse that should be at the heart of argument. By checking for logical fallacies in a published argument that you're analyzing, you can identify weak points; by checking for fallacies in your own writing, you can revise to strengthen your argument. It's more important that you notice these fallacies and be able to describe what you see than it is to be able to label them by their technical names. The concepts are more important than the terms.

Fallacies of Relevance

One characteristic of evidence we have just discussed is relevance. Fallacies that result from using evidence that's irrelevant to the claim fall under the general heading of red herrings. (The term derives from the dried fish that trainers used to distract dogs when teaching them to hunt foxes.) A **red herring** occurs when a speaker skips to a new and irrelevant topic in order to avoid the topic of discussion. If Politician X says, "We can debate these regulations until the cows come home, but what the American people want to know is, when are we going to end this partisan bickering?" she has effectively avoided providing evidence on the benefits or detriments of the regulations by trying to change the subject to that of partisanship.

One common type of red herring is an ***ad hominem* fallacy**. *Ad hominem* is Latin for "to the man"; the phrase refers to the diversionary tactic of switching the argument from the issue at hand to the character of the other speaker. If you argue that a park in your community should not be renovated because the person supporting it was arrested during a domestic dispute, then you are guilty of *ad hominem* — arguing against the person rather than addressing the issue. This fallacy is frequently misunderstood to mean that *any* instance of questioning someone's character is *ad hominem*. Not so. It is absolutely valid to call a person's character into question if it is *relevant* to the topic at hand. For example, if a court case hinges on the testimony of a single witness and that person happens to be a con artist, then his character is absolutely relevant in deciding whether he is a credible witness.

Analogy is the most vulnerable type of evidence because it is always susceptible to the charge that two things are not comparable, resulting in a **faulty analogy**. However, some analogies are more vulnerable than others, particularly those that focus on irrelevant or inconsequential similarities between two things. Whenever analogy is used, it's important to gauge whether the dissimilarities outweigh the similarities. Advertisements sometimes draw faulty analogies to appeal to pathos; for example, an ad for a very expensive watch might picture a well-known athlete or a ballet dancer and draw an analogy between the precision and artistry of (1) the person and (2) the mechanism. When writers use analogy to add drama to a claim, it's important to question whether the similarities really fit and illuminate the point or simply add emotional appeal. For instance, to argue that "we put animals who are in irreversible pain out of their misery, so we should do the same for people" asks the reader to ignore significant and profound differences between animals and humans. The analogy may at first glance appeal to emotions, but it is questionable.

Fallacies of Accuracy

Using evidence that is either intentionally or unintentionally inaccurate will result in a fallacy. The most common example of inaccurate evidence resulting in a fallacy is one called the straw man. A **straw man fallacy** occurs when a speaker chooses a deliberately poor or oversimplified example in order to ridicule and refute an opponent's viewpoint. For example, consider the following scenario. Politician X proposes that we put astronauts on Mars in the next four years. Politician Y ridicules this proposal by saying that his opponent is looking for "little green men in outer space." Politician Y is committing a straw man fallacy by inaccurately representing Politician X's proposal, which is about space exploration and scientific experimentation, not "little green men."

Another fallacy that results from using inaccurate evidence is the **either/or fallacy**, also called a **false dilemma**. In this fallacy, the speaker presents two extreme options as the only possible choices. For instance:

Either we agree to higher taxes, or our grandchildren will be mired in debt.

This statement offers only two ways to view the issue, and both are extreme.

Fallacies of Insufficiency

Perhaps the most common of fallacies occurs when evidence is insufficient. We call this a **hasty generalization**, meaning that there is not enough evidence to support a particular conclusion. For instance: "Smoking isn't bad for you; my great-aunt smoked a pack a day and lived to be ninety." It could be that the story of the speaker's aunt is true, but this single anecdote does not provide enough evidence to discredit the results of years of medical research.

Another fallacy resulting from insufficient evidence is circular reasoning. **Circular reasoning** involves repeating the claim as a way to provide evidence, resulting in no evidence at all. For instance, a student who asserts, "You can't give me a C; I'm an A student" is guilty of circular reasoning; that is, the "evidence" that she should get an A is that she is an A student. The so-called evidence is insufficient because it is a mere repetition of the claim. You can frequently spot circular reasoning in advertising. For instance: "Buy this shampoo because it's the best shampoo!" or "Shop at this store because it's a shopper's paradise."

We will discuss other common logical fallacies as we examine specific types of evidence.

First-Hand Evidence

First-hand evidence is something you *know*, whether it's from personal experience, anecdotes you've heard from others, observations, or your general knowledge of events.

Personal Experience

The most common type of first-hand evidence is personal experience. Bringing in personal experience adds a human element and can be an effective way to appeal to pathos. For example, when writing about whether you do or do not support single-sex classrooms, you might describe your experience as a student, or you might use your observations about your school or classmates to inform your argument. Personal experience is a great way to make an abstract issue more human, and it is an especially effective technique in the introduction and conclusion of an argument. Personal experience can interest readers and draw them in, but they'll need more than just your perspective to be persuaded.

Personal experience works best if the writer can speak as an insider. For instance, you can speak knowledgeably about the issue of single-sex classrooms because you have inside knowledge about classrooms and how they work. In the following essay about the environmentalist movement, Jennifer Oladipo argues that minorities need to become more involved: "The terms *environmentalist* and *minority* conjure two distinct images in most people's minds — a false dichotomy that seriously threatens any chance of pulling the planet out of its current ecological tailspin." As a member of a minority group herself, she uses her personal experience as both an entrance into the essay and a source of evidence.

Why Can't Environmentalism Be Colorblind?
JENNIFER OLADIPO

In nearly two years of volunteering and working at an urban nature preserve, I have never seen another face like mine come through our doors. At least, I've not seen another black woman come for a morning hike or native-wildlife program. The few I do encounter are teachers and chaperones with school groups, or aides assisting people with disabilities. When I commute by bus to the preserve, located in the middle of Louisville, Kentucky, I disembark with blacks and other minorities. Yet none of them ever seems to make it to the trails.

I might have assumed they simply weren't interested, but then I saw that none of the center's newsletters were mailed to predominantly minority areas of town, nor did any press releases go to popular minority radio stations or newspapers. Not ever, as far as I could tell. Although the nature center seeks a stronger community presence and feels the same budget pinch as other small nonprofits, it has missed large swaths of the community with its message.

The terms *environmentalist* and *minority* conjure two distinct images in most people's minds — a false dichotomy that seriously threatens any chance of pulling the planet out of its current ecological tailspin. Some people think this country is on the precipice of a societal shift that will make environmental stewardship an integral part of our collective moral code. But that is not going to happen as long as we as a nation continue to think and act as if "green" automatically means "white."

Assumptions about who is amenable to conservation values cost the environmental movement numbers and dollars. Religion, capitalism, and even militarism learned ages ago to reach actively across the racial spectrum. In terms of winning over minorities, they have left environmentalism in the dust. Not until I joined an environmental-journalism organization was my mailbox flooded with information about serious environmental issues — even though I have been volunteering in organic gardens, hiking, and camping for years. I had received solicitations for credit cards and political parties, fast-food coupons, and a few Books of Mormon — but I had to seek out environmental groups.

Minorities make up one-third of the population, and we are growing as an   5 economic and financial force as our numbers increase. We are a key to maintaining the energy that environmentalism has gained as a result of intense mainstream attention. That momentum will peter out without more people to act on the present sense of urgency. Imagine the power of 100 million Asians, African Americans, Latinos, and Native Americans invested in sustainable living, joining green organizations, voting for politicians and laws that protect the environment.

Nobody benefits from the perception that enjoying and caring for the environment is an exclusively white lifestyle. The truth is that brown, yellow, red, and black people like to go backpacking, too. Those of us with the means are buying organic, local, and hybrid. If environmentalism continues to appear mostly white and well-off, it will continue to be mostly white and well-off, even as racial and economic demographics change. The environmental movement will continue to overlook the nuances, found in diversity of experience, that reveal multiple facets of environmental problems — and their solutions.

Sooner or later, even global warming will be pushed off magazine covers, television screens, and the congressional floor. Before that time, we need to have in place something even more impressive: a racially diverse, numerically astounding mass of environmentalists ready to pick up the ball and run with it.

(2007)

Oladipo writes most of her essay around her personal experience working in a Kentucky nature preserve, explaining why she chose the work and pointing out the lack of "another face like mine" (par. 1) in that setting. She also describes her experience working for an "environmental-journalism organization" (par. 4) and spending time outdoors. Although she primarily draws on her own experiences in her essay, she also uses some statistics and a reasonable tone to make a persuasive case.

> ## FALLACY ALERT: *Hasty* Generalization
>
> As we described previously (p. 103), a hasty generalization is a fallacy in which there is not enough evidence to support a particular conclusion. When using personal experience as evidence, it is important to remember that while it might provide some ethos to speak on a topic and it may be an effective way to appeal to pathos, personal experience is rarely universal proof.
>
> EXAMPLE   Pulling wisdom teeth is just another unnecessary and painful medical procedure. I still have all of mine, and they haven't given me any problems.

Anecdotes

First-hand evidence also includes **anecdotes** about other people that you've either observed or been told about. Like personal experience, anecdotes can be a useful way to appeal to pathos.

In the following excerpt from an op-ed piece, Fabiola Santiago argues against the policy that children born in the United States to immigrants, including those who are undocumented, must be treated as nonresidents when it comes to receiving state services. To make the case about the specific unfairness of imposing out-of-state tuition on Florida residents who fall into this category, Santiago uses an anecdote as part of her evidence.

In College, These American Citizens Are Not Created Equal
FABIOLA SANTIAGO

> "I lift my lamp beside the golden door!" — Lady Liberty
>
> On Saturday, the day after its 125th anniversary celebration, the Statue of Liberty will close its doors for a year-long, $27 million renovation of the monument's interior. One could only hope that the nation's soul will undergo some transformation as well. Emma Lazarus, the descendant of Sephardic Jews expelled from Spain who wrote in 1883 "The New Colossus," the moving sonnet at the base of the statue in New York harbor, would shed mournful tears at the lack of compassion for immigrants these days. She would weep at the ease with which words of disdain are spoken by some who lead and aspire to lead, and at the underhanded way in which ill-willed actions are taken against immigrants and their children.

Lady Liberty's "golden door" is not only jammed, slammed shut, or slightly ajar depending on where you come from, but we've fallen so low on the scale of our founding values that in the United States of America of today not all U.S. citizens are created equal. There are states like Florida, Alabama, and Arizona where politicians and bureaucrats use the system to discriminate, to create classes of Americans, to disenfranchise some of the most deserving among us. The latest low blow was unveiled by a class-action lawsuit and a bill filed in the Florida Legislature last week. Under rules established by the state's Department of Education and the university system's Board of Governors, students like Wendy Ruiz — born and raised in Miami — have to pay out-of-state tuition at rates that are more than three times what other Florida resident students pay for their education. Ruiz has lived in the state all her life. She has a Florida birth certificate, a Florida driver's license, and is registered to vote in Florida. But while other Miami Dade College students pay about $1,266 per term in tuition, she must pay $4,524 because the state considers her a dependent of nonresidents. Here's an institution that is supposed to defend education punishing a young American for the sins of her parents, who are undocumented immigrants. But we should all aspire to have neighbors like the Ruizes, who raised a daughter like Wendy, willing to work three part-time jobs to pay her tuition while maintaining a 3.7 grade-point average. "I know that I will be successful because I have never wanted something so bad in my life like I want this," Ruiz said of her education. Who knows what more Wendy Ruiz might accomplish, what more she could become if she were able to pay all of her attention to her education without the unfair financial burden of paying extravagantly unfair fees.

(2011)

Santiago could have provided facts and figures about the legislative policy in question. Instead, she focuses on one person, Wendy Ruiz. Santiago points out that Ruiz "has lived in the state all her life. She has a Florida birth certificate, a Florida driver's license, and is registered to vote in Florida." Santiago then explains the difference in tuition for residents versus nonresidents, noting that Wendy is a model citizen "willing to work three part-time jobs to pay her tuition." She even quotes Wendy's comments about the premium she places on education. In this example, Santiago is not writing about herself, but she is telling an anecdote about another person that gives a human face to the argument. She appeals to pathos by describing the situation of Wendy Ruiz, being careful to point out that her situation typifies that of others who would suffer from a proposed policy.

Current Events

References to current events are accessed first-hand through observation. Staying abreast of what is happening locally, nationally, and globally ensures a store of information that can be used as evidence in arguments. Remember that current events can be interpreted in many ways, so seek out multiple perspectives and be on the lookout for bias. Here is an example from an essay by the political analyst Fareed Zakaria about the plight of the American education system. He wrote the article around the time of the death of Steve Jobs, the founder of Apple, when details of Jobs's life were in the national news. In "When Will We Learn?" Zakaria argues for the improvement of our public education system, citing Jobs and his partner, Steve Wozniak, as evidence of the impact of a strong high school education.

> For the past month, we have all marveled at the life of Steve Jobs, the adopted son of working-class parents, who dropped out of college and became one of the great technologists and businessmen of our time. How did he do it? He was, of course, an extraordinary individual, and that explains much of his success, but his environment might also have played a role. Part of the environment was education. And it is worth noting that Jobs got a great secondary education. The school he attended, Homestead High in Cupertino, Calif., was a first-rate public school that gave him a grounding in both the liberal arts and technology. It did the same for Steve Wozniak, the more technically oriented co-founder of Apple Computer, whom Jobs met at that same school.
>
> In 1972, the year Jobs graduated, California's public schools were the envy of the world. They were generally rated the finest in the country, well funded and well run, with excellent teachers. These schools were engines of social mobility that took people like Jobs and Wozniak and gave them an educational grounding that helped them rise.
>
> *(2011)*

Second-Hand Evidence

Second-hand evidence is evidence that is accessed through research, reading, and investigation. It includes factual and historical information, expert opinion, quantitative data, and sometimes literary sources. Any time you cite what someone else knows, not what you know, you are using second-hand evidence. While citing second-hand evidence may occasionally appeal to pathos and certainly may establish a writer's ethos, the central appeal is to logos — reason and logic.

Historical Information

A common type of second-hand evidence is historical information — verifiable facts that a writer knows from research. This kind of evidence can provide background and context to current debates; it also can help establish the writer's ethos because it shows that he or she has taken the time and effort to research the matter and become informed. One possible pitfall is that historical events are complicated. You'll want to keep your description of the events brief, but be sure not to misrepresent the events. In the following paragraph from *Hate Speech: The History of an American Controversy* (1994), author Samuel Walker provides historical information to establish the "intolerance" of the 1920s era.

> The 1920s are remembered as a decade of intolerance. Bigotry was as much a symbol of the period as Prohibition, flappers, the stock market boom, and Calvin

Coolidge. It was the only time when the Ku Klux Klan paraded en masse through the nation's capital. In 1921 Congress restricted immigration for the first time in American history, drastically reducing the influx of Catholics and Jews from southern and eastern Europe, and the nation's leading universities adopted admission quotas to restrict the number of Jewish students. The Sacco and Vanzetti case, in which two Italian American anarchists were executed for robbery and murder in a highly questionable prosecution, has always been one of the symbols of the anti-immigrant tenor of the period.

(1994)

To support the claim that the 1920s was a period characterized by bigotry, Walker cites a series of historical examples: the KKK, immigration laws, restriction targeting certain ethnicities, and a high-profile court case.

Historical information is often used to develop a point of comparison or contrast to a more contemporary situation. In the following paragraph from Charles Krauthammer's op-ed "The 9/11 'Overreaction'? Nonsense," the political commentator does exactly that by comparing the War on Terror to previous military campaigns in U.S. history.

True, in both [the Iraq and Afghanistan] wars there was much trial, error, and tragic loss. In Afghanistan, too much emphasis on nation-building. In Iraq, the bloody middle years before we found our general and our strategy. But cannot the same be said of, for example, the Civil War, the terrible years before Lincoln found his general? Or the Pacific campaign of World War II, with its myriad miscalculations, its often questionable island-hopping, that cost infinitely more American lives?

(2011)

Notice that Krauthammer's historical evidence is brief but detailed enough to both show his grasp of the history and explicitly lay out his comparison. Simply saying, "These wars are no different from the Civil War or World War II" would have been far too vague and thus ineffective.

FALLACY ALERT: *Post Hoc Ergo Propter Hoc*

The name of the *post hoc ergo propter hoc* fallacy is Latin for "after which therefore because of which." What that means is that it is incorrect to claim that something is a cause just because it happened earlier. In other words, correlation does not imply causation.

EXAMPLE   We elected Johnson as president and look where it got us: hurricanes, floods, stock market crashes.

That's a simple example, but in reality causality is very tricky to prove because few things have only one cause. When using historical evidence, you should be especially aware of this fallacy. Check your facts. Consider the complexity of the situation. Proceed with caution.

Expert Opinion

Most everyone is an expert on something! And how often do we bolster our viewpoint by pointing out that so-and-so agrees with us? Expert opinion is a more formal variation on that common practice. An expert is someone who has published research on a topic or whose job or experience gives him or her specialized knowledge. Sometimes, you might cite the viewpoint of an individual who is an "expert" in a local matter but who is not widely recognized. If, for instance, you are writing about school policy, you might cite the opinion of a teacher or student government officer. The important point is to make certain that your expert is seen as credible by your audience so that his or her opinion will add weight to your argument.

Following is an excerpt from "What's Wrong with Cinderella?," by Peggy Orenstein, in which she critiques what she calls "the princess culture" that Disney promotes. In this paragraph, she is commenting on the phenomenon of "Supergirl." Note the use of an expert — and how that expert is identified — as evidence.

> The princess as superhero is not irrelevant. Some scholars I spoke with say that given its post-9/11 timing, princess mania is a response to a newly dangerous world. "Historically, princess worship has emerged during periods of uncertainty and profound social change," observes Miriam Forman-Brunell, a historian at the University of Missouri–Kansas City. Francis Hodgson Burnett's original *Little Princess* was published at a time of rapid urbanization, immigration and poverty; Shirley Temple's film version was a hit during the Great Depression. "The original folk tales themselves," Forman-Brunell says, "spring from medieval and early modern European culture that faced all kinds of economic and demographic and social upheaval — famine, war, disease, terror of wolves. Girls play savior during times of economic crisis and instability." That's a heavy burden for little shoulders. Perhaps that's why the magic wand has become an essential part of the princess get-up. In the original stories — even the Disney versions of them — it's not the girl herself who's magic: it's the fairy godmother. Now if Forman-Brunell is right, we adults have become the cursed creatures whom girls have the thaumaturgic [miraculous] power to transform.
>
> *(2006)*

Orenstein is careful to present credentials (in this case, through quoting a university professor) and to quote and paraphrase the relevant information as evidence. She quotes Forman-Brunell and then comments on this expert's viewpoint. Orenstein may have held the same opinion about fairy godmothers and their impact on girls' views of themselves, but the findings of a researcher add credibility to the argument.

FALLACY ALERT: Appeal to False Authority

Appeal to false authority occurs when someone who has no expertise to speak on an issue is cited as an authority. A TV star, for instance, is not a medical

expert, even though pharmaceutical advertisements often use celebrity endorsements. When choosing whom to cite as an expert, be sure to verify the person's
background and qualifications.

Quantitative Evidence

Quantitative evidence includes things that can be represented in numbers: statistics,
surveys, polls, census information. This type of evidence can be persuasive in its appeal
to logos. Amy Domini cites numerical evidence in her essay to support her contention that "[f]ast food is a way of life. In America, the average person eats it more than
150 times a year. In 2007, sales for the 400 largest U.S.-based fast-food chains totaled
$277 billion, up 7 percent from 2006" (see p. 87).

Quantitative evidence need not be all percentages and dollar figures, however. In
an article on American education, Fareed Zakaria compares the education situation of
the United States with that of other countries by citing quantitative information without a lot of numbers and figures.

> U.S. schoolchildren spend less time in school than their peers abroad. They have
> shorter school days and a shorter school year. Children in South Korea will spend
> almost two years more in school than Americans by the end of high school. Is it
> really so strange that they score higher on tests?
>
> If South Korea teaches the importance of hard work, Finland teaches another
> lesson. Finnish students score near the very top on international tests, yet they do
> not follow the Asian model of study, study and more study. Instead they start school
> a year later than in most countries, emphasize creative work and shun tests for most
> of the year. But Finland has great teachers, who are paid well and treated with the
> same professional respect that is accorded to doctors and lawyers. They are found
> and developed through an extremely competitive and rigorous process. All teach-
> ers are required to have master's degrees, and only 1 in 10 applicants is accepted
> to the country's teacher-training programs.

Zakaria includes quantitative data — two more years of school for Korean students
than their American counterparts, a highly competitive process for teacher-training
programs that accept only one of every ten applicants — as part of his overall discussion. He could have cited dollar amounts as evidence of how well paid teachers are in
Finland, but in the context of this column he makes the point and moves on; perhaps
if he were writing for a more scholarly or skeptical audience, he would have thought
it necessary to provide even more information.

FALLACY ALERT: Bandwagon Appeal

Bandwagon appeal (or *ad populum* **fallacy**) occurs when evidence boils down
to "everybody's doing it, so it must be a good thing to do." Sometimes, statistics

can be used to prove that "everybody's doing it" and thus give a bandwagon appeal the appearance of cold, hard fact.

> EXAMPLE   You should vote to elect Rachel Johnson — she has a strong lead in the polls!

Polling higher does not necessarily make Senator Johnson the "best" candidate, only the most popular.

Literary Sources

Like professional writers, you can use poetry and fiction as evidence to support an argument or as sources in a synthesis essay. Sometimes professional writers cite poets, novelists, and playwrights whose work is well-known enough that their names, and the names of their characters, carry weight; of course, name-dropping isn't enough. Literary sources can help writers establish ethos by presenting themselves as educated and well-read. They acknowledge common ground between reader and writer. They provide depth, nuance, and interest. In a March 2013 *New York Times* op-ed piece, for instance, Jennifer Glass challenges Yahoo chairperson Marissa Mayer's dictate that employees can no longer work from home.

> [E]mployees, creative or not, get older, marry, bear children, watch their parents grow infirm, and want lives outside the workplace. And despite companies' best efforts to replace family and simulate home life by providing cafeterias, game rooms, and concierge services for dry cleaning, most people eventually learn the hard way that companies will not care for you when times are hard; they will cut your pay or forgo your 401(k) match in economic downturns, and will dispose of you when you become ill or disabled. As Robert Frost reminds us, home is the place where they have to take you in. Work is not that place.
>
> *(2013)*

Glass paraphrases lines from Robert Frost's "The Death of the Hired Man" — which reads, "Home is the place where, when you have to go there, / They have to take you in" — to support her claim that work is not the same as home. She assumes her audience is familiar with the poem and uses it as a cultural touchstone. More important, the lines' meaning is an apt and succinct addition to Glass's argument.

Literary texts can be used to introduce an idea or issue. In "The End of White America," published in the *Atlantic* magazine in January/February 2009, writer Hua Hsu argues that Caucasians becoming the minority is "a cultural and demographic inevitability." He opens his essay with a scene from *The Great Gatsby* by F. Scott Fitzgerald.

> *"Civilization's going to pieces," he remarks. He is in polite company, gathered with friends around a bottle of wine in the late-afternoon sun, chatting and gossiping. "I've gotten to be a terrible pessimist about things. Have you read* The Rise of the Colored Empires *by this man Goddard?" They hadn't. "Well, it's a fine book, and*

everybody ought to read it. The idea is if we don't look out the white race will be — will be utterly submerged. It's all scientific stuff; it's been proved."

He is Tom Buchanan, a character in F. Scott Fitzgerald's *The Great Gatsby*, a book that nearly everyone who passes through the American education system is compelled to read at least once. Although *Gatsby* doesn't gloss as a book on racial anxiety — it's too busy exploring a different set of anxieties entirely — Buchanan was hardly alone in feeling besieged. The book by "this man Goddard" had a real-world analogue: Lothrop Stoddard's *The Rising Tide of Color Against White World-Supremacy*, published in 1920, five years before *Gatsby*. Nine decades later, Stoddard's polemic remains oddly engrossing. He refers to World War I as the "White Civil War" and laments the "cycle of ruin" that may result if the "white world" continues its infighting. The book features a series of foldout maps depicting the distribution of "color" throughout the world and warns, "Colored migration is a universal peril, menacing every part of the white world."

(2009)

This scene from *Gatsby* is the hook Hsu uses to grab his reader's attention. His readers will be drawn in by the familiar *Gatsby* reference. It helps him establish that this issue has history, and it allows him to note that the Lothrop Stoddard book actually existed. So, this literary source serves several functions for Hsu. But notice how Hsu qualifies his literary example: "*Gatsby* doesn't gloss as a book on racial anxiety." He will move in his essay into real-life examples, using interviews, anecdotes, and quantitative evidence to develop his argument. Hsu can use *Gatsby* to introduce the idea that the 1920s were a time when Caucasians were "feeling besieged" by the "rising tide of color" (to borrow Stoddard's title), but he has to move on to real-life examples because a fictional character alone is not sufficient evidence.

In *Lincoln at Gettysburg*, a book-length analysis of the Gettysburg Address, author Gary Wills illustrates Abraham Lincoln's tendency to use "one prejudice against another" — in this case the American prejudice against monarchies to fight against slavery — with an example from Mark Twain's *Huckleberry Finn*:

One cannot own human beings, and one should not be in the position of king over human beings. Mark Twain, too, relied on this latter prejudice when he introduced fake royalty onto Huck's raft, to deepen the relationship between Huck and Jim. The King and the Dauphin demand servile labor from their "subjects," who must kneel to their "betters" when bringing them food. Paradoxically, the man already a slave is the first to rebel: "Dese [two] is all I kin stan." Huck and Jim are made allies yearning for a joint freedom from "royalty," and it is in this situation that Huck, hearing the story of Jim's deaf daughter, first makes the startling admission: "I do believe he cared just as much for his people as white folks does for their'n."

(1992)

While Wills acknowledges that the purpose of this scene in the novel is to strengthen Huck and Jim's relationship, he uses the literary source to comment on Lincoln's understanding of human nature and how it helped him achieve his goals. Wills uses many types of sources in his book, both primary and secondary, but an iconic and well-known character like Huck Finn can certainly provide credible evidence of the values and beliefs of a particular time period. Literature is very useful for acknowledging common ground, commenting on culture, and introducing or illustrating key issues, but it should not be your only evidence. You need real-life examples from several different types of primary and secondary sources, such as the ones we've talked about above.

• ACTIVITY •

Identify the logical fallacy in each of the following examples.

1. What's the problem? All my friends have a curfew of midnight!

2. A person who is honest will not steal, so my client, an honest person, clearly is not guilty of theft.

3. Her economic plan is impressive, but remember: this is a woman who spent six weeks in the Betty Ford Center getting treatment for alcoholism.

4. Since Mayor Perry has been in office, our city has had a balanced budget; if he were governor, the state budget would finally be balanced.

5. If we outlaw guns, only outlaws will have guns.

6. Smoking is dangerous because it is harmful to your health.

7. He was last year's MVP, and he drives a Volvo. That must be a great car.

8. A national study of grades 6–8 showed that test scores went down last year and absenteeism was high; this generation is going to the dogs.

• ACTIVITY •

Annotate the essay below by identifying the different types of first- and second-hand evidence presented to develop the argument. Analyze how each type of evidence appeals to ethos, logos, pathos, or a combination of those. Be on the lookout for logical fallacies, and explain how they weaken Thomas's argument.

Terror's Purse Strings
DANA THOMAS

Luxury fashion designers are busily putting final touches on the handbags they will present during the spring-summer 2008 women's wear shows, which begin next week in New York City's Bryant Park. To understand the importance of the handbag in fashion today consider this: According to consumer surveys conducted by Coach, the average American woman was buying two new handbags a year in 2000; by 2004, it was more than four. And the average luxury bag retails for 10 to 12 times its production cost.

"There is a kind of an obsession with bags," the designer Miuccia Prada told me. "It's so easy to make money."

Counterfeiters agree. As soon as a handbag hits big, counterfeiters around the globe churn out fake versions by the thousands. And they have no trouble selling them. Shoppers descend on Canal Street in New York, Santee Alley in Los Angeles and flea markets and purse parties around the country to pick up knockoffs for one-tenth the legitimate bag's retail cost, then pass them off as real.

"Judges, prosecutors, defense attorneys shop here," a private investigator told me as we toured the counterfeit section of Santee Alley. "Affluent people from Newport Beach." According to a study by the British law firm Davenport Lyons, two-thirds of British consumers are "proud to tell their family and friends" that they bought fake luxury fashion items.

At least 11 percent of the world's clothing is fake, according to 2000 figures from the Global Anti-Counterfeiting Group in Paris. Fashion is easy to copy: counterfeiters buy the real items, take them apart, scan the pieces to make patterns and produce almost-perfect fakes.

Most people think that buying an imitation handbag or wallet is harmless, a victimless crime. But the counterfeiting rackets are run by crime syndicates that also deal in narcotics, weapons, child prostitution, human trafficking and terrorism. Ronald K. Noble, the secretary general of Interpol, told the House of Representatives Committee on International Relations that profits from the sale of counterfeit goods have gone to groups associated with Hezbollah, the Shiite terrorist group, paramilitary organizations in Northern Ireland and FARC, the Revolutionary Armed Forces of Colombia.

Sales of counterfeit T-shirts may have helped finance the 1993 World Trade Center bombing, according to the International AntiCounterfeiting Coalition. "Profits from counterfeiting are one of the three main sources of income supporting international terrorism," said Magnus Ranstorp, a terrorism expert at the University of St. Andrews, in Scotland.

Most fakes today are produced in China, a good many of them by children. Children are sometimes sold or sent off by their families to work in clandestine factories that produce counterfeit luxury goods. Many in the West consider this an urban myth. But I have seen it myself.

On a warm winter afternoon in Guangzhou, I accompanied Chinese police officers on a factory raid in a decrepit tenement. Inside, we found two dozen children, ages 8 to 13, gluing and sewing together fake luxury-brand handbags. The police confiscated everything, arrested the owner and sent the children out. Some punched their timecards, hoping to still get paid. (The average Chinese factory worker earns about $120 a month; the counterfeit factory worker earns half that or less.) As we made our way back to the police

5

vans, the children threw bottles and cans at us. They were now jobless and, because the factory owner housed them, homeless. It was *Oliver Twist* in the 21st century.

What can we do to stop this? Much like the war on drugs, the effort to protect luxury brands must go after the source: the counterfeit manufacturers. The company that took me on the Chinese raid is one of the only luxury-goods makers that works directly with Chinese authorities to shut down factories, and it has one of the lowest rates of counterfeiting.

Luxury brands also need to teach consumers that the traffic in fake goods has many victims. But most companies refuse to speak publicly about counterfeiting — some won't even authenticate questionable items for concerned customers — believing, like Victorians, that acknowledging despicable actions tarnishes their sterling reputations.

So it comes down to us. If we stop knowingly buying fakes, the supply chain will dry up and counterfeiters will go out of business. The crime syndicates will have far less money to finance their illicit activities and their terrorist plots. And the children? They can go home.

(2008)

• ESSAY IN PROGRESS: Using Evidence •

Choose one of the thesis statements you developed on page 101, and write three paragraphs of support, using a different type of evidence in each. You will probably have to do some research if you want to use historical information, expert testimony, or quantitative data.

Shaping Argument

The shape of an argument — that is, the organization or arrangement — reflects a host of factors, including audience and purpose, but it usually follows one of several patterns. We'll discuss classical oration, induction and deduction, and the Toulmin model as four common ways to structure an argument. Keep in mind that writers often modify these structures as needed. The essential point to remember is that the organization should fit the ideas, rather than forcing ideas to fit into a prescribed organizational pattern.

The Classical Oration

Classical rhetoricians outlined a five-part structure for an oratory, or speech, that writers still use today, although perhaps not always consciously:

- The **introduction (exordium)** introduces the reader to the subject under discussion. In Latin, *exordium* means "beginning a web," which is an apt description for an introduction. Whether it is a single paragraph or several, the introduction draws the readers into the text by piquing their interest, challenging them, or otherwise getting their attention. Often the introduction is where the writer establishes ethos.

- The **narration (narratio)** provides factual information and background material on the subject at hand, thus beginning the developmental paragraphs, or establishes why the subject is a problem that needs addressing. The level of detail a writer uses in this section depends largely on the audience's knowledge of the subject. Although classical rhetoric describes narration as appealing to logos, in actuality it often appeals to pathos because the writer attempts to evoke an emotional response about the importance of the issue being discussed.

- The **confirmation (confirmatio)**, usually the major part of the text, includes the development or the proof needed to make the writer's case — the nuts and bolts of the essay, containing the most specific and concrete detail in the text. The confirmation generally makes the strongest appeal to logos.

- The **refutation (refutatio)**, which addresses the counterargument, is in many ways a bridge between the writer's proof and conclusion. Although classical rhetoricians recommended placing this section at the end of the text as a way to anticipate objections to the proof given in the confirmation section, this is not a hard-and-fast rule. If opposing views are well-known or valued by the audience, a writer will address them before presenting his or her own argument. The counterargument's appeal is largely to logos.

- The **conclusion (peroratio)**, sometimes called the peroration — whether it is one paragraph or several — brings the essay to a satisfying close. Here the writer usually appeals to pathos and reminds the reader of the ethos established earlier. Rather than simply repeating what has gone before, the conclusion brings all the writer's ideas together and answers the question, so what? Writers should remember the classical rhetoricians' advice that the last words and ideas of a text are those the audience is most likely to remember.

An example of the classical model at work is the piece below written in 2006 by Sandra Day O'Connor, a former Supreme Court justice, and Roy Romer, then superintendent of the Los Angeles Unified School District.

Not by Math Alone
Sandra Day O'Connor and Roy Romer

Fierce global competition prompted President Bush to use the State of the Union address to call for better math and science education, where there's evidence that many schools are falling short. | Introduction

We should be equally troubled by another shortcoming in American schools: Most young people today simply do not have an adequate understanding of how our government and political system work, and they are thus not well prepared to participate as citizens.

This country has long exemplified democratic practice to the rest of the world. With the attention we are paying to advancing democracy abroad, we ought not neglect it at home.

Two-thirds of 12th-graders scored below "proficient" on the last national civics assessment in 1998, and only 9 percent could list two ways a democracy benefits from citizen participation. Yes, young people remain highly patriotic, and many volunteer in their communities. But most are largely disconnected from current events and issues.

A healthy democracy depends on the participation of citizens, and that participation is learned behavior; it doesn't just happen. As the 2003 report "The Civic Mission of Schools" noted: "Individuals do not automatically become free and responsible citizens, but must be educated for citizenship." That means civic learning — educating students for democracy — needs to be on par with other academic subjects.   *Narration*   5

This is not a new idea. Our first public schools saw education for citizenship as a core part of their mission. Eighty years ago, John Dewey said, "Democracy needs to be reborn in every generation and education is its midwife."

But in recent years, civic learning has been pushed aside. Until the 1960s, three courses in civics and government were common in American high schools, and two of them ("civics" and "problems of democracy") explored the role of citizens and encouraged students to discuss current issues. Today those courses are very rare.

What remains is a course on "American government" that usually spends little time on how people can — and why they should — participate. The effect of reduced civic learning on civic life is not theoretical. Research shows that the better people   *Confirmation* understand our history and system of government, the more likely they are to vote and participate in the civic life.

We need more and better classes to impart the knowledge of government, history, law and current events that students need to understand and participate in a democratic republic. And we also know that much effective civic learning takes place beyond the classroom — in extracurricular activity, service work that is connected to class work, and other ways students experience civic life.

Preserving our democracy should be reason enough to pro-   10
mote civic learning. But there are other benefits. Understanding
society and how we relate to each other fosters the attitudes essential for success in college, work and communities; it enhances
student learning in other subjects.

Economic and technological competitiveness are essential,
and America's economy and technology have flourished because
of the rule of law and the "assets" of a free and open society.
Democracy has been good for business and for economic well-
being. By the same token, failing to hone the civic tools of democracy will have economic consequences.

Bill Gates — a top business and technology leader — argues
strongly that schools have to prepare students not only for college
and career but for citizenship as well.

None of this is to diminish the importance of improving math
and science education. This latest push, as well as the earlier
emphasis on literacy, deserves support. It should also be the occa-   *Refutation*
sion for a broader commitment, and that means restoring education
for democracy to its central place in school.

We need more students proficient in math, science and engineering. We also need them to be prepared for their role as citizens. Only then can self-government work. Only then will we not   *Conclusion*
only be more competitive but also remain the beacon of liberty in
a tumultuous world.

*Sandra Day O'Connor retired as an associate justice of the
Supreme Court. Roy Romer, a former governor of Colorado, is
superintendent of the Los Angeles Unified School District. They
are co-chairs of the national advisory council of the Campaign
for the Civic Mission of Schools.*

(2006)

Sandra Day O'Connor and Roy Romer follow the classical model very closely. The
opening two paragraphs are an introduction to the main idea the authors develop. In
fact, the one-sentence paragraph 2 contains their two-part claim, or thesis: "Most
young people today simply do not have an adequate understanding of how our government and political system work, and they are thus not well prepared to participate
as citizens." O'Connor's position as a former Supreme Court justice establishes her
ethos as a reasonable person, an advocate for justice, and a concerned citizen. Romer's
biographical note at the end of the article suggests similar qualities. The authors use the
pronoun "we" in the article to refer not only to themselves but to all of "us" who are
concerned about American society. The opening phrase, "Fierce global competition,"
connotes a sense of urgency, and the warning that we are not adequately preparing our

young people to participate as citizens is sure to evoke an emotional response of concern, even alarm.

In paragraphs 3–6—the narration—the authors provide background information, including facts that add urgency to their point. They cite statistics, quote from research reports, even call on the well-known educator John Dewey. They also include a definition of "civic learning," a key term in their argument. Their facts-and-figures appeal is largely to logos, though the language of "a healthy democracy" certainly engages the emotions.

Paragraphs 7–12 present the bulk of the argument—the confirmation—by offering reasons and examples to support the case that young people lack the knowledge necessary to be informed citizens. The authors link civic learning to other subjects as well as to economic development. They quote Bill Gates, chairman of Microsoft, who has spoken about the economic importance of a well-informed citizenry.

In paragraph 13, O'Connor and Romer briefly address a major objection—the refutation—that we need to worry more about math and science education than about civic learning. While they concede the importance of math, science, and literacy, they point out that it is possible to increase civic education without undermining the gains made in those other fields.

The final paragraph—the conclusion—emphasizes the importance of a democracy to a well-versed citizenry, a point that stresses the shared values of the authors with their audience. The appeal to pathos is primarily through the vivid language, particularly the final sentence with its emotionally charged description "beacon of liberty," a view of their nation that most Americans hold dear.

Induction and Deduction

Induction and deduction are ways of reasoning, but they are often effective ways to structure an entire argument as well.

Induction

Induction (from the Latin *inducere*, "to lead into") means arranging an argument so that it leads from particulars to universals, using specific cases to draw a conclusion. For instance:

> Regular exercise promotes weight loss.
>
> Exercise lowers stress levels.
>
> Exercise improves mood and outlook.
>
> GENERALIZATION   Exercise contributes to better health.

We use induction in our everyday lives. For example, if your family and friends have owned several cars made by Subaru that have held up well, then you are likely to conclude inductively that Subaru makes good cars. Yet induction is also used in more technical situations. Even the scientific method is founded on inductive reasoning. Scientists use experiments to determine the effects in certain cases, and from there they might infer a universal scientific principle. For instance, if bases neutralize acids in every experiment conducted, then it can reasonably be inferred that all bases neutralize acids. The process of induction involves collecting evidence and then drawing an inference based on that evidence in order to reach a conclusion.

When you write a full essay developed entirely by reasons, one after another supporting the main point, then your entire argument is inductive. For instance, suppose you are asked to take a position on whether the American Dream is alive and well today. As you examine the issue, you might think of examples from your own community that demonstrate that the Dream is not a reality for the average citizen; you might study current events and think about the way societal expectations have changed; you might use examples from fiction you have read, such as the novel *Tortilla Curtain* by T. Corraghessan Boyle or movies such as *Boyz N the Hood*, where economic pressures limit the characters' horizons. All of this evidence together supports the inference that the American Dream no longer exists for the average person. To write that argument, you would support your claim with a series of reasons explained through concrete examples: you would argue inductively.

Arguments developed inductively can never be said to be true or false, right or wrong. Instead, they can be considered strong or weak, so it's important to consider possible vulnerabilities — in particular, the exception to the rule. Let's consider an example from politics. An argument written in favor of a certain political candidate might be organized inductively around reasons that she is the best qualified person for the job because of her views on military spending, financial aid for college students, and states' rights. However, the argument is vulnerable to an objection that her views on, for instance, the death penalty or environmental issues weaken her qualifications. Essentially, an argument structured inductively cannot lead to certainty, only to probability.

Let's look at an excerpt from *Outliers* by Malcolm Gladwell for an example of how an argument can be structured largely by induction. Gladwell uses various types of evidence here to support his conclusion that "[w]hen it comes to math . . . Asians have a built-in advantage."

from *Outliers*
MALCOLM GLADWELL

> Take a look at the following list of numbers: 4, 8, 5, 3, 9, 7, 6. Read them out loud. Now look away and spend twenty seconds memorizing that sequence before saying them out loud again.
>
> If you speak English, you have about a 50 percent chance of remembering that sequence perfectly. If you're Chinese, though, you're almost certain to get it right every time. Why is that? Because as human beings we store digits in a memory loop that runs for about two seconds. We most easily memorize whatever we can say or read within that two-second span. And Chinese speakers get that list of

numbers — 4, 8, 5, 3, 9, 7, 6 — right almost every time because, unlike English, their language allows them to fit all those seven numbers into two seconds.

That example comes from Stanislas Dehaene's book *The Number Sense*. As Dehaene explains:

> Chinese number words are remarkably brief. Most of them can be uttered in less than one-quarter of a second (for instance, 4 is "si" and 7 "qi"). Their English equivalents — "four," "seven," — are longer: pronouncing them takes about one-third of a second. The memory gap between English and Chinese apparently is entirely due to this difference in length. In languages as diverse as Welsh, Arabic, Chinese, English and Hebrew, there is a reproducible correlation between the time required to pronounce numbers in a given language and the memory span of its speakers. In this domain, the prize for efficacy goes to the Cantonese dialect of Chinese, whose brevity grants residents of Hong Kong a rocketing memory span of about 10 digits.

It turns out that there is also a big difference in how number-naming systems in Western and Asian languages are constructed. In English, we say fourteen, sixteen, seventeen, eighteen, and nineteen, so one might expect that we would also say oneteen, twoteen, threeteen, and fiveteen. But we don't. We use a different form: eleven, twelve, thirteen, and fifteen. Similarly, we have forty and sixty, which sound like the words they are related to (four and six). But we also say fifty and thirty and twenty, which sort of sound like five and three and two, but not really. And, for that matter, for numbers above twenty, we put the "decade" first and the unit number second (twenty-one, twenty-two), whereas for the teens, we do it the other way around (fourteen, seventeen, eighteen). The number system in English is highly irregular. Not so in China, Japan, and Korea. They have a logical counting system. Eleven is ten-one. Twelve is ten-two. Twenty-four is two-tens-four and so on.

That difference means that Asian children learn to count much faster than   5
American children. Four-year-old Chinese children can count, on average, to forty. American children at that age can count only to fifteen, and most don't reach forty until they're five. By the age of five, in other words, American children are already a *year* behind their Asian counterparts in the most fundamental of math skills.

The regularity of their number system also means that Asian children can perform basic functions, such as addition, far more easily. Ask an English-speaking seven-year-old to add thirty-seven plus twenty-two in her head, and she has to convert the words to numbers (37 + 22). Only then can she do the math: 2 plus 7 is 9 and 30 and 20 is 50, which makes 59. Ask an Asian child to add three-tens-seven and two-tens-two, and then the necessary equation is right there, embedded in the sentence. No number translation is necessary: It's five-tens-nine.

"The Asian system is transparent," says Karen Fuson, a Northwestern University psychologist who has closely studied Asian-Western differences. "I think that it makes the whole attitude toward math different. Instead of being a rote learning thing, there's a pattern I can figure out. There is an expectation that I can do this. There is an expectation that it's sensible. For fractions, we say three-fifths. The Chinese is literally 'out of five parts, take three.' That's telling you conceptually what a fraction is. It's differentiating the denominator and the numerator."

The much-storied disenchantment with mathematics among Western children starts in the third and fourth grades, and Fuson argues that perhaps a part of that disenchantment is due to the fact that math doesn't seem to make sense; its linguistic structure is clumsy; its basic rules seem arbitrary and complicated.

Asian children, by contrast, don't feel nearly the same bafflement. They can hold more numbers in their heads and do calculations faster, and the way fractions are expressed in their languages corresponds exactly to the way a fraction actually is — and maybe that makes them a little more likely to enjoy math, and maybe because they enjoy math a little more, they try a little harder and take more math classes and are more willing to do their homework, and on and on, in a kind of virtuous circle.

When it comes to math, in other words, Asians have a built-in advantage.   10

(2008)

In each paragraph, Gladwell provides reasons backed by evidence. He begins in the opening two paragraphs by drawing in the reader with an anecdotal example that (he assumes) will demonstrate his point: if you speak English, you won't do as well as if you speak Chinese. In paragraph 3, he provides additional support by citing an expert who has written a book entitled *The Number Sense.* In the next two paragraphs, he discusses differences in the systems of Western and Asian languages that explain why Asian children learn certain basic skills that put them ahead of their Western counterparts at an early age. In paragraphs 6 and 7, he raises another issue — attitude toward problem solving — and provides evidence from an expert to explain the superiority of Asian students. By this point, Gladwell has provided enough specific information — from facts, experts, examples — to support an inference that is a generalization. In this case, he concludes that "[w]hen it comes to math . . . Asians have a built-in advantage." Gladwell's reasoning and the structure of his argument are inductive.

Deduction

When you argue using **deduction**, you reach a conclusion by starting with a general principle or universal truth (a major premise) and applying it to a specific case (a minor premise). Deductive reasoning is often structured as a **syllogism**, a logical structure that uses the major premise and minor premise to reach a necessary conclusion. Let's use the same example about exercise that we used to demonstrate induction, but now we'll develop a syllogism to argue deductively:

MAJOR PREMISE	Exercise contributes to better health.
MINOR PREMISE	Yoga is a type of exercise.
CONCLUSION	Yoga contributes to better health.

The strength of deductive logic is that if the first two premises are true, then the conclusion is logically valid. Keep in mind, though, that if either premise is false (or questionable in any way), then the conclusion is subject to challenge. Consider the following:

MAJOR PREMISE	Celebrities are role models for young people.
MINOR PREMISE	Lindsey Lohan is a celebrity.
CONCLUSION	Lindsey Lohan is a role model for young people.

As you can see in this example, the conclusion is logically valid — but is it true? You can challenge the conclusion by challenging the veracity of the major premise — that is, whether all celebrities are role models for young people.

Deduction is a good way to combat stereotypes that are based on faulty premises. Consider this one:

MAJOR PREMISE	Women are poor drivers.
MINOR PREMISE	Ellen is a woman.
CONCLUSION	Ellen is a poor driver.

Breaking this stereotype down into a syllogism clearly shows the faulty logic. Perhaps some women, just as some men, are poor drivers, but to say that women in general drive poorly is to stereotype by making a hasty generalization. Breaking an idea down into component parts like this helps expose the basic thinking, which then can yield a more nuanced argument. This example might be qualified, for instance, by saying that *some* women are poor drivers; thus, Ellen *might* be a poor driver.

• ESSAY IN PROGRESS: Shaping an Argument •

Write an outline that shows how you could structure the argument you are crafting either inductively or deductively. If you are using induction, cite at least four specifics that lead to your generalization (claim). If using deduction, break the overall reasoning of the essay into a syllogism with both a major and a minor premise and a conclusion.

Combining Induction and Deduction

While some essays are either completely inductive or completely deductive, it's more common for an essay to combine these methods depending on the situation. Often, induction — a series of examples — is used to verify a minor premise, then that premise can become the foundation for deductive reasoning. Let's take a look at a brief excerpt from a book by political philosophy professor and author Michael J. Sandel that does just that.

from *Justice: What's the Right Thing to Do?*
Michael J. Sandel

Some philosophers who would tax the rich to help the poor argue in the name of utility; taking a hundred dollars from a rich person and giving it to a poor person will diminish the rich person's happiness only slightly, they speculate, but greatly increase the happiness of the poor person. John Rawls also defends redistribution, but on the grounds of hypothetical consent. He argues that if we imagined a hypothetical social contract in an original position of equality, everyone would agree to a principle that would support some form of redistribution.

But there is a third, more important reason to worry about the growing inequality of American life: Too great a gap between rich and poor undermines the solidarity that democratic citizenship requires. Here's how: as inequality deepens, rich and poor live increasingly separate lives. The affluent send their children to private schools (or to public schools in wealthy suburbs), leaving urban public schools to the children of families who have no alternative. A similar trend leads to the secession by the privileged from other public institutions and facilities. Private health clubs replace municipal recreation centers and swimming pools. Upscale residential communities hire private security guards and rely less on public police protection. A second or third car removes the need to rely on public transportation. And so on. The affluent secede from public places and services, leaving them to those who can't afford anything else.

This has two bad effects, one fiscal, the other civic. First, public services deteriorate, as those who no longer use those services become less willing to support them with their taxes. Second, public institutions such as schools, parks, playgrounds, and community centers cease to be places where citizens from different walks of life encounter one another. Institutions that once gathered people together and served as informal schools of civic virtue become few and far between. The hollowing out of the public realm makes it difficult to cultivate the solidarity and sense of community on which democratic citizenship depends.

So, quite apart from its effects on utility or consent, inequality can be corrosive to civic virtue. Conservatives enamored of markets and liberals concerned with redistribution overlook this loss.

If the erosion of the public realm is the problem, what is the solution? A politics 5 of the common good would take as one of its primary goals the reconstruction of the infrastructure of civic life. Rather than focus on redistribution for the sake of broadening access to private consumption, it would tax the affluent to rebuild public institutions and services so that rich and poor alike would want to take advantage of them.

(2009)

The argument of this passage can be distilled into this syllogism:

MAJOR PREMISE   Our democracy depends on a feeling of solidarity among all citizens.

MINOR PREMISE   The gap between the rich and the poor is growing in America, producing greater inequality and reducing solidarity. (Supported inductively with evidence)

CONCLUSION   To preserve democracy, we should work to close the gap.

The major premise supplies the general principle on which the argument hinges, that a shared feeling of solidarity among all citizens is fundamental to the success of our democracy. While the argument follows the deductive path of the syllogism, the minor premise is supported inductively with evidence. Sandel says, "as inequality deepens, rich and poor live increasingly separate lives" (par. 2). He offers evidence about schooling, transportation, recreational facilities; he explains how "inequality can be corrosive to civic virtue" (par. 4); and he states that we should "rebuild public institutions and services so that rich and poor alike would want to take advantage of them" (par. 5). The evidence is convincing. Our democracy is in trouble; inequality is a major cause; we should close the wealth gap if we are to preserve democracy.

Using the Toulmin Model

A useful way of both analyzing and structuring an argument is through the **Toulmin model**, an approach to argument created by British philosopher Stephen Toulmin in his book *The Uses of Argument* (1958). The Toulmin model is an effective tool in uncovering the assumptions that underlie arguments. Although at first this method — particularly its terminology — may seem complicated, it is actually very practical because it helps with analysis, structuring, qualifying a thesis, and understanding abstract arguments. Once mastered, it can be a very powerful tool.

The Toulmin model has six elements: claim, support (evidence), warrant (the assumption), backing, qualifier, and reservation. We have already discussed claims, which are arguable assertions. Toulmin defined a claim as "a conclusion whose merits we are seeking to establish." You have also already learned about support or evidence. A **warrant** expresses the **assumption** necessarily shared by the speaker and the audience. Similar to the minor premise of a syllogism, the assumption links the claim to the evidence; in other words, if the speaker and audience do not share the same assumption regarding the claim, all the evidence in the world won't be enough to sway them. **Backing** consists of further assurances or data without which the assumption lacks authority. The **qualifier**, when used (for example, *usually, probably, maybe, in most cases, most likely*), tempers the claim a bit, making it less absolute. The **reservation** explains the terms and conditions necessitated by the qualifier. In many cases, the argument will contain a **rebuttal** that gives voice to objections.

The following diagram illustrates the Toulmin model at work:

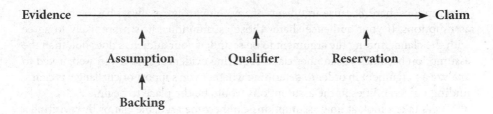

A Toulmin analysis will follow this form:

> Because (evidence as support), therefore (claim), since (assumption), on account of (backing), unless (reservation).

If there is a qualifier (such as *usually* or *maybe*), it will precede the claim. In our examples, we will put "therefore" in parentheses to indicate that you would omit the word in your writing. Here is a simple illustration:

> Because it is raining, (therefore) I should take my umbrella, since it will keep me dry.

You will immediately recognize the tacit assumption (that an umbrella will keep you dry) given explicit expression in the warrant. The backing would be "on account of the fact that the material is waterproof," and the reservation might be "unless there is a hole in it." In this case, the backing and reservation are so obvious that they don't need to be stated. The diagram below illustrates this argument — a simple one indeed, but one that demonstrates the process:

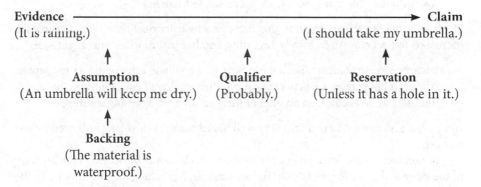

Fully expressed, this Toulmin argument would read:

> Because it is raining, (therefore) I should probably take my umbrella, since it will keep me dry on account of its waterproof material, unless, of course, there is a hole in it.

Analyzing Assumptions

You will note how the Toulmin model gives expression to the usually unspoken but necessary assumption. The Toulmin model shows us that assumptions are the link between a claim and the evidence used to support it. And, really, we should say "assumptions" here, because arguments of any complexity are always based on multiple assumptions. If your audience shares those assumptions, it is more likely to agree with the claim, finding the argument to be sound; if your audience does not, then the assumption becomes yet another claim requiring evidence. And if you were asked to analyze an argument in order to determine whether you support or challenge its claim, finding vulnerabilities in the assumptions would be the place to begin.

Let's take a look at how assumptions can become arguable claims by revisiting a piece that you read earlier in this chapter, Amy Domini's article "Why Investing in Fast Food May Be a Good Thing." We will see that by using the Toulmin method you could paraphrase her argument as follows:

> Because the fast-food industry continues to grow and is not going away, (therefore) even those of us who support Slow Food should invest in it, since investing has the power to persuade businesses to change.

The last part expresses one of the assumptions the audience must agree on in order for Domini's argument to be persuasive. Does investing have the power to persuade business to change?

Two examples from the education article extract by Fareed Zakaria will further illustrate the method. Paraphrased according to Toulmin, one of Zakaria's arguments would run as follows:

> Because Chinese and South Korean children spend almost two years more in school than do Americans, (therefore) they outperform Americans on tests, since increased instructional time is responsible for increased test scores.

Do you agree with the assumption that increased instructional time is responsible for increased test scores? Alternatively, revealing another assumption, one might say:

> Because foreign students spend more time in school and achieve higher test scores, (therefore) they receive a better education, since quality of education and learning is indicated by test scores, on account of their accuracy in assessing learning.

Again, the assumption here might very well be debatable. Is learning indicated by test scores?

Sometimes, in the development of an argument, claims are presented implicitly early in the piece and more explicitly later. For an example, let's return to "The C Word in the Hallways" by Anna Quindlen. In the article, she makes several claims and supports them with credible evidence. Still, if you are to agree with her position, it is necessary to agree with the assumptions on which her arguments rest. Using the Toulmin model can help you to discover what they are, especially when the claim is implicit, as in the following:

> So many have already been lost. This month Kip Kinkel was sentenced to life in prison in Oregon for the murders of his parents and a shooting rampage at his high school that killed two students. A psychiatrist who specializes in the care of adolescents testified that Kinkel, now 17, had been hearing voices since he was 12. Sam Manzie is also 17. He is serving a 70-year sentence for luring an 11-year-old boy named Eddie Werner into his New Jersey home and strangling him with the cord of

an alarm clock because his Sega Genesis was out of reach. Manzie had his first psychological evaluation in the first grade.

Using the Toulmin model, Quindlen's implicit argument here might be paraphrased as follows:

> Because Kinkel's and Manzie's mental illnesses were known for several years before they committed murder, (therefore) mental health care could have saved lives, since psychological intervention would have prevented them from committing these heinous acts.

As you finish the article, you come to realize that the entire argument rests on that assumption. Indeed, would psychological intervention have had that result? It certainly provokes discussion, which means that it is perhaps a point of vulnerability in Quindlen's argument.

• ACTIVITY •

For each of the following statements, identify the assumption that would link the claim to its support. Use the following format to discover the assumption: "Because (support), therefore (claim), since (assumption), on account of (backing), unless (reservation)." Decide whether each of the statements would require a qualifier.

1. Grades should be abolished because they add stress to the learning experience.
2. Until you buy me a diamond, I won't know that you love me!
3. Everyone should read novels because they make us more understanding of human foibles and frailties.
4. If we want to decrease gang violence, we should legalize drugs.
5. Don't get married if you believe that familiarity breeds contempt.
6. WiFi should be available to everyone without cost since the Internet has become a vital part of our lives.
7. You must obey her because she is your mother.
8. Because improving the educational system in this country is essential to competing with the other industrialized nations, we need to equip all classrooms with the latest computer technology.

From Reading to Writing

The Toulmin model can help you not only analyze the arguments that you read but also to bring logic and order to those that you write. Of course, the Toulmin language shouldn't be used directly in your essays because it often sounds stiff and lacks the nuance of more natural writing. Eliminating some of the artificial constructions and awkward phrasings — because, therefore, since — can create a strong thesis statement, or at least help you think through the logic of your argument fully so that you can compose one that is strong and persuasive.

Let's walk through the process of refining an argument topic using the Toulmin model. We'll begin by responding to an argument about the increased visual nature of our print media, including textbooks:

> One reason education in this country is so bad is that the textbooks are crammed full of fluff like charts and graphs and pictures.

Let's restate this argument using the Toulmin model and look at its component parts, omitting the redundant "therefore."

> Because textbook authors are filling their books with charts, graphs, and pictures, therefore the quality of education is declining in this country, since less written information equals less learning.

Evidence ————————————————————→ **Claim**
(Textbooks contain charts, graphs, pictures.)   (Education is declining.)

↑

Assumption
(Learning comes from written text.)

↑

Backing
(Traditionally, students have been learning from written text.)

Studying the argument this way, we find that the original argument has a vulnerability in that it assumes students only learn from printed text and not from visual material.

We can also use Toulmin to craft a response, using a simple template such as this: "Because _____, (therefore) _____, since _____, on account of _____, unless _____." Just because it's a template doesn't mean it has to tie your hands intellectually. You can put forth any viewpoint you like. Here is one response, just as an example (again, deleting the "therefore"):

> Because charts, graphs, and pictures provide information, therefore they do not hinder the education system, since that information is a supplement to written text.

In this case, we did not include a qualifier or a reservation.

Evidence ————————————————————→ **Claim**
(Charts, graphs, pictures provide information.)   (Visuals do not hinder education.)

↑

Assumption
(Visual information supplements written text.)

↑

Backing
(Students learn from a variety of media.)

You would then use that statement to develop your position and to write the thesis for your essay. The following example presents the claim but doesn't argue with the data: it acknowledges its validity, as far as it goes (this creates a reasonable tone and appeals to ethos and logos), and then zeros in on the assumption with a pair of rhetorical questions:

> Much of the argument is indisputable; however, some of it can be interpreted in different ways. Take, for instance, the criticism of textbooks for using too many visuals, particularly of a map replacing a topographical description. Is the map really a bad thing? Are any of the charts and graphs bad things?

The essay would then go on to argue the value of visuals not as replacements for but as enhancements to written texts, developing a qualified and reasoned argument.

• ACTIVITY •

Complete each of the following templates, using an argument from this chapter (e.g., "Crazed Rhetoric" by Tom Toles, "Why Investing in Fast Food May Be a Good Thing" by Amy Domini, or "*Star Wars*" by Roger Ebert). Use at least two different texts.

1. In his/her argument, _____ concludes _____ and supports the conclusion with such evidence as _____ and _____. To link this conclusion with the evidence, he/she makes the assumption that _____.

2. Although what _____ says about _____ may be true in some cases, his/her position fails to take _____ into account. A closer look at _____ reveals _____.

3. While the position advanced by _____ may seem reasonable, it assumes _____. If that were so, then _____. It might be more reasonable to consider _____.

4. One way to look at _____ would be to say _____; but if that were the case, then _____. Of course, another view might be _____. Yet another way to consider _____ might be _____.

5. Position _____ would be sound only if we chose to ignore _____. When we consider _____, then _____. In addition, _____.

6. Wouldn't it be wonderful if we could all agree about _____? The trouble is, _____. _____ says _____ and _____ says _____. How can we come to a compromise that recognizes _____?

Analyzing Literary Texts as Arguments

Let's talk about a part of a novel, a speech that you're probably familiar with: Atticus Finch's closing argument to the all white, all male jury in the trial of Tom Robinson in *To Kill a Mockingbird* by Harper Lee. You will likely recall that Atticus, father of Scout, the novel's narrator, is a lawyer in Maycomb County, Alabama, in the 1930s. He has been assigned by the court to defend Tom Robinson, a black man accused of raping Mayella Ewell, a white woman. We see all of the action through Scout's eyes and she has come into court in the middle of her father's closing statement. She watches horrified as Atticus "unbuttoned his collar, loosened his tie and took off his coat." She and her brother were shocked at this unprecedented informality. She recounts that he was "talking to the jury as if they were folks on the post office corner."

Atticus begins his closing by reminding the jury that they must be sure "beyond all reasonable doubt as to the guilt of the defendant." He adds that the case should never have come to trial, noting that the case is "as simple as black and white." According to Atticus, the state has not provided any evidence that the crime took place. He questions the credibility of the state's witnesses, whose testimony has been contradicted by Tom Robinson, the defendant. He goes so far as to say that someone — not Tom Robinson — in the court is guilty.

Atticus remarks that he pities the chief witness for the state, Mayella Ewell. He pities her for her poverty and ignorance and offers a psychological explanation for her behavior: she has made the accusation against Tom "in an effort to get rid of her own guilt" — the guilt Atticus believes she feels about her attraction to a black man. Atticus restates his own conviction that Mayella's father witnessed Mayella's attempt to seduce Tom Robinson, and suggests, based on circumstantial evidence, that it was Bob Ewell himself who beat Mayella. He says, "Mayella Ewell was beaten savagely by someone who led almost exclusively with his left" and then reminds the jury that Tom Robinson took his oath with his only good hand: his right.

Atticus summarizes the case and addresses "the evil assumption" he says is shared by both the state's witnesses and the jury: "that *all* Negroes lie, that *all* Negroes are basically immoral beings, that *all* Negro men are not to be trusted around our women, an assumption that one associates with minds of their caliber." He qualifies this "truth" by reminding the jury, "some Negroes lie, some Negroes are immoral, some Negro men are not to be trusted around women — black or white. But this is a truth that applies to the human race and to no particular race of men. There is not a person in this courtroom who has never told a lie, who has never done an immoral thing, and there is no man living who has never looked upon a woman without desire."

Atticus finishes this way:

"One more thing, gentlemen, before I quit. Thomas Jefferson once said that all men are created equal, a phrase that the Yankees and the distaff side of the

Executive branch in Washington are fond of hurling at us. There is a tendency in this year of grace, 1935, for certain people to use this phrase out of context, to satisfy all conditions. The most ridiculous example I can think of is that the people who run public education promote the stupid and idle along with the industrious — because all men are created equal, educators will gravely tell you, the children left behind suffer terrible feelings of inferiority. We know all men are not created equal in the sense some people would have us believe — some people are smarter than others, some people have more opportunity because they're born with it, some men make more money than others, some ladies make better cakes than others — some people are born gifted beyond the normal scope of most men.

"But there is one way in this country in which all men are created equal — there is one human institution that makes a pauper the equal of a Rockefeller, the stupid man the equal of an Einstein, and the ignorant man the equal of any college president. That institution, gentlemen, is a court. It can be the Supreme Court of the United States or the humblest J.P. court in the land, or this honorable court which you serve. Our courts have their faults, as does any human institution, but in this country our courts are the great levelers, and in our courts all men are created equal.

"I'm no idealist to believe firmly in the integrity of our courts and in the jury system — that is no ideal to me, it is a living, working reality. Gentlemen, a court is no better than each man of you sitting before me on this jury. A court is only as sound as its jury, and a jury is only as sound as the men who make it up. I am confident that you gentlemen will review without passion the evidence you have heard, come to a decision, and restore this defendant to his family. In the name of God, do your duty."

(1960)

Atticus builds his argument deliberately, using the organization of a classical oration. His opening remarks from the introduction (*exordium*), in which Atticus reminds the jurors of what they're there for — to decide whether Tom Robinson is guilty beyond a reasonable doubt. He ends his introduction with a claim of fact that will set the tone for the rest of the speech: this trial is about race, "as simple as black and white." Atticus then reviews the major facts in his narration (*narratio*) revealing that there is not "one iota of medical evidence to the effect that the crime Tom Robinson is charged with ever took place" and that the state has depended on "the testimony of two witnesses whose evidence has not only been called into serious question on cross-examination, but has been flatly contradicted by the defendant."

Atticus transitions to his confirmation with a claim of fact: "The defendant is not guilty, but somebody in this courtroom is." In the confirmation, Atticus presents the main points and evidence in his argument as he tries to convince the jury that Mayella's guilt about her attraction to Tom Robinson prompted the rape accusation. Atticus then builds his case, not against Mayella Ewell, but against the social pressures that compelled her to press charges. He begins with an appeal to pathos. Rather than trying to demonize Mayella Ewell, he says he has "nothing but pity in [his] heart" for her and calls her a "victim of cruel poverty and ignorance." He then takes the jury through the mental steps Mayella took to assuage the guilt she felt about her attraction to Tom Robinson. Atticus appeals to logos with the factual evidence of the right-handedness of Tom Robinson versus the left-handedness of Mayella's father, who in all likelihood had beaten and maybe even raped her.

Atticus addresses the counterargument in his refutation (*refutatio*), which is introduced with "the evil assumption — that *all* Negroes lie." Without using the term, he is identifying the counterargument as a **slippery slope** fallacy. He makes a claim of value about Tom Robinson, reminding the jury that the odds are against him — a black man's word against the words of two white people. Nevertheless, he asks the jury to recall the cynical assumptions made by all the state's witnesses (except the sheriff) that Tom is guilty for the mere reason that he is black. He refutes those assumptions in the following paragraph, noting that there is "not a person in this courtroom who has never told a lie, who has never done an immoral thing, and there is no man living who has never looked upon a woman without desire." He even concedes to the jury that he doesn't really believe that all men are created equal — except in one notable way.

In the last part of his closing statement (the conclusion, or *peroratio*), Atticus develops the claims of value and policy that are his — and Harper Lee's — thesis. He makes the claim of value that "our courts have their faults, as does any human institution, but in this country our courts are the great levelers, and in our courts all men are created equal." He exhorts the jury to let the court do its job, and he expresses his confidence in the men of the jury sitting before him. His claim of policy is implicit: let the court do its job. Atticus ends with an appeal to pathos, pleading with the jury to send Tom Robinson home to his family.

A courtroom speech in a novel is a very direct application of argument, but some arguments are more subtle. Let's take a look at the poem "Success is counted sweetest," by Emily Dickinson.

Success is counted sweetest
EMILY DICKINSON

> Success is counted sweetest
> By those who ne'er succeed.
> To comprehend a nectar
> Requires sorest need.
>
> Not one of all the purple Host 5
> Who took the Flag today
> Can tell the definition
> So clear of Victory
>
> As he defeated — dying —
> On whose forbidden ear   10

The distant strains of triumph
Burst agonized and clear!

(1859)

Read the first two lines of the poem carefully and you will see that the statement of the poem's theme happens to be a claim of fact and value. It is a paradoxical statement: we would expect that winners would appreciate success more than losers do. Lines 3 and 4 contain an analogy that serves as logical evidence to back up the initial claim: we most appreciate the sweetness of nectar when we need it the most.

The next two stanzas provide the occasion, as well as a specific example used as evidence to support the speaker's claim. We usually assume that Emily Dickinson is the speaker in her poetry; here she is talking about war: the "purple Host / Who took the Flag today" are the victors in a battle. The first part of her evidence is that not one of that purple (a color associated with royalty) host (a word that means a large group) can understand the sweetness of victory. Then she narrows on an example, the single warrior in the last stanza, "defeated — dying," who understands it all too well. He is the evidence for Dickinson's assertion. He lies dying — his ear "forbidden" the joyful sounds of victory; nevertheless, he hears the "distant strains of triumph / Burst agonized and clear." In Dickinson's wonderfully compact way, she makes a clear argument, while at the same time, especially in that last stanza, she appeals to pathos and recreates for the reader the tragedy of dying in battle with the tantalizing sweetness, the "distant strains," of success held just out of reach.

• ACTIVITY •

Read Langston Hughes's "Mother to Son" carefully, attending to its occasion, its audience, and its language. Then analyze the argument it makes. Do you think the speaker — a mother talking to her son — makes a different argument from that of the poet, Langston Hughes? Explain why or why not.

Well, son, I'll tell you:
Life for me ain't been no crystal stair.
It's had tacks in it,
And splinters,
And boards torn up,   5
And places with no carpet on the floor —
Bare.
But all the time
I'se been a-climbin' on,
And reachin' landin's,   10
And turnin' corners,
And sometimes goin' in the dark

Where there ain't been no light.
So boy, don't you turn back.
Don't you set down on the steps   15
'Cause you finds it's kinder hard.
Don't you fall now —
For I'se still goin', honey,
I'se still climbin',
And life for me ain't been no crystal stair.   20

(1922)

Analyzing Visual Texts as Arguments

In this section, we'll focus on how to analyze visual texts that present arguments. A visual argument can be an advertisement, a political cartoon, a photograph, a bumper sticker, a T-shirt, a hat, a Web page, or even a piece of fine art. Yet the tools to analyze argument — identifying the claims, analyzing the way evidence is used, thinking critically about the artist's assumptions, examining how the piece is structured, considering appeals to ethos, pathos, and logos — are fairly similar for both visual and written arguments.

Although the tools that artists use to make their arguments are primarily visual strategies, such as the placement of figures and objects and the use of color, the process of analysis is the same as with any text: look carefully, take note of every detail, make connections about your observations, and draw conclusions. Again, as with any written text, it's important to know what occasioned the visual image and, if possible, who the artist intended as his or her audience.

Following is a checklist to use with any visual text:

- Where did the visual first appear? Who is the audience? Who is the speaker or artist? Does this person have political or organizational affiliations that are important to understanding the text?

- What do you notice first? Where is your eye drawn? What is your overall first impression?

- What topic does the visual address or raise? What claim does the visual make about that topic?

- Does the text tell or suggest a narrative or story? If so, what is the point?

- What aspects of the image evoke emotions? Look especially at color, light and dark, shadow, realistic versus distorted or caricatured figures, and visual allusions.

Let's use this checklist to analyze a four-frame cartoon entitled *Rat Race* that appeared on the United Kingdom Web site polyp.org.uk.

Courtesy of Polyp

(See color insert, Image 8.)

- **Where did the visual first appear? Who is the audience? Who is the speaker? Does this person have political or organizational affiliations that are important to understanding the text?** This cartoon first appeared in *Ethical Consumer* magazine, a publication whose mission is to provide information to consumers about products and brands that are socially and environmentally responsible. The magazine has an obvious bias against buying products for the sake of status rather than of necessity and against companies or organizations motivated primarily by profit. The readers of *Ethical Consumer* are likely to be practical or even frugal, to frown on materialism, and to be skeptical of big business.

- **What do you notice first? Where is your eye drawn? What is your overall first impression?** Although there's quite a bit going on in these frames, your eye is probably drawn most immediately to the written text that is in bold: WORK HARDER / EARN MORE MONEY / BUY MORE THINGS / KEEP GOING. Since the written text appears in the same place within each frame, it also might be seen as a way to structure the piece.

- **What topic does the visual address or raise? Does the visual make a claim about that topic?** With rats racing all over the place within frames and from frame to frame, clearly the topic is the rat race — an allusion to the well-known expression. Even at this early stage of analysis, the artist's claim that the rat race is a never-ending cycle of working to earn money to buy material possessions becomes pretty clear.

- **Does the text tell or suggest a narrative or story? If so, what is the point?** The frames constitute a story, a narrative: the key "characters" are rats that seem to be caught in a maze; the idea of a trap is emphasized by the rats' bodies appearing in pieces, fragmented, with only one example of a whole body being in the picture. The sign at the top ("Happiness is just around the corner!") is repeated in each frame, a slogan that seems to cheer the rats on and keep them on task.

- **What aspects of the image evoke emotions? Look especially at color, shades of light and dark, shadow, realistic versus distorted or caricatured figures, and visual allusions.** You might feel a range of emotions being evoked. First of all, it's hard not to see something comic about the bug-eyed rats with human expressions who are frantically running from or toward something, though it's not clear what. Red usually evokes alarm. The background is a little more subtle, but the closer you look, the world beyond the "maze" goes from lighter to darker shades us the frames progress, suggesting a workday, the morning-until-night routine. That background does not have any trees or natural shapes but, rather, industrial-looking smokestacks and buildings. The rats themselves are caricatures, distortions with huge heads and eyes. They are depicted as looking at the signs or maybe watching one another; however, there's no contact between or among them. We've already noted the overarching allusion to "the rat race," a common expression people use to refer to a situation that involves ceaseless activity with little meaning. In addition, the signs on the walls of each frame remind us of advertisements that entice us to buy things or acquire luxuries. They're promises of a better physical appearance or lifestyle.

- **What claim does the visual make about the issue(s) it addresses?** Let's take stock of what we have observed thus far and connect some of those observations. We have exaggerated images of rats in a maze working to make money to buy things that require them to continue working to make money to pay for those things and the next things that promise happiness. The red color and the exaggerated characteristics of the rats signal a fevered urgency that the cartoon's overall message mocks. The rats live crowded, frantic lives driven by the pursuit of material goods and fueled by ads, slogans, and other external stimuli. It's true that we are making an inferential leap, but given all these specifics, we can fairly conclude that the artist's claim is one of value: "The rat race just isn't worth it!" Or, to state it more formally, "the constant striving to make money in order to spend money can never bring satisfaction, only more striving."

If we think about this analysis in the terms of argument we have used throughout this chapter, each of the four frames might be thought of as a paragraph. In each one, the artist refutes a counterargument: happiness is just around the corner if you work harder, if you earn more money, if you buy more things, if you keep going. These slogans become assertions that the drawings refute as the rats become increasingly frantic within the confines of the maze and as day turns to night. The argument seems to be organized inductively because as each slogan (assertion) is refuted by the images of the rats, who are anything but happy as they face yet another "corner," the viewer draws the conclusion that the rat race is thankless, useless, and never a route to happiness.

Photographs are another type of visual text that can make powerful arguments. How often do we look at the photograph on the front page of a newspaper or news site before we read the lead story? The photo in that case may greatly influence how we read the written text by shaping our attitude toward the piece or even by leading us to form conclusions before reading so much as a single word.

In fact, photographic images carry additional power because they seem "real," authentic images of truth frozen in time. No political cartoon has ever claimed to be "reality." But it is important to understand that while photographs may be more "real" than a drawing, they nevertheless are artificial. The photographer must decide how to light a scene, what to focus on, when to take the picture, what to put inside the frame and outside of it, and how to compose the shot in order to convey the desired meaning. Unfortunately, combining the power of the photographic image has at times resulted in the irresistible temptation to pose or construct an image to make a point. But even if the image is not doctored, a photograph is constructed to tell a story, evoke emotions, and make a strong argument.

Let's examine an iconic photograph called *The Steerage*, taken in 1907 by photographer Alfred Stieglitz (see the next page). We might start with a definition of *steerage*, which is the cheapest accommodation on a passenger ship—originally the compartments containing the steering apparatus. Stieglitz did not take the photograph for a particular publication because by this point he was already a highly regarded artist who championed the relatively new medium of photography as an art form. The context is the early twentieth century, when immigration to the United States was at a high point. The photograph depicts the wealthier classes aboard ship on the deck above the poorer classes, who are housed in the steerage. Notice how your eye is immediately drawn to the empty gangway that separates the two groups. This point of focus raises the issue of separation, even segregation.

This time, instead of going through the checklist step-by-step as we did with *Rat Race*, let's just think about how the style of this photo might be seen as evidence used to make its claim. In what ways might that gangway be symbolic? Why would Stieglitz choose the moment when it is empty? What story is this photograph telling? Note the similarities and differences between the two groups depicted. Stieglitz juxtaposes them. Some differences, such as dress, are stark; yet what similarities do you see? How does Stieglitz want his audience—his viewers—to experience the people in this scene? Why do you suppose we see the group in the top more straight on, face-to-face, while the people in the lower level in many instances have their backs to us? Think about the time period, and ask yourself what cultural values the viewers—those who frequent art galleries and are familiar with artists of the day—bring to this image.

Granted, the technology did not make color photos an option, but notice the many shades of light and dark, the shadows, the highlighted areas: What mood does this moment frozen in time suggest? How does the evocation of mood add to the pathos of the scene? What claim — or claims — is Stieglitz making through this visual image?

The Metropolitan Museum of Art. Image source: Art Resource, NY. © 2013 Georgia O'Keeffe Museum/Artists Rights Society (ARS), New York.

• ACTIVITY •

The photograph seen here was taken by photographer Sian Kennedy in Sulphur, Louisiana, in 2005 after the destruction wrought by Hurricane Katrina. Analyze the photograph's argument. If you like, you may use the list of questions that appears on page 136 as a starting point for your analysis.

Sian Kennedy/cultura/Corbis

(See color insert, Image 9.)

• ESSAY IN PROGRESS: Using Visual Evidence •

Find a visual text — a political cartoon, an advertisement, a photograph, or the like — that supports or enhances the argument you have been developing. Write a paragraph or two explaining how the visual text makes its own argument.

• CULMINATING ACTIVITY •

The following texts — an excerpt from an essay, a poem, and an advertisement — all make claims about body image. What claim does each of these texts make? How is the claim developed? How does each appeal to its audience?

from *Celebrity Bodies*
DANIEL HARRIS

This excerpt is from an essay originally published in *Southwest Review*, the literary magazine of Southern Methodist University, in 2008.

A vision of the female body dictated by male desire would be far healthier and more attractive than one dictated by the imperatives of the closet, by manufacturers whose primary concern is showing off their goods to the best effect.

How much influence does this aesthetic have on the general public? Such well-known personalities as the withered Nicole Richie or the cadaverous Victoria "Posh" Beckham, a.k.a. "Skeletal Spice," are often cited as the chief culprits behind the endemic of eating disorders among the young but the fact remains that, while as many as one hundred thousand teenage girls suffer from excessive dieting, two out of three Americans are overweight and an estimated sixty million, or 20 percent of the population, are obese. Are Hollywood and the fashion world responsible for our ever-increasing girth or is the effect of our obsession with what many have dubbed "the rich and famished" as open to debate as the influence of television violence and the Xbox on actual crime statistics? Does Lindsay Lohan's waspish waistline make us skip meals and induce vomiting just as Mortal Kombat presumably makes us pick up assault rifles and open fire? How direct *is* the impact of Hollywood on our bodies, as direct as the *Daily Mirror* recently suggested when it ran a photograph of the emaciated Keira Knightley next to the headline "If Pictures Like This One of Keira Carried a Health Warning, My Darling Daughter Might Have Lived"? If many adolescents seek "thin-spiration" from such desiccated waifs as Jessica Alba, who has admitted to being on a diet since age twelve, or Elisa Donovan, who dwindled to a mere 90 pounds after eating nothing but coffee, water, and toast for two years, the majority of Americans seem to be following the lead of reformed foodaholic Tom Arnold who, until he began taking the diet aid Xenical, regularly splurged on McDonald's and then hid his half-dozen Big Macs and Quarter Pounders from his equally gluttonous wife Roseanne, not out of shame, but because he didn't want to share.

What is dangerous about the influence of popular culture on our state of physical health is not how slavishly we imitate the stars, attempting to acquire Hilary Swank's lats, Jennifer Lopez's glutes, and Beyoncé's quads, but how little they affect us at all, how they have turned us into quiescent spectators who worship an unattainable ideal so remote from our daily affairs that its exemplars seem to belong to another species. Celebrities are like athletes, a class of surrogates who live vigorous, aerobic lives while we develop diabetes and arteriosclerosis on our sofas. Hollywood didn't create fat, anxious

Americans; fat, anxious Americans created Hollywood, a vision of humanity that bears little resemblance to the typical dissipated physique, sagging from too many processed foods and sedentary hours watching lithe beauties cavort in haute couture. Fantasy worlds, like those inhabited by celebrities, are never fashioned in the image of the dreamer. The dreamer imagines an existence as unlike his own as possible and is content to admire this world from afar, not as a possible destination but as a wonderland all the more enticing the more unapproachable and exclusionary. Our fantasies engender a paralyzing awe that instills in us despair, a sense of hopelessness about maintaining our bodies, about achieving the buff perfections of stars spoon-fed by studio dieticians who force them to nibble on rice cakes and celery sticks and submit to grueling regimens of Pilates and kickboxing. In fact, we would almost certainly be healthier if we *did* imitate Hollywood, if we *did* work out and diet as compulsively as they do, if, like supermodel Dayle Haddon, we performed leg lifts while washing the dishes, side bends while standing in line at Starbucks, and thigh resistance exercises in the elevators of our four-star hotels.

We blame pop culture for turning us into diet-crazed bulimics, but how can celebrities be "role models," however derelict, when almost no one seems to imitate them, when we get fatter even as they get skinnier, exercise less even as they train like triathletes? Granted, we are preoccupied with celebrities, follow the evolution of their hair styles, take tours past the gates of their estates, make wild surmises about their sexual preferences, but obsession does not necessarily, or even usually, entail imitation. This does not keep us, however, from penalizing them with an unjust double standard, insisting that, in the name of public hygiene, they maintain scrupulously healthy diets, drink abstemiously, engage in unerringly faithful relations with their spouses, and indignantly turn down film roles in which they are asked to participate in such iniquitous activities as smoking. Never before have we demanded that popular culture be as virtuous as we have in the last forty years, that our stars, in the mistaken belief that they manufacture the moral templates of our lives, beat their breasts in remorse and enroll in rehab every time they fail a breathalyzer test, stumble on the red carpet, or light a cigarette in public.

(2008)

homage to my hips
LUCILLE CLIFTON

This poem is from Lucille Clifton's 1987 collection, *Good Woman*.

these hips are big hips.
they need space to

move around in.
they don't fit into little
petty places, these hips   5
are free hips.
they don't like to be held back.
these hips have never been enslaved,
they go where they want to go
they do what they want to do.   10
these hips are mighty hips.
these hips are magic hips.
i have known them
to put a spell on a man and
spin him like a top!   15

(1987)

Michael Jackson with and without Plastic Surgery

The image on the left is a simulation of what Michael Jackson might have looked like at age fifty without plastic surgery. The image was created using a young presurgery picture of Jackson and aging simulation software. The image on the right shows Jackson as he actually looked at age fifty.

Brenda Chase/Getty Images

© Mirrorpix/Splash News./Corbis

• **ESSAY IN PROGRESS: First Draft** •

Write a full argument that includes at least three different types of evidence and a visual text. You have been developing this essay throughout the chapter: use the texts and drafts you've developed thus far, as you like, but do not hesitate to rethink and revise. Suggested length: 500–700 words

4

Synthesizing Sources
Entering the Conversation

W e all draw on the ideas of others as we develop our own positions, regardless of the topic. Whether you are explaining your opinion about an issue specific to your community (such as whether to allow skateboarding in public parks) or you are developing a position on a national or global issue (such as whether to change immigration policies), you should know as much as possible about the topic. Rather than make a quick response that reflects an opinion based only on what you already know, you'll want to research and read sources — what others have written. Then you can develop your own *informed* opinion, a measured response that considers multiple perspectives and possibilities. We call this process **synthesis**; it involves considering various viewpoints in an effort to create a new and more informed position.

Philosopher Kenneth Burke compared this process to showing up late to a party. There are a dozen different conversations going on. If you were to approach one group of people having a heated debate, you'd need to listen for a while to understand what the specific topic is, what has already been said, who is taking what side, and what they're not saying. Then, by either expanding on what others are saying, challenging what others are saying, or filling in a gap in their understanding, you would begin to enter the conversation and make your own contribution. And that's what synthesis is all about: entering the conversation that society is having about a topic. You enter the conversation by carefully reading and understanding multiple viewpoints and ideas surrounding an issue, examining your own ideas on the matter, and then synthesizing these perspectives into a more informed position than the one you began with.

When you're learning about a subject, look for reliable sources. Be aware of the **bias** that a source brings to the topic. Consider the speaker: What does he or she believe in? How might the speaker's position lead to personal gain? Don't look for a pro-and-con debate that represents only polarized views; look for a range of viewpoints. This might sound like a lot to keep in mind, but don't worry; you work with sources all the time. For instance, when you decide to buy a new smartphone, you gather information by exploring different sources. You might consult *Consumer Reports* and other technology magazines, compare prices and technical specs, ask friends for their opinions and experiences, and go to an electronics store to talk with experts. You might also read reviews online or use electronic forums as a quick source for many opinions. But you might choose not to ask a friend who has an old flip phone; nor would you want to get all your information from a salesperson, who likely works on commission. The final result of this type of inquiry would be a purchase, not an essay, but you would have had to synthesize a range of sources in order to make the argument to yourself that the phone you chose was the best fit for you.

> ### • ACTIVITY •
>
> Write a brief paragraph about a time when you used multiple sources to help make a decision. You can choose a decision as simple as which movie you saw or which shoes you purchased or as serious as which colleges you applied to. Discuss how each source contributed to your decision and how you evaluated which sources were more, or less, influential.

Using Sources to Inform an Argument

As we discussed in Chapter 3, many different types of evidence can be used to support an argument. But it is important to remember that your sources should enhance, not replace, your argument. You may worry that the ideas of others are so persuasive that you have nothing new to say. Or you may think that the more sources you cite, the more impressed your reader (especially your teacher) will be. But as you develop your skills in writing synthesis essays, you will find that sources are most persuasive when they inform your own ideas and demonstrate your understanding of opposing views. What *you* have to say is the main event; *your* position is central.

In the following example, Laura Hillenbrand, author of *Seabiscuit*, a Pulitzer Prize–winning book about a champion racehorse who beat the odds, maintains her own voice throughout, even when she uses the work of experts to help make a point. (She identifies those sources in a section at the end of her book.) But whether she is quoting directly or paraphrasing, she never gets lost in the sources or allows them to overwhelm her ideas.

from *Seabiscuit*
LAURA HILLENBRAND

> To pilot a racehorse is to ride a half-ton catapult. It is without question one of the most formidable feats in sport. The extraordinary athleticism of the jockey is unparalleled: A study of the elements of athleticism conducted by Los Angeles exercise physiologists and physicians found that of all major sports competitors, jockeys may be, pound for pound, the best overall athletes. They have to be. To begin with, there are the demands on balance, coordination, and reflex. A horse's body is a constantly shifting topography, with a bobbing head and neck and roiling muscle over the shoulders, back, and rump. On a running horse, a jockey does not sit in the saddle, he crouches over it, leaning all of his weight on his toes, which rest on the thin metal

bases of stirrups dangling about a foot from the horse's topline. When a horse is in full stride, the only parts of the jockey that are in continuous contact with the animal are the insides of the feet and ankles — everything else is balanced in midair. In other words, jockeys squat on the pitching backs of their mounts, a task much like perching on the grille of a car while it speeds down a twisting, potholed freeway in traffic. The stance is, in the words of University of North Carolina researchers, "a situation of dynamic imbalance and ballistic opportunity." The center of balance is so narrow that if jockeys shift only slightly rearward, they will flip right off the back. If they tip more than a few inches forward, a fall is almost inevitable. A thoroughbred's neck, while broad from top to bottom, is surprisingly narrow in width, like the body of a fish. Pitching up and down as the horse runs, it offers little for the jockey to grab to avoid plunging to the ground and under the horse's hooves.

Notes

Jockey (video), Tel-Air Productions, 1980.

A. E. Waller et al., "Jockey Injuries in the United States," *Journal of the American Medical Association*, 2000; vol. 283, no. 10.

(2001)

Rather than citing her sources within the text, Hillenbrand includes the information about the sources she cites in the endnotes section of her book. The first item is a videotape about the study by Los Angeles exercise physiologists and physicians; the second is an article in a medical journal. The inclusion of both acknowledges that she turned to authorities — sources — to deepen and supplement her knowledge about the mechanics and physics of how a racehorse and a jockey move as one entity.

Using Sources in Literary Analysis

Sources are often a key part of your analysis of, discussion of, and arguments related to literary texts. You might cite literary criticism, reviews, debates about the merit of a poem or novel, or biographical studies. You also might cite an author's letters, autobiographical writings, or even archival sources. Following is an excerpt from an essay by Jane Smiley that appeared in *Harper's* magazine in 1996, entitled "Say It Ain't So, Huck: Second Thoughts on Mark Twain's Masterpiece."

Although Huck had his fans at publication, his real elevation into the pantheon was worked out early in the Propaganda Era, between 1948 and 1955, by Lionel Trilling, Leslie Fiedler, T. S. Eliot, Joseph Wood Krutch, and some lesser lights, in the introductions to American and British editions of the novel and in such journals as *Partisan Review* and *The New York Times Book Review*. The requirements of Huck's installation rapidly revealed themselves: the failure of the last twelve chapters (in which Huck finds Jim imprisoned on the Phelps plantation and Tom Sawyer is reintroduced and elaborates a cruel and unnecessary scheme for Jim's liberation) had to be diminished, accounted for, or forgiven; after that, the novel's special qualities had to be placed in the context first of other American novels (to their detriment) and then of world literature. The best bets here seemed to be Twain's style and the river setting, and the critics invested accordingly: Eliot, who had never read the novel as a boy, traded on his own childhood beside the big river, elevating Huck to the Boy, and the Mississippi to the River God, therein finding the sort of mythic resonance that he admired. Trilling liked the river god idea, too, though he didn't bother to capitalize it. He also thought that Twain, through Huck's lying, told truths, one of them being (I kid you not) that "something . . . had gone out of American life after the [Civil War], some simplicity, some innocence, some peace." What Twain himself was proudest of in the novel — his style — Trilling was glad to dub "not less than definitive in American literature. The prose of *Huckleberry Finn* established for written prose the virtues of American colloquial speech. . . . He is the master of the style that escapes the fixity of the printed page, that sounds in our ears with the immediacy of the heard voice, the very voice of unpretentious truth." The last requirement was some quality that would link Huck to other, though "lesser," American novels such as Herman Melville's *Moby-Dick*, that would possess some profound insight into the American character. Leslie Fiedler obligingly provided it when he read homoerotic attraction into the relationship between Huck and Jim, pointing out the similarity of this to such other white man–dark man friendships as those between Ishmael and Queequeg in *Moby-Dick* and Natty Bumppo and Chingachgook in James Fenimore Cooper's *Last of the Mohicans*.

The canonization proceeded apace: great novel (Trilling, 1950), greatest novel (Eliot, 1950), world-class novel (Lauriat Lane Jr., 1955). Sensible naysayers, such as Leo Marx, were lost in the shuffle of propaganda. But, in fact, *Adventures of Huckleberry Finn* has little to offer in the way of greatness. There is more to be learned about the American character *from* its canonization than *through* its canonization.

(1996)

The paragraphs here are the second and third paragraphs of Smiley's essay, in which she debunks the claim that *The Adventures of Huckleberry Finn* is the novel "all American literature grows out of." She establishes herself as well-read on the subject of Twain's novel by reviewing the literature about the novel before she embarks on her own claims that the "canonization" of *The Adventures of Huckleberry Finn* is more interesting as a comment on the American character than the book itself. She cites literary experts such as critics Leslie Fiedler and Lionel Trilling, as well as writers such as T. S. Eliot. She names the publications in which their commentary appeared — *Partisan Review, New York Times Book Review* — and both quotes and paraphrases the ideas of these writers. Smiley takes on the big names in American literature criticism, but her argument would be much weaker had she not acknowledged the praise of those who had, as she notes, elevated *The Adventures of Huckleberry Finn* into the "pantheon" of great American literature.

• ACTIVITY •

In the following passage from *A Level Playing Field: African American Athletes and the Republic of Sports*, Gerald L. Early discusses the complex character of Jackie Robinson, the first black athlete to play in major league baseball. What is the purpose of the sources Early chooses to include? How do they enhance or detract from his own voice? What is the purpose of each of the notes documenting the sources?

from *A Level Playing Field*
GERALD L. EARLY

But 1949 was also Robinson's year of liberation. According to Branch Rickey, known as the Mahatma by sportswriters, the Dodgers executive who signed Robinson and who pushed for integration: "For three years [that was the agreement] this boy was to turn the other cheek. He did, day after day, until he had no other to turn. They were both beat off. There were slight slip-ups on occasion in that first year in Montreal."[1]

Robinson had agreed to ignore all slights, insults, and abuses that he endured on the playing field during his first three years as a professional ballplayer in the white leagues. This generated, naturally, a certain public sympathy, as Robinson did, indeed, endure much abuse, and he did not have a natural or an easy camaraderie with most of his white teammates. He became almost a perfect Gandhi-like figure of sacrifice and forbearance, and he created the paradigm for how integration was to proceed in the United States in the 1950s and early 1960s — the Noble Negro who, through his nobility, a mystical product of his American heritage of suffering but enduring devotion to the foundational principles of American life, legitimates white institutions as he integrates them. As the *New York Times* put it in 1950, "The going wasn't easy. Jackie Robinson met open or covert hostility with the spirit of a gallant gentleman. He kept his temper, he kept his poise and he played good baseball. Now he has won his battle. No fan threatens to riot, no player threatens to go on strike when Jackie Robinson, or any one of several Negroes, takes the field."[2] This is the Robinson that is always remembered when his career is reexamined today. He is almost always sentimentalized.

But it must be remembered that Robinson played major league baseball with the Dodgers for ten years, only two of which were under this agreement. (The agreement also included the year in Montreal.) So for most of his career as a big league ballplayer, Robinson did not act in any sort of self-sacrificing nonviolent way. He was a tough, almost chip-on-the-shoulder player, a

---

[1]Branch Rickey, with Robert Riger, *The American Diamond: A Documentary of the Game of Baseball* (New York: Simon & Schuster, 1965), p. 46.
[2]"Jackie Robinson's New Honor," *New York Times*, December 8, 1950.

> particularly aggressive athlete who usually took umbrage at the least slight or unfairness he felt on the field. He understood that high-performance sports were about intimidation, and he was not about to be intimidated.[3]
>
> *(2011)*

Using Sources to Appeal to an Audience

If you were writing an in-class essay, would you take the time to put together a bibliography? Of course not. But you would prepare a bibliography for a formal research paper because that type of writing has a different purpose and the audience has different expectations. A writer must analyze the rhetorical situation in order to determine what is appropriate, even when it comes to sources and documentation. (See The Rhetorical Triangle, p. 3.)

Now let's consider a topic and examine how sources were used and identified for three different audiences. The following excerpts are from three pieces about indirect speech by the linguist and cognitive scientist Steven Pinker.

The first example is from an article in *Time* magazine written for a general audience of readers interested primarily in understanding the basics of Pinker's ideas.

from *Words Don't Mean What They Mean*
STEVEN PINKER

> Why don't people just say what they mean? The reason is that conversational partners are not modems downloading information into each other's brains. People are very, very touchy about their relationships. Whenever you speak to someone, you are presuming the two of you have a certain degree of familiarity — which your words might alter. So every sentence has to do two things at once: convey a message and continue to negotiate that relationship.
>
> The clearest example is ordinary politeness. When you are at a dinner party and want the salt, you don't blurt out, "Gimme the salt." Rather, you use what linguists call a whimperative, as in "Do you think you could pass the salt?" or "If you could pass the salt, that would be awesome."
>
> Taken literally, these sentences are inane. The second is an overstatement, and the answer to the first is obvious. Fortunately, the hearer assumes that the speaker is rational and listens between the lines. Yes, your point is to request the salt, but you're doing it in such a way that first takes care to establish what linguists call "felicity conditions," or the prerequisites to making a sensible request. The

---

[3]"In 1950, and the years to come, Jack battled with umpires over matters not simply of judgment but of ethics, in his growing belief that the umpires, all white, were abusing their power in order to put him in his place." See Rampersad, *Jackie Robinson*, p. 229; see also Jackie Robinson, "Now I Know Why They Boo Me!" *Look*, January 25, 1955, pp. 22–28.

underlying rationale is that the hearer not be given a command but simply be asked or advised about one of the necessary conditions for passing the salt. Your goal is to have your need satisfied without treating the listener as a flunky who can be bossed around at will.

(2007)

Note that there are no formal sources cited. The terms that are introduced — *whimperative* and *felicity conditions* — are more playful than technical, and Pinker makes no attempt to cite the academic origin of these terms or the other ideas in this article. He does not delve into the research that led to the conclusions he outlines. His goal in this brief article for the general reader is to inform and keep moving.

The audience for Pinker's book *The Stuff of Thought: Language as a Window into Human Nature* is interested in exploring his subject more deeply, and his use and citation of sources becomes correspondingly more extensive and formal.

from *The Stuff of Thought*
Steven Pinker

The double message conveyed with an implicature is nowhere put to greater use than in the commonest kind of indirect speech of all, politeness. Politeness in linguistics does not refer to social etiquette, like eating your peas without using your knife, but to the countless adjustments that speakers make to avoid the equally countless ways that their listeners might be put off. People are very, very touchy, and speakers go to great lengths not to step on their toes. In their magisterial work *Politeness: Some Universals in Language Use*, the anthropologists Penelope Brown and Stephen Levinson . . . extended Grice's theory by showing how people all over the world use politeness to lubricate their social interactions.[1]

Politeness Theory begins with Erving Goffman's observation that when people interact they constantly worry about maintaining a nebulous yet vital commodity called "face" (from the idiom "to save face").[2] Goffman defined face as a positive social value that a person claims for himself. Brown and Levinson divide it into positive face, the desire to be approved (specifically, that other people want for you what you want for yourself), and negative face, the desire to be unimpeded or autonomous. The terminology, though clumsy, points to a fundamental duality in social life, which has been discovered in many guises and goes by many names: solidarity and status, connection and autonomy, communion and agency, intimacy and power, communal sharing and authority ranking.[3]

(2007)

---

[1]Brown & Levinson, 1987b. See also Brown, 1987; Brown & Gilman, 1972; Fraser, 1990; Green, 1996; Holtgraves, 2002.
[2]Goffman, 1967.
[3]Fiske, 1992; Fiske, 2004; Haslam, 2004; Holtgraves, 2002.

While this is not a scientific study, it is also not a brief and breezy article in a magazine with a very wide readership. The audience for a book of this sort has some interest in the topic — they have chosen to read a whole book on linguistics and cognition — and because of that Pinker feels comfortable not just summarizing the latest thinking in the field but introducing terminology common to research in linguistics and tracing the origins of concepts back to their academic roots. He also formally (and fully) cites his sources using extensive endnotes that appear at the back of the book.

Finally, take a look at the next selection from a scholarly article by Pinker in the academic journal *Intercultural Pragmatics*.

from *The Evolutionary Social Psychology of Off-Record Indirect Speech Acts*
STEVEN PINKER

The double message conveyed with an implicature is nowhere put to greater use than in the commonest kind of indirect speech, politeness. In their seminal work *Politeness: Some Universals in Language Use*, Brown and Levinson (1987b) extended Grice's theory by showing how people in many (perhaps all) cultures use politeness to lubricate their social interactions.

Politeness Theory begins with Goffman's (1967) observation that when people interact they constantly worry about maintaining a commodity called "face" (from the idiom "to save face"). Goffman defined face as a positive social value that a person claims for himself. Brown and Levinson divide it into positive face, the desire to be approved (specifically, that other people want for you what you want for yourself), and negative face, the desire to be unimpeded or autonomous. The terminology points to a fundamental duality in social life which goes by many names: solidarity and status, connection and autonomy, communion and agency, intimacy and power, communal sharing and authority ranking (Fiske 1992, 2004; Haslam 2004; Holtgraves 2002). Later we will see how these wants come from two of the three major social relations in human life.

Brown and Levinson argue that Grice's Cooperative Principle applies to the maintenance of face as well as to the communication of data. Conversationalists work together, each trying to maintain his own face and the face of his partner. The challenge is that most kinds of speech pose at least some threat to the face of the hearer. The mere act of initiating a conversation imposes a demand on the hearer's time and attention. Issuing an imperative challenges her status and autonomy. Making a request puts her in the position where she might have to refuse, earning her a reputation as stingy or selfish. Telling something to someone implies that she was ignorant of the fact in the first place. And then there are criticisms, boasts, interruptions, outbursts, the telling of bad news, and the broaching of divisive topics, all of which can injure the hearer's face directly.

At the same time, people have to get on with the business of life, and in doing so they have to convey requests and news and complaints. The solution is to make amends with politeness: the speaker sugarcoats his utterances with niceties that reaffirm his concern for the hearer or that acknowledge her autonomy. Brown and Levinson call the stratagems positive and negative politeness, though better terms are sympathy and deference.

References

Brown, Penelope, and Stephen C. Levinson. 1987a. Introduction to the reissue: A review of recent work. In *Politeness: Some universals in language use*. New York: Cambridge University Press.

---. 1987b. *Politeness: Some universals in language usage*. New York: Cambridge University Press.

Fiske, Alan P. 1992. The four elementary forms of sociality: Framework for a unified theory of social relations. *Psychological Review*, 99: 689–723.

---. 2004. Four modes of constituting relationships: Consubstantial assimilation; space, magnitude, time, and force; Concrete procedures; Abstract symbolism. In N. Haslam (ed.), *Relational models theory: A contemporary overview*. Mahwah: Erlbaum Associates.

Goffman, Erving. 1959. *The presentation of self in everyday life*. New York: Doubleday.

---. 1967. On face-work: An analysis of ritual elements in social interaction. In *Interaction ritual: Essays on face-to-face behavior*. New York: Random House.

Grice, Herbert P. 1975. Logic and conversation. In P. Cole & J. L. Morgan (eds.), *Syntax & Semantics* Vol. 3: Speech acts. New York: Academic Press.

Haslam, Nick. (ed.). 2004. *Relational models theory: A contemporary overview*. Mahwah: Erlbaum Associates.

Holtgraves, Tom M. 2002. *Language as social action*. Mahwah: Erlbaum Associates.

(2007)

Notice that for this academic audience of researchers and scholars who bring a good deal of prior knowledge to the text, Pinker chooses other scholarly works as his sources and documents them thoroughly in a style that gives those sources more emphasis. Rather than just putting the citations at the back of the book, he embeds the source names throughout for direct reference and then includes a detailed works cited or list of references at the end of the article. Many of his readers, likely already familiar with these sources, will find Pinker's text more authoritative because he has included them.

As you can see, the type of evidence and the way it is documented depend on audience and situation. But what does all of this have to do with the writing you will be doing? The texts we have examined in this chapter were written by journalists, professors, and scholars; the sources they use and the ways they document them are appropriate for their audiences. In school, you have probably written essays for which you were required to use outside sources, sources that were assigned to you, or sources that were part of your classroom readings. Keep in mind that your goal in a synthesis essay is the same as that of professional writers: to use sources to support and illustrate your own ideas and to establish your credibility as a reasonable and informed writer. Whether your teacher wants you to make informal in-text citations or use formal in-text parenthetical documentation and an end-of-paper works cited list, you must document sources to give credit where credit is due.

• ACTIVITY •

To set themselves apart, columnists for print and online publications establish a viewpoint and style. The types of sources they use and the way they use them are part of that style. Using three columns by one writer, analyze the columnist's audience by examining the type of sources he or she uses. For your columnist, you might consider a political commentator from a national or local publication, a sportswriter, a movie or music reviewer, a professional blogger, or even an amateur blogger.

Conversation

Education: The Civil Rights Issue of Our Time?

In this section, we will walk you through the process of writing a synthesis essay: understanding the task, analyzing a series of readings, and writing an argument using them. Here is your prompt:

> Declining test scores, low rankings of K–12 schools in comparison to their international counterparts, and mounting debt from college tuition are among the factors that have led to severe criticism of the U.S. education system from preschool through the university. In fact, many have described public education as "the civil rights issue of our time." Using the text by Horace Mann and at least three other sources, write an essay explaining why you agree or disagree with this characterization of education.

What does this prompt direct you to do? It opens with a statement of fact about criticism being leveled at education in America. The second sentence introduces a viewpoint—that is, education is the civil rights issue of our time. What are "civil rights"? You might think immediately of the civil rights movement that fought for racial equality under the law—particularly during the 1960s. But here the term refers to the freedoms and rights granted to all citizens that make "life, liberty, and the pursuit of happiness" a reality. Although education is not specifically mentioned in the Constitution, or in any of its amendments, every state has compulsory education laws requiring young people to attend school, and the Fourteenth Amendment states, "No State shall make or enforce any law which shall abridge the privileges or immunities of citizens of the United States; nor shall any State deprive any person of life, liberty, or property, without due process of law; nor deny to any person within its jurisdiction the equal protection of the laws." Could equal protection be interpreted as requiring an equal quality of education? Could flaws in the educational system be interpreted as depriving a person of "life, liberty, or property"? In the third sentence of the prompt, you are asked to explain why you agree or disagree with the statement that education today is not just "a" civil rights issue but "the" civil rights issue of our time. Notice, too, that the definition of "education" is left open; there is no specific level of education mentioned. The third sentence also instructs you to use particular sources in your essay.

Before reading the texts, think about how the sources will help you complete the assignment. As we've discussed, sources can illustrate or support your own ideas. If your initial response to the prompt is that disparities in educational opportunities make public education a civil rights issue, then you can look to your sources to help you make that point. But it's important not to summarily reject texts that disagree with your position or are not directly relevant to it. In fact, you might use a text that presents an opposing opinion as a counterargument and then concede and refute it. Most important, keep an open mind while you read the sources so that your thesis shows that you understand the complexity of the subject of education as well as the implications of describing the contemporary system of education as a "civil rights issue."

Sources

Horace Mann, from *Report of the Massachusetts Board of Education* (1848)
Norman Rockwell, *The Problem We All Live With* (1964)
Edward P. Jones, *The First Day* (1992)
Antonio Alvarez, *Out of My Hands* (2008)
Blake Ellis, *Average Student Loan Debt Nears $27,000* (2012)
David Kirp, *The Secret to Fixing Bad Schools* (2013)
Ross Douthat, *The Secrets of Princeton* (2013)
Caroline M. Hoxby and Christopher Avery, from *The Missing "One-Offs": The Hidden Supply of High-Achieving, Low-Income Students* (2013)

from *Report of the Massachusetts Board of Education*

HORACE MANN

The following selection is taken from an official 1848 policy document by Horace Mann (1796–1859), who is known as the father of American public education.

Intellectual Education as a Means of Removing Poverty, and Securing Abundance

According to the European theory, men are divided into classes, — some to toil and earn, others to seize and enjoy. According to the Massachusetts theory, all are to have an equal chance for earning, and equal security in the enjoyment of what they earn. The latter tends to equality of condition; the former, to the grossest inequalities. . . .

But is it not true that Massachusetts, in some respects, instead of adhering more and more closely to her own theory, is becoming emulous of the baneful examples of Europe? The distance between the two extremes of society is lengthening, instead of being abridged. With every generation, fortunes increase on the one hand, and some new privation is added to poverty on the other. We are verging towards those extremes of opulence and of penury, each of which unhumanizes the human mind. A perpetual struggle for the bare necessaries of life, without the ability to obtain them, makes men wolfish. Avarice, on the other hand, sees, in all the victims of misery around it, not objects for pity and succor, but only crude materials to be worked up into more money.

I suppose it to be the universal sentiment of all those who mingle any ingredient of benevolence with their notions on political economy, that vast and overshadowing private fortunes are among the greatest dangers to which the happiness of the people in a republic can be subjected. Such fortunes would create a feudalism of a new kind, but one more oppressive and unrelenting than that of the middle ages. The feudal lords in England and on the Continent never held their retainers in a more abject condition of servitude than the great majority of foreign manufacturers and capitalists hold their operatives and laborers at the present day. The means employed are different; but the similarity in results is striking. What force did then, money does now. The villein[1] of the middle ages had no spot of earth on which he could live, unless one were granted to him by his lord. The operative or laborer of the present day has no employment, and therefore no bread, unless the capitalist will accept his services. The vassal had no shelter but such as his master provided for him. Not one in five thousand of English operatives or farm-laborers is able to build or own even a hovel; and therefore they must accept such shelter as capital offers them. The baron prescribed his own terms to his retainers: those terms were peremptory, and the serf must submit or perish. The British manufacturer or farmer prescribes the rate of wages he will give to his work-people; he reduces these wages under whatever pretext he pleases; and they, too, have no alternative but submission or starvation. In some respects, indeed, the condition of the modern dependent is more forlorn than that of the corresponding serf class in former times. Some attributes of the patriarchal relation did spring up between the lord and his lieges to soften the harsh relations subsisting between them. Hence came some oversight of the condition of children, some relief in sickness, some protection and support in the decrepitude of age. But only in instances comparatively few have kindly offices smoothed the rugged relation between British capital and British labor. The children of the work-people are abandoned to their fate; and notwithstanding the privations they suffer, and the dangers they threaten, no power in the realm has yet been able to secure them an education; and when the adult laborer is prostrated by sickness, or eventually worn out by toil and age, the poorhouse, which has all along been his destination, becomes his destiny. . . .

Now, surely nothing but universal education can counterwork this tendency to the domination of capital and servility of labor. If one class possesses all the wealth and the education, while the residue of society is ignorant and poor, it matters not by what name the relation between them may be called: the latter, in fact and in truth, will be the servile dependants and subjects of the former. But, if education

---

[1]In a feudal society, a serf who has the right to own property. — Eds.

be equably diffused, it will draw property after it by the strongest of all attractions, for such a thing never did happen, and never can happen, as that an intelligent and practical body of men should be permanently poor. Property and labor in different classes are essentially antagonistic; but property and labor in the same class are essentially fraternal. The people of Massachusetts have, in some degree, appreciated the truth, that the unexampled prosperity of the State — its comfort, its competence, its general intelligence and virtue — is attributable to the education, more or less perfect, which all its people have received: but are they sensible of a fact equally important; namely, that it is to this same education that two-thirds of the people are indebted for not being today the vassals of as severe a tyranny, in the form of capital, as the lower classes of Europe are bound to in the form of brute force?

Education, then, beyond all other devices of human origin, is the great equalizer of   5
the conditions of men, — the balance-wheel of the social machinery. I do not here mean that it so elevates the moral nature as to make men disdain and abhor the oppression of their fellow-men. This idea pertains to another of its attributes. But I mean that it gives each man the independence and the means by which he can resist the selfishness of other men. It does better than to disarm the poor of their hostility towards the rich: it prevents being poor. Agrarianism is the revenge of poverty against wealth. The wanton destruction of the property of others — the burning of hay-ricks and corn-ricks, the demolition of machinery because it supersedes hand-labor, the sprinkling of vitriol on rich dresses — is only agrarianism run mad. Education prevents both the revenge and the madness. On the other hand, a fellow-feeling for one's class or caste is the common instinct of hearts not wholly sunk in selfish regards for person or for family. The spread of education, by enlarging the cultivated class or caste, will open a wider area over which the social feelings will expand; and, if this education should be universal and complete, it would do more than all things else to obliterate factitious distinctions in society. . . .

For the creation of wealth, then, — for the existence of a wealthy people and a wealthy nation, — intelligence is the grand condition. The number of improvers will increase as the intellectual constituency, if I may call it, increases. In former times, and in most parts of the world even at the present day, not one man in a million has ever had such a development of mind as made it possible for him to become a contributor to art or science. Let this development precede, and contributions, numberless, and of inestimable value, will be sure to follow. That political economy, therefore, which busies itself about capital and labor, supply and demand, interest and rents, favorable and unfavorable balances of trade, but leaves out of account the element of a widespread mental development, is nought but stupendous folly. The greatest of all the arts in political economy is to change a consumer into a producer; and the next greatest is to increase the producer's producing power, — an end to be directly attained by increasing his intelligence. For mere delving, an ignorant man is but little better than a swine, whom he so much resembles in his appetites, and surpasses in his powers of mischief.

(1848)

The text by Horace Mann is a primary nonfiction document from the mid-nineteenth century, a period when the country was formalizing democratic policies at the same time that events that would lead to the Civil War were unfolding. Mann contrasts the class system in England with the "theory" that "all are to have an equal chance for earning, and equal security in the enjoyment of what they earn" (par. 1). Yet, he points out the increasing "distance between the two extremes of society" as "fortunes increase on the one hand, and some new privation is added to poverty on the other" (par. 2). He believes the most effective force against this dangerous tendency is "universal education": "the great equalizer of the conditions of men, — the balance-wheel of the social machinery" (par. 5). Mann expresses profound faith in the potential of intelligence and "widespread mental development" (par. 6) to create a community of individuals working toward the common good. Although the specific focus is the state of Massachusetts, Mann's text establishes the philosophical and ideological basis for the belief that education available to all is essential to a functioning democracy: "The number of improvers will increase as the intellectual constituency . . . increases" (par. 6). Do you find this belief more idealistic than practical? To what extent do you think it is a realistic goal for the entire country today?

The Problem We All Live With

NORMAN ROCKWELL

> Popular artist Norman Rockwell made this painting of Ruby Bridges, the six-year-old African American girl who was escorted by U.S. Marshals into an all-white school in New Orleans as part of desegregation legislation. Originally published in the January 14, 1964, issue of *Look* magazine, the painting was installed in the White House outside the Oval Office of President Barack Obama for several months in 2011.

This iconic image is probably familiar to you. The artist, Norman Rockwell, known for his warm celebration of small-town and family life, addressed the far more volatile subject of desegregation in the mid-1960s in this depiction of an African American girl, seen in silhouette, surrounded by federal marshals as she makes what would otherwise be a simple walk to school. Rockwell's use of color dramatizes the black-white tension, which is further heightened by the barely legible derogatory word scrawled on the wall and punctuated by the red splat of a thrown tomato. This work raises many questions, such as whether the marshals are protecting Ruby or boxing her in. What is the significance of depicting them without heads and faces? What is "the problem" in Rockwell's title: Racism? Segregation? Race relations? Does the phrase "we all live with" suggest that we should just live with it, as the saying goes, or is Rockwell suggesting that we "all" bear responsibility for addressing or resolving "the problem"? The fact that the first African American president paid tribute to the painting adds to the authority of this visual text as a symbol of the civil rights

Printed by permission of the Norman Rockwell Family Agency. Copyright © the Norman Rockwell Family Entities, Norman Rockwell Museum Collections

NORMAN ROCKWELL, *THE PROBLEM WE ALL LIVE WITH*, 1964, OIL ON CANVAS, 36" × 58". ILLUSTRATION FOR *LOOK* MAGAZINE, JANUARY 14, 1964.

(SEE COLOR INSERT, IMAGE 11.)

movement in America. How does President Obama's action change or contribute to your interpretation of the painting?

Like the painting just discussed, fiction can comment indirectly on social and political issues. Let's look at a short story by Edward P. Jones.

The First Day

EDWARD P. JONES

> Edward P. Jones (b. 1951) won the Pulitzer Prize for Fiction in 2003 for his novel *The Known World.* The following story appeared in his first book, a collection of short stories entitled *Lost in the City* (1992).

On an otherwise unremarkable September morning, long before I learned to be ashamed of my mother, she takes my hand and we set off down New Jersey Avenue to begin my very first day of school. I am wearing a checkeredlike blue-and-green cotton dress, and scattered about these colors are bits of yellow and white and brown. My mother has uncharacteristically spent nearly an hour on my hair that morning, plaiting and replaiting so that now my scalp tingles. Whenever I turn my head quickly, my nose fills with the faint smell of Dixie Peach hair grease. The smell is somehow a soothing one now and I will reach for it time and time again before the morning ends. All the plaits, each with a blue barrette near the tip and each twisted into an uncommon sturdiness, will last until I go to bed that night, something that has never happened before. My stomach is full of milk and oatmeal sweetened with brown sugar. Like everything else I have on, my pale green slip and underwear are new, the underwear having come three to a plastic package with a little girl on the front who appears to be dancing. Behind my ears, my mother, to stop my whining, has dabbed the stingiest bit of her gardenia perfume, the last present my father gave her before he disappeared into memory. Because I cannot smell it, I have only her word that the perfume is there. I am also wearing yellow socks trimmed with thin lines of black and white around the tops. My shoes are my greatest joy, black patent-leather miracles, and when one is nicked at the toe later that morning in class, my heart will break.

I am carrying a pencil, a pencil sharpener, and a small ten-cent tablet with a black-and-white speckled cover. My mother does not believe that a girl in kindergarten needs such things, so I am taking them only because of my insistent whining and because they are presents from our neighbors, Mary Keith and Blondelle Harris. Miss Mary and Miss Blondelle are watching my two younger sisters until my mother returns. The women are as precious to me as my mother and sisters. Out playing one day, I have overheard an older child, speaking to another child, call Miss Mary and Miss Blondelle a word that is brand new to me. This is my mother: When I say the word in fun to one of my sisters, my mother slaps me across the mouth and the word is lost for years and years.

All the way down New Jersey Avenue, the sidewalks are teeming with children. In my neighborhood, I have many friends, but I see none of them as my mother and I walk. We cross New York Avenue, we cross Pierce Street, and we cross L and K, and still I see no one who knows my name. At I Street, between New Jersey Avenue and Third Street, we enter Seaton Elementary School, a time-worn, sad-faced building across the street from my mother's church, Mt. Carmel Baptist.

Just inside the front door, women out of the advertisements in *Ebony* are greeting other parents and children. The woman who greets us has pearls thick as jumbo marbles that come down almost to her navel, and she acts as if she had known me all my life, touching my shoulder, cupping her hand under my chin. She is enveloped in a perfume that I only know is not gardenia. When, in answer to her question, my mother tells her that we live at 1227 New Jersey Avenue, the woman first seems to be picturing in her head where we live. Then she shakes her head and says that we are at the wrong school, that we should be at Walker-Jones.

My mother shakes her head vigorously. "I want her to go here," my mother says.   5
"If I'da wanted her someplace else, I'da took her there." The woman continues to act as if she has known me all my life, but she tells my mother that we live beyond the area that Seaton serves. My mother is not convinced and for several more minutes she questions the woman about why I cannot attend Seaton. For as many Sundays as I can remember, perhaps even Sundays when I was in her womb, my mother has pointed across I Street to Seaton as we come and go to Mt. Carmel. "You gonna go there and learn about the whole world." But one of the guardians of that place is say-

ing no, and no again. I am learning this about my mother: The higher up on the scale of respectability a person is — and teachers are rather high up in her eyes — the less she is liable to let them push her around. But finally, I see in her eyes the closing gate, and she takes my hand and we leave the building. On the steps, she stops as people move past us on either side.

"Mama, I can't go to school?"

She says nothing at first, then takes my hand again and we are down the steps quickly and nearing New Jersey Avenue before I can blink. This is my mother: She says, "One monkey don't stop no show."

Walker-Jones is a larger, newer school and I immediately like it because of that. But it is not across the street from my mother's church, her rock, one of her connections to God, and I sense her doubts as she absently rubs her thumb over the back of her hand. We find our way to the crowded auditorium where gray metal chairs are set up in the middle of the room. Along the wall to the left are tables and other chairs. Every chair seems occupied by a child or adult. Somewhere in the room a child is crying, a cry that rises above the buzz-talk of so many people. Strewn about the floor are dozens and dozens of pieces of white paper, and people are walking over them without any thought of picking them up. And seeing this lack of concern, I am all of a sudden afraid.

"Is this where they register for school?" my mother asks a woman at one of the tables.

The woman looks up slowly as if she has heard this question once too often.   10
She nods. She is tiny, almost as small as the girl standing beside her. The woman's hair is set in a mass of curlers and all of those curlers are made of paper money, here a dollar bill, there a five-dollar bill. The girl's hair is arrayed in curls, but some of them are beginning to droop and this makes me happy. On the table beside the woman's pocketbook is a large notebook, worthy of someone in high school, and looking at me looking at the notebook, the girl places her hand possessively on it. In her other hand she holds several pencils with thick crowns of additional erasers.

"These the forms you gotta use?" my mother asks the woman, picking up a few pieces of the paper from the table. "Is this what you have to fill out?"

The woman tells her yes, but that she need fill out only one.

"I see," my mother says, looking about the room. Then: "Would you help me with this form? That is, if you don't mind."

The woman asks my mother what she means.

"This form. Would you mind helpin me fill it out?"   15

The woman still seems not to understand.

"I can't read it. I don't know how to read or write, and I'm askin you to help me." My mother looks at me, then looks away. I know almost all of her looks, but this one is brand new to me. "Would you help me, then?"

The woman says Why sure, and suddenly she appears happier, so much more satisfied with everything. She finishes the form for her daughter and my mother and I step aside to wait for her. We find two chairs nearby and sit. My mother is now diseased, according to the girl's eyes, and until the moment her mother takes her and the form to the front of the auditorium, the girl never stops looking at my mother. I stare back at her. "Don't stare," my mother says to me. "You know better than that."

Another woman out of the *Ebony* ads takes the woman's child away. Now, the woman says upon returning, let's see what we can do for you two.

My mother answers the questions the woman reads off the form. They start with my last name, and then on to the first and middle names. This is school, I think. This is going to school. My mother slowly enunciates each word of my name. This is my mother: As the questions go on, she takes from her pocketbook document after document, as if they will support my right to attend school, as if she has been saving them up for just this moment. Indeed, she takes out more papers than I have ever seen her do in other places: my birth certificate, my baptismal record, a doctor's letter concerning my bout with chicken pox, rent receipts, records of immunization, a letter about our public assistance payments, even her marriage license — every single paper that has anything even remotely to do with my five-year-old life. Few of the papers are needed here, but it does not matter and my mother continues to pull out the documents with the purposefulness of a magician pulling out a long string of scarves. She has learned that money is the beginning and end of everything in this world, and when the woman finishes, my mother offers her fifty cents, and the woman accepts it without hesitation. My mother and I are just about the last parent and child in the room.   20

My mother presents the form to a woman sitting in front of the stage, and the woman looks at it and writes something on a white card, which she gives to my mother. Before long, the woman who has taken the girl with the drooping curls appears from behind us, speaks to the sitting woman, and introduces herself to my mother and me. She's to be my teacher, she tells my mother. My mother stares.

We go into the hall, where my mother kneels down to me. Her lips are quivering. "I'll be back to pick you up at twelve o'clock. I don't want you to go nowhere. You just wait right here. And listen to every word she say." I touch her lips and press them together. It is an old, old game between us. She puts my hand down at my side, which is not part of the game. She stands and looks a second at the teacher, then she turns and walks away. I see where she has darned one of her socks the night before. Her shoes make loud sounds in the hall. She passes through the doors and I can still hear the loud sounds of her shoes. And even when the teacher turns me toward the classrooms and I hear what must be the singing and talking of all the children in the world, I can still hear my mother's footsteps above it all.

(1992)

Although Edward P. Jones does not actually state his faith in education as Mann does, the actions of the characters in this story suggest a similar belief. The mother, who has little formal education and cannot read, is determined that her daughter will have the advantages of schooling and is confident that her daughter has a right to an education. She risks being embarrassed or even laughed at when she admits she cannot read and asks another mother to help her fill out the forms. The mother in the story leaves her daughter with the parting advice to listen to everything the teacher has to say: education is serious business with high stakes. Yet, we know from the first lines of the story that education can have negative consequences as well: in this case, as the daughter narrates the story from the future, she reminds us (or herself) that this first day of school occurred "before [she] learned to be ashamed of [her] mother." Has the education that opened doors for the daughter distanced her from her mother? Is that an inevitable process, or has education become one more way to distinguish haves from have-nots?

Out of My Hands

Antonio Alvarez

> The federal DREAM Act (acronym for Development, Relief, and Education for Alien Minors) was originally proposed in 2001 to offer a pathway to citizenship for any undocumented immigrant who enters the United States as a minor, graduates from high school in this country, and completes a minimum of two years of college or university studies or serves for at least two years in the military. Kent Wong, director of UCLA's Center for Labor Studies and Education, compiled narratives written by students about their experiences as undocumented immigrants. The following is one of those stories, which was published in *Underground Undergrads: UCLA Undocumented Immigrant Students Speak Out* (2008).

As I ran downstairs from the third floor, I looked forward to playing with the other children living in our apartment building. Some of my friends were playing with *trompos* (a top spun with yarn, like a dreidel), others with marbles, and some of the girls were jumping rope. I noticed that one of the children had a water gun very similar to mine. I approached the boy, took a closer look at the toy, and realized that it actually was mine. I asked the boy why he had taken my water gun and told him that he needed to return it. He said, "No, your mother sold it to me because you guys are leaving. You guys are moving away, somewhere else." This was when I first knew that I was going to the United States. I was four years old.

My father, Antonio, said that he decided to go to the United States "to be able to have a better life, a better future, in being able to realize our dreams, the American dream." Similarly my mother, Alida, "did not see a future for us in Mexico" and viewed the United States as the answer to our problems. During the 1980s, Mexico underwent a major economic crisis, leaving my father without a stable job to support our family. The instinct to survive led both of my parents to view immigration as their only option. My father left in mid-1988, and the rest of the family — me, my mother, two-year-old brother Isai, and eight-month-old sister Alida — left in late December 1989.

The plan was for my father to work in the United States and send money back home to support us and hopefully to accumulate enough to start up our own business. My mother grew impatient in Mexico when my father did not return however. She believed he needed to see his children. She decided to migrate with the entire family to the United States without giving prior notice to my father. . . .

My parents' plan was not to permanently settle in the United States; however, as time passed, they decided to stay. One of our goals became, and continues to be, to adjust our residential status from undocumented to documented permanent residents. My father filled out numerous applications to adjust his residential status, and the process was long and arduous. He began in 1992, but due to a mistake of addresses when we changed residences, and a long waiting list, it took my father about fourteen years to adjust his status. He obtained a work permit in 2003 and finally his permanent residency in 2006. Now he has petitioned for permanent residency for me, my siblings, and my mother, but the waiting list is so long — a lifetime for us.

Along with our residential status, anti-immigrant laws have shaped our lives in the   5
United States. My parents said that the laws that have affected us most severely include California's Proposition 187,[1] which was approved by voters in 1994. My mother believed it was not fair to keep children out of public schools and to keep them from receiving medical treatment. We were surprised at how much support the proposition gained and that an overwhelming majority of Californians voted for it. My mother told me that I would probably not be able to attend school any more if my undocumented status was reported by anyone on the school staff. Though the proposition passed, it was struck down as unconstitutional by the courts, and I continued to attend school.

I remember the 1996 driver's license legislation's passing and going into effect, because my dad was worried to death by it. He was mortified because at that time and up until 2006, he had been working two jobs — one of them as a pizza delivery worker for different pizza chains, which required a valid driver's license. It was hard watching how much stress he had because he knew renewing his driver's license would be impossible, since the new law prohibited undocumented immigrants from receiving licenses or renewing them. By the time my father had to renew his license, however, he had received his work permit. It allowed him to renew his driver's license without any legal trouble.

Though I remember these laws as severe obstacles for our family's livelihood, legislation affecting higher education opportunities for undocumented students stand out in my memory most prominently. I realized that I was an immigrant and that something was not right during the Proposition 187 campaign but until I reached high school, I did not understand that my future would be seriously limited. During my freshman year, I discovered that I could not obtain a license because I was undocumented, and during my junior year, I realized the hardships I would face upon entering college. I had achieved almost a 4.0 grade point average up until my sophomore year, but when I learned that I could not receive any federal or state financing to attend a four-year university, I became demoralized, and my grades suffered from it. I thought there was no point to continuing to work so hard in high school if attending a community college — where my high school grades would be irrelevant — was my only option.

---

[1] A ballot initiative that denied education, nonemergency health care, and other social services to undocumented immigrants. It was overturned by the Supreme Court in 1995. — Eds.

My outlook changed a few months before high school graduation. I talked to one of my teachers who was once an undocumented immigrant student but is now a permanent resident. He told me about AB 540 and explained that it would allow me to pay in-state tuition at UC, CSU, and community college. Though I was accepted to CSU Los Angeles and CSU Fullerton, he recommended I first attend a community college for its affordability, complete my first two years there, save money, and then transfer to a four-year university.

I took his advice and enrolled at East Los Angeles College (ELAC) in the summer of 2003 and quickly followed this by searching for a job. As a result of my undocumented status, I could not work anywhere I wanted and was limited to low-wage jobs that did not require identification or background checks. I was hired at a market, where I worked over thirty hours a week. I now had a goal. My plan at ELAC was to work and go to school and then to transfer to a CSU because the UCs and private schools were too expensive and required longer commutes. Though it was a good plan, it saddened me because my ideal dream from years before — ever since I had visited the UCLA campus during an elementary school field trip — had been to attend a top university.

I enjoyed the schooling I received at ELAC, and I flourished. I took sociology   10
classes and fell in love with the subject. It was then that I realized that I wanted a career in helping others, specifically individuals whose voices were muted in society. Impressed by my work, both my sociology and English professors told me I needed to include a UC in my future. When I finally did apply to transfer, I was accepted to every university I applied to: USC, UC San Diego, UC Berkeley, and UCLA. I decided to attend UCLA, where I struggle for the thousands of dollars to finance my education. I will graduate with a degree in sociology and Chicana/o studies.

Being undocumented has been a way of life for me, my family, and millions of others. When I apply for jobs that I know I am overqualified for but that do not include background checks, I experience strong feelings of detachment and frustration, followed by hints of helplessness. I work these jobs to pay for a college experience that does not include semesters abroad and living in a dorm and other experiences that "normal" students have. I hope that by sharing some of my family's history and experiences — as undocumented immigrants, undocumented workers, undocumented students, undocumented people, and second-class human beings — I can help produce an emphatic and humanistic approach to immigration that vigorously rejects the notion that a human can be illegal.

(2008)

This source is a personal narrative by a college student who immigrated to the United States from Mexico. After describing the obstacles his family encountered trying to realize their dreams of becoming U.S. citizens, he tells the story of his own experiences as he navigated the policies and laws governing his eligibility for financial support for a university education and constraining his employment opportunities. Writing as a student, at the University of California at Los Angeles, he states that he "will graduate" with a BA degree, though he has struggled to finance his education. Do you think that Antonio Alvarez's story confirms the power of education to uplift and transform, as Mann hoped, or is it evidence that Mann's belief in education as a "balance wheel" has not proved to be true?

Average Student Loan Debt Nears $27,000

Blake Ellis

This excerpt appeared in CNN Money on October 18, 2012.

Two-thirds of the class of 2011 held student loans upon graduation, and the average borrower owed $26,600, according to a report from the Institute for College Access & Success' Project on Student Debt. That's up 5% from 2010 and is the highest level of debt in the seven years the report has been published.

The increase comes at a time when unemployment has remained stubbornly high for college graduates — it was at 8.8% for 2011. Those without a college degree are more than twice as likely to end up without jobs, however. The unemployment rate for recent high school graduates was 19.1% last year.

Many students in the class of 2011 also entered college right before the recession hit, with many families suddenly finding themselves unable to afford the tuition payments. At the same time, many public colleges have hiked tuition significantly in response to state budget cuts, while private colleges have also been **increasing tuition.**

One thing that has likely kept student debt loads from growing even larger in recent years is increased federal financial aid, the report said.

"In these tough times, a college degree is still your best bet for getting a job and   5 decent pay," said TICAS President Lauren Asher. "But, as debt levels rise, fear of loans can prevent students from getting the education they need to succeed."

The school you choose matters: The amount of debt a student has upon graduation can vary dramatically depending on the school they attend.

Of the 1,057 colleges in the study, average debt per graduate ranged from $3,000 to $55,250. At 114 colleges, graduates had average debt above $35,000, while 64 colleges said that more than 90% of seniors graduate with debt.

Tuition, fees, the availability of financial aid and the cost of living all factor into the amount of debt students wind up with, the report found.

"Students and parents need to know that, even at similar looking schools, debt levels can be wildly different," said Asher.

While Indiana University of Pennsylvania and Clarion University of Pennsylvania   10 are both public four-year colleges and charge annual tuition and fees of roughly $7,500, for example, graduates of Indiana University of Pennsylvania had average debt of $32,416 while Clarion University graduates had average debt of only $3,815.

The Project on Student Debt said since certain schools didn't submit data, it didn't have enough information to rank colleges by their debt, but it did highlight "high debt" schools and "low debt" schools.

The schools where students graduated with the highest average debt loads — between $31,900 and $46,700 — include Franklin Pierce University in New Hampshire, La Salle

University in Pennsylvania, Morgan State University in Maryland and Kentucky State University.

Franklin Pierce graduates, for example, owed an average of $44,702, while Kentucky State graduates owed an average of $36,293.

Schools with the lowest average debt—between $3,000 and $9,750—include Williams College in Massachusetts, Yale University in Connecticut, Pomona College in California, College of the Ozarks in Missouri and Berea College in Kentucky.

(2012)

This source is a straightforward newspaper article reporting on college student debt for the class of 2011. In addition to citing statistics that indicate the magnitude of debt that students often must accumulate, the article points out the double bind that college students face: steady increases in their tuition at the same time that chances for employment are bleak if they do not earn a college degree. If, then, education is more accessible to those with wealthy parents, is it "universal education," as Mann characterized it? Or does the civil right to public education end after the K–12 level? Since college, by definition, requires selection based on achievement of various kinds (e.g., academic or extracurricular), are economic variables acceptable or even expected?

The Secret to Fixing Bad Schools

David Kirp

Professor of public policy at the University of California–Berkeley, David Kirp is the author of *Improbable Scholars: The Rebirth of a Great American School System and a Strategy for America's Schools.* This article, which is excerpted from that book, appeared in the *New York Times* in February 2013.

What would it really take to give students a first-rate education? Some argue that our schools are irremediably broken and that charter schools offer the only solution. The striking achievement of Union City, N.J.—bringing poor, mostly immigrant kids into the educational mainstream—argues for reinventing the public schools we have.

Union City makes an unlikely poster child for education reform. It's a poor community with an unemployment rate 60 percent higher than the national average. Three-quarters of the students live in homes where only Spanish is spoken. A quarter are thought to be undocumented, living in fear of deportation.

Public schools in such communities have often operated as factories for failure. This used to be true in Union City, where the schools were once so wretched that state officials almost seized control of them. How things have changed. From third grade through high school, students' achievement scores now approximate the statewide average. What's more, in 2011, Union City boasted a high school graduation rate of 89.5 percent—roughly 10 percentage points higher than the national average. Last year, 75 percent of Union City graduates enrolled in college, with top students winning scholarships to the Ivies.

As someone who has worked on education policy for four decades, I've never seen the likes of this. After spending a year in Union City working on a book, I believe its transformation offers a nationwide strategy.

Ask school officials to explain Union City's success and they start with pre-kindergarten, which enrolls almost every 3- and 4-year-old. There's abundant research showing the lifetime benefits of early education. Here, seeing is believing.

One December morning the lesson is making latkes, the potato pancakes that are a Hanukkah staple. Everything that transpires during these 90 minutes could be called a "teachable moment" — describing the smell of an onion ("Strong or light? Strong — duro. Will it smell differently when we cook it? We'll have to find out."); pronouncing the "p" in pepper and pimento; getting the hang of a food processor ("When I put all the ingredients in, what will happen?").

Cognitive and noncognitive, thinking and feeling; here, this line vanishes. The good teacher is always on the lookout for both kinds of lessons, always aiming to reach both head and heart. "My goal is to do for these kids what I do with my own children," the teacher, Susana Rojas, tells me. "It's all about exposure to concepts — wide, narrow, long, short. I bring in breads from different countries. 'Let's do a pie chart showing which one you liked the best.' I don't ask them to memorize 1, 2, 3 — I could teach a monkey to count."

From pre-K to high school, the make-or-break factor is what the Harvard education professor Richard Elmore calls the "instructional core" — the skills of the teacher, the engagement of the students and the rigor of the curriculum. To succeed, students must become thinkers, not just test-takers.

When Alina Bossbaly greets her third grade students, ethics are on her mind. "Room 210 is a pie — un pie — and each of us is a slice of that pie." The pie offers a down-to-earth way of talking about a community where everyone has a place. Building character and getting students to think is her mission. From Day 1, her kids are writing in their journals, sifting out the meaning of stories and solving math problems. Every day, Ms. Bossbaly is figuring out what's best for each child, rather than batch-processing them.

Though Ms. Bossbaly is a star, her philosophy pervades the district. Wherever I went, these schools felt less like impersonal institutions than the simulacrum[1] of an extended family.

Until recently, Union City High bore the scarlet-letter label, "school in need of improvement." It has taken strong leadership from its principal, John Bennetti, to turn things around — to instill the belief that education can be a ticket out of poverty.

On Day 1, the principal lays out the house rules. Everything is tied to a single theme — pride and respect in "our house" — that resonates with the community culture of family, unity and respect. "Cursing doesn't showcase our talents. Breaking the

---

[1] An imitation, representation, or substitute. — Eds.

dress code means we're setting a tone that unity isn't important, coming in late means missing opportunities to learn." Bullying is high on his list of nonnegotiables: "We are about caring and supporting."

These students sometimes behave like college freshmen, as in a seminar where they're parsing Toni Morrison's *Beloved*. They can be boisterously jokey with their teachers. But there's none of the note-swapping, gum-chewing, wisecracking, talking-back rudeness you'd anticipate if your opinions about high school had been shaped by movies like *Dangerous Minds*.

And the principal is persuading teachers to raise their expectations. "There should be more courses that prepare students for college, not simply more work but higher-quality work," he tells me. This approach is paying off big time: Last year, in a study of 22,000 American high schools, *U.S. News & World Report* and the American Institutes for Research ranked Union City High in the top 22 percent.

What makes Union City remarkable is, paradoxically, the absence of pizazz. It   15 hasn't followed the herd by closing "underperforming" schools or giving the boot to hordes of teachers. No Teach for America recruits toil in its classrooms, and there are no charter schools.

A quarter-century ago, fear of a state takeover catalyzed a transformation. The district's best educators were asked to design a curriculum based on evidence, not hunch. Learning by doing replaced learning by rote. Kids who came to school speaking only Spanish became truly bilingual, taught how to read and write in their native tongue before tackling English. Parents were enlisted in the cause. Teachers were urged to work together, the superstars mentoring the stragglers and coaches recruited to add expertise. Principals were expected to become educational leaders, not just disciplinarians and paper-shufflers.

From a loose confederacy, the schools gradually morphed into a coherent system that marries high expectations with a "we can do it" attitude. "The real story of Union City is that it didn't fall back," says Fred Carrigg, a key architect of the reform. "It stabilized and has continued to improve."

To any educator with a pulse, this game plan sounds so old-school obvious that it verges on platitude. That these schools are generously financed clearly makes a difference — not every community will decide to pay for two years of prekindergarten — but too many districts squander their resources.

School officials flock to Union City and other districts that have beaten the odds, eager for a quick fix. But they're on a fool's errand. These places — and there are a host of them, largely unsung — didn't become exemplars by behaving like magpies, taking shiny bits and pieces and gluing them together. Instead, each devised a long-term strategy reaching from preschool to high school. Each keeps learning from experience and tinkering with its model. Nationwide, there's no reason school districts — big or small; predominantly white, Latino or black — cannot construct a system that, like the schools of Union City, bends the arc of children's lives.

(2013)

Public policy scholar David Kirp offers a contrasting perspective to the gloom-and-doom view that public schools are "factories for failure" (par. 3). The public schools in Union City, New Jersey, where the unemployment rate is 60 percent more than over the national average and 75 percent of the students are nonnative speakers of English, have been transformed. The high-school graduation rate in 2011 was 89.5 percent, with 75 percent of graduates going on to college. Employing "old-school" strategies, Union City schools have instilled in their students "the belief that education can be a ticket out of poverty" (par. 11). What qualities are responsible for the success of Union City schools? To what extent is this system a realistic model for reform of public schools in general and especially for those serving low-income communities?

The Secrets of Princeton

Ross Douthat

> In this selection, *New York Times* columnist Ross Douthat responds to a letter published in the *Daily Princetonian* (March 29, 2013) from Susan Patton, which had offered the following advice to Princeton women students: "Find a husband on campus before you graduate."

Susan Patton, the Princeton alumna who became famous for her letter urging Ivy League women to use their college years to find a mate, has been denounced as a traitor to feminism, to coeducation, to the university ideal. But really she's something much more interesting: a traitor to her class.

Her betrayal consists of being gauche enough to acknowledge publicly a truth that everyone who's come up through Ivy League culture knows intuitively — that elite universities are about connecting more than learning, that the social world matters far more than the classroom to undergraduates, and that rather than an escalator elevating the best and brightest from every walk of life, the meritocracy as we know it mostly works to perpetuate the existing upper class.

Every elite seeks its own perpetuation, of course, but that project is uniquely difficult in a society that's formally democratic and egalitarian and colorblind. And it's even more difficult for an elite that prides itself on its progressive politics, its social conscience, its enlightened distance from hierarchies of blood and birth and breeding.

Thus the importance, in the modern meritocratic culture, of the unacknowledged mechanisms that preserve privilege, reward the inside game, and ensure that the advantages enjoyed in one generation can be passed safely onward to the next.

The intermarriage of elite collegians is only one of these mechanisms — but it's an enormously important one. The outraged reaction to her comments notwithstanding, Patton wasn't telling Princetonians anything they didn't already understand. *Of course* Ivy League schools double as dating services. *Of course* members of elites — yes, gender egalitarians, the males as well as the females — have strong incentives to marry one another, or at the very least find a spouse from within the wider

5

meritocratic circle. What better way to double down on our preexisting advantages? What better way to minimize, in our descendants, the chances of the dread phenomenon known as "regression to the mean"?

That this "assortative mating," in which the best-educated Americans increasingly marry one another, also ends up perpetuating existing inequalities seems blindingly obvious, which is no doubt why it's considered embarrassing and reactionary to talk about it too overtly. We all know what we're supposed to do — our mothers don't have to come out and say it!

Why, it would be like telling elite collegians that they should all move to similar cities and neighborhoods, surround themselves with their kinds of people and gradually price everybody else out of the places where social capital is built, influence exerted and great careers made. No need — that's what we're already doing! (What Richard Florida called "the mass relocation of highly skilled, highly educated, and highly paid Americans to a relatively small number of metropolitan regions, and a corresponding exodus of the traditional lower and middle classes from these same places" is one of the striking social facts of the modern meritocratic era.) We don't need well-meaning parents lecturing us about the advantages of elite self-segregation, and giving the game away to everybody else. . . .

Or it would be like telling admissions offices at elite schools that they should seek a form of student-body "diversity" that's mostly cosmetic, designed to flatter multicultural sensibilities without threatening existing hierarchies all that much. They don't need to be told — that's how the system already works! The "holistic" approach to admissions, which privileges résumé-padding and extracurriculars over raw test scores or G.P.A.'s, has two major consequences: It enforces what looks suspiciously like de facto discrimination against Asian applicants with high SAT scores, while disadvantaging talented kids — often white and working class and geographically dispersed — who don't grow up in elite enclaves with parents and friends who understand the system. The result is an upper class that looks superficially like America, but mostly reproduces the previous generation's elite.

But don't come out and say it! Next people will start wondering why the names in the *U.S. News* rankings change so little from decade to decade. Or why the American population gets bigger and bigger, but our richest universities admit the same size classes every year. Or why in a country of 300 million people and countless universities, we can't seem to elect a president or nominate a Supreme Court justice who doesn't have a Harvard or Yale degree.

No, it's better for everyone when these questions aren't asked too loudly. The days of noblesse oblige are long behind us, so our elite's entire claim to legitimacy rests on theories of equal opportunity and upward mobility and the promise that "merit" correlates with talents and deserts.

That the actual practice of meritocracy mostly involves a strenuous quest to avoid any kind of downward mobility, for oneself or for one's kids, is something every upper-class American understands deep in his or her highly educated bones.

But really, Susan Patton, do we have to talk about it?

(2013)

Ross Douthat takes the unpopular position that elite schools perpetuate elitism — deliberately, consistently, and effectively — at the same time they pay lip service to the concept of meritocracy. He argues that Americans claim to believe in "theories of equal opportunity and upward mobility" (par. 10), yet elite universities' attempts to "diversify" and reflect a more egalitarian society mostly reproduce "the previous generation's elite" (par. 8). Do you agree that what he calls "assortative mating" is "blindingly obvious" (par. 6)? Do you find the fact that "in a country of 300 million people and countless universities, we can't seem to elect a president or nominate a Supreme Court justice who doesn't have a Harvard or Yale degree" (par. 9) evidence of elitism? Is the concept of the United States as a meritocracy — that is, a system in which people's success in life depends primarily on their own intelligence and hard work rather than on birthright — an ideal more than a reality? Do you find Douthat's position (and tone) in this essay too cynical?

from *The Missing "One-Offs"*
The Hidden Supply of High-Achieving, Low-Income Students
CAROLINE M. HOXBY AND CHRISTOPHER AVERY

Caroline M. Hoxby of Stanford University and Christopher Avery of Harvard University studied college application patterns of low-income students with top test scores and grades. Following is a summary of their research and a chart based on their findings.

Abstract

We show that the vast majority of very high-achieving students who are low-income do not apply to any selective college or university. This is despite the fact that selective institutions would often cost them less, owing to generous financial aid, than the resource-poor two-year and non-selective four-year institutions to which they actually apply. Moreover, high-achieving, low-income students who do apply to selective institutions are admitted and graduate at high rates. We demonstrate that these low-income students' application behavior differs greatly from that of their high-income counterparts who have similar achievement. The latter group generally follows the advice to apply to a few "par" colleges, a few "reach" colleges, and a couple of "safety" schools. We separate the low-income, high-achieving students into those whose application behavior is similar to that of their high-income counterparts ("achievement-typical" behavior) and those whose apply to no selective institutions ("income-typical" behavior). We show that income-typical students do not come from families or neighborhoods that are more disadvantaged than those of achievement-typical students. However, in contrast to the achievement-typical students, the income-typical students come from districts too small to support selective public high schools, are not in a critical mass of fellow high achievers, and are unlikely to encounter a teacher or schoolmate from an older cohort who attended a selective college. We demonstrate that widely-used policies — college admissions staff recruiting, college campus visits, college access programs — are likely to be ineffective with income-typical students, and we suggest policies that will be effective must depend less on geographic concentration of high achievers.

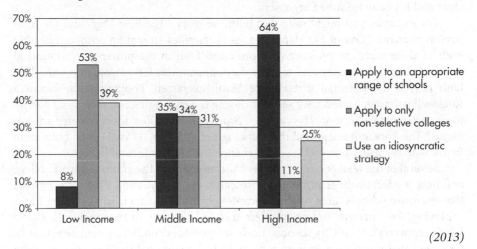

(2013)

Writing a Synthesis Essay

Now that you have read the sources in this chapter's Conversation on whether education is the civil rights issue of our time, let's walk through the process of synthesizing the sources and writing a synthesis essay. As you move from reading and analyzing the sources to integrating them into your own writing, you will engage in a process of selection. This is often a complex step in which, ideally, you explore the individual texts and start to see connections between and among them. Essential to this process is your willingness to understand each text on its own terms, even if you disagree with its ideas or position; in fact, texts that present viewpoints different from those you initially hold are often the ones that become most important to the development of your argument.

Formulating Your Position

Before you formulate your own position, you should take stock of the issues. Try not to divide the sources into "pro" and "con" positions because that will just create a dividing line between agreement and disagreement rather than allow you to delve into more subtle ideas. Your goal when you read sources provided for you or when you research on your own is to look for multiple perspectives — a range of ways to consider a topic or subject. It's especially important to be open to positions that you find less appealing or actually disagree with, at least at the beginning of your research. What would be the purpose of consulting sources if all you want to do is validate your own position? You may, in fact, find sources that do just that, but in the process of reading and analyzing, you are likely to gain a more in-depth understanding of the complexity of your subject. The more ways you consider an issue, the more likely you are to write a clear and logically informed argument.

For example, you might note that both the story "The First Day" and the first-person narrative "Out of My Hands" focus on families struggling economically. Yet both of these texts are evidence of a profound faith in the power of education to improve financial security and to provide opportunities for personal growth. That faith reflects the potential that Horace Mann expressed. Looking at the Norman Rockwell painting, however, we see that during the civil rights era, race was a barrier to equal access to education. Has *Brown v. Board of Education* made segregated schools illegal? The Rockwell image and the autobiographical "Out of My Hands" both seem to ask whether legislation and laws can change social attitudes and behavior.

Several of the texts focus on money in terms of both the affordability of college and how it affects college admissions. Research in "The Missing 'One-Offs'" shows that exclusive schools often offer applicants substantial financial support, yet high-achieving, low-income students are less inclined to apply to those schools. David Kirp's report on Union City schools, however, provides conflicting evidence: that is, he shows that given high expectations and high-quality instruction, students who are not born into affluent, well-educated families can start their own tradition of graduating from college. Will these Union City graduates, then, break the spell of "elite self-segregation" that Ross Douthat argues prevails at such competitive institutions?

Now that you've begun to explore the texts through the lens of multiple perspectives, a series of issues should emerge. It's often useful to restate issues as questions. Consider the following and develop at least three other questions of your own:

- In the past, has education been a viable means for citizens to exercise their rights of personal liberty — particularly the potential for upward mobility?
- What influence does socioeconomic status play in opportunities in K–12 education? In access to colleges and universities?
- Does delivery of an inadequate K–12 education that limits the choices students have in higher education constitute a violation of civil rights?
- Does the availability of quality K–12 education in public schools correlate with family income level?
- Did Horace Mann intend that "universal education" be extended to include equal access at the college and university level?

These questions — and others you might have — illustrate the complexity of the issue and ensure that you do not develop an argument that is one-sided, polarized between "yes" and "no," or the written equivalent of a shouting match. Instead, you want to present your viewpoint in an essay that reflects the complexities surrounding the topic.

The fact is, you can rarely change a reader's mind radically or immediately. But you can aim for creating a compelling argument that leaves the reader thinking, questioning, considering, and reconsidering. To do this, you have to acknowledge that the issue at hand is a complex one with no easy solutions and that a variety of valid perspectives on the matter exist. You want to present a reasonable idea in a voice that is logical, informed, and sincere. To write a qualified argument, you must anticipate objections to your position and recognize and respect the complexities of multiple perspectives.

With these questions and issues in mind, you can begin to formulate a thesis, or claim, that captures your position on the topic. Consider the following working thesis statements:

> Limits on opportunity because of race, gender, and ethnicity have been to a large extent eliminated, yet the vastly different quality of education students receive in today's public schools makes education the most pressing civil rights issue of our day.

> Obstacles to achieving admission to selective colleges exist today, but the opportunities are available for anyone who has the intelligence, drive, and determination to succeed.

> Although Horace Mann's vision of education as the "balance wheel of the social machinery" has been realized in our system of K–12 public education, the inequalities at the college and university level are evidence that education today is the civil rights issue of our time.

> Characterizing our current educational system as "the civil rights issue of our time" is a deceptive attempt to equate a serious but practical and solvable problem with a true moral crisis that the civil rights movement represented.

Although you might want to tailor one of these working thesis statements to use in your essay, each one suggests a clear focus while acknowledging the complexities of the issue.

• ACTIVITY •

Of the thesis statements above, select one you *disagree — or at least partially disagree — with*. Then, using the readings in the Conversation, find three pieces of evidence that support that thesis.

Framing Quotations

When writing with sources, it's important not to simply summarize or paraphrase them. You need to use the sources to strengthen your own argument. One effective way to make sure the sources are working for you is to include a sentence or two of explanation or commentary with each quotation. You might use a lead-in sentence, so your readers know what to look for, as in the following:

> Family income need not limit the quality of education in public schools; nor is it essential to have state-of-the-art technology and a cadre of teachers proven to be the best and the brightest. Using the example of Union City, New Jersey, pre-K through 12 schools, David Kirp reports that there is an "absence of pizazz" but an abundance of strategies committed to a "coherent system that marries high expectations with a 'we can do it' attitude."

Alternatively, you might follow a quotation with a sentence or two of commentary to remind readers of your point and how the quotation reinforces it, as you see here:

> Key to making Mann's concept of "universal education" a reality is creating a positive environment for learning with the shared values embodied in Union City Schools. Kirp describes a "single theme — pride and respect in 'our house' — that resonates with the community culture of family, unity, and respect." Thus, specific behaviors such as adhering to dress codes, not participating in bullying, and avoiding curse words uphold the commitment to the stated values. Similarly, seminar-like class discussions demonstrate those values at work as students show respect for their teachers, classmates, and themselves even as they engage in lively debate.

And, of course, be careful not to represent ideas or words as your own if they are not: give credit where it is due!

Integrating Quotations

When using multiple sources in your writing, it becomes even more important to incorporate the quotations in a way that is both clear and interesting. You want the transition from your own voice to others' words and ideas to be smooth and natural sounding. The most effective way to accomplish this is to integrate the quotations into your own sentences. This may be a bit challenging, but the benefit is seamless prose. When you integrate quotations in this way, the reader can follow your ideas and see the sources in the context of your argument. Be sure that the result is a grammatically correct and syntactically fluent sentence. For instance, suppose you want to use the ideas in these two sentences from David Kirp:

Cognitive and noncognitive, thinking and feeling; here, this line vanishes. The good teacher is always on the lookout for both kinds of lessons, always aiming to reach both head and heart.

In an effort to paraphrase and include some direct quotations, you might draft this sentence:

> In Union City, the distinction between "cognitive and noncognitive, thinking and feeling" "vanishes" because of "aiming to reach both head and heart."

This sentence has a couple of problems, starting with a heavy load of quoted phrases at the beginning: the writer's own voice doesn't have a chance to be heard. Then, the second part of the sentence veers off without a subject: Who is "aiming"? An improved sentence uses fewer quotations and syntax that allows for accurate quoting:

> David Kirp explains that in Union City, the usual dichotomy of thought and feeling "vanishes" as teachers develop instruction "aiming to reach both head and heart."

• ACTIVITY •

Below you will find a paragraph using the excerpt from Horace Mann as a source. Read the paragraph, and then revise it in order to make more effective use of the source.

> In the "Report of the Massachusetts Board of Education," Horace Mann expresses his belief in the power of "universal education" to counteract the "tendency to the domination of capital and servility of labor." If society is split between those who are "ignorant and poor" and those who hold "all the wealth and the education," then the latter are powerful and the former are both powerless and hopeless. Education must be made available to all, he believes, because it is "beyond all other devices of human origin . . . the great equalizer of the conditions of men, — the balance-wheel of the social machinery." Access to education "will open a wider area over which the social feelings will expand; and, if this education should be universal and complete, it would do more than all things else to obliterate factitious distinctions in society." Mann shows himself to be an idealist as well as a pragmatist when he argues that there is a direct correlation between increasing intelligence through education and increasing the wealth of a society: "The greatest of all the arts in political economy is to change a consumer into a producer; and the next greatest is to increase the producer's producing power, — an end to be directly attained by increasing his intelligence."

Citing Sources

Since you will be quoting from several works, you have to keep track of your sources for your reader. In timed situations, you'll probably include only the source number or the author's name in parentheses after the quotation or paraphrase, as shown below:

> Recent research reveals that many ("probably the vast majority") of very high-achieving high school students from low-income families do not even apply to selective colleges; in fact, only 8 percent of these students apply to a variety of schools that include high reach and so-called "safe" choices, while 35 percent of their middle-income counterparts and 64 percent of high-income students apply to the full range (Hoxby and Avery).

You need to cite the source of paraphrases as well as direct quotations. Any time you use other people's ideas, you must give them credit.

Another, more elegant option is to mention the author and title of the work in the sentence introducing or including the quotation:

> In their study published in 2013, researchers Caroline Hoxby and Christopher Avery report that only 8 percent of high-achieving students from low-income families apply to a variety of colleges, including selective institutions and so-called "safe" choices, while 35 percent of their middle-income counterparts and 64 percent of high-income students apply to the full range.

If you are writing a more formal research paper, you will likely need to follow Modern Language Association (MLA) documentation procedures, including providing a works cited page. Ask your teacher if you are unclear about what is required for an assignment. Guidelines for MLA documentation appear in the back of this book.

As you go through the readings and selections in the following chapters, you will join conversations on a range of topics and reflect on and integrate the ideas of writers from different times and places into your own thinking and writing. Each chapter includes three Conversations in which you will practice synthesizing with a series of texts (including visuals) related to the chapter's readings. You should also be aware of the conversations going on around you all the time. How do people call on sources to reinforce their positions? And how do people enter an ongoing conversation and move it forward?

A Sample Synthesis Essay

Following is a complete synthesis essay responding to the prompt that asks whether education is the civil rights issue of our time. Read it carefully, and then consider its effectiveness by responding to the questions that follow.

You Gotta Fight for Your Right . . . to Education

Mackenzie Broderick

When Horace Mann wrote his report for the Massachusetts Board of Education in 1848, he envisioned a society where everyone in the United States, regardless of background or economic status, would have an opportunity — an equal opportunity — to acquire an education. Tied to the concept of liberty as defined in the Constitution and Declaration of Independence, public education from elementary grades through high school became a "civil right." Although today most of us think of the "civil rights movement" as an era that ended racial segregation, including "separate but equal" schools, education as a "civil right" still needs safeguarding. Unfortunately, during the second decade of the twenty-first century, Mann's vision for a populace enjoying the civil right of equal access to education has been achieved only to a limited extent in primary and secondary schools, and the inequalities he lamented as privileging the wealthiest citizens are starkly apparent in colleges and universities.

To some extent, the egalitarian dreams of Mann have come true. He witnessed the effects of the Industrial Revolution on American society; instead of attending school, many children were sent to work in factories alongside their parents; many child-labor laws would not even be considered until the next century. But the advent of free and compulsory education took children out of the factory and placed them in the schoolhouse. A free education offered the opportunity for many to rise above the station they were born into, resulting in a large middle class that was almost nonexistent in Mann's time. Furthermore, even the simple ability to read helped create the fraternity Mann championed because a population that is literate is able to make more informed decisions, from voting to creating labor unions. While education has traditionally been more difficult for women and minorities to achieve, the fact that the disenfranchised still managed to change the status quo speaks to the power of education.

We see the struggle to grasp the civil right of education continuing well into the twentieth century. Norman Rockwell's iconic painting entitled *The Problem We All Live With* dramatizes the school desegregation battles that occurred even after *Brown v. Board of Education* declared the "separate but equal" policy of schools reserved for African Americans to be illegal. The little girl looks toward her future as she walks into her school building carrying the book and ruler that symbolize her readiness to start class, but she has to be guarded by federal marshals in order to make her journey across racial divides. Even later on, we see disparity in opportunities that are class rather than race based. In the short story "The First Day," another girl makes her start in school thanks to the determined efforts of her mother, who can neither read nor write. But author Edward P. Jones reminds us of the socioeconomic factors that govern which school a child attends. When the mother and daughter try to enroll in the school across from their church, they are told firmly that they do not belong: "my mother tells her [the teacher greeting students] that we live at 1227 New Jersey Avenue, the woman first seems to be picturing in her head where we live. Then she shakes her head and says that we are at the wrong school, that we should be at Walker-Jones." The mother wants more than anything for her daughter to attend school, a place to "learn about the whole world," so she has no choice but to take her to the designated school.

While the feudal system Mann wrote of is a relic of the past, the divide between the rich and the rest is widening today. Those already wealthy can afford to send their children to top-notch private schools if the neighborhood ones are inadequate — as many of our urban schools are — or hire private counselors and tutors to supplement their education and prepare them for high-stakes tests that open or close college doors. Schools such as the one described in David Kirp's article about Union City, New Jersey, that have brought "poor, mostly immigrant kids into the educational mainstream" are praiseworthy but exceptional. Without the advantage of a rigorous K–12 education, what hope do most students have of being admitted to a good college, let alone receiving a scholarship?

The economic divide is most apparent at the college level. Although we have an extensive system of public universities, they are by no means free or "universal," as Mann described. Even applying to colleges can be more than $1,000 with the cost of standardized tests and application fees. A recent research study showed that low-income students who are also high achievers in terms of high school grades and test scores are less likely to even apply to selective schools: only 8 percent of low-income, high-achieving students know enough about the application process to apply to a variety of colleges, while 64 percent of their high-income counterparts apply to a full range, from safe to highly selective colleges and universities (Hoxby and Avery). Plus, when students graduate from college, and not just exceedingly expensive private ones, inequality takes a stronger hold: the average student loan debt in 2011 was $27,000, according to a CNN report (Ellis); today, it is even higher, making the choice to attend college for all but the very affluent a trade-off between debt and degree.

Civil rights are those rights guaranteed to all citizens, especially the right to equality in social, political, and economic rights. If education is the means to social mobility, political influence, and a higher income level — as Mann believed it should and would be — then in today's world of inadequate public schools and out-of-control college costs, education definitely is the civil rights issue of our time.

Questions

1. How effectively do you think Mackenzie Broderick uses Horace Mann's selection as a source? To what extent has she integrated it into the bigger picture of education as a civil rights issue?
2. Where in the essay do you think Mackenzie uses sources especially well? Where do you think their use could be improved? Are there any instances where your interpretation of a source differs from Mackenzie's? Explain your responses.
3. How effectively does Mackenzie address the counterargument?
4. Why do you think the conclusion is or is not effective? Does it answer the "so what" question? How might it be improved?
5. Mackenzie uses first person occasionally, yet she does not draw on her personal experience in this essay. Do you think that developing one or more of her points with a personal anecdote about her own experience or that of a family member would strengthen the essay, or would it detract from a more objective tone?
6. If you were talking to Mackenzie as a peer critic, what would you tell her is the main strength of her essay? What one suggestion would you make for her to revise and improve her work?

Culminating Activity

Leon Botstein, president of Bard College, proposed that high school as we know it should be abolished. After reading his proposal, which was published as an article in the *New York Times* in 1999, write an essay explaining what you believe are the chief issues that must be addressed in order to improve America's high schools. Develop your argument by drawing on your own experience and at least two of the sources you have just read.

Let Teenagers Try Adulthood
LEON BOTSTEIN

> The national outpouring after the Littleton [Columbine High School] shootings has forced us to confront something we have suspected for a long time: the American high school is obsolete and should be abolished. In the . . . month [after the shootings] high school students present and past [came] forward with stories about cliques and the artificial intensity of a world defined by insiders and outsiders, in which the insiders hold sway because of superficial definitions of good looks and attractiveness, popularity and sports prowess.
>
> The team sports of high school dominate more than student culture. A community's loyalty to the high school system is often based on the extent to which varsity teams succeed. High school administrators and faculty members are often former coaches, and the coaches themselves are placed in a separate, untouchable

category. The result is that the culture of the inside elite is not contested by the adults in the school. Individuality and dissent are discouraged.

But the rules of high school turn out not to be the rules of life. Often the high school outsider becomes the more successful and admired adult. The definitions of masculinity and femininity go through sufficient transformation to make the game of popularity in high school an embarrassment. No other group of adults young or old is confined to an age-segregated environment, much like a gang in which individuals of the same age group define each other's world. In no workplace, not even in colleges or universities, is there such a narrow segmentation by chronology.

Given the poor quality of recruitment and training for high school teachers, it is no wonder that the curriculum and the enterprise of learning hold so little sway over young people. When puberty meets education and learning in modern America, the victory of puberty masquerading as popular culture and the tyranny of peer groups based on ludicrous values meet little resistance.

By the time those who graduate from high school go on to college and realize   5
what really is at stake in becoming an adult, too many opportunities have been lost and too much time has been wasted. Most thoughtful young people suffer the high school environment in silence and in their junior and senior years mark time waiting for college to begin. The Littleton killers, above and beyond the psychological demons that drove them to violence, felt trapped in the artificiality of the high school world and believed it to be real. They engineered their moment of undivided attention and importance in the absence of any confidence that life after high school could have a different meaning.

Adults should face the fact that they don't like adolescents and that they have used high school to isolate the pubescent and hormonally active adolescent away from both the picture-book idealized innocence of childhood and the more accountable world of adulthood. But the primary reason high school doesn't work anymore, if it ever did, is that young people mature substantially earlier in the late 20th century than they did when the high school was invented. For example, the age of first menstruation has dropped at least two years since the beginning of this century, and not surprisingly, the onset of sexual activity has dropped in proportion. An institution intended for children in transition now holds young adults back well beyond the developmental point for which high school was originally designed.

Furthermore, whatever constraints to the presumption of adulthood among young people may have existed decades ago have now fallen away. Information and images, as well as the real and virtual freedom of movement we associate with adulthood, are now accessible to every 15- and 16-year-old.

Secondary education must be rethought. Elementary school should begin at age 4 or 5 and end with the sixth grade. We should entirely abandon the concept of the middle school and junior high school. Beginning with the seventh grade, there should be four years of secondary education that we may call high school. Young people should graduate at 16 rather than 18.

They could then enter the real world, the world of work or national service, in which they would take a place of responsibility alongside older adults in mixed company. They could stay at home and attend junior college, or they could go away to college. For all the faults of college, at least the adults who dominate the world of colleges, the faculty, were selected precisely because they were exceptional and different, not because they were popular. Despite the often cavalier attitude toward teaching in college, at least physicists know their physics, mathematicians know and love their mathematics, and music is taught by musicians, not by graduates of education schools, where the disciplines are subordinated to the study of classroom management.

For those 16-year-olds who do not want to do any of the above, we might   10
construct new kinds of institutions, each dedicated to one activity, from science to dance, to which adolescents could devote their energies while working together with professionals in those fields.

At 16, young Americans are prepared to be taken seriously and to develop the motivations and interests that will serve them well in adult life. They need to enter a world where they are not in a lunchroom with only their peers, estranged from other age groups and cut off from the game of life as it is really played. There is nothing utopian about this idea; it is immensely practical and efficient, and its implementation is long overdue. We need to face biological and cultural facts and not prolong the life of a flawed institution that is out of date.

(1999)

5

A Meeting of Old and New Worlds
Beginnings to 1750

The philosopher George Santayana once said of Christopher Columbus, "He gave the world another world." But the so-called New World was not really new at all. Humans have populated the continents of the Americas since as early as 30,000 B.C.E., so any date we choose as the starting point of our national body of literature is arbitrary; in fact, many of the pieces in this chapter were not written by "Americans" as we understand the term today, since neither the original inhabitants of the American continents nor the earliest European explorers and settlers considered themselves Americans. When Columbus landed in this new world, the land that became America was inhabited by an estimated 5 million natives, living in hundreds of tribes, many with rich traditions of myths and legends. "How the World Was Made" and "The Earth on Turtle's Back" are two origin stories in this chapter that exemplify this oral tradition. Beyond the vibrant cultural life found in native tribes, many of them had developed sophisticated social structures. Perhaps the most impressive of these was the Iroquois Confederacy, an alliance of six nations governed by the Iroquois Constitution, a document so democratic in philosophy that Benjamin Franklin reportedly presented it as a model when the Founding Fathers began drafting the U.S. Constitution.

Many American schoolchildren learn that "in 1492, Columbus sailed the ocean blue." But Columbus never actually set foot on North America, nor was he the first European explorer to reach the American continents — Leif Eriksson led a Nordic expedition to Newfoundland in the eleventh century. Nevertheless, Columbus remains a key figure in America's history and imagination. This chapter includes a group of texts considering his legacy, and the national holiday that bears his name. Columbus's four voyages across the Atlantic Ocean galvanized Europe's interest in and awareness of the American continent and initiated a period of fierce competition to colonize "the New World." In the 150 years after Columbus first set sail, Amerigo Vespucci explored Brazil and the West Indies; John Cabot sought the Northwest Passage; Hernando de Soto charted the southern region of North America; Hernán Cortés and Francisco Pizarro, respectively, conquered the Aztecs and the Incas of South America; George Weymouth explored New England; Henry Hudson sailed the river that now bears his name; and the Pilgrims reached Plymouth Rock. From the fifteenth to the early eighteenth century, America was little more than a loose collection of

Woodcut for the cover of a pamphlet, printed in Florence, 1493. Photo: akg-images.

This woodcut from a 1493 pamphlet printed in Florence, Italy, shows King Ferdinand of Spain dispatching Columbus's fleet for the New World.

settlements, some commissioned by European monarchs for economic and imperial purposes, some privately funded for farming and trading, and others composed of religious dissenters seeking refuge from discrimination in their native lands.

This heady period of discovery was also a time when cultures clashed violently. Waves of settlers brought with them disease and destruction that eradicated a large percentage of the indigenous population of the Americas. Acknowledgment of the damage done, respect for the cultures eradicated, and curiosity about the ways of life now lost have been relatively recent phenomena. One notable exception to this rule can be found in the writings of the Spanish explorer Cabeza de Vaca, whose account of his harrowing journey through the American south is a unique, and comparatively sympathetic, anthropological exploration of the native populations he encountered.

Nova Britannia.

OFFRING MOST

Excellent fruites by Planting in
VIRGINIA.

Exciting all such as be well affected
to further the same.

C. 2263.

LONDON

Printed for SAMUEL MACHAM, and are to be sold at
his Shop in Pauls Church-yard, at the
Signe of the Bul-head.
1609.

English School, (17th century)/Private Collection/The Bridgeman Art Library

This is the title page of a pamphlet by the Virginia Company, whose aim was to entice investors to buy stock in the enterprise. It reads: "Nova Brittania. Offering most excellent fruits by planting in Virginia. Exciting all such as be well affected to further the same."

This chapter includes many pieces that explore the tension between Native Americans and white settlers. Most are told from the perspective of the colonists, chronicling the genuine dangers of colonial life. One such narrative by Mary Rowlandson, a colonist in the Massachusetts Bay Colony, tells her story of captivity by Native Americans in 1676 and her eventual ransom. When it was published in 1682, it became the first best seller of American literature. Another group of texts revolving around Pocahontas examines the divide between the real woman, who was a daughter of a Native American chief and who married a white settler, and the mythical icon of popular culture. The texts question why Pocahontas is still important to our culture, what she represents, and how she is and has been represented, both textually and graphically.

Library of Congress

NATHANIEL CURRIER, *THE LANDING OF THE PILGRIMS AT PLYMOUTH, 11TH DECEMBER 1620,* C. 1840, COLOR LITHOGRAPH.

Arguably the most famous group of settlers was the Pilgrims, who founded Plymouth Colony, in present-day Massachusetts, after arriving at Plymouth Rock on the *Mayflower* in 1620. The Pilgrims were a branch of English Puritans who advocated not just reform of the Church of England, as most Puritans did, but total separation from it. Religious dissent in England was illegal, with fines and imprisonment for those who did not attend Church of England services or who held their own. The Pilgrims fled England both to avoid punishment and to pursue the freedom to worship as they saw fit.

Soon, other religious dissenters in England followed the Pilgrims' path across the Atlantic. Between 1620 and 1640, approximately 21,000 Puritans made the journey. Puritan settlers in the colonies of New England, particularly in the Massachusetts Bay Colony, lived extremely strict, religious lives. The colonies banned nonreligious entertainment, games, alcohol, and even the celebration of Christmas. They valued education, frugality, family, and hard work—values that would come to typify the American way of life. In this chapter, the poetry of Edward Taylor provides glimpses into the Puritan mind-set and helps us understand colonial life from a religious and spiritual perspective, while Anne Bradstreet's work explores the struggles of being a woman, and particularly a literary woman, within the confines of the rigid and hierarchical Puritan society.

American School, (19th century)/Private Collection/The Bridgeman Art Library

WITCHCRAFT AT SALEM VILLAGE, 1883, ENGRAVING, FROM *THE ROMANCE AND TRAGEDY OF PIONEER LIFE* BY AUGUSTUS L. MASON.

This chapter also explores an ignominious series of events during the Puritan era. The Salem Witch Trials, which occurred in colonial Massachusetts in 1692–1693, are seen through sermons and speeches by Cotton Mather, calling for his fellow Puritans to root out what he and many others believed was the work of the devil, and John Hale, reflecting on the aftermath when the community sought to find a way to heal from the hysteria and injustice.

In the Conversation on the American Jeremiad—a jeremiad being a style of writing and oration that laments a decline while celebrating the possibility of an ideal—you will study more of the sermons of this period. Puritan ministers utilized the rhetorical strategy of the jeremiad to strike fear — and hope — in the hearts and minds of colonists; politicians, religious leaders, and journalists still use it today. When you read the jeremiads, some of which were written centuries apart, you will have an opportunity to think about the ways Puritan literature, culture, and thought remain alive in the contemporary United States.

In this chapter, you will explore the earliest literature of a chaotic new world, formed as two old worlds collided. In this transitional period, a wide assortment of religious refugees, explorers, imperialists, merchants, and indigenous people coexisted — sometimes in harmony, sometimes in conflict — for more than two centuries before anything resembling the United States of America was born. And out of this chaos we begin to see the formation of narratives that define the national character: the Puritan work ethic, a deep spiritual devotion, the pioneering spirit, the self-reliance, and even a nascent feminism, as expressed in the work of Anne Bradstreet. These narratives continue to echo down the corridors of American history.

NATIVE AMERICAN ORIGIN STORIES

The tribes that inhabited the land that would become America held a wide variety of beliefs but also shared some commonalities. Most tribes recognized a supreme creator, although by different names and with different attributes. Most tribes also held beliefs that would now be called *animism*, which maintains that animals, plants, and other aspects of nature have a sacred or spiritual aspect. Included here are origin stories that show how two tribes explain the beginning of life on earth. It is important to remember that what remains of these stories is fragmentary and in written form, thus lacking the power of performance that was, and is, a fundamental part of the oral tradition. The first, "How the World Was Made," comes to us from the Cherokee tradition. The Cherokee were originally a southeastern tribe, but they were forcibly relocated to Arkansas and Oklahoma in the 1830s on the now infamous route known as the Trail of Tears. Today, the Cherokee Nation, the federally recognized government of the Cherokee people, is based in Tahlequah, Oklahoma. The second story, "The Earth on Turtle's Back," is from the Onondaga tribe, or "People of the Hill." Originally from northern New York, the Onondaga were one of the five original tribes of the Iroquois Nation. Members of the Onondaga tribe currently reside on the Six Nations Reserve in Onondaga County, New York, and in Ontario, Canada.

How the World Was Made

The earth is a great island floating in a sea of water, and suspended at each of the four cardinal points by a cord hanging down from the sky vault, which is of solid rock. When the world grows old and worn out, the people will die and the cords will break and let the earth sink down into the ocean, and all will be water again. The Indians are afraid of this.

When all was water, the animals were above in Gălûñ´lătĭ,[1] beyond the arch; but it was very much crowded, and they were wanting more room. They wondered what was below the water, and at last Dâyuni´sĭ, "Beaver's Grandchild," the little Water-beetle, offered to go and see if it could learn. It darted in every direction over the surface of the water, but could find no firm place to rest. Then it dived to the bottom and came up with some soft mud, which began to grow and spread on every side until it became the island which we call the earth. It was afterward fastened to the sky with four cords, but no one remembers who did this.

At first the earth was flat and very soft and wet. The animals were anxious to get down, and sent out different birds to see if it was yet dry, but they found no place to alight and came back again to Gălûñ´lătĭ. At last it seemed to be time, and they sent out the Buzzard and told him to go and make ready for them. This was the Great Buzzard, the father of all the buzzards we see now. He flew all over the earth, low down near the ground, and it was still soft. When he reached the Cherokee country, he was very tired, and his wings began to flap and strike the ground, and wherever they struck the earth there was a valley, and where they turned up again there was a mountain. When the animals above saw this, they were afraid that the whole world would be mountains, so they called him back, but the Cherokee country remains full of mountains to this day.

When the earth was dry and the animals came down, it was still dark, so they got the sun and set it in a track to go every day across the island from east to west, just overhead. It was too hot this way, and Tsiska´gĭlĭ´, the Red Crawfish, had his shell scorched a bright red, so that his meat was spoiled; and the Cherokee do not eat it. The conjurers put the sun another handbreadth higher in the air, but it was still too hot. They raised it another time, and another, until it was seven handbreadths high and just under the sky arch. Then it was right, and they left it so. This is why the conjurers call the highest place Gûlkwâ´gine Di´gălûñ´lătiyûñ´, "the seventh height," because it is seven handbreadths above the earth. Every day the sun goes along under this arch, and returns at night on the upper side to the starting place.

There is another world under this, and it is like ours in everything — animals, plants, and people — save that the seasons are different. The streams that come down from the mountains are the trails by which we reach this underworld, and the springs at their heads are the doorways by which we enter it, but to do this one must fast and go to water and have one of the underground people for a guide. We know that the seasons in the underworld are different from ours, because the water in the springs is always warmer in winter and cooler in summer than the outer air.

When the animals and plants were first made — we do not know by whom — they were told to watch and keep awake for seven nights, just as young men now fast and keep awake when they pray to their medicine. They tried to do this, and nearly all were awake through the first night, but the next night several dropped off to sleep,

5

---

[1]The sky vault where all creatures lived before the world was created. — Eds.

and the third night others were asleep, and then others, until, on the seventh night, of all the animals only the owl, the panther, and one or two more were still awake. To these were given the power to see and to go about in the dark, and to make prey of the birds and animals which must sleep at night. Of the trees only the cedar, the pine, the spruce, the holly, and the laurel were awake to the end, and to them it was given to be always green and to be greatest for medicine, but to the others it was said: "Because you have not endured to the end you shall lose your hair every winter."

Men came after the animals and plants. At first there were only a brother and sister until he struck her with a fish and told her to multiply, and so it was. In seven days a child was born to her, and thereafter every seven days another, and they increased very fast until there was danger that the world could not keep them. Then it was made that a woman should have only one child in a year, and it has been so ever since.

The Earth on Turtle's Back

Before this Earth existed, there was only water. It stretched as far as one could see, and in that water there were birds and animals swimming around. Far above, in the clouds, there was a Skyland. In that Skyland there was a great and beautiful tree. It had four white roots which stretched to each of the sacred directions, and from its branches all kinds of fruits and flowers grew.

There was an ancient chief in the Skyland. His young wife was expecting a child, and one night she dreamed that she saw the Great Tree uprooted. The next morning she told her husband the story.

He nodded as she finished telling her dream. "My wife," he said, "I am sad that you had this dream. It is clearly a dream of great power and, as is our way, when one has such a powerful dream we must do all that we can to make it true. The Great Tree must be uprooted."

Then the ancient chief called the young men together and told them that they must pull up the tree. But the roots of the tree were so deep, so strong, that they could not budge it. At last the ancient chief himself came to the tree. He wrapped his arms around it, bent his knees and strained. At last, with one great effort, he uprooted the tree and placed it on its side. Where the tree's roots had gone deep into the Skyland there was now a big hole. The wife of the chief came close and leaned over to look down, grasping the tip of one of the Great Tree's branches to steady her. It seemed as if she saw something down there, far below, glittering like water. She leaned out further to look and, as she leaned, she lost her balance and fell into the hole. Her grasp slipped off the tip of the branch, leaving her with only a handful of seeds as she fell, down, down, down, down.

Far below, in the waters, some of the birds and animals looked up.   5

"Someone is falling toward us from the sky," said one of the birds.

"We must do something to help her," said another. Then two Swans flew up. They caught the Woman From the Sky between their wide wings. Slowly, they began to bring her down toward the water, where the birds and animals were watching.

"She is not like us," said one of the animals. "Look, she doesn't have webbed feet. I don't think she can live in the water."

"What shall we do, then?" said another of the water animals.

"I know," said one of the water birds. "I have heard that there is Earth far below   10 the waters. If we dive down and bring up Earth, then she will have a place to stand."

So the birds and animals decided that someone would have to bring up Earth. One by one they tried.

The Duck dove down first, some say. He swam down and down, far beneath the surface, but could not reach the bottom and floated back up. Then the Beaver tried. He went even deeper, so deep that it was all dark, but he could not reach the bottom, either. The Loon tried, swimming with his strong wings. He was gone a long long time, but he, too, failed to bring up Earth. Soon it seemed that all had tried and all had failed. Then a small voice spoke up.

"I will bring up Earth or die trying."

They looked to see who it was. It was the tiny Muskrat. She dove down and swam and swam. She was not as strong or as swift as the others, but she was determined. She went so deep that it was all dark, and still she swam deeper. She went so deep that her lungs felt ready to burst, but she swam deeper still. At last, just as she was becoming unconscious, she reached out one small paw and grasped at the bottom, barely touching it before she floated up, almost dead.

When the other animals saw her break the surface they thought she had failed.   15 Then they saw her right paw was held tightly shut.

"She has the Earth," they said. "Now where can we put it?"

"Place it on my back," said a deep voice. It was the Great Turtle, who had come up from the depths.

They brought the Muskrat over to the Great Turtle and placed her paw against his back. To this day there are marks at the back of the Turtle's shell which were made by Muskrat's paw. The tiny bit of Earth fell on the back of the turtle. Almost immediately, it began to grow larger and larger and larger until it became the whole world.

Then the two Swans brought the Sky Woman down. She stepped onto the new Earth and opened her hand, letting the seeds fall onto the bare soil. From those seeds the trees and grass sprang up. Life on Earth had begun.

Exploring the Text

1. What phenomenon or practice does each story seek to explain? Pay close attention to the power relationships.
2. How does each story shed light on the specific tribe's understanding of the relationship between humans, supernatural forces, and the natural world?
3. What element(s) of human behavior are explained or analyzed by each story? Consider gender and familial roles.

NATIVE AMERICAN TRICKSTER STORIES

The trickster in Native American stories is a complex cultural figure who often combines conflicting characteristics: he is shrewd yet foolish, mean yet kind, cunning yet careless. The trickster takes the form of different animals, but the coyote is the most common. The first tale reprinted here, "A Satisfying Meal," comes from the Hopi tribe. Members of a federally recognized sovereign nation, the Hopi Indians live primarily on a reservation in northeastern Arizona. They were first encountered by the Spaniards in the sixteenth century and claim ancestry from the Anasazi Indians, who lived in cliff pueblos found throughout the Four Corners area (now New Mexico, Utah, Arizona, and Colorado). The second tale in this section, "Coyote Gets Stuck," comes from the Shasta (or Casta) tribe, members of which continue to live in their traditional homeland in northwestern California and southwestern Oregon.

A Satisfying Meal

Coyote and Fox are not very fond of each other because they are always competing for the same kind of food. So whenever he has a chance to play a trick on Fox, Coyote will do it.

One day Fox managed to catch a prairie dog. He killed it. He said: "This is a fine, fat prairie dog. It will make a tasty meal."

Fox got some wood and made a fire. When the wood had been reduced to glowing embers, Fox pushed the prairie dog under the hot ashes to roast it. "It will take a while until the meat is done," Fox said to himself. "I think I'll have a little nap in the meantime." So he went to sleep.

Not far away, Coyote came walking along, scrounging for something to eat, sniffing around. The wind brought to him a scent of roasted meat. Coyote's nose quivered with delight. "Ah," he said, "I am smelling something good."

Following his nose, Coyote came to the spot where Fox was sleeping. He dug out the prairie dog from under the still-glowing embers. He ate it up in no time at all. He said: "This meat is very tender, cooked just the way I like it." He left only the bare bones. He took a little of the fat and smeared it around Fox's mouth. Then Coyote went off laughing.

Fox woke up. He noticed that his mouth was greasy. He said: "I must have eaten the prairie dog. Funny, I don't remember it." He dug underneath the ashes and pulled out what was left — the prairie dog's bones. "I was right," he said, "I did eat the meat, even though I don't remember it."

Fox sat down on a rock. He was thinking. He said to himself: "If I had eaten that prairie dog, I should feel sated. Instead I am hungry, very hungry. Therefore I did not eat that meat." He jumped up: "Now I know what happened. That evil trickster, that no good Coyote, has stolen my meat. I will find him and kill him!"

Fox followed Coyote's tracks. Coyote saw him coming. Coyote said to himself: "Fox is faster than I am. I cannot get rid of him by running away." So Coyote stood up and leaned against an overhanging cliff. Fox came running. "Watch out, Coyote, you miserable trickster," he cried. "I've come to kill you!"

"Fool," Coyote cried. "Half-wit! Don't you see that I'm holding up this overhanging cliff, which is about to crush us both to death? Here, you lean against the cliff and hold it up while I go for a tree trunk to wedge against this rock wall, so that we both can get out from under it without being crushed. Lean against it real hard or it will flatten you. I'll be right back!" Fox leaned against the cliff real hard. He waited and waited, but Coyote did not come back. "This evil Coyote has tricked me again," said Fox, as he jumped away from the rock wall, still looking up to see whether it would fall down on him. "Yes, Coyote has made a fool out of me."

Once more, Fox followed Coyote's tracks. He found him sitting on a tree stump   10
near a stream. Again Coyote did not try to flee. Fox came running, foaming at the mouth: "Watch out, Coyote, this time I'll make an end of you, once and for all. I'll tear your throat out!"

It was sunset. The red setting sun was reflected in the stream's water. "Nitwit!" Coyote shouted, pointing at the sun's reflection. "Idiot, look at this hunk of fine red meat in the water. Instead of bothering me, you should try to get it before the current sweeps it away. Here, I'll hold on to your tail to pull you up after you've grabbed the meat!"

Fox fell for it. As he jumped into the water, Coyote quickly tied a heavy rock to Fox's tail. Fox drowned. "Finally I'm rid of this pest," said Coyote. But of course he was wrong. No matter how often Coyote and Fox kill each other, they always come to life again.

Coyote Gets Stuck

Coyote was roaming. He encountered Pitch. Coyote greeted him: "How are you, uncle?" Pitch did not answer. Coyote said: "Did you not hear me?" Pitch remained silent. Coyote was annoyed: "Hey, I am speaking to you. Why don't you answer?" Pitch said nothing.

Now Coyote was really angry: "You rude, impolite fellow, don't you hear me? Are you deaf?" There was still no answer. Coyote was furious. "I'll teach you a lesson!" he cried. Coyote struck Pitch with his right fist. It got stuck.

Coyote growled: "Let me go or I'll kick you." Pitch did not move.

Coyote kicked him with his right foot, which got stuck. Coyote tried to balance himself on one leg.

He shook his left fist into Pitch's face and threatened: "You evil, no-good fellow,   5
I'll knock you senseless!" He gave Pitch a good whack, but now his left hand was stuck.

Coyote got more and more frustrated. "I'll knock you with my other foot," he shouted. He got no reaction. He kicked with all his might and his left foot was stuck.

Coyote shouted: "You nasty lump! I shall whip you with my tail!" He struck Pitch with his tail, but it, too, got stuck.

Finally Coyote threatened Pitch: "My teeth are sharp. I will bite you to death!" Pitch still did not react. Coyote sank his teeth deep into Pitch and, of course, his mouth got stuck. He was helpless, glued to Pitch, unable to move. He could hardly breathe. He croaked: "Oh, my aunt! Help me!"

Coyote's aunt was powerful. She came running to his aid. "Set fire to him! Set fire to him!" Coyote cried. Aunt took a burning stick and plunged it into Pitch's side. As soon as the flame touched Pitch, he grew soft. He began to melt. Then Coyote could extricate himself. Coyote told his defeated opponent: "You will be nothing but pitch. People will call you pitch. Now you are no longer a person, you are just a gooey, sticky, unpleasant lump." Then Coyote and his aunt went off to attend to some matter.

Exploring the Text

1. In each of these stories, the coyote goes through a series of tricks (either tricking or being tricked). What point is made by having a sequence of adventures or trials rather than a single one?
2. The trickster embodies contradiction and paradox. How does the coyote's interaction with the fox in the first tale and with Pitch in the second show conflicting traits rather than just a single one?
3. Trickster tales serve both to entertain and to instruct. Discuss these two functions in terms of one of these stories.
4. Author and folklorist Howard Norman has said of the trickster in Native American cultures: "His presence demands, cries out for, compassion and generosity toward existence itself. Trickster is a celebrator of life, a celebration of life, because by rallying against him a community discovers its own resilience and protective skills." How does this description apply to one of the tales you've just read?

TALKBACK

N. Scott Momaday

Navarre Scott Momaday was born in 1934 at the Kiowa-Comanche Indian Hospital in Lawton, Oklahoma. He is a member of the Kiowa tribe but has Cherokee heritage on his mother's side, and he was raised on Navajo and Apache reservations in New Mexico and Arizona. Momaday's novel *House Made of Dawn* won the Pulitzer Prize for Fiction in 1969 and has influenced two subsequent generations of Native American writers. President George W. Bush awarded Momaday a National Medal of the Arts in 2007, and in the same year he was named Poet Laureate of Oklahoma.

The Becoming of the Native
Man in America Before Columbus

Momaday's essay "The Becoming of the Native: Man in America Before Columbus" is the first chapter of the anthology *America in 1492: The World of the Indian Peoples Before the Arrival of Columbus*.

> THURSDAY, 11 OCTOBER 1492
> *The moon, in its third quarter, rose in the east shortly before midnight. I estimate that we were making about 9 knots and had gone some 67½ miles between the beginning of night and 2 o'clock in the morning. Then, at two hours after midnight, the* Pinta *fired a cannon, my prearranged signal for the sighting of land.*

> FRIDAY, 12 OCTOBER 1492
> *At dawn we saw naked people. . . .*
> — THE LOG OF CHRISTOPHER COLUMBUS

It was not until 1498, when he explored what is now Venezuela, that Columbus realized he had touched upon a continent. On his last voyage, in 1502, he reached Central America. It is almost certain that he never knew of the great landmass to the north, an expanse that reached almost to Asia and to the top of the world, or that he had found a great chain of land that linked two of the earth's seven continents. In the little time that remained to him (he died in 1506) the enormity of his discovery was virtually unknown and unimagined. Christopher Columbus, the Admiral of the Ocean Sea, went to his grave believing he had reached Asia. But his accomplishment was even greater than he dreamed. He had in fact sailed beyond the *orbis*, the circle believed to describe the limits of the earth, and beyond medieval geography. His voyage to the New World was a navigation in time; it was a passage from the Middle Ages to the Renaissance.

There are moments in history to which one can point and say, "At this hour, on this day, the history of the world was changed forever." Such a moment occurred at two o'clock on the morning of October 12, 1492, when a cannon, fired from the Spanish caravel *Pinta*, announced the sighting of land. The land sighted was probably Samana Cay in the Bahamas. It was the New World.

It is this term, "New World," with which I should like to begin this discussion, not only because it is everywhere a common designation of the Americas but also because it represents one of the great anomalies of history. The British writer J. B. Priestley, after visiting the United States, commented that "New World" is a misnomer. The American Southwest seemed to him the oldest landscape he had ever seen. Indeed, the New World is ancient. Here is a quintessential irony.

For Americans in general, a real part of the irony consists of their Eurocentric understanding of history. Columbus and his Old World contemporaries knew a good deal about the past, the past that was peculiarly theirs, for it had been recorded in writing. It was informed by a continuity that could be traced back to the story of Creation in the Old Testament. Most Americans have inherited that same understanding of the past. American history, therefore, as distinct from other histories, begins in the popular mind with the European intercession in the "New World." Relatively little is known of the Americas and their peoples before Columbus, although we are learning more all the time. On the far side of 1492 in the Americas there is a prehistoric darkness in which are mysteries as profound and provocative as are those of Stonehenge and Lascaux and Afrasiab.[1]

Who were the "naked people" Columbus and his men observed at dawn on that autumn day five hundred years ago? Columbus, the first ethnographer in the New World, tells us a few things about them. They were broad in the forehead, straight and well-proportioned. They were friendly and bore gifts to their visitors. They were skilled boat-builders and boatmen. They painted their faces and their bodies. They made clothes and hammocks out of cotton. They lived in sturdy houses. They had dogs. And they too lived their daily lives in the element of language; they traded in words and names. We do not know what name or names they conferred upon their seafaring guests, but on October 17, on the sixth day of his sojourn among them, Columbus referred to them in his log as "Indios."

In 1492 the "Indians" were widespread in North, Central, and South America. They were the only human occupants of a third of the earth's land surface. And by the year 1492 they had been in the New World for untold thousands of years.

The "Paleo-Indians," as they are known, the ancestors of modern American Indians, came from Asia and entered upon the continent of North America by means of the Bering land bridge, a wide corridor of land, now submerged, connecting Siberia and Alaska. During the last glaciation (20,000 to 14,000 years ago) the top of the world was dominated by ice. Even so, most of Asia and most of Beringia were unglaciated. From Alaska to the Great Plains of the present United States ran a kind of corridor between the Cordilleran and Laurentide ice sheets, a thoroughfare for the migration of hunters and the animals they hunted. It is known that human bands had reached the Lena River drainage in northeastern Siberia at least 18,000 years ago. Over the next 7,000 years these nomads crossed the Bering bridge and dispersed widely throughout the Americas.

This dispersal is one of the great chapters in the story of mankind. It was an explosion, a revolution on a scale scarcely to be imagined. By 1492 there were untold numbers of indigenous human societies in the New World, untold numbers of languages and dialects, architecture to rival any monument of the Old World, astronomical observatories and solar calendars, a profound knowledge of

5

---

[1]Lascaux and Afrasiab are ancient archaeological sites. The cave paintings of Lascaux, in France, date to c. 15,000 B.C.E., while the wall paintings of Afrasiab, in Uzbekistan, date to the seventh century C.E. — Eds.

natural medicine and the healing arts, very highly developed oral traditions, dramas, ceremonies, and — above all — a spiritual comprehension of the universe, a sense of the natural and supernatural, a sense of the sacred. Here was every evidence of man's long, inexorable ascendancy to civilization.

It is appropriate that I interject here my particular point of view. I am an American Indian, and I believe that I can therefore speak to the question of America before Columbus with a certain advantage of ancestral experience, a cultural continuity that reaches far back in time. My forebears have been in North America for many thousands of years. In my blood I have a real sense of that occupation. It is worth something to me, as indeed that long, unbroken tenure is worth something to every Native American.

I am Kiowa. The Kiowas are a Plains Indian people who reside now in   10
Oklahoma. But they are newcomers to the Southern Plains, not having ventured below the Arkansas River until the eighteenth century. In 1492 they were near the headwaters of the Yellowstone River, in what is now western Montana. Their migration to the Southern Plains is the most recent migration of all those which have described the great dispersal of native peoples, and their Plains culture is the last culture to evolve in North America.

According to their origin myth, the Kiowas entered the world through a hollow log. Where was the log, I wonder. And what was at the other end? When I imagine my blood back through generations to the earliest man in America, I see in my mind's eye a procession of shamanistic figures,[2] like those strange anthropomorphic forms painted on the cliffs of Barrier Canyon, Utah, emerging from the mists. They proceed, it seems, from the source of geology itself, from timelessness into time.

When man set foot on the continent of North America he was surely an endangered species. His resources were few, as we think of them from our vantage point in the twentieth century. He was almost wholly at the mercy of the elements, and the world he inhabited was hard and unforgiving. The simple accomplishment of survival must have demanded all of his strength. But he had certain indispensable resources. He knew how to hunt. He possessed tools and weapons, however crude. He could make fire. He probably had dogs and travois,[3] perhaps sleds. He had some sense of society, of community, of cooperation. And, alone among the creatures of the earth, he could think and speak. He had a human sense of morality, an irresistible craving for order, beauty, appropriate behavior. He was intensely spiritual.

The Kiowas provide us with a fortunate example of migration and dispersal, I believe. Although their migration from the Yellowstone to the Wichita Mountains is recent (nonetheless prehistoric in the main), it was surely preceded by

---

[2]In Native American tradition, shamans are mystics and healers who enter trances in order to interact with the spirit world. — Eds.
[3]A simple sling made up of two poles and a piece of fabric that is pulled behind an animal. — Eds.

countless migrations of the same kind in the same landscape, generally speaking, over a period of some thousands of years. The experience of the Kiowas, then, from earliest evidence to the present, may serve to indicate in a general way the experience of other tribes and other cultures. It may allow us to understand something about the American Indian and about the condition of his presence in America in 1492.

The hollow log of the Kiowa origin myth is a not uncommon image in comparative mythology. The story of the tree of life is found throughout the world, and in most instances it is symbolic of passage, origination, evolution. It is tempting to associate the hollow log with the passage to America, the peopling of the Americas, to find in it a metaphorical reflection of the land bridge.

We tell stories in order to affirm our being and our place in the scheme of   15
things. When the Kiowas entered upon the Great Plains they had to tell new stories of themselves, stories that would enable them to appropriate an unknown and intimidating landscape to their experience. They were peculiarly vulnerable in that landscape, and they told a story of dissension, finally of a schism in the tribe, brought about by a quarrel between two great chiefs. They encountered awesome forces and features in nature, and they explained them in story too. And so they told the story of Man-Ka-Ih, the storm spirit, which speaks the Kiowa language and does the Kiowas no harm, and they told of the tree that bore the seven sisters into the sky, where they became the stars of the Big Dipper. In so doing they not only accounted for the great monolith that is Devils Tower, Wyoming (in Kiowa, Tsoai, "rock tree"), but related themselves to the stars in the process. When they came upon the Plains they were befriended by the Crows, who gave them the sun-dance fetish Tai-Me, which was from that time on their most powerful medicine, and they told a story of the coming of Tai-Me in their hour of need. Language was their element. Words, spoken words, were the manifestations of their deepest belief, of their deepest feelings, of their deepest life. When Europeans first came to America, having had writing for hundreds of years and lately the printing press, they could not conceive of the spoken word as sacred, could not understand the American Indian's profound belief in the efficacy of language.

I have told the story of the arrowmaker many times. When I was a child I heard it told more times than I can say. It was at the center of my oral tradition long before I knew what that tradition was, and that is as it should be. The story had never been written down. It had existed, perhaps hundreds of years, at the level of the human voice.

If an arrow is well made, it will have tooth marks upon it. That is how you know. The Kiowas made fine arrows and straightened them in their teeth. Then they drew them to the bow to see that they were straight. Once there was a man and his wife. They were alone at night in their tipi. By the light of a fire the man was making arrows. After a while he caught sight of something. There was a small opening in the tipi where two hides were sewn together. Someone was there on the outside, looking in. The man went on with his work, but he said to his wife, "Someone is standing outside. Do not be afraid. Let us talk easily, as of ordinary things." He took up an arrow and straightened it in his teeth; then, as it was right for him to do, he drew it to the bow and took aim, first in this direction and then in that. And all the while he was talking, as if to his wife. But this is how he spoke: "I know that you are there on the outside, for I can feel your eyes upon me. If you are a Kiowa, you will understand what I am saying, and you will speak your name." But there was no answer, and the man went on in the same way, pointing the arrow all around. At last his aim fell upon the place where his enemy stood, and he let go of the string. The arrow went straight to the enemy's heart.

Only after I had lived with the story for many years did I understand that it is about language. The storyteller is anonymous and illiterate, but he exists in his words, and he has survived for untold generations. The arrowmaker is a man made of words, and he too is a storyteller. He achieves victory over his enemy by exerting the force of language upon the unknown. What he does is far less important than what he says. His arrows are words. His enemy (and the presence outside *is* an enemy, for the storyteller tells us so) is vanquished by the word. The story is concise, beautiful, and alive. I know of nothing in literature that is more intensely alive.

Concurrent with the evolution of an oral tradition is the rise of ceremony. The sun dance was the preeminent expression of the spiritual life of the Plains culture. And it was a whole and intricate and profound expression.

And within the symmetry of this design of language and religion there came art. Universal in the world of the American Indian is a profound aesthetic sense. From ancient rock paintings to contemporary theater, through such forms as beadwork, featherwork, leathercraft, wood carving, ceramics, ledger-book drawing, music, and dance, American Indian art has rivaled other great art of the world. In museums and galleries around the globe are treasures of that art that are scarcely to be imagined.

These various expressions of the human spirit, emblematic of the American Indian today and five hundred years ago and long before that, are informed by an equation of man and the landscape that has had to be perceived, if neither appreciated nor acknowledged, by every society that has made contact with it. The naked people Columbus saw in 1492 were the members of a society altogether worthy and well made, a people of the everlasting earth, possessed of honor and dignity and a generosity of spirit unsurpassed. 20

(1993)

Exploring the Text

1. What does N. Scott Momaday mean when he describes Christopher Columbus's voyage as "a passage from the Middle Ages to the Renaissance" (par. 1)?
2. Momaday discusses the "irony" of the term "New World" (pars. 3–4). What are his reasons for this characterization?

3. Nearly halfway through the essay, Momaday introduces himself: "It is appropriate that I interject here my particular point of view" (par. 9). What ethos does he establish in the next several paragraphs? Why do you think he chose not to "interject" his viewpoint earlier in the essay?

4. What does Momaday mean when he says of the hollow log origin story: "It is tempting to associate the hollow log with the passage to America, the peopling of the Americas, to find in it a metaphorical reflection of the land bridge" (par. 14)?

5. What is the importance of the story of the arrowmaker that Momaday tells near the end of the essay?

6. Momaday begins and ends his essay with a reference to an entry in Columbus's log that refers to Native inhabitants as "naked people." Why does Momaday find this description so significant?

7. Momaday states that Native Americans "tell stories in order to affirm our being and our place in the scheme of things" (par. 15). What affirmation is in the stories in this essay, including his personal narrative?

Making Connections

1. Momaday writes that the diverse cultures referred to as Native American "tell stories in order to affirm [their] being and [their] place in the scheme of things" (par. 15). How do the Native American origin stories and trickster stories (pp. 192–98) included in this chapter illustrate that purpose? Discuss at least two of them.

2. Momaday characterizes the early inhabitants of North America as having "had some sense of society, of community, of cooperation . . . a human sense of morality, an irresistible craving for order, beauty, appropriate behavior" and as "intensely spiritual" (par. 12). Support that characterization with examples and details from the Native American origin stories and trickster stories.

3. What stereotypes of Native Americans and the New World does Momaday challenge? Discuss two of them in terms of the Native American origin stories and trickster stories.

IROQUOIS CONFEDERACY

The Iroquois, or "People of the Longhouse," were a coalition of six tribes: the Onondaga, Cayuga, Mohawk, Oneida, Seneca, and Tuscarora. When exactly the original confederacy formed is a matter of debate among historians, but the most popular theory suggests 1142, well before contact with European explorers. The Tuscarora tribe joined the confederacy much later, in the early eighteenth century. At the height of their power, the Iroquois controlled land from the Hudson to the Illinois Rivers and from the Ottawa to the Tennessee Rivers, though most of the population was based in what is now New York State. The confederacy dissolved in the eighteenth century, following the Revolutionary War.

from *The Iroquois Constitution*

The constitution of the Iroquois Confederacy, also called the Great Binding Law, or Gayanashagowa, which means "the Great Law of Peace," is a transcription of a set of laws communicated orally and codified by wampum, strands of shell beads that convey symbolic meaning. Scholars continue to debate to what extent the laws and form of government described in the Iroquois Constitution influenced the Founding Fathers of the United States.

1. I am Dekanawidah and with the Five Nations' Confederate Lords I plant the Tree of Great Peace. I plant it in your territory, Adodarhoh, and the Onondaga Nation, in the territory of you who are Fire Keepers.

   I name the tree the Tree of the Great Long Leaves. Under the shade of this Tree of the Great Peace we spread the soft white feathery down of the globe thistle as seats for you, Adodarhoh, and your cousin Lords.

   We place you upon those seats, spread soft with the feathery down of the globe thistle, there beneath the shade of the spreading branches of the Tree of Peace. There shall you sit and watch the Council Fire of the Confederacy of the Five Nations, and all the affairs of the Five Nations shall be transacted at this place before you, Adodarhoh, and your cousin Lords, by the Confederate Lords of the Five Nations.

2. Roots have spread out from the Tree of the Great Peace, one to the north, one to the east, one to the south and one to the west. The name of these roots is the Great White Roots and their nature is Peace and Strength.

   If any man or any nation outside the Five Nations shall obey the laws of the Great Peace and make known their disposition to the Lords of the Confederacy, they may trace the Roots to the Tree and if their minds are clean and they are obedient and promise to obey the wishes of the Confederate Council, they shall be welcomed to take shelter beneath the Tree of the Long Leaves.

   We place at the top of the Tree of the Long Leaves an Eagle who is able to see afar. If he sees in the distance any evil approaching or any danger threatening he will at once warn the people of the Confederacy. . . .

9. All the business of the Five Nations Confederate Council shall be conducted by the two combined bodies of Confederate Lords. First the question shall be passed upon by the Mohawk and Seneca Lords, then it shall be discussed and passed by the Oneida and Cayuga Lords. Their decisions shall then be referred to the Onondaga Lords (Fire Keepers), for final judgment.

   The same process shall obtain when a question is brought before the council by an individual or a War Chief. . . .

19. If at any time it shall be manifest that a Confederate Lord has not in mind the welfare of the people or disobeys the rules of this Great Law, the men or women of the Confederacy, or both jointly, shall come to the Council and upbraid the erring Lord through his War Chief. If the complaint of the people through the War Chief is not heeded the first time it shall be uttered again and then if no attention is given a third complaint and warning shall be given. If the Lord is contumacious, the matter shall go to the council of War Chiefs. The War Chiefs shall then divest the erring Lord of his title by order of the women in whom the titleship is vested.[1] When the Lord is deposed the women shall notify the Confederate Lords through their War Chief, and the Confederate Lords shall sanction the act. The women will then select another of their sons as a candidate and the Lords shall elect him. Then shall the chosen one be installed by the Installation Ceremony. . . .

26. It shall be the duty of all of the Five Nations Confederate Lords, from time to time as occasion demands, to act as mentors and spiritual guides of their people and remind them of their Creator's will and words. They shall say: 10

    "Hearken, that peace may continue unto future days!

    "Always listen to the words of the Great Creator, for he has spoken.

    "United people, let not evil find lodging in your minds.

    "For the Great Creator has spoken and the cause of Peace shall not become old.

    "The cause of peace shall not die if you remember the Great Creator." 15

    Every Confederate Lord shall speak words such as these to promote peace.

27. All Lords of the Five Nations Confederacy must be honest in all things. They must not idle or gossip, but be men possessing those honorable qualities that make true royaneh.[2] It shall be a serious wrong for anyone to lead a Lord into trivial affairs, for the people must ever hold their Lords high in estimation out of respect to their honorable positions.

28. When a candidate Lord is to be installed he shall furnish four strings of shells (or wampum) one span in length bound together at one end. Such will constitute the evidence of his pledge to the Confederate Lords that he will live according to the constitution of the Great Peace and exercise justice in all affairs.

    When the pledge is furnished the Speaker of the Council must hold the shell strings in his hand and address the opposite side of the Council Fire and he shall commence his address saying:

    "Now behold him. He has now become a Confederate Lord. See how splendid he looks." 20

    An address may then follow. At the end of it he shall send the bunch of shell strings to the opposite side and they shall be received as evidence of the pledge. Then shall the opposite side say:

---

[1] Iroquois society was matrilineal, with descent traced through the female line. Male war chiefs were nominated by the women of the tribe, and could be removed by them as well. — Eds.
[2] Nobility. — Eds.

"We now do crown you with the sacred emblem of the deer's antlers, the emblem of your Lordship. You shall now become a mentor of the people of the Five Nations. The thickness of your skin shall be seven spans — which is to say that you shall be proof against anger, offensive actions and criticism. Your heart shall be filled with peace and good will and your mind filled with a yearning for the welfare of the people of the Confederacy. With endless patience you shall carry out your duty and your firmness shall be tempered with tenderness for your people. Neither anger nor fury shall find lodgement in your mind and all your words and actions shall be marked with calm deliberation. In all of your deliberations in the Confederate Council, in your efforts at lawmaking, in all your official acts, self interest shall be cast into oblivion. Cast not over your shoulder behind you the warnings of the nephews and nieces should they chide you for any error or wrong you may do, but return to the way of the Great Law which is just and right. Look and listen for the welfare of the whole people and have always in view not only the present but also the coming generations, even those whose faces are yet beneath the surface of the ground — the unborn of the future Nation." . . .

55. A large bunch of shell strings, in the making of which the Five Nations Confederate Lords have equally contributed, shall symbolize the completeness of the union and certify the pledge of the nations represented by the Confederate Lords of the Mohawk, the Oneida, the Onondaga, the Cayuga and the Seneca, that all are united and formed into one body or union called the Union of the Great Law, which they have established.

A bunch of shell strings is to be the symbol of the council fire of the Five Nations Confederacy. . . .

Every five years the Five Nations Confederate Lords and the people shall   25
assemble together and shall ask one another if their minds are still in the same spirit of unity for the Great Binding Law and if any of the Five Nations shall not pledge continuance and steadfastness to the pledge of unity then the Great Binding Law shall dissolve. . . .

57. Five arrows shall be bound together very strong and each arrow shall represent one nation. As the five arrows are strongly bound this shall symbolize the complete union of the nations. Thus are the Five Nations united completely and enfolded together, united into one head, one body and one mind. Therefore they shall labor, legislate and council together for the interest of future generations.

The Lords of the Confederacy shall eat together from one bowl the feast of cooked beaver's tail. While they are eating they are to use no sharp utensils for if they should they might accidentally cut one another and bloodshed would follow. All measures must be taken to prevent the spilling of blood in any way. . . .

60. A broad dark belt of wampum of thirty-eight rows, having a white heart in the center, on either side of which are two white squares all connected with the heart by white rows of beads shall be the emblem of the unity of the Five Nations.

The first of the squares on the left represents the Mohawk nation and its territory; the second square on the left and the one near the heart, represents the Oneida nation and its territory; the white heart in the middle represents the

Onondaga nation and its territory, and it also means that the heart of the Five Nations is single in its loyalty to the Great Peace, that the Great Peace is lodged in the heart (meaning the Onondaga Lords), and that the Council Fire is to burn there for the Five Nations, and further, it means that the authority is given to advance the cause of peace whereby hostile nations out of the Confederacy shall cease warfare; the white square to the right of the heart represents the Cayuga nation and its territory and the fourth and last white square represents the Seneca nation and its territory.

White shall here symbolize that no evil or jealous thoughts shall creep into the minds of the Lords while in Council under the Great Peace. White, the emblem of peace, love, charity and equity surrounds and guards the Five Nations. . . . 30

92. If a nation, part of a nation, or more than one nation within the Five Nations should in any way endeavor to destroy the Great Peace by neglect or violating its laws and resolve to dissolve the Confederacy, such a nation or such nations shall be deemed guilty of treason and called enemies of the Confederacy and the Great Peace.

It shall then be the duty of the Lords of the Confederacy who remain faithful to resolve to warn the offending people. They shall be warned once and if a second warning is necessary they shall be driven from the territory of the Confederacy by the War Chiefs and his men. . . .

117. Three strings of shell one span in length shall be employed in addressing the assemblage at the burial of the dead. The speaker shall say:

"Hearken you who are here, this body is to be covered. Assemble in this place again ten days hence for it is the decree of the Creator that mourning shall cease when ten days have expired. Then shall a feast be made."

Then at the expiration of ten days the speaker shall say: 35

"Continue to listen you who are here. The ten days of mourning have expired and your minds must now be freed of sorrow as before the loss of a relative. The relatives have decided to make a little compensation to those who have assisted at the funeral. It is a mere expression of thanks. This is to the one who did the cooking while the body was lying in the house. Let her come forward and receive this gift and be dismissed from the task." In substance this shall be repeated for every one who assisted in any way until all have been remembered.

(c. 1142)

Exploring the Text

1. What elements of a democratic decision-making process are incorporated into the Iroquois Constitution?
2. What symbols and rituals are prescribed in this document? How might these contribute to establishing a sense of community among the individual tribes? Pay special attention to the Tree of the Great Peace.
3. What qualifications, particularly of character, are recommended for those who assume positions of authority?

4. What procedures and safeguards are included to ensure fair and just resolution of disagreements, including questionable behavior of the lords?
5. What guidelines for everyday life experiences are offered in this document? How are these related to public issues of governance?
6. Historian Gerald Murphy made the following assertion:

> During the bicentennial year of the Constitution of the United States, a number of books were written concerning the origin of that long-revered document. One of these, *The Genius of the People*, alleged that after the many weeks of debate a committee sat to combine the many agreements into one formal document. The chairman of the committee was John Rutledge of South Carolina. He had served in an earlier time, along with Ben Franklin and others, at the Stamp Act Congress, held in Albany, New York. This Committee of Detail was having trouble deciding just how to formalize the many items of discussion into one document that would satisfy one and all. Rutledge proposed they model the new government they were forming into something along the lines of the Iroquois League of Nations, which had been functioning as a democratic government for hundreds of years, and which he had observed in Albany. While there were many desirable, as well as undesirable, models from ancient and modern histories in Europe and what we know now as the Middle East, only the Iroquois had a system that seemed to meet most of the demands espoused by the many parties to the debates. *The Genius of the People* alleged that the Iroquois had a Constitution which began: "We the people, to form a union. . . ." That one sentence was enough to light a fire under me, and cause me to do some deep research into ancient Iroquoian lore. I never did find that one sentence backed up in what writings there are concerning the ancient Iroquois. But I DID find sufficient data and evidence to convince me that the Iroquois most certainly did have a considerable influence on the drafting of our own Constitution, and we present-day Americans owe them a very large debt.

Murphy summarizes the position of other historians and scholars who have argued the influence of the Iroquois Constitution on the U.S. Constitution. What evidence in this selection from the Iroquois Constitution supports his position?

Álvar Núñez Cabeza de Vaca

Álvar Núñez Cabeza de Vaca (1488/90–1557/58) was a Spanish explorer of the New World, who wrote detailed accounts of his expeditions and the native peoples he encountered. In 1527, Cabeza de Vaca embarked from Spain as treasurer of the royally commissioned Narváez expedition of the North American mainland. The ill-fated expedition lost two ships in a hurricane off Cuba and another on the way to Tampa Bay, Florida. The party then split up, with Cabeza de Vaca's faction fighting their way overland through the swamps of Florida, harried by attacks from the native population. Desperate to escape, the explorers crafted makeshift boats and once again set out to sea, only to be washed up on Galveston Island, Texas. Those of the expedition who remained wandered throughout Texas, northeastern Mexico, New Mexico, and Arizona for years, facing starvation, disease, poverty, and even enslavement. Cabeza de Vaca was one of only four survivors of the original 600-man party. He returned to Europe in 1537, but he was quickly asked to turn back to establish settlements in South America. Because of his generous attitude toward the indigenous population and the failure of one of his settlements at Buenos Aires, in present-day Argentina, Cabeza de Vaca was arrested for poor administration in 1544 and returned to Spain for trial in 1545. He was exonerated.

from *The Relation of Cabeza de Vaca*

La relación que dio Álvar Núñez Cabeza de Vaca was first published in 1542 as a formal report to Emperor Charles V of Spain. A second edition, published in 1555, was translated into several languages, but an English version did not appear until 1625 as part of a collection of travel literature. The sections below include the *proem* or preface; a description of his initial encounter with native inhabitants after he washed up on Galveston Island; an account of his captivity when he was separated from others in his party; and a narrative of his later encounter with Spanish slave hunters.

Proem

S acred Caesarian Catholic Majesty:

Among the many who have held sway, I think no prince can be found whose service has been attended with the ardor and emulation shown for that of your Highness at this time. The inducement is evident and powerful: men do not pursue together the same career without motive, and strangers are observed to strive with those who are equally impelled by religion and loyalty.

Although ambition and love of action are common to all, as to the advantages that each may gain, there are great inequalities of fortune, the result not of conduct, but only accident, nor caused by the fault of any one, but coming in the providence of God and solely by His will. Hence to one arises deeds more signal than he thought to achieve; to another the opposite in every way occurs, so that he can show no higher proof of purpose than his effort, and at times even this is so concealed that it cannot of itself appear.

As for me, I can say in undertaking the march I made on the main by the royal authority, I firmly trusted that my conduct and services would be as evident and distinguished as were those of my ancestors[1] and that I should not have to speak in

---

[1] Cabeza de Vaca's grandfather Pedro de Vera was instrumental in helping Spain conquer the Canary Islands off the west coast of Africa. — Eds.

order to be reckoned among those who for diligence and fidelity in affairs your Majesty honors. Yet, as neither my counsel nor my constancy availed to gain aught for which we set out, agreeably to your interests, for our sins, no one of the many armaments that have gone into those parts has been permitted to find itself in straits great like ours, or come to an end alike forlorn and fatal. To me, one only duty remains, to present a relation of what was seen and heard in the ten years I wandered lost and in privation through many and remote lands. Not merely a statement of positions and distances, animals and vegetation, but of the diverse customs of the many and very barbarous people with whom I talked and dwelt, as well as all other matters I could hear of and discern, that in some way I may avail your Highness. My hope of going out from among those nations was always small, still my care and diligence were none the less to keep in particular remembrance everything, that if at any time God our Lord should will to bring me where I now am, it might testify to my exertion in the royal behalf.

As the narrative is in my opinion of no trivial value to those who in your name go to subdue those countries and bring them to a knowledge of the true faith and true Lord, and under the imperial dominion, I have written this with much exactness; and although in it may be read things very novel and for some persons difficult to believe, nevertheless they may without hesitation credit me as strictly faithful. Better than to exaggerate, I have lessened in all things, and it is sufficient to say the relation is offered to your Majesty for truth. I beg it may be received in the name of homage, since it is the most that one could bring who returned thence naked. . . .

Chapter 14

To this island we gave the name Malhado. The people we found there are large and well formed; they have no other arms than bows and arrows, in the use of which they are very dexterous. The men have one of their nipples bored from side to side, and some have both, wearing a cane in each, the length of two palms and a half, and the thickness of two fingers. They have the under lip also bored, and wear in it a piece of cane the breadth of half a finger. Their women are accustomed to great toil. The stay they make on the island is from October to the end of February. Their subsistence then is the root I have spoken of, got from under the water in November and December. They have weirs of cane and take fish only in this season; afterwards they live on the roots. At the end of February, they go into other parts to seek food; for then the root is beginning to grow and is not food.

Those people love their offspring the most of any in the world, and treat them with the greatest mildness. When it occurs that a son dies, the parents and kindred weep as does everybody; the wailing continuing for him a whole year. They begin before dawn every day, the parents first and after them the whole town. They do the same at noon and at sunset. After a year of mourning has passed, the rites of the dead are performed; then they wash and purify themselves from the stain of smoke. They lament all the deceased in this manner, except the aged, for whom they show no regret, as they say that their season has passed, they having no enjoyment, and that living they would occupy the earth and take aliment from the young. Their custom is to bury the dead, unless it be those among them who have been physicians. These they burn. While the fire kindles they are all dancing and making high festivity, until the bones become powder. After the lapse of a year the funeral honors are celebrated, every one taking part in them, when that dust is presented in water for the relatives to drink.

Every man has an acknowledged wife. The physicians are allowed more freedom: they may have two or three wives, among whom exist the greatest friendship and harmony. From the time a daughter marries, all that he who takes her to wife kills in hunting or catches in fishing, the woman brings to the house of her father, without daring to eat or take any part of it, and thence victuals are taken to the husband. From that time neither her father nor mother enters his house, nor can he enter theirs, nor the houses of their children; and if by chance they are in the direction of meeting, they turn aside, and pass the distance of a crossbow shot from each other, carrying the head low the while, the eyes cast on the ground; for they hold it improper to see or to speak to each other. But the woman has liberty to converse and communicate with the parents and relatives of her husband. The custom exists from this island the distance of more than fifty leagues inland. . . .

Chapter 15

On an island of which I have spoken, they wished to make us physicians without examination or inquiring for diplomas. They cure by blowing upon the sick, and with that breath and the imposing of hands they cast out infirmity. They ordered that we also should do this, and be of use to them in some way. We laughed at what they did, telling them it was folly, that we knew not how to heal. In consequence, they withheld food from us until we should practise what they required. Seeing our persistence, an Indian told me I knew not what I uttered, in saying that what he knew availed nothing; for stones and other matters growing about in the fields have virtue, and that passing a pebble along the stomach would take away pain and restore health, and certainly then we who were extraordinary men must possess power and efficacy over all other things. At last, finding ourselves in great want we were constrained to obey; but without fear lest we should be blamed for any failure or success.

Their custom is, on finding themselves sick to send for a physician, and after he has applied the cure, they give him not only all they have, but seek among their relatives for more to give. The practitioner scarifies[2] over the seat of pain, and then sucks about the wound. They make cauteries[3] with fire, a remedy among them in high repute, which I have tried on myself and found benefit from it. They afterwards blow on the spot, and having finished, the patient considers that he is relieved.

---

[2]Scarifying involves making numerous small cuts around a wound. — Eds.
[3]Cauteries are instruments used for cauterizing wounds. Cauterizing is a means of closing a wound by burning it. — Eds.

Our method was to bless the sick, breathing upon them, and recite a Pater- 10
noster and an Ave-Maria, praying with all earnestness to God our Lord that he would
give health and influence them to make us some good return. In his clemency he
willed that all those for whom we supplicated, should tell the others that they were
sound and in health, directly after we made the sign of the blessed cross over them.
For this the Indians treated us kindly; they deprived themselves of food that they
might give to us, and presented us with skins and some trifles.

So protracted was the hunger we there experienced, that many times I was three
days without eating. The natives also endured as much; and it appeared to me a thing
impossible that life could be so prolonged, although afterwards I found myself in
greater hunger and necessity, which I shall speak of farther on.

The Indians who had Alonzo del Castillo, Andrés Dorantes, and the others that
remained alive, were of a different tongue and ancestry from these, and went to the
opposite shore of the main to eat oysters, where they stayd until the first day of April,
when they returned. The distance is two leagues in the widest part. The island is half
a league in breadth and five leagues in length.

The inhabitants of all this region go naked. The women alone have any part
of their persons covered, and it is with a wool that grows on trees. The damsels
dress themselves in deer-skin. The people are generous to each other of what they
possess. They have no chief. All that are of a lineage keep together. They speak two
languages; those of one are called Capoques, those of the other, Han. They have a
custom when they meet, or from time to time when they visit, of remaining half an
hour before they speak, weeping; and, this over, he that is visited first rises and gives
the other all he has, which is received, and after a little while he carries it away, and
often goes without saying a word. They have other strange customs; but I have told
the principal of them, and the most remarkable, that I may pass on and further relate
what befell us.

Chapter 16

After Dorantes and Castillo returned to the island, they brought together the
Christians, who were somewhat separated, and found them in all to be fourteen. As I
have said, I was opposite on the main, where my Indians had taken me, and where so
great sickness had come upon me, that if anything before had given me hopes of life,
this were enough to have entirely bereft me of them.

When the Christians heard of my condition, they gave an Indian the cloak of 15
marten skins we had taken from the cacique, as before related, to pass them over to
where I was that they might visit me. Twelve of them crossed; for two were so feeble
that their comrades could not venture to bring them. . . .

I was obliged to remain with the people belonging to the island more than a year,
and because of the hard work they put upon me and the harsh treatment, I resolved
to flee from them and go to those of Charruco, who inhabit the forests and country
of the main, the life I led being insupportable. Besides much other labor, I had to get
out roots from below the water, and from among the cane where they grew in the

ground. From this employment I had my fingers so worn that did a straw but touch them they would bleed. Many of the canes are broken, so they often tore my flesh, and I had to go in the midst of them with only the clothing on I have mentioned.

Accordingly, I put myself to contriving how I might get over to the other Indians, among whom matters turned somewhat more favorably for me. I set to trafficking, and strove to make my employment profitable in the ways I could best contrive, and by that means I got food and good treatment. The Indians would beg me to go from one quarter to another for things of which they have need; for in consequence of incessant hostilities, they cannot traverse the country, nor make many exchanges. With my merchandise and trade I went into the interior as far as I pleased, and travelled along the coast forty or fifty leagues. The principal wares were cones and other pieces of sea-snail, conchs used for cutting, and fruit like a bean of the highest value among them, which they use as a medicine and employ in their dances and festivities. Among other matters were sea-beads. Such were what I carried into the interior; and in barter I got and brought back skins, ochre with which they rub and color the face, hard canes of which to make arrows, sinews, cement and flint for the heads, and tassels of the hair of deer that by dyeing they make red. This occupation suited me well; for the travel allowed me liberty to go where I wished, I was not obliged to work, and was not a slave. Wherever I went I received fair treatment, and the Indians gave me to eat out of regard to my commodities. My leading object, while journeying in this business, was to find out the way by which I should go forward, and I became well known. The inhabitants were pleased when they saw me, and I had brought them what they wanted; and those who did not know me sought and desired the acquaintance, for my reputation. The hardships that I underwent in this were long to tell, as well of peril and privation as of storms and cold. Oftentimes they overtook me alone and in the wilderness; but I came forth from them all by the great mercy of God our Lord. Because of them I avoided pursuing the business in winter, a season in which the natives themselves retire to their huts and ranches, torpid and incapable of exertion.

I was in this country nearly six years, alone among the Indians, and naked like them. . . .

Chapter 33

When we saw sure signs of Christians, and heard how near we were to them, we gave thanks to God our Lord for having chosen to bring us out of a captivity so melancholy and wretched. The delight we felt let each one conjecture, when he shall remember the length of time we were in that country, the suffering and perils we underwent. That night I entreated my companions that one of them should go back three days' journey after the Christians who were moving about over the country, where we had given assurance of protection. Neither of them received this proposal well, excusing themselves because of weariness and exhaustion; and although either might have done better than I, being more youthful and athletic, yet seeing their unwillingness, the next morning I took the negro with eleven Indians, and, following the Christians by their trail, I travelled ten leagues, passing three villages, at which they had slept.

The day after I overtook four of them on horseback, who were astonished at the sight of me, so strangely habited as I was, and in company with Indians. They stood staring at me a length of time, so confounded that they neither hailed me nor drew near to make an inquiry. I bade them take me to their chief: accordingly we went together half a league to the place where was Diego de Alcaraz, their captain.

After we had conversed, he stated to me that he was completely undone; he had not been able in a long time to take any Indians; he knew not which way to turn, and his men had well begun to experience hunger and fatigue. I told him of Castillo and Dorantes, who were behind, ten leagues off, with a multitude that conducted us. He thereupon sent three cavalry to them, with fifty of the Indians who accompanied him. The negro returned to guide them, while I remained. I asked the Christians to give me a certificate of the year, month, and day I arrived there, and of the manner of my coming, which they accordingly did. From this river to the town of the Christians, named San Miguel, within the government of the province called New Galicia, are thirty leagues.

Chapter 34

Five days having elapsed, Andrés Dorantes and Alonzo del Castillo arrived with those who had been sent after them. They brought more than six hundred persons of that community, whom the Christians had driven into the forests, and who had wandered in concealment over the land. Those who accompanied us so far had drawn them out, and given them to the Christians, who thereupon dismissed all the others they had brought with them. Upon their coming to where I was, Alcaraz begged that we would summon the people of the towns on the margin of the river, who straggled about under cover of the woods, and order them to fetch us something to eat. This last was unnecessary, the Indians being ever diligent to bring us all they could. Directly we sent our messengers to call them, when there came six hundred souls, bringing us all the maize in their possession. They fetched it in certain pots, closed with clay, which they had concealed in the earth. They brought us whatever else they had; but we, wishing only to have the provision, gave the rest to the Christians, that they might divide among themselves. After this we had many high words with them; for they wished to make slaves of the Indians we brought.

In consequence of the dispute, we left at our departure many bows of Turkish shape we had along with us and many pouches. The five arrows with the points of emerald were forgotten among others, and we lost them. We gave the Christians a store of robes of cowhide and other things we brought. We found it difficult to induce the Indians to return to their dwellings, to feel no apprehension and plant maize. They were willing to do nothing until they had gone with us and delivered us into the hands of other Indians, as had been the custom; for, if they returned without doing so, they were afraid they should die, and, going with us, they feared neither Christians nor lances. Our countrymen became jealous at this, and caused their interpreter to tell the Indians that we were of them, and for a long time we had been lost; that they were the lords of the land who must be obeyed and served, while we were persons of mean condition and small force. The Indians cared little or nothing for what was told them; and conversing among themselves said the Christians lied: that we had come whence the sun rises, and they whence it goes down; we healed the sick, they killed the sound; that we had come naked and barefooted, while they had arrived in clothing and on horses with lances; that we were not covetous of anything, but all that was given to us we directly turned to give, remaining with nothing; that the others had the only purpose to rob whomsoever they found, bestowing nothing on any one.

In this way they spoke of all matters respecting us, which they enhanced by contrast with matters concerning the others, delivering their response through the interpreter of the Spaniards. To other Indians they made this known by means of one among them through whom they understood us. Those who speak that tongue we discriminately call Primahaitu, which is like saying Vasconyados.[4] We found it in use over more than four hundred leagues of our travel, without another over that whole extent. Even to the last, I could not convince the Indians that we were of the Christians; and only with great effort and solicitation we got them to go back to their residences. We ordered them to put away apprehension, establish their towns, plant and cultivate the soil.

From abandonment the country had already grown up thickly in trees. It is, no doubt, the best in all these Indias, the most prolific and plenteous in provisions. Three times in the year it is planted. It produces great variety of fruit, has beautiful rivers, with many other good waters. There are ores with clear traces of gold and silver. The people are well disposed: they serve such Christians as are their friends, with great good will. They are comely, much more so than the Mexicans. Indeed, the land needs no circumstance to make it blessed. 25

The Indians, at taking their leave, told us they would do what we commanded, and would build their towns, if the Christians would suffer them; and this I say and affirm most positively, that, if they have not done so, it is the fault of the Christians. . . .

(1542)

Exploring the Text

1. In the "proem," what purpose or purposes does Álvar Núñez Cabeza de Vaca claim for his narrative? What ethos does he establish? Pay special attention to

---

[4] *Vasconyados* is a term for the Basque people (*Vasco*, in Spanish), who live in a region of northern Spain and southern France. The Basques are named for the language they speak, just as Cabeza de Vaca named the Primahaitu after the language they spoke. — Eds.

his qualification that "neither my counsel nor my constancy availed to gain aught for which we set out" (par. 3) and his ending plea that the narrative be "received in the name of homage, since it is the most that one could bring who returned thence naked" (par. 4).

2. What details of the customs and practices of the indigenous people does Cabeza de Vaca emphasize? In his descriptions of the different cultures he encounters, what evidence do you find of his admiration? Of his criticism or disapproval? Of uncertainty or ambivalence?

3. What is the response of Cabeza de Vaca and his crew to the expectation that they would act as physicians or healers (pars. 8–10)? What different views of "healing" are revealed in this account?

4. Cabeza de Vaca learns to appreciate cultures and rituals different from his own, yet there are lines — for example, "other strange customs" (par. 13) — that his own background and beliefs will not allow him to cross. Identify two examples and explain the nature of his resistance.

5. Since he does not outright renounce his Christian beliefs, how does Cabeza de Vaca reconcile the behavior of his fellow Christians? To what extent does the behavior of the Spanish slave traders in Chapters 33 and 34 shake the faith of Cabeza de Vaca?

6. In what instances do you find Cabeza de Vaca portraying himself and members of his expedition in a particularly flattering light? Do these detract from his relatively enlightened view of the indigenous peoples' behavior and beliefs?

7. Cabeza de Vaca is seen in many different roles in this narrative, among them as conquistador, shaman, captive, diplomat, and missionary. From these excerpts, do you see him juggling multiple, in some cases contradictory, roles, or do you read the narrative as a journey of spiritual growth from one role to a very different one? Cite specific passages to support your viewpoint.

8. What strategies does Cabeza de Vaca employ to establish authenticity in his narrative? As you respond, consider his stated audience — Emperor Charles V — and his larger audience of people becoming acquainted with the New World through this narrative.

9. Cabeza de Vaca's narrative is simultaneously a documentary account of a lived experience and an attempt to interpret it and give it meaning. Identify one or two places where the more anthropological style of the account gives way to interpretation, and discuss the effect of these two rhetorical purposes in combination. Is the result a confusing or a more powerful description?

10. Cabeza de Vaca continues to be the subject of discussion, debate, and reconstruction. Following is an image of him by the twentieth-century southwestern artist Ted DeGrazía (1909–1982). DeGrazía did a series of paintings about Cabeza de Vaca and his journey. What elements of the explorer's personality and narrative does the artist emphasize in this interpretation? To what extent does the visual depiction capture Cabeza de Vaca as you imagine him from your reading?

Courtesy of DeGrazia Gallery in the Sun, DeGrazia Foundation, Tucson, Arizona. All Rights Reserved.

ETTORE (TED) DEGRAZÍA, *TRADING, TRAVELING, AND MOSQUITOES*,
1973, OIL ON CANVAS, 8" x 11".

RICHARD FRETHORNE

Richard Frethorne was an Englishman who came to America in 1622 as an indentured servant and settled near the Jamestown colony in Virginia. Farmers, planters,
and even shopkeepers in early seventeenth-century America found it very difficult
to hire workers. They were unsuccessful in enslaving the local Indian population,
and it was very easy for potential workers to set up their own farms. Therefore,
they recruited laborers — primarily from England, Ireland, and Germany — as
indentured servants, who signed contracts for terms of uncompensated servitude in
exchange for passage to America.

Letter to Father and Mother

Though very little is known about Frethorne's life, the letters he wrote to his parents provide a unique record of the hardships of colonial America, especially for indentured servants.

L oving and kind father and mother:

My most humble duty remembered to you, hoping in God of your good health, as I myself am at the making hereof. This is to let you understand that I your child am in a most heavy case by reason of the nature of the country, [which] is such that it causeth much sickness, [such] as the scurvy and the bloody flux and diverse other diseases, which maketh the body very poor and weak. And when we are sick there is nothing to comfort us; for since I came out of the ship I never ate anything but peas, and loblollie (that is, water gruel). As for deer or venison I never saw any since I came into this land. There is indeed some fowl, but we are not allowed to go and get it, but must work hard both early and late for a mess of water gruel and a mouthful of bread and beef. A mouthful of bread for a penny loaf must serve for four men which is most pitiful. [You would be grieved] if you did know as much as I [do], when people cry out day and night — Oh! that they were in England without their limbs — and would not care to lose any limb to be in England again, yea, though they beg from door to door. For we live in fear of the enemy every hour, yet we have had a combat with them on the Sunday before Shrovetide, and we took two alive and made slaves of them. But it was by policy, for we are in great danger; for our plantation is very weak by reason of the death and sickness of our company. For we came but twenty for the merchants, and they are half dead just; and we look every hour when two more should go. Yet there came some four other men yet to live with us, of which there is but one alive; and our Lieutenant is dead, and [also] his father and his brother. And there was some five or six of the last year's twenty, of which there is but three left, so that we are fain[1] to get other men to plant with us; and yet we are but 32 to fight against 3000 if they should come. And the nighest help that we have is ten miles of us, and when the rogues overcame this place [the] last [time] they slew 80 persons. How then shall we do, for we lie even in their teeth? They may easily take us, but [for the fact] that God is merciful and can save with few as well as with many, as he showed to Gilead. And like Gilead's soldiers, if they lapped water, we drink water which is but weak.

And I have nothing to comfort me, nor there is nothing to be gotten here but sickness and death, except [in the event] that one had money to lay out in some things for profit. But I have nothing at all — no, not a shirt to my back but two rags (2), nor no clothes but one poor suit, nor but one pair of shoes, but one pair of stockings, but one cap, [and] but two bands. My cloak is stolen by one of my own fellows,

---

[1]Compelled. — Eds.

and to his dying hour [he] would not tell me what he did with it; but some of my fellows saw him have butter and beef out of a ship, which my cloak, I doubt [not], paid for. So that I have not a penny, nor a penny worth, to help me to either spice or sugar or strong waters, without the which one cannot live here. For as strong beer in England doth fatten and strengthen them, so water here doth wash and weaken these here [and] only keeps [their] life and soul together. But I am not half [of] a quarter so strong as I was in England, and all is for want of victuals; for I do protest unto you that I have eaten more in [one] day at home than I have allowed me here for a week. You have given more than my day's allowance to a beggar at the door; and if Mr. Jackson had not relieved me, I should be in a poor case. But he like a father and she like a loving mother doth still help me.

For when we go up to Jamestown (that is 10 miles of us) there lie all the ships that come to land, and there they must deliver their goods. And when we went up to town [we would go], as it may be, on Monday at noon, and come there by night, [and] then load the next day by noon, and go home in the afternoon, and unload, and then away again in the night, and [we would] be up about midnight. Then if it rained or blowed never so hard, we must lie in the boat on the water and have nothing but a little bread. For when we go into the boat we [would] have a loaf allowed to two men, and it is all [we would get] if we stayed there two days, which is hard; and [we] must lie all that while in the boat. But that Goodman Jackson pitied me and made me a cabin to lie in always when I [would] come up, and he would give me some poor jacks [to take] home with me, which comforted me more than peas or water gruel. Oh, they be very godly folks, and love me very well, and will do anything for me. And he much marvelled that you would send me a servant to the Company; he saith I had been better knocked on the head. And indeed so I find it now, to my great grief and misery; and [I] saith that if you love me you will redeem me suddenly, for which I do entreat and beg. And if you cannot get the merchants to redeem me for some little money, then for God's sake get a gathering or entreat some good folks to lay out some little sum of money in meal and cheese and butter and beef. Any eating meat will yield great profit. Oil and vinegar is very good; but, father, there is great loss in leaking. But for God's sake send beef and cheese and butter, or the more of one sort and none of another. But if you send cheese, it must be very old cheese; and at the cheesemonger's you may buy very good cheese for twopence farthing or half-penny, that will be liked very well. But if you send cheese, you must have a care how you pack it in barrels; and you must put cooper's chips between every cheese, or else the heat of the hold will rot them. And look whatsoever you send me—be it never so much—look, what[ever] I make of it, I will deal truly with you. I will send it over and beg the profit to redeem me; and if I die before it come, I have entreated Goodman Jackson to send you the worth of it, who hath promised he will. If you send, you must direct your letters to Goodman Jackson, at Jamestown, a gunsmith. (You must set down his freight, because there be more of his name there.) Good father, do not forget me, but have mercy and pity my miserable case. I know if you did but see me, you would weep to see me; for I have but one suit. (But [though] it is a strange one, it is very well guarded.) Wherefore, for God's sake, pity me. I pray you to remember my love to all my friends and kindred. I hope all my brothers and sisters are in good health, and as for my part I have set down my resolution that certainly will be; that is, that the answer of this letter will be life or death to me. Therefore, good father, send as soon as you can; and if you send me any thing let this be the mark. ROT

Richard Frethorne
(March 20, April 2, 3, 1623)

Exploring the Text

1. Who is "the enemy" (par. 1) in Richard Frethorne's account? Who are the "rogues" (par. 1)?
2. What are the terms and conditions, according to Frethorne's account, that contribute to his "miserable case" (par. 3)?
3. How might the fact that he is writing to his parents influence the picture he presents of his life in Virginia? Note that he addresses the letter to both of his parents yet ends with an entreaty to his "good father."
4. From this letter, what inferences can you draw about the life of the poor in England during the early 1600s?
5. Following is the final paragraph from an essay on indentured servitude by historian Richard Hofstadter. In what way does Frethorne's letter support or challenge Hofstadter's view?

> Thoreau, brooding over the human condition in the relatively idyllic precincts of Concord and Walden Pond, was convinced that the mass of men lead lives of quiet desperation. His conviction quickens to life again when we contemplate the human costs of what historians sometimes lightly refer to as the American experiment. It is true that thousands came to the colonies in search of freedom or plenty and with a reasonably good chance of finding them, and that the colonies harbored a force of free white workers whose wages and conditions might well have been the envy of their European counterparts. Yet these fortunate men were considerably outnumbered by persons, white or black, who came to America in one kind of servitude or another. It is also true that for some servants, especially for those who already had a skill, a little cash, or some intelligence or education or gentility, servitude in America might prove not a great deal worse than an ordinary apprenticeship, despite the special tribulations and hazards it inflicted. But when one thinks of the great majority of those who came during the long span of time between the first settlements and the disappearance of white servitude in the early nineteenth century—bearing in mind the poverty and the ravaged lives which they left in Europe, the cruel filter of the Atlantic crossing, the high mortality of the crossing and the seasoning, and the many years of arduous toil that lay between the beginning of servitude and the final realization of tolerable comfort — one is deeply impressed by the

measure to which the sadness that is natural to life was overwhelmed in the condition of servitude by the stark miseries that seem all too natural to the history of the poor. For a great many the journey across the Atlantic proved in the end to have been only an epitome of their journey through life. And yet there must have seemed to be little at risk because there was so little at stake. They had so often left a scene of turbulence, crime, exploitation, and misery that there could not have been much hope in most of them; and as they lay in their narrow bedsteads listening to the wash of the rank bilge water below them, sometimes racked with fever or lying in their own vomit, few could have expected very much from American life, and those who did were too often disappointed. But with white servants we have only begun to taste the anguish of the early American experience.

ANNE BRADSTREET

In 1630, Anne Bradstreet (1612/13–1678) and her husband Simon, the son of a nonconformist minister, sailed to Massachusetts with Anne's parents on the *Arabella*, the flagship of the Massachusetts Bay Company. With *The Tenth Muse Lately Sprung Up in America* (1650) — published in England, possibly without her knowledge — she became the first female poet in America. Because the Puritan community disdained female intellectual ambition, it was thought advisable to append the words "By a Gentle Woman in Those Parts," to reassure readers that Bradstreet was a diligent Puritan mother. Bradstreet's remarkable poetry consists of thirty-five short reflective poems, explicit in their description of familial and marital love. Some of these appeared in the 1678 edition of *The Tenth Muse*; others remained hidden in her notebook until they were published in 1867. The twentieth century saw a resurgence of interest in Bradstreet, with new editions of her work in 1967 and 1981 and a 2005 scholarly biography by Charlotte Gordon, entitled *Mistress Bradstreet: The Untold Life of America's First Poet*. Both of the following poems, published in *The Tenth Muse*, address the problematic role of a female poet in seventeenth-century America.

The Prologue

1

To sing of wars, of captains, and of kings,
Of cities founded, commonwealths begun,
For my mean pen are too superior things:
Or how they all, or each their dates have run
Let poets and historians set these forth,   5
My obscure lines shall not so dim their worth.

2

But when my wond'ring eyes and envious heart
Great Bartas' sugared lines[1] do but read o'er,
Fool I do grudge the Muses did not part
'Twixt him and me that overfluent store;   10
A Bartas can do what a Bartas will
But simple I according to my skill.

3

From schoolboy's tongue no rhet'ric we expect,
Nor yet a sweet consort from broken strings,
Nor perfect beauty where's a main defect: 15
My foolish, broken, blemished Muse so sings,
And this to mend, alas, no art is able,
'Cause nature made it so irreparable.

4

Nor can I, like that fluent sweet tongued Greek,[2]
Who lisped at first, in future times speak plain.   20
By art he gladly found what he did seek,
A full requital of his striving pain.
Art can do much, but this maxim's most sure:
A weak or wounded brain admits no cure.

5

I am obnoxious to each carping tongue   25
Who says my hand a needle better fits,
A poet's pen all scorn I should thus wrong,
For such despite they cast on female wits:
If what I do prove well, it won't advance,
They'll say it's stol'n, or else it was by chance.   30

6

But sure the antique Greeks were far more mild
Else of our sex, why feigned they those nine
And poesy made Calliope's own child;[3]

---

[1]Guillaume du Bartas (1544–1590), French epic poet. — Eds.
[2]Demosthenes, an Athenian orator who put stones in his mouth to improve his
enunciation. — Eds.
[3]In Greek mythology, Calliope was the Muse of epic poetry. — Eds.

So 'mongst the rest they placed the arts divine:
But this weak knot they will full soon untie,   35
The Greeks did nought, but play the fools and lie.

7

Let Greeks be Greeks, and women what they are
Men have precedency and still excel,
It is but vain unjustly to wage war;
Men can do best, and women know it well.   40
Preeminence in all and each is yours;
Yet grant some small acknowledgement of ours.

8

And oh ye high flown quills that soar the skies,
And ever with your prey still catch your praise,
If e'er you deign these lowly lines your eyes,   45
Give thyme or parsley wreath, I ask no bays;
This mean and unrefined ore of mine
Will make your glist'ring gold but more to shine.

(1650)

Exploring the Text

1. In the opening stanza, how does Anne Bradstreet as the speaker in the poem address the concerns her largely male audience is likely to have? What does she claim is outside the scope of her work?
2. In the second stanza, what does Bradstreet mean by "I do grudge the Muses did not part / 'Twixt [Great Bartas] and me that overfluent store" (ll. 9–10)?
3. How does Bradstreet characterize her own talents in stanza 3? What has "nature" made "so irreparable"?
4. How do you interpret Bradstreet's concluding lines in stanza 4: "Art can do much, but this maxim's most sure: / A weak or wounded brain admits no cure" (ll. 23–24)?
5. What shift in attitude does the fifth stanza introduce (ll. 25–30)? Check the archaic definitions of *obnoxious* and *despite*. Who is Bradstreet referring to as "they" in line 28?
6. What is the point Bradstreet makes in stanzas 6 and 7 in her reference to "the antique Greeks"? Does she undermine her own argument when she writes, "Men can do best, and women know it well" (l. 40)? Why or why not?
7. Thyme and parsley are herbs used in cooking, and bays are laurel leaves that were used in ancient Greece and Rome to crown triumphant athletes or great artists. Why in the final stanza does she ask for a "thyme or parsley wreath" but "no bays" (l. 46)?

8. This poem was the prologue to *The Tenth Muse* when it was first published in England in 1650. Think about its purpose as an introduction to the collection. How would you characterize the complex tone? Is the speaker rebellious? Apologetic? Humble? Sarcastic? Aggressive? Conciliatory? Cite specific phrases and lines to support your response.

9. What was the rhetorical situation of Bradstreet and her readers? Analyze the poem, which is often read as an argument that Bradstreet builds stanza by stanza, by considering formal characteristics such as claim, assumptions, counterargument, and evidence.

The Author to Her Book

Thou ill-formed offspring of my feeble brain,
Who after birth didst by my side remain,
Till snatched from thence by friends, less wise than true,
Who thee abroad, exposed to public view,
Made thee in rags, halting to th' press to trudge,   5
Where errors were not lessened (all may judge).
At thy return my blushing was not small,
My rambling brat (in print) should mother call,
I cast thee by as one unfit for light,
Thy visage was so irksome in my sight;   10
Yet being mine own, at length affection would
Thy blemishes amend, if so I could:
I washed thy face, but more defects I saw,
And rubbing off a spot still made a flaw.
I stretched thy joints to make thee even feet,   15
Yet still thou run'st more hobbling than is meet;
In better dress to trim thee was my mind,
But nought save homespun cloth i' th' house I find.
In this array 'mongst vulgars mayst thou roam.
In critic's hands beware thou dost not come,   20
And take thy way where yet thou art not known;
If for thy father asked, say thou hadst none;
And for thy mother, she alas is poor,
Which caused her thus to send thee out of door.

                                                                (1678)

Exploring the Text

1. The title signals the extended metaphor — or conceit — of the poem. What is it? Identify several specific characteristics that the two elements being compared share.

2. Why does Anne Bradstreet describe her "offspring" as "ill-formed" (l. 1)?

3. How does Bradstreet characterize the process of revision? Cite specific details and descriptions to support your response.

4. What point does Bradstreet make by juxtaposing "vulgars" (l. 19) with "critic[s]" (l. 20)?

5. What are two possible interpretations of the speaker's admonition, "If for thy father asked, say thou hadst none" (l. 22)?

6. During this period, women who wrote often faced social censure for stepping outside what was considered their "place" — that is, the domestic sphere of wife and mother. In what ways does Bradstreet address this prevailing cultural viewpoint at the same time she asserts her identity as a poet? Do you think her choice of the motherhood metaphor undermines or celebrates her authority as a writer in a patriarchal society?

7. Taken together, how do "Prologue" and "The Author to Her Book" stake a claim for the woman artist in seventeenth-century America?

 **TALKBACK**

Eavan Boland

Eavan Boland (b. 1944) spent the first six years of her life in Dublin, moving to London when her father was appointed Irish ambassador and then to New York when he was appointed president of the UN General Assembly. Boland returned to Dublin for college, earning a BA in English and Latin from Trinity College Dublin. She has taught at Stanford University since 1996. Boland established her reputation with her collection *In Her Own Image* (1980) and has published regularly since then. She is a feminist and a poet but, she maintains, not a feminist poet. She sees a fundamental difference between the "ethic" of feminism and the "aesthetic" of poetry, arguing that feminism is a definite moral position, whereas poetry, like all art, begins where certainty ends.

Becoming Anne Bradstreet

Boland wrote the following poem for a chapbook called *Shakespeare's Sisters*, a series of poems by contemporary poets commissioned to complement the Folger Shakespeare Library's 2012 exhibit *Shakespeare's Sisters: Voices of English and European Women Writers, 1500–1700*.

It happens again
As soon as I take down her book and open it.

I turn the page.
My skies rise higher and hang younger stars.

The ship's rail freezes.   5
Mare Hibernicum[1] leads to Anne Bradstreet's coast.

---

[1] Latin for "Irish Sea," the body of water that separates Ireland from Great Britain. — Eds.

A blackbird leaves her pine trees
And lands in my spruce trees.

I open my door on a Dublin street.
Her child/her words are staring up at me: 10

In better dress to trim thee was my mind,
But nought save home-spun cloth, i' th' house I find.

We say *home truths*
Because her words can be at home anywhere —

At the source, at the end and whenever   15
The book lies open and I am again

An Irish poet watching an English woman
Become an American poet.

(2012)

Exploring the Text

1. How do you interpret the title? What relationship is Eavan Boland, as the speaker of the poem, suggesting?
2. In what ways does "*Mare Hibernicum* [lead] to Anne Bradstreet's coast"? What is Boland suggesting by this statement?
3. Why do you think Boland chose to include two lines (ll. 11–12) from "The Author to Her Book" in her own poem? Why might those particular lines appeal to Boland?
4. To whom does "We" refer (l. 13)?

Making Connections

1. What connections with Bradstreet does Boland as speaker of her poem suggest when she writes, "My skies rise higher and hang younger stars" (l. 4)? What symbolic links do these lines suggest: "A blackbird leaves her pine trees / And lands in my spruce trees" (ll. 7–8)?
2. Boland's poem ends with a description of transformation: "An Irish poet watching an English woman / Become an American poet" (ll. 17–18). In what ways does the historical relationship between England and Ireland and between England and the North American colony of Bradstreet's time contribute to the bond between Bradstreet and Boland?
3. Would you characterize Boland's poem as a tribute to Anne Bradstreet, a eulogy, a reflection on her importance in a tradition of literature, a defense of the quality of her work, a dialogue between two artists who have faced similar challenges, or a combination of these — or as something else entirely?

4. In "Becoming Anne Bradstreet," Boland asserts that Bradstreet's "words can be at home anywhere" (l. 14), including, obviously, the present. Discuss the extent to which you agree, using "Prologue" and "The Author to Her Book" as evidence for your viewpoint.

ANONYMOUS
Mrs. Elizabeth Freake and Baby Mary

This portrait by an anonymous painter depicts Elizabeth Freake (1642–1713), the wife of John Freake, a wealthy merchant and attorney who lived in Boston, Massachusetts, and their daughter Mary, the youngest of their six children. It is believed that this portrait was painted in 1671; an earlier version depicted only the mother, with baby Mary added three years later. Around ten surviving portraits painted between 1670 and 1674 are attributed to this painter.

Worcester Art Museum, Massachusetts, USA/The Bridgeman Art Library

ANONYMOUS, *MRS. ELIZABETH FREAKE AND BABY MARY*, C. 1671, OIL ON CANVAS, 42½" × 36¾", WORCESTER ART MUSEUM, WORCESTER, MASSACHUSETTS.
(See color insert, Image 12.)

Exploring the Text

1. What does this portrayal of a mother and her child tell you about early New England attitudes toward children and child raising? Use evidence from the painting to support your interpretation.

2. Strict Puritan New Englanders followed sumptuary laws that forbade them to wear bright colors and ornate materials. How do you explain the outfits of the mother and daughter portrayed here? Hint: consider the social and economic status of the subjects.

3. Art historian Milton Brown has described this painting as having "a surprisingly authentic psychological mood." Explain what that mood is and cite details in the portrait that contribute to it.

4. Art historians have alternately identified the painter as an untrained artist, a Dutch itinerant from New York, and even an artist working in the French style. What elements in the painting can you identify that suggest formal artistic training? What examples suggest that the painter was most likely self-taught?

5. Look at the portrait below of a mother and child painted more than a hundred years before the Freake portrait by the Italian painter Agnolo Bronzino. What are the differences between the two portraits? Do you see any similarities? How might you explain the different skill level demonstrated by the Italian painter?

De Agostini Picture Library/A. Dagli Orti/The Bridgeman Art Library

AGNOLO BRONZINO, *ELEONORA OF TOLEDO WITH HER SON GIOVANNI*, c. 1545, OIL ON WOOD, 45¼" × 37⅞", UFFIZI GALLERY, FLORENCE, ITALY.
(See color insert, Image 13.)

EDWARD TAYLOR

A Protestant dissenter in England, Edward Taylor (1642–1729) immigrated to the Massachusetts Bay Colony in 1668 after refusing to sign England's Act of Uniformity and losing his teaching position in Leicestershire. Taylor chronicled his Atlantic crossing and began studying at Harvard upon his arrival in the colonies. He trained as both a pastor and a physician and settled on the western frontier of Massachusetts. Taylor left strict instructions to his heirs that none of his writing ever be published; as a result, his work was forgotten for two centuries, until a 7,000-page manuscript of his poems was discovered in the Yale University library in 1937. This unearthing established him as one of colonial America's foremost poets.

Huswifery

Taylor's poem "Huswifery" is characteristic of his poetry, which reflects his deeply held religious views. His style shows his admiration of seventeenth-century British metaphysical poets, such as John Donne and George Herbert, who often employed extended metaphor or conceits in their work. The title "Huswifery" refers to household duties, usually those of a wife, in this case cloth making. Taylor assumes his audience is familiar with a spinning wheel. With a spinning wheel, raw material fibers, such as flax (linen), cotton, or wool, are gathered onto a stick, or distaff. These fibers are then fed onto a spool that spins and twists the fibers into thread. This thread is gathered using a flyer that evenly winds it onto a reel. The thread can then be woven into cloth with a loom and cleaned, or "fulled," at a fulling mill.

Make me, O Lord, thy Spining Wheele compleate.
   Thy Holy Worde my Distaff make for mee.
Make mine Affections thy Swift Flyers neate
   And make my Soule thy holy Spoole to bee.
    My Conversation make to be thy Reele   5
    And reele the yarn thereon spun of thy Wheele.

Make me thy Loome then, knit therein this Twine:
   And make thy Holy Spirit, Lord, winde quills:
Then weave the Web thyselfe. The yarn is fine.
    Thine Ordinances make my Fulling Mills.   10
    Then dy the same in Heavenly Colours Choice,
    All pinkt with Varnisht Flowers of Paradise.

Then cloath therewith mine Understanding, Will,
   Affections, Judgment, Conscience, Memory
My Words, and Actions, that their shine may fill   15
   My wayes with glory and thee glorify.

Then mine apparell shall display before yee
That I am Cloathd in Holy robes for glory.

(c. 1680)

Exploring the Text

1. In the first six lines, the speaker equates each part of the spinning wheel with an aspect of spiritual life. What is the correspondence with the distaff (a piece of wood on which flax or wool is spun into thread), the "Swift Flyers" (a device to regulate the action of the spinner), the "Spoole" (the instrument that twists the yarn into consistent cords), and the "Reele" (the instrument that winds the finished thread)?

2. In the second stanza, the speaker compares himself to a loom — that is, a mechanism on which to weave the thread into cloth. What is he asking when he implores, "Make me thy Loome" (l. 7)? What is the role of the Holy Spirit and the Lord in this process suggested by the conceit? (Note that "quills" are spindles on which thread is woven; "Fulling Mills" are where cloth is cleansed and prepared for dyeing.)

3. According to stanza 3, what role does the speaker believe he can play once he is attired in the elaborate garment — "Holy robes for glory" — described in stanza 2?

4. The conceit of a mundane task, one usually reserved for women, roots the poem in everyday human experience in the physical world, yet its subject is spirituality and the relationship with the Divine. How does Edward Taylor bring the human and the spiritual together without appearing to be inappropriate or, possibly, heretical?

5. Taylor approached writing poetry not only as an artistic expression but also as an act of devotion. In what ways can this poem be interpreted as a prayer?

MARY ROWLANDSON

Mary Rowlandson (c. 1637–1711) was abducted and held captive for three months by Wampanoag Indians in 1676 during what was known as Metacomet's (or King Philip's) War, named for the Wampanoag Indian leader. The war, which spanned from 1675 to 1678, was caused by territorial disputes between Euro-American settlers and the Algonquin Indian tribes. During an attack on the small town of Lancaster, Massachusetts, Indians seized Rowlandson, her three children, and nineteen of their neighbors. During the next three months, she witnessed the death of her young daughter and other English colonists. Rowlandson was sold by her captor to Quannopin, who became her "master," and his three wives became her "mistresses." On May 2, 1676, Rowlandson's captors, who were themselves starving and uprooted, agreed to the ransom her husband, a minister, offered.

from *A Narrative of the Captivity and Restoration of Mrs. Mary Rowlandson*

In 1682, six years after her release, Rowlandson published a narrative about her captivity experience, entitled *The Sovereignty and Goodness of God: Being a Narrative of the Captivity and Restoration of Mrs. Mary Rowlandson.* She claimed that she wrote it for her children. The first North American captivity narrative with a woman as the central figure, it went through four printings in a short time and gained a wide readership in both New England and London. The following excerpts reflect Rowlandson's division of her narrative into twenty "removes," her designation for the occasions when she and her captors traveled from one geographical location or camp to another.

On the tenth of *February*, 1675. came the *Indians* with great numbers upon *Lancaster.* Their first coming was about Sun-rising. Hearing the noise of some Guns, we looked out; several Houses were burning, and the Smoke ascending to Heaven. There were five Persons taken in one House, the Father, and the Mother, and a sucking Child they knock'd on the head; the other two they took, and carried away alive. There were two others, who being out of their Garrison upon some occasion, were set upon; one was knock'd on the head, the other escaped. Another there was who running along was shot and wounded, and fell down; he begged of them his Life, promising them Money (as they told me); but they would not hearken to him, but knock'd him on the head, stripped him naked, and split open his Bowels. Another seeing many of the *Indians* about his Barn, ventured and went out, but was quickly shot down. There were three others belonging to the same Garrison who were killed. The *Indians* getting up upon the Roof of the Barn, had advantage to shoot down upon them over their Fortification. Thus these murtherous Wretches went on, burning and destroying before them.

At length they came and beset our own House, and quickly it was the dolefullest day that ever mine eyes saw. The House stood upon the edge of a Hill; some of the *Indians* got behind the Hill, others into the Barn, and others behind any thing that would shelter them: from all which Places they shot against the *House*, so that the Bullets seemed to fly like Hail: and quickly they wounded one Man among us, then another, and then a third. About two Hours (according to my observation in that amazing time) they had been about the House, before they could prevail to fire it, (which they did with Flax and Hemp which they brought out of the Barn, and there being no Defence about the House, onely two Flankers, at two opposite Corners, and one of them not finished.) They fired it once, and one ventured out and quenched it; but they quickly fired it again, and that took. Now is that dreadful Hour come, that I have often heard of, (in the time of the War, as it was the Case of others) but now mine Eyes see it. Some in our House were fighting for their Lives, others wallowing in their Blood; the House on fire over our Heads, and the bloody Heathen ready to knock us on the Head if we stirred out. Now might we hear Mothers and Children crying out for themselves, and one another, *Lord, what shall we do!* Then I took my

Children (and one of my Sisters, hers) to go forth and leave the House: But as soon as we came to the Door and appeared, the *Indians* shot so thick; that the Bullets ratled against the House, as if one had taken an handful of Stones and threw them; so that we were fain to give back. We had six stout Dogs belonging to our Garrison, but none of them would stir, though another time, if an *Indian* had come to the Door, they were ready to fly upon him, and tear him down. The Lord hereby would make us the more to acknowledge his Hand, and to see that our Help is always in him. But out we must go, the Fire increasing, and coming along behind us roaring, and the *Indians* gaping before us with their Guns, Spears, and Hatchets, to devour us. No sooner were we out of the House, but my Brother-in-Law (being before wounded (in defending the House) in or near the Throat) fell down dead, whereat the *Indians* scornfully shouted, and hallowed, and were presently upon him, stripping off his Clothes. The Bullets flying thick, one went thorow my Side, and the same (as would seem) thorow the Bowels and Hand of my dear Child in my Arms. One of my eldest Sisters Children (named *William*) had then his Leg broken, which the *Indians* perceiving, they knock'd him on the head. Thus were we butchered by those merciless Heathen, standing amazed, with the Blood running down to our Heels. My elder Sister being yet in the House, and seeing those woful Sights, the Infidels haling Mothers one way, and Children another, and some wallowing in their Blood, and her elder son telling her that (her Son) *William* was dead, and my self was wounded; she said, And *Lord, let me die with them*: Which was no sooner said, but she was struck with a Bullet, and fell down dead over the Threshold. . . . The *Indians* laid hold of us, pulling me one way, and the Children another, and said, *Come, go along with us*: I told them, they would kill me: They answered, *If I were willing to go along with them, they would not hurt me*.

O the doleful Sight that now was to behold at this House! *Come, behold the Works of the Lord, what desolation he has made in the Earth*. Of thirty seven Persons who were in this one House, none escaped either present Death, or a bitter Captivity, save onely one, who might say as he, *Job* 1. 15. *And I onely am escaped alone to tell the News*. There were twelve killed, some shot, some stabb'd with their Spears, some knock'd down with their Hatchets. When we are in prosperity, Oh the Little that we think of such dreadful Sights, and to see our dear Friends and Relations lie bleeding out their Heart-blood upon the Ground! There was one who was chopp'd into the Head with a Hatchet, and stripp'd naked, and yet was crawling up and down. It is a solemn Sight to see so many Christians lying in their Blood, some here, and some there, like a company of Sheep torn by Wolves. All of them stript naked by a company of hell-hounds, roaring, singing, ranting and insulting, as if they would have torn our very hearts out, yet the Lord by his Almighty power, preserved a number of us from death, for there were twenty four of us taken alive: and carried Captive.

I had often before this said, that if the *Indians* should come, I should chuse rather to be killed by them, than taken alive: but when it came to the trial my mind changed: their glittering Weapons so daunted my Spirit, that I chose rather to go along with those (as I may say) ravenous Bears, than that moment to end my daies. And that I may the better declare what happened to me during that grievous Captivity, I shall particularly speak of the several Removes we had up and down the Wilderness.

The First Remove

Now away we must go with those Barbarous Creatures, with our bodies wounded   5
and bleeding, and our hearts no less than our bodies. About a mile we went that
night; up upon a hill within sight of the Town where they intended to lodge. There
was hard by a vacant house (deserted by the English before, for fear of the *Indians*) I
asked them whether I might not lodge in the house that night? to which they
answered, what will you love *English-men* still? this was the dolefullest night that
ever my eyes saw. Oh the roaring, and singing, and dancing, and yelling of those
black creatures in the night, which made the place a lively resemblance of hell: And
as miserable was the waste that was there made, of Horses, Cattle, Sheep, Swine,
Calves, Lambs, Roasting Pigs, and Fowls (which they had plundered in the Town)
some roasting, some lying and burning, and some boyling, to feed our merciless
Enemies; who were joyful enough though we were disconsolate. To add to the dole-
fulness of the former day, and the dismalness of the present night, my thoughts ran
upon my losses and sad bereaved condition. All was gone, my Husband gone (at
least separated from me, he being in the Bay; and to add to my grief, the *Indians* told
me they would kill him as he came homeward) my Children gone, my Relations and
Friends gone, our house and home, and all our comforts within door, and without, all was gone (except my life) and I knew not but the next moment that might
go too.

There remained nothing to me but one poor wounded Babe, and it seemed at present worse than death, that it was in such a pitiful condition, bespeaking Compassion,
and I had no refreshing for it, nor suitable things to revive it. Little do many think, what
is the savageness and bruitishness of this barbarous Enemy! . . .

The Second Remove

But now (the next morning) I must turn my back upon the Town, and travel with
them into the vast and desolate Wilderness, I know not whither. It is not my tongue,
or pen can express the sorrows of my heart, and bitterness of my spirit, that I had at
this departure: But God was with me, in a wonderful manner, carrying me along, and
bearing up my Spirit, that it did not quite fail. One of the *Indians* carried my poor
wounded Babe upon a horse: it went moaning all a long, I shall die, I shall die. I went
on foot after it, with sorrow that cannot be exprest. At length I took it off the Horse,
and carried it in my arms, till my strength failed, and *I* fell down with it. Then they
set me upon a horse, with my wounded Child in my lap, and there being no Furniture
upon the horse back; as we were going down a steep hill, we both fell over the horses
head, at which they like inhuman creatures laught, and rejoiced to see it, though I
thought we should there have ended our dayes, as overcome with so many difficulties. But the Lord renewed my strength still, and carried me along, that I might see
more of his power, yea, so much that *I* could never have thought of, had *I* not
experienced it.

The Third Remove

... Thus nine dayes I sat upon my knees, with my babe in my lap, till my flesh was raw again: my child being even ready to depart this sorrowful world, they bid me carry it out, to another Wigwam: (I suppose because they would not be troubled with such spectacles.) Whither I went with a very heavy heart, and down I sate with the picture of death in my lap. About two hours in the Night, my sweet Babe like a Lamb departed this life, on *Feb.* 18. 1675. it being about six years and five months old. It was nine dayes (from the first wounding) in this Miserable condition, without any refreshing of one nature or other, except a little cold water. I cannot but take notice, how at another time I could not bear to be in the room where any dead person was, but now the case is changed: I must and could lye down by my dead Babe, side by side, all the night after. I have thought since of the wonderful goodness of God to me, in preserving me so in the use of my reason and senses, in that distressed time, that I did not use wicked and violent means to end my own miserable life. In the morning, when they understood that my child was dead, they sent for me home to my Masters Wigwam: (by my Master in this writing must be understood *Quannopin*, who was a Saggamore and married King *Philips* wives Sister; not that he first took me, but I was sold to him by another *Narrhaganset Indian*, who took me when first I came out of the Garrison.) I went to take up my dead Child in my arms to carry it with me, but they bid me let it alone: there was no resisting, but go I must and leave it. When I had been a while at my Masters wigwam, I took the first opportunity I could get, to go look after my dead child: when *I* came I asked them what they had done with it? they told me it was upon the hill: then they went and shewed me where it was, where I saw the ground was newly digged, and there they told me they had buried it. ...

The Fourteenth Remove

Now must we pack up and be gone from this Thicket, bending our course towards the Bay-Towns. I having nothing to eat by the way this day, but a few crumbs of Cake, that an *Indian* gave my Girl, the same day we were taken. She gave it me, and I put it into my pocket: there it lay till it was so mouldy (for want of good baking) that one could not tell what it was made of; it fell all to crumbs, and grew so dry and hard, that it was like little flints; and this refreshed me many times, when I was ready to faint. It was in my thoughts when I put it into my mouth, that if ever I returned, I would tell the World, what a blessing the Lord gave to such mean food. As we went along, they killed a *Deer*, with a young one in her: they gave me a piece of the *Fawn*, and it was so young and tender, that one might eat the bones as well as the flesh, and yet I thought it very good. When night came on we sate down, it rained, but they quickly got up a Bark Wigwam, where I lay dry that night. I looked out in the morning, and many of them had lain in the rain all night, I saw by their Reeking. Thus the Lord dealt mercifully with me many times: and I fared better than many of them. In the morning they took the blood of the *Deer*, and put it into the Paunch, and so boiled it I could eat nothing of that, though they ate it sweetly. And yet they were so nice in other things, that when I had fetcht water, and had put the Dish I dipt the water with, into the Kittle of water which I brought, they would say, they would knock me down; for they said, it was a sluttish[1] trick. . . .

The Nineteenth Remove

My Master had three Squaws: living sometimes with one, and sometimes with another. One, this old Squaw at whose Wigwam I was, and with whom my Master had been those three weeks. Another was *Wettimore*, with whom I had lived and served all this while. A severe and proud Dame she was; bestowing every day in dressing herself near as much time as any of the Gentry of the land: powdering her hair and painting her face, going with her Neck-laces, with Jewels in her ears, and bracelets upon her hands. When she had dressed herself, her Work was to make Girdles of Wampom and Beads. The third Squaw was a younger one, by whom he had two Papooses.[2] By that time I was refresht by the old Squaw, with whom my Master was, *Wettimores* Maid came to call me home, at which I fell a weeping; then the old Squaw told me, to encourage me, that if I wanted victuals, I should come to her, and that I should lye there in her Wigwam. Then I went with the Maid, and quickly came again and lodged there. The Squaw laid a Mat under me, and a good Rugg over me; the first time I had any such Kindness shewed me. I understood that *Wettimore* thought, that if she should let me go and serve with the old Squaw, she would be in danger to lose not only my service but the redemption-pay also. And I was not a little glad to hear this; being by it raised in my hopes, that in Gods due time there would be an end of this sorrowful hour. Then came an *Indian*, and asked me to knit him three pair of Stockins, for which I had a Hat, and a silk Handker chief. Then another asked me to make her a shift, for which she gave me an Apron. . . .

The Twentieth Remove

But before I go any further, I would take leave to mention a few remarkable passages of Providence; which I took special notice of in my afflicted time. . . .

5. Another, thing that I would observe is, the strange providence of God in turning things about when the *Indians were at the highest*, and the *English at the lowest*. I was with the Enemy eleven weeks and five days; and not one Week passed without the fury of the Enemy, and some desolation by fire and sword upon one place or other. They mourned (with their black faces) for their own losses: yet triumphed and rejoyced in their inhumane (and many times devillish cruelty) to the

---

[1]Dirty or slovenly. — Eds.
[2]Narragansett word for *baby*. — Eds.

English. They would boast much of their Victories; saying, that in two hours time, they had destroyed such a Captain, and his Company, in such a place; and such a Captain, and his Company, in such a place; and such a Captain, and his Company, in such a place: and boast how many Towns they had destroyed, and then scoff, and say, they had done them a good turn, to send them to Heaven so soon. Again they would say, this Summer they would knock all the Rogues in the head, or drive them into the Sea, or make them flie the Country: thinking surely, *Agag-like*,[3] *The bitterness of Death is past.* Now the *Heathen* begin to think that all is their own, and the poor *Christians* hopes to fail (as to man) and now their eyes are more to God, and their hearts sigh heaven-ward: and to say in good earnest, *Help Lord, or we perish*; when the Lord had brought his People to this, that they saw no help in any thing but himself; then he takes the quarrel into his own hand: and though they had made a pit (in their own imaginations) as deep as hell for the *Christians* that Summer; yet the Lord hurll'd themselves into it. And the Lord had not so many wayes before, to preserve them, but now he hath as many to destroy them.

But to return again to my going home: where we may see a remarkable change of providence: at first they were all against it, except my Husband would come for me; but afterwards they assented to it, and seemed much to rejoyce in it: some asking me to send them some Bread, others some Tobacco, others shaking me by the hand, offering me a Hood and Scarf to ride in; not one moving hand or tongue against it. Thus hath the Lord answered my poor desires, and the many earnest requests of others put up unto God for me. In my Travels an *Indian* came to me, and told me, if I were willing, he and his Squaw would run away, and go home along with me. I told him, No, I was not willing to run away, but desired to wait Gods time, that I might go home quietly, and without fear. And now God hath granted me my desire. . . .

I can remember the time, when I used to sleep quietly without workings in my thoughts, whole nights together: but now it is otherwise with me. When all are fast about me, and no eye open, but his who ever waketh, my thoughts are upon things past, upon the awful dispensations of the Lord towards us: upon his wonderful power and might in carrying us through so many difficulties, in returning us in safety, and suffering none to hurt us. I remember in the night season, how the other day I was in the midst of thousands of enemies, and nothing but death before me: it was then hard work to perswade my self that ever I should be satisfied with bread again. But now we are fed with the finest of the Wheat, and (as I may so say) with honey out of the rock: instead of the husks, we have the fatted Calf: the thoughts of these things in the particulars of them, and of the love and goodness of God towards us, make it true of me, what *David* said of himself, *Psal.* 6. 6. *I water my Couch with my tears.* Oh the wonderful power of God that mine eyes have seen, affording matter enough for my thoughts to run in, that when others are sleeping mine eyes are weeping.

---

[3]A reference to 1 Samuel 15:32. King Saul killed all of Agag's people but spared the king, in violation of the Lord's orders. Agag thought he had been spared, but Samuel killed him soon thereafter. — Eds.

I have seen the extream vanity of this World: one hour I have been in health, and 15 wealth, wanting nothing: but the next hour in sickness, and wounds, and death, having nothing but sorrow and affliction.

Before I knew what affliction meant, I was ready sometimes to wish for it. When I lived in prosperity; having the comforts of this World about me, my Relations by me, and my heart chearful: and taking little care for any thing; and yet seeing many (whom I preferred before my self) under many trials and afflictions, in sickness, weakness, poverty, losses, crosses, and cares of the World, I should be sometimes jealous least I should have my portion in this life; and that Scripture would come to my mind, *Heb.* 12. 6. *For whom the Lord loveth he chasteneth, and scourgeth every Son whom he receiveth*: but now I see the Lord had his time to scourge and chasten me. The portion of some is to have their Affliction by drops, now one drop and then another: but the dregs of the Cup, the wine of astonishment, like a sweeping rain that leaveth no food, did the Lord prepare to be my portion. Affliction I wanted, and Affliction I had, full measure (I thought) pressed down and running over: yet I see when God calls a person to any thing, and through never so many difficulties, yet he is fully able to carry them through, and make them see and say they have been gainers thereby. And I hope I can say in some measure, as *David* did, *It is good for me that I have been afflicted.* The Lord hath shewed me the vanity of these outward things, that they are the *Vanity of vanities, and vexation of spirit*; that they are but a shadow, a blast, a bubble, and things of no continuance; that we must rely on God himself, and our whole dependance must be upon him. If trouble from smaller matters begin to arise in me, I have something at hand to check my self with, and say when I am troubled, It was but the other day, that if I had had the world, I would have given it for my Freedom, or to have been a Servant to a *Christian*. I have learned to look beyond present and smaller troubles, and to be quieted under them, as *Moses* said, *Exod.* 14. 13. *Stand still, and see the salvation of the Lord.*

(1682)

Exploring the Text

1. The full title of the surviving American second edition of this text is *The Sovereignty and Goodness of God. Together with the Faithfulness of His Promises Displayed: Being a Narrative of the Captivity and Restoration of Mrs. Mary Rowlandson.* In a note on the title page, Mary Rowlandson states that she wrote the account for her "private use" and that it was "made public at the earnest Desire of some Friends, and for the Benefit of the afflicted." In what ways are the title and this statement of purpose appropriate for the colonial audience?

2. Imagine yourself a seventeenth-century reader in London, someone with little or no first-hand experience of Native Americans. What "knowledge" would you gain about Indian culture and values? Pay close attention to the terms that Rowlandson uses to describe the Indians and their cultural practices.

3. In the opening sections, how does Rowlandson combine action-packed storytelling with reflective commentary to characterize her captivity as a battle between good and evil? How do both spiritual trial and physical torment contribute to this struggle?

4. One scholar of this period interprets the narrative as follows: "For Rowlandson, it was the situation of her captivity rather than native culture as such that inverted the proper order of things." How do her descriptions of Quannopin and his wives, as well as her captors' customs, support or challenge this interpretation?

5. Does Rowlandson in any way change her attitude toward her Indian captors from the start to the end of the narrative? If so, how? If you believe she does not, what instances of kindness or even mercy do you note that she does not acknowledge?

6. Rowlandson sees events of her captivity as representing a biblical drama in which she is a participant much like various characters in the Old and New Testaments. Choose two or three key events or series of events from the narrative. How do they reveal Rowlandson interpreting her experiences through the lens of her Puritan belief in God's providence and sovereignty? How do her scriptural quotations contribute to the power of her narrative?

7. Captivity narratives—an early form of travel literature and a forerunner of fiction—have three common plotline characteristics: a separation, a transformation, and a return. Generally the longest part, the transformation includes adventures, as captives journey into the wilderness, encounter various obstacles and trials, and become more familiar with their captors' way of life. Explain these structural components in Rowlandson's narrative.

8. When Rowlandson's narrative was first published in 1682, it was framed by two documents: a preface that was anonymous but thought to have been written by the Puritan minister Increase Mather and her late husband's last sermon. The preface included this analysis of Rowlandson's intent:

> This narrative was penned by the Gentlewoman her self, to be to her a memorandum of Gods dealing with her, that she might never forget, but remember the same, and the several circumstances thereof, all the days of her life. A pious scope which deserves both commendation and imitation: Some friends having obtained a sight of it, could not but be so much affected with the many passages of working providence discovered therein as to judge it worthy of public view, and although unmeet that such works of God should be hid from the present and future Generations: And therefore though this Gentlewomans modesty would not thrust it into the Press, yet her gratitude unto God made her not hardly persuadable to let it pass, that God might have his due glory and others benefit by it as well as herself.

In light of this explanation in the preface and the framing of Rowlandson's narrative by two male sponsors, what evidence do you find in the narrative of her defense and reinforcement of the male patriarchy of Puritan society? To what extent do you find evidence that might challenge the traditional gender roles of the time?

9. The following woodcut illustrated Rowlandson's captivity narrative when it was reprinted in *Pioneers in the Settlement of America*, by William A. Crafts, in 1876. What is the artist's interpretation of this encounter in *Mrs. Rowlandson and Her Indian Captors*? Cite specific details of lighting, composition, and expression to support your response.

⟳ TALKBACK

Louise Erdrich

Born in 1954, Louise Erdrich is a graduate of Dartmouth College and the author of best-selling novels, volumes of poetry, and children's books. Erdrich's father was German American, but she is Native American on her mother's side and a member of the Turtle Mountain Band of Chippewa Indians. Her work, which often contains multiple narrators and moves backward and forward in time, concerns the political and social struggles of Native Americans. Erdrich has received the O. Henry Award, the Pushcart Prize for Poetry, a Guggenheim Fellowship, and the National Book Critics Circle Award for Fiction, among many other awards. In 2007, she turned down an honorary doctorate from the University of North Dakota in protest of the university's "Fighting Sioux" mascot; she received an honorary doctorate from her alma mater, Dartmouth, in 2009.

Captivity

A response to Mary Rowlandson's captivity narrative, Erdrich's poem "Captivity" explores a captive's fear — and misunderstanding — of her captors. The poem is from her collection *Jacklight* (1991).

*He (my captor) gave me a bisquit, which I put in my pocket, and not daring to eat
it, buried it under a log, fearing he had put something in it to make me love him.*
— From the narrative of the captivity of Mrs. Mary Rowlandson,
who was taken prisoner by the Wampanoag when Lancaster,
Massachusetts, was destroyed, in the year 1676

The stream was swift, and so cold
I thought I would be sliced in two.
But he dragged me from the flood
by the ends of my hair.
I had grown to recognize his face.   5
I could distinguish it from the others.
There were times I feared I understood
his language, which was not human,
and I knelt to pray for strength.

We were pursued by God's agents   10
or pitch devils, I did not know.
Only that we must march.
Their guns were loaded with swan shot.
I could not suckle and my child's wail
put them in danger.   15
He had a woman
with teeth black and glittering.
She fed the child milk of acorns.
The forest closed, the light deepened.

I told myself that I would starve   20
before I took food from his hands
but I did not starve.
One night
he killed a deer with a young one in her
and gave me to eat of the fawn.   25
It was so tender,
the bones like the stems of flowers,
that I followed where he took me.
The night was thick. He cut the cord
that bound me to the tree.   30

After that the birds mocked.
Shadows gaped and roared
and the trees flung down
their sharpened lashes.
He did not notice God's wrath.   35

God blasted fire from half-buried stumps.
I hid my face in my dress, fearing He would burn us all
but this, too, passed.

Rescued, I see no truth in things.
My husband drives a thick wedge   40
through the earth, still it shuts
to him year after year.
My child is fed of the first wheat.
I lay myself to sleep
on a Holland-laced pillowbeer.[1]   45
I lay to sleep.
And in the dark I see myself
as I was outside their circle.

They knelt on deerskins, some with sticks,
and he led his company in the noise   50
until I could no longer bear
the thought of how I was.
I stripped a branch
and struck the earth,
in time, begging it to open   55
to admit me
as he was
and feed me honey from the rock.

(1991)

Exploring the Text

1. Who is the speaker, the "I" of the poem? What is the effect of this choice on the poem's impact? Who are "we" in lines 10 and 12?

2. In line 2, the speaker says she thought she would be "sliced in two." What other images of division or conflict do you find in the poem? How do they contribute to your understanding of a central idea Louise Erdrich is developing in the poem?

3. Who is "he" (l. 3)? Why does the speaker say, "There were times I feared I understood / his language" (ll. 7–8)?

4. How are the Indians depicted in the poem? Pay particular attention to their relationship to the natural world and the final characterization of the man leading "his company" (l. 50).

5. How would you describe the speaker's relationship with her God and religion? Cite specific lines to support your response.

---

[1]Pillowcase. — Eds.

6. From the opening epigraph, Erdrich gives details about food and eating. What are they? How do they work together to contribute to overall meaning?

7. To what extent and in what ways does your knowledge of Erdrich's mixed European American and Native American heritage influence your interpretation of the poem?

Making Connections

1. Traditionally, when a contemporary author revisits an older work, a person spoken about becomes the speaker: thus, we say that the person gains "voice." For instance, a story about a woman that was originally told from a man's point of view might be retold in the woman's voice. Erdrich does not do this. Why do you think it would or would not have been more effective if she had written her poem in the voice of a Native American?

2. In what ways does the ending of Erdrich's poem challenge or even reverse the ending of Rowlandson's captivity narrative?

3. Compare and contrast Mary Rowlandson's version of her captivity with that of the speaker in "Captivity." Pay attention to the specifics of event, setting, and language that Erdrich uses from the original text (e.g., Rowlandson's Fourteenth Remove and Erdrich's stanza 3, beginning "I told myself that I would starve"). What is the significance of the similarities and differences?

4. Read the short story "Captivity," from *First Indian on the Moon*, by Sherman Alexie. In one section, Alexie writes, "It's too late, Mary Rowlandson, for us to sit together and dig up the past you buried under a log, salvage whatever else you had left behind." What does he mean? How would Erdrich respond to that assertion? Explain your response within the context of her poem "Captivity."

Cotton Mather

Cotton Mather (1663–1728) was a Puritan clergyman, writer, and historian from Boston, Massachusetts, who is best remembered for persecuting witches during the late 1600s. During the Salem Witch Trials (1692–1693), Mather served as an advisor to Boston magistrates, attended the trials, wrote sermons against witchcraft, and investigated many of the cases himself. He was, however, a complex thinker and prolific writer on many political and social, as well as scientific, issues. A graduate of Harvard College and recipient of an honorary degree from the University of Glasgow, Mather was elected Fellow of the Royal Society of London and held progressive views for the time; for instance, he advocated for inoculation against smallpox, a position that was opposed by many physicians of the day. Furthermore, in his work *Christian Philosopher* (1721), he attempted to provide a rational foundation for Christianity by reconciling scientific and theological principles.

Wonders of the Invisible World
A Hortatory and Necessary Address to a Country Now Extraordinarily Alarum'd by the Wrath of the Devil

In one of his most famous works, *Wonders of the Invisible World*, Mather gives detailed descriptions of each case in the Salem Witch Trials. In all, nineteen women were accused, tried, and executed and several others were incarcerated for witchcraft.

L et us now make a good and a right use of the prodigious *descent* which the *Devil* in *Great Wrath* is at this day making upon our Land. Upon the Death of a Great Man once, an Orator call'd the Town together, crying out, *Concurrite Cives, Dilapsa sunt vestra Mœnio!* that is, *Come together, Neighbours, your Town-Walls are fallen down!* But such is the descent of the Devil at this day upon our selves, that I may truly tell you, *The Walls of the whole World are broken down!* The usual *Walls* of defence about mankind have such a Gap made in them, that the very *Devils* are broke in upon us, to seduce the *Souls*, torment the *Bodies*, sully the *Credits*, and consume the *Estates* of our Neighbours, with Impressions both as *real* and as *furious*, as if the *Invisible* World were becoming *Incarnate*, on purpose for the vexing of us. And what use ought now to be made of so tremendous a dispensation? We are engaged in a *Fast* this day; but shall we try to fetch *Meat out of the Eater*, and make the *Lion* to afford some *Hony* for our *Souls*?

That the Devil is *come down unto us with great Wrath*, we find, we feel, we now deplore. In many ways, for many years hath the Devil been assaying to Extirpate the Kingdom of our Lord Jesus here. *New-England* may complain of the Devil, as in *Psal.* 129 · 1, 2, *Many a time have they afflicted me, from my Youth, may* New-England *now say; many a time have they afflicted me from my Youth; yet they have not prevailed against me.* But now there is a more than ordinary *affliction*, with which the *Devil* is Galling of us: and such an one as is indeed Unparallelable. The things confessed by *witches*, and the things endured by *Others*, laid together, amount unto this account of our Affliction. The *Devil*, Exhibiting himself ordinarily as a small *Black man*, has decoy'd a fearful knot of proud, froward, ignorant, envious and malicious creatures, to lift themselves in his horrid Service, by entring their Names in a *Book* by him tendred unto them. These *Witches*, whereof above a Score have now *Confessed*, and *shown their Deeds*, and some are now tormented by the Devils, for *Confessing*, have met in Hellish *Randezvouzes*, wherein the Confessors do say, they have had their Diabolical Sacraments, imitating the *Baptism* and the *Supper* of our Lord. In these hellish meetings, these Monsters have associated themselves to do no less a thing than, *To destroy the Kingdom of our Lord Jesus Christ, in these parts of the World*; and in order hereunto, First they each of them have their *Spectres*, or Devils, commission'd by them, & representing of them, to be the Engines of their Malice. By these wicked *Spectres*, they seize poor people about the Country, with various & bloudy *Torments*; and of those evidently Preternatural torments there are some have dy'd. They have bewitched some, even so far as to make *Self-destroyers*: and others are in many Towns here and there languishing under their *Evil hands*. The people thus afflicted, are miserably scratched and bitten, so that the Marks are most visible to all the World, but the causes utterly invisible; and the same Invisible Furies do most visibly stick Pins into the bodies of the afflicted, and *scale* them, and hideously distort, and disjoint all their members, besides a thousand other sorts of Plagues beyond these of any natural diseases which they give unto them. Yea, they sometimes drag the poor people out of their chambers, and carry them over Trees and Hills, for divers miles together. A large part of the persons tortured by these Diabolical *Spectres*, are horribly tempted by them, sometimes with fair promises, and sometimes with hard threatnings, but always with felt miseries, to sign the *Devils Laws* in a Spectral Book laid before them; which two or three of these poor Sufferers, being by their tiresome sufferings overcome to do, they have immediately been released from all their miseries and they appear'd in *Spectre* then to Torture those that were before their Fellow-Sufferers. The *Witches* which by their covenant with the Devil, are become Owners of *Spectres*, are oftentimes by their own *Spectres* required and compelled to give their consent, for the molestation of some, which they had no mind otherwise to fall upon; and cruel depredations are then made upon the Vicinage.[2] In the Prosecution of these Witchcrafts, among a thousand other unaccountable things, the *Spectres* have an odd faculty of cloathing the most substantial and corporeal Instruments of Torture, with Invisibility, while the wounds thereby given have been the most palpable things in the World; so that the Sufferers assaulted with Instruments of Iron, wholly unseen to the standers by, though, to their cost, seen by themselves, have, upon snatching, wrested the Instruments out of the *Spectres* hands, and every one has then immediately not only *beheld*, but *handled*, an Iron Instrument taken by a Devil from a Neighbour. These wicked *Spectres* have proceeded so far, as to steal several quantities of Mony from divers people, part of which Money, has, before sufficient Spectators, been dropt out of the Air into the Hands of the Sufferers, while the *Spectres* have been urging them to subscribe their *Covenant with Death*. In such extravagant ways have these Wretches propounded, the *Dragooning*[3] of as many as they can, in their own Combination, and the *Destroying* of others, with lingring, spreading, deadly diseases; till our Countrey should at last become too hot for us. Among the Ghastly Instances of the *success* which those Bloody Witches have had, we have seen even some of their own Children, so dedicated unto the Devil, that in their Infancy, it is found, the *Imps* have sucked them, and rendred them Venomous to a Prodigy. We have also seen the Devils first batteries upon the Town, where the first Church of our Lord in this Colony was gathered, producing those distractions, which have almost ruin'd the Town. We have seen likewise the *Plague* reaching afterwards into other Towns far and near, where the Houses of good Men have the Devils filling of them with terrible Vexations!

This is the Descent, which, it seems, the Devil has now made upon us. But that which makes this Descent the more formidable, is; The *multitude* and *quality* of Persons accused of an interest in this *Witchcraft*, by the Efficacy of the *Spectres* which

---

[1]Those who live in the vicinity. — Eds.
[2]Compel through violence. — Eds.

take their Name and shape upon them; causing very many good and wise Men to fear, That many *innocent*, yea, and some *vertuous* persons, are by the Devils in this matter, imposed upon; That the Devils have obtain'd the power, to take on them the likeness of harmless people, and in that likeness to afflict other people, and be so abused by Præstigious *Dæmons*, that upon their look or touch, the afflicted shall be odly affected. Arguments from the *Providence of God*, on the one side, and from our *Charity* towards *Man* on the other side, have made this now to become a most agitated Controversie among us. There is an *Agony* produced in the Minds of Men, lest the Devil should sham us with *Devices*, of perhaps a finer Thred, than was ever yet practised upon the World. The whole business is become hereupon so *Snarled*, and the determination of the Question one way or another, so *dismal*, that our Honourable Judges have a Room for *Jehoshaphat's* Exclamation, *We know not what to do!* They have used, as Judges have heretofore done, the *Spectral Evidences*, to introduce their further Enquiries into the *Lives* of the persons accused; and they have thereupon, by the wonderful Providence of God, been so strengthened with *other evidences*, that some of the *Witch Gang* have been fairly Executed. But what shall be done, as to those against whom the *evidence* is chiefly founded in the *dark world*? Here they do solemnly demand our Addresses to the *Father of Lights*, on their behalf. But in the mean time, the Devil improves the *Darkness* of this Affair, to push us into a *Blind Mans Buffet*, and we are even ready to be *sinfully*, yea, hotly, and madly, mauling one another in the *dark*.

The consequence of these things, every *considerate* Man trembles at; and the more, because the frequent cheats of Passion, and Rumour, do precipitate so many, that I wish I could say, The most were *considerate*.

But that which carries on the formidableness of our Trials, unto that which may be   5
called, *A wrath unto the uttermost*, is this: It is not without the *wrath* of the Almighty *God* himself, that the *Devil* is permitted thus to come down upon us in *wrath*. It was said, in *Isa.* 9 · 19, *Through the wrath of the Lord of Hosts, the Land is darkned.* Our Land is *darkned* indeed; since the *Powers of Darkness* are turned in upon us: 'tis a *dark time*, yea a black night indeed, now the *Ty-dogs* of the Pit are abroad among us: but, *It is through the wrath of the Lord of Hosts!* Inasmuch as the *Fire-brands* of *Hell* it self are used for the scorching of us, with cause enough may we cry out, *What means the heat of this anger?* Blessed Lord! Are all the other Instruments of thy Vengeance, too good for the chastisement of such transgressors as we are? Must the very *Devils* be sent out of *Their own place*, to be our Troublers: Must we be lash'd with *Scorpions*, fetch'd from the *Place of Torment*? Must this *Wilderness* be made a Receptacle for the *Dragons of the Wilderness*? If a *Lapland* should nourish in it vast numbers, the successors of the old *Biarmi*, who can with looks or words bewitch other people, or sell Winds to Marriners, and have their *Familiar Spirits* which they bequeath to their Children when they die, and by their Enchanted Kettle-Drums can learn things done a Thousand Leagues off; If a *Swedeland* should afford a Village, where some scores of Haggs, may not only have their Meetings with *Familiar Spirits*, but also by their Enchantments drag many scores of poor children out of their Bed-chambers, to be spoiled at those Meetings; This, were not altogether a

© Peabody Essex Museum, Salem, Massachusetts, USA/The Bridgeman Art Library

TOMPKINS HARRISON MATTESON, *THE TRIAL OF GEORGE JACOBS, 5TH AUGUST, 1692*, 1855, OIL ON CANVAS, PEABODY ESSEX MUSEUM, SALEM, MASSACHUSETTS.

In 1855, American artist Tompkins Harrison Matteson (1813–1884) painted this depiction of the courtroom trial of George Jacobs, who was accused of witchcraft by his granddaughter, found guilty, and hanged.
(See color insert, Image 14).

matter of so much wonder! But that *New-England* should this way be harassed! They are not *Chaldeans*, that *Bitter and Hasty Nation*, but they are, *Bitter and Burning Devils*; They are not *Swarthy Indians*, but they are *Sooty Devils*; that are let loose upon us. Ah, Poor *New-England*! Must the plague of *Old Ægypt* come upon thee? Whereof we read in *Psal.* 78 · 49, *He cast upon them the fierceness of his Anger, Wrath, and Indignation, and Trouble, by sending Evil Angels among them.* What, O what must next be looked for? Must that which is there next mentioned, be next encountered? *He spared not their soul from death, but gave their life over to the Pestilence.* For my part, when I consider what *Melancthon* says, in one of his Epistles, *That these Diabolical Spectacles are often Prodigies*; and when I consider, how often people have been by *Spectres* called upon, just before their Deaths; I am verily afraid, lest some wasting *Mortality* be among the things, which this Plague is the *Forerunner* of. I pray God prevent it!

(1693)

Exploring the Text

1. In the opening paragraph, Cotton Mather speaks as a Puritan minister to his congregation — or flock — telling them they are in danger. What rhetorical strategies does he use to impress on them the urgency of the situation?

2. Throughout the speech, Mather makes use of biblical references and passages as evidence. Select at least three and discuss how they support the argument he is making.

3. In this speech, Mather proceeds from a general warning that the devil has come into the community to increasingly specific and frightening allegations of the manifestations of the evil. What are they? How is each calculated to escalate the level of fear?

4. Selecting either paragraph 2 or 3, analyze how through his choice of language Mather dramatizes the battle between the forces of good and evil; note his use of specific words as well as images.

5. During the Salem Witch Trials, a key issue was the inclusion of "spectral evidence" — that is, evidence that cannot be seen. As expressed in this address, what is Mather's position on the use and usefulness of such evidence?

6. What is it that Mather claims "makes this Descent [of the Devil into the community] the more formidable" (par. 3)?

7. What is the "*wrath unto the uttermost*" (par. 5)? What is the reasoning Mather develops to support his claim?

8. How does Mather characterize "New-England" as the site of this conflict between opposing forces? What significance is there to the fact that "*New-England* should this way be harassed!" (par. 5)?

9. A "hortatory" address calls the audience to action — that is, it exhorts them. What action is Mather urging his Salem community to take, and what rhetorical strategies does he use to encourage them?

10. As a Puritan minister, Mather believed that God had chosen him for a special mission in the New World: to root out evil and establish the kingdom of God. Where in his text do you find evidence of this sense of personal destiny?

11. Look at the painting on page 247. How does it capture the fear and hysteria that Mather calls on in his speech?

JOHN HALE

Reverend John Hale (1636–1700) was a prominent clergyman associated with the Salem Witch Trials who famously reconsidered his support of the trials after his own wife was accused of witchcraft in November 1692. Although the last trial was held in May 1693, the community was left to address legal issues of compensation and the reconciliation of accusers and the accused. In addition, public confidence in authority had been eroded by the magistrates' willingness to convict on the basis of problematic evidence. Hale, a minister for over thirty years, was one of the leaders trying to bring about healing in the aftermath of the Salem Witch Trials.

from *A Modest Inquiry into the Nature of Witchcraft*

In 1697, Hale wrote *A Modest Inquiry into the Nature of Witchcraft*, a book that challenged the legal precedents and morality used by the court during the witch trials. The following excerpts are from this book, which was published in 1702, two years after his death. In "The Preface to the Christian Reader," Hale explains his decision to come forward and address the issue; in Chapter XVIII, he attempts to put the tragic events in both scriptural and historical context.

The Preface to the Christian Reader

The Holy Scriptures inform us that the Doctrine of Godliness is a great Mystery, containing the Mysteries of the Kingdom of Heaven: Mysteries which require great search for the finding out: And as the Lord hath his Mysteries to bring us to Eternal Glory; so Satan hath his Mysteries to bring us to Eternal Ruine: Mysteries not easily understood, whereby the depths of Satan are managed in hidden wayes. So the Whore of Babylon makes the Inhabitants of the Earth drunk with the Wine of her Fornication, by the Mystery of her abominations, Rev. 17. 2. And the man of Sin hath his Mystery of iniquity whereby he deceiveth men through the working of Satan in signes and lying wonders, 2 Thes. 2. 3, 7, 9.

And among Satans Mysteries of iniquity, this of Witchcraft is one of the most difficult to be searched out by the Sons of men; as appeareth by the great endeavours of Learned and Holy men to search it out, and the great differences that are found among them, in the rules laid down for the bringing to light these hidden works of darkness. So that it may seem presumption in me to undertake so difficult a Theam, and to lay down such rules as are different from the Sentiments of many Eminent writers, and from the Presidents and practices of able Lawyers; yea and from the Common Law it self.

But my Apology for this undertaking is;

1. That there hath been such a dark dispensation by the Lord, letting loose upon us the Devil, *Anno* 1691 and 1692, as we never experienced before: And thereupon apprehending and condemning persons for Witchcraft; and nextly acquitting others no less liable to such a charge; which evidently shew we were in the dark, and knew not what to do; but have gone too far on the one or other side, if not on both. Hereupon I esteemed it necessary for some person to Collect a Summary of that affair, with some animadversions[1] upon it, which might at least give some light to

---

[1]Criticisms. — Eds.

them which come after, to shun those Rocks by which we were bruised, and nar-rowly escaped Shipwrack upon. And I have waited five years for some other per-son to undertake it, who might doe it better than I can, but find none; and judge it better to do what I can, than that such a work should be left undone. Better sincerely though weakly done, then not at all, or with such a byas of prejudice as will put false glosses upon that which was managed with uprightness of heart, though there was not so great a spirit of discerning, as were to be wished in so weighty a Concernment.

2. I have been present at several Examinations and Tryals, and knew sundry of those   5
   that Suffered upon that account in former years, and in this last affair, and so have more advantages than a stranger, to give account of these Proceedings.

3. I have been from my Youth trained up in the knowledge and belief of most of those principles I here question as unsafe to be used. The first person that suffered on this account in New-England, about Fifty years since, was my Neighbour, and I heard much of what was charged upon her, and others in those times; and the reverence I bore to aged, learned and judicious persons, caused me to drink in their principles in these things, with a kind of Implicit Faith. *Quo semel est imbuta recens servabit odorem, Testa diu.*[2] A Child will not easily forsake the prin-ciples he hath been trained up in from his Cradle.

   But observing the Events of that sad Catastrophe, *Anno* 1692, I was brought to a more strict scanning of the principles I had imbibed, and by scanning, to question, and by questioning at length to reject many of them, upon the reasons shewed in the ensuing Discourse. It is an approved saying *Nihil certius, quam quod ex dubio fit certum*; No truth more certain to a man, than that which he hath for-merly doubted or denied, and is recovered from his error, by the convincing evi-dence of Scripture and reason. Yet I know and am sensible, that while we know but in part, man is apt in flying from a discovered error, to run into the contrary extream.

   Incidit in Scyllam qui vult vitare Charybdim.[3]

   The middle way is commonly the way of truth. And if any can shew me a better middle way than I have here laid down, I shall be ready to embrace it: But the con-viction must not be by vinegar or drollery, but by strength of argument.

4. I have had a deep sence of the sad consequence of mistakes in matters Capital; and their impossibility of recovering when compleated. And what grief of heart it brings to a tender conscience, to have been unwittingly encouraging of the Sufferings of the innocent. And I hope a zeal to prevent for the future such suffer-ings is pardonable, although there should be much weakness, and some errors in the pursuit thereof.

---

[2]Quote from the Roman poet Horace that reads, "The jar will long retain the odor of that with which it was once filled." — Eds.

[3]Latin. "Into Scylla falls he who tries to keep clear of Charybdis." A reference to Homer's *Odyssey*, in which Odysseus and his crew must navigate the narrow strait between Scylla (a rock) and Charybdis (a whirlpool). — Eds.

5. I observe the failings that have been on the one hand, have driven some into that which is indeed an extream on the other hand, and of dangerous consequences, *viz.* To deny any such persons to be under the New Testament, who by the Devils aid discover Secrets, or do work wonders. Therefore in the latter part of this discourse, I have taken pains to prove the Affirmative, yet with brevity, because it hath been done already by Perkins of *Witchcraft*. Glanvil his *Saducismus Triumphatus*, Pt. 1. p. 1 to 90 and Pt. 2. p. 1 to 80. Yet I would not be understood to justify all his notions in those discourses, but acknowledge he hath strongly proved the being of Witches.

6. I have special reasons moving me to bear my testimony about these matters, before I go hence and be no more; the which I have here done, and I hope with some assistance of his Spirit, to whom I commit my self and this my labour, even that God whose I am and whom I serve: Desiring his Mercy in Jesus Christ to Pardon all the Errors of his People in the day of darkness; and to enable us to fight with Satan by Spiritual Weapons, putting on the whole Armour of God.

   And tho' Satan by his Messengers may buffet Gods Children, yet there's a promise upon right *Resisting, he shall flee from them*, Jam. 4. 7. *And that all things shall work together for the good of those that Love the Lord*, Rom. 8. 28. So that I believe Gods Children shall be gainers by the assaults of Satan, which occasion'd this Discourse; which that they may, is the Prayer of, Thine in the Service of the Gospel.

Chapter XVIII

I shall conclude this Discourse with some Application of the whole.

1. We may hence see ground to fear, that there hath been a great deal of innocent blood shed in the Christian World, by proceeding upon unsafe principles, in condemning persons for Malefick Witchcraft. . . .

3. But to come nigher home, we have cause to be humbled for the mistakes and errors which have been in these Colonies, in their Proceedings against persons for this crime, above fourty years ago and downwards, upon insufficient presumptions and presidents of our Nation, whence they came. I do not say, that all those were innocent, that suffered in those times upon this account. But that such grounds were then laid down to proceed upon, which were too slender to evidence the crime they were brought to prove; and thereby a foundation laid to lead into error those that came after. May we not say in this matter, as it is, Psal. 106. 6. *We have sinned with our fathers?* And as, Lam. 5. 7. *Our fathers have sinned and are not, and we have born their iniquities?* And whether this be not one of the sins the Lord hath been many years contending with us for, is worthy our serious enquiry. If the Lord punished Israel with famine three years for a sin of misguided zeal fourty years before that, committed by the breach of a Covenant made four hundred years before that: 2 Sam. 21. 1, 2, Why may not the Lord visit upon us the misguided zeal of our Predecessors about Witchcraft above fourty years ago, even when that Generation is gathered to their Fathers.

4. But I would come yet nearer to our own times, and bewail the errors and mistakes that have been in the year 1692. In the apprehending too many we may believe were innocent, and executing of some, I fear, not to have been condemned; by following such traditions of our fathers, maxims of the Common Law, and Presidents and Principles, which now we may see weighed in the balance of the Sanctuary, are found too light. I heartily concur with that direction for our publick prayers, emitted December 17, 1696, by our General Assembly, in an order for a general Fast, *viz.* "That God would shew us what we know not, and help us wherein we have done amiss, to do so no more: And especially that whatever mistakes on either hand, have been fallen into, either by the body of this people, or any order of men, referring to the late tragedy raised among us by Satan and his Instruments, through the awful Judgment of God: He would humble us therefore, and pardon all the errors of his Servants and People, that desire to love his Name, and be attoned to his land." I am abundantly satisfyed that those who were most concerned to act and judge in those matters, did not willingly depart from the rules of righteousness. But such was the darkness of that day, the tortures and lamentations of the afflicted, and the power of former presidents, that we walked in the clouds, and could not see our way. And we have most cause to be humbled for error on that hand, which cannot be retrieved. So that we must beseech the Lord, that if any innocent blood hath been shed, in the hour of temptation, the Lord will not lay it to our charge, but be merciful to his people whom he hath redeemed, Deut. 21. 8, And that in the day when he shall visit, he will not visit this sin upon our land, but blot it out, and wash it away with the blood of Jesus Christ.

5. I would humbly propose whether it be not expedient, that some what more should be publickly done then yet hath, for clearing the good name and reputation of some that have suffered upon this account, against whom the evidence of their guilt was more slender, and the grounds for charity for them more convincing. And this (in order to our obtaining from the Lord farther reconciliation to our land,) and that none of their surviving relations, may suffer reproach upon that account. I have both read and heard of several in England, that have been executed for Capital crimes, and afterwards upon sence of an error in the process against them, have been restored in blood and honour by some publick act. . . .

9. Another extream we must beware of, is, *viz.* Because our fathers in the beginning times of this Land, did not see so far into these mysteries of iniquity, as hath been since discovered, Let us not undervalue the good foundations they laid for God and his people, and for us in Church and Civil Government. For Paul that eminent Apostle knew but in part; no wonder then, if our Fathers were imperfect men. In the purest times in Israel, there were some Clouds of ignorance over-shadowing of them. . . .

Now he that shall reject all the good in doctrine and practice, which was maintained, professed and practiced by so many Godly leaders, because of some few errors found among them, will be found to fight against God. A dwarf upon a giants shoulders, can see farther than the giant.

It was a glorious enterprize of the beginners of these Colonies, to leave their native Country to propagate the Gospel: And a very high pitch of faith, zeal, and 20 courage that carried them forth, to follow the Lord into this wilderness, into a land that was not sown. Then was New England holiness to the Lord, and all that did devour them, or attempted so to do, did offend, and evil did come upon them. And the Lord did graciously remember this kindness of their Youth, and love of their Espousals; In granting them many eminent tokens of his favour; by his presence with them in his Ordinances, for the Conversion of Souls, and edifying and comforting the hearts of his Servants: By signal answering their prayers in times of difficulty: By protecting them from their Enemies; By guiding of, and providing for them in a Desert. And the Lord will still remember this their kindness unto their Posterity, unless that by their Apostasy from the Lord, they vex his Holy Spirit, to turn to be their Enemy: And thereby cut off the Entail of his Covenant Mercies; which God forbid. *Oh that the Lord may be with us, as he was with our Fathers; and that he may not leave us, nor forsake us!*

Finis.

(1697, 1702)

Exploring the Text

1. What is the purpose of John Hale's opening paragraph? Why does he include so many quotations from the Bible?
2. In the following paragraphs, Hale details why he believes he is qualified "for this undertaking" (par. 3). What are the grounds he describes to establish his ethos with his Puritan audience?
3. Why does Hale emphasize from the outset that this discourse in the aftermath of the Salem Witch Trials must proceed "by strength of argument" (par. 8)?
4. What does Hale mean by the "misguided zeal of our Predecessors" (par. 15)? Is this description sufficiently strong for the occasion, or should he have used a more condemnatory phrase?
5. While Hale is concerned with the larger theological issues of repentance and redemption, he also recommends some very practical measures to prevent further suffering of individuals within the community. What are these?
6. What does Hale mean in this statement, "A dwarf upon a giants shoulders, can see farther than the giant" (par. 19)?
7. What was the "glorious enterprize" that Hale reminds his readers of at the end (par. 20)? Why does he raise this point near the end of his text?
8. Historians emphasize the anguish Hale felt about the witch hunt, the trials, and, most of all, the executions. Where in this text do you find evidence of his personal regret?
9. Reverend John Hale wrote this apologia not in the heat of debate or battle but as a reflection. In it he fully acknowledges the burden he and other leaders must bear for the hysteria, the division, and the executions. What rhetorical strategies does he employ in this document to promote healing within the community of Salem? Include in your analysis a discussion of his tone in this document.

Conversation

The American Jeremiad

The following selections are examples of American jeremiads — sermons, speeches, visual texts, or essays that, in the words of the scholar Sacvan Bercovitch, "unify a people by creating tension between ideal social life and its real manifestation." The traditional jeremiad presents a biblical or spiritual ideal for behavior, then describes the ways individuals and communities have fallen from those standards, and finally provides a vision for an ideal public life that will result from a return to these high standards. It is named after the biblical lamentations of the prophet Jeremiah, who prophesied the destruction of Jerusalem because the Israelites had turned their back on the Lord and were worshipping false idols. Speaking through Jeremiah, God said, "I had planted thee a noble vine, wholly a right seed: how then art thou turned into the degenerate plant of a strange vine unto me?" (Jeremiah 2:21). The American version of the jeremiad began as a rhetorical strategy of Puritan preachers looking to set high standards and high hopes in the New World, but the form has continued to find a home in American discourse because of the lofty ideals outlined in the nation's founding documents and a strongly optimistic belief in progress.

Sources

John Winthrop, from *A Modell of Christian Charity* (1630)
Jonathan Edwards, from *Sinners in the Hands of an Angry God* (1741)
Frederick Douglass, from *What, to the Slave, Is the Fourth of July?* (1852)
Robert F. Kennedy, *The Mindless Menace of Violence* (1968)
Ronald Reagan, from *Farewell Address* (1989)
Stephen H. Webb, *How Soccer Is Ruining America: A Jeremiad* (2009)
American Lung Association, *Sandwich. Snack. Arsenic.* (2011)
Barack Obama, *Tucson Memorial Speech* (2011)

from *A Modell of Christian Charity*

JOHN WINTHROP

John Winthrop (1588–1649) was governor of the Massachusetts Bay Colony, a settlement founded by a group of entrepreneurs who left Europe for opportunities in the New World. He was a Puritan, like most of the members of the group, and central to their vision was an ideal community in which all citizens would focus their lives on the word of God. Interestingly, this pursuit of a perfect society based on the teachings of the Bible resulted in tremendous secular success as well. Winthrop gave this speech on board the ship *Arabella*, on its way from England to the New World in 1630. The speech was, in some ways, a pep talk — to calm the immigrants' fears about what they would face in the New World — but it was also an exhortation to create an ideal community based on their covenant with God.

It rests now to make some application of this discourse by the present design, which gave the occasion of writing of it. Herein are four things to be propounded: first, the persons; secondly, the work; thirdly, the end; fourthly, the means.

First for the persons. We are a company professing ourselves fellow members of Christ, in which respect only though we were absent from each other many miles, and had our imployments as far distant, yet we ought to account ourselves knit together by this bond of love, and live in the exercise of it, if we would have comfort of our being in Christ. This was notorious in the practice of the Christians in former times; as is testified of the Waldenses, from the mouth of one of the adversaries *Æneas Sylvius*, "mutuo [ament] pene antequam norunt," they use to love any of their own religion even before they were acquainted with them.

Secondly for the work we have in hand. It is by a mutual consent, through a special overvaluing providence and a more than an ordinary approbation of the churches of Christ, to seek out a place of cohabitation and consortship under a due form of government both civil and ecclesiastical. In such cases as this, the care of the public must oversway all private respects, by which not only conscience but mere civil policy doth bind us. For it is a true rule that particular estates cannot subsist in the ruin of the public.

Thirdly, the end is to improve our lives to do more service to the Lord; the comfort and encrease of the body of Christ whereof we are members; that ourselves and posterity may be the better preserved from the common corruptions of this evil world, to serve the Lord and work out our salvation under the power and purity of his holy ordinances.

Fourthly, for the means whereby this must be effected. They are twofold, a conformity with the work and end we aim at. These we see are extraordinary, therefore we must not content ourselves with usual ordinary means. Whatsoever we did or ought to have done when we lived in England, the same must we do, and more also, where we go. That which the most in their churches maintain as a truth in profession only, we must bring into familiar and constant practice, as in this duty of love. We must love brotherly without dissimulation; we must love one another with a pure heart fervently. We must bear one another's burthens. We must not look only on our own things, but also on the things of our brethren, neither must we think that the Lord will bear with such failings at our hands as he doth from those among whom we have lived; and that for three reasons: 5

First, in regard of the more near bond of marriage between him and us, wherein he hath taken us to be his after a most strict and peculiar manner, which will make him the more jealous of our love and obedience. So he tells the people of Israel, "You only have I known of all the families of the earth, therefore will I punish you for your transgressions." Secondly, because the Lord will be sanctified in them that come near him. We know that there were many that corrupted the service of the Lord, some setting up altars before his own, others offering both strange fire and strange sacrifices also; yet there came no fire from heaven or other sudden judgment upon them, as did upon Nadab and Abihu, who yet we may think did not sin presumptuously. Thirdly, when God gives a special commission he looks to have it strictly observed in every article. When he gave Saul a commission to destroy Amalek, he indented with him upon certain articles, and because he failed in one of the least, and that upon a fair pretense, it lost him the kingdom which should have been his reward if he had observed his commission.

Thus stands the cause between God and us. We are entered into covenant with him for this work. We have taken out a commission, the Lord hath given us leave to draw our own articles. We have professed to enterprise these actions, upon these and those ends, we have hereupon besought him of favor and blessing. Now if the Lord shall please to hear us, and bring us in peace to the place we desire, then hath he ratified this covenant and sealed our commission, [and] will expect a strict performance of the articles contained in it. But if we shall neglect the observation of these articles which are the ends we have propounded and, dissembling with our God, shall fall to embrace this present world and prosecute our carnal intentions, seeking great things for ourselves and our posterity, the Lord will surely break out in wrath against us, be revenged of such a perjured people, and make us know the price of the breach of such a covenant.

Now the only way to avoid this shipwreck, and to provide for our posterity, is to follow the counsel of Micah, to do justly, to love mercy, to walk humbly with our God. For this end, we must be knit together in this work as one man. We must entertain each other in brotherly affection, we must be willing to abridge ourselves of our superfluities, for the supply of others' necessities. We must uphold a familiar commerce together in all meekness, gentleness, patience, and liberality. We must delight in each other, make others' conditions our own, rejoice together, mourn together, labor and suffer together, always having before our eyes our commission and community in the work, our community as members of the same body. So shall we keep the unity of the spirit in the bond of peace. The Lord will be our God, and delight to dwell among us as his own people, and will command a blessing upon us in all our ways, so that we shall see much more of his wisdom, power, goodness, and truth, than formerly we have been acquainted with. We shall find that the God of Israel is among us, when ten of us shall be able to resist a thousand of our enemies; when he shall make us a praise and glory that men shall say of succeeding plantations, "the Lord make it like that of New England." For we must consider that we shall be as a city upon a hill. The eyes of all people are upon us, so that if we shall deal falsely with our God in this work we have undertaken, and so cause him to withdraw his present help from us, we shall be made a story and a by-word through the world. We shall open the mouths of enemies to speak evil of the ways of God, and all professors for God's sake. We shall shame the faces of many of God's worthy servants, and cause their prayers to be turned into curses upon us till we be consumed out of the good land whither we are agoing.

And to shut up this discourse with that exhortation of Moses, that faithful servant of the Lord, in his last farewell to Israel, Deuteronomy 30: Beloved, there is now set before us life and good, death and evil, in that we are commanded this day to love the Lord our God, and to love one another, to walk in his ways and to keep his commandments and his ordinance and his laws, and the articles of our covenant with him, that we may live and be multiplied, and that the Lord our God may bless us in the land whither we go to possess it. But if our hearts shall turn away, so that we will not obey, but shall be seduced, and worship other gods, our pleasures and profits, and serve them; it is propounded unto us this day, we shall surely perish out of the good land whither we pass over this vast sea to possess it.

> Therefore let us choose life,
> that we and our seed
> may live by obeying his
> voice and cleaving to him,
> for he is our life and
> our prosperity.

(1630)

Questions

1. As you read, look for the words and images that Governor John Winthrop uses to create a sense of community in his audience. How does he use them to develop his vision of an ideal community? Have you run across these words and images in other sermons and public speeches? If so, explain.
2. Look carefully at the two metaphors — the shipwreck and the shining city on the hill — in paragraph 8. How does each one help the speech fit the requirements of a jeremiad?
3. What do you think Winthrop means when he says that "the care of the public must oversway all private respects" (par. 3)? What suggestions does he make for ensuring the "care of the public"?
4. What contrasts does Winthrop set up in his speech? How do they help guide his instructions for creating a colonial enterprise that balances religion and commerce?
5. How does Winthrop address what the new colonists are leaving behind? How does he focus them on the future?

from *Sinners in the Hands of an Angry God*

JONATHAN EDWARDS

Preached on July 8, 1741, in Enfield, Massachusetts (now Connecticut), this sermon was written by the Yale-educated Jonathan Edwards (1703–1758). Edwards was a Congregational minister whose education was influenced both by the open-mindedness of the Enlightenment and the strict Calvinist theology of Puritanism. "Sinners in the Hands of an Angry God" is considered typical of sermons of the Great Awakening, a movement that emphasized both the positive and the negative images of God's power, especially the belief that hell was real rather than metaphorical and that it was the fate of those who did not embrace the majesty of God.

This that you have heard is the case of everyone of you that are out of Christ. That world of misery, that lake of burning brimstone is extended abroad under you. There is the dreadful pit of the glowing flames of the wrath of God; there is hell's wide gaping mouth open; and you have nothing to stand upon, nor anything to take hold of: there is nothing between you and hell but the air; 'tis only the power and mere pleasure of God that holds you up.

You probably are not sensible of this; you find you are kept out of hell, but don't see the hand of God in it, but look at other things, as the good state of your bodily constitution, your care of your own life, and the means you use for your own preservation. But indeed these things are nothing; if God should withdraw his hand, they would avail no more to keep you from falling, than the thin air to hold up a person that is suspended in it.

Your wickedness makes you as it were heavy as lead, and to tend downwards with great weight and pressure towards hell; and if God should let you go, you would immediately sink and swiftly descend and plunge into the bottomless gulf, and your healthy constitution, and your own care and prudence, and best contrivance, and all your righteousness, would have no more influence to uphold you and keep you out of hell, than a spider's web would have to stop a falling rock. . . . There are the black clouds of God's wrath now hanging directly over your heads, full of the dreadful storm, and big with thunder; and were it not for the restraining hand of God it would immediately burst forth upon you. The sovereign pleasure of God for the present stays his rough wind; otherwise it would come with fury, and your destruction would come like a whirlwind, and you would be like the chaff of the summer threshing floor.

The wrath of God is like great waters that are dammed for the present; they increase more and more, and rise higher and higher, till an outlet is given, and the longer the stream is stopped, the more rapid and mighty is its course, when once it is let loose. 'Tis true, that judgment against your evil works has not been executed hitherto; the floods of God's vengeance have been withheld; but your guilt in the meantime is constantly increasing, and you are every day treasuring up more wrath; the waters are continually rising and waxing more and more mighty; and there is nothing but the mere pleasure of God that holds the waters back that are unwilling to be stopped, and press hard to go forward; if God should only withdraw his hand from the floodgate, it would immediately fly open, and the fiery floods of the fierceness and wrath of God would rush forth with inconceivable fury, and would come upon you with omnipotent power; and if your strength were ten thousand times greater than it is, yea, ten thousand times greater than the strength of the stoutest, sturdiest devil in hell, it would be nothing to withstand or endure it. . . .

And now you have an extraordinary opportunity, a day wherein Christ has flung the door of mercy wide open, and stands in the door calling and crying with a loud

5

voice to poor sinners; a day wherein many are flocking to him, and pressing into the kingdom of God; many are daily coming from the east, west, north and south; many that were very lately in the same miserable condition that you are in, are in now an happy state, with their hearts filled with love to him that has loved them and washed them from their sins in his own blood, and rejoicing in hope of the glory of God. How awful is it to be left behind at such a day! To see so many others feasting, while you are pining and perishing! To see so many rejoicing and singing for joy of heart, while you have cause to mourn for sorrow of heart, and howl for vexation of spirit! How can you rest one moment in such a condition? Are not your souls as precious as the souls of the people at Suffield,[4] where they are flocking from day to day to Christ?

(1741)

Questions

1. How does Jonathan Edwards personalize hell for his listeners?
2. In addition to the terrifying description of hell, what other ways does Edwards appeal to his audience to heed his warnings and turn to Christ?
3. Historians consider the sermons of Edwards and other Great Awakening revivalists to have helped sow the seeds of the American Revolution. What is it about a sermon like this that might have encouraged disassociation from English authority?
4. What evidence do you find in this sermon that Edwards knew about the newly recognized physical property of gravity, discovered by Isaac Newton?
5. The American lawyer Clarence Darrow said of Jonathan Edwards, "Nothing but a distorted or diseased mind could have produced his 'Sinners in the Hands of an Angry God.' Nothing but the puritanical, cruel generation in which he lived could have tolerated it." And yet, we continue to read it today and consider it a classic of early American literature. What does it have to offer a modern reader? What does it tell us about the important transitions in American history? How does it connect old and new ideas, such as individual freedom versus political or clerical authority, even science versus scripture?

from *What, to the Slave, Is the Fourth of July?*

Frederick Douglass

> Frederick Douglass (1818–1895), an escaped slave who became a passionate orator and crusader against slavery, gave this speech — arguably his most famous — in Rochester, New York, at a Fourth of July celebration, an event many American cities marked with readings of the Declaration of Independence. The speech was distributed later in pamphlet form and appeared in Douglass's newspaper, *Frederick Douglass Paper*, on July 9, 1852.

---

[1]The neighboring town. — Eds.

Fellow-citizens; above your national, tumultuous joy, I hear the mournful wail of millions! whose chains, heavy and grievous yesterday, are, to-day, rendered more intolerable by the jubilee shouts that reach them. If I do forget, if I do not faithfully remember those bleeding children of sorrow this day, "may my right hand forget her cunning, and may my tongue cleave to the roof of my mouth!" To forget them, to pass lightly over their wrongs, and to chime in with the popular theme, would be treason most scandalous and shocking, and would make me a reproach before God and the world. My subject, then fellow-citizens, is AMERICAN SLAVERY. I shall see, this day, and its popular characteristics, from the slave's point of view. Standing, there, identified with the American bondman, making his wrongs mine, I do not hesitate to declare, with all my soul, that the character and conduct of this nation never looked blacker to me than on this 4th of July! Whether we turn to the declarations of the past, or to the professions of the present, the conduct of the nation seems equally hideous and revolting. America is false to the past, false to the present, and solemnly binds herself to be false to the future. Standing with God and the crushed and bleeding slave on this occasion, I will, in the name of humanity which is outraged, in the name of liberty which is fettered, in the name of the constitution and the Bible, which are disregarded and trampled upon, dare to call in question and to denounce, with all the emphasis I can command, everything that serves to perpetuate slavery—the great sin and shame of America! "I will not equivocate; I will not excuse;" I will use the severest language I can command; and yet not one word shall escape me that any man, whose judgment is not blinded by prejudice, or who is not at heart a slaveholder, shall not confess to be right and just.

But I fancy I hear some one of my audience say, it is just in this circumstance that you and your brother abolitionists fail to make a favorable impression on the public mind. Would you argue more, and denounce less, would you persuade more, and rebuke less, your cause would be much more likely to succeed. But, I submit, where all is plain there is nothing to be argued. What point in the antislavery creed would you have me argue? On what branch of the subject do the people of this country need light? Must I undertake to prove that the slave is a man? That point is conceded already. Nobody doubts it. The slaveholders themselves acknowledge it in the enactment of laws for their government. They acknowledge it when they punish disobedience on the part of the slave. There are seventy-two crimes in the State of Virginia, which, if committed by a black man, (no matter how ignorant he be), subject him to the punishment of death; while only two of the same crimes will subject a white man to the like punishment. What is this but the acknowledgement that the slave is a moral, intellectual and responsible being? The manhood of the slave is conceded. It is admitted in the fact that Southern statute books are covered with enactments forbidding, under severe fines and penalties, the teaching of the slave to read or to write. When you can point to any such laws, in reference to the beasts of the field, then I may consent to argue the manhood of the slave. When the dogs in your streets, when the fowls of the air, when the cattle on your hills, when the fish of the sea, and the reptiles that crawl, shall be unable to distinguish the slave from a brute, then will I argue with you that the slave is a man!

For the present, it is enough to affirm the equal manhood of the Negro race. Is it not astonishing that, while we are ploughing, planting and reaping, using all kinds of mechanical tools, erecting houses, constructing bridges, building ships, working in metals of brass, iron, copper, silver and gold; that, while we are reading, writing and cyphering, acting as clerks, merchants and secretaries, having among us lawyers, doctors, ministers, poets, authors, editors, orators and teachers; that, while we are engaged in all manner of enterprises common to other men, digging gold in California, capturing the whale in the Pacific, feeding sheep and cattle on the hill-side, living, moving, acting, thinking, planning, living in families as husbands, wives and children, and, above all, confessing and worshipping the Christian's God, and looking hopefully for life and immortality beyond the grave, we are called upon to prove that we are men!

Would you have me argue that man is entitled to liberty? that he is the rightful owner of his own body? You have already declared it. Must I argue the wrongfulness of slavery? Is that a question for Republicans? Is it to be settled by the rules of logic and argumentation, as a matter beset with great difficulty, involving a doubtful application of the principle of justice, hard to be understood? How should I look to-day, in the presence of Americans, dividing, and subdividing a discourse, to show that men have a natural right to freedom? speaking of it relatively, and positively, negatively, and affirmatively. To do so, would be to make myself ridiculous, and to offer an insult to your understanding. There is not a man beneath the canopy of heaven, that does not know that slavery is wrong for him.

What, am I to argue that it is wrong to make men brutes, to rob them of their   5
liberty, to work them without wages, to keep them ignorant of their relations to their fellow men, to beat them with sticks, to flay their flesh with the lash, to load their limbs with irons, to hunt them with dogs, to sell them at auction, to sunder their families, to knock out their teeth, to burn their flesh, to starve them into obedience and submission to their masters? Must I argue that a system thus marked with blood, and stained with pollution, is wrong? No! I will not. I have better employments for my time and strength than such arguments would imply.

What, then, remains to be argued? Is it that slavery is not divine; that God did not establish it; that our doctors of divinity are mistaken? There is blasphemy in the thought. That which is inhuman, cannot be divine! Who can reason on such a proposition? They that can, may; I cannot. The time for such argument is past.

At a time like this, scorching irony, not convincing argument, is needed. O! had I the ability, and could I reach the nation's ear, I would, to-day, pour out a fiery stream of biting ridicule, blasting reproach, withering sarcasm, and stern rebuke. For it is not light that is needed, but fire; it is not the gentle shower, but thunder. We need the storm, the whirlwind, and the earthquake. The feeling of the nation must be quickened; the conscience of the nation must be roused; the propriety of the nation must be startled; the hypocrisy of the nation must be exposed; and its crimes against God and man must be proclaimed and denounced.

What, to the American slave, is your 4th of July? I answer: a day that reveals to him, more than all other days in the year, the gross injustice and cruelty to which he is the constant victim. To him, your celebration is a sham; your boasted liberty, an unholy license; your national greatness, swelling vanity; your sounds of rejoicing are empty and heartless; your denunciations of tyrants, brass fronted impudence; your shouts of liberty and equality, hollow mockery; your prayers and hymns, your sermons and thanksgivings, with all your religious parade, and solemnity, are, to him, mere bombast, fraud, deception, impiety, and hypocrisy — a thin veil to cover up crimes which would disgrace a nation of savages. There is not a nation on the earth guilty of practices, more shocking and bloody, than are the people of these United States, at this very hour.

Go where you may, search where you will, roam through all the monarchies and despotisms of the old world, travel through South America, search out every abuse, and when you have found the last, lay your facts by the side of the everyday practices of this nation, and you will say with me, that, for revolting barbarity and shameless hypocrisy, America reigns without a rival.

(1852)

Questions

1. How does Frederick Douglass use religious language in this speech? Find examples and explain what they add to his argument.
2. What three issues, usually used by abolitionists to denounce slavery, does Douglass examine? What conclusions does he come to? What is the tone of his conclusions?
3. In what way does this excerpt from Douglass's speech fit the definition of a jeremiad? Does it provide a standard? Does it show the ways in which the community has fallen from the standard? Does it provide a vision? Or does it adapt the traditional form of the jeremiad to serve Douglass's specific purpose? Explain your answer, using examples from the speech.
4. The audience for Douglass's speech probably shared his beliefs in regard to slavery. In what ways does the speech acknowledge that shared ground? In what ways does Douglass set himself apart from the audience?

The Mindless Menace of Violence

Robert F. Kennedy

Senator Robert F. Kennedy (1925–1968) made these remarks to the Cleveland City Club, in Cleveland, Ohio, on April 5, 1968, the day after the assassination of Dr. Martin Luther King Jr. Just hours after King had been shot, Kennedy had spoken extemporaneously at a rally in Indianapolis, Indiana, where he broke the news that King was dead. He had been warned that the police might not be able to protect him if the crowd rioted. But he reminded the audience of King's message and also spoke publicly for the first time about the assassination of his brother,

John F. Kennedy. His words had a calming effect, and the crowd left quietly. There were riots in many other parts of the country — and Robert Kennedy would himself be assassinated two months later.

This is a time of shame and sorrow. It is not a day for politics. I have saved this one opportunity to speak briefly to you about this mindless menace of violence in America which again stains our land and every one of our lives.

It is not the concern of any one race. The victims of the violence are black and white, rich and poor, young and old, famous and unknown. They are, most important of all, human beings whom other human beings loved and needed. No one — no matter where he lives or what he does — can be certain who will suffer from some senseless act of bloodshed. And yet it goes on and on.

Why? What has violence ever accomplished? What has it ever created? No martyr's cause has ever been stilled by his assassin's bullet.

No wrongs have ever been righted by riots and civil disorders. A sniper is only a coward, not a hero; and an uncontrolled, uncontrollable mob is only the voice of madness, not the voice of the people.

Whenever any American's life is taken by another American unnecessarily — 5 whether it is done in the name of the law or in the defiance of law, by one man or a gang, in cold blood or in passion, in an attack of violence or in response to violence — whenever we tear at the fabric of life which another man has painfully and clumsily woven for himself and his children, the whole nation is degraded.

"Among free men," said Abraham Lincoln, "there can be no successful appeal from the ballot to the bullet; and those who take such appeal are sure to lose their cause and pay the costs."

Yet we seemingly tolerate a rising level of violence that ignores our common humanity and our claims to civilization alike. We calmly accept newspaper reports of civilian slaughter in far off lands. We glorify killing on movie and television screens and call it entertainment. We make it easy for men of all shades of sanity to acquire weapons and ammunition they desire.

Too often we honor swagger and bluster and the wielders of force; too often we excuse those who are willing to build their own lives on the shattered dreams of others. Some Americans who preach nonviolence abroad fail to practice it here at home. Some who accuse others of inciting riots have by their own conduct invited them.

Some look for scapegoats, others look for conspiracies, but this much is clear: violence breeds violence, repression brings retaliation, and only a cleaning of our whole society can remove this sickness from our soul.

For there is another kind of violence, slower but just as deadly, destructive as 10 the shot or the bomb in the night. This is the violence of institutions; indifference and inaction and slow decay. This is the violence that afflicts the poor, that poisons relations between men because their skin has different colors. This is a slow destruction of a child by hunger, and schools without books and homes without heat in the winter.

This is the breaking of a man's spirit by denying him the chance to stand as a father and as a man among other men. And this too afflicts us all. I have not come here to propose a set of specific remedies nor is there a single set. For a broad and adequate outline we know what must be done. When you teach a man to hate and fear his brother, when you teach that he is a lesser man because of his color or his beliefs or the policies he pursues, when you teach that those who differ from you threaten your freedom or your job or your family, then you also learn to confront others not as fellow citizens but as enemies—to be met not with cooperation but with conquest, to be subjugated and mastered.

We learn, at the last, to look at our brothers as aliens, men with whom we share a city, but not a community, men bound to us in common dwelling, but not in common effort. We learn to share only a common fear—only a common desire to retreat from each other—only a common impulse to meet disagreement with force. For all this there are no final answers.

Yet we know what we must do. It is to achieve true justice among our fellow citizens. The question is now what programs we should seek to enact. The question is whether we can find in our own midst and in our own hearts that leadership of human purpose that will recognize the terrible truths of our existence.

We must admit the vanity of our false distinctions among men and learn to find our own advancement in the search for the advancement of all. We must admit in ourselves that our own children's future cannot be built on the misfortunes of others. We must recognize that this short life can neither be ennobled or enriched by hatred or revenge.

Our lives on this planet are too short and the work to be done too great to let this   15
spirit flourish any longer in our land. Of course we cannot vanish it with a program, nor with a resolution.

But we can perhaps remember—even if only for a time—that those who live with us are our brothers, that they share with us the same short moment of life, that they seek—as we do—nothing but the chance to live out their lives in purpose and happiness, winning what satisfaction and fulfillment they can.

Surely this bond of common faith, this bond of common goal, can begin to teach us something. Surely we can learn, at least, to look at those around us as fellow men and surely we can begin to work a little harder to bind up the wounds among us and to become in our hearts brothers and countrymen once again.

(1968)

Questions

1. What purposes do you think this speech served? In what ways does it serve the traditional purpose of the jeremiad, which is to restore social stability? What else might the occasion have demanded of Robert F. Kennedy?
2. What patterns can you see in the speech—parallel structures, repeated images—that helped Kennedy achieve the purposes of the speech?
3. How does Kennedy establish common ground with his audience?

4. A jeremiad has been described as a rhetorical appeal that calls for its audience to affirm rather than to question the reasons for their problems. John M. Murphy, writing about this address in *Quarterly Journal of Speech*, notes, "The [American] jeremiad deflects attention away from the possible institutional or systemic flaws and toward considerations of individual sin. Redemption is achieved through the efforts of the American people, not through a change in the system itself. . . . The jeremiad, then, serves as a rhetoric of social control." How does this speech draw a direct connection between the self and society? How does this speech encourage social control?

5. How does Kennedy connect his plea for nonviolence to his social agenda?

from *Farewell Address*

Ronald Reagan

> Ronald Reagan (1911–2004) was the fortieth president of the United States. What follows is a portion of the address he gave at the end of his second term in 1989.

There is a great tradition of warnings in Presidential farewells, and I've got one that's been on my mind for some time.

But oddly enough it starts with one of the things I'm proudest of in the past eight years: the resurgence of national pride that I called "the new patriotism." This national feeling is good, but it won't count for much, and it won't last unless it's grounded in thoughtfulness and knowledge.

An informed patriotism is what we want. And are we doing a good enough job teaching our children what America is and what she represents in the long history of the world? Those of us who are over 35 or so years of age grew up in a different America. We were taught, very directly, what it means to be an American, and we absorbed almost in the air a love of country and an appreciation of its institutions. If you didn't get these things from your family you got them from the neighborhood, from the father down the street who fought in Korea or the family who lost someone at Anzio. Or you could get a sense of patriotism from school. And if all else failed, you could get a sense of patriotism from the popular culture. The movies celebrated democratic values and implicitly reinforced the idea that America was special. TV was like that, too, through the mid-Sixties.

But now we're about to enter the Nineties, and some things have changed. Younger parents aren't sure that an unambivalent appreciation of America is the right thing to teach modern children. And as for those who create the popular culture, well-grounded patriotism is no longer the style.

Our spirit is back, but we haven't reinstitutionalized it. We've got to do a better job of getting across that America is freedom — freedom of speech, freedom of religion, freedom of enterprise — and freedom is special and rare. It's fragile; it needs protection. 5

We've got to teach history based not on what's in fashion but what's important: Why the Pilgrims came here, who Jimmy Doolittle was, and what those 30 seconds over Tokyo meant. You know, four years ago, on the 40th anniversary of D-Day, I read a letter from a young woman writing to her late father, who'd fought on Omaha Beach. Her name was Lisa Zanatta Henn, and she said, "We will always remember, we will never forget what the boys of Normandy did." Well, let's help her keep her word.

If we forget what we did, we won't know who we are. I am warning of an eradication of that — of the American memory that could result, ultimately, in an erosion of the American spirit. Let's start with some basics — more attention to American history and a greater emphasis of civic ritual. And let me offer lesson No. 1 about America: All great change in America begins at the dinner table. So tomorrow night in the kitchen I hope the talking begins. And children, if your parents haven't been teaching you what it means to be an American — let 'em know and nail 'em on it. That would be a very American thing to do.

And that's about all I have to say tonight. Except for one thing.

The past few days when I've been at that window upstairs, I've thought a bit of the shining "city upon a hill." The phrase comes from John Winthrop, who wrote it to describe the America he imagined. What he imagined was important, because he was an early Pilgrim — an early "Freedom Man." He journeyed here on what today we'd call a little wooden boat, and, like the other pilgrims, he was looking for a home that would be free.

I've spoken of the shining city all my political life, but I don't know if I ever quite   10
communicated what I saw when I said it. But in my mind, it was a tall proud city built on rocks stronger than oceans, wind swept, God blessed, and teeming with people of all kinds living in harmony and peace — a city with free ports that hummed with commerce and creativity, and if there had to be city walls, the walls had doors, and the doors were open to anyone with the will and the heart to get here.

That's how I saw it, and see it still.

And how stands the city on this winter night? More prosperous, more secure and happier than it was eight years ago. But more than that: after 200 years, two centuries, she still stands strong and true on the granite ridge, and her glow has held steady no matter what storm. And she's still a beacon, still a magnet for all who must have freedom, for all the Pilgrims from all the lost places who are hurtling through the darkness, toward home.

We've done our part. And as I "walk off into the city streets," a final word to the men and women of the Reagan Revolution — the men and women across America who for eight years did the work that brought America back:

My friends, we did it. We weren't just marking time, we made a difference. We made the city stronger — we made the city freer — and we left her in good hands.

All in all, not bad. Not bad at all.   15

And so, goodbye.

God bless you. And God bless the United States of America.

(1989)

Questions

1. How does Ronald Reagan characterize John Winthrop? Why might he have described him as an "early Pilgrim" traveling to the New World in a "little wooden boat" (par. 9)?
2. How does Reagan use Winthrop's "city upon a hill" metaphor to describe the goals of his own political career? How does Reagan answer the question, "How stands the city?" (par. 12)?
3. How would you describe Reagan's persona in this speech? How does he create that persona?
4. What aspects of Reagan's speech fit the definition of a jeremiad? What parts don't?
5. Critics have noted that the American jeremiad is essentially conservative, even as it calls for change. What aspects of Reagan's speech are conservative? What aspects encourage change?

How Soccer Is Ruining America: A Jeremiad

STEPHEN H. WEBB

> Stephen H. Webb is a professor of religion and philosophy. This essay was posted on the Web site *First Things* in 2009.

Soccer is running America into the ground, and there is very little anyone can do about it. Social critics have long observed that we live in a therapeutic society that treats young people as if they can do no wrong. Every kid is a winner, and nobody is ever left behind, no matter how many times they watch the ball going the other way. Whether the dumbing down of America or soccer came first is hard to say, but soccer is clearly an important means by which American energy, drive, and competitiveness is being undermined to the point of no return.

What other game, to put it bluntly, is so boring to watch? (Bowling and golf come to mind, but the sound of crashing pins and the sight of the well-attired strolling on perfectly kept greens are at least inherently pleasurable activities.) The linear, two-dimensional action of soccer is like the rocking of a boat but without any storm and while the boat has not even left the dock. Think of two posses pursuing their prey in opposite directions without any bullets in their guns. Soccer is the fluoridation of the American sporting scene.

For those who think I jest, let me put forth four points, which is more points than most fans will see in a week of games — and more points than most soccer players have scored since their pee-wee days.

1. Any sport that limits you to using your feet, with the occasional bang of the head, has something very wrong with it. Indeed, soccer is a liberal's dream of tragedy: It creates an egalitarian playing field by rigorously enforcing a uniform

disability. Anthropologists commonly define man according to his use of hands. We have the thumb, an opposable digit that God gave us to distinguish us from animals that walk on all fours. The thumb lets us do things like throw baseballs and fold our hands in prayer. We can even talk with our hands. Have you ever seen a deaf person trying to talk with their feet? When you are really angry and acting like an animal, you kick out with your feet. Only fools punch a wall with their hands. The Iraqi who threw his shoes at President [George W.] Bush was following his primordial instincts. Showing someone your feet, or sticking your shoes in someone's face, is the ultimate sign of disrespect. Do kids ever say, "Trick or Treat, smell my hands"? Did Jesus wash his disciples' hands at the Last Supper? No, hands are divine (they are one of the body parts most frequently attributed to God), while feet are in need of redemption. In all the portraits of God's wrath, never once is he pictured as wanting to step on us or kick us; he does not stoop that low.

2. Sporting should be about breaking kids down before you start building them up. 5 Take baseball, for example. When I was a kid, baseball was the most popular sport precisely because it was so demanding. Even its language was intimidating, with bases, bats, strikes, and outs. Striding up to the plate gave each of us a chance to act like we were starring in a Western movie, and tapping the bat to the plate gave us our first experience with inventing self-indulgent personal rituals. The boy chosen to be the pitcher was inevitably the first kid on the team to reach puberty, and he threw a hard ball right at you.

   Thus, you had to face the fear of disfigurement as well as the statistical probability of striking out. The spectacle of your failure was so public that it was like having all of your friends invited to your home to watch your dad forcing you to eat your vegetables. We also spent a lot of time in the outfield chanting, "Hey batter batter!" as if we were Buddhist monks on steroids. Our chanting was compensatory behavior, a way of making the time go by, which is surely why at soccer games today it is the parents who do all of the yelling.

3. Everyone knows that soccer is a foreign invasion, but few people know exactly what is wrong with that. More than having to do with its origin, soccer is a European sport because it is all about death and despair. Americans would never invent a sport where the better you get the less you score. Even the way most games end, in sudden death, suggests something of an old-fashioned duel. How could anyone enjoy a game where so much energy results in so little advantage, and which typically ends with a penalty kick out, as if it is the audience that needs to be put out of its misery. Shootouts are such an anticlimax to the game and are so unpredictable that the teams might as well flip a coin to see who wins — indeed, they might as well flip the coin before the game, and not play at all.

4. And then there is the question of gender. I know my daughter will kick me when she reads this, but soccer is a game for girls. Girls are too smart to waste an entire day playing baseball, and they do not have the bloodlust for football. Soccer penalizes shoving and burns countless calories, and the margins of victory are almost

always too narrow to afford any gloating. As a display of nearly death-defying stamina, soccer mimics the paradigmatic feminine experience of childbirth more than the masculine business of destroying your opponent with insurmountable power.

Let me conclude on a note of despair appropriate to my topic. There is no way to run away from soccer, if only because it is a sport all about running. It is as relentless as it is easy, and it is as tiring to play as it is tedious to watch. The real tragedy is that soccer is a foreign invasion, but it is not a plot to overthrow America. For those inclined toward paranoia, it would be easy to blame soccer's success on the political left, which, after all, worked for years to bring European decadence and despair to America. The left tried to make existentialism, Marxism, post-structuralism, and deconstructionism fashionable in order to weaken the clarity, pragmatism, and drive of American culture. What the left could not accomplish through these intellectual fads, one might suspect, they are trying to accomplish through sport.

Yet this suspicion would be mistaken. Soccer is of foreign origin, that is certainly   10
true, but its promotion and implementation are thoroughly domestic. Soccer is a self-inflicted wound. Americans have nobody to blame but themselves. Conservative suburban families, the backbone of America, have turned to soccer in droves. Baseball is too intimidating, football too brutal, and basketball takes too much time to develop the required skills. American parents in the past several decades are overworked and exhausted, but their children are overweight and neglected. Soccer is the perfect antidote to television and video games. It forces kids to run and run, and everyone can play their role, no matter how minor or irrelevant to the game. Soccer and television are the peanut butter and jelly of parenting.

I should know. I am an overworked teacher, with books to read and books to write, and before I put in a video for the kids to watch while I work in the evenings, they need to have spent some of their energy. Otherwise, they want to play with me! Last year all three of my kids were on three different soccer teams at the same time. My daughter is on a traveling team, and she is quite good. I had to sign a form that said, among other things, I would not do anything embarrassing to her or the team during the game. I told the coach I could not sign it. She was perplexed and worried. "Why not?" she asked. "Are you one of those parents who yells at their kids?" "Not at all," I replied. "I read books on the sidelines during the game, and this embarrasses my daughter to no end." That is my one way of protesting the rise of this pitiful sport. Nonetheless, I must say that my kids and I come home from a soccer game a very happy family.

(2009)

Questions

1. At what point did you know that this piece is satirical? What was the giveaway?
2. What aspects of American society is Stephen H. Webb criticizing through the lens of his jeremiad against soccer?

3. The Web site *First Things* is published by the Institute on Religion and Public Life, "an interreligious, nonpartisan research and education institute whose purpose is to advance a religiously informed public philosophy for the ordering of society." What particular part of that audience do you think Webb is addressing? Explain your answer.

4. What aspects of this piece fit the definition of a jeremiad? What aspects do not? Do you think Webb has the right to call it a jeremiad? Explain your answer.

5. Why do you think Webb ends his piece by noting that he and his kids "come home from a soccer game a very happy family"? How does that ending reinforce — or contradict — Webb's jeremiad against soccer?

Sandwich. Snack. Arsenic.

AMERICAN LUNG ASSOCIATION

The following 2011 public service announcement (PSA) is by the American Lung Association, an organization dedicated to improving lung health and preventing lung disease.

Sandwich.
Snack.
Arsenic.

A new report, *Toxic Air: The Case for Cleaning up Coal-fired Power Plants*, from the American Lung Association finds that coal-fired power plants in the U.S. expose our kids to 386,000 tons of 84 dangerous pollutants, like mercury, arsenic, hydrogen chloride and formaldehyde. Many of these pollutants trigger asthma attacks in kids.

We can put a stop to those threats. In fact, many power plants already use technology to clean up hazardous pollution before it gets in the air. It's time for the EPA to make sure all power plants do.

Then we can all breathe a little easier.

Courtesy of the American Lung Association

‡ AMERICAN LUNG ASSOCIATION.
Fighting for Air
www.LungUSA.org

Caption reads:

A new report, *Toxic Air: The Case for Cleaning up Coal-fired Power Plants*, from the American Lung Association finds that coal-fired power plants in the U.S. expose our kids to 386,000 tons of 84 dangerous pollutants, like mercury, arsenic, hydrogen chloride and formaldehyde. Many of these pollutants trigger asthma attacks in kids.

We can put a stop of those threats. In fact, many power plants already use technology to clean up hazardous pollution before it gets in the air. It's time for the EPA to make sure all power plants do.

Then we can all breathe a little easier.

(See color insert, Image 15.)

Questions

1. Consider the point of view from which you see the lunch box in this ad. Why do you think it is photographed from directly above? Why is part of it out of the frame of the photo? What does that "bird's-eye" view add? What does the cutoff suggest?
2. In what ways does the photo hark back to simpler, and possibly healthier, times? Is there anything else in the picture besides the test tube marked "POISON" that suggests or hints at hazards for children? Explain your answer.
3. Find online the report mentioned in the ad. How do you think this ad summarizes the points that the report makes? Who is the audience for the PSA? Who is probably the audience for the report?
4. How does this ad fit — or not fit — the definition of a jeremiad? Does it set a standard? Does it describe how we have fallen from the standard? Does it provide a vision to help us return to that standard? Explain your answers.

Tucson Memorial Speech

Barack Obama

On January 12, 2011, forty-fourth president of the United States Barack Obama made these remarks at the memorial service for the victims of the shooting in Tuscson, Arizona, that occurred four days earlier. Congresswoman Gabrielle Giffords was among those shot. She survived; six others did not. In the aftermath of the shooting, much national and international attention was given to the harsh political rhetoric of the United States.

To the families of those we've lost; to all who called them friends; to the students of this university, the public servants who are gathered here, the people of Tucson and the people of Arizona: I have come here tonight as an American who, like all Americans, kneels to pray with you today and will stand by you tomorrow.

There is nothing I can say that will fill the sudden hole torn in your hearts. But know this: The hopes of a nation are here tonight. We mourn with you for the fallen. We join you in your grief. And we add our faith to yours that Representative Gabrielle Giffords and the other living victims of this tragedy will pull through.

Scripture tells us:

There is a river whose streams make glad the city of God,
the holy place where the Most High dwells.
God is within her, she will not fall;
God will help her at break of day.

On Saturday morning, Gabby, her staff and many of her constituents gathered outside a supermarket to exercise their right to peaceful assembly and free speech. They were fulfilling a central tenet of the democracy envisioned by our founders —

representatives of the people answering questions to their constituents, so as to carry their concerns back to our nation's capital. Gabby called it "Congress on Your Corner" — just an updated version of government of and by and for the people.

And that quintessentially American scene, that was the scene that was shattered   5 by a gunman's bullets. And the six people who lost their lives on Saturday — they, too, represented what is best in us, what is best in America.

Judge John Roll served our legal system for nearly 40 years. A graduate of this university and a graduate of this law school, Judge Roll was recommended for the federal bench by John McCain 20 years ago, appointed by President George H. W. Bush and rose to become Arizona's chief federal judge.

His colleagues described him as the hardest-working judge within the Ninth Circuit. He was on his way back from attending Mass, as he did every day, when he decided to stop by and say hi to his representative. John is survived by his loving wife, Maureen, his three sons and his five beautiful grandchildren.

George and Dorothy Morris — "Dot" to her friends — were high school sweethearts who got married and had two daughters. They did everything together — traveling the open road in their RV, enjoying what their friends called a 50-year honeymoon. Saturday morning, they went by the Safeway to hear what their congresswoman had to say. When gunfire rang out, George, a former Marine, instinctively tried to shield his wife. Both were shot. Dot passed away.

A New Jersey native, Phyllis Schneck retired to Tucson to beat the snow. But in the summer, she would return East, where her world revolved around her three children, her seven grandchildren and 2-year-old great-granddaughter. A gifted quilter, she'd often work under a favorite tree, or sometimes she'd sew aprons with the logos of the Jets and the Giants to give out at the church where she volunteered. A Republican, she took a liking to Gabby, and wanted to get to know her better.

Dorwan and Mavy Stoddard grew up in Tucson together — about 70 years ago.   10 They moved apart and started their own respective families. But after both were widowed they found their way back here, to, as one of Mavy's daughters put it, "be boyfriend and girlfriend again."

When they weren't out on the road in their motor home, you could find them just up the road, helping folks in need at the Mountain Avenue Church of Christ. A retired construction worker, Dorwan spent his spare time fixing up the church along with his dog, Tux. His final act of selflessness was to dive on top of his wife, sacrificing his life for hers.

Everything — everything — Gabe Zimmerman did, he did with passion. But his true passion was helping people. As Gabby's outreach director, he made the cares of thousands of her constituents his own, seeing to it that seniors got the Medicare benefits that they had earned, that veterans got the medals and the care that they deserved, that government was working for ordinary folks. He died doing what he loved — talking with people and seeing how he could help. And Gabe is survived by his parents, Ross and Emily, his brother, Ben, and his fiancée, Kelly, who he planned to marry next year.

And then there is nine-year-old Christina Taylor Green. Christina was an A student; she was a dancer; she was a gymnast; she was a swimmer. She decided that she wanted to be the first woman to play in the Major Leagues, and as the only girl on her Little League team, no one put it past her.

She showed an appreciation for life uncommon for a girl her age. She'd remind her mother, "We are so blessed. We have the best life." And she'd pay those blessings back by participating in a charity that helped children who were less fortunate.

Our hearts are broken by their sudden passing. Our hearts are broken — and yet,   15
our hearts also have reason for fullness.

Our hearts are full of hope and thanks for the 13 Americans who survived the shooting, including the congresswoman many of them went to see on Saturday.

I have just come from the University Medical Center, just a mile from here, where our friend Gabby courageously fights to recover even as we speak. And I want to tell you — her husband Mark is here and he allows me to share this with you — right after we went to visit, a few minutes after we left her room and some of her colleagues in Congress were in the room, Gabby opened her eyes for the first time. Gabby opened her eyes for the first time.

Gabby opened her eyes. Gabby opened her eyes, so I can tell you she knows we are here. She knows we love her. And she knows that we are rooting for her through what is undoubtedly going to be a difficult journey. We are there for her.

Our hearts are full of thanks for that good news, and our hearts are full of gratitude for those who saved others. We are grateful to Daniel Hernandez — a volunteer in Gabby's office.

And, Daniel, I'm sorry, you may deny it, but we've decided you are a hero because   20
you ran through the chaos to minister to your boss, and tended to her wounds and helped keep her alive.

We are grateful to the men who tackled the gunman as he stopped to reload. Right over there. We are grateful for petite Patricia Maisch, who wrestled away the killer's ammunition, and undoubtedly saved some lives. And we are grateful for the doctors and nurses and first responders who worked wonders to heal those who'd been hurt. We are grateful to them.

These men and women remind us that heroism is found not only on the fields of battle. They remind us that heroism does not require special training or physical strength. Heroism is here, in the hearts of so many of our fellow citizens, all around us, just waiting to be summoned — as it was on Saturday morning. Their actions, their selflessness poses a challenge to each of us. It raises a question of what, beyond prayers and expressions of concern, is required of us going forward. How can we honor the fallen? How can we be true to their memory?

You see, when a tragedy like this strikes, it is part of our nature to demand explanations — to try to impose some order on the chaos and make sense out of that which seems senseless. Already we've seen a national conversation commence, not only about the motivations behind these killings, but about everything from the merits of gun safety laws to the adequacy of our mental health system. And much of this process, of debating what might be done to prevent such tragedies in the future, is an essential ingredient in our exercise of self-government.

But at a time when our discourse has become so sharply polarized — at a time when we are far too eager to lay the blame for all that ails the world at the feet of those who happen to think differently than we do — it's important for us to pause for a moment and make sure that we're talking with each other in a way that heals, not in a way that wounds.

Scripture tells us that there is evil in the world, and that terrible things happen   25 for reasons that defy human understanding. In the words of Job, "When I looked for light, then came darkness." Bad things happen, and we have to guard against simple explanations in the aftermath.

For the truth is none of us can know exactly what triggered this vicious attack. None of us can know with any certainty what might have stopped these shots from being fired, or what thoughts lurked in the inner recesses of a violent man's mind. Yes, we have to examine all the facts behind this tragedy. We cannot and will not be passive in the face of such violence. We should be willing to challenge old assumptions in order to lessen the prospects of such violence in the future. But what we cannot do is use this tragedy as one more occasion to turn on each other. That we cannot do. That we cannot do.

As we discuss these issues, let each of us do so with a good dose of humility. Rather than pointing fingers or assigning blame, let's use this occasion to expand our moral imaginations, to listen to each other more carefully, to sharpen our instincts for empathy and remind ourselves of all the ways that our hopes and dreams are bound together.

After all, that's what most of us do when we lose somebody in our family — especially if the loss is unexpected. We're shaken out of our routines. We're forced to look inward. We reflect on the past: Did we spend enough time with an aging parent, we wonder. Did we express our gratitude for all the sacrifices that they made for us? Did we tell a spouse just how desperately we loved them, not just once in a while but every single day?

So sudden loss causes us to look backward — but it also forces us to look forward; to reflect on the present and the future, on the manner in which we live our lives and nurture our relationships with those who are still with us.

We may ask ourselves if we've shown enough kindness and generosity and com-   30 passion to the people in our lives. Perhaps we question whether we're doing right by our children, or our community, whether our priorities are in order.

We recognize our own mortality, and we are reminded that in the fleeting time we have on this Earth, what matters is not wealth, or status, or power, or fame — but rather, how well we have loved and what small part we have played in making the lives of other people better.

And that process — that process of reflection, of making sure we align our values with our actions — that, I believe, is what a tragedy like this requires.

For those who were harmed, those who were killed — they are part of our family, an American family 300 million strong. We may not have known them personally, but surely we see ourselves in them. In George and Dot, in Dorwan and Mavy, we sense the abiding love we have for our own husbands, our own wives, our own life partners. Phyllis — she's our mom or our grandma; Gabe our brother or son. In Judge Roll, we recognize not only a man who prized his family and doing his job well, but also a man who embodied America's fidelity to the law.

And in Gabby — in Gabby, we see a reflection of our public-spiritedness; that desire to participate in that sometimes frustrating, sometimes contentious, but always necessary and never-ending process to form a more perfect union.

And in Christina — in Christina we see all of our children. So curious, so trusting,   35
so energetic, so full of magic. So deserving of our love. And so deserving of our good example.

If this tragedy prompts reflection and debate — as it should — let's make sure it's worthy of those we have lost. Let's make sure it's not on the usual plane of politics and point-scoring and pettiness that drifts away in the next news cycle.

The loss of these wonderful people should make every one of us strive to be better. To be better in our private lives, to be better friends and neighbors and coworkers and parents. And if, as has been discussed in recent days, their death helps usher in more civility in our public discourse, let us remember it is not because a simple lack of civility caused this tragedy — it did not — but rather because only a more civil and honest public discourse can help us face up to the challenges of our nation in a way that would make them proud.

We should be civil because we want to live up to the example of public servants like John Roll and Gabby Giffords, who knew first and foremost that we are all Americans, and that we can question each other's ideas without questioning each other's love of country and that our task, working together, is to constantly widen the circle of our concern so that we bequeath the American Dream to future generations.

They believed — they believed, and I believe that we can be better. Those who died here, those who saved life here — they help me believe. We may not be able to stop all evil in the world, but I know that how we treat one another, that's entirely up to us.

And I believe that for all our imperfections, we are full of decency and goodness,   40
and that the forces that divide us are not as strong as those that unite us.

That's what I believe, in part because that's what a child like Christina Taylor Green believed.

Imagine — imagine for a moment, here was a young girl who was just becoming aware of our democracy; just beginning to understand the obligations of citizenship; just starting to glimpse the fact that some day she, too, might play a part in shaping her nation's future. She had been elected to her student council. She saw public service as something exciting and hopeful. She was off to meet her congresswoman, someone she was sure was good and important and might be a role model. She saw all this through the eyes of a child, undimmed by the cynicism or vitriol that we adults all too often just take for granted.

I want to live up to her expectations. I want our democracy to be as good as Christina imagined it. I want America to be as good as she imagined it. All of us — we should do everything we can to make sure this country lives up to our children's expectations.

As has already been mentioned, Christina was given to us on September 11th, 2001, one of 50 babies born that day to be pictured in a book called "Faces of Hope." On either side of her photo in that book were simple wishes for a child's life. "I hope you help those in need," read one. "I hope you know all the words to the National Anthem and sing it with your hand over your heart." "I hope you jump in rain puddles."

If there are rain puddles in Heaven, Christina is jumping in them today. And here   45
on this Earth — here on this Earth, we place our hands over our hearts, and we commit ourselves as Americans to forging a country that is forever worthy of her gentle, happy spirit.

May God bless and keep those we've lost in restful and eternal peace. May He love and watch over the survivors. And may He bless the United States of America.

(2011)

Questions

1. How does Barack Obama's speech consider the occasion? What aspects of the speech make it uniquely a memorial speech?
2. What is the purpose of the minibiographies of those who died in the shooting? How do they set the tone for Obama's speech?
3. Obama says that some think the shooting may "usher in more civility in our public discourse" (par. 37). How does he enlarge on that idea? Why does he believe it is so important? How is it connected to what he believes we must do going forward?
4. Some people have criticized this speech as being too sentimental or too centrist. They believe Obama's speech on this occasion should have been a stronger call for action. Do you agree or disagree? Explain your answer.
5. Do you think this speech qualifies as a jeremiad? In what ways does or doesn't it?

Making Connections

1. John Winthrop's "A Modell of Christian Charity" (p. 254) and Jonathan Edwards's "Sinners in the Hands of an Angry God" (p. 257) are both considered masterpieces of early American literature and are often presented together even though about a hundred years separates their creation. What do they have in common? What do you see as the greatest difference between them? What does that difference suggest about the religious and spiritual life of pre–Revolutionary War Americans?
2. Robert F. Kennedy's "The Mindless Menace of Violence" speech (p. 262) and Barack Obama's Tucson memorial speech (p. 271) are both responses to violence. How is each one's response and solution similar? How are they different?

3. According to *New York Times* essayist Wen Stephenson, a jeremiad should be "simultaneously lamenting a declension and celebrating a national dream." What declension and national dream do Kennedy, Ronald Reagan (p. 265) and Obama lament and celebrate?

4. In what ways is Obama's Tucson memorial speech similar to Winthrop's "A Modell of Christian Charity"? Look carefully at the ways each evokes the idea of faith in American ideals.

5. Do you think Stephen H. Webb's "How Soccer Is Ruining America: A Jeremiad" (p. 267) is closer in its intent and language to Reagan's farewell address or to Kennedy's "The Mindless Menace of Violence"? Explain your answer. Be sure to consider occasion and speaker in your response.

6. David Howard Pitney, in his book *The Afro-American Jeremiad*, defines the black jeremiad as "both radical and conservative." In comparing it to the traditional American jeremiad, he notes that "the jeremiad typically voiced by national black leaders seems consistently . . . more searching in examining American social faults and bolder in prescribing reforms than its usual white counterparts." Contrast the excerpt from Frederick Douglass's Fourth of July speech (p. 259) to another speech in this Conversation, noting the differences between a traditional American jeremiad and what Pitney calls an Afro-American jeremiad.

Entering the Conversation

As you respond to the following prompts, support your position with appropriate evidence, including at least three sources in this Conversation on the American jeremiad, unless otherwise indicated.

1. Write an essay in which you assess the effectiveness of the jeremiads in this Conversation. You might begin by discussing the effectiveness of jeremiads in general. In what ways can they be tools that encourage civility, engagement, and personal growth?

2. Write an essay in which you examine the rhetorical moves that the jeremiads in this Conversation share.

3. In his essay "With God on His Side," Gary Wills notes that the "dynamics of the jeremiad move from rebuke to reform." Write an essay in which you trace and analyze that path in at least three of the pieces included here. Be sure to look for other patterns that connect (or separate) the speeches.

4. Michael Tomasky, writing in *American Prospect*, says that the jeremiad is effective when it is based not on religious faith but on "faith in America and its potential to do good." Conversely, American historian George McKenna suggests that it

works when it "shock[s] the congregation into recognizing the enormity of their sin . . . but also . . . remind[s] them that God chastens those he loves." What do you think? Is the nonreligious jeremiad as powerful as the jeremiad that evokes God? Write an essay in which you examine that question.

5. Defend, challenge, or qualify the assertion that the American jeremiad remains a central component to the rhetoric of public life.

6. It has been argued that the "city upon the hill" of Winthrop's speech given on the *Arabella* was the beginning of America's "corporate identity" (as Sacvan Bercovitch calls it): its view of itself as separate and distinct from human history. Find other examples, either explicit or implicit, in modern public discourse of the idea of America as a city on a hill. In what ways do they argue for American exceptionalism? Do they have other purposes as well? How do they express them? Write a roundtable discussion that includes Winthrop and Reagan from this Conversation along with at least two other writers who have alluded to the city on the hill.

7. In his essay "American Jeremiad: A Manifesto," Wen Stephenson suggests that *The Great Gatsby*, Thoreau's *Walden*, the lyrics of Bob Dylan, and poetry by the Beats are all examples of jeremiads. Choose one of these works or another work that you think fills the qualifications of a jeremiad and write an essay explaining why. Refer to at least three of the examples in this Conversation to support your analysis.

Conversation

The Columbus Day Controversy

In five thousand years of recorded history, scarcely another figure has ignited as much controversy. . . . Christopher Columbus, rediscoverer of America, was a visionary explorer. He was a harbinger of genocide. He was a Christianizing messiah. He was a pitiless slave master. He was a lionhearted seaman, a rapacious plunderer, a masterly navigator, a Janus-faced schemer, a liberator of oppressed tribes, a delusional megalomaniac.   — IAN W. TOLL

So begins a review of a 2011 biography of Christopher Columbus (1451–1506), who set out for India under the patronage of King Ferdinand and Queen Isabella of Spain. Believing he had reached the East Indies, Columbus claimed islands in the Caribbean for Spain; he made four voyages between 1492 and 1498, exploring Caribbean islands and areas of Central and South America. A heroic icon to many in the United States, Columbus is commemorated with a national holiday. While his explorations were indisputably a turning point in European expansion and, many argue, the start of a new global era, several centuries of scholarship have revealed Columbus as a complex and controversial figure whose accomplishments have been oversimplified, possibly even fictionalized, but certainly glorified. The following Conversation includes texts that comment on the reality and image of Columbus and present a range of perspectives on the meaning and appropriateness of the national holiday that honors his legacy.

Sources

Christopher Columbus, from *Journal of the First Voyage to America* (1492)
King Ferdinand of Spain, *The Requierimiento* (1513)
John Vanderlyn, *Landing of Columbus* (1847)
Walt Whitman, *Prayer of Columbus* (1874)
Jack Weatherford, *Examining the Reputation of Christopher Columbus* (1989)
Michael S. Berliner, *The Christopher Columbus Controversy* (1991)
National Public Radio, *Wilma Mankiller Reflects on Columbus Day* (2008)
William J. Connell, *What Columbus Day Really Means* (2010)
Laurence Bergreen, from *Columbus: The Four Voyages* (2011)

from *Journal of the First Voyage to America*

CHRISTOPHER COLUMBUS

> Christopher Columbus kept a record of his first seven-month voyage to the New World, recording details of navigation as well as perceptions of the people and landscapes he encountered. When he returned to Spain, he presented it to the king and queen as a gift.
>
> After the original journal in Columbus's handwriting disappeared, a priest transcribed, summarized, and occasionally quoted from the copy in the 1530s. The copy subsequently vanished, and what remains is the priest's manuscript. Thus, the shifts between first and third person in the remaining document reflect direct quotations from Columbus, along with occasional paraphrases.

Thursday, 11 October

... What follows are the very words of the Admiral [Christopher Columbus] in his book about his first voyage to, and discovery of, these Indies. I, he says, in order that they would be friendly to us — because I recognized that they were people who would be better freed [from error] and converted to our Holy Faith by love than by force — to some of them I gave red caps, and glass beads which they put on their chests, and many other things of small value, in which they took so much pleasure and became so much our friends that it was a marvel. Later they came swimming to the ships' launches where we were and brought us parrots and cotton thread in balls and javelins and many other things, and they traded them to us for other things which we gave them, such as small glass beads and bells. In sum, they took everything and gave of what they had very willingly. But it seemed to me that they were a people very poor in everything. All of them go around as naked as their mothers bore them; and the women also, although I did not see more than one quite young girl. And all those that I saw were young people, for none did I see of more than 30 years of age. They are very well formed, with handsome bodies and good faces. Their hair [is] coarse — almost like the tail of a horse — and short. They wear their hair down over their eyebrows except for a little in the back which they wear long and never cut. Some of them paint themselves with black, and they are of the color of the Canarians, neither black nor white; and some of them paint themselves with white, and some of them with red, and some of them with whatever they find. And some of them paint their faces, and some of them the whole body, and some of them only the eyes, and some of them only the nose. They do not carry arms nor are they acquainted with them, because I showed them swords and they took them by the edge and through ignorance cut themselves. They have no iron. Their javelins are shafts without iron and some of them have at the end a fish tooth and others of other things. All of them alike are of good-sized stature and carry themselves well. I saw some who had marks of wounds on their bodies and I made signs to them asking what they were; and they showed me how people from other islands nearby came there and tried to take them, and how they defended themselves; and I believed and believe that they come here from tierra firme to take them captive. They should be good and intelligent servants, for I see that they say very quickly everything that is said to them; and I believe that they would become Christians very easily, for it seemed to me that they had no religion. Our Lord pleasing, at the time of my departure I will take six of them from here to Your Highnesses in order that they may learn to speak. No animal of any kind did I see on this island except parrots. All are the Admiral's words.

Saturday, 13 October

As soon as it dawned, many of these people came to the beach — all young as I have said, and all of good stature — very handsome people, with hair not curly but straight and coarse, like horsehair; and all of them very wide in the forehead and head, more so than any other race that I have seen so far. And their eyes are very handsome and not small; and none of them are black, but of the color of the Canary Islanders. . . . All alike have straight legs and no belly but are very well formed. They came to the ship with dugouts that are made from the trunk of one tree, like a long boat, and all of one piece, and worked marvelously in the fashion of the land, and so big that in some of them 40 and 45 men came. And others smaller, down to some in which came one man alone. They row with a paddle like that of a baker and go marvelously. And if it capsizes on them they then throw themselves in the water, and they right and empty it with calabashes that they carry. They brought balls of spun cotton and parrots and javelins and other little things that it would be tiresome to write down, and they gave everything for anything that was given to them. I was attentive and labored to find out if there was any gold; and I saw that some of them wore a little piece hung in a hole that they have in their noses. And by signs I was able to understand that, going to the south or rounding the island to the south, there was there a king who had large vessels of it and had very much gold. I strove to get them to go there and later saw that they had no intention of going. I decided to wait until the afternoon of the morrow and then depart for the southwest, for, as many of them showed me, they said there was land to the south and to the southwest and to the northwest and that these people from the northwest came to fight them many times. And so I will go to the southwest to seek gold and precious stones. . . . And these people are very gentle, and because of their desire to have some of our things, and believing that nothing will be given to them without their giving something, and not having anything, they take what they can and then throw themselves into the water to swim. But everything they have they give for anything given to them, for they traded even for pieces of bowls and broken glass cups. . . . And also the gold that they wear hung in their noses originates here; but in order not to lose time I want to go to see if I can find the island of Cipango [Japan]. Now, since night had come, all the Indians went ashore in their dugouts.

Sunday, 14 October

As soon as it dawned I ordered the ship's boat and the launches of the caravels made ready and went north-northeast along the island in order to see what there was in the other part, which was the eastern part. And also to see the villages, and I soon saw two or three, as well as people, who all came to the beach calling to us and giving thanks to God. Some of them brought us water; others, other things to eat; others, when they saw that I did not care to go ashore, threw themselves into the sea swimming and came to us, and we understood that they were asking us if we had come from the heavens. And one old man got into the ship's boat, and others in loud voices called to all the men and women: Come see the men who came from the heavens. Bring them something to eat and drink. Many men came, and many women, each one with something, giving thanks to God, throwing themselves on the ground; and they raised their hands to heaven, and afterward they called to us in loud voices to come ashore. . . . [T]hese people are very naive about weapons, as Your Highnesses will see from the seven that I caused to be taken in order to carry them away to you and to learn our language and to return them. Except that, whenever Your Highnesses may command, all of them can be taken to Castile or held captive in this same island; because with 50 men all of them could be held in subjection and can be made to do whatever one might wish. . . . I . . . returned to the ship and set sail, and I saw so many islands that I did not know how to decide which one I would go to first. And those men whom I had taken told me by signs that they were so very many that they were numberless. . . .

Tuesday and Wednesday, 16 October

. . . I came to a village where I anchored and to which had come that man whom I found mid-sea yesterday in that dugout. He had given so many good reports about us that during the whole night there was no lack of dugouts alongside the ship, to which they brought us water and of what they had. I ordered something given to each one, that is to say ten or twelve little glass beads on a thread, and some brass jingles of the sort that in Castile are worth a maravedi[1] each, and some metal lace-ends, all of which they considered of the greatest excellence. And also I ordered them given food, in order that they might eat when they came to the ship, and molasses. And later . . . I sent the ship's boat to shore for water. And the natives very willingly showed my people where the water was, and they themselves brought the filled barrels to the boat and delighted in pleasing us. This island is exceedingly large and I have decided to sail around it, because according to my understanding, on or near it there is a gold mine. . . . These people are like those of the . . . [other] islands in speech and customs except that these now appear somewhat more civilized and given to commerce and more astute. Because I see that they have brought cotton here to the ship and other little things for which they know better how to bargain payment than the others did. And in this island I even saw cotton cloths made like small cloaks, and the people are more intelligent, and the women wear in front of their bodies a little thing of cotton that scarcely covers their genitals. . . . I do not detect in them any religion and I believe that they would become Christians very quickly because they are of very good understanding. . . .

Monday, 22 October

All this night and today I stayed waiting [to see] if the king of this place or other persons would bring gold or something else of substance; and there came many of these people, like the others of the other islands, naked and painted, some of them with white, some with red, some with black, and so on in many fashions. They brought javelins and balls of cotton to barter, which they traded here with some sailors for pieces of broken glass cups and for pieces of clay bowls. Some of them were wearing pieces of gold hanging from their noses, and they willingly gave it for a bell of the sort [put] on the foot of a sparrow hawk and for small glass beads; but it is so little that it is nothing. For it is true that any little thing given to them, as well as our coming, they considered great marvels; and they believed that we had come from the heavens.

Friday, 15 March

Yesterday, after sunset, she went on her course with little wind, and at sunrise she was off Saltes. At noon, with the tide rising, they crossed the bar of Saltes, and reached the port which they had left on the 3rd of August of the year before.[2] The Admiral says that so ends this journal, unless it becomes necessary to go to Barcelona by sea, having received news that their Highnesses are in that city, to give an account of all his voyage

---

[1]Gold coin. — eds.
[2]Having been absent 225 days.

which our Lord had permitted him to make, and saw fit to set forth in him. For, assuredly, he held with a firm and strong knowledge that his high Majesty made all things good, and that all is good except sin. Nor can he value or think of anything being done without His consent. "I know respecting this voyage," says the Admiral, "that he has miraculously shown his will, as may be seen from this journal, setting forth the numerous miracles that have been displayed in the voyage, and in me who was so long at the court of your Highnesses, working in opposition to and against the opinions of so many chief persons of your household, who were all against me, looking upon this enterprise as folly. But I hope, in our Lord, that it will be a great benefit to Christianity, for so it has ever appeared." These are the final words of the Admiral Don Cristoval Colon respecting his first voyage to the Indies and their discovery.

(1492)

Questions

1. Christopher Columbus carefully recounts his observations of the New World, describing a people and place that others would be unfamiliar with. Where does he report objectively and where does he draw value judgments? Selecting one passage, analyze the different types of descriptions.

2. What led Columbus to conclude that the native population was "asking us if we had come from the heavens" (par. 3)?

3. What are some of the details that Columbus cites to show, intentionally or unintentionally, that the natives are inferior to the Europeans? Consider the motives he ascribes to them in specific instances.

4. Overall, how does Columbus characterize the indigenous population? Does his opinion change as the days go by? How do you reconcile, for instance, his conclusion that they are "a people very poor in everything" (par. 1), yet they are "somewhat more civilized and given to commerce and more astute" (par. 4) than other islanders?

5. Following is an excerpt from a formal letter that Columbus wrote to the secretary to the royal court of Spain, which he intended to be read by the king and queen. He reports similar information and events as he does in the October entries of his journal, yet there are differences. What are they? How do these differences reflect his appeal to a specific audience with the intent of gaining continued support for his journeys?

> They do not hold any creed nor are they idolaters; but they all believe that power and good are in the heavens and were very firmly convinced that I, with these ships and men, came from the heavens, and in this belief they everywhere received me after they had mastered their fear. This belief is not the result of ignorance, for they are, on the contrary, of a very acute intelligence and they are men who navigate all those seas, so that it is amazing how good an account they give of everything. It is because they have never seen people clothed or ships of such a kind.

As soon as I arrived in the Indies, in the first island which I found, I took some of the natives by force, in order that they might learn and might give me information of whatever there is in these parts. And so it was that they soon understood us, and we them, either by speech or by signs, and they have been very serviceable. At present, those I bring with me are still of the opinion that I come from Heaven, for all the intercourse which they have had with me. They were the first to announce this wherever I went, and the others went running from house to house, and to the neighbouring towns, with loud cries of, "Come! Come! See the men from Heaven!" So all came, men and women alike, when their minds were set at rest concerning us, not one, small or great, remaining behind, and they all brought something to eat and drink, which they gave with extraordinary affection. . . .

In all these islands, I saw no great diversity in the appearance of the people or in their manners and language. On the contrary, they all understand one another, which is a very curious thing, on account of which I hope that their Highnesses will determine upon their conversion to our holy faith, towards which they are very inclined.

The Requierimiento

KING FERDINAND OF SPAIN

The Requierimiento is a written document that "required" or "demanded" that the local populations of the Americas accept Spanish rule and Christianity. This document was supposed to be read, in Spanish, to indigenous populations before any act of conquest. Its legal and moral authority was debated and criticized by many, including clerical missionaries, and it was abolished in 1556.

On the part of the King, Don Fernando, and of Doña Juana, his daughter, Queen of Castile and León, subduers of the barbarous nations, we their servants notify and make known to you, as best we can, that the Lord our God, living and eternal, created the heaven and the earth, and one man and one woman, of whom you and we, and all the men of the world, were and are all descendants, and all those who come after us.

Of all these nations God our Lord gave charge to one man, called St. Peter, that he should be lord and superior of all the men in the world, that all should obey him, and that he should be the head of the whole human race, wherever men should live, and under whatever law, sect, or belief they should be; and he gave him the world for his kingdom and jurisdiction.

One of these pontiffs, who succeeded St. Peter as lord of the world in the dignity and seat which I have before mentioned, made donation of these isles and Terrafirma to the aforesaid King and Queen and to their successors, our lords, with all that there are in these territories,

Wherefore, as best we can, we ask and require you that you consider what we have said to you, and that you take the time that shall be necessary to understand and deliberate upon it, and that you acknowledge the Church as the ruler and superior of the whole world,

But if you do not do this, and maliciously make delay in it, I certify to you that, with the help of God, we shall powerfully enter into your country, and shall make war against you in all ways and manners that we can, and shall subject you to the yoke and obedience of the Church and of their highnesses; we shall take you, and your wives, and your children, and shall make slaves of them, and as such shall sell and dispose of them as their highnesses may command; and we shall take away your goods, and shall do you all the mischief and damage that we can, as to vassals who do not obey, and refuse to receive their lord, and resist and contradict him: and we protest that the deaths and losses which shall accrue from this are your fault, and not that of their highnesses, or ours, nor of these cavaliers who come with us.

(1513)

Questions

1. Keeping in mind that this document is a translation from the original Spanish, how is the Catholic Church and its authority characterized? Cite specific language choices.
2. What are the terms that the Requierimiento offers to the indigenous populations if they "acknowledge the Church as the ruler and superior of the whole world" (par. 4) and thus accept the authority of the pope and the king and queen of Spain as his surrogates?
3. What are the promised consequences if the indigenous populations do not accept this authority?
4. This document may be viewed as a series of claims, assumptions, and conclusions. Outline the logical structure of the argument. As you do this, remember the distinction between logical validity and truth.

Landing of Columbus

JOHN VANDERLYN

In 1836, Congress commissioned American neoclassicist painter John Vanderlyn (1775–1852) to paint the *Landing of Columbus* for the Capitol rotunda, where it was installed in 1847. The painting depicts Christopher Columbus and members of his crew, newly landed from his flagship *Santa Maria*, on a beach in the West Indies on October 12, 1492.

Architect of the Capitol

JOHN VANDERLYN, *LANDING OF COLUMBUS*, 1847, OIL ON CANVAS, 12' × 18' U.S. CAPITOL ROTUNDA, WASHINGTON, D.C.
(See color insert, Image 16.)

Questions

1. What details — such as composition, color, demeanor, action — give this portrayal of Columbus its heroic qualities? What details suggest a triumphant conquest?
2. What symbolic elements do you note in the painting? Consider the royal banner of Aragon and Castile, which Columbus raises in his left hand, along with other symbols of church and state.
3. Where and how are the native West Indians positioned in the painting? How are they depicted?
4. Based on this painting alone, complete one of these statements: "Columbus's landing in the New World was a moment of _____."
   (or) "Columbus's landing in the West Indies heralded _____."
   Explain your statement, referring to specific elements in the painting to support your position.
5. Analyze the painting rhetorically. As part of your discussion, consider that the painting was commissioned for a specific place and time, make note of who the primary and secondary audiences were, and review the historical context of the 1830s.

Prayer of Columbus

WALT WHITMAN

American poet Walt Whitman (1819–1892) wrote "Prayer of Columbus" near the end of his life. Richard Wilbur, himself a poet and the editor of a collection of Whitman's poetry, wrote: "The figure of Columbus is one that possessed the imagination of Whitman in his later years. He identified himself with that other discoverer of America who was, like him, neglected in his old age. . . . [The] poem was written in 1873–74, in the midst of despair." Whitman included with the poem this introductory note: "It was near the close of his indomitable and pious life . . . when nearly seventy years of age — that Columbus, to save his two remaining ships from foundering in the Caribbean Sea in a terrible storm, had to run them ashore . . . he was taken very sick . . . his men revolted, and death seem'd daily imminent; though he was eventually rescued, and sent home to Spain to die, unrecognized, neglected and in want. . . ."

A batter'd, wreck'd old man,
Thrown on this savage shore, far, far from home,
Pent by the sea and dark rebellious brows, twelve dreary months,
Sore, stiff with many toils, sicken'd and nigh to death,
I take my way along the island's edge,   5
Venting a heavy heart.

I am too full of woe!
Haply I may not live another day;
I cannot rest O God, I cannot eat or drink or sleep,
Till I put forth myself, my prayer, once more to Thee,   10
Breathe, bathe myself once more in Thee, commune with Thee,
Report myself once more to Thee.

Thou knowest my years entire, my life,
My long and crowded life of active work, not adoration merely;
Thou knowest the prayers and vigils of my youth,   15
Thou knowest my manhood's solemn and visionary meditations,
Thou knowest how before I commenced I devoted all to come to Thee,
Thou knowest I have in age ratified all those vows and strictly kept them,
Thou knowest I have not once lost nor faith nor ecstasy in Thee,
In shackles, prison'd, in disgrace, repining not,   20
Accepting all from Thee, as duly come from Thee.

All my emprises[1] have been fill'd with Thee,
My speculations, plans, begun and carried on in thoughts of Thee,

---

[1]Adventurous enterprise. — Eds.

Sailing the deep or journeying the land for Thee;
Intentions, purports, aspirations mine, leaving results to Thee.   25

O I am sure they really came from Thee,
The urge, the ardor, the unconquerable will,
The potent, felt, interior command, stronger than words,
A message from the Heavens whispering to me even in sleep,
These sped me on.   30

By me and these the work so far accomplish'd,
By me earth's elder cloy'd and stifled lands uncloy'd, unloos'd,
By me the hemispheres rounded and tied, the unknown to the known.

The end I know not, it is all in Thee,
Or small or great I know not — haply what broad fields, what lands,   35
Haply the brutish measureless human undergrowth I know,
Transplanted there may rise to stature, knowledge worthy Thee,
Haply the swords I know may there indeed be turn'd to reaping-tools,
Haply the lifeless cross I know, Europe's dead cross, may bud and
    blossom there.

One effort more, my altar this bleak sand;   40
That Thou O God my life hast lighted,
With ray of light, steady, ineffable, vouchsafed of Thee,
Light rare untellable, lighting the very light,
Beyond all signs, descriptions, languages;
For that O God, be it my latest word, here on my knees,   45
Old, poor, and paralyzed, I thank Thee.

My terminus near,
The clouds already closing in upon me,
The voyage balk'd, the course disputed, lost,
I yield my ships to Thee.   50

My hands, my limbs grow nerveless,
My brain feels rack'd, bewilder'd,
Let the old timbers part, I will not part,
I will cling fast to Thee, O God, though the waves buffet me,
Thee, Thee at least I know.   55

Is it the prophet's thought I speak, or am I raving?
What do I know of life? what of myself?
I know not even my own work past or present,
Dim ever-shifting guesses of it spread before me,

Of newer better worlds, their mighty parturition,[2]   60
Mocking, perplexing me.

And these things I see suddenly, what mean they?
As if some miracle, some hand divine unseal'd my eyes,
Shadowy vast shapes smile through the air and sky,
And on the distant waves sail countless ships,   65
And anthems in new tongues I hear saluting me.

(1874)

Questions

1. The poem is presented as a prayer that Christopher Columbus makes to his God. What does he pray for?
2. In lines 31–39, what does the speaker mean when he says, "By me and these the work so far accomplish'd . . . blossom there"? What is "Europe's dead cross"?
3. Why does Walt Whitman have Columbus characterize his "own work past or present" (l. 58) as "Mocking, perplexing" (l. 61) him?
4. What are the "anthems in new tongues I hear saluting me" in the final line?
5. Overall, how does Whitman characterize Columbus and his life's work?
6. In 1995, when the Washington, D.C., Metropolitan Area Transit Authority unveiled a large wall sculpture in a subway station honoring the memory of Columbus, the program notes described this poem as celebrating "the faith and piety" of Columbus. Explain why you agree or disagree with this interpretation.

Examining the Reputation of Christopher Columbus

Jack Weatherford

> This article appeared in the *Baltimore Evening News* in 1989. Jack Weatherford, an anthropologist at Macalaster College, is the author of *Indian Givers: How the Indians of the Americas Transformed the World* and *Native Roots: How Indians Enriched America.*

Christopher Columbus' reputation has not survived the scrutiny of history, and today we know that he was no more the discoverer of America than Pocahontas was the discoverer of Great Britain. Native Americans had built great civilizations with many millions of people long before Columbus wandered lost into the Caribbean.

---

[1]Birth. — Eds.

Columbus' voyage has even less meaning for North Americans than for South Americans because Columbus never set foot on our continent, nor did he open it to European trade. Scandinavian Vikings already had settlements here in the eleventh century, and British fishermen probably fished the shores of Canada for decades before Columbus. The first European explorer to thoroughly document his visit to North America was the Italian explorer Giovanni Caboto, who sailed for England's King Henry VII and became known by his anglicized name, John Cabot. Caboto arrived in 1497 and claimed North America for the English sovereign while Columbus was still searching for India in the Caribbean. After three voyages to America and more than a decade of study, Columbus still believed that Cuba was a part of the continent of Asia, South America was only an island, and the coast of Central America was close to the Ganges River.

Unable to celebrate Columbus' exploration as a great discovery, some apologists now want to commemorate it as the great "cultural encounter." Under this interpretation, Columbus becomes a sensitive genius thinking beyond his time in the passionate pursuit of knowledge and understanding. The historical record refutes this, too.

Contrary to popular legend, Columbus did not prove that the world was round; educated people had known that for centuries. The Egyptian-Greek scientist Erastosthenes, working for Alexandria and Aswan, already had measured the circumference and diameter of the world in the third century B.C. Arab scientists had developed a whole discipline of geography and measurement, and in the tenth century A.D., Al Maqdisi described the earth with 360 degrees of longitude and 180 degrees of latitude. The Monastery of St. Catherine in the Sinai still has an icon — painted five hundred years before Columbus — which shows Jesus ruling over a spherical earth. Nevertheless, Americans have embroidered many such legends around Columbus, and he has become part of a secular mythology for schoolchildren. Autumn would hardly be complete in any elementary school without construction-paper replicas of the three cute ships that Columbus sailed to America, or without drawings of Queen Isabella pawning her jewels to finance Columbus' trip.

This myth of the pawned jewels obscures the true and more sinister story of how   5
Columbus financed his trip. The Spanish monarch invested in his excursion, but only on the condition that Columbus would repay this investment with profit by bringing back gold, spices, and other tribute from Asia. This pressing need to repay his debt underlies the frantic tone of Columbus' diaries as he raced from one Caribbean island to the next, stealing anything of value.

After he failed to contact the emperor of China, the traders of India or the merchants of Japan, Columbus decided to pay for his voyage in the one important commodity he had found in ample supply — human lives. He seized 1,200 Taino Indians from the island of Hispaniola, crammed as many onto his ships as would fit and sent them to Spain, where they were paraded naked through the streets of Seville and sold as slaves in 1495.

Columbus tore children from their parents, husbands from wives. On board Columbus' slave ships, hundreds died; the sailors tossed the Indian bodies into the Atlantic. Because Columbus captured more Indian slaves than he could transport to

Spain in his small ships, he put them to work in mines and plantations which he, his family and followers created throughout the Caribbean. His marauding band hunted Indians for sport and profit — beating, raping, torturing, killing, and then using the Indian bodies as food for their hunting dogs. Within four years of Columbus' arrival on Hispaniola, his men had killed or exported one-third of the original Indian population of 300,000. Within another fifty years, the Taino people had been made extinct, the first casualties of the holocaust of American Indians. The plantation owners then turned to the American mainland and to Africa for new slaves to follow the tragic path of the Taino.

This was the great cultural encounter initiated by Christopher Columbus. This is the event we celebrate each year on Columbus Day. The United States honors only two men with federal holidays bearing their names. In January we commemorate the birth of Martin Luther King Jr., who struggled to lift the blinders of racial prejudice and to cut the remaining bonds of slavery in America. In October, we honor Christopher Columbus, who opened the Atlantic slave trade and launched one of the greatest waves of genocide known in history.

(1989)

Questions

1. What is the tone of the opening paragraph? Given this beginning, what assumptions does Jack Weatherford seem to be making about his readers?
2. What is the overall claim that Weatherford makes in this argument?
3. What is the primary type of evidence the author cites? Explain why you do or do not find it persuasive.
4. What does Weatherford mean by "a secular mythology for schoolchildren" (par. 4)?
5. Identify the verbs the author uses in sentences about Columbus. What conclusions can you draw about his attitude based on the verbs alone?
6. Is the conclusion, with its reference to the Martin Luther King Jr. holiday, effective? Explain your response.

The Christopher Columbus Controversy

MICHAEL S. BERLINER

Michael S. Berliner is cochair of the board of directors of the Ayn Rand Institute, an organization that promotes Rand's philosophy of objectivism, which values individualism, freedom, and reason. First published in the *Los Angeles Times* in 1991, this article was republished in periodicals throughout the country nearly every year for more than a decade.

Columbus Day approaches, but to the "politically correct" this is no cause for celebration. On the contrary, they view the arrival of Christopher Columbus in 1492 as an occasion to be mourned. They have mourned, they have attacked, and they have intimidated schools across the country into replacing Columbus Day celebrations with "ethnic diversity" days.

The politically correct view is that Columbus did not discover America, because people had lived here for thousands of years. Worse yet, it's claimed, the main legacy of Columbus is death and destruction. Columbus is routinely vilified as a symbol of slavery and genocide, and the celebration of his arrival likened to a celebration of Hitler and the Holocaust. The attacks on Columbus are ominous, because the actual target is Western civilization.

Did Columbus "discover" America? Yes—in every important respect. This does not mean that no human eye had been cast on America before Columbus arrived. It does mean that Columbus brought America to the attention of the civilized world, i.e., to the growing, scientific civilizations of Western Europe. The result, ultimately, was the United States of America. It was Columbus' discovery for Western Europe that led to the influx of ideas and people on which this nation was founded—and on which it still rests. The opening of America brought the ideas and achievements of Aristotle, Galileo, Newton, and the thousands of thinkers, writers, and inventors who followed.

Prior to 1492, what is now the United States was sparsely inhabited, unused, and undeveloped. The inhabitants were primarily hunter-gatherers, wandering across the land, living from hand-to-mouth and from day-to-day. There was virtually no change, no growth for thousands of years. With rare exception, life was nasty, brutish, and short: there was no wheel, no written language, no division of labor, little agriculture and scant permanent settlement; but there were endless, bloody wars. Whatever the problems it brought, the vilified Western culture also brought enormous, undreamed-of benefits, without which most of today's Indians would be infinitely poorer or not even alive.

Columbus should be honored, for in so doing, we honor Western civilization.   5
But the critics do not want to bestow such honor, because their real goal is to denigrate the values of Western civilization and to glorify the primitivism, mysticism, and collectivism embodied in the tribal cultures of American Indians. They decry the glorification of the West as "Eurocentrism." We should, they claim, replace our reverence for Western civilization with multiculturalism, which regards all cultures as morally equal. In fact, they aren't. Some cultures are better than others: a free society is better than slavery; reason is better than brute force as a way to deal with other men; productivity is better than stagnation. In fact, Western civilization stands for man at his best. It stands for the values that make human life possible: reason, science, self-reliance, individualism, ambition, productive achievement. The values of Western civilization are values for all men; they cut across gender, ethnicity, and geography. We should honor Western civilization not for the ethnocentric reason that some of us happen to have European ancestors but because it is the objectively superior culture.

Underlying the political collectivism of the anti-Columbus crowd is a racist view of human nature. They claim that one's identity is primarily ethnic: if one thinks his ancestors were good, he will supposedly feel good about himself; if he thinks his ancestors were bad, he will supposedly feel self-loathing. But it doesn't work; the achievements or failures of one's ancestors are monumentally irrelevant to one's actual worth as a person. Only the lack of a sense of self leads one to look to others to provide what passes for a sense of identity. Neither the deeds nor misdeeds of others are his own; he can take neither credit nor blame for what someone else chose to do. There are no racial achievements or racial failures, only individual achievements and individual failures. One cannot inherit moral worth or moral vice. "Self-esteem through others" is a self-contradiction.

Thus the sham of "preserving one's heritage" as a rational life goal. Thus the cruel hoax of "multicultural education" as an antidote to racism: it will continue to create more racism.

Individualism is the only alternative to the racism of political correctness. We must recognize that everyone is a sovereign entity, with the power of choice and independent judgment. That is the ultimate value of Western civilization, and it should be proudly proclaimed.

(1991)

Questions

1. What does Michael S. Berliner believe is the "'politically correct'" (par. 1) view of Columbus Day?
2. What evidence does Berliner provide to support his claim that the "actual target" (par. 2) of such a view is not Columbus Day itself but Western civilization?
3. Why does Berliner put *discover* (par. 3) in quotation marks? What is his definition of the term as he uses it in his argument?
4. According to Berliner, what are the hallmarks of an "objectively superior culture" (par. 5)?
5. Why does he believe that "'multicultural education' . . . will continue to create more racism" (par. 7)?
6. Why, ultimately, does Berliner think we should celebrate Columbus Day?

Wilma Mankiller Reflects on Columbus Day

NATIONAL PUBLIC RADIO

The following is an excerpt from the transcript of an interview with Wilma Mankiller on National Public Radio in 2008. An activist and advocate for Native American rights, Mankiller (1945–2010) was the first female chief of the Cherokee Nation, serving from 1985 to 1995, and a recipient of the Presidential Medal of Freedom.

MICHEL MARTIN (Host): I'm Michel Martin, and you're listening to *Tell Me More* from NPR News. . . .

It's Columbus Day, and, if you have the day off, you may be catching up on sleep, errands, or time with loved ones. Some people mark Columbus Day by going to parades that honor the man, who schoolchildren have long been taught discovered America.

But not everyone is celebrating. For people who trace their ancestry to those displaced and marginalized by the European journey to this continent, this is a day of somber reflection, even mourning. Joining us to talk about this, as well as whatever else is on her mind, is Wilma Mankiller.

She was the first woman to become chief of the Cherokee Nation. She's a longtime activist and advocate for Native American rights and human rights. Wilma Mankiller, welcome to the program. Thank you so much for joining us.

Ms. WILMA MANKILLER (Chief, Cherokee Nation; Activist, Native American Rights):   5
Thank you. I'm very happy to be here.

MARTIN: You know, I think so much of how Americans view Columbus Day is still based on what we learned in elementary school. I still remember that rhyme, "In 1492 Columbus sailed the ocean blue." Do you remember how you were taught about this day?

Ms. MANKILLER: You know, I was taught the same way other students are. That Columbus discovered America. And, all students enter maybe I think it's about the third grade, when you start learning about American history.

And you know, we learned that there was this great, new world discovered by Columbus, with beautiful oceans, and bodies of water, and abundant forest, and foodstuffs. Well, you know, it certainly wasn't a new world to the millions of people that had lived here for thousands of years, and there's no discussion of that at all.

MARTIN: Do you remember that being sort of a crisis for you? Do you know how there's a point at which the reality that you know, and what you have learned either through ancestors or through your own research kind of bumps up against the narrative that you were presented? Do you remember when that happened for you? And was that a crisis for you?

Ms. MANKILLER: I think it probably happened to me in 1969. We were living in San   10
Francisco at that time. You know, I think it was the first time I heard the story that the Iroquois Confederacy, which is kind of an international group, was founded before Columbus arrived.

So, I began to think about what existed in the Americas before the arrival of Columbus, and others who claimed to have discovered our lands. So, I think probably that period of activism in the late 1960s was sort of the watershed moment for me, when I realized how unfortunate it was that most Americans who have been living in our, you know, towns and villages for hundreds of years, know so little about us.

MARTIN: Do you think that the basic American narrative that's been taught about Columbus has evolved over the years? Because there has been, I think I would argue — I don't know if you agree — but since that time, since the period of Native American activism, a lot of Americans became interested in, you know, first peoples, and what their lives and experiences have been. So do you think that the narrative's changed over time?

Ms. MANKILLER: I think it's evolved somewhat, and I wish I could say that it had evolved more. I think that in virtually every sector of society, native people, whether they're in tribal government or whether they're in the private sector or an artist, they encounter people every day who have such enormously stupid, ridiculous, stereotypes about native people, and have so little accurate information about either the history of native people or their contemporary lives.

And so, all of us who are active in our communities and active in the country, and engage with a lot of people every time we get together, our native people, we talk about that, what kind of stupid questions were you asked recently? What can we do? Do we need to do more forums? Do we need to have more native journalists? Do we have to create more native films? What can we do to change this? And actually, all those things are being done. So, I'm guardedly optimistic that it will change in the future.

MARTIN: Can I ask you what stupid questions you've been asked lately? Hopefully not right now.   15

(Soundbite of laughter)

Ms. MANKILLER: Well, I can't think of one I've been asked lately, but I remember one time a reporter with an English accent — very clipped English accent — called me at my home in rural Oklahoma and asked me if I rode a horse to work.

(Soundbite of laughter)

So — and I thought, you know what, I'm just going to take this guy for a ride.

MARTIN: Oh, dear.

Ms. MANKILLER: So I told him, yes, I did. I rode a horse to work. I described the horse. And I said, my husband and I live in a tepee along the edge of a river, and he fished and hunted every day, and this guy was writing the stuff down.

MARTIN: Oh, my. But on the other hand, how do you respond to those who say that   20
the desire to explore other worlds is also human, and that Columbus can't be blamed for what happened after?

Ms. MANKILLER: Well, I think that obviously the desire to explore a new world is human. I'm not sure the desire to conquer other lands is necessarily the best human attribute, or to kill indigenous people and exploit their natural resources is a human attribute that many of us would find very admirable.

MARTIN: How do you think we should talk about Columbus Day?

Ms. MANKILLER: I think in a balanced view. And I really think that Columbus Day can be used as a — just as you're doing. It can be used as an opportunity to have a conversation, and to provide a little more education to people about the indigenous people that were here before Columbus.

And to give — make sure that Americans have some sort of historical and cultural context for understanding our contemporary issues. It's really hard to understand contemporary Native American issues if you have no historical or cultural context. So I think that Columbus can be discussed in a balanced way, and it can provide an enormous opportunity for education, for conversations. . . .

MARTIN: And so — and of course, this is a conversation that happens both within com-   25
munities and outside of communities and among communities. You know, within

the communities some leaders would say, well, you know, is focusing on the painful history and victimization really the best idea?

This is distracting. It's harmful. Does this kind of conversation also go on, I think, among Native Americans at a time like this, when we're thinking about a painful history?

Ms. MANKILLER: It does go on. But I think that whether it's family history, or political history, or a history of what I would characterize genocide, I think that you have to acknowledge it. I think you have to acknowledge it, and talk about it in order to move forward in a good way together as human beings.

But to hide it, or pretend it doesn't exist, is not a good idea. I don't think that necessarily means that we need to go around every day with anger in our hearts and about what happened to us historically. I think—but I think it's important to acknowledge it, and think about it.

(2008)

Questions

1. What does interviewer Michel Martin mean by "the basic American narrative that's been taught about Columbus" (par. 12)?
2. What stereotypes about Native Americans and Christopher Columbus does Wilma Mankiller discuss and dispute?
3. What does Mankiller mean by a "balanced view" (par. 23) of Columbus Day? Why do you think she does *not* call for the abolition of this holiday?

What Columbus Day Really Means

WILLIAM J. CONNELL

> This article appeared in the *American Scholar*, a publication of the Phi Beta Kappa Society, in 2010. William J. Connell, a professor of history at Seton Hall University, specializes in the history of Italy and early modern Europe.

During the run-up to Columbus Day I usually get a call from at least one and sometimes several newspaper reporters who are looking for the latest on what has become one of the most controversial of our national holidays. Rather than begin with whatever issues the media are covering—topics like the number of deaths in the New World caused by the European discovery; or the attitude of Columbus toward the indigenous inhabitants of the Caribbean (whom he really did want to use as forced laborers); or whether syphilis really came from the Americas to Europe; or whether certain people (the cast of *The Sopranos*, Supreme Court Justice Antonin Scalia) deserve to be excluded from or honored in the parade in New York—I always try to remind the reporters that Columbus Day is just a holiday.

Leave the parades aside. The most evident way in which holidays are celebrated is by taking a day off from work or school. Our system of holidays, which developed gradually over time and continues to evolve, is founded upon the recognition that weekends are not sufficient, that some jobs don't offer much time off, and that children and teachers need a break now and then in the course of the school year. One characteristic of holidays is that unless they are observed widely, which is to say by almost everyone, many of us wouldn't take them. There are so many incremental reasons for not taking time off (to make some extra money, to impress the boss, or because we're our own bosses and can't stop ourselves) that a lot of us would willingly do without a day's vacation that would have been good both for us and for society at large if we had taken it. That is why there are legal holidays.

But which days should be holidays? Another way of posing the question would be to say, "Given that holidays are necessary, but that left to their own devices people would simply work, how do you justify a legal holiday so that it does not appear completely arbitrary, and so that people will be encouraged to observe it?" Most of the media noise around the Columbus Day holiday is about the holiday's excuse, not the holiday itself. Realizing that helps to put matters in perspective.

In a country of diverse religious faiths and national origins like the United States, it made sense to develop a holiday system that was not entirely tied to a religious calendar. (Christmas survives here, of course, but in law it's a secular holiday much like New Year's Day.) So Americans do not all leave for the shore on August 15th, the Feast of the Assumption of the Blessed Virgin, the way Italians do; and while St. Patrick's Day is celebrated by many Americans, it is not a legal holiday in any of the states. The American system of holidays was constructed mostly around a series of great events and persons in our nation's history. The aim was to instill a feeling of civic pride. Holidays were chosen as occasions to bring everyone together, not for excluding certain people. They were supposed to be about the recognition of our society's common struggles and achievements. *Civic religion* is often used to describe the principle behind America's calendar of public holidays.

Consider the range and variability of the meanings of our holidays. Certainly they have not always been occasions for celebration: Memorial Day and Veterans Day involve mourning for the dead and wounded. Labor Day commemorated significant hardships in the decades when unions were struggling to organize. Having grown up in the 1960s I remember how Abraham Lincoln's birthday (now lumped in with Presidents' Day, and with some of its significance transferred to Martin Luther King Jr. Day) took on special meaning during the Civil Rights movement and after the JFK assassination. 5

When thinking about the Columbus Day holiday it helps to remember the good intentions of the people who put together the first parade in New York. Columbus Day was first proclaimed a national holiday by President Benjamin Harrison in 1892, 400 years after Columbus's first voyage. The idea, lost on present-day critics of the holiday, was that this would be a national holiday that would be special for recognizing both Native Americans, who were here before Columbus, and the many immigrants — including Italians — who were just then coming to this country in astounding numbers. It was to be a national holiday that was *not* about the Founding Fathers or the Civil War, but about the *rest* of American history. Like the Columbian Exposition dedicated in Chicago that year and opened in 1893, it was to be about our land and all its people. Harrison especially designated the schools as centers of the Columbus celebration because universal public schooling, which had only recently taken hold, was seen as essential to a democracy that was seriously aiming to include everyone and not just preserve a governing elite.

You won't find it in the public literature surrounding the first Columbus Day in 1892, but in the background lay two recent tragedies, one involving Native Americans, the other involving Italian Americans. The first tragedy was the massacre by U.S. troops of between 146 and 200 Lakota Sioux, including men, women and children, at Wounded Knee, South Dakota, on December 29, 1890. Shooting began after a misunderstanding involving an elderly, deaf Sioux warrior who hadn't heard and therefore did not understand that he was supposed to hand over his rifle to the U.S. Cavalry. The massacre at Wounded Knee marked the definitive end of Indian resistance in the Great Plains. The episode was immediately seen by the government as potentially troubling, although there was much popular sentiment against the Sioux. An inquiry was held, the soldiers were absolved, and some were awarded medals that Native Americans to this day are seeking to have rescinded.

A second tragedy in the immediate background of the 1892 Columbus celebration took place in New Orleans. There, on March 14, 1891 — only 10 weeks after the Wounded Knee Massacre — 11 Italians were lynched in prison by a mob led by prominent Louisiana politicians. A trial for the murder of the New Orleans police chief had ended in mistrials for three of the Italians and the acquittal of the others who were brought to trial. Unhappy with the verdict and spurred on by fear of the "Mafia" (a word that had only recently entered American usage), civic leaders organized an assault on the prison to put the Italians to death. This episode was also troubling to the U.S. government. These were legally innocent men who had been killed. But Italians were not very popular, and even Theodore Roosevelt was quoted as saying that he thought the New Orleans Italians "got what they deserved." A grand jury was summoned, but no one was charged with a crime. President Harrison, who would proclaim the Columbus holiday the following year, was genuinely saddened by the case, and over the objections of some members of Congress he paid reparations to the Italian government for the deaths of its citizens.

Whenever I hear of protests about the Columbus Day holiday — protests that tend to pit Native Americans against Italian Americans — I remember these tragedies that occurred so soon before the first Columbus Day holiday, and I shake my head. President Harrison did not allude to either of these sad episodes in his proclamation of the holiday, but the idea for the holiday involved a vision of an America that would get beyond the prejudice that had led to these deaths. Columbus Day was supposed to recognize the greatness of all of America's people, but especially Italians and Native Americans.

Consider how the first Columbus Day parade in New York was described in the   10
newspapers. It consisted mostly of about 12,000 public school students grouped into
20 regiments, each commanded by a principal. The boys marched in school uniforms
or their Sunday best, while the girls, dressed in red, white and blue, sat in bleachers.
Alongside the public schoolers there were military drill squads and 29 marching
bands, each of 30 to 50 instruments. After the public schools, there followed 5,500
students from the Catholic schools. Then there were students from the private
schools wearing school uniforms. These included the Hebrew Orphan Asylum, the
Barnard School Military Corps, and the Italian and American Colonial School.
The Dante Alighieri Italian College of Astoria was dressed entirely in sailor outfits.
These were followed by the Native American marching band from the Carlisle
Indian School in Pennsylvania, which, according to one description, included "300
marching Indian boys and 50 tall Indian girls." That the Native Americans came right
after the students from the Dante Alighieri School speaks volumes about the spirit of
the original Columbus Day.

I teach college kids, and since they tend to be more skeptical about Columbus
Day than younger students, it's nice to point out that the first Columbus Day parade
had a "college division." Thus 800 New York University students played kazoos and
wore mortarboards. In between songs they chanted "Who are we? Who are we? New
York Universitee!" The College of Physicians and Surgeons wore skeletons on their
hats. And the Columbia College students marched in white hats and white sweaters,
with a message on top of their hats that spelled out "We are the People."

So Columbus Day is for all Americans. It marks the first encounter that brought
together the original Americans and the future ones. A lot of suffering followed, and
a lot of achievement too. That a special role has been reserved for Italians in keeping the parades and the commemoration alive for well over a century seems right,
since Columbus was Italian — although even in the 1890s his nationality was being
contested. Some people, who include respectable scholars, still argue, based on elements of his biography and family history, that Columbus must really have been
Spanish, Portuguese, Jewish, or Greek, instead of, or in addition to, Italian. One
lonely scholar in the 1930s even wrote that Columbus, because of a square jaw and
dirty blond hair in an old portrait, must have been Danish. The consensus, however,
is that he was an Italian from outside of Genoa.

So much for his ethnicity. What about his moral standing? In the late 19th century an international movement, led by a French priest, sought to have Columbus
canonized for bringing Christianity to the New World. To the Catholic Church's
credit, this never got very far. It sometimes gets overlooked in current discussions that
we neither commemorate Columbus's birthday (as was the practice for Presidents
Washington and Lincoln, and as we now do with Martin Luther King Jr.) nor his death
date (which is when Christian saints are memorialized), but rather the date of his
arrival in the New World. The historical truth about Columbus — the short version
suitable for reporters who are pressed for time — is that Columbus *was* Italian, but he
was no saint.

The holiday marks the event, not the person. What Columbus gets criticized for nowadays are attitudes that were typical of the European sailing captains and merchants who plied the Mediterranean and the Atlantic in the 15th century. Within that group he was unquestionably a man of daring and unusual ambition. But what really mattered was his landing on San Salvador, which was a momentous, world-changing occasion such as has rarely happened in human history. Sounds to me like a pretty good excuse for taking a day off from work.

(2010)

Questions

1. William J. Connell bases his argument on a premise of a specific viewpoint toward holidays. What is it?
2. What does Connell mean by "civic religion" (par. 4) with regard to American holidays? Explain whether you agree or disagree that there is such a thing.
3. What evidence does Connell provide to support his claim that originally the Columbus Day holiday "was *not* about the Founding Fathers or the Civil War, but about the *rest* of American history" (par. 6)? How persuasive do you find his reasoning?
4. Connell discusses two "tragedies" (par. 7) that had occurred very close to the 1892 initiation of the Columbus Day holiday: the massacre at Wounded Knee and the lynching of eleven Italians in a Louisiana prison. How does he connect these events with the holiday? How effective is he in making the connection?
5. What point does Connell make about Columbus's "moral standing" (par. 13)? Why does he raise the effort made to have Columbus canonized?
6. Examine the logic of the final paragraph. What links does Connell make between and among his points that the "holiday marks the event, not the person," the person was "unquestionably a man of daring and unusual ambition," and "what really mattered" was his landing on San Salvador in 1492? How effective is this conclusion?

from *Columbus*
The Four Voyages

LAURENCE BERGREEN

A graduate of Harvard University, Laurence Bergreen (b. 1950) has published numerous biographies, including *Over the Edge of the World: Magellan's Terrifying Circumnavigation of the Globe* (2003) and *Marco Polo: From Venice to Xanadu* (2007). He has written for the *New York Times*, the *Wall Street Journal*, and *Esquire* magazine and is a featured historian on the History Channel. The following excerpt is the epilogue from his best-selling biography *Columbus: The Four Voyages* (2011).

The drastic devaluation of Columbus seems a recent phenomenon, but it originated at the time of his voyages. The Spanish judicial investigator, Francisco de Bobadilla, sent him home in chains. King Ferdinand disdained him. Bishop Fonseca's intense dislike for Columbus was widely known. Amerigo Vespucci fostered the impression that he, rather than Columbus, had discovered a New World, and gave his name to the continent. His former lieutenant, Alonso de Ojeda, laid claim to territories first visited by Columbus. Nicolás de Ovando, who succeeded Columbus as governor of Hispaniola, endangered his life and mocked him. The Porras brothers, Francisco Roldán, and others who sailed with Columbus staged mutinies with little or no retribution.

The most lasting damage to Columbus's reputation came from the pen of Bartolomé de Las Casas. Arriving in Hispaniola with the new governor, Nicolás de Ovando, in 1502, Las Casas began as a slave owner. In 1510, he became the first priest to be ordained in the Americas, often called the "Apostle to the Indians." In his influential jeremiad, *A Short Account of the Destruction of the Indies* (*Brevísima relación de la destrucción de las Indias*), written in 1542, he laid out the torture and genocidal practices of the Spanish colonialists who followed Columbus.

Las Casas championed the nearly extinct victims of this outrage — "the simplest people in the world," he wrote of the Taíno Indians, "long suffering, unassertive, and submissive, . . . without malice or guile, utterly faithful and obedient" — in short, the kind of subjects the Spanish crown would want to have. Yet instead of cultivating these gentle and intelligent people, "we know for sure our fellow-countrymen have, through their cruelty and wickedness, depopulated and laid waste an area which boasted more than ten kingdoms, each of them larger than the Iberian Peninsula." They slaughtered their children, "on occasion running through a mother and her baby with a single thrust of their swords." The Spaniards were even more brutal with the Indians' leaders, whom they lashed to a "griddle consisting of sticks resting on pitchforks driven into the ground and then grill[ed] them over a slow fire, with the result that they howled in agony and despair as they died a lingering death."

All this Las Casas witnessed. He estimated that "the despotic and diabolical behavior of the Christians has, over the last forty years, led to the unjust and totally unwarranted deaths of more than twelve million souls, women and children among them." Indeed, he believed fifteen million to be a more accurate tally of deaths caused by Christians resorting to torture, wholesale slaughter, and "the harshest and most iniquitous and brutal slavery that man has ever devised for his fellow men." Las Casas's figures have long been debated, but even conservative estimates are stark: of 250,000 Indians under Spanish rule, only 40,000 survived after fifteen years. After a few decades, only a few hundred survived. Many died from infectious diseases caused by exposure to germs borne by the Europeans or their livestock, against which the inhabitants of the New World were defenseless.

And the reason for this tragedy? In his words, "Purely and simply greed." 5

Las Casas's indictment found a receptive audience in Spain's nascent rival, England, where it took root as the Spanish "Black Legend." For centuries thereafter, Spain and the explorers who sailed under the Spanish flag were widely condemned as murderers and thieves. The shadow of the Black Legend hung over Columbus as it did over other explorers from Spain. Explorers who sailed under the Spanish flag were widely condemned as murderers and thieves who habitually resorted to inhuman extremes of cruelty. Without meaning to, Las Casas's account served as a call to arms for Spain's mostly Protestant rivals to save the New World from further horrors. The surviving Indians became pawns in a geopolitical struggle beyond their comprehension. Even religion offered little guidance concerning the explorers' deeds and the acquisition of empire. Both Las Casas and Spain's pious rulers believed God was on their side, as did England.

In 1510, eight years after arriving in Hispaniola, Las Casas became a missionary to the Taínos of Cuba. For a time he exploited Indian labor, then renounced the practice, and by 1514 declared his opposition to the Spanish Enterprise of the Indies, even while encouraging the conversion of the Indians to Christianity. In his later years, he formulated the Doctrine of Self-Determination. It stated, simply, that all power derives from the people, that the people delegate power to rulers to serve the interests of their people, and that significant government deeds require popular approval. "No state, king, or emperor can alienate territories, or change their political system without the express approval of their inhabitants," he affirmed. Las Casas lived on until July 17, 1566, and died at age ninety-two.

Not everyone was hostile to Columbus or indifferent to his suffering and accomplishments. His loyal friend Diego Méndez always considered his desperate rescue mission in a modified canoe across the open sea to Hispaniola as his life's great adventure. In his will, dated June 19, 1536, he directed his executors to erect a tomb made of stone — "the best to be had" — to commemorate the event. In the middle of the stone, he ordered, "let there be a canoe, which is a hollowed log in which the Indians navigate, since in one such I navigated 300 leagues, and above it let them carve merely the letters which read CANOA."

Nowadays, Columbus the explorer is everywhere. Sculptures, monuments, and memorials of Columbus abound in public squares in Genoa, Barcelona, Madrid, Mexico City, Seville, and in cities throughout the Caribbean and the Americas. From street level these statues reveal themselves by turns as heroic, grotesque, and fearsome; they portray a gargoyle of conquest. Rivers, cities, towns, thoroughfares, and the nation of Colombia have been named in his honor.

In the United States especially, his example and his voyages answered an unceasing need for self-definition and identity. Beginning in the eighteenth century, his name was given to the capital of South Carolina, the capital of Ohio, and the mighty Columbia River in the Pacific Northwest. Through an act of Congress in 1871, the site of the nation's capital was named the District of Columbia. New York City has Columbia University, Columbus Circle, and Columbus Avenue. 10

His marble statue sits atop a seventy-foot granite column rising above Columbus Circle. Designed by Gaetano Russo in 1892, the monument's marble base proclaims:

To
CHRISTOPHER COLUMBUS
The Italians Resident in America,
Scoffed at Before,
During the Voyage, Menaced,
After It, Chained,
As Generous As Oppressed,
To the World He Gave a World.

Columbus held up a mirror to the Old World, revealing and magnifying its inhumanity and greed along with its piety, curiosity, and exuberance. Columbus's voyages revealed many harsh truths about the limits of human understanding, but it is too late to undo the consequences of these voyages. Their crimson thread is now woven deeply into the fabric of European and global history.

For all the scorn Columbus engendered, his four voyages constitute one of the greatest adventure stories in history. Although he was not the first explorer to glimpse or visit the distant shores of the Americas, his was the discovery that permanently planted the reality of the New World in the imagination — and political schemes — of the Old. Columbus forever changed the idea of what a European empire could be. He had the vision — and, at times, the delusion — to imagine, and to persuade himself and others that he had found something immense, important, and lasting.

For all their accomplishments and liabilities, Columbus's voyages were just the beginning, setting in motion consequences — political, cultural, and scientific — that persist to this day. In its complexity and powerful contradictions, his example speaks more urgently than ever to our contentious era.

(2011)

Questions

1. What is the "most lasting damage to Columbus's reputation" (par. 2) according to Laurence Bergreen? Why did this indictment find "a receptive audience in Spain's nascent rival, England" (par. 6)?
2. What do you think Bergreen means when he claims that Columbus's "example and his voyages answered an unceasing need for self-definition and identity" (par. 10) for Americans?
3. Do you agree with Bergreen that "it is too late to undo the consequences of these voyages" (par. 12)?
4. What point is Bergreen making by his reference to the Columbus Monument in New York City's Columbus Circle, and specifically to its inscription? How does knowing that Italian sculptor Gaetano Russo undertook the statue of Christopher Columbus in honor of the four hundredth anniversary of his New World discovery inform your response?
5. Overall, what is Bergreen's opinion of the legacy of Columbus in "our contentious era" (par. 14)?

Making Connections

1. What are the major differences between the arguments of Jack Weatherford (p. 289) and William J. Connell (p. 296)? Carefully examine the assumptions on which they base their arguments.

2. How would Wilma Mankiller (p. 293) likely respond to Columbus's *Journal* (p. 279)?

3. In what ways does Walt Whitman's poem (p. 287) embody the view of Columbus depicted in John Vanderlyn's painting (p. 286), and in what ways does the poem challenge that view? Cite specific details to support your response.

4. To what extent do you think Michael S. Berliner (p. 291) would be critical of the politics and philosophy of the Requierimiento (p. 284)?

5. Defend Connell's argument by citing evidence from Columbus's *Journal*. How do Columbus's perceptions make the case that it is the event, not the man, that the holiday celebrates?

6. What common ground do you find between Berliner and Laurence Bergreen (p. 300)? Consider assumptions they might share as well as explicit viewpoints.

7. Bergreen uses lines 1–6 and the last three stanzas of Whitman's "Prayer of Columbus" as the epigraph to his biography of Columbus. Why do you think he chose that poem for his epigraph?

Entering the Conversation

As you respond to each of the following prompts, support your position with appropriate evidence, including at least three sources in this Conversation on the Columbus Day controversy, unless otherwise indicated.

1. Should the United States continue its celebration of the Columbus Day holiday? Write an essay explaining your position. In your essay, assess proposals for alternative celebrations, such as South Dakota's Native American Day or California's Indigenous People's Day.

2. In his article "What Columbus Day Really Means," Connell asserts, "Most of the media noise around the Columbus Day holiday is about the holiday's excuse, not the holiday itself" (par. 3). Write an essay explaining why you agree or disagree with this statement about the celebration of Columbus Day. Use two of the secondary sources along with Columbus's *Journal* and/or the Requierimiento to bolster your argument.

3. Given the current controversy, should the Vanderlyn painting be removed from the Capitol rotunda? Write an essay explaining your response, using at least three of the texts from this Conversation.

4. In 1912, the Columbus Memorial Fountain was dedicated. Situated in front of historic Union Station in Washington, D.C, it features a globe on top of a monument surrounded by figures, including that of a Native American, representing the Old and the New worlds; a statue of Columbus is in the center, and the following inscription appears on the back of the monument: "To the memory of Christopher Columbus, whose high faith and indomitable courage gave to mankind a new world." After researching the background of and funding for this monument, write an essay arguing for or against its worth as part of the Washington, D.C., landscape. Use at least three of the sources in this Conversation to develop your argument.

5. One argument in defense of maintaining the Columbus Day holiday is that it is unfair to judge events and persons from an earlier time period — in this case, a fifthteenth-century man — by twenty-first-century standards. Explain why you agree or disagree with this perspective.

Conversation

Pocahontas: A Woman, a Movie, a Myth?

Who was Pocahontas? How is it that from a period of history in which relations between European settlers and the indigenous population were marked by a combination of tension, distrust, exploitation, and violence, there emerged the story of a young Native American girl who mercifully saved a white settler from death and later married another. What about this story captured the national imagination at the time and continues to do so? Is it simply a feel-good love story? Is it a way to whitewash a brutal history by focusing on one positive event, whether it actually happened or not? Who has Pocahontas become? When we hear or see her name, do we think of the historical figure? The literary and cinematic character? The mythic being? What is it about her that continues to grip the American imagination? What is the purpose and effect of the narrative that defines her?

Sources
Daniel Richter, *Living with Europeans* (2002)
Simon van de Passe, *Matoaka als Rebecca* (1616)
Captain John Smith, *Letter to Queen Anne of Great Britain* (1616)
John Gadsby Chapman, *The Baptism of Pocahontas* (1839)
George P. Morris, *The Chieftain's Daughter: A Ballad* (1840)

Howard Chandler Christy, *Pocahontas* (1911)
Paula Gunn Allen, *Pocahontas to Her English Husband, John Rolfe* (1988)
Gary Edgerton and Kathy Merlock Jackson, from *Redesigning Pocahontas: Disney, the "White Man's Indian," and the Marketing of Dreams* (1996)
Paula Gunn Allen, from *Pocahontas: Medicine Woman, Spy, Entrepreneur, Diplomat* (2004)

Living with Europeans

DANIEL RICHTER

> Daniel Richter (b. 1962) is director of the McNeil Center for Early American
> Studies at the University of Pennsylvania. The following selection is from his 2002
> book, *Facing East from Indian Country: A Native History of Early America*, which
> was a finalist for the 2002 Pulitzer Prize for History.

It is much easier to reconstruct the abstract forces that constrained the seventeenth-century Native world than it is to recover the personal experiences of the people who struggled to give that world human shape. Early colonists recorded countless Indian names (as best they could reproduce them in the Latin alphabet) and glimpsed the activities of Indian people who visited them or in whose villages they sojourned, but they seldom developed any real understanding of their subjects' motives or broader experiences — and so, in most cases, neither can we. Nonetheless, a handful of individuals do emerge strikingly from fragmentary references in documents preserved from the period. Among them are three whose stories have been told repeatedly since then: the Virginia Algonquian "princess" Pocahontas, the Mohawk Roman Catholic candidate for sainthood Kateri Tekakwitha, and the Wampanoag Metacom, or "King Philip," who inspired a bloody war against Puritan New England. Verifiable evidence about these figures is so scant that it may never be possible to determine the "truth" about their lives, but enough information is available to reveal how each confronted the forces of material change and tried to incorporate Europeans into an Indian world on indigenous terms. Their stories illuminate the dilemmas that all seventeenth-century Native people faced.

Every North American schoolchild knows — or thinks she knows — the story of Pocahontas:

> A beautiful Indian princess welcomed the English colonists to Jamestown in 1607 and fell in love with the dashing young Captain John Smith. When Smith was captured by her father, the great chief Powhatan, she risked her life to save her lover from a brutal execution. Thereafter a frequent visitor to the English settlement, she brought the colonists food and thwarted her father's plans to do them in. When Smith was injured in a gunpowder explosion and forced to return to England, Pocahontas pined away, but ultimately fell in love with another colonist, John Rolfe. She was baptized a Christian, took the name Rebecca (recalling

the biblical matriarch who left her own people to marry Isaac and become the mother of a nation), and married Rolfe, with whom she had a son named Thomas. On a visit to England in 1616, she tragically died and was buried in a village church at Gravesend. But her legacy of love that triumphed over racial barriers lived on in the numerous Virginian descendants of her son.

Almost every particular of this familiar story — or, rather, the two distinct tales of Pocahontas and Smith and Pocahontas and Rolfe that animators from Disney Studios reconflated not long ago — is either incorrect or misleading.[1] References to a girl or woman named Pocahontas appear in the writings of at least four seventeenth-century English chroniclers: London courtier John Chamberlain, Virginia colonists William Strachey and Ralph Hamor, and, most importantly, the colony's sometime president and lifelong historian Smith.[2] Their works reveal that "Pocahontas" was a nickname, or perhaps even just a descriptive term, meaning something to the effect of "playful one" or "mischievous girl." It is possible, therefore, that not every Pocahontas they mention was the one who later became famous. That person's formal public name was Amonute; her personal, secret name, known only to her kin until revealed to a literate English audience, was Matoaka.[3]

Little is known about her life prior to the establishment of Jamestown. She was born in 1595 or 1596 as one of perhaps ten daughters and twenty sons of Powhatan, the *mamanatowick*, or paramount chief, who presided over the approximately thirty local communities and 15,000 people of Tsenacommacah, the "densely inhabited land" later called the Virginia Tidewater. Her mother was one of numerous wives of Powhatan, but the older woman's identity is otherwise a mystery. The missing information is crucial for evaluating Pocahontas' status as a "princess," for among her people, as among most Native societies in eastern North America, political office descended in the female line. Thus neither Pocahontas nor her potential husband would have had any hereditary claim to Powhatan's chiefdom; as Smith observed, "her marriage could no way have entitled [her spouse] by any right to the kingdom," which would descend to the *mamanatowick*'s maternal nephews, not to his own children.[4] What-ever exalted social status she may have inherited through her mother's line, there is no particular reason to assume that she was her father's favorite. Indeed Strachey identified her youngest half-sister as the "great darling of the king's."[5]

There is no evidence that Pocahontas met Smith or any other English person before the end of 1607, when the captain's exploratory party was captured, he was brought to her father's village, and she supposedly rescued him from death. At the time, Pocahontas was a prepubescent girl of about twelve; Smith was a squat bearded man in his late twenties. Whether the Englishman's life was actually in danger on that occasion, whether Pocahontas acted on her own or on her father's or others' instruc-tions, or even whether the girl intervened at all are matters of debate, in part because of the contradictory accounts Smith himself wrote. His early books give no hint that his life was in peril when he was held prisoner, but after Pocahontas became famous for her marriage to Rolfe he published increasingly elaborate stories of how "she hazarded the beating out of her own brains to save" his.[6] Still, the most likely inter-pretation of what happened is that the "execution" and "rescue" were part of an

elaborately staged ceremony, designed to establish Powhatan's life-and-death authority over Smith, to incorporate the English as subordinate people within the *mamanatowick*'s realm, and to make Pocahontas an intermediary between the two leaders and
their communities.[7]

Such a relationship is suggested by the fact that Pocahontas subsequently appeared
in Jamestown several times accompanying parties bearing food and messages from
Powhatan to his English tributaries. These trips were not all business, however;
Jamestown residents told tales of how a youngster wearing the non-garb traditional
for children in her society would "get the boys forth with her into the market place
and make them wheel, falling on their hands turning their heels upwards, whom she
would follow, and wheel her self naked as she was all the Fort over." *Au naturel* cartwheels notwithstanding, there was no romance between Smith and Pocahontas, who
at best shared the fondness of an older man for a younger girl he later described as
"the very nonpareil of [Powhatan's] kingdom."[8] After Smith's departure—more the
result of a revolt against his leadership than of concern for his health, which could not
have been improved by a long ocean voyage—she apparently went about her life
much as she would have if the English had never arrived. In about 1610, at the age of
fourteen or fifteen, she married a "private captain called Kocoum" and went to live
with him in an outlying town in Powhatan's domain.[9]

Her relationship to John Rolfe began some three years later with another
capture, this time of Pocahontas by the English. War between colonists and the
Powhatans had broken out shortly after Smith's departure, largely because of incessant English demands for food tribute. Also in dispute were English claims to land in
an area at the heart of Powhatan's chiefdom stretching fifty miles up the James River
from Jamestown to the outpost of Henrico, which the colonists established in 1611.
Following a policy of divide and rule, the English had made peace with one of the
constituent elements of Powhatan's paramount chiefdom, the Patawomecks. In their
country in April 1613, Englishman Samuel Argall convinced one of that nation's
headmen to lure Pocahontas—who was on an extended visit to her father's erstwhile
tributaries—on board his vessel.[10] The young captive spent most of the next year as
a hostage at Jamestown, under the supervision of Deputy Governor Thomas Dale,
and at Henrico, in the house of the Reverend Alexander Whitaker. During that period
she received instruction—indoctrination might be a better word—in Christianity.
Dale, promulgator of the colony's infamously draconian "Laws Divine, Moral and
Martial," was hardly known for his light touch; during a previous term as governor
he had sentenced some English wrongdoers "to be hanged, some burned, some to be
broken upon wheels, others to be staked, and some to be shot to death."[11] Whitaker's
approach may have been no more subtle. He wrote approvingly that "Sir Thomas
Dale had labored a long time to ground in her" a rote knowledge of the Apostles'
Creed, the Lord's Prayer, and the Ten Commandments in English.[12]

During her captivity Pocahontas came to know John Rolfe, a twenty-eight-year-
old bachelor who had recently shipped to England a trial sample of the tobacco he
had been experimenting with since first importing seeds from the West Indies in
1611.[13] Rolfe became smitten with the then-eighteen-year-old woman, "to whom," he

said, "my hearty and best thoughts are, and have for a long time been so entangled, and enthralled in so intricate a labyrinth, that I was even awearied to unwind myself thereout." Whether Pocahontas requited her suitor's love is unknown. Perhaps at first he simply represented a way out of the oppressive tutelage of Whitaker and Dale. In any event, what Rolfe feared might be only "the unbridled desire of carnal affection" was, he convinced himself, outweighed by the higher goals of the "good of this plantation for the honor of our country, for the glory of God for my own salvation and for the converting to the true knowledge of God and Jesus Christ, an unbelieving creature."[14]

In March 1614, as Rolfe sorted out his feelings, Dale took Pocahontas with him when he marched an army into the heart of Powhatan's domain, "burned . . . some forty houses, and . . . made freeboot and pillage" to demonstrate who was in charge. Despite this show of force, Powhatan balked at Dale's efforts to impose a peace treaty until, in the midst of negotiations, Rolfe wrote a letter to the governor confessing his attraction to Pocahontas and suggesting a diplomatic marriage to seal an alliance. Powhatan — who had several weeks earlier proposed "that his daughter should be [Dale's] child, and ever dwell with [him], desiring to be ever friends" — agreed to the match immediately. Pocahontas, having, according to Dale, "made some good progress" in her catechism, hastily received baptism, and within ten days the union was blessed with Anglican rites at Jamestown. No one seemed to worry about the bride's inconvenient previous marriage to Kocoum.[15]

Two years later, with Indians and English seemingly enjoying an age of peace   10
and colonists madly planting Rolfe's tobacco everywhere, the couple and their infant son traveled to England. The family was accompanied by a man named Uttamatomakkin (whom English sources described as an adviser to her father) and perhaps ten other people from Tsenacommacah. Sometime after their arrival in June 1616, Smith (who Pocahontas had been told was dead) went to see her in her lodgings and wrote for her a letter of introduction to Queen Anne, in which he told the rescue story in public for the first time.[16] In January 1617 the Indians were ceremonially received at court, where they were "graciously used" by King James I. They also sat "well placed" at a performance of a theatrical work by Ben Jonson, amid grumbling by some courtiers that Pocahontas was "no fair lady," despite "her tricking up and high style and titles." Two months later she succumbed to an unidentified ailment at Gravesend, as she prepared to travel home on a ship commanded by the same Samuel Argall who had captured her.[17]

Hopes for the kind of peaceful ethnic relations the Rolfe-Pocahontas marriage symbolized expired with her. Powhatan died in early 1618, leaving his paramount chieftainship to a series of elderly relatives. Effective leadership, however, passed long before his death to the Pamunkey chief Opechancanough and a charismatic religious figure named Nemattanew, or "Jack of the Feather," who promised his followers that European musket shots would do them no harm. In November 1621, as the two were mobilizing forces to resist English expansionism, Nemattanew got into a scuffle with colonists who accused him of murdering an Englishman and took a fatal shot from one of the guns to which he claimed immunity. His movement lived on, however, and in March of the next year Opechancanough planned a series of carefully coordinated assaults that killed at least 330 English — perhaps one quarter of the colony's population — in a single day. A decade of brutal retaliatory warfare ensued, until the exhausted English imposed peace terms.[18]

The conceptual distance the victors had traveled since the days of the Rolfe-Pocahontas marriage is perhaps best measured by comments made during the war by Virginia governor Francis Wyatt. "Our first work is expulsion of the savages to gain the free range of the country for increase of Cattle, swine, etc.," he wrote. "It is infinitely better to have no heathen among us, who at best were but as thorns in our sides, than to be at peace and league with them."[19] So things stood until 1644, when Opechancanough — reputedly 100 years old and unable to walk unassisted — was carried into the field on a litter to lead his people in a final desperate campaign against the English. In March 1646 English forces captured him and displayed him in a cage at Jamestown. Despite his disabilities and "eye-lids . . . so heavy that he could not see," he defiantly protested the indignity until one of his guards shot him in the back.[20]

What might we make of these intertwined tales and their murderous end? Euro-Americans have usually faced west to focus on what the narratives mean for them and their own story. From this perspective, Pocahontas' main purpose was to make possible the survival of the Jamestown colony, and thus the future development of the United States. Her story conveys lessons about a road not taken, about an intercultural cooperation that should have been, about a Native American who not only welcomed colonizers with open arms but so thoroughly assimilated to their ways that she changed her name and her religion in order to become one with them. As a twentieth-century biographer put it, "Pocahontas did not share her people's hostility, and it is that fact that catapulted her into history. . . . Encountering a new culture, she responded with curiosity and concern, and she accepted the potential for change and development within herself. She rose, surely and dramatically, above the ignorance and savagery of her people."[21] Opechancanough presumably did not.

An eastward-facing perspective on the limited documentary evidence about Pocahontas, however, suggests a very different meaning for her stories. What if we think of her not as the sexy savior of Jamestown but instead as "a young exile, who died at age twenty-two in a foreign country"?[22] Significantly, the only attempt to record Pocahontas' own words was made by that less-than-reliable source John Smith after his visit with her in England in 1616. When her old acquaintance first encountered her, "she turned about, obscured her face, as not seeming well contented." Hours later, after Smith had begun to doubt her ability even to speak English, Pocahontas finally

> began to talk, and remembered me well what courtesies she had done, saying, "You did promise Powhatan [that] what was yours should be his, and he the like to you; you called him father being in his land a stranger, and by the same reason so must I do you," which though I [Smith] would have excused, I durst not allow of that title, because she was a king's daughter. With a well set countenance she said, "Were you not afraid to come into my father's country, and

caused fear in him and all his people (but me) and fear you here I should call you father? I tell you then I will, and you shall call me child, and so I will be for ever and ever your countryman. They did tell us always you were dead, and I knew no other till I came to Plymouth [England]; yet Powhatan did command Uttamatomakkin to seek you, and know the truth, because your countrymen will lie much."[23]

If Smith's version of Pocahontas' words is accurate, at least three powerful   15
messages emerge. First is a pervasive tone of profound sadness — if not embittered disillusionment. This is not the song of an enlightened savage happy to live in civilization at last, but rather the lament of a "stranger" trapped by duty far from home in a world of congenital liars. Yet duty strongly emerges as the second message conveyed by Pocahontas' words, if they are her words. She conveys a firm sense of her social role and how she must play it. She defines that role neither as the Christian convert Rebecca nor as the wife of John Rolfe; instead, she is the one obligated to call Smith "father" and "be for ever and ever" his "countryman." In Native eastern North America, obligations were always supposed to be reciprocal. The third message, therefore, is the failure of Smith and his mendacious countrymen to uphold the standard of reciprocity. He refuses to let her call him "father" and has apparently forgotten his pledge to "Powhatan [that] what was yours should be his, and he the like to you."

So it seems plausible that, far from being a youthful rebel who defied her father's will to join the English invaders, Pocahontas was a dutiful child who fulfilled a very traditional function in Native politics and diplomacy.[24] Her role in whatever happened during Smith's 1608 captivity defined him as her adoptive parent, and thus also established kinship relations between him and her biological father and, presumably, her mother's clan as well. (There would be nothing odd about having two or more "fathers." Virginia Algonquian children probably used the same term of respect — which only imperfectly translates into English — to address both a male parent and his brothers.) Pocahontas' later marriage to Rolfe — a match both sides understood as an act of diplomatic alliance — vastly strengthened already existing connections. Through her, the English and the Powhatans became fictive kin, and the ceremonial, political, and economic basis for peace, as people of Tsenacommacah understood that concept, became possible. Thus, a month after the marriage, Powhatan "inquire[d] how his brother Sir Thomas Dale fared, after that of his daughter's welfare, her marriage, his unknown son, and how they liked, lived, and loved together." When told all was well, "he laughed heartily, and said he was very glad of it."[25]

We need not idealize either the motives of Powhatan or the unanimity of his people to appreciate the genuine, if fragile, potential that Pocahontas' adoption and marriage represented or the ways in which that potential resonated with traditional Native practices. When Pocahontas took the name Rebecca and went to live among Europeans, she did so not to abandon her culture but to incorporate the English into her Native world, to make it possible for them to live in Indian country by Indian rules. In this light, it could not be more wrong to assert that she broke decisively with her people. To the contrary, Pocahontas played a familiar diplomatic role and may in fact have had very little choice in either her casting or her performance. Nor need we demonize the English to appreciate the tragedy that resulted from their failure to fulfill reciprocal obligations of kinship that they did not — or would not — understand. "Your king gave me nothing," Uttamatomakkin complained to Smith after an audience with James I that inexplicably included none of the gifts that any chief worthy of the name should have bestowed to display his power and largesse. Not surprisingly, when he returned to Tsenacommacah after Pocahontas' death, Powhatan's agent had little good to say about the English.[26] The story of Pocahontas, then, does represent a road of intercultural cooperation that tragically was not taken — but a road toward cooperation on Indian, rather than English, terms. To take that road, Smith and others in positions of authority over European colonists would have had to acknowledge that they were living in Indian country, that what they called "Virginia" was not theirs alone to govern. Whether that acknowledgment would have been enough — whether Powhatans and English could ever have found a way to share Tsenacommacah on mutually advantageous terms — will never be known. But Pocahontas' diplomatic marriage suggests that there was a genuine moment when an alternative history might have been made. Perhaps that is the deepest tragedy of her story.

Notes

1. On the 1995 film *Pocahontas*, see Gary Edgerton and Kathy Merlock Jackson, "Redesigning Pocahontas: Disney, the 'White Man's Indian,' and the Marketing of Dreams," *Journal of Popular Film and Television* 24, no. 2 (Summer 1996): 90–98; and Jill Lepore, Review of *The Scarlet Letter* and *Pocahontas*, *American Historical Review* 101 (1996): 1166–68. On the biblical resonance of the name Rebecca see Frances Mossiker, *Pocahontas: The Life and the Legend* (New York: Knopf, 1976), 169–170. The career of the Pocahontas myth in American culture is traced in Ann Uhry Abrams, *The Pilgrims and Pocahontas: Rival Myths of American Origin* (Boulder: Westview Press, 1999).

2. *The Letters of John Chamberlain*, ed. Norman Egbert McClure, 2 vols. (Philadelphia: American Philosophical Society, 1939); William Strachey, *The Historie of Travell into Virginia Britania* (1612), ed. Louis B. Wright and Virginia Freund, Publications of the Hakluyt Society, 2d ser., vol. 103 (London, 1953); Raphe Hamor, *A True Discourse of the Present State of Virginia, and the Successe of the Affaires There till the 18 of June, 1614* (London, 1615); *The Complete Works of Captain John Smith (1580–1631)*, ed. Philip L. Barbour, 3 vols. (Chapel Hill: University of North Carolina Press, 1986).

3. Helen Rountree, *The Powhatan Indians of Virginia: Their Traditional Culture* (Norman: University of Oklahoma Press, 1989), 80.

4. Barbour, *Complete Works of Smith*, 2: 274 (quotation); Helen C. Rountree, *Pocahontas's People: The Powhatan Indians of Virginia through Four Centuries* (Norman: University of Oklahoma Press, 1990), 8–10; Frederic W. Gleach, *Powhatan's World and Colonial Virginia: A Conflict of Cultures* (Lincoln: University of Nebraska Press, 1997), 22–35.

Kathleen M. Brown notes that Powhatan — perhaps in violation of traditional patterns — arranged to have numerous male offspring of his wives and what may have been 100 or more shorter-term liaisons made subordinate chiefs in various villages that were part of his domain, but many of these may have also had some claim on office through their high-status mothers; Brown, *Good Wives, Nasty Wenches, and Anxious Patriarchs* (Chapel Hill: University of North Carolina Press, 1996), 51–53. It should also be noted that many of those described in English sources as Powhatan's "sons" may in fact have been his maternal nephews.

5. Strachey, *Historie of Travell*, 62.
6. Barbour, *Complete Works of Smith*, 2: 259. For an overview of the evidence, see J. A. Leo LeMay, *Did Pocahontas Save Captain John Smith?* (Athens: University of Georgia Press, 1992).
7. Frederic W. Gleach, "Controlled Speculation: Interpreting the Saga of Pocahontas and Captain John Smith," in *Reading beyond Words: Contexts for Native History*, ed. Jennifer S. H. Brown and Elizabeth Vibert (Peterborough, Ont.: Broadview Press, 1996), 34.
8. Barbour, *Complete Works of Smith*, 1: 274.
9. Strachey, *Historie of Travell*, 72.
10. McClure, *Letters of John Chamberlain*, 1: 470–471.
11. Quoted in Edmund S. Morgan, *American Slavery, American Freedom: The Ordeal of Colonial Virginia* (New York: W. W. Norton, 1975), 74.
12. Quoted in Grace Steele Woodward, *Pocahontas* (Norman: University of Oklahoma Press, 1969), 159.
13. Alden T. Vaughan. *American Genesis: Captain John Smith and the Founding of Virginia* (Boston: Little, Brown, 1975), 99.
14. Hamor, *True Discourse*, 63.
15. Ibid., 54, 6–11.
16. Barbour, *Complete Works of Smith*, 2: 258–262.
17. McClure, *Letters of John Chamberlain*, 2: 12, 50 (first quotation), 56–57 (second quotation), 66.
18. J. Frederick Fausz, "Opechancanough: Indian Resistance Leader," in *Struggle and Survival in Colonial America*, ed. David G. Sweet and Gary B. Nash (Berkeley: University of California Press, 1981), 21–37.
19. Quoted in Vaughan, *American Genesis*, 163.
20. Quoted in Fausz, "Opechancanough," 34–35.
21. Woodward, *Pocahontas*, 6–7.
22. Robert S. Tilton, *Pocahontas: The Evolution of an American Narrative* (New York: Cambridge University Press, 1994), 186.
23. Barbour, ed., *Complete Works of Smith*, vol. 2, p. 261.
24. Bernd C. Peyer, *The Tutor'd Mind: Indian Missionary-Writers in Antebellum America* (Amherst: University of Massachusetts Press, 1997), 27–30.
25. Hamor, *True Discourse*, 40.
26. Barbour, *Complete Works of Smith*, 2: 261 (quotation); Brown, *Good Wives*, 42–45, 69–72.

(2002)

Questions

1. Daniel Richter writes, "Every North American schoolchild knows — or thinks she knows — the story of Pocahontas" (par. 2). How closely does the brief account he provides match what you know (or thought you knew) about Pocahontas? Where does it diverge? What is your response to his claim that that story is "either incorrect or misleading" (par. 3)?

2. Richter says that as a historian it is difficult to provide an accurate account of the story of Pocahontas "in part because of the contradictory accounts Smith himself wrote" (par. 5). What does this suggest about history itself and also about this particular story?

3. Richter makes two strong claims: in paragraph 5, he supplies "the most likely interpretation of what happened," and in the next paragraph he states that "there was no romance between Smith and Pocahontas." What is your response to these, perhaps surprising, claims?

4. How does Richter distinguish between westward- and eastward-facing perspectives regarding historical narrative? Which one provides greater insight into the story of Pocahontas? Explain.

5. Richter begins paragraph 15 with "If Smith's version of Pocahontas' words is accurate, at least three powerful messages emerge." Briefly recount the three messages and discuss how they influence your understanding of Pocahontas and Smith.

6. In the final two paragraphs, Richter offers his interpretation of the meaning of Pocahontas, and concludes: "Perhaps that is the deepest tragedy of her story." What is your response to Richter's interpretation?

7. What is the overall rhetorical effect of Richter's footnotes?

Matoaka als Rebecca

Simon van de Passe

The engraving on the next page, the only known contemporaraneous portrait of "Pocahontas," was made in 1616 by Dutch engraver Simon van de Passe. It was commissioned by the Virginia Company, which was established by King James of England in 1606 to create settlements in America. The Latin words around the portrait may be translated as "Matoaka, alias Rebecca, daughter of the most powerful prince of the Powhatan Empire of Virginia."

Questions

1. What is your first impression of this picture? How old does "Matoaka, alias Rebecca," look? Pocahontas is said to have been twenty-one, or twenty-two at the oldest, when she died. Considering that this is the only contemporaraneous portrait of her, how accurate is it likely to be?

2. Look carefully at the details: the face, the clothing, the eyes, and the hand. What do you find striking or surprising?

MATOAKA ALS REBECCA FILIA POTENTISS PRINC POWHATANI IMP. VIRGINIA.

Ætatis suæ 21. A.
1616

Matoaks als Rebecka daughter to the mighty Prince Powhatan Emperour of Attanoughkomouck als virginia converted and baptized in the Christian faith, and wife to the wor.ll Mr. Joh. Rolff.

Private Collection / The Bridgeman Art Library

3. How did the Virginia Company wish Pocahontas to be regarded? Why would they want her to be seen as depicted here?

Letter to Queen Anne of Great Britain

CAPTAIN JOHN SMITH

> The following letter was written in 1616 by Captain John Smith of the Virginia Company; in it he introduces Pocahontas to the queen of England.

To the most high and virtuous princess, Queen Anne of Great Britain

Most admired Queen,

The love I bear my God, my King and country, hath so oft emboldened me in the worst of extreme dangers, that now honesty doth constrain me to presume thus far beyond myself, to present your Majesty this short discourse: if ingratitude be a deadly poison to all honest virtues, I must be guilty of that crime if I should omit any means to be thankful.

So it is, that some ten years ago being in Virginia, and taken prisoner by the power of Powhatan their chief King, I received from this great Salvage exceeding great courtesy, especially from his son Nantaquaus, the most manliest, comeliest, boldest spirit, I ever saw in a Salvage, and his sister Pocahontas, the Kings most dear and well-beloved daughter, being but a child of twelve or thirteen years of age, whose compassionate pitiful heart, of my desperate estate, gave me much cause to respect her: I being the first Christian this proud King and his grim attendants ever saw: and thus enthralled in their barbarous power, I cannot say I felt the least occasion of want that was in the power of those my mortal foes to prevent, notwithstanding all their threats. After some six weeks fatting amongst those Salvage courtiers, at the minute of my execution, she hazarded the beating out of her own brains to save mine; and not only that, but so prevailed with her father, that I was safely conducted to Jamestown: where I found about eight and thirty miserable poor and sick creatures, to keep possession of all those large territories of Virginia; such was the weakness of this poor commonwealth, as had the Salvages not fed us, we directly had starved. And this relief, most gracious Queen, was commonly brought us by this Lady Pocahontas.

Notwithstanding all these passages, when inconstant fortune turned our peace to war, this tender virgin would still not spare to dare to visit us, and by her our jars have been oft appeased, and our wants still supplied; were it the policy of her father thus to employ her, or the ordinance of God thus to make her his instrument, or her extraordinary affection to our nation, I know not: but of this I am sure; when her father with the utmost of his policy and power, sought to surprise me, having but eighteen with me, the dark night could not affright her from coming through the irksome woods, and with watered eyes gave me intelligence, with her best advice to escape his fury; which had he known, he had surely slain her.

Jamestown with her wild train she as freely frequented, as her fathers habitation; and during the time of two or three years, she next under God, was still the instrument to preserve this colony from death, famine and utter confusion; which if in those times, had once been dissolved, Virginia might have lain as it was at our first arrival to this day. Since then, this business having been turned and varied by many accidents from that I left it at: it is most certain, after a long and troublesome war after my departure, betwixt her father and our colony; all which time she was not heard of.

About two years after she herself was taken prisoner, being so detained near two years longer, the colony by that means was relieved, peace concluded; and at last rejecting her barbarous condition, she was married to an English Gentleman, with whom at this present she is in England; the first Christian ever of that Nation, the first Virginian ever spoke English, or had a child in marriage by an Englishman: a matter surely, if my meaning be truly considered and well understood, worthy a Princes understanding. 5

Thus, most gracious Lady, I have related to your Majesty, what at your best leisure our approved Histories will account you at large, and done in the time of your Majesty's life; and however this might be presented you from a more worthy pen, it cannot from a more honest heart, as yet I never begged anything of the state, or any:

and it is my want of ability and her exceeding desert; your birth, means and authority; her birth, virtue, want and simplicity, doth make me thus bold, humbly to beseech your Majesty to take this knowledge of her, though it be from one so unworthy to be the reporter, as myself, her husbands estate not being able to make her fit to attend your Majesty. The most and least I can do, is to tell you this, because none so oft hath tried it as myself, and the rather being of so great a spirit, however her stature: if she should not be well received, seeing this Kingdom may rightly have a Kingdom by her means; her present love to us and Christianity might turn to such scorn and fury, as to divert all this good to the worst of evil; whereas finding so great a Queen should do her some honor more than she can imagine, for being so kind to your servants and subjects, would so ravish her with content, as endear her dearest blood to effect that, your Majesty and all the Kings honest subjects most earnestly desire.

And so I humbly kiss your gracious hands,
Captain John Smith, 1616

Questions

1. How does Captain John Smith characterize Powhatan, Nantaquaus, and Pocahontas?
2. Were you surprised by the brevity of Smith's account of his supposed rescue by Pocahontas? How does Smith's account as delivered here match your understanding of his interaction with Pocahontas, based on your familiarity with the legend and your reading of Richter (p. 306)?
3. What is Smith's tone in the final sentence of the letter?
4. What are Smith's motives? What is the purpose of his letter to the queen?
5. In Smith's 1608 account, which contains no mention of a rescue, he describes Pocahontas as a "child of ten years old." Eight years later, in this 1616 letter to Queen Anne of Great Britain, he writes, "at the minute of my execution, she hazarded the beating out of her own brains to save mine" (par. 2). Then in 1624, he elaborates on the event in this account:

> At his entrance before the king, all the people gave a great shout. The queen of Appamatuck was appointed to bring him water to wash his hands, and another brought him a bunch of feathers, instead of a towel to dry them: having feasted him after their best barbarous manner they could, a long consultation was held, but the conclusion was, two great stones were brought before Powhatan: then as many as could laid hands on him, dragged him to them, and thereon laid his head, and being ready with their clubs, to beat out his brains, Pocahontas the king's dearest daughter, when no entreaty could prevail, got his head in her arms, and laid her own upon his to save him from death: whereat the Emperor was contented he should live to make him hatchets, and her bells, beads, and copper; for they thought him as well of all occupations as themselves.

Finally, six years after that, in a 1630 account, Smith tells a similar story of having been rescued by a young girl in Hungary in 1602. What do Smith's different versions suggest to you about the story?

The Baptism of Pocahontas

JOHN GADSBY CHAPMAN

> The following painting, commissioned by the U.S. Congress in 1839, was hung
> in the U.S. Capitol rotunda among paintings of other American heroes.

JOHN GADSBY CHAPMAN, *THE BAPTISM OF POCAHONTAS*, 1839, OIL ON CANVAS, 12' × 18',
U.S. CAPITOL ROTUNDA, WASHINGTON, D.C.

(See color insert, Image 17.)

Architect of the Capitol

Questions

1. Why would the U.S. Congress decide in 1839 to commission such a painting to
   hang among representations of other American heroes in the Capitol rotunda?
   Consider events that took place in the country at the time — for example, passage
   of the Indian Removal Act of 1830 and the infamous "Trail of Tears" that Native
   Americans were forced to travel.
2. What are your first impressions of this painting? How are the central figures of the
   minister, John Rolfe, and Pocahontas depicted?
3. What is your impression of the Native American figures, particularly Pocahontas's
   sister — who is holding a baby, her brother Nantaquaus — who is turning away,
   and her uncle Opechancanough — who is seated, facing the viewer? How do they
   contrast with the English figures and with Pocahontas? What is the rhetorical
   effect of these depictions?

4. In 1863 and again in 1875, this image was engraved on the back of $20 U.S. banknotes. What does this suggest about the prominence of this depiction? What features made it so important?

The Chieftain's Daughter
A Ballad

GEORGE P. MORRIS

> George P. Morris was an editor and author of popular poems, songs, and hymns. His most famous piece was "Woodsman, Spare That Tree." The following 1840 ballad, said to have been the most popular poem about Pocahontas in the nineteenth century, was put to music by Henry Russell, an English composer.

Upon the barren sand
  A single captive stood,
Around him came, with bow and brand,
  The red men of the wood.
Like him of old, his doom he hears,   5
  Rock-bound on ocean's rim: —
The chieftain's daughter knelt in tears,
  And breathed a prayer for him.

Above his head in air,
  The savage war-club swung,   10
The frantic girl, in wild despair,
  Her arms about him flung.
Then shook the warriors of the shade,
  Like leaves on aspen limb,
Subdued by that heroic maid   15
  Who breathed a prayer for him.

"Unbind him?" gasp'd the chief,
  "Obey your king's decree!"
He kiss'd away her tears of grief,
  And set the captive free.   20
'Tis ever thus, when in life's storm,
  Hope's star to man grows dim,
An angel kneels in woman's form,
  And breathes a prayer for him.

(1840)

Questions

1. What is the central irony that George P. Morris develops in the second stanza?
2. How would you describe Morris's overall tone in this poem?
3. How do the last four lines of the poem differ from those that precede them? What is their rhetorical effect?
4. How does the repetition of "breathed a prayer for him" at the end of each stanza influence the meaning of the poem?
5. What about this poem might account for its great popularity in its time?
6. Go online to find the sheet music for this ballad, or listen to a recording. How does reading the music or listening to the song affect your understanding and estimation of the piece?

Pocahontas

HOWARD CHANDLER CHRISTY

Howard Chandler Christy was a prolific artist, contributing realistic illustrations to magazines such as *Scribner's* and *Harper's*, and patriotic posters for use by the U.S. Navy and Marine Corps. You would probably recognize his famous recruiting poster showing a young lady in a naval uniform with the caption: "Gee!! I Wish I Were a Man. I'd Join the Navy." The 1911 painting on the next page is the first of a series of eight "Christy Girl" paintings that suggest not only who the idealized American heroic woman was but also what American beauty was. The eight include: *Pocahontas*, the *Puritan Girl*, the *Colonial Girl*, the *Revolutionary Girl*, the *Pioneer Girl*, the *Dixie Girl*, the *Western Girl*, and the *American Girl*. Each one depicts a beautiful, independent American woman.

Questions

1. This painting seems to depict a proposal. The kneeling figure is not identified; is he likely to be Captain John Smith? Pocahontas's Indian husband Kocoum? John Rolfe? Explain the reason for your choice.
2. Look carefully at the figure of Pocahontas. How is she depicted? Consider her posture, her clothing, and her countenance. How would you describe the attitude portrayed?
3. As the first of the series of eight "Christy Girl" paintings, what are this painting's symbolic suggestions? How does this painting reflect the image of women in 1911?
4. How does this painting contribute to the developing myth of Pocahontas in its time? What does it suggest about contemporaneous conceptions of women?

© Copyright 2013 National Museum of American Illustration™, Newport RI Photos courtesy Archives of the American Illustrators Gallery™ NYC

HOWARD CHANDLER CHRISTY, *POCAHONTAS*, 1911, OIL ON CANVAS, 69" × 49", AMERICAN ILLUSTRATORS GALLERY, NEW YORK.

(See color insert, Image 18.)

Pocahontas to Her English Husband, John Rolfe

PAULA GUNN ALLEN

Well-known as a poet and writer of fiction, Paula Gunn Allen, of mixed European American and Native American Pueblo Laguna descent, was a professor of English and American Indian Studies at UCLA. In the following 1988 poem, the poet speaks in the imagined voice of Pocahontas.

In a way, then, Pocahontas was a kind of traitor to her people. . . . Perhaps I am being a little too hard on her. The crucial point, it seems to me, is to remember that Pocahontas was a hostage. Would she have converted freely to Christianity if she had not been in captivity? There is no easy answer to this question other than to note that

once she was free to do what she wanted, she avoided her own people like the
plague. . . .

Pocahontas was a white dream—a dream of cultural superiority.

—CHARLES LARSON, *American Indian Fiction*

Had I not cradled you in my arms,
oh beloved perfidious one,
you would have died.
And how many times did I pluck you
from certain death in the wilderness—   5
my world through which you stumbled
as though blind?
Had I not set you tasks,
your masters far across the sea
would have abandoned you—   10
did abandon you, as many times
they left you
to reap the harvest of their lies.
Still you survived, oh my fair husband,
and brought them gold   15
wrung from a harvest I taught you
to plant. Tobacco.
It is not without irony that by this crop
your descendants die, for other
powers than you know   20
take part in this as in all things.
And indeed I did rescue you—
not once but a thousand thousand times
and in my arms you slept, a foolish child,
and under my protecting gaze you played,   25
chattering nonsense about a God
you had not wit to name. I'm sure
you wondered at my silence, saying I was
a simple wanton, a savage maid,
dusky daughter of heathen sires   30
who cartwheeled naked through the muddy towns
learning the ways of grace only
by your firm guidance, through
your husbandly rule:
no doubt, no doubt.   35
I spoke little, you said.
And you listened less,
but played with your gaudy dreams

and sent ponderous missives to the throne
striving thereby to curry favor   40
with your king.
I saw you well. I
understood your ploys and still
protected you, going so far as to die
in your keeping — a wasting,   45
putrefying Christian death — and you,
deceiver, whiteman, father of my son,
survived, reaping wealth greater
than any you had ever dreamed
from what I taught you   50
and from the wasting of my bones.

(1988)

Questions

1. The poet assumes the voice of Pocahontas and addresses her husband: "oh beloved perfidious one" (l. 2). Why would she use such an oxymoronic phrase at the beginning of the poem? What is its effect? How do that phrase and the rhetorical question that follows contribute to her tone?
2. How effectively does Paula Gunn Allen develop the "irony" she mentions in line 19? How does the irony in lines 33–34 ("learning the ways of grace only / by your firm guidance") contribute to the poem?
3. How does Allen's juxtaposition of Pocahontas as protector with Rolfe's characterization of her as "a simple wanton, a savage maid, / dusky daughter of heathen sires" (ll. 29–30) serve to undermine stereotypes regarding Native Americans?
4. In line 31, Allen refers to the famous passage from William Strachey's 1615 book, *History of Travaile into Virginia Britannica* (one of the very few sources from which we draw information about Pocahontas): "Pocahuntas, a well-featured but wanton young girle . . . of the age of eleven or twelve years, get the boyes forth into the market place, and make them wheele, falling on their hands, turning their heels upwards, whom she would followe, and wheele so herself, naked as she was, all the fort over." Although Strachey probably never actually *saw* Pocahontas himself, his description is widely accepted as accurate. How does Allen interpret his account in this poem?
5. What is the argument that Allen advances in the poem? What is her view of Pocahontas?

from *Redesigning Pocahontas*
Disney, the "White Man's Indian," and the Marketing of Dreams

GARY EDGERTON AND KATHY MERLOCK JACKSON

> The following selection is from a 1996 critical article on the Disney film *Pocahontas*. Gary Edgerton is professor and chair of the Communication and Theater Arts Department at Old Dominion University. Kathy Merlock Jackson is professor and coordinator of communications at Virginia Wesleyan College.

It is a story that is fundamentally about racism and intolerance and we hope that people will gain a greater understanding of themselves and of the world around them. It's also about having respect for each other's cultures.

— THOMAS SCHUMACHER, SENIOR VICE PRESIDENT OF
DISNEY FEATURE ANIMATION (*POCAHONTAS* 35)

The challenge was how to do a movie with such themes and make it interesting, romantic, fun.

— PETER SCHNEIDER, PRESIDENT OF
DISNEY FEATURE ANIMATION (*POCAHONTAS* 37)

Don't Know Much about History

Artists and authors have actually been reshaping Pocahontas and her history for nearly four centuries. In *Pocahontas: Her Life and Legend*, William M. S. Rasmussen and Robert S. Tilton surveyed literally dozens of depictions, beginning during Pocahontas's lifetime, when she was "living proof that American natives could be Christianized and civilized" (7). Fact and fiction were blended at the outset into this legendary personality who symbolized friendly and advantageous relations between American Indians and English settlers from a distinctly Anglo-American point of view. Disney's animators are merely part of that longer tradition, the latest in a series of story-tellers, painters, poets, sculptors, and commercial artists who have taken liberties with Pocahontas's historical record for their own purposes (Rasmussen and Tilton).

Disney's *Pocahontas* is, once again, a parable of assimilation, although this time the filmmakers hinted at a change in outlook. Producer James Pentecost for instance reported that

> "Colors of the Wind" perhaps best sums up the entire spirit and essence of the film . . . this song was written before anything else. It set the tone of the movie and defined the character of Pocahontas. Once Alan [Menken] and Stephen [Schwartz] wrote that song, we knew what the film was about. (*Pocahontas* 51–52)

Schwartz agreed with Pentecost, adding that his lyrics were inspired by Chief Seattle's famous speech to the United States Congress that challenged white ascendancy in America and the appropriation of American Indian lands (*Pocahontas* 52).

"Colors of the Wind" functions as a rousing anthem for Pocahontas, extolling the virtues of tolerance, cross-cultural sensitivity, and respect for others and the natural environment:

> You think you own whatever land you
> land on
> The earth is just a dead thing you can
> claim
> But I know ev'ry rock and tree and
> creature
> Has a life, has a spirit, has a name
> You think the only people who are
> people
> Are the people who think and look like
> you
> But if you walk the footsteps of a stranger
> You'll learn things you never knew
> You never knew.

These lofty sentiments, however, are down-played by the film's overriding com-   5
mitment to romantic fantasy. Pocahontas, for example, sings "Colors of the Wind" in response to John Smith's remark that her people are "savages," but the rest of the technically stirring sequence plays more like an adolescent seduction than a lesson teaching Smith those "things [he] never knew [he] never knew."

Pocahontas's search for her "dream," a classic Disney plot device, is a case in point. A great deal of dramatic energy is spent on Pocahontas's finding her "true path." She is sprightly, though troubled, in her conversations with Grandmother Willow. She is struggling with her own youthful uncertainties as well as her father's very definite plans for her:

> Should I choose the smoothest course
> Steady as a beating drum
> Should I marry Kocoum
> Is all my dreaming at an end?
> Or do you still wait for me, dreamgiver
> Just around the river bend?

Unsure of Kocoum, but regarding love and marriage as her only options, Pocahontas finally finds her answer in John Smith.

What this development discloses, of course, is the conventional viewpoint of the filmmakers: Pocahontas essentially falls in love with the first white man she sees. The film's scriptwriters chose certain episodes from her life, invented others, and in the process shaped a narrative that highlights some events, ideas, and values, while suppressing others. The historical Pocahontas and John Smith were never lovers, she was twelve and he was twenty-seven when they met in 1607. In relying so completely on their romantic coupling, however, Disney's animators minimize the many challenging issues that they raise — racism, colonialism, environmentalism, and spiritual alienation.

The entire plot structure is similarly calculated to support the Disney game plan. The film begins in London in 1607 with John Smith and the Virginia Company crew setting out for the New World, and it concludes with Smith's return trip to England in 1609, although the duration of the movie seems to span weeks rather than years. The scriptwriters, nevertheless, terminate the narrative at the most expedient juncture, avoiding the more tragic business of Pocahontas's kidnapping by the English; her isolation from her people for a year; her ensuing conversion to Christianity; her marriage and name change to Lady Rebecca Rolfe; and her untimely death from tuberculosis at age twenty-one in England (Barbour; Fritz; Mossiker; Woodward). Disney's filmmakers did, in fact, research those details of Pocahontas's life before starting production, but obviously their aim was to keep audiences as comfortable as possible by providing a predictable product.

Co-director Eric Goldberg later claimed that "it's important for us as filmmakers to be able to say not everything was entirely hunky-dory by the end . . . which it usually is in a traditionally Disneyesque movie" (Mallory 24). Given the eventual fate of Pocahontas and the Algonquins, though, Disney's animators could hardly have opted for the usual "happily ever after" finale. The filmmakers, after all, were genuinely trying to offend no one, including the Native American community and their consultants. 10

Pocahontas's climactic sequence further establishes the film's dominant, love-story narrative, albeit with some variations of the classic Disney formula. After English settler Thomas shoots and kills Kocoum, tensions between the American Indians and the British mount. John Smith is captured by Kocoum's companions, blamed for his death, and immediately slated for execution. In a replay of the legendary rescue scene, Pocahontas risks her life to save John Smith, catalyzing peace between the English and the American Indians. In the process, the film's animators and scriptwriters complete their upgrade of the Indian princess characterization by making Pocahontas more assertive, determined to realize her "dream," and according to her father, "wis[e] beyond her years."

The film, moreover, concludes with Pocahontas standing alone on a rocky summit, watching the ship carrying a wounded John Smith sail for England. She has presumably resolved to stay behind in Virginia and take her rightful place alongside her father as a peacemaker, even though her actions in the previous eighty minutes of the film suggest that her "path" lies elsewhere. Pocahontas thus reinforces another resilient stereotype that the main purpose of a Disney heroine is to further the interests of love, notwithstanding the bittersweet coda. Pocahontas's newfound ambition to become a mediator, then, is a workable if somewhat disingenuous solution, especially considering the latent historical realities percolating beneath this romantic plotline.

The questions then arise: Can a Disney animated feature be substantive as well as entertaining? Can race, gender, and the rest of [the] Pocahontas postmodernist agenda be presented in a thought-provoking way that still works for the animation audience, especially children? We believe the answer is yes, but we also believe the

Everett Collection

A scene from Disney's 1995 movie *Pocahontas*.

studio has an obligation to create a more forward-looking alternative to existing stereotypes and to deal more fully and maturely with the serious issues and charged imagery that it addresses.

Consider the redesigning of the character of Pocahontas. Supervising animator Glen Keane remembered how former studio chairman Jeffrey Katzenberg charged him with reshaping Pocahontas as "the finest creature the human race has to offer" (Kim 24). He also admitted, "I don't want to say a rut, but we've been doing mainly Caucasian faces" (Cochran 42). Keane, in turn, drew on four successive women for inspiration, beginning with paintings of Pocahontas herself; then Native American consultant Shirley "Little Dove" Custalow McGowan; then twenty-one-year-old Filipino model Dyna Taylor; and finally white supermodel Christy Turlington (Cochran 42). After studio animators spent months sketching her, their Pocahontas emerged as a multicultural pastiche. They started with Native American faces but eventually gravitated to the more familiar and Anglicized looks of the statuesque Turlington. Not surprisingly, all the key decision makers and supervising artists on *Pocahontas* were white males. Disney and Keane's "finest creature" clearly is the result of a very conventional viewpoint.

Accordingly, what of avoiding old stereotypes? Native American actors were cast in all the native roles in the film; still, Pocahontas's screen image is less American Indian than fashionably exotic. Many critics, for example *Newsweek*'s Laura Shapiro, refer to the makeover as "Native American Barbie" (Shapiro and Chang 57) — in   15 other words, Indian features, such as Pocahontas's eyes, skin color, and wardrobe, only provide a kind of Native American styling to an old stereotype.

The British colonists also replace the Indians as stock villains in *Pocahontas*, with Governor Ratcliffe, in particular, singing about gold, riches, and power in the appropriately titled song "Mine, Mine, Mine." The film's final impression, therefore, is that, with Ratcliffe bound, gagged, and headed back to England, American Indians and Europeans are now free to coexist peacefully. Race is a dramatic or stylistic device, but the more profound consequences of institutional racism are never allowed even momentarily to invade the audience's comfort zone.

Perhaps the Disney studio should trust its patrons more. Fairy tales and fantasies have traditionally challenged children (and adults) with the unpleasant realities lurking just beneath their placid exteriors. Audiences are likely to enjoy added depth and suggestiveness enough to buy plenty of tickets and merchandise. Disney's *Pocahontas* raises important issues but does not fully address them; it succeeds as a king-sized commercial vehicle, but fails as a half-hearted revision.

Contested Meanings

> *The meaning of a text is always the site of a struggle.*
>
> —LAWRENCE GROSSBERG (86)

> *History is always interpreted. I'm not saying this film is accurate, but it is a start. I grew up being called Pocahontas as a derogatory term. They hissed that name at me, as if it was something dirty. Now, with this film, Pocahontas can reach a larger culture as a heroine. No, it doesn't make up for five hundred years of genocide, but it is a reminder that we will have to start telling our own stories.*
>
> —IRENE BEDARD (QTD. IN VINCENT E5)

The comments of Irene Bedard, the Native American actress who plays the voice of Pocahontas, augment many of the critical responses that surfaced after the release of *Pocahontas* in the summer of 1995. She offers audiences some valuable insights into the Native American perspective, especially with her painful recollection of being ridiculed with the surprising taunt, "Pocahontas." As she says, this film signals a welcomed counterbalance to such insults; most significantly, she calls for the emergence and development of a truly American Indian cinema that is the next needed step for fundamentally improving depictions of Native Americans on film.

Until that time, however, we can extend our understanding of Pocahontas, in particular, and established and alternative views toward Indian people in general, by examining the spectrum of critical reactions that the animated film engendered. The most striking aspect of *Pocahontas*'s critical reception is the contradictory nature of the responses: the film is alternately described as progressive or escapist, enlightened or racist, feminist or retrograde—depending on the critic. Inherently fraught with contradictions, Disney's *Pocahontas* sends an abundance of mixed messages, which probably underscores the limits of reconstructing the Native American image at Disney or, perhaps, any other major Hollywood studio that operates first and foremost as a marketer of conventional dreams and a seller of related consumer products.

Works Cited

Barbour, Philip L. *Pocahontas and Her World*. Boston: Houghton Mifflin, 1970. Print.

Cochran, Jason. "What Becomes a Legend Most?" *Entertainment Weekly* 16 June 1995: 42. Print.

Fritz, Jean. *The Double Life of Pocahontas*. New York: Puffin, 1983. Print.

Grossberg, Lawrence. "Reply to the Critics." *Critical Studies in Mass Communication* 3 (1983): 86–95. Print.

Kim, Albert. "Whole New World?" *Entertainment Weekly* 23 June 1995: 22–25. Print.

Mallory, Michael. "American History Makes Animation History." *The Disney Magazine* Spring 1995: 22–24. Print.

Mossiker, Frances. *Pocahontas*. New York: Knopf, 1976. Print.

"*Pocahontas*: Press Kit." Burbank: Walt Disney Pictures, 1995. Print.

Rasmussen, William M. S., and Robert S. Tilton. *Pocahontas: Her Life and Legend*. Richmond: Virginia Historical Society, 1994. Print.

Shapiro, Laura, and Yahlin Chang. "The Girls of Summer." *Newsweek* 22 May 1995: 56–57. Print.

Vincent, Mall. "Disney vs. History . . . Again." *Virginian-Pilot and Ledger-Star* 20 June 1995: E1, E5. Print.

———. "'Pocahontas': Discarding the History, It's still a Terrific Show." *Virginian-Pilot and Ledger-Star* 24 June 1995: E1 E2. Print.

Woodward, Grace Steele. *Pocahontas*. Norman: U of Oklahoma P, 1969. Print.

(1996)

Questions

1. What is the rhetorical purpose of the opening quotations from Thomas Schumacher and Peter Schneider? How do they contribute to the argument made by the authors?

2. In the second paragraph, Gary Edgerton and Kathy Merlock Jackson state that the film *Pocahontas* is "a parable of assimilation." What do they mean by that?

3. The authors say that the "lofty sentiments" of the song "Colors of the Wind" are "down-played by the film's overriding commitment to romantic fantasy" (par. 5). *Is* the movie overly romantic? If so, does that romanticism undermine the value and effect of the song? Explain.

4. The authors write: "The film's scriptwriters chose certain episodes from her life, invented others, and in the process shaped a narrative that highlights some events, ideas, and values, while suppressing others" (par. 7). For example, historians deny the love story portrayed between Smith and Pocahontas. In addition, the song has Pocahontas asking herself: "Should I marry Kocoum?" Historical accounts tell us that Pocahontas *did* marry him. Why would the filmmakers decide

to do what Edgerton and Jackson claim? Is it true that the filmmakers "terminate the narrative at the most expedient juncture," avoiding the awful realities of history "to keep audiences as comfortable as possible by providing a predictable product" (par. 8)?

5. What is the meaning and purpose of the textual citation in paragraph 8: (Barbour; Fritz; Mossiker; Woodward)?

6. Does the film reinforce stereotypes, as the authors claim, or does it enlighten its viewers about racism and intolerance, as Thomas Schumacher suggests in the epigraph to the article? Explain.

7. In paragraph 13, the authors ask, "Can a Disney animated feature be substantive as well as entertaining?" Is that a rhetorical question? If so, what does it imply? If not, how would you answer it?

8. In the final paragraph, the authors write that "the film is alternately described as progressive or escapist, enlightened or racist, feminist or retrograde." Must the film be regarded as an either-or experience? What is your position on these juxtaposed responses? Explain.

from *Pocahontas*
Medicine Woman, Spy, Entrepreneur, Diplomat

PAULA GUNN ALLEN

> The following selection is excerpted from a 2004 biography of Pocahontas by Paula Gunn Allen (p. 321).

Fluidity of Identity

A part of the culture of individualism, a name is considered unchanging: it identifies one from cradle to grave; only one per customer is allowed. With many Native Nations, it was a different matter, and among many it still is. The figure frozen in history bears the child name: Pocahontas. It was her familiar or informal name, but it wasn't meant to hang on as her identity; these people took (and take) a name to be indicative of one's state — and childhood is a state. When Pocahontas became a woman — menstruating, pubic-haired, married — her name was no longer Pocahontas, although those of her close family who knew her best might still use the appellation affectionately. Even among modern Americans a child's baby name is often used by the parents, siblings, grandparents, or aunts and uncles as a way of recalling familial ties, shared history, and affection.

It was as Pocahontas that John Smith knew her, and much of our knowledge about her comes from his quill. He ever referred to her as "Pocahuntis," as he spelled the name, even years after her death, and Pocahontas she remained; only the spelling changed. That modern peoples know her only as a child says a great deal about white–American Indian relations, and it reveals volumes about Anglo-European consciousness. We read our culture and believe that we are reading about something other than ourselves; it is a common enough characteristic of a race that relies on early childhood learning for understanding everything that comes along for the rest of one's life. The race I refer to here is neither Indian nor Anglo; it is human. The words *Pocahontas*, *Powhatan*, and *Indians* are familiar enough to many Americans. But the ideas and images they evoke differ greatly from community to community and from period to period. What *Indian* means to a person who is American Indian bears little resemblance to what it signifies in the minds of other Americans. Similarly, a narrative convention in one system often makes little sense in one that is at great variance from it. So the American Indian narrative tradition and the Indo-European one differ in a number of ways. This is a fact that certainly complicates understanding the one in the terms of the other.

That the difference is as basic as a name — name of person, place, or phenomenon — forces those intent on bridging the distance between one culture's worldview and another's to beware the easy categorization of either. *Pocahontas: Medicine Woman, Spy, Entrepreneur, Diplomat* is first and last an Indian story, requiring that readers keep in mind that the bridge we must negotiate in considering Pocahontas's life began in the Algonquin forests of the *manitowinini*. The story crosses over the sea from there, just as our hero, Matoaka, nicknamed Pocahontas and baptized Rebecca, went from *manitowinini* to Faerie, from *tsenacommacah* to England, and from child to legend.

Pocahontas, the child, is the persona who entered history when as a prepubescent girl she threw her arms around Smith and signaled that he would be adopted, or remade, into her clan. Her age at that time is reckoned at about eleven years. A few years later, she was abducted by the English and held at a rudimentary boarding school — the first of many devoted to the purpose of "civilizing Indians" — that was distant from James Fort, as the English version has it. However, from an Algonquin point of view, it is more likely that she went to them voluntarily, letting them believe whatever they would. She went as Matoaka (or Matoaks), which was her adult name. When she was adopted, was remade, to enter the Virginia Company clan, she traded her Indian name, Matoaka, for an English name, Rebecca. In Powhatan terms, in which remaking a person into another person was familiar, she was no longer Matoaka; she had become Lady Rebecca, and as Lady Rebecca she died. If we were to keep to the cultural customs of the subject, we would refer to Pocahontas as Lady Rebecca.

Lady Rebecca had another name and role or identity: Amonute. This was her   5
medicine name, identifying her as Beloved Woman, shaman-priestess, sorcerer, adept of high degree. It was a name shared only once with the English, and as such is questioned in the pages of biographers. However, it is highly probable that she was a member of the *midéwewin*, the Medicine Lodge or Great Medicine Dance, a spiritual discipline widespread among the Algonquins all over North America. This society, or spiritual discipline, was concerned with various kinds of magic, healing being only one. The term *medicine*, like the newer word *shaman*, signifies that something Native is going on. Analogous words — that is, words that signify much of what these

shamans and medicine people do — abound: in non-Native contexts such people are usually identified as seers, priestesses, priests, or wizards. Many of the actions these trained spiritual adepts take do things that defy our present understanding of how things work, do things that material laws of the old physics don't account for. Among these are teleporting objects, soul walking, rain bringing, clear seeing, prophecy, finding water or any lost object or person, even protecting soldiers from a particular community. Carrying out a World Renewal Ceremony, while not a common practice, is sufficiently widespread among Native practitioners to make it likely that it was such a ceremony, on an almost unimaginable scale, that Amonute, Pocahontas as high priestess, along with the *matchacómoco*, the Great Council of the Powhatan Alliance, was engaged in. . . .

Old Men's Tales

As it has been recorded in history, film, fiction, poetry, and biography, the story of Pocahontas is largely a story about the heroic John Smith and the survival of a hardy band of English Christians who came to the *tsenacommacah* ("Virginia," as the newcomers named it). They came to bring civilization to the savage, Christianity to the heathen, and to light the flame of personal liberty, democracy, and the American way of life.

They were aided and abetted in this noble enterprise by a single Indian maiden named Matoaka, but usually called by her nickname, Pocahontas. This "little wanton," as some translated her nickname, sided with the bearded strangers despite the king, her father, Powhatan's anger. She remained loyal to the strangers despite their depredations against her own people, even despite the cruel rejection from Captain John Smith, the man she loved so truly. It is a story told and retold; its outlines are as familiar to Americans as our ideas about the American way of life. . . .

So Pocahontas entered Western history; the Beloved Woman, shaman-priestess and eventual *weroanskaa* (female leader) of the Powhatan Alliance. She was a woman of many roles and heroic stature, and her four names contain her life's history. Her familiar name, the one she is most known by, was Pocahontas. Her clan or personal name was Matoaka or Matoaks. Her sacred or priestess name was Amonute. Her Christian name was Lady Rebecca Rolfe. Thus began the great ceremony that would lead to the formation of the largest and wealthiest nation the world has yet seen.

In the short span of her life, which was a bit more than twenty years, she would set in motion a chain of events that would ensure the dominance of the *manito-aki* in global life and affairs, usher in a period of terrible decline for her people, liberate the starving and miserable peoples of Europe and beyond, and introduce to a world awakening from feudalist absolutism the idea of egalitarianism, personal responsibility, and autonomy and the initiation of peaceful methods as a way of negotiating national and cultural differences. She would be involved in a great world change in these ways because it was the role of a Beloved Woman to do these things, and, because it was a time of vast change, it was the responsibility of a particularly able

Beloved Woman to do so. That woman, as the manito seem to have decreed, was Pocahontas. Among the several roles she filled, the primary one may have been her role as Beloved Woman. Particularly important during times of conflict between the community and its external adversaries, a woman who held this office would find herself called on to decide whether any captives — leaders and warriors alike — would be executed. Her decision was final; no man or woman could override it. The universal symbol of office for such women was one or more white feathers. In the case of the *manitowinini,* this badge of office would have been seen as connecting to the sacred story of Sky Woman, whose plummet through the void was arrested by waterfowl — symbolized by white feathers or, on prepubescent women, by white down.

Because Pocahontas is always depicted with white feathers, the major symbol of   10
the office of Beloved Woman, and because of the role she played in the ceremony during which John Smith's fate — and that of his fellow travelers — was decided, and because he specifically mentioned that the girl who saved him had her hair adorned with white down feathers, we can safely identify her as one who held the office.

In historic times there were fewer Beloved Women than it seems were present during Pocahontas's lifetime. This is because, or so one supposes, this was the time before the precipitous decline in the population of Algonquin and other Native Nations in the Southeast. These were, however, times in which conflict was increasing and strangers were seen, or reported, throughout the regions where the office of Beloved Woman was common practice. In turn, this widespread sense of threat was dramatically intensified by prophecies of imminent doom well known among them. So, for a variety of reasons, Pocahontas was not the only Beloved Woman (or Beloved Woman in training) among the Powhatans. Significantly, she was the one who, for whatever reason, flung her small body over Smith's and in that gesture determined that he would live. . . .

(2004)

Questions

1. Paula Gunn Allen discusses the four names of the person we know as Pocahontas. She comments: "That modern peoples know her only as a child says a great deal about white–American Indian relations, and it reveals volumes about Anglo-European consciousness" (par. 2). What *does* that fact say, and what are the *volumes* she suggests that it speaks?
2. Allen writes, "If we were to keep to the cultural customs of the subject, we would refer to Pocahontas as Lady Rebecca" (par. 4). Why *don't* we refer to her by her proper name? What does that suggest about how we use the story of Pocahontas?
3. How does Allen characterize the "story of Pocahontas" in paragraphs 6 and 7? Is that how you view the story? Explain.
4. Consider Allen's diction where she writes that the English Christians were "aided and abetted in this noble enterprise" (par. 7). How would you describe the tone created by her choice of language? What is the rhetorical effect of that tone on her account?

5. What is the "chain of events" that Allen claims Pocahontas "set in motion" (par. 9)? Do you agree that she could be responsible for so much? How does Allen's account differ from others with which you are familiar?

Making Connections

1. Most of what we know of the "historic" Pocahontas comes from the writings of Captain John Smith. Compare the perspectives of historian Daniel Richter (p. 306) and biographer Paula Gunn Allen (p. 330) with what Captain John Smith reports (p. 315).

2. The poem by George P. Morris (p. 319) and the painting by John Gadsby Chapman (p. 318) are almost exactly contemporaneous. What features do they share? What values do they esteem? What do the similarities between the two suggest about American attitudes at that time?

3. What similarities and differences do you see among the visual representations of Pocahontas by Simon van de Passe (p. 315), Chapman, and Howard Chandler Christy (p. 321)? How can you account for such radically different portrayals? How do the earlier portrayals compare with the later ones?

4. Look carefully at the portrayals of Pocahontas in the verses by Morris and Allen (p. 321), and in "Colors of the Wind" (p. 325). What similarities and differences do you find? Which verses idealize and romanticize Pocahontas? Which are critical? Which one or two do you like more? Why? How might Allen respond to those written by the others?

5. Morris, author of "The Chieftain's Daughter," has written, "Every part of the brief but glorious life of Pocahontas is calculated to produce a thrill of admiration, and to reflect the highest honor of her name." Which of the selections reflect Morris's perspective?

6. *Pocahontas: Medicine Woman, Spy, Entrepreneur, Diplomat*, by Allen, appeared two years after Richter's book *Facing East from Indian Country: A Native History of Early America*. How might Richter respond to Allen's account of the Pocahontas story?

7. Write a response to "Pocahontas to Her English Husband, John Rolfe" in Rolfe's voice.

Entering the Conversation

As you respond to each of the following prompts, support your position with appropriate evidence, including at least three sources in this Conversation on Pocahontas, unless otherwise indicated.

1. Much of what we read and see about "Pocahontas" is hagiographic; that is, it ideal-izes her as a mythic figure. In the American conciousness, Pocahontas, or Matoaka, is a person more mythic than real. As historians William M. S. Rasmussen and Robert S. Tilton state, "She has been called America's Joan of Arc because of her saintlike virtue and her courage to risk death for a noble cause. She has even been revered as the 'mother' of the nation, the female counterpart to George Washington." Why has she been so mythologized? Why has she become such an important figure to Americans? How do the texts in the Conversation contribute to or interrogate this hagiographic portrayal?

2. In his book *The Hero with a Thousand Faces*, Joseph Campbell writes, "Wherever the poetry of myth is interpreted as biography, history, or science, it is killed." Write an essay about Pocahontas in which you support, refute, or qualify Campbell's state-ment.

3. Historian and critic Charles Larson, in his 1978 book, *American Indian Fiction*, writes of Pocahontas: "She was an Indian we created solely out of our ethnocentric imaginations. She was the shadow of the great forest." Consider what he means by "our ethnocentric imaginations" and by "the shadow of the great forest." Then write an essay that defends, challenges, or qualifies the validity of Larson's statement.

4. Regarding Pocahontas and others, historian Daniel Richter writes, "It is much easier to reconstruct the abstract forces that constrained the seventeenth-century Native world than it is to recover the personal experiences of the people who struggled to give that world human shape. . . . Verifiable evidence about these figures is so scant that it may never be possible to determine the 'truth' about their lives. . . ." Write an essay about Pocahontas that explores the validity of Richter's statement.

5. In his 1981 book, *Simulacra and Simulation*, French philosopher Jean Beaudrillard analyzes the progression of an image in four stages: "It is the reflection of a pro-found reality; it masks and denatures a profound reality; it masks the *absence* of a profound reality; it has no relation to any reality whatsoever: it is its own pure simulacrum." A simulacrum differs from a representation or a simulation in that it may be considered a copy without an original, producing what Beaudrillard calls a "hyperreality." Consider the implications of Beaudrillard's ideas as they relate to our conception of Pocahontas. Are we dealing with reality or hyper-reality if what we "know" about Pocahontas comes mainly from an animated Disney movie?

6. View the 2009 film *Avatar*, and write an essay that compares and contrasts it with the Disney film *Pocahontas* and with the mythic figure you have learned about throughout this Conversation.

Grammar as Rhetoric and Style
Subordination in the Complex Sentence

One way that writers build longer sentences that are logical and clear is through subordination. **Subordination** is the use of a subordinating conjunction to make the meaning of one clause dependent on another clause. Although there are different types of subordination, involving both clauses and phrases, we are focusing here on the **complex sentence** — that is, a sentence formed by an **independent clause** and a **dependent clause** that begins with a subordinating conjunction.

Just because a clause is subordinate does not mean that what it says is unimportant. The ideas in both clauses contribute to the meaning of the sentence. It is the job of subordination to tell us how those ideas are related. This ability to connect ideas is the reason subordination is so effective; by using *because*, you tell your reader that one thing causes another; by using *when*, you indicate that two things are related chronologically. Thus, you can show the logical relationships in a rather lengthy sentence without impeding clarity.

Note the relationship between the dependent and independent clauses in the following sentence:

> After he failed to contact the emperor of China, the traders of India or the merchants of Japan, Columbus decided to pay for his voyage in the one important commodity he had found in ample supply — human lives.
>
> — JACK WEATHERFORD

In this example, Weatherford uses the subordinate clause to establish the chronology of events that lead to the main action of the sentence — that is, Columbus's decision to pay for his voyage with human beings.

Subordinating conjunctions can be classified by the relationships they indicate:

Contrast or concession   *although, even though, though, while, whereas*

> Although he was not the first explorer to glimpse or visit the distant shores of the Americas, his was the discovery that permanently planted the reality of the New World in the imagination — and political schemes — of the old.
>
> — LAURENCE BERGREEN

Cause and effect or reason   *because, since, so that*

> Because Columbus captured more Indian slaves than he could transport to Spain in his small ships, he put them to work in mines and plantations which he, his family and followers created throughout the Caribbean.
>
> — JACK WEATHERFORD

Condition   *if, once, unless, should, whether*

> And if any can shew me a better middle way than I have here laid down, I shall
> be ready to embrace it. . . .   — JOHN HALE

> Whether the dumbing down of America or soccer came first is hard to say, but
> soccer is clearly an important means by which American energy, drive, and
> competitiveness is being undermined to the point of no return.
> — STEPHEN H. WEBB

Time   *when, whenever, after, before, as, once, since, while, until*

> Sporting should be about breaking kids down before you start building
> them up.   — STEPHEN H. WEBB

Correct punctuation adds clarity to longer sentences. The rule of thumb is to use a comma to set off a subordinate clause that opens a sentence unless that sentence is very short. Notice that each of the opening clauses in the preceding examples from Weatherford, Edgerton and Jackson, Hale, and Webb is set off with a comma. Note that the comma comes not after the subordinating conjunction but after the entire clause. If you read the examples aloud, you'll probably find yourself naturally pausing at the end of the subordinate clause. Of course, these rules are not rigid; they are matters of style. Notice that the opening clauses in the first five examples from Weatherford, Edgerton and Jackson, Hale, and Webb are set off with a comma.

When the subordinate clause follows the independent clause — as it does in the last example from Webb on the previous page — it gets a little trickier. Most of the time there is no comma at all because the dependent clause is necessary to the meaning of the sentence; this is called a *restrictive clause*. The sentence you just read is an example: the clause "because the dependent clause is necessary . . ." is essential to the meaning of the sentence. In some cases, however, the dependent clause adds information but is not necessary to the meaning of the sentence. For example:

> Relatively little is known of the Americas and their peoples before Columbus,
> although we are learning more all the time.   — N. SCOTT MOMADAY

Here the subordinate clause is not essential to the meaning of the sentence, so it is set off with a comma; this is called a *nonrestrictive clause*. This all may sound a bit familiar to you. In the discussion of appositives in Chapter 6 (p. 535) we will talk about using commas with essential and nonessential elements. Here the rule is the same: essential information must be included and thus should not be set off with a comma; nonessential information that can be excluded should be set off with a comma.

Keep in mind that a dependent clause cannot stand alone. When you begin with a subordinating conjunction, be careful not to end up with a sentence fragment — that is, a dependent clause followed by a period. To correct such a sentence fragment, simply attach it to an independent clause by using a subordinating conjunction.

Rhetorical and Stylistic Strategy

One rhetorical strategy is to use subordination to blend shorter sentences into more graceful, longer sentences. Consider the following two sentences:

> I imagine my blood back through generations to the earliest man in America. I see in my mind's eye a procession of shamanistic figures, like those strange anthropomorphic forms painted on the cliffs of Barrier Canyon. . . .

Both are complete sentences. As readers, we understand them easily. The relationship between the two is temporal. But consider the difference with the addition of a subordinating conjunction:

> When I imagine my blood back through generations to the earliest man in America, I see in my mind's eye a procession of shamanistic figures, like those strange anthropomorphic forms painted on the cliffs of Barrier Canyon. . . .
> — N. Scott Momaday

Here the conjunction *when* indicates a temporal relationship — one of simultaneous action: Momaday indicates that in the act of imagining, he sees an image of the past. Combining the two short sentences does not make the resulting sentence more difficult to understand; on the contrary, the longer sentence is easier to understand because it leaves nothing to chance.

Another rhetorical decision a writer has to make is which clause should be dependent and which should be independent in a complex sentence. One clause may be just as important as the other, yet the independent clause usually carries the most force; in that case, you should put the idea you want to emphasize in an independent clause. Sometimes, the choice is obvious because the relationship is chronological or cause and effect, but other times either clause could be independent.

In the example of the restrictive clause above, note that Momaday could have switched the two clauses. He wrote:

> Relatively little is known of the Americas and their peoples before Columbus, although we are learning more all the time.   — N. Scott Momaday

What would be the difference in effect if he had reversed the clauses?

> Although relatively little is known of the Americas and their peoples before Columbus, we are learning more all the time.

This altered sentence opens with a subordinate clause about the amount of knowledge we have of the Americas prior to Columbus, and the independent clause emphasizes that the knowledge base is steadily increasing. But Momaday's point is that we know very little; he adds that knowledge is growing. By making the current level of knowledge the independent clause, Momaday stresses that point but then acknowledges that what we do know continues to expand.

Where to place the subordinate clause is another choice a writer has. Consider the following example from President Barack Obama's Tucson memorial speech:

> [A]t a time when our discourse has become so sharply polarized — at a time when we are far too eager to lay the blame for all that ails the world at the feet of those who think differently than we do — it's important for us to pause for a moment and make sure that we're talking with each other in a way that heals, not in a way that wounds.   — BARACK OBAMA

What would the difference in effect have been if President Obama had said the following?

> It's important for us to pause for a moment and make sure that we're talking with each other in a way that heals, not in a way that wounds, at a time when our discourse has become so sharply polarized — at a time when we are far too eager to lay the blame for all that ails the world at the feet of those who happen to think differently than we do.

Both examples indicate that the relationship between the two clauses is one of time — signaled by "when." But the second example leads with the need for momentary reflection and adds the element of time. The sentence that was actually delivered emphasizes the "time" — "a time when our discourse has become . . . polarized," "when we are . . . eager to lay . . . blame."

• EXERCISE 1 •

Using subordination, combine each of the following pairs of sentences into one sentence. You might shift the order of the sentences, and in some cases you may have to change the wording slightly. Be sure to punctuate correctly.

1. The investigators have gathered and analyzed all the evidence. We may expect a full report.
2. Tom had listened to the music of Bruce Springsteen for years. He had no idea a live performance could be so exciting.
3. The team has suffered its share of injuries this year. It could have improved its performance by giving Flynn more time on the field.
4. We will not be able to resolve this situation amicably. We must be willing to leave our prejudices at the door.
5. The crime rate has escalated near the mall. Many people have stopped shopping at the mall.
6. Rose Henderson has the qualifications to become a first-rate senator. Most of us knew she did not have a good chance to be elected. We worked hard on her campaign.

7. Lan Cao is a law professor. She is also the author of the novel *Monkey Bridge*.

8. I'm not feeling well today. I plan to leave the office early.

9. Apple offered a free iPod with every MacBook. Sales of the MacBook improved dramatically.

10. The affluent population of Dallas, Texas, is increasing steadily. Housing prices are rising beyond what someone with a middle-class salary can afford.

11. We all realize the necessity for increased security. We need to protect our civil liberties.

12. Thousands of vacationers travel to our national parks in search of solitude and fresh air. Other people prefer the excitement of casinos and amusement parks.

• EXERCISE 2 •

Identify each subordinate clause in the following sentences, and explain its effect. Pay special attention to the placement of the subordinate clauses. All examples are direct quotations from the readings in this chapter.

1. It was not until 1498, when he explored what is now Venezuela, that Columbus realized he had touched upon a continent.
   — N. Scott Momaday

2. It is this term, "New World," with which I should like to begin this discussion, not only because it is everywhere a common designation of the Americas but also because it represents one of the great anomalies of history.
   — N. Scott Momaday

3. Whenever I hear of protests about the Columbus Day holiday — protests that tend to pit Native Americans against Italian Americans — I remember these tragedies that occurred so soon before the first Columbus Day holiday, and I shake my head.
   — William J. Connell

4. I teach college kids, and since they tend to be more skeptical about Columbus Day than younger students, it's nice to point out that the first Columbus Day had a "college division."
   — William J. Connell

5. But indeed these things are nothing; if God should withdraw his hand, they would avail no more to keep you from falling, than the thin air to hold up a person that is suspended in it.
   — Jonathan Edwards

6. Whenever any American's life is taken by another American unnecessarily — whether it is done in the name of the law or in the defiance of law, by one man or a gang, in cold blood or in passion, in an attack of violence or

in response to violence — whenever we tear at the fabric of life which another man has painfully and clumsily woven for himself and his children, the whole nation is degraded.   — ROBERT F. KENNEDY

7. When you teach a man to hate and fear his brother, when you teach that he is a lesser man because of his color or his beliefs or the policies he pursues, when you teach that those who differ from you threaten your freedom or your job or your family, then you also learn to confront others not as fellow citizens but as enemies — to be met not with cooperation but with conquest, to be subjugated and mastered.

— ROBERT F. KENNEDY

8. This national feeling is good, but it won't count for much, and it won't last unless it's grounded in thoughtfulness and knowledge.

— RONALD REAGAN

9. We are a company professing ourselves fellow members of Christ, in which respect only though we were absent from each other many miles, and had our imployments as far distant, yet we ought to account ourselves knit together by this bond of love and live in the exercise of it, if we would have comfort of our being in Christ.   — JOHN WINTHROP

10. Disney's *Pocahontas* is, once again, a parable of assimilation, although this time the filmmakers hinted at a change in outlook.

— GARY EDGERTON AND KATHY MERLOCK JACKSON

• EXERCISE 3 •

Analyze the use of subordinate clauses in the following passages from seventeenth-century writers. Pay particular attention to how subordination calls attention to specific types of relationships between and among ideas.

1. Thirdly, when God gives a special commission he looks to have it strictly observed in every article. When he gave Saul a commission to destroy Amalek, he indented with him upon certain articles, and because he failed in one of the least, and that upon a fair pretense, it lost him the kingdom which should have been his reward if he had observed his commission.

— JOHN WINTHROP

2. Now if the Lord shall please to hear us, and bring us in peace to the place we desire, then hath he ratified this covenant and sealed our commission, [and] will expect a strict performance of the articles contained in it. But if we shall neglect the observation of these articles which are the ends we have propounded and, dissembling with our God, shall fall to embrace this

present world and prosecute our carnal intentions, seeking great things for ourselves and our posterity, the Lord will surely break out in wrath against us, be revenged of such a perjured people, and make us know the price of the breach of such a covenant.   — JOHN WINTHROP

3. 'Tis true, that judgment against your evil works has not been executed hitherto; the floods of God's vengeance have been withheld; but your guilt in the meantime is constantly increasing, and you are every day treasuring up more wrath; the waters are continually rising and waxing more and more mighty; and there is nothing but the mere pleasure of God that holds the waters back that are unwilling to be stopped, and press hard to go forward; if God should only withdraw his hand from the floodgate, it would immediately fly open, and the fiery floods of the fierceness and wrath of God would rush forth with inconceivable fury, and would come upon you with omnipotent power; and if your strength were ten thousand times greater than it is, yea, ten thousand times greater than the strength of the stoutest, sturdiest devil in hell, it would be nothing to withstand or endure it.   — JONATHAN EDWARDS

4. The most and least I can do, is to tell you this, because none so oft hath tried it as myself, and the rather being of so great a spirit, however her stature: if she should not be well received, seeing this Kingdom may rightly have a Kingdom by her means; her present love to us and Christianity might turn to such scorn and fury, as to divert all this good to the worst of evil; whereas finding so great a Queen should do her some honor more than she can imagine, for being so kind to your servants and subjects, would so ravish her with content, as endear her dearest blood to effect that, your Majesty and all the Kings honest subjects most earnestly desire.

— CAPTAIN JOHN SMITH

• EXERCISE 4 •

Examine some of your own writing — at least 300 words in length. Identify any examples of subordination. Then, revise the writing by adding subordinate conjunctions that make the relationship among ideas more specific and precise. In what ways has the overall effect of the writing changed? Is it more effective? Why or why not?

Suggestions for Writing
A Meeting of Old and New Worlds

1. A key theme during the time period covered by this chapter, which spans several centuries, is the collision of old worlds and new. What cultures and value systems are in conflict in the readings? Compare and contrast the bases for two conflicts.

2. The seventeenth century saw the emergence of women as critical voices in the New World — in both positive and negative ways. By studying the work by and about women of this era, what issues, questions, and values of gender roles do you see surfacing?

3. Travel writing has become its own field of study, with scholarly journals and numerous books dedicated to the subject. After reading a contemporary travel writer, discuss how his or her work is similar to or different from the travel writing by Cabeza de Vaca, Christopher Columbus, Captain John Smith, and Mary Rowlandson included in this chapter. Pay special attention to audience and purpose in your analysis.

4. The historical figure Tituba was one of the first people in Salem to be accused of witchcraft. Different accounts have identified her ethnicity as Native American, West Indian, and African; she has been the subject of scholarly articles as well as fictional accounts (e.g., *Tituba of Salem Village*, by Ann Petry, and *I, Tituba, Black Witch of Salem*, by Maryse Conde), and she plays a key role in Arthur Miller's play *The Crucible*. After researching Tituba, including how she is visually represented, discuss what insights into the phenomenon of the Salem Witch Trials you gained through studying the historical interest in and controversy about her.

5. Bruce Goebel, author of *Reading Native American Literature* (2004), makes the following criticism of the treatment of Native Americans in high-school history textbooks:

> First, economy of stereotype is the favored technique. From Columbus's own shallow perception of these early tributes, the historians select a few key images — innocence and passivity, gold jewelry — which contribute to and do not question the mytho-heroic narrative about Columbus.... Second, a strategy of invisibility ... seems to pervade most accounts. While various Indian tribes may at some point in a thousand-page textbook receive a subchapter's worth of attention, those whose history is poorly known or whose experience conflicts too greatly with traditional perceptions of heroic men and events are simply left out....

After examining two different history textbooks (a recently published one and another published one or two decades earlier), write an essay that supports, challenges, or qualifies Goebel's viewpoint.

6. How does this early era in the development of the United States manifest itself today? Choose one issue, conflict, idea, or viewpoint from this era and discuss how it continues to influence today's national narrative.

6

A New Republic
1750–1830

"We hold these truths to be self-evident, that all men are created equal, that they are endowed by their Creator with certain unalienable Rights, that among these are Life, Liberty and the pursuit of Happiness." With these words, on July 4, 1776, the United States of America declared its independence from England, and our nation was born. Commissioned by the Continental Congress and written by Thomas Jefferson with help from John Adams and Benjamin Franklin, the Declaration of Independence was first published as a broadside — a large sheet of paper meant for mass distribution — and distributed throughout the colonies to be read aloud. At once a rallying cry against oppression and tyranny and, according to Jefferson, an "expression of the American mind," the Declaration of Independence, one of the documents you will read in this chapter, still strikes a chord in us almost two and a half centuries later. Now, of course, we read the document as much more than simply a declaration of our independence; it is at once an extraordinary statement on human rights, moral principles, and the right to revolt and also an essential piece of American literature.

Revolutionary sentiment had been brewing in the colonies for a decade and a half prior to the declaration, articulated by writers and thinkers such as Patrick Henry and Thomas Paine, who built the moral and intellectual case for revolution and for the war that it would cause. John Adams would later reflect, "But what do we mean by the American Revolution? Do we mean the American War? The Revolution was effected before the War commenced. The Revolution was in the minds and hearts of the people; a change in their religious sentiments, of their duties and obligations . . . this radical change in the principles, opinions, sentiments, and affections of the people, was the real American Revolution."

But the war would surely come. As King George III issued taxes that placed financial burdens on the colonists and passed laws that limited their freedoms, the rallying cry "no taxation without representation" spread throughout the colonies. The Boston Massacre of 1770, in which British soldiers fired into a crowd of protestors and killed five civilians, further strained Britain's relationship with the colonies. Three years later, colonial resistance culminated in the Boston Tea Party. The destruction of three shiploads of taxed tea was a pivotal moment in the run-up to what we now call the Revolutionary War, triggering more protests against the British

Library of Congress, Prints and Photographs Division

This 1770 engraving by Paul Revere depicts the Boston Massacre, an event that helped propel the colonists to war.

and leading to the First Continental Congress. It was still another five years before the first military actions of the war began at the battles of Lexington and Concord on April 19, 1775; its first shot was immortalized in Ralph Waldo Emerson's poem "Concord Hymn" as "the shot heard round the world." Paine's *Common Sense* of January 1776 and *Crisis* pamphlets that followed, perhaps more than any other documents, helped American soldiers find the strength necessary to maintain the fight.

The Art Archive at Art Resource, NY

In this circa 1776 etching, New Yorkers pull down a statue of King George III after a reading of the Declaration of Independence. The statue was melted down to make bullets for the Continental army.

The Revolutionary War lasted until 1781, when the British finally surrendered to colonial forces at Yorktown, and officially concluded with the signing of the Treaty of Paris in 1783, but internal struggles persisted. Independence did not necessarily guarantee equitable and just governance. The declaration promised life, liberty, and the pursuit of happiness, but it would be up to the colonists whom we now call the Founding Fathers to secure those promises. What, precisely, would the new government be like? How should states be represented? And how much power would fall to the federal government rather than to the states? In their famous *Federalist* papers, published under the name Publius, Alexander Hamilton, James Madison, and John Jay argued for the Federalist cause and for the adoption of the Constitution. Anti-Federalists were concerned with the primacy of states' rights; most prominent among them, Samuel Adams of Massachusetts and Patrick Henry of Virginia, feared that the Constitution would grant the central government too much power. And now, well over two centuries later, we find that such debates continue.

The Constitution called for a president to head the executive branch of government and be the commander in chief of the armed forces. The nation chose not Thomas Jefferson or Benjamin Franklin but the war hero General George Washington, perhaps the ideal candidate to assume the role of first president. Equally powerful as a man and a myth, he embodied the American ideals of strength and courage, both physical and moral. This chapter includes a group of texts that explore how the myth of George Washington was created and how it continues to be part of our national identity.

The authors of our founding documents were children of the Enlightenment, influenced by the philosophical and scientific ideas of such thinkers and "natural philosophers" (the word *scientist* would not be used until 1833) as Isaac Newton and John Locke. Many of the Founding Fathers (two notable exceptions being the afore-mentioned Patrick Henry and Samuel Adams) were "Deists," rationalists who looked to the world itself rather than to scripture for an understanding of God and the universe. More concerned with tolerance than with orthodoxy, they enshrined religious tolerance in the Constitution by writing "Congress shall make no law respecting an establishment of religion, or prohibiting the free exercise thereof." America was, and is, a very religious nation. Most Americans at the time read little more than the Bible. And even if most of the Founding Fathers were Deists, that doesn't mean the population was. This chapter includes a Conversation that will ask you to compare the ideal of religious tolerance with the reality.

Once the revolution was accomplished, the Constitution ratified, and a president chosen, the citizens of the new nation began forging a new identity. What did it mean to be an American? That is the question addressed by Hector St. John de Crèvecoeur in his 1782 *Letters from an American Farmer*. Looking at America, Crèvecoeur saw a new land where a diverse population lived in freedom and equality, fulfilling the promise of Jefferson's declaration.

America was a new kind of nation where "all men are equally citizens." But what does "men" mean in the declaration? Clearly it does not mean "mankind," since that would include women. Nor did it refer to black men, most of whom were slaves, or to Native Americans. By 1804, the Northern states had abolished slavery, and by 1808 our third president, Thomas Jefferson, had outlawed the importation of slaves. But these measures didn't guarantee equality. Thus America, founded on the notion of equality, paradoxically remained a nation of inequality. In this chapter, this paradox is addressed by such writers as Judith Sargent Murray, who addressed women's rights as early as 1790; by Benjamin Banneker, who wrote to Thomas Jefferson about slavery in 1791; and by Chief Red Jacket and Chief Tecumseh, who addressed Native American rights in the first decade of the 1800s. Some scholars would add Phillis Wheatley to this list of dissenters. The first African American woman to publish a book, her political and poetic legacy continues to be the subject of debate, one that you will enter in this chapter's Conversation on the influence of Phillis Wheatley, in which you will consider such questions as these: Did she embed subtle protests against slavery in her poetry? Should she have called for freedom more forcefully? Did her poetry change the way early Americans thought of African Americans?

As America moved into the nineteenth century, it saw a period of unprecedented growth. The Louisiana Purchase of 1803 doubled the size of the country, and by 1830 the nation had increased from the original thirteen colonies to twenty-four states (half slave states and half free) with a population of over 12 million people, including nearly 2 million slaves. In addition, there were over 100,000 native Indians residing in the states, 50,000 Indians having been "removed" to Indian Territory. As the nation grew, so too did the ideological rifts—Federalism versus states' rights, freedom versus slavery, American ideals versus reality—that would threaten the very truths proclaimed in the Declaration of Independence. The literature in this chapter shows a new nation struggling with those rifts, one struggling to fulfill the promise of its birth.

Library of Congress Prints and Photographs Division

John J. Barralet (illustrator) and Benjamin Tanner (engraver), *America Guided by Wisdom,* 1815.

This allegorical image uses classical allusions to express optimism in the American democratic experiment. The artists described the image as follows: "On the fore ground Minerva, the goddess of Wisdom, is pointing to a Shield, supported by the Genius of America, bearing the Arms of the United States, with the motto UNION AND INDEPENDENCE, by which the country enjoys the prosperity signaled by the horn of plenty at the feet of America. The second ground is occupied by an Equestrian Statue of WASHINGTON placed in front, indicating the progress of the liberal arts. Commerce is represented by the figure of Mercury, with one foot resting on bales of American manufactures, pointing out the advantages of encouraging and protecting Navigation, signified by an armed vessel under sail, to Ceres, who is seated with implements of Agriculture near her. The Bee Hive is emblematic of industry, and the female spinning at the cottage door, shows the first and most useful of domestic manufactures."

Benjamin Franklin

Benjamin Franklin (1706–1790) was a scholar, a diplomat, an author, a scientist, a businessman, and an inventor. One of the Founding Fathers, he helped draft the Declaration of Independence and was a delegate to the Constitutional Convention. Considered by many to be the quintessential American and chief among the Founding Fathers — with perhaps only George Washington standing with him — Franklin is the only person to have signed the Declaration of Independence, the Treaty of Alliance with France against Britain, the Treaty of Paris (which concluded the Revolutionary War), and the U.S. Constitution. In 1741, he began publishing *Poor Richard's Almanac*, a very popular and influential magazine that established his reputation (under a pseudonym) as a satirist and secured his fortune. He made important contributions to science, especially in the understanding of electricity. He was ambassador to France from 1776 to 1785 and governor of Pennsylvania from 1785 to 1788. Toward the end of his life, he became a prominent abolitionist.

The Speech of Miss Polly Baker

The following essay initially appeared in 1747 in a London paper. Subsequently, American publications picked it up. For several decades, the story was accepted as having been written by a woman named Polly Baker, but eventually Franklin admitted that he had written it to criticize a legal system that penalized mothers, but not fathers, for having children out of wedlock. Although there has been some controversy, most scholars accept Franklin as the author, including the editors of *The Papers of Benjamin Franklin*, published by the American Philosophical Society and Yale University.

The Speech of Miss Polly Baker, before a Court of Judicature, at Connecticut near Boston in New-England; where she was prosecuted the Fifth Time, for having a Bastard Child: Which influenced the Court to dispense with her Punishment, and induced one of her Judges to marry her the next Day.

May it please the Honourable Bench to indulge me in a few Words: I am a poor unhappy Woman, who have no Money to fee Lawyers to plead for me, being hard put to it to get a tolerable Living. I shall not trouble your Honours with long Speeches; for I have not the Presumption to expect, that you may, by any Means, be prevailed on to deviate in your Sentence from the Law, in my Favour. All I humbly hope is, That your Honours would charitably move the Governor's Goodness on my Behalf, that my Fine may be remitted. This is the Fifth Time, Gentlemen, that I have been dragged before your Court on the same Account; twice I have paid heavy Fines, and twice have been brought to Publick Punishment, for want of Money to pay those Fines. This may have been agreeable to the Laws, and I don't dispute it; but since Laws are sometimes unreasonable in themselves, and therefore repealed, and others bear too hard on the Subject in particular Circumstances; and therefore there is left a Power somewhat to dispense with the Execution of them; I take the Liberty to say, That I think this Law, by which I am punished, is both unreasonable in itself, and particularly severe with regard to me, who have always lived an inoffensive Life in the Neighbourhood where I was born, and defy my Enemies (if I have any) to say I ever wronged Man, Woman, or Child.

Abstracted from the Law, I cannot conceive (may it please your Honours) what the Nature of my Offence is. I have brought Five fine Children into the World, at the Risque of my Life; I have maintained them well by my own Industry, without burthening the Township, and would have done it better, if it had not been for the heavy

Charges and Fines I have paid. Can it be a Crime (in the Nature of Things I mean) to add to the Number of the King's Subjects, in a new Country that really wants People? I own it, I should think it a Praise-worthy, rather than a punishable Action. I have debauched no other Woman's Husband, nor enticed any Youth; these Things I never was charged with, nor has any one the least Cause of Complaint against me, unless, perhaps, the Minister, or Justice, because I have had Children without being married, by which they have missed a Wedding Fee. But, can ever this be a Fault of mine?

I appeal to your Honours. You are pleased to allow I don't want Sense; but I must be stupified to the last Degree, not to prefer the Honourable State of Wedlock, to the Condition I have lived in. I always was, and still am willing to enter into it; and doubt not my behaving well in it, having all the Industry, Frugality, Fertility, and Skill in Economy, appertaining to a good Wife's Character. I defy any Person to say, I ever refused an Offer of that Sort: On the contrary, I readily consented to the only Proposal of Marriage that ever was made me, which was when I was a Virgin; but too easily confiding in the Person's Sincerity that made it, I unhappily lost my own Honour, by trusting to his; for he got me with Child, and then forsook me: That very Person you all know; he is now become a Magistrate of this Country; and I had Hopes he would have appeared this Day on the Bench, and have endeavoured to moderate the Court in my Favour; then I should have scorned to have mentioned it; but I must now complain of it, as unjust and unequal, That my Betrayer and Undoer, the first Cause of all my faults and Miscarriages (if they must be deemed such) should be advanced to Honour and Power in the Government, that punishes my Misfortunes with Stripes and Infamy.

I should be told, 'tis like, That were there no Act of Assembly in the Case, the   5
Precepts of Religion are violated by my Transgressions. If mine, then, is a religious Offence, leave it to religious Punishments. You have already excluded me from the Comforts of your Church-Communion. Is not that sufficient? You believe I have offended Heaven, and must suffer eternal Fire: Will not that be sufficient? What Need is there, then, of your additional Fines and Whipping?

I own, I do not think as you do; for, if I thought what you call a Sin, was really such, I could not presumptuously commit it. But, how can it be believed, that Heaven is angry at my having Children, when to the little done by me towards it, God has been pleased to add his Divine Skill and admirable Workmanship in the Formation of their Bodies, and crowned it, by furnishing them with rational and immortal Souls. Forgive me, Gentlemen, if I talk a little extravagantly on these Matters; I am no Divine, but if you, Gentlemen, must be making Laws, do not turn natural and useful Actions into Crimes, by your Prohibitions. But take into your wise Consideration, the great and growing Number of Batchelors in the Country, many of whom from the mean Fear of the Expences of a Family, have never sincerely and honourably courted a Woman in their Lives; and by their Manner of Living, leave unproduced (which is little better than Murder) Hundreds of their Posterity to the Thousandth Generation. Is not this a greater Offence against the Publick Good, than mine? Compel them, then, by Law, either to Marriage, or to pay double the Fine of Fornication every Year.

What must poor young Women do, whom Custom have forbid to solicit the Men, and Who cannot force themselves upon Husbands, when the Laws take no Care to provide them any; and yet severely punish them if they do their Duty without them; the Duty of the first and great Command of Nature, and of Nature's God, *Encrease and Multiply.* A Duty, from the steady Performance of which, nothing has been able to deter me; but for its Sake, I have hazarded the Loss of the Publick Esteem, and have frequently endured Publick Disgrace and Punishment; and therefore ought, in my humble Opinion, instead of a Whipping, to have a Statue erected to my Memory.

(1747)

Exploring the Text

1. How does Benjamin Franklin develop Polly Baker into a sympathetic character? What ethos does the character establish at the outset?
2. What is the basic argument that Polly makes? Try explaining it through a syllogism, a series of syllogisms, or the Toulmin model (see Chapter 3).
3. What evidence does Polly present in her defense?
4. How does Polly anticipate counterarguments? What examples of concession and refutation do you find?
5. What is the effect of the rhetorical questions Polly asks? Refer to specific examples in your response.
6. Does Polly tailor her argument to the particular audience of magistrates? If so, how? If not, explain why.
7. Outline the logic of Polly's argument that she should, in fact, be rewarded instead of punished. Go a step further, and show how she turns the law's logic on itself to argue that the bachelors in the community are the ones guilty of "a greater Offence against the Publick Good" (par. 6).
8. What instances of a double standard does Polly point out? Pay close attention to the examples of men's behavior being seen in an entirely different light than women's in the same situation.
9. How do the diction and syntax establish Polly as a humble, obedient woman?
10. If you did not know that Polly was a fictional character created by an author whose intent is to criticize a practice or system, what clues might you notice that suggest something is below the surface? Consider elements of satire such as hyperbole, understatement, connotative language, double entendres, and puns.
11. What does Franklin achieve by writing in the voice of a woman and creating this fictional scenario rather than simply writing a straightforward criticism of a system that he believes treats women unfairly?

from *The Autobiography of Benjamin Franklin*

Although Benjamin Franklin began writing his autobiography in 1771, it was first published in France in 1791, a year after his death, and then in England in 1793. It might be seen as ironic that the first complete edition of this quintessential American life story was not published in the United States until 1868.

Not having any Copy here of what is already written, I know not whether an Account is given of the means I used to establish the Philadelphia publick Library, which from a small Beginning is now become so considerable, though I remember to have come down to near the Time of that Transaction, 1730. I will therefore begin here, with an Account of it, which may be struck out if found to have been already given.

At the time I establish'd my self in Pensylvania, there was not a good Bookseller's Shop in any of the Colonies to the Southward of Boston. In New-York & Philad[a] the Printers were indeed Stationers, they sold only Paper, &c. Almanacks, Ballads, and a few common School Books. Those who lov'd Reading were oblig'd to send for their Books from England. The Members of the Junto had each a few. We had left the Alehouse where we first met, and hired a Room to hold our Club in. I propos'd that we should all of us bring our Books to that Room, where they would not only be ready to consult in our Conferences, but become a common Benefit, each of us being at Liberty to borrow such as he wish'd to read at home. This was accordingly done, and for some time contented us. Finding the Advantage of this little Collection, I propos'd to render the Benefit from Books more common by commencing a Public Subscription Library. I drew a Sketch of the Plan and Rules that would be necessary, and got a skilful Conveyancer Mr Charles Brockden to put the whole in Form of Articles of Agreement to be subscribed, by which each Subscriber engag'd to pay a certain Sum down for the first Purchase of Books and an annual Contribution for encreasing them. So few were the Readers at that time in Philadelphia, and the Majority of us so poor, that I was not able with great Industry to find more than Fifty Persons, mostly young Tradesmen, willing to pay down for this purpose Forty shillings each, & Ten Shillings per Annum. On this little Fund we began. The Books were imported. The Library was open one Day in the Week for lending them to the Subscribers, on their Promisory Notes to pay Double the Value if not duly returned. The Institution soon manifested its Utility, was imitated by other Towns and in other Provinces, the Librarys were augmented by Donations, Reading became fashionable, and our People having no publick Amusements to divert their Attention from Study became better acquainted with Books, and in a few Years were observ'd by Strangers to be better instructed & more intelligent than People of the same Rank generally are in other Countries.

When we were about to sign the above-mentioned Articles, which were to be binding on us, our Heirs, &c for fifty Years, Mr Brockden, the Scrivener, said to us, "You are young Men, but it is scarce probable that any of you will live to see the Expiration of the Term fix'd in this Instrument." A Number of us, however, are yet living: But the Instrument was after a few Years rendered null by a Charter that incorporated & gave Perpetuity to the Company.

The Objections, & Reluctances I met with in Soliciting the Subscriptions, made me soon feel the Impropriety of presenting one's self as the Proposer of any useful Project that might be suppos'd to raise one's Reputation in the smallest degree above that of one's Neighbours, when one has need of their Assistance to accomplish that Project. I therefore put my self as much as I could out of sight, and stated it as a Scheme of *a Number of Friends*, who had requested me to go about and propose it to such as they thought Lovers of Reading. In this way my Affair went on more smoothly, and I ever after practis'd it on such Occasions; and from my frequent Successes, can heartily recommend it. The present little Sacrifice of your Vanity will afterwards be amply repaid. If it remains a while uncertain to whom the Merit belongs, some one more vain than yourself will be encourag'd to claim it, and then even Envy will be dispos'd to do you Justice, by plucking those assum'd Feathers, & restoring them to their right Owner.

This Library afforded me the Means of Improvement by constant Study, for   5
which I set apart an Hour or two each Day; and thus repair'd in some Degree the Loss of the Learned Education my Father once intended for me. Reading was the only Amusement I allow'd my self. I spent no time in Taverns, Games, or Frolicks of any kind. And my Industry in my Business continu'd as indefatigable as it was necessary. I was in debt for my Printing-house, I had a young Family coming on to be educated, and I had to contend with for Business two Printers who were establish'd in the Place before me. My Circumstances however grew daily easier: my original Habits of Frugality continuing. And My Father having among his Instructions to me when a Boy, frequent-ly repeated a Proverb of Solomon, *"Seest thou a Man diligent in his Calling, he shall stand before Kings, he shall not stand before mean Men."* I from thence consider'd Industry as a Means of obtaining Wealth and Distinction, which encourag'd me; tho' I did not think that I should ever literally stand before Kings, which however has since happened. for I have stood before five, & even had the honour of sitting down with one, the King of Denmark, to Dinner.

We have an English Proverb that says,

> He that would thrive
> Must ask his Wife;

it was lucky for me that I had one as much dispos'd to Industry & Frugality as my self. She assisted me chearfully in my Business, folding & stitching Pamphlets, tending Shop, purchasing old Linen Rags for the Paper-makers, &c &c. We kept no idle Servants, our Table was plain & simple, our Furniture of the cheapest. For instance my Breakfast was a long time Bread & Milk, (no Tea,) and I ate it out of a twopenny earthen Porringer with a Pewter Spoon. But mark how Luxury will enter Families, and make a Progress, in Spite of Principle. Being Call'd one Morning to Breakfast, I found it in a China Bowl with a Spoon of Silver. They had been bought for me without my Knowledge by my Wife, and had cost her the enormous Sum of three and twenty Shillings for which she had no other Excuse or Apology to make, but that she thought *her* Husband deserv'd a Silver Spoon & China Bowl as well as any of his Neighbours. This was the first Appearance of Plate & China in our House, which afterwards in a Course of Years as our Wealth encreas'd, augmented gradually to several Hundred Pounds in Value.

I had been religiously educated as a Presbyterian; and tho' some of the Dogmas of that Persuasion, such as the Eternal Decrees of God, Election, Reprobation, &c. appear'd to me unintelligible, others doubtful, & I early absented myself from the Public Assemblies of the Sect, Sunday being my Studying-Day, I never was without some religious Principles; I never doubted, for instance, the Existance of the Deity, that he made the World, & govern'd it by his Providence; that the most acceptable Service of God was the doing Good to Man; that our Souls are immortal; and that all Crime will be punished & Virtue rewarded either here or hereafter; these I esteem'd the Essentials of every Religion, and being to be found in all the Religions we had in our Country I respected them all, tho' with different degrees of Respect as I found them more or less mix'd with other Articles which without any Tendency to inspire, promote or confirm Morality, serv'd principally to divide us & make us unfriendly to one another. This Respect to all, with an Opinion that the worst had some good Effects, induc'd me to avoid all Discourse that might tend to lessen the good Opinion another might have of his own Religion; and as our Province increas'd in People and new Places of worship were continually wanted, & generally erected by voluntary Contribution, my Mite for such purpose, whatever might be the Sect, was never refused.

Tho' I seldom attended any Public Worship, I had still an Opinion of its Propriety, and of its Utility when rightly conducted, and I regularly paid my annual Subscription for the Support of the only Presbyterian Minister or Meeting we had in Philadelphia. He us'd to visit me sometimes as a Friend, and admonish me to attend his Administrations, and I was now and then prevail'd on to do so, once for five Sundays successively. Had he been, *in my Opinion*, a good Preacher perhaps I might have continued, notwithstanding the occasion I had for the Sunday's Leisure in my Course of Study: But his Discourses were chiefly either polemic Arguments, or Explications of the peculiar Doctrines of our Sect, and were all to me very dry, uninteresting and unedifying, since not a single moral Principle was inculcated or enforc'd, their Aim seeming to be rather to make us Presbyterians than good Citizens. At length he took for his Text that Verse of the 4th Chapter of Philippians, *Finally, Brethren, Whatsoever Things are true, honest, just, pure, lovely, or of good report, if there be any virtue, or any praise, think on these Things*; & I imagin'd in a Sermon on such a Text, we could not miss of having some Morality: But he confin'd himself to five Points only as meant by the Apostle, viz. 1. Keeping holy the Sabbath Day. 2. Being diligent in Reading the Holy Scriptures. 3. Attending duly the Publick Worship. 4. Partaking of the Sacrament. 5. Paying a due Respect to God's Ministers. These might be all good Things, but as they were not the kind of good Things that I expected from that Text, I despaired of ever meeting with them from any other, was disgusted, and attended his Preaching no more. I had some Years before compos'd a little Liturgy or Form of Prayer for my own private Use, viz. in 1728. entitled, *Articles of Belief & Acts of Religion*. I return'd to the Use of this, and went no more to the public Assemblies. My Conduct might be blameable, but I leave it without attempting farther to excuse it, my present purpose being to relate Facts, and not to make Apologies for them.

It was about this time that I conceiv'd the bold and arduous Project of arriving at moral Perfection. I wish'd to live without committing any Fault at any time; I would conquer all that either Natural Inclination, Custom, or Company might lead me into. As I knew, or thought I knew, what was right and wrong, I did not see why I might not *always* do the one and avoid the other. But I soon found I had undertaken a Task of more Difficulty than I had imagined: While my Care was employ'd in guarding against one Fault, I was often surpriz'd by another. Habit took the Advantage of Inattention. Inclination was sometimes too strong for Reason. I concluded at length, that the mere speculative Conviction that it was our Interest to be compleatly virtuous, was not sufficient to prevent our Slipping, and that the contrary Habits must be broken and goodness acquired and established, before we can have any Dependance on a steady uniform Rectitude of Conduct. For this purpose I therefore contriv'd the following Method.

In the various Enumerations of the moral Virtues I had met with in my Reading,   10 I found the Catalogue more or less numerous, as different Writers included more or fewer Ideas under the same Name. Temperance, for Example, was by some confin'd to Eating & Drinking, while by others it was extended to mean the moderating every other Pleasure, Appetite, Inclination or Passion, bodily or mental, even to our Avarice & Ambition. I propos'd to myself, for the sake of Clearness, to use rather more Names with fewer Ideas annex'd to each, than a few Names with more Ideas; and I included under Thirteen Names of Virtues all that at that time occurr'd to me as necessary or desirable, and annex'd to each a short Precept, which fully express'd the Extent I gave to its Meaning.

These Names of Virtues with their Precepts were

1. TEMPERANCE. Eat not to Dulness. Drink not to Elevation.
2. SILENCE. Speak not but what may benefit others or your self. Avoid trifling Conversation.
3. ORDER. Let all your Things have their Places. Let each Part of your Business have its Time.
4. RESOLUTION. Resolve to perform what you ought. Perform without fail what you resolve.
5. FRUGALITY. Make no Expence but to do good to others or yourself: i.e. Waste nothing.
6. INDUSTRY. Lose no Time. Be always employed in something useful. Cut off all unnecessary Actions.
7. SINCERITY. Use no hurtful Deceit. Think innocently and justly; and, if you speak; speak accordingly.
8. JUSTICE. Wrong none, by doing Injuries or omitting the Benefits that are your Duty.
9. MODERATION. Avoid Extreams. Forbear resenting Injuries so much as you think they deserve.
10. CLEANLINESS. Tolerate no Uncleanness in Body, Cloaths or Habitation.
11. TRANQUILITY. Be not disturbed at Trifles, or at Accidents common or unavoidable.
12. CHASTITY. Rarely use Venery but for Health or Offspring; Never to Dulness, Weakness, or the Injury of your own or another's Peace or Reputation.
13. HUMILITY. Imitate Jesus and Socrates.

My intention being to acquire the *Habitude* of all these Virtues, I judg'd it would be well not to distract my Attention by attempting the whole at once, but to fix it on one of them at a time, and when I should be Master of that, then to proceed to another, and so on till I should have gone thro' the thirteen. And as the previous Acquisition of some might facilitate the Acquisition of certain others, I arrang'd them with that View as they stand above. *Temperance* first, as it tends to procure that Coolness & Clearness of Head, which is so necessary where constant Vigilance was to be kept up, and Guard maintained, against the unremitting Attraction, of ancient Habits, and the Force of perpetual Temptations. This being acquir'd & establish'd, *Silence* would be more easy, and my Desire being to gain Knowledge at the same time that I improv'd in Virtue, and considering that in Conversation it was obtain'd rather by the Use of the Ears than of the Tongue, & therefore wishing to break a Habit I was getting into of Prattling, Punning & Joking, which only made me acceptable to trifling Company, I gave *Silence* the second Place. This, and the next, *Order*, I expected would allow me more Time for attending to my Project and my Studies; RESOLUTION once become habitual, would keep me firm in my Endeavours to obtain all the subsequent Virtues; *Frugality & Industry*, by freeing me from my remaining Debt, & producing Affluence & Independance would make more easy the Practice of *Sincerity* and *Justice*, &c. &c. Conceiving then that agreeable to the Advice of Pythagoras in his Golden Verses, daily Examination would be necessary, I contriv'd the following Method for conducting that Examination.[1]

I made a little Book in which I allotted a Page for each of the Virtues. I rul'd each Page with red Ink so as to have seven Columns, one for each Day of the Week, marking each Column with a Letter for the Day. I cross'd these Columns with thirteen red Lines, marking the Beginning of each Line with the first Letter of one of the Virtues,

---

[1] *Let not the stealing God of Sleep surprize,*
Nor creep in Slumbers on thy weary Eyes,
Ere ev'ry Action of the former Day,
Strictly thou dost, and righteously survey.
With Rev'rence at thy own Tribunal stand,
And answer justly to thy own Demand
Where have I been? In what have I transgrest?
What Good or Ill has this Day's Life exprest?
Where have I fail'd in what I ought to do?
In what to GOD, to Man, or to myself I owe?
Inquire severe whate'er from first to last,
From Morning's Dawn till Ev'nings Gloom has past.
If Evil were thy Deeds, repenting mourn,
And let thy Soul with strong Remorse be torn:
[If Good, the Good with Peace of Mind repay,
And to thy secret Self with Pleasure say,
Rejoice, my Heart, for all went well to Day.]

[Franklin's note]

on which line & in its proper Column I might mark by a little black Spot every Fault I found upon Examination, to have been committed respecting that Virtue upon that Day.

TEMPERANCE.						
Eat not to Dulness.						
Drink not to Elevation.						
S	M	T	W	T	F	S

	S	M	T	W	T	F	S
T							
S	●●	●		●		●	
O	●	●	●		●	●	
R			●			●	
F		●					
I			●				
S							
J							
M							
Cl.							
T							
Ch							
H							

Form of the Pages

I determined to give a Week's strict Attention to each of the Virtues successively. Thus in the first Week my great Guard was to avoid every the least Offence against Temperance, leaving the other Virtues to their ordinary Chance, only marking every Evening the Faults of the Day. Thus if in the first Week I could keep my first line marked T clear of Spots, I suppos'd the Habit of that Virtue so much strengthen'd and its opposite weaken'd, that I might venture extending my Attention to include the next, and for the following Week keep both Lines clear of Spots. Proceeding thus to the last, I could go thro' a Course compleat in Thirteen Weeks, and four Courses in a Year. And like him who having a Garden to weed, does not attempt to eradicate all the bad Herbs at once, which would exceed his Reach and his Strength, but works on one of the Beds at a time, & having accomplish'd the first proceeds to a second; so I should have, (I hoped) the encouraging Pleasure of seeing on my Pages the Progress I made in Virtue, by clearing successively my Lines of their Spots, till in the End by a Number of Courses, I should be happy in viewing a clean Book after a thirteen Weeks daily Examination.

This my little Book had for its Motto these Lines from *Addison's Cato;* 15

> *Here will I hold: If there is a Pow'r above us,*
> *(And that there is, all Nature cries aloud*
> *Thro' all her Works) he must delight in Virtue,*
> *And that which he delights in must be happy.*

Another from *Cicero.*

O Vitae Philosophia Dux! O Virtutum indagatrix, expultrixque vitiorum! Unus dies bene, & ex preceptis tuis actus, peccanti immortalitati est anteponendus.[2]

Another from the Proverbs of Solomon speaking of Wisdom or Virtue;

Length of Days is in her right hand, and in her Left Hand Riches and Honours; Her Ways are Ways of Pleasantness, and all her Paths are Peace. III, 16, 17.

---

[2]Latin. "O Philosophy, guide of life! O seeker of virtue and expeller of vices! One day lived well and in accordance with your precepts is better than an eternity of sin." — Eds.

And conceiving God to be the Fountain of Wisdom, I thought it right and necessary to solicit his Assistance for obtaining it; to this End I form'd the following little Prayer, which was prefix'd to my Tables of Examination; for daily Use.

O Powerful Goodness! bountiful Father! merciful Guide! Increase in me that Wisdom which discovers my truest Interests; Strengthen my Resolutions to perform what that Wisdom dictates. Accept my kind Offices to thy other Children, as the only Return in my Power for thy continual Favours to me.

I us'd also sometimes a little Prayer which I took from *Thomson's* Poems. viz

Father of Light and Life, thou Good supreme,
O teach me what is good, teach me thy self!
Save me from Folly, Vanity and Vice,
From every low Pursuit, and fill my Soul
With Knowledge, conscious Peace, & Virtue pure,
Sacred, substantial, neverfading Bliss!

The Precept of *Order* requiring that *every Part of my Business should have its allot-*   20
ted Time, one Page in my little Book contain'd the following Scheme of Employment for the Twenty-four Hours of a natural Day,

The Morning Question, What Good Shall I do this Day?	5	Rise, wash, and address *Powerful Goodness*; contrive Day's Business and take the Resolution of the Day; prosecute the present Study: and breakfast?—
	6	
	7	
	8	
	9	Work.
	10	
	11	
	12	Read, or overlook my Accounts, and dine.
	1	
	2	
	3	Work.
	4	
	5	
	6	
Evening Question, What Good have I done to day?	7	Put Things in their Places, Supper, Musick, or Diversion, or Conversation, Examination of the Day.
	8	
	9	
	10	
	11	
	12	
	1	Sleep—
	2	
	3	
	4	

I enter'd upon the Execution of this Plan for Self Examination, and continu'd it with occasional Intermissions for some time. I was surpriz'd to find myself so much fuller of Faults than I had imagined, but I had the Satisfaction of seeing them diminish. To avoid the Trouble of renewing now & then my little Book, which by scraping out the Marks on the Paper of old Faults to make room for new Ones in a new Course, became full of Holes: I transferr'd my Tables & Precepts to the Ivory Leaves of a Memorandum Book, on which the Lines were drawn with red Ink that made a durable Stain, and on those Lines I mark'd my Faults with a black Lead Pencil, which Marks I could easily wipe out with a wet Sponge. After a while I went thro' one Course only in a Year, and afterwards only one in several Years; till at length I omitted them entirely, being employ'd in Voyages & Business abroad with a Multiplicity of Affairs, that interfered. But I always carried my little Book with me. My Scheme of ORDER, gave me the most Trouble, and I found, that tho' it might be practicable where a Man's Business was such as to leave him the Disposition of his Time, that of a Journeyman Printer for instance, it was not possible to be exactly observ'd by a Master, who must mix with the World, and often receive People of Business at their own Hours. *Order* too, with regard to Places for Things, Papers, &c. I found extreamly difficult to acquire. I had not been early accustomed to it, & having an exceeding good Memory, I was not so sensible of the Inconvenience attending Want of Method. This Article therefore cost me so much painful Attention & my Faults in it vex'd me so much, and I made so little Progress in Amendment, & had such frequent Relapses, that I was almost ready to give up the Attempt, and content my self with a faulty Character in that respect. Like the Man who in buying an Ax of a Smith my Neighbour, desired to have the whole of its Surface as bright as the Edge; the Smith consented to grind it bright for him if he would turn the Wheel. He turn'd while the Smith press'd the broad Face of the Ax hard & heavily on the Stone, which made the Turning of it very fatiguing. The Man came every now & then from the Wheel to see how the Work went on; and at length would take his Ax as it was without farther Grinding. No, says the Smith, Turn on, turn on; we shall have it bright by and by; as yet 'tis only speckled. Yes, says the Man; but *I think I like a speckled Ax best*. And I believe this may have been the Case with many who having for want of some such Means as I employ'd found the Difficulty of obtaining good, & breaking bad Habits, in other Points of Vice & Virtue, have given up the Struggle, & concluded that *a speckled Ax was best*. For something that pretended to be Reason was every now and then suggesting to me, that such extream Nicety as I exacted of my self might be a kind of Foppery in Morals, which if it were known would make me ridiculous; that a perfect Character might be attended with the Inconvenience of being envied and hated; and that a benevolent Man should allow a few Faults in himself, to keep his Friends in Countenance. In Truth I found myself incorrigible with respect to *Order*; and now I am grown old, and my Memory bad, I feel very sensibly the want of it. But on the whole, tho' I never arrived at the Perfection I had been so ambitious of obtaining, but fell far short of it, yet I was by the

Endeavour made a better and a happier Man than I otherwise should have been, if I had not attempted it; As those who aim at perfect Writing by imitating the engraved Copies, tho' they never reach the wish'd for Excellence of those Copies, their Hand is mended by the Endeavour, and is tolerable while it continues fair & legible.

And it may be well my Posterity should be informed, that to this little Artifice, with the Blessing of God, their Ancestor ow'd the constant Felicity of his Life down to his 79th Year in which this is written. What Reverses may attend the Remainder is in the Hand of Providence: But if they arrive the Reflection on past Happiness enjoy'd ought to help his Bearing them with more Resignation. To *Temperance* he ascribes his long-continu'd Health, & what is still left to him of a good Constitution. To *Industry* and *Frugality* the early Easiness of his Circumstances, & Acquisition of his Fortune, with all that Knowledge which enabled him to be an useful Citizen, and obtain'd for him some Degree of Reputation among the Learned. To *Sincerity & Justice* the Confidence of his Country, and the honourable Employs it conferr'd upon him. And to the joint Influence of the whole Mass of the Virtues, even in their imperfect State he was able to acquire them, all that Evenness of Temper, & that Chearfulness in Conversation which makes his Company still sought for, & agreable even to his younger Acquaintance. I hope therefore that some of my Descendants may follow the Example & reap the Benefit.

It will be remark'd that, tho' my Scheme was not wholly without Religion there was in it no mark of any of the distinguishing Tenets of any particular Sect. I had purposely avoided them; for being fully persuaded of the Utility and Excellency of my Method, and that it might be serviceable to People in all Religions, and intending some time or other to publish it, I would not have any thing in it that should prejudice any one of any Sect against it. I purposed writing a little Comment on each Virtue, in which I would have shown the Advantages of possessing it, & the Mischiefs attending its opposite Vice; and I should have called my Book the ART *of Virtue*, because it would have shown the *Means & Manner* of obtaining Virtue; which would have distinguish'd it from the mere Exhortation to be good, that does not instruct & indicate the Means; but is like the Apostle's Man of verbal Charity, who only, without showing to the Naked & the Hungry *how* or where they might get Cloaths or Victuals, exhorted them to be fed & clothed. *James* II, 15, 16.

But it so happened that my Intention of writing & publishing this Comment was never fulfilled. I did indeed, from time to time put down short Hints of the Sentiments, Reasonings, &c. to be made use of in it; some of which I have still by me: But the necessary close Attention to private Business in the earlier part of Life, and public Business since, have occasioned my postponing it. For it being connected in my Mind with a *great and extensive Project* that required the whole Man to execute, and which an unforeseen Succession of Employs prevented my attending to, it has hitherto remain'd unfinish'd.

In this Piece it was my Design to explain and enforce this Doctrine, that vicious   25
Actions are not hurtful because they are forbidden, but forbidden because they are
hurtful, the Nature of Man alone consider'd: That it was therefore every ones Interest
to be virtuous, who wish'd to be happy even in this World. And I should from this
Circumstance, there being always in the World a Number of rich Merchants, Nobility,
States and Princes, who have need of honest Instruments for the Management of
their Affairs, and such being so rare, have endeavoured to convince young Persons,
that no Qualities were so likely to make a poor Man's Fortune as those of Probity &
Integrity.

My List of Virtues contain'd at first but twelve: But a Quaker Friend having
kindly inform'd me that I was generally thought proud; that my Pride show'd itself
frequently in Conversation; that I was not content with being in the right when
discussing any Point, but was overbearing & rather insolent; of which he convinc'd
me by mentioning several Instances; I determined endeavouring to cure myself
if I could of this Vice or Folly among the rest, and I added *Humility* to my List,
giving an extensive Meaning to the Word. I cannot boast of much Success in
acquiring the *Realty* of this Virtue; but I had a good deal with regard to the
Appearance of it. I made it a Rule to forbear all direct Contradiction to the Sentiments
of others, and all positive Assertion of my own. I even forbid myself agreable
to the old Laws of our Junto, the Use of every Word or Expression in the Language
that imported a fix'd Opinion; such as *certainly, undoubtedly,* &c. and I adopted
instead of them, *I conceive, I apprehend,* or *I imagine* a thing to be so or so, or it
so appears to me at present. When another asserted something that I thought an
Error, I deny'd my self the Pleasure of contradicting him abruptly, and of showing
immediately some Absurdity in his Proposition; and in answering I began by
observing that in certain Cases or Circumstances his Opinion would be right, but
that in the present case there *appear'd* or *seem'd* to me some Difference, &c. I soon
found the Advantage of this Change in my Manners. The Conversations I engag'd
in went on more pleasantly. The modest way in which I propos'd my Opinions,
procur'd them a readier Reception and less Contradiction; I had less Mortification
when I was found to be in the wrong, and I more easily prevail'd with others to
give up their Mistakes & join with me when I happen'd to be in the right. And
this Mode, which I at first put on, with some violence to natural Inclination,
became at length so easy & so habitual to me, that perhaps for these Fifty Years
past no one has ever heard a dogmatical Expression escape me. And to this Habit
(after my Character of Integrity) I think it principally owing, that I had early so
much Weight with my Fellow Citizens, when I proposed new Institutions, or
Alterations in the old; and so much Influence in public Councils when I became
a Member. For I was but a bad Speaker, never eloquent, subject to much Hesitation
in my choice of Words, hardly correct in Language, and yet I generally carried my
Points.

In reality there is perhaps no one of our natural Passions so hard to subdue as
Pride. Disguise it, struggle with it, beat it down, stifle it, mortify it as much as one

pleases, it is still alive, and will every now and then peep out and show itself. You will see it perhaps often in this History. For even if I could conceive that I had compleatly overcome it, I should probably be proud of my Humility.

Thus far written at Passy 1784

Exploring the Text

1. Considering what you know about the Founding Fathers — that is, their Enlightenment values and respect for learning — are you surprised by what Benjamin Franklin says about the scarcity of books in the colonies? Explain.
2. As reported in paragraph 4, what is the lesson that Franklin has learned? Does it apply merely to his circumstances, or do you see it as timelessly universal, applying to our own lives now? Explain.
3. Knowing Franklin's liberal views toward women (as you may have inferred from reading "The Speech of Miss Polly Baker" on p. 350), why do you suppose his mention of his wife is so brief (par. 6)?
4. What is Franklin's attitude toward religion? Make specific reference to the text as you characterize his view.
5. In his essay "Circles," Ralph Waldo Emerson writes, "There is no virtue which is final; all are initial. The virtues of society are the vices of the saint. The terror of reform is the discovery that we must cast away our virtues, or what we have always esteemed such, into the same pit that has contained our grosser vices." In his autobiography, Franklin writes, "It was about this time that I conceiv'd the bold and arduous Project of arriving at moral Perfection" (par. 9). How would you compare the two views of virtue held by these writers? Is an enterprise such as achieving moral perfection even possible? Explain.
6. Read carefully Franklin's list of thirteen virtues, with their precepts (par. 11). Which two or three do you think are the most important? Which two or three would be the most difficult to achieve? Why?
7. Consider the schedule that Franklin made in his "little Book" (par. 13). What inferences can you make about Franklin from a close reading of his list of virtues and his schedule?
8. Franklin uses one analogy in paragraph 14 and two in paragraph 21. How do they help Franklin achieve his purpose? Which of the three is most successful? Why?
9. How would Franklin's employment schedule (par. 20) compare with that of a young person today? With your own?
10. Are you surprised to read that a friend told Franklin that he was "generally thought proud" (par. 26)? Why or why not? Franklin concludes the final paragraph with a paradox. How effective is it? Do you find it revealing? Amusing? Appropriate? Ironic? Explain.

◐ TALKBACK

D. H. LAWRENCE

David Herbert Lawrence was born in 1885 in a mining village in England. His father was a miner, and his mother was a schoolteacher. With his mother's encouragement, Lawrence was educated and became a schoolteacher himself, escaping life in the mines. His works include the novels *Sons and Lovers* (1912), *The Rainbow* (1915), and *Women in Love* (1920), as well as and several collections of poetry and short stories. Lawrence often felt as though the forces of modern civilization were against him; he was no friend of "progress" through industrialization, which he thought inimical to man's natural being. Some of his books were banned because of their graphic love scenes, and he had trouble with the British authorities because his wife was German and because he objected to British foreign policy.

from *Benjamin Franklin*

Lawrence's interest in America and its literature is manifest in his 1923 book, *Studies in Classic American Literature*, from which the following selection is excerpted.

The Perfectibility of Man! Ah heaven, what a dreary theme! The perfectibility of the Ford car! The perfectibility of which man? I am many men. Which of them are you going to perfect? I am not a mechanical contrivance.

Education! Which of the various me's do you propose to educate, and which do you propose to suppress?

Anyhow, I defy you. I defy you, oh society, to educate me or to suppress me, according to your dummy standards.

The ideal man! And which is he, if you please? Benjamin Franklin or Abraham Lincoln? The ideal man! Roosevelt or Porfirio Diaz[1]?

There are other men in me, besides this patient ass who sits here in a tweed   5
jacket. What am I doing, playing the patient ass in a tweed jacket? Who am I talking to? Who are you, at the other end of this patience?

Who are you? How many selves have you? And which of these selves do you want to be?

Is Yale College going to educate the self that is in the dark of you, or Harvard College?

The ideal self! Oh, but I have a strange and fugitive self shut out and howling like a wolf or a coyote under the ideal windows. See his red eyes in the dark? This is the self who is coming into his own.

The perfectibility of man, dear God! When every man as long as he remains alive is in himself a multitude of conflicting men. Which of these do you choose to perfect, at the expense of every other?

---

[1]Mexican president from 1876 to 1911. His reign brought peace and prosperity but also repression. — Eds.

Old Daddy Franklin will tell you. He'll rig him up for you, the pattern   10
American. Oh, Franklin was the first downright American. He knew what he
was about, the sharp little man. He set up the first dummy American.

At the beginning of his career this cunning little Benjamin drew up for
himself a creed that should "satisfy the professors of every religion, but shock
none."

Now wasn't that a real American thing to do? . . .

The soul of man is a dark forest. The Hercynian Wood[2] that scared the Romans
so, and out of which came the white-skinned hordes of the next civilization.

Who knows what will come out of the soul of man? The soul of man is a
dark vast forest, with wild life in it. Think of Benjamin fencing it off!

Oh, but Benjamin fenced a little tract that he called the soul of man, and   15
proceeded to get it into cultivation. Providence, forsooth. And they think that bit
of barbed wire is going to keep us in pound for ever? More fools they.

This is Benjamin's barbed wire fence. He made himself a list of virtues,
which he trotted inside like a grey nag in a paddock. . . .

A Quaker friend told Franklin that he, Benjamin, was generally considered
proud, so Benjamin put in the Humility touch as an afterthought. The amusing
part is the sort of humility it displays. "Imitate Jesus and Socrates," and mind you
don't outshine either of these two. One can just imagine Socrates and Alcibiades[3]
roaring in their cups over Philadelphian Benjamin, and Jesus looking at him a
little puzzled, and murmuring: "Aren't you wise in your own conceit, Ben?" . . .

Which brings us right back to our question, what's wrong with Benjamin,
that we can't stand him? Or else, what's wrong with us, that we find fault with such
a paragon?

Man is a moral animal. All right. I am a moral animal. And I'm going to
remain such. I'm not going to be turned into a virtuous little automaton as
Benjamin would have me. "This is good, that is bad. Turn the little handle and let
the good tap flow," saith Benjamin, and all America with him. . . .

I am a moral animal. But I am not a moral machine. I don't work with a   20
little set of handles or levers. The Temperance-silence-order-resolution-frugality-
industry-sincerity-justice-moderation-cleanliness-tranquility-chastity-humility

---

[2]European forest so large and dense that it blocked the northern expansion of the
Roman Empire. It was said to spread north from the Danube and east from the Rhine,
covering most of Germany and what is now considered Eastern Europe. — Eds.
[3]Ancient Greek statesman and general who was said to have been very handsome and
arrogant. He appears as a character in a Socratic dialogue called *First Alcibiades*, in
which Socrates slowly convinces him that he has much to learn about politics and
justice. — Eds.

keyboard is not going to get me going. I'm really not just an automatic piano with a moral Benjamin getting tunes out of me.

Here's my creed, against Benjamin's. This is what I believe:

"That I am I."

"That my soul is a dark forest."

"That my known self will never be more than a little clearing in the forest."

"That gods, strange gods, come forth from the forest into the clearing of my known self, and then go back."

"That I must have the courage to let them come and go."

"That I will never let mankind put anything over me, but that I will try always to recognize and submit to the gods in me and the gods in other men and women."

There is my creed. He who runs may read. He who prefers to crawl, or to go by gasoline, can call it rot.

Then for a "list." It is rather fun to play at Benjamin.

1. TEMPERANCE. Eat and carouse with Bacchus, or munch dry bread with Jesus, but don't sit down without one of the gods.
2. SILENCE. Be still when you have nothing to say; when genuine passion moves you, say what you've got to say, and say it hot.
3. ORDER. Know that you are responsible to the gods inside you and to the men in whom the gods are manifest. Recognize your superiors and your inferiors, according to the gods. This is the root of all order.
4. RESOLUTION. Resolve to abide by your own deepest promptings, and to sacrifice the smaller thing to the greater. Kill when you must, and be killed the same: the must coming from the gods inside you, or from the men in whom you recognize the Holy Ghost.
5. FRUGALITY. Demand nothing; accept what you see fit. Don't waste your pride or squander your emotion.
6. INDUSTRY. Lose no time with ideals; serve the Holy Ghost; never serve mankind.
7. SINCERITY. To be sincere is to remember that I am I, and that the other man is not me.
8. JUSTICE. The only justice is to follow the sincere intuition of the soul, angry or gentle. Anger is just, and pity is just, but judgment is never just.
9. MODERATION. Beware of absolutes. There are many gods.
10. CLEANLINESS. Don't be too clean. It impoverishes the blood.
11. TRANQUILITY. The soul has many motions, many gods come and go. Try and find your deepest issue, in every confusion, and abide by that. Obey the man in whom you recognize the Holy Ghost; command when your honour comes to command.
12. CHASTITY. Never "use" venery at all. Follow your passional impulse, if it be answered in the other being; but never have any motive in mind, neither offspring nor health nor even pleasure, nor even service. Only know that

"venery" is of the great gods. An offering-up of yourself to the very great gods, the dark ones, and nothing else.

13. HUMILITY. See all men and women according to the Holy Ghost that is within them. Never yield before the barren.

There's my list. I have been trying dimly to realize it for a long time, and only America and old Benjamin have at last goaded me into trying to formulate it.

And now I, at least, know why I can't stand Benjamin. He tries to take away 25 my wholeness and my dark forest, my freedom. For how can any man be free, without an illimitable background? And Benjamin tries to shove me into a barbed wire paddock and make me grow potatoes or Chicagoes.

(1923)

Exploring the Text

1. Why does D. H. Lawrence refer to the idea of the perfectibility of man as a "dreary theme" (par. 1)?

2. How would you describe Lawrence's tone? Select a passage that you found particularly acid tongued and enjoyable and describe the rhetorical flourishes that made it so effective. How do those features contribute to Lawrence's overall point?

3. In criticizing the ideas of Franklin, Lawrence writes, "There are other men in me" (par. 5) and that "every man as long as he remains alive is in himself a multitude of conflicting men" (par. 9). These words evoke Ralph Waldo Emerson ("Speak what you think now in hard words, and to-morrow speak what to-morrow thinks in hard words again, though it contradict everything you said to-day"), Henry David Thoreau ("I am a parcel of vain strivings tied / By a chance bond together"), and especially Walt Whitman ("Do I contradict myself? / Very well then I contradict myself; / I am large, I contain multitudes"), all Romantic writers who influenced Lawrence's thought and work. How does this kinship with classic American writers contribute to Lawrence's piece? How does it appeal to ethos, logos, and pathos? Explain.

4. What is the effect of such language as "little automaton" (par. 19), "moral machine" (par. 20), and "Temperence-silence-order-resolution-frugality-industry-sincerity-justice-moderation-cleanliness-tranquility-chastity-humility keyboard" (par. 20)?

5. What can you infer about Lawrence's values based on your reading of his own list of virtues (par. 23)?

Making Connections

1. Why would D. H. Lawrence, an iconic British modernist writer, react so vehemently to the work of Benjamin Franklin, an American writer from more than a century earlier?

2. Whose list of virtues appeals more to you, Franklin's or Lawrence's? Which one speaks more clearly and cogently to our time? Why?

3. Lawrence responded to Franklin. Now respond to both of them by making your own list. Which of Franklin's virtues would you keep? Would you delete any? What order would they be in? How much would Lawrence's list affect your thinking?

4. Franklin and Lawrence take very different perspectives regarding moral virtue. Do you believe in the perfectibility of man's moral virtues, or do you think it is a "dreary theme"? Explain.

5. In F. Scott Fitzgerald's 1925 novel, *The Great Gatsby*, Gatsby's father, Mr. Gatz, finds in his son's childhood copy of a book called *Hopalong Cassidy* the printed word SCHEDULE and the date September 12, 1906. And underneath:

Rise from bed	6.00	A.M.
Dumbbell exercise and wall-scaling	6.15–6.30	"
Study electricity, etc.	7.15–8.15	"
Work	8.30–4.30	P.M.
Baseball and sports	4.30–5.00	"
Practice elocution, poise and how to attain it	5.00–6.00	"
Study needed inventions	7.00–9.00	"

GENERAL RESOLVES

No wasting time at Shatters or [a name, indecipherable]
No more smokeing or chewing.
Bath every other day
Read one improving book or magazine per week
Save $5.00 [crossed out] $3.00 per week
Be better to parents

What is Fitzgerald's purpose in revealing Gatsby as a child having been influenced by Benjamin Franklin? Which writer, Lawrence or Fitzgerald, provides the more effective response to Franklin? Explain.

BENJAMIN WEST

Benjamin West (1738–1820) was an American painter of international renown. Born in what is now Swarthmore, Pennsylvania, West was not formally educated; he claimed in his memoirs that Native Americans taught him to create his own paints by mixing clay from the riverbank with bear grease. West made his early reputation by painting portraits around Pennsylvania. His work caught the eye of several wealthy Pennsylvanians, who commissioned his work and sponsored his artistic education and travel. After traveling in Italy in the early 1760s, West arrived in London to paint portraits of the royal family for King George III; in 1772, the king appointed him the court's official history painter. He founded England's Royal Academy of the Arts from 1792 to 1820 and served as its second president. West was one of the first American-born artists to find fame in Europe, but he remained connected to his native country, overseeing the training of many American artists who visited England to study.

Best known for his paintings of historical subjects, West depicted significant historical events in a monumental fashion: on a large scale, in vivid color and detail, and populated by vast numbers of characters.

William Penn's Treaty with the Indians

William Penn, who was raised as an Anglican but became a Quaker at twenty-two, founded the Province of Pennsylvania, the British colony that ultimately became the state of Pennsylvania. Benjamin West's painting, *William Penn's Treaty with the Indians*, depicts an encounter between Penn and the Native Americans.

Friends' House, Euston, London, UK/The Bridgeman Art Library

BENJAMIN WEST, *PENN'S TREATY WITH THE INDIANS*, 1772, OIL ON CANVAS, 75½" × 107¾", PENNSYLVANIA ACADEMY OF THE FINE ARTS.
(SEE COLOR INSERT, IMAGE 19.)

Exploring the Text

1. The painting depicts a meeting that took place in Philadelphia. Notice the use of light colors on the left and dark pigments on the right. How might the shading be symbolic?
2. How are the Quaker colonists depicted? How are the Indians depicted? What attitudes do these depictions suggest?
3. How do the two figures at the far left differ from the Quakers? Who might they be? What might they represent?
4. Benjamin West was a close friend of King George III, who would often visit him in his studio to discuss art and contemporary affairs. Does that information affect or alter your response to the painting? Why or why not?
5. What is the painter's attitude toward William Penn? This painting was comissioned by Thomas Penn, the son of the central figure. How might that commission have influenced the depiction of Penn? Be specific in your answer.
6. What is the mood of the painting? How does it make you feel while looking at it?
7. Traditionally, paintings of historical events tended to be idealized, heroic, and allegorical rather than historically accurate. In his time, West was criticized for going against that tradition. However, modern historians and art historians have pointed out that West's paintings are not strictly historically accurate. Historian and art critic Simon Schama writes, "West rejected literalism and embraced rhetoric." How might this view apply to *William Penn's Treaty with the Indians*? How realistic does the event depicted in this painting look to you? Explain the relationships between fiction and history and between realism and symbolism in the painting.

PAUL REVERE

Most famous for his "midnight ride" that alerted the colonial militia of the approach of British forces prior to the battles of Lexington and Concord in 1775, Paul Revere (1734–1818) was a printer, an engraver, a silversmith, and an industrialist. He was responsible for engraving and/or printing some of the most influential political cartoons of the revolutionary period.

The Able Doctor, or America Swallowing the Bitter Draught

Though it was first published in *London Magazine* in April 1774, this cartoon of the Boston Tea Party became famous when a copy of it, created by Paul Revere, appeared in the *Royal American Magazine* in June of the same year. It was created at the time of the Boston Port Bill, which was signed into law on March 31, 1774, and by which Britain officially closed Boston Harbor as punishment for the

Boston Tea Party. According to the Library of Congress, the cartoon shows Lord North, with the "Boston Port Bill" extending from a pocket, forcing tea (the Intolerable Acts) down the throat of a partially draped Native American female figure representing "America" whose arms are restrained by Lord Mansfield, while Lord Sandwich, a notorious womanizer, restrains her feet and peeks up her skirt. "Britannia," standing behind "America," turns away and shields her face with her left hand as figures representing France and Spain look on from the left and a figure holding "military law" stands to the right.

Exploring the Text

1. In *The Able Doctor*, sticking out of Lord North's pocket we see the Boston Port Bill, a bill that would close Boston Harbor in response to the Boston Tea Party. A month after the cartoon appeared in England, Paul Revere copied the engraving for the *Royal American Magazine*. The only change he made was to add the word "TEA" to the pot held by the prime minister. Why would Revere make such a change?

2. Each of the figures in Revere's engraving may be regarded as allegorical. Look carefully at the central figures: Brittania, Prime Minister North, Chief Justice Mansfield, Lord of the Admiralty Sandwich, and "America." How are they depicted? What are they doing? What do their actions suggest?

3. What is the attitude of the original artist (and of Paul Revere) toward the subject of the cartoon? How does the cartoon make you feel? What was the likely reaction of the colonists who saw it in 1774?

4. The image below is a 1774 British engraving entitled *The Bostonians Paying the Excise-Man, or Tarring and Feathering,* which depicts colonists punishing Boston commissioner of customs John Malcolm, the collector of tea taxes. The Boston Tea Party is visible in the background. Notice other details. For example, what does the noose hanging from the "Liberty Tree" suggest? Why is the sign on the tree upside down? Why are the colonists pouring a pot of tea into the mouth of the tarred and feathered central figure? Notice the similarities between this engraving and Paul Revere's *The Able Doctor.* How are they visually alike? How do they differ? How would you describe the difference in perspective of each?

Album/Art Resource, NY

Patrick Henry

Patrick Henry (1736–1799) was an attorney, a politician, an orator, and a Founding Father. He served as a colonel in the First Virginia Regiment during the Revolutionary War and as the first and sixth governor of postrevolutionary Virginia. Henry vigorously opposed the Stamp Act of 1765 and promoted revolution and independence for the American colonies. As a fierce supporter of states' and individuals' rights, Henry strongly opposed the United States Constitution, fearing the document would give too much power to the federal government. He encouraged the adoption of the Bill of Rights — amendments to the Constitution — to help uphold the liberties of the states and the people.

Speech to the Second Virginia Convention

In 1775, during a debate in the Virginia House of Burgesses over whether or not the colonies should mobilize for military action in response to Britain's encroaching forces, Henry gave this famous speech, in which he exclaims, "Give me liberty, or give me death!"

No man thinks more highly than I do of the patriotism, as well as abilities, of the very worthy gentlemen who have just addressed the House. But different men often see the same subject in different lights; and, therefore, I hope it will not be thought disrespectful to those gentlemen if, entertaining as I do opinions of a character very opposite to theirs, I shall speak forth my sentiments freely and without reserve. This is no time for ceremony. The question before the House is one of awful moment to this country. For my own part, I consider it as nothing less than a question of freedom or slavery; and in proportion to the magnitude of the subject ought to be the freedom of the debate. It is only in this way that we can hope to arrive at truth, and fulfill the great responsibility which we hold to God and our country. Should I keep back my opinions at such a time, through fear of giving offense, I should consider myself as guilty of treason towards my country, and of an act of disloyalty toward the Majesty of Heaven, which I revere above all earthly kings.

Mr. President, it is natural to man to indulge in the illusions of hope. We are apt to shut our eyes against a painful truth, and listen to the song of that siren till she transforms us into beasts. Is this the part of wise men, engaged in a great and arduous struggle for liberty? Are we disposed to be of the number of those who, having eyes, see not, and, having ears, hear not, the things which so nearly concern their temporal salvation? For my part, whatever anguish of spirit it may cost, I am willing to know the whole truth; to know the worst, and to provide for it.

I have but one lamp by which my feet are guided, and that is the lamp of experience. I know of no way of judging of the future but by the past. And judging by the past, I wish to know what there has been in the conduct of the British ministry for the last ten years to justify those hopes with which gentlemen have been pleased to solace themselves and the House. Is it that insidious smile with which our petition has been lately received? Trust it not, sir; it will prove a snare to your feet. Suffer not yourselves to be betrayed with a kiss. Ask yourselves how this gracious reception of our petition comports with those warlike preparations which cover our waters and darken our land. Are fleets and armies necessary to a work of love and reconciliation? Have we shown ourselves so unwilling to be reconciled that force must be called in to win back our love? Let us not deceive ourselves, sir. These are the implements of war and subjugation; the last arguments to which kings resort. I ask gentlemen, sir, what means this martial array, if its purpose be not to force us to submission? Can gentlemen assign any other possible motive for it? Has Great Britain any enemy, in this quarter of the world, to call for all this accumulation of navies and armies? No, sir, she has none. They are meant for us: they can be meant for no other. They are sent over to bind and rivet upon us those chains which the British ministry have been so long forging. And what have we to oppose to them? Shall we try argument? Sir, we have been trying that for the last ten years. Have we anything new to offer upon the subject? Nothing. We have held the subject up in every light of which it is capable; but it has been all in vain. Shall we resort to entreaty and humble supplication? What terms shall we find which have not been already exhausted? Let us not, I beseech you, sir, deceive ourselves. Sir, we have done everything that could be done to avert the storm which is now coming on. We have petitioned; we have remonstrated; we have supplicated; we have prostrated ourselves before the throne, and have implored its interposition to arrest the tyrannical hands of the ministry and Parliament. Our petitions have been slighted; our remonstrances have produced additional violence and insult; our supplications have been disregarded; and we have been spurned, with contempt, from the foot of the throne! In vain, after these things, may we indulge the fond hope of peace and reconciliation. There is no longer any room for hope. If we wish to be free — if we mean to preserve inviolate those inestimable privileges for which we have been so long contending — if we mean not basely to abandon the noble struggle in which we have been so long engaged, and which we have pledged ourselves never to abandon until the glorious object of our contest shall be obtained — we must fight! I repeat it, sir, we must fight! An appeal to arms and to the God of hosts is all that is left us!

They tell us, sir, that we are weak; unable to cope with so formidable an adversary. But when shall we be stronger? Will it be the next week, or the next year? Will it be when we are totally disarmed, and when a British guard shall be stationed in every house? Shall we gather strength by irresolution and inaction? Shall we acquire the means of effectual resistance by lying supinely on our backs and hugging the delusive phantom of hope, until our enemies shall have bound us hand and foot? Sir, we are not weak if we make a proper use of those means which the God of nature hath placed in our power. The millions of people, armed in the holy cause of liberty, and in such a country as that which we possess, are invincible by any force which our enemy can send against us. Besides, sir, we shall not fight our battles alone. There is a just God who presides over the destinies of nations, and who will raise up friends to fight our battles for us. The battle, sir, is not to the strong alone; it is to the vigilant, the active, the brave. Besides, sir, we have no election. If we were base enough to desire it, it is now too late to retire from the contest. There is no retreat but in submission and slavery! Our chains are forged! Their clanking may be heard on the plains of Boston! The war is inevitable — and let it come! I repeat it, sir, let it come.

It is in vain, sir, to extenuate the matter. Gentlemen may cry, Peace, Peace — but   5 there is no peace. The war is actually begun! The next gale that sweeps from the north will bring to our ears the clash of resounding arms! Our brethren are already in the field! Why stand we here idle? What is it that gentlemen wish? What would they have? Is life so dear, or peace so sweet, as to be purchased at the price of chains and slavery? Forbid it, Almighty God! I know not what course others may take; but as for me, give me liberty or give me death!

(1775)

Exploring the Text

1. What is the nature of the chief appeal that Patrick Henry makes at the beginning of his speech? Why would he begin this way?
2. How would you describe Henry's tone throughout the speech?
3. Henry discusses hope in three different places. Identify each example. How does he characterize hope? Why? What is the effect of this characterization?
4. Select two allusions that Henry makes. What is their rhetorical effect?
5. A prominent feature of Henry's speech is his use of the rhetorical question. Select three examples. How do they contribute to his argument?
6. Why does Henry focus on the urgency of "now"?
7. Select three examples of figurative language. How do they contribute to Henry's purpose?
8. Select three examples of Henry's appeals to pathos. How do they serve the rhetorical triangle introduced in Chapter 1?

THOMAS PAINE

Thomas Paine (1737–1809) was born in Great Britain but immigrated to the colonies in 1774 to participate in the American Revolution. A political activist and theorist, Paine is best known for his literary contributions to the revolutionary cause — his pamphlets *Common Sense* and *The American Crisis*. Paine promoted human rights and decried tyranny, monarchy, and slavery in America, Great

Britain, and France. This brought him both admirers and enemies. In 1779, he was expelled from the Congressional Committee on Foreign Affairs after secretly negotiating with France; in 1792, he was tried for seditious libel in Great Britain after the publication of his *Rights of Man*, an attempt to expose the "fraud . . . of monarchy." He was elected to the French National Convention (despite not speaking French) but in 1793 was arrested after Robespierre excluded foreigners from serving; he claimed that George Washington conspired with the French to imprison him. Paine ultimately criticized Christianity and organized religion in *The Age of Reason*. Although received warmly by Thomas Jefferson when he returned to America, Paine died in obscurity. Only six people, apparently all black freed slaves, attended his funeral.

from *Common Sense*

Common Sense was a best seller in the colonies and encouraged the idea of republicanism, enthusiasm for the revolutionary cause, and recruitment to the Continental army. Even John Adams said, "Without the pen of the author of *Common Sense*, the sword of Washington would have been raised in vain." In this publication, Thomas Paine appeals to the "common sense" of the American people to argue for independence from England.

Some writers have so confounded society with government, as to leave little or no distinction between them; whereas they are not only different, but have different origins. Society is produced by our wants, and government by our wickedness; the former promotes our happiness *positively* by uniting our affections, the latter *negatively* by restraining our vices. The one encourages intercourse, the other creates distinctions. The first is a patron, the last a punisher.

Society in every state is a blessing, but government even in its best state is but a necessary evil; in its worst state an intolerable one; for when we suffer, or are exposed to the same miseries *by a government*, which we might expect in a country *without government*, our calamity is heightened by reflecting that we furnish the means by which we suffer. Government, like dress, is the badge of lost innocence; the palaces of kings are built on the ruins of the bowers of paradise. For were the impulses of conscience clear, uniform, and irresistably obeyed, man would need no other lawgiver; but that not being the case, he finds it necessary to surrender up a part of his property to furnish means for the protection of the rest; and this he is induced to do by the same prudence which in every other case advises him out of two evils to choose the least. *Wherefore*, security being the true design and end of government, it unanswerably follows that whatever *form* thereof appears most likely to ensure it to us, with the least expence and greatest benefit, is preferable to all others.

In order to gain a clear and just idea of the design and end of government, let us suppose a small number of persons settled in some sequestered part of the earth, unconnected with the rest, they will then represent the first peopling of any country, or of the world. In this state of natural liberty, society will be their first thought. A thousand motives will excite them thereto, the strength of one man is so unequal to his wants, and his mind so unfitted for perpetual solitude, that he is soon obliged to seek assistance and relief of another, who in his turn requires the same. Four or five united would be able to raise a tolerable dwelling in the midst of a wilderness, but *one* man might labour out the common period of life without accomplishing any thing; when he had felled his timber he could not remove it, nor erect it after it was removed; hunger in the mean time would urge him from his work, and every different want call him a different way. Disease, nay even misfortune would be death, for though neither might be mortal, yet either would disable him from living, and reduce him to a state in which he might rather be said to perish than to die.

Thus necessity, like a gravitating power, would soon form our newly arrived emigrants into society, the reciprocal blessings of which, would supersede, and render the obligations of law and government unnecessary while they remained perfectly just to each other; but as nothing but heaven is impregnable to vice, it will unavoidably happen, that in proportion as they surmount the first difficulties of emigration, which bound them together in a common cause, they will begin to relax in their duty and attachment to each other; and this remissness, will point out the necessity, of establishing some form of government to supply the defect of moral virtue.

Some convenient tree will afford them a State-House, under the branches of which, the whole colony may assemble to deliberate on public matters. It is more than probable that their first laws will have the title only of REGULATIONS, and be enforced by no other penalty than public disesteem. In this first parliament every man, by natural right, will have a seat.

But as the colony increases, the public concerns will increase likewise, and the distance at which the members may be separated, will render it too inconvenient for all of them to meet on every occasion as at first, when their number was small, their habitations near, and the public concerns few and trifling. This will point out the convenience of their consenting to leave the legislative part to be managed by a select number chosen from the whole body, who are supposed to have the same concerns at stake which those have who appointed them, and who will act in the same manner as the whole body would act were they present. If the colony continue increasing, it will become necessary to augment the number of the representatives, and that the interest of every part of the colony may be attended to, it will be found best to divide the whole into convenient parts, each part sending its proper number; and that the *elected* might never form to themselves an interest separate from the *electors*, prudence will point out the propriety of having elections often; because as the *elected* might by that means return and mix again with the general body of the *electors* in a few months, their fidelity to the public will be secured by the prudent reflexion of not making a rod for themselves. And as this frequent interchange will establish a common interest with every part of the community, they will mutually and naturally support each other, and on this (not on the unmeaning name of king) depends the *strength of government, and the happiness of the governed.*

Here then is the origin and rise of government; namely, a mode rendered necessary by the inability of moral virtue to govern the world; here too is the design and end of government, viz. freedom and security. And however our eyes may be dazzled with show, or our ears deceived by sound; however prejudice may warp our wills, or interest darken our understanding, the simple voice of nature and of reason will say, it is right.

(1776)

Exploring the Text

1. In the first paragraph, what are the purpose and effect of the juxtapositions that Thomas Paine uses to characterize the differences between society and government?
2. How does the use of imagery, figurative language, and analogy contribute to Paine's position in the second paragraph?
3. How does Paine characterize "society" in paragraphs 2 and 3?
4. How accurately does Paine's hypothetical account anticipate the future United States under the Constitution?
5. Paine writes of the "frequent interchange" that will "establish a common interest with every part of the community" (par. 6). Is this what we have in American politics today? To what extent have we kept the promise that he identified?
6. Paine states, "Here then is the origin and rise of government; namely, a mode rendered necessary by the inability of moral virtue to govern the world; here too is the design and end of government, viz. freedom and security" (par. 7). Do you agree with his characterization of government? Is it accurate today? Explain.
7. What is the rhetorical effect of the figurative language at the end of paragraph 7?

from *The Crisis, I*

Thomas Paine wrote *The Crisis, I* on a drumhead by campfire light while accompanying General Washington's troops in retreat from seemingly overpowering British forces in New Jersey. On December 23, 1776, Washington had it read to the troops. It not only inspired them before the Battle of Trenton, but it also inspired the nation.

These are the times that try men's souls: The summer soldier and the sunshine patriot will, in this crisis, shrink from the service of his country; but he that stands it NOW, deserves the love and thanks of man and woman. Tyranny, like hell, is not easily conquered; yet we have this consolation with us, that the harder the conflict, the more glorious the triumph. What we obtain too cheap, we esteem too lightly: — 'Tis dearness only that gives every thing its value. Heaven knows how to set a proper price upon its goods; and it would be strange indeed, if so celestial an article as FREEDOM should not be highly rated. Britain, with an army to enforce her tyranny, has declared, that she has a right (*not only to* TAX) but "*to* BIND *us in* ALL CASES WHATSOEVER," and if being *bound in that manner* is not slavery, then is there not such a thing as slavery upon earth. Even the expression is impious, for so unlimited a power can belong only to GOD.

Whether the Independence of the Continent was declared too soon, or delayed too long, I will not now enter into as an argument; my own simple opinion is, that had it been eight months earlier, it would have been much better. We did not make a proper use of last winter, neither could we, while we were in a dependent state. However, the fault, if it were one, was all our own; we have none to blame but ourselves. But no great deal is lost yet; all that Howe[1] has been doing for this month past is rather a ravage than a conquest, which the spirit of the Jersies a year ago would have quickly repulsed, and which time and a little resolution will soon recover.

I have as little superstition in me as any man living, but my secret opinion has ever been, and still is, that GOD almighty will not give up a people to military destruction, or leave them unsupportedly to perish, who had so earnestly and so repeatedly sought to avoid the calamities of war, by every decent method which wisdom could invent. Neither have I so much of the infidel in me, as to suppose, that HE has relinquished the government of the world, and given us up to the care of devils; and as I do not, I cannot see on what grounds the king of Britain can look up to heaven for help against us: A common murderer, a highwayman, or a housebreaker, has as good a pretence as he.

(1776)

Exploring the Text

1. Note how rich the first paragraph is in rhetorical and literary devices. How does Thomas Paine use imagery, parallel structures, juxtapositions, and figurative language to engage the reader?
2. How does your knowledge of the pamphlet's occasion affect your reading and understanding of the piece?
3. Paine writes, "we have none to blame but ourselves" (par. 2). How does that statement appeal to both ethos and pathos?
4. What does Paine mean by "superstition" (par. 3)? What is the rhetorical effect of the juxtaposition of that with "the infidel"?
5. How effectively does the phrase "[a] common murderer, a highwayman, or a housebreaker" (par. 3) serve Paine's purpose?
6. Political writer and thinker Christopher Hitchens reminds us that when President Franklin Roosevelt "made his great speech to rally the American people against fascism after the attack on Pearl Harbor, he quoted an entire paragraph from Paine's *The Crisis* beginning: 'These are the times that try men's souls. . . .'" Speaking

---

[1]General Sir William Howe (1729–1814), the fifth Viscount Howe, was commander of British forces during the Revolutionary War. — Eds.

of our own time of "crisis," Hitchens goes on to say, "In a time when both rights and reason are under several kinds of open and covert attack, the life and writing of Thomas Paine will always be part of the arsenal on which we shall need to depend." What crises do we face today? Do you agree with Hitchens regarding Paine's importance? Why or why not?

from *The Final Crisis, XIII*

In this 1783 text, the last in the series called *The Crisis,* Thomas Paine reflects on the success of the revolution and the future of the new nation.

The times that tried men's souls are over — and the greatest and completest revolution the world ever knew, gloriously and happily accomplished.

But to pass from the extremes of danger to safety — from the tumult of war to the tranquillity of peace, though sweet in contemplation, requires a gradual composure of the senses to receive it. Even calmness has the power of stunning when it opens too instantly upon us. The long and raging hurricane that should cease in a moment would leave us in a state rather of wonder than enjoyment; and some moments of recollection must pass before we could be capable of tasting the felicity of repose. There are but few instances in which the mind is fitted for sudden transitions: It takes in its pleasures by reflection and comparison, and those must have time to act before the relish for new scenes is complete.

In the present case — the mighty magnitude of the object — the various uncertainties of fate it has undergone — the numerous and complicated dangers we have suffered or escaped — the eminence we now stand on, and the vast prospect before us, must all conspire to impress us with contemplation.

To see it in our power to make a world happy — to teach mankind the art of being so — to exhibit, on the theater of the universe, a character hitherto unknown — and to have, as it were, a new creation entrusted to our hands, are honors that command reflection and can neither be too highly estimated nor too gratefully received.

In this pause then of recollection — while the storm is ceasing, and the long agitated mind vibrating to a rest, let us look back on the scenes we have passed, and learn from experience what is yet to be done.

Never, I say, had a country so many openings to happiness as this. Her setting out into life, like the rising of a fair morning, was unclouded and promising. Her cause was good. Her principles just and liberal. Her temper serene and firm. Her conduct regulated by the nicest steps, and everything about her wore the mark of honor.

It is not every country (perhaps there is not another in the world) that can boast so fair an origin. Even the first settlement of America corresponds with the character of the revolution. Rome, once the proud mistress of the universe, was originally a band of ruffians. Plunder and rapine made her rich, and her oppression of millions made her great. But America need never be ashamed to tell her birth nor relate the stages by which she rose to empire.

The remembrance then of what is past, if it operates rightly, must inspire her with the most laudable of all ambition, that of adding to the fair fame she began with. The world has seen her great in adversity. Struggling, without a thought of yielding beneath accumulated difficulties. Bravely, nay proudly, encountering distress and rising in resolution as the storm increased. All this is justly due to her, for her fortitude has merited the character. Let, then, the world see that she can bear prosperity: and that her honest virtue in time of peace is equal to the bravest virtue in time of war.

She is now descending to the scenes of quiet and domestic life. Not beneath the cypress shade of disappointment, but to enjoy in her own land, and under her own vine, the sweet of her labors and the reward of her toil. — In this situation, may she never forget that a fair national reputation is of as much importance as independence. That it possesses a charm that wins upon the world, and makes even enemies civil. That it gives a dignity which is often superior to power, and commands reverence where pomp and splendor fail.

It would be a circumstance ever to be lamented, and never to be forgotten, were   10 a single blot from any cause whatever suffered to fall on a revolution which to the end of time must be an honor to the age that accomplished it: and which has contributed more to enlighten the world and diffuse a spirit of freedom and liberality among mankind than any human event (if this may be called one) that ever preceded it.

It is not among the least of the calamities of a long continued war that it unhinges the mind from those nice sensations which at other times appear so amiable. The continual spectacle of woe blunts the finer feelings, and the necessity of bearing with the sight renders it familiar. In like manner are many of the moral obligations of society weakened till the custom of acting by necessity becomes an apology where it is truly a crime. Yet let but a nation conceive rightly of its character, and it will be chastely just in protecting it. None ever began with a fairer [character] than America and none can be under a greater obligation to preserve it.

The debt which America has contracted, compared with the cause she has gained and the advantages to flow from it, ought scarcely to be mentioned. She has it in her choice to do, and to live, as happily as she pleases. The world is in her hands. She has no foreign power to monopolize her commerce, perplex her legislation, or control her prosperity. The struggle is over, which must one day have happened, and, perhaps, never could have happened at a better time.* And instead of a domineering master, she has gained an *ally* whose exemplary greatness and universal liberality have extorted a confession even from her enemies.

---

*That the revolution began at the exact period of time best fitted to the purpose is sufficiently proved by the event — But the great hinge on which the whole machine turned, is the UNION OF THE STATES: and this union was naturally produced by the inability of any one state to support itself against any foreign enemy without the assistance of the rest.

Had the states severally been less able than they were when the war began, their united strength would not have been equal to the undertaking, and they must, in all human probability, have failed. — And, on the other hand, had they severally been more able, they might

With the blessings of peace, independence, and a universal commerce, the states, individually and collectively, will have leisure and opportunity to regulate and establish their domestic concerns, and to put it beyond the power of calumny to throw the least reflection on their honor. Character is much easier kept than recovered; and that man, if any such there be, who, from sinister views or littleness of soul, lends unseen his hand to injure it, contrives a wound it will never be in his power to heal.

(1783)

Exploring the Text

1. Note that Thomas Paine begins with a reference to his *Crisis, I*, written seven years earlier, at the start of what we now call the Revolutionary War. What do you think was the likely response of his readers to that reference?
2. What is the rhetorical effect of the use of metaphor and imagery in the second paragraph?
3. Why would the "honors" to which Paine refers "command reflection" (par. 4)? What kind of reflection do they command? Why? What is Paine's concern?
4. Paine says of the United States that "everything about her wore the mark of honor" (par. 6). To what extent do you think the United States still wears that "mark of honor"? Explain.

---

not have seen, or, what is more, might not have felt, the necessity of uniting: and either by attempting to stand alone or in small confederacies would have been separately conquered.

Now, as we cannot see a time (and many years must pass away before it can arrive) when the strength of any one state, or several united, can be equal to the whole of the present United States, and as we have seen the extreme difficulty of collectively prosecuting the war to a successful issue, and preserving our national importance in the world, therefore, from the experience we have had, and the Knowledge we have gained, we must, unless we make a waste of wisdom, be strongly impressed with the advantage as well as the necessity of strengthening that happy union which has been our salvation, and without which we should have been a ruined people.

While I was writing this note, I cast my eye on the pamphlet COMMON SENSE, from which I shall make an extract, as it exactly applies to the case. It is as follows:

"I have never met with a man, either in England or America, who has not confessed his opinion that a separation between the countries would take place one time or other; And there is no instance in which we have shown less judgment than in endeavoring to describe what we call the ripeness or fitness of the continent for independence.

"As all men allow the measure and differ only in their opinion of the time, let us, in order to remove mistakes, take a general survey of things and endeavor, if possible, to find out the VERY TIME. But we need not to go far, the inquiry ceases at once, for THE TIME HAS FOUND US. The general concurrence, the glorious union of all things prove the fact.

"It is not in numbers but in a union that our great strength lies. The continent is just arrived at that pitch of strength in which no single colony is able to support itself, and the whole, when united, can accomplish the matter: and either more or less than this, might be fatal in its effects."

— Pamphlet COMMON SENSE

5. Paine hopes that America will "never forget that a fair national reputation is of as much importance as independence" (par. 9). Why would that be so? How accurately does it describe America's place in the world today? Explain.
6. Paine writes, "The continual spectacle of woe blunts the finer feelings, and the necessity of bearing with the sight renders it familiar" (par. 11). What does he mean? Is he lamenting, or is he admonishing?
7. How would you paraphrase the final paragraph? What is your personal response to Paine's position?

from *The Age of Reason*

In this, his most controversial work, Thomas Paine defends his belief in God but denies the authority of the Bible and of any organized religion. While sympathetic to its Deist ideas, even Thomas Jefferson advised Paine against publishing it, viewing it as too radical for its time.

It has been my intention, for several years past, to publish my thoughts upon religion. I am well aware of the difficulties that attend the subject, and from that consideration, had reserved it to a more advanced period of life. I intended it to be the last offering I should make to my fellow-citizens of all nations, and that at a time when the purity of the motive that induced me to it, could not admit of a question, even by those who might disapprove the work.

The circumstance that has now taken place in France of the total abolition of the whole national order of priesthood, and of everything appertaining to compulsive systems of religion, and compulsive articles of faith, has not only precipitated my intention, but rendered a work of this kind exceedingly necessary, lest in the general wreck of superstition, of false systems of government, and false theology, we lose sight of morality, of humanity, and of the theology that is true.

As several of my colleagues and others of my fellow-citizens of France have given me the example of making their voluntary and individual profession of faith, I also will make mine; and I do this with all that sincerity and frankness with which the mind of man communicates with itself.

I believe in one God, and no more; and I hope for happiness beyond this life.

I believe in the equality of man; and I believe that religious duties consist in   5
doing justice, loving mercy, and endeavoring to make our fellow-creatures happy.

But, lest it should be supposed that I believe in many other things in addition to these, I shall, in the progress of this work, declare the things I do not believe, and my reasons for not believing them.

I do not believe in the creed professed by the Jewish church, by the Roman church, by the Greek church, by the Turkish church, by the Protestant church, nor by any church that I know of. My own mind is my own church.

All national institutions of churches, whether Jewish, Christian or Turkish, appear to me no other than human inventions, set up to terrify and enslave mankind, and monopolize power and profit.

I do not mean by this declaration to condemn those who believe otherwise; they have the same right to their belief as I have to mine. But it is necessary to the happiness of man, that he be mentally faithful to himself. Infidelity does not consist in believing, or in disbelieving; it consists in professing to believe what he does not believe.

It is impossible to calculate the moral mischief, if I may so express it, that mental   10
lying has produced in society. When a man has so far corrupted and prostituted the chastity of his mind, as to subscribe his professional belief to things he does not believe, he has prepared himself for the commission of every other crime. He takes up the trade of a priest for the sake of gain, and in order to qualify himself for that trade, he begins with a perjury. Can we conceive any thing more destructive to morality than this?

Soon after I had published the pamphlet *Common Sense*, in America, I saw the exceeding probability that a revolution in the system of government would be followed by a revolution in the system of religion. The adulterous connection of church and state, wherever it had taken place, whether Jewish, Christian, or Turkish, had so effectually prohibited by pains and penalties, every discussion upon established creeds, and upon first principles of religion, that until the system of government should be changed, those subjects could not be brought fairly and openly before the world; but that whenever this should be done, a revolution in the system of religion would follow. Human inventions and priestcraft would be detected; and man would return to the pure, unmixed and unadulterated belief of one God, and no more.

(1794)

Exploring the Text

1. How does Thomas Paine appeal to ethos and pathos in the first two paragraphs?
2. After the publication of *The Age of Reason*, Paine was vilified as an unbeliever, an infidel, a blasphemer, and an atheist. His fall from grace commenced, and he died in poverty. We may look to the example of Samuel Adams, who wrote to Paine on November 30, 1802:

> I have frequently with pleasure reflected on your services to my native, and your adopted country. Your *Common Sense*, and your *Crisis* unquestionably awakened the public mind, and led the people loudly to call for a declaration of our national independence. I therefore esteemed you as a warm friend of the liberty, & lasting welfare of the human race. But when I heard, that you had turned your mind to a defence of infidelity, I felt myself much astonished, and more grieved, that you had attempted a measure so injurious to the feelings, and so repugnant to the true interest of so great a part of the citizens of the United States.

Is Paine defending infidelity? Consider especially paragraphs 4, 5, and 9 of this excerpt. Notice that Adams writes eight years after the publication of the book he discusses (evidently without having read it). Why do you suppose the reaction to Paine's last book was so strong?

3. Why does Paine state — along with what he believes — what he *does not* believe?

4. How does Paine characterize "institutions of churches" (par. 8)? What is your response to his distinction between the institution of a church and religious belief?

5. In the final paragraph, Paine defines *infidelity*. Do you agree with his definition? Why or why not?

6. In 2012, Louis Lapham, former editor of *Harper's* magazine and current editor of *Lapham's Quarterly*, said this about Thomas Paine:

> Paine was the most famous political thinker of his day, his books in the late eighteenth century selling more copies than the Bible, but after the Americans had won their War of Independence, his notions of democracy were deemed unsuitable to the work of dividing up the spoils. The proprietors of their new-found estate claimed the privilege of apportioning its freedom, and they remembered that Paine opposed the holding of slaves and the denial to women of the same sorts of rights awarded to men. A man too much given to plain speaking, on too familiar terms with the lower classes of society, and therefore not to be trusted.

How accurately do you think Lapham characterizes Paine's place in American history? Was Paine simply ahead of his time?

ABIGAIL AND JOHN ADAMS

John Adams (1735–1826), one of America's Founding Fathers, was the second president of the United States. His wife, Abigail Smith Adams (1744–1818), was also dedicated to the cause of liberty. They corresponded frequently about topics ranging from politics to conditions on the home front during the war.

Letters

Boston was held by the British for most of the war but liberated by George Washington's army just before these letters were written. In the following two letters, Abigail writes to her husband in Philadelphia, where he is serving in the Continental Congress, and John responds as both a husband and a politician. Abigail presses her husband to "Remember the Ladies" as he and his colleagues discuss freedom from tyranny. Given the time period, her exhortation did not refer to women's suffrage but rather to laws regarding such matters as inheritance and spousal abuse.

From Abigail to John

Braintree, March 31, 1776

I wish you would ever write me a Letter half as long as I write you; and tell me if you may where your Fleet are gone? What sort of Defence Virginia can make against our common Enemy? Whether it is so situated as to make an able Defence? Are not the Gentery Lords and the common people vassals, are they not like the uncivilized Natives Brittain represents us to be? I hope their Riffel Men who have shewen themselves very savage and even Blood thirsty; are not a specimen of the Generality of the people.

I . . . am willing to allow the Colony great merrit for having produced a Washington but they have been shamefully duped by a Dunmore.[1]

I have sometimes been ready to think that the passion for Liberty cannot be Eaquelly Strong in the Breasts of those who have been accustomed to deprive their fellow Creatures of theirs. Of this I am certain that it is not founded upon that generous and christian principal of doing to others as we would that others should do unto us.

Do not you want to see Boston; I am fearfull of the small pox, or I should have been in before this time. I got Mr. Crane to go to our House and see what state it was in. I find it has been occupied by one of the Doctors of a Regiment, very dirty, but no other damage has been done to it. The few things which were left in it are all gone. Cranch has the key which he never deliverd up. I have wrote to him for it and am determined to get it cleand as soon as possible and shut it up. I look upon it a new acquisition of property, a property which one month ago I did not value at a single Shilling, and could with pleasure have seen it in flames.

The Town in General is left in a better state than we expected, more oweing to a   5 percipitate flight than any Regard to the inhabitants, tho some individuals discoverd a sense of honour and justice and have left the rent of the Houses in which they were, for the owners and the furniture unhurt, or if damaged sufficent to make it good.

Others have committed abominable Ravages. The Mansion House of your President is safe and the furniture unhurt whilst both the House and Furniture of the Solisiter General have fallen a prey to their own merciless party. Surely the very Fiends feel a Reverential awe for Virtue and patriotism, whilst they Detest the paricide[2] and traitor.

I feel very differently at the approach of spring to what I did a month ago. We knew not then whether we could plant or sow with safety, whether when we had toild we could reap the fruits of our own industery, whether we could rest in our own Cottages, or whether we should not be driven from the sea coasts to seek shelter in the wilderness, but now we feel as if we might sit under our own vine and eat the good of the land.

---

[1]The Fourth Earl of Dunmore (John Murray) was the British colonial governor of Virginia from 1771 to 1776. He opposed independence for the colonies and was forced to return to England. — Eds.

[2]A son who murdered his father, also known as a *patricide*. — Eds.

I feel a gaieti de Coar[3] to which before I was a stranger. I think the Sun looks brighter, the Birds sing more melodiously, and Nature puts on a more chearfull countanance. We feel a temporary peace, and the poor fugitives are returning to their deserted habitations.

Tho we felicitate ourselves, we sympathize with those who are trembling least the Lot of Boston should be theirs. But they cannot be in similar circumstances unless pusilanimity and cowardise should take possession of them. They have time and warning given them to see the Evil and shun it. — I long to hear that you have declared an independency — and by the way in the new Code of Laws which I suppose it will be necessary for you to make I desire you would Remember the Ladies, and be more generous and favourable to them than your ancestors. Do not put such unlimited power into the hand of the Husbands. Remember all Men would be tyrants if they could. If perticuliar care and attention is not paid to the Ladies we are determined to foment a Rebelion, and will not hold ourselves bound by any Laws in which we have no voice, or Representation.

That your Sex are Naturally Tyrannical is a Truth so thoroughly established as to admit of no dispute, but such of you as wish to be happy willingly give up the harsh title of Master for the more tender and endearing one of Friend. Why then, not put it out of the power of the vicious and the Lawless to use us with cruelty and indignity with impunity. Men of Sense in all Ages abhor those customs which treat us only as the vassals of your Sex. Regard us then as Beings placed by providence under your protection and in immitation of the Supreem Being make use of that power only for our happiness.

From John to Abigail

April 14, 1776
You justly complain of my short Letters, but the critical State of Things and the Multiplicity of Avocations must plead my Excuse. You ask where the Fleet is. The inclosed Papers will inform you. You ask what Sort of Defence Virginia can make. I believe they will make an able Defence. Their Militia and minute Men have been some time employed in training them selves and they have Nine Battallions of regulars as they call them, maintained among them, under good Officers, at the Continental Expence. They have set up a Number of Manufactories of Fire Arms, which are busily employed. They are tolerably supplied with Powder, and are successfull and assiduous, in making Salt Petre. Their neighbouring Sister or rather Daughter Colony of North Carolina, which is a warlike Colony, and has several Battallions at the Continental Expence, as well as a pretty good Militia, are ready to assist them, and they are in very good Spirits, and seem determined to make a brave Resistance. — The Gentry are very rich, and the common People very poor.

This Inequality of Property, gives an Aristocratical Turn to all their Proceedings, and occasions a strong Aversion in their Patricians, to Common Sense. But the Spirit of these Barons, is coming down, and it must submit.

---

[3]French (correctly spelled gaieté de coeur) for happiness of heart. — Eds.

It is very true, as you observe they have been duped by Dunmore. But this is a Common Case. All the Colonies are duped, more or less, at one Time and another. A more egregious Bubble was never blown up, than the Story of Commissioners coming to treat with the Congress. Yet it has gained Credit like a Charm, not only without but against the clearest Evidence. I never shall forget the Delusion, which seized our best and most sagacious Friends the dear Inhabitants of Boston, the Winter before last. Credulity and the Want of Foresight, are Imperfections in the human Character, that no Politician can sufficiently guard against.

You have given me some Pleasure, by your Account of a certain House in Queen Street. I had burned it, long ago, in Imagination. It rises now to my View like a Phoenix. — What shall I say of the Solicitor General? I pity his pretty Children, I pity his Father, and his sisters. I wish I could be clear that it is no moral Evil to pity him and his Lady. Upon Repentance they will certainly have a large Share in the Compassions of many. But . . . let Us take Warning and give it to our Children. Whenever Vanity, and Gaiety, a Love of Pomp and Dress, Furniture, Equipage, Buildings, great Company, expensive Diversions, and elegant Entertainments get the better of the Principles and Judgments of Men or Women there is no knowing where they will stop, nor into what Evils, natural, moral, or political, they will lead us.

Your Description of your own Gaiety de Coeur, charms me. Thanks be to God you have just Cause to rejoice — and may the bright Prospect be obscured by no Cloud. 15

As to Declarations of Independency, be patient. Read our Privateering Laws, and our Commercial Laws. What signifies a Word.

As to your extraordinary Code of Laws, I cannot but laugh. We have been told that our Struggle has loosened the bands of Government every where. That Children and Apprentices were disobedient — that schools and Colledges were grown turbulent — that Indians slighted their Guardians and Negroes grew insolent to their Masters.

But your Letter was the first Intimation that another Tribe more numerous and powerfull than all the rest were grown discontented. — This is rather too coarse a Compliment but you are so saucy, I wont blot it out.

Depend upon it, We know better than to repeal our Masculine systems. Altho they are in full Force, you know they are little more than Theory. We dare not exert our Power in its full Latitude. We are obliged to go fair, and softly, and in Practice you know We are the subjects. We have only the Name of Masters, and rather than give up this, which would compleatly subject Us to the Despotism of the Peticoat, I hope General Washington, and all our brave Heroes would fight. I am sure every good Politician would plot, as long as he would against Despotism, Empire, Monarchy, Aristocracy, Oligarchy, or Ochlocracy.[4] — A fine Story indeed. I begin to think the Ministry as deep as they are wicked. After stirring up Tories, Landjobbers,[5] Trimmers,[6]

---

[4]Mob rule. — Eds.
[5]Those who make their living buying and selling land. — Eds.
[6]Those who change their opinions to suit the period or audience. — Eds.

Bigots, Canadians, Indians, Negroes, Hanoverians,[7] Hessians,[8] Russians, Irish Roman Catholicks, Scotch Renegadoes,[9] at last they have stimulated the [women] to demand new Priviledges and threaten to rebell.

Exploring the Text

1. What ethos does Abigail Adams establish in the opening paragraph? How do the questions contribute to the persona she presents?
2. Abigail describes Boston in considerable detail. What is the general impression she tries to convey? Why do you think she chose the details she did?
3. When Abigail exhorts John Adams to "Remember the Ladies," she also points out that "all Men would be tyrants if they could" (par. 9) and that "your Sex are Naturally Tyrannical" (par. 10). How does she make such statements without sounding accusatory or alienating her husband? Explain.
4. When John tells Abigail that he "cannot but laugh" (par. 17) at her suggestions for laws, is he dismissing her? Is he disrespectful to her? Explain.
5. Is the last paragraph of John's letter written tongue in cheek, or is he serious? What does he mean by "the Despotism of the Peticoat" (par. 19)? How do you interpret this ending?
6. Describe the overall tone of each of these letters. Based on the tone and the information in the letters, describe the relationship between John and Abigail Adams. What evidence of intimacy do you find in each letter?
7. Imagine that Abigail and John Adams had access to e-mail, and rewrite these two letters as e-mail correspondence.

THOMAS JEFFERSON

Thomas Jefferson (1743–1826) was born to high social standing in Albemarle County, Virginia. The son of a planter and surveyor, Jefferson became a lawyer, a promoter of the revolutionary cause, and the third president of the United States. Politically, Jefferson was a leader of the first Republican Party — he promoted states' rights and opposed a strong central government; he sympathized with the French Revolution, but this view led him into conflict with Alexander Hamilton and, eventually, to resign as George Washington's secretary of state. Jefferson was elected vice president in 1796 and then served two terms as president, from 1801

---

[7]Members of supporters of the House of Hanover, which at the time included the British royal family. — Eds.

[8]German mercenaries hired by the British during the Revolutionary War. — Eds.

[9]Protestant Scottish immigrants who came to America to flee the persecution by Catholics in Ireland. — Eds.

to 1809. During his presidency, Jefferson oversaw the Louisiana Purchase, an acquisition of French territory that doubled the geographic size of the United States. Retiring from politics to his estate at Monticello, in Charlottesville, Virginia, Jefferson planned and founded the University of Virginia in 1819. Jefferson himself summarized his accomplishments thus on his gravestone: "Here was buried Thomas Jefferson, Author of the Declaration of American Independence, of the Statute of Virginia for religious freedom, and Father of the University of Virginia."

The Declaration of Independence

The task of writing the Declaration of Independence was put to the "Committee of Five": John Adams, Roger Sherman, Benjamin Franklin, Robert Livingston, and Thomas Jefferson. Jefferson drafted it, and Adams and Franklin made some changes to it. The Declaration of Independence is the document that formally severed the American colonies' ties with the British crown and initiated the revolution.

In CONGRESS, July 4, 1776

The unanimous Declaration of the thirteen united States of America

When in the Course of human events it becomes necessary for one people to dissolve the political bands which have connected them with another and to assume among the powers of the earth, the separate and equal station to which the Laws of Nature and of Nature's God entitle them, a decent respect to the opinions of mankind requires that they should declare the causes which impel them to the separation.

We hold these truths to be self-evident, that all men are created equal, that they are endowed by their Creator with certain unalienable Rights, that among these are Life, Liberty and the pursuit of Happiness. — That to secure these rights, Governments are instituted among Men, deriving their just powers from the consent of the governed, — That whenever any Form of Government becomes destructive of these ends, it is the Right of the People to alter or to abolish it, and to institute new Government, laying its foundation on such principles and organizing its powers in such form, as to them shall seem most likely to effect their Safety and Happiness. Prudence, indeed, will dictate that Governments long established should not be changed for light and transient causes; and accordingly all experience hath shewn that mankind are more disposed to suffer, while evils are sufferable than to right themselves by abolishing the forms to which they are accustomed. But when a long train of abuses and usurpations, pursuing invariably the same Object evinces a design to reduce them under absolute Despotism, it is their right, it is their duty, to throw off such Government, and to provide new Guards for their Future security. — Such has been the patient sufferance of these Colonies; and such is now the necessity which constrains them to alter their former Systems of Government. The history of the present King of Great Britain is a history of repeated injuries and usurpations, all having in direct object the establishment of an absolute Tyranny over these States. To prove this, let Facts be submitted to a candid world.

He has refused his Assent to Laws, the most wholesome and necessary for the public good.

He has forbidden his Governors to pass Laws of immediate and pressing importance, unless suspended in their operation till his Assent should be obtained; and when so suspended, he has utterly neglected to attend to them.

He has refused to pass other Laws for the accommodation of large districts 5 of people, unless those people would relinquish the right of Representation in the Legislature, a right inestimable to them and formidable to tyrants only.

He has called together legislative bodies at places unusual, uncomfortable, and distant from the depository of their Public Records, for the sole purpose of fatiguing them into compliance with his measures.

He has dissolved Representative Houses repeatedly, for opposing with manly firmness his invasions on the rights of the people.

He has refused for a long time, after such dissolutions, to cause others to be elected, whereby the Legislative Powers, incapable of Annihilation, have returned to the People at large for their exercise; the State remaining in the mean time exposed to all the dangers of invasion from without, and convulsions within.

He has endeavoured to prevent the population of these States; for that purpose obstructing the Laws for Naturalization of Foreigners; refusing to pass others to encourage their migrations hither, and raising the conditions of new Appropriations of Lands.

He has obstructed the Administration of Justice by refusing his Assent to Laws 10 for establishing Judiciary Powers.

He has made Judges dependent on his Will alone for the tenure of their offices, and the amount and payment of their salaries.

He has erected a multitude of New Offices, and sent hither swarms of Officers to harass our people and eat out their substance.

He has kept among us, in times of peace, Standing Armies without the Consent of our legislatures.

He has affected to render the Military independent of and superior to the Civil Power.

He has combined with others to subject us to a jurisdiction foreign to our con- 15 stitution, and unacknowledged by our laws; giving his Assent to their Acts of pretended Legislation:

For quartering large bodies of armed troops among us:

For protecting them, by a mock Trial from punishment for any Murders which they should commit on the Inhabitants of these States:

For cutting off our Trade with all parts of the world:

For imposing Taxes on us without our Consent:

For depriving us in many cases, of the benefit of Trial by Jury: 20

For transporting us beyond Seas to be tried for pretended offences:

For abolishing the free System of English Laws in a neighbouring Province, establishing therein an Arbitrary government, and enlarging its Boundaries so as to render it at once an example and fit instrument for introducing the same absolute rule into these Colonies:

For taking away our Charters, abolishing our most valuable Laws and altering fundamentally the Forms of our Governments:

For suspending our own Legislatures, and declaring themselves invested with power to legislate for us in all cases whatsoever.

He has abdicated Government here, by declaring us out of his Protection and   25
waging War against us.

He has plundered our seas, ravaged our coasts, burnt our towns, and destroyed the lives of our people.

He is at this time transporting large Armies of foreign Mercenaries to compleat the works of death, desolation, and tyranny, already begun with circumstances of Cruelty & Perfidy scarcely paralleled in the most barbarous ages, and totally unworthy the Head of a civilized nation.

He has constrained our fellow Citizens taken Captive on the high Seas to bear Arms against their Country, to become the executioners of their friends and Brethren, or to fall themselves by their Hands.

He has excited domestic insurrections amongst us, and has endeavoured to bring on the inhabitants of our frontiers, the merciless Indian Savages whose known rule of warfare, is an undistinguished destruction of all ages, sexes and conditions.

In every stage of these Oppressions We have Petitioned for Redress in the most   30
humble terms: Our repeated Petitions have been answered only by repeated injury. A Prince, whose character is thus marked by every act which may define a Tyrant, is unfit to be the ruler of a free people.

Nor have We been wanting in attentions to our British brethren. We have warned them from time to time of attempts by their legislature to extend an unwarrantable jurisdiction over us. We have reminded them of the circumstances of our emigration and settlement here. We have appealed to their native justice and magnanimity, and we have conjured them by the ties of our common kindred to disavow these usurpations, which would inevitably interrupt our connections and correspondence. They too have been deaf to the voice of justice and of consanguinity. We must, therefore, acquiesce in the necessity, which denounces our Separation, and hold them, as we hold the rest of mankind, Enemies in War, in Peace Friends.

We, therefore, the Representatives of the united States of America, in General Congress, Assembled, appealing to the Supreme Judge of the world for the rectitude of our intentions, do, in the Name, and by Authority of the good People of these Colonies, solemnly publish and declare, That these united Colonies are, and of Right ought to be Free and Independent States, that they are Absolved from all Allegiance to the British Crown, and that all political connection between them and the State of Great Britain, is and ought to be totally dissolved; and that as Free and Independent States, they have full Power to levy War, conclude Peace, contract Alliances, establish Commerce, and to do all other Acts and Things which Independent States may of right do. — And for the support of this Declaration, with a firm reliance on the protection of Divine Providence, we mutually pledge to each other our Lives, our Fortunes, and our sacred Honor.

Exploring the Text

1. What are the subject and the predicate of the first sentence of the declaration?
2. What is a major assumption underlying the statement made in the first sentence? Explain the rhetorical principle at work.
3. What are each of the "truths" and "rights" indicated by Thomas Jefferson?
4. What effect does the phrase "self-evident" have in the second sentence? How does that phrase help support Jefferson's position?
5. Why does Jefferson begin with an appeal to "respect" as a value before stating his claim? Why not simply begin by declaring his position?
6. How does Jefferson appeal to logos, ethos, and pathos? Identify and explain two examples for each.
7. Read carefully the second and third "truths" that Jefferson states. At that time, was it a historical fact that governments were instituted for the purpose Jefferson states? Consult or do some research on the topic to help you formulate your answer.
8. What is the effect of the rhetorical parallelism with which Jefferson concludes the declaration?
9. Where is Jefferson's argument inductive? Where is it deductive? Explain.
10. Jefferson states that "all men are created equal" (par. 2). What does he mean by "all men"? Who is excluded? How do these exclusions influence your response to the declaration? Explain.

 **TALKBACK**

Elizabeth Cady Stanton

Elizabeth Cady Stanton (1815–1902) was an American activist and a leading figure of the early women's rights movement. In 1848, Stanton and fellow activist Lucretia Mott organized the first convention to address women's rights and issues in Seneca Falls, New York — an event now known as the Seneca Falls Convention.

Declaration of Sentiments

At the Seneca Falls Convention, Stanton presented her Declaration of Sentiments, modeled after the U.S. Declaration of Independence, which boldly demanded that the individual rights of women be acknowledged and respected by society. The document was signed by 68 women and 32 men — 100 people out of the nearly 300 attendees of the conference.

When, in the course of human events, it becomes necessary for one portion of the family of man to assume among the people of the earth a position different from that which they have hitherto occupied, but one to which the laws of nature and of nature's God entitle them, a decent respect to the opinions of mankind requires that they should declare the causes that impel them to such a course.

We hold these truths to be self-evident: that all men and women are created equal; that they are endowed by their Creator with certain inalienable rights; that among these are life, liberty, and the pursuit of happiness; that to secure these rights governments are instituted, deriving their just powers from the consent of the governed. Whenever any form of Government becomes destructive of these ends, it is the right of those who suffer from it to refuse allegiance to it, and to insist upon the institution of a new government, laying its foundation on such principles, and organizing its powers in such form as to them shall seem most likely to effect their safety and happiness. Prudence, indeed, will dictate that governments long established should not be changed for light and transient causes; and accordingly, all experience hath shown that mankind are more disposed to suffer, while evils are sufferable, than to right themselves by abolishing the forms to which they are accustomed. But when a long train of abuses and usurpations, pursuing invariably the same object, evinces a design to reduce them under absolute despotism, it is their duty to throw off such government, and to provide new guards for their future security. Such has been the patient sufferance of the women under this government, and such is now the necessity which constrains them to demand the equal station to which they are entitled.

The history of mankind is a history of repeated injuries and usurpations on the part of man toward woman, having in direct object the establishment of an absolute tyranny over her. To prove this, let facts be submitted to a candid world.

He has never permitted her to exercise her inalienable right to the elective franchise.

He has compelled her to submit to laws, in the formation of which she had   5
no voice.

He has withheld from her rights which are given to the most ignorant and degraded men — both natives and foreigners.

Having deprived her of this first right of a citizen, the elective franchise, thereby leaving her without representation in the halls of legislation, he has oppressed her on all sides.

He has made her, if married, in the eye of the law, civilly dead.

He has taken from her all right in property, even to the wages she earns.

He has made her, morally, an irresponsible being, as she can commit many   10
crimes with impunity, provided they be done in the presence of her husband. In the covenant of marriage, she is compelled to promise obedience to her husband, he becoming, to all intents and purposes, her master — the law giving him power to deprive her of her liberty, and to administer chastisement.

He has so framed the laws of divorce, as to what shall be the proper causes of divorce; in case of separation, to whom the guardianship of the children shall be given; as to be wholly regardless of the happiness of women — the law, in all cases, going upon the false supposition of the supremacy of man, and giving all power into his hands.

After depriving her of all rights as a married woman, if single and the owner of property, he has taxed her to support a government which recognizes her only when her property can be made profitable to it.

He has monopolized nearly all the profitable employments, and from those she is permitted to follow, she receives but a scanty remuneration.

He closes against her all the avenues to wealth and distinction, which he considers most honorable to himself. As a teacher of theology, medicine, or law, she is not known.

He has denied her the facilities for obtaining a thorough education — all   15
colleges being closed against her.

He allows her in Church as well as State, but a subordinate position, claiming Apostolic authority for her exclusion from the ministry, and, with some exceptions, from any public participation in the affairs of the Church.

He has created a false public sentiment, by giving to the world a different code of morals for men and women, by which moral delinquencies which exclude women from society, are not only tolerated but deemed of little account in man.

He has usurped the prerogative of Jehovah himself, claiming it as his right to assign for her a sphere of action, when that belongs to her conscience and her God.

He has endeavored, in every way that he could to destroy her confidence in her own powers, to lessen her self-respect, and to make her willing to lead a dependent and abject life.

Now, in view of this entire disfranchisement of one-half the people of this   20
country, their social and religious degradation, — in view of the unjust laws above mentioned, and because women do feel themselves aggrieved, oppressed, and fraudulently deprived of their most sacred rights, we insist that they have immediate admission to all the rights and privileges which belong to them as citizens of these United States.

In entering upon the great work before us, we anticipate no small amount of misconception, misrepresentation, and ridicule; but we shall use every instrumentality within our power to effect our object. We shall employ agents, circulate tracts, petition the State and national Legislatures, and endeavor to enlist the pulpit and the press in our behalf. We hope this Convention will be followed by a series of Conventions, embracing every part of the country.

(1848)

Exploring the Text

1. How does Elizabeth Cady Stanton establish her ethos?
2. Why does Stanton call her declaration one of "sentiments" and not "independence"?
3. Clearly, Stanton's declaration is based very closely on Jefferson's — especially at the beginning. How is it specifically different from his in the first three paragraphs?

4. Which of Stanton's facts and resolutions do you find most compelling? Choose three of each and explain the reasons for your choices. How much might your response be influenced by your gender? Explain.
5. How do you think such a declaration might have been regarded by the men of the time? Explain your answer.
6. Does Stanton appeal most to ethos, logos, or pathos? Explain.

Ho Chi Minh

Ho Chi Minh (1890–1969) was a Communist revolutionary who became president and prime minister of the Democratic Republic of Vietnam (North Vietnam). Educated in France, Minh was integral in founding the Democratic Republic of Vietnam, the People's Army of Vietnam, and the Viet Cong, the organization and army that fought the South Vietnamese and the United States during the Vietnam War. Ho Chi Minh is so significant in the history of his country that after his death, the capital city of Vietnam, Saigon, was renamed Ho Chi Minh City. In the manner of other legendary Communist leaders, his embalmed body is on display at the Ho Chi Minh Mausoleum in Hanoi.

Proclamation of Independence of the Democratic Republic of Vietnam

From 1941 onward, Ho Chi Minh led the Vietnamese fight for independence from the French, who had controlled northern Vietnam since 1884. On August 19, 1945, protests and riots against French colonial rule broke out across Vietnam, and on September 2, Minh issued a Proclamation of Independence of the Democratic Republic of Vietnam, appealing to the free world as his country resisted French imperialism. In the 1950s the United States began supporting the French and in 1965 sent troops to invade Vietnam, beginning a war that would be waged for the next ten years.

"All men are created equal. They are endowed by their Creator with certain unalienable rights, among these are Life, Liberty and the pursuit of happiness."

This immortal statement was made in the Declaration of Independence of the United States of America in 1776. Now if we enlarge the sphere of our thoughts, this statement conveys another meaning: All the peoples on the earth are equal from birth, all the peoples have a right to live, be happy and free.

The Declaration of the Rights of Man and of the Citizen of the French Revolution in 1791 also states: "All men are born free and with equal rights, and must always be free and have equal rights."

Those are undeniable truths.

Nevertheless, for more than eighty years, the French imperialists deceit- 5 fully raising the standard of Liberty, Equality, and Fraternity, have violated our Fatherland and oppressed our fellow-citizens. They have acted contrarily to the ideals of humanity and justice.

In the province of politics, they have deprived our people of every liberty.

They have enforced inhuman laws; to ruin our unity and national consciousness, they have carried out three different policies in the North, the Center, and the
South of Vietnam.

They have founded more prisons than schools. They have mercilessly slain
our patriots; they have deluged our revolutionary areas with innocent blood.
They have fettered public opinion; they have promoted illiteracy.

To weaken our race they have forced us to use their manufactured opium
and alcohol.

In the province of economics, they have stripped our fellow-citizens of every-   10
thing they possessed, impoverishing the individual and devastating the land.

They have robbed us of our rice fields, our mines, our forests, our raw
materials. They have monopolized the printing of bank-notes, the import and
export trade; they have invented numbers of unlawful taxes, reducing our
people, especially our countryfolk, to a state of extreme poverty.

They have stood in the way of our businessmen and stifled all their under-
takings; they have extorted our working classes in a most savage way.

In the Autumn of the year 1940, when the Japanese fascists violated Indochina's
territory to get one more foothold in their fight against the Allies, the French imperialists fell on their knees and surrendered, handing over our country to the Japanese, adding Japanese fetters to the French ones. From that day on the Vietnamese
people suffered hardships yet unknown in the history of mankind. The result
of this double oppression was terrific: from Quangtri to the Northern border
two million people were starved to death in the early months of 1945.

On the 9th of March 1945 the French troops were disarmed by the Japanese.
Once more the French either fled, or surrendered unconditionally, showing thus
that not only were they incapable of "protecting" us, but that they twice sold us
to the Japanese.

Yet, many times before the month of March, the Vietminh[1] had urged the   15
French to ally with them against the Japanese. The French colonists never answered. On the contrary they intensified their terrorizing policy. Before taking
their flight they even killed a great number of our patriots who had been imprisoned at Yenbay and Caobang.

Nevertheless, towards the French people our fellow-citizens have always
manifested an attitude pervaded with toleration and humanity. Even after the
Japanese putsch of March 1945 the Vietminh have helped many Frenchmen to
reach the frontier, have delivered some of them from the Japanese jails, and
never failed to protect their lives and properties.

The truth is that since the Autumn of 1940 our country had ceased to be a
French colony and had become a Japanese outpost. After the Japanese had surrendered to the Allies our whole people rose to conquer political power and
institute the Republic of Vietnam.

---

[1]Abbreviated form of Vietnam Doc Lap Dong Minh Hoi, or League for the Independence of Vietnam. — Eds.

The truth is that we have wrested our independence from the Japanese and not from the French. The French have fled, the Japanese have capitulated, Emperor Bao Dai has abdicated, our people has broken the fetters which for over a century have tied us down; our people has at the same time overthrown the monarchic constitution that had reigned supreme for so many centuries and instead has established the present Republican Government.

For these reasons, we, members of the provisional Government, representing the whole population of Vietnam, have declared and renew here our declaration that we break off all relations with the French people and abolish all the special rights the French have unlawfully acquired on our Fatherland.

The whole population of Vietnam is united in a common allegiance to the   20
Republican Government and is linked by a common will which is to annihilate the dark aims of the French imperialists.

We are convinced that the Allied nations which have acknowledged at Teheran and San Francisco the principles of self-determination and equality of status will not refuse to acknowledge the independence of Vietnam.

A people that has courageously opposed French domination for more than eighty years, a people that has fought by the Allies' side these last years against the fascists, such a people must be free, such a people must be independent.

For these reasons we, members of the Provisional Government of Vietnam, declare to the world that Vietnam has the right to be free and independent, and has in fact become a free and independent country. We also declare that the Vietnamese people is determined to make the heaviest sacrifices to maintain its independence and its Liberty.

(1945)

Exploring the Text

1. Why does Ho Chi Minh begin by quoting both the U.S. Declaration of Independence and the declaration of the French Revolution? What is the rhetorical effect of such a beginning?
2. In Ho Chi Minh's proclamation he includes a great deal of historical background. Why did he do that? What does that suggest about his audience?
3. Does Minh appeal most to ethos, logos, or pathos? Explain.
4. U.S. troops invaded Vietnam in 1965, waging war until 1975. How does a reading of this declaration affect your view of the Vietnam War (or of the "American War," as the Vietnamese call it)?

Making Connections

1. Read carefully paragraphs 1 and 2 of the declarations by Thomas Jefferson (p. 389) and Elizabeth Cady Stanton (p. 393). Explain how the writers use rhetorical strategies to develop their arguments.

2. Defend or challenge Jefferson's and Stanton's characterizations of the "self-evident truths" that they proclaim.
3. How are Jefferson's and Ho Chi Minh's (p. 396) declarations similar? How are they different?
4. Jefferson recounts the "crimes" of King George III of England. Whose "crimes" are recounted by Stanton and by Minh? Explain.
5. If Jefferson were alive in the twentieth century, how do you think he would have responded to Minh's proclamation? How might he have responded to Stanton's declaration if he had been alive when it was drafted?
6. Why do you suppose the Declaration of Independence has had such a huge influence on the writing and thinking of others?
7. Read carefully H. L. Mencken's "Declaration of Independence in American," from his book *The American Language*. Write a piece in which you convey Jefferson's, Stanton's, or Minh's thoughts and ideas in the slang of the 1950s, '60s, '80s, or today, as Mencken did using the slang of 1921.

HECTOR ST. JOHN DE CRÈVECOEUR

Hector St. John de Crèvecoeur (1735–1813) was born in Normandy, France, and immigrated to North America in 1755. He served in the French colonial militia during the French and Indian Wars, and upon Britain's defeat of France, he moved to New York and became a citizen. Crèvecoeur embarked on a prosperous second career as a farmer in Orange County, New York, and wrote about his experiences in the colonies and the blossoming American society. Crèvecoeur returned to London in 1779, after three months' imprisonment by the British on suspicion of being an American spy.

from *Letters from an American Farmer*

Upon his return to London, Crèvecoeur published *Letters from an American Farmer*, a volume of essays that became the first best seller by an American in Europe. In his third letter, Crèvecoeur asks the pertinent question, "What is American?"

I wish I could be acquainted with the feelings and thoughts which must agitate the heart and present themselves to the mind of an enlightened Englishman, when he first lands on this continent. He must greatly rejoice that he lived at a time to see this fair country discovered and settled; he must necessarily feel a share of national pride, when he views the chain of settlements which embellishes these extended shores. When he says to himself, this is the work of my countrymen, who, when convulsed by factions, afflicted by a variety of miseries and wants, restless and impatient, took refuge here. They brought along with them their national genius, to which they principally owe what liberty they enjoy, and what substance they possess. Here he sees the industry of his native country displayed in a new manner, and traces in their works the embrios of all the arts, sciences, and ingenuity which flourish in Europe. Here he beholds fair cities, substantial villages, extensive fields, an immense country filled with decent houses, good roads, orchards, meadows, and bridges, where an hundred years ago all was wild, woody and uncultivated! What a train of pleasing ideas this fair spectacle must suggest: it is a prospect which must inspire a good citizen with the most heartfelt pleasure. The difficulty consists in the manner of viewing so extensive a scene. He is arrived on a new continent; a modern society offers itself to his contemplation, diffèrent from what he had hitherto seen. It is not composed, as in Europe, of great lords who possess every thing, and of a herd of people who have nothing. Here are no aristocratical families, no courts, no kings, no bishops, no ecclesiastical dominion, no invisible power giving to a few a very visible one; no great manufacturers employing thousands, no great refinements of luxury. The rich and the poor are not so far removed from each other as they are in Europe. Some few towns excepted, we are all tillers of the earth, from Nova Scotia to West Florida. We are a people of cultivators, scattered over an immense territory, communicating with each other by means of good roads, and navigable rivers, united by the silken bands of mild government, all respecting the laws, without dreading their power, because they are equitable. We are all animated with the spirit of an industry which is unfettered and unrestrained, because each person works for himself. If he travels through our rural districts he views not the hostile castle, and the haughty mansion, contrasted with the clay-built hut and miserable cabbin, where cattle and men help to keep each other warm, and dwell in meanness, smoke, and indigence. A pleasing uniformity of decent competence appears throughout our habitations. The meanest of our log-houses is a dry and comfortable habitation. Lawyer or merchant are the fairest titles our towns afford; that of a farmer is the only appellation of the rural inhabitants of our country. It must take some time ere he can reconcile himself to our dictionary, which is but short in words of dignity, and names of honour. There, on a Sunday, he sees a congregation of respectable farmers and their wives, all clad in neat homespun, well mounted, or riding in their own humble waggons. There is not among them an esquire, saving the unlettered magistrate. There he sees a parson as simple as his flock, a farmer who does not riot on the labour of others. We have no princes, for whom we toil, starve, and bleed: we are the most perfect society now existing in the world. Here man is free as he ought to be; nor is this pleasing equality so transitory as many others are. Many ages will not see the shores of our great lakes replenished with inland nations, nor the unknown bounds of North America entirely peopled. Who can tell how far it extends? Who can tell the millions of men whom it will feed and contain? for no European foot has as yet travelled half the extent of this mighty continent!

The next wish of this traveller will be to know whence came all these people? they are a mixture of English, Scotch, Irish, French, Dutch, Germans, and Swedes. From this promiscuous breed, that race now called Americans have arisen. The eastern provinces must indeed be excepted, as being the unmixed descendents of Englishmen. I have heard many wish that they had been more intermixed also: for my part, I am no wisher, and think it much better as it has happened. They exhibit a most conspicuous figure in this great and variegated picture; they too enter for a great share in the pleasing perspective displayed in these thirteen provinces. I know it is fashionable to reflect on them, but I respect them for what they have done; for the accuracy and wisdom with which they have settled their territory; for the decency of their manners; for their early love of letters; their ancient college,[1] the first in this hemisphere; for their industry; which to me who am but a farmer, is the criterion of everything. There never was a people, situated as they are, who with so ungratful a soil have done more in so short a time. Do you think that the monarchical ingredients which are more prevalent in other governments, have purged them from all foul stains? Their histories assert the contrary.

In this great American asylum, the poor of Europe have by some means met together, and in consequence of various causes; to what purpose should they ask one another what countrymen they are? Alas, two thirds of them had no country. Can a wretch who wanders about, who works and starves, whose life is a continual scene of sore affliction or pinching penury; can that man call England or any other kingdom his country? A country that had no bread for him, whose fields procured him no harvest, who met with nothing but the frowns of the rich, the severity of the laws, with jails and punishments; who owned not a single foot of the extensive surface of this planet? No! urged by a variety of motives, here they came. Every thing has tended to regenerate them; new laws, a new mode of living, a new social system; here they are become men: in Europe they were as so many useless plants, wanting vegitative mould, and refreshing showers; they withered, and were mowed down by want, hunger, and war; but now by the power of transplantation, like all other plants they have taken root and flourished! Formerly they were not numbered in any civil lists of their country, except in those of the poor; here they rank as citizens. By what invisible power has this surprising metamorphosis been performed? By that of the laws and that of their industry. The laws, the indulgent laws, protect them as they arrive, stamping on them the symbol of adoption; they receive ample rewards for their labours; these accumulated rewards procure them lands; those lands confer on them the title of freemen, and to that title every benefit is affixed which men can possibly require. This is the great operation daily performed by our laws. From whence proceed these laws? From our government. Whence the government? It is derived from the original genius and strong desire of the people ratified and confirmed by the crown. This is the great chain which links us all, this is the picture which every province exhibits, Nova Scotia excepted.[2] There the crown has done all; either there were no people who had genius, or it was not much attended to: the consequence is, that the province is very thinly inhabited indeed; the power of the crown in conjunction

---

[1]Harvard College, founded 150 years earlier in 1636. — Eds.
[2]A reference to the Great Expulsion of 1755, when the French Acadians in Nova Scotia were forcibly relocated to other colonies or back to France, as a British military strategy during the French and Indian Wars. Many Acadians deported to France returned to America and settled in the Louisiana area, where the word *Acadian* morphed into the word *Cajun*. — Eds.

with the musketos has prevented men from settling there. Yet some parts of it flourished once, and it contained a mild harmless set of people. But for the fault of a few leaders, the whole were banished. The greatest political error the crown ever committed in America, was to cut off men from a country which wanted nothing but men!

What attachment can a poor European emigrant have for a country where he had nothing? The knowledge of the language, the love of a few kindred as poor as himself, were the only cords that tied him: his country is now that which gives him land, bread, protection, and consequence: *Ubi panis ibi patria*,[3] is the motto of all emigrants. What then is the American, this new man? He is either an European, or the descendant of an European, hence that strange mixture of blood, which you will find in no other country. I could point out to you a family whose grandfather was an Englishman, whose wife was Dutch, whose son married a French woman, and whose present four sons have now four wives of different nations. *He* is an American, who leaving behind him all his ancient prejudices and manners, receives new ones from the new mode of life he has embraced, the new government he obeys, and the new rank he holds. He becomes an American by being received in the broad lap of our great *Alma Mater.* Here individuals of all nations are melted into a new race of men, whose labours and posterity will one day cause great changes in the world. Americans are the western pilgrims, who are carrying along with them that great mass of arts, sciences, vigour, and industry which began long since in the east; they will finish the great circle. The Americans were once scattered all over Europe; here they are incorporated into one of the finest systems of population which has ever appeared, and which will hereafter become distinct by the power of the different climates they inhabit. The American ought therefore to love this country much better than that wherein either he or his forefathers were born. Here the rewards of his industry follow with equal steps the progress of his labour; his labour is founded on the basis of nature, *self-interest*; can it want a stronger allurement? Wives and children, who before in vain demanded of him a morsel of bread, now, fat and frolicsome, gladly help their father to clear those fields whence exuberant crops are to arise to feed and to clothe them all; without any part being claimed, either by a despotic prince, a rich abbot, or a mighty lord. Here religion demands but little of him; a small voluntary salary to the minister, and gratitude to God; can he refuse these? The American is a new man, who acts upon new principles; he must therefore entertain new ideas, and form new opinions. From involuntary idleness, servile dependence, penury, and useless labour, he has passed to toils of a very different nature, rewarded by ample subsistence. — This is an American.

(1782)

Exploring the Text

1. Which of the appeals — ethos, logos, or pathos — is strongest in this piece? Explain. What are the main differences between Americans and Europeans as Hector St. John de Crèvecoeur describes them?

---

[3]Latin. "Where there is bread, there is my country." — Eds.

2. Which do you regard as Crèvecoeur's most compelling observation in the first paragraph? Why?

3. How does the "promiscuous breed" to which Crèvecoeur refers at the beginning of the second paragraph compare with Americans today? How might he characterize Americans in our time?

4. Crèvecoeur poses several questions in this letter. Which are rhetorical questions? Which are not? What is the effect of those that are not?

5. How are Crèvecoeur's own values revealed in his characterization of "an American"?

6. In *Rights of Man* (1791), Thomas Paine makes the following observation about America:

> If there is a country in the world, where concord, according to common calculation, would be least expected, it is America. Made up, as it is, of people from different nations, accustomed to different forms and habits of government, speaking different languages, and more different in their modes of worship, it would appear that the union of such a people was impracticable; but by the simple operation of constructing government on the principles of society and the rights of man, every difficulty retires, and all the parts are brought into cordial unison. There, the poor are not oppressed, the rich are not privileged. Industry is not mortified by the splendid extravagance of a court rioting at its expence. Their taxes are few, because their government is just; and as there is nothing to render them wretched, there is nothing to engender riots and tumults.

Compare Paine's observation with what Crèvecoeur writes in paragraph 4 of his letter. What similarities and differences do you find?

7. In her 2010 book, *The History of White People*, African American historian Nell Irvin Painter responds to Crèvecoeur's final paragraph:

> This "new man" escapes old Europe's oppression, embraces new opportunity, and glories in freedom of thought and economic mobility. Now a classic description of *the* American, Crèvecoeur's paragraph constantly appears as an objective eyewitness account of American identity. But letter 3 is only one part of the story. When other classes, races, sexes, and the South entered Crèvecoeur's picture, all sorts of revisions became necessary.

What might some of those necessary revisions be? Does Painter's statement alter your view of Crèvecoeur? Explain.

8. Crèvecoeur writes of America: "Here individuals of all nations are melted into a new race of men, whose labours and posterity will one day cause great changes in the world" (par. 4). Considering that he wrote that statement in 1782, how accurate was his prediction? Provide specific examples.

Alexander Hamilton, James Madison, and John Jay

Alexander Hamilton (c. 1755–1804) represented New York at the Constitutional Convention in 1787 and became the first secretary of the Treasury, serving from 1789 to 1795. James Madison (1751–1836) was a member of the U.S. House of Representatives from 1789 to 1797, secretary of state from 1801 to 1809, and ultimately the fourth president of the United States. John Jay (1745–1829) was a Founding Father who served as president of the Continental Congress, governor of the state of New York, and first chief justice of the Supreme Court.

from *The Federalist* Papers

The Federalist papers are a series of eighty-five articles written by Alexander Hamilton, James Madison, and John Jay under the pseudonym Publius to promote and justify the ratification of the United States Constitution. Seventy-seven of these essays were first published in the *Independent Journal* and the *New York Packet* in 1787 and 1788. In 1788, with eight additional essays they were compiled into a book and published in two volumes under the title *The Federalist*.

The Federalist No. 1

"The Federalist No. 1" was published in the *Independent Journal* on October 27, 1787. Historians have identified Alexander Hamilton as the primary author of this essay.

To the People of the State of New York:

After an unequivocal experience of the inefficiency of the subsisting federal government, you are called upon to deliberate on a new Constitution for the United States of America. The subject speaks its own importance; comprehending in its consequences nothing less than the existence of the UNION, the safety and welfare of the parts of which it is composed, the fate of an empire in many respects the most interesting in the world. It has been frequently remarked that it seems to have been reserved to the people of this country, by their conduct and example, to decide the important question, whether societies of men are really capable or not of establishing good government from reflection and choice, or whether they are forever destined to depend for their political constitutions on accident and force. If there be any truth in the remark, the crisis at which we are arrived may with propriety be regarded as the era in which that decision is to be made; and a wrong election of the part we shall act may, in this view, deserve to be considered as the general misfortune of mankind.

This idea will add the inducements of philanthropy to those of patriotism, to heighten the solicitude which all considerate and good men must feel for the event. Happy will it be if our choice should be directed by a judicious estimate of our true interests, unperplexed and unbiased by considerations not connected with the public good. But this is a thing more ardently to be wished than seriously to be expected. The plan offered to our deliberations affects too many particular interests, innovates upon too many local institutions, not to involve in its discussion a variety of objects foreign to its merits, and of views, passions, and prejudices little favorable to the discovery of truth.

Among the most formidable of the obstacles which the new Constitution will have to encounter may readily be distinguished the obvious interest of a certain class of men in every State to resist all changes which may hazard a diminution of the power, emolument, and consequence of the offices they hold under the State establishments; and the perverted ambition of another class of men, who will either hope to aggrandize themselves by the confusions of their country, or will flatter themselves with fairer prospects of elevation from the subdivision of the empire into several partial confederacies than from its union under one government.

It is not, however, my design to dwell upon observations of this nature. I am well aware that it would be disingenuous to resolve indiscriminately the opposition of any set of men (merely because their situations might subject them to suspicion) into interested or ambitious views. Candor will oblige us to admit that even such men may be actuated by upright intentions; and it cannot be doubted that much of the opposition which has made its appearance, or may hereafter make its appearance, will spring from sources, blameless at least, if not respectable — the honest errors of minds led astray by preconceived jealousies and fears. So numerous indeed and so powerful are the causes which serve to give a false bias to the judgment, that we, upon many occasions, see wise and good men on the wrong as well as on the right side of questions of the first magnitude to society. This circumstance, if duly attended to, would furnish a lesson of moderation to those who are ever so much persuaded of their being in the right in any controversy. And a further reason for caution, in this respect, might be drawn from the reflection that we are not always sure that those who advocate the truth are influenced by purer principles than their antagonists. Ambition, avarice, personal animosity, party opposition, and many other motives not more laudable than these, are apt to operate as well upon those who support as those who oppose the right side of a question. Were there not even these inducements to moderation, nothing could be more ill-judged than that intolerant spirit which has, at all times, characterized political parties. For in politics, as in religion, it is equally absurd to aim at making proselytes by fire and sword. Heresies in either can rarely be cured by persecution.

And yet, however just these sentiments will be allowed to be, we have already 5 sufficient indications that it will happen in this as in all former cases of great national discussion. A torrent of angry and malignant passions will be let loose. To judge from the conduct of the opposite parties, we shall be led to conclude that they will mutually hope to evince the justness of their opinions, and to increase the number of their converts by the loudness of their declamations and the bitterness of their invectives. An enlightened zeal for the energy and efficiency of government will be stigmatized as the offspring of a temper fond of despotic power and hostile to the principles of liberty. An over-scrupulous jealousy of danger to the rights of the people, which is more commonly the fault of the head than of the heart, will be represented as mere pretense and artifice, the stale bait for popularity at the expense of the public good. It will be forgotten, on the one hand, that jealousy is the usual concomitant of love, and that the noble enthusiasm of liberty is apt to be infected with a spirit of narrow and illiberal distrust. On the other hand, it will be equally forgotten that the vigor of government is essential to the security of liberty; that, in the contemplation of a sound and well-informed judgment, their interest can never be separated; and that a dangerous ambition more often lurks behind the specious mask of zeal for the rights of the people than under the forbidden appearance of zeal for the firmness and efficiency of government. History will teach us that the former has been found a much more certain road to the introduction of despotism than the latter, and that of those men who have overturned the liberties of republics, the greatest number have begun their career by paying an obsequious court to the people; commencing demagogues, and ending tyrants.

In the course of the preceding observations, I have had an eye, my fellow-citizens, to putting you upon your guard against all attempts, from whatever quarter, to influence your decision in a matter of the utmost moment to your welfare, by any impressions other than those which may result from the evidence of truth. You will, no doubt, at the same time, have collected from the general scope of them, that they proceed from a source not unfriendly to the new Constitution. Yes, my countrymen, I own to you that, after having given it an attentive consideration, I am clearly of opinion it is your interest to adopt it. I am convinced that this is the safest course for your liberty, your dignity, and your happiness. I affect not reserves which I do not feel. I will not amuse you with an appearance of deliberation when I have decided. I frankly acknowledge to you my convictions, and I will freely lay before you the reasons on which they are founded. The consciousness of good intentions disdains ambiguity. I shall not, however, multiply professions on this head. My motives must remain in the depository of my own breast. My arguments will be open to all, and may be judged of by all. They shall at least be offered in a spirit which will not disgrace the cause of truth.

PUBLIUS
(1787)

Exploring the Text

1. How does Alexander Hamilton establish the gravity of the situation he addresses in the first paragraph?

2. What are the chief reasons for caution and moderation that Hamilton offers in paragraphs 2 through 4?
3. How would you explain the nature of the two main obstacles Hamilton addresses? Which one is more important? Explain.
4. How effective is the comparison that he makes between politics and religion (par. 4)?
5. How does Hamilton characterize the "great national discussion" (par. 5)?
6. Why might "zeal for the rights of the people" be a "specious mask" while the appearance of "zeal for the firmness and efficiency of government" be "forbidden" (par. 5)? Do you find this ironic? Why would Hamilton suggest the former as more dangerous? Explain.
7. How does Hamilton appeal to ethos in paragraph 6?
8. Hamilton has been regarded by some as holding a pessimistic view of human nature. In "Federalist No. 6" Hamilton writes that "men are ambitious, vindictive, and rapacious." But in "Federalist No. 76" he states, "The supposition of universal venality in human nature is little less an error in political reasoning than the supposition of universal rectitude." And in the same paper he recommends that a citizen "view human nature as it is, without either flattering its virtues, or exaggerating its vices." Would you characterize Hamilton as optimistic, pessimistic, or merely realistic? Explain.

The Federalist No. 10

"The Federalist No. 10" was published in the *Daily Adviser* on November 22, 1787. Historians have identified James Madison as the primary author of this essay.

To the people of the state of New-York:

... By a faction I understand a number of citizens, whether amounting to a majority or minority of the whole, who are united and actuated by some common impulse of passion, or of interest, adverse to the rights of other citizens, or to the permanent and aggregate interests of the community.

There are two methods of curing the mischiefs of faction: the one, by removing its causes; the other, by controling its effects.

There are again two methods of removing the causes of faction: the one by destroying the liberty which is essential to its existence; the other, by giving to every citizen the same opinions, the same passions, and the same interests.

It could never be more truly said than of the first remedy, that it is worse than the disease. Liberty is to faction, what air is to fire, an aliment without which it instantly expires. But it could not be a less folly to abolish liberty, which is essential to political life, because it nourishes faction, than it would be to wish the annihilation of air, which is essential to animal life, because it imparts to fire its destructive agency.

The second expedient is as impracticable, as the first would be unwise. As long 5
as the reason of man continues fallible, and he is at liberty to exercise it, different
opinions will be formed. As long as the connection subsists between his reason and
his self-love, his opinions and his passions will have a reciprocal influence on each
other; and the former will be objects to which the latter will attach themselves. The
diversity in the faculties of men from which the rights of property originate, is not
less an insuperable obstacle to a uniformity of interests. The protection of these faculties is the first object of Government. From the protection of different and unequal
faculties of acquiring property, the possession of different degrees and kinds of property immediately results: and from the influence of these on the sentiments and views
of the respective proprietors, ensues a division of the society into different interests
and parties.

The latent causes of faction are thus sown in the nature of man; and we see them
every where brought into different degrees of activity, according to the different circumstances of civil society. A zeal for different opinions concerning religion, concerning Government, and many other points, as well of speculation as of practice; an
attachment to different leaders ambitiously contending for pre-eminence and power;
or to persons of other descriptions whose fortunes have been interesting to the
human passions, have in turn divided mankind into parties, inflamed them with
mutual animosity, and rendered them much more disposed to vex and oppress each
other, than to co-operate for their common good. So strong is this propensity of
mankind to fall into mutual animosities, that where no substantial occasion presents
itself, the most frivolous and fanciful distinctions have been sufficient to kindle their
unfriendly passions, and excite their most violent conflicts. But the most common
and durable source of factions, has been the various and unequal distribution of
property. Those who hold, and those who are without property, have ever formed
distinct interests in society. Those who are creditors, and those who are debtors, fall
under a like discrimination. A landed interest, a manufacturing interest, a mercantile
interest, a monied interest, with many lesser interests, grow up of necessity in civilized nations, and divide them into different classes, actuated by different sentiments
and views. The regulation of these various and interfering interests forms the principal task of modern Legislation, and involves the spirit of party and faction in the
necessary and ordinary operations of Government. . . .

It is in vain to say, that enlightened statesmen will be able to adjust these clashing
interests, and render them all subservient to the public good. Enlightened statesmen
will not always be at the helm: Nor, in many cases, can such an adjustment be made
at all, without taking into view indirect and remote considerations, which will rarely
prevail over the immediate interest which one party may find in disregarding the
rights of another, or the good of the whole.

The inference to which we are brought, is, that the *causes* of faction cannot be
removed; and that relief is only to be sought in the means of controling its *effects*.

If a faction consists of less than a majority, relief is supplied by the republican
principle, which enables the majority to defeat its sinister views by regular vote: It
may clog the administration, it may convulse the society; but it will be unable to

execute and mask its violence under the forms of the Constitution. When a majority is included in a faction, the form of popular government on the other hand enables it to sacrifice to its ruling passion or interest, both the public good and the rights of other citizens. To secure the public good, and private rights, against the danger of such a faction, and at the same time to preserve the spirit and the form of popular government, is then the great object to which our enquiries are directed: Let me add that it is the great desideratum, by which alone this form of government can be rescued from the opprobrium under which it has so long labored, and be recommended to the esteem and adoption of mankind.

By what means is this object attainable? Evidently by one of two only. Either the   10 existence of the same passion or interest in a majority at the same time, must be prevented; or the majority, having such co-existent passion or interest, must be rendered, by their number and local situation, unable to concert and carry into effect schemes of oppression. If the impulse and the opportunity be suffered to coincide, we well know that neither moral nor religious motives can be relied on as an adequate control. They are not found to be such on the injustice and violence of individuals, and lose their efficacy in proportion to the number combined together; that is, in proportion as their efficacy becomes needful. . . .

A Republic, by which I mean a Government in which the scheme of representation takes place, opens a different prospect, and promises the cure for which we are seeking. Let us examine the points in which it varies from pure Democracy, and we shall comprehend both the nature of the cure, and the efficacy which it must derive from the Union.

The two great points of difference between a Democracy and a Republic are, first, the delegation of the Government, in the latter, to a small number of citizens elected by the rest: secondly, the greater number of citizens, and greater sphere of country, over which the latter may be extended.

The effect of the first difference is, on the one hand to refine and enlarge the public views, by passing them through the medium of a chosen body of citizens, whose wisdom may best discern the true interest of their country, and whose patriotism and love of justice, will be least likely to sacrifice it to temporary or partial considerations. Under such a regulation, it may well happen that the public voice pronounced by the representatives of the people, will be more consonant to the public good, than if pronounced by the people themselves convened for the purpose. On the other hand, the effect may be inverted. Men of factious tempers, of local prejudices, or of sinister designs, may by intrigue, by corruption or by other means, first obtain the suffrages, and then betray the interests of the people. The question resulting is, whether small or extensive Republics are most favorable to the election of proper guardians of the public weal; and it is clearly decided in favor of the latter by two obvious considerations.

In the first place it is to be remarked that however small the Republic may be, the Representatives must be raised to a certain number, in order to guard against the cabals of a few; and that however large it may be, they must be limited to a certain number, in order to guard against the confusion of a multitude. Hence the number of Representatives in the two cases, not being in proportion to that of the Constituents, and being proportionally greatest in the small Republic, it follows, that if the proportion of fit characters, be not less, in the large than in the small Republic, the former will present a greater option, and consequently a greater probability of a fit choice.

In the next place, as each Representative will be chosen by a greater number of citizens in the large than in the small Republic, it will be more difficult for unworthy candidates to practise with success the vicious arts, by which elections are too often carried; and the suffrages of the people being more free, will be more likely to centre on men who possess the most attractive merit, and the most diffusive and established characters.

It must be confessed, that in this, as in most other cases, there is a mean, on both sides of which inconveniencies will be found to lie. By enlarging too much the number of electors, you render the representative too little acquainted with all their local circumstances and lesser interests; as by reducing it too much, you render him unduly attached to these, and too little fit to comprehend and pursue great and national objects. The Federal Constitution forms a happy combination in this respect; the great and aggregate interests being referred to the national, the local and particular, to the state legislatures.

The other point of difference is, the greater number of citizens and extent of territory which may be brought within the compass of Republican, than of Democratic Government; and it is this circumstance principally which renders factious combinations less to be dreaded in the former, than in the latter. The smaller the society, the fewer probably will be the distinct parties and interests composing it; the fewer the distinct parties and interests, the more frequently will a majority be found of the same party; and the smaller the number of individuals composing a majority, and the smaller the compass within which they are placed, the more easily will they concert and execute their plans of oppression. Extend the sphere, and you take in a greater variety of parties and interests; you make it less probable that a majority of the whole will have a common motive to invade the rights of other citizens; or if such a common motive exists, it will be more difficult for all who feel it to discover their own strength, and to act in unison with each other. Besides other impediments, it may be remarked, that where there is a consciousness of unjust or dishonorable purposes, communication is always checked by distrust, in proportion to the number whose concurrence is necessary.

Hence it clearly appears, that the same advantage, which a Republic has over a Democracy, in controling the effects of faction, is enjoyed by a large over a small Republic — is enjoyed by the Union over the States composing it. Does this advantage consist in the substitution of Representatives, whose enlightened views and virtuous sentiments render them superior to local prejudices, and to schemes of injustice? It will not be denied, that the Representation of the Union will be most likely to possess these requisite endowments. Does it consist in the greater security afforded by a greater variety of parties, against the event of any one party being able to outnumber and oppress the rest? In an equal degree does the encreased variety of parties, comprised within the Union, encrease this security. Does it, in fine, consist in the greater obstacles opposed to the concert and accomplishment of the secret wishes of an unjust and interested majority? Here, again, the extent of the Union gives it the most palpable advantage.

The influence of factious leaders may kindle a flame within their particular States, but will be unable to spread a general conflagration through the other States: a religious sect, may degenerate into a political faction in a part of the Confederacy; but the variety of sects dispersed over the entire face of it, must secure the national Councils against any danger from that source: a rage for paper money, for an abolition of debts, for an equal division of property, or for any other improper or wicked project, will be less apt to pervade the whole body of the Union, than a particular member of it; in the same proportion as such a malady is more likely to taint a particular county or district, than an entire State.

In the extent and proper structure of the Union, therefore, we behold a   20 Republican remedy for the diseases most incident to Republican Government. And according to the degree of pleasure and pride, we feel in being Republicans, ought to be our zeal in cherishing the spirit, and supporting the character of Federalists.

(1787)

Exploring the Text

1. How does James Madison characterize "faction" (par. 1)? Do you see examples of such extremes in American politics today? Explain.
2. What analogy does Madison use in paragraph 4? How does it contribute to his argument?
3. What are the "faculties" that Madison discusses in paragraph 5? Do you agree with his statement that the "protection of these faculties is the first object of Government"?
4. What, according to Madison, is the chief cause of faction? Why does he believe that the causes cannot be removed?
5. Madison states, "If the impulse and the opportunity be suffered to coincide, we well know that neither moral nor religious motives can be relied on as an adequate control" (par. 10). What assumptions about human nature underlie such an assertion? Do you agree with Madison? Why or why not?
6. According to Madison, what are the effects of the major differences between a republic and a pure democracy?
7. Madison says that the Constitution forms a "happy combination" (par. 16). What does he mean by that?
8. What is the effect of the rhetorical questions Madison employs as he moves toward his conclusion?
9. In "Federalist No. 55," Madison states:

> As there is a degree of depravity in mankind which requires a certain degree of circumspection and distrust, so there are other qualities in human nature which justify a certain portion of esteem and confidence. Republican government presupposes the existence of these qualities in a higher degree than any other form.

Do you agree with his characterization? Why or why not?

Preamble to the United States Constitution and the Bill of Rights

In 1787, several years after the United States won its independence from Britain in the Revolutionary War, the Federal Convention met in Philadelphia to lay the foundations for a new autonomous government and to draft the United States Constitution. Responding to opponents of the Constitution, who warned that the proposed central government could lead to tyranny — similar to what was experienced under British rule — in 1789 the First Congress of the United States presented the state legislatures with twelve amendments that spelled out the individual rights of citizens. Out of the twelve, only ten amendments were ratified by the states; these are now known as the Bill of Rights. More a declaration of national principles than a meticulous plan of governmental operation, the Constitution separates and balances governmental powers to protect the interests of majority rule and minority rights, of liberty and equality, and of the central and state governments. The U.S. Constitution was ratified in 1789.

Preamble to the United States Constitution

We the people of the United States, in order to form a more perfect union, establish justice, insure domestic tranquility, provide for the common defense, promote the general welfare, and secure the blessings of liberty to ourselves and our posterity, do ordain and establish this Constitution for the United States of America.

Bill of Rights

Amendment I

Congress shall make no law respecting an establishment of religion, or prohibiting the free exercise thereof; or abridging the freedom of speech, or of the press; or the right of the people peaceably to assemble, and to petition the Government for a redress of grievances.

Amendment II

A well regulated Militia, being necessary to the security of a free State, the right of the people to keep and bear Arms, shall not be infringed.

Amendment III

No Soldier shall, in time of peace be quartered in any house, without the consent of the Owner, nor in time of war, but in a manner to be prescribed by law.

Amendment IV

The right of the people to be secure in their persons, houses, papers, and effects, against unreasonable searches and seizures, shall not be violated, and no Warrants shall issue, but upon probable cause, supported by Oath or affirmation, and particularly describing the place to be searched, and the persons or things to be seized.

Amendment V

No person shall be held to answer for a capital, or otherwise infamous crime, unless on a presentment or indictment of a Grand Jury, except in cases arising in the land or naval forces, or in the Militia, when in actual service in time of War or public danger; nor shall any person be subject for the same offence to be twice put in jeopardy of life or limb; nor shall be compelled in any criminal case to be a witness against himself, nor be deprived of life, liberty, or property, without due process of law; nor shall private property be taken for public use, without just compensation.

Amendment VI

In all criminal prosecutions, the accused shall enjoy the right to a speedy and public trial, by an impartial jury of the State and district wherein the crime shall have been committed, which district shall have been previously ascertained by law, and to be informed of the nature and cause of the accusation; to be confronted with the witnesses against him; to have compulsory process for obtaining witnesses in his favor, and to have the Assistance of Counsel for his defence.

Amendment VII

In Suits at common law, where the value in controversy shall exceed twenty dollars, the right of trial by jury shall be preserved, and no fact tried by a jury, shall be otherwise reexamined in any Court of the United States, than according to the rules of the common law.

Amendment VIII

Excessive bail shall not be required, nor excessive fines imposed, nor cruel and unusual punishments inflicted.

Amendment IX

The enumeration in the Constitution, of certain rights, shall not be construed to deny or disparage others retained by the people.

Amendment X

The powers not delegated to the United States by the Constitution, nor prohibited by it to the States, are reserved to the States respectively, or to the people.

(1789)

Exploring the Text

1. According to the preamble, what are the six reasons that the Constitution should be established? How would you list them in order of priority? Why?
2. What is the significance of beginning with the phrase "We the people"?
3. How would you paraphrase each of the ten amendments in the Bill of Rights?
4. Notice that in some of the amendments the language is quite general. Some people might say, for example, that such language as "probable cause" in the Fourth Amendment and "excessive" and "cruel and unusual" in the Eighth Amendment is ambiguous or vague — and certainly open to interpretation. Why do you think the framers were not more specific? Should they have been? Why or why not?
5. Which three or four amendments in the Bill of Rights seem most important to you? Why?

 TALKBACK

Sanford Levinson

Sanford Levinson (b. 1941) is an expert on constitutional law and an American law and government professor at the University of Texas. He is the author of six books, including *Wrestling with Diversity* (2003), *Our Undemocratic Constitution: Where the Constitution Goes Wrong (And How We the People Can Correct It)* (2006), and *Framed: America's 51 Constitutions and the Crisis of Governance* (2012).

Our Imbecilic Constitution

In his essay "Our Imbecilic Constitution," which was published in the *New York Times* on May 28, 2012, Levinson discusses the Constitution's role in modern politics.

Advocating the adoption of the new Constitution drafted in Philadelphia, the authors of *The Federalist Papers* mocked the "imbecility" of the weak central government created by the Articles of Confederation.

Nearly 225 years later, critics across the spectrum call the American political system dysfunctional, even pathological. What they don't mention, though, is the role of the Constitution itself in generating the pathology.

Ignore, for discussion's sake, the clauses that helped to entrench chattel slavery until it was eliminated by a brutal Civil War. Begin with the Senate and its assignment of equal voting power to California and Wyoming; Vermont and Texas; New York and North Dakota. Consider that, although a majority of Americans since World War II have registered opposition to the Electoral College, we will participate this year in yet another election that "battleground states" will dominate while the three largest states will be largely ignored.

Our vaunted system of "separation of powers" and "checks and balances" — a legacy of the founders' mistrust of "factions" — means that we rarely have anything that can truly be described as a "government." Save for those rare instances when one party has hefty control over four branches — the House of Representatives, the Senate, the White House and the Supreme Court — gridlock threatens. Elections are increasingly meaningless, at least in terms of producing results commensurate with the challenges facing the country.

But if one must choose the worst single part of the Constitution, it is surely 5
Article V, which has made our Constitution among the most difficult to amend of any in the world. The last truly significant constitutional change was the 22nd Amendment, added in 1951, to limit presidents to two terms. The near impossibility of amending the national Constitution not only prevents needed reforms; it also makes discussion seem futile and generates a complacent denial that there is anything to be concerned about.

It was not always so. In the election of 1912, two presidents — past and future — seriously questioned the adequacy of the Constitution. Theodore Roosevelt would have allowed Congress to override Supreme Court decisions invalidating federal laws, while Woodrow Wilson basically supported a parliamentary system and, as president, tried to act more as a prime minister than as an agent of Congress. The next few years saw the enactment of amendments establishing the legitimacy of the federal income tax, direct election of senators, Prohibition and women's right to vote.

No such debate is likely to take place between Barack Obama and Mitt Romney. They, like most contemporary Americans, have seemingly lost their capacity for thinking seriously about the extent to which the Constitution serves us well. Instead, the Constitution is enveloped in near religious veneration. (Indeed, Mormon theology treats it as God-given.)

What might radical reform mean?

We might look to the 50 state constitutions, most of which are considerably easier to amend. There have been more than 230 state constitutional conventions; each state has had an average of almost three constitutions. (New York, for example, is on its fifth Constitution, adopted in 1938.) This year Ohioans will be voting on whether to call a new constitutional convention; its Constitution, like 13 others, including New York's, gives voters the chance to do so at regular intervals, typically 20 years.

Another reform would aim to fix congressional gridlock. We could permit 10
each newly elected president to appoint 50 members of the House and 10 members of the Senate, all to serve four-year terms until the next presidential election. Presidents would be judged on actual programs, instead of hollow rhetoric.

If enhanced presidential power seems too scary, then the solution might lie in reducing, if not eliminating, the president's power to veto legislation and to return to true bicameralism, instead of the tricameralism we effectively operate under. We might allow deadlocks between the two branches of Congress to be broken by, say, a supermajority of the House or of Congress voting as a whole.

One might also be inspired by the states to allow at least some aspects of direct democracy. California — the only state with a constitution more dysfunctional than that of the United States — allows constitutional amendment at the ballot box. Maine, more sensibly, allows its citizenry to override legislation they deem objectionable. Might we not be far better off to have a national referendum on "Obamacare" instead of letting nine politically unaccountable judges decide?

Even if we want to preserve judicial review of national legislation, something Justice Oliver Wendell Holmes Jr. believed could be dispensed with, perhaps we should emulate North Dakota or Nebraska, which require supermajorities of their court to invalidate state legislation. Why shouldn't the votes of, say, seven of the nine Supreme Court justices be required to overturn national legislation?

Or consider the fact that almost all states have rejected the model of judges nominated by the president and then confirmed by the Senate. Most state judges are electorally accountable in some way, and almost all must retire at a given age. Many states have adopted commissions to limit the politicization of the appointment process.

What was truly admirable about the framers was their willingness to critique, indeed junk, the Articles of Confederation. One need not believe that the Constitution of 1787 should be discarded in quite the same way to accept that we are long overdue for a serious discussion about its own role in creating the depressed (and depressing) state of American politics. 15

(2012)

Letters to the Editor

To the Editor:

As Prof. Sanford Levinson points out, the Constitution is in several respects a deeply flawed document. But its flaws are a result of compromises that were necessary to establish the new government.

Compromises are by their very nature untidy and frustrating to true believers who insist on maintaining their ideological purity. Without compromises, however, stalemate is inevitable.

As Abraham Lincoln stated, "We could not secure the good we did secure if we grasped for more."

The current paralysis of our political system is not attributable to constitutional flaws but instead to the failure of both parties to approach crucial issues with the same spirit of compromise that made the nation possible.

Earl E. Pollock
Sarasota, Fla., May 29, 2012

The writer is a lawyer and the author of
The Supreme Court and American Democracy.

To the Editor:

Although there are certainly practical problems posed by applying our venerable Constitution to modern American life, these are minuscule compared with the monstrosity that would likely emerge from a new Constitutional Convention, circa 2012. Can you imagine what would happen when the delegates financed by the vegan lobby clash with those financed by the meat lobby, not to mention when several thousand other divisive voices of the American public start clashing with their counterparts?

If not terminal gridlock (probably the better alternative), what would likely result would be a ponderous mountain of claptrap.

Our Constitution, like the Common Law of England, is a short statement of fundamental principles that govern behavior. It elegantly balances power between the states and the federal government and between the government and the governed. No good would come from throwing it into the dustbin of history.

Frederic N. Smalkin
Cockeysville, Md., May 29, 2012

The writer, a retired district court judge, is jurist in residence
at the University of Baltimore School of Law.

To the Editor:

Our Constitution has endured for 225 years. It has its faults. It was written by human beings, who by definition are imperfect. However, it has protected our democracy through all sorts of crises — political, economic, social and military.

Leave the Constitution alone. Gridlock in Washington will not last forever, but with the Constitution, our freedom will.

Garry S. Sklar
North Woodmere, N.Y., May 29, 2012

Exploring the Text

1. Why does Sanford Levinson write, "Ignore, for discussion's sake, the clauses that helped to entrench chattel slavery until it was eliminated by a brutal Civil War" (par. 3)? What is his rhetorical purpose?
2. What are the problematic effects of the Constitution that Levinson points out in paragraphs 3 and 4?
3. What do you think of the proposal that Levinson makes regarding congressional gridlock in paragraph 10? How would Americans respond to such a proposal?
4. In paragraphs 4 and 12, Levinson argues in opposition to the position that James Madison establishes in "Federalist No. 10" (p. 418). Do you think that Levinson makes valid points? Explain, with reference to Madison's text.
5. Which of Levinson's proposals seem most reasonable? Which seem least reasonable? Explain.
6. How does the biographical information provided for Earl E. Pollock and Frederic N. Smalkin affect your response to their letters to the editor?
7. In their letters to the editor, Pollock, Smalkin, and Garry S. Sklar respond to Levinson's argument. What do their positions share?
8. Which of the three letters to the editor makes the most compelling case? Explain.

Making Connections

1. Levinson writes of the "near impossibility of amending the national Constitution" (par. 5). Why do you suppose we Americans hold the Constitution sacrosanct, as it were, as if it cannot be changed?
2. In a 1788 speech before the Senate, Alexander Hamilton said, "Constitutions should consist only of general provisions; the reason is that they must necessarily be permanent, and that they cannot calculate for the possible change of things." Nearly a century later, in his 1850 speech before the Senate, Henry Clay stated, "The Constitution of the United States was made not merely for the generation that then existed, but for posterity — unlimited, undefined, endless, perpetual posterity." Do you think the Constitution should be changed? Why or why not? If so, how? Defend, challenge, or qualify the validity of the opinions of either Hamilton or Clay regarding the unchanging nature of the Constitution.
3. The First and Second Amendments in the Bill of Rights continue to be controversial, with Americans engaged in an ongoing debate about just what they mean. Why do you think those two amendments continue to be so controversial? Should they be amended in an attempt at clarity of meaning? Why or why not?
4. Levinson concludes, "What was truly admirable about the framers was their willingness to critique, indeed junk, the Articles of Confederation. One need not believe that the Constitution of 1787 should be discarded in quite the

same way to accept that we are long overdue for a serious discussion about its own role in creating the depressed (and depressing) state of American politics." What is the primary implication of this statement for us today?

JUDITH SARGENT MURRAY

Judith Sargent Murray (1751–1820) was an essayist, a poet, and one of America's first women's rights activists. Born in Gloucester, Massachusetts, Murray first noticed gender inequality when her younger brother, Winthrop, began studying the classics — a subject that she, as a young female, was barred from pursuing. Though Murray learned to read and write in English and French, she saw that her brother's education was far superior to her own; she realized from a very young age that women are just as capable as men but, lacking in education and self-confidence, could not thrive. In order not to have her ideas dismissed, Murray began to write under the pseudonyms "Mr. Vigilius" and "The Gleaner," and she published her first book of essays and plays, *The Gleaner*, in 1798. Her work championed equality of the sexes, economic independence and education for women, nonviolence, philanthropy, civic duty, and the virtues of the new American republic.

from *On the Equality of the Sexes*

Murray's essay "On the Equality of the Sexes" was published in *Massachusetts Magazine* in March and April 1790, predating Mary Wollstonecraft's "A Vindication of the Rights of Women," often considered the first work of women's rights activism, by two years.

Is it upon mature consideration we adopt the idea, that nature is thus partial in her distributions? Is it indeed a fact, that she hath yielded to one half of the human species so unquestionable a mental superiority? I know that to both sexes elevated understandings, and the reverse, are common. But, suffer me to ask, in what the minds of females are so notoriously deficient, or unequal. May not the intellectual powers be ranged under these four heads — imagination, reason, memory and judgment. The province of imagination hath long since been surrendered to us, and we have been crowned and undoubted sovereigns of the regions of fancy. Invention is perhaps the most arduous effort of the mind; this branch of imagination hath been particularly ceded to us, and we have been time out of mind invested with that creative faculty. Observe the variety of fashions (here I bar the contemptuous smile) which distinguish and adorn the female world: how continually are they changing, insomuch that they almost render the wise man's assertion problematical, and we are ready to say, *there is something new under the sun. . . .*

Another instance of our creative powers, is our talent for slander; how ingenious are we at inventive scandal? what a formidable story can we in a moment fabricate merely from the force of a prolifick imagination? how many reputations, in the fertile brain of a female, have been utterly despoiled? how industrious are we at improving a hint? suspicion how easily do we convert into conviction, and conviction, embellished by the power of eloquence, stalks abroad to the surprise and confusion of unsuspecting innocence. Perhaps it will be asked if I furnish these facts as instances of excellency in our sex. Certainly not; but as proofs of a creative faculty, of a lively imagination. Assuredly great activity of mind is thereby discovered, and was this activity properly directed, what beneficial effects would follow. Is the needle and kitchen sufficient to employ the operations of a soul thus organized? I should conceive not, Nay, it is a truth that those very departments leave the intelligent principle vacant, and at liberty for speculation. Are we deficient in reason? we can only reason from what we know, and if an opportunity of acquiring knowledge hath been denied us, the inferiority of our sex cannot fairly be deduced from thence. Memory, I believe, will be allowed us in common. . . .

"But our judgment is not so strong — we do not distinguish so well." — Yet it may be questioned, from what doth this superiority, in this determining faculty of the soul, proceed. May we not trace its source in the difference of education, and continued advantages? Will it be said that the judgment of a male of two years old, is more sage than that of a female's of the same age? I believe the reverse is generally observed to be true. But from that period what partiality! how is the one exalted, and the other depressed, by the contrary modes of education which are adopted! the one is taught to aspire, and the other is early confined and limitted. As their years increase, the sister must be wholly domesticated, while the brother is led by the hand through all the flowery paths of science. Grant that their minds are by nature equal, yet who shall wonder at the *apparent* superiority, if indeed custom becomes *second nature*. . . . At length arrived at womanhood, the uncultivated fair one feels a void, which the employments allotted her are by no means capable of filling. What can she do? to books she may not apply; or if she doth, *to those only of the novel kind*, lest she merit the appellation of a *learned lady*; and what ideas have been affixed to this term, the observation of many can testify. Fashion, scandal, and sometimes what is still more reprehensible, are then called in to her relief; and who can say to what lengths the liberties she takes may proceed. Meantimes she herself is most unhappy; she feels the want of a cultivated mind. Is she single, she in vain seeks to fill up time from sexual employments or amusements. Is she united to a person whose soul nature made equal to her own, education hath set him so far above her, that in those entertainments which are productive of such rational felicity, she is not qualified to accompany him. She experiences a mortifying consciousness of inferiority, which embitters every enjoyment. Doth the person to whom her adverse fate hath consigned her, possess a mind incapable of improvement, she is equally wretched, in being so closely connected with an individual whom she cannot but despise. Now, was she permitted the same instructors as her brother, (with an eye however to their particular departments) for the employment of a rational mind an ample field would be opened. . . . A mind, thus filled, would have little room for the trifles with which our sex are, with too much justice, accused of amusing themselves, and they would thus be rendered fit companions for those, who should one day wear them as their crown. Fashions, in their variety, would then give place to conjectures, which might perhaps conduce to the improvements of the literary world; and there would be no leisure for slander or detraction. Reputation would not then be blasted, but serious speculations would occupy the lively imaginations of the sex. Unnecessary visits would only be indulged by way of relaxation, or to answer the demands of consanguinity and friendship. Females would become discreet, their judgments would be invigorated, and their partners for life being circumspectly chosen, an unhappy Hymen[1] would then be as rare, as is now the reverse.

Will it be urged that those acquirements would supersede our domestick duties. I answer that every requisite in female economy is easily attained; and, with truth I can add, that when once attained, they require no further *mental attention*. Nay, while we are pursuing the needle, or the superintendency of the family, I repeat, that our minds are at full liberty for reflection; that imagination may exert itself in full vigor; and that if a just foundation is early laid, our ideas will then be worthy of rational beings. If we were industrious we might easily find time to arrange them upon paper, or should avocations press too hard for such an indulgence, the hours allotted for conversation would at least become more refined and rational. Should it still be vociferated, "Your domestick employments are sufficient" — I would calmly ask, is it reasonable, that a candidate for immortality, for the joys of heaven, an intelligent being, who is to spend an eternity in contemplating the works of the Deity, should at present be so degraded, as to be allowed no other ideas, than those which are suggested by the mechanism of a pudding, or the sewing the seams of a garment? . . .

Yes, ye lordly, ye haughty sex, our souls are by nature *equal* to yours; the same   5
breath of God animates, enlivens, and invigorates us; and that we are not fallen lower than yourselves, let those witness who have greatly towered above the various discouragements by which they have been so heavily oppressed; and though I am unacquainted with the list of celebrated characters on either side, yet from the observations I have made in the contracted circle in which I have moved, I dare confidently believe, that from the commencement of time to the present day, there hath been as many females, as males, who, by the *mere force of natural powers*, have merited the crown of applause; who, *thus unassisted*, have seized the wreath of fame. . . . But waving this . . . advantage, for *equality only*, we wish to contend. . . .

The exquisite delicacy of the female mind proclaimeth the exactness of its texture, while its nice sense of honour announceth its innate, its native grandeur. And indeed, in one respect, the preeminence seems to be tacitly allowed us; for after an education which limits and confines, and employments and recreations which naturally tend to enervate the body, and debilitate the mind; after we have from early youth been adorned with ribbons, and other gewgaws, dressed out like the ancient victims previous to a sacrifice, being taught by the care of our parents in collecting the most showy materials that the ornamenting our exteriour ought to be the principal object of our attention; after, I say, fifteen years thus spent, we are introduced into the world, amid the united adulation of every beholder. Praise is sweet to the soul; we are immediately intoxicated by large draughts of flattery, which being plentifully administered, is to the pride of our hearts, the most acceptable incense. It is expected

---

[1]Greek god of marriage. — Eds.

that with the other sex we should commence immediate war, and that we should triumph over the machinations of the most artful. We must be constantly upon our guard; prudence and discretion must be our characteristiks; and we must rise superiour to, and obtain a complete victory over those who have been long adding to the native strength of their minds, by an unremitted study of men and books, and who have, moreover, conceived from the loose characters which they have seen portrayed in the extensive variety of their reading, a most contemptible opinion of the sex. . . . And if we are allowed an equality of acquirements, let serious studies equally employ our minds, and we will bid our souls arise to equal strengths. We will meet upon even ground, the despot man; we will rush with alacrity to the combat, and, crowned by success, we shall then answer the exalted expectations, which are formed. . . .

[S]ensibility, soft compassion, and gentle commiseration, are inmates in the female bosom. . . . If we meet an equal, a sensible friend, we will reward him with the hand of amity, and through life we will be assiduous to promote his happiness; but from every deep laid scheme, for our ruin, retiring into ourselves, amid the flowery paths of science, we will indulge in all the refined and sentimental pleasures of contemplation: And should it still be urged, that the studies thus insisted upon would interfere with our more peculiar department, I must further reply, that *early hours*, and close application, will do wonders; and to her who is from the first dawn of reason taught to fill up time rationally, both the requisites will be easy. I grant that niggard[2] fortune is too generally unfriendly to the mind; and that much of that valuable treasure, time, is necessarily expended upon the wants of the body; but it should be remembered; that in embarrassed circumstances our companions have as little leisure for literary improvements, as is afforded to us. . . . Nay, we have even more leisure for sedentary pleasures, as our avocations are more retired, much less laborious, and, as hath been observed, by no means require that avidity of attention which is proper to the employments of the other sex. In high life, or, in other words, where the parties are in possession of affluence, the objection respecting time is wholly obviated, and of course falls to the ground; and it may also be repeated, that many of those hours which are at present swallowed up in fashion and scandal, might be redeemed, were we habituated to useful reflections. But in one respect, O ye arbiters of our fate! we confess that the superiority is indubitably yours; you are by nature formed for our protectors; we pretend not to vie with you in bodily strength; upon this point we will never contend for victory. Shield us then, we beseech you, from external evils, and in return we will transact *your* domestick affairs. Yes, *your*, for are you not equally interested in those matters with ourselves?

(1790)

Exploring the Text

1. How effective are the rhetorical questions in the opening of Judith Sargent Murray's essay? Explain.

---

[2]Stingy. — Eds.

2. Murray states that "intellectual powers [may] be ranged under these four heads — imagination, reason, memory and judgment" (par. 1) Do you agree? How would you order them in importance?

3. What might be viewed as ironic in her discussion of imagination? Does that irony help or harm her argument? Explain.

4. Murray asks, "Are we deficient in reason?" (par. 2). Analyze the argument she offers in response to her own question. Is it cogent? Explain.

5. What does she imply by saying, "Memory, I believe, will be allowed us in common" (par. 2)?

6. In paragraph 3, Murray presents a hypothetical situation: "Now, was she permitted the same instructors as her brother . . ." What she offers as conjecture regarding education of the sexes in her time has in fact transpired since then. To what extent do women now benefit from the results she indicates?

7. What is the rhetorical effect of the parallelisms in the second sentence of paragraph 6?

8. While Murray argues for the equality of the sexes in terms of the intellect and the soul, she acknowledges some differences as well. What are they? How does her acknowledgment affect the cogency of her argument?

 TALKBACK

H. L. Mencken

Known as the "Sage of Baltimore," Henry Louis Mencken (1888–1956) was an American journalist and essayist famous for his sardonic wit and scathing satire. The ultimate skeptic, he interrogated the authority of all institutions, whether they were social, governmental, religious, or educational. Among his most famous and influential books are *The American Language* (1919) and the six volumes of essays, titled *Prejudices*, published from 1919 to 1927. He was immortalized as the character E. K. Hornbeck in the play *Inherit the Wind*.

from *In Defense of Women*

This selection comes from the first chapter, "The Feminine Mind," of Mencken's book *In Defense of Women* (1918). As you read, you might ask whether this is a defense of women or an attack on men.

That it should be necessary, at this late stage in the senility of the human race, to argue that women have a fine and fluent intelligence is surely an eloquent proof of the defective observation, incurable prejudice, and general imbecility of their lords and masters. Women, in fact, are not only intelligent; they have almost a monopoly of certain of the subtler and more utile forms of intelligence. The thing itself, indeed, might be reasonably described as a special feminine character; there is in it, in more than one of its manifestations, a femaleness as palpable as the femaleness of cruelty, masochism or rouge. Men are strong. Men are brave in physical combat. Men are romantic, and love what they conceive to be virtue and beauty. Men incline to faith, hope and charity. Men know how to sweat and endure. Men are amiable and fond. But in so far as they show the true fundamentals of intelligence — in so far as they reveal a capacity for discovering the kernel of eternal verity in the husk of delusion and hallucination and a passion for bringing it forth — to that extent, at least, they are feminine, and still nourished by the milk of their mothers. The essential traits and qualities of the male, the hall-marks of the unpolluted masculine, are at the same time the hall-marks of the numskull. The caveman is all muscles and mush. Without a woman to rule him and think for him, he is a truly lamentable spectacle: a baby with whiskers, a rabbit with the frame of an aurochs, a feeble and preposterous caricature of God. . . .

Men, as everyone knows, are disposed to question this superior intelligence of women; their egoism demands the denial, and they are seldom reflective enough to dispose of it by logical and evidential analysis. Moreover, there is a certain specious appearance of soundness in their position; they have forced upon women an artificial character which well conceals their real character, and women have found it profitable to encourage the deception. But though every normal man thus cherishes the soothing unction that he is the intellectual superior of all women, and particularly of his wife, he constantly gives the lie to his pretension by consulting and deferring to what he calls her intuition. That is to say, he knows by experience that her judgment in many matters of capital concern is more subtle and searching than his own, and, being disinclined to accredit this greater sagacity to a more competent intelligence, he takes refuge behind the doctrine that it is due to some impenetrable and intangible talent for guessing correctly, some half mystical supersense, some vague (and, in essence, infra-human) instinct.

The true nature of this alleged instinct, however, is revealed by an examination of the situations which inspire a man to call it to his aid. These situations do not arise out of the purely technical problems that are his daily concern, but out of the rarer and more fundamental, and hence enormously more difficult problems which beset him only at long and irregular intervals, and so offer a test, not of his mere capacity for being drilled, but of his capacity for genuine ratiocination. No man, I take it, save one consciously inferior and hen-pecked, would consult his wife about hiring a clerk, or about extending credit to some paltry customer, or about some routine piece of tawdry swindling; but not even the most egoistic man would fail to sound the sentiment of his wife about taking a partner into his business, or about standing for public office, or about marrying off their daughter. Such things are of massive importance; they lie at the foundation of well-being; they call for the best thought that the man confronted by them can muster; the perils hidden in a wrong decision overcome even the clamors of vanity. It is in such situations that the superior mental grasp of women is of obvious utility, and has to be admitted. It is here that they rise above the insignificant sentimentalities, superstitions and formulæ of men, and apply to the business their singular talent for separating the appearance from the substance, and so exercise what is called their intuition.

Intuition? Bosh! Women, in fact, are the supreme realists of the race. Apparently illogical, they are the possessors of a rare and subtle super-logic. Apparently whimsical, they hang to the truth with a tenacity which carries them through every phase of its incessant, jelly-like shifting of form. Apparently un-observant and easily deceived, they see with bright and horrible eyes. . . . In men, too, the same merciless perspicacity sometimes shows itself — men recognized to be more aloof and uninflammable than the general — men of special talent for the logical — sardonic men, cynics. Men, too, sometimes have brains. But that is a rare, rare man, I venture, who is as steadily intelligent, as constantly sound in judgment, as little put off by appearances, as the average multipara of forty-eight.

(1918)

Exploring the Text

1. How would you characterize H. L. Mencken's tone in the first sentence?
2. Mencken begins by praising female intelligence and then speaks of "the female-ness of cruelty, masochism or rouge." Were those words surprising to read? What is the effect of such diction?
3. How does Mencken characterize men? What is the effect of the parallelisms he uses?
4. Throughout the piece, Mencken uses highly varied word choice. Provide several examples of diction that is colloquial and diction that is elevated. What is the effect of such a contrast?
5. Mencken writes that "there is a certain specious appearance of soundness in their position; they have forced upon women an artificial character which well conceals their real character, and women have found it profit-able to encourage the deception" (par. 2). What does he mean by that state-ment? Explain.
6. What distinctions does Mencken make in paragraph 3?
7. How does Mencken characterize women in paragraph 4? What is the effect of the parallel structures he uses?
8. In this piece, Mencken "praises" women. Consider the likely response of women readers. If you are female, what is your response? Do you feel praised? If you are male, how do you suppose women would respond to the piece?

Making Connections

1. What similarities do you find in the first two paragraphs of Judith Sargent Murray's (p. 419) and H. L. Mencken's (p. 423) selections regarding their views of women?
2. How would you compare Murray's attitude toward men with Mencken's?

3. Murray states "ye lordly, ye haughty sex" (par. 5) when she refers to men. How would Mencken view such a characterization?

4. How might Murray regard Mencken's recognition of "a certain specious appearance of soundness" (par. 2) in the position men hold regarding women?

5. How might Murray respond to Mencken's piece overall? Would she agree with him? Would she be amused? Would she feel challenged? Explain.

6. How do you think men living in Murray's time would regard Mencken's piece? Explain.

BENJAMIN BANNEKER

Benjamin Banneker (1731–1806) was a free African American who worked as a farmer, an astronomer, an almanac author, and a mathematician. Legend has it that Banneker's maternal grandparents, a European woman named Molly Walsh and a slave named Banneka, collaborated to found a farm near Ellicott City, Maryland, then married. Little information has been verified about Banneker's parents, his youth, or his upbringing, though he spent much of his life on his family's farm and acquired an informal but comprehensive education along the way. Quakers established a school near the Banneker family's farm, and a farmer named Peter Heinrichs shared his personal library with young Benjamin and introduced him to Quaker beliefs in a formal classroom setting. On the farm, Banneker learned to read the stars, made elaborate astronomical and mathematical observations and calculations, and maintained journals and almanacs. Abolitionists and abolitionist groups promoted Banneker's almanacs, which became best sellers. His first almanac, published in 1792, included weather forecasts, harvest and tide tables, dates for yearly feasts, and home treatments for illnesses.

Letter to Thomas Jefferson

In his 1793 almanac, Banneker published his correspondence with the then secretary of state Thomas Jefferson, in which he expressed his views on slavery and racial equality in the United States.

Baltimore County, Maryland, August 19, 1791

S ir,

I am fully sensible of the greatness of that freedom, which I take with you on the present occasion; a liberty which seemed to me scarcely allowable, when I reflected on that distinguished and dignified station in which you stand, and the almost general prejudice and prepossession, which is so prevalent in the world against those of my complexion.

I suppose it is a truth too well attested to you, to need a proof here, that we are a race of beings, who have long labored under the abuse and censure of the world; that we have long been looked upon with an eye of contempt; and that we have long been considered rather as brutish than human, and scarcely capable of mental endowments.

Sir, I hope I may safely admit, in consequence of that report which hath reached me, that you are a man far less inflexible in sentiments of this nature, than many others; that you are measurably friendly, and well disposed towards us; and that you are willing and ready to lend your aid and assistance to our relief, from those many distresses, and numerous calamities, to which we are reduced. Now Sir, if this is founded in truth, I apprehend you will embrace every opportunity, to eradicate that train of absurd and false ideas and opinions, which so generally prevails with respect to us; and that your sentiments are concurrent with mine, which are, that one universal Father hath given being to us all; and that he hath not only made us all of one flesh, but that he hath also, without partiality, afforded us all the same sensations and endowed us all with the same faculties; and that however variable we may be in society or religion, however diversified in situation or color, we are all of the same family, and stand in the same relation to him.

Sir, if these are sentiments of which you are fully persuaded, I hope you cannot but acknowledge, that it is the indispensible duty of those, who maintain for themselves the rights of human nature, and who possess the obligations of Christianity, to extend their power and influence to the relief of every part of the human race, from whatever burden or oppression they may unjustly labor under; and this, I apprehend, a full conviction of the truth and obligation of these principles should lead all to. Sir, I have long been convinced, that if your love for yourselves, and for those inestimable laws, which preserved to you the rights of human nature, was founded on sincerity, you could not but be solicitous, that every individual, of whatever rank or distinction, might with you equally enjoy the blessings thereof; neither could you rest satisfied short of the most active effusion of your exertions, in order to their promotion from any state of degradation, to which the unjustifiable cruelty and barbarism of men may have reduced them.

Sir, I freely and cheerfully acknowledge, that I am of the African race, and in that   5
color which is natural to them of the deepest dye; and it is under a sense of the most profound gratitude to the Supreme Ruler of the Universe, that I now confess to you, that I am not under that state of tyrannical thraldom, and inhuman captivity, to which too many of my brethren are doomed, but that I have abundantly tasted of the fruition of those blessings, which proceed from that free and unequalled liberty with which you are favored; and which, I hope, you will willingly allow you have mercifully received, from the immediate hand of that Being, from whom proceedeth every good and perfect Gift.

Sir, suffer me to recal to your mind that time, in which the arms and tyranny of the British crown were exerted, with every powerful effort, in order to reduce you to a state of servitude: look back, I entreat you, on the variety of dangers to which you were exposed; reflect on that time, in which every human aid appeared unavailable, and in which even hope and fortitude wore the aspect of inability to the conflict, and you cannot but be led to a serious and grateful sense of your miraculous and providential preservation; you cannot but acknowledge, that the present freedom and tranquility which you enjoy you have mercifully received, and that it is the peculiar blessing of Heaven.

This, Sir, was a time when you clearly saw into the injustice of a state of slavery, and in which you had just apprehensions of the horrors of its condition. It was now that your abhorrence thereof was so excited, that you publicly held forth this true and invaluable doctrine, which is worthy to be recorded and remembered in all succeeding ages: "We hold these truths to be self-evident, that all men are created equal; that they are endowed by their Creator with certain unalienable rights, that among these are life, liberty, and the pursuit of happiness." Here was a time, in which your tender feelings for yourselves had engaged you thus to declare, you were then impressed with proper ideas of the great violation of liberty, and the free possession of those blessings, to which you were entitled by nature; but, Sir, how pitiable is it to reflect, that although you were so fully convinced of the benevolence of the Father of Mankind, and of his equal and impartial distribution of these rights and privileges, which he hath conferred upon them, that you should at the same time counteract his mercies, in detaining by fraud and violence so numerous a part of my brethren, under groaning captivity and cruel oppression, that you should at the same time be found guilty of that most criminal act, which you professedly detested in others, with respect to yourselves.

I suppose that your knowledge of the situation of my brethren, is too extensive to need a recital here; neither shall I presume to prescribe methods by which they may be relieved, otherwise than by recommending to you and all others, to wean yourselves from those narrow prejudices which you have imbibed with respect to them, and as Job proposed to his friends, "put your soul in their souls' stead;" thus shall your hearts be enlarged with kindness and benevolence towards them; and thus shall you need neither the direction of myself or others, in what manner to proceed herein. And now, Sir, although my sympathy and affection for my brethren hath caused my enlargement thus far, I ardently hope, that your candor and generosity will plead with you in my behalf, when I make known to you, that it was not originally my design; but having taken up my pen in order to direct to you, as a present, a copy of an Almanac, which I have calculated for the succeeding year, I was unexpectedly and unavoidably led thereto.

This calculation is the production of my arduous study, in this my advanced stage of life; for having long had unbounded desires to become acquainted with the secrets of nature, I have had to gratify my curiosity herein, through my own assiduous application to Astronomical Study, in which I need not recount to you the many difficulties and disadvantages, which I have had to encounter.

And although I had almost declined to make my calculation for the ensuing year, 10 in consequence of that time which I had allotted therefor, being taken up at the Federal Territory, by the request of Mr. Andrew Ellicott, yet finding myself under several engagements to Printers of this state, to whom I had communicated my design, on my return to my place of residence, I industriously applied myself thereto, which I hope I have accomplished with correctness and accuracy; a copy of which I have taken the liberty to direct to you, and which I humbly request you will favorably receive; and although you may have the opportunity of perusing it after its publication, yet I choose to send it to you in manuscript previous thereto, that thereby you might not only have an earlier inspection, but that you might also view it in my own hand writing.

And now, Sir, I shall conclude, and subscribe myself, with the most profound respect, Your most obedient humble servant,

Benjamin Banneker

Response from Thomas Jefferson

Philadelphia, August 30, 1791.

Sir,

I thank you, sincerely, for your letter of the 19th instant, and for the Almanac it contained. No body wishes more than I do, to see such proofs as you exhibit, that nature has given to our black brethren talents equal to those of the other colors of men; and that the appearance of the want of them, is owing merely to the degraded condition of their existence, both in Africa and America. I can add with truth, that no body wishes more ardently to see a good system commenced, for raising the condition, both of their body and mind, to what it ought to be, as far as the imbecility of their present existence, and other circumstances, which cannot be neglected, will admit.

I have taken the liberty of sending your Almanac to Monsieur de Condozett, Secretary of the Academy of Sciences at Paris, and Member of the Philanthropic Society, because I considered it as a document, to which your whole color had a right for their justification, against the doubts which have been entertained of them.

I am with great esteem, Sir, Your most obedient Humble Servant,

Thomas Jefferson

Exploring the Text

1. How would you describe Benjamin Banneker's stance in his letter? What tone does he use to create this stance with respect to his missive to Thomas Jefferson? Explain.
2. What are some of the values to which Banneker appeals? How do they contribute to his use of ethos and pathos?

3. Provide three examples of religious references in the letter. How do they contribute to Banneker's purpose?
4. What is the comparison Banneker makes in paragraph 6? What is the likely effect on his reader, Secretary of State Jefferson?
5. Banneker quotes Jefferson directly in paragraph 7. What is the rhetorical effect of this strategy?
6. In paragraph 7, Banneker accuses Jefferson of criminal cruelty and hypocrisy. How does Banneker's stance and use of language aid his purpose? Is his approach likely to be persuasive or dissuasive? Explain.
7. What is the main topic of Jefferson's letter? Does it surprise you? Are you surprised at the brevity of Jefferson's reply? Explain.
8. Jefferson writes, "I can add with truth, that no body wishes more ardently to see a good system commenced" (par. 1). Considering the powerful nature of Jefferson's position, how might Banneker respond to Jefferson's choice of the verb *wishes*? Might Banneker be disappointed with Jefferson's message? Explain.

CHIEF TECUMSEH

Tecumseh (1768–1813) was a leader of the Shawnee tribe and the large group of tribes known as Tecumseh's Confederacy. He actively opposed the United States, beginning with the rebellion he staged, known as Tecumseh's War, which evolved into the War of 1812. Tecumseh was brought up in present-day Ohio amidst constant warfare — first the American Revolutionary War and later the Northwest Indian War (1785–1795). During the War of 1812, a conflict between the United States and the British Empire, Tecumseh's Confederacy allied with the British to block America's expansion into Canada. Abandoned by British troops, Tecumseh was shot and killed by American forces during the Battle of the Thames, on October 5, 1813, near Moraviantown, Ontario; his forces quickly surrendered to William Henry Harrison.

Address to General William Henry Harrison

Tecumseh's address to general and future president William Henry Harrison took place during a diplomatic meeting between the Indian leader and the then governor of the Indiana Territory. Tecumseh demanded passionately that Indian lands be returned.

Brother: I wish you to listen to me well. I wish to reply to you now explicitly. As I think you do not clearly understand what I before said to you, I will explain it again. . . .

Brother, since the peace was made, you have killed some of the Shawnees, Winnebagoes, Delawares, and Miamis, and you have taken our land from us, and I do not see how we can remain at peace with you if you continue to do so. You have given goods to the Kickapoos for the sale of their land to you which has been cause of many deaths among them. You have promised us assistance, but I do not see that you have given us any. You try to force the red people to do some injury. It is you that are pushing them on to do mischief. You endeavor to make distinctions. You wish to prevent the Indians doing as we wish them — to unite, and let them consider their lands as the common property of the whole; you take tribes aside and advise them not to come into this measure; and until our design is accomplished we do not wish to accept of your invitation to go and see the President. The reason I tell you this, you want, by your distinctions of Indian tribes in allotting to each a particular tract of land, to make them to war with each other. You never see an Indian come and endeavor to make the white people do so. You are continually driving the red people; when, at last, you will drive them into the Great Lake, where they can't either stand or walk.

Brother, you ought to know what you are doing with the Indians. Perhaps it is by direction of the President to make those distinctions. It is a very bad thing, and we do not like it. Since my residence at Tippecanoe[1] we have endeavored to level all distinctions — to destroy village chiefs, by whom all mischief is done. It is they who sell our lands to the Americans. Our object is to let our affairs be transacted by warriors.

Brother, this land that was sold and the goods that were given for it were only done by a few. The treaty was afterwards brought here, and the Weas were induced to give their consent because of their small numbers. The treaty at Fort Wayne was made through the threats of Winnemac; but in future we are prepared to punish those chiefs who may come forward to propose to sell the land. If you continue to purchase of them it will produce war among the different tribes, and at last, I do not know what will be the consequence to the white people.

Brother, I was glad to hear your speech. You said that if we could show that the land was sold by people that had no right to sell, you would restore it. Those that did sell did not own it. It was me. These tribes set up a claim, but the tribes with me will not agree with their claim. If the land is not restored to us you will see, when we return to our homes, how it will be settled. We shall have a great council, at which all the tribes will be present, when we shall show to those who sold that they had no right to the claim that they set up; and we will see what will be done to those chiefs that did sell the land to you. I am not alone in this determination; it is the determination of all the warriors and red people that listen to me. I now wish you to listen to

5

---

[1]The headquarters of the confederacy of tribes assembled by Tecumseh was in a village called Prophetstown, of Tippecanoe. This was the site of a battle between Tecumseh and Harrison's forces in 1811. — Eds.

me. If you do not, it will appear as if you wished me to kill all the chiefs that sold you the land. I tell you so because I am authorized by all the tribes to do so. I am the head of them all; I am a warrior, and all the warriors will meet together in two or three moons from this; then I will call for those chiefs that sold you the land and shall know what to do with them. If you do not restore the land, you will have a hand in killing them. . . .

Brother, I wish you would take pity on the red people and do what I have requested. If you will not give up the land and do cross the boundary of your present settlement, it will be very hard, and produce great troubles among us. How can we have confidence in the white people? When Jesus Christ came on earth, you killed him and nailed him on a cross. You thought he was dead, but you were mistaken. You have Shakers among you, and you laugh and make light of their worship. Everything I have said to you is the truth. The Great Spirit has inspired me, and I speak nothing but the truth to you. . . .

Brother, I hope you will confess that you ought not to have listened to those bad birds who bring you bad news. I have declared myself freely to you, and if any explanation should be required from our town, send a man who can speak to us. If you think proper to give us any presents, and we can be convinced that they are given through friendship alone, we will accept them. As we intend to hold our council at the Huron village, that is near the British, we may probably make them a visit. Should they offer us any presents of goods, we will not take them; but should they offer us powder and the tomahawk, we will take the powder and refuse the tomahawk. I wish you, brother, to consider everything I have said as true, and that it is the sentiment of all the red people that listen to me.

(1810)

Exploring the Text

1. What is Chief Tecumseh's purpose in this speech? How would you describe the stance he takes regarding Governor Harrison? How would you describe his tone?
2. What analogy does Tecumseh develop in paragraph 3? How does it contribute to his argument?
3. What is the rhetorical effect of beginning nearly every paragraph with "Brother"?
4. How does Tecumseh illustrate the cultural divide between Indians and whites?
5. How do Tecumseh's comparisons, particularly his rhetorical question in paragraph 6, contribute to his argument?
6. Near the end of the speech Tecumseh says that "we will take the powder and refuse the tomahawk" (par. 7). What does he mean? What are the implications of that statement?
7. Identify two places in the speech where Tecumseh seems to be delivering a threat. Identify two places where the speech seems an earnest plea. Overall, would you characterize the speech as more of a sincere plea or a veiled threat? Explain.

Francis Scott Key

Francis Scott Key (1779–1843) was an American poet and lawyer who wrote the poem that became the lyrics for the U.S. national anthem, "The Star-Spangled Banner." He also served as U.S. district attorney from 1833 to 1841. Key was born in what is now Carroll County, Maryland; his father served in the Continental army during the Revolutionary War. Key studied law at St. John's College in Annapolis, Maryland.

The Star-Spangled Banner

During the War of 1812, Key participated in negotiations to release American prisoners of war from the British; as part of the talks, Key and two other Americans dined as guests aboard a British ship. The Americans became familiar with British plans to attack Baltimore and were not allowed off the ship. Throughout the night of September 13, 1814, they were forced to watch the British bombardment of Fort McHenry, during the Battle of Baltimore. In the morning, Key saw the American flag still standing on the shore, reported this news to the prisoners below deck, and was inspired to write a poem about the experience. He published the poem in the *Patriot* on September 20, 1814, and later set the words to the tune of John Stafford Smith's "To Anacreon in Heaven." In 1914, President Woodrow Wilson issued an executive order declaring Key's song, which became known as "The Star-Spangled Banner," the national anthem.

O say can you see, by the dawn's early light,
What so proudly we hail'd at the twilight's last gleaming,
Whose broad stripes and bright stars through the perilous fight
O'er the ramparts we watch'd were so gallantly streaming?
And the rocket's red glare, the bomb bursting in air,   5
Gave proof through the night that our flag was still there,
O say does that star-spangled banner yet wave
O'er the land of the free and the home of the brave?

On the shore dimly seen through the mists of the deep
Where the foe's haughty host in dread silence reposes,   10
What is that which the breeze, o'er the towering steep,
As it fitfully blows, half conceals, half discloses?
Now it catches the gleam of the morning's first beam,
In full glory reflected now shines in the stream,
'Tis the star-spangled banner — O long may it wave   15
O'er the land of the free and the home of the brave!

And where is that band who so vauntingly swore,
That the havoc of war and the battle's confusion
A home and a Country should leave us no more?
Their blood has wash'd out their foul footstep's pollution.   20
No refuge could save the hireling and slave
From the terror of flight or the gloom of the grave,
And the star-spangled banner in triumph doth wave
O'er the land of the free and the home of the brave.

O thus be it ever when freemen shall stand   25
Between their lov'd home and the war's desolation!
Blest with vict'ry and peace may the heav'n rescued land
Praise the power that hath made and preserv'd us a nation!
Then conquer we must, when our cause it is just,
And this be our motto — "In God is our trust,"   30
And the star-spangled banner in triumph shall wave
O'er the land of the free and the home of the brave.

(1814)

Exploring the Text

1. Read stanza 1 (which you have doubtless heard many times) very carefully. How would you describe the imagery? What, if anything, do you find surprising? Explain.
2. What is the nature of the appeal created by the rhetorical question at the end of the first stanza? Why do you suppose Key doesn't end the other stanzas with rhetorical questions?
3. To whom does the "band" (l. 17) refer? What has become of them?
4. How does Key use contrasts throughout the poem? Choose two of them and describe the effect of each.
5. Most Americans know — or are at least highly familiar with — the first stanza of the poem; in fact, many think that is the whole poem or song. Do you think the first stanza is the most appropriate one for the national anthem? Make an argument for the use of a different stanza at ceremonial occasions.
6. Many people have suggested that our national anthem should not be about war and bloodshed (not to mention that it uses the tune of a nineteenth-century British drinking song) but rather should be about something more inspirational, such as is found in songs like "America, the Beautiful," "God Bless America," "This Land Is Your Land," "My Country, 'Tis of Thee," or even "Don't Fence Me In." Do you think "The Star-Spangled Banner" should remain our national anthem? Offer an alternative if you think it should be changed. Provide textual evidence from your choice.

WASHINGTON IRVING

Often regarded as America's first man of letters, Washington Irving (1783–1859) was a writer, historian, and diplomat. Over the course of his career, Irving wrote biographies of Christopher Columbus (1828), Muhammad (1850), and George Washington (1859) — for whom he was named — and histories of New York (1809), fifteenth-century Spain (1829), and the Alhambra (1832). He served as U.S. ambassador to Spain from 1842 to 1846. He began publishing observational letters in the *Morning Chronicle* in 1802. After moving to England in 1819, he published *The Sketch Book of Geoffrey Crayon, Gentleman,* an international best seller that included such tales as "Rip Van Winkle" and "The Legend of Sleepy Hollow."

Rip Van Winkle

Irving's most famous story, "Rip Van Winkle" is a frame tale, or story within a story; actually, we might say it's a frame tale framed. Published in *The Sketch Book of Geoffrey Crayon, Gentleman* in 1820, it purports to be a tale found among the papers of one Diedrich Knickerbocker, author of the 1809 *History of New York.* The note at the end says that the story "is an absolute fact, narrated with his [Knickerbocker's] usual fidelity." And the final word is left to Knickerbocker: "The story, therefore, is beyond the possibility of doubt." Set in the Catskill Mountains, the tale takes place in the years surrounding the American Revolution.

[The following Tale was found among the papers of the late Diedrich Knickerbocker, an old gentleman of New-York, who was very curious in the Dutch history of the province, and the manners of the descendants from its primitive settlers. His historical researches, however, did not lay so much among books, as among men; for the former are lamentably scanty on his favourite topics; whereas he found the old burghers, and still more, their wives, rich in that legendary lore, so invaluable to true history. Whenever, therefore, he happened upon a genuine Dutch family, snugly shut up in its low-roofed farm house, under a spreading sycamore, he looked upon it as a little clasped volume of black-letter,[1] and studied it with the zeal of a bookworm.

The result of all these researches was a history of the province, during the reign of the Dutch governors, which he published some years since. There have been various opinions as to the literary character of his work, and, to tell the truth, it is not a whit better than it should be. Its chief merit is its scrupulous accuracy, which, indeed, was a little questioned, on its first appearance, but has since been completely

---

[1] An ornate font used in medieval manuscripts. — Eds.

established; and it is now admitted into all historical collections, as a book of unquestionable authority.[2]

The old gentleman died shortly after the publication of his work, and now, that he is dead and gone, it cannot do much harm to his memory, to say, that his time might have been much better employed in weightier labours. He, however, was apt to ride his hobby his own way; and though it did now and then kick up the dust a little in the eyes of his neighbours, and grieve the spirit of some friends, for whom he felt the truest deference and affection; yet his errors and follies are remembered "more in sorrow than in anger,"[3] and it begins to be suspected, that he never intended to injure or offend. But however his memory may be appreciated by critics, it is still held dear among many folk, whose good opinion is well worth having; particularly certain biscuit bakers, who have gone so far as to imprint his likeness on their new year cakes, and have thus given him a chance for immortality, almost equal to being stamped on a Waterloo medal, or a Queen Anne's farthing.[4]]

Rip Van Winkle

A Posthumous Writing of Diedrich Knickerbocker

> *By Woden, God of Saxons,*
> *From whence comes Wensday, that is Wodensday,*
> *Truth is a thing that ever I will keep*
> *Unto thylke day in which I creep into*
> *My sepulchre —*
>
> — Cartwright[5]

Whoever has made a voyage up the Hudson, must remember the Kaatskill mountains. They are a dismembered branch of the great Appalachian family, and are seen away to the west of the river, swelling up to a noble height, and lording it over the surrounding country. Every change of season, every change of weather, indeed, every hour of the day, produces some change in the magical hues and shapes of these mountains, and they are regarded by all the good wives, far and near, as perfect barometers. When the weather is fair and settled, they are clothed in blue and purple, and print their bold outlines on the clear evening sky; but some times, when the rest of the landscape is cloudless, they will gather a hood of gray vapours about their summits, which, in the last rays of the setting sun, will glow and light up like a crown of glory.

At the foot of these fairy mountains, the voyager may have descried the light   5
smoke curling up from a village, whose shingle roofs gleam among the trees, just where

---

[2]Irving is referring to his own deliberately inaccurate *History of New York* (1809). — Eds.
[3]Quotation from *Hamlet* 1.1.231–32. — Eds.
[4]Relatively rare collectible coin. — Eds.
[5]Lines from *The Ordinary* by William Cartwright (1611–1643). — Eds.

the blue tints of the upland melt away into the fresh green of the nearer landscape. It is a little village of great antiquity, having been founded by some of the Dutch colonists, in the early times of the province, just about the beginning of the government of the good Peter Stuyvesant,[6] (may he rest in peace!) and there were some of the houses of the original settlers standing within a few years, with lattice windows, gable fronts surmounted with weathercocks, and built of small yellow bricks brought from Holland.

In that same village, and in one of these very houses, (which, to tell the precise truth, was sadly time worn and weather beaten,) there lived many years since, while the country was yet a province of Great Britain, a simple good natured fellow, of the name of Rip Van Winkle. He was a descendant of the Van Winkles who figured so gallantly in the chivalrous days of Peter Stuyvesant, and accompanied him to the siege of Fort Christina.[7] He inherited, however, but little of the martial character of his ancestors. I have observed that he was a simple good natured man; he was moreover a kind neighbour, and an obedient, henpecked husband. Indeed, to the latter circumstance might be owing that meekness of spirit which gained him such universal popularity; for those men are most apt to be obsequious and conciliating abroad, who are under the discipline of shrews at home. Their tempers, doubtless, are rendered pliant and malleable in the fiery furnace of domestic tribulation, and a curtain lecture[8] is worth all the sermons in the world for teaching the virtues of patience and long suffering. A termagant[9] wife may, therefore, in some respects, be considered a tolerable blessing; and if so, Rip Van Winkle was thrice blessed.

Certain it is, that he was a great favourite among all the good wives of the village, who, as usual with the amiable sex, took his part in all family squabbles, and never failed, whenever they talked those matters over in their evening gossippings, to lay all the blame on Dame Van Winkle. The children of the village, too, would shout with joy whenever he approached. He assisted at their sports, made their playthings, taught them to fly kites and shoot marbles, and told them long stories of ghosts, witches, and Indians. Whenever he went dodging about the village, he was surrounded by a troop of them, hanging on his skirts, clambering on his back, and playing a thousand tricks on him with impunity; and not a dog would bark at him throughout the neighbourhood.

The great error in Rip's composition was an insuperable aversion to all kinds of profitable labour. It could not be for the want of assiduity or perseverance; for he would sit on a wet rock, with a rod as long and heavy as a Tartar's lance,[10] and fish all day without a murmur, even though he should not be encouraged by a single nibble.

---

[6]Peter Stuyvesant (1592–1672) was the last Dutch director-general of New Netherland, before it was turned over to the British in 1664 and renamed New York. — Eds.
[7]Swedish fort in Delaware conquered by Stuyvesant in 1655. — Eds.
[8]Lecture of a wife to her husband in private (behind closed curtains). — Eds.
[9]Quarrelsome. — Eds.
[10]Russian (Tartar) cavalry were famous for using a relatively short, light lance that was roughly eight feet long. — Eds.

He would carry a fowling piece on his shoulder, for hours together, trudging through woods and swamps, and up hill and down dale, to shoot a few squirrels or wild pigeons. He would never even refuse to assist a neighbour in the roughest toil, and was a foremost man at all country frolicks for husking Indian corn, or building stone fences; the women of the village, too, used to employ him to run their errands, and to do such little odd jobs as their less obliging husbands would not do for them; — in a word, Rip was ready to attend to any body's business but his own; but as to doing family duty, and keeping his farm in order, it was impossible.

In fact, he declared it was no use to work on his farm; it was the most pestilent little piece of ground in the whole country; every thing about it went wrong, and would go wrong, in spite of him. His fences were continually falling to pieces; his cow would either go astray, or get among the cabbages; weeds were sure to grow quicker in his fields than any where else; the rain always made a point of setting in just as he had some out-door work to do. So that though his patrimonial estate had dwindled away under his management, acre by acre, until there was little more left than a mere patch of Indian corn and potatoes, yet it was the worst conditioned farm in the neighbourhood.

His children, too, were as ragged and wild as if they belonged to nobody. His son   10
Rip, an urchin begotten in his own likeness, promised to inherit the habits, with the old clothes of his father. He was generally seen trooping like a colt at his mother's heels, equipped in a pair of his father's cast-off galligaskins,[11] which he had much ado to hold up with one hand, as a fine lady does her train in bad weather.

Rip Van Winkle, however, was one of those happy mortals, of foolish, well-oiled dispositions, who take the world easy, eat white bread or brown, which ever can be got with least thought or trouble, and would rather starve on a penny than work for a pound. If left to himself, he would have whistled life away, in perfect contentment; but his wife kept continually dinning in his ears about his idleness, his carelessness, and the ruin he was bringing on his family. Morning, noon, and night, her tongue was incessantly going, and every thing he said or did was sure to produce a torrent of household eloquence. Rip had but one way of replying to all lectures of the kind, and that, by frequent use, had grown into a habit. He shrugged his shoulders, shook his head, cast up his eyes, but said nothing. This, however, always provoked a fresh volley from his wife, so that he was fain to draw off his forces, and take to the outside of the house — the only side which, in truth, belongs to a henpecked husband.

Rip's sole domestic adherent was his dog Wolf, who was as much henpecked as his master; for Dame Van Winkle regarded them as companions in idleness, and even looked upon Wolf with an evil eye, as the cause of his master's so often going astray. True it is, in all points of spirit befitting an honourable dog, he was as courageous an animal as ever scoured the woods — but what courage can withstand the ever-during and all-besetting terrors of a woman's tongue? The moment Wolf entered the house, his crest fell, his tail drooped to the ground, or curled between his legs, he sneaked about with a gallows air, casting many a sidelong glance at Dame Van

---

[11]Loose-fitting pants that stop just below the knee and are worn with long socks. — Eds.

Winkle, and at the least flourish of a broomstick or ladle, would fly to the door with yelping precipitation.

Times grew worse and worse with Rip Van Winkle as years of matrimony rolled on; a tart temper never mellows with age, and a sharp tongue is the only edge tool that grows keener by constant use. For a long while he used to console himself, when driven from home, by frequenting a kind of perpetual club of the sages, philosophers, and other idle personages of the village, that held its sessions on a bench before a small inn, designated by a rubicund[12] portrait of his majesty George the Third. Here they used to sit in the shade, of a long lazy summer's day, talk listlessly over village gossip, or tell endless sleepy stories about nothing. But it would have been worth any statesman's money to have heard the profound discussions that sometimes took place, when by chance an old newspaper fell into their hands, from some passing traveller. How solemnly they would listen to the contents, as drawled out by Derrick Van Bummel, the schoolmaster, a dapper learned little man, who was not to be daunted by the most gigantic word in the dictionary; and how sagely they would deliberate upon public events some months after they had taken place.

The opinions of this junto[13] were completely controlled by Nicholas Vedder, a patriarch of the village, and landlord of the inn, at the door of which he took his seat from morning till night, just moving sufficiently to avoid the sun, and keep in the shade of a large tree; so that the neighbours could tell the hour by his movements as accurately as by a sun dial. It is true, he was rarely heard to speak, but smoked his pipe incessantly. His adherents, however, (for every great man has his adherents,) perfectly understood him, and knew how to gather his opinions. When any thing that was read or related displeased him, he was observed to smoke his pipe vehemently, and send forth short, frequent, and angry puffs; but when pleased, he would inhale the smoke slowly and tranquilly, and emit it in light and placid clouds, and sometimes taking the pipe from his mouth, and letting the fragrant vapour curl about his nose, would gravely nod his head in token of perfect approbation.

From even this strong hold the unlucky Rip was at length routed by his termagant wife, who would suddenly break in upon the tranquillity of the assemblage, call the members all to nought, nor was that august personage, Nicholas Vedder himself, sacred from the daring tongue of this terrible virago, who charged him outright with encouraging her husband in habits of idleness.

Poor Rip was at last reduced almost to despair; and his only alternative to escape from the labour of the farm and the clamour of his wife, was to take gun in hand, and stroll away into the woods. Here he would sometimes seat himself at the foot of a tree, and share the contents of his wallet[14] with Wolf, with whom he sympathised as a fellow sufferer in persecution. "Poor Wolf," he would say, "thy mistress leads thee a dogs' life of it; but never mind, my lad, while I live thou shalt never want a friend to stand

15

---

[12]Ruddy; having a rosy complexion. — Eds.
[13]Secret group. — Eds.
[14]Bag of food and supplies. — Eds.

by thee!" Wolf would wag his tail, look wistfully in his master's face, and if dogs can feel pity, I verily believe he reciprocated the sentiment with all his heart.

In a long ramble of the kind on a fine autumnal day, Rip had unconsciously scrambled to one of the highest parts of the Kaatskill mountains. He was after his favourite sport of squirrel shooting, and the still solitudes had echoed and re-echoed with the reports of his gun. Panting and fatigued, he threw himself, late in the afternoon, on a green knoll, covered with mountain herbage, that crowned the brow of a precipice. From an opening between the trees, he could overlook all the lower country for many a mile of rich woodland. He saw at a distance the lordly Hudson, far, far below him, moving on its silent but majestic course, the reflection of a purple cloud, or the sail of a lagging bark, here and there sleeping on its glassy bosom, and at last losing itself in the blue highlands.

On the other side he looked down into a deep mountain glen, wild, lonely, and shagged, the bottom filled with fragments from the impending cliffs, and scarcely lighted by the reflected rays of the setting sun. For some time Rip lay musing on this scene, evening was gradually advancing, the mountains began to throw their long blue shadows over the valleys, he saw that it would be dark long before he could reach the village, and he heaved a heavy sigh when he thought of encountering the terrors of Dame Van Winkle.

As he was about to descend, he heard a voice from a distance, hallooing, "Rip Van Winkle! Rip Van Winkle!" He looked around, but could see nothing but a crow winging its solitary flight across the mountain. He thought his fancy must have deceived him, and turned again to descend, when he heard the same cry ring through the still evening air; "Rip Van Winkle! Rip Van Winkle!" — at the same time Wolf bristled up his back, and giving a low growl, skulked to his master's side, looking fearfully down into the glen. Rip now felt a vague apprehension stealing over him; he looked anxiously in the same direction, and perceived a strange figure slowly toiling up the rocks, and bending under the weight of something he carried on his back. He was surprised to see any human being in this lonely and unfrequented place, but supposing it to be some one of the neighbourhood in need of his assistance, he hastened down to yield it.

On nearer approach, he was still more surprised at the singularity of the stranger's appearance. He was a short square built old fellow, with thick bushy hair, and a grizzled beard. His dress was of the antique Dutch fashion — a cloth jerkin[15] strapped round the waist — several pair of breeches, the outer one of ample volume, decorated with rows of buttons down the sides, and bunches at the knees. He bore on his shoulder a stout keg, that seemed full of liquor, and made signs for Rip to approach and assist him with the load. Though rather shy and distrustful of this new acquaintance, Rip complied with his usual alacrity, and mutually relieving each other, they clambered up a narrow gully, apparently the dry bed of a mountain torrent. As they ascended, Rip every now and then heard long rolling peals, like distant thunder, that seemed to issue out of a deep ravine, or rather cleft between lofty rocks, toward which

20

---

[15]Close-fitting jacket. — Eds.

their rugged path conducted. He paused for an instant, but supposing it to be the muttering of one of those transient thunder showers which often take place in mountain heights, he proceeded. Passing through the ravine, they came to a hollow, like a small amphitheatre, surrounded by perpendicular precipices, over the brinks of which impending trees shot their branches, so that you only caught glimpses of the azure sky, and the bright evening cloud. During the whole time, Rip and his companion had laboured on in silence; for though the former marvelled greatly what could be the object of carrying a keg of liquor up this wild mountain, yet there was something strange and incomprehensible about the unknown, that inspired awe, and checked familiarity.

On entering the amphitheatre, new objects of wonder presented themselves. On a level spot in the centre was a company of odd-looking personages playing at ninepins. They were dressed in a quaint, outlandish fashion: some wore short doublets,[16] others jerkins, with long knives in their belts, and most had enormous breeches, of similar style with that of the guide's. Their visages, too, were peculiar: one had a large head, broad face, and small piggish eyes; the face of another seemed to consist entirely of nose, and was surmounted by a white sugarloaf hat,[17] set off with a little red cockstail. They all had beards, of various shapes and colours. There was one who seemed to be the commander. He was a stout old gentleman, with a weather-beaten countenance; he wore a laced doublet, broad belt and hanger,[18] high crowned hat and feather, red stockings, and high heeled shoes, with roses in them. The whole group reminded Rip of the figures in an old Flemish painting, in the parlour of Dominie[19] Van Schaick, the village parson, and which had been brought over from Holland at the time of the settlement.

What seemed particularly odd to Rip, was, that though these folks were evidently amusing themselves, yet they maintained the gravest faces, the most mysterious silence, and were, withal, the most melancholy party of pleasure he had ever witnessed. Nothing interrupted the stillness of the scene, but the noise of the balls, which, whenever they were rolled, echoed along the mountains like rumbling peals of thunder.

As Rip and his companion approached them, they suddenly desisted from their play, and stared at him with such fixed statue-like gaze, and such strange, uncouth, lack lustre countenances, that his heart turned within him, and his knees smote together. His companion now emptied the contents of the keg into large flagons, and made signs to him to wait upon the company. He obeyed with fear and trembling; they quaffed the liquor in profound silence, and then returned to their game.

By degrees, Rip's awe and apprehension subsided. He even ventured, when no eye was fixed upon him, to taste the beverage, which he found had much of the

---

[16]Men's padded jacket, originally worn under armor to make it more comfortable. — Eds.
[17]Tall brimless hat. — Eds.
[18]Short sword. — Eds.
[19]Title for a clergyman. — Eds.

flavour of excellent Hollands.[20] He was naturally a thirsty soul, and was soon tempted to repeat the draught. One taste provoked another, and he reiterated his visits to the flagon so often, that at length his senses were overpowered, his eyes swam in his head, his head gradually declined, and he fell into a deep sleep.

On awaking, he found himself on the green knoll from whence he had first seen   25
the old man of the glen. He rubbed his eyes — it was a bright sunny morning. The birds were hopping and twittering among the bushes, and the eagle was wheeling aloft, and breasting the pure mountain breeze. "Surely," thought Rip, "I have not slept here all night." He recalled the occurrences before he fell asleep. The strange man with the keg of liquor — the mountain ravine — the wild retreat among the rocks — the wo-begone party at nine-pins — the flagon — "Oh! that flagon! that wicked flagon!" thought Rip — "what excuse shall I make to Dame Van Winkle?"

He looked round for his gun, but in place of the clean well-oiled fowling-piece, he found an old firelock lying by him, the barrel encrusted with rust, the lock falling off, and the stock worm-eaten. He now suspected that the grave roysters[21] of the mountain had put a trick upon him, and having dosed him with liquor, had robbed him of his gun. Wolf, too, had disappeared, but he might have strayed away after a squirrel or partridge. He whistled after him, shouted his name, but all in vain; the echoes repeated his whistle and shout, but no dog was to be seen.

He determined to revisit the scene of the last evening's gambol, and if he met with any of the party, to demand his dog and gun. As he arose to walk he found himself stiff in the joints, and wanting in his usual activity. "These mountain beds do not agree with me," thought Rip, "and if this frolick should lay me up with a fit of the rheumatism, I shall have a blessed time with Dame Van Winkle." With some difficulty he got down into the glen: he found the gully up which he and his companion had ascended the preceding evening, but to his astonishment a mountain stream was now foaming down it, leaping from rock to rock, and filling the glen with babbling murmurs. He, however, made shift to scramble up its sides, working his toilsome way through thickets of birch, sassafras, and witch hazle, and sometimes tripped up or entangled by the wild grape vines that twisted their coils and tendrils from tree to tree, and spread a kind of network in his path.

At length he reached to where the ravine had opened through the cliffs, to the amphitheatre; but no traces of such opening remained. The rocks presented a high impenetrable wall, over which the torrent came tumbling in a sheet of feathery foam, and fell into a broad deep basin, black from the shadows of the surrounding forest. Here, then, poor Rip was brought to a stand. He again called and whistled after his dog; he was only answered by the cawing of a flock of idle crows, sporting high in air about a dry tree that overhung a sunny precipice; and who, secure in their elevation, seemed to look down and scoff at the poor man's perplexities. What was to be done? the morning was passing away, and Rip felt famished for his breakfast. He grieved to give up his dog and gun; he dreaded to meet his wife; but it would not do to starve

---

[20]Dutch gin. — Eds.
[21]Boisterous men. — Eds.

among the mountains. He shook his head, shouldered the rusty firelock, and, with a heart full of trouble and anxiety, turned his steps homeward.

As he approached the village, he met a number of people, but none that he knew, which somewhat surprised him, for he had thought himself acquainted with every one in the country round. Their dress, too, was of a different fashion from that to which he was accustomed. They all stared at him with equal marks of surprise, and whenever they cast eyes upon him, invariably stroked their chins. The constant recurrence of this gesture, induced Rip, involuntarily, to do the same, when, to his astonishment, he found his beard had grown a foot long!

He had now entered the skirts of the village. A troop of strange children ran at   30
his heels, hooting after him, and pointing at his gray beard. The dogs, too, not one of which he recognized for his old acquaintances, barked at him as he passed. The very village seemed altered: it was larger and more populous. There were rows of houses which he had never seen before, and those which had been his familiar haunts had disappeared. Strange names were over the doors — strange faces at the windows — every thing was strange. His mind now began to misgive him, that both he and the world around him were bewitched. Surely this was his native village, which he had left but the day before. There stood the Kaatskill mountains — there ran the silver Hudson at a distance — there was every hill and dale precisely as it had always been — Rip was sorely perplexed — "That flagon last night," thought he, "has addled my poor head sadly!"

It was with some difficulty he found the way to his own house, which he approached with silent awe, expecting every moment to hear the shrill voice of Dame Van Winkle. He found the house gone to decay — the roof fallen in, the windows shattered, and the doors off the hinges. A half starved dog, that looked like Wolf, was skulking about it. Rip called him by name, but the cur snarled, showed his teeth, and passed on. This was an unkind cut indeed — "My very dog," sighed poor Rip, "has forgotten me!"

He entered the house, which, to tell the truth, Dame Van Winkle had always kept in neat order. It was empty, forlorn, and apparently abandoned. This desolateness overcame all his connubial[22] fears — he called loudly for his wife and children — the lonely chambers rung for a moment with his voice, and then all again was silence.

He now hurried forth, and hastened to his old resort, the little village inn — but it too was gone. A large ricketty wooden building stood in its place, with great gaping windows, some of them broken, and mended with old hats and petticoats, and over the door was painted, "The Union Hotel, by Jonathan Doolittle." Instead of the great tree that used to shelter the quiet little Dutch inn of yore, there now was reared a tall naked pole, with something on top that looked like a red night cap,[23] and from it was fluttering a flag, on which was a singular assemblage of stars and stripes — all this was strange and incomprehensible. He recognised on the sign, however, the ruby face of King George, under which he had smoked so many a peaceful pipe, but even this was

---

[22]Having to do with marriage. — Eds.
[23]Symbol used by the revolutionaries during the American Revolution. — Eds.

singularly metamorphosed. The red coat was changed for one of blue and buff,[24] a sword was stuck in the hand instead of a sceptre, the head was decorated with a cocked hat, and underneath was painted in large characters, GENERAL WASHINGTON.

There was, as usual, a crowd of folk about the door, but none that Rip recollected. The very character of the people seemed changed. There was a busy, bustling, disputatious tone about it, instead of the accustomed phlegm and drowsy tranquillity. He looked in vain for the sage Nicholas Vedder, with his broad face, double chin, and fair long pipe, uttering clouds of tobacco smoke instead of idle speeches; or Van Bummel, the schoolmaster, doling forth the contents of an ancient newspaper. In place of these, a lean bilious looking fellow, with his pockets full of handbills, was haranguing vehemently about rights of citizens — election — members of congress — liberty — Bunker's hill — heroes of seventy-six — and other words, that were a perfect Babylonish jargon[25] to the bewildered Van Winkle.

The appearance of Rip, with his long grizzled beard, his rusty fowling piece, his 35 uncouth dress, and the army of women and children that had gathered at his heels, soon attracted the attention of the tavern politicians. They crowded around him, eyeing him from head to foot, with great curiosity. The orator bustled up to him, and drawing him partly aside, inquired "which side he voted?" Rip stared in vacant stupidity. Another short but busy little fellow pulled him by the arm, and raising on tiptoe, inquired in his ear, "whether he was Federal or Democrat." Rip was equally at a loss to comprehend the question; when a knowing, self-important old gentleman, in a sharp cocked hat, made his way through the crowd, putting them to the right and left with his elbows as he passed, and planting himself before Van Winkle, with one arm akimbo, the other resting on his cane, his keen eyes and sharp hat penetrating, as it were, into his very soul, demanded, in an austere tone, "what brought him to the election with a gun on his shoulder, and a mob at his heels, and whether he meant to breed a riot in the village?" "Alas! gentlemen," cried Rip, somewhat dismayed, "I am a poor quiet man, a native of the place, and a loyal subject of the King, God bless him!"

Here a general shout burst from the bystanders — "A tory! a tory! a spy! a refugee! hustle him! away with him!" It was with great difficulty that the self-important man in the cocked hat restored order; and having assumed a tenfold austerity of brow, demanded again of the unknown culprit, what he came there for, and whom he was seeking. The poor man humbly assured them that he meant no harm; but merely came there in search of some of his neighbours, who used to keep about the tavern.

"Well — who are they? — name them."

Rip bethought himself a moment, and inquired, "where's Nicholas Vedder?"

There was a silence for a little while, when an old man replied, in a thin piping voice, "Nicholas Vedder? why he is dead and gone these eighteen years! There was a wooden tombstone in the church yard that used to tell all about him, but that's rotted and gone too."

---

[24]Colors worn by the revolutionaries during the American Revolution. — Eds.
[25]Gibberish. — Eds.

"Where's Brom Dutcher?"   40

"Oh, he went off to the army in the beginning of the war; some say he was killed at the battle of Stoney-Point — others say he was drowned in a squall, at the foot of Antony's Nose. I don't know — he never came back again."

"Where's Van Bummel, the schoolmaster?"

"He went off to the wars too, was a great militia general, and is now in Congress."

Rip's heart died away, at hearing of these sad changes in his home and friends, and finding himself thus alone in the world. Every answer puzzled him, too, by treating of such enormous lapses of time, and of matters which he could not understand: war — congress — Stoney-Point; — he had no courage to ask after any more friends, but cried out in despair, "does nobody here know Rip Van Winkle?"

"Oh, Rip Van Winkle!" exclaimed two or three, "Oh, to be sure! that's Rip Van   45
Winkle yonder, leaning against the tree."

Rip looked, and beheld a precise counterpart of himself, as he went up the mountain: apparently as lazy, and certainly as ragged. The poor fellow was now completely confounded. He doubted his own identity, and whether he was himself or another man. In the midst of his bewilderment, the man in the cocked hat demanded who he was, and what was his name?

"God knows," exclaimed he, at his wit's end; "I'm not myself — I'm somebody else — that's me yonder — no — that's somebody else, got into my shoes — I was myself last night, but I fell asleep on the mountain, and they've changed my gun, and every thing's changed, and I'm changed, and I can't tell what's my name, or who I am!"

The bystanders began now to look at each other, nod, wink significantly, and tap their fingers against their foreheads. There was a whisper, also, about securing the gun, and keeping the old fellow from doing mischief. At the very suggestion of which, the self-important man in the cocked hat retired with some precipitation. At this critical moment a fresh likely woman pressed through the throng to get a peep at the gray-bearded man. She had a chubby child in her arms, which, frightened at his looks, began to cry. "Hush, Rip," cried she, "hush, you little fool, the old man won't hurt you." The name of the child, the air of the mother, the tone of her voice, all awakened a train of recollections in his mind. "What is your name, my good woman?" asked he.

"Judith Gardenier."

"And your father's name?"   50

"Ah, poor man, his name was Rip Van Winkle; it's twenty years since he went away from home with his gun, and never has been heard of since — his dog came home without him; but whether he shot himself, or was carried away by the Indians, nobody can tell. I was then but a little girl."

Rip had but one question more to ask; but he put it with a faltering voice:

"Where's your mother?"

Oh, she too had died but a short time since; she broke a blood vessel in a fit of passion at a New-England pedlar.

There was a drop of comfort, at least, in this intelligence. The honest man could   55
contain himself no longer. He caught his daughter and her child in his arms. "I am

your father!" cried he — "Young Rip Van Winkle once — old Rip Van Winkle now! — Does nobody know poor Rip Van Winkle!"

All stood amazed, until an old woman, tottering out from among the crowd, put her hand to her brow, and peering under it in his face for a moment, exclaimed, "Sure enough! it is Rip Van Winkle — it is himself. Welcome home again, old neighbour — Why, where have you been these twenty long years?"

Rip's story was soon told, for the whole twenty years had been to him but as one night. The neighbours stared when they heard it; some were seen to wink at each other, and put their tongues in their cheeks; and the self-important man in the cocked hat, who, when the alarm was over, had returned to the field, screwed down the corners of his mouth, and shook his head — upon which there was a general shaking of the head throughout the assemblage.

It was determined, however, to take the opinion of old Peter Vanderdonk, who was seen slowly advancing up the road. He was a descendant of the historian of that name, who wrote one of the earliest accounts of the province. Peter was the most ancient inhabitant of the village, and well versed in all the wonderful events and traditions of the neighbourhood. He recollected Rip at once, and corroborated his story in the most satisfactory manner. He assured the company that it was a fact, handed down from his ancestor the historian, that the Kaatskill mountains had always been haunted by strange beings. That it was affirmed that the great Hendrick Hudson, the first discoverer of the river and country, kept a kind of vigil there every twenty years, with his crew of the Half-moon, being permitted in this way to revisit the scenes of his enterprize, and keep a guardian eye upon the river, and the great city called by his name. That his father had once seen them in their old Dutch dresses playing at nine-pins in a hollow of the mountain; and that he himself had heard, one summer afternoon, the sound of their balls, like long peals of thunder.

To make a long story short, the company broke up, and returned to the more important concerns of the election. Rip's daughter took him home to live with her; she had a snug, well-furnished house, and a stout cheery farmer for a husband, whom Rip recollected for one of the urchins that used to climb upon his back. As to Rip's son and heir, who was the ditto of himself, seen leaning against the tree, he was employed to work on the farm; but evinced an hereditary disposition to attend to any thing else but his business.

Rip now resumed his old walks and habits; he soon found many of his former 60 cronies, though all rather the worse for the wear and tear of time; and preferred making friends among the rising generation, with whom he soon grew into great favour.

Having nothing to do at home, and being arrived at that happy age when a man can do nothing with impunity, he took his place once more on the bench, at the inn door, and was reverenced as one of the patriarchs of the village, and a chronicle of the old times "before the war." It was some time before he could get into the regular track of gossip, or could be made to comprehend the strange events that had taken place during his torpor. How that there had been a revolutionary war — that the country had thrown off the yoke of old England — and that, instead of being a subject of his Majesty George the Third, he was now a free citizen of the United States. Rip, in fact, was no politician; the changes of states and empires made but little impression on him. But there was one species of despotism under which he had long groaned, and that was — petticoat government. Happily, that was at an end; he had got his neck out of the yoke of matrimony, and could go in and out whenever he pleased, without dreading the tyranny of Dame Van Winkle. Whenever her name was mentioned, however, he shook his head, shrugged his shoulders, and cast up his eyes; which might pass either for an expression of resignation to his fate, or joy at his deliverance.

He used to tell his story to every stranger that arrived at Mr. Doolittle's hotel. He was observed, at first, to vary on some points every time he told it, which was, doubtless, owing to his having so recently awaked. It at last settled down precisely to the tale I have related, and not a man, woman, or child in the neighbourhood, but knew it by heart. Some always pretended to doubt the reality of it, and insisted that Rip had been out of his head, and that this was one point on which he always remained flighty. The old Dutch inhabitants, however, almost universally gave it full credit. Even to this day they never hear a thunder storm of a summer afternoon, about the Kaatskill, but they say Hendrick Hudson and his crew are at their game of nine-pins; and it is a common wish of all henpecked husbands in the neighbourhood, when life hangs heavy on their hands, that they might have a quieting draught out of Rip Van Winkle's flagon.

Note

The foregoing tale, one would suspect, had been suggested to Mr. Knickerbocker by a little German superstition about Charles V. and the Kypphauser mountain;[26] the subjoined note, however, which he had appended to the tale, shows that it is an absolute fact, narrated with his usual fidelity:

The story of Rip Van Winkle may seem incredible to many, but nevertheless I give it my full belief, for I know the vicinity of our old Dutch settlements to have been very subject to marvellous events and appearances. Indeed, I have heard many stranger stories than this, in the villages along the Hudson; all of which were too well authenticated to admit of a doubt. I have even talked with Rip Van Winkle myself, who, when last I saw him, was a very venerable old man, and so perfectly rational and consistent on every other point, that I think no conscientious person could refuse to take this into the bargain; nay, I have seen a certificate on the subject taken before a country justice, and signed with a cross, in the justice's own hand writing. The story, therefore, is beyond the possibility of doubt.

D. K.

---

[26]Irving is referring to a German iteration of the archetypal "King in the Mountain" legend, in which a popular or powerful ruler is said to not be dead but waiting within a nearby mountain to return to his people. Arthurian legends sometimes take on this trope, and the Grimm Brothers used it in tales featuring Frederick Barbarossa and Charlemagne. — Eds.

Postscript

The following are travelling notes from a memorandum-book of Mr. Knickerbocker: 65

The Kaatsberg, or Catskill Mountains, have always been a region full of fable. The Indians considered them the abode of spirits, who influenced the weather, spreading sunshine or clouds over the landscape, and sending good or bad hunting seasons. They were ruled by an old squaw spirit, said to be their mother. She dwelt on the highest peak of the Catskills, and had charge of the doors of day and night to open and shut them at the proper hour. She hung up the new moons in the skies, and cut up the old ones into stars. In times of drought, if properly propitiated, she would spin light summer clouds out of cobwebs and morning dew, and send them off from the crest of the mountain, flake after flake, like flakes of carded cotton, to float in the air; until, dissolved by the heat of the sun, they would fall in gentle showers, causing the grass to spring, the fruits to ripen, and the corn to grow an inch an hour. If displeased, however, she would brew up clouds black as ink, sitting in the midst of them like a bottle-bellied spider in the midst of its web; and when these clouds broke, wo betide the valleys!

In old times, say the Indian traditions, there was a kind of Manitou or Spirit, who kept about the wildest recesses of the Catskill Mountains, and took a mischievous pleasure in wreaking all kinds of evils and vexations upon the red men. Sometimes he would assume the form of a bear, a panther, or a deer; lead the bewildered hunter a weary chase through tangled forests and among ragged rocks; and then spring off with a loud ho! ho! leaving him aghast on the brink of a beetling precipice or raging torrent.

The favorite abode of this Manitou is still shown. It is a great rock or cliff in the loneliest part of the mountains, and, from the flowering vines which clamber about it, and the wild flowers which abound in its neighborhood, is known by the name of the Garden Rock. Near the foot of it is a small lake, the haunt of the solitary bittern, with water-snakes basking in the sun on the leaves of the pond-lilies which lie on the surface. This place was held in great awe by the Indians, insomuch that the boldest hunter would not pursue his game within its precincts. Once upon a time, however, a hunter who had lost his way, penetrated to the garden rock, where he beheld a number of gourds placed in the crotches of trees. One of these he seized and made off with it, but in the hurry of his retreat he let it fall among the rocks, when a great stream gushed forth, which washed him away and swept him down precipices, where he was dashed to pieces, and the stream made its way to the Hudson, and continues to flow to the present day; being the identical stream known by the name of the Kaaters-kill.

(1820)

Exploring the Text

1. We know, of course, that in his "frame tale" Washington Irving is pretending, having invented everything: Crayon, Knickerbocker, and the story itself. Why

does Irving present this story in such a fashion? What effect does the framing have on the story?

2. Note the rich imagery in the opening paragraphs of the story. What is its effect? How does it establish the mood of the story?

3. How is Rip characterized in paragraphs 6 through 11? Is he a "hero" or an anti-hero? Explain. How is Derrick Van Bummel characterized in paragraph 13? What is Irving's tone in each of these characterizations?

4. Regarding Rip's encounter on the mountain, Irving writes that "there was something strange and incomprehensible about the unknown, that inspired awe, and checked familiarity" (par. 20). Does Irving's remark apply merely to Rip, or is there something universal about the condition he describes? Explain.

5. After Rip gets used to his new surroundings, he assumes the role of storyteller, a "historian" of sorts. What might Irving be implying here?

6. What does the final paragraph of the story suggest about the relationship between reality and the imagination?

7. William Cullen Bryant says of Irving: "If there are touches of satire in his writings, he is the best natured and most amiable of satirists, amiable beyond Horace; and in his irony — for there is a vein of playful irony running through many of his works — there is no tinge of bitterness." Find examples of irony and satire in "Rip Van Winkle." Do you agree with Bryant's characterization? Why or why not?

8. In *The Hero with a Thousand Faces*, scholar Joseph Campbell contends that the classic pattern of a hero's journey is the departure from home, a strange experience that transforms the hero, and a return. Of "Rip Van Winkle," he writes:

> The story of Rip Van Winkle is an example of the delicate case of the returning hero. Rip moved into the adventurous realm unconsciously, as we all do every night when we go to sleep. . . . [W]e return, like Rip, with nothing to show for the experience but our whiskers. . . . The returning hero, to complete his adventure, must survive the impact of the world. Rip Van Winkle never knew what he had experienced; his return was a joke.

If "Rip Van Winkle" is not a true hero's journey, is it instead a satire of the hero's journey story? Is it a story about transformation, not that of a person but rather that of a country? Or is it just a fun story? Be specific in your answer.

9. "Van Winkle," from "Powhatan's Daughter," part 2 of *The Bridge*, Hart Crane's 1930 epic poem about America, begins:

> MACADAM,[1] gun-grey as the tunny's[2] belt,
> Leaps from Far Rockaway to Golden Gate:

---

[1] Early road-making material consisting of layers of small stones held together with a cement-like binder. Invented by John McAdam in 1820. — Eds.
[2] Tuna. — Eds.

Listen! the miles a hurdy-gurdy grinds —
Down gold arpeggios mile on mile unwinds.

Times earlier, when you hurried off to school
— It is the same hour though a later day —
You walked with Pizarro in a copybook,
And Cortez rode up, reining tautly in —
Firmly as coffee grips the taste, — and away!

There was Priscilla's cheek close in the wind,
And Captain Smith, all heard and certainty,
And Rip Van Winkle bowing by the way, —
"Is this Sleepy Hollow, friend — ?" And he —

> *And Rip forgot the office hours,*
> *and he forgot the pay;*
> *Van Winkle sweeps a tenement*
> *way down on Avenue A,–*

In his poem, Crane makes use of historical and mythic figures from America's past as he simultaneously explores his dual journey: backward into his childhood memories, delivered in the third person, and forward through the growth and development of the country. Why would Crane choose Rip Van Winkle as his guide on both journeys? Explain.

10. Imagine Rip's story taking place more recently — that is, imagine he slept through the Civil War, the Great Depression, World War II, the civil rights era, or the last twenty years. How would he respond to the changes he would encounter when he awoke?

Conversation

The Myth of George Washington

In his eulogy on behalf of Congress and the nation, Henry Lee praised George Washington as being "first in war, first in peace, and first in the hearts of his countrymen." He was also perhaps the first American hero. The classic strong silent type, George Washington was an imposing figure, well over six feet tall, and a man of few precisely chosen words. Edward G. Lengel, author of *Inventing George Washington*, says:

> George Washington is an elusive quarry. The closer he seems, the more easily he slips away. Washington fostered this with his own demeanor. Conscious of his role

as an actor on the public stage, he crafted an outward persona that obscured his private being. He deliberately hid certain elements of his inner life, and carried them with him to the grave. Even so, he wanted to be known. He preserved the bulk of his correspondence and records, public and private, for posterity, and he fretted endlessly about how his countrymen would remember him after he was gone.

Washington served as commander in chief of the Continental army during the American Revolution, but as soon after the British surrender as possible, he retired "victorious from the field of War to the field of agriculture." He was tapped for the first presidency of the new republic, serving two terms and refusing to serve another, further enhancing his reputation as a man who put country first and his ambitions second.

It seems that every generation has invented its own George Washington, a figure who can be held up as the paragon of so many American virtues. And it may be that the elusive quality that makes him difficult to pin down is what allows his legacy to help each generation of Americans explain who they are and what's important to them. In this Conversation, you will read and view texts that ask not just who George Washington was but what his mythology means to the nation.

Sources

George Washington, *Letter to Colonel Lewis Nicola* (1782)
George Washington, from *Farewell Address* (1796)
Gilbert Stuart, *George Washinton — Lansdowne Portrait* (1796)
Mason Locke Weems, from *A History of the Life and Death, Virtues and Exploits of General George Washington* (1799)
Horatio Greenough, *George Washington* (1832)
Emanuel Leutze, *Washington Crossing the Delaware* (1851)
Jane Addams, *Tribute to George Washington* (1903)
Frank O'Hara, *On Seeing Larry Rivers'* Washington Crossing the Delaware *at the Museum of Modern Art* (1957)
Jill Lepore, from *His Highness* (2010)
Dodge Motor Company, *This Is the Car You Buy* . . . (2010)
Edward G. Lengel, from *Inventing George Washington* (2011)

Letter to Colonel Lewis Nicola

GEORGE WASHINGTON

After the British surrendered at Yorktown in 1781, the Continental troops under Washington's command stayed on their guard, partly because many British troops remained in the colonies but mostly because Congress was having difficulty raising money to pay the army. The Articles of Confederation, which allowed Congress to create an army, did not require it to levy taxes to pay for it; that was the job of the states. One solution, proposed by officers who believed this situation highlighted the weakness of a republic, was a constitutional monarchy modeled after England's.

They asked Washington — who could do no wrong in their eyes — to take the title of king. Here is Washington's reply.

Sir:

With a mixture of great surprise and astonishment I have read with attention the Sentiments you have submitted to my perusal. Be assured Sir, no occurrence in the course of the War, has given me more painful sensations than your information of there being such ideas existing in the Army as you have expressed, and I must view with abhorrence, and reprehend with severity. For the present, the communication of them will rest in my own bosom, unless some further agitation of the matter shall make a disclosure necessary.

I am much at a loss to conceive what part of my conduct could have given encouragement to an address which to me seems big with the greatest mischief that can befall my Country. If I am not deceived in the knowledge of myself, you could not have found a person to whom your schemes are more disagreeable; at the same time in justice to my own feelings I must add, that no Man possesses a more sincere wish to see ample justice done to the Army than I do, and as far as my powers and influence, in a constitutional way extend, they shall be employed to the utmost of my abilities to effect it, should there be any occasion. Let me conjure you then, if you have any regard for your Country, concern for yourself or posterity, or respect for me, to banish these thoughts from your Mind, and never communicate, as from yourself, or any one else, a sentiment of the like Nature. With esteem I am.

George Washington
(1782)

Questions

1. Describe the tone of George Washington's response.
2. What assumptions has Colonel Lewis Nicola made about Washington? How does Washington address them?
3. How does this letter add to what you already know about Washington?

from *Farewell Address*

George Washington

This address, published as a letter first in the *American Daily Advertiser* in 1796 and then in newspapers across the country, was drafted by Washington with help from James Madison and Alexander Hamilton. It announces that he will not serve a third term as president of the United States.

To the efficacy and permanency of Your Union, a Government for the whole is indispensable. No Alliances however strict between the parts can be an adequate substitute. They must inevitably experience the infractions & interruptions which all Alliances in all times have experienced. Sensible of this momentous truth, you have improved upon your first essay, by the adoption of a Constitution of Government, better calculated than your former for an intimate Union, and for the efficacious management of your common concerns. This government, the offspring of our own choice uninfluenced and unawed, adopted upon full investigation & mature deliberation, completely free in its principles, in the distribution of its powers, uniting security with energy, and containing within itself a provision for its own amendment, has a just claim to your confidence and your support. Respect for its authority, compliance with its Laws, acquiescence in its measures, are duties enjoined by the fundamental maxims of true Liberty. The basis of our political Systems is the right of the people to make and to alter their Constitutions of Government. But the Constitution which at any time exists, 'till changed by an explicit and authentic act of the whole People, is sacredly obligatory upon all. The very idea of the power and the right of the People to establish Government presupposes the duty of every Individual to obey the established Government.

All obstructions to the execution of the Laws, all combinations and Associations, under whatever plausible character, with the real design to direct, controul counteract, or awe the regular deliberation and action of the Constituted authorities are distructive of this fundamental principle and of fatal tendency. They serve to Organize faction, to give it an artificial and extraordinary force — to put in the place of the delegated will of the Nation, the will of a party; often a small but artful and enterprizing minority of the Community; and, according to the alternate triumphs of different parties, to make the public Administration the Mirror of the ill concerted and incongruous projects of faction, rather than the Organ of consistent and wholesome plans digested by common councils and modefied by mutual interests. However combinations or Associations of the above description may now & then answer popular ends, they are likely, in the course of time and things, to become potent engines, by which cunning, ambitious and unprincipled men will be enabled to subvert the Power of the People, & to usurp for themselves the reins of Government; destroying afterwards the very engines which have lifted them to unjust dominion.

Towards the preservation of your Government and the permanency of your present happy state, it is requisite, not only that you steadily discountenance irregular oppositions to its acknowledged authority, but also that you resist with care the spirit of innovation upon its principles however specious the pretexts. One method of assault may be to effect, in the forms of the Constitution, alterations which will impair the energy of the system, and thus to undermine what cannot be directly overthrown. In all the changes to which you may be invited, remember that time and habit are at least as necessary to fix the true character of Governments, as of other human institutions — that experience is the surest standard, by which to test the real tendency of the existing Constitution of a Country — that facility in changes upon the credit of mere hypotheses & opinion exposes to perpetual change, from the endless variety of hypotheses and opinion: and remember, especially, that for the efficient management of your common interests, in a country so extensive as ours, a Government of as much vigour as is consistent with the perfect security of Liberty is indispensable — Liberty itself will find in such a Government, with powers properly distributed and adjusted, its surest Guardian. It is indeed little else than a name, where the Government is too feeble to withstand the enterprises of faction, to confine each member of the Society within the limits prescribed by the laws & to maintain all in the secure & tranquil enjoyment of the rights of person & property.

(1796)

Questions

1. What message does George Washington give regarding the Constitution?
2. What does Washington see as the reciprocal obligations of the people and the government?
3. What does Washington see as the biggest danger in political parties?
4. What does this address reveal about the ways Washington will come to be seen by future generations?

George Washington—Lansdowne Portrait

GILBERT STUART

Commissioned by Senator William Bingham of Pennsylvania and his wife, Anne, in 1796, the painting on the facing page was a gift to the former British prime minister William Petty FitzMaurice (the first Marquess of Lansdowne) in recognition of his brokering a lasting peace between Britain and America. In 2001, a foundation committed $30 million to create a permanent home for the painting in the National Portrait Gallery of the Smithsonian Institution.

Questions

1. Explain what you think the picture's symbolism means. Look carefully at Washington's sword, the medallion on the chair, the weather outside the window, the books, the items on the desk, the decoration on the leg of the table, among other bits of iconography.
2. What can you read in the picture about Washington's personality and state of mind? Hint: his clenched expression may be the result of new false teeth.
3. America's image of Washington is largely the result of three paintings by Gilbert Stuart: this one, called the *Lansdowne Portrait*, and two others, the *Athenaeum* and the *Vaughn*, which just show his head. Apparently, Washington hated sitting for

National Portrait Gallery, Smithsonian Institution/Art Resource, NY

GILBERT STUART, *GEORGE WASHINGTON—LANSDOWNE PORTRAIT*, 1796, OIL ON CANVAS, 8'×5', NATIONAL PORTRAIT GALLERY OF THE SMITHSONIAN INSTITUTION, WASHINGTON, D.C. (SEE COLOR INSERT, IMAGE 20.)

portraits; Stuart used a stand-in to model Washington's body. In addition, at the time of the sitting Washington was having trouble: he was squabbling with his cabinet over relations with England; the press portrayed him as a monarch in the style of France's Louis XIV; and he was in discomfort from his false teeth. Look carefully at the details of this portrait and consider whether Stuart was sympathetic to Washington's woes — or not.

from *A History of the Life and Death, Virtues and Exploits of General George Washington*

MASON LOCKE WEEMS

> Mason Locke Weems, an itinerant preacher and bookseller, wrote a biography of Washington that was based largely on anecdote, if not outright fantasy, entitled *A History of the Life and Death, Virtues and Exploits of General George Washington*. Published just after Washington's death in 1799, it was wildly popular.

Never did the wise Ulysses take more pains with his beloved Telemachus, than did Mr. Washington with George, to inspire him with an *early love of truth*.

"Truth, George" (said he) "is the loveliest quality of youth. I would ride fifty miles, my son, to see the little boy whose heart is so *honest*, and his lips so *pure*, that we may depend on every word he says. O how lovely does such a child appear in the eyes of every body! His parents doat on him; his relations glory in him; they are constantly praising him to their children, whom they beg to imitate him. They are often sending for him, to visit them; and receive him, when he comes, with as much joy as if he were a little angel, come to set pretty examples to their children."

"But, Oh! how different, George, is the case with the boy who is so given to lying, that nobody can believe a word he says! He is looked at with aversion wherever he goes, and parents dread to see him come among their children. Oh, George! my son! rather than see you come to this pass, dear as you are to my heart, gladly would I assist to nail you up in your little coffin, and follow you to your grave. Hard, indeed, would it be to me to give up my son, whose little feet are always so ready to run about with me, and whose fondly looking eyes and sweet prattle make so large a part of my happiness: but still I would give him up, rather than see him a common liar."

"Pa, (said George very seriously) do I ever tell lies?"

"No, George, I *thank God* you do not, my son; and I rejoice in the hope you never   5 will. At least, you shall never, from me, have cause to be guilty of so shameful a thing. Many parents, indeed, even compel their children to this vile practice, by barbarously beating them for every little fault; hence, on the next offence, the little terrified creature slips out a *lie!* just to escape the rod. But as to yourself, George, you know I have *always* told you, and now tell you again, that, whenever by accident you do any thing wrong, which must often be the case, as you are but a poor little boy yet, without *experience* or *knowledge*, never tell a falsehood to conceal it; but come *bravely* up, my son, like a *little man*, and tell me of it: and instead of beating you, George, I will but the more honour and love you for it, my dear."

This, you'll say, was sowing good seed! — Yes, it was: and the crop, thank God, was, as I believe it ever will be, where a man acts the true parent, that is, the *Guardian Angel*, by his child.

The following anecdote is a *case in point*. It is too valuable to be lost, and too true to be doubted; for it was communicated to me by the same excellent lady to whom I am indebted for the last.

"When George," said she, "was about six years old, he was made the wealthy master of a *hatchet!* of which, like most little boys, he was immoderately fond, and was constantly going about chopping every thing that came in his way. One day, in the garden, where he often amused himself hacking his mother's pea-sticks, he unluckily tried the edge of his hatchet on the body of a beautiful young English cherry-tree, which he barked so terribly, that I don't believe the tree ever got the better of it. The next morning the old gentleman finding out what had befallen his tree, which, by the by, was a great favourite, came into the house, and with much warmth asked for the mischievous author, declaring at the same time, that he would not have taken five guineas for his tree. Nobody could tell him any thing about it. Presently George and his hatchet made their appearance. *George*, said his father, *do you know who killed that beautiful little cherry-tree yonder in the garden?* This was a *tough question*; and George staggered under it for a moment; but quickly recovered himself: and looking at his father, with the sweet face of youth brightened with the inexpressible charm of all-conquering truth, he bravely cried out, *"I can't tell a lie, Pa; you know I can't tell a lie. I did cut it with my hatchet."* — *Run to my arms, you dearest boy,* cried his father in transports, *run to my arms; glad am I, George, that you killed my tree; for you have paid me for it a thousand fold. Such an act of heroism in my son, is more worth than a thousand trees, though blossomed with silver, and their fruits of purest gold.*

(1799)

Questions

1. Although he claimed, "It was related to me twenty years ago by an aged lady who was a distant relative," the famous story of Washington and the cherry tree is considered Mason Locke Weems's invention. Do you think it matters whether or not this story is true? Explain your answer.
2. What particularly American values does this story celebrate? Why is Washington mythologized in this way? Why does this story have so much staying power?
3. Why do you think this story is the one that every schoolchild learns? What does it tell us about American values when it comes to raising children?
4. Do you think this story is good for Washington's image or bad for it? Explain your answer.

George Washington

HORATIO GREENOUGH

The marble statue on the following page was commissioned in 1832 by Congress to celebrate the centennial of George Washington's birthday. It was intended for the rotunda in the Capitol building. From the minute it arrived, however, according to the Web site of the Smithsonian Institution Press, it "attracted controversy and criticism." Modeled after a classical Greek statue of Zeus, this half-naked Washington seemed either offensive or comical to many Americans, some of whom joked that he is reaching for his clothes. The statue has been in several locations since then, including the lawn of the Capitol, and now resides in the new National Museum of American History.

Smithsonian American Art Museum, Washington, DC/Art Resource, NY

Questions

1. What is your reaction to the statue? Do you find it uplifting? Do you find it comical? Explain your answer.
2. What do you think the position of Washington's hands represents? How do these gestures square with the myth of Washington?
3. Washington was often compared to Cincinnatus, a legendary Roman who was called from his plow to rescue Rome. He took up command of the army, vanquished the enemy, and returned to his farm when the danger had passed. How does this statue allude to Cincinnatus?

Washington Crossing the Delaware

EMANUEL LEUTZE

> Painted in 1851 by Emanuel Leutze, a German American, this painting commemorates Washington's crossing of the Delaware River in December 1776, part of a surprise attack on the Hessian forces at Trenton, New Jersey. The original painting was part of the collection in a museum in Germany and was destroyed during an air raid in 1942. A replica hangs in the Metropolitan Museum of Art.

Metropolitan Museum of Art, New York, USA/The Bridgeman Art library

EMANUEL LEUTZE, *WASHINGTON CROSSING THE DELAWARE*, 1851, OIL ON CANVAS, 149" × 255", METROPOLITAN MUSEUM OF ART, NEW YORK.
(SEE COLOR INSERT, IMAGE 21.)

Questions

1. This painting is well known for its historical inaccuracies. The flag, for example, was a design that didn't actually fly until more than a year after the crossing. The crossing was in the middle of the night, yet the light in the painting makes it look like early morning. Explain whether you think these inaccuracies detract from or add to the painting's message.
2. Look carefully at the people in the boat. Why did the artist render such a diverse group?
3. What message does the painting send about Washington's leadership qualities? How does it contribute to Washington's mythical status?

Tribute to George Washington

JANE ADDAMS

This speech by Jane Addams, a social reformer and cofounder of Hull House, was given in honor of George Washington in 1903 in celebration of his birthday.

We meet together upon those birthdays of our great men not only to review their lives, but to revive and cherish our own patriotism. This matter is a difficult task. In the first place, we are prone to think that by merely reciting these great deeds we get a reflected glory, and that the future is secure to us because the past has been so fine. In the second place, we are apt to think that we inherit the fine qualities of those great men simply because we have had a common descent and are living in the same territory.

As for the latter, we know full well that the patriotism of common descent is the mere patriotism of the clan — the early patriotism of the tribe. We know that the possession of a like territory is merely an advance upon that, and that both of them are unworthy to be the patriotism of a great cosmopolitan nation, whose patriotism must be large enough to obliterate racial distinction and to forget that there are such things as surveyor's lines. Then when we come to the study of great men it is easy to think only of their great deeds, and not to think enough of their spirit. What is a great man who has made his mark upon history? Every time, if we think far enough, he is a man who has looked through the confusion of the moment and has seen the moral issue involved; he is a man who has refused to have his sense of justice distorted; he has listened to his conscience until conscience becomes a trumpet call to likeminded men, so that they gather about him, and together, with mutual purpose and mutual aid, they make a new period in history.

Let us assume for a moment that if we are going to make this day of advantage to us, we will have to appeal to the present as well as to the past. We will have to rouse our national consciences as well as our national pride, and we will all have to remember that it lies with the young people of this nation whether or not it is going to go on to a finish in any way worthy of its beginning.

If we go back to George Washington, and ask what he would be doing were he bearing our burdens now and facing our problems at this moment, we would, of course, have to study his life bit by bit — his life as a soldier, as a statesman, and as a simple Virginia planter.

First, as a soldier. What is it that we admire about the soldier? It certainly is not that he goes into battle. What we admire about the soldier is that he has the power of losing his own life for the life of a larger cause; that he holds his personal suffering of no account; that he flings down in the rage of battle his all and says, "I will stand or fall with this cause." That, it seems to me, is the glorious thing we most admire, and if we are going to preserve that same spirit of the soldier, we will have to found a similar spirit in the civil life of the people, the same pride in civil warfare, the spirit of courage, and the spirit of self-surrender which lies back of this.

5

If we look out upon our national perspective, do we not see certainly one great menace which calls for patriotism? We see all around us a spirit of materialism — an undue emphasis put upon material possessions, an inordinate desire to win wealth, an inordinate desire to please those who are the possessors of wealth. Now, let us say, if we feel that this is a menace, that with all our power, with all the spirit of a soldier, we will arouse high-minded youth of this country against this spirit of materialism. We will say today that we will not count the opening of markets the one great field which our nation is concerned in, but that when our flag flies everywhere it shall fly for righteousness as well as for increased commercial prosperity; that we will see to it that no sin of commercial robbery shall be committed where it floats; that we shall see to it that nothing in our commercial history will not bear the most careful scrutiny and investigation; that we will restore a commercial life, however complicated, to such honor and simple honesty as George Washington expressed in his business dealings.

Let us take, for a moment, George Washington as a statesman. What was it he did, during those days when they were framing a Constitution, when they were meeting together night after night, and trying to adjust the rights and privileges of every class in the community? What was it that sustained him during all those days, all those weeks, during all those months and years? It was the belief that they were founding a nation on the axiom that all men are created free and equal. What would George Washington say if he found that, among us, there were causes constantly operating against that equality? If he knew that any child which is thrust prematurely into industry has no chance in life with children who are preserved from that pain and sorrow? If he knew that every insanitary street, and every insanitary house, cripples a man so that he has no health and no vigor with which to carry on his life labor? If he knew that all about us are forces making against skill, making against the best manhood and womanhood? What would he say? He would say that if the spirit of equality means anything, it means like opportunity, and if we once lose like opportunity we lose the only chance we have toward equality throughout the nation.

Let us take George Washington as a citizen. What did he do when he retired from office, because he was afraid holding office any longer might bring a wrong to himself and harm to his beloved nation? We say that he went back to his plantation on the Potomac. What were his thoughts during the all too short days that he lived there? He thought of many possibilities, but, looking out over his country, did he fear that there should rise up a crowd of men who held office not for their country's good, but for their own good? Would he not have foreboded evil if he had known that among us were groups and hordes of professional politicians who, without any blinking or without any pretense that they did otherwise, apportioned the spoils of office, and considered an independent man as a mere intruder, as a mere outsider? If he had seen that the original meaning of office holding and the function of government had become indifferent to us, that we were not using our foresight and our conscience in order to find out this great wrong which was sapping the foundations of self-government? He would tell us that anything which makes for better civic service, which makes for a merit system, which makes for fitness for office, is the only thing which will tell against this wrong, and that this course is the wisest patriotism. What did he write in his last correspondence? He wrote that he felt very unhappy on the subject of slavery, that there was, to his mind, a great menace in the holding of slaves. We know that he neither bought nor sold slaves himself, and that he freed his own slaves in his will. That was a century ago. A man who a century ago could do that, would he, do you think, be indifferent now to the great questions of social maladjustment which we feel all around us? His letters breathe a yearning for a better condition for the slaves as the letters of all great men among us breathe a yearning for the better condition of the unskilled and underpaid. A wise patriotism, which will take hold of these questions by careful, legal enactment, by constant and vigorous enforcement, because of the belief that if the meanest man in the republic is deprived of his rights, then every man in the republic is deprived of his rights, is the only patriotism by which public-spirited men and women, with a thoroughly aroused conscience, can worthily serve this republic. Let us say again that the lessons of great men are lost unless they reinforce upon our minds the highest demands which we make upon ourselves; that they are lost unless they drive our sluggish wills forward in the direction of their highest ideals.

(1903)

Questions

1. What does Jane Addams warn as a danger of focusing on the "great deeds" (par. 2) of famous men?
2. How does Addams connect the example set by George Washington to the social ills of her own time?
3. Do you think Addams uses the message of Washington's Farewell Address (see p. 452) to good effect in this speech? Explain your answer.
4. Do you think this speech adds to the mythmaking about Washington? Explain why or why not.

On Seeing Larry Rivers' Washington Crossing the Delaware *at the Museum of Modern Art*

Frank O'Hara

> Poet Frank O'Hara and painter Larry Rivers were close friends. This poem was inspired by Rivers's 1957 painting — a revision of the Emanuel Leutze painting — that hangs in the Museum of Modern Art in New York City, where O'Hara worked as an assistant curator.

Now that our hero has come back to us
in his white pants and we know his nose
trembling like a flag under fire,

we see the calm cold river is supporting
our forces, the beautiful history.   5

To be more revolutionary than a nun
is our desire, to be secular and intimate
as, when sighting a redcoat, you smile
and pull the trigger. Anxieties
and animosities, flaming and feeding   10

on theoretical considerations and
the jealous spiritualities of the abstract,
the robot? they're smoke, billows above
the physical event. They have burned up.
See how free we are! as a nation of persons.   15

Dear father of our country, so alive
you must have lied incessantly to be
immediate, here are your bones crossed
on my breast like a rusty flintlock,
a pirate's flag, bravely specific   20

and ever so light in the misty glare
of a crossing by water in winter to a shore
other than that the bridge reaches for.
Don't shoot until, the white of freedom glinting
on your gun barrel, you see the general fear.   25

(1957)

Questions

1. What myths about George Washington does Frank O'Hara invoke in this poem?
2. Find a reproduction of Larry Rivers's *Washington Crossing the Delaware* online.
   In what ways is the poem about Rivers's painting? In what ways is it about George
   Washington? Is there a point at which they connect?

from *His Highness*

JILL LEPORE

> This article appeared in the *New Yorker* in 2010 as a review of Ron Chernow's
> biography of George Washington, *Washington: A Life.*

Jared Sparks, thirty-seven, and known for his editorial eye, reached Mount Vernon
by carriage just before sunset on March 14, 1827. He made no note of the grounds,
the house, the stables, the slope of the hill. He sought only George Washington's

papers. It had taken him years to get permission to see them, finally securing it from Washington's nephew and literary executor, the Supreme Court Justice Bushrod Washington, by pledging discretion, and, no less important, agreeing to split the profits from publishing an edition of Washington's writings. A former chaplain of Congress, Sparks was the editor and owner of the United States' first literary magazine, the *North American Review*, which, under his direction, was distinguished for its judiciousness. A man better suited to the work of editing Washington's papers and writing his biography would have been hard to find, which makes it all the stranger that what Sparks did to those papers was, in his lifetime, called one of the most flagrant injuries ever inflicted by an editor upon a writer or by a biographer upon his subject — some swipe, even making allowances for hyperbole.

No one could have seen that coming when Sparks made his way from the carriage and into the house where he cloistered himself for more than a month. Diaries, notebooks, scraps, and some forty thousand letters: a biographer's harem. He wrote to a friend that he was in Paradise. No one bothered him. "I have been here entirely alone," he wrote in his journal, and you can almost hear his heart beating. In a garret, he pried open a chest: "Discovered some new and valuable papers to-day, particularly a small manuscript book containing an original journal of Washington, written in the year 1748, March and April, when he was barely sixteen years old." Everything was a find. "It is quite certain that no writer of Washington's biography has seen this book." Maybe, at long last, Washington's secrets would be revealed.

No biographer of George Washington has failed to remark on his inscrutability. In *Washington: A Life* . . . Ron Chernow calls Washington "the most famously elusive figure in American history." Sparks eventually published eleven volumes of Washington's writings, together with a one-volume biography. In 1893, Worthington C. Ford published the last installment of a fourteen-volume set. An edition of thirty-nine volumes was completed in 1940. Of the University of Virginia Press's magnificent "Papers of George Washington," begun in 1968, sixty-two volumes have been published so far. But, for all those papers, Washington rarely revealed himself on the page. Even his few surviving letters to his wife are formal and strained. Those diaries? Here is Washington's entire diary entry for October 24, 1774, a day that he was in Philadelphia, as a delegate to the Continental Congress, debating, among other things, a petition to be sent to the King: "Dined with Mr. Mease & Spent the Evening at the New Tavern." Here is how John Adams's diary entry for that same day *begins*:

> In Congress, nibbling and quibbling, as usual.
>
> There is no greater mortification than to sit with half a dozen Witts, deliberating upon a Petition, Address, or Memorial. These great Witts, these subtle Cricks, these refined Genius's, these learned Lawyers, these wise Statesmen, are so fond of shewing their Parts and Powers, as to make their Consultations very tedius.
>
> Young Ned Rutledge is a perfect Bob o' Lincoln — a Swallow — a Sparrow — a Peacock — excessively vain, excessively weak, and excessively variable and unsteady — jejune, inane, and puerile.
>
> Mr. Dickinson is very modest, delicate, and timid.

Aside from chucking Washington in favor of writing about Adams, what's a biographer to do?

Washington's contemporaries saw in him what they wanted to see. So have his biographers, of whom there have been many, including a delegate to the Continental Congress (David Ramsay), a U.S. senator (Henry Cabot Lodge), a Chief Justice of the Supreme Court (John Marshall), and an American President (Woodrow Wilson). There have always been Washington killjoys. Abigail Adams was troubled by the beatification of Washington: "To no one Man in America belongs the Epithet of *Saviour*," she believed. Mark Twain once said that while Washington couldn't tell a lie, Twain could, and didn't, which made Twain the better man. The first Washington-was-a-fraud biography was published in 1926. Its author, William E. Woodward, had, in his 1923 novel, *Bunk*, coined the word "debunk." Woodward argued, mostly, that the father of our country was dim-witted: "Washington possessed the superb self-confidence that comes only to those men whose inner life is faint." The *Times* called Woodward's biography tittle-tattle.

Every generation must have its Washington; ours is fated to choose among dozens. Ronald Reagan, in his first Inaugural Address, looked at the obelisk across the Mall and spoke about "the monument to a monumental man." Since 1990, major American publishing houses have brought out no fewer than eighteen Washington biographies, a couple of them very fine, to say nothing of the slew of boutique-y books about the man's military career, his moral fortitude, his friendship with Lafayette, his faith in God, his betrayal by Benedict Arnold, his "secret navy," his inspiring words, his leadership skills, his business tips, his kindness to General William Howe's dog, and his journey home to Mount Vernon for Christmas in 1783. *George*, a magazine of celebrity and politics featuring on its cover stars dressed up as Washington, was launched in 1995. By now, just about every Presidential historian and potboiler-maker in the business has churned out a biography of Washington. And still they keep coming. At nine hundred and twenty-eight pages, Chernow's is the longest single-volume biography of Washington ever published.

George Washington was born in Westmoreland County, Virginia, in 1732. His father died when he was eleven. When he was sixteen, he went on a surveying trip in the Shenandoah Valley — during which he kept the diary that Sparks found — and, three years later, travelled to the West Indies. At twenty, he assumed his first military command; his reckless and often failed but indisputably bold campaigns, in the seventeen-fifties, gained him a reputation for invincibility. He was tall and imposing, at once powerful and graceful, and he rode a horse exceptionally well. "Well turned" is what people said in the eighteenth century about a man like that, which makes you picture God laboring at a lathe. More recent descriptions range from the fabulous to the immoderate. Woodrow Wilson, in his 1896 biography, made it sound as if Washington had grown up in Sherwood Forest: "All the land knew him and loved him for gallantry and brave capacity; he carried himself like a prince." Chernow dwells on Washington's manliness, describing him, every few pages or so, as "a superb physical specimen, with a magnificent physique," "an exceptionally muscular and vigorous young man," with an "imposing face and virile form," "powerfully rough-hewn and endowed with matchless strength," not excepting his "wide, flaring hips with muscular thighs." (Chernow finds even Washington's prose "muscular.") The mar to his beauty was his terrible teeth, which were replaced by unsuccessful transplant surgery and by dentures made from ivory and from teeth pulled from the mouths of his slaves.

Washington was elected to the Virginia Assembly in 1758 and was married the next year. Until the passage of the Intolerable Acts, he occupied himself managing his vast estate and wasn't much animated by the colonies' growing struggle with Parliamentary authority. But then he threw himself into it, serving as a delegate to the First Continental Congress, in 1774. The next year, he was appointed commander-in-chief of the Continental Army and rode to Cambridge to take command. During the war, and, even more, after it, Washington came to embody the new nation's vision of itself: virtuous, undaunted, and incorruptible. Nothing earned him deserved admiration more than his surrendering of his command at the end of the war. That resignation — relinquishing power when he could so easily have seized it — saved the republic. He returned to public life in 1787, to preside over the Constitutional Convention, where he played a largely ceremonial but nonetheless crucial role. Washington knew the difference between ceremony and pomposity, and kept to one side of it.

He was elected President by a unanimous vote of the electoral college. In his Inaugural Address (likely drafted by James Madison), he said that "the preservation of the sacred fire of liberty and the destiny of the republican model of government" were fated by "the eternal rules of order and right which Heaven itself has ordained" and staked, finally, deeply, "on the experiment entrusted to the hands of the American people." Charged with leading a wholly new form of government, wherein his every decision set a precedent, he began holding, in 1791, what came to be called cabinet meetings.

His Presidency was marked by much debate about how he ought to be treated, 10 and even how he should be addressed. (Adams had wanted to call him His Most Benign Highness, and Washington was fond of His High Mightiness.) Owen Wister began his 1907 biography of Washington with a story about what happened on Washington's sixtieth birthday: "On the 22d of February, 1792, Congress was sitting in Philadelphia, and to many came the impulse to congratulate the President. . . . Therefore a motion was made to adjourn for half an hour, that this civility might be paid. The motion was bitterly opposed, as smacking of idolatry and as leaning toward monarchy." (A century later, Washington's birthday became a national holiday, now commemorated as a great time to buy a new car.)

Washington was a very good President, and an unhappy one. Distraught by growing factionalism within and outside his Administration, especially by the squabbling of Hamilton and Jefferson and the rise of a Jeffersonian opposition, he served another term only reluctantly. His second Inaugural Address was just a hundred and thirty-five words long; he said, more or less, Please, I'm doing my best. In 1796, in his enduringly eloquent Farewell Address (written by Madison and

Hamilton), he cautioned the American people about party rancor: "The alternate domination of one faction over another, sharpened by the spirit of revenge, natural to party dissension, which in different ages and countries has perpetrated the most horrid enormities, is itself a frightful despotism." And then he went back to Mount Vernon. He freed his slaves in his will, possibly hoping that this, too, would set a precedent. It did not.

Washington isn't like Adams, effusively cantankerous; he's not like Jefferson, a cabinet of contradictions. He's not funny like Franklin or capacious like Madison. If critics said that his inner life glowed but faintly, Chernow, who calls him "the most interior of the founders," thinks his inner life was red hot, burning with pent-up passion. Washington wasn't a tortured man, though, nor was he enigmatic. He was a staged man, shrewd, purposeful, and effective. Not surprisingly for an eighteenth-century military man, he held himself at a considerable remove from his men. But he also held himself at this remove from just about everyone else.

He played a role, surpassingly well. He dressed for the part (he was obsessed with his clothes), and studied for it (as a boy, he copied out a set of sixteenth-century Italian "Rules of Civility," which read like stage directions: "Bedew no mans face with your Spittle by approaching too near to him when you Speak"). Washington's theatrical reserve can look, now, like mysteriousness. But what he was going for was an imperturbability that had to do with eighteenth-century notions of honor, gentility, and manliness; its closest surviving kin, today, is what's called military bearing. Chernow's aim is to make of Washington something other than a "lifeless waxwork," an "impossibly stiff and wooden figure, composed of too much marble to be quite human." That has been the aim of every Washington biographer, and none of them have achieved it. Sparks, so far from doing it, only made things worse. "Setting Washington on stilts" is what Sparks was charged with, although, really, Washington was already up there, leaning on legs of wood.

(2010)

Questions

1. How would you describe the tone of Jill Lepore's review? Do you think she is respectful of Ron Chernow's work? Is she respectful of George Washington? Explain your answer.
2. The "flagrant" injury Lepore claims Jared Sparks caused (par. 1) turns out to be Sparks's editing of Washington's papers. According to Lepore, he "corrected Washington's spelling and punctuation. What he found badly expressed, he rewrote." Do you think it is appropriate to edit the words of a president? Why do you think Sparks rewrote Washington's words?
3. Why do you think Lepore spends so much time discussing other biographies of Washington in this review of Chernow's book?

This Is the Car You Buy Because You Can't Buy a Bald Eagle

Dodge Motor Company

This poster was part of a 2010 Dodge ad campaign titled "Let Freedom Rev."

Dodge and Challenger are registered trademarks of Chrysler Group LLC.

Questions

1. The caption on this ad reads, "This is the car you buy because you can't buy a bald eagle," while another version says, "Let freedom rev." What do the words add to the effect of the poster? What do you think they explain, if anything?
2. What is the mood of the ad? How is it created? Consider the composition (where the figures and the car are located in relation to each other) as well as the expressions on the faces of the figures.
3. Why do you think Dodge chose an image of George Washington for its advertising campaign? What aspects of the Washington myth are particularly well suited to automobile advertising?

from *Inventing George Washington*

Edward G. Lengel

The following excerpt is from a chapter titled "Washington's Visions" in Edward G. Lengel's book *Inventing George Wastington*. Lengel examines some of the spiritual and religious myths and traditions associated with George Washington, such as his praying at Valley Forge, the subject of several famous pieces of artwork including *The Prayer at Valley Forge* (1866) by Henry Brueckner, *The Prayer at Valley Forge* (1976) by Arnold Friberg, and the stained-glass window in the Congressional Prayer Room in Washington, D.C.

Not all the religious traditions of Washington at Valley Forge are Christian. In the 1880s and 1890s, some books claimed that Washington had visited one Daniel Hart, a Jew living in Philadelphia. The visit probably never took place — there is no primary evidence for it — but in this simple form the story amounted to just another of the relatively harmless "George Washington slept here" stories common in local folklore. But it did not end there. Sometime in the twentieth century stories circulated — probably orally — that Washington had told Hart of an episode at Valley Forge on the evening of Christmas Day 1777. Entering a shack where some soldiers had bedded down, the story goes, Washington noticed a young soldier off in a corner, softly crying. The general asked the lad what troubled him and noticed that he held a strange lamp. The soldier replied that it was his Hanukkah lamp and that he was a Jew recently arrived from Poland. He then told Washington about how the lamp commemorated the victory of a small band of Israelites over a much larger foe and explained that he had cried in hopes that the Continental army would experience the same kind of victory. The experience, Washington allegedly told Hart, inspired him to fight on against all odds. Taking hold among the Jewish American immigrant community, the legend spread and appeared in several books — most recently Stephen Krensky's award-winning children's book, *Hanukkah at Valley Forge* (2006). The story, says Krensky, "is based on facts, but the tale itself must be taken on faith."[1]

(2011)

Questions

1. Why do you think Edward Lengel is so sure this event never took place? Does it matter whether the event can be authenticated?
2. What purpose does the footnote serve?
3. What does this anecdote tell us about the mythology of George Washington in that a children's book could be written about his meeting with and his becoming inspired by a Jewish soldier?

Making Connections

1. Historian and critic Garry Wills writes, in *Cincinnatus, George Washington and the Enlightenment*, "Generations of Americans grew up admiring the Washington of Parson Weems, who trivializes the man, in our eyes, by turning him into a

[1] J. L. Bell, "Washington's Hanukkah: An Oral Tradition," Boston 1775 Blog, February 7, 2007; Penny Schwartz, "By George, It's a New Spin on Hanukkah," *Boston Globe*, December 10, 2006.

moral fable. Horatio Greenough, by contrast, deprives us of the human by rendering the god. Weems deflates, Greenough inflates; the result is the same." What do you think Wills means by "the result is the same"? Which version of Washington do you think is the most important and fitting for the "father of our country"?

2. Both his letter to Colonel Nicola (p. 451) and his Farewell Address (p. 452) are considered examples of how Washington controlled his own image during his lifetime. What do you think he wants the public to take away from these two documents? Are those values still associated with Washington?

3. How much fact or history is there in Gilbert Stuart's *Landsdowne Portrait* (p. 454) or in Emanuel Leutze's *Washington Crossing the Delaware* (p. 459)? Does it matter? Do you think visual texts, such as paintings, should provide accurate historical information? If not, what purpose do they serve?

4. What would Jane Addams (p. 460) think of Frank O'Hara's poem (p. 462)? Do Addams and O'Hara share the same views of the American values personified by Washington? How are their views the same? How are they different?

5. Mason Locke Weems (p. 456) says his anecdote about Washington and the cherry tree is "too valuable to be lost, and too true to be doubted" (par. 7), What would Jill Lepore (p. 463) think of Weems's skill as a biographer? What do you think?

6. Lepore calls Washington's Farewell Address "enduringly eloquent" (par. 11). How do you think it holds up to other presidential addresses that you have read? Think of Abraham Lincoln's second inaugural (p. 695) or John F. Kennedy's inaugural (p. 77). Respond to Lepore with your opinion of the Farewell Address.

7. Do you think the portrayal of Washington in the Dodge Challenger poster is closer to the way he is portrayed by Weems, by Stuart, or by Horatio Greenough (p. 458)? Explain your answer.

Entering the Conversation

As you respond to each of the following prompts, support your position with appropriate evidence, including at least three sources in this Conversation on the myth of George Washington, unless otherwise indicated.

1. In his review of *Washington: A Life*, by Ron Chernow, for the Web site Daily Beast, retired four-star general Wesley Clark writes, "How incredibly fortunate America was to have someone like George Washington emerge as a young man and mature into the extraordinary and towering figure who personified our country and its virtues." Write an essay in which you examine Clark's statement, agreeing with, disagreeing with, or qualifying it based on information from the sources here.

2. To what do you credit George Washington's mythic status? Write an essay in which you analyze the qualities that Washington has come to represent. Discuss why you think those qualities are particularly American.

3. In "George Washington, Genius in Leadership," Richard C. Stazesky, president emeritus of the George Washington Society of Delaware, wrote:

> I believe that the answer points again to the fact that he was eminently successful as the Father of the Country, a title bestowed on him but one which he also appropriated and lived. A truly successful and effective father is one who never claims credit for his achievements in being the father and who inculcates his ideas and values in his offspring so well that they, in fact, do not realize themselves from whence these came; they, therefore, tend just to take them for granted or to credit themselves for them. We all know the story of the college sophomore who was amazed at how seemingly uninformed, even stupid, was his father, only to discover later how informed, bright, and wise his father had become. The ideas that Washington had and lived became so imbued in American institutions and culture, because of his skill as a visionary leader, that we have failed to realize from whence they came, namely, from our national Father, George Washington.

Use the sources here — and other information about Washington — to address the question of George Washington as both a literal and a figurative father figure.

4. Professor William M. Etter, writing about the myth of George Washington's wooden teeth in the *Encyclopedia of George Washington's Mount Vernon*, notes:

> Washington did actually experience great discomfort and facial distortion with his cumbersome metal and ivory dentures. Moreover, the belief that Washington had to use teeth made out of ordinary wood — as opposed to the technologically advanced and expensive contraptions he actually did wear — helps make Washington more accessible to the general public as a common person with everyday struggles. Perhaps this myth has endured because it balances Washington's imposing status in American history and the idealized images of the man presented in other myths like the Cherry Tree legend and, in doing so, humanizes an individual who may often seem remote and statuesque.

In what other ways do we see Washington humanized? Do those efforts work? Do you think it's important for a public figure to be brought down to size, or should he or she be "larger than life"? Write an essay in which you discuss the pros and cons of Washington's larger-than-life status. Consider today's public figures and the ways in which they are at times humanized and at times blown up larger than life.

Conversation

Religious Tolerance

Religious freedom and tolerance are central principles on which the United States of America was founded, as the country was settled largely by religious dissidents looking to worship as they saw fit. The First Amendment to the U.S. Constitution (1789) states: "Congress shall make no law respecting an establishment of religion, or prohibiting the free exercise thereof," and article 6 of the U.S. Constitution states that "no religious Test shall ever be required as a Qualification to any Office or public Trust under the United States." Even as our country has become increasingly diverse, the vast majority of Americans refer to themselves as Christians. There are many who argue that the United States is indeed a Christian nation in terms of its origins and the values held by both its Founding Fathers and the majority of its citizens. Unfortunately, as we look through our history, we find that religious tolerance might be an ideal more than a practice. Whether we're considering Baptists, Native Americans, Catholics, Muslims, Jews, or members of any other sect, Americans have found tolerance to be a challenge. In this Conversation, we'll explore these issues and look at selections that will help us answer one of the questions most fundamental to American identity: To what extent is America a nation that practices religious tolerance and freedom?

Sources

Kenneth C. Davis, *America's True History of Religious Tolerance* (2010)

James Madison, from *Memorial and Remonstrance against Religious Assessments* (1785)

Thomas Jefferson, *The Virginia Act for Establishing Religious Freedom* (1779)

George Washington, *To the Hebrew Congregation in Newport, Rhode Island* (1790)

Red Jacket, *Defense of Native American Religion* (1805)

John F. Kennedy, *Address to the Greater Houston Ministerial Association* (1960)

Jeff Jacoby, *The Role of Religion in Government: Invoking Jesus at the Inauguration* (2001)

Diane L. Eck, from *A New Religious America: How a "Christian Country" Has Become the World's Most Religiously Diverse Nation* (2001)

Gary Tramontina, *Ten Commandments Courthouse Controversy* (2003)

Michael Bloomberg, *Ground Zero Mosque Speech* (2010)

John Fea, from *Was America Founded as a Christian Nation?* (2011)

America's True History of Religious Tolerance

Kenneth C. Davis

> Kenneth C. Davis is the best-selling author of the Don't Know Much about History series. The following essay appeared in the October 2010 issue of *Smithsonian* magazine.

Wading into the controversy surrounding an Islamic center planned for a site near New York City's Ground Zero memorial this past August, President Obama declared: "This is America. And our commitment to religious freedom must be unshakeable. The principle that people of all faiths are welcome in this country and that they will not be treated differently by their government is essential to who we are." In doing so, he paid homage to a vision that politicians and preachers have extolled for more than two centuries — that America historically has been a place of religious tolerance. It was a sentiment George Washington voiced shortly after taking the oath of office just a few blocks from Ground Zero.

But is it so?

In the storybook version most of us learned in school, the Pilgrims came to America aboard the *Mayflower* in search of religious freedom in 1620. The Puritans soon followed, for the same reason. Ever since these religious dissidents arrived at their shining "city upon a hill," as their governor John Winthrop called it, millions from around the world have done the same, coming to an America where they found a welcome melting pot in which everyone was free to practice his or her own faith.

The problem is that this tidy narrative is an American myth. The real story of religion in America's past is an often awkward, frequently embarrassing and occasionally bloody tale that most civics books and high-school texts either paper over or shunt to the side. And much of the recent conversation about America's ideal of religious freedom has paid lip service to this comforting tableau.

From the earliest arrival of Europeans on America's shores, religion has often   5
been a cudgel, used to discriminate, suppress and even kill the foreign, the "heretic" and the "unbeliever" — including the "heathen" natives already here. Moreover, while it is true that the vast majority of early-generation Americans were Christian, the pitched battles between various Protestant sects and, more explosively, between Protestants and Catholics, present an unavoidable contradiction to the widely held notion that America is a "Christian nation."

First, a little overlooked history: the initial encounter between Europeans in the future United States came with the establishment of a Huguenot (French Protestant) colony in 1564 at Fort Caroline (near modern Jacksonville, Florida). More than half a century before the *Mayflower* set sail, French pilgrims had come to America in search of religious freedom.

The Spanish had other ideas. In 1565, they established a forward operating base at St. Augustine and proceeded to wipe out the Fort Caroline colony. The Spanish commander, Pedro Menéndez de Avilés, wrote to the Spanish King Philip II that he had "hanged all those we had found in [Fort Caroline] because . . . they were scattering the odious Lutheran doctrine in these Provinces." When hundreds of survivors of a shipwrecked French fleet washed up on the beaches of Florida, they were put to the sword, beside a river the Spanish called Matanzas ("slaughters"). In other words, the first encounter between European Christians in America ended in a blood bath.

The much-ballyhooed arrival of the Pilgrims and Puritans in New England in the early 1600s was indeed a response to persecution that these religious dissenters had experienced in England. But the Puritan fathers of the Massachusetts Bay

Colony did not countenance tolerance of opposing religious views. Their "city upon a hill" was a theocracy that brooked no dissent, religious or political.

The most famous dissidents within the Puritan community, Roger Williams and Anne Hutchinson, were banished following disagreements over theology and policy. From Puritan Boston's earliest days, Catholics ("Papists") were anathema and were banned from the colonies, along with other non-Puritans. Four Quakers were hanged in Boston between 1659 and 1661 for persistently returning to the city to stand up for their beliefs.

Throughout the colonial era, Anglo-American antipathy toward Catholics — especially French and Spanish Catholics — was pronounced and often reflected in the sermons of such famous clerics as Cotton Mather and in statutes that discriminated against Catholics in matters of property and voting. Anti-Catholic feelings even contributed to the revolutionary mood in America after King George III extended an olive branch to French Catholics in Canada with the Quebec Act of 1774, which recognized their religion.   10

When George Washington dispatched Benedict Arnold on a mission to court French Canadians' support for the American Revolution in 1775, he cautioned Arnold not to let their religion get in the way. "Prudence, policy and a true Christian Spirit," Washington advised, "will lead us to look with compassion upon their errors, without insulting them." (After Arnold betrayed the American cause, he publicly cited America's alliance with Catholic France as one of his reasons for doing so.)

In newly independent America, there was a crazy quilt of state laws regarding religion. In Massachusetts, only Christians were allowed to hold public office, and Catholics were allowed to do so only after renouncing papal authority. In 1777, New York State's constitution banned Catholics from public office (and would do so until 1806). In Maryland, Catholics had full civil rights, but Jews did not. Delaware required an oath affirming belief in the Trinity. Several states, including Massachusetts and South Carolina, had official, state-supported churches.

In 1779, as Virginia's governor, Thomas Jefferson had drafted a bill that guaranteed legal equality for citizens of all religions — including those of no religion — in the state. It was around then that Jefferson famously wrote, "But it does me no injury for my neighbor to say there are twenty gods or no God. It neither picks my pocket nor breaks my leg." But Jefferson's plan did not advance — until after Patrick ("Give Me Liberty or Give Me Death") Henry introduced a bill in 1784 calling for state support for "teachers of the Christian religion."

Future president James Madison stepped into the breach. In a carefully argued essay titled "Memorial and Remonstrance Against Religious Assessments," the soon-to-be father of the Constitution eloquently laid out reasons why the state had no business supporting Christian instruction. Signed by some 2,000 Virginians, Madison's argument became a fundamental piece of American political philosophy, a ringing endorsement of the secular state that "should be as familiar to students of American history as the Declaration of Independence and the Constitution," as Susan Jacoby has written in *Freethinkers*, her excellent history of American secularism.

Among Madison's 15 points was his declaration that "the Religion then of every 15 man must be left to the conviction and conscience of every . . . man to exercise it as these may dictate. This right is in its nature an unalienable right."

Madison also made a point that any believer of any religion should understand: that the government sanction of a religion was, in essence, a threat to religion. "Who does not see," he wrote, "that the same authority which can establish Christianity, in exclusion of all other Religions, may establish with the same ease any particular sect of Christians, in exclusion of all other Sects?" Madison was writing from his memory of Baptist ministers being arrested in his native Virginia.

As a Christian, Madison also noted that Christianity had spread in the face of persecution from worldly powers, not with their help. Christianity, he contended, "disavows a dependence on the powers of this world . . . for it is known that this Religion both existed and flourished, not only without the support of human laws, but in spite of every opposition from them."

Recognizing the idea of America as a refuge for the protester or rebel, Madison also argued that Henry's proposal was "a departure from that generous policy, which offering an Asylum to the persecuted and oppressed of every Nation and Religion, promised a lustre to our country."

After long debate, Patrick Henry's bill was defeated, with the opposition outnumbering supporters 12 to 1. Instead, the Virginia legislature took up Jefferson's plan for the separation of church and state. In 1786, the Virginia Act for Establishing Religious Freedom, modified somewhat from Jefferson's original draft, became law. The act is one of three accomplishments Jefferson included on his tombstone, along with writing the Declaration and founding the University of Virginia. (He omitted his presidency of the United States.) After the bill was passed, Jefferson proudly wrote that the law "meant to comprehend, within the mantle of its protection, the Jew, the Gentile, the Christian and the Mahometan, the Hindoo and Infidel of every denomination."

Madison wanted Jefferson's view to become the law of the land when he went to 20 the Constitutional Convention in Philadelphia in 1787. And as framed in Philadelphia that year, the U.S. Constitution clearly stated in Article VI that federal elective and appointed officials "shall be bound by Oath or Affirmation, to support this Constitution, but no religious Test shall ever be required as a Qualification to any Office or public Trust under the United States."

This passage — along with the facts that the Constitution does not mention God or a deity (except for a pro forma "year of our Lord" date) and that its very first amendment forbids Congress from making laws that would infringe of the free exercise of religion — attests to the founders' resolve that America be a secular republic. The men who fought the Revolution may have thanked Providence and attended church regularly — or not. But they also fought a war against a country in which the head of state was the head of the church. Knowing well the history of religious warfare that led to America's settlement, they clearly understood both the dangers of that system and of sectarian conflict.

It was the recognition of that divisive past by the founders — notably Washington, Jefferson, Adams, and Madison — that secured America as a secular republic. As president, Washington wrote in 1790: "All possess alike liberty of conscience and immunity of citizenship. . . . For happily the Government of the United States, which gives to bigotry no sanction, to persecution no assistance, requires only that they who live under its protection, should demean themselves as good citizens."

He was addressing the members of America's oldest synagogue, the Touro Synagogue in Newport, Rhode Island (where his letter is read aloud every August). In closing, he wrote specifically to the Jews a phrase that applies to Muslims as well: "May the children of the Stock of Abraham, who dwell in this land, continue to merit and enjoy the good will of the other inhabitants, while every one shall sit in safety under his own vine and fig tree, and there shall be none to make him afraid."

As for Adams and Jefferson, they would disagree vehemently over policy, but on the question of religious freedom they were united. "In their seventies," Jacoby writes, "with a friendship that had survived serious political conflicts, Adams and Jefferson could look back with satisfaction on what they both considered their greatest achievement — their role in establishing a secular government whose legislators would never be required, or permitted, to rule on the legality of theological views."

Late in his life, James Madison wrote a letter summarizing his views: "And I have no doubt that every new example, will succeed, as every past one has done, in shewing that religion & Govt. will both exist in greater purity, the less they are mixed together." 25

While some of America's early leaders were models of virtuous tolerance, American attitudes were slow to change. The anti-Catholicism of America's Calvinist past found new voice in the 19th century. The belief widely held and preached by some of the most prominent ministers in America was that Catholics would, if permitted, turn America over to the pope. Anti-Catholic venom was part of the typical American school day, along with Bible readings. In Massachusetts, a convent — coincidentally near the site of the Bunker Hill Monument — was burned to the ground in 1834 by an anti-Catholic mob incited by reports that young women were being abused in the convent school. In Philadelphia, the City of Brotherly Love, anti-Catholic sentiment, combined with the country's anti-immigrant mood, fueled the Bible Riots of 1844, in which houses were torched, two Catholic churches were destroyed and at least 20 people were killed.

At about the same time, Joseph Smith founded a new American religion — and soon met with the wrath of the mainstream Protestant majority. In 1832, a mob tarred and feathered him, marking the beginning of a long battle between Christian America and Smith's Mormonism. In October 1838, after a series of conflicts over land and religious tension, Missouri Governor Lilburn Boggs ordered that all Mormons be expelled from his state. Three days later, rogue militiamen massacred 17 church members, including children, at the Mormon settlement of Haun's Mill. In 1844, a mob murdered Joseph Smith and his brother Hyrum while they were jailed in Carthage, Illinois. No one was ever convicted of the crime.

Even as late as 1960, Catholic presidential candidate John F. Kennedy felt compelled to make a major speech declaring that his loyalty was to America, not the pope. (And as recently as the 2008 Republican primary campaign, Mormon candidate Mitt Romney felt compelled to address the suspicions still directed toward the Church of Jesus Christ of Latter-day Saints.) Of course, America's anti-Semitism was practiced institutionally as well as socially for decades. With the great threat of "godless" Communism looming in the 1950s, the country's fear of atheism also reached new heights.

America can still be, as Madison perceived the nation in 1785, "an Asylum to the persecuted and oppressed of every Nation and Religion." But recognizing that deep religious discord has been part of America's social DNA is a healthy and necessary step. When we acknowledge that dark past, perhaps the nation will return to that "promised . . . lustre" of which Madison so grandiloquently wrote.

(2010)

Questions

1. What is Kenneth C. Davis's essay occasioned by? How does that incident serve to highlight the issue he addresses?
2. Davis refers to the idea that "America historically has been a place of religious tolerance" (par. 1) as "an American myth" (par. 4). What evidence does he provide to support that characterization? How convincing is it?
3. Davis discusses an early history of divisiveness in America and states: "It was the recognition of that divisive past by the founders — notably Washington, Jefferson, Adams, and Madison — that secured America as a secular republic" (par. 22). Whether America is or is not a secular nation is a much-debated topic. Do you think that it is? Why or why not?
4. Davis provides examples of anti-Catholicism, anti-Semitism, and anti-Mormonism. What other instances of religious intolerance do you know of? Which are prominent today?
5. How would you characterize Davis's perspective in the final paragraph? Do you agree with it? Why or why not?

from *Memorial and Remonstrance against Religious Assessments*

James Madison

In 1785, James Madison, co-author of the *Federalist* papers and future president of the United States, published a reaction to Patrick Henry's proposed Assessment Bill, which would have provided public funding for Anglican ministers. Following is an excerpt.

To the Honorable the General Assembly of the Commonwealth of Virginia
A Memorial and Remonstrance Against Religious Assessments

We the subscribers, citizens of the said Commonwealth, having taken into serious consideration, a Bill printed by order of the last Session of General Assembly, entitled "A Bill establishing a provision for Teachers of the Christian Religion," and conceiving that the same if finally armed with the sanctions of a law, will be a dangerous abuse of power, are bound as faithful members of a free State to remonstrate against it, and to declare the reasons by which we are determined. We remonstrate against the said Bill,

1. **Because** we hold it for a fundamental and undeniable truth, "that religion or the duty which we owe to our Creator and the manner of discharging it, can be directed only by reason and conviction, not by force or violence." The Religion then of every man must be left to the conviction and conscience of every man; and it is the right of every man to exercise it as these may dictate. This right is in its nature an unalienable right. It is unalienable, because the opinions of men, depending only on the evidence contemplated by their own minds cannot follow the dictates of other men: It is unalienable also, because what is here a right towards men, is a duty towards the Creator. It is the duty of every man to render to the Creator such homage and such only as he believes to be acceptable to him. This duty is precedent, both in order of time and in degree of obligation, to the claims of Civil Society. Before any man can be considerd as a member of Civil Society, he must be considered as a subject of the Governour of the Universe: And if a member of Civil Society, who enters into any subordinate Association, must always do it with a reservation of his duty to the General Authority; much more must every man who becomes a member of any particular Civil Society, do it with a saving of his allegiance to the Universal Sovereign. We maintain therefore that in matters of Religion, no man's right is abridged by the institution of Civil Society and that Religion is wholly exempt from its cognizance. True it is, that no other rule exists, by which any question which may divide a Society, can be ultimately determined, but the will of the majority; but it is also true that the majority may trespass on the rights of the minority.

2. **Because** Religion be exempt from the authority of the Society at large, still less can it be subject to that of the Legislative Body. The latter are but the creatures and vicegerents of the former. Their jurisdiction is both derivative and limited: it is limited with regard to the co-ordinate departments, more necessarily is it limited with regard to the constituents. The preservation of a free Government requires not merely, that the metes and bounds which separate each department of power be invariably maintained; but more especially that neither of them be suffered to overleap the great Barrier which defends the rights of the people. The Rulers who are guilty of such an encroachment, exceed the commission from which they derive their authority, and are Tyrants. The People who submit to it are governed by laws made neither by themselves nor by an authority derived from them, and are slaves.

3. **Because** it is proper to take alarm at the first experiment on our liberties. We hold this prudent jealousy to be the first duty of Citizens, and one of the noblest

characteristics of the late Revolution. The free men of America did not wait till usurped power had strengthened itself by exercise, and entangled the question in precedents. They saw all the consequences in the principle, and they avoided the consequences by denying the principle. We revere this lesson too much soon to forget it. Who does not see that the same authority which can establish Christianity, in exclusion of all other Religions, may establish with the same ease any particular sect of Christians, in exclusion of all other Sects? that the same authority which can force a citizen to contribute three pence only of his property for the support of any one establishment, may force him to conform to any other establishment in all cases whatsoever?

4. **Because** the Bill violates the equality which ought to be the basis of every law, and which is more indispensible, in proportion as the validity or expediency of any law is more liable to be impeached. If "all men are by nature equally free and independent," all men are to be considered as entering into Society on equal conditions; as relinquishing no more, and therefore retaining no less, one than another, of their natural rights. Above all are they to be considered as retaining an "equal title to the free exercise of Religion according to the dictates of Conscience." Whilst we assert for ourselves a freedom to embrace, to profess and to observe the Religion which we believe to be of divine origin, we cannot deny an equal freedom to those whose minds have not yet yielded to the evidence which has convinced us. If this freedom be abused, it is an offence against God, not against man: To God, therefore, not to man, must an account of it be rendered. As the Bill violates equality by subjecting some to peculiar burdens, so it violates the same principle, by granting to others peculiar exemptions. Are the quakers and Menonists the only sects who think a compulsive support of their Religions unnecessary and unwarrantable? can their piety alone be entrusted with the care of public worship? Ought their Religions to be endowed above all others with extraordinary privileges by which proselytes may be enticed from all others? We think too favorably of the justice and good sense of these demoninations to believe that they either covet pre-eminences over their fellow citizens or that they will be seduced by them from the common opposition to the measure.

5. **Because** the Bill implies either that the Civil Magistrate is a competent Judge of Religious Truth; or that he may employ Religion as an engine of Civil policy. The first is an arrogant pretension falsified by the contradictory opinions of Rulers in all ages, and throughout the world: the second an unhallowed perversion of the means of salvation.

6. **Because** the establishment proposed by the Bill is not requisite for the support of the Christian Religion. To say that it is, is a contradiction to the Christian Religion itself, for every page of it disavows a dependence on the powers of this world: it is a contradiction to fact; for it is known that this Religion both existed and flourished, not only without the support of human laws, but in spite of every opposition from them, and not only during the period of miraculous aid, but long after it had been left to its own evidence and the ordinary care of Providence. Nay, it is a contradiction in terms; for a Religion not invented by human policy,

must have pre-existed and been supported, before it was established by human policy. It is moreover to weaken in those who profess this Religion a pious confidence in its innate excellence and the patronage of its Author; and to foster in those who still reject it, a suspicion that its friends are too conscious of its fallacies to trust it to its own merits.

7. **Because** experience witnesseth that eccelsiastical establishments, instead of maintaining the purity and efficacy of Religion, have had a contrary operation. During almost fifteen centuries has the legal establishment of Christianity been on trial. What have been its fruits? More or less in all places, pride and indolence in the Clergy, ignorance and servility in the laity, in both, superstition, bigotry and persecution. Enquire of the Teachers of Christianity for the ages in which it appeared in its greatest lustre; those of every sect, point to the ages prior to its incorporation with Civil policy. Propose a restoration of this primitive State in which its Teachers depended on the voluntary rewards of their flocks, many of them predict its downfall. On which Side ought their testimony to have greatest weight, when for or when against their interest?

8. **Because** the establishment in question is not necessary for the support of Civil Government. If it be urged as necessary for the support of Civil Government only as it is a means of supporting Religion, and it be not necessary for the latter purpose, it cannot be necessary for the former. If Religion be not within the cognizance of Civil Government how can its legal establishment be necessary to Civil Government? What influence in fact have ecclesiastical establishments had on Civil Society? In some instances they have been seen to erect a spiritual tyranny on the ruins of the Civil authority; in many instances they have been seen upholding the thrones of political tyranny: in no instance have they been seen the guardians of the liberties of the people. Rulers who wished to subvert the public liberty, may have found an established Clergy convenient auxiliaries. A just Government instituted to secure & perpetuate it needs them not. Such a Government will be best supported by protecting every Citizen in the enjoyment of his Religion with the same equal hand which protects his person and his property; by neither invading the equal rights of any Sect, nor suffering any Sect to invade those of another.

(1785)

Questions

1. What is a remonstrance? What is James Madison's purpose in calling this piece by that name?
2. How does Madison characterize religious rights in sections 1 and 2?
3. What fear does he address with the rhetorical questions in section 3?
4. In section 4, Madison writes, "As the Bill violates equality by subjecting some to peculiar burdens, so it violates the same principle, by granting to others peculiar exemptions." What does he mean by this? Do you agree?

5. In section 8, how does Madison compare government protection of a citizen's religion with that of "his person and his property"? Is it a reasonable comparison? Explain.
6. Currently, religious institutions receive tax breaks from the government. Are such exemptions in violation of Madison's principles? Explain.

The Virginia Act for Establishing Religious Freedom

THOMAS JEFFERSON

> The following bill was written in 1779 and passed in 1786. On his tombstone, Jefferson cited composing it along with establishing the University of Virginia and writing the Declaration of Independence as his three crowning achievements (and neglected to mention his tenure as an American president).

I.

Whereas Almighty God hath created the mind free; that all attempts to influence it by temporal punishments or burdens, or by civil incapacitations, tend only to beget habits of hypocrisy and meanness, and are a departure from the plan of the Holy Author of our religion, who being Lord both of body and mind, yet chose not to propagate it by coercions on either, as was in his Almighty power to do; that the impious presumption of legislators and rulers, civil as well as ecclesiastical, who, being themselves but fallible and uninspired men, have assumed dominion over the faith of others, setting up their own opinions and modes of thinking as the only true and infallible, and as such endeavoring to impose them on others, hath established and maintained false religions over the greatest part of the world, and through all time; that to compel a man to furnish contributions of money for the propagation of opinions which he disbelieves, is sinful and tyrannical; that even the forcing him to support this or that teacher of his own religious persuasion, is depriving him of the comfortable liberty of giving his contributions to the particular pastor whose morals he would make his pattern, and whose powers he feels most persuasive to righteousness, and is withdrawing from the ministry those temporal rewards, which proceeding from an approbation of their personal conduct, are an additional incite-ment to earnest and unremitting labors for the instruction of mankind; that our civil rights have no dependence on our religious opinions, more than our opinions in physics or geometry; that, therefore, the proscribing any citizen as unworthy the public confidence by laying upon him an incapacity of being called to the offices of trust and emolument, unless he profess or renounce this or that religious opinion, is depriving him injuriously of those privileges and advantages to which in common with his fellow citizens he has a natural right; that it tends also to corrupt the prin-ciples of that very religion it is meant to encourage, by bribing, with a monopoly of worldly honors and emoluments, those who will externally profess and conform to it; that though indeed these are criminal who do not withstand such temptation, yet neither are those innocent who lay the bait in their way; that to suffer the civil magistrate to intrude his powers into the field of opinion and to restrain the profession or propagation of principles, on the supposition of their ill tendency, is a dangerous fallacy, which at once destroys all religious liberty, because he being of course judge of that tendency, will make his opinions the rule of judgment, and approve or condemn the sentiments of others only as they shall square with or differ from his own; that it is time enough for the rightful purposes of civil government, for its officers to interfere when principles break out into overt acts against peace and good order; and finally, that truth is great and will prevail if left to herself, that she is the proper and sufficient antagonist to error, and has nothing to fear from the conflict, unless by human interposition disarmed of her natural weapons, free argument and debate, errors ceasing to be dangerous when it is permitted freely to contradict them.

II.

Be it therefore enacted by the General Assembly, That no man shall be compelled to frequent or support any religious worship, place, or ministry whatsoever, nor shall be enforced, restrained, molested, or burdened in his body or goods, nor shall otherwise suffer on account of his religious opinions or belief; but that all men shall be free to profess, and by argument to maintain, their opinions in matters of religion, and that the same shall in nowise diminish, enlarge, or affect their civil capacities.

III.

And though we well know this Assembly, elected by the people for the ordinary purposes of legislation only, have no power to restrain the acts of succeeding Assemblies constituted with powers equal to our own and that therefore to declare this act irrevocable would be of no effect in law, yet we are free to declare, and do declare, that the rights hereby asserted are of the natural rights of mankind, and that if any act shall be hereafter passed to repeal the present or to narrow its operation, such act will be an infringement of natural right.

(1779)

Questions

1. In a succession of noun clauses, section 1 of the bill lists fifteen propositions of which the General Assembly of Virginia is aware and proffers them as reasons to adopt the bill. Select the three that you see as most compelling and explain why.
2. How would you paraphrase section 2?
3. What does section 3 add to the bill? What is Thomas Jefferson's purpose in including it?

To the Hebrew Congregation in Newport, Rhode Island

GEORGE WASHINGTON

> In 1790, Moses Seixas, warden of the Hebrew Congregation in Newport, Rhode Island, wrote to President George Washington. In his letter, he praised the "Government, which to bigotry gives no sanction, to persecution no assistance, . . . this so ample and extensive Federal Union whose basis is Philanthropy, Mutual confidence and Public Virtue," and gratefully welcomed Washington to Newport. The following letter is the president's response.

Gentlemen:

While I receive with much satisfaction, your Address replete with expressions of affection and esteem, I rejoice in the opportunity of answering you, that I shall always retain, a grateful remembrance of the cordial welcome I experienced in my visit to Newport, from all classes of Citizens.

The reflection on the days of difficulty and danger which are past, is rendered the more sweet, from a consciousness that they are succeeded by days of uncommon prosperity and security. If we have wisdom to make the best use of the advantages with which we are now favored, we cannot fail, under the just administration of a good Government, to become a great and a happy people.

The Citizens of the United States of America have a right to applaud themselves for having given to mankind examples of an enlarged and liberal policy: a policy worthy of imitation. All possess alike liberty of conscience and immunities of citizenship. It is now no more that toleration is spoken of, as if it was by the indulgence of one class of people, that another enjoyed the exercise of their inherent natural rights. For happily the Government of the United States, which gives to bigotry no sanction, to persecution no assistance, requires only that they who live under its protection, should demean themselves as good citizens, in giving it on all occasions their effectual support. It would be inconsistent with the frankness of my character not to avow that I am pleased with your favorable opinion of my administration, and fervent wishes for my felicity. May the Children of the Stock of Abraham, who dwell in this land, continue to merit and enjoy the good will of the other inhabitants, while every one shall sit in safety under his own vine and fig tree, and there shall be none to make him afraid. May the father of all mercies scatter light and not darkness in our paths, and make us all in our several vocations useful here, and in his own due time and way everlastingly happy.

George Washington
(1790)

Questions

1. What is George Washington's purpose in responding the way he does?
2. What does Washington mean by the "immunities of citizenship" (par. 3)?

3. Washington writes, in 1790, that "[i]t is now no more that toleration is spoken of" and that the government "gives to bigotry no sanction, to persecution no assistance" (par. 3). To what extent was that so then? Is it so today?

Defense of Native American Religion

RED JACKET

> Chief Sagoyewatha of the Senecas, members of the Iroquois Confederation, was known as Red Jacket from his habit of wearing red coats given to him by the British, on whose side the Senecas fought in the American Revolution. After the war, Red Jacket, acting as a mediator between the U.S. government and the Senecas, led a delegation that met with George Washington.
>
> The text below is his response to a Boston missionary society that wanted to proselytize among the Iroquois.

Friend and brother; it was the will of the Great Spirit that we should meet together this day. He orders all things, and he has given us a fine day for our council. He has taken his garment from before the sun, and caused it to shine with brightness upon us; our eyes are opened, that we see clearly; our ears are unstopped, that we have been able to hear distinctly the words that you have spoken; for all these favors we thank the Great Spirit, and him only.

Brother, this council fire was kindled by you; it was at your request that we came together at this time; we have listened with attention to what you have said. You requested us to speak our minds freely; this gives us great joy, for we now consider that we stand upright before you, and can speak what we think; all have heard your voice, and all speak to you as one man; our minds are agreed.

Brother, you say you want an answer to your talk before you leave this place. It is right you should have one, as you are a great distance from home, and we do not wish to detain you; but we will first look back a little, and tell you what our fathers have told us, and what we have heard from the white people.

Brother, listen to what we say. There was a time when our forefathers owned this great island. Their seats extended from the rising to the setting sun. The Great Spirit had made it for the use of Indians. He had created the buffalo, the deer, and other animals for food. He made the bear and the beaver, and their skins served us for clothing. He had scattered them over the country, and taught us how to take them. He had caused the earth to produce corn for bread. All this he had done for his red children because he loved them. If we had any disputes about hunting grounds, they were generally settled without the shedding of much blood. But an evil day came upon us; your forefathers crossed the great waters, and landed on this island. Their numbers were small; they found friends, and not enemies; they told us they had fled from their own country for fear of wicked men, and come here to enjoy their religion. They asked for a small seat; we took pity on them, granted their request, and they sat down amongst us; we gave them corn and meat; they gave us poison in return. The white people had now found our country; tidings were carried back, and more came amongst us; yet we did not fear them, we took them to be friends; they called us brothers; we believed them, and gave them a larger seat. At length, their numbers had greatly increased; they wanted more land; they wanted our country. Our eyes were opened, and our minds became uneasy. Wars took place; Indians were hired to fight against Indians, and many of our people were destroyed. They also brought strong liquor among us; it was strong and powerful, and has slain thousands.

Brother, our seats were once large, and yours were very small; you have now   5 become a great people, and we have scarcely a place left to spread our blankets; you have got our country, but are not satisfied; you want to force your religion upon us.

Brother, continue to listen. You say you are sent to instruct us how to worship the Great Spirit agreeably to his mind, and if we do not take hold of the religion which you white people teach, we shall be unhappy hereafter. You say that you are right, and we are lost; how do we know this to be true? We understand that your religion is written in a book; if it was intended for us as well as you, why has not the Great Spirit given it to us, and not only to us, but why did he not give to our forefathers the knowledge of that book, with the means of understanding it rightly? We only know what you tell us about it. How shall we know when to believe, being so often deceived by the white people?

Brother, you say there is but one way to worship and serve the Great Spirit; if there is but one religion, why do you white people differ so much about it? Why not all agree, as you can all read the book?

Brother, we do not understand these things. We are told that your religion was given to your forefathers, and has been handed down from father to son. We also have a religion which was given to our forefathers, and has been handed down to us their children. We worship that way. It teacheth us to be thankful for all the favors we receive; to love each other, and to be united. We never quarrel about religion.

Brother, the Great Spirit has made us all; but he has made a great difference between his white and red children; he has given us a different complexion, and different customs; to you he has given the arts; to these he has not opened our eyes; we know these things to be true. Since he has made so great a difference between us in other things, why may we not conclude that he has given us a different religion according to our understanding. The Great Spirit does right; he knows what is best for his children; we are satisfied.

Brother, we do not wish to destroy your religion, or take it from you; we only   10 want to enjoy our own.

Brother, you say you have not come to get our land or our money, but to enlighten our minds. I will now tell you that I have been at your meetings, and saw you collecting money from the meeting. I cannot tell what this money was intended for, but suppose it was for your minister; and if we should conform to your way of thinking, perhaps you may want some from us.

Brother, we are told that you have been preaching to the white people in this place. These people are our neighbors; we are acquainted with them; we will wait a little while and see what effect your preaching has upon them. If we find it does them good, makes them honest and less disposed to cheat Indians, we will then consider again what you have said.

Brother, you have now heard our answer to your talk, and this is all we have to say at present. As we are going to part, we will come and take you by the hand, and hope the Great Spirit will protect you on your journey, and return you safe to your friends.

(1805)

Questions

1. Notice how Red Jacket begins each paragraph. How does this approach appeal to both ethos and pathos?
2. How would you characterize Red Jacket's tone in the second and third paragraphs?
3. What is Red Jacket's rhetorical purpose in paragraphs 6 through 12, where he says "we are told" and repeats the phrase "you say" several times. How does this repetition serve his purpose?
4. How effectively does Red Jacket use rhetorical questions? Imagine the audience's response to each of them.
5. Near the end, Red Jacket makes a promise. Is it a sincere one? Is it similar to a rhetorical question, in that Red Jacket already knows the result of what he suggests? Explain.
6. What does Red Jacket's speech say about religious tolerance in America? Explain.

Address to the Greater Houston Ministerial Association

John F. Kennedy

On September 12, 1960, the then presidential candidate John F. Kennedy delivered the following speech to the Greater Houston Ministerial Association. Kennedy would become the first Roman Catholic to be elected president of the United States.

Reverend Meza, Reverend Reck, I'm grateful for your generous invitation to state my views.

While the so-called religious issue is necessarily and properly the chief topic here tonight, I want to emphasize from the outset that I believe that we have far more critical issues in the 1960 campaign; the spread of Communist influence, until it now festers only 90 miles from the coast of Florida—the humiliating treatment of our President and Vice President by those who no longer respect our power—the hungry children I saw in West Virginia, the old people who cannot pay their doctors' bills, the families forced to give up their farms—an America with too many slums, with too few schools, and too late to the moon and outer space. These are the real issues which should decide this campaign. And they are not religious issues — for war and hunger and ignorance and despair know no religious barrier.

But because I am a Catholic, and no Catholic has ever been elected President, the real issues in this campaign have been obscured — perhaps deliberately, in some quarters less responsible than this. So it is apparently necessary for me to state once again — not what kind of church I believe in, for that should be important only to me — but what kind of America I believe in.

I believe in an America where the separation of church and state is absolute; where no Catholic prelate would tell the President — should he be Catholic — how to act, and no Protestant minister would tell his parishioners for whom to vote; where no church or church school is granted any public funds or political preference, and where no man is denied public office merely because his religion differs from the President who might appoint him, or the people who might elect him.

I believe in an America that is officially neither Catholic, Protestant, nor Jewish;   5 where no public official either requests or accepts instructions on public policy from the Pope, the National Council of Churches, or any other ecclesiastical source; where no religious body seeks to impose its will directly or indirectly upon the general populace or the public acts of its officials; and where religious liberty is so indivisible that an act against one church is treated as an act against all.

For while this year it may be a Catholic against whom the finger of suspicion is pointed, in other years it has been — and may someday be again — a Jew, or a Quaker, or a Unitarian, or a Baptist. It was Virginia's harassment of Baptist preachers, for example, that led to Jefferson's statute of religious freedom. Today, I may be the victim, but tomorrow it may be you — until the whole fabric of our harmonious society is ripped apart at a time of great national peril.

Finally, I believe in an America where religious intolerance will someday end, where all men and all churches are treated as equals, where every man has the same right to attend or not to attend the church of his choice, where there is no Catholic vote, no anti-Catholic vote, no bloc voting of any kind, and where Catholics, Protestants, and Jews, at both the lay and the pastoral levels, will refrain from those attitudes of disdain and division which have so often marred their works in the past, and promote instead the American ideal of brotherhood.

That is the kind of America in which I believe. And it represents the kind of Presidency in which I believe, a great office that must be neither humbled by making it the instrument of any religious group nor tarnished by arbitrarily withholding its occupancy from the members of any one religious group. I believe in a President whose views on religion are his own private affair, neither imposed upon him by the nation, nor imposed by the nation upon him as a condition to holding that office.

I would not look with favor upon a President working to subvert the First Amendment's guarantees of religious liberty; nor would our system of checks and balances permit him to do so. And neither do I look with favor upon those who would work to subvert Article VI of the Constitution by requiring a religious test — even by indirection — for if they disagree with that safeguard, they should be openly working to repeal it.

I want a Chief Executive whose public acts are responsible to all and obligated to   10
none, who can attend any ceremony, service, or dinner his office may appropriately
require of him; and whose fulfillment of his presidential office is not limited or conditioned by any religious oath, ritual, or obligation.

This is the kind of America I believe in — and this is the kind of America I fought
for in the South Pacific, and the kind my brother died for in Europe. No one suggested then that we might have a "divided loyalty," that we did "not believe in liberty,"
or that we belonged to a disloyal group that threatened — I quote — "the freedoms for
which our forefathers died."

And in fact this is the kind of America for which our forefathers did die when
they fled here to escape religious test oaths that denied office to members of less
favored churches — when they fought for the Constitution, the Bill of Rights, the
Virginia Statute of Religious Freedom — and when they fought at the shrine I visited
today, the Alamo. For side by side with Bowie and Crockett died Fuentes, and
McCafferty, and Bailey, and Badillo, and Carey — but no one knows whether they
were Catholics or not. For there was no religious test there.

I ask you tonight to follow in that tradition — to judge me on the basis of 14 years
in the Congress, on my declared stands against an Ambassador to the Vatican, against
unconstitutional aid to parochial schools, and against any boycott of the public
schools — which I attended myself. And instead of doing this, do not judge me on the
basis of these pamphlets and publications we all have seen that carefully select quotations out of context from the statements of Catholic church leaders, usually in other
countries, frequently in other centuries, and rarely relevant to any situation here. And
always omitting, of course, the statement of the American Bishops in 1948 which
strongly endorsed Church-State separation, and which more nearly reflects the views
of almost every American Catholic.

I do not consider these other quotations binding upon my public acts. Why should
you?

But let me say, with respect to other countries, that I am wholly opposed to the   15
State being used by any religious group, Catholic or Protestant, to compel, prohibit,
or prosecute the free exercise of any other religion. And that goes for any persecution, at any time, by anyone, in any country. And I hope that you and I condemn with
equal fervor those nations which deny their Presidency to Protestants, and those
which deny it to Catholics. And rather than cite the misdeeds of those who differ, I
would also cite the record of the Catholic Church in such nations as France and
Ireland, and the independence of such statesmen as De Gaulle and Adenauer.

But let me stress again that these are my views.

For contrary to common newspaper usage, I am not the Catholic candidate for
President.

I am the Democratic Party's candidate for President who happens also to be a
Catholic.

I do not speak for my church on public matters; and the church does not speak
for me. Whatever issue may come before me as President, if I should be elected, on

birth control, divorce, censorship, gambling, or any other subject, I will make my decision in accordance with these views — in accordance with what my conscience tells me to be in the national interest, and without regard to outside religious pressure or dictates. And no power or threat of punishment could cause me to decide otherwise.

But if the time should ever come — and I do not concede any conflict to be 20 remotely possible — when my office would require me to either violate my conscience or violate the national interest, then I would resign the office; and I hope any other conscientious public servant would do likewise.

But I do not intend to apologize for these views to my critics of either Catholic or Protestant faith; nor do I intend to disavow either my views or my church in order to win this election.

If I should lose on the real issues, I shall return to my seat in the Senate, satisfied that I'd tried my best and was fairly judged.

But if this election is decided on the basis that 40 million Americans lost their chance of being President on the day they were baptized, then it is the whole nation that will be the loser, in the eyes of Catholics and non-Catholics around the world, in the eyes of history, and in the eyes of our own people.

But if, on the other hand, I should win this election, then I shall devote every effort of mind and spirit to fulfilling the oath of the Presidency — practically identical, I might add, with the oath I have taken for 14 years in the Congress. For without reservation, I can, and I quote, "solemnly swear that I will faithfully execute the office of President of the United States, and will to the best of my ability preserve, protect, and defend the Constitution — so help me God."

(1960)

Questions

1. What is the effect of beginning the speech with references to poverty, hunger, education, space, and the threat of war?
2. Does it seem surprising that an American presidential candidate should even think it necessary to address such an issue as John F. Kennedy does here? Do you believe, as Kennedy states, that a president's "views on religion are his own private affair" (par. 8)? Why or why not?
3. Kennedy describes several times the kind of America he believes in. Since the time of this speech, has America become that place?
4. Kennedy states, "For contrary to common newspaper usage, I am not the Catholic candidate for President. I am the Democratic Party's candidate for President who happens also to be a Catholic" (pars. 17–18). What is the distinction that he makes? Why is it important to make it?
5. How would you describe Kennedy's tone in the speech, especially toward its conclusion?

The Role of Religion in Government
Invoking Jesus at the Inauguration

JEFF JACOBY

> Jeff Jacoby (b. 1959) is a conservative columnist for the *Boston Globe*, whose columns are syndicated around the United States. The following editorial appeared in that newspaper on February 1, 2001, and in many other newspapers across the country thereafter.

Jesus was at the inauguration. Not everyone was pleased. While the Rev. Franklin Graham began his invocation with the nondenominational words of King David's last blessing — "Yours, O God, is the greatness and the power and the glory and the majesty and the splendor" — he ended with something more sectarian: "We pray this in the name of the Father, and of the Son, the Lord Jesus Christ, and of the Holy Spirit. Amen."

A second clergyman sounded a similar note. "We respectfully submit this humble prayer," the Rev. Kirbyjon Caldwell concluded his benediction, "in the name that's above all other names, Jesus the Christ. Let all who agree say 'amen.'"

But not all of us do agree. Some 15 percent of Americans are either non-Christian or nonbelievers and would find it impossible to answer "amen" to any prayer proclaiming the supremacy of Jesus. And so, you won't be surprised to hear, there were objections.

The inaugural prayers were "inappropriate and insensitive," says Barry Lynn, who heads Americans United for the Separation of Church and State. Caldwell's prayer in particular was "astonishing" for being so "exclusionary" — for creating "a two-tiered system for Americans: those able to say amen — Christians — and those who can't."

Alan Dershowitz is offended, too. "The first act by the new administration was in   5
defiance of our Constitution," he fumes in a *Los Angeles Times* column. The preachers' "parochial language" was a slap at Muslims, Jews, Buddhists, and others — a "plain message" that "Bush's America is a Christian nation and that non-Christians are welcome [only] as a tolerated minority rather than as fully equal citizens."

Equally outraged is the *New Republic*. It execrates the Jesus talk as "crushing Christological thuds" that "barred millions of Americans from their own amens," exposing as hollow "the spirit of inclusion in which the conservatives propound their religiosity."

No doubt this ire is sincere. Still, I wonder: Would Dershowitz or *TNR* have been as appalled by prayers in Jesus' name if Al Gore had been the one taking the oath? Or is open devotion to Jesus a problem only when it is associated with Republicans?

Think back to all the commentary, much of it mocking or disapproving, when Bush said during a debate that the thinker he most identified with was "Christ, because he changed my heart." But there was no distress — and no snickering — when Gore declared that the "bedrock" of his approach to "any important question" is to ask "WWJD . . . what would Jesus do?"

Nor do I recall any Dershowitz blast at the incoming Clinton administration in 1993 after the Rev. Billy Graham offered an inaugural prayer "in the name of the one who was called Wonderful Counselor, the mighty God, the everlasting Father, the Prince of Peace" (a passage from Isaiah that Christians read as a reference to Jesus). And when, at the 1997 Clinton-Gore inaugural, Graham prayed "in the name of the Father, the Son, and the Holy Spirit," the *New Republic* did not protest his "crushing Christological thuds."

I am not saying that all antipathy to Jesus-specific prayer is in reality just a disguise for antipathy to Republicans. I know from firsthand experience that many American Jews feel genuine unease when they hear appeals to Jesus, especially when they are uttered in an official setting. Some resent the reminder that they are different from their neighbors. Some, like Dershowitz, are offended by the implication that America is a Christian country, or that "normal" Americans embrace Christianity. Still others find Jesus-talk vaguely threatening, a hint that they are not really welcome here — perhaps, at some level, not really safe.

But none of these attitudes justifies telling Christians not to pray as Christians. Like it or not, American Jews — like American Muslims, Buddhists, Hindus, and atheists — are different from their neighbors. This is a Christian country — it was founded by Christians and built on broad Christian principles. Threatening? Far from it: It is in precisely this Christian country that Jews have known the most peaceful, prosperous, and successful existence in their long history.

In America, a non-Christian need not answer "amen" to an explicitly Christian prayer. This is a society where members of minority faiths live and worship without fear, secure in the hospitality and liberty America extends to all religions. If a rabbi, invited to deliver a public prayer, invoked "the God of our fathers Abraham, Isaac, and Jacob" — or if an imam opened "in the name of Allah, the merciful and compassionate" — no reasonable Christian would object. Why then should anyone take it amiss when a Christian prays in the name of Jesus?

Religious diversity does not mean no American should ever have to listen to prayers that are different from his own. On the contrary: It means no American should try to suppress the prayers of others. "Jesus" should not be a forbidden word in this land. Not even at a presidential inauguration.

(2001)

Questions

1. Why does Jeff Jacoby begin with such a dramatic opening statement? What is its rhetorical effect?
2. Is Reverend Graham's invocation truly "nondenominational," beginning with words from the Bible? What might a non-Christian or non-Jew think?
3. How does Jacoby characterize the critics of the inaugural prayers? Is he being fair? Is he extreme? Explain.
4. How do the concessions in paragraphs 7 and 10 contribute to Jacoby's argument?

5. Do you find it ironic or appropriate that a Jewish writer should take the position that Jacoby does? Explain.
6. Do you agree with Jacoby's explanation of what "religious diversity" (par. 13) means? Explain.

from *A New Religious America*
How a "Christian Country" Has Become the World's Most Religiously Diverse Nation

DIANE L. ECK

Diane L. Eck is professor of comparative religion at Harvard University. The following selection addresses the issue of religious practice in the workplace.

Working It Out: The Workplace and Religious Practice

One of the places we most commonly encounter religious difference in America today is the workplace. What religious attire may one wear? A cross? Yarmulke? Head scarf? Turban? Where and when is it appropriate to pray? What facilities do employers need to provide, and what policies do they need to implement? Religious difference is a question not just for theological schools and religious institutions but increasingly for businesses and corporations, offices and factories. These are the places where "we the people" most frequently meet, and how we manage our encounters here might be far more important than how we cope with imaginary encounters in the realm of theologies and beliefs.

The most common workplace issues have traditionally concerned working on the Sabbath, which is Saturday for Jews and Seventh-Day Adventists. Consider the case of a computer operator at a hospital in Fort Smith, Arkansas. Although he is a Seventh-Day Adventist and asked not to work on Saturdays, he was placed on call on Saturdays. When he refused to make himself available on his Sabbath, the hospital fired him. Title VII of the Civil Rights Act of 1964 prohibits discrimination on the basis of race, color, religion, national origin, or sex. In interpreting the act in relation to the religious practices of workers, the employer must try to make "reasonable accommodation" of religious practice, at least as long as it does not impose an "undue hardship" on the employer. In this case, the court ruled that the hospital was in violation of the Civil Rights Act. But just what constitutes "reasonable accommodation" and "undue hardship" is the thorny issue as each case comes forward.

In the past ten years the Equal Employment Opportunity Commission (EEOC), which considers workplace complaints that may violate the Civil Rights Act, has reported a 31 percent rise in complaints of religious discrimination in the workplace. This is not surprising, given the number of new immigrants in the workforce and the range of questions their attire, their holidays, and their religious life bring to the workplace environment. [In a previous chapter we] looked at the incivility and prejudice

Muslim women wearing the *hijah* may encounter. But sometimes incivility slides up the scale toward discrimination. For example, in 1996 Rose Hamid, a twelve-year veteran flight attendant with U.S. Air, became increasingly serious about her faith in the wake of some health problems and made the decision to wear a head scarf. Her first day at work, she was ordered to take it off because it was not part of the uniform of a flight attendant, and when she refused she was put on unpaid leave. Rose filed a complaint with the Equal Employment Opportunity Commission. What is reasonable accommodation in Rose's case? Rose had modeled different ways in which the colors of her uniform would be duplicated in her scarf, and some would argue that reasonable accommodation would mean allowing some flexibility in the uniform as long as it was readily recognizable. But U.S. Air moved Rose to a job that did not require a uniform and hence put her out of public visibility. The issue was resolved in a slightly different way by Domino's Pizza in 1998. That year, a convert to Islam who showed up at work wearing a head scarf was told by her employer at Domino's, "Unless you take that stupid thing off you have to leave."[1] The employer soon learned his response to her was more than just rude. It was against the law. Here, the Council on American Islamic Relations called attention to the case. The employers reached what they believed was a reasonable accommodation: wearing the signature Domino's baseball cap over a red and blue head scarf. . . .

Prayer in the workplace is another issue that has gained complexity with the new immigration. A Christian group might gather at 7:15 to pray together before work. A Buddhist meditation group might spend part of its lunch hour in sitting practice. In the spring of 1998 I received a CAIR bulletin with information on three similar cases of workplace prayer accommodation in manufacturing plants around Nashville. Whirlpool Corporation reportedly had refused to allow Muslim employees to offer obligatory prayers on the job. One Muslim employee quit, and the others continued to perform their obligatory midday prayer secretly during bathroom breaks. When CAIR intervened, contacted the managers, and began a dialogue, together they envisioned a solution: the Muslim employees could perhaps customize their coffee breaks so that they could fit an Islamic prayer schedule. Today, Muslim organizations, including CAIR, are taking the initiative in providing the kind of information that might head off the endless round of discrimination cases. They have published a booklet called *An Employer's Guide to Islamic Religious Practices*, detailing what employers might need to know about the obligations of Muslim workers. . . .

See You in Court

The American Constitution guarantees that there will be "no establishment" of religion and that the "free exercise" of religion will be protected. As we have seen, these twin principles have guided church-state relations in the United States for the past two hundred years. But the issues have become increasingly complex in a multi-religious America, where the church in question may now be the mosque, the

5

---

[1]Katherine Roth, "God on the Job," *Working Woman*, February 1998, 65.

Buddhist temple, the Hindu temple, or the Sikh gurdwara. Every religious tradition has its own questions. Can a Muslim schoolteacher wear her head covering on the job as a public school teacher? Can a Sikh student wear the *kirpan*, the symbolic knife required of all initiated Sikhs, to school, or a Sikh worker wear a turban on a hard-hat job, in apparent violation of safety regulations? Should a crèche be displayed in the Christmas season on public property? Can the sanctity of Native lands be protected from road building? Should the taking of peyote[2] by Native Americans be protected as the free exercise of religion? Can a city council pass an ordinance prohibiting the sacrifice of animals by the adherents of the Santería faith?

These difficult questions make clear that one vital arena of America's new pluralism is the courts. Since about 1960, church-state issues in America have been increasingly on court agendas. Just as the "church" is not a single entity in multireligious America, the "state" is multiple too, with zoning boards, city councils, state governments, and the federal government. At all levels, courts hear disputes and offer interpretations of laws and regulations and the constitutional principles that undergird them.

The First Amendment principles of nonestablishment of religion and the free exercise of religion sometimes almost seem to be in tension: the free exercise of religion calling for the protection of religious groups, while the nonestablishment of religion prohibiting any such special treatment.

(2001)

Questions

1. Diane L. Eck asks, "What religious attire may one wear? A cross? Yarmulke? Head scarf? Turban?" (par. 1). What is the rhetorical effect of the order in which she has chosen to list the items?
2. How much authority do you think schools and businesses should have regarding what students and employees wear? What has your observation and experience taught you about this issue?
3. What are your responses to the ways issues regarding religious practice were resolved by U.S. Air, Domino's Pizza, and Whirlpool? Explain.
4. Notice that the six questions in paragraph 5 are not what we would call rhetorical. Can we answer these questions? Explain.
5. Eck concludes, "The First Amendment principles of nonestablishment of religion and the free exercise of religion sometimes almost seem to be in tension: the free exercise of religion calling for the protection of religious groups, while the nonestablishment of religion prohibiting any such special treatment" (par. 7). To what extent does tolerance of religious difference extend to accommodation of religious practices and rituals?

---

[2]Cactus that grows in the American Southwest and is used by some Native Americans in religious ceremonies because of its psychoactive effects.

Ten Commandments Courthouse Controversy

GARY TRAMONTINA

In August 2003, a federal court ordered the removal of a monument of the Ten Commandments from the rotunda of the state Judicial Building in Montgomery, Alabama. Alabama chief justice Roy Moore defied the order and appealed the decision but eventually lost. The photos below and on the following page were taken by Gary Tramontina, a professional freelance photographer from Birmingham, Alabama.

Ken Cornelius and Carol Moore display signs during a protest in front of the state Judicial Building on August 16, 2003, in Montgomery, Alabama. A rally, blocks away, attracted thousands of supporters of Alabama chief justice Roy Moore's decision to defy a federal judge's order to remove a monument of the Ten Commandments from the judicial building.

Questions

1. What does each of the photos depict? How would you describe the subjects of each photo?
2. What values do the subjects appeal to in each of the photos?
3. People who have prayed at the monument have been criticized by some for having worshipped a graven image and having defied the Constitution; they have been

Gary Tramontina/Getty Images

Workers pause in preparation to move the Ten Commandments monument from the rotunda of the state Judicial Building on August 27, 2003, in Montgomery, Alabama. The monument, which was inside the building, was ordered removed by federal courts. Alabama chief justice Roy Moore was suspended for refusing to comply with the order.

praised by others for having prayed to defend morality and American values. Do you agree with either of these views? Why or why not?

4. How would you describe the conflict depicted in the signs held by Ken Cornelius and Carol Moore in the first photo? How would you describe the conflict suggested in the second photo? In which of the photos do the people present a stronger case? Explain.

5. Should religious images and monuments be displayed by government institutions and in public places? Do such displays reflect the beliefs of the Founding Fathers and the values that Americans share? Or do they go against the Constitution by favoring one religion over another? Explain.

Ground Zero Mosque Speech

Michael Bloomberg

The following is the text of a speech by Michael Bloomberg, the mayor of New York City, delivered on August 3, 2010, regarding the construction of a mosque and an Islamic center in Lower Manhattan, near the site of the World Trade Center.

We have come here to Governors Island to stand where the earliest settlers first set foot in New Amsterdam, and where the seeds of religious tolerance were first planted. We've come here to see the inspiring symbol of liberty that, more than 250 years later, would greet millions of immigrants in the harbor, and we come here to state as strongly as ever — this is the freest City in the world. That's what makes New York special and different and strong.

Our doors are open to everyone — everyone with a dream and a willingness to work hard and play by the rules. New York City was built by immigrants, and it is sustained by immigrants — by people from more than a hundred different countries speaking more than two hundred different languages and professing every faith. And whether your parents were born here, or you came yesterday, you are a New Yorker.

We may not always agree with every one of our neighbors. That's life and it's part of living in such a diverse and dense city. But we also recognize that part of being a New Yorker is living with your neighbors in mutual respect and tolerance. It was exactly that spirit of openness and acceptance that was attacked on 9/11.

On that day, 3,000 people were killed because some murderous fanatics didn't want us to enjoy the freedom to profess our own faiths, to speak our own minds, to follow our own dreams and to live our own lives.

Of all our precious freedoms, the most important may be the freedom to wor-   5
ship as we wish. And it is a freedom that, even here in a city that is rooted in Dutch tolerance, was hard-won over many years. In the mid-1650s, the small Jewish community living in Lower Manhattan petitioned Dutch Governor Peter Stuyvesant for the right to build a synagogue — and they were turned down.

In 1657, when Stuyvesant also prohibited Quakers from holding meetings, a group of non-Quakers in Queens signed the Flushing Remonstrance, a petition in defense of the right of Quakers and others to freely practice their religion. It was perhaps the first formal, political petition for religious freedom in the American colonies — and the organizer was thrown in jail and then banished from New Amsterdam.

In the 1700s, even as religious freedom took hold in America, Catholics in New York were effectively prohibited from practicing their religion — and priests could be arrested. Largely as a result, the first Catholic parish in New York City was not established until the 1780s — St. Peter's on Barclay Street, which still stands just one block north of the World Trade Center site and one block south of the proposed mosque and community center.

This morning, the City's Landmark Preservation Commission unanimously voted not to extend landmark status to the building on Park Place where the mosque and community center are planned. The decision was based solely on the fact that there was little architectural significance to the building. But with or without landmark designation, there is nothing in the law that would prevent the owners from opening a mosque within the existing building. The simple fact is this building is private property, and the owners have a right to use the building as a house of worship.

The government has no right whatsoever to deny that right — and if it were tried, the courts would almost certainly strike it down as a violation of the U.S. Constitution.

Whatever you may think of the proposed mosque and community center, lost in the heat of the debate has been a basic question — should government attempt to deny private citizens the right to build a house of worship on private property based on their particular religion? That may happen in other countries, but we should never allow it to happen here. This nation was founded on the principle that the government must never choose between religions or favor one over another.

The World Trade Center Site will forever hold a special place in our City, in our   10
hearts. But we would be untrue to the best part of ourselves — and who we are as New Yorkers and Americans — if we said "no" to a mosque in Lower Manhattan.

Let us not forget that Muslims were among those murdered on 9/11 and that our Muslim neighbors grieved with us as New Yorkers and as Americans. We would betray our values — and play into our enemies' hands — if we were to treat Muslims differently than anyone else. In fact, to cave to popular sentiment would be to hand a victory to the terrorists — and we should not stand for that.

For that reason, I believe that this is an important test of the separation of church and state as we may see in our lifetime — as important a test — and it is critically important that we get it right.

On September 11, 2001, thousands of first responders heroically rushed to the scene and saved tens of thousands of lives. More than 400 of those first responders did not make it out alive. In rushing into those burning buildings, not one of them asked "What God do you pray to?" "What beliefs do you hold?"

The attack was an act of war — and our first responders defended not only our City but also our country and our Constitution. We do not honor their lives by denying the very constitutional rights they died protecting. We honor their lives by defending those rights — and the freedoms that the terrorists attacked.

Of course, it is fair to ask the organizers of the mosque to show some special   15
sensitivity to the situation — and in fact, their plan envisions reaching beyond their walls and building an interfaith community. By doing so, it is my hope that the mosque will help to bring our City even closer together and help repudiate the false and repugnant idea that the attacks of 9/11 were in any way consistent with Islam. Muslims are as much a part of our City and our country as the people of any faith and they are as welcome to worship in Lower Manhattan as any other group. In fact, they have been worshipping at the site for the better part of a year, as is their right.

The local community board in Lower Manhattan voted overwhelmingly to support the proposal and if it moves forward, I expect the community center and mosque will add to the life and vitality of the neighborhood and the entire City.

Political controversies come and go, but our values and our traditions endure — and there is no neighborhood in this City that is off limits to God's love and mercy, as the religious leaders here with us today can attest.

(2010)

Questions

1. How does Mayor Michael Bloomberg characterize New York City in the first three paragraphs?

2. Bloomberg refers to the 9/11 attackers as "murderous fanatics" (par. 4) rather than suicide bombers, 911 highjackers, Muslim extremists, Islamic terrorists, or similar descriptions used by others and the media. What is the effect of Bloomberg's diction?
3. Bloomberg writes, "Of all our precious freedoms, the most important may be the freedom to worship as we wish" (par. 5). What are our other "precious freedoms"? Do you agree with what he says?
4. What are some of the values to which Bloomberg appeals in paragraphs 8 and 9? How do they contribute to the effectiveness of his argument?
5. What appeals to pathos does Bloomberg make in paragraphs 13 and 14? How does he appeal to ethos and logos in paragraph 14?
6. Bloomberg says that "this is an important a test of the separation of church and state as we may see in out lifetime . . . and it is critically important that we get it right" (par. 12). Do you agree? Why or why not?

from *Was America Founded as a Christian Nation?*

JOHN FEA

> John Fea is associate professor and chair of the History Department at Messiah College, a Christian college in Mechanicsburgh, Pennsylvania. This selection comes from his 2011 book, *Was America Founded as a Christian Nation?*

> *The Government of the United States of America is not, in any sense, founded on the Christian religion.*

So begins Article 11 of the Treaty of Tripoli, a 1797 agreement between the United States and Tripoli, a Muslim nation located on the Barbary Coast of northern Africa. The treaty was necessary because Barbary pirates, under the sanction of Tripoli, were capturing American ships and selling crew members into slavery. The Muslim states of the Barbary Coast (Tripoli, Algiers, Morocco, and Tunis) had long used piracy to control Mediterranean trade routes. Any nation that wanted to trade freely in the region was forced to negotiate a peace treaty with the Barbary States, which usually included some kind of monetary tribute. During the colonial era, American vessels were protected from the Barbary pirates by British warships, but after the Revolution the United States would need to work out its own treaty with these countries. The Treaty of Tripoli, which included the assertion that the United States was not founded on the Christian religion, was signed by President John Adams and ratified unanimously by the Senate. The text of the treaty was published in several newspapers, and there was no public opposition to it.

The American negotiators of this treaty did not want the religious differences between the United States and Tripoli to hinder attempts at reaching a trade agreement. Claiming that the United States was not "founded on the Christian religion" probably made negotiations proceed more smoothly. But today this brief religious reference in a rather obscure treaty in the history of American diplomacy has played a prominent role in the debate over whether the United States was founded as a Christian nation. It has become one of the most deadly arrows in the quiver of those who oppose the idea that the country was founded on Christian principles.[1]

If the Treaty of Tripoli is correct, and the United States was not "founded on the Christian religion," then someone forgot to tell the American people. Most Americans who followed events in the Mediterranean viewed the struggle between the United States and the Barbary nations — a struggle that would last well into the nineteenth century — as a kind of holy war. Americans published poems and books describing Muslims as "children of Ishmael" who posed a threat to Christian civilization. Captivity narratives describing Christians who were forced to convert to Islam only heightened these popular beliefs.[2] In fact, the sentiment expressed in the Treaty of Tripoli — that the United States was not "founded on the Christian religion" — can hardly be reconciled with the way that politicians, historians, clergy, educators, and other writers perceived the United States in the first one hundred years of its existence. The idea that the United States was a "Christian nation" was central to American identity in the years between the Revolution and the Civil War.

Nineteenth-century Americans who believed that the United States was a Christian nation made their case in at least three different ways. First, they appealed to divine providence. The United States had a special place in God's plan for the world. The success of the American Revolution confirmed it. Second, they argued that the founders were Christians and thus set out to create a nation that reflected their personal beliefs. Third, they made the case that the U.S. government and the documents upon which it was founded were rooted in Christian ideas. Today's Christian nationalists have a good portion of American history on their side.

Christian Nationalism in the Early American Republic

If the United States was ever a "Christian nation," it was so during the period between   5
the ratification of the Constitution (1789) and the start of the Civil War (1861). While the Constitution made clear that there would be no official or established religion in America, and the states were gradually removing religious requirements for office-holders, Christianity, and particularly Protestant evangelicalism, defined the culture.

When ministers, politicians, and writers during these years described the United States as a "Christian nation," they were usually referring to the beliefs and character of the majority of its citizens. The United States was populated by Christians. This meant that it was not a "Muslim nation" or a "Buddhist nation" or a "Hindu nation." Indeed, the people of most Western European nations in the nineteenth century would have used the phrase "Christian nation" to describe the countries to which they belonged. But in America the phrase "Christian nation" could also carry a deeper meaning. It was often used as a way of describing the uniqueness of the American experiment. It was freighted with the idea that the United States had a special role to play in the plan of God, thus making it a special or privileged Christian nation. Moreover, when nineteenth-century Americans talked about living in a "Christian nation" they rarely used the term in a polemical way. In other words, they were not trying to defend the label against those who did not believe the United States was a Christian nation. Instead, they used the phrase as if it were a well-known, generally accepted fact.[3]

One of the main reasons that people could describe the United States as a Christian nation during this period was because the country was experiencing a massive revival of Protestant evangelicalism.[4] Known as the Second Great Awakening, this religious revival stressed salvation through faith in the atoning work of Jesus Christ and was quite compatible with the democratic spirit of the early nineteenth century. Humans were no longer perceived as waiting passively for a sovereign and distant God who, on his own terms and in his own timing, offered select individuals the gift of eternal life. Instead, ordinary American citizens took an active role in their own salvation. Theology moved away from a Calvinism that stressed humankind's inability to save itself and toward a free-will or democratic theology, preached most powerfully and popularly by revivalist Charles Finney. The new theology empowered individuals to decide their own religious fate by accepting or rejecting the gospel message.[5]

This revival of religion owed a lot to the First Amendment (1791). By forbidding Congress from making laws "respecting an establishment of religion, or prohibiting the free exercise thereof," religion became voluntary. If churches could no longer rely on state support, they would need to craft their message in such a way that would attract people to their pews. Long-established denominations such as Episcopalians, Presbyterians, and Congregationalists gave way to more democratic, enthusiastic, and evangelical groups such as Baptists and Methodists. New sects such as the Mormons and the Disciples of Christ emerged with force. Religious services continued to be conducted in churches, but they were also being held in camp meetings like the one in Cane Ridge, Kentucky, in 1801. Writing in 1855, church historian Philip Schaff quoted an Austrian writer who observed, "The United States are by far the most religious and Christian country in the world . . . because religion is there most free."[6] When Thomas Jefferson claimed smugly in 1822 that Unitarianism would soon be "the religion of the majority from north and south," he could not have been more wrong.[7] Apparently Jefferson did not leave Monticello very much during the final years of his life, for America was fast becoming the most evangelical Christian country on the face of the earth. . . .

Religion and the First Amendment

While some Anti-Federalists opposed the Constitution for its failure to affirm a religious test for national office or its failure to reference Almighty God, others opposed it for its failure to affirm liberty of conscience in matters of religion. Centinel, a Philadelphia Anti-Federalist, wrote that the Constitution had "no declaration, that all men have a natural and unalienable right to worship Almighty God, according to the dictates of their own consciences and understanding." Recalling the long history of religious persecution in Europe, another Philadelphia Anti-Federalist, "An Old Whig," demanded a "*bill of rights* to secure, in the first place by the most express stipulations, the sacred right of conscience." "Sydney," a New York Anti-Federalist, wondered why the U.S. Constitution did not include a statement protecting citizens from religious persecution in the way that the New York state constitution had done.[8]

Anti-Federalist demands for a formal statement defending the right to liberty of conscience in matters of religion came to fruition when the First Amendment to the U.S. Constitution went into effect in 1791. The amendment was part of ten amendments, known today as the Bill of Rights, passed by the first U.S. Congress in 1789 and ratified, as per the Constitution, by three-fourths of the states. The First Amendment stated that "Congress shall make no law respecting an establishment of religion, or prohibiting the free exercise thereof." The amendment's religious clause has drawn much discussion throughout the course of American history. Contemporary debate over the meaning of the amendment has centered on whether the federal government can limit public displays of Christmas manger scenes or the Ten Commandments in federal buildings. While such debates are certainly worthwhile, our intention here is to explore the meaning of the First Amendment in the historical context in which it was written.

Most interpreters of the First Amendment agree that it forbids Congress from passing a law that privileges a particular religious group over any other. Unlike many of the British-American colonies and some of the states, the U.S. government does not promote a specific religious group or use federal funds to support a particular sect. As we saw above, the "noestablishment" clause applied only to the national government. The First Amendment also forbids the national government from inhibiting the "free exercise" of religion. It protects individuals from government intrusion into their religious practices. The First Amendment was written to secure the individual right to worship according to one's conscience. It was not meant as a means of protecting government from the religious beliefs of its citizens.

(2011)

Notes

1. See, for example, Brooke Allen, "Our Godless Constitution," *The Nation* (Feb. 3, 2005); idem, accessed September 10, 2010, at www.thenation.com/article/our-godless-constitution?; "The Great Debate of Our Season," *Mother Jones* (December 2005), accessed September 10, 2010, at motherjones.com/politics/2005/12/great-debate/our-seaso1.

2. Thomas Kidd, *American Christians and Islam: Evangelical Culture and Muslims from the Colonial Period to the Age of Terrorism* (Princeton: Princeton University Press, 2008), 22–23.

3. These conclusions are based on the reading of hundreds of references to "Christian nation" in early-nineteenth-century print available through Google Books.

4. George Marsden describes a "massive evangelical consensus" in nineteenth-century America. See Marsden, *Reforming Fundamentalism: Fuller Seminary and the New Evangelicalism* (Grand Rapids: Eerdmans, 1988), 119.

5. The best treatment of this is Nathan Hatch, *The Democratization of American Christianity* (New Haven: Yale University Press, 1991).

6. Philip Schaff, *America: A Sketch of Its Political, Social, and Religious Character* (1855; repr., Cambridge: Belknap, 1961), 11, cited in Roger Finke and Rodney Stark, *The Churching of America, 1776–2005: Winners and Losers in Our Religious Economy*, 2nd ed. (New Brunswick, NJ: Rutgers University Press, 2005), 6.

7. Thomas Jefferson to Thomas Cooper, November 2, 1822, accessed at the University of Virginia Electronic Text Center.

8. Horace Bushnell, "Popular Government by Divine Right," November 24, 1864, in *"God Ordained This War": Sermons on the Sectional Crisis, 1830–1865*, ed. David B. Chesebrough (Columbia: University of South Carolina Press, 1991), quotation, 106; cf. 117; Albert Barnes, *The Love of Country* (Philadelphia: C. Sherman & Sons, 1861), 38–40.

Questions

1. How does the information in the headnote contribute to understanding John Fea's ethos? How does that knowledge influence your response to this selection?
2. According to Fea, what was the purpose of the Treaty of Tripoli? What was the intent of the statement, "The Government of the United States of America is not, in any sense, founded on the Christian religion"?
3. Fea writes, "If the Treaty of Tripoli is correct, and the United States was not 'founded on the Christian religion,' then someone forgot to tell the American people" (par. 3), and he characterizes America as a Christian nation. How can we reconcile the two positions? Explain.
4. How does Fea characterize the relationship between religion and the First Amendment? What are the implications of his two concluding sentences?
5. How would you paraphrase Fea's position? What does it suggest about religious tolerance in America today?
6. What is the rhetorical effect of Fea's footnotes?

Making Connections

1. How does "America's True History of Religious Tolerance" by Kenneth C. Davis (p. 472) serve as a thematic connection among the pieces in this Conversation? Include details from three particular selections in your answer.

2. What similarities do you find in the writing of James Madison (p. 477), Thomas Jefferson (p. 481), and George Washington (p. 483) as depicted by Davis?

3. Which of the fifteen clauses in section 1 of "The Virginia Act for Establishing Religious Freedom" are echoed and reinforced in John F. Kennedy's speech (p. 486)?

4. How do you think Red Jacket (p. 484) would respond if he could read the pieces by Jeff Jacoby (p. 490) and Michael Bloomberg (p. 496)? In his voice, write a response to the ideas that they address.

5. What common issues are addressed in Madison's 1789 "Memorial and Remonstrance against Religious Assessments" and in the selection from Diane L. Eck's book *A New Religious America* (p. 492) published in 2001?

6. What comparisons and contrasts can be made between the then senator and future U.S. president John F. Kennedy's 1960 speech and New York City mayor Michael Bloomberg's 2010 speech?

7. How would you compare the perspectives of Bloomberg, Eck, and Jacoby regarding religious matters in contemporary America?

8. How would Jacoby regard the photographs by Gary Tramontina (pp. 495–96)? How do you think Washington, Jefferson, or Madison would respond to the issue surrounding the monument of the Ten Commandments?

Entering the Conversation

As you respond to each of the following prompts, support your position with appropriate evidence, including at least three sources in this Conversation on religious tolerance, unless otherwise indicated.

1. Have the fears that Madison expressed in "Memorial and Remonstrance against Religious Assessments" continued to plague our society today or have we moved beyond them?

2. In 1802, Samuel Adams accused Thomas Paine of writing (in his book *The Age of Reason*, a volume which Adams admitted he had not read) a "defence of infidelity." Paines's letter in response concludes:

   > The key to heaven is not in the keeping of any sect, nor ought the road to it be obstructed by any. Our relation to each other in this world is as men, and the man who is a friend to man and to his rights, let his religious opinions be what they may, is a good citizen to who, I can give, as I ought to do, and as every other ought, the right hand of fellowship, and to none with more hearty good will, my dear friend, than to you.

   Write an essay that explores Paine's remarks as they relate to religious tolerance.

3. In his speech, Kennedy mentions Catholics, Protestants, and Jews. Whom does he leave out? What other religious peoples would a contemporary president feel it necessary to include? Write an essay that explains how Kennedy's speech might differ if it were given today.

4. In theses lines from paragraphs 5 and 17 of his speech, Mayor Bloomberg states the following:

   > Of all our precious freedoms, the most important may be the freedom to worship as we wish. . . . Political controversies come and go, but our values and our tradi-

tions endure — and there is no neighborhood in this city that is off limits to God's love and mercy, as the religious leaders here with us today can attest.

Write an essay that explores the validity of what Bloomberg says about the freedom to worship, about political controversies, and about our values and traditions.

5. In her book *A New Religious America*, Eck writes about the influence of stereotypes regarding religion:

> After race, the most visible signal of difference is dress, and this is where religious minorities become visible minorities. Many Muslim women wear *hijab*, either a simple head scarf or a full outer garment. A few even wear a face covering called a *nikab*. Muslim men may wear a beard, and Sikh men may wear not only a beard but also a turban wrapper around their uncut hair. Jewish men may wear a yarmulke, or skullcap. Buddhist monks may wear saffron, maroon, black, or gray robes, depending on their culture of origin. In all these cases looking different may sometimes trigger uneasiness and even fear — the fear that we do not know who "they" are or perhaps that we do not know who "we" are. As Americans, we are literally afraid of ourselves.

Do you agree with Eck that we Americans are afraid of ourselves? Write an essay that answers that question.

6. Annapolis graduate and former professor of constitutional law Carl Pearlston writes:

> Can America still be called a Christian nation? It is certainly a more religiously pluralistic and diverse society than it was during the 18th, 19th, and early 20th centuries. There are increasing numbers of non-Christians immigrating to this country, and there has been a rapid rise in adherents to Islam among our population. There are millions of Muslims, Jews, Buddhists, Shintoists, Unitarians, Hindus, Wiccans, Naturists, Agnostics, and Atheists, but Christians comprise roughly 84% of the population. Our constitutional legal system is still based on the Jewish/Christian Bible, not the Koran or other holy book. We still observe Sunday, the Christian Sabbath, as an official holiday. Easter and Christmas still have a special place in the holiday lexicon. The Ten Commandments are still on the wall behind the Supreme Court justices when they take the bench. Our coins still display the motto "In God We Trust." The US is still firmly part of a Western Civilization fashioned by a Judeo-Christian religious ethic and heritage. Alexis de Tocqueville observed more than a century and a half ago, "There is no country in the world, where the Christian religion retains a greater influence over the souls of men than in America." That is still true today. We live, not under a Christian government, but in a nation where all are free to practice their particular religion, in accommodation with other religions, and in accordance with the basic principles of the nation, which are Christian in origin. It is in that sense that America may properly be referred to as a Christian nation.

Is the United States of America a Christian nation? Write an essay that explores that question.

7. The idea of the "separation between church and state" has a long history. Roger Williams (c. 1603–1684), who founded Plymouth Plantation, the first Baptist church in America, and Rhode Island as the first government without an official religion, was an abolitionist and a proponent of religious freedom who spoke of a "hedge of separation between the garden of the church and the wilderness of the world." Explore the idea of the "separation of church and state" that is so revered in American society. Write an essay that explores the extent to which church and state should be separate or how high that "hedge" should be.

8. Consider the following question: Is the United States of America now, or has it ever been, a nation that believes in and practices religious tolerance? If your answer is no, explain your position, using appropriate evidence. If it is yes, to what extent has the country lived up to its founding ideals regarding religious freedom and tolerance? Provide evidence to support your position.

Conversation

The Influence of Phillis Wheatley

Both an enigmatic and a controversial figure, Phillis Wheatley (c. 1753–1784) was the first African American woman to have a book published. She was born in Africa, likely in what is now Senegal, and sold into slavery at age seven to John and Susannah Wheatley of Boston. She became the personal servant of Susannah, who taught her English and Christianity along with Latin, history, geography, and Western mythology. As early as 1765, she began to write poetry, which the family encouraged. By age thirteen, she published her first poem, "On Messrs. Hussey and Coffin," based on the true story of two men who nearly drowned at sea. The next year, she published "An Elegiac Poem, on the Death of the Celebrated Divine George Whitefield," which brought her more attention. Although publishers in Boston declined her work, with the Wheatley's son she traveled to London, where the Countess of Huntingdon supported publication of *Poems on Various Subjects, Religious and Moral* (1773), the first book written by a black woman in America and the second to be written by any woman in America.

When she returned from London, she was emancipated by John Wheatley. Both he and his wife died in 1778, the year Phillis Wheatley married John Peters, a free black man, in Boston. During the next years, two of their children died, and in 1784, Wheatley died in childbirth with her third child, who survived her only briefly.

While the seriousness of Wheatley's efforts has never been called into question, the significance of her contribution has been the source of controversy for more than two centuries. In fact, the authenticity of her work was called into question at various junctures during her own lifetime and subsequently. In addition, many critics have dismissed her style — characterized by classical allusions, formal diction, and strict patterns of rhyme and rhythm — as derivative of other eighteenth-century poets, such as Alexander Pope. Others have seen her work as groundbreaking, pointing to her confident literary persona, shrewd determination to gain a wide readership, and skill at encoding antislavery views in seemingly conventional structures.

The following documents include poetry and letters written by Wheatley along with recent analyses of her work and her influence by prominent African American intellectuals and artists.

Sources

Phillis Wheatley, *On Being Brought from Africa to America* (1773)
To S.M. a Young African *Painter, on Seeing His Works* (1773)
To the University of Cambridge, in New-England (1773)
To His Excellency General Washington (1776) (along with letters)
Letter to Reverend Samson Occom (1774)
Kevin Young, *Homage to Phillis Wheatley* (1998)
June Jordan, from *The Difficult Miracle of Black Poetry in America* (2002)
Henry Louis Gates Jr., *Mr. Jefferson and the Trials of Phillis Wheatley* (2002)

On Being Brought from Africa to America

Phillis Wheatley

'Twas mercy brought me from my *Pagan* land,
Taught my benighted soul to understand
That there's a God, that there's a *Saviour* too:
Once I redemption neither sought nor knew.
Some view our sable race with scornful eye,   5
"Their colour is a diabolic die."
Remember, *Christians*, *Negros*, black as *Cain*,
May be refin'd, and join th' angelic train.

(1773)

Questions

1. What argument does the speaker of this poem make against the prevailing view of Africans during this time period?
2. In line 3, what is the significance of Phillis Wheatley's distinction between "a God" and "a *Saviour* too"?
3. Consider connotations and multiple meanings of word choices that Wheatley makes. What difference would it have made if she had used "heathen" instead of

"*Pagan*" (l. 1)? What ambiguity is there in the word "benighted" (l. 2)? What is the impact of her description of her color as "sable" (l. 5)?

4. What tone does the speaker take when she addresses her audience with the imperative, "Remember, *Christians*" (l. 7)? What way might that line be read other than as a direct address to her Christian readers?

5. In his biography of Wheatley, Vincent Carretta admonishes those who read this poem as Wheatley's rejection of her African heritage as "confus[ing] accommodation with appropriation." What do you think he means by that statement? Explain why you agree or disagree.

To S.M. a Young African Painter, on Seeing His Works

PHILLIS WHEATLEY

The engraving used as the frontispiece for Phillis Wheatley's book, *Poems on Various Subjects, Religious and Moral* (1773), was based on a painting by Scipio Moorhead, a slave owned by a Boston minister. The portrait was commissioned by the Countess of Huntingdon, a noblewoman and abolitionist to whom the book was dedicated. In his biography *Phillis Wheatley: Portrait of a Genius in Bondage*, Vincent Carretta contends that this frontispiece portrait "of a woman of Wheatley's status and ethnicity was unprecedented" and is the first instance of a colonial American woman having her portrait printed with her writing. When Wheatley

PHILLIS WHEATLEY, 1773, ENGRAVING
BASED ON A PORTRAIT BY SCIPIO
MOORHEAD.

Library of Congress Rare Book and Special Collections Division saw this image, she wrote the following poem, which appeared as part of the published book.

To show the lab'ring bosom's deep intent,
And thought in living characters to paint,
When first thy pencil did those beauties give,
And breathing figures learnt from thee to live,
How did those prospects give my soul delight,   5
A new creation rushing on my sight?
Still, wond'rous youth! each noble path pursue,
On deathless glories fix thine ardent view:
Still may the painter's and the poet's fire
To aid thy pencil, and thy verse conspire!   10
And may the charms of each seraphic[1] theme
Conduct thy footsteps to immortal fame!
High to the blissful wonders of the skies
Elate thy soul, and raise thy wishful eyes.
Thrice happy, when exalted to survey   15
That splendid city, crown'd with endless day,
Whose twice six gates on radiant hinges ring:
Celestial *Salem*[2] blooms in endless spring.

   Calm and serene thy moments glide along,
And may the muse inspire each future song!   20
Still, with the sweets of contemplation bless'd,
May peace with balmy wings your soul invest!
But when these shades of time are chas'd away,
And darkness ends in everlasting day,
On what seraphic pinions shall we move,   25
And view the landscapes in the realms above?
There shall thy tongue in heav'nly murmurs flow,
And there my muse with heav'nly transport glow:
No more to tell of *Damon's*[3] tender sighs,
Or rising radiance of *Aurora's*[4] eyes,   30
For nobler themes demand a nobler strain,
And purer language on th' ethereal plain.
Cease, gentle muse! the solemn gloom of night
Now seals the fair creation from my sight.

                                        (1773)

---

[1]Angelic. — Eds.
[2]Short for Jerusalem. — Eds.
[3]In Greek mythology, Damon offered his life in exchange for his friend Pythias's, who had been sentenced to death. — Eds.
[4]Roman goddess of the dawn. — Eds.

Questions

1. What question does the speaker ask in the opening six lines? Try phrasing them as a statement. How does doing so change the tone?
2. What does the speaker mean by "deathless glories" (l. 8)? What phrase that follows in the next few lines reemphasizes the idea?
3. In the first stanza, what are the two types of happiness the speaker urges Scipio Moorhead to aspire to?
4. How is imagination depicted in this poem? What images and descriptions does Phillis Wheatley use to convey its power?
5. Who is the "gentle muse" (l. 33) the speaker addresses?
6. The second stanza is filled with images of light and dark, sun and shade. How do these images contribute to the ideas Wheatley expresses? What subtext might she be suggesting to her audience, the painter, through these images?
7. Wheatley's readers would be familiar with her classical references. Not just ornamentation, however, these add to the authority Wheatley claims for her speaker. Specifically, what purpose(s) do these allusions serve?
8. How does the rhetorical situation of speaker to audience — that is, slave to slave, artist to artist — affect the tone of the poem? Does the intimacy of this relationship bring readers of the poem closer to or distance them from the emotional power of the poem?

To the University of Cambridge, in New-England

Phillis Wheatley

> Wheatley assumes a persona of authority in the following poem addressed to students at the University of Cambridge, which later became Harvard College.

While an intrinsic ardor prompts to write,
The muses promise to assist my pen;
'Twas not long since I left my native shore
The land of errors, and *Egyptian* gloom.
Father of mercy, 'twas thy gracious hand   5
Brought me in safety from those dark abodes.

   Students, to you 'tis giv'n to scan the heights
Above, to traverse the ethereal space,
And mark the systems of revolving worlds.
Still more, ye sons of science ye receive   10
The blissful news by messengers from heav'n,
How *Jesus*' blood for your redemption flows.
See him with hands out-stretcht upon the cross;
Immense compassion in his bosom glows;

He hears revilers, nor resents their scorn: 15
What matchless mercy in the Son of God!
When the whole human race by sin had fall'n,
He deign'd to die that they might rise again,
And share with him in the sublimest skies,
Life without death, and glory without end.   20

   Improve your privileges while they stay,
Ye pupils, and each hour redeem, that bears
Or good or bad report of you to heav'n.
Let sin, that baneful evil to the soul,
By you be shunn'd, nor once remit your guard;   25
Suppress the deadly serpent in its egg.
Ye blooming plants of human race divine,
An *Ethiop* tells you 'tis your greatest foe;
Its transient sweetness turns to endless pain,
And in immense perdition sinks the soul.   30

                                               (1773)

Questions

1. In the opening two lines, the speaker establishes her authority to address her audience. What is the nature of that authority? What common ground does she establish between herself and the audience?
2. Following are the first few lines of an earlier version of this poem, written in 1767. How does this original draft compare with the revised poem? What impact do you think the association of "*Egyptian* gloom" (l. 4) adds in the final version?

> While an intrinsic ardor bids me write
> The muse doth promise to assist my pen.
> 'Twas but e'en now I left my native Shore
> The sable Land of errors' darkest night
> There, sacred Nine! For you no place was found,
> Parent of mercy, 'twas thy Powerfull hand
> Brought me in Safety from the dark abode.

3. What are the responsibilities that the speaker reminds her elite audience of university students that they must accept? (Keep in mind that many of the young men at the University of Cambridge during that time were studying to become ministers.)
4. What elements of Christianity does Wheatley stress in this poem?
5. Why do you think the speaker identifies herself as "An *Ethiop*" (l. 28) rather than an African or another phrase descriptive of her race? What is the impact of that description?

6. In what ways does this poem resemble a commencement address? What persona does Wheatley assume in order to communicate with these young students, who were likely to be heirs of prominence and privilege?
7. In the last seven lines, Wheatley warns her audience not to submit to the temptations of sin. Some have interpreted these lines as an antislavery argument questioning why conversion to Christianity would not change the social status of slaves. To what extent do you agree with this interpretation?

To His Excellency General Washington

Phillis Wheatley

> Wheatley sent the following letter to George Washington with her poem; he responded to her with an invitation that she should visit. Phillis Wheatley and George Washington met at the Continental army's headquarters at Cambridge in March 1776. The poem was published that same year in the *Virginia Gazette* and the *Pennsylvania Magazine.*

Sir,

I have taken the freedom to address your Excellency in the enclosed poem, and entreat your acceptance, though I am not insensible of its inaccuracies. Your being appointed by the Grand Continental Congress to be Generalissimo of the armies of North America, together with the fame of your virtues, excite sensations not easy to suppress. Your generosity, therefore, I presume, will pardon the attempt. Wishing your Excellency all possible success in the great cause you are so generously engaged in. I am, Your Excellency's most obedient humble servant,

Phillis Wheatley

Cambridge, February 28, 1776.

Mrs. Phillis,

Your favour of the 26th of October did not reach my hands 'till the middle of December. Time enough, you will say, to have given an answer ere this. Granted. But a variety of important occurrences, continually interposing to distract the mind and withdraw the attention, I hope will apologize for the delay, and plead my excuse for the seeming, but not real neglect.

I thank you most sincerely for your polite notice of me, in the elegant Lines you enclosed; and however undeserving I may be of such encomium and panegyrick, the style and manner exhibit a striking proof of your great poetical Talents. In honour of which, and as a tribute justly due to you, I would have published the Poem, had I not been apprehensive, that, while I only meant to give the World this new instance of your genius, I might have incurred the imputation of Vanity. This and nothing else, determined me not to give it place in the public Prints.

If you should ever come to Cambridge, or near Head Quarters, I shall be happy to see a person so favoured by the Muses, and to whom Nature has been so liberal and beneficent in her dispensations.

I am, with great Respect, etc.

George Washington

Celestial choir! enthron'd in realms of light,
Columbia's scenes of glorious toils I write.
While freedom's cause her anxious breast alarms,
She flashes dreadful in refulgent arms.
See mother earth her offspring's fate bemoan,   5
And nations gaze at scenes before unknown!
See the bright beams of heaven's revolving light
Involved in sorrows and the veil of night!
The goddess comes, she moves divinely fair,
Olive and laurel binds her golden hair: 10
Wherever shines this native of the skies,
Unnumber'd charms and recent graces rise.
Muse! bow propitious while my pen relates
How pour her armies through a thousand gates:
As when Eolus[1] heaven's fair face deforms,   15
Enwrapp'd in tempest and a night of storms;
Astonish'd ocean feels the wild uproar,
The refluent surges beat the sounding shore;
Or thick as leaves in Autumn's golden reign,
Such, and so many, moves the warrior's train.   20
In bright array they seek the work of war,
Where high unfurl'd the ensign waves in air.
Shall I to Washington their praise recite?
Enough thou know'st them in the fields of fight.
Thee, first in place and honours, — we demand   25
The grace and glory of thy martial band.
Fam'd for thy valour, for thy virtues more,
Hear every tongue thy guardian aid implore!
One century scarce perform'd its destin'd round,
When Gallic powers Columbia's fury found;   30
And so may you, whoever dares disgrace
The land of freedom's heaven-defended race!
Fix'd are the eyes of nations on the scales,
For in their hopes Columbia's arm prevails.
Anon Britannia droops the pensive head,   35
While round increase the rising hills of dead.

---

[1]In Greek mythology, Eolus was the keeper of the winds. — Eds.

Ah! cruel blindness to Columbia's state!
Lament thy thirst of boundless power too late.
   Proceed, great chief, with virtue on thy side,
Thy ev'ry action let the goddess guide.   40
A crown, a mansion, and a throne that shine,
With gold unfading, WASHINGTON! be thine.

(1776)

Questions

1. How do the letters that accompany the poem affect your reading of it? What do the letters suggest about Phillis Wheatley?
2. How does the speaker in this poem characterize the struggle for Columbia's (the colonies') independence in the opening twelve lines? Who is the "goddess" in line 9?
3. Who is George Washington, as he is depicted in lines 13–28? Consider specific descriptions as well as image patterns.
4. How do you interpret the reference to "The land of freedom's heaven-defended race!" (l. 32)?
5. In the last two lines, what role does Wheatley predict for Washington?
6. In what ways does this poem suggest a connection between the desire for American independence and the slave's desire for freedom?

Letter to Reverend Samson Occom

PHILLIS WHEATLEY

> Wheatley wrote this letter to Reverend Samson Occom, a Mohegan Indian ordained a Presbyterian minister, in 1774, after she had gained her own freedom. Reverend Occom had written an indictment of the hypocrisy of Christian ministers who were slaveholders.

Rev'd and honor'd Sir,

I have this Day received your obliging kind Epistle, and am greatly satisfied with your Reasons respecting the Negroes, and think highly reasonable what you offer in Vindication of their natural Rights: Those that invade them cannot be insensible that the divine Light is chasing away the thick Darkness which broods over the Land of Africa; and the Chaos which has reign'd so long, is converting into beautiful Order, and [r]eveals more and more clearly, the glorious Dispensation of civil and religious Liberty, which are so inseparably united, that there is little or no Enjoyment of one without the other: Otherwise, perhaps, the Israelites had been less solicitous for their Freedom from Egyptian slavery; I do not say they would have been contented without it, by no means, for in every human Breast, God has implanted a Principle, which we call Love of Freedom; it is impatient of Oppression, and pants for Deliverance;

and by the Leave of our modern Egyptians I will assert, that the same Principle lives in us. God grant Deliverance in his own Way and Time, and get him honour upon all those whose Avarice impels them to countenance and help forward the Calamities of their fellow Creatures. This I desire not for their Hurt, but to convince them of the strange Absurdity of their Conduct whose Words and Actions are so diametrically opposite. How well the Cry for Liberty, and the reverse Disposition for the exercise of oppressive Power over others agree, — I humbly think it does not require the Penetration of a Philosopher to determine.

(1774)

Questions

1. What are the "natural Rights" to which Phillis Wheatley refers in the opening sentence?
2. How does she yoke "civil and religious Liberty" throughout this letter?
3. Who does Wheatley characterize as "our modern Egyptians"?
4. What is the argument she makes in her accusation of the "Absurdity of their Conduct whose Words and Actions are so diametrically opposite"?

Homage to Phillis Wheatley
Poet & Servant to Mr. Wheatley of Boston, on her Maiden Voyage to Britain

KEVIN YOUNG

> Born in 1970 in Nebraska, Kevin Young is the author of seven collections of poetry. He holds a BA from Harvard University and an MFA in creative writing from Brown University and is currently the Atticus Haygood Professor of English and Creative Writing at Emory University. His poetry collection *Jelly Roll: A Blues* was a finalist for the National Book Award in 2003. This poem appeared in the anthology *Giant Steps: The New Generation of African American Writers* (2000), edited by Young.

There are days I can understand
why you would want to board
broad back of some ship
and sail: venture, not homeward
but toward Civilization's   5

Cold seat, — having from wild
been stolen, and sent into more wild
of Columbia, our exiles
and Christians clamoring upon
the cobblestones of Bostontown —   10

Sail across an Atlantic (this time) mild,
the ship's polite and consumptive
passengers proud. Your sickness
quit soon as you disembarked in mist
of England — free, finally, of our Republic's   15

Rough clime, its late converts who thought
they would not die, or die simply
in struggle, martyr to some God, —
you know of gods there
are many, who is really only   20

One — and that sleep, restless fever
would take most you loved. Why
fate fight? Death, dark mistress,
would come a-heralding silent
the streets, — no door to her closed,   25

No stair (servant or front) too steep.
Gen. Washington, whom you praise,
victorious, knows this — will even admit
you to his parlor. Who could resist a Negress
who can recite Latin and speak the Queen's?   30

Docked among the fog and slight sun
of London, you know who you are not
but that is little new. Native
of nowhere, — you'll stay a spell, return,
write, grow still. I wake with you   35

In my mind, leaning, learning
to write — your slight profile
that long pull of lower lip, its pout
proving you rescued by
some sadness too large to name.   40

My Most Excellence, my quill
and ink lady, you spill such script
no translation it needs —
your need is what's missing, unwritten
wish to cross back but not back   45

Into that land (for you) of the dead —
you want to see from above
deck the sea, to pluck from wind

a sense no Land can
give: drifting, looking not   50

For Leviathan's breath, nor waves
made of tea, nor for mermen half-
out of water (as you) — down
in the deep is not the narwhal enough real?
Beneath our wind-whipt banner you smile   55

At Sea which owns no country.

(1998)

Questions

1. What do you think is the purpose of the poem's subtitle, "Poet & Servant to Mr. Wheatley of Boston, on her Maiden Voyage to Britain"? Why is it fitting that Kevin Young chose this particular situation to focus on in his poem?
2. How do you interpret "Who could resist a Negress / who can recite Latin and speak the Queen's" (ll. 29–30)? Is Young being serious? Sarcastic? Support your response by citing specific phrases and lines.
3. In lines 31–40, Young interprets the feelings and motivations of Wheatley. What conclusions does he draw? Do you agree with him?
4. What question does Young ask in lines 51–54? Is it a rhetorical question or one he is asking her? Explain your response.
5. What is the effect of separating the final line — which is part of a sentence that begins in the previous stanza?
6. What examples do you find of Young using language more appropriate to Wheatley's milieu than to his own contemporary one? How does that language help you understand why Young wrote this poem as a dialogue between himself and Wheatley?
7. On the basis of this poem, what is the connection Young feels to Wheatley?

from *The Difficult Miracle of Black Poetry in America*
Or Something like a Sonnet for Phillis Wheatley

JUNE JORDAN

> June Jordan (1936–2002) authored many books of poetry — including *Kissing God Goodbye: Poems 1991–1997* (1997), *Living Room* (1985), and *Haruko/ Love Poems* (1994) — as well as children's books, plays, a novel, and collections of political essays. A recipient of a Rockefeller Foundation grant and fellowships from the National Endowment for the Arts and the New York Foundation for the Arts, she taught at the University of California–Berkeley.

It was not natural. And she was the first. Come from a country of many tongues tortured by rupture, by theft, by travel like mismatched clothing packed down into the cargo hold of evil ships sailing, irreversible, into slavery. Come to a country to be docile and dumb, to be big and breeding, easily, to be turkey/horse/cow, to be cook/ carpenter/plow, to be 5′6″ 140 lbs., in good condition and answering to the name of Tom or Mary: to be bed bait: to be legally spread legs for rape by the master/the master's son/the master's overseer/the master's visiting nephew: to be nothing human nothing family nothing from nowhere nothing that screams nothing that weeps nothing that dreams nothing that keeps anything/anyone deep in your heart to live forcibly illiterate, forcibly itinerant: to live eyes lowered head bowed: to be worked without rest, to be worked without pay, to be worked without thanks, to be worked day up to nightfall: to be three-fifths of a human being at best: to be this valuable/this hated thing among strangers who purchased your life and then cursed it unceasingly: to be a slave: to be a slave. Come to this country a slave and how should you sing? After the flogging the lynch rope the general terror and weariness what should you know of a lyrical life? How could you, belonging to no one, but property to those despising the smiles of your soul, how could you dare to create yourself: a poet?

A poet can read. A poet can write.

A poet is African in Africa, or Irish in Ireland, or French on the left bank of Paris, or white in Wisconsin. A poet writes in her own language. A poet writes of her own people, her own history, her own vision, her own room, her own house where she sits at her own table quietly placing one word after another word until she builds a line and a movement and an image and a meaning that somersaults all of these into the singing, the absolutely individual voice of the poet at liberty. A poet is somebody free. A poet is someone at home.

How should there be Black poets in America?

It was not natural. And she was the first. It was 1761 — so far back before the   5
revolution that produced these United States, so far back before the concept of freedom disturbed the insolent crimes of this continent — in 1761, when seven year old Phillis stood, as she must, when she stood nearly naked, as small as a seven year old, by herself, standing on land at last, at last after the long, annihilating horrors of the Middle Passage. Phillis, standing on the auctioneer's rude platform: Phillis For Sale.

Was it a nice day?

Does it matter? Should she muse on the sky or remember the sea? Until then Phillis had been somebody's child. Now she was about to become somebody's slave.

Suzannah and John Wheatley finished their breakfast and ordered the carriage brought 'round. They would ride to the auction. This would be an important outing. They planned to buy yet another human being to help with the happiness of the comfortable life in Boston. You don't buy a human being, you don't purchase a slave, without thinking ahead. So they had planned this excursion. They were dressed for the occasion, and excited, probably. And experienced, certainly. The Wheatleys already owned several slaves. They had done this before; the transaction would not startle or confound or embarrass or appall either one of them.

Was it a nice day?

When the Wheatleys arrived at the auction they greeted their neighbors, they   10
enjoyed this business of mingling with other townsfolk politely shifting about the
platform, politely adjusting positions for gain of a better view of the bodies for sale.
The Wheatleys were good people. They were kind people. They were openminded
and thoughtful. They looked at the bodies for sale. They looked and they looked.
This one could be useful for that. That one might be useful for this. But then they
looked at that child, that Black child standing nearly naked, by herself. Seven or
eight years old, at the most, and frail. Now that was a different proposal! Not a strong
body, not a grown set of shoulders, not a promising wide set of hips, but a little body,
a delicate body, a young, surely terrified face! John Wheatley agreed to the whim of
his wife, Suzannah. He put in his bid. He put down his cash. He called out the numbers. He competed successfully. He had a good time. He got what he wanted. He
purchased yet another slave. He bought that Black girl standing on the platform,
nearly naked. He gave this new slave to his wife and Suzannah Wheatley was delighted. She and her husband went home. They rode there by carriage. They took that new
slave with them. An old slave commanded the horses that pulled the carriage that
carried the Wheatleys home, along with the new slave, that little girl they named
Phillis.

Why did they give her that name?

Was it a nice day?

Does it matter?

It was not natural. And she was the first. Phillis Miracle: Phillis Miracle
Wheatley: the first Black human being to be published in America. She was the second female to be published in America.

And the miracle begins in Africa. It was there that a bitterly anonymous man   15
and a woman conjoined to create this genius, this lost child of such prodigious aptitude and such beguiling attributes that she very soon interposed the reality of her
particular, dear life between the Wheatleys' notions about slaves and the predictable
outcome of such usual blasphemies against Black human beings.

Seven year old Phillis changed the slaveholding Wheatleys. She altered their
minds. She entered their hearts. She made them see her and when they truly saw her,
Phillis, darkly amazing them with the sweetness of her spirit and the alacrity of her
forbidden, strange intelligence, they in their own way, loved her as a prodigy, as a girl
mysterious but godly.

Sixteen months after her entry into the Wheatley household Phillis was talking
the language of her owners. Phillis was fluently reading the Scriptures. At eight and
a half years of age, this Black child, or "Africa's Muse," as she would later describe
herself, was fully literate in the language of this slaveholding land. She was competent
and eagerly asking for more: more books, more and more information. And Suzannah
Wheatley loved this child of her whimsical good luck. It pleased her to teach and to
train and to tutor this Black girl, this Black darling of God. And so Phillis delved into
kitchen studies commensurate, finally, to a classical education available to young
white men at Harvard.

She was nine years old.

What did she read? What did she memorize? What did the Wheatleys give to this African child? Of course, it was white, all of it white. It was English, most of it, from England. It was written, all of it, by white men taking their pleasure, their walks, their pipes, their pens and their paper, rather seriously, while somebody else cleaned the house, washed the clothes, cooked the food, watched the children: probably not slaves, but possibly a servant, or, commonly, a wife. It was written, this white man's literature of England, while somebody else did the other things that have to be done. And that was the literature absorbed by the slave, Phillis Wheatley. That was the writing, the thoughts, the nostalgia, the lust, the conceits, the ambitions, the mannerisms, the games, the illusions, the discoveries, the filth and the flowers that filled up the mind of the African child.

At fourteen, Phillis published her first poem, "To the University of Cambridge":   20 not a brief limerick or desultory teenager's verse, but thirty-two lines of blank verse telling those fellows what for and whereas, according to their own strict Christian codes of behavior. It is in that poem that Phillis describes the miracle of her own Black poetry in America:

> While an intrinsic ardor bids me write
> the muse doth promise to assist my pen

She says that her poetry results from "an intrinsic ardor," not to dismiss the extraordinary kindness of the Wheatleys, and not to diminish the wealth of white men's literature with which she found herself quite saturated, but it was none of these extrinsic factors that compelled the labors of her poetry. It was she who created herself a poet, notwithstanding and in despite of everything around her.

Two years later, Phillis Wheatley, at the age of sixteen, had composed three additional, noteworthy poems. This is one of them, "On Being Brought from Africa to America":

> 'Twas mercy brought me from my Pagan land,
> Taught my benighted soul to understand
> That there's a God, that there's a Savior too:
> Once I redemption neither sought nor knew
> Some view our sable race with scornful eye,
> "Their color is a diabolic die."
> Remember, *Christians*, Negroes, black as Cain,
> May be refin'd, and join the angelic train.

Where did Phillis get these ideas?

It's simple enough to track the nonsense about herself "benighted": *benighted* means surrounded and preyed upon by darkness. That clearly reverses what had happened to that African child, surrounded by and captured by the greed of white men. Nor should we find puzzling her depiction of Africa as "Pagan" versus somewhere "refined." Even her bizarre interpretation of slavery's theft of Black life as a merciful rescue should not bewilder anyone. These are regular kinds of iniquitous nonsense found in white literature, the literature that Phillis Wheatley assimilated, with no choice in the matter.

But here, in this surprising poem, this first Black poet presents us with some- 25 thing wholly her own, something entirely new. It is her matter of fact assertion that, "Once I redemption neither sought nor knew," as in once I existed beyond and without these terms under consideration. *Once I existed on other than your terms.* And, she says, *but* since we are talking your talk about good and evil/redemption and damnation, let me tell you something you had better understand. I am Black as Cain *and* I may very well be an angel of the Lord. Take care not to offend the Lord!

Where did that thought come to Phillis Wheatley?

Was it a nice day?

Does it matter?

Following her "intrinsic ardor," and attuned to the core of her own person, this girl, the first Black poet in America, had dared to redefine herself from house slave to, possibly, an angel of the Almighty.

She was making herself at home. 30

And, depending whether you estimated that nearly naked Black girl on the auction block to be seven or eight years old, in 1761, by the time she was eighteen or nineteen, she had published her first book of poetry, *Poems on Various Subjects, Religious and Moral.* It was published in London, in 1773, and the American edition appeared, years later, in 1786. Here are some examples from the poems of Phillis Wheatley:

From "On the Death of Rev. Dr. Sewell":

Come let us all behold with wishful eyes
The saint ascending to his native skies.

From "On the Death of the Rev. Mr. George Whitefield":

Take him, ye Africans, he longs for you,
Impartial Savior is his title due,
Washed in the fountain of redeeming blood,
You shall be sons and kings, and priest to God.

Here is an especially graceful and musical couplet, penned by the first Black poet in America:

But, see the softly stealing tears apace,
Pursue each other down the mourner's face;

This is an especially awful, virtually absurd set of lines by Ms. Wheatley: 35

"Go Thebons! Great nations will obey
And pious tribute to her altars pay:
With rights divine, the goddess be implor'd,
Nor be her sacred offspring nor ador'd."

Thus Manto spoke. The Thebon maids obey.
And pious tribute to the goddess pay.

Awful, yes. Virtually absurd; well, yes, except, consider what it took for that young African to undertake such personal abstraction and mythologies a million million miles remote from her own ancestry, and her own darkly formulating face! Consider what might meet her laborings, as poet, should she, instead, invent a vernacular precise to Senegal, precise to slavery, and, therefore, accurate to the secret wishings of her lost and secret heart?

If she, this genius teenager, should, instead of writing verse to comfort a white man upon the death of his wife, or a white woman upon the death of her husband, or verse commemorating weirdly fabled white characters bereft of children diabolically dispersed; if she, instead composed a poetry to speak her pain, to say her grief, to find her parents, or to stir her people into insurrection, what would we now know about God's darling girl, that Phillis?

Who would publish that poetry, then?

But Phillis Miracle, she managed, nonetheless, to write, sometimes, towards the personal truth of her experience.

For example, we find in a monumental poem entitled "Thoughts on the Works   40 of Providence," these five provocative lines, confirming every suspicion that most of the published Phillis Wheatley represents a meager portion of her concerns and inclinations.

As reason's pow'rs by day our God disclose,
So we may trace him in the night's repose.
Say what is sleep? And dreams how passing strange!
When action ceases, and ideas range
Licentious and unbounded o'er the plains.

And, concluding this long work, there are these lines:

Infinite *love* whene'er we turn our eyes
Appears: this ev'ry creature's wants supplies,
This most is heard in Nature's constant voice.
This makes the morn, and this the eve rejoice,
This bids the fost'ring rains and dews descend
To nourish all, to serve one gen'ral end,
The good of man: Yet man ungrateful pays
But little homage, and but little praise.

Now and again and again these surviving works of the genius Phillis Wheatley veer incisive and unmistakable, completely away from the verse of good girl Phillis ever compassionate upon the death of someone else's beloved, pious Phillis modestly enraptured by the glorious trials of virtue on the road to Christ, arcane Phillis intent upon an "Ode to Neptune," or patriotic Phillis penning an encomium to General George Washington ("Thee, first in peace and honor"). Then do we find that "Ethiop," as she once called herself, that "Africa's muse," knowledgeable, but succinct, on "dreams how passing strange! / When action ceases, and ideas range / Licentious and unbounded o'er the plains."

Phillis Licentious Wheatley?

Phillis Miracle Wheatley in contemplation of love and want of love?

Was it a nice day? 45

It was not natural. And she was the first.

Repeatedly singing for liberty, singing against the tyrannical, repeatedly avid in her trusting support of the American Revolution (how could men want freedom enough to die for it but then want slavery enough to die for that?) repeatedly lifting witness to the righteous and the kindly factors of her days, this was no ordinary teen-aged poet, male or female, Black or white. Indeed, the insistently concrete content of her tribute to the revolutionaries who would forge America, an independent nation state, indeed the specific daily substance of her poetry establishes Phillis Wheatley as the first decidedly American poet on this continent, Black or white, male or female.

Nor did she only love the ones who purchased her, a slave, those ones who loved her, yes, but with astonishment. Her lifelong friend was a young Black woman, Obour Tanner, who lived in Newport, Rhode Island, and one of her few poems dedicated to a living person, neither morbid nor ethereal, was written to the young Black visual artist Scipio Moorhead, himself a slave. It is he who crafted the portrait of Phillis that serves as her frontispiece profile in her book of poems. Here are the opening lines from her poem, "To S.M., A Young *African* Painter, On Seeing His Works."

> To show the lab'ring bosom's deep intent,
> And thought in living characters to paint.
> When first thy pencil did those beauties give,
> And breathing figures learnt from thee to live,
> How did those prospects give my soul delight,
> A new creation rushing on my sight?
>
> Still, wondrous youth! each noble path pursue,
> On deathless glories fix thine ardent view:
> Still may the painter's and the poet's fire
> To aid thy pencil, and thy verse conspire!
> And may the charms of each seraphic theme
> Conduct thy footsteps to immortal fame!

Remember that the poet so generously addressing the "wondrous youth" is certainly no older than eighteen, herself! And this, years before the American Revolution, and how many many years before the 1960s! This is the first Black poet of America addressing her Brother Artist not as so-and-so's Boy, but as "Scipio Moorhead, A Young African Painter."

Where did Phillis Miracle acquire this consciousness? 50

Was it a nice day?

It was not natural. And she was the first.

But did she — we may persevere, critical from the ease of the 1980s — did she love, did she need, freedom?

In the poem (typically titled at such length and in such deferential rectitude as to discourage most readers from scanning what follows), in the poem tided "To the Right Honorable William, Earl of Dartmouth, His Majesty's Principal Secretary of State for North America, etc.," Phillis Miracle has written these irresistible, authentic, felt lines:

> No more America in mournful strain
> Of wrongs, and grievance unredress'd complain,
> No longer shalt Thou dread the iron chain,
> Which wanton tyranny with lawless head
> Had made, and with it meant t' enslave the land.
> Should you, my Lord, while you peruse my song,
> Wonder from whence my love of Freedom sprung,
> Whence flow these wishes for the common good,
> By feeling hearts alone best understood,
> I, young in life, by seeming cruel of fate
> Was snatch'd from Afric's fancy'd happy seat.
> What pangs excruciating must molest
> What sorrows labour in my parent's breast?
>
> Steel'd was that soul and by no misery mov'd
> That from a father seized his babe belov'd
> Such, such my case. And can I then but pray
> Others may never feel tyrannic sway?

So did the darling girl of God compose her thoughts, prior to 1776.   55
And then.
And then her poetry, these poems, were published in London.
And then, during her twenty-first year, Suzannah Wheatley, the white woman slaveholder who had been changed into the white mother, the white mentor, the white protector of Phillis, died.

Without that white indulgence, that white love, without that white sponsorship, what happened to the young African daughter, the young African poet?
No one knows for sure.   60
With the death of Mrs. Wheatley, Phillis came of age, a Black slave in America.
Where did she live?
How did she eat?
No one knows for sure.
But four years later she met and married a Black man, John Peters. Mr. Peters   65
apparently thought well of himself, and of his people. He comported himself with dignity, studied law, argued for the liberation of Black people, and earned the every-day dislike of white folks. His wife bore him three children; all of them died.
His wife continued to be Phillis Miracle.

His wife continued to obey the "intrinsic ardor" of her calling and she never ceased the practice of her poetry. She hoped, in fact, to publish a second volume of her verse.

This would be the poetry of Phillis the lover of John, Phillis the woman, Phillis the wife of a Black man pragmatically premature in his defiant self-respect, Phillis giving birth to three children, Phillis, the mother, who must bury the three children she delivered into American life.

None of these poems was ever published.

This would have been the poetry of someone who had chosen herself free, and   70
brave to be free in a land of slavery

When she was thirty-one years old, in 1784, Phillis Wheatley, the first Black poet in America, she died.

Her husband, John Peters, advertised and begged that the manuscript of her poems she had given to someone, please be returned. But no one returned them.

And I believe we would not have seen them, anyway. I believe no one would have published the poetry of Black Phillis Wheatley, that grown woman who stayed with her chosen Black man. I believe that the death of Suzannah Wheatley, coincident with the African poet's twenty-first birthday, signalled, decisively, the end of her status as a child, as a dependent. From there we would hear from an independent Black woman poet in America.

Can you imagine that, in 1775?

Can you imagine that, today?   75

America has long been tolerant of Black children, compared to its reception of independent Black men and Black women.

She died in 1784.

Was it a nice day?

It was not natural. And she was the first.

Last week, as the final judge for this year's Loft McKnight Awards in creative   80
writing, awards distributed in Minneapolis, Minnesota, I read through sixteen manuscripts of rather fine poetry.

These are the terms, the lexical items, that I encountered there:

Rock, moon, star, roses, chimney, Prague, elms, lilac, railroad tracks, lake, lilies, snow geese, crow, mountain, arrow feathers, ear of corn, marsh, sandstone, rabbit-bush, gulley, pumpkins, eagle, tundra, dwarf willow, dipper-bird, brown creek, lizards, sycamores, glacier, canteen, skate eggs, birch, spruce, pumphandle

Is anything about that listing odd? I didn't suppose so. These are the terms, the lexical items accurate to the specific white Minnesota daily life of those white poets.

And so I did not reject these poems, I did not despise them saying, "How is this possible? Sixteen different manuscripts of poetry written in 1985 and not one of them uses the terms of my own Black life! Not one of them writes about the police murder of Eleanor Bumpurs or the Bernard Goetz shooting of four Black boys or apartheid in South Africa, or unemployment, or famine in Ethiopia, or rape, or fire escapes, or cruise missiles in the New York harbor, or medicare, or alleyways, or napalm, or $4.00 an hour, and no time off for lunch."

I did not and I would not presume to impose my urgencies upon white poets writing in America. But the miracle of Black poetry in America, the *difficult* miracle of Black poetry in America, is that we have been rejected and we are frequently dismissed as "political" or "topical" or "sloganeering" and "crude" and "insignificant" because, like Phillis Wheatley, we have persisted for freedom. We will write against South Africa and we will seldom pen a poem about wild geese flying over Prague, or grizzlies at the rain barrel under the dwarf willow trees. We will write, published or not, however we may, like Phillis Wheatley, of the terror and the hungering and the quandaries of our African lives on this North American soil. And as long as we study white literature, as long as we assimilate the English language and its implicit English values, as long as we allude and defer to gods we "neither sought nor knew," as long as we, Black poets in America, remain the children of slavery, as long as we do not come of age and attempt, then to speak the truth of our difficult maturity in an alien place, then we will be beloved, and sheltered, and published.

But not otherwise. And yet we persist.   85

And it was not natural. And she was the first.

This is the difficult miracle of Black poetry in America: that we persist, published or not, and loved or unloved: we persist.

And this is "Something Like A Sonnet for Phillis Miracle Wheatley":

Girl from the realm of birds florid and fleet
flying full feather in far or near weather
Who fell to a dollar lust coffled like meat
Captured by avarice and hate spit together
Trembling asthmatic alone on the slave block
built by a savagery travelling by carriage
viewed like a species of flaw in the livestock:
A child without safety of mother or marriage
Chosen by whimsy but born to surprise
They taught you to read but you learned how to write
Begging the universe into your eyes:
They dressed you in light but you dreamed
with the night.
From Africa singing of justice and grace,
Your early verse sweetens the fame of our Race.

And because we Black people in North America persist in an irony profound, Black poetry persists in this way:

Like the trees of winter and
like the snow which has no power
makes very little sound
but comes and collects itself

edible light on the black trees
The tall black trees of winter
lifting up a poetry of snow
so that we may be astounded
by the poems of Black
trees inside a cold environment

(2002)

Questions

1. What is June Jordan's purpose in writing this essay? How would you classify it — as biography? Literary criticism? Political analysis? Polemic? Tribute? Other?
2. What is the effect of Jordan's repetition of certain sentences, such as "It was not natural"? How is she using the word *natural*? Why does she repeatedly ask, "Was it a nice day?"
3. What evidence does Jordan provide to support her statement that "Phillis Miracle, she managed, nonetheless, to write, sometimes, towards the personal truth of her experience" (par. 39)?
4. Where in the essay does Jordan address counterarguments? What does she concede? How does she refute those arguments?
5. Identify places in the essay where Jordan focuses on her own experience. Do these add to the interest and authenticity of the essay, or does the subjectivity lessen the credibility of her argument? Consider Jordan's own poetry at the end of the essay as part of your response.
6. Why does Wheatley appeal so powerfully to Jordan? What is the nature of the relationship between these two women, as Jordan characterizes it?

Mr. Jefferson and the Trials of Phillis Wheatley

Henry Louis Gates Jr.

According to the Web site of the National Endowment for the Arts, "The Jefferson Lecture in the Humanities recognizes an individual who has made significant scholarly contributions to the humanities and who has the ability to communicate the knowledge and wisdom of the humanities in a broadly appealing way." Henry Louis Gates Jr. (b. 1950), currently the Alphonse Fletcher University Professor and director of the W. E. B. DuBois Institute for African and African American Research at Harvard University, delivered the lecture in 2002. Gates opened by pointing out the irony of his topic at an event named for Thomas Jefferson, who was a slaveholder and critic of Phillis Wheatley. Jefferson asserted, "Religion, indeed, has produced a Phillis Wheatley; but it could not produce a poet. The compositions published under her name are below the dignity of criticism." Dr. Gates began his lecture by establishing his ethos: "I stand here as a fellow countryman of Thomas Jefferson, in several senses: as a citizen, like all of you, of the republic of letters; as an American who believes deeply in the soaring promise of the Declaration of Independence . . . and hence, in a broad sense, a fellow Virginian. . . . For all of us, white and black, alike, Jefferson remains an essential ancestor." In the following excerpt from the end of the lecture, Gates examines the criticism Jefferson leveled at Wheatley as a poet and the response of more recent African American intellectuals and artists who were also skeptical of Wheatley's contribution to American literature.

[W]hat's important, for our purposes, is that even black authors accepted the premise that a group, a "race," had to *demonstrate* its equality through the creation of literature. When the historian David Levering Lewis aptly calls the Harlem Renaissance of the 1920s "art as civil rights," it is Jefferson who stands as the subtext for this formulation. Or listen to these words from James Weldon Johnson, written in 1922:

> A people may become great through many means, but there is only one measure by which its greatness is recognized and acknowledged. The final measure of the greatness of all peoples is the amount and standard of the literature and art they have produced. . . . No people that has produced great literature and art has ever been looked upon by the world as distinctly inferior.

In their efforts to prove Jefferson wrong, in other words, black writers created a body of literature, one with a prime political motive: to demonstrate black equality. Surely this is one of the oddest origins of a bellestric tradition in the history of world literature. Indeed, when Wole Soyinka received the Nobel Prize for Literature in 1986, a press release on behalf of the Nigerian government declared that — because of this prize — no longer could the world see Africans as distinctly inferior. The specter of Thomas Jefferson haunts even there, in Africa in 1986, as does the shadow of Phillis Wheatley.

Now, given all of the praise and attention that Wheatley received, given her unprecedented popularity and fame, one might be forgiven for thinking that Wheatley's career took off with the publication of her poems in 1773, and that she lived happily ever after. She did not: she died in 1784 in abject poverty, preceded in death by her three children, surrounded by filth, and abandoned, apparently, by her husband, John Peters, a fast-talking small businessman who affected the airs and dress of a gentleman and who would later sell off Phillis's proposed second volume of poetry — the one to have been dedicated to Franklin — which has never been recovered. Am I the only scholar who dreams of finding this lost manuscript?

And what happens to her literary legacy after she dies? Interwoven through Phillis Wheatley's intriguing and troubling afterlife is a larger parable about the politics of authenticity. For, as I've said, those rituals of validation scarcely died with Phillis Wheatley; on the contrary, they would become a central theme in the abolitionist era, where the publication of the slave narratives by and large also depended on letters of authentication that testified to the veracity and capacities of the ex-slave author who had written this work "by himself" or "by herself."

One might be forgiven, too, for imagining that Phillis Wheatley would be among   5
the most venerated names among black Americans today, as celebrated as Frederick
Douglass, Rosa Parks, or Dr. King. It was probably true that, as one writer claimed
several years ago, "historically throughout black America, more YMCAs, schools, dor-
mitories and libraries have been named for Phillis Wheatley than for any other black
woman." And, indeed, I can testify to the presence before 1955 of Phillis Wheatley
Elementary School in Ridgeley, West Virginia, a couple of hours up the Potomac, near
Piedmont, where I grew up — though it took until college for me to learn just who Miss
Wheatley was.

That Phillis Wheatley is not a household word within the black community is
owing largely to one poem that she wrote, an eight-line poem entitled "On Being
Brought from Africa to America." The poem was written in 1768, just seven years after
Phillis was purchased by Susanna Wheatley. Phillis was about fourteen years old.

The eight-line poem reads as follows:

> 'Twas mercy brought me from my Pagan land,
> Taught my benighted soul to understand
> That there's a God, that there's a Saviour too:
> Once I redemption neither sought nor knew.
> Some view our sable race with scornful eye,
> "Their colour is a diabolic die,"
> Remember, Christians, Negros, black as Cain,
> May be refin'd, and join th' angelic train.

This, it can be safely said, has been the most reviled poem in African American
literature. To speak in such glowing terms about the "mercy" manifested by the slave
trade was not exactly going to endear Miss Wheatley to black power advocates in
the 1960s. No Angela Davis[1] she! But as scholars such as Robinson, Julian Mason,
and John Shields point out, her political detractors ignore the fact that Wheatley
elsewhere in her poems complained bitterly about the human costs of the slave
trade, as in this example from her famous poem, "To the Right Honourable William,
Earl of Dartmouth."

> Should you, my lord, while you peruse my song,
> Wonder from whence my love of Freedom sprung,
> Whence flow these wishes for the common good,
> By feeling hearts alone best understood,
> I, young in life, by seeming cruel fate
> Was snatch'd from Afric's fancy'd happy seat:
> What pangs excruciating must molest,
> What sorrows labour in my parent's breast
> Steel'd was that soul and by no misery mov'd

---

[1]Former professor at the University of California, Santa Cruz, and a prominent feminist and
Civil Rights activist. — Eds.

That from a father seiz'd his babe belov'd:
Such, such my case. And can I then but pray
Others may never feel tyrannic sway?

And there is Wheatley's letter to the Reverend Sampson Occom, "a converted Mohegan Indian Christian Minister" who was the eighteenth century's most distinguished graduate from Moor's Charity Indian School of Lebanon, Connecticut, which would relocate in 1770 to Hanover, New Hampshire, where it would be renamed after the Earl of Dartmouth (and its student body broadened, against many protests, to include white students). Wheatley's letter about the evils of slavery was printed in the *Massachusetts Spy* on March 24, 1774; it reads in part:

> [I]n every [human] Breast, God has implanted a Principle, which we call Love of Freedom; it is impatient of Oppression, and pants for Deliverance; and by the Leave of our modern Egyptians I will assert, that the same Principle lives in us. God grant Deliverance in his own Way and Time, and get him honour upon all those whose Avarice impels them to countenance and help [forward] the Calamities of their fellow Creatures. This I desire not for their Hurt, but to convince them of the strange Absurdity of their Conduct whose Words and actions are so diametrically opposite. How well the Cry for Liberty, and the reverse Disposition for the exercise of oppressive Power over others agree, — I humbly think it does not require the Penetration of a Philosopher to determine.

Despite sentiments such as these, the fact that Wheatley's short poem has been   10
so widely anthologized in this century has made her something of a pariah in black political and critical circles, especially in the militant 1960s, where critics had a field day mocking her life and her works (most of which they had not read). . . .

Amiri Baraka, father of the Black Arts movement, in his seminal collection of essays entitled *Home* (1966), says that Wheatley's "pleasant imitations of 18th century English poetry are far, and finally, ludicrous departures from the huge black voices that splintered southern nights with their hollers, chants, arwhoolies, and ballits." For him, of course, these chants represent the authentic spirit of black creativity.

Stephen Henderson, writing in *The Militant Black Writer* (1969), argues that "it is no wonder that many black people have . . . rejected Phillis Wheatley," because her work reflects "the old self-hatred that one hears in the *Dozens* and in the blues. It is, frankly," he concludes, "the nigger component of the Black Experience." Dudley Randall wrote in that same year that "whatever references she made to her African heritage were derogatory, reflecting her status as a favored house slave and a curiosity."

Addison Gayle, a major black aesthetic critic, wrote in *The Way of the World* (1975) that Wheatley was the first black writer "to accept the images and symbols of degradation passed down from the South's most intellectual lights and the first to speak from a sensibility finely tuned by close approximation to their oppressors." Wheatley, in sum, "had surrendered the right to self-definition to others."

And the assaults continued, the critical arrows arriving in waves. This once most revered figure in black letters would, in the sixties, become the most reviled figure. Angelene Jamison argued in 1974 that Wheatley and her poetry were "too white," a sentiment that Ezekiel Mphalele echoed two years later when he indicted her for having "a white mind," and said he felt "too embarrassed even to mention her in passing" in a study of black literature. Similarly, Eleanor Smith maintained that Wheatley was "taught by whites to think," thus she had "a white mind" and "white orientations." Here we're given Phillis Wheatley as Uncle Tom's mother.

And examples could be multiplied. But it's clear enough what we're witnessing. The Jeffersonian critique has been recuperated and recycled by successive generations of black writers and critics. Precisely the sort of mastery of the literary craft and themes that led to her vindication before the Boston town-hall tribunal,[2] was now summoned as proof that she was, culturally, an impostor. Phillis Wheatley, having been painstakingly authenticated in her own time, now stands as a symbol of falsity, artificiality, of spiritless and rote convention. As new cultural vanguards sought to police and patrol the boundaries of black art, Wheatley's glorious carriage would become a tumbril.

Meet Phillis Wheatley, race traitor. . . .

And this has not merely turned out to be a sixties phenomenon. Those haunting questions of identity linger with us still, much to the devastation of inner-city youth. I read with dismay the results of a poll published a few years ago. The charge of "acting white" was applied to speaking standard English, getting straight A's, or even visiting the Smithsonian! Think about it: we have moved from a situation where Phillis Wheatley's acts of literacy could be used to demonstrate our people's inherent humanity and their inalienable right to freedom, to a situation where acts of literacy are stigmatized somehow as acts of racial betrayal. Phillis Wheatley, so proud to the end of her hard-won attainments, would weep. So would Douglass; so would DuBois. In reviving the ideology of "authenticity" — especially in a Hip-Hop world where too many of our children think it's easier to become Michael Jordan than Vernon Jordan — we have ourselves reforged the manacles of an earlier, admittedly racist era.

And, even now, so the imperative remains: to cast aside the mine-and-thine rhetoric of cultural ownership. For cultures can no more be owned than people can. As W.E.B. DuBois put it so poignantly:

> I sit with Shakespeare and he winces not. Across the color line I move arm and arm with Balzac and Dumas, where smiling men and welcoming women glide in gilded halls. From out the caves of evening that swing between the strong-limbed earth and the tracery of the stars, I summon Aristotle and Aurelius and what soul I will, and they come all graciously with no scorn nor condescension. So, wed with Truth, I dwell above the veil.

---

[2]Wheatley was allegedly brought before a tribunal of Boston luminaries and asked to prove that she and she alone wrote her poetry. After the oral examination, the tribunal released the following statement: "We whose Names are under-written, do assure the World, that the Poems specified in the following Page, were (as we verily believe) written by Phillis, a young Negro Girl, who was but a few Years since, brought an uncultivated Barbarian from Africa, and has ever since been, and now is, under the Disadvantage of serving as a Slave in a Family in this Town. She has been examined by some of the best judges, and is thought qualified to write them." —Eds.

This is the vision that we must embrace, as full and equal citizens of the republic of letters, a republic whose citizenry must always embrace both Phillis Wheatley and Thomas Jefferson.

Frederick Douglass recognized this clearly; in a speech delivered in 1863, at the height of the Civil War, Douglass argued that his contemporaries in the Confederacy selectively cited Jefferson's proslavery writings when convenient, ignoring the rest. For Douglass, black Americans were the true patriots, because they fully embraced Jeffersonian democracy; they were the most Jeffersonian Americans of all, allowing us to witness a new way to appreciate the miracle that is America. Here was Jefferson, whom Douglass called "the sage of the Old Dominion," cast as the patron saint of the black freedom struggle. 20

If Frederick Douglass could recuperate and champion Thomas Jefferson, during the Civil War of all times, is it possible for us to do the same for a modest young poet named Phillis Wheatley? What's required is only that we recognize that there are no "white minds" or "black minds": there are only minds, and yes, they are, as that slogan has it, a terrible thing to waste. What would happen if we ceased to stereotype Wheatley but, instead, read her, read her with all the resourcefulness that she herself brought to her craft? I can already hear the skeptics: that's all well and good, they'll say, but how is it possible to read Wheatley's "On Being Brought from Africa to America"? But, of course, there are few things that cannot be redeemed by those of charitable inclination. And just a few days after a recent Fourth of July, I received a fax, sent from a public fax machine in Madison, Connecticut, from a man named Walter Grigo.

Mr. Grigo — a freelance writer — had evidently become fascinated with anagrams, and wished to alert me to quite a stunning anagram indeed. "On Being Brought from Africa to America," this eight-line poem, was, in its entirety, an anagram, he pointed out. If you simply rearranged the letters, you got the following plea:

> Hail, Brethren in Christ! Have ye
> Forgotten God's word? Scriptures teach
> Us that bondage is wrong. His own greedy
> Kin sold Joseph into slavery. "Is there
> No balm in Gilead?" God made us all.
> Aren't African men born to be free? So
> Am I. Ye commit so brute a crime
> On us. But we can change thy attitude.
> America, manumit our race. I thank the
> Lord.

It's indeed the case that every letter in Wheatley's poem can be rearranged to produce an entirely new work, one with the reverse meaning of the apologetic and infamous original. "Could it be that Phillis Wheatley was this devious?" Mr. Grigo asked me. And it's fun to think that the most scorned poem in the tradition, all this time, was a secret, coded love letter to freedom, hiding before our very eyes. I don't claim that this stratagem was the result of design, but we're free to find significance, intended or no, where we uncover it. And so we're reminded of our task, as readers: to learn to read Wheatley anew, unblinkered by the anxieties of her time and ours. The challenge isn't to read white, or read black; it is to read. If Phillis Wheatley stood for anything, it was the creed that culture was, could be, the equal possession of all humanity. It was a lesson she was swift to teach, and that we have been slow to learn. But the learning has begun. Almost two and a half centuries after a schooner brought this African child to our shores, we can finally say: Welcome home, Phillis; welcome home.

(2002)

Questions

1. Why does Henry Louis Gates Jr. object to the "premise that . . . a 'race' . . . [has] to *demonstrate* its equality through the creation of literature" (par. 1)?
2. How does Gates use Wheatley's own writings (poems and letters) as evidence in his argument? How convincing is his claim that one text offsets or disputes another?
3. What are the chief criticisms of Wheatley that Gates cites? On what basis does he call them into question?
4. Why does Gates link "haunting questions" (par. 17) regarding Wheatley's identity to similar questions that linger in the twenty-first century? Specifically, what does he mean by this statement: "we have moved from a situation where Phillis Wheatley's acts of literacy could be used to demonstrate our people's inherent humanity and their inalienable right to freedom, to a situation where acts of literacy are stigmatized somehow as acts of racial betrayal" (par. 17)?
5. What, finally, does Gates believe is the lasting influence of Wheatley?

Making Connections

1. What similarities are there in Phillis Wheatley's poems "On Being Brought from Africa to America" (p. 507) and "To the University of Cambridge, in New-England" (p. 510)?

2. How does the persona of Wheatley's speaker in "To S.M." (p. 508) differ from that in her poem to George Washington (p. 512)?

3. In which of her poems does Wheatley express ideas similar to those in her letter to the Reverend Samson Occom (p. 514)?

4. With thirty-four years between them, June Jordan (p. 517) and Kevin Young (p. 515) represent different generations of African American poets. Despite this gap, what is there about Wheatley that intrigues both of them? What are a few differences in their views of her?

5. Would Henry Louis Gates Jr. (p. 527) more closely share the views of Young or Jordan?

6. What similarities and differences do you see in Gates's and Jordan's analyses of "On Being Brought from Africa to America"?

Entering the Conversation

As you respond to each of the following prompts, support your position with appropriate evidence, including at least two of Wheatley's poems and two other sources from this Conversation on the influence of Phillis Wheatley, unless otherwise indicated.

1. Was Wheatley a conventional thinker who emulated the style and structure of eighteenth-century British poets to appeal to a white readership, or was she a subversive artist who shrewdly cloaked her rebellious thoughts in a form most likely to gain her an admiring readership? Explain why you see her in one of these opposing characterizations or in another way.

2. Defend, challenge, or qualify the following statement by Gates in the 2002 Jefferson Lecture in the Humanities: "If Phillis Wheatley stood for anything, it was the creed that culture was, could be, the equal possession of all humanity" (par. 23).

3. Discuss the claim made by scholar Mary McAleer Balkun that Wheatley wrote poems intended for a Christian audience, yet these poems use a variety of literary techniques to take "the audience from a position of initial confidence and agreement to confusion and uncertainty, to a new ideological position at the conclusion of each poem."

4. In *Giant Steps: The New Generation of African American Writers* edited by Young, he ends with his own poem "Homage to Phillis Wheatley." Explain why you believe that this tribute to Wheatley is or is not a fitting coda to a collection of writing by contemporary young African American poets.

5. Some argue that Wheatley's poems are significant primarily as artifacts of history, while others take the position that they represent artistic genius. Explain your view on the influence and reputation of the poetry of Phillis Wheatley.

6. Research and read one or more children's or young adult books on Wheatley (e.g., *Phillis Wheatley: Young Revolutionary Poet* or *A Voice of Her Own: The Story of Phillis Wheatley*) and discuss how she is characterized. How accurate or fair do you find these perspectives?

7. In his biography of Wheatley, scholar Vincent Carretta describes "the nadir of this movement" to discredit the contribution of Wheatley as "the accusations that Wheatley had 'a white mind,' and was 'not sensitive enough to the needs of her own people to demonstrate a kinship to Blacks in her life or writings.'" Write an argument refuting such accusations.

Grammar as Rhetoric and Style

Appositives

An appositive is a noun or noun phrase that tells you more about a preceding noun, pronoun, or noun phrase. The appositive and the word or phrase to which it refers may be said to be in apposition. In each sentence below, the appositive is printed in blue. The arrow points to the noun, pronoun, or noun phrase to which the appositive refers.

The essential traits and qualities of the male, the hall-marks of the unpolluted masculine, are at the same time the hall-marks of the numskull.

—H. L. MENCKEN

When she was thirty-one years old, in 1784, Phillis Wheatley, the first Black poet in America, she died.

—JUNE JORDAN

In Philadelphia, the City of Brotherly Love, anti-Catholic sentiment, combined with the country's anti-immigrant mood, fueled the Bible Riots of 1844, in which houses were torched, two Catholic churches were destroyed, and at least twenty people were killed.

—KENNETH C. DAVIS

Future President James Madison stepped into the breach.

—KENNETH C. DAVIS

Punctuation and Appositives

Choosing Punctuation

The last example given does not use punctuation to set off the appositive from the rest of the sentence, but the others do. Here's why: if the appositive is not essential to the meaning of the sentence but is more of an aside or a parenthetical remark (the technical term is *nonrestrictive*), then the writer uses punctuation to set it off. If the appositive *is* essential to the meaning of the sentence (*restrictive*), then the writer does *not* set it off with punctuation marks. Simply put, include what is essential; exclude what is not. In the first and second examples given above, the appositives for "essential traits and qualities of the male" and for "Phillis Wheatley" further identifiy each of them, but not in a way that is essential to the sentences, so H. L. Mencken and June Jordan set off the appositives with commas. In the final sentences, Kenneth C. Davis thought it essential that he tell the reader *which* future president he is writing about, so he does not punctuate the appositive.

If your appositive needs punctuation, you can set it off in one of three ways. First, you can use one or two commas.

"We respectfully submit this humble prayer," the Rev. Kirbyjon Caldwell

concluded his benediction, "in the name that's above all other names, Jesus the Christ."   — JEFF JACOBY

Second, you can use one or two dashes.

Most Americans who followed events in the Mediterranean viewed

the struggle between the United States and the Barbary nations — a struggle that would last well into the nineteenth century — as a kind of holy war.
— JOHN FEA

Third, you can use a colon.

Caldwell's prayer in particular was "astonishing" for being so "exclusionary" —

for creating "a two-tiered system for Americans: those able to say amen — Christians — and those who can't."   — JEFF JACOBY

Dashes emphasize the appositive more than commas do. Furthermore, if an appositive contains its own internal commas, then one dash, two dashes, or a colon makes it easier to read the complete sentence.

Position of Appositive: Before or After a Proper Noun?

All the examples so far in this lesson have shown an appositive coming *after* the proper noun or pronoun it details. Proper nouns in apposition usually come first, with the appositive following.

"To S.M. a Young *African* Painter, on Seeing His Works"
— PHILLIS WHEATLEY

The proper noun may also follow, depending on the writer's choice.

"To His Excellency General Washington"   — PHILLIS WHEATLEY

I drew a Sketch of the Plan and Rules that would be necessary, and got

a skilful Conveyancer Mr Charles Brockden to put the whole in Form of
Articles of Agreement. . . . — Benjamin Franklin

Whether you put the appositive before or after the noun it details is a stylistic choice. If in doubt, read the sentence aloud with several surrounding sentences to determine which placement sounds better. Of course, sometimes a writer may alternate placement in a sentence.

Rhetorical and Stylistic Strategy

Appositives generally serve two rhetorical and stylistic functions:

- First, an appositive can *clarify* a term by providing a proper noun or a synonym for the term, by defining or explaining the term, or by getting more specific.

PROPER NOUN   He was addressing the members of America's oldest synagogue,

the Touro Synagogue in Newport, Rhode Island (where his letter is read aloud every August). — Kenneth C. Davis

SYNONYM   What then is the American, this new man?
— Hector St. John de Crèvecoeur

If we meet an equal, a sensible friend, we will reward him with the hand of amity, and through life we will be assiduous to promote his happiness. . . . — Judith Sargent Murray

DEFINITION   So begins Article 11 of the Treaty of Tripoli, a 1797 agreement

between the United States and Tripoli, a Muslim nation located on the Barbary coast of northern Africa. — John Fea

EXPLANATION   An over-scrupulous jealousy of danger to the rights of the people, which is more commonly the fault of the head than of the heart, will be presented as mere pretense and artifice, the

stale bait for popularity at the expense of the public good.
— Alexander Hamilton

Liberty is to faction, what air is to fire, an ailment without which it instantly expires. — James Madison

SPECIFICITY   Here is Washington's entire diary entry for October 24, 1774,
a day that he was in Philadelphia, as a delegate to the
Continental Congress, debating, among other things, a
petition to be sent to the King: "Dined with Mr. Mease &
Spent the Evening at the New Tavern."   —JILL LEPORE

The most famous dissidents within the Puritan community,
Roger Williams and Anne Hutchinson, were banished
following disagreements over theology and policy.
                                                —KENNETH C. DAVIS

TO IDENTIFY   We the people of the United States, in order to form a more
WITH OR   perfect union, establish justice, insure domestic tranquility,
TO ADDRESS   provide for the common defense, promote the general
welfare, and secure the blessings of liberty to ourselves and
our posterity, do ordain and establish this Constitution for
the United States of America.
            — PREAMBLE TO THE UNITED STATES CONSTITUTION

• Second, an appositive can smooth choppy writing. Note how stilted and
wooden the sentences below sound without appositives.

NO APPOSITIVE   The most famous dissidents within the Puritan community
were Roger Williams and Anne Hutchinson. They were
banished following disagreements over theology and policy.

APPOSITIVE   The most famous dissidents within the Puritan community,
Roger Williams and Anne Hutchinson, were banished
following disagreements over theology and policy.
                                                —KENNETH C. DAVIS

NO APPOSITIVE   Philadelphia is the City of Brotherly Love. In that city,
anti-Catholic sentiment, combined with the country's
anti-immigrant mood, fueled the Bible Riots of 1844, in
which houses were torched, two Catholic churches were
destroyed, and at least twenty people were killed.

APPOSITIVE   In Philadelphia, the City of Brotherly Love, anti-Catholic
sentiment, combined with the country's anti-immigrant mood,
fueled the Bible Riots of 1844, in which houses were torched,
two Catholic churches were destroyed, and at least twenty
people were killed.   —KENNETH C. DAVIS

NO APPOSITIVE   James Madison was a future president. He stepped into the
breach.

APPOSITIVE   Future President James Madison stepped into the breach.
— KENNETH C. DAVIS

Sometimes a sentence will contain a double appositive; that is, there will be an appositive for an earlier appositive.

Even the Franco Englishman, W. L. George, one of the most sharp-witted of the faculty, wastes a whole book up on the demonstration, and then, with a great air of uttering something new, gives it the humourless title of "The Intelligence of Women."
— H. L. MENCKEN

Notice that W. L. George is in apposition with "the Franco Englishman," providing his name; then the noun phrase "one of the most sharp-witted of the faculty" further describes him in another appositive. Be on the lookout for a few examples like this one as you work through the exercises.

• EXERCISE 1 •

Each of the following is a direct quotation from a selection in this chapter. Identify the appositive in each and the word or phrase it details. Note that at least one of the examples contains a double appositive.

1. It was written, this white man's literature of England, while somebody else did the other things that have to be done. And that was the literature absorbed by the slave, Phillis Wheatley.   — JUNE JORDAN

2. If she, this genius teenager, should, instead of writing verse to comfort a white man upon the death of his wife, or a white woman upon the death of her husband, or verse commemorating weirdly fabled white characters bereft of children diabolically dispersed; if she, instead composed a poetry to speak her pain, to say her grief, to find her parents, or to stir her people into insurrection, what would we now know about God's darling girl, that Phillis?   — JUNE JORDAN

3. Addison Gayle, a major black aesthetic critic, wrote in *The Way of the World* (1975) that Wheatley was the first black writer "to accept the images and symbols of degradation passed down from the South's most intellectual lights and the first to speak from a sensibility finely tuned by close approximation to their oppressors."   — HENRY LOUIS GATES JR.

4. 'Twas not long since I left my native shore
The land of errors, and *Egyptian* gloom.   — PHILLIS WHEATLEY

5. Amiri Baraka, father of the Black Arts movement, in his seminal collection of essays entitled *Home* (1966), says that Wheatley's "pleasant imitations of 18th century English poetry are far, and finally, ludicrous departures from

the huge black voices that splintered southern nights with their hollers, chants, arwhoolies, and ballits." — HENRY LOUIS GATES JR.

6. [B]ut I must now complain of it, as unjust and unequal, That my Betrayer and Undoer, the first Cause of all my faults and Miscarriages (if they must be deemed such) should be advanced to Honour and Power in the Government, that punishes my Misfortunes with Stripes and Infamy.
— BENJAMIN FRANKLIN

7. Can a Sikh student wear the *kirpan*, the symbolic knife required of all initiated Sikhs, to school, or a Sikh worker wear a turban on a hard-hat job, in apparent violation of safety regulations? — DIANE L. ECK

8. If we meet an equal, a sensible friend, we will reward him with the hand of amity, and through life we will be assiduous to promote his happiness.
— JUDITH SARGENT MURRAY

9. We, therefore, the Representatives of the united States of America, in General Congress, Assembled, appealing to the Supreme Judge of the world for the rectitude of our intentions . . . — THOMAS JEFFERSON

• EXERCISE 2 •

Provide the correct punctuation for each of the following sentences by using dashes, commas, or colons to separate appositives from the rest of the sentences. If a sentence does not need punctuation around the appositive, write "NP" for "no punctuation." Be ready to explain why your choice of punctuation is the most effective in each case.

1. Several West African countries Nigeria, Ghana, Benin, Cameroon, and Togo were at some time in their history under colonial rule.

2. The mayoral candidate's rally opened to throngs of people an unusually large turnout for a cold, rainy day.

3. The British parliamentary system has two branches the House of Lords and the House of Commons.

4. The fifth canon of rhetoric style includes a writer's choices of diction and syntax.

5. One of our most popular poets Billy Collins is also one of our most gifted.

6. The surgeons reconstructed his hand the most damaged part of his body.

7. The rewards of hard work both physical and mental are often intangible.

8. Nadine Gordimer a white South African author won the Nobel Prize in Literature in 1991 when the country was still under the rule of apartheid.

9. Don't you think that businesses should close on July 4 the birthday of our country?

• EXERCISE 3 •

Combine each of the following pairs of sentences into one more fluent and coherent sentence by using an appositive. Be sure to punctuate correctly.

1. The *Times* is a world-renowned newspaper. It is delivered to my house every day.

2. Dolores Cunningham is the first mayor in our town's history to increase jobs during her four-year term. She is an advocate of the supply-side theory of economics.

3. A major health problem for teenagers is bulimia. Bulimia is a potentially life-threatening eating disorder.

4. My car is in the parking lot. It's an old blue station wagon with a dent in the fender.

5. That call was from Bridget. She's the top student in my calculus class.

6. The Edwardsville Tigers are the only baseball team ever to lose a series that it had led three games to none. They will be forever remembered for this colossal choke.

7. Warren G. Harding defeated James Cox in the 1920 presidential election by 26 percentage points. This was the biggest landslide victory in the history of U.S. presidential elections.

8. The service opened to the choir's rendition of Handel's "Hallelujah Chorus." That performance was a smashing success.

• EXERCISE 4 •

Identify the appositives in the following sentences from "Rip Van Winkle," by Washington Irving, and explain their effect. Note that all are direct quotations.

1. The Following Tale was found among the papers of the late Diedrich Knickerbocker, an old gentleman of New-York, who was very curious in the Dutch history of the province, and the manners of the descendants from its primitive settlers.

2. This, however, always provoked a fresh volley from his wife, so that he was fain to draw off his forces, and take to the outside of the house — the only side which, in truth, belongs to a henpecked husband.

3. Rip's sole domestic adherent was his dog Wolf. . . .

4. The opinions of this junto were completely controlled by Nicholas Vedder, a patriarch of the village, and landlord of the inn, at the door of which he took his seat from morning till night. . . .

5. He looked in vain for the sage Nicholas Vedder, with his broad face, double chin, and fair long pipe, uttering clouds of tobacco smoke instead of idle speeches; or Van Bummel, the schoolmaster, doling forth the contents of an ancient newspaper.

6. That it was affirmed that the great Hendrick Hudson, the first discoverer of the river and country, kept a kind of vigil there every twenty years, with his crew of the Half-moon, being permitted in this way to revisit the scenes of his enterprize, and keep a guardian eye upon the river, and the great city called by his name.

7. His son Rip, an urchin begotten in his own likeness, promised to inherit the habits, with the old clothes of his father.

8. "Alas! gentlemen," cried Rip, somewhat dismayed, "I am a poor quiet man, a native of the place, and a loyal subject of the King, God bless him!"

• EXERCISE 5 •

Each of the following comes from a selection in the chapter and includes one or more appositives. Identify the appositives, explain their effect, and then write a sentence of your own using that sentence as a model.

1. Even as late as 1960, Catholic presidential candidate John F. Kennedy felt compelled to make a major speech declaring that his loyalty was to America, not the pope. (And as recently as the 2008 Republican primary campaign, Mormon candidate Mitt Romney felt compelled to address the suspicions still directed toward the Church of Jesus Christ of Latter-day Saints.)

— KENNETH C. DAVIS, PAR. 28

2. I believe no one would have published the poetry of Black Phillis Wheatley, that grown woman who stayed with her chosen Black man.

— JUNE JORDAN, PAR. 73

3. For example, in 1996 Rose Hamid, a twelve-year veteran flight attendant with U.S. Air, became increasingly serious about her faith in the wake of some health problems and made the decision to wear a head scarf.

— DIANE L. ECK, PAR. 3

4. In men, too, the same merciless perspicacity sometimes shows itself — men recognized to be more aloof and uninflammable than the general — men of special talent for the logical — sardonic men, cynics.

— H. L. MENCKEN, PAR. 4

5. Meet Phillis Wheatley, race traitor.   — HENRY LOUIS GATES JR., PAR. 16

6. Should it still be vociferated, "Your domestick employments are sufficient" — I would calmly ask, is it reasonable, that a candidate for immortality, for the joys of heaven, an intelligent being, who is to spend an eternity in contemplating the works of the Deity, should at present be so degraded, as to be allowed no other ideas, than those which are suggested by the mechanism of a pudding, or the sewing the seams of a garment?

— JUDITH SARGENT MURRAY, PAR. 4

7. Our vaunted system of "separation of powers" and "checks and balances" — a legacy of the founders' mistrust of "factions" — means that we rarely have anything that can truly be described as a "government."

— SANFORD LEVINSON, PAR. 4

8. And there is Wheatley's letter to the Reverend Sampson Occom, "a converted Mohegan Indian Christian Minister" who was the eighteenth century's most distinguished graduate from Moor's Charity Indian School of Lebanon, Connecticut, which would relocate in 1770 to Hanover, New Hampshire, where it would be renamed after the Earl of Dartmouth (and its student body broadened, against many protests, to include white students).   — HENRY LOUIS GATES JR., PAR. 9

9. In fact, the sentiment expressed in the Treaty of Tripoli — that the United States was not "founded on the Christian religion" — can hardly be reconciled with the way that politicians, historians, clergy, educators, and other writers perceived the United States in the first one hundred years of its existence.   — JOHN FEA, PAR. 3

10. These are the implements of war and subjugation; the last arguments to which kings resort.   — PATRICK HENRY, PAR. 3

Suggestions for Writing
A New Republic

Now that you have read and studied a variety of selections centering on America's colonial beginnings and its transformation into a new republic, explore the significance of that time period by synthesizing your own thoughts and ideas with those expressed in the readings.

1. Thomas Paine states in *Rights of Man*:

   > When it shall be said in any country in the world my poor are happy; neither ignorance nor distress is to be found among them; my jails are empty of prisoners, my streets of beggars; the aged are not in want; the taxes are not oppressive; the rational world is my friend, because I am a friend of its happiness: when these things can be said, then may that country boast its constitution and its government.

   We can certainly say that it was the hope of Paine and the Founding Fathers that that statement could be said of the United States. To what extent do you think the statement holds true today?

2. Native Americans are central figures in *William Penn's Treaty with the Indians* (p. 369), the painting by Benjamin West, and also in the speech by Chief Tecumseh (p. 430). Compare the attitudes of West and Tecumseh toward their subjects. Pay particular attention to the intended audience for each piece.

3. In this chapter, we have two exchanges by letter: one between Benjamin Banneker and Thomas Jefferson (p. 426) and one between John and Abigail Adams (p. 385). Compare and contrast the exchanges, taking particular note of their appeals to ethos, logos, and pathos.

4. It might seem peculiar that despite being such a dramatic period in American history, we begin and end the chronological section of this chapter with humorous pieces, that is, Benjamin Franklin's "The Speech of Miss Polly Baker" (p. 349) and Washington Irving's "Rip Van Winkle" (p. 435). How effectively does humor frame the serious content of the chapter? Is the contrast appropriate? Explain.

5. Compare and contrast the uses of irony in the satirical pieces in this chapter by Franklin, H. L. Mencken (p. 423), and Irving. Which delivers the most sardonic tone? Which is mildest in its use of irony? Which is the most successful satire? Explain.

6. This chapter contains several speeches and addresses: those by "Miss Polly Baker," Patrick Henry (p. 373), George Washington (p. 452), Red Jacket (p. 484), Tecumseh, Jane Addams (p. 460), John F. Kennedy (p. 486), and Michael Bloomberg (p. 496). Compare and contrast three of the speeches in terms of how effectively they address the components of Aristotle's rhetorical triangle.

7. Women and women's rights are central to the selections by Franklin, Abigail Adams, Elizabeth Cady Stanton (p. 393), and Judith Sargent Murray (p. 419). Compare and contrast how three of these writers use rhetorical strategies to establish their positions regarding women in America.

8. Now that you have carefully read the Second Amendment to the Constitution, how do you interpret its meaning as it relates to current discussions and arguments regarding firearms?

9. In a 1933 speech, Alfred E. Smith said, "All the ills of democracy can be cured by more democracy." What might be some of the "ills" of democracy? How would James Madison (p. 407), Alexander Hamilton (p. 404), Jefferson (p. 389), and Paine (p. 375) respond to Smith's remark? Compose an imaginary discussion among the four about this topic.

10. In the November 30, 2012, issue of the *New York Times*, historian and law professor Paul Finkelman wrote,

> We are endlessly fascinated with Jefferson, in part because we seem unable to reconcile the rhetoric of liberty in his writing with the reality of slave owning and his lifetime support for slavery. Time and again, we play down the latter in favor of the former, or write off the paradox as somehow indicative of his complex depths. . . . There is, it is true, a compelling paradox about Jefferson: when he wrote the Declaration of Independence, announcing the "self-evident" truth that all men are "created equal," he owned some 175 slaves. Too often, scholars and readers use those facts as a crutch, to write off Jefferson's inconvenient views as products of the time and the complexities of the human condition.

But at that same time there were some men — for example, Paine — who would not own slaves and spoke out against slavery. Finkelman reminds us that many of Jefferson's contemporaries freed their slaves during or after the Revolution — even Washington freed them in his will — while Jefferson did not. Even after his death, his will emancipated only five of his slaves. Write an essay that defends, challenges, or qualifies Finkelman's ideas regarding Jefferson.

11. How have the readings in this chapter expanded your understanding of early American history of the founding fathers? Refer specifically to several selections to support your answer.

America in Conflict
1830–1865

As America entered the mid-nineteenth century, the nation was experiencing widespread expansion in almost every conceivable way. In 1830, nearly all land west of the Missouri border was either unorganized territory or controlled by Mexico, but by 1865, the United States would control the continent from shore to shore. America's population grew at unprecedented rates during this period, from 13 million people to more than 30 million. Expansion in territory and population went hand in hand with technological innovations and massive infrastructure improvements. The Erie Canal, finished in 1825, enabled shipping from New York Harbor into the middle of the country via the Great Lakes, turning New York City into the nation's most important port. Steamboats and steam locomotives became viable forms of transportation, and thirty-five thousand miles of railroad track were laid down across the country. Steam-powered manufacturing equipment was invented, including printing presses for books and newspapers. And yet, this industrialization and urbanization was not uniform across the nation: while cities and manufacturing boomed in Northern states, the Southern economy remained largely agrarian, slave based, and highly lucrative for landowners thanks to cotton, a cash crop that would account for roughly 60 percent of America's exports.

The promise of economic opportunity and cheap farmland lured millions of emigrants from Europe, particularly from Ireland, Germany, Scandinavia, and Central Europe. America's westward expansion drew settlers into uncharted territory as wagon trains braved the Oregon Trail. The discovery of gold in California in the late 1840s initiated a gold rush, drawing even more people west. One group of people, however, did not go by choice. As the American population continued to grow, the Native American populations in the East were driven onto reservations and Indian Territories in the West. The Indian Removal Act of 1830, signed by President Andrew Jackson, relocated the Cherokee, Seminole, Muscogee (Creek), Chickasaw, and Choctaw tribes from their homelands in the American Southeast to what would become Oklahoma. The thousand-mile journey was long and arduous, and each tribe would suffer heavy losses from disease, exposure to the elements, and insufficient rations, though perhaps none suffered as much as the Cherokee, who lost nearly half of their population. The route of the forced relocation would come to be called the "Trail of Tears." One important voice regarding the treatment of Native Americans

EMANUEL LEUTZE, *WESTWARD THE COURSE OF EMPIRE TAKES ITS WAY*, 1861, 20' × 30'; MURAL IN THE U.S. CAPITOL, HOUSE OF REPRESENTATIVES CHAMBER.

during this period was that of Chief Seattle, whose defiant message to President Franklin Pierce in 1854 is included in this chapter.

Increasing industrialization, along with an expanding frontier, created a shifting natural landscape as wilderness became increasingly settled and developed. A new adventurous and romantic spirit began to express itself in American arts, especially in the poetry of William Cullen Bryant and in the paintings of Thomas Cole and Asher B. Durand. An "American Renaissance," in the words of literary critic F. O. Matthiessen, began in Concord, Massachusetts, and its hopeful optimism flourished in the writings of transcendentalists Henry David Thoreau and Ralph Waldo Emerson and in the poetry of Walt Whitman. Emerson, the "sage of Concord," would become the most influential writer of the century, and his essay "Self-Reliance" is regarded as the quintessential expression of the American spirit. The darker, more skeptical side of romanticism could be seen in the brooding fiction of such writers as Edgar Allan Poe, Nathaniel Hawthorne (who called his fictional works not stories and novels but "tales" and "romances"), and Herman Melville, the author of *Moby-Dick*, a book considered by many modern critics to be the greatest American novel, the only other contender from the nineteenth century being *The Adventures of Huckleberry Finn* by Mark Twain. In this chapter, you will encounter readings by these writers and enter a Conversation about Henry David Thoreau, the transcendentalist writer who temporarily rejected urban society in Massachusetts for a solitary life in the woods near Walden Pond. Readings by and about Thoreau will ask you to investigate how and why he still matters and why his ideas resonate today.

While romanticism ran through much of early American literature, its hopeful optimism could hardly be said to express the feelings or conditions of three groups of Americans: slaves, Native Americans, and women. They were simply excluded from the American promise. At the same time, this period also became one of immense social reform. Public schools were instituted, prisons were reenvisioned as institutions of reform rather than punishment, debtors' prisons were abolished, and women's rights became a serious issue, which you will find expressed in the writings of Sojourner Truth and Margaret Fuller included in this chapter.

Doubtless the most active reformers were the abolitionists. Abolitionist groups and newspapers such as the *Liberator* flourished in the Northeast. Slave narratives by Harriet Jacobs and Frederick Douglass, and Harriet Beecher Stowe's novel *Uncle Tom's Cabin* (1852), revealed the horrors of slavery to a wide reading public and helped make the moral case for abolition. In 1850, the brutal Fugitive Slave Act established that escaped slaves must be returned to their masters, and in 1857 the *Dred Scott* decision in the Supreme Court declared that Africans in America held no constitutional rights. A Conversation in this chapter explores one controversial abolitionist whose dramatic actions arguably lit the fuse that started the American Civil

An advertisement for Harriet Beecher Stowe's *Uncle Tom's Cabin,* c. 1860.

War and ended slavery in the United States. In 1859, John Brown raided the arsenal at Harpers Ferry, Virginia, in an effort to arm a slave rebellion in the South. His small band was overwhelmed by troops, and Brown was captured, convicted, and hanged. In "The Last Days of John Brown" (1860), Thoreau writes, "They all called him crazy then; who calls him crazy now?" Was John Brown a hero fighting to abolish an inhumane practice and free an enslaved people, or a madman and terrorist who attacked his own nation? These are questions you will consider as you read the sources in the Conversation on this controversial figure from the nineteenth century.

Having campaigned on a platform against the expansion of slavery beyond states in which it already existed, Abraham Lincoln was elected president in 1860. The next year, representatives of the Southern slave states formed the Confederate States of America. Prior to Lincoln's inauguration as president, the first seven Confederate states — South Carolina, Mississippi, Florida, Alabama, Georgia, Louisiana, and Texas — declared their secession from the Union in the early months of 1861. Then Confederate forces fired on the United States military base at Fort Sumter, South Carolina, on April 12, 1861, and Virginia, Arkansas, Tennessee, and North Carolina seceded quickly thereafter.

Barely a century after the signing of the Declaration of Independence and the completion of the American Revolution, the American republic was torn asunder by a deadly civil war. The United States of America — its mission, its principles, and its future — was in jeopardy. In 1863, at the height of the national crisis, President Abraham Lincoln commemorated a cemetery on the site of the battlefield at Gettysburg with these famous words: "We here highly resolve that these dead shall not

Library of Congress Prints and Photographs Division

President Lincoln at the Battle of Antietam.

have died in vain — that this nation, under God, shall have a new birth of freedom — and that government of the people by the people for the people, shall not perish from the earth." Lincoln's speech, a mere ten sentences long, expressed the president's determination to preserve the Republic and gave hope to the young and fragile nation. In this chapter, you will read more of Lincoln's works and reflections from thinkers both then and now in a Conversation on the president whom many have come to call the Great Emancipator.

Over the course of four years, the American Civil War took the lives of over 1 million people, approximately 700,000 of them soldiers. But perhaps, as Lincoln had hoped, those million did not die in vain — the Emancipation Proclamation freed approximately 3.5 million slaves in the Southern states, and the Thirteenth Amendment, adopted several months after the war's conclusion, outlawed slavery in the United States. On April 9, 1865, at Appomattox, Virginia, General Robert E. Lee surrendered his Army of Northern Virginia to Ulysses S. Grant, and as the news spread, Confederate forces throughout the South surrendered over the following days. Then, five days after Lee's submission, in one of the greatest tragedies in American history, President Lincoln was shot and killed by John Wilkes Booth, a Southern sympathizer.

The America of this chapter is one that is emerging from great promise and great conflict into a multifaceted and complex nation, and through its literature, we can examine its triumphs, its tragedies, its growing pains, and its rebirth.

WILLIAM CULLEN BRYANT

William Cullen Bryant (1794–1878), a poet and an editor, was born in Cummington, Massachusetts. He attended Williams College and studied law. His interest in poetry stemmed from his exposure to it in childhood. Under the tutelage of his father, a doctor and politician, Bryant translated classical verse and wrote poems emulating British poets such as William Wordsworth and Alexander Pope. In 1827, Bryant became assistant editor of the *New York Evening Post*; after one year he became editor in chief and part owner, the position in which he remained for the next half century. Despite his early aversion to the politics of Jefferson, Bryant became a staunch supporter of the progressive, populist Republican Party, and he was an early proponent of Abraham Lincoln's.

Thanatopsis

Bryant began writing "Thanatopsis," arguably his most famous poem, at the age of seventeen, and it was published five years later, in 1817, in the *North American Review*. In 1821, the poet added new introductory and concluding lines, which are included here, and the work was republished in the collection *Thanatopsis and Other Poems*.

To him who in the love of Nature holds
Communion with her visible forms, she speaks
A various language; for his gayer hours
She has a voice of gladness, and a smile
And eloquence of beauty, and she glides   5
Into his darker musings, with a mild
And healing sympathy, that steals away
Their sharpness, ere he is aware. When thoughts
Of the last bitter hour come like a blight
Over thy spirit, and sad images   10
Of the stern agony, and shroud, and pall,
And breathless darkness, and the narrow house,
Make thee to shudder, and grow sick at heart; —
Go forth, under the open sky, and list
To Nature's teachings, while from all around —   15
Earth and her waters, and the depths of air, —
Comes a still voice — Yet a few days, and thee
The all-beholding sun shall see no more
In all his course; nor yet in the cold ground,
Where thy pale form was laid, with many tears,   20
Nor in the embrace of ocean, shall exist
Thy image. Earth, that nourished thee, shall claim
Thy growth, to be resolved to earth again,
And, lost each human trace, surrendering up
Thine individual being, shalt thou go   25
To mix for ever with the elements,
To be a brother to the insensible rock
And to the sluggish clod, which the rude swain
Turns with his share, and treads upon. The oak
Shall send his roots abroad, and pierce thy mould.   30

   Yet not to thine eternal resting-place
Shalt thou retire alone — nor couldst thou wish
Couch more magnificent. Thou shalt lie down
With patriarchs of the infant world — with kings,
The powerful of the earth — the wise, the good,   35
Fair forms, and hoary seers of ages past,
All in one mighty sepulchre. — The hills
Rock-ribbed and ancient as the sun, — the vales
Stretching in pensive quietness between;
The venerable woods — rivers that move   40
In majesty, and the complaining brooks
That make the meadows green; and, poured round all,
Old ocean's gray and melancholy waste, —
Are but the solemn decorations all

Of the great tomb of man. The golden sun,   45
The planets, all the infinite host of heaven,
Are shining on the sad abodes of death,
Through the still lapse of ages. All that tread
The globe are but a handful to the tribes
That slumber in its bosom. — Take the wings   50
Of morning — and the Barcan desert pierce,
Or lose thyself in the continuous woods
Where rolls the Oregan, and hears no sound,
Save his own dashings — yet — the dead are there:
And millions in those solitudes, since first   55
The flight of years began, have laid them down
In their last sleep — the dead reign there alone.
So shalt thou rest — and what if thou withdraw
Unheeded by the living, and no friend
Take note of thy departure? All that breathe   60
Will share thy destiny. The gay will laugh
When thou art gone, the solemn brood of care
Plod on, and each one as before will chase
His favourite phantom; yet all these shall leave
Their mirth and their employments, and shall come,   65
And make their bed with thee. As the long train
Of ages glide away, the sons of men,
The youth in life's green spring, and he who goes
In the full strength of years, matron, and maid,
And the sweet babe, and the gray-headed man,   70
Shall one by one be gathered to thy side,
By those, who in their turn shall follow them.

    So live, that when thy summons comes to join
The innumerable caravan, that moves
To that mysterious realm, where each shall take   75
His chamber in the silent halls of death,
Thou go not like the quarry-slave at night,
Scourged to his dungeon, but, sustained and soothed
By an unfaltering trust, approach thy grave,
Like one who wraps the drapery of his couch   80
About him, and lies down to pleasant dreams.

(1817)

Exploring the Text

1. "Thanatopsis" is notable for its use of syntactical inversions, which can at first
   make understanding difficult. What is the subject of the first sentence, which
   runs through line 8?

2. Why is nature's voice "various" (l. 3)? What is the speaker's attitude toward nature as expressed in lines 1–17?

3. In this poem, William Cullen Bryant develops several stunning metaphors. What is the meaning of the "last bitter hour" (l. 9), the "narrow house" (l. 12), the "Couch more magnificent" (l. 33), and "innumerable caravan" (l. 74)? How do these metaphors contribute to the poem?

4. What are the antecedents of the pronouns *their* (l. 8) and *his* (l. 19)? How does identifying them aid your understanding of the poem?

5. Identify three examples of personification in the poem. What are their effects?

6. This poem employs several contrasts. Identify three prominent ones. What is their effect?

7. What is the meaning of lines 22–30? Is the circumstance they recount still true today? Explain.

8. What is the primary implication of lines 48–50?

9. How would you describe Bryant's tone in this poem?

10. The poem's title, "Thanatopsis," takes its meaning from the Greek *thanatos*, death, and *opsis*, vision or sight, and is often called "A Meditation on Death." The poem is indeed about death and mortality. Is it gloomy? Depressing? How would you describe the mood of the poem?

To Cole, the Painter, Departing for Europe
A Sonnet

This poem was occasioned by the departure of poet William Cullen Bryant's friend Thomas Cole for Europe to study painting.

Thine eyes shall see the light of distant skies:
    Yet, COLE! thy heart shall bear to Europe's strand
    A living image of thy native land,
Such as on thine own glorious canvas lies;
Lone lakes — savannas where the bison roves —   5
    Rocks rich with summer garlands — solemn streams —
    Skies, where the desert eagle wheels and screams —
Spring bloom and autumn blaze of boundless groves.
Fair scenes shall greet thee where thou goest — fair,
    But different — everywhere the trace of men,   10
    Paths, homes, graves, ruins, from the lowest glen
To where life shrinks from the fierce Alpine air,
    Gaze on them, till the tears shall dim thy sight,
    But keep that earlier, wilder image bright.

(1829)

Exploring the Text

1. How would you paraphrase the first four lines of this sonnet? What does William Cullen Bryant say that Cole's "eyes shall see" (l. 1) and "heart shall bear" (l. 2)?
2. How does Bryant characterize the subjects of Cole's art? According to Bryant, what will be the main difference between Cole's art and what he will see in Europe? What is Bryant's attitude toward that difference? Explain.
3. At the end of the poem, what does Bryant enjoin Cole to do? Why?

THOMAS COLE

Thomas Cole (1801–1848) was born in Lancashire, England, and immigrated to the United States in 1818. Cole is famous for founding the Hudson River school, an artistic movement that was influenced by romanticism and that tried to capture the beauty of the Hudson River valley.

View from Mount Holyoke, Northampton, Massachusetts, after a Thunderstorm — The Oxbow

One of Thomas Cole's most well-known paintings, The Oxbow (as it is commonly called) is regarded as a masterpiece of American romantic landscape painting. (See the next page.)

Exploring the Text

1. How would you describe the images depicted on the left side of the painting? What mood or atmosphere do they create for the viewer? How would you describe those to the right? What mood or atmosphere do they create? What is the effect of the contrast that Thomas Cole presents between the two sides of the painting?
2. What is suggested by the presence of the figure in the lower right? If it is the painter himself, why does the figure play such a seemingly insignificant role in the painting?
3. Cole painted The Oxbow after returning from the European trip that William Jennings Bryant refers to in his sonnet "To Cole, the Painter, Departing for Europe." In what way could this painting be a response to his friend's poem? Refer specifically to the text of the poem and to details in the painting.

Metropolitan Museum of Art, New York, USA/Photo © Boltin Picture Library/
The Bridgeman Art Library

THOMAS COLE, *THE OXBOW*, 1836, OIL ON CANVAS, 51.5" × 76", METROPOLITAN MUSEUM OF ART, NEW YORK.
(See color insert, Image 22.)

ASHER B. DURAND

Asher B. Durand (1796–1886), a successful engraver, was inspired by Thomas Cole to become a painter; he became a major representative of the Hudson River school of painting.

Kindred Spirits

Durand's *Kindred Spirits* is regarded as a masterpiece of American landscape painting. It depicts premier American landscape artist Thomas Cole (1801–1848) and romantic poet William Cullen Bryant (1794–1878) in the Catskill Mountains of New York State in 1849. Bryant's eulogy at Cole's funeral inspired Durand to paint a picture depicting their friendship in the natural world that they both loved so well.

Francis G. Mayer/Corbis

Asher B. Durand, *Kindred Spirits*, 1849, oil on canvas, 44" × 36", Crystal Bridges Museum of American Art, Arkansas.
(See color insert, Image 23.)

Exploring the Text

1. What do you notice first in this painting? Is it pleasing? Why or why not?
2. What might the painter be suggesting with the overarching tree limb?

3. The phrase *kindred spirits* is taken from "Sonnet to Solitude," a poem about the healing power of nature by English romantic poet John Keats. It expresses a theme dear to both Cole and Bryant, and may be meant to refer to the two figures in the painting. Might nature be a third kindred spirit? Why or why not?
4. What is Asher B. Durand's attitude toward the human figures he depicts? What is his attitude toward the scene as a whole?

Nathaniel Hawthorne

One of America's major voices of the nineteenth century, Nathaniel Hawthorne was born in Salem, Massachusetts, into a family whose ancestors had participated in the Salem Witch Trials of the seventeenth century. He graduated from Bowdoin College in Maine, where his classmates included the poet Henry Wadsworth Longfellow and future president of the United States Franklin Pierce, who appointed Hawthorne American consul in Liverpool, England. In 1832, Hawthorne published a volume of stories, *Twice-Told Tales*, followed by *Mosses from an Old Manse*, named for his house, which had belonged to Ralph Waldo Emerson. The years 1850 and 1851 saw the publication of his major works, *The Scarlet Letter* and *The House of the Seven Gables*.

My Kinsman, Major Molineux

Hawthorne's work is often allegorical and contains many of the elements of the supernatural; in fact, he referred to his books as "romances" rather than as novels. Many of his characters struggle with identity as they confront the nature of evil, pride, guilt, and temptation. Among his most famous stories are "Rappaccini's Daughter," "Young Goodman Brown," and "My Kinsman, Major Molineux" (1832), which is included here.

A fter the kings of Great Britain had assumed the right of appointing the colonial governors, the measures of the latter seldom met with the ready and general approbation, which had been paid to those of their predecessors, under the original charters. The people looked with most jealous scrutiny to the exercise of power, which did not emanate from themselves, and they usually rewarded the rulers with slender gratitude, for the compliances, by which, in softening their instructions from beyond the sea, they had incurred the reprehension of those who gave them. The annals of Massachusetts Bay will inform us, that of six governors, in the space of about forty years from the surrender of the old charter, under James II., two were imprisoned by a popular insurrection; a third, as Hutchinson[1] inclines to believe, was driven from the

---

[1]Thomas Hutchinson (1711–1780), the last governor of the province of Massachusetts Bay, wrote *The History of the Colony and Province of Massachusetts-Bay* (1764). — Eds.

province by the whizzing of a musket ball; a fourth, in the opinion of the same historian, was hastened to his grave by continual bickerings with the house of representatives; and the remaining two, as well as their successors, till the Revolution, were favored with few and brief intervals of peaceful sway. The inferior members of the court party, in times of high political excitement, led scarcely a more desirable life. These remarks may serve as preface to the following adventures, which chanced upon a summer night, not far from a hundred years ago. The reader, in order to avoid a long and dry detail of colonial affairs, is requested to dispense with an account of the train of circumstances, that had caused much temporary inflammation of the popular mind.

It was near nine o'clock of a moonlight evening, when a boat crossed the ferry with a single passenger, who had obtained his conveyance, at that unusual hour, by the promise of an extra fare. While he stood on the landing-place, searching in either pocket for the means of fulfilling his agreement, the ferryman lifted a lantern, by the aid of which, and the newly risen moon, he took a very accurate survey of the stranger's figure. He was a youth of barely eighteen years, evidently country-bred, and now, as it should seem, upon his first visit to town. He was clad in a coarse grey coat, well worn, but in excellent repair; his under garments were durably constructed of leather, and sat tight to a pair of serviceable and well-shaped limbs; his stockings of blue yarn, were the incontrovertible handiwork of a mother or a sister; and on his head was a three-cornered hat, which in its better days had perhaps sheltered the graver brow of the lad's father. Under his left arm was a heavy cudgel, formed of an oak sapling, and retaining a part of the hardened root; and his equipment was completed by a wallet,[2] not so abundantly stocked as to incommode the vigorous shoulders on which it hung. Brown curly hair, well-shaped features, and bright, cheerful eyes, were nature's gifts, and worth all that art could have done for his adornment.

The youth, one of whose names was Robin, finally drew from his pocket the half of a little province-bill of five shillings, which, in the depreciation of that sort of currency, did but satisfy the ferryman's demand, with the surplus of a sexangular piece of parchment valued at three pence. He then walked forward into the town, with as light a step, as if his day's journey had not already exceeded thirty miles, and with as eager an eye, as if he were entering London city, instead of the little metropolis of a New England colony. Before Robin had proceeded far, however, it occurred to him, that he knew not whither to direct his steps; so he paused, and looked up and down the narrow street, scrutinizing the small and mean wooden buildings, that were scattered on either side.

"This low hovel cannot be my kinsman's dwelling," thought he, "nor yonder old house, where the moonlight enters at the broken casement; and truly I see none hereabouts that might be worthy of him. It would have been wise to inquire my way of the ferryman, and doubtless he would have gone with me, and earned a shilling from the Major for his pains. But the next man I meet will do as well."

He resumed his walk, and was glad to perceive that the street now became wider, and the houses more respectable in their appearance. He soon discerned a figure moving on moderately in advance, and hastened his steps to overtake it. As Robin drew nigh, he saw that the passenger was a man in years, with a full periwig of grey

[2]Knapsack. — Eds.

hair, a wide-skirted coat of dark cloth, and silk stockings rolled about his knees. He carried a long and polished cane, which he struck down perpendicularly before him, at every step; and at regular intervals he uttered two successive hems, of a peculiarly solemn and sepulchral intonation. Having made these observations, Robin laid hold of the skirt of the old man's coat, just when the light from the open door and windows of a barber's shop, fell upon both their figures.

"Good evening to you, honored Sir," said he, making a low bow, and still retaining his hold of the skirt. "I pray you to tell me whereabouts is the dwelling of my kinsman, Major Molineux?"

The youth's question was uttered very loudly; and one of the barbers, whose razor was descending on a well-soaped chin, and another who was dressing a Ramillies wig,[3] left their occupations, and came to the door. The citizen, in the meantime, turned a long favored countenance upon Robin, and answered him in a tone of excessive anger and annoyance. His two sepulchral hems, however, broke into the very centre of his rebuke, with most singular effect, like a thought of the cold grave obtruding among wrathful passions.

"Let go my garment, fellow! I tell you. I know not the man you speak of. What! I have authority, I have — hem, hem — authority; and if this be the respect you show your betters, your feet shall be brought acquainted with the stocks, by daylight, tomorrow morning!"

Robin released the old man's skirt, and hastened away, pursued by an ill-mannered roar of laughter from the barber's shop. He was at first considerably surprised by the result of his question, but, being a shrewd youth, soon thought himself able to account for the mystery.

"This is some country representative," was his conclusion, "who has never seen the inside of my kinsman's door, and lacks the breeding to answer a stranger civilly. The man is old, or verily — I might be tempted to turn back and smite him on the nose. Ah, Robin, Robin! even the barber's boys laugh at you, for choosing such a guide! You will be wiser in time, friend Robin."

He now became entangled in a succession of crooked and narrow streets, which crossed each other, and meandered at no great distance from the water-side. The smell of tar was obvious to his nostrils, the masts of vessels pierced the moonlight above the tops of the buildings, and the numerous signs, which Robin paused to read, informed him that he was near the centre of business. But the streets were empty, the shops were closed, and lights were visible only in the second stories of a few dwelling-houses. At length, on the corner of a narrow lane, through which he was passing, he beheld the broad countenance of a British hero swinging before the door of an inn, whence proceeded the voices of many guests. The casement of one of the lower windows was thrown back, and a very thin curtain permitted Robin to distinguish a party at supper, round a well-furnished table. The fragrance of the good cheer

10

---

[3] A typical wig of the era, with curls above the ears and a braid down the back. Named after a British victory over the French in Ramillies, Belgium, during the War of Spanish Succession, May 23, 1706. — Eds.

steamed forth into the outer air, and the youth could not fail to recollect, that the last remnant of his travelling stock of provision had yielded to his morning appetite, and that noon had found, and left him, dinnerless.

"Oh, that a parchment three-penny might give me a right to sit down at yonder table," said Robin, with a sigh. "But the Major will make me welcome to the best of his victuals; so I will even step boldly in, and inquire my way to his dwelling."

He entered the tavern, and was guided by the murmur of voices, and fumes of tobacco, to the public room. It was a long and low apartment, with oaken walls, grown dark in the continual smoke, and a floor, which was thickly sanded, but of no immaculate purity. A number of persons, the larger part of whom appeared to be mariners, or in some way connected with the sea, occupied the wooden benches, or leather-bottomed chairs, conversing on various matters, and occasionally lending their attention to some topic of general interest. Three or four little groups were draining as many bowls of punch, which the great West India trade had long since made a familiar drink in the colony. Others, who had the aspect of men who lived by regular and laborious handicraft, preferred the insulated bliss of an unshared potation, and became more taciturn under its influence. Nearly all, in short, evinced a predilection for the Good Creature[4] in some of its various shapes, for this is a vice, to which, as the Fast-day sermons of a hundred years ago will testify, we have a long hereditary claim. The only guests to whom Robin's sympathies inclined him, were two or three sheepish countrymen, who were using the inn somewhat after the fashion of a Turkish Caravansary; they had gotten themselves into the darkest corner of the room, and, heedless of the Nicotian atmosphere, were supping on the bread of their own ovens, and the bacon cured in their own chimney-smoke. But though Robin felt a sort of brotherhood with these strangers, his eyes were attracted from them, to a person who stood near the door, holding whispered conversation with a group of ill-dressed associates. His features were separately striking almost to grotesqueness, and the whole face left a deep impression in the memory. The forehead bulged out into a double prominence, with a vale between; the nose came boldly forth in an irregular curve, and its bridge was of more than a finger's breadth; the eyebrows were deep and shaggy, and the eyes glowed beneath them like fire in a cave.

While Robin deliberated of whom to inquire respecting his kinsman's dwelling, he was accosted by the innkeeper, a little man in a stained white apron, who had come to pay his professional welcome to the stranger. Being in the second generation from a French protestant, he seemed to have inherited the courtesy of his parent nation; but no variety of circumstance was ever known to change his voice from the one shrill note in which he now addressed Robin.

"From the country, I presume, Sir?" said he, with a profound bow. "Beg to congratulate you on your arrival, and trust you intend a long stay with us. Fine town   15

---

[4]A reference to alcohol, based on a quotation from Increase Mather's *Wo to Drunkards* (1673): "Drink is in itself a good creature of God, and to be received with thankfulness, but the abuse of drink is from Satan, the wine is from God, but the drunkard is from the Devil." — Eds.

here, Sir, beautiful buildings, and much that may interest a stranger. May I hope for the honor of your commands in respect to supper?"

"The man sees a family likeness! the rogue has guessed that I am related to the Major!" thought Robin, who had hitherto experienced little superfluous civility.

All eyes were now turned on the country lad, standing at the door, in his worn three-cornered hat, grey coat, leather breeches, and blue yarn stockings, leaning on an oaken cudgel, and bearing a wallet on his back. Robin replied to the courteous innkeeper, with such an assumption of consequence, as befitted the Major's relative.

"My honest friend," he said, "I shall make it a point to patronise your house on some occasion, when—" here he could not help lowering his voice—"I may have more than a parchment three-pence in my pocket. My present business," continued he, speaking with lofty confidence, "is merely to inquire the way to the dwelling of my kinsman, Major Molineux."

There was a sudden and general movement in the room, which Robin interpreted as expressing the eagerness of each individual to become his guide. But the innkeeper turned his eyes to a written paper on the wall, which he read, or seemed to read, with occasional recurrences to the young man's figure.

"What have we here?" said he, breaking his speech into little dry fragments.   20
"'Left the house of the subscriber, bounden servant, Hezekiah Mudge—had on when he went away, grey coat, leather breeches, master's third best hat. One pound currency reward to whoever shall lodge him in any jail in the province.' Better trudge, boy, better trudge."

Robin had began to draw his hand towards the lighter end of the oak cudgel, but a strange hostility in every countenance, induced him to relinquish his purpose of breaking the courteous innkeeper's head. As he turned to leave the room, he encountered a sneering glance from the bold-featured personage whom he had before noticed; and no sooner was he beyond the door, than he heard a general laugh, in which the innkeeper's voice might be distinguished, like the dropping of small stones into a kettle.

"Now is it not strange," thought Robin, with his usual shrewdness, "is it not strange, that the confession of an empty pocket, should outweigh the name of my kinsman, Major Molineux? Oh, if I had one of these grinning rascals in the woods, where I and my oak sapling grew up together, I would teach him that my arm is heavy, though my purse be light!"

On turning the corner of the narrow lane, Robin found himself in a spacious street, with an unbroken line of lofty houses on each side, and a steepled building at the upper end, whence the ringing of a bell announced the hour of nine. The light of the moon, and the lamps from numerous shop windows, discovered people promenading on the pavement, and amongst them, Robin hoped to recognise his hitherto inscrutable relative. The result of his former inquiries made him unwilling to hazard another, in a scene of such publicity, and he determined to walk slowly and silently up the street, thrusting his face close to that of every elderly gentleman, in search of the Major's lineaments. In his progress, Robin encountered many gay and gallant figures. Embroidered garments, of showy colors, enormous periwigs, gold-laced hats, and silver hilted swords, glided past him and dazzled his optics. Travelled youths, imitators of the European fine gentlemen of the period, trod jauntily along, half-dancing to the fashionable tunes which they hummed, and making poor Robin ashamed of his quiet and natural gait. At length, after many pauses to examine the gorgeous display of goods in the shop windows, and after suffering some rebukes for the impertinence of his scrutiny into people's faces, the Major's kinsman found himself near the steepled building, still unsuccessful in his search. As yet, however, he had seen only one side of the thronged street; so Robin crossed, and continued the same sort of inquisition down the opposite pavement, with stronger hopes than the philosopher seeking an honest man,[5] but with no better fortune. He had arrived about midway towards the lower end, from which his course began, when he overheard the approach of some one, who struck down a cane on the flag-stones at every step, uttering, at regular intervals, two sepulchral hems.

"Mercy on us!" quoth Robin, recognising the sound.

Turning a corner, which chanced to be close at his right hand, he hastened to   25
pursue his researches, in some other part of the town. His patience was now wearing low, and he seemed to feel more fatigue from his rambles since he crossed the ferry, than from his journey of several days on the other side. Hunger also pleaded loudly within him, and Robin began to balance the propriety of demanding, violently and with lifted cudgel, the necessary guidance from the first solitary passenger, whom he should meet. While a resolution to this effect was gaining strength, he entered a street of mean appearance, on either side of which, a row of ill-built houses was straggling towards the harbor. The moonlight fell upon no passenger along the whole extent, but in the third domicile which Robin passed, there was a half-opened door, and his keen glance detected a woman's garment within.

"My luck may be better here," said he to himself.

Accordingly, he approached the door, and beheld it shut closer as he did so; yet an open space remained, sufficing for the fair occupant to observe the stranger, without a corresponding display on her part. All that Robin could discern was a strip of scarlet petticoat, and the occasional sparkle of an eye, as if the moonbeams were trembling on some bright thing.

"Pretty mistress," — for I may call her so with a good conscience, thought the shrewd youth, since I know nothing to the contrary — "my sweet pretty mistress, will you be kind enough to tell me whereabouts I must seek the dwelling of my kinsman, Major Molineux?"

Robin's voice was plaintive and winning, and the female, seeing nothing to be shunned in the handsome country youth, thrust open the door, and came forth into the moonlight. She was a dainty little figure, with a white neck, round arms, and a slender waist, at the extremity of which her scarlet petticoat jutted out over a hoop, as if she were standing in a balloon. Moreover, her face was oval and pretty, her hair dark beneath the little cap, and her bright eyes possessed a sly freedom, which triumphed over those of Robin.

---

[5]A reference to the Greek philosopher Diogenes (412–323 B.C.E.), who would carry a lamp with him during the daytime and say that he was searching for an honest man. — Eds.

"Major Molineux dwells here," said this fair woman.   30

Now her voice was the sweetest Robin had heard that night, the airy counterpart of a stream of melted silver; yet he could not help doubting whether that sweet voice spoke gospel truth. He looked up and down the mean street, and then surveyed the house before which they stood. It was a small, dark edifice of two stories, the second of which projected over the lower floor; and the front apartment had the aspect of a shop for petty commodities.

"Now truly I am in luck," replied Robin, cunningly, "and so indeed is my kinsman, the Major, in having so pretty a housekeeper. But I prithee trouble him to step to the door; I will deliver him a message from his friends in the country, and then go back to my lodgings at the inn."

"Nay, the Major has been a-bed this hour or more," said the lady of the scarlet petticoat; "and it would be to little purpose to disturb him to-night, seeing his evening draught was of the strongest. But he is a kind-hearted man, and it would be as much as my life's worth, to let a kinsman of his turn away from the door. You are the good old gentleman's very picture, and I could swear that was his rainy-weather hat. Also, he has garments very much resembling those leather — But come in, I pray, for I bid you hearty welcome in his name."

So saying, the fair and hospitable dame took our hero by the hand; and though the touch was light, and the force was gentleness, and though Robin read in her eyes what he did not hear in her words, yet the slender waisted woman, in the scarlet petticoat, proved stronger than the athletic country youth. She had drawn his half-willing footsteps nearly to the threshold, when the opening of a door in the neighborhood, startled the Major's housekeeper, and, leaving the Major's kinsman, she vanished speedily into her own domicile. A heavy yawn preceded the appearance of a man, who, like the Moonshine of Pyramus and Thisbe,[6] carried a lantern, needlessly aiding his sister luminary in the heavens. As he walked sleepily up the street, he turned his broad, dull face on Robin, and displayed a long staff, spiked at the end.

"Home, vagabond, home!" said the watchman, in accents that seemed to fall asleep   35
as soon as they were uttered. "Home, or we'll set you in the stocks by peep of day!"

"This is the second hint of the kind," thought Robin. "I wish they would end my difficulties, by setting me there to-night."

Nevertheless, the youth felt an instinctive antipathy towards the guardian of midnight order, which at first prevented him from asking his usual question. But just when the man was about to vanish behind the corner, Robin resolved not to lose the opportunity, and shouted lustily after him—

"I say, friend! will you guide me to the house of my kinsman, Major Molineux?"

The watchman made no reply, but turned the corner and was gone; yet Robin seemed to hear the sound of drowsy laughter stealing along the solitary street. At that

---

[6]In act 5 of Shakespeare's *A Midsummer Night's Dream*, amateurs produce a hilarious version of the tragic tale of Pyramus and Thisbe in which one character dresses as the moon and carries a lantern in order to represent the moonshine under which the lovers meet. — Eds.

moment, also, a pleasant titter saluted him from the open window above his head; he looked up, and caught the sparkle of a saucy eye; a round arm beckoned to him, and next he heard light footsteps descending the staircase within. But Robin, being of the household of a New England clergyman, was a good youth, as well as a shrewd one; so he resisted temptation, and fled away.

He now roamed desperately, and at random, through the town, almost ready to believe that a spell was on him, like that, by which a wizard of his country, had once kept three pursuers wandering, a whole winter night, within twenty paces of the cottage which they sought. The streets lay before him, strange and desolate, and the lights were extinguished in almost every house. Twice, however, little parties of men, among whom Robin distinguished individuals in outlandish attire, came hurrying along, but though on both occasions they paused to address him, such intercourse did not at all enlighten his perplexity. They did but utter a few words in some language of which Robin knew nothing, and perceiving his inability to answer, bestowed a curse upon him in plain English, and hastened away. Finally, the lad determined to knock at the door of every mansion that might appear worthy to be occupied by his kinsman, trusting that perseverance would overcome the fatality which had hitherto thwarted him. Firm in this resolve, he was passing beneath the walls of a church, which formed the corner of two streets, when, as he turned into the shade of its steeple, he encountered a bulky stranger, muffled in a cloak. The man was proceeding with the speed of earnest business, but Robin planted himself full before him, holding the oak cudgel with both hands across his body, as a bar to further passage.

"Halt, honest man, and answer me a question," said he, very resolutely. "Tell me, this instant, whereabouts is the dwelling of my kinsman, Major Molineux?"

"Keep your tongue between your teeth, fool, and let me pass," said a deep, gruff voice, which Robin partly remembered. "Let me pass, I say, or I'll strike you to the earth!"

"No, no, neighbor!" cried Robin, flourishing his cudgel, and then thrusting its larger end close to the man's muffled face. "No, no, I'm not the fool you take me for, nor do you pass, till I have an answer to my question. Whereabouts is the dwelling of my kinsman, Major Molineux?"

The stranger, instead of attempting to force his passage, stept back into the moonlight, unmuffled his own face and stared full into that of Robin.

"Watch here an hour and Major Molineux will pass by," said he.

Robin gazed with dismay and astonishment, on the unprecedented physiognomy of the speaker. The forehead with its double prominence, the broad-hooked nose, the shaggy eyebrows, and fiery eyes, were those which he had noticed at the inn, but the man's complexion had undergone a singular, or more properly, a two-fold change. One side of the face blazed of an intense red, while the other was black as midnight, the division line being in the broad bridge of the nose; and a mouth, which seemed to extend from ear to ear, was black or red, in contrast to the color of the cheek. The effect was as if two individual devils, a fiend of fire and a fiend of darkness, had united themselves to form this infernal visage. The stranger grinned in Robin's face, muffled his party-colored features, and was out of sight in a moment.

40

45

"Strange things we travellers see!" ejaculated Robin.

He seated himself, however, upon the steps of the church-door, resolving to wait the appointed time for his kinsman's appearance. A few moments were consumed in philosophical speculations, upon the species of the *genus homo*, who had just left him, but having settled this point shrewdly, rationally, and satisfactorily, he was compelled to look elsewhere for amusement. And first he threw his eyes along the street; it was of more respectable appearance than most of those into which he had wandered, and the moon, "creating, like the imaginative power, a beautiful strangeness in familiar objects," gave something of romance to a scene, that might not have possessed it in the light of day. The irregular, and often quaint architecture of the houses, some of whose roofs were broken into numerous little peaks; while others ascended, steep and narrow, into a single point; and others again were square; the pure milk-white of some of their complexions, the aged darkness of others, and the thousand sparklings, reflected from bright substances in the plastered walls of many; these matters engaged Robin's attention for awhile, and then began to grow wearisome. Next he endeavored to define the forms of distant objects, starting away with almost ghostly indistinctness, just as his eye appeared to grasp them; and finally he took a minute survey of an edifice, which stood on the opposite side of the street, directly in front of the church-door, where he was stationed. It was a large square mansion, distinguished from its neighbors by a balcony, which rested on tall pillars, and by an elaborate Gothic window, communicating therewith.

"Perhaps this is the very house I have been seeking," thought Robin.

Then he strove to speed away the time, by listening to a murmur, which swept continually along the street, yet was scarcely audible, except to an unaccustomed ear like his; it was a low, dull, dreamy sound, compounded of many noises, each of which was at too great a distance to be separately heard. Robin marvelled at this snore of a sleeping town, and marvelled more, whenever its continuity was broken, by now and then a distant shout, apparently loud where it originated. But altogether it was a sleep-inspiring sound, and to shake off its drowsy influence, Robin arose, and climbed a window-frame, that he might view the interior of the church. There the moonbeams came trembling in, and fell down upon the deserted pews, and extended along the quiet aisles. A fainter, yet more awful radiance, was hovering round the pulpit, and one solitary ray had dared to rest upon the opened page of the great bible. Had Nature, in that deep hour, become a worshipper in the house, which man had builded? Or was that heavenly light the visible sanctity of the place, visible because no earthly and impure feet were within the walls? The scene made Robin's heart shiver with a sensation of loneliness, stronger than he had ever felt in the remotest depths of his native woods; so he turned away, and sat down again before the door. There were graves around the church, and now an uneasy thought obtruded into Robin's breast. What if the object of his search, which had been so often and so strangely thwarted, were all the time mouldering in his shroud? What if his kinsman should glide through yonder gate, and nod and smile to him in passing dimly by?

"Oh, that any breathing thing were here with me!" said Robin.

50

Recalling his thoughts from this uncomfortable track, he sent them over forest, hill, and stream, and attempted to imagine how that evening of ambiguity and weariness, had been spent by his father's household. He pictured them assembled at the door, beneath the tree, the great old tree, which had been spared for its huge twisted trunk, and venerable shade, when a thousand leafy brethren fell. There, at the going down of the summer sun, it was his father's custom to perform domestic worship, that the neighbors might come and join with him like brothers of the family, and that the wayfaring man might pause to drink at that fountain, and keep his heart pure by freshening the memory of home. Robin distinguished the seat of every individual of the little audience; he saw the good man in the midst, holding the scriptures in the golden light that shone from the western clouds; he beheld him close the book, and all rise up to pray. He heard the old thanksgiving for daily mercies, the old supplications for their continuance, to which he had so often listened in weariness, but which were now among his dear remembrances. He perceived the slight inequality of his father's voice when he came to speak of the Absent One; he noted how his mother turned her face to the broad and knotted trunk, how his elder brother scorned, because the beard was rough upon his upper lip, to permit his features to be moved; how his younger sister drew down a low hanging branch before her eyes; and how the little one of all, whose sports had hitherto broken the decorum of the scene, understood the prayer for her playmate, and burst into clamorous grief. Then he saw them go in at the door; and when Robin would have entered also, the latch tinkled into its place, and he was excluded from his home.

"Am I here, or there?" cried Robin, starting; for all at once, when his thoughts had become visible and audible in a dream, the long, wide, solitary street shone out before him.

He aroused himself, and endeavored to fix his attention steadily upon the large edifice which he had surveyed before. But still his mind kept vibrating between fancy and reality; by turns, the pillars of the balcony lengthened into the tall, bare stems of pines, dwindled down to human figures, settled again in their true shape and size, and then commenced a new succession of changes. For a single moment, when he deemed himself awake, he could have sworn that a visage, one which he seemed to remember, yet could not absolutely name as his kinsman's, was looking towards him from the Gothic window. A deeper sleep wrestled with, and nearly overcame him, but fled at the sound of footsteps along the opposite pavement. Robin rubbed his eyes, discerned a man passing at the foot of the balcony, and addressed him in a loud, peevish, and lamentable cry.

"Halloo, friend! must I wait here all night for my kinsman, Major Molineux?" 55

The sleeping echoes awoke, and answered the voice; and the passenger, barely able to discern a figure sitting in the oblique shade of the steeple, traversed the street to obtain a nearer view. He was himself a gentleman in his prime, of open, intelligent, cheerful, and altogether prepossessing countenance. Perceiving a country youth, apparently homeless and without friends, he accosted him in a tone of real kindness, which had become strange to Robin's ears.

"Well, my good lad, why are you sitting here?" inquired he. "Can I be of service to you in any way?"

"I am afraid not, Sir," replied Robin, despondingly; "yet I shall take it kindly, if you'll answer me a single question. I've been searching half the night for one Major Molineux; now, Sir, is there really such a person in these parts, or am I dreaming?"

"Major Molineux! The name is not altogether strange to me," said the gentleman, smiling. "Have you any objection to telling me the nature of your business with him?"

Then Robin briefly related that his father was a clergyman, settled on a small salary, at a long distance back in the country, and that he and Major Molineux were brothers' children. The Major, having inherited riches, and acquired civil and military rank, had visited his cousin in great pomp a year or two before; had manifested much interest in Robin and an elder brother, and, being childless himself, had thrown out hints respecting the future establishment of one of them in life. The elder brother was destined to succeed to the farm, which his father cultivated, in the interval of sacred duties; it was therefore determined that Robin should profit by his kinsman's generous intentions, especially as he had seemed to be rather the favorite, and was thought to possess other necessary endowments. 60

"For I have the name of being a shrewd youth," observed Robin, in this part of his story.

"I doubt not you deserve it," replied his new friend, good naturedly; "but pray proceed."

"Well, Sir, being nearly eighteen years old, and well grown, as you see," continued Robin, raising himself to his full height, "I thought it high time to begin the world. So my mother and sister put me in handsome trim, and my father gave me half the remnant of his last year's salary, and five days ago I started for this place, to pay the Major a visit. But would you believe it, Sir? I crossed the ferry a little after dusk, and have yet found nobody that would show me the way to his dwelling; only an hour or two since, I was told to wait here, and Major Molineux would pass by."

"Can you describe the man who told you this?" inquired the gentleman.

"Oh, he was a very ill-favored fellow, Sir," replied Robin, "with two great bumps on his forehead, a hook nose, fiery eyes, and, what struck me as the strangest, his face was of two different colors. Do you happen to know such a man, Sir?" 65

"Not intimately," answered the stranger, "but I chanced to meet him a little time previous to your stopping me. I believe you may trust his word, and that the Major will very shortly pass through this street. In the mean time, as I have a singular curiosity to witness your meeting, I will sit down here upon the steps, and bear you company."

He seated himself accordingly, and soon engaged his companion in animated discourse. It was but of brief continuance, however, for a noise of shouting, which had long been remotely audible, drew so much nearer, that Robin inquired its cause.

"What may be the meaning of this uproar?" asked he. "Truly, if your town be always as noisy, I shall find little sleep, while I am an inhabitant."

"Why, indeed, friend Robin, there do appear to be three or four riotous fellows abroad to-night," replied the gentleman. "You must not expect all the stillness of your native woods, here in our streets. But the watch will shortly be at the heels of these lads, and—"

"Aye, and set them in the stocks by peep of day," interrupted Robin, recollecting his own encounter with the drowsy lantern-bearer. "But, dear Sir, if I may trust my ears, an army of watchmen would never make head against such a multitude of riot-ers. There were at least a thousand voices went to make up that one shout."

"May not one man have several voices, Robin, as well as two complexions?" said his friend.

"Perhaps a man may; but heaven forbid that a woman should!" responded the shrewd youth, thinking of the seductive tones of the Major's housekeeper.

The sounds of a trumpet in some neighboring street, now became so evident and continual, that Robin's curiosity was strongly excited. In addition to the shouts, he heard frequent bursts from many instruments of discord, and a wild and confused laughter filled up the intervals. Robin rose from the steps, and looked wistfully towards a point, whither several people seemed to be hastening.

"Surely some prodigious merrymaking is going on," exclaimed he. "I have laughed very little since I left home, Sir, and should be sorry to lose an opportunity. Shall we just step round the corner by that darkish house, and take our share of the fun?"

"Sit down again, sit down, good Robin," replied the gentleman, laying his hand on the skirt of the grey coat. "You forget that we must wait here for your kinsman; and there is reason to believe that he will pass by, in the course of a very few moments."

The near approach of the uproar had now disturbed the neighborhood; windows flew open on all sides; and many heads, in the attire of the pillow, and confused by sleep suddenly broken, were protruded to the gaze of whoever had leisure to observe them. Eager voices hailed each other from house to house, all demanding the expla-nation, which not a soul could give. Half-dressed men hurried towards the unknown commotion, stumbling as they went over the stone steps, that thrust themselves into the narrow foot-walk. The shouts, the laughter, and the tuneless bray, the antipodes of music, came onward with increasing din, till scattered individuals, and then denser bodies, began to appear round a corner, at the distance of a hundred yards.

"Will you recognise your kinsman, Robin, if he passes in this crowd?" inquired the gentleman.

"Indeed, I can't warrant it, Sir; but I'll take my stand here, and keep a bright look out," answered Robin, descending to the outer edge of the pavement.

A mighty stream of people now emptied into the street, and came rolling slowly towards the church. A single horseman wheeled the corner in the midst of them, and close behind him came a band of fearful wind-instruments, sending forth a fresher discord, now that no intervening buildings keep it from the ear. Then a redder light disturbed the moonbeams, and a dense multitude of torches shone along the street, concealing by their glare whatever object they illuminated. The single horseman, clad in a military dress, and bearing a drawn sword, rode onward as the leader, and, by his fierce and variegated countenance, appeared like war personified; the red of one cheek was an emblem of fire and sword; the blackness of the other betokened the mourning which attends them. In his train, were wild figures in the Indian dress, and many fantastic shapes without a model, giving the whole march a visionary air, as if a dream had broken forth from some feverish brain, and were sweeping visibly through the midnight streets. A mass of people, inactive, except as applauding spectators, hemmed the procession in, and several women ran along the sidewalks, piercing the confusion of heavier sounds, with their shrill voices of mirth or terror.

"The double-faced fellow has his eye upon me," muttered Robin, with an indefi-   80
nite but uncomfortable idea, that he was himself to bear a part in the pageantry.

The leader turned himself in the saddle, and fixed his glance full upon the country youth, as the steed went slowly by. When Robin had freed his eyes from those fiery ones, the musicians were passing before him, and the torches were close at hand; but the unsteady brightness of the latter formed a veil which he could not penetrate. The rattling of wheels over the stones sometimes found its way to his ear, and confused traces of a human form appeared at intervals, and then melted into the vivid light. A moment more, and the leader thundered a command to halt; the trumpets vomited a horrid breath, and held their peace; the shouts and laughter of the people died away, and there remained only an universal hum, nearly allied to silence. Right before Robin's eyes was an uncovered cart. There the torches blazed the brightest, there the moon shone out like day, and there, in tar-and-feathery dignity, sat his kinsman, Major Molineux!

He was an elderly man, of large and majestic person, and strong, square features, betokening a steady soul; but steady as it was, his enemies had found the means to shake it. His face was pale as death, and far more ghastly; the broad forehead was contracted in his agony, so that the eyebrows formed one dark grey line; his eyes were red and wild, and the foam hung white upon his quivering lip. His whole frame was agitated by a quick, and continual tremor, which his pride strove to quell, even in those circumstances of overwhelming humiliation. But perhaps the bitterest pang of all was when his eyes met those of Robin; for he evidently knew him on the instant, as the youth stood witnessing the foul disgrace of a head that had grown grey in honor. They stared at each other in silence, and Robin's knees shook, and his hair bristled, with a mixture of pity and terror. Soon, however, a bewildering excitement began to seize upon his mind; the preceding adventures of the night, the unexpected appearance of the crowd, the torches, the confused din, and the hush that followed, the spectre of his kinsman reviled by that great multitude, all this, and more than all, a perception of tremendous ridicule in the whole scene, affected him with a sort of mental inebriety. At that moment a voice of sluggish merriment saluted Robin's ears; he turned instinctively, and just behind the corner of the church stood the lantern-bearer, rubbing his eyes, and drowsily enjoying the lad's amazement. Then he heard a peal of laughter like the ringing of silvery bells; a woman twitched his arm, a saucy eye met his, and he saw the lady of the scarlet petticoat. A sharp, dry cachinnation appealed to his memory, and, standing on tiptoe in the crowd, with his white apron over his head, he beheld the courteous little innkeeper. And lastly, there sailed over the heads of the multitude a great, broad laugh, broken in the midst by two deep sepulchral hems; thus —

"Haw, haw, haw — hem, hem — haw, haw, haw, haw!"

The sound proceeded from the balcony of the opposite edifice, and thither Robin turned his eyes. In front of the Gothic window stood the old citizen, wrapped in a wide gown, his grey periwig exchanged for a nightcap, which was thrust back from his forehead, and his silk stockings hanging down about his legs. He supported himself on his polished cane in a fit of convulsive merriment, which manifested itself on his solemn old features, like a funny inscription on a tomb-stone. Then Robin seemed to hear the voices of the barbers; of the guests of the inn; and of all who had made sport of him that night. The contagion was spreading among the multitude, when, all at once, it seized upon Robin, and he sent forth a shout of laughter that echoed through the street; every man shook his sides, every man emptied his lungs, but Robin's shout was the loudest there. The cloud-spirits peeped from their silvery islands, as the congregated mirth went roaring up the sky! The Man in the Moon heard the far bellow; "Oho," quoth he, "the old Earth is frolicsome to-night!"

When there was a momentary calm in that tempestuous sea of sound, the leader 85 gave the sign, and the procession resumed its march. On they went, like fiends that throng in mockery round some dead potentate, mighty no more, but majestic still in his agony. On they went, in counterfeited pomp, in senseless uproar, in frenzied merriment, trampling all on an old man's heart. On swept the tumult, and left a silent street behind.

"Well, Robin, are you dreaming?" inquired the gentleman, laying his hand on the youth's shoulder.

Robin started, and withdrew his arm from the stone post, to which he had instinctively clung, while the living stream rolled by him. His cheek was somewhat pale, and his eye not quite so lively as in the earlier part of the evening.

"Will you be kind enough to show me the way to the Ferry?" said he, after a moment's pause.

"You have then adopted a new subject of inquiry?" observed his companion, with a smile.

"Why, yes, Sir," replied Robin, rather dryly. "Thanks to you, and to my other 90 friends, I have at last met my kinsman, and he will scarce desire to see my face again. I begin to grow weary of a town life, Sir. Will you show me the way to the Ferry?"

"No, my good friend Robin, not to-night, at least," said the gentleman. "Some few days hence, if you continue to wish it, I will speed you on your journey. Or, if you prefer to remain with us, perhaps, as you are a shrewd youth, you may rise in the world, without the help of your kinsman, Major Molineux."

(1832)

Exploring the Text

1. What is the purpose of the opening paragraph of the story?
2. How does Nathaniel Hawthorne describe the protagonist in the second paragraph? Why does Hawthorne present him this way?

3. What might be significant about Robin's name? Why is it significant that he has come from the country to the town and that he has arrived by ferry, across the water?

4. At first, Robin seems filled with both self-confidence and uncertainty. Find evidence of both qualities. Identify at least three assumptions that he holds and three misunderstandings that he makes as he wanders through the town in search of his kinsman.

5. In terms of Robin's understanding of his own identity, what is the significance in paragraph 53 of his question, "Am I here, or there?"

6. How many times in the story is Robin characterized as "shrewd"? Is the characterization ironic? Describe and discuss the significance of each instance.

7. When Robin finally meets his kinsman, Hawthorne describes the encounter: "They stared at each other in silence, and Robin's knees shook, and his hair bristled, with a mixture of pity and terror" (par. 82). In his *Poetics*, Aristotle defined tragedy as "an imitation of action" that arouses "pity and terror" in its audience. Why would Hawthorne use those exact words? Does the meeting provide the catharsis that Aristotle discusses? Explain.

8. What has become of Robin's kinsman? What is significant in that, as Robin witnesses Major Molineux's fate, "Robin's shout was the loudest there" (par. 84)?

9. What does Robin learn from his experience about his own identity? Will he return home? Why or why not?

10. How does Hawthorne use this story as an exploration of the nature of temptation and guilt? Explain, using the experience of Robin to support your conclusions.

11. In *The Experience of Literature* (1967), acclaimed scholar Lionel Trilling states:

> Regarding "My Kinsman, Major Molineux": Can we suppose that a man like Hawthorne, a man notable for his gentleness, is saying that the dark and evil impulses of the savage mob have some beneficent part in the young man's development? Can he be telling us that the experience of evil is necessary to the understanding and practice of good, or that what is thought bad by gentle and pious people is not really, or not wholly, bad? The questions that press upon us cannot be answered with any assurance that we are responding with precise understanding to what the author means.

Do you agree that these questions cannot be answered? As a symbol, what might the kinsman, Major Molineux, represent? What might be the significance of the grotesque leader of the procession and the kindly stranger? How might Robin's quest serve as an allegory for the development of the American character?

12. Professor Agnes Donohue, in her 1962 book, *A Casebook on the Hawthorne Question*, states:

> The ambiguity in Hawthorne's stories is at once his triumph and, for some literalist critics, his failure. The tension it creates is a dramatic asset. Many of the

tales, or romances as he thought of them, are multi-leveled ironic explorations of the human psyche — capable of endless extensions of meaning and of stimulating repeated analysis and interpretation.

Do you regard the ambiguity of Hawthorne's work as a triumph or a failure? Explain.

HENRY WADSWORTH LONGFELLOW

Henry Wadsworth Longfellow (1807–1882) was born in Portland, Maine, and educated at Bowdoin College. He lived most of his life in Cambridge, Massachusetts, traveled extensively in Europe, and later taught at both Bowdoin and Harvard Colleges. A staunch abolitionist and vocal supporter of reconciliation between the Northern and Southern states following the Civil War, Longfellow was a central figure in New England social, intellectual, and political circles. He published his first volumes of poetry, *Voices of the Night* and *Ballads and Other Poems*, in 1839 and 1841, respectively. In 1868, with the help of his friends William Dean Howells, James Russell Lowell, and Charles Eliot Norton — a group known as "The Dante Club" — Longfellow published the first translation by an American of Dante's *Divine Comedy*. He was also a member of the Fireside Poets, a group of five American poets best known for their popular, populist works, meant to entertain families gathered around the household fire. During his lifetime, Longfellow enjoyed incomparable commercial success both at home and abroad: by 1874, he was earning as much as $3,000 per poem, and his work was translated into Italian, French, and German. His most popular works include the short poems included here as well as "Paul Revere's Ride" (1860), "The Wreck of the Hesperus" (1841), and the epic poems *The Song of Hiawatha* (1855) and *Evangeline* (1847).

A Psalm of Life

First published in the *Knickerbocker*, "A Psalm of Life" was reprinted in his collection *Voices of the Night* in 1839.

What the heart of the young man said to the psalmist.

Tell me not, in mournful numbers,
  "Life is but an empty dream!"
For the soul is dead that slumbers,
  And things are not what they seem.

Life is real! Life is earnest!   5
  And the grave is not its goal;

"Dust thou art, to dust returnest,"
 Was not spoken of the soul.

Not enjoyment, and not sorrow,
 Is our destined end or way;   10
But to act, that each to-morrow
 Find us farther than to-day.

Art is long, and Time is fleeting,
 And our hearts, though stout and brave,
Still, like muffled drums, are beating   15
 Funeral marches to the grave.

In the world's broad field of battle,
 In the bivouac of Life,
Be not like dumb, driven cattle!
 Be a hero in the strife!   20

Trust no Future, howe'er pleasant!
 Let the dead Past bury its dead!
Act, — act in the living Present!
 Heart within, and God o'erhead!

Lives of great men all remind us   25
 We can make our lives sublime,
And, departing, leave behind us
 Footsteps on the sands of time;

Footprints, that perhaps another,
 Sailing o'er life's solemn main,   30
A forlorn and shipwrecked brother,
 Seeing, shall take heart again.

Let us, then, be up and doing,
 With a heart for any fate;
Still achieving, still pursuing,   35
 Learn to labor and to wait.

(1838)

Exploring the Text

1. How would you describe the tone established by Henry Wadsworth Longfellow's direct address to the reader in the first stanza? Where else in the poem does he do the same? What is the effect of his use of the imperative mood?
2. How do you interpret the meaning of stanza 3?

3. What is the effect of the figurative language in the fifth stanza?
4. How does the imagery developed in stanzas 7 and 8 contribute to the meaning and effect of the poem?
5. How would you paraphrase the meaning of the poem? How do you respond to the advice that the final stanza proffers? How can its message be seen as an expression of the American spirit?

Nature

"Nature" was published in *Keramos and Other Poems (A Book of Sonnets)* in 1878.

As a fond mother, when the day is o'er,
  Leads by the hand her little child to bed,
  Half willing, half reluctant to be led,
  And leave his broken playthings on the floor,
Still gazing at them through the open door,   5
  Nor wholly reassured and comforted
  By promises of others in their stead,
  Which, though more splendid, may not please
      him more;
So Nature deals with us, and takes away
  Our playthings one by one, and by the hand   10
  Leads us to rest so gently, that we go
Scarce knowing if we wished to go or stay,
  Being too full of sleep to understand
  How far the unknown transcends the what we
      know.

(1878)

Exploring the Text

1. How would you briefly paraphrase the analogy on which the entire poem depends?
2. How would you describe the tone of this poem? How is it created?
3. What is the meaning of the final two lines?
4. Why do you think Henry Wadsworth Longfellow chose to write this poem as a sonnet? Which characteristics of the sonnet work particularly well for the ideas he wishes to present?
5. This poem was composed nearly forty years after "A Psalm of Life." How do the two poems differ? Are they expressive of the thoughts and attitudes of a younger and then an older man? Explain.
6. How would you compare this poem with William Cullen Bryant's "Thanatopsis" (p. 551)? How would each author regard the other's poem? Explain.

EDGAR ALLAN POE

Edgar Allan Poe (1809–1849) was born in Boston but lived most of his life in Baltimore, Maryland. He briefly attended West Point Military Academy and later worked as a journalist and well-respected literary critic. Poe was an accomplished romantic poet but is chiefly known as a writer of psychologically gripping horror stories. He arguably invented the detective-story genre with "Murder at the Rue Morgue" (1841), which featured the character Detective C. August Dupin. He was also one of the first American writers to work in the new genre of science fiction. Among his most famous works are the poems "The Raven" (1845) and "Annabel Lee" (1849) and the short stories "The Pit and the Pendulum" (1842), "The Tell-Tale Heart" (1843), "The Cask of Amontillado" (1846), and "The Fall of the House of Usher" (1839).

The Fall of the House of Usher

First published in September 1839 in *Burton's Gentleman's Magazine*, "The Fall of the House of Usher" was included the following year in Poe's collection *Tales of the Grotesque and Arabesque*. The story contains the poem "The Haunted Palace," which had been published in the April 1839 issue of *Baltimore Museum* magazine.

Son cœur est un luth suspendu;
Sitôt qu'on le touche il résonne.[1]

—DE BÉRANGER

D uring the whole of a dull, dark, and soundless day in the autumn of the year, when the clouds hung oppressively low in the heavens, I had been passing alone, on horseback, through a singularly dreary tract of country, and at length found myself, as the shades of the evening drew on, within view of the melancholy House of Usher. I know not how it was — but, with the first glimpse of the building, a sense of insufferable gloom pervaded my spirit. I say insufferable; for the feeling was unrelieved by any of that half-pleasurable, because poetic, sentiment, with which the mind usually receives even the sternest natural images of the desolate or terrible. I looked upon the scene before me — upon the mere house, and the simple landscape features of the domain — upon the bleak walls — upon the vacant eye-like windows — upon a few rank sedges — and upon a few white trunks of decayed trees — with an utter depression of soul which I can compare to no earthly sensation more properly than to the after-dream of the reveller upon opium — the bitter lapse into every-day life — the hideous dropping off of the veil. There was an iciness, a sinking, a sickening of the heart — an unredeemed dreariness of thought which no goading of the imagi-

---

[1]His heart is a suspended lute; / As soon as it is touched, it resounds. — Eds.

nation could torture into aught of the sublime. What was it — I paused to think — what was it that so unnerved me in the contemplation of the House of Usher? It was a mystery all insoluble; nor could I grapple with the shadowy fancies that crowded upon me as I pondered. I was forced to fall back upon the unsatisfactory conclusion, that while, beyond doubt, there *are* combinations of very simple natural objects which have the power of thus affecting us, still the analysis of this power lies among considerations beyond our depth. It was possible, I reflected, that a mere different arrangement of the particulars of the scene, of the details of the picture, would be sufficient to modify, or perhaps to annihilate its capacity for sorrowful impression; and, acting upon this idea, I reined my horse to the precipitous brink of a black and lurid tarn that lay in unruffled lustre by the dwelling, and gazed down — but with a shudder even more thrilling than before — upon the remodelled and inverted images of the gray sedge, and the ghastly tree-stems, and the vacant and eye-like windows.

Nevertheless, in this mansion of gloom I now proposed to myself a sojourn of some weeks. Its proprietor, Roderick Usher, had been one of my boon companions in boyhood; but many years had elapsed since our last meeting. A letter, however, had lately reached me in a distant part of the country — a letter from him — which, in its wildly importunate nature, had admitted of no other than a personal reply. The MS. gave evidence of nervous agitation. The writer spoke of acute bodily illness — of a mental disorder which oppressed him — and of an earnest desire to see me, as his best, and indeed his only personal friend, with a view of attempting, by the cheerfulness of my society, some alleviation of his malady. It was the manner in which all this, and much more, was said — it was the apparent *heart* that went with his request — which allowed me no room for hesitation; and I accordingly obeyed forthwith what I still considered a very singular summons.

Although, as boys, we had been even intimate associates, yet I really knew little of my friend. His reserve had been always excessive and habitual. I was aware, however, that his very ancient family had been noted, time out of mind, for a peculiar sensibility of temperament, displaying itself, through long ages, in many works of exalted art, and manifested, of late, in repeated deeds of munificent yet unobtrusive charity, as well as in a passionate devotion to the intricacies, perhaps even more than to the orthodox and easily recognizable beauties, of musical science. I had learned, too, the very remarkable fact, that the stem of the Usher race, all time-honoured as it was, had put forth, at no period, any enduring branch; in other words, that the entire family lay in the direct line of descent, and had always, with very trifling and very temporary variation, so lain. It was this deficiency, I considered, while running over in thought the perfect keeping of the character of the premises with the accredited character of the people, and while speculating upon the possible influence which the one, in the long lapse of centuries, might have exercised upon the other — it was this deficiency, perhaps of collateral issue, and the consequent undeviating transmission, from sire to son, of the patrimony with the name, which had, at length, so identified the two as to merge the original title of the estate in the quaint and equivocal appellation of the "House of Usher" — an appellation which seemed to include, in the minds of the peasantry who used it, both the family and the family mansion.

I have said that the sole effect of my somewhat childish experiment — that of looking down within the tarn — had been to deepen the first singular impression. There can be no doubt that the consciousness of the rapid increase of my superstition — for why should I not so term it? — served mainly to accelerate the increase itself. Such, I have long known, is the paradoxical law of all sentiments having terror as a basis. And it might have been for this reason only, that, when I again uplifted my eyes to the house itself, from its image in the pool, there grew in my mind a strange fancy — a fancy so ridiculous, indeed, that I but mention it to show the vivid force of the sensations which oppressed me. I had so worked upon my imagination as really to believe that about the whole mansion and domain there hung an atmosphere peculiar to themselves and their immediate vicinity — an atmosphere which had no affinity with the air of heaven, but which had reeked up from the decayed trees, and the gray wall, and the silent tarn — a pestilent and mystic vapour, dull, sluggish, faintly discernible, and leaden-hued.

Shaking off from my spirit what *must* have been a dream, I scanned more narrowly the real aspect of the building. Its principal feature seemed to be that of an excessive antiquity. The discoloration of ages had been great. Minute fungi overspread the whole exterior, hanging in a fine tangled web-work from the eaves. Yet all this was apart from an extraordinary dilapidation. No portion of the masonry had fallen; and there appeared to be a wild inconsistency between its still perfect adaptation of parts, and the crumbling condition of the individual stones. In this there was much that reminded me of the specious totality of the old woodwork which has rotted for long years in some neglected vault, with no disturbance from the breath of the external air. Beyond this indication of extensive decay, however, the fabric gave little token of instability. Perhaps the eye of a scrutinizing observer might have discovered a barely perceptible fissure, which, extending from the roof of the building in front, made its way down the wall in a zigzag direction, until it became lost in the sullen waters of the tarn.

Noticing these things, I rode over a short causeway to the house. A servant in waiting took my horse, and I entered the Gothic archway of the hall. A valet, of stealthy step, thence conducted me, in silence, through many dark and intricate passages in my progress to the *studio* of his master. Much that I encountered on the way contributed, I know not how, to heighten the vague sentiments of which I have already spoken. While the objects around me — while the carvings of the ceilings, the sombre tapestries of the walls, the ebon blackness of the floors, and the phantasmagoric armorial trophies which rattled as I strode, were but matters to which, or to such as which, I had been accustomed from my infancy — while I hesitated not to acknowledge how familiar was all this — I still wondered to find how unfamiliar were the fancies which ordinary images were stirring up. On one of the staircases, I met the physician of the family. His countenance, I thought, wore a mingled expression of low cunning and perplexity. He accosted me with trepidation and passed on. The valet now threw open a door and ushered me into the presence of his master.

The room in which I found myself was very large and lofty. The windows were long, narrow, and pointed, and at so vast a distance from the black oaken floor as to

5

be altogether inaccessible from within. Feeble gleams of encrimsoned light made their way through the trellised panes, and served to render sufficiently distinct the more prominent objects around; the eye, however, struggled in vain to reach the remoter angles of the chamber, or the recesses of the vaulted and fretted ceiling. Dark draperies hung upon the walls. The general furniture was profuse, comfortless, antique, and tattered. Many books and musical instruments lay scattered about, but failed to give any vitality to the scene. I felt that I breathed an atmosphere of sorrow. An air of stern, deep, and irredeemable gloom hung over and pervaded all.

Upon my entrance, Usher arose from a sofa on which he had been lying at full length, and greeted me with a vivacious warmth which had much in it, I at first thought, of an overdone cordiality — of the constrained effort of the *ennuyé* man of the world. A glance, however, at his countenance convinced me of his perfect sincerity. We sat down; and for some moments, while he spoke not, I gazed upon him with a feeling half of pity, half of awe. Surely, man had never before so terribly altered, in so brief a period, as had Roderick Usher! It was with difficulty that I could bring myself to admit the identity of the wan being before me with the companion of my early boyhood. Yet the character of his face had been at all times remarkable. A cadaverousness of complexion; an eye large, liquid, and luminous beyond comparison; lips somewhat thin and very pallid, but of a surpassingly beautiful curve; a nose of a delicate Hebrew model, but with a breadth of nostril unusual in similar formations; a finely moulded chin, speaking, in its want of prominence, of a want of moral energy; hair of a more than web-like softness and tenuity; these features, with an inordinate expansion above the regions of the temple, made up altogether a countenance not easily to be forgotten. And now in the mere exaggeration of the prevailing character of these features, and of the expression they were wont to convey, lay so much of change that I doubted to whom I spoke. The now ghastly pallor of the skin, and the now miraculous lustre of the eye, above all things startled and even awed me. The silken hair, too, had been suffered to grow all unheeded, and as, in its wild gossamer texture, it floated rather than fell about the face, I could not, even with effort, connect its Arabesque expression with any idea of simple humanity.

In the manner of my friend I was at once struck with an incoherence — an inconsistency; and I soon found this to arise from a series of feeble and futile struggles to overcome an habitual trepidancy — an excessive nervous agitation. For something of this nature I had indeed been prepared, no less by his letter, than by reminiscences of certain boyish traits, and by conclusions deduced from his peculiar physical conformation and temperament. His action was alternately vivacious and sullen. His voice varied rapidly from a tremulous indecision (when the animal spirits seemed utterly in abeyance) to that species of energetic concision — that abrupt, weighty, unhurried, and hollow-sounding enunciation — that leaden, self-balanced, and perfectly modulated guttural utterance, which may be observed in the lost drunkard, or the irreclaimable eater of opium, during the periods of his most intense excitement.

It was thus that he spoke of the object of my visit, of his earnest desire to see me, and of the solace he expected me to afford him. He entered, at some length, into what he conceived to be the nature of his malady. It was, he said, a constitutional and a family evil, and one for which he despaired to find a remedy — a mere nervous affection, he immediately added, which would undoubtedly soon pass off. It displayed itself in a host of unnatural sensations. Some of these, as he detailed them, interested and bewildered me; although, perhaps, the terms and the general manner of their narration had their weight. He suffered much from a morbid acuteness of the senses; the most insipid food was alone endurable; he could wear only garments of certain texture; the odours of all flowers were oppressive; his eyes were tortured by even a faint light; and there were but peculiar sounds, and these from stringed instruments, which did not inspire him with horror.

To an anomalous species of terror I found him a bounden slave. "I shall perish," said he, "I *must* perish in this deplorable folly. Thus, thus, and not otherwise, shall I be lost. I dread the events of the future, not in themselves, but in their results. I shudder at the thought of any, even the most trivial, incident, which may operate upon this intolerable agitation of soul. I have, indeed, no abhorrence of danger, except in its absolute effect — in terror. In this unnerved — in this pitiable condition — I feel that the period will sooner or later arrive when I must abandon life and reason together, in some struggle with the grim phantasm, FEAR."

I learned, moreover, at intervals, and through broken and equivocal hints, another singular feature of his mental condition. He was enchained by certain superstitious impressions in regard to the dwelling which he tenanted, and whence, for many years, he had never ventured forth — in regard to an influence whose suppositious force was conveyed in terms too shadowy here to be re-stated — an influence which some peculiarities in the mere form and substance of his family mansion had, by dint of long sufferance, he said, obtained over his spirit — an effect which the *physique* of the gray wall and turrets, and of the dim tarn into which they all looked down, had, at length, brought about upon the *morale* of his existence.

He admitted, however, although with hesitation, that much of the peculiar gloom which thus afflicted him could be traced to a more natural and far more palpable origin — to the severe and long-continued illness — indeed to the evidently approaching dissolution — of a tenderly beloved sister, his sole companion for long years, his last and only relative on earth. "Her decease," he said, with a bitterness which I can never forget, "would leave him (him the hopeless and the frail) the last of the ancient race of the Ushers." While he spoke, the lady Madeline (for so was she called) passed slowly through a remote portion of the apartment, and, without having noticed my presence, disappeared. I regarded her with an utter astonishment not unmingled with dread — and yet I found it impossible to account for such feelings. A sensation of stupor oppressed me, as my eyes followed her retreating steps. When a door, at length, closed upon her, my glance sought instinctively and eagerly the countenance of the brother — but he had buried his face in his hands, and I could only perceive that a far more than ordinary wanness had overspread the emaciated fingers through which trickled many passionate tears.

The disease of the lady Madeline had long baffled the skill of her physicians. A settled apathy, a gradual wasting away of the person, and frequent although transient affections of a partially cataleptical character were the unusual diagnosis. Hitherto she had steadily borne up against the pressure of her malady, and had not betaken herself finally to bed; but on the closing in of the evening of my arrival at the house, she succumbed (as her brother told me at night with inexpressible agitation) to the prostrating power of the destroyer; and I learned that the glimpse I had obtained of her person would thus probably be the last I should obtain — that the lady, at least while living, would be seen by me no more.

For several days ensuing, her name was unmentioned by either Usher or myself: and during this period I was busied in earnest endeavours to alleviate the melancholy of my friend. We painted and read together, or I listened, as if in a dream, to the wild improvisations of his speaking guitar. And thus, as a closer and still closer intimacy admitted me more unreservedly into the recesses of his spirit, the more bitterly did I perceive the futility of all attempt at cheering a mind from which darkness, as if an inherent positive quality, poured forth upon all objects of the moral and physical universe in one unceasing radiation of gloom. 15

I shall ever bear about me a memory of the many solemn hours I thus spent alone with the master of the House of Usher. Yet I should fail in any attempt to convey an idea of the exact character of the studies, or of the occupations, in which he involved me, or led me the way. An excited and highly distempered ideality threw a sulphureous lustre over all. His long improvised dirges will ring forever in my ears. Among other things, I hold painfully in mind a certain singular perversion and amplification of the wild air of the last waltz of Von Weber. From the paintings over which his elaborate fancy brooded, and which grew, touch by touch, into vagueness at which I shuddered the more thrillingly, because I shuddered knowing not why; — from these paintings (vivid as their images now are before me) I would in vain endeavour to educe more than a small portion which should lie within the compass of merely written words. By the utter simplicity, by the nakedness of his designs, he arrested and overawed attention. If ever mortal painted an idea, that mortal was Roderick Usher. For me at least — in the circumstances then surrounding me — there arose out of the pure abstractions which the hypochondriac contrived to throw upon his canvas, an intensity of intolerable awe, no shadow of which I felt ever yet in the contemplation of the certainly glowing yet too concrete reveries of Fuseli.

One of the phantasmagoric conceptions of my friend, partaking not so rigidly of the spirit of abstraction, may be shadowed forth, although feebly, in words. A small picture presented the interior of an immensely long and rectangular vault or tunnel, with low walls, smooth, white, and without interruption or device. Certain accessory points of the design served well to convey the idea that this excavation lay at an exceeding depth below the surface of the earth. No outlet was observed in any portion of its vast extent, and no torch or other artificial source of light was discernible; yet a flood of intense rays rolled throughout, and bathed the whole in a ghastly and inappropriate splendour.

I have just spoken of that morbid condition of the auditory nerve which rendered all music intolerable to the sufferer, with the exception of certain effects of stringed instruments. It was, perhaps, the narrow limits to which he thus confined himself upon the guitar, which gave birth, in great measure, to the fantastic character of his performances. But the fervid *facility* of his *impromptus* could not be so accounted for. They must have been, and were, in the notes, as well as in the words of his wild fantasias (for he not unfrequently accompanied himself with rhymed verbal improvisations), the result of that intense mental collectedness and concentration to which I have previously alluded as observable only in particular moments of the highest artificial excitement. The words of one of these rhapsodies I have easily remembered. I was, perhaps, the more forcibly impressed with it, as he gave it, because, in the under or mystic current of its meaning, I fancied that I perceived, and for the first time, a full consciousness on the part of Usher, of the tottering of his lofty reason upon her throne. The verses, which were entitled "The Haunted Palace," ran very nearly, if not accurately, thus:

I

In the greenest of our valleys,
 By good angels tenanted,
Once a fair and stately palace —
 Radiant palace — reared its head.
In the monarch Thought's dominion —
 It stood there!
Never seraph spread a pinion
 Over fabric half so fair.

II

Banners yellow, glorious, golden,
 On its roof did float and flow;
(This — all this — was in the olden
 Time long ago)
And every gentle air that dallied,
 In that sweet day,
Along the ramparts plumed and pallid,
 A winged odour went away.

III

Wanderers in that happy valley
 Through two luminous windows saw
Spirits moving musically
 To a lute's well-tunèd law,
Round about a throne, where sitting
 (Porphyrogene!)

In state his glory well befitting,
    The ruler of the realm was seen.

IV

And all with pearl and ruby glowing
    Was the fair palace door,
Through which came flowing, flowing,
    flowing
And sparkling evermore,
A troop of Echoes whose sweet duty
    Was but to sing,
In voices of surpassing beauty,
    The wit and wisdom of their king.

V

But evil things, in robes of sorrow,
    Assailed the monarch's high estate;
(Ah, let us mourn, for never morrow
    Shall dawn upon him, desolate!)
And, round about his home, the glory
    That blushed and bloomed
Is but a dim-remembered story
    Of the old time entombed.

VI

And travellers now within that valley,
    Through the red-litten windows see
Vast forms that move fantastically
    To a discordant melody;
While, like a rapid ghastly river,
    Through the pale door,
A hideous throng rush out forever,
    And laugh — but smile no more.

I well remember that suggestions arising from this ballad led us into a train of thought wherein there became manifest an opinion of Usher's which I mention not so much on account of its novelty (for other men[2] have thought thus), as on account

---

[2]Watson, Dr. Percival, Spallanzani, and especially the Bishop of Landaff. — See *Chemical Essays,* vol. v.

of the pertinacity with which he maintained it. This opinion, in its general form, was that of the sentience of all vegetable things. But, in his disordered fancy, the idea had assumed a more daring character, and trespassed, under certain conditions, upon the kingdom of inorganization. I lack words to express the full extent, or the earnest *abandon* of his persuasion. The belief, however, was connected (as I have previously hinted) with the gray stones of the home of his forefathers. The conditions of the sentience had been here, he imagined, fulfilled in the method of collocation of these stones — in the order of their arrangement, as well as in that of the many *fungi* which overspread them, and of the decayed trees which stood around — above all, in the long undisturbed endurance of this arrangement, and in its reduplication in the still waters of the tarn. Its evidence — the evidence of the sentience — was to be seen, he said (and I here started as he spoke), in the gradual yet certain condensation of an atmosphere of their own about the waters and the walls. The result was discoverable, he added, in that silent yet importunate and terrible influence which for centuries had moulded the destinies of his family, and which made *him* what I now saw him — what he was. Such opinions need no comment, and I will make none.

Our books — the books which, for years, had formed no small portion of the   20 mental existence of the invalid — were, as might be supposed, in strict keeping with his character of phantasm. We pored together over such works as the Ververt et Chartreuse of Gresset; the Belphegor of Machiavelli; the Heaven and Hell of Swedenborg; the Subterranean Voyage of Nicholas Klimm of Holberg; the Chiromancy of Robert Flud, of Jean D'Indaginé, and of De la Chambre; the Journey into the Blue Distance of Tieck; and the City of the Sun of Campanella. One favourite volume was a small octavo edition of the *Directorium Inquisitorum,*[3] by the Dominican Eymeric de Gironne; and there were passages in Pomponius Mela, about the old African Satyrs and Ægipans, over which Usher would sit dreaming for hours. His chief delight, however, was found in the perusal of an exceedingly rare and curious book in quarto Gothic — the manual of a forgotten church — the *Vigiliæ Mortuorum secundum Chorum Ecclesiæ Maguntinæ.*[4]

I could not help thinking of the wild ritual of this work, and of its probable influence upon the hypochondriac, when, one evening, having informed me abruptly that the lady Madeline was no more, he stated his intention of preserving her corpse for a fortnight (previously to its final interment), in one of the numerous vaults within the main walls of the building. The worldly reason, however, assigned for this singular proceeding, was one which I did not feel at liberty to dispute. The brother had been led to his resolution (so he told me) by consideration of the unusual character of the malady of the deceased, of certain obtrusive and eager inquiries on the part of her medical men, and of the remote and exposed situation of the burial-ground of the family. I will not deny that when I called to mind the sinister countenance of the person whom I met upon the staircase, on the day of my arrival at the house, I had

---

[3]*Directory for the Inquisitors.* — Eds.
[4]*Vigils for the Dead according to the Use of the Church of Mainz.* — Eds.

no desire to oppose what I regarded as at best but a harmless, and by no means an unnatural, precaution.

At the request of Usher, I personally aided him in the arrangements for the temporary entombment. The body having been encoffined, we two alone bore it to its rest. The vault in which we placed it (and which had been so long unopened that our torches, half smothered in its oppressive atmosphere, gave us little opportunity for investigation) was small, damp, and entirely without means of admission for light; lying, at great depth, immediately beneath that portion of the building in which was my own sleeping apartment. It had been used, apparently, in remote feudal times, for the worst purposes of a donjon-keep, and, in later days, as a place of deposit for powder, or some other highly combustible substance, as a portion of its floor, and the whole interior of a long archway through which we reached it, were carefully sheathed with copper. The door, of massive iron, had been, also, similarly protected. Its immense weight caused an unusually sharp grating sound, as it moved upon its hinges.

Having deposited our mournful burden upon tressels within this region of horror, we partially turned aside the yet unscrewed lid of the coffin, and looked upon the face of the tenant. A striking similitude between the brother and sister now first arrested my attention; and Usher, divining, perhaps, my thoughts, murmured out some few words from which I learned that the deceased and himself had been twins, and that sympathies of a scarcely intelligible nature had always existed between them. Our glances, however, rested not long upon the dead — for we could not regard her unawed. The disease which had thus entombed the lady in the maturity of youth, had left, as usual in all maladies of a strictly cataleptical character, the mockery of a faint blush upon the bosom and the face, and that suspiciously lingering smile upon the lip which is so terrible in death. We replaced and screwed down the lid, and, having secured the door of iron, made our way, with toil, into the scarcely less gloomy apartments of the upper portion of the house.

And now, some days of bitter grief having elapsed, an observable change came over the features of the mental disorder of my friend. His ordinary manner had vanished. His ordinary occupations were neglected or forgotten. He roamed from chamber to chamber with hurried, unequal, and objectless step. The pallor of his countenance had assumed, if possible, a more ghastly hue — but the luminousness of his eye had utterly gone out. The once occasional huskiness of his tone was heard no more; and a tremulous quaver, as if of extreme terror, habitually characterized his utterance. There were times, indeed, when I thought his unceasingly agitated mind was labouring with some oppressive secret, to divulge which he struggled for the necessary courage. At times, again, I was obliged to resolve all into the mere inexplicable vagaries of madness, for I beheld him gazing upon vacancy for long hours, in an attitude of the profoundest attention, as if listening to some imaginary sound. It was no wonder that his condition terrified — that it infected me. I felt creeping upon me, by slow yet certain degrees, the wild influences of his own fantastic yet impressive superstitions.

It was, especially, upon retiring to bed late in the night of the seventh or eighth day after the placing of the lady Madeline within the donjon, that I experienced the full power of such feelings. Sleep came not near my couch — while the hours waned and waned away. I struggled to reason off the nervousness which had dominion over me. I endeavoured to believe that much, if not all of what I felt, was due to the bewildering influence of the gloomy furniture of the room — of the dark and tattered draperies, which, tortured into motion by the breath of a rising tempest, swayed fitfully to and fro upon the walls, and rustled uneasily about the decorations of the bed. But my efforts were fruitless. An irrepressible tremour gradually pervaded my frame; and, at length, there sat upon my very heart an incubus of utterly causeless alarm. Shaking this off with a gasp and a struggle, I uplifted myself upon the pillows, and, peering earnestly within the intense darkness of the chamber, hearkened — I know not why, except that an instinctive spirit prompted me — to certain low and indefinite sounds which came, through the pauses of the storm, at long intervals, I knew not whence. Overpowered by an intense sentiment of horror, unaccountable yet unendurable, I threw on my clothes with haste (for I felt that I should sleep no more during the night), and endeavoured to arouse myself from the pitiable condition into which I had fallen, by pacing rapidly to and fro through the apartment.

I had taken but few turns in this manner, when a light step on an adjoining staircase arrested my attention. I presently recognised it as that of Usher. In an instant afterward he rapped, with a gentle touch, at my door, and entered, bearing a lamp. His countenance was, as usual, cadaverously wan — but, moreover, there was a species of mad hilarity in his eyes — an evidently restrained *hysteria* in his whole demeanour. His air appalled me — but anything was preferable to the solitude which I had so long endured, and I even welcomed his presence as a relief.

"And you have not seen it?" he said abruptly, after having stared about him for some moments in silence—"you have not then seen it? — but, stay! you shall." Thus speaking, and having carefully shaded his lamp, he hurried to one of the casements, and threw it freely open to the storm.

The impetuous fury of the entering gust nearly lifted us from our feet. It was, indeed, a tempestuous yet sternly beautiful night, and one wildly singular in its terror and its beauty. A whirlwind had apparently collected its force in our vicinity; for there were frequent and violent alterations in the direction of the wind; and the exceeding density of the clouds (which hung so low as to press upon the turrets of the house) did not prevent our perceiving the life-like velocity with which they flew careering from all points against each other, without passing away into the distance. I say that even their exceeding density did not prevent our perceiving this — yet we had no glimpse of the moon or stars — nor was there any flashing forth of the lightning. But the under surfaces of the huge masses of agitated vapour, as well as all terrestrial objects immediately around us, were glowing in the unnatural light of a faintly luminous and distinctly visible gaseous exhalation which hung about and enshrouded the mansion.

"You must not — you shall not behold this!" said I, shudderingly, to Usher, as I led him, with a gentle violence, from the window to a seat. "These appearances, which bewilder you, are merely electrical phenomena not uncommon — or it may be that they have their ghastly origin in the rank miasma of the tarn. Let us close this casement; — the air is chilling and dangerous to your frame. Here is one of your favourite romances. I will read, and you shall listen; — and so we will pass away this terrible night together."

The antique volume which I had taken up was the "Mad Trist" of Sir Launcelot 30 Canning; but I had called it a favourite of Usher's more in sad jest than in earnest; for, in truth, there is little in its uncouth and unimaginative prolixity which could have had interest for the lofty and spiritual ideality of my friend. It was, however, the only book immediately at hand; and I indulged a vague hope that the excitement which now agitated the hypochondriac might find relief (for the history of mental disorder is full of similar anomalies) even in the extremeness of the folly which I could read. Could I have judged, indeed, by the wild overstrained air of vivacity with which he hearkened, or apparently hearkened, to the words of the tale, I might well have congratulated myself upon the success of my design.

I had arrived at that well-known portion of the story where Ethelred, the hero of the Trist, having sought in vain for peaceable admission into the dwelling of the hermit, proceeds to make good an entrance by force. Here, it will be remembered, the words of the narrative run thus:

"And Ethelred, who was by nature of a doughty heart, and who was now mighty withal, on account of the powerfulness of the wine which he had drunken, waited no longer to hold parley with the hermit, who, in sooth, was of an obstinate and maliceful turn, but, feeling the rain upon his shoulders, and fearing the rising of the tempest, uplifted his mace outright, and, with blows, made quickly room in the plankings of the door for his gauntleted hand; and now pulling therewith sturdily, he so cracked, and ripped, and tore all asunder, that the noise of the dry and hollow-sounding wood alarmed and reverberated throughout the forest."

At the termination of this sentence I started and, for a moment, paused; for it appeared to me (although I at once concluded that my excited fancy had deceived me) — it appeared to me that, from some very remote portion of the mansion, there came, indistinctly, to my ears, what might have been, in its exact similarity of character, the echo (but a stifled and dull one certainly) of the very cracking and ripping sound which Sir Launcelot had so particularly described. It was, beyond doubt, the coincidence alone which had arrested my attention; for, amid the rattling of the sashes of the casements, and the ordinary commingled noises of the still increasing storm, the sound, in itself, had nothing, surely, which should have interested or disturbed me. I continued the story:

"But the good champion Ethelred, now entering within the door, was sore enraged and amazed to perceive no signal of the maliceful hermit; but, in the stead thereof, a dragon of a scaly and prodigious demeanour, and of a fiery tongue, which sate in guard before a palace of gold, with a floor of silver; and upon the wall there hung a shield of shining brass with this legend enwritten—

Who entereth herein, a conqueror hath bin;
Who slayeth the dragon, the shield he shall win.

And Ethelred uplifted his mace, and struck upon the head of the dragon, which 35 fell before him, and gave up his pesty breath, with a shriek so horrid and harsh, and withal so piercing, that Ethelred had fain to close his ears with his hands against the dreadful noise of it, the like whereof was never before heard."

Here again I paused abruptly, and now with a feeling of wild amazement—for there could be no doubt whatever that, in this instance, I did actually hear (although from what direction it proceeded I found it impossible to say) a low and apparently distant, but harsh, protracted, and most unusual screaming or grating sound—the exact counterpart of what my fancy had already conjured up for the dragon's unnatural shriek as described by the romancer.

Oppressed, as I certainly was, upon the occurrence of the second and most extraordinary coincidence, by a thousand conflicting sensations, in which wonder and extreme terror were predominant, I still retained sufficient presence of mind to avoid exciting, by any observation, the sensitive nervousness of my companion. I was by no means certain that he had noticed the sounds in question; although, assuredly, a strange alteration had, during the last few minutes, taken place in his demeanour. From a position fronting my own, he had gradually brought round his chair, so as to sit with his face to the door of the chamber; and thus I could but partially perceive his features, although I saw that his lips trembled as if he were murmuring inaudibly. His head had dropped upon his breast—yet I knew that he was not asleep, from the wide and rigid opening of the eye as I caught a glance of it in profile. The motion of his body, too, was at variance with this idea—for he rocked from side to side with a gentle yet constant and uniform sway. Having rapidly taken notice of all this, I resumed the narrative of Sir Launcelot, which thus proceeded:

"And now, the champion, having escaped from the terrible fury of the dragon, bethinking himself of the brazen shield, and of the breaking up of the enchantment which was upon it, removed the carcass from out of the way before him, and approached valorously over the silver pavement of the castle to where the shield was upon the wall; which in sooth tarried not for his full coming, but fell down at his feet upon the silver floor, with a mighty great and terrible ringing sound."

No sooner had these syllables passed my lips, than—as if a shield of brass had indeed, at the moment, fallen heavily upon a floor of silver—I became aware of a distinct, hollow, metallic, and clangorous, yet apparently muffled reverberation. Completely unnerved, I leaped to my feet; but the measured rocking movement of Usher was undisturbed. I rushed to the chair in which he sat. His eyes were bent fixedly before him, and throughout his whole countenance there reigned a stony rigidity. But, as I placed my hand upon his shoulder, there came a strong shudder over his whole person; a sickly smile quivered about his lips; and I saw that he spoke in a low, hurried, and gibbering murmur, as if unconscious of my presence. Bending closely over him, I at length drank in the hideous import of his words.

"Not hear it?—yes, I hear it, and *have* heard it. Long—long—long—many minutes, many hours, many days, have I heard it—yet I dared not—oh, pity me, miserable wretch that I am!—I dared not—I *dared* not speak! *We have put her living in the tomb!* Said I not that my senses were acute? I *now* tell you that I heard her first feeble movements in the hollow coffin. I heard them—many, many days ago—yet I dared

40

not — I *dared not speak!* And now — to-night — Ethelred — ha! ha! — the breaking of the hermit's door, and the death-cry of the dragon, and the clangour of the shield! — say, rather, the rending of her coffin, and the grating of the iron hinges of her prison, and her struggles within the coppered archway of the vault! Oh whither shall I fly? Will she not be here anon? Is she not hurrying to upbraid me for my haste? Have I not heard her footsteps on the stair? Do I not distinguish that heavy and horrible beating of her heart? MADMAN!" — here he sprang furiously to his feet, and shrieked out his syllables, as if in the effort he were giving up his soul—"MADMAN! I TELL YOU THAT SHE NOW STANDS WITHOUT THE DOOR!"

As if in the superhuman energy of his utterance there had been found the potency of a spell — the huge antique panels to which the speaker pointed threw slowly back, upon the instant, their ponderous and ebony jaws. It was the work of the rushing gust — but then without those doors there *did* stand the lofty and enshrouded figure of the lady Madeline of Usher. There was blood upon her white robes, and the evidence of some bitter struggle upon every portion of her emaciated frame. For a moment she remained trembling and reeling to and fro upon the threshold, then, with a low moaning cry, fell heavily inward upon the person of her brother, and in her violent and now final death-agonies, bore him to the floor a corpse, and a victim to the terrors he had anticipated.

From that chamber, and from that mansion, I fled aghast. The storm was still abroad in all its wrath as I found myself crossing the old causeway. Suddenly there shot along the path a wild light, and I turned to see whence a gleam so unusual could have issued; for the vast house and its shadows were alone behind me. The radiance was that of the full, setting, and blood-red moon, which now shone vividly through that once barely discernible fissure, of which I have before spoken as extending from the roof of the building, in a zigzag direction, to the base. While I gazed, this fissure rapidly widened — there came a fierce breath of the whirlwind — the entire orb of the satellite burst at once upon my sight — my brain reeled as I saw the mighty walls rushing asunder — there was a long tumultuous shouting sound like the voice of a thousand waters — and the deep and dank tarn at my feet closed sullenly and silently over the fragments of the "HOUSE OF USHER."

(1839)

Exploring the Text

1. How does Edgar Allan Poe use vivid details and sensory images to describe the opening scene — and especially the house? How does the description contribute to the sense of "insufferable gloom" (par. 1) that the narrator feels?

2. How is Roderick Usher described? What is your impression of him? How does your impression compare with that of the narrator?

3. For such an important figure in the story, Madeline's presence is brief. What impression does she make on the reader?

4. What implications for the story do you see in the first stanza of "The Haunted Palace," one of the "rhapsodies" that Usher sings? What parallels do you see between the poem and the story as a whole?

5. The narrator states, "Such opinions need no comment, and I will make none" (par. 19). To which opinions does he refer? Why does he make that statement? What does it imply?

6. Why does the narrator assist Usher with the entombment of Madeline? Are there suggestions in the text that she might still be alive at the time? Explain.

7. What parallels do you see between the story as a whole and the tale of Ethelred? How do they contribute to the effectiveness of the story?

8. How do the Usher lineage, the house, and Madeline serve as counterparts to or parallels for Roderick Usher the man? How do those parallels support what you see as the theme of the story?

9. Regarding the description of the demise of Madeline and Roderick, modern British writer D. H. Lawrence (p. 1262) writes, "It is lurid and melodramatic, but it is true. It is a ghastly psychological truth of what happens in the last stages of this beloved love, which cannot be separate, cannot be isolate." Do you agree with Lawrence? Why or why not?

10. What might the fissure represent—the fissure that was "barely perceptible" (par. 5) and "barely discernible" before it "rapidly widened" as the House of Usher—the building itself—was torn asunder at the conclusion of the story (par. 42)?

11. Ambrose Bierce (p. 875) regarded "The Fall of the House of Usher" as the greatest American short story. What features of the story might account for such a high estimation? Would you agree? Why or why not?

RALPH WALDO EMERSON

Ralph Waldo Emerson (1803–1882) was one of America's most influential thinkers and writers. After graduating from Harvard Divinity School, he followed nine generations of his family into the ministry but practiced for only a few years. In 1836, he and other like-minded intellectuals, including Henry David Thoreau, founded the Transcendental Club, and that same year, he published his influential essay "Nature" (1836). Known as a great orator, Emerson made his living as a popular lecturer on a wide range of topics. From 1821 to 1826, he taught in city and country schools and later served on a number of school boards, including the Concord school committee and the board of overseers of Harvard College.

from *Self-Reliance*

"Self-Reliance," a portion of which is included here, is widely regarded as Emerson's most important and influential expression of the American spirit. It was originally published in 1841, in Emerson's first collection of essays.

I read the other day some verses written by an eminent painter[1] which were original and not conventional. Always the soul hears an admonition in such lines, let the subject be what it may. The sentiment they instil is of more value than any thought they may contain. To believe your own thought, to believe that what is true for you in your private heart, is true for all men, — that is genius. Speak your latent conviction and it shall be the universal sense; for always the inmost becomes the outmost, — and our first thought is rendered back to us by the trumpets of the Last Judgment. Familiar as the voice of the mind is to each, the highest merit we ascribe to Moses, Plato, and Milton, is that they set at naught books and traditions, and spoke not what men but what they thought. A man should learn to detect and watch that gleam of light which flashes across his mind from within, more than the lustre of the firmament of bards and sages. Yet he dismisses without notice his thought, because it is his. In every work of genius we recognise our own rejected thoughts: they come back to us with a certain alienated majesty. Great works of art have no more affecting lesson for us than this. They teach us to abide by our spontaneous impression with good humored inflexibility then most when the whole cry of voices is on the other side. Else, to-morrow a stranger will say with masterly good sense precisely what we have thought and felt all the time, and we shall be forced to take with shame our own opinion from another.

There is a time in every man's education when he arrives at the conviction that envy is ignorance; that imitation is suicide; that he must take himself for better, for worse, as his portion; that though the wide universe is full of good, no kernel of nourishing corn can come to him but through his toil bestowed on that plot of ground which is given to him to till. The power which resides in him is new in nature, and none but he knows what that is which he can do, nor does he know until he has tried. Not for nothing one face, one character, one fact makes much impression on him, and another none. It is not without preestablished harmony, this sculpture in the memory. The eye was placed where one ray should fall, that it might testify of that particular ray. Bravely let him speak the utmost syllable of his confession. We but half express ourselves, and are ashamed of that divine idea which each of us represents. It may be safely trusted as proportionate and of good issues, so it be faithfully imparted, but God will not have his work made manifest by cowards. It needs a divine man to exhibit any thing divine. A man is relieved and gay when he has put his heart into his work and done his best; but what he has said or done otherwise, shall give him no peace. It is a deliverance which does not deliver. In the attempt his genius deserts him; no muse befriends; no invention, no hope.

Trust thyself: every heart vibrates to that iron string. Accept the place the divine Providence has found for you; the society of your contemporaries, the connexion of events. Great men have always done so and confided themselves childlike to the genius of their age, betraying their perception that the Eternal was stirring at their heart, working through their hands, predominating in all their being. And we are now men, and must accept in the highest mind the same transcendent destiny; and

---

[1]Washington Allston (1779–1843). — Eds.

not pinched in a corner, not cowards fleeing before a revolution, but redeemers and benefactors, pious aspirants to be noble clay plastic under the Almighty effort, let us advance and advance on Chaos and the Dark.

What pretty oracles nature yields us on this text in the face and behavior of children, babes and even brutes. That divided and rebel mind, that distrust of a sentiment because our arithmetic has computed the strength and means opposed to our purpose, these have not. Their mind being whole, their eye is as yet unconquered, and when we look in their faces, we are disconcerted. Infancy conforms to nobody: all conform to it, so that one babe commonly makes four or five out of the adults who prattle and play to it. So God has armed youth and puberty and manhood no less with its own piquancy and charm, and made it enviable and gracious and its claims not to be put by, if it will stand by itself. Do not think the youth has no force because he cannot speak to you and me. Hark! in the next room, who spoke so clear and emphatic? Good Heaven! it is he! it is that very lump of bashfulness and phlegm which for weeks has done nothing but eat when you were by, that now rolls out these words like bell-strokes. It seems he knows how to speak to his contemporaries. Bashful or bold, then, he will know how to make us seniors very unnecessary.

The nonchalance of boys who are sure of a dinner, and would disdain as much   5
as a lord to do or say aught to conciliate one, is the healthy attitude of human nature. How is a boy the master of society; independent, irresponsible, looking out from his corner on such people and facts as pass by, he tries and sentences them on their merits, in the swift summary way of boys, as good, bad, interesting, silly, eloquent, troublesome. He cumbers himself never about consequences, about interests: he gives an independent, genuine verdict. You must court him: he does not court you. But the man is, as it were, clapped into jail by his consciousness. As soon as he has once acted or spoken with éclat, he is a committed person, watched by the sympathy or the hatred of hundreds whose affections must now enter into his account. There is no Lethe for this. Ah, that he could pass again into his neutral, godlike independence! Who can thus lose all pledge, and having observed, observe again from the same unaffected, unbiased, unbribable, unaffrighted innocence, must always be formidable, must always engage the poet's and the man's regards. Of such an immortal youth the force would be felt. He would utter opinions on all passing affairs, which being seen to be not private but necessary, would sink like darts into the ear of men, and put them in fear.

These are the voices which we hear in solitude, but they grow faint and inaudible as we enter into the world. Society everywhere is in conspiracy against the manhood of every one of its members. Society is a joint-stock company in which the members agree for the better securing of his bread to each shareholder, to surrender the liberty and culture of the eater. The virtue in most request is conformity. Self-reliance is its aversion. It loves not realities and creators, but names and customs.

Whoso would be a man must be a nonconformist. He who would gather immortal palms must not be hindered by the name of goodness, but must explore if it be goodness. Nothing is at last sacred but the integrity of our own mind. Absolve you to yourself, and you shall have the suffrage of the world. I remember an answer which when quite young I was prompted to make to a valued adviser who was wont to importune me with the dear old doctrines of the church. On my saying, What have I to do with the sacredness of traditions, if I live wholly from within? my friend suggested — "But these impulses may be from below, not from above." I replied, "They do not seem to me to be such; but if I am the devil's child, I will live then from the devil." No law can be sacred to me but that of my nature. Good and bad are but names very readily transferable to that or this; the only right is what is after my constitution, the only wrong what is against it. A man is to carry himself in the presence of all opposition as if every thing were titular and ephemeral but he. I am ashamed to think how easily we capitulate to badges and names, to large societies and dead institutions. Every decent and well-spoken individual affects and sways me more than is right. I ought to go upright and vital, and speak the rude truth in all ways. . . .

Virtues are in the popular estimate rather the exception than the rule. There is the man *and* his virtues. Men do what is called a good action, as some piece of courage or charity, much as they would pay a fine in expiation of daily non-appearance on parade. Their works are done as an apology or extenuation of their living in the world, — as invalids and the insane pay a high board. Their virtues are penances. I do not wish to expiate, but to live. My life is not an apology, but a life. It is for itself and not for a spectacle. I much prefer that it should be of a lower strain, so it be genuine and equal, than that it should be glittering and unsteady. I wish it to be sound and sweet, and not to need diet and bleeding. My life should be unique; it should be an alms, a battle, a conquest, a medicine. I ask primary evidence that you are a man, and refuse this appeal from the man to his actions. I know that for myself it makes no difference whether I do or forbear those actions which are reckoned excellent. I cannot consent to pay for a privilege where I have intrinsic right. Few and mean as my gifts may be, I actually am, and do not need for my own assurance or the assurance of my fellows any secondary testimony.

What I must do, is all that concerns me, not what the people think. This rule, equally arduous in actual and in intellectual life, may serve for the whole distinction between greatness and meanness. It is the harder, because you will always find those who think they know what is your duty better than you know it. It is easy in the world to live after the world's opinion; it is easy in solitude to live after our own; but the great man is he who in the midst of the crowd keeps with perfect sweetness the independence of solitude.

The objection to conforming to usages that have become dead to you, is, that it   10
scatters your force. It loses your time and blurs the impression of your character. If you maintain a dead church, contribute to a dead Bible-Society, vote with a great party either for the Government or against it, spread your table like base housekeepers, — under all these screens, I have difficulty to detect the precise man you are. And, of course, so much force is withdrawn from your proper life. But do your thing, and I shall know you. Do your work, and you shall reinforce yourself. A man must consider what a blind-man's-buff is this game of conformity. If I know your sect, I anticipate your argument. I hear a preacher announce for his text and topic the expediency of one of the institutions of his church. Do I not know beforehand that not possibly can he say

a new and spontaneous word? Do I not know that with all this ostentation of examining the grounds of the institution, he will do no such thing? Do I not know that he is pledged to himself not to look but at one side; the permitted side, not as a man, but as a parish minister? He is a retained attorney, and these airs of the bench are the emptiest affectation. Well, most men have bound their eyes with one or another handkerchief, and attached themselves to some one of these communities of opinion. This conformity makes them not false in a few particulars, authors of a few lies, but false in all particulars. Their every truth is not quite true. Their two is not the real two, their four not the real four: so that every word they say chagrins us, and we know not where to begin to set them right. Meantime nature is not slow to equip us in the prison-uniform of the party to which we adhere. We come to wear one cut of face and figure, and acquire by degrees the gentlest asinine expression. There is a mortifying experience in particular which does not fail to wreak itself also in the general history; I mean, "the foolish face of praise,"[2] the forced smile which we put on in company where we do not feel at ease in answer to conversation which does not interest us. The muscles, not spontaneously moved, but moved by a low usurping wilfulness, grow tight about the outline of the face and make the most disagreeable sensation, a sensation of rebuke and warning which no brave young man will suffer twice.

For non-conformity the world whips you with its displeasure. And therefore a man must know how to estimate a sour face. The bystanders look askance on him in the public street or in the friend's parlor. If this aversation had its origin in contempt and resistance like his own, he might well go home with a sad countenance; but the sour faces of the multitude, like their sweet faces, have no deep cause, — disguise no god, but are put on and off as the wind blows, and a newspaper directs. Yet is the discontent of the multitude more formidable than that of the senate and the college. It is easy enough for a firm man who knows the world to brook the rage of the cultivated classes. Their rage is decorous and prudent, for they are timid as being very vulnerable themselves. But when to their feminine rage the indignation of the people is added, when the ignorant and the poor are aroused, when the unintelligent brute force that lies at the bottom of society is made to growl and mow, it needs the habit of magnanimity and religion to treat it godlike as a trifle of no concernment.

The other terror that scares us from self-trust is our consistency; a reverence for our past act or word, because the eyes of others have no other data for computing our orbit than our past acts, and we are loath to disappoint them.

But why should you keep your head over your shoulder? Why drag about this monstrous corpse of your memory, lest you contradict somewhat you have stated in this or that public place? Suppose you should contradict yourself; what then? It seems to be a rule of wisdom never to rely on your memory alone, scarcely even in acts of pure memory, but bring the past for judgment into the thousand-eyed present, and live ever in a new day. Trust your emotion. In your metaphysics you have denied personality to the Deity: yet when the devout motions of the soul come, yield to them

---

[2]Alexander Pope (1688–1744), "Epistle to Dr. Arbuthnot," line 212. — Eds.

heart and life, though they should clothe God with shape and color. Leave your theory as Joseph his coat in the hand of the harlot, and flee.[3]

A foolish consistency is the hobgoblin of little minds, adored by little statesmen and philosophers and divines. With consistency a great soul has simply nothing to do. He may as well concern himself with his shadow on the wall. Out upon your guarded lips! Sew them up with packthread, do. Else, if you would be a man, speak what you think today in words as hard as cannon balls, and to-morrow speak what to-morrow thinks in hard words again, though it contradict every thing you said to-day. Ah, then, exclaim the aged ladies, you shall be sure to be misunderstood. Misunderstood! It is a right fool's word. Is it so bad then to be misunderstood? Pythagoras was misunderstood, and Socrates, and Jesus, and Luther, and Copernicus, and Galileo, and Newton, and every pure and wise spirit that ever took flesh. To be great is to be misunderstood.

I suppose no man can violate his nature. All the sallies of his will are rounded in   15 by the law of his being as the inequalities of Andes and Himalayas are insignificant in the curve of the sphere. Nor does it matter how you gauge and try him. A character is like an acrostic or Alexandrian stanza; — read it forward, backward, or across, it still spells the same thing. In this pleasing contrite wood-life which God allows me, let me record day by day my honest thought without prospect or retrospect, and, I cannot doubt, it will be found symmetrical, though I mean it not, and see it not. My book should smell of pines and resound with the hum of insects. The swallow over my window should interweave that thread or straw he carries in his bill into my web also. We pass for what we are. Character teaches above our wills. Men imagine that they communicate their virtue or vice only by overt actions and do not see that virtue or vice emit a breath every moment. . . .

Man is timid and apologetic. He is no longer upright. He dares not say "I think," "I am," but quotes some saint or sage. He is ashamed before the blade of grass or the blowing rose. These roses under my window make no reference to former roses or to better ones; they are for what they are; they exist with God to-day. There is no time to them. There is simply the rose; it is perfect in every moment of its existence. Before a leaf-bud has burst, its whole life acts; in the full-blown flower, there is no more; in the leafless root, there is no less. Its nature is satisfied, and it satisfies nature, in all moments alike. There is no time to it. But man postpones or remembers; he does not live in the present, but with reverted eye laments the past, or, heedless of the riches that surround him, stands on tiptoe to foresee the future. He cannot be happy and strong until he too lives with nature in the present, above time.

This should be plain enough. Yet see what strong intellects dare not yet hear God himself, unless he speak the phraseology of I know not what David, or Jeremiah, or Paul. We shall not always set so great a price on a few texts, on a few lives. We are like

---

[3]In the Old Testament account, Joseph is sold into slavery by his brothers and becomes the servant of Potiphar, the Pharaoh of Egypt's captain of the guard. Potiphar's wife tempts Joseph and grabs his cloak. In his haste to get away, he leaves his cloak in her hands and flees (Genesis 39). — Eds.

children who repeat by rote the sentences of grandames and tutors, and, as they grow older, of the men of talents and character they chance to see, — painfully recollecting the exact words they spoke; afterwards, when they come into the point of view which those had who uttered these sayings, they understand them, and are willing to let the words go; for, at any time, they can use words as good, when occasion comes. So was it with us, so will it be, if we proceed. If we live truly, we shall see truly. It is as easy for the strong man to be strong, as it is for the weak to be weak. When we have new perception, we shall gladly disburthen the memory of its hoarded treasures as old rubbish. When a man lives with God, his voice shall be as sweet as the murmur of the brook and the rustle of the corn.

And now at last the highest truth on this subject remains unsaid; probably, cannot be said; for all that we say is the far off remembering of the intuition. That thought, by what I can now nearest approach to say it, is this. When good is near you, when you have life in yourself, — it is not by any known or appointed way; you shall not discern the foot-prints of any other; you shall not see the face of man; you shall not hear any name; — the way, the thought, the good shall be wholly strange and new. It shall exclude all other being. You take the way from man not to man. All persons that ever existed are its fugitive ministers. There shall be no fear in it. Fear and hope are alike beneath it. It asks nothing. There is somewhat low even in hope. We are then in vision. There is nothing that can be called gratitude nor properly joy. The soul is raised over passion. It seeth identity and eternal causation. It is a perceiving that Truth and Right are. Hence it becomes a Tranquillity out of the knowing that all things go well. Vast spaces of nature; the Atlantic Ocean, the South Sea; vast intervals of time, years, centuries, are of no account. This which I think and feel, underlay that former state of life and circumstances, as it does underlie my present, and will always all circumstance, and what is called life, and what is called death.

Life only avails, not the having lived. Power ceases in the instant of repose; it resides in the moment of transition from a past to a new state; in the shooting of the gulf; in the darting to an aim. This one fact the world hates, that the soul *becomes*; for, that forever degrades the past; turns all riches to poverty; all reputation to a shame; confounds the saint with the rogue; shoves Jesus and Judas equally aside. Why then do we prate of self-reliance? Inasmuch as the soul is present, there will be power not confident but agent. To talk of reliance, is a poor external way of speaking. Speak rather of that which relies, because it works and is. Who has more soul than I, masters me, though he should not raise his finger. Round him I must revolve by the gravitation of spirits; who has less, I rule with like facility. We fancy it rhetoric when we speak of eminent virtue. We do not yet see that virtue is Height, and that a man or a company of men plastic and permeable to principles, by the law of nature must overpower and ride all cities, nations, kings, rich men, poets, who are not. . . .

I must be myself. I will not hide my tastes or aversions. I will so trust that what   20
is deep is holy, that I will do strongly before the sun and moon whatever inly rejoices me, and the heart appoints. If you are noble, I will love you; if you are not, I will not hurt you and myself by hypocritical attentions. If you are true, but not in the same

truth with me, cleave to your companions; I will seek my own. I do this not selfishly but humbly and truly. It is alike your interest and mine and all men's, however long we have dwelt in lies, to live in truth. Does this sound harsh to-day? You will soon love what is dictated by your nature as well as mine, and if we follow the truth, it will bring us out safe at last. — But so you may give these friends pain. Yes, but I cannot sell my liberty and my power, to save their sensibility. Besides, all persons have their moments of reason when they look out into the region of absolute truth; then will they justify me and do the same thing.

The populace think that your rejection of popular standards is a rejection of all standard, and mere antinomianism; and the bold sensualist will use the name of philosophy to gild his crimes. But the law of consciousness abides. There are two confessionals, in one or the other of which we must be shriven. You may fulfil your round of duties by clearing yourself in the *direct*, or, in the *reflex* way. Consider whether you have satisfied your relations to father, mother, cousin, neighbor, town, cat, and dog; whether any of these can upbraid you. But I may also neglect this reflex standard, and absolve me to myself. I have my own stern claims and perfect circle. It denies the name of duty to many offices that are called duties. But if I can discharge its debts, it enables me to dispense with the popular code. If any one imagines that this law is lax, let him keep its commandment one day.

And truly it demands something godlike in him who has cast off the common motives of humanity, and has ventured to trust himself for a task-master. High be his heart, faithful his will, clear his sight, that he may in good earnest be doctrine, society, law to himself, that a simple purpose may be to him as strong as iron necessity is to others.

If any man consider the present aspects of what is called by distinction *society*, he will see the need of these ethics. The sinew and heart of man seem to be drawn out, and we are become timorous desponding whimperers. We are afraid of truth, afraid of fortune, afraid of death, and afraid of each other. Our age yields no great and perfect persons. We want men and women who shall renovate life and our social state, but we see that most natures are insolvent; cannot satisfy their own wants, have an ambition out of all proportion to their practical force, and so do lean and beg day and night continually. Our housekeeping is mendicant, our arts, our occupations, our marriages, our religion we have not chosen, but society has chosen for us. We are parlor soldiers. The rugged battle of fate, where strength is born, we shun.

If our young men miscarry in their first enterprizes, they lose all heart. If the young merchant fails, men say he is *ruined*. If the finest genius studies at one of our colleges, and is not installed in an office within one year afterwards in the cities or suburbs of Boston or New York, it seems to his friends and to himself that he is right in being disheartened and in complaining the rest of his life. A sturdy lad from New Hampshire or Vermont, who in turn tries all the professions, who *teams it, farms it, peddles*, keeps a school, preaches, edits a newspaper, goes to Congress, buys a township, and so forth, in successive years, and always, like a cat, falls on his feet, is worth a hundred of these city dolls. He walks abreast with his days, and feels no shame in not "studying a profession," for he does not postpone his life, but lives already. He has not one chance, but a hundred chances. Let a stoic[4] arise who shall reveal the resources of man, and tell men they are not leaning willows, but can and must detach themselves; that with the exercise of self-trust, new powers shall appear; that a man is the word made flesh, born to shed healing to the nations, that he should be ashamed of our compassion, and that the moment he acts from himself, tossing the laws, the books, idolatries, and customs out of the window, — we pity him no more but thank and revere him, — and that teacher shall restore the life of man to splendor, and make his name dear to all History.

It is easy to see that a greater self-reliance, — a new respect for the divinity in   25
man, — must work a revolution in all the offices and relations of men; in their religion; in their education; in their pursuits; their modes of living; their association; in their property; in their speculative views. . . .

Society never advances. It recedes as fast on one side as it gains on the other. Its progress is only apparent, like the workers of a treadmill. It undergoes continual changes: it is barbarous, it is civilized, it is christianized, it is rich, it is scientific; but this change is not amelioration. For every thing that is given, something is taken. Society acquires new arts and loses old instincts. What a contrast between the well-clad, reading, writing, thinking American, with a watch, a pencil, and a bill of exchange in his pocket, and the naked New Zealander, whose property is a club, a spear, a mat, and an undivided twentieth of a shed to sleep under. But compare the health of the two men, and you shall see that his aboriginal strength the white man has lost. If the traveller tell us truly, strike the savage with a broad axe, and in a day or two the flesh shall unite and heal as if you struck the blow into soft pitch, and the same blow shall send the white to his grave.

The civilized man has built a coach, but has lost the use of his feet. He is supported on crutches, but loses so much support of muscle. He has got a fine Geneva watch, but he has lost the skill to tell the hour by the sun. A Greenwich nautical almanac he has, and so being sure of the information when he wants it, the man in the street does not know a star in the sky. The solstice he does not observe; the equinox he knows as little; and the whole bright calendar of the year is without a dial in his mind. His notebooks impair his memory; his libraries overload his wit; the insurance office increases the number of accidents; and it may be a question whether machinery does not encumber; whether we have not lost by refinement some energy, by a christianity entrenched in establishments and forms, some vigor of wild virtue. For every stoic was a stoic; but in Christendom where is the Christian?

There is no more deviation in the moral standard than in the standard of height or bulk. No greater men are now than ever were. A singular equality may be observed between the great men of the first and of the last ages; nor can all the science, art, religion and philosophy of the nineteenth century avail to educate greater men than Plutarch's heroes, three or four and twenty centuries ago. Not in time is the race progressive. Phocion, Socrates, Anaxagoras, Diogenes, are great men, but they leave no

---

[4]Adherent of Greek school of philosophy that encouraged being attuned with one's inner self and being content with one's present state of being. — Eds.

class. He who is really of their class will not be called by their name, but be wholly his own man, and, in his turn the founder of a sect. The arts and inventions of each period are only its costume, and do not invigorate men. The harm of the improved machinery may compensate its good. Hudson and Behring[5] accomplished so much in their fishing-boats, as to astonish Parry and Franklin,[6] whose equipment exhausted the resources of science and art. Galileo, with an opera-glass, discovered a more splendid series of facts than any one since. Columbus found the New World in an undecked boat. It is curious to see the periodical disuse and perishing of means and machinery which were introduced with loud laudation, a few years or centuries before. The great genius returns to essential man. We reckoned the improvements of the art of war among the triumphs of science, and yet Napoleon conquered Europe by the Bivouac, which consisted of falling back on naked valor, and disencumbering it of all aids. The Emperor held it impossible to make a perfect army, says Las Cases,[7] "without abolishing our arms, magazines, commissaries, and carriages, until in imitation of the Roman custom, the soldier should receive his supply of corn, grind it in his hand-mill, and bake his bread himself."

Society is a wave. The wave moves onward, but the water of which it is composed, does not. The same particle does not rise from the valley to the ridge. Its unity is only phenomenal. The persons who make up a nation to-day, next year die, and their experience with them.

And so the reliance on Property, including the reliance on governments which protect it, is the want of self-reliance. Men have looked away from themselves and at things so long, that they have come to esteem what they call the soul's progress, namely, the religious, learned, and civil institutions, as guards of property, and they deprecate assaults on these, because they feel them to be assaults on property. They measure their esteem of each other, by what each has, and not by what each is. But a cultivated man becomes ashamed of his property, ashamed of what he has, out of new respect for his being. Especially he hates what he has, if he see that it is accidental, — came to him by inheritance, or gift, or crime; then he feels that it is not having; it does not belong to him, has no root in him, and merely lies there, because no revolution or no robber takes it away. But that which a man is, does always by necessity acquire, and what the man acquires is permanent and living property, which does not wait the beck of rulers, or mobs, or revolutions, or fire, or storm, or bankruptcies, but perpetually renews itself wherever the man is put. "Thy lot or portion of life," said the Caliph Ali,[8] "is seeking after thee; therefore be at rest from seeking after it." Our dependence on these foreign goods leads us to our slavish respect for numbers. The political parties meet in numerous conventions; the greater the concourse, and with each new uproar of

30

---

[5]Navigators Henry Hudson (d. 1611) and Vitus Jonassen Bering (1680–1741). — Eds.
[6]Arctic explorers Sir William Edward Perry (1790–1855) and Sir John Franklin (1786–1847). — Eds.
[7]Comte Emmanuel de Las Cases (1766–1842), author of an eight-volume biography of Napoleon. — Eds.
[8]Caliph Ali (602?–661), first leader of the Shiite branch of Islam. — Eds.

announcement, The delegation from Essex! The Democrats from New Hampshire! The Whigs of Maine! the young patriot feels himself stronger than before by a new thousand of eyes and arms. In like manner the reformers summon conventions, and vote and resolve in multitude. But not so, O friends! will the God deign to enter and inhabit you, but by a method precisely the reverse. It is only as a man puts off from himself all external support, and stands alone, that I see him to be strong and to prevail. He is weaker by every recruit to his banner. Is not a man better than a town? Ask nothing of men, and in the endless mutation, thou only firm column must presently appear the upholder of all that surrounds thee. He who knows that power is in the soul, that he is weak only because he has looked for good out of him and elsewhere, and so perceiving, throws himself unhesitatingly on his thought, instantly rights himself, stands in the erect position, commands his limbs, works miracles; just as a man who stands on his feet is stronger than a man who stands on his head.

So use all that is called Fortune. Most men gamble with her, and gain all, and lose all, as her wheel rolls. But do thou leave as unlawful these winnings, and deal with Cause and Effect, the chancellors of God. In the Will work and acquire, and thou hast chained the wheel of Chance, and shalt always drag her after thee. A political victory, a rise of rents, the recovery of your sick, or the return of your absent friend, or some other quite external event, raises your spirits, and you think good days are preparing for you. Do not believe it. It can never be so. Nothing can bring you peace but yourself. Nothing can bring you peace but the triumph of principles.

(1841)

Exploring the Text

1. What "admonition" does Ralph Waldo Emerson refer to in the second sentence? What does he mean?
2. What are the rhetorical strategies that Emerson uses in the first paragraph of "Self-Reliance"? Identify three examples and explain their effects.
3. Paragraph 3 begins with a direct address: "Trust thyself: every heart vibrates to that iron string." What does this metaphor mean, and how does it serve as an apt introductory phrase for what follows in paragraphs 3 through 6?
4. What analogies does Emerson employ in paragraphs 4 and 5? Select one of them and explain how it helps Emerson develop his ideas.
5. "If I know your sect, I anticipate your argument" (par. 10), writes Emerson. What does he mean? How might his idea apply to society today?
6. Emerson writes, "These roses under my window make no reference to former roses or to better ones; they are for what they are; they exist with God to-day" (par. 16). What does he mean? How does the image of the roses contribute to Emerson's main idea?
7. Emerson criticizes what he calls "our age" (the early to mid-nineteenth century) (par. 23). To what extent do Emerson's observations apply to life in "our age" today?

8. How do Emerson's juxtapositions in paragraph 27 contribute to the selection as a whole?

9. What analogy does Emerson develop in paragraph 29? Explain how it contributes to his argument.

10. One prominent feature of Emerson's writing is his use of short and dense paragraphs that may be regarded as key passages — for example, paragraphs 9, 14, 16, 20, 21, 27, and 31. Select two that appeal most to you. How does Emerson use rhetorical strategies to develop his ideas in those paragraphs?

11. Emerson is well-known for his pithy, timeless, epigrammatic statements — for example, "Trust thyself: every heart vibrates to that iron string" (par. 3), "No law can be sacred to me but that of my nature" (par. 7), "If I know your sect, I anticipate your argument" (par. 10), "A foolish consistency is the hobgoblin of little minds" (par. 14), "To be great is to be misunderstood" (par. 14), "The civilized man has built a coach, but has lost the use of his feet" (par. 27), "They measure their esteem of each other, by what each has, and not by what each is" (par. 30), and "Nothing can bring you peace but yourself. Nothing can bring you peace but the triumph of principles" (par. 31). Select two of these statements and discuss the extent to which they apply to our life and time. Be specific in your discussion.

12. In the penultimate paragraph, Emerson discusses man's attitude toward property:

> They measure their esteem of each other, by what each has, and not by what each is. But a cultivated man becomes ashamed of his property, ashamed of what he has, out of new respect for his being. Especially he hates what he has, if he see that it is accidental, — came to him by inheritance, or gift, or crime; then he feels that it is not having; it does not belong to him, has no root in him, and merely lies there, because no revolution or no robber takes it away.

Do you agree with what Emerson says of the "cultivated" man? Defend or challenge his remark, using your observation and experience to support your position.

13. How effectively does paragraph 31 serve as a conclusion to the essay? Be specific in your answer.

14. Thomas Paine begins *Common Sense* (p. 376):

> Some writers have so confounded society with government, as to leave little or no distinction between them; whereas they are not only different, but have different origins. Society is produced by our wants, and government by our wickedness; the former promotes our happiness *positively* by uniting our affections, the latter *negatively* by restraining our vices. The one encourages intercourse, the other creates distinctions. The first is a patron, the last a punisher. Society in every state is a blessing . . .

Emerson writes, "Society everywhere is in conspiracy against the manhood of every one of its members" (par. 6) and characterizes "society" throughout "Self-Reliance." What does each writer mean by *society*? How would you compare and contrast Emerson's and Paine's different perspectives on it? Explain.

TALKBACK

BENJAMIN ANASTAS

Benjamin Anastas was born in 1969 in Gloucester, Massachusetts. A graduate of the Iowa Writers' Workshop, Anastas has published both fiction and nonfiction in a wide variety of national publications. He is the author of two novels, *An Underachiever's Diary* (1998) and *The Faithful Narrative of a Pastor's Disappearance* (2002), and a memoir, *Too Good to Be True* (2012).

The Foul Reign of Emerson's "Self-Reliance"

His article "The Foul Reign of Emerson's 'Self-Reliance'" was published in the *New York Times Magazine* on December 4, 2011.

My first exposure to the high-flown pap of Ralph Waldo Emerson's "Self-Reliance" came in a basement classroom at the private boys' school where I enrolled to learn the secrets of discipline and because I wanted, at age 14, to wear a tie. The class was early American literature, the textbook an anthology with the heft of a volume of the Babylonian Talmud; a ribbon for holding your place between "Rip Van Winkle," by Washington Irving, and "Young Goodman Brown," by Nathaniel Hawthorne; and a slick hardcover the same shade of green as the backside of a dollar bill.

Our teacher, let's call him Mr. Sideways, had a windblown air, as if he had just stepped out of an open coupe, and the impenetrable self-confidence of someone who is convinced that he is liked. (He was not.) "Whoso would be a man," he read aloud to a room full of slouching teenage boys in button-down shirts and ties stained with sloppy Joes from the dining hall, "must be a nonconformist. He who would gather immortal palms must not be hindered by the name of goodness. . . . Nothing is at last sacred but the integrity of your own mind." And then he let loose the real hokum: "Absolve you to yourself," he read, "and you shall have the suffrage of the world."

I am sure that Mr. Sideways lectured dutifully on transcendentalism and its founding ideas — Emerson's "transparent eyeball" and its gift of X-ray sight; Thoreau's flight from a life of "quiet desperation" in society to the stillness of Walden Pond; the starred ceiling of the heavens that Ralph Waldo called the "Over-Soul," uniting us with its magnetic beams — but what I remember most about that English class was the week that Mr. Sideways told us to leave our anthologies at home so that he could lead us in a seminar in how to make a fortune in real estate by tapping the treasure trove he referred to as "O.P.M.," or Other People's Money. He drew pyramids and pie charts on the blackboard. He gave us handouts.

For years I blamed Mr. Sideways — and the money fever of the 1980s — for this weird episode of hucksterism in English class. But that was being unfair. Our teacher had merely fallen under the spell, like countless others before and after, of the most pernicious piece of literature in the American canon. The whim that inspired him to lead a seminar in house-flipping to a stupefied under-age audience was Emerson's handiwork. "All that Adam had," he goads in his essay "Nature," "all that Caesar could, you have and can do." Oh, the deception! The rank insincerity! It's just like the Devil in Mutton Chops to promise an orgiastic communion fit for the gods, only to deliver a gospel of "self-conceit so intensely intellectual," as Melville complained, "that at first one hesitates to call it by its right name."

The excessive love of individual liberty that debases our national politics? It found its original poet in Ralph Waldo. The plague of devices that keep us staring into the shallow puddle of our dopamine reactions, caressing our touch screens for another fix of our own importance? That's right: it all started with Emerson's "Self-Reliance." Our fetish for the authentically homespun and the American affliction of ignoring volumes of evidence in favor of the flashes that meet the eye, the hunches that seize the gut? It's Emerson again, skulking through Harvard Yard in his cravat and greasy undertaker's waistcoat, while in his mind he's trailing silken robes fit for Zoroaster[1] and levitating on the grass.

Before it does another generation's worth of damage to the American psyche, let's put an end to the foul reign of "Self-Reliance" and let the scholars pick over the meaning of its carcass. One question first, though: Is there anything worth salvaging among the spiritualist ramblings, obscure metaphysics and aphorisms so pandering that Joel Osteen[2] might think twice about delivering them? Is there an essential part of Emerson's signature essay that we've somehow lost sight of?

"There is a time in every man's education," Emerson writes, presuming, with his usual élan, to both personify his young country and issue a decree for its revival, "when he arrives at the conviction that envy is ignorance; that imitation is suicide; that he must take himself for better, for worse, as his portion; that though the wide universe is full of good, no kernel of nourishing corn can come to him but through his toil bestowed on the plot of ground which is given him to till."

As the story in our high-school anthology went, the citizenry that the Bard of Concord met on his strolls through the town green in the 1830s were still cowed by the sermons of their Puritan forefathers — we had read Jonathan Edwards's "Sinners in the Hands of an Angry God" to get a taste — prone to awe when it came to the literature of distant foreign empires and too complacent on the biggest moral issues of the day: the institution of slavery and the genocide of the Indians. (At least Emerson saw well enough with his transparent eye to criticize both.) The country had every bit of God-given energy and talent and latent conviction that it needed to produce genius, he believed, but too much

5

---

[1]Zoroaster, also called Zarathustra, an ancient Persian prophet. — Eds.
[2]Joel Osteen (b. 1963), an American televangelist. — Eds.

kowtowing to society and the approval of elders had tamed his fellows of their natural gifts (the "aboriginal Self," he called it) and sapped them of their courage.

"[M]ost men have bound their eyes with one or another handkerchief," a disenchanted Emerson observed, "and attached themselves to . . . communities of opinion. This conformity makes them not false in a few particulars, but false in all particulars." Society operates like a corporation that requires its shareholders to sacrifice their rights for the comfort of all, Emerson believed. Instead of "realities and creators," it gives men "names and customs."

So what is his cure for the country's ailing soul, his recipe for our deliverance from civilization and its discontents? This is the aim of "Self-Reliance," which Emerson culled from a series of lectures he delivered at the Masonic Temple of Boston — his "Divinity School Address" at Harvard in 1838, denounced by one listener as "an incoherent rhapsody," had already caused an outcry — and published in his collection *Essays: First Series in 1841*. Cornel West has praised Emerson for his "dynamic perspective" and for his "prescription for courageous self-reliance by means of nonconformity and inconsistency." Harold Bloom noted, in an article for the *Times*, that by " 'self-reliance' Emerson meant the recognition of the God within us, rather than the worship of the Christian godhead." This is the essay's greatest virtue for its original audience: it ordained them with an authority to speak what had been reserved for only the powerful, and bowed to no greater human laws, social customs or dictates from the pulpit. "Trust thyself: every heart vibrates to that iron string." Or: "No law can be sacred to me but that of my nature." Some of the lines are so ingrained in us that we know them by heart. They feel like natural law.

There is a downside to ordaining the self with divine authority, though. We humans are fickle creatures, and natures — however sacred — can mislead us. That didn't bother Emerson. "Speak what you think now in hard words," Emerson exhorted, "and tomorrow speak what tomorrow thinks in hard words again, though it contradict every thing you said today." (Memo to Mitt Romney: no more apologies for being "as consistent as human beings can be." You're Emersonian!)

The larger problem with the essay, and its more lasting legacy as a cornerstone of the American identity, has been Emerson's tacit endorsement of a radically self-centered worldview. It's a lot like the Ptolemaic model of the planets that preceded Copernicus; the sun, the moon and the stars revolve around our portable reclining chairs, and whatever contradicts our right to harbor misconceptions — whether it be Birtherism, climate-science denial or the conviction that Trader Joe's sells good food — is the prattle of the unenlightened majority and can be dismissed out of hand.

"A man is to carry himself in the presence of all opposition," Emerson advises, "as if every thing were titular and ephemeral but he." If this isn't the official motto of the 112th Congress of the United States, well, it should be. The gridlock, grandstanding, rule manipulating and inability to compromise aren't symptoms of national decline. We're simply coming into our own as Emerson's republic.

10

Just recently I was watching the original "Think Different" spot that reversed Apple Computer's fortunes when it was first shown in 1997 and marked the first real triumph for Steve Jobs after returning from the wilderness to the company he helped to found. The echoes of Emerson in the ad are striking, especially in the famous voice-over narration by Richard Dreyfuss, reading a poem now known by historians and Apple's legion of fans as "Here's to the Crazy Ones." The message was already familiar when it first met our ears.

In calling out to all the misfits and the rebels and the troublemakers, the   15
"round pegs in square holes" who "see things differently" and have trouble with the rules, the ad evokes the ideal first created by Emerson of a rough-hewed outsider who changes the world through a combination of courage, tenacity, resourcefulness and that God-given wild card, genius. While Dreyfuss narrates, archival footage of the "crazy ones" flickers on the screen in black and white: Albert Einstein leads the way, followed by Bob Dylan, the Rev. Martin Luther King Jr., a jubilant Richard Branson shaking a Champagne bottle in a flight suit.

This is the problem when the self is endowed with divinity, and it's a weakness that Emerson acknowledged: if the only measure of greatness is how big an iconoclast you are, then there really is no difference between coming up with the theory of relativity, plugging in an electric guitar, leading a civil rights movement, or spending great gobs of your own money to fly a balloon across the Atlantic. In "Self-Reliance," Emerson addresses this potentially fatal flaw to his thinking with a principle he calls "the law of consciousness." (It is not convincing.) Every one of us has two confessionals, he writes. At the first, we clear our actions in the mirror (a recapitulation of the dictum "trust thyself"). At the second, we consider whether we've fulfilled our obligations to our families, neighbors, communities and—here Emerson can't resist a bit of snark—our cats and dogs. Which confessional is the higher one? To whom do we owe our ultimate allegiance? It's not even a contest.

"I have my own stern claims and perfect circle," Emerson writes. With this one fell swoop, Emerson tips the scales in favor of his own confessional, and any hope he might have raised for creating a balance to the self's divinity is lost. Ever since, we've been misreading him, or at least misapplying him. As a sad result, it has been the swagger of a man's walk that makes his measure, and Americans' right to love ourselves before any other that trumps all.

(2011)

Exploring the Text

1. Note three or four examples of highly charged diction in the first two paragraphs. How do those choices and Benjamin Anastas's use of hyperbole contribute to the tone he establishes right away?
2. A sensitive reader might say that Anastas commits several fallacies in this short piece. For example, might "Mr. Sideways," as characterized in paragraphs

3 and 4, be regarded as a "straw man"? Does the speaker "beg the question" in paragraph 5? And does he overgeneralize in paragraph 10? Analyze each of these examples. Does the reader's determination of them as fallacies depend on the extent to which that reader agrees with Anastas's position? Explain.

3. In paragraph 8, Anastas makes a parenthetical statement: "(At least Emerson saw well enough with his transparent eye to criticize both.)" Here "both" refers to "the institution of slavery and the genocide of the Indians." How does such a "concession" contribute to the effectiveness of his argument? Explain.

4. How would you analyze Anastas's rhetoric in paragraph 10? Is the paragraph effective? Explain why or why not.

5. How would you describe the overall tone of this piece? How does it contribute to the success of the writer's argument?

Making Connections

1. How accurately does Anastas represent Ralph Waldo Emerson's ideas as articulated in "Self-Reliance"?

2. Have we in our modern age become too egocentric? And if so, is Emerson to blame? Anastas writes, "The larger problem with the essay, and its more lasting legacy as a cornerstone of American identity, has been Emerson's tacit endorsement of a radically self-centered worldview" (par. 12). Do you agree with Anastas that an Emersonian view encourages us "to harbor misconceptions" and assures us that it is our right to do so?

3. If he could, how might Emerson respond to "The Foul Reign of Emerson's 'Self-Reliance'"? Write a reply to Anastas in Emerson's voice.

4. According to Anastas, what are some of the ills that plague modern life and discourse in America? Do you agree with his view? Would Emerson? Why or why not?

5. Emerson concludes "Self-Reliance" by writing, "Nothing can bring you peace but yourself. Nothing can bring you peace but the triumph of principles." He implies that reliance on the self is based on a reliance on principles. Based on your reading of the piece by Anastas, do you think he would agree? Find two or three statements from "Self-Reliance" that you think Anastas would approve of. Discuss whether or not Anastas is too dismissive of Emerson.

6. Anastas makes a very strong claim, stating that "Self-Reliance" is "the most pernicious piece of literature in the American canon" (par. 4). If you agree with Anastas, explain why, using specific evidence from Emerson's text. If you disagree, make a case for what you see as the "most pernicious" text you have had to read. You might imitate Anastas's rhetoric as you develop your argument. Be sure to refer specifically to the text of the piece you attack.

MARGARET FULLER

Margaret Fuller (1810–1850) was a scholar, a literary critic, an editor, a journalist, a teacher, and a political activist and often hailed as America's first true feminist. A pioneer of the transcendentalist movement, she numbered among her friends and colleagues many of the intellectual revolutionaries of the day, including Ralph Waldo Emerson, Henry David Thoreau, Bronson Alcott, Horace Greeley, and Thomas Carlyle. In 1839, Fuller began hosting a series of conversations at Elizabeth Peabody's West Street bookshop in Boston, which provided an open forum for women to discuss topics such as classical mythology, education, ethics, the fine arts, and women's rights. Fuller joined Emerson in 1840 as editor of the influential transcendentalist journal the *Dial*.

from *Woman in the Nineteenth Century*

In 1843, Fuller published an essay entitled "The Greatest Lawsuit: Man vs. Men and Woman vs. Women." In 1845, she expanded it into a book, which was published as *Woman in the Nineteenth Century*. Horace Greeley later wrote that "it was the loftiest and most commanding assertion yet made of the right of Woman to be regarded and treated as an independent, intelligent, rational being."

Here, as elsewhere, the gain of creation consists always in the growth of individual minds, which live and aspire, as flowers bloom and birds sing, in the midst of morasses; and in the continual development of that thought, the thought of human destiny, which is given to eternity adequately to express, and which ages of failure only seemingly impede. Only seemingly, and whatever seems to the contrary, this country is as surely destined to elucidate a great moral law, as Europe was to promote the mental culture of man.

Though the national independence be blurred by the servility of individuals, though freedom and equality have been proclaimed only to leave room for a monstrous display of slave-dealing and slave-keeping; though the free American so often feels himself free, like the Roman, only to pamper his appetites and his indolence through the misery of his fellow beings, still it is not in vain, that the verbal statement has been made, "All men are born free and equal." There it stands, a golden certainty wherewith to encourage the good, to shame the bad. The new world may be called clearly to perceive that it incurs the utmost penalty, if it reject or oppress the sorrowful brother. And, if men are deaf, the angels hear. But men cannot be deaf. It is inevitable that an external freedom, an independence of the encroachments of other men, such as has been achieved for the nation, should be so also for every member of it. That which has once been clearly conceived in the intelligence cannot fail sooner or later to be acted out. It has become a law as irrevocable as that of the

Medes[1] in their ancient dominion; men will privately sin against it, but the law, as expressed by a leading mind of the age,

> *"Tutti fatti a sembianza d'un Solo,*
> *Figli tutti d'un solo riscatto,*
> *In qual'ora, in qual parte del suolo*
> *Trascorriamo quest' aura vital,*
> *Siam fratelli, siam stretti ad un patto:*
> *Maladetto colui che lo infrange,*
> *Che s'innalza sul fiacco che piange*
> *Che contrista uno spirto immortal."*[2]

> "All made in the likeness of the One,
>   All children of one ransom,
> In whatever hour, in whatever part of the soil,
>   We draw this vital air,
> We are brothers; we must be bound by one compact,
>   Accursed he who infringes it,
> Who raises himself upon the weak who weep,
>   Who saddens an immortal spirit."

This law cannot fail of universal recognition. Accursed be he who willingly saddens an immortal spirit, doomed to infamy in later, wiser ages, doomed in future stages of his own being to deadly penance, only short of death. Accursed be he who sins in ignorance, if that ignorance be caused by sloth.

We sicken no less at the pomp than the strife of words. We feel that never were lungs so puffed with the wind of declamation, on moral and religious subjects, as now. We are tempted to implore these "word-heroes," these word-Catos,[3] word-Christs, to beware of cant[4, 5] above all things; to remember that hypocrisy is the most hopeless as well as the meanest of crimes, and that those must surely be polluted by it, who do not reserve a part of their morality and religion for private use. Landor[6] says that he cannot have a great deal of mind who cannot afford to let the larger part of it lie fallow, and what is true of genius is not less so of virtue. The tongue is a valuable member, but

---

[1]In the sixth century B.C.E., the Medes ruled the area from present-day Azerbaijan to Central Asia and Afghanistan. — Eds.

[2]Alessandro Manzoni (1785–1873), Italian poet and novelist. — Eds.

[3]Marcus Porcius Cato (Cato the Elder) (234–149 B.C.E.), Roman statesman and orator. — Eds.

[4]Statements, especially on religious and moral subjects, that are not sincerely believed by the person making them; hypocritical talk. — Eds.

[5]Dr. [Samuel] Johnson's one piece of advice should be written on every door; "Clear your mind of cant." But Byron, to whom it was so acceptable, in clearing away the noxious vine, shook down the building. Sterling's emendation is worthy of honor: "Realize your cant, not cast it off."

[6]Walter Savage Landor (1775–1864), English poet. — Eds.

should appropriate but a small part of the vital juices that are needful all over the body. We feel that the mind may "grow black and rancid in the smoke" even "of altars." We start up from the harangue to go into our closet and shut the door. There inquires the spirit, "Is this rhetoric the bloom of healthy blood or a false pigment artfully laid on?" And yet again we know where is so much smoke, must be some fire; with so much talk about virtue and freedom, must be mingled some desire for them; that it cannot be in vain that such have become the common topics of conversation among men, rather than schemes for tyranny and plunder, that the very newspapers see it best to proclaim themselves Pilgrims, Puritans, Heralds of Holiness. The king that maintains so costly a retinue cannot be a mere boast, or Carabbas fiction.[7] We have waited here long in the dust; we are tired and hungry, but the triumphal procession must appear at last.

Of all its banners, none has been more steadily upheld, and under none have more valor and willingness for real sacrifices been shown, than that of the champions of the enslaved African. And this band it is, which, partly from a natural following out of principles, partly because many women have been prominent in that cause, makes, just now, the warmest appeal in behalf of woman.

Though there has been a growing liberality on this subject, yet society at large is not so prepared for the demands of this party, but that they are and will be for some time, coldly regarded as the Jacobins[8] of their day.

"Is it not enough," cries the irritated trader, "that you have done all you could to break up the national union, and thus destroy the prosperity of our country, but now you must be trying to break up family union, to take my wife away from the cradle and the kitchen hearth to vote at polls, and preach from a pulpit? Of course, if she does such things, she cannot attend to those of her own sphere. She is happy enough as she is. She has more leisure than I have, every means of improvement, every indulgence."

"Have you asked her whether she was satisfied with these *indulgences*?"

"No, but I know she is. She is too amiable to wish what would make me unhappy, and too judicious to wish to step beyond the sphere of her sex. I will never consent to have our peace disturbed by any such discussions."

"'Consent — you?' it is not consent from you that is in question, it is assent from your wife."

"Am not I the head of my house?"

"You are not the head of your wife. God has given her a mind of her own."

"I am the head and she the heart."

"God grant you play true to one another then. I suppose I am to be grateful that you did not say she was only the hand. If the head represses no natural pulse of the heart, there can be no question as to your giving your consent. Both will be of one accord, and there needs but to present any question to get a full and true answer.

---

[7]The Marquess of Carabbas was the name the cat gave his master in the popular French story "Puss in Boots" by Charles Perrault (1628–1703). — Eds.
[8]The political club that became a radical republican organization during the French Revolution. — Eds.

There is no need of precaution, of indulgence, or consent. But our doubt is whether the heart does consent with the head, or only obeys its decrees with a passiveness that precludes the exercise of its natural powers, or a repugnance that turns sweet qualities to bitter, or a doubt that lays waste the fair occasions of life. It is to ascertain the truth, that we propose some liberating measures."

Thus vaguely are these questions proposed and discussed at present. But their being proposed at all implies much thought and suggests more. Many women are considering within themselves, what they need that they have not, and what they can have, if they find they need it. Many men are considering whether women are capable of being and having more than they are and have, *and*, whether, if so, it will be best to consent to improvement in their condition.   15

This morning, I open the Boston "*Daily Mail*," and find in its "poet's corner," a translation of Schiller's "Dignity of Woman." In the advertisement of a book on America, I see in the table of contents this sequence, "Republican Institutions. American Slavery. American Ladies."

I open the "*Deutsche Schnellpost*," published in New-York, and find at the head of a column, *Juden- und Frauen-emancipation in Ungarn*. Emancipation of Jews and Women in Hungary.

The past year has seen action in the Rhode-Island legislature, to secure married women rights over their own property, where men showed that a very little examination of the subject could teach them much; an article in the Democratic Review on the same subject more largely considered, written by a woman, impelled, it is said, by glaring wrong to a distinguished friend having shown the defects in the existing laws, and the state of opinion from which they spring; and an answer from the revered old man, J. Q. Adams, in some respects the Phocion[9] of his time, to an address made him by some ladies. To this last I shall again advert in another place.

These symptoms of the times have come under my view quite accidentally: one who seeks, may, each month or week, collect more.

The numerous party, whose opinions are already labelled and adjusted too much   20
to their mind to admit of any new light, strive, by lectures on some model-woman of bride-like beauty and gentleness, by writing and lending little treatises, intended to mark out with precision the limits of woman's sphere, and woman's mission, to prevent other than the rightful shepherd from climbing the wall, or the flock from using any chance to go astray.

Without enrolling ourselves at once on either side, let us look upon the subject from the best point of view which to-day offers. No better, it is to be feared, than a high house-top. A high hill-top or at least a cathedral spire, would be desirable.

It may well be an Anti-Slavery party that pleads for woman, if we consider merely that she does not hold property on equal terms with men; so that, if a husband dies without making a will, the wife, instead of taking at once his place as head of the family, inherits only a part of his fortune, often brought him by herself, as if she were a child, or ward only, not an equal partner.

---

[9]Phocion (402–318 B.C.E.), Athenian ruler known for his powerful speeches. — Eds.

We will not speak of the innumerable instances in which profligate and idle men live upon the earnings of industrious wives; or if the wives leave them, and take with them the children, to perform the double duty of mother and father, follow from place to place, and threaten to rob them of the children, if deprived of the rights of a husband, as they call them, planting themselves in their poor lodgings, frightening them into paying tribute by taking from them the children, running into debt at the expense of these otherwise so overtasked helots. Such instances count up by scores within my own memory. I have seen the husband who had stained himself by a long course of low vice, till his wife was wearied from her heroic forgiveness, by finding that his treachery made it useless, and that if she would provide bread for herself and her children, she must be separate from his ill fame. I have known this man come to instal himself in the chamber of a woman who loathed him and say she should never take food without his company. I have known these men steal their children whom they knew they had no means to maintain, take them into dissolute company, expose them to bodily danger, to frighten the poor woman, to whom, it seems, the fact that she alone had borne the pangs of their birth, and nourished their infancy, does not give an equal right to them. I do believe that this mode of kidnapping, and it is frequent enough in all classes of society, will be by the next age viewed as it is by Heaven now, and that the man who avails himself of the shelter of men's laws to steal from a mother her own children, or arrogate any superior right in them, save that of superior virtue, will bear the stigma he deserves, in common with him who steals grown men from their mother land, their hopes, and their homes.

I said, we will not speak of this now, yet I have spoken, for the subject makes me feel too much. I could give instances that would startle the most vulgar and callous, but I will not, for the public opinion of their own sex is already against such men, and where cases of extreme tyranny are made known, there is private action in the wife's favor. But she ought not to need this, nor, I think, can she long. Men must soon see that, on their own ground, that woman is the weaker party, she ought to have legal protection, which would make such oppression impossible. But I would not deal with "atrocious instances" except in the way of illustration, neither demand from men a partial redress in some one matter, but go to the root of the whole. If principles could be established, particulars would adjust themselves aright. Ascertain the true destiny of woman, give her legitimate hopes, and a standard within herself; marriage and all other relations would by degrees be harmonized with these.

But to return to the historical progress of this matter. Knowing that there exists   25 in the minds of men a tone of feeling towards women as towards slaves, such as is expressed in the common phrase, "Tell that to women and children," that the infinite soul can only work through them in already ascertained limits; that the gift of reason, man's highest prerogative, is allotted to them in much lower degree; that they must be kept from mischief and melancholy by being constantly engaged in active labor, which is to be furnished and directed by those better able to think, &c., &c.; we need not multiply instances, for who can review the experience of last week without recall-ing words which imply, whether in jest or earnest, these views or views like these; knowing this, can we wonder that many reformers think that measures are not likely to be taken in behalf of women, unless their wishes could be publicly represented by women?

That can never be necessary, cry the other side. All men are privately influenced by women; each has his wife, sister, or female friends, and is too much biased by these relations to fail of representing their interests, and, if this is not enough, let them propose and enforce their wishes with the pen. The beauty of home would be destroyed, the delicacy of the sex be violated, the dignity of halls of legislation degraded by an attempt to introduce them there. Such duties are inconsistent with those of a mother; and then we have ludicrous pictures of ladies in hysterics at the polls, and senate chambers filled with cradles.

But if, in reply, we admit as truth that woman seems destined by nature rather for the inner circle, we must add that the arrangements of civilized life have not been, as yet, such as to secure it to her. Her circle, if the duller, is not the quieter. If kept from "excitement," she is not from drudgery. Not only the Indian squaw carries the burdens of the camp, but the favorites of Louis the Fourteenth accompany him in his journeys, and the washerwoman stands at her tub and carries home her work at all seasons, and in all states of health. Those who think the physical circumstances of woman would make a part in the affairs of national government unsuitable, are by no means those who think it impossible for the negresses to endure field work, even during pregnancy, or the sempstresses to go through their killing labors.

As to the use of the pen, there was quite as much opposition to woman's possessing herself of that help to free agency, as there is now to her seizing on the rostrum or the desk; and she is likely to draw, from a permission to plead her cause that way, opposite inferences to what might be wished by those who now grant it.

As to the possibility of her filling with grace and dignity, any such position, we should think those who had seen the great actresses, and heard the Quaker preachers of modern times, would not doubt, that woman can express publicly the fulness of thought and creation, without losing any of the peculiar beauty of her sex. What can pollute and tarnish is to act thus from any motive except that something needs to be said or done. Women could take part in the processions, the songs, the dances of old religion; no one fancied their delicacy was impaired by appearing in public for such a cause.

As to her home, she is not likely to leave it more than she now does for balls, theatres, meetings for promoting missions, revival meetings, and others to which she flies, in hope of an animation for her existence, commensurate with what she sees enjoyed by men. Governors of ladies' fairs are no less engrossed by such a change, than the Governor of the state by his; presidents of Washingtonian societies no less away from home than presidents of conventions. If men look straitly to it, they will find that, unless their lives are domestic, those of the women will not be. A house is no home unless it contain food and fire for the mind as well as for the body. The female Greek, of our day, is as much in the street as the male to cry, What news? We doubt not it was the same in Athens of old. The women, shut out from the market place, made up for it at the religious festivals. For human beings are not so constituted that they can live without expansion. If they do not get it one way, they must another, or perish.

30

As to men's representing women fairly at present, while we hear from men who owe to their wives not only all that is comfortable or graceful, but all that is wise in the arrangement of their lives, the frequent remark, "You cannot reason with a woman," when from those of delicacy, nobleness, and poetic culture, the contemptuous phrase "women and children," and that in no light sally of the hour, but in works intended to give a permanent statement of the best experiences, when not one man, in the million, shall I say? no, not in the hundred million, can rise above the belief that woman was made *for man*, when such traits as these are daily forced upon the attention, can we feel that man will always do justice to the interests of woman? Can we think that he takes a sufficiently discerning and religious view of her office and destiny, *ever* to do her justice, except when prompted by sentiment, accidentally or transiently, that is, for the sentiment will vary according to the relations in which he is placed. The lover, the poet, the artist, are likely to view her nobly. The father and the philosopher have some chance of liberality; the man of the world, the legislator for expediency, none.

Under these circumstances, without attaching importance, in themselves, to the changes demanded by the champions of woman, we hail them as signs of the times. We would have every arbitrary barrier thrown down. We would have every path laid open to woman as freely as to man. Were this done and a slight temporary fermentation allowed to subside, we should see crystallizations more pure and of more various beauty. We believe the divine energy would pervade nature to a degree unknown in the history of former ages, and that no discordant collision, but a ravishing harmony of the spheres would ensue.

Yet, then and only then, will mankind be ripe for this, when inward and outward freedom for woman as much as for man shall be acknowledged as a right, not yielded as a concession. As the friend of the negro assumes that one man cannot by right, hold another in bondage, so should the friend of woman assume that man cannot, by right, lay even well-meant restrictions on women. If the negro be a soul, if the woman be a soul, appareled in flesh, to one Master only are they accountable. There is but one law for souls, and if there is to be an interpreter of it, he must come not as man, or son of man, but as son of God.

(1845)

Exploring the Text

1. Identify two contrasts or juxtapositions in the first four paragraphs. How do they contribute to Margaret Fuller's position?
2. How does the transition from paragraph 4 to paragraph 5 prepare the reader for the main idea of the piece?
3. What is the rhetorical purpose and effect of the dialogue in paragraphs 7–14?
4. What is the distinction that Fuller makes between men and women in paragraph 15? Does that distinction still exist today? Explain why or why not.
5. What are the "symptoms" (par. 19) that Fuller discusses?

6. What rhetorical strategies does Fuller use in paragraph 23? How do they contribute to her argument?

7. Paraphrase the prediction that Fuller makes at the end of paragraph 23. Was she accurate? Explain.

8. Fuller writes, "I said, we will not speak of this now, yet I have spoken, for the subject makes me feel too much" (par. 24). What is her purpose? What appeals does she make with that statement?

9. How would you paraphrase Fuller's intended answer to the lengthy rhetorical question that she poses in paragraph 25?

10. What rhetorical appeals does Fuller make in the final paragraphs of this selection? How do they serve to address some of the obstacles to women's rights in the nineteenth century?

Frederick Douglass

Frederick Douglass (1818–1895) was an African American orator, social reformer, and writer. Born into slavery near Hillsboro, Maryland, he taught himself to read and write in his teenage years and secretly spread his knowledge to fellow slaves. After he escaped from slavery in 1838, he became an instrumental figure of the abolitionist movement. Famous for his eloquent speeches and dazzling rhetoric, he was considered to be the leading black intellectual of his day. Douglass wrote several autobiographies about his experiences, including *Narrative of the Life of Frederick Douglass, an American Slave, Written by Himself* (1845) and *Life and Times of Frederick Douglass* (1881). In his speech "Men of Color, to Arms," which he delivered in Rochester, New York, in 1863, he urged free African Americans to enlist in the Union army during the Civil War.

from *Narrative of the Life of Frederick Douglass, an American Slave, Written by Himself*

Published in 1845, this memoir is the most well-known and highly regarded of the slave narratives. It established its author as a prominent figure in American letters and in the abolitionist movement.

Chapter I

I was born in Tuckahoe, near Hillsborough, and about twelve miles from Easton, in Talbot county, Maryland. I have no accurate knowledge of my age, never having seen any authentic record containing it. By far the larger part of the slaves know as little of their age as horses know of theirs, and it is the wish of most masters within my knowledge to keep their slaves thus ignorant. I do not remember to have ever met a slave who could tell of his birthday. They seldom come nearer to it than planting-time, harvest-time, cherry-time, spring-time, or fall-time. A want of information concerning my own was a source of unhappiness to me even during childhood. The white children could tell their ages. I could not tell why I ought to be deprived of the same privilege. I was not allowed to make any inquiries of my master concerning it. He deemed all such inquiries on the part of a slave improper and impertinent, and evidence of a restless spirit. The nearest estimate I can give makes me now between twenty-seven and twenty-eight years of age. I come to this, from hearing my master say, some time during 1835, I was about seventeen years old.

My mother was named Harriet Bailey. She was the daughter of Isaac and Betsey Bailey, both colored, and quite dark. My mother was of a darker complexion than either my grandmother or grandfather.

My father was a white man. He was admitted to be such by all I ever heard speak of my parentage. The opinion was also whispered that my master was my father; but of the correctness of this opinion, I know nothing; the means of knowing was withheld from me. My mother and I were separated when I was but an infant — before I knew her as my mother. It is a common custom, in the part of Maryland from which I ran away, to part children from their mothers at a very early age. Frequently, before the child has reached its twelfth month, its mother is taken from it, and hired out on some farm a considerable distance off, and the child is placed under the care of an old woman, too old for field labor. For what this separation is done, I do not know, unless it be to hinder the development of the child's affection toward its mother, and to blunt and destroy the natural affection of the mother for the child. This is the inevitable result.

I never saw my mother, to know her as such, more than four or five times in my life; and each of these times was very short in duration, and at night. She was hired by a Mr. Stewart, who lived about twelve miles from my home. She made her journeys to see me in the night, travelling the whole distance on foot, after the performance of her day's work. She was a field hand, and a whipping is the penalty of not being in the field at sunrise, unless a slave has special permission from his or her master to the contrary — a permission which they seldom get, and one that gives to him that gives it the proud name of being a kind master. I do not recollect of ever seeing my mother by the light of day. She was with me in the night. She would lie down with me, and get me to sleep, but long before I waked she was gone. Very little communication ever took place between us. Death soon ended what little we could have while she lived, and with it her hardships and suffering. She died when I was about seven years old, on one of my master's farms, near Lee's Mill. I was not allowed to be present during her illness, at her death, or burial. She was gone long before I knew any thing about it. Never having enjoyed, to any considerable extent, her soothing presence, her tender and watchful care, I received the tidings of her death with much the same emotions I should have probably felt at the death of a stranger.

Called thus suddenly away, she left me without the slightest intimation of who my father was. The whisper that my master was my father, may or may not be true; 5

and, true or false, it is of but little consequence to my purpose whilst the fact remains, in all its glaring odiousness, that slaveholders have ordained, and by law established, that the children of slave women shall in all cases follow the condition of their mothers; and this is done too obviously to administer to their own lusts, and make a gratification of their wicked desires profitable as well as pleasurable; for by this cunning arrangement, the slaveholder, in cases not a few, sustains to his slaves the double relation of master and father.

I know of such cases; and it is worthy of remark that such slaves invariably suffer greater hardships, and have more to contend with, than others. They are, in the first place, a constant offence to their mistress. She is ever disposed to find fault with them; they can seldom do any thing to please her; she is never better pleased than when she sees them under the lash, especially when she suspects her husband of showing to his mulatto children favors which he withholds from his black slaves. The master is frequently compelled to sell this class of his slaves, out of deference to the feelings of his white wife; and, cruel as the deed may strike any one to be, for a man to sell his own children to human flesh-mongers, it is often the dictate of humanity for him to do so; for, unless he does this, he must not only whip them himself, but must stand by and see one white son tie up his brother, of but few shades darker complexion than himself, and ply the gory lash to his naked back; and if he lisp one word of disapproval, it is set down to his parental partiality, and only makes a bad matter worse, both for himself and the slave whom he would protect and defend.

Every year brings with it multitudes of this class of slaves. It was doubtless in consequence of a knowledge of this fact, that one great statesman of the south predicted the downfall of slavery by the inevitable laws of population. Whether this prophecy is ever fulfilled or not, it is nevertheless plain that a very different-looking class of people are springing up at the south, and are now held in slavery, from those originally brought to this country from Africa; and if their increase will do no other good, it will do away the force of the argument, that God cursed Ham, and therefore American slavery is right. If the lineal descendants of Ham are alone to be scripturally enslaved, it is certain that slavery at the south must soon become unscriptural; for thousands are ushered into the world, annually, who, like myself, owe their existence to white fathers, and those fathers most frequently their own masters.

I have had two masters. My first master's name was Anthony. I do not remember his first name. He was generally called Captain Anthony — a title which, I presume, he acquired by sailing a craft on the Chesapeake Bay. He was not considered a rich slaveholder. He owned two or three farms, and about thirty slaves. His farms and slaves were under the care of an overseer. The overseer's name was Plummer. Mr. Plummer was a miserable drunkard, a profane swearer, and a savage monster. He always went armed with a cowskin and a heavy cudgel. I have known him to cut and slash the women's heads so horribly, that even master would be enraged at his cruelty, and would threaten to whip him if he did not mind himself. Master, however, was not a humane slaveholder. It required extraordinary barbarity on the part of an overseer to affect him. He was a cruel man, hardened by a long life of slaveholding. He would at times seem to take great pleasure in whipping a slave. I have often been awakened at the dawn of day by the most heart-rending shrieks of an own aunt of mine, whom he used to tie up to a joist, and whip upon her naked back till she was literally covered with blood. No words, no tears, no prayers, from his gory victim, seemed to move his iron heart from its bloody purpose. The louder she screamed, the harder he whipped; and where the blood ran fastest, there he whipped longest. He would whip her to make her scream, and whip her to make her hush; and not until overcome by fatigue, would he cease to swing the blood-clotted cowskin. I remember the first time I ever witnessed this horrible exhibition. I was quite a child, but I well remember it. I never shall forget it whilst I remember any thing. It was the first of a long series of such outrages, of which I was doomed to be a witness and a participant. It struck me with awful force. It was the blood-stained gate, the entrance to the hell of slavery, through which I was about to pass. It was a most terrible spectacle. I wish I could commit to paper the feelings with which I beheld it.

This occurrence took place very soon after I went to live with my old master, and under the following circumstances. Aunt Hester went out one night, — where or for what I do not know, — and happened to be absent when my master desired her presence. He had ordered her not to go out evenings, and warned her that she must never let him catch her in company with a young man, who was paying attention to her belonging to Colonel Lloyd. The young man's name was Ned Roberts, generally called Lloyd's Ned. Why master was so careful of her, may be safely left to conjecture. She was a woman of noble form, and of graceful proportions, having very few equals, and fewer superiors, in personal appearance, among the colored or white women of our neighborhood.

Aunt Hester had not only disobeyed his orders in going out, but had been found   10
in company with Lloyd's Ned; which circumstance, I found, from what he said while whipping her, was the chief offence. Had he been a man of pure morals himself, he might have been thought interested in protecting the innocence of my aunt; but those who knew him will not suspect him of any such virtue. Before he commenced whipping Aunt Hester, he took her into the kitchen, and stripped her from neck to waist, leaving her neck, shoulders, and back, entirely naked. He then told her to cross her hands, calling her at the same time a d —— d b —— h. After crossing her hands, he tied them with a strong rope, and led her to a stool under a large hook in the joist, put in for the purpose. He made her get upon the stool, and tied her hands to the hook. She now stood fair for his infernal purpose. Her arms were stretched up at their full length, so that she stood upon the ends of her toes. He then said to her, "Now, you d —— d b —— h, I'll learn you how to disobey my orders!" and after rolling up his sleeves, he commenced to lay on the heavy cowskin, and soon the warm, red blood (amid heart-rending shrieks from her, and horrid oaths from him) came dripping to the floor. I was so terrified and horror-stricken at the sight, that I hid myself in a closet, and dared not venture out till long after the bloody transaction was over. I expected it would be my turn next. It was all new to me. I had never seen any thing like it before. I had always lived with my grandmother on the outskirts of the plantation, where she was put to raise the children of the younger women. I had therefore been, until now, out of the way of the bloody scenes that often occurred on the plantation.

Chapter II

My master's family consisted of two sons, Andrew and Richard; one daughter, Lucretia, and her husband, Captain Thomas Auld. They lived in one house, upon the home plantation of Colonel Edward Lloyd. My master was Colonel Lloyd's clerk and superintendent. He was what might be called the overseer of the overseers. I spent two years of childhood on this plantation in my old master's family. It was here that I witnessed the bloody transaction recorded in the first chapter; and as I received my first impressions of slavery on this plantation, I will give some description of it, and of slavery as it there existed. The plantation is about twelve miles north of Easton, in Talbot county, and is situated on the border of Miles River. The principal products raised upon it were tobacco, corn, and wheat. These were raised in great abundance; so that, with the products of this and the other farms belonging to him, he was able to keep in almost constant employment a large sloop, in carrying them to market at Baltimore. This sloop was named Sally Lloyd, in honor of one of the colonel's daughters. My master's son-in-law, Captain Auld, was master of the vessel; she was otherwise manned by the colonel's own slaves. Their names were Peter, Isaac, Rich, and Jake. These were esteemed very highly by the other slaves, and looked upon as the privileged ones of the plantation; for it was no small affair, in the eyes of the slaves, to be allowed to see Baltimore.

Colonel Lloyd kept from three to four hundred slaves on his home plantation, and owned a large number more on the neighboring farms belonging to him. The names of the farms nearest to the home plantation were Wye Town and New Design. "Wye Town" was under the overseership of a man named Noah Willis. New Design was under the overseership of a Mr. Townsend. The overseers of these, and all the rest of the farms, numbering over twenty, received advice and direction from the managers of the home plantation. This was the great business place. It was the seat of government for the whole twenty farms. All disputes among the overseers were settled here. If a slave was convicted of any high misdemeanor, became unmanageable, or evinced a determination to run away, he was brought immediately here, severely whipped, put on board the sloop, carried to Baltimore, and sold to Austin Woolfolk, or some other slave-trader, as a warning to the slaves remaining.

Here, too, the slaves of all the other farms received their monthly allowance of food, and their yearly clothing. The men and women slaves received, as their monthly allowance of food, eight pounds of pork, or its equivalent in fish, and one bushel of corn meal. Their yearly clothing consisted of two coarse linen shirts, one pair of linen trousers, like the shirts, one jacket, one pair of trousers for winter, made of coarse negro cloth, one pair of stockings, and one pair of shoes; the whole of which could not have cost more than seven dollars. The allowance of the slave children was given to their mothers, or the old women having the care of them. The children unable to work in the field had neither shoes, stockings, jackets, nor trousers, given to them; their clothing consisted of two coarse linen shirts per year. When these failed them, they went naked until the next allowance-day. Children from seven to ten years old, of both sexes, almost naked, might be seen at all seasons of the year.

There were no beds given the slaves, unless one coarse blanket be considered such, and none but the men and women had these. This, however, is not considered a very great privation. They find less difficulty from the want of beds, than from the want of time to sleep; for when their day's work in the field is done, the most of them having their washing, mending, and cooking to do, and having few or none of the ordinary facilities for doing either of these, very many of their sleeping hours are consumed in preparing for the field the coming day; and when this is done, old and young, male and female, married and single, drop down side by side, on one common bed, — the cold, damp floor, — each covering himself or herself with their miserable blankets; and here they sleep till they are summoned to the field by the driver's horn. At the sound of this, all must rise, and be off to the field. There must be no halting; every one must be at his or her post; and woe betides them who hear not this morning summons to the field; for if they are not awakened by the sense of hearing, they are by the sense of feeling: no age nor sex finds any favor. Mr. Severe, the overseer, used to stand by the door of the quarter, armed with a large hickory stick and heavy cowskin, ready to whip any one who was so unfortunate as not to hear, or, from any other cause, was prevented from being ready to start for the field at the sound of the horn.

Mr. Severe was rightly named: he was a cruel man. I have seen him whip a   15 woman, causing the blood to run half an hour at the time; and this, too, in the midst of her crying children, pleading for their mother's release. He seemed to take pleasure in manifesting his fiendish barbarity. Added to his cruelty, he was a profane swearer. It was enough to chill the blood and stiffen the hair of an ordinary man to hear him talk. Scarce a sentence escaped him but that was commenced or concluded by some horrid oath. The field was the place to witness his cruelty and profanity. His presence made it both the field of blood and of blasphemy. From the rising till the going down of the sun, he was cursing, raving, cutting, and slashing among the slaves of the field, in the most frightful manner. His career was short. He died very soon after I went to Colonel Lloyd's; and he died as he lived, uttering, with his dying groans, bitter curses and horrid oaths. His death was regarded by the slaves as the result of a merciful providence.

Mr. Severe's place was filled by a Mr. Hopkins. He was a very different man. He was less cruel, less profane, and made less noise, than Mr. Severe. His course was characterized by no extraordinary demonstrations of cruelty. He whipped, but seemed to take no pleasure in it. He was called by the slaves a good overseer.

The home plantation of Colonel Lloyd wore the appearance of a country village. All the mechanical operations for all the farms were performed here. The shoemaking and mending, the blacksmithing, cartwrighting, coopering, weaving, and grain-grinding, were all performed by the slaves on the home plantation. The whole place wore a business-like aspect very unlike the neighboring farms. The number of houses, too, conspired to give it advantage over the neighboring farms. It was called by the slaves the *Great House Farm*. Few privileges were esteemed higher, by the slaves of the out-farms, than that of being selected to do errands at the Great House Farm. It was associated in their minds with greatness. A representative could not be prouder of his election to a seat in the American Congress, than a slave on one of the out-farms would be of his election to do errands at the Great House Farm. They regarded it as evidence of great confidence reposed in them by their overseers; and it was on this account, as well as a constant desire to be out of the field from under the driver's lash, that they esteemed it a high privilege, one worth careful living for. He was called the smartest and most trusty fellow, who had this honor conferred upon him the most frequently. The competitors for this office sought as diligently to please their overseers, as the office-seekers in the political parties seek to please and deceive the people. The same traits of character might be seen in Colonel Lloyd's slaves, as are seen in the slaves of the political parties.

The slaves selected to go to the Great House Farm, for the monthly allowance for themselves and their fellow-slaves, were peculiarly enthusiastic. While on their way, they would make the dense old woods, for miles around, reverberate with their wild songs, revealing at once the highest joy and the deepest sadness. They would compose and sing as they went along, consulting neither time nor tune. The thought that came up, came out;—if not in the word, in the sound;—and as frequently in the one as in the other. They would sometimes sing the most pathetic sentiment in the most rapturous tone, and the most rapturous sentiment in the most pathetic tone. Into all of their songs they would manage to weave something of the Great House Farm. Especially would they do this, when leaving home. They would then sing most exult-ingly the following words: —

I am going away to the Great House Farm!
O, yea! O, yea! O!

This they would sing, as a chorus, to words which to many would seem unmeaning jargon, but which, nevertheless, were full of meaning to themselves. I have some-times thought that the mere hearing of those songs would do more to impress some minds with the horrible character of slavery, than the reading of whole volumes of philosophy on the subject could do.

I did not, when a slave, understand the deep meaning of those rude and apparently incoherent songs. I was myself within the circle; so that I neither saw nor heard as those without might see and hear. They told a tale of woe which was then altogether beyond my feeble comprehension; they were tones loud, long, and deep; they breathed the prayer and complaint of souls boiling over with the bitterest anguish. Every tone was a testimony against slavery, and a prayer to God for deliverance from chains. The hearing of those wild notes always depressed my spirit, and filled me with ineffable sadness. I have frequently found myself in tears while hearing them. The mere recurrence to those songs, even now, afflicts me; and while I am writing these lines, an expression of feeling has already found its way down my cheek. To those songs I trace my first glimmering conception of the dehumanizing character of slavery. I can never get rid of that concep-tion. Those songs still follow me, to deepen my hatred of slavery, and quicken my sympathies for my brethren in bonds. If any one wishes to be impressed with the soul-killing effects of slavery, let him go to Colonel Lloyd's plantation, and, on allowance-day, place himself in the deep pine woods, and there let him, in silence, analyze the sounds that shall pass through the chambers of his soul,—and if he is not thus impressed, it will only be because "there is no flesh in his obdurate heart."[1]

I have often been utterly astonished, since I came to the north, to find persons who could speak of the singing, among slaves, as evidence of their contentment and happiness. It is impossible to conceive of a greater mistake. Slaves sing most when they are most unhappy. The songs of the slave represent the sorrows of his heart; and he is relieved by them, only as an aching heart is relieved by its tears. At least, such is my experience. I have often sung to drown my sorrow, but seldom to express my happiness. Crying for joy, and singing for joy, were alike uncommon to me while in the jaws of slavery. The singing of a man cast away upon a desolate island might be as appropriately considered as evidence of contentment and happiness, as the singing of a slave; the songs of the one and of the other are prompted by the same emotion.

Chapter III

. . . To describe the wealth of Colonel Lloyd would be almost equal to describing the riches of Job. He kept from ten to fifteen house-servants. He was said to own a thousand slaves, and I think this estimate quite within the truth. Colonel Lloyd owned so many that he did not know them when he saw them; nor did all the slaves of the out-farms know him. It is reported of him, that, while riding along the road one day, he met a colored man, and addressed him in the usual manner of speaking to colored people on the public highways of the south: "Well, boy, whom do you belong to?" "To Colonel Lloyd," replied the slave. "Well, does the colonel treat you well?" "No, sir," was the ready reply. "What, does he work you too hard?" "Yes, sir." "Well, don't he give you enough to eat?" "Yes, sir, he gives me enough, such as it is."

The colonel, after ascertaining where the slave belonged, rode on; the man also went on about his business, not dreaming that he had been conversing with his master. He thought, said, and heard nothing more of the matter, until two or three weeks afterwards. The poor man was then informed by his overseer that, for having found fault with his master, he was now to be sold to a Georgia trader. He was immediately chained and handcuffed; and thus, without a moment's warning, he was snatched away, and forever sundered, from his family and friends, by a hand more unrelenting than death. This is the penalty of telling the truth, of telling the simple truth, in answer to a series of plain questions.

It is partly in consequence of such facts, that slaves, when inquired of as to their condition and the character of their masters, almost universally say they are contented, and that their masters are kind. The slaveholders have been known to send in spies among their slaves, to ascertain their views and feelings in regard to their condition. The frequency of this has had the effect to establish among the slaves the maxim, that a still tongue makes a wise head. They suppress the truth rather than take the consequences of telling it, and in so doing prove themselves a part of the

---

[1]Book 2, line 8, of *The Task* (1785), by English poet William Cowper (1731–1800). — Eds.

human family. If they have any thing to say of their masters, it is generally in their masters' favor, especially when speaking to an untried man. I have been frequently asked, when a slave, if I had a kind master, and do not remember ever to have given a negative answer; nor did I, in pursuing this course, consider myself as uttering what was absolutely false; for I always measured the kindness of my master by the standard of kindness set up among slaveholders around us. Moreover, slaves are like other people, and imbibe prejudices quite common to others. They think their own better than that of others. Many, under the influence of this prejudice, think their own masters are better than the masters of other slaves; and this, too, in some cases, when the very reverse is true. Indeed, it is not uncommon for slaves even to fall out and quarrel among themselves about the relative goodness of their masters, each contending for the superior goodness of his own over that of the others. At the very same time, they mutually execrate their masters when viewed separately. It was so on our plantation. When Colonel Lloyd's slaves met the slaves of Jacob Jepson, they seldom parted without a quarrel about their masters; Colonel Lloyd's slaves contending that he was the richest, and Mr. Jepson's slaves that he was the smartest, and most of a man. Colonel Lloyd's slaves would boast his ability to buy and sell Jacob Jepson. Mr. Jepson's slaves would boast his ability to whip Colonel Lloyd. These quarrels would almost always end in a fight between the parties, and those that whipped were supposed to have gained the point at issue. They seemed to think that the greatness of their masters was transferable to themselves. It was considered as being bad enough to be a slave; but to be a poor man's slave was deemed a disgrace indeed!

Chapter IV

Mr. Hopkins remained but a short time in the office of overseer. Why his career was so short, I do not know, but suppose he lacked the necessary severity to suit Colonel Lloyd. Mr. Hopkins was succeeded by Mr. Austin Gore, a man possessing, in an eminent degree, all those traits of character indispensable to what is called a first-rate overseer. Mr. Gore had served Colonel Lloyd, in the capacity of overseer, upon one of the out-farms, and had shown himself worthy of the high station of overseer upon the home or Great House Farm.

Mr. Gore was proud, ambitious, and persevering. He was artful, cruel, and obdu- 25
rate. He was just the man for such a place, and it was just the place for such a man. It afforded scope for the full exercise of all his powers, and he seemed to be perfectly at home in it. He was one of those who could torture the slightest look, word, or gesture, on the part of the slave, into impudence, and would treat it accordingly. There must be no answering back to him; no explanation was allowed a slave, showing himself to have been wrongfully accused. Mr. Gore acted fully up to the maxim laid down by slaveholders, — "It is better that a dozen slaves suffer under the lash, than that the overseer should be convicted, in the presence of the slaves, of having been at fault." No matter how innocent a slave might be — it availed him nothing, when accused by Mr. Gore of any misdemeanor. To be accused was to be convicted, and to be convicted was to be punished; the one always following the other with immutable cer-

tainty. To escape punishment was to escape accusation; and few slaves had the fortune to do either, under the overseership of Mr. Gore. He was just proud enough to demand the most debasing homage of the slave, and quite servile enough to crouch, himself, at the feet of the master. He was ambitious enough to be contented with nothing short of the highest rank of overseers, and persevering enough to reach the height of his ambition. He was cruel enough to inflict the severest punishment, artful enough to descend to the lowest trickery, and obdurate enough to be insensible to the voice of a reproving conscience. He was, of all the overseers, the most dreaded by the slaves. His presence was painful; his eye flashed confusion; and seldom was his sharp, shrill voice heard, without producing horror and trembling in their ranks.

Mr. Gore was a grave man, and, though a young man, he indulged in no jokes, said no funny words, seldom smiled. His words were in perfect keeping with his looks, and his looks were in perfect keeping with his words. Overseers will sometimes indulge in a witty word, even with the slaves; not so with Mr. Gore. He spoke but to command, and commanded but to be obeyed; he dealt sparingly with his words, and bountifully with his whip, never using the former where the latter would answer as well. When he whipped, he seemed to do so from a sense of duty, and feared no consequences. He did nothing reluctantly, no matter how disagreeable; always at his post, never inconsistent. He never promised but to fulfill. He was, in a word, a man of the most inflexible firmness and stone-like coolness.

His savage barbarity was equalled only by the consummate coolness with which he committed the grossest and most savage deeds upon the slaves under his charge. Mr. Gore once undertook to whip one of Colonel Lloyd's slaves, by the name of Demby. He had given Demby but few stripes, when, to get rid of the scourging, he ran and plunged himself into a creek, and stood there at the depth of his shoulders, refusing to come out. Mr. Gore told him that he would give him three calls, and that, if he did not come out at the third call, he would shoot him. The first call was given. Demby made no response, but stood his ground. The second and third calls were given with the same result. Mr. Gore then, without consultation or deliberation with any one, not even giving Demby an additional call, raised his musket to his face, taking deadly aim at his standing victim, and in an instant poor Demby was no more. His mangled body sank out of sight, and blood and brains marked the water where he had stood.

A thrill of horror flashed through every soul upon the plantation, excepting Mr. Gore. He alone seemed cool and collected. He was asked by Colonel Lloyd and my old master, why he resorted to this extraordinary expedient. His reply was, (as well as I can remember,) that Demby had become unmanageable. He was setting a dangerous example to the other slaves, — one which, if suffered to pass without some such demonstration on his part, would finally lead to the total subversion of all rule and order upon the plantation. He argued that if one slave refused to be corrected, and escaped with his life, the other slaves would soon copy the example; the result of which would be, the freedom of the slaves, and the enslavement of the whites. Mr. Gore's defence was satisfactory. He was continued in his station as overseer upon the home plantation. His fame as an overseer went abroad. His horrid crime was not even submitted to judicial investigation. It was committed in the presence of slaves, and they of course could neither institute a suit, nor testify against him; and thus the guilty perpetrator of one of the bloodiest and most foul murders goes unwhipped of justice, and uncensured by the community in which he lives. Mr. Gore lived in St. Michael's, Talbot county, Maryland, when I left there; and if he is still alive, he very probably lives there now; and if so, he is now, as he was then, as highly esteemed and as much respected as though his guilty soul had not been stained with his brother's blood.

I speak advisedly when I say this, — that killing a slave, or any colored person, in Talbot county, Maryland, is not treated as a crime, either by the courts or the community. Mr. Thomas Lanman, of St. Michael's, killed two slaves, one of whom he killed with a hatchet, by knocking his brains out. He used to boast of the commission of the awful and bloody deed. I have heard him do so laughingly, saying, among other things, that he was the only benefactor of his country in the company, and that when others would do as much as he had done, we should be relieved of "the d——d niggers."

The wife of Mr. Giles Hick, living but a short distance from where I used to live, murdered my wife's cousin, a young girl between fifteen and sixteen years of age, mangling her person in the most horrible manner, breaking her nose and breastbone with a stick, so that the poor girl expired in a few hours afterward. She was immediately buried, but had not been in her untimely grave but a few hours before she was taken up and examined by the coroner, who decided that she had come to her death by severe beating. The offence for which this girl was thus murdered was this: — She had been set that night to mind Mrs. Hick's baby and during the night she fell asleep, and the baby cried. She, having lost her rest for several nights previous, did not hear the crying. They were both in the room with Mrs. Hicks. Mrs. Hicks, finding the girl slow to move, jumped from her bed, seized an oak stick of wood by the fireplace, and with it broke the girl's nose and breastbone, and thus ended her life. I will not say that this most horrid murder produced no sensation in the community. It did produce sensation, but not enough to bring the murderess to punishment. There was a warrant issued for her arrest, but it was never served. Thus she escaped not only punishment, but even the pain of being arraigned before a court for her horrid crime.

Whilst I am detailing bloody deeds which took place during my stay on Colonel Lloyd's plantation, I will briefly narrate another, which occurred about the same time as the murder of Demby by Mr. Gore.

Colonel Lloyd's slaves were in the habit of spending a part of their nights and Sundays in fishing for oysters, and in this way made up the deficiency of their scanty allowance. An old man belonging to Colonel Lloyd, while thus engaged, happened to get beyond the limits of Colonel Lloyd's, and on the premises of Mr. Beal Bondly. At this trespass, Mr. Bondly took offence, and with his musket came down to the shore, and blew its deadly contents into the poor old man.

Mr. Bondly came over to see Colonel Lloyd the next day, whether to pay him for his property, or to justify himself in what he had done, I know not. At any rate, this whole fiendish transaction was soon hushed up. There was very little said about it at all, and nothing done. It was a common saying, even among little white boys, that it was worth a half-cent to kill a "nigger," and a half-cent to bury one.

(1845)

Exploring the Text

1. "My father was a white man," abruptly states Frederick Douglass (par. 3). Were you startled or surprised by that statement? Explain.
2. What appeals to ethos, logos, and pathos does Douglass make in the first few paragraphs? Which one is most prominent?
3. Of the whipping he observed, Douglass writes, "It was a most terrible spectacle. I wish I could commit to paper the feelings with which I beheld it" (par. 8). Read the paragraph carefully. How successfully do you think Douglass *has* committed his feelings to paper? Explain.
4. Chapter 2 begins with a description of Colonel Lloyd's plantation. What is your impression of the conditions there?
5. Douglass writes of Mr. Hopkins: "He whipped, but seemed to take no pleasure in it. He was called by the slaves a good overseer" (par. 16). How would you describe Douglass's tone in that statement? What does it suggest about the relationship between slaves and their masters?
6. Douglass writes, "I was myself within the circle; so that I neither saw nor heard as those without might see and hear" (par. 19). Ralph Waldo Emerson (p. 590), in his 1841 essay "Circles," states, "The field cannot be well seen from within the field." Douglass seems to be elaborating on Emerson's metaphor. What is the nature of the appeal that Douglass makes with this reference? How does the remark aid the reader's understanding of Douglass's situation?
7. In Chapter 3, what is the chief irony that Douglass develops regarding slaves?
8. How does Douglass use rhetorical strategies to characterize Mr. Gore in the second and third paragraphs of Chapter 4? (Consider such features of style and rhetoric as juxtaposition, antithesis, antimetabole, contrasts, irony, and parallelism.)
9. Douglass states, "Mr. Gore's defence was satisfactory" (par. 28). What is the effect of that understatement?
10. From your reading of the first four chapters, what is your overall impression of Douglass's life as a slave? Be specific.

SOJOURNER TRUTH

Sojourner Truth (c. 1797–1883), born Isabella Baumfree, was an African American abolitionist and women's rights advocate. Born into slavery in New York, she escaped with her infant daughter in 1826. The next year, she went to court and succeeded in winning the freedom of her son, who had been sold into slavery in Alabama, since New York law had emancipated its slaves in 1827. In 1843, she officially changed her name to Sojourner Truth, and in 1844, she joined the Northampton Association of Education and Industry, a Massachusetts-based organization that was funded by abolitionists and supported women's rights and religious tolerance. In 1850, abolitionist William Lloyd Garrison privately published her autobiography,

The Narrative of Sojourner Truth: A Northern Slave, and she bought her first home in Northampton, Massachusetts. She became a well-known speaker, appearing at women's rights conventions all over the country.

Ain't I a Woman?

Sojouner Truth delivered the following speech, "Ain't I a Woman?," in 1851 at the Ohio Women's Rights Convention.

Well, children, where there is so much racket there must be something out of kilter. I think that 'twixt the negroes of the South and the women of the North, all talking about rights, the white men will be in a fix pretty soon. But what's all this here talking about?

That man over there says that women need to be helped into carriages, and lifted over ditches, and to have the best place everywhere. Nobody ever helps me into carriages, or over mud-puddles, or gives me any best place! And ain't I a woman? Look at me! Look at my arm! I have ploughed and planted, and gathered into barns, and no man could head me! And ain't I a woman? I could work as much and eat as much as a man — when I could get it — and bear the lash as well! And ain't I a woman? I have borne thirteen children, and seen them most all sold off to slavery, and when I cried out with my mother's grief, none but Jesus heard me! And ain't I a woman?

Then they talk about this thing in the head; what's this they call it? [Intellect, someone whispers.] That's it, honey. What's that got to do with women's rights or negro's rights? If my cup won't hold but a pint, and yours holds a quart, wouldn't you be man not to let me have my little half-measure full?

Then that little man in black there, he says women can't have as much rights as men, 'cause Christ wasn't a woman! Where did your Christ come from? Where did your Christ come from? From God and a woman! Man had nothing to do with Him.

If the first woman God ever made was strong enough to turn the world upside down all alone, these women together ought to be able to turn it back, and get it right side up again! And now they is asking to do it, the men better let them.

Obliged to you for hearing me, and now old Sojourner ain't got nothing more to say.

(1851)

Exploring the Text

1. How does Sojourner Truth's opening paragraph set the tone for her speech? Is referring to her audience as "children" likely to antagonize them?
2. What is the effect of her repeated question, "And ain't I a woman?" How does this question appeal to ethos?

3. What is her appeal in paragraphs 2–5? What would be the effect of omitting any one of her examples? Could their order be changed?
4. What is the ratio of questions to declarative sentences in this speech? What conclusions can you draw from that information? Rewrite Truth's speech, turning all the questions into statements. Read it aloud. What effect does this change make?
5. Go through the speech and mark the appeals to ethos, logos, and pathos. Discuss one example in which all three coincide.
6. How does Truth use religion in her speech? Does she risk being accused of blasphemy?
7. How would you characterize Truth's presentation of herself in the final sentence?

HARRIET BEECHER STOWE

Harriet Elizabeth Beecher was born on June 14, 1811, in Litchfield, Connecticut, one of thirteen children born to religious leader Lyman Beecher and his wife, Roxanna Foote Beecher. Harriet's seven brothers grew up to be ministers, and included among them was the famous leader and abolitionist Henry Ward Beecher. Her sister Catharine was an author and a teacher, and her sister Isabella became a leader in the cause of women's rights. At twenty-one, Harriet moved to Cincinnati, Ohio, where she met seminary teacher Calvin Ellis Stowe. They were married on January 6, 1836, and eventually moved to a cottage in Brunswick, Maine, close to Bowdoin College. In 1851, the first installment of her novel *Uncle Tom's Cabin* appeared in the *National Era*. With the book's publication the next year, Stowe achieved national fame. The book has become one of the most influential novels in American literature. Stowe died in Hartford, Connecticut, on July 6, 1896.

from *Uncle Tom's Cabin*
or Life among the Lowly

The selection here is Chapter 12 from Harriet Beecher Stowe's novel *Uncle Tom's Cabin*, a book poet Langston Hughes called a "moral battle cry for freedom." It was the most popular book in its time and certainly one of the most influential and controversial. In their 1973 work, *American Literature: The Makers and the Making*, renowned scholars and writers Cleanth Brooks, R. W. B. Lewis, and Robert Penn Warren write, "The political effects of *Uncle Tom's Cabin* were momentous: it provided for the imagination concrete and passionately conceived scenes in which the vague general dislike for slavery could realize itself. . . . It may be true that President Lincoln, on meeting Mrs. Stowe, said: 'So this is the little lady who made this big war.'"

Chapter XII: Select Incident of Lawful Trade

In Ramah there was a voice heard, — weeping, and lamentation, and great mourning; Rachel weeping for her children, and would not be comforted.[1]

Mr. Haley and Tom jogged onward in their wagon, each, for a time, absorbed in his own reflections. Now, the reflections of two men sitting side by side are a curious thing, — seated on the same seat, having the same eyes, ears, hands and organs of all sorts, and having pass before their eyes the same objects, — it is wonderful what a variety we shall find in these same reflections!

As, for example, Mr. Haley: he thought first of Tom's length, and breadth, and height, and what he would sell for, if he was kept fat and in good case till he got him into market. He thought of how he should make out his gang; he thought of the respective market value of certain *supposititious* men and women and children who were to compose it, and other kindred topics of the business; then he thought of himself, and how humane he was, that whereas other men chained their "niggers" hand and foot both, he only put fetters on the feet, and left Tom the use of his hands, as long as he behaved well; and he sighed to think how ungrateful human nature was, so that there was even room to doubt whether Tom appreciated his mercies. He had been taken in so by "niggers" whom he had favored; but still he was astonished to consider how good-natured he yet remained!

As to Tom, he was thinking over some words of an unfashionable old book, which kept running through his head, again and again, as follows: "We have here no continuing city, but we seek one to come; wherefore God himself is not ashamed to be called our God; for he hath prepared for us a city." These words of an ancient volume, got up principally by "ignorant and unlearned men," have, through all time, kept up, somehow, a strange sort of power over the minds of poor, simple fellows, like Tom. They stir up the soul from its depths, and rouse, as with trumpet call, courage, energy, and enthusiasm, where before was only the blackness of despair.

Mr. Haley pulled out of his pocket sundry newspapers, and began looking over their advertisements, with absorbed interest. He was not a remarkably fluent reader, and was in the habit of reading in a sort of recitative half-aloud, by way of calling in his ears to verify the deductions of his eyes. In this tone he slowly recited the following paragraph:

EXECUTOR'S SALE, — NEGROES! — Agreeably to order of court, will be sold, on Tuesday, February 20, before the Court-house door, in the town of Washington, Kentucky, the following negroes: Hagar, aged 60; John, aged 30; Ben, aged 21; Saul, aged 25; Albert, aged 14. Sold for the benefit of the creditors and heirs of the estate of Jesse Blutchford, Esq.

Samuel Morris,
Thomas Flint,
Executors.

---

[1]Matthew 2:18. King James Bible. — Eds.

"This yer I must look at," said he to Tom, for want of somebody else to talk to.

"Ye see, I'm going to get up a prime gang to take down with ye, Tom; it'll make   5
it sociable and pleasant like, — good company will, ye know. We must drive right
to Washington first and foremost, and then I'll clap you into jail, while I does the
business."

Tom received this agreeable intelligence quite meekly; simply wondering, in his
own heart, how many of these doomed men had wives and children, and whether
they would feel as he did about leaving them. It is to be confessed, too, that the naive,
off-hand information that he was to be thrown into jail by no means produced an
agreeable impression on a poor fellow who had always prided himself on a strictly
honest and upright course of life. Yes, Tom, we must confess it, was rather proud of
his honesty, poor fellow, — not having very much else to be proud of; — if he had
belonged to some of the higher walks of society, he, perhaps, would never have been
reduced to such straits. However, the day wore on, and the evening saw Haley and
Tom comfortably accommodated in Washington, — the one in a tavern, and the other
in a jail.

About eleven o'clock the next day, a mixed throng was gathered around the courthouse steps, — smoking, chewing, spitting, swearing, and conversing, according to
their respective tastes and turns, — waiting for the auction to commence. The men and
women to be sold sat in a group apart, talking in a low tone to each other. The woman
who had been advertised by the name of Hagar was a regular African in feature and
figure. She might have been sixty, but was older than that by hard work and disease,
was partially blind, and somewhat crippled with rheumatism. By her side stood her
only remaining son, Albert, a bright-looking little fellow of fourteen years. The boy
was the only survivor of a large family, who had been successively sold away from her
to a southern market. The mother held on to him with both her shaking hands, and
eyed with intense trepidation every one who walked up to examine him.

"Don't be feard, Aunt Hagar," said the oldest of the men, "I spoke to Mas'r Thomas
'bout it, and he thought he might manage to sell you in a lot both together."

"Dey needn't call me worn out yet," said she, lifting her shaking hands. "I can
cook yet, and scrub, and scour, — I'm wuth a buying, if I do come cheap; — tell em
dat ar, — you *tell* em," she added, earnestly.

Haley here forced his way into the group, walked up to the old man, pulled his   10
mouth open and looked in, felt of his teeth, made him stand and straighten himself,
bend his back, and perform various evolutions to show his muscles; and then passed
on to the next, and put him through the same trial. Walking up last to the boy, he felt
of his arms, straightened his hands, and looked at his fingers, and made him jump,
to show his agility.

"He an't gwine to be sold widout me!" said the old woman, with passionate eagerness; "he and I goes in a lot together; I 's rail strong yet, Mas'r, and can do heaps o'
work, — heaps on it, Mas'r."

"On plantation?" said Haley, with a contemptuous glance. "Likely story!" and, as
if satisfied with his examination, he walked out and looked, and stood with his hands
in his pocket, his cigar in his mouth, and his hat cocked on one side, ready for action.

"What think of 'em?" said a man who had been following Haley's examination, as if to make up his own mind from it.

"Wal," said Haley, spitting, "I shall put in, I think, for the youngerly ones and the boy."

"They want to sell the boy and the old woman together," said the man.   15

"Find it a tight pull; — why, she's an old rack o' bones, — not worth her salt."

"You wouldn't then?" said the man.

"Anybody 'd be a fool 't would. She's half blind, crooked with rheumatis, and foolish to boot."

"Some buys up these yer old crittur, and ses there's a sight more wear in 'em than a body 'd think," said the man, reflectively.

"No go, 't all," said Haley; "wouldn't take her for a present, — fact, — I've *seen*,   20
now."

"Wal, 't is kinder pity, now, not to buy her with her son, — her heart seems so sot on him, — s'pose they fling her in cheap."

"Them that's got money to spend that ar way, it's all well enough. I shall bid off on that ar boy for a plantation-hand; — wouldn't be bothered with her, no way, not if they'd give her to me," said Haley.

"She'll take on desp't," said the man.

"Nat'lly, she will," said the trader, coolly.

The conversation was here interrupted by a busy hum in the audience; and the   25
auctioneer, a short, bustling, important fellow, elbowed his way into the crowd. The old woman drew in her breath, and caught instinctively at her son.

"Keep close to yer mammy, Albert, — close, — dey'll put us up togedder," she said.

"O, mammy, I'm feard they won't," said the boy.

"Dey must, child; I can't live, no ways, if they don't," said the old creature, vehemently.

The stentorian tones of the auctioneer, calling out to clear the way, now announced that the sale was about to commence. A place was cleared, and the bidding began. The different men on the list were soon knocked off at prices which showed a pretty brisk demand in the market; two of them fell to Haley.

"Come, now, young un," said the auctioneer, giving the boy a touch with his   30
hammer, "be up and show your springs, now."

"Put us two up togedder, togedder, — do please, Mas'r," said the old woman, holding fast to her boy.

"Be off," said the man, gruffly, pushing her hands away; "you come last. Now, darkey, spring;" and, with the word, he pushed the boy toward the block, while a deep, heavy groan rose behind him. The boy paused, and looked back; but there was no time to stay, and, dashing the tears from his large, bright eyes, he was up in a moment.

His fine figure, alert limbs, and bright face, raised an instant competition, and half a dozen bids simultaneously met the ear of the auctioneer. Anxious, half-frightened, he looked from side to side, as he heard the clatter of contending bids, — now here, now there, — till the hammer fell. Haley had got him. He was pushed from the block toward his new master, but stopped one moment, and looked back, when his poor old mother, trembling in every limb, held out her shaking hands toward him.

"Buy me too, Mas'r, for de dear Lord's sake! — buy me, — I shall die if you don't!"

"You'll die if I do, that's the kink of it," said Haley, — "no!" And he turned on his heel.   35

The bidding for the poor old creature was summary. The man who had addressed Haley, and who seemed not destitute of compassion, bought her for a trifle, and the spectators began to disperse.

The poor victims of the sale, who had been brought up in one place together for years, gathered round the despairing old mother, whose agony was pitiful to see.

"Couldn't dey leave me one? Mas'r allers said I should have one, — he did," she repeated over and over, in heart-broken tones.

"Trust in the Lord, Aunt Hagar," said the oldest of the men, sorrowfully.

"What good will it do?" said she, sobbing passionately.   40

"Mother, mother, — don't! don't!" said the boy. "They say you 's got a good master."

"I don't care, — I don't care. O, Albert! oh, my boy! you 's my last baby. Lord, how ken I?"

"Come, take her off, can't some of ye?" said Haley, dryly; "don't do no good for her to go on that ar way."

The old men of the company, partly by persuasion and partly by force, loosed the poor creature's last despairing hold, and, as they led her off to her new master's wagon, strove to comfort her.

"Now!" said Haley, pushing his three purchases together, and producing a bundle   45
of handcuffs, which he proceeded to put on their wrists; and fastening each handcuff to a long chain, he drove them before him to the jail.

A few days saw Haley, with his possessions, safely deposited on one of the Ohio boats. It was the commencement of his gang, to be augmented, as the boat moved on, by various other merchandise of the same kind, which he, or his agent, had stored for him in various points along shore.

The La Belle Rivière, as brave and beautiful a boat as ever walked the waters of her namesake river, was floating gayly down the stream, under a brilliant sky, the stripes and stars of free America waving and fluttering over head; the guards crowded with well-dressed ladies and gentlemen walking and enjoying the delightful day. All was full of life, buoyant and rejoicing; — all but Haley's gang, who were stored, with other freight, on the lower deck, and who, somehow, did not seem to appreciate their various privileges, as they sat in a knot, talking to each other in low tones.

"Boys," said Haley, coming up, briskly, "I hope you keep up good heart, and are cheerful. Now, no sulks, ye see; keep stiff upper lip, boys; do well by me, and I'll do well by you."

The boys addressed responded the invariable "Yes, Mas'r," for ages the watch-word of poor Africa; but it's to be owned they did not look particularly cheerful; they had their various little prejudices in favor of wives, mothers, sisters, and children, seen for the last time, — and though "they that wasted them required of them mirth," it was not instantly forthcoming.

"I've got a wife," spoke out the article enumerated as "John, aged thirty," and he   50
laid his chained hand on Tom's knee,—"and she don't know a word about this, poor
girl!"

"Where does she live?" said Tom.

"In a tavern a piece down here," said John; "I wish, now, I *could* see her once
more in this world," he added.

Poor John! It *was* rather natural; and the tears that fell, as he spoke, came as
naturally as if he had been a white man. Tom drew a long breath from a sore heart,
and tried, in his poor way, to comfort him.

And over head, in the cabin, sat fathers and mothers, husbands and wives; and
merry, dancing children moved round among them, like so many little butterflies,
and everything was going on quite easy and comfortable.

"O, mamma," said a boy, who had just come up from below, "there's a negro   55
trader on board, and he's brought four or five slaves down there."

"Poor creatures!" said the mother, in a tone between grief and indignation.

"What's that?" said another lady.

"Some poor slaves below," said the mother.

"And they've got chains on," said the boy.

"What a shame to our country that such sights are to be seen!" said another lady.   60

"O, there's a great deal to be said on both sides of the subject," said a genteel
woman, who sat at her state-room door sewing, while her little girl and boy were
playing round her. "I've been south, and I must say I think the negroes are better off
than they would be to be free."

"In some respects, some of them are well off, I grant," said the lady to whose
remark she had answered. "The most dreadful part of slavery, to my mind, is its outrages on the feelings and affections, —the separating of families, for example."

"That *is* a bad thing, certainly," said the other lady, holding up a baby's dress she
had just completed, and looking intently on its trimmings; "but then, I fancy, it don't
occur often."

"O, it does," said the first lady, eagerly; "I've lived many years in Kentucky and
Virginia both, and I've seen enough to make any one's heart sick. Suppose, ma'am,
your two children, there, should be taken from you, and sold?"

"We can't reason from our feelings to those of this class of persons," said the   65
other lady, sorting out some worsteds on her lap.

"Indeed, ma'am, you can know nothing of them, if you say so," answered the first
lady, warmly. "I was born and brought up among them. I know they *do* feel, just as
keenly, —even more so, perhaps, —as we do."

The lady said "Indeed!" yawned, and looked out the cabin window, and finally
repeated, for a finale, the remark with which she had begun, —"After all, I think they
are better off than they would be to be free."

"It's undoubtedly the intention of Providence that the African race should be
servants, —kept in a low condition," said a grave-looking gentleman in black, a clergyman, seated by the cabin door. "'Cursed be Canaan; a servant of servants shall he
be,' the scripture says."

"I say, stranger, is that ar what that text means?" said a tall man, standing by.

"Undoubtedly. It pleased Providence, for some inscrutable reason, to doom the race to bondage, ages ago; and we must not set up our opinion against that." 70

"Well, then, we'll all go ahead and buy up niggers," said the man, "if that's the way of Providence, — won't we, Squire?" said he, turning to Haley, who had been standing, with his hands in his pockets, by the stove and intently listening to the conversation.

"Yes," continued the tall man, "we must all be resigned to the decrees of Providence. Niggers must be sold, and trucked round, and kept under; it's what they's made for. 'Pears like this yer view's quite refreshing, an't it, stranger?" said he to Haley.

"I never thought on 't," said Haley, "I couldn't have said as much, myself; I ha'nt no larning. I took up the trade just to make a living; if 'tan't right, I calculated to 'pent on 't in time, *ye* know."

"And now you'll save yerself the trouble, won't ye?" said the tall man. "See what 't is, now, to know scripture. If ye'd only studied yer Bible, like this yer good man, ye might have know'd it before, and saved ye a heap o' trouble. Ye could jist have said, 'Cussed be' — what's his name?—'and 't would all have come right.'" And the stranger . . . sat down, and began smoking, with a curious smile on his long, dry face.

A tall, slender young man, with a face expressive of great feeling and intelligence, 75 here broke in, and repeated the words, "'All things whatsoever ye would that men should do unto you, do ye even so unto them.' I suppose," he added, "*that* is scripture, as much as 'Cursed be Canaan.'"

"Wal, it seems quite *as* plain a text, stranger," said John the drover, "to poor fellows like us, now;" and John smoked on like a volcano.

The young man paused, looked as if he was going to say more, when suddenly the boat stopped, and the company made the usual steamboat rush, to see where they were landing.

"Both them ar chaps parsons?" said John to one of the men, as they were going out.

The man nodded.

As the boat stopped, a black woman came running wildly up the plank, darted 80 into the crowd, flew up to where the slave gang sat, and threw her arms round that unfortunate piece of merchandise before enumerate—"John, aged thirty," and with sobs and tears bemoaned him as her husband.

But what needs tell the story, told too oft, — every day told, — of heart-strings rent and broken, — the weak broken and torn for the profit and convenience of the strong! It needs not to be told; — every day is telling it, — telling it, too, in the ear of One who is not deaf, though he be long silent.

The young man who had spoken for the cause of humanity and God before stood with folded arms, looking on this scene. He turned, and Haley was standing at his side. "My friend," he said, speaking with thick utterance, "how can you, how dare you, carry on a trade like this? Look at those poor creatures! Here I am, rejoicing in my heart that I am going home to my wife and child; and the same bell which is a signal to carry me onward towards them will part this poor man and his wife forever. Depend upon it, God will bring you into judgment for this."

The trader turned away in silence.

"I say, now," said the drover, touching his elbow, "there's differences in parsons, an't there? 'Cussed be Canaan' don't seem to go down with this 'un, does it?"

Haley gave an uneasy growl. 85

"And that ar an't the worst on 't," said John; "mabbe it won't go down with the Lord, neither, when ye come to settle with Him, one o' these days, as all on us must, I reckon."

Haley walked reflectively to the other end of the boat.

"If I make pretty handsomely on one or two next gangs," he thought, "I reckon I'll stop off this yer; it's really getting dangerous." And he took out his pocket-book, and began adding over his accounts,— a process which many gentlemen besides Mr. Haley have found a specific for an uneasy conscience.

The boat swept proudly away from the shore, and all went on merrily, as before. Men talked, and loafed, and read, and smoked. Women sewed, and children played, and the boat passed on her way.

One day, when she lay to for a while at a small town in Kentucky, Haley went up 90 into the place on a little matter of business.

Tom, whose fetters did not prevent his taking a moderate circuit, had drawn near the side of the boat, and stood listlessly gazing over the railings. After a time, he saw the trader returning, with an alert step, in company with a colored woman, bearing in her arms a young child. She was dressed quite respectably, and a colored man followed her, bringing along a small trunk. The woman came cheerfully onward, talking, as she came, with the man who bore her trunk, and so passed up the plank into the boat. The bell rung, the steamer whizzed, the engine groaned and coughed, and away swept the boat down the river.

The woman walked forward among the boxes and bales of the lower deck, and, sitting down, busied herself with chirruping to her baby.

Haley made a turn or two about the boat, and then, coming up, seated himself near her, and began saying something to her in an indifferent undertone.

Tom soon noticed a heavy cloud passing over the woman's brow; and that she answered rapidly, and with great vehemence.

"I don't believe it, — I won't believe it!" he heard her say. "You're jist a foolin' 95 with me."

"If you won't believe it, look here!" said the man, drawing out a paper; "this yer's the bill of sale, and there's your master's name to it; and I paid down good solid cash for it, too, I can tell you, — so, now!"

"I don't believe Mas'r would cheat me so; it can't be true!" said the woman, with increasing agitation.

"You can ask any of these men here, that can read writing. Here!" he said, to a man that was passing by, "jist read this yer, won't you! This yer gal won't believe me, when I tell her what 't is."

"Why, it's a bill of sale, signed by John Fosdick," said the man, "making over to you the girl Lucy and her child. It's all straight enough, for aught I see."

The woman's passionate exclamations collected a crowd around her, and the   100
trader briefly explained to them the cause of the agitation.

"He told me that I was going down to Louisville, to hire out as cook to the same tavern where my husband works, — that's what Mas'r told me, his own self; and I can't believe he'd lie to me," said the woman.

"But he has sold you, my poor woman, there's no doubt about it," said a good-natured looking man, who had been examining the papers; "he has done it, and no mistake."

"Then it's no account talking," said the woman, suddenly growing quite calm; and, clasping her child tighter in her arms, she sat down on her box, turned her back round, and gazed listlessly into the river.

"Going to take it easy, after all!" said the trader. "Gal's got grit, I see."

The woman looked calm, as the boat went on; and a beautiful soft summer breeze   105
passed like a compassionate spirit over her head, — the gentle breeze, that never inquires whether the brow is dusky or fair that it fans. And she saw sunshine sparkling on the water, in golden ripples, and heard gay voices, full of ease and pleasure, talking around her everywhere; but her heart lay as if a great stone had fallen on it. Her baby raised himself up against her, and stroked her cheeks with his little hands; and, springing up and down, crowing and chatting, seemed determined to arouse her. She strained him suddenly and tightly in her arms, and slowly one tear after another fell on his wondering, unconscious face; and gradually she seemed, and little by little, to grow calmer, and busied herself with tending and nursing him.

The child, a boy of ten months, was uncommonly large and strong of his age, and very vigorous in his limbs. Never, for a moment, still, he kept his mother constantly busy in holding him, and guarding his springing activity.

"That's a fine chap!" said a man, suddenly stopping opposite to him, with his hands in his pockets. "How old is he?"

"Ten months and a half," said the mother.

The man whistled to the boy, and offered him part of a stick of candy, which he eagerly grabbed at, and very soon had it in a baby's general depository, to wit, his mouth.

"Rum fellow!" said the man "Knows what's what!" and he whistled, and walked   110
on. When he had got to the other side of the boat, he came across Haley, who was smoking on top of a pile of boxes.

The stranger produced a match, and lighted a cigar, saying, as he did so,

"Decentish kind o' wench you've got round there, stranger."

"Why, I reckon she *is* tol'able fair," said Haley, blowing the smoke out of his mouth.

"Taking her down south?" said the man.

Haley nodded, and smoked on.   115

"Plantation hand?" said the man.

"Wal," said Haley, "I'm fillin' out an order for a plantation, and I think I shall put her in. They told me she was a good cook; and they can use her for that, or set her at the cotton-picking. She's got the right fingers for that; I looked at 'em. Sell well, either way;" and Haley resumed his cigar.

"They won't want the young 'un on the plantation," said the man.

"I shall sell him, first chance I find," said Haley, lighting another cigar.

"S'pose you'd be selling him tol'able cheap," said the stranger, mounting the pile   120
of boxes, and sitting down comfortably.

"Don't know 'bout that," said Haley; "he's a pretty smart young 'un, straight, fat, strong; flesh as hard as a brick!"

"Very true, but then there's the bother and expense of raisin'."

"Nonsense!" said Haley; "they is raised as easy as any kind of critter there is going; they an't a bit more trouble than pups. This yer chap will be running all around, in a month."

"I've got a good place for raisin', and I thought of takin' in a little more stock," said the man. "One cook lost a young 'un last week, — got drownded in a washtub, while she was a hangin' out the clothes, — and I reckon it would be well enough to set her to raisin' this yer."

Haley and the stranger smoked a while in silence, neither seeming willing to   125
broach the test question of the interview. At last the man resumed:

"You wouldn't think of wantin' more than ten dollars for that ar chap, seeing you *must* get him off yer hand, any how?"

Haley shook his head, and spit impressively.

"That won't do, no ways," he said, and began his smoking again.

"Well, stranger, what will you take?"

"Well, now," said Haley, "I *could* raise that ar chap myself, or get him raised; he's   130
oncommon likely and healthy, and he'd fetch a hundred dollars, six months hence; and, in a year or two, he'd bring two hundred, if I had him in the right spot; I shan't take a cent less nor fifty for him now."

"O, stranger! that's rediculous, altogether," said the man.

"Fact!" said Haley, with a decisive nod of his head.

"I'll give thirty for him," said the stranger, "but not a cent more."

"Now, I'll tell ye what I will do," said Haley, spitting again, with renewed decision. "I'll split the difference, and say forty-five; and that's the most I will do."

"Well, agreed!" said the man, after an interval.   135

"Done!" said Haley. "Where do you land?"

"At Louisville," said the man.

"Louisville," said Haley. "Very fair, we get there about dusk. Chap will be asleep, — all fair, — get him off quietly, and no screaming, — happens beautiful, — I like to do everything quietly, — I hates all kind of agitation and fluster." And so, after a transfer of certain bills had passed from the man's pocket-book to the trader's, he resumed his cigar.

It was a bright, tranquil evening when the boat stopped at the wharf at Louisville. The woman had been sitting with her baby in her arms, now wrapped in a heavy sleep. When she heard the name of the place called out, she hastily laid the child down in a little cradle formed by the hollow among the boxes, first carefully spreading under it her cloak; and then she sprung to the side of the boat, in hopes that, among the various hotel-waiters who thronged the wharf, she might see her husband. In this hope, she pressed forward to the front rails, and, stretching far over them, strained her eyes intently on the moving heads on the shore, and the crowd pressed in between her and the child.

"Now's your time," said Haley, taking the sleeping child up, and handing him to the stranger. "Don't wake him up, and set him to crying, now; it would make a devil of a fuss with the gal." The man took the bundle carefully, and was soon lost in the crowd that went up the wharf.   140

When the boat, creaking, and groaning, and puffing, had loosed from the wharf, and was beginning slowly to strain herself along, the woman returned to her old seat. The trader was sitting there, — the child was gone!

"Why, why, — where?" she began, in bewildered surprise.

"Lucy," said the trader, "your child's gone; you may as well know it first as last. You see, I know'd you couldn't take him down south; and I got a chance to sell him to a first-rate family, that'll raise him better than you can."

The trader had arrived at that stage of Christian and political perfection which has been recommended by some preachers and politicians of the north, lately, in which he had completely overcome every humane weakness and prejudice. His heart was exactly where yours, sir, and mine could be brought, with proper effort and cultivation. The wild look of anguish and utter despair that the woman cast on him might have disturbed one less practised; but he was used to it. He had seen that same look hundreds of times. You can get used to such things, too, my friend; and it is the great object of recent efforts to make our whole northern community used to them, for the glory of the Union. So the trader only regarded the mortal anguish which he saw working in those dark features, those clenched hands, and suffocating breathings, as necessary incidents of the trade, and merely calculated whether she was going to scream, and get up a commotion on the boat; for, like other supporters of our peculiar institution, he decidedly disliked agitation.

But the woman did not scream. The shot had passed too straight and direct through the heart, for cry or tear.   145

Dizzily she sat down. Her slack hands fell lifeless by her side. Her eyes looked straight forward, but she saw nothing. All the noise and hum of the boat, the groaning of the machinery, mingled dreamily to her bewildered ear; and the poor, dumb-stricken heart had neither cry nor tear to show for its utter misery. She was quite calm.

The trader, who, considering his advantages, was almost as humane as some of our politicians, seemed to feel called on to administer such consolation as the case admitted of.

"I know this yer comes kinder hard, at first, Lucy," said he; "but such a smart, sensible gal as you are, won't give way to it. You see it's *necessary*, and can't be helped!"

"O! don't, Mas'r, don't!" said the woman, with a voice like one that is smothering.

"You're a smart wench, Lucy," he persisted; "I mean to do well by ye, and get ye a nice place down river; and you'll soon get another husband, — such a likely gal as you—"   150

"O! Mas'r, if you *only* won't talk to me now," said the woman, in a voice of such quick and living anguish that the trader felt that there was something at present in the case beyond his style of operation. He got up, and the woman turned away, and buried her head in her cloak.

The trader walked up and down for a time, and occasionally stopped and looked at her.

"Takes it hard, rather," he soliloquized, "but quiet, tho'; — let her sweat a while; she'll come right, by and by!"

Tom had watched the whole transaction from first to last, and had a perfect understanding of its results. To him, it looked like something unutterably horrible and cruel, because, poor, ignorant black soul! he had not learned to generalize, and to take enlarged views. If he had only been instructed by certain ministers of Christianity, he might have thought better of it, and seen in it an every-day incident of a lawful trade; a trade which is the vital support of an institution which an American divine[2] tells us has "*no evils but such as are inseparable from any other relations in social and domestic life.*" But Tom, as we see, being a poor, ignorant fellow, whose reading had been confined entirely to the New Testament, could not comfort and solace himself with views like these. His very soul bled within him for what seemed to him the *wrongs* of the poor suffering thing that lay like a crushed reed on the boxes; the feeling, living, bleeding, yet immortal *thing*, which American state law coolly classes with the bundles, and bales, and boxes, among which she is lying.

Tom drew near, and tried to say something; but she only groaned. Honestly, and with tears running down his own cheeks, he spoke of a heart of love in the skies, of a pitying Jesus, and an eternal home; but the ear was deaf with anguish, and the palsied heart could not feel.

Night came on, — night calm, unmoved, and glorious, shining down with her innumerable and solemn angel eyes, twinkling, beautiful, but silent. There was no speech nor language, no pitying voice or helping hand, from that distant sky. One after another, the voices of business or pleasure died away; all on the boat were sleeping, and the ripples at the prow were plainly heard. Tom stretched himself out on a box, and there, as he lay, he heard, ever and anon, a smothered sob or cry from the prostrate creature, —"O! what shall I do? O Lord! O good Lord, do help me!" and so, ever and anon, until the murmur died away in silence.

At midnight, Tom waked, with a sudden start. Something black passed quickly by him to the side of the boat, and he heard a splash in the water. No one else saw or heard anything. He raised his head, — the woman's place was vacant! He got up, and sought about him in vain. The poor bleeding heart was still, at last, and the river rippled and dimpled just as brightly as if it had not closed above it.

Patience! patience! ye whose hearts swell indignant at wrongs like these. Not one throb of anguish, not one tear of the oppressed, is forgotten by the Man of Sorrows, the Lord of Glory. In his patient, generous bosom he bears the anguish of a world.

155

---

[1]Dr. Joel Parker of Philadelphia.

Bear thou, like him, in patience, and labor in love; for sure as he is God, "the year of his redeemed *shall* come."

The trader waked up bright and early, and came out to see to his live stock. It was now his turn to look about in perplexity.

"Where alive is that gal?" he said to Tom.   160

Tom, who had learned the wisdom of keeping counsel, did not feel called upon to state his observations and suspicions, but said he did not know.

"She surely couldn't have got off in the night at any of the landings, for I was awake, and on the look-out, whenever the boat stopped. I never trust these yer things to other folks."

This speech was addressed to Tom quite confidentially, as if it was something that would be specially interesting to him. Tom made no answer.

The trader searched the boat from stem to stern, among boxes, bales and barrels, around the machinery, by the chimneys, in vain.

"Now, I say, Tom, be fair about this yer," he said, when, after a fruitless search,   165
he came where Tom was standing. "You know something about it, now. Don't tell me, — I know you do. I saw the gal stretched out here about ten o'clock, and ag'in at twelve, and ag'in between one and two; and then at four she was gone, and you was a sleeping right there all the time. Now, you know something, — you can't help it."

"Well, Mas'r," said Tom, "towards morning something brushed by me, and I kinder half woke; and then I hearn a great splash, and then I clare woke up, and the gal was gone. That's all I know on 't."

The trader was not shocked nor amazed; because, as we said before, he was used to a great many things that you are not used to. Even the awful presence of Death struck no solemn chill upon him. He had seen Death many times, — met him in the way of trade, and got acquainted with him, — and he only thought of him as a hard customer, that embarrassed his property operations very unfairly; and so he only swore that the gal was a baggage, and that he was devilish unlucky, and that, if things went on in this way, he should not make a cent on the trip. In short, he seemed to consider himself an ill-used man, decidedly; but there was no help for it, as the woman had escaped into a state which *never will* give up a fugitive, — not even at the demand of the whole glorious Union. The trader, therefore, sat discontentedly down, with his little account-book, and put down the missing body and soul under the head of *losses!*

"He's a shocking creature, isn't he, — this trader? so unfeeling! It's dreadful, really!"

"O, but nobody thinks anything of these traders! They are universally despised, — never received into any decent society."

But who, sir, makes the trader? Who is most to blame? The enlightened, culti-   170
vated, intelligent man, who supports the system of which the trader is the inevitable result, or the poor trader himself? You make the public statement that calls for his trade, that debauches and depraves him, till he feels no shame in it; and in what are you better than he?

Are you educated and he ignorant, you high and he low, you refined and he coarse, you talented and he simple?

In the day of a future judgment, these very considerations may make it more tolerable for him than for you.

In concluding these little incidents of lawful trade, we must beg the world not to think that American legislators are entirely destitute of humanity, as might, perhaps, be unfairly inferred from the great efforts made in our national body to protect and perpetuate this species of traffic.

Who does not know how our great men are outdoing themselves, in declaiming against the *foreign* slave-trade. There are a perfect host of Clarksons and Wilberforces[3] risen up among us on that subject, most edifying to hear and behold. Trading negroes from Africa, dear reader, is so horrid! It is not to be thought of! But trading them from Kentucky, — that's quite another thing!

(1852)

Exploring the Text

1. What ironies does Harriet Beecher Stowe develop in the first seven paragraphs? Provide three examples and explain their effects.
2. What is Stowe's rhetorical purpose? How does the imagery in paragraphs 47–54 contribute to that purpose?
3. Read carefully the conversation that runs from paragraphs 50–76. How would you characterize the attitudes of the speakers? How does the conversation contribute to the chapter as a whole?
4. What is the effect of such diction as "the article enumerated as 'John, aged thirty'" (par. 50) and "that unfortunate piece of merchandise before enumerate" (par. 80)?
5. Stowe writes, "And he took out his pocket-book, and began adding over his accounts, — a process which many gentlemen besides Mr. Haley have found a specific for an uneasy conscience" (par. 88). What does she mean? What is Stowe's tone in that sentence?
6. Read paragraph 144 carefully. What is the effect of Stowe's direct address to the reader? How does it make you feel?
7. How would you describe Stowe's tone in paragraph 154? How does it serve her rhetorical purpose?
8. What is the rhetorical shift that Stowe develops between paragraphs 164 and 165? From that point on, how does she use rhetorical strategies to conclude the episode?

---

[2]Thomas Clarkson (1760–1846) and William Wilberforce (1759–1833) were British politicians and abolitionists who succeeded in first abolishing the slave trade in the British Empire in 1807 and then abolishing slavery entirely in 1833. — Eds.

HISTORIC FREDERICKSBURG FOUNDATION

The following images are from the Historic Fredericksburg Foundation. Fredericksburg, Virginia, located halfway between Washington, D.C., and Richmond, Virginia — the capitals of the Union and the Confederacy, respectively — was the site of the Battle of Fredericksburg (December 11–15, 1862) and the Second Battle of Fredericksburg (May 3, 1863). The first battle resulted in a Confederate victory; the second was won by Union forces. It is the location of the Fredericksburg and Spotsylvania National Military Park.

Auction Block Monument

This monument, a three-foot-high block of sandstone with a step hewn into one side, stands at the corner of William and Charles Streets, in Fredericksburg, Virginia. It marks the location where auctions of property and of slaves took place. Slaves offered for sale would stand on the block for inspection.

Courtesy of Franklin Thomas.

The auction block monument at the corner of William and Charles Streets, Fredericksburg, Virginia.

Courtesy of Franklin Thomas.

The auction block and plaque, which reads "Auction Block, Fredericksburg's Principal Auction Site in Pre-Civil War Days for Slaves and Property. 1984. HFFI" (Historical Fredericksburg Foundation, Inc.).

Exploring the Text

1. This pre–Civil War auction block was used to buy and sell many items, including slaves. The Historic Fredericksburg Foundation plaque is dated 1984. What might be the foundation's rhetorical purpose in creating this plaque and turning this auction block into a monument? Explain.
2. How does the monument appeal to ethos, logos, and pathos? Which one is primary?
3. How might different viewers — residents, tourists, whites, blacks, old, young — regard the grim reminder of our nation's past that the monument provides? Do you think such a monument is appropriate to have on a city street corner? Explain.

HERMAN MELVILLE

Herman Melville (1819–1891) was born in New York City. After working as a clerk in a bank and as a schoolteacher, he went to sea in 1841. He traveled to Liverpool, England, on his first voyage and then on a whaling ship to the Marquesas Islands and other parts of the South Seas. Based on his experiences there, he wrote the novels *Typee* and *Omoo*, which were published in 1847. In 1849, he wrote

Redburn, an autobiographical novel based on his first voyage. Largely self-educated, Melville read widely, and after his adventures, he began to write more complex books, including *Moby-Dick*.

from *Moby-Dick;*
or, *The Whale*

Among those who greatly influenced Melville's writing are Shakespeare and Ralph Waldo Emerson, both of whom can be detected in Melville's novel *Moby-Dick*, which he completed in 1851. In the book, Melville's narrator, Ishmael, tells of the epic quest of Captain Ahab after the white whale. Now widely regarded as one of the greatest novels of American literature for its gripping epic adventure and profound metaphysical journey, it was not well received in its time. Nor were his later novels, *Pierre* and *The Confidence Man*. The following selection, "Loomings," is the first chapter of *Moby-Dick*.

Call me Ishmael. Some years ago — never mind how long precisely — having little or no money in my purse, and nothing particular to interest me on shore, I thought I would sail about a little and see the watery part of the world. It is a way I have of driving off the spleen, and regulating the circulation. Whenever I find myself growing grim about the mouth; whenever it is a damp, drizzly November in my soul; whenever I find myself involuntarily pausing before coffin warehouses, and bringing up the rear of every funeral I meet; and especially whenever my hypos get such an upper hand of me, that it requires a strong moral principle to prevent me from deliberately stepping into the street, and methodically knocking people's hats off — then, I account it high time to get to sea as soon as I can. This is my substitute for pistol and ball. With a philosophical flourish Cato[1] throws himself upon his sword; I quietly take to the ship. There is nothing surprising in this. If they but knew it, almost all men in their degree, some time or other, cherish very nearly the same feelings towards the ocean with me.

There now is your insular city of the Manhattoes, belted round by wharves as Indian isles by coral reefs — commerce surrounds it with her surf. Right and left, the streets take you waterward. Its extreme down-town is the battery, where that noble mole is washed by waves, and cooled by breezes, which a few hours previous were out of sight of land. Look at the crowds of water-gazers there.

Circumambulate the city of a dreamy Sabbath afternoon. Go from Corlears Hook to Coenties Slip, and from thence, by Whitehall, northward. What do you see? — Posted like silent sentinels all around the town, stand thousands upon thousands of mortal men fixed in ocean reveries. Some leaning against the spiles; some seated upon the pier heads; some looking over the bulwarks of ships from China; some high aloft in the rigging, as if striving to get a still better seaward peep. But these are all landsmen;

---

[1]Cato the Younger (95 BCE–46 CE) was a Roman aristocrat who resisted Julius Caesar's rise to power and fell on his own sword rather than live under Caesar's rule. — Eds.

of week days pent up in lath and plaster—tied to counters, nailed to benches, clinched to desks. How then is this? Are the green fields gone? What do they here?

But look! here come more crowds, pacing straight for the water, and seemingly bound for a dive. Strange! Nothing will content them but the extremest limit of the land; loitering under the shady lee of yonder warehouses will not suffice. No. They must get just as nigh the water as they possibly can without falling in. And there they stand—miles of them—leagues. Inlanders all, they come from lanes and alleys, streets and avenues—north, east, south, and west. Yet here they all unite. Tell me, does the magnetic virtue of the needles of the compasses of all those ships attract them thither?

Once more. Say, you are in the country; in some high land of lakes. Take almost any path you please, and ten to one it carries you down in a dale, and leaves you there by a pool in the stream. There is magic in it. Let the most absent-minded of men be plunged in his deepest reveries—stand that man on his legs, set his feet a-going, and he will infallibly lead you to water, if water there be in all that region. Should you ever be athirst in the great American desert, try this experiment, if your caravan happen to be supplied with a metaphysical professor. Yes, as every one knows, meditation and water are wedded for ever.

But here is an artist. He desires to paint you the dreamiest, shadiest, quietest, most enchanting bit of romantic landscape in all the valley of the Saco. What is the chief element he employs? There stand his trees, each with a hollow trunk, as if a hermit and a crucifix were within; and here sleeps his meadow, and there sleep his cattle; and up from yonder cottage goes a sleepy smoke. Deep into distant woodlands winds a mazy way, reaching to overlapping spurs of mountains bathed in their hill-side blue. But though the picture lies thus tranced, and though this pine-tree shakes down its sighs like leaves upon this shepherd's head, yet all were vain, unless the shepherd's eye were fixed upon the magic stream before him. Go visit the Prairies in June, when for scores on scores of miles you wade knee-deep among Tiger-lilies—what is the one charm wanting?—Water—there is not a drop of water there! Were Niagara but a cataract of sand, would you travel your thousand miles to see it? Why did the poor poet of Tennessee, upon suddenly receiving two handfuls of silver, deliberate whether to buy him a coat, which he sadly needed, or invest his money in a pedestrian trip to Rockaway Beach? Why is almost every robust healthy boy with a robust healthy soul in him, at some time or other crazy to go to sea? Why upon your first voyage as a passenger, did you yourself feel such a mystical vibration, when first told that you and your ship were now out of sight of land? Why did the old Persians hold the sea holy? Why did the Greeks give it a separate deity, and own brother of Jove? Surely all this is not without meaning. And still deeper the meaning of that story of Narcissus, who because he could not grasp the tormenting, mild image he saw in the fountain, plunged into it and was drowned. But that same image, we ourselves see in all rivers and oceans. It is the image of the ungraspable phantom of life; and this is the key to it all.

Now, when I say that I am in the habit of going to sea whenever I begin to grow hazy about the eyes, and begin to be over conscious of my lungs, I do not mean to have it inferred that I ever go to sea as a passenger. For to go as a passenger you must needs have a purse, and a purse is but a rag unless you have something in it. Besides, passengers get sea-sick—grow quarrelsome—don't sleep of nights—do not enjoy themselves

5

much, as a general thing;—no, I never go as a passenger; nor, though I am something of a salt, do I ever go to sea as a Commodore, or a Captain, or a Cook. I abandon the glory and distinction of such offices to those who like them. For my part, I abominate all honorable respectable toils, trials, and tribulations of every kind whatsoever. It is quite as much as I can do to take care of myself, without taking care of ships, barques, brigs, schooners, and what not. And as for going as cook,—though I confess there is considerable glory in that, a cook being a sort of officer on shipboard—yet, somehow, I never fancied broiling fowls;—though once broiled, judiciously buttered, and judgmatically salted and peppered, there is no one who will speak more respectfully, not to say reverentially, of a broiled fowl than I will. It is out of the idolatrous dotings of the old Egyptians upon broiled ibis and roasted river horse, that you see the mummies of those creatures in their huge bake-houses the pyramids.

No, when I go to sea, I go as a simple sailor, right before the mast, plumb down into the forecastle, aloft there to the royal mast-head. True, they rather order me about some, and make me jump from spar to spar, like a grasshopper in a May meadow. And at first, this sort of thing is unpleasant enough. It touches one's sense of honor, particularly if you come of an old established family in the land, the Van Rensselaers, or Randolphs, or Hardicanutes. And more than all, if just previous to your putting your hand into the tarpot, you have been lording it as a country schoolmaster, making the tallest boys stand in awe of you. The transition is a keen one, I assure you, from a schoolmaster to a sailor, and requires a strong decoction of Seneca and the Stoics[2] to enable you to grin and bear it. But even this wears off in time.

What of it, if some old hunks of a sea-captain orders me to get a broom and sweep down the decks? What does that indignity amount to, weighed, I mean, in the scales of the New Testament? Do you think the archangel Gabriel thinks anything the less of me, because I promptly and respectfully obey that old hunks in that particular instance? Who ain't a slave? Tell me that. Well, then, however the old sea-captains may order me about—however they may thump and punch me about, I have the satisfaction of knowing that it is all right; that everybody else is one way or other served in much the same way—either in a physical or metaphysical point of view, that is; and so the universal thump is passed round, and all hands should rub each other's shoulder-blades, and be content.

Again, I always go to sea as a sailor, because they make a point of paying me for   10
my trouble, whereas they never pay passengers a single penny that I ever heard of. On the contrary, passengers themselves must pay. And there is all the difference in the world between paying and being paid. The act of paying is perhaps the most uncomfortable infliction that the two orchard thieves entailed upon us. But *being paid*,—what will compare with it? The urbane activity with which a man receives money is really marvellous, considering that we so earnestly believe money to be the root of all earthly ills, and that on no account can a monied man enter heaven. Ah! how cheerfully we consign ourselves to perdition!

---

[2]Greek school of philosophy that encouraged being attuned with one's inner self and being content with one's present state of being. Seneca (4 BCE–65 CE) was a Roman statesman and Stoic philosopher.—Eds.

Finally, I always go to sea as a sailor, because of the wholesome exercise and pure air of the forecastle deck. For as in this world, head winds are far more prevalent than winds from astern (that is, if you never violate the Pythagorean maxim[3]), so for the most part the Commodore on the quarterdeck gets his atmosphere at second hand from the sailors on the forecastle. He thinks he breathes it first; but not so. In much the same way do the commonalty lead their leaders in many other things, at the same time that the leaders little suspect it. But wherefore it was that after having repeatedly smelt the sea as a merchant sailor, I should now take it into my head to go on a whaling voyage; this the invisible police officer of the Fates, who has the constant surveillance of me, and secretly dogs me, and influences me in some unaccountable way — he can better answer than any one else. And, doubtless, my going on this whaling voyage, formed part of the grand programme of Providence that was drawn up a long time ago. It came in as a sort of brief interlude and solo between more extensive performances. I take it that this part of the bill must have run something like this:

"*Grand Contested Election for the Presidency of the United States.*
"WHALING VOYAGE BY ONE ISHMAEL.
"BLOODY BATTLE IN AFGHANISTAN."

Though I cannot tell why it was exactly that those stage managers, the Fates, put me down for this shabby part of a whaling voyage, when others were set down for magnificent parts in high tragedies, and short and easy parts in genteel comedies, and jolly parts in farces — though I cannot tell why this was exactly; yet, now that I recall all the circumstances, I think I can see a little into the springs and motives which being cunningly presented to me under various disguises, induced me to set about performing the part I did, besides cajoling me into the delusion that it was a choice resulting from my own unbiased freewill and discriminating judgment.

Chief among these motives was the overwhelming idea of the great whale himself. Such a portentous and mysterious monster roused all my curiosity. Then the wild and distant seas where he rolled his island bulk; the undeliverable, nameless perils of the whale; these, with all the attending marvels of a thousand Patagonian sights and sounds, helped to sway me to my wish. With other men, perhaps, such things would not have been inducements; but as for me, I am tormented with an everlasting itch for things remote. I love to sail forbidden seas, and land on barbarous coasts. Not ignoring what is good, I am quick to perceive a horror, and could still be social with it — would they let me — since it is but well to be on friendly terms with all the inmates of the place one lodges in.

By reason of these things, then, the whaling voyage was welcome; the great floodgates of the wonder-world swung open, and in the wild conceits that swayed me to my purpose, two and two there floated into my inmost soul, endless processions of the whale, and, mid most of them all, one grand hooded phantom, like a snow hill in the air.

(1851)

---

[3]Pythagoras (570 BCE) was a mathematician, philosopher, and founder of the religion of Pythagoreanism that included strict rules for living well, including avoiding eating beans to prevent flatulence (or "winds from astern" as Melville calls them). — Eds.

Exploring the Text

1. How would you describe the tone that the speaker uses to present himself in the first paragraph?
2. Throughout this selection, Herman Melville uses a great deal of figurative language and vivid imagery. Select two examples. How do they contribute to his purpose?
3. Briefly recount Ishmael's three reasons for going to sea. Which one do you find most compelling? Why?
4. How would you describe the speaker's attitude toward life as revealed in paragraphs 9 and 12?
5. How would you characterize the speaker based on his use of language?
6. Melville employs many references to the Bible and to ancient Greek myth and philosophy. How do these allusions contribute to his purpose?
7. Historian Nathaniel Philbrick, author of the 2000 National Book Award–winning book, *In the Heart of the Sea*, which tells the story of the *Essex*, a whaling ship whose adventure inspired Melville's *Moby-Dick*, recounts his experience with Melville's novel as a young man and the son of an English professor. "Even though I hadn't read a word, I grew up hating *Moby-Dick*," he writes. "I resisted until my senior year in high school when my English teacher made it clear that I had no choice. . . . The voice of Ishmael, the novel's narrator, caught me completely by surprise. I had expected to be bored to death, but Ishmael sounded like the best friend I had always hoped to find." Philbrick cites the opening chapter as having hooked him in. Based on your reading of "Loomings," how would you evaluate Philbrick's remarks?
8. Does "Loomings" make you want to read the novel *Moby-Dick*? Why or why not?

Shiloh: A Requiem (April, 1862)

The battle of Shiloh, or Pittsburg Landing, was fought in southwestern Tennessee near the Mississippi border on April 6–7, 1862. It resulted in a Union victory and left 23,000 casualties. At that point, it was the bloodiest battle of the Civil War. The battle site is commemorated as the Shiloh National Military Park. *Shiloh*, "a place of peace," was the ancient capital of Israel before Jerusalem, and it also refers to the Messiah, meaning the "peaceful one."

Skimming lightly, wheeling still,
  The swallows fly low
Over the field in clouded days,
  The forest-field of Shiloh —
Over the field where April rain   5
Solaced the parched ones stretched in pain
Through the pause of night
That followed the Sunday fight

Around the church of Shiloh —
The church so lone, the log-built one,   10
That echoed to many a parting groan
    And natural prayer
Of dying foemen mingled there —
Foemen at morn, but friends at eve —
    Fame or country least their care: 15
(What like a bullet can undeceive!)
    But now they lie low,
While over them the swallows skim,
    And all is hushed at Shiloh.

(1862)

Exploring the Text

1. Note that Herman Melville subtitled this poem "A Requiem." How does that affect your interpretation of it?
2. Identify at least three images that Melville uses to describe the setting. How does the imagery contribute to the tone and mood of the poem? How would you describe the tone and mood?
3. Consider the juxtaposition in line 14: "Foemen at morn, but friends at eve." Look for other juxtapositions in the poem. What do they add to the meaning of the poem as a whole? Are they apt for a poem about war in general? Are they particularly so for this war? Explain.
4. How do you interpret line 16? Why did Melville cast it as a parenthetical statement? Does it ask a rhetorical question? Explain.
5. Listen to the poem as you read it, noting especially the long *o* sounds in "low," "Shiloh," "followed," "lone," and so on, and the onomatopoeia of such words as "groan" and "hushed." How does the assonance affect your reading of the poem? How does it make you feel as you read?
6. Why does the poem begin and end with the swallows? What are the implications of the final line?

 **TALKBACK**

WILLIAM STAFFORD

William Stafford (1914–1993) was born in Kansas and earned his BA and MA at the University of Kansas. He was drafted into the military in 1941, but as a conscientious objector he instead was sent to the Civilian Public Service camps and did work in forestry and soil conservation. He earned his PhD at the University of Iowa in 1954. His first book of poetry, *Traveling Through the Dark* (1962), earned the National Book Award in 1963. In 1970, Stafford was named consultant in poetry to the Library of Congress, a position now known as poet laureate.

At the Un-National Monument along the Canadian Border

"At the Un-National Monument along the Canadian Border" was written in 1975 and included in the 1998 collection *The Way It Is: New and Selected Poems*. It reflects William Stafford's lifelong pacifist beliefs.

This is the field where the battle did not happen,
where the unknown soldier did not die.
This is the field where grass joined hands,
where no monument stands,
and the only heroic thing is the sky.   5

Birds fly here without any sound,
unfolding their wings across the open.
No people killed — or were killed — on this ground
hallowed by neglect and an air so tame
that people celebrate it by forgetting its name.   10

                                                                                    (1975)

Exploring the Text

1. What is the significance of the title of this poem? Why does William Stafford set the poem along the Canadian border?
2. How would you describe the tone of the poem? What details serve to reveal the speaker's attitude?
3. Why is the sky called heroic?
4. What is the effect of the dashes in line 8?
5. This poem presents a basic paradox: a place is being defined by what is not there and what did *not* happen there. How would you describe the paradox of the last line, "that people celebrate it by forgetting its name"?
6. How would you paraphrase the poem as a whole?

Making Connections

1. Compare the imagery presented in the two poems. How are the two poems alike? How are they different? Which of the two poems speaks more powerfully to you? Why?
2. Look carefully at the word *mingled* (l.13) in "Shiloh" (p. 648) and at *joined* (l. 3) in "At the Un-National Monument along the Canadian Border." What is the effect of each? How does each contribute to the poem as a whole? Compare how the two poets use these similar verbs.

3. If they could, how would Stafford and Herman Melville respond to each other's poems? Explain.

4. Imagine seeing the "Un-National Monument" — with the text of Stafford's poem on the memorial plaque — fronting a field across from Antietam, Shiloh, Gettysburg, or another war memorial with which you are familiar. What impressions would it make on visitors? What might be its effect?

5. How does this poem evoke both Melville's "Shiloh" and Abraham Lincoln's "Gettysburg Address" (p. 692)? Do you think the references were conscious? Did Stafford intend his readers to think of those pieces? Explain.

CHIEF SEATTLE

Chief Seattle (c. 1786–1866), or Satala, was born in the Pacific Northwest. He became chief of the Suquamish and Duwamish tribes in what is now Washington State. He converted to Catholicism in the late 1840s. An advocate of peace who promoted trade with the "white man," he became so prominent that the city of Seattle was named for him.

Message to President Franklin Pierce

This selection is Chief Seattle's reply to a treaty offered by Governor Isaac Stevens, commissioner of Indian Affairs. Since the text was delivered orally, there are several versions of it in existence. The version included here is the 1891 copy printed in Frederick James Grant's *History of Seattle, Washington*, which is believed to be the most complete and accurate version still in existence.

Yonder sky has wept tears of compassion on our fathers for centuries untold, and which, to us, looks eternal, may change. To-day it is fair, to-morrow it may be overcast with clouds. My words are like the stars that never set. What Seattle says the great chief, Washington, . . . can rely upon, with as much certainty as our pale-face brothers can rely upon the return of the seasons. The son of the white chief says his father sends us greetings of friendship and good-will. This is kind, for we know he has little need of our friendship in return, because his people are many. They are like the grass that covers the vast prairies, while my people are few, and resemble the scattering trees of a storm-swept plain.

The great, and I presume also good, white chief sends us word that he wants to buy our lands but is willing to allow us to reserve enough to live on comfortably. This indeed appears generous, for the red man no longer has rights that he need respect, and the offer may be wise, also, for we are no longer in need of a great country. There was a time when our people covered the whole land as the waves of a wind-ruffled sea cover its shell-paved floor. But that time has long since passed away with the greatness of tribes almost forgotten. I will not mourn over our untimely decay, nor reproach my pale-face brothers with hastening it, for we, too, may have been somewhat to blame.

When our young men grow angry at some real or imaginary wrong and disfigure their faces with black paint, their hearts, also are disfigured and turn black, and then their cruelty is relentless and knows no bounds, and our old men are not able to restrain them.

But let us hope that hostilities between the red man and his pale-face brothers may never return. We would have everything to lose and nothing to gain.

True it is that revenge, with our young braves, is considered gain, even at the cost   5
of their own lives, but old men who stay at home in times of war, and old women who have sons to lose, know better.

Our great father Washington, for I presume he is now our father as well as yours, since George has moved his boundaries to the north, our great and good father, I say, sends us word by his son, who, no doubt, is a great chief among his people, that if we do as he desires, he will protect us. His brave armies will be to us a bristling wall of strength, and his great ships of war will fill our harbors so that our ancient enemies far to the northward, the Simsiams and Hydas, will no longer frighten our women and old men. Then he will be our father and we will be his children. But can this ever be? Your God loves your people and hates mine; he folds his strong arms lovingly around the white man and leads him as a father leads his infant son, but he has forsaken his red children; he makes your people wax strong every day, and soon they will fill the land; while our people are ebbing away like a fast-receding tide, that will never flow again. The white man's God cannot love his red children or he would protect them. They seem to be orphans and can look nowhere for help. How then can we become brothers? How can your father become our father and bring us prosperity and awaken in us dreams of returning greatness?

Your God seems to us to be partial. He came to the white man. We never saw Him; never even heard His voice; He gave the white man laws but He had no word for His red children whose teeming millions filled this vast continent as the stars fill the firmament. No, we are two distinct races and must ever remain so. There is little in common between us. The ashes of our ancestors are sacred and their final resting place is hallowed ground, while you wander away from the tombs of your fathers seemingly without regret.

Your religion was written on tables of stone by the iron finger of an angry God, lest you might forget it. The red man could never remember nor comprehend it.

Our religion is the traditions of our ancestors, the dreams of our old men, given them by the great Spirit, and the visions of our sachems, and is written in the hearts of our people.

Your dead cease to love you and the homes of their nativity as soon as they pass   10
the portals of the tomb. They wander far off beyond the stars, are soon forgotten and

never return. Our dead never forget the beautiful world that gave them being. They still love its winding rivers, its great mountains and its sequestered vales, and they ever yearn in tenderest affection over the lonely hearted living and often return to visit and comfort them.

Day and night cannot dwell together. The red man has ever fled the approach of the white man, as the changing mists on the mountain side flee before the blazing morning sun.

However, your proposition seems a just one, and I think my folks will accept it and will retire to the reservation you offer them, and we will dwell apart and in peace, for the words of the great white chief seem to be the voice of nature speaking to my people out of the thick darkness that is fast gathering around them like a dense fog floating inward from a midnight sea.

It matters but little where we pass the remainder of our days. They are not many. The Indian's night promises to be dark. No bright star hovers about the horizon. Sad-voiced winds moan in the distance. Some grim Nemesis of our race is on the red man's trail, and wherever he goes he will still hear the sure approaching footsteps of the fell destroyer and prepare to meet his doom, as does the wounded doe that hears the approaching footsteps of the hunter. A few more moons, a few more winters and not one of all the mighty hosts that once filled this broad land or that now roam in fragmentary bands through these vast solitudes will remain to weep over the tombs of a people once as powerful and as hopeful as your own.

But why should we repine? Why should I murmur at the fate of my people? Tribes are made up of individuals and are no better than they. Men come and go like the waves of the sea. A tear, a tamanamus, a dirge, and they are gone from our long-ing eyes forever. Even the white man, whose God walked and talked with him, as friend to friend, is not exempt from the common destiny. We *may* be brothers after all. We shall see.

We will ponder your proposition, and when we have decided we will tell you. But should we accept it, I here and now make this the first condition: That we will not be denied the privilege, without molestation, of visiting at will the graves of our ances-tors and friends. Every part of this country is sacred to my people. Every hillside, every valley, every plain and grove has been hallowed by some fond memory or some sad experience of my tribe. Even the rocks that seem to lie dumb as they swelter in the sun along the silent seashore in solemn grandeur thrill with memories of past events connected with the fate of my people, and the very dust under your feet responds more lovingly to our footsteps than to yours, because it is the ashes of our ancestors, and our bare feet are conscious of the sympathetic touch, for the soil is rich with the life of our kindred. 15

The sable braves, and fond mothers, and glad-hearted maidens, and the little children who lived and rejoiced here, and whose very names are now forgotten, still love these solitudes, and their deep fastnesses at eventide grow shadowy with the presence of dusky spirits. And when the last red man shall have perished from the earth and his memory among white men shall have become a myth, these shores shall swarm with the invisible dead of my tribe, and when your children's children shall think themselves alone in the field, the store, the shop, upon the highway or in the silence of the woods they will not be alone. In all the earth there is no place dedicated to solitude. At night, when the streets of your cities and villages shall be silent, and you think them deserted, they will throng with the returning hosts that once filled and still love this beautiful land. The white man will never be alone. Let him be just and deal kindly with my people, for the dead are not altogether power-less.

(1854)

Exploring the Text

1. According to Chief Seattle, what are several differences between the "white man" and the "red man"?
2. If the message included here is a reply to a treaty offered by Governor Isaac Stevens, commissioner of Indian Affairs, why do you think Chief Seattle writes not to Stevens but to President Pierce? What does this suggest about the impor-tance of audience?
3. How might President Pierce respond, if he were to do so?
4. The speech included here is one of many versions. Many are apocryphal, and this one might be inauthentic in part. Read a few versions on the Internet. Which one do you think might be closest to what Seattle actually said? Explain.
5. How does Seattle's admonition of the white man speak to us in the twenty-first century? Is it still valid? Explain why or why not.

TALKBACK

Dr. Rayna Green

Rayna Green (b. 1942), a scholar, a poet, and an essayist of German and Cherokee descent, is associated with the Smithsonian Institution's National Museum of American History in Washington, D.C. Though Green was born in Dallas, Texas, and raised mainly by her mother's family, who are descendants of German settlers, she was deeply influenced by her father's Native American heritage and the Cherokee music and cultural traditions her paternal grandmother taught her at a young age. Green received a PhD in American studies from Indiana University in 1973. She has taught English, the social sciences, American studies, and Native American studies at many institutions, including the University of Arkansas, the University of Maryland, Yale University, George Washington University, and Dartmouth College. She has published many articles and poems about Native American culture and history, and she has served as an advocate for the improve-ment of tribal health, education, and development for the Cherokee Nation of Oklahoma.

from *A Modest Proposal*
The Museum of the Plains White Person

Rayna Green delivered the following "after feast speech" before hundreds of native women at a 1981 conference on educational equity in Tahlequah, Oklahoma, nine years before President George Herbert Walker Bush signed legislation protecting Indian grave sites on federal lands.

The thing I'm most excited about recently is the grand project. This is a multimillion-dollar project, it's been funded by all the major foundations in the country. It's very exciting. As you know, all over the country, the Cherokee Nation and many of the Indian nations all over the country have established their own museums. I've done a great deal of museum consulting for the National Endowment and for the tribal museums, for the Indian Museum Association. But I had found a real lack of a particular kind of museum that I really feel we need. And this is going to be a major cultural institution. I want to tell you about it because I am so thrilled to be part of this. This idea, I have to give credit, was originally hatched up by the ex-chairman of the Winnebago Tribe, Louis LaRose, and myself, late one night in a serious scholarly discussion in Albuquerque. Basically what we want to develop is a unique, cultural institution. I know you will be thrilled. This is an institution that is meant for Indian people. It is something we've been needing for a long time. It's something that is particularly needed to meet a very special critical need. The museum is called THE MUSEUM OF THE PLAINS WHITE PERSON. It meets this critical need that I spoke of. It's very serious. You see, we began to be very worried. As you know their (White people's) culture is dying out. Very soon, very soon there will be very few surviving White persons. We worry about this. What will the last surviving White persons do when they have no one to ask what their language was like, what their customs and clothes were like. So, we began to worry about this and we came up with the idea of the MUSEUM OF THE PLAINS WHITE PERSON. As I said, it's been met with great reception all over the country. Foundations have rushed to pour money in. Indian people have given money for it. I can't tell you how many shawl and blanket raffles have gone on to pay for this museum. And I want to tell you something about the museum and perhaps this will inspire some of you to go to those few White people that you know are living out there and quickly acquire artifacts from them before they disappear. Because, you know, they don't know how to take care of them. We worry about this. It's quite serious.

The first big collection that we are working on, and this is really inspiring, is the bone collection. As you know, all museums have to have a bone collection. We have begun a national campaign to acquire the bones of famous White people. We want little Indian children to be able to come in and study these and Indian scholars want to pore over them, the different skull shapes and so forth. And, of course, when we do acquire them we will acquire them permanently. As you know, they cannot be given back once they have been handled. We do need to study them for years. And so we are acquiring these. We have just acquired, I think, what is a quite moving find. One of the most important ones. We have just acquired the bones of John Wayne. As you realize what great significance this can have for the scholars, what a study of his bones will tell us about these people and what their lives were like. Well, so that's very important.

There are a number of other famous bones that we want to acquire and I am sure you can begin to guess whose we have our sights on. It's going to be thrilling. The collection will be quite large, of course. We have planned to make the collection as large as it needs to be with as many samples. So, we are going to begin a massive grave excavation all over the country. We have, through our legal offices, which have become very sophisticated, as you know, acquired clear title to at least eighty percent of all the graves in White cemeteries all over the country. We plan to move in with steam shovels right away. We've acquired Mr. Peabody's big coal shovel which did strip mining up at Northern Cheyenne in order to begin and it's going to be an amazing project.

I'll tell you a few things about some of the other collections that I think are quite exciting. We are going to have collections of their food, for example — their food ways. We are going to reconstruct a McDonald's in its entirety. In that we're going to have true-to-life plastic exhibits of white bread, mayonnaise, iceberg lettuce and peanut butter which will be everywhere — smeared all over everything. Primarily stuck to the roof of everyone's mouth. We are going to have several exhibits about their customs. We want to have some performing arts there and we have found the last of a number of White people who know their dances and songs and who have preserved these intact and we are going to have everyday, living exhibits of the two-step, the fox-trot, the disco and other dances. This is going to be very exciting when children come to visit, particularly.

We have acquired exhibits of their costumes. In fact, in the condominium   5 that we are going to reconstruct in its entirety, inside the museum, there will be a typical little family with the gentleman in the three-piece suit and a briefcase and all the other artifacts of their civilization.

We have found one very unusual thing that I do want to tell you about. It's an archaeological remain that we have found somewhat in the vicinity of what used to be called "Los Angeles." It's very interesting. It proves that their culture was very flighty. They seemed to change rulers quite regularly. It's kind of interesting. In fact, we found an archaeological artifact that indicates that they changed rulers regularly. It's a big thing they used to call a neon sign — and it says QUEEN FOR A DAY.[1] We are going to do some more excavation to determine just how they did depose their rulers and how they transferred power.

---

[1] "Queen for a Day" was the name of a radio and television game show that ran in the 1950s and 1960s. — Eds.

Well, I think you'll agree that this is one of the most exciting things that Indian people have done — one of the most exciting contributions that we could make. As young Indian scholars we are deeply pleased to be able to make this.

(1981)

Exploring the Text

1. Rayna Green is director of the American Indian Program at the Smithsonian Institution's National Museum of American History in Washington, D.C. How does knowing that affect your reading of her proposal?
2. How would you describe Green's tone at the beginning of the piece?
3. How does Green use "shawl and blanket raffles" (par. 1) to satirize white culture?
4. Which artifacts in the proposed museum does Green use to criticize actual Indian museums? Explain.
5. Are you amused by Green's proposal? Offended? Explain.
6. Take note of Green's audience. What might have been their likely response? How might the response differ, if at all, if the address were delivered to a "white persons" audience? Explain.

Making Connections

1. What are some instances of irony that you see in both texts? How do the texts differ in their use of irony?
2. It might be said that Chief Seattle and Green have similar purposes in their texts. In what ways are they similar? How do they differ?
3. How would you compare and contrast the pieces in terms of the tones that the speakers use?
4. How would you compare the two texts in terms of the ways they address the wide gulf between whites and Native Americans?
5. Imagine that people — both Native Americans and whites — from 1855 could witness what has happened between the groups since then. How would they respond to Green's piece? How do you think Chief Seattle might respond if he were in Green's 1981 audience?
6. In Alexis de Tocqueville's 1835 book, *Democracy in America*, he states:

   > Before the arrival of the white men in the new world, the inhabitants of North America lived quietly in their woods, enduring the vicissitudes and practicing the virtues and vices common to savage nations. The Europeans having dispersed the Indian tribes and driven them into the deserts, condemned them to a wandering life, full of inexpressible sufferings.

   How would Chief Seattle respond to that statement? How would Green? How do you?

WALT WHITMAN

Walt Whitman (1819–1892) was born on Long Island, New York. Early in his life, he worked as a country schoolteacher and printer and served as writer and editor for the *Brooklyn Eagle* newspaper. He continued in a variety of jobs, writing and working as a carpenter, and published his now famous *Leaves of Grass* in 1855. Whitman would continue to revise and add to *Leaves of Grass* until his death. Regarded as offensive and vulgar at the time for its outspoken sexual content, the poems celebrated individuality and the richness of life. In 1862, Whitman went to Virginia to find his brother George, who had been wounded in the Civil War. He was shocked to witness the horrors of war firsthand and was deeply moved by the suffering of the wounded. He worked as an aide in army hospitals in Washington, caring first for his brother and then for other soldiers as well. Among Whitman's most well-known poems from this time are "O Captain! My Captain!" (p. 659) and "When Lilacs Last in the Dooryard Bloom'd," both about Abraham Lincoln

There Was a Child Went Forth

This poem was published without a title in the first edition of *Leaves of Grass* (1855). Later it became known as "Poem of the Child That Went Forth, and Always Goes Forth, Forever and Forever," and finally as "There Was a Child Went Forth."

There was a child went forth every day,
And the first object he looked upon and received with wonder or pity or love or dread, that object he became,
And that object became part of him for the day or a certain part of the day . . . . or for many years or stretching cycles of years.

The early lilacs became part of this child,
And grass, and white and red morningglories, and white and red clover, and the song   5
of the phœbe-bird,
And the March-born lambs, and the sow's pink-faint litter, and the mare's foal, and the cow's calf, and the noisy brood of the barnyard or by the mire of the pond-side . . and the fish suspending themselves so curiously below there . . and the beautiful curious liquid . . and the water-plants with their graceful flat heads . . all became part of him.

And the field-sprouts of April and May became part of him . . . . wintergrain sprouts, and those of the light-yellow corn, and of the esculent roots of the garden,
And the appletrees covered with blossoms, and the fruit afterward . . . . and wood-berries . . and the commonest weeds by the road;
And the old drunkard staggering home from the outhouse of the tavern whence he had lately risen,

And the schoolmistress that passed on her way to the school . . and the friendly boys   10
    that passed . . and the quarrelsome boys . . and the tidy and freshcheeked girls . .
    and the barefoot negro boy and girl,
And all the changes of city and country wherever he went.

His own parents . . he that had propelled the fatherstuff at night, and fathered him . .
    and she that conceived him in her womb and birthed him . . . . they gave this child
    more of themselves than that,
They gave him afterward every day . . . . they and of them became part of him.

The mother at home quietly placing the dishes on the suppertable,
The mother with mild words . . . . clean her cap and gown . . . . a wholesome odor   15
    falling off her person and clothes as she walks by:
The father, strong, selfsufficient, manly, mean, angered, unjust,
The blow, the quick loud word, the tight bargain, the crafty lure,
The family usages, the language, the company, the furniture . . . . the yearning and
    swelling heart,
Affection that will not be gainsayed . . . . The sense of what is real . . . . the thought if
    after all it should prove unreal,
The doubts of daytime and the doubts of nighttime . . . the curious whether and   20
    how,
Whether that which appears so is so . . . . Or is it all flashes and specks?
Men and women crowding fast in the streets . . if they are not flashes and specks what
    are they?
The streets themselves, and the facades of houses . . . . the goods in the windows,
Vehicles . . teams . . the tiered wharves, and the huge crossing at the ferries;
The village on the highland seen from afar at sunset . . . . the river between,   25
Shadows . . aureola and mist . . light falling on roofs and gables of white or brown,
    three miles off,
The schooner near by sleepily dropping down the tide . . the little boat slacktowed
    astern,
The hurrying tumbling waves and quickbroken crests and slapping;
The strata of colored clouds . . . . the long bar of maroontint away solitary by it-
    self . . . . the spread of purity it lies motionless in,
The horizon's edge, the flying seacrow, the fragrance of saltmarsh and shoremud;   30
These became part of that child who went forth every day, and who now goes and will
    always go forth every day,
And these become of him or her that peruses them now.

(1855)

Exploring the Text

1. What does Walt Whitman mean by "that object he became, / And that object
became part of him" (ll. 2–3)?

2. What does the word *there* do in line 6? How does it affect the image Whitman creates?

3. Note how particular the images are in the second and third stanzas of the poem. Select three that appeal to you. How does their vivid quality contribute to the poem's meanings? What do they reveal about the speaker?

4. What is the nature of the shift in line 9? What does it suggest about the objects that the boy sees and becomes?

5. What is the effect of the parallelism in the poem?

6. Which of the poet's observations resonate with your own experience? Explain why they might be significant.

7. How does Whitman make the personal experience of the child become universal?

8. What implications does the poem have for education and for the ways that we teach and learn?

9. Whitman writes, "The horizon's edge, the flying seacrow, the fragrance of salt-marsh and shoremud" (l. 30). How does he use sensory imagery to link the near and the far off?

10. To whom does "him or her" refer in the final line? What are the implications of the final two lines?

11. Find the 1871 version of this poem online or at the library and read it. Analyze the probable reasons for the revisions in the final form. Which version do you prefer? Why?

O Captain! My Captain!

Inspired by Abraham Lincoln and occasioned by his assassination, this poem was published in New York's *Saturday Press* in November of 1865. It was widely reprinted and became Whitman's most popular poem.

O Captain! my Captain! our fearful trip is done,
The ship has weather'd every rack, the prize we sought is won,
The port is near, the bells I hear, the people all exulting,
While follow eyes the steady keel, the vessel grim and daring:
    But O heart! heart! heart!   5
      O the bleeding drops of red,
        Where on the deck my Captain lies,
        Fallen cold and dead.

O Captain! my Captain! rise up and hear the bells;
Rise up — for you the flag is flung — for you the bugle trills,   10
For you bouquets and ribbon'd wreaths — for you the shores
    a-crowding,
For you they call, the swaying mass, their eager faces turning;

Here Captain! dear father!
  This arm beneath your head!
    It is some dream that on the deck,   15
    You've fallen cold and dead.

My Captain does not answer, his lips are pale and still,
My father does not feel my arm, he has no pulse nor will,
The ship is anchor'd safe and sound, its voyage closed and done,
From fearful trip the victor ship comes in with object won;   20
  Exult O shores, and ring O bells!
    But I with mournful tread,
      Walk the deck my Captain lies,
        Fallen cold and dead.

(1865)

Exploring the Text

1. What is the extended metaphor that runs throughout the poem? Explain how it operates in the poem. What is its rhetorical effect?
2. How do contrasting images of achievement and success, on the one hand, and images suggesting loss, on the other, contribute to the effect of the poem?
3. What is the tone of the poem? What is the speaker's attitude toward his subject? Explain.
4. In *American Literature: The Makers and the Making* (1973), Cleanth Brooks, R. W. B. Lewis, and Robert Penn Warren discuss how scholars, critics, and poets have esteemed Walt Whitman's work and state, "But as a poet, for most readers and over too long a period of time, Whitman was chiefly known as the author of 'O Captain! My Captain!' the worst and least characteristic poem he ever wrote." Do you see the poem as they do? Might there have been good reason for Whitman to use a simple and popular form for this poem? Support, qualify, or refute the position taken by these scholars. Use analysis of this poem and others by Whitman as evidence.

Crossing Brooklyn Ferry

This poem first appeared as "Sun-Down Poem" in the second edition of *Leaves of Grass* (1856). Walt Whitman gave it its present title in 1860 and revised it repeatedly. The version included here is the final one, from the "Death Bed" edition of January 1892, two months before Whitman's death. Henry David Thoreau named this poem along with *Song of Myself* as his favorite poems by Whitman.

1

Flood-tide below me! I see you face to face!
Clouds of the west — sun there half an hour high — I see you also face
    to face.
Crowds of men and women attired in the usual costumes, how curious
    you are to me!
On the ferry-boats the hundreds and hundreds that cross, returning
    home, are more curious to me than you suppose,
And you that shall cross from shore to shore years hence are more to   5
    me, and more in my meditations, than you might suppose.

2

The impalpable sustenance of me from all things at all hours of the day,
The simple, compact, well-join'd scheme, myself disintegrated, every one
    disintegrated yet part of the scheme,
The similitudes of the past and those of the future,
The glories strung like beads on my smallest sights and hearings, on the
    walk in the street and the passage over the river,
The current rushing so swiftly and swimming with me far away,   10
The others that are to follow me, the ties between me and them,
The certainty of others, the life, love, sight, hearing of others.

Others will enter the gates of the ferry and cross from shore to shore,
Others will watch the run of the flood-tide,
Others will see the shipping of Manhattan north and west, and the heights   15
    of Brooklyn to the south and east,
Others will see the islands large and small;
Fifty years hence, others will see them as they cross, the sun half an hour
    high,
A hundred years hence, or ever so many hundred years hence, others will
    see them,
Will enjoy the sunset, the pouring-in of the flood-tide, the falling-back to
    the sea of the ebb-tide.

3

It avails not, time nor place — distance avails not,   20
I am with you, you men and women of a generation, or ever so many
    generations hence,
Just as you feel when you look on the river and sky, so I felt,
Just as any of you is one of a living crowd, I was one of a crowd,

Just as you are refresh'd by the gladness of the river and the bright flow,
    I was refresh'd,
Just as you stand and lean on the rail, yet hurry with the swift current,   25
    I stood yet was hurried,
Just as you look on the numberless masts of ships and the thick-stemm'd
    pipes of steamboats, I look'd.

I too many and many a time cross'd the river of old,
Watched the Twelfth-month sea-gulls, saw them high in the air floating
    with motionless wings, oscillating their bodies,
Saw how the glistening yellow lit up parts of their bodies and left the rest
    in strong shadow,
Saw the slow-wheeling circles and the gradual edging toward the south,   30
Saw the reflection of the summer sky in the water,
Had my eyes dazzled by the shimmering track of beams,
Look'd at the fine centrifugal spokes of light round the shape of my head in
    the sunlit water,
Look'd on the haze on the hills southward and south-westward,
Look'd on the vapor as it flew in fleeces tinged with violet,   35
Look'd toward the lower bay to notice the vessels arriving,
Saw their approach, saw aboard those that were near me,
Saw the white sails of schooners and sloops, saw the ships at anchor,
The sailors at work in the rigging or out astride the spars,
The round masts, the swinging motion of the hulls, the slender serpentine   40
    pennants,
The large and small steamers in motion, the pilots in their pilot-houses,
The white wake left by the passage, the quick tremulous whirl of the wheels,
The flags of all nations, the falling of them at sunset,
The scallop-edged waves in the twilight, the ladled cups, the frolicsome crests
    and glistening,
The stretch afar growing dimmer and dimmer, the gray walls of the granite   45
    storehouses by the docks,
On the river the shadowy group, the big steam-tug closely flank'd on each
    side by the barges, the hay-boat, the belated lighter,
On the neighboring shore the fires from the foundry chimneys burning
    high and glaringly into the night,
Casting their flicker of black contrasted with wild red and yellow light over
    the tops of houses, and down into the clefts of streets.

4

These and all else were to me the same as they are to you,
I loved well those cities, loved well the stately and rapid river,   50
The men and women I saw were all near to me,

Others the same — others who look back on me because I look'd forward to them,
(The time will come, though I stop here to-day and to-night.)

5

What is it then between us?
What is the count of the scores or hundreds of years between us?   55

Whatever it is, it avails not — distance avails not, and place avails not,
I too lived, Brooklyn of ample hills was mine,
I too walk'd the streets of Manhattan island, and bathed in the waters
    around it,
I too felt the curious abrupt questionings stir within me,
In the day among crowds of people sometimes they came upon me,   60
In my walks home late at night or as I lay in my bed they came upon me,
I too had been struck from the float forever held in solution,
I too had receiv'd identity by my body,
That I was I knew was of my body, and what I should be I knew
    I should be of my body.

6

It is not upon you alone the dark patches fall,   65
The dark threw its patches down upon me also,
The best I had done seem'd to me blank and suspicious,
My great thoughts as I supposed them, were they not in reality meagre?
Nor is it you alone who know what it is to be evil,
I am he who knew what it was to be evil,   70
I too knitted the old knot of contrariety,
Blabb'd, blush'd, resented, lied, stole, grudg'd,
Had guile, anger, lust, hot wishes I dared not speak,
Was wayward, vain, greedy, shallow, sly, cowardly, malignant,
The wolf, the snake, the hog, not wanting in me,   75
The cheating look, the frivolous word, the adulterous wish, not wanting,
Refusals, hates, postponements, meanness, laziness, none of these wanting,
Was one with the rest, the days and haps of the rest,
Was call'd by my nighest name by clear loud voices of young men as they
    saw me approaching or passing,
Felt their arms on my neck as I stood, or the negligent leaning of their flesh   80
    against me as I sat,
Saw many I loved in the street or ferry-boat or public assembly, yet never told
    them a word,
Lived the same life with the rest, the same old laughing, gnawing, sleeping,
Play'd the part that still looks back on the actor or actress,

The same old role, the role that is what we make it, as great as we like,
Or as small as we like, or both great and small.   85

7

Closer yet I approach you,
What thought you have of me now, I had as much of you — I laid in my stores
    in advance,
I consider'd long and seriously of you before you were born.

Who was to know what should come home to me?
Who knows but I am enjoying this?   90
Who knows, for all the distance, but I am as good as looking at you now, for all you
    cannot see me?

8

Ah, what can ever be more stately and admirable to me than mast-hemm'd
    Manhattan?
River and sunset and scallop-edg'd waves of flood-tide?
The sea-gulls oscillating their bodies, the hay-boat in the twilight, and the
    belated lighter?
What gods can exceed these that clasp me by the hand, and with voices I love   95
    call me promptly and loudly by my nighest name as I approach?
What is more subtle than this which ties me to the woman or man that looks
    in my face?
Which fuses me into you now, and pours my meaning into you?

We understand then do we not?
What I promis'd without mentioning it, have you not accepted?
What the study could not teach — what the preaching could not accomplish is   100
    accomplish'd, is it not?

9

Flow on, river! flow with the flood-tide, and ebb with the ebb-tide!
Frolic on, crested and scallop-edg'd waves!
Gorgeous clouds of the sunset! drench with your splendor me, or the men and
    women generations after me!
Cross from shore to shore, countless crowds of passengers!
Stand up, tall masts of Mannahatta! stand up, beautiful hills of Brooklyn!   105
Throb, baffled and curious brain! throw out questions and answers!
Suspend here and everywhere, eternal float of solution!
Gaze, loving and thirsting eyes, in the house or street or public assembly!
Sound out, voices of young men! loudly and musically call me by my nighest name!

Live, old life! play the part that looks back on the actor or actress! 110
Play the old role, the role that is great or small according as one makes it!
Consider, you who peruse me, whether I may not in unknown ways be looking
    upon you;
Be firm, rail over the river, to support those who lean idly, yet haste with the
    hasting current;
Fly on, sea-birds! fly sideways, or wheel in large circles high in the air;
Receive the summer sky, you water, and faithfully hold it till all downcast eyes 115
    have time to take it from you!
Diverge, fine spokes of light, from the shape of my head, or any one's head,
    in the sunlit water!
Come on, ships from the lower bay! pass up or down, white-sail'd schooners,
    sloops, lighters!
Flaunt away, flags of all nations! be duly lower'd at sunset!
Burn high your fires, foundry chimneys! cast black shadows at nightfall! cast
    red and yellow light over the tops of the houses!
Appearances, now or henceforth, indicate what you are, 120
You necessary film, continue to envelop the soul,
About my body for me, and your body for you, be hung out divinest aromas,
Thrive, cities — bring your freight, bring your shows, ample and sufficient rivers,
Expand, being than which none else is perhaps more spiritual,
Keep your places, objects than which none else is more lasting. 125

You have waited, you always wait, you dumb, beautiful ministers,
We receive you with free sense at last, and are insatiate henceforward.
Not you any more shall be able to foil us, or withhold yourselves from us,
We use you, and do not cast you aside — we plant you permanently within us,
We fathom you not — we love you — there is perfection in you also, 130
You furnish your parts toward eternity,
Great or small, you furnish your parts toward the soul.

(1856, 1892)

Exploring the Text

1. In Part 1 of the poem, what does the speaker report that he sees? What does he think about?
2. What ironies does the poet develop in Part 2?
3. In Part 3, the speaker addresses the reader directly: "Just as you feel when you look on the river and sky, so I felt" (l. 22). What is different about the direct address here as opposed to other examples with which you are famliar? What is the poet's purpose?
4. Walt Whitman presents a catalogue of metaphoric images of objects both natural and man-made. Part 3, especially, asks the reader to *see*. Through which of these visions in Part 3 do you recognize your own experience?

5. Part 4 begins: "These and all else were to me the same as they are to you" (l. 49). Perhaps the expected order would be the reverse: these are the same to you as they were to me. Why does Whitman write the line as he does? How does the meaning differ?

6. What might be some of the "abrupt questionings" that stir in Part 5? What does he mean by, "I too had been struck from the float forever held in solution" (l. 62)? What does the speaker anticipate as he moves into Part 6? What does he confess? What effects do these strategies have on the reader?

7. What purpose do the questions serve in Parts 7 and 8?

8. Notice that Part 9 shifts to the imperative mood. What is its effect on meaning and tone? How would you describe the tone of lines 101–125?

9. Who are the "dumb, beautiful ministers" (l. 126)? What is the poet's attitude toward them?

10. In this poem, Whitman develops a series of contrasts: between the reader and the speaker; Brooklyn and Manhattan; river and shore; great and small; natural and man-made; light and dark; past and future; life and death; unity and separation; ebb and flood; and so on. How do these contrasts contribute to the poem as a whole? Choose two or three to discuss in your response.

11. What is the speaker's attitude toward the future? Explain.

12. What does Whitman suggest about the power of the poem itself? Consider carefully what he writes at the end of Parts 5 and 8.

↻ TALKBACK

ALLEN GINSBERG

Allen Ginsberg (1926–1997) was born in Newark, New Jersey. As a teenager, he began to read Walt Whitman, who, along with William Carlos Williams (p. 1106) and English and Romantic poet William Blake, exerted an enormous influence on his writing. Ginsberg went to Columbia University on a scholarship to study law but changed his major to English. He became a major voice in the Beat movement, which included poets Gregory Corso and Lawrence Ferlinghetti and novelists William S. Burroughs and Jack Kerouac, author of *On the Road* (1957). Ginsberg led a varied, unconventional life: he worked as a dishwasher, welder, and university professor; he was arrested several times for participating in political protests; he spent time in a psychiatric institution; and he toured with Bob Dylan's band. Ginsberg's work is notable for its free expression and rejection of conformity and materialism. *Howl* (1955) created intense interest and controversy for both its style and its content. In 1957, the poem's publisher was charged with obscenity; however, the case was thrown out when the presiding judge ruled that *Howl* was of "redeeming social consequence." Ginsberg's other works include *Kaddish and Other Poems* (1961), which many regard as his finest collection, and the mixed-genre volume *The Fall of America*, which won a National Book Award in 1973.

A Supermarket in California

This poem is from Ginsberg's collection *Howl and Other Poems* (1956). Written in 1955, it was intended as a celebration of the centennial anniversary of *Leaves of Grass*. It is considered one of the major expressions of the "Beat Generation."

What thoughts I have of you tonight, Walt Whitman, for I walked down the side-streets under the trees with a headache self-conscious looking at the full moon.

In my hungry fatigue, and shopping for images, I went into the neon fruit supermarket, dreaming of your enumerations!

What peaches and what penumbras! Whole families shopping at night! Aisles full of husbands! Wives in the avocados, babies in the tomatoes! — and you, García Lorca, what were you doing down by the watermelons?

I saw you, Walt Whitman, childless, lonely old grubber, poking among the meats in the refrigerator and eyeing the grocery boys.

I heard you asking questions of each: Who killed the pork chops? What   5
price bananas? Are you my Angel?

I wandered in and out of the brilliant stacks of cans following you, and followed in my imagination by the store detective.

We strode down the open corridors together in our solitary fancy tasting artichokes, possessing every frozen delicacy, and never passing the cashier.

Where are we going, Walt Whitman? The doors close in an hour. Which way does your beard point tonight?

(I touch your book and dream of our odyssey in the supermarket and feel absurd.)

Will we walk all night through solitary streets? The trees add shade to shade,   10
lights out in the houses, we'll both be lonely.

Will we stroll dreaming of the lost America of love past blue automobiles in driveways, home to our silent cottage?

Ah, dear father, graybeard, lonely old courage-teacher, what America did you have when Charon quit poling his ferry and you got out on a smoking bank and stood watching the boat disappear on the black waters of Lethe?[1]

(1955)

Exploring the Text

1. In the first section of the poem, we find a variety of images — for example, the "sidestreets" under the "full moon," the "neon fruit supermarket," and "[w]hat peaches and what penumbras." What is the effect of these images? What do they suggest thematically?

---

[1]In Greek mythology, Charon was the ferryman who would take the dead across the River Styx to Hades. Lethe, also in Hades, is the river of oblivion or forgetfulness. — Eds.

2. How does Allen Ginsberg describe the supermarket? Why is García Lorca there?
3. What makes the speaker think of Walt Whitman? Why would Whitman ask the questions in line 5? What is the speaker suggesting by these questions?
4. How would you describe Whitman as he is characterized in the poem?
5. Why would the speaker imagine being followed "by the store detective" (l. 6)?
6. What does the speaker suggest is "lost" about America? What do the references to Hades suggest about the meaning of the poem? How does Ginsberg's tone at the end of the poem contribute to that meaning?

Making Connections

1. Walking plays a major role in both "A Supermarket in California" and "Crossing Brooklyn Ferry." What is the purpose and importance of walking in each of these poems? Explain.
2. Each of these two poems presents a vision from a first-person point of view — one looking forward, the other back — directly addressing the audience as "you." Compare and contrast the perspectives of the two poems.
3. What do both Whitman and Ginsberg suggest about the value and power of poetic vision? Do you agree? Why or why not? Is there another poet or poem that provides such value to you? Explain.
4. In *Studies in Classic American Literature*, D. H. Lawrence (p. 1262) writes, "Whitman is a very great poet, of the end of life. A very great post-mortem poet, of the transitions of the soul as it loses its integrity. The poet of the soul's last shout and shriek, on the confines of death." Lawrence's remark might also be applicable to Ginsberg. How would you compare and contrast Ginsberg's poem with "Crossing Brooklyn Ferry" regarding their attitudes toward mortality?
5. Imagine that Whitman could reply to Ginsberg's poem. What would he say? Explain.

JEFFERSON DAVIS

Jefferson Davis (1808–1889) was an American statesman and president of the Confederate States of America during the Civil War, from 1861 to 1865. Davis was raised in Kentucky and graduated from the United States Military Academy (West Point) in 1828. After fighting in the Mexican-American War, Davis represented the state of Mississippi as a Democratic U.S. senator. In 1853, President Franklin Pierce named Davis secretary of war, and when Pierce failed to win reelection in 1857, Davis returned to his position as a senator for Mississippi. He resigned from the Senate in 1861, and in the same year he was elected to a six-year term as the provisional president of the Confederate States of America. The Union army captured Davis in 1865, signaling the defeat of the Confederacy and the end of the Civil War. Davis was charged with, but never tried for, treason.

Inaugural Address

Jefferson Davis was inaugurated as provisional president of the Confederate States of America on February 18, 1861, in the Confederacy's first capital, Montgomery, Alabama. In his inaugural address, Davis appeals to the ideals of the Founding Fathers and the American Revolution against tyranny.

Gentlemen of the Congress of the Confederate States of America:

Called to the difficult and responsible station of Executive Chief of the Provisional Government which you have instituted, I approach the discharge of the duties assigned me with an humble distrust of my abilities, but with a sustaining confidence in the wisdom of those who are to aid and guide me in the administration of public affairs, and an abiding faith in the patriotism and virtue of the people. Looking forward to the speedy establishment of a provisional government to take the place of the present one, and which, by its great moral and physical powers, will be better able to contend with the difficulties which arise from the conflicting incidents of separate nations, I enter upon the duties of the office for which I have been chosen with the hope that the beginning of our career as a Confederacy may not be obstructed by hostile opposition to the enjoyment of that separate and independent existence which we have asserted, and which, with the blessing of Providence, we intend to maintain.

Our present position has been achieved in a manner unprecedented in the history of nations. It illustrates the American idea that government rests upon the consent of the governed, and that it is the right of the people to alter or abolish a government whenever it becomes destructive of the ends for which it was established. The declared purposes of the compact of Union from which we have withdrawn were to establish justice, insure domestic tranquillity, to provide for the common defence, to promote the general welfare, and to secure the blessings of liberty for ourselves and our posterity; and when in the judgment of the sovereign States now comprising this Confederacy it had been perverted from the purposes for which it was ordained, and had ceased to answer the ends for which it was established, an appeal to the ballot box declared that so far as they were concerned the government created by that compact should cease to exist. In this they merely asserted a right which the Declaration of Independence of 1776 defined to be inalienable. Of the time and occasion for its exercise, they, as sovereign, were the final judges each for itself. The impartial and enlightened verdict of mankind will vindicate the rectitude of our conduct, and He who knows the hearts of men will judge the sincerity with which we have labored to preserve the government of our fathers, in its spirit and in those rights inherent in it, which were solemnly proclaimed at the birth of the States, and which have been affirmed and reaffirmed in the Bills of Rights of the several States. When they entered into the Union of 1789, it was with the undeniable recognition of the power of the people to resume the authority delegated for the purposes of that government whenever, in their opinion, its functions were perverted and its ends defeated. By virtue of this authority, the time and occasion requiring them to exercise it having arrived, the sovereign States here represented have seceded from that Union, and it is a gross abuse of language to denominate the act rebellion or revolution. They have formed a new alliance, but in each State its government has remained as before. The rights of person and property have not been disturbed. The agency through which they have communicated with foreign powers has been changed, but this does not necessarily interrupt their international relations.

Sustained by a consciousness that our transition from the former Union to the present Confederacy has not proceeded from any disregard on our part of our just obligations, or any failure to perform every constitutional duty — moved by no intention or design to invade the rights of others — anxious to cultivate peace and commerce with all nations — if we may not hope to avoid war, we may at least expect that posterity will acquit us of having needlessly engaged in it. We are doubly justified by the absence of wrong on our part, and by wanton aggression on the part of others. There can be no cause to doubt that the courage and patriotism of the people of the Confederate States will be found equal to any measure of defence which may be required for their security. Devoted to agricultural pursuits, their chief interest is the export of a commodity required in every manufacturing country. Our policy is peace, and the freest trade our necessities will permit. It is alike our interest, and that of all those to whom we would sell and from whom we would buy, that there should be the fewest practicable restrictions upon interchange of commodities. There can be but little rivalry between us and any manufacturing or navigating community, such as the Northwestern States of the American Union.

It must follow, therefore, that mutual interest would invite good will and kindness between them and us. If, however, passion or lust of dominion should cloud the judgment and inflame the ambition of these States, we must prepare to meet the emergency, and maintain, by the final arbitrament of the sword, the position we have assumed among the nations of the earth. We have now entered upon our career of independence, and it must be inflexibly pursued.

Through many years of controversy with our late associates, the Northern States, we have vainly endeavored to secure tranquillity and obtain respect for the rights to which we were entitled. As a necessity, not a choice we have resorted to separation, and henceforth our energies must be devoted to the conducting of our own affairs, and perpetuating the Confederacy we have formed. If a just perception of mutual interest shall permit us peaceably to pursue our separate political career, my most earnest desire will have been fulfilled. But if this be denied us, and the integrity and jurisdiction of our territory be assailed, it will but remain for us with a firm resolve to appeal to arms and invoke the blessings of Providence upon a just cause.

As a consequence of our new constitution, and with a view to meet our anticipated wants, it will be necessary to provide a speedy and efficient organization of the several branches of the executive departments having special charge of our foreign intercourse, financial and military affairs, and postal service. For purposes of defence, the Confederate States may, under ordinary circumstances, rely mainly upon their militia; but it is deemed advisable, in the present condition of affairs, that there should be a well instructed, disciplined army, more numerous than would be usually required for a peace establishment.

I also suggest that for the protection of our harbors and commerce on the high seas, a navy adapted to those objects be built up. These necessities have doubtless engaged the attention of Congress.

With a constitution differing only in form from that of our forefathers, in so far as it is explanatory of their well known intents, freed from sectional conflicts which have so much interfered with the pursuits of the general welfare, it is not unreasonable to expect that the States from which we have parted may seek to unite their fortunes with ours under the government we have instituted. For this your constitution has made adequate provision, but beyond this, if I mistake not the judgment and will of the people, our reunion with the States from which we have separated is neither practicable nor desirable. To increase power, develop the resources, and promote the happiness of this Confederacy, it is necessary that there should be so much homogeneity as that the welfare of every portion be the aim of the whole. When this homogeneity does not exist, antagonisms are engendered which must and should result in separation.

Actuated solely by a desire to protect and preserve our own rights and promote our own welfare, the secession of the Confederate States has been marked by no aggression upon others, and followed by no domestic convulsion. Our industrial pursuits have received no check; the cultivation of our fields has progressed as heretofore; and even should we be involved in war, there would be no considerable diminution in the production of the great staple which constitutes our exports, and in which the commercial world has an interest scarcely less than our own. This common interest of producer and consumer can only be interrupted by external force, which would obstruct shipments to foreign markets — a course of conduct which would be detrimental to manufacturing and commercial interests abroad. Should reason guide the action of the government from which we have separated, a policy so injurious to the civilized world, the Northern States included, could not be dictated even by the strongest desire to inflict injury upon us; but if otherwise, a terrible responsibility will rest upon it, and the suffering of millions will bear testimony to the folly and wickedness of our aggressors. In the meantime there will remain to us, besides the ordinary remedies before suggested, the well known resources for retaliation upon the commerce of our enemy.

Experience in public stations of subordinate grade to this which your kindness has conferred on me, has taught me that care and toil and disappointments are the price of official elevation. You will have many errors to forgive, many deficiencies to tolerate, but you will not find in me either a want of zeal or fidelity to a cause that has my highest hopes and most enduring affection. Your generosity has bestowed upon me an undeserved distinction, one which I neither sought nor desired. Upon the continuance of that sentiment, and upon your wisdom and patriotism, I rely to direct

10

and support me in the performance of the duties required at my hands. We have changed the constituent parts, not the system of our government. The constitution formed by our fathers is the constitution of the "Confederate States." In *their* exposition of it, and in the judicial constructions it has received, it has a light that reveals its true meaning. Thus instructed as to the just interpretations of that instrument, and ever remembering that all public offices are but trusts, held for the benefit of the people, and that delegated powers are to be strictly construed, I will hope that by due diligence in the discharge of my duties, though I may disappoint your expectations, yet to retain, when retiring, something of the good will and confidence which welcome my entrance into office. It is joyous in perilous times to look around upon a people united in heart, who are animated and actuated by one and the same purpose and high resolve, with whom the sacrifices to be made are not weighed in the balance against honor, right, liberty and equality. Obstacles may retard, but cannot prevent their progressive movements. Sanctified by justice and sustained by a virtuous people, let me reverently invoke the God of our fathers to guide and protect us in our efforts to perpetuate the principles which by HIS blessing they were able to vindicate, establish and transmit to their posterity, and with the continuance of HIS favor, ever to be gratefully acknowledged, let us look hopefully forward to success, to peace, and to prosperity.

(1861)

Exploring the Text

1. Identify appeals to ethos, logos, and pathos in the first paragraph. Which one is most prominent? Explain.
2. How accurately does Jefferson Davis paraphrase the Declaration of Independence at the beginning of the second paragraph? What is the purpose of this reference? How effective is it?
3. Davis states that "the sovereign States here represented have seceded from that Union, and it is a gross abuse of language to denominate the act rebellion or revolution" (par. 2). Apply the Toulmin model (as described in Chapter 3) to his claim. Do you find his argument sound? Would his audience have found it sound? Explain.
4. According to Davis, what has changed for the Confederate states? What has remained the same?
5. What distinctions does Davis make between the North and the South in the third paragraph?
6. Davis writes, "To increase power, develop the resources, and promote the happiness of this Confederacy, it is necessary that there should be so much homogeneity as that the welfare of every portion be the aim of the whole. When this homogeneity does not exist, antagonisms are engendered which must and should result in separation" (par. 8). What are some of the implications of such a position? Do you think it is true that welfare and equality depend on homogeneity? Explain.

7. What appeals does Davis make as he concludes his argument? How effective would they have been with his original audience?
8. If he were able, how might Thomas Jefferson (p. 389) respond to the argument put forth by Davis?

ALFRED M. GREEN

Alfred M. Green was an African American schoolteacher working in Philadelphia during the Civil War.

Let Us Take Up the Sword

In the following speech, delivered at a meeting of African Americans in Philadelphia in April 1861 (the first month of the Civil War), Green urges blacks to join the Union army and fight to abolish slavery in America.

The time has arrived in the history of the great Republic when we may again give evidence to the world of the bravery and patriotism of a race in whose hearts burns the love of country, of freedom, and of civil and religious toleration. It is these grand principles that enable men, however proscribed, when possessed of true patriotism, to say, "My country, right or wrong, I love thee still!"

It is true, the brave deeds of our fathers, sworn and subscribed to by the immortal Washington of the Revolution of 1776, and by Jackson and others in the War of 1812, have failed to bring us into recognition as citizens, enjoying those rights so dearly bought by those noble and patriotic sires.

It is true that our injuries in many respects are great; fugitive-slave laws, Dred Scott decisions, indictments for treason, and long and dreary months of imprisonment. The result of the most unfair rules of judicial investigation has been the pay we have received for our solicitude, sympathy and aid in the dangers and difficulties of those "days that tried men's souls."

Our duty, brethren, is not to cavil over past grievances. Let us not be derelict to duty in the time of need. While we remember the past and regret that our present position in the country is not such as to create within us that burning zeal and enthusiasm for the field of battle which inspires other men in the full enjoyment of every civil and religious emolument, yet let us endeavor to hope for the future and improve the present auspicious moment for creating anew our claims upon the justice and honor of the Republic; and, above all, let not the honor and glory achieved by our fathers be blasted or sullied by a want of true heroism among their sons.

Let us, then, take up the sword, trusting in God, who will defend the right, remembering that these are other days than those of yore; that the world today is on the side   5 of freedom and universal political equality; that the war cry of the howling leaders of Secession and treason is: "Let us drive back the advance guard of civil and religious freedom; let us have more slave territory; let us build stronger the tyrant system of slavery in the great American Republic." Remember, too, that your very presence among the troops of the North would inspire your oppressed brethren of the South with zeal for the overthrow of the tyrant system, and confidence in the armies of the living God — the God of truth, justice and equality to all men.

(1861)

Exploring the Text

1. How does Alfred M. Green appeal to ethos, logos, and pathos? Identify an appeal to each and explain how it contributes to his argument. Which of the appeals is the strongest? Explain.
2. What is the effect of the concessions that Green makes in paragraphs 2 and 3?
3. Which values likely held by his audience does Green appeal to? Which negative qualities, or vices, does he appeal to? Be specific.
4. What rhetorical effect does the word *brethren* (par. 4) have?
5. What point does Green make in the final sentence of his speech?
6. Analyze Green's argument according to the Toulmin model (as described in Chapter 3). Is the argument cogent? Would his original audience have found it persuasive? Explain.

ANONYMOUS

No More Auction Block for Me
or, Many Thousands Gone

> This traditional song was sung by slaves during the Civil War. Its authorship is unknown. The tune was adapted by Bob Dylan for his song "Blowin' in the Wind."

Exploring the Text

1. What is the tone and mood of this song?
2. How does each of the opening lines reflect the slave experience? What is the effect of the repetition of lines 2, 3, and 4 throughout?
3. There are several recorded versions of this song available online, including the one by Bob Dylan. Listen to a few of them. Which one do you like best? Why?

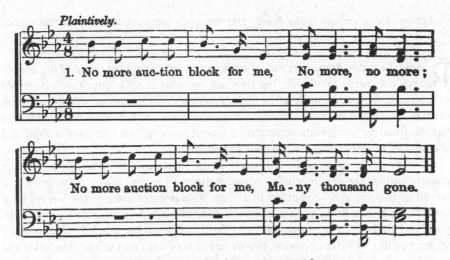

Plaintively.

1. No more auc-tion block for me,   No more,   no more;

No more auction block for me,   Ma-ny   thousand   gone.

2. **No more peck o' corn for me, &c.**
3. **No more driver's lash for me, &c.**
4. **No more pint o' salt for me, &c.**
5. **No more hundred lash for me, &c.**
6. **No more mistress' call for me, &c.**

HARRIET JACOBS

Harriet Ann Jacobs (1813–1897) was an African American writer, abolitionist, and reformer. Born a slave in Edenton, North Carolina, she fled from her owner in 1835, spending seven years hiding in the tiny attic above her grandmother's house before finally escaping to freedom in 1842. She moved to Rochester, New York, where she became an active and well-known member of the abolitionist movement, and used her fame during the Civil War to raise money for black refugees and improve conditions for recently freed slaves.

from *Incidents in the Life of a Slave Girl, Written by Herself*

In her autobiography, *Incidents in the Life of a Slave Girl, Written by Herself*, which was published in 1861, Jacobs recounts her struggle for freedom and the abuse she endured as a female slave. Because the Fugitive Slave Act was still in effect, making it illegal to not return a runaway slave to the owner, Harriet Jacobs changed all the names of the people in the book, including her own. The main character is named Linda Brent, and the book was published under that pseudonym.

Reader, be assured this narrative is no fiction. I am aware that some of my adventures may seem incredible; but they are, nevertheless, strictly true. I have not exaggerated the wrongs inflicted by Slavery; on the contrary, my descriptions fall far short of the facts. I have concealed the names of places, and given persons fictitious names. I had no motive for secrecy on my own account, but I deemed it kind and considerate towards others to pursue this course.

I wish I were more competent to the task I have undertaken. But I trust my readers will excuse deficiencies in consideration of circumstances. I was born and reared in Slavery; and I remained in a Slave State twenty-seven years. Since I have been at the North, it has been necessary for me to work diligently for my own support, and the education of my children. This has not left me much leisure to make up for the loss of early opportunities to improve myself; and it has compelled me to write these pages at irregular intervals, whenever I could snatch an hour from household duties.

When I first arrived in Philadelphia, Bishop Paine advised me to publish a sketch of my life, but I told him I was altogether incompetent to such an undertaking. Though I have improved my mind somewhat since that time, I still remain of the same opinion; but I trust my motives will excuse what might otherwise seem presumptuous. I have not written my experiences in order to attract attention to myself; on the contrary, it would have been more pleasant to me to have been silent about my own history. Neither do I care to excite sympathy for my own sufferings. But I do earnestly desire to arouse the women of the North to a realizing sense of the condition of two millions of women at the South, still in bondage, suffering what I suffered, and most of them far worse. I want to add my testimony to that of abler pens to convince the people of the Free States what Slavery really is. Only by experience can any one realize how deep, and dark, and foul is that pit of abominations. May the blessing of God rest on this imperfect effort in behalf of my persecuted people!

Linda Brent

VII. The Lover

Why does the slave ever love? Why allow the tendrils of the heart to twine around objects which may at any moment be wrenched away by the hand of violence? When separations come by the hand of death, the pious soul can bow in resignation, and say, "Not my will, but thine be done, O Lord!" But when the ruthless hand of man strikes the blow, regardless of the misery he causes, it is hard to be submissive. I did not reason thus when I was a young girl. Youth will be youth. I loved, and I indulged the hope that the dark clouds around me would turn out a bright lining. I forgot that in the land of my birth the shadows are too dense for light to penetrate.

A land

> "Where laughter is not mirth; nor thought the mind;
> Nor words a language; nor e'en men mankind.
> Where cries reply to curses, shrieks to blows,
> And each is tortured in his separate hell."

There was in the neighborhood a young colored carpenter; a free born man. We had been well acquainted in childhood, and frequently met together afterwards. We became mutually attached, and he proposed to marry me. I loved him with all the ardor of a young girl's first love. But when I reflected that I was a slave, and that the laws gave no sanction to the marriage of such, my heart sank within me. My lover wanted to buy me; but I knew that Dr. Flint was too wilful and arbitrary a man to consent to that arrangement. From him, I was sure of experiencing all sorts of opposition, and I had nothing to hope from my mistress. She would have been delighted to have got rid of me, but not in that way. It would have relieved her mind of a burden if she could have seen me sold to some distant state, but if I was married near home I should be just as much in her husband's power as I had previously been, — for the husband of a slave has no power to protect her. Moreover, my mistress, like many others, seemed to think that slaves had no right to any family ties of their own; that they were created merely to wait upon the family of the mistress. I once heard her abuse a young slave girl, who told her that a colored man wanted to make her his wife. "I will have you peeled and pickled, my lady," said she, "if I ever hear you mention that subject again. Do you suppose that I will have you tending *my* children with the children of that nigger?" The girl to whom she said this had a mulatto child, of course not acknowledged by its father. The poor black man who loved her would have been proud to acknowledge his helpless offspring.

Many and anxious were the thoughts I revolved in my mind. I was at a loss what to do. Above all things, I was desirous to spare my lover the insults that had cut so deeply into my own soul. I talked with my grandmother about it, and partly told her my fears. I did not dare to tell her the worst. She had long suspected all was not right, and if I confirmed her suspicions I knew a storm would rise that would prove the overthrow of all my hopes.

This love-dream had been my support through many trials; and I could not bear to run the risk of having it suddenly dissipated. There was a lady in the neighborhood, a particular friend of Dr. Flint's, who often visited the house. I had a great respect for her, and she had always manifested a friendly interest in me. Grandmother thought she would have great influence with the doctor. I went to this lady, and told her my story. I told her I was aware that my lover's being a free-born man would prove a great objection; but he wanted to buy me; and if Dr. Flint would consent to that arrangement, I felt sure he would be willing to pay any reasonable price. She knew that Mrs. Flint disliked me; therefore, I ventured to suggest that perhaps my mistress would approve of my being sold, as that would rid her of me. The lady listened with kindly sympathy, and promised to do her utmost to promote my wishes. She had an interview with the doctor, and I believe she pleaded my cause earnestly; but it was all to no purpose.

How I dreaded my master now! Every minute I expected to be summoned to his presence; but the day passed, and I heard nothing from him. The next morning, a message was brought to me: "Master wants you in his study." I found the door ajar, and I stood a moment gazing at the hateful man who claimed a right to rule me, body and soul. I entered, and tried to appear calm. I did not want him to know how my heart was bleeding. He looked fixedly at me, with an expression which seemed to say, "I have half a mind to kill you on the spot." At last he broke the silence, and that was a relief to both of us.

"So you want to be married, do you?" said he, "and to a free nigger."

"Yes, sir."   10

"Well, I'll soon convince you whether I am your master, or the nigger fellow you honor so highly. If you *must* have a husband, you may take up with one of my slaves."

What a situation I should be in, as the wife of one of *his* slaves, even if my heart had been interested!

I replied, "Don't you suppose, sir, that a slave can have some preference about marrying? Do you suppose that all men are alike to her?"

"Do you love this nigger?" said he, abruptly.

"Yes, sir."   15

"How dare you tell me so!" he exclaimed, in great wrath. After a slight pause, he added, "I supposed you thought more of yourself; that you felt above the insults of such puppies."

I replied, "If he is a puppy I am a puppy, for we are both of the negro race. It is right and honorable for us to love each other. The man you call a puppy never insulted me, sir; and he would not love me if he did not believe me to be a virtuous woman."

He sprang upon me like a tiger, and gave me a stunning blow. It was the first time he had ever struck me; and fear did not enable me to control my anger. When I had recovered a little from the effects, I exclaimed, "You have struck me for answering you honestly. How I despise you!"

There was silence for some minutes. Perhaps he was deciding what should be my punishment; or, perhaps, he wanted to give me time to reflect on what I had said, and to whom I had said it. Finally, he asked, "Do you know what you have said?"

"Yes, sir; but your treatment drove me to it."   20

"Do you know that I have a right to do as I like with you, — that I can kill you, if I please?"

"You have tried to kill me, and I wish you had; but you have no right to do as you like with me."

"Silence!" he exclaimed, in a thundering voice. "By heavens, girl, you forget yourself too far! Are you mad? If you are, I will soon bring you to your senses. Do you think any other master would bear what I have borne from you this morning? Many masters would have killed you on the spot. How would you like to be sent to jail for your insolence?"

"I know I have been disrespectful, sir," I replied; "but you drove me to it; I couldn't help it. As for the jail, there would be more peace for me there than there is here."

"You deserve to go there," said he, "and to be under such treatment, that you   25
would forget the meaning of the word *peace*. It would do you good. It would take
some of your high notions out of you. But I am not ready to send you there yet, notwithstanding your ingratitude for all my kindness and forbearance. You have been
the plague of my life. I have wanted to make you happy, and I have been repaid with
the basest ingratitude; but though you have proved yourself incapable of appreciating my kindness, I will be lenient towards you, Linda. I will give you one more
chance to redeem your character. If you behave yourself and do as I require, I will
forgive you and treat you as I always have done; but if you disobey me, I will punish
you as I would the meanest slave on my plantation. Never let me hear that fellow's
name mentioned again. If I ever know of your speaking to him, I will cowhide you
both; and if I catch him lurking about my premises, I will shoot him as soon as I
would a dog. Do you hear what I say? I'll teach you a lesson about marriage and free
niggers! Now go, and let this be the last time I have occasion to speak to you on this
subject."

Reader, did you ever hate? I hope not. I never did but once, and I trust I never
shall again. Somebody has called it "the atmosphere of hell;" and I believe it is so.

For a fortnight the doctor did not speak to me. He thought to mortify me; to
make me feel that I had disgraced myself by receiving the honorable addresses of a
respectable colored man, in preference to the base proposals of a white man. But
though his lips disdained to address me, his eyes were very loquacious. No animal
ever watched its prey more narrowly than he watched me. He knew that I could write,
though he had failed to make me read his letters; and he was now troubled lest I
should exchange letters with another man. After a while he became weary of silence;
and I was sorry for it. One morning, as he passed through the hall, to leave the house,
he contrived to thrust a note into my hand. I thought I had better read it, and spare
myself the vexation of having him read it to me. It expressed regret for the blow he
had given me, and reminded me that I myself was wholly to blame for it. He hoped
I had become convinced of the injury I was doing myself by incurring his displeasure.
He wrote that he had made up his mind to go to Louisiana; that he should take several slaves with him, and intended I should be one of the number. My mistress would
remain where she was; therefore I should have nothing to fear from that quarter. If I
merited kindness from him, he assured me that it would be lavishly bestowed. He
begged me to think over the matter, and answer the following day.

The next morning I was called to carry a pair of scissors to his room. I laid them
on the table with the letter beside them. He thought it was my answer, and did not
call me back. I went as usual to attend my young mistress to and from school. He met
me in the street, and ordered me to stop at his office on my way back. When I entered,
he showed me his letter, and asked me why I had not answered it. I replied, "I am
your daughter's property, and it is in your power to send me, or take me, wherever you
please." He said he was very glad to find me so willing to go, and that we should start
early in the autumn. He had a large practice in the town, and I rather thought he had
made up the story merely to frighten me. However that might be, I was determined
that I would never go to Louisiana with him.

Summer passed away, and early in the autumn Dr. Flint's eldest son was sent to Louisiana to examine the country, with a view to emigrating. That news did not disturb me. I knew very well that I should not be sent with *him*. That I had not been taken to the plantation before this time, was owing to the fact that his son was there. He was jealous of his son; and jealousy of the overseer had kept him from punishing me by sending me into the fields to work. Is it strange that I was not proud of these protectors? As for the overseer, he was a man for whom I had less respect than I had for a bloodhound.

Young Mr. Flint did not bring back a favorable report of Louisiana, and I heard no more of that scheme. Soon after this, my lover met me at the corner of the street, and I stopped to speak to him. Looking up, I saw my master watching us from his window. I hurried home, trembling with fear. I was sent for, immediately, to go to his room. He met me with a blow. "When is mistress to be married?" said he, in a sneering tone. A shower of oaths and imprecations followed. How thankful I was that my lover was a free man! that my tyrant had no power to flog him for speaking to me in the street!

Again and again I revolved in my mind how all this would end. There was no hope that the doctor would consent to sell me on any terms. He had an iron will, and was determined to keep me, and to conquer me. My lover was an intelligent and religious man. Even if he could have obtained permission to marry me while I was a slave, the marriage would give him no power to protect me from my master. It would have made him miserable to witness the insults I should have been subjected to. And then, if we had children, I knew they must "follow the condition of the mother." What a terrible blight that would be on the heart of a free, intelligent father! For *his* sake, I felt that I ought not to link his fate with my own unhappy destiny. He was going to Savannah to see about a little property left him by an uncle; and hard as it was to bring my feelings to it, I earnestly entreated him not to come back. I advised him to go to the Free States, where his tongue would not be tied, and where his intelligence would be of more avail to him. He left me, still hoping the day would come when I could be bought. With me the lamp of hope had gone out. The dream of my girlhood was over. I felt lonely and desolate.

Still I was not stripped of all. I still had my good grandmother, and my affectionate brother. When he put his arms round my neck, and looked into my eyes, as if to read there the troubles I dared not tell, I felt that I still had something to love. But even that pleasant emotion was chilled by the reflection that he might be torn from me at any moment, by some sudden freak of my master. If he had known how we loved each other, I think he would have exulted in separating us. We often planned together how we could get to the north. But, as William remarked, such things are easier said than done. My movements were very closely watched, and we had no means of getting any money to defray our expenses. As for grandmother, she was strongly opposed to her children's undertaking any such project. She had not forgotten poor Benjamin's sufferings, and she was afraid that if another child tried to escape, he would have a similar or a worse fate. To me, nothing seemed more dreadful than my present life. I said to myself, "William *must* be free. He shall go to the north, and I will follow him." Many a slave sister has formed the same plans.

30

X. A Perilous Passage in the Slave Girl's Life

After my lover went away, Dr. Flint contrived a new plan. He seemed to have an idea that my fear of my mistress was his greatest obstacle. In the blandest tones, he told me that he was going to build a small house for me, in a secluded place, four miles away from the town. I shuddered; but I was constrained to listen, while he talked of his intention to give me a home of my own, and to make a lady of me. Hitherto, I had escaped my dreaded fate, by being in the midst of people. My grandmother had already had high words with my master about me. She had told him pretty plainly what she thought of his character, and there was considerable gossip in the neighborhood about our affairs, to which the open-mouthed jealousy of Mrs. Flint contributed not a little. When my master said he was going to build a house for me, and that he could do it with little trouble and expense, I was in hopes something would happen to frustrate his scheme; but I soon heard that the house was actually begun. I vowed before my Maker that I would never enter it. I had rather toil on the plantation from dawn till dark; I had rather live and die in jail, than drag on, from day to day, through such a living death. I was determined that the master, whom I so hated and loathed, who had blighted the prospects of my youth, and made my life a desert, should not, after my long struggle with him, succeed at last in trampling his victim under his feet. I would do any thing, every thing, for the sake of defeating him. What *could* I do? I thought and thought, till I became desperate, and made a plunge into the abyss.

And now, reader, I come to a period in my unhappy life, which I would gladly forget if I could. The remembrance fills me with sorrow and shame. It pains me to tell you of it; but I have promised to tell you the truth and I will do it honestly, let it cost me what it may. I will not try to screen myself behind the plea of compulsion from a master; for it was not so. Neither can I plead ignorance or thoughtlessness. For years, my master had done his utmost to pollute my mind with foul images, and to destroy the pure principles inculcated by my grandmother, and the good mistress of my childhood. The influences of slavery had had the same effect on me that they had on other young girls; they had made me prematurely knowing, concerning the evil ways of the world. I knew what I did, and I did it with deliberate calculation.

But, O, ye happy women, whose purity has been sheltered from childhood, who have been free to choose the objects of your affection, whose homes are protected by law, do not judge the poor desolate slave girl too severely! If slavery had been abolished, I, also, could have married the man of my choice; I could have had a home shielded by the laws; and I should have been spared the painful task of confessing what I am now about to relate; but all my prospects had been blighted by slavery. I wanted to keep myself pure; and, under the most adverse circumstances, I tried hard to preserve my self-respect; but I was struggling alone in the powerful grasp of the demon Slavery; and the monster proved too strong for me. I felt as if I was forsaken by God and man; as if all my efforts must be frustrated; and I became reckless in my despair.

I have told you that Dr. Flint's persecutions and his wife's jealousy had given rise to some gossip in the neighborhood. Among others, it chanced that a white unmarried gentleman had obtained some knowledge of the circumstances in which I was placed. He knew my grandmother, and often spoke to me in the street. He became interested for me, and asked questions about my master, which I answered in part. He expressed a great deal of sympathy, and a wish to aid me. He constantly sought opportunities to see me, and wrote to me frequently. I was a poor slave girl, only fifteen years old.

So much attention from a superior person was, of course, flattering; for human nature is the same in all. I also felt grateful for his sympathy, and encouraged by his kind words. It seemed to me a great thing to have such a friend. By degrees, a more tender feeling crept into my heart. He was an educated and eloquent gentleman; too eloquent, alas, for the poor slave girl who trusted in him. Of course I saw whither all this was tending. I knew the impassable gulf between us; but to be an object of interest to a man who is not married, and who is not her master, is agreeable to the pride and feelings of a slave, if her miserable situation has left her any pride or sentiment. It seems less degrading to give one's self, than to submit to compulsion. There is something akin to freedom in having a lover who has no control over you, except that which he gains by kindness and attachment. A master may treat you as rudely as he pleases, and you dare not speak; moreover, the wrong does not seem so great with an unmarried man, as with one who has a wife to be made unhappy. There may be sophistry in all this; but the condition of a slave confuses all principles of morality, and, in fact, renders the practice of them impossible.

When I found that my master had actually begun to build the lonely cottage, other feelings mixed with those I have described. Revenge, and calculations of interest, were added to flattered vanity and sincere gratitude for kindness. I knew nothing would enrage Dr. Flint so much as to know that I favored another; and it was something to triumph over my tyrant even in that small way. I thought he would revenge himself by selling me, and I was sure my friend, Mr. Sands, would buy me. He was a man of more generosity and feeling than my master, and I thought my freedom could be easily obtained from him. The crisis of my fate now came so near that I was desperate. I shuddered to think of being the mother of children that should be owned by my old tyrant. I knew that as soon as a new fancy took him, his victims were sold far off to get rid of them; especially if they had children. I had seen several women sold, with his babies at the breast. He never allowed his offspring by slaves to remain long in sight of himself and his wife. Of a man who was not my master I could ask to have my children well supported; and in this case, I felt confident I should obtain the boon. I also felt quite sure that they would be made free. With all these thoughts revolving in my mind, and seeing no other way of escaping the doom I so much dreaded, I made a headlong plunge. Pity me, and pardon me, O virtuous reader! You never knew what it is to be a slave; to be entirely unprotected by law or custom; to have the laws reduce you to the condition of a chattel, entirely subject to the will of another. You never exhausted your ingenuity in avoiding the snares, and eluding the power of a hated tyrant; you never shuddered at the sound of his footsteps, and trembled within hearing of his voice. I know I did wrong. No one can feel it more sensibly than I do. The painful and humiliating memory will haunt me to my dying day. Still, in looking back, calmly, on the events of my life, I feel that the slave woman ought not to be judged by the same standard as others.

The months passed on. I had many unhappy hours. I secretly mourned over the sorrow I was bringing on my grandmother, who had so tried to shield me from harm. I knew that I was the greatest comfort of her old age, and that it was a source of pride to her that I had not degraded myself, like most of the slaves. I wanted to confess to her that I was no longer worthy of her love; but I could not utter the dreaded words.

As for Dr. Flint, I had a feeling of satisfaction and triumph in the thought of telling *him*. From time to time he told me of his intended arrangements, and I was silent. At last, he came and told me the cottage was completed, and ordered me to go to it. I told him I would never enter it. He said, "I have heard enough of such talk as that. You shall go, if you are carried by force; and you shall remain there."

I replied, "I will never go there. In a few months I shall be a mother."

He stood and looked at me in dumb amazement, and left the house without a word. I thought I should be happy in my triumph over him. But now that the truth was out, and my relatives would hear of it, I felt wretched. Humble as were their circumstances, they had pride in my good character. Now, how could I look them in the face? My self-respect was gone! I had resolved that I would be virtuous, though I was a slave. I had said, "Let the storm beat! I will brave it till I die." And now, how humiliated I felt!

I went to my grandmother. My lips moved to make confession, but the words stuck in my throat. I sat down in the shade of a tree at her door and began to sew. I think she saw something unusual was the matter with me. The mother of slaves is very watchful. She knows there is no security for her children. After they have entered their teens she lives in daily expectation of trouble. This leads to many questions. If the girl is of a sensitive nature, timidity keeps her from answering truthfully and this well-meant course has a tendency to drive her from maternal counsels. Presently, in came my mistress, like a mad woman, and accused me concerning her husband. My grandmother, whose suspicions had been previously awakened, believed what she said. She exclaimed, "O Linda! has it come to this? I had rather see you dead than to see you as you now are. You are a disgrace to your dead mother." She tore from my fingers my mother's wedding ring and her silver thimble. "Go away!" she exclaimed, "and never come to my house, again." Her reproaches fell so hot and heavy, that they left me no chance to answer. Bitter tears, such as the eyes never shed but once, were my only answer. I rose from my seat, but fell back again, sobbing. She did not speak to me; but the tears were running down her furrowed cheeks, and they scorched me like fire. She had always been so kind to me! *So* kind! How I longed to throw myself at her feet, and tell her all the truth! But she had ordered me to go, and never to come there again. After a few minutes, I mustered strength, and started to obey her. With what feelings did I now close that little gate, which I used to open with such an eager hand in my childhood! It closed upon me with a sound I never heard before.

Where could I go? I was afraid to return to my master's. I walked on recklessly, not caring where I went, or what would become of me. When I had gone four or five miles, fatigue compelled me to stop. I sat down on the stump of an old tree. The stars were shining through the boughs above me. How they mocked me, with their bright, calm light! The hours passed by, and as I sat there alone a chilliness and deadly sickness came over me. I sank on the ground. My mind was full of horrid thoughts. I prayed to die; but the prayer was not answered. At last, with great effort I roused myself, and walked some distance further, to the house of a woman who had been a friend of my mother. When I told her why I was there, she spoke soothingly to me; but I could not be comforted. I thought I could bear my shame if I could only be reconciled to my grandmother. I longed to open my heart to her. I thought if she could know the real state of the case, and all I had been bearing for years, she would perhaps judge me less harshly. My friend advised me to send for her. I did so; but days of agonizing suspense passed before she came. Had she utterly forsaken me? No. She came at last. I knelt before her, and told her the things that had poisoned my life; how long I had been persecuted; that I saw no way of escape; and in an hour of extremity I had become desperate. She listened in silence. I told her I would bear any thing and do any thing, if in time I had hopes of obtaining her forgiveness. I begged of her to pity me, for my dead mother's sake. And she did pity me. She did not say, "I forgive you;" but she looked at me lovingly, with her eyes full of tears. She laid her old hand gently on my head, and murmured, "Poor child! Poor child!"

(1861)

Exploring the Text

1. What effect does the preface have on the reader? What appeals does it make?
2. How would you describe Harriet Jacobs's tone at the beginning of Chapter 7?
3. Were you surprised by Jacobs's replies to Dr. Flint's demands (pars. 13–24)? What do they suggest about her character?
4. Jacobs writes, "Reader, did you ever hate? I hope not. I never did but once; and I trust I never shall again. Somebody has called it 'the atmosphere of hell;' and I believe it is so" (par. 26). On what does she base her belief in the validity of that statement? Are you surprised that she would say that she hated only once? Explain.
5. How successfully does Jacobs create suspense in Chapter 7?
6. In Chapter 10, Jacobs pleads her case with the reader. What is the rhetorical effect of her use of direct address in paragraph 34? How does the direct address in the next paragraph (par. 35) differ? How do both instances contribute to her narrative?
7. Jacobs writes, "I was a poor slave girl, only fifteen years old" (par. 36). How does knowledge of her age affect your response to the narrative?

8. Jacobs concludes paragraph 38: "I feel that the slave woman ought not to be judged by the same standard as others." In that paragraph, how does she use rhetorical strategies to prepare the reader for that claim?

9. What irony does Jacobs use to conclude Chapter 10? Explain. How does the irony contribute to the overall effect of the narrative?

ALEXANDER GARDNER

Photographer Alexander Gardner lived from 1821 to 1882. The following photograph is from the 1866 collection *Gardner's Photographic Sketchbook of the War.*

Confederate Dead before the Dunker Church

This photograph was taken after the Battle of Antietam, a few miles north of Harpers Ferry, which lies on the border of Maryland and West Virginia. The battle took place on September 17, 1862, and was the bloodiest single day of the Civil War — and, in fact, in all of American history. Approximately four thousand soldiers were killed and nearly twenty thousand others were wounded or missing after twelve hours of fighting.

Prints and Photographs Division, Library of Congress

Exploring the Text

1. What do you see in the photograph? Comment on all its details.
2. Notice that this photograph is framed as a painting would be. How does the "place-ment" of the objects — from the photographer's perspective — influence the mean-ing of the photograph? What impression does the photographer evidently wish to create? What is your impression?
3. What might be viewed as ironic about the photograph?
4. Does this photograph remind you of Herman Melville's poem "Shiloh" (p. 647), written just five months before the photograph was taken? How would you com-pare and contrast the two pieces?

TIMOTHY O'SULLIVAN

Timothy O'Sullivan (c. 1840–1882) was born in Ireland and immigrated to New York City with his parents. As a photographer, he was widely known for his work related to the Civil War.

A Harvest of Death

While Antietam saw the single bloodiest day of the Civil War, the Battle of Gettysburg, a major turning point in the Civil War, was the bloodiest battle over-

Prints and Photographs Division, Library of Congress

all, with a total of fifty-one thousand casualties. The battle was fought over three days, July 1–3, 1863. Printed in Alexander Gardner's 1866 collection, *Gardner's Photographic Sketchbook of the War*, this photograph was taken by Sullivan on the battlefield.

Exploring the Text

1. This photograph was taken after the first day of the battle. How does knowing that two more gruesome days would follow affect your viewing of the photo?
2. Look carefully at the photograph. What do you see? Consider all the visual features, including the soldiers and the setting.
3. How do the contrasts between light and dark and the living and the dead contribute to the photograph's effect? What is the mood created by the photograph? What details contribute to that mood?
4. How would you compare this photograph with the one taken at Antietam? Which one leaves a stronger impression? Why?

SUPERVISORY COMMITTEE FOR RECRUITING COLORED REGIMENTS

During the last two years of the Civil War, many African Americans, newly freed by Abraham Lincoln's 1862 Emancipation Proclamation, were recruited by the Union army and became known as the United States Colored Troops (USCT). One organization responsible for recruitment and training of troops was the Supervisory Committee for Recruiting Colored Regiments, based in Philadelphia.

Come and Join Us Brothers

The following poster from 1863, entitled "Come and Join Us Brothers," is an example of propaganda used by the Union army to recruit African Americans to replenish its dwindling ranks. The 178,000 free blacks and freedmen who enlisted bolstered the Union war effort at a very critical time, and by the war's end, they composed nearly one-tenth of all Union troops.

COME AND JOIN US BROTHERS.

PUBLISHED BY THE SUPERVISORY COMMITTEE FOR RECRUITING COLORED REGIMENTS
1210 CHESTNUT ST. PHILADELPHIA.

Division of Home and Community Life, National Museum of American History, Smithsonian Institution. Harry T. Peters, "America on Stone" Lithography Collection.

(See color insert, Image 24.)

Exploring the Text

1. Read the title carefully. Does it invite, urge, enjoin, plead, or command the audience? Which verb do you consider most appropriate? Explain why.
2. How does the poster appeal to ethos, logos, and pathos? Which one is the strongest appeal?
3. What are the values of the audience that the creator of the lithograph wishes to evoke?
4. Submit the claims suggested by this piece to the Toulmin model (see Chapter 3). What does that analysis reveal about the argument presented?
5. This poster was published by the Supervisory Committee for Recruiting Colored Regiments from Philadelphia, Pennsylvania, in 1863, two years after Alfred M. Green (p. 673) gave his speech in that city. It is very likely that at least part of the audience for both pieces was the same. Which piece do you think was more persuasive? Why?

Conversation

Abraham Lincoln: The Great Emancipator

Abraham Lincoln (1809–1865) was born in rural Kentucky and raised in rural Indiana before settling in Illinois, where he held various jobs before becoming a member of the state legislature. In 1860, he was elected as the sixteenth president of the United States of America. He was re-elected in 1864 in the midst of the Civil War, which began in 1861. Every child knows the Abraham Lincoln story: "honest Abe" who lived in a log cabin and learned to write on the back of a shovel because his family was too poor to have paper; the hardworking rail-splitter who embodied the American Dream by becoming a self-taught lawyer, successful politician, and president; the Great Emancipator who freed the slaves; the strong, laconic, wise leader who led the Union to victory in the Civil War; and finally, the great martyr for liberty, assassinated while attending the theater with his wife on April 14, 1865. While Lincoln's place among the greatest of American heroes is surely secure, we might ask how much of the story is true to life and how much is mythic. How much of his story is biography and how much hagiography? *Hagiography* is a term that originally referred to biographies of saints, but has come to mean any bibliography that turns the subject into a saint while ignoring any flaws. To what degree is hagiography appropriate for such a grand figure?

As you read these texts by and about him, think carefully about Abraham Lincoln as a man, as a president, as a writer, and as a legacy. How much does the Lincoln you thought you knew resemble the Lincoln you know when you finish these readings?

Sources

Abraham Lincoln, *The Emancipation Proclamation* (1863)
   The Gettysburg Address (1863)
   Letter to Albert G. Hodges (1864)
   Second Inaugural Address (1865)
Henry W. Herrick, *Reading the Emancipation Proclamation in the Slaves' Cabin* (1864)
Thomas Ball, *Freedman's Memorial to Abraham Lincoln* (1876)
Frederick Douglass, from *Reminiscences of Abraham Lincoln by Distinguished Men of His Time* (1886)
Mario M. Cuomo, from *Abraham Lincoln and Our "Unfinished Work"* (1986)
James McPherson, from *Who Freed the Slaves?* (1996)
Ira Berlin, from *Who Freed the Slaves? Emancipation and Its Meaning* (1997)
Peter Norvig, *The Gettysburg PowerPoint Presentation* (2003)

The Emancipation Proclamation

ABRAHAM LINCOLN

> On January 1, 1863, President Abraham Lincoln delivered the Emancipation Proc-
> lamation, which freed all slaves residing in states in rebellion against the United
> States of America.

By the President of the United States of America:

A Proclamation.

Whereas, on the twentysecond day of September, in the year of our Lord one
thousand eight hundred and sixty two, a proclamation was issued by the President of
the United States, containing, among other things, the following, to wit:

"That on the first day of January, in the year of our Lord one thousand eight
hundred and sixty-three, all persons held as slaves within any State or designated
part of a State, the people whereof shall then be in rebellion against the United States,
shall be then, thenceforward, and forever free; and the Executive Government of the
United States, including the military and naval authority thereof, will recognize and
maintain the freedom of such persons, and will do no act or acts to repress such
persons, or any of them, in any efforts they may make for their actual freedom.

"That the Executive will, on the first day of January aforesaid, by proclamation,   5
designate the States and parts of States, if any, in which the people thereof, respectively, shall then be in rebellion against the United States; and the fact that any State,
or the people thereof, shall on that day be, in good faith, represented in the Congress
of the United States by members chosen thereto at elections wherein a majority of the
qualified voters of such State shall have participated, shall, in the absence of strong
countervailing testimony, be deemed conclusive evidence that such State, and the
people thereof, are not then in rebellion against the United States."

Now, therefore I, Abraham Lincoln, President of the United States, by virtue of
the power in me vested as Commander-in-Chief, of the Army and Navy of the
United States in time of actual armed rebellion against authority and government of
the United States, and as a fit and necessary war measure for suppressing said rebellion, do, on this first day of January, in the year of our Lord one thousand eight
hundred and sixty three, and in accordance with my purpose so to do publicly proclaimed for the full period of one hundred days, from the day first above mentioned,
order and designate as the States and parts of States wherein the people thereof
respectively, are this day in rebellion against the United States, the following, to wit:

Arkansas, Texas, Louisiana, (except the Parishes of St. Bernard, Plaquemines,
Jefferson, St. Johns, St. Charles, St. James[,] Ascension, Assumption, Terrebonne,
Lafourche, St. Mary, St. Martin, and Orleans, including the City of New-Orleans)
Mississippi, Alabama, Florida, Georgia, South-Carolina, North-Carolina, and Virginia,
(except the fortyeight counties designated as West Virginia, and also the counties of

Berkley, Accomac, Northampton, Elizabeth-City, York, Princess Ann, and Norfolk, including the cities of Norfolk & Portsmouth [)]; and which excepted parts are, for the present, left precisely as if this proclamation were not issued.

And by virtue of the power, and for the purpose aforesaid, I do order and declare that all persons held as slaves within said designated States, and parts of States, are, and henceforward shall be free; and that the Executive government of the United States, including the military and naval authorities thereof, will recognize and maintain the freedom of said persons.

And I hereby enjoin upon the people so declared to be free to abstain from all violence, unless in necessary self-defence; and I recommend to them that, in all cases when allowed, they labor faithfully for reasonable wages.

And I further declare and make known, that such persons of suitable condition, 10 will be received into the armed service of the United States to garrison forts, positions, stations, and other places, and to man vessels of all sorts in said service.

And upon this act, sincerely believed to be an act of justice, warranted by the Constitution, upon military necessity, I invoke the considerate judgment of mankind, and the gracious favor of Almighty God.

In witness whereof, I have hereunto set my hand and caused the seal of the United States to be affixed.

Done at the City of Washington, this first day of January, in the year of our Lord one thousand eight hundred and sixty three, and of the Independence of the United States of America the eighty-seventh.

By the President: Abraham Lincoln

(1863)

Questions

1. Of the three classic appeals, to ethos, logos, and pathos, which is most prominent in this text? Explain.
2. What are the two things proclaimed in paragraph 4? Briefly paraphrase them.
3. In the proclamation, where does Abraham Lincoln address those who are freed? What does he say to them?
4. How does Lincoln characterize the proclamation in paragraph 6? Why does he do so in that way?
5. In the final sentence, Lincoln evokes the Declaration of Independence. Why does he refer to it this way? What is the effect of the reference?
6. In his 2008 book, *Lincoln: The Biography of a Writer*, biographer and scholar Fred Kaplan characterizes the Emancipation Proclamation: "Lawyerly, concise, and unliterary, it was admirably suited to its purpose, and paradoxically, perhaps the single most consequential document of Lincoln's presidency, an act of dictate rather than of commentary or persuasion." Do you agree? Defend or challenge Kaplan's position, using Lincoln's text and your knowledge of American history as evidence.

The Gettysburg Address

ABRAHAM LINCOLN

Approximately fifty thousand soldiers were casualties during the Battle of Gettysburg, waged in July of 1863. Four months later, President Lincoln delivered the rightly famous Gettysburg Address at the dedication of the Soldiers' National Cemetery at the battle site in Gettysburg, Pennsylvania.

Four score and seven years ago our fathers brought forth on this continent a new nation, conceived in liberty, and dedicated to the proposition that all men are created equal.

Now we are engaged in a great civil war, testing whether that nation, or any nation, so conceived and so dedicated, can long endure. We are met on a great battle-field of that war. We have come to dedicate a portion of that field, as a final resting place for those who here gave their lives that that nation might live. It is altogether fitting and proper that we should do this.

But, in a larger sense, we can not dedicate, we can not consecrate, we can not hallow this ground. The brave men, living and dead, who struggled here, have consecrated it, far above our poor power to add or detract. The world will little note, nor long remember what we say here, but it can never forget what they did here. It is for us the living, rather, to be dedicated here to the unfinished work which they who fought here have thus far so nobly advanced. It is rather for us to be here dedicated to the great task remaining before us — that from these honored dead we take increased devotion to that cause for which they gave the last full measure of devotion — that we here highly resolve that these dead shall not have died in vain — that this nation, under God, shall have a new birth of freedom — and that government of the people, by the people, for the people, shall not perish from the earth.

(1863)

Questions

1. How would you describe the tone of the speech? Use a two-word phrase, an adjective-noun combination ("angry sarcasm," for example), or a combination of adjectives (such as "melancholy and wistful") to do so.
2. When Abraham Lincoln delivered the Gettysburg Address, the audience was surprised by how short the speech was: a mere 272 words. What is the rhetorical effect of such brevity?
3. How does Lincoln use diction about life and death in this speech? What is the effect?
4. Considering the immense importance of this speech, note how ironic it is that Lincoln said, "The world will little note, nor long remember what we say here" (par. 3). Why do you think this speech has endured? Explain.
5. Note the word *perish* in the final sentence of the speech. How do its connotations differ from *die*, for example, or *fade* or *pass away*?

6. In such a short speech, the final sentence is notable for its length (82 words) and complexity. What is the rhetorical effect of concluding the speech with such a sentence?

7. In his 1992 book, *Lincoln at Gettysburg: The Words That Remade America*, historian Garry Wills writes:

> The Gettysburg Address has become an authoritative expression of the American spirit — as authoritative as the Declaration [of Independence] itself, and perhaps even more influential, since it determines how we read the Declaration. For most people now, the Declaration means what Lincoln told us it means, as a way of correcting the Constitution itself without overthrowing it. It is this correction of the spirit, this intellectual revolution, that makes attempts to go back beyond Lincoln to some earlier version so feckless. . . . By accepting the Gettysburg Address, its concept of a single people dedicated to a proposition, we have been changed. Because of it, we live in a different America.

How accurately does Wills characterize the importance of the Gettysburg Address? Based on the text itself, and your knowledge of American history, how would you evaluate Wills's claims?

Letter to Albert G. Hodges

ABRAHAM LINCOLN

In a conversation that President Lincoln had with Governor Thomas E. Bramlette, Senator Archibald Dixon, and Albert G. Hodges, all from Kentucky, a slave state that did not secede from the Union, Bramlette protested the recruiting of black soldiers in Kentucky. In response to a request from Hodges, editor of the *Frankfort Commonwealth*, Lincoln wrote a letter on April 4, 1864, in which he summarized the conversation.

My dear Sir:

You ask me to put in writing the substance of what I verbally said the other day, in your presence, to Governor Bramlette and Senator Dixon. It was about as follows:

I am naturally anti-slavery. If slavery is not wrong, nothing is wrong. I can not remember when I did not so think, and feel. And yet I have never understood that the Presidency conferred upon me an unrestricted right to act officially upon this judgment and feeling. It was in the oath I took that I would, to the best of my ability, preserve, protect, and defend the Constitution of the United States. I could not take the office without taking the oath. Nor was it my view that I might take an oath to get power, and break the oath in using the power. I understood, too, that in ordinary civil administration this oath even forbade me to practically indulge my primary abstract judgment on the moral question of slavery. I had publicly declared this many times, and in many ways. And I aver that, to this day, I have done no official act in mere deference to my abstract judgment and feeling on slavery. I did understand however, that my oath to preserve the Constitution to the best of my ability, imposed upon me the duty of preserving, by every indispensable means, that government — that nation — of which that Constitution was the organic law. Was it possible to lose the nation, and yet preserve the Constitution? By general law life *and* limb must be protected; yet often a limb must be amputated to save a life; but a life is never wisely given to save a limb. I felt that measures, otherwise unconstitutional, might become lawful, by becoming indispensable to the preservation of the Constitution, through the preservation of the nation. Right or wrong, I assumed this ground, and now avow it. I could not feel that, to the best of my ability, I had even tried to preserve the Constitution, if, to save slavery, or any minor matter, I should permit the wreck of government, country, and Constitution all together. When, early in the war, Gen. Fremont attempted military emancipation, I forbade it, because I did not then think it an indispensable necessity. When a little later, Gen. Cameron, then Secretary of War, suggested the arming of blacks, I objected, because I did not yet think it an indispensable necessity. When, still later, Gen. Hunter attempted military emancipation, I again forbade it, because I did not yet think the indispensable necessity had come. When, in March, and May, and July 1862 I made earnest, and successive appeals to the border states to favor compensated emancipation, I believed the indispensable necessity for military emancipation, and arming the blacks would come, unless averted by that measure. They declined the proposition; and I was, in my best judgment, driven to the alternative of either surrendering the Union, and with it, the Constitution, or of laying strong hand upon the colored element. I chose the latter. In choosing it, I hoped for greater gain than loss; but of this, I was not entirely confident. More than a year of trial now shows no loss by it in our foreign relations, none in our home popular sentiment, none in our white military force, — no loss by it any how or any where. On the contrary, it shows a gain of quite a hundred and thirty thousand soldiers, seamen, and laborers. These are palpable facts, about which, as facts, there can be no cavilling. We have the men; and we could not have had them, without the measure.

And now let any Union man who complains of the measure, test himself by writing down in one line that he is for subduing the rebellion by force of arms; and in the next, that he is for taking these hundred and thirty thousand men from the Union side, and placing them where they would be but for the measure he condemns. If he can not face his case so stated, it is only because he can not face the truth.

I add a word which was not in the verbal conversation. In telling this tale I attempt no compliment to my own sagacity. I claim not to have controlled events, but confess plainly that events have controlled me. Now, at the end of three years struggle the nation's condition is not what either party, or any man devised, or expected. God alone can claim it. Whither it is tending seems plain. If God now wills the removal of a great wrong, and wills also that we of the North as well as you of the South, shall pay fairly for our complicity in that wrong, impartial history will find therein new cause to attest and revere the justice and goodness of God.

Yours truly

A. Lincoln

(1864)

Questions

1. What distinctions does Abraham Lincoln make between his feeling and his judgment, on the one hand, and his duty, on the other?
2. What is the purpose and effect of the analogy that Lincoln develops in the first paragraph of his summary statement?
3. What reasons does Lincoln give for having forbidden emancipation in the past? What convinced him that the "indispensable necessity" had finally come?
4. What is the purpose of the brief paragraph 2 of his summary?
5. How does Lincoln appeal to ethos in the concluding paragraph of the letter?

Second Inaugural Address

ABRAHAM LINCOLN

After being re-elected to the presidency in 1884 for a second term, Abraham Lincoln delivered his second inaugural address on March 4, 1865. At the time, it was evident that the war would soon be over. In the speech, the president reflects on the meaning and purpose of the war and the prospects for peace and reconstruction.

At this second appearing to take the oath of the presidential office, there is less occasion for an extended address than there was at the first. Then a statement, somewhat in detail, of a course to be pursued, seemed fitting and proper. Now, at the expiration of four years, during which public declarations have been constantly called forth on every point and phase of the great contest which still absorbs the attention, and engrosses the energies of the nation, little that is new could be presented. The progress of our arms, upon which all else chiefly depends, is as well known to the public as to myself; and it is, I trust, reasonably satisfactory and encouraging to all. With high hope for the future, no prediction in regard to it is ventured.

On the occasion corresponding to this four years ago, all thoughts were anxiously directed to an impending civil-war. All dreaded it — all sought to avert it. While the inaugural address was being delivered from this place, devoted altogether to *saving* the Union without war, insurgent agents were in the city seeking to *destroy* it without war — seeking to dissolve the Union, and divide effects, by negotiation. Both parties deprecated war; but one of them would *make* war rather than let the nation survive; and the other would *accept* war rather than let it perish. And the war came.

One eighth of the whole population were colored slaves, not distributed generally over the Union, but localized in the Southern part of it. These slaves constituted a peculiar and powerful interest. All knew that this interest was, somehow, the cause of the war. To strengthen, perpetuate, and extend this interest was the object for which the insurgents would rend the Union, even by war; while the government claimed no right to do more than to restrict the territorial enlargement of it. Neither party expected for the war, the magnitude, or the duration, which it has already attained. Neither anticipated that the *cause* of the conflict might cease with, or even before, the conflict itself should cease. Each looked for an easier triumph, and a result less fundamental and astounding. Both read the same Bible, and pray to the same God; and each invokes His aid against the other. It may seem strange that any men should dare to ask a just God's assistance in wringing their bread from the sweat of other men's faces; but let us judge not that we be not judged. The prayers of both could not be answered; that of neither has been answered fully. The Almighty has His own purposes. "Woe unto the world because of offences! for it must needs be that offences come; but woe to that man by whom the offence cometh!" If we shall suppose that American Slavery is one of those offences which, in the providence of God, must needs come, but which, having continued through His appointed time, He now wills to remove, and that He gives to both North and South, this terrible war, as the woe due to those by whom the offence came, shall we discern therein any departure from those divine attributes which the believers in a Living God always ascribe to Him? Fondly do we hope — fervently do we pray — that this mighty scourge of war may speedily pass away. Yet, if God wills that it continue, until all the wealth piled by the bond-man's two hundred and fifty years of unrequited toil shall be sunk, and until every drop of blood drawn with the lash, shall be paid by another drawn with the sword, as was said three thousand years ago, so still it must be said "the judgments of the Lord, are true and righteous altogether."

With malice toward none; with charity for all; with firmness in the right, as God gives us to see the right, let us strive on to finish the work we are in; to bind up the nation's wounds; to care for him who shall have borne the battle, and for his widow, and his orphan — to do all which may achieve and cherish a just, and a lasting peace, among ourselves, and with all nations.

(1865)

Questions

1. How would you describe President Abraham Lincoln's tone at the beginning of the speech? How does it change by the end?
2. Notice that in the second paragraph Lincoln uses many contrasts and juxtapositions to create distinctions, and in the third paragraph, he makes comparisons to point to similarities. How do these strategies contribute to his rhetorical purpose?

Considering the fact that he was addressing not only his Union supporters but also the entire audience, what likely effect did these strategies have on his audience?

3. Lincoln says, "It may seem strange that any men should dare to ask a just God's assistance in wringing their bread from the sweat of other men's faces; but let us judge not that we be not judged" (par. 3). What does that statement imply?

4. Explain the rhetorical question that Lincoln poses in paragraph 3.

5. Which of the classic appeals, to ethos, logos, or pathos, is most prominent in this speech? Explain.

Reading the Emancipation Proclamation in the Slaves' Cabin

Henry W. Herrick

> Also known as *The Midnight Hour*, this 1864 engraving by J. W. Watts is based on a scene by New Hampshire artist Henry W. Herrick. It is thought to depict the night of January 1, 1863, the day of the signing of the Emancipation Proclamation.

EMANCIPATION   PROCLAMATION.

Division of Rare and Manuscript Collections, Cornell University Library

Questions

1. Note the various figures in the engraving. Who is reading the proclamation? What is significant about the soldier's presence? Is he a Union or a Confederate soldier? Explain.
2. Look carefully at the facial expressions of the people in the cabin, particularly at the man behind the soldier, the old woman on the left, the man with his hands clasped on the right, and the young mother in the foreground. If you were to give voice to their thoughts based on their expressions, what would each one say?
3. Why did the artist depict Abraham Lincoln's portrait at the bottom of the engraving? Does it enhance the experience of looking at the scene? Does it detract from it? Explain.
4. What do you think Henry W. Herrick would say if you could ask him why he composed his painting as he did?

Freedman's Memorial to Abraham Lincoln

THOMAS BALL

> The Freedman's Memorial to Abraham Lincoln, also known as the Emancipation Memorial, a statue commissioned by African American donors and designed and

Courtesy of Terrence Restivo.

sculpted by Thomas Ball, was completed in 1876. Depicted is the fugitive slave Archer Alexander being freed by the Great Emancipator, President Lincoln. The memorial stands in Lincoln Park in the Capitol Hill area of Washington, D.C.

Questions

1. Look carefully at the statue. How would you describe the figures depicted? Note such particular details as the hands of the figures, their postures, and their facial expressions.
2. Thomas Ball was asked to depict Lincoln as "helping to break the chain that had bound him [the slave]." How does that information affect your view of the memorial?
3. The memorial met with general approval, especially from white citizens, but Frederick Douglass complained that the statue "showed the Negro on his knees when a more manly attitude would have been indicative of freedom." How do you feel about the scene captured by the statue? Is it appropriate? Explain.
4. How does this image contribute to your understanding of Abraham Lincoln's legacy?

from *Reminiscences of Abraham Lincoln by Distinguished Men of His Time*

FREDERICK DOUGLASS

A decade after his speech at the dedication of the Freedman's Memorial to Abraham Lincoln, Frederick Douglass wrote this piece for *Reminiscences of Abraham Lincoln by Distinguished Men of His Time*, a collection edited by Allen Thorndike Rice of the influential scholarly journal *North American Review*.

I do not know more about Mr. Lincoln than is known by countless thousands of Americans who have met the man. But I am quite willing to give my recollections of him and the impressions made by him upon my mind as to his character.

My first interview with him was in the summer of 1863, soon after the Confederate States had declared their purpose to treat colored soldiers as insurgents, and their purpose not to treat any such soldiers as prisoners of war subject to exchange like other soldiers. My visit to Mr. Lincoln was in reference to this threat of the Confederate States. I was at the time engaged in raising colored troops, and I desired some assurances from President Lincoln that such troops should be treated as soldiers of the United States, and when taken prisoners exchanged like other soldiers; that when any of them were hanged or enslaved the President should retaliate. I was introduced to Mr. Lincoln on this occasion by Senator Pomeroy, of Kansas; I met him at the Executive Mansion.

I was somewhat troubled with the thought of meeting one so august and high in authority, especially as I had never been in the White House before, and had never spoken to a President of the United States before. But my embarrassment soon vanished when I met the face of Mr. Lincoln. When I entered he was seated in a low chair, surrounded by a multitude of books and papers, his feet and legs were extended in front of his chair. On my approach he slowly drew his feet in from the different parts of the room into which they had strayed, and he began to rise, and continued to rise until he looked down upon me, and extended his hand and gave me a welcome. I began, with some hesitation, to tell him who I was and what I had been doing, but he soon stopped me, saying in a sharp, cordial voice:

"You need not tell me who you are, Mr. Douglass, I know who you are. Mr. Sewell has told me all about you."

He then invited me to take a seat beside him. Not wishing to occupy his time   5
and attention, seeing that he was busy, I stated to him the object of my call at once. I said:

"Mr. Lincoln, I am recruiting colored troops. I have assisted in fitting up two regiments in Massachusetts, and am now at work in the same way in Pennsylvania, and have come to say this to you, sir, if you wish to make this branch of the service successful you must do four things:

"First — You must give colored soldiers the same pay that you give white soldiers.

"Second — You must compel the Confederate States to treat colored soldiers, when taken prisoners, as prisoners of war.

"Third — When any colored man or soldier performs brave, meritorious exploits in the field, you must enable me to say to those that I recruit that they will be promoted for such service, precisely as white men are promoted for similar service.

"Fourth — In case any colored soldiers are murdered in cold blood and taken   10
prisoners, you should retaliate in kind."

To this little speech Mr. Lincoln listened with earnest attention and with very apparent sympathy, and replied to each point in his own peculiar, forcible way. First he spoke of the opposition generally to employing negroes as soldiers at all, of the prejudice against the race, and of the advantage to colored people that would result from their being employed as soldiers in defense of their country. He regarded such an employment as an experiment, and spoke of the advantage it would be to the colored race if the experiment should succeed. He said that he had difficulty in getting colored men into the United States uniform; that when the purpose was fixed to employ them as soldiers, several different uniforms were proposed for them, and that it was something gained when it was finally determined to clothe them like other soldiers.

Now, as to the pay, we had to make some concession to prejudice. There were threats that if we made soldiers of them at all white men would not enlist, would not fight beside them. Besides, it was not believed that a negro could make a good soldier, as good a soldier as a white man, and hence it was thought that he should not have the same pay as a white man. But said he,

"I assure you, Mr. Douglass, that in the end they shall have the same pay as white soldiers."

As to the exchange and general treatment of colored soldiers when taken prisoners of war, he should insist to their being entitled to all privileges of such prisoners.

Mr. Lincoln admitted the justice of my demand for the promotion of colored soldiers for good conduct in the field, but on the matter of retaliation he differed from me entirely. I shall never forget the benignant expression of his face, the tearful look of his eye and the quiver in his voice, when he deprecated a resort to retaliatory measures.

"Once begun," said he, "I do not know where such a measure would stop." 15

He said he could not take men out and kill them in cold blood for what was done by others. If he could get hold of the persons who were guilty of killing the colored prisoners in cold blood, the case would be different, but he could not kill the innocent for the guilty.

Before leaving Mr. Lincoln, Senator Pomeroy said:

"Mr. President, Mr. Stanton is going to make Douglass Adjutant-General to General Thomas, and is going to send him down the Mississippi to recruit."

Mr. Lincoln said in answer to this:

"I will sign any commission that Mr. Stanton will give Mr. Douglass." 20

At this point we parted.

I met Mr. Lincoln several times after this interview.

I was once invited by him to take tea with him at the Soldiers' Home. On one occasion, while visiting him at the White House, he showed me a letter he was writing to Horace Greeley in reply to some of Greeley's criticisms against protracting the war. He seemed to feel very keenly the reproaches heaped upon him for not bringing the war to a speedy conclusion; said he was charged with making it an Abolition war instead of a war for the Union, and expressed his desire to end the war as soon as possible. While I was talking with him Governor Buckingham sent in his card, and I was amused by his telling the messenger, as well as by the way he expressed it, to "tell Governor Buckingham to wait, I want to have a long talk with my friend Douglass."

He used those words. I said: "Mr. Lincoln, I will retire." "Oh, no, no, you shall not, I want Governor Buckingham to wait," and he did wait for at least a half hour. When he came in I was introduced by Mr. Lincoln to Governor Buckingham, and the Governor did not seem to take it amiss at all that he had been required to wait.

I was present at the inauguration of Mr. Lincoln, the 4th of March, 1865. I felt 25 then that there was murder in the air, and I kept close to his carriage on the way to the Capitol, for I felt that I might see him fall that day. It was a vague presentiment.

At that time the Confederate cause was on its last legs, as it were, and there was deep feeling. I could feel it in the atmosphere here. I did not know exactly what it was, but I just felt as if he might be shot on his way to the Capitol. I cannot refer to any incident, in fact, to any expression that I heard, it was simply a presentiment that Lincoln might fall that day. I got right in front of the east portico of the Capitol, listened to his inaugural address, and witnessed his being sworn in by Chief Justice Chase. When he came on the steps he was accompanied by Vice-President Johnson. In looking out in the crowd he saw me standing near by, and I could see he was pointing me out to Andrew Johnson. Mr. Johnson, without knowing perhaps that I saw the movement, looked quite annoyed that his attention should be called in that direction. So I got a peep into his soul. As soon as he saw me looking at him, suddenly he assumed rather an amicable expression of countenance. I felt that, whatever else the man might be, he was no friend to my people.

I heard Mr. Lincoln deliver this wonderful address. It was very short; but he answered all the objections raised to his prolonging the war in one sentence — it was a remarkable sentence.

"Fondly do we hope, profoundly do we pray, that this mighty scourge of war shall soon pass away, yet if God wills it continue until all the wealth piled up by two hundred years of bondage shall have been wasted, and each drop of blood drawn by the lash shall have been paid for by one drawn by the sword, we must still say, as was said three thousand years ago, the judgments of the Lord are true and righteous altogether."

For the first time in my life, and I suppose the first time in any colored man's life, I attended the reception of President Lincoln on the evening of the inauguration. As I approached the door I was seized by two policemen and forbidden to enter. I said to them that they were mistaken entirely in what they were doing, that if Mr. Lincoln knew that I was at the door he would order my admission, and I bolted in by them. On the inside I was taken charge of by two other policemen, to be conducted as I supposed to the President, but instead of that they were conducting me out the window on a plank.

"Oh," said I, "this will not do, gentlemen," and as a gentleman was passing in I   30 said to him, "Just say to Mr. Lincoln that Fred. Douglass is at the door."

He rushed in to President Lincoln, and almost in less than a half a minute I was invited into the East Room of the White House. A perfect sea of beauty and elegance, too, it was. The ladies were in very fine attire, and Mrs. Lincoln was standing there. I could not have been more than ten feet from him when Mr. Lincoln saw me; his countenance lighted up, and he said in a voice which was heard all around: "Here comes my friend Douglass." As I approached him he reached out his hand, gave me a cordial shake, and said: "Douglass, I saw you in the crowd to-day listening to my inaugural address. There is no man's opinion that I value more than yours: what do you think of it?" I said: "Mr. Lincoln, I cannot stop here to talk with you, as there are thousands waiting to shake you by the hand;" but he said again: "What did you think of it?" I said: "Mr. Lincoln, it was a sacred effort," and then I walked off. "I am glad you liked it," he said. That was the last time I saw him to speak with him.

In all my interviews with Mr. Lincoln I was impressed with his entire freedom from popular prejudice against the colored race. He was the first great man that I talked with in the United States freely, who in no single instance reminded me of the difference between himself and myself, of the difference of color, and I thought that all the more remarkable because he came from a State where there were black laws. I account partially for his kindness to me because of the similarity with which I had fought my way up, we both starting at the lowest round of the ladder. . . .

There was one thing concerning Lincoln that I was impressed with, and that was that a statement of his was an argument more convincing than any amount of logic. He had a happy faculty of stating a proposition, of stating it so that it needed no argument. It was a rough kind of reasoning, but it went right to the point. Then, too, there was another feeling that I had with reference to him, and that was that while I felt in his presence I was in the presence of a very great man, as great as the greatest, I felt as though I could go and put my hand on him if I wanted to, to put my hand on his shoulder. Of course I did not do it, but I felt that I could. I felt as though I was in the presence of a big brother, and that there was safety in his atmosphere.

It was often said during the war that Mrs. Lincoln did not sympathize fully with her husband in his anti-slavery feeling, but I never believed this concerning her, and have good reason for being confirmed in my impression of her by the fact that, when Mr. Lincoln died and she was about leaving the White House, she selected his favorite walking cane and said: "I know of no one that would appreciate this more than Fred. Douglass." She sent it to me at Rochester, and I have it in my house to-day, and expect to keep it there as long as I live.

Frederick Douglass.
(1886)

Questions

1. Frederick Douglass begins, "I do not know more about Mr. Lincoln than is known by countless thousands of Americans who have met the man." Do you think that is true? Is Douglass being disingenuous? Why would he begin this way?
2. How satisfied is Douglass with Lincoln's responses to his concerns? Be specific as you explain.
3. On which point do Douglass and Lincoln disagree (par. 14)? Notice that Douglass doesn't state his response. Why not? What do you think his response was? Explain.
4. In paragraph 28, Douglass quotes from Lincoln's second inaugural address. Clearly this passage struck Douglass powerfully. Why would he select this particular passage to include in this piece? Explain.
5. How does Douglass characterize Abraham Lincoln? Be specific in your answer.
6. Douglass writes, "There was one thing concerning Lincoln that I was impressed with, and that was that a statement of his was an argument more convincing than any amount of logic. He had a happy faculty of stating a proposition, of stating it so that it needed no argument" (par. 33). Based on your reading of four texts by Lincoln, do you agree? Select a brief passage from one of the texts as evidence to defend or challenge Douglass's statement.

from *Abraham Lincoln and Our "Unfinished Work"*

MARIO M. CUOMO

Mario M. Cuomo (b. 1932) served three terms as governor of New York State, from 1983 through 1994. The following excerpt is from a speech he gave before the Abraham Lincoln Association in Springfield, Missouri, on February 12, 1986.

Lincoln believed, with every fibre of his being, that this place, America, could offer a dream to all mankind, different than any other in the annals of history. More generous, more compassionate, more inclusive. No one knew better than Lincoln, our sturdiness, the ability of most of us to make it on our own given the chance. But at the same time, no one knew better the idea of family, the idea that unless we helped one another, there were some who would never make it.

One person climbs the ladder of personal ambition, reaches his dream, and then turns — and pulls the ladder up. Another reaches the place he has sought, turns, and reaches down for the person behind him. With Lincoln, it was that process of turning and reaching down, that commitment to keep lifting people up the ladder, which defined the American character, stamping us forever with a mission that reached even beyond our borders to embrace the world. Lincoln's belief in America, in the American people, was broader, deeper, more daring than any other person's of his age — and perhaps, ours too. And this is the near-unbelievable greatness of the man: that with that belief, he not only led us, he created us.

His personal mythology became our national mythology. It is as if Homer not only chronicled the siege of Troy, but conducted the siege as well. As if Shakespeare set his playwrighting aside to lead the English against the Armada. Because Lincoln embodied his age in his actions and in his words.

Words, even and measured, hurrying across three decades, calling us to our destiny. Words he prayed, and troubled over — more than a million words in his speeches and writings. Words that chronicled the search for his own identity as he searched for a nation's identity. Words that were, by turns, as chilling as the night sky and as assuring as home. Words his reason sharpened into steel, and his heart softened into an embrace. Words filled with all the longings of his soul and of his century. Words wrung from his private struggle, spun to capture the struggle of a nation. Words out of his own pain to heal that struggle. Words of retribution, but never of revenge. Words that judged, but never condemned. Words that pleaded, cajoled for the one belief — that the promise must be kept — that the dream must endure and grow, until it embraces everyone. Words ringing down into the present. All the hope and the pain of that epic caught, somehow, by his cadences: the tearing away, the binding together, the leaving behind, the reaching beyond. As individuals, as a people, we are still reaching up, for a better job, a better education, even for the stars, just as Lincoln did. But because of Lincoln, we do it in a way that is unique to this world.

What other people on earth have ever claimed a quality of character that resided not in a way of speaking, dressing, dancing, praying, but in an idea? What other people on earth have ever refused to set the definitions of their identity by anything other than that idea? No, we have not learned quickly or easily that the dream of America endures only so long as we keep faith with the struggle to include. But Lincoln — through his words and his works — has etched that message forever into our consciousness.

Lincoln showed us, for all time, what unites us. He taught us that we cannot rest until the promise of equality and opportunity embraces every region, every race, every religion, every nationality, . . . and every class. Until it includes, "the penniless beginner" and the "poor man seeking his chance."[1]

In his time Lincoln saw that as long as one in every seven Americans was enslaved, our identity as a people was hostage to that enslavement. He faced that injustice. He fought it. He gave his life to see it righted.

Time and again, since then, we have had to face challenges that threatened to divide us. And time and again, we have conquered them. We reached out — hesitantly at times, sometimes only after great struggle — but always we reached out, to include impoverished immigrants, the farmer and the factory worker, women, the disabled.

To all those whose only assets were their great expectations, America found ways to meet those expectations, and to create new ones. Generations of hard-working people moved into the middle class and beyond. We created a society as open and free as any on earth. And we did it Lincoln's way: by founding that society on a belief in the boundless enterprise of the American people. Always, we have extended the promise, moving toward the light, toward our declared purpose as a people: "to form a more perfect union," to overcome all that divides us because we believe that ancient wisdom that Lincoln believed: "A house divided against itself cannot stand."[2] Step-by-step, our embrace grows wider. The old bigotries seem to be dying. The old stereotypes and hatreds, that denied so many their full share of an America they helped build, have gradually given way to acceptance, fairness and civility.

But still, great challenges remain. Suddenly, ominously, a new one has emerged.   10
In Lincoln's time, one of every seven Americans was a slave. Today, for all our affluence and might, despite what every day is described as our continuing economic recovery, nearly one in every seven Americans lives in poverty, not in chains — because Lincoln saved us from that   but trapped in a cycle of despair that is its own enslavement. Today, while so many of us do so well, one of every two minority children is born poor, many of them to be oppressed for a lifetime by inadequate education and the suffocating influence of broken families and social disorientation. Our identity as a people is hostage to the grim facts of more than thirty-three million Americans for whom equality and opportunity is not yet an attainable reality, but only an illusion.

Some people look at these statistics and the suffering people behind them, and deny them, pretending instead we are all one great "shining city on a hill." Lincoln told us for a lifetime — and for all time to come — that there can be no shining city

---

[1]In a speech in Chicago on December 10, 1856, Lincoln said: "Public opinion, on any subject, always has a 'central idea,' from which all its minor thoughts radiate. The 'central idea' in our public opinion at the beginning was . . . 'the equality of all men.' And although it has always submitted patiently to whatever of inequality there seemed to be as a matter of actual necessity, its constant working has been a steady progress toward the practical equality of all men," (*Collected Works*, 2:385). Speaking again in Chicago on July 10, 1858, Lincoln spoke of the "electric cord" in the Declaration of Independence "that links the hearts of patriotic and liberty-loving men together. . . ." (*Collected Works*, 2:499–500).

[2]House Divided Speech, Springfield, Illinois, 16 June 1858, *Collected Works*, 2:461.

when one in seven of us is denied the promise of the declaration. He tells us today that we are justly proud of all that we have accomplished, but that for all our progress, for all our achievement, for all that so properly makes us proud, we have no right to rest, content. Nor justification for turning from the effort, out of fear or lack of confidence.

We have met greater challenges with fewer resources. We have faced greater perils with fewer friends. It would be a desecration of our belief and an act of ingratitude for the good fortune we have had, to end the struggle for inclusion because it is over for some of us.

So, this evening, we come to pay you our respects, Mr. Lincoln. Not just by recalling your words and revering your memory, which we do humbly and with great pleasure. This evening, we offer you more Mr. President: we offer you what you have asked us for, a continuing commitment to live your truth, to go forward painful step by painful step, enlarging the greatness of this nation with patient confidence in the ultimate justice of the people.

Because—as you have told us Mr. President—there is no better or equal hope in the world. Thank you.

(1986)

Questions

1. In the first section of this piece, how does Governor Mario M. Cuomo characterize Abraham Lincoln? Be specific.
2. What is the effect of the rhetorical questions in paragraph 5?
3. How effective is the analogy between slavery and poverty that Cuomo makes in paragraph 10?
4. Note that Cuomo concludes by directly addressing Lincoln. What is the rhetorical effect of this decision?

from *Who Freed the Slaves?*

James McPherson

> James McPherson (b. 1936) is a professor of history at Princeton University and author of the Pulitzer Prize–winning *Battle Cry of Freedom: The Civil War Era,* among many other highly acclaimed books. In his essay "Who Freed the Slaves?" he assesses Abraham Lincoln's role as the Great Emancipator.

If we were to go out on the streets of almost any town in America and ask the question posed by the title of this essay, probably nine out of ten respondents would answer unhesitatingly, "Abraham Lincoln." Most of them would cite the Emancipation Proclamation as the key document. Some of the more reflective and better informed respondents would add the Thirteenth Amendment and point to Lincoln's important role in its adoption. And a few might qualify their answer by noting that without

Union military victory the Emancipation Proclamation and Thirteenth Amendment would never have gone into effect, or at least would not have applied to the states where most of the slaves lived. But, of course, Lincoln was commander in chief of Union armies, so the credit for their victories would belong mainly to him. The answer would still be the same: Lincoln freed the slaves.

In recent years, though, this answer has been challenged as another example of elitist history, of focusing only on the actions of great white males and ignoring the actions of the overwhelming majority of the people, who also make history. If we were to ask our question of professional historians, the reply would be quite different. For one thing, it would not be simple or clear-cut. Many of them would answer along the lines of "On the one hand . . . but on the other. . . ." They would speak of ambivalence, ambiguity, nuances, paradox, irony. They would point to Lincoln's gradualism, his slow and apparently reluctant decision for emancipation, his revocation of emancipation orders by Generals John C. Frémont and David Hunter, his exemption of border states and parts of the Confederacy from the Emancipation Proclamation, his statements seemingly endorsing white supremacy. They would say that the whole issue is more complex than it appears — in other words many historians, as is their wont, would not give a straight answer to the question.

But of those who did, a growing number would reply, as did a historian speaking to the Civil War Institute at Gettysburg College in 1991: "THE SLAVES FREED THEMSELVES."[1] They saw the Civil War as a potential war for abolition well before Lincoln did. By flooding into Union military camps in the South, they forced the issue of emancipation on the Lincoln administration. By creating a situation in which Northern officials would either have to return them to slavery or acknowledge their freedom, these "contrabands," as they came to be called, "acted resolutely to place their freedom — and that of their posterity — on the wartime agenda." Union officers, then Congress, and finally Lincoln decided to confiscate this human property belonging to the enemy and put it to work for the Union in the form of servants, teamsters, laborers, and eventually soldiers in Northern armies. Weighed in the scale of war, these 190,000 black soldiers and sailors (and probably a larger number of black army laborers) tipped the balance in favor of Union victory. Even deep in the Confederate interior remote from the fighting fronts, with the departure of masters and overseers to the army, "leaving women and old men in charge, the balance of power gradually shifted in favor of slaves, undermining slavery on farms and plantations far from the line of battle."[2]

One of the leading exponents of the black self-emancipation thesis is the historian and theologian Vincent Harding, whose book *There Is a River: The Black Struggle for Freedom in America* has become almost a Bible for the argument. "While Lincoln

---

[1]Robert F. Engs, "The Great American Slave Rebellion," lecture delivered to the Civil War Institute at Gettysburg College. June 27, 1991, p. 3.
[2]Ira Berlin, Barbara J. Fields, Thavolia Glymph, Joseph P. Reidy, and Leslie S. Rowland, eds., *Freedom: A Documentary History of Emancipation 1861–1867*, Ser. I, Vol. I, *The Destruction of Slavery* (Cambridge, 1985), pp. 2. 10.

continued to hesitate about the legal, constitutional, moral, and military aspects of the matter," Harding writes, "the relentless movement of the self-liberated fugitives into the Union lines" soon "approached and surpassed every level of force previously known. . . . Making themselves an unavoidable military and political issue . . . this overwhelming human movement . . . of self-freed men and women . . . took their freedom into their own hands." The Emancipation Proclamation, when it finally and belatedly came, merely "confirmed and gave ambiguous legal standing to the freedom which black people had already claimed through their own surging, living proclamations."[3]

During the 1980s this self-emancipation theme achieved the status of orthodoxy   5 among social historians. The largest scholarly enterprise on the history of emancipation and the transition from a slave to a free society during the Civil War era, the Freedmen and Southern Society project at the University of Maryland, stamped its imprimatur on the interpretation. The slaves, wrote the editors of this project, were "the prime movers in securing their own liberty." . . .

How valid are these statements? First, we must recognize the considerable degree of truth in the main thesis. By coming into Union lines, by withdrawing their labor from Confederate owners, by working for the Union army and fighting as soldiers in it, slaves did play an active part in achieving their own freedom and, for that matter, in preserving the Union. Like workers, immigrants, women, and other non-elites, slaves were neither passive victims nor pawns of powerful white males who loom so large in our traditional image of American history. They too played a part in determining their own destiny; they too made a history that historians have finally discovered. That is all to the good. But by challenging the "myth" that Lincoln freed the slaves, proponents of the self-emancipation thesis are in danger of creating another myth — that he had little to do with it. It may turn out, upon close examination, that the traditional answer to the question "Who Freed the Slaves?" is closer to being the right answer than is the new and currently more fashionable answer.

First, one must ask what was the sine qua non of emancipation in the 1860s — the essential condition, the one thing without which it would not have happened. The clear answer is the war. Without the Civil War there would have been no confiscation act, no Emancipation Proclamation, no Thirteenth Amendment (not to mention the Fourteenth and Fifteenth), certainly no self-emancipation, and almost certainly no end of slavery for several more decades at least. Slavery had existed in North America for more than two centuries before 1861, but except for a tiny fraction of slaves who fought in the Revolution, or escaped, or bought their freedom, there had been no self-emancipation during that time. Every slave insurrection or insurrection conspiracy failed in the end. On the eve of the Civil War, plantation agriculture was more profitable, slavery more entrenched, slave owners more prosperous, and the "slave power" more dominant within the South if not in the nation at large than it had ever

---

[3]Vincent Harding, *There Is a River: The Black Struggle for Freedom in America* (New York, 1981), pp. 231, 230, 225, 226, 228, 235.

been. Without the war, the door to freedom would have remained closed for an indeterminate length of time.

What brought the war and opened that door? The answer, of course, is complex as well as controversial. A short and simplified summary is that secession and the refusal of the United States government to recognize the legitimacy of secession brought on the war. In both of these matters Abraham Lincoln moves to center stage. Seven states seceded and formed the Confederacy because he won election to the presidency on an antislavery platform; four more seceded after shooting broke out when he refused to evacuate Fort Sumter; the shooting escalated to full-scale war because he called out the troops to suppress rebellion. The common denominator in all of the steps that opened the door to freedom was the active agency of Abraham Lincoln as antislavery political leader, president-elect, president, and commander in chief. . . .

But, we must ask, would not the election of *any* Republican in 1860 have provoked secession? Probably not, if the candidate had been Edward Bates[4] — who might conceivably have won the election but had no chance of winning the nomination. Yes, almost certainly, if William H. Seward had been the nominee. Seward's earlier talk of a "higher law" and an "irrepressible conflict" had given him a more radical reputation than Lincoln. But Seward might not have won the election. More to the point, if he had won, seven states would undoubtedly have seceded but Seward would have favored compromises and concessions to keep others from going out and perhaps to lure those seven back in. Most important of all, he would have evacuated Fort Sumter and thereby extinguished the spark that threatened to flame into war.

As it was, Seward did his best to compel Lincoln into concessions and evacua-   10
tion of the fort. But Lincoln stood firm. When Seward flirted with the notion of supporting the Crittenden Compromise,[5] which would have repudiated the Republican platform by permitting the expansion of slavery, Lincoln stiffened the backbones of Seward and other key Republican leaders. "Entertain no proposition for a compromise in regard to the *extension* of slavery," he wrote to them. "The tug has to come, & better now, than any time hereafter." Crittenden's compromise "would lose us everything we gained by the election." It "acknowledges that slavery has equal rights with liberty, and surrenders all we have contended for. . . . We have just carried an election on principles fairly stated to the people. Now we are told in advance, the government shall be broken up, unless we surrender to those we have beaten. . . . If we surrender, it is the end of us. They will repeat the experiment upon us *ad libitum.* A year will not pass, till we shall have to take Cuba as a condition upon which they will stay in the Union."[6]

---

[4]Conservative Republican lawyer from Missouri whom Lincoln appointed as attorney general. — Eds.

[5]Kentucky senator John J. Crittenden's proposal to reestablish the Missouri Compromise line, with slavery prohibited north of it and allowed south of it. — Eds.

[6]Roy P. Basler, ed., *The Collected Works of Abraham Lincoln*, 9 vols. (New Brunswick, N.J., 1953–1955). IV, 149–51, 154, 183, 155, 172.

It is worth emphasizing here that the common denominator in these letters from Lincoln to Republican leaders was slavery. To be sure, on the matters of slavery where it already existed and enforcement of the fugitive slave provision of the Constitution, Lincoln was willing to reassure the South. But on the crucial issue of 1860, slavery in the territories, he refused to compromise, and this refusal kept his party in line. . . . As Lincoln expressed it in a private letter to his old friend Alexander Stephens, "You think slavery is *right* and ought to be extended; while we think it is *wrong* and ought to be restricted. That I suppose is the rub."

It was indeed the rub. Even more than in his election to the presidency, Lincoln's refusal to compromise on the expansion of slavery or on Fort Sumter proved decisive. If another person had been in his place, the course of history — and of emancipation — would have been different. Here again we have without question a sine qua non.

It is quite true that once the war started, Lincoln moved more slowly and apparently more reluctantly toward making it a war for emancipation than black leaders, abolitionists, radical Republicans, and the slaves themselves wanted him to move. He did reassure Southern whites that he had no intention and no constitutional power to interfere with slavery in the states. In September 1861 and May 1862 he revoked orders by Generals Frémont and Hunter freeing the slaves of Confederates in their military districts. In December 1861 he forced Secretary of War Simon Cameron to delete from his annual report a paragraph recommending the freeing and arming of slaves. And though Lincoln signed the confiscation acts of August 1861 and July 1862 that freed some slaves owned by Confederates, this legislation did not come from his initiative. Out in the field it was the slaves who escaped to Union lines and officers like General Benjamin Butler who accepted them as "contraband of war" that took the initiative.

All of this appears to support the thesis that slaves emancipated themselves and that Lincoln's image as emancipator is a myth. But let us take a closer look. It seems clear today, as it did in 1861, that no matter how many thousands of slaves came into Union lines, the ultimate fate of the millions who did not, as well as the fate of the institution of slavery itself, depended on the outcome of the war. If the North won, slavery would be weakened if not destroyed; if the Confederacy won, slavery would survive and perhaps grow stronger from the postwar territorial expansion of an independent and confident slave power. Thus Lincoln's emphasis on the priority of Union had positive implications for emancipation, while precipitate or premature actions against slavery might jeopardize the cause of Union and therefore boomerang in favor of slavery.

Lincoln's chief concern in 1861 was to maintain a united coalition of War Democrats and border-state Unionists as well as Republicans in support of the war effort. To do this he considered it essential to define the war as being waged solely for Union, which united this coalition, and not a war against slavery, which would fragment it. When General Frémont issued his emancipation edict in Missouri on August 30, 1861, the political and military efforts to prevent Kentucky, Maryland, and Missouri from seceding and to cultivate Unionists in western Virginia and eastern

Tennessee were at a crucial stage, balancing on a knife edge. To keep his fragile coalition from falling apart, therefore, Lincoln rescinded Frémont's order.

Almost certainly this was the right decision at the time. Lincoln's greatest skills as a political leader were his sensitivity to public opinion and his sense of timing. Within six months of his revocation of Frémont's order, he began moving toward a stronger antislavery position. During the spring and early summer of 1862 he alternately coaxed and prodded border-state Unionists toward recognition of the inevitable escalation of the conflict into a war against slavery and toward acceptance of his plan for compensated emancipation in their states. He warned them that the "friction and abrasion" of a war that had by this time swept every institution into its maelstrom could not leave slavery untouched. But the border states remained deaf to Lincoln's warnings and refused to consider his offer of federally compensated emancipation.

By July 1862, Lincoln turned a decisive corner toward abolition. He made up his mind to issue an emancipation proclamation. Whereas a year earlier, even three months earlier, Lincoln had believed that avoidance of such a drastic step was necessary to maintain that knife-edge balance in the Union coalition, things had now changed. The escalation of the war in scope and fury had mobilized all the resources of both sides, including the slave labor force of the Confederacy. . . . The risks of alienating the border states and Northern Democrats, Lincoln now believed, were outweighed by the opportunity to energize the Republican majority and to mobilize part of the slave population for the cause of Union — and freedom. When Lincoln told his cabinet on July 22, 1862, that he had decided to issue an emancipation proclamation, [Postmaster General] Montgomery Blair, speaking for the forces of conservatism in the North and border states, warned of the consequences among these groups if he did so. But Lincoln was done conciliating them. He had tried to make the border states see reason; now "we must make the forward movement" without them. "They [will] acquiesce, if not immediately, soon." As for the Northern Democrats, "their clubs would be used against us take what course we might."[7]

Two years later, speaking to a visiting delegation of abolitionists, Lincoln explained why he had moved more slowly against slavery than they had urged. Having taken an oath to preserve and defend the Constitution, which protected slavery, "I did not consider that I had a *right* to touch the 'State' institution of 'Slavery' until all other measures for restoring the Union had failed. . . . The moment came when I felt that slavery must die that the nation might live! . . . Many of my strongest supporters urged *Emancipation* before I thought it indispensable, and, I may say, before I thought the country ready for it. It is my conviction that, had the proclamation been issued even six months earlier than it was, public sentiment would not have sustained it."[8]

---

[7]John G. Nicolay and John Hay, *Abraham Lincoln: A History*, 10 vols. (New York, 1890), VI, 158–63.

[8]Francis B. Carpenter, *Six Months at the White House with Abraham Lincoln* (New York, 1866), pp. 76–77.

Lincoln actually could have made a case that the country had not been ready for the Emancipation Proclamation in September 1862, even in January 1863. Democratic gains in the Northern congressional elections of 1862 resulted in part from a voter backlash against the preliminary Emancipation Proclamation. The morale crisis in Union armies and swelling Copperhead strength during the winter of 1863 grew in part from a resentful conviction that Lincoln had unconstitutionally transformed the purpose of the war from restoring the Union to freeing the slaves. Without question, this issue bitterly divided the Northern people and threatened fatally to erode support for the war effort — the very consequence Lincoln had feared in 1861 and Montgomery Blair had warned against in 1862. Not until after the twin military victories at Gettysburg and Vicksburg[9] did this divisiveness diminish and emancipation gain a clear mandate in the off-year elections of 1863. In his annual message of December 1863, Lincoln conceded that the Emancipation Proclamation a year earlier had been "followed by dark and doubtful days." But now, he added, "the crisis which threatened to divide the friends of the Union is past."[10]

Even that statement turned out to be premature and overoptimistic. In the summer of 1864, Northern morale again plummeted and the emancipation issue once more threatened to undermine the war effort. By August, Grant's campaign in Virginia had bogged down in the trenches after enormous casualties. Sherman seemed similarly thwarted before Atlanta and smaller Union armies elsewhere appeared to be accomplishing nothing. War weariness and defeatism corroded the will of Northerners as they contemplated the staggering cost of this conflict in the lives of their young men. Lincoln came under enormous pressure to open peace negotiations to end the slaughter. Even though Jefferson Davis insisted that Confederate independence was his essential condition for peace, Northern Democrats managed to convince many Northern people that only Lincoln's insistence on emancipation blocked peace. A typical Democratic newspaper editorial declared that "tens of thousands of white men must yet bite the dust to allay the negro mania of the President."[11]

Even Republicans like Horace Greeley, who had criticized Lincoln two years earlier for slowness to embrace emancipation, now criticized him for refusing to abandon it as a precondition for negotiations. The Democratic national convention adopted a platform for the 1864 presidential election calling for peace negotiations to restore the Union with slavery. Every political observer, including Lincoln himself, believed in August that the Republicans would lose the election. The *New York Times* editor and Republican national chairman Henry Raymond told Lincoln that "two special causes are assigned [for] this great reaction in public sentiment, — the want of military success, and the impression . . . that we *can* have peace with Union

20

---

[9]The day after the Battle of Gettysburg, Confederate soldiers surrendered at Vicksburg, Mississippi. — Eds.
[10]Basler, ed., *Collected Works of Lincoln*, VII, 49–50.
[11]*Columbus Crisis*, Aug. 3. 1864.

if we would . . . [but that you are] fighting not for Union but for the abolition of slavery."[12]

The pressure on Lincoln to back down on emancipation caused him to waver temporarily but not to buckle. Instead, he told weak-kneed Republicans that "no human power can subdue this rebellion without using the Emancipation lever as I have done." More than one hundred thousand black soldiers and sailors were fighting for the Union, said Lincoln. They would not do so if they thought the North intended to "betray them. . . . If they stake their lives for us they must be prompted by the strongest motive . . . the promise of freedom. And the promise being made, must be kept. . . . There have been men who proposed to me to return to slavery the black warriors" who had fought for the Union. "I should be damned in time & in eternity for so doing. The world shall know that I will keep my faith to friends and enemies, come what will."[13]

When Lincoln said this, he fully expected to lose the election. In effect, he was saying that he would rather be right than president. In many ways this was his finest hour. As matters turned out, of course, he was both right and president. Sherman's capture of Atlanta, [General Philip] Sheridan's victories in the Shenandoah Valley, and military success elsewhere transformed the Northern mood from deepest despair in August 1864 to determined confidence by November, and Lincoln was triumphantly reelected. He won without compromising one inch on the emancipation question.

It is instructive to consider two possible alternatives to this outcome. If the Democrats had won, at best the Union would have been restored without a Thirteenth Amendment; at worst the Confederacy would have achieved its independence. In either case, the institution of slavery would have survived. That this did not happen was owing more to the steadfast purpose of Abraham Lincoln than to any other single factor.

The proponents of the self-emancipation thesis, however, would avow that all of this is irrelevant. . . . But I disagree. The tide of freedom could have been swept back. On numerous occasions during the war, it was. . . . The editors of the Freedmen's and Southern Society project, the most scholarly advocates of the self-emancipation thesis, acknowledge that "Southern armies could recapture black people who had already reached Union lines. . . . Indeed, any Union retreat could reverse the process of liberation and throw men and women who had tasted freedom back into bondage. . . . Their travail testified to the link between the military success of the Northern armies and the liberty of Southern slaves."[14]

Precisely. That is the crucial point. Slaves did not emancipate themselves; they were liberated by Union armies. Freedom quite literally came from the barrel of a gun. And who was the commander in chief that called these armies into being, appointed

25

---

[12]Raymond to Lincoln, Aug. 22, 1864, in Basler, ed., *Collected Works of Lincoln*, VII, 518.
[13]Lincoln to Charles D. Robinson, Aug. 17, 1864; interview of Lincoln with Alexander W. Randall and Joseph T. Mills, Aug. 19, 1864, both in ibid., 500, 506–7.
[14]Berlin et al., eds., *The Destruction of Slavery*, pp. 35–36.

their generals, and gave them direction and purpose? There, indubitably, is our sine qua non.

But let us grant that once the war was carried into slave territory, no matter how it came out the ensuing "friction and abrasion" would have enabled thousands of slaves to escape to freedom. In that respect, a degree of self-emancipation did occur. But even on a large scale, such emancipation was very different from *the abolition of the institution of slavery*. During the American Revolution almost as large a percentage of the slaves won freedom by coming within British lines as achieved liberation by coming within Union lines during the Civil War. Yet slavery survived the Revolution. Ending the institution of bondage required Union victory; it required Lincoln's reelection in 1864; it required the Thirteenth Amendment. Lincoln played a vital role, indeed the central role, in all of these achievements. It was also his policies and his skillful political leadership that set in motion the processes by which the reconstructed or Unionist states of Louisiana, Arkansas, Tennessee, Maryland, and Missouri abolished the institution in those states during the war itself.

Regrettably, Lincoln did not live to see the final ratification of the Thirteenth Amendment. But if he had never lived, it seems safe to say that we would not have had a Thirteenth Amendment in 1865. In that sense, the traditional answer to the question "Who Freed the Slaves?" is the right answer. Lincoln did not accomplish this in the manner sometimes symbolically portrayed, breaking the chains of helpless and passive bondsmen with the stroke of a pen by signing the Emancipation Proclamation. But by pronouncing slavery a moral evil that must come to an end and then winning the presidency in 1860, provoking the South to secede, by refusing to compromise on the issue of slavery's expansion or on Fort Sumter, by careful leadership and timing that kept a fragile Unionist coalition together in the first year of war and committed it to emancipation in the second, by refusing to compromise this policy once he had adopted it, and by prosecuting the war to unconditional victory as commander in chief of an army of liberation, Abraham Lincoln freed the slaves.

(1996)

Questions

1. Analyze the argument that James McPherson makes in the first two paragraphs. How convincing is it? Explain.
2. Why, according to McPherson, did President Lincoln rescind General Frémont's order of emancipation (par. 15)?
3. McPherson quotes Lincoln extensively in paragraphs 10 and 18. How effectively does he use Lincoln's words to support his own positions? Explain.
4. In paragraphs 20 and 21, McPherson begins three sentences with the word *even*. How does the use of this word help him to develop his position?
5. Notice the emphatic parallelisms that McPherson uses in paragraph 28. How do they contribute to the effectiveness of his argument?
6. What is McPherson's central thesis? Paraphrase it in a sentence or two. How convincing is it? Do you agree? Why or why not?

from *Who Freed the Slaves? Emancipation and Its Meaning*

IRA BERLIN

Ira Berlin (b. 1941) is a professor at the University of Maryland and author of many books, including *Many Thousands Gone: The First Two Centuries of Slavery in North America,* which takes its title from the traditional 1860s song "No More Auction Block for Me," or "Many Thousands Gone" (p. 674). In "Who Freed the Slaves?," Berlin responds to James McPherson's essay (p. 706).

The debate over the origins of Civil War emancipation in the American South can be parsed in such a way as to divide historians into two camps: those who understand emancipation primarily as the product of the slaves' struggle to free themselves, and those who see the Great Emancipator's hand at work. James McPherson made precisely such a division. While acknowledging the role of the slaves in their own liberation, he came down heavily on the side of Lincoln's authorship of emancipation, a fact he maintained most ordinary Americans grasped intuitively but one that eluded some scholars whose taste for the complex, the nuanced, and the ironic had blinded them to the obvious. McPherson characterized the critics of Lincoln's preeminence — advocates of what he called the "self-emancipation thesis" — as scholarly populists whose stock in trade was a celebration of the "so-called 'non-elite.'" Such scholars, McPherson implied, denied the historical role of "white males," and perhaps all regularly constituted authority, in a misguided celebration of the masses.

McPherson singled out Vincent Harding as the high priest of the self-emancipationists, declaring Harding's *There Is a River: The Black Struggle for Freedom in America* "almost a Bible" for the revisionists.[1] But there were other culprits, among them Robert F. Engs and myself and my colleagues on the Freedmen and Southern Society Project at the University of Maryland, whose multivolume documentary history, *Freedom,* he termed "the largest scholarly enterprise on the history of emancipation."[2]

---

[1]Vincent Harding, *There Is a River: The Black Struggle for Freedom in America* (New York: Harcourt, Brace, Jovanovich, 1981).

[2]Since most historical scholarship is carried on in the solitary artisan tradition, it is easy to exaggerate the numbers involved in collaborative historical research. Sad to say, "the largest scholarly enterprise on the history of emancipation" bears little resemblance to the Manhattan Project or major research projects in the social sciences. Since its inception in 1976, fewer than a dozen historians have been associated with the project — never more than five at any one time. Besides myself, the editors of the four volumes in print are Barbara Jeanne Fields, Thavolia Glymph, Steven Miller, Joseph P. Reidy, Leslie S. Rowland, and Julie Saville.

The project's main work has been published by Cambridge Univ. Press under the title *Freedom: A Documentary History of Emancipation.* Thus far four volumes are in print: *The Destruction of Slavery* (1985); *The Wartime Genesis of Free Labor: The Upper South* (1993); *The Wartime Genesis of Free Labor: The Lower South* (1991); and *The Black Military Experience* (1982). In 1992, the New Press published an abridgment of the first four volumes entitled *Free at Last: A Documentary History of Slavery, Freedom, and the Civil War,* and Cambridge has issued a volume entitled *Slaves No More.*

He gave special attention to Barbara Jeanne Fields, a member of the project who had articulated many of *Freedom*'s themes on Ken Burns's TV documentary *The Civil War*.[3] Together, these historians were responsible for elevating the "self-emancipation thesis" into what McPherson called "a new orthodoxy." . . .

Lincoln's proclamation of January 1, 1863, as its critics have noted, freed not a single slave who was not already entitled to freedom under legislation passed by Congress the previous year. It applied only to the slaves in territories then beyond the reach of Federal authority. It specifically exempted Tennessee and Union-occupied portions of Louisiana and Virginia, and it left slavery in the loyal border states — Delaware, Maryland, Kentucky, and Missouri — untouched. Indeed, in a strict sense, the Proclamation went no further than the Second Confiscation Act of July 1862, which freed all slaves who entered Union lines professing that their owners were disloyal, as well as those slaves who fell under Federal control as Union troops occupied Confederate territory. Moreover, at its fullest, the Emancipation Proclamation rested upon the president's wartime power as commander in chief and was subject to constitutional challenge. Lincoln recognized the limitations of his ill-defined wartime authority, and, as his commitment to emancipation grew firmer in 1863 and 1864, he pressed for passage of a constitutional amendment to affirm slavery's destruction.

What then was the point of the Proclamation? It spoke in muffled tones that heralded not the dawn of universal liberty but the compromised and piecemeal arrival of an undefined freedom. Indeed, the Proclamation's flat prose, ridiculed by the late Richard Hofstadter as having "all the moral grandeur of a bill of lading," suggests that the true authorship of African American freedom lies elsewhere — not at the top of American society but at its base.[4] McPherson . . . and others are correct in noting that the editors of the Freedmen and Southern Society Project and other revisionists built upon this insight.

From the first guns at Fort Sumter, the strongest advocates of emancipation were   5 the slaves themselves. Lacking political standing or a public voice, forbidden access to the weapons of war, slaves nevertheless tossed aside the grand pronouncements of Lincoln and other Union leaders that the sectional conflict was only a war for national unity. Instead, they moved directly to put their own freedom — and that of their posterity — atop the national agenda. Steadily, as opportunities arose, slaves risked their all for freedom. By abandoning their owners, coming uninvited into Union lines, and offering their lives and labor in the Federal cause, slaves forced Federal soldiers at the lowest level to recognize their importance to the Union's success. That understanding traveled quickly up the chain of command. In time, it became evident

---

[3]Barbara Jeanne Fields, "Who Freed the Slaves?" in *The Civil War: An Illustrated History*, ed. Geoffrey C. Ward with Ken Burns and Ric Burns (New York: Knopf, 1990); 178–81. One particularly unfortunate aspect of the debate is the tendency to divide the participants along racial lines and to identify black scholars as the proponents of the slave's agency. See James M. McPherson, "Liberating Lincoln," *New York Review of Books*, Apr. 21, 1994.

[4]Richard Hofstadter, *The American Political Tradition and the Men Who Made It* (New York: Vintage, 1948), 132.

to even the most obtuse Federal commanders that every slave who crossed into Union lines was a double gain: one subtracted from the Confederacy and one added to the Union. The slaves' resolute determination to secure their liberty converted many white Northern Americans — soldiers and civilians alike — to the view that the security of the Union depended upon the destruction of slavery. Eventually, this belief tipped the balance in favor of freedom, even among Yankees who displayed little interest in the question of slavery and no affection for black people.

Slaves were not without allies. Abolitionists, black and white, dismissed the Republican doctrine that slavery should be respected and given constitutional protection where it existed. Instead, abolitionists, like the slaves, saw the war as an opportunity to assault a system they believed was immoral and pressed for its extradition. Rather than condemn slavery from the comfort of their drawing rooms, some radical opponents of slavery volunteered to fight slavery on its own terrain, strapped on their haversacks, and marched south as part of the Union army. But soldiering was young men's work and sex, age, condition, and circumstance barred many radicals from the Federal army. Most abolitionists could only fume against slavery in petitions, editorials, and sermons. Although their campaign on behalf of emancipation laid the foundation for congressional and then presidential action against slavery, the majority of abolitionists had but slender means to attack slavery directly. Only slaves had both the commitment and the opportunity to initiate the assault on slavery.

Some slaves did not even wait for the war to begin. In March 1861, before the first shots at Fort Sumter, eight runaways presented themselves at Fort Pickens, a federal installation in Florida, "entertaining the idea" — in the words of the fort's commander — that Federal forces "were placed here to protect them and grant them their freedom." The commander believed otherwise and delivered the slaves to the local sheriff, who returned them to their owner.[5] Although their mission failed, these eight runaways were only the first to evince publicly a conviction that eventually became widespread throughout the slave community.

In making the connection between the war and freedom, slaves also understood that a Union victory was imperative. They did what they could to secure it, throwing their full weight behind the Federal cause, volunteering their services as teamsters, stable hands, and boatmen; butchers, bakers, and cooks; nurses, orderlies, and laundresses; blacksmiths, coopers, and carpenters; and, by the tens of thousands, as common laborers. Slaves "tabooed" those few in their ranks who shunned the effort.[6] Hundreds of thousands of black men and women would work for the Union army, and more than 135,000 slave men became Union soldiers. Even deep within the Confederacy, where escape to Federal lines was impossible, slaves did what they could to

---

[5]U.S. War Department, *The War of the Rebellion: A Compilation of the Official Records of the Union and Confederate Armies*, 128 vols. (Washington, D.C.: GPO, 1880–1901), ser. 2, vol. 1, 750 (hereafter cited as *OR*).

[6]*Freedom: A Documentary History of Emancipation, 1861–1867*, ser. 1, vol. 2, *The Wartime Genesis of Free Labor: The Upper South*, ed. Ira Berlin, Steven F. Miller, Joseph P. Reidy, and Leslie S. Rowland (Cambridge: Cambridge University Press, 1993), 123–26.

undermine the Confederacy and strengthen the Union—from aiding escaped Northern prisoners of war to praying for Northern military success. With their loyalty, their labor, and their lives, slaves provided crucial muscle and blood in support of the Federal war effort. No one was more responsible for smashing the shackles of slavery than the slaves.

Still, slaves could not free themselves. Nowhere in the four volumes of *Freedom* do the editors of the Freedmen and Southern Society Project claim they did. Nowhere in the four volumes of *Freedom* is the term *self-emancipation* employed. . . . Slaves could—and they did—put the issue of freedom on the wartime agenda; they could—and they did—make certain that the question of their liberation did not disappear in the complex welter of the war; they could—and they did—ensure that there was no retreat from the commitment to emancipation once the issue was drawn. In short, they did what was in their power to do with the weapons they had. They could not vote, pass laws, issue field orders, or promulgate great proclamations. That was the realm of citizens, legislators, military officers, and the president. However, the actions of the slaves made it possible and necessary for citizens, legislators, military officers, and the president to act. Slaves were the prime movers in the emancipation drama, not the sole movers. Slaves set others in motion, including many who would never have moved if left to their own devices. How they did so is nothing less than the story of emancipation.[7]

Among the slaves' first students were Union soldiers of the lowest rank. Arriving in the South with little direct knowledge of slavery and often contemptuous of black people, Federal soldiers encountered slaves who were eager to test their owners' fulminations against Yankee abolitionists and black Republicans. Union soldiers soon found their camps inundated with slaves, often breathless, tattered, and bearing marks of abuse who were seeking sanctuary and offering to assist them in any way possible. In so doing, slaves took a considerable risk. They not only faced sure punishment if captured, but Union soldiers often turned upon them violently.

Still, some gained entry into Federal lines, where they found work aplenty. Sometimes the slaves' labor cut to the heart of the soldiers' military mission, as slaves understood that the enemy of their enemy was their friend and were pleased to impart information about Confederate troop movements, assist in the construction of Federal fortifications, and guide Union troops through a strange countryside. But just as often, slaves ingratiated themselves with Federal troops in ways that had no particular military significance. They foraged for firewood, cooked food, cleaned camps, and did dozens of onerous jobs that otherwise would have fallen to the soldiers themselves.

Northern soldiers did not have to be Free-Soilers, abolitionists, or even radical egalitarians to appreciate these valuable services. Thus, soldiers were dismayed to discover that they had violated orders by harboring the fugitives. They were more upset when the men and women who cleaned their camps and cooked their food were dragged off to certain punishment by angry masters or mistresses. Indeed, even those

---

[7]The argument is fully explicated in *The Destruction of Slavery*.

soldiers who stoutly maintained that they fought only for Union bitterly resented being implicated in the punishment of men and women who had done nothing more than do them a good turn in exchange for a blanket and a few morsels of food. "I don't care a damn for the darkies," declared one midwestern volunteer in March 1862, "but I couldn't help to send a runaway nigger back. I'm blamed if I could."[8] The "blame" many Union soldiers felt at being implicated in slavery was compounded by their outrage when they discovered that the very same men and women they had returned to bondage were being mobilized by the Confederate enemy against them. To Union soldiers, the folly of denying themselves the resources that their enemy used freely—indeed, assisting their enemy in maintaining those resources—seemed senseless to the point of absurdity. . . .

Faced with conflicting demands—the need for labor versus the requirements of Federal policy; the desire to protect hapless fugitives versus the demands of Unionist owners—many Union soldiers and officers searched for ways to stand clear of the entire business, to be, in the idiom of the day, neither slave catcher nor slave stealer. Union policy toward slaves beginning in the fall of 1861 through the spring of 1862 was designed to eliminate the "devilish nigger question," as one Maryland official called it, by excluding fugitive slaves from Union lines. But slaves refused to surrender their belief that the Federal army was a refuge from slavery; they would not allow Federal soldiers to evade the central reality of the war.

Slaves continued to press themselves on soldiers, bringing gifts of food, information, and of course labor. There always seemed to be a few Yankee soldiers who, for whatever reason, sheltered runaways, and a handful who encouraged slave flight. But even when the fugitives were denied entry to Federal lines, they camped outside, just far enough away to avoid expulsion by Union commanders, just close enough to avoid capture by Confederate soldiers. Meanwhile, alert for ways to turn the military conflict to their own advantage, slaves continued to search the seams of Federal policy looking for an opening: the ascent of a sympathetic commander or a crisis that might inflate the value of their knowledge or their muscle. Many learned the letter of the law so that they could seemingly recite from memory passages from the House Resolution of 1861,[9] the additional Article of War of March 1862,[10] the First Confiscation Act of August 1861,[11] or the Second Confiscation Act of July 1862.[12]

---

[8]Quoted in James M. McPherson, *What They Fought For, 1861–1865* (Baton Rouge: Louisiana State Univ. Press, 1994), 59.
[9]The Crittenden-Johnson Resolution (not to be confused with the Crittenden Compromise mentioned on p. 709) stated that the purpose of the war was not to overthrow or interfere with "the rights of established institutions," meaning slavery. The resolution passed in both houses of Congress in July, but was then defeated in December as antislavery sentiment grew.—Eds.
[10]This article forbade the military from returning fugitive slaves to their owners.—Eds.
[11]Permitted the military to confiscate property used to support the Confederacy, including slaves.—Eds.
[12]Stated that any Confederate (military or civilian) who did not surrender would have his slaves freed via criminal proceedings.—Eds.

Time and time again, slaves forced Federal soldiers and officers to make the choice, a choice that became easier as the Union army's need for labor grew. Change did not come at once, but it came.

The lessons slaves taught soldiers and soldiers taught officers slowly ascended the Union chain of command and in November 1861 reached Lincoln's cabinet for the first time. Secretary of War Simon Cameron publicly endorsed a proposal to arm slaves to fight for the Union and freedom.[13] Lincoln quieted Cameron and packed him off to Russia as minister, but the slaves continued undeterred to press their case.

The slow shift in Federal policy gained momentum as the Union army penetrated deeper into the Confederacy, where slaveholders were not reluctant Unionists but outright rebels. In these circumstances, some field commanders became quick learners. Their respect for the old order yielded to a willingness to challenge the rights of the master and finally to a firm determination to extirpate slavery. Others learned slowly, imperfectly, or not at all. However, before long, the most obdurate generals began to disappear from places of high command, and the quick studies rose to the top.

The broad outline of the story was always the same. Slaves forced the issue: what should be done with them? Deciding the matter was always difficult, for it required a choice between the contradictory interests of the master and of the slave. At first slaveholders held the upper hand, but in time the advantage slipped to the slaves. When the slaves' loyalty became more valuable than the masters' in the eyes of Federal authorities, the Federal army became the slaves' willing partner rather than its reluctant enemy. The process by which the Union army became an army of liberation was in its essence political and reveals how black people had been incorporated into American politics long before they had the vote, the right to petition, or independent standing at law. . . .

The lesson that slaves taught common soldiers, that common soldiers taught officers, that officers taught field commanders, that field commanders taught their desk-bound superiors in Washington, and that resonated in the North was not wasted on Abraham Lincoln. In many ways, Lincoln was a slow learner, but he learned.

Lincoln was no friend of slavery. He believed, as he said many times, that "if slavery is not wrong, nothing is wrong." But, as president, Lincoln also believed he had a constitutional obligation not to interfere with slavery where it existed. Shortly before his inauguration, he offered to support a proposed constitutional amendment that would have prohibited any subsequent amendment authorizing Congress "to abolish or interfere . . . with the domestic institutions" of any state, including slavery."[14] As wartime leader, he feared the disaffection of the loyal slave states, which he understood to be critical to the success of the Union. He crafted much of his wartime policy

15

---

[13]Edward McPherson, *The Political History of the United States of America during the Great Rebellion, 1860–1865*, 2d ed. (Washington, D.C.: Philip & Solomons, 1865), 249, 416.
[14]For the proposed amendment, see ibid., 59; Abraham Lincoln, *Collected Works of Abraham Lincoln*, ed. Roy P. Basler, 9 vols. (New Brunswick, N.J.: Rutgers Univ. Press, 1953–55), 4:421–41.

respecting slavery to avoid alienating loyal slaveholders, especially in Kentucky, Missouri, and Maryland. . . .

Where others led on emancipation, Lincoln followed. Lincoln responded slowly   20
to demands for emancipation as they rose through the military chain of command and as they echoed on the Northern home front. Even as pressure for emancipation grew in the spring of 1862, Lincoln continued to urge gradual, compensated emancipation. The compensation would be to slaveholders for property lost, not to slaves for labor stolen. In late September 1862, even while announcing that he would proclaim emancipation on January 1 if the rebellious states did not return to the Union, he again called for gradual, compensated emancipation in the border states and compensation for loyal slaveholders elsewhere. The preliminary emancipation proclamation also reiterated his support for colonizing freed slaves "upon this continent or elsewhere."[15] While some pressed for the enlistment of black soldiers, Lincoln doubted the capacity of black men for military service, fearing that former slaves would simply turn their guns over to their old masters.

As black laborers became essential to the Union war effort and as demands to enlist black men in the Federal army mounted, the pressure for emancipation became inexorable. By the summer of 1862, Lincoln understood the importance of the sable arm as well as any. On July 12, making yet another plea for gradual, compensated emancipation in the Union's own slave states, Lincoln bluntly warned border-state congressmen that slavery was doomed "by mere friction and abrasion — by the mere incidents of the war," and that it would be impossible to restore the Union with slavery in place.[16] Ignored once again, Lincoln acted on his own advice. In late July 1862, five days after signing the Second Confiscation and the Militia acts, he issued an executive order translating the new legislation into instructions for the Union army and navy. He authorized military commanders operating in the seceded states to "seize and use any property, real or personal, which may be necessary or convenient for . . . military purposes," and he instructed them to "employ as laborers . . . so many persons of African descent as can be advantageously used for military and naval purposes." Although he also reiterated the customary injunctions against wanton or malicious destruction of private property, there was no mistaking the import of Lincoln's order.[17]

Lincoln had decided to act. On July 22, he informed the cabinet of his intention to issue a proclamation of general emancipation. The slaves' determination had indeed made every policy short of emancipation untenable.[18] . . .

---

[15] U.S. *Statutes at Large*, 12 (Washington, D.C.: GPO, 1863): 1267–68.

[16] Lincoln, *Collected Works*, 5:317–19, quotation on p. 318.

[17] Lincoln's executive order, dated July 22, 1862, was promulgated to the armies in the field by a War Department order dated August 16. *OR*, ser. 3, 2:397.

[18] As Lincoln later put it, "No human power can subdue this rebellion without using the Emancipation lever as I have done." Lincoln, *Collected Works*, 7:499–502, 506–8, quotation on p. 507.

On January 1, 1863, Lincoln fulfilled his promise to free all slaves in the states still in rebellion. Had another Republican been in Lincoln's place, that person doubtless would have done the same. Without question, some would have acted more expeditiously and with greater bravado. Without question, some would have acted more cautiously and with lesser resolve. In the end, Lincoln did what needed to be done. Others might be left behind; Lincoln would not. It does no disservice to Lincoln — or to anyone else — to say that his claim to greatness rests upon his willingness to act when the moment was right.

When Lincoln finally acted, he moved with confidence and determination. He stripped the final Emancipation Proclamation of any reference to compensation for former slaveholders or colonization for former slaves.[19] He added provisions that allowed for the service of black men in the Union army and navy. The Proclamation opened the door to the eventual enlistment of more than 179,000 black men, most of them former slaves. More than anything else, the enlistment of black men, slave as well as free, transformed the Federal army into an army of liberation. At war's end, the number of black men in Federal uniform was larger than the number of soldiers in Lee's Army of Northern Virginia. Military enlistment became the surest solvent of slavery, extending to places the Emancipation Proclamation did not reach, especially the loyal slave states. Once slave men entered the Union army, they were free and they made it clear that they expected their families to be free as well. In March 1865, Congress confirmed this understanding and provided for the freedom of the immediate families of all black soldiers. Lincoln's actions, however tardy, gave force to all that the slaves had risked. The Emancipation Proclamation transformed the war in ways only the president could. After January 1, 1863, the Union army marched for freedom, and Lincoln was its commander.[20]

Lincoln understood the importance of his role, both politically and morally — just   25
as the slaves had understood theirs.[21] Having determined to free the slaves, Lincoln declared he would not take back the Emancipation Proclamation even when military failure and political reversals threatened that policy. He repudiated his misgivings

---

[19]Lincoln, who had declared in his second annual message to Congress, "I cannot make it better known than it already is, that I strongly favor colonization," never made another public appeal for the scheme. Don E. Fehrenbacher, "Only His Stepchildren: Lincoln and the Negro," *Civil War History* 30 (1974): 308.

[20]At times, McPherson appears to argue that the preeminence of Lincoln's role in the process of emancipation derived from the simple fact that he was the Republican candidate, wartime president, and commander in chief of the Union army, for freedom could not be achieved without Southern secession, civil war, and Union victory. If that is the pith of the case, it is easy enough to concede. Indeed, the first sentence of *The Black Military Experience* asserts: "Freedom came to most American slaves only through force of arms."

[21]Although he makes no case for the slaves' role in emancipation, Don Fehrenbacher reaches a similar conclusion respecting Lincoln's role. "Emancipation itself, as [Lincoln] virtually acknowledged, came out of the logic of events, not his personal volition, but the time and manner of its coming were largely his choice." "Only His Stepchildren," 306.

about the military abilities of black soldiers and became one of their great supporters. Lincoln praised the role of black soldiers in preserving the Union and ending chattel bondage and vowed not to "betray" them. The growing presence of black men in the Union army deepened Lincoln's commitment to emancipation. "There have been men who proposed to me to return to slavery the black warriors of Port Hudson & Olustee to . . . conciliate the South," Lincoln reflected in August 1864. "I should be damned in time & in eternity for doing so."[22] Lincoln later suggested that black soldiers might have the vote, perhaps his greatest concession to racial equality.[23] To secure the freedom that his proclamation had promised, Lincoln pressed for the final liquidation of slavery in the Union's own slave states where diehards obstructed and delayed. To that end and to write freedom into the nation's highest charter, Lincoln promoted passage of the Thirteenth Amendment, although he did not live to see its ratification.

The Emancipation Proclamation's place in the drama of emancipation is thus secure — as is Lincoln's. To deny it is to ignore the intense struggle by which freedom arrived. It is to ignore the Union soldiers who sheltered slaves, the abolitionists who stumped for emancipation, and the thousands of men and women who, like Lincoln, changed their minds as slaves made the case for universal liberty. Reducing the Emancipation Proclamation to a nullity and Lincoln to a cipher denies human agency just as personifying emancipation in a larger-than-life Great Emancipator denies the agency of the slaves and many others, and trivializes the process by which the slaves were freed. And, as in many other cases, process is critical. . . .

Emphasizing that emancipation was not the work of one hand underscores the force of contingency, the crooked course by which universal freedom arrived. It captures the ebb and flow of events which, at times, placed Lincoln among the opponents of emancipation and then propelled him to the forefront of freedom's friends. It emphasizes the clash of wills that is the essence of politics, whether it involves enfranchised legislators or voteless slaves. Politics, perforce, necessitates an on-the-ground struggle among different interests, not the unfolding of a single idea or perspective, whether that of an individual or an age. Lincoln, no less than the meanest slave, acted upon changing possibilities as he understood them. The very same events — secession and war — that gave the slaves' actions new meaning also gave Lincoln's actions new meaning. To think that Lincoln could have anticipated these changes — or, more strangely still, somehow embodied them — imbues him with a power over the course of events that no human being has ever enjoyed. Lincoln was

---

[22]Lincoln, *Collected Works*, 7:499–502, 506–8, quotation on p. 507.
[23]"I barely suggest for your private consideration," Lincoln wrote to the Unionist governor of Louisiana in March 1864, "whether some of the colored people may not be let in [to the suffrage] — as, for instance, the very intelligent, and especially those who have fought gallantly in our ranks. They would probably help," he added, "in some trying times to come, to keep the jewel of liberty within the family of freedom." Lincoln, *Collected Works*, 7:243.

part of history, not above it. Whatever he believed about slavery in 1861, Lincoln did not see the war as an instrument of emancipation.[24] The slaves did. Lincoln's commitment to emancipation changed with time because it had to. The slaves' commitment to universal freedom never wavered because it could not.

Complexity — contrary to McPherson — is not ambivalence or ambiguity. To tell the whole story, to follow that crooked course, does not diminish the clarity of an argument or mystify it into a maze of "nuance, paradox, or irony." Telling the entire tale is not a form of obfuscation. If done right, it clarifies precisely because it consolidates the mass of competing claims under a single head. Elegance or simplicity of argument is useful only when it encompasses all of the evidence, not when it excludes or narrows it.

In the perennial tests in which constituted authority searches for the voice of the people and when the people are testing the measure of their leaders, it is well to recall the relationship of both to securing freedom's greatest victory. In this sense, slaves were right in celebrating January 1, 1863, as the Day of Jubilee. As Loretta Hanes noted 130 years later, "It meant so much to people because it was a ray of light, the hope of a new day coming. And it gave them courage."[25] Indeed, the Emancipation Proclamation reminds all — both those viewing its faded pages and those studying it — that real change derives both from the actions of the people and from the imprimatur of constituted authority. It teaches that "social" history is no less political than "political" history, for it too rests upon the bending of wills, which is the essence of politics, and that no political process is determined by a single individual. If the Emancipation Proclamation speaks to the central role of constituted authority — in the person of Abraham Lincoln — in making history, it speaks no less loudly to the role of ordinary men and women, seizing the moment to make the world according to their own understanding of justice and human decency. The connection between the two should not be forgotten.

(1997)

---

[24]If there is a tendency in one brand of social history to emphasize the agency of the disfranchised, there is a similar tendency in one brand of political history to emphasize the omnipotence and clairvoyance of the great leader. The hero sees farthest, first. While combating the former fallacy, McPherson succumbs to the latter. From the beginning of the war, McPherson maintains, "Lincoln demurred from turning the war for Union into a war for slavery because the war for Union united Northern people while premature emancipation would divide them and lose the war." Lincoln, in other words, understood the Civil War as a struggle for emancipation from the beginning. He waited, however, for the right moment to spring the news on those not quite as farseeing. "With an acute sense of timing," McPherson continues, "Lincoln first proclaimed emancipation only as a *means* to win the war (to gain moderate and conservative support) and ultimately as an *end* — to give America 'a new birth of freedom,' as Lincoln said at Gettysburg."

[25]*USA Today*, Dec. 30, 1992.

Questions

1. How does Ira Berlin characterize Abraham Lincoln in the first four paragraphs of his piece?
2. Berlin writes, "The slaves' determination had indeed made every policy short of emancipation untenable" (par. 22). What is Berlin implying? What claim does this statement support?
3. Berlin quotes extensively from Lincoln. Select two direct quotations. How effectively does Berlin use them to support his position? Explain.
4. Analyze the argument that Berlin makes in paragraph 23. How convincing is it? Explain.
5. What is the relationship between footnotes 16 through 18 and the text of paragraphs 21 and 22? How do they contribute to Berlin's argument? Be specific.
6. What is the rhetorical purpose of paragraph 26? How does it relate to Berlin's overall argument? Explain.

The Gettysburg PowerPoint Presentation

Peter Norvig

> A director of research at Google, Inc., Peter Norvig put together a PowerPoint version of the Gettysburg Address. It was published in the June/July 2003 issue of *American Heritage* magazine.

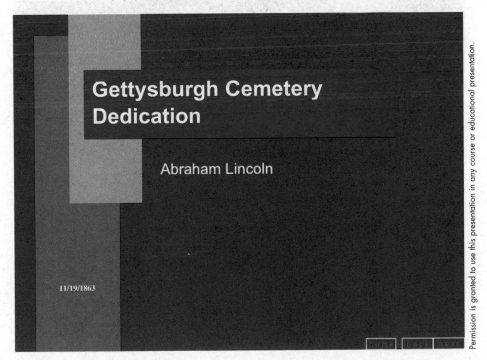

Permission is granted to use this presentation in any course or educational presentation.

Agenda

- Met on battlefield (great)
- Dedicate portion of field - fitting!
- Unfinished work (great tasks)

11/19/1863

home back next

Not on Agenda!

- Dedicate
- Consecrate
- Hallow
  (in narrow sense)
- Add or detract
- Note or remember what we say

11/19/1863

home back next

Review of Key Objectives & Critical Success Factors

- What makes nation unique
  - Conceived in Liberty
  - Men are equal
- Shared vision
  - New birth of freedom
  - Gov't of/for/by the people

11/19/1863

home back next

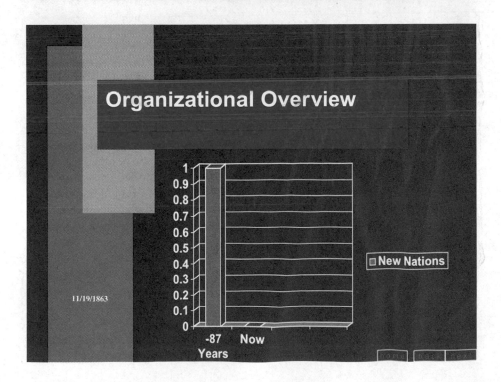

Organizational Overview

11/19/1863

□ New Nations

1
0.9
0.8
0.7
0.6
0.5
0.4
0.3
0.2
0.1
0

-87   Now
Years

home back next

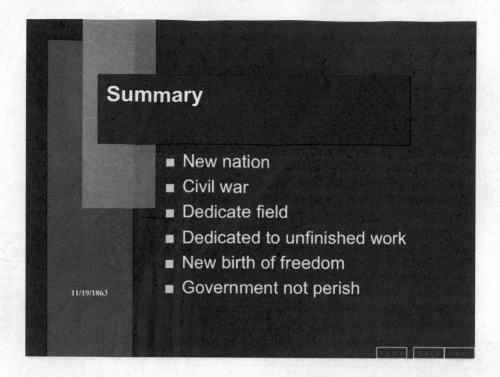

Questions

1. How would you describe Peter Norvig's tone in the text of Lincoln's introduction?
2. What is similar between the text of Lincoln's speech and that of Norvig's PowerPoint presentation? What is different?
3. What is your attitude toward Norvig's PowerPoint? What do you think is the attitude of the editors at *American Heritage* magazine? Explain.
4. Norvig describes the idea behind this text as follows: "How many of us have been frustrated at seeing too many presentations where PowerPoint or other visual aids obscure rather than enhance the point? After one too many bad presentations at a meeting in January 2000, I decided to see if I could *do* something about it. Back in my hotel room I imagined what Abe Lincoln might have done if he had used PowerPoint rather than the power of oratory at Gettysburg." Does he achieve his purpose? Does your experience with PowerPoint resemble Norvig's? Explain.

Making Connections

1. What themes and rhetorical features are shared by the four primary texts by Abraham Lincoln? How are they different? Which one is your favorite? Why?

2. Imagine that you are doing a presentation for your class (or for a middle-school class) about the Emancipation Proclamation and that you may include one visual as a slide. Which would you choose, the engraving by Henry W. Herrick (p. 697) or the sculpture by Thomas Ball (p. 698)? Compare and contrast the two and explain why you would choose one over the other.

3. This conversation includes two personal essays on Lincoln that were written more than a century apart, one by Frederick Douglass (p. 699), a former slave, and the other by Mario M. Cuomo (p. 703), then governor of New York State. Compare and contrast their views of Lincoln. Do they seem to be discussing the same man? Why or why not?

4. In his letter to Albert G. Hodges (p. 693), President Lincoln discusses his reasons for postponing emancipation. Ira Berlin (p. 715) discusses Lincoln's reasoning and criticizes his delay saying, "Where others led on emancipation, Lincoln followed" (par. 20). Considering what Lincoln himself says in his letter, evaluate Berlin's position.

5. Cuomo begins a number of his statements with *words*. Select two of those statements that appeal to you, and apply them to the texts that you have read by Lincoln. How does each of them serve as an illustration of Lincoln's words? Be specific as you explain.

6. Analyze and evaluate Berlin's argument in response to James McPherson's (p. 706). How might McPherson respond to Berlin if the exchange were to continue?

7. Imagine that Douglass, Cuomo, McPherson, Berlin, and Lincoln were sitting in an auditorium watching Peter Norvig's PowerPoint presentation. What would their responses be?

8. In his 1992 book, *Lincoln at Gettysburg: The Words That Remade America*, historian Garry Wills says of Lincoln's second inaugural address that it "complements and completes the Gettysburg Address" (which Wills regards as Lincoln's finest). He contends that the second inaugural "is the only speech worthy to stand with it." Historian Ronald C. White Jr., in his 2002 book, *Lincoln's Greatest Speech, the Second Inaugural*, claims that Lincoln himself considered the latter speech his best and writes, "For too long the Second Inaugural Address has lived within the shadow of the Gettysburg Address." Who is right? Do you agree with Wills or with White? Defend the position of one of these historians, using the texts of both speeches and your knowledge of American history.

Entering the Conversation

As you respond to each of the following prompts, support your position with appropriate evidence, including at least three sources in this Conversation on Abraham Lincoln, unless otherwise indicated.

1. In his annual remarks to Congress on December 1, 1862, a month before the Emancipation Proclamation, Abraham Lincoln said: "We know how to save the Union. The world knows we do know how to save it. We — even *we here* — hold the power, and bear the responsibility. In *giving* freedom to the *slave*, we *assure* freedom to the *free*, — honorable alike in what we give, and what we preserve. We shall nobly save, or meanly lose, the last best hope of earth." Write an essay that supports this claim.

2. In 1880 in the *North American Review*, James C. Welling wrote, "It was a day of elemental stir, and the ground is still quaking beneath our feet, under the throes and convulsions of that great social and political change which was first definitely foreshadowed to the world by the Emancipation Proclamation of Abraham Lincoln." It might be said that "the ground is still quaking" under our feet today. Write an essay that examines the extent to which Welling's statement still applies to our time.

3. Do you agree, as Cuomo (p. 703) states, that the work Lincoln inspires us to do is "unfinished"? Write an essay that explores Cuomo's idea.

4. View the 2012 film *Lincoln*, produced and directed by Steven Spielberg. Compare how Abraham Lincoln is depicted in the film with how he is depicted in the sources in this Conversation.

5. President Lincoln preserved the Union. President Lincoln freed the slaves. Was Abraham Lincoln a visionary who strove to ensure for all Americans, white and black alike, what the Declaration of Independence promised? Was he a great and dutiful statesman and politician who took the pragmatic route to save the Union at all costs? There are those who see Lincoln as the Great Emancipator (of slaves) and those who see him as the Great Preserver (of the Union). Write an essay that defends or qualifies one of those positions.

6. Read "O Captain! My Captain!" (p. 659), a poem about Abraham Lincoln by Walt Whitman. Write an essay that discusses and evaluates Whitman's view of Lincoln, referring to several texts in this Conversation. You might also read "When Lilacs Last in the Dooryard Bloom'd," another Whitman poem about Lincoln.

7. In paragraph 9 of "Abraham Lincoln and Our 'Unfinished Work'" (p. 703), Cuomo writes, "The old bigotries seem to be dying." Do you agree? What are the "old bigotries"? Are there new bigotries as well? How can the example of Abraham Lincoln and his legacy help guide us past new bigotries as well as old?

Conversation

John Brown: Patriot or Terrorist?

John Brown (1800–1859) was born into a deeply religious family in Connecticut and moved to Ohio when he was five. He made his living variously as a farmer, tanner, and land speculator; he fathered six children with his first wife, who died in childbirth, and thirteen with his second. He was always a committed abolitionist who, despite significant financial difficulties, contributed to antislavery causes, gave land to fugitive slaves, and participated in the Underground Railroad. In his fifties, he and five of his sons went to Kansas to fight pro-slavery forces. During what became known as the Pottawatomie Massacre and the Battle of Osawatomie, Brown assumed the role of abolitionist leader and led violent attacks against proponents of slavery. When he returned from Kansas, he began raising money to support his plan to free slaves in Virginia. On October 16, 1859, at Harpers Ferry, Virginia, Brown led a raid on the federal arsenal, motivated by his belief that the system of slavery could only be overthrown by arming the slaves themselves. Many of the twenty-one men with him were captured or killed, including two of his sons, and Brown was imprisoned, tried, and hanged within a few months.

Whether the raid at Harpers Ferry can be said to have caused the Civil War is a matter of continuing debate, but there is strong agreement that it was a catalyst. John Brown's often-quoted last words predicted the brutal conflict that followed: "I, John Brown, am now quite certain that the crimes of this guilty land can never be purged away but with blood." From the beginning, responses to Brown have been polarized, from Southern denunciations of him as a deranged zealot to Northern endorsements of him as a heroic prophet. African American leaders, including Frederick Douglass, eulogized him; poets, such as Langston Hughes and Robert Hayden, memorialized him; and W. E. B. DuBois wrote a laudatory biography. Nonetheless, the violence of his methods — despite an indisputably noble cause — has been called into question, and the accusations, particularly after September 11, 2001, that he was a "terrorist" have intensified the controversy surrounding his reputation and legacy more than 150 years after his death.

Sources
John Brown, *Last Speech* (1859)
John Brown, *Last Letter to His Family* (1859)
Frances Ellen Watkins Harper, *Letter to John Brown* (1859)
Henry David Thoreau, from *A Plea for Captain John Brown* (1859)
Thomas Hovenden, *The Last Moments of John Brown* (c. 1882)
Ken Chowder, *The Father of American Terrorism* (2000)
Robert E. McGlone, *The "Madness" of John Brown* (2009)
David Reynolds, *Freedom's Martyr* (2009)
Tony Horwitz, *The 9/11 of 1859* (2009)

Last Speech

JOHN BROWN

John Brown gave this speech at the conclusion of his trial, about a month before his execution in Charlestown, West Virginia.

I have, may it please the Court, a few words to say.

In the first place, I deny everything but what I have all along admitted, of a design on my part to free the slaves. I intended certainly to have made a clean thing of that matter, as I did last winter, when I went into Missouri and there took slaves without the snapping of a gun on either side, moved them through the country, and finally left them in Canada. I designed to have done the same thing again, on a larger scale. That was all I intended. I never did intend murder, or treason, or the destruction of property, or to excite or incite slaves to rebellion, or to make insurrection.

I have another objection; and that is, it is unjust that I should suffer such a penalty. Had I interfered in the manner which I admit, and which I admit has been fairly proved (for I admire the truthfulness and candor of the greater portion of the witnesses who have testified in this case), — had I so interfered in behalf of the rich, the powerful, the intelligent, the so-called great, or in behalf of any of their friends, — either father, mother, brother, sister, wife, or children, or any of that class, — and suffered and sacrificed what I have in this interference, it would have been all right; and every man in this court would have deemed it an act worthy of reward rather than punishment.

This court acknowledges, as I suppose, the validity of the law of God. I see a book kissed here which I suppose to be the Bible, or at least the New Testament. That teaches me that all things whatsoever I would that men should do to me, I should do even so to them. It teaches me, further, to "remember them that are in bonds, as bound with them." I endeavored to act up to that instruction. I say, I am yet too young to understand that God is any respecter of persons. I believe that to have interfered as I have done — in behalf of His despised poor, was not wrong, but right. Now, if it is deemed necessary that I should forfeit my life for the furtherance of the ends of justice, and mingle my blood further with the blood of my children and with the blood of millions in this slave country whose rights are disregarded by wicked, cruel, and unjust enactments, — I submit; so let it be done!

Let me say one word further.

I feel entirely satisfied with the treatment I have received on my trial. Considering all the circumstances, it has been more generous than I expected. But I feel no consciousness of guilt. I have stated from the first what was my intention, and what was not. I never have had any design against the life of any person, nor any disposition to commit treason, or excite slaves to rebel, or make any general insurrection. I never encouraged any man to do so, but always discouraged any idea of that kind.

Let me say, also, a word in regard to the statements made by some of those connected with me. I hear it has been stated by some of them that I have induced them

5

to join me. But the contrary is true. I do not say this to injure them, but as regretting their weakness. There is not one of them but joined me of his own accord, and the greater part of them at their own expense. A number of them I never saw, and never had a word of conversation with, till the day they came to me; and that was for the purpose I have stated.

Now I have done.

(1859)

Questions

1. Clearly, John Brown knew his death sentence would not be changed; in fact, many argue that he wanted to die a martyr. What, then, is the chief purpose of this speech?
2. What does he mean by the phrase "a clean thing of that matter" (par. 2)?
3. In paragraph 3, Brown offers a series of qualifications ("Had I interfered . . . had I so interfered") to support an assertion. What is his point? Do you find his support sufficient for the claim?
4. In what ways does he call on religion? Does he refer to "the law of God" (par. 4) to justify his actions? Does he ask forgiveness from a higher power?
5. Which allegations does he admit to? Which does he deny?
6. What ethos does Brown establish in this speech? Cite specific words and images he uses to develop his persona.
7. How would you describe the tone of this speech?

Last Letter to His Family

JOHN BROWN

> Brown wrote the following letter to his children and second wife from Charlestown Prison two days before his execution.

Charlestown, Prison, Jefferson Co. Va. 30th Nov. 1859

My Dearly beloved Wife, Sons: & Daughters, *every one*

As I now begin what is probably the last letter I shall ever write to any of you; I conclude to write you all at the same time. I will mentions [sic] some little matters particularly applicable to little property concerns in another place. I yesterday received a letter from my wife from near Philadelphia: dated Nov 27th, by which it would seem that she has about given up the idea of seeing me again. I had written her to come on; if *she* felt equal to the undertaking; but I do not know as she will get my letter in time. It was on her *own account chiefly* that I asked her to stay *back* at first. I had a most strong desire to see her again; but there appeared to be very serious objections; & should we never meet in *this life*; I trust she will in the end be satisfied it was *for the best at least*; if not most for her comfort. I enclosed in my last letter to her a Draft of $50, Fifty Dollars from John Jay made payable to her order. I have now another to send her from my excellent old friend Edward Harris of Woonsocket Rhode Island for $100, One Hundred Dollars; which I shall *also make payable to her* order. I am writing the hour of my public *murder* with great composure of mind, & cheerfulness; feeling the strongest assurance that in no other possible way could I be used to so much advance the cause of God; & of humanity; & that nothing that either I or all my family have sacrificed or suffered: *will be lost.* The reflection that a *wise, & merciful, as well as Just, & holy God*: rules not only the affairs of *this world*; but of all worlds; is a rock to set our feet upon; under all circumstances; *even* those more severely *trying ones*: into which our own follies; & [w]rongs have placed us. I have now no doubt but that our seeming *disaster*: will ultimately result in the most *glorious success.* So my dear *shattered; & broken* family; be of good cheer; & believe & trust in God; "with all your heart; & with all your soul; for *he* doeth *All things well.*" Do not feel ashamed on my account; nor *for one moment* despair of the cause; or grow *weary* of *well doing.* I bless God; I never felt stronger confidence in the certain & near approach of a *bright Morning; & glorious day*; then I have felt; & do now feel; since my confinement here. I am endeavouring to "return" like a "poor Prodigal" *as I am*; to my Father: against whom I have *always* sined [*sic*]: *in the hope*; that he may kindly, & forgivingly "meet me: though; *a verry* [*sic*] *great way off.*" Oh my dear Wife & Children would "to God" you could know how I have been "traveling in birth for you" all; that no one of you "may fail of the grace of God, through Jesus Christ": that no one of you may be blind to the truth: & glorious "light of *his* word"; in which Life; & Immortality; are brought to light." I beseech you *every one* to make the bible your *dayly* [*sic*] *& Nightly study*; with a *childlike honest, candid, teachable spirit*: out of love and respect for your Husband; & Father: & I beseech *the God* of *my Fathers*; to open all your eyes to a discovery of *the truth.* You *cannot imagine* how much *you* may *soon need* the consolations of the Christian religion.

Circumstances like my own; for more than a month past; convince me beyound [*sic*] *all doubt* of our great need: of something more to rest our hopes on; than merely our own vague theories framed up, while our *prejudices* are excited; *or* our *Vanity* worked up to its highest pitch. Oh do not trust your eternal all uppon [*sic*] the boisterous Ocean, without *even a Helm*; or *Compass* to *aid* you in steering. I do *not ask any* of you; to throw *away your reason*: I only *ask* you, to make a candid, & sober *use of your reason*: My dear younger children will you listen to this last poor admonition of one who can *only* love you? Oh be determined at once to give your whole hearts to God; & let *nothing shake; or alter;* that resolution. You need have no fear *of* REGRETING [*sic*] it. Do not be in vain; and thoughtless: but *sober minded.* And let me entreat you all to love *the whole remnant* of our once great family: "with a pure *heart fervently.*" Try to *build again*: your broken walls: & to make *the utmost* of every *stone* that is left. Nothing can so tend to make life a blessing as the consciousness that you *love; & are beloved:* & "love ye the stranger" *still.* It is a ground of the utmost comfort to *my mind*: to know that so many of you as have had *the opportunity;* have given full proof of your fidelity to the great family of man. *Be faithful* until *death.* From the exercise of habitual love to man: *it cannot* be very *hard:* to *learn to love* his *maker.* I must *yet* insert a reason for my firm belief in the Divine inspiration of the Bible: notwithstanding I am (perhaps naturally) skeptical. (certainly not, *credulous.*) I wish you all to consider *it most thoroughly;* when you read that blessed book; & see whether you *can not* discover such evidence yourselves. It is the purity of *heart, feeling, or motive:* as well as *word, & action* which is every where insisted on; that distinguish it from *all other teachings;* that *commends it* to *my conscience:* whether *my heart* be "willing, & obedient" *or not.* The inducements that it holds out; are another reason *of my conviction* or its *truth: & genuineness;* that I cannot here *omit;* in this my *last argument,* for the Bible *Eternal life:* is that my soul *is* "panting after" this moment. I mention this; as reason for endeavouring to leave a valuable copy of the Bible to be carefully *preserved* in remembrance *of me:* to so many of my posterity; *instead of* some *other* thing: of equal *cost.* I beseech you all to live in habitual contentment with verry [*sic*] *moderate* circumstances: & gains, of *worldly store:* & most earnestly to teach this: to your *children; & Childrens, Children;* after you: by *example: as well:* as precept. Be determined to know by experience *as soon as may be:* whether bible instruction is of *Divine origin* or not; *which says;* "Owe no man *anything but* to love one another." John Rogers wrote to his children, "Abhor that arrant whore of Rome." John Brown writes to his children to abhor with *undiing hatred,* also: that "sum of all vilanies;" Slavery. *Remember* that "he that is *slow* to *anger* is *better* than the mighty: and he that ruleth his *spirit;* than he that taketh a city." Remember also: *that* "they that be *wise* shall *shine:* and they that *turn* many to *righteousness:* as the stars forever; & ever." And now dearly beloved *Farewell* To God & the word of his grace I comme[n]d you all.

Your Affectionate Husband & Father, John Brown

(1859)

Questions

1. In this letter, John Brown writes to his entire immediate family rather than to any one individual, even his wife. How does this collective audience influence the content of his letter?
2. What point is Brown making in this sentence: "Circumstances like my own; for more than a month past; convince me . . . *Vanity* worked up to its highest pitch" (par. 2)?
3. Brown frames much of this letter in terms of the teachings and "the consolations of the Christian religion" (par. 1). Which elements does he emphasize?
4. What practical advice does he impart in the letter?
5. What warnings does he make?
6. How would you define the legacy Brown wishes to pass on to his children?

Letter to John Brown

FRANCES ELLEN WATKINS HARPER

Frances Ellen Watkins Harper (1825–1911) was the author of many poems, includ-ing "Bury Me in a Free Land" (1858), and the novel *Iola Leroy* (1892). Born to free parents in Baltimore, she taught at Union Seminary in Wilberforce, Ohio, and was a popular lecturer for the American Anti-Slavery Society. After the raid on Harpers Ferry, she wrote letters and raised money on behalf of the captured men and their families. The following open letter was published in a number of news-papers and was reputedly smuggled into Brown's prison cell.

Kendalville, Indiana, Nov. 25.

Dear Friend: Although the hands of Slavery throw a barrier between you and me, and it may not be my privilege to see you in your prison-house, Virginia has no bolts or bars through which I dread to send you my sympathy. In the name of the young girl sold from the warm clasp of a mother's arms to the clutches of a libertine or a profligate, — in the name of the slave mother, her heart rocked to and fro by the agony of her mournful separations, — I thank you, that you have been brave enough to reach out your hands to the crushed and blighted of my race. You have rocked the bloody Bastile; and I hope that from your sad fate great good may arise to the cause of freedom. Already from your prison has come a shout of triumph against the giant sin of our country. The hemlock is distilled with victory when it is pressed to the lips of Socrates. The Cross becomes a glorious ensign when Calvary's pale-browed suf-ferer yields up his life upon it. And, if Universal Freedom is ever to be the dominant power of the land, your bodies may be only her first stepping stones to dominion. I would prefer to see Slavery go down peaceably by men breaking off their sins by righ-teousness and their iniquities by showing justice and mercy to the poor; but we cannot tell what the future may bring forth. God writes national judgments upon national sins; and what may be slumbering in the storehouse of divine justice we do not know. We may earnestly hope that your fate will not be a vain lesson, that it will intensify our hatred of Slavery and love of freedom, and that your martyr grave will be a sacred altar upon which men will record their vows of undying hatred to that system which tramples on man and bids defiance to God. I have written to your dear wife, and sent her a few dollars, and I pledge myself to you that I will continue to assist her. May the ever-blessed God shield you and your fellow-prisoners in the darkest hours. Send my sympathy to your fellow-prisoners; tell them to be of good courage; to seek a refuge in the Eternal God, and lean upon His everlasting arms for a sure support. If any of them, like you, have a wife or children that I can help, let them send me word. . . .

    Yours in the cause of freedom,

F. E. W.
(1859)

Questions

1. What ethos does Frances Ellen Watkins Harper establish in the first two sentences? Cite specific language and images to support your response.
2. What does she mean with her allusion to Socrates in this sentence: "The hemlock is distilled with victory when it is pressed to the lips of Socrates"?
3. What is the likely effect of Harper's religious references — both on Brown and on the readers at the time?
4. How does Harper characterize the violent methods of Brown's raid on Harpers Ferry?
5. What is (or are) the purpose(s) of Harper's letter?

from *A Plea for Captain John Brown*

HENRY DAVID THOREAU

> Henry David Thoreau delivered this speech in Concord, Massachusetts, two weeks after the raid on Harpers Ferry in 1859. His unequivocal defense and admiration of Brown stood against popular opinion of the time, much of it mirroring the characterization by the abolitionist newspaper the *Liberator* as "a misguided, wild, and apparently insane effort." The following excerpt is the final third of the speech.

"All is quiet at Harper's Ferry," say the journals. What is the character of that calm which follows when the law and the slaveholder prevail? I regard this event as a touchstone designed to bring out, with glaring distinctness, the character of this government. We needed to be thus assisted to see it by the light of history. It needed to see itself. When a government puts forth its strength on the side of injustice, as ours to maintain Slavery and kill the liberators of the slave, it reveals itself a merely brute force, or worse, a demoniacal force. It is the head of the Plug Uglies. It is more manifest than ever that tyranny rules. I see this government to be effectually allied with France and Austria in oppressing mankind. There sits a tyrant holding fettered four millions of slaves; here comes their heroic liberator. This most hypocritical and diabolical government looks up from its seat on the gasping four millions, and inquires with an assumption of innocence, "What do you assault me for? Am I not an honest man? Cease agitation on this subject, or I will make a slave of you, too, or else hang you."

We talk about a *representative* government; but what a monster of a government is that where the noblest faculties of the mind, and the *whole* heart, are not *represented*. A semi-human tiger or ox, stalking over the earth, with its heart taken out and the top of its brain shot away. Heroes have fought well on their stumps when their legs were shot off, but I never heard of any good done by such a government as that.

The only government that I recognize, — and it matters not how few are at the head of it, or how small its army, — is that power that establishes justice in the land, never that which establishes injustice. What shall we think of a government to which all the truly brave and just men in the land are enemies, standing between it and those whom it oppresses? A government that pretends to be Christian and crucifies a million Christs every day!

Treason! Where does such treason take its rise? I cannot help thinking of you as you deserve, ye governments. Can you dry up the fountains of thought? High treason, when it is resistance to tyranny here below, has its origin in, and is first committed by the power that makes and forever recreates man. When you have caught and hung all these human rebels, you have accomplished nothing but your own guilt, for you have not struck at the fountain head. You presume to contend with a foe against whom West Point cadets and rifled cannon *point* not. Can all the art of the cannon-founder tempt matter to turn against its maker? Is the form in which the founder thinks he casts it more essential than the constitution of it and of himself?

The United States have a coffle[1] of four millions of slaves. They are determined to keep them in this condition; and Massachusetts is one of the confederated overseers to prevent their escape. Such are not all the inhabitants of Massachusetts, but such are they who rule and are obeyed here. It was Massachusetts, as well as Virginia, that put down this insurrection at Harper's Ferry. She sent the marines there, and she will have to pay the penalty of her sin.

Suppose that there is a society in this State that out of its own purse and magnanimity saves all the fugitive slaves that run to us, and protects our colored fellow-citizens, and leaves the other work to the Government, so-called. Is not that government fast losing its occupation, and becoming contemptible to mankind? If private men are obliged to perform the offices of government, to protect the weak and dispense justice, then the government becomes only a hired man, or clerk, to perform menial or indifferent services. Of course, that is but the shadow of a government whose existence necessitates a Vigilant Committee. What should we think of the oriental Cadi[2] even, behind whom worked in secret a vigilant committee? But such is the character of our Northern States generally; each has its Vigilant Committee. And, to a certain extent, these crazy governments recognize and accept this relation. They say, virtually, "We'll be glad to work for you on these terms, only don't make a noise about it." And thus the government, its salary being insured, withdraws into the back shop, taking the constitution with it, and bestows most of its labor on repairing that. When I hear it at work sometimes, as I go by, it reminds me, at best, of those farmers who in winter contrive to turn a penny by following the coopering business. And what kind of spirit is their barrel made to hold? They speculate in stocks, and bore holes in mountains, but they are not competent to lay out even a decent highway. The only *free* road, the Underground Railroad, is owned and managed by the Vigilant Committee. *They* have tunnelled under the whole breadth of the land. Such a government is losing its power and respectability as surely as water runs out of a leaky vessel, and is held by one that can contain it.

5

---

[1]A group chained in a line — usually referring to animals, prisoners, or slaves. — Eds.
[2]A Muslim judge who rules based on Islamic religious law. Also spelled *Qadi.* — Eds.

I hear many condemn these men because they were so few. When were the good and the brave ever in a majority? Would you have had him wait till that time came? — till you and I came over to him? The very fact that he had no rabble or troop of hirelings about him, would alone distinguish him from ordinary heroes. His company was small indeed, because few could be found worthy to pass muster. Each one who there laid down his life for the poor and oppressed was a picked man, culled out of many thousands, if not millions; apparently a man of principle, of rare courage and devoted humanity; ready to sacrifice his life at any moment for the benefit of his fellow-man. It may be doubted if there were as many more their equals in these respects in all the country — I speak of his followers only — for their leader, no doubt, scoured the land far and wide, seeking to swell his troop. These alone were ready to step between the oppressor and the oppressed. Surely they were the very best men you could select to be hung. That was the greatest compliment which this country could pay them. They were ripe for her gallows. She has tried a long time, she has hung a good many, but never found the right one before.

When I think of him, and his six sons, and his son-in-law, — not to enumerate the others, — enlisted for this fight, proceeding coolly, reverently, humanely to work, for months, if not years, sleeping and waking upon it, summering and wintering the thought, without expecting any reward but a good conscience, while almost all America stood ranked on the other side, I say again, that it affects me as a sublime spectacle. If he had had any journal advocating "*his cause*," any organ, as the phrase is, monotonously and wearisomely playing the same old tune, and then passing round the bat, it would have been fatal to his efficiency. If he had acted in any way so as to be let alone by the government, he might have been suspected. It was the fact that the tyrant must give place to him, or he to the tyrant, that distinguished him from all the reformers of the day that I know.

It was his peculiar doctrine that a man has a perfect right to interfere by force with the slaveholder, in order to rescue the slave. I agree with him. They who are continually shocked by slavery have some right to be shocked by the violent death of the slaveholder, but no others. Such will be more shocked by his life than by his death. I shall not be forward to think him mistaken in his method who quickest succeeds to liberate the slave. I speak for the slave when I say, that I prefer the philanthropy of Captain Brown to that philanthropy which neither shoots me nor liberates me. At any rate, I do not think it is quite sane for one to spend his whole life in talking or writing about this matter, unless he is continuously inspired, and I have not done so. A man may have other affairs to attend to. I do not wish to kill nor to be killed, but I can foresee circumstances in which both these things would be by me unavoidable. We preserve the so-called peace of our community by deeds of petty violence every day. Look at the policeman's billy and handcuffs! Look at the jail! Look at the gallows! Look at the chaplain of the regiment! We are hoping only to live safely on the outskirts of *this* provisional army. So we defend ourselves and our hen-roosts, and maintain slavery. I know that the mass of my countrymen think that the only righteous use that can be made of Sharpe's rifles and revolvers is to fight duels with them, when we are insulted by other nations, or to hunt Indians, or shoot fugitive slaves with them, or the like. I think that for once the Sharpe's rifles and the revolvers were employed in a righteous cause. The tools were in the hands of one who could use them.

The same indignation that is said to have cleared the temple once will clear it again. The question is not about the weapon, but the spirit in which you use it. No man has appeared in America, as yet, who loved his fellow-man so well, and treated him so tenderly. He lived for him. He took up his life and he laid it down for him. What sort of violence is that which is encouraged, not by soldiers but by peaceable citizens, not so much by laymen as by ministers of the gospel, not so much by the fighting sects as by the Quakers, and not so much by Quaker men as by Quaker women?

This event advertises me that there is such a fact as death — the possibility of a man's dying. It seems as if no man had ever died in America before, for in order to die you must first have lived. I don't believe in the hearses, and palls, and funerals that they have had. There was no death in the case, because there had been no life; they merely rotted or sloughed off, pretty much as they had rotted or sloughed along. No temple's vail was rent, only a hole dug somewhere. Let the dead bury their dead. The best of them fairly ran down like a clock. Franklin — Washington — they were let off without dying; they were merely missing one day. I hear a good many pretend that they are going to die; or that they have died, for aught that I know. Nonsense! I'll defy them to do it. They haven't got life enough in them. They'll deliquesce[3] like fungi, and keep a hundred eulogists mopping the spot where they left off. Only half a dozen or so have died since the world began. Do you think that you are going to die, sir? No! there's no hope of you. You haven't got your lesson yet. You've got to stay after school. We make a needless ado about capital punishment — taking lives, when there is no life to take. *Memento mori!*[4] We don't understand that sublime sentence which some worthy got sculptured on his gravestone once. We've interpreted it in a grovelling and snivelling sense; we've wholly forgotten how to die.

But be sure you do die, nevertheless. Do your work, and finish it. If you know how to begin, you will know when to end.

These men, in teaching us how to die, have at the same time taught us how to live. If this man's acts and words do not create a revival, it will be the severest possible satire on the acts and words that do. It is the best news that America has ever heard. It has already quickened the feeble pulse of the North, and infused more and more generous blood into her veins and heart, than any number of years of what is called commercial and political prosperity could. How many a man who was lately contemplating suicide has now something to live for!

One writer says that Brown's peculiar monomania made him to be "dreaded by the Missourians as a supernatural being." Sure enough, a hero in the midst of us cowards is always so dreaded. He is just that thing. He shows himself superior to nature. He has a spark of divinity in him.

10

---

[3]Liquefy, specifically due to decomposition and decay. — Eds.
[4]Latin. "Remember you will die." An object or piece of art that reminds the audience of the inevitability of death. — Eds.

"Unless above himself he doth erect himself,
How poor a thing is man!"

Newspaper editors argue also that it is a proof of his *insanity* that he thought he   15
was appointed to do this work which he did—that he did not suspect himself for a
moment! They talk as if it were impossible that a man could be "divinely appointed" in
these days to do any work whatever; as if vows and religion were out of date as connected with any man's daily work,—as if the agent to abolish Slavery could only be
somebody appointed by the President, or by some political party. They talk as if a man's
death were a failure, and his continued life, be it of whatever character, were a success.

When I reflect to what a cause this man devoted himself, and how religiously, and
then reflect to what cause his judges and all who condemn him so angrily and fluently
devote themselves, I see that they are as far apart as the heavens and earth are asunder.

The amount of it is, our "*leading men*" are a harmless kind of folk, and they know
well enough that *they* were not divinely appointed, but elected by the votes of their party.

Who is it whose safety requires that Captain Brown be hung? Is it indispensable
to any Northern man? Is there no resource but to cast these men also to the Mino-
taur? If you do not wish it, say so distinctly. While these things are being done, beauty
stands veiled and music is a screeching lie. Think of him—of his rare qualities! such
a man as it takes ages to make, and ages to understand; no mock hero, nor the representative of any party. A man such as the sun may not rise upon again in this benighted land. To whose making went the costliest material, the finest adamant; sent
to be the redeemer of those in captivity; and the only use to which you can put him
is to hang him at the end of a rope! You who pretend to care for Christ crucified,
consider what you are about to do to him who offered himself to be the saviour of
four millions of men.

Any man knows when he is justified, and all the wits in the world cannot
enlighten him on that point. The murderer always knows that he is justly punished; but when a government takes the life of a man without the consent of his
conscience, it is an audacious government, and is taking a step towards its own
dissolution. Is it not possible that an individual may be right and a government
wrong? Are laws to be enforced simply because they were made? or declared by
any number of men to be good, if they are *not* good? Is there any necessity for a
man's being a tool to perform a deed of which his better nature disapproves? Is it
the intention of law-makers that *good* men shall be hung ever? Are judges to interpret the law according to the letter, and not the spirit? What right have *you* to enter
into a compact with yourself that you *will* do thus or so, against the light within
you? Is it for *you* to *make up* your mind—to form any resolution whatever—and
not accept the convictions that are forced upon you, and which ever pass your
understanding? I do not believe in lawyers, in that mode of attacking or defending
a man, because you descend to meet the judge on his own ground, and, in cases
of the highest importance, it is of no consequence whether a man breaks a human
law or not. Let lawyers decide trivial cases. Business men may arrange that among
themselves. If they were the interpreters of the everlasting laws which rightfully

bind man, that would be another thing. A counterfeiting law-factory, standing half in a slave land and half in a free! What kind of laws for free men can you expect from that?

I am here to plead his cause with you. I plead not for his life, but for his character — his immortal life; and so it becomes your cause wholly, and is not his in the least. Some eighteen hundred years ago Christ was crucified; this morning, perchance, Captain Brown was hung. These are the two ends of a chain which is not without its links. He is not Old Brown any longer; he is an angel of light.

I see now that it was necessary that the bravest and humanest man in all the country should be hung. Perhaps he saw it himself. I *almost fear* that I may yet hear of his deliverance, doubting if a prolonged life, if *any* life, can do as much good as his death.

"Misguided"! "Garrulous"! "Insane"! Vindictive"! So ye write in your easy chairs, and thus he wounded responds from the floor of the Armory, clear as a cloudless sky, true as the voice of nature is: "No man sent me here; it was my own prompting and that of my Maker. I acknowledge no master in human form."

And in what a sweet and noble strain he proceeds, addressing his captors, who stand over him: "I think, my friends, you are guilty of a great wrong against God and humanity, and it would be perfectly right for any one to interfere with you so far as to free those you wilfully and wickedly hold in bondage."

And referring to his movement: "It is, in my opinion, the greatest service a man can render to God."

"I pity the poor in bondage that have none to help them; that is why I am here; not to gratify any personal animosity, revenge, or vindictive spirit. It is my sympathy with the oppressed and the wronged, that are as good as you, and as precious in the sight of God."

You don't know your testament when you see it.

"I want you to understand that I respect the rights of the poorest and weakest of colored people, oppressed by the slave power, just as much as I do those of the most wealthy and powerful."

"I wish to say, furthermore, that you had better, all you people at the South, prepare yourselves for a settlement of that question, that must come up for settlement sooner than you are prepared for it. The sooner you are prepared the better. You may dispose of me very easily. I am nearly disposed of now; but this question is still to be settled — this negro question, I mean; the end of that is not yet."

I foresee the time when the painter will paint that scene, no longer going to Rome for a subject; the poet will sing it; the historian record it; and, with the Landing of the Pilgrims and the Declaration of Independence, it will be the ornament of some future national gallery, when at least the present form of Slavery shall be no more here. We shall then be at liberty to weep for Captain Brown. Then, and not till then, we will take our revenge.

(1859)

Questions

1. In the opening six paragraphs, how does Henry David Thoreau characterize the government? How does he lead to his final statement, "Such a government is losing its power and respectability as surely as water runs out of a leaky vessel, and is held by one that can contain it" (par. 6)?
2. Why does Thoreau assert that hanging the men, including Brown, for their part in the raid was "the greatest compliment which this country could pay them" (par. 7)?
3. What point is Thoreau trying to make when he states, "I speak for the slave when I say, that I prefer the philanthropy of Captain Brown to that philanthropy which neither shoots me nor liberates me" (par. 9)?
4. Thoreau makes extensive references to the New Testament in this speech. How would these references likely appeal to the audience of his time?
5. Identify three accusations that had been leveled at Brown. How does Thoreau respond to each? How effective is he in challenging each?
6. What does Thoreau mean by this statement: "I am here to plead his cause with you. I plead not for his life, but for his character — his immortal life; and so it becomes your cause wholly, and is not his in the least" (par. 20)?
7. What is the reasoning that leads Thoreau to conclude that Brown's execution was "necessary" (par. 21)?
8. What is the effect Thoreau achieves by quoting Brown's own words so extensively in the last section of the speech?

The Last Moments of John Brown

THOMAS HOVENDEN

> An influential Irish painter of everyday scenes and human figures, Thomas Hovenden (1840–1895) was commissioned by New York businessman Robbins Battell to paint what became known as *The Last Moments of John Brown* (1882). This work, which is currently in the Metropolitan Museum of Art, inaugurated a series of paintings by Hovenden dealing with American history and culture, including *Breaking Home Ties* (1890), considered his masterwork.

Questions

1. How is Brown depicted in this painting? As a viewer of his "last moments" in this work, how would you remember him? Cite specific details to support your response.
2. What visual allusions do you find in the painting? What do they add to your interpretation?
3. Some believe that Thomas Hovenden read the following account that appeared in the *New York Tribune* on December 5, 1859:

THOMAS HOVENDEN, *THE LAST MOMENTS OF JOHN BROWN*, C. 1882, OIL ON CANVAS, 77" × 66", METROPOLITAN MUSEUM OF ART, NEW YORK.
(See color insert, Image 25.)

On leaving the Jail, John Brown had on his face an expression of calmness and serenity characteristic of the patriot who is about to die with a living consciousness that he is laying his life down for the good of his fellow-creatures. . . . As he stepped out of the door a black woman, with her little child in arms, stood near his way. The twain were of the despised race, for whose emancipation and elevation to the dig-

Copyright © The Metropolitan Museum of Art. Image source: Art Resource, NY.

nity of children of God, he was about to lay down his life. . . . He stopped for a moment in his course, stooped over, and, with the tenderness of one whose love is as broad as the brotherhood of man, kissed [the child] affectionately.

Even though historians doubt that the account is accurate (for example, civilians, such as the woman and baby, were not allowed in the area of Brown's hanging because of rumored plans for escape), how does Hovenden's painting capture the tone of the description?

The Father of American Terrorism

KEN CHOWDER

> Ken Chowder is an award-winning filmmaker who wrote the documentary John Brown's Holy War. This article appeared in American Heritage magazine (February/March 2000); the following excerpt is the final section, which focuses on the raid on Harpers Ferry.

But what about that Harpers Ferry plan — a tiny band attacking the U.S. government, hoping to concoct a revolution that would carry across the South? Clearly that was crazy.

Elements on both the far left and the far right are at this moment vitally interested in his story.

Yes and no. If it was crazy, it was not unique. Dozens of people, often bearing arms, had gone South to rescue slaves. Secret military societies flourished on both sides, plotting to expand or destroy the system of slavery by force. Far from being the product of a singular cracked mind, the plan was similar to a number of others, including one by a Boston attorney named Lysander Spooner. James Horton, a leading African American history scholar, offers an interesting scenario. "Was Brown crazy to assume he could encourage slave rebellion? . . . Think about the possibility of Nat Turner well-armed, well-equipped. . . . Nat Turner might have done some pretty amazing things," Horton says. "It was perfectly rational and reasonable for John Brown to believe he could encourage slaves to rebel."

But the question of Brown's sanity still provokes dissension among experts. Was he crazy? "He was obsessed," Bruce Olds says, "he was fanatical, he was monomaniacal, he was a zealot, and . . . psychologically unbalanced." Paul Finkelman disagrees: Brown "is a bad tactician, he's a bad strategist, he's a bad planner, he's not a very good general — but he's not crazy."

Some believe that there is a very particular reason why Brown's reputation as a madman has clung to him. Russell Banks and James Horton make the same argument. "The reason white people think he was mad," Banks says, "is because he was a white man and he was willing to sacrifice his life in order to liberate black Americans." "We should be very careful," Horton says, "about assuming that a white man who is willing to put his life on the line for black people is, of necessity, crazy."

5

Perhaps it is reasonable to say this: A society where slavery exists is by nature one where human values are skewed. America before the Civil War was a violent society, twisted by slavery. Even sober and eminent people became firebrands. John Brown had many peculiarities of his own, but he was not outside his society; to a great degree, he represented it, in its many excesses.

The past, as always, continues to change, and the spinning of John Brown's story goes on today. The same events — the raid on Harpers Ferry or the Pottawatomie Massacre — are still seen in totally different ways. What is perhaps most remarkable is that elements at both the left and right ends of American society are at this moment vitally interested in the story of John Brown.

On the left is a group of historical writers and teachers called Allies for Freedom. This group believes that the truth about the Harpers Ferry raid has been buried by the conventions of history. Its informal leader, Jean Libby, author of *John Brown Mysteries*, says, "What we think is that John Brown was a black nationalist. His ultimate goal was the creation of an independent black nation." The Allies for Freedom believes, too, that far from being the folly of a lunatic, Brown's plan was not totally unworkable, that it came much closer to succeeding than historians have pictured. Libby thinks that many slaves and free blacks did join the uprising — perhaps as many as fifty. Why would history conceal the fact of active black participation in Harpers Ferry? "The South was anxious to cover up any indication that the raid might have been successful," Libby says, "so slaves would never again be tempted to revolt."

Go a good deal farther to the left, and there has long been admiration for John Brown. In 1975 the Weather Underground put out a journal called *Osawatomie*. In the late 1970s a group calling itself the John Brown Brigade engaged in pitched battles with the Ku Klux Klan; in one confrontation in Greensboro, North Carolina, in 1979, five members of the John Brown Brigade were shot and killed. Writers also continue to draw parallels between John Brown and virtually any leftist who uses political violence, including the Symbionese Liberation Army (the kidnappers of Patty Hearst in the 1970s), the Islamic terrorists who allegedly set off a bomb in the World Trade Center in Manhattan, and Ted Kaczynski, the Unabomber.

At the same time, John Brown is frequently compared to those at the far opposite   10
end of the political spectrum. Right-to-life extremists have bombed abortion clinics and murdered doctors; they have, in short, killed for a cause they believed in, just as John Brown did. Paul Hill was convicted of murdering a doctor who performed abortions; it was, Hill said, the Lord's bidding: "There's no question in my mind that it was what the Lord wanted me to do, to shoot John Britton to prevent him from killing unborn children." If that sounds quite like John Brown, it was no accident. From death row Hill wrote to the historian Dan Stowell that Brown's "example has and continues to serve as a source of encouragement to me. . . . Both of us looked to the scriptures for direction, [and] the providential similarities between the oppressive circumstances we faced and our general understandings of the appropriate means to deliver the oppressed have resulted in my being encouraged to pursue a path which is in many ways similar to his." Shortly before his execution Hill wrote

that "the political impact of Brown's actions continues to serve as a powerful paradigm in my understanding of the potential effects the use of defensive force may have for the unborn."

Nor was the murder Hill committed the only right-wing violence that has been compared to Brown's. The Oklahoma City bombing in 1995 was a frontal attack on a U.S. government building, just like the Harpers Ferry raid. Antiabortion murders, government bombings, anarchist bombs in the mail — nearly every time political violence surfaces, it gets described in the press as a part of a long American tradition of terrorism, with John Brown as a precursor and hero, a founding father of principled violence.

He gets compared to anarchists, leftist revolutionaries, and right-wing extremists. The spinning of John Brown, in short, is still going strong. But what does that make him? This much, at least, is certain: John Brown is a vital presence for all sorts of people today. In February PBS's *The American Experience* is broadcasting a ninety-minute documentary about him. Russell Banks's novel *Cloudsplitter* was a critical success and a bestseller as well. On the verge of his two hundredth birthday (this May 9), John Brown is oddly present. Perhaps there is one compelling reason for his revival in this new millennium: perhaps the violent, excessive, morally torn society John Brown represents so aptly was not just his own antebellum America but this land, now.

(2000)

Questions

1. In the opening paragraphs, Ken Chowder discusses the debate over John Brown's sanity. What conclusion does he reach?
2. According to Chowder, how does "the left" in the late twentieth and early twenty-first centuries view Brown? How does "the right" view him?
3. Ultimately, why does Chowder believe that, on his two-hundredth birthday, Brown remains "oddly present" in the American consciousness?

from *The "Madness" of John Brown*

Robert E. McGlone

Associate professor of history at the University of Hawaii, Robert McGlone is the author of the biography *John Brown's War against Slavery* (2009). The selection that appears here was taken from an article in the *Civil War Times* in October 2009.

[A]s Brown himself understood, the claim that he was "insane" threatened the very meaning of his life. Thus at his trial he emphatically rejected an insanity plea to spare him from the hangman. When an Akron newspaperman telegraphed Brown's court-appointed attorneys in Richmond that insanity was prevalent in Brown's maternal family, Brown declared in court that he was "perfectly unconscious of insanity" in himself.

As Brown understood it, the "greatest and principal object" of his life — his quest to destroy slavery — would be seen as delusional if he were declared insane. The sacrifices he and his supporters had made would count for nothing. The deaths of his men and the bereavement of his wife would be doubly tragic and the attack on Harpers Ferry robbed of heroism, its purpose discredited.

In letters to his wife and children, Brown acknowledged that his raid had ended in a "calamity" or a "seeming disaster." But he urged them all to have faith and to feel no shame over his impending fate.

While his half brother Jeremiah helped gather affidavits supposedly attesting to Brown's "monomania," or single minded fixation on eradicating slavery, John's brother Frederick went on a lecture tour in his support. Neither Jeremiah nor anyone else in John Brown's large family renounced the raid.

When it comes to Brown's war against slavery, the question of his mental balance   5
must nevertheless be addressed. By the time of the Harpers Ferry raid, some of his contemporaries had already begun to question his sanity. As they insisted, was not the raid itself evidence of an "unhinged" mind? Wasn't Brown "crazy" to suppose he could overthrow American slavery by commencing a movement on so grand a scale with just 21 active fighters?

No one can doubt that Brown sought to elevate the status of African Americans. Throughout his adult life, he conceived projects to help them gain entry into the privileged world of whites. As a youth he helped fugitive slaves on the Underground Railroad; as a prospering farmer and town builder, he proposed adopting black children and founding schools for them. In 1849 he moved his family to North Elba, N.Y., to teach fugitives how to maintain a farm.

He held a two-day convention in Canada to secure the participation of fugitive American blacks in his planned war on slavery. He wrote a declaration of independence on their behalf. He respected and raised money for "General" Harriet Tubman and called his friend Frederick Douglass "the first great national Negro leader." Yet to the extent that in his projects he envisioned himself as a mentor, leader, or commander in chief, Brown's embrace of egalitarianism was, paradoxically, paternalistic. He solicited support from blacks for the war against slavery but not their counsel in shaping it.

Despite that, his black allies never called seizing Harpers Ferry crazy. Although Brown had been hanged for his actions, Douglass insisted the raid had lit the fire that consumed slavery. Brown chose to open his war against slavery at Harpers Ferry, W.E.B. Du Bois wrote in 1909, because the capture of a U.S. arsenal would create a "dramatic climax to the inception of his plan" and because it was the "safest natural entrance to the Great Black Way" through the mountains from slavery to freedom in the North.

Harpers Ferry wasn't Brown's first foray onto the national stage. In 1857 his band of men had killed several proslavery settlers in "Bleeding Kansas," hacking to death five men along Pottawatomie Creek with short, heavy swords. Scholars differ on whether the killings should be considered murders or acts of war following the pro-slavery sack of Lawrence just days before. I have found evidence that Brown and his sons saw their attack as a kind of preemptive strike against men who had threatened violence against freestaters. But to understand is not necessarily to justify or excuse. How a deeply religious man could commit such an act is a question one cannot ignore in assessing Brown's mind.

Du Bois understood that Brown's recourse to violence in killing "border ruffians" in   10
Kansas and his attempt to seize the armory at Harpers Ferry in order to arm slaves had caused "bitter debate as to how far force and violence can bring peace and good will."

But Du Bois, a co-founder of the NAACP, did not think slavery could have been ended without the Civil War. He concluded that "the violence which John Brown led made Kansas a free state" and his plan to put arms in the hands of slaves hastened the end of slavery. Du Bois's book *John Brown* was a "tribute to the man who of all Americans has perhaps come nearest to touching the real souls of black folk." African-American historians, artists and activists have long eulogized Brown as an archetype of self-sacrifice. "If you are for me and my problems," Malcolm X declared in 1965, "then you have to be willing to do as old John Brown did."

Blacks' reverence for the memory of Brown has not inspired those mainstream historians uncomfortable with Brown's reliance on violence. The belief that he may have suffered from a degree of "madness" has echoed down through the decades in Brown biographical literature. In his popular 1959 narrative *The Road to Harpers Ferry*, J.C. Furnas argued that Brown was consumed by a widespread "Spartacus[1] complex."

But Furnas also found that "certain details of Old Brown's career" and writings evidenced psychiatric illness. Brown might have been "intermittently 'insane' . . . for years before Harpers Ferry," Furnas speculated, "sometimes able to cope with practicalities but eventually betrayed by his strange inconsistencies leading up to and during the raid — his disease then progressing into the egocentric exaltation that so edified millions between his capture and death."

Careful historians like David M. Potter reaffirmed the centrality of the slavery issue in his posthumously published synthesis *The Impending Crisis, 1848–1861*, but even Potter conceded that Brown "was not a well-adjusted man" — despite the fact many abolitionists shared his belief that the slaves were restive.

In 1970 historian Stephen B. Oates sought to bridge the rival biographical tradi-   15
tions by depicting Brown as a religious obsessive in an era of intense political conflict. Oates' Brown was not the Cromwellian warrior of early legend builders. Nor was he the greedy, self-deluded soldier of fortune of debunkers.

He was a curious, somewhat schizoid amalgam of the legend builders' martyr and his evil doppelganger. This Brown possessed courage, energy, compassion and indomitable faith in his call to free the slaves. He was also egotistical, inept, cruel, intolerant and self-righteous, "always exhibit[ing] a puritanical obsession with the wrongs of others."

---

[1]Spartacus (109–71 BCE) was a gladiator who led a slave uprising against the Roman Republic. — Eds.

Oates was doubtful that historians might ever persuasively identify psychosis in a subject they studied. He repudiated historian Allan Nevins's belief that Brown suffered from "reasoning insanity" and "ambitious paranoia," but he declared that Brown was not "normal," "well adjusted" or "sane" either (later dismissing these terms as meaningless).

But reference to Brown's "glittering eye"—a telltale mark of insanity in 19th-century popular culture—invited Oates' readers to conclude that Brown was touched with madness after all. Finding in Brown an "angry, messianic mind," Oates straddled the two biographical traditions. For three decades, his portrait of Brown has perpetuated the image of mental instability.

(2009)

Questions

1. Why did Brown address and deny the charges that he was "insane" rather than using insanity as a defense?
2. What arguments claiming that Brown was mentally unbalanced does Robert E. McGlone discuss?
3. How does he address and refute these?
4. How effective do you find prominent African Americans' testimony as evidence to establish Brown's sanity?
5. What are the "rival biographical traditions" (par. 15) historian Stephen B. Oates attempts to correct? How does his interpretation seek to "bridge" them?

Freedom's Martyr

DAVID REYNOLDS

David Reynolds, professor of English and American studies at the City University of New York, is the author of the biography *John Brown, Abolitionist: The Man Who Killed Slavery, Sparked the Civil War, and Seeded Civil Rights* (2005). This essay appeared as an op-ed piece in the *New York Times* in 2009.

It's important for Americans to recognize our national heroes, even those who have been despised by history. Take John Brown.

Today is the 150th anniversary of Brown's hanging—the grim punishment for his raid weeks earlier on Harpers Ferry, Va. With a small band of abolitionists, Brown had seized the federal arsenal there and freed slaves in the area. His plan was to flee with them to nearby mountains and provoke rebellions in the South. But he stalled too long in the arsenal and was captured. He was brought to trial in a Virginia court, convicted of treason, murder, and inciting an insurrection, and hanged on December 2, 1859.

It's a date we should hold in reverence. Yes, I know the response: Why remember a misguided fanatic and his absurd plan for destroying slavery?

There are compelling reasons. First, the plan was not absurd. Brown reasonably saw the Appalachians, which stretch deep into the South, as an ideal base for a guerrilla war. He had studied the Maroon rebels of the West Indies, black fugitives who had used mountain camps to battle colonial powers on their islands. His plan was to create panic by arousing fears of a slave rebellion, leading Southerners to view slavery as dangerous and impractical.

Second, he was held in high esteem by many great men of his day. Ralph Waldo   5
Emerson compared him to Jesus, declaring that Brown would "make the gallows as glorious as the cross." Henry David Thoreau placed Brown above the freedom fighters of the American Revolution. Frederick Douglass said that while he had lived for black people, John Brown had died for them. A later black reformer, W. E. B. Du Bois, called Brown the white American who had "come nearest to touching the real souls of black folk."

Du Bois was right. Unlike nearly all other Americans of his era, John Brown did not have a shred of racism. He had long lived among African Americans, trying to help them make a living, and he wanted blacks to be quickly integrated into American society. When Brown was told he could have a clergyman to accompany him to the gallows, he refused, saying he would be more honored to go with a slave woman and her children.

By the time of his hanging, John Brown was so respected in the North that bells tolled in many cities and towns in his honor. Within two years, the Union troops marched southward singing, "John Brown's body lies a-mouldering in the grave, but his soul keeps marching on." Brown remained a hero to the North right up through Reconstruction.

However, he fell from grace during the long, dark period of Jim Crow. The attitude was, who cares about his progressive racial views, except a few blacks? His reputation improved a bit with the civil rights movement, but he is still widely dismissed as a deranged cultist. This is an injustice to a forward-thinking man dedicated to the freedom and political participation of African-Americans.

O.K., some might say, but how about the blotches on his record, especially the murders and bloody skirmishes in Kansas in the 1850s? Brown considered himself a soldier at war. His attacks on pro-slavery forces were part of an escalating cycle of pre-emptive and retaliatory violence that most historians now agree were in essence the first engagements of the Civil War.

Besides, none of the heroes from that period is unblemished. Lincoln was the   10
Great Emancipator, but he shared the era's racial prejudices, and even after the war started thought that blacks should be shipped out of the country once they were freed. Andrew Jackson was the man of his age, but in addition to being a slaveholder, he has the extra infamy of his callous treatment of Native Americans, for which some hold him guilty of genocide. John Brown comes with "buts" — but in that he has plenty of company. He deserves to be honored today.

For starters, he should be pardoned. Technically, Gov. Tim Kaine of Virginia would have to do this, since Brown was tried on state charges and executed there. Such a posthumous pardon by a state occurred just this October, when South Carolina pardoned two black men who were executed 94 years ago for murdering a Confederate veteran.

A presidential pardon, however, would be more meaningful. Posthumous pardons are by definition symbolic. They're intended to remove stigma or correct injustice. While the president cannot grant pardons for state crimes, a strong argument can be made for a symbolic exception in Brown's case.

By today's standards, his crime was arguably of a federal nature, as his attack was on a federal arsenal in what is now West Virginia. His actions were prompted by federal slavery rulings he considered despicable, especially the Supreme Court's *Dred Scott* decision. Brown was captured by federal troops under Robert E. Lee. And the Virginia court convicted him of treason against Virginia even though he was not a resident. (He was tried in Virginia at the orders of its governor, probably to avert Northern political pressure on the federal government.)

There is precedent for presidential pardons of the deceased; in 1999, Bill Clinton pardoned Henry O. Flipper, an African-American lieutenant who was court-martialed in 1881 for misconduct. Last year, George W. Bush gave a posthumous pardon to Charles Winters, an American punished for supplying B-17 bombers to Israel in the late 1940s. In October, Senator John McCain and Representative Peter King petitioned President Obama to pardon Jack Johnson, the black boxing champion, who was convicted a century ago of transporting a white woman across state lines for immoral purposes.

Justice would be served, belatedly, if President Obama and Governor Kaine   15
found a way to pardon a man whose heroic effort to free four million enslaved blacks helped start the war that ended slavery. Once and for all, rescue John Brown from the loony bin of history.

(2009)

Questions

1. What occasioned this essay?
2. David Reynolds asks, in paragraph 3, "Why remember a misguided fanatic and his absurd plan for destroying slavery?" What is his answer?
3. Reynolds asserts that Brown "did not have a shred of racism" (par. 6). To what extent do you find this an important defense of his actions?
4. Which counterarguments does Reynolds address? Identify two and discuss how effectively you believe he concedes and refutes them.
5. Why does Reynolds believe it is important to establish that "Brown considered himself a soldier at war" (par. 9)?
6. How does Reynolds support his claim that a posthumous presidential pardon for Brown would be appropriate and significant? To what extent do you agree?
7. Reynolds ends by calling for the "rescue" of Brown from the "loony bin of history." Does this characterization undermine or emphasize his argument? Explain your response.

The 9/11 of 1859

TONY HORWITZ

Award-winning reporter Tony Horwitz has been a fellow at the Radcliffe Institute for Advanced Study at Harvard University and a visiting scholar at Brown University. *Midnight Rising*, a biography of John Brown, won the 2012 William Henry Seward Award for Excellence in Civil War Biography. This essay appeared as an op-ed piece in the *New York Times* on the same day as the previous piece by David Reynolds. Horwitz is responding to the decision to try Khalid Shaikh Mohammed in a civilian rather than a military court; the decision was subsequently overturned.

Charles Town, West Virginia

One hundred and fifty years ago today, the most successful terrorist in American history was hanged at the edge of this Shenandoah Valley town. Before climbing atop his coffin for the wagon ride to the gallows, he handed a note to one of his jailers: "I, John Brown, am now quite certain that the crimes of this guilty land will never be purged away but with blood."

Eighteen months later, Americans went to war against each other, with soldiers marching into battle singing "John Brown's Body." More than 600,000 men died before the sin of slavery was purged.

Few if any Americans today would question the justness of John Brown's cause: the abolition of human bondage. But as the nation prepares to try Khalid Shaikh Mohammed, who calls himself the architect of the 9/11 attacks, it may be worth pondering the parallels between John Brown's raid in 1859 and Al Qaeda's assault in 2001.

Brown was a bearded fundamentalist who believed himself chosen by God to destroy the institution of slavery. He hoped to launch his holy war by seizing the United States armory at Harpers Ferry, Va., and arming blacks for a campaign of liberation. Brown also chose his target for shock value and symbolic impact. The only federal armory in the South, Harpers Ferry was just 60 miles from the capital, where "our president and other leeches," Brown wrote, did the bidding of slave owners. The first slaves freed and armed by Brown belonged to George Washington's great-grandnephew.

Brown's strike force was similar in size and makeup to that of the 9/11 hijackers. 5
He led 21 men, all but two in their 20s, and many of them radicalized by guerrilla fighting in Bleeding Kansas, the abolitionists' Afghanistan. Brown also relied on covert backers — not oil-rich Saudis, but prominent Yankees known as the Secret Six. Brown used aliases and coded language and gathered his men at a mountain hideout. But, like the 9/11 bombers, Brown's men were indiscreet, disclosing their plan to family and sweethearts. A letter warning of the plot even reached the secretary of war. It arrived in August, the scheme seemed outlandish, and the warning was ignored.

Brown and his men were prepared to die, and most did, in what quickly became a suicide mission. Trapped in Harpers Ferry, the raiders fought for 24 hours until Robert E. Lee ordered marines to storm the building where the survivors had holed up. Ten raiders were killed, including two of Brown's sons, and seven more hanged. No slaves won their freedom. The first civilian casualty was a free black railroad worker, shot in the back while fleeing the raiders.

This fiasco might have been a footnote of history if Brown had died of his wounds or been immediately executed. Instead, he survived, and was tried under tight security in a civilian court in Charles Town, near Harpers Ferry. Rather than challenge the evidence, or let his lawyers plead insanity, Brown put the South on trial. Citing the biblical injunction to "remember them that are in bonds," he declared his action "was not wrong, but right."

"If it is deemed necessary that I should forfeit my life for the furtherance of the ends of justice," he said, "and mingle my blood further with the blood of my children and with the blood of millions in this slave country whose rights are disregarded by wicked, cruel and unjust enactments — I submit; so let it be done!" He was hanged a month later, before a crowd that included John Wilkes Booth, who later wrote of the "terroriser" with a mix of contempt and awe.

Brown's courage and eloquence made him a martyr-hero for many in the North. This canonization, in turn, deepened Southern rage and alarm over the raid. Though Brown occupied the far fringe of abolitionism — a "wild and absurd freak," *The New York Times* called him — Southern firebrands painted his raid as part of a broad conspiracy. An already polarized nation lurched closer to violent divorce. "The time for compromise was gone," Frederick Douglass later observed. "The armed hosts of freedom stood face to face over the chasm of a broken Union, and the clash of arms was at hand." This was exactly what Brown had predicted in his final note.

Khalid Shaikh Mohammed is no John Brown. The 9/11 attack caused mass, 10 indiscriminate slaughter, for inscrutable ends. Brown fed breakfast to his hostages; the hijackers slit throats with box cutters. Any words Mr. Mohammed may offer in his own defense will likely strike Americans as hateful and unpersuasive. In any event, the judge probably won't grant him an ideological platform.

But perhaps he doesn't need one. In 1859, John Brown sought not only to free slaves in Virginia but to terrorize the South and incite a broad conflict. In this he triumphed: panicked whites soon mobilized, militarized and marched double-quick toward secession. Brown's raid didn't cause the Civil War, but it was certainly a catalyst.

It may be too early to say if 9/11 bred a similar overreaction. But last night President Obama vowed to increase our efforts in Afghanistan — one of two wars that, eight years on, have killed nearly twice as many Americans as the hijacked planes. The nation, beset by the wars' burden, will continue to find its domestic and foreign policy options hobbled.

Show trial or no trial, terrorists sometimes win.

(2009)

Questions

1. What is the effect of Tony Horowitz's characterization of Brown as "the most successful terrorist in American history" (par. 1) even before he states Brown's name? Do you think he assumes his readers would agree with him, or is he deliberately trying to provoke them?
2. What "parallels" (par. 3) does Horowitz claim between John Brown's raid in 1859 and Al Qaeda's assault in 2001? What differences does he acknowledge?
3. Why does Horowitz believe that the raid, which he calls a "fiasco," "might have been a footnote of history" (par. 7) if Brown had not had a public trial and execution?
4. Why do you think the reference to John Wilkes Booth (par. 8) strengthens or weakens Horowitz's argument?
5. Finally, what is the purpose of Horowitz's argument? Include consideration of the final sentence in your response. To what extent do you believe he achieved his purpose?

Making Connections

1. What evidence do you find in John Brown's final letter (p. 733) or final speech (p. 732) to support any claims of his mental instability that Robert E. McGlone presents (p. 747)?

2. What similarities do you find between Frances Ellen Watkins Harper's (p. 736) and Henry David Thoreau's (p. 737) views of Brown?

3. Do you think the image of Brown in Thomas Hovenden's painting (p. 743) is more similar to that presented by Thoreau or by David Reynolds (p. 750)? Cite specific details of both written and visual texts to support your response.

4. In what ways does Ken Chowder (p. 745) share Thoreau's view of American society?

5. What is the basic disagreement between Reynolds and Tony Horowitz (p. 753) in their op-ed columns? What common ground, if any, do they have?

6. How might Brown respond to the way Horowitz characterizes him?

7. What point(s) of agreement do you find among Chowder, Horowitz, and McGlone?

Entering the Conversation

As you respond to each of the following prompts, support your position with appropriate evidence, including at least three sources in this Conversation on John Brown, unless otherwise indicated.

1. Taken together, these sources present a survey of the controversy surrounding John Brown. Using a minimum of four of them, explain what the main points of contention and interpretations are and how each is supported.

2. In these source materials and others, Brown is referred to in numerous ways: "freedom's martyr," "an American hero," "noble abolitionist," "misguided fanatic," "anarchy incarnate," "heroic liberator," "deranged cultist," "cold-blooded terrorist," "angel of light." Using at least three of the sources, including one of the primary documents by Brown, develop and support your own characterization of John Brown.

3. In his Address at the Fourteenth Anniversary of Storer College in Harpers Ferry (May 30, 1881), Frederick Douglass described Brown as follows: "To the outward eye of men, John Brown was a criminal, but to their inward eye he was a just man and true. His deeds might be disowned, but the spirit which made those deeds possible was worthy [of] highest honor." Explain why you agree or disagree with Douglass's assessment; cite at least three sources to support your position.

4. Central to the controversy about John Brown is the extent to which violence can ever be justified. Explain when, if ever, you believe that violent actions are appropriate or necessary. Do you believe that "principled violence," as Ken Chowder describes it, exists?

5. The legend of John Brown, to some degree, was created by the popular images, poems, and songs about him. Research one of these and discuss how it supports or challenges at least three of the views of Brown presented in the sources here.

6. Nicole Etcheson, history professor at Ball State University, concludes her article "John Brown, Terrorist?" (*American Nineteenth Century History*, March 2009) with a comparison of Brown and Abraham Lincoln:

   > While still a candidate for president, Abraham Lincoln repudiated Brown's attack on Harpers Ferry. He agreed with Brown "in thinking slavery wrong," but "that cannot excuse violence, bloodshed, and treason." Ironically, Lincoln would preside over a war that accomplished Brown's goals — the abolition of slavery — although by even greater violence. Lincoln's Second Inaugural, which warned that the war might continue "until every drop of blood drawn with the lash, shall be paid by another drawn with the sword," echoes Brown's own belief that the crimes of this guilty land would be purged with blood. And Lincoln agreed with Brown about the sinfulness of slavery, the awfulness of God's judgment on the nation, and the redemptive power of blood sacrifice. No one, however, characterizes Abraham Lincoln's views as terrorism. Instead, we acknowledge such views as those of a chief of state during a terrible and bloody civil conflict that liberated the nation from a heinous institution. Were Brown's aims so different from Lincoln's?

Write a response to Etcheson's final question, based on your knowledge of Lincoln and at least three sources in this Conversation.

6. The Quaker poet John Greenleaf Whittier wrote the following poem valorizing Brown three weeks after his death:

> John Brown of Ossawatomie spake on his dying day:
> "I will not have to shrive my soul a priest in Slavery's pay.
> But let some poor slave-mother whom I have striven to free,
> With her children, from the gallows-stair put up a prayer for me!"
>
> John Brown of Ossawatomie, they led him out to die;
> And lo! a poor slave-mother with her little child pressed nigh.
> Then the bold, blue eye grew tender, and the old harsh face grew mild,
> As he stooped between the jeering ranks and kissed the negro's child!
>
> The shadows of his stormy life that moment fell apart;
> And they who blamed the bloody hand forgave the loving heart.
> That kiss from all its guilty means redeemed the good intent,
> And round the grisly fighter's hair the martyr's aureole bent!
>
> Perish with him the folly that seeks through evil good!
> Long live the generous purpose unstained with human blood!
> Not the raid of midnight terror, but the thought which underlies;
> Not the borderer's pride of daring, but the Christian's sacrifice.
>
> Nevermore may yon Blue Ridges the Northern rifle hear,
> Nor see the light of blazing homes flash on the negro's spear.
> But let the free-winged angel Truth their guarded passes scale,
> To teach that right is more than might, and justice more than mail!
>
> So vainly shall Virginia set her battle in array;
> In vain her trampling squadrons knead the winter snow with clay.
> She may strike the pouncing eagle, but she dares not harm the dove;
> And every gate she bars to Hate shall open wide to Love!

The poem is based on the same newspaper account of Brown's final moments as Thomas Hovenden's painting is thought to have been. Discuss the similarities and differences between the two depictions of Brown in the painting and the poem, and explain how these depictions reflect attitudes toward Brown examined in two of the sources.

Conversation

The Legacy of Henry David Thoreau

Henry David Thoreau is one of the most important and influential writers and thinkers that America — if not the world — has produced. Brilliant, provocative, eccentric, independent, he left a legacy that is immense and might be described as fivefold. First, Thoreau exemplified personal independence and self-reliance. Some go so far as to suggest that what Ralph Waldo Emerson preached, Thoreau practiced. As contemporary historian Jay Parini says in his 2008 book, *Promised Land: Thirteen Books That Changed America*, "Henry David Thoreau defines American Independence."

Thoreau also exemplified political independence and integrity. He spoke out against slavery and the Mexican war — in fact he was jailed for refusing to pay taxes supporting those evils. (He had no objection to paying the highway tax, he humorously remarked.) It is this political independence that influenced so profoundly such figures as Mahatma Gandhi and Martin Luther King Jr., the counterculture movement of the 1960s, and many of those who speak "truth to power" today.

He was also a transcendentalist, one who, in Emerson's words, strove to discover "an original relation to the universe." For Thoreau, the pathway was through nature. "God exhibits himself to the walker in a frosted-bush today, as much as in a burning one to Moses of old," he wrote in his journal in January of 1853. His ideas and words live on in those who seek spiritual enlightenment in nature.

Thoreau's legacy is equally strong in the environmental movement. He was a naturalist, a keen observer of the natural world who believed in the renewing power of nature and in the importance of conservation. He wrote in his journal on October 15, 1859: "Each town should have a park, or rather a primitive forest, of five hundred or a thousand acres, where a stick should never be cut for fuel, a common possession forever, for instruction and recreation." It is not surprising that Thoreau's remark "in wilderness is the preservation of the world" would become a motto of the Sierra Club, one of the most prominent environmentalist groups today. Thoreau influenced the environmentalism of John Muir and Aldo Leopold and lives on today in the works of Wendell Berry, Barry Lopez, E. O. Wilson, Annie Dillard, Bill McKibben, Richard Louv, and countless others.

Finally, Thoreau has taken on new relevance as a visionary and a critic of contemporary reliance on technology. In any consideration of the effects of the rapid pace of modern life, it seems almost a requirement to refer to the ideas of and to quote passages from Thoreau. As we find ourselves careening down the information superhighway, plugged in to smartphones, voicemail, text messages, the Internet, video games, IMs, Facebook, Twitter (or the next thing beyond 2013, when this introduction was written) while bouncing between classes, homework, extracurricular activities, sports, clubs, and work, the message of this excerpt from *Walden* seems more timely than ever: "Simplify, simplify." While some of us may find Thoreau's positions extreme, we nonetheless find his attitudes appealing.

Five enduring legacies — not bad for a man who was born nearly two hundred years ago. In this Conversation, you will read excerpts from three essential chapters of *Walden* (but we recommend that you read the whole book on your own) and a selection of modern and contemporary sources — some by the voices mentioned above — that exemplify and discuss the living legacy of Henry David Thoreau.

Sources

Bill McKibben, from *Walden: Living Deliberately* (2008)
Henry David Thoreau, from *Walden* (1854)
E. B. White, from *Walden* (1939)
Robert Crumb, *A Short History of America* (1979)
Annie Dillard, *Living like Weasels* (1982)
E. O. Wilson, from *The Future of Life* (2002)
Sue Monk Kidd, *Doing Nothing* (2008)
William Powers, from *Hamlet's BlackBerry* (2010)
Crispin Sartwell, *My Walden, My Walmart* (2012)
Ken Ilgunas, from *Walden on Wheels: On the Open Road from Debt to Freedom* (2013)

from *Walden*
Living Deliberately

BILL McKIBBEN

> Most well-known for *The End of Nature*, published in 1989 and one of the first books to address global warming and climate change, environmentalist and essayist Bill McKibben is the editor of *American Earth: Environmental Writing since Thoreau*, published by the Library of America in 2008. The passage below, written as an introduction to an edition of *Walden*, also appeared in the Summer 2012 edition of *Lapham's Quarterly*.

Understanding the whole of *Walden* is a hopeless task. Its writing resembles nothing so much as Scripture; ideas are condensed to epigrams, four or five to a paragraph. Its magic density yields dozens of different readings: psychological, spiritual, literary, political, cultural. To my mind though, at the beginning of the twenty-first century, it is most crucial to read *Walden* as a practical environmentalist's volume and to search for Thoreau's heirs among those trying to change our relation to the planet. We need to understand that when Thoreau sat in the dooryard of his cabin "from sunrise till noon, rapt in a reverie, amidst the pines and hickories and sumachs, in undisturbed solitude and stillness, while the birds sang around or flitted noiseless through the house," he was offering counsel and example exactly suited for our critical moment in time.

Born in 1817, Thoreau studied at Harvard and then eventually returned to his native Concord in 1837. It was here that he fell in with Ralph Waldo Emerson and

Bronson Alcott — and through them with the whole Transcendental world, including Margaret Fuller, editor of *The Dial,* the start-up Transcendentalist periodical that first put the young Thoreau in print. He worked odd jobs as a surveyor, a tutor, and in his family's pencil business until the spring of 1845, when he built the small cabin a mile and a half from his boyhood home on the shore of Walden Pond. Save for frequent trips back to town for dinner, a night in the Concord jail for nonpayment of taxes — the inspiration for his famous essay, "Civil Disobedience" — and a trip to the Maine woods to climb Mount Katahdin, he stayed in the cabin for two years, two months, and two days. But when he came to write his great book, he collapsed this stretch of time into a single year, resulting in one of the great American books, a volume that launched what would become the environmental idea. In it he tackled questions that had previously seemed obvious: How much do we need? How should we live? What were we built for? He was not an organizer, not an environmentalist — it is unlikely he would have joined the Sierra Club or the Audubon Society — but he sensed a century early the questions that would one day define the counterculture and the environmental era. . . .

And it is here that Thoreau comes to the rescue. He posed two intensely practical questions that must come to dominate this age if we're to make real change: How much is enough? How do I know what I want? For him, I repeat, those were not environmental questions; they were not even practical questions, exactly. If you could answer them you might improve your own life, but that was the extent of his concern. Simplicity, calmness, quiet — these were the preconditions for a moral life, a true life, a philosophic life. "He will live with the license of a higher order of beings in proportion as he simplifies his life." Thoreau believed in the same intense self-examination as any lotus-positioned wispy-bearded ascetic. Happily, though, he went about it in very American ways — he was Buddha with a receipt from the hardware store. And it is that prosaic streak that makes him indispensable now. . . .

If "How much is enough?" is the subversive question for the consumer society, "How do I know what I want?" is the key assault on the Information Age. How can I hear my own heart? What is my true desire?

To understand Thoreau's genius, remember that he raised this question in a time   5
and place that would seem to us almost unbelievably silent. The communications revolution had barely begun. Advertising was not yet a business, but the few shop signs in Concord, which we now preserve as quaint markers of a vanished age, appeared already to Thoreau as eyesores "hung out on all sides to allure him; some to catch him by the appetite, as the tavern and victualling cellar; some by the fancy, as the dry goods store and the jeweller's; and others by the hair or the feet or the skirts, as the barber, the shoemaker, or the tailor." No Internet, no television, no radio, no telephone, no phonograph; and yet somehow he sensed all that this would one day mean to us. He did not need to see someone babbling into a hands-free cell phone to sense that we'd gone too far. He was so hypersensitive, such an alert antenna, that he was worried before Alexander Graham Bell was eight years old. "We are in great haste to construct a magnetic telegraph from Maine to Texas," he

writes. "But Maine and Texas, it may be, have nothing important to communicate." While in the Adirondack woods, Emerson wrote a laudatory poem upon the occasion of hearing the great news that the trans-Atlantic telegraph cable had at last been laid. Thoreau dryly quipped, "perchance the first news that will leak through into the broad, flapping American ear will be that the Princess Adelaide has the whooping cough." . . .

"Let us spend one day as deliberately as Nature, and not be thrown off the track by every nutshell and mosquito's wing that falls on the rails," writes Thoreau. "Let us settle ourselves, and work and wedge our feet downward through the mud and slush of opinion, and prejudice, and tradition, and delusion, and appearance . . . till we come to a hard bottom and rocks in place, which we can call reality, and say, 'This is, and no mistake.'" Only when we have some of that granite to stand on — that firm identity rooted in the *reality* of the natural world — only then can we distinguish between the things we're supposed to want and the things we actually do want. Only then can we say how much is enough and have some hope of really knowing.

In the 154 years since *Walden*, Thoreau has become ever more celebrated in theory and ever more ignored in practice. "Men think that it is essential that the Nation have commerce, and export ice, and talk through a telegraph, and ride thirty miles an hour," he writes. How sleepy that protest sounds to an age that thinks we must travel supersonically, communicate instantaneously, and trade globally. Then again, how sound it seems to an age when we are distracted, depressed, alienated, and over-rushed. He would have understood the jail sentence imposed hourly by the cascade of emails into the inbox or the backlog of messages on the voicemail.

He is the American incarnation in a line of crackpots and gurus from Buddha on. Jesus, St. Francis of Assisi, Gandhi, and the holy men and women of every branch of the ethical religious tradition share the same outlook: simplicity is good for the soul, good for the right relationship with God. In the Christian formulation: do not lay up treasure here on earth; you can't serve both God and money; give away all that you have and follow me. These are not injunctions we've tried very hard to put into practice. We've adopted the competing religious worldview, the one that worships an ever-growing economy. But such spiritual notions have not disappeared; they've flowed like a small but steady river through world history, never completely drying up.

Thoreau helped add a new tributary to that stream. His nature writing is raw, wild, and haunting. He comes to the marsh at night to hear the hooting owls: "All day the sun has shone on the surface of some savage swamp, where the single spruce stands hung with usnea lichens, and small hawks circulate above, and the chicadee lisps amid the evergreens, and the partridge and the rabbit skulk beneath; but now a more dismal and fitting day dawns, and a different race of creatures awakes to express the meaning of Nature there." In his wildness he harks back to the ancient pantheistic traditions, older by far than the Buddha and still alive in remnant form among some native peoples, traditions that might have understood his eagerness to eat a woodchuck raw. He presaged the twentieth-century American-led boom in his affection for nature, for its ability to provide a solid bottom. When he wrote, most of the civilized world still regarded the forest and the mountain with fear and trepidation. In his wake came Walt Whitman, John Burroughs, John Muir. Right behind them came a million people toting backpacks. If lakeshore cottages and the backcountry subdivision can be numbered among his legacies, so can the national parks and wildernesses. This stream grew even larger as the concern for the right relationship with God joined with a love for the physical world. It was still not large enough to jump its banks and flood the city where Economy sat enthroned, but more and more people could hear the roar of its rapids.

Now, quite suddenly, at the beginning of the twenty-first century, a whole new waterway of thought swells that countercultural river. The saints in their robes and the nature lovers in their Gore-Tex jackets are suddenly joined by men and women in lab coats clutching computer printouts. The students of the largest environmental changes taking place around us come with a message eerily similar to those we've heard before. When the International Panel on Climate Change reported in 2001 that humans were likely to raise the earth's surface temperature five degrees Fahrenheit this century, and that they had begun to alter the most basic forces of the planet's surface, the implication of their graphs and charts and data sets was: simplify, simplify, simplify. Not because it's good for your relationship with God, but because if you don't, the temperature of the planet will be higher by 2100 than it's been for hundreds of millions of years, which means crop-withering heat waves, daunting hurricanes, rising seas, and dying forests. They were calling for community — not because it's good for the soul but because without it there's little chance we'll become efficient enough in our use of energy or materials. The math is hard to argue with; business as usual and growth as usual spell an end to the world as usual. This is the one overwhelming fact of our lifetimes — Thoreau knew nothing of it, and yet he knew it all.

10

(2008)

Questions

1. In the second paragraph, Bill McKibben mentions three questions that Thoreau asks and then focuses on two of them. Why does he omit the third?
2. Describing Thoreau, McKibben writes that "he was Buddha with a receipt from the hardware store" (par. 3). What does that description suggest?
3. Why does McKibben say that "How much is enough?" (par. 4) is a subversive question? Why does he refer to "How do I know what I want?" as the "key assault on the Information Age" (par. 4)?
4. What, according to McKibben, is Thoreau's "genius" (par. 5)?
5. What is ironic about Thoreau's "legacies" that McKibben indicates (par. 9)?
6. McKibben concludes with a paradox: "Thoreau knew nothing of it, and yet he knew it all." What is McKibben suggesting about Thoreau and about *Walden*?

from *Walden*

HENRY DAVID THOREAU

from Economy

When I wrote the following pages, or rather the bulk of them, I lived alone, in the woods, a mile from any neighbor, in a house which I had built myself, on the shore of Walden Pond, in Concord, Massachusetts, and earned my living by the labor of my hands only. I lived there two years and two months. At present I am a sojourner in civilized life again.

I should not obtrude my affairs so much on the notice of my readers if very particular inquiries had not been made by my townsmen concerning my mode of life, which some would call impertinent, though they do not appear to me at all impertinent, but, considering the circumstances, very natural and pertinent. Some have asked what I got to eat; if I did not feel lonesome; if I was not afraid; and the like. Others have been curious to learn what portion of my income I devoted to charitable purposes; and some, who have large families, how many poor children I maintained. I will therefore ask those of my readers who feel no particular interest in me to pardon me if I undertake to answer some of these questions in this book. In most books, the *I*, or first person, is omitted; in this it will be retained; that, in respect to egotism, is the main difference. We commonly do not remember that it is, after all, always the first person that is speaking. I should not talk so much about myself if there were any body else whom I knew as well. Unfortunately, I am confined to this theme by the narrowness of my experience. Moreover, I, on my side, require of every writer, first or last, a simple and sincere account of his own life, and not merely what he has heard of other men's lives; some such account as he would send to his kindred from a distant land; for if he has lived sincerely, it must have been in a distant land to me. Perhaps these pages are more particularly addressed to poor students. As for the rest of my readers, they will accept such portions as apply to them. I trust that none will stretch the seams in putting on the coat, for it may do good service to him whom it fits.

I would fain say something, not so much concerning the Chinese and Sandwich Islanders[1] as you who read these pages, who are said to live in New England; something about your condition, especially your outward condition or circumstances in this world, in this town, what it is, whether it is necessary that it be as bad as it is, whether it cannot be improved as well as not. I have travelled a good deal in Concord; and every where, in shops, and offices, and fields, the inhabitants have appeared to me to be doing penance in a thousand remarkable ways. What I have heard of Bramins[2] sitting exposed to four fires and looking in the face of the sun; or hanging suspended, with their heads downward, over flames; or looking at the heavens over their shoulders

---

[1] Hawaiians. — Eds.
[2] The highest-ranking social caste in Hindu India, which traditionally is made up of priests. — Eds.

"until it becomes impossible for them to resume their natural position, while from the twist of the neck nothing but liquids can pass into the stomach"; or dwelling, chained for life, at the foot of a tree; or measuring with their bodies, like caterpillars, the breadth of vast empires; or standing on one leg on the tops of pillars, — even these forms of conscious penance are hardly more incredible and astonishing than the scenes which I daily witness. The twelve labors of Hercules were trifling in comparison with those which my neighbors have undertaken; for they were only twelve, and had an end; but I could never see that these men slew or captured any monster or finished any labor. They have no friend Iolas to burn with a hot iron the root of the hydra's head, but as soon as one head is crushed, two spring up.

I see young men, my townsmen, whose misfortune it is to have inherited farms, houses, barns, cattle, and farming tools; for these are more easily acquired than got rid of. Better if they had been born in the open pasture and suckled by a wolf, that they might have seen with clearer eyes what field they were called to labor in. Who made them serfs of the soil? Why should they eat their sixty acres, when man is condemned to eat only his peck of dirt? Why should they begin digging their graves as soon as they are born? They have got to live a man's life, pushing all these things before them, and get on as well as they can. How many a poor immortal soul have I met well nigh crushed and smothered under its load, creeping down the road of life, pushing before it a barn seventy-five feet by forty, its Augean stables never cleansed, and one hundred acres of land, tillage, mowing, pasture, and wood-lot! The portionless, who struggle with no such unnecessary inherited encumbrances, find it labor enough to subdue and cultivate a few cubic feet of flesh. . . .

The mass of men lead lives of quiet desperation. What is called resignation is 5 confirmed desperation. From the desperate city you go into the desperate country, and have to console yourself with the bravery of minks and muskrats. A stereotyped but unconscious despair is concealed even under what are called the games and amusements of mankind. There is no play in them, for this comes after work. But it is a characteristic of wisdom not to do desperate things. . . .

The greater part of what my neighbors call good I believe in my soul to be bad, and if I repent of any thing, it is very likely to be my good behavior. What demon possessed me that I behaved so well? You may say the wisest thing you can old man, — you who have lived seventy years, not without honor of a kind, — I hear an irresistible voice which invites me away from all that. One generation abandons the enterprises of another like stranded vessels.

I think that we may safely trust a good deal more than we do. We may waive just so much care of ourselves as we honestly bestow elsewhere. Nature is as well adapted to our weakness as to our strength. The incessant anxiety and strain of some is a well nigh incurable form of disease. We are made to exaggerate the importance of what work we do; and yet how much is not done by us! or, what if we had been taken sick? How vigilant we are! determined not to live by faith if we can avoid it; all the day long on the alert, at night we unwillingly say our prayers and commit ourselves to uncertainties. So thoroughly and sincerely are we compelled to live, reverencing our life, and denying the possibility of change. This is the only way, we say; but there are as many ways as there can be drawn radii from one centre. All change is a miracle to contemplate; but it is a miracle which is taking place every instant. Confucius said, "To know that we know what we know, and that we do not know what we do not know, that is true knowledge." When one man has reduced a fact of the imagination to be a fact to his understanding, I foresee that all men will at length establish their lives on that basis. . . .

Let us consider for a moment what most of the trouble and anxiety which I have referred to is about, and how much it is necessary that we be troubled, or, at least, careful. It would be some advantage to live a primitive and frontier life, though in the midst of an outward civilization, if only to learn what are the gross necessaries of life and what methods have been taken to obtain them; or even to look over the old day-books of the merchants, to see what it was that men most commonly bought at the stores, what they stored, that is, what are the grossest groceries. For the improvements of ages have had but little influence on the essential laws of man's existence; as our skeletons, probably, are not to be distinguished from those of our ancestors.

By the words, *necessary of life*, I mean whatever, of all that man obtains by his own exertions, has been from the first, or from long use has become, so important to human life that few, if any, whether from savageness, or poverty, or philosophy, ever attempt to do without it. To many creatures there is in this sense but one necessary of life, Food. To the bison of the prairie it is a few inches of palatable grass, with water to drink; unless he seeks the Shelter of the forest or the mountain's shadow. None of the brute creation requires more than Food and Shelter. The necessaries of life for man in this climate may, accurately enough, be distributed under the several heads of Food, Shelter, Clothing, and Fuel; for not till we have secured these are we prepared to entertain the true problems of life with freedom and a prospect of success. Man has invented, not only houses, but clothes and cooked food; and possibly from the accidental discovery of the warmth of fire, and the consequent use of it, at first a luxury, arose the present necessity to sit by it. We observe cats and dogs acquiring the same second nature. By proper Shelter and Clothing we legitimately retain our own internal heat; but with an excess of these, or of Fuel, that is, with an external heat greater than our own internal, may not cookery properly be said to begin? Darwin, the naturalist, says of the inhabitants of Tierra del Fuego,[3] that while his own party, who were well clothed and sitting close to a fire, were far from too warm, these naked savages, who were farther off, were observed, to his great surprise, "to be streaming with perspiration at undergoing such a roasting." So, we are told, the New Hollander goes naked with impunity, while the European shivers in his clothes. Is it impossible to combine the hardiness of these savages with the intellectualness of the civilized man? According to Liebig, man's body is a stove, and food the fuel which keeps up the internal combustion in the lungs. In cold weather we eat more, in warm less. The animal heat is the result of a slow combustion, and disease and death take place when this is too rapid; or for want of fuel, or from some defect in the draught, the fire goes out. Of course the vital heat is not to be confounded with fire; but so much for analogy. It appears, therefore, from the above list, that the expression, *animal life*, is nearly synonymous with the expression, *animal heat*; for while Food may be regarded

---

[3]Spanish. "Land of Fire." The archipelago at the very southern tip of South America. — Eds.

as the Fuel which keeps up the fire within us, — and Fuel serves only to prepare that Food or to increase the warmth of our bodies by addition from without, — Shelter and Clothing also serve only to retain the *heat* thus generated and absorbed. . . .

Most of the luxuries, and many of the so called comforts of life, are not only not 10 indispensable, but positive hinderances to the elevation of mankind. With respect to luxuries and comforts, the wisest have ever lived a more simple and meagre life than the poor. The ancient philosophers, Chinese, Hindoo, Persian, and Greek, were a class than which none has been poorer in outward riches, none so rich in inward. We know not much about them. It is remarkable that *we* know so much of them as we do. The same is true of the more modern reformers and benefactors of their race. None can be an impartial or wise observer of human life but from the vantage ground of what *we* should call voluntary poverty. Of a life of luxury the fruit is luxury, whether in agriculture, or commerce, or literature, or art. There are nowadays professors of philosophy, but not philosophers. Yet it is admirable to profess because it was once admirable to live. To be a philosopher is not merely to have subtle thoughts, nor even to found a school, but so to love wisdom as to live according to its dictates, a life of simplicity, independence, magnanimity, and trust. It is to solve some of the problems of life, not only theoretically, but practically. The success of great scholars and thinkers is commonly a courtier-like success, not kingly, not manly. They make shift to live merely by conformity, practically as their fathers did, and are in no sense the progenitors of a nobler race of men. But why do men degenerate ever? What makes families run out? What is the nature of the luxury which enervates and destroys nations? Are we sure that there is none of it in our own lives? The philosopher is in advance of his age even in the outward form of his life. He is not fed, sheltered, clothed, warmed, like his contemporaries. How can a man be a philosopher and not maintain his vital heat by better methods than other men?

When a man is warmed by the several modes which I have described, what does he want next? Surely not more warmth of the same kind, as more and richer food, larger and more splendid houses, finer and more abundant clothing, more numerous incessant and hotter fires, and the like. When he has obtained those things which are necessary to life, there is another alternative than to obtain the superfluities; and that is, to adventure on life now, his vacation from humbler toil having commenced. The soil, it appears, is suited to the seed, for it has sent its radicle downward, and it may now send its shoot upward also with confidence. Why has man rooted himself thus firmly in the earth, but that he may rise in the same proportion into the heavens above? — for the nobler plants are valued for the fruit they bear at last in the air and light, far from the ground, and are not treated like the humbler esculents, which, though they may be biennials, are cultivated only till they have perfected their root, and often cut down at top for this purpose, so that most would not know them in their flowering season.

I do not mean to prescribe rules to strong and valiant natures, who will mind their own affairs whether in heaven or hell, and perchance build more magnificently and spend more lavishly than the richest, without ever impoverishing themselves, not knowing how they live, — if, indeed, there are any such, as has been dreamed; nor to those who find their encouragement and inspiration in precisely the present condition of things, and cherish it with the fondness and enthusiasm of lovers, — and, to some extent, I reckon myself in this number; I do not speak to those who are well employed, in whatever circumstances, and they know whether they are well employed or not; — but mainly to the mass of men who are discontented, and idly complaining of the hardness of their lot or of the times, when they might improve them. There are some who complain most energetically and inconsolably of any, because they are, as they say, doing their duty. I also have in my mind that seemingly wealthy, but most terribly impoverished class of all, who have accumulated dross, but know not how to use it, or get rid of it, and thus have forged their own golden or silver fetters.

If I should attempt to tell how I have desired to spend my life in years past, it would probably surprise those of my readers who are somewhat acquainted with its actual history; it would certainly astonish those who know nothing about it. I will only hint at some of the enterprises which I have cherished.

In any weather, at any hour of the day or night, I have been anxious to improve the nick of time, and notch it on my stick too; to stand on the meeting of two eternities, the past and future, which is precisely the present moment; to toe that line. You will pardon some obscurities, for there are more secrets in my trade than in most men's, and yet not voluntarily kept, but inseparable from its very nature. I would gladly tell all that I know about it, and never paint "No Admittance" on my gate.

I long ago lost a hound, a bay horse, and a turtle-dove, and am still on their trail. 15
Many are the travellers I have spoken concerning them, describing their tracks and what calls they answered to. I have met one or two who had heard the hound, and the tramp of the horse, and even seen the dove disappear behind a cloud, and they seemed as anxious to recover them as if they had lost them themselves.

To anticipate, not the sunrise and the dawn merely, but, if possible, Nature herself! How many mornings, summer and winter, before yet any neighbor was stirring about his business, have I been about mine! No doubt, many of my townsmen have met me returning from this enterprise, farmers starting for Boston in the twilight, or woodchoppers going to their work. It is true, I never assisted the sun materially in his rising, but, doubt not, it was of the last importance only to be present at it.

So many autumn, ay, and winter days, spent outside the town, trying to hear what was in the wind, to hear and carry it express! I well-nigh sunk all my capital in it, and lost my own breath into the bargain, running in the face of it. If it had concerned either of the political parties, depend upon it, it would have appeared in the Gazette with the earliest intelligence. At other times watching from the observatory of some cliff or tree, to telegraph any new arrival; or waiting at evening on the hill-tops for the sky to fall, that I might catch something, though I never caught much, and that, manna-wise, would dissolve again in the sun.

For a long time I was reporter to a journal, of no very wide circulation, whose editor has never yet seen fit to print the bulk of my contributions, and, as is too common with writers, I got only my labor for my pains. However, in this case my pains were their own reward.

For many years I was self-appointed inspector of snow storms and rain storms, and did my duty faithfully; surveyor, if not of highways, then of forest paths and all across-lot routes, keeping them open, and ravines bridged and passable at all seasons, where the public heel had testified to their utility.

I have looked after the wild stock of the town, which give a faithful herdsman a good deal of trouble by leaping fences; and I have had an eye to the unfrequented nooks and corners of the farm; though I did not always know whether Jonas or Solomon worked in a particular field to-day; that was none of my business. I have watered the red huckleberry, the sand cherry and the nettle tree, the red pine and the black ash, the white grape and the yellow violet, which might have withered else in dry seasons.

In short, I went on thus for a long time, I may say it without boasting, faithfully minding my business, till it became more and more evident that my townsmen would not after all admit me into the list of town officers, nor make my place a sinecure with a moderate allowance. My accounts, which I can swear to have kept faithfully, I have, indeed, never got audited, still less accepted, still less paid and settled. However, I have not set my heart on that.

Not long since, a strolling Indian went to sell baskets at the house of a well-known lawyer in my neighborhood. "Do you wish to buy any baskets?" he asked. "No, we do not want any," was the reply. "What!" exclaimed the Indian as he went out the gate, "do you mean to starve us?" Having seen his industrious white neighbors so well off, — that the lawyer had only to weave arguments, and by some magic wealth and standing followed, he had said to himself; I will go into business; I will weave baskets; it is a thing which I can do. Thinking that when he had made the baskets he would have done his part, and then it would be the white man's to buy them. He had not discovered that it was necessary for him to make it worth the other's while to buy them, or at least make him think that it was so, or to make something else which it would be worth his while to buy. I too had woven a kind of basket of a delicate texture, but I had not made it worth any one's while to buy them. Yet not the less, in my case, did I think it worth my while to weave them, and instead of studying how to make it worth men's while to buy my baskets, I studied rather how to avoid the necessity of selling them. The life which men praise and regard as successful is but one kind. Why should we exaggerate any one kind at the expense of the others?

Finding that my fellow-citizens were not likely to offer me any room in the court house, or any curacy or living any where else, but I must shift for myself, I turned my face more exclusively than ever to the woods, where I was better known. I determined to go into business at once, and not wait to acquire the usual capital, using such slender means as I had already got. My purpose in going to Walden Pond was not to live cheaply nor to live dearly there, but to transact some private business with the fewest obstacles; to be hindered from accomplishing which for want of a little common sense, a little enterprise and business talent, appeared not so sad as foolish. . . .

Near the end of March, 1845, I borrowed an axe and went down to the woods by Walden Pond, nearest to where I intended to build my house, and began to cut down some tall arrowy white pines, still in their youth, for timber. It is difficult to begin without borrowing, but perhaps it is the most generous course thus to permit your fellow-men to have an interest in your enterprise. The owner of the axe, as he released his hold on it, said that it was the apple of his eye; but I returned it sharper than I received it. It was a pleasant hillside where I worked, covered with pine woods, through which I looked out on the pond, and a small open field in the woods where pines and hickories were springing up. The ice in the pond was not yet dissolved, though there were some open spaces, and it was all dark colored and saturated with water. There were some slight flurries of snow during the days that I worked there; but for the most part when I came out on to the railroad, on my way home, its yellow sand heap stretched away gleaming in the hazy atmosphere, and the rails shone in the spring sun, and I heard the lark and pewee and other birds already come to commence another year with us. They were pleasant spring days, in which the winter of man's discontent was thawing as well as the earth, and the life that had lain torpid began to stretch itself. One day, when my axe had come off and I had cut a green hickory for a wedge, driving it with a stone, and had placed the whole to soak in a pond hole in order to swell the wood, I saw a striped snake run into the water, and he lay on the bottom, apparently without inconvenience, as long as I staid there, or more than a quarter of an hour; perhaps because he had not yet fairly come out of the torpid state. It appeared to me that for a like reason men remain in their present low and primitive condition; but if they should feel the influence of the spring of springs arousing them, they would of necessity rise to a higher and more ethereal life. I had previously seen the snakes in frosty mornings in my path with portions of their bodies still numb and inflexible, waiting for the sun to thaw them. On the 1st of April it rained and melted the ice, and in the early part of the day, which was very foggy, I heard a stray goose groping about over the pond and cackling as if lost, or like the spirit of the fog.

So I went on for some days cutting and hewing timber, and also studs and rafters,   25 all with my narrow axe, not having many communicable or scholar-like thoughts, singing to myself,—

> Men say they know many things;
> But lo! they have taken wings,—
> The arts and sciences,
> And a thousand appliances;
> The wind that blows
> Is all that any body knows.

. . . At Cambridge College the mere rent of a student's room, which is only a little larger than my own, is thirty dollars each year, though the corporation had the advantage of building thirty-two side by side and under one roof, and the occupant suffers the inconvenience of many and noisy neighbors, and perhaps a residence in the fourth story. I cannot but think that if we had more true wisdom in these respects, not only less education would be needed, because, forsooth, more would already have been acquired, but the pecuniary expense of getting an education would in a great measure vanish. Those conveniences which the student requires at Cambridge or elsewhere cost him or somebody else ten times as great a sacrifice of life as they would with proper management on both sides. Those things for which the most money is demanded are never the things which the student most wants. Tuition, for instance, is an important item in the term bill, while for the far more valuable education which he gets by associating with the most cultivated of his contemporaries no charge is made. The mode of founding a college is, commonly, to get up a subscription of dollars and cents, and then following blindly the principles of a division of labor to its extreme, a principle which should never be followed but with circumspection, — to call in a contractor who makes this a subject of speculation, and he employs Irishmen or other operatives actually to lay the foundations, while the students that are to be are said to be fitting themselves for it; and for these oversights successive generations have to pay. I think that it would be *better than this*, for the students, or those who desire to be benefited by it, even to lay the foundation themselves. The student who secures his coveted leisure and retirement by systematically shirking any labor necessary to man obtains but an ignoble and unprofitable leisure, defrauding himself of the experience which alone can make leisure fruitful. "But," says one, "you do not mean that the students should go to work with their hands instead of their heads?" I do not mean that exactly, but I mean something which he might think a good deal like that; I mean that they should not *play* life, or *study* it merely, while the community supports them at this expensive game, but earnestly *live* it from beginning to end. How could youths better learn to live than by at once trying the experiment of living? Methinks this would exercise their minds as much as mathematics. If I wished a boy to know something about the arts and sciences, for instance, I would not pursue the common course, which is merely to send him into the neighborhood of some professor, where any thing is professed and practised but the art of life; — to survey the world through a telescope or a microscope, and never with his natural eye; to study chemistry, and not learn how his bread is made, or mechanics, and not learn how it is earned; to discover new satellites to Neptune, and not detect the motes in his eyes, or to what vagabond he is a satellite himself; or to be devoured by the monsters that swarm all around him, while contemplating the monsters in a drop of vinegar. Which would have advanced the most at the end of a month, — the boy who had made his own jackknife from the ore which he had dug and smelted, reading as much as would be necessary for this, — or the boy who had attended the lectures on metallurgy at the Institute in the mean while, and had received a Rogers' penknife from his father? Which would be most likely to cut his fingers? . . . To my astonishment I was informed on leaving college that I had studied navigation! — why, if I had taken one turn down the harbor I should have known more about it. Even the *poor* student studies and is taught only *political* economy, while that economy of living which is synonymous with philosophy is not even sincerely professed in our colleges. The consequence is, that while he is reading Adam Smith,[4] Ricardo,[5] and Say,[6] he runs his father in debt irretrievably.

---

[4]Adam Smith, eighteenth-century Scottish philosopher and economist. — Eds.
[5]David Ricardo, nineteenth-century British economist. — Eds.
[6]Jean-Baptiste Say, nineteenth-century French economist. — Eds.

As with our colleges, so with a hundred "modern improvements;" there is an illusion about them; there is not always a positive advance. The devil goes on exacting compound interest to the last for his early share and numerous succeeding investments in them. Our inventions are wont to be pretty toys, which distract our attention from serious things. They are but improved means to an unimproved end, an end which it was already but too easy to arrive at; as railroads lead to Boston or New York. We are in great haste to construct a magnetic telegraph from Maine to Texas; but Maine and Texas, it may be, have nothing important to communicate. Either is in such a predicament as the man who was earnest to be introduced to a distinguished deaf woman, but when he was presented, and one end of her ear trumpet was put into his hand, had nothing to say. As if the main object were to talk fast and not to talk sensibly. We are eager to tunnel under the Atlantic and bring the old world some weeks nearer to the new; but perchance the first news that will leak through into the broad, flapping American ear will be that the Princess Adelaide has the whooping cough. . . .

from Where I Lived, and What I Lived For

The present was my next experiment of this kind, which I purpose to describe more at length; for convenience, putting the experience of two years into one. As I have said, I do not propose to write an ode to dejection, but to brag as lustily as chanticleer in the morning, standing on his roost, if only to wake my neighbors up.

When first I took up my abode in the woods, that is, began to spend my nights as well as days there, which, by accident, was on Independence day, or the fourth of July, 1845, my house was not finished for winter, but was merely a defence against the rain, without plastering or chimney, the walls being of rough weather-stained boards, with wide chinks, which made it cool at night. The upright white hewn studs and freshly planed door and window casings gave it a clean and airy look, especially in the morning, when its timbers were saturated with dew, so that I fancied that by noon some sweet gum would exude from them. To my imagination it retained throughout the day more or less of this auroral character, reminding me of a certain house on a mountain which I had visited the year before. This was an airy and unplastered cabin, fit to entertain a travelling god, and where a goddess might trail her garments. The winds which passed over my dwelling were such as sweep over the ridges of mountains, bearing the broken strains, or celestial parts only, of terrestrial music. The morning wind forever blows, the poem of creation is uninterrupted; but few are the ears that hear it. Olympus is but the outside of the earth every where. . . .

I went to the woods because I wished to live deliberately, to front only the essential facts of life, and see if I could not learn what it had to teach, and not, when I came to die, discover that I had not lived. I did not wish to live what was not life, living is so dear; nor did I wish to practice resignation, unless it was quite necessary. I wanted to live deep and suck out all the marrow of life, to live so sturdily and Spartan-like as to put to rout all that was not life, to cut a broad swath and shave close, to drive life into a corner, and reduce it to its lowest terms, and, if it proved to be mean, why then

30

to get the whole and genuine meanness of it, and publish its meanness to the world; or if it were sublime, to know it by experience, and be able to give a true account of it in my next excursion. For most men, it appears to me, are in a strange uncertainty about it, whether it is of the devil or of God, and have *somewhat hastily* concluded that it is the chief end of man here to "glorify God and enjoy him forever."[7]

Still we live meanly, like ants; though the fable tells us that we were long ago changed into men; like pygmies we fight with cranes;[8] it is error upon error, and clout upon clout, and our best virtue has for its occasion a superfluous and evitable wretchedness. Our life is frittered away by detail. An honest man has hardly need to count more than his ten fingers, or in extreme cases he may add his ten toes, and lump the rest. Simplicity, simplicity, simplicity! I say, let your affairs be as two or three, and not a hundred or a thousand; instead of a million count half a dozen, and keep your accounts on your thumb-nail. In the midst of this chopping sea of civilized life, such are the clouds and storms and quicksands and thousand-and-one items to be allowed for, that a man has to live, if he would not founder and go to the bottom and not make his port at all, by dead reckoning, and he must be a great calculator indeed who succeeds. Simplify, simplify. Instead of three meals a day, if it be necessary eat but one; instead of a hundred dishes, five; and reduce other things in proportion. Our life is like a German Confederacy, made up of petty states, with its boundary forever fluctuating, so that even a German cannot tell you how it is bounded at any moment. The nation itself, with all its so-called internal improvements, which, by the way are all external and superficial, is just such an unwieldy and overgrown establishment, cluttered with furniture and tripped up by its own traps, ruined by luxury and heedless expense, by want of calculation and a worthy aim, as the million households in the land; and the only cure for it, as for them, is in a rigid economy, a stern and more than Spartan simplicity of life and elevation of purpose. It lives too fast. Men think that it is essential that the *Nation* have commerce, and export ice, and talk through a telegraph, and ride thirty miles an hour, without a doubt, whether *they* do or not; but whether we should live like baboons or like men, is a little uncertain. If we do not get out sleepers,[9] and forge rails, and devote days and nights to the work, but go to tinkering upon our *lives* to improve *them*, who will build railroads? And if railroads are not built, how shall we get to heaven in season? But if we stay at home and mind our business, who will want railroads? We do not ride on the railroad; it rides upon us. Did you ever think what those sleepers are that underlie the railroad? Each one is a man, an Irishman, or a Yankee man. The rails are laid on them, and they are covered with sand, and the cars run smoothly over them. They are sound sleepers, I assure you. And every few years a new lot is laid down and run over, so that, if some have

---

[7]The first question and answer in the Westminster Catechism, a statement of religious doctrine that came out of the Protestant Reformation, is "Q: What is the chief end of man? A: To glorify God and enjoy him forever." — Eds.

[8]Allusions to the Greek fable of the Myrmidons (ant-people), and to Book III of the *Iliad*, respectively. The *Iliad* draws a parallel between the Trojan War and the mythological war between the cranes and the pygmies. — Eds.

[9]Here, *sleepers* means "railroad ties." — Eds.

the pleasure of riding on a rail, others have the misfortune to be ridden upon. And when they run over a man that is walking in his sleep, a supernumerary sleeper in the wrong position, and wake him up, they suddenly stop the cars, and make a hue and cry about it, as if this were an exception. I am glad to know that it takes a gang of men for every five miles to keep the sleepers down and level in their beds as it is, for this is a sign that they may sometimes get up again.

Why should we live with such hurry and waste of life? We are determined to be starved before we are hungry. Men say that a stitch in time saves nine, and so they take a thousand stitches today to save nine tomorrow. As for *work*, we haven't any of any consequence. We have the Saint Vitus' dance,[10] and cannot possibly keep our heads still. If I should only give a few pulls at the parish bell-rope, as for a fire, that is, without setting the bell, there is hardly a man on his farm in the outskirts of Concord, notwithstanding that press of engagements which was his excuse so many times this morning, nor a boy, nor a woman, I might almost say, but would foresake all and follow that sound, not mainly to save property from the flames, but, if we will confess the truth, much more to see it burn, since burn it must, and we, be it known, did not set it on fire—or to see it put out, and have a hand in it, if that is done as handsomely; yes, even if it were the parish church itself. Hardly a man takes a half-hour's nap after dinner, but when he wakes he holds up his head and asks, "What's the news?" as if the rest of mankind had stood his sentinels. Some give directions to be waked every half-hour, doubtless for no other purpose; and then, to pay for it, they tell what they have dreamed. After a night's sleep the news is as indispensable as the breakfast. "Pray tell me anything new that has happened to a man anywhere on this globe"—and he reads it over his coffee and rolls, that a man has had his eyes gouged out this morning on the Wachito River; never dreaming the while that he lives in the dark unfathomed mammoth cave of this world, and has but the rudiment of an eye himself.

For my part, I could easily do without the post-office. I think that there are very few important communications made through it. To speak critically, I never received more than one or two letters in my life—I wrote this some years ago—that were worth the postage. The penny-post is, commonly, an institution through which you seriously offer a man that penny for his thoughts which is so often safely offered in jest. And I am sure that I never read any memorable news in a newspaper. If we read of one man robbed, or murdered, or killed by accident, or one house burned, or one vessel wrecked or one steamboat blown up, or one cow run over on the Western Railroad, or one mad dog killed, or one lot of grasshoppers in the winter—we never need read of another. One is enough. If you are acquainted with the principle, what do you care for a myriad instances and applications? To a philosopher all *news*, as it is called, is gossip, and they who edit and read it are old women over their tea. Yet not a few are greedy after this gossip. There was such a rush, as I hear, the other day at one of the offices to learn the foreign news by the last arrival, that several large squares of plate glass belonging to the establishment were broken by the pressure—news which I seriously think a ready wit might write a twelvemonth, or twelve

---

[10]A disease that causes the victim to twitch uncontrollably. St. Vitus is the patron saint of dancers. —Eds.

years, beforehand with sufficient accuracy. As for Spain, for instance, if you know how to throw in Don Carlos and the Infanta, and Don Pedro and Seville and Granada, from time to time in the right proportions — they may have changed the names a little since I saw the papers — and serve up a bullfight when other entertainments fail, it will be true to the letter, and give us as good an idea of the exact state or ruin of things in Spain as the most succinct and lucid reports under this head in the newspapers; and as for England, almost the last significant scrap of news from that quarter was the revolution of 1649; and if you have learned the history of her crops for an average year, you never need attend to that thing again, unless your speculations are of a merely pecuniary character. If one may judge who rarely looks into the newspapers, nothing new does ever happen in foreign parts, a French revolution not excepted.

What news! how much more important to know what that is which was never old! "Kieou-pe-yu (great dignitary of the state of Wei) sent a man to Khoung-tseu to know his news. Khoung-tseu caused the messenger to be seated near him, and questioned him in these terms: What is your master doing? The messenger answered with respect: My master desires to diminish the number of his faults, but he cannot come to the end of them. The messenger being gone, the philosopher remarked: What a worthy messenger! What a worthy messenger!" The preacher, instead of vexing the ears of drowsy farmers on their day of rest at the end of the week — for Sunday is the fit conclusion of an ill-spent week, and not the fresh and brave beginning of a new one — with this one other draggle-tail of a sermon, should shout with thundering voice, "Pause! Avast! Why so seeming fast, but deadly slow?"

Shams and delusions are esteemed for soundless truths, while reality is fabulous. 35
If men would steadily observe realities only, and not allow themselves to be deluded, life, to compare it with such things as we know, would be like a fairy tale and the Arabian Nights' Entertainments. If we respected only what is inevitable and has a right to be, music and poetry would resound along the streets. When we are unhurried and wise, we perceive that only great and worthy things have any permanent and absolute existence, that petty fears and petty pleasures are but the shadow of the reality. This is always exhilarating and sublime. . . .

If you stand right fronting and face to face to a fact, you will see the sun glimmer on both its surfaces, as if it were a cimeter,[11] and feel its sweet edge dividing you through the heart and marrow, and so you will happily conclude your mortal career. Be it life or death, we crave only reality. If we are really dying, let us hear the rattle in our throats and feel cold in the extremities; if we are alive, let us go about our business.

Time is but the stream I go afishing in. I drink at it; but while I drink I see the sandy bottom and detect how shallow it is. Its thin current slides away but eternity remains. I would drink deeper; fish in the sky, whose bottom is pebbly with stars. I cannot count one. I know not the first letter of the alphabet. I have always been regretting that I was not as wise as the day I was born. The intellect is a cleaver; it

---

[11]Also known as a *scimeter* or *scimitar*, a curved-blade sword traditionally used in the Middle East. — Eds.

discerns and rifts its way into the secret of things. I do not wish to be any more busy with my hands than is necessary. My head is hands and feet. I feel all my best faculties concentrated in it. My instinct tells me that my head is an organ for burrowing, as some creatures use their snout and fore paws, and with it I would mine and burrow my way through these hills. I think that the richest vein is somewhere hereabouts, so by the divining-rod and thin rising vapors, I judge; and here I will begin to mine.

from Conclusion

I left the woods for as good a reason as I went there. Perhaps it seemed to me that I had several more lives to live, and could not spare any more time for that one. It is remarkable how easily and insensibly we fall into a particular route, and make a beaten track for ourselves. I had not lived there a week before my feet wore a path from my door to the pond-side; and though it is five or six years since I trod it, it is still quite distinct. It is true, I fear that others may have fallen into it, and so helped to keep it open. The surface of the earth is soft and impressible by the feet of men; and so with the paths which the mind travels. How worn and dusty, then, must be the highways of the world, how deep the ruts of tradition and conformity! I did not wish to take a cabin passage, but rather to go before the mast and on the deck of the world, for there I could best see the moonlight amid the mountains. I do not wish to go below now.

I learned this, at least, by my experiment; that if one advances confidently in the direction of his dreams, and endeavors to live the life which he has imagined, he will meet with success unexpected in common hours. He will put some things behind, will pass an invisible boundary; new, universal, and more liberal laws will begin to establish themselves around and within him; or the old laws be expanded, and interpreted in his favor in a more liberal sense, and he will live with the license of a higher order of beings. In proportion as he simplifies his life, the laws of the universe will appear less complex, and solitude will not be solitude, nor poverty poverty, nor weakness weakness. If you have built castles in the air, your work need not be lost; that is where they should be. Now put the foundations under them.

It is a ridiculous demand which England and America make, that you shall speak so that they can understand you. Neither men nor toad-stools grow so. As if that were important, and there were not enough to understand you without them. As if Nature could support but one order of understandings, could not sustain birds as well as quadrupeds, flying as well as creeping things, and *hush* and *who*, which Bright can understand, were the best English. As if there were safety in stupidity alone. I fear chiefly lest my expression may not be *extra-vagant* enough, may not wander far enough beyond the narrow limits of my daily experience, so as to be adequate to the truth of which I have been convinced. *Extra vagance!* it depends on how you are yarded. The migrating buffalo, which seeks new pastures in another latitude, is not extravagant like the cow which kicks over the pail, leaps the cow-yard fence, and runs after her calf, in milking time. I desire to speak somewhere *without* bounds; like a man in a waking moment, to men in their waking moments; for I am convinced

40

that I cannot exaggerate enough even to lay the foundation of a true expression. Who that has heard a strain of music feared then lest he should speak extravagantly any more forever? In view of the future or possible, we should live quite laxly and undefined in front, our outlines dim and misty on that side; as our shadows reveal an insensible perspiration toward the sun. The volatile truth of our words should continually betray the inadequacy of the residual statement. Their truth is instantly *translated*; its literal monument alone remains. The words which express our faith and piety are not definite; yet they are significant and fragrant like frankincense to superior natures.

Why level downward to our dullest perception always, and praise that as common sense? The commonest sense is the sense of men asleep, which they express by snoring. Sometimes we are inclined to class those who are once-and-a-half witted with the half-witted, because we appreciate only a third part of their wit. Some would find fault with the morning-red, if they ever got up early enough. "They pretend," as I hear, "that the verses of Kabir have four different senses; illusion, spirit, intellect, and the exoteric doctrine of the Vedas," but in this part of the world it is considered a ground for complaint if a man's writings admit of more than one interpretation. While England endeavors to cure the potato-rot, will not any endeavor to cure the brain-rot, which prevails so much more widely and fatally?

I do not suppose that I have attained to obscurity, but I should be proud if no more fatal fault were found with my pages on this score than was found with the Walden ice. Southern customers objected to its blue color, which is the evidence of its purity, as if it were muddy, and preferred the Cambridge ice, which is white, but tastes of weeds. The purity men love is like the mists which envelop the earth, and not like the azure ether beyond.

Some are dinning in our ears that we Americans, and moderns generally, are intellectual dwarfs compared with the ancients, or even the Elizabethan men. But what is that to the purpose? A living dog is better than a dead lion.[12] Shall a man go and hang himself because he belongs to the race of pygmies, and not be the biggest pygmy that he can? Let every one mind his own business, and endeavor to be what he was made.

Why should we be in such desperate haste to succeed, and in such desperate enterprises? If a man does not keep pace with his companions, perhaps it is because he hears a different drummer. Let him step to the music which he hears, however measured or far away. It is not important that he should mature as soon as an apple-tree or an oak. Shall he turn his spring into summer? If the condition of things which we were made for is not yet, what were any reality which we can substitute? We will not be shipwrecked on a vain reality. Shall we with pains erect a heaven of blue glass over ourselves, though when it is done we shall be sure to gaze still at the true ethereal heaven far above, as if the former were not? . . .

Rather than love, than money, than fame, give me truth. I sat at a table where were   45 rich food and wine in abundance, and obsequious attendance, but sincerity and truth were not; and I went away hungry from the inhospitable board. The hospitality was as cold as the ices. I thought that there was no need of ice to freeze them. They talked to

---

[12]Ecclesiastes 9:4.

me of the age of the wine and the fame of the vintage; but I thought of an older, a newer, and purer wine, of a more glorious vintage, which they had not got, and could not buy. The style, the house and grounds and "entertainment" pass for nothing with me. I called on the king, but he made me wait in his hall, and conducted like a man incapacitated for hospitality. There was a man in my neighborhood who lived in a hollow tree. His manners were truly regal. I should have done better had I called on him. . . .

There is an incessant influx of novelty into the world, and yet we tolerate incredible dulness. I need only suggest what kind of sermons are still listened to in the most enlightened countries. There are such words as joy and sorrow, but they are only the burden of a psalm, sung with a nasal twang, while we believe in the ordinary and mean. We think that we can change our clothes only. It is said that the British Empire is very large and respectable, and that the United States are a first-rate power. We do not believe that a tide rises and falls behind every man which can float the British Empire like a chip, if he should ever harbor it in his mind. Who knows what sort of seventeen-year locust will next come out of the ground? The government of the world I live in was not framed, like that of Britain, in after-dinner conversations over the wine.

The life in us is like the water in the river. It may rise this year higher than man has ever known it, and flood the parched uplands; even this may be the eventful year, which will drown out all our muskrats. It was not always dry land where we dwell. I see far inland the banks which the stream anciently washed, before science began to record its freshets. Every one has heard the story which has gone the rounds of New England, of a strong and beautiful bug which came out of the dry leaf of an old table of apple-tree wood, which had stood in a farmer's kitchen for sixty years, first in Connecticut, and afterward in Massachusetts, — from an egg deposited in the living tree many years earlier still, as appeared by counting the annual layers beyond it, which was heard gnawing out for several weeks, hatched perchance by the heat of an urn. Who does not feel his faith in a resurrection and immortality strengthened by hearing of this? Who knows what beautiful and winged life, whose egg has been buried for ages under many concentric layers of woodenness in the dead dry life of society, deposited at first in the alburnum of the green and living tree, which has been gradually converted into the semblance of its well-seasoned tomb, — heard perchance gnawing out now for years by the astonished family of man, as they sat round the festive board, — may unexpectedly come forth from amidst society's most trivial and handselled furniture, to enjoy its perfect summer life at last!

I do not say that John or Jonathan will realize all this; but such is the character of that morrow which mere lapse of time can never make to dawn. The light which puts out our eyes is darkness to us. Only that day dawns to which we are awake. There is more day to dawn. The sun is but a morning star.

(1854)

Questions

1. How does Henry David Thoreau characterize life in New England at the time he went to live at Walden? How do you regard that characterization? To what extent might it apply to life today?

2. About the different ways in which people live their lives, Thoreau writes, "This is the only way, we say; but there are as many ways as there can be drawn radii from one centre" (par. 7). Do you agree? Why or why not?

3. Being extremely economical in his assessment even for his own time, Thoreau denotes what he calls "necessary of life" and what he considers near necessities (par. 9). He writes, "Most of the luxuries, and many of the so called comforts of life, are not only not indispensable, but positive hinderances to the elevation of mankind" (par. 10). Do you agree with this statement? What would we add to his list today? Which things that Thoreau considered luxuries do we now deem necessities?

4. Thoreau writes, "There are nowadays professors of philosophy, but not philosophers. Yet it is admirable to profess because it was once admirable to live" (par. 10). What does he mean? To what extent does he speak to our time as well as to his own?

5. How would you describe Thoreau's tone in the first two sentences of paragraph 11? How is his attitude relevant to our current economy?

6. Thoreau says that he will talk about how he has spent his life in years past and "hint at some of the enterprises which I have cherished" (par. 13). How would you paraphrase the account that he provides in the next eight paragraphs (pars. 14–21)?

7. Who is Thoreau's intended audience in paragraph 2? How does he characterize that audience? Who is it in paragraph 12? Which one is more likely to attend to his message? Is such an audience living today?

8. What is the purpose of the example that Thoreau introduces in paragraph 22? Do you agree with the lesson that he draws from it? Explain.

9. How does Thoreau characterize himself in paragraphs 23–25?

10. Thoreau calls student life at "Cambridge College" (Harvard University, from which Thoreau had graduated) as "this expensive game" (par. 26). Do you agree with Thoreau's ideas about education? Make specific references to the text of paragraph 26 in your answer.

11. What is Thoreau calling for when he writes, "Simplicity, simplicity, simplicity!" and enjoins his readers to "simplify, simplify" (par. 31)? Explain.

12. Thoreau writes, "We do not ride on the railroad; it rides upon us" (par. 31). Consider an electronic device (such as a laptop computer, a smartphone, a tablet, an MP3 player, or such social networks as Facebook and Twitter). What would Thoreau say about it? Has this device helped simplify our lives or has it had a negative impact on them? Explain.

13. Thoreau writes, "What news! how much more important to know what that is which was never old!" (par. 34). Write an essay in which you evaluate Thoreau's own writing according to this thought. Consider how this essay appeals to two audiences: the contemporaneous and the contemporary.

14. What does Thoreau mean by the phrase "starved before we are hungry" (par. 32)? What other examples of paradox do you find in this excerpt from *Walden*? How do they contribute to Thoreau's main ideas?

15. How do you interpret Thoreau's assertion that "[s]hams and delusions are esteemed for soundless truths, while reality is fabulous" (par. 35)? Using that statement as a topic sentence, develop the idea with examples from your own experience.

16. Thoreau speaks of the "government of the world I live in" (par. 46). What does he mean? How would you describe the world that he lives in? What governs it?

17. One of the rhetorical techniques that Thoreau uses most is analogy (he even states at one point, "so much for analogy"). Identify three examples of his use of analogy and explain which one you find most compelling or effective.

18. Thoreau concludes *Walden* as follows: "The light which puts out our eyes is darkness to us. Only that day dawns to which we are awake. There is more day to dawn. The sun is but a morning star" (par. 48). Do you see this as a fitting conclusion? Explain what Thoreau means. Why does he conclude this way?

19. Do you think Thoreau's advice and sentiments are meant as recommendations for living one's entire life or as suggestions for periodically reflecting on life's true meaning? Is he suggesting isolation as a way of life? Explain.

20. Thoreau is known for his epigrammatic statements, some of which have become so popular and familiar that they adorn posters, bumper stickers, and coffee mugs. Select your favorite one from the reading and explain why you find it so compelling.

from *Walden*

E. B. WHITE

E. B. White (1899–1985) was an editor, an essayist, and a writer of children's books who lived in New York and Maine. He is best known for his essay "Once More to the Lake," for his children's books *Stuart Little* (1945) and *Charlotte's Web* (1952), and for his revision of William Strunk Jr.'s *The Elements of Style* (1959). In the essay included here, White composes a letter to Thoreau, intending to bring him up to date regarding Concord, Massachusetts.

Miss Nims, take a letter to Henry David Thoreau. Dear Henry: I thought of you the other afternoon as I was approaching Concord doing fifty on Route 62. That is a high speed at which to hold a philosopher in one's mind, but in this century we are a nimble bunch.

On one of the lawns in the outskirts of the village a woman was cutting the grass with a motorized lawn mower. What made me think of you was that the machine had rather got away from her, although she was game enough, and in the brief glimpse I had of the scene it appeared to me that the lawn was mowing the lady. She kept a tight grip on the handles, which throbbed violently with every explosion of the one-cylinder motor, and as she sheered around bushes and lurched along at a reluctant trot behind her impetuous servant, she looked like a puppy who had grabbed something that was too much for him. Concord hasn't changed much, Henry; the farm implements and the animals still have the upper hand.

I may as well admit that I was journeying to Concord with the deliberate intention of visiting your woods; for although I have never knelt at the grave of a philosopher nor placed wreaths on moldy poets, and have often gone a mile out of my way to avoid some place of historical interest, I have always wanted to see Walden Pond. The account which you left of your sojourn there is, you will be amused to learn, a document of increasing pertinence; each year it seems to gain a little headway, as the world loses ground. We may all be transcendental yet, whether we like it or not. As our common complexities increase, any tale of individual simplicity (and yours is the best written and the cockiest) acquires a new fascination; as our goods accumulate, but not our well being, your report of an existence without material adornment takes on a certain awkward credibility.

My purpose in going to Walden Pond, like yours, was not to live cheaply or to live dearly there, but to transact some private business with the fewest obstacles. Approaching Concord, doing forty, doing forty-five, doing fifty, the steering wheel held snug in my palms, the highway held grimly in my vision, the crown of the road now serving me (on the righthand curves), now defeating me (on the lefthand curves), I began to rouse myself from the stupefaction which a day's motor journey induces. It was a delicious evening, Henry, when the whole body is one sense, and imbibes delight through every pore, if I may coin a phrase. Fields were richly brown where the harrow, drawn by the stripped Ford, had lately sunk its teeth; pastures were green; and overhead the sky had that same everlasting great look which you will find on Page 144 of the Oxford pocket edition. I could feel the road entering me, through tire, wheel, spring, and cushion; shall I not have intelligence with earth too? Am I not partly leaves and vegetable mold myself? —a man of infinite horsepower, yet partly leaves.

Stay with me on 62 and it will take you into Concord. As I say, it was a delicious   5
evening. The snake had come forth to die in a bloody S on the highway, the wheel upon its head, its bowels flat now and exposed. The turtle had come up too to cross the road and die in the attempt, its hard shell smashed under the rubber blow, its intestinal yearning (for the other side of the road) forever squashed. There was a sign by the wayside which announced that the road had a "cotton surface." You wouldn't know what that is, but neither, for that matter, did I. There is a cryptic ingredient in many of our modern improvements —we are awed and pleased without knowing quite what we are enjoying. It is something to be traveling on a road with a cotton surface.

The civilization round Concord today is an odd distillation of city, village, farm, and manor. The houses, yards, fields look not quite suburban, not quite rural. Under the bronze beech and the blue spruce of the departed baron grazes the milch goat of the heirs. Under the porte-cochère stands the reconditioned station wagon; under the grape arbor sit the puppies for sale. (But why do men degenerate ever? What makes families run out?)

It was June and everywhere June was publishing her immemorial stanza; in the lilacs, in the syringa, in the freshly edged paths and the sweetness of moist beloved gardens, and the little wire wickets that preserve the tulips' front. Farmers were already moving the fruits of their toil into their yards, arranging the rhubarb, the asparagus, the strictly fresh eggs on the painted stands under the little shed roofs with the patent shingles. And though it was almost a hundred years since you had taken your ax and started cutting out your home on Walden Pond, I was interested to observe that the philosophical spirit was still alive in Massachusetts: in the center of a vacant lot some boys were assembling the framework of the rude shelter, their whole mind and skill concentrated in the rather inauspicious helter-skeleton of studs and rafters. They too were escaping from town, to live naturally, in a rich blend of savagery and philosophy.

That evening, after supper at the inn, I strolled out into the twilight to dream my shapeless transcendental dreams and see that the car was locked up for the night (first open the right front door, then reach over, straining, and pull up the handles of the left rear and the left front till you hear the click, then the handle of the right rear, then shut the right front but open it again, remembering that the key is still in the ignition switch, remove the key, shut the right front again with a bang, push the tiny keyhole cover to one side, insert key, turn, and withdraw). It is what we all do, Henry. It is called locking the car. It is said to confuse thieves and keep them from making off with the laprobe. Four doors to lock behind one robe. The driver himself never uses a laprobe, the free movement of his legs being vital to the operation of the vehicle; so that when he locks the car it is a pure and unselfish act. I have in my life gained very little essential heat from laprobes, yet I have ever been at pains to lock them up. . . .

A fire engine, out for a trial spin, roared past Emerson's house, hot with readiness for public duty. Over the barn roofs the martins dipped and chittered. A swarthy daughter of an asparagus grower, in culottes, shirt, and bandanna, pedalled past on her bicycle. It was indeed a delicious evening, and I returned to the inn (I believe it was your house once) to rock with the old ladies on the concrete veranda.

Next morning early I started afoot for Walden, out Main Street and down Thoreau, past the depot and the Minuteman Chevrolet Company. The morning was fresh, and in a bean field along the way I flushed an agriculturalist, quietly studying his beans. Thoreau Street soon joined Number 126, an artery of the State. We number our highways nowadays, our speed being so great we can remember little of their quality or character and are lucky to remember their number. (Men have an indistinct notion that if they keep up this activity long enough all will at length ride somewhere, in next to no time.) Your pond is on 126. 10

I knew I must be nearing your woodland retreat when the Golden Pheasant lunchroom came into view — Sealtest ice cream, toasted sandwiches, hot frankfurters, waffles, tonics, and lunches. Were I the proprietor, I should add rice, Indian meal, and molasses — just for old time's sake. The Pheasant, incidentally, is for sale: a chance for some nature lover who wishes to set himself up beside a pond in the Concord atmosphere and live deliberately, fronting only the essential facts of life on Number 126. Beyond the Pheasant was a place called Walden Breezes, an oasis whose porch pillars were made of old green shutters sawed into lengths. On the porch was a distorting mirror, to give the traveler a comical image of himself, who had miraculously learned to gaze in an ordinary glass without smiling. Behind the Breezes, in a sunparched clearing, dwelt your philosophical descendants in their trailers, each trailer the size of your hut, but all grouped together for the sake of congeniality. Trailer people leave the city, as you did, to discover solitude and in any weather, at any hour of the day or night, to improve the nick of time; but they soon collect in villages and get bogged deeper in the mud than ever. The camp behind Walden Breezes was just rousing itself to the morning. The ground was packed hard under the heel, and the sun came through the clearing to bake the soil and enlarge the wry smell of cramped housekeeping. Cushman's bakery truck had stopped to deliver an early basket of rolls. A camp dog, seeing me in the road, barked petulantly. A man emerged from one of the trailers and set forth with a bucket to draw water from some forest tap.

Leaving the highway I turned off into the woods toward the pond, which was apparent through the foliage. The floor of the forest was strewn with dried old oak leaves and *Transcripts*. From beneath the flattened popcorn wrapper (*granum explosum*) peeped the frail violet. I followed a footpath and descended to the water's edge. The pond lay clear and blue in the morning light, as you have seen it so many times. In the shallows a man's waterlogged shirt undulated gently. A few flies came out to greet me and convoy me to your cove, past the No Bathing signs on which the fellows and the girls had scrawled their names. I felt strangely excited suddenly to be snooping around your premises, tiptoeing along watchfully, as though not to tread by mistake upon the intervening century. Before I got to the cove I heard something which seemed to me quite wonderful: I heard your frog, a full, clear *troonk*, guiding me, still hoarse and solemn, bridging the years as the robins had bridged them in the sweetness of the village evening. But he soon quit, and I came on a couple of young boys throwing stones at him.

Your front yard is marked by a bronze tablet set in a stone. Four small granite posts, a few feet away, show where the house was. On top of the tablet was a pair of faded blue bathing trunks with a white stripe. Back of it is a pile of stones, a sort of cairn, left by your visitors as a tribute I suppose. It is a rather ugly little heap of stones, Henry. In fact the hillside itself seems faded, browbeaten; a few tall skinny pines, bare of lower limbs, a smattering of young maples in suitable green, some birches and oaks, and a number of trees felled by the last big wind. It was from the bole of one of these fallen pines, torn up by the roots, that I extracted the stone which I added to the cairn—a sentimental act in which I was interrupted by a small terrier from a nearby picnic group, who confronted me and wanted to know about the stone.

I sat down for a while on one of the posts of your house to listen to the bluebottles and the dragonflies. The invaded glade sprawled shabby and mean at my feet, but the flies were tuned to the old vibration. There were the remains of a fire in your ruins, but I doubt that it was yours; also two beer bottles trodden into the soil and become part of earth. A young oak had taken root in your house, and two or three ferns, unrolling like the ticklers at a banquet. The only other furnishings were a DuBarry pattern sheet, a page torn from a picture magazine, and some crusts in wax paper.

Before I quit I walked clear round the pond and found the place where you used to sit on the northeast side to get the sun in the fall, and the beach where you got sand for scrubbing your floor. On the eastern side of the pond, where the highway borders it, the State has built dressing rooms for swimmers, a float with diving towers, drinking fountains of porcelain, and rowboats for hire. The pond is in fact a State Preserve, and carries a twenty-dollar fine for picking wild flowers, a decree signed in all solemnity by your fellow-citizens Walter C. Wardwell, Erson B. Barlow, and Nathaniel I. Bowditch. There was a smell of creosote where they had been building a wide

15

wooden stairway to the road and the parking area. Swimmers and boaters were arriving; bodies plunged vigorously into the water and emerged wet and beautiful in the bright air. As I left, a boatload of town boys were splashing about in mid-pond, kidding and fooling, the young fellows singing at the tops of their lungs in a wild chorus:

> *Amer-ica, Amer-ica, God shed his grace on thee,*
> *And crown thy good with brotherhood*
> *From sea to shi-ning sea!*

I walked back to town along the railroad, following your custom. The rails were expanding noisily in the hot sun, and on the slope of the roadbed the wild grape and the blackberry sent up their creepers to the track.

The expense of my brief sojourn in Concord was:

Canvas shoes	$1.95
Baseball bat	.25 } gifts to take back
Left-handed fielder's glove	1.25 } to a boy
Hotel and meals	4.25
	———
In all	$7.70

As you see, this amount was almost what you spent for food for eight months. I cannot defend the shoes or the expenditure for shelter and food: they reveal a meanness and grossness in my nature which you would find contemptible. The baseball equipment, however, is the kind of impediment with which you were never on even terms. You must remember that the house where you practiced the sort of economy which I respect was haunted only by mice and squirrels. You never had to cope with a shortstop.

(1939)

Questions

1. How many direct references to the text of *Walden* do you find in E. B. White's essay? Choose the three that you find most interesting. How do they contribute to the effectiveness of the piece?
2. What is White's attitude toward progress? Explain.
3. Note two instances of irony. What is their rhetorical effect?
4. How would you describe White's overall tone?

A Short History of America

ROBERT CRUMB

Born in 1943, Robert Crumb was one of the originators of "underground" comics, creating such characters as Mr. Natural and Fritz the Cat. The comic strip included here first appeared in *CoEvolution Quarterly* in 1979.

(See color insert, Image 26.)

Questions

1. How would you paraphrase the narrative sequence depicted in the twelve frames?
2. Imagine that you are living in the time depicted in one of the frames. In a letter to someone living in an earlier frame, write about the progress the country has made. Or, write a warning to future generations who might occupy later frames.
3. What can you infer about Robert Crumb's attitude toward the progress depicted in the cartoon? Do you agree with his perspective? Why or why not?
4. Write an answer to the question "What next?" posed at the end of the final frame. Then create your own visual that supports your response. You can create your visual in one of three ways: draw the next frame or sequence of frames, take photos that depict the next frame or sequence, or find images online or in magazines that do so.
5. Which frame most accurately depicts a scene contemporaneous to Thoreau's time? Explain.
6. Select three frames from the cartoon sequence. For each one, find a quotation from *Walden* that could serve as a caption for the cartoon. Explain the reasons for your choices.

Living like Weasels

ANNIE DILLARD

> The following essay is from Annie Dillard's book *Teaching a Stone to Talk: Expeditions and Encounters* (1982). Dillard (b. 1945) is a Pulitzer Prize–winning author, professor of English, and philosopher of nature who writes in the tradition of Thoreau, and whose master's thesis was on *Walden*.

A weasel is wild. Who knows what he thinks? He sleeps in his underground den, his tail draped over his nose. Sometimes he lives in his den for two days without leaving. Outside, he stalks rabbits, mice, muskrats, and birds, killing more bodies than he can eat warm, and often dragging the carcasses home. Obedient to instinct, he bites his prey at the neck, either splitting the jugular vein at the throat or crunching the brain at the base of the skull, and he does not let go. One naturalist refused to kill a weasel who was socketed into his hand deeply as a rattlesnake. The man could in no way pry the tiny weasel off, and he had to walk half a mile to water, the weasel dangling from his palm, and soak him off like a stubborn label.

And once, says Ernest Thompson Seton[1] — once, a man shot an eagle out of the sky. He examined the eagle and found the dry skull of a weasel fixed by the jaws to his throat. The supposition is that the eagle had pounced on the weasel and the weasel

---

[1] A founding chair of the Boy Scouts of America, Ernest Thompson Seton (1860–1946) was a British wildlife illustrator, naturalist, and writer. — Eds.

swiveled and bit as instinct taught him, tooth to neck, and nearly won. I would like to have seen that eagle from the air a few weeks or months before he was shot. Was the whole weasel still attached to his feathered throat, a fur pendant? Or did the eagle eat what he could reach, gutting the living weasel with his talons before his breast, bending his beak, cleaning the beautiful airborne bones?

I have been reading about weasels because I saw one last week. I startled a weasel who startled me, and we exchanged a long glance.

Near my house in Virginia is a pond — Hollins Pond. It covers two acres of bottomland near Tinker Creek with six inches of water and six thousand lily pads. There is a fifty-five mph highway at one end of the pond, and a nesting pair of wood ducks at the other. Under every bush is a muskrat hole or a beer can. The far end is an alternating series of fields and woods, fields and woods, threaded everywhere with motorcycle tracks — in whose bare clay wild turtles lay eggs.

One evening last week at sunset, I walked to the pond and sat on a downed log   5
near the shore. I was watching the lily pads at my feet tremble and part over the thrusting path of a carp. A yellow warbler appeared to my right and flew behind me. It caught my eye; I swiveled around — and the next instant, inexplicably, I was looking down at a weasel, who was looking up at me.

Weasel! I'd never seen one wild before. He was ten inches long, thin as a curve, a muscled ribbon, brown as fruitwood, soft-furred, alert. His face was fierce, small and pointed as a lizard's; he would have made a good arrowhead. There was just a dot of chin, maybe two brown hairs' worth, and then the pure white fur began that spread down his underside. He had two black eyes I didn't see, any more than you see a window.

The weasel was stunned into stillness as he was emerging from beneath an enormous shaggy wild rose bush four feet away. I was stunned into stillness twisted backward on the tree trunk. Our eyes locked, and someone threw away the key.

Our look was as if two lovers, or deadly enemies, met unexpectedly on an overgrown path when each had been thinking of something else: a clearing blow to the gut. It was also a bright blow to the brain, or a sudden beating of brains, with all the charge and intimate grate of rubbed balloons. It emptied our lungs. It felled the forest, moved the fields, and drained the pond; the world dismantled and tumbled into that black hole of eyes. If you and I looked at each other that way, our skulls would split and drop to our shoulders. But we don't. We keep our skulls.

He disappeared. This was only last week, and already I don't remember what shattered the enchantment. I think I blinked, I think I retrieved my brain from the weasel's brain, and tried to memorize what I was seeing, and the weasel felt the yank of separation, the careening splashdown into real life and the urgent current of instinct. He vanished under the wild rose. I waited motionless, my mind suddenly full of data and my spirit with pleadings, but he didn't return.

Please do not tell me about "approach-avoidance conflicts." I tell you I've been in   10
that weasel's brain for sixty seconds, and he was in mine. Brains are private places,

muttering through unique and secret tapes — but the weasel and I both plugged into another tape simultaneously, for a sweet and shocking time. Can I help it if it was a blank?

What goes on in his brain the rest of the time? What does a weasel think about? He won't say. His journal is tracks in clay, a spray of feathers, mouse blood and bone: uncollected, unconnected, loose-leaf, and blown.

I would like to learn, or remember, how to live. I come to Hollins Pond not so much to learn how to live as, frankly, to forget about it. That is, I don't think I can learn from a wild animal how to live in particular — shall I suck warm blood, hold my tail high, walk with my footprints precisely over the prints of my hands? — but I might learn something of mindlessness, something of purity of living in the physical senses and the dignity of living without bias or motive. The weasel lives in necessity and we live in choice, hating necessity and dying at the last ignobly in its talons. I would like to live as I should, as the weasel lives as he should. And I suspect that for me the way is like the weasel's: open to time and death painlessly, noticing everything, remembering nothing, choosing the given with a fierce and pointed will.

I missed my chance. I should have gone for the throat. I should have lunged for that streak of white under the weasel's chin and held on, held on through mud and into the wild rose, held on for a dearer life. We could live under the wild rose wild as weasels, mute and uncomprehending. I could very calmly go wild. I could live two days in the den, curled, leaning on mouse fur, sniffing bird bones, blinking, licking, breathing musk, my hair tangled in the roots of grasses. Down is a good place to go, where the mind is single. Down is out, out of your ever-loving mind and back to your careless senses. I remember muteness as a prolonged and giddy fast, where every moment is a feast of utterance received. Time and events are merely poured, unremarked, and ingested directly, like blood pulsed into my gut through a jugular vein. Could two live that way? Could two live under the wild rose, and explore by the pond, so that the smooth mind of each is as everywhere present to the other, and as received and as unchallenged, as falling snow?

We could, you know. We can live any way we want. People take vows of poverty, chastity, and obedience — even of silence — by choice. The thing is to stalk your calling in a certain skilled and supple way, to locate the most tender and live spot and plug into that pulse. This is yielding, not fighting. A weasel doesn't "attack" anything; a weasel lives as he's meant to, yielding at every moment to the perfect freedom of single necessity.

I think it would be well, and proper, and obedient, and pure, to grasp your one 15 necessity and not let it go, to dangle from it limp wherever it takes you. Then even death, where you're going no matter how you live, cannot you part. Seize it and let it seize you up aloft even, till your eyes burn out and drop; let your musky flesh fall off in shreds, and let your very bones unhinge and scatter, loosened over fields, over fields and woods, lightly, thoughtless, from any height at all, from as high as eagles.

(1982)

Questions

1. What comes to mind when you hear the word *weasel*? What are the qualities of a weasel that Annie Dillard admires?
2. Dillard uses a great deal of figurative language, hyperbole, and even alliteration in her writing. How do these features contribute to the effectiveness of the essay?
3. Dillard writes "we" in the third paragraph, indicating the first of several times she identifies with the weasel. What are the others? What is the effect of these identifications?
4. Notice Dillard's careful attention to detail and style. How do the juxtapositions in paragraph 5 and the particular details — especially in paragraphs 4 and 6 — contribute to her purpose?
5. Dillard uses the phrase "under the wild rose" several times in the essay. What effect does this repetition have on the piece as a whole?
6. What does Dillard mean by "the perfect freedom of single necessity" (par. 14)? She continues, "I think it would be well, and proper, and obedient, and pure, to grasp your one necessity and not let it go, to dangle from it limp wherever it takes you" (par. 15). What does she mean? What might be your "one necessity"? Do you agree with what she says about grasping it? Explain.

from *The Future of Life*

E. O. WILSON

> In the following excerpt, from *The Future of Life* (2002), acclaimed scientist Edward O. Wilson composes a "letter" to Henry David Thoreau in which he considers Thoreau's relevance to our time.

Henry!

May I call you by your Christian name? Your words invite familiarity and make little sense otherwise. How else to interpret your insistent use of the first personal pronoun? *I* wrote this account, you say, here are *my* deepest thoughts, and no third person placed between us could ever be so well represented. Although *Walden* is sometimes oracular in tone, I don't read it, the way some do, as an oration to the multitude. Rather, it is a work of art, the testament of a citizen of Concord, in New England, from one place, one time, and one writer's personal circumstance that manages nevertheless to reach across five generations to address accurately the general human condition. Can there be a better definition of art? . . .

Now, prophet of the conservation movement, mentor of Gandhi and Martin Luther King Jr., accept this tribute tardily given. Keen observer of the human condition, scourge of the philistine culture, Greek stoic adrift in the New World, you are reborn in each generation and vested with new meaning and nuance. Sage of Concord — Saint Henry, they sometimes call you — you've fairly earned your place in history.

On the other hand, you were not a great naturalist. (Forgive me!) Even had you kept entirely to natural history during your short life, you would have ranked well below William Bartram, Louis Agassiz, and that prodigious collector of North American plants John Torrey, and be scarcely remembered today. With longer life it would likely have been different, because you were building momentum in natural history rapidly when you left us. And to give you full credit, your ideas on succession and other properties of living communities pointed straight toward the modern science of ecology.

That doesn't matter now. I understand why you came to Walden Pond; your words are clear enough on that score. Granted, you chose this spot primarily to study nature. But you could have done that as easily and far more comfortably on daily excursions from your mother's house in Concord Center, half an hour's walk away, where in fact you did frequently repair for a decent meal. Nor was your little cabin meant to be a wilderness hermitage. No wilderness lay within easy reach anyway, and even the woods around Walden Pond had shrunk to their final thin margins by the 1840s. You called solitude your favorite companion. You were not afraid, you said, to be left to the mercy of your own thoughts. Yet you craved humanity passionately, and your voice is anthropocentric in mood and philosophy. Visitors to the Walden cabin were welcomed. Once a group of twenty-five or more crowded into the solitary room of the tiny house, shoulder to shoulder. You were not appalled by so much human flesh pressed together (but I am). You were lonely at times. The whistle of a passing train on the Fitchburg track and the distant rumble of oxcarts crossing a bridge must have given you comfort on cold, rainy days. Sometimes you went out looking for someone, anyone, in spite of your notorious shyness, just to have a conversation. You fastened on them, as you put it, like a bloodsucker.

In short, you were far from the hard-eyed frontiersman bearing pemmican and   5
a long rifle. Frontiersmen did not saunter, botanize, and read Greek. So how did it happen that an amateur naturalist perched in a toy house on the edge of a ravaged woodland became the founding saint of the conservation movement? Here is what I believe happened. Your spirit craved an epiphany. You sought enlightenment and fulfillment the Old Testament way, by reduction of material existence to the fundamentals. The cabin was your cave on the mountainside. You used poverty to purchase a margin of free existence. It was the only method you could devise to seek the meaning in a life otherwise smothered by quotidian necessity and haste. You lived at Walden, as you said (I dare not paraphrase),

> to front only the essential facts of life, and see if I could not learn what it had to teach, and not, when I came to die, discover that I had not lived . . . to live deep

and suck out all the marrow of life, to live so sturdily and Spartan-like as to put to rout all that was not life, to cut a broad swath and shave close, to drive life into a corner, and reduce it to its lowest terms, and, if it proved to be mean, why then to get the whole and genuine meanness of it, and publish its meanness to the world; or if it were sublime, to know it by experience, and be able to give a true account of it in my next excursion.

You were mistaken, I think, to suppose that there are as many ways of life possible as radii that can be drawn from the center of a circle, and your choice just one of them. On the contrary, the human mind can develop along only a very few pathways imaginable. They are selected by satisfactions we instinctively seek in common. The sturdiness of human nature is the reason people plant flowers, gods live on high mountains, and a lake is the eye of the world through which — your metaphor — we can measure our own souls.

It is exquisitely human to search for wholeness and richness of experience. When these qualities are lost among the distracting schedules of everyday life, we seek them elsewhere. When you stripped your outside obligations to the survivable minimum, you placed your trained and very active mind in an unendurable vacuum. And this is the essence of the matter: in order to fill the vacuum, you discovered the human proclivity to embrace the natural world.

Your childhood experience told you exactly where to go. It could not be a local cornfield or gravel pit. Nor the streets of Boston, which, however vibrant as the hub of a growing nation, might cost a layabout his dignity and even his life. It had to be a world both tolerant of poverty and rich and beautiful enough to be spiritually rewarding. Where around Concord could that possibly be but a woodlot next to a lake?

You traded most of the richness of social existence for an equivalent richness of the natural world. The choice was entirely logical, for the following reason. Each of us finds a comfortable position somewhere along the continuum that ranges from complete withdrawal and self-absorption at one end to full civic engagement and reciprocity at the other. The position is never fixed. We fret, vacillate, and steer our lives through the riptide of countervailing instincts that press from both ends of the continuum. The uncertainty we feel is not a curse. It is not a confusion on the road out of Eden. It is just the human condition. We are intelligent mammals, fitted by evolution — by God, if you prefer — to pursue personal ends through cooperation. Our priceless selves and family first, society next. In this respect we are the polar opposite of your cabinside ants, bound together as replaceable parts of a superorganism. Our lives are therefore an insoluble problem, a dynamic process in search of an indefinable goal. They are neither a celebration nor a spectacle but rather, as a later philosopher put it, a predicament. Humanity is the species forced by its basic nature to make moral choices and seek fulfillment in a changing world by any means it can devise.

You searched for essence at Walden and, whether successful in your own mind 10 or not, you hit upon an ethic with a solid feel to it; nature is ours to explore forever;

it is our crucible and refuge; it is our natural home; it is all these things. Save it, you said: in wildness is the preservation of the world.

Now, in closing this letter, I am forced to report bad news. (I put it off till the end.) The natural world in the year 2001 is everywhere disappearing before our eyes — cut to pieces, mowed down, slowed under, gobbled up, replaced by human artifacts.

No one in your time could imagine a disaster of this magnitude. Little more than a billion people were alive in the 1840s. They were overwhelmingly agricultural, and few families needed more than two or three acres to survive. The American frontier was still wide open. And far away on continents to the south, up great rivers, beyond unclimbed mountain ranges, stretched unspoiled equatorial forests brimming with the maximum diversity of life. These wildernesses seemed as unattainable and time-less as the planets and stars. That could not last, because the mood of Western civili-zation is Abrahamic. The explorers and colonists were guided by a biblical prayer: May we take possession of this land that God has provided and let it drip milk and honey into our mouths, forever.

Now, more than six billion people fill the world. The great majority are very poor; nearly one billion exist on the edge of starvation. All are struggling to raise the quality of their lives any way they can. That unfortunately includes the conver-sion of the surviving remnants of the natural environment. Half of the great tropi-cal forests have been cleared. The last frontiers of the world are effectively gone. Species of plants and animals are disappearing a hundred or more times faster than before the coming of humanity, and as many as half may be gone by the end of this century. An Armageddon is approaching at the beginning of the third millennium. But it is not the cosmic war and fiery collapse of mankind foretold in sacred scrip-ture. It is the wreckage of the planet by an exuberantly plentiful and ingenious humanity.

The race is now on between the technoscientific forces that are destroying the living environment and those that can be harnessed to save it. We are inside a bottle-neck of overpopulation and wasteful consumption. If the race is won, humanity can emerge in far better condition than when it entered, and with most of the diversity of life still intact.

The situation is desperate — but there are encouraging signs that the race can be   15
won. Population growth has slowed, and, if the present trajectory holds, is likely to peak between eight and ten billion people by century's end. That many people, experts tell us, can be accommodated with a decent standard of living, but just barely: the amount of arable land and water available per person, globally, is already declining. In solving the problem, other experts tell us, it should also be possible to shelter most of the vulnerable plant and animal species.

In order to pass through the bottleneck, a global land ethic is urgently needed. Not just any land ethic that might happen to enjoy agreeable sentiment, but one based on the best understanding of ourselves and the world around us that science and technology can provide. Surely the rest of life matters. Surely our stewardship is its only hope. We will be wise to listen carefully to the heart, then act with rational intention and all the tools we can gather and bring to bear.

Henry, my friend, thank you for putting the first element of that ethic in place. Now it is up to us to summon a more encompassing wisdom. The living world is dying; the natural economy is crumbling beneath our busy feet. We have been too self-absorbed to foresee the long-term consequences of our actions, and we will suffer a terrible loss unless we shake off our delusions and move quickly to a solution. Science and technology led us into this bottleneck. Now science and technology must help us find our way through and out.

You once said that old deeds are for old people, and new deeds are for new. I think that in historical perspective it is the other way around. You were the new and we are the old. Can we now be the wiser? For you, here at Walden Pond, the lamentation of the mourning dove and the green frog's *t-r-r-oonk!* across the predawn water were the true reason for saving this place. For us, it is an exact knowledge of what that truth is, all that it implies, and how to employ it to best effect. So, two truths. We will have them both, you and I and all those now and forever to come who accept the stewardship of nature.

Affectionately yours,
Edward
(2002)

Questions

1. Do you agree with E. O. Wilson's characterization of *Walden* as a work of art? Why or why not?
2. While Wilson's essay praises Thoreau, there are places where he is critical of the Thoreau "myth." Choose two. How does Wilson's critical attitude affect his ethos? Is it effective with the reader? Explain.
3. In paragraphs 7–9, Wilson discusses Thoreau's purpose. How accurate do you find his account? Use references to *Walden* to support your position.
4. Note the rhetorical shift in paragraph 11. How do you suppose Thoreau might react to this shift? How might he respond to Wilson's "bad news"?
5. Notice that Wilson begins his peroration by addressing his reader, "Henry, my friend." While Henry David Thoreau is nominally his audience, we know that the actual audience consists of contemporary twenty-first-century readers. How does Wilson's attitude toward his audience differ when addressing those different audiences? Be specific.
6. How would you paraphrase Wilson's main idea? Be specific.

Doing Nothing

SUE MONK KIDD

> The following blog post, which considers the influence of Thoreau, is by Sue Monk Kidd, an author best known for her novels *The Secret Life of Bees* (2002) and *The Invention of Wings* (2013).

Last fall, after I finished writing *The Mermaid Chair*, I began to think fondly of doing nothing. I'd been working at a pretty high pitch for several years, writing, speaking and traveling, and I'd loved every moment of it, but honestly, now I felt tired down in my bones, in the wrinkles of gray matter in my brain. I was what you call spent.

The other day someone told me about seeing a prime time television commercial urging the American people to please, please take their vacations. Apparently the time we take for rest and renewal is shrinking; apparently we place our work at the top of the food chain and it tends to swallow up everything else.

In *The Secret Life of Bees* (page 57 to be exact), there's a line in which Lily says, "Next to Shakespeare, I love Thoreau best." I love Thoreau best, too. I read *Walden* when I was fifteen. Along with Kate Chopin's novel, *The Awakening*, it made the biggest impression on me of any book I read in my adolescence. As you probably know, *Walden* is Thoreau's account of seeking spiritual awakening by returning to a simple life beside Walden Pond in the New England woods. It is strange the way certain sentences from the book are still alive in me. Like this one:

> I went to the woods because I wished to live deliberately, to . . . see if I could not learn what it had to teach, and not, when I came to die, discover that I had not lived.

Since fifteen, I've harbored a secret and, I admit, highly romantic fantasy of going off like Thoreau to my own Walden Pond.

But as I considered an entire winter of doing nothing, I told my husband we better leap before I started looking around too much at all the things I had to do, before the urge to write the next book got to me. We ended up on an island along the coast of Florida, in a place by the sea where I leave the doors flung open to the sound of the waves, where early in the morning pelicans lap through the salted fog and dolphins spew their breath beyond the jetty. Every day I tell myself that I came here to see if I could live deliberately and learn what this place has to teach me.

I have been here seven weeks now. Of course my Thoreau experiment got the romance knocked out of it pretty early on. My car battery went dead—it did not distinguish between my regular life and my contemplative life. And so it seems to unfold nearly every day—the complexity and demands of life on earth intrude and I am pulled away from doing nothing to doing something. But still . . . still I am finding a slower rhythm establishing itself in me.

At the moment, I am writing to you from the lanai. In Georgia where I grew up, this would be called the porch; in Charleston, the piazza. What these things all have

5

in common is that you sit on them and observe the breathing world. This newsletter is coming along slowly because I keep peering out at the water where the sun is hovering on the horizon. The first time I observed it sink into the gulf, I explained to my husband that it looked like a big orange, fizzing tablet that drops into the water and dissolves. He said by all means not to use that terrible metaphor in the newsletter. I am anyway because it makes me laugh. And because as bad as it is, the metaphor is apt. After the sun hits the water, light will splash up in effervescent patterns, moving across the sky. Most evenings I sit right here watching all this till I'm enclosed in darkness and awe.

I know now there really is a kind of loitering that is good for us. In *Walden*, Thoreau describes how he sat in his doorway for hours watching the pines and hickories and sumacs — essentially doing nothing — and proclaimed the experience far better than any work of his hands. Can you think of anything that seems more out of touch with the rushing world? Yet, he proclaims there's value in sitting there. Even when you recognize its value, it can be hard to practice this sort of thing. I understand that. I spent the first two weeks of my "nothing doing retreat" (as a friend of mine labeled it) fighting off the recurring idea that I was wasting time, that watching sun cycles and water heave itself onto the shore in repetitive sameness for hours on end is irrelevant.

Then one day on the lanai, I watched a vast migration of stingrays. They floated in the water for hours like great dark lily pads, and I watched with the vague sense of coming into sync with a deeper, slower, truer rhythm than the one I usually lived by. I began to see the relevance of doing nothing.

It's clear to me that the human soul is meant to move at a much slower pace than the world around it. When we lose touch with this pace, we can get what has been referred to in medical circles as "hurry sickness." It shows up in a whole array of symptoms and diseases. Since coming here my blood pressure has sunk to new lows.

And it is not just my body and spirit that need this episode of lavish rest, but my creativity.   10

It waxed for such a long season, but now it needed to wane in order to renew itself. I read an article years ago that said the mind had to rest in order for the brain to produce the chemicals necessary to think dynamic, new thoughts, otherwise we just keep recycling the same old tired ones. I have no idea if this is really true, but I think it must be. Right now, my creative mind is lying empty and fallow. I have plowed under all my ideas. With each day that passes, the feeling grows in me that the seed for my next book is lying in a fertile crevice deep inside, incubating. Waiting.

Meanwhile, here on the lanai, I notice the sun has finally disappeared and the afterglow is darkening toward night. I can no longer see my scribbles on the legal pad. I think, though, I've said what I wanted to say to you: how beautiful nothing can be.

(2008)

Questions

1. Do you think that Americans work too much, as Sue Monk Kidd suggests? Is there "a kind of loitering that is good for us" (par. 7)? Should we slow down, contemplate, and sometimes "do nothing," as she recommends?
2. Kidd says that Thoreau's *Walden* and Chopin's *The Awakening* were the books that made the strongest impressions on her when she was an adolescent. Which books have done that for you? From what you have read of *Walden*, how likely is it that it might be an important book for you?
3. In paragraph 3, Kidd quotes a famous passage from *Walden*: "I went to the woods because I wished to live deliberately, to . . . see if I could not learn what it had to teach, and not, when I came to die, discover that I had not lived." How does this particular statement express Kidd's purpose in her own life? Explain.
4. Kidd writes, "It's clear to me that the human soul is meant to move at a much slower pace than the world around it. When we lose touch with this pace, we can get what has been referred to in medical circles as 'hurry sickness.' It shows up in a whole array of symptoms and diseases" (par. 9). Have you experienced "hurry sickness"? Have you observed it? Do you agree with Kidd that slowing down can ameliorate its symptoms? Explain.

from *Hamlet's BlackBerry*

William Powers

The following passage is excerpted from "The Walden Zone," a chapter in *Hamlet's BlackBerry: A Practical Philosophy for Building a Good Life in the Digital Age* (2010), by contemporary journalist William Powers.

At a time of rapidly growing connectedness, Thoreau disconnected. He was the great escape artist, and escape would seem to be his message. If you want to take back your life, Get out! Or, as he puts it in *Walden*:

> I went to the woods because I wished to live deliberately, to front only the essential facts of life, and see if I could not learn what it had to teach, and not, when I came to die, discover that I had not lived. . . . I wanted to live deep and suck out all the marrow of life.

The essential problem hasn't changed, nor has the goal. Who doesn't want to live the fullest, deepest life they possibly can? For the overconnected soul wishing to apply Thoreau's message, however, the sticking point is his method. As a practical matter, not many people have the freedom to escape society — jobs, family, and other obligations — and hole up in the woods. In any case, very few of us want the pure solitude that Thoreau seems to be advocating when he writes, "I love to be alone. I never found the companion that was so companionable as solitude."

It's the rare person whose ideal of home is a cabin for one in a neighborhood without neighbors. Part of what's always been special and invigorating about the typical home is that it makes solitude available *within* the context of the larger social environment. It's an intermittent respite, a space into which one retreats briefly at regular intervals, to emerge later refreshed.

Today there's another factor that makes Thoreau's approach seem not just unappealing but downright pointless. Even if we wanted to run away physically from society, in a digital world there's no place to go. With ubiquitous mobile connectivity, you can't use geography to escape what he called society, because it's everywhere. If you have a screen of any kind with you—and who doesn't these days?—you haven't left society at all.

But to dismiss Thoreau for these reasons is to miss the whole point of *Walden*   5 and its relevance to our time. In fact, he wasn't trying to escape civilization, and what he created at Walden Pond was not even close to pure solitude. As for ubiquitous technology, it's true that the world was a lot less connected in the middle of the nineteenth century than it is today. However, Thoreau lived through a major technological shift, the arrival of instant communication, that foreshadowed the current one. The woods weren't wireless in his era, but for the first time in history they were getting *wired*, and the wires were carrying information around the world at unimaginable speeds. Thoreau saw the enormous human implications of this change, and he structured the Walden experiment so that it spoke not just to his own time but to the technological future he saw coming.

In a world where it's increasingly hard to escape the crowd, can you still build a refuge, a place to go inward and reclaim all the things that a too-busy life takes away? Thoreau says you can, and he offers a practical construct for making it happen....

But can we apply *Walden* to our time? Thoreau may have been close to town, but he wasn't holed up with the rest of the planet, as we are with our screens. Given that digital technology has so altered the landscape of modern life, and particularly life at home, is it a stretch to think Thoreau could have anything useful to say to us?

Not at all. Though it's true that he lived in a very different information environment from today's, he and his friends and neighbors really *were* living close to the rest of the planet in a new way. Previously, information could travel only as quickly as the swiftest mode of physical transportation, which was trains. With the arrival of the telegraph in the 1840s, messages could suddenly dart from place to place instantaneously. Oceans, deserts, and mountain ranges were no longer barriers. All it took was a wire. The notion that one could now theoretically keep up with anything and everything happening on Earth, and around the clock, was both thrilling and unsettling. An East Coast American of Thoreau's generation wasn't just increasingly connected to the wide world, he was increasingly immersed in it, and he needed to manage that immersion. What to read? What to care about?

This was a subtle but significant shift in the nature of inward life, and everyone was grappling with it. "A slender wire has become the highway of thought," observed the *New York Times* in an editorial published on September 14, 1852.

Messages follow each other in quick succession. Joy spreads on the track of sorrow. The arrival of a ship, news of a revolution, or a battle, the price of pork, the state of foreign and domestic markets, missives of love, the progress of courts, the success or discomfiture of disease, the result of elections, and an innumerable host of social, political and commercial details, all chase each other over the slender and unconscious wires.

With a little updating of the language, this could be a description of the moment-by-moment randomness now offered by any digital screen. There was simply a great deal more information bearing down on everyone, and even the home was no safe haven. In *The Victorian Internet*, a history of the telegraph, Tom Standage quotes W. E. Dodge, a prominent telegraph-era businessman from New York, describing the plight of a family man battling information overload:

> The merchant goes home after a day of hard work and excitement to a late dinner, trying amid the family circle to forget business, when he is interrupted by a telegram from London, directing, perhaps, the purchase in San Francisco of 20,000 barrels of flour, and the poor man must dispatch his dinner as hurriedly as possible in order to send off his message to California. The businessman of the present day must be continually on the jump.

In other words, the telegraph was the latest agent of the "quiet desperation" that Thoreau saw all around him and felt in himself. Devices meant to relieve burdens were imposing new ones, pulling people away from life's most meaningful experiences, including the family dinner table. "But lo! men have become the tools of their tools," he wrote, and though he wasn't specifically referring to the telegraph, elsewhere in *Walden* he made it clear that the slender wire could make tools out of people. New technologies, he said, are often just "pretty toys, which distract our attention from serious things. . . . We are in great haste to construct a magnetic telegraph from Maine to Texas; but Maine and Texas, it may be, have nothing important to communicate." Yet at other times, he wrote about the telegraph in a hopeful, lyrical way, suggesting he saw the wonder of the technology and perhaps its potential to do good. "As I went under the new telegraph wire, I heard it vibrating like a harp high overhead," he noted in his journal. "It was as the sound of a far-off glorious life."

Naturalist that he was, it's often assumed that Thoreau loathed technology. In fact he was a sophisticated user, and occasionally a designer, of technologies. He never made much money from writing and supported himself by working in two different tool-intensive fields: as a surveyor and in the pencil-manufacturing business owned by his family. At one point he took on the ambitious project of reengineering the Thoreau pencil so it might fare better in a competitive marketplace. He worked hard on it, conducting extensive research into why certain European-made pencils were so superior to their American counterparts. Based on what he learned, he changed the materials, design, and manufacturing process of his company's pencils, essentially developing a brand-new product. His efforts were a great success, producing "the very best lead pencils manufactured in America" at the time, according to Henry Petroski's *The Pencil*, a history of the tool.

Thoughtful student of technology that he was, Thoreau saw that as the latest connective devices extended their reach into the lives of individuals, they were exacting huge costs. They're the same costs we're paying today—extreme busyness and a consequent loss of depth. The more wired people became, the more likely they were to fill up their minds with junk and trivia. What if we built this fabulous global telegraph network, he wondered, and then used it only to keep up on gossip about *celebrities*? "We are eager to tunnel under the Atlantic and bring the Old World some weeks nearer to the New; but perchance the first news that will leak through into the broad, flapping American ear will be that the Princess Adelaide has the whooping cough. After all, the man whose horse trots a mile a minute does not carry the most important messages."

That is, he saw that instant communication had the potential to exacerbate the very problem he had gone to Walden to solve, the superficial, short-attention-span approach to life that afflicted his friends and neighbors and often himself. They were all living from one emergency to the next, he writes at one point, consumed by their work, always checking the latest news. . . .

Once the consciousness was hooked on busyness and external stimuli, Thoreau saw, it was hard to break the habit. Never mind the telegraph, even the post office could become an addiction, as he observed in a speech:

> Surface meets surface. When our life ceases to be inward and private, conversation degenerates into mere gossip. . . . In proportion as our inward life fails, we go more constantly and desperately to the post-office. You may depend on it, that the poor fellow who walks away with the greatest number of letters proud of his extensive correspondence has not heard from himself this long while.

This is the problem of *our* time, too, of course. And it's what he went to *Walden* to solve. The mission: to see if, by building a home at a slight distance from society—disconnected, yet still connected in many ways—and living there thoughtfully, he could go back inward, regaining the depth and joy that was being leached out of everyday life.

Among all those who were struggling with this challenge in the mid–nineteenth century, Thoreau was unusually well situated to find an answer. Concord was the center of American Transcendentalism, a philosophical movement that provided a rich vein of pertinent ideas. Transcendentalists believed that true enlightenment does not come from other people or outward sources such as organized religion, scientific observation, and books; rather, it comes from within. The profoundest truths about existence are available to each of us through intuition and reflection.

It was a philosophy that spoke directly to a time when trains and telegraph lines, as well as industrialization and other forces of modernity, were pulling people in exactly the opposite direction—outward. The crowd seemed terribly important and powerful in those days, just as it does now, and it was hard to resist its influence. It was as if you had no choice but to submit, fall in line. The Transcendentalists believed

15

that resistance was crucial. Emerson, the movement's leading figure, wrote in his great essay "Self-Reliance" that to be truly happy and productive, you have to tune out the crowd and listen to "the voices which we hear in solitude." In another piece, Emerson described a Transcendentalist as a person who essentially wakes up one day and realizes, "My life is superficial, takes no root in the deep world." And then does something about it.

Guided by this philosophy, the Walden project was really an exercise in practical reengineering. In this case, the device that needed redesigning wasn't a pencil but life itself. Thoreau's method was to strip away the layers of complexity that outer life imposes, to "Simplify, simplify," as he wrote, and, in so doing, recover that lost depth. As Thoreau scholar Bradley P. Dean puts it, "By simplifying our outward lives, we are freer and better able to expand and enrich our inward lives."

The heart of the effort, serving as both headquarters and object lesson, was   20
Thoreau's tiny house and the life he constructed there. It was seriously spartan, reflecting the simplicity creed. But there was another kind of simplicity that mattered even more than the material kind: simplicity of the mind. Though the house was right in the midst of civilization, close to town, in sight of the railroad, and within easy reach of visitors, he defined it as a *zone* of inwardness, and that's what it became. . . .

Zoning is way overdue for a comeback, a digital revival, and it's surprising it hasn't happened yet. Thoreau could be the model. Our situation is different from his, in that the crowd is no longer just nearby — it's right in the home, wherever there's a screen. So our zoning has to be interior. Every home could have at least one Walden Zone, a room where no screens of any kind are allowed. Households that take their tranquillity seriously, and have sufficient room, might designate such a space for each person. There could be a shelf or cabinet outside the doorway where, upon entering, all smart phones and laptops are turned off and put away.

The wireless signals in those rooms won't go away, of course, and that's a problem. But as with Thoreau, the point of the zone is to use an idea as a constraint on behavior. For a Walden Zone to work, you first have to *believe* it's a good idea; once you do, it's a lot easier to resist temptation. The mind puts up an invisible wall, which blocks the invisible signal. Technology could help, too. Perhaps a canny entrepreneur with an eye to the Thoreauvian future will come up with a device that scrambles wireless signals in any designated space.

The opposite of a Walden Zone would be a Crowd Zone, any room specifically designated for screen life. Home offices would be automatic Crowd Zones for most people. Since the kitchen is a natural gathering place in many homes, it's a good Crowd Zone candidate. In a thoughtfully zoned house, a kitchen with floor-to-ceiling wall screens begins to make sense. Connectedness is much more appealing and rewarding when you know there's a place nearby to get away to.

Another option is whole-house zoning, in which the entire dwelling becomes a Walden Zone during certain times of the day or certain days of the week. This requires more commitment, as it means truly swearing off screens during designated times. The advantage of this approach is that it creates a genuine refuge, as Thoreau's house must have been on quiet winter nights when the town seemed a thousand miles away. My family has had great success with a regimen of this kind. . . .

The point is not to withdraw *from* the world but *within* the world. It's funny that   25 Thoreau, of all people, should be the source of this wisdom. But remember, Walden was just a two-year experiment. When it was done, he returned to society and lived the rest of his life there. But he took a valuable piece of knowledge with him: you *can* go home again, whenever you need sanctuary, so long as you have a home that serves this purpose. It doesn't have to be far off in the woods or up in the mountains or anywhere special. It's not the place that matters, it's the philosophy. To be happy in the crowd, everyone needs a little Walden.

"You think that I am impoverishing myself by withdrawing from men," Thoreau once wrote in his journal, "but in my solitude I have woven for myself a silken web or *chrysalis*, and, nymph-like, shall ere long burst forth a more perfect creature, fitted for a higher society."

(2010)

Questions

1. William Powers writes, "But to dismiss Thoreau for these reasons is to miss the whole point of *Walden* and its relevance to our time" (par. 5). What are "these reasons" to which he refers? Briefly summarize them. Do you agree with him?
2. Why does Powers call Thoreau's stay at Walden Pond the "Walden experiment" (par. 5)?
3. Powers asks, "But can we apply *Walden* to our time? . . . [I]s it a stretch to think Thoreau could have anything useful to say to us?" and then answers, "Not at all" (pars. 7–8). How adequately does Powers support his own answer to what seems to be a rhetorical question? Be specific.
4. Powers quotes from an 1852 *New York Times* editorial and from *The Victorian Internet*, a history of the telegraph, and writes of the editorial, "With a little updating . . . , this could be a description of the moment-by-moment randomness now offered by any digital screen" (par. 10). Rewrite both passages, updating the details. Then assess the validity of Powers's claim.
5. Powers writes, "Devices meant to relieve burdens were imposing new ones, pulling people away from life's most meaningful experiences" (par. 11). Have you observed or experienced this phenomenon? Do you agree with what Powers writes about our modern, "plugged-in" world: that we suffer from "extreme busyness and a consequent loss of depth" and that "[t]he more wired people became, the more likely they were to fill up their minds with junk and trivia" (par. 13)? Explain.
6. What does Powers mean by "simplicity of the mind" (par. 20)?
7. Do you agree with Powers that having a "Walden Zone" (par. 21) would be a good thing? Why or why not?
8. As he concludes this selection, Powers writes, "It doesn't have to be far off in the woods or up in the mountains or anywhere special. It's not the place that matters, it's the philosophy. To be happy in the crowd, everyone needs a little Walden"

(par. 25). "In "Self-Reliance" (p. 590), Thoreau's friend and neighbor Ralph Waldo Emerson writes, "It is easy in the world to live after the world's opinion; it is easy in solitude to live after our own; but the great man is he who in the midst of the crowd keeps with perfect sweetness the independence of solitude." Compare the ideas expressed in those statements. Do you agree with them? Explain.

My Walden, My Walmart

CRISPIN SARTWELL

The following op-ed piece by philosophy professor and writer Crispin Sartwell appeared in the *New York Times* on May 2, 2012.

I'm a Thoreauvian philosopher. I realize that sounds pretentious, but I do live more or less alone in the woods, in an old one-room schoolhouse amid orchards, trying to "front" nature. I've actually had several Waldens here in central Pennsylvania, though as it happens, none of them have ever been too far from a Walmart. And since I'm constantly in there, I probably shouldn't pretend I hate it.

One day, somewhere near the peanut butter, I ran into my occasional acquaintance Greg.

"Hey, man!" I said. "Nice day."

"Is it? I can't deal with it, nice or not," Greg offered in return, tossing piles of two-for-one items into the cart, as one does when one has three daughters at home. "It's the change. I'm not ready." It turned out he was referring to the simultaneous menopause of his wife and puberty of his middle girl. Nothing he could say or do, he claimed, didn't cause the people he loved to scream in his face, burst into tears and run to their rooms.

Now, the degree of intimacy Greg and I mustered near the peanut butter might appear excessive, though it was encouraged by the fact that we are both guys and share, though not with Thoreau, the experience of raising daughters.

It was also made possible by the excellent social vibe of a Walmart in small-town America. I'm liable to see Greg again sometime around Christmas. I'll tell him I'm having prostate issues, or that I'm under indictment, or whatever it may be that day.

We are at a cultural moment when living in close proximity and having many close friends and a ceaseless embracing community are thought to be unalloyed goods. "Bowling alone" is our shorthand for personal despair and social disintegration.

However, as I dare say you — like Jean-Paul Sartre[1] — have noticed, people can be annoying. We need distance from, as much as we need association with, one another. Thoreau tried for both: he would walk from Walden Pond to Concord, hang out with

5

---

[1]Twentieth-century French existentialist writer and philosopher who included in his play *No Exit* the famous line "Hell is other people." — Eds.

his dear friends the Emersons and the Alcotts, and then retreat to his hovel to be fairly happily alone.

If on such occasions Thoreau was thinking in his reflective way that human beings are animals and that what we do is natural, then he did not consider his stroll into Concord a departure from nature but an exploration of a bit of it. And this is the way I feel about Walmart, which — big-box island in a blacktop sea — is a perfectly natural object, as much an environment as my woods.

Walmart is no Concord. And if Greg will pardon my saying so, he is no   10
Emerson or Alcott, though possibly he is a better golfer than either. Then again, he is also not my dear friend. He's just a guy I'm happy to run across in Walmart. He's generous enough to give me sudden access to his life, without placing me under an obligation to do anything more than giggle and cluck. Ours is a perfectly good, serviceable relationship, shaped as it is by long aisles of distracting merchandise and extensive shopping lists.

Like Thoreau, I am an anarchist berry picker. Like Thoreau, I lack both easy charm and extreme social desperation, the very features of personality that fit human beings for society. Like Thoreau, I am trying to reduce my expenses to something close to my income.

Unlike Thoreau, I have cable. Yet Thoreau and I commune, more or less the same way that Greg and I do, across space and time. And that's how I can assure you that, if Thoreau were around today, he'd be pushing a cart through a Walmart three miles from Walden Pond with a bag of socks, a gallon of milk and a Blu-ray player, nodding pleasantly at people he sort of recognizes.

(2012)

Questions

1. How does Crispin Sartwell's use of humor contribute to the effectiveness of this piece?
2. How does Sartwell compare Concord with Walmart? Is he making an analogy between Henry David Thoreau and himself? Explain.
3. Do you agree with Sartwell's concluding remark? Why or why not?
4. What is Sartwell's main point? Do you agree with him?

from *Walden on Wheels*
On the Open Road from Debt to Freedom

KEN ILGUNAS

Adapted from *Walden on Wheels: On the Open Road from Debt to Freedom* (2013), a memoir by Ken Ilgunas, the following article appeared in the *New York Times* on April 10, 2013.

Could I live in a van? I looked over the Craigslist ads, took a bus to John's used car dealership in Raleigh, N.C., and scanned the rows of sedans, trucks and SUVs in search of my new home. And there it was. A giant 1994 Ford Econoline coated with a burgundy sheen, the sun turning its black-tinted windows a blinding white. It looked out of place among the shiny, spotless SUVs, whose bumpers proudly faced away, as if exhibiting a juvenile disdain for their ponderous elder. Its distended underbelly hung vulnerably low — so low I wondered if it would scrape its undercarriage when climbing up and over speed bumps.

It was big, it was beautiful and, best of all, it was only $1,500.

While the ad promised that the van "drives great," it had more than enough problems to justify its price tag: one of the two side doors wouldn't open, there were large patches on the windows where the tint had peeled off, and the tires were bald — so bald that, later on, when I went to buy a part at Sears, a couple of mechanics doubled over in laughter when I asked them if they thought the tires would pass inspection.

"I'll take it," I told John anyway, unable to hold back my grin. Despite its deformities, it was love at first sight.

I had been accepted into Duke's graduate liberal studies program, but I couldn't 5 afford it. I had just paid off my $32,000 undergraduate debt, I was nearly broke, and the prospect of taking out loans was unthinkable. Going back into debt made about as much sense as running out of a burning building just to run into another.

Today, the cost of higher education is ridiculous. Average tuition at a public university, in state, is $8,655. At a private, it's $29,056. My program would cost, in total, a reasonable $11,000 after grant aid. But it's not just tuition that puts students into debt; it's room and board. At Duke, where rates are similar to universities across the country, a non-air-conditioned dorm with two roommates costs $5,464 an academic year. The cheapest meal plan for freshmen is a ghastly $5,540, or $27 a day.

When I added up the costs of tuition, books, transportation, food, housing, not to mention car insurance, utilities and, dare I say, a date, I felt hopeless. I had only $4,000 to my name and no possessions except a backpack full of camping gear. But as desperate as I was, I was determined to go back to school.

Which brought me back to: *Could I live in a van?*

The van-dwelling lifestyle, I figured, would eliminate many of the costs. For Internet and electricity, I'd use the library. For showers, I'd buy a cheap campus gym membership. For food, I'd cook my own meals. For rent, well, I wouldn't have any rent. For dates, well, I probably wouldn't have any of them, either.

Seven and a half years before, when I had enrolled at the University at Buffalo as 10 an undergraduate, I wasn't the sort of person who would have done something as bold and weird and possibly illegal as secretly living in a big creepy van on a college campus. But something had changed on my journey to get out of debt.

Along with owing $32,000, I'd graduated with an unmarketable degree in history and English. Naturally, I struggled to find work and wound up taking a $9-an-hour job as a tour guide and cook at a remote truck stop called Coldfoot in Alaska's Arctic. But while I took the job out of desperation, I'd accidentally placed myself in a near-ideal situation to pay off my debt. In Coldfoot, the nearest store was 250 miles away (eliminating all temptations to buy stuff), there was no cellphone reception (making a phone plan unnecessary), and workers got free room and board (no food, rent or utility costs). After a year, I had paid off $18,000. A year later, I got a better-paying seasonal job with the Park Service. After two and a half years of work, I was debt free.

But my journey wasn't just a financial awakening. I had learned about subsistence living in Arctic villages, and worked with a 74-year-old maintenance man who lived in his 1980 Chevy Suburban year-round. I began to bring into question what passed for "normal" down in the lower 48, especially when it often led to a lifetime of work, bills and Bed Bath & Beyond purchases. Out of debt, I felt for the first time that my life was my own, and that I could do whatever I wished with it.

And more than anything I wished to use this freedom to continue the liberal arts education that had put me into so much debt. While the cost of my education had chained my ankles to the steel balls of debt, the liberal arts had freed some other part of me. Between a Thoreauvian van-dwelling experiment and studying the great thinkers, I thought Duke would help me become a better person. Living in a van wouldn't just be a way for me to afford school. It would be an adventure. It would be my "Walden on Wheels."

"Could I live in a van?" I asked myself one last time. *Why the hell not?*

The spring semester would start in just a couple of days, so I spent a day making the van as comfortable as I could. I removed the two middle pilot seats to create living space, brought in a plastic storage container to hold my possessions, neatly folded all my clothes into my suitcase, and bought a big black cloth to hang behind my driver and passenger seats so that no one could see me inside. 15

I knew I had the personality for van dwelling. I'd developed a comfort with tight quarters, a sixth sense for cheapness and a tolerance for squalor that was (I hate to brag) unequaled. I had the physical constitution for it, too: I was blessed with a high tolerance for cold temperatures, practically no sense of smell and a bladder (I hate to brag) the size of a football.

But the first few weeks didn't match up with my romantic vision of a Waldenesque life of ancient texts and quiet solitude. I was assigned to the Mill Lot, a parking lot in the middle of a busy shopping district, a mile from campus, in the heart of Durham. I parked in between a college bar and an apartment building within eyeshot of office windows where men and women in business attire, I worried, might discover me.

Although the lot was rarely visited, I was constantly paranoid about getting discovered. Because I didn't know what Duke would say if it learned of my experiment, I was determined to keep the van a secret. I wouldn't tell anyone. And to ensure "stealth," as van dwellers call it (see the Yahoo message board "VanDwellers"), each morning I lifted up the blinds and looked out the windows to make sure no one saw me leave the van, and I didn't re-enter until late at night. Whenever the subject of my home came up in conversations with fellow students, I lied my pants off.

My secret was making it impossible to make friends, I was sleeping in temperatures as low as 10 degrees, and as a bachelor living in tight quarters, I was constantly inhaling air riddled with strange odors. Worst of all, I felt a terrible loneliness settle deep into me. To compensate, I began to sing and talk to myself with unprecedented frequency.

My main concern, though, was my dwindling money supply. After my first week [20] of purchases — the van, books, school fees, car insurance, food and a cellphone bill — I had less than $1,000 left in savings and $2,000 to pay in tuition. I had nothing else to cut back on, so I tried to eat as little as possible. Walking back from the library one night, I spotted a few mangled slices of pizza lying in a box on the lawn. A savage hunger roared in my belly. Has it already come to this?

My worries were temporarily alleviated when I became a paid "study participant" for Duke's neuroscience department. Several times a week, for $10 an hour, I was zapped by electrodes, pricked by needles and dazed by pharmaceuticals. Shamelessly, I donated three of my four primary bodily fluids. Later, I found out about studies that paid $20 an hour to perform cognitive tests inside an M.R.I.

Though the van-dwelling lifestyle had its share of hardships, I adapted. On my isobutane backpacking stove, I cooked lavish meals each night, usually some combination of vegetables, noodles and peanut butter. I had only one pot, so all my meals were stews: spaghetti stew, rice and bean stew, vegetable stew, with healthy, calorie-dense dollops of peanut butter mixed in. For breakfast, I'd have cereal with powdered milk, and for lunch I'd make sandwiches and carry them to campus. At the gym, I showered, shaved and brushed my teeth, and filled up large water bottles for cooking.

I washed my clothes every few weeks at a laundromat a short walk from my parking space, and I did all of my studying at the campus library, where I used the free Wi-Fi and charged up my electronics. The van offered no protection from the cold, but once I shivered into my thermal underwear and slipped into my sleeping bag, burritoed in my own body heat, I'd fall into a deep and peaceful slumber.

The van-dwelling lifestyle proved to be as affordable as I'd suspected. I was able to eat for $4.34 a day and I lived on $103 a week. My finances became even more manageable when I got a part-time job tutoring at an inner-city elementary school.

I didn't buy my first meal at a restaurant until more than halfway through the [25] semester, on a weeklong trip to a field station for my "Biodiversity in North Carolina" class. The day before I was to go, my mother sent me an e-mail reminding me about my tax return. I'd get a refund! It was a $1,600 golden ticket that Uncle Sam was going to slip into my bank account. I was rich. This was a turning point, I realized. I had financial security for the first time in months. I'm not poor anymore, I thought nostalgically.

Knowing that my tax refund was coming, I slackened my Spartan standards: I bought a case of beer, I dined at a restaurant twice, and at the field station I slept in a heated room on a comfortable bed. But treating myself made me feel a strange sense of guilt, as if I'd cut some corner I promised myself I wouldn't cut. During my third night at the station, beleaguered with self-reproach, I dragged my sleeping bag outside and slept on the pavement under the stars. I didn't need these things. The beer, the food or even the bed. I didn't even really want them. I was buying stuff simply because I could afford it. If you put a man in a country club, he'll feel the need for a yacht. But if you drop him in the wilderness, his desires will be only those essential to his survival. I had decided not to take out loans for graduate school in part because I knew that if I allowed myself access to easy money, I'd again fall victim to the consumerist trap. I'd be indiscreet with my money. I'd begin to pay for and rely on things I thought I needed but didn't. I'd lose perspective. I didn't want to once again be swallowed whole by the dominant culture, accepting its norms and values and desires as my own.

I knew what I was missing in my life. It wasn't things. It wasn't heat, plumbing, an iPhone or a plasma-screen TV. It was people. It was a community. It was a meaningful role to play in society. And these were things — as much as I wanted them — that I knew I could temporarily do without.

When not at work or in class, I would lie in bed for hours, reading, thinking, doing nothing, enjoying the solitude, staring at the ceiling, idly musing, unworried about feeling industrious or useful. I pondered everything from the Milky Way to the fallen crumb on my floor.

Oh, and the liberal arts. Studying liberal arts, after years spent working at far-flung camps that didn't have as much as a stack of used books, felt like vital fare for a famished soul. I read Rousseau and Diogenes and Thoreau, and my liberal arts education, as well as the education of living in a van, came together like two rivers meeting at a confluence and flowing together as one.

After the semester, I went back to Alaska for the summer, where I worked and filled up my depleted bank account. As the fall approached, I looked up rates of apartments around Duke. But I began to think of how my van had begun to feel less like an experiment and more like a real home. I remembered the half-dozen dogwood trees that shadowed my parking spot and bore branches heavy with thick, lustrous white flowers, and how they buzzed with a million bumblebees and smelled of a woman's hair. I'd remember how, on mornings, I'd awake to a medley of birdsong so loud and cheery you'd think my little hermitage was tucked away in a copse of trees at Walden Pond.   30

To me, Thoreau's cabin wasn't just a home; it was the reimagining of a life; it was the conviction that we can turn the wildest figments of our imagination into something real. And I knew that whether I'd come to live in a home on wheels or in one fastened to the ground, I'd in some sense be a van dweller for life.

That fall semester, I asked myself, "Could I live in a van?"

Could I not?

(2013)

Questions

1. What are Ken Ilgunas's reasons for living in a van? How do they compare with Thoreau's reasons for living in a cabin? Why does Ilgunas call his enterprise a "Thoreauvian van-dwelling experiment" (par. 13)? Why would he title his book *Walden on Wheels*?

2. When Ilgunas received his tax refund, he spent his money on what Thoreau would call "luxuries," only to report, "I didn't need these things" (par. 26). What does Ilgunas's experiment teach him about "economy," as Thoreau saw it?

3. Ilgunas writes, "To me, Thoreau's cabin wasn't just a home; it was the reimagining of a life; it was the conviction that we can turn the wildest figments of our imagination into something real" (par. 31). Near the end of *Walden*, Thoreau writes, "If you have built castles in the air, your work need not be lost; that is where they should be. Now put the foundations under them." Compare those two statements. To what extent does Ilgunas's experiment respond to what Thoreau enjoins?

4. What is the main point Ilgunas wishes to leave with his readers? What is your overall response to his piece? Is it admirable? Realistic? Could you see yourself becoming a Thoreau for our time, as Ilgunas has? Explain.

Making Connections

1. Imagine that Bill McKibben (p. 759) and Annie Dillard (p. 785) could respond to "A Short History of America" by Robert Crumb (p. 783). What might each of them say?

2. Compare and contrast the perspectives on Thoreau presented by McKibben and William Powers (p. 795).

3. Compare and contrast E. B. White's (p. 779) and E. O. Wilson's (p. 788) "letters" to Thoreau. Which one do you prefer? Why?

4. Sue Monk Kidd (p. 793) writes about her "Thoreau experiment"; Powers discusses "the Walden experiment"; Ken Ilgunas (p. 802) writes about his "Thoreauvian van-dwelling experiment." What is the significance of the word choice in each case?

5. In two different places in her essay, Dillard deliberately evokes Thoreau's *Walden*. Identify the passages and discuss their effect on her meaning.

6. Compare Kidd and Ilgunas on their ideas of "doing nothing."

7. Compare the perspectives of Wilson, Kidd, and Powers. What ideas do they share? How do they differ?

Entering the Conversation

As you respond to each of the following prompts, support your position with appropriate evidence, including at least three of the sources in this Conversation on the legacy of Thoreau, unless otherwise indicated.

1. In his 2008 book, *Promised Land: Thirteen Books That Changed America*, Jay Parini writes, "*Walden* presents a challenge on every page, as Thoreau lays down

the gauntlet, saying: Look at me. Then look at yourself. Are you living up to your potential? Are you learning from life what it really has to teach? Have you fronted the essentials in your own fashion?" Do you feel that challenge as you read *Walden*? Write an essay that examines the validity of Parini's claim.

2. In *The Thoreau You Didn't Know* (2009), Robert Sullivan imagines Thoreau in modern America, and asks:

> Would he blog? Would he but fish only from sustainable industries when ordering seafood at a restaurant? Would he use Google or Yahoo! Or another web browser, since Google depends on hydroelectric power that affects salmon runs in the Pacific Northwest, and would he use a Blackberry in a restaurant or wait until he got outside or back to his hotel room? Most crucially, perhaps, what kind of car would Thoreau drive?

Why do you suppose the legacy of Thoreau is so strong that a writer would even pose such questions? How would you answer two of them?

3. "In one book . . . he surpasses everything we have had in America," Robert Frost said of Thoreau. Based on your knowledge of American literature, defend or challenge Frost's claim.

4. An 1854 review of *Walden* in the *Boston Daily Journal* begins, "This is a remarkable book." The review concludes, "But while many will be fascinated by its contents, few will be improved . . . the best that can be said of the work in its probable effects is, that while many will be charmed by the descriptive powers of the author, and will smile at his extravagant ideas, few will be influenced by his opinions. This is a negative virtue in a book which might do much mischief if the author could establish a bond of sympathy with the reader." What do you suppose could be the "mischief" that the book might do? Write an essay that supports or refutes the assertions made in the review.

5. "The Criminalization of Natural Play," a chapter from *Last Child in the Woods* (2008) by contemporary environmentalist and educator Richard Louv, begins with an epigraph from *Walden*: "For many years I was self-appointed inspector of snowstorms and rainstorms." Complaining about ever-increasing restrictions on play and access to nature for children, Louv writes, "They want to let their imaginations run; they want to see where a stream of water takes them." Why would the example of Henry David Thoreau serve as a good one for children today?

6. Thoreau discusses "modern improvements" (note that he puts the phrase in quotation marks) and says, "As if the main object were to talk fast and not to talk sensibly. We are eager to tunnel under the Atlantic and bring the old world some weeks nearer to the new: but perchance the first news that will leak through into the broad, flapping American ear will be that the Princess Adelaide has the whooping cough" (par. 27). Later on, he disparages the telegraph and the post office. One might wonder whether Neil Postman had Thoreau in mind when writing in *Amusing Ourselves to Death* that "the contribution of the telegraph to public discourse was to dignify irrelevance and amplify impotence." Write an essay in

which you consider the implications of Thoreau's and Postman's statements as they relate to contemporary society. Use your own observation and experience as evidence to support your argument.

7. As noted in the introduction to this Conversation, Thoreau's legacy may be seen as fivefold: he is a model of self-reliance, of political integrity, of transcendentalist belief, of environmentalist concern, and of visionary thinking. Which of these do you see as the most important? Explain why.

8. In "*Walden*: Living Deliberately," Bill McKibben writes, "In the 154 years since *Walden*, Thoreau has become ever more celebrated in theory and ever more ignored in practice" (par. 7). Write an essay in which you defend, challenge, or qualify McKibben's assertion.

Grammar as Rhetoric and Style
Cumulative, Periodic, and Inverted Sentences

Most of the time, writers of English use the following standard sentence patterns:

Subject/Verb (SV)

    S   V

The man nodded.   —Harriet Beecher Stowe

Subject/Verb/Subject complement (SVC)

    S   V   C

Society is a wave.   —Ralph Waldo Emerson

Subject/Verb/Direct object (SVO)

    S   V   O

Haley gave an uneasy growl.   —Harriet Beecher Stowe

Subject/Verb/Indirect object/Direct object (SVIO)

     S   V   I   O

[*you* understood] Tell me that.   —Herman Melville

To make longer sentences, writers often coordinate two or more of the standard sentence patterns or subordinate one sentence pattern to another. To make longer sentences, writers often coordinate two or more of the standard sentence patterns using a coordinating conjunction such as *and*, *but*, or *so*, or subordinate one sentence pattern or another. (See the grammar lesson about subordination on p. 836.) Here are examples of both techniques.

Coordinating patterns

                        S   V   O

The woman's passionate exclamations collected a crowd around her, and the

 S   V   O

trader briefly explained to them the cause of the agitation.

                                              —HARRIET BEECHER STOWE

       S   V

A mass of people, inactive, except as applauding spectators, hemmed the

   O   S   V

procession in, and several women ran along the sidewalks, piercing the
confusion of heavier sounds, with their shrill voices of mirth or terror.

                                             —NATHANIEL HAWTHORNE

          S V   O   S V   C

At last he broke the silence, and that was a relief to both of us.

                                             —HARRIET JACOBS

Subordinating one pattern to another

S V   C   S   V

It was a bright, tranquil evening when the boat stopped at the wharf at Louisville.

                                           —HARRIET BEECHER STOWE

            S   V ┌───────────────────O───────────────┐

While the editors argue that the slaves were in fact the prime movers of emancipation,

                S   V ┌───O───┐

nowhere do they deny Lincoln's centrality to the events that culminated in universal
freedom.   —IRA BERLIN

       S V   O   S V   C

When I wrote the following pages, or rather the bulk of them, I lived alone, in the
woods, a mile from any neighbor, in a house which I had built myself, on the shore

                                  V   O

of Walden Pond, in Concord, Massachusetts, and earned my living by the labor of
my hands only.   —HENRY DAVID THOREAU

                                                   ┌───S───┐

Approaching Concord, doing forty, doing forty-five, doing fifty, the steering wheel

 V   O   V   S

held snug in my palms, the highway held grimly in my vision, the crown of the
road now serving me (on the righthand curves), now defeating me (on the lefthand

S┌─── V ───┐   O

curves), I began to rouse myself from the stupefaction which a day's motor journey induces.
—E. B. WHITE

One disadvantage of sticking with standard sentence patterns, coordinating them or subordinating them, is that several standard sentences in a row become monotonous. So writers break out of the standard patterns now and then by using a more unusual pattern, such as the **cumulative sentence**, the **periodic sentence**, or the **inverted sentence**. When you use one of these sentence patterns, you call attention to that sentence because its pattern contrasts significantly with those of the sentences surrounding it. You can use unusual sentence patterns to emphasize a point, as well as to control sentence rhythm, increase tension, or create a dramatic impact. In other words, using an unusual pattern helps you avoid monotony in your writing.

Cumulative Sentence

The cumulative, or "loose," sentence begins with a standard sentence pattern (shown here in blue) and adds multiple details *after* it. The details can take the form of subordinate clauses or different kinds of phrases. These details accumulate, or pile up — hence, the name *cumulative*.

> He now roamed desperately, and at random, through the town, almost ready to believe that a spell was on him, like that, by which a wizard of his country, had once kept three pursuers wandering, a whole winter night, within twenty paces of the cottage which they sought.
> —NATHANIEL HAWTHORNE

> It is rather for us to be here dedicated to the great task remaining before us — that from these honored dead we take increased devotion to that cause for which they gave the last full measure of devotion — that we here highly resolve that these dead shall not have died in vain — that this nation, under God, shall have a new birth of freedom — and that government of the people, by the people, for the people, shall not perish from the earth.
> —ABRAHAM LINCOLN

> We ended up on an island along the coast of Florida, in a place by the sea where I leave the doors flung open to the sound of the waves, where early in the morning pelicans flap through the salted fog and dolphins spew their breath beyond the jetty.
> —SUE MONK KIDD

In the cumulative sentence from Sue Monk Kidd, the independent clause focuses on place, an island in Florida. Then the sentence accumulates a string of modifiers that describe that place with sensory details. Using a cumulative sentence allows Kidd to include all of these modifiers in one smooth sentence rather than use a series of shorter sentences that repeat "island." Furthermore, this accumulation of modifiers takes the reader into the scene just as the writer experiences it: one detail at a time.

Periodic Sentence

The periodic sentence *begins* with multiple details and holds off a standard sentence pattern — the subject and predicate (shown here in blue) — until the end.

In the following periodic sentence, Henry David Thoreau begins with several modifiers that detail his thoughts of John Brown. The independent clause comes at the end.

> When I think of him, and his six sons, and his son-in-law, — not to enumerate the others, — enlisted for this fight, proceeding coolly, reverently, humanely to work, for months, if not years, sleeping and waking upon it, summering and wintering the thought, without expecting any reward but a good conscience, while almost all America stood ranked on the other side, I say again, that it affects me as a sublime spectacle.   —HENRY DAVID THOREAU

In the following periodic sentence, Herman Melville packs the front of the sentence with phrases providing elaborate detail. His modifiers describe the circumstances that propel him to "go to sea," with the independent clause containing the subject and the predicate coming at the end.

> Whenever I find myself growing grim about the mouth; whenever it is a damp, drizzly November in my soul; whenever I find myself involuntarily pausing before coffin warehouses, and bringing up the rear of every funeral I meet; and especially whenever my hypos get such an upper hand of me, that it requires a strong moral principle to prevent me from deliberately stepping into the street, and methodically knocking people's hats off — then, I account it high time to get to sea as soon as I can.   —HERMAN MELVILLE

The vivid descriptions and figurative language engage us, so that by the end of the sentence we can feel (or at least imagine) what Ishmael, Melville's narrator, feels about going to sea. By placing the descriptions at the beginning of the sentence, Melville demonstrates how a series of impressions and circumstances can lead to a decision to act. Could Melville have written this as a cumulative sentence? He probably could have by moving things around—"I account it high time to get to sea as soon as I can whenever..."—and then providing the details. The impact of the descriptive detail would be similar in some ways but not exactly the same. Clearly, Melville preferred the periodic to the cumulative in this case.

Whether you choose to place detail at the beginning or the end of a sentence often depends on the surrounding sentences. Unless you have a good reason, though, you probably should not put one cumulative sentence after another or one periodic sentence after another. Instead, by shifting sentence patterns, you can vary sentence length and change the rhythm of your sentences.

Finally, perhaps the most famous example of the periodic sentence in modern English prose is the fourth sentence in paragraph 14 of Martin Luther King Jr.'s "Letter from Birmingham Jail." It can be found on page 1345.

Inverted Sentence

In every standard English sentence pattern, the subject comes before the verb (SV). But if a writer chooses, he or she can invert the standard sentence pattern and put the verb before the subject (VS) or the object before the subject or verb (OVS). This is called an **inverted sentence**. Inversion is more common in poetry than prose, as the following examples illustrate:

>   V   S   O
> Comes a still voice — Yet a few days, and thee
>   S   ⌐V⌐
> The all-beholding sun shall see no more
> In all his course . . .
>
>   —WILLIAM CULLEN BRYANT

>   S V C   O S V
> The port is near, the bells I hear, the people all exulting,
>   V   S   O
> While follow eyes the steady keel, the vessel grim and daring . . .
>
>   —WALT WHITMAN

Here are three prose examples:

>   C   C
> A settled apathy, a gradual wasting away of the person, and frequent although
>   C   V   S
> transient affections of a partially cataleptical character were the unusual diagnosis.
>
>   —EDGAR ALLAN POE

>   C   V S   V
> Accursed be he who willingly saddens an immortal spirit, doomed to infamy in
>   V
> later, wiser ages, doomed in future stages of his own being to deadly penance, only
> short of death.   —MARGARET FULLER

>   ⌐V⌐   ⌐   S   ⌐
> Already from your prison has come a shout of triumph against the giant sin of our
> country.   —FRANCES ELLEN WATKINS HARPER

The inverted sentence pattern slows the reader down because it is simply more difficult to comprehend inverted word order. Take this example from Ralph Waldo Emerson.

> High be his heart, faithful his will, clear his sight, that he may in good earnest be doctrine, society, law to himself, that a simple purpose may be to him as strong as iron necessity is to others.   —RALPH WALDO EMERSON

In this example, Emerson calls attention to the adjectives (the subject complements "high, "faithful," and "clear") that describe his subject's condition, placing attention on those features while avoiding beginning with the repetitive "his." Consider the difference had he written the following:

> His heart is high, his will faithful, his sight clear . . .

This "revised" version is easier to read quickly, and even though the meaning is essentially the same, the emphasis is different. In fact, to understand the full impact, we need to consider the sentence as a whole. The virtues extolled at the beginning (loftiness, faith, and loyalty, clarity of vision) are those necessary for strength of purpose and self-reliance. The emphasis on the virtues that the inversion provides, rather than on the hypothetical man whom they describe, serves Emerson's purpose.

A Word about Punctuation

It is important to follow the normal rules of comma use when punctuating unusual sentence patterns. In a cumulative sentence, the descriptors that follow the main clause generally need to be set off from it and one another with commas, as in the examples from Hawthorne and Kidd on page 811. Likewise, in a periodic sentence, the series of clauses or phrases that precede the subject should be set off from the subject and one another by commas, as in the example from Thoreau on page 812. When writing an inverted sentence, you may be tempted to insert a comma between the verb and the subject because of the unusual order — but do not the comma insert!

• EXERCISE 1 •

For each of the following, craft a periodic, a cumulative, or an inverted sentence by filling in the blanks. Identify each sentence by type.

1. Among the tangle of weeds and brush were _____.

2. Hoping, knowing _____, but realizing _____, the candidate _____.

3. All his life, he would remember that fateful moment when the fish _____, _____, _____.

4. If you _____ and if you _____, then _____.

5. Into the clouds soared _____.

6. Only when _____ will _____.

• EXERCISE 2 •

The following paragraph from *Who Freed the Slaves?* by James M. McPherson consists of five sentences: a simple declarative sentence; then a complex sentence that begins with a conjunction and an adverbial clause; another simple declarative sentence; next a short cumulative sentence; and finally a lengthy periodic sentence. Keep the first and third sentences as they are. Reverse the order of sentence two, beginning with the main clause and ending with the subordinate clause, and then rewrite the cumulative sentence as periodic and the periodic as cumultive. Compare the two paragraphs. Discuss the relationship among the sentences in each paragraph and the rhetorical effect of syntax on each.

Regrettably, Lincoln did not live to see the final ratification of the Thirteenth Amendment. But if he had never lived, it seems safe to say that we would not have had a Thirteenth Amendment in 1865. In that sense, the traditional answer to the question "Who Freed the Slaves?" is the right answer. Lincoln did not accomplish this in the manner sometimes symbolically portrayed, breaking the chains of helpless and passive bondsmen with the stroke of a pen by signing the Emancipation Proclamation. But by pronouncing slavery a moral evil that must come to an end and then winning the presidency in 1860, provoking the South to secede, by refusing to compromise on the issue of slavery's expansion or on Fort Sumter, by careful leadership and timing that kept a fragile Unionist coalition together in the first year of war and committed it to emancipation in the second, by refusing to compromise this policy once he had adopted it, and by prosecuting the war to unconditional victory as commander in chief of an army of liberation, Abraham Lincoln freed the slaves.

• EXERCISE 3 •

Identify each of the following sentences as periodic, cumulative, or inverted, and discuss the impact of using that pattern. (Each sentence is a direct quotation from essays in this chapter, so you might want to check the context of the sentence to appreciate its impact more fully.) Note that some sentences use more than one unusual pattern.

1. It was June and everywhere June was publishing her immemorial stanza; in the lilacs, in the syringa, in the freshly edged paths and the sweetness of moist beloved gardens, and the little wire wickets that preserve the tulips' front.
   —E. B. WHITE

2. About eleven o'clock the next day, a mixed throng was gathered around the court-house steps, — smoking, chewing, spitting, swearing, and conversing, according to their respective tastes and turns, — waiting for the auction to commence.
   —HARRIET BEECHER STOWE

3. While the objects around me — while the carvings of the ceilings, the sombre tapestries of the walls, the ebon blackness of the floors, and the phantasmagoric armorial trophies which rattled as I strode, were but matters to which, or to such as which, I had been accustomed from my infancy — while I hesitated not to acknowledge how familiar was all this — I still wondered to find how unfamiliar were the fancies which ordinary images were stirring up.   —Edgar Allan Poe

4. Let us, then, take up the sword, trusting in God, who will defend the right, remembering that these are other days than those of yore; that the world today is on the side of freedom and universal political equality; that the war cry of the howling leaders of Secession and treason is: "Let us drive back the advance guard of civil and religious freedom; let us have more slave territory; let us build stronger the tyrant system of slavery in the great American Republic."   —Alfred M. Green

5. Now, at the expiration of four years, during which public declarations have been constantly called forth on every point and phase of the great contest which still absorbs the attention, and engrosses the energies of the nation, little that is new could be presented.   —Abraham Lincoln

6. To this little speech Mr. Lincoln listened with earnest attention and with very apparent sympathy, and replied to each point in his own peculiar, forcible way.   —Frederick Douglass

7. I endeavoured to believe that much, if not all of what I felt, was due to the bewildering influence of the gloomy furniture of the room — of the dark and tattered draperies, which, tortured into motion by the breath of a rising tempest, swayed fitfully to and fro upon the walls, and rustled uneasily about the decorations of the bed.   —Edgar Allan Poe

8. Though the national independence be blurred by the servility of individuals, though freedom and equality have been proclaimed only to leave room for a monstrous display of slave-dealing and slave-keeping; though the free American so often feels himself free, like the Roman, only to pamper his appetites and his indolence through the misery of his fellow beings, still it is not in vain, that the verbal statement has been made, "All men are born free and equal."   —Margaret Fuller

9. Sustained by a consciousness that our transition from the former Union to the present Confederacy has not proceeded from any disregard on our part of our just obligations, or any failure to perform every constitutional duty — moved by no intention or design to invade the rights of others — anxious to cultivate peace and commerce with all nations — if we may not hope to avoid war, we may at least expect that posterity will acquit us of having needlessly engaged in it.   —Jefferson Davis

10. Under these circumstances, without attaching importance, in themselves, to the changes demanded by the champions of woman, we hail them as signs of the times. —MARGARET FULLER

11. I felt creeping upon me, by slow yet certain degrees, the wild influences of his own fantastic yet impressive superstitions.   —EDGAR ALLAN POE

• EXERCISE 4 •

Following are several examples of unusual sentence patterns. Using each one as a model, write your own sentence about texts or issues from this chapter, imitating the syntax of each.

1. Night came on, — night calm, unmoved, and glorious, shining down with her innumerable and solemn angel eyes, twinkling, beautiful, but silent.
   —HARRIET BEECHER STOWE

2. If we shall suppose that American Slavery is one of those offences which, in the providence of God, must needs come, but which, having continued through His appointed time, He now wills to remove, and that He gives to both North and South, this terrible war, as the woe due to those by whom the offence came, shall we discern therein any departure from those divine attributes which the believers in a Living God always ascribe to Him?
   —ABRAHAM LINCOLN

3. Now, if it is deemed necessary that I should forfeit my life for the furtherance of the ends of justice, and mingle my blood further with the blood of my children and with the blood of millions in this slave country whose rights are disregarded by wicked, cruel, and unjust enactments, — I submit; so let it be done!   —JOHN BROWN

4. In front of the Gothic window stood the old citizen, wrapped in a wide gown, his grey periwig exchanged for a nightcap, which was thrust back from his forehead, and his silk stockings hanging down about his legs.
   —NATHANIEL HAWTHORNE

5. The rugged battle of fate, where strength is born, we shun.
   —RALPH WALDO EMERSON

6. Fondly do we hope — fervently do we pray — that this mighty scourge of war may speedily pass away.   —ABRAHAM LINCOLN

7. At length, after many pauses to examine the gorgeous display of goods in the shop windows, and after suffering some rebukes for the impertinence

of his scrutiny into people's faces, the Major's kinsman found himself near the steepled building, still unsuccessful in his search.

—NATHANIEL HAWTHORNE

8. During the whole of a dull, dark, and soundless day in the autumn of the year, when the clouds hung oppressively low in the heavens, I had been passing alone, on horseback, through a singularly dreary tract of country, and at length found myself, as the shades of the evening drew on, within view of the melancholy House of Usher.   —EDGAR ALLAN POE

9. When first I took up my abode in the woods, that is, began to spend my nights as well as days there, which, by accident, was on Independence day, or the fourth of July, 1845, my house was not finished for winter, but was merely a defence against the rain, without plastering or chimney, the walls being of rough weather-stained boards, with wide chinks, which made it cool at night.   —HENRY DAVID THOREAU

10. I went to the woods because I wished to live deliberately, to front only the essential facts of life, and see if I could not learn what it had to teach, and not, when I came to die, discover that I had not lived.

—HENRY DAVID THOREAU

• EXERCISE 5 •

In this chapter, you have learned about sentence structure, or syntax—specifically, about cumulative, periodic, and inverted sentences. Write a paragraph that includes at least one example of each type. Also include a simple sentence and one that uses either coordination or subordination. Then, rewrite your cumulative sentence as periodic, your periodic as cumulative, and your inverted sentence in normal word order (SVO). Carefully consider the rhetorical effects of each pattern. Finally, rewrite your paragraph using those patterns that you deem most effective. Explain the reasons for your choices.

Suggestions for Writing

America in Conflict

1. Women's rights and the status of women are central issues in the selections by Margaret Fuller (p. 607), Sojourner Truth (p. 625), and Harriet Jacobs (p. 675). Compare and contrast how the three writers use rhetorical strategies to establish their positions about women in America.

2. Consider the contrasting visual images found at the beginning and end of the chronological portion of this chapter: the romantic visions depicted by Thomas Cole (p. 556) and Asher B. Durand (p. 557) and the reports of grim reality by Alexander Gardner (p. 685) and Timothy O'Sullivan (p. 686). How effectively do these contrasting visuals serve to frame, or bookend, the period covered by the chapter?

3. In his *Journal* entry of March 1845, Ralph Waldo Emerson writes: "Poetry must be new as foam, and as old as the rock." In his essay "Circles," he writes, "The poets are thus liberating gods." This chapter contains the work of six poets: William Cullen Bryant, Henry Wadsworth Longfellow, Walt Whitman, Allen Ginsberg, Herman Melville, and William Stafford. Select one of Emerson's statements and write an essay that defends or challenges its application to three of the poets in the chapter.

4. Compare and contrast the narratives of Frederick Douglass (p. 614) and Harriet Jacobs (p. 675). Which one is more compelling? Why?

5. Slavery is addressed directly by the autobiographical works of Douglass and Jacobs, by Harriet Beecher Stowe's fictional account (p. 627), by Alfred M. Green's speech (p. 673), by the song "No More Auction Block for Me" (p. 674), and by the auction block monument (p. 641). Compare and contrast three of these texts as they address the institution of slavery.

6. Select one of the following statements from Alexis de Tocqueville's 1835 book, *Democracy in America*. Write an essay that defends, challenges, or qualifies the statement's validity, using at least three texts from the chapter to support your position.

> I know no country in which there is so little independence of mind and freedom of discussion as in America.

> The great advantages of the Americans consists in their being able to commit faults which they may afterwards repair.

> The great advantage of the Americans is that they have arrived at a state of democracy without having to endure a democratic revolution; and that they are born equal, instead of becoming so.

> It is by the enjoyment of a dangerous freedom that the Americans learn the art of rendering the danger of freedom less formidable.

7. It is often suggested that the works of many of the writers in this period represent a tension between optimism and pessimism, between hope and mystery, between the exploration of evil and the possibility of good, between darkness and light. On one side would be Emerson, Thoreau, and Whitman; on the other we would have Hawthorne, Poe, and Melville. Consider the following statements — the first, about Hawthorne, and the second, about Melville — from

historian Vernon Louis Parrington's 1927 work, *Main Currents in American Thought*:

> And so while the Concord thinkers were proclaiming man to be the indubitable child of God, Hawthorne was critically examining the question of evil as it appeared in the light of his own experience. It was the central, fascinating problem of his intellectual life, and in pursuit of a solution he probed curiously into the hidden, furtive recesses of the soul.

> All the powers of darkness fought over him. They drove him down into the gloom of his tormented soul, and if they did not conquer, they left him maimed and stricken. The golden dreams of transcendental faith, that buoyed up Emerson and gave hope to Thoreau, turned to ashes in his mouth; the white gleams of mysticism that now and then lighted up his path died out and left him in darkness.

Select one of Parrington's statements and support, qualify, or challenge its validity, using the work of three or four writers from this chapter as evidence.

8. "Be ashamed to die unless you have won some victory for humanity!" stated Horace Mann in his commencement address at Antioch College in 1859. Write an essay about those writers and texts in this chapter that express a victory for humanity. Refer to at least three texts.

9. Many of the texts in this chapter might be said to be about the meeting of and conflict among three races: white, black, and Native American. In Alexis de Tocqueville's 1835 book, *Democracy in America*, he writes: "The human beings who are scattered over [the United States] . . . do not form, as in Europe, so many branches of the same stock. Three races, naturally distinct, and, I might almost say, hostile to each other, are discoverable among them at the first glance. Almost insurmountable barriers had been raised between them by education and law, as well as by their origin and outward characteristics, but fortune has brought them together on the same soil, where, although they are mixed, they do not amalgamate, and each race fulfills its destiny apart." Consider the implications of that statement for the texts in this chapter. Using references to at least three texts, assess the validity of the statement regarding race in America.

10. On December 2, 1841, in his *Lecture on the Times*, Ralph Waldo Emerson stated, "But turn it how we will, as we ponder this meaning of the times, every new thought drives us to the deep fact, that the Time is the child of the Eternity. The main interest which any aspects of the Times can have for us, is the great spirit which gazes through them, the light which they can shed on the wonderful questions, What we are? and Whither we tend? We do not wish to be deceived. Here we drift, like white sail across the wild ocean, now bright on the wave, now darkling in the trough of the sea; — but from what port did we sail? Who knows? Or to what port are we bound? Who knows?" Consider Emerson's statement care-

fully. Write an essay that explores Emerson's thoughts and ideas as they relate to at least three selections from the chapter.

11. Many of the works in this chapter are about the Civil War. Consider those by John Brown and Abraham Lincoln and the works by Jefferson Davis, Alfred M. Green, Harriet Beecher Stowe, Herman Meville, Timothy O'Sullivan; the song "No More Auction Block for Me"; and the recruitment poster. Write an essay about what these texts have done to enhance your understanding of that war. Refer to at least three of the texts in your response.

12. The period covered by this chapter is often called the "American Renaissance," in literary scholar F. O. Matthiessen's words, or the age of American romanticism. The chief features of romanticism are its favoring of the imagination, emotion, and intuition over reason and order; the importance of the individual and self-reliance over authority, tradition, and conformity; trust in subjectivity over objectivity; belief in the innocence of youth over the corruptions and compromises of age; a preference for the natural world, the frontier, and primitivism over civilization and urbanity; and a high regard for the rebel over the conservative. A reaction against orthodoxy, the romantic view esteems the democratic spirit, the quest for beauty and truth, and a delight in mystery and adventure and looks to nature as a source of knowledge, power, and enlightenment. The chief figures of romanticism in this chapter are William Cullen Bryant, Thomas Cole, Asher B. Durand, Nathaniel Hawthorne, Ralph Waldo Emerson, Edgar Allan Poe, Henry David Thoreau, Herman Melville, and Walt Whitman. Select three of these writers and write an essay that demonstrates them to be major voices in American romanticism. Which single writer best expresses the romantic spirit? Explain.

8

Reconstructing America
1865–1913

After the Civil War, the United States grappled with its aftermath, both joyous and mournful. How should the newly unified nation ensure the rights of millions of newly freed slaves? How should it rebuild the South and its political systems while reuniting the nation? What should be done with the leaders of the Confederacy? Presidents Abraham Lincoln, Andrew Johnson, and Ulysses S. Grant implemented policies to tackle these questions, policies that collectively came to be called Reconstruction. The issue of ensuring the rights of newly freed slaves was addressed by the ratification of the Thirteenth, Fourteenth, and Fifteenth Amendments, which outlawed slavery and granted African Americans citizenship, the right to vote, the rights of due process, and equal protection under the law. After the war, the Southern states came under the authority of the Union army, and with Reconstruction, they began again to self-govern and to have representation in the U.S. Congress. These new governments, often biracial, established public schools and charitable institutions, and raised taxes to support public works such as construction projects and transportation networks.

Despite what most believe were the good intentions of Reconstruction, the decade following the Civil War remained a period of violence and division. Racial tensions and discrimination flourished, as groups such as the Ku Klux Klan, the White League, and the Red Shirts terrorized African Americans, while regressive white politicians regained enough power to institute the discriminatory Jim Crow laws. In this chapter, readings by Paul Laurence Dunbar and Ida B. Wells-Barnett explore the pain and suffering of the African American population during this time, and correspondence between the newly freed Jourdon Anderson and his former master reveals a new American power structure. Writings by Booker T. Washington and W. E. B. DuBois highlight contrasting approaches to the education and leadership of African Americans as they assumed their full rights and responsibilities as citizens.

America experienced its most rapid westward expansion in this post–Civil War period. The Homestead Act of 1862 provided opportunities for Americans to own undeveloped federal land west of the Mississippi at no cost. This, along with mining, ranching, and the spirit of exploration and adventure, drew Americans westward. Between 1862 and 1934, 1.6 million homesteads were granted, privatizing 420,000 square miles of American land — about 10 percent of the land in the United States.

Prints and Photographs Division, Library of Congress

This woodcut, originally titled *Reconstruction of the South*, depicts a literal turning of swords into ploughshares as both the South and the Union are reconstructed following the Civil War. The center of the image features entrepreneur and philanthropist George Peabody, who gave $2 million to support education in the South through his Peabody Education Fund.

Applicants for homesteads were required to be the heads of their households or at least twenty-one years old; they had to live on the land for at least five years, build a home, and start a farm or ranch. Conditions in the American "Wild West" were notoriously difficult, and only about 40 percent of homestead applicants completed their five-year commitment and received the title to their land.

Much of this westward expansion was facilitated by the completion of the transcontinental railroad in 1869, which made travel to the West much faster and safer than it had been by wagon train. While seen as a reflection of technological innovation and inevitable "progress," the transcontinental railroad relied on cheap labor primarily provided by Chinese immigrants. At one point, 8,000 of the 10,000 men toiling for the Central Pacific Railroad were Chinese. Public concern about the impact of these workers on the labor force led to passage of the Chinese Exclusion Act in 1882, which prohibited immigration from China for the next ten years.

Westward expansion occurred at the expense of Native American populations, who were dislocated and relocated to make room for settlers. Both the settlers and the U.S. Army sent to protect them frequently met with resistance from displaced tribes, leading to skirmishes and outright battles. These conflicts have since been elevated by

Prints and Photographs Division, Library of Congress

John Gast, *American Progress*, 1872, color lithograph from an oil painting by the same title. This painting was commissioned by publisher George Crofutt and used to promote his travel guides to the American West. It appeared as a woodcut on the frontispiece of his *Transcontinental Tourist's Guide*, and copies of the color lithograph were given to each subscriber of his publication *Western World*.

Hollywood and storytellers to the level of American mythology, particularly the figure of the American cowboy. Romanticized as a brave loner who embodied the "rugged individualist" of the dime novels that popularized this image, the cowboy became a powerful part of the national narrative. A Conversation in this chapter explores the evolution of this mythic figure and considers his impact on the national character, as well as his more contemporary incarnations.

In his groundbreaking speech in 1893 at the World's Columbian Exposition, a celebration of the four hundredth anniversary of Columbus's arrival in the New World, Frederick Jackson Turner lamented the "closing" of the frontier and what that loss of a sense of infinite boundaries would mean for the national identity. His "Frontier Thesis" provided a foundation for manifest destiny, an ideology that justified territorial expansion to the Pacific Ocean and annexation of Pacific territories.

As the nation expanded, so too did its population. From the 1850s to the 1860s, immigration nearly doubled, and it continued to increase steadily until the 1930s. In this period, immigrants were primarily Europeans lured to America by the promise of freedom and prosperity. A Conversation about immigration in this chapter will ask you to consider "the lure of America" and reflect on attitudes toward immigrants both then and now.

Much of the immigrant population clustered in American urban metropolises, driven there in large part by jobs created by rapid industrial growth. In the years approaching the turn of the twentieth century, America was leading the world in the production of iron and steel, producing half of the world's cotton, corn, and oil, and mining a third of its gold and coal. As industrialization flourished, products became cheaper, giving Americans unprecedented buying power. For some, rapid industrialization meant economic prosperity and cheaper consumer goods. This resulted in the growth of a new middle class, a group who worked to live but also enjoyed leisure time, vacations, and entertainment ranging from sporting events to vaudeville shows to carnival amusements. Department stores and mail-order catalogs became prevalent. Advances in electricity revolutionized America's living and working spaces. The trolley car and the train transported Americans with extraordinary speed and convenience.

But despite these advances, most Americans were not wealthy, and urban life was particularly harsh in this period. Inhabitants of the cities experienced extreme overcrowding, crushing poverty, and disease. Children and adults toiled in factories. Schooling was still a luxury. Governments provided no social safety nets for

Prints and Photographs Division, Library of Congress

This photograph and others by photographer and social reformer Lewis Wickes Hine led to outrage over child-labor practices in America — and eventually to reforms. This particular shot was taken in Bib Mill No. 1, Macon, Georgia, in 1909. Of this photo Hine said, "Some boys were so small they had to climb up on the spinning frame to mend the broken threads and put back the empty bobbins."

their constituents. The gap between the rich and the poor became so vast that, as the saying goes, "one half of the world does not know how the other half lives." Jacob Riis took that old saying as the inspiration for his groundbreaking work of photojournalism, *How the Other Half Lives*, which illustrated the squalid conditions of New York's slums and tenement houses and exposed the country's middle and upper classes to these images for the first time. A selection of his writing, along with some of his stunning photographs, can be found in this chapter. Also included in this chapter are excerpts from Upton Sinclair's *The Jungle*, a fictional — though appallingly realistic — depiction of the treatment of workers in a Chicago meatpacking plant, and *Twenty Years at Hull House*, the memoir of Jane Addams, a social reformer and founder of one of America's first settlement houses. She writes of the poverty and abuse that pervaded Chicago and her hope to uplift her city and community through progressive reform, democratic and egalitarian social and political institutions, and suffrage and economic opportunity for all.

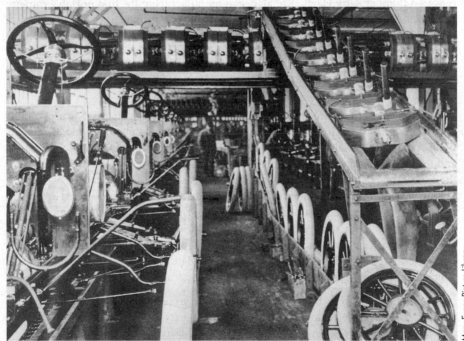

Mary Evans Picture Library

In 1913, Henry Ford installed the first moving assembly line in his Highland Park factory (in Detroit, Michigan) and revolutionized the automobile industry by producing a car every ninety-three minutes. By 1918, the plant was turning out ten thousand cars a day. The efficiency of the plant made the Ford Model T the world's first affordable automobile, making car ownership a reality for the middle class.

During this period, workers facing low wages, long hours, and dreadful living conditions collided with growing corporations that amassed enormous wealth for a few individuals. Movements emerged to improve working conditions and address growing economic inequality. Laborers organized to fight for wages, benefits, and rights. The Federation of Organized Trades and Labor Unions (later to become the American Federation of Labor) was founded in 1881. Though child labor did not formally come to an end until the 1930s, the National Child Labor Committee formed in 1904 and dedicated itself to eradicating the practice. Women began calling for full voting rights that would, for one thing, ensure they had a stronger influence over working conditions for children and for themselves. While the Nineteenth Amendment giving women the right to vote was not ratified until 1920, political and social activism during the late 1800s and early 1900s laid the foundation for passage of that legislation.

Despite the hardships endured during this period, it was also an exciting time of technological progress that would forever change Americans' way of life. The automobile began to be mass manufactured in 1901 by the Ransom E. Olds company, which would later become Oldsmobile. The Wright Brothers completed the first powered flight at Kitty Hawk. Kodak began manufacturing the first portable camera. Guglielmo Marconi sent the first successful radio communication. Thomas Edison invented the alkaline battery, the lightbulb, the phonograph, and the kinetophone — or talking motion picture. Einstein published his theory of special relativity in 1905, which, among other things, explained gravity as a curvature in space-time and laid the groundwork for the field of nuclear physics by revealing the relationship between mass and energy: $E = mc^2$.

Our national literature flourished in this era. Technologies such as the use of automated presses and the invention of the linotype machine resulted in wide dissemination of printed materials. These advances along with the rapid growth of public libraries and increased literacy rates made reading a national pastime — and a big business. By the end of the century, the term "best seller" had entered the American vernacular.

Though some of the wounds of the Civil War had been healed, westward expansion was giving way to imperialistic calls for a global presence, and changing demographics brought demands for more equitable political and social conditions. On July 4, 1913, the nation symbolically looked both backward and forward when more than fifty thousand veterans came together to commemorate the Battle of Gettysburg. In his Independence Day speech, President Woodrow Wilson struck a conciliatory note, saying:

> Do not put uniforms by. Put the harness of the present on. Lift your eyes to the great tracts of life yet to be conquered in the interest of righteous peace, of that prosperity which lies in a people's hearts and outlasts all wars and errors of men.

Yet the harmonious respite was brief; one year later, on August 14, 1914, the United States entered World War I.

JOURDON ANDERSON

Jourdon Anderson (c. 1825–1907) was an African American slave from Tennessee who was freed in 1864 by the Union army during the Civil War. Soon after his emancipation, Anderson and his family settled in Dayton, Ohio, where he worked various jobs before becoming sexton for a local church, a position he held until his death.

To My Old Master

Although there has been some doubt about the authenticity of this letter, it appears in *The Freedman's Book* (1865), by Lydia Maria Child, with the note "written just as he dictated it." The letter was also published in the *Cincinnati Commercial* and the *New York Tribune*.

Dayton, Ohio, August 7, 1865.

To my old Master, Colonel P. H. Anderson, Big Spring, Tennessee.

Sir: I got your letter, and was glad to find that you had not forgotten Jourdon, and that you wanted me to come back and live with you again, promising to do better for me than anybody else can. I have often felt uneasy about you. I thought the Yankees would have hung you long before this, for harboring Rebs they found at your house. I suppose they never heard about your going to Colonel Martin's to kill the Union soldier that was left by his company in their stable. Although you shot at me twice before I left you, I did not want to hear of your being hurt, and am glad you are still living. It would do me good to go back to the dear old home again, and see Miss Mary and Miss Martha and Allen, Esther, Green, and Lee. Give my love to them all, and tell them I hope we will meet in the better world, if not in this. I would have gone back to see you all when I was working in the Nashville Hospital, but one of the neighbors told me that Henry intended to shoot me if he ever got a chance.

I want to know particularly what the good chance is you propose to give me. I am doing tolerably well here. I get twenty-five dollars a month, with victuals and clothing; have a comfortable home for Mandy, — the folks call her Mrs. Anderson, — and the children — Milly, Jane, and Grundy — go to school and are learning well. The teacher says Grundy has a head for a preacher. They go to Sunday school, and Mandy and me attend church regularly. We are kindly treated. Sometimes we over-hear others saying, "Them colored people were slaves" down in Tennessee. The children feel hurt when they hear such remarks; but I tell them it was no disgrace in Tennessee to belong to Colonel Anderson. Many darkeys would have been proud, as I used to be, to call you master. Now if you will write and say what wages you will give me, I will be better able to decide whether it would be to my advantage to move back again.

As to my freedom, which you say I can have, there is nothing to be gained on that score, as I got my free papers in 1864 from the Provost-Marshal-General of the Department of Nashville. Mandy says she would be afraid to go back without some proof that you were disposed to treat us justly and kindly; and we have concluded to test your sincerity by asking you to send us our wages for the time we served you. This will make us forget and forgive old scores, and rely on your justice and friendship in the future. I served you faithfully for thirty-two years, and Mandy twenty years. At twenty-five dollars a month for me, and two dollars a week for Mandy, our earnings would amount to eleven thousand six hundred and eighty dollars. Add to this the interest for the time our wages have been kept back, and deduct what you paid for our clothing, and three doctor's visits to me, and pulling a tooth for Mandy, and the balance will show what we are in justice entitled to. Please send the money by Adams's Express, in care of V. Winters, Esq., Dayton, Ohio. If you fail to pay us for faithful labors in the past, we can have little faith in your promises in the future. We trust the good Maker has opened your eyes to the wrongs which you and your fathers have done to me and my fathers, in making us toil for you for generations without recompense. Here I draw my wages every Saturday night; but in Tennessee there was never any pay-day for the negroes any more than for the horses and cows. Surely there will be a day of reckoning for those who defraud the laborer of his hire.

In answering this letter, please state if there would be any safety for my Milly and   5
Jane, who are now grown up, and both good-looking girls. You know how it was with poor Matilda and Catherine. I would rather stay here and starve — and die, if it come to that — than have my girls brought to shame by the violence and wickedness of their young masters. You will also please state if there has been any schools opened for the colored children in your neighborhood. The great desire of my life now is to give my children an education, and have them form virtuous habits.

Say howdy to George Carter, and thank him for taking the pistol from you when you were shooting at me.

From your old servant,
Jourdon Anderson.
(1865)

Exploring the Text

1. What information about his "old Master" does Jourdon Anderson recall in the letter? What impression does the recollection of these details suggest about the ethos Jourdon is establishing? How do you imagine Colonel Anderson might respond when reminded, for instance, of his "harboring Rebs" (par. 1)?
2. What evidence does Jourdon provide — implicitly or explicitly — of the dignity and respectful treatment he and his family enjoy in their midwestern home?
3. What does Jourdon require in order for him to "forget and forgive old scores, and rely on [Colonel Anderson's] justice and friendship in the future" (par. 3)? What

other assurance(s) does Jourdon ask of Colonel Anderson? Based on language in the text, what do you think Jourdon believes the odds are that Colonel Anderson will meet his terms?

4. How would you describe the tone of the letter? How do irony and understatement contribute to achieving that tone?

WINSLOW HOMER

Winslow Homer (1836–1910) is considered one of the most significant American painters of the nineteenth century. Born in Boston, Massachusetts, and mainly self-taught, Homer started his career as a commercial illustrator. During the Civil War (1861–1865) he was sent to the front lines to sketch battle scenes and camp life for *Harper's* magazine.

The Veteran in a New Field

Homer completed the following painting in 1865, a few months after the end of the Civil War.

Image copyright © The Metropolitan Museum of Art. Image source: Art Resource, NY.

WINSLOW HOMER, *THE VETERAN IN A NEW FIELD*, 1865, OIL ON CANVAS, 24⅛" × 38⅛", METROPOLITAN MUSEUM OF ART, NEW YORK.
(See color insert, Image 27.)

Exploring the Text

1. What strikes you first and most powerfully about the painting? Is it a specific detail or a general feeling?
2. What does the composition of the painting suggest about its meaning? Consider the division of space, the colors, and the placement of the figure.
3. What is the effect of the central figure having his back to us, the viewers? Do you think Winslow Homer is making a statement about "turning his back" on something or someone, or does this perspective lead the viewer to a particular attitude toward the scene? Explain.
4. What biblical associations does wheat have? How might specific scriptures inform your understanding of the painting?
5. The veteran in this painting holds a scythe that was out-of-date even during this period. If you look carefully, you can see the multiple blades of a more modern cradle scythe that Homer deliberately painted over in favor of the archaic single-bladed scythe. Why might the artist have done that? What is the impact of the veteran using an old-fashioned single-bladed scythe to mow the field?
6. What is the narrative of this painting — that is, what story does it tell? Is it optimistic? Sad? Redemptive? Ambivalent? Is it a story of new beginnings, or is it an elegy? Explain your response by citing details from the painting and your understanding of its historical context.
7. Many of the Civil War's bloodiest battles were fought in fields of grain, and in Chapter 7 (p. 686) you analyzed an image of one of them in *A Harvest of Death*. That photo, like many others, pictures corpses lying on a field. Given this information, along with the details of Homer's painting, how do you interpret the title Homer chose?

 TALKBACK

Natasha Trethewey

Appointed poet laureate in 2012, Natasha Trethewey was born in Gulfport, Mississippi, in 1966 and earned an MA in literature at Hollins University in Virginia and an MFA in poetry at the University of Massachusetts. She is currently a professor of English and creative writing at Emory University in Atlanta, Georgia. Her first collection of poetry, *Domestic Work* (2000), was selected by Rita Dove as the winner of the inaugural Cave Canem Poetry Prize for the best first book by an African American poet.

Again, the Fields
After Winslow Homer

"Again, the Fields" is from *Native Guard* (2006), the book for which Trethewey was awarded the Pulitzer Prize in 2007.

the dead they lay long the lines like sheaves of Wheat I could have walked on the
boddes all most from one end too the other

No more muskets, the bone-drag
weariness of marching, the trampled
grass, soaked earth red as the wine

of sacrament. Now, the veteran
turns toward a new field, bright   5
as domes of the republic. Here,

he has shrugged off the past — his jacket
and canteen flung down in the corner.
At the center of the painting, he anchors

the trinity, joining earth and sky.   10
The wheat falls beneath his scythe —
a language of bounty — the swaths

like scripture on the field's open page.
Boundless, the wheat stretches beyond
the frame, as if toward a distant field —   15

the white canvas where sky and cotton
meet, where another veteran toils,
his hands the color of dark soil.

                                                    (2006)

Exploring the Text

1. Natasha Trethewey subtitles her poem "After Winslow Homer" and begins it
   with an epigraph quoting a Civil War soldier's letter to his father. How do
   these two introductory elements inform your reading of the poem?
2. Read the first sentence aloud, noting the line breaks as the poet indicates.
   What emotions are evoked? What tone do the first four lines establish?
3. What biblical images and associations does Trethewey include in the poem?
   What is the effect of references to "the trinity" (l. 10) or the simile "like scripture on the field's open page" (l. 13)?
4. What is the "language of bounty" (l. 12)? Consider the actual reference that
   the appositive structure indicates as well as the metaphoric meaning.
5. The "distant field" of the last three lines introduces a scene that happens
   outside the frame of the painting. What is that scene? Were you surprised
   by this turn in the poem? Why or why not? Reread the poem and consider the ways that Trethewey might be preparing the reader for the final
   stanza.

Making Connections

1. The speaker in the poem both describes and interprets Homer's painting. Which are the literal descriptions; which are interpretive?
2. How would you describe Trethewey's attitude toward Homer's painting? Is she critical? Appreciative? Admiring? Ironic? Nostalgic? Ambivalent?
3. In his announcement of Trethewey as U.S. Poet Laureate in 2012, James Billington, the librarian of Congress, said that the language of her poetry "reminds you that the experience of great art, of great poetry, is something that stretches beyond the frame it comes to you in." In what ways does "Again, the Fields" stretch beyond the frame of Homer's canvas? Discuss to what extent you think it fair to hypothesize or point out what is *not* included or addressed in a work from an earlier time period.
4. An *elegy* is a tribute to, lamentation for, or serious reflection on the dead. Compare and contrast Homer's painting and Trethewey's poem as elegies.
5. Imagine that Homer could read "Again, the Fields." What might his response be? Research Homer's participation in the Civil War; then, in his voice, write a letter to Trethewey.

EMILY DICKINSON

Born into a prominent family in Amherst, Massachusetts, Emily Dickinson (1830–1886) received some formal education at Amherst Academy and Mary Lyons Mount Holyoke Female Seminary (which became Mount Holyoke College). Dickinson was a famously shy and reclusive person who preferred to remain within her close family circle, though some contemporary scholars have begun to question that characterization. In 1862, she enclosed four poems in a letter to literary critic and abolitionist Thomas Wentworth Higginson, who had written a piece in the *Atlantic Monthly* that included practical advice for young writers. Her letter began, "Mr. Higginson, — Are you too deeply occupied to say if my verse is alive? The mind is so near itself it cannot see distinctly, and I have none to ask. Should you think it breathed, and had you the leisure to tell me, I should feel quick gratitude." Dickinson didn't sign the letter, but instead enclosed her name on a card inside a smaller envelope. Dickinson wrote more than seventeen hundred poems, but only ten were published in her lifetime.

"Hope" is the thing with feathers —

"Hope" is the thing with feathers —
That perches in the soul —
And sings the tune without the words —
And never stops — at all —

And sweetest — in the Gale — is heard —   5
And sore must be the storm —
That could abash the little Bird
That kept so many warm —

I've heard it in the chillest land —
And on the strangest Sea —   10
Yet, never, in Extremity,
It asked a crumb — of Me.

(c. 1861)

Exploring the Text

1. What associations — even archetypes — does Emily Dickinson evoke with her image of "Hope" as a bird?
2. Why would Dickinson, a brilliant poet, use such a general, sometimes derogatory, word as "thing" (l. 1)? What difference would it make to say, for instance, that Hope is the "creature" with feathers, or that Hope "wears" feathers?
3. Of what importance is it that Hope sings the "tune without the words" (l. 3) — that is, Hope does not use verbal language?
4. What is the meaning of "abash" (l. 7)? What does the sound of this term add to the meaning?
5. In what ways might you read the phrase "in Extremity" (l. 11) as ambiguous? To whom or what does it refer?
6. How does the repeated four-part structure of the three stanzas reinforce the poem's meaning?

The Soul selects her own Society —

The Soul selects her own Society —
Then — shuts the Door —
To her divine Majority —
Present no more —

Unmoved — she notes the Chariots — pausing —   5
At her low Gate —
Unmoved — an Emperor be kneeling
Upon her Mat —

I've known her — from an ample nation —
Choose One —   10
Then — close the Valves of her attention —
Like Stone —

(c. 1862)

Exploring the Text

1. What aspects of the human being does the Soul represent in this poem? Of what importance is it that the Soul is referred to as a "she" in this poem?
2. What is the "divine Majority" (l. 3)? What are the multiple meanings of "majority," and which ones might apply here?
3. In the second stanza, who is "Unmoved"? What is the effect of the words indicating status?
4. In the third stanza, what association do the "Valves" evoke? What does this image suggest?
5. How is the Soul characterized in this poem? As coldly self-sufficient? Confidently independent? Angry and distant? Proudly self-assured? Explain.
6. How do the rhythm and rhyme of this poem contribute to its meaning? Consider the paired lines within each stanza. How does the final line create an appropriate effect for the meaning of this poem?
7. Following is an analysis of the poem by contemporary critic Camille Paglia:

   > This is Emily Dickinson's declaration of independence, a manifesto of artistic vocation and mission. It is stern, flat, and implacable. Yet its emotions are intense and stretched to the limit.... Tenderness or compassion would compromise her artistic integrity and endanger her enterprise.... [W]ith militant resolve, she negates the entire world to preserve her small, proud kingdom of art.

   Do you agree or disagree with this analysis? Discuss which parts of this interpretation your understanding of the poem supports or challenges or which require qualification.

After great pain, a formal feeling comes —

After great pain, a formal feeling comes —
The Nerves sit ceremonious, like Tombs —
The stiff Heart questions was it He, that bore,
And Yesterday, or Centuries before?

The Feet, mechanical, go round —   5
Of Ground, or Air, or Ought —
A Wooden way
Regardless grown,
A Quartz contentment, like a stone —

This is the Hour of Lead —   10
Remembered, if outlived,
As Freezing persons, recollect the Snow —
First — Chill — then Stupor — then the letting go —

                                        (c. 1862)

Exploring the Text

1. In the opening stanza, what is "a formal feeling"?
2. What connotations are associated with "formal," "ceremonious," and "stiff" — the language used in stanza 1? What words in subsequent lines carry similar connotations?
3. Who is the "He" in line 3? How does that reference connect with line 4?
4. What stage of grief is described in the second stanza? How does the sufferer experience it? Is there any kind of peace or relief suggested by the oxymoron "Quartz contentment" (l. 9)?
5. What are the various meanings of the word "Ought" (l. 6)? Which meaning do you think is most fitting here — and why?
6. What are the possibilities for the final stage of grief, as described in the third stanza? How does the metaphor Emily Dickinson develops illuminate those?
7. Dickinson does not give us a first-person speaker, nor does she anywhere in the poem refer to the grief-stricken person as a whole human being. How, instead, does she refer to those who are grieving? What is the effect of this choice?
8. Dickinson does not indicate the specific event that causes the grief in this poem. What is the impact of not creating a more specific context? Does the abstraction add to or diminish the power of the poem?
9. How would you describe the tone of the poem? Cite specific lines and phrases to support your description.

I heard a Fly buzz — when I died —

I heard a Fly buzz — when I died —
The Stillness in the Room
Was like the Stillness in the Air —
Between the Heaves of Storm —

The Eyes around — had wrung them dry —   5
And Breaths were gathering firm
For that last Onset — when the King
Be witnessed — in the Room —

I willed my Keepsakes — Signed away
What portion of me be   10
Assignable — and then it was
There interposed a Fly —

With Blue — uncertain stumbling Buzz —
Between the light — and me —
And then the Windows failed — and then   15
I could not see to see —

(c. 1862)

Exploring the Text

1. What is the actual scene or setting being described in this poem? Who is the speaker?
2. What is the effect in the opening line of juxtaposing two events that are, at least on the surface, of such different magnitude?
3. What is meant by line 5: "The Eyes around — had wrung them dry — "? What is the antecedent of "them"?
4. Who is "the King" (l. 7)? What are at least two possibilities? Provide plausible support for each.
5. Look up the definition of "interposed" (par. 12) to explore multiple meanings. What do various meanings add to your understanding of the poem?
6. The fourth stanza has puzzled readers and critics alike. How do you interpret that stanza, and how does your interpretation affect your reading of the poem as a whole?
7. What do you make of the choice to use a fly in this poem? Is Dickinson simply using the fly as typical of a small, minor living creature, one we casually swat away without thinking? Since flies feed on dead flesh (maggots consume corpses), does it serve as a reminder that life ends in decay? Does the fly represent Satan's lieutenant Beelzebub, known also as the Lord of the Flies? Is the fly a symbol of death? Or is there another view? Explain how your understanding of the fly guides your interpretation of the poem.

My Life had stood — a Loaded Gun —

My Life had stood — a Loaded Gun —
In Corners — till a Day
The Owner passed — identified —
And carried Me away —

And now We roam in Sovreign Woods —   5
And now We hunt the Doe —
And every time I speak for Him —
The Mountains straight reply —

And do I smile, such cordial light
Upon the Valley glow —   10
It is as a Vesuvian face
Had let its pleasure through —

And when at Night — Our good Day done —
I guard My Master's Head —
'Tis better than the Eider-Duck's[1]   15
Deep Pillow — to have shared —

---

[1] Arctic duck famed for its down feathers, which were often used for pillows and blankets. — Eds.

To foe of His — I'm deadly foe —
None stir the second time —
On whom I lay a Yellow Eye —
Or an emphatic Thumb —   20

Though I than He — may longer live
He longer must — than I —
For I have but the power to kill,
Without — the power to die —

(c. 1863)

Exploring the Text

1. Who is the speaker — the "Me" (l. 4) — in the poem? What are the pronoun referents in line 7, "I speak for Him"?

2. In stanza 2, why are the woods "Sovreign" (l. 5)?

3. How does the "cordial light" of the "smile" (l. 9) contrast with the "Vesuvian face" (l. 11)? What does Dickinson suggest through this juxtaposition?

4. Why is it "better" to "guard My Master's Head" than to lie sharing the "Eider-Duck's / Deep Pillow" (ll. 14–16)?

5. Poet and feminist critic Adrienne Rich (1929–2010) has called this "a central poem in understanding Emily Dickinson, and ourselves, and the condition of the woman artist, particularly in the nineteenth century. It seems likely that the nineteenth-century woman poet, especially, felt the medium of poetry as dangerous. . . . [T]he poem grows out of her anger at the narrow life allowed to Dickinson by her society and by her father." In what ways do you see this as a poem about the anger of an artist?

6. Another way to look at this poem is through a historical lens. Writing to refute a more symbolic interpretation of the poem, British poet Herbert Lomas reminds readers that the poem was written two years after the start of the Civil War, near the time of the Battle of Gettysburg (1863). He argues that the gun is literal, which, he claims, explains the final stanza: "The personified gun says it may well outlive its Master (in a gun-room and in the poem). Its Master, however, can and may well die in battle — but 'must longer' live than the gun: for the Owner/Master is an immortal soul, and killer of other immortal souls." Explain why you agree or disagree with this interpretation. What other parts of the poem support or challenge this interpretation?

7. The previous two questions explain interpretations by literary critics. How do you interpret this complicated poem? What resources of language does Dickinson employ to develop the meaning you see in the text?

TALKBACK

Hans Ostrom

Hans Ostrom (b. 1954) grew up in Sierra City, California. His grandfather, a Swedish immigrant, worked in gold mines in the Sierra Nevada range. Ostrom, Distinguished Professor of English at the University of Puget Sound, teaches composition, creative writing, rhetoric, and literature and is codirector of African American studies. He is the author of *Langston Hughes: A Study of the Short Fiction* (1993) and *A Langston Hughes Encyclopedia* (2001). Ostrom's articles, poems, and short stories have appeared in a variety of magazines and journals. He is also the author of the novels *Three to Get Ready* (1991) and *Honoring Juanita* (2010), as well as two poetry collections, *Subjects Apprehended* (2000) and *The Coast Starlight: Collected Poems, 1976–2006* (2006).

Emily Dickinson and Elvis Presley in Heaven

They call each other E. Elvis picks
wildflowers near the river and brings
them to Emily. She explains half-rhymes to him.

In heaven Emily wears her hair long, sports
Levis and western blouses with rhinestones.   5
Elvis is lean again, wears baggy trousers

and T-shirts, a letterman's jacket from Tupelo High.
They take long walks and often hold hands.
She prefers they remain just friends. Forever.

Emily's poems now contain naugahyde, Cadillacs,   10
Electricity, jets, TV, Little Richard and Richard
Nixon. The rock-a-billy rhythm makes her smile.

Elvis likes himself with style. This afternoon
he will play guitar and sing "I Taste a Liquor
Never Brewed" to the tune of "Love Me Tender."   15

Emily will clap and harmonize. Alone
in their cabins later, they'll listen to the river
and nap. They will not think of Amherst

or Las Vegas. They know why God made them
roommates. It's because America   20
was their hometown. It's because

God is a thing
without feathers. It's because
God wears blue suede shoes.

(2006)

Exploring the Text

1. Hans Ostrom's poem depends on the reader understanding references to both Emily Dickinson's and Elvis Presley's works. What resonances does he expect his readers to have with the following allusions related to Elvis and his era: "lean again" (l. 6), "Tupelo High" (l. 7), "naugahyde" (l. 10), "Little Richard and Richard / Nixon" (ll. 11–12), "Love Me Tender" (l. 15), and "Las Vegas" (l. 19)?
2. What is the intention and effect of the period after "friends" in line 9?
3. In nearly every stanza, Ostrom uses enjambment — a stylistic device in which one line ends without a pause and continues to the next line to complete its meaning. What is the effect of this device in Ostrom's poem?
4. What does Ostrom's pairing of Presley and Dickinson suggest about the poet's idea of heaven?

Making Connections

1. What qualities of these two people — one a classic poet, the other a pop-culture icon — and our understanding of and response to them does Hans Ostrom's poem suggest?
2. What technical qualities of Dickinson's poetry does Ostrom incorporate into this poem? Why?
3. Is Ostrom mocking, poking fun at, paying tribute to, or being disrespectful of Dickinson and the stereotype of her as a reclusive spinster? Cite both her poems and his as you explain what you believe his intent and tone are in this poem.
4. How does Ostrom argue that the Belle of Amherst and the King of Rock and Roll are both undeniably American? To what extent is he suggesting that they are equally important in terms of their influence on American culture — or is he?

FRANK LESLIE'S ILLUSTRATED NEWSPAPER

This cartoon was created by a staff cartoonist for the popular weekly news and literary publication *Frank Leslie's Illustrated Newspaper*, later renamed *Leslie's Weekly*.

Does Not Such a Meeting Make Amends?

On July 1, 1862, President Abraham Lincoln signed into law the Pacific Railway Act, which provided federal support to construct a railway system that would extend from the Missouri River to the Pacific Ocean. Such a system, when combined with the existing railroads operating in the East, would create the first transcontinental railroad. Construction by the Union Pacific Railroad began in Iowa and worked its way west, while the Central Pacific Railroad started in San Francisco and proceeded east. On May 10, 1869, rails of the Union Pacific and Central Pacific railways were joined at Promontory Point, Utah, thus connecting the nation from coast to coast. A ceremony was held to drive in the Golden Spike, a symbol of completion. The wood engraving shown here appeared on May 29, 1869.

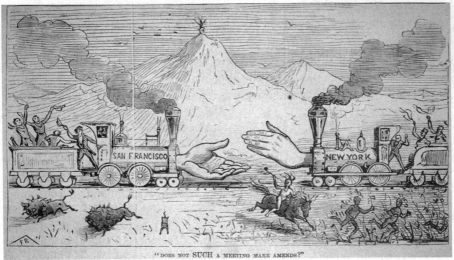

"DOES NOT SUCH A MEETING MAKE AMENDS?"

Prints and Photographs Division, Library of Congress

Exploring the Text

1. What is the narrative of this illustration? Identify the different characters who are involved. How is the landscape depicted? Which elements function as symbols? Start with where your eye is drawn and then move out into the surrounding fields as you analyze this complex image.

2. What "amends" does this illustration suggest need to be made? How would this event make amends? Look up the definition of "amends" and consider multiple meanings.
3. Are the specific contemporary issues that needed to be amended depicted in the illustration, or did the artist assume that the audience knew what they were? If you see them in the illustration, identify them.
4. *Frank Leslie's Illustrated Newspaper* was known for its patriotic stances on most issues. To what extent do you find this illustration patriotic? How does it "answer" the question that is its caption: "Does not SUCH a meeting making amends?"

RED CLOUD

Makhpiya-Luta (1822–1909), known as Red Cloud, was chief of the largest tribe of the Oglala Sioux. He successfully resisted development of Powder River Country in Wyoming and Montana from 1866 to 1868, a period known as Red Cloud's War.

Speech on Indian Rights

On November 6, 1868, Red Cloud signed a treaty that ended Red Cloud's War, ceded tribal lands, and established the Great Sioux Reservation, which encompassed all of South Dakota west of the Missouri River. This treaty marked the end of the Oglala Sioux's nearly decade-long efforts to maintain their land in the Yellowstone and Powder River valleys. In 1870, Red Cloud traveled to New York and Washington, D.C., to clarify the treaty, whose terms authorized U.S. government agents as administrators of the reservation, and to speak in defense of the Sioux. His speeches, which aroused public opinion, resulted in the government revising the treaty. Although Red Cloud remained a critic of the government, and especially of agents of the Bureau of Indian Affairs, he counseled his tribe to remain peaceful, fearing that additional wars would result in further losses — a position not entirely appreciated by younger, more radical members of his tribe. Following is a speech he gave at Cooper Union, a private college in New York City, on July 16, 1870, at a reception in his honor.

My Brothers and my Friends who are before me today: God Almighty has made us all, and He is here to hear what I have to say to you today. The Great Spirit made us both. He gave us lands and He gave you lands. You came here and we received you as brothers. When the Almighty made you, He made you all white and clothed you. When He made us He made us with red skins and poor. When you first came we were very many and you were few. Now you are many and we are few. You do not know who appears before you to speak. He is a representative of the original American race, the first people of this continent. We are good, and not bad. The reports which you get about us are all on one side. You hear of us only as murderers and thieves. We are not so. If we had more lands to give to you we would give them, but we have no more. We are driven into a very little island, and we want you, our dear friends, to help us with the Government of the United States. The Great Spirit made us poor and ignorant. He made you rich and wise and skillful in things which we know nothing about. The good Father made you to eat tame game and us to eat wild game. Ask any one who has gone through to California. They will tell you we have treated them well. You have children. We, too, have children, and we wish to bring them up well. We ask you to help us do it. At the mouth of Horse Creek, in 1852, the Great Father[1] made a treaty with us. We agreed to let him pass through our territory unharmed for fifty-five years. We kept our word. We committed no murders, no depredations, until the troops came there. When the troops were sent there trouble and disturbance arose. Since that time there have been various goods sent from time to time to us, but only once did they reach us, and soon the Great Father took away the only good man he had sent us, Col. Fitzpatrick. The Great Father said we must go to farming, and some of our men went to farming near Fort Laramie, and were treated very badly indeed. We came to Washington to see our Great Father that peace might be continued. The Great Father that made us both wishes peace to be kept; we want to keep peace. Will you help us? In 1808 men came out and brought papers. We could not read them, and they did not tell us truly what was in them. We thought the treaty was to remove the forts, and that we should then cease from fighting. But they wanted to send us traders on the Missouri. We did not want to go on the Missouri, but wanted traders where we were. When I reached Washington the Great Father explained to me what the treaty was, and showed me that the interpreters had deceived me. All I want is right and justice. I have tried to get from the Great Father what is right and just. I have not altogether succeeded. I want you to help me to get what is right and just. I represent the whole Sioux nation, and they will be bound by what I say. I am no Spotted Tail, to say one thing one day and be bought for a pin the next. Look at me. I am poor and naked, but I am the Chief of the nation. We do not want riches, but we want to train our children right. Riches would do us no good. We could not take them with us to the other world. We do not want riches, we want peace and love.

The riches that we have in this world, Secretary Cox[2] said truly, we cannot take with us to the next world. Then I wish to know why Commissioners are sent out to us who do nothing but rob us and get the riches of this world away from us? I was brought up among the traders, and those who came out there in the early times treated me well and I had a good time with them. They taught us to wear clothes and to use tobacco and ammunition. But, by and by, the Great Father sent out a different kind of men; men who cheated and drank whisky; men who were so bad that the Great Father could not keep them at home and so sent them out there. I have sent a great many words to the Great Father but they never reached him. They were drowned on the way, and I was afraid the

---

[1] Red Cloud uses this term to refer to the president of the United States. — Eds.

[2] Jacob Dolson Cox (1828–1900) was the United States Secretary of the interior from 1869–70. — Eds.

words I spoke lately to the Great Father would not reach you, so I came to speak to you myself; and now I am going away to my home. I want to have men sent out to my people whom we know and can trust. I am glad I have come here. You belong in the East and I belong in the West, and I am glad I have come here and that we could understand one another. I am very much obliged to you for listening to me. I go home this afternoon. I hope you will think of what I have said to you. I bid you all an affectionate farewell.

(1870)

Exploring the Text

1. What common ground does Red Cloud establish at the outset with his audience? What differences does he acknowledge?
2. What is the stated purpose of his speech? What evidence does he provide to support his intentions?
3. What specific allegations does he make against the U.S. government? What are the most serious transgressions, according to his view? What actions does he recommend to address the problems he identifies?
4. Red Cloud insists that he wants only peace. What evidence do you find of his sincerity through both his literal statements and his rhetorical strategies?
5. How would you describe the tone of the speech? Use a phrase that includes a contrast word (such as *but* or *yet*) to capture the complexity of the tone.
6. At the end of this speech, Red Cloud was given a standing ovation. Why would his audience have been so moved by his message and the way he presented it? In your response, consider the following description of Cooper Union's founder:

> Peter Cooper's abolitionism was consistent with his generally progressive social views. He was a strong advocate for the rights of Native Americans and lobbied President Grant to adopt a peace policy in the west. In the 1870s, at a time when Indians were widely regarded as enemy savages, great leaders like Red Cloud, of the Lakota Sioux, and Little Raven, chief of the Arapaho, were given the lectern at the Great Hall. Cooper was also a fighter for women's rights who opened the doors of his institute to Susan B. Anthony and Elizabeth Cady Stanton.

THOMAS NAST

Thomas Nast (1840–1902) has been called "the father of American caricature" because of his influential political cartoons. He was known for his legendary campaign against New York City's Boss Tweed and the Tammany Hall political machine. He popularized the political symbols of the elephant for the Republican Party and the donkey for the Democratic Party. Between 1859 and 1896, he drew more than 2,200 political cartoons for *Harper's Weekly*.

Worse than Slavery

The following image appeared in *Harper's Weekly* in 1874. Note that the White League, founded in Louisiana in 1874, was a paramilitary group committed to white supremacy. While it had some links to the Ku Klux Klan, the White League operated much more openly: members (many of whom were former Confederate soldiers) did not hide their identities, and the group generally acted through mainstream political channels.

Prints and Photographs Division, Library of Congress

Exploring the Text

1. What precisely is going on in this image? Identify each of the characters, the symbols, and the allusions. What "story" or narrative is Thomas Nast telling?

2. How do the structure, placement of characters, proportions, and use of space in this visual image contribute to the narrative?

3. What tensions does Nast emphasize in this cartoon? Consider his depiction through its use of both visual images and written text.

4. Nast uses little humor in this cartoon, yet he does employ caricature. What elements of caricature do you notice? How does caricature contribute to his argument?

5. How does Nast support his claim that African Americans in the South were facing something "Worse than Slavery"? Explain in terms of evidence presented to prove a claim. Does Nast address a counterargument? Qualify or modify his claim? How persuasive do you think he would have been to readers of *Harper's Weekly* in 1874?

MARK TWAIN

Mark Twain (1835–1910) is the pseudonym of Samuel Langhorne Clemens. Best known as a novelist — *The Adventures of Huckleberry Finn* (1884), *Tom Sawyer* (1876), and *A Connecticut Yankee in King Arthur's Court* (1889) are among Twain's most famous novels — Twain also worked as a typesetter, a riverboat pilot, a miner, a reporter, and an editor. His early writings reflect his pre–Civil War upbringing in their idyllic images as well as in their reminders of some of America's least acceptable social realities. Twain spent his life observing and reporting on his surroundings, and his work provides a glimpse into the mind-set of people who lived in the late nineteenth century.

from *Life on the Mississippi*

Life on the Mississippi (1883), a mixture of autobiography and travel narrative, recounts Twain's experiences as a riverboat pilot on the Mississippi River traveling from St. Louis to New Orleans. What follows are Chapter VIII, "Perplexing Lessons," and Chapter IX, "Continued Perplexities," which appear early in the memoir and describe the young Twain's training as a "cub" steamboat pilot under the tutelage of Mr. Bixby.

Chapter VIII: Perplexing Lessons

At the end of what seemed a tedious while, I had managed to pack my head full of islands, towns, bars, "points," and bends; and a curiously inanimate mass of lumber it was, too. However, inasmuch as I could shut my eyes and reel off a good long string of these names without leaving out more than ten miles of river in every fifty, I began to feel that I could take a boat down to New Orleans if I could make her skip those little gaps. But of course my complacency could hardly get start enough to lift my nose a trifle into the air, before Mr. Bixby would think of something to fetch it down again. One day he turned on me suddenly with this settler:

"What is the shape of Walnut Bend?"

He might as well have asked me my grandmother's opinion of protoplasm. I reflected respectfully, and then said I didn't know it had any particular shape. My gunpowdery chief went off with a bang, of course, and then went on loading and firing until he was out of adjectives.

I had learned long ago that he only carried just so many rounds of ammunition, and was sure to subside into a very placable and even remorseful old smooth-bore as soon as they were all gone. That word "old" is merely affectionate; he was not more than thirty-four. I waited. By and by he said:

"My boy, you've got to know the *shape* of the river perfectly. It is all there is left   5 to steer by on a very dark night. Every thing else is blotted out and gone. But mind you, it hasn't the same shape in the night that it has in the daytime."

"How on earth am I ever going to learn it, then?"

"How do you follow a hall at home in the dark? Because you know the shape of it. You can't see it."

"Do you mean to say that I've got to know all the million trifling variations of shape in the banks of this interminable river as well as I know the shape of the front hall at home?"

"On my honor, you've got to know them *better* than any man ever did know the shapes of the halls in his own house."

"I wish I was dead!"   10

"Now I don't want to discourage you, but —— "

"Well, pile it on me; I might as well have it now as another time."

"You see, this has got to be learned; there isn't any getting around it. A clear starlight night throws such heavy shadows that, if you didn't know the shape of a shore perfectly, you would claw away from every bunch of timber, because you would take the black shadow of it for a solid cape; and you see you would be getting scared to death every fifteen minutes by the watch. You would be fifty yards from shore all the time when you ought to be within fifty feet of it. You can't see a snag in one of those shadows, but you know exactly where it is, and the shape of the river tells you when you are coming to it. Then there's your pitch-dark night; the river is a very different shape on a pitch-dark night from what it is on a starlight night. All shores seem to be straight lines, then, and mighty dim ones, too; and you'd *run* them for straight lines, only you know better. You boldly drive your boat right into what seems to be a solid, straight wall (you knowing very well that in reality there is a curve there), and that wall falls back and makes way for you. Then there's your gray mist. You take a night when there's one of these grisly, drizzly, gray mists, and then there isn't *any* particular shape to a shore. A gray mist would tangle the head of the oldest man that ever lived. Well, then, different kinds of *moonlight* change the shape of the river in different ways. You see —— "

"Oh, don't say any more, please! Have I got to learn the shape of the river according to all these five hundred thousand different ways? If I tried to carry all that cargo in my head it would make me stoop-shouldered."

"*No!* you only learn *the* shape of the river; and you learn it with such absolute   15 certainty that you can always steer by the shape that's *in your head*, and never mind the one that's before your eyes."

"Very well, I'll try it; but, after I have learned it, can I depend on it? Will it keep the same form and not go fooling around?"

Before Mr. Bixby could answer, Mr. W. came in to take the watch, and he said:

"Bixby, you'll have to look out for President's Island, and all that country clear away up above the Old Hen and Chickens. The banks are caving and the shape of the shores changing like every thing. Why, you wouldn't know the point above 40. You can go up inside the old sycamore snag, now."[1]

So that question was answered. Here were leagues of shore changing shape. My spirits were down in the mud again. Two things seemed pretty apparent to me. One was, that in order to be a pilot a man had got to learn more than any one man ought to be allowed to know; and the other was, that he must learn it all over again in a different way every twenty-four hours.

That night we had the watch until twelve. Now it was an ancient river custom for 20 the two pilots to chat a bit when the watch changed. While the relieving pilot put on his gloves and lit his cigar, his partner, the retiring pilot, would say something like this:

"I judge the upper bar is making down a little at Hale's Point; had quarter twain with the lower lead and mark twain[2] with the other."

"Yes, I thought it was making down a little, last trip. Meet any boats?"

"Met one abreast the head of 21, but she was away over hugging the bar, and I couldn't make her out entirely. I took her for the *Sunny South* — hadn't any skylights forward of the chimneys."

And so on. And as the relieving pilot took the wheel his partner would mention that we were in such-and-such a bend, and say we were abreast of such-and-such a man's wood-yard or plantation. This was courtesy; I supposed it was *necessity*. But Mr. W. came on watch full twelve minutes late on this particular night — a tremendous breach of etiquette; in fact, it is the unpardonable sin among pilots. So Mr. Bixby gave him no greeting whatever, but simply surrendered the wheel and marched out of the pilot-house without a word. I was appalled; it was a villainous night for blackness, we were in a particularly wide and blind part of the river, where there was no shape or substance to any thing, and it seemed incredible that Mr. Bixby should have left that poor fellow to kill the boat, trying to find out where he was. But I resolved that I would stand by him any way. He should find that he was not wholly friendless. So I stood around, and waited to be asked where we were. But Mr. W. plunged on serenely through the solid firmament of black cats that stood for an atmosphere, and never opened his mouth. "Here is a proud devil!" thought I; "here is a limb of Satan that would rather send us all to destruction than put himself under obligations to me, because I am not yet one of the salt of the earth and privileged to snub captains and lord it over every thing dead and alive in a steamboat." I presently climbed up on the bench; I did not think it was safe to go to sleep while this lunatic was on watch.

---

[1] It may not be necessary, but still it can do no harm to explain that "inside" means between the snag and the shore. — M. T.

[2] Archaic word for *two*; in this context, it means two fathoms deep (about 12 feet) and safe for passage by a riverboat. — Eds.

However, I must have gone to sleep in the course of time, because the next thing   25
I was aware of was the fact that day was breaking, Mr. W. gone, and Mr. Bixby at the
wheel again. So it was four o'clock and all well — but me; I felt like a skinful of dry
bones, and all of them trying to ache at once.

Mr. Bixby asked me what I had stayed up there for. I confessed that it was to do
Mr. W. a benevolence — tell him where he was. It took five minutes for the entire pre-
posterousness of the thing to filter into Mr. Bixby's system, and then I judge it filled
him nearly up to the chin; because he paid me a compliment — and not much of a
one either. He said:

"Well, taking you by and large, you do seem to be more different kinds of an ass
than any creature I ever saw before. What did you suppose he wanted to know for?"

I said I thought it might be a convenience to him.

"Convenience! D —— nation! Didn't I tell you that a man's got to know the river
in the night the same as he'd know his own front hall?"

"Well, I can follow the front hall in the dark if I know it *is* the front hall; but sup-   30
pose you set me down in the middle of it in the dark and not tell me which hall it is;
how am *I* to know?"

"Well, you've *got* to, on the river!"

"All right. Then I'm glad I never said any thing to Mr. W."

"I should say so! Why, he'd have slammed you through the window and utterly
ruined a hundred dollars' worth of window-sash and stuff."

I was glad this damage had been saved, for it would have made me unpopular
with the owners. They always hated any body who had the name of being careless and
injuring things.

I went to work now to learn the shape of the river; and of all the eluding and   35
ungraspable objects that ever I tried to get mind or hands on, that was the chief. I
would fasten my eyes upon a sharp, wooded point that projected far into the river
some miles ahead of me, and go to laboriously photographing its shape upon my
brain; and just as I was beginning to succeed to my satisfaction, we would draw up
toward it and the exasperating thing would begin to melt away and fold back into the
bank! If there had been a conspicuous dead tree standing upon the very point of
the cape, I would find that tree inconspicuously merged into the general forest, and
occupying the middle of a straight shore, when I got abreast of it! No prominent hill
would stick to its shape long enough for me to make up my mind what its form really
was, but it was as dissolving and changeful as if it had been a mountain of butter in
the hottest corner of the tropics. Nothing ever had the same shape when I was coming
down-stream that it had borne when I went up. I mentioned these little difficulties to
Mr. Bixby. He said:

"That's the very main virtue of the thing. If the shapes didn't change every three
seconds they wouldn't be of any use. Take this place where we are now, for instance.
As long as that hill over yonder is only one hill, I can boom right along the way I'm
going; but the moment it splits at the top and forms a V, I know I've got to scratch
to starboard in a hurry, or I'll bang this boat's brains out against a rock; and then
the moment one of the prongs of the V swings behind the other, I've got to waltz to

larboard again, or I'll have a misunderstanding with a snag that would snatch the keelson out of this steamboat as neatly as if it were a sliver in your hand. If that hill didn't change its shape on bad nights there would be an awful steamboat grave-yard around here inside of a year."

It was plain that I had got to learn the shape of the river in all the different ways that could be thought of, — upside down, wrong end first, inside out, fore-and-aft, and "thort-ships," — and then know what to do on gray nights when it hadn't any shape at all. So I set about it. In the course of time I began to get the best of this knotty lesson, and my self-complacency moved to the front once more. Mr. Bixby was all fixed, and ready to start it to the rear again. He opened on me after this fashion:

"How much water did we have in the middle crossing at Hole-in-the-Wall, trip before last?"

I considered this an outrage. I said:

"Every trip, down and up, the leadsmen are singing through that tangled place   40
for three-quarters of an hour on a stretch. How do you reckon I can remember such a mess as that?"

"My boy, you've got to remember it. You've got to remember the exact spot and the exact marks the boat lay in when we had the shoalest water, in every one of the five hundred shoal places between St. Louis and New Orleans; and you mustn't get the shoal soundings and marks of one trip mixed up with the shoal soundings and marks of another, either, for they're not often twice alike. You must keep them separate."

When I came to myself again, I said:

"When I get so that I can do that, I'll be able to raise the dead, and then I won't have to pilot a steamboat to make a living. I want to retire from this business. I want a slush-bucket and a brush; I'm only fit for a roustabout. I haven't got brains enough to be a pilot; and if I had I wouldn't have strength enough to carry them around, unless I went on crutches."

"Now drop that! When I say I'll learn[3] a man the river, I mean it. And you can depend on it, I'll learn him or kill him."

Chapter IX: Continued Perplexities

There was no use in arguing with a person like this. I promptly put such a strain on   45
my memory that by and by even the shoal water and the countless crossing-marks began to stay with me. But the result was just the same. I never could more than get one knotty thing learned before another presented itself. Now I had often seen pilots gazing at the water and pretending to read it as if it were a book; but it was a book that told me nothing. A time came at last, however, when Mr. Bixby seemed to think me far enough advanced to bear a lesson on water-reading. So he began:

"Do you see that long, slanting line on the face of the water? Now, that's a reef. Moreover, it's a bluff reef. There is a solid sand-bar under it that is nearly as straight

---

[3]"Teach" is not in the river vocabulary. — M. T.

up and down as the side of a house. There is plenty of water close up to it, but mighty little on top of it. If you were to hit it, you would knock the boat's brains out. Do you see where the line fringes out at the upper end and begins to fade away?"

"Yes, sir."

"Well, that is a low place; that is the head of the reef. You can climb over there, and not hurt any thing. Cross over, now, and follow along close under the reef — easy water there — not much current."

I followed the reef along till I approached the fringed end. Then Mr. Bixby said:

"Now get ready. Wait till I give the word. She won't want to mount the reef; a boat   50
hates shoal water. Stand by — wait — *wait* — keep her well in hand. *Now* cramp her down! Snatch her! snatch her!"

He seized the other side of the wheel and helped to spin it around until it was hard down, and then we held it so. The boat resisted, and refused to answer for a while, and next she came surging to starboard, mounted the reef, and sent a long, angry ridge of water foaming away from her bows.

"Now watch her; watch her like a cat, or she'll get away from you. When she fights strong and the tiller slips a little, in a jerky, greasy sort of way, let up on her a trifle; it is the way she tells you at night that the water is too shoal; but keep edging her up, little by little, toward the point. You are well up on the bar now; there is a bar under every point, because the water that comes down around it forms an eddy and allows the sediment to sink. Do you see those fine lines on the face of the water that branch out like the ribs of a fan? Well, those are little reefs; you want to just miss the ends of them, but run them pretty close. Now look out — look out! Don't you crowd that slick, greasy-looking place; there ain't nine feet there; she won't stand it. She begins to smell it; look sharp, I tell you! Oh, blazes, there you go! Stop the starboard wheel! Quick! Ship up to back! Set her back!"

The engine bells jingled and the engines answered promptly, shooting white columns of steam far aloft out of the 'scape-pipes, but it was too late. The boat had "smelt" the bar in good earnest; the foamy ridges that radiated from her bows suddenly disappeared, a great dead swell came rolling forward, and swept ahead of her, she careened far over to larboard, and went tearing away toward the shore as if she were about scared to death. We were a good mile from where we ought to have been when we finally got the upper hand of her again.

During the afternoon watch the next day, Mr. Bixby asked me if I knew how to run the next few miles. I said:

"Go inside the first snag above the point, outside the next one, start out from the   55
lower end of Higgins's wood-yard, make a square crossing, and —— "

"That's all right. I'll be back before you close up on the next point."

But he wasn't. He was still below when I rounded it and entered upon a piece of river which I had some misgivings about. I did not know that he was hiding behind a chimney to see how I would perform. I went gayly along, getting prouder and prouder, for he had never left the boat in my sole charge such a length of time before. I even got to "setting" her and letting the wheel go entirely, while I vaingloriously turned my back and inspected the stern marks and hummed a tune, a sort of easy indifference which I had prodigiously admired in Bixby and other great pilots. Once I inspected rather long, and when I faced to the front again my heart flew into my mouth so suddenly that if I hadn't clapped my teeth together I should have lost it. One of those frightful bluff reefs was stretching its deadly length right across our bows! My head was gone in a moment; I did not know which end I stood on; I gasped and could not get my breath; I spun the wheel down with such rapidity that it wove itself together like a spider's web; the boat answered and turned square away from the reef, but the reef followed her! I fled, but still it followed, still it kept — right across my bows! I never looked to see where I was going, I only fled. The awful crash was imminent. Why didn't that villain come? If I committed the crime of ringing a bell I might get thrown overboard. But better that than kill the boat. So in blind desperation I started such a rattling "shivaree" down below as never had astounded an engineer in this world before, I fancy. Amidst the frenzy of the bells the engines began to back and fill in a furious way, and my reason forsook its throne — we were about to crash into the woods on the other side of the river. Just then Mr. Bixby stepped calmly into view on the hurricane deck. My soul went out to him in gratitude. My distress vanished; I would have felt safe on the brink of Niagara with Mr. Bixby on the hurricane deck. He blandly and sweetly took his toothpick out of his mouth between his fingers, as if it were a cigar, — we were just in the act of climbing an overhanging big tree, and the passengers were scudding astern like rats, — and lifted up these commands to me ever so gently:

"Stop the starboard! Stop the larboard! Set her back on both!"

The boat hesitated, halted, pressed her nose among the boughs a critical instant, then reluctantly began to back away.

"Stop the larboard! Come ahead on it! Stop the starboard! Come ahead on it! 60 Point her for the bar!"

I sailed away as serenely as a summer's morning. Mr. Bixby came in and said, with mock simplicity:

"When you have a hail, my boy, you ought to tap the big bell three times before you land, so that the engineers can get ready."

I blushed under the sarcasm, and said I hadn't had any hail.

"Ah! Then it was for wood, I suppose. The officer of the watch will tell you when he wants to wood up."

I went on consuming, and said I wasn't after wood. 65

"Indeed? Why, what could you want over here in the bend, then? Did you ever know of a boat following a bend up-stream at this stage of the river?"

"No, sir — and _I_ wasn't trying to follow it. I was getting away from a bluff reef."

"No, it wasn't a bluff reef; there isn't one within three miles of where you were."

"But I saw it. It was as bluff as that one yonder."

"Just about. Run over it!" 70

"Do you give it as an order?"

"Yes. Run over it!"

"If I don't, I wish I may die."

"All right; I am taking the responsibility."

I was just as anxious to kill the boat, now, as I had been to save it before. I impressed 75 my orders upon my memory, to be used at the inquest, and made a straight break for the reef. As it disappeared under our bows I held my breath; but we slid over it like oil.

"Now, don't you see the difference? It wasn't any thing but a *wind* reef. The wind does that."

"So I see. But it is exactly like a bluff reef. How am I ever going to tell them apart?"

"I can't tell you. It is an instinct. By and by you will just naturally *know* one from the other, but you never will be able to explain why or how you know them apart."

It turned out to be true. The face of the water, in time, became a wonderful book — a book that was a dead language to the uneducated passenger, but which told its mind to me without reserve, delivering its most cherished secrets as clearly as if it uttered them with a voice. And it was not a book to be read once and thrown aside, for it had a new story to tell every day. Throughout the long twelve hundred miles there was never a page that was void of interest, never one that you could leave unread without loss, never one that you would want to skip, thinking you could find higher enjoyment in some other thing. There never was so wonderful a book written by man; never one whose interest was so absorbing, so unflagging, so sparklingly renewed with every reperusal. The passenger who could not read it was charmed with a peculiar sort of faint dimple on its surface (on the rare occasions when he did not overlook it altogether); but to the pilot that was an *italicized* passage; indeed, it was more than that, it was a legend of the largest capitals, with a string of shouting exclamation points at the end of it, for it meant that a wreck or a rock was buried there that could tear the life out of the strongest vessel that ever floated. It is the faintest and simplest expression the water ever makes, and the most hideous to a pilot's eye. In truth, the passenger who could not read this book saw nothing but all manner of pretty pictures in it, painted by the sun and shaded by the clouds, whereas to the trained eye these were not pictures at all, but the grimmest and most dead-earnest of reading matter.

Now when I had mastered the language of this water, and had come to know 80 every trifling feature that bordered the great river as familiarly as I knew the letters of the alphabet, I had made a valuable acquisition. But I had lost something, too. I had lost something which could never be restored to me while I lived. All the grace, the beauty, the poetry, had gone out of the majestic river! I still kept in mind a certain wonderful sunset which I witnessed when steamboating was new to me. A broad expanse of the river was turned to blood; in the middle distance the red hue brightened into gold, through which a solitary log came floating, black and conspicuous; one place a long, slanting mark lay sparkling upon the water; in another the surface was broken by boiling, tumbling rings, that were as many-tinted as an opal; where the ruddy flush was faintest, was a smooth spot that was covered with graceful circles and radiating lines, ever so delicately traced; the shore on our left was densely wooded, and the sombre shadow that fell from this forest was broken in one place by a long, ruffled trail that shone like silver; and high above the forest wall a clean-stemmed dead tree waved a single leafy bough that glowed like a flame in the unobstructed splendor that was flowing from the sun. There were graceful curves, reflected images, woody heights, soft distances; and over the whole scene, far and near, the dissolving lights drifted steadily, enriching it every passing moment with new marvels of coloring.

I stood like one bewitched. I drank it in, in a speechless rapture. The world was new to me, and I had never seen any thing like this at home. But as I have said, a day came when I began to cease from noting the glories and the charms which the moon and the sun and the twilight wrought upon the river's face; another day came when I ceased altogether to note them. Then, if that sunset scene had been repeated, I should have looked upon it without rapture, and should have commented upon it, inwardly, after this fashion: "This sun means that we are going to have wind to-morrow; that floating log means that the river is rising, small thanks to it; that slanting mark on the water refers to a bluff reef which is going to kill somebody's steamboat one of these nights, if it keeps on stretching out like that; those tumbling 'boils' show a dissolving bar and a changing channel there; the lines and circles in the slick water over yonder are a warning that that troublesome place is shoaling up dangerously; that silver streak in the shadow of the forest is the 'break' from a new snag, and he has located himself in the very best place he could have found to fish for steamboats; that tall dead tree, with a single living branch, is not going to last long, and then how is a body ever going to get through this blind place at night without the friendly old land-mark?"

No, the romance and the beauty were all gone from the river. All the value any feature of it had for me now was the amount of usefulness it could furnish toward compassing the safe piloting of a steamboat. Since those days, I have pitied doctors from my heart. What does the lovely flush in a beauty's cheek mean to a doctor but a "break" that ripples above some deadly disease? Are not all her visible charms sown thick with what are to him the signs and symbols of hidden decay? Does he ever see her beauty at all, or doesn't he simply view her professionally, and comment upon her unwholesome condition all to himself? And doesn't he sometimes wonder whether he has gained most or lost most by learning his trade?

(1883)

Exploring the Text

1. What kind of a student is young Mark Twain as he portrays himself in the first chapter, "Perplexing Lessons"? Consider his interactions with both Mr. Bixby and Mr. W.

2. Twain explains in a footnote that Mr. Bixby uses the term "learn" instead of "teach" because the latter is "not in the river vocabulary"; for example, Bixby states, "When I say I'll learn a man the river, I mean it" (par. 44). What does this distinction say about Bixby's attitude toward the process of education on the river?

3. Throughout these two chapters, Twain focuses on his early education as an apprentice steamboat pilot. What are the primary lessons he learns from Bixby? How would you describe Bixby's teaching methods? What, for instance, does he mean when he explains the necessity of knowing "all the million trifling variations

of shape in the banks of this interminable river . . . *better* than any man ever did know the shapes of the halls in his own house" (pars. 8–9)?

4. Known for his biting wit and satire, Twain once wrote, "Humor is the good natured side of a truth." Do you see evidence of such use of humor in *Life on the Mississippi*? Find at least three examples of humor in this excerpt, including both sharp and gentle, and discuss what effect(s) Twain achieves through humor. How does Twain use it to express his version of the truth?

5. Twain portrays the Mississippi River as a character as much as he portrays Mr. Bixby, Mr. W., and others. What are the qualities of this character? What is Twain's attitude toward "her," as he refers to the river? Do you think he is romanticizing the river and the surrounding community and environment?

6. What does Twain mean when he writes, "The face of the water, in time, became a wonderful book" (par. 79)? What details does he offer to expand on and explore this metaphor?

7. Why does Twain believe that once he "had mastered the language of this water . . . [a]ll the grace, the beauty, the poetry, had gone out of the majestic river" (par. 80)?

8. Like all memoir, these two chapters include the voice of the young remembered self along with that of the more mature remembering self. What are the different narrative strategies of each of these voices? Consider dialogue, action, reflection, and tone in your response.

Sarah Orne Jewett

Sarah Orne Jewett (1849–1909) was born in Maine. As a young girl, she accompanied her father, a country doctor, on his visits to patients, an experience that, at least in part, inspired her to write stories about rural New England. She began writing as a child, and at nineteen she had a story published in the *Atlantic Monthly*. One major theme in Jewett's work is the powerful influence of nature. *A White Heron and Other Stories*, published in 1886, and *The Country of the Pointed Firs*, published a decade later, are her best known works.

A White Heron

Following is "A White Heron" (1886), the most popular of Jewett's short stories.

I

The woods were already filled with shadows one June evening, just before eight o'clock, though a bright sunset still glimmered faintly among the trunks of the trees. A little girl was driving home her cow, a plodding, dilatory, provoking creature in her behavior, but a valued companion for all that. They were going away from whatever light there was, and striking deep into the woods, but their feet were familiar with the path, and it was no matter whether their eyes could see it or not.

There was hardly a night the summer through when the old cow could be found waiting at the pasture bars; on the contrary, it was her greatest pleasure to hide herself away among the high huckleberry bushes, and though she wore a loud bell she had made the discovery that if one stood perfectly still it would not ring. So Sylvia had to hunt for her until she found her, and call Co'! Co'! with never an answering Moo, until her childish patience was quite spent. If the creature had not given good milk and plenty of it, the case would have seemed very different to her owners. Besides, Sylvia had all the time there was, and very little use to make of it. Sometimes in pleasant weather it was a consolation to look upon the cow's pranks as an intelligent attempt to play hide and seek, and as the child had no playmates she lent herself to this amusement with a good deal of zest. Though this chase had been so long that the wary animal herself had given an unusual signal of her whereabouts, Sylvia had only laughed when she came upon Mistress Moolly at the swamp-side, and urged her affec- tionately homeward with a twig of birch leaves. The old cow was not inclined to wander farther, she even turned in the right direction for once as they left the pasture, and stepped along the road at a good pace. She was quite ready to be milked now, and seldom stopped to browse. Sylvia wondered what her grandmother would say because they were so late. It was a great while since she had left home at half-past five o'clock, but everybody knew the difficulty of making this errand a short one. Mrs. Tilley had chased the hornéd torment too many summer evenings herself to blame any one else for lingering, and was only thankful as she waited that she had Sylvia, nowadays, to give such valuable assistance. The good woman suspected that Sylvia loitered occa- sionally on her own account; there never was such a child for straying about out-of- doors since the world was made! Everybody said that it was a good change for a little maid who had tried to grow for eight years in a crowded manufacturing town, but, as for Sylvia herself, it seemed as if she never had been alive at all before she came to live at the farm. She thought often with wistful compassion of a wretched geranium that belonged to a town neighbor.

"'Afraid of folks,'" old Mrs. Tilley said to herself, with a smile, after she had made the unlikely choice of Sylvia from her daughter's houseful of children, and was return- ing to the farm. "'Afraid of folks,' they said! I guess she won't be troubled no great with 'em up to the old place!" When they reached the door of the lonely house and stopped to unlock it, and the cat came to purr loudly, and rub against them, a deserted pussy, indeed, but fat with young robins, Sylvia whispered that this was a beautiful place to live in, and she never should wish to go home.

The companions followed the shady wood-road, the cow taking slow steps and the child very fast ones. The cow stopped long at the brook to drink, as if the pasture were not half a swamp, and Sylvia stood still and waited, letting her bare feet cool themselves in the shoal water, while the great twilight moths struck softly against her. She waded on through the brook as the cow moved away, and listened to the thrushes with a heart that beat fast with pleasure. There was a stirring in the great boughs over- head. They were full of little birds and beasts that seemed to be wide awake, and going

Sylvia's heart gave a wild beat; she knew that strange white bird, and had once stolen softly near where it stood in some bright green swamp grass, away over at the other side of the woods. There was an open place where the sunshine always seemed strangely yellow and hot, where tall, nodding rushes grew, and her grandmother had warned her that she might sink in the soft black mud underneath and never be heard of more. Not far beyond were the salt marshes just this side the sea itself, which Sylvia wondered and dreamed much about, but never had seen, whose great voice could sometimes be heard above the noise of the woods on stormy nights.

"I can't think of anything I should like so much as to find that heron's nest," the handsome stranger was saying. "I would give ten dollars to anybody who could show it to me," he added desperately, "and I mean to spend my whole vacation hunting for it if need be. Perhaps it was only migrating, or had been chased out of its own region by some bird of prey."

Mrs. Tilley gave amazed attention to all this, but Sylvia still watched the toad, not divining, as she might have done at some calmer time, that the creature wished to get to its hole under the door-step, and was much hindered by the unusual spectators at that hour of the evening. No amount of thought, that night, could decide how many wished-for treasures the ten dollars, so lightly spoken of, would buy. 25

The next day the young sportsman hovered about the woods, and Sylvia kept him company, having lost her first fear of the friendly lad, who proved to be most kind and sympathetic. He told her many things about the birds and what they knew and where they lived and what they did with themselves. And he gave her a jack-knife, which she thought as great a treasure as if she were a desert-islander. All day long he did not once make her troubled or afraid except when he brought down some unsuspecting singing creature from its bough. Sylvia would have liked him vastly better without his gun; she could not understand why he killed the very birds he seemed to like so much. But as the day waned, Sylvia still watched the young man with loving admiration. She had never seen anybody so charming and delightful; the woman's heart, asleep in the child, was vaguely thrilled by a dream of love. Some premonition of that great power stirred and swayed these young creatures who traversed the solemn woodlands with soft-footed silent care. They stopped to listen to a bird's song; they pressed forward again eagerly, parting the branches, — speaking to each other rarely and in whispers; the young man going first and Sylvia following, fascinated, a few steps behind, with her gray eyes dark with excitement.

She grieved because the longed-for white heron was elusive, but she did not lead the guest, she only followed, and there was no such thing as speaking first. The sound of her own unquestioned voice would have terrified her, — it was hard enough to answer yes or no when there was need of that. At last evening began to fall, and they drove the cow home together, and Sylvia smiled with pleasure when they came to the place where she heard the whistle and was afraid only the night before.

II

Half a mile from home, at the farther edge of the woods, where the land was highest, a great pine-tree stood, the last of its generation. Whether it was left for a boundary mark, or for what reason, no one could say; the woodchoppers who had felled its mates were dead and gone long ago, and a whole forest of sturdy trees, pines and oaks and maples, had grown again. But the stately head of this old pine towered above them all and made a landmark for sea and shore miles and miles away. Sylvia knew it well. She had always believed that whoever climbed to the top of it could see the ocean; and the little girl had often laid her hand on the great rough trunk and looked up wistfully at those dark boughs that the wind always stirred, no matter how hot and still the air might be below. Now she thought of the tree with a new excitement, for why, if one climbed it at break of day, could not one see all the world, and easily discover from whence the white heron flew, and mark the place, and find the hidden nest?

What a spirit of adventure, what wild ambition! What fancied triumph and delight and glory for the later morning when she could make known the secret! It was almost too real and too great for the childish heart to bear.

All night the door of the little house stood open and the whippoorwills came and sang upon the very step. The young sportsman and his old hostess were sound asleep, but Sylvia's great design kept her broad awake and watching. She forgot to think of sleep. The short summer night seemed as long as the winter darkness, and at last when the whippoorwills ceased, and she was afraid the morning would after all come too soon, she stole out of the house and followed the pasture path through the woods, hastening toward the open ground beyond, listening with a sense of comfort and companionship to the drowsy twitter of a half-awakened bird, whose perch she had jarred in passing. Alas, if the great wave of human interest which flooded for the first time this dull little life should sweep away the satisfactions of an existence heart to heart with nature and the dumb life of the forest! 30

There was the huge tree asleep yet in the paling moonlight, and small and silly Sylvia began with utmost bravery to mount to the top of it, with tingling, eager blood coursing the channels of her whole frame, with her bare feet and fingers, that pinched and held like bird's claws to the monstrous ladder reaching up, up, almost to the sky itself. First she must mount the white oak tree that grew alongside, where she was almost lost among the dark branches and the green leaves heavy and wet with dew; a bird fluttered off its nest, and a red squirrel ran to and fro and scolded pettishly at the harmless housebreaker. Sylvia felt her way easily. She had often climbed there, and knew that higher still one of the oak's upper branches chafed against the pine trunk, just where its lower boughs were set close together. There, when she made the dangerous pass from one tree to the other, the great enterprise would really begin.

She crept out along the swaying oak limb at last, and took the daring step across into the old pine-tree. The way was harder than she thought; she must reach far and hold fast, the sharp dry twigs caught and held her and scratched her like angry talons, the pitch made her thin little fingers clumsy and stiff as she went round and round the tree's great stem, higher and higher upward. The sparrows and robins in the woods below were beginning to wake and twitter to the dawn, yet it seemed much lighter there aloft in the pine-tree, and the child knew she must hurry if her project were to be of any use.

The tree seemed to lengthen itself out as she went up, and to reach farther and farther upward. It was like a great main-mast to the voyaging earth; it must truly have been amazed that morning through all its ponderous frame as it felt this determined spark of human spirit wending its way from higher branch to branch. Who knows how steadily the least twigs held themselves to advantage this light, weak creature on her way! The old pine must have loved his new dependent. More than all the hawks, and bats, and moths, and even the sweet voiced thrushes, was the brave, beating heart of the solitary gray-eyed child. And the tree stood still and frowned away the winds that June morning while the dawn grew bright in the east.

Sylvia's face was like a pale star, if one had seen it from the ground, when the last thorny bough was past, and she stood trembling and tired but wholly triumphant, high in the tree-top. Yes, there was the sea with the dawning sun making a golden dazzle over it, and toward that glorious east flew two hawks with slow-moving pinions. How low they looked in the air from that height when one had only seen them before far up, and dark against the blue sky. Their gray feathers were as soft as moths; they seemed only a little way from the tree, and Sylvia felt as if she too could go flying away among the clouds. Westward, the woodlands and farms reached miles and miles into the distance; here and there were church steeples, and white villages, truly it was a vast and awesome world.

The birds sang louder and louder. At last the sun came up bewilderingly bright. 35
Sylvia could see the white sails of ships out at sea, and the clouds that were purple and rose-colored and yellow at first began to fade away. Where was the white heron's nest in the sea of green branches, and was this wonderful sight and pageant of the world the only reward for having climbed to such a giddy height? Now look down again, Sylvia, where the green marsh is set among the shining birches and dark hemlocks; there where you saw the white heron once you will see him again; look, look! a white spot of him like a single floating feather comes up from the dead hemlock and grows larger, and rises, and comes close at last, and goes by the landmark pine with steady sweep of wing and outstretched slender neck and crested head. And wait! wait! do not move a foot or a finger, little girl, do not send an arrow of light and consciousness from your two eager eyes, for the heron has perched on a pine bough not far beyond yours, and cries back to his mate on the nest and plumes his feathers for the new day!

The child gives a long sigh a minute later when a company of shouting cat-birds comes also to the tree, and vexed by their fluttering and lawlessness the solemn heron goes away. She knows his secret now, the wild, light, slender bird that floats and wavers, and goes back like an arrow presently to his home in the green world beneath. Then Sylvia, well satisfied, makes her perilous way down again, not daring to look far below the branch she stands on, ready to cry sometimes because her fingers ache and her lamed feet slip. Wondering over and over again what the stranger would say to her, and what he would think when she told him how to find his way straight to the heron's nest.

"Sylvy, Sylvy!" called the busy old grandmother again and again, but nobody answered, and the small husk bed was empty and Sylvia had disappeared.

The guest waked from a dream, and remembering his day's pleasure hurried to dress himself that might it sooner begin. He was sure from the way the shy little girl looked once or twice yesterday that she had at least seen the white heron, and now she must really be made to tell. Here she comes now, paler than ever, and her worn old frock is torn and tattered, and smeared with pine pitch. The grandmother and the sportsman stand in the door together and question her, and the splendid moment has come to speak of the dead hemlock-tree by the green marsh.

But Sylvia does not speak after all, though the old grandmother fretfully rebukes her, and the young man's kind, appealing eyes are looking straight in her own. He can make them rich with money; he has promised it, and they are poor now. He is so well worth making happy, and he waits to hear the story she can tell.

No, she must keep silence! What is it that suddenly forbids her and makes her   40 dumb? Has she been nine years growing and now, when the great world for the first time puts out a hand to her, must she thrust it aside for a bird's sake? The murmur of the pine's green branches is in her ears, she remembers how the white heron came flying through the golden air and how they watched the sea and the morning together, and Sylvia cannot speak; she cannot tell the heron's secret and give its life away.

Dear loyalty, that suffered a sharp pang as the guest went away disappointed later in the day, that could have served and followed him and loved him as a dog loves! Many a night Sylvia heard the echo of his whistle haunting the pasture path as she came home with the loitering cow. She forgot even her sorrow at the sharp report of his gun and the sight of thrushes and sparrows dropping silent to the ground, their songs hushed and their pretty feathers stained and wet with blood. Were the birds better friends than their hunter might have been, — who can tell? Whatever treasures were lost to her, woodlands and summer-time, remember! Bring your gifts and graces and tell your secrets to this lonely country child!

(1886)

Exploring the Text

1. What is the effect of the imagery in the first paragraph?
2. Look up *sylvan* in the dictionary. What does Sarah Orne Jewett suggest by using *Sylvia* as the name of her protagonist?
3. In paragraph 2, Jewett writes, "The good woman suspected that Sylvia loitered occasionally on her own account; there never was such a child for straying about out-of-doors since the world was made!" In terms of the voice, what is the relationship between the two clauses that make up this sentence?
4. How does Sylvia regard the stranger and his request (par. 8)?
5. How has Jewett characterized the hunter so that he is not simply a villain or an evil force for Sylvia to resist? For instance, what is the significance of his being an ornithologist? What other details and descriptions does Jewett use to make his portrayal more complex?
6. Jewett concludes paragraph 30 by writing, "Alas, if the great wave of human interest which flooded for the first time this dull little life should sweep away the satisfactions of an existence heart to heart with nature and the dumb life of the forest!"

Considering especially such diction as "dull," "little," and "dumb," what is Jewett's attitude toward Sylvia?

7. What is the effect of Jewett's use of personification throughout the story?

8. "A White Heron" may be read as a hero's journey that follows the traditional pattern of a central figure who is cast out from familiar surroundings, undertakes a journey, encounters obstacles, and experiences a significant change, leading to some sort of redemption. Discuss Sylvia's journey from this perspective.

9. Some have characterized Jewett as a local colorist. That is, they view her work, including this story, as regionalist literature that focuses on specific features such as the dialect, customs, and landscape of a geographical area. Regionalist works are thus valued more as reflections of a particular place than as depictions of larger universal themes. Do you see "A White Heron" as primarily an example of regionalism? Explain your answer with specific references to the text of the story.

Albert Bierstadt

Albert Bierstadt (1830–1902) was a German American painter best known for his depictions of the nineteenth-century American West. Having grown up in New Bedford, Massachusetts, where his family settled when they immigrated in 1831, Bierstadt returned to Germany in his twenties to study with members of the highly acclaimed Düsseldorf school of painting. He moved back to America in 1857, and soon after was contracted by the U.S. government to travel west with a land surveyor to create sketches and drawings of the region. Upon his return to the East, Bierstadt converted many of the sketches into finished paintings, and his interest in the American West continued throughout his career.

The Last of the Buffalo

In the following painting from 1888, Bierstadt laments the pending extinction of the buffalo, which had become a pressing issue in the late 1880s as a result of westward expansion. The painting raised awareness of the problem, and following an official government census, a conservation plan was implemented.

Exploring the Text

1. Albert Bierstadt's paintings are often described as epic works showing grand vistas. What elements in this depiction of the American landscape fit these descriptions?

2. What two symbols of the American West are at the center of the painting? How are the fates of these two connected?

Corcoran Gallery of Art, Washington D.C., USA/Gift of Mary (Mrs. Albert) Bierstadt/The Bridgeman Art Library

ALBERT BIERSTADT, *THE LAST OF THE BUFFALO*, 1888, OIL ON CANVAS, 71" × 118¾", CORCORAN GALLERY, WASHINGTON, D.C.
(See color insert, Image 28.)

3. If you read the painting as a narrative, what story is Bierstadt telling? In addition to the central conflict, consider the buffalo in the foreground, the skulls and bones in the left foreground, and the lighting.
4. One critic has described this painting as "a lament for the West that has passed." What specific elements of the painting would you cite to support this interpretation? Do you find such an interpretation realistic? Harsh? Sentimental? Explain your answer.

ANDREW CARNEGIE

Andrew Carnegie (1835–1919) came to America from Scotland at the age of thirteen. In a classic rags-to-riches tale, he rose from poverty to become one of the nation's wealthiest industrialists. After working in entry-level positions for the railroads, Carnegie worked his way up the ladder, eventually noticing the need for sturdy iron bridges for trains, which led to his founding of the Keystone Bridge Company. This emphasis on iron bridges and steel train rails drew him into the steel industry in earnest; he founded Carnegie Steel, which would later become U.S. Steel — at that time the most valuable company in the world. Carnegie devoted the last two decades of his life to philanthropy, encouraging education through public libraries and Carnegie Mellon University and peace through the Carnegie Endowment for International Peace.

from *The Gospel of Wealth*

In this selection written in 1889, when wealth was increasingly being concentrated in the hands of an elite group of industrialists, Carnegie argues that the rich understand best how to use their wealth for the common good. Following is an excerpt from his essay, which was published in the *North American Review*, a highly regarded literary magazine.

The problem of our age is the proper administration of wealth, that the ties of brotherhood may still bind together the rich and poor in harmonious relationship. The conditions of human life have not only been changed, but revolutionized, within the past few hundred years. In former days there was little difference between the dwelling, dress, food, and environment of the chief and those of his retainers. The Indians are today where civilized man then was. . . . The contrast between the palace of the millionaire and the cottage of the laborer with us to-day measures the change which has come with civilization. This change, however, is not to be deplored, but welcomed as highly beneficial. It is well, nay, essential, for the progress of the race that the houses of some should be homes for all that is highest and best in literature and the arts, — and for all the refinements of civilization, rather than that none should be so. Much better this great irregularity than universal squalor. . . . The "good old times" were not good old times. Neither master nor servant was as well situated then as to-day. A relapse to old conditions would be disastrous to both — not the least so to him who serves — and would sweep away civilization with it. But whether the change be for good or ill, it is upon us, beyond our power to alter, and, therefore, to be accepted and made the best of. It is a waste of time to criticize the inevitable.

It is easy to see how the change has come. . . . In the manufacture of products we have the whole story. . . . Formerly, articles were manufactured at the domestic hearth, or in small shops which formed part of the household. The master and his apprentices worked side by side, the latter living with the master, and therefore subject to the same conditions. When these apprentices rose to be masters, there was little or no change in their mode of life, and they, in turn, educated succeeding apprentices in the same routine. There was, substantially, social equality, and even political equality, for those engaged in industrial pursuits had then little or no voice in the State.

The inevitable result of such a mode of manufacture was crude articles at high prices. To-day the world obtains commodities of excellent quality at prices which even the preceding generation would have deemed incredible. . . . The poor enjoy what the rich could not before afford. What were the luxuries have become the necessaries of life. The laborer has now more comforts than the farmer had a few generations ago. The farmer has more luxuries than the landlord had, and is more richly clad and better housed. The landlord has books and pictures rarer and appointments more artistic than the king could then obtain.

The price we pay for this salutary change is, no doubt, great. We assemble thousands of operatives in the factory, and in the mine, of whom the employer can know little or nothing, and to whom he is little better than a myth. All intercourse between them is at an end. Rigid castes are formed, and, as usual, mutual ignorance breeds mutual distrust. Each caste is without sympathy with the other, and ready to credit anything disparaging in regard to it. Under the law of competition, the employer of thousands is forced into the strictest economies, among which the rates paid to labor figure prominently, and often there is friction between the employer and the employed, between capital and labor, between rich and poor. Human society loses homogeneity.

The price which society pays for the law of competition, like the price it pays for cheap comforts and luxuries, is also great; but the advantages of this law are also greater still than its cost — for it is to this law that we owe our wonderful material development, which brings improved conditions in its train. But, whether the law be benign or not, we must say of it, as we say of the change in the conditions of men to which we have referred: It is here; we cannot evade it; no substitutes for it have been found; and while the law may be sometimes hard for the individual, it is best for the race, because it insures the survival of the fittest in every department. We accept and welcome, therefore, as conditions to which we must accommodate ourselves, great inequality of environments; the concentration of business, industrial and commercial, in the hands of a few; and the law of competition between these, as being not only beneficial, but essential to the future progress of the race. . . .

What is the proper mode of administering wealth after the laws upon which civilization is founded have thrown it into the hands of the few? And it is of this great question that I believe I offer the true solution. It will be understood that fortunes are here spoken of, not moderate sums saved by many years of effort, the returns from which are required for the comfortable maintenance and education of families. This is not wealth, but only competence, which it should be the aim of all to acquire, and which it is for the best interests of society should be acquired. . . .

There remains . . . only one mode of using great fortunes; . . . in this we have the true antidote for the temporary unequal distribution of wealth, the reconciliation of the rich and the poor — a reign of harmony. . . . It is founded upon the present most intense Individualism, and the race is prepared to put it in practice by degrees whenever it pleases. Under its sway we shall have an ideal State, in which the surplus wealth of the few will become, in the best sense, the property of the many, because administered for the common good; and this wealth, passing through the hands of the few, can be made a much more potent force for the elevation of our race than if distributed in small sums to the people themselves. Even the poorest can be made to see this, and to agree that great sums gathered by some of their fellow-citizens and spent for public purposes, from which the masses reap the principal benefit, are more valuable to them than if scattered among themselves in trifling amounts through the course of many years. . . .

Poor and restricted are our opportunities in this life, narrow our horizon, our best work most imperfect; but rich men should be thankful for one inestimable boon. They have it in their power during their lives to busy themselves in organizing benefactions from which the masses of their fellows will derive lasting advantage, and thus dignify their own lives. The highest life is probably to be reached, not by such imitation of the life of Christ as Count Tolstoi[1] gives us, but, while animated by Christ's spirit, by recognizing the changed conditions of this age, and adopting modes of expressing this spirit suitable to the changed conditions under which we live, still laboring for the good of our fellows, which was the essence of his life and teaching, but laboring in a different manner.

This, then, is held to be the duty of the man of wealth: To set an example of modest, unostentatious living, shunning display or extravagance; to provide moderately for the legitimate wants of those dependent upon him; and, after doing so, to consider all surplus revenues which come to him simply as trust funds, which he is called upon to administer, and strictly bound as a matter of duty to administer in the manner which, in his judgment, is best calculated to produce the most beneficial results for the community — the man of wealth thus becoming the mere trustee and agent for his poorer brethren, bringing to their service his superior wisdom, experience, and ability to administer, doing for them better than they would or could do for themselves. . . .

[O]ne of the serious obstacles to the improvement of our race is indiscriminate   10
charity. It were better for mankind that the millions of the rich were thrown into the sea than so spent as to encourage the slothful, the drunken, the unworthy. Of every thousand dollars spent in so-called charity to-day; it is probable that nine hundred and fifty dollars is unwisely spent — so spent, indeed, as to produce the very evils which it hopes to mitigate or cure. . . .

[T]he best means of benefiting the community is to place within its reach the ladders upon which the aspiring can rise — free libraries, parks, and means of recreation, by which men are helped in body and mind; works of art, certain to give pleasure and improve the public taste; and public institutions of various kinds, which will improve the general condition of the people; in this manner returning their surplus wealth to the mass of their fellows in the forms best calculated to do them lasting good.

Thus is the problem of rich and poor to be solved. The laws of accumulation will be left free, the laws of distribution free. Individualism will continue, but the millionaire will be but a trustee for the poor, intrusted for a season with a great part of the increased wealth of the community, but administering it for the community far better than it could or would have done for itself. . . .

Such, in my opinion, is the true gospel concerning wealth, obedience to which is destined some day to solve the problem of the rich and the poor, and to bring "Peace on earth, among men good will."

(1889)

Exploring the Text

1. What does Andrew Carnegie mean by this statement in the opening paragraph: "Much better this great irregularity than universal squalor"? How does this statement lay the foundation for the argument that follows?

---

[1]Russian author Leo Tolstoy (1828–1910), whose later works tried to distinguish between Christian doctrine and the true teachings of Jesus. — Eds.

2. What forces and changes does Carnegie consider "inevitable" (par. 1) and why? In what ways does this perspective lay the foundation for his overall argument?

3. What is the logic that Carnegie uses to conclude that the advantages of the "law of competition" (par. 5) outweigh any disadvantages? You might explain his logic through the use of a syllogism or Toulmin analysis.

4. Carnegie uses a number of familiar words that he either defines in narrow terms or assumes his audience understands. What is the meaning of each of the following terms in the context of Carnegie's article: "civilization/civilized" (par. 1), "caste" (par. 4), "race" (par. 5), "progress" (par. 5), "trust fund" (par. 9), and "duty" (par. 9)?

5. How does Carnegie believe the "reign of harmony" (par. 7) between rich and poor will be brought about? Why, according to him, must "indiscriminate charity" (par. 10) be eliminated to achieve such a reconciliation?

6. Identify at least two counterarguments that Carnegie addresses. How effectively does he concede and refute each?

7. On what basis does Carnegie invoke Christian beliefs as part of his argument? What is the effect of calling his beliefs about wealth a "gospel"?

8. To what extent has Carnegie's belief that the wealthiest members of the community should be "trustee[s] for the poor" (par. 12) become an accepted tenet of American culture today?

JACOB RIIS

Jacob Riis (1849–1914) was a Danish American social reformer, journalist, and photographer. Riis emigrated from Denmark to America when he was twenty-one years old and settled in New York, where he first found work as a carpenter and then began his career in journalism. As a police reporter for the *New York Tribune*, Riis focused on the impoverished New Yorkers who populated the slums of the city and with articles and photographs exposed their poor living conditions to the middle and upper classes.

The Mixed Crowd

In 1889, Riis published a magazine article about the harsh realities of the New York City slums, including candid photographs of the tenements and their residents. In response to the article's popularity, Riis expanded it into a book entitled *How the Other Half Lives: Studies among the Tenements of New York*. The book is credited with having contributed to reforms, including New York State's landmark Tenement House Act of 1901. Included here is Chapter 3 from *How the Other Half Lives*, accompanied by two of Riis's groundbreaking photographs.

When once I asked the agent of a notorious Fourth Ward alley how many people might be living in it I was told: One hundred and forty families, one hundred Irish, thirty-eight Italian, and two that spoke the German tongue. Barring the agent herself, there was not a native-born individual in the court. The answer was characteristic of the cosmopolitan character of lower New York, very nearly so of the whole of it, wherever it runs to alleys and courts. One may find for the asking an Italian, a German, a French, African, Spanish, Bohemian, Russian, Scandinavian, Jewish, and Chinese colony. Even the Arab, who peddles "holy earth" from the Battery[1] as a direct importation from Jerusalem, has his exclusive preserves at the lower end of Washington Street. The one thing you shall vainly ask for in the chief city of America is a distinctively American community. There is none; certainly not among the tenements. Where have they gone to, the old inhabitants? I put the question to one who might fairly be presumed to be of the number, since I had found him sighing for the "good old days" when the legend "no Irish need apply" was familiar in the advertising columns of the newspapers. He looked at me with a puzzled air. "I don't know," he said. "I wish I did. Some went to California in '49, some to the war and never came back. The rest, I expect, have gone to heaven, or somewhere. I don't see them 'round here."

Whatever the merit of the good man's conjectures, his eyes did not deceive him. They are not here. In their place has come this queer conglomerate mass of heterogeneous elements, ever striving and working like whiskey and water in one glass, and with the like result final union and a prevailing taint of whiskey. The once unwelcome Irishman has been followed in his turn by the Italian, the Russian Jew, and the Chinaman, and has himself taken a hand at opposition, quite as bitter and quite as ineffectual, against these later hordes. Wherever these have gone they have crowded him out, possessing the block, the street, the ward with their denser swarms. But the Irishman's revenge is complete. Victorious in defeat over his recent as over his more ancient foe, the one who opposed his coming no less than the one who drove him out, he dictates to both their politics, and, secure in possession of the offices, returns the native his greeting with interest, while collecting the rents of the Italian whose house he has bought with the profits of his saloon. As a landlord he is picturesquely autocratic. An amusing instance of his methods came under my notice while writing these lines. An inspector of the Health Department found an Italian family paying a man with a Celtic name twenty-five dollars a month for three small rooms in a ramshackle rear tenement — more than twice what they were worth — and expressed his astonishment to the tenant, an ignorant Sicilian laborer. He replied that he had once asked the landlord to reduce the rent, but he would not do it.

"Well! What did he say?" asked the inspector.

---

[1]The southern shoreline of Manhattan, which was used as a cannon battery to defend the Dutch settlement of New Amsterdam; it served that role in later wars as well. — Eds.

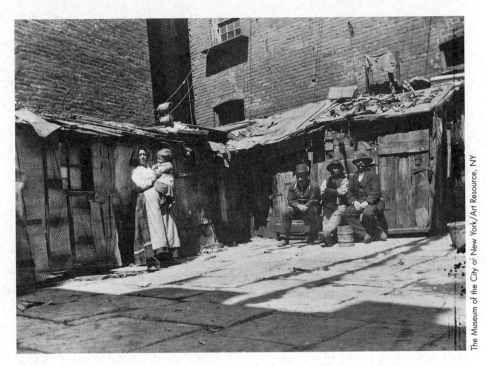

The Museum of the City of New York/Art Resource, NY

It Costs a Dollar a Month to Sleep in These Sheds (c. 1902).

"'Damma, man!' he said; 'if you speaka thata way to me, I fira you and your things in the streeta.'" And the frightened Italian paid the rent.

In justice to the Irish landlord it must be said that like an apt pupil he was   5
merely showing forth the result of the schooling he had received, re-enacting, in his own way, the scheme of the tenements. It is only his frankness that shocks. The Irishman does not naturally take kindly to tenement life, though with characteristic versatility he adapts himself to its conditions at once. It does violence, nevertheless, to the best that is in him, and for that very reason of all who come within its sphere soonest corrupts him. The result is a sediment, the product of more than a generation in the city's slums, that, as distinguished from the larger body of his class, justly ranks at the foot of tenement dwellers, the so-called "low Irish."

It is not to be assumed, of course, that the whole body of the population living in the tenements, of which New Yorkers are in the habit of speaking vaguely as "the poor," or even the larger part of it, is to be classed as vicious or as poor in the sense of verging on beggary.

New York's wage-earners have no other place to live, more is the pity. They are truly poor for having no better homes; waxing poorer in purse as the exorbitant rents to which they are tied, as ever was serf to soil, keep rising. The wonder is that they are not all corrupted, and speedily, by their surroundings. If, on the contrary, there be a steady working up, if not out of the slough, the fact is a powerful argument for the optimist's belief that the world is, after all, growing better, not worse, and would go far toward disarming apprehension, were it not for the steadier growth of the sediment of the slums and its constant menace. Such an impulse toward better things there certainly is. The German rag-picker of thirty years ago, quite as low in the scale as his Italian successor, is the thrifty tradesman or prosperous fanner[2] of to-day.[3]

The Italian scavenger of our time is fast graduating into exclusive control of the corner fruit-stands, while his black-eyed boy monopolizes the boot-blacking industry in which a few years ago he was an intruder. The Irish hod-carrier[4] in the second generation has become a brick-layer, if not the Alderman of his ward, while the Chinese coolie[5] is in almost exclusive possession of the laundry business. The reason is obvious. The poorest immigrant comes here with the purpose and ambition to better himself and, given half a chance, might be reasonably expected to make the most of it. To the false plea that he prefers the squalid homes in which his kind are housed there could be no better answer. The truth is, his half chance has too long been wanting, and for the bad result he has been unjustly blamed.

As emigration from east to west follows the latitude, so does the foreign influx in New York distribute itself along certain well-defined lines that waver and break only under the stronger pressure of a more gregarious race or the encroachments of inexorable business. A feeling of dependence upon mutual effort, natural to strangers in a strange land, unacquainted with its language and customs, sufficiently accounts for this.

The Irishman is the true cosmopolitan immigrant. All-pervading, he shares his   10
lodging with perfect impartiality with the Italian, the Greek, and the "Dutchman," yielding only to sheer force of numbers, and objects equally to them all. A map of the city, colored to designate nationalities, would show more stripes than on the skin of a zebra, and more colors than any rainbow. The city on such a map would fall into two great halves, green for the Irish prevailing in the West Side tenement districts, and blue for the Germans on the East Side. But intermingled with these ground colors would be an odd variety of tints that would give the whole the appearance of an extraordinary crazy-quilt. From down in the Sixth Ward, upon the site of the old Collect Pond that in the days of the fathers drained the hills which are no more, the red of the Italian would be seen forcing its way northward along the line of Mulberry Street to the quarter of the French purple on Bleecker Street and South Fifth Avenue, to lose itself and reappear, after a lapse of miles, in the "Little Italy" of Harlem, east

---

[2]Someone who winnows or cleans grain using a fan to blow away dirt and husks. — Eds.
[3]The Sheriff Street Colony of rag-pickers, long since gone, is an instance in point. The thrifty Germans saved up money during years of hard work in squalor and apparently wretched poverty to buy a township in a Western State, and the whole colony moved out there in a body. There need be no doubt about their thriving there. — Riis
[4]Coal carrier, but also a general term for an unskilled laborer. — Eds.
[5]Term for Chinese and Indian laborers that, in current usage, is derogatory. — Eds.

Image copyright © The Metropolitan Museum of Art. Image source: Art Resource, NY.

Baby in a Slum Tenement (c. 1889).

of Second Avenue. Dashes of red, sharply defined, would be seen strung through the Annexed District, northward to the city line. On the West Side the red would be seen overrunning the old Africa of Thompson Street, pushing the black of the negro rapidly uptown, against querulous but unavailing protests, occupying his home, his church, his trade and all, with merciless impartiality. There is a church in Mulberry Street that has stood for two generations as a sort of milestone of these migrations. Built originally for the worship of staid New Yorkers of the "old stock," it was engulfed by the colored tide, when the draft-riots drove the negroes out of reach of Cherry Street and the Five Points. Within the past decade the advance wave of the Italian onset reached it, and to-day the arms of United Italy adorn its front. The negroes have made a stand at several points along Seventh and Eighth Avenues; but their main body, still pursued by the Italian foe, is on the march yet, and the black mark will be found overshadowing to-day many blocks on the East Side, with One Hundredth Street as the centre, where colonies of them have settled recently.

Hardly less aggressive than the Italian, the Russian and Polish Jew, having overrun the district between Rivington and Division Streets, east of the Bowery, to the point of suffocation, is filling the tenements of the old Seventh Ward to the river front, and disputing with the Italian every foot of available space in the back alleys of Mulberry Street. The two races, differing hopelessly in much, have this in common: they carry their slums with them wherever they go, if allowed to do it. Little Italy already rivals its parent, the "Bend," in foulness. Other nationalities that begin at the bottom make a fresh start when crowded up the ladder. Happily both are manageable, the one by rabbinical, the other by the civil law. Between the dull gray of the Jew, his favorite color, and the Italian red, would be seen squeezed in on the map a sharp streak of yellow, marking the narrow boundaries of Chinatown. Dovetailed in with the German population, the poor but thrifty Bohemian might be picked out by the sombre hue of his life as of his philosophy, struggling against heavy odds in the big human bee-hives of the East Side. Colonies of his people extend northward, with long lapses of space, from below the Cooper Institute[6] more than three miles. The Bohemian is the only foreigner with any considerable representation in the city who counts no wealthy man of his race, none who has not to work hard for a living, or has got beyond the reach of the tenement.

(1890)

Exploring the Text

1. In the first paragraph, Jacob Riis writes, "The one thing you shall vainly ask for in the chief city of America is a distinctly American community." Do you find that statement ironic? Do you find it characteristic of our idea of the "melting pot"? Explain.
2. Riis, in paragraphs 2 and 3, describes the "picturesquely autocratic" Irish landlord; in paragraph 5, he states, "In justice to the Irish landlord it must be said that like an apt pupil he was merely showing forth the result of the schooling he had received, re-enacting, in his own way, the scheme of the tenements." What does Riis mean by that last statement? What is his larger point that this example of the Irish serves to support?
3. Riis refers to the "German rag-picker," the "Italian scavenger," the "Irish hod-carrier," and the "Chinese coolie" (pars. 7 and 8). Do you read these phrases as stereotypes? Are they offensive? Why or why not? Why has Riis chosen to use these examples?
4. How does Riis characterize the immigrant in paragraph 8? Is this characterization inconsistent or consistent with the previous paragraphs? Explain.
5. Look very carefully at the diction and imagery Riis uses in paragraphs 10 and 11. How do his rhetorical choices characterize the immigrant's struggle? How do these choices reflect the relationship between Riis and his likely audience?
6. What do you see as Riis's purpose in this piece? To what extent do you believe he succeeds in achieving that purpose?
7. What is most striking about the photos that accompany this essay? What argument is Riis making through them? Cite specific details that support his claim(s).

---

[6]Founded by Peter Cooper, the Cooper Institute (now called Cooper Union) is a private college located in New York's East Village neighborhood. — Eds.

8. Although Riis did feature individuals, especially children, in some of his photos, more often he chose to depict a group image. Why? What is the impact of de-emphasizing the individual in these group portraits?

9. In the introduction to *How the Other Half Lives*, Riis wrote the following:

> Long ago it was said that "one half of the world does not know how the other half lives." That was true then. It did not know because it did not care. The half that was on top cared little for the struggles, and less for the fate, of those who were underneath, so long as it was able to hold them there and keep its own seat.

In what ways does this essay with the accompanying photographs insist that the "half that was on top" pay attention to and care about the "struggles" and "fate" of the "other half"? How does Riis appeal to the conscience and fears of the middle- and upper-class viewer?

AMBROSE BIERCE

Ambrose Bierce (1842–c. 1914) was an American journalist, critic, and short-story writer from Meigs County, Ohio. When the Civil War broke out in 1861, Bierce enlisted in the Union army, where he served as a topographer and fought in many well-known battles such as Shiloh, Pickett's Mill, and Chickamauga. He resigned from the army in 1865 and moved to California, where he began his writing career, becoming a regular columnist and editorialist for the *San Francisco Examiner*. Bierce also wrote novels, poems, and fables, but is most famous for his *Devil's Dictionary*, which includes sardonic definitions of common words, for instance: Bride, n., A woman with a fine prospect of happiness behind her. Hoping to report firsthand on Pancho Villa and the Mexican Revolution, Bierce traveled to Mexico in 1913; he disappeared in 1914 and was never seen again.

An Occurrence at Owl Creek Bridge

This short story, Bierce's most famous, was originally published in the *San Francisco Examiner* in 1890.

I

A man stood upon a railroad bridge in Northern Alabama, looking down into the swift waters twenty feet below. The man's hands were behind his back, the wrists bound with a cord. A rope loosely encircled his neck. It was attached to a stout cross-timber above his head, and the slack fell to the level of his knees. Some loose boards laid upon the sleepers supporting the metals of the railway supplied a footing for him and his executioners — two private soldiers of the Federal army, directed by a sergeant, who in civil life may have been a deputy sheriff. At a short remove upon the same temporary platform was an officer in the uniform of his rank, armed. He was a captain. A sentinel at each end of the bridge stood with his rifle in the position known as "support," that is to say, vertical in front of the left shoulder, the hammer resting on the forearm thrown straight across the chest — a formal and unnatural position, enforcing an erect carriage of the body. It did not appear to be the duty of these two men to know what was occurring at the centre of the bridge; they merely blockaded the two ends of the foot plank which traversed it.

Beyond one of the sentinels nobody was in sight; the railroad ran straight away into a forest for a hundred yards, then, curving, was lost to view. Doubtless there was an outpost further along. The other bank of the stream was open ground — a gentle acclivity crowned with a stockade of vertical tree trunks, loop-holed for rifles, with a single embrasure through which protruded the muzzle of a brass cannon commanding the bridge. Midway of the slope between bridge and fort were the spectators — a single company of infantry in line, at "parade rest," the butts of the rifles on the ground, the barrels inclining slightly backward against the right shoulder, the hands crossed upon the stock. A lieutenant stood at the right of the line, the point of his sword upon the ground, his left hand resting upon his right. Excepting the group of four at the centre of the bridge not a man moved. The company faced the bridge, staring stonily, motionless. The sentinels, facing the banks of the stream, might have been statues to adorn the bridge. The captain stood with folded arms, silent, observing the work of his subordinates but making no sign. Death is a dignitary who, when he comes announced, is to be received with formal manifestations of respect, even by those most familiar with him. In the code of military etiquette silence and fixity are forms of deference.

The man who was engaged in being hanged was apparently about thirty-five years of age. He was a civilian, if one might judge from his dress, which was that of a planter. His features were good — a straight nose, firm mouth, broad forehead, from which his long, dark hair was combed straight back, falling behind his ears to the collar of his well-fitted frock coat. He wore a moustache and pointed beard, but no whiskers; his eyes were large and dark grey and had a kindly expression which one would hardly have expected in one whose neck was in the hemp. Evidently this was no vulgar assassin. The liberal military code makes provision for hanging many kinds of people, and gentlemen are not excluded.

The preparations being complete, the two private soldiers stepped aside and each drew away the plank upon which he had been standing. The sergeant turned to the captain, saluted and placed himself immediately behind that officer, who in turn moved apart one pace. These movements left the condemned man and the sergeant standing on the two ends of the same plank, which spanned three of the cross-ties of the bridge. The end upon which the civilian stood almost, but not quite, reached a fourth. This plank had been held in place by the weight of the captain; it was now held by that of the sergeant. At a signal from the former, the latter would step aside, the plank would tilt and the condemned man go down between two ties. The arrangement commended itself to his judgment as simple and effective. His face had not been covered nor his eyes bandaged. He looked a moment at his "unsteadfast footing," then let his gaze wander to the swirling water of the stream racing madly beneath his feet. A piece of dancing driftwood caught his attention and his eyes followed it down the current. How slowly it appeared to move! What a sluggish stream!

He closed his eyes in order to fix his last thoughts upon his wife and children. The water, touched to gold by the early sun, the brooding mists under the banks at some distance down the stream, the fort, the soldiers, the piece of drift — all had distracted him. And now he became conscious of a new disturbance. Striking through the thought of his dear ones was a sound which he could neither ignore nor understand, a sharp, distinct, metallic percussion like the stroke of a blacksmith's hammer upon the anvil; it had the same ringing quality. He wondered what it was, and whether immeasurably distant or near by — it seemed both. Its recurrence was regular, but as slow as the tolling of a death knell. He awaited each stroke with impatience and — he knew not why — apprehension. The intervals of silence grew progressively longer; the delays became maddening. With their greater infrequency the sounds increased in strength and sharpness. They hurt his ear like the thrust of a knife; he feared he would shriek. What he heard was the ticking of his watch. 5

He unclosed his eyes and saw again the water below him. "If I could free my hands," he thought, "I might throw off the noose and spring into the stream. By diving I could evade the bullets, and, swimming vigorously, reach the bank, take to the woods, and get away home. My home, thank God, is as yet outside their lines; my wife and little ones are still beyond the invader's farthest advance."

As these thoughts, which have here to be set down in words, were flashed into the doomed man's brain rather than evolved from it, the captain nodded to the sergeant. The sergeant stepped aside.

II

Peyton Farquhar was a well-to-do planter, of an old and highly respected Alabama family. Being a slave owner, and, like other slave owners, a politician, he was naturally an original secessionist and ardently devoted to the Southern cause. Circumstances of an imperious nature which it is unnecessary to relate here, had prevented him from taking service with the gallant army which had fought the disastrous campaigns ending with the fall of Corinth,[1] and he chafed under the inglorious restraint, longing for the release of his energies, the larger life of the soldier, the opportunity for distinction. That opportunity, he felt, would come, as it comes to all in war time. Meanwhile he did what he could. No service was too humble for him to perform in aid of the South, no adventure too perilous for him to undertake if consistent with the character of a civilian who was at heart a soldier, and who in good faith and without too much qualification assented to at least a part of the frankly villainous dictum that all is fair in love and war.

---

[1]Corinth, Mississippi, was taken by the Union army in May 1862. — Eds.

One evening while Farquhar and his wife were sitting on a rustic bench near the entrance to his grounds, a grey-clad soldier rode up to the gate and asked for a drink of water. Mrs. Farquhar was only too happy to serve him with her own white hands. While she was gone to fetch the water, her husband approached the dusty horseman and inquired eagerly for news from the front.

"The Yanks are repairing the railroads," said the man, "and are getting ready for 10 another advance. They have reached the Owl Creek bridge, put it in order, and built a stockade on the other bank. The commandant has issued an order, which is posted everywhere, declaring that any civilian caught interfering with the railroad, its bridges, tunnels, or trains, will be summarily hanged. I saw the order."

"How far is it to the Owl Creek bridge?" Farquhar asked.

"About thirty miles."

"Is there no force on this side the creek?"

"Only a picket post half a mile out, on the railroad, and a single sentinel at this end of the bridge."

"Suppose a man—a civilian and student of hanging—should elude the picket 15 post and perhaps get the better of the sentinel," said Farquhar, smiling, "what could he accomplish?"

The soldier reflected. "I was there a month ago," he replied. "I observed that the flood of last winter had lodged a great quantity of driftwood against the wooden pier at this end of the bridge. It is now dry and would burn like tow."

The lady had now brought the water, which the soldier drank. He thanked her ceremoniously, bowed to her husband, and rode away. An hour later, after nightfall, he repassed the plantation, going northward in the direction from which he had come. He was a Federal scout.

III

As Peyton Farquhar fell straight downward through the bridge, he lost consciousness and was as one already dead. From this state he was awakened—ages later, it seemed to him—by the pain of a sharp pressure upon his throat, followed by a sense of suffocation. Keen, poignant agonies seemed to shoot from his neck downward through every fibre of his body and limbs. These pains appeared to flash along well-defined lines of ramification, and to beat with an inconceivably rapid periodicity. They seemed like streams of pulsating fire heating him to an intolerable temperature. As to his head, he was conscious of nothing but a feeling of fullness—of congestion. These sensations were unaccompanied by thought. The intellectual part of his nature was already effaced; he had power only to feel, and feeling was torment. He was conscious of motion. Encompassed in a luminous cloud, of which he was now merely the fiery heart, without material substance, he swung through unthinkable arcs of oscillation, like a vast pendulum. Then all at once, with terrible suddenness, the light about him shot upward with the noise of a loud plash; a frightful roaring was in his ears, and all was cold and dark. The power of thought was restored; he knew that the rope had broken and he had fallen into the stream. There was no additional strangulation; the noose about his neck was already suffocating him, and kept the water from his lungs.

To die of hanging at the bottom of a river — the idea seemed to him ludicrous. He opened his eyes in the blackness and saw above him a gleam of light, but how distant, how inaccessible! He was still sinking, for the light became fainter and fainter until it was a mere glimmer. Then it began to grow and brighten, and he knew that he was rising toward the surface — knew it with reluctance, for he was now very comfortable. "To be hanged and drowned," he thought, "that is not so bad; but I do not wish to be shot. No; I will not be shot; that is not fair."

He was not conscious of an effort, but a sharp pain in his wrist apprised him that he was trying to free his hands. He gave the struggle his attention, as an idler might observe the feat of a juggler, without interest in the outcome. What splendid effort! — what magnificent, what superhuman strength! Ah, that was a fine endeavor! Bravo! The cord fell away; his arms parted and floated upward, the hands dimly seen on each side in the growing light. He watched them with a new interest as first one and then the other pounced upon the noose at his neck. They tore it away and thrust it fiercely aside, its undulations resembling those of a water-snake. "Put it back, put it back!" He thought he shouted these words to his hands, for the undoing of the noose had been succeeded by the direst pang which he had yet experienced. His neck arched horribly; his brain was on fire; his heart, which had been fluttering faintly, gave a great leap, trying to force itself out at his mouth. His whole body was racked and wrenched with an insupportable anguish! But his disobedient hands gave no heed to the command. They beat the water vigorously with quick, downward strokes, forcing him to the surface. He felt his head emerge; his eyes were blinded by the sunlight; his chest expanded convulsively, and with a supreme and crowning agony his lungs engulfed a great draught of air, which instantly he expelled in a shriek!

He was now in full possession of his physical senses. They were, indeed, preter- 20 naturally keen and alert. Something in the awful disturbance of his organic system had so exalted and refined them that they made record of things never before perceived. He felt the ripples upon his face and heard their separate sounds as they struck. He looked at the forest on the bank of the stream, saw the individual trees, the leaves and the veining of each leaf — saw the very insects upon them, the locusts, the brilliant-bodied flies, the grey spiders stretching their webs from twig to twig. He noted the prismatic colors in all the dewdrops upon a million blades of grass. The humming of the gnats that danced above the eddies of the stream, the beating of the dragon flies' wings, the strokes of the water spiders' legs, like oars which had lifted their boat — all these made audible music. A fish slid along beneath his eyes and he heard the rush of its body parting the water.

He had come to the surface facing down the stream; in a moment the visible world seemed to wheel slowly round, himself the pivotal point, and he saw the bridge, the fort, the soldiers upon the bridge, the captain, the sergeant, the two privates, his executioners. They were in silhouette against the blue sky. They shouted and gesticulated, pointing at him; the captain had drawn his pistol, but did not fire; the others were unarmed. Their movements were grotesque and horrible, their forms gigantic.

Suddenly he heard a sharp report and something struck the water smartly within a few inches of his head, spattering his face with spray. He heard a second report, and saw one of the sentinels with his rifle at his shoulder, a light cloud of blue smoke rising from the muzzle. The man in the water saw the eye of the man on the bridge gazing into his own through the sights of the rifle. He observed that it was a grey eye, and remembered having read that grey eyes were keenest and that all famous marksmen had them. Nevertheless, this one had missed.

A counter swirl had caught Farquhar and turned him half round; he was again looking into the forest on the bank opposite the fort. The sound of a clear, high voice in a monotonous singsong now rang out behind him and came across the water with a distinctness that pierced and subdued all other sounds, even the beating of the ripples in his ears. Although no soldier, he had frequented camps enough to know the dread significance of that deliberate, drawling, aspirated chant; the lieutenant on shore was taking a part in the morning's work. How coldly and pitilessly — with what an even, calm intonation, presaging and enforcing tranquility in the men — with what accurately-measured intervals fell those cruel words:

"Attention, company. . . . Shoulder arms. . . . Ready. . . . Aim. . . . Fire."

Farquhar dived — dived as deeply as he could. The water roared in his ears like   25
the voice of Niagara, yet he heard the dulled thunder of the volley, and rising again toward the surface, met shining bits of metal, singularly flattened, oscillating slowly downward. Some of them touched him on the face and hands, then fell away, continuing their descent. One lodged between his collar and neck; it was uncomfortably warm, and he snatched it out.

As he rose to the surface, gasping for breath, he saw that he had been a long time under water; he was perceptibly farther down stream — nearer to safety. The soldiers had almost finished reloading; the metal ramrods flashed all at once in the sunshine as they were drawn from the barrels, turned in the air, and thrust into their sockets. The two sentinels fired again, independently and ineffectually.

The hunted man saw all this over his shoulder; he was now swimming vigorously with the current. His brain was as energetic as his arms and legs; he thought with the rapidity of lightning.

"The officer," he reasoned, "will not make the martinet's error a second time. It is as easy to dodge a volley as a single shot. He has probably already given the command to fire at will. God help me, I cannot dodge them all!"

An appalling plash within two yards of him, followed by a loud rushing sound, *diminuendo*, which seemed to travel back through the air to the fort and died in an explosion which stirred the very river to its deeps! A rising sheet of water, which curved over him, fell down upon him, blinded him, strangled him! The cannon had taken a hand in the game. As he shook his head free from the commotion of the smitten water, he heard the deflected shot humming through the air ahead, and in an instant it was cracking and smashing the branches in the forest beyond.

"They will not do that again," he thought; "the next time they will use a charge   30
of grape. I must keep my eye upon the gun; the smoke will apprise me — the report arrives too late; it lags behind the missile. It is a good gun."

Suddenly he felt himself whirled round and round — spinning like a top. The water, the banks, the forest, the now distant bridge, fort, and men — all were commingled and blurred. Objects were represented by their colors only; circular horizontal streaks of color — that was all he saw. He had been caught in a vortex and was being whirled on with a velocity of advance and gyration which made him giddy and sick. In a few moments he was flung upon the gravel at the foot of the left bank of the stream — the southern bank — and behind a projecting point which concealed him from his enemies. The sudden arrest of his motion, the abrasion of one of his hands on the gravel, restored him and he wept with delight. He dug his fingers into the sand, threw it over himself in handfuls and audibly blessed it. It looked like gold, like diamonds, rubies, emeralds; he could think of nothing beautiful which it did not resemble. The trees upon the bank were giant garden plants; he noted a definite order in their arrangement, inhaled the fragrance of their blooms. A strange, roseate light shone through the spaces among their trunks, and the wind made in their branches the music of æolian harps.[2] He had no wish to perfect his escape, was content to remain in that enchanting spot until retaken.

A whizz and rattle of grapeshot among the branches high above his head roused him from his dream. The baffled cannoneer had fired him a random farewell. He sprang to his feet, rushed up the sloping bank, and plunged into the forest.

All that day he travelled, laying his course by the rounding sun. The forest seemed interminable; nowhere did he discover a break in it, not even a woodman's road. He had not known that he lived in so wild a region. There was something uncanny in the revelation.

By nightfall he was fatigued, footsore, famishing. The thought of his wife and children urged him on. At last he found a road which led him in what he knew to be the right direction. It was as wide and straight as a city street, yet it seemed untravelled. No fields bordered it, no dwelling anywhere. Not so much as the barking of a dog suggested human habitation. The black bodies of the great trees formed a straight wall on both sides, terminating on the horizon in a point, like a diagram in a lesson in perspective. Overhead, as he looked up through this rift in the wood, shone great golden stars looking unfamiliar and grouped in strange constellations. He was sure they were arranged in some order which had a secret and malign significance. The wood on either side was full of singular noises, among which — once, twice, and again — he distinctly heard whispers in an unknown tongue.

His neck was in pain, and, lifting his hand to it, he found it horribly swollen. He 35 knew that it had a circle of black where the rope had bruised it. His eyes felt congested; he could no longer close them. His tongue was swollen with thirst; he relieved its fever by thrusting it forward from between his teeth into the cool air. How softly the turf had carpeted the untravelled avenue! He could no longer feel the roadway beneath his feet!

Doubtless, despite his suffering, he fell asleep while walking, for now he sees another scene — perhaps he has merely recovered from a delirium. He stands at the gate of his own home. All is as he left it, and all bright and beautiful in the morning sunshine. He must have travelled the entire night. As he pushes open the gate and passes up the wide white walk, he sees a flutter of female garments; his wife, looking

---

[2]In Greek mythology, stringed musical instruments played by the wind. — Eds.

fresh and cool and sweet, steps down from the verandah to meet him. At the bottom of the steps she stands waiting, with a smile of ineffable joy, an attitude of matchless grace and dignity. Ah, how beautiful she is! He springs forward with extended arms. As he is about to clasp her, he feels a stunning blow upon the back of the neck; a blinding white light blazes all about him, with a sound like a shock of a cannon — then all is darkness and silence!

Peyton Farquhar was dead; his body, with a broken neck, swung gently from side to side beneath the timbers of the Owl Creek bridge.

(1890)

Exploring the Text

1. Consider the title of the story: "An Occurrence at Owl Creek Bridge." Why "an" and not "the"? Why the general, objective word "occurrence"? Note a few other examples of the flat, objective nature of the narration. What effect(s) does Ambrose Bierce achieve by choosing to narrate in this way?

2. This story is notable for the vivid quality of its description. Find three examples of strong visual description. How do such appeals to the sense of sight contribute to the author's purpose?

3. What is the purpose of section II of the story, which shifts in time from sections I and III?

4. To what extent were you surprised by the ending of the story? Specifically, what was your reaction to the final sentence? What do you think that Bierce intended or did not intend this story to be about?

5. What clues to the ending of the story did you find as you first read it? Upon rereading, what additional clues do you see? Pay particular attention to paragraphs 18–20.

6. Reviewing a new collected edition of Bierce's works in the May 2012 edition of the *New York Review of Books*, literary critic Michael Dirda writes:

   > Throughout these gruesome episodes of war, there is no armor against fate, as seeming coincidence assumes the character of tragic destiny. Bierce himself always insisted that most of his Civil War fiction was based on fact. As he wrote in a letter, "It commonly occurs that in my poor little battle-yarns the incidents that come in for special reprobation by the critics as 'improbable' and even 'impossible' are transcripts from memory — things that actually occurred before my eyes." The Battle of Shiloh, for instance, took place near Owl Creek.

   Do you regard the story as "improbable" or "impossible"? Or do you see it as realistic? What in the story would lead the reader to regard it as having been based on fact? Explain.

7. Modern American writer Kurt Vonnegut Jr. called "An Occurrence at Owl Creek Bridge" the greatest American short story. What might account for his estimation? Do you agree? Why or why not?

8. Watch French director Robert Enrico's 1962 short film (24 minutes) "An Occurrence at Owl Creek Bridge," which aired on *The Twilight Zone* in 1964. The film won awards at both the Cannes Film Festival and the Academy Awards. Compare and contrast the film with the short story.

Ida B. Wells-Barnett

The daughter of slaves, Ida B. Wells-Barnett (1862–1931) was born in Mississippi and raised six of her siblings after both her parents and their youngest child died in a yellow fever epidemic in 1878. She worked as a teacher and journalist, becoming the editor and part owner of the *Memphis Free Speech* at age twenty-seven. She became increasingly committed to uncovering the brutality of lynching after three African American business owners, including a friend of hers, were lynched in Memphis in 1892.

from *Southern Horrors*
Lynch Law in All Its Phases

Wells-Barnett expanded a seven-column article written for the *New York Age* into a pamphlet entitled "Southern Horrors: Lynch Law in All Its Phases." The "lynch law" referred to the practice of punishment through mob action without due process of law. Following is the preface and a selection from that pamphlet.

Preface

The greater part of what is contained in these pages was published in the New York *Age* June 25, 1892, in explanation of the editorial which the Memphis whites considered sufficiently infamous to justify the destruction of my paper, *The Free Speech*.

Since the appearance of that statement, requests have come from all parts of the country that "Exiled," (the name under which it then appeared) be issued in pamphlet form. Some donations were made, but not enough for that purpose. The noble effort of the ladies of New York and Brooklyn . . . have enabled me to comply with this request and give the world a true, unvarnished account of the causes of lynch law in the South.

This statement is not a shield for the despoiler of virtue, nor altogether a defense for the poor blind Afro-American Sampsons who suffer themselves to be betrayed by white Delilahs. It is a contribution to truth, an array of facts, the perusal of which it is hoped will stimulate this great American Republic to demand that justice be done though the heavens fall.

It is with no pleasure I have dipped my hands in the corruption here exposed. Somebody must show that the Afro-American race is more sinned against than sinning, and it seems to have fallen upon me to do so. The awful death-roll that Judge

Lynch is calling every week is appalling, not only because of the lives it takes, the rank cruelty and outrage to the victims, but because of the prejudice it fosters and the stain it places against the good name of a weak race.

The Afro-American is not a bestial race. If this work can contribute in any way   5 toward proving this, and at the same time arouse the conscience of the American people to a demand for justice to every citizen, and punishment by law for the lawless, I shall feel I have done my race a service. Other considerations are of minor importance.

Ida B. Wells.

New York City, Oct. 26, 1892.

To the Afro-American women of New York and Brooklyn, whose race love, earnest zeal and unselfish effort at Lyric Hall, in the City of New York, on the night of October 5th, 1892, — made possible its publication, this pamphlet is gratefully dedicated by the author.

Chapter V: The South's Position

Henry W. Grady[1] in his well-mannered speeches in New England and New York pictured the Afro-American as incapable of self-government. Through him and other leading men the cry of the South to the country has been "Hands off! Leave us to solve our problem." To the Afro-American the South says, "the white man must and will rule." There is little difference between the Ante-bellum South and the New South.

Her white citizens are wedded to any method however revolting, any measure however extreme, for the subjugation of the young manhood of the race. They have cheated him out of his ballot, deprived him of civil rights or redress therefor in the civil courts, robbed him of the fruits of his labor, and are still murdering, burning and lynching him.

The result is a growing disregard of human life. Lynch law has spread its insidious influence till men in New York State, Pennsylvania and on the free Western plains feel they can take the law in their own hands with impunity, especially where an Afro-American is concerned. The South is brutalized to a degree not realized by its own inhabitants, and the very foundation of government, law and order, are imperilled.

Public sentiment has had a slight "reaction" though not sufficient to stop the crusade of lawlessness and lynching. The spirit of Christianity of the great M. E. Church[2] was aroused to the frequent and revolting crimes against a weak people, enough to pass strong condemnatory resolutions at its General Conference in Omaha last May. The spirit of justice of the grand old party asserted itself sufficiently to secure

---

[1]Henry W. Grady (1850–1889) was a prominent Southern journalist who used articles in the *Atlanta Constitution* to define a vision of the New South — one dependent on neither slavery nor agriculture for its survival. — Eds.

[2]Methodist Episcopal Church. — Eds.

a denunciation of the wrongs, and a feeble declaration of the belief in human rights in the Republican platform at Minneapolis, June 7th. Some of the great dailies and weeklies have swung into line declaring that lynch law must go. The President of the United States issued a proclamation that it be not tolerated in the territories over which he has jurisdiction. Governor Northern and Chief Justice Bleckley of Georgia have proclaimed against it. . . .

The strong arm of the law must be brought to bear upon lynchers in severe pun- 10
ishment, but this cannot and will not be done unless a healthy public sentiment demands and sustains such action.

The men and women in the South who disapprove of lynching and remain silent on the perpetration of such outrages, are *particeps criminis*, accomplices, accessories before and after the fact, equally guilty with the actual law-breakers who would not persist if they did not know that neither the law nor militia would be employed against them.

Chapter VI: Self Help

In the creation of this healthier public sentiment, the Afro-American can do for himself what no one else can do for him. The world looks on with wonder that we have conceded so much and remain law-abiding under such great outrage and provocation.

To Northern capital and Afro-American labor the South owes its rehabilitation. If labor is withdrawn capital will not remain. The Afro-American is thus the backbone of the South. A thorough knowledge and judicious exercise of this power in lynching localities could many times effect a bloodless revolution. The white man's dollar is his god, and to stop this will be to stop outrages in many localities.

The Afro-Americans of Memphis denounced the lynching of three of their best citizens, and urged and waited for the authorities to act in the matter and bring the lynchers to justice. No attempt was made to do so, and the black men left the city by thousands, bringing about great stagnation in every branch of business. Those who remained so injured the business of the street car company by staying off the cars, that the superintendent, manager and treasurer called personally on the editor of the *Free Speech*, asked them to urge our people to give them their patronage again. Other business men became alarmed over the situation and the *Free Speech* was run away that the colored people might be more easily controlled. A meeting of white citizens in June, three months after the lynching, passed resolutions for the first time, condemning it. *But they did not punish the lynchers.* Every one of them was known by name, because they had been elected to do the dirty work, by some of the very citizens who passed these resolutions. Memphis is fast losing her black population, who proclaim as they go that there is no protection for the life and property of any Afro-American citizen in Memphis who is not a slave.

The Afro-American citizens of Kentucky, whose intellectual and financial 15
improvement has been phenomenal, have never had a separate car law until now. Delegations and petitions poured into the Legislature against it, yet the bill passed and the Jim Crow Car of Kentucky is a legalized institution. Will the great mass of Negroes continue to patronize the railroad? A special from Covington, Ky., says:

Covington, June 13th. — The railroads of the State are beginning to feel very markedly, the effects of the separate coach bill recently passed by the Legislature. No class of people in the State have so many and so largely attended excursions as the blacks. All these have been abandoned, and regular travel is reduced to a minimum. A competent authority says the loss to the various roads will reach $1,000,000 this year.

A call to a State Conference in Lexington, Ky., last June had delegates from every country in the State. Those delegates, the ministers, teachers, heads of secret and others orders, and the head of every family should [pass] the word around for every member of the race in Kentucky to stay off railroads unless obliged to ride. If they did so, and their advice was followed persistently the convention would not need to petition the Legislature to repeal the law or raise money to file a suit. The railroad corporations would be so effected they would in self-defense lobby to have the separate car law repealed. On the other hand, as long as the railroads can get Afro-American excursions they will always have plenty of money to fight all the suits brought against them. They will be aided in so doing by the same partisan public sentiment which passed the law. White men passed the law, and white judges and juries would pass upon the suits against the law, and render judgment in line with their prejudices and in deference to the greater financial power.

The appeal to the white man's pocket has ever been more effectual than all the appeals ever made to his conscience. Nothing, absolutely nothing, is to be gained by a further sacrifice of manhood and self-respect. By the right exercise of his power as the industrial factor of the South, the Afro-American can demand and secure his rights, the punishment of lynchers, and a fair trial for accused rapists.

Of the many inhuman outrages of this present year, the only case where the proposed lynching did *not* occur, was where the men armed themselves in Jacksonville, Fla., and Paducah, Ky., and prevented it. The only times an Afro-American who was assaulted got away has been when he had a gun and used it in self-defense.

The lesson this teaches and which every Afro-American should ponder well, is that a Winchester rifle should have a place of honor in every black home, and it should be used for that protection which the law refuses to give. When the white man who is always the aggressor knows he runs as great risk of biting the dust every time his Afro-American victim does, he will have greater respect for Afro-American life. The more the Afro-American yields and cringes and begs, the more he has to do so, the more he is insulted, outraged and lynched.

The assertion has been substantiated throughout these pages that the press con- 20 tains unreliable and doctored reports of lynchings, and one of the most necessary things for the race to do is to get these facts before the public. The people must know before they can act, and there is no educator to compare with the press.

The Afro-American papers are the only ones which will print the truth, and they lack means to employ agents and detectives to get at the facts. The race must rally a mighty host to the support of their journals, and thus enable them to do much in the way of investigation.

A lynching occurred at Port Jarvis, N.Y., the first week in June. A white and colored man were implicated in the assault upon a white girl. It was charged that the white man paid the colored boy to make the assault, which he did on the public highway in broad day time, and was lynched. This, too, was done by "parties unknown." The white man in the case still lives. He was imprisoned and promises to fight the case on trial. At the preliminary examination, it developed that he had been a suitor of the girl's. She had repulsed and refused him, yet had given him money, and he had sent threatening letters demanding more.

The day before this examination she was so wrought up, she left home and wandered miles away. When found she said she did so because she was afraid of the man's testimony. Why should she be afraid of the prisoner? Why should she yield to his demands for money if not to prevent him exposing something he knew? It seems explainable only on the hypothesis that a *liaison* existed between the colored boy and the girl, and the white man knew of it. The press is singularly silent. Has it a motive? We owe it to ourselves to find out.

Near Vicksburg, Miss., a murder was committed by a gang of burglars. Of course it must have been done by Negroes, and Negroes were arrested for it. It is believed that 2 men, Smith Tooley and John Adams belonged to a gang controlled by white men and, fearing exposure, on the night of July 4th, they were hanged in the Court House yard by those interested in silencing them. Robberies since committed in the same vicinity have been known to be by white men who had their faces blackened. We strongly believe in the innocence of these murdered men, but we have no proof. No other news goes out to the world save that which stamps us as a race of cut-throats, robbers and lustful wild beasts. So great is Southern hate and prejudice, they legally (?) hung poor little thirteen year old Mildred Brown at Columbia, S.C., Oct. 7th, on the circumstantial evidence that she poisoned a white infant. If her guilt had been proven unmistakably, had she been white, Mildred Brown would never have been hung.

The country would have been aroused and South Carolina disgraced forever for   25 such a crime. The Afro-American himself did not know as he should have known as his journals should be in a position to have him know and act.

Nothing is more definitely settled than he must act for himself. I have shown how he may employ the boycott, emigration and the press, and I feel that by a combination of all these agencies can be effectually stamped out lynch law, that last relic of barbarism and slavery. "The gods help those who help themselves."

(1892)

Exploring the Text

1. What ethos does Ida B. Wells-Barnett establish in the preface? How do the diction and imagery of this opening section appeal to the pathos of her audience?
2. How does Wells-Barnett support her claim that "[t]here is little difference between the Ante-bellum South and the New South" (par. 6)?
3. What efforts to stop the "insiduous influence" (par. 8) of lynch laws does she acknowledge? Why does she believe those efforts have been largely ineffective?

4. Wells-Barnett argues that "the Afro-American can do for himself what no one else can do for him" (par. 12). What specific strategies does she advocate? Which appeal to economic interests? Which are based on an-eye-for-an-eye justice? Which seem most feasible to you?

5. Why does Wells-Barnett claim that "there is no educator to compare with the press" (par. 20)? Does she refer to a specific press or to the press in general?

6. What impact do the examples — that is, the actual cases — that she cites have? Do you think these serve as effective support for the claims she makes? Why or why not?

7. To what extent has Wells-Barnett made the case that the lynch law is "that last relic of barbarism and slavery" (par. 26), as she describes it? Has she sufficiently prepared her audience for such strong rhetoric? Explain your response with specific reference to the text.

KATE CHOPIN

Born Katherine O'Flaherty in St. Louis, Missouri, Kate Chopin (1850–1904) is best known for her novel *The Awakening* (1899), which is now recognized as an American classic but was controversial when originally published. Most of Chopin's work is set in Louisiana, where she settled after marrying New Orleans business-man Oscar Chopin. After his early death in 1883, she was determined to earn her living as a writer. She published short stories in magazines such as the *Atlantic*, *New Century*, and *Vogue*. Although some of her earlier work received positive responses as sketches with local and regional appeal, Chopin was criticized for her frank depiction of women's desire for personal freedom, a theme that received full expression in *The Awakening*.

The Story of an Hour

"The Story of an Hour" was initially rejected by both *Century* and *Vogue* maga-zines because of its potentially controversial themes; after the critical success of a collection of Chopin's short fiction, *Vogue* published it in 1894. The story enjoyed even greater popularity in the mid-twentieth century when it was regarded as an early feminist text.

Knowing that Mrs. Mallard was afflicted with a heart trouble, great care was taken to break to her as gently as possible the news of her husband's death.

It was her sister Josephine who told her, in broken sentences; veiled hints that revealed in half concealing. Her husband's friend Richards was there, too, near her. It was he who had been in the newspaper office when intelligence of the railroad disas-ter was received, with Brently Mallard's name leading the list of "killed." He had only taken the time to assure himself of its truth by a second telegram, and had hastened to forestall any less careful, less tender friend in bearing the sad message.

She did not hear the story as many women have heard the same, with a paralyzed inability to accept its significance. She wept at once, with sudden, wild abandonment, in her sister's arms. When the storm of grief had spent itself she went away to her room alone. She would have no one follow her.

There stood, facing the open window, a comfortable, roomy armchair. Into this she sank, pressed down by a physical exhaustion that haunted her body and seemed to reach into her soul.

She could see in the open square before her house the tops of trees that were all 5 aquiver with the new spring life. The delicious breath of rain was in the air. In the street below a peddler was crying his wares. The notes of a distant song which some one was singing reached her faintly, and countless sparrows were twittering in the eaves.

There were patches of blue sky showing here and there through the clouds that had met and piled one above the other in the west facing her window.

She sat with her head thrown back upon the cushion of the chair, quite motion-less, except when a sob came up into her throat and shook her, as a child who has cried itself to sleep continues to sob in its dreams.

She was young, with a fair, calm face, whose lines bespoke repression and even a certain strength. But now there was a dull stare in her eyes, whose gaze was fixed away off yonder on one of those patches of blue sky. It was not a glance of reflection, but rather indicated a suspension of intelligent thought.

There was something coming to her and she was waiting for it, fearfully. What was it? She did not know; it was too subtle and elusive to name. But she felt it, creeping out of the sky, reaching toward her through the sounds, the scents, the color that filled the air.

Now her bosom rose and fell tumultuously. She was beginning to recognize this 10 thing that was approaching to possess her, and she was striving to beat it back with her will — as powerless as her two white slender hands would have been.

When she abandoned herself a little whispered word escaped her slightly parted lips. She said it over and over under her breath: "free, free, free!" The vacant stare and the look of terror that had followed it went from her eyes. They stayed keen and bright. Her pulses beat fast, and the coursing blood warmed and relaxed every inch of her body.

She did not stop to ask if it were or were not a monstrous joy that held her. A dear and exalted perception enabled her to dismiss the suggestion as trivial.

She knew that she would weep again when she saw the kind, tender hands folded in death; the face that had never looked save with love upon her fixed and gray and dead. But she saw beyond that bitter moment a long procession of years to come that would belong to her absolutely. And she opened and spread her arms out to them in welcome.

There would be no one to live for her during those coming years; she would live for herself. There would be no powerful will bending hers in that blind persistence with which men and women believe they have a right to impose a private will upon a fellow-creature. A kind intention or a cruel intention made the act seem no less a crime as she looked upon it in that brief moment of illumination.

And yet she had loved him — sometimes. Often she had not. What did it matter!   15 What could love, the unsolved mystery, count for in face of this possession of self-assertion which she suddenly recognized as the strongest impulse of her being!

"Free! Body and soul free!" she kept whispering.

Josephine was kneeling before the closed door with her lips to the keyhole, imploring for admission. "Louise, open the door! I beg; open the door — you will make yourself ill. What are you doing, Louise? For heaven's sake open the door."

"Go away. I am not making myself ill." No; she was drinking in a very elixir of life through that open window.

Her fancy was running riot along those days ahead of her. Spring days, and summer days, and all sorts of days that would be her own. She breathed a quick prayer that life might be long. It was only yesterday she had thought with a shudder that life might be long.

She arose at length and opened the door to her sister's importunities. There was   20 a feverish triumph in her eyes, and she carried herself unwittingly like a goddess of Victory. She clasped her sister's waist, and together they descended the stairs. Richards stood waiting for them at the bottom.

Some one was opening the front door with a latchkey. It was Brently Mallard who entered, a little travel-stained, composedly carrying his gripsack and umbrella. He had been far from the scene of accident, and did not even know there had been one. He stood amazed at Josephine's piercing cry; at Richards' quick motion to screen him from the view of his wife.

But Richards was too late.

When the doctors came they said she had died of heart disease — of joy that kills.

(1894)

Exploring the Text

1. What ambiguities do you find in paragraph 3; that is, what descriptions and details have potential multiple meanings?
2. What tension between the interior world of Mrs. Mallard and the world outside the window does Kate Chopin develop in paragraphs 4–6?
3. How do you interpret the meaning of the description that Mrs. Mallard's gaze was "not a glance of reflection, but rather indicated a suspension of intelligent thought" (par. 8)?
4. What is the "monstrous joy" (par. 12) that Mrs. Mallard feels?
5. Mrs. Mallard remembers that her husband "had never looked save with love upon her" (par. 13); she reflects that "she had loved him — sometimes. Often she had not" (par. 15). What do these conflicting descriptions suggest about their relationship?
6. What is the freedom that Mrs. Mallard seems to long for in this story?

7. What does Chopin mean when she refers to Mrs. Mallard as carrying herself "unwittingly like a goddess of Victory" (par. 20)?
8. What details, including passages, would you cite to support an interpretation of this story as a criticism of the institution of marriage? Are there indications that Mrs. Mallard was or was not a dutiful wife? Does Chopin characterize Brently Mallard as a good husband?
9. Who is the victim and who is the victimizer in this story? Or is this terminology inappropriate?

BOOKER T. WASHINGTON

Born a slave in West Virginia, Booker T. Washington (1856–1915) was an influential educator and the founder of Tuskegee Normal and Industrial Institute in Alabama. After emancipation, he worked in salt mines and coal mines and then literally walked two hundred miles to attend the Hampton Institute in Virginia, which was then an industrial school for African Americans and Native Americans. There, he paid his tuition and board by working as a janitor. Graduating with honors in 1875, Washington taught at the Hampton Institute until 1881.

The Atlanta Exposition Address

Stressing the importance of learning a trade and developing self-confidence, Washington's pragmatism appealed to African Americans living in the post-Reconstruction South. He was criticized by the NAACP and other organizations for promoting accommodation rather than resistance to Southern white supremacy. He worked behind the scenes, however, to sponsor civil rights suits and advocate on behalf of Historically Black Colleges and Universities. Washington delivered the following speech in 1895 before the Cotton States and International Exposition in Atlanta to promote the economic ascendancy of the South.

M r. President and Gentlemen of the Board of Directors and Citizens.

One-third of the population of the South is of the Negro race. No enterprise seeking the material, civil, or moral welfare of this section can disregard this element of our population and reach the highest success. I but convey to you, Mr. President and Directors, the sentiment of the masses of my race when I say that in no way have the value and manhood of the American Negro been more fittingly and generously recognized than by the managers of this magnificent Exposition at every stage of its progress. It is a recognition that will do more to cement the friendship of the two races than any occurrence since the dawn of our freedom.

Not only this, but the opportunity here afforded will awaken among us a new era of industrial progress. Ignorant and inexperienced, it is not strange that in the first years of our new life we began at the top instead of at the bottom; that a seat in Congress or the state legislature was more sought than real estate or industrial skill; that the political convention of stump speaking had more attractions than starting a dairy farm or truck garden.

A ship lost at sea for many days suddenly sighted a friendly vessel. From the mast of the unfortunate vessel was seen a signal, "Water, water; we die of thirst!" The answer from the friendly vessel at once came back, "Cast down your bucket where you are." A second time the signal, "Water, water; send us water!" ran up from the distressed vessel, and was answered, "Cast down your bucket where you are." And a third and fourth signal for water was answered, "Cast down your bucket where you are." The captain of the distressed vessel, at last heeding the injunction, cast down his bucket, and it came up full of fresh, sparkling water from the mouth of the Amazon River. To those of my race who depend on bettering their condition in a foreign land or who underestimate the importance of cultivating friendly relations with the Southern white man, who is their next-door neighbour, I would say: "Cast down your bucket where you are" — cast it down in making friends in every manly way of the people of all races by whom we are surrounded.

Cast it down in agriculture, mechanics, in commerce, in domestic service, and in the professions. And in this connection it is well to bear in mind that whatever other sins the South may be called to bear, when it comes to business pure and simple, it is in the South that the Negro is given a man's chance in the commercial world, and in nothing is this Exposition more eloquent than in emphasizing this chance. Our greatest danger is that in the great leap from slavery to freedom we may overlook the fact that the masses of us are to live by the productions of our hands, and fail to keep in mind that we shall prosper in proportion as we learn to dignify and glorify common labour and put brains and skill into the common occupations of life; shall prosper in proportion as we learn to draw the line between the superficial and the substantial, the ornamental gewgaws of life and the useful. No race can prosper till it learns that there is as much dignity in tilling a field as in writing a poem. It is at the bottom of life we must begin, and not at the top. Nor should we permit our grievances to overshadow our opportunities.

To those of the white race who look to the incoming of those of foreign birth and strange tongue and habits for the prosperity of the South, were I permitted I would repeat what I say to my own race, "Cast down your bucket where you are." Cast it down among the eight millions of Negroes whose habits you know, whose fidelity and love you have tested in days when to have proved treacherous meant the ruin of your firesides. Cast down your bucket among these people who have, without strikes and labour wars, tilled your fields, cleared your forests, builded your railroads and cities, and brought forth treasures from the bowels of the earth, and helped make possible this magnificent representation of the progress of the South. Casting down your bucket among my people, helping and encouraging them as you are doing on these grounds, and to education of head, hand, and heart, you will find that they will buy your surplus land, make blossom the waste places in your fields, and run your factories. While doing this, you can be sure in the future, as in the past,

5

that you and your families will be surrounded by the most patient, faithful, law-abiding, and unresentful people that the world has seen. As we have proved our loyalty to you in the past, in nursing your children, watching by the sickbed of your mothers and fathers, and often following them with tear-dimmed eyes to their graves, so in the future, in our humble way, we shall stand by you with a devotion that no foreigner can approach, ready to lay down our lives, if need be, in defence of yours, interlacing our industrial, commercial, civil, and religious life with yours in a way that shall make the interests of both races one. In all things that are purely social we can be as separate as the fingers, yet one as the hand in all things essential to mutual progress.

There is no defence or security for any of us except in the highest intelligence and development of all. If anywhere there are efforts tending to curtail the fullest growth of the Negro, let these efforts be turned into stimulating, encouraging, and making him the most useful and intelligent citizen. Effort or means so invested will pay a thousand per cent interest. These efforts will be twice blessed—"blessing him that gives and him that takes."

There is no escape through law of man or God from the inevitable:—

The laws of changeless justice bind
  Oppressor with oppressed;
And close as sin and suffering joined
  We march to fate abreast.

Nearly sixteen millions of hands will aid you in pulling the load upward, or they will pull against you the load downward. We shall constitute one-third and more of the ignorance and crime of the South, or one-third its intelligence and progress; we shall contribute one-third to the business and industrial prosperity of the South, or we shall prove a veritable body of death, stagnating, depressing, retarding every effort to advance the body politic.

Gentlemen of the Exposition, as we present to you our humble effort at an exhibition of our progress, you must not expect overmuch. Starting thirty years ago with ownership here and there in a few quilts and pumpkins and chickens (gathered from miscellaneous sources), remember the path that has led from these to the inventions and production of agricultural implements, buggies, steam-engines, newspapers, books, statuary, carving, paintings, the management of drugstores and banks, has not been trodden without contact with thorns and thistles. While we take pride in what we exhibit as a result of our independent efforts, we do not for a moment forget that our part in this exhibition would fall far short of your expectations but for the constant help that has come to our educational life, not only from the Southern states, but especially from Northern philanthropists, who have made their gifts a constant stream of blessing and encouragement.

The wisest among my race understand that the agitation of questions of social equality is the extremest folly, and that progress in the enjoyment of all the privileges that will come to us must be the result of severe and constant struggle rather than of

10

artificial forcing. No race that has anything to contribute to the markets of the world is long in any degree ostracized. It is important and right that all privileges of the law be ours, but it is vastly more important that we be prepared for the exercises of these privileges. The opportunity to earn a dollar in a factory just now is worth infinitely more than the opportunity to spend a dollar in an opera-house.

In conclusion, may I repeat that nothing in thirty years has given us more hope and encouragement, and drawn us so near to you of the white race, as this opportunity offered by the Exposition; and here bending, as it were, over the altar that represents the results of the struggles of your race and mine, both starting practically empty-handed three decades ago, I pledge that in your effort to work out the great and intricate problem which God has laid at the doors of the South, you shall have at all times the patient, sympathetic help of my race; only let this be constantly in mind, that, while from representations in these buildings of the product of field, of forest, of mine, of factory, letters, and art, much good will come, yet far above and beyond material benefits will be that higher good, that, let us pray God, will come, in a blotting out of sectional differences and racial animosities and suspicions, in a determination to administer absolute justice, in a willing obedience among all classes to the mandates of law. This, then, coupled with our material prosperity, will bring into our beloved South a new heaven and new earth.

(1895)

Exploring the Text

1. What are Booker T. Washington's goals as articulated in this speech? What does he believe is the best way to achieve them?
2. What appeals to ethos does Washington make in the opening paragraphs? What additional appeals to ethos does he make as the speech proceeds?
3. What is the point of the story Washington tells in paragraph 3 about a "ship lost at sea"? What is the rhetorical effect?
4. This speech has come to be known by the sentence "Cast down your bucket where you are" (par. 3). What does Washington mean by this exhortation?
5. In what types of work does Washington believe African Americans should engage? What is the logic that leads him to this belief?
6. How do you interpret Washington's concluding statement in paragraph 5: "In all things that are purely social we can be as separate as the fingers, yet one as the hand in all things essential to mutual progress"?
7. Why is the Shakespeare quotation in paragraph 7 (" 'blessing him that gives and him that takes' ") appropriate to the point Washington is making?
8. Discuss two possible — and contrasting — interpretations of Washington's assertion: "The opportunity to earn a dollar in a factory just now is worth infinitely more than the opportunity to spend a dollar in an opera-house" (par. 10). In today's age of globalization and outsourcing, when many of our factory jobs have gone to foreign workers, does this statement still apply? Rewrite the sentence,

replacing "factory" with a contemporary place of employment. Does the new sentence effectively update the idea? Why or why not?

9. Where in this speech does Washington implicitly argue against racial stereotypes and advocate American values of rugged individualism and a strong work ethic? How have racial stereotypes changed since then? Is our work ethic as strong now as it once was?

10. Discuss the importance of the occasion and audience of this speech. How do these factors influence its form and content?

11. In the introduction to Washington's autobiography, *Up from Slavery*, Henry Louis Gates Jr. and Nellie McKay make the following observation: "To some, Washington's autobiography seems to paper over centuries of accumulated white responsibility for the evils of slavery, and instead of demanding the reform of white American institutions, it calls for African American conformity to the dominant myth of individualism in the United States. To other readers, however, Washington's message in *Up from Slavery* puts its priorities exactly where they had to be — on the necessity of self-help within the African American community" (*Norton Anthology of African American Literature*). Which view is closer to yours? Cite specific passages to support your position.

Paul Laurence Dunbar

Paul Laurence Dunbar (1872–1906) was the first African American to gain national popularity as a poet. Born and raised in Dayton, Ohio, and the son of ex-slaves, Dunbar published his first poems in Dayton's local newspaper, the *Herald*, in 1888. In 1891, when his formal schooling ended, he began work as an elevator operator, and he used this position to publicize and sell copies of his first collection of poetry, *Oak and Ivy*, which was written half in traditional verse and half in African American dialect. He gained international fame for his second book of poems, *Majors and Minors* (1896), and in his career he went on to publish ten more books of poetry, four short-story collections, five novels, and one play. He also wrote the lyrics for the first Broadway musical written and performed solely by African Americans. Titled *In Dahomey*, the musical appeared on Broadway in 1903 and became one of the most successful productions of the time period.

We Wear the Mask

"We Wear the Mask" is considered by many to be the best of Dunbar's work. Published in 1895, it anticipates the concept of "the veil" that W. E. B. DuBois explores in *The Souls of Black Folk* (1903) and presages many seminal works by later African American writers, including the novel *Invisible Man* by Ralph Ellison (p. 1201).

We wear the mask that grins and lies,
It hides our cheeks and shades our eyes, —
This debt we pay to human guile;
With torn and bleeding hearts we smile,
And mouth with myriad subtleties.   5

Why should the world be over-wise,
In counting all our tears and sighs?
Nay, let them only see us, while
   We wear the mask.

We smile, but, O great Christ, our cries   10
To thee from tortured souls arise.
We sing, but oh the clay is vile
Beneath our feet, and long the mile;
But let the world dream otherwise,
   We wear the mask!   15

(1896)

Exploring the Text

1. What does Paul Laurence Dunbar mean by "This debt we pay to human guile" (l. 3)? What are the "myriad subtleties" (l. 5)?
2. Who are the "tortured souls" (l. 11)? How do you interpret "the clay is vile / Beneath our feet, and long the mile" (ll. 12–13)?
3. In both stanzas 2 and 3, the speaker contrasts appearance and reality in two different situations (and with two different examples). What do they have in common?
4. What is the relationship between the speaker and the audience? What is the effect of using first-person plural?
5. How would you characterize the tone of this poem?
6. Imagine that you did not know that Dunbar was African American or that the poem is generally understood within a racial context. In what ways could the poem be about the "mask(s)" that most humans present to the exterior world?
7. Dunbar has been severely criticized by other African American writers for his dialect poetry, which many feel perpetuates racial stereotypes. Critic Joanne Braxton looks to "We Wear the Mask" to counter such criticism, making the point that here Dunbar is writing about the mask he was forced to wear to conceal the truth behind "his comic drama, his witty lyricism, and his use of irony" in those poems. How might you interpret the poem as Dunbar's defense of the poetic mask he wore in order to appeal to a wide readership?

Douglass

Dunbar's poem "Douglass," from his 1903 collection, *Lyrics of Love and Laughter*, is an apostrophe to African American leader Frederick Douglass, whom Dunbar met in 1893 while promoting his first collection of poetry, *Oak and Ivy*. Douglass admired Dunbar's work and hired him to manage the Haitian exhibit at the World's Columbian Exposition in Chicago.

Ah, Douglass, we have fall'n on evil days,
  Such days as thou, not even thou didst know,
  When thee, the eyes of that harsh long ago
Saw, salient, at the cross of devious ways,
And all the country heard thee with amaze.   5
  Not ended then, the passionate ebb and flow,
  The awful tide that battled to and fro;
We ride amid a tempest of dispraise.
Now, when the waves of swift dissension swarm,
  And Honor, the strong pilot, lieth stark,   10
Oh, for thy voice high-sounding o'er the storm,
  For thy strong arm to guide the shivering bark,
The blast-defying power of thy form,
  To give us comfort through the lonely dark.

(1903)

Exploring the Text

1. Why does Paul Laurence Dunbar, the speaker of the poem, call on Douglass at this particular time in history? How does he characterize the moment? What qualities of Douglass does Dunbar believe are sorely needed at the moment in history when the poem was written?
2. What is the central metaphor that Dunbar develops in this poem? Cite specific lines and phrases that dramatize the crisis Dunbar depicts through this metaphor.
3. How does the sonnet structure reinforce the meaning of this poem?
4. Dunbar wrote a poem entitled "Frederick Douglass" in 1895 when he first heard of his friend's death. Compare and contrast "Douglass" with that earlier poem. How are the two different occasions that inspired the poems reflected in the verse? Which poem do you believe is more effective? Why?

↻ TALKBACK

ROBERT HAYDEN

Born Asa Bundy Sheffey in Detroit, Michigan, Robert Hayden (1913–1980) attended Detroit City College (now Wayne State University) before studying under W. H. Auden (p. 1169) in the graduate English program at the University of Michigan. In 1976, Hayden was appointed consultant in poetry to the Library of Congress, a post that was the forerunner to that of poet laureate. His first volume, *Heart-Shape in the Dust* (1940), took its voice from the Harlem Renaissance. Later work continued to garner critical praise, including Hayden's epic poem on the *Amistad* mutiny, "Middle Passage," and *A Ballad of Remembrance* (1962).

Frederick Douglass

This poem first appeared in the *Atlantic Monthly* in 1947.

When it is finally ours, this freedom, this liberty, this beautiful
and terrible thing, needful to man as air,
usable as earth; when it belongs at last to all,
when it is truly instinct, brain matter, diastole, systole,
reflex action; when it is finally won; when it is more   5
than the gaudy mumbo jumbo of politicians:
this man, this Douglass, this former slave, this Negro
beaten to his knees, exiled, visioning a world
where none is lonely, none hunted, alien,
this man, superb in love and logic, this man   10
shall be remembered. Oh, not with statues' rhetoric,
not with legends and poems and wreaths of bronze alone,
but with the lives grown out of his life, the lives
fleshing his dream of the beautiful, needful thing.

(1947)

Exploring the Text

1. The poem consists of one long periodic sentence and a fragment. What is the main clause of the sentence? What is the effect of the multiple dependent clauses and modifiers leading to the independent clause?
2. What is the effect of Robert Hayden referring to liberty as "this beautiful and terrible thing" (ll. 1–2)?
3. What is "the gaudy mumbo jumbo of politicians" (l. 6)?
4. What other abstractions (such as "this beautiful and terrible thing") do you find in the poem? How does Hayden manage to make Frederick Douglass a vital presence when he uses such abstractions to recall him?

5. Lines 11–14, while technically a sentence fragment, are, in fact, an explanation. What is Hayden explaining, and how these lines are linked to the previous sentence?

6. In the *Norton Anthology of African American Literature*, editors Henry Louis Gates Jr. and Nellie McKay point out that Hayden's poetry fell out of favor with many of the young black nationalists of the 1960s who felt that it did not speak directly enough to the more radical politics of civil rights. Yet, they continue, the "beat" of a poem such as "Frederick Douglass" testifies to his "vision of human possibility that bet its hand on the redemptive occasions of the future." In what ways might the "beat" of the poem contribute to its being interpreted as a call to action? Consider anaphora, enjambment, and repetition in your response.

Making Connections

1. These two poems about Frederick Douglass were written more than four decades apart, obviously during very different political eras. What qualities of Douglass do both Paul Laurence Dunbar and Hayden stress? How do the differences in the characteristics each poet emphasizes reflect the poet's historical context?

2. How would you describe each of these poems? Are they a tribute to Douglass? A meditation on Douglass? A lamentation of his passing? A personal remembrance? A celebration of his influence? A memorial to his greatness? An adulatory praise song? Cite specific passages to support your response, including consideration of the different titles.

3. Both Dunbar and Hayden chose to use the sonnet form for these poems, though in very different ways. How does each poet's approach to this conventional structure contribute to the tone of his poem?

4. Dunbar calls on Douglass for guidance during "a tempest of dispraise" (l. 8). Hayden asserts that "this man / shall be remembered" (ll. 10–11). To what extent do you think Hayden's assertion suggests that the memory of Douglass, so strong and unquestionable to Dunbar, is in jeopardy? Base your response on these poems as well as on your knowledge of the political time periods.

Stephen Crane

Stephen Crane (1871–1900) was an American novelist, short-story writer, and journalist and considered to be one of the most innovative writers of his time. Born in Newark, New Jersey, Crane began writing at a young age, publishing his first articles when he was sixteen. In 1891, he quit school to become a freelance reporter and writer, writing for various New York City publications, including the *Tribune*. His first novel, *Maggie: A Girl of the Streets*, won him literary acclaim in

1893, and in 1895 he published *The Red Badge of Courage,* a Civil War novel that made him internationally famous.

The Open Boat
A Tale Intended to Be After the Fact. Being the Experience of Four Men from the Sunk Steamer Commodore

Crane based "The Open Boat" on his experience as a war correspondent aboard the *Commodore,* a steamship that shipwrecked off the coast of Florida on its way to Cuba with munitions for the insurgents who were rebelling against Spanish rule. Crane and three others spent thirty hours in a ten-foot dinghy before washing ashore near Daytona Beach, Florida. His report of the incident was published in the *New York Press* on January 7, 1897, less than a week after his rescue. This story, which appeared in the June 1897 issue of *Scribner's* magazine, has been widely praised by writers such as Ernest Hemingway and Joseph Conrad and is considered by many to be Crane's best work.

I

None of them knew the color of the sky. Their eyes glanced level, and were fastened upon the waves that swept toward them. These waves were of the hue of slate, save for the tops, which were of foaming white, and all of the men knew the colors of the sea. The horizon narrowed and widened, and dipped and rose, and at all times its edge was jagged with waves that seemed thrust up in points like rocks.

Many a man ought to have a bath-tub larger than the boat which here rode upon the sea. These waves were most wrongfully and barbarously abrupt and tall, and each froth-top was a problem in small boat navigation.

The cook squatted in the bottom and looked with both eyes at the six inches of gunwale which separated him from the ocean. His sleeves were rolled over his fat forearms, and the two flaps of his unbuttoned vest dangled as he bent to bail out the boat. Often he said: "Gawd! That was a narrow clip." As he remarked it he invariably gazed eastward over the broken sea.

The oiler, steering with one of the two oars in the boat, sometimes raised himself suddenly to keep clear of water that swirled in over the stern. It was a thin little oar and it seemed often ready to snap.

The correspondent, pulling at the other oar, watched the waves and wondered why he was there. 5

The injured captain, lying in the bow, was at this time buried in that profound dejection and indifference which comes, temporarily at least, to even the bravest and most enduring when, willy nilly, the firm fails, the army loses, the ship goes down. The mind of the master of a vessel is rooted deep in the timbers of her, though he command for a day or a decade, and this captain had on him the stern impression of a scene in the grays of dawn of seven turned faces, and later a stump of a top-mast with a white ball on it that slashed to and fro at the waves, went low and lower, and down. Thereafter there was something strange in his voice. Although steady, it was deep with mourning, and of a quality beyond oration or tears.

"Keep'er a little more south, Billie," said he.

"'A little more south,' sir," said the oiler in the stern.

A seat in this boat was not unlike a seat upon a bucking broncho, and, by the same token, a broncho is not much smaller. The craft pranced and reared, and plunged like an animal. As each wave came, and she rose for it, she seemed like a horse making at a fence outrageously high. The manner of her scramble over these walls of water is a mystic thing, and, moreover, at the top of them were ordinarily these problems in white water, the foam racing down from the summit of each wave, requiring a new leap, and a leap from the air. Then, after scornfully bumping a crest, she would slide, and race, and splash down a long incline and arrive bobbing and nodding in front of the next menace.

A singular disadvantage of the sea lies in the fact that after successfully surmount-   10
ing one wave you discover that there is another behind it just as important and just as nervously anxious to do something effective in the way of swamping boats. In a ten-foot dingey one can get an idea of the resources of the sea in the line of waves that is not probable to the average experience, which is never at sea in a dingey. As each slaty wall of water approached, it shut all else from the view of the men in the boat, and it was not difficult to imagine that this particular wave was the final outburst of the ocean, the last effort of the grim water. There was a terrible grace in the move of the waves, and they came in silence, save for the snarling of the crests.

In the wan light, the faces of the men must have been gray. Their eyes must have glinted in strange ways as they gazed steadily astern. Viewed from a balcony, the whole thing would doubtlessly have been weirdly picturesque. But the men in the boat had no time to see it, and if they had had leisure there were other things to occupy their minds. The sun swung steadily up the sky, and they knew it was broad day because the color of the sea changed from slate to emerald-green, streaked with amber lights, and the foam was like tumbling snow. The process of the breaking day was unknown to them. They were aware only of this effect upon the color of the waves that rolled toward them.

In disjointed sentences the cook and the correspondent argued as to the difference between a life-saving station and a house of refuge. The cook had said: "There's a house of refuge just north of the Mosquito Inlet Light, and as soon as they see us, they'll come off in their boat and pick us up."

"As soon as who see us?" said the correspondent.

"The crew," said the cook.

"Houses of refuge don't have crews," said the correspondent. "As I understand   15
them, they are only places where clothes and grub are stored for the benefit of ship-wrecked people. They don't carry crews."

"Oh, yes, they do," said the cook.

"No, they don't," said the correspondent.

"Well, we're not there yet, anyhow," said the oiler, in the stern.

"Well," said the cook, "perhaps it's not a house of refuge that I'm thinking of as being near Mosquito Inlet Light. Perhaps it's a life-saving station."

"We're not there yet," said the oiler, in the stern.   20

II

As the boat bounced from the top of each wave, the wind tore through the hair of the hatless men, and as the craft plopped her stern down again the spray slashed past them. The crest of each of these waves was a hill, from the top of which the men surveyed, for a moment, a broad tumultuous expanse; shining and wind-riven. It was probably splendid. It was probably glorious, this play of the free sea, wild with lights of emerald and white and amber.

"Bully good thing it's an on-shore wind," said the cook. "If not, where would we be? Wouldn't have a show."

"That's right," said the correspondent.

The busy oiler nodded his assent.

Then the captain, in the bow, chuckled in a way that expressed humor, contempt,   25
tragedy, all in one. "Do you think we've got much of a show, now, boys?" said he.

Whereupon the three were silent, save for a trifle of hemming and hawing. To express any particular optimism at this time they felt to be childish and stupid, but they all doubtless possessed this sense of the situation in their mind. A young man thinks doggedly at such times. On the other hand, the ethics of their condition was decidedly against any open suggestion of hopelessness. So they were silent.

"Oh, well," said the captain, soothing his children, "we'll get ashore all right."

But there was that in his tone which made them think, so the oiler quoth: "Yes! If this wind holds!"

The cook was bailing: "Yes! If we don't catch hell in the surf."

Canton flannel gulls flew near and far. Sometimes they sat down on the sea, near   30
patches of brown sea-weed that rolled over the waves with a movement like carpets on a line in a gale. The birds sat comfortably in groups, and they were envied by some in the dingey, for the wrath of the sea was no more to them than it was to a covey of prairie chickens a thousand miles inland. Often they came very close and stared at the men with black beadlike eyes. At these times they were uncanny and sinister in their unblinking scrutiny, and the men hooted angrily at them, telling them to be gone. One came, and evidently decided to alight on the top of the captain's head. The bird flew parallel to the boat and did not circle, but made short sidelong jumps in the air in chicken-fashion. His black eyes were wistfully fixed upon the captain's head. "Ugly brute," said the oiler to the bird. "You look as if you were made with a jackknife." The cook and the correspondent swore darkly at the creature. The captain naturally wished to knock it away with the end of the heavy painter, but he did not dare do it, because anything resembling an emphatic gesture would have capsized this freighted boat, and so with his open hand, the captain gently and carefully waved the gull away. After it had been discouraged from the pursuit the captain breathed easier on account of his hair, and others breathed easier because the bird struck their minds at this time as being somehow grewsome and ominous.

In the meantime the oiler and the correspondent rowed. And also they rowed.

They sat together in the same seat, and each rowed an oar. Then the oiler took both oars; then the correspondent took both oars; then the oiler; then the correspondent. They rowed and they rowed. The very ticklish part of the business was when the time came for the reclining one in the stern to take his turn at the oars. By the very last star of truth, it is easier to steal eggs from under a hen than it was to change seats in the dingey. First the man in the stern slid his hand along the thwart and moved with care, as if he were of Sèvres. Then the man in the rowing seat slid his hand along the other thwart. It was all done with the most extraordinary care. As the two sidled past each other, the whole party kept watchful eyes on the coming wave, and the captain cried: "Look out now! Steady there!"

The brown mats of sea-weed that appeared from time to time were like islands, bits of earth. They were travelling, apparently, neither one way nor the other. They were, to all intents, stationary. They informed the men in the boat that it was making progress slowly toward the land.

The captain, rearing cautiously in the bow, after the dingey soared on a great swell, said that he had seen the lighthouse at Mosquito Inlet. Presently the cook remarked that he had seen it. The correspondent was at the oars, then, and for some reason he too wished to look at the lighthouse, but his back was toward the far shore and the waves were important, and for some time he could not seize an opportunity to turn his head. But at last there came a wave more gentle than the others, and when at the crest of it he swiftly scoured the western horizon.

"See it?" said the captain.   35

"No," said the correspondent, slowly, "I didn't see anything."

"Look again," said the captain. He pointed. "It's exactly in that direction."

At the top of another wave, the correspondent did as he was bid, and this time his eyes chanced on a small still thing on the edge of the swaying horizon. It was precisely like the point of a pin. It took an anxious eye to find a lighthouse so tiny.

"Think we'll make it, captain?"

"If this wind holds and the boat don't swamp, we can't do much else," said the   40
captain.

The little boat, lifted by each towering sea, and splashed viciously by the crests, made progress that in the absence of sea-weed was not apparent to those in her. She seemed just a wee thing wallowing, miraculously, top-up, at the mercy of five oceans. Occasionally, a great spread of water, like white flames, swarmed into her.

"Bail her, cook," said the captain, serenely.

"All right, captain," said the cheerful cook.

III

It would be difficult to describe the subtle brotherhood of men that was here established on the seas. No one said that it was so. No one mentioned it. But it dwelt in the boat, and each man felt it warm him. They were a captain, an oiler, a cook, and a correspondent, and they were friends, friends in a more curiously iron-bound degree than may be common. The hurt captain, lying against the water-jar in the bow, spoke always in a low voice and calmly, but he could never command a more ready and swiftly obedient crew than the motley three of the dingey. It was more than a mere recognition of what was best for the common safety. There was surely in it a quality that was personal and heartfelt. And after this devotion to the commander of the boat there was this comradeship that the correspondent, for instance, who had been taught to be cynical of men, knew even at the time was the best experience of his life. But no one said that it was so. No one mentioned it.

"I wish we had a sail," remarked the captain. "We might try my overcoat on the   45
end of an oar and give you two boys a chance to rest." So the cook and the correspondent held the mast and spread wide the overcoat. The oiler steered, and the little boat made good way with her new rig. Sometimes the oiler had to scull sharply to keep a sea from breaking into the boat, but otherwise sailing was a success.

Meanwhile the light-house had been growing slowly larger. It had now almost assumed color, and appeared like a little gray shadow on the sky. The man at the oars could not be prevented from turning his head rather often to try for a glimpse of this little gray shadow.

At last, from the top of each wave the men in the tossing boat could see land. Even as the light-house was an upright shadow on the sky, this land seemed but a long black shadow on the sea. It certainly was thinner than paper. "We must be about opposite New Smyrna," said the cook, who had coasted this shore often in schooners. "Captain, by the way, I believe they abandoned that life-saving station there about a year ago."

"Did they?" said the captain.

The wind slowly died away. The cook and the correspondent were not now obliged to slave in order to hold high the oar. But the waves continued their old impetuous swooping at the dingey, and the little craft, no longer under way, struggled woundily over them. The oiler or the correspondent took the oars again.

Shipwrecks are *apropos* of nothing. If men could only train for them and have   50
them occur when the men had reached pink condition, there would be less drowning at sea. Of the four in the dingey none had slept any time worth mentioning for two days and two nights previous to embarking in the dingey, and in the excitement of clambering about the deck of a foundering ship they had also forgotten to eat heartily.

For these reasons, and for others, neither the oiler nor the correspondent was fond of rowing at this time. The correspondent wondered ingenuously how in the name of all that was sane could there be people who thought it amusing to row a boat. It was not an amusement; it was a diabolical punishment, and even a genius of mental aberrations could never conclude that it was anything but a horror to the muscles and a crime against the back. He mentioned to the boat in general how the amusement of rowing struck him, and the weary-faced oiler smiled in full sympathy. Previously to the foundering, by the way, the oiler had worked double-watch in the engine-room of the ship.

"Take her easy, now, boys," said the captain. "Don't spend yourselves. If we have to run a surf you'll need all your strength, because we'll sure have to swim for it. Take your time."

Slowly the land arose from the sea. From a black line it became a line of black and a line of white, trees, and sand. Finally, the captain said that he could make out a house on the shore. "That's the house of refuge, sure," said the cook. "They'll see us before long, and come out after us."

The distant light-house reared high. "The keeper ought to be able to make us out now, if he's looking through a glass," said the captain. "He'll notify the life-saving people."

"None of those other boats could have got ashore to give word of the wreck," said the oiler, in a low voice. "Else the life-boat would be out hunting us." 55

Slowly and beautifully the land loomed out of the sea. The wind came again. It had veered from the northeast to the southeast. Finally, a new sound struck the ears of the men in the boat. It was the low thunder of the surf on the shore. "We'll never be able to make the light-house now," said the captain. "Swing her head a little more north, Billie," said the captain.

" 'A little more north,' sir," said the oiler.

Whereupon the little boat turned her nose once more down the wind, and all but the oarsman watched the shore grow. Under the influence of this expansion doubt and direful apprehension was leaving the minds of the men. The management of the boat was still most absorbing, but it could not prevent a quiet cheerfulness. In an hour perhaps, they would be ashore.

Their back-bones had become thoroughly used to balancing in the boat and they now rode this wild colt of a dingey like circus men. The correspondent thought that he had been drenched to the skin, but happening to feel in the top pocket of his coat, he found therein eight cigars. Four of them were soaked with sea-water; four were perfectly scatheless. After a search, somebody produced three dry matches, and thereupon the four waifs rode in their little boat, and with an assurance of an impending rescue shining in their eyes, puffed at the big cigars and judged well and ill of all men. Everybody took a drink of water.

IV

"Cook," remarked the captain, "there don't seem to be any signs of life about your house of refuge." 60

"No," replied the cook. "Funny they don't see us!"

A broad stretch of lowly coast lay before the eyes of the men. It was of low dunes topped with dark vegetation. The roar of the surf was plain, and sometimes they could see the white lip of a wave as it spun up the beach. A tiny house was blocked out black upon the sky. Southward, the slim light-house lifted its little gray length.

Tide, wind, and waves were swinging the dingey northward. "Funny they don't see us," said the men.

The surf's roar was here dulled, but its tone was, nevertheless, thunderous and mighty. As the boat swam over the great rollers, the men sat listening to this roar.

"We'll swamp sure," said everybody. 65

It is fair to say here that there was not a life-saving station within twenty miles in either direction, but the men did not know this fact and in consequence they made dark and opprobrious remarks concerning the eyesight of the nation's life-savers. Four scowling men sat in the dingey and surpassed records in the invention of epithets.

"Funny they don't see us."

The light-heartedness of a former time had completely faded. To their sharpened minds it was easy to conjure pictures of all kinds of incompetency and blindness and, indeed, cowardice. There was the shore of the populous land, and it was bitter and bitter to them that from it came no sign.

"Well," said the captain, ultimately, "I suppose we'll have to make a try ourselves. If we stay out here too long we'll none of us have strength left to swim after the boat swamps."

And so the oiler, who was at the oars, turned the boat straight for the shore. 70 There was a sudden tightening of muscles. There was some thinking.

"If we don't all get ashore—" said the captain. "If we don't all get ashore, I suppose you fellows know where to send news of my finish?"

They then briefly exchanged some addresses and admonitions. As for the reflections of the men, there was a great deal of rage in them. Perchance they might be formulated thus: "If I am going to be drowned—if I am going to be drowned—if I am going to be drowned, why, in the name of the seven mad gods who rule the sea, was I allowed to come thus far and contemplate sand and trees? Was I brought here merely to have my nose dragged away as I was about to nibble the sacred cheese of life? It is preposterous. If this old ninny-woman, Fate, cannot do better than this, she should be deprived of the management of men's fortunes. She is an old hen who knows not her intention. If she has decided to drown me, why did she not do it in the beginning and save me all this trouble. The whole affair is absurd. . . . But, no, she cannot mean to drown me. She dare not drown me. She cannot drown me. Not after all this work." Afterward the man might have had an impulse to shake his fist at the clouds: "Just you drown me, now, and then hear what I call you!"

The billows that came at this time were more formidable. They seemed always just about to break and roll over the little boat in a turmoil of foam. There was a preparatory and long growl in the speech of them. No mind unused to the sea would have concluded that the dingey could ascend these sheer heights in time. The shore was still afar. The oiler was a wily surfman. "Boys," he said, swiftly, "she won't live three minutes more and we're too far out to swim. Shall I take her to sea again, captain?"

"Yes! Go ahead!" said the captain.

This oiler, by a series of quick miracles, and fast and steady oarsmanship, turned 75 the boat in the middle of the surf and took her safely to sea again.

There was a considerable silence as the boat bumped over the furrowed sea to deeper water. Then somebody in gloom spoke. "Well, anyhow, they must have seen us from the shore by now."

The gulls went in slanting flight up the wind toward the gray desolate east. A squall, marked by dingy clouds, and clouds brick-red, like smoke from a burning building, appeared from the southeast.

"What do you think of those life-saving people? Ain't they peaches?"

"Funny they haven't seen us."

"Maybe they think we're out here for sport! Maybe they think we're fishin'. Maybe 80 they think we're damned fools."

It was a long afternoon. A changed tide tried to force them southward, but wind and wave said northward. Far ahead, where coast-line, sea, and sky formed their mighty angle, there were little dots which seemed to indicate a city on the shore.

"St. Augustine?"

The captain shook his head. "Too near Mosquito Inlet."

And the oiler rowed, and then the correspondent rowed. Then the oiler rowed. It was a weary business. The human back can become the seat of more aches and pains than are registered in books for the composite anatomy of a regiment. It is a limited area, but it can become the theatre of innumerable muscular conflicts, tangles, wrenches, knots, and other comforts.

"Did you ever like to row, Billie?" asked the correspondent.   85

"No," said the oiler. "Hang it."

When one exchanged the rowing-seat for a place in the bottom of the boat, he suffered a bodily depression that caused him to be careless of everything save an obligation to wiggle one finger. There was cold sea-water swashing to and fro in the boat, and he lay in it. His head, pillowed on a thwart, was within an inch of the swirl of a wave crest, and sometimes a particularly obstreperous sea came in-board and drenched him once more. But these matters did not annoy him. It is almost certain that if the boat had capsized he would have tumbled comfortably out upon the ocean as if he felt sure that it was a great soft mattress.

"Look! There's a man on the shore!"

"Where?"

"There! See 'im? See 'im?"   90

"Yes, sure! He's walking along."

"Now he's stopped. Look! He's facing us!"

"He's waving at us!"

"So he is! By thunder!"

"Ah, now, we're all right! Now we're all right! There'll be a boat out here for us   95
half an hour."

"He's going on. He's running. He's going up to that house there."

The remote beach seemed lower than the sea, and it required a searching glance to discern the little black figure. The captain saw a floating stick and they rowed to it. A bath-towel was by some weird chance in the boat, and, tying this on the stick, the captain waved it. The oarsman did not dare turn his head, so he was obliged to ask questions.

"What's he doing now?"

"He's standing still again. He's looking, I think. . . . There he goes again. Toward the house. . . . Now he's stopped again."

"Is he waving at us?"   100

"No, not now! he was, though."

"Look! There comes another man!"

"He's running."

"Look at him go, would you."

"Why, he's on a bicycle. Now he's met the other man. They're both waving at us.   105
Look!"

"There comes something up the beach."

"What the devil is that thing?"

"Why, it looks like a boat."

"Why, certainly it's a boat."

"No, it's on wheels."   110

"Yes, so it is. Well, that must be the life-boat. They drag them along shore on a wagon."

"That's the life-boat, sure."

"No, by —, it's — it's an omnibus."

"I tell you it's a life-boat."

"It is not! It's an omnibus. I can see it plain. See? One of these big hotel omni-   115
buses."

"By thunder, you're right. It's an omnibus, sure as fate. What do you suppose they are doing with an omnibus? Maybe they are going around collecting the life-crew, hey?"

"That's it, likely. Look! There's a fellow waving a little black flag. He's standing on the steps of the omnibus. There come those other two fellows. Now they're all talking together. Look at the fellow with the flag. Maybe he ain't waving it."

"That ain't a flag, is it? That's his coat. Why, certainly, that's his coat."

"So it is. It's his coat. He's taken it off and is waving it around his head. But would you look at him swing it."

"Oh, say, there isn't any life-saving station there. That's just a winter resort hotel   120
omnibus that has brought over some of the boarders to see us drown."

"What's that idiot with the coat mean? What's he signaling, anyhow?"

"It looks as if he were trying to tell us to go north. There must be a life-saving station up there."

"No! He thinks we're fishing. Just giving us a merry hand. See? Ah, there, Willie."

"Well, I wish I could make something out of those signals. What do you suppose he means?"

"He don't mean anything. He's just playing."   125

"Well, if he'd just signal us to try the surf again, or to go to sea and wait, or go north, or go south, or go to hell — there would be some reason in it. But look at him. He just stands there and keeps his coat revolving like a wheel. The ass!"

"There come more people."

"Now there's quite a mob. Look! Isn't that a boat?"

"Where? Oh, I see where you mean. No, that's no boat."

"That fellow is still waving his coat."   130

"He must think we like to see him do that. Why don't he quit it. It don't mean anything."

"I don't know. I think he is trying to make us go north. It must be that there's a life-saving station there somewhere."

"Say, he ain't tired yet. Look at 'im wave."

"Wonder how long he can keep that up. He's been revolving his coat ever since he caught sight of us. He's an idiot. Why aren't they getting men to bring a boat out.

A fishing boat — one of those big yawls — could come out here all right. Why don't he do something?"

"Oh, it's all right, now."

"They'll have a boat out here for us in less than no time, now that they've seen us."

A faint yellow tone came into the sky over the low land. The shadows on the sea slowly deepened. The wind bore coldness with it, and the men began to shiver.

"Holy smoke!" said one, allowing his voice to express his impious mood, "if we keep on monkeying out here! If we've got to flounder out here all night!"

"Oh, we'll never have to stay here all night! Don't you worry. They've seen us now, and it won't be long before they'll come chasing out after us."

The shore grew dusky. The man waving a coat blended gradually into this gloom, and it swallowed in the same manner the omnibus and the group of people. The spray, when it dashed uproariously over the side, made the voyagers shrink and swear like men who were being branded.

"I'd like to catch the chump who waved the coat. I feel like soaking him one, just for luck."

"Why? What did he do?"

"Oh, nothing, but then he seemed so damned cheerful."

In the meantime the oiler rowed, and then the correspondent rowed, and then the oiler rowed. Gray-faced and bowed forward, they mechanically, turn by turn, plied the leaden oars. The form of the light-house had vanished from the southern horizon, but finally a pale star appeared, just lifting from the sea. The streaked saffron in the west passed before the all-merging darkness, and the sea to the east was black. The land had vanished, and was expressed only by the low and drear thunder of the surf.

"If I am going to be drowned — if I am going to be drowned — if I am going to drowned, why, in the name of the seven mad gods, who rule the sea, was I allowed to come thus far and contemplate sand and trees? Was I brought here merely to have my nose dragged away as I was about to nibble the sacred cheese of life?"

The patient captain, drooped over the water-jar, was sometimes obliged to speak to the oarsman.

"Keep her head up! Keep her head up!"

" 'Keep her head up,' sir." The voices were weary and low.

This was surely a quiet evening. All save the oarsman lay heavily and listlessly in the boat's bottom. As for him, his eyes were just capable of noting the tall black waves that swept forward in a most sinister silence, save for an occasional subdued growl of a crest.

The cook's head was on a thwart, and he looked without interest at the water under his nose. He was deep in other scenes. Finally he spoke. "Billie," he murmured, dreamfully, "what kind of pie do you like best?"

V

"Pie," said the oiler and the correspondent, agitatedly. "Don't talk about those things, blast you!"

"Well," said the cook, "I was just thinking about ham sandwiches, and — "

A night on the sea in an open boat is a long night. As darkness settled finally, the shine of the light, lifting from the sea in the south, changed to full gold. On the northern horizon a new light appeared, a small bluish gleam on the edge of the waters. These two lights were the furniture of the world. Otherwise there was nothing but waves.

Two men huddled in the stern, and distances were so magnificent in the dingey that the rower was enabled to keep his feet partly warmed by thrusting them under his companions. Their legs indeed extended far under the rowing-seat until they touched the feet of the captain forward. Sometimes, despite the efforts of the tired oarsman, a wave came piling into the boat, an icy wave of the night, and the chilling water soaked them anew. They would twist their bodies for a moment and groan, and sleep the dead sleep once more, while the water in the boat gurgled about them as the craft rocked.

The plan of the oiler and the correspondent was for one to row until he lost the   155
ability, and then arouse the other from his sea-water couch in the bottom of the boat.

The oiler plied the oars until his head drooped forward, and the overpowering sleep blinded him. And he rowed yet afterward. Then he touched a man in the bottom of the boat, and called his name. "Will you spell me for a little while?" he said, meekly.

"Sure, Billie," said the correspondent, awakening and dragging himself to a sitting position. They exchanged places carefully, and the oiler, cuddling down in the sea-water at the cook's side, seemed to go to sleep instantly.

The particular violence of the sea had ceased. The waves came without snarling. The obligation of the man at the oars was to keep the boat headed so that the tilt of the rollers would not capsize her, and to preserve her from filling when the crests rushed past. The black waves were silent and hard to be seen in the darkness. Often one was almost upon the boat before the oarsman was aware.

In a low voice the correspondent addressed the captain. He was not sure that the captain was awake, although this iron man seemed to be always awake. "Captain, shall I keep her making for that light north, sir?"

The same steady voice answered him. "Yes. Keep it about two points off the port   160
bow."

The cook had tied a life-belt around himself in order to get even the warmth which this clumsy cork contrivance could donate, and he seemed almost stove-like when a rower, whose teeth invariably chattered wildly as soon as he ceased his labor, dropped down to sleep.

The correspondent, as he rowed, looked down at the two men sleeping under foot. The cook's arm was around the oiler's shoulders, and, with their fragmentary clothing and haggard faces, they were the babes of the sea, a grotesque rendering of the old babes in the wood.

Later he must have grown stupid at his work, for suddenly there was a growling of water, and a crest came with a roar and a swash into the boat, and it was a wonder that it did not set the cook afloat in his life-belt. The cook continued to sleep, but the oiler sat up, blinking his eyes and shaking with the new cold.

"Oh, I'm awful sorry, Billie," said the correspondent, contritely.

"That's all right, old boy," said the oiler, and lay down again and was asleep.   165

Presently it seemed that even the captain dozed, and the correspondent thought that he was the one man afloat on all the oceans. The wind had a voice as it came over the waves, and it was sadder than the end.

There was a long, loud swishing astern of the boat, and a gleaming trail of phosphorescence, like blue flame, was furrowed on the black waters. It might have been made by a monstrous knife.

Then there came a stillness, while the correspondent breathed with the open mouth and looked at the sea.

Suddenly there was another swish and another long flash of bluish light, and this time it was alongside the boat, and might almost have been reached with an oar. The correspondent saw an enormous fin speed like a shadow through the water, hurling the crystalline spray and leaving the long glowing trail.

The correspondent looked over his shoulder at the captain. His face was hidden, and he seemed to be asleep. He looked at the babes of the sea. They certainly were asleep. So, being bereft of sympathy, he leaned a little way to one side and swore softly into the sea. 170

But the thing did not then leave the vicinity of the boat. Ahead or astern, on one side or the other, at intervals long or short, fled the long sparkling streak, and there was to be heard the whiroo of the dark fin. The speed and power of the thing was greatly to be admired. It cut the water like a gigantic and keen projectile.

The presence of this biding thing did not affect the man with the same horror that it would if he had been a picnicker. He simply looked at the sea dully and swore in an undertone.

Nevertheless, it is true that he did not wish to be alone with the thing. He wished one of his companions to awaken by chance and keep him company with it. But the captain hung motionless over the water-jar and the oiler and the cook in the bottom of the boat were plunged in slumber.

VI

"If I am going to be drowned — if I am going to be drowned — if I am going to be drowned, why, in the name of the seven mad gods, who rule the sea, was I allowed to come thus far and contemplate sand and trees?"

During this dismal night, it may be remarked that a man would conclude that it was really the intention of the seven mad gods to drown him, despite the abominable injustice of it. For it was certainly an abominable injustice to drown a man who had worked so hard. The man felt it would be a crime most unnatural. Other people had drowned at sea since galleys swarmed with painted sails, but still —— 175

When it occurs to a man that nature does not regard him as important, and that she feels she would not maim the universe by disposing of him, he at first wishes to throw bricks at the temple, and hates deeply the fact that there are no bricks and no temples. Any visible expression of nature would surely be pelleted with his jeers.

Then, if there be no tangible thing to hoot he feels, perhaps, the desire to confront a personification and indulge in pleas, bowed to one knee, and with hands supplicant, saying: "Yes, but I love myself."

A high cold star on a winter's night is the word he feels that she says to him. Thereafter he knows the pathos of his situation.

The men in the dingey had not discussed these matters, but each had, no doubt, reflected upon them in silence and according to his mind. There was seldom any expression upon their faces save the general one of complete weariness. Speech was devoted to the business of the boat.

To chime the notes of his emotion, a verse mysteriously entered the correspondent's head. He had even forgotten that he had forgotten this verse, but it suddenly was in his mind. 180

> A soldier of the Legion lay dying in Algiers,
> There was lack of woman's nursing, there was dearth of woman's tears;
> But a comrade stood beside him, and he took that comrade's hand
> And he said: "I shall never see my own, my native land."

In his childhood, the correspondent had been made acquainted with the fact that a soldier of the Legion lay dying in Algiers, but he had never regarded the fact as important. Myriads of his school-fellows had informed him of the soldier's plight, but the dinning had naturally ended by making him perfectly indifferent. He had never considered it his affair that a soldier of the Legion lay dying in Algiers, nor had it appeared to him as a matter for sorrow. It was less to him than the breaking of a pencil's point.

Now, however, it quaintly came to him as a human, living thing. It was no longer merely a picture of a few throes in the breast of a poet, meanwhile drinking tea and warming his feet at the grate; it was an actuality — stern, mournful, and fine.

The correspondent plainly saw the soldier. He lay on the sand with his feet out straight and still. While his pale left hand was upon his chest in an attempt to thwart the going of his life, the blood came between his fingers. In the far Algerian distance, a city of low square forms was set against a sky that was faint with the last sunset hues. The correspondent, plying the oars and dreaming of the slow and slower movements of the lips of the soldier, was moved by a profound and perfectly impersonal comprehension. He was sorry for the soldier of the Legion who lay dying in Algiers.

The thing which had followed the boat and waited had evidently grown bored at the delay. There was no longer to be heard the slash of the cut-water, and there was no longer the flame of the long trail. The light in the north still glimmered, but it was apparently no nearer to the boat. Sometimes the boom of the surf rang in the correspondent's ears, and he turned the craft seaward then and rowed harder. Southward, someone had evidently built a watch-fire on the beach. It was too low and too far to be seen, but it made a shimmering, roseate reflection upon the bluff back of it, and this could be discerned from the boat. The wind came stronger, and sometimes a wave suddenly raged out like a mountain-cat and there was to be seen the sheen and sparkle of a broken crest.

The captain, in the bow, moved on his water-jar and sat erect. "Pretty long night," 185
he observed to the correspondent. He looked at the shore. "Those life-saving people
take their time."

"Did you see that shark playing around?"

"Yes, I saw him. He was a big fellow, all right."

"Wish I had known you were awake."

Later the correspondent spoke into the bottom of the boat.

"Billie!" There was a slow and gradual disentanglement. "Billie, will you spell me?" 190

"Sure," said the oiler.

As soon as the correspondent touched the cold comfortable sea-water in the
bottom of the boat, and had huddled close to the cook's life-belt he was deep in sleep,
despite the fact that his teeth played all the popular airs. This sleep was so good to
him that it was but a moment before he heard a voice call his name in a tone that
demonstrated the last stages of exhaustion. "Will you spell me?"

"Sure, Billie."

The light in the north had mysteriously vanished, but the correspondent took his
course from the wide-awake captain.

Later in the night they took the boat farther out to sea, and the captain directed 195
the cook to take one oar at the stern and keep the boat facing the seas. He was to call
out if he should hear the thunder of the surf. This plan enabled the oiler and the correspondent to get respite together. "We'll give those boys a chance to get into shape
again," said the captain. They curled down and, after a few preliminary chatterings
and trembles, slept once more the dead sleep. Neither knew they had bequeathed to
the cook the company of another shark, or perhaps the same shark.

As the boat caroused on the waves, spray occasionally bumped over the side
and gave them a fresh soaking, but this had no power to break their repose. The
ominous slash of the wind and the water affected them as it would have affected
mummies.

"Boys," said the cook, with the notes of every reluctance in his voice, "she's drifted
in pretty close. I guess one of you had better take her to sea again." The correspondent,
aroused, heard the crash of the toppled crests.

As he was rowing, the captain gave him some whiskey and water, and this steadied
the chills out of him. "If I ever get ashore and anybody shows me even a photograph of
an oar ——"

At last there was a short conversation.

"Billie. . . . Billie, will you spell me?" 200

"Sure," said the oiler.

VII

When the correspondent again opened his eyes, the sea and the sky were each of the
gray hue of the dawning. Later, carmine and gold was painted upon the waters. The
morning appeared finally, in its splendor, with a sky of pure blue, and the sunlight
flamed on the tips of the waves.

On the distant dunes were set many little black cottages, and a tall white wind-mill reared above them. No man, nor dog, nor bicycle appeared on the beach. The cottages might have formed a deserted village.

The voyagers scanned the shore. A conference was held in the boat. "Well," said the captain, "if no help is coming, we might better try a run through the surf right away. If we stay out here much longer we will be too weak to do anything for ourselves at all." The others silently acquiesced in this reasoning. The boat was headed for the beach. The correspondent wondered if none ever ascended the tall wind-tower, and if then they never looked seaward. This tower was a giant, standing with its back to the plight of the ants. It represented in a degree, to the correspondent, the serenity of nature amid the struggles of the individual — nature in the wind, and nature in the vision of men. She did not seem cruel to him then, nor beneficent, nor treacherous, nor wise. But she was indifferent, flatly indifferent. It is, perhaps, plausible that a man in this situation pressed with the unconcern of the universe, should see the innumerable flaws of his life and have them taste wickedly in his mind and wish for another chance. A distinction between right and wrong seems absurdly clear to him, then, in this new ignorance of the grave-edge, and he understands that if he were given another opportunity he would mend his conduct and his words, and be better and brighter during an introduction, or at a tea.

"Now, boys," said the captain, "she is going to swamp sure. All we can do is to work her in as far as possible, and then when she swamps, pile out and scramble for the beach. Keep cool now and don't jump until she swamps sure." 205

The oiler took the oars. Over his shoulders he scanned the surf. "Captain," he said, "I think I'd better bring her about, and keep her head-on to the seas and back her in."

"All right, Billie," said the captain. "Back her in." The oiler swung the boat then and, seated in the stern, the cook and the correspondent were obliged to look over their shoulders to contemplate the lonely and indifferent shore.

The monstrous inshore rollers heaved the boat high until the men were again enabled to see the white sheets of water scudding up the slanted beach. "We won't get in very close," said the captain. Each time a man could wrest his attention from the rollers, he turned his glance toward the shore, and in the expression of the eyes during this contemplation there was a singular quality. The correspondent, observing the others, knew that they were not afraid, but the full meaning of their glances was shrouded.

As for himself, he was too tired to grapple fundamentally with the fact. He tried to coerce his mind into thinking of it, but the mind was dominated at this time by the muscles, and the muscles said they did not care. It merely occurred to him that if he should drown it would be a shame.

There were no hurried words, no pallor, no plain agitation. The men simply looked at the shore. "Now, remember to get well clear of the boat when you jump," said the captain. 210

Seaward the crest of a roller suddenly fell with a thunderous crash, and the long white comber came roaring down upon the boat.

"Steady now," said the captain. The men were silent. They turned their eyes from the shore to the comber and waited. The boat slid up the incline, leaped at the furious top, bounced over it, and swung down the long back of the waves. Some water had been shipped and the cook bailed it out.

But the next crest crashed also. The tumbling boiling flood of white water caught the boat and whirled it almost perpendicular. Water swarmed in from all sides. The correspondent had his hands on the gunwale at this time, and when the water entered at that place he swiftly withdrew his fingers, as if he objected to wetting them.

The little boat, drunken with this weight of water, reeled and snuggled deeper into the sea.

"Bail her out, cook! Bail her out," said the captain.   215

"All right, captain," said the cook.

"Now, boys, the next one will do for sure," said the oiler. "Mind to jump clear of the boat."

The third wave moved forward, huge, furious, implacable. It fairly swallowed the dingey, and almost simultaneously the men tumbled into the sea. A piece of life-belt had lain in the bottom of the boat, and as the correspondent went overboard he held this to his chest with his left hand.

The January water was icy, and he reflected immediately that it was colder than he had expected to find it off the coast of Florida. This appeared to his dazed mind as a fact important enough to be noted at the time. The coldness of the water was sad; it was tragic. This fact was somehow mixed and confused with his opinion of his own situation that it seemed almost a proper reason for tears. The water was cold.

When he came to the surface he was conscious of little but the noisy water.   220
Afterward he saw his companions in the sea. The oiler was ahead in the race. He was swimming strongly and rapidly. Off to correspondent's left, the cook's great white and corked back bulged out of the water, and in the rear the captain was hanging with his one good hand to the keel of the overturned dingey.

There is a certain immovable quality to a shore, and the correspondent wondered at it amid the confusion of the sea.

It seemed also very attractive, but the correspondent knew that it was a long journey, and he paddled leisurely. The piece of life-preserver lay under him, and sometimes he whirled down the incline of a wave as if he were on a hand-sled.

But finally he arrived at a place in the sea where travel was beset with difficulty. He did not pause swimming to inquire what manner of current had caught him, but there his progress ceased. The shore was set before him like a bit of scenery on a stage, and he looked at it and understood with his eyes each detail of it.

As the cook passed, much farther to the left, the captain was calling to him, "Turn over on your back, cook! Turn over on your back and use the oar."

"All right, sir." The cook turned on his back, and, paddling with an oar, went   225
ahead as if he were a canoe.

Presently the boat also passed to the left of the correspondent with the captain clinging with one hand to the keel. He would have appeared like a man raising himself to look over a board fence, if it were not for the extraordinary gymnastics of the boat. The correspondent marvelled that the captain could still hold it.

They passed on, nearer to shore — the oiler, the cook, the captain — and following them went the water-jar, bouncing gayly over the seas.

The correspondent remained in the grip of this strange new enemy — a current. The shore, with its white slope of sand and its green bluff, topped with little silent cottages, was spread like a picture before him. It was very near to him then, but he was impressed as one who in a gallery looks at a scene from Brittany or Algiers.

He thought: "I am going to drown? Can it be possible? Can it be possible? Can it be possible?" Perhaps an individual must consider his own death to be the final phenomenon of nature.

But later a wave perhaps whirled him out of this small deadly current, for he found suddenly that he could again make progress toward the shore. Later still, he was aware that the captain, clinging with one hand to the keel of the dingey, had his face turned away from the shore and toward him, and was calling his name. "Come to the boat! Come to the boat!" 230

In his struggle to reach the captain and the boat, he reflected that when one gets properly wearied, drowning must really be a comfortable arrangement, a cessation of hostilities accompanied by a large degree of relief, and he was glad of it, for the main thing in his mind for some moments had been horror of the temporary agony. He did not wish to be hurt.

Presently he saw a man running along the shore. He was undressing with most remarkable speed. Coat, trousers, shirt, everything flew magically off him.

"Come to the boat," called the captain.

"All right, captain." As the correspondent paddled, he saw the captain let himself down to bottom and leave the boat. Then the correspondent performed his one little marvel of the voyage. A large wave caught him and flung him with ease and supreme speed completely over the boat and far beyond it. It struck him even then as an event in gymnastics, and a true miracle of the sea. An overturned boat in the surf is not a plaything to a swimming man.

The correspondent arrived in water that reached only to his waist, but his condition did not enable him to stand for more than a moment. Each wave knocked him into a heap, and the under-tow pulled at him. 235

Then he saw the man who had been running and undressing, and undressing and running, come bounding into the water. He dragged ashore the cook, and then waded toward the captain, but the captain waved him away, and sent him to the correspondent. He was naked, naked as a tree in winter, but a halo was about his head, and he shone like a saint. He gave a strong pull, and a long drag, and a bully heave at the correspondent's hand. The correspondent, schooled in the minor formulae, said: "Thanks, old man." But suddenly the man cried: "What's that?" He pointed a swift finger. The correspondent said: "Go."

In the shallows, face downward, lay the oiler. His forehead touched sand that was periodically, between each wave, clear of the sea.

The correspondent did not know all that transpired afterward. When he achieved safe ground he fell, striking the sand with each particular part of his body. It was as if he had dropped from a roof, but the thud was grateful to him.

It seems that instantly the beach was populated with men with blankets, clothes, and flasks, and women with coffee-pots and all the remedies sacred to their minds. The welcome of the land to the men from the sea was warm and generous, but a still and dripping shape was carried slowly up the beach, and the land's welcome for it could only be the different and sinister hospitality of the grave.

When it came night, the white waves paced to and fro in the moonlight, and the wind brought the sound of the great sea's voice to the men on shore, and they felt that they could then be interpreters.

240

(1897)

Exploring the Text

1. What is the effect of the opening paragraph? How does it set the scene for the entire story?

2. What is the narrative stance in this story? How do you account for conditional statements — set here in italic — such as "In the wan light, the faces of the men *must have been* gray. Their eyes *must have* glinted" (par. 11) and "It was *probably* splendid. It was *probably* glorious, this play of the free sea, wild with lights of emerald and white and amber" (par. 21)? Why does Stephen Crane introduce such uncertainty?

3. What is "the subtle brotherhood of men" (par. 44) that Crane's narrator refers to? How is this camaraderie developed into a theme in the story?

4. What is the importance of the narrator's imagined "reflections of the men," which "might be formulated thus: 'If I am going to be drowned — if I am going to be drowned . . . She dare not drown me. She cannot drown me. Not after all this work'" (par. 72)?

5. Why does the correspondent "mysteriously" recall a verse he "had even forgotten that he had forgotten" (par. 180)? What is the meaning of the description that he was moved "by a profound and perfectly impersonal comprehension" (par. 183)?

6. Why are the characters referred to by their function rather than their given names in most of the story? Why is the oiler, Billie, the exception?

7. The story is divided into seven sections or chapters. What is the structural principle governing these divisions? What titles might you give each?

8. The ocean dominates this story from the very first paragraph to the last. How does Crane portray the sea in this story? Cite specific passages of description, paying close attention to figurative language.

9. Early in the story, we are told that the captain "chuckled in a way that expressed humor, contempt, tragedy, all in one" (par. 25). Identify at least one passage and discuss how Crane shows the complexity of feeling multiple emotions simultaneously, especially conflicting emotions. Consider instances that include humor in this life-and-death situation.

10. Crane does not depict nature as an entirely hostile force in "The Open Boat"; he shows how it both impedes and assists the four men. What details illustrate

the varying roles nature plays in this story? Ultimately, what conclusion does the correspondent reach about the relationship between humans and nature? Consider the ending in your response.

11. Explain why you believe that the worldview Crane presents in this story is ultimately optimistic or pessimistic.

12. Following is a section from Crane's account of the sinking of the *Commodore*. How does it differ in style and tone from the short story? What seeds of the story do you detect in this nonfiction report?

> The cook let go of the line.
>
> We rowed around to see if we could not get a line from the chief engineer, and all this time, mind you, there were no shrieks, no groans, but silence, silence and silence, and then the *Commodore* sank. She lurched to windward, then swung afar back, righted and dove into the sea, and the rafts were suddenly swallowed by this frightful maw of the ocean. And then by the men on the ten-foot dingy were words said that were still not words, something far beyond words.
>
> The lighthouse of Mosquito Inlet stuck up above the horizon like the point of a pin. We turned our dingy toward the shore. The history of life in an open boat for thirty hours would no doubt be very instructive for the young, but none is to be told here now. For my part I would prefer to tell the story at once, because from it would shine the splendid manhood of Captain Edward Murphy and of William Higgins, the oiler, but let it suffice at this time to say that when we were swamped in the surf and making the best of our way toward the shore the captain gave orders amid the wildness of the breakers as clearly as if he had been on the quarterdeck of a battleship.
>
> John Kitchell of Daytona came running down the beach, and as he ran the air was filled with clothes. If he had pulled a single lever and undressed, even as the fire horses harness, he could not to me seem to have stripped with more speed. He dashed into the water and grabbed the cook. Then he went after the captain, but the captain sent him to me, and then it was that we saw Billy Higgins lying with his forehead on sand that was clear of the water, and he was dead.

E. A. ROBINSON

Edwin Arlington Robinson (1869–1935) was a Pulitzer Prize–winning American poet born in Maine. Robinson studied at Harvard University, where he published his first poems in the *Harvard Advocate*. He moved to New York City in the 1890s, and in 1896 he published his first volume of poetry, *The Torrent and the Night*, at his own expense. Unable to make a living as a poet, Robinson took a job as an inspector for the New York City subway system. He gained little attention for his poetry until 1902, when President Theodore Roosevelt wrote a magazine article praising Robinson's poetry collection *Captain Craig and Other Poems.* Soon after, Roosevelt offered Robinson a position in a U.S. Customs House, a job that he kept from 1905 to 1910. *The Man against the Sky* (1916) became his first major success. In 1922, he won a Pulitzer Prize for *Collected Poems,* and in 1925 he won another Pulitzer Prize for *The Man Who Died Twice.* He was awarded his third and final Pulitzer Prize in 1928 for a trilogy of poems based on Arthurian legends.

Richard Cory

This poem was published in Robinson's 1897 collection, *The Children of the Night.*

Whenever Richard Cory went down town,
We people on the pavement looked at him:
He was a gentleman from sole to crown,
Clean favored, and imperially slim.

And he was always quietly arrayed,   5
And he was always human when he talked;
But still he fluttered pulses when he said,
"Good-morning," and he glittered when he walked.

And he was rich — yes, richer than a king —
And admirably schooled in every grace: 10
In fine, we thought that he was everything
To make us wish that we were in his place.

So on we worked, and waited for the light,
And went without the meat, and cursed the bread;
And Richard Cory, one calm summer night,   15
Went home and put a bullet through his head.

(1897)

Exploring the Text

1. How would you characterize the speaker in this poem?
2. What specific information does the poem provide about the appearance and demeanor of Richard Cory?
3. What is meant by his being "quietly arrayed" (l. 5) and "always human" (l. 6)?
4. Line 13 opens with the conjunction "So," which suggests causality. What is the cause-effect relationship between stanza 3 and the first two lines of stanza 4?
5. The ending of the poem is surprising, even shocking, when first read, and we have not even a hint of why Richard Cory took such desperate action. Do you think it

is more effective that we know nothing of the circumstances or turmoil that might have led him to commit suicide?

6. Explain how situational irony works in this poem.

Miniver Cheevy

This poem was first published in Robinson's collection *The Town Down the River* (1910).

Miniver Cheevy, child of scorn,
    Grew lean while he assailed the seasons;
He wept that he was ever born,
    And he had reasons.

Miniver loved the days of old   5
    When swords were bright and steeds were prancing;
The vision of a warrior bold
    Would set him dancing.

Miniver sighed for what was not,
    And dreamed, and rested from his labors;   10
He dreamed of Thebes and Camelot,
    And Priam's[1] neighbors.

Miniver mourned the ripe renown
    That made so many a name so fragrant;
He mourned Romance, now on the town,   15
    And Art, a vagrant.

Miniver loved the Medici,[2]
    Albeit he had never seen one;
He would have sinned incessantly
    Could he have been one.   20

Miniver cursed the commonplace
    And eyed a khaki suit with loathing;
He missed the mediaeval grace
    Of iron clothing.

---

[1]King of Troy during the Trojan War. — Eds.
[2]Italian political and banking dynasty that ruled the city-state of Florence and other parts of Tuscany from the fourteenth to the eighteenth century. The family boasts four popes, two queens of France, and a host of other royalty. — Eds.

Miniver scorned the gold he sought,   25
　　But sore annoyed was he without it;
Miniver thought, and thought, and thought,
　　And thought about it.

Miniver Cheevy, born too late,
　　Scratched his head and kept on thinking;   30
Miniver coughed, and called it fate,
　　And kept on drinking.

(1910)

Exploring the Text

1. What is the ambiguity in the description "child of scorn" (l. 1)? What are two possible meanings?
2. The words used to describe Cheevy's view of "the days of old" (l. 5) are fairly clichéd: "When swords were bright and steeds were prancing; / The vision of a warrior bold" (ll. 6–7). What effect does E. A. Robinson achieve by choosing such hackneyed expressions?
3. Why does Cheevy dream of "Thebes and Camelot, / And Priam's neighbors" (ll. 11–12)? What do these examples have in common?
4. What is the "khaki suit" (l. 22)? What is "iron clothing" (l. 24)?
5. How do you interpret these lines: "Miniver scorned the gold he sought, / But sore annoyed was he without it" (ll. 25–26)?
6. What examples of humor do you find in this poem? Consider elements such as word choice, alliteration, repetition, and allusion as well as patterns of rhyme and rhythm. How would you characterize the humor? Is it gentle sarcasm? Bitter irony? Playful wit?
7. Do you think that Miniver Cheevy's inability to fit into his own era is a consequence of history (i.e., he was born at the wrong time) or the result of his own character failings? Make your case with concrete references to the text of the poem.
8. What is the tone of the poem? Cite specific words and lines to support your response.

THEODORE ROOSEVELT

Theodore Roosevelt (1858–1919) was only forty-two when he became the twenty-sixth president of the United States following William McKinley's assassination in 1901. During his first term, he spearheaded the construction of the Panama Canal, and during his second, he won the Nobel Peace Prize — the first American to do so — for his mediation in the Russo-Japanese War of 1904–1905. Prior to holding office, he commanded the famed Rough Riders, an all-volunteer cavalry that led the charge on San Juan Hill in the Spanish-American War, for which he was awarded the Congressional Medal of Honor. Roosevelt led what he called the "strenuous life," which included working on his ranch in the Dakotas, going on safari in Africa, and exploring the Amazon basin.

The Strenuous Life

Included here is the first part of the speech Roosevelt delivered in 1899 to Chicago's Hamilton Club, a private organization, after the Senate had ratified the treaty with Spain that established the Philippines as a colony of the United States. In the remainder of the speech, Roosevelt defends American imperialism as much on the basis of his definition of the American character as on the country's political and economic interests.

In speaking to you, men of the greatest city of the West, men of the State which gave to the country Lincoln and Grant, men who preëminently and distinctly embody all that is most American in the American character, I wish to preach, not the doctrine of ignoble ease, but the doctrine of the strenuous life, the life of toil and effort, of labor and strife; to preach that highest form of success which comes, not to the man who desires mere easy peace, but to the man who does not shrink from danger, from hardship, or from bitter toil, and who out of these wins the splendid ultimate triumph.

A life of slothful ease, a life of that peace which springs merely from lack either of desire or of power to strive after great things, is as little worthy of a nation as of an individual. I ask only that what every self-respecting American demands from himself and from his sons shall be demanded of the American nation as a whole. Who among you would teach your boys that ease, that peace, is to be the first consideration in their eyes — to be the ultimate goal after which they strive? You men of Chicago have made this city great, you men of Illinois have done your share, and more than your share, in making America great, because you neither preach nor practise such a doctrine. You work yourselves, and you bring up your sons to work. If you are rich and are worth your salt, you will teach your sons that though they may have leisure, it is not to be spent in idleness; for wisely used leisure merely means that those who possess it, being free from the necessity of working for their livelihood, are all the more bound to carry on some kind of non-remunerative work in science, in letters, in art, in exploration, in historical research — work of the type we most need in this country, the successful carrying out of which reflects most honor upon the nation.

We do not admire the man of timid peace. We admire the man who embodies victorious effort; the man who never wrongs his neighbor, who is prompt to help a friend, but who has those virile qualities necessary to win in the stern strife of actual life. It is hard to fail, but it is worse never to have tried to succeed. In this life we get nothing save by effort. Freedom from effort in the present merely means that there has been stored up effort in the past. A man can be freed from the necessity of work only by the fact that he or his fathers before him have worked to good purpose. If the freedom thus purchased is used aright, and the man still does actual work, though of a different kind, whether as a writer or a general, whether in the field of politics or in the field of exploration and adventure, he shows he deserves his good fortune. But if he treats this period of freedom from the need of actual labor as a period, not of preparation, but of mere enjoyment, even though perhaps not of vicious enjoyment, he shows that he is simply a cumberer of the earth's surface, and he surely unfits himself to hold his own with his fellows if the need to do so should again arise. A mere life of ease is not in the end a very satisfactory life, and, above all, it is a life which ultimately unfits those who follow it for serious work in the world.

In the last analysis a healthy state can exist only when the men and women who make it up lead clean, vigorous, healthy lives; when the children are so trained that they shall endeavor, not to shirk difficulties, but to overcome them; not to seek ease, but to know how to wrest triumph from toil and risk. The man must be glad to do a man's work, to dare and endure and to labor; to keep himself, and to keep those dependent upon him. The woman must be the housewife, the helpmeet of the home-maker, the wise and fearless mother of many healthy children. In one of Daudet's powerful and melancholy books he speaks of "the fear of maternity, the haunting terror of the young wife of the present day." When such words can be truthfully written of a nation, that nation is rotten to the heart's core. When men fear work or fear righteous war, when women fear motherhood, they tremble on the brink of doom; and well it is that they should vanish from the earth, where they are fit subjects for the scorn of all men and women who are themselves strong and brave and high-minded,

As it is with the individual, so it is with the nation. It is a base untruth to say that   5
happy is the nation that has no history. Thrice happy is the nation that has a glorious history. Far better it is to dare mighty things, to win glorious triumphs, even though checkered by failure, than to take rank with those poor spirits who neither enjoy much nor suffer much, because they live in the gray twilight that knows not victory nor defeat. If in 1861 the men who loved the Union had believed that peace was the end of all things, and war and strife the worst of all things, and had acted up to their belief, we would have saved hundreds of thousands of lives, we would have saved hundreds of millions of dollars. Moreover, besides saving all the blood and treasure we then lavished, we would have prevented the heartbreak of many women, the dissolution of many homes, and we would have spared the country those months of gloom and shame when it seemed as if our armies marched only to defeat. We could have avoided all this suffering simply by shrinking from strife. And if we had thus avoided it, we would have shown that we were weaklings, and that we were unfit to stand among the great nations of the earth. Thank God for the iron in the blood of our fathers, the men who upheld the wisdom of Lincoln, and bore sword or rifle in the armies of Grant! Let us, the children of the men who proved themselves equal to the mighty days, let us, the children of the men who carried the great Civil War to a triumphant conclusion, praise the God of our fathers that the ignoble counsels of peace were rejected; that the suffering and loss, the blackness of sorrow and despair, were

unflinchingly faced, and the years of strife endured; for in the end the slave was freed, the Union restored, and the mighty American republic placed once more as a helmeted queen among nations.

We of this generation do not have to face a task such as that our fathers faced, but we have our tasks, and woe to us if we fail to perform them! We cannot, if we would, play the part of China, and be content to rot by inches in ignoble ease within our borders, taking no interest in what goes on beyond them, sunk in a scrambling commercialism; heedless of the higher life, the life of aspiration, of toil and risk, busying ourselves only with the wants of our bodies for the day, until suddenly we should find, beyond a shadow of question, what China has already found, that in this world the nation that has trained itself to a career of unwarlike and isolated ease is bound, in the end, to go down before other nations which have not lost the manly and adventurous qualities. If we are to be a really great people, we must strive in good faith to play a great part in the world. We cannot avoid meeting great issues. All that we can determine for ourselves is whether we shall meet them well or ill. In 1898 we could not help being brought face to face with the problem of war with Spain. All we could decide was whether we should shrink like cowards from the contest, or enter into it as beseemed a brave and high-spirited people; and, once in, whether failure or success should crown our banners.

So it is now. We cannot avoid the responsibilities that confront us in Hawaii, Cuba, Porto Rico, and the Philippines. All we can decide is whether we shall meet them in a way that will redound to the national credit, or whether we shall make of our dealings with these new problems a dark and shameful page in our history. To refuse to deal with them at all merely amounts to dealing with them badly. We have a given problem to solve. If we undertake the solution, there is, of course, always danger that we may not solve it aright; but to refuse to undertake the solution simply renders it certain that we cannot possibly solve it aright.

The timid man, the lazy man, the man who distrusts his country, the over-civilized man, who has lost the great fighting, masterful virtues, the ignorant man, and the man of dull mind, whose soul is incapable of feeling the mighty lift that thrills "stern men with empires in their brains" — all these, of course, shrink from seeing the nation undertake its new duties; shrink from seeing us build a navy and an army adequate to our needs; shrink from seeing us do our share of the world's work, by bringing order out of chaos in the great, fair tropic islands from which the valor of our soldiers and sailors has driven the Spanish flag. These are the men who fear the strenuous life, who fear the only national life which is really worth leading. They believe in that cloistered life which saps the hardy virtues in a nation, as it saps them in the individual; or else they are wedded to that base spirit of gain and greed which recognizes in commercialism the be-all and end-all of national life, instead of realizing that, though an indispensable element, it is, after all, but one of the many elements that go to make up true national greatness. No country can long endure if its foundations are not laid deep in the material prosperity which comes from thrift, from business energy and enterprise, from hard, unsparing effort in the fields of industrial activity; but neither was any nation ever yet truly great if it relied upon material prosperity alone. All honor must be paid to the architects of our material prosperity, to the great captains of industry who have built our factories and our railroads, to the strong men who toil for wealth with brain or hand; for great is the debt of the nation to these and their kind. But our debt is yet greater to the men whose highest type is to be found in a statesman like Lincoln, a soldier like Grant. They showed by their lives that they recognized the law of work, the law of strife; they toiled to win a competence for themselves and those dependent upon them; but they recognized that there were yet other and even loftier duties — duties to the nation and duties to the race.

We cannot sit huddled within our own borders and avow ourselves merely an assemblage of well-to-do hucksters who care nothing for what happens beyond. Such a policy would defeat even its own end; for as the nations grow to have ever wider and wider interests, and are brought into closer and closer contact, if we are to hold our own in the struggle for naval and commercial supremacy, we must build up our power without our own borders. We must build the isthmian canal,[1] and we must grasp the points of vantage which will enable us to have our say in deciding the destiny of the oceans of the East and the West. . . .

I preach to you, then, my countrymen, that our country calls not for the life of ease but for the life of strenuous endeavor. The twentieth century looms before us big with the fate of many nations. If we stand idly by, if we seek merely swollen, slothful ease and ignoble peace, if we shrink from the hard contests where men must win at hazard of their lives and at the risk of all they hold dear, then the bolder and stronger peoples will pass us by, and will win for themselves the domination of the world. Let us therefore boldly face the life of strife, resolute to do our duty well and manfully; resolute to uphold righteousness by deed and by word; resolute to be both honest and brave, to serve high ideals, yet to use practical methods. Above all, let us shrink from no strife, moral or physical, within or without the nation, provided we are certain that the strife is justified, for it is only through strife, through hard and dangerous endeavor, that we shall ultimately win the goal of true national greatness.

(1899)

Exploring the Text

1. The rhetorical situation for this speech is that Theodore Roosevelt, one of the Rough Riders in the Spanish-American War of 1898 (the invitation to the banquet referred to him as "Colonel Roosevelt") and newly elected governor of New York, was being honored at a banquet by the Hamilton Club, an exclusive members-only organization established in 1890. How does he tailor his speech to this audience (which was all male)? What ethos does he establish?
2. What is the relationship among freedom, leisure, idleness, and work as Roosevelt uses those terms in the third paragraph?

---

[1]What would become the Panama Canal. — Eds.

3. How does Roosevelt define gender roles in this speech? Consider his definition of "man's work" and a woman's role as described in paragraph 4. How do these assumptions guide Roosevelt's argument about the qualities most essential for national vigor and vitality?

4. How does Roosevelt interpret the Civil War as demonstrating that America was not a nation of "weaklings" (par. 5)?

5. Ultimately, what does Roosevelt believe is "most American in the American character" (par. 1)? What are "those virile qualities necessary to win in the stern strife of actual life" (par. 3)?

6. What purpose does Roosevelt achieve through his example of China (par. 6)?

7. How does Roosevelt make the transition from exhorting the virtues of "the strenuous life" for individuals to arguing that similar characteristics are necessary in the life of the nation? How convincing do you find this analogy? Consider the concluding paragraph of the excerpt in your analysis.

8. The Hamilton Club, organized in 1890, catered to an exclusive membership selected through an application process governed by its leadership. The club's objective was stated as follows: "This Club is incorporated for the advancement of political science; to promote good government — local, state and national; to develop the growth and spread of patriotism and of Republican principles; and to cultivate friendly and social relations among its members." How does Roosevelt's speech reflect these goals?

9. Roosevelt ends this exuberant speech by claiming that "our country calls not for the life of ease but for the life of strenuous endeavor" if the country is to achieve "true national greatness." To what extent do you see his perspective in today's national discourse?

JANE ADDAMS

Jane Addams (1860–1935) was an American writer, women's rights activist, and social settlement pioneer. A daughter of Senator John Addams, she grew up in Illinois and graduated from the prestigious Rockford Female Seminary in 1881. In 1889, with her partner Ellen Gates Starr, Addams founded Hull House, a social settlement in Chicago, which brought educated middle-class and upper-middle-class "settlers" to live in poor neighborhoods and provide free services, such as day care, education, and health care, to the impoverished urban residents. From Hull House, where she lived for the rest of her life, Addams helped raise national awareness about the issues of women's rights, public health, and child welfare. In the early 1900s, she became involved in the peace movement, attending the International Congress of Women at The Hague in 1915 and helping found the Women's Peace Party (WILPF) in 1919. In 1931, Addams became the first American woman to receive the Nobel Peace Prize.

from *The Subtle Problem of Charity*

In "The Subtle Problem of Charity," published in the *Atlantic Monthly* in 1899, Addams discusses the ethics of philanthrophy in a democracy that, she believed, places too high a premium on economic success. In this excerpt, she focuses on the development of mutual understanding between those in a position to provide assistance and those in need of it.

Probably there is no relation in life which our democracy is changing more rapidly than the charitable relation, — that relation which obtains between benefactor and beneficiary: at the same time, there is no point of contact in our modern experience which reveals more clearly the lack of that equality which democracy implies. We have reached the moment when democracy has made such inroads upon this relationship that the complacency of the old-fashioned charitable man is gone forever; while the very need and existence of charity deny us the consolation and freedom which democracy will at last give.

We find in ourselves the longing for a wider union than that of family or class, and we say that we have come to include all men in our hopes; but we fail to realize that all men are hoping, and are part of the same movement of which we are a part. Many of the difficulties in philanthropy come from an unconscious division of the world into the philanthropists and those to be helped. It is an assumption of two classes, and against this class assumption our democratic training revolts as soon as we begin to act upon it.

The trouble is that the ethics of none of us are clearly defined, and we are continually obliged to act in circles of habit based upon convictions which we no longer hold. Thus, our estimate of the effect of environment and social conditions has doubtless shifted faster than our methods of administering charity have changed. Formerly when it was believed that poverty was synonymous with vice and laziness, and that the prosperous man was the righteous man, charity was administered harshly with a good conscience; for the charitable agent really blamed the individual for his poverty, and the very fact of his own superior prosperity gave him a certain consciousness of superior morality. Since then we have learned to measure by other standards, and the money-earning capacity, while still rewarded out of all proportion to any other, is not respected as exclusively as it was; and its possession is by no means assumed to imply the possession of the highest moral qualities. We have learned to judge men in general by their social virtues as well as by their business capacity, by their devotion to intellectual and disinterested aims, and by their public spirit, and we naturally resent being obliged to judge certain individuals solely upon the industrial side for no other reason than that they are poor. Our democratic instinct constantly takes alarm at this consciousness of two standards.

Of the various struggles which a decade of residence in a settlement implies, none have made a more definite impression on my mind than the incredibly painful difficulties which involve both giver and recipient when one person asks charitable aid of another.

An attempt is made in this paper to show what are some of the perplexities which   5
harass the mind of the charity worker; to trace them to ethical survivals which are
held not only by the benefactor, but by the recipients of charity as well; and to suggest
wherein these very perplexities may possibly be prophetic. . . .

The charity visitor, let us assume, is a young college woman, well-bred and open-
minded. When she visits the family assigned to her, she is embarrassed to find herself
obliged to lay all the stress of her teaching and advice upon the industrial virtues, and
to treat the members of the family almost exclusively as factors in the industrial system. She insists that they must work and be self-supporting; that the most dangerous
of all situations is idleness; that seeking one's own pleasure, while ignoring claims and
responsibilities, is the most ignoble of actions. The members of her assigned family
may have charms and virtues, — they may possibly be kind and affectionate and
considerate of one another, generous to their friends; but it is her business to stick to
the industrial side. As she daily holds up these standards, it often occurs to the mind
of the sensitive visitor, whose conscience has been made tender by much talk of
brotherhood and equality which she has heard at college, that she has no right to say
these things; that she herself has never been self-supporting; that, whatever her virtues may be, they are not the industrial virtues; that her untrained hands are no more
fitted to cope with actual conditions than are those of her broken-down family. . . .

Added to this is a consciousness in the mind of the visitor of a genuine misunderstanding of her motives by the recipients of her charity and by their neighbors.
Let us take a neighborhood of poor people, and test their ethical standards by those
of the charity visitor, who comes with the best desire in the world to help them out of
their distresses. A most striking incongruity, at once apparent, is the difference between
the emotional kindness with which relief is given by one poor neighbor to another poor
neighbor, and the guarded care with which relief is given by a charity visitor to a charity recipient. The neighborhood mind is immediately confronted not only by the difference of method, but also by an absolute clashing of two ethical standards.

A very little familiarity with the poor districts of any city is sufficient to show how
primitive and frontier-like are the neighborly relations. There is the greatest willingness to lend or borrow anything, and each resident of a given tenement house knows
the most intimate family affairs of all the others. The fact that the economic condition
of all alike is on a most precarious level makes the ready outflow of sympathy and
material assistance the most natural thing in the world. There are numberless instances of heroic self-sacrifice quite unknown in the circles where greater economic advantages make that kind of intimate knowledge of one's neighbors impossible. . . .

The charity visitor may blame the women for lack of gentleness toward their children,
for being hasty and rude to them, until she learns to reflect that the standard of
breeding is not that of gentleness toward the children so much as the observance of
certain conventions, such as the punctilious wearing of mourning garments after the
death of a child. The standard of gentleness each mother has to work out largely by
herself, assisted only by the occasional shamefaced remark of a neighbor, that "they
do better when you are not too hard on them"; but the wearing of mourning garments is sustained by the definitely expressed sentiment of every woman in the street.

The mother would have to bear social blame, a certain social ostracism, if she failed to comply with that requirement. It is not comfortable to outrage the conventions of those among whom we live, and if our social life be a narrow one, it is still more difficult. The visitor may choke a little when she sees the lessened supply of food and the scanty clothing provided for the remaining children, in order that one may be conventionally mourned. But she does not talk so strongly against it as she would have done during her first month of experience with the family since bereaved.

The subject of clothes, indeed, perplexes the visitor constantly, and the result of her   10
reflections may be summed up something in this wise: The girl who has a definite social standing, who has been to a fashionable school or to a college, whose family live in a house seen and known by all her friends and associates, can afford to be very simple or even shabby as to her clothes, if she likes. But the working girl, whose family lives in a tenement or moves from one small apartment to another, who has little social standing, and has to make her own place, knows full well how much habit and style of dress have to do with her position. Her income goes into her clothing out of all proportion to that which she spends upon other things. But if social advancement is her aim, it is the most sensible thing which she can do. She is judged largely by her clothes. . . . Have we worked out our democracy in regard to clothes farther than in regard to anything else?

The charity visitor has been rightly brought up to consider it vulgar to spend much money upon clothes, to care so much for "appearances." . . . The poor naturally try to bridge the [class] difference[s] by reproducing the street clothes which they have seen; they therefore imitate, sometimes in more showy and often in more trying colors, in cheap and flimsy material, in poor shoes and flippant hats, the extreme fashion of the well-to-do. They are striving to conform to a common standard which their democratic training presupposes belongs to us all. The charity visitor may regret that the Italian peasant woman has laid aside her picturesque kerchief, and substituted a cheap street hat. But it is easy to recognize the first attempt toward democratic expression. . . .

A certain charity visitor is peculiarly appealed to by the weakness and pathos of forlorn old age. She is responsible for the well-being of perhaps a dozen old women, to whom she sustains a sincere and simple and almost filial relation. Some of them learn to take her benefactions quite as if they came from their own relatives, grumbling at all she does, and scolding her with a family freedom. One of these poor old women was injured in a fire years ago. She has but the fragment of a hand left, and is grievously crippled in her feet. Through years of pain she had become addicted to opium, and when she first came under the residents' care was held from the poorhouse only by the awful thought that she would there perish without her drug. Five years of tender care have done wonders for her. She lives in two neat little rooms, where with a thumb and two fingers she makes innumerable quilts, which she sells and gives away with the greatest delight. Her opium is regulated to a set amount taken each day, and she has been drawn away from much drinking. She is a voracious reader, and has her head full of strange tales made up from books and her own imagination. . . . Her neighbors are constantly shocked by the fact that she is supported and comforted by "a charity lady," while at the same time she occasionally "rushes the growler," scolding at the boys lest they jar her in her tottering walk. The care of her has broken through even that second standard, which the neighborhood had learned to recognize as the standard of charitable societies, that only the "worthy poor" are to be helped. . . . In order to disarm them, and at the same time to explain what would otherwise seem loving-kindness so colossal as to be abnormal, she tells them that during her sojourn in the suburb she discovered an awful family secret, a horrible scandal connected with the long-suffering charity visitor; that it is in order to prevent the divulgence of this that the ministrations are continued. Some of her perplexed neighbors accept this explanation as simple and offering a solution of a vexed problem. . . .

Of what use is all this striving and perplexity? Has the experience any value? It is obviously genuine, for it induces an occasional charity visitor to live in a tenement house as simply as the other tenants do. It drives others to give up visiting the poor altogether, because, they claim, the situation is untenable. . . . [T]he young charity visitor who goes from a family living upon a most precarious industrial level to her own home in a prosperous part of the city, if she is sensitive at all, is never free from perplexities which our growing democracy forces upon her.

For most of the years during a decade of residence in a settlement, my mind was sore and depressed over the difficulties of the charitable relationship. The incessant clashing of ethical standards, which had been honestly gained from widely varying industrial experience, — the misunderstandings inevitable between people whose conventions and mode of life had been so totally unlike, — made it seem reasonable to say that nothing could be done until industrial conditions were made absolutely democratic. The position of a settlement, which attempts at one and the same time to declare its belief in this eventual, industrial democracy, and to labor toward that end, to maintain a standard of living, and to deal humanely and simply with those in actual want, often seems utterly untenable and preposterous. Recently, however, there has come to my mind the suggestion of a principle, that while the painful condition of administering charity is the inevitable discomfort of a transition into a more democratic relation, the perplexing experiences of the actual administration have a genuine value of their own. . . .

The Hebrew prophet made three requirements from those who would join the great forward-moving procession led by Jehovah. "To love mercy," and at the same time "to do justly," is the difficult task. To fulfill the first requirement alone is to fall into the error of indiscriminate giving, with all its disastrous results; to fulfill the second exclusively is to obtain the stern policy of withholding, and it results in such a dreary lack of sympathy and understanding that the establishment of justice is impossible. It may be that the combination of the two can never be attained save as we fulfill still the third requirement, "to walk humbly with God," which may mean to walk for many dreary miles beside the lowliest of his creatures, not even in peace of mind, that the companionship of the humble is popularly supposed to give, but rather with the pangs and misgivings to which the poor human understanding is subjected whenever it attempts to comprehend the meaning of life.

(1899)

Exploring the Text

1. What occasioned this article, according to Jane Addams's explanation in the opening paragraphs?

2. What are the "difficulties in philanthropy" (par. 2) and the "incessant clashing of ethical standards" (par. 14) on which Addams focuses? Discuss how she reveals these complexities in at least one of the examples she provides.

3. Where in the text does Addams speak primarily as a scientific observer of social conditions? Where does she speak more as a passionate advocate of social reform? Do you think these voices complement or undercut each other? Cite specific text to support your responses.

4. How would you describe the ethos Addams establishes? Pay particular attention to how she presents (or avoids presenting) her own privileged background as the daughter of a wealthy family.

5. How does Addams manage to question the values of an increasingly market-driven and competitive society without criticizing American values? Or does she?

6. Identify passages or specific language choices in this essay that may have sounded condescending to Addams's audience or that you find patronizing or condescending from a contemporary perspective. In what ways is she trying to avoid ethical absolutes in her discussion of the poor, especially when referring to immigrants? Does she succeed?

7. Addams frames her discussion of the "problems of charity" in two traditions: democracy and Christianity. What purpose(s) does she achieve by threading the discussion of democracy throughout the essay but referring to Christian texts only at the end? Keep her audience in mind as you consider this question.

8. Have we solved what Addams saw as the "clashing" of ethics and morality in the relationship between benefactor and beneficiary? What tone do we attach to the word "charity" today? Is the belief that wealthy people should also be philanthropists more or less a part of our current expectations than it was a century ago? Discuss your view on these issues, using examples from contemporary life.

KATHARINE LEE BATES

Katharine Lee Bates (1859–1929) was an American poet and songwriter born in Falmouth, Massachusetts. After graduating from Wellesley College in 1880, she remained at her alma mater for many years as a professor of English literature. During her lifetime, Bates became known for her poetry, travel books, and children's books, and she was a regular contributor to various periodicals, including the *Atlantic Monthly*, the *Congregationalist*, the *Boston Evening Transcript*, and the *Christian Century*. Her poem "Goody Santa Claus on a Sleigh Ride," which she published in 1889, is said to have first popularized Mrs. Claus.

America the Beautiful

Bates was inspired to write the original version of this poem after seeing Pikes Peak in the summer of 1893, during a teaching stint in Colorado Springs. Bates described her experience thus: "One day some of the other teachers and I decided to go on a trip to 14,000-foot Pikes Peak. We hired a prairie wagon. Near the top we had to leave the wagon and go the rest of the way on mules. I was very tired. But when I saw the view, I felt great joy. All the wonder of America seemed displayed there, with the sea-like expanse."

The poem went through several revisions after its original publication on July 4, 1895, in the weekly journal called the *Congregationalist.* It appeared in the *Boston Evening Transcript* on November 19, 1904, and in her book *America the Beautiful and Other Poems* (1912). The version below is from that collection.

O beautiful for spacious skies,
   For amber waves of grain,
For purple mountain majesties
   Above the fruited plain!
     America! America!   5
   God shed His grace on thee
And crown thy good with brotherhood
   From sea to shining sea!

O beautiful for pilgrim feet,
   Whose stern, impassioned stress   10
A thoroughfare for freedom beat
   Across the wilderness!
     America! America!
   God mend thine every flaw,
Confirm thy soul in self-control,   15
   Thy liberty in law!

O beautiful for heroes proved
   In liberating strife,
Who more than self their country loved,
   And mercy more than life!   20
     America! America!
   May God thy gold refine,
Till all success be nobleness,
   And every gain divine!

O beautiful for patriot dream   25
   That sees beyond the years
Thine alabaster cities gleam

Undimmed by human tears!
  America! America!
God shed His grace on thee   30
And crown thy good with brotherhood
  From sea to shining sea!

                                   (1912)

Exploring the Text

1. What element(s) of America does Katharine Lee Bates celebrate in this poem? What are the primary sources of her inspiration?
2. What is Bates calling for in the lines that read, "God mend thine every flaw, / Confirm thy soul in self-control, / Thy liberty in law!" (ll. 14–16)?
3. How do you interpret the following lines: "May God thy gold refine, / Till all success be nobleness, / And every gain divine!" (ll. 22–25)?
4. What phrases or images from the poem have become part of the national idiom, often quoted even by those who may not know their source as being this poem? Why do you think a specific phrase or image is particularly memorable or appealing?
5. Following is the original version of the poem, entitled "America." What changes do you note between this version and the revised poem that appeared in Bates's collection of poetry? What are the effects of these changes?

> ### America. A Poem for July 4.
> O beautiful for halcyon skies,
> For amber waves of grain,
> For purple mountain majesties
> Above the enameled plain!
> America! America!   5
> God shed His grace on thee,
> Till souls wax fair as earth and air
> And music-hearted sea!
>
> O beautiful for pilgrim feet
> Whose stern, impassioned stress   10
> A thoroughfare for freedom beat
> Across the wilderness!
> America! America!
> God shed His grace on thee
> Till paths be wrought through wilds of thought 15
> By pilgrim foot and knee!
>
> O beautiful for glory-tale
> Of liberating strife,

When once or twice, for man's avail,
Men lavished precious life!   20
America! America!
God shed His grace on thee
Till selfish gain no longer stain,
The banner of the free!

O beautiful for patriot dream   25
That sees beyond the years
Thine alabaster cities gleam
Undimmed by human tears!
America! America!
God shed His grace on thee   30
Till nobler men keep once again
Thy whiter jubilee!

6. Many have championed and continue to champion "America the Beautiful" to be designated as a national anthem; some even argue that it should replace "The Star-Spangled Banner," which was named the official national anthem by congressional resolution in 1931. Lynn Sherr, author of *America the Beautiful: The Stirring True Story behind Our Nation's Favorite Song* (2001), supports that position: "I think it's simple, I think it's emotional, and I think it talks about a country, a land and its people — not just about a flag, not just about a battle. It doesn't talk about conquest. It talks about the possibilities of this nation." What is your view? You might research some of the arguments offered over the past century, including current efforts on behalf of "America the Beautiful."

7. Research different recordings of "America the Beautiful" and discuss artists' interpretations of it. Ray Charles and Buffy St. Marie are two artists whose renditions are very popular.

Zitkala-Ša

Zitkala-Ša (1876–1938), also known as Gertrude Simmons Bonnin, was a Native American writer, musician, and political activist. Born on a Sioux reservation in South Dakota and educated by Quaker missionaries in Indiana, she spent her life torn between her Sioux heritage and the dominant white culture of the time. Zitkala-Ša was awarded her first diploma from the Quaker school in 1895, and in the same year she won a scholarship to attend Earlham College in Richmond, Indiana, where she became known for her oratory talents. She moved to Boston, Massachusetts, where she played violin with the New England Conservatory of Music from 1897 to 1899. For the rest of her career, Zitkala-Ša taught English and music at various schools and became a prolific writer. Her works brought traditional Native American stories to a widespread readership, and she published several works that chronicled her struggles to reconcile her Native American culture with mainstream American culture. An avid lobbyist and supporter of Native American rights, she founded the National Council of American Indians in 1926 to advocate for Native Americans to gain American citizenship.

from *The School Days of an Indian Girl*

Zitkala-Ša published her autobiographical articles in the *Atlantic Monthly* between 1900 and 1902. Following are three sections, entitled "The Big Red Apples," "The Land of Red Apples," and "The Cutting of My Long Hair."

The Big Red Apples

The first turning away from the easy, natural flow of my life occurred in an early spring. It was in my eighth year; in the month of March, I afterward learned. At this age I knew but one language, and that was my mother's native tongue.

From some of my playmates I heard that two paleface missionaries were in our village. They were from that class of white men who wore big hats and carried large hearts, they said. Running direct to my mother, I began to question her why these two strangers were among us. She told me, after I had teased much, that they had come to take away Indian boys and girls to the East. My mother did not seem to want me to talk about them. But in a day or two, I gleaned many wonderful stories from my play-fellows concerning the strangers.

"Mother, my friend Judéwin is going home with the missionaries. She is going to a more beautiful country than ours; the palefaces told her so!" I said wistfully, wishing in my heart that I too might go.

Mother sat in a chair, and I was hanging on her knee. Within the last two seasons my big brother Dawée had returned from a three years' education in the East, and his coming back influenced my mother to take a farther step from her native way of living. First it was a change from the buffalo skin to the white man's canvas that covered our wigwam. Now she had given up her wigwam of slender poles, to live, a foreigner, in a home of clumsy logs.

"Yes, my child, several others besides Judéwin are going away with the palefaces. Your brother said the missionaries had inquired about his little sister," she said, watching my face very closely.   5

My heart thumped so hard against my breast, I wondered if she could hear it.

"Did he tell them to take me, mother?" I asked, fearing lest Dawée had forbidden the palefaces to see me, and that my hope of going to the Wonderland would be entirely blighted.

With a sad, slow smile, she answered: "There! I knew you were wishing to go, because Judéwin has filled your ears with the white man's lies. Don't believe a word they say! Their words are sweet, but, my child, their deeds are bitter. You will cry for me, but they will not even soothe you. Stay with me, my little one! Your brother Dawée says that going East, away from your mother, is too hard an experience for his baby sister."

Thus my mother discouraged my curiosity about the lands beyond our eastern horizon; for it was not yet an ambition for Letters that was stirring me. But on the following day the missionaries did come to our very house. I spied them coming up the footpath leading to our cottage. A third man was with them, but he was not my brother Dawée. It was another, a young interpreter, a paleface who had a smattering of the Indian language. I was ready to run out to meet them, but I did not dare to displease my mother. With great glee, I jumped up and down on our ground floor. I begged my mother to open the door, that they would be sure to come to us. Alas! They came, they saw, and they conquered!

Judéwin had told me of the great tree where grew red, red apples; and how we could reach out our hands and pick all the red apples we could eat. I had never seen apple trees. I had never tasted more than a dozen red apples in my life; and when I heard of the orchards of the East, I was eager to roam among them. The missionaries smiled into my eyes and patted my head. I wondered how mother could say such hard words against him. 10

"Mother, ask them if little girls may have all the red apples they want, when they go East," I whispered aloud, in my excitement.

The interpreter heard me, and answered: "Yes, little girl, the nice red apples are for those who pick them; and you will have a ride on the iron horse if you go with these good people."

I had never seen a train, and he knew it.

"Mother, I am going East! I like big red apples, and I want to ride on the iron horse! Mother, say yes!" I pleaded.

My mother said nothing. The missionaries waited in silence; and my eyes began to blur with tears, though I struggled to choke them back. The corners of my mouth twitched, and my mother saw me. 15

"I am not ready to give you any word," she said to them. "Tomorrow I shall send you my answer by my son."

With this they left us. Alone with my mother, I yielded to my tears, and cried aloud, shaking my head so as not to hear what she was saying to me. This was the first time I had ever been so unwilling to give up my own desire that I refused to hearken to my mother's voice.

There was a solemn silence in our home that night. Before I went to bed I begged the Great Spirit to make my mother willing I should go with the missionaries.

The next morning came, and my mother called me to her side. "My daughter, do you still persist in wishing to leave your mother?" she asked.

"Oh, mother, it is not that I wish to leave you, but I want to see the wonderful Eastern land," I answered. 20

My dear old aunt came to our house that morning, and I heard her say, "Let her try it."

I hoped that, as usual, my aunt was pleading on my side. My brother Dawée came for mother's decision. I dropped my play, and crept close to my aunt.

"Yes, Dawée, my daughter, though she does not understand what it all means, is anxious to go. She will need an education when she is grown, for then there will be fewer real Dakotas, and many more palefaces. This tearing her away, so young, from her mother is necessary, if I would have her an educated woman. The palefaces, who owe us a large debt for stolen lands, have begun to pay a tardy justice in offering some education to our children. But I know my daughter must suffer keenly in this experiment. For her sake, I dread to tell you my reply to the missionaries. Go, tell them that they may take my little daughter, and that the Great Spirit shall not fail to reward them according to their hearts."

Wrapped in my heavy blanket, I walked with my mother to the carriage that was soon to take us to the iron horse. I was happy. I met my playmates, who were also wearing their best thick blankets. We showed one another our new beaded moccasins, and the width of the belts that girdled our new dresses. Soon we were being drawn rapidly away by the white man's horses. When I saw the lonely figure of my mother vanish in the distance, a sense of regret settled heavily upon me. I felt suddenly weak, as if I might fall limp to the ground. I was in the hands of strangers whom my mother did not fully trust. I no longer felt free to be myself, or to voice my own feelings. The tears trickled down my cheeks, and I buried my face in the folds of my blanket. Now the first step, parting me from my mother, was taken, and all my belated tears availed nothing.

Having driven thirty miles to the ferryboat, we crossed the Missouri in the evening. Then riding again a few miles eastward, we stopped before a massive brick building. I looked at it in amazement, and with a vague misgiving, for in our village I had never seen so large a house. Trembling with fear and distrust of the palefaces, my teeth chattering from the chilly ride, I crept noiselessly in my soft moccasins along the narrow hall, keeping very close to the bare wall. I was as frightened and bewildered as the captured young of a wild creature.

The Land of Red Apples

There were eight in our party of bronzed children who were going East with the missionaries. Among us were three young braves, two tall girls, and we three little ones, Judéwin, Thowin, and I.

We had been very impatient to start on our journey to the Red Apple Country, which, we were told, lay a little beyond the great circular horizon of the Western prairie. Under a sky of rosy apples we dreamt of roaming as freely and happily as we had chased the cloud shadows on the Dakota plains. We had anticipated much pleasure from a ride on the iron horse, but the throngs of staring palefaces disturbed and troubled us.

On the train, fair women, with tottering babies on each arm, stopped their haste and scrutinized the children of absent mothers. Large men, with heavy bundles in their hands, halted near by, and riveted their glassy blue eyes upon us.

I sank deep into the corner of my seat, for I resented being watched. Directly in front of me, children who were no larger than I hung themselves upon the backs of their seats, with their bold white faces toward me. Sometimes they took their forefingers out of their mouths and pointed at my moccasined feet. Their mothers, instead of reproving such rude curiosity, looked closely at me, and attracted their children's further notice to my blanket. This embarrassed me, and kept me constantly on the verge of tears.

I sat perfectly still, with my eyes downcast, daring only now and then to shoot 30 long glances around me. Chancing to turn to the window at my side, I was quite breathless upon seeing one familiar object. It was the telegraph pole which strode by at short paces. Very near my mother's dwelling, along the edge of a road thickly bordered with wild sunflowers, some poles like these had been planted by white men. Often I had stopped, on my way down the road, to hold my ear against the pole, and, hearing its low moaning, I used to wonder what the paleface had done to hurt it. Now I sat watching for each pole that glided by to be the last one.

In this way I had forgotten my uncomfortable surroundings, when I heard one of my comrades call out my name. I saw the missionary standing very near, tossing candies and gums into our midst. This amused us all, and we tried to see who could catch the most of the sweetmeats.

Though we rode several days inside of the iron horse, I do not recall a single thing about our luncheons.

It was night when we reached the school grounds. The lights from the windows of the large buildings fell upon some of the icicled trees that stood beneath them. We were led toward an open door, where the brightness of the lights within flooded out over the heads of the excited palefaces who blocked our way. My body trembled more from fear than from the snow I trod upon.

Entering the house, I stood close against the wall. The strong glaring light in the large whitewashed room dazzled my eyes. The noisy hurrying of hard shoes upon a bare wooden floor increased the whirring in my ears. My only safety seemed to be in keeping next to the wall. As I was wondering in which direction to escape from all this confusion, two warm hands grasped me firmly, and in the same moment I was tossed high in midair. A rosy-cheeked paleface woman caught me in her arms. I was both frightened and insulted by such trifling. I stared into her eyes, wishing her to let me stand on my own feet, but she jumped me up and down with increasing enthusiasm. My mother had never made a plaything of her wee daughter. Remembering this I began to cry aloud.

They misunderstood the cause of my tears, and placed me at a white table loaded 35 with food. There our party were united again. As I did not hush my crying, one of the older ones whispered to me, "Wait until you are alone in the night."

It was very little I could swallow besides my sobs, that evening.

"Oh, I want my mother and my brother Dawée! I want to go to my aunt!" I pleaded; but the ears of the palefaces could not hear me.

From the table we were taken along an upward incline of wooden boxes, which I learned afterward to call a stairway. At the top was a quiet hall, dimly lighted. Many narrow beds were in one straight line down the entire length of the wall. In them lay sleeping brown faces, which peeped just out of the coverings. I was tucked into bed with one of the tall girls, because she talked to me in my mother tongue and seemed to soothe me.

I had arrived in the wonderful land of rosy skies, but I was not happy, as I had thought I should be. My long travel and the bewildering sights had exhausted me. I fell asleep, heaving deep, tired sobs. My tears were left to dry themselves in streaks, because neither my aunt nor my mother was near to wipe them away.

The Cutting of My Long Hair

The first day in the land of apples was a bitter-cold one; for the snow still covered the 40
ground, and the trees were bare. A large bell rang for breakfast, its loud metallic voice
crashing through the belfry overhead and into our sensitive ears. The annoying clatter of shoes on bare floors gave us no peace. The constant clash of harsh noises, with
an undercurrent of many voices murmuring an unknown tongue, made a bedlam
within which I was securely tied. And though my spirit tore itself in struggling for its
lost freedom, all was useless.

A paleface woman, with white hair, came up after us. We were placed in a line of
girls who were marching into the dining room. These were Indian girls, in stiff shoes
and closely clinging dresses. The small girls wore sleeved aprons and shingled hair.
As I walked noiselessly in my soft moccasins, I felt like sinking to the floor, for my
blanket had been stripped from my shoulders. I looked hard at the Indian girls, who
seemed not to care that they were even more immodestly dressed than I, in their
tightly fitting clothes. While we marched in, the boys entered at an opposite door. I
watched for the three young braves who came in our party. I spied them in the rear
ranks, looking as uncomfortable as I felt.

A small bell was tapped, and each of the pupils drew a chair from under the table.
Supposing this act meant they were to be seated, I pulled out mine and at once slipped
into it from one side. But when I turned my head, I saw that I was the only one seated,
and all the rest at our table remained standing. Just as I began to rise, looking shyly
around to see how chairs were to be used, a second bell was sounded. All were seated at
last, and I had to crawl back into my chair again. I heard a man's voice at one end of
the hall, and I looked around to see him. But all the others hung their heads over their
plates. As I glanced at the long chain of tables, I caught the eyes of a paleface woman
upon me. Immediately I dropped my eyes, wondering why I was so keenly watched by
the strange woman. The man ceased his mutterings, and then a third bell was tapped.
Every one picked up his knife and fork and began eating. I began crying instead, for
by this time I was afraid to venture anything more.

But this eating by formula was not the hardest trial in that first day. Late in the
morning, my friend Judéwin gave me a terrible warning. Judéwin knew a few words
of English; and she had overheard the paleface woman talk about cutting our long,
heavy hair. Our mothers had taught us that only unskilled warriors who were captured had their hair shingled by the enemy. Among our people, short hair was worn
by mourners, and shingled hair by cowards!

We discussed our fate some moments, and when Judéwin said, "We have to
submit, because they are strong," I rebelled.

"No, I will not submit! I will struggle first!" I answered. 45

I watched my chance, and when no one noticed I disappeared. I crept up the stairs
as quietly as I could in my squeaking shoes, — my moccasins had been exchanged for
shoes. Along the hall I passed, without knowing whither I was going. Turning aside
to an open door, I found a large room with three white beds in it. The windows were
covered with dark green curtains, which made the room very dim. Thankful that no

one was there, I directed my steps toward the corner farthest from the door. On my hands and knees I crawled under the bed, and cuddled myself in the dark corner.

From my hiding place I peered out, shuddering with fear whenever I heard footsteps near by. Though in the hall loud voices were calling my name, and I knew that even Judéwin was searching for me, I did not open my mouth to answer. Then the steps were quickened and the voices became excited. The sounds came nearer and nearer. Women and girls entered the room. I held my breath and watched them open closet doors and peep behind large trunks. Some one threw up the curtains, and the room was filled with sudden light. What caused them to stoop and look under the bed I do not know. I remember being dragged out, though I resisted by kicking and scratching wildly. In spite of myself, I was carried downstairs and tied fast in a chair.

I cried aloud, shaking my head all the while until I felt the cold blades of the scissors against my neck, and heard them gnaw off one of my thick braids. Then I lost my spirit. Since the day I was taken from my mother I had suffered extreme indignities. People had stared at me. I had been tossed about in the air like a wooden puppet. And now my long hair was shingled like a coward's! In my anguish I moaned for my mother, but no one came to comfort me. Not a soul reasoned quietly with me, as my own mother used to do; for now I was only one of many little animals driven by a herder.

(1900)

Exploring the Text

1. In the opening section, "The Big Red Apples," Zitkala-Ša acknowledges that "it was not yet an ambition for Letters that was stirring me" (par. 9). What, then, does motivate her desire to leave her mother and familiar circumstances to travel east with the missionaries?

2. Why does her mother oppose her daughter's wish to leave? At what point does the narrator realize that her mother's fears are coming true?

3. In "The Land of Red Apples," what happens that causes Zitkala-Ša to doubt her decision?

4. Having her hair cut was the most dramatic of the "extreme indignities" (par. 48) that the narrator describes, but what other measures are taken by the missionaries to distance her (and her peers) from her native culture?

5. What role does language play in the experience of young Zitkala-Ša? In what instances does she show that she is most aware of the importance of her own language?

6. Throughout these autobiographical pieces, Zitkala-Ša takes readers to the immediacy of her childhood experiences, yet these are filtered through her adult consciousness. In the opening section, for instance, discussing the missionaries she says, "Alas! They came, they saw, and they conquered!" (par. 9). What other examples of the adult "interpreter" do you find?

7. The author began her life with the given name Gertrude Simmons, reflecting the influence of her European American father, her mother's second husband, who abandoned the family soon after the birth of his daughter. She took the Lakota name Zitkala-Ša, which means Red Bird, when she began to write around 1900. After her

marriage to Raymond Bonnin, she used Gertrude Simmons Bonnin as her legal name and in her dealings with the Bureau of Indian Affairs; that is the name on her grave in Arlington National Cemetery. Today, some books identify her as Gertrude Bonnin, others as Zitkala-Ša. Which name do you believe is the more appropriate primary designation for her?

8. In her book *Tender Violence: Domestic Visions in an Age of U.S. Imperialism* (2000), scholar Laura Wexler characterizes the assimilationist education efforts of seemingly well-intentioned missionaries as "tender violence." Using Zitkala-Ša's autobiographical writings as a source, to what extent do you think that term captures the experience?

9. Below are two portraits of Zitkala-Ša, both taken in 1898, by the American photographer Gertrude Käsebier (1852–1934). The women became friends, and Käsebier is said to have encouraged her to select what she wanted to wear and how she wanted to pose in the portraits. How do each of these images depict Zitkala-Ša's multiple identities? What representations of both her Native American and European American cultures do you note? Does she seem to privilege one over the other or embody a blended balance? Cite specifics in the photographs to support your response, including her expression and the material objects within each image.

Gertrude Käsebier Collection, Division of Culture & the Arts, National Museum of American History, Smithsonian Institution

JAMES WELDON JOHNSON

Born in Jacksonville, Florida, James Weldon Johnson (1871–1938) graduated from Atlanta University in 1894. In 1897, he passed the Florida bar exam, and for the next forty years, he served in various public capacities as an educator, a diplomat, a civil rights activist, and a writer. In the early 1900s, President Theodore Roosevelt appointed him United States consul to Venezuela and Nicaragua, and from 1916 to 1929, he served as executive secretary of the National Association for the Advancement of Colored People (NAACP).

Lift Ev'ry Voice and Sing

Johnson wrote the following poem during his tenure as principal of the segregated Stanton School in Jacksonville, Florida, and it was first performed in 1900 as part of a celebration of Lincoln's birthday. A year later, his brother, Rosamond, set it to music. It gained enormous popularity and became known as the "Negro National Anthem."

Lift ev'ry voice and sing,
Till earth and heaven ring,
Ring with the harmonies of Liberty;
Let our rejoicing rise
High as the list'ning skies,   5
Let it resound loud as the rolling sea.
Sing a song full of the faith that the dark past has taught us,
Sing a song full of the hope that the present has brought us;
Facing the rising sun of our new day begun,
Let us march on till victory is won.   10

Stony the road we trod,
Bitter the chast'ning rod.
Felt in the days when hope unborn had died;
Yet with a steady beat,
Have not our weary feet   15
Come to the place for which our fathers sighed?
We have come over a way that with tears has been watered,
We have come, treading our path through the blood of the
  slaughtered,
Out from the gloomy past,
Till now we stand at last   20
Where the white gleam of our bright star is cast.

God of our weary years,
God of our silent tears,
Thou who hast brought us thus far on the way;
Thou who hast by Thy might,   25
Led us into the light,
Keep us forever in the path, we pray.

Lest our feet stray from the places, our God, where we met Thee,
Lest our hearts, drunk with the wine of the world, we forget Thee;
Shadowed beneath Thy hand,   30
May we forever stand,
True to our God,
True to our native land.

(1900)

Exploring the Text

1. Without referencing actual events, the poem alludes to the history of African Americans. What particulars of that historical experience might be linked to specific lines in the poem?
2. The poem is filled with tensions and dualities. Cite at least two and explain how they are developed. Do they resolve themselves into a balance, or does one triumph?
3. How would you describe the tone of the poem? Consider the final three lines in your explanation.
4. Listen to a recording or performance of "Lift Ev'ry Voice and Sing." How does the music match your understanding of the poem, or does it change it? Explain with reference to specific lines or passages.
5. In *Lift Ev'ry Voice and Sing: A Celebration of the Negro National Anthem* (2000), editors Julian Bond and Sondra Kathryn Wilson distinguish between an anthem and a "hymn":

> As a college student, Johnson had realized the glaring contradictions between white America's actions and the true aims of the United States Constitution. He believed that the Constitution meant exactly what it said, and it was his inexorable faith in the founding principles of America that inspired him to write "Lift Every Voice and Sing" not as an anthem but as a hymn. He did not conceive the song as an anthem, and at no time did he refer to it in that manner. By the 1920s the song was being pasted inside the back covers of hymnal books across the South and in many parts of the North. It is likely that around this time the "anthem" label evolved through folklore, thus sealing the song's permanent status among African Americans as their "Negro National Anthem."
>
> James Weldon Johnson was the chief executive officer of the NAACP during the 1920s, when the organization made "Lift Every Voice and Sing" its "official song." Because of his strong belief that "a nation can have but one anthem" and the NAACP's fundamental ideology of integration, labeling the song an "anthem" would have been antithetical to the organization's central objective. Johnson's main task as NAACP leader was to legally abolish the fiendish acts of lynchings that were increasingly occurring; he called for the saving of black America's bodies and white America's souls. He certainly understood that when the wide-ranging forces of racism struck, his people needed something to fall back on. And

it was clear to him that African Americans made the song what they needed it to be — their anthem of hope and prayer.

After looking up the definition of the terms, explain Bond and Wilson's reasoning and why you believe that "Lift Ev'ry Voice and Sing" is best characterized as an anthem or as a hymn.

6. In 2008, jazz singer Rene Martin was invited to perform the national anthem at a city event in Denver, Colorado. She sang the lyrics to "Lift Ev'ry Voice and Sing" to the music of "The Star Spangled Banner." As a member of the listening audience, how would you have responded?

W. E. B. DuBois

Intellectual, philosopher, political activist, scholar, and writer W. E. B. DuBois (1868–1963) was born in Great Barrington, Massachusetts, and educated at Fisk University, Harvard University (where he earned his PhD in history in 1895), and the University of Berlin. Although during the early part of his career, he agreed with Booker T. Washington (p. 891) on issues of racial solidarity and economic autonomy, by the turn of the century DuBois had become more militant, criticizing Washington's commitment to vocational education as an accommodationist approach to change. In his seminal work, *The Souls of Black Folk* (1903), DuBois denounced Washington's approach to racial equality (in "Of Mr. Booker T. Washington and Others") and argued in "Of the Training of Black Men" for a cadre of liberally educated leadership. DuBois was influential as a writer as well as a founding member of the National Association for the Advancement of Colored People and editor of the *Crisis*, the official publication of the group. He spent his long life in efforts to solve what he called "the problem of the twentieth century" — "the color line."

The Talented Tenth

The following excerpt is from "The Talented Tenth," an essay published in *The Negro Problem* (1903), an anthology of writings by African American scholars.

The Negro race, like all races, is going to be saved by its exceptional men. The problem of education, then, among Negroes must first of all deal with the Talented Tenth; it is the problem of developing the Best of this race that they may guide the mass away from the contamination and death of the Worst, in their own and other races. Now the training of men is a difficult and intricate task. Its technique is a matter for educational experts, but its object is for the vision of seers. If we make money the object of man-training, we shall develop money-makers but not necessarily men; if we make technical skill the object of education, we may possess artisans but not, in nature, men. Men we shall have only as we make manhood the object of the work of the schools—intelligence, broad sympathy, knowledge of the world that was and is, and of the relation of men to it—this is the curriculum of that Higher Education which must underlie true life. On this foundation we may build bread winning, skill of hand and quickness of brain, with never a fear lest the child and man mistake the means of living for the object of life.

If this be true—and who can deny it—three tasks lay before me; first to show from the past that the Talented Tenth as they have risen among American Negroes have been worthy of leadership; secondly, to show how these men may be educated and developed; and thirdly, to show their relation to the Negro problem. . . .

From the very first it has been the educated and intelligent of the Negro people that have led and elevated the mass, and the sole obstacles that nullified and retarded their efforts were slavery and race prejudice. . . .

And so we come to the present—a day of cowardice and vacillation, of strident wide-voiced wrong and faint hearted compromise; of double-faced dallying with Truth and Right. Who are to-day guiding the work of the Negro people? The "exceptions" of course. And yet so sure as this Talented Tenth is pointed out, the blind worshippers of the Average cry out in alarm: "These are exceptions, look here at death, disease and crime—these are the happy rule." Of course they are the rule, because a silly nation made them the rule: Because for three long centuries this people lynched Negroes who dared to be brave, raped black women who dared to be virtuous, crushed dark-hued youth who dared to be ambitious, and encouraged and made to flourish servility and lewdness and apathy. But not even this was able to crush all manhood and chastity and aspiration from black folk. A saving remnant continually survives and persists, continually aspires, continually shows itself in thrift and ability and character. Exceptional it is to be sure, but this is its chiefest promise; it shows the capability of Negro blood, the promise of black men. Do Americans ever stop to reflect that there are in this land a million men of Negro blood, well-educated, owners of homes, against the honor of whose womanhood no breath was ever raised, whose men occupy positions of trust and usefulness, and who, judged by any standard, have reached the full measure of the best type of modern European culture? Is it fair, is it decent, is it Christian to ignore these facts of the Negro problem, to belittle such aspiration, to nullify such leadership and seek to crush these people back into the mass out of which by toil and travail, they and their fathers have raised themselves?

Can the masses of the Negro people be in any possible way more quickly raised   5
than by the effort and example of this aristocracy of talent and character? Was there ever a nation on God's fair earth civilized from the bottom upward? Never; it is, ever was and ever will be from the top downward that culture filters. The Talented Tenth rises and pulls all that are worth the saving up to their vantage ground. This is the history of human progress. . . .

How then shall the leaders of a struggling people be trained and the hands of the risen few strengthened? There can be but one answer: The best and most capable of their youth must be schooled in the colleges and universities of the land. . . .

All men cannot go to college but some men must; every isolated group or nation must have its yeast, must have for the talented few centers of training where men are not so mystified and befuddled by the hard and necessary toil of earning a living, as to have no aims higher than their bellies, and no God greater than Gold. This is true training, and thus in the beginning were the favored sons of the freedmen trained. Out of the colleges of the North came, after the blood of war, Ware, Cravath, Chase, Andrews, Bumstead and Spence[1] to build the foundations of knowledge and civilization in the black South. Where ought they to have begun to build? At the bottom, of course, quibbles the mole with his eyes in the earth. Aye! truly at the bottom, at the very bottom; at the bottom of knowledge, down in the very depths of knowledge there where the roots of justice strike into the lowest soil of Truth. And so they did begin; they founded colleges, and up from the colleges shot normal schools, and out from the normal schools went teachers, and around the normal teachers clustered other teachers to teach the public schools; the college trained in Greek and Latin and mathematics, 2,000 men; and these men trained full 50,000 others in morals and manners, and they in turn taught thrift and the alphabet to nine millions of men, who to-day hold $300,000,000 of property. It was a miracle — the most wonderful peace-battle of the 19th century, and yet to-day men smile at it, and in fine superiority tell us that it was all a strange mistake; that a proper way to found a system of education is first to gather the children and buy them spelling books and hoes; afterward men may look about for teachers, if haply they may find them; or again they would teach men Work, but as for Life — why, what has Work to do with Life, they ask vacantly. . . .

The college-bred Negro . . . is, as he ought to be, the group leader, the man who sets the ideals of the community where he lives, directs its thoughts and heads its social movements. It need hardly be argued that the Negro people need social leadership more than most groups; that they have no traditions to fall back upon, no long established customs, no strong family ties, no well defined social classes. All these things must be slowly and painfully evolved. The preacher was, even before the war, the group leader of the Negroes, and the church their greatest social institution. Naturally this preacher was ignorant and often immoral, and the problem of replacing the older type by better educated men has been a difficult one. Both by direct work and by direct influence on other preachers, and on congregations, the college-bred preacher has an opportunity for reformatory work and moral inspiration, the value of which cannot be overestimated.

It has, however, been in the furnishing of teachers that the Negro college has found its peculiar function. Few persons realize how vast a work, how mighty a revolution has been thus accomplished. To furnish five millions and more of ignorant people with teachers of their own race and blood, in one generation, was not only a very difficult undertaking, but a very important one, in that, it placed before the eyes of almost every Negro child an attainable ideal. It brought the masses of the blacks in contact with modern civilization, made black men the leaders of their com-

---

[1]Founders and presidents of Historically Black Colleges and Universities. — Eds.

munities and trainers of the new generation. In this work college-bred Negroes were first teachers, and then teachers of teachers. And here it is that the broad culture of college work has been of peculiar value. Knowledge of life and its wider meaning, has been the point of the Negro's deepest ignorance, and the sending out of teachers whose training has not been simply for bread winning, but also for human culture, has been of inestimable value in the training of these men. . . .

The main question, so far as the Southern Negro is concerned, is: What under the present circumstance, must a system of education do in order to raise the Negro as quickly as possible in the scale of civilization? The answer to this question seems to me clear: It must strengthen the Negro's character, increase his knowledge and teach him to earn a living. Now it goes without saying, that it is hard to do all these things simultaneously or suddenly, and that at the same time it will not do to give all the attention to one and neglect the others; we could give black boys trades, but that alone will not civilize a race of ex-slaves; we might simply increase their knowledge of the world, but this would not necessarily make them wish to use this knowledge honestly; we might seek to strengthen character and purpose, but to what end if this people have nothing to eat or to wear? . . . If then we start out to train an ignorant and unskilled people with a heritage of bad habits, our system of training must set before itself two great aims — the one dealing with knowledge and character, the other part seeking to give the child the technical knowledge necessary for him to earn a living under the present circumstances. These objects are accomplished in part by the opening of the common schools on the one, and of the industrial schools on the other. But only in part, for there must also be trained those who are to teach these schools — men and women of knowledge and culture and technical skill who understand modern civilization, and have the training and aptitude to impart it to the children under them. There must be teachers, and teachers of teachers, and to attempt to establish any sort of a system of common and industrial school training, without *first* (and I say *first* advisedly) without *first* providing for the higher training of the very best teachers, is simply throwing your money to the winds. . . . Nothing, in these latter days, has so dampened the faith of thinking Negroes in recent educational movements, as the fact that such movements have been accompanied by ridicule and denouncement and decrying of those very institutions of higher training which made the Negro public school possible, and make Negro industrial schools thinkable. . . .

I would not deny, or for a moment seem to deny, the paramount necessity of teaching the Negro to work, and to work steadily and skillfully; or seem to depreciate in the slightest degree the important part industrial schools must play in the accomplishment of these ends, but I *do* say, and insist upon it, that it is industrialism drunk with its vision of success, to imagine that its own work can be accomplished without providing for the training of broadly cultured men and women to teach its own teachers, and to teach the teachers of the public schools.

But I have already said that human education is not simply a matter of schools; it is much more a matter of family and group life — the training of one's home, of one's daily companions, of one's social class. Now the black boy of the South moves in a black world — a world with its own leaders, its own thoughts, its own ideals. In this world he gets by far the larger part of his life training, and through the eyes of this dark world he peers into the veiled world beyond. Who guides and determines the education which he receives in his world? His teachers here are the group-leaders of the Negro people — the physicians and clergymen, the trained fathers and mothers, the influential and forceful men about him of all kinds; here it is, if at all, that the culture of the surrounding world trickles through and is handed on by the graduates of the higher schools. Can such culture training of group leaders be neglected? Can we afford to ignore it? . . . You have no choice; either you must help furnish this race from within its own ranks with thoughtful men of trained leadership, or you must suffer the evil consequences of a headless misguided rabble.

I am an earnest advocate of manual training and trade teaching for black boys, and for white boys, too. I believe that next to the founding of Negro colleges the most valuable addition to Negro education since the war, has been industrial training for black boys. Nevertheless, I insist that the object of all true education is not to make men carpenters, it is to make carpenters men; there are two means of making the carpenter a man, each equally important: the first is to give the group and community in which he works, liberally trained teachers and leaders to teach him and his family what life means; the second is to give him sufficient intelligence and technical skill to make him an efficient workman; the first object demands the Negro college and college-bred men — not a quantity of such colleges, but a few of excellent quality; not too many college-bred men, but enough to leaven the lump, to inspire the masses, to raise the Talented Tenth to leadership; the second object demands a good system of common schools, well-taught, conveniently located and properly equipped. . . .

Further than this, after being provided with group leaders of civilization, and a foundation of intelligence in the public schools, the carpenter, in order to be a man, needs technical skill. This calls for trade schools. . . .

[M]odern industry has taken great strides since the war, and the teaching of trades is no longer a simple matter. Machinery and long processes of work have greatly changed the work of the carpenter, the ironworker and the shoemaker. A really efficient workman must be to-day an intelligent man who has had good technical training in addition to thorough common school, and perhaps even higher training. . . .   15

Thus, again, in the manning of trade schools and manual training schools we are thrown back upon the higher training as its source and chief support. There was a time when any aged and wornout carpenter could teach in a trade school. But not so to-day. Indeed the demand for college-bred men by a school like Tuskegee, ought to make Mr. Booker T. Washington the firmest friend of higher training. Here he has as helpers the son of a Negro senator, trained in Greek and the humanities, and graduated at Harvard; the son of a Negro congressman and lawyer, trained in Latin and mathematics, and graduated at Oberlin; he has as his wife, a woman who read Virgil and Homer in the same class room with me; he has as college chaplain, a classical graduate of Atlanta University; as teacher of science, a graduate of Fisk; as teacher of history, a graduate of Smith, — indeed some thirty of his chief teachers are college graduates, and instead of studying French grammars in the midst of weeds, or buying pianos for dirty cabins, they are at Mr. Washington's right hand helping him in a noble work. And yet one of the effects of Mr. Washington's propaganda has been to throw doubt upon the expediency of such training for Negroes, as these persons have had.

Men of America, the problem is plain before you. Here is a race transplanted through the criminal foolishness of your fathers. Whether you like it or not the millions are here, and here they will remain. If you do not lift them up, they will pull you down. Education and work are the levers to uplift a people. Work alone will not do it unless inspired by the right ideals and guided by intelligence. Education must not simply teach work—it must teach Life. The Talented Tenth of the Negro race must be made leaders of thought and missionaries of culture among their people. No others can do this work and Negro colleges must train men for it. The Negro race, like all other races, is going to be saved by its exceptional men.

(1903)

Exploring the Text

1. What is the claim W. E. B. DuBois makes in the opening paragraph? What assumptions underlie this claim?
2. What does DuBois mean by "exceptional" (par. 1)? Is this term synonymous with the "aristocracy of talent and character" (par. 5) that DuBois describes?
3. In paragraph 7, DuBois lists a number of educators who came from Northern colleges "after the blood of war." What point is he making by the following rhetorical question and image: "Where ought they to have begun to build? At the bottom, of course, quibbles the mole with his eyes in the earth"?
4. What, according to DuBois, is the "peculiar function" of "the Negro college" (par. 9)?
5. To what extent does DuBois argue that education for "knowledge and character" is incompatible with "the technical knowledge necessary . . . to earn a living under the present circumstances" (par. 10)? Explain why you agree or disagree with this duality in 1903 or even now.
6. In the paragraph beginning, "I would not deny, or for a moment seem to deny, the paramount necessity of teaching the Negro to work" (par. 11), how does DuBois address the counterargument by concession and refutation? Where else in this essay does he address the arguments of Booker T. Washington and his followers?
7. DuBois warns that "either you must help furnish this race from within its own ranks with thoughtful men of trained leadership, or you must suffer the evil consequences of a headless misguided rabble" (par. 12). Is this statement a logical conclusion from support previously provided, or is it an either-or fallacy? Explain your response with references to the text.
8. How—specifically—does DuBois develop the figurative assertion that "the object of all true education is not to make men carpenters, it is to make carpenters men" (par. 13)?

9. Who is the intended audience DuBois addresses in this essay? Identify specific passages and use of language to support your response. How effective do you imagine he would have been at reaching this audience? Why?

WILLA CATHER

Willa Cather (1873–1947) was an American novelist best known for depictions of frontier life on the Great Plains. Raised in Nebraska, she graduated from the University of Nebraska in 1894 and moved to Pittsburgh two years later to write for a women's magazine called *Home Monthly*. She continued to write for various magazines and publications, and in 1906 she got a job at *McClure's* magazine in New York City, where her first novel, *Alexander's Bridge*, was published. She published three more novels — known as her Prairie Trilogy — between 1913 and 1918, and in 1922 she won the Pulitzer Prize for *One of Ours*, a World War I novel.

The Sculptor's Funeral

"The Sculptor's Funeral" (1905) was published in *McClure's* magazine early in her career. It explores many of the themes Cather would develop further in the following decades.

A group of the townspeople stood on the station siding of a little Kansas town, awaiting the coming of the night train, which was already twenty minutes overdue. The snow had fallen thick over everything; in the pale starlight the line of bluffs across the wide, white meadows south of the town made soft, smoke-colored curves against the clear sky. The men on the siding stood first on one foot and then on the other, their hands thrust deep into their trousers pockets, their overcoats open, their shoulders screwed up with the cold; and they glanced from time to time toward the southeast, where the railroad track wound along the river shore. They conversed in low tones and moved about restlessly, seeming uncertain as to what was expected of them. There was but one of the company who looked as though he knew exactly why he was there, and he kept conspicuously apart, walking to the far end of the platform, returning to the station door, then pacing up the track again, his chin sunk in the high collar of his overcoat, his burly shoulders drooping forward, his gait heavy and dogged. Presently he was approached by a tall, spare, grizzled man clad in a faded Grand Army suit, who shuffled out from the group and advanced with a certain deference, craning his neck forward until his back made the angle of a jack-knife three-quarters open.

"I reckon she's a-goin' to be pretty late agin to-night, Jim," he remarked in a squeaky falsetto. "S'pose it's the snow?"

"I don't know," responded the other man with a shade of annoyance, speaking from out an astonishing cataract of red beard which grew fiercely and thickly in all directions.

The spare man shifted the quill toothpick he was chewing to the other side of his mouth. "It ain't likely that anybody from the East will come with the corpse, I s'pose?" he went on reflectively.

"I don't know," responded the other, more curtly than before.   5

"It's too bad he didn't belong to some lodge or other. I like an order funeral myself. They seem more appropriate for people of some reputation," the spare man continued, with an ingratiating concession in his shrill voice, as he carefully placed his toothpick in his vest pocket. He always carried the flag at the G. A. R. funerals in the town.

The heavy man turned on his heel without replying, and walked up the siding. The spare man shuffled back to the uneasy group. "Jim's ez full ez a tick, ez ushel," he commented commiseratingly.

Just then a distant whistle sounded, and there was a shuffling of feet on the platform. A number of lanky boys of all ages appeared as suddenly and slimily as eels wakened by the crack of thunder; some came from the waiting-room, where they had been warming themselves by the red stove, or half asleep on the slat benches; others uncoiled themselves from baggage trucks or slid out of express wagons. Two clambered down from the driver's seat of a hearse that stood backed up against the siding. They straightened their stooping shoulders and lifted their heads, and a flash of momentary animation kindled their dull eyes at that cold, vibrant scream, the world-wide call for men. It stirred them like the note of a trumpet, just as it had often stirred in his boyhood the man who was coming home to-night.

The night express shot, red as a rocket, out of the eastward marsh lands, and wound along the river shore under the long lines of shivering poplars that sentineled the meadows, the escaping steam hanging in gray masses against the still, pale sky and blotting out the Milky Way. In a moment the red glare from the headlight streamed up the snow-covered track before the siding and glittered on the wet, black rails. The burly man with the disheveled red beard walked swiftly up the platform toward the approaching train, uncovering his head as he went. The group of men behind him hesitated, glanced questioningly at one another, and awkwardly followed his example. The train stopped, and the crowd shuffled up to the express car just as the door was thrown open, the spare man in the G. A. R. suit thrusting his head forward with curiosity. The express messenger appeared in the doorway, accompanied by a young man in a long ulster[1] and traveling-cap.

"Are Mr. Merrick's friends here?" inquired the young man.   10

The group on the platform swayed and shuffled uneasily. Philip Phelps, the banker, responded with dignity: "We have come to take charge of the body. Mr. Merrick's father is very feeble and can't be about."

"Send the agent out here," growled the express messenger, "and tell the operator to lend a hand."

---

[1]Long overcoat that includes a short cape around the shoulders. — Eds.

The coffin was got out of its rough box and down on the snowy platform. The townspeople drew back enough to make room for it and then formed a close semi-circle about it, looking curiously at the palm-leaf which lay across the black cover. No one said anything. The baggageman stood by his truck, waiting to get at the trunks. The engine panted heavily, and the fireman dodged in and out among the wheels with his yellow torch and long oil-can, snapping the spindle boxes. The young Bostonian, one of the dead sculptor's pupils, who had come with the body, looked about him help-lessly. He turned to the banker, the only one of that black, uneasy, stoop-shouldered group who seemed enough of an individual to be addressed.

"None of Mr. Merrick's brothers are here?" he asked uncertainly.

The man with the red beard for the first time stepped up and joined the group.   15
"No, they have not come yet; the family is scattered. The body will be taken directly to the house." He stooped and took hold of one of the handles of the coffin.

"Take the long hill road up, Thompson; it will be easier on the horses," called the liveryman, as the undertaker snapped the door of the hearse and prepared to mount to the driver's seat.

Laird, the red-bearded lawyer, turned again to the stranger: "We didn't know whether there would be any one with him or not," he explained. "It's a long walk, so you'd better go up in the hack." He pointed to a single battered conveyance, but the young man replied stiffly: "Thank you, but I think I will go up with the hearse. If you don't object," turning to the undertaker, "I'll ride with you."

They clambered up over the wheels and drove off in the starlight up the long, white hill toward the town. The lamps in the still village were shining from under the low, snow-burdened roofs; and beyond, on every side, the plains reached out into emptiness, peaceful and wide as the soft sky itself, and wrapped in a tangible, white silence.

When the hearse backed up to a wooden sidewalk before a naked, weather-beaten frame house, the same composite, ill-defined group that had stood upon the station siding was huddled about the gate. The front yard was an icy swamp, and a couple of warped planks, extending from the sidewalk to the door, made a sort of rickety foot-bridge. The gate hung on one hinge, and was opened wide with difficulty. Steavens, the young stranger, noticed that something black was tied to the knob of the front door.

The grating sound made by the casket, as it was drawn from the hearse, was   20
answered by a scream from the house; the front door was wrenched open, and a tall, corpulent woman rushed out bareheaded into the snow and flung herself upon the coffin, shrieking: "My boy, my boy! And this is how you've come home to me!"

As Steavens turned away and closed his eyes with a shudder of unutterable repul-sion, another woman, also tall, but flat and angular, dressed entirely in black, darted out of the house and caught Mrs. Merrick by the shoulders, crying sharply: "Come, come, mother; you mustn't go on like this!" Her tone changed to one of obsequious solemnity as she turned to the banker: "The parlor is ready, Mr. Phelps."

The bearers carried the coffin along the narrow boards, while the undertaker ran ahead with the coffin-rests. They bore it into a large, unheated room that smelled of dampness and disuse and furniture polish, and set it down under a hanging lamp ornamented with jingling glass prisms and before a "Rogers group" of John Alden and Priscilla, wreathed with smilax.[2] Henry Steavens stared around him with the sickening conviction that there had been some horrible mistake, and that he had somehow arrived at the wrong destination. He looked painfully about over the clover-green Brussels, the fat plush upholstery; among the hand-painted china plaques and panels and vases, for some mark of identification, for something that might once have conceivably belonged to Harvey Merrick. It was not until he recognized his friend in the crayon portrait of a little boy in kilts and curls, hanging over the piano, that he felt willing to let any of these people approach the coffin.

"Take the lid off, Mr. Thompson; let me see my boy's face," wailed the elder woman between her sobs. This time Steavens looked fearfully, almost beseechingly, into her face, red and swollen under its masses of strong, black, shiny hair. He flushed, dropped his eyes, and then, almost incredulously, looked again. There was a kind of power about her face—a kind of brutal handsomeness, even; but it was scarred and furrowed by violence, and so colored and coarsened by fiercer passions that grief seemed never to have laid a gentle finger there. The long nose was distended and knobbed at the end, and there were deep lines on either side of it; her heavy, black brows almost met across her forehead, her teeth were large and square, and set far apart—teeth that could tear. She filled the room; the men were obliterated, seemed tossed about like twigs in an angry water, and even Steavens felt himself being drawn into the whirlpool.

The daughter—the tall, raw-boned woman in crêpe, with a mourning-comb in her hair which curiously lengthened her long face—sat stiffly upon the sofa, her hands, conspicuous for their large knuckles, folded in her lap, her mouth and eyes drawn down, solemnly awaiting the opening of the coffin. Near the door stood a mulatto woman, evidently a servant in the house, with a timid bearing and an emaciated face pitifully sad and gentle. She was weeping silently, the corner of her calico apron lifted to her eyes, occasionally suppressing a long, quivering sob. Steavens walked over and stood beside her.

Feeble steps were heard on the stairs, and an old man, tall and frail, odorous of   25 pipe smoke, with shaggy, unkempt gray hair and a dingy beard, tobacco-stained about the mouth, entered uncertainly. He went slowly up to the coffin and stood rolling a blue cotton handkerchief between his hands, seeming so pained and embarrassed by his wife's orgy of grief that he had no consciousness of anything else.

"There, there, Annie, dear, don't take on," he quavered timidly, putting out a shaking hand and awkwardly patting her elbow. She turned with a cry, and sank upon his shoulder with such violence that he tottered a little. He did not even glance toward the coffin, but continued to look at her with a dull, frightened, appealing expression, as a spaniel looks at the whip. His sunken cheeks slowly reddened and burned with miserable shame. When his wife rushed from the room, her daughter strode after her with set lips. The servant stole up to the coffin, bent over it for a moment, and then slipped

---

[2]Genus of climbing flowering plants. — Eds.

away to the kitchen, leaving Steavens, the lawyer, and the father to themselves. The old man stood trembling and looking down at his dead son's face. The sculptor's splendid head seemed even more noble in its rigid stillness than in life. The dark hair had crept down upon the wide forehead; the face seemed strangely long, but in it there was not that beautiful and chaste repose which we expect to find in the faces of the dead. The brows were so drawn that there were two deep lines above the beaked nose, and the chin was thrust forward defiantly. It was as though the strain of life had been so sharp and bitter that death could not at once wholly relax the tension and smooth the countenance into perfect peace — as though he were still guarding something precious and holy which might even yet be wrested from him.

The old man's lips were working under his stained beard. He turned to the lawyer with timid deference: "Phelps and the rest are comin' back to set up with Harve, ain't they?" he asked. "Thank 'ee, Jim, thank 'ee." He brushed the hair back gently from his son's forehead. "He was a good boy, Jim; always a good boy. He was ez gentle ez a child and the kindest of 'em all — only we didn't none of us ever onderstand him." The tears trickled slowly down his beard and dropped upon the sculptor's coat.

"Martin, Martin — Oh, Martin! come here," his wife wailed from the top of the stairs. The old man started timorously: "Yes, Annie, I'm coming." He turned away, hesitated, stood for a moment in miserable indecision; then reached back and patted the dead man's hair softly, and stumbled from the room.

"Poor old man, I didn't think he had any tears left. Seems as if his eyes would have gone dry long ago. At his age nothing cuts very deep," remarked the lawyer.

Something in his tone made Steavens glance up. While the mother had been in the room the young man had scarcely seen anyone else; but now, from the moment he first glanced into Jim Laird's florid face and blood-shot eyes, he knew that he had found what he had been heart-sick at not finding before — the feeling, the understanding, that must exist in some one, even here.   30

The man was red as his beard, with features swollen and blurred by dissipation, and a hot, blazing blue eye. His face was strained — that of a man who is controlling himself with difficulty — and he kept plucking at his beard with a sort of fierce resentment. Steavens, sitting by the window, watched him turn down the glaring lamp, still its jangling pendants with an angry gesture, and then stand with his hands locked behind him, staring down into the master's face. He could not help wondering what link there could have been between the porcelain vessel and so sooty a lump of potter's clay.

From the kitchen an uproar was sounding; when the dining-room door opened, the import of it was clear. The mother was abusing the maid for having forgotten to make the dressing for the chicken salad which had been prepared for the watchers. Steavens had never heard anything in the least like it: it was injured, emotional, dramatic abuse, unique and masterly in its excruciating cruelty, as violent and unrestrained as had been her grief of twenty minutes before. With a shudder of disgust, the lawyer went into the dining-room and closed the door into the kitchen.

"Poor Roxy's getting it now," he remarked when he came back. "The Merricks took her out of the poor-house years ago; and if her loyalty would let her, I guess the poor old thing could tell tales that would curdle your blood. She's the mulatto woman who was standing in here a while ago, with her apron to her eyes. The old woman is a fury; there never was anybody like her for demonstrative piety and ingenious cruelty. She made Harvey's life a hell for him when he lived at home; he was so sick ashamed of it. I never could see how he kept himself so sweet."

"He was wonderful," said Steavens slowly, "wonderful; but until to-night I have never known how wonderful."

"That is the true and eternal wonder of it, anyway; that it can come even from   35 such a dung-heap as this," the lawyer cried, with a sweeping gesture which seemed to indicate much more than the four walls within which they stood.

"I think I'll see whether I can get a little air. The room is so close I am beginning to feel rather faint," murmured Steavens, struggling with one of the windows. The sash was stuck, however, and would not yield, so he sat down dejectedly and began pulling at his collar. The lawyer came over, loosened the sash with one blow of his red fist, and sent the window up a few inches. Steavens thanked him, but the nausea which had been gradually climbing into his throat for the last half hour left him with but one desire — a desperate feeling that he must get away from this place with what was left of Harvey Merrick. Oh, he comprehended well enough now the gentle bitterness of the smile that he had seen so often on his master's lips!

He remembered that once, when Merrick returned from a visit home, he brought with him a singularly feeling and suggestive bas-relief of a thin, faded old woman, sitting and sewing something pinned to her knee; while a full-lipped, full-blooded little urchin, his trousers sustained by a single gallows,[3] stood beside her impatiently twitching her gown to call her attention to a butterfly he had caught. Steavens, impressed by the tender and delicate modeling of the thin, tired face, had asked him if it were his mother. He remembered the dull flush that had burned up in the sculptor's face.

The lawyer was sitting in a rocking-chair beside the coffin, his head thrown back and his eyes closed. Steavens looked at him earnestly, puzzled at the line of the chin, and wondering why a man should conceal a feature of such distinction under that disfiguring shock of red beard. Suddenly, as though he felt the young sculptor's keen glance, he opened his eyes.

"Was he always a good deal of an oyster?" he asked abruptly. "He was terribly shy as a boy."

"Yes, he was an oyster, since you put it so," rejoined Steavens. "Although he   40 could be very fond of people, he always gave one the impression of being detached. He disliked violent emotion; he was reflective, and rather distrustful of himself — except, of course, as regarded his work. He was sure-footed enough there. He distrusted men pretty thoroughly, and women even more, yet somehow without believing ill of them. He was determined, indeed, to believe the best, but he seemed afraid to investigate."

"A burnt dog dreads the fire," said the lawyer grimly, and closed his eyes.

---

[3]Suspender. — Eds.

Steavens went on and on, reconstructing that whole miserable boyhood. All this raw, biting ugliness had been the portion of the man whose tastes were refined beyond the limits of the reasonable — whose mind was an exhaustless gallery of beautiful impressions, so sensitive that the mere shadow of a poplar leaf flickering against a sunny wall would be etched and held there forever. Surely, if ever a man had the magic wand in his finger-tips, it was Merrick. Whatever he touched, he revealed its holiest secret; liberated it from enchantment and restored it to its pristine loveliness, like the Arabian prince who fought the enchantress, spell for spell. Upon whatever he had come in contact with, he had left a beautiful record of the experience — a sort of ethereal signature; a scent, a sound, a color that was his own.

Steavens understood now the real tragedy of his master's life; neither love nor wine, as many had conjectured, but a blow which had fallen earlier and cut deeper than these could have done — a shame not his, and yet so unescapably his, to hide in his heart from his very boyhood. And without, the frontier warfare; the yearning of a boy, cast ashore upon a desert of newness and ugliness and sordidness, for all that is chastened and old, and noble with traditions.

At eleven o'clock the tall, flat woman in black crêpe entered and announced that the watchers were arriving, and asked them "to step into the dining-room." As Steavens rose, the lawyer said dryly: "You go on — it'll be a good experience for you, doubtless; as for me, I'm not equal to that crowd to-night; I've had twenty years of them."

As Steavens closed the door after him, he glanced back at the lawyer, sitting by   45
the coffin in the dim light, with his chin resting on his hand.

The same misty group that had stood before the door of the express-car shuffled into the room. In the light of the kerosene lamp they separated and became individuals. The minister, a pale, feeble-looking man with white hair and blond chin-whiskers, took his seat beside a small table, and placed his Bible upon it. The Grand Army man took a seat behind the stove and tilted his chair back comfortably against the wall, fishing his quill toothpick from his waistcoat pocket. The two bankers, Phelps and Elder, sat off in a corner behind the dinner-table, where they could finish their discussion of the new usury law and its effect on chattel security loans. The real estate agent, an old man with a smiling, hypocritical face, soon joined them. The coal and lumber dealer and the cattle shipper sat on opposite sides of the hard coal burner, their feet on the nickel-work. Steavens took a book from his pocket and began to read. The talk around him ranged through various topics of local interest while the house was quieting down. When it was clear that the members of the family were in bed, the Grand Army man hitched his shoulders, and untangling his long legs, caught his heels on the rounds of his chair.

"S'pose there'll be a will, Phelps?" he queried in his weak falsetto.

The banker laughed disagreeably, and began trimming his nails with a pearl-handled pocket-knife.

"There'll scarcely be any need for one, will there?" he queried in his turn.

The restless Grand Army man shifted his position again, getting his knees still   50
nearer his chin. "Why, the ole man says Harve's done right well lately," he chirped.

The other banker spoke up, "I reckon he means by that Harve ain't asked him to mortgage any more farms lately so as he could go on with his education."

"Seems like my mind don't reach back to a time when Harve wasn't bein' edy-cated," tittered the Grand Army man.

There was a general chuckle. The minister took out his handkerchief and blew his nose sonorously. Banker Phelps closed his knife with a snap. "It's too bad the old man's sons didn't turn out better," he remarked, with reflective authority. "They never hung together. He spent money enough on Harve to stock a dozen cattle-farms, and he might as well have poured it into Sand Creek. If Harve had stayed at home and helped nurse what little they had, and gone into stock on the old man's bottom farm, they might all have been well fixed. But the old man had to trust everything to tenants and was cheated right and left."

"Harve never could have handled stock none," interposed the cattleman. "He hadn't it in him to be sharp. Do you remember when he bought Sander's mules for eight-year olds, when everybody in town knew that Sander's father-in-law give 'em to his wife for a wedding present eighteen years before, an' they was full-grown mules then?"

Every one chuckled, and the Grand Army man rubbed his knees with a spasm of childish delight.

"Harve never was much account for anything practical, and he shore was never fond of work," began the coal and lumber dealer. "I mind the last time he was home; the day he left, when the old man was out to the barn helpin' his hand hitch up to take Harve to the train, and Cal. Moots was patchin' up the fence, Harve, he come out on the step and sings out, in his ladylike voice: 'Cal. Moots, Cal. Moots! please come cord my trunk.'"

"That's Harve for you," approved the Grand Army man gleefully. "I kin hear him howlin' yet, when he was a big feller in long pants, and his mother used to whale him with a rawhide in the barn for lettin' the cows git foundered in the cornfield when he was drivin' 'em home from pasture. He killed a cow of mine that-a-way once — a pure Jersey and the best milker I had, an' the ole man had to put up for her. Harve, he was watchin' the sun set acrost the marshes when the anamile got away; he argued that sunset was oncommon fine."

"Where the old man made his mistake was in sending the boy East to school," said Phelps, stroking his goatee and speaking in a deliberate, judicial tone. "There was where he got his head full of trapseing to Paris and all such folly. What Harve needed, of all people, was a course in some first-class Kansas City business college."

The letters were swimming before Steavens's eyes. Was it possible that these men did not understand, that the palm on the coffin meant nothing to them? The very name of their town would have remained forever buried in the postal guide, had it not been now and again mentioned in the world in connection with Harvey Merrick's. He remembered what his master had said to him on the day of his death, after the congestion of both lungs had shut off any probability of recovery, and the sculptor had asked his pupil to send his body home. "It's not a pleasant place to be lying while the world is moving and doing and bettering," he had said, with a feeble smile: "but it rather seems as though we ought to go back to the place we came from in the end. The townspeople will come in for a look at me; and after they have had their say, I shan't have much to fear from the judgment of God. The wings of the Victory, in there" — with a weak gesture toward his studio — "will not shelter me."

The cattleman took up the comment. "Forty's young for a Merrick to cash in; they usually hang on pretty well. Probably he helped it along with whisky." 60

"His mother's people were not long-lived, and Harvey never had a robust constitution," said the minister mildly. He would have liked to say more. He had been the boy's Sunday-school teacher, and had been fond of him; but he felt that he was not in a position to speak. His own sons had turned out badly, and it was not a year since one of them had made his last trip home in the express-car, shot in a gambling-house in the Black Hills.

"Nevertheless, there is no disputin' that Harve frequently looked upon the wine when it was red, also variegated, and it shore made an oncommon fool of him," moralized the cattleman.

Just then the door leading into the parlor rattled loudly, and everyone started involuntarily, looking relieved when only Jim Laird came out. His red face was convulsed with anger, and the Grand Army man ducked his head when he saw the spark in his blue, blood-shot eye. They were all afraid of Jim; he was a drunkard, but he could twist the law to suit his client's needs as no other man in all Western Kansas could do; and there were many who tried. The lawyer closed the door gently behind him, leaned back against it, and folded his arms, cocking his head a little to one side. When he assumed this attitude in the court-room, ears were always pricked up, as it usually foretold a flood of withering sarcasm.

"I've been with you gentlemen before," he began in a dry, even tone, "when you've sat by the coffins of boys born and raised in this town; and, if I remember rightly, you were never any too well satisfied when you checked them up. What's the matter, anyhow? Why is it that reputable young men are as scarce as millionaires in Sand City? It might almost seem to a stranger that there was some way something the matter with your progressive town. Why did Reuben Sayer, the brightest young lawyer you ever turned out, after he had come home from the university as straight as a die, take to drinking, and forge a check and shoot himself? Why did Bill Merrit's son die of the shakes in a saloon in Omaba? Why was Mr. Thomas's son, here, shot in a gambling-house? Why did young Adams burn his mill to beat the insurance companies, and go to the pen?"

The lawyer paused and unfolded his arms, laying one clenched fist quietly on the table. "I'll tell you why: because you drummed nothing but money and knavery into their ears from the time they wore knickerbockers; because you carped away at them as you've been carping here to-night, holding our friends Phelps and Elder up to them for their models, as our grandfathers held up George Washington and John Adams. But the boys, worse luck, were young, and raw at the business you put them to; and how could they match coppers with such artists as Phelps and Elder? You wanted them to be successful rascals; they were only unsuccessful ones — that's all the difference. There was only one boy ever raised in this borderland between ruffian- 65 ism and civilization who didn't come to grief, and you hated Harvey Merrick more for winning out than you hated all the other boys who got under the wheels. Lord, Lord, how you did hate him! Phelps, here, is fond of saying that he could buy and sell us all out any time he's a mind to; but he knew Harve wouldn't have given a tinker's damn for his bank and all his cattle-farms put together; and a lack of appreciation, that way, goes hard with Phelps.

"Old Nimrod, here, thinks Harve drank too much; and this from such as Nimrod and me!

"Brother Elder says Harve was too free with the old man's money — fell short in filial consideration, maybe. Well, we can all remember the very tone in which Brother Elder swore his own father was a liar, in the county court; and we all know that the old man came out of that partnership with his son as bare as a sheared lamb. But maybe I'm getting personal, and I'd better be driving ahead at what I want to say."

The lawyer paused a moment, squared his heavy shoulders, and went on: "Harvey Merrick and I went to school together, back East. We were in dead earnest, and we wanted you all to be proud of us some day. We meant to be great men. Even I, and I haven't lost my sense of humor, gentlemen, I meant to be a great man. I came back here to practise, and I found you didn't in the least want me to be a great man. You wanted me to be a shrewd lawyer — oh, yes! Our veteran here wanted me to get him an increase of pension, because he had dyspepsia; Phelps wanted a new county survey that would put the widow Wilson's little bottom farm inside his, south line; Elder wanted to lend money at 5 per cent a month and get it collected; old Stark here wanted to wheedle old women up in Vermont into investing their annuities in real-estate mortgages that are not worth the paper they are written on. Oh, you needed me hard enough, and you'll go on needing me; and that's why I'm not afraid to plug the truth home to you this once.

"Well, I came back here and became the damned shyster you wanted me to be. You pretend to have some sort of respect for me; and yet you'll stand up and throw mud at Harvey Merrick, whose soul you couldn't dirty, and whose hands you couldn't tie. Oh, you're a discriminating lot of Christians! There have been times when the sight of Harvey's name in some Eastern paper has made me hang my head like a whipped dog; and, again, times when I liked to think of him off there in the world, away from all this hog-wallow, doing his great work, and climbing the big, clean up-grade he'd set for himself.

"And we? Now that we've fought and lied and sweated and stolen and hated, as 70 only the disappointed strugglers in a bitter, dead little Western town know how to do, what have we got to show for it? Harvey Merrick wouldn't have given one sunset over your marshes for all you've got put together, and you know it. It's not for me to say why, in the inscrutable wisdom of God, a genius should ever have been called from this place of hatred and bitter waters; but I want this Boston man to know that the drivel he's been hearing here to-night is the only tribute any truly great man could ever have from such a lot of sick, side-tracked, burnt-dog, land-poor sharks as the here-present financiers of Sand City — upon which town may God have mercy!"

The lawyer thrust out his hand to Steavens as he passed him, caught up his overcoat in the hall, and had left the house before the Grand Army man had found time to lift his ducked head and crane his long neck about at his fellows.

Next day Jim Laird was drunk and unable to attend the funeral services. Steavens called twice at his office, but was compelled to start East without seeing him. He had a presentiment that he would hear from him again, and left his address on the lawyer's table; but if Laird found it, he never acknowledged it. The thing in him that Harvey Merrick had loved must have gone under ground with Harvey Merrick's coffin; for it never spoke again, and Jim got the cold he died of driving across the Colorado mountains to defend one of Phelps's sons, who had got into trouble out there by cutting government timber.

(1905)

Exploring the Text

1. What is the impact of the descriptive opening scene? What mood is established? Who are the "lanky boys" who appear "slimily as eels wakened by the crack of thunder" (par. 8)? How are they connected to the story that is unfolding?

2. What physical details does Willa Cather provide of the Merricks' home — both inside and outside — that characterize the psychological environment?

3. Harvey Merrick's mother is a key figure in the story, both past and present. How does Cather depict her appearance and her personality? Is her "orgy of grief" (par. 25) at her son's death typical of her behavior? Are we led to believe it is genuine? Do you find her a three-dimensional or stereotyped character? Why?

4. What purpose does Roxy, a minor character, play in developing the themes of this story? Consider Cather's description of her, what others say of her, and her actions.

5. When we first see Merrick in his coffin, Cather writes, "It was as though the strain of life had been so sharp and bitter that death could not at once wholly relax the tension and smooth the countenance into perfect peace — as though he were still guarding something precious and holy which might even yet be wrested from him" (par. 26). What does this sentence mean? From whose perspective is it written?

6. When the "same misty group" (par. 46) of men who were at the station are in the dining room of the Merrick home, they talk about Harvey Merrick. What values do they reveal about themselves, particularly those that Harvey did not share or validate? In what ways is Jim Laird's speech a rebuke and rebuttal to this community?

7. Who is Jim Laird? This character, who is present in nearly every moment of the story from start to finish, parallels Harvey in some ways yet diverges from him in others. Why do you think Cather develops him as such a significant figure in the story?

8. Although the story is told in the third person, the perspective of Henry Steavens trying to understand his friend and mentor Merrick is closest to the reader's view. What "clues" and insights does Cather gradually reveal as Steavens tries to combine what he already knows of Merrick with the new knowledge he gained in Sand City? What, finally, does he determine was "the real tragedy of his master's life" (par. 43)?

9. Harvey Merrick's dying wish was that his body be sent "home" to Sand City because "it rather seems as though we ought to go back to the place we came from in the end" (par. 59). Given the events of the story, do you think that Cather agrees with this view? Cite specific passages and actions to support your response.

10. "The Sculptor's Funeral" challenges a romantic view of "America's heartland," as a place of plainspoken people with a strong work ethic and moral compassion. Yet, do you think that Cather categorically indicts the Midwest for hypocrisy and small-mindedness? What evidence of ambivalence toward the Midwest, specifically small-town communities, do you find in the story?

UPTON SINCLAIR

Upton Sinclair (1878–1968) was an American novelist and politician and one of the most influential muckraker journalists of the 1900s. Born in Baltimore, Maryland, he taught himself to read at the age of five and at fourteen enrolled at New York City College. After his graduation in 1897, he attended Columbia University's law school but dropped out to pursue a writing career. Sinclair became a member of the Socialist Party in 1902, and in 1906 he was nominated as a Socialist candidate for Congress from New Jersey. During his career, he wrote many novels and articles that focused on reform and political issues, and in 1933 he ran for governor of California. After his defeat at the polls, he went on to write an eleven-volume novel series that chronicled the dealings of the U.S. government between 1913 and 1949.

from *The Jungle*

The following excerpt is from Sinclair's 1906 novel, *The Jungle*, which is his most famous work and centers on the experiences of Lithuanian immigrant Jurgis Rudkus and his family. Sinclair's purpose in *The Jungle* was to expose the harsh lives of immigrants, especially the grim working conditions in a capitalist economy. The public responded most viscerally to his descriptions of the meatpacking industry; calls for reform resulted in the passage of the Pure Food and Drug Act by President Theodore Roosevelt in 1906, legislation that Sinclair himself disavowed because taxpayer dollars would be used to implement regulations. The following selection is taken from Chapter 9 of the novel.

A nd shortly afterward one of these, a physician, made the discovery that the carcasses of steers which had been condemned as tubercular by the government inspectors, and which therefore contained ptomaines,[1] which are deadly poisons, were left upon an open platform and carted away to be sold in the city; and so he insisted that these carcasses be treated with an injection of kerosene[2] — and was ordered to resign the same week! So indignant were the packers that they went farther, and compelled the mayor to abolish the whole bureau of inspection; so that since then there has not been even a pretence of any interference with the graft. There was said to be two thousand dollars a week hush-money from the tubercular steers alone; and as much again from the hogs which had died of cholera on the trains, and which you might see any day being loaded into box-cars and hauled away to a place called Globe, in Indiana, where they made a fancy grade of lard.

Jurgis heard of these things little by little, in the gossip of those who were obliged to perpetrate them. It seemed as if every time you met a person from a new department, you heard of new swindles and new crimes. There was, for instance, a Lithuanian who was a cattle-butcher for the plant where Marija had worked, which killed meat for canning only; and to hear this man describe the animals which came to his place would have been worth while for a Dante or a Zola.[3] It seemed that they must have agencies all over the country, to hunt out old and crippled and diseased cattle to be canned. There were cattle which had been fed on "whiskey-malt," the refuse of the breweries, and had become what the men called "steerly" — which means covered with boils. It was a nasty job killing these, for when you plunged your knife into them they would burst and splash foul-smelling stuff into your face; and when a man's sleeves were smeared with blood, and his hands steeped in it, how was he ever to wipe his face, or to clear his eyes so that he could see? It was stuff such as this that made the "embalmed beef" that had killed several times as many United States soldiers as all the bullets of the Spaniards; only the army beef, besides, was not fresh canned, it was old stuff that had been lying for years in the cellars.

Then one Sunday evening, Jurgis sat puffing his pipe by the kitchen stove, and talking with an old fellow whom Jonas had introduced, and who worked in the canning-rooms at Durham's; and so Jurgis learned a few things about the great and only Durham canned goods, which had become a national institution. They were regular alchemists at Durham's; they advertised a mushroom-catsup, and the men who made it did not know what a mushroom looked like. They advertised "potted chicken," — and it was like the boarding-house soup of the comic papers, through which a chicken had walked with rubbers on. Perhaps they had a secret process for

---

[1]Compounds created by bacteria during the decomposition of protein. — Eds.
[2]Kerosene was used to intentionally taint rotten meat to ensure that it did not get into the food supply. — Eds.
[3]Emile Zola (1840–1902) was a popular French writer who wrote realistic portraits of the lives of the poor and persecuted. — Eds.

making chickens chemically—who knows? said Jurgis's friend; the things that went into the mixture were tripe, and the fat of pork, and beef suet, and hearts of beef, and finally the waste ends of veal, when they had any. They put these up in several grades, and sold them at several prices; but the contents of the cans all came out of the same hopper. And then there was "potted game" and "potted grouse," "potted ham," and "devilled ham"—de-vyled, as the men called it. "De-vyled" ham was made out of the waste ends of smoked beef that were too small to be sliced by the machines; and also tripe, dyed with chemicals so that it would not show white; and trimmings of hams and corned beef; and potatoes, skins and all, and finally the hard cartilaginous gullets of beef, after the tongues had been cut out. All this ingenious mixture was ground up and flavored with spices to make it taste like something. Anybody who could invent a new imitation had been sure of a fortune from old Durham, said Jurgis's informant; but it was hard to think of anything new in a place where so many sharp wits had been at work for so long; where men welcomed tuberculosis in the cattle they were feeding, because it made them fatten more quickly; and where they bought up all the old rancid butter left over in the grocery-stores of a continent, and "oxidized" it by a forced-air process, to take away the odor, rechurned it with skim-milk, and sold it in bricks in the cities! Up to a year or two ago it had been the custom to kill horses in the yards—ostensibly for fertilizer; but after long agitation the newspapers had been able to make the public realize that the horses were being canned. Now it was against the law to kill horses in Packingtown, and the law was really complied with—for the present, at any rate. Any day, however, one might see sharp-horned and shaggy-haired creatures running with the sheep—and yet what a job you would have to get the public to believe that a good part of what it buys for lamb and mutton is really goat's flesh!

There was another interesting set of statistics that a person might have gathered in Packingtown—those of the various afflictions of the workers. When Jurgis had first inspected the packing-plants with Szedvilas, he had marvelled while he listened to the tale of all the things that were made out of the carcasses of animals, and of all the lesser industries that were maintained there; now he found that each one of these lesser industries was a separate little inferno, in its way as horrible as the killing-beds, the source and fountain of them all. The workers in each of them had their own peculiar diseases. And the wandering visitor might be sceptical about all the swindles, but he could not be sceptical about these, for the worker bore the evidence of them about on his own person—generally he had only to hold out his hand.

There were the men in the pickle-rooms, for instance, where old Antanas had gotten his death; scarce a one of these that had not some spot of horror on his person. Let a man so much as scrape his finger pushing a truck in the pickle-rooms, and he might have a sore that would put him out of the world; all the joints in his fingers might be eaten by the acid, one by one. Of the butchers and floorsmen, the beef-boners and trimmers, and all those who used knives, you could scarcely find a person who had the use of his thumb; time and time again the base of it had been slashed, till it was a mere lump of flesh against which the man pressed the knife to hold it. The hands of these men would be criss-crossed with cuts, until you could no longer pretend to count them or to trace them. They would have no nails, — they had worn them off pulling hides; their knuckles were swollen so that their fingers spread out like a fan. There were men who worked in the cooking-rooms, in the midst of steam and sickening odors, by artificial light; in these rooms the germs of tuberculosis might live for two years, but the supply was renewed every hour. There were the beef-luggers, who carried two-hundred-pound quarters into the refrigerator-cars; a fearful kind of work, that began at four o'clock in the morning, and that wore out the most powerful men in a few years. There were those who worked in the chilling-rooms, and whose special disease was rheumatism; the time-limit that a man could work in the chilling-rooms was said to be five years. There were the wool-pluckers, whose hands went to pieces even sooner than the hands of the pickle-men; for the pelts of the sheep had to be painted with acid to loosen the wool, and then the pluckers had to pull out this wool with their bare hands, till the acid had eaten their fingers off. There were those who made the tins for the canned-meat; and their hands, too, were a maze of cuts, and each cut represented a chance for blood-poisoning. Some worked at the stamping-machines, and it was very seldom that one could work long there at the pace that was set, and not give out and forget himself, and have a part of his hand chopped off. There were the "hoisters," as they were called, whose task it was to press the lever which lifted the dead cattle off the floor. They ran along upon a rafter, peering down through the damp and the steam; and as old Durham's architects had not built the killing-room for the convenience of the hoisters, at every few feet they would have to stoop under a beam, say four feet above the one they ran on; which got them into the habit of stooping, so that in a few years they would be walking like chimpanzees. Worst of any, however, were the fertilizer-men, and those who served in the cooking-rooms. These people could not be shown to the visitor, — for the odor of a fertilizer-man would scare any ordinary visitor at a hundred yards, and as for the other men, who worked in tank-rooms full of steam, and in some of which there were open vats near the level of the floor, their peculiar trouble was that they fell into the vats; and when they were fished out, there was never enough of them left to be worth exhibiting, — sometimes they would be overlooked for days, till all but the bones of them had gone out to the world as Durham's Pure Leaf Lard!

(1906)

Exploring the Text

1. In the opening paragraph, Upton Sinclair describes the outrage of workers at the physician's insistence that kerosene be used on spoiled meat. What is their chief concern?
2. What does Sinclair mean by the description "regular alchemists" (par. 3)?
3. What is the "separate little inferno, in its way as horrible as the killing-beds, the source and fountain of them all" (par. 4)?

4. How does Sinclair develop and support his argument that the work in these factories is dehumanizing because of both the nature of the work and the powerlessness of the workers?

5. What unsafe practices does Sinclair emphasize in this section? How would you characterize his descriptions? Are they exaggerated? Gruesome? Detached? Melodramatic?

6. In a 1906 issue of *Cosmopolitan* magazine, Sinclair wrote of his disappointment that the American public focused on food reform rather than on the larger social critique of the difficult lives of workers: "I aimed at the public's heart, and by accident I hit it in the stomach." How does this quote demonstrate Sinclair's point? Or does it?

 **TALKBACK**

ERIC SCHLOSSER

Born in 1959 and raised in New York and Los Angeles, Eric Schlosser graduated from Princeton University with a degree in American history and studied British history at Oxford University. In addition to working as a correspondent for the *Atlantic*, he has published articles in such periodicals as the *New Yorker*, the *Nation*, *Rolling Stone*, and *Vanity Fair*. His 2001 book about the food industry, *Fast Food Nation: The Dark Side of the American Meal*, became a best seller and was adapted into a film directed by Richard Linklater in 2006. Schlosser also participated in making the 2009 documentary film *Food Inc.* His second best seller, *Reefer Madness: Sex, Drugs, and Cheap Labor in the American Black Market* (2003), grew out of his articles on the enforcement of marijuana laws and illegal immigration in California. His latest book, *Command and Control* (2013), discusses nuclear nonproliferation.

from *Fast Food Nation*

The following selection from Chapter 8 of *Fast Food Nation*, "The Most Dangerous Job," discusses the meatpacking industry.

One night I visit a slaughterhouse somewhere in the High Plains. The slaughterhouse is one of the nation's largest. About five thousand head of cattle enter it every day, single file, and leave in a different form. Someone who has access to the plant, who's upset by its working conditions, offers to give me a tour. The slaughterhouse is an immense building, gray and square, about three stories high, with no windows on the front and no architectural clues to what's happening inside. My friend gives me a chain-mail apron and gloves, suggesting I try them on. Workers on the line wear about eight pounds of chain mail beneath their white coats, shiny steel armor that covers their hands, wrists, stomach, and back. The chain mail's designed to protect workers from cutting themselves and from being cut by other workers. But knives somehow manage to get past it. My host hands me some Wellingtons, the kind of knee-high rubber boots that English gentlemen wear in the countryside. "Tuck your pants into the boots," he says. "We'll be walking through some blood."

I put on a hardhat and climb a stairway. The sounds get louder, factory sounds, the noise of power tools and machinery, bursts of compressed air. We start at the end of the line, the fabricating room. Workers call it "fab." When we step inside, fab seems familiar: steel catwalks, pipes along the walls, a vast room, a maze of conveyor belts. This could be the Lamb Weston plant in Idaho, except hunks of red meat ride the belts instead of french fries. Some machines assemble cardboard boxes, others vacuum-seal subprimals of beef in clear plastic. The workers look extremely busy, but there's nothing unsettling about this part of the plant. You see meat like this all the time in the back of your local supermarket.

The fab room is cooled to about 40 degrees, and as you head up the line, the feel of the place starts to change. The pieces of meat get bigger. Workers — about half of them women, almost all of them young and Latino — slice meat with long slender knives. They stand at a table that's chest high, grab meat off a conveyor belt, trim away fat, throw meat back on the belt, toss the scraps onto a conveyer belt above them, and then grab more meat, all in a matter of seconds. I'm now struck by how many workers there are, hundreds of them, pressed close together, constantly moving, slicing. You see hardhats, white coats, flashes of steel. Nobody is smiling or chatting, they're too busy, anxiously trying not to fall behind. An old man walks past me, pushing a blue plastic barrel filled with scraps. A few workers carve the meat with Whizzards, small electric knives that have spinning round blades. The Whizzards look like the Norelco razors that Santa rides in the TV ads. I notice that a few of the women near me are sweating, even though the place is freezing cold.

Sides of beef suspended from an overhead trolley swing toward a group of men. Each worker has a large knife in one hand and a steel hook in the other. They grab the meat with their hooks and attack it fiercely with their knives. As they hack away, using all their strength, grunting, the place suddenly feels different, primordial. The machinery seems beside the point, and what's going on before me has been going on for thousands of years — the meat, the hook, the knife, men straining to cut more meat.

On the kill floor, what I see no longer unfolds in a logical manner. It's one   5 strange image after another. A worker with a power saw slices cattle into halves as though they were two-by-fours, and then the halves swing by me into the cooler. It feels like a slaughterhouse now. Dozens of cattle, stripped of their skins, dangle on chains from their hind legs. My host stops and asks how I feel, if I want to go any further. This is where some people get sick. I feel fine, determined to see the whole process, the world that's been deliberately hidden. The kill floor is hot and humid. It stinks of manure. Cattle have a body temperature of about 101 degrees, and there are a lot of them in the room. Carcasses swing so fast along the rail that you have to keep an eye on them constantly, dodge them, watch your step, or one will slam you and throw you onto the bloody concrete floor. It happens to workers all the time.

I see: a man reach inside cattle and pull out their kidneys with his bare hands, then drop the kidneys down a metal chute, over and over again, as each animal passes by him; a stainless steel rack of tongues; Whizzards peeling meat off decapitated heads, picking them almost as clean as the white skulls painted by Georgia O'Keeffe. We wade through blood that's ankle deep and that pours down drains into huge vats below us. As we approach the start of the line, for the first time I hear the steady *pop*, *pop*, *pop* of live animals being stunned.

Now the cattle suspended above me look just like the cattle I've seen on ranches for years, but these ones are upside down swinging on hooks. For a moment, the sight seems unreal; there are so many of them, a herd of them, lifeless. And then I see a few hind legs still kicking, a final reflex action, and the reality comes hard and clear.

For eight and a half hours, a worker called a "sticker" does nothing but stand in a river of blood, being drenched in blood, slitting the neck of a steer every ten seconds or so, severing its carotid artery. He uses a long knife and must hit exactly the right spot to kill the animal humanely. He hits that spot again and again. We walk up a slippery metal stairway and reach a small platform, where the production line begins. A man turns and smiles at me. He wears safety goggles and a hardhat. His face is splattered with gray matter and blood. He is the "knocker," the man who welcomes cattle to the building. Cattle walk down a narrow chute and pause in front of him, blocked by a gate, and then he shoots them in the head with a captive bolt stunner — a compressed-air gun attached to the ceiling by a long hose — which fires a steel bolt that knocks the cattle unconscious. The animals keep strolling up, oblivious to what comes next, and he stands over them and shoots. For eight and a half hours, he just shoots. As I stand there, he misses a few times and shoots the same animal twice. As soon as the steer falls, a worker grabs one of its hind legs, shackles it to a chain, and the chain lifts the huge animal into the air. . . .

Some of the most dangerous jobs in meatpacking today are performed by the late-night cleaning crews. A large proportion of these workers are illegal immigrants. They are considered "independent contractors," employed not by the meatpacking firms but by sanitation companies. They earn hourly wages that are about one-third lower than those of regular production employees. And their work is so hard and so horrendous that words seem inadequate to describe it. The men and women who now clean the nation's slaughterhouses may arguably have the worst job in the United States. "It takes a really dedicated person," a former member of a cleaning crew told me, "or a really desperate person to get the job done."

When a sanitation crew arrives at a meatpacking plant, usually around midnight, it faces a mess of monumental proportions. Three to four thousand cattle, each weighing about a thousand pounds, have been slaughtered there that day.

The place has to be clean by sunrise. Some of the workers wear water-resistant clothing; most don't. Their principal cleaning tool is a high-pressure hose that shoots a mixture of water and chlorine heated to about 180 degrees. As the water is sprayed, the plant fills with a thick, heavy fog. Visibility drops to as little as five feet. The conveyer belts and machinery are running. Workers stand on the belts, spraying them, riding them like moving sidewalks, as high as fifteen feet off the ground. Workers climb ladders with hoses and spray the catwalks. They get under tables and conveyer belts, climbing right into the bloody muck, cleaning out grease, fat, manure, leftover scraps of meat.

Glasses and safety goggles fog up. The inside of the plant heats up; temperatures soon exceed 100 degrees. "It's hot, and it's foggy, and you can't see anything," a former sanitation worker said. The crew members can't see or hear each other when the machinery's running. They routinely spray each other with burning hot, chemical-laden water. They are sickened by the fumes. Jesus, a soft-spoken employee of DCS Sanitation Management, Inc., the company that IBP uses in many of its plants, told me that every night on the job he gets terrible headaches. "You feel it in your head," he said. "You feel it in your stomach, like you want to throw up." A friend of his vomits whenever they clean the rendering area. Other workers tease the young man as he retches. Jesus says the stench in rendering is so powerful that it won't wash off; no matter how much soap you use after a shift, the smell comes home with you, seeps from your pores.

One night while Jesus was cleaning, a coworker forgot to turn off a machine, lost two fingers, and went into shock. An ambulance came and took him away, as everyone else continued to clean. He was back at work the following week. "If one hand is no good," the supervisor told him, "use the other." Another sanitation worker lost an arm in a machine. Now he folds towels in the locker room. The scariest job, according to Jesus, is cleaning the vents on the roof of the slaughterhouse. The vents become clogged with grease and dried blood. In the winter, when everything gets icy and the winds pick up, Jesus worries that a sudden gust will blow him off the roof into the darkness.

Although official statistics are not kept, the death rate among slaughterhouse sanitation crews is extraordinarily high. They are the ultimate in disposable workers: illegal, illiterate, impoverished, untrained. The nation's worst job can end in just about the worst way. Sometimes these workers are literally ground up and reduced to nothing.

(2002)

Exploring the Text

1. How do the details of clothing (e.g., "chain-mail apron and gloves") and sounds set the scene in the opening paragraph? What feeling do the first three paragraphs establish?

2. What details and descriptions, especially in paragraphs 4 and 5, does Eric Schlosser use to help convey his vision? How would you describe his vision?

3. This chapter is written in first person. What impact does that have on the reader? Note places where Schlosser calls attention to his own reaction or "interprets" the scene. Why do you think Schlosser chose *not* to report in a more objective voice?

4. How does Schlosser support the claim that the "men and women who now clean the nation's slaughterhouses may arguably have the worst job in the United States" (par. 9)?

5. In the opening section of his chapter, Schlosser does not discuss any specific person, but in the second section he focuses on a member of the crew named Jesus. What effect does Schlosser achieve by describing and quoting this individual?

Making Connections

1. Compare and contrast the arguments that Upton Sinclair (p. 961) and Eric Schlosser (p. 965) develop. What are their central point(s) and major purpose(s)? How do they support these? Consider their use of authorial viewpoint, appeals to pathos and logos, and descriptive detail.

2. After researching the term "muckraker," discuss Sinclair and Schlosser as muckrakers of their time. To what extent is the term considered (and would be considered by these individuals) as pejorative or complimentary? You might address whether fiction or nonfiction is more effective when used to expose unfair practices and corruption.

3. In 2012, on the tenth anniversary of the publication of *Fast Food Nation*, Schlosser published an article in the *Daily Beast* lamenting that the book is still relevant. It included these paragraphs:

> In 2002 the Occupational Safety and Health Administration changed the form that meatpacking companies must use to report injuries. The new form had no space to report musculoskeletal disorders caused by repetitive trauma — thereby preventing a whole category of serious injury from being counted. Instantly, as if by magic, the injury rate in meatpacking dropped by almost 50 percent. "Recordable safety incident rate in plants cut in half since 1996," the American Meat Institute proudly announced in a press release, without ever mentioning that the decline was due to the change in record keeping. In a scathing report on the exploitation of American meatpacking workers, Human Rights Watch suggested that the AMI had deliberately chosen the year 1996, as a basis of comparison, to mislead the public. "A 50 percent drop in meat and poultry industry injury rates in a single year would be implausible," the report noted, "but reaching back six years creates an impressive but fictitious improvement in plant safety."
>
> A few years later the AMI claimed that "recordable injuries" had actually fallen by 70 percent, thanks to the meatpacking industry's concern for worker

safety. The claim was made in an AMI pamphlet commemorating the 100th anniversary of *The Jungle*'s publication.

The title of the pamphlet — "If Upton Sinclair Were Alive Today . . . He'd Be Amazed by the U.S. Meat Industry" — was perhaps its most accurate assertion. Sinclair would no doubt be amazed. He would be amazed by how little has fundamentally changed over the past century, by how poor immigrant workers are still routinely being injured, and by how the industry's lies, no matter how brazen, are still said with a straight face.

After researching on your own, explain whether you agree or disagree with the final sentence in Schlosser's article, asserting that Sinclair "would be amazed by how little has fundamentally changed." Refer to both excerpts in this TalkBack as part of your response.

4. What would Sinclair and Schlosser have to say to one another? Write a dialogue between the two on the topic of food safety, fast food, or a more contemporary issue, such as the slow food movement. Be creative in choosing the setting for your dialogue (e.g., a McDonald's restaurant) and the format (e.g., e-mails) it takes.

5. Assuming the persona of a contemporary muckraker, write a brief piece on a current issue. You can choose to write fiction or nonfiction, but use at least two of the rhetorical strategies that Sinclair and Schlosser employ.

Conversation

The Changing Roles of Women

With the ratification of the Nineteenth Amendment on August 18, 1920, women gained the right to vote. The amendment proclaims, "The right of citizens of the United States to vote shall not be denied or abridged by the United States or by any State on account of sex." The campaign for female enfranchisement, however, began decades earlier in 1848 at Seneca Falls with the *Declaration of Sentiments* (p. 393) and developed into a national, often heated, conversation during the next decades. The question of both the rights and the role of women in a rapidly changing social and political environment was a complex one. Some claimed that the Constitution already granted the vote to women, who need only seize their legal right; others took up economic and psychological issues related to gender identity; others looked to women's impact on the growing labor force, and that of their children as well. In this Conversation, you will explore all of these issues and investigate the changing roles of women in America through the women's rights movement of the 1960s and 1970s and into the present day.

Sources

Susan B. Anthony, *Sentencing Statement* (1872)

Charlotte Perkins Gilman, from *Women and Economics* (1898)

Thorstein Veblen, from *The Theory of the Leisure Class* (1899)

Edith Wharton, from *The House of Mirth* (1905)

Florence Kelley, *Speech on Child Labor* (1905)

Dunston-Weiler Lithograph Company, *Suffragette Madonna* and *Uncle Sam, Suffragee* (1909)

Bertha M. Boye, *Votes for Women* (1911)

Marie Jenney Howe, *An Anti-Suffrage Monologue* (1913)

Gail Collins, from *When Everything Changed: The Amazing Journey of American Women from 1950 to the Present* (2009)

Madeleine M. Kunin, from *The New Feminist Agenda* (2012)

Sentencing Statement

SUSAN B. ANTHONY

> Born into an activist Quaker family, Susan B. Anthony (1820–1906) was a staunch abolitionist, advocate for women's suffrage, and proponent of women's labor organizations. She attended the Seneca Falls convention, where she met Elizabeth Cady Stanton, but at that time she was committed to the temperance movement. Frustrated because women were not permitted to speak at rallies, she joined the women's rights movement in 1852. In 1872, after she and sixteen other women tried to vote in a federal election in New York State, she was arrested and put on trial. She was found guilty, though without a jury's verdict, and ordered to pay a fine of $100 and the costs of prosecution. Following is a transcript of the exchange between Anthony and Judge Ward Hunt during the sentencing.

JUDGE HUNT: (Ordering the defendant to stand up), Has the prisoner anything to say why sentence shall not be pronounced?

MISS ANTHONY: Yes, your honor, I have many things to say; for in your ordered verdict of guilty, you have trampled under foot every vital principle of our government. My natural rights, my civil rights, my political rights, my judicial rights, are all alike ignored. Robbed of the fundamental privilege of citizenship, I am degraded from the status of a citizen to that of a subject; and not only myself individually, but all of my sex, are, by your honor's verdict, doomed to political subjection under this, so-called, form of government.

JUDGE HUNT: The Court cannot listen to a rehearsal of arguments the prisoner's counsel has already consumed three hours in presenting.

MISS ANTHONY: May it please your honor, I am not arguing the question, but simply stating the reasons why sentence cannot, in justice, be pronounced against me. Your denial of my citizen's right to vote, is the denial of my right of consent as one of the governed, the denial of my right of representation as one of the taxed, the denial of my right to a trial by a jury of my peers as an offender against law, therefore, the denial of my sacred rights to life, liberty, property and —

JUDGE HUNT: The Court cannot allow the prisoner to go on.   5

MISS ANTHONY: But your honor will not deny me this one and only poor privilege of protest against this high-handed outrage upon my citizen's rights. May it please the Court to remember that since the day of my arrest last November, this is the first time that either myself or any person of my disfranchised class has been allowed a word of defense before judge or jury —

JUDGE HUNT: The prisoner must sit down — the Court cannot allow it.

MISS ANTHONY: All of my prosecutors, from the 8th ward corner grocery politician, who entered the complaint, to the United States Marshal, Commissioner, District Attorney, District Judge, your honor on the bench, not one is my peer, but each and all are my political sovereigns; and had your honor submitted my case to the jury, as was clearly your duty, even then I should have had just cause of protest, for not one of those men was my peer; but, native or foreign born, white or black, rich or poor, educated or ignorant, awake or asleep, sober or drunk, each and every man of them was my political superior; hence, in no sense, my peer. Even, under such circumstances, a commoner of England, tried before a jury of Lords, would have far less cause to complain than should I, a woman, tried before a jury of men. Even my counsel, the Hon. Henry R. Selden, who has argued my cause so ably, so earnestly, so unanswerably before your honor, is my political sovereign. Precisely as no disfranchised person is entitled to sit upon a jury, and no woman is entitled to the franchise, so, none but a regularly admitted lawyer is allowed to practice in the courts, and no woman can gain admission to the bar — hence, jury, judge, counsel, must all be of the superior class.

JUDGE HUNT: The Court must insist — the prisoner has been tried according to the established forms of law.

MISS ANTHONY: Yes, your honor, but by forms of law all made by men, interpreted   10 by men, administered by men, in favor of men, and against women; and hence, your honor's ordered verdict of guilty, against a United States citizen for the exercise of "*that citizen's right to vote*," simply because that citizen was a woman and not a man. But, yesterday, the same man made forms of law, declared it a crime punishable with $1,000 fine and six months' imprisonment, for you, or me, or any of us, to give a cup of cold water, a crust of bread, or a night's shelter to a panting fugitive as he was tracking his way to Canada. And every man or woman in whose veins coursed a drop of human sympathy violated that wicked law, reckless of consequences, and was justified in so doing. As then, the slaves who got their freedom must take it over, or under, or through the unjust forms of law, precisely so, now, must women, to get their right to a voice in this government, take it; and I have taken mine, and mean to take it at every possible opportunity.

JUDGE HUNT: The Court orders the prisoner to sit down. It will not allow another word.

MISS ANTHONY: When I was brought before your honor for trial, I hoped for a broad and liberal interpretation of the Constitution and its recent amendments, that should declare all United States citizens under its protecting ægis — that should declare equality of rights the national guarantee to all persons born or naturalized in the United States. But failing to get this justice — failing, even, to get a trial by a jury *not* of my peers — I ask not leniency at your hands — but rather the full rigors of the law.

JUDGE HUNT: The Court must insist —
(Here the prisoner sat down.)

JUDGE HUNT: The prisoner will stand up.
(Here Miss Anthony arose again.)
The sentence of the Court is that you pay a fine of one hundred dollars and the   15
costs of the prosecution.

MISS ANTHONY: May it please your honor, I shall never pay a dollar of your unjust penalty. All the stock in trade I possess is a $10,000 debt, incurred by publishing my paper — *The Revolution* — four years ago, the sole object of which was to educate all women to do precisely as I have done, rebel against your man-made, unjust, unconstitutional forms of law, that tax, fine, imprison and hang women, while they deny them the right of representation in the government; and I shall work on with might and main to pay every dollar of that honest debt, but not a penny shall go to this unjust claim. And I shall earnestly and persistently continue to urge all women to the practical recognition of the old revolutionary maxim, that "Resistance to tyranny is obedience to God."

(1872)

Questions

1. On what grounds does Susan B. Anthony claim that having a jury would still not have made her trial fair and just?
2. What is the basic logic of Anthony's stance? Develop the logic through a Toulmin analysis.
3. How would you describe Anthony's attitude toward the judge and the trial in general? Cite specific words and images to characterize the tone.
4. Anthony's arguments appeal to both logic and emotion. Which of her appeals do you find more effective and why? Do the appeals work together to further her purpose, or does one undermine the other?
5. In this exchange, do you think that Anthony primarily adds to a divide of men versus women or invokes the egalitarian tenets of democracy?

from *Women and Economics*

CHARLOTTE PERKINS GILMAN

> Charlotte Perkins Gilman (1860–1935) came from a long line of feminists and
> suffragists, including her grandaunt, Harriet Beecher Stowe, the author of *Uncle Tom's
> Cabin*. Born in Hartford, Connecticut, Gilman was educated mostly at home and
> briefly at the Rhode Island School of Design. She wrote her famous short story, "The
> Yellow Wallpaper" (1892), as an indictment of the rest cure prescribed to her for
> postpartum depression after the birth of her daughter. Following is an excerpt from
> Gilman's book *Women and Economics*, in which she makes the argument that
> "the economic independence and specialization of women is essential to the
> improvement of marriage, motherhood, domestic industry, and racial improvement."
> She promoted the social reform and change in cultural identity that would make
> women full economic partners with men by allowing them to work outside of the
> home.

When we make plain to ourselves that a pure, lasting, monogamous sex-union can
exist without bribe or purchase, without the manacles of economic dependence, and
that men and women so united in sex-relation will still be free to combine with others in economic relation, we shall not regard devotion to humanity as an unnatural
sacrifice, nor collective prosperity as a thing to fear.

Besides this maintenance of primeval individualism in the growing collectivity
of social economic process and the introduction of the element of sex-combat into
the narrowing field of industrial competition, there is another side to the evil influence of the sexuo-economic relation upon social development. This is in the attitude
of woman as a non-productive consumer.

In the industrial evolution of the human race, that marvellous and subtle drawing
out and interlocking of special functions which constitute the organic life of society,
we find that production and consumption go hand in hand; and production comes
first. One cannot consume what has not been produced. Economic production is the
natural expression of human energy, — not sex-energy at all, but race-energy, — the
unconscious functioning of the social organism. Socially organized human beings
tend to produce, as a gland to secrete: it is the essential nature of the relation. The
creative impulse, the desire to make, to express the inner thought in outer form, "just
for the work's sake, no use at all i' the work!" this is the distinguishing character of
humanity. "I want to mark!" cries the child, demanding the pencil. He does not want
to eat. He wants to mark. He is not seeking to get something into himself, but to put
something out of himself. He generally wants to do whatever he sees done, — to make
pie-crust or to make shavings, as it happens. The pie he may eat, the shavings not; but
he likes to make both. This is the natural process of production, and is followed by the
natural process of consumption, where practicable. But consumption is not the main
end, the governing force. Under this organic social law, working naturally, we have the
evolution of those arts and crafts in the exercise of which consists our human living,

and on the product of which we live. So does society evolve within itself—secrete as it were—the social structure with all its complex machinery; and we function therein as naturally as so many glands, other things being equal.

But other things are not equal. Half the human race is denied free productive expression, is forced to confine its productive human energies to the same channels as its reproductive sex-energies. Its creative skill is confined to the level of immediate personal bodily service, to the making of clothes and preparing of food for individuals. No social service is possible. While its power of production is checked, its power of consumption is inordinately increased by the showering upon it of the "unearned increment" of masculine gifts. For the woman there is, first, no free production allowed; and, second, no relation maintained between what she does produce and what she consumes. She is forbidden to make, but encouraged to take. Her industry is not the natural output of creative energy, not the work she does because she has the inner power and strength to do it; nor is her industry even the measure of her gain. She has, of course, the natural desire to consume; and to that is set no bar save the capacity or the will of her husband.

Thus we have painfully and laboriously evolved and carefully maintain among us an enormous class of non-productive consumers,—a class which is half the world, and mother of the other half. We have built into the constitution of the human race the habit and desire of taking, as divorced from its natural precursor and concomitant of making. We have made for ourselves this endless array of "horse-leech's daughters, crying, Give! give!" To consume food, to consume clothes, to consume houses and furniture and decorations and ornaments and amusements, to take and take and take forever,—from one man if they are virtuous, from many if they are vicious, but always to take and never to think of giving anything in return except their womanhood,—this is the enforced condition of the mothers of the race. What wonder that their sons go into business "for what there is in it"! What wonder that the world is full of the desire to get as much as possible and to give as little as possible! What wonder, either, that the glory and sweetness of love are but a name among us, with here and there a strange and beautiful exception, of which our admiration proves the rarity!

Between the brutal ferocity of excessive male energy struggling in the marketplace as in a battlefield and the unnatural greed generated by the perverted condition of female energy, it is not remarkable that the industrial evolution of humanity has shown peculiar symptoms. One of the minor effects of this last condition—this limiting of female industry to close personal necessities, and this tendency of her over-developed sex-nature to overestimate the so-called "duties of her position"— has been to produce an elaborate devotion to individuals and their personal needs,—not to the understanding and developing of their higher natures, but to the intensification of their bodily tastes and pleasure. The wife and mother, pouring the rising tide of racial power into the same old channels that were allowed her primitive ancestors, constantly ministers to the physical needs of her family with a ceaseless and concentrated intensity. They like it, of course. But it maintains in the individuals of the race an exaggerated sense of the importance of food and clothes and ornaments to themselves, without at all including a knowledge of their right use and value to us all. It developes personal selfishness.

Again, the consuming female, debarred from any free production, unable to estimate the labor involved in the making of what she so lightly destroys, and her consumption limited mainly to those things which minister to physical pleasure, creates a market for sensuous decoration and personal ornament, for all that is luxurious and enervating, and for a false and capricious variety in such supplies, which operates as a most deadly check to true industry and true art. As the priestess of the temple of consumption, as the limitless demander of things to use up, her economic influence is reactionary and injurious. Much, very much, of the current of useless production in which our economic energies run waste — man's strength poured out like water on the sand — depends on the creation and careful maintenance of this false market, this sink into which human labor vanishes with no return. Woman, in her false economic position, reacts injuriously upon industry, upon art, upon science, discovery, and progress. The sexuo-economic relation in its effect on the constitution of the individual keeps alive in us the instincts of savage individualism which we should otherwise have well outgrown. . . .

(1898)

Questions

1. What is the relationship between consumption and production that is fundamental to Charlotte Perkins Gilman's argument? Why does Gilman believe that the woman "is forbidden to make, but encouraged to take" (par. 4)?
2. What are the consequences that Gilman envisions when a society includes "an enormous class of non-productive consumers" (par. 5)?
3. Gilman decries "the priestess of the temple of consumption, as the limitless demander of things to use up, [whose] economic influence is reactionary and injurious" (par. 7). To what extent do you think she is blaming women for their situation? Is she blaming the victim?
4. What does Gilman mean in the final paragraph by "this false market" and women's "false economic position"?
5. Why is Gilman so vehemently opposed to what she calls "savage individualism" (par. 7)? What is the alternative?

from *The Theory of the Leisure Class*

THORSTEIN VEBLEN

Thorstein Veblen (1857–1929) was an economist best known for his book *The Theory of the Leisure Class* (1899). He introduced the term "conspicuous consumption," which means consuming simply to demonstrate one's accomplishments or economic status. In the following excerpt, from Chapter 3 of that book, Veblen *discusses the newly emerging middle class and the role of women as conspicuous consumers.*

[H]ere occurs a curious inversion. It is a fact of common observation that in this lower middle class there is no pretence of leisure on the part of the head of the household. Through force of circumstances it has fallen into disuse. But the middle-class wife still carries on the business of vicarious leisure, for the good name of the household and its master. In descending the social scale in any modern industrial community, the primary fact — the conspicuous leisure of the master of the household — disappears at a relatively high point. The head of the middle-class household has been reduced by economic circumstances to turn his hand to gaining a livelihood by occupations which often partake largely of the character of industry, as in the case of the ordinary business man of to-day. But the derivative fact — the vicarious leisure and consumption rendered by the wife, and the auxiliary vicarious performance of leisure by menials — remains in vogue as a conventionality which the demands of reputability will not suffer to be slighted. It is by no means an uncommon spectacle to find a man applying himself to work with the utmost assiduity, in order that his wife may in due form render for him that degree of vicarious leisure which the common sense of the time demands.

The leisure rendered by the wife in such cases is, of course, not a simple manifestation of idleness or indolence. It almost invariably occurs disguised under some form of work or household duties or social amenities, which prove on analysis to serve little or no ulterior end beyond showing that she does not and need not occupy herself with anything that is gainful or that is of substantial use. As has already been noticed under the head of manners, the greater part of the customary round of domestic cares to which the middle-class housewife gives her time and effort is of this character. Not that the results of her attention to household matters, of a decorative and mundificatory character, are not pleasing to the sense of men trained in middle-class proprieties; but the taste to which these effects of household adornment and tidiness appeal is a taste which has been formed under the selective guidance of a canon of propriety that demands just these evidences of wasted effort. The effects are pleasing to us chiefly because we have been taught to find them pleasing. There goes into these domestic duties much solicitude for a proper combination of form and colour, and for other ends that are to be classed as æsthetic in the proper sense of the term; and it is not denied that effects having some substantial æsthetic value are sometimes attained. Pretty much all that is here insisted on is that, as regards these amenities of life, the housewife's efforts are under the guidance of traditions that have been shaped by the law of conspicuously wasteful expenditure of time and substance. If beauty or comfort is achieved, — and it is a more or less fortuitous circumstance if they are, — they must be achieved by means and methods that commend themselves to the great economic law of wasted effort. The more reputable, "presentable" portion of middle-class household paraphernalia are, on the one hand, items of conspicuous consumption, and on the other hand, apparatus for putting in evidence the vicarious leisure rendered by the housewife.

The requirement of vicarious consumption at the hands of the wife continues in force even at a lower point in the pecuniary scale than the requirement of vicarious leisure. At a point below which little if any pretence of wasted effort, in ceremonial cleanness and the like, is observable, and where there is assuredly no conscious attempt at ostensible leisure, decency still requires the wife to consume some goods conspicuously for the reputability of the household and its head. So that, as the latter-day outcome of this evolution of an archaic institution, the wife, who was at the outset the drudge and chattel of the man, both in fact and in theory, — the producer of goods for him to consume, — has become the ceremonial consumer of goods which he produces. But she still quite unmistakably remains his chattel in theory; for the habitual rendering of vicarious leisure and consumption is the abiding mark of the unfree servant.

(1899)

Questions

1. What is the irony of the "derivative fact" that Thorstein Veblen refers to in paragraph 1?
2. If the "leisure rendered by the wife" is "not a simple manifestation of idleness or indolence" (par. 2), then what is it, according to Veblen?
3. What vicious cycle is Veblen pointing out in the following two sentences: "Not that the results of her attention to household matters . . . are not pleasing. [They are] because we have been taught to find them pleasing" (par. 2)?
4. What is "the great economic law of wasted effort" (par. 2)?
5. What does Veblen mean by such descriptive phrases as "vicarious leisure" (par. 1), "conspicuous leisure" (par. 1), and "vicarious consumption" (par. 3), which he uses throughout this excerpt? Are these phrases synonymous?
6. What is the "archaic institution" (par. 3)? Why does this institution result in women who are wives remaining "chattel in theory" and having no choice but to act as "the unfree servant"?
7. What precisely is the argument Veblen is making in this excerpt? To what extent do you agree with his reasoning?

from *The House of Mirth*

EDITH WHARTON

> Edith Wharton (1862–1937) was a Pulitzer Prize–winning American novelist and short-story writer. In this excerpt from early in *The House of Mirth* (1905), the impoverished central character, Lily Bart, reflects on the financial advantages she expects to enjoy as the wife of Percy Gryce, a member of the 1890s New York aristocracy.

Seating herself on the upper step of the terrace, Lily leaned her head against the honeysuckles wreathing the balustrade. The fragrance of the late blossoms seemed an emanation of the tranquil scene, a landscape tutored to the last degree of rural elegance. In the foreground glowed the warm tints of the gardens. Beyond the lawn, with its pyramidal pale-gold maples and velvety firs, sloped pastures dotted with cattle; and through a long glade the river widened like a lake under the silver light of September. Lily did not want to join the circle about the tea-table. They represented the future she had chosen, and she was content with it, but in no haste to anticipate its joys. The certainty that she could marry Percy Gryce when she pleased had lifted a heavy load from her mind, and her money troubles were too recent for their removal not to leave a sense of relief which a less discerning intelligence might have taken for happiness. Her vulgar cares were at an end. She would be able to arrange her life as she pleased, to soar into that empyrean[1] of security where creditors cannot penetrate. She would have smarter gowns than Judy Trenor, and far, far more jewels than Bertha Dorset. She would be free forever from the shifts, the expedients, the humiliations of the relatively poor. Instead of having to flatter, she would be flattered; instead of being grateful, she would receive thanks. There were old scores she could pay off as well as old benefits she could return. And she had no doubts as to the extent of her power. She knew that Mr. Gryce was of the small chary type most inaccessible to impulses and emotions. He had the kind of character in which prudence is a vice, and good advice the most dangerous nourishment. But Lily had known the species before: she was aware that such a guarded nature must find one huge outlet of egoism, and she determined to be to him what his Americana had hitherto been: the one possession in which he took sufficient pride to spend money on it. She knew that this generosity to self is one of the forms of meanness, and she resolved so to identify herself with her husband's vanity that to gratify her wishes would be to him the most exquisite form of self-indulgence. The system might at first necessitate a resort to some of the very shifts and expedients from which she intended it should free her; but she felt sure that in a short time she would be able to play the game in her own way. How should she have distrusted her powers? Her beauty itself was not the mere ephemeral possession it might have been in the hands of inexperience: her skill in enhancing it, the care she took of it, the use she made of it, seemed to give it a kind of permanence. She felt she could trust it to carry her through to the end.

And the end, on the whole, was worth while. Life was not the mockery she had thought it three days ago. There was room for her, after all, in this crowded selfish world of pleasure whence, so short a time since, her poverty had seemed to exclude her. These people whom she had ridiculed and yet envied were glad to make a place for her in the charmed circle about which all her desires revolved. They were not as brutal and self-engrossed as she had fancied — or rather, since it would no longer be necessary to flatter and humour them, that side of their nature became less conspicuous. Society is a revolving body which is apt to be judged according to its place in each man's heaven; and at present it was turning its illuminated face to Lily.

In the rosy glow it diffused her companions seemed full of amiable qualities. She liked their elegance, their lightness, their lack of emphasis: even the self-assurance which at times was so like obtuseness now seemed the natural sign of social ascendency.

---

[1]In Greek philosophy, the highest layer of the heavens. — Eds.

They were lords of the only world she cared for, and they were ready to admit her to their ranks and let her lord it with them. Already she felt within her a stealing allegiance to their standards, an acceptance of their limitations, a disbelief in the things they did not believe in, a contemptuous pity for the people who were not able to live as they lived.

The early sunset was slanting across the park. Through the boughs of the long avenue beyond the gardens she caught the flash of wheels, and divined that more visitors were approaching. There was a movement behind her, a scattering of steps and voices: it was evident that the party about the tea-table was breaking up. Presently she heard a tread behind her on the terrace. She supposed that Mr. Gryce had at last found means to escape from his predicament, and she smiled at the significance of his coming to join her instead of beating an instant retreat to the fire-side.

(1905)

Questions

1. What does Edith Wharton suggest with her observation that Lily's "vulgar cares were at an end. She would be able to arrange her life as she pleased, to soar into that empyrean of security where creditors cannot penetrate" (par. 1)?
2. What do you think Lily means by her reference to "the relatively poor" (par. 1)?
3. How does Lily define herself as the wife of Gryce? What was she "determined to be to him" (par. 1)?
4. What source(s) of power does Lily understand will be hers to wield as well as nurture when she is Gryce's wife?
5. What shift in attitude does the narrator portray in this passage in which Lily imagines herself as a member of the social aristocracy, a sphere which she initially thought of as a "crowded selfish world of pleasure" (par. 2)?
6. Based on this excerpt, how would you describe Wharton's view of marriage in the society of her time?

Speech on Child Labor

Florence Kelley

> An early advocate of women's suffrage, Florence Kelley (1859–1932) was a social reformer known for her work against sweatshops and her efforts to pass legislation for eight-hour workdays and restrictions on child labor. She delivered the following speech before the National American Woman Suffrage Association on July 22, 1905, in Philadelphia.

We have, in this country, two million children under the age of sixteen years who are earning their bread. They vary in age from six and seven years (in the cotton mills of

Georgia) and eight, nine and ten years (in the coal-breakers of Pennsylvania), to four-teen, fifteen and sixteen years in more enlightened states. No other portion of the wage earning class increased so rapidly from decade to decade as the young girls from fourteen to twenty years. Men increase, women increase, youth increase, boys increase in the ranks of the breadwinners; but no contingent so doubles from census period to census period (both by percent and by count of heads), as does the contingent of girls between twelve and twenty years of age. They are in commerce, in offices, in manufacturing.

Tonight while we sleep, several thousand little girls will be working in textile mills, all the night through, in the deafening noise of the spindles and the looms spinning and weaving cotton and wool, silks and ribbons for us to buy.

In Alabama the law provides that a child under sixteen years of age shall not work in a cotton mill at night longer than eight hours, and Alabama does better in this respect than any other southern state. North and South Carolina and Georgia place no restriction upon the work of children at night; and while we sleep little white girls will be working tonight in the mills in those states, working eleven hours at night. In Georgia there is no restriction whatever! A girl of six or seven years, just tall enough to reach the bobbins, may work eleven hours by day or by night. And they will do so tonight, while we sleep. Nor is it only in the South that these things occur. Alabama does better than New Jersey. For Alabama limits the children's work at night to eight hours, while New Jersey permits it all night long. Last year New Jersey took a long backward step. A good law was repealed which had required women and [chil-dren] to stop work at six in the evening and at noon on Friday. Now, therefore, in New Jersey, boys and girls, after their fourteenth birthday, enjoy the pitiful privilege of working all night long.

In Pennsylvania, until last May it was lawful for children, thirteen years of age, to work twelve hours at night. A little girl, on her thirteenth birthday, could start away from her home at half past five in the afternoon, carrying her pail of midnight luncheon as happier people carry their midday luncheon, and could work in the mill from six at night until six in the morning, without violating any law of the Commonwealth.

If the mothers and the teachers in Georgia could vote, would the Georgia legis- 5 lature have refused at every session for the last three years to stop the work in the mills of children under twelve years of age?

Would the New Jersey Legislature have passed that shameful repeal bill enabling girls of fourteen years to work all night, if the mothers in New Jersey were enfran-chised? Until the mothers in the great industrial states are enfranchised, we shall none of us be able to free our consciences from participation in this great evil. No one in this room tonight can feel free from such participation. The children make our shoes in the shoe factories; they knit our stockings, our knitted underwear in the knitting factories. They spin and weave our cotton underwear in the cotton mills. Children braid straw for our hats, they spin and weave the silk and velvet wherewith we trim our hats. They stamp buckles and metal ornaments of all kinds, as well as pins and hat-pins. Under the sweating system, tiny children make artificial flowers and neckwear for us to buy. They carry bundles of garments from the factories to the tenements, little beasts of burden, robbed of school life that they may work for us.

We do not wish this. We prefer to have our work done by men and women. But we are almost powerless. Not wholly powerless, however, are citizens who enjoy the right of petition. For myself, I shall use this power in every possible way until the right to the ballot is granted, and then I shall continue to use both. What can we do to free our consciences? There is one line of action by which we can do much. We can enlist the workingmen on behalf of our enfranchisement just in proportion as we strive with them to free the children. No labor organization in this country ever fails to respond to an appeal for help in the freeing of the children.

For the sake of the children, for the Republic in which these children will vote after we are dead, and for the sake of our cause, we should enlist the workingmen voters, with us, in this task of freeing the children from toil!

(1905)

Questions

1. What appeals to logos does Florence Kelley make right at the start of her speech? Why? What relationship does this establish with her audience?
2. When does Kelley appeal to pathos? What strategies does she use to make this appeal?
3. How does her explanation of conditions in Alabama and New Jersey (par. 3) anticipate (and refute) a counterargument?
4. Kelley does not get to her central claim until almost the middle of the speech (par. 5). What is her thesis? Why do you think she withheld it for so long?
5. Throughout her speech, Kelley uses the pronoun "we." What connection is she making with her audience? Why does she shift to "I" in the penultimate paragraph?
6. What do you believe is Kelley's purpose in the final two paragraphs? Is it effective to have waited until this point, or is it too late to add another issue?
7. How does Kelley balance logical and emotional appeals in this speech? Does one finally outweigh the other? How does this balance — or shifting balance — help achieve her purpose?

Suffragette Madonna
and
Uncle Sam, Suffragee

Dunston-Weiler Lithograph Company

As the movement to enfranchise women gained a following in the early 1900s, antisuffragette images frequently played on fears that traditional gender roles (including appearance) would be at risk. As popular means to send short, often humorous communications, some postcards in the early 1900s also presented a visual commentary about voting rights for women. In 1909, the Dunston-Weiler Lithograph Company of New York produced twelve full-color lithographic postcards presenting visual arguments against women's suffrage. The two examples on the following page are from that collection.

© 2013 Washington State History Society. All rights reserved. Website by SiteCrafting.

SUFFRAGETTE SERIES Nº 1.

SUFFRAGETTE SERIES Nº 6.

·SUFFRAGETTE MADONNA·
COPYRIGHT 1909 BY DUNSTON-WEILER LITHOGRAPH CO.

UNCLE SAM, SUFFRAGEE.

Courtesy of the Alice Marshall Women's History Collection, Series VII: Postcards, AKM 91/1.2, Archives and Special Collections, Penn State Harrisburg Library, University Libraries, Pennsylvania State University.

(See color insert, Image 29.)

(See color insert, Image 30.)

Questions

1. The *Suffragette Madonna* image was particularly popular during this time, and there were many different versions made. Why would this particular visual representation be so appealing to those who opposed enfranchisement of women?

2. How does the composition — use of space, color, placement of objects — add to the emotional appeal of this visual text? How does the expression on the baby's face contribute to this appeal?

3. In what ways is the physical appearance of the man in *Suffragette Madonna* feminized? Pay attention to his clothing, gaze, expression, and facial characteristics.

4. *Uncle Sam, Suffragee* is a parody of the Uncle Sam depictions commonly used during the period. What elements are especially noteworthy here? Consider the costume, stance, and facial expression.

5. In what ways is the feminization of Uncle Sam the same as and different from that of the man in *Suffragette Madonna*?

6. What exactly is the tone of the comedy in each of these postcards? Is it sarcastic humor, bitter irony, playful wit, or something else? Cite specifics from each postcard to support your perspective.

7. Are these two postcards making similar visual arguments, or do you see differences in claims or strategies? Is the chief purpose of each to discredit and denigrate women, to mock men who support enfranchising women, or something else?

Votes for Women

BERTHA M. BOYE

> Graphic artist Bertha M. Boye (1883–1930) won the contest for most beautiful image of the suffragette cause sponsored by the state of California to advertise the 1911 suffrage referendum. This image is an art nouveau graphic of a woman in front of the Golden Gate, the opening between San Francisco Bay and the Pacific Ocean.

Questions

1. How would you describe the mood of this poster? How do the colors, symmetry, overall setting, and representational figure contribute to the mood?

2. What does the sun symbolize in this image? Consider how its shape, placement, and color suggest multiple meanings.

3. What associations does the central statue-like figure evoke? Is she an allegorical figure? If so, allegorical of what?

4. With which negative stereotypes of suffragettes does the central figure of the painting contrast? How might she be viewed as reinforcing any of the stereotypes?

5. An art critic interpreted the banner that the figure holds as follows: "The poster's slogan appears not as an argument or battle cry, but as an unassailable truth, an 'inalienable right' whose time had come." Explain why and how your interpretation supports, challenges, or qualifies this view.

(See color insert, Image 31.)

Schlesinger Library, Radcliffe Institute, Harvard University

An Anti-Suffrage Monologue

Marie Jenney Howe

Marie Jenney Howe (1871–1934) was a Unitarian minister and founder in 1912 of the Heterodoxy Club of Greenwich Village, a group of women intellectuals. She wrote this satiric "Anti-Suffrage Monologue" in 1913 to be performed by the New York Woman's Suffrage Party's drama group.

Please do not think of me as old-fashioned. I pride myself on being a modern up-to-date woman. I believe in all kinds of broad-mindedness, only I do not believe in woman suffrage because to do that would be to deny my sex.

Woman suffrage is the reform against nature. Look at these ladies sitting on the platform. Observe their physical inability, their mental disability, their spiritual instability and general debility! Could they walk up to the ballot box, mark a ballot, and drop it in? Obviously not. Let us grant for the sake of argument that they could mark a ballot. But could they drop it in? Ah, no. All nature is against it. The laws of man cry out against it. The voice of God cries out against it — and so do I.

Enfranchisement is what makes man man. Disfranchisement is what makes woman woman. If women were enfranchised every man would be just like every woman and every woman would be just like every man. There would be no difference between them. And don't you think this would rob life of just a little of its poetry and romance?

Man must remain man. Woman must remain woman. If man goes over and tries to be like woman, if woman goes over and tries to be like man, it will become so very confusing and so difficult to explain to our children. Let us take a practical example. If a woman puts on a man's coat and trousers, takes a man's cane and hat and cigar, and goes out on the street, what will happen to her? She will be arrested and thrown into jail. Then why not stay at home?

I know you begin to see how strongly I *feel* on this subject, but I have some rea-   5
sons as well. These reasons are based on logic. Of course, I am not logical. I am a creature of impulse, instinct, and intuition — and I glory in it. But I know that these reasons are based on logic because I have culled them from the men whom it is my privilege to know.

My first argument against suffrage is that the women would not use it if they had it. You couldn't drive them to the polls. My second argument is, if the women were enfranchised they would neglect their homes, desert their families, and spend all their time at the polls. You may tell me that the polls are only open once a year. But I know women. They are creatures of habit. If you let them go to the polls once a year, they will hang round the polls all the rest of the time.

I have arranged these arguments in couplets. They go together in such a way that if you don't like one you can take the other. This is my second anti-suffrage couplet. If the women were enfranchised they would vote exactly as their husbands do and only double the existing vote. Do you like that argument? If not, take this one. If the women were enfranchised they would vote against their own husbands, thus creating dissension, family quarrels, and divorce.

My third anti-suffrage couplet is — women are angels. Many men call me an angel and I have a strong instinct which tells me it is true; that is why I am an anti, because "I want to be an angel and with the angels stand." And if you don't like that argument take this one. Women are depraved. They would introduce into politics a vicious element which would ruin our national life.

Fourth anti-suffrage couplet: women cannot understand politics. Therefore there would be no use in giving women political power, because they would not know what to do with it. On the other hand, if the women were enfranchised, they would mount rapidly into power, take all the offices from all the men, and soon we would have women governors of all our states and dozens of women acting as President of the United States.

Fifth anti-suffrage couplet: women cannot band together. They are incapable of   10
organization. No two women can even be friends. Women are cats. On the other hand,

if women were enfranchised, we would have all the women banded together on one side and all the men banded together on the other side, and there would follow a sex war which might end in bloody revolution.

Just one more of my little couplets: the ballot is greatly over-estimated. It has never done anything for anybody. Lots of men tell me this. And the corresponding argument is — the ballot is what makes man man. It is what gives him all his dignity and all of his superiority to women. Therefore if we allow women to share this privilege, how could a woman look up to her own husband? Why, there would be nothing to look up to.

I have talked to many woman suffragists and I find them very unreasonable. I say to them: "Here I am, convince me." I ask for proof. Then they proceed to tell me of Australia and Colorado and other places where women have passed excellent laws to improve the condition of working women and children. But I say, "What of it?" These are facts. I don't care about facts. I ask for proof.

Then they quote the eight million women of the United States who are now supporting themselves, and the twenty-five thousand married women in the City of New York who are self-supporting. But I say again, what of it? These are statistics. I don't believe in statistics. Facts and statistics are things which no truly womanly woman would ever use.

I wish to prove anti-suffrage in a womanly way — that is, by personal example. This is my method of persuasion. Once I saw a woman driving a horse, and the horse ran away with her. Isn't that just like a woman? Once I read in the newspapers about a woman whose house caught on fire, and she threw the children out of the window and carried the pillows downstairs. Does that show political acumen, or does it not? Besides, look at the hats that women wear! And have you ever known a successful woman governor of a state? Or have you ever known a really truly successful woman president of the United States? Well, if they could they would, wouldn't they? Then, if they haven't, doesn't that show they couldn't? As for the militant suffragettes, they are all hyenas in petticoats. Now do you want to be a hyena and wear petticoats?

Now, I think I have proved anti-suffrage; and I have done it in a womanly way — 15 that is, without stooping to the use of a single fact or argument or a single statistic. . . .

I know the suffragists reply that all our activities have been taken out of the home. The baking, the washing, the weaving, the spinning are all long since taken out of the home. But I say, all the more reason that something should stay in the home. Let it be woman. Besides, think of the great modern invention, the telephone. That has been put into the home. Let woman stay at home and answer the telephone.

We antis have so much imagination! Sometimes it seems to us that we can hear the little babies in the slums crying to us. We can see the children in factories and mines reaching out their little hands to us, and the working women in the sweated industries, the underpaid, underfed women, reaching out their arms to us — all, all crying as with one voice, "Save us, save us, from Woman Suffrage." Well may they make this appeal to us, for who knows what woman suffrage might not do for such as these. It might even alter the conditions under which they live.

We antis do not believe that any conditions should be altered. We want everything to remain just as it is. All is for the best. Whatever is, is right. . . .

(1913)

Questions

1. What stereotypes does Marie Jenney Howe play on in this monologue? Cite specific passages for at least four different characteristics that would argue against women becoming responsible voters.
2. What examples of logical fallacies do you find in this monologue? Consider circular reasoning, red herring, hasty generalization, false dilemma, bandwagon appeal, and others.
3. What elements of satire — such as understatement, hyperbole, and humor — do you find in this monologue?
4. What does Howe mean by her repeated phrase "a womanly way"?
5. An effective satire causes us to laugh, but it also causes us to think; its purpose is to bring about some kind of change, usually social or political. What exactly is Howe satirizing? How effective do you believe her satire is?

from *When Everything Changed*

The Amazing Journey of American Women from 1950 to the Present

Gail Collins

> With a BA in journalism and an MA in government, Gail Collins (b. 1945) became the first woman to serve as editor of the *New York Times* editorial page (2001–2007). She continues today as an op-ed columnist. Collins is the author of several books, including *Scorpion Tongues: Gossip, Celebrity and American Politics* (1998); and *America's Women: Four Hundred Years of Dolls, Drudges, Helpmates, and Heroines* (2003). The following is an excerpt from Chapter 1 of her 2009 book, *When Everything Changed: The Amazing Journey of American Women from 1950 to the Present.*

1. Repudiating Rosie

"Some of you DO wear a cautious face."

In January 1960, *Mademoiselle* welcomed in a new decade for America's young women by urging them to be . . . less boring. "Some of you do wear a cautious face," the editors admitted. "But are you really—cautious, unimaginative, determined to play it safe at any price?" *Mademoiselle* certainly hoped not. But its readers had good reason to set their sights low. The world around them had been drumming one message into their heads since they were babies: women are meant to marry and let their husbands take care of all the matters relating to the outside world. They were not supposed to have adventures or compete with men for serious rewards. ("I think that when women are encouraged to be competitive too many of them become disagreeable," said Dr. Benjamin Spock, whose baby book had served as the bible for the postwar generation of mothers.) *Newsweek*, decrying a newly noticed phenomenon of dissatisfied housewives in 1960, identified the core of the issue: menstruation. "From the beginning of time, the female cycle has defined and confined woman's role," the newsmagazine wrote. "As Freud was credited with saying: 'Anatomy is destiny.'"

Though no group of women has ever pushed aside these natural restrictions as far as the American wife, it seems that she still cannot accept them in good grace. Most girls grew up without ever seeing a woman doctor, lawyer, police officer, or bus driver. Jo Freeman, who went to Berkeley in the early '60s, realized only later that while she had spent four years "in one of the largest institutions of higher education in the world — and one with a progressive reputation," she had never once had a female professor. "I never even saw one. Worse yet, I didn't notice." If a young woman expressed interest in a career outside the traditional teacher/nurse/secretary, her mentors carefully shepherded her back to the proper path. As a teenager in Pittsburgh, Angela Nolfi told her guidance counselor that she wanted to be an interior decorator, but even that very feminine pursuit apparently struck her adviser as too high-risk or out of the ordinary. "He said, 'Why don't you be a home-economics teacher?'" she recalled. And once *Mademoiselle* had finished urging its readers to shoot for the sky, it celebrated the end of the school year with an article on careers that seemed to suggest most new college graduates would be assuming secretarial duties, and ended with tips on "pre-job hand-beautifying" for a new generation of typists.

Whenever things got interesting, women seemed to vanish from the scene. There was no such thing as a professional female athlete — even in schools, it was a given that sports were for boys. An official for the men-only Boston Marathon opined that it was "unhealthy for women to run long distances." When *Mademoiselle* selected seven "headstrong people who have made names for themselves lately" to comment on what the 1960s would bring, that magazine for young women managed to find only one headstrong woman to include in the mix — playwright Lorraine Hansberry, who did double duty as the panel's only minority.

"Women used to be the big stars, but these days it's men."

Nothing sent the message about women's limited options more forcefully than television, which had just finished conquering the nation with a speed that made Alexander the Great look like an underachiever. In 1950 only about 9 percent of American homes boasted a set, but by 1960 nearly 90 percent of families had a TV, and those who didn't were feeling very deprived indeed. Beverly Burton, a Wyoming farm wife, had been estranged throughout the 1950s from a mother who had once told her she was sorry Beverly had ever been born. When her mother decided to mend fences, she sent Burton a note saying, "I hope this will cover the past" — attached to a television set. And it did indeed become a turning point in the relationship.

The postwar generation that was entering adolescence in the 1960s had grown up   5
watching *Howdy Doody*, the must-see TV for the first wave of baby boomers. *Howdy* was a raucous puppet show in which the human performers interspersed broad physical comedy with endless pitches for the sponsors' products. "But all the slapstick

stopped when they brought out Princess Summerfall Winterspring," remembered Stephen Davis, a childhood fan whose father worked on the show. The princess, played by a teenage singer named Judy Tyler, was the only long-running female character in *Howdy Doody*'s crowded cast. The role had been created when a producer realized "we could sell a lot of dresses if only we had a girl on the show," and the princess spent most of her time expressing concern about plot developments taking place while she was offstage. Adults approved. "The harshness and crudeness which so many parents objected to in *Howdy Doody* now appears to have largely been a case of too much masculinity," said *Variety*. But the stuff that made kids love the show — the broad comedy and bizarre plots — was all on the male side of the equation. Princess Summerfall Winterspring sang an occasional song — and watched.

The more popular and influential television became, the more efficiently women were swept off the screen. In the 1950s, when the medium was still feeling its way, there were a number of shows built around women — mainly low-budget comedies such as *Our Miss Brooks*, *Private Secretary*, and *My Little Margie*. None of the main characters were exactly role models — Miss Brooks was a teacher who spent most of her time mooning over a hunky biology instructor, and Margie lived off her rich father. Still, the shows were unquestionably about them. And the most popular program of all was *I Love Lucy*, in which Lucille Ball was the focus of every plotline, ever striving to get out of her three-room apartment and into her husband Ricky's nightclub show.

But by 1960 television was big business, and if women were around at all, they were in the kitchen, where they decorously stirred a single pot on the stove while their husbands and children dominated the action. (In 1960 the nominees for the Emmy for best comedy series were *The Bob Cummings Show*, *The Danny Thomas Show*, *The Jack Benny Show*, *The Red Skelton Show*, *The Phil Silvers Show*, and *Father Knows Best*.) When a script did turn its attention to the wife, daughter, or mother, it was frequently to remind her of her place and the importance of letting boys win. On *Father Knows Best*, younger daughter Kathy was counseled by her dad on how to deliberately lose a ball game. Teenage daughter Betty found happiness when she agreed to stop competing with a male student for a junior executive job at the local department store and settled for the more gender-appropriate task of modeling bridal dresses.

In dramatic series, women stood on the sidelines, looking worried. When Betty Friedan asked why there couldn't be a female lead in *Mr. Novak* — which was, after all, a series about a high school teacher — she said the producer explained, "For drama, there has to be action, conflict. . . . For a woman to make decisions, to triumph over anything, would be unpleasant, dominant, masculine." Later in the decade, the original *Star Trek* series would feature a story about a woman so desperate to become a starship captain — a post apparently restricted to men — that she arranged to have her brain transferred into Captain Kirk's body. The crew quickly noticed that the captain was manicuring his nails at the helm and having hysterics over the least little thing.

Cowboy action series were the best-loved TV entertainment in 1960. Eleven of the top twenty-five shows were Westerns, and they underlined the rule that women did not have adventures, except the ones that involved getting kidnapped or caught in a natural disaster. "Women used to be the big stars, but these days it's men," said Michael Landon, one of the leads in *Bonanza*, the long-running story of an all-male family living on a huge Nevada ranch after the Civil War. Perhaps to emphasize their heterosexuality, the Cartwright men had plenty of romances. But the scriptwriters killed their girlfriends off at an extraordinarily speedy clip. The family patriarch, Ben, had been widowed three times, and his three sons all repeatedly got married or engaged, only to quickly lose their mates to the grim reaper. A rather typical episode began with Joe (Landon) happily dancing with a new fiancée. Before the first commercial, the poor girl was murdered on her way home from the hoedown.

(2009)

Questions

1. What preconceptions about the role of women does Gail Collins allude to in the opening paragraph? What authorities does she cite to support her allegations?
2. Although Collins gives *Mademoiselle*, a magazine geared to young women, some credit for encouraging its readers to look beyond society's expectations, she also indicates ways the magazine reflects those expectations. What evidence does she cite to illustrate what she perceives as *Mademoiselle's* ambivalence toward the changing role of women in the 1960s?
3. What examples does she cite to support her assertion that "[n]othing sent the message about women's limited options more forcefully than television" (par. 4)?
4. To what extent do women in today's television shows challenge the stereotypes Collins describes? Cite at least one program or series that does challenge and another that is a remnant of the late 1950s shows Collins refers to.

from *The New Feminist Agenda*

MADELEINE M. KUNIN

> Madeleine M. Kunin (b. 1933) was the first woman governor of Vermont and the first woman in the United States to serve three terms. Author of *Living a Political Life* (1994), she served as the ambassador to Switzerland from 1996 to 1999 and currently is a professor at the University of Vermont. Following is "Time for a Revolution," the opening chapter of *The New Feminist Agenda: Defining the Next Revolution for Women, Work, and Family* (2012).

Five of us were meeting for lunch and reminiscing about the women's movement. "I was never one of those angry women," one said. "I'm still angry," I blurted. My reaction surprised both me and my friends. Where did that come from? A source I hadn't tapped before. Upon reflection, I realized that I'm not angry enough to carry a placard down hot macadam streets in front of the nation's Capitol, like I did in my thirties when I marched for women's rights. But now in my seventies I'm still dissatisfied with the status quo and harbor a passion for change. Old age allows me the luxury of being impatient — there is not so much time left — and it permits me to say what I think, to be demanding, and, best of all, to imagine a different world where there is true gender equality in the workplace, the home, and the political arena.

Why the anger? What did I expect?

I expected that the women's movement of the 1970s would give me a good answer to the question my students regularly asked: how do you manage to have a family *and* a career?

I expected that affordable, quality child care would be widely available, that paid family leave would be the law, and that equal pay for equal work would be a reality. I did not expect that women would still make 77 cents for every dollar that men earn.

I expected that one-third to one-half of our Congress, governors, state legisla-   5
tures, and mayors would be female. I did not expect that in 2010 that number would be 17 percent in the Congress, and the United States would be tied at 69th place in the percentage of women in parliaments, out of 178 countries.

I expected that one-third to one-half of corporate board members would be women. I did not expect to see that proportion stuck at 17 percent.

I expected that a high percentage of the Fortune 500 companies would be led by women. I did not expect that figure to be 3 percent.

I expected that misogyny, rape, and other acts of violence against women would be widely condemned and sharply reduced. I did not expect that a female journalist could be sexually abused in the middle of Cairo's Tahrir Square and then blamed for bringing it on herself, as Lara Logan of CBS News experienced in February 2011.

I expected that *Roe v. Wade* would remain the law of the land. I did not expect that it would be eroded, state by state.

I expected that by the year 2011 grandmothers like myself would be able to tell   10
their grandchildren of how life used to be "long ago," when families had to figure out for themselves how to be both wage earners and caregivers.

Some changes occurred that I had not expected and could not have imagined: that women would comprise nearly 60 percent of college undergraduates, that women would comprise half of the medical and law students, that women would enter the workforce in record numbers, and that the traditional family supported by the father would be overtaken by the two-wage-earner family.

That's the good news. The bad news is that many women who have careers that we never could have imagined for ourselves are still flummoxed by the most age-old problem: how to have a job and take care of the children, the elderly, the sick, and the disabled. Until we find a way to sort out how to share these responsibilities — between spouses, partners, employers, and governments — gender equality will remain an elusive goal. Progress for women will remain stalled. But it's not only about gender anymore. As I write, Italy is in an economic crisis, in danger of defaulting on its government debt. One reason given for its economic woes is that it has the lowest percentage of women in the workforce in all of Europe. Why? Whether because of the country's macho culture or lack of family support programs, Italy offers little in the way of encouragement or assistance for working families.

Time for Change, Again

The countries that do support working families benefit from greater productivity and social well-being. It is time for another social revolution, not for the benefit of women alone, but for the most traditional of reasons: for the sake of the family. We need to reweave the fabric of society to provide the love and care necessary for the more fragile members of our families. The workplace must be reconfigured to harmonize with these responsibilities. The urgency for change is felt by families at all income levels, even those who are able to negotiate flexibility for themselves and can afford to pay for quality child care. Middle- and low-income employees are most starkly affected by today's work/life stress. They cannot make ends meet, financially or emotionally. They experience a severe time deficit that does not allow them to give enough of themselves at work or at home. These frustrations are commonplace. If the kitchen table, the water cooler, or Twitter could talk, these stories would overwhelm all other conversation. If one family's text messages about who is picking up the children or shopping for dinner were gathered in a book over a few years, it would be too heavy to lift.

The question families ponder is: how can we be better parents and employees without neglecting either our families or our jobs? We are beginning to understand the individual cost that the schism between work and family exacts. We have not added up the national cost. Our reluctance, or outright refusal, to enact policies that would bridge the gap between family and work has contributed to disturbing national statistics: alarmingly high child poverty rates, declining college graduation rates and test scores, and a growing chasm between the rich, the middle class, and the poor. Our inability — for political, economic, or cultural reasons — to invest in families leaves us vulnerable to being reduced to second-rate status in the global economy. Impossible to measure, but not to be ignored, is the moral cost we pay by depriving so many young Americans of the chance to realize the American Dream.

It is time to mobilize a constituency for change. Who is to be charged with calling   15
a halt to the "push-me, pull-me" tug-of-war game that families are forced to play? The obvious answer is: women, as part of a broad coalition, attending to the unfinished business of feminism.

As *New York Times* columnist Gail Collins concluded in her book *When Everything Changed*, "The feminist movement of the late twentieth century created a new United States in which women ran for president, fought for their country, argued before the Supreme Court, performed heart surgery, directed movies, and flew into space. But it did not resolve the tensions of trying to raise children and hold down a job at the same time. . . . They had not remade the world the way the revolutionaries had hoped."

Do feminists have an obligation to complete their mission of gender equality? Yes, but not single-handedly. The issue of accommodating both work and family has outgrown the parameters of our current perception of feminism. The entire family is affected when women and men cannot find equanimity in their lives: women, men, children, grandparents, and uncles and aunts. The new constituency for work/life policies is inclusive. We have left the female ghetto of family/work issues and moved into every neighborhood.

Women have traditionally led the charge on family issues, in part because of experience: fatigue from too many late-night feedings, red knees from too much scrubbing, and creased brows from too much worrying about where the children are and what they might be doing. Women spoke up because they knew what they were talking about, but more often they were out front because no one else would volunteer. Women remain the key sponsors of legislation affecting women and families, both in Congress and in state legislatures, because they understand the chapters of their own lives. But women alone can no longer complete the mission. We need that other half — men — to march at our sides, linked arm-in arm as we approach the Capitol steps. What demands will we make? Let's translate the easy rhetoric of "family values" into tough action. Enough sweet talk; we want results that will enable us to be good parents, good caregivers, and good workers.

When women try to figure out the conundrum of finding a good match between work and family, we believe it is only a question of balance. We add an ounce or two on one side of the work/life scale, and subtract an ounce from the other. Perfect — for one moment, but not for the next, when a child gets sick or a new supervisor changes the schedule, or there is an unexpected pregnancy. Suddenly we're out of kilter. And the responsibility for being out of balance is ours and ours alone. We have failed.

We are not alone. When we fall, we bring our families down with us. They bear the consequences of either less income or less care, or both. A minority of highly skilled, highly paid women can negotiate paid family leave and flexible schedules, but the majority cannot because they don't have the power to ask without fear of losing their jobs, and they rightly fear that they are easily replaceable. 20

One by one, women's and men's requests for policies that support families have been denied. Demands made by a broad and diverse coalition are harder to ignore. This has been the pattern of change throughout history: when the "I" becomes "we," a cause begins to move from the fringe to the center, as has been exemplified by the social changes brought about by movements for disability rights and gay and lesbian civil rights.

Who are "we"? We are the disparate constituencies — children, women (all women, not only those who call themselves feminists, but also those who shudder at the idea of being called feminists), the elderly, the handicapped, the sick — who can give one loud shout out for change. Such a large chorus will increase the volume, but noise is not enough. To build strong bonds among constituencies that have not often worked together, we have to start by redefining ourselves. Can we mobilize under the banner of Feminists for Families?

(2012)

Questions

1. Madeleine M. Kunin begins with an anecdote about herself and her friends in which she calls attention to her history as a feminist and, hence, her age. What ethos is she establishing with this personal opening?

2. What rhetorical strategies is she employing in paragraphs 2–10 when she lists all the things she "expected"?

3. What concessions does she make to possible counterarguments? How effective is her refutation?

4. What is Kunin's principal claim? This is an argument of policy that calls for a change. What is that change?

5. What does she mean when she writes that we "are beginning to understand the individual cost that the schism between work and family exacts. We have not added up the national cost" (par. 14)? Does she support her statement later in that same paragraph that our inability "to invest in families leaves us vulnerable to being reduced to second-rate status in the global economy"?

6. How does she answer her question, "Do feminists have an obligation to complete their mission of gender equality" (par. 17)?

7. How effective do you find her analogy that her call to action for policies "that support families" is similar to "the social changes brought about by movements for disability rights and gay and lesbian civil rights" (par. 21)?

Making Connections

1. Would Susan B. Anthony (p. 971) more likely be in agreement with the thinking of Florence Kelley (p. 980) or of Marie Jenney Howe (p. 985)? Are there areas of agreement among all three of these women?

2. What similarities do you find between the arguments of Charlotte Perkins Gilman (p. 974) and Thorstein Veblen (p. 976)?

3. In what ways does the passage from *The House of Mirth* by Edith Wharton (p. 978) illustrate the ideas of Gilman or Veblen?

4. What concerns do Kelley and Madeleine M. Kunin (p. 991) share, despite their separation in time of more than a century?

5. In what ways are the graphics *Suffragette Madonna* (p. 983) and *Votes for Women* (p. 985) alike and different in terms of viewpoint and rhetorical strategy?

6. Which of the stereotypes that Howe satirizes do you see in the antisuffragette postcards?

7. Which issues raised by either Anthony or Wharton are touched upon again in Gail Collins's analysis (p. 988) of society's expectations of women at the start of the 1960s?

Entering the Conversation

As you respond to each of the following prompts, support your position with appropriate evidence, including at least three sources in this Conversation on the changing roles of women, unless otherwise indicated.

1. Which of the goals of the early advocates for a more meaningful political and economic role and personal life for women do you believe have been achieved?

2. Some of the authors during the late 1800s and early 1900s advocated social change by arguing that the enfranchisement of women would strengthen the existing culture rather than overturn or even change it. Discuss at least three different arguments put forth to articulate this position. Which do you find the most effective and why?

3. Many of the suffragists emphasized the plight of the working woman and, implicitly or explicitly, argued for a natural alliance between the suffragists and workers. Discuss how the texts in this Conversation argue that the women's suffrage movement would not only benefit women but also all workers and, thus, the entire economy.

4. In the 1960s, during the so-called Women's Liberation Movement, the Virginia Slims cigarette manufacturers launched an advertising campaign with the slogan, "You've come a long way, baby!" This campaign continued for more than a decade, with many of the ads depicting fictional historical events involving women during the suffrage period of the early nineteenth century. Many showed women smoking as an act of rebellion and poked fun at the men who tried to censure them. Ultimately, concern over the health risks of smoking led to shifts in approaches to the ads, but during their heyday this campaign was very successful. Find some of these ads online and discuss how images of women's suffrage were interpreted to serve the purposes of the advertiser.

5. In "The End of Men," an article by Hanna Rosin in the *Atlantic* in 2012, she asks, "What if the postindustrial economy is simply more congenial to women than to men?" Rosin cites the fact that during the recession of 2008, "three quarters of the eight million jobs lost were lost by men," and that many of those jobs in construction and manufacturing are unlikely to return to a position of prominence. Further, Rosin points out that today women outnumber men in colleges and professional schools and that the qualities most valued in the early twenty-first century economy — "social intelligence, open communication, the ability to sit still and focus" — are qualities that women, because of society's prevailing values, are more likely than men to develop. She concludes:

> Yes, the U.S. still has a wage gap, one that can be convincingly explained — at least in part — by discrimination. Yes, women still do most of the child care. And yes,

the upper reaches of society are still dominated by men. But given the power of the forces pushing at the economy, this setup feels like the last gasp of a dying age rather than the permanent establishment. Dozens of college women I interviewed for this story assumed that they very well might be the ones working while their husbands stayed at home, either looking for work or minding the children. Guys, one [college] senior remarked to me, "are the new ball and chain." It may be happening slowly and unevenly, but it's unmistakably happening: in the long view, the modern economy is becoming a place where women hold the cards.

Explain why you agree or disagree with Rosin's argument that the workplace has shifted to favor women.

Conversation

Immigration: The Lure of America

America is a land of immigrants. Unless you are a native American Indian, you are descended from immigrants. While the seventeenth and eighteenth centuries saw fewer than one million immigrants to the United States, most of them from the British Isles, the numbers increased dramatically in the middle of the nineteenth century. During the period between 1840 and 1930, nearly thirty million Europeans came to settle in America. In the first decade of the twentieth century, over a million people came per year.

But immigrants were not always welcome, and throughout our history certain groups have been excluded and citizenship restricted. The U.S. Naturalization Law of 1790 states that "any Alien being a free white person, who shall have resided within the limits and under the jurisdiction of the United States for the term of two years, may be admitted to become a citizen thereof." In 1875, the Page Act, named for California congressman Horace F. Page, specifically restricted Asian immigration in order to end "cheap Chinese labor." The 1882 Chinese Exclusion Act was even more restrictive.

While these early restrictions were attempts to exclude Asians and Africans, new restrictions would apply to Southern and Eastern Europeans. In order to "preserve" the national and ethnic character of the country, the 1921 Emergency Immigration Act restricted the number of immigrants admitted from any country annually to "3 percent of the number of residents from that same country living in the United States," and the Immigration Act of 1924 reduced that to 2 percent.

A national debate on this issue continues to rage today. How open do we want our borders to be? How restrictive should we be? How welcome are immigrants today? What threats do we perceive from immigrants? What contributions can we expect? Is the United States still a melting pot? Is this still the "Promised Land"? What continues to be the lure of America? Consider these questions as you read the sources and enter this Conversation on immigration and the lure of America.

Sources

Emma Lazarus, *The New Colossus* (1883)

Dennis Kearney and H. L. Knight, *Appeal from California. The Chinese Invasion. Workingman's Address* (1878)

Joseph McDonnell, *The Chinese Must Go* (1878)

Joseph Keppler, *Looking Backward* (1893)

Robert H. Clancy, *An Un-American Bill* (1924)

Ellison DuRant Smith, *Shut the Door* (1924)

Mary Gordon, *More than Just a Shrine* (1985)

Charles Bowden, *Our Wall* (2007)

Christoph Niemann, *Promised Land* (2011)

Walter Russell Mead, *America's New Tiger Immigrants* (2012)

The New Colossus

EMMA LAZARUS

> Written in 1883 and engraved on a bronze plaque inside the Statue of Liberty in New York Harbor in 1903, the following sonnet is by Jewish American poet Emma Lazarus (1849–1887).

Not like the brazen giant of Greek fame,
With conquering limbs astride from land to land;
Here at our sea-washed, sunset gates shall stand
A mighty woman with a torch, whose flame
Is the imprisoned lightning, and her name   5
Mother of Exiles. From her beacon-hand
Glows world-wide welcome; her mild eyes command
The air-bridged harbor that twin cities frame.
"Keep, ancient lands, your storied pomp!" cries she
With silent lips. "Give me your tired, your poor,   10
Your huddled masses yearning to breathe free,
The wretched refuse of your teeming shore.
Send these, the homeless, tempest-tost to me,
I lift my lamp beside the golden door!"

(1883)

Questions

1. Notice that Emma Lazarus begins with an image of what the Statue of Liberty is *not* like. How does its contrast with the ancient Colossus of Rhodes affect the meaning of the poem?
2. How do the statue's welcoming words to the oppressed contribute to the American idea of the country as a "melting pot"?
3. Do you see an irony in welcoming the "huddled masses" (l. 11) and "wretched refuse" (l. 12) through the "golden door" (l. 14)? Do you think Americans still hold to that welcoming idea today? Why or why not?

Appeal from California. The Chinese Invasion. Workingman's Address

Dennis Kearney and H. L. Knight

> Dennis Kearney and H. L. Knight were labor leaders, respectively president and secretary of California's Workingmen's Party. In this article, which appeared in the *Indianapolis Times* on February 28, 1878, they argue for the exclusion of Chinese workers.

Our moneyed men have ruled us for the past thirty years. Under the flag of the slave-holder they hoped to destroy our liberty. Failing in that, they have rallied under the banner of the millionaire, the banker and the land monopolist, the railroad king and the false politician, to effect their purpose.

We have permitted them to become immensely rich against all sound republican policy, and they have turned upon us to sting us to death. They have seized upon the government by bribery and corruption. They have made speculation and public robbery a science. They have loaded the nation, the state, the county, and the city with debt. They have stolen the public lands. They have grasped all to themselves, and by their unprincipled greed brought a crisis of unparalleled distress on forty millions of people, who have natural resources to feed, clothe, and shelter the whole human race.

Such misgovernment, such mismanagement, may challenge the whole world for intense stupidity, and would put to shame the darkest tyranny of the barbarous past.

We, here in California, feel it as well as you. We feel that the day and hour has come for the Workingmen of America to depose capital and put Labor in the Presidential chair, in the Senate and Congress, in the State House, and on the Judicial Bench. We are with you in this work. Workingmen must form a party of their own, take charge of the government, dispose gilded fraud, and put honest toil in power.

In our golden state all these evils have been intensified. Land monopoly has   5
seized upon all the best soil in this fair land. A few men own from ten thousand to two hundred thousand acres each. The poor Laborer can find no resting place, save

on the barren mountain, or in the trackless desert. Money monopoly has reached its grandest proportions. Here, in San Francisco, the palace of the millionaire looms up above the hovel of the starving poor with as wide a contrast as anywhere on earth.

To add to our misery and despair, a bloated aristocracy has sent to China — the greatest and oldest despotism in the world — for a cheap working slave. It rakes the slums of Asia to find the meanest slave on earth — the Chinese coolie — and imports him here to meet the free American in the Labor market, and still further widen the breach between the rich and the poor, still further to degrade white Labor.

These cheap slaves fill every place. Their dress is scant and cheap. Their food is rice from China. They hedge twenty in a room, ten by ten. They are whipped curs, abject in docility, mean, contemptible, and obedient in all things. They have no wives, children, or dependents.

They are imported by companies, controlled as serfs, worked like slaves, and at last go back to China with all their earnings. They are in every place, they seem to have no sex. Boys work, girls work; it is all alike to them.

The father of a family is met by them at every turn. Would he get work for himself? Ah! A stout Chinaman does it cheaper. Will he get a place for his oldest boy? He can not. His girl? Why, the Chinaman is in her place too! Every door is closed. He can only go to crime or suicide, his wife and daughter to prostitution, and his boys to hoodlumism and the penitentiary.

Do not believe those who call us savages, rioters, incendiaries, and outlaws. We   10
seek our ends calmly, rationally, at the ballot box. So far good order has marked all our proceedings. But, we know how false, how inhuman, our adversaries are. We know that if gold, if fraud, if force can defeat us, they will all be used. And we have resolved that they shall not defeat us. We shall arm. We shall meet fraud and falsehood with defiance, and force with force, if need be.

We are men, and propose to live like men in this free land, without the contamination of slave labor, or die like men, if need be, in asserting the rights of our race, our country, and our families.

California must be all American or all Chinese. We are resolved that it shall be American, and are prepared to make it so. May we not rely upon your sympathy and assistance?

> With great respect for the Workingman's Party of California.
> Dennis Kearney, President
> H.L. Knight, Secretary
> *(1878)*

Questions

1. Identify three appeals that Dennis Kearney and H. L. Knight make in paragraphs 1–3. How do they contribute to the effectiveness of the argument?

2. How do the authors characterize American workers? How do they characterize Chinese workers?
3. Where do the authors exaggerate? How does the hyperbole affect their position? Is it helpful or dissuasive? Explain.
4. In paragraph 10, the authors shift their stance to address the readers directly. Do you read that paragraph more as a promise or a threat? Explain.
5. What in the piece elicits your sympathy? What elicits your aversion? To what extent do you agree or disagree with the argument presented? Explain.
6. Apply the Toulmin model to the selection. How does that analysis affect your view of the argument?

The Chinese Must Go

JOSEPH McDONNELL

Born in Ireland, Joseph McDonnell became an American labor leader. In this June 30, 1878, editorial in the *New York Labor Standard,* he defends the rights of all workers and argues against exclusion based on nationality.

The cry that the "Chinese must go" is both narrow and unjust. It represents no broad or universal principle. It is merely a repetition of the cry that was raised years ago by native Americans against the immigration of Irishmen, Englishmen, Germans and others from European nations. It now ill becomes those, or the descendants of those, against whom this cry was raised in past years, to raise a similar tocsin against a class of foreigners who have been degraded by ages of oppression.

The "Know Nothing" movement had its REAL origin in the dread of native workmen that they would be undersold in the labor market by the cheap labor of Great Britain, Germany and other European countries. The American workingmen were accustomed to wear better clothes, live in better habitations, eat better food, and consequently, received better wages than the workingmen of Europe. For these reasons they dreaded the immigration of Europeans, whose habits were not so independent, and whose style of living was so inferior, because they saw clearly that the new comers would be satisfied with a rate of wages that would provide them with the class of living they had been accustomed to.

The feeling at the bottom of the "Know Nothing" movement IN ITS EARLY DAYS was certainly a general one against low wages, and if it had raised the cry: "No low wages," "No cheap labor!" instead of sounding the intolerant, silly and shameful cry against Irishmen, Englishmen, Germans and all other "foreigners," it would have accomplished incalculable good. As it was it fell into the hands of infamous, scheming politicians, who pandered to the worst prejudices of the masses by raising a cry against men of various religious faiths and foreign nationalities. This policy suited them; it raised them to prominence and office and allowed what they IN THEIR HEARTS desired, the onward march of low wages.

In our day we must commit no such blunders. We have certainly a right to protect and use every available means against the capitalistic combinations through which thousands of poor and ill-fed beings are imported to this country from China, Italy and elsewhere, but we have no right to raise a cry against any class of human beings because of their nationality. The workingmen of England have given us an example in this respect which we would do well to follow. Instead of raising a cry throughout all England against the American Chinese who have been brought over there to cut down wages, the workingmen have distinctly stated that they welcome workingmen from all nations, and that their warfare is only against the system of low wages and all who support it.

Let us do in a like manner. Let us organize and raise our voices against low wages 5 and long hours. Let us use our organized power against the capitalistic combinations which carry on a slave trade between this country and China and elsewhere, by importing thousands for the purpose of reducing wages in America. Let our first stand be against those rich and intelligent thieves who strive to perpetuate and establish a system of overwork and starvation pay. And then against all those, whether they be Chinese or American, Irish or English, French or German, Spanish or Italian who refuse to cooperate with us for their good and ours, and that of the whole human family.

We must not forget that in Pennsylvania, and other States, where there are no Chinese, there is absolutely a worse state of affairs than exists even in China, and furthermore that America is now doing unto England, what China has been doing unto America.

We favor every effort against the conspiracy of the rich to import cheap labor from Europe and Asia, but we warn the workingmen that no action but International Labor action, and no cry but that of high wages and short hours will lead us into the promised land of peace, plenty and happiness.

(1878)

Questions

1. What is the basis of Joseph McDonnell's appeal in the first paragraph?
2. McDonnell attacks demands for exclusion of Chinese workers. How effectively does his editorial address the argument made by Dennis Kearney and H. L. Knight (p. 999)?
3. Identify the features of classical arrangement (pp. 116–17) that you find in McDonnell's argument. How do they contribute to its effectiveness?
4. McDonnell is an immigrant. How does that information affect his ethos? Explain.
5. What do you consider McDonnell's most compelling statement? Explain why you find it so powerful.
6. Apply the Toulmin model to McDonnell's editorial. How does that analysis affect your view of his argument?

Looking Backward

JOSEPH KEPPLER

The following political cartoon by Vienna-born Austrian American cartoonist Joseph Keppler (1838–1894) appeared on January 11, 1893, in *Puck*, a magazine of humor and satire founded by Keppler and published in St. Louis, Missouri.

(See color insert, Image 32.)

Questions

1. How would you describe the man on the gangplank? The men on the dock? What do the characters depict?
2. What do the shadows behind the figures represent? Explain.
3. How does Joseph Keppler's use of irony contribute to the argument that the cartoon presents?
4. This cartoon was originally accompanied by a caption that read, "They would close to the new-comer the bridge that carried them and their fathers over." Apply the Toulmin model to it. How would you paraphrase the meaning of the cartoon after such an analysis?

An Un-American Bill

ROBERT H. CLANCY

> The following speech was delivered on April 8, 1924, by Congressman Robert H. Clancy of Michigan during the debate over the Johnson Reed Act, which would become U.S. immigration law in 1924. The new law would establish quotas and restrict immigration much more than previous legislation had, effectively banning immigration from Asia.

Since the foundations of the American commonwealth were laid in colonial times over 300 years ago, vigorous complaint and more or less bitter persecution have been aimed at newcomers to our shores. Also the congressional reports of about 1840 are full of abuse of English, Scotch, Welsh immigrants as paupers, criminals, and so forth.

Old citizens in Detroit of Irish and German descent have told me of the fierce tirades and propaganda directed against the great waves of Irish and Germans who came over from 1840 on for a few decades to escape civil, racial, and religious persecution in their native lands.

The "Know-Nothings,"[1] lineal ancestors of the Ku-Klux Klan, bitterly denounced the Irish and Germans as mongrels, scum, foreigners, and a menace to our institutions, much as other great branches of the Caucasian race of glorious history and antecedents are berated to-day. All are riff-raff, unassimilables, "foreign devils," swine not fit to associate with the great chosen people — a form of national pride and hallucination as old as the division of races and nations.

But to-day it is the Italians, Spanish, Poles, Jews, Greeks, Russians, Balkanians, and so forth, who are the racial lepers. And it is eminently fitting and proper that so many Members of this House with names as Irish as Paddy's pig, are taking the floor these days to attack once more as their kind has attacked for seven bloody centuries the fearful fallacy of chosen peoples and inferior peoples. The fearful fallacy is that one is made to rule and the other to be abominated. . . .

In this bill we find racial discrimination at its worst — a deliberate attempt to go back 34 years in our census taken every 10 years so that a blow may be aimed at peoples of eastern and southern Europe, particularly at our recent allies in the Great War — Poland and Italy. 5

Jews in Detroit Are Good Citizens

Of course the Jews too are aimed at, not directly, because they have no country in Europe they can call their own, but they are set down among the inferior peoples. Much of the animus against Poland and Russia, old and new, with the countries that

---

[1] A nineteenth-century anti-immigrant political party. Members who were asked about the secret organization were supposed to respond, "I know nothing." — Eds.

have arisen from the ruins of the dead Czar's European dominions, is directed against the Jew.

We have many American citizens of Jewish descent in Detroit, tens of thousands of them — active in every profession and every walk of life. They are particularly active in charities and merchandising. One of our greatest judges, if not the greatest, is a Jew. Surely no fair-minded person with a knowledge of the facts can say the Jews of Detroit are a menace to the city's or the country's well-being. . . .

Italian Citizens Are Not Inferior

Forty or fifty thousand Italian-Americans live in my district in Detroit. They are found in all walks and classes of life — common hard labor, the trades, business, law, medicine, dentistry, art, literature, banking, and so forth.

They rapidly become Americanized, build homes, and make themselves into good citizens. They brought hardihood, physique, hope, and good humor with them from their outdoor life in Sunny Italy, and they bear up under the terrific strain of life and work in busy Detroit.

One finds them by thousands digging streets, sewers, and building foundations, 10 and in the automobile and iron and steel fabric factories of various sorts. They do the hard work that the native-born American dislikes. Rapidly they rise in life and join the so-called middle and upper classes. . . .

The Italian-Americans of Detroit played a glorious part in the Great War. They showed themselves as patriotic as the native born in offering the supreme sacrifice.

In all, I am informed, over 300,000 Italian-speaking soldiers enlisted in the American Army, almost 10 per cent of our total fighting force. Italians formed about 4 per cent of the population of the United States and they formed 10 per cent of the American military force. Their casualties were 12 per cent. . . .

Detroit Satisfied with the Poles

I wish to take the liberty of informing the House that from my personal knowledge and observation of tens of thousands of Polish-Americans living in my district in Detroit that their Americanism and patriotism are unassailable from any fair or just standpoint.

The Polish-Americans are as industrious and as frugal and as loyal to our institutions as any class of people who have come to the shores of this country in the past 300 years. They are essentially home builders, and they have come to this country to stay. They learn the English language as quickly as possible, and take pride in the rapidity with which they become assimilated and adopt our institutions.

Figures available to all show that in Detroit in the World War the proportion of 15 American volunteers of Polish blood was greater than the proportion of Americans of any other racial descent. . . .

Polish-Americans do not merit slander nor defamation. If not granted charitable or sympathetic judgment, they are at least entitled to justice and to the high place they have won in American and European history and citizenship.

The forces behind the Johnson bill and some of its champions in Congress charge that opposition to the racial discrimination feature of the 1890 quota basis arises from "foreign blocs." They would give the impression that 100 per cent Americans are for it and that the sympathies of its opponents are of the "foreign-bloc" variety, and bear stigma of being "hyphenates." I meet that challenge willingly. I feel my Americanism will stand any test.

Every American Had Foreign Ancestors

The foreign born of my district writhe under the charge of being called "hyphenates." The people of my own family were all hyphenates — English-Americans, German-Americans, Irish-Americans. They began to come in the first ship or so after the *Mayflower*. But they did not come too early to miss the charge of anti-Americanism. Roger Williams was driven out of the Puritan colony of Salem to die in the wilderness because he objected "violently" to blue laws and the burning or hanging of rheumatic old women on witchcraft charges. He would not "assimilate" and was "a grave menace to American institutions and democratic government."

My family put 11 men and boys into the Revolutionary War, and I am sure they and their women and children did not suffer so bitterly and sacrifice until it hurt to establish the autocracy of bigotry and intolerance which exists in many quarters to-day in this country. Some of these men and boys shed their blood and left their bodies to rot on American battle fields. To me real Americanism and the American flag are the product of the blood of men and of the tears of women and children of a different type than the rampant "Americanizers" of to-day.

My mother's father fought in the Civil War, leaving his six small children in Detroit when he marched away to the southern battle fields to fight against racial distinctions and protect his country. 20

My mother's little brother, about 14 years old, and the eldest child, fired by the traditions of his family, plodded off to the battle fields to do his bit. He aspired to be a drummer boy and inspire the men in battle, but he was found too small to carry a drum and was put at the ignominious task of driving army mules, hauling cannons and wagons.

I learned more of the spirit of American history at my mother's knee than I ever learned in my four years of high-school study of American history and in my five and a half years of study at the great University of Michigan.

All that study convinces me that the racial discriminations of this bill are un-American. . . .

It must never be forgotten also that the Johnson bill, although it claims to favor the northern and eastern European peoples only, does so on a basis of comparison with the southern and eastern European peoples. The Johnson bill cuts down materially the number of immigrants allowed to come from northern and western Europe, the so-called Nordic peoples. . . .

Then I would be true to the principles for which my forefathers fought and true   25
to the real spirit of the magnificent United States of to-day. I can not stultify myself by voting for the present bill and overwhelm my country with racial hatreds and racial lines and antagonisms drawn even tighter than they are to-day. [Applause.]

(1924)

Questions

1. In the fourth paragraph, Congressman Robert H. Clancy refers to "Italians, Spanish, Poles, Jews, Greeks, Russians, Balkanians, and so forth, who are the racial lepers." Why do you think he uses the phrase "racial lepers"? Is such language appropriate? What might be the response if a congressperson used such language today? Explain.
2. Clancy specifically considers the cases of Jews, Italians, and Poles. How effectively do these examples support his position?
3. What is the rhetorical effect of Clancy's reference to Roger Williams (par. 18)?
4. Does Clancy's reference to his own family appeal to ethos, logos, or pathos? Explain.
5. Congressman Clancy says that "the racial discriminations of this bill are un-American" (par. 23). How effectively has he supported that claim?

Shut the Door

Ellison DuRant Smith

The following speech was delivered on April 9, 1924, by Senator Ellison DuRant Smith of South Carolina during the debate over the Johnson Reed Act, which would become U.S. immigration law in 1924.

It seems to me the point as to this measure — and I have been so impressed for several years — is that the time has arrived when we should shut the door. We have been called the melting pot of the world. We had an experience just a few years ago, during the great World War, when it looked as though we had allowed influences to enter our borders that were about to melt the pot in place of us being the melting pot.

I think that we have sufficient stock in America now for us to shut the door, Americanize what we have, and save the resources of America for the natural increase of our population. We all know that one of the most prolific causes of war is the desire for increased land ownership for the overflow of a congested population. We are increasing at such a rate that in the natural course of things in a comparatively few years the landed resources, the natural resources of the country, shall be taken up by the natural increase of our population. It seems to me the part of wisdom now that we have throughout the length and breadth of continental America a population which is beginning to encroach upon the reserve and virgin resources of the country to keep it in trust for the multiplying population of the country.

I do not believe that political reasons should enter into the discussion of this very vital question. It is of greater concern to us to maintain the institutions of America, to maintain the principles upon which this Government is founded, than to develop and exploit the undeveloped resources of the country. There are some things that are dearer to us, fraught with more benefit to us, than the immediate development of the undeveloped resources of the country. I believe that our particular ideas, social, moral, religious, and political, have demonstrated, by virtue of the progress we have made and the character of people that we are, that we have the highest ideals of any member of the human family or any nation. We have demonstrated the fact that the human family, certainly the predominant breed in America, can govern themselves by a direct government of the people. If this Government shall fail, it shall fail by virtue of the terrible law of inherited tendency. Those who come from the nations which from time immemorial have been under the dictation of a master fall more easily by the law of inheritance and the inertia of habit into a condition of political servitude than the descendants of those who cleared the forests, conquered the savage, stood at arms and won their liberty from their mother country, England.

I think we now have sufficient population in our country for us to shut the door and to breed up a pure, unadulterated American citizenship. I recognize that there is a dangerous lack of distinction between people of a certain nationality and the breed of the dog. Who is an American? Is he an immigrant from Italy? Is he an immigrant from Germany? If you were to go abroad and some one were to meet you and say, "I met a typical American," what would flash into your mind as a typical American, the typical representative of that new Nation? Would it be the son of an Italian immigrant, the son of a German immigrant, the son of any of the breeds from the Orient, the son of the denizens of Africa? We must not get our ethnological distinctions mixed up with our anthropological distinctions. It is the breed of the dog in which I am interested. I would like for the Members of the Senate to read that book just recently published by Madison Grant, *The Passing of a Great Race*. Thank God we have in America perhaps the largest percentage of any country in the world of the pure, unadulterated Anglo-Saxon stock; certainly the greatest of any nation in the Nordic breed. It is for the preservation of that splendid stock that has characterized us that I would make this not an asylum for the oppressed of all countries, but a country to assimilate and perfect that splendid type of manhood that has made America the foremost Nation in her progress and in her power, and yet the youngest of all the nations. I myself believe that the preservation of her institutions depends upon us now taking counsel with our condition and our experience during the last World War.

Without offense, but with regard to the salvation of our own, let us shut the door and assimilate what we have, and let us breed pure American citizens and develop our own American resources. I am more in favor of that than I am of our quota proposition. Of course, it may not meet the approbation of the Senate that we shall shut the door — which I unqualifiedly and unreservedly believe to be our duty — and develop what we have, assimiliate and digest what we have into pure Americans, with American aspirations, and thoroughly familiar with the love of American institutions, rather than the importation of any number of men from other countries. If we may not have that, then I am in favor of putting the quota down to the lowest possible point, with every selective element in it that may be.

The great desideratum of modern times has been education not alone book knowledge, but that education which enables men to think right, to think logically, to think truthfully, men equipped with power to appreciate the rapidly developing conditions that are all about us, that have converted the world in the last 50 years into a brand new world and made us masters of forces that are revolutionizing production. We want men not like dumb, driven cattle from those nations where the progressive thought of the times has scarcely made a beginning and where they see men as mere machines; we want men who have an appreciation of the power of the individual and a like appreciation of the responsibility brought about by the manifestation of the power of that individual. We have not that in this country to-day. We have men here to-day who are selfishly utilizing the enormous forces discovered by genius, and if we are not careful as statesmen, if we are not careful in our legislation, these very masters of the tremendous forces that have been made available to us will bring us under their domination and control by virtue of the power they have in multiplying their wealth.

We are struggling to-day against the organized forces of man's brain multiplied a million times by materialized thought in the form of steam and electricity as applied in the everyday affairs of man. We have enough in this country to engage the brain of every lover of his country in solving the problems of a democratic government in the midst of the imperial power that genius is discovering and placing in the hands of man. We have population enough to-day without throwing wide our doors and jeopardizing the interests of this country by pouring into it men who willingly become the slaves of those who employ them in manipulating these forces of nature, and they few reap the enormous benefits that accrue therefrom.

We ought to Americanize not only our population but our forces. We ought to Americanize our factories and our vast material resources, so that we can make each contribute to the other and have an abundance for us under the form of the government laid down by our fathers.

The Senator from Georgia [Mr. Harris] has introduced an amendment to shut the door. It is not a question of politics. It is a question of maintaining that which has made you and me the beneficiaries of the greatest hope that ever burned in the human breast for the most splendid future that ever stood before mankind, where the boy in the gutter can look with confidence to the seat of the Presidency of the United States; where the boy in the gutter can look forward to the time when, paying the price of a proper citizen, he may fill a seat in this hall; where the boy to-day poverty-stricken, standing in the midst of all the splendid opportunities of America, should have and, please God, if we do our duty, will have an opportunity to enjoy the marvelous wealth that the genius and brain of our country is making possible for us all.

We do not want to tangle the skein of America's progress by those who imperfectly understand the genius of our Government and the opportunities that lie about

10

us. Let us keep what we have, protect what we have, make what we have the realization of the dream of those who wrote the Constitution.

I am more concerned about that than I am about whether a new railroad shall be built or whether there shall be diversified farming next year or whether a certain coal mine shall be mined. I would rather see American citizenship refined to the last degree in all that makes America what we hope it will be than to develop the resources of America at the expense of the citizenship of our country. The time has come when we should shut the door and keep what we have for what we hope our own people to be.

(1924)

Questions

1. In the third paragraph, Ellison DuRant Smith mentions four ideas. What are they? In your view, which of them are supported by the content of his speech?
2. Look particularly closely at the diction Senator Smith uses in paragraph 4. List several examples of powerful diction. What is the nature of the imagery developed by his word choices? How do you respond to them? How do you think his audience might have reacted to them?
3. Does Senator Smith offer to compromise? Explain.
4. What appeals does Smith make in paragraph 9? How effective are they?
5. What assumptions does Smith make in paragraphs 3, 6, and 10? How do they affect the cogency of his arguments?

More than Just a Shrine

MARY GORDON

> The following essay by journalist and novelist Mary Gordon appeared in the *New York Times Magazine* on November 3, 1985.

I once sat in a hotel in Bloomsbury trying to have breakfast alone. A Russian with a habit of compulsively licking his lips asked if he could join me. I was afraid to say no; I thought it might be bad for detente. He explained to me that he was a linguist, and that he always liked to talk to Americans to see if he could make any connection between their speech and their ethnic background. When I told him about my mixed ancestry — my mother is Irish and Italian, my father a Lithuanian Jew — he began jumping up and down in his seat, rubbing his hands together and licking his lips even more frantically.

"Ah," he said, "so you are really somebody who comes from what is called the boiling pot of America." Yes, I told him, yes I was, but I quickly rose to leave. I thought it would be too hard to explain to him the relation of the boiling potters to the main course, and I wanted to get to the British Museum. I told him that the only thing I could think of that united people whose backgrounds, histories, and points of view were utterly diverse was that their people had landed at a place called Ellis Island.

I didn't tell him that Ellis Island was the only American landmark I'd ever visited. How could I describe to him the estrangement I'd always felt from the kind of traveler who visits shrines to America's past greatness, those rebuilt forts with muskets behind glass and sabers mounted on the walls and gift shops selling maple sugar candy in the shape of Indian headdresses, those reconstructed villages with tables set for 50 and the Paul Revere silver gleaming? All that Americana — Plymouth Rock, Gettysburg, Mount Vernon, Valley Forge — it all inhabits for me a zone of blurred abstraction with far less hold on my imagination than the Bastille or Hampton Court. I suppose I've always known that my uninterest in it contains a large component of the willed: I am American, and those places purport to be my history. But they are not mine.

Ellis Island is, though; it's the one place I can be sure my people are connected to. And so I made a journey there to find my history, like any Rotarian[1] traveling in his Winnebago to Antietam to find his. I had become part of that humbling democracy of people looking in some site for a past that has grown unreal. The monument I traveled to was not, however, a tribute to some old glory. The minute I set foot upon the island I could feel all that it stood for: insecurity, obedience, anxiety, dehumanization, the terrified and careful deference of the displaced. I hadn't traveled to the Battery and boarded a ferry across from the Statue of Liberty to raise flags or breathe a richer, more triumphant air. I wanted to do homage to the ghosts.

I felt them everywhere, from the moment I disembarked and saw the building with its high-minded brick, its hopeful little lawn, its ornamental cornices. The place was derelict when I arrived; it had not functioned for more than 30 years — almost as long as the time it had operated at full capacity as a major immigration center. I was surprised to learn what a small part of history Ellis Island had occupied. The main building was constructed in 1892, then rebuilt between 1898 and 1900 after a fire. Most of the immigrants who arrived during the latter half of the 19th century, mainly northern and western Europeans, landed not at Ellis Island but on the western tip of the Battery at Castle Garden, which had opened as a receiving center for immigrants in 1855.

By the 1880s the facilities at Castle Garden had grown scandalously inadequate. Officials looked for an island on which to build a new immigration center because they thought that on an island immigrants could be more easily protected from swindlers and quickly transported to railroad terminals in New Jersey. Bedloe's Island was considered, but New Yorkers were aghast at the idea of a "Babel" ruining their beautiful new treasure, *Liberty Enlightening the World*. The statue's sculptor, Frederic Auguste Bartholdi, reacted to the prospect of immigrants landing near his masterpiece in horror; he called it a "monstrous plan." So much for Emma Lazarus.

Ellis Island was finally chosen because the citizens of New Jersey petitioned the federal government to remove from the island an old naval powder magazine that

[1]Member of the Rotary Club, a popular service organization. — Eds.

5

they thought dangerously close to the Jersey shore. The explosives were removed; no one wanted the island for anything. It was the perfect place to build an immigration center.

I thought about the island's history as I walked into the building and made my way to the room that was the center in my imagination of the Ellis Island experience: the Great Hall. It had been made real for me in the stark, accusing photographs of Louis Hine and others who took those pictures to make a point. It was in the Great Hall that everyone had waited — waiting, always, the great vocation of the dispossessed. The room was empty, except for me and a handful of other visitors and the Park Ranger who showed us around. I felt myself grow insignificant in that room, with its huge semicircular windows, its air, even in dereliction, of solid and official probity.

I walked in the deathlike expansiveness of the room's disuse and tried to think of what it might have been like, filled and swarming. More than 16 million immigrants came through that room; approximately 250,000 were rejected. Not really a large proportion, but the implications for the rejected were dreadful. For some, there was nothing to go back to, or there was certain death; for others, who left as adventurers, to return would be to adopt in local memory the fool's role, and the failure's. No wonder that the island's history includes reports of 3,000 suicides.

Sometimes immigrants could pass through Ellis Island in mere hours, though for some the process took days. The particulars of the experience in the Great Hall were often influenced by the political events and attitudes on the mainland. In the 1890s and the first years of the new century, when cheap labor was needed, the newly built receiving center took in its immigrants with comparatively little question. But as the century progressed, the economy worsened, eugenics became both scientifically respectable and popular and World War I made American xenophobia seem rooted in fact.

Immigration acts were passed; newcomers had to prove, besides moral correctness and financial solvency, their ability to read. Quota laws came into effect, limiting the number of immigrants from southern and eastern Europe to less than 14 percent of the total quota. Intelligence tests were biased against all non-English-speaking persons and medical examinations became increasingly strict, until the machinery of immigration nearly collapsed under its own weight. The Second Quota Law of 1924 provided that all immigrants be inspected and issued visas at American consular offices in Europe, rendering the center almost obsolete.

On the day of my visit, my mind fastened upon the medical inspections, which had always seemed to me most emblematic of the ignominy and terror the immigrants endured. The medical inspectors, sometimes dressed in uniforms like soldiers, were particularly obsessed with a disease of the eyes called trachoma, which they checked for by flipping back the immigrants' top eyelids with a hook used for buttoning gloves — a method that sometimes resulted in the transmission of the disease to healthy people. Mothers feared that if their children cried too much, their red eyes would be mistaken for a symptom of the disease and the whole family would be sent

10

home. Those immigrants suspected of some physical disability had initials chalked on their coats. I remembered the photographs I'd seen of people standing, dumb-struck and innocent as cattle, with their manifest numbers hung around their necks and initials marked in chalk upon their coats: "E" for eye trouble, "K" for hernia, "L" for lameness, "X" for mental defects, "H" for heart disease.

I thought of my grandparents as I stood in the room; my 17-year-old grand-mother, coming alone from Ireland in 1896, vouched for by a stranger who had found her a place as a domestic servant to some Irish who had done well. I tried to imagine the assault it all must have been for her; I've been to her hometown, a collec-tion of farms with a main street — smaller than the athletic field of my local public school. She must have watched the New York skyline as the first- and second-class passengers were whisked off the gangplank with the most cursory of inspections while she was made to board a ferry to the new immigration center.

What could she have made of it — this buff-painted wooden structure with its towers and its blue slate roof, a place *Harper's Weekly* described as "a latter-day water-ing place hotel"? It would have been the first time she'd have heard people speaking something other than English. She would have mingled with people carrying baskets on their heads and eating foods unlike any she had ever seen — dark-eyed people, like the Sicilian she would marry 10 years later, who came over with his family at 13, the man of the family, responsible even then for his mother and sister. I don't know what they thought, my grandparents, for they were not expansive people, nor romantic; they didn't like to think of what they called "the hard times," and their trip across the ocean was the single adventurous act of lives devoted after landing to security, respect-ability and fitting in.

What is the potency of Ellis Island for someone like me — an American, obvi-   15
ously, but one who has always felt that the country really belonged to the early settlers, that, as J. F. Powers wrote in *Morte D'Urban*, it had been "handed down to them by the Pilgrims, George Washington and others, and that they were taking a risk in letting you live in it." I have never been the victim of overt discrimination; nothing I have wanted has been denied me because of the accidents of blood. But I suppose it is part of being an American to be engaged in a somewhat tiresome but always self-absorbing process of national definition. And in this process, I have found in traveling to Ellis Island an important piece of evidence that could remind me I was right to feel my differentness. Something had happened to my people on that island, a result of the eternal wrongheadedness of American protectionism and the predictabilities of simple greed. I came to the island, too, so I could tell the ghosts that I was one of them, and that I honored them — their stoicism, and their innocence, the fear that turned them inward, and their pride. I wanted to tell them that I liked them better than the Americans who made them pass through the Great Hall and stole their names and chalked their weaknesses in public on their clothing. And to tell the ghosts what I have always thought: that American history was a very classy party that was not much fun until they arrived, brought the good food, turned up the music and taught everyone to dance.

(1985)

Questions

1. How does Mary Gordon establish her ethos in the first paragraph?
2. How does the author characterize Ellis Island? Based on your reading or experience, does her description of the place match your impression?
3. What is the rhetorical effect of Gordon's shift to personal experience in paragraph 13?
4. Gordon writes, "But I suppose it is part of being an American to be engaged in a somewhat tiresome but always self-absorbing process of national definition" (par. 15). Do you agree? Why or why not?
5. What does Gordon imply about America with her final sentence?

Our Wall

CHARLES BOWDEN

The following is an excerpt from an essay by American journalist Charles Bowden that appeared in *National Geographic* magazine in May 2007.

A border wall seems to violate a deep sense of identity most Americans cherish. We see ourselves as a nation of immigrants with our own goddess, the Statue of Liberty, a symbol so potent that dissident Chinese students fabricated a version of it in 1989 in Tiananmen Square as the visual representation of their yearning for freedom.

Walls are curious statements of human needs. Sometimes they are built to keep restive populations from fleeing. The Berlin Wall was designed to keep citizens from escaping from communist East Germany. But most walls are for keeping people out. They all work for a while, until human appetites or sheer numbers overwhelm them. The Great Wall of China, built mostly after the mid-14th century, kept northern tribes at bay until the Manchu conquered China in the 17th century. Hadrian's Wall, standing about 15 feet (5 meters) high, 9 feet (3 meters) wide, and 73 miles (117 kilometers) long, kept the crazed tribes of what is now Scotland from running amok in Roman Britain — from A.D. 122 until it was overrun in 367. Then you have the Maginot Line, a series of connected forts built by France after World War I to keep the German army from invading. It was a success, except for one flaw: The troops of the Third Reich simply went around its northwestern end and invaded France through the Netherlands and Belgium. Now tourists visit its labyrinth of tunnels and underground barracks.

In 1859 a rancher named Thomas Austin released 24 rabbits in Australia because, he noted, "the introduction of a few rabbits could do little harm and might provide a touch of home, in addition to a spot of hunting." By that simple act, he launched one of the most extensive barriers ever erected by human beings: the rabbit fences of Australia, which eventually reached 2,023 miles (3,256 kilometers). Within 35 years, the rabbits had overrun the continent, a place lacking sufficient and dedicated rabbit predators. For a century and a half, the Australian government has tried various solutions: imported fleas, poisons, trappers. Nothing has dented the new immigrants. The fences themselves failed almost instantly — rabbits expanded faster than the barriers could be built, careless people left gates open, holes appeared, and, of course, the rabbits simply dug under them.

In Naco all the walls of the world are present in one compact bundle. You have Hadrian's Wall or the Great Wall of China because the barrier is intended to keep people out. You have the Maginot Line because a 15-minute walk takes you to the end of the existing steel wall. You have the rabbit fences of Australia because people still come north illegally, as do the drugs.

Perhaps the closest thing to the wall going up on the U.S.-Mexico border is the   5
separation wall being built by Israel in the West Bank. Like the new American wall, it is designed to control the movement of people, but it faces the problem of all walls — rockets can go over it, tunnels can go under it. It offends people, it comforts people, it fails to deliver security. And it keeps expanding.

Rodolfo Santos Esquer puts out *El Mirador*, a weekly newspaper in Naco, Sonora, and he finds the wall hateful. He stands in his cramped office — a space he shares with a small shop peddling underwear — and says, "It looks like the Berlin Wall. It is horrible. It is ugly. You feel more racism now. It is a racist wall. If people get close to the wall, the Border Patrol calls the Mexican police, and they go and question people."

And then he lightens up because he is a sunny man, and he says it actually hasn't changed his life or the lives of most people in town. Except that the coyotes[1] now drive to the end of the wall before crossing. And as the wall grows in length, the coyotes raise their rates. Santos figures half the town is living off migrants going north — either feeding them and housing them or guiding them into the U.S. Passage to Phoenix, about 200 miles (320 kilometers) away, is now $1,500 and rising. He notes that after the wall went up in 1996, the migration mushroomed. He wonders if there is a connection, if the wall magically beckons migrants. Besides, he says, people just climb over it with ropes.

Santos fires up his computer and shows an image he snapped in the cemetery of a nearby town. There, there, he points as he enlarges a section of the photo. Slowly a skull-shaped blur floats into view against the black of the night — a ghost, he believes. The border is haunted by ghosts — the hundreds who die each year from heat and cold, the ones killed in car wrecks as the packed vans of migrants flee the Border Patrol, and the increasing violence erupting between smugglers and the agents of Homeland Security. Whenever heat is applied to one part of the border, the migration simply moves to another part. The walls in southern California drove immigrants into the Arizona desert and, in some cases, to their deaths. We think of walls as statements of foreign policy, and we forget the intricate lives of the people we wall in and out.

---

[1] People who smuggle immigrants across the border for a fee. — Eds.

Emanuel Castillo Erúnez, 23, takes crime and car wreck photos for *El Mirador*. He went north illegally when he was 17, walked a few days, then was picked up and returned to Mexico. He sits on a bench in the plaza, shielded by a New York Yankees cap, and sums up the local feeling about the wall simply: "Some are fine with it, some are not." He thinks of going north again, but then he thinks of getting caught again. And so he waits.

There is a small-town languor about Naco, Sonora, and the wall becomes 10 unnoticeable in this calm. The Minutemen and National Guard terrify people. At the Hospedaje Santa María, four people wait for a chance to go over the wall and illegally enter the wealth of the United States. It is a run-down, two-story building, one of many boarding houses for migrants in Naco. Salvador Rivera, a solid man in his early 30, has been here about a year. He worked in Washington State, but, when his mother fell ill, he returned home to Nayarit, Mexico, and is now having trouble getting past the increased security. He left behind an American girlfriend he can no longer reach.

"For so many years, we Mexicans have gone to the U.S. to work. I don't understand why they put up a wall to turn us away. It's not like we're robbing anybody over there, and they don't pay us very much."

But talk of the wall almost has to be prompted. Except for those engaged in smuggling drugs or people, border crossers in Naco, Sonora, continue to enter through the main gate, as they always have. They visit relatives on the other side, as they always have. What has changed is this physical statement, a big wall lined with bright lights, that says, yes, we are two nations.

Jesús Gastelum Ramírez lives next door to the wall, makes neon signs, and looks like Willie Nelson. He watches people climb the wall and he understands a reality forgotten by most U.S. lawmakers — that simply to go through the wire instantly raises a person's income tenfold. Gastelum knows many of his neighbors smuggle people, and he understands.

Until recently, a volleyball team from the Mexican Naco and a team from the U.S. Naco used to meet once a year at the point where the wall ends on the west side of town, put up a net on the line, bring kegs of beer, and play a volleyball game. People from both Nacos would stream out to the site and watch. And then the wall would no longer exist for a spell. But it always confronts the eye.

Dan Duley, 50, operates heavy equipment and is a native of the Naco area. He 15 was living in Germany after serving in the Air Force when the Berlin Wall came down, and he thought that was a fine thing. But here he figures something has to be done. "We need help," he says. "We're being invaded. They've taken away our jobs, our security. I'm just a blue-collar man living in a small town. And I just wish the government cared about a man who was blue."

But then, as in many conversations on the border, the rhetoric calms down. Duley, along with many other Naco residents, believes the real solution has to be economic, that jobs must be created in Mexico. There is an iron law on this border: The closer one gets to the line, the more rational the talk becomes because everyone has personal ties to people on the other side. Everyone realizes the wall is a police solution to an economic problem. The Mexicans will go over it, under it, or try to tear holes in it. Or, as is often the case, enter legally with temporary visiting papers and then melt into American communities. Of the millions of illegal immigrants living in the United States, few would have come if there wasn't a job waiting for them.

(2007)

Questions

1. Why does Charles Bowden begin with a discussion of different borders and walls before focusing on the wall between the United States and Mexico?
2. Bowden offers the perspectives of Rodolfo Santos Esquer, Emanuel Castillo Erúnez, Salvador Rivera, and Dan Duley. How do those perspectives differ? Which one resonates most with you? Why?
3. Bowden says that there is "a reality forgotten by most U.S. lawmakers — that simply to go through the wire instantly raises a person's income tenfold" (par. 13). He also says, "Everyone realizes the wall is a police solution to an economic problem" (par. 16). What are the implications of these statements? Do you think the tension on the Mexico-U.S. border is an issue of law and order or of economics? Explain.
4. What does the wall suggest about American identity and character?

Promised Land

CHRISTOPH NIEMANN

The cartoon on the next page by illustrator and author Christoph Niemann appeared on the cover of the *New Yorker* magazine on November 28, 2011.

Questions

1. What do you see in the cartoon? How would you describe what it depicts?
2. How does the cartoon use analogy to make its point?
3. About *Promised Land*, Christoph Niemann says, "Too often in politics, very complex subjects are being turned into sound bites, so it's easy to take them apart. . . . Cartoonists, not politicians, should be the ones who condense political discussions into simple images." Has the cartoonist succeeded with his stated objective? Explain.
4. How would you paraphrase the message of the cartoon according to the Toulmin model?
5. What might a Native American say about *Promised Land*? Explain.

Copyright © Condé Nast. From *The New Yorker* Magazine. All rights reserved. Cover by Christoph Niemann. Reprinted by Permission.

(See color insert, Image 33.)

America's New Tiger Immigrants

WALTER RUSSELL MEAD

Walter Russell Mead is professor of foreign affairs at Bard College and editor at large of *American Interest* magazine. The following article appeared in the *Wall Street Journal* on June 30, 2012.

No Country on earth is in the same league as the U.S. when it comes to the quantity of immigrants who have come here and the quality of their contributions. But lately, in our generally sour mood, Americans have been questioning the benefits of immigration. Many worry that today's immigrants differ from those of the past: less ambitious, less skilled, less willing and able to assimilate.

The conventional picture is of an unstoppable wave of unskilled, mostly Spanish-speaking workers — many illegal — coming across the Mexican border. People who see immigration this way fear that, instead of America assimilating the immigrants, the immigrants will assimilate us. But this picture is both out of date and factually wrong.

A report released this month by the Pew Research Center shows just how much the face of immigration has changed in the past few years. Since 2008, more newcomers to the U.S. have been Asian than Hispanic (in 2010, it was 36% of the total, versus 31%). Today's typical immigrant is not only more likely to speak English and have a college education, but also to have come to the U.S. legally, with a job already in place.

What's responsible for the change? The reasons include a rapidly falling birthrate in Mexico, dramatic economic growth there and the collapse of the U.S. residential construction industry — a traditional market for low-skilled, non-English speaking immigrants whose documentation was often subject to question.

A great deal of mythology has grown up around American immigration. Images of 5 Irish and Italians forced by starvation to emigrate, Jews fleeing Russian persecution — this was all real, but just part of the story. Waves of educated and professional middle-class people also arrived — men like Albert Gallatin fleeing the radicalism of the French Revolution, disappointed liberals abandoning Europe after the failure of the revolutions of 1848, and of course the generations of educated exiles from the terrible totalitarianisms of the 20th century.

America needs and benefits from both kinds of immigration. Like all waves, the Asian influx mixes the skilled and the unskilled. But overall it resembles earlier waves of educated and already urbanized immigrants more than the desperate and often unskilled rural groups from Europe and Latin America.

The Pew study found that the new Asian immigrants identify themselves, surprisingly, as 22% Protestant and 19% Catholic, but whatever their religion, most of them have in spades what Max Weber called the Protestant work ethic. Arguably, in America's long history of immigration, the group that the new immigrants resemble most is the original cohort of Puritans who settled New England.

Like them, the Asians tend to be better-educated than most of the people in their countries of origin. Steeped in the culture of enterprise and capitalism, they're more likely than native-born Americans to have a bachelor of arts degree. While family sponsorship is still the most important entry route for Asians (as for all immigrants), this group is three times more likely than other recent immigrants to come to the U.S. on visas arranged through employers.

In many cases, they're not coming to the U.S. because of the economic conditions back home. After all, places like China, Korea, and India have experienced jumps in prosperity and an explosion in opportunity for the skilled and the hardworking. But most of the new immigrants like it here and want to stay (only 12% wish they had stayed home).

More Asian-Americans (69%) than other Americans (58%) believe that you will   10
get ahead with hard work. Also 93% say that their ethnic group is "hardworking."

There also seems to be some truth in the "Tiger Mom" syndrome described by author Amy Chua. While 39% of Asian-Americans say their group puts "too much" pressure on kids to succeed in school, 60% of Asian-Americans think that other Americans don't push their kids hard enough.

Other family values are strong as well, according to Pew. Only 16% of Asian-American babies are born out of wedlock, in contrast to 41% for the general population. In the U.S., 63% of all children grow up in a household with two parents; the figure for Asian-Americans is 80%. Some 66% of Asian-Americans believe parents should have some input into what careers their children select and 61% think that parents have something useful to say about their children's choice of a spouse. The hard work and strong family values appear to pay off: Asian-Americans' median household income is $66,000 (national median: $49,800) and their median household wealth is $83,500 (national median: $68,529).

Nor does the community seem to be inward-looking or unwilling to assimilate. While just over half of first-generation Asian immigrants say that they speak English "very well," 95% of those born in the U.S. say they do. Only 17% of second-generation Asian-Americans say that their friends are mostly members of their own ethnic group.

Perhaps reflecting this social integration, Asian-Americans are the most likely of all American racial groups to marry outside their own race: 29% married non-Asians between 2008 and 2010; the comparable figure for Hispanics was 26%, for blacks 17% and for whites 9%.

Immigration from Asia wasn't always this smooth, and for many years the fed-   15
eral government, often prodded by politicians from the West Coast, tried to keep Asians out. By 1870, Chinese workers accounted for 20% of California's labor force; the Chinese Exclusion Act of 1882 cut Chinese immigration from 39,500 that year to just 10 people in 1887.

With the Chinese excluded, thousands of Japanese, Koreans and Indians replaced them as cheap labor, but public opinion soon turned against these immigrants as well. In 1906 the San Francisco school board ordered the segregation of Japanese students in its public schools. The news sparked riots in Japan, and President Theodore Roosevelt scrambled to make what was called the "Gentleman's Agreement" by which the Japanese government agreed to stop immigration to the U.S. In 1917 India was added to the "Pacific-Barred Zone" from which no immigrants to the U.S. were allowed, and from 1924 until 1965 Asian immigration into the United States was essentially banned.

The ensuing 37 years of legal immigration are making an impact. In 1965, Asian-Americans accounted for less than 1% of the population; today they are almost at 6% and growing, with the biggest numbers from China, the Philippines and India, followed by Vietnam, Korea and Japan. (Almost one out of four Asian-Americans has roots in either mainland China or Taiwan.)

The honor roll of American immigration is long. Names like Alexander Hamilton, Albert Einstein, Andrew Carnegie, Madeleine Albright and Sergey Brin speak for themselves. Those who worry today whether we have what it takes to meet the challenges of this new and difficult century need to look at the people who continue to join their fates to ours. The world's best, the world's hardest-working and the world's most ambitious are still coming our way.

(2012)

Questions

1. Walter Russell Mead says that the conventional picture Americans have regarding immigration is "both out of date and factually wrong" (par. 2). How effectively does he support that assertion?

2. Do you agree with Mead that "America needs and benefits from both kinds of immigration" (par. 6)? Why or why not?

3. Despite the restrictions and hardships inflicted on would-be Asian immigrants throughout U.S. history, as Mead reports (pars. 15–17), they continue to come to America and have in fact surpassed Hispanics or Latinos as the largest and fastest-growing group to do so. Are you surprised to learn this? Why do you suppose it is so?

4. Mead concludes, "The world's best, the world's hardest-working and the world's most ambitious are still coming our way." What is the effect of the word "still" in that sentence? Do you agree with Mead? What does this piece suggest about the future of immigration in the United States?

Making Connections

1. Compare Senator Ellison DuRant Smith's descriptions of immigrants (p. 1007) with those by Dennis Kearney and H. L. Knight (p. 999). What similarities do you see?

2. Compare the perspective of Congressman Robert H. Clancy (p. 1004) with that of Joseph McDonnell (p. 1001). How are they similar or different?

3. Compare the similarities and differences between the 1893 cartoon *Looking Backward* (p. 1003) and the 2011 cartoon *Promised Land* (p. 1018)? How might you paraphrase the message of both in a single sentence?

4. Compare the rhetorical purposes of Joseph Keppler's cartoon and Congressman Clancy's speech. How might Clancy respond to *Looking Backward*? How might Senator Smith?

5. How might Mary Gordon (p. 1010) or Walter Russell Mead (p. 1019) respond to the speeches by Senator Smith and Congressman Clancy?

6. How might Mead respond to the article by Kearney and Knight? How might he respond to the editorial by McDonnell?

Entering the Conversation

As you respond to each of the following prompts, support your position with appropriate evidence, including at least three sources in this Conversation on immigration and the lure of America, unless otherwise indicated.

1. To distinguish it from others throughout history, Charles Bowden (p. 1014) calls the wall between Mexico and the United States "*our* wall." What else does he suggest through the use of "our"? How does the barrier made by the wall compare with the "world-wide welcome" (l. 7) promised in "The New Colossus" (p. 998)? Or with the "process of national definition" (par. 15) that Gordon undergoes at Ellis Island? How can we reconcile as expressions of our national identity the values of freedom and security expressed by the Statue of Liberty on the one hand and the border wall and other barriers, both literal and figurative, on the other?

2. In his 1791 book, *The Rights of Man*, Thomas Paine made the following observation about America:

> If there is a country in the world, where concord, according to common calculation, would be least expected, it is America. Made up, as it is, of people from different nations*, accustomed to different forms and habits of government, speaking different languages, and more different in their modes of worship, it would appear that the union of such a people was impracticable; but by the simple operation of constructing government on the principles of society and the rights of man, every difficulty retires, and all the parts are brought into cordial unison.

---

*That part of America which is generally called New-England, including New Hampshire, Rhode Island, and Connecticut, is peopled chiefly by English descendants. In the state of New York, about half are Dutch, the rest English, Scotch, and Irish. In New-Jersey, a mixture of English and Dutch, with some Scotch and Irish. In Pennsylvania, about one third are English, another Germans, and the remainder are Scotch and Irish, with some Swedes. The states to the southward have a greater proportion of English than the middle states, but in all of them there is a mixture; and besides those enumerated, there are a considerable number of French, and some few of all the European nations lying on the coast. The most numerous religious denomination are the Presbyterians; but no one sect is established above another, and all men are equally citizens.

Today we might be amused at what Paine saw as great diversity in 1791. (We might note that even such a progressive thinker as Paine — perhaps ahead of his time, he was against slavery and for women's rights — does not mention Blacks or Native Americans.) He could not imagine the great "melting pot" that America would become. Write an essay in which you examine the extent to which Paine's observations hold true today.

3. As Gordon wittily reminds us in her essay, America is known worldwide as a nation of immigrants. What is the lure of America? Despite hardships, why do people keep coming to the United States today?

4. Angel Island operated as the immigration center in San Francisco Bay from 1910 to 1940. Sometimes called the "Ellis Island of the West," it was the chief entrance point for immigrants from Asia, many of whom were detained for days, weeks, and in a few cases, years. Research the history of Angel Island and its significance for Asian Americans, considering the conditions of the center and taking particular note of the poetry that the detainees carved on the walls. Write an essay on Angel Island's place in the story of American immigration.

5. This Conversation explores not only the lure of America but also efforts throughout our nation's history to stem the tide of immigration. How has this historical perspective influenced your views on the current immigration debate? Should we continue to expand inclusiveness? Should we restrict the number of immigrants that we accept into the country? Develop a position on the issue.

6. How does immigration in the United States today compare with that in other countries? Are other countries experiencing tension between their citizenry and people from other countries and cultures who wish to enter? Choose a foreign country and compare the immigration issues there with those in the United States.

7. Paul Taylor, executive vice president of the Pew Research Center and co-author of the 2012 Pew Report "The Rise of Asian Americans," writes: "Like immigrants throughout American history, the new arrivals from Asia are strivers. What's distinctive about them is their educational credentials. These aren't the tired, poor, huddled masses of Emma Lazarus's famous inscription on the Statue of Liberty. They are the highly skilled workforce of the 21st century." Compare the issues and realities of immigration today with those of over a century ago.

Conversation
The American Cowboy

Whether fact, fiction, or a little of both, the cowboy is a complex figure in American history and popular culture. Few know of the cowboy's origins in the vaquero tradition of Mexico that was brought to California in the seventeenth century, or the role of African American cowboys after the Civil War. When they think of a cowboy, many people picture a gunslinger of the Wild West, a loner, an adventurer, and often a rebel. Yet the reality is that most cowboys were hired by ranchers to manage, protect, and drive cattle herds. The "range wars" of the late 1870s and 1880s contributed to the view of cowboys as the gunslingers of the American West. Land ownership was not as clear-cut in that period, leading many ranchers to fight over control of open range. Perhaps the cowboy is best known to us through movies: the Western is the quintessential American genre, starting in 1903 with *The Great Train Robbery* and continuing up to the present day in the interpretations of directors like Quentin Tarantino and the Coen brothers. Film stars such as John Wayne and Clint Eastwood are synonymous with the Western. Cowboys in film and literature have influenced our definition of manhood, and the battles between "cowboys and Indians" in cinema and print are responsible, many would argue, for damaging stereotypes that persist.

The written and visual texts you'll explore in this Conversation, ranging from the late nineteenth to the twenty-first century, may challenge your perspective or enlarge it and, ideally, will lead you to consider who the cowboy was or is and why it matters to our national identity. Your investigations might even explain why contemporary Western singers Waylon Jennings and Willie Nelson advise, "Mammas, don't let your babies grow up to be cowboys."

Sources

Joseph Nimmo Jr., from *The American Cowboy* (1886)

Frederic S. Remington, *A Dash for the Timber* (1889)

Frederick Jackson Turner, from *The Significance of the Frontier in American History* (1893)

Buffalo Bill Cody, *Buffalo Bill's Wild West* (program, 1893)

Owen Wister, from *The Virginian: A Horseman of the Plains* (1902)

E. E. Cummings, *Buffalo Bill 's* (1920)

Leonard McCombe, *Marlboro Man* (1949)

Gretel Ehrlich, *About Men* (1984)

Sherman Alexie, *My Heroes Have Never Been Cowboys* (1993)

Joy Kasson, *Buffalo Bill's Wild West: Celebrity, Memory, and Popular History* (2000)

Benjamin Percy, The Virginian *Teaches the Merit of a Man* (2007)

from *The American Cowboy*

JOSEPH NIMMO JR.

Joseph Nimmo Jr. (1830–1909) was a statistician, an economist, and a civil engineer who served as chief of both the United States Division of Internal Commerce and the Bureau of Statistics. A selection from his article "The American Cowboy" follows. It was published in 1886 in *Harper's New Monthly* magazine, the nineteenth-century version of today's *Harper's*.

During the last fifteen years the American cow-boy has occupied a place sufficiently important to entitle him to a considerable share of public attention. His occupation is unique. In the exercise of his function he is always a man on horseback. His duty as a worker in the cattle business is at times to ride over the range in order to see that straying cattle do not rove too far from the assigned limits of the herd of which he has charge; at times to drive the herd from one locality to another; and at times to "round up" the dispersed cattle, by which is meant to collect them together for the purpose of branding calves, or of selecting beef cattle, which latter are driven to railroad stations for shipment to market. The chief qualifications of efficiency in this calling are courage, physical alertness, ability to endure exposure and fatigue, horsemanship, and skill in the use of the lariat.

The original cow-boy of this country was essentially a creature of circumstance, and mainly a product of western and southwestern Texas. Armed to the teeth, booted and spurred, long-haired, and covered with the broad-brimmed sombrero — the distinctive badge of his calling — his personal appearance proclaimed the sort of man he was.

The Texas cow-boys were frontiersmen, accustomed from their earliest childhood to the alarms and the struggles incident to forays of Indians of the most ferocious and warlike nature. The section of the State in which they lived was also for many years exposed to incursions of bandits from Mexico, who came with predatory intent upon the herds and the homes of the people of Texas. The carrying of fire-arms and other deadly weapons was consequently a prevalent custom among them. And being scattered over vast areas, and beyond the efficient protection and restraints of civil law, they of necessity became a law unto themselves.

It is not a strange thing that such an occupation and such environment should have developed a class of men whom persons accustomed to the usages of cultivated society would characterize as ruffians of the most pronounced type. But among the better disposed of the Texas cow-boys, who constitute, it is believed, much more than a majority of them, there were true and trusty men, in whom the dangers and fortunes of their lives developed generous and heroic traits of character. The same experiences, however, led the viciously inclined to give free vent to the worst passions. Upon slight provocation they would shoot down a fellow-man with almost as little compunction as they fired upon the wild beasts.

But the peculiar characteristics of the Texas cow-boys qualified them for an important public service. By virtue of their courage and recklessness of danger, their excellent horsemanship, and skill in the use of fire-arms, and by virtue also of the influence which they have exerted upon their gentler brethren of the northern ranges, they have been an efficient instrumentality in preventing Indian outbreaks, and in protecting the frontier settlements of the entire range and ranch cattle area against predatory incursions and massacres by Indians. This has been a natural result of the fact that the cowboys constitute throughout that region a corps of mounted scouts, armed and equipped, twenty thousand strong. They traverse vast ranges, ford rivers, and search for cattle amid mountain fastnesses and in lurking places of the river bottoms. . . .

5

It is only twenty years since the discovery was made that between the line of settlement in Dakota, Nebraska, and Kansas at the east, and the Sierra Nevada and Coast ranges at the west, there was an area as large as the portion of the United States which is situated east of the Mississippi River, throughout which cattle could be raised and fattened on the open range, seeking their own food, water, and shelter without any aid from man, from the time they were dropped until they were in condition to be driven to a railroad station for shipment to market. This discovery, greater in its importance than the discovery of gold in California, or silver in Nevada, or petroleum in Pennsylvania, happened, according to the most reliable accounts, in this wise. Early in December, 1864, a government trader, with a wagon train of supplies drawn by oxen, was on his way west to Camp Douglas, in the Territory of Utah, but being overtaken on the Laramie Plains by an unusually severe snowstorm, he was compelled at once to go into winter-quarters. He turned his cattle adrift, expecting, as a matter of course, they would soon perish from exposure and starvation, but they remained about the camp, and as the snow was blown off the highlands the dried grass afforded them an abundance of forage. When the spring opened they were found to be in even better condition than when turned out to die four months previously. This at once led to the experiment of herding cattle on the northern ranges. But it was for years a slow and hazardous business. At that time it was the custom to allow the Indians upon the reservations to wander off during the summer months throughout the present range and ranch cattle area, in order that they might hunt buffaloes and other large game, and thus sustain themselves in their accustomed way until the approach of winter, when they returned to their reservations to be again provided for by the government. Permission to depart on these expeditions was always given upon the promise made to the military and civil officers of the United States that while absent they would be "good Indians." But as cattle were more easily caught than buffaloes, they found it greatly to their advantage to swoop down upon the herds, stampede them, and slaughter at their leisure as many as their needs required. Oftentimes, by way of amusement, they lifted the scalp of a stray cowboy. In many instances they massacred whole camps of settlers, whose chief occupation was cattle herding. Occasionally these "wards of the nation" so far forgot themselves as to put on war-paint and set the United States at defiance. The massacre of General Custer and his detachment, on the 25th of June, 1876, at Little Big Horn, Dakota, near the present location of Fort Custer, led, however, to the adoption of a more stringent policy on the part of the United States government with respect to requiring the Indians to remain upon their reservations. During the five years following that tragic event our valiant little army, widely scattered over a vast area, had many bloody encounters with the savages. At last the spirit of resistance was broken, and Montana, Idaho, and Dakota became comparatively safe for the introduction of the range cattle business, which had already become known in Colorado and Wyoming as a highly attractive enterprise and a speedy avenue to wealth. As the work of the army drew nigh to completion the cow-boy galloped in, and became the mounted policeman of a vast area, always on patrol.

But even after the red man had retired to his reservation the lot of the cattle-men was not entirely serene. From time immemorial the horse-thief and the cattle-thief seem to have been a sort of parasitic growth upon frontier life, apparently begotten of its conditions. So it was on the range. For several years the entire region from Kansas and Colorado at the south to Montana and Dakota at the north was infested by cattle-thieves. The country afforded apparently illimitable scope for this nefarious traffic. It seemed at one time somewhat a matter of doubt as to which should prosper most, the herdsmen or the cattle-thieves. As the cattle of many proprietors intermingled freely on vast ranges, it was comparatively easy and safe for a few marauders to pounce down upon detached groups of cattle here and there separated from the main body of the herds, and drive them off over some mountain range to a distant valley or range where grazing was abundant, and there brand the calves with a chosen hieroglyphic representative of a separate ownership, and change the marks of cattle already branded, by one or more dashes with a red-hot iron. It was clearly seen that in order to stamp out this new and threatening evil recourse must be had to a drastic remedy. Accordingly the various cattle associations organized a detective service, composed mainly of brave and trusty cow-boys, who were charged with the duty of reconnoitring the whole country in order to discover the miscreants in their lairs, also to watch for altered and surreptitious brands at the railroad shipping stations. In this way a large number of stolen cattle was recovered, and many cattle-thieves were apprehended. When the latter were arrested within the limits of the efficient administration of the law, they were handed over to the civil authorities. But when caught beyond the limits of organized counties, administrative justice was extemporized. The cattle-men and the cow-boys themselves supplied judges, jurymen, witnesses, attorneys, constables, and executioners. Sometimes a level-headed cow-boy was placed upon the judicial bench. The cattle-men assert that the extreme and only penalty was never inflicted except upon the clearest evidence of guilt.

When the verdict of guilty was pronounced, a short shrift, and a stout rope, and a grave without a coffin or a winding-sheet, ended the proceedings.

But a great change has taken place. On the northern ranges cattle stealing has become almost entirely a thing of the past. . . .

(1886)

Questions

1. Why does Joseph Nimmo Jr. open the article with an explanation of the "function" of the cowboy and his "qualifications" rather than with a discussion of the cowboy's temperament and personality traits? What does this approach suggest about Nimmo's intended purpose?

2. As he develops the article, Nimmo explains to his reading audience, who were largely Easterners at this point in the magazine's history, the kind of man drawn to the life of the mid-nineteenth-century cowboy. What are these qualities?

3. Nimmo emphasizes the work of the cowboys as a group — "a class of men" (par. 4) — rather than as individuals. Why? What is it that they do as "an important public service" (par. 5)?

4. How are Native Americans depicted in this article? What motivation does Nimmo attribute to their actions? Cite specific passages to support your response.
5. Nimmo builds an argument in this passage about cowboys and violence. What is his major claim? How does he support it? Where does he address counterarguments?
6. How does the diction of this passage suggest a mythic struggle between good and evil? Refer to specific words and images to explain your response. Why do you believe such language would or would not have been persuasive to his audience?

A Dash for the Timber

Frederic S. Remington

An influential painter and sculptor of the American West, Frederic S. Remington (1861–1909) grew up in New York State and received his artistic training at Yale College of Art and the Art Students League in New York City. He made his first trip to the western United States as a twenty-year-old vacationing in Montana. He lived for a few years in Kansas but returned to New York City in 1885 as an illustrator for *Harper's Weekly*. He traveled to the American Southwest several times between 1885 and 1888, primarily to cover the U.S. cavalry and the Apache Indians. In *A Dash for the Timber* (1889), a classic Western battle ensues as the cowboys rush for cover. The painting appealed to the American public who felt nostalgic for a rapidly disappearing world of action and adventure in the so-called Wild West, and it launched Remington's career as a major painter.

Amon Carter Museum of American Art, Fort Worth, Texas

FREDERIC S. REMINGTON, *A DASH FOR THE TIMBER*, 1889, OIL ON CANVAS, 84" × 48", AMON CARTER MUSEUM OF AMERICAN ART, FORT WORTH, TEXAS. (See color insert, Image 34.)

Questions

1. What is the narrative, or the story line, of this scene? Pay attention to the figures, the spatial arrangement and color, and the interaction among landscape, humans, and animals. How does the title relate to the narrative?
2. During his trips West, Frederic S. Remington is reputed to have kept detailed diaries, made numerous field sketches, and taken photographs with the latest equipment of the day. How does the painting reflect his commitment to a realistic depiction of the action and geography of this scene?
3. The Web site of the Amon Carter Museum of American Art, which owns this painting, describes the "truly cinematic" effect of the piece and the influence of Remington's Western images on "the popular imagination." In what ways is this still image "cinematic"? What examples of the influence of this image can you identify in popular culture today or from the twentieth century?
4. From its inception at the turn of the century through the present, this painting has been criticized by some as being sentimental and even racist. Why? What specific details in the painting might support such an interpretation? Do you agree or disagree with that interpretation? Explain.

from *The Significance of the Frontier in American History*

Frederick Jackson Turner

A prominent scholar of U.S. history, Frederick Jackson Turner (1861–1932) was born in Wisconsin and received his doctorate from Johns Hopkins University. He was a professor of history at the University of Wisconsin and at Harvard University. Turner delivered his lecture "The Significance of the Frontier in American History" to a gathering of the American Historical Society in 1893, at the World's Columbian Exposition, a vast fair that celebrated the four hundredth anniversary of Columbus's voyage. Dubbed the "Frontier Thesis," Turner's argument that westward expansion shaped American individualistic democracy and the national character is one of the most influential as well as most debated interpretations of U.S. history. In it, he reflects on the role of the frontier in shaping the "dominant individualism" of American character and warns that "the closing of a great historical movement" would have dire consequences on that character. Following is an excerpt from the speech, which was expanded and published as a book in 1920.

In a recent bulletin of the Superintendent of the Census for 1890 appear these significant words: "Up to and including 1880 the country had a frontier of settlement, but at present the unsettled area has been so broken into by isolated bodies of settlement that there can hardly be said to be a frontier line. In the discussion of its extent, its westward movement, etc., it can not, therefore, any longer have a place in the census reports." This brief official statement marks the closing of a great historic movement. Up to our own day American history has been in a large degree the history of the colonization of the Great West. The existence of an area of free land, its continuous recession, and the advance of American settlement westward, explain American development.

Behind institutions, behind constitutional forms and modifications, lie the vital forces that call these organs into life and shape them to meet changing conditions. The peculiarity of American institutions is the fact that they have been compelled to adapt themselves to the changes of an expanding people — to the changes involved in crossing a continent, in winning a wilderness, and in developing at each area of this progress out of the primitive economic and political conditions of the frontier into the complexity of city life. Said Calhoun in 1817, "We are great, and rapidly — I was about to say fearfully — growing!"[1] So saying, he touched the distinguishing feature of American life. All peoples show development; the germ theory of politics has been sufficiently emphasized. In the case of most nations, however, the development has occurred in a limited area; and if the nation has expanded, it has met other growing peoples whom it has conquered. But in the case of the United States we have a different phenomenon. Limiting our attention to the Atlantic coast, we have the familiar phenomenon of the evolution of institutions in a limited area, such as the rise of representative government; the differentiation of simple colonial governments into complex organs; the progress from primitive industrial society, without division of labor, up to manufacturing civilization. But we have in addition to this a recurrence of the process of evolution in each western area reached in the process of expansion. Thus American development has exhibited not merely advance along a single line, but a return to primitive conditions on a continually advancing frontier line, and a new development for that area. American social development has been continually beginning over again on the frontier. This perennial rebirth, this fluidity of American life, this expansion westward with its new opportunities, its continuous touch with the simplicity of primitive society, furnish the forces dominating American character. The true point of view in the history of this nation is not the Atlantic coast, it is the Great West. Even the slavery struggle, which is made so exclusive an object of attention by writers . . . , occupies its important place in American history because of its relation to westward expansion.

In this advance, the frontier is the outer edge of the wave — the meeting point between savagery and civilization. Much has been written about the frontier from the point of view of border warfare and the chase, but as a field for the serious study of the economist and the historian it has been neglected. . . .

In the settlement of America we have to observe how European life entered the continent, and how America modified and developed that life and reacted on Europe. Our early history is the study of European germs developing in an American environment. Too exclusive attention has been paid by institutional students to the Germanic origins, too little to the American factors. The frontier is the line of most rapid and effective Americanization. The wilderness masters the colonist. It finds him a European in dress, industries, tools, modes of travel, and thought. It takes him from the railroad car and puts him in the birch canoe. It strips off the garments of civilization and arrays him in the hunting shirt and the moccasin. It puts him in the log cabin of the Cherokee and Iroquois and runs an Indian palisade around him. Before long he

---

[1]"Abridgment of Debates of Congress," v, p. 706.

has gone to planting Indian corn and plowing with a sharp stick; he shouts the war cry and takes the scalp in orthodox Indian fashion. In short, at the frontier the environment is at first too strong for the man. He must accept the conditions which it furnishes, or perish, and so he fits himself into the Indian clearings and follows the Indian trails. Little by little he transforms the wilderness, but the outcome is not the old Europe, not simply the development of Germanic germs, any more than the first phenomenon was a case of reversion to the Germanic mark. The fact is, that here is a new product that is American. At first, the frontier was the Atlantic coast. It was the frontier of Europe in a very real sense. Moving westward, the frontier became more and more American. As successive terminal moraines result from successive glaciations, so each frontier leaves its traces behind it, and when it becomes a settled area the region still partakes of the frontier characteristics. Thus the advance of the frontier has meant a steady movement away from the influence of Europe, a steady growth of independence on American lines. And to study this advance, the men who grew up under these conditions, and the political, economic, and social results of it, is to study the really American part of our history. . . .

But the most important effect of the frontier has been in the promotion of democ- 5
racy here and in Europe. As has been indicated, the frontier is productive of individualism. Complex society is precipitated by the wilderness into a kind of primitive organization based on the family. The tendency is anti-social. It produces antipathy to control, and particularly to any direct control. The tax-gatherer is viewed as a representative of oppression. Prof. Osgood, in an able article,[2] has pointed out that the frontier conditions prevalent in the colonies are important factors in the explanation of the American Revolution, where individual liberty was sometimes confused with absence of all effective government. The same conditions aid in explaining the difficulty of instituting a strong government in the period of the confederacy. The frontier individualism has from the beginning promoted democracy.

So long as free land exists, the opportunity for a competency exists, and economic power secures political power. But the democracy born of free land, strong in selfishness and individualism, intolerant of administrative experience and education, and pressing individual liberty beyond its proper bounds, has its dangers as well as its benefits. Individualism in America has allowed a laxity in regard to governmental affairs which has rendered possible the spoils system and all the manifest evils that follow from the lack of a highly developed civic spirit. In this connection may be noted also the influence of frontier conditions in permitting lax business honor, inflated paper currency, and wild-cat banking. The colonial and revolutionary frontier was the region whence emanated many of the worst forms of an evil currency.[3] The West in the War of 1812 repeated the phenomenon on the frontier of that day, while the speculation and wild-cat banking of the period of the crisis of 1837 occurred on the new frontier belt of the next tier of States. Thus each one of the periods of lax financial integrity coincides with periods when a new set of frontier communities had arisen, and coincides in area

---

[2] *Political Science Quarterly*, ii, p. 457. Compare Sumner, "Alexander Hamilton," chs. ii–vii.
[3] On the relation of frontier conditions to Revolutionary taxation, see Sumner, "Alexander Hamilton," ch. iii.

with these successive frontiers, for the most part. The recent Populist agitation is a case in point. Many a State that now declines any connection with the tenets of the Populists, itself adhered to such ideas in an earlier stage of the development of the State. A primitive society can hardly be expected to show the intelligent appreciation of the complexity of business interests in a developed society. The continual recurrence of these areas of paper-money agitation is another evidence that the frontier can be isolated and studied as a factor in American history of the highest importance.[4]

The East has always feared the result of an unregulated advance of the frontier, and has tried to check and guide it. The English authorities would have checked settlement at the headwaters of the Atlantic tributaries and allowed the "savages to enjoy their deserts in quiet lest the peltry trade should decrease." This called out Burke's[5] splendid protest:

> If you stopped your grants, what would be the consequence? The people would occupy without grants. They have already so occupied in many places. You can not station garrisons in every part of these deserts. If you drive the people from one place, they will carry on their annual tillage and remove with their flocks and herds to another. Many of the people in the back settlements are already little attached to particular situations. Already they have topped the Appalachian Mountains. From thence they behold before them an immense plain, one vast, rich, level meadow; a square of five hundred miles. Over this they would wander without a possibility of restraint; they would change their manners with their habits of life; would soon forget a government by which they were disowned; would become hordes of English Tartars; and, pouring down upon your unfortified frontiers a fierce and irresistible cavalry, become masters of your governors and your counselers, your collectors and comptrollers, and of all the slaves that adhered to them. Such would, and in no long time must, be the effect of attempting to forbid as a crime and to suppress as an evil the command and blessing of Providence, "Increase and multiply." Such would be the happy result of an endeavor to keep as a lair of wild beasts that earth which God, by an express charter, has given to the children of men. . . .

From the conditions of frontier life came intellectual traits of profound importance. The works of travelers along each frontier from colonial days onward describe

---

[4]I have refrained from dwelling on the lawless characteristics of the frontier, because they are sufficiently well known. The gambler and desperado, the regulators of the Carolinas, and the vigilantes of California, are types of that line of scum that the waves of advancing civilization bore before them, and of the growth of spontaneous organs of authority where legal authority was absent. Compare Barrows, "United States of Yesterday and To-morrow"; Shinn, "Mining Camps"; and Bancroft, "Popular Tribunals." The humor, bravery, and rude strength, as well as the vices of the frontier in its worst aspect, have left traces on American character, language, and literature, not soon to be effaced.

[5]Edmund Burke (1729–1797), Irish statesman and philosopher who supported the American Revolution. — Eds.

certain common traits, and these traits have, while softening down, still persisted as survivals in the place of their origin, even when a higher social organization succeeded. The result is that to the frontier the American intellect owes its striking characteristics. That coarseness and strength combined with acuteness and inquisitiveness; that practical, inventive turn of mind, quick to find expedients; that masterful grasp of material things, lacking in the artistic but powerful to effect great ends; that restless, nervous energy;[6] that dominant individualism, working for good and for evil, and withal that buoyancy and exuberance which comes with freedom — these are traits of the frontier, or traits called out elsewhere because of the existence of the frontier. Since the days when the fleet of Columbus sailed into the waters of the New World, America has been another name for opportunity, and the people of the United States have taken their tone from the incessant expansion which has not only been open but has even been forced upon them. He would be a rash prophet who should assert that the expansive character of American life has now entirely ceased. Movement has been its dominant fact, and, unless this training has no effect upon a people, the American energy will continually demand a wider field for its exercise. But never again will such gifts of free land offer themselves. For a moment, at the frontier, the bonds of custom are broken and unrestraint is triumphant. There is not *tabula rasa*. The stubborn American environment is there with its imperious summons to accept its conditions; the inherited ways of doing things are also there; and yet, in spite of environment, and in spite of custom, each frontier did indeed furnish a new field of opportunity, a gate of escape from the bondage of the past; and freshness, and confidence, and scorn of older society, impatience of its restraints and its ideas, and indifference to its lessons, have accompanied the frontier. What the Mediterranean Sea was to the Greeks, breaking the bond of custom, offering new experiences, calling out new institutions and activities, that, and more, the ever retreating frontier has been to the United States directly, and to the nations of Europe more remotely. And now, four centuries from the discovery of America, at the end of a hundred years of life under the Constitution, the frontier has gone, and with its going has closed the first period of American history.

(1893, 1920)

Questions

1. What was the rhetorical situation of this speech when it was delivered at the World's Columbian Exposition? How does that context affect the approach Frederick Jackson Turner takes and the tone he uses? Pay special attention to the relationship between him and his initial audience.

---

[6]Colonial travelers agree in remarking on the phlegmatic characteristics of the colonists. It has frequently been asked how such a people could have developed that strained nervous energy now characteristic of them. Compare Sumner, "Alexander Hamilton," p. 98, and Adams, "History of the United States," i, p. 60; ix, pp. 240, 241. The transition appears to become marked at the close of the War of 1812, a period when interest centered upon the development of the West, and the West was noted for restless energy. Grund, "Americans," ii, ch. i.

2. Turner uses the word "primitive" with relative frequency. What does it mean in this essay? Is it a synonym for "savagery"? How does its juxtaposition with "civilization" add to its meaning?

3. What does Turner mean in the following statement: "The frontier is the line of most rapid and effective Americanization. The wilderness masters the colonist" (par. 4)? In what way is this point fundamental to Turner's argument?

4. How, according to Turner, has "frontier individualism . . . promoted democracy" (par. 5)? What are the "dangers as well as . . . benefits" of this "democracy born of free land" (par. 6)?

5. What point does Turner emphasize with the lengthy quotation from Edmund Burke's 1775 "Speech for Conciliation with America" (par. 7)?

6. Turner claims that "the American intellect owes its striking characteristics" (par. 8) to the frontier. What are those characteristics, and what are their consequences to Turner's claim about American "exceptionalism" — that is, the distinctive American character? What evidence does he provide for his argument?

7. Turner bookends his speech-turned-essay with references to "the closing of a great historic movement" (par. 1) and "the ever retreating frontier" (par. 8). Is his essay more of an elegy for the West, a celebration of the opportunities of the present moment, or an argument to move on to the next "frontier"? Cite two specific passages to support your response.

Buffalo Bill's Wild West

Buffalo Bill Cody

> Born William Cody (1846–1917), Buffalo Bill Cody was a soldier, a gold prospector, a Pony Express rider, a showman, and an impresario. Born in Ohio, he lived in Canada and the Kansas Territory while growing up. He received the Medal of Honor in 1872 for service as a scout in the army. During that same year, Ned Buntline, author of a number of Westerns and creator of the character Buffalo Bill, persuaded Cody to go onstage portraying himself. In 1883, Cody organized Buffalo Bill's Wild West, a show that proved enormously successful in the United States and Europe. It included dramatizations of such Wild West scenes as a buffalo hunt with real buffaloes, Custer's Last Stand with some Lakota who had actually fought in the battle, and colorful figures and sharpshooters such as Annie Oakley and Wild Bill Hickok. The image on the following page is the cover of an 1893 program from Buffalo Bill's Wild West.

Questions

1. How is the West portrayed in this poster? Specifically, how are cowboys and Native Americans depicted?

2. Based on his image in this advertisement, how do you think Cody sees himself?

3. What are the values prized in the West according to this image?

The Newberry Library, Chicago

(See color insert, Image 35.)

4. Cody insisted that his show be called simply "The Wild West" or "Buffalo Bill's Wild West" without the word "Show." Why? To what extent was this choice a wise one on the part of this consummate showman?

from *The Virginian*
A Horseman of the Plains

OWEN WISTER

Owen Wister (1860–1938) was born into an affluent Philadelphia family, worked for a while in a bank, went to Harvard College, and was preparing to enter Harvard Law School when he suffered a series of mysterious health problems, including vertigo and hallucinations. In 1885, at his doctor's urging to travel west to restore his health, he went to Wyoming, where, as a 2002 article in *Harvard Magazine* says, his "real life was about to begin." He made additional trips over the next fifteen years as he began writing short fiction, and in 1902, he published *The Virginian*. The novel sold 200,000 copies its first year, making its author an instant celebrity, and has never gone out of print; it has been made into five movies and a television series. Following are selections from Chapters 1 and 2 of *The Virginian*, which is narrated by an unnamed easterner on his first westward journey.

I. Enter the Man

Some notable sight was drawing the passengers, both men and women, to the window; and therefore I rose and crossed the car to see what it was. I saw near the track an enclosure, and round it some laughing men, and inside it some whirling dust, and amid the dust some horses, plunging, huddling, and dodging. They were cow ponies in a corral, and one of them would not be caught, no matter who threw the rope. We had plenty of time to watch this sport, for our train had stopped that the engine might take water at the tank before it pulled us up beside the station platform of Medicine Bow. We were also six hours late, and starving for entertainment. The pony in the corral was wise, and rapid of limb. Have you seen a skilful boxer watch his antagonist with a quiet, incessant eye? Such an eye as this did the pony keep upon whatever man took the rope. The man might pretend to look at the weather, which was fine; or he might affect earnest conversation with a bystander: it was bootless. The pony saw through it. No feint hoodwinked him. This animal was thoroughly a man of the world. His undistracted eye stayed fixed upon the dissembling foe, and the gravity of his horse-expression made the matter one of high comedy. Then the rope would sail out at him, but he was already elsewhere; and if horses laugh, gayety must have abounded in that corral. Sometimes the pony took a turn alone; next he had slid in a flash among his brothers, and the whole of them like a school of playful fish whipped round the corral, kicking up the fine dust, and (I take it) roaring with laughter. Through the window-glass of our Pullman the thud of their mischievous hoofs reached us, and the strong, humorous curses of the cow-boys. Then for the first time I noticed a man who sat on the high gate of the corral, looking on. For he now climbed down with the undulations of a tiger, smooth and easy, as if his muscles flowed beneath his skin. The others had all visibly whirled the rope, some of them even shoulder high. I did not see his arm lift or move. He appeared to hold the rope down low, by his leg. But like a sudden snake I saw the noose go out its length and fall true; and the thing was done. As the captured pony walked in with a sweet, church-door expression, our train moved slowly on to the station, and a passenger remarked, "That man knows his business."

But the passenger's dissertation upon roping I was obliged to lose, for Medicine Bow was my station. I bade my fellow-travellers good-by, and descended, a stranger, into the great cattle land. And here in less than ten minutes I learned news which made me feel a stranger indeed.

My baggage was lost; it had not come on my train; it was adrift somewhere back in the two thousand miles that lay behind me. And by way of comfort, the baggage-man remarked that passengers often got astray from their trunks, but the trunks mostly found them after a while. Having offered me this encouragement, he turned whistling to his affairs and left me planted in the baggage-room at Medicine Bow. I stood deserted among crates and boxes, blankly holding my check, furious and for-lorn. I stared out through the door at the sky and the plains; but I did not see the antelope shining among the sage-brush, nor the great sunset light of Wyoming. Annoyance blinded my eyes to all things save my grievance: I saw only a lost trunk. And I was muttering half-aloud, "What a forsaken hole this is!" when suddenly from outside on the platform came a slow voice: —

"Off to get married *again*? Oh, don't!"

The voice was Southern and gentle and drawling; and a second voice came in   5
immediate answer, cracked and querulous: —

"It ain't again. Who says it's again? Who told you, anyway?"

And the first voice responded caressingly: —

"Why, your Sunday clothes told me, Uncle Hughey. They are speakin' mighty loud o' nuptials."

"You don't worry me!" snapped Uncle Hughey, with shrill heat.

And the other gently continued, "Ain't them gloves the same yu' wore to your last   10
weddin'?"

"You don't worry me! You don't worry me!" now screamed Uncle Hughey.

Already I had forgotten my trunk; care had left me; I was aware of the sunset, and had no desire but for more of this conversation. For it resembled none that I had heard in my life so far. I stepped to the door and looked out upon the station platform.

Lounging there at ease against the wall was a slim young giant, more beautiful than pictures. His broad, soft hat was pushed back; a loose-knotted, dull-scarlet hand-kerchief sagged from his throat; and one casual thumb was hooked in the cartridge-belt that slanted across his hips. He had plainly come many miles from somewhere across the vast horizon, as the dust upon him showed. His boots were white with it. His overalls were gray with it. The weather-beaten bloom of his face shone through it duskily, as the ripe peaches look upon their trees in a dry season. But no dinginess of travel or shabbiness of attire could tarnish the splendor that radiated from his youth and strength. The old man upon whose temper his remarks were doing such deadly work was combed and curried to a finish, a bridegroom swept and garnished; but alas for age! Had I been the bride, I should have taken the giant, dust and all.

He had by no means done with the old man. . . .

II. "When You Call Me That, *Smile*!"

. . . I think that Steve was more curious even than myself. Time was on the wing. His   15
bet must be decided, and the drinks enjoyed. He stood against the grocery counter, contemplating the Virginian. But it was to me that he spoke. The Virginian, however, listened to every word.

"Your first visit to this country?"

I told him yes.

"How do you like it?"

I expected to like it very much.

"How does the climate strike you?"   20

I thought the climate was fine.

"Makes a man thirsty though."

This was the sub-current which the Virginian plainly looked for. But he, like Steve, addressed himself to me.

"Yes," he put in, "thirsty while a man's soft yet. You'll harden."

"I guess you'll find it a drier country than you were given to expect," said Steve.   25

"If your habits have been frequent that way," said the Virginian.

"There's parts of Wyoming," pursued Steve, "where you'll go hours and hours before you'll see a drop of wetness."

"And if yu' keep a-thinkin' about it," said the Virginian, "it'll seem like days and days."

Steve, at this stroke, gave up, and clapped him on the shoulder with a joyous chuckle. "You old son-of-a——!" he cried affectionately.

"Drinks are due now," said the Virginian. "My treat, Steve. But I reckon your   30
suspense will have to linger a while yet."

Thus they dropped into direct talk from that speech of the fourth dimension where they had been using me for their telephone.

"Any cyards going to-night?" inquired the Virginian.

"Stud and draw," Steve told him. "Strangers playing."

"I think I'd like to get into a game for a while," said the Southerner. "Strangers, yu' say?"

And then, before quitting the store, he made his toilet for this little hand at poker.   35
It was a simple preparation. He took his pistol from its holster, examined it, then shoved it between his overalls and his shirt in front, and pulled his waistcoat over it. He might have been combing his hair for all the attention any one paid to this, except myself. Then the two friends went out, and I bethought me of that epithet which Steve again had used to the Virginian as he clapped him on the shoulder. Clearly this wild country spoke a language other than mine — the word here was a term of endearment. Such was my conclusion.

The drummers had finished their dealings with the proprietor, and they were gossiping together in a knot by the door as the Virginian passed out.

"See you later, old man!" This was the American drummer accosting his prospective bed-fellow.

"Oh, yes," returned the bed-fellow, and was gone.

The American drummer winked triumphantly at his brethren. "He's all right," he observed, jerking a thumb after the Virginian. "He's easy. You got to know him to work him. That's all."

"Und vat is your point?" inquired the German drummer.   40

"Point is — he'll not take any goods off you or me; but he's going to talk up the killer to any consumptive he runs acrost. I ain't done with him yet. Say," (he now addressed the proprietor), "what's her name?"

"Whose name?"

"Woman runs the eating-house."

"Glen. Mrs. Glen."

"Ain't she new?"   45

"Been settled here about a month. Husband's a freight conductor."

"Thought I'd not seen her before. She's a good-looker."

"Hm! Yes. The kind of good looks I'd sooner see in another man's wife than mine."

"So that's the gait, is it?"

"Hm! well, it don't seem to be. She come here with that reputation. But there's   50
been general disappointment."

"Then she ain't lacked suitors any?"

"Lacked! Are you acquainted with cow-boys?"

"And she disappointed 'em? Maybe she likes her husband?"

"Hm! well, how are you to tell about them silent kind?"

"Talking of conductors," began the drummer. And we listened to his anecdote. It   55
was successful with his audience; but when he launched fluently upon a second I
strolled out. There was not enough wit in this narrator to relieve his indecency, and
I felt shame at having been surprised into laughing with him.

I left that company growing confidential over their leering stories, and I sought
the saloon. It was very quiet and orderly. Beer in quart bottles at a dollar I had never
met before; but saving its price, I found no complaint to make of it. Through folding
doors I passed from the bar proper with its bottles and elk head back to the hall with
its various tables. I saw a man sliding cards from a case, and across the table from him
another man laying counters down. Near by was a second dealer pulling cards from
the bottom of a pack, and opposite him a solemn old rustic piling and changing coins
upon the cards which lay already exposed.

But now I heard a voice that drew my eyes to the far corner of the room.

"Why didn't you stay in Arizona?"

Harmless looking words as I write them down here. Yet at the sound of them I
noticed the eyes of the others directed to that corner. What answer was given to them
I did not hear, nor did I see who spoke. Then came another remark.

"Well, Arizona's no place for amatures."   60

This time the two card dealers that I stood near began to give a part of their attention to the group that sat in the corner. There was in me a desire to leave this room. So far my hours at Medicine Bow had seemed to glide beneath a sunshine of merriment, of easy-going jocularity. This was suddenly gone, like the wind changing to north in the middle of a warm day. But I stayed, being ashamed to go.

Five or six players sat over in the corner at a round table where counters were piled. Their eyes were close upon their cards, and one seemed to be dealing a card at a time to each, with pauses and betting between. Steve was there and the Virginian; the others were new faces.

"No place for amatures," repeated the voice; and now I saw that it was the dealer's. There was in his countenance the same ugliness that his words conveyed.

"Who's that talkin'?" said one of the men near me, in a low voice.

"Trampas." 65

"What's he?"

"Cow-puncher, bronco-buster, tin-horn, most anything."

"Who's he talkin' at?"

"Think it's the black-headed guy he's talking at."

"That ain't supposed to be safe, is it?" 70

"Guess we're all goin' to find out in a few minutes."

"Been trouble between 'em?"

"They've not met before. Trampas don't enjoy losin' to a stranger."

"Fello's from Arizona, yu' say?"

"No. Virginia. He's recently back from havin' a look at Arizona. Went down there 75 last year for a change. Works for the Sunk Creek outfit." And then the dealer lowered his voice still further and said something in the other man's ear, causing him to grin. After which both of them looked at me.

There had been silence over in the corner; but now the man Trampas spoke again.

"*And* ten," said he, sliding out some chips from before him. Very strange it was to hear him, how he contrived to make those words a personal taunt. The Virginian was looking at his cards. He might have been deaf.

"*And* twenty," said the next player, easily.

The next threw his cards down.

It was now the Virginian's turn to bet, or leave the game, and he did not speak at 80 once.

Therefore Trampas spoke. "Your bet, you son-of-a ——."

The Virginian's pistol came out, and his hand lay on the table, holding it unaimed. And with a voice as gentle as ever, the voice that sounded almost like a caress, but drawling a very little more than usual, so that there was almost a space between each word, he issued his orders to the man Trampas: —

"When you call me that, *smile*." And he looked at Trampas across the table.

Yes, the voice was gentle. But in my ears it seemed as if somewhere the bell of death was ringing; and silence, like a stroke, fell on the large room. All men present, as if by some magnetic current, had become aware of this crisis. In my ignorance, and the total stoppage of my thoughts, I stood stock-still, and noticed various people crouching, or shifting their positions.

"Sit quiet," said the dealer, scornfully to the man near me. "Can't you see he don't want to push trouble? He has handed Trampas the choice to back down or draw his steel." 85

Then, with equal suddenness and ease, the room came out of its strangeness. Voices and cards, the click of chips, the puff of tobacco, glasses lifted to drink, — this level of smooth relaxation hinted no more plainly of what lay beneath than does the surface tell the depth of the sea.

For Trampas had made his choice. And that choice was not to "draw his steel." If it was knowledge that he sought, he had found it, and no mistake! We heard no further reference to what he had been pleased to style "amatures." In no company would the black-headed man who had visited Arizona be rated a novice at the cool art of self-preservation.

One doubt remained: What kind of a man was Trampas? A public back-down is an unfinished thing, — for some natures at least. I looked at his face, and thought it sullen, but tricky rather than courageous.

Something had been added to my knowledge also. Once again I had heard applied to the Virginian that epithet which Steve so freely used. The same words, identical to the letter. But this time they had produced a pistol. "When you call me that, *smile!*" So I perceived a new example of the old truth, that the letter means nothing until the spirit gives it life.

(1902)

Questions

1. How does the opening scene characterize the Virginian? Consider the way he is described (physical appearance and personality traits) and his interaction with other characters. What is so alluring about him?

2. In the second chapter, how does Owen Wister portray the Medicine Bow community? How does the dialogue contribute to this portrayal?

3. Wister is said to have based the scene in Chapter 2 on a remark he actually overheard in a similar setting. Why do you think the remark made such an impression on him? What values do you see revealed in the way the Virginian responds to the same "epithet" in the two different contexts? What insight does the narrator gain from the two incidents?

4. The Virginian is from the South and of an age that he could have fought for the Confederacy during the Civil War. What does Wister achieve by giving him this background rather than making him a New Englander?

5. The narrator is an easterner, a city person unfamiliar with the customs and culture of the West. What evidence does Wister give to emphasize the narrator's outsider status? Why might Wister have chosen a narrator with this background rather than use a Westerner or an omniscient narrator?

6. In his introduction to the novel, Wister writes of the "vanished world" of the West during the last quarter of the nineteenth century:

> What is become of the horseman, the cow-puncher, the last romantic figure upon our soil? For he was romantic. Whatever he did, he did with his might. The bread that he earned was earned hard, the wages that he squandered were squandered hard, — half a year's pay sometimes gone in a night, — "blown in," as he expressed it, or "blowed in," to be perfectly accurate. Well, he will be here among us always, invisible, waiting his chance to live and play as he would like. His wild kind has been among us, since the beginning: a young man with his temptations, a hero without wings.

What does Wister mean in his answer to the question he poses at the start of this paragraph? How do the society of Medicine Bow in general and the Virginian in particular illustrate the point(s) he is making?

7. Writing in *Harvard Magazine*, Castle Freeman Jr. calls *The Virginian* "the template on which every Western since has been cut" — a viewpoint echoed by numerous readers and critics as well as filmmakers. Why? What characteristics of the cowboy and the American Western genre do you see in this selection that make this novel a "template"?

Buffalo Bill 's

E. E. Cummings

Edward Estlin (E. E.) Cummings (1894–1962) was a prolific poet famous for defying traditional rules of typography, capitalization, and punctuation in pursuit of poetry that is both provocative and whimsical. "Buffalo Bill 's" was published in the *Dial* in 1920, three years after the death of William Cody.

Buffalo Bill 's
defunct
    who used to
    ride a watersmooth-silver
                stallion   5
and break onetwothreefourfive pigeonsjustlikethat
                         Jesus

he was a handsome man
               and what i want to know is
how do you like your blueeyed boy   10
Mister Death

(1920)

Questions

1. Characterize the speaker in this poem. What is his attitude toward Buffalo Bill (aka William Cody)? Is the poem meant to admire or disparage him? Explain your answer by referring to specific words and images in the text.
2. What is the difference between "Buffalo Bill is dead" and "Buffalo Bill 's defunct" (ll. 1–2)? How does the word "defunct" work in collaboration with (or opposition to) the lines that follow — about riding a stallion and shooting clay pigeons?
3. What is the effect of the isolated single-word line "Jesus" (l. 7)? How can it be read in several different ways?
4. Literary critic David Ray comments that "though the poem appears to be a simple elegy, it must be placed in the context of Cummings's obstinate attitude of hatred toward an American culture that invites children (and even men) to create an unworthy gallery of heroes. . . . [H]e has long attacked our society's worst indulgences in materialism, hypocrisy . . . and the following of false heroes and tawdry ideals." Taking into account how you would characterize the tone of this poem, support, challenge, or qualify Ray's interpretation.

Marlboro Man

LEONARD McCOMBE

This iconic photograph, taken by Leonard McCombe, was used by the Philip Morris Company to transform Marlboro cigarettes from the feminine appeal of being "Mild as May" to a more rugged image that appealed to men. When this campaign

Leonard McCombe/Getty Images

began in 1955, sales were at $5 billion; by 1957, they had jumped to $20 billion despite growing health concerns over cigarettes. McCombe took this photo of Clarence Hailey Long, a ranch foreman in Texas, in 1949.

Questions

1. How does the composition of the photograph contribute to its effect? Why is the focus exclusively on the face rather than a longer shot that would include the entire body?
2. What is the effect of the subject's gaze not meeting the eyes of the viewer?
3. *Life* magazine assigned McCombe to do a story that dispelled the glamorous image of cowboys seen in Hollywood movies of the period and, instead, documented the hardworking life of ranchers. What stereotypes about cowboys or the West does the photo exploit — or combat?
4. Why do you think that this photo caught the eye of legendary advertising executive Leo Burnett as a good choice for his campaign to transform the image of Marlboro cigarettes?

About Men

Gretel Ehrlich

> In the following essay from *The Solace of Open Spaces* (1984), author and documentary filmmaker Gretel Ehrlich compares the popular view of the cowboy with the cowboys she knows from her own experiences living in Wyoming.

When I'm in New York but feeling lonely for Wyoming I look for the Marlboro ads in the subway. What I'm aching to see is horseflesh, the glint of a spur, a line of distant mountains, brimming creeks, and a reminder of the ranchers and cowboys I've ridden with for the last eight years. But the men I see in those posters with their stern, humorless looks remind me of no one I know here. In our hell-bent earnestness to romanticize the cowboy we've ironically disesteemed his true character. If he's "strong and silent" it's because there's probably no one to talk to. If he "rides away into the sunset" it's because he's been on horseback since four in the morning moving cattle and he's trying, fifteen hours later, to get home to his family. If he's "a rugged individualist" he's also part of a team: ranch work is teamwork and even the glorified open-range cowboys of the 1880s rode up and down the Chisholm Trail in the company of twenty or thirty other riders. Instead of the macho, trigger-happy man our culture has perversely wanted him to be, the cowboy is more apt to be convivial, quirky, and softhearted. To be "tough" on a ranch has nothing to do with conquests and displays of power. More often than not, circumstances — like the colt he's riding or an unexpected blizzard — are overpowering him. It's not toughness but "toughing it out" that counts. In other words, this macho, cultural artifact the cowboy has become is simply a man who possesses resilience, patience, and an instinct for survival. "Cowboys are just like a pile of rocks — everything happens to them. They get climbed on, kicked, rained and snowed on, scuffed up by wind. Their job is 'just to take it,'" one old-timer told me.

A cowboy is someone who loves his work. Since the hours are long — ten to fifteen hours a day — and the pay is $30 he has to. What's required of him is an odd mixture of physical vigor and maternalism. His part of the beef-raising industry is to birth and nurture calves and take care of their mothers. For the most part his work is done on horseback and in a lifetime he sees and comes to know more animals than people. The iconic myth surrounding him is built on American notions of heroism: the index of a man's value as measured in physical courage. Such ideas have perverted manliness into a self-absorbed race for cheap thrills. In a rancher's world, courage has less to do with facing danger than with acting spontaneously — usually on behalf of an animal or another rider. If a cow is stuck in a boghole he throws a loop around her neck, takes his dally (a half hitch around the saddle horn), and pulls her out with horsepower. If a calf is born sick, he may take her home, warm her in front of the kitchen fire, and massage her legs until dawn. One friend, whose favorite horse was trying to swim a lake with hobbles on, dove under water and cut her legs loose with a knife, then swam her to shore, his arm around her neck lifeguard-style, and saved her from drowning. Because these incidents are usually linked to someone or something outside himself, the westerner's courage is selfless, a form of compassion.

The physical punishment that goes with cowboying is greatly underplayed. Once fear is dispensed with, the threshold of pain rises to meet the demands of the job. When Jane Fonda asked Robert Redford (in the film *Electric Horseman*) if he was sick as he struggled to his feet one morning, he replied, "No, just bent." For once the movies had it right. The cowboys I was sitting with laughed in agreement. Cowboys are rarely complainers; they show their stoicism by laughing at themselves.

If a rancher or cowboy has been thought of as a "man's man" — laconic, harddrinking, inscrutable — there's almost no place in which the balancing act between male and female, manliness and femininity, can be more natural. If he's gruff, handsome, and physically fit on the outside, he's androgynous at the core. Ranchers are midwives, hunters, nurturers, providers, and conservationists all at once. What we've interpreted as toughness — weathered skin, calloused hands, a squint in the eye, and a growl in the voice — only masks the tenderness inside. "Now don't go telling me these lambs are cute," one rancher warned me the first day I walked into the footballfield-sized lambing sheds. The next thing I knew he was holding a black lamb. "Ain't this little rat good-lookin'?"

So many of the men who came to the West were southerners — men looking for work and a new life after the Civil War — that chivalrousness and strict codes of honor were soon thought of as western traits. There were very few women in Wyoming during territorial days, so when they did arrive (some as mail-order brides from places like Philadelphia) there was a stand-offishness between the sexes and a formality that persists now. Ranchers still tip their hats and say, "Howdy, ma'am" instead of shaking hands with me.

5

Even young cowboys are often evasive with women. It's not that they're Jekyll and Hyde creatures — gentle with animals and rough on women — but rather, that they don't know how to bring their tenderness into the house and lack the vocabulary to express the complexity of what they feel. Dancing wildly all night becomes a metaphor for the explosive emotions pent up inside, and when these are, on occasion, released, they're so battery-charged and potent that one caress of the face or one "I love you" will peal for a long while.

The geographical vastness and the social isolation here make emotional evolution seem impossible. Those contradictions of the heart between respectability, logic, and convention on the one hand, and impulse, passion, and intuition on the other, played out wordlessly against the paradisical beauty of the West, give cowboys a wide-eyed but drawn look. Their lips pucker up, not with kisses but with immutability. They may want to break out, staying up all night with a lover just to talk, but they don't know how and can't imagine what the consequences will be. Those rare occasions when they do bare themselves result in confusion. "I feel as if I'd sprained my heart," one friend told me a month after such a meeting.

My friend Ted Hoagland wrote, "No one is as fragile as a woman but no one is as fragile as a man." For all the women here who use "fragileness" to avoid work or as a sexual ploy, there are men who try to hide theirs, all the while clinging to an adolescent dependency on women to cook their meals, wash their clothes, and keep the ranch house warm in winter. But there is true vulnerability in evidence here. Because these men work with animals, not machines or numbers, because they live outside in landscapes of torrential beauty, because they are confined to a place and a routine embellished with awesome variables, because calves die in the arms that pulled others into life, because they go to the mountains as if on a pilgrimage to find out what makes a herd of elk tick, their strength is also a softness, their toughness, a rare delicacy.

(1984)

Questions

1. Gretel Ehrlich opens with a reference to the Marlboro Man (p. 1043), a lone and rugged-looking cowboy who represented Marlboro in its cigarette advertising for many years. With this reference and her description of the Wyoming landscape, what effect does she achieve in the first three sentences of her essay?

2. In the first paragraph, Ehrlich claims that by romanticizing the cowboy, we have "disesteemed his true character" (par. 1). How does she define that "true character"?

3. What does Ehrlich mean when she calls the cowboy "an odd mixture of physical vigor and maternalism" (par. 2)?

4. In paragraphs 5 and 6, Ehrlich analyzes the cowboy's relationship with women. How has the cowboy's history defined the way he interacts with women?

5. How does the paradoxical statement by Ted Hoagland that "[n]o one is as fragile as a woman but no one is as fragile as a man" (par. 8) distill the points Ehrlich makes throughout the essay?

My Heroes Have Never Been Cowboys

SHERMAN ALEXIE

Sherman J. Alexie Jr. (b. 1966), a member of the Spokane and the Coeur d'Alene tribes, grew up on the Spokane Reservation in Washington State. A graduate of Washington State University, he has published more than twenty books, most notably *The Lone Ranger and Tonto Fistfight in Heaven* (1993), *The Absolutely True Diary of a Part-Time Indian* (2007), and *War Dances* (2009), which won the PEN/Faulkner Award for best American fiction. One of the stories in the *Lone Ranger* collection was the basis for the movie *Smoke Signals* (1999), for which Alexie wrote the screenplay. The following selection appeared in *First Indian on the Moon*, a collection of poetry and short prose published in 1993.

1.

In the reservation textbooks, we learned Indians were invented in 1492 by a crazy mixed-blood named Columbus. Immediately after class dismissal, the Indian children traded in those American stories and songs for a pair of tribal shoes. *These boots are made for walking, babe, and that's just what they'll do. One of these days these boots are gonna walk all over you.*

2.

Did you know that in 1492 every Indian instantly became an extra in the Great American Western? But wait, I never wondered what happened to Randolph Scott or Tom Mix. The Lone Ranger was never in my vocabulary. On the reservation, when we played Indians and cowboys, all of us little Skins fought on the same side against the cowboys in our minds. We never lost.

3.

Indians never lost their West, so how come I walk into the supermarket and find a dozen cowboy books telling me *How The West Was Won*? Curious, I travel to the world's largest shopping mall, find the Lost and Found Department. "Excuse me," I say. "I seem to have lost the West. Has anybody turned it in?" The clerk tells me I can find it in the Sears Home Entertainment Department, blasting away on fifty televisions.

4.

On Saturday morning television, the cowboy has fifty bullets in his six-shooter; he never needs to reload. It's just one more miracle for this country's heroes.

5.

My heroes have never been cowboys; my heroes carry guns in their minds.   5

6.

Win their hearts and minds and we win the war. Can you hear that song echo across history? If you give the Indian a cup of coffee with six cubes of sugar, he'll be your servant. If you give the Indian a cigarette and a book of matches, he'll be your friend. If you give the Indian a can of commodities, he'll be your lover. He'll hold you tight in his arms, cowboy, and two-step you outside.

7.

Outside it's cold and a confused snow falls in May. I'm watching some western on TBS, colorized, but the story remains the same. Three cowboys string telegraph wire across the plains until they are confronted by the entire Sioux nation. The cowboys, 19th century geniuses, talk the Indians into touching the wire, holding it in their hands and mouths. After a dozen or so have hold of the wire, the cowboys crank the portable generator and electrocute some of the Indians with a European flame and chase the rest of them away, bareback and burned. All these years later, the message tapped across my skin remains the same.

8.

It's the same old story whispered on the television in every HUD house on the reservation. It's 500 years of that same screaming song, translated from the American.

9.

Lester FallsApart found the American dream in a game of Russian Roulette: one bullet and five empty chambers. "It's Manifest Destiny," Lester said just before he pulled the trigger five times quick. "I missed," Lester said just before he reloaded the pistol: one empty chamber and five bullets. "Maybe we should call this Reservation Roulette," Lester said just before he pulled the trigger once at his temple and five more times as he pointed the pistol toward the sky.

10.

Looking up into the night sky, I asked my brother what he thought God looked like   10
and he said "God probably looks like John Wayne."

11.

We've all killed John Wayne more than once. When we burned the ant pile in our backyard, my brother and I imagined those ants were some cavalry or another. When Brian, that insane Indian boy from across the street, suffocated neighborhood dogs and stuffed their bodies into the reservation high school basement, he must have imagined those dogs were cowboys, come back to break another treaty.

12.

Every frame of the black and white western is a treaty; every scene in this elaborate serial is a promise. But what about the reservation home movies? What about the reservation heroes? I remember this: Down near Bull's Pasture, Eugene stood on the pavement with a gallon of tequila under his arm. I watched in the rearview mirror as he raised his arm to wave goodbye and dropped the bottle, glass and dreams of the weekend shattered. After all these years, that moment is still the saddest of my whole life.

13.

Your whole life can be changed by the smallest pain.

14.

Pain is never added to pain. It multiplies. Arthur, here we are again, you and I, fancy-dancing through the geometric progression of our dreams. Twenty years ago, we never believed we'd lose. Twenty years ago, television was our way of finding heroes and spirit animals. Twenty years ago, we never knew we'd spend the rest of our lives in the reservation of our minds, never knew we'd stand outside the gates of the Spokane Indian Reservation without a key to let ourselves back inside. From a distance, that familiar song. Is it country and western? Is it the sound of hearts breaking? Every song remains the same here in America, this country of the Big Sky and Manifest Destiny, this country of John Wayne and broken treaties. Arthur, I have no words which can save our lives, no words approaching forgiveness, no words flashed across the screen at the reservation drive-in, no words promising either of us top billing. Extras, Arthur, we're all extras.

(1993)

Questions

1. What does Sherman Alexie mean by the statement, "On the reservation, when we played Indians and cowboys, all of us little Skins fought on the same side against the cowboys in our minds" (par. 2)?
2. In this text, Alexie refers to "Manifest Destiny" (pars. 9 and 12). How would you define this term or concept from his perspective?

3. How do you interpret his assertion that "[e]very frame of the black and white western is a treaty; every scene in this elaborate serial is a promise" (par. 12)?
4. Violence — physical, emotional, and psychological — pervades this text. Identify examples of each type. What is Alexie's purpose in invoking violence?
5. Alexie refers to "the cowboys in our minds" (par. 2) and "the reservation of our minds" (par. 14). What is the significance of this division between the external perceived reality of his life and his internal understandings? How do film and references to film stars, such as John Wayne, help the author develop this conflict?
6. How does Alexie link the cowboy as symbol with his references to "story"?
7. Critic Ron McFarland describes Alexie's work as "a rhetoric . . . that reflects pain and anger, a rhetoric that could give way to bitterness. What keeps that from happening and makes the pain and anger bearable for the reader . . . is not so much the hope, love, and compassion . . . but humor. Predictably, this humor is rarely gentle or playful (though it can be that at times), but most often satirical." To what extent do you agree with this assessment? Refer to specifics in the text to support your response.

Buffalo Bill's Wild West
Celebrity, Memory, and Popular History

Joy Kasson

> Joy Kasson (b. 1944), author of several books on American history, is professor of American studies and English at the University of North Carolina, Chapel Hill. She received her BA from Radcliffe College and her PhD from Yale University and was a Fulbright Scholar. Following is an excerpt from the concluding chapter, "Performing National Identity," from her book *Buffalo Bill's Wild West: Celebrity, Memory, and Popular History* (2000).

Buffalo Bill's Wild West helped to shape both the substance of an American national identity and the tools for its cultural dissemination. Before Frederick Jackson Turner wrote a word about the frontier, and before Theodore Roosevelt established that the virtues of the strenuous life should be the basis for national pride and political success, Buffalo Bill had brilliantly propounded the thesis that American identity was founded on the Western experience: triumphant conquest of wildness through virtue, skill, and firepower. At the same time, and equally important, the Wild West sanitized this narrative. In its fictionalized historical representation, Americans could savor the thrill of danger without risking its consequences, could believe that struggle and conflict inflicted no lasting wounds, and could see for themselves that the enemy "other" would rise from the dust, wave to the crowd, and sell souvenir photographs at the end of the day.

Buffalo Bill's frontier thesis was never an explicit, coherent theory about what America was. Rather, its power came from being a spectacle so gripping, so encompassing, so sensuous that it became part of its spectators' own experience. Buffalo Bill's showmanship *created* American memory through the medium of popular entertainment. In doing so, it heralded the opening of a new age in mass communications in which both political and economic authority would accrue to those who could most effectively spin a message, sell a product, and shape popular perceptions. Not only did Buffalo Bill's Wild West promulgate a particular interpretation of American identity, but it also demonstrated the power of mass media to formulate values.

The substance of Buffalo Bill's frontier thesis infused American thinking for most of the twentieth century. From patriotic parades to football cheers, from tourist promotions to cigarette advertising, the image of the virile Western hero never lost its allure as a symbol of the American spirit. A recent book featuring beautiful photographs of artifacts from the largest private collection of Buffalo Bill memorabilia makes plain its authors' nostalgia for the Wild West's notion of American life. The authors acknowledge their love for the "romance and ethos of the Old West." That ethos seems to them still operative: "Not only is American culture the richer and more fascinating because of [Buffalo Bill's] unique legacy, but so is the rest of the world's." At the same time, these admiring collectors specifically associate the legacy of the Old West with a set of values threatened by late-twentieth-century transformations, those of their own childhood, when nation and family seemed to follow the script so carefully crafted by Cody and his associates: "an age of heroes, when there was still widespread respect for parental authority."[1] As the authors tacitly acknowledge, the considerable cynicism in public life in the late twentieth century worked against the tradition of uncritical hero worship. A chorus of voices raised questions about the values that underlay the romance of the Old West — from Stanley Kubrick, whose *Dr. Strangelove* envisioned the doomsday nuclear bomb falling with a hat-waving cowboy riding it like a bucking bronco, to critics of the Vietnam War who associated American military arrogance with the Wild West Texas drawl of President Lyndon Johnson.[2] Yet Ronald Reagan, the most popular of American presidents after the Vietnam War, took office on the strength of a cowboy image and a promise to make America ride "tall in the saddle" once again. . . .

The romance of the West has also been memorably transmitted to the present through twentieth-century America's most influential medium: motion pictures. More than seven thousand Western films and thousands more television Westerns have been produced, viewed, and re-viewed around the world.[3] Not only did Cody participate in the making of early Westerns himself, but the plot, characters, incidents, and personnel of the Wild West made an almost seamless leap from the arena to the early film studio. Edwin Porter's 1903 *Great Train Robbery* drew on the familiar Wild West story of the robbery of the stagecoach. Scenes from the Indian wars, narratives of captivity and rescue, Indian attack and cavalry charge, all set pieces from Buffalo Bill's Wild West, formed the backbone of many early film Westerns.

Similarly, Buffalo Bill's Wild West provided many of the performers for early Western films. Not coincidentally, a leading producer named his company the Bison Company when it moved its operations to California in 1909. Its paraphernalia and personnel were supplied by an entertainment organization that drew upon and competed with Cody's exhibitions, the Miller Brothers 101 Ranch Wild West Show, based

5

in Oklahoma. Miller Brothers hired many show Indians from the same Pine Ridge and Rosebud reservations where Cody recruited.[4] Within a few years, Bison productions were also using the same stock and materials spectators had seen in Buffalo Bill's Wild West. Miller Brothers and Bison were among the major buyers of animals and equipment at the bankruptcy sale after the failure of the Two Bills show.[5]

The marks of Buffalo Bill's Wild West are everywhere on the film Western. The generalized "Indian" dressed in feather headdress, war paint, and mounted on a racing pony moved directly into film from the Wild West, where differences between tribes were minimized and all Indians took on a generalized Plains Indian identity. The Stetson hat, which Buffalo Bill popularized (and advertised), became part of the standard costume for the Western film star. As Western films took on a life of their own at the mid-century, they began to depart from the Wild West's cast of characters. The figure of the cowboy, the focus for Western films and novels, had occupied a relatively small place in Buffalo Bill's Wild West, and the gunfighter, a Western film and television staple, never appeared. But to the extent that he was heroic, the Western film protagonist presented the frontier virtues that Buffalo Bill's performances had made famous: masculinity, courage, self-possession. As the critic Lee Clark Mitchell has written, the Western film is defined by "a set of problems recurring in endless combination: the problem of progress, . . . the problem of honor, . . . the problem of law or justice, . . . the problem of violence, . . . and subsuming all, the problem of what it means to be a man."[6] Thematically, Buffalo Bill's Wild West had set the stage for all these preoccupations. . . .

The substance of Buffalo Bill's legacy, then, lies in the dramatization of the cultural issues that have been basic to American national identity: the use of violence and conquest in the formation of the American nation, Americans' love-hate relationship with unspoiled nature and native peoples, gender and the meaning of heroism, and the role of the individual in an increasingly urban, industrial, and corporate society. But the Wild West's importance also lies in its very form: a mass medium that blurs the lines between fact and fiction, history and melodrama, truth and entertainment. Buffalo Bill's Wild West *became* the truth about America when it was *believed as* the truth by Americans and others around the world.

The organizers and promoters of Buffalo Bill's Wild West understood and deployed techniques of image creation, salesmanship, and promotion that would soon become standard for everything from breakfast cereal to political candidates. They created a thoroughly modern celebrity and made him into a brand name, instantly recognizable around the world. The sophisticated mass media of the twentieth century extended and elaborated upon the Wild West's ability to convince viewers they had seen "the real thing." By the time of Cody's death, Edward L. Bernays had embarked on his trailblazing career in "publicity direction," and the advertising boom of the 1920s transformed the ways in which products were marketed and designed. . . .

Despite his claims to historical significance, Buffalo Bill finally knew that he would be remembered as a showman: "Let my show go on," he was supposed to have said on his deathbed.[7] Certainly, Cody tried until the very end to keep alive not only his mortal body but his heroic self as well. Always hoping a fortune would be just around the corner, always eager to provide a good show and to connect with the public, he played those last seasons not just to pay the bills but, perhaps more importantly, to sustain the narrative of his life. Performing in Iowa in 1915, Cody gallantly stayed in the ring to help spectators endangered by a sudden flood while four hundred workers and performers fled to higher ground.[8] If the real man had become the stage persona, the opposite was also true.

Cody's position, subsumed into his own constructed image, was remarkably modern, a fact that was recognized in a tribute by one of the most self-conscious of modernist poets, E. E. Cummings. One of Cummings's first published poems, printed in the *Dial* in January 1920, was an elegy to Buffalo Bill:

> Buffalo Bill 's
> defunct
>   who used to
>   ride a watersmooth-silver
>   stallion
> and break onetwothreefourfive pigeonsjustlikethat
>   Jesus
>
> he was a handsome man
>   and what i want to know is
> how do you like your blueeyed boy
> Mister Death[9]

Manuscript pages of notes show that Cummings began the poem early in 1917, probably in response to a newspaper headline announcing Buffalo Bill's death.[10] As a child, Cummings had gone to circuses and made up his own animal acts. His library included a book about Buffalo Bill, and his childhood drawings included a picture of Sitting Bull and Buffalo Bill.[11] The poem evokes the energy and glamour of the Wild West, and suggests his own childhood fascination with performance and a willingness to be swept up in the excitement. The coinage *watersmooth-silver* suggests both the color and the rippling motion of Cody's big gray horse, Isham, his favorite mount in his later years, and the run-on phrases *onetwothreefourfive* and *pigeonsjustlikethat* suggest the breathlessness of an admiring fan.

The poem, simple and straightforward as it may first appear, resonates with the complexity of Buffalo Bill's own position in American culture. Cummings opens the poem with a worldly, ironic, modern voice. The word *defunct*, with its detached, clinical sound, also seems deflationary and harsh. Cummings's notes show that he first jotted down the phrase "Buffalo Bill is Dead," which he could have read in a newspaper.[12] The poem's terse, gruff opening refuses to participate in the heroic vocabulary with which Buffalo Bill identified himself with his own myth or in the gushingly sentimental accounts of his death.

But in the final three lines the irreverent modernist creates his own mythicized fantasy, imagining Buffalo Bill entering the afterlife, still the favored, blue-eyed boy, now performing not for the cheering public but for the mysterious "Mister Death."

The famous buffalo hunter and Indian fighter has always been the killer, but now he has become the prey. Yet the star is not knocked off his horse, dragged unceremoniously offstage and deprived of a red flannel scalp. In the courtly formality of the final phrase, Cummings suggests a Buffalo Bill whose heroism survives his death. Not a defunct corpse now but a handsome man who will be a blue-eyed boy forever, Cummings's hero rides offstage, radiating complexity, not unlike the living showman. Lighting out for the territory like Huck Finn, "going West" in the colloquial sense of dying, Cummings's Buffalo Bill is indeed an apt hero for the modern era, an age when images have become indistinguishable from what they purport to represent and the content of national identity seems identical to its performance.

Notes

1. R. L. Wilson, with Greg Martin, *Buffalo Bill's Wild West, An American Legend* (New York: Random House, 1998), pp. vii, 256.
2. Stanley Kubrick, dir., *Dr. Strangelove, or, How I Learned to Stop Worrying and Love the Bomb*, 1964; J. William Fulbright, *The Arrogance of Power* (New York: Random House, 1967).
3. Edward Buscombe, ed., *The BFI Companion to the Western* (London: André Deutsch, Ltd., 1988), p. 13.
4. L. C. Moses, *Wild West Shows and the Images of American Indians 1883–1933* (Albuquerque: University of New Mexico Press, 1996), p. 179.
5. Don Russell, *The Lives and Legends of Buffalo Bill* (Norman: University of Oklahoma Press, 1960), p. 456.
6. Lee Clark Mitchell, *Westerns: Making the Man in Fiction and Film* (Chicago: University of Chicago Press, 1996), p. 3.
7. Russell reports this claim, but doubts its accuracy, in *Lives and Legends*, p. 473.
8. Ibid., p. 460.
9. E. E. Cummings, *Complete Poems: 1904–1962*, Edited by George James Firmage (New York: Liveright, 1923, 1951, 1991), p. 90. Reprinted by permission of Liveright Publishing Corporation.
10. Rushworth M. Kidder, "'Buffalo Bill's' — An Early Cummings Manuscript," *Harvard Library Bulletin* 24 (Oct. 1976), pp. 373–80.
11. Richard S. Kennedy, *Dreams in the Mirror: A Biography of E. E. Cummings* (New York: Liveright, 1980), pp. 23, 31, 32.
12. Kidder, "'Buffalo Bill's.'" plate 1.

(2000)

Questions

1. What does Joy Kasson mean when she states that the Wild West show "sanitized" (par. 1) the narrative of the Western experience?
2. According to Kasson, what is "the script so carefully crafted by Cody and his associates" (par. 3)?

3. What influences of Buffalo Bill's Wild West does Kasson see in the cowboy of Western films? What qualities does she ascribe to the cowboy as film protagonist?
4. What is the purpose of Kasson's analysis of the poem on Buffalo Bill by E. E. Cummings? In what ways does it serve as evidence for a point she is making?
5. What does Kasson see as the "legacy" of Buffalo Bill? What is the logic behind her claim that his show "*became* the truth about America when it was *believed as* the truth by Americans and others around the world" (par. 7)? How persuasive do you find this interpretation?
6. What is Kasson's attitude toward William Cody/Buffalo Bill? Would you describe it as admiring, critical, ambivalent, objective, something other, or a combination of these?

The Virginian *Teaches the Merit of a Man*

Benjamin Percy

> Benjamin Percy (b. 1979) is the author of the novels *Red Moon* (2013) and *The Wilding* (2010) and the short-story collections *Refresh, Refresh* (2010) and *The Language of Elk* (2007). Following is a transcript of a segment from *All Things Considered* on National Public Radio in 2007.

My father was 50, mustached, and as deeply tan as a piece of jerky. The book was just as weather-beaten. He handed it to me and said, "Reading this will make a man out of you."

He had said the same when whipping fastball after fastball at me, teaching me to stand tough in the batter's box. Have to admit, I greeted *The Virginian* with as much enthusiasm as a knuckleball to the teeth.

But he pestered me and I began it. And once I began, the pages fluttered by so swiftly they made a breeze on my face. Then, more than anything, I wanted to tug on my metaphorical chaps and spur my horse forward at such a speed his hooves would rise off the pasture and we would be flying — 150 years into the past — when poker games inevitably went sour, when the six-shooter was the tool to fix all problems, when "days [looked] alike, and often [lost] their very names in the quiet depths of Cattle Land."

I don't know how to say it any better than this: the book made me ridiculously happy.

Published in 1902, Owen Wister's *The Virginian* is the first fully realized Western. 5 The mythical cowboy figure — the man of few words, the man who gets the girl and brings justice to the frontier, the man we know from countless films and pulp novels — first appears here.

He is the Virginian, a nameless and "slim young giant," who has "plainly come many miles from . . . across the vast horizon." If you imagine a yellowed map of the United States, and if you imagine a red arrow moving across it — accompanied by old-time piano music — tracing the passage of the thousands who heard the call "Go West!" and went, you have the Virginian's journey to Wyoming.

Immediately I felt a profound jealousy for the way the Virginian lights off for the territories, where every breath is "pure as water and strong as wine," and where he earns a reputation as a horseman.

By God, I wanted that!

I was 18 at the time, a legal adult — but a man? Could I be called that in earnest?

Owen Wister, like some great and terrible Moses draped in leather and carrying   10
a buffalo gun, taught me to re-examine what it meant to be a man. It meant more than earning a diploma or getting married or buying a house. It meant living simply, respecting women, holding congress with nature. It meant making decisions informed by a moral code so that you were never the one to start trouble, but oh, could you finish it. In our world of hydrogenated soybean oil and sport utility vehicles and Pottery Barn and grubless lawns, the novel is a welcome shot to the arm, a much needed antidote to all the plastic and phoniness.

Reading *The Virginian* helps me better appreciate honor and nature and life and testosterone, in the same way the Bible helps so many better appreciate God.

When trying to explain to his beloved why he must gunplay with a no-good rotten scoundrel of a cattle-thief, the Virginian says, "Can't yu' see how it must be about a man?" In many ways *this* is the novel's central concern — the merit of a man — and for a long time I have wandered in the Virginian's incompatible world, comparing myself to him. Quick draw, talented horseman, resilient drinker, feared by men and cherished by women. I like to think of us — together — hunting buffalo or warming beans over a campfire. Whenever I crack open the book, it almost seems possible — I am *almost* there.

(2007)

Questions

1. What is it about *The Virginian* that appealed to a young, twenty-first-century reader? Why does the book make Benjamin Percy "ridiculously happy" (par. 4)?
2. Percy says the novel made him "re-examine what it meant to be a man" (par. 10). What is his conclusion about what it does mean, and how does the character of the Virginian, "[t]he mythical cowboy figure" (par. 5), guide him to this understanding?
3. Do you find any of these descriptions hyperbolic: "Reading *The Virginian* helps me better appreciate honor and nature and life and testosterone, in the same way the Bible helps so many better appreciate God" (par. 11); Owen Wister was "like some great and terrible Moses draped in leather and carrying a buffalo gun" (par. 10); "In our world of hydrogenated soybean oil and sport utility vehicles and Pottery Barn and grubless lawns, the novel is a welcome shot to the arm, a much needed antidote to all the plastic and phoniness" (par. 10)? Why do you think these are or are not exaggerations? In what ways are they effective?
4. Based on Percy's response and the excerpts you read from *The Virginian* (p. 1036), why do you agree or disagree that the novel offers insights on what manhood means in the twenty-first century?

Making Connections

1. Is Frederic S. Remington's depiction of the West (p. 1028) more congruent with that of Joseph Nimmo Jr. in "The American Cowboy" (p. 1024) or of Owen Wister in *The Virginian* (p. 1036)?

2. Based on his poem "Buffalo Bill 's" (p. 1042), would E. E. Cummings be more in agreement with Frederick Jackson Turner's (p. 1029) or Sherman Alexie's (p. 1047) view of the cowboy?

3. How would Joy Kasson (p. 1050) view the *Marlboro Man* (p. 1043)? What might be her analysis of the photo's appeal?

4. How do you think Alexie would respond to Gretel Ehrlich's (p. 1044) depiction of the American cowboy?

5. Why do you agree or disagree with Kasson's assertion that Cummings's poem "resonates with the complexity of Buffalo Bill's own position in American culture" (par. 11)?

6. Used as an adjective, the word "cowboy" can be a pejorative, meaning someone who acts irresponsibly without regard for consequences (e.g., cowboy diplomacy). Do you find more support for this negative meaning in the selection by Nimmo or by Wister?

Entering the Conversation

As you respond to each of the following prompts, support your position with appropriate evidence, including at least three sources in this Conversation on the American cowboy, unless otherwise indicated.

1. Consider the following thoughts on the difference between myth and history from historian John Mack Faragher:

   Think of the word "myth" here not as a synonym for erroneous belief, but as the body of tales, fables, and fantasies that help a people make sense of its history. Like history, myth finds meaning in the events of the past. But unlike history, myth is less concerned with facts than with ideological essences.

   How much of what we know — and feel — about the American cowboy is myth and how much is fact? Is it important to distinguish between the two?

2. How have the myth and reality of the cowboy shaped today's definition of masculinity? Consider examples from popular culture along with at least two of the texts in this Conversation.

3. View a classic Western film — such as *The Oxbow Incident* (1943), *High Noon* (1952), *The Searchers* (1956), or *True Grit* (1969, 2010) — and discuss the characterization of

the cowboy in the American West. How does the film's depiction of this figure reflect or dispute at least three of the texts in this Conversation?

4. Other countries, particularly those in South America, have figures analogous to American cowboys: e.g., gauchos on the plains of the southern cone of South America; the *llaneros* on the plains of Colombia and Venezuela; the *vaqueiros* of the Brazilian northeast; and the Mexican *vaqueros*. Research one or more of these and discuss in what respects they are similar to and different from the myth and/or reality of the American cowboy.

5. What about the cowgirls? The National Cowgirl Museum and Hall of Fame explains its mission: to "honor and celebrate women, past and present, whose lives exemplify the courage, resilience, and independence that helped shape the American West, and foster an appreciation of the ideals and spirit of self-reliance they inspire." Who were these women? What made them famous? After researching this topic, compare and contrast the depiction of the cowgirl and that of the cowboy in American popular culture.

6. Imagine Sherman Alexie going to Buffalo Bill's Wild West. Write a monologue from Alexie's viewpoint, describing what he sees. You might do additional research into William Cody to inform your response.

Grammar as Rhetoric and Style
Modifiers

A modifier may be a one-word adverb or adjective; a phrase, such as a prepositional or participial phrase; or a clause, such as an adjective clause. At its best, a modifier describes, focuses, or qualifies the nouns, pronouns, and verbs it modifies. But when a writer overuses or incorrectly uses modifiers, the result may be verbose or even flowery writing.

Notice how Theodore Roosevelt uses modifiers to describe the virtues of "The Strenuous Life":

> We do not admire the man of timid peace. We admire the man who embodies victorious effort; the man who never wrongs his neighbor, who is prompt to help a friend, but who has those virile qualities necessary to win in the stern strife of actual life.

With simple but precise adjectives, he sets up a contrast: the man of "*timid* peace" versus one of "*victorious* effort." He follows with three relative clauses further defining the admirable man ("who . . . who . . . but who . . ."). He stresses at the end of the sentence the "*virile* qualities" of such a person and adds alliteration to the adjective-noun combination to leave us thinking about the "*stern* strife of *actual* life." Roosevelt's subject itself argues for muscular, concise writing as he defines an ethic of masculinity. His careful use of modifiers establishes a tension between passive and active responses to life's struggles.

In *Life on the Mississippi*, Mark Twain employs modifiers to convey the difficulty of learning "the shape of the river" when he was a cub riverboat pilot:

> I went to work now to learn the shape of the river; and of all the eluding and ungraspable objects that ever I tried to get mind or hands on, that was the chief. I would fasten my eyes upon a sharp, wooded point that projected far into the river some miles ahead of me, and go to laboriously photographing its shape upon my brain; and just as I was beginning to succeed to my satisfaction, we would draw up toward it and the exasperating thing would begin to melt away and fold back into the bank! If there had been a conspicuous dead tree standing upon the very point of the cape, I would find that tree inconspicuously merged into the general forest, and occupying the middle of a straight shore, when I got abreast of it! No prominent hill would stick to its shape long enough for me to make up my mind what its form really was, but it was as dissolving and changeful as if it had been a mountain of butter in the hottest corner of the tropics.

Twain seems almost to struggle to find the language to describe the river: trying to plumb its mysteries is more difficult than understanding any of "the *eluding* and *ungraspable* objects" he has encountered. The adjectives "eluding" and "ungraspable" evoke the difficulty and contrast with "a *sharp, wooded* point" that he sees miles ahead, a point whose shape he tries "*laboriously*" to photograph on his brain. Twain juxtaposes two words — an adjective and an adverb — with opposite meanings to emphasize his frustration: "a *conspicuous dead* tree standing upon the very point" that seems a "tree *inconspicuously* merged into the *general* forest." These modifiers help us feel what seems to him like a mirage, a "dissolving and changeful" form that echoes the "eluding and ungraspable objects" at the start of this description. The final simile may be the most striking image in the passage, but the modifiers have given us as readers a sense of how inadequate Twain feels trying to navigate what seems like the dreamscape of the Mississippi River.

Rhetorical and Stylistic Strategy

Like most language choices skilled writers make, picking the right modifiers contributes to achieving a particular effect and purpose. A clinical modifier has a different rhetorical effect than a lyrical one. Further, rhetorical strategies such as repetition and parallel structure apply to adjectives and adverbs, participial and prepositional phrases, and relative clauses.

Modifiers can enliven, focus, or qualify ideas. In this passage from *Fast Food Nation*, Eric Schlosser brings the scene in the slaughterhouse to life for his readers through modifiers that appeal to the senses:

> Sides of beef suspended from an overhead trolley swing toward a group of men. Each worker has a large knife in one hand and a steel hook in the other. They grab the meat with their hooks and attack it fiercely with their knives. As they hack away, using all their strength, grunting, the place suddenly feels different, primordial. The machinery seems beside the point, and what's going on before me has been going on for thousands of years — the meat, the hook, the knife, men straining to cut more meat.

In the first few sentences, Schlosser appeals to our visual and aural sensibilities to give us a vivid rendering of the gruesome scene. The sides of beef are "suspended from an *overhead* trolley." Each worker is armed with a "*large* knife . . . and a *steel* hook" that allow him to attack the meat "*fiercely*." We hear workers "grunting" as they hack at the meat until Schlosser says that despite the up-to-date machinery, the slaughterhouse feels "*primordial*" — a modifier meaning at the beginning of time, in an original state. Such an unusual modifier is likely to make us stop for a moment to think about the scene. Is Schlosser suggesting primordial as merely ancient, or does the word suggest a savagery out of sync with contemporary times?

Modifiers can add precision to a simple statement. In "The Subtle Problems of Charity," Jane Addams describes the affluent woman who wants to be of assistance to the poor:

> The charity visitor, let us assume, is a young college woman, well-bred and open-minded.

A few sentences later, Addams describes this woman's awareness that

> whatever her virtues may be, they are not the industrial virtues; that her untrained hands are no more fitted to cope with actual conditions than are those of her broken-down family.

In the first sentence, "*young college* woman" would identify the person, but the modifiers "*well-bred* and *open-minded*" give us a better sense of the perspective she brings to her situation. Similarly, in the second example, "*untrained*" and "*broken-down*" add vividness to the point Addams is making. Without the modifiers, we could understand the ideas Addams is expressing, but the emphasis and immediacy brought by those descriptive details would be missing.

Modifiers add concrete detail in both of the previous examples, but they can also add a sort of poetry to description and narration. In *Life on the Mississippi*, Mark Twain reflects on his loss of wonder for and sense of mystery about the river once he became a skilled pilot.

> All the grace, the beauty, the poetry, had gone out of the majestic river! I still kept in mind a certain wonderful sunset which I witnessed when steamboating

was new to me. A broad expanse of the river was turned to blood; in the middle distance the red hue brightened into gold, through which a solitary log came floating, black and conspicuous; one place a long, slanting mark lay sparkling upon the water; in another the surface was broken by boiling, tumbling rings, that were as many-tinted as an opal; where the ruddy flush was faintest, was a smooth spot that was covered with graceful circles and radiating lines, ever so delicately traced; the shore on our left was densely wooded, and the somber shadow that fell from this forest was broken in one place by a long, ruffled trail that shone like silver; and high above the forest wall a clean-stemmed dead tree waved a single leafy bough that glowed like a flame in the unobstructed splendor that was flowing from the sun. There were graceful curves, reflected images, woody heights, soft distances; and over the whole scene, far and near, the dissolving lights drifted steadily, enriching it every passing moment with new marvels of coloring.

Twain describes the sunset through the eyes of the boy who was awed by the mystery of the landscape. The ordinary, even vague adjective "wonderful" is qualified by the description that follows: "red hue brightened into gold," a "*solitary* log" that was "black and conspicuous," and a mark that "lay *sparkling*." Twain describes patterns on the water's surface being "broken by *boiling, tumbling* rings" and "*graceful* circles and *radiating* lines, ever so delicately traced." Throughout the passage, these modifiers lead us to see the "new marvels of coloring" that the sunset impressed on the young Twain.

Modifiers can work through juxtaposition to emphasize contrast and through parallel structure to add emphasis. Let's look at this passage by Joy Kasson about Buffalo Bill Cody:

Despite his claims to historical significance, Buffalo Bill finally knew that he would be remembered as a showman: "Let my show go on," he was supposed to have said on his deathbed. Certainly, Cody tried until the very end to keep alive not only his mortal body but his heroic self as well. Always hoping a fortune would be just around the corner, always eager to provide a good show and to connect with the public, he played those last seasons not just to pay the bills but, perhaps more importantly, to sustain the narrative of his life.

Through juxtaposition of contrasting adjectives, she emphasizes the contrast of Cody's "*mortal* body" with his "*heroic* self" — that is, his physical presence versus the legend. She emphasizes similarity by repeating the adverb "always" before two participial phrases: "Always hoping" and "always eager."

Cautions

Studying how accomplished writers use modifiers helps us understand how to use them effectively. Following are some cautions to keep in mind when using modifiers in your own writing.

1. *Do not use too many modifiers.* Mark Twain gives a clear image of how he felt as a cub pilot on the mighty Mississippi River. However, less experienced writers may overwrite by including too many adjectives, as shown in the following example:

> The bright yellow compact car with the pun-laden, out-of-state vanity plates was like beautiful, warm sunshine on the gray, dreary Tuesday afternoon.

2. *Do not rely on adjectives when strong verbs would be more effective.* Instead of writing "Elani walked with a confident and quick stride," perhaps write, "Elani strutted."

3. *Beware of adding too many qualifiers.* Be especially careful about *really* and *very.* "Troy felt really sad" might be expressed as "Troy felt discouraged" or "despondent." Or it might simply be stated as "Troy felt sad." Similarly, "The mockingbird's song is very beautiful" is probably just as well stated as "The mockingbird's song is beautiful" or, introducing a strong verb, as "The mockingbird serenades."

You need not avoid qualifiers altogether, but if you find yourself using them over and over, it's time to check whether they're *really very* effective.

• EXERCISE 1 •

Rewrite each of the following sentences to make the modifiers more effective.

1. Dolores offered a perfectly unique view of the situation.
2. I really had difficulty understanding my teacher because he talked so quickly and softly.
3. Michael was so very excited about the beginning of lacrosse season that he could barely sleep.
4. Susan talked with self-assurance about movies she hadn't even seen.
5. The skyline was amazing on the beautiful evening.

• EXERCISE 2 •

Identify the modifiers, both words and phrases, in the following paragraphs from "The Cutting of My Long Hair" by Zitkala-Ša. Are the modifiers effective or excessive? Cite specific examples to support your view of whether the modifiers support or distract from Zitkala-Ša's achieving her purpose.

The first day in the land of apples was a bitter-cold one; for the snow still covered the ground, and the trees were bare. A large bell rang for breakfast, its loud metallic voice crashing through the belfry overhead and into our sensitive ears. The annoying clatter of shoes on bare floors gave us no peace. The constant clash of harsh noises, with an undercurrent of many voices murmuring an unknown tongue, made a bedlam within which I was securely tied. And though my spirit tore itself in struggling for its lost freedom, all was useless.

A paleface woman, with white hair, came up after us. We were placed in a line of girls who were marching into the dining room. These were Indian girls, in stiff shoes and closely clinging dresses. The small girls wore sleeved aprons and shingled hair. As I walked noiselessly in my soft moccasins, I felt like sinking to the floor, for my blanket had been stripped from my shoulders. I looked hard at the Indian girls, who seemed not to care that they were even more immodestly dressed than I, in their tightly fitting clothes.

• EXERCISE 3 •

Focus on the use of modifiers in the following passage from "The Talented Tenth" by W. E. B. DuBois. Look carefully at the adjectives he uses to characterize the present moment as well as the past. Consider how the use of repetition and parallel structure adds to the impact of adjective clauses and adverbs. How do the modifiers contribute to the dramatic effect DuBois builds?

And so we come to the present—a day of cowardice and vacillation, of strident wide-voiced wrong and fainthearted compromise; of double-faced dallying with Truth and Right. Who are to-day guiding the work of the Negro people? The "exceptions" of course. And yet so sure as this Talented Tenth is pointed out, the blind worshippers of the Average cry out in alarm: "These are exceptions, look here at death, disease and crime—these are the happy rule." Of course they are the rule, because a silly nation made them the rule: Because for three long centuries this people lynched Negroes who dared to be brave, raped black women who dared to be virtuous, crushed dark-hued youth who dared to be ambitious, and encouraged and made to flourish servility and lewdness and apathy. But not even this was able to crush all manhood and chastity and aspiration from black folk. A saving remnant continually survives and persists, continually aspires, continually shows itself in thrift and ability and character.

• EXERCISE 4 •

We have removed many of the modifiers in the following passage from *Life on the Mississippi*, in which Mark Twain describes how he felt as a young pilot taking the helm on his own, unaware that his mentor Mr. Bixby was watching nearby.

- Read the paragraph aloud, and listen to its cadence (the combination of the text's rhythm with the rise and fall in the inflection of the speaker's voice).
- Add the following modifiers: *frightful, easy, calmly, deadly, blind, vaingloriously, sole, gaily, awful, entirely, prodigiously.* (Check the meaning of any unfamiliar words.) Use these adjectives and adverbs to improve the paragraph's effectiveness.
- Compare your version to the original (see pp. 852–53, par. 57).
- Discuss the rhetorical effect of the modifiers in this passage.

I did not know that he was hiding behind a chimney to see how I would perform. I went along, getting prouder and prouder, for he had never left the boat in my charge such a length of time before. I even got to "setting" her and letting the wheel go, while I turned my back and inspected the stern marks and hummed a tune, a sort of indifference which I had admired in Bixby and other great pilots. Once I inspected rather long, and when I faced to the front again my heart flew into my mouth so suddenly that if I hadn't clapped my teeth together I should have lost it. One of those bluff reefs was stretching its length right across our bows! My head was gone in a moment; I did not know which end I stood on; I gasped and could not get my breath; I spun the wheel down with such rapidity that it wove itself together like a spider's web; the boat answered and turned square away from the reef, but the reef followed her! I fled, but still it followed, still it kept — right across my bows! I never looked to see where I was going, I only fled. The crash was imminent. Why didn't that villain come? If I committed the crime of ringing a bell I might get thrown overboard. But better that than kill the boat. So in desperation I started such a rattling "shivaree" down below as never had astounded an engineer in this world before, I fancy. Amidst the frenzy of the bells the engines began to back and fill in a furious way, and my reason forsook its throne — we were about to crash into the woods on the other side of the river. Just then Mr. Bixby stepped into view on the hurricane deck.

• EXERCISE 5 •

Following are examples of authors' skillful use of modifiers, both single words and phrases. In each, identify the modifier or modifiers, and discuss the effect they create. Then write a sentence or passage of your own, emulating the writer's technique.

1. [W]e shall contribute one-third to the business and industrial prosperity of the South, or we shall prove a veritable body of death, stagnating, depressing, retarding every effort to advance the body politic.
   — BOOKER T. WASHINGTON

2. Although official statistics are not kept, the death rate among slaughter-house sanitation crews is extraordinarily high. They are the ultimate in disposable workers: illegal, illiterate, impoverished, untrained.

— ERIC SCHLOSSER

3. A thorough knowledge and judicious exercise of this power in lynching localities could many times effect a bloodless revolution.

— IDA B. WELLS-BARNETT

4. The injured captain, lying in the bow, was at this time buried in that profound dejection and indifference which comes, temporarily at least, to even the bravest and most enduring when, willy nilly, the firm fails, the army loses, the ship goes down.

— STEPHEN CRANE

5. We are beginning to understand the individual cost that the schism between work and family exacts. We have not added up the national cost.

— MADELEINE M. KUNIN

6. Instead of the macho, trigger-happy man our culture has perversely wanted him to be, the cowboy is more apt to be convivial, quirky, and softhearted.

— GRETEL EHRLICH

7. Half a mile from home, at the farther edge of the woods, where the land was highest, a great pine-tree stood, the last of its generation.

— SARAH ORNE JEWETT

Suggestions for Writing
Reconstructing America

1. This period in U.S. history is often characterized as a time of "a loss of innocence" brought about by the divisions and bloodshed of the Civil War. How would you define that phrase in this context? Write an essay explaining how the literature of the era reflects "a loss of innocence" in the spirit of the nation. Feel free to use texts that pose or suggest a counterargument.

2. During the era covered by this chapter, fiction flourished, and with the growth of periodicals, the short story gained enormous popularity and influence. Using at least three of the pieces of fiction from this chapter, write an essay discussing why you believe short stories had such popular appeal for the American public.

3. Immigration, industrialization, and urbanization characterize this time period and widened social divisions based on wealth, religion, race, and ethnicity. Write an essay discussing the increasing divides in American culture as illustrated in several of the texts in this chapter.

4. With newly freed African Americans and a growing immigrant population, educating a larger populace that was more diverse than an elite group of affluent white men became problematic for the states. What approaches were suggested, or tried, during this era? What were the main issues that educating an expanding democracy posed? Refer to several of the texts in this chapter in your response.

5. After the Civil War, how did Americans promote the idea of "re-union" — of bringing the nation back together? Develop a discussion that includes at least four authors from this period who address the question, How can the wounds of war be healed?

6. One of the tensions during this period was between the desire to assimilate into mainstream culture and the desire to preserve tradition and heritage. In some instances, assimilation was made more difficult because of discrimination. Based on the texts you've read in this chapter, discuss how this tension manifested itself and at least two different responses to it. Which inclination do you think ultimately dominated this period?

7. A powerful symbol of western expansion, the railroad, particularly the transcontinental railroad, was both idealized and demonized. While to many it demonstrated America's technological prowess and the power of industrialization, to others it brought into high relief exploitation of low-cost labor, including immigrants, that resulted from corporate greed. Using texts from this chapter and others from your research, discuss how the building of railroads to link the established East and the developing West embodied both of these perspectives.

8. Following is an excerpt from the *Brooklyn Daily Eagle* on May 23, 1883, celebrating the opening of the Brooklyn Bridge, one of the most amazing engineering feats of its day:

> Brooklyn, if not New York also, will turn aside from all ordinary business tomorrow to celebrate one of the noblest achievements of modern times. The bridge about to be opened to the public is a work as characteristic of our civilization as the Pyramid of Cheops was of Egypt. The colossal pile of stone which still excites the wonder of travelers in the land of the Pharaohs recalls the magnificence of a tyrannical dynasty, the vast influence of a hierarchy buttressed by superstition and the practical enslavement of millions of industrious people. The bridge is a monument to the skill of a free people, to the arts of peace, to liberal thought and to the spirit which makes the promotion of the common welfare the chief end of government. It is possible for the Americans to rear pyramids if he were so minded; it was not possible for the combined intellect of

antiquity to spin a yard of the 14,361 miles of wire by which two cities are bound together.

Discuss how this description of the Brooklyn Bridge defined America's sense of itself in the world at that time. How does this view compare with other perspectives, similar or different, in other texts you've read in this chapter?

9. In a previous chapter you analyzed the history and lyrics of "The Star-Spangled Banner," and in this chapter you read "America the Beautiful" and "Lift Ev'ry Voice and Sing." We have a history of debate over the concept and choice of a national anthem in this country. Some argue that "The Star-Spangled Banner" places too strong an emphasis on war and that "America the Beautiful" would, thus, be preferable. Others argue that the diversity of the country makes any single national anthem inappropriate and meaningless. Discuss whether the current national anthem should be retained, replaced, or abandoned entirely. If you believe change is appropriate, what do you suggest should be the U.S. anthem?

10. In 1872, John Gast painted *American Progress* (p. 825), commissioned by George Crofutt, who published a popular series of western travel guides. Discuss how this image reflects or disputes "progress" as defined during this period in American history.

America in the Modern World

1913–1945

The decades surrounding the turn of the twentieth century were a time of unprecedented change. The world was still wrestling with the groundbreaking ideas of the late nineteenth century: Sigmund Freud's notion of the unconscious mind (the id), Karl Marx's socialism, Charles Darwin's theory of evolution, and Friedrich Nietzsche's nihilist mantra "God is dead" that announced a growing secularization in society. Meanwhile, the United States, and much of the Western world, was experiencing rapid industrialization, a boom in urban populations, and a flurry of scientific and technological breakthroughs that would lay the foundation for modern life. Inasmuch as humanity had ever been confident that it understood itself, life, or the world we live in, these destabilizing forces shattered that confidence. Traditional art forms suddenly seemed incapable of representing the mystery, complexity, and uncertainty of modern life. Not to mention the fact that Kodak's invention of the simple, affordable "Brownie" camera in 1900 meant that making representative visual art no longer required years of training, but just a simple click of the shutter. The response to these changes was a movement called modernism — marked by abstract art, symbolic poetry, and stream-of-consciousness prose — that tried to represent the subjective experience of modern life rather than the objective reality of it. It was driven by innovation in form and content. As poet Ezra Pound declared, "Make it new!" The unofficial starting point of modernism in America was the 1913 Armory Show, officially titled the International Exhibition of Modern Art, which introduced American audiences to the works of European modern artists such as Henri Matisse, Marcel Duchamp, and Pablo Picasso. In this chapter, you will study works by Ezra Pound, Marsden Hartley, Wallace Stevens, T. S. Eliot, William Carlos Williams, Charles Demuth, and other modernist pioneers who made American art and literature new.

Amid this cultural tumult came what President Woodrow Wilson called "the war to end all wars." Urging Congress to declare war on Germany in 1917, Wilson called for America to spread liberty across the world, which must be "made safe for democracy." World War I was one of the bloodiest wars in recorded history, with a deadly combination of primitive trench-warfare tactics and modern weaponry taking nearly 9 million lives. It was also one of the most politically bewildering, beginning as a struggle between the Austro-Hungarian Empire and Serbia before a tangled web of alliances dragged Russia, Great Britain, France, Germany, Italy, the Ottoman

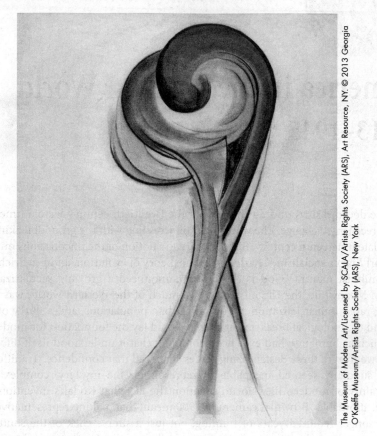

The Museum of Modern Art/Licensed by SCALA/Artists Rights Society (ARS), Art Resource, NY. © 2013 Georgia O'Keeffe Museum/Artists Rights Society (ARS), New York

GEORGIA O'KEEFE, *NO. 12 SPECIAL*, 1916, CHARCOAL ON PAPER, 24"×19", MUSEUM OF MODERN ART, NEW YORK.

Empire, Japan, Bulgaria, and ultimately the United States into the conflict. Although World War I began in 1914, the United States did not get involved until April 1917, spurred to action by the 1915 German sinking of the British ocean liner *Lusitania*, which killed 128 Americans, and the sinking of seven American merchant ships in January 1917. The United States remained actively engaged in the conflict until its conclusion in November 1918, mobilizing more than 4 million troops and suffering approximately 110,000 casualties — 43,000 of which stemmed from an influenza epidemic. World War I ushered in a new era of American military might and American industrialization; through its presence in the war, America made good on Wilson's promise, as it spread its principles of reform, freedom, and democracy.

The United States emerged from World War I into a period of relative peace and prosperity. Cities were burgeoning, reforms were taking hold, and success in the war gave rise to a feeling of American security and self-confidence. The so-called Roaring Twenties epitomized this sentiment. The 1920s saw a dramatic increase in Americans'

Corbis

American troops on the front line in the Meuse valley, north of Verdun, France, in 1916.

use of cars, telephones, and electricity; we turned our attention to celebrity culture through the movies and sports through the construction of giant stadiums. Industries boomed as American consumers demanded new and better innovations. Women gained the right to vote in 1920, giving them a voice in American political life for the first time. "Flapper" culture encouraged women to shake off the constraints of nineteenth-century fashion; women stopped wearing corsets, showed off their arms and legs, cut their hair short, and wore makeup.

During the 1920s, American literature, art, and music changed dramatically. New York City's uptown Harlem neighborhood was the center of the New Negro Movement, later called the Harlem Renaissance, as art, literature, and music by African Americans found new expression. Harlem was a destination for many migrant African Americans seeking work and economic opportunity; it was also home to a new African American middle class. The works by Langston Hughes, Claude McKay, Zora Neale Hurston, and Richard Wright in this chapter will ask you to consider issues of equality, racial pride, stereotyping, integration, and identity. In this chapter's Conversation on the influence of jazz, we will explore the cultural impact of this music and how other arts were inspired by its new, experimental, and genuinely American form of expression.

Bettmann/Corbis

A "Hooverville" of makeshift shacks in New York City's Central Park, c. 1931.

The Roaring Twenties came to a screeching halt when the stock market crashed on October 29, 1929, the day known as "Black Tuesday." Wall Street collapsed, and the United States slipped into a severe economic downturn that led to the Great Depression. The Great Depression dragged on throughout the 1930s, with unemployment rates reaching nearly 25 percent. To make matters worse, a catastrophic drought and erosion from poor farming practices caused a dust bowl in the American Midwest, where agricultural production halted and farmers were displaced from their land.

President Franklin Delano Roosevelt was inaugurated in 1933, and his series of progressive reforms and programs, known as the New Deal, slowly began to improve the lives of suffering Americans. Roosevelt's second inaugural address and his First Lady Eleanor Roosevelt's speech "What Libraries Mean to the Nation" will help you understand the circumstances of American life during the Great Depression, as well as the enduring role of literature throughout difficult periods of our history. Works by John Steinbeck and William Faulkner also explore rural American life during the 1930s.

By the end of the 1930s, another war was raging throughout Europe. As in the previous conflict, the United States at first chose not to engage in the war. However, on December 7, 1941, Japan attacked the American naval fleet stationed at Pearl Harbor, Hawaii, and thrust America into the Second World War, fighting against Japan, Germany, and Italy. World War II ended up being the deadliest, costliest, and most sprawling war in recorded history. Over 16 million Americans fought in the military—290,000 were killed and 670,000 were wounded. Randall Jarrell's famous poem "The Death of the Ball Turret Gunner" takes us into the world of one soldier.

Everyday life on the home front was dramatically altered during World War II. Food, clothing, and gas were rationed. Women joined the war effort by taking jobs as electricians, riveters, and welders in factories producing goods for the war. The lives of Japanese Americans were shattered when they were forced into internment camps on the off chance they might be spies, a wartime policy now universally regarded as one of the most egregious stains on our nation's history and reputation. A cluster of texts in this chapter asks you to investigate the internment of Japanese Americans and to consider if it is possible to right the wrongs of the past through reparations.

The Second World War ended with a bang. And that bang would change the world forever. Atomic bombs dropped by the United States on Hiroshima and Nagasaki not only ended the war in the Pacific but also propelled the nation into the atomic age.

A view of Hiroshima after the explosion of the atomic bomb.

Bettmann/Corbis

In this chapter, you will read the speech President Harry S Truman gave announcing this destructive event and the arrival of America as a global superpower.

As it turned out, despite the great loss of life and widespread destruction, World War II was exactly the economic stimulus that America needed to end the Great Depression. The country emerged from the war as a global military and economic superpower primed for a new era of prosperity.

EZRA POUND

Ezra Pound (1885–1972) was an American poet, critic, and editor and a major figure of the early modernist movement. Though he was born in Hailey, Idaho, it wasn't until he moved to Europe in 1908 that he published several books of poetry and found success. In the early twentieth century, while working in London as a foreign editor for several American literary magazines, Pound heralded a modernist movement in English and American literature, helping to discover and shape the work of contemporaries such as T. S. Eliot, James Joyce, Robert Frost, and Ernest Hemingway. Pound moved to Italy after World War I, where his pro-Fascist broadcasts and publications led to his arrest by American forces in 1945 and more than a decade of incarceration. His most famous works include *Ripostes* (1912), *Hugh Selwyn Mauberley* (1920), and his unfinished 120-section epic, *The Cantos* (1917–1969), some sections of which he wrote in prison.

In a Station of the Metro

Published in January 1913 in the magazine *Poetry*, "In a Station of the Metro" describes Pound's experience in a Paris subway (called the Metro) station.

The apparition of these faces in the crowd;
Petals on a wet, black bough.

(1913)

Exploring the Text

1. Do you think this poem is happy or sad? Explain your answer.
2. What sensory associations do you make when you read this poem?
3. What exactly do you think the speaker is looking at? Explain your answer.
4. What is the effect of juxtaposing flowers with a subway station?
5. You may recognize this poem as a form of haiku (or hokku, as Ezra Pound called it). In what ways is it like a traditional haiku and in what ways is it different? Hint: consider the function of the title.

6. Pound was an imagist, one of a group of English and American poets who wrote free verse and believed in the simple clarity of an image. "In a Station of the Metro" is considered a prime example of imagism. Looking at this brief poem, consider how Pound uses metaphor to make us see something new in a train station and how it came to be an iconic imagist poem.

A Few Don'ts by an Imagiste

Ezra Pound coined the term "imagist" when he was editing the work of his friend Hilda Doolittle (HD). In part a rebellion against the rules of rhyme and meter in traditional English poetry, the imagist's goal was to allow the images to create the poem. Up until this time, literary movements originated in France, which was why Pound gave the new movement a French name in this piece. "A Few Don'ts by an Imagiste" was published in *Poetry* magazine, just a couple of months after "In a Station of the Metro," in March 1913.

An "Image" is that which presents an intellectual and emotional complex in an instant of time. I use the term "complex" rather in the technical sense employed by the newer psychologists, such as Hart, though we might not agree absolutely in our application.

It is the presentation of such a "complex" instantaneously which gives that sense of sudden liberation; that sense of freedom from time limits and space limits; that sense of sudden growth, which we experience in the presence of the greatest works of art.

It is better to present one Image in a lifetime than to produce voluminous works.

All this, however, some may consider open to debate. The immediate necessity is to tabulate A LIST OF DON'TS for those beginning to write verses. But I can not put all of them into Mosaic negative.

To begin with, consider the three rules recorded by Mr. Flint, not as dogma — never consider anything as dogma — but as the result of long contemplation, which, even if it is some one else's contemplation, may be worth consideration.

Pay no attention to the criticism of men who have never themselves written a notable work. Consider the discrepancies between the actual writing of the Greek poets and dramatists, and the theories of the Graeco-Roman grammarians, concocted to explain their metres.

5

Language

Use no superfluous word, no adjective, which does not reveal something.

Don't use such an expression as "dim lands *of peace*." It dulls the image. It mixes an abstraction with the concrete. It comes from the writer's not realizing that the natural object is always the *adequate* symbol.

Go in fear of abstractions. Don't retell in mediocre verse what has already been done in good prose. Don't think any intelligent person is going to be deceived when you try to shirk all the difficulties of the unspeakably difficult art of good prose by chopping your composition into line lengths.

What the expert is tired of today the public will be tired of tomorrow. 10

Don't imagine that the art of poetry is any simpler than the art of music, or that you can please the expert before you have spent at least as much effort on the art of verse as the average piano teacher spends on the art of music.

Be influenced by as many great artists as you can, but have the decency either to acknowledge the debt outright, or to try to conceal it.

Don't allow "influence" to mean merely that you mop up the particular decorative vocabulary of some one or two poets whom you happen to admire. A Turkish war correspondent was recently caught red-handed babbling in his dispatches of "dove-gray" hills, or else it was "pearl-pale," I can not remember.

Use either no ornament or good ornament.

Rhythm and Rhyme

Let the candidate fill his mind with the finest cadences he can discover, preferably in 15 a foreign language so that the meaning of the words may be less likely to divert his attention from the movement; e.g., Saxon charms, Hebridean Folk Songs,[1] the verse of Dante, and the lyrics of Shakespeare — if he can dissociate the vocabulary from the cadence. Let him dissect the lyrics of Goethe coldly into their component sound values, syllables long and short, stressed and unstressed, into vowels and consonants.

It is not necessary that a poem should rely on its music, but if it does rely on its music that music must be such as will delight the expert.

Let the neophyte know assonance and alliteration, rhyme immediate and delayed, simple and polyphonic, as a musician would expect to know harmony and counterpoint and all the minutiae of his craft. No time is too great to give to these matters or to any one of them, even if the artist seldom have need of them.

Don't imagine that a thing will "go" in verse just because it's too dull to go in prose.

Don't be "viewy" — leave that to the writers of pretty little philosophic essays. Don't be descriptive; remember that the painter can describe a landscape much better than you can, and that he has to know a deal more about it.

When Shakespeare talks of the "Dawn in russet mantle clad" he presents some- 20 thing which the painter does not present. There is in this line of his nothing that one can call description; he presents.

Consider the way of the scientists rather than the way of an advertising agent for a new soap.

The scientist does not expect to be acclaimed as a great scientist until he has *discovered* something. He begins by learning what has been discovered already. He goes from that point onward. He does not bank on being a charming fellow personally. He does not expect his friends to applaud the results of his freshman class work. Freshmen in poetry are unfortunately not confined to a definite and recognizable

---

[1]The Hebrides are a series of islands off the northwest tip of Scotland. — Eds.

class room. They are "all over the shop." Is it any wonder "the public is indifferent to poetry"?

Don't chop your stuff into separate *iambs*. Don't make each line stop dead at the end, and then begin every next line with a heave. Let the beginning of the next line catch the rise of the rhythm wave, unless you want a definite longish pause.

In short, behave as a musician, a good musician, when dealing with that phase of your art which has exact parallels in music. The same laws govern, and you are bound by no others.

Naturally, your rhythmic structure should not destroy the shape of your words, or their natural sound, or their meaning. It is improbable that, at the start, you will be able to get a rhythm-structure strong enough to affect them very much, though you may fall a victim to all sorts of false stopping due to line ends and caesurae. 25

The musician can rely on pitch and the volume of the orchestra. You can not. The term harmony is misapplied to poetry; it refers to simultaneous sounds of different pitch. There is, however, in the best verse a sort of residue of sound which remains in the ear of the hearer and acts more or less as an organ-base. A rhyme must have in it some slight element of surprise if it is to give pleasure; it need not be bizarre or curious, but it must be well used if used at all.

Vide[2] further Vildrac and Duhamel's notes on rhyme in *Technique Poetique*.

That part of your poetry which strikes upon the imaginative *eye* of the reader will lose nothing by translation into a foreign tongue; that which appeals to the ear can reach only those who take it in the original.

Consider the definiteness of Dante's presentation, as compared with Milton's rhetoric. Read as much of Wordsworth as does not seem too unutterably dull.

If you want the gist of the matter go to Sappho, Catullus, Villon, Heine when he is in the vein, Gautier when he is not too frigid; or, if you have not the tongues, seek out the leisurely Chaucer. Good prose will do you no harm, and there is good discipline to be had by trying to write it. 30

Translation is likewise good training, if you find that your original matter "wobbles" when you try to rewrite it. The meaning of the poem to be translated can not "wobble."

If you are using a symmetrical form, don't put in what you want to say and then fill up the remaining vacuums with slush.

Don't mess up the perception of one sense by trying to define it in terms of another. This is usually only the result of being too lazy to find the exact word. To this clause there are possibly exceptions.

The first three simple proscriptions will throw out nine-tenths of all the bad poetry now accepted as standard and classic; and will prevent you from many a crime of production.

". . . *Mais d'abord il faut etre un poete*,"[3] as MM. Duhamel and Vildrac have said at the end of their little book, *Notes sur la Technique Poetique*; but in an American one 35

---

[2] Latin. "See." — Eds.
[3] French. "But first you have to be a poet." — Eds.

takes that at least for granted, otherwise why does one get born upon that august continent!

(1913)

Exploring the Text

1. Describe the tone of "A Few Don'ts by an Imagiste."
2. What do you think is the purpose of this essay?
3. We know that Ezra Pound had a long (and controversial) career as a poet, a critic, and an editor. He was only twenty-eight when he wrote this essay. How does he establish ethos?
4. Do you think Pound's ideas in this essay are conservative or revolutionary? Explain your answer.
5. English poet and critic F. S. Flint (par. 5) put forth three rules to write good poetry: (1) to directly treat the "thing," whether subjectively or objectively; (2) to use absolutely no word that does not contribute to the presentation; and (3) with regard to rhythm, to compose in sequence of the musical phrase, not in sequence of the metronome. What other rules does Pound lay out in this essay? In what ways do they support Flint's rules and in what ways do they run counter to them?
6. In what ways does Pound suggest applying his suggestions and rules to areas other than poetry? What other applications can you think of? How might you apply them to your own writing, for example?

ROBERT FROST

Though Robert Frost (1874–1963) is considered the quintessential New England poet, he was born in San Francisco. After the death of his father when Frost was eleven years old, the family moved to Massachusetts. Frost attended Dartmouth College and Harvard University, but in both cases he left early to support his family. He delivered newspapers, farmed, worked in a factory, and taught high school and college, but he considered poetry his true calling. Frost won four Pulitzer Prizes for his collections *New Hampshire: A Poem with Notes and Grace Notes* (1924), *Collected Poems* (1931), *A Further Range* (1937), and *A Witness Tree* (1943). In 1961, Frost recited one of his poems at the inauguration of President John F. Kennedy.

Reluctance

Published in 1914, "Reluctance" was inspired somewhat by a trip Frost made to North Carolina's Dismal Swamp after Elinor White, who later became his wife, refused his first marriage proposal.

Out through the fields and the woods
   And over the walls I have wended;
I have climbed the hills of view
   And looked at the world, and descended;
I have come by the highway home,   5
   And lo, it is ended.

The leaves are all dead on the ground,
   Save those that the oak is keeping
To ravel them one by one
   And let them go scraping and creeping   10
Out over the crusted snow,
   When others are sleeping.

And the dead leaves lie huddled and still,
   No longer blown hither and thither;
The last lone aster is gone;   15
   The flowers of the witch hazel wither;
The heart is still aching to seek,
   But the feet question "Whither?"

Ah, when to the heart of man
   Was it ever less than a treason   20
To go with the drift of things,
   To yield with a grace to reason,
And bow and accept the end
   Of a love or a season?

(1914)

Exploring the Text

1. How does Robert Frost use the natural world to make an argument?
2. What do you make of the play on words with "wither" (l. 16) and "whither" (l. 18)? What do you think is the answer to the question of "Whither," which means "where"?
3. Frost is considered a modernist poet, which means, among other things, that his work has an economy and a directness to it. On the other hand, he used many of the traditional tools of the nineteenth-century poets — this poem rhymes, for example. Does "Reluctance" seem to be a contemporary, or modern, poem or does it feel old-fashioned to you? Explain.
4. What is the tone of "Reluctance"? Does the tone jibe with the poem's subject or is there a bit of a disconnect? Explain your answer.
5. Poet and critic William Stafford said of Frost's poetry that "the bland voice quietly carrying readers across chasms cannot prevent terrible glimpses. The poems

often veil and, at the same time, hint at elements too abrupt, too full of hurt, for direct presentation." Does this description apply to "Reluctance"? Explain why or why not.

Mending Wall

"Mending Wall" was the opening poem in Frost's second collection, *North of Boston*, published in 1914.

Something there is that doesn't love a wall,
That sends the frozen-ground-swell under it,
And spills the upper boulders in the sun;
And makes gaps even two can pass abreast.
The work of hunters is another thing: 5
I have come after them and made repair
Where they have left not one stone on a stone,
But they would have the rabbit out of hiding,
To please the yelping dogs. The gaps I mean,
No one has seen them made or heard them made,   10
But at spring mending-time we find them there.
I let my neighbor know beyond the hill;
And on a day we meet to walk the line
And set the wall between us once again.
We keep the wall between us as we go.   15
To each the boulders that have fallen to each.
And some are loaves and some so nearly balls
We have to use a spell to make them balance:
"Stay where you are until our backs are turned!"
We wear our fingers rough with handling them.   20
Oh, just another kind of outdoor game,
One on a side. It comes to little more:
There where it is we do not need the wall:
He is all pine and I am apple orchard.
My apple trees will never get across   25
And eat the cones under his pines, I tell him.
He only says, "Good fences make good neighbors."
Spring is the mischief in me, and I wonder
If I could put a notion in his head:
"*Why* do they make good neighbors? Isn't it   30
Where there are cows? But here there are no cows.
Before I built a wall I'd ask to know
What I was walling in or walling out,
And to whom I was like to give offense.

Something there is that doesn't love a wall,   35
That wants it down." I could say "Elves" to him,
But it's not elves exactly, and I'd rather
He said it for himself. I see him there
Bringing a stone grasped firmly by the top
In each hand, like an old-stone savage armed.   40
He moves in darkness as it seems to me,
Not of woods only and the shade of trees.
He will not go behind his father's saying,
And he likes having thought of it so well
He says again, "Good fences make good neighbors."   45

(1914)

Exploring the Text

1. Is there a conflict in the poem? Explain.
2. Read lines 12–15 carefully. How could the different meanings of the word "between," which is repeated twice, change the meaning of the poem?
3. Why do you think Robert Frost allows the neighbor to offer the proverb "Good fences make good neighbors" twice? Do you think the speaker agrees with this adage? Why do you think the neighbor gets the last word?
4. "Mending Wall" questions whether a wall that has no function in the modern world still fulfills a ritualistic need. When Frost was asked about the poem's meaning, he said his poems are "all set to trip the reader head foremost into the boundless." In what way does trying to answer the poem's question trip you "into the boundless"? Which of the poem's two characters trips "into the boundless"?
5. When President Kennedy visited the Berlin Wall, he quoted the first line of "Mending Wall." His audience knew what he meant, of course. Later, when Frost visited Russia, he found that the Russian translation of the poem left off the first line. He said he could have done better for them by saying: "Something there is that doesn't love a wall, / Something there is that does." Does that potential change alter the meaning of the poem for you? Explain.

Fire and Ice

"Fire and Ice" was first published in *Harper's* magazine in December 1920.

Some say the world will end in fire,
Some say in ice.
From what I've tasted of desire
I hold with those who favor fire.

But if it had to perish twice,   5
I think I know enough of hate
To say that for destruction ice
Is also great
And would suffice.

(1920)

Exploring the Text

1. What do you think "fire" and "ice" represent in this poem?
2. What is the effect of the repetition "Some say" in the first two lines?
3. Do you think "Fire and Ice" is about the end of the world or about something else altogether? Explain your answer.
4. Characterize the speaker of "Fire and Ice." Try reading the poem aloud a few different ways, changing your intonation to put stress on different parts of each line. What effect does that have on your perception of the speaker?
5. Frost scholar Tom Hansen refutes the claim of Harlow Shapley, an American astronomer and teacher, that his conversation with Robert Frost about the possible ways the world might end inspired "Fire and Ice." Hansen instead believes that the poem is "an astute diagnosis of the chronic malfunction of the human heart." What do you think? Which interpretation resonates more with you?

Marsden Hartley

Marsden Hartley (1877–1943) was an American modernist painter. Originally from Lewiston, Maine, Hartley was raised in Cleveland, Ohio, but he traveled extensively throughout his life and studied at various institutions, including the Cleveland School of Art and the National Academy of Design. His work went through several stylistic phases, including neoimpressionist, expressionist, cubist, and representational. His most well-known works are part of a series of German military paintings, entitled *The War Motifs*, which he painted during the first years of World War I while living in Berlin, Germany.

Portrait of a German Officer

Portrait of a German Officer (1914) is an example of Hartley's use of both the geometric juxtapositions of cubism and the coarse brushwork and dramatic hues of German expressionism. In honor of his friend Karl von Freyburg, a cavalry officer who was killed in action during the war, Hartley included in this painting Freyburg's initials (Kv.F), his regiment number (4), and his age (24).

Image copyright © The Metropolitan Museum of Art. Image source: Art Resource, NY.

MARSDEN HARTLEY, *PORTRAIT OF A GERMAN OFFICER*, 1914, OIL ON CANVAS, 68¼" × 41⅜",
METROPOLITAN MUSEUM OF ART, NEW YORK.
(See color insert, Image 36.)

Exploring the Text

1. Look first at the painting's lines, shapes, colors, and composition (where and
   how the objects are placed on the canvas). What is your first impression? Then
   look at the iconography (the recognizable objects). Do they change your first
   impression?

2. *Portrait of a German Officer* is one of a series of abstract portraits of German officers. What evidence of war do you see in the painting? What do you think Marsden Hartley's opinion was of the military and the war culture he saw in Berlin during those years?
3. What do you think this painting says about Karl von Freyburg? About Hartley's relationship with him?
4. How did Hartley communicate emotion in this painting?
5. This painting is inspired by both cubism (visual fragments composed as if in a collage) and German expressionism (coarse brushwork and bright colors contrasted with black). What is the effect of this combination of techniques? Consider both the physical and the psychological effects of the work.

WALLACE STEVENS

Wallace Stevens (1879–1955), an important American modernist poet, was born in Reading, Pennsylvania, studied at Harvard University, and graduated from New York Law School. He worked as a lawyer in New York and became vice president of one of the largest insurance companies in Hartford, Connecticut. In addition to being a successful businessman, Stevens is considered one of the great poets of the twentieth century. His poetry collections include *Harmonium* (1923), *The Man with the Blue Guitar and Other Poems* (1937), *A Primitive like an Orb* (1948), and *Transport to Summer* (1947). *Collected Poems* (1954) brought Stevens both a Pulitzer Prize and the National Book Award. Stevens's work is often described as meditative and philosophical. He was a poet of ideas, with a strong belief in the poet as someone with heightened powers. Stevens favored precision of imagery and clear, sharp language, rejecting the sentiment favored by the Romantic and the Victorian poets.

Thirteen Ways of Looking at a Blackbird

With its haiku-like austerity and abstract form, "Thirteen Ways of Looking at a Blackbird" has been associated with the cubist painters, such as Pablo Picasso and Georges Braque, whose work depicted subjects from many viewpoints by breaking them up and reassembling them in an abstract form.

I

Among twenty snowy mountains
The only moving thing
Was the eye of the blackbird.

II

I was of three minds,
Like a tree   5
In which there are three blackbirds.

III

The blackbird whistled in the autumn winds.
It was a small part of the pantomime.

IV

A man and a woman
Are one.   10
A man and a woman and a blackbird
Are one.

V

I do not know which to prefer,
The beauty of inflections
Or the beauty of innuendoes,   15
The blackbird whistling
Or just after.

VI

Icicles filled the long window
With barbaric glass.
The shadow of the blackbird   20
Crossed it, to and fro.
The mood
Traced in the shadow
An indecipherable cause.

VII

O thin men of Haddam,   25
Why do you imagine golden birds?
Do you not see how the blackbird
Walks around the feet
Of the women about you?

VIII

I know noble accents   30
And lucid, inescapable rhythms;
But I know, too,
That the blackbird is involved
In what I know.

IX

When the blackbird flew out of sight,   35
It marked the edge
Of one of many circles.

X

At the sight of blackbirds
Flying in a green light,
Even the bawds of euphony   40
Would cry out sharply.

XI

He rode over Connecticut
In a glass coach.
Once, a fear pierced him,
In that he mistook   45
The shadow of his equipage
For blackbirds.

XII

The river is moving.
The blackbird must be flying.

XIII

It was evening all afternoon.   50
It was snowing
And it was going to snow.
The blackbird sat
In the cedar-limbs.

(1917)

Exploring the Text

1. Each of the thirteen stanzas of "Thirteen Ways of Looking at a Blackbird" might be a complete poem. What, besides the blackbird, connects them?
2. "Thirteen Ways of Looking at a Blackbird" has a cinematic quality that is introduced in the first stanza, when the eye of the speaker moves from a long establishing shot of snowy mountains to a close-up of the eye of a blackbird. What other film techniques do you find as you work through the poem? Consider the use of framing, close-ups, even sound.
3. Haddam, a town in Connecticut, is mentioned in stanzas VII and XI. What are some possible explanations for the Connecticut references? What comment might Stevens be making by contrasting Connecticut life to blackbirds?
4. Is there logic to the order of the stanzas? Try reshuffling them to see if the meaning of the poem changes.
5. Wallace Stevens said that this group of poems was "not meant to be a collection of epigrams or of ideas, but of sensations." What sensations does the poem produce in you as you read it? How does Stevens achieve his purpose of creating sensations?

TALKBACK

Aaron A. Abeyta

A graduate of the MFA program at Colorado State University and professor of English at Adams State College, Aaron A. Abeyta (b. 1971) is the author of *Colcha* (2001); *As Orion Falls* (2005); and *Rise, Do Not Be Afraid* (2007).

Thirteen Ways of Looking at a Tortilla

"Thirteen Ways of Looking at a Tortilla" is from Abeyta's 2001 collection *Colcha*, which received an American Book Award and the Colorado Book Award.

i.

among twenty different tortillas
the only thing moving
was the mouth of the niño

ii.

i was of three cultures
like a tortilla   5
for which there are three bolios

iii.

the tortilla grew on the wooden table
it was a small part of the earth

iv.

a house and a tortilla
are one   10
a man a woman and a tortilla
are one

v.

i do not know which to prefer
the beauty of the red wall
or the beauty of the green wall   15
the tortilla fresh
or just after

vi.

tortillas filled the small kitchen
with ancient shadows
the shadow of Maclovia   20
cooking long ago
the tortilla
rolled from the shadow
the innate roundness

vii.

o thin viejos of chimayo   25
why do you imagine biscuits
do you not see how the tortilla
lives with the hands
of the women about you

viii.

i know soft corn   30
and beautiful inescapable sopapillas
but i know too
that the tortilla
has taught me what i know

ix.

when the tortilla is gone   35
it marks the end
of one of many tortillas

x.

at the sight of tortillas
browning on a black comal
even the pachucos of española   40
would cry out sharply

xi.

he rode over new mexico
in a pearl low rider
once he got a flat
in that he mistook   45
the shadow of his spare
for a tortilla

xii.

the abuelitas are moving
the tortilla must be baking

xiii.

it was cinco de mayo all year   50
it was warm
and it was going to get warmer
the tortilla sat
on the frijolito plate

(2001)

Exploring the Text

1. Why do you think Aaron A. Abeyta chose the tortilla as his subject for a "Thirteen Ways" poem?
2. How does he introduce the tortilla? What do the "twenty different tortillas" in the first verse suggest to you? How is the image extended with the open mouth of the niño (child)? How does it set up one of the themes of the poem?

3. Identify some of the poem's images. How does Abeyta create them? What senses do the images appeal to?
4. Abeyta made the decision not to translate some Spanish expressions into English. How does that affect your reading of the poem? Try translating them and see how that changes the poem's meaning and form.

Making Connections

1. Aside from the subject matter, what do you think is the biggest difference between "Thirteen Ways of Looking at a Blackbird" (p. 1084) and "Thirteen Ways of Looking at a Tortilla" (p. 1087)?
2. Is Aaron A. Abeyta's purpose to honor the Wallace Stevens poem or to satirize it? Or is it a combination of the two? Explain your answer.
3. Stevens locates at least part of his poem in Connecticut; Abeyta places his in Chimayo, a small village near Santa Fe, New Mexico. How are these two settings different? Are there any similarities? How do they add layers of meaning to the two poems? How do they separate the two poems?
4. Using these poems as a model, write your own version that looks at a familiar object thirteen different ways.

EDNA ST. VINCENT MILLAY

Edna St. Vincent Millay (1892–1950) was born in Maine. In 1912, she entered her poem "Renascence" in a competition, winning fourth place and inclusion in *The Lyric Year*, which earned her acclaim and a scholarship to Vassar College. The poem would be included in her first collection, *Renascence and Other Poems*, published in 1917. After graduating, Vincent (as she insisted on being called) moved to Greenwich Village — then New York City's bohemian district. To this period belong her poetry collection *A Few Figs from Thistles* (1920); her first verse play, *The Lamp and the Bell* (1921); and a play in one act, *Aria da Capo* (1920). After an extended trip to Europe, she returned to New York and published *The Harp Weaver and Other Poems* (1923). That year she won the Pulitzer Prize for Poetry, the first woman to be so honored. She also wrote the libretto of one of the few American grand operas, *The King's Henchman* (1927). Sympathetic to Marxism-Leninism, she was active in protests against the execution of Sacco and Vanzetti, addressing the issue in *Buck in the Snow* (1928).

First Fig

This poem was originally published in *Poetry* in June 1918 and then collected in the book *A Few Figs from Thistles* (1920).

My candle burns at both ends;
   It will not last the night;
But ah, my foes, and oh, my friends —
   It gives a lovely light!

(1918)

Exploring the Text

1. What is the effect of the poem's rhyme? Do you think it contradicts the poem's meaning or supports it? Explain your answer.
2. The phrase "burn the candle at both ends" used to be a reference to waste: candles were expensive and valuable — not to be used carelessly. It has since come to refer to a life lived frantically, in which one enjoys oneself late into the night only to begin again the next morning. How do both of these meanings work in this short poem?
3. Why do you think Edna St. Vincent Millay used "ah" to address her foes and "oh" to address her friends?
4. Millay wrote the following poem, called "Second Fig":

    Safe upon the solid rock the ugly houses stand:
    Come and see my shining palace built upon the sand.

    What does it have in common with "First Fig"? Why do you think she called it "Second Fig"? What connections do you make with figs? Why do you think Millay used *fig* twice in her titles?
5. Critic Carl Van Doren wrote that since the ancient Greek poet Sappho few women had "written as outspokenly as Millay." Why might this poem have been considered outspoken? Could "Second Fig," found in question 4, also be considered outspoken? How do you think these poems hold up to that characterization today?

MARIANNE MOORE

Marianne Moore (1887–1972) was an American modernist poet born in Kirkwood, Missouri. After graduating from Pennsylvania's Bryn Mawr College in 1909, she eventually moved to New York City, where she took a job at the New York Public Library in 1921 and befriended fellow poets such as William Carlos Williams and Wallace Stevens. Moore's poems appeared in prestigious literary magazines such as the *Egoist* and the *Dial*, where she served as editor from 1925 to 1929. In 1921, Moore's first book, *Poems*, was published by fellow poet and Bryn Mawr classmate Hilda Doolittle. Among Moore's many honors were the Bollingen Prize, the National Book Award, and the Pulitzer Prize, all for her 1951 work, *Collected Poems*.

Poetry

One of Moore's most well-known poems, "Poetry" is famous for having been revised and republished many times, changing from a five-stanza to a one-stanza poem and back again. The version here is from 1919 and was published in the collection *Others*.

I too, dislike it: there are things that are important
          beyond all this fiddle.
  Reading it, however, with a perfect contempt for it,
         one discovers that there is in
it after all, a place for the genuine.   5
   Hands that can grasp, eyes
    that can dilate, hair that can rise
      if it must, these things are important not because a

high sounding interpretation can be put upon them
          but because they are   10
  useful; when they become so derivative as to
         become unintelligible, the
same thing may be said for all of us — that we
   do not admire what
   we cannot understand. The bat,   15
    holding on upside down or in quest of something to

eat, elephants pushing, a wild horse taking a roll,
         a tireless wolf under
a tree, the immovable critic twinkling his skin like a
         horse that feels a flea, the base-   20
ball fan, the statistician — case after case
   could be cited did
   one wish it; nor it is valid
    to discriminate against "business documents and

school-books"; all these phenomena are important.   25
         One must make a distinction
  however: when dragged into prominence by half poets,
         the result is not poetry,
  nor till the autocrats among us can be
    "literalists of   30
    the imagination" — above
      insolence and triviality and can present

for inspection, "imaginary gardens with real toads
         in them," shall we have

it. In the meantime, if you demand on one hand, 35
       in defiance of their opinion —
the raw material of poetry in
   all its rawness and
    that which is on the other hand,
      genuine then you are interested in poetry. 40

(1919)

Exploring the Text

1. What argument does Marianne Moore make about poetry in this poem?
2. Read "Poetry" grammatically. That is, read it in complete sentences without paying attention to line breaks. What changes? What stays the same? Why do you think Moore broke the lines as she did?
3. In lines 30–31, Moore paraphrases William Butler Yeats, who described the poet William Blake as a "literalist of the imagination." The other places she uses quotations marks, such as "imaginary gardens with real toads in them" (l. 32) are from her imagination. What do you think is the effect of this combination? How might it suit Moore's purpose?
4. "[T]he vastness of the particular" is how poet William Carlos Williams described Moore's signature mode. "So that in looking at some apparently small object, one feels the swirl of great events," he added. How does "Poetry" illustrate Williams's observation?
5. Moore was well-known for being a baseball fan. How does her allusion to baseball in lines 20–21 help her develop her ideas about what poetry is and isn't?
6. This version of the poem was published in 1919. In 1967, Moore revised it, reducing the poem to just three lines:

> I, too, dislike it.
> Reading it, however with a perfect contempt for it, one discovers in it, after all, a place for the genuine.

How do the two versions "annotate, challenge, and criticize one another," as poet Robert Pinsky suggests?

CLAUDE MCKAY

Poet, novelist, and journalist Claude McKay was born in 1890 in Jamaica. The youngest of eleven children, he was sent to live with an older brother — a schoolteacher — who took charge of his education, introducing him to the classics of British literature, such as works by John Milton, Alexander Pope, and the

Romantics. McKay began writing poetry at the age of ten, and by the time he immigrated to the United States at age twenty-two, he had published two volumes of verse. In America, McKay faced the harsh realities of racism and, despite his education, took on menial jobs to make a living. McKay became known for his protest poetry, which spoke directly about racial issues and the trials of the working class. Langston Hughes and Countee Cullen considered McKay an inspirational voice during the Harlem Renaissance. McKay's novels include *Home to Harlem* (1922), *Banjo: A Story without a Plot* (1929), and *Banana Bottom* (1933). He lived abroad, in England and France, on and off for years, but returned to the United States in 1934, where he worked in Chicago as a journalist, writing mostly for left-leaning publications. McKay died in 1948, having never returned to Jamaica.

If We Must Die

Inspired by a wave of lynchings, "If We Must Die" encourages resistance, even if a fight seems doomed. While some people believe that Winston Churchill quoted lines from "If We Must Die," there is no evidence to support that claim. Nevertheless, "If We Must Die," first published in the July 1919 issue of the *Liberator*, shares many qualities with Churchill's World War II speeches.

If we must die, let it not be like hogs
Hunted and penned in an inglorious spot,
While round us bark the mad and hungry dogs,
Making their mock at our accursèd lot.
If we must die, O let us nobly die,   5
So that our precious blood may not be shed
In vain; then even the monsters we defy
Shall be constrained to honor us though dead!
O Kinsmen! we must meet the common foe!
Though far outnumbered let us show us brave,   10
And for their thousand blows deal one deathblow!
What though before us lies the open grave?
Like men we'll face the murderous, cowardly pack,
Pressed to the wall, dying, but fighting back!

(1919)

Exploring the Text

1. Identify the form of "If We Must Die." Why do you think Claude McKay chose that form for his message? How does the rhyme scheme add a level of meaning to the poem?
2. Who do you think is the speaker of "If We Must Die"? What is his persona?

3. What argument does McKay make by beginning "If We Must Die" with images of animals and starting the penultimate line with "Like men we'll face the murderous, cowardly pack" (l. 13)?
4. McKay wrote this poem in response to a series of antiblack riots and lynchings in the summer of 1919. How do you think the poem was received by whites? By blacks?
5. Do you think "If We Must Die" is a plea for martyrdom? How else might it be explained?
6. Critic William Maxwell notes that though "If We Must Die" is considered to be the "inaugural address of the Harlem Renaissance," McKay unveiled it first to the black employees of the Pennsylvania Railroad, where McKay was a waiter. Why do you think he chose them as his first audience?

THEODORE DREISER

Novelist and journalist Theodore Dreiser (1871–1945) was born in Terre Haute, Indiana. A prolific writer in many genres, he is most famous for his frank (and at the time, shocking) novels about urban life, *Sister Carrie* (1900) and *An American Tragedy* (1925). His fiction was frequently inspired by his lifelong work as a journalist. Dreiser is considered one of the greatest American naturalist writers. Naturalism was an offshoot of realism that tried to faithfully reproduce human events and experiences and also explain how they were influenced by heredity, social conditions, or the environment.

A Certain Oil Refinery

This article was first published in *New York Call*, a socialist daily paper, in 1919 under the title "The Standard Oil Works of Bayonne." It was retitled in Dreiser's collected writings, *The Colors of the Great City*, in 1923.

There is a section of land very near New York, lying at the extreme southern point of the peninsula known as Bayonne, which is given up to a peculiar business. The peninsula is a long neck of land lying between those two large bays which extend a goodly distance on either hand, one toward the city of Newark, the other toward the vast and restless ocean beyond Brooklyn. Stormy winds sweep over it at many periods of the year. The seagull and the tern fly high over its darksome roof-tops. Tall stacks and bare, red buildings and scores of rounded tanks spread helter-skelter over its surface, give it a dreary, unkempt and yet not wholly inartistic appearance which appeals, much as a grotesque deformity appeals or a masque intended to represent pain.

This section is the seat of a most prosperous manufacturing establishment, a single limb of a many-branched tree, and its business is the manufacturing, or rather refining, of oil. Of an ordinary business day you would not want a more inspiring picture of that which is known as manufacture. Great ships, inbound and outbound, from all ports of the world, lie anchored at its docks. Long trains of oil cars are backed in on many spurs of tracks, which branch from main-line arteries and stand like caravans of steel, waiting to carry new burdens of oil to the uttermost parts of the land. There are many buildings and outhouses of all shapes and dimensions which are continually belching forth smoke in a solid mass, and if you stand and look in any direction on a gloomy day you may see red fires which burn and gleam in a steady way, giving a touch of somber richness to a scene which is otherwise only a mass of black and gray.

This region is remarkable for the art, as for the toil of it, if nothing more. A painter could here find a thousand contrasts in black and gray and red and blue, which would give him ample labor for his pen or brush. These stacks are so tall, the building from which they spring so low. Spread out over a marshy ground which was once all sea-weed and which now shows patches of water stained with iridescent oil, broken here and there with other patches of black earth to match the blacker buildings which abound upon it, you have a combination in shades and tones of one color which no artist could resist. A Whistler could make wonderful blacks and whites of this. A Vierge or a Shinn could show us what it means to catch the exact image of darkness at its best. A casual visitor, if he is of a sensitive turn, shudders or turns away with a sense of depression haunting him. It is a great world of gloom, done in lines of splendid activity, but full of the pathos of faint contrasts in gray and black.

At that, it is not so much the art of it that is impressive as the solemn life situation which it represents. These people who work in it — and there are thousands of them — are of an order which you would call commonplace. They are not very bright intellectually, of course, or they would not work here. They are not very attractive physically, for nature suits body to mind in most instances, and these bodies as a rule reflect the heaviness of the intelligence which guides them. They are poor Swedes and Poles, Hungarians and Lithuanians, people who in many instances do not speak our tongue as yet, and who are used to conditions so rough and bare that those who are used to conditions of even moderate comfort shudder at the thought of them. They live in tumbledown shacks next to "the works" and they arrange their domestic economies heaven only knows how. Wages are not high (a dollar or a dollar and a half a day is good pay in most instances), and many of them have families to support, large families, for children in all the poorer sections are always numerous. There are dark, minute stores, and as dark and meaner saloons, where many of them (the men) drink. Looking at the homes and the saloons hereabout, it would seem to you as though any grade of intelligence ought to do better than this, as if an all-wise, directing intelligence, which we once assumed nature to possess, could not allow such homely, clap-trap things to come into being. And yet here they are.

Taken as a mass, however, and in extreme heat or cold, under rain or snow, when 5
the elements are beating about them, they achieve a swart solemnity, rise or fall to a somber dignity or misery for which nature might well be praised. They look so grim, so bare, so hopeless. Artists ought to make pictures of them. Writers ought to write of

them. Musicians should get their inspiration for what is antiphonal and contra-puntal from such things. They are of the darker moods of nature, its meanest inspiration.

However, it is not of these houses alone that this picture is to be made, but of the work within the plant, its nature, its grayness, its intricacy, its rancidity, its commonplaceness, its mental insufficiency; for it is a routine, a process, lacking from one year's end to another any trace of anything creative — the filling of one vat and another, for instance, and letting the same settle; introducing into one vat and another a given measure of chemicals which are known to bring about separation and purifications or, in other words, the process called refining; opening gates in tubes and funnels which drain the partially refined oils into other vats and finally into barrels and tanks, which are placed on cars or ships. You may find the how of it in any encyclopedia. But the interesting thing to me is that men work and toil here in a sickening atmosphere of blackness and shadow, of vile odors, of vile substances, of vile surroundings. You could not enter this yard, nor glance into one of these buildings, nor look at these men tramping by, without feeling that they were working in shadow and amid foul odors and gases, which decidedly are not conducive to either health or the highest order of intelligence.

Refuse tar, oil, and acids greet the nostrils and sight everywhere. The great chimneys on either hand are either belching huge columns of black or blue smoke, or vapory blue gases, which come in at the windows. The ground under your feet is discolored by oil, and all the wagons, cars, implements, machinery, buildings, and the men, of course, are splotched and spotted with it. There seems to be no escape. The very air is full of smoke and oil.

It is in this atmosphere that thousands of men are working. You may see them trudging in in the morning, their buckets or baskets over their arms, a consistent pallor overspreading their faces, an irritating cough in some instances indicating their contact with the smoke and fumes; and you may see them trudging out again at night, marked with the same pallor, coughing with the same cough; a day of peculiar duties followed by a night in the somber, gray places which they call home. Another line of men is always coming in as they go out. It is a line of men which straggles over all of two miles and is coming or going during an hour, either of the morning or the night. There is no gayety in it, no enthusiasm. You may see depicted on these faces only the mental attitude which ensues where one is compelled to work at some thing in which there is nothing creative. It is really, when all is said and done, not a pleasant picture.

I will not say, however, that it is an unrelieved hardship for men to work so. "The Lord tempereth the wind to the shorn lamb" is an old proverb and unquestionably a true one. Indubitably these men do not feel as keenly about these things as some of the more exalted intellectual types in life, and it is entirely possible that a conception of what we know as "atmosphere" may never have found lodgment in their brains. Nevertheless, it is true that their physical health is affected to a certain extent, and it is also true that the home life to which they return is what it is, whether this be due to low intelligence or low wages, or both. The one complements the other, of course. If any attempt were made to better their condition physically or mentally, it might well be looked upon by them as meddling. At the same time it is true that up to this time nothing has been done to improve their condition. Doing anything more for them than paying them wages is not thought of.

A long trough, for instance, a single low wooden tub, in a small boarded-off space, in the boss teamsters' shanty, with neither soap nor towels and only the light that comes from a low door, is all the provision made for the host of "still-cleaners," the men who are engaged in the removal of the filthy refuse — tar, acids, and vile residuums from the stills and agitators. In connection with the boiler-room, where over three hundred men congregate at noontime and at night, there is to be found nothing better. You may see rows of grimy men congregate at noontime and at night, to eat their lunch or dinner, there is to be found nothing better. You may see rows of grimy men in various departments attempting to clean themselves under such circumstances, and still others walking away without any attempt at cleaning themselves before leaving. It takes too long. The idea of furnishing a clean dining-room in which to eat or a place to hang coats has never occurred to any one. They bring their food in buckets.

However, that vast problem, the ethics of employment, is not up for discussion in this instance: only the picture which this industry presents. On a gray day or a stormy one, if you have a taste for the somber, you have here all the elements of a gloomy labor picture which may not long endure, so steadily is the world changing. On the one hand, masters of great force and wealth, penurious to a degree, on the other the victims of this same penuriousness and indifference, dumbly accepting it, and over all this smoke and gas and these foul odors about all these miserable chambers. Truly, I doubt if one could wish a better hell for one's enemies than some of the wretched chambers here, where men rove about like troubled spirits in a purgatory of man's devising; nor any mental state worse than that in which most of these victims of Mother Nature find themselves. At the bottom nothing but darkness and thickness of wit, and dullness of feeling, let us say, and at the top the great brilliant blooms known to the world as the palaces and the office buildings and the private cars and the art collections of the principal owners of the stock of this concern. For those at the top, the brilliancy of the mansions of Fifth Avenue, the gorgeousness of the resorts of Newport and Palm Beach, the delights of intelligence and freedom; for those beneath, the dark chamber, the hanging smoke, pallor, foul odors, wretched homes. Yet who shall say that this is not the foreordained order of life? Can it be changed? Will it ever be, permanently? Who is to say?

(1919)

Exploring the Text

1. What do you think is Theodore Dreiser's purpose in this piece?
2. Do you consider "A Certain Oil Refinery" a sketch or an exposé? Explain your answer, keeping Dreiser's purpose in mind.
3. Examine the way Dreiser uses contrasts in "A Certain Oil Refinery." What is the effect of the contrasts?

4. What do you make of the aesthetic considerations in this piece? Why do you think Dreiser suggests that artists, such as James McNeill Whistler, Everett Shinn, and Daniel Vierge, might have been inspired by the setting to create works of art? Do you think those suggestions are appropriate to the purpose of the piece? Explain why or why not.
5. What picture does Dreiser paint of the refinery workers? Where does he place them on the social scale? What suggestions or hope for improving their conditions does Dreiser offer?
6. Dreiser was what we might call a social Darwinist, someone who applied Charles Darwin's ideas about evolution to human behavior and interaction. What evidence do you see in this piece of Dreiser's ideas about the "survival of the fittest"?

E. E. CUMMINGS

Edward Estlin (E. E.) Cummings (1894–1962) was a prolific poet famous for his experimental style. Born and raised in an affluent family in Cambridge, Massachusetts, he graduated from Cambridge Latin High School and received both a BA and an MA in English and classical studies from Harvard University. Before the United States entered World War I, Cummings, an avowed pacifist, volunteered as an ambulance driver in France, where he was held for a time in a detention camp — an experience that deepened his distrust of authority. *The Enormous Room* (1922), his first published work, is a fictional account of his imprisonment, which was followed in 1923 by his first collection of poems, *Tulips and Chimneys*.

in Just-

Cummings is famous for defying traditional rules of typography, capitalization, and punctuation in pursuit of poetry that is both provocative and whimsical. Originally published in the *Dial* in May 1920, "in Just-" is a fine example of his iconoclastic style.

in Just-
spring   when the world is mud-
luscious the little
lame balloonman

whistles   far   and wee   5

and eddieandbill come
running from marbles and
piracies and it's
spring

when the world is puddle-wonderful   10

the queer
old balloonman whistles
far   and   wee
and bettyandisbel come dancing

from hop-scotch and jump-rope and   15

it's
spring
and

   the

         goat-footed   20

balloonMan   whistles
far
and
wee

                                                (1920)

Exploring the Text

1. Characterize the speaker of "in Just-." Try to describe him or her in as much detail as possible.
2. What games does this poem play with rhythm? Look especially at the spacing, or lack of spacing, between words. What is the effect of the rhythmic changes?
3. E. E. Cummings is known for his unconventional punctuation and typography. Identify the ways that the arrangement of the words functions as punctuation.
4. According to critic Albert C. Labriola, "in Just-" is grouped with poems called "Chansons Innocentes," an allusion to William Blake's *Songs of Innocence* and its partner *Songs of Experience*. What aspects of the poem do you consider innocent? What parts are more about experience?

LANGSTON HUGHES

Langston Hughes (1902–1967) was born in the African American community of Joplin, Missouri, and raised in Lawrence, Kansas. He spent a year at Columbia University and became involved with the Harlem Renaissance movement but was shocked by the endemic racial prejudice at the university and subsequently left.

Hughes traveled for several years, spending some time in Paris before returning to the United States. He completed his BA at Pennsylvania's Lincoln University in 1929, after which he returned to Harlem for the remainder of his life. Hughes was prolific in verse, prose, and drama. His first volume of poetry, *The Weary Blues*, was published in 1926. His first novel, *Not Without Laughter* (1930), won the Harmon Gold Medal for literature. He is remembered for his celebration of the uniqueness of African American culture, which found expression in "The Negro Artist and the Racial Mountain" (1926), published in the *Nation*, and in the poem "The Negro Speaks of Rivers."

The Negro Speaks of Rivers

"The Negro Speaks of Rivers" was Langston Hughes's first published poem — in the *Crisis*, in 1921 — written when he was eighteen. It was later included in his first volume of poetry, *The Weary Blues* (1926). Hughes dedicated it to activist and historian W. E. B. DuBois.

I've known rivers:
I've known rivers ancient as the world and older than the
   flow of human blood in human veins.

My soul has grown deep like the rivers.

I bathed in the Euphrates when dawns were young.   5
I built my hut near the Congo and it lulled me to sleep.
I looked upon the Nile and raised the pyramids above it.
I heard the singing of the Mississippi when Abe Lincoln
   went down to New Orleans, and I've seen its muddy
   bosom turn all golden in the sunset.   10

I've known rivers:
Ancient, dusky rivers.

My soul has grown deep like the rivers.

(1921)

Exploring the Text

1. Who do you think is the "I" of the poem?
2. What is the central metaphor of this poem? Are there secondary metaphors? Describe them.
3. What do three of the four rivers Hughes mentions have in common? Why is the fourth one different? What does this tell us about Hughes's purpose in "The Negro Speaks of Rivers"?

4. Characterize the diction of "The Negro Speaks of Rivers."
5. Abraham Lincoln is said to have formed his antislavery views after boat trips down the Mississippi to New Orleans, where he saw the slave trade firsthand. How does Hughes characterize that connection in lines 8–9?
6. What arguments does "The Negro Speaks of Rivers" make about the African American experience in the United States? How does the structure of the poem help Hughes develop them?

The Negro Artist and the Racial Mountain

In 1926, the *Nation* published "The Negro-Art Hokum," by conservative African American journalist George Schuyler, who argued that African American artists should not limit themselves to working with subject matter or genres that were racially specific or traditional. He said, "Negroes and whites from the same localities in this country talk, think, and act about the same. Because a few writers with a paucity of themes have seized upon imbecilities of the Negro rustics and clowns and palmed them off as authentic and characteristic Aframerican behavior, the common notion that the black American is so 'different' from his white neighbor has gained wide currency." A week later, the magazine published Hughes's response, which appears here.

One of the most promising of the young Negro poets said to me once, "I want to be a poet — not a Negro poet," meaning, I believe, "I want to write like a white poet"; meaning subconsciously, "I would like to be a white poet"; meaning behind that, "I would like to be white." And I was sorry the young man said that, for no great poet has ever been afraid of being himself. And I doubted then that, with his desire to run away spiritually from his race, this boy would ever be a great poet. But this is the mountain standing in the way of any true Negro art in America — this urge within the race toward whiteness, the desire to pour racial individuality into the mold of American standardization, and to be as little Negro and as much American as possible.

But let us look at the immediate background of this young poet. His family is of what I suppose one would call the Negro middle class: people who are by no means rich yet never uncomfortable nor hungry — smug, contented, respectable folk, members of the Baptist church. The father goes to work every morning. He is a chief steward at a large white club. The mother sometimes does fancy sewing or supervises parties for the rich families of the town. The children go to a mixed school. In the home they read white papers and magazines. And the mother often says "Don't be like niggers" when the children are bad. A frequent phrase from the father is, "Look how well a white man does things." And so the word *white* comes to be unconsciously a symbol of all the virtues. It holds for the children beauty, morality, and money. The whisper of "I want to be white" runs silently through their minds. This young poet's home is, I believe, a fairly typical home of the colored middle class. One sees immediately how difficult it would be for an artist born in such a home to interest himself in interpreting the beauty of his own people. He is never taught to see that beauty. He is taught rather not to see it, or if he does, to be ashamed of it when it is not according to Caucasian patterns.

For racial culture the home of a self-styled "high-class" Negro has nothing better to offer. Instead there will perhaps be more aping of things white than in a less cultured or less wealthy home. The father is perhaps a doctor, lawyer, landowner, or politician. The mother may be a social worker, or a teacher, or she may do nothing and have a maid. Father is often dark but he has usually married the lightest woman he could find. The family attend a fashionable church where few really colored faces are to be found. And they themselves draw a color line. In the North they go to white theaters and white movies. And in the South they have at least two cars and a house "like white folks." Nordic manners, Nordic faces, Nordic hair, Nordic art (if any), and an Episcopal heaven. A very high mountain indeed for the would-be racial artist to climb in order to discover himself and his people.

But then there are the low-down folks, the so-called common element, and they are the majority — may the Lord be praised! The people who have their nip of gin on Saturday nights and are not too important to themselves or the community, or too well fed, or too learned to watch the lazy world go round. They live on Seventh Street in Washington or State Street in Chicago and they do not particularly care whether they are like white folks or anybody else. Their joy runs, bang! into ecstasy. Their religion soars to a shout. Work maybe a little today, rest a little tomorrow. Play awhile. Sing awhile. O, let's dance! These common people are not afraid of spirituals, as for a long time their more intellectual brethren were, and jazz is their child. They furnish a wealth of colorful, distinctive material for any artist because they still hold their own individuality in the face of American standardizations. And perhaps these common people will give to the world its truly great Negro artist, the one who is not afraid to be himself. Whereas the better-class Negro would tell the artist what to do, the people at least let him alone when he does appear. And they are not ashamed of him — if they know he exists at all. And they accept what beauty is their own without question.

Certainly there is, for the American Negro artist who can escape the restrictions   5
the more advanced among his own group would put upon him, a great field of unused material ready for his art. Without going outside his race, and even among the better classes with their "white" culture and conscious American manners, but still Negro enough to be different, there is sufficient matter to furnish a black artist with a lifetime of creative work. And when he chooses to touch on the relations between Negroes and whites in this country with their innumerable overtones and undertones, surely, and especially for literature and the drama, there is an inexhaustible supply of themes at hand. To these the Negro artist can give his racial individuality, his heritage of rhythm and warmth, and his incongruous humor that so often, as in the Blues, becomes ironic laughter mixed with tears. But let us look again at the mountain.

A prominent Negro clubwoman in Philadelphia paid eleven dollars to hear Raquel Meller sing Andalusian popular songs. But she told me a few weeks before she would not think of going to hear "that woman," Clara Smith, a great black artist, sing Negro folksongs. And many an upper-class Negro church, even now, would not dream of employing a spiritual in its services. The drab melodies in white folks' hymnbooks are much to be preferred. "We want to worship the Lord correctly and quietly. We don't believe in 'shouting.' Let's be dull like the Nordics," they say, in effect.

The road for the serious black artist, then, who would produce a racial art is most certainly rocky and the mountain is high. Until recently he received almost no encouragement for his work from either white or colored people. The fine novels of Chestnutt go out of print with neither race noticing their passing. The quaint charm and humor of Dunbar's dialect verse brought to him, in his day, largely the same kind of encouragement one would give a sideshow freak (A colored man writing poetry! How odd!) or a clown (How amusing!).

The present vogue in things Negro, although it may do as much harm as good for the budding colored artist, has at least done this: it has brought him forcibly to the attention of his own people among whom for so long, unless the other race had noticed him beforehand, he was a prophet with little honor. I understand that Charles Gilpin acted for years in Negro theaters without any special acclaim from his own, but when Broadway gave him eight curtain calls, Negroes, too, began to beat a tin pan in his honor. I know a young colored writer, a manual worker by day, who had been writing well for the colored magazines for some years, but it was not until he recently broke into the white publications and his first book was accepted by a prominent New York publisher that the "best" Negroes in his city took the trouble to discover that he lived there. Then almost immediately they decided to give a grand dinner for him. But the society ladies were careful to whisper to his mother that perhaps she'd better not come. They were not sure she would have an evening gown.

The Negro artist works against an undertow of sharp criticism and misunderstanding from his own group and unintentional bribes from the whites. "O, be respectable, write about nice people, show how good we are," say the Negroes. "Be stereotyped, don't go too far, don't shatter our illusions about you, don't amuse us too seriously. We will pay you," say the whites. Both would have told Jean Toomer not to write "Cane." The colored people did not praise it. The white people did not buy it. Most of the colored people who did read "Cane" hate it. They are afraid of it. Although the critics gave it good reviews the public remained indifferent. Yet (excepting the work of DuBois) "Cane" contains the finest prose written by a Negro in America. And like the singing of Robeson, it is truly racial.

But in spite of the Nordicized Negro intelligentsia and the desires of some white   10
editors we have an honest American Negro literature already with us. Now I await the rise of the Negro theater. Our folk music, having achieved world-wide fame, offers itself to the genius of the great individual American Negro composer who is to come. And within the next decade I expect to see the work of a growing school of colored artists who paint and model the beauty of dark faces and create with new technique the expressions of their own soul-world. And the Negro dancers who will dance like flame and the singers who will continue to carry our songs to all who listen — they will be with us in even greater numbers tomorrow.

Most of my own poems are racial in theme and treatment, derived from the life I know. In many of them I try to grasp and hold some of the meanings and rhythms of jazz. I am sincere as I know how to be in these poems and yet after every reading I answer questions like these from my own people: Do you think Negroes should always write about Negroes? I wish you wouldn't read some of your poems to white folks. How do you find anything interesting in a place like a cabaret? Why do you write about black people? You aren't black. What makes you do so many jazz poems?

But jazz to me is one of the inherent expressions of Negro life in America: the eternal tom-tom beating in the Negro soul — the tom-tom of revolt against weariness in a white world, a world of subway trains, and work, work, work; the tom-tom of joy and laughter, and pain swallowed in a smile. Yet the Philadelphia clubwoman is ashamed to say that her race created it and she does not like me to write about it. The old subconscious "white is best" runs through her mind. Years of study under white teachers, a lifetime of white books, pictures, and papers, and white manners, morals, and Puritan standards made her dislike the spirituals. And now she turns up her nose at jazz and all its manifestations — likewise almost everything else distinctly racial. She doesn't care for the Winold Reiss portraits of Negroes because they are "too Negro." She does not want a true picture of herself from anybody. She wants the artist to flatter her, to make the white world believe that all Negroes are as smug and as near white in soul as she wants to be. But, to my mind, it is the duty of the younger Negro artist, if he accepts any duties at all from outsiders, to change through the force of his art that old whispering "I want to be white," hidden in the aspirations of his people, to "Why should I want to be white? I am a Negro — and beautiful!"

So I am ashamed for the black poet who says, "I want to be a poet, not a Negro poet," as though his own racial world were not as interesting as any other world. I am ashamed, too, for the colored artist who runs from the painting of Negro faces to the painting of sunsets after the manner of the academicians because he fears the strange un-whiteness of his own features. An artist must be free to choose what he does, certainly, but he must also never be afraid to do what he might choose.

Let the blare of Negro jazz bands and the bellowing voice of Bessie Smith singing Blues penetrate the closed ears of the colored near-intellectuals until they listen and perhaps understand. Let Paul Robeson singing "Water Boy," and Rudolph Fisher writing about the streets of Harlem, and Jean Toomer holding the heart of Georgia in his hands, and Aaron Douglas drawing strange black fantasies cause the smug Negro middle class to turn from their white, respectable, ordinary books and papers to catch a glimmer of their own beauty. We younger Negro artists who create now intend to express our individual dark-skinned selves without fear or shame. If white people are pleased we are glad. If they are not, it doesn't matter. We know we are beautiful. And ugly too. The tom-tom cries and the tom-tom laughs. If colored people are pleased we are glad. If they are not, their displeasure doesn't matter either. We build our temples for tomorrow, strong as we know how, and we stand on top of the mountain, free within ourselves.

(1926)

Questions

1. Langston Hughes opens his essay by introducing a quote from a "promising . . . young Negro" poet who said that he wanted to "be a poet — not a Negro poet." Why do you think Hughes begins his argument with this young man's declaration? How does he carry that thread through the piece? Do you agree with Hughes's take on the quote from the young poet? How might the quote be interpreted differently?
2. What is the "mountain" that Hughes refers to in the title of his essay? How does he sustain that metaphor throughout the essay?
3. What two different types of African Americans does Hughes compare and contrast? Which one does he believe has more influence on the arts? Why?
4. What or who is the "clubwoman in Philadelphia" in paragraph 6 meant to represent? What purpose does she serve in Hughes's argument?
5. What part does Hughes suggest that jazz plays in the way he describes his art and the art of African Americans that he admires?
6. What do you think? Should artists base their choice of genre and subject on their race? Is race an effective way to classify art? What do you think defines African American art and culture? Is it a matter of subject, or is it more a matter of style, as cultural critic Cornel West has suggested?

WILLIAM CARLOS WILLIAMS

William Carlos Williams (1883–1963) was a doctor, a poet, an essayist, a novelist, and a playwright famous for his unique and succinct modernist poems. Williams studied medicine at the University of Pennsylvania, where he befriended Ezra Pound, whose imagist ideas greatly influenced Williams's early work. Later in his writing career, Williams forged his own path, trying to create a uniquely American poetry that emphasized the importance of the everyday. His most influential collections include *Spring and All* (1923), *The Desert Music and Other Poems* (1954), *Pictures from Brueghel and Other Poems* (1962), and his six-book epic, *Paterson* (1963).

The Great Figure

William Carlos Williams's poem "The Great Figure" was published in *Sour Grapes: A Book of Poems* in 1921.

Among the rain
and lights
I saw the figure 5
in gold

on a red   5
firetruck
moving
tense
unheeded
to gong clangs   10
siren howls
and wheels rumbling
through the dark city.

(1921)

Exploring the Text

1. What is the central image of the poem? What are the secondary images? How did William Carlos Williams create the imagery in this very short poem?

2. Do you consider "The Great Figure" literal or figurative — or a little bit of both? Explain your answer by describing which aspects of the poem are figurative and which are literal.

3. What expectations does the poem's title, "The Great Figure," create? In what ways are those expectations met in the poem? In what ways are they defied?

4. Compare this poem to Ezra Pound's "In a Station of the Metro" (p. 1074). Both examine "found" moments. How are the poems the same? How are they different?

5. According to Williams's autobiography, he was on his way to visit the painter Marsden Hartley when he "heard a great clatter of bells and the roar of a fire engine passing the end of the street down Ninth Avenue. [He] turned just in time to see a golden figure 5 on a red background flash by. The impression was so sudden and forceful that [he] took a piece of paper out of [his] pocket and wrote a short poem about it." Do you see any evidence of a connection in style between Williams and Hartley, whose work is on page 1082? Consider also the work by Charles Demuth featured in the following TalkBack.

 **TALKBACK**

CHARLES DEMUTH

Charles Demuth (1883–1935) was an American painter from Lancaster, Pennsylvania. He graduated from Franklin and Marshall Academy and went on to study at Drexel University and the Pennsylvania Academy of Fine Arts. As a young man, he traveled to Paris, where he attended the Académie Colarossi and the Académie Julian and became a part of the avant-garde art movement. Though he was plagued by illness throughout his life, Demuth produced more than one thousand works of art and was able to live on the proceeds of his work.

I Saw the Figure 5 in Gold

Demuth's painting *I Saw the Figure Five in Gold* (1928), one of a series of eight abstract portraits of his friends, was inspired by William Carlos Williams's poem "The Great Figure."

CHARLES DEMUTH, *I SAW THE FIGURE 5 IN GOLD*, 1928, 35½" × 30", OIL ON CARDBOARD, METROPOLITAN MUSEUM OF ART, NEW YORK.
(See color insert, Image 37.)

Exploring the Text

1. What aspects of *I Saw the Figure 5 in Gold* make it a portrait? What aspects make it abstract?
2. Charles Demuth was part of a group of artists called the precisionists, who were interested in the precision of industrialization and the modernization of the American landscape. How is this painting both a landscape and a meditation on industrialization?

3. What is the effect of the geometric shapes? How does Demuth use them to re-create the motion of the fire engine from William Carlos Williams's poem, "The Great Figure" (p. 1106)?

4. *I Saw the Figure 5 in Gold* is considered a precursor to pop art, a twentieth-century genre that challenged the traditions of fine art by using imagery from popular culture — such as is seen in Andy Warhol's paintings of Campbell soup cans. How does Demuth's painting challenge the traditions of fine art?

Making Connections

1. In what ways is Demuth's *I Saw the Figure 5 in Gold* (p. 1108) an illustration of Williams's "The Great Figure"? In what ways does it depart from the poem?

2. What stylistic choices did Demuth make to illustrate Williams's poem? Consider Demuth's use of color, shape, line, perspective, and light.

3. *Ekphrasis* is a term used to describe a piece of writing that comments on another art form — for example, a poem about a piece of artwork or a novel about a film. In the case of these two works, the writing came first. How precisely does the painting comment on the poem?

4. Why do you think Demuth painted the number 5 three times? What part of Williams's poem does that particular element illustrate?

5. According to Peter Halter in *The Revolution in the Visual Arts and the Poetry of William Carlos Williams*, when Demuth sent *I Saw the Figure 5 in Gold* to the photographer and promoter of modern art Alfred Stieglitz, Demuth said, "I hope you like it. It looks almost American." What do you think he meant? Why do you think it was important to Demuth that his work look American?

WILLIAM CARLOS WILLIAMS

This Is Just to Say

"This Is Just to Say" appeared in Williams's *Collected Poems 1921–1931* (1934).

I have eaten
the plums
that were in
the icebox

and which   5
you were probably

saving
for breakfast

Forgive me
they were delicious   10
so sweet
and so cold

(1934)

Exploring the Text

1. How would you describe the tone of "This Is Just to Say"?
2. This poem is notable for its complete lack of punctuation. What effect does that have on the tone of "This Is Just to Say"?
3. "This Is Just to Say" is considered a "found" poem. It takes the form of a note left on a kitchen table. Its very informal nature leaves its theme wide open. What do you think is its message?
4. What effect does the poem's typography (the way it looks on the page) have?
5. William Carlos Williams is considered an imagist, a poet who writes in free verse and believes first and foremost in the simple clarity of an image. How does this poem fit that definition? How does it compare to Ezra Pound's "In a Station of the Metro" (p. 1074)?
6. Love notes between husbands and wives are often the subject or even the form of poetry. Could "This Is Just to Say" be considered a love note? Explain your answer.
7. Williams's wife, Florence, wrote the following reply to "This Is Just to Say":

> Reply
>
> (crumped on her desk)
>
> Dear Bill: I've made a
> couple of sandwiches for you.
> In the ice-box you'll find
> blue-berries — a cup of grapefruit
> a glass of cold coffee.
>
> On the stove is the tea-pot
> with enough tea leaves
> for you to make tea if you
> prefer — Just light the gas —
> boil the water and put it in the tea
>
> Plenty of bread in the bread-box
> and butter and eggs —

I didn't know just what to
make for you. Several people
called up about office hours—

See you later. Love. Floss.

Please switch off the telephone.

Compare and contrast Florence's note with "This Is Just to Say." Can you make a case that Florence's note is also a poem? Explain your answer.

TALKBACK

KENNETH KOCH

Kenneth Koch (1925–2002) was considered part of the New York school of poetry, a group of poets that included Frank O'Hara and that moved away from the introspective poetry of the early twentieth century. Koch graduated from Harvard and taught at Columbia University for over forty years. In addition to *The Art of Love: Poems* (1975), *On the Great Atlantic Railway: Selected Poems 1950–1988* (1994), and *One Train* (1994), for which he won the Bollingen Prize, Koch is also well-known for *Wishes, Lies and Dreams: Teaching Children to Write Poetry* (1970).

Variations on a Theme by William Carlos Williams

This poem first appeared in Koch's 1962 collection *Thank You and Other Poems*. When an interviewer asked about the playfulness of his work, Koch responded, "I don't intend for my poetry to be mainly funny or satiric, but it seems to me that high spirits and sort of a comic view are part of being serious."

1

I chopped down the house that you had been saving to live in next
    summer.
I am sorry, but it was morning, and I had nothing to do
and its wooden beams were so inviting.

2

We laughed at the hollyhocks together
and then I sprayed them with lye.
Forgive me. I simply do not know what I am doing.   5

3

I gave away the money that you had been saving to live on for the
    next ten years.
The man who asked for it was shabby
and the firm March wind on the porch was so juicy and cold.

4

Last evening we went dancing and I broke your leg.   10
Forgive me. I was clumsy, and
I wanted you here in the wards, where I am the doctor!

(1962)

Exploring the Text

1. What is the tone of "Variations on a Theme by William Carlos Williams"?
2. The expression "variations on a theme" comes from music, where it means that material is repeated in an altered form. Why do you think Kenneth Koch called his parody of the William Carlos Williams poem a variation on a theme?
3. Do you consider this poem a love note? Explain your reasons.
4. Williams was a doctor. How does knowing that change the meaning of the last line of Koch's poem?
5. What is the effect of the undertone of violence in this poem?

Making Connections

1. The Koch poem (p. 111) is punctuated quite conventionally, while Williams's poem (p. 1109) has no punctuation at all. Compare and contrast the effects of the punctuation choices. How do those choices affect each poem's tone?
2. Compare the speakers in the two poems. As you compare, consider whether the speakers are men or women. What other qualities are revealed about them? How can you tell?
3. The Williams poem's title is also its first line — "This is just to say" being a way we sometimes start notes or e-mails — while the Koch poem forgoes that nicety. How does that difference affect meaning in the two poems?
4. Do you think the Koch poem is more than just a parody? How do you think the speaker feels about Williams?
5. Compose a couple of your own versions of "This Is Just to Say." Make one a straightforward "love note"; make another a parody.

T. S. ELIOT

Poet, dramatist, and critic Thomas Stearns Eliot (1888–1965) was born and raised in St. Louis, Missouri. He moved to England when he was twenty-five and eventually became a British subject. He once said that his poetry was a combination of American and British influences but that "in its sources, in its emotional springs, it comes from America." Eliot studied philosophy at Harvard and Oxford, even learning Sanskrit to study Buddhism and other Indic religions. He later worked at Lloyds Bank in London and eventually became a director of Faber & Faber, an English publishing house. His most famous works include "The Love Song of J. Alfred Prufrock" (1917), *The Waste Land* (1922), "Ash Wednesday" (1930), "Burnt Norton" (1941), "Little Gidding" (1942), *The Four Quartets* (1943), and the play *Murder in the Cathedral* (1935). The musical *Cats* was based on Eliot's *Old Possum's Book of Practical Cats* (1939), which earned him posthumous Tony Awards in 1983 for best book and best score. He was awarded the Nobel Prize for Literature in 1948. Eliot is considered one of the great poetic innovators of the twentieth century and is closely associated with the modernist movement — especially with regard to his use of stream of consciousness.

The Hollow Men

Published in 1925 in Eliot's *Poems: 1909–1925*, some people consider "The Hollow Men" an addendum to Eliot's famous poem *The Waste Land* (1922). Four of the five sections of "The Hollow Men" had been previously published in literary journals, such as the *Dial*.

> *Mistah Kurtz — he dead.*[1]
> *A penny for the Old Guy*[2]

I

We are the hollow men
We are the stuffed men
Leaning together
Headpiece filled with straw. Alas!
Our dried voices, when   5

---

[1]Line from Joseph Conrad's *Heart of Darkness* announcing the death of Kurtz, the ivory hunter whom the novel's protagonist has been searching for in Africa. — Eds.
[2]Common saying in England around Guy Fawkes Day, as children beg for money for fireworks. Guy Fawkes was implicated in the failed Gunpowder Plot of 1605, in which he attempted to blow up the British Parliament. His capture and demise are celebrated every year with fireworks and bonfires used to burn straw effigies. — Eds.

We whisper together
Are quiet and meaningless
As wind in dry grass
Or rats' feet over broken glass
In our dry cellar   10

Shape without form, shade without colour,
Paralysed force, gesture without motion;

Those who have crossed
With direct eyes, to death's other Kingdom
Remember us — if at all — not as lost   15
Violent souls, but only
As the hollow men
The stuffed men.

II

Eyes I dare not meet in dreams
In death's dream kingdom   20
These do not appear:
There, the eyes are
Sunlight on a broken column
There, is a tree swinging
And voices are   25
In the wind's singing
More distant and more solemn
Than a fading star.

Let me be no nearer
In death's dream kingdom   30
Let me also wear
Such deliberate disguises
Rat's coat, crowskin, crossed staves
In a field
Behaving as the wind behaves   35
No nearer —

Not that final meeting
In the twilight kingdom

III

This is the dead land
This is cactus land   40

Here the stone images
Are raised, here they receive
The supplication of a dead man's hand
Under the twinkle of a fading star.

Is it like this   45
In death's other kingdom
Waking alone
At the hour when we are
Trembling with tenderness
Lips that would kiss   50
Form prayers to broken stone.

IV

The eyes are not here
There are no eyes here
In this valley of dying stars
In this hollow valley   55
This broken jaw of our lost kingdoms

In this last of meeting places
We grope together
And avoid speech
Gathered on this beach of the tumid river   60

Sightless, unless
The eyes reappear
As the perpetual star
Multifoliate rose
Of death's twilight kingdom   65
The hope only
Of empty men.

V

Here we go round the prickly pear
Prickly pear prickly pear
Here we go round the prickly pear   70
At five o'clock in the morning.

Between the idea
And the reality
Between the motion
And the act   75

Falls the Shadow
    For Thine is the Kingdom

Between the conception
And the creation
Between the emotion   80
And the response
Falls the Shadow
    Life is very long

Between the desire
And the spasm   85
Between the potency
And the existence
Between the essence
And the descent
Falls the Shadow   90
    For Thine is the Kingdom
For Thine is
Life is
For Thine is the

This is the way the world ends   95
This is the way the world ends
This is the way the world ends
Not with a bang but a whimper.

                (1925)

Exploring the Text

1. How would you describe the mood or atmosphere of "The Hollow Men"?
2. What image patterns do you notice in "The Hollow Men"? Consider how often each one is repeated. How do the images — and their repetition — add to the deeper meaning of the poem?
3. "The Hollow Men" has two epigraphs. How do you think these are connected to the rest of the poem?
4. "The Hollow Men" borrows from several genres. What "sampling" can you pick out? In what ways does this technique help T. S. Eliot develop his ideas?
5. How does the last section of "The Hollow Men" differ from the first four sections? Why do you think "prickly pear" (a kind of cactus) replaces "mulberry bush" in his rewording of the nursery rhyme?
6. In "Tradition and the Individual Talent," Eliot writes, "To proceed to a more intelligible exposition of the relation of the poet to the past: he can neither take the past as a lump, an indiscriminate bolus, nor can he form himself wholly on one or

two private admirations, nor can he form himself wholly upon one preferred period. The first course is inadmissible, the second is an important experience of youth, and the third is a pleasant and highly desirable supplement." How does "The Hollow Men" illustrate this idea?

7. Some critics consider "The Hollow Men" a response to World War I, while others see it as a reflection of Eliot's failing marriage and personal religious crisis. What are your thoughts about those two possibilities? Could the poem be both? Explain your answer.

ZORA NEALE HURSTON

Zora Neale Hurston (1891–1960) came to prominence in the 1920s during the Harlem Renaissance. A novelist, a folklorist, and an anthropologist, she first gained attention with her short stories, including "Sweat" and "Spunk." She is best known for her novel *Their Eyes Were Watching God* (1937), set in Eatonville, Florida, where Hurston grew up; the town was the first incorporated African American community in the United States. Hurston graduated from Barnard College and lived most of her life in the New York area, though she traveled extensively in the Caribbean doing anthropological research. Her writing is known for its celebration of African American folk culture, as well as its use of authentic vernacular speech. Hurston, who died in poverty, was all but forgotten until Alice Walker took an interest in her. Walker's 1971 essay "Looking for Zora" describes her personal journey to find Hurston's unmarked grave. The publication of that essay prompted a resurgence of interest in Hurston, including republication of many of her books.

How It Feels to Be Colored Me

"How It Feels to Be Colored Me" was first published in *The World Tomorrow* in May 1928.

I am colored but I offer nothing in the way of extenuating circumstances except the fact that I am the only Negro in the United States whose grandfather on the mother's side was *not* an Indian chief.

I remember the very day that I became colored. Up to my thirteenth year I lived in the little Negro town of Eatonville, Florida. It is exclusively a colored town. The only white people I knew passed through the town going to or coming from Orlando. The native whites rode dusty horses, the Northern tourists chugged down the sandy village road in automobiles. The town knew the Southerners and never stopped cane chewing when they passed. But the Northerners were something else again. They were peered at cautiously from behind curtains by the timid. The more venturesome would come out on the porch to watch them go past and got just as much pleasure out of the tourists as the tourists got out of the village.

The front porch might seem a daring place for the rest of the town, but it was a gallery seat for me. My favorite place was atop the gate-post. Proscenium box for a born first-nighter. Not only did I enjoy the show, but I didn't mind the actors knowing that I liked it. I usually spoke to them in passing. I'd wave at them and when they returned my salute, I would say something like this: "Howdy-do-well-I-thank-you-where-you-goin'?" Usually automobile or the horse paused at this, and after a queer exchange of compliments, I would probably "go a piece of the way" with them, as we say in farthest Florida. If one of my family happened to come to the front in time to see me, of course negotiations would be rudely broken off. But even so, it is clear that I was the first "welcome-to-our-state" Floridian, and I hope the Miami Chamber of Commerce will please take notice.

During this period, white people differed from colored to me only in that they rode through town and never lived there. They liked to hear me "speak pieces" and sing and wanted to see me dance the parse-me-la, and gave me generously of their small silver for doing these things, which seemed strange to me for I wanted to do them so much that I needed bribing to stop. Only they didn't know it. The colored people gave no dimes. They deplored any joyful tendencies in me, but I was their Zora nevertheless. I belonged to them, to the nearby hotels, to the county — everybody's Zora.

But changes came in the family when I was thirteen, and I was sent to school in Jacksonville. I left Eatonville, the town of the oleanders, as Zora. When I disembarked from the river-boat at Jacksonville, she was no more. It seemed that I had suffered a sea change. I was not Zora of Orange County any more, I was now a little colored girl. I found it out in certain ways. In my heart as well as in the mirror, I became a fast brown — warranted not to rub nor run. 5

But I am not tragically colored. There is no great sorrow dammed up in my soul, nor lurking behind my eyes. I do not mind at all. I do not belong to the sobbing school of Negrohood who hold that nature somehow has given them a lowdown dirty deal and whose feelings are all hurt about it. Even in the helter-skelter skirmish that is my life, I have seen that the world is to the strong regardless of a little pigmentation more or less. No, I do not weep at the world — I am too busy sharpening my oyster knife.

Someone is always at my elbow reminding me that I am the granddaughter of slaves. It fails to register depression with me. Slavery is sixty years in the past. The operation was successful and the patient is doing well, thank you. The terrible struggle that made me an American out of a potential slave said "On the line!" The Reconstruction said "Get set!"; and the generation before said "Go!" I am off to a flying start and I must not halt in the stretch to look behind and weep. Slavery is the price I paid for civilization, and the choice was not with me. It is a bully adventure and worth all that I have paid through my ancestors for it. No one on earth ever had a greater chance for glory. The world to be won and nothing to be lost. It is thrilling to think — to know that for any act of mine, I shall get twice as much praise or twice as much blame. It is quite exciting to hold the center of the national stage, with the spectators not knowing whether to laugh or to weep.

The position of my white neighbor is much more difficult. No brown specter pulls up a chair beside me when I sit down to eat. No dark ghost thrusts its leg against mine in bed. The game of keeping what one has is never so exciting as the game of getting.

I do not always feel colored. Even now I often achieve the unconscious Zora of Eatonville before the Hegira.[1] I feel most colored when I am thrown against a sharp white background.

For instance at Barnard. "Beside the waters of the Hudson" I feel my race. Among the thousand white persons, I am a dark rock surged upon, and overswept, but through it all, I remain myself. When covered by the waters, I am; and the ebb but reveals me again.   10

Sometimes it is the other way around. A white person is set down in our midst, but the contrast is just as sharp for me. For instance, when I sit in the drafty basement that is The New World Cabaret with a white person, my color comes. We enter chatting about any little nothing that we have in common and are seated by the jazz waiters. In the abrupt way that jazz orchestras have, this one plunges into a number. It loses no time in circumlocutions, but gets right down to business. It constricts the thorax and splits the heart with its tempo and narcotic harmonies. This orchestra grows rambunctious, rears on its hind legs and attacks the tonal veil with primitive fury, rending it, clawing it until it breaks through to the jungle beyond. I follow those heathen—follow them exultingly. I dance wildly inside myself; I yell within, I whoop; I shake my assegai[2] above my head, I hurl it true to the mark *yeeeeooww!* I am in the jungle and living in the jungle way. My face is painted red and yellow and my body is painted blue. My pulse is throbbing like a war drum. I want to slaughter something—give pain, give death to what, I do not know. But the piece ends. The men of the orchestra wipe their lips and rest their fingers. I creep back slowly to the veneer we call civilization with the last tone and find the white friend sitting motionless in his seat, smoking calmly.

"Good music they have here," he remarks, drumming the table with his fingertips.

Music. The great blobs of purple and red emotion have not touched him. He has only heard what I felt. He is far away and I see him but dimly across the ocean and the continent that have fallen between us. He is so pale with his whiteness then and I am *so* colored.

At certain times I have no race, I am *me*. When I set my hat at a certain angle and saunter down Seventh Avenue, Harlem City, feeling as snooty as the lions in front of the Forty-Second Street Library, for instance. So far as my feelings are concerned,

---

[1]Journey to escape danger. Specifically, Muhammad's departure from Mecca in 622 C.E. to escape an assassination plot. — Eds.
[2]African spear. — Eds.

Peggy Hopkins Joyce[3] on the Boule Mich[4] with her gorgeous raiment, stately carriage, knees knocking together in a most aristocratic manner, has nothing on me. The cosmic Zora emerges. I belong to no race nor time. I am the eternal feminine with its string of beads.

I have no separate feeling about being an American citizen and colored. I am   15
merely a fragment of the Great Soul that surges within the boundaries. My country, right or wrong.

Sometimes, I feel discriminated against, but it does not make me angry. It merely astonishes me. How *can* any deny themselves the pleasure of my company? It's beyond me.

But in the main, I feel like a brown bag of miscellany propped against a wall. Against a wall in company with other bags, white, red, and yellow. Pour out the contents, and there is discovered a jumble of small things priceless and worthless. A first-water diamond, an empty spool, bits of broken glass, lengths of string, a key to a door long since crumbled away, a rusty knife-blade, old shoes saved for a road that never was and never will be, a nail bent under the weight of things too heavy for any nail, a dried flower or two still a little fragrant. In your hand is the brown bag. On the ground before you is the jumble it held — so much like the jumble in the bags, could they be emptied, that all might be dumped in a single heap and the bags refilled without altering the content of any greatly. A bit of colored glass more or less would not matter. Perhaps that is how the Great Stuffer of Bags filled them in the first place — who knows?

(1928)

Exploring the Text

1. What is the function of the first paragraph of "How It Feels to Be Colored Me" in setting the tone of the essay? What is its effect on you, the reader?
2. What arguments does Zora Neale Hurston counter in this essay?
3. What is the effect of Hurston's metaphor describing the end of slavery in paragraph 7?
4. How would you characterize the language Hurston uses in paragraph 11 to describe her reaction to the music in the New World Cabaret?
5. Hurston divides her essay into four sections. What is the purpose of these divisions?
6. Who do you think is Hurston's audience for this essay?
7. The term *colored* was considered somewhat pejorative even during Hurston's time. Why does Hurston use it in her title and throughout her essay? Note other words and descriptions of skin color. What might Hurston be suggesting by the range of terms she uses?

---

[3] American actress known for her extravagant lifestyle, including a famous million-dollar shopping spree in 1920. — Eds.
[4] Boulevard Saint-Michel, one of the main streets in Paris's Latin Quarter. — Eds.

ERNEST HEMINGWAY

American novelist, journalist, and short-story writer Ernest Hemingway (1899–1961) was born in Illinois and became a reporter for the *Kansas City Star* after high school. During World War I, he volunteered as an ambulance driver in Italy, where he was wounded and hospitalized. After the war, Hemingway worked as a reporter for American newspapers and then as a foreign correspondent in Europe. Among his most famous works are the novels *The Sun Also Rises* (1926), *A Farewell to Arms* (1929), and *The Old Man and the Sea* (1955). He was awarded the Nobel Prize for Literature in 1954, and the influence of his "simple," "journalistic" style on modern writing has been incalculable.

A Clean, Well-Lighted Place

This short story was first published in *Scribner's* magazine in 1933.

It was late and everyone had left the café except an old man who sat in the shadow the leaves of the tree made against the electric light. In the day time the street was dusty, but at night the dew settled the dust and the old man liked to sit late because he was deaf and now at night it was quiet and he felt the difference. The two waiters inside the café knew that the old man was a little drunk, and while he was a good client they knew that if he became too drunk he would leave without paying, so they kept watch on him.

"Last week he tried to commit suicide," one waiter said.

"Why?"

"He was in despair."

"What about?"

"Nothing."   5

"How do you know it was nothing?"

"He has plenty of money."

They sat together at a table that was close against the wall near the door of the café and looked at the terrace where the tables were all empty except where the old man sat in the shadow of the leaves of the tree that moved slightly in the wind. A girl and a soldier went by in the street. The street light shone on the brass number on his collar. The girl wore no head covering and hurried beside him.

"The guard will pick him up," one waiter said.   10

"What does it matter if he gets what he's after?"

"He had better get off the street now. The guard will get him. They went by five minutes ago."

The old man sitting in the shadow rapped on his saucer with his glass. The younger waiter went over to him.

"What do you want?"

The old man looked at him. "Another brandy," he said. 15

"You'll be drunk," the waiter said. The old man looked at him. The waiter went away.

"He'll stay all night," he said to his colleague. "I'm sleepy now. I never get into bed before three o'clock. He should have killed himself last week."

The waiter took the brandy bottle and another saucer from the counter inside the café and marched out to the old man's table. He put down the saucer and poured the glass full of brandy.

"You should have killed yourself last week," he said to the deaf man. The old man motioned with his finger. "A little more," he said. The waiter poured on into the glass so that the brandy slopped over and ran down the stem into the top saucer of the pile. "Thank you," the old man said. The waiter took the bottle back inside the café. He sat down at the table with his colleague again.

"He's drunk now," he said. 20

"He's drunk every night."

"What did he want to kill himself for?"

"How should I know."

"How did he do it?"

"He hung himself with a rope." 25

"Who cut him down?"

"His niece."

"Why did they do it?"

"Fear for his soul."

"How much money has he got?" 30

"He's got plenty."

"He must be eighty years old."

"Anyway I should say he was eighty."

"I wish he would go home. I never get to bed before three o'clock. What kind of hour is that to go to bed?"

"He stays up because he likes it." 35

"He's lonely. I'm not lonely. I have a wife waiting in bed for me."

"He had a wife once too."

"A wife would be no good to him now."

"You can't tell. He might be better with a wife."

"His niece looks after him. You said she cut him down." 40

"I know."

"I wouldn't want to be that old. An old man is a nasty thing."

"Not always. This old man is clean. He drinks without spilling. Even now, drunk. Look at him."

"I don't want to look at him. I wish he would go home. He has no regard for those who must work."

The old man looked from his glass across the square, then over at the waiters. 45

"Another brandy," he said, pointing to his glass. The waiter who was in a hurry came over.

"Finished," he said, speaking with that omission of syntax stupid people employ when talking to drunken people or foreigners. "No more tonight. Close now."

"Another," said the old man.

"No. Finished." The waiter wiped the edge of the table with a towel and shook his head.

The old man stood up, slowly counted the saucers, took a leather coin purse from his pocket and paid for the drinks, leaving half a peseta tip.

The waiter watched him go down the street, a very old man walking unsteadily but with dignity.

"Why didn't you let him stay and drink?" the unhurried waiter asked. They were putting up the shutters. "It is not half-past two."

"I want to go home to bed."

"What is an hour?"

"More to me than to him."

"An hour is the same."

"You talk like an old man yourself. He can buy a bottle and drink at home."

"It's not the same."

"No, it is not," agreed the waiter with a wife. He did not wish to be unjust. He was only in a hurry.

"And you? You have no fear of going home before your usual hour?"

"Are you trying to insult me?"

"No, hombre, only to make a joke."

"No," the waiter who was in a hurry said, rising from pulling down the metal shutters. "I have confidence. I am all confidence."

"You have youth, confidence, and a job," the older waiter said. "You have everything."

"And what do you lack?"

"Everything but work."

"You have everything I have."

"No. I have never had confidence and I am not young."

"Come on. Stop talking nonsense and lock up."

"I am of those who like to stay late at the café," the older waiter said. "With all those who do not want to go to bed. With all those who need a light for the night."

"I want to go home and into bed."

"We are of two different kinds," the older waiter said. He was now dressed to go home. "It is not only a question of youth and confidence although those things are very beautiful. Each night I am reluctant to close up because there may be some one who needs the café."

"Hombre, there are bodegas open all night long."

"You do not understand. This is a clean and pleasant café. It is well lighted. The light is very good and also, now, there are shadows of the leaves."

"Good night," said the younger waiter.

"Good night," the other said. Turning off the electric light he continued the conversation with himself. It is the light of course but it is necessary that the place be

50

55

60

65

70

75

clean and pleasant. You do not want music. Certainly you do not want music. Nor can you stand before a bar with dignity although that is all that is provided for these hours. What did he fear? It was not fear or dread. It was a nothing that he knew too well. It was all a nothing and a man was nothing too. It was only that and light was all it needed and a certain cleanness and order. Some lived in it and never felt it but he knew it was nada y pues nada y pues nada.[1] Our nada who art in nada, nada be thy name thy kingdom nada thy will be nada in nada as it is in nada. Give us this nada our daily nada and nada us our nada as we nada our nadas and nada us not into nada but deliver us from nada; pues nada. Hail nothing full of nothing, nothing is with thee. He smiled and stood before a bar with a shining steam pressure coffee machine.

"What's yours?" asked the barman.

"Nada."

"Otro loco más,"[2] said the barman and turned away.

"A little cup," said the waiter.   80

The barman poured it for him.

"The light is very bright and pleasant but the bar is unpolished," the waiter said.

The barman looked at him but did not answer. It was too late at night for conversation.

"You want another copita?" the barman asked.

"No, thank you," said the waiter and went out. He disliked bars and bodegas. A   85
clean, well-lighted café was a very different thing. Now, without thinking further, he would go home to his room. He would lie in the bed and finally, with daylight, he would go to sleep. After all, he said to himself, it is probably only insomnia. Many must have it.

(1933)

Exploring the Text

1. Describe the setting of "A Clean, Well-Lighted Place."
2. Describe the story's six characters. What do they have in common? What differentiates them?
3. Look carefully at the story's mentions of light and dark. What patterns emerge? How do those patterns develop the deeper meanings of "A Clean, Well-Lighted Place"?
4. Why do you think the older waiter inserts the word "nada" (*nothing*, in Spanish) in the Lord's Prayer and at the beginning of the Hail Mary? What words has he replaced with "nada"? Read the two prayers in their original form and compare them to the versions here.
5. What do you think the old man's deafness represents in "A Clean, Well-Lighted Place"?

---

[1] Spanish. "Nothing, and then nothing, and then nothing." — Ed.
[2] Spanish. "Another crazy one." — Eds.

6. Compare and contrast the two waiters based on the dialogue between them. How are their needs different? What does each one represent?
7. This story takes place in a café in Europe. In what ways are its themes American? In what ways might you consider them European?
8. James Joyce is said to have considered "A Clean, Well-Lighted Place" one of the best short stories ever written. He said that Ernest Hemingway "reduced the veil between literature and life." Do you agree with Joyce? Explain your answer.

 **TALKBACK**

YIYUN LI

Originally from Beijing, China, Yiyun Li (b. 1972) moved to the United States in 1996 to study immunology and writing at the University of Iowa. She made a name for herself with her first collection of short stories, the award-winning *A Thousand Years of Good Prayers* (2005). This was followed by a novel, *The Vagrants* (2009), and another collection of stories, *Golden Boy, Emerald Girl* (2010). Li currently lives in Oakland, California, and teaches at the University of California–Davis.

A Clean, Well-Lighted Place

This piece was published in the April 18, 2011, issue of the *New Yorker*, which was dedicated to journeys, in a section called "Coming to America."

"Here's a fact for you America-philes," a certain Major Tang, in the Army in which I had once served, liked to say when he caught us memorizing English vocabulary. "The moon in America is no bigger or brighter than the moon in China." A scientifically sound statement, though what a surprise it was to find that the moon in Iowa, where I landed in 1996 to go to graduate school, did seem much bigger and brighter. In my native Beijing, the moon looked faded behind the smog, remote and melancholy.

Equally astonishing was American lighting: in many places, lights stayed on from morning till night. At home, our family, conscious of saving every penny, would not turn on a single lamp until the last ray of daylight had vanished. Lights in public places were sound-controlled. The residents in our building had developed the habit of clapping or stomping to turn on a lamp, and to announce their presence; a few, like me, preferred a stealthy, unnoticeable passing in the dark.

How does one live in such a well-lighted country? Before I left China, I had prepared myself with a four-cassette course in American English. Phrases like "Be there or be square" and "Stop running around like a chicken with its head cut off" stayed with me because of their imperativeness.

No one told me to "be there or be square," but everyone I met, it seemed, expected me to have fun. After I had planned a set of immunology experiments with my adviser, he said, "Have fun." The nurse I met biweekly over a six-month period, because I had not passed the TB skin test required for enrollment at the university, always wished me a "good time" with the pills. A sorority mother in her sixties, a member of a local group that befriended international students, asked repeatedly, "Did you have fun?" after I visited the sorority house and dined with her girls. How could I explain that it was not memories of fun that would stay with me but what I saw in her bedroom: an oil painting of her, at eighteen, riding a prize horse; a black-and-white wedding photograph of her and her husband, a Navy officer who had died four years earlier; the thirty-seven stuffed animals on her bed, one for each year of her marriage?

As part of a program to help foreign students understand America, I signed   5 up to patrol the town with the police on a shift between midnight and 3 A.M. An officer drove us around and talked about his family: his wife, who had grown up in Correctionville, Iowa; his childhood, in a farmhouse outside the Quad Cities; their three children. He asked about my studies at the university, and about China. When we had exhausted those topics, we cruised in silence.

A little before two that morning, a call came in. A man had been seen buying cold medicine on two consecutive nights. The officer sped to a Walmart at the edge of town, where three more police cars arrived within minutes. The man in question, we were told, was playing pinball in the store. After half an hour, he walked out of the store, a plastic bag with a yellow smiley face dangling from his hand. Just as he unlocked his car, the four police vehicles surrounded him.

From where I sat, I could not see much besides the officers in their black uniforms, worn over bulky bulletproof vests. Twenty minutes passed. Finally, two of the officers moved their cars, and the man drove away.

The store's undercover security guard, the officer explained when he returned, had noticed a hypodermic needle at the entrance of the store. He had not seen the man drop it, but he suspected that he had. "We ran a search of his vehicle registration," the officer said. "If there's one thing coming up, we could bring him back for more questions. Or if the security guard saw him with the needle. As it stands now . . ." He shrugged, and then said it was time I ended my shift.

In parting, I said goodbye to the officer, and he wished me "a fun time in America."

What a strange country, I thought, where fun, like good lighting, seemed   10 mandatory. Was it fun that had kept the man at the pinball machine when he could have left with his suspicious purchase before the police arrived? Had someone told the security guard to have fun before he went to work, watching sleepless souls wander among the aisles? The other people I had seen on this night shift — the few customers in the diner where we stopped for coffee, the custodian of a water plant, a man behind the counter in a gas station — looked as though they had walked out of the paintings of Edward Hopper, yet the characters in those paintings, lacking an escape from the harsh, hard-edged light, had the choice of silence. They did not exhort one another to have a good time; they did not need to step out of their loneliness to tackle the task of having fun.

(2011)

Exploring the Text

1. How does the first paragraph set up expectations for the rest of "A Clean, Well-Lighted Place"? Does the essay fulfill those expectations or defy them? Explain your answer.
2. What meaning does "American lighting" (par. 2) have for Yiyun Li?
3. What do the phrases Li remembers from her "four-cassette course in American English" (par. 3) have in common with the very American expectation to have fun that she encounters everywhere? Why do you think that connection is significant to her?
4. Do you think Li answers the question she asks in paragraph 3: "How does one live in such a well-lighted country?" Explain your answer.
5. Edward Hopper is known for his paintings of landscapes and people that highlight their isolation. *Nighthawks*, his painting of a coffee shop late at night, in which four people seem to be in their own worlds, is especially famous. How does Li's allusion to Hopper help her comment on what she finds strange about life in America?

Making Connections

1. Why do you think Yiyun Li titled her essay "A Clean, Well-Lighted Place"?
2. Both Ernest Hemingway's story (p. 1121) and Li's essay (p. 1125) make assumptions about the values of others. How are those assumptions similar? How are they different?
3. Do you think the well-lighted Walmart in Li's piece has anything to do with the well-lit café in Hemingway's story? Explain your answer.

EDITH WHARTON

Edith Wharton (1862–1937) was a Pulitzer Prize–winning American novelist and short-story writer. Between 1900 and 1938, Wharton published twenty-two novels, including *The House of Mirth* (1905), which first gained her literary fame, and *The Age of Innocence* (1920), for which she won a Pulitzer Prize, the first awarded to a woman for literature. During World War I (1914–1918), Wharton stayed in Paris and devoted her time to helping those displaced by the war. Her efforts included finding (and, in some cases, providing) employment for refugees, opening tuberculosis hospitals, and serving as a founder of the American Hostels for Belgian refugees. When the war ended in 1918, Wharton officially moved to France, returning to America only once more in her lifetime to receive an honorary doctorate from Yale University in 1923.

Roman Fever

"Roman Fever" was first published in *Liberty* in 1934; its title plays on the multiple meanings of Roman fever: in a literal sense, malaria — caught from mosquitoes in the damp Roman ruins — but also the "misbehavior" that American women might have indulged in when they were away from the stultifying mores and traditions of home.

I

From the table at which they had been lunching two American ladies of ripe but well-cared-for middle age moved across the lofty terrace of the Roman restaurant and, leaning on its parapet, looked first at each other, and then down on the outspread glories of the Palatine and the Forum, with the same expression of vague but benevolent approval.

As they leaned there a girlish voice echoed up gaily from the stairs leading to the court below. "Well, come along, then," it cried, not to them but to an invisible companion, "and let's leave the young things to their knitting" and a voice as fresh laughed back: "Oh, look here, Babs, not actually *knitting*—" "Well, I mean figuratively," rejoined the first. "After all, we haven't left our poor parents much else to do . . ." and at that point the turn of the stairs engulfed the dialogue.

The two ladies looked at each other again, this time with a tinge of smiling embarrassment, and the smaller and paler one shook her head and colored slightly.

"Barbara!" she murmured, sending an unheard rebuke after the mocking voice in the stairway.

The other lady, who was fuller, and higher in color, with a small determined nose supported by vigorous black eyebrows, gave a good-humored laugh. "That's what our daughters think of us!" 5

Her companion replied by a deprecating gesture. "Not of us individually. We must remember that. It's just the collective modern idea of Mothers. And you see — " Half guiltily she drew from her handsomely mounted black handbag a twist of crimson silk run through by two fine knitting needles. "One never knows," she murmured. "The new system has certainly given us a good deal of time to kill; and sometimes I get tired just looking — even at this." Her gesture was now addressed to the stupendous scene at their feet.

The dark lady laughed again, and they both relapsed upon the view, contemplating it in silence, with a sort of diffused serenity which might have been borrowed from the spring effulgence of the Roman skies. The luncheon-hour was long past, and the two had their end of the vast terrace to themselves. At its opposite extremity a few groups, detained by a lingering look at the outspread city, were gathering up guidebooks and fumbling for tips. The last of them scattered, and the two ladies were alone on the air-washed height.

"Well, I don't see why we shouldn't just stay here," said Mrs. Slade, the lady of the high color and energetic brows. Two derelict basket-chairs stood near, and she pushed them into the angle of the parapet, and settled herself in one, her gaze upon the Palatine. "After all, it's still the most beautiful view in the world."

"It always will be, to me," assented her friend Mrs. Ansley, with so slight a stress on the "me" that Mrs. Slade, though she noticed it, wondered if it were not merely accidental, like the random underlinings of old-fashioned letter-writers.

"Grace Ansley was always old-fashioned," she thought; and added aloud, with a retrospective smile: "It's a view we've both been familiar with for a good many years. When we first met here we were younger than our girls are now. You remember?"

"Oh, yes, I remember," murmured Mrs. Ansley, with the same undefinable stress—"There's that head-waiter wondering," she interpolated. She was evidently far less sure than her companion of herself and of her rights in the world.

"I'll cure him of wondering," said Mrs. Slade, stretching her hand toward a bag as discreetly opulent-looking as Mrs. Ansley's. Signing to the head-waiter, she explained that she and her friend were old lovers of Rome, and would like to spend the end of the afternoon looking down on the view—that is, if it did not disturb the service? The head-waiter, bowing over her gratuity, assured her that the ladies were most welcome, and would he still more so if they would condescend to remain for dinner. A full moon night, they would remember. . . .

Mrs. Slade's black brows drew together, as though references to the moon were out-of-place and even unwelcome. But she smiled away her frown as the head-waiter retreated. "Well, why not? We might do worse. There's no knowing, I suppose, when the girls will be back. Do you even know back from *where*? I don't!"

Mrs. Ansley again colored slightly. "I think those young Italian aviators we met at the Embassy invited them to fly to Tarquinia for tea. I suppose they'll want to wait and fly back by moonlight."

"Moonlight—moonlight! What a part it still plays. Do you suppose they're as sentimental as we were?"

"I've come to the conclusion that I don't in the least know what they are," said Mrs. Ansley. "And perhaps we didn't know much more about each other."

"No; perhaps we didn't."

Her friend gave her a shy glance. "I never should have supposed you were sentimental, Alida."

"Well, perhaps I wasn't." Mrs. Slade drew her lids together in retrospect; and for a few moments the two ladies, who had been intimate since childhood, reflected how little they knew each other. Each one, of course, had a label ready to attach to the other's name; Mrs. Delphin Slade, for instance, would have told herself, or any one who asked her, that Mrs. Horace Ansley, twenty-five years ago, had been exquisitely lovely—no, you wouldn't believe it, would you? . . . though, of course, still charming, distinguished. . . . Well, as a girl she had been exquisite; far more beautiful than her daughter Barbara, though certainly Babs, according to the new standards at any rate, was more effective—had more *edge*, as they say. Funny where she got it, with those two nullities as parents. Yes; Horace Ansley was—well, just the duplicate of his wife. Museum specimens of old New York. Good-looking, irreproachable, exemplary. Mrs. Slade and Mrs. Ansley had lived opposite each other—actually as well as figuratively—for years. When the drawing-room curtains in No. 20 East 73rd Street were renewed, No. 23, across the way, was always aware of it. And of all the movings, buyings, travels, anniversaries, illnesses — the tame chronicle of an estimable pair. Little of it escaped Mrs. Slade. But she had grown bored with it by the time her husband made his big *coup* in Wall Street, and when they bought in upper Park Avenue had already begun to think: "I'd rather live opposite a speakeasy for a change; at least one might see it raided." The idea of seeing Grace raided was so amusing that (before the move) she launched it at a woman's lunch. It made a hit, and went the rounds — she sometimes wondered if it had crossed the street, and reached Mrs. Ansley. She hoped not, but didn't much mind. Those were the days when respectability was at a discount, and it did the irreproachable no harm to laugh at them a little.

A few years later, and not many months apart, both ladies lost their husbands. 20 There was an appropriate exchange of wreaths and condolences, and a brief renewal of intimacy in the half-shadow of their mourning; and now, after another interval, they had run across each other in Rome, at the same hotel, each of them the modest appendage of a salient daughter. The similarity of their lot had again drawn them together, lending itself to mild jokes, and the mutual confession that, if in old days it must have been tiring to "keep up" with daughters, it was now, at times, a little dull not to.

No doubt, Mrs. Slade reflected, she felt her unemployment more than poor Grace ever would. It was a big drop from being the wife of Delphin Slade to being his widow. She had always regarded herself (with a certain conjugal pride) as his equal in social gifts, as contributing her full share to the making of the exceptional couple they were: but the difference after his death was irremediable. As the wife of the famous corporation lawyer, always with an international case or two on hand, every day brought its exciting and unexpected obligation: the impromptu entertaining of eminent colleagues from abroad, the hurried dashes on legal business to London, Paris or Rome, where the entertaining was so handsomely reciprocated; the amusement of hearing in her wake: "What, that handsome woman with the good clothes and the eyes is Mrs. Slade — *the* Slade's wife? Really? Generally the wives of celebrities are such frumps."

Yes; being *the* Slade's widow was a dullish business after that. In living up to such a husband all her faculties had been engaged; now she had only her daughter to live up to, for the son who seemed to have inherited his father's gifts had died suddenly in boyhood. She had fought through that agony because her husband was there, to be helped and to help; now, after the father's death, the thought of the boy had become unbearable. There was nothing left but to mother her daughter; and dear Jenny was such a perfect daughter that she needed no excessive mothering. "Now with Babs Ansley I don't know that I *should* be so quiet," Mrs. Slade sometimes half-enviously reflected; but Jenny, who was younger than her brilliant friend, was that rare accident, an extremely pretty girl who somehow made youth and prettiness seem as safe as their absence. It was all perplexing — and to Mrs. Slade a little boring. She wished that Jenny would fall in love — with the wrong man, even; that she might have to be watched, out-manœuvred, rescued. And instead, it was Jenny who watched her mother, kept her out of draughts, made sure that she had taken her tonic....

Mrs. Ansley was much less articulate than her friend, and her mental portrait of Mrs. Slade was slighter, and drawn with fainter touches. "Alida Slade's awfully brilliant;

but not as brilliant as she thinks," would have summed it up; though she would have added, for the enlightenment of strangers, that Mrs. Slade had been an extremely dashing girl; much more so than her daughter, who was pretty, of course, and clever in a way, but had none of her mother's — well, "vividness," some one had once called it. Mrs. Ansley would take up current words like this, and cite them in quotation marks, as unheard-of audacities. No; Jenny was not like her mother. Sometimes Mrs. Ansley thought Alida Slade was disappointed; on the whole she had had a sad life. Full of failures and mistakes; Mrs. Ansley had always been rather sorry for her. . . .

So these two ladies visualized each other, each through the wrong end of her little telescope.

II

For a long time they continued to sit side by side without speaking. It seemed as   25
though, to both, there was a relief in laying down their somewhat futile activities in the presence of the vast Memento Mori which faced them. Mrs. Slade sat quite still, her eyes fixed on the golden slope of the Palace of the Caesars, and after a while Mrs. Ansley ceased to fidget with her bag, and she too sank into meditation. Like many intimate friends, the two ladies had never before had occasion to be silent together, and Mrs. Ansley was slightly embarrassed by what seemed, after so many years, a new stage in their intimacy, and one with which she did not yet know how to deal.

Suddenly the air was full of that deep clangor of bells which periodically covers Rome with a roof of silver. Mrs. Slade glanced at her wristwatch. "Five o'clock already," she said, as though surprised.

Mrs. Ansley suggested interrogatively: "There's bridge at the Embassy at five." For a long time Mrs. Slade did not answer. She appeared to be lost in contemplation, and Mrs. Ansley thought the remark had escaped her. But after a while she said, as if speaking out of a dream: "Bridge, did you say? Not unless you want to. . . . But I don't think I will, you know."

"Oh, no," Mrs. Ansley hastened to assure her. "I don't care to at all. It's so lovely here; and so full of old memories, as you say." She settled herself in her chair, and almost furtively drew forth her knitting. Mrs. Slade took sideway note of this activity, but her own beautifully cared-for hands remained motionless on her knee.

"I was just thinking," she said slowly, "what different things Rome stands for to each generation of travelers. To our grandmothers, Roman fever; to our mothers, sentimental danger — how we used to be guarded! — to our daughters, no more dangers than the middle of Main Street. They don't know it — but how much they're missing!"

The long golden light was beginning to pale, and Mrs. Ansley lifted her knitting   30
a little closer to her eyes. "Yes; how we were guarded!"

"I always used to think," Mrs. Slade continued, "that our mothers had a much more difficult job than our grandmothers. When Roman fever stalked the streets it must have been comparatively easy to gather in the girls at the danger hour; but when you and I were young, with such beauty calling us, and the spice of disobedience thrown in, and no worse risk than catching cold during the cool hour after sunset, the mothers used to be put to it to keep us in — didn't they?"

She turned again toward Mrs. Ansley, but the latter had reached a delicate point in her knitting. "One, two, three — slip two; yes, they must have been," she assented, without looking up.

Mrs. Slade's eyes rested on her with a deepened attention. "She can knit — in the face of *this*! How like her. . . ."

Mrs. Slade leaned back, brooding, her eyes ranging from the ruins which faced her to the long green hollow of the Forum, the fading glow of the church fronts beyond it, and the outlying immensity of the Colosseum. Suddenly she thought: "It's all very well to say that our girls have done away with sentiment and moonlight. But if Babs Ansley isn't out to catch that young aviator — the one who's a Marchese[1] — then I don't know anything. And Jenny has no chance beside her. I know that too. I wonder if that's why Grace Ansley likes the two girls to go everywhere together? My poor Jenny as a foil — !" Mrs. Slade gave a hardly audible laugh, and at the sound Mrs. Ansley dropped her knitting.

"Yes — ?"   35

"I — oh, nothing. I was only thinking how your Babs carries everything before her. That Campolieri boy is one of the best matches in Rome. Don't look so innocent, my dear — you know he is. And I was wondering, ever so respectfully, you understand . . . wondering how two such exemplary characters as you and Horace had managed to produce anything quite so dynamic." Mrs. Slade laughed again, with a touch of asperity.

Mrs. Ansley's hands lay inert across her needles. She looked straight out at the great accumulated wreckage of passion and splendor at her feet. But her small profile was almost expressionless. At length she said: "I think you overrate Babs, my dear."

Mrs. Slade's tone grew easier. "No; I don't. I appreciate her. And perhaps envy you. Oh, my girl's perfect; if I were a chronic invalid I'd — well, I think I'd rather be in Jenny's hands. There must be times . . . but there! I always wanted a brilliant daughter . . . and never quite understood why I got an angel instead."

Mrs. Ansley echoed her laugh in a faint murmur. "Babs is an angel too."

"Of course — of course! But she's got rainbow wings. Well, they're wandering by   40
the sea with their young men; and here we sit . . . and it all brings back the past a little too acutely."

Mrs. Ansley had resumed her knitting. One might almost have imagined (if one had known her less well, Mrs. Slade reflected) that, for her also, too many memories rose from the lengthening shadows of those august ruins. But no; she was simply absorbed in her work. What was there for her to worry about? She knew that Babs would almost certainly come back engaged to the extremely eligible Campolieri. "And she'll sell the New York house, and settle down near them in Rome, and never be in their way . . . she's much too tactful. But she'll have an excellent cook, and just the right people in for bridge and cocktails . . . and a perfectly peaceful old age among her grandchildren."

---

[1]Italian nobleman. — Eds.

Mrs. Slade broke off this prophetic flight with a recoil of self-disgust. There was no one of whom she had less right to think unkindly than of Grace Ansley. Would she never cure herself of envying her? Perhaps she had begun too long ago.

She stood up and leaned against the parapet, filling her troubled eyes with the tranquilizing magic of the hour. But instead of tranquilizing her the sight seemed to increase her exasperation. Her gaze turned toward the Colosseum. Already its golden flank was drowned in purple shadow, and above it the sky curved crystal clear, without light or color. It was the moment when afternoon and evening hang balanced in mid-heaven.

Mrs. Slade turned back and laid her hand on her friend's arm. The gesture was so abrupt that Mrs. Ansley looked up, startled.

"The sun's set. You're not afraid, my dear?"   45

"Afraid — ?"

"Of Roman fever or pneumonia? I remember how ill you were that winter. As a girl you had a very delicate throat, hadn't you?"

"Oh, we're all right up here. Down below, in the Forum, it does get deathly cold, all of a sudden . . . but not here."

"Ah, of course you know because you had to be so careful." Mrs. Slade turned back to the parapet. She thought: "I must make one more effort not to hate her." Aloud she said: "Whenever I look at the Forum from up here I remember that story about a great-aunt of yours, wasn't she? A dreadfully wicked great-aunt?"

"Oh yes; Great-aunt Harriet. The one who was supposed to have sent her young   50
sister out to the Forum after sunset to gather a night-blooming flower for her album. All our great-aunts and grandmothers used to have albums of dried flowers."

Mrs. Slade nodded. "But she really sent her because they were in love with the same man —"

"Well, that was the family tradition. They said Aunt Harriet confessed it years afterward. At any rate, the poor little sister caught the fever and died. Mother used to frighten us with the story when we were children."

"And you frightened *me* with it, that winter when you and I were here as girls. The winter I was engaged to Delphin."

Mrs. Ansley gave a faint laugh. "Oh, did I? Really frightened you? I don't believe you're easily frightened."

"Not often; but I was then. I was easily frightened because I was too happy. I   55
wonder if you know what that means?"

"I — yes. . . ." Mrs. Ansley faltered.

"Well, I suppose that was why the story of your wicked aunt made such an impression on me. And I thought: 'There's no more Roman fever, but the Forum is deathly cold after sunset — especially after a hot day. And the Colosseum's even colder and damper.'"

"The Colosseum — ?"

"Yes. It wasn't easy to get in, after the gates were locked for the night. Far from easy. Still, in those days it could be managed; it was managed, often. Lovers met there who couldn't meet elsewhere. You knew that?"

"I — I daresay. I don't remember."   60

"You don't remember? You don't remember going to visit some ruins or other one
evening, just after dark, and catching a bad chill? You were supposed to have gone to
see the moon rise. People always said that expedition was what caused your illness."

There was a moment's silence; then Mrs. Ansley rejoined: "Did they? It was all
so long ago."

"Yes. And you got well again — so it didn't matter. But I suppose it struck your
friend — the reason given for your illness, I mean — because everybody knew you
were so prudent on account of your throat, and your mother took such care of
you. . . . You *had* been out late sight-seeing, hadn't you, that night?"

"Perhaps I had. The most prudent girls aren't always prudent. What made you
think of it now?"

Mrs. Slade seemed to have no answer ready. But after a moment she broke out: 65
"Because I simply can't bear it any longer — "

Mrs. Ansley lifted her head quickly. Her eyes were wide and very pale. "Can't
bear what?"

"Why — your not knowing that I've always known why you went."

"Why I went — ?"

"Yes. You think I'm bluffing, don't you? Well, you went to meet the man I was
engaged to — and I can repeat every word of the letter that took you there."

While Mrs. Slade spoke Mrs. Ansley had risen unsteadily to her feet. Her bag,   70
her knitting and gloves, slid in a panic-stricken heap to the ground. She looked at
Mrs. Slade as though she were looking at a ghost.

"No, no — don't," she faltered out.

"Why not? Listen, if you don't believe me. 'My one darling, things can't go on like
this. I must see you alone. Come to the Colosseum immediately after dark tomorrow.
There will be somebody to let you in. No one whom you need fear will suspect' — but
perhaps you've forgotten what the letter said?"

Mrs. Ansley met the challenge with an unexpected composure. Steadying herself
against the chair she looked at her friend, and replied: "No; I know it by heart too."

"And the signature? 'Only *your* D.S.' Was that it? I'm right, am I? That was the
letter that took you out that evening after dark?"

Mrs. Ansley was still looking at her. It seemed to Mrs. Slade that a slow struggle   75
was going on behind the voluntarily controlled mask of her small quiet face. "I
shouldn't have thought she had herself so well in hand," Mrs. Slade reflected, almost
resentfully. But at this moment Mrs. Ansley spoke, "I don't know how you knew. I
burnt that letter at once."

"Yes; you would, naturally — you're so prudent!" The sneer was open now. "And
if you burnt the letter you're wondering how on earth I know what was in it. That's it,
isn't it?"

Mrs. Slade waited, but Mrs. Ansley did not speak.

"Well, my dear, I know what was in that letter because I wrote it!"

"You wrote it?"

"Yes."

The two women stood for a minute staring at each other in the last golden light. Then Mrs. Ansley dropped back into her chair. "Oh," she murmured, and covered her face with her hands.

Mrs. Slade waited nervously for another word or movement. None came, and at length she broke out: "I horrify you."

Mrs. Ansley's hands dropped to her knee. The face they uncovered was streaked with tears. "I wasn't thinking of you. I was thinking—it was the only letter I ever had from him!"

"And I wrote it. Yes; I wrote it! But I was the girl he was engaged to. Did you happen to remember that?"

Mrs. Ansley's head dropped again. "I'm not trying to excuse myself.... I remembered...."

"And still you went?"

"Still I went."

Mrs. Slade stood looking down on the small bowed figure at her side. The flame of her wrath had already sunk, and she wondered why she had ever thought there would be any satisfaction in inflicting so purposeless a wound on her friend. But she had to justify herself.

"You do understand? I'd found out—and I hated you, hated you. I knew you were in love with Delphin—and I was afraid; afraid of you, of your quiet ways, your sweetness... your... well, I wanted you out of the way, that's all. Just for a few weeks; just till I was sure of him. So in a blind fury I wrote that letter.... I don't know why I'm telling you now."

"I suppose," said Mrs. Ansley slowly, "it's because you've always gone on hating me."

"Perhaps. Or because I wanted to get the whole thing off my mind." She paused. "I'm glad you destroyed the letter. Of course I never thought you'd die."

Mrs. Ansley relapsed into silence, and Mrs. Slade, leaning above her, was conscious of a strange sense of isolation, of being cut off from the warm current of human communion. "You think me a monster!"

"I don't know.... It was the only letter I had, and you say he didn't write it?"

"Ah, how you care for him still!"

"I cared for that memory," said Mrs. Ansley.

Mrs. Slade continued to look down on her. She seemed physically reduced by the blow—as if, when she got up, the wind might scatter her like a puff of dust. Mrs. Slade's jealousy suddenly leapt up again at the sight. All these years the woman had been living on that letter. How she must have loved him, to treasure the mere memory of its ashes! The letter of the man her friend was engaged to. Wasn't it she who was the monster?

"You tried your best to get him away from me, didn't you? But you failed; and I kept him. That's all."

"Yes. That's all."

"I wish now I hadn't told you. I'd no idea you'd feel about it as you do; I thought you'd be amused. It all happened so long ago, as you say; and you must do me the justice to remember that I had no reason to think you'd ever taken it seriously. How could I, when you were married to Horace Ansley two months afterward? As soon as you could get out of bed your mother rushed you off to Florence and married you. People were rather surprised — they wondered at its being done so quickly; but I thought I knew. I had an idea you did it out of *pique* — to be able to say you'd got ahead of Delphin and me. Girls have such silly reasons for doing the most serious things. And your marrying so soon convinced me that you'd never really cared."

"Yes. I suppose it would," Mrs. Ansley assented. 100

The clear heaven overhead was emptied of all its gold. Dusk spread over it, abruptly darkening the Seven Hills. Here and there lights began to twinkle through the foliage at their feet. Steps were coming and going on the deserted terrace — waiters looking out of the doorway at the head of the stairs, then reappearing with trays and napkins and flasks of wine. Tables were moved, chairs straightened. A feeble string of electric lights flickered out. Some vases of faded flowers were carried away, and brought back replenished. A stout lady in a dust-coat suddenly appeared, asking in broken Italian if any one had seen the elastic band which held together her tattered Baedeker.[2] She poked with her stick under the table at which she had lunched, the waiters assisting.

The corner where Mrs. Slade and Mrs. Ansley sat was still shadowy and deserted. For a long time neither of them spoke. At length Mrs. Slade began again: "I suppose I did it as a sort of joke —"

"A joke?"

"Well, girls are ferocious sometimes, you know. Girls in love especially. And I remember laughing to myself all that evening at the idea that you were waiting around there in the dark, dodging out of sight, listening for every sound, trying to get in — Of course I was upset when I heard you were so ill afterward."

Mrs. Ansley had not moved for a long time. But now she turned slowly toward 105 her companion. "But I didn't wait. He'd arranged everything. He was there. We were let in at once," she said.

Mrs. Slade sprang up from her leaning position. "Delphin there? They let you in? — Ah, now you're lying!" she burst out with violence.

Mrs. Ansley's voice grew clearer, and full of surprise. "But of course he was there. Naturally he came —"

"Came? How did he know he'd find you there? You must be raving!"

Mrs. Ansley hesitated, as though reflecting. "But I answered the letter. I told him I'd be there. So he came."

Mrs. Slade flung her hands up to her face. "Oh, God — you answered! I never 110 thought of your answering. . . ."

"It's odd you never thought of it, if you wrote the letter."

---

[2]Travel guide. — Eds.

"Yes. I was blind with rage."

Mrs. Ansley rose, and drew her fur scarf about her. "It is cold here. We'd better go. . . . I'm sorry for you," she said as she clasped the fur about her throat.

The unexpected words sent a pang through Mrs. Slade. "Yes; we'd better go." She gathered up her bag and cloak. "I don't know why you should be sorry for me," she muttered.

Mrs. Ansley stood looking away from her toward the dusky secret mass of the   115
Colosseum. "Well — because I didn't have to wait that night."

Mrs. Slade gave an unquiet laugh. "Yes; I was beaten there. But I oughtn't to begrudge it to you, I suppose. At the end of all these years. After all, I had everything; I had him for twenty-five years. And you had nothing but that one letter that he didn't write."

Mrs. Ansley was again silent. At length she turned toward the door of the terrace. She took a step, and turned back, facing her companion.

"I had Barbara," she said, and began to move ahead of Mrs. Slade toward the stairway.

(1934)

Exploring the Text

1. How does the setting of "Roman Fever" provide both a literal and a figurative backdrop for the story's conflicts?
2. How does Edith Wharton develop the characters of Alida Slade and Grace Ansley? Are there hints at the beginning of the story about how things will turn out? Were you surprised by the ending? Explain your answer.
3. In what ways do each of the women visualize the other "through the wrong end of her little telescope" (par. 24)? Is either Alida or Grace correct in her view?
4. What are the differences between Alida's and Grace's daughters, Jenny and Barbara? How do we learn of their differences? Is there evidence in the story to support those observations?
5. Alida Slade remarks on the "different things Rome stands for to each generation of travelers. To our grandmothers, Roman fever; to our mothers, sentimental danger — how we used to be guarded! — to our daughters, no more dangers than the middle of Main Street. They don't know it — but how much they're missing!" (par. 29). What does she think the daughters are missing? What else might the dangers of Rome mean to women who travel there? What comment might Wharton be making about the limitations women faced in her world?
6. How can "Roman Fever" be considered social commentary? How might it move beyond social commentary into the realm of morality?
7. What do you think is the greatest irony in this story fraught with irony?
8. To your mind, which woman has the upper hand? Explain your answer.

ELEANOR ROOSEVELT

Eleanor Roosevelt (1884–1962) was the wife of Franklin D. Roosevelt and First Lady of the United States from 1933 to 1945. She was best known for her devotion to civil rights and her advocacy for working women. After her husband died in 1945, Roosevelt served as one of the United States' first delegates to the United Nations, where, as a chairwoman, she drafted and approved the Universal Declaration of Human Rights in 1948. In 1961, during John F. Kennedy's administration, Roosevelt chaired the Presidential Commission on the Status of Women; she went on to assist in the establishment of the state of Israel and to attempt negotiations with the Soviet Union.

What Libraries Mean to the Nation

Roosevelt delivered the following speech on April 1, 1936, at the District of Columbia Library Association dinner.

It has been a great pleasure to be here this evening and to hear all the things that have been said about libraries in the district and in general, and the librarians, without whom the libraries would be of little use, I am afraid. But as I sat here I fear that I have thought a good deal about the fact that there are so many places in the United States that have no libraries and that have no way of getting books.

What the libraries mean to the nation is fairly obvious to all of us, especially to those who are here this evening. We know that without libraries, without education, which is based largely on libraries, we cannot have an educated people who will carry on successfully our form of government, and it seems to me that what we really are interested in is how we can make this country more conscious of what it has not got, because we do pat ourselves on the back for the things that we have and that we do. I was looking over some maps which were sent to me and I longed to have these maps very much enlarged and put up in many, many places throughout this country, because I do not think that many people know how many states do not spend more than ten cents per capita for library books a year, and how many states have large areas, particularly rural areas, where one cannot get books.

One of the things that I have been particularly grateful for in the years of the depression — and, of course, I think, sad as it has been, we have some things to be grateful for — is that we have discovered so many things that we had not known before. These facts have come to the knowledge of a great many people who had simply passed them by before, because they did not happen to think about them, and one of these things, that we used to be able to hide, is the areas of the country which are not served in any way by libraries. I have seen photographs, for instance, of girls going out on horseback with libraries strapped on behind them, taking books to children and grown people in places that have been without libraries. We know a good deal about Mrs. Breckinridge's nursing service in Kentucky, but we know very little about the libraries that go out in the same way that her nurses do, on horseback.

I have lived a great deal in the country, in a state which prides itself in spending much money on education, and I am quite sure that some people think there is no lack of education and no lack of library facilities, and sometimes I long to take people and let them see some of the back country districts that I know, in New York State. I know one place in the northern part of the state where I camped for a while in the summer, and I went to the school and talked to the teachers. They are using school books which have been passed down from one child to another. They have practically no books outside of the textbooks. The children in the district are so poor and some of them so pathetic that I suppose the struggle to live has been so great you could not think much about what you fed the mind, but I came away feeling that right there, in one of the biggest and richest states in the country, we had a big area that needed books and needed libraries to help these schools in the education of the children, and, even more, to help the whole community to learn to live through their minds.

We are doing a tremendous amount through the home economics colleges to help   5
people to learn how to live in their homes, to better their standards of material living. We have got to think in exactly the same way about helping them to live mentally and to attain better standards, and we can do it only through the children. We can do ground work with the children; we must begin with them; but we have got to do a tremendous amount with the older people.

I had a letter the other day which was pathetic. It was from a man who said he was 74 years old. He wrote to ask me to see that the adult education classes in that particular community were not stopped, because it had meant so much to him to learn to read. He did not think that I could understand what it meant never to have been able to understand a word on the printed page. He said, "I am not the only one. My next door neighbor is 81 and he learned to read last winter, and it has just made life over for us." It gave you the feeling that there is a good deal of education that is not being done in this country, in spite of all that *is* done.

We have come a long way. We have done a great deal, but we still have a lot that can be done to improve our educational system, and we still have a tremendous amount to do with our libraries. We have got to make our libraries the center of a new life in the mind, because people are hungry to use their minds.

A New Era Ahead

We are facing a great change in civilization, and the responsibility, I think, for what we do with our leisure time is a very great responsibility for all of us who have intellectual interests. Somebody said to me, "I would not be so worried and I would not mind facing the fact that we are working fewer hours, if I only knew what people would do with their free time. I would not know what to do myself if I had only to work six hours a day."

That is a challenge. We, here in this country, ought to know what to do with our time, if we have it. I do not know whether we are going to have it, but if we are going to have more leisure time, it is the library, and people who live in the libraries and work in libraries, who are going to lead the way, who are going to give other people the curiosity and the vision of useful things, and pleasant things, and amusing things which can be done in those hours in which we may not have to work in the ways in which we have worked before. It is a very great responsibility, but it is also a very great interest.

Now, I think here in the city of Washington, and in nearly all big cities, the prob- 10 lem is a different one from the one I know so well in the country districts. I think that perhaps there are more facilities and, for that reason, there are more stimulating people engaged in solving the different problems that affect education in cities. But there is a great need, a very great need, in rural America. There is a great need for imagination in the ways used to stir the interest of old and young to use what library facilities they have, and to insist that they shall have more and to make them willing to pay for more, because, in the end, they will get something that they want out of it.

The more I have thought about the problem, the more I have felt that we do not use all our opportunities to stimulate an interest in books. Everything today in which people are interested, the radio, the movies — all of these — should, if properly used, stimulate the use of books. For instance, if there is a remarkably good movie, like *The Life of Pasteur*, it seems to me that it should be used by people in our rural schools and rural libraries to create an interest in the life of Pasteur, the things that Pasteur did, the people around him, and all the discoveries that have come from that time on. I am sure that if we put our minds on it, there are a great many ways in which we can use the things which are coming constantly into the lives of people through-out the country to stimulate an interest in the oldest and most interesting recreation there is.

But you do have to learn to love books, you do have to learn how to read them, you do have to learn that a book is a companion, and this is done in a great many different ways. I think we can do a great deal by having more copies of the same book, perhaps less expensive books, in the libraries so that we can have a good many people reading the same books and coming together for discussion.

I know, for instance, that even in a small group, like a family, we all want to read one book at the same time, and we all want to tear each other's hair out when we can't get a copy. It seems to me that here is something we should be thinking about, to stimulate the reading of books in families and large groups of people. I think the CCC[1] has made me realize this. One boy said to me, "Do you know about that book? I am so glad to be able to talk about it. . . . You know, it takes such a long time to get a book around." Now, if there had been a dozen or more copies of that book, the group would have talked about that book and it would have been a valuable contribution. It would have stimulated their intellectual thought.

I feel that the care of libraries and the use of books, and the knowledge of books, is a tremendously vital thing, and that we who deal with books and who love books

------

[1]The Civilian Conservation Corps provided manual labor jobs for young men during the Great Depression. — Eds.

have a great opportunity to bring about something in this country which is more vital here than anywhere else, because we have the chance to make a democracy that will be a real democracy, that will fulfill the vision that Senator King has just given us. It will take on our part imagination and patience and constant interest in awakening interest in other people. But, if we do, I think we shall find that our love of books will bring us a constantly widening audience and constantly more interesting contacts in whatever part of the country we may go.

(1936)

Exploring the Text

1. Describe the tone of Eleanor Roosevelt's remarks. How does the tone show awareness and consideration of her audience?
2. How does Roosevelt establish credibility beyond the fact that she is First Lady of the United States?
3. What assumptions does Roosevelt make about her audience? Find sentences in the speech in which those assumptions are most obvious.
4. What kind of evidence does Roosevelt provide to support her claim that the country needs more libraries? Classify them as claims of fact, value, and policy. Does one type dominate?
5. What do you think of Roosevelt's argument that rural areas need more libraries and that libraries need to stock multiple copies of popular books? Do those arguments stand up today?
6. In this digital age, what do you think is the primary answer to the question of what libraries mean to the nation?

WORKS PROGRESS ADMINISTRATION

Part of Roosevelt's New Deal, the Works Progress Administration (WPA) was designed to stimulate the economy through public-works projects such as building roads, bridges, buildings, and schools. At its height, the initiative employed over 3 million people. It also commissioned works from visual artists, designers, and photographers under the Federal Art Project.

Bookmobile, Louisiana

The following photo, taken circa 1938, of the bookmobile at Bayou de Large, fifteen miles south of Houma, Louisiana, is part of the Franklin Delano Roosevelt Library and comes from the WPA archives.

National Archives

Exploring the Text

1. What strikes you first in the photograph? Explain why you find it striking.
2. What emotions does the photo capture? How are those emotions expressed?
3. What is the effect of the diagonal line created by the boat moving from the bottom left toward the upper right in the photo?
4. What does this photograph remind you of? Are there literary or mythological connections to be made?
5. What do you think the bookmobile meant to the people in the photo? What can you tell from their body language and placement in the picture?

Franklin Delano Roosevelt

Franklin Delano Roosevelt (1882–1945) was the thirty-second president of the United States (1933–1945) and the only American president elected to more than two terms. Roosevelt led the nation through two of its most challenging periods, the Great Depression and World War II. Roosevelt's New Deal — a series of programs that provided government jobs for the unemployed, boosted economic growth, and regulated the financial and transportation industries — helped America begin to recover from the Great Depression. After the attack on Pearl Harbor in 1941 and throughout World War II (1939–1945), Roosevelt worked with Winston Churchill and Joseph Stalin to lead the Allies against Germany, Italy, and Japan, and he sanctioned the development of the world's first atomic bomb.

Second Inaugural Address: One-Third of a Nation

After being re-elected by a landslide, Roosevelt gave this speech on January 20, 1937, the first time the presidential inauguration was held in January rather than in March.

When four years ago we met to inaugurate a President, the Republic, single-minded in anxiety, stood in spirit here. We dedicated ourselves to the fulfillment of a vision — to speed the time when there would be for all the people that security and peace essential to the pursuit of happiness. We of the Republic pledged ourselves to drive from the temple of our ancient faith those who had profaned it; to end by action, tireless and unafraid, the stagnation and despair of that day. We did those first things first.

Our covenant with ourselves did not stop there. Instinctively we recognized a deeper need — the need to find through government the instrument of our united purpose to solve for the individual the ever-rising problems of a complex civilization. Repeated attempts at their solution without the aid of government had left us baffled and bewildered. For, without that aid, we had been unable to create those moral controls over the services of science which are necessary to make science a useful servant instead of a ruthless master of mankind. To do this we knew that we must find practical controls over blind economic forces and blindly selfish men.

We of the Republic sensed the truth that democratic government has innate capacity to protect its people against disasters once considered inevitable, to solve problems once considered unsolvable. We would not admit that we could not find a way to master economic epidemics just as, after centuries of fatalistic suffering, we had found a way to master epidemics of disease. We refused to leave the problems of our common welfare to be solved by the winds of chance and the hurricanes of disaster.

In this we Americans were discovering no wholly new truth; we were writing a new chapter in our book of self-government.

This year marks the one hundred and fiftieth anniversary of the Constitutional Convention which made us a nation. At that Convention our forefathers found the way out of the chaos which followed the Revolutionary War; they created a strong government with powers of united action sufficient then and now to solve problems utterly beyond individual or local solution. A century and a half ago they established the federal government in order to promote the general welfare and secure the blessings of liberty to the American people.

Today we invoke those same powers of government to achieve the same objectives.

Four years of new experience have not belied our historic instinct. They hold out the clear hope that government within communities, government within the separate States, and government of the United States can do the things the times

5

require, without yielding its democracy. Our tasks in the last four years did not force democracy to take a holiday.

Nearly all of us recognize that as intricacies of human relationships increase, so power to govern them also must increase — power to stop evil; power to do good. The essential democracy of our Nation and the safety of our people depend not upon the absence of power, but upon lodging it with those whom the people can change or continue at stated intervals through an honest and free system of elections. The Constitution of 1787 did not make our democracy impotent.

In fact, in these last four years, we have made the exercise of all power more democratic; for we have begun to bring private autocratic powers into their proper subordination to the public's government. The legend that they were invincible — above and beyond the processes of a democracy — has been shattered. They have been challenged and beaten.

Our progress out of the depression is obvious. But that is not all that you and I   10 mean by the new order of things. Our pledge was not merely to do a patchwork job with second-hand materials. By using the new materials of social justice we have undertaken to erect on the old foundations a more enduring structure for the better use of future generations.

In that purpose we have been helped by achievements of mind and spirit. Old truths have been relearned; untruths have been unlearned. We have always known that heedless self-interest was bad morals; we know now that it is bad economics. Out of the collapse of a prosperity whose builders boasted their practicality has come the conviction that in the long run economic morality pays. We are beginning to wipe out the line that divides the practical from the ideal; and in so doing we are fashioning an instrument of unimagined power for the establishment of a morally better world.

This new understanding undermines the old admiration of worldly success as such. We are beginning to abandon our tolerance of the abuse of power by those who betray for profit the elementary decencies of life.

In this process evil things formerly accepted will not be so easily condoned. Hard-headedness will not so easily excuse hard-heartedness. We are moving toward an era of good feeling. But we realize that there can be no era of good feeling save among men of good will.

For these reasons I am justified in believing that the greatest change we have witnessed has been the change in the moral climate of America.

Among men of good will, science and democracy together offer an ever-richer   15 life and ever-larger satisfaction to the individual. With this change in our moral climate and our rediscovered ability to improve our economic order, we have set our feet upon the road of enduring progress.

Shall we pause now and turn our back upon the road that lies ahead? Shall we call this the promised land? Or, shall we continue on our way? For "each age is a dream that is dying, or one that is coming to birth."

Many voices are heard as we face a great decision. Comfort says, "Tarry a while." Opportunism says, "This is a good spot." Timidity asks, "How difficult is the road ahead?"

True, we have come far from the days of stagnation and despair. Vitality has been preserved. Courage and confidence have been restored. Mental and moral horizons have been extended.

But our present gains were won under the pressure of more than ordinary circumstance. Advance became imperative under the goad of fear and suffering. The times were on the side of progress.

To hold to progress today, however, is more difficult. Dulled conscience, irresponsibility, and ruthless self-interest already reappear. Such symptoms of prosperity may become portents of disaster! Prosperity already tests the persistence of our progressive purpose. 20

Let us ask again: Have we reached the goal of our vision of that fourth day of March, 1933? Have we found our happy valley?

I see a great nation, upon a great continent, blessed with a great wealth of natural resources. Its hundred and thirty million people are at peace among themselves; they are making their country a good neighbor among the nations. I see a United States which can demonstrate that, under democratic methods of government, national wealth can be translated into a spreading volume of human comforts hitherto unknown, and the lowest standard of living can be raised far above the level of mere subsistence.

But here is the challenge to our democracy: In this nation I see tens of millions of its citizens — a substantial part of its whole population — who at this very moment are denied the greater part of what the very lowest standards of today call the necessities of life.

I see millions of families trying to live on incomes so meager that the pall of family disaster hangs over them day by day.

I see millions whose daily lives in city and on farm continue under conditions labeled indecent by a so-called polite society half a century ago. 25

I see millions denied education, recreation, and the opportunity to better their lot and the lot of their children.

I see millions lacking the means to buy the products of farm and factory and by their poverty denying work and productiveness to many other millions.

I see one-third of a nation ill-housed, ill-clad, ill-nourished.

It is not in despair that I paint you that picture. I paint it for you in hope — because the Nation, seeing and understanding the injustice in it, proposes to paint it out. We are determined to make every American citizen the subject of his country's interest and concern; and we will never regard any faithful, law-abiding group within our borders as superfluous. The test of our progress is not whether we add more to the abundance of those who have much; it is whether we provide enough for those who have too little.

If I know aught of the spirit and purpose of our Nation, we will not listen to Comfort, Opportunism, and Timidity. We will carry on. 30

Overwhelmingly, we of the Republic are men and women of good will; men and women who have more than warm hearts of dedication; men and women who have cool heads and willing hands of practical purpose as well. They will insist that every agency of popular government use effective instruments to carry out their will.

Government is competent when all who compose it work as trustees for the whole people. It can make constant progress when it keeps abreast of all the facts. It can obtain justified support and legitimate criticism when the people receive true information of all that government does.

If I know aught of the will of our people, they will demand that these conditions of effective government shall be created and maintained. They will demand a nation uncorrupted by cancers of injustice and, therefore, strong among the nations in its example of the will to peace.

Today we reconsecrate our country to long-cherished ideals in a suddenly changed civilization. In every land there are always at work forces that drive men apart and forces that draw men together. In our personal ambitions we are individualists. But in our seeking for economic and political progress as a nation, we all go up, or else we all go down, as one people.

To maintain a democracy of effort requires a vast amount of patience in dealing with differing methods, a vast amount of humility. But out of the confusion of many voices rises an understanding of dominant public need. Then political leadership can voice common ideals, and aid in their realization.

In taking again the oath of office as President of the United States, I assume the solemn obligation of leading the American people forward along the road over which they have chosen to advance.

While this duty rests upon me I shall do my utmost to speak their purpose and to do their will, seeking Divine guidance to help us each and every one to give light to them that sit in darkness and to guide our feet into the way of peace.

(1937)

Exploring the Text

1. Whom do you think President Franklin Delano Roosevelt speaks for in this address?
2. Do you consider this speech optimistic or pessimistic? Using support from the selection, explain your answer.
3. Do you think Roosevelt depends most on claims of fact, of value, or of policy? Try to find examples of each, and then consider why he might have depended on one type of claim over the others.
4. What contrasts does Roosevelt set up in this speech? What do you think their purpose is?
5. How does Roosevelt answer the question he asks in paragraph 21: "Have we found our happy valley?"
6. Roosevelt uses figurative language sparingly, but effectively, in this speech. Find examples and explain why he might have chosen to speak figuratively rather than literally at those moments.

JOHN STEINBECK

John Steinbeck (1902–1968) was a Pulitzer and Nobel Prize–winning American writer and the author of twenty-seven books. Born and raised in California, Steinbeck briefly attended Stanford University but dropped out before graduating to pursue a freelance writing career in New York in 1925. When that failed, he returned to California, where he continued to write, and he finally found fame in 1935 with the publication of *Tortilla Flat*, a collection of humorous stories. With his later novels — *Of Mice and Men* (1937), *The Grapes of Wrath* (1939), and *East of Eden* (1952) — Steinbeck established a reputation for social criticism because his writing focused on the impoverished lives of rural laborers in California during the early to mid-1900s. He won the Pulitzer Prize for Fiction in 1940 for *The Grapes of Wrath*, and in 1962 he received the Nobel Prize for Literature.

The Chrysanthemums

"The Chrysanthemums" was published in the October 1937 edition of *Harper's* magazine.

The high grey-flannel fog of winter closed off the Salinas Valley from the sky and from all the rest of the world. On every side it sat like a lid on the mountains and made of the great valley a closed pot. On the broad, level land floor the gang plows bit deep and left the black earth shining like metal where the shares had cut. On the foothill ranches across the Salinas River, the yellow stubble fields seemed to be bathed in pale cold sunshine, but there was no sunshine in the valley now in December. The thick willow scrub along the river flamed with sharp and positive yellow leaves.

It was a time of quiet and of waiting. The air was cold and tender. A light wind blew up from the southwest so that the farmers were mildly hopeful of a good rain before long; but fog and rain do not go together.

Across the river, on Henry Allen's foothill ranch there was little work to be done, for the hay was cut and stored and the orchards were plowed up to receive the rain deeply when it should come. The cattle on the higher slopes were becoming shaggy and rough-coated.

Elisa Allen, working in her flower garden, looked down across the yard and saw Henry, her husband, talking to two men in business suits. The three of them stood by the tractor shed, each man with one foot on the side of the little Fordson. They smoked cigarettes and studied the machine as they talked.

Elisa watched them for a moment and then went back to her work. She was thirty-five. Her face was lean and strong and her eyes were as clear as water. Her figure looked blocked and heavy in her gardening costume, a man's black hat pulled low down over her eyes, clod-hopper shoes, a figured print dress almost completely covered by a big

5

corduroy apron with four big pockets to hold the snips, the trowel and scratcher, the seeds, and the knife she worked with. She wore heavy leather gloves to protect her hands while she worked.

She was cutting down the old year's chrysanthemum stalks with a pair of short and powerful scissors. She looked down toward the men by the tractor shed now and then. Her face was eager and mature and handsome; even her work with the scissors was overeager, overpowerful. The chrysanthemum stems seemed too small and easy for her energy.

She brushed a cloud of hair out of her eyes with the back of her glove, and left a smudge of earth on her cheek in doing it. Behind her stood the neat white farm house with red geraniums close-banked around it as high as the windows. It was a hard-swept looking little house with hard-polished windows, and a clean mud-mat on the front steps.

Elisa cast another glance toward the tractor shed. The strangers were getting into their Ford coupe. She took off a glove and put her strong fingers down into the forest of new green chrysanthemum sprouts that were growing around the old roots. She spread the leaves and looked down among the close-growing stems. No aphids were there, no sowbugs or snails or cutworms. Her terrier fingers destroyed such pests before they could get started.

Elisa started at the sound of her husband's voice. He had come near quietly, and he leaned over the wire fence that protected her flower garden from cattle and dogs and chickens.

"At it again," he said. "You've got a strong new crop coming."   10

Elisa straightened her back and pulled on the gardening glove again. "Yes. They'll be strong this coming year." In her tone and on her face there was a little smugness.

"You've got a gift with things," Henry observed. "Some of those yellow chrysanthemums you had this year were ten inches across. I wish you'd work out in the orchard and raise some apples that big."

Her eyes sharpened. "Maybe I could do it, too. I've a gift with things, all right. My mother had it. She could stick anything in the ground and make it grow. She said it was having planters' hands that knew how to do it."

"Well, it sure works with flowers," he said.

"Henry, who were those men you were talking to?"   15

"Why, sure, that's what I came to tell you. They were from the Western Meat Company. I sold thirty head of three-year-old steers. Got nearly my own price, too."

"Good," she said. "Good for you."

"And I thought," he continued, "I thought how it's Saturday afternoon, and we might go into Salinas for dinner at a restaurant, and then to a picture show — to celebrate, you see."

"Good," she repeated. "Oh, yes. That will be good."

Henry put on his joking tone. "There's fights tonight. How'd you like to go to the   20
fights?"

"Oh, no," she said breathlessly. "No, I wouldn't like fights."

"Just fooling, Elisa. We'll go to a movie. Let's see. It's two now. I'm going to take Scotty and bring down those steers from the hill. It'll take us maybe two hours. We'll go in town about five and have dinner at the Cominos Hotel. Like that?"

"Of course I'll like it. It's good to eat away from home."

"All right, then. I'll go get up a couple of horses."

She said, "I'll have plenty of time to transplant some of these sets, I guess."   25

She heard her husband calling Scotty down by the barn. And a little later she saw the two men ride up the pale yellow hillside in search of the steers.

There was a little square sandy bed kept for rooting the chrysanthemums. With her trowel she turned the soil over and over, and smoothed it and patted it firm. Then she dug ten parallel trenches to receive the sets. Back at the chrysanthemum bed she pulled out the little crisp shoots, trimmed off the leaves at each one with her scissors, and laid it on a small orderly pile.

A squeak of wheels and plod of hoofs came from the road. Elisa looked up. The country road ran along the dense bank of willows and cottonwoods that bordered the river, and up this road came a curious vehicle, curiously drawn. It was an old spring-wagon, with a round canvas top on it like the corner of a prairie schooner. It was drawn by an old bay horse and a little grey-and-white burro. A big stubble-bearded man sat between the cover flaps and drove the crawling team. Underneath the wagon, between the hind wheels, a lean and rangy mongrel dog walked sedately. Words were painted on the canvas, in clumsy, crooked letters. "Pots, pans, knives, sisors, lawn mores, Fixed." Two rows of articles, and the triumphantly definitive "Fixed" below. The black paint had run down in little sharp points beneath each letter.

Elisa, squatting on the ground, watched to see the crazy, loose-jointed wagon pass by. But it didn't pass. It turned into the farm road in front of her house, crooked old wheels skirling and squeaking. The rangy dog darted from between the wheels and ran ahead. Instantly the two ranch shepherds flew out at him. Then all three stopped, and with stiff and quivering tails, with taut straight legs, with ambassadorial dignity, they slowly circled, sniffing daintily. The caravan pulled up to Elisa's wire fence and stopped. Now the newcomer dog, feeling outnumbered, lowered his tail and retired under the wagon with raised hackles and bared teeth.

The man on the seat called out, "That's a bad dog in a fight when he gets started."   30

Elisa laughed. "I see he is. How soon does he generally get started?"

The man caught up her laughter and echoed it heartily. "Sometimes not for weeks and weeks," he said. He climbed stiffly down, over the wheel. The horse and the donkey drooped like unwatered flowers.

Elisa saw that he was a very big man. Although his hair and beard were greying, he did not look old. His worn black suit was wrinkled and spotted with grease. The laughter had disappeared from his face and eyes the moment his laughing voice ceased. His eyes were dark, and they were full of the brooding that gets in the eyes of teamsters and of sailors. The calloused hands he rested on the wire fence were cracked, and every crack was a black line. He took off his battered hat.

"I'm off my general road, ma'am," he said. "Does this dirt road cut over across the river to the Los Angeles highway?"

Elisa stood up and shoved the thick scissors in her apron pocket. "Well, yes, it 35
does, but it winds around and then fords the river. I don't think your team could pull
through the sand."

He replied with some asperity, "It might surprise you what them beasts can pull
through."

"When they get started?" she asked.

He smiled for a second. "Yes. When they get started."

"Well," said Elisa, "I think you'll save time if you go back to the Salinas road and
pick up the highway there."

He drew a big finger down the chicken wire and made it sing. "I ain't in any 40
hurry, ma'am. I go from Seattle to San Diego and back every year. Takes all my time.
About six months each way. I aim to follow nice weather."

Elisa took off her gloves and stuffed them in the apron pocket with the scissors.
She touched the under edge of her man's hat, searching for fugitive hairs. "That
sounds like a nice kind of a way to live," she said.

He leaned confidentially over the fence. "Maybe you noticed the writing on my
wagon. I mend pots and sharpen knives and scissors. You got any of them things
to do?"

"Oh, no," she said, quickly. "Nothing like that." Her eyes hardened with resistance.

"Scissors is the worst thing," he explained. "Most people just ruin scissors trying
to sharpen 'em, but I know how. I got a special tool. It's a little bobbit kind of thing,
and patented. But it sure does the trick."

"No. My scissors are all sharp." 45

"All right, then. Take a pot," he continued earnestly, "a bent pot, or a pot with a
hole. I can make it like new so you don't have to buy no new ones. That's a savings
for you."

"No," she said shortly. "I tell you I have nothing like that for you to do."

His face fell to an exaggerated sadness. His voice took on a whining undertone.
"I ain't had a thing to do today. Maybe I won't have no supper tonight. You see I'm off
my regular road. I know folks on the highway clear from Seattle to San Diego. They
save their things for me to sharpen up because they know I do it so good and save
them money."

"I'm sorry," Elisa said irritably. "I haven't anything for you to do."

His eyes left her face and fell to searching the ground. They roamed about until 50
they came to the chrysanthemum bed where she had been working. "What's them
plants, ma'am?"

The irritation and resistance melted from Elisa's face. "Oh, those are chrysanthemums, giant whites and yellows. I raise them every year, bigger than anybody around
here."

"Kind of a long-stemmed flower? Looks like a quick puff of colored smoke?" he
asked.

"That's it. What a nice way to describe them."

"They smell kind of nasty till you get used to them," he said.

"It's a good bitter smell," she retorted, "not nasty at all."   55

He changed his tone quickly, "I like the smell myself."

"I had ten-inch blooms this year," she said.

The man leaned farther over the fence. "Look. I know a lady down the road a piece, has got the nicest garden you ever seen. Got nearly every kind of flower but no chrysanthemums. Last time I was mending a copper-bottom washtub for her (that's a hard job but I do it good), she said to me, 'If you ever run acrost some nice chrysanthemums I wish you'd try to get me a few seeds.' That's what she told me."

Elisa's eyes grew alert and eager. "She couldn't have known much about chrysanthemums. You *can* raise them from seed, but it's much easier to root the little sprouts you see there."

"Oh," he said. "I s'pose I can't take none to her, then."   60

"Why yes you can," Elisa cried. "I can put some in damp sand, and you can carry them right along with you. They'll take root in the pot if you keep them damp. And then she can transplant them."

"She'd sure like to have some, ma'am. You say they're nice ones?"

"Beautiful," she said. "Oh, beautiful." Her eyes shone. She tore off the battered hat and shook out her dark pretty hair. "I'll put them in a flower pot, and you can take them right with you. Come into the yard."

While the man came through the picket gate Elisa ran excitedly along the geranium-bordered path to the back of the house. And she returned carrying a big red flower pot. The gloves were forgotten now. She kneeled on the ground by the starting bed and dug up the sandy soil with her fingers and scooped it into the bright new flower pot. Then she picked up the little pile of shoots she had prepared. With her strong fingers she pressed them into the sand and tamped around them with her knuckles. The man stood over her. "I'll tell you what to do," she said. "You remember so you can tell the lady."

"Yes, I'll try to remember."   65

"Well, look. These will take root in about a month. Then she must set them out, about a foot apart in good rich earth like this, see?" She lifted a handful of dark soil for him to look at. "They'll grow fast and tall. Now remember this: In July tell her to cut them down, about eight inches from the ground."

"Before they bloom?" he asked.

"Yes, before they bloom." Her face was tight with eagerness. "They'll grow right up again. About the last of September the buds will start."

She stopped and seemed perplexed. "It's the budding that takes the most care," she said hesitantly. "I don't know how to tell you." She looked deep into his eyes, searchingly. Her mouth opened a little, and she seemed to be listening. "I'll try to tell you," she said. "Did you ever hear of planting hands?"

"Can't say I have, ma'am."   70

"Well, I can only tell you what it feels like. It's when you're picking off the buds you don't want. Everything goes right down into your fingertips. You watch your fingers work. They do it themselves. You can feel how it is. They pick and pick the buds. They never make a mistake. They're with the plant. Do you see? Your fingers and the plant. You can feel that, right up your arm. They know. They never make a mistake. You can feel it. When you're like that you can't do anything wrong. Do you see that? Can you understand that?"

She was kneeling on the ground looking up at him. Her breast swelled passionately.

The man's eyes narrowed. He looked away self-consciously. "Maybe I know," he said. "Sometimes in the night in the wagon there — "

Elisa's voice grew husky. She broke in on him, "I've never lived as you do, but I know what you mean. When the night is dark — why, the stars are sharp-pointed, and there's quiet. Why, you rise up and up! Every pointed star gets driven into your body. It's like that. Hot and sharp and — lovely."

Kneeling there, her hand went out toward his legs in the greasy black trousers. 75
Her hesitant fingers almost touched the cloth. Then her hand dropped to the ground. She crouched low like a fawning dog.

He said, "It's nice, just like you say. Only when you don't have no dinner, it ain't."

She stood up then, very straight, and her face was ashamed. She held the flower pot out to him and placed it gently in his arms. "Here. Put it in your wagon, on the seat, where you can watch it. Maybe I can find something for you to do."

At the back of the house she dug in the can pile and found two old and battered aluminum saucepans. She carried them back and gave them to him. "Here, maybe you can fix these."

His manner changed. He became professional. "Good as new I can fix them." At the back of his wagon he set a little anvil, and out of an oily tool box dug a small machine hammer. Elisa came through the gate to watch him while he pounded out the dents in the kettles. His mouth grew sure and knowing. At a difficult part of the work he sucked his underlip.

"You sleep right in the wagon?" Elisa asked. 80

"Right in the wagon, ma'am. Rain or shine I'm dry as a cow in there."

"It must be nice," she said. "It must be very nice. I wish women could do such things."

"It ain't the right kind of a life for a woman."

Her upper lip raised a little, showing her teeth. "How do you know? How can you tell?" she said.

"I don't know, ma'am," he protested. "Of course I don't know. Now here's your 85 kettles, done. You don't have to buy no new ones."

"How much?"

"Oh, fifty cents'll do. I keep my prices down and my work good. That's why I have all them satisfied customers up and down the highway."

Elisa brought him a fifty-cent piece from the house and dropped it in his hand. "You might be surprised to have a rival some time. I can sharpen scissors, too. And I can beat the dents out of little pots. I could show you what a woman might do."

He put his hammer back in the oily box and shoved the little anvil out of sight. "It would be a lonely life for a woman, ma'am, and a scary life, too, with animals creeping under the wagon all night." He climbed over the singletree, steadying himself with a hand on the burro's white rump. He settled himself in the seat, picked up the lines. "Thank you kindly, ma'am," he said. "I'll do like you told me; I'll go back and catch the Salinas road."

"Mind," she called, "if you're long in getting there, keep the sand damp." 90

"Sand, ma'am? . . . Sand? Oh, sure. You mean around the chrysanthemums. Sure I will." He clucked his tongue. The beasts leaned luxuriously into their collars. The mongrel dog took his place between the back wheels. The wagon turned and crawled out the entrance road and back the way it had come, along the river.

Elisa stood in front of her wire fence watching the slow progress of the caravan. Her shoulders were straight, her head thrown back, her eyes half-closed, so that the scene came vaguely into them. Her lips moved silently, forming the words "Goodbye — good-bye." Then she whispered, "That's a bright direction. There's a glowing there." The sound of her whisper startled her. She shook herself free and looked about to see whether anyone had been listening. Only the dogs had heard. They lifted their heads toward her from their sleeping in the dust, and then stretched out their chins and settled asleep again. Elisa turned and ran hurriedly into the house.

In the kitchen she reached behind the stove and felt the water tank. It was full of hot water from the noonday cooking. In the bathroom she tore off her soiled clothes and flung them into the corner. And then she scrubbed herself with a little block of pumice, legs and thighs, loins and chest and arms, until her skin was scratched and red. When she had dried herself she stood in front of a mirror in her bedroom and looked at her body. She tightened her stomach and threw out her chest. She turned and looked over her shoulder at her back.

After a while she began to dress, slowly. She put on her newest underclothing and her nicest stockings and the dress which was the symbol of her prettiness. She worked carefully on her hair, penciled her eyebrows and rouged her lips.

Before she was finished she heard the little thunder of hoofs and the shouts of 95 Henry and his helper as they drove the red steers into the corral. She heard the gate bang shut and set herself for Henry's arrival.

His step sounded on the porch. He entered the house calling, "Elisa, where are you?"

"In my room, dressing. I'm not ready. There's hot water for your bath. Hurry up. It's getting late."

When she heard him splashing in the tub, Elisa laid his dark suit on the bed, and shirt and socks and tie beside it. She stood his polished shoes on the floor beside the bed. Then she went to the porch and sat primly and stiffly down. She looked toward the river road where the willow-line was still yellow with frosted leaves so that under the high grey fog they seemed a thin band of sunshine. This was the only color in the grey afternoon. She sat unmoving for a long time. Her eyes blinked rarely.

Henry came banging out of the door, shoving his tie inside his vest as he came. Elisa stiffened and her face grew tight. Henry stopped short and looked at her. "Why — why, Elisa. You look so nice!"

"Nice? You think I look nice? What do you mean by 'nice'?"   100

Henry blundered on. "I don't know. I mean you look different, strong and happy."

"I am strong? Yes, strong. What do you mean 'strong'?"

He looked bewildered. "You're playing some kind of a game," he said helplessly. "It's a kind of a play. You look strong enough to break a calf over your knee, happy enough to eat it like a watermelon."

For a second she lost her rigidity. "Henry! Don't talk like that. You didn't know what you said." She grew complete again. "I'm strong," she boasted, "I never knew before how strong."

Henry looked down toward the tractor shed, and when he brought his eyes back   105
to her, they were his own again. "I'll get out the car. You can put on your coat while I'm starting."

Elisa went into the house. She heard him drive to the gate and idle down his motor, and then she took a long time to put on her hat. She pulled it here and pressed it there. When Henry turned the motor off she slipped into her coat and went out.

The little roadster bounced along on the dirt road by the river, raising the birds and driving the rabbits into the brush. Two cranes flapped heavily over the willow-line and dropped into the river-bed.

Far ahead on the road Elisa saw a dark speck. She knew.

She tried not to look as they passed it, but her eyes would not obey. She whispered to herself sadly, "He might have thrown them off the road. That wouldn't have been much trouble, not very much. But he kept the pot," she explained. "He had to keep the pot. That's why he couldn't get them off the road."

The roadster turned a bend and she saw the caravan ahead. She swung full   110
around toward her husband so she could not see the little covered wagon and the mismatched team as the car passed them.

In a moment it was over. The thing was done. She did not look back.

She said loudly, to be heard above the motor. "It will be good, tonight, a good dinner."

"Now you're changed again," Henry complained. He took one hand from the wheel and patted her knee. "I ought to take you in to dinner oftener. It would be good for both of us. We get so heavy out on the ranch."

"Henry," she asked, "could we have wine at dinner?"

"Sure we could. Say! That will be fine."   115

She was silent for a while; then she said, "Henry, at those prize fights, do the men hurt each other very much?"

"Sometimes a little, not often. Why?"

"Well, I've read how they break noses, and blood runs down their chests. I've read how the fighting gloves get heavy and soggy with blood."

He looked around at her. "What's the matter, Elisa? I didn't know you read things like that." He brought the car to a stop, then turned to the right over the Salinas River bridge.

"Do any women ever go to the fights?" she asked.   120

"Oh, sure, some. What's the matter Elisa? Do you want to go? I don't think you'd like it, but I'll take you if you really want to go."

She relaxed limply in the seat. "Oh, no. No. I don't want to go. I'm sure I don't." Her face was turned away from him. "It will be enough if we can have wine. It will be plenty." She turned up her coat collar so he could not see that she was crying weakly — like an old woman.

(1937)

Exploring the Text

1. Describe the relationship Elisa has with her husband. Explain why you came to the conclusion you did.
2. What do you think the chrysanthemums Elisa grows represent in the story? How do the different characters' reactions to them help develop those characters?
3. What do you think is the main conflict in this story? How does John Steinbeck set it up?
4. How does the backdrop of the natural world help Steinbeck develop the themes in this story? Consider especially what the setting means for each character and the interactions with each other.
5. In what ways does Elisa change when she is with the tinker? What do you think those changes represent?
6. Critics have considered this story an early example of a woman trying to gain equality in a man's world. Charles A. Sweet Jr., writing in 1974 in *Modern Fiction Studies*, says that Elisa is "the representative of the feminine ideal of equality and its inevitable defeat." Do you consider that a viable reading of the story? How might we read it differently in the twenty-first century? Or would we?

WILLIAM FAULKNER

William Faulkner (1897–1962) is considered one of the finest American writers of the twentieth century. Born in New Albany, Mississippi, Faulkner grew bored with education in his early teens, joining first the Canadian and then the British Royal Air Force during the First World War. While living in New Orleans, Faulkner wrote his first novel, *Soldier's Pay* (1926). Over the next three years, he published *Mosquitoes* (1927) and *The Sound and the Fury* (1929), which established his reputation. The following decade saw Faulkner at his most prolific. *As I Lay Dying* (1930), *Sanctuary* (1931), and *Light in August* (1932), together with collections of poems and short stories, preceded publication of *Absalom, Absalom!* in 1936. During spells in Hollywood, he also established himself as a masterful screenwriter. In 1949, he was awarded the Nobel Prize for Literature.

Barn Burning

Published in *Harper's* magazine in June 1939, "Barn Burning" is one of Faulkner's most popular stories. Members of the Snopes family appear in several other works by Faulkner, all of which are set in the fictional Yoknapatawpha County in Mississippi.

The store in which the Justice of the Peace's court was sitting smelled of cheese. The boy, crouched on his nail keg at the back of the crowded room, knew he smelled cheese, and more: from where he sat he could see the ranked shelves close-packed with the solid, squat, dynamic shapes of tin cans whose labels his stomach read, not from the lettering which meant nothing to his mind but from the scarlet devils and the silver curve of fish — this, the cheese which he knew he smelled and the hermetic meat which his intestines believed he smelled coming in intermittent gusts momentary and brief between the other constant one, the smell and sense just a little of fear because mostly of despair and grief, the old fierce pull of blood. He could not see the table where the Justice sat and before which his father and his father's enemy (*our enemy* he thought in that despair; *ourn! mine and hisn both! He's my father!*) stood, but he could hear them, the two of them that is, because his father had said no word yet:

"But what proof have you, Mr. Harris?"

"I told you. The hog got into my corn. I caught it up and sent it back to him. He had no fence that would hold it. I told him so, warned him. The next time I put the hog in my pen. When he came to get it I gave him enough wire to patch up his pen. The next time I put the hog up and kept it. I rode down to his house and saw the wire I gave him still rolled on to the spool in his yard. I told him he could have the hog when he paid me a dollar pound fee. That evening a nigger came with the dollar and got the hog. He was a strange nigger. He said, 'He say to tell you wood and hay kin burn.' I said, 'What?' 'That whut he say to tell you,' the nigger said. 'Wood and hay kin burn.' That night my barn burned. I got the stock out but I lost the barn."

"Where is the nigger? Have you got him?"

"He was a strange nigger, I tell you. I don't know what became of him."

"But that's not proof. Don't you see that's not proof?"

"Get that boy up here. He knows." For a moment the boy thought too that the man meant his older brother until Harris said, "Not him. The little one. The boy," and, crouching, small for his age, small and wiry like his father, in patched and faded jeans even too small for him, with straight, uncombed, brown hair and eyes gray and wild as storm scud, he saw the men between himself and the table part and become a lane of grim faces, at the end of which he saw the Justice, a shabby, collarless, graying man in spectacles, beckoning him. He felt no floor under his bare feet; he seemed to walk beneath the palpable weight of the grim turning faces. His father, stiff in his black Sunday coat donned not for the trial but for the moving, did not even look at him. *He aims for me to lie*, he thought, again with that frantic grief and despair. *And I will have to do hit.*

5

"What's your name, boy?" the Justice said.

"Colonel Sartoris Snopes," the boy whispered.

"Hey?" the Justice said. "Talk louder. Colonel Sartoris? I reckon anybody named   10
for Colonel Sartoris in this country can't help but tell the truth, can they?" The boy
said nothing. *Enemy! Enemy!* he thought; for a moment he could not even see, could
not see that the Justice's face was kindly nor discern that his voice was troubled when
he spoke to the man named Harris: "Do you want me to question this boy?" But he
could hear, and during those subsequent long seconds while there was absolutely no
sound in the crowded little room save that of quiet and intent breathing it was as if he
had swung outward at the end of a grape vine, over a ravine, and at the top of the swing
had been caught in a prolonged instant of mesmerized gravity, weightless in time.

"No!" Harris said violently, explosively. "Damnation! Send him out of here!"
Now time, the fluid world, rushed beneath him again, the voices coming to him again
through the smell of cheese and sealed meat, the fear and despair and the old grief of
blood:

"This case is closed. I can't find against you, Snopes, but I can give you advice.
Leave this country and don't come back to it."

His father spoke for the first time, his voice cold and harsh, level, without
emphasis: "I aim to. I don't figure to stay in a country among people who . . ." he said
something unprintable and vile, addressed to no one.

"That'll do," the Justice said. "Take your wagon and get out of this country before
dark. Case dismissed."

His father turned, and he followed the stiff black coat, the wiry figure walking a   15
little stiffly from where a Confederate provost's man's musket ball had taken him in the
heel on a stolen horse thirty years ago, followed the two backs now, since his older
brother had appeared from somewhere in the crowd, no taller than the father but
thicker, chewing tobacco steadily, between the two lines of grim-faced men and out of
the store and across the worn gallery and down the sagging steps and among the dogs
and half-grown boys in the mild May dust, where as he passed a voice hissed:

"Barn burner!"

Again he could not see, whirling; there was a face in a red haze, moonlike, bigger
than the full moon, the owner of it half again his size, he leaping in the red haze toward
the face, feeling no blow, feeling no shock when his head struck the earth, scrabbling
up and leaping again, feeling no blow this time either and tasting no blood, scrabbling up to see the other boy in full flight and himself already leaping into pursuit as
his father's hand jerked him back, the harsh, cold voice speaking above him: "Go get
in the wagon."

It stood in a grove of locusts and mulberries across the road. His two hulking
sisters in their Sunday dresses and his mother and her sister in calico and sunbonnets
were already in it, sitting on and among the sorry residue of the dozen and more
movings which even the boy could remember — the battered stove, the broken beds
and chairs, the clock inlaid with mother-of-pearl, which would not run, stopped at
some fourteen minutes past two o'clock of a dead and forgotten day and time, which
had been his mother's dowry. She was crying, though when she saw him she drew

her sleeve across her face and began to descend from the wagon. "Get back," the father said.

"He's hurt. I got to get some water and wash his . . ."

"Get back in the wagon," his father said. He got in too, over the tail-gate. His father mounted to the seat where the older brother already sat and struck the gaunt mules two savage blows with the peeled willow, but without heat. It was not even sadistic; it was exactly that same quality which in later years would cause his descendants to over-run the engine before putting a motor car into motion, striking and reining back in the same movement. The wagon went on, the store with its quiet crowd of grimly watching men dropped behind; a curve in the road hid it. *Forever* he thought. *Maybe he's done satisfied now, now that he has . . .* stopping himself, not to say it aloud even to himself. His mother's hand touched his shoulder.

"Does hit hurt?" she said.

"Naw," he said. "Hit don't hurt. Lemme be."

"Can't you wipe some of the blood off before hit dries?"

"I'll wash to-night," he said. "Lemme be, I tell you."

The wagon went on. He did not know where they were going. None of them ever did or ever asked, because it was always somewhere, always a house of sorts waiting for them a day or two days or even three days away. Likely his father had already arranged to make a crop on another farm before he . . . Again he had to stop himself. He (the father) always did. There was something about his wolflike independence and even courage when the advantage was at least neutral which impressed strangers, as if they got from his latent ravening ferocity not so much a sense of dependability as a feeling that his ferocious conviction in the rightness of his own actions would be of advantage to all whose interest lay with his.

That night they camped, in a grove of oaks and beeches where a spring ran. The nights were still cool and they had a fire against it, of a rail lifted from a nearby fence and cut into lengths — a small fire, neat, niggard almost, a shrewd fire; such fires were his father's habit and custom always, even in freezing weather. Older, the boy might have remarked this and wondered why not a big one; why should not a man who had not only seen the waste and extravagance of war, but who had in his blood an inherent voracious prodigality with material not his own, have burned everything in sight? Then he might have gone a step farther and thought that that was the reason: that niggard blaze was the living fruit of nights passed during those four years in the woods hiding from all men, blue or gray, with his strings of horses (captured horses, he called them). And older still, he might have divined the true reason: that the element of fire spoke to some deep mainspring of his father's being, as the element of steel or of powder spoke to other men, as the one weapon for the preservation of integrity, else breath were not worth the breathing, and hence to be regarded with respect and used with discretion.

But he did not think this now and he had seen those same niggard blazes all his life. He merely ate his supper beside it and was already half asleep over his iron plate when his father called him, and once more he followed the stiff back, the stiff and ruthless limp, up the slope and on to the starlit road where, turning, he could see his father against the stars but without face or depth — a shape black, flat, and bloodless as though cut from tin in the iron folds of the frockcoat which had not been made for him, the voice harsh like tin and without heat like tin:

"You were fixing to tell them. You would have told him." He didn't answer. His father struck him with the flat of his hand on the side of the head, hard but without heat, exactly as he had struck the two mules at the store, exactly as he would strike either of them with any stick in order to kill a horse fly, his voice still without heat or anger: "You're getting to be a man. You got to learn. You got to learn to stick to your own blood or you ain't going to have any blood to stick to you. Do you think either of them, any man there this morning, would? Don't you know all they wanted was a chance to get at me because they knew I had them beat? Eh?" Later, twenty years later, he was to tell himself, "If I had said they wanted only truth, justice, he would have hit me again." But now he said nothing. He was not crying. He just stood there. "Answer me," his father said.

"Yes," he whispered. His father turned.

"Get on to bed. We'll be there tomorrow."   30

To-morrow they were there. In the early afternoon the wagon stopped before a paintless two-room house identical almost with the dozen others it had stopped before even in the boy's ten years, and again, as on the other dozen occasions, his mother and aunt got down and began to unload the wagon, although his two sisters and his father and brother had not moved.

"Likely hit ain't fitten for hawgs," one of the sisters said.

"Nevertheless, fit it will and you'll hog it and like it," his father said. "Get out of them chairs and help your Ma unload."

The two sisters got down, big, bovine, in a flutter of cheap ribbons; one of them drew from the jumbled wagon bed a battered lantern, the other a worn broom. His father handed the reins to the older son and began to climb stiffly over the wheel. "When they get unloaded, take the team to the barn and feed them." Then he said, and at first the boy thought he was still speaking to his brother: "Come with me."

"Me?" he said.   35

"Yes," his father said. "You."

"Abner," his mother said. His father paused and looked back — the harsh level stare beneath the shaggy, graying, irascible brows.

"I reckon I'll have a word with the man that aims to begin to-morrow owning me body and soul for the next eight months."

They went back up the road. A week ago — or before last night, that is — he would have asked where they were going, but not now. His father had struck him before last night but never before had he paused afterward to explain why; it was as if the blow and the following calm, outrageous voice still rang, repercussed, divulging nothing to him save the terrible handicap of being young, the light weight of his few years, just heavy enough to prevent his soaring free of the world as it seemed to be ordered but not heavy enough to keep him footed solid in it, to resist it and try to change the course of its events.

Presently he could see the grove of oaks and cedars and the other flowering trees   40
and shrubs where the house would be, though not the house yet. They walked beside a fence massed with honeysuckle and Cherokee roses and came to a gate swinging

open between two brick pillars, and now, beyond a sweep of drive, he saw the house for the first time and at that instant he forgot his father and the terror and despair both, and even when he remembered his father again (who had not stopped) the terror and despair did not return. Because, for all the twelve movings, they had sojourned until now in a poor country, a land of small farms and fields and houses, and he had never seen a house like this before. *Hit's big as a courthouse* he thought quietly, with a surge of peace and joy whose reason he could not have thought into words, being too young for that: *They are safe from him. People whose lives are a part of this peace and dignity are beyond his touch, he no more to them than a buzzing wasp: capable of stinging for a little moment but that's all; the spell of this peace and dignity rendering even the barns and stable and cribs which belong to it impervious to the puny flames he might contrive . . .* this, the peace and joy, ebbing for an instant as he looked again at the stiff black back, the stiff and implacable limp of the figure which was not dwarfed by the house, for the reason that it had never looked big anywhere and which now, against the serene columned backdrop, had more than ever that impervious quality of something cut ruthlessly from tin, depthless, as though, sidewise to the sun, it would cast no shadow. Watching him, the boy remarked the absolutely undeviating course which his father held and saw the stiff foot come squarely down in a pile of fresh droppings where a horse had stood in the drive and which his father could have avoided by a simple change of stride. But it ebbed only for a moment, though he could not have thought this into words either, walking on in the spell of the house, which he could even want but without envy, without sorrow, certainly never with that ravening and jealous rage which unknown to him walked in the ironlike black coat before him: *Maybe he will feel it too. Maybe it will even change him now from what maybe he couldn't help but be.*

They crossed the portico. Now he could hear his father's stiff foot as it came down on the boards with clocklike finality, a sound out of all proportion to the displacement of the body it bore and which was not dwarfed either by the white door before it, as though it had attained to a sort of vicious and ravening minimum not to be dwarfed by anything — the flat, wide, black hat, the formal coat of broadcloth which had once been black but which had now that friction-glazed greenish cast of the bodies of old house flies, the lifted sleeve which was too large, the lifted hand like a curled claw. The door opened so promptly that the boy knew the Negro must have been watching them all the time, an old man with neat grizzled hair, in a linen jacket, who stood barring the door with his body, saying, "Wipe yo foots, white man, fo you come in here. Major ain't home nohow."

"Get out of my way, nigger," his father said, without heat too, flinging the door back and the Negro also and entering, his hat still on his head. And now the boy saw the prints of the stiff foot on the doorjamb and saw them appear on the pale rug behind the machinelike deliberation of the foot which seemed to bear (or transmit) twice the weight which the body compassed. The Negro was shouting "Miss Lula! Miss Lula!" somewhere behind them, then the boy, deluged as though by a warm wave by a suave turn of carpeted stair and a pendant glitter of chandeliers and a mute gleam of gold frames, heard the swift feet and saw her too, a lady — perhaps he had never seen her like before either — in a gray, smooth gown with lace at the throat and an apron tied at the waist and the sleeves turned back, wiping cake or biscuit dough from her hands with a towel as she came up the hall, looking not at his father at all but at the tracks on the blond rug with an expression of incredulous amazement.

"I tried," the Negro cried. "I tole him to . . ."

"Will you please go away?" she said in a shaking voice. "Major de Spain is not at home. Will you please go away?"

His father had not spoken again. He did not speak again. He did not even look   45
at her. He just stood stiff in the center of the rug, in his hat, the shaggy iron-gray brows twitching slightly above the pebble-colored eyes as he appeared to examine the house with brief deliberation. Then with the same deliberation he turned; the boy watched him pivot on the good leg and saw the stiff foot drag round the arc of the turning, leaving a final long and fading smear. His father never looked at it, he never once looked down at the rug. The Negro held the door. It closed behind them, upon the hysteric and indistinguishable woman-wail. His father stopped at the top of the steps and scraped his boot clean on the edge of it. At the gate he stopped again. He stood for a moment, planted stiffly on the stiff foot, looking back at the house. "Pretty and white, ain't it?" he said. "That's sweat. Nigger sweat. Maybe it ain't white enough yet to suit him. Maybe he wants to mix some white sweat with it."

Two hours later the boy was chopping wood behind the house within which his mother and aunt and the two sisters (the mother and aunt, not the two girls, he knew that; even at this distance and muffled by walls the flat loud voices of the two girls emanated an incorrigible idle inertia) were setting up the stove to prepare a meal, when he heard the hooves and saw the linen-clad man on a fine sorrel mare, whom he recognized even before he saw the rolled rug in front of the Negro youth following on a fat bay carriage horse — a suffused, angry face vanishing, still at full gallop, beyond the corner of the house where his father and brother were sitting in the two tilted chairs; and a moment later, almost before he could have put the axe down, he heard the hooves again and watched the sorrel mare go back out of the yard, already galloping again. Then his father began to shout one of the sisters' names, who presently emerged backward from the kitchen door dragging the rolled rug along the ground by one end while the other sister walked behind it.

"If you ain't going to tote, go on and set up the wash pot," the first said.

"You, Sarty!" the second shouted. "Set up the wash pot!" His father appeared at the door, framed against that shabbiness, as he had been against that other bland perfection, impervious to either, the mother's anxious face at his shoulder.

"Go on," the father said. "Pick it up." The two sisters stooped, broad, lethargic; stooping, they presented an incredible expanse of pale cloth and a flutter of tawdry ribbons.

"If I thought enough of a rug to have to git hit all the way from France I wouldn't   50
keep hit where folks coming in would have to tromp on hit," the first said. They raised the rug.

"Abner," the mother said. "Let me do it."

"You go back and git dinner," his father said. "I'll tend to this."

From the woodpile through the rest of the afternoon the boy watched them, the rug spread flat in the dust beside the bubbling wash pot, the two sisters stooping over it with that profound and lethargic reluctance, while the father stood over them in turn, implacable and grim, driving them though never raising his voice again. He could smell the harsh homemade lye they were using; he saw his mother come to the door once and look toward them with an expression not anxious now but very like despair; he saw his father turn, and he fell to with the axe and saw from the corner of his eye his father raise from the ground a flattish fragment of field stone and examine it and return to the pot, and this time his mother actually spoke: "Abner. Abner. Please don't. Please, Abner."

Then he was done too. It was dusk; the whippoorwills had already begun. He could smell coffee from the room where they would presently eat the cold food remaining from the mid-afternoon meal, though when he entered the house he realized they were having coffee again probably because there was a fire on the hearth, before which the rug now lay spread over the backs of the two chairs. The tracks of his father's foot were gone. Where they had been were now long, water-cloudy scoriations resembling the sporadic course of a lilliputian mowing machine.

It still hung there while they ate the cold food and then went to bed, scattered without order or claim up and down the two rooms, his mother in one bed, where his father would later lie, the older brother in the other, himself, the aunt, and the two sisters on pallets on the floor. But his father was not in bed yet. The last thing the boy remembered was the depthless, harsh silhouette of the hat and coat bending over the rug and it seemed to him that he had not even closed his eyes when the silhouette was standing over him, the fire almost dead behind it, the stiff foot prodding him awake. "Catch up the mule," his father said. 55

When he returned with the mule his father was standing in the black door, the rolled rug over his shoulder. "Ain't you going to ride?" he said.

"No. Give me your foot."

He bent his knee into his father's hand, the wiry, surprising power flowed smoothly, rising, he rising with it, on to the mule's bare back (they had owned a saddle once; the boy could remember it though not when or where) and with the same effortlessness his father swung the rug up in front of him. Now in the starlight they retraced the afternoon's path, up the dusty road rife with honeysuckle, through the gate and up the black tunnel of the drive to the lightless house, where he sat on the mule and felt the rough warp of the rug drag across his thighs and vanish.

"Don't you want me to help?" he whispered. His father did not answer and now he heard again that stiff foot striking the hollow portico with that wooden and clocklike deliberation, that outrageous overstatement of the weight it carried. The rug, hunched, not flung (the boy could tell that even in the darkness) from his father's shoulder struck the angle of wall and floor with a sound unbelievably loud, thunderous, then the foot again, unhurried and enormous; a light came on in the house and the boy sat, tense, breathing steadily and quietly and just a little fast, though the foot itself did not increase its beat at all, descending the steps now; now the boy could see him.

"Don't you want to ride now?" he whispered. "We kin both ride now," the light 60
within the house altering now, flaring up and sinking. *He's coming down the stairs
now*, he thought. He had already ridden the mule up beside the horse block; presently his father was up behind him and he doubled the reins over and slashed the
mule across the neck, but before the animal could begin to trot the hard, thin arm
came round him, the hard, knotted hand jerking the mule back to a walk.

In the first red rays of the sun they were in the lot, putting plow gear on the
mules. This time the sorrel mare was in the lot before he heard it at all, the rider collarless and even bareheaded, trembling, speaking in a shaking voice as the woman in
the house had done, his father merely looking up once before stooping again to the
hame he was buckling, so that the man on the mare spoke to his stooping back:

"You must realize you have ruined that rug. Wasn't there anybody here, any of
your women . . ." he ceased, shaking, the boy watching him, the older brother leaning
now in the stable door, chewing, blinking slowly and steadily at nothing apparently.
"It cost a hundred dollars. But you never had a hundred dollars. You never will. So I'm
going to charge you twenty bushels of corn against your crop. I'll add it in your contract
and when you come to the commissary you can sign it. That won't keep Mrs. de Spain
quiet but maybe it will teach you to wipe your feet off before you enter her house again."

Then he was gone. The boy looked at his father, who still had not spoken or even
looked up again, who was now adjusting the logger-head in the hame.

"Pap," he said. His father looked at him — the inscrutable face, the shaggy brows
beneath which the gray eyes glinted coldly. Suddenly the boy went toward him, fast,
stopping as suddenly. "You done the best you could!" he cried. "If he wanted hit done
different why didn't he wait and tell you how? He won't git no twenty bushels! He
won't git none! We'll gether hit and hide hit! I kin watch . . ."

"Did you put the cutter back in that straight stock like I told you?" 65

"No, sir," he said.

"Then go do it."

That was Wednesday. During the rest of that week he worked steadily, at what
was within his scope and some which was beyond it, with an industry that did not
need to be driven nor even commanded twice; he had this from his mother, with the
difference that some at least of what he did he liked to do, such as splitting wood with
the half-size axe which his mother and aunt had earned, or saved money somehow,
to present him with at Christmas. In company with the two older women (and on
one afternoon, even one of the sisters), he built pens for the shoat and the cow which
were a part of his father's contract with the landlord, and one afternoon, his father
being absent, gone somewhere on one of the mules, he went to the field.

They were running a middle buster now, his brother holding the plow straight
while he handled the reins, and walking beside the straining mule, the rich black soil
shearing cool and damp against his bare ankles, he thought *Maybe this is the end of
it. Maybe even that twenty bushels that seems hard to have to pay for just a rug will be
a cheap price for him to stop forever and always from being what he used to be*; thinking, dreaming now, so that his brother had to speak sharply to him to mind the mule:

Maybe he even won't collect the twenty bushels. Maybe it will all add up and balance and vanish — corn, rug, fire; the terror and grief, the being pulled two ways like between two teams of horses — gone, done with for ever and ever.

Then it was Saturday; he looked up from beneath the mule he was harnessing and saw his father in the black coat and hat. "Not that," his father said. "The wagon gear." And then, two hours later, sitting in the wagon bed behind his father and brother on the seat, the wagon accomplished a final curve, and he saw the weathered paint-less store with its tattered tobacco- and patent-medicine posters and the tethered wagons and saddle animals below the gallery. He mounted the gnawed steps behind his father and brother, and there again was the lane of quiet, watching faces for the three of them to walk through. He saw the man in spectacles sitting at the plank table and he did not need to be told this was a Justice of the Peace; he sent one glare of fierce, exultant, partisan defiance at the man in collar and cravat now, whom he had seen but twice before in his life, and that on a galloping horse, who now wore on his face an expression not of rage but of amazed unbelief which the boy could not have known was at the incredible circumstance of being sued by one of his own tenants, and came and stood against his father and cried at the Justice: "He ain't done it! He ain't burnt . . ." 70

"Go back to the wagon," his father said.

"Burnt?" the Justice said. "Do I understand this rug was burned too?"

"Does anybody here claim it was?" his father said. "Go back to the wagon." But he did not, he merely retreated to the rear of the room, crowded as that other had been, but not to sit down this time, instead, to stand pressing among the motionless bodies, listening to the voices:

"And you claim twenty bushels of corn is too high for the damage you did to the rug?"

"He brought the rug to me and said he wanted the tracks washed out of it. I washed the tracks out and took the rug back to him." 75

"But you didn't carry the rug back to him in the same condition it was in before you made the tracks on it."

His father did not answer, and now for perhaps half a minute there was no sound at all save that of breathing, the faint, steady suspiration of complete and intent listening.

"You decline to answer that, Mr. Snopes?" Again his father did not answer. "I'm going to find against you, Mr. Snopes. I'm going to find that you were responsible for the injury to Major de Spain's rug and hold you liable for it. But twenty bushels of corn seems a little high for a man in your circumstances to have to pay. Major de Spain claims it cost a hundred dollars. October corn will be worth about fifty cents. I figure that if Major de Spain can stand a ninety-five dollar loss on something he paid cash for, you can stand a five-dollar loss you haven't earned yet. I hold you in damages to Major de Spain to the amount of ten bushels of corn over and above your contract with him, to be paid to him out of your crop at gathering time. Court adjourned."

It had taken no time hardly, the morning was but half begun. He thought they would return home and perhaps back to the field, since they were late, far behind all other farmers. But instead his father passed on behind the wagon, merely indicating with his hand for the older brother to follow with it, and crossed the road toward the blacksmith shop opposite, pressing on after his father, overtaking him, speaking, whispering up at the harsh, calm face beneath the weathered hat: "He won't git no ten bushels neither. He won't git one. We'll . . ." until his father glanced for an instant down at him, the face absolutely calm, the grizzled eyebrows tangled above the cold eyes, the voice almost pleasant, almost gentle:

"You think so? Well, we'll wait till October anyway."

80

The matter of the wagon — the setting of a spoke or two and the tightening of the tires — did not take long either, the business of the tires accomplished by driving the wagon into the spring branch behind the shop and letting it stand there, the mules nuzzling into the water from time to time, and the boy on the seat with the idle reins, looking up the slope and through the sooty tunnel of the shed where the slow hammer rang and where his father sat on an upended cypress bolt, easily, either talking or listening, still sitting there when the boy brought the dripping wagon up out of the branch and halted it before the door.

"Take them on to the shade and hitch," his father said. He did so and returned. His father and the smith and a third man squatting on his heels inside the door were talking, about crops and animals; the boy, squatting too in the ammoniac dust and hoof-parings and scales of rust, heard his father tell a long and unhurried story out of the time before the birth of the older brother even when he had been a professional horse-trader. And then his father came up beside him where he stood before a tattered last year's circus poster on the other side of the store, gazing rapt and quiet at the scarlet horses, the incredible poisings and convolutions of tulle and tights and the painted leers of comedians, and said, "It's time to eat."

But not at home. Squatting beside his brother against the front wall, he watched his father emerge from the store and produce from a paper sack a segment of cheese and divide it carefully and deliberately into three with his pocket knife and produce crackers from the same sack. They all three squatted on the gallery and ate, slowly, without talking; then in the store again, they drank from a tin dipper tepid water smelling of the cedar bucket and of living beech trees. And still they did not go home. It was a horse lot this time, a tall rail fence upon and along which men stood and sat and out of which one by one horses were led, to be walked and trotted and then cantered back and forth along the road while the slow swapping and buying went on and the sun began to slant westward, they — the three of them — watching and listening, the older brother with his muddy eyes and his steady, inevitable tobacco, the father commenting now and then on certain of the animals, to no one in particular.

It was after sundown when they reached home. They ate supper by lamplight, then, sitting on the doorstep, the boy watched the night fully accomplish, listening to the whippoorwills and the frogs, when he heard his mother's voice: "Abner! No! No! Oh, God. Oh, God. Abner!" and he rose, whirled, and saw the altered light through the door where a candle stub now burned in a bottle neck on the table and his father, still in the hat and coat, at once formal and burlesque as though dressed carefully for some shabby and ceremonial violence, emptying the reservoir of the lamp back into the five-gallon kerosene can from which it had been filled, while the mother tugged at his arm until he shifted the lamp to the other hand and flung her back, not savagely or viciously, just hard, into the wall, her hands flung out against the wall for balance, her mouth open and in her face the same quality of hopeless despair as had been in her voice. Then his father saw him standing in the door.

"Go to the barn and get that can of oil we were oiling the wagon with," he said. 85 The boy did not move. Then he could speak.

"What . . ." he cried. "What are you . . ."

"Go get that oil," his father said. "Go."

Then he was moving, running, outside the house, toward the stable: this the old habit, the old blood which he had not been permitted to choose for himself, which had been bequeathed him willy nilly and which had run for so long (and who knew where, battening on what of outrage and savagery and lust) before it came to him. *I could keep on*, he thought. *I could run on and on and never look back, never need to see his face again. Only I can't. I can't*, the rusted can in his hand now, the liquid sploshing in it as he ran back to the house and into it, into the sound of his mother's weeping in the next room, and handed the can to his father.

"Ain't you going to even send a nigger?" he cried. "At least you sent a nigger before!"

This time his father didn't strike him. The hand came even faster than the blow 90 had, the same hand which had set the can on the table with almost excruciating care flashing from the can toward him too quick for him to follow it, gripping him by the back of his shirt and on to tiptoe before he had seen it quit the can, the face stooping at him in breathless and frozen ferocity, the cold, dead voice speaking over him to the older brother who leaned against the table, chewing with that steady, curious, side-wise motion of cows:

"Empty the can into the big one and go on. I'll catch up with you."

"Better tie him up to the bedpost," the brother said.

"Do like I told you," the father said. Then the boy was moving, his bunched shirt and the hard, bony hand between his shoulder-blades, his toes just touching the floor, across the room and into the other one, past the sisters sitting with spread heavy thighs in the two chairs over the cold hearth, and to where his mother and aunt sat side by side on the bed, the aunt's arms about his mother's shoulders.

"Hold him," the father said. The aunt made a startled movement. "Not you," the father said. "Lennie. Take hold of him. I want to see you do it." His mother took him by the wrist. "You'll hold him better than that. If he gets loose don't you know what he is going to do? He will go up yonder." He jerked his head toward the road. "Maybe I'd better tie him."

"I'll hold him," his mother whispered. 95

"See you do then." Then his father was gone, the stiff foot heavy and measured upon the boards, ceasing at last.

Then he began to struggle. His mother caught him in both arms, he jerking and wrenching at them. He would be stronger in the end, he knew that. But he had no time to wait for it. "Lemme go!" he cried. "I don't want to have to hit you!"

"Let him go!" the aunt said. "If he don't go, before God, I am going up there myself!"

"Don't you see I can't?" his mother cried. "Sarty! Sarty! No! No! Help me, Lizzie!"

Then he was free. His aunt grasped at him but it was too late. He whirled, running, his mother stumbled forward on to her knees behind him, crying to the nearer sister: "Catch him, Net! Catch him!" But that was too late too, the sister (the sisters were twins, born at the same time, yet either of them now gave the impression of being, encompassing as much living meat and volume and weight as any other two of the family) not yet having begun to rise from the chair, her head, face, alone merely turned, presenting to him in the flying instant an astonishing expanse of young female features untroubled by any surprise even, wearing only an expression of bovine interest. Then he was out of the room, out of the house, in the mild dust of the starlit road and the heavy rifeness of honeysuckle, the pale ribbon unspooling with terrific slowness under his running feet, reaching the gate at last and turning in, running, his heart and lungs drumming, on up the drive toward the lighted house, the lighted door. He did not knock, he burst in, sobbing for breath, incapable for the moment of speech; he saw the astonished face of the Negro in the linen jacket without knowing when the Negro had appeared.

"De Spain!" he cried, panted. "Where's . . ." then he saw the white man too emerging from a white door down the hall. "Barn!" he cried. "Barn!"

"What?" the white man said. "Barn?"

"Yes!" the boy cried. "Barn!"

"Catch him!" the white man shouted.

But it was too late this time too. The Negro grasped his shirt, but the entire sleeve, rotten with washing, carried away, and he was out that door too and in the drive again, and had actually never ceased to run even while he was screaming into the white man's face.

Behind him the white man was shouting, "My horse! Fetch my horse!" and he thought for an instant of cutting across the park and climbing the fence into the road, but he did not know the park nor how high the vine-massed fence might be and he dared not risk it. So he ran on down the drive, blood and breath roaring; presently he was in the road again though he could not see it. He could not hear either: the galloping mare was almost upon him before he heard her, and even then he held his course, as if the very urgency of his wild grief and need must in a moment more find him wings, waiting until the ultimate instant to hurl himself aside and into the weed-choked roadside ditch as the horse thundered past and on, for an instant in furious silhouette against the stars, the tranquil early summer night sky which, even before the shape of the horse and rider vanished, stained abruptly and violently upward: a long, swirling roar incredible and soundless, blotting the stars, and he springing up and into the road again, running again, knowing it was too late yet still running even after he heard the shot and, an instant later, two shots, pausing now without knowing he had ceased to run, crying "Pap! Pap!", running again before he knew he had begun to run, stumbling, tripping over something and scrabbling up again without ceasing to run, looking backward over his shoulder at the glare as he got up, running on among the invisible trees, panting, sobbing, "Father! Father!"

At midnight he was sitting on the crest of a hill. He did not know it was midnight and he did not know how far he had come. But there was no glare behind him now and he sat now, his back toward what he had called home for four days anyhow, his face toward the dark woods which he would enter when breath was strong again, small, shaking steadily in the chill darkness, hugging himself into the remainder of his thin, rotten shirt, the grief and despair now no longer terror and fear but just grief and despair. *Father. My father*, he thought. "He was brave!" he cried suddenly, aloud but not loud, no more than a whisper: "He was! He was in the war! He was in Colonel Sartoris' cav'ry!" not knowing that his father had gone to that war a private in the fine old European sense, wearing no uniform, admitting the authority of and giving fidelity to no man or army or flag, going to war as Malbrouck himself did: for booty — it meant nothing and less than nothing to him if it were enemy booty or his own.

The slow constellations wheeled on. It would be dawn and then sun-up after a while and he would be hungry. But that would be to-morrow and now he was only cold, and walking would cure that. His breathing was easier now and he decided to get up and go on, and then he found that he had been asleep because he knew it was almost dawn, the night almost over. He could tell that from the whippoorwills. They were everywhere now among the dark trees below him, constant and inflectioned and ceaseless, so that, as the instant for giving over to the day birds drew nearer and nearer, there was no interval at all between them. He got up. He was a little stiff, but walking would cure that too as it would the cold, and soon there would be the sun. He went on down the hill, toward the dark woods within which the liquid silver voices of the birds called unceasing — the rapid and urgent beating of the urgent and quiring heart of the late spring night. He did not look back.

(1939)

Exploring the Text

1. Describe the techniques William Faulkner uses to set the scene in the story's first paragraph.
2. What are some of the recurring images in "Barn Burning"? How do they connect to the story's theme?
3. How does Faulkner develop the characters of Sarty and his father, Abner? How does the character development differ? How is it the same?
4. Why do you think Abner Snopes feels he can walk into Major de Spain's house even though de Spain's servant and wife have told him not to (pars. 41–44)? What does that attitude tell us about his background?
5. What is the central conflict in "Barn Burning"? What are the secondary conflicts?
6. In what ways can "Barn Burning" be considered a coming-of-age story?
7. Why do you think Faulkner made the decision not to identify the victims of the gunshots at the end of the story? Who do you think is shot?
8. Both Abner Snopes and Sarty's older brothers show up in later works by Faulkner, while Sarty does not. Does knowing that change your view of "Barn Burning"? Why do you think Faulkner might not have wanted to reprise young Sarty?
9. Why is the burning of a barn so fraught with meaning? What do you think it means to Abner Snopes? To his neighbors and family?

W. H. AUDEN

Born in northern England to a doctor and a nurse, Wystan Hugh Auden (1907–1973) earned a scholarship to Oxford to study engineering. While there, he became interested in poetry — especially the modernist poetry of T. S. Eliot — and studied English instead. He was part of a group of poets known as the Oxford Group (and later, the Auden Generation), which included Stephen Spender and Louis MacNeice. During the 1930s, Auden traveled to Spain and China; became involved in political causes; and wrote prose, poetry, and plays. In 1939, Auden left England and became a U.S. citizen. *Another Time* (1940), the first book he wrote in America, contains some of his most famous poems, including "Musée des Beaux Arts." He won a Pulitzer Prize for *The Age of Anxiety* (1947) and a National Book Award for *The Shield of Achilles* (1955).

The Unknown Citizen

"The Unknown Citizen" was published in the *New Yorker* magazine in 1939, shortly after Auden moved from England to the United States.

(To JS/07 M 378
This Marble Monument
Is Erected by the State)

He was found by the Bureau of Statistics to be
One against whom there was no official complaint,
And all the reports on his conduct agree
That, in the modern sense of an old-fashioned word, he was a saint,
For in everything he did he served the Greater Community.   5
Except for the War till the day he retired,
He worked in a factory and never got fired,
But satisfied his employers, Fudge Motors Inc.
Yet he wasn't a scab or odd in his views.
For his Union reports that he paid his dues,   10
(Our report on his Union shows it was sound)
And our Social Psychology workers found
That he was popular with his mates and liked a drink.
The Press are convinced that he bought a paper every day
And that his reactions to advertisements were normal in every way.   15
Policies taken out in his name prove that he was fully insured,
And his Health-card shows he was once in a hospital but left it cured.
Both Producers Research and High-Grade Living declare
He was fully sensible to the advantages of the Instalment Plan

And had everything necessary to the Modern Man,   20
A phonograph, a radio, a car and a frigidaire.
Our researchers into Public Opinion are content
That he held the proper opinions for the time of year;
When there was peace, he was for peace: when there was war, he went.
He was married and added five children to the population,   25
Which our Eugenist says was the right number for a parent of his generation.
And our teachers report that he never interfered with their education.
Was he free? Was he happy? The question is absurd:
Had anything been wrong, we should certainly have heard.

                                                          (1939)

Exploring the Text

1. What does the title remind you of? How is it allusive? How is it a play on words? Explain whether or not it has personal meaning for you. What might it have meant in W. H. Auden's time?
2. What is the effect of the rhyme in "The Unknown Citizen"?
3. Note the list of possessions in line 21: "A phonograph, a radio, a car and a frigidaire." What would that list consist of if the poem were written today?
4. What do you think Auden means in line 27: "And our teachers report that he never interfered with their education"?
5. What argument does "The Unknown Citizen" make on the subject of citizenship? How does Auden support his claim?
6. This poem is considered satirical. What are the targets of the satire?

RICHARD WRIGHT

Richard Nathaniel Wright (1908–1960) was an African American writer and poet who helped redefine ideas of racial relations in the United States during the early to mid-twentieth century. Born on a plantation near Natchez, Mississippi — to an illiterate sharecropper father and an educated schoolteacher mother — Wright went to school only through the ninth grade, yet he published his first short story in a local black newspaper at the age of sixteen. He moved to Chicago in 1927, and after the Great Depression left him jobless, he joined the Communist Party in 1932. He moved to New York City in 1937 to serve as an editor of the Communist newspaper *Daily Worker*, and in 1940 he published the novel *Native Son*, which brought him instant fame. His autobiography, *Black Boy*, a moving account of his experiences as an impoverished African American growing up in twentieth-century America, was published in 1945 to high acclaim.

The Man Who Was Almost a Man

"The Man Who Was Almost a Man" appeared originally as "Almos' a Man" in the January 1940 edition of *Harper's Bazaar*, a fashion magazine known for publishing new fiction. Wright revised and retitled the story; it was included in a posthumous collection of stories entitled *Eight Men*, published in 1961.

Dave struck out across the fields, looking homeward through paling light. Whut's the use talkin wid em niggers in the field? Anyhow, his mother was putting supper on the table. Them niggers can't understan nothing. One of these days he was going to get a gun and practice shooting, then they couldn't talk to him as though he were a little boy. He slowed, looking at the ground. Shucks, Ah ain scareda them even ef they are biggern me! Aw, Ah know whut Ahma do. Ahm going by ol Joe's sto n git that Sears Roebuck catlog n look at them guns. Mebbe Ma will lemme buy one when she gits mah pay from ol man Hawkins. Ahma beg her t gimme some money. Ahm ol ernough to hava gun. Ahm seventeen. Almost a man. He strode, feeling his long loose-jointed limbs. Shucks, a man oughta hava little gun aftah he done worked hard all day.

He came in sight of Joe's store. A yellow lantern glowed on the front porch. He mounted steps and went through the screen door, hearing it bang behind him. There was a strong smell of coal oil and mackerel fish. He felt very confident until he saw fat Joe walk in through the rear door, then his courage began to ooze.

"Howdy, Dave! Whutcha want?"

"How yuh, Mistah Joe? Aw, Ah don wanna buy nothing. Ah jus wanted t see ef yuhd lemme look at tha catlog erwhile."

"Sure! You wanna see it here?" 5

"Nawsuh. Ah wants t take it home wid me. Ah'll bring it back termorrow when Ah come in from the fiels."

"You plannin on buying something?"

"Yessuh."

"Your ma lettin you have your own money now?"

"Shucks. Mistah Joe, Ahm gittin t be a man like anybody else!" 10

Joe laughed and wiped his greasy white face with a red bandanna.

"Whut you plannin on buyin?"

Dave looked at the floor, scratched his head, scratched his thigh, and smiled. Then he looked up shyly.

"Ah'll tell yuh, Mistah Joe, ef yuh promise yuh won't tell."

"I promise." 15

"Waal, Ahma buy a gun."

"A gun? What you want with a gun?"

"Ah wanna keep it."

"You ain't nothing but a boy. You don't need a gun."

"Aw, lemme have the catlog, Mistah Joe. Ah'll bring it back." 20

Joe walked through the rear door. Dave was elated. He looked around at barrels of sugar and flour. He heard Joe coming back. He craned his neck to see if he were bringing the book. Yeah, he's got it. Gawddog, he's got it!

"Here, but be sure you bring it back. It's the only one I got."

"Sho, Mistah Joe."

"Say, if you wanna buy a gun, why don't you buy one from me? I gotta gun to sell."

"Will it shoot?"   25

"Sure it'll shoot."

"Whut kind is it?"

"Oh, it's kinda old . . . a left-hand Wheeler. A pistol. A big one."

"Is it got bullets in it?"

"It's loaded."   30

"Kin Ah see it?"

"Where's your money?"

"What yuh wan fer it?"

"I'll let you have it for two dollars."

"Just two dollahs? Shucks, Ah could buy tha when Ah git mah pay."   35

"I'll have it here when you want it."

"Awright, suh. Ah be in fer it."

He went through the door, hearing it slam again behind him. Ahma git some money from Ma n buy me a gun! Only two dollahs! He tucked the thick catalogue under his arm and hurried.

"Where yuh been, boy?" His mother held a steaming dish of black-eyed peas.

"Aw, Ma, Ah jus stopped down the road t talk wid the boys."   40

"Yuh know bettah t keep suppah waitin."

He sat down, resting the catalogue on the edge of the table.

"Yuh git up from there and git to the well n wash yosef! Ah ain feedin no hogs in mah house!"

She grabbed his shoulder and pushed him. He stumbled out of the room, then came back to get the catalogue.

"Whut this?"   45

"Aw, Ma, it's jusa catlog."

"Who yuh git it from?"

"From Joe, down at the sto."

"Waal, thas good. We kin use it in the outhouse."

"Naw, Ma." He grabbed for it. "Gimme ma catlog, Ma."   50

She held onto it and glared at him.

"Quit hollerin at me! Whut's wrong wid yuh? Yuh crazy?"

"But Ma, please. It ain mine! It's Joe's! He tol me t bring it back t im termorrow."

She gave up the book. He stumbled down the back steps, hugging the thick book under his arm. When he had splashed water on his face and hands, he groped back to the kitchen and fumbled in a corner for the towel. He bumped into a chair; it clattered to the floor. The catalogue sprawled at his feet. When he had dried his eyes he snatched up the book and held it again under his arm. His mother stood watching him.

"Now, ef yuh gonna act a fool over that ol book, Ah'll take it n burn it up." 55

"Naw, Ma, please."

"Waal, set down n be still!"

He sat down and drew the oil lamp close. He thumbed page after page, unaware of the food his mother set on the table. His father came in. Then his small brother.

"Whutcha got there, Dave?" his father asked.

"Jusa catlog," he answered, not looking up. 60

"Yeah, here they is!" His eyes glowed at blue-and-black revolvers. He glanced up, feeling sudden guilt. His father was watching him. He eased the book under the table and rested it on his knees. After the blessing was asked, he ate. He scooped up peas and swallowed fat meat without chewing. Buttermilk helped to wash it down. He did not want to mention money before his father. He would do much better by cornering his mother when she was alone. He looked at his father uneasily out of the edge of his eye.

"Boy, how come yuh don quit foolin wid tha book n eat yo suppah?"

"Yessuh."

"How you n ol man Hawkins gitten erlong?"

"Suh?" 65

"Can't yuh hear? Why don yuh lissen? Ah ast yu how wuz yuh n ol man Hawkins gittin erlong?"

"Oh, swell, Pa. Ah plows mo lan than anybody over there."

"Waal, yuh oughta keep you mind on whut yuh doin."

"Yessuh."

He poured his plate full of molasses and sopped it up slowly with a chunk of 70 cornbread. When his father and brother had left the kitchen, he still sat and looked again at the guns in the catalogue, longing to muster courage enough to present his case to his mother. Lawd, ef Ah only had tha pretty one! He could almost feel the slickness of the weapon with his fingers. If he had a gun like that he would polish it and keep it shining so it would never rust. N Ah'd keep it loaded, by Gawd!

"Ma?" His voice was hesitant.

"Hunh?"

"Ol man Hawkins give yuh mah money yit?"

"Yeah, but ain no usa yuh thinking bout throwin nona it erway. Ahm keeping tha money sos yuh kin have cloes t go to school this winter."

He rose and went to her side with the open catalogue in his palms. She was wash- 75 ing dishes, her head bent low over a pan. Shyly he raised the book. When he spoke, his voice was husky, faint.

"Ma, Gawd knows Ah wans one of these."

"One of whut?" she asked, not raising her eyes.

"One of these," he said again, not daring even to point. She glanced up at the page, then at him with wide eyes.

"Nigger, is yuh gone plumb crazy?"

"Aw, Ma—" 80

"Git outta here! Don yuh talk t me bout no gun! Yuh a fool!"

"Ma, Ah kin buy one fer two dollahs."

"Not ef Ah knows it, yuh ain!"

"But yuh promised me one—"

"Ah don care what Ah promised! Yuh ain nothing but a boy yit!"

"Ma, ef yuh lemme buy one Ah'll *never* ast yuh fer nothing no mo."

"Ah tol yuh t git outta here! Yuh ain gonna toucha penny of tha money fer no gun! Thas how come Ah has Mistah Hawkins t pay yo wages t me, 'cause Ah knows yuh ain got no sense."

"But, Ma, we needa gun. Pa ain got no gun. We needa gun in the house. Yuh kin never tell whut might happen."

"Now don yuh try to maka fool outta me, boy! Ef we did hava gun, yuh wouldn't have it!"

He laid the catalogue down and slipped his arm around her waist.

"Aw, Ma, Ah done worked hard alla summer n ain ast yuh fer nothing, is Ah, now?"

"Thas whut yuh spose t do!"

"But Ma, Ah wans a gun. Yuh kin lemme have two dollahs outta mah money. Please, Ma. I kin give it to Pa. . . . Please, Ma! Ah loves yuh, Ma."

When she spoke her voice came soft and low.

"What yu wan wida gun, Dave? Yuh don need no gun. Yuh'll git in trouble. N ef yo pa jus thought Ah let yuh have money t buy a gun he'd hava fit."

"Ah'll hide it, Ma. It ain but two dollahs."

"Lawd, chil, whut's wrong wid yuh?"

"Ain nothin wrong, Ma. Ahm almos a man now. Ah wans a gun."

"Who gonna sell yuh a gun?"

"Ol Joe at the sto."

"N it don cos but two dollahs?"

"Thas all, Ma. Jus two dollahs. Please, Ma."

She was stacking the plates away; her hands moved slowly, reflectively. Dave kept an anxious silence. Finally, she turned to him.

"Ah'll let yuh git tha gun ef yuh promise me one thing."

"What's tha, Ma?"

"Yuh bring it straight back t me, yuh hear? It be fer Pa."

"Yessum! Lemme go now, Ma."

She stooped, turned slightly to one side, raised the hem of her dress, rolled down the top of her stocking, and came up with a slender wad of bills.

"Here," she said. "Lawd knows yuh don need no gun. But yer pa does. Yuh bring it right back t me, yuh hear? Ahma put it up. Now ef yuh don, Ahma have yuh pa lick yuh so hard yuh won fergit it."

"Yessum."

He took the money, ran down the steps, and across the yard.

"Dave! Yuuuuuh Daaaaave!"

He heard, but he was not going to stop now. "Now, Lawd!"

The first movement he made the following morning was to reach under his pillow for the gun. In the gray light of dawn he held it loosely, feeling a sense of power. Could kill a man with a gun like this. Kill anybody, black or white. And if he were holding his gun in his hand, nobody could run over him; they would have to respect him. It was a big gun, with a long barrel and a heavy handle. He raised and lowered it in his hand, marveling at its weight.

He had not come straight home with it as his mother had asked; instead he had stayed out in the fields, holding the weapon in his hand, aiming it now and then at some imaginary foe. But he had not fired it; he had been afraid that his father might hear. Also he was not sure he knew how to fire it.

To avoid surrendering the pistol he had not come into the house until he knew that they were all asleep. When his mother had tiptoed to his bedside late that night and demanded the gun, he had first played possum; then he had told her that the gun was hidden outdoors, that he would bring it to her in the morning. Now he lay turning it slowly in his hands. He broke it, took out the cartridges, felt them, and then put them back.

He slid out of bed, got a long strip of old flannel from a trunk, wrapped the gun in it, and tied it to his naked thigh while it was still loaded. He did not go in to breakfast. Even though it was not yet daylight, he started for Jim Hawkins' plantation. Just as the sun was rising he reached the barns where the mules and plows were kept.

"Hey! That you, Dave?"

He turned. Jim Hawkins stood eying him suspiciously.

"What're yuh doing here so early?"

"Ah didn't know Ah wuz gittin up so early, Mistah Hawkins. Ah wuz fixin t hitch up ol Jenny n take her t the fiels."

"Good. Since you're so early, how about plowing that stretch down by the woods?"

"Suits me, Mistah Hawkins."

"O.K. Go to it!"

He hitched Jenny to a plow and started across the fields. Hot dog! This was just what he wanted. If he could get down by the woods, he could shoot his gun and nobody would hear. He walked behind the plow, hearing the traces creaking, feeling the gun tied tight to his thigh.

When he reached the woods, he plowed two whole rows before he decided to take out the gun. Finally, he stopped, looked in all directions, then untied the gun and held it in his hand. He turned to the mule and smiled.

"Know whut this is, Jenny? Naw, yuh wouldn know! Yuhs jusa ol mule! Anyhow, this is a gun, n it kin shoot, by Gawd!"

He held the gun at arm's length. Whut t hell, Ahma shoot this thing! He looked at Jenny again.

"Lissen here, Jenny! When Ah pull this ol trigger, Ah don wan yuh t run n acka fool now!"

Jenny stood with head down, her short ears pricked straight. Dave walked off about twenty feet, held the gun far out from him at arm's length, and turned his head. Hell, he told himself, Ah ain afraid. The gun felt loose in his fingers; he waved it wildly for a moment. Then he shut his eyes and tightened his forefinger. Bloom! A report half deafened him and he thought his right hand was torn from his arm. He

115

120

125

130

heard Jenny whinnying and galloping over the field, and he found himself on his knees, squeezing his fingers hard between his legs. His hand was numb; he jammed it into his mouth, trying to warm it, trying to stop the pain. The gun lay at his feet. He did not quite know what had happened. He stood up and stared at the gun as though it were a living thing. He gritted his teeth and kicked the gun. Yuh almos broke mah arm! He turned to look for Jenny; she was far over the fields, tossing her head and kicking wildly.

"Hol on there, ol mule!"

When he caught up with her she stood trembling, walling her big white eyes at him. The plow was far away; the traces had broken. Then Dave stopped short, looking, not believing. Jenny was bleeding. Her left side was red and wet with blood. He went closer. Lawd, have mercy! Wondah did Ah shoot this mule? He grabbed for Jenny's mane. She flinched, snorted, whirled, tossing her head.

"Hol on now! Hol on."

Then he saw the hole in Jenny's side, right between the ribs. It was round, wet, red. A crimson stream streaked down the front leg, flowing fast. Good Gawd! Ah wuzn't shootin at tha mule. He felt panic. He knew he had to stop that blood, or Jenny would bleed to death. He had never seen so much blood in all his life. He chased the mule for half a mile, trying to catch her. Finally she stopped, breathing hard, stumpy tail half arched. He caught her mane and led her back to where the plow and gun lay. Then he stopped and grabbed handfuls of damp black earth and tried to plug the bullet hole. Jenny shuddered, whinnied, and broke from him.

"Hol on! Hol on now!"   135

He tried to plug it again, but blood came anyhow. His fingers were hot and sticky. He rubbed dirt into his palms, trying to dry them. Then again he attempted to plug the bullet hole, but Jenny shied away, kicking her heels high. He stood helpless. He had to do something. He ran at Jenny; she dodged him. He watched a red stream of blood flow down Jenny's leg and form a bright pool at her feet.

"Jenny . . . Jenny," he called weakly.

His lips trembled. She's bleeding t death! He looked in the direction of home, wanting to go back, wanting to get help. But he saw the pistol lying in the damp black clay. He had a queer feeling that if he only did something, this would not be; Jenny would not be there bleeding to death.

When he went to her this time, she did not move. She stood with sleepy, dreamy eyes; and when he touched her she gave a low-pitched whinny and knelt to the ground, her front knees slopping in blood.

"Jenny . . . Jenny . . ." he whispered.   140

For a long time she held her neck erect; then her head sank, slowly. Her ribs swelled with a mighty heave and she went over.

Dave's stomach felt empty, very empty. He picked up the gun and held it gingerly between his thumb and forefinger. He buried it at the foot of a tree. He took a stick to cover the pool of blood with dirt — but what was the use? There was Jenny lying with her mouth open and her eyes walled and glassy. He could not tell Jim Hawkins he had shot his mule. But he had to tell something. Yeah, Ah'll tell em Jenny started gittin wil n fell on the joint of the plow. . . . But that would hardly happen to a mule. He walked across the field slowly, head down.

It was sunset. Two of Jim Hawkins' men were over near the edge of the woods digging a hole in which to bury Jenny. Dave was surrounded by a knot of people, all of whom were looking down at the dead mule.

"I don't see how in the world it happened," said Jim Hawkins for the tenth time.

The crowd parted and Dave's mother, father, and small brother pushed into the 145 center.

"Where Dave?" his mother called.

"There he is," said Jim Hawkins.

His mother grabbed him.

"Whut happened, Dave? Whut yuh done?"

"Nothin." 150

"C mon, boy, talk," his father said.

Dave took a deep breath and told the story he knew nobody believed.

"Waal," he drawled. "Ah brung ol Jenny down here sos Ah could do mah plowin. Ah plowed bout two rows, just like yuh see." He stopped and pointed at the long rows of upturned earth. "Then somethin musta been wrong wid ol Jenny. She wouldn ack right a-tall. She started snortin n kickin her heels. Ah tried t hol her, but she pulled erway, rearin n goin in. Then when the point of the plow was stickin up in the air, she swung erroun n twisted herself back on it. . . . She stuck herself n started t bleed. N fo Ah could do anything, she wuz dead."

"Did you ever hear of anything like that in all your life?" asked Jim Hawkins.

There were white and black standing in the crowd. They murmured. Dave's mother 155 came close to him and looked hard into his face. "Tell the truth, Dave," she said.

"Looks like a bullet hole to me," said one man.

"Dave, whut yuh do wid the gun?" his mother asked.

The crowd surged in, looking at him. He jammed his hands into his pockets, shook his head slowly from left to right, and backed away. His eyes were wide and painful.

"Did he hava gun?" asked Jim Hawkins.

"By Gawd, Ah tol yuh tha wuz a gun wound," said a man, slapping his thigh. 160

His father caught his shoulders and shook him till his teeth rattled.

"Tell whut happened, yuh rascal! Tell whut. . . ."

Dave looked at Jenny's stiff legs and began to cry.

"Whut yuh do wid tha gun?" his mother asked.

"What wuz he doin wida gun?" his father asked. 165

"Come on and tell the truth," said Hawkins. "Ain't nobody going to hurt you. . . ."

His mother crowded close to him.

"Did yuh shoot tha mule, Dave?"

Dave cried, seeing blurred white and black faces.

"Ahh ddinn gggo tt sshooot hher. . . . Ah ssswear ffo Gawd Ahh ddin. . . . Ah wuz 170 a-tryin t sssee ef the old gggun would sshoot —"

"Where yuh git the gun from?" his father asked.

"Ah got it from Joe, at the sto."

"Where yuh git the money?"

"Ma give it t me."

"He kept worryin me, Bob. Ah had t. Ah tol im t bring the gun right back t me. . . . 175
It was fer yuh, the gun."

"But how yuh happen to shoot that mule?" asked Jim Hawkins.

"Ah wuzn shootin at the mule, Mistah Hawkins. The gun jumped when Ah pulled the trigger. . . . N fo Ah knowed anythin Jenny was there a-bleedin."

Somebody in the crowd laughed. Jim Hawkins walked close to Dave and looked into his face.

"Well, looks like you have bought you a mule, Dave."

"Ah swear fo Gawd, Ah didn go t kill the mule, Mistah Hawkins!" 180

"But you killed her!"

All the crowd was laughing now. They stood on tiptoe and poked heads over one another's shoulders.

"Well, boy, looks like yuh done bought a dead mule! Hahaha!"

"Ain tha ershame."

"Hohohohoho." 185

Dave stood, head down, twisting his feet in the dirt.

"Well, you needn't worry about it, Bob," said Jim Hawkins to Dave's father. "Just let the boy keep on working and pay me two dollars a month."

"Whut yuh wan fer yo mule, Mistah Hawkins?"

Jim Hawkins screwed up his eyes.

"Fifty dollars." 190

"Whut yuh do wid tha gun?" Dave's father demanded.

Dave said nothing.

"Yuh wan me t take a tree n beat yuh till yuh talk!"

"Nawsuh!"

"Whut yuh do wid it?" 195

"Ah throwed it erway."

"Where?"

"Ah . . . Ah throwed it in the creek."

"Waal, c mon home. N firs thing in the mawnin git to tha creek n fin tha gun."

"Yessuh." 200

"Whut yuh pay fer it?"

"Two dollahs."

"Take tha gun n git yo money back n carry it to Mistah Hawkins, yuh hear? N don fergit Ahma lam you black bottom good fer this! Now march yosef on home, suh!"

Dave turned and walked slowly. He heard people laughing. Dave glared, his eyes welling with tears. Hot anger bubbled in him. Then he swallowed and stumbled on.

That night Dave did not sleep. He was glad that he had gotten out of killing the mule 205
so easily, but he was hurt. Something hot seemed to turn over inside him each time

he remembered how they had laughed. He tossed on his bed, feeling his hard pillow. N Pa says he's gonna beat me. . . . He remembered other beatings, and his back quivered. Naw, naw, Ah sho don wan im t beat me tha way no mo. Dam em all! Nobody ever gave him anything. All he did was work. They treat me like a mule, n then they beat me. He gritted his teeth. N Ma had t tell on me.

Well, if he had to, he would take old man Hawkins that two dollars. But that meant selling the gun. And he wanted to keep that gun. Fifty dollars for a dead mule.

He turned over, thinking how he had fired the gun. He had an itch to fire it again. Ef other men kin shoota gun, by Gawd, Ah kin! He was still, listening. Mebbe they all sleepin now. The house was still. He heard the soft breathing of his brother. Yes, now! He would go down and get that gun and see if he could fire it! He eased out of bed and slipped into overalls.

The moon was bright. He ran almost all the way to the edge of the woods. He stumbled over the ground, looking for the spot where he had buried the gun. Yeah, here it is. Like a hungry dog scratching for a bone, he pawed it up. He puffed his black cheeks and blew dirt from the trigger and barrel. He broke it and found four cartridges unshot. He looked around; the fields were filled with silence and moonlight. He clutched the gun stiff and hard in his fingers. But, as soon as he wanted to pull the trigger, he shut his eyes and turned his head. Naw, Ah can't shoot wid mah eyes closed n mah head turned. With effort he held his eyes open; then he squeezed. *Blooooom!* He was stiff, not breathing. The gun was still in his hands. Dammit, he'd done it! He fired again. *Blooooom!* He smiled. *Blooooom! Blooooom! Click, click.* There! It was empty. If anybody could shoot a gun, he could. He put the gun into his hip pocket and started across the fields.

When he reached the top of a ridge he stood straight and proud in the moonlight, looking at Jim Hawkins' big white house, feeling the gun sagging in his pocket. Lawd, ef Ah had just one mo bullet Ah'd taka shot at tha house. Ah'd like t scare ol man Hawkins jusa little. . . . Jusa enough t let im know Dave Saunders is a man.

To his left the road curved, running to the tracks of the Illinois Central. He jerked ²¹⁰ his head, listening. From far off came a faint *hoooof-hoooof; hoooof-hoooof.* . . . He stood rigid. Two dollahs a mont. Les see now. . . . Tha means it'll take bout two years. Shucks! Ah'll be dam!

He started down the road, toward the tracks. Yeah, here she comes! He stood beside the track and held himself stiffly. Here she comes, erroun the ben. . . . C mon, yuh slow poke! C mon! He had his hand on his gun; something quivered in his stomach. Then the train thundered past, the gray and brown box cars rumbling and clinking. He gripped the gun tightly; then he jerked his hand out of his pocket. Ah betcha Bill wouldn't do it! Ah betcha. . . . The cars slid past, steel grinding upon steel. Ahm ridin yuh ternight, so hep me Gawd! He was hot all over. He hesitated just a moment; then he grabbed, pulled atop of a car, and lay flat. He felt his pocket; the gun was still there. Ahead the long rails were glinting in the moonlight, stretching away, away to somewhere, somewhere where he could be a man. . . .

(1940, 1961)

Exploring the Text

1. What do you think Richard Wright's purpose is in this story?
2. What is the point of view in "The Man Who Was Almost a Man"? How does it help Wright achieve his purpose?
3. Why do you think Wright chose to use dialect for Dave's inner monologue and for the story's dialogue? What are some of the effects of that choice?
4. The gun has, of course, a literal meaning in "The Man Who Was Almost a Man," but it also carries symbolic weight. What are some of the gun's symbolic meanings?
5. Look carefully at the paragraphs in which Dave is trying to get his mother to give him money to buy the gun (pars. 76–113). What qualities does he use to convince her? How does that scene develop or extend his characterization?
6. What is the effect on Dave when, near the end of the story, he fires the gun successfully?
7. What does it mean to Dave to be a man? What does it mean to you? Are there similarities?
8. Did you find this story funny? Explain your answer.

Randall Jarrell

Randall Jarrell (1914–1965) was born in Nashville, Tennessee. He earned his BA and MA at Vanderbilt University and taught at Kenyon College. In 1939, he went to teach at the University of Texas. He enlisted in the Army Air Corps in 1942 and served in World War II. He trained as a flying cadet but did not qualify as a pilot; instead, he worked as a celestial navigation tower operator and trainer, spending most of the war in Tucson, Arizona. After the war, he taught at Sarah Lawrence College and the University of North Carolina at Greensboro. Jarrell's fame and influence as a deft and acerbic literary critic is as great as his reputation as a poet.

The Death of the Ball Turret Gunner

"The Death of the Ball Turret Gunner" is from Jarrell's first book, *Little Friend, Little Friend* (1945). It was inspired by his service in the war and is perhaps his most famous poem. Jarrell provided this explanatory note:

> A ball turret was a Plexiglass sphere set into the belly of a B-17 or B-24, and inhabited by two .50 caliber machine guns and one man, a short small man. When this gunner tracked with his machine guns a fighter attacking his bomber from below, he revolved with the turret; hunched upside down in his little sphere. The fighters which attacked him were armed with cannon firing explosive shells. The hose was a steam hose.

From my mother's sleep I fell into the State
And I hunched in its belly till my wet fur froze.
Six miles from earth, loosed from its dream of life,
I woke to black flak and the nightmare fighters.
When I died they washed me out of the turret with a hose.

(1945)

Exploring the Text

1. Who is the speaker in this poem? Describe him as well as you can.
2. Trace the verbs in the "The Death of the Ball Turret Gunner." What kind of pattern do you see? Who is creating the action in each verb? How is the pattern related to the meaning of the poem?
3. What associations do you make with the word "State" (l. 1)?
4. How do the sounds of the words "black flak" (l. 4) function as onomatopoeia — the use of a word that refers to a sound and whose pronunciation mimics that sound? What is their effect?
5. What argument does Randall Jarrell make in "The Death of the Ball Turret Gunner"? How does he support his claim?

HARRY S TRUMAN

Harry S Truman (1884–1972) was the thirty-third president of the United States, serving from 1945 to 1953, a span that included the final years of World War II, the Korean War, and the beginnings of the Cold War. The last president to not hold a college degree, Truman worked as a farmer and a clerk before enlisting in the army to fight in World War I. He rose to the rank of captain, and his remarkable record and leadership skills allowed him to transition into politics upon his return home. Truman served as the U.S. senator from Missouri from 1935 to 1945 and as vice president from January 1945 to April 1945, when President Franklin Delano Roosevelt's death while in office made Truman president.

Statement by the President of the United States

While the conflict in the European theater of operations during World War II had ended with Germany's surrender on May 8, 1945, the war in the Pacific continued. Japan stood strong, ignoring Allied demands for an unconditional surrender made later that summer at the Potsdam Conference. With an invasion of mainland Japan destined to be bloody and drawn out, Truman decided on another strategy. On August 6, 1945, the American bomber *Enola Gay* dropped an atomic bomb, code-named "Little Boy," on the port city of Hiroshima. Nine days later, another atomic bomb would be dropped on Nagasaki. In this speech, Truman announces the bombing of Hiroshima to the nation and to the world.

THE WHITE HOUSE
Washington, D. C.

IMMEDIATE RELEASE

STATEMENT BY THE PRESIDENT OF THE UNITED STATES

Sixteen hours ago an American airplane dropped one bomb on [Hiroshima] and destroyed its usefulness to the enemy. That bomb had more power than 20,000 tons of T.N.T. It had more than two thousand times the blast power of the British "Grand Slam" which is the largest bomb ever yet used in the history of warfare.

The Japanese began the war from the air at Pearl Harbor. They have been repaid many fold. And the end is not yet. With this bomb we have now added a new and revolutionary increase in destruction to supplement the growing power of our armed forces. In their present form these bombs are now in production and even more powerful forms are in development.

It is an atomic bomb. It is a harnessing of the basic power of the universe. The force from which the sun draws its power has been loosed against those who brought war to the Far East.

Before 1939, it was the accepted belief of scientists that it was theoretically possible to release atomic energy. But no one knew any practical method of doing it. By 1942, however, we knew that the Germans were working feverishly to find a way to add atomic energy to the other engines of war with which they hoped to enslave the world. But they failed. We may be grateful to Providence that the Germans got the V-1's and V-2's late and in limited quantities and even more grateful that they did not get the atomic bomb at all.

The battle of the laboratories held fateful risks for us as well as the battles of the air, land and sea, and we have now won the battle of the laboratories as we have won the other battles.

Beginning in 1940, before Pearl Harbor, scientific knowledge useful in war was pooled between the United States and Great Britain, and many priceless helps to our victories have come from that arrangement. Under that general policy the research on the atomic bomb was begun. With American and British scientists working together we entered the race of discovery against the Germans.

The United States had available the large number of scientists of distinction in the many needed areas of knowledge. It had the tremendous industrial and financial resources necessary for the project and they could be devoted to it without undue impairment of other vital war work. In the United States the laboratory work and the production plants, on which a substantial start had already been made, would be out of reach of enemy bombing, while at that time Britain was exposed to constant air attack and was still threatened with the possibility of invasion. For these reasons Prime

Minister Churchill and President Roosevelt agreed that it was wise to carry on the project here. We now have two great plants and many lesser works devoted to the production of atomic power. Employment during peak construction numbered 125,000 and over 65,000 individuals are even now engaged in operating the plants. Many have worked there for two and a half years. Few know what they have been producing. They see great quantities of material going in and they see nothing coming out of these plants, for the physical size of the explosive charge is exceedingly small. We have spent two billion dollars on the greatest scientific gamble in history—and won.

But the greatest marvel is not the size of the enterprise, its secrecy, nor its cost, but the achievement of scientific brains in putting together infinitely complex pieces of knowledge held by many men in different fields of science into a workable plan. And hardly less marvellous has been the capacity of industry to design, and of labor to operate, the machines and methods to do things never done before so that the brainchild of many minds came forth in physical shape and performed as it was supposed to do. Both science and industry worked under the direction of the United States Army, which achieved a unique success in managing so diverse a problem in the advancement of knowledge in an amazingly short time. It is doubtful if such another combination could be got together in the world. What has been done is the greatest achievement of organized science in history. It was done under high pressure and without failure.

We are now prepared to obliterate more rapidly and completely every productive enterprise the Japanese have above ground in any city. We shall destroy their docks, their factories, and their communications. Let there be no mistake; we shall completely destroy Japan's power to make war.

It was to spare the Japanese people from utter destruction that the ultimatum of July 26 was issued at Potsdam. Their leaders promptly rejected that ultimatum. If they do not now accept our terms they may expect a rain of ruin from the air, the like of which has never been seen on this earth. Behind this air attack will follow sea and land forces in such numbers and power as they have not yet seen and with the fighting skill of which they are already well aware. 10

The Secretary of War, who has kept in personal touch with all phases of the project, will immediately make public a statement giving further details.

His statement will give facts concerning the sites at Oak Ridge near Knoxville, Tennessee, and at Richland near Pasco, Washington, and an installation near Santa Fe, New Mexico. Although the workers at the sites have been making materials to be used in producing the greatest destructive force in history they have not themselves been in danger beyond that of many other occupations, for the utmost care has been taken of their safety.

The fact that we can release atomic energy ushers in a new era in man's understanding of nature's forces. Atomic energy may in the future supplement the power that now comes from coal, oil, and falling water, but at present it cannot be produced on a basis to compete with them commercially. Before that comes there must be a long period of intensive research.

It has never been the habit of the scientists of this country or the policy of this Government to withhold from the world scientific knowledge. Normally, therefore, everything about the work with atomic energy would be made public.

But under present circumstances it is not intended to divulge the technical pro-   15
cesses of production or all the military applications, pending further examination of
possible methods of protecting us and the rest of the world from the danger of sudden
destruction.

I shall recommend that the Congress of the United States consider promptly the
establishment of an appropriate commission to control the production and use of atomic
power within the United States. I shall give further consideration and make further
recommendations to the Congress as to how atomic power can become a powerful and
forceful influence towards the maintenance of world peace.

(1945)

Exploring the Text

1. There were several different audiences for this speech. Identify them and explain
   how Harry S Truman appeals to each of them in different sections of the speech.
2. How would you describe the style of Truman's statement?
3. Truman's speech focuses on several different subjects. Trace the path of his focus
   and analyze why you think he might have chosen the order he used.
4. What type of sentence dominates Truman's statement? What is its effect?
5. Look carefully at the adjectives Truman uses. What do they have in common?
   Why might they have been chosen?
6. Do you think the speech inspires confidence? How might a speech on a similar
   topic be different today? Or would it?
7. There has always been tremendous debate about the use of the atomic bomb to
   bring World War II to an end, but Truman defended it and claimed to have no
   regrets about the decision, for which he took full responsibility. What qualities in
   this statement show his resolve? Do you sense any second-guessing or defensive-
   ness? Explain your answer.

 TALKBACK

Jonathan Schell

Jonathan Schell (b. 1943) is an author, educator, and activist known primarily for
advocating against the proliferation of nuclear weapons. He was a staff writer for
the *New Yorker* for twenty years and has written for both *Newsweek* and the
Nation. His most famous book is *The Fate of the Earth* (1982).

from *The Fate of the Earth*

The election of Ronald Reagan in 1980 brought with it a significant shift in foreign
policy toward the Soviet Union, including an end to détente, or the thaw in Cold
War tensions, which had been brokered by President Richard Nixon in 1971, and
a tough new stance focused on bringing down what Reagan would later call the

"Evil Empire." As a result, the threat of nuclear war in the early 1980s was as imminent as it had been at any time since the Cuban missile crisis of 1962. In 1982, Schell wrote a series of three essays for the *New Yorker* magazine entitled "The Fate of the Earth." These essays were later collected in a book of the same name, which was nominated for the Pulitzer Prize, the National Book Award, and the National Book Critics Circle Award. The selection that appears here is from the end of the first essay, subtitled "A Republic of Insects and Grass."

To say that human extinction is a certainty would, of course, be a misrepresentation — just as it would be a misrepresentation to say that extinction can be ruled out. To begin with, we know that a holocaust may not occur at all. If one does occur, the adversaries may not use all their weapons. If they do use all their weapons, the global effects, in the ozone and elsewhere, may be moderate. And if the effects are not moderate but extreme, the ecosphere may prove resilient enough to withstand them without breaking down catastrophically. These are all substantial reasons for supposing that mankind will not be extinguished in a nuclear holocaust, or even that extinction in a holocaust is unlikely, and they tend to calm our fear and to reduce our sense of urgency. Yet at the same time we are compelled to admit that there *may* be a holocaust, that the adversaries *may* use all their weapons, that the global effects, including effects of which we are as yet unaware, *may* be severe, that the ecosphere *may* suffer catastrophic breakdown, and that our species *may* be extinguished. We are left with uncertainty, and are forced to make our decisions in a state of uncertainty. If we wish to act to save our species, we have to muster our resolve in spite of our awareness that the life of the species may not now in fact be jeopardized. On the other hand, if we wish to ignore the peril, we have to admit that we do so in the knowledge that the species may be in danger of imminent self-destruction. When the existence of nuclear weapons was made known, thoughtful people everywhere in the world realized that if the great powers entered into a nuclear-arms race the human species would sooner or later face the possibility of extinction. They also realized that in the absence of international agreements preventing it an arms race would probably occur. They knew that the path of nuclear armament was a dead end for mankind. The discovery of the energy in mass — of "the basic power of the universe" — and of a means by which man could release that energy altered the relationship between man and the source of his life, the earth. In the shadow of this power, the earth became small and the life of the human species doubtful. In that sense, the question of human extinction has been on the political agenda of the world ever since the first nuclear weapon was detonated, and there was no need for the world to build up its present tremendous arsenals before starting to worry about it. At just what point the species crossed, or will have crossed, the boundary between merely having the technical knowledge to destroy itself and actually having the arsenals at hand, ready to be used at any second, is not precisely knowable. But it is clear that at present, with some twenty thousand megatons of nuclear explosive power in existence, and with more being added every day, we have entered into the zone of uncertainty, which is to say the zone of risk of extinction. But the mere risk of extinction has a significance that is categorically different from, and immeasurably greater than, that of any other risk, and as we make our decisions we have to take that significance into account. Up to now, every risk has been contained within the frame of life; extinction would shatter the frame. It represents not the defeat of some purpose but an abyss in which all human purposes would be drowned for all time. We have no right to place the possibility of this limitless, eternal defeat on the same footing as risks that we run in the ordinary conduct of our affairs in our particular transient moment of human history. To employ a mathematical analogy, we can say that although the risk of extinction may be fractional, the stake is, humanly speaking, infinite, and a fraction of infinity is still infinity. In other words, once we learn that a holocaust *might* lead to extinction we have no right to gamble, because if we lose, the game will be over, and neither we nor anyone else will ever get another chance. Therefore, although, scientifically speaking, there is all the difference in the world between the mere possibility that a holocaust will bring about extinction and the certainty of it, morally they are the same, and we have no choice but to address the issue of nuclear weapons as though we knew for a certainty that their use would put an end to our species. In weighing the fate of the earth and, with it, our own fate, we stand before a mystery, and in tampering with the earth we tamper with a mystery. We are in deep ignorance. Our ignorance should dispose us to wonder, our wonder should make us humble, our humility should inspire us to reverence and caution, and our reverence and caution should lead us to act without delay to withdraw the threat we now pose to the earth and to ourselves.

In trying to describe possible consequences of a nuclear holocaust, I have mentioned the limitless complexity of its effects on human society and on the ecosphere — a complexity that sometimes seems to be as great as that of life itself. But if these effects should lead to human extinction, then all the complexity will give way to the utmost simplicity — the simplicity of nothingness. We — the human race — shall cease to be.

(1982)

Exploring the Text

1. How does Jonathan Schell maintain a measured and reasonable tone when the subject is the possibility of the destruction of life on earth? Why do you think he does this?
2. How does Schell appeal to logos in this excerpt?
3. Who do you think is the audience for this piece? How can you tell?
4. Consider the way Schell uses "we" and "I." Do you see a pattern? Why might he have switched from one to the other?
5. Analyze the sentence that ends the first paragraph of this excerpt. How does it deliver its impact? Do you find it convincing? Explain your answer.

Making Connections

1. Compare and contrast the ways that Harry S Truman (p. 1181) and Jonathan Schell (p. 1184) design their arguments. Are any common to both writers? What are the differences? How do the differences serve the purpose of each document?
2. Schell continues to be an ardent campaigner against nuclear weapons. He is a columnist and teacher and mentions Truman in nearly everything he writes, both for Truman's role in the dropping of atomic bombs to end World War II and for his role in trying to ban nuclear weapons worldwide. Imagine a conversation between the two men. On what grounds might they agree? On what issues would they differ?
3. During the Korean War, a war that was, according to Schell, "long, wearying, poorly understood, and publicly disliked," Harry S Truman fired General Douglas MacArthur, who had proposed using nuclear weapons. MacArthur had announced, "There can be no substitute for victory." How does this action square with the Truman who released the statement regarding having used an atomic weapon on Japan? Do you think this theme of what Schell calls "thwarted U.S. greatness" still resonates? Explain your answer.

Conversation

The Influence of Jazz

You might associate jazz with "easy listening" or "old-timey music," or you might play in a jazz band or be an ardent collector of jazz music. Wherever you enter this Conversation, it's important to remember that jazz was one of the most important artistic movements of the twentieth century, beginning in the 1920s in New Orleans, having roots in Africa, and being inspired by tribal drumming, slavery field chants, gospel, ragtime, and the blues. The 1920s are known as the Jazz Age, a term coined by F. Scott Fitzgerald, and jazz's influence spread all over the United States and Europe. Jazz musicians work to find a distinct sound and style through improvisation; thus, every recording — even of the same song — will sound different. In fact, the interplay between the group and the individual soloist is one of the things that makes jazz unique and has led to its extensive influence on visual arts and literature. It's difficult, of course, to talk and write about music without having listened to it. The recommended listening list (p. 1188) provides you with examples of excellent jazz from several periods. Try listening before you begin work on this Conversation, in which we introduce connections among jazz, literature, and art.

Sources

Gerald Early, from *Jazz and the African American Literary Tradition* (2010)
Robert O'Meally, from *Seeing Jazz* (1997)
Langston Hughes, *Jazzonia* (1923)
Stuart Davis, *Swing Landscape* (1938)
William Henry Johnson, *Jitterbugs VI* (1941)
Ralph Ellison, from *Invisible Man* (1952)
Whitney Balliett, *Daddy-O* (1958)
Donald Barthelme, *The King of Jazz* (1958)
Jayne Cortez, *Jazz Fan Looks Back* (2002)
Michael Segell, from *The Devil's Horn* (2005)
Evelyn Toynton, from *Jackson Pollock* (2012)

Recommended Listening

What Is Jazz?

These pieces illustrate jazz improvisation in a range of popular songs. You'll recognize the melodies. Listen to what else is going on.

> Charlie Parker (alto saxophone) and Kenny Dorham (trumpet), "White Christmas"
> Lester Young (tenor saxophone), "I Got Rhythm"
> Dizzy Gillespie (trumpet), "Dizzy Atmosphere"
> Ethan Iverson (piano) and David King (drums), "Heart of Glass"

Origins

These are some of the examples of the music from New Orleans that came to be called jazz.

> King Oliver (cornet), "Weather Bird Rag"
> Louis Armstrong (trumpet), "West End Blues"

From Hot to Cool

In the early days, jazz, with its thumping rhythm, was said to be "hot." Later, jazz was played in a more relaxed way, and the musicians who played it came to be called "cool."

> Count Basie (piano) with Carl Smith (trumpet) and Lester Young (tenor saxophone), "Oh Lady Be Good"
> Billie Holiday (vocals), "Now They Call It Swing"

Big Bands = Pure Power

Fifteen musicians, eight of them brass, big drum set. Need we say more?

Count Basie Orchestra, "Jumpin' at the Woodside"
Duke Ellington Orchestra and Paul Gonsalves (tenor saxophone),
    "Diminuendo in Blue and Crescendo in Blue"

Modern Voices

These musicians moved away from recognizable melodies into something more abstract: original music that came to be known as bebop and hard bop.

Charlie Parker (alto saxophone) and Dizzy Gillespie (trumpet), "KoKo"
Miles Davis (trumpet) and John Coltrane (tenor saxophone), "If I Were a Bell"
Thelonious Monk (piano) and Charlie Rouse (tenor saxophone), "Hackensack"
Grant Green (guitar), "Oleo"
Clifford Brown (trumpet) with Richie Powell (piano) and Max Roach (drums),
    "Land's End"
Sonny Clark (piano) and Ike Quebec (tenor saxophone), "Deep in a Dream"

Jazz Now

A sampling of today's jazz artists.

Jason Moran (piano), "You've Got to Be Modernistic"
Robert Glasper (piano), "Smells Like Teen Spirit"
Miquel Zenón (alto saxophone), "Esta Plena"
Esperanza Spalding (vocals, bass), "I Know You Know"
Greg Osby (saxophone), "Mob Job"

from *Jazz and the African American Literary Tradition*

Gerald Early

> The following introduction to jazz was written by Gerald Early (b. 1952) for the Web site of the National Humanities Center. Early is a professor at Washington University in St. Louis and the author of many books of cultural criticism, including *The Culture of Bruising: Essays on Prizefighting, Literature, and Modern American Culture*, which won the National Book Critics Circle Award for criticism. Early won a Grammy for Best Album Notes for the collection *Rhapsodies in Black: Music and Words from the Harlem Renaissance.*

Both blacks and whites (as well as Latinos) in the United States performed jazz and the audience was diverse, although in large measure now, the audience for this music is mostly white. Historically, jazz was largely the creation of black Americans as they have figured disproportionately among the major innovators of this musical expression. This has created two forms of tensions within jazz: that whites have not been given sufficient credit for their contributions to this art which has had white participation since its earliest days; and, second, between black performers and the whites who mostly constituted the critics, writers, venue and record company owners who described, analyzed, promoted, publicized, recorded, and distributed this music. This latter tension was especially felt during the 1950s and 1960s, when racial discord in the United States was more pronounced because of the civil rights movement, the violence it spawned, and the intensely politicized battle over the re-definition of race and the end of white hegemony in the United States and around the colonized world at the time.

But jazz was more than just music; at the height of its influence, jazz was a cultural movement, particularly influencing the young in dress, language, and attitude. It was, in this respect, a prototype for both rock and roll and hip hop because it was so viscerally hated by the bourgeoisie and the musical establishment of the day. Jazz was associated with interracial sex (many jazz nightclubs were open to patrons of any race) and with illegal drugs, in the early days, marijuana, and during the 1950s, with heroin. Visual artists and writers were frequently inspired by jazz, many thinking its sense of spontaneity, its dissonance, its anti-bourgeois attitude embodied compelling aspects of modernism. Jazz deeply influenced artists such as Romare Bearden and Jackson Pollock. Many filmmakers, both in the United States and Europe — from the 1930s through the 1960s — used jazz in either nightclub scenes, as source music, or as part of the musical score in films and animated features. Jazz was used extensively in film noir and crime movies, and occasionally in psychological dramas.

Jazz's roots are in the city: New Orleans, Chicago, New York, Kansas City, Los Angeles, Philadelphia, and Detroit have at various times been major incubators for jazz. Jazz has always been an urban music, tied to urban nightlife, Prohibition, vice zones, dance halls, inner city neighborhoods, and concert stages. Its history coincides not only with the urbanization of America itself but particularly with the urbanization of African Americans, dating from their movement from the South starting around the beginning of World War I when job opportunities in industry opened up for them.

Jazz broke on the scene at the same time as the arrival of the New Negro Renaissance, also known as the Harlem Renaissance, a period covering from 1919 to 1939. This period in African American life featured a self-conscious attempt by black leaders like W. E. B. Du Bois, James Weldon Johnson, Charles S. Johnson, and Alain Locke to create a school of black literature because they firmly believed that in order for blacks to achieve greatness as a people, they had to produce great art. But it must be remembered that this period was not just about art: important black political leaders were spawned during the Renaissance including black nationalist Marcus Garvey and his Universal Negro Improvement Association, A. Philip Randolph, an agitating socialist who became the head of the Pullman Porters union, and Du Bois himself who, through his editorship of *The Crisis*, the magazine of the National Association for the Advancement of Colored People, continued to push for civil rights and a form of Pan Africanism that was antagonistic to Garvey's.

The African American response to jazz during this era was mixed. For many middle class, educated blacks, jazz was considered low class, secular (the devil's music), played in dives and joints that morally disfigured black communities. The only black writer of the Renaissance who was truly taken with jazz was Langston Hughes (1902–1967), who, during the course of his career, not only wrote many poems about it but also on occasion read his poems against a jazz backdrop, even recording with bassist Charles Mingus, a creative partnership that Mingus found unsatisfying. Frank Marshall Davis (1905–1987), a poet and journalist from Chicago, also voiced a fondness for jazz in his writing. Jazz figured in two Claude McKay (1889–1948) novels: *Home to Harlem* (1928) and *Banjo* (1929), which is about a roving seaman who is also a musician, a banjo player, an instrument still played by African Americans at the time and frequently featured in small jazz bands. Considering the impact of jazz, it is surprising how little impact the music had on African American letters in the 1920s and 1930s.

Jazz became much more prominent in black letters after World War II, when the music became much more self-consciously an "art" music designed for listening rather than for dancing. Many consider Ralph Ellison's monumental novel, *Invisible Man* (1952), winner of the National Book Award, to be one of the most successful "jazz" novels ever written, although the book is not about a musician and music does not figure in it a great deal. Ellison himself studied both composition and trumpet as a student in his hometown of Oklahoma City and at Tuskegee Institute, where, in fact, he majored in music. So, unlike most black writers, Ellison actually knew music technically. He also felt that music was central to understanding race in America: "The music, the dances that Americans do are greatly determined by Negro American style, by a Negro American sense of elegance, by an American Negro sense of what the American experience should be, by what Negroes feel about how an American should move, should express himself." But he also understood music, black music particularly, as something equally metaphorical, historical, and cultural. This is evident in his essays on jazz such as "Living with Music," "The Charlie Christian Story," and "On Bird, Bird-Watching and Jazz" that were collected for his 1964 volume of essays, *Shadow and Act*.

Louis Armstrong's recording of "What Did I Do (To Be So Black and Blue)" figures significantly in the beginning of *Invisible Man* and is, in some ways, one of the major themes of the novel; the other being how the Negro is a central figure and actor in American cultural life, that the black American is indeed American in a vital sense. The scene where the protagonist listens to Armstrong sing this song conveys this symbolically as he eats vanilla ice cream (white) drenched in sloe gin (red) while the blues play on his phonograph. This scene also emphasizes how significant the creation of African American art is to Ellison's act of creating his novel.

But generally most critics think of the novel as jazz-like in its experimental structure, the sense of improvisation that the prose of the novel suggests, particularly the increasing improvisational nature of the Invisible Man's speeches, the slightly weird, off-kilter way that the characters relate to one another and to the narrative itself. Was the entire novel the narrator's hallucination? The novel certainly suggests that jazz is a part of a larger tapestry of black creativity, founded in black folk life, including black speech and sermonizing, black styles of dress, and black eating habits. And this thread of black creativity has had largely a liberating effect on American life even as it, ironically, represents a form of discipline on the part of its inventors.

Other novels dealing directly with the lives of jazz musicians that appeared a few years after *Invisible Man* were John A. Williams's *Night Song* (1961), based loosely on the life of saxophonist Charlie Parker (in 1967 a film version was made entitled *Sweet Love, Bitter*, starring Dick Gregory), and William Melvin Kelley's *A Drop of Patience* (1965), both novels prominently feature interracial romances between black male musicians and white women. Poet and painter Ted Joans (1928–2003) also arrived on the scene at this time, achieving notoriety as a graffiti artist spray-painting "Bird Lives" on city walls immediately after the death of Charlie Parker in 1955, he spent his entire career writing poems about jazz or that imitated jazz playing. His most famous jazz poem is "Jazz Is My Religion." In this brief excerpt, devotion to a pure, non-commercial jazz is seen as a form of piety, the purity of the commitment matching the purity of the art, a common feeling among many jazz fans and musicians of the post–World War II era:

> Jazz is my religion and it alone do I dig the jazz
> Clubs are my houses of worship and sometimes the
> Concert halls but some holy places are too commercial
> like churches) so I don't dig the sermons there

Also emerging at the same time as Joans was Beat poet Bob Kaufman (1925–1986), whose poetry was often improvised on the spot, frequently not written down, in much the spirit of the jazz musician. This excerpt from "Crootey Songo," one of his most famous poems, shows how he fashioned the words to resemble or imitate a scat singer's or a saxophonist's improvisation and also to suggest a distinct language or linguistic system, not unlike the speech of the jazz hipster:

> DERRAT SLEGELATIONS FLO GOOF BABER,
> SCRASH SHO DUBIES WAGO WAILO WAILO
> GEED BOP NAVA GLIED, NAVA GLIED NAVA,
> SPLEERIEDER, HUYEDIST, HEDACAZ, AX ---, O, O.

The 1960s was the era of the Black Arts Movement, when younger black writers, fired by both Black Nationalism and Marxism, wrote passionately for race solidarity and denounced not only racism but virtually everything white. Many of these writers were poets and a good many jazz poems were written in homage to specific jazz artists, especially saxophonist John Coltrane, who was probably the most popular jazz musician among the black intelligentsia at this time, or in imitation of the flow and spontaneity of jazz. This was probably the last time in American society when a significant portion of young people were still taken by jazz, in part, because it was now an art music with intellectual and spiritual pretensions. Unlike rhythm and blues or 1960s soul music, jazz at this time, seemed a music that took itself seriously, and was not merely a diversion, and jazz was, in good measure, passionately anti-commercial. Poet, playwright, and essayist, former Beat Amiri Baraka (LeRoi Jones) was the leader of this school of writing, a long-time jazz aficionado, who began his jazz writing career providing notes for jazz albums. Baraka produced an important study of black music entitled *Blues People* (1963), which is partly about jazz. His collection of essays, *Black Music* (1967), is devoted almost entirely to avant-garde jazz and was instrumental in introducing a young audience to this music. Baraka produced a number of noted jazz poems including "AM/Trak," a poem for John Coltrane, and "Pres Spoke in a Language," for saxophonist Lester Young. Other noted Black Arts Movement poets who wrote jazz poetry include Etheridge Knight, Sonia Sanchez, and Haki Madhubuti (Don L. Lee). Other African American poets of the 1960s and 1970s who were known for writing jazz poetry but were not directly associated with the Black Arts Movement were Michael S. Harper, Quincy Troupe, and Al Young.

Among the black writers on the scene today, essayist and novelist Stanley Crouch, poet and fiction writer Nathaniel Mackey, and poet Yusef Komunyakaa are the most associated with jazz, a music whose presence and influence has diminished over the last 35 years, especially among young people. Crouch has written many first-rate essays about jazz and is considered to be the nation's leading jazz critic; in addition, his novel, *Don't the Moon Look Lonesome* (2000), about a young white jazz singer and her African American saxophonist husband, offers the reader an insider's view not only of the jazz world but of the intricacies of music-making from the point of view of a professional musician. The book, in some ways like *Invisible Man*, is built around several speeches or speech-acts delivered or performed by various characters, lessons in creative improvisation and creative narrative that suggest music, which intensifies the book's extraordinary jazz sensibility. Komunyakaa, a Pulitzer Prize winner, has not only written a number of jazz poems but also co-edited with Sascha Feinstein *The Jazz Poetry Anthology* (1991) and *The Second Set: The Jazz Poetry Anthology* (1996). Mackey, an avant gardist, editor of the magazine *Hambone*, and radio DJ, has written a number of jazz poems. Indeed, jazz particularly and music in general is the main inspiration of his writing. He has also written four novels as part of a series about a fictional Los Angeles musical collective called *The Mystic Horns*.

(2010)

Questions

1. How does Gerald Early describe the reaction of the African American middle class to the early days of jazz music? What was the basis of their view? Have things changed? Explain why or why not.
2. When and why does Early see a change in the relationship between jazz and literature — what he calls "black letters" (par. 6)? What changes in the music led to changes in that relationship?
3. What does Early see as some of the social effects of jazz music?

from *Seeing Jazz*

ROBERT O'MEALLY

> In the introduction to his book *Seeing Jazz* (1997), a collection of works of art and
> literature inspired by jazz, professor of American literature and director of the Jazz
> Study Group at Columbia University Robert O'Meally discusses what he calls the
> three definitive aspects of jazz — rhythm, improvisation, and call and response — pro-
> viding examples of artists and writers who have captured those elements in their
> work.

Rhythm

Examples of *rhythm* veer toward the mystical: the first thunders that drummed the
world into being, the dance of the spheres and of the sea, the ebb and flow of desire and
procreation, the cadence of blood through human veins. Jazz music's rhythms echo
these primal sounds along with those of its origins as an American music owing debts
to Europe, Asia, Native America, and Africa — especially Africa, where the music's
polyrhythmic character and drum and dance-beat attitudes found their beginnings.

Jazz crystallized at the turn of the 19th to the 20th century in the black communities of the United States, and if we listen closely as Sidney Bechet advises, we hear its
history deeply drumming. We hear spirituals, blues, vendor's cries, marching bands,
street corner idlers telling lies. We hear the sound of trains — wheels on tracks, whistles,
brakes, conductors' calls, easy (and uneasy) riders. In the music of Mary Lou Williams,
for example, we hear modern city rhythms — steady and winging in one instance,
barbwire jagged and discontinuous in the next.

The rhythms of jazz have also inspired poets and visual artists. Both depict the
drama of jazz players in action. Both accept the harder task of capturing in line and
image the feeling and the meaning of the music. Both *see* jazz and make their audiences see it, too.

But how does one *see* jazz in this sense? How does one *write* or *draw* the rhythms
of this music? Writers like Toni Morrison, Ntozake Shange, Amiri Baraka, Albert
Murray, Michael Harper, and Rita Dove (just to name some leaders in the literary jazz
aesthetic) not only tell the stories of jazz characters but pace their lines to approximate
the dance-beat cadences and other rhythmic features of jazz music. Through playfully
syncopated repetitions, their words perform a jazz dance on the page. No wonder
Langston Hughes specified that one of his books, *Ask Your Mama*, be read aloud to
jazz accompaniment; the words for him were solo notes sounded and scored in a jazz-
rhythm pattern.

Through much of the century, visual artists literally have drawn jazz musicians,   5
dancers, instruments, and sheet music. Henri Matisse, Piet Mondrian, and Jean Dubuffet
make jazz music sound through their paintings, make us *see* the music. These and many
others have created visual jazz compositions through their manipulation of *lines, figures,
tones, structures, colors,* and *rhythms.* Note how the language of aesthetics overlaps
from art form to art form. In some sense, do not all artists — whether dancers or
architects, sculptors or poets — desire that their works have rhythm?

In visual art, a jazz rhythm may be visible in repeated images or human figures (with variations from image to image). Thus do the artists follow jazz's impulse to play 4/4 along with 3/4 or 6/8, to mirror jazz's complexly swinging, polyrhythmic character. Like writers, some visual artists divide their work into sections that approximate the structures of jazz: the A section swinging into the B section and back to A before onto C (the *vamp, chorus, riff, solo space, outchorus*, etc.) with rhythm always at the base. Stuart Davis and Romare Bearden describe the effort to achieve a sense of the *jazz interval* in their works, the *skip tones, jump spaces*, and silences in anticipation of the next sound. Others achieve a percussive sense of color — jazz drum songs for the eye.

Perhaps most profoundly, writers and visual artists who project jazz rhythms into their art express a jazz timekeeper's bass-clef sense of life. The feeling, as Ralph Ellison once put it, that as blues-beset as life may be . . . the real secret is somehow to make life *swing*, to survive by staying in the groove.

Improvisation

The word *improvisation* derives from the Latin *im + provisus*, meaning "not provided" or "not foreseen." In some sense, all artistic creation depends on the ability to improvise, to extemporize an unscripted drama, to blow a note not heard before, to fill the blank canvas of the moment. But in the making of jazz music, improvisation is a definitive hallmark, a *sine qua non*: a something without which, *not*. Jazz is substantially a performer's art where any charts or notations are provisional guideposts, notes indicating a work's general direction but never its final lines or last word. It is a music in the oral tradition, one in which a composer/arranger's latest changes may be shouted out during on-stage performance and where the performer may introduce a shift in direction while playing, in the unforeseen moment of jazz creation.

Jazz's improvised character is balanced with the fact that it is never a free-for-all; it has both an improvised freshness as well as a composer/arranger's sense of completeness and finish. Duke Ellington told his band to plan the notes as written but also "to keep some dirt in there, somewhere." In other words, even when Ellington's band played pieces with no solo spaces indicated, he wanted his players to keep the made-up-on-the-spot dimension, something the score expected but did not ask for explicitly, something of the performers' improvised own, some "dirt."

At their best, jazz compositions sound like frozen improvisations, just as solos by such jazz artists as Thelonious Monk and Miles Davis sound like liquid compositions. The jazz improvisor's solo statement not only tells the soloist's own story . . . but must complement the composer/arranger's overall conceptions. In other words, true jazz musicians are co-composers of every work they play. The audience delights just as much in a particular composition as in a particular band's or player's treatment of it on a given day.

All of which has implications and challenges for the other arts. . . . Romare Bearden insisted that, like a jazz soloist, he played with the possibilities within the framework of his conception: he soloed, he improvised. Jean-Michel Basquiat, Alexis De Boeck, and others gave their work a swingingly improvised dimension. They kept "some dirt in there, somewhere," too.

This in-the-moment quality is most obvious in the work of jazz photographers like William Claxton, Herman Leonard, and Anthem Barboza. Like jazz players, jazz photographers must be so well trained that they can see an image, have an idea, and execute instantly. As Ornette Coleman advises, they "forget about the changes in key and just play." And when it comes to jazz art (musical, literary, or visual) the ability to play is the thing. Technique, however painfully hard earned, is taken for granted and "forgotten." When the bandleader points to you, can you create a composition on the spot? With little or nothing formally provided, are you composed? Can you improvise? Can you play?

Call and Response

Call and response refers to the Sunday service: "Say 'Amen' somebody"—"AMEN!" This interaction between preachers and congregations all over black America has become an integral feature of cultural expression in the United States. Born in West and Central Africa, where one experiences it in exchanges among singers and instrumentalists (as well as dancers and sculptors), in the U.S. this pattern occurs in church songs and sermons and also in word songs, play songs (such as "Little Sally Walker"), blues, rags, and in jazz. You say something; I say something back.

Call and response in jazz may consist of a two-part song within the single self—a dialogue between the pianist's right hand and the left; an instrumentalist/singer's exchange between the voice and the accompanying *box* or *axe*.

Jazz call and response also identifies complicated exchanges between a single   15
voice and other voices: soloist and the chorus of other players; soloist and the congregation of listeners and dancers. These conversations in the language of jazz may be friendly or exhortative in the mode of the preacher and the amening congregation. They may be mutual praise songs or friendly games of leap frog.

They may also involve knock-down competitions, challenges, games of innuendo, ritual insult, mockery. Sometimes signifying contests (also called "cutting contests") involve big-mouthing and virtuoso sounding off. Dizzy Gillespie and Roy Eldridge were fearsome cutting contestants because, while they loved to whisper and pray through their horns, they also knew how to lie, wrangle, cuss an opponent down and, if need be, out. Call and response could be sweet, call and response could be rough.

It is a fascinating phenomenon that the call and response circle in jazz often widens to include dancers and listeners who are not dancing, but whose rapt attention and well-timed foot tapping become part of the total performance. In our (post-) modern world, jazz listeners respond to musicians' calls sent by radio or record (and C.D.) players. The hearer's response to jazz music may be to think things over yet again; the response may be to push back the furniture and dance or to turn the lights down low and have a very private party. Like jazz improvisers who transform every composition they play, listeners add their own sweet or bitter notes to the music and make it their own.

To the jazz musician, the "call" of jazz may come from an almost indescribably subtle attitude of a dancer. It may come from the example of Louis Armstrong, sounding like a century-full of music buzz-toned through the barrel of a single magic horn.

Visual and literary artists are parties to this dynamic process of jazz calling and responding. For not only do they respond to the work of people in their own fields (novelist Ellison to novelist Dostoevski, muralist James Phillips to the muralists of Mexico), they also call and respond to jazz music and its makers. This book's sections on rhythm and improvisation tell part of the story of how this process works. A jazz rhythm by Max Roach (a call) becomes a rhythm of color in a Roland Jean collage (a response); an improvisation by Charlie Parker becomes an improvised line in a Norman Lewis sketch. Writers hear the call of the music and respond with words that swing and chapters that take a jazz shape. Call, countercall; call, recall; call, response.

Perhaps above all, these writers and visual artists respond to jazz music's beauti- 20 ful call for unequivocal excellence. "If I could write a poem as perfect as Parker's solo or paint a picture as evocative as Ellington's 'Mood Indigo,'" these works seem to say, "well then maybe, wherever they are, Bird and Duke would respond to me across the distances of space and time, would give to me a full-throated, full-spirited *amen*."

(1997)

Questions

1. According to Robert O'Meally, how do artists and writers depict rhythm? What are the differences in the ways visual artists and writers depict it? What are the similarities?
2. Put O'Meally's definitions of improvisation in your own words. Where might you see improvisation other than in music? Do you use it in your own work — or play? Explain.
3. What are some contemporary examples of call and response?

Jazzonia

Langston Hughes

This poem was originally published in 1923 with several other of Hughes's early poems in the *Crisis*, the official publication of the National Association for the Advancement of Colored People (NAACP). For more biographical information on Langston Hughes, see page 1100.

Oh, silver tree!
Oh, shining rivers of the soul!

In a Harlem cabaret
Six long-headed jazzers play.
A dancing girl whose eyes are bold   5
Lifts high a dress of silken gold.

Oh, singing tree!
Oh, shining rivers of the soul!

Were Eve's eyes
In the first garden   10
Just a bit too bold?
Was Cleopatra gorgeous
In a gown of gold?

Oh, shining tree!
Oh, silver rivers of the soul!   15

In a whirling cabaret
Six long-headed jazzers play.

(1923)

Questions

1. What associations does Langston Hughes make with jazz in this poem? Consider the words as well as the rhythm and syntax in the poem.
2. What do the women mentioned in the poem — the dancing girl, Eve, and Cleopatra — have in common? What does that common ground say about jazz?
3. What does it mean that Hughes moves the setting of the poem from "In a Harlem cabaret" (l. 3) to "In a whirling cabaret" (l. 16)?

Swing Landscape

STUART DAVIS

Stuart Davis (1892–1964) began his career painting realistic scenes of jazz saloons, but by the 1930s, as recorded music brought jazz to the masses, Davis's work reflected not just the music but also the technological communication of jazz through movies and the radio. This painting was commissioned by the Federal Arts Project, part of President Franklin D. Roosevelt's Works Progress Administration, which provided artists, musicians, and actors with employment during the Great Depression. It depicts the seaport of Gloucester, Massachusetts, transforming it into what looks like a jazz-inspired billboard.

Questions

1. What is recognizable in this painting? What is abstract? In what ways does this painting disorient the viewer?
2. What elements of urban life does Stuart Davis depict in what is supposed to be a quaint seaport scene?

Museum purchase with funds from the Hope fund Indiana University Art Museum, 42.1. Photograph by: Michael Cavanagh and Kevin Montague.

STUART DAVIS, *SWING LANDSCAPE*, 1938, 86¾" × 172⅞", OIL ON CANVAS, INDIANA UNIVERSITY ART MUSEUM, BLOOMINGTON.
(See color insert, Image 38.)

3. How does *Swing Landscape* visually depict the rhythm and syncopation (the shifting of a musical accent by stressing a normally unstressed beat) of jazz? Look carefully at the way Davis uses repetition and the juxtaposition of geometric shapes and colors.

Jitterbugs VI

WILLIAM HENRY JOHNSON

William Henry Johnson (1901–1970) was an African American painter who was born in South Carolina and moved to New York when he was seventeen. He studied in New York and on Cape Cod before moving to France in 1926 to study art. Returning to the United States in 1946, Johnson was assigned by the Works Progress Administration to teach at the Harlem Community Art Center.

Questions

1. The jitterbug is a dance — very fast, very complex — that came out of Harlem and was part of the swing craze of the late 1930s and 1940s. How does William Henry Johnson's print re-create the speed and energy of the jitterbug?
2. What is the effect of the hard angles in the painting? What is the effect of their repetition?

Whitney Museum of American Art

WILLIAM HENRY JOHNSON, *JITTERBUGS VI*, C. 1941, HAND-COLORED SCREENPRINT, 17 1/16" × 11 1/4",
WHITNEY MUSEUM OF AMERICAN ART, NEW YORK.
(See color insert, Image 39.)

3. What elements of graphic art, or even pop art (art that depicts scenes of everyday
   life using techniques of commercial art and illustration), do you see in this
   work?

from *Invisible Man*

RALPH ELLISON

Ralph Waldo Ellison (1914–1994) was an African American novelist and scholar born in Oklahoma City, Oklahoma. In 1933, he enrolled at the Tuskegee Institute in Alabama on a scholarship to study music, and after his third year he moved to New York City to study sculpture and photography. There he met novelist Richard Wright in 1937 and soon shifted his focus to writing, publishing short stories, book reviews, and articles in newspapers and magazines, such as *New Challenge* and *New Masses*. In 1952, Ellison published his first and most famous novel, *Invisible Man*, which won the National Book Award in 1953. Considered one of the great American novels, *Invisible Man* is about a young black man's search for self-knowledge; its central metaphor is the invisibility of African Americans in white society. The following selection is from the novel's prologue.

Now I have one radio-phonograph; I plan to have five. There is a certain acoustical deadness in my hole, and when I have music I want to feel its vibration, not only with my ear but with my whole body. I'd like to hear five recordings of Louis Armstrong playing and singing "What Did I Do to Be so Black and Blue" — all at the same time. Sometimes now I listen to Louis while I have my favorite dessert of vanilla ice cream and sloe gin. I pour the red liquid over the white mound, watching it glisten and the vapor rising as Louis bends that military instrument into a beam of lyrical sound. Perhaps I like Louis Armstrong because he's made poetry out of being invisible. I think it must be because he's unaware that he is invisible. And my own grasp of invisibility aids me to understand his music. Once when I asked for a cigarette, some jokers gave me a reefer, which I lighted when I got home and sat listening to my phonograph. It was a strange evening. Invisibility, let me explain, gives one a slightly different sense of time, you're never quite on the beat. Sometimes you're ahead and sometimes behind. Instead of the swift and imperceptible flowing of time, you are aware of its nodes, those points where time stands still or from which it leaps ahead. And you slip into the breaks and look around. That's what you hear vaguely in Louis' music.

Once I saw a prizefighter boxing a yokel. The fighter was swift and amazingly scientific. His body was one violent flow of rapid rhythmic action. He hit the yokel a hundred times while the yokel held up his arms in stunned surprise. But suddenly the yokel, rolling about in the gale of boxing gloves, struck one blow and knocked science, speed and footwork as cold as a well-digger's posterior. The smart money hit the canvas. The long shot got the nod. The yokel had simply stepped inside of his opponent's sense of time. So under the spell of the reefer I discovered a new analytical way of listening to music. The unheard sounds came through, and each melodic line existed of itself, stood out clearly from all the rest, said its piece, and waited patiently for the other voices to speak.

(1952)

Questions

1. In paragraph 7 of the excerpt from Gerald Early's *Jazz and the African American Literary Tradition* (p. 1189), Early mentions that the symbolic aspect of this excerpt (the black man eating white ice cream with red syrup on it) as well as the music he's listening to ("What Did I Do to Be So Black and Blue?") emphasizes the difficult process of making art, especially for a black man. How does the anecdote about the prizefighter and the yokel (par. 2) expand on that theme?

2. What aspects of the three elements of jazz — rhythm, improvisation, call and response — that Robert O'Meally (p. 1194) identifies are present in Ellison's excerpt?

3. What does the narrator of *Invisible Man* say about what we might call negative space? How does it connect to what jazz trumpeter Miles Davis once said, "Don't play what's there; play what's not there"?

Daddy-O

WHITNEY BALLIETT

Whitney Balliett (1926–2007) was the jazz critic of the *New Yorker* magazine from 1957 to 2001. This piece appeared in the *New Yorker* in 1958.

Kenneth Rexroth, the fifty-two-year-old poet, translator (modern Greek, ancient Greek, Latin, Spanish, Chinese, Japanese), anthologist, painter (abstract), and critic (literary, music), who has also been a hobo, range cook, horse wrangler, cab driver, and sheepherder, was born in South Bend, Indiana, but has lived for much of the past thirty years in San Francisco, where he has become a leader of that city's ongoing poetry revival. He has also helped found a poetry-read-to-jazz movement there, and the other day he opened in New York at the Five Spot Café, a Saroyan bar-and-grill at the south end of Cooper Square, for a couple of weeks of readings with the Pepper Adams Quintet. I had lunch with him on the day of his début, and found him a nervous, medium-sized man with short gray hair, a mustache, a towering forehead, and eyes that slope like a sharply peaked roof when his face is in repose. He has a voice that is apt to move in mid-syllable from a whisper to a roar, and he often erupts into machine-gun laughter, delivered in a low monotone. He was dressed in a gray-black suit, a transparent white silk shirt, and a blue-and-white polka-dot string tie. After he had ordered oysters, shad roe, vegetables ("Waiter, I don't care *which* vegetables, so long as they're *fresh*"), salad, and dark beer, he looked down at the table and said, "I've been supporting myself since I was thirteen. I've only had five years of school. In fact, I've *lived* in the kind of world that Jack Kerouac *imagines* he has lived in." His eyes shot up, and he sprayed a dozen rounds of laughter about the room. "A good many people, including the musicians I work with, think of jazz poetry at first as something only a weedhead would do. Not long ago, I worked with a symphony bassist, and he told me afterward, 'You know, I was really scared, but it's been one of the greatest musical experiences of my life.' I didn't start this thing. Renegade monks were doing it in the Middle Ages. Charles Cros, a nineteenth-century poet, read his stuff (things like '*Le Hareng Saur*': 'There was a great white wall, bare, bare, bare' — ha-ha-ha-ha-ha-ha) to *bal-musette*[1] bands. There have been countless talking-blues singers in the South. Maxwell Bodenheim did it in the twenties and Langston Hughes in the thirties, and even I did it in the twenties, at the Green Mask, in Chicago, with Frank Melrose, a K.C. pianist. I've been reading poetry to jazz for two years now, starting in The Cellar, in San Francisco, with a quintet. Since then, I've done all of the West Coast, St. Louis, Chicago, Minneapolis. The most important instrument in my accompaniment is the bass. The bass goes right up your leg and sends out the voice. Modern jazz has outgrown everything. The audience can't get into the music without verbal contact. The poetry gives you that, and the jazz gets the poetry out of those seminars taught by aging poets for budding poets in corn-belt colleges. I plan a good deal of the musical accompaniment, which isn't all jazz by any means. I use bits of Satie, Webern, Boccherini. Each musician has a copy of what I'm reciting, with cues and musical notations on it. I read Ruthven Todd, Larry Durrell, Ferlinghetti, and some of my own stuff, including a lot of translations. A friend warned me about New York. 'You've got to be careful, man,' he said. 'They've been having meetings to keep Rexroth out.' Ha-ha-ha-ha-ha-ha-ha!"

Rexroth asked me to stop in at the Five Spot before his first show that night, and I was met there by Ivan Black, a stocky, black-mustached representative of the Five Spot, who ushered me to a table near the bandstand, a raised platform roughly the size of a large window seat. "I've got to go and wake Rexroth up," he told us. "He's sleeping at a friend's, over on Second Avenue. I'll be right back." The Five Spot is long and narrow, with a bar, sheltered by a fringed canopy, running down most of one wall; three gold-colored macelike objects suspended from a maroon ceiling; and the rest of the wall space spattered with posters and programs of various sorts. "He wasn't asleep at all," Black's voice said after a while, in a relieved way, and Rexroth, wearing impenetrable dark glasses, sat down beside me. "These shades protect you in a club," he said. "I've decided they relax you. I read my stuff. You can't do it out of your head. You get swinging, and you don't know what you're talking about."

Rexroth then said it was time to begin. Black excused himself and, while squeezing onto the platform to introduce Rexroth, accidentally brushed a thick sheaf of manuscripts off a wobbly music stand.

"Damn it, Ivan! What are you doing?" Rexroth bellowed as Black backed and filled on the manuscripts.

The manuscripts were replaced, a drum roll crashed out, and Black introduced Rexroth as a horse wrangler and the Daddy-O of the jazz-poetry movement.

5

---

[1]Style of French dance music that became popular in the 1880s. Once played with a musette, an instrument similar to bagpipes, it is now generally played with an accordion. — Eds.

Rexroth got up on the platform, plunged his left hand into his left coat pocket, took as wide a stance as space permitted, stuck his stomach out, and read, in a strong singsong voice, a Ruthven Todd poem; Carl Sandburg's "Mag," accompanied by an Ellington blues; a poem by Pablo Neruda; a poem of his own; and a twelfth-century Chinese poem, accompanied only by the bass, which played long passages between such lines as "But why do the birds all hate me?," "Why do the flowers betray me?," "Why do the peach and cherry blossoms prostrate me?"

(1958)

Questions

1. How does poet Kenneth Rexroth explain the relationship between poetry and jazz?
2. In what ways does Whitney Balliett use elements of jazz in this piece?
3. Rexroth once said, "It is important to get poetry out of the hands of the professors and out of the hands of the squares. If we can get poetry out into the life of the country, it can be creative. Homer, or the guy who recited Beowulf, was show business. We simply want to make poetry part of 'show business.'" Do you think that reading poetry to jazz music is an effective way to "get poetry out into the life of the country"? Explain your answer.
4. Are rap and hip-hop the present-day equivalent to poetry read to music? Why or why not?

The King of Jazz

DONALD BARTHELME

> Donald Barthelme (1931–1989), known especially for his short fiction, grew up in Houston, Texas, and attended college there. He never received a degree, however, and spent much of his time in Houston's jazz clubs. This story was published in the *New Yorker* in 1958.

Well I'm the king of jazz now, thought Hokie Mokie to himself as he oiled the slide on his trombone. Hasn't been a 'bone man been king of jazz for many years. But now that Spicy MacLammermoor, the old king, is dead, I guess I'm it. Maybe I better play a few notes out of this window here, to reassure myself.

"Wow!" said somebody standing on the sidewalk. "Did you hear that?"

"I did," said his companion.

"Can you distinguish our great homemade American jazz performers, each from the other?"

"Used to could."

"Then who was that playing?"

5

"Sounds like Hokie Mokie to me. Those few but perfectly selected notes have the real epiphanic glow."

"The what?"

"The real epiphanic glow, such as is obtained only by artists of the calibre of Hokie Mokie, who's from Pass Christian, Mississippi. He's the king of jazz, now that Spicy MacLammermoor is gone."

Hokie Mokie put his trombone in its trombone case and went to a gig. At the gig 10
everyone fell back before him, bowing.

"Hi Bucky! Hi Zoot! Hi Freddie! Hi George! Hi Thad! Hi Roy! Hi Dexter! Hi Jo! Hi Willie! Hi Greens!"

"What we gonna play, Hokie? You the king of jazz now, you gotta decide."

"How 'bout 'Smoke'?"

"Wow!" everybody said. "Did you hear that? Hokie Mokie can just knock a fella out, just the way he pronounces a word. What a intonation on that boy! God Almighty!"

"I don't want to play 'Smoke,'" somebody said. 15

"Would you repeat that, stranger?"

"I don't want to play 'Smoke.' 'Smoke' is dull. I don't like the changes. I refuse to play 'Smoke.'"

"He refuse to play 'Smoke'! But Hokie Mokie is the king of jazz and he says 'Smoke'!"

"Man, you from outa town or something? What do you mean you refuse to play 'Smoke'? How'd you get on this gig anyhow? Who hired you?"

"I am Hideo Yamaguchi, from Tokyo, Japan." 20

"Oh, you're one of those Japanese cats, eh?"

"Yes I'm the top trombone man in all of Japan."

"Well you're welcome here until we hear you play. Tell me, is the Tennessee Tea Room still the top jazz place in Tokyo?"

"No, the top jazz place in Tokyo is the Square Box now."

"That's nice. O.K., now we gonna play 'Smoke' just like Hokie said. You ready, 25
Hokie? O.K., give you four for nothin'. One! Two! Three! Four!"

The two men who had been standing under Hokie's window had followed him to the club. Now they said:

"Good God!"

"Yes, that's Hokie's famous 'English sunrise' way of playing. Playing with lots of rays coming out of it, some red rays, some blue rays, some green rays, some green stemming from a violet center, some olive stemming from a tan center —"

"That young Japanese fellow is pretty good, too."

"Yes, he is pretty good. And he holds his horn in a peculiar way. That's frequently 30
the mark of a superior player."

"Bent over like that with his head between his knees — good God, he's sensational!"

He's sensational, Hokie thought. Maybe I ought to kill him.

But at that moment somebody came in the door pushing in front of him a four-and-one-half-octave marimba. Yes, it was Fat Man Jones, and he began to play even before he was fully in the door.

"What're we playing?"

"'Billie's Bounce.'" 35

"That's what I thought it was. What're we in?"

"F."

"That's what I thought we were in. Didn't you use to play with Maynard?"

"Yeah I was on that band for a while until I was in the hospital."

"What for?" 40

"I was tired."

"What can we add to Hokie's fantastic playing?"

"How 'bout some rain or stars?"

"Maybe that's presumptuous?"

"Ask him if he'd mind." 45

"You ask him, I'm scared. You don't fool around with the king of jazz. That young Japanese guy's pretty good, too."

"He's sensational."

"You think he's playing in Japanese?"

"Well I don't think it's English."

This trombone's been makin' my neck green for thirty-five years, Hokie thought. 50 How come I got to stand up to yet another challenge, this late in life?

"Well, Hideo—"

"Yes, Mr. Mokie?"

"You did well on both 'Smoke' and 'Billie's Bounce.' You're just about as good as me, I regret to say. In fact, I've decided you're *better* than me. It's a hideous thing to contemplate, but there it is. I have only been the king of jazz for twenty-four hours, but the unforgiving logic of this art demands we bow to Truth, when we hear it."

"Maybe you're mistaken?"

"No, I got ears. I'm not mistaken. Hideo Yamaguchi is the new king of jazz." 55

"You want to be king emeritus?"

"No, I'm just going to fold up my horn and steal away. This gig is yours, Hideo. You can pick the next tune."

"How 'bout 'Cream'?"

"O.K., you heard what Hideo said, it's 'Cream.' You ready, Hideo?"

"Hokie, you don't have to leave. You can play too. Just move a little over to the 60 side there—"

"Thank you, Hideo, that's very gracious of you. I guess I will play a little, since I'm still here. Sotto voce, of course."

"Hideo is wonderful on 'Cream'!"

"Yes, I imagine it's his best tune."

"What's that sound coming in from the side there?"

"Which side?" 65

"The left."

"You mean that sound that sounds like the cutting edge of life? That sounds like polar bears crossing Arctic ice pans? That sounds like a herd of musk ox in full flight? That sounds like male walruses diving to the bottom of the sea? That sounds like fumaroles smoking on the slopes of Mt. Katmai? That sounds like the wild turkey walking through the deep, soft forest? That sounds like beavers chewing trees in an Appalachian marsh? That sounds like an oyster fungus growing on an aspen trunk? That sounds like a mule deer wandering a montane of the Sierra Nevada? That sounds like prairie dogs kissing? That sounds like witchgrass tumbling or a river meandering? That sounds like manatees munching seaweed at Cape Sable? That sounds like coatimundis moving in packs across the face of Oklahoma? That sounds like—"

"Good God, it's Hokie! Even with a cup mute on, he's blowing Hideo right off the stand!"

"Hideo's playing on his knees now! Good God, he's reaching into his belt for a large steel sword— Stop him!"

"Wow! That was the most exciting 'Cream' ever played! Is Hideo all right?" 70

"Yes, somebody is getting him a glass of water."

"You're my man, Hokie! That was the dadblangedest thing I ever saw!"

"You're the king of jazz once again!"

"Hokie Mokie is the most happening thing there is!"

"Yes, Mr. Hokie sir, I have to admit it, you blew me right off the stand. I see I have 75
many years of work and study before me still."

"That's O.K., son. Don't think a thing about it. It happens to the best of us. Or it almost happens to the best of us. Now I want everybody to have a good time because we're gonna play 'Flats.' 'Flats' is next."

"With your permission, sir, I will return to my hotel and pack. I am most grateful for everything I have learned here."

"That's O.K., Hideo. Have a nice day. He-he. Now, 'Flats.'"

(1958)

Questions

1. What elements of jazz appear in this story?
2. What do you think Donald Barthelme is satirizing in this story? How does he do it?
3. Do you find the story funny? Why or why not?

Jazz Fan Looks Back

Jayne Cortez

Jayne Cortez (1934–2012) was a poet and spoken-word performance artist. She lived in Dakar, Senegal, and New York City. In her obituary in the *New York Times*, her work was described as "[m]eant for the ear even more than for the eye, her words combine a hurtling immediacy with an incantatory orality."

I crisscrossed with Monk
Wailed with Bud
Counted every star with Stitt
Sang "Don't Blame Me" with Sarah
Wore a flower like Billie   5
Screamed in the range of Dinah
& scatted "How High the Moon" with Ella Fitzgerald
as she blew roof off the Shrine Auditorium
   Jazz at the Philharmonic

I cut my hair into a permanent tam   10
Made my feet rebellious metronomes
Embedded record needles in paint on paper
Talked bopology talk
Laughed in high-pitched saxophone phrases
Became keeper of every Bird riff   15
every Lester lick
as Hawk melodicized my ear of infatuated tongues
& Blakey drummed militant messages in
soul of my applauding teeth
& Ray hit bass notes to the last love seat in my bones   20
I moved in triple time with Max
Grooved high with Diz
Perdidoed with Pettiford
Flew home with Hamp
Shuffled in Dexter's Deck   25
Squatty-rooed with Peterson
Dreamed a "52nd Street Theme" with Fats
& scatted "Lady Be Good" with Ella Fitzgerald
as she blew roof off the Shrine Auditorium
   Jazz at the Philharmonic   30

(2002)

Questions

1. In "Jazz Fan Looks Back," the speaker names famous jazz musicians: Thelonious
   Monk, Bud Powell, Sonny Stitt, Sarah Vaughan, Dinah Washington, Billie Holiday,
   Ella Fitzgerald, Charlie (Bird) Parker, Lester Young, Coleman Hawkins, Max
   Roach, Dizzy Gillespie, Oscar Pettiford, Lionel Hampton, Dexter Gordon, and Fats
   Navarro. Choose two or three of the musicians in the poem and listen to some of
   their work. What do they have in common? Do you know of jazz musicians whom
   Jayne Cortez does not mention? Why might she have left them out?
2. Try reading this poem aloud. How does the meaning change?

3. Jazz at the Philharmonic was a series of famous concerts that took place at the Philharmonic Auditorium in Los Angeles. What do you think it means that Cortez repeats "Jazz at the Philharmonic" twice? What is she saying about what a jazz fan hears when he or she looks back?
4. What elements of jazz do you find in this poem?

from *The Devil's Horn*

MICHAEL SEGELL

This excerpt comes from Michael Segell's *The Devil's Horn: The Story of the Saxophone from Noisy Novelty to King of Cool*, published in 2005. Segell is an amateur musician and a professional writer and music lover.

When he released *A Love Supreme*, John Coltrane said that "as long as there is some feeling of communication, it isn't necessary that it be understood." But that hasn't deterred modern music psychologists from trying to tease out which performance and acoustical cues most effectively aid that communication. In the past decade, researchers have conducted more than a hundred studies that explore music's ability to evoke in the listener the five "basic" emotions — happiness, sadness, anger, fear, and love/tenderness, which appear in musical scores as, respectively, *festoso, dolente, furloso, amoroso,* and *teneramente* — or the hundreds of subsets of those emotions. Patrik N. Juslin and Petri Laukka, psychologists at Uppsala University in Sweden, have done meta-analyses of studies examining expressive musical cues, including tempo, sound level, timing, intonation, articulation, timbre, vibrato, tone attacks, tone decays, and pauses. Sadness, they have found, is associated with slow tempo, low sound level, legato articulation, small articulation variability, slow tone attacks, and dull timbre. Happiness is associated with fast tempo, high sound level, staccato articulation, large articulation variability, fast tone attacks, and bright timbre. The combination of cues that is most expressive, according to listeners — and very similar to the combination that evokes sadness and tenderness — includes legato articulation, soft spectrum, slow tempo, high sound level, and slow tone attacks. Sounds that mimicked so-called separation calls — sobs, cries, and moans — were the most poignant of all. Some instruments, obviously, are more capable than others of delivering these cues. Arguably, the saxophone, with the sounds of dozens of instruments tucked into its complex wave form, can deliver almost all of them.

For at least one saxophonist, little distinction exists between the expressive cues he issues on the instrument and the weight and meaning of his words. In fact, the poet Robert Pinsky says, when he plays the saxophone — he has played the horn, semi-professionally and recreationally, all his life — he's trying to do the same thing he does when he "fits the words together" in a poem.

"The horn is connected to what I do as a writer because it's on a completely physical scale and an infinite scale," says Pinsky, who was poet laureate of the United

States between 1997 and 2000. "Theoretically, the cone of a saxophone goes on forever, giving the sounds that come from it an infinite quality. But it's given its expression by a human. I try to do something with the vowels and consonants of words that makes them musical — infinite — but the medium is my voice, or anybody's voice who is reading the poem, which means that the medium is inherently on a human scale — on a physical scale, like the saxophone.

"I would trade everything I've written if I could play the saxophone the way I want to. If I could sell my soul and just be tremendous, a monster, I'd be a tenor player. But I can't. I'm not musical enough. The closest I can come to what the saxophone can do is with words."

(2005)

Questions

1. What does Michael Segell think of the capacity for music — in particular the music created by the saxophone — to communicate emotion?
2. Why might Segell have cited John Coltrane, a saxophone player considered by many to be in the forefront of avant-garde jazz, even though he refutes what Coltrane says?
3. What is Segell's purpose in quoting Robert Pinsky, former poet laureate of the United States?

from *Jackson Pollock*

Evelyn Toynton

> Evelyn Toynton's work has appeared in the *Atlantic Monthly*, the *New York Times Book Review*, the *American Scholar*, and other publications. She is the author of *Modern Art*, a novel based on Jackson Pollock and his wife, the painter Lee Krasner. This excerpt is from a biography of Pollock (1912–1956), who is considered one of the great American abstract expressionist painters. He is known for his large canvases, which lay on the floor as he splattered, dripped, and applied paint from above.

The nineteenth-century English aesthete Walter Pater said that "all art constantly aspires to the condition of music. . . . In its ideal, consummate moments, the end is not distinct from the means, the form from the matter, the subject from the expression." Or, as the critic George Steiner has written, "The energy that is music puts us in felt relation to the energy that is life; it puts us in a relation of experienced immediacy with the abstractly and verbally inexpressible, but wholly palpable, primary fact of being."[1] Beginning with the mural he painted for Guggenheim, Pollock's work got closer and closer to the condition of music — specifically, to jazz, the one indubitably, quintessentially American art form, which Pater might not have recognized as music at all.

Image copyright © The Metropolitan Museum of Art. Image source: Art Resource, NY. © 2013 The Pollock-Krasner Foundation/Artists Rights Society (ARS), New York.

Jackson Pollock, *One: Number 31, 1950,* oil and enamel on canvas, 8' 10" × 17' 5⅝", Museum of Modern Art, New York.

The form of the drip paintings emerged as Pollock worked on them; he did not make sketches or work out in his mind beforehand what he intended the finished canvas to look like. Instead, like a jazz musician improvising on a theme, he relied on his instinctive sense of what worked, what the painting itself called for, once the process of making it was under way: "When I am *in* my painting, I am not aware of what I am doing . . . the painting has a life of its own. I try to let it come through."[2]

Also like a jazz musician, he made use of accident and chance, though Pollock, understandably defensive about suspicions of his artistry, was at pains to minimize the role these played in his process: "I *can* control the flow of paint; there is no accident," he said, and "I don't use the accident — 'cause I deny the accident."[3] Yet, as we have seen, he used whatever materials happened to fall on the canvas as he worked, incorporating cigarette ash, cigarette butts, and dead insects into the work at various junctures, as well as the broken glass and sand "and other foreign matter" that he added deliberately.

The freer his paintings became, the more they seemed to tap into some of the same "primitive," preverbal impulses as jazz — to express, like jazz, the workings of the unconscious, not through the use of symbols but directly. Like jazz, they convey a sense of exultation, of urgent, rhapsodic feeling just barely contained — the Nietzschean tension between wildness and form. (It is telling that Nietzsche identified that state of ecstasy and wildness with Dionysus, the god of wine; jazz musicians are more notorious even than Pollock for their use of consciousness-altering substances of various kinds.)

Like jazz, the drip paintings give the impression of freewheeling immediacy and spontaneity — a distinctively American quality — while exhibiting the same high-wire discipline necessary to avoid spinning out of control. Neither Pollock nor a great jazz musician improvises from scratch; there is a huge fund of skill and knowledge,

5

of knowing the moves, that is being drawn on in the act itself. But perhaps the most striking point of resemblance is the way both are governed by rhythm.

A passionate aficionado, Pollock told Krasner that jazz was "the only *other* creative thing happening in the country."[4] But though it is always progressive jazz that his work is likened to — especially the edgy, radically experimental music of Charlie Parker, who like Pollock renewed the art form in which he worked through his own originality and daring — when it came to jazz, Pollock was a conservative. Rather than Parker and bebop, he listened to the more traditional musicians he had first heard when he was young, people like Louis Armstrong and Count Basie and Duke Ellington.

Notes

1. Pater, *The Renaissance*, pp. 95, 98; Steiner, *Real Presences*, p. 196.
2. O'Connor, *Jackson Pollock*, p. 40.
3. Quoted in Karmel, *Jackson Pollock: Interviews, Articles, and Reviews*, pp. 138, 22 (interview with William Wright).
4. O'Meally, *Jazz Cadence of American Culture*, p. 179.

(2012)

Questions

1. How does Evelyn Toynton compare the way Jackson Pollock paints to the way a jazz musician plays? How does she qualify the comparison?
2. Toynton quotes several experts in this selection. Which one do you find most convincing or interesting? Explain your answer.
3. Toynton makes the point that Pollock's work is compared to bebop, the most progressive jazz of his time period, though he liked the music of more traditional jazz artists, such as Louis Armstrong and Duke Ellington. Listen to some of the jazz that came after bebop — free jazz, for example. In what way might that genre have been influenced by Pollock's work?
4. What elements of jazz do you see in Pollock's *One: Number 31, 1950*?

Making Connections

1. Compare and contrast Langston Hughes's "Jazzonia" (p. 1197) and Jayne Cortez's "Jazz Fan Looks Back" (p. 1207). What do they have in common? What separates them? Both are considered jazz poems; do you agree? Explain.

2. Imagine the scene at the poetry reading set to jazz that Whitney Balliett describes in "Daddy-O" (p. 1202). How might it be similar to the scene Donald Barthelme sets in "The King of Jazz" (p. 1204)? What seems genuine in each? What might be pretentious?

3. The poet Robert Pinsky, quoted in Michael Segall's *The Devil's Horn* (p. 1209), said in an interview, "In jazz, as in poetry, there's always the play between what's regular

and what's wild." What might Robert O'Meally (p. 1194) consider to be the "play between what's regular and what's wild" in both poetry and jazz?

4. Looking at the selection from the prologue of *Invisible Man* (p. 1201), try to identify some of the qualities that caused Gerald Early (p. 1189) to consider it the quintessential "'jazz' novel" (par. 6).

5. Compare and contrast William Henry Johnson's *Jitterbuggers VI* (p. 1200) to Stuart Davis's *Swing Landscape* (p. 1199). How do they reflect the changes in jazz music as it moved from the familiar tunes of the American songbook to the abstractions of bebop and hard bop?

Entering the Conversation

As you respond to each of the following prompts, support your position with appropriate evidence, including at least three sources in this Conversation on the influence of jazz, unless otherwise indicated.

1. Choose one of the poems, excerpts from fiction, or works of art in this Conversation and analyze its style using the three elements Robert O'Meally considers essential to jazz. Make an argument for or against the piece as a work of jazz.

2. Winthrop Sargeant was the *New Yorker*'s critic for both jazz and classical music for many years. He was notoriously crotchety and very hard on jazz. In the conclusion of his 1946 book, *Jazz, Hot and Hybrid*, he concludes, "Meanwhile jazz, as a rip-snorting stimulant to the social life of a restless, energetic people, need offer no apologies. It is rapidly becoming the world's most universally welcomed popular art form. And there can be no doubt that the world is the richer for it." Analyze this statement, looking carefully for a subtext or second layer of meaning, and then write an essay in which you support, challenge, or qualify Sargeant's conclusion about jazz. Use the sources here, as well as your own listening experiences, as evidence.

3. The poet and essayist Kevin Young writes in *The Grey Album*, a collection of his essays, that modernism often

> masked a form of anxiety. Rather than a comfort with progress—that American ideal—modernism itself may represent an apprehension about precisely that progress. Part of the blues' brood, jazz was and remains for many a site of this anxiety. While the music was seen as hectic, jumpy, and symptomatic, jazz is actually the diagnosis: we've all come down with a serious case of modernism. In its self-consciousness jazz mirrors modernism; in its willingness to refer to itself (especially later, in bebop), jazz foreshadows the growing self-reflexivity found in the postmodern era and art over the course of the last century.

Using the sources here, as well as your knowledge of music and art of the twentieth and twenty-first centuries, write an essay about how anxiety is both depicted in art and music and, perhaps, how anxiety drives the creation of art and music.

4. In *The History of Jazz*, Ted Gioia notes the influence of the mythology of jazz, one that he says "romanticized the jazz life and celebrated its leading practitioners as defiant, rebellious youths determined to go their own way in music, as in other pursuits." What evidence do you see of that sense of rebellion in the works in this Conversation? Consider that several of the artists and musicians discussed here had problems with drug or alcohol abuse or lived on the margins of society, some even dying unknown and impoverished. Write an essay in which you argue for or against the idea that an artist's difficult personal life adds credence or value to his or her art.

5. Most fans of jazz agree that the most universally appealing quality of the music is its sense of swing, which is hard to define but might be that quality that makes you tap your feet or nod your head. Write an essay about how the works in this Conversation, and other jazz-inspired works you know, "swing."

Conversation

Japanese Internment and Reparations: Making It Right?

The Japanese bombing of Pearl Harbor on the morning of December 7, 1941, precipitated the entrance of the United States into World War II; it also began a series of events that resulted in 120,000 Japanese Americans being interned in camps operated by the War Relocation Authority. Soon after the bombing, more than two thousand men suspected of espionage or sabotage — "enemy aliens," as these Japanese Americans were called — were arrested by the FBI. Within a few months, fear that Japanese Americans' loyalty lay with Japan increased, stoked by comments such as that of Lieutenant General John L. DeWitt, commander of the Western Defense Command, who said, "The Japanese race is an enemy race, and racial affinities are not severed by migration." Early in 1942, President Franklin D. Roosevelt issued Executive Order 9066, authorizing the war department to designate military areas from which "any and all persons may be excluded."

After the war, most of these interned citizens returned to their homes, having suffered financial losses, disruption of education and careers, and deep psychological wounds. Court cases questioning the constitutionality of the relocation camps reached as high as the Supreme Court. In *Korematsu v. United States*, the Court did not rule the action unconstitutional but did issue the precedent-setting statement that "all legal restrictions which curtail the civil rights of a single racial group are immediately suspect. . . . Courts must subject them to the most rigid scrutiny."

Ultimately, it was in 1988, with the passage of the Civil Liberties Act, that Congress authorized a presidential apology to Japanese Americans. The act acknowledges that "a grave injustice was done to both citizens and permanent resident aliens of Japanese ancestry" and that ". . . these actions were carried out without adequate security reasons and without any acts of espionage or sabotage documented . . . and were motivated largely by racial prejudice, wartime hysteria, and a failure of political leadership." In compensation for the "enormous damages, both material and intangible," the act also provided for payment of $20,000 in reparations for each surviving internee.

Many argue that the case of Japanese Americans sets a precedent and that other groups who have suffered unjust treatment, such as African Americans, also deserve reparations. The texts in this Conversation will acquaint you with the circumstances and viewpoints surrounding the Japanese internment, will present several arguments both for and against reparations for African Americans, and will ask you to explore whether it is possible to right the wrongs of the past and whether providing financial compensation to wronged individuals or institutions is an appropriate and effective way to do so.

Sources

Franklin Delano Roosevelt, *Executive Order No. 9066* (1942)

Western Defense Command, *Evacuation Order* (1942)

Dorothea Lange, *I Am an American* (1942)

Julie Otsuka, from *When the Emperor Was Divine* (2002)

George H. W. Bush, *Letter of Apology* (1991)

Eric K. Yamamoto, from *Racial Reparations: Japanese American Redress and African American Claims* (1998)

Brent Staples, *The Slave Reparations Movement Adopts the Rhetoric of Victimhood* (2001)

Charles Ogletree Jr., *Litigating the Legacy of Slavery* (2002)

Henry Louis Gates Jr., *Ending the Slavery Blame-Game* (2010)

Executive Order No. 9066

FRANKLIN DELANO ROOSEVELT

Franklin Delano Roosevelt (1882–1945) was the thirty-second president of the United States (1933–1945) and led the nation through World War II. Following is the legal document he signed that allowed for the internment of Japanese Americans in militarily sensitive areas, a designation that, according to General John DeWitt, encompassed the "Pacific Coast" and "the vicinity thereof."

The President has signed the following Executive Order:

AUTHORIZING THE SECRETARY OF WAR TO PRESCRIBE
MILITARY AREAS
9066

WHEREAS the successful prosecution of the war requires every possible protection against espionage and against sabotage to national-defense material, national-defense premises, and national-defense utilities as defined in Section 4, Act of April 20, 1918, 40 Stat. 533, as amended by the Act of November 30, 1940, 54 Stat. 1220, and the Act of August 21, 1941, 55 Stat. 655 (U.S.C., Title 50, Sec. 104):

NOW, THEREFORE, by virtue of the authority vested in me as President of the United States, and Commander in Chief of the Army and Navy, I hereby authorize and direct the Secretary of War, and the Military Commanders whom he may from time to time designate, whenever he or any designated Commander deems such action necessary or desirable, to prescribe military areas in such places and of such extent as he or the appropriate Military Commander may determine, from which any or all persons may be excluded, and with respect to which, the right of any person to enter, remain in, or leave shall be subject to whatever restrictions the Secretary of War or the appropriate Military Commander may impose in his discretion. The Secretary of War is hereby authorized to provide for residents of any such area who are excluded therefrom, such transportation, food, shelter, and other accommodations as may be necessary, in the judgment of the Secretary of War or the said Military Commander, and until other arrangements are made, to accomplish the purpose of this order. The designation of military areas in any region or locality shall supersede designations of prohibited and restricted areas by the Attorney General under the Proclamations of December 7 and 8, 1941, and shall supersede the responsibility and authority of the Attorney General under the said Proclamations in respect of such prohibited and restricted areas.

I hereby further authorize and direct the Secretary of War and the said Military Commanders to take such other steps as he or the appropriate Military Commander may deem advisable to enforce compliance with the restrictions applicable to each Military area hereinabove authorized to be designated, including the use of Federal troops and other Federal Agencies, with authority to accept assistance of state and local agencies.

I hereby further authorize and direct all Executive Departments, independent establishments and other Federal Agencies, to assist the Secretary of War or the said Military Commanders in carrying out this Executive Order, including the furnishing of medical aid, hospitalization, food, clothing, transportation, use of land, shelter, and other supplies, equipment, utilities, facilities, and services.

This order shall not be construed as modifying or limiting in any way the author- 5 ity heretofore granted under Executive Order No. 8972, dated December 12, 1941, nor shall it be construed as limiting or modifying the duty and responsibility of the Federal Bureau of Investigation, with respect to the investigation of alleged acts of sabotage or the duty and responsibility of the Attorney General and the Department of Justice under the Proclamations of December 7 and 8, 1941, prescribing regulations for the conduct and control of alien enemies, except as such duty and responsibility is superseded by the designation of Military areas hereunder.

> Franklin D. Roosevelt
> The White House,
> February 19, 1942.

Questions

1. What justification for this executive order does President Roosevelt cite?
2. This document was issued nearly two months after the United States declared war on Japan. What domestic actions does the president as commander in chief authorize in this document?
3. What responsibilities does the president designate to assure the protection and care of those affected by this order?
4. Why do you think that a particular ethnic group, such as the Japanese, is never mentioned in this order? Does that omission lessen the impact of the prejudice against them?
5. Given the official and legal language of this document, what leeway does the secretary of war have in the treatment of "alien enemies" (par. 5)?

Evacuation Order

WESTERN DEFENSE COMMAND

During the spring of 1942, 108 evacuation orders directed the removal of Japanese Americans in California, Washington, Oregon, and parts of Arizona. These were issued under the name of General John L. DeWitt, head of the Western Defense Command. Some of these notices appeared in newspapers, but most were posted in high-visibility places, such as on billboards and community buildings. Families were given one week to prepare. The two-step process began with the affected Japanese being transported to one of sixteen "assembly centers" near their homes and then sent to one of ten "relocation centers." The following evacuation order was issued in San Francisco on May 7, 1942.

WESTERN DEFENSE COMMAND AND FOURTH ARMY
WARTIME CIVIL CONTROL ADMINISTRATION

Presidio of San Francisco, California
May 7, 1942

INSTRUCTIONS TO ALL PERSONS OF
JAPANESE
ANCESTRY
Living in the Following Area:

All of the City of Sacramento, State of California.

Pursuant to the provisions of Civilian Exclusion Order No. 52, this Headquarters, dated May 7, 1942, all persons of Japanese ancestry, both alien and non-alien, will be evacuated from the above area by 12 o'clock noon P.W.T, Saturday, May 16, 1942.

No Japanese person living in the above area will be permitted to change residence after 12 o'clock noon, P.W.T, Thursday, May 7, 1942, without obtaining special permission from the representative of the Commanding General, Northern California Sector, at the Civil Control Station located at:

> Civic Memorial Auditorium,
> Fifteenth and I Streets,
> Sacramento, California.

Such permits will only be granted for the purpose of uniting members of a family, or in cases of grave emergency.

The Civil Control Station is equipped to assist the Japanese population affected by this evacuation in the following ways:

1. Give advice and instructions on the evacuation.
2. Provide services with respect to the management, leasing, sale, storage or other disposition of most kinds of property including real estate, business and professional equipment, household goods, boats, automobiles and livestock.
3. Provide temporary residence elsewhere for all Japanese in family groups.
4. Transport persons and a limited amount of clothing and equipment to their new residence.

The Following Instructions Must Be Observed:

1. A responsible member of each family, preferably the head of the family, or the person in whose name most of the property is held, and each individual living alone, will report to the Civil Control Station to receive further instructions. This must be done between 8:00 a.m. and 5:00 p.m. on Friday, May 8, 1942, or between 8:00 a.m. and 5 p.m. on Saturday, May 9, 1942, or between 8:00 a.m. and 5 p.m. on Sunday, May 10, 1942.
2. Evacuees must carry with them on departure for the Assembly Center, the following property:
   (a) Bedding and linens (no mattress) for each member of the family;

(b) Toilet articles for each member of the family;

(c) Extra clothing for each member of the family;

(d) Sufficient knives, forks, spoons, plates, bowls and cups for each member of the family;

(e) Essential personal effects for each member of the family.

All items carried will be securely packaged, tied and plainly marked with the name of the owner and numbered in accordance with instructions received at the Civil Control Station. The size and number of packages is limited to that which can be carried by the individual or family group.

No contraband items as described in paragraph 6, Public Proclamation No. 3, Headquarters Western Defense Command and Fourth Army, dated March 24, 1942, will be carried.

3. No pets of any kind will be permitted.

4. No personal items and no household goods will be shipped to the Assembly Center.

5. The United States Government through its agencies will provide for the storage, at the sole risk of the owner, of the more substantial household items, such as iceboxes, washing machines, pianos and other heavy furniture. Cooking utensils and other small items will be accepted if crated, packed and plainly marked with the name and address of the owner. Only one name and address will be used by a given family.

6. Each family, and individual living alone, will be furnished transportation to the Assembly Center or will be authorized to travel by private automobile in a supervised group. All instructions pertaining to the movement will be obtained at the Civil Control Station.

Go to the Civil Control Station between the hours of 8:00 a.m. and 5:00 p.m., Friday, May 8, 1942, or between the hours of 8:00 a.m. and 5 p.m., Saturday, May 9, 1942, or between the hours of 8:00 a.m. and 5 p.m., Sunday, May 10, 1942, to receive further instructions.

J. L. DeWitt
Lieutenant General, U.S. Army
Commanding

Questions

1. What is the meaning of the designation "all persons of Japanese ancestry, both alien and non-alien"?

2. According to this document, in what ways is the Civil Control Station able "to assist the Japanese population"?

3. How long does each family have to "register" at the Civil Control Center?

4. What is each family permitted to take with them? What provision is made for belongings and property that cannot be taken along?

5. What recourse do Japanese individuals or families who wish to request an exception or accommodation have, according to this document?

6. What euphemisms do you note in this document?

I Am an American

DOROTHEA LANGE

Dorothea Lange (1895–1965) was a famous documentary-style photographer, known for her work with the Farm Security Administration during the Depression era. This photograph was taken in March 1942. The owner of the store, a Japanese American and graduate of the University of California, placed the sign in his window the day after the bombing of Pearl Harbor; he was later sent to one of the relocation camps.

Prints and Photographs Division, Library of Congress

Questions

1. What do you see in this photograph? Describe it as objectively as possible without relying on any background knowledge.
2. This is a still photo, not one taken in a hurried moment to capture action in progress. What issues, ideas, or meaning do you think Dorothea Lange suggests through her composition?
3. This photo has achieved iconic status in photojournalism and in the story of the Japanese internment. Why? What makes it so memorable — and representative?

from *When the Emperor Was Divine*
JULIE OTSUKA

> Julie Otsuka (b. 1962) is an award-winning Japanese American author who grew up in California and received a BA from Yale University and an MFA from Columbia University. "Evacuation Order No. 19" is the opening chapter of her first novel, *When the Emperor Was Divine* (2002), which is based on her family history: her grandfather was arrested by the FBI as a suspected spy for Japan the day after the bombing of Pearl Harbor, and her grandmother, mother, and uncle spent three years in an internment camp in Topaz, Utah. Otsuka's most recent novel is *The Buddha in the Attic* (2011).

The sign had appeared overnight. On billboards and trees and the backs of the bus-stop benches. It hung in the window of Woolworth's. It hung by the entrance to the YMCA. It was stapled to the door of the municipal court and nailed, at eye level, to every telephone pole along University Avenue. The woman was returning a book to the library when she saw the sign in a post office window. It was a sunny day in Berkeley in the spring of 1942 and she was wearing new glasses and could see everything clearly for the first time in weeks. She no longer had to squint but she squinted out of habit anyway. She read the sign from top to bottom and then, still squinting, she took out a pen and read the sign from top to bottom again. The print was small and dark. Some of it was tiny. She wrote down a few words on the back of a bank receipt, then turned around and went home and began to pack.

When the overdue notice from the library arrived in the mail nine days later she still had not finished packing. The children had just left for school and boxes and suitcases were scattered across the floor of the house. She tossed the envelope into the nearest suitcase and walked out the door.

Outside the sun was warm and the palm fronds were clacking idly against the side of the house. She pulled on her white silk gloves and began to walk east on Ashby. She crossed California Street and bought several bars of Lux soap and a large jar of face cream at the Rumford Pharmacy. She passed the thrift shop and the boarded-up grocery but saw no one she knew on the sidewalk. At the newsstand on the corner of Grove she bought a copy of the *Berkeley Gazette*. She scanned the headlines quickly. The Burma Road had been severed and one of the Dionne quintuplets — Yvonne — was still recovering from an ear operation. Sugar rationing would begin on Tuesday. She folded the paper in half but was careful not to let the ink darken her gloves.

At Lundy's Hardware she stopped and looked at the display of victory garden shovels in the window. They were well-made shovels with sturdy metal handles and she thought, for a moment, of buying one — the price was right and she did not like to pass up a bargain. Then she remembered that she already had a shovel at home in the shed. In fact, she had two. She did not need a third. She smoothed down her dress and went into the store.

"Nice glasses," Joe Lundy said the moment she walked through the door.

5

"You think?" she asked. "I'm not used to them yet." She picked up a hammer and gripped the handle firmly. "Do you have anything bigger?" she asked. Joe Lundy said that what she had in her hand was the biggest hammer he had. She put the hammer back on the rack.

"How's your roof holding out?" he asked her.

"I think the shingles are rotting. It just sprung another leak."

"It's been a wet year."

The woman nodded. "But we've had some nice days." She walked past the vene-   10
tian blinds and the blackout shades to the back of the store. She picked out two rolls of tape and a ball of twine and brought them back to the register. "Every time it rains I have to set out the bucket," she said. She put down two quarters on the counter.

"Nothing wrong with a bucket," said Joe Lundy. He pushed the quarters back toward her across the counter but he did not look at her. "You can pay me later," he said. Then he began to wipe the side of the register with a rag. There was a dark stain there that would not go away.

"I can pay you now," said the woman.

"Don't worry about it," said Joe Lundy. He reached into his shirt pocket and gave her two caramel candies wrapped in gold foil. "For the children," he said. She slipped the caramels into her purse but left the money. She thanked him for the candy and walked out of the store.

"That's a nice red dress," he called out after her.

She turned around and squinted at him over the top of her glasses. "Thank you,"   15
she said. "Thank you, Joe." Then the door slammed behind her and she was alone on the sidewalk and she realized that in all the years she had been going to Joe Lundy's store she had never before called him by his name. Joe. It sounded strange to her. Wrong, almost. But she had said it. She had said it out loud. She wished she had said it earlier.

She wiped her forehead with her handkerchief. The sun was bright and she did not like to sweat in public. She took off her glasses and crossed to the shady side of the street. At the corner of Shattuck she took the streetcar downtown. She got off at Kittredge and went into J. F. Hink's department store and asked the salesman if they had any duffel bags but they did not, they were all sold out. He had sold the last one a half-hour ago. He suggested she try J. C. Penney's but they were sold out of duffel bags there too. They were sold out of duffel bags all over town.

When she got home the woman took off her red dress and put on her faded blue one — her housedress. She twisted her hair up into a bun and put on an old pair of comfortable shoes. She had to finish packing. She rolled up the Oriental rug in the living room. She took down the mirrors. She took down the curtains and shades. She carried the tiny bonsai tree out into the yard and set it down on the grass beneath the eaves where it would not get too much shade or too much sun but just the right amount of each. She brought the wind-up Victrola and the Westminster chime clock downstairs to the basement.

Upstairs, in the boy's room, she unpinned the One World One War map of the world from the wall and folded it neatly along the crease lines. She wrapped up his stamp collection and the painted wooden Indian with the long headdress he had won at the Sacramento State Fair. She pulled out the *Joe Palooka* comic books from under his bed. She emptied the drawers. Some of his clothes — the clothes he would need — she left out for him to put into his suitcase later. She placed his baseball glove on his pillow. The rest of his things she put into boxes and carried into the sunroom.

The door to the girl's room was closed. Above the doorknob was a note that had not been there the day before. It said DO NOT DISTURB. The woman did not open the door. She went down the stairs and removed the pictures from the walls. There were only three: the painting of Princess Elizabeth that hung in the dining room, the picture of Jesus in the foyer, and in the kitchen, a framed reproduction of Millet's *The Gleaners*. She placed Jesus and the little Princess together facedown in a box. She made sure to put Jesus on top. She took *The Gleaners* out of its frame and looked at the picture one last time. She wondered why she had let it hang in the kitchen for so long. It bothered her, the way those peasants were forever bent over above that endless field of wheat. "Look up" she wanted to say to them. "Look up, look up!" *The Gleaners*, she decided, would have to go. She set the picture outside with the garbage.

In the living room she emptied all the books from the shelves except Audubon's *Birds of America*. In the kitchen she emptied the cupboards. She set aside a few things for later that evening. Everything else — the china, the crystal, the set of ivory chopsticks her mother had sent to her fifteen years ago from Kagoshima on her wedding day — she put into boxes. She taped the boxes shut with the tape she had bought from Lundy's Hardware and carried them one by one up the stairs to the sunroom. When she was done she locked the door with two padlocks and sat down on the landing with her dress pushed up above her knees and lit a cigarette. Tomorrow she and the children would be leaving. She did not know where they were going or how long they would be gone or who would be living in their house while they were away. She knew only that tomorrow they had to go. 20

There were things they could take with them: bedding and linen, forks, spoons, plates, bowls, cups, clothes. These were the words she had written down on the back of the bank receipt. Pets were not allowed. That was what the sign had said.

It was late April. It was the fourth week of the fifth month of the war and the woman, who did not always follow the rules, followed the rules. She gave the cat to the Greers next door. She caught the chicken that had been running wild in the yard since the fall and snapped its neck beneath the handle of a broomstick. She plucked out the feathers and set the carcass into a pan of cold water in the sink.

By early afternoon her handkerchief was soaked. She was breathing hard and her nose was itching from the dust. Her back ached. She slipped off her shoes and massaged the bunions on her feet, then went into the kitchen and turned on the radio. Enrico Caruso was singing *"La donna è mobile"* again. His voice was full and sweet. She opened the icebox and took out a plate of rice balls stuffed with pickled plums. She ate them slowly as she listened to the tenor sing. The plums were dark and sour. They were just the way she liked them.

When the aria was over she turned off the radio and put two rice balls into a blue bowl. She cracked an egg over the bowl and added some salmon she had cooked the night before. She brought the bowl outside to the back porch and set it down on the steps. Her back was throbbing but she stood up straight and clapped her hands three times.

A small white dog came limping out of the trees. 25

"Eat up, White Dog," she said. White Dog was old and ailing but he knew how to eat. His head bobbed up and down above the bowl. The woman sat down beside him and watched. When the bowl was empty he looked up at her. One of his eyes was clouded over. She rubbed his stomach and his tail thumped against the wooden steps.

"Good dog," she said.

She stood up and walked across the yard and White Dog followed her. The narcissus in the garden were white with mildew and the irises were beginning to wilt. Weeds were everywhere. The woman had not mowed the grass for months. Her husband usually did that. She had not seen her husband since his arrest last December. First he had been sent to Fort Missoula, Montana, on a train and then he had been transferred to Fort Sam Houston, Texas. Every few days he was allowed to write her a letter. Usually he told her about the weather. The weather at Fort Sam Houston was fine. On the back of every envelope was stamped "Censored, War Department," or "Detained Alien Enemy Mail."

The woman sat down on a rock beneath the persimmon tree. White Dog lay at her feet and closed his eyes. "White Dog," she said, "look at me." White Dog raised his head. The woman was his mistress and he did whatever she asked. She put on her white silk gloves and took out a roll of twine. "Now just keep looking at me," she said. She tied White Dog to the tree. "You've been a good dog," she said. "You've been a good white dog."

Somewhere in the distance a telephone rang. White Dog barked. "Hush," she said. 30
White Dog grew quiet. "Now roll over," she said. White Dog rolled over and looked up at her with his good eye. "Play dead," she said. White Dog turned his head to the side and closed his eyes. His paws went limp. The woman picked up the large shovel that was leaning against the trunk of the tree. She lifted it high in the air with both hands and brought the blade down swiftly on his head. White Dog's body shuddered twice and his hind legs kicked out into the air, as though he were trying to run. Then he grew still. A trickle of blood seeped out from the corner of his mouth. She untied him from the tree and let out a deep breath. The shovel had been the right choice. Better, she thought, than a hammer.

Beneath the tree she began to dig a hole. The soil was hard on top but soft and loamy beneath the surface. It gave way easily. She plunged the shovel into the earth again and again until the hole was deep. She picked up White Dog and dropped him into the hole. His body was not heavy. It hit the earth with a quiet thud. She pulled off her gloves and looked at them. They were no longer white. She dropped them into the hole and picked up the shovel again. She filled up the hole. The sun was hot and the only place there was any shade was beneath the trees. The woman was standing beneath the trees. She was forty-one and tired. The back of her dress was drenched with sweat.

The author's family at the Tanforan Assembly Center (Dorothea Lange/National Archives)

National Archives photo

She brushed her hair out of her eyes and leaned against the tree. Everything looked the same except the earth was a little darker where the hole had been. Darker and wetter. She plucked a leaf from a low-hanging branch and went back inside the house.

When the children came home from school she reminded them that early the next morning they would be leaving. Tomorrow they were going on a trip. They could bring with them only what they could carry.

"I already know that," said the girl. She wore a white cotton frock with tiny blue anchors and her hair was pulled back in two tight black braids. She tossed her books onto the sofa and told the woman that her teacher, Mr. Rutherford, had talked for an entire hour about prime numbers and coniferous trees.

"Do you know what a coniferous tree is?" the girl asked.

The woman had to admit that she did not. "Tell me," she said, but the girl just   35
shook her head no.

"I'll tell you later," said the girl. She was ten years old and she knew what she liked. Boys and black licorice and Dorothy Lamour. Her favorite song on the radio was "Don't Fence Me In." She adored her pet macaw. She went to the bookshelf and took down *Birds of America*. She balanced the book on her head and walked slowly, her spine held erect, up the stairs to her room.

A few seconds later there was a loud thump and the book came tumbling back down the stairs. The boy looked up at his mother. He was seven and a small black fedora was tilted to one side of his head. "She has to stand up straighter," he said softly. He went to the foot of the stairs and stared at the book. It had landed face open to a picture of a small brown bird. A marsh wren. "You have to stand up straighter," he shouted.

"It's not that," came the girl's reply, "it's my head."

"What's wrong with your head?" shouted the boy.

"Too round. Too round on *top*."   40

He closed the book and turned to his mother. "Where's White Dog?" he asked.

He went out to the porch and clapped his hands three times.

"White Dog?" he yelled. He clapped his hands again. "White Dog!" He called out several more times, then went back inside and stood beside the woman in the kitchen. She was slicing apples. Her fingers were long and white and they knew how to hold a knife. "That dog just gets deafer every day," he said.

He sat down and turned the radio on and off, on and off, while she arranged the apples on a plate. The Radio City Symphony was performing the last movement of Tchaikovsky's *1812 Overture*. Cymbals were crashing. Cannons boomed. She set the plate down in front of the boy. "Eat," she said. He reached for a slice of apple just as the audience burst into applause. "Bravo," they shouted, "bravo, bravo!" The boy turned the dial to see if he could find *Speaking of Sports* but all he could find was the news and a Sammy Kaye serenade. He turned off the radio and took another slice of apple from the plate.

"It's so hot in here," he said.   45

"Take off your hat then," said the woman but the boy refused. The hat was a present from his father. It was big on him but the boy wore it every day. She poured him a glass of cold barley water and he drank it all in one gulp.

The girl came into the kitchen and went to the macaw's cage by the stove. She leaned over and put her face close to the bars. "Tell me something," she said.

The bird fluffed his wings and danced from side to side on his perch. "Baaaak," he said.

"That's not what I wanted to hear," said the girl.

"Take off your hat," said the bird.   50

The girl sat down and the woman gave her a glass of cold barley water and a long silver spoon. The girl licked the spoon and stared at her reflection. Her head was upside down. She dipped the spoon into the sugar bowl.

"Is there anything wrong with my face?" she asked.

"Why?" said the woman.

"People were staring."

"Come over here," said the woman. 55

The girl stood up and walked over to her mother.

"Let me look at you."

"You took down the mirrors," the girl said.

"I had to. I had to put them away."

"Tell me how I look." 60

The woman ran her hands across the girl's face. "You look fine," she said. "You have a fine nose."

"What else?" asked the girl.

"You have a fine set of teeth."

"Teeth don't count."

"Teeth are essential." 65

The woman began to rub the girl's shoulders. She told the girl to lean back and close her eyes and then she pressed her fingers deep into the girl's neck until she felt her begin to relax. "If there was something wrong with my face," the girl asked, "would you tell me?"

"Turn around," the woman said.

The girl turned around.

"Now look at me."

The girl looked at her. 70

"You have the most beautiful face I have ever seen."

"You're just saying that."

"No, I mean it."

The boy turned on the radio. The weatherman was giving the forecast for the next day. He was predicting rain and cooler temperatures. "Sit down and drink your water," the boy said to his sister. "Don't forget to take your umbrella tomorrow," said the weatherman.

The girl sat down. She drank her barley water and began to tell the woman all 75 about coniferous trees. Most of them were evergreens but some were just shrubs. Not all of them had cones. Some of them, like the yew, only had seedpods.

"That's good to know," said the woman. Then she stood up and told the girl it was time to practice the piano for Thursday's lesson.

"Do I have to?"

The woman thought for a moment. "No," she said, "only if you want to."

"Tell me I have to."

"I can't." 80

The girl went out to the living room and sat down on the piano bench. "The metronome's gone," she called out.

"Just count to yourself then," said the woman.

"... Three, five, seven ..." The girl put down her knife and paused. They were eating supper at the table. Outside it was dusk. The sky was dark purple and a breeze was blowing in off the bay. Hundreds of jays were twittering madly in the Greers' magnolia tree next door. A drop of rain fell on the ledge above the kitchen sink and the woman stood up and closed the window.

"Eleven, thirteen," said the girl. She was practicing her prime numbers for Monday's test.

"Sixteen?" said the boy.   85

"No," said the girl. "Sixteen's got a square root."

"I forgot," said the boy. He picked up a drumstick and began to eat.

"You never knew," said the girl.

"Forty-one," said the boy. "Eighty-six." He wiped his mouth with a napkin. "Twelve," he added.

The girl looked at him. Then she turned to her mother. "There's something wrong   90
with this chicken," she said. "It's too tough." She put down her fork. "I can't swallow another bite."

"Don't, then," said the woman.

"I'll eat it," said the boy. He plucked a wing from his sister's plate and put it into his mouth. He ate the whole thing. Then he spit out the bones and asked his mother where they were going the next day.

"I don't know," the woman said.

The girl stood up and left the table. She sat down at the piano and began to play a piece by Debussy from memory. "Golliwogg's Cake Walk." The melody was slow and simple. She had played it at a recital the summer before. Her father had sat in the front row of the audience and when she was finished he had clapped and clapped. She played the piece all the way through without missing a note. When she began to play it a second time the boy got up and went to his room and began to pack.

The first thing he put inside of his suitcase was his baseball glove. He slipped it   95
into the large pocket with the red satin lining. The pocket bulged. He threw in his clothes and tried to close the lid but the suitcase was very full. He sat on top of it and the lid sank down slowly. Suddenly he stood up again. The lid sprang open. There was something he had forgotten. He went to the closet in the hall and brought back his polka-dotted umbrella. He held it out at arm's length and shook his head sadly. The umbrella was too long. There was no way it would fit inside the suitcase.

The woman stood alone in the kitchen, washing her hands. The children had gone to bed and the house was quiet. The pipes were still hot from the day and the water from the faucet was warm. She could hear thunder in the distance — thunder and, from somewhere far off in the night, the faint wail of a siren. She looked out the window above the sink. The sky was still clear and she could see a full moon through the branches of the maple tree. The maple was a sapling with delicate leaves that turned bright red in the fall. Her husband had planted it for her four summers ago. She turned off the tap and looked around for the dish towel but it was not there. She had already packed the towels. They were in the suitcase by the door in the hall.

She dried her hands on the front of her dress and went to the birdcage. She lifted off the green cloth and undid the wire clasp on the door. "Come on out," she said. The bird stepped cautiously onto her hand and looked at her. "It's only me," she said. The bird blinked. His eyes were black and bulbous. They had no center.

"Get over here," he said, "get over here now." He sounded just like her husband. If she closed her eyes she could easily imagine that her husband was right there in the room with her.

The woman did not close her eyes. She knew exactly where her husband was. He was sleeping on a cot — a cot or maybe a bunk bed — somewhere in a tent at Fort Sam Houston where the weather was always fine. She pictured him lying there with one arm flung across his eyes and then she kissed the top of the bird's head.

"I am right here," she said. "I am right here, right now."   100

She gave the bird a sunflower seed and he cracked the shell open in his beak. "Get over here," he said again.

She opened the window and set the bird out on the ledge.

"You're all right," the bird said.

She stroked the underside of his chin and he closed his eyes. "Silly bird," she whispered. She closed the window and locked it. Now the bird was outside on the other side of the glass. He tapped the pane three times with his claw and said something but she did not know what it was. She could not hear him anymore.

She rapped back.   105

"Go," she said. The bird flapped his wings and flew up into the maple tree. She grabbed the broom from behind the stove and went outside and shook the branches of the tree. A spray of water fell from the leaves. "Go," she shouted. "Get on out of here."

The bird spread his wings and flew off into the night.

She went back inside the kitchen and took out a bottle of plum wine from beneath the sink. Without the bird in the cage, the house felt empty. She sat down on the floor and put the bottle to her lips. She swallowed once and looked at the place on the wall where *The Gleaners* had hung. The white rectangle was glowing in the moonlight. She stood up and traced around its edges with her finger and began to laugh — quietly at first, but soon her shoulders were heaving and she was gasping for breath. She put down the bottle and waited for the laughter to stop but it would not, it kept on coming until finally the tears were running down her cheeks. She picked up the bottle again and drank. The wine was dark and sweet. She had made it herself last fall. She took out her handkerchief and wiped her mouth. Her lips left a dark stain on the cloth. She put the cork back into the bottle and pushed it in as far as it would go. "*La donna è mobile*," she sang to herself as she went down the stairs to the basement. She hid the bottle behind the old rusted furnace where no one would ever find it.

In the middle of the night the boy crawled into her bed and asked her, over and over again, "What is that funny noise? What is that funny *noise*?"

The woman smoothed down his black hair. "Rain," she whispered.   110

The boy understood. He fell asleep at once. The thunder had come and gone and except for the sound of the rain the house was now quiet. The woman lay awake worrying about the leaky roof. Her husband had meant to fix it but he never had. She got up and placed a tin bucket on the floor to catch the water. She felt better after she did that. She climbed back into bed beside the boy and pulled the blanket up around his shoulders. He was chewing in his sleep and she wondered if he was hungry. Then she remembered the candy in her purse. The caramels. She had forgotten about the caramels. What would Joe Lundy say? He would tell her she was wearing a nice red dress. He would tell her not to worry about it. She knew that. She closed her eyes. She would give the caramels to the children in the morning. That was what she would do. She whispered a silent prayer to herself and drifted off to sleep as the water dripped steadily into the bucket. The boy shrugged off the blanket and rolled up against the wall where it was cool. In a few hours he and the girl and their mother would wake up and go to the Civil Control Station at the First Congregational Church on Channing Way. Then they would pin their identification numbers to their collars and grab their suitcases and climb up onto the bus and go to wherever it was they had to go.

(2002)

Questions

1. This introductory chapter opens with a reference to a "sign," though Otsuka does not reveal its import. At the end of the first paragraph, do you as a reader have any idea what the sign is about or foretells? When do you begin to realize that something about this seemingly ordinary "sunny day in Berkeley in the spring of 1942" is definitely not ordinary?

2. The mother gives the family's cat away and frees their pet bird, but she kills and buries the dog. Why? Why do you think Otsuka provides such a graphic description of the act?

3. Otsuka juxtaposes everyday events, such as going to the hardware store, with strange, sometimes ominous details, such as stores "all over town" being "sold out of duffel bags" (par. 16). What other odd juxtapositions begin to alert the reader that something sinister is occurring or is about to occur?

4. After the children have gone to bed, the mother drinks plum wine and begins to laugh, "quietly at first, but soon her shoulders were heaving and she was gasping for breath" (par. 108). She laughs until she cries. What does this uncharacteristic behavior say about her state of mind at this point?

5. Instead of giving her characters specific names, Otsuka refers to them here (and throughout the novel) as "the woman," "the girl," "the boy," and "the father." How does this lack of a particular name affect your relationship to each character?

6. How does the language — word choice and syntax — in this opening chapter of the novel contribute to the impression that the woman's control over the situation at hand and her own emotions is precarious?

Letter of Apology

George H. W. Bush

In 1988, the Civil Liberties Act was passed, calling for a formal presidential apology and authorizing reparations of $20,000 for each surviving internee who was a U.S. citizen or legal resident immigrant at the time of internment. The following letter accompanied each $20,000 check.

A monetary sum and words alone cannot restore lost years or erase painful memories; neither can they fully convey our Nation's resolve to rectify injustice and to uphold the rights of individuals. We can never fully right the wrongs of the past. But we can take a clear stand for justice and recognize that serious injustices were done to Japanese Americans during World War II.

In enacting a law calling for restitution and offering a sincere apology, your fellow Americans have, in a very real sense, renewed their traditional commitment to the ideals of freedom, equality, and justice. You and your family have our best wishes for the future.

Sincerely,
George Bush
President of the United States
(1991)

Questions

1. How would you describe the tone of this letter? Cite specific words and structural elements. What is the effect of including the phrase "in a very real sense" (par. 2)?
2. What acknowledgment does the letter make? What does it not acknowledge? Is emphasis placed on the individual or the community — in terms of both responsibility and restitution?
3. President Ronald Reagan, who signed the Civil Liberties Act of 1988, made the following comment: "Yes, the nation was then at war, struggling for its survival. And it's not for us today to pass judgment upon those who may have made mistakes while engaged in that great struggle. Yet we must recognize that the internment of Japanese Americans was just that, a mistake." Do you think that this comment (or a paraphrase expressing the same point) should have been included as part of the letter? Why or why not?

from *Racial Reparations*
Japanese American Redress and African American Claims

ERIC K. YAMAMOTO

> Eric K. Yamamoto holds the Korematsu Professorship of Law and Social Justice at the University of Hawaii at Manoa. He was part of the legal team in the Supreme Court case *Korematsu v. United States*, has won numerous teaching awards, and has written books and articles on racial justice and redress. The following excerpts are taken from a special issue of the Boston College *Third World Law Journal* on "The Long Shadow of Korematsu."

In 1991 the United States Office of Redress Administration presented the first $20,000 reparations check to the oldest Hawai'i survivor of the Japanese American internment camps. I attended the stately ceremony. The mood, while serious, was decidedly up-beat. Tears of relief mixed with sighs of joy. Freed at last.

Amidst the celebration I reflected on the Japanese American redress process and wondered about its impacts over time. The process had been arduous, with twists and turns. Many Japanese Americans contributed,[1] and their communities overwhelm-ingly considered reparations a great victory, as did I.

Other racial groups lent support, often in the form of political endorsements. Support also came as ringing oratory—for instance, the moving speech on the floor of the House of Representatives by African American Congressperson Ron Dellums.[2] Yet some of the support seemed begrudging. One African American scholar observed,

> [t]he apology [to Japanese Americans] was so appropriate and the payment so justified . . . that the source of my ambivalent reaction was at first difficult to iden-tify. After some introspection, I guiltily discovered that my sentiments were related to a very dark, brooding feeling that I had fought long and hard to conquer—inferiority. A feeling that took first root in the soil of "Why them and not me."[3]

This confession led me to ask about what political role Japanese Americans might play in future struggles for racial justice in America. That question then led to my essay in 1992 about the social meanings of Japanese American redress. The essay started with the recognition that Japanese American beneficiaries of reparations benefited personally, sometimes profoundly. The trauma of racial incarceration, without charges or trial, and the lingering self-doubt over two generations left scars on the soul. The government's apology and bestowal of symbolic reparations fostered long overdue healing for many. As I observed then, redress was:

> cathartic for internees. A measure of dignity was restored. Former internees could finally talk about the internment. Feelings long repressed, surfaced. One woman,

---

[1]*See* Takeshi Nakayma, *Historic Chapter Closes*, RAFU SHIMPO, Aug. 10, 1998, 1, 3. Con-tributors to Japanese American redress included the Japanese American Citizens League (JACL), the National Coalition for Japanese American Redress, numerous elected officials, and grassroots organizers.
[2]*See* 133 CONG. REC. H7555, H7576–77 (daily ed. Sept. 17, 1987) (statement of Rep. Dellums), 135 CONG. REC. H7597, H7626–27 (daily ed. Aug. 4, 1988) (statement of Rep. Dellums). In support of an amendment to the Related Agencies Appropriations Act of 1990 concerning the Civil Liberties Act of 1988, Dellums recalled:
> I participated in the debate that gave rise to the authorizing legislation. For some of us in this Chamber, that was a very painful debate for me, a very emotional debate. Hopefully, for all of us it was a debate full of principle[,] integrity and compassion. . . .
> Mr. Speaker, I urge support of the amendment before us. This is a matter of high principle, and those of us who recall the debate on the floor remember there were tears in the House Chamber, and there was conflict, agony, and pain in this Chamber.
135 CONG. REC. H7595–02, H7626-27 (daily ed. Oct. 26, 1989) (statement of Rep. Dellums).
[3]Vincene Verdun, *If the Shoe Fits, Wear It: An Analysis of Reparations to African Americans*, 67 TUL. L. REV. 597, 647 (1993).

now in her sixties, stated that she always felt the internment was wrong, but that, after being told by the military, the President and the Supreme Court that it was a necessity, she had come seriously to doubt herself. Redress and reparations and the recent successful court challenges, she said, had now freed her soul.

But, I wondered, what were the long-term societal effects of reparations — the social   5 legacy of Japanese American redress beyond personal benefits? Would societal attitudes toward Asian Americans and other racial minorities change? Would institutions, especially those that curtailed civil liberties in the name of national security, be restructured? Would Japanese American reparations serve as a catalyst for redress for others?

I identified and critiqued two emerging and seemingly contradictory views of reparations for Japanese Americans and then offered a third. The first view was that redress demonstrates that America does the right thing, that the Constitution works (if belatedly) and that the United States is far along on its march to racial justice for all. I criticized that view as unrealistically bright.

> The criticism is not that reparations are insignificant for recipients; the criticism is that they can lead to an "adjustment of individual attitudes" towards the historical injustice of the internment without giving current "consideration to the fundamental realities of power." The "danger lies in the possibility of enabling people to 'feel good' about each other" for the moment, "while leaving undisturbed the attendant social realities" creating the underlying conflict.

The second view was that "reparations legislation has the potential of becoming a civil rights law that at best delivers far less than it promises and that at worst creates illusions of progress, functioning as a hegemonic device to preserve the status quo." I criticized that view as overly dark.

As part of this critique, and drawing upon critical race theory insights, I offered a third view.

> [R]eparations legislation and court rulings in cases such as [the] *Korematsu* [*coram nobis* case] do not . . . inevitably lead to a restructuring of governmental institutions, a changing of societal attitudes or a transformation of social relationships, and the dangers of illusory progress and co-optation are real. At the same time, reparations claims, and the rights discourse they engender in attempts to harness the power of the state, can and should be appreciated as intensely powerful and calculated political acts that challenge racial assumptions underlying past and present social arrangements. They bear potential for contributing to institutional and attitudinal restructuring. . . .[4]

---

[4]The *Korematsu coram nobis* litigation in 1983–84 reopened the United States Supreme Court's decision in the original *Korematsu* case in 1944 which upheld the constitutionality of the internment. *Korematsu v. U.S.*, 584 F. Supp. 1406 (N.D.Cal. 1984). Based on recently discovered World War II documents showing the absence of military necessity for the internment and the Justice Department's wilful misrepresentations to the Court, the federal district court found a manifest injustice and set aside Fred Korematsu's conviction for refusing to abide by the military's exclusion orders. *See id.* at 1417.

In light of this third view, I posited that the social meaning of Japanese American redress was yet to be determined. I suggested that the key to the legacy of redress was how Japanese Americans acted when faced with continuing racial subordination of African Americans, Native Americans, Native Hawaiians, Latinas/os, and Asian Americans. Would we draw upon the lessons of the reparations movement and work to end all forms of societal oppression, or would we close up shop because we got ours?

Six years have passed. During that time, the United States, indeed the world, has gone apology crazy. Japanese American redress has stimulated a spate of race apologies. Some apologies appear to reflect heartfelt recognition of historical and current injustice and are backed by reparations. Other apologies appear empty, as strategic maneuvers to release pent-up social pressure.

Amidst this phenomenon African Americans have renewed their call for reparations for the legally sanctioned harms of slavery and Jim Crow oppression. These renewed claims have gained momentum, perhaps more so than at any time since Reconstruction — when Congress and the President sought to confiscate Southern land and provide freed slaves with forty acres and a mule. The Florida legislature recently approved reparations for survivors and descendants of the 1923 Rosewood massacre.[5] The African American victims of the Tuskegee syphilis experiment received reparations and a presidential apology in 1997. One reparations lawsuit was filed on the West Coast and a reparations class action is contemplated on the East Coast. Representative John Conyers' resolution calling for a Congressional Reparations Study Commission, reintroduced every year since 1989, has garnered endorsements from an impressive array of political organizations.

And in every African American reparations publication, in every legal argument, in almost every discussion, the topic of Japanese American redress surfaces. Sometimes as legal precedent. Sometimes as moral compass. Sometimes as political guide. . . .

Reparations, if thoughtfully conceived, offered and administered, can be transformative. They can help change material conditions of group life and send political messages about societal commitment to principles of equality. When reparations stimulate change, however, they also generate resistance. Proponents suffer backlash. Thus, when reparations claims are treated seriously, they tend to re-create victimhood by inflaming old wounds and triggering regressive reactions. This is the dilemma of reparations.

Seeing these dual possibilities in all redress movements, Joe Singer describes the potential for further victimization in two contemporary situations.[6] He recounts

10

---

[5]In 1995, each of the nine African American survivors of the mayhem as a result of a white woman's false rape charge was awarded $150,000 in reparations; the descendants of Rosewood residents received between $375 and $22,535 for loss of property. *See* Lori Robinson, *Righting a Wrong Among Black Americans: The Debate is Escalating over Whether an Apology for Slavery Is Enough*, Seattle Post-Intelligencer, June 29, 1997, *available in* 1997 WL 3200157.

[6]See generally Joseph William Singer, *Reparation* (1997) (unpublished manuscript, on file with author).

Jews' highly publicized demands in 1997 that Swiss banks account for and restore Jewish money and gold held by the banks for Nazis during World War II. Bank acknowledgment and restitution treats Jews as worthy human beings with rights, including the right to own property. Restitution counters the anti-Semitic myth of Jews misappropriating the property of others. Jewish "victimhood is acknowledged, but Jews are not treated as mere victims, but as agents calling the Swiss banks to account. . . ."

One problem, however, is that Jewish demands for monetary restitution resur-   15
rect for some the harsh historical stereotypes of Jews "as money-grubbing, as having both accumulated secret bank accounts in the past and as caring now about nothing more than money. . . ." Another, and broader, problem is that additional Jewish reparations claims may spark resentment among other groups whose reparations claims have gone unmet (such as Hungarian gypsies who were exterminated by Nazis in Auschwitz and elsewhere).

Singer also describes reparations demands for African Americans. Some understand those demands as a call for redress of past injustice; others understand the demands as a "refusal to grow up." The result, evident in the volatile affirmative action debates, is that "calls to repair the current effects of past injustice are met with derisory denials that continuing injustice exists and that the problems of African Americans are now purely of their own making." As Singer observes about mixed healing potential in both situations, the "very thing that restoration is intended to combat may be the result of the demand for restoration." . . .

The socio-psychological benefits of apologies and reparations are often significant for recipients.[7] As previously mentioned, one woman said the Japanese American redress process had "freed her soul." Other beneficiaries responded with a collective sigh of relief. Ben Takeshita, for instance, expressed the sentiments of many when he said that although monetary payments "could not begin to compensate . . . for his . . . lost freedom, property, livelihood, or the stigma of disloyalty," the reparations demonstrated the sincerity of the government's apology.[8]

In light of both the dangers and the transformative potential of reparations, I offer two insights into specific reparations efforts, insights drawn from Japanese American redress that bear on the shape of African American reparations claims and strategy.

---

[7]According to clinical psychologist Susan Heitler, "[a]n apology is a much more complex and powerful phenomenon than most people realize[.]" Additionally, psychologist Susan T. Fisk observes,

> An apology for slavery would say it may not have been me, but it was my people or my government that did this and we now see that it was really a crime and sin. It is potentially healing. It shares responsibility for ending racism and it acknowledges that slavery has some relevance to today.

Id. See also Sharon Cohen, *Americans to be Compensated for Horrors of Holocaust: Survivors Say Reparations Won't End Nightmares,* SAN DIEGO UNION-TRIB., Apr. 6, 1997, *available in* 1997 WL 3126022 (for concentration camp survivor, "[r]eceiving reparations . . . would be a psychological boost").

[8]Nicholas Tavuchis, *Mea Culpa: A Sociology of Apology and Reconciliation* 107 (1991).

One is normative: reparations by government or groups should be aimed at a restructuring of the institutions and relationships that gave rise to the underlying justice grievance. Otherwise, as a philosophical and practical matter, reparations cannot be effective in addressing root problems of misuse of power, particularly in the maintenance of oppressive systemic structures, or integrated symbolically into a group's (or government's) moral foundation for responding to intergroup conflicts or for urging others to restructure oppressive relationships. This means that monetary reparations are important, but not simply as individual compensation. Money is important to facilitate the process of personal and community "repair" discussed below.

A second insight is descriptive: restructuring those institutions and changing societal attitudes will not flow naturally and inevitably from reparations itself. Dominant interests, whether governmental or private, will cast reparations in ways that tend to perpetuate existing power structures and relationships. Indeed, traditionally framed, American interests in racial reparations, including international credibility and domestic peace, tend to reinforce the social status quo.

Those seeking reparations need to draw on the moral force of their claims (and not frame it legally out of existence) while simultaneously radically recasting reparations in a way that both materially benefits those harmed and generally furthers some larger interests of mainstream America. Moreover, those benefiting from reparations in the past need to draw upon the material benefits of reparations and the political insights and commitments derived from their particular reparations process and join with others to push for bureaucratic, legal and attitudinal restructuring — to push for material change. And their efforts must extend beyond their own reparations to securing reparations for others.

These insights point toward a reframing of the prevailing reparations paradigm — a new framing embracing the notion of reparations as "repair." Indeed, reparation, in singular, means repair. It encompasses both acts of repairing damage to the material conditions of racial group life — distributing money to those in need and transferring land ownership to those dispossessed, building schools, churches, community centers and medical clinics, creating tax incentives and loan programs for businesses owned by inner city residents — and acts of restoring injured human psyches — enabling those harmed to live with, but not in, history. Reparations, as collective actions, foster the mending of tears in the social fabric, the repairing of breaches in the polity.

For example, slavery, Jim Crow apartheid and mainstream resistance to integration inflicted horrendous harms upon African American individuals and their communities, harms now exacerbated by the increasing resegregation of America. Reparations directly improving the material conditions of life for African Americans and their communities are especially appropriate. In addition, the racial harm to African Americans also wounded the American polity. It grated on America's sense of morality (do we really believe in freedom, equality and justice?), destabilized the American psyche (are we really oppressors?), generated personal discomfort and fear in daily interactions (will there be retribution?), and continues to do so. As Harlon Dalton observes, "perpetuating racial hierarchy in a society that professes to be

20

egalitarian is destructive of the spirit as well as of the body politic."[9] Reparations for African Americans, conceived as repair, can help mend this larger tear in the social fabric for the benefit of both blacks and mainstream America.

So viewed, reparations are potentially transformative. Reparations can avoid "the traps of individualism, neutrality and indeterminacy that plague many mainstream concepts of rights or legal principles."[10] Reparations are grounded in group, rather than individual, rights and responsibilities and provide tangible benefits to those wronged by those in power. As Mari Matsuda observes, properly cast, reparations target substantive barriers to liberty and equality. In addition, coupled with acknowledgment and apology, reparations are potentially transformative because of what they symbolize for both bestower and beneficiary: reparations "condemn exploitation and adopt a vision of a more just world."[11]

(1998)

Questions

1. What is the purpose of quoting African American congressperson Ron Dellums and scholar Vincene Verdun in the opening of this essay (par. 3)?
2. What two attitudes toward "the social meanings of Japanese American redress" (par. 4) does Eric K. Yamamoto present? What is the third—his own—viewpoint?
3. What does Yamamoto believe is "the dilemma of reparations" (par. 13)? How is it demonstrated in the example of restitution for Jews victimized by Nazi Germany?
4. Why does Yamamoto argue that "monetary reparations are important, but not simply as individual compensation" (par. 18)?
5. What does Yamamoto mean when he calls for "a reframing of the prevailing reparations paradigm" (par. 21)?
6. Under what circumstances and terms does Yamamoto believe that "reparations are potentially transformative" (par. 23)?

The Slave Reparations Movement Adopts the Rhetoric of Victimhood

Brent Staples

An editorial writer for the *New York Times*, Brent Staples (b. 1951) is author of the award-winning memoir *Parallel Times: Growing Up in Black and White* (1994). The following essay appeared as an op-ed piece in the *New York Times* on September 2, 2001.

---

[9] Harlon L. Dalton, *Racial Healing: Confronting the Fear Between Blacks and Whites* 4 (1995).
[10] Mari J. Matsuda, *Looking to the Bottom: Critical Legal Studies and Reparations*, 22 HARV. C.R-C.L. L. REV. 323, 373–88 (1987).
[11] *See id.* at 394.

My great-grandfather John Wesley Staples was born in Bedford County, Va., on July 4, 1865. Independence Day of that year was laden with symbolism because it heralded the end of slavery through the 13th Amendment. Family legend has it that John Wesley was one of the first free Negroes born in his county. But three of his siblings were born into slavery, as was his mother, Somerville, who was known in the family as an Ethiopian.

Slavery is nearer to us in time than most Americans understand. My eldest uncle, who turns 84 this year, has often recalled meeting former slaves when he was a boy at John Wesley's farm in Troutville, Va. Had John Wesley lived to my uncle's age, he would had seen the beginning of the civil rights movement and met the great-grandson who would later become an editorial writer for *The New York Times.*

The post-slavery South was especially brutal for elderly black people who had given their working lives to their masters and could no longer care for themselves. Freedom, such as it was, was further circumscribed during the late 19th century, when Southern states were writing Negroes out of the state constitutions, denying them the right to vote, hold office or attend school. The trend was deepened by sharecropping and other forms of bondage.

Black Americans often suppressed slave memories out of horror and shame. But the Staples family embraced its story out of pride in how well John Wesley and his wife, Eliza, managed to fare in the aggressively racist environment of the South in the late 19th century and early 20th century. My great-grandparents had the benefit of a strong extended family, allowing them to pool resources, including manpower. The Staples family protected the farm and John Wesley's wholesaling business with shotguns and pistols that were evident even at the dinner table. With no school available for black children, John Wesley and Eliza joined with their neighbors and built one in a field at the intersection of their three properties.

The teacher is listed in my great-aunt Sophronia's grade school composition book as a "Miss Marion B. Brown." She worked at the one-room school in return for room and board from the families. When John Wesley died in 1940, he left behind a literate family, a thriving farm and $40,000 in cash — a small fortune by standards of the time. This achievement paved the way for my father's generation and mine, which included the first college-bound members of the Staples family line. 5

Black Americans made spectacular progress beginning in the decades after slavery, moving from cotton fields to the boardroom in just over a century. But the recent debate about reparations for slavery has introduced a different narrative in which black people are cast as a victim class seeking compensation for the suffering of ancestors. The most popular version of the reparations proposal is found in *The Debt: What America Owes to Blacks*, by the Africa analyst Randall Robinson. The book has gained surprising credibility on the political left while generating a considerable backlash among moderate and conservative black intellectuals.

Targeted compensation is legal and morally just. The state of Florida made the right gesture in 1994 when it gave college scholarships to descendants from the black community of Rosewood, which was destroyed by whites in 1923 while the state did nothing.[1] The federal government has rightly compensated modern-day Native Americans for lands taken from them in the last century. Supporters of reparations have at least a moral case when they argue that companies that enriched themselves in slavery should attempt restitution when documents are specific enough to permit it.

But the sweeping notion that individual black Americans are owed a "debt" for slavery is a bridge too far. Black families have made and lost fortunes just as white families have. There is in addition no provable connection between 19th-century bondage and specific cases of 21st-century destitution. For these reasons, a publicly financed reparations program based on ancestry is not sustainable politically.

Such a program would logically be open to millions of people who have lived as "white" for generations but are descended from enslaved black people. The program would also be available to the descendants of black slave owners, who were far more common than many people like to admit. Black masters in South Carolina, for example, were confined to the margins of society but held many of the same attitudes about race as whites. Black masters continued to hold slaves even as the Union Army prepared for its terrible march through South Carolina.

The reparations debate is part of a burgeoning discussion about the role of slavery in American history. But by blaming history alone for modern-day social ills like poverty, illiteracy and unemployment, reparations advocates are unwittingly saying that these problems are so deeply rooted as to be unsolvable. They are also subverting the true story of black people in the United States. This story is one of extraordinary achievement in the face of gargantuan obstacles. It begins in the waning hours of slavery and continues to this very day.

10

(2001)

Questions

1. What ethos does Brent Staples establish in the opening paragraphs of the essay?
2. Why do you think Staples uses the term "targeted compensation" (par. 7) instead of "reparations"? What does he mean by his claim that "reparations advocates are . . . subverting the true story of black people in the United States" (par. 10)?
3. What concessions does he make to the counterargument—that is, support for reparations?
4. Why do you agree or disagree with Staples's statement that there is "no provable connection between 19th-century bondage and specific cases of 21st-century destitution" (par. 8)?
5. Following is a response in the *New York Times* to Staples's column. What parts of Staples's argument does Martin Kilson question? What evidence does he provide?

---

[1]Rosewood, Florida, was the site of the Rosewood Massacre, in which a white mob from nearby Sumner tried to pursue an escaped prisoner who allegedly beat and raped a white woman. By the end of the incident, twenty blacks had been murdered and the entire town of Rosewood had been burned down. — Eds.

How effectively does he challenge Staples's position? Consider the analogy he makes in his final statement.

> To the Editor:
>
> Brent Staples's pride in the achievements of his great-grandfather and other farmland-owning post-Emancipation Negroes (Editorial Observer, Sept. 2) is refreshing. But his appraisal of black social mobility as "spectacular progress" is bizarre.
>
> By 1940, when blacks numbered 12 million, there were 63,697 teachers, 3,524 doctors and 1,052 lawyers, according to the Census Bureau. Was this spectacular progress? A generation and a half later, in 1970, when blacks numbered 20 million, there were 235,436 teachers, 6,106 doctors and 3,728 lawyers. Spectacular progress?
>
> For Mr. Staples, reparations activists fake a narrative of blacks "as a victim class." But historical scholarship documents the horrendous victimization of blacks — for example, unpaid labor of millions that was key to American capital accumulation.
>
> Just as American Jews uniformly supported reparations from Germany, so do African Americans uniformly support reparations for American slavery's victimization of their ancestors.
>
> — Martin Kilson, Dublin, N.H., Sept. 3, 2001

Litigating the Legacy of Slavery

Charles Ogletree Jr.

Charles Ogletree Jr. (b. 1952) is the Jesse Climenko Professor at Harvard Law School and founder of the school's Charles Hamilton Houston Institute for Race and Justice. He is the author of numerous books, including *All Deliberate Speed: Reflections on the First Half-Century of* Brown v. Board of Education (2004) and *The Presumption of Guilt: The Arrest of Henry Louis Gates Jr. and Race, Class, and Crime in America* (2010). The following essay was first published in the *New York Times* on March 21, 2002.

Last Tuesday, a group of lawyers filed a federal class-action lawsuit in New York on behalf of all African-American descendants of slaves. The lawsuit seeks compensation from a number of defendants for profits earned through slave labor and the slave trade.

This lawsuit is limited to FleetBoston, Aetna, CSX and other to-be-named companies. The broader reparations movement seeks to explore the historical role that other private institutions and government played during slavery and the era of legal racial discrimination that followed. The goal of these historical investigations is to bring American society to a new reckoning with how our past affects the current conditions of African-Americans and to make America a better place by helping the truly disadvantaged.

The Reparations Coordinating Committee, of which I am a co-chairman, will proceed with its own plans to file wide-ranging reparations lawsuits late this autumn. The committee is a group of lawyers, academics, public officials and activists that has conducted extensive research and begun to identify parties to sue and claims to be raised.

The shape of a reparations strategy can already be seen. Among private defendants, corporations will be prominent, as last week's lawsuit shows. Other private institutions — Brown University, Yale University and Harvard Law School — have made headlines recently as the beneficiaries of grants and endowments traced back to slavery and are probable targets. Naming the government as a defendant is also central to any reparations strategy; public officials guaranteed the viability of slavery and the segregation that followed it.

A number of recent examples illustrate the possibilities for making reparations   5
claims nationally and internationally. In South Africa, reparations have been part of the work of the Truth and Reconciliation Commission, which seeks to compensate people with clear material needs who suffered under apartheid because of their race. It was also in South Africa that, in the final documents of a racism conference sponsored by the United Nations, slavery was defined as a "crime against humanity," a legal determination that may enable the reparations movement to extend its reach to international forums.

In the United States, just three years ago the federal government reached a consent decree with a class of over 20,000 black farmers to compensate for years of discrimination by the Department of Agriculture. The case represents the largest civil-rights settlement by the government ever, with a likely payout of about $2 billion. Previously, the government also approved significant compensation for Japanese-Americans interned during World War II and paid reparations to black survivors of the Rosewood, Fla., race riots.

Although these precedents differ from a slavery-based reparations claim in that they involved classes of individuals who were both alive and easily identified, they nonetheless indicate government willingness to acknowledge past wrongs and remedy them. It is important that in each case the government waived its immunity from suit, thereby lifting the ordinary bar that prevents lawsuits against a sovereign.

Bring[ing] the government into litigation will also generate a public debate on slavery and the role its legacy continues to play in our society. The opportunity to use expert witnesses and conduct extensive discovery, to get facts and documentation, makes the courtroom an ideal venue for this debate.

A full and deep conversation on slavery and its legacy has never taken place in America; reparations litigation will show what slavery meant, how it was profitable and how it has continued to affect the opportunities of millions of black Americans.

Litigation is required to promote this discussion because political accountability   10
has not been forthcoming. In each Congressional session since 1989, Representative John Conyers has introduced a bill to study slavery reparations and it has quickly died each time.

Though claims for slavery reparations have moved near the front of national and international policy discussions in the past few years, the movement has deep historical roots. Those roots go back at least as far as the unkept promise in 1864 of "40 acres and a mule" to freed slaves, which acknowledged our country's debt to the newly emancipated.

Indeed, the civil rights movement has long been organized, in part, around the notion that slavery and the century of legal discrimination that followed have had enduring and detrimental effects on American minorities.

The reparations movement should not, I believe, focus on payments to individuals. The damage has been done to a group — African-American slaves and their descendants — but it has not been done equally within the group. The reparations movement must aim at undoing the damage where that damage has been most severe and where the history of race in America has left its most telling evidence. The legacy of slavery and racial discrimination in America is seen in well-documented racial disparities in access to education, health care, housing, insurance, employment and other social goods. The reparations movement must therefore focus on the poorest of the poor — it must finance social recovery for the bottom-stuck, providing an opportunity to address comprehensively the problems of those who have not substantially benefited from integration or affirmative action.

The root of "reparations" is "to repair." This litigation strategy could give us an opportunity to fully address the legacy of slavery in a spirit of repair.

(2002)

Questions

1. Charles Ogletree Jr. approaches his argument, as lawyers do, through precedent— that is, previous cases that established a principle or rule. What precedents does he cite to support his advocacy of reparations?
2. What does he mean when he states that the U.S. government "waived its immunity from suit, thereby lifting the ordinary bar that prevents lawsuits against a sovereign" (par. 7)? Why is this point significant?
3. Ogletree claims that litigation is required to promote a public discussion of slavery and its legacy. To what extent do you agree with this claim?
4. What remedy does Ogletree propose instead of direct cash payments to individuals? Why does he not favor a monetary payment?
5. To what extent do you agree that the litigation strategy Ogletree supports would "give us an opportunity to fully address the legacy of slavery in a spirit of repair" (par. 14)?

Ending the Slavery Blame-Game

HENRY LOUIS GATES JR.

Scholar, literary critic, and writer Henry Louis Gates Jr. (b. 1950) is the Alphonse Fletcher University Professor and director of the W. E. B. DuBois Institute for African and African American Research at Harvard University. This essay appeared in the *New York Times* on April 23, 2010.

Thanks to an unlikely confluence of history and genetics — the fact that he is African American and president — Barack Obama has a unique opportunity to reshape the debate over one of the most contentious issues of America's racial legacy: reparations, the idea that the descendants of American slaves should receive compensation for their ancestors' unpaid labor and bondage.

There are many thorny issues to resolve before we can arrive at a judicious (if symbolic) gesture to match such a sustained, heinous crime. Perhaps the most vexing is how to parcel out blame to those directly involved in the capture and sale of human beings for immense economic gain.

While we are all familiar with the role played by the United States and the European colonial powers like Britain, France, Holland, Portugal and Spain, there is very little discussion of the role Africans themselves played. And that role, it turns out, was a considerable one, especially for the slave-trading kingdoms of western and central Africa. These included the Akan of the kingdom of Asante in what is now Ghana, the Fon of Dahomey (now Benin), the Mbundu of Ndongo in modern Angola and the Kongo of today's Congo, among several others.

For centuries, Europeans in Africa kept close to their military and trading posts on the coast. Exploration of the interior, home to the bulk of Africans sold into bondage at the height of the slave trade, came only during the colonial conquests, which is why Henry Morton Stanley's pursuit of Dr. David Livingstone in 1871 made for such compelling press: he was going where no (white) man had gone before.

How did slaves make it to these coastal forts? The historians John Thornton and Linda Heywood of Boston University estimate that 90 percent of those shipped to the New World were enslaved by Africans and then sold to European traders. The sad truth is that without complex business partnerships between African elites and European traders and commercial agents, the slave trade to the New World would have been impossible, at least on the scale it occurred.

Advocates of reparations for the descendants of those slaves generally ignore this untidy problem of the significant role that Africans played in the trade, choosing to believe the romanticized version that our ancestors were all kidnapped unawares by evil white men, like Kunta Kinte was in *Roots*. The truth, however, is much more complex: slavery was a business, highly organized and lucrative for European buyers and African sellers alike.

The African role in the slave trade was fully understood and openly acknowledged by many African-Americans even before the Civil War. For Frederick Douglass, it was an argument against repatriation schemes for the freed slaves. "The savage chiefs of the western coasts of Africa, who for ages have been accustomed to selling their captives into bondage and pocketing the ready cash for them, will not more readily accept our moral and economical ideas than the slave traders of Maryland and Virginia," he warned. "We are, therefore, less inclined to go to Africa to work against the slave trade than to stay here to work against it."

To be sure, the African role in the slave trade was greatly reduced after 1807, when abolitionists, first in Britain and then, a year later, in the United States, succeeded in banning the importation of slaves. Meanwhile, slaves continued to be bought and sold within the United States, and slavery as an institution would not be abolished until 1865. But the culpability of American plantation owners neither erases nor supplants that of the African slavers. In recent years, some African leaders have become more comfortable discussing this complicated past than African-Americans tend to be.

In 1999, for instance, President Mathieu Kerekou of Benin astonished an all-black congregation in Baltimore by falling to his knees and begging African-Americans' forgiveness for the "shameful" and "abominable" role Africans played in the trade. Other African leaders, including Jerry Rawlings of Ghana, followed Mr. Kerekou's bold example.

Our new understanding of the scope of African involvement in the slave trade is 10 not historical guesswork. Thanks to the *Trans-Atlantic Slave Trade Database*, directed by the historian David Eltis of Emory University, we now know the ports from which more than 450,000 of our African ancestors were shipped out to what is now the United States (the database has records of 12.5 million people shipped to all parts of the New World from 1514 to 1866). About 16 percent of United States slaves came from eastern Nigeria, while 24 percent came from the Congo and Angola.

Through the work of Professors Thornton and Heywood, we also know that the victims of the slave trade were predominantly members of as few as 50 ethnic groups. This data, along with the tracing of blacks' ancestry through DNA tests, is giving us a fuller understanding of the identities of both the victims and the facilitators of the African slave trade.

For many African-Americans, these facts can be difficult to accept. Excuses run the gamut, from "Africans didn't know how harsh slavery in America was" and "Slavery in Africa was, by comparison, humane" or, in a bizarre version of "The devil made me do it," "Africans were driven to this only by the unprecedented profits offered by greedy European countries."

But the sad truth is that the conquest and capture of Africans and their sale to Europeans was one of the main sources of foreign exchange for several African kingdoms for a very long time. Slaves were the main export of the kingdom of Kongo; the Asante Empire in Ghana exported slaves and used the profits to import gold. Queen Njinga, the brilliant 17th-century monarch of the Mbundu, waged wars of resistance against the Portuguese but also conquered polities as far as 500 miles inland and sold her captives to the Portuguese. When Njinga converted to Christianity, she sold African traditional religious leaders into slavery, claiming they had violated her new Christian precepts.

Did these Africans know how harsh slavery was in the New World? Actually, many elite Africans visited Europe in that era, and they did so on slave ships following the prevailing winds through the New World. For example, when Antonio Manuel, Kongo's ambassador to the Vatican, went to Europe in 1604, he first stopped in Bahia, Brazil, where he arranged to free a countryman who had been wrongfully enslaved.

African monarchs also sent their children along these same slave routes to be   15
educated in Europe. And there were thousands of former slaves who returned to
settle Liberia and Sierra Leone. The Middle Passage, in other words, was sometimes
a two-way street. Under these circumstances, it is difficult to claim that Africans were
ignorant or innocent.

Given this remarkably messy history, the problem with reparations may not be
so much whether they are a good idea or deciding who would get them; the larger
question just might be from whom they would be extracted.

So how could President Obama untangle the knot? In David Remnick's new
book *The Bridge: The Life and Rise of Barack Obama*, one of the president's former
students at the University of Chicago comments on Mr. Obama's mixed feelings
about the reparations movement: "He told us what he thought about reparations. He
agreed entirely with the theory of reparations. But in practice he didn't think it was
really workable."

About the practicalities, Professor Obama may have been more right than he
knew. Fortunately, in President Obama, the child of an African and an American, we
finally have a leader who is uniquely positioned to bridge the great reparations divide.
He is uniquely placed to publicly attribute responsibility and culpability where they
truly belong, to white people and black people, on both sides of the Atlantic, com-
plicit alike in one of the greatest evils in the history of civilization. And reaching that
understanding is a vital precursor to any just and lasting agreement on the divisive
issue of slavery reparations.

(2010)

Questions

1. What does Henry Louis Gates Jr. believe is the "most vexing" of the "many thorny
   issues to resolve" (par. 2) in the reparations controversy?
2. What is his position on the issue of reparations for African Americans as stated in
   this essay?
3. What evidence does he cite to support his position? What is the predominant type
   of evidence?
4. What does he mean by "this remarkably messy history" (par. 16)?
5. Why does he believe that President Barack Obama is "a leader who is uniquely
   positioned to bridge the great reparations divide" (par. 18)? To what extent do you
   agree?

Making Connections

1. How do you think Julie Otsuka, or the woman in "Evacuation Order No. 19"
   (p. 1221) would respond to the photo with the sign "I Am an American" (p. 1220),
   by Dorothea Lange? With sympathy? Anger? Skepticism?

2. In what ways might Charles Ogletree Jr. (p. 1240) or Henry Louis Gates Jr. (p. 1242) argue that the evacuation order treats Japanese American citizens as property?

3. How might Gates, Ogletree, or Brent Staples (p. 1237) respond to an apology to African Americans similar to the one President George H. W. Bush signed for Japanese Americans (p. 1230)?

4. Where in his article does Eric K. Yamamoto (p. 1231) reflect the viewpoint of Ogletree? Where does he reflect that of Staples? With which one would he agree more fully?

5. With what part(s) of Staples's argument would Ogletree most strenuously disagree?

6. What common ground do you find between Staples and Gates?

Entering the Conversation

As you respond to each of the following prompts, support your position with appropriate evidence, including at least three sources in this Conversation on Japanese American internment and reparations, unless otherwise indicated.

1. To what extent are the arguments for African American reparations analogous to the arguments that led to monetary reparations for Japanese Americans interned during World War II? Discuss points of both comparison and contrast.

2. What does Eric K. Yamamoto mean by the "dangers and the transformative potential of reparations" (par. 18)? Taking this distinction into account, explain why you believe that African Americans should or should not receive reparations today. If not, why not? If so, what form should reparations take?

3. Explain why you agree or disagree with the following assertion of Yamamoto: "Reparations for African Americans, conceived as repair, can help mend this larger tear in the social fabric [of the United States] for the benefit of both blacks and mainstream America" (par. 22).

4. Now that the United States has elected an African American president to two terms, is the reparations debate still viable or even relevant? Why or why not?

5. Different terms for "reparations" are used in the various source documents for this Conversation. These include "targeted compensation," "compensation," "redress," "repair," and "restitution." How do different terms represent different attitudes toward "reparations" and what it means to the community at issue as well as to the larger society?

Conversation

What Is American Literature?
. . . .

As early as the turn of the nineteenth century, writers and critics were asking, What is American literature? Having brought the English language to the New World, were Americans burdened with the traditions of English literature, or were they free to develop their own literary traditions? We ask you to consider what makes American literature distinctly American, how that label has changed over the years, and what, exactly, it means to call a work a piece of American literature. The following nine selections will help you give that subject some thought.

Sources

Walt Whitman, from *Letter to Ralph Waldo Emerson* (1856)
Emma Lazarus, *American Literature* (1881)
John Macy, from *The Spirit of American Literature* (1913)
Sherwood Anderson, from *An Apology for Crudity* (1917)
Amy Lowell, from *On "New Poetry"* (1917)
Bliss Perry, from *The American Spirit in Literature* (1920)
D. H. Lawrence, from *The Spirit of Place* (1923)
Tom Wolfe, from *Why They Aren't Writing the Great American Novel Anymore* (1972)
Margaret Atwood, *Hello, Martians. Let* Moby-Dick *Explain* (2012)

from *Letter to Ralph Waldo Emerson*

WALT WHITMAN

> Walt Whitman sent a first edition of *Leaves of Grass* to Ralph Waldo Emerson, who responded with an enthusiastic letter of admiration, calling it the "most extraordinary piece of wit and wisdom that America has yet contributed." Without asking permission, Whitman published the letter in the *New York Tribune* as an advertisement for his book, included it as an appendix to the second edition, and stamped its best line ("I greet you at the beginning of a great career") in gold leaf on the second edition's spine. The second edition also included an open letter to Emerson about the development of literature in America, parts of which appear here.

Swiftly, on limitless foundations, the United States too are founding a literature. It is all as well done, in my opinion, as could be practicable. Each element here is in condition. Every day I go among the people of Manhattan Island, Brooklyn, and other cities, and among the young men, to discover the spirit of them, and to refresh myself. These are to be attended to; I am myself more drawn here than to those authors, publishers, importations, reprints, and so forth. I pass coolly through those, understanding them perfectly well, and that they do the indispensable service, outside of men like me, which nothing else could do. In poems, the young men of The States shall be represented, for they out-rival the best of the rest of the earth.

The lists of ready-made literature which America inherits by the mighty inheritance of the English language—all the rich repertoire of traditions, poems, histories, metaphysics, plays, classics, translations, have made, and still continue, magnificent preparations for that other plainly signified literature, to be our own, to be electric, fresh, lusty, to express the full-sized body, male and female—to give the modern meanings of things, to grow up beautiful, lasting, commensurate with America, with all the passions of home, with the inimitable sympathies of having been boys and girls together, and of parents who were with our parents.

What else can happen The States, even in their own despite? That huge English flow, so sweet, so undeniable, has done incalculable good here, and is to be spoken of for its own sake with generous praise and with gratitude. Yet the price The States have had to lie under for the same has not been a small price. Payment prevails; a nation can never take the issues of the needs of other nations for nothing. America, grandest of lands in the theory of its politics, in popular reading, in hospitality, breadth, animal beauty, cities, ships, machines, money, credit, collapses quick as lightning at the repeated, admonishing, stern words, Where are any mental expressions from you, beyond what you have copied or stolen? Where the born throngs of poets, literats, orators, you promised? Will you but tag after other nations? They struggled long for their literature, painfully working their way, some with deficient languages, some with priest-craft, some in the endeavor just to live—yet achieved for their times, works, poems, perhaps the only solid consolation left to them through ages afterward of shame and decay. You are young, have the perfectest of dialects, a free press, a free government, the world forwarding its best to be with you. As justice has been strictly done to you, from this hour do strict justice to yourself. Strangle the singers who will not sing you loud and strong. Open the doors of The West. Call for new great masters to comprehend new arts, new perfections, new wants. Submit to the most robust bard till he remedy your barrenness. Then you will not need to adopt the heirs of others; you will have true heirs, begotten of yourself, blooded with your own blood. . . .

All current nourishments to literature serve. Of authors and editors I do not know how many there are in The States, but there are thousands, each one building his or her step to the stairs by which giants shall mount. Of the twenty-four modern mammoth two-double, three-double, and four-double cylinder presses now in the world, printing by steam, twenty-one of them are in These States. The twelve thousand large and small shops for dispensing books and newspapers—the same number of public libraries, any one of which has all the reading wanted to equip a man or woman for American reading—the three thousand different newspapers, the nutriment of the imperfect ones coming in just as usefully as any—the story papers, various, full of strong-flavored romances, widely circulated—the one-cent and two-cent journals—the political ones, no matter what side—the weeklies in the country—the sporting and pictorial papers — the monthly magazines, with plentiful imported feed — the sentimental novels, numberless copies of them — the low-priced flaring tales, adventures, biographies — all are prophetic; all waft rapidly on. I see that they swell wide, for reasons. I am not troubled at the movement of them, but greatly pleased. I see plying shuttles, the active ephemeral myriads of books also, faithfully weaving the garments of a generation of men, and a generation of women, they do not perceive or know. What a progress popular reading and writing has made in fifty years! What a progress fifty years hence! The time is at hand when inherent literature will be a main part of These States, as general and real as steam-power, iron, corn, beef, fish. First-rate American persons are to be supplied. Our perennial materials for fresh thoughts, histories, poems, music, orations, religions, recitations, amusements, will then not be disregarded, any more than our perennial fields, mines, rivers, seas. Certain things are established, and are immovable; in those things millions of years stand justified. The mothers and fathers of whom modern centuries have come, have not existed for nothing; they too had brains and hearts. Of course all literature, in all nations and years, will share marked attributes in common, as we all, of all ages, share the common human attributes. America is to be kept coarse and broad. What is to be done is to withdraw from precedents, and be directed to men and women — also to The States in their federalness; for the union of the parts of the body is not more necessary to their life than the union of These States is to their life.

A profound person can easily know more of the people than they know of them-   5
selves. Always waiting untold in the souls of the armies of common people, is stuff better than anything that can possibly appear in the leadership of the same. That gives final verdicts. In every department of These States, he who travels with a coterie, or with selected persons, or with imitators, or with infidels, or with the owners of slaves, or with that which is ashamed of the body of a man, or with that which is ashamed of the body of a woman, or with any thing less than the bravest and the openest, travels straight for the slopes of dissolution. The genius of all foreign literature is clipped and cut small, compared to our genius, and is essentially insulting to our usages, and to the organic compacts of These States. Old forms, old poems, majestic and proper in their own lands here in this land are exiles; the air here is very strong. Much that stands well and has a little enough place provided for it in the small scales of European kingdoms, empires, and the like, here stands haggard, dwarfed, ludicrous, or has no place little enough provided for it. Authorities, poems, models, laws, names, imported into America, are useful to America today to destroy them, and so more disencumbered to great works, great days.

(1856)

Questions

1. What does Walt Whitman consider to be America's inheritance? What does he consider to be its purpose?

2. What advantages does Whitman think American writers have? What exhortations does Whitman give about those advantages?
3. In what ways does paragraph 4 reflect what Whitman envisions as American literature? What does his style suggest about what he sees as our "inherent literature"?
4. Do you think American literature has, as Whitman predicts, kept "coarse and broad" (par. 4)?

American Literature

EMMA LAZARUS

> Known best for her sonnet "The New Colossus," some lines of which are inscribed on the base of the Statue of Liberty, Emma Lazarus (1849–1887) grew up in New York City and Newport, Rhode Island. This essay was published in the *Critic* in 1881 in response to an article by literary critic George Woodberry.

In the May number of the *Fortnightly Review* Mr. George Edward Woodberry dogmatizes in a singular way concerning the "Fortunes of Literature under the American Republic." "Among us," he writes, "literature has no continuous tradition; where the torch fell, it was extinguished. Irving, it is true, had imitators who came to nothing; but our fiction does not seem to be different because Hawthorne lived; no poet has caught the music of Longfellow; no thinker carries forward the conclusions of Emerson. These men have left no lineage. . . . We have not earned the right to claim them as a national possession." The merest tyro[1] in the study of American literature can unravel this flimsy web of sophistries. In the first place we have yet to learn that in the sense of producing imitators, the influence of a man of genius is beneficial. On the contrary, we consider the shoal of imitators of the few first-class living poets of England — Tennyson, Morris, Swinburne, and Browning — one of the worst pests of contemporary literature. Who cares a fig for the imitators of Thackeray, of Dickens, of Carlyle? All these great men have marked mannerisms of style which make them the easy prey of a host of petty tricksters, who do all in their power by a cheap imitation of the outward form to disgust the world with the original, inimitable thought. The modern novel was invented, not by an Englishman, but by Balzac: Thackeray did not take up the torch extinguished in the hands of Scott, but appropriated what was his own in the immense world discovered by the Frenchman. It may be remembered, too, that contemporary English criticism declared Dickens's early work to be imitative of an American's — Irving. What would be said of an American who placed himself so conspicuously and shamelessly under the guidance of foreign leaders, as did Carlyle under the banner of Germany? The language which we share in common with England gives a false air of resemblance to productions that have infinitely less

---

[1]Novice. — Eds.

in common than have those of Carlyle with the works of Jean-Paul and the German romantic school.

Emerson stands isolated by his superiority in the sense that all men of genius are isolated, even from their followers; but whoever fails to see in Emerson's works the flowering of a distinctively American school of thought and habit of life, fails to understand the essential spirit of his teachings. Moreover, "his conclusions" *are* "carried forward," and to their extreme development, by a fellow-townsman of his own, only second to him in intellectual force, and with a still stronger local flavor — the poet-naturalist, Henry Thoreau. Again, in our own generation it is difficult to conceive of, otherwise than as a successor of these two, the keen-eyed observer of Nature and charming reporter of her open secrets, John Burroughs. Individual and sincere though he be, the influence of Emerson and Thoreau is strongly felt through his writings, which could have been produced nowhere else than in America. Let Mr. Woodberry take up any number of the *Atlantic Monthly*, any volume of New England essays or poetry, and judge whether the influence, as subtle as it is strong, of the transcendental idealist Emerson has not penetrated through all superficial practicalities and vulgarities to the very fibre of our best intellectual life. Is Mr. Woodberry quite fair in selecting Donatello as the representative type of Hawthorne's genius, and adding, "Except for the accident of the author's birth, the character would be as welcome in England as in America"? This is as if we should choose "Romola" for our example, and say, "Except for the accident of George Eliot's birth, she would be as welcome in Italy as in England." In each case we unjustly exclude the essentially national and even more powerful works of the same author. What foreigner could have given us the inside view of New England Puritanism presented in the *Scarlet Letter*, or have created the character of Hester Prynne? Did not the history of Salem "contribute an important element to the growth of Hawthorne's genius," which we *have* "a right to claim as a national possession"? Why does Mr. Woodberry persistently put forward, as the only American poet, Longfellow, and ignore (except as a writer of sensational tales) Edgar Poe, "whose cup was small, but who drank from his own glass," as emphatically as did Alfred de Musset, or Keats, or Tennyson? Is it by accident that Walt Whitman was born in America, or Lowell, or Holmes, or Bret Harte, or the author of *Uncle Tom's Cabin*, or, to come down to the present moment, the men who wrote the *Fool's Errand*, and *Creole Days*? "To-day," affirms Mr. Woodberry, "American authors make their reputation by English criticism, and American magazines are rivals for English pens." It is surprising that so ridiculously obsolete a tradition as this should still endeavor to pass current. The *Atlantic Monthly* has never depended for its reputation upon foreign contributions, and it is notorious that the success of *Scribner's Monthly* and of *Harper's* has been based upon their national character.

For evils that do not exist, Mr. Woodberry is at no loss to discover causes equally mythical. He complains of the lack of good critics, and describes the habit of American critics as being simply to "give a synopsis of the work before them": yet, after reading French, German, Italian, and English articles, amid the flood of criticisms upon Carlyle, with which the world has been deluged since his death, we found by far the most discriminating and intelligent analysis of his genius among the essays of an

American — Mr. Lowell; while one of the most just and sympathetic estimates of Carlyle's personality appeared in a Boston magazine over the signature of the elder Henry James; and Emerson's reminiscences, published in a New York monthly, painted a portrait that could have come only from the hand of a master. Mr. Stedman, in his criticisms of American and English poets, Mr. Henry James, Jr., in his volume on the French poets and novelists, and, in their more elaborate and critical articles, Mr. Stoddard and Mr. Howells, compare favorably with the leading European critics. So far from true is it that "American authors make their reputation by English criticism" that we do not hesitate to reject and ridicule the English verdict of men whom we consider ourselves better fitted to understand — as in the case of a certain poet, whom all the lion hunters of London could not foist upon America as anything higher than a second-rate singer. On the other hand, in some instances, American critics have founded the reputation of English books. Carlyle's now hackneyed sentence "I hear many echoes, but only one voice — from Concord," ascribes to the right quarter the first rumor of his fame. It is less well-known, but equally true, that the same authoritative voice was among the first to proclaim the greatness of the authors of the "Idylls of the King," and "Peg Woffington." In short, we cannot help thinking that the literary history of the past fifty years in America contrasts favorably with that of the past fifty years in England — the only period with which it can, with any show of justice, be compared.

(1881)

Questions

1. What counterargument does Emma Lazarus acknowledge and refute in this essay?
2. How does Lazarus develop and support her own argument?
3. What influences on American literature does Lazarus consider distinctly American? What is distinctly American about them?

from *The Spirit of American Literature*

John Macy

> John Macy (1877–1932) was an author, a critic, a teacher, and a poet. Unhappily married to and mostly separated from Anne Sullivan, the famous teacher of Helen Keller, he helped Keller and Sullivan write *The Story of My Life,* Keller's best-selling autobiography. This excerpt is from the first chapter of his influential survey of major American writers from Washington Irving to Henry James, *The Spirit of American Literature,* published in 1913.

American literature is a branch of English literature, as truly as are English books written in Scotland or South Africa. Our literature lies almost entirely in the nineteenth century when the ideas and books of the western world were freely interchanged among the nations and became accessible to an increasing number of readers. In literature nationality is determined by language rather than by blood or geography. M. Maeterlinck, born a subject of King Leopold, belongs to French literature. Mr. Joseph Conrad, born in Poland, is already an English classic. Geography, much less important in the nineteenth century than before, was never, among modern European nations, so important as we sometimes are asked to believe. Of the ancestors of English literature "Beowulf" is scarcely more significant, and rather less graceful, than our tree-inhabiting forebears with prehensile toes; the true progenitors of English literature are Greek, Latin, Hebrew, Italian, and French.

American literature and English literature of the nineteenth century are parallel derivatives from preceding centuries of English literature. Literature is a succession of books from books. Artistic expression springs from life ultimately but not immediately. It may be likened to a river which is swollen throughout its course by new tributaries and by the seepages of its banks; it reflects the life through which it flows, taking colour from the shores; the shores modify it, but its power and volume descend from distant headwaters and affluents far up stream. Or it may be likened to the race-life which our food nourishes or impoverishes, which our individual circumstances foster or damage, but which flows on through us, strangely impersonal and beyond our power to kill or create.

It is well for a writer to say: "Away with books! I will draw my inspiration from life!" For we have too many books that are simply better books diluted by John Smith. At the same time, literature is not born spontaneously out of life. Every book has its literary parentage, and students find it so easy to trace genealogies that much criticism reads like an Old Testament chapter of "begats." Every novel was suckled at the breasts of older novels, and great mothers are often prolific of anæmic offspring. The stock falls off and revives, goes a-wandering, and returns like a prodigal. The family records get blurred. But of the main fact of descent there is no doubt.

American literature is English literature made in this country. Its nineteenth-century characteristics are evident and can be analyzed and discussed with some degree of certainty. Its "American" characteristics — no critic that I know has ever given a good account of them. You can define certain peculiarities of American politics, American agriculture, American public schools, even American religion. But what is uniquely American in American literature? Poe is just as American as Mark Twain; Lanier is just as American as Whittier. The American spirit in literature is a myth, like American valour in war, which is precisely like the valour of Italians and Japanese. The American, deluded by a falsely idealized image which he calls America, can say that the purity of Longfellow represents the purity of American home life. An Irish Englishman, Mr. Bernard Shaw, with another falsely idealized image of America, surprised that a fact does not fit his image, can ask: "What is Poe doing in that galley?" There is no answer. You never can tell. Poe could not help it. He was born in Boston, and lived in Richmond, New York, Baltimore, Philadelphia. Professor Van Dyke says that Poe was a maker of "decidedly un-American cameos," but I do not understand what that means. Facts are uncomfortable consorts of prejudices and emotional generalities; they spoil domestic peace, and when there is a separation they sit solid at home while the other party goes. Irving, a shy, sensitive gentleman, who wrote with fastidious care, said: "It has been a matter of marvel, to European readers, that a man from the wilds of America should express himself in tolerable English." It is a matter of marvel, just as it is a marvel that Blake and Keats flowered in the brutal city of London a hundred years ago.

The literary mind is strengthened and nurtured, is influenced and mastered, by the accumulated riches of literature. In the last century the strongest thinkers in our language were Englishmen, and not only the traditional but the contemporary influences on our thinkers and artists were British. This may account for one negative characteristic of American literature — its lack of American quality. True, our records must reflect our life. Our poets, enamoured of nightingales and Persian gardens, have not altogether forgotten the mocking-bird and the woods of Maine. Fiction, written by inhabitants of New York, Ohio, and Massachusetts, does tell us something of the ways of life in those mighty commonwealths, just as English fiction written by Lancashire men about Lancashire people is saturated with the dialect, the local habits and scenery of that county. But wherever an English-speaking man of imagination may dwell, in Dorset or Calcutta or Indianapolis, he is subject to the strong arm of the empire of English literature; he cannot escape it; it tears him out of his obscure bed and makes a happy slave of him. He is assigned to the department of the service for which his gifts qualify him, and his special education is undertaken by drill-masters and captains who hail from provinces far from his birthplace.

Dickens, who writes of London, influences Bret Harte, who writes of California, and Bret Harte influences Kipling, who writes of India. Each is intensely local in subject matter. The affinity between them is a matter of temperament, manifested, for example, in the swagger and exaggeration characteristic of all three. California did not "produce" Bret Harte; the power of Dickens was greater than that of the Sierras and the Golden Gate. Bret Harte created a California that never existed, and Indian gentlemen, Caucasian and Hindoo, tell us that Kipling invented an army and an empire unknown to geographers and war-offices.

The ideas at work among these English men of letters are world-encircling and fly between book and brain. The dominant power is on the British Islands, and the prevailing stream of influence flows west across the Atlantic. Sometimes it turns and runs the other way. Poe influenced Rossetti; Whitman influenced Henley. For a century Cooper has been in command of the British literary marine. Literature is reprehensibly unpatriotic, even though its votaries are, as individual citizens, afflicted with local prides and hostilities. It takes only a dramatic interest in the guns of Yorktown. Its philosophy was nobly uttered by Gaston Paris in the Collège de France in 1870, when the city was beleaguered by the German armies: "Common studies, pursued in the same spirit, in all civilized countries, form, beyond the restrictions of diverse and often hostile nationalities, a great country which no war profanes, no conqueror menaces, where souls find that refuge and unity which in former times was offered them by the city of God." The catholicity of English language and literature transcends the temporal boundaries of states.

(1913)

Questions

1. Why does John Macy think that American literature is a "branch of English literature" (par. 1)? Do you agree or disagree with him? Explain your answer.
2. Describe the metaphor Macy uses in paragraph 2 to explain artistic expression.
3. Why does Macy believe there is no such thing as a "uniquely American" (par. 4) quality to American literature? What evidence does he use to support his argument?

from *An Apology for Crudity*

SHERWOOD ANDERSON

> Sherwood Anderson (1876–1941) was a novelist and short-story writer whose most important work is the short-story sequence *Winesburg, Ohio*. His work is said to have influenced the American writers Ernest Hemingway, William Faulkner, Norman Mailer, and Studs Turkel. This essay was published in the literary journal the *Dial* in 1917.

For a long time I have believed that crudity is an inevitable quality in the production of a really significant present-day American literature. How indeed is one to escape the obvious fact that there is as yet no native subtlety of thought or living among us? And if we are a crude and childlike people how can our literature hope to escape the influence of that fact? Why indeed should we want it to escape?

If you are in doubt as to the crudity of thought in America, try an experiment. Come out of your offices, where you sit writing and thinking, and try living with us. Get on a train at Pittsburg and go west to the mountains of Colorado. Stop for a time in our towns and cities. Stay for a week in some Iowa corn-shipping town and for another week in one of the Chicago clubs. As you loiter about read our newspapers and listen to our conversations, remembering, if you will, that as you see us in the towns and cities, so we are. We are not subtle enough to conceal ourselves and he who runs with open eyes through the Mississippi Valley may read the story of the Mississippi Valley.

It is a marvelous story and we have not yet begun to tell the half of it. A little, I think I know why. It is because we who write have drawn ourselves away. We have not had faith in our people and in the story of our people. If we are crude and childlike, that is our story and our writing men must learn to dare to come among us until they know the story. The telling of the story depends, I believe, upon their learning that lesson and accepting that burden.

To my room, which is on a street near the loop in the city of Chicago, come men who write. They talk and I talk. We are fools. We talk of writers of the old world and the beauty and subtlety of the work they do. Below us the roaring city lies like a great animal on the prairies, but we do not run out to the prairies. We stay in our rooms and talk.

And so, having listened to talk and having myself talked overmuch, I grow weary 5
of talk and walk in the streets. As I walk alone, an old truth comes home to me and
I know that we shall never have an American literature until we return to faith in
ourselves and to the facing of our own limitations. We must, in some way, become
in ourselves more like our fellows, more simple and real.

For surely it does not follow that because we Americans are a people without
subtlety, we are a dull or uninteresting people. Our literature is dull, but we are not.
One remembers how Dostoevsky had faith in the simplicity of the Russians and what
he achieved. He lived and he expressed the life of his time and people. The thing that
he did brings hope of achievement for our men.

But let us first of all accept certain truths. Why should we Americans aspire to a
subtlety that belongs not to us but to old lands and places? Why talk of intellectuality and of intellectual life when we have not accepted the life that we have? There is
death on that road and following it has brought death into much of American writing. Can you doubt what I say? Consider the smooth slickness of the average magazine story. There is often great subtlety of plot and phrase, but there is no reality. Can
such work live? The answer is that the most popular magazine story or novel does not
live in our minds for a month.

And what are we to do about it? To me it seems that as writers we shall have to
throw ourselves with greater daring into the life here. We shall have to begin to write
out of the people and not for the people. We shall have to find within ourselves a
little of that courage. To continue along the road we are travelling is unthinkable. To
draw ourselves apart, to live in little groups and console ourselves with the thought
that we are achieving intellectuality, is to get nowhere. By such a road we can hope
only to go on producing a literature that has nothing to do with life as it is lived in
these United States.

To be sure, the doing of the thing I am talking about will not be easy. America is
a land of objective writing and thinking. New paths will have to be made. The subjective impulse is almost unknown to us. Because it is close to life, it works out into
crude and broken forms. It leads along a road that such American masters of prose as
James and Howells did not want to take, but if we are to get anywhere, we shall have
to travel that road.

(1917)

Questions

1. What does Sherwood Anderson mean by "crudity"? Explain how you think he feels
   about it.
2. Why does Anderson think American literature needs to become less "dull" (par. 6)?
   How does he suggest making that happen?
3. What is your view of crudity in literature? Do you think literature should reveal
   our worst habits and instincts or should those aspects be cleaned up? What would
   Anderson think of the "gross out" comedy in some of today's films? Might he think
   we've gone too far?

from *On "New Poetry"*

Amy Lowell

> Amy Lowell (1874–1925) was an American poet and critic. She was awarded
> a posthumous Pulitzer Prize for *What O'Clock* (1926). This selection is from
> *Tendencies in Modern American Poetry*, Lowell's study of American poets such as
> Robert Frost and Carl Sandburg, which was published in 1917.

When people speak of the "New Poetry," they generally mean that poetry which is
written in the newer, freer forms. But such a distinction is misleading in the extreme,
for, after all, forms are merely forms, of no particular value unless they are the necessary and adequate clothing to some particular manner of thought.

There is a "New Poetry" to-day, and the new forms are a part of its attire, but the
body is more important than the clothing and existed before it. All real changes are
a matter of slow growth, of evolution. The beginnings of a change are almost imperceptible, the final stages, on the other hand, being so radical that everyone remarks
them, and with such astonishment that the cry of "freak," "charlatan," is almost sure
to be raised by ignorant readers.

A great artistic movement is as inevitable a thing as the growth of a race. But, as
in races, individuals possess differing characteristics, so the various artists whose
work represents a revolt may differ most widely one from another, and yet, in varying
still more widely from artists of other epochs, they create what critics call a "movement." . . .

A poetic movement may be compared to a braid of woven strands. Of the six poets
of whom I shall speak, each is an exemplar, and I think the most typical exemplar, of a
strand. But one particular tinge is peculiar to all the strands, and that particular tinge
is revolt against the immediate past.

We shall see these poets revolting against stilted phrases and sentimentality; we   5
shall see them endeavouring to express themselves, and the new race which America
is producing; we shall see them stepping boldly from realism to far flights of imagination. We shall see them ceding more and more to the influence of other, alien, peoples,
and fusing exotic modes of thought with their Anglo-Saxon inheritance. This is indeed
the melting pot, and its fumes affect the surrounding company as well as the ingredients
in the crucible.

To understand the change which is going on in American poetry, it is necessary
to glance back for a moment to earlier conditions.

If we examine the state of American poetry from, let us say, 1830 until the Civil
War, we shall be struck with one thing. That is, with the racial homogeneity of our
poets. They are all of good English stock, in their work, I mean. It is true that two
great geniuses flung themselves up out of this mass of cultivated endeavour. But that
is no exception to the Anglo-Saxon rule, for no literature is richer in geniuses than is
the English. But these two geniuses, Edgar Allan Poe and Walt Whitman, were too
far ahead of their times to have much effect upon their contemporaries. They are

better understood, and have more followers, in the America of to-day. Wordsworth on the one hand, Byron on the other, were the main springs of American poetry.

Good poetry, if not strikingly great poetry, marked the epoch of Whittier, Bryant, Emerson, Lowell, Longfellow, and Holmes. They were English provincial poets, in the sense that America was still a literary province of the Mother Country.

But from the Civil War until almost the present day, the literary sponsors of American verse were much less worthy of disciples. The robustness of Byron gave place to the sugared sentimentality of Tennyson; the moral strength of Wordsworth made way for the frozen didacticism of Matthew Arnold. But worse was to follow, for technique usurped the place of emotion, and words, mere words, were exalted out of all due proportion. Swinburne and Rossetti are not good masters to follow, no matter with what skill they themselves wrought. Only those of our poets who kept solidly to the Shakespearean tradition achieved any measure of success. But Keats was the last great exponent of that tradition, and we all know how thin, how lacking in charm, the copies of Keats have become. No matter how beautiful a piece of music may be, we cannot hear it indefinitely without satiety, and the same piece rendered by a phonograph soon becomes unbearable. Our poets were largely phonographs to greater English poets dead and gone, as the pages of our magazines of twenty years ago will abundantly prove.

Art is like politics. Any theory carried too far ends in sterility, and freshness is only gained by following some other line. Faultless, flowing verses, raised about a worn-out, threadbare idea — fine moral sentiments expressed in the weak, innocuous language of the hymn-books — had no resemblance to the temper of modern American life. Publishers still printed poetry, but not with any idea of its answering a demand; editors accepted it to round out short pages, but they hardly expected to have more attention accorded it than an ornamental scroll would have received. Readers found more sustenance in Browning, and bewailed the fact that he was dead, and, alas, English! America was not a country for poets, said the wiseacres, it was given over to materialism, and materialism could never produce art.

This was tantamount to saying that art was an artificial thing, whereas making steel harrows was a natural thing. Of course, that is a ridiculous point of view. Art, true art, is the desire of a man to express himself, to record the reactions of his personality to the world he lives in. Great emotion always tends to become rhythmic, and out of that tendency the forms of art have been evolved. Art becomes artificial only when the forms take precedence over the emotion.

Now here was a great country practically dumb. Here was a virile race, capable of subduing a vast continent in an incredibly short time, with no tongue to vent its emotion. How should such a race express itself by the sentiments appropriate to a highly civilized country no bigger than New York State, and of that country some fifty years earlier, to boot?

I would not be construed into saying that the larger the country, the more profound the emotions. That would be absurd. I only mean that the material conditions under which Americans lived — the great unoccupied spaces, the constant warring

10

and overcoming of nature, the fluid state of the social fabric — all made a different speech necessary, if they were really to express the thoughts that were in them.

There was one other element in the constitution of the American people, quite as important as these I have mentioned. That element was, and is, the ingrained Puritanism which time and place do so little to eradicate. Of course, the dwellers in large cities, worked upon from their earliest childhood by modern conditions, were able to modify the Puritan sentiment, to cast out what of poison remained in it. For Puritanism, at this late day, has resolved itself into a virulent poison which saps vitality and brings on the convulsions of despair.

Puritanism was always a drastic, soul-searching, joyless religion. It was itself a   15
revolt against a licence that had become unbearable. But no student of history can fail to be struck with the vigour and healthy-mindedness of a race which can live under such an incubus and retain its sanity. There is no more horrible page to the student than that of the early times in New England, when nervous little children were tortured with exhortations to declare their faith and escape the clutches of the devil, and senile old women were hanged for witches. Moloch and his sacrifices of human victims is no more revolting. Yet, in spite of much infant mortality, and many of the weaker members of a community going insane, the people as a whole lived and throve under this threatening horror, with the vitality of a race born to endure.

Indeed, my simile of a drug is no idle comparison. For Puritanism undoubtedly did much to strengthen the fibre of the early settlers, but its prolonged effect has been to produce anæmia and atrophy, and where these do not follow, where the strength of the individual keeps him fighting for the cause of individuality against the composite thought of a race, the result is an innate cynicism, a dreadful despair which will not let him be.

The age of Bryant and Longfellow was singularly free from these negative, but powerful, results of the Puritanic poison. Didactic and moral these poets undoubtedly were, but with them the paternal tradition was diluted by nothing more violent than time. They were in sympathy with its main trend only; like fruits set in the sun, the substance itself had mellowed and sweetened. Living in a highly educated community, they modified with it, and only so far as it, too, modified. They were not at war with their times, their surroundings, or their fellow citizens.

In the case of smaller places, the result is very different. Here, Puritanism held sway quite out of time. It persisted long after it had become an anachronism to New England at large. An individual brought up in one of the small towns scattered over the country was therefore obliged to reproduce suddenly in himself the evolution of three hundred years. In so far as he was advanced mentally beyond his fellows, he suffered the pangs of growth and misunderstanding. And his evolution carried with it the farther torture of consciousness. Sudden change can never accomplish the result of a long, slow process. What large cities like Boston lived into, the clever youths of smaller towns were thrust violently upon.

We must never forget that all inherited prejudice and training pulls one way, in these unfortunate cases; the probing, active mind pulls another. The result is a profound melancholy, tinged with cynicism. Self-analysis has sapped joy, and the impossibility of constructing an ethical system in accordance both with desire and with tradition has twisted the mental vision out of all true proportion. It takes the lifetime of more than one individual to throw off a superstition, and the effort to do so is not made without sacrifice.

(1917)

Questions

1. What does Amy Lowell think ties the work of the writers of "New Poetry" together? What are her criticisms of earlier American poetry?
2. How does Lowell counter the critics who say that America can't produce art because the country is too materialistic?
3. How does Lowell think Puritanism affects American poetry?

from *The American Spirit in Literature*

BLISS PERRY

> Bliss Perry (1860–1954) was a literary critic, writer, and teacher who wrote extensively about American literature. He was the editor of the *Atlantic Monthly* and taught at Williams College, Princeton University, and Harvard University. This is an excerpt from Chapter 10 of *The American Spirit in Literature*, published in 1920.

Perhaps the truth is that although we are a reading people we are not yet a book-loving people. The American newspaper and magazine have been successful in making their readers fancy that newspaper and magazine are an equivalent for books. Popular orators and popular preachers confirm this impression, and colleges and universities have often emphasized a vocational choice of books — in other words, books that are not books at all, but treatises. It is not, of course, that American journalism, whether of the daily or monthly sort, has consciously set itself to supplant the habit of book-reading. A thousand social and economic factors enter into such a problem. But few observers will question the assertion that the influence of the American magazine, ever since its great period of national literary service in the eighties and nineties, has been more marked in the field of conduct and of artistic taste than in the stimulation of a critical literary judgment. An American schoolhouse of today owes its improvement in appearance over the schoolhouse of fifty years ago largely to the popular diffusion, through the illustrated magazines, of better standards of artistic taste. But whether the judgment of school-teachers and school-children upon a piece of literature is any better than it was in the red schoolhouse of fifty years ago is a disputable question.

But we must stop guessing, or we shall never have done. The fundamental problem of our literature, as this book has attempted to trace it, has been to obtain from a mixed population dwelling in sections as widely separated as the peoples of Northern and Southern Europe, an integral intellectual and spiritual activity which could express, in obedience to the laws of beauty and truth, the emotions stimulated by our national life. It has been assumed in the preceding chapters that American literature is something different from English literature written in America. Canadian and Australian literatures have indigenous qualities of their own, but typically they belong to the colonial literature of Great Britain. This can scarcely be said of the writings of Franklin and Jefferson, and it certainly cannot be said of the writings of Cooper, Hawthorne, Emerson, Thoreau, Whitman, Lowell, Lincoln, Mark Twain, and Mr. Howells. In the pages of these men and of hundreds of others less distinguished, there is a revelation of a new national type. That the full energies of this nation have been back of our books, giving them a range and vitality and unity commensurate with the national existence, no one would claim. There are other spheres of effort in which American character has been more adequately expressed than in words. Nevertheless the books are here, in spite of every defect in national discipline, every flaw in national character; and they deserve the closest attention from all those who are trying to understand the American mind.

If the effort toward an expression of a peculiarly complex national experience has been the problem of our literary past, the literary problem of the future is the expression of the adjustment of American ideals to the standards of civilization. "Patriotism," said the martyred Edith Cavell[1] just before her death, "is not enough." Nationality and the instincts of national separatism now seem essential to the preservation of the political units of the world-state, precisely as a healthy individualism must be the basis of all enduring social fellowship. Yet it is clear that civilization is a larger, more ultimate term than nationality. Chauvinism is nowhere more repellent than in the things of the mind. It is difficult for some Americans to think internationally even in political affairs — to construe our national policy and duty in terms of obligation to civilization. Nevertheless the task must be faced, and we are slowly realizing it.

In the field of literature, likewise, Americanism is not a final word either of blame or praise. It is a word of useful characterization. Only American books, and not books written in English in America, can adequately represent our national contribution to the world's thinking and feeling. So argued Emerson and Whitman, long ago. But the younger of these two poets came to realize in his old age that the New World and the Old World are fundamentally one. The literature of the New World will inevitably have an accent of its own, but it must speak the mother-language of civilization, share in its culture, accept its discipline.

It has been said disparagingly of Longfellow and his friends: "The houses of the Brahmins had only eastern windows. The souls of the whole school lived in the old lands of culture, and they visited these lands as often as they could, and, returning, brought back whole libraries of books which they eagerly translated." But even if   5

---

[1]British nurse who helped smuggle Allied soldiers out of German-occupied Belgium during World War I. She was tried for treason by the Germans and executed, despite international condemnation of her sentence. — Eds.

Longfellow and his friends had been nothing more than translators and diffusers of European culture, their task would have been justified. They kept the ideals of civilization from perishing in this new soil. Through those eastern windows came in, and still comes in, the sunlight to illumine the American spirit. To decry the literatures of the Orient and of Greece and Rome as something now outgrown by America, is simply to close the eastern windows, to narrow our conception of civilization to merely national and contemporaneous terms. It is as provincial to attempt this restriction in literature as it would be in world-politics. We must have all the windows open in our American writing, free access to ideas, knowledge of universal standards, perception of universal law.

(1920)

Questions

1. What does Bliss Perry think about the effect of magazines on American reading habits?
2. Why does Perry think it is important to have "all the windows open in our American writing" (par. 5)?
3. Why does Perry think American literature deserves close attention even though the American spirit has shown itself stronger in areas other than literature?

from *The Spirit of Place*

D. H. LAWRENCE

> This essay is the opening chapter of *Studies in Classic American Literature* (1923), by the British writer David Herbert Lawrence (1885–1930). Lawrence is the author of *The Rainbow* (1915), *Women in Love* (1920), and *Lady Chatterley's Lover* (1928), among other works.

We like to think of the old-fashioned American classics as children's books. Just childishness, on our part. The old American art-speech contains an alien quality, which belongs to the American continent and to nowhere else. But, of course, so long as we insist on reading the books as children's tales, we miss all that.

One wonders what the proper high-brow Romans of the third and fourth or later centuries read into the strange utterances of Lucretius or Apuleius or Tertullian, Augustine or Athanasius. The uncanny voice of Iberian Spain, the weirdness of old Carthage, the passion of Libya and North Africa; you may bet the proper old Romans never heard these at all. They read old Latin inference over the top of it, as we read old European inference over the top of Poe or Hawthorne.

It is hard to hear a new voice, as hard as it is to listen to an unknown language. We just don't listen. There is a new voice in the old American classics. The world has declined to hear it, and has babbled about children's stories.

Why? — Out of fear. The world fears a new experience more than it fears anything. Because a new experience displaces so many old experiences. And it is like trying to use muscles that have perhaps never been used, or that have been going stiff for ages. It hurts horribly.

The world doesn't fear a new idea. It can pigeon-hole any idea. But it can't pigeon-hole a real new experience. It can only dodge. The world is a great dodger, and the Americans the greatest. Because they dodge their own very selves.

There is a new feeling in the old American books, far more than there is in the modern American books, which are pretty empty of any feeling, and proud of it. There is a "different" feeling in the old American classics. It is the shifting over from the old psyche to something new, a displacement. And displacements hurt. This hurts. So we try to tie it up, like a cut finger. Put a rag round it.

It is a cut too. Cutting away the old emotions and consciousness. Don't ask what is left.

Art-speech is the only truth. An artist is usually a damned liar, but his art, if it be art, will tell you the truth of his day. And that is all that matters. Away with eternal truth. Truth lives from day to day, and the marvellous Plato of yesterday is chiefly bosh today.

The old American artists were hopeless liars. But they were artists, in spite of themselves. Which is more than you can say of most living practitioners.

And you can please yourself, when you read *The Scarlet Letter*, whether you accept what that sugary, blue-eyed little darling of a Hawthorne has to say for himself, false as all darlings are, or whether you read the impeccable truth of his art-speech.

The curious thing about art-speech is that it prevaricates so terribly, I mean it tells such lies. I suppose because we always all the time tell ourselves lies. And out of a pattern of lies art weaves the truth. Like Dostoevsky posing as a sort of Jesus, but most truthfully revealing himself all the while as a little horror.

Truly art is a sort of subterfuge. But thank God for it, we can see through the subterfuge if we choose. Art has two great functions. First, it provides an emotional experience. And then, if we have the courage of our own feelings, it becomes a mine of practical truth. We have had the feelings *ad nauseam*. But we've never dared dig the actual truth out of them, the truth that concerns us, whether it concerns our grandchildren or not.

The artist usually sets out — or used to — to point a moral and adorn a tale. The tale, however, points the other way, as a rule. Two blankly opposing morals, the artist's and the tale's. Never trust the artist. Trust the tale. The proper function of a critic is to save the tale from the artist who created it.

Now we know our business in these studies; saving the American tale from the American artist.

(1923)

Questions

1. Why does D. H. Lawrence say that the world is hesitant to accept American literature? How does he put American literature into a world context?

2. Why does Lawrence say, "Never trust the artist. Trust the tale" (par. 13).
3. Later in this essay, Lawrence says, "Every continent has its own great spirit of place. Every people is polarized in some particular locality, which is home, the homeland. Different places on the face of the earth have different vital effluence, different vibration, different chemical exhalation, different polarity with different stars: call it what you like. But the spirit of place is a great reality." Does this belief resonate today or does it seem outdated? Explain your answer.

from *Why They Aren't Writing the Great American Novel Anymore*

Tom Wolfe

> This essay appeared in *Esquire* magazine in 1972. In it Tom Wolfe examines the development of New Journalism, writing in which journalists and authors use the tools of fiction in their reporting and nonfiction.

The similarity between the early days of the novel and the early days of the New Journalism is not merely coincidental. In both cases we are watching the same process. We are watching a group of writers coming along, working in a genre regarded as Lower Class (the novel before the 1850's, slick-magazine journalism before the 1960's), who discover the joys of detailed realism and its strange powers. Many of them seem to be in love with realism for its own sake; and never mind the "sacred callings" of literature. They seem to be saying: "Hey! Come here! This is the way people are living now—just the way I'm going to show you! It may astound you, disgust you, delight you or arouse your contempt or make you laugh. . . . Nevertheless, this is what it's like! It's *all* right here! You won't be bored! Take a look!"

As I hardly have to tell you, that is not exactly the way serious novelists regard the task of the novel today. In this decade, the Seventies, The Novel will be celebrating the one-hundredth anniversary of its canonization as *the* spiritual genre. Novelists today keep using words like "myth," "fable" and "magic." That state of mind known as "the sacred office of the novelist" had originated in Europe in the 1870's and didn't take hold in the American literary world until after the Second World War. But it soon made up for lost time. What kind of novel should a sacred officer write? In 1948 Lionel Trilling presented the theory that the novel of social realism (which had flourished in America throughout the 1930's) was finished because the freight train of history had passed it by. The argument was that such novels were a product of the rise of the bourgeoisie in the nineteenth century at the height of capitalism. But now bourgeois society was breaking up, fragmenting. A novelist could no longer portray a part of that society and hope to capture the Zeitgeist; all he would be left with was one of the broken pieces. The only hope was a new kind of novel (his candidate was the novel of ideas). This theory caught on among young novelists with an astonishing grip. Whole careers were altered. All those writers hanging out in the literary pubs in New York such as the White Horse Tavern rushed off to write every kind of novel you could imagine, so long as it wasn't the so-called "big novel" of manners and society. The next thing one knew, they were into novels of ideas, Freudian novels, surrealistic novels ("black comedy"), Kafkaesque novels and, more recently, the cata-tonic novel or novel of immobility, the sort that begins: "In order to get started, he went to live alone on an island and shot himself." (Opening line of a Robert Coover short story.)

As a result, by the Sixties, about the time I came to New York, the most serious, ambitious and, presumably, talented novelists had abandoned the richest terrain of the novel: namely, society, the social tableau, manners and morals, the whole busi-ness of "the way we live now," in Trollope's phrase. There is no novelist who will be remembered as the novelist who captured the Sixties in America, or even in New York, in the sense that Thackeray was the chronicler of London in the 1840's and Balzac was the chronicler of Paris and all of France after the fall of the Empire. Balzac prided himself on being "the secretary of French society." Most serious American novelists would rather cut their wrists than be known as "the secretary of American society," and not merely because of ideological considerations. With fable, myth and the sacred office to think about — who wants such a menial role?

That was marvelous for journalists — I can tell you that. The Sixties was one of the most extraordinary decades in American history in terms of manners and morals. Manners and morals *were* the History of the Sixties. A hundred years from now when historians write about the 1960's in America (always assuming, to paraphrase Céline, that the Chinese will still give a damn about American history), they won't write about it as the decade of the war in Vietnam or of space exploration or of political assassina-tions . . . but as the decade when manners and morals, styles of living, attitudes toward the world changed the country more crucially than any political events . . . all the changes that were labeled, however clumsily, with such tags as "the generation gap," "the counter culture," "black consciousness," "sexual permissiveness," "the death of God," . . . the abandonment of proprieties, pieties, decorums connoted by "go-go funds," "fast money," swinger groovy hippie drop-out pop Beatles Andy Baby Jane Bernie Huey Eldridge LSD marathon encounter stone underground rip-off. . . . This whole side of American life that gushed forth when postwar American affluence finally blew the lid off — all this novelists simply turned away from, gave up by default. That left a huge gap in American letters, a gap big enough to drive an ungainly Reo rig like the New Journalism through.

When I reached New York in the early Sixties, I couldn't believe the scene I saw 5 spread out before me. New York was pandemonium with a big grin on. Among people with money — and they seemed to be multiplying like shad — it was the wild-est, looniest time since the 1920's . . . a universe of creamy forty-five-year-old fashion-able fatties with walnut-shell eyes out on the giblet slab wearing the hip-huggers and the minis and the Little Egypt eyes and the sideburns and the boots and the bells and the love beads, doing the Watusi and the Funky Broadway and jiggling and grinning and sweating and sweating and grinning and jiggling until the onset of dawn or saline depletion, whichever came first. . . . It was a hulking carnival. But what really amazed me was that as a writer I had it practically all to myself. As fast as I could possibly do it, I was turning out articles on this amazing spectacle that I saw bubbling and screaming right there in front of my wondering eyes — New York! — and all the while I just knew that some enterprising novelist was going to come along and *do* this whole marvelous scene with one gigantic daring bold stroke. It was so ready, so *ripe* — beckoning . . . but it never happened. To my great amazement New York simply remained the journalist's bonanza. For that matter, novelists seemed to shy away from the life of the great cities altogether. The thought of tackling such a subject seemed to terrify them, confuse them, make them doubt their own powers. And besides, it would have meant tackling social realism as well.

To my even greater amazement I had the same experience when I came upon 1960's California. This was the very incubator of new styles of living, and these styles were right there for all to see, ricocheting off every eyeball — and again a few amazed journalists working in the new form had it all to themselves, even the psychedelic movement, whose waves are still felt in every part of the country, in every grammar school even, like the intergalactic pulse. I wrote *The Electric Kool-Aid Acid Test* and then waited for the novels that I was sure would come pouring out of the psychedelic experience . . . but they never came forth, either. I learned later that publishers had been waiting, too. They had been practically crying for novels by the new writers who must be out there somewhere, the new writers who would do the big novels of the hippie life or campus life or radical movements or the war in Vietnam or dope or sex or black militancy or encounter groups or the whole whirlpool all at once. They waited, and all they got was the Prince of Alienation . . . sailing off to Lonesome Island on his Tarot boat with his back turned and his Timeless cape on, reeking of camphor balls.

Amazing, as I say. If nothing else had done it, that would have. The — New Journalists — Parajournalists — had the whole crazed obscene uproarious Mammon-faced drug-soaked mau-mau; lust oozing Sixties in America all to themselves.

(1972)

Questions

1. What does Tom Wolfe think early novelists and practitioners of New Journalism have in common?
2. In what ways does Wolfe believe the American novel has changed by the time he writes this in the 1970s? According to him, how did that change open the way for New Journalism?
3. How does this excerpt reflect some of the elements of New Journalism?
4. Do you consider examples of New Journalism, such as Truman Capote's *In Cold Blood*, to be literature? Explain why or why not.

Hello, Martians. Let Moby-Dick *Explain*

Margaret Atwood

This essay by Canadian novelist, poet, and environmental activist Margaret Atwood (b. 1939) was published in the *New York Times* in 2012. Short-listed five times and winner once of the Man Booker Prize, Atwood is the author of *The Handmaid's Tale* (1985), *Cat's Eye* (1988), and *The Blind Assassin* (2000), among other books.

Last night the Martians touched down in the backyard. They were oval and bright pink, with two antlike antennae topped by eyes fringed with sea-anemone lashes. They said they'd come to study America.

"Why ask me?" I said. "America is farther south."

"You are an observer," they said. "Please tell us: Does America have a different 'flavor' from that of other countries? Is it the center of the cultural world? How does it look to outsiders?"

"America has always been different from Europe," I said, "having begun as a utopian religious community. Some have seen it as a dream world where you can be what you choose, others as a mirage that lures, exploits and disappoints. Some see it as a land of spiritual potential, others as a place of crass and vulgar materialism. Some see it as a mecca for creative entrepreneurs, others as a corporate oligarchy where the big eat the small and inventions helpful to the world are stifled. Some see it as the home of freedom of expression, others as a land of timorous conformity and mob-opinion rule."

"Thank you," said the Martians, after looking up "thank you" on translate.google .com™. "How may we best discover the essence of America?" 5

"Through its literature, would be my choice," I said, "but I'm biased."

"O.K.," said the Martians. "What should we read first? Can we have marshmal-lows?"

"Let's start with two stories by Nathaniel Hawthorne," I said. "'The Maypole of Merry Mount,' and 'Young Goodman Brown.' Here are your marshmallows."

Their pink antennae waved excitedly. They stored away the marshmallows as rare American artifacts. Then they read the stories, very quickly, as Martians do. "What do these mean to contemporary America?" they asked.

"In 'The Maypole of Merry Mount,'" I said, "some people having a fun party in 10 the woods are disrupted by the Puritans, who consider them immoral. Both groups have come to America in search of 'freedom.' The Merry Mounters interpret 'freedom' as sexual and individual freedom, the Puritans as freedom to practice their own religion while outlawing the behavior of others. This fight is still going on in America: the same issues come up in every election. In my novel *The Handmaid's Tale*," I added modestly, "I've included them as 'freedom to' and 'freedom from.'"

"We took that in high school," said the Martians. "What about 'Young Goodman Brown'?"

"So, in 'Young Goodman Brown,'" I said, "this Puritan goes for a walk at night and discovers that all his neighbors and relations — including his young wife, Faith — are members of a satanic witchcraft group. He wakes up in the morning wondering if he's had a bad dream. But ever afterward he distrusts the neighbors; and so do all Americans, because how do you know whether the neighbors are who they claim to be? Every once in a while America has a Salem-style witch hunt, during which hysteria takes over and people are tagged with the satanic label of the moment. Right now it's mostly 'terrorism,' though in some quarters it's 'liberalism' or even 'evil-green-dragon environmentalism.'"

The Martians decided to eat one marshmallow each to see what it tasted like. Their mouths were underneath: they dealt with food by hopping onto it. "Can we have popcorn now? Orville Redenbacher's™?" they said. "And a Coke™?"

"How do you know about those things?" I said.

"We watch American TV and Internet," they said, "like everyone else in the universe. Though American cultural hegemony is slipping, we perceive: newly rich countries such as India and Brazil have developed their own mass media. Also, America's promise of democracy and egalitarianism — the mainstay of its cultural capital, widely understood — is being squandered. America is viewed as riddled with internal contradictions, what with vote suppression, the economic inequality protested by Occupy Wall Street, the impact of the mortgage meltdown, and the public's loss of confidence in political institutions. So, the popcorn? We can do the microwaving." They took out their ray guns.   15

"After you've read the next book," I said. "It's Melville's *Moby-Dick*."

The Martians riffled through *Moby-Dick* at top speed. Then they consulted translate.google.com™ for an expression that would best convey their reaction. "Holy crap!" they said. "Does this mean what we think it means?" they said.

"What do you think it means?" I said. "I'll do the popcorn myself: you might get the wavelength wrong."

"*Moby-Dick* is about the oil industry," they said. "And the Ship of American State. The owners of the *Pequod* are rapacious and stingy religious hypocrites. The ship's business is to butcher whales and turn them into an industrial energy product. The mates are the middle management. The harpooners, who are from races colonized by America one way or another, are supplying the expert tech labor. Elijah the prophet — from the American artist caste — foretells the *Pequod*'s doom, which comes about because the chief executive, Ahab, is a megalomaniac who wants to annihilate nature.

"Nature is symbolized by a big white whale, which has interfered with Ahab's   20 personal freedom by biting off his leg and refusing to be slaughtered and boiled. The narrator, Ishmael, represents journalists; his job is to warn America that it's controlled by psychotics who will destroy it, because they hate the natural world and don't grasp the fact that without it they will die. That's enough literature for now. Can we have popcorn?"

After inhaling the popcorn, they slurped up their Cokes™, then asked me to take an Instagram™ on their cellphones of them with the bottles.

"Now we are going to Las Vegas to do some gambling," they said, "because it's a very American thing. After that we will buzz the Grand Canyon, and then we'll go to the Boot Hill Museum in Kansas and get pictures of ourselves dressed as Wild West cowboys and honky-tonk floozies."

"I think you should be careful," I said.

"Why?" the Martians asked.

"Forgive me for pointing this out, but you look a lot like diagrams of the human 25 female uterus," I said. "Complete with fallopian tubes and ovaries."

A human being might be insulted to be told this, but it didn't seem to bother the Martians. Having looked up "uterus" on translate.google.com™, they said, "Isn't the uterus a good thing? The life force and so on?"

"In some parts of America," I said, "the men are obsessed with uteri. They feel that having one is potentially demonic. It's a hangover from 'Young Goodman Brown.' If they saw you hopping around — worse still, eating popcorn — they'd go completely berserk, and pronounce you pregnant, and put you in jail."

"Maybe we will go to Radio City Music Hall instead," the Martians said.

"Good choice," I said. "You won't stand out in New York, or not much. If anyone bothers you, accuse them of being specist. Throw in that you're vegans."

"O.K.," they said. "When we get back to Mars, we will start an American book 30 club. We wish to read David Foster Wallace, not to mention Edith Wharton and Raymond Carver and tons of others. It is the writers who convey the inner truth about a nation, despite themselves, yes? Will you join us on video?"

"A pleasure," I said. "Any reader is a friend of mine."

(2012)

Questions

1. Besides the fact that she's a writer, why do you think Margaret Atwood suggests literature as the way to "best discover the essence of America" (par. 5)?
2. Based on the stories Atwood suggests, what does she consider to be the most important influence in both American literature and politics?
3. Do you think Atwood believes that there is such a thing as American literature? Explain your answer.

Making Connections

1. Both Amy Lowell (p. 1257) and Margaret Atwood (p. 1267) discuss the influence of Puritanism on American literature. In what ways are their views similar? In what ways are they different?
2. Emma Lazarus (p. 1250) argues that the influence of "a man of genius" is beneficial, noting that "contemporary English criticism declared [Charles] Dickens's early work to be imitative of an American's — [Washington] Irving" (par. 1). What might

she say to Walt Whitman (p. 1247) about his exhortation to "[c]all for new great masters to comprehend new arts, new perfections, new wants" (par. 3)?

3. Compare and contrast the excerpts from John Macy (p. 1252) and Bliss Perry (p. 1260), both of which address the spirit of American literature.

4. What do you think Sherwood Anderson (p. 1255) would say to Atwood's visiting Martians?

5. Tom Wolfe (p. 1264) suggests that writers in the twentieth century were interested only in novels of ideas, not in novels of manners and society. Would D. H. Lawrence (p. 1262) agree? How does he see the obligation of the American writer? What "tale" did he think writers should tell?

Entering the Conversation

As you respond to each of the following prompts, support your position with appropriate evidence, including at least three sources in this Conversation on American literature, unless otherwise indicated.

1. What makes American literature distinctly American? What aspects of our nation, our storytelling, our language, our culture, or the genres in which we work make our literature exceptionally American?

2. Coined by the French writer on America, Alexis de Tocqueville, "American exceptionalism" is a term used to describe the telling of the American story as a grand and unique narrative. Some think that American exceptionalism has contributed to a limited national identity, marginalizing those whose stories do not fit the narrative. Consider the views of the writers here, as well as your reading in American literature, and write an essay in which you support, challenge, or qualify the concept of American exceptionalism.

3. Consider one of the American novels you have read this year. Write an essay in which you analyze it as being representative of American literature. Refer to at least three of the sources here for ideas about what might or might not define American literature.

4. Rice University scholar Caroline Levander suggests we ask, Where is American literature? rather than What is American literature? She says that American literature has emerged over space as well as over time and that another way to look at American literature is as a "collaborative undertaking occurring throughout the nation's shifting geographic margins and centers." Use Levander's lens to imagine a round-table discussion in which the writers here consider the question, Where is American literature?

5. What's ahead for the great American novel? Maria Konnikova, writing in *Slate*, says,

> Today's American soul is a far cry from that of the mid-1800s. With transla-
> tions and multiculturalism, fluid borders, constant travel, and cultural inter-
> mingling, what does it even mean, American? Race, slavery, these are all indelible
> parts of the picture. But increasingly, racial history may be becoming one of
> an array of ever-mingling, ever-changing, ever-shifting possibilities. Surely, just
> as apt a modern-day contender for the title would be someone like Teju Cole
> or Junot Diaz or Jhumpa Lahiri — someone who embodies America's flow of
> identities, the reimagining of the American Dream. That, in a way, would be
> far more akin to the spirit of the GAN [Great American Novel] — the vista that
> tries to capture what it means to be *American*, in contrast to being anything
> else.

Write an essay in which you predict the future of American literature, focusing
on, as Konnikova says, what it means to be American.

Grammar as Rhetoric and Style
Direct, Precise, and Active Verbs

Direct, precise, active verbs energize writing. Consider this description with verbs in
blue from "The Chrysanthemums" by John Steinbeck (p. 1147, pars. 7–8):

> She brushed a cloud of hair out of her eyes with the back of her glove, and left a
> smudge of earth on her cheek in doing it. Behind her stood the neat white farm
> house with red geraniums close-banked around it as high as the windows. It
> was a hard-swept looking little house with hard-polished windows, and a clean
> mud-mat on the front steps.
> Elisa cast another glance toward the tractor shed. The strangers were getting
> into their Ford coupe. She took off a glove and put her strong fingers down into
> the forest of new green chrysanthemum sprouts that were growing around the
> old roots. She spread the leaves and looked down among the close-growing
> stems. No aphids were there, no sowbugs or snails or cutworms. Her terrier
> fingers destroyed such pests before they could get started.

The simple verb forms and strong active verbs in Steinbeck's description of Elisa
help develop her character as confident, precise, and definitive when she works on
her chrysanthemums. It is easy to visualize her and her actions as she notices, but
doesn't dwell on, the men getting into the car.

Now consider another passage, from Edith Wharton's "Roman Fever" (p. 1127, par. 7). The verbs are in blue:

> The dark lady laughed again, and they both relapsed upon the view, contemplating it in silence, with a sort of diffused serenity which might have been borrowed from the spring effulgence of the Roman skies. The luncheon-hour was long past, and the two had their end of the vast terrace to themselves. At its opposite extremity a few groups, detained by a lingering look at the outspread city, were gathering up guide-books and fumbling for tips. The last of them scattered, and the two ladies were alone on the air-washed height.

Wharton uses active and passive verbs to give a sense of the transitional nature of the scene. The last two sentences have four different action verbs, but the last part — in which the two ladies are left to the view — relies solely on a passive verb form of "to be." The women are quite isolated from the hustle and bustle of the tourists, as that verb form suggests.

Direct Verbs

Use forms of *to be* and other linking verbs sparingly and with a specific reason. Often you can change a form of *to be* followed by a predicate adjective or a predicate noun (also called nominalization) into an action verb. Consider how the second sentence in the pairs below sports a stronger verb than the first:

> The high grey-flannel fog of winter was closing off the Salinas Valley from the sky and from all the rest of the world.

> The high grey-flannel fog of winter closed off the Salinas Valley from the sky and from all the rest of the world. — JOHN STEINBECK

> It is the presentation of such a "complex" instantaneously which gives that sense of sudden liberation; that sense of freedom from time limits and space limits; that sense of sudden growth, which is the experience we have in the presence of the greatest works of art.

> It is the presentation of such a "complex" instantaneously which gives that sense of sudden liberation; that sense of freedom from time limits and space limits; that sense of sudden growth, which we experience in the presence of the greatest works of art. — EZRA POUND

> During this period, white people were different from colored to me only in that they rode through town and never lived there.

During this period, white people differed from colored to me only in that they rode through town and never lived there. — ZORA NEALE HURSTON

Precise Verbs

While there is nothing wrong with the verbs *got* and *put* in the first sentence below, consider the precision of the verbs in the second sentence.

He got out of bed and put on his overalls.

He eased out of bed and slipped into overalls. — RICHARD WRIGHT

Similarly, in the first sentence that follows, *keep* and *comes* are perfectly serviceable verbs — until you compare them with the more precise verbs that the writer selects.

To keep a democracy of effort requires a vast amount of patience in dealing with differing methods, a vast amount of humility. But out of the confusion of many voices comes an understanding of dominant public need.

To maintain a democracy of effort requires a vast amount of patience in dealing with differing methods, a vast amount of humility. But out of the confusion of many voices rises an understanding of dominant public need.
— FRANKLIN DELANO ROOSEVELT

Active Verbs

In addition to selecting a verb that is direct and creates a precise image, use verbs in the active voice — with an easy-to-picture subject doing something — unless you have a specific purpose for using the passive voice, where the subject is acted on. Here, for example, in a sentence from "How It Feels to Be Colored Me," Zora Neale Hurston makes good use of the passive voice (p. 1117, par. 9):

I feel most colored when I am thrown against a sharp white background.

In this sentence, Hurston is acted on. Why? Perhaps because she wanted to create a sense of helplessness.

By and large, though, strong writers stick with the active voice, as Ernest Hemingway does when he describes what's going on outside the café in "A Clean, Well-Lighted Place" (p. 1121, par. 9):

A girl and a soldier went by in the street. The street light shone on the brass number on his collar. The girl wore no head covering and hurried beside him.
— ERNEST HEMINGWAY

Hemingway could have cast that sentence in the passive voice, as follows:

> They were passed by a girl and a soldier. The brass number on his collar was lit by the street light. The girl's head was not covered and she was hurrying beside him.

As is often the case, and as this example demonstrates, use of the passive voice muddies the picture.

• EXERCISE 1 •

Improve the following sentences by replacing one or more verbs in each with a more effective one — that is, a more vivid, precise, and active verb.

1. My first college visit will always be remembered by me.
2. There are many technological advances available to make our lives easier.
3. In the middle of the night, sirens could be heard.
4. It was not very long before she regretted buying the expensive handbag.
5. The Graham technique is little esteemed by modern dancers today.
6. The college advisor said she could not make a suggestion about which school to apply to because she didn't know his SAT scores.
7. The team captain is responsible for scheduling practices and communicating with team members.
8. A decision was reached by the arbitration panel.
9. The local sheriff gave a warning to the college students about walking around with open containers.
10. The chief of surgery took the opportunity to thank the volunteers.
11. Do your children have fears about going away to camp?
12. Antigone was very protective of Oedipus in *Oedipus at Colonus*.

• EXERCISE 2 •

Identify the verbs in the following passages. Discuss how these verbs affect the tone of the passages.

> To my room, which is on a street near the loop in the city of Chicago, come men who write. They talk and I talk. We are fools. We talk of writers of the Old World

and the beauty and subtlety of the work they do. Below us the roaring city lies like a great animal on the prairies, but we do not run out to the prairies. We stay in our rooms and talk.

And so, having listened to talk and having myself talked overmuch, I grow weary of talk and walk in the streets. As I walk alone, an old truth comes home to me and I know that we shall never have an American literature until we return to faith in ourselves and to the facing of our own limitations. We must, in some way, become in ourselves more like our fellows, more simple and real.

— SHERWOOD ANDERSON, *An Apology for Crudity*

It is an atomic bomb. It is a harnessing of the basic power of the universe. The force from which the sun draws its power has been loosed against those who brought war to the Far East.

—HARRY S TRUMAN, Statement by the President of the United States

• EXERCISE 3 •

Analyze the verbs in the first two paragraphs (p. 1143) of Franklin Delano Roosevelt's second inaugural address, One-Third of a Nation. How would you describe the verbs FDR uses? How do they set the tone for the subject of his address? Do the verbs he uses provide a hint that his address has a message that goes beyond the usual inauguration speech? Cite specific examples to support your view.

When four years ago we met to inaugurate a President, the Republic, single-minded in anxiety, stood in spirit here. We dedicated ourselves to the fulfillment of a vision — to speed the time when there would be for all the people that security and peace essential to the pursuit of happiness. We of the Republic pledged ourselves to drive from the temple of our ancient faith those who had profaned it; to end by action, tireless and unafraid, the stagnation and despair of that day. We did those first things first.

Our covenant with ourselves did not stop there. Instinctively we recognized a deeper need — the need to find through government the instrument of our united purpose to solve for the individual the ever-rising problems of a complex civilization. Repeated attempts at their solution without the aid of government had left us baffled and bewildered. For, without that aid, we had been unable to create those moral controls over the services of science which are necessary to make science a useful servant instead of a ruthless master of mankind. To do this we knew that we must find practical controls over blind economic forces and blindly selfish men.

> **• EXERCISE 4 •**
>
> Count the verbs in one of the passages in Exercise 2 or 3. Then categorize them as linking verbs or more vivid action verbs and calculate the ratio of one to the other. Do the same for several paragraphs of your own writing. Are you relying more on linking verbs, or are most of your verbs direct and precise action verbs?

Suggestions for Writing
America in the Modern World

Now that you have examined a number of texts from the period between the two world wars, explore aspects of this era in America's history by synthesizing your own ideas and the readings. You might want to do additional research or use readings from other classes as you write.

1. Write an essay in which you discuss whether or not the poetry of American imagist William Carlos Williams (p. 1106) follows the rules set out by Ezra Pound in "A Few Don'ts by an Imagiste" (p. 1075).

2. Actor, poet, director, and activist Ossie Davis said this about Langston Hughes:

   > Langston Hughes belongs to whoever is listening. A possession in common, like the sights and sounds of a streetcorner hangout, or the barbershop debate over pretty girls' legs, and baseball players: Open your ears and your heart if you've got one; Langston will walk right in and do the rest. His thoughts come naked, conceived in the open, only at home in the public domain. Free, without charge, like water, like air — like salted peanuts at a Harlem rent party. Come in, have one on me — that's Langston's style; a great host; a perfect bartender; dishing it up, iambic pentameter, on the rocks and on the house, fresh wrote this morning. Dead now, but still alive. Ol' Langston in the corners of my mind.

   Do you agree with Davis about Hughes's accessibility or do you find him harder to understand? Explain in an essay your own experience reading the work of Langston Hughes, starting with the poems (pp. 1101, 1197) and also looking at his essay (p. 1102) in this chapter.

3. Research the group of women known as the "pack horse librarians" of Kentucky and write about how they lived the ideas and ideals of Eleanor Roosevelt's speech about what libraries mean to the nation (p. 1138). Create a pitch for a film about them: imagine whom you would cast, where you would shoot, and how you would tell their story in film.

4. This chapter includes many pieces that could be defined as representing modernism, a movement marked by abstract art, symbolic poetry, and stream-of-consciousness prose. Peter Watson, the New York correspondent for the *London Times*, wrote in his book *A Terrible Beauty*, "One of the many innovations of modernism was the new demands it placed on the audience. Music, painting, literature, even architecture, would never be quite so 'easy' as they had been." Write an essay in which you analyze one or more works in this chapter through the lens of Watson's comment.

5. The works in this chapter are bookended by two world wars. Write an essay in which you trace the influences of war on the literature of the time.

10

Redefining America
1945 to the Present

On August 6 and August 9, 1945, the United States dropped atomic bombs on the Japanese cities of Hiroshima and Nagasaki, simultaneously marking the end of World War II and the beginning of a new era in which America would become the world's foremost economic, military, and cultural power.

Reluctant allies during the war, America and the Soviet Union emerged from World War II as the sole remaining superpowers, separated by a profound ideological divide between capitalism and Communism, democracy and totalitarianism. As Europe recovered physically and politically, the two superpowers vied for influence over its fate. Western Europe was rebuilt with U.S. help via the Marshall Plan, while the Soviet Union quickly stepped in to seize control of Eastern Europe, setting up satellite states in Poland, Romania, Czechoslovakia, Bulgaria, Albania, and Hungary. Caught between the two superpowers, Germany and its capital, Berlin, were divided into East and West, Communist and democratic. Alarmed by the Soviet Union's expansionist policies in Eastern Europe and beyond, the United States and its allies adopted a policy of containment to stop the spread of Communism. The Cold War had begun, and it would affect American life until the Soviet Union fell in 1991.

The Soviet Union raised the stakes of the Cold War in 1949, when they shocked the world by successfully testing a nuclear weapon. The Cold War became an arms race, with the threat of nuclear war hanging over American life like a dark cloud. Children learned to duck and cover under school desks in case of a nuclear attack. Families built fallout shelters in their backyards. As William Faulkner said in his Nobel Prize acceptance speech, "There are no longer problems of the spirit. There is only the question: When will I be blown up?" Adding further paranoia to this Cold War anxiety, a spy ring was uncovered within the Los Alamos nuclear facility. The ring had been relaying top-secret nuclear weapons plans to the Soviets. The threat of Communist infiltration, global Communism, and nuclear war set off a panic, often called the Red Scare, that had Congress searching for Communists within the government, in unions, in education, and in Hollywood. In this chapter, you will read a series of texts about the anxieties of the atomic age and their impact on the present day, including a piece by playwright Arthur Miller in which he explains how commonalities between the hunt for Communists and the Salem Witch Trials inspired him to write *The Crucible*.

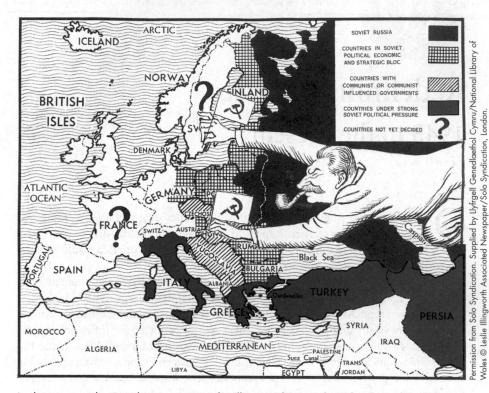

In this cartoon by British cartoonist Leslie Illingworth, Joseph Stalin spreads Communism throughout Eastern Europe.

Despite the anxiety, the United States emerged from World War II into a period of previously unimaginable prosperity. Wartime spending and production had pulled the nation out of the economic depression of the 1930s and transformed it into a manufacturing juggernaut that produced newly developed consumer goods, including plastics, passenger jets, dishwashers, refrigerators, washing machines, air conditioners, and televisions. Employment in both white- and blue-collar sectors skyrocketed, as did the American standard of living. The economy grew by a startling 37 percent during the 1950s, and the gross domestic product (GDP) rose by 250 percent between 1940 and 1960. The 1950s saw a corresponding swell in income levels across the board, but particularly in the middle class. In this chapter, you will read a Conversation on the American middle class that asks you to consider the factors that led to its rise during the postwar boom and to reflect on the impact that growing income inequality might have on its future.

Perhaps no product symbolizes the prosperity of the postwar era more than the automobile. Cars and trucks were no longer luxuries or tools but a part of the American way of life, a tangible expression of freedom. By the mid-1950s, there were more than 60 million automobiles on American roads. With the rise of the automobile came

Walter Kiddie Nuclear Laboratories, Inc. Packaged Shelter, Bettmann/Corbis.

The fear of nuclear attack during the Cold War brought a rise in the purchase and installation of bomb shelters such as this one, which were stocked with enough food and water to sustain a family for three to five days.

an increase in single-family homes (as opposed to apartment buildings or homes intended for extended families), which were often grouped together on the outskirts of a city in suburbs. And as suburbs grew, urban populations declined for the first time in America's history. In this chapter, you will enter a Conversation about America's love affair with the automobile. Is it over? Has the impact of suburban sprawl begun to outweigh the call of the open road? Has the automobile's place in our hearts been replaced by other technologies, or will the open road always be a part of our national identity?

Gary Leonard/Corbis

Despite the exuberance of the postwar boom, not everyone shared in the prosperity of the 1950s and 1960s. Jim Crow laws made discrimination the law of the land throughout the American South, though de facto segregation existed all over America. In this chapter, you will read James Baldwin's "Notes of a Native Son" which gives a glimpse of the emotional toll racial discrimination takes on its victims. Things began to change in 1954, with the heroic efforts of the civil rights movement. The Selma-to-Montgomery marches, the Montgomery Bus Boycott begun by Rosa Parks, the simple ordering of a cup of coffee at a segregated Woolworth's lunch counter in Greensboro, North Carolina — these are iconic events in our nation's history. In this chapter, poet Rita Dove brings Rosa Parks's actions to life in her poem "Rosa." In the spring of 1963, during a protest to desegregate the shops in downtown Birmingham, Alabama, Martin Luther King Jr. and thousands of others were arrested. In jail, on smuggled scraps of paper, King wrote his famous "Letter from Birmingham Jail." which you will read in this chapter. It is paired with a TalkBack essay by Malcolm Gladwell, who contends that Twitter and other social networks are not capable of generating the dramatic campaigns and lasting change that the civil rights movement achieved.

Throughout the 1960s, the Cold War continued to smolder. The Cuban Missile Crisis brought the world as close as it has ever come to all-out nuclear war. And in Asia, the United States sent troops into Vietnam ostensibly to prevent a Communist takeover of South Vietnam by the Soviet-backed North Vietnamese. Despite protests at home — especially on college campuses — the United States supported its actions based on a belief in the domino theory, which held that if one country in a region fell to Communism, others would follow. The Vietnam War lasted for more than a decade

In this August 28, 1963, file photo, Dr. Martin Luther King Jr. (*center front*) marches for civil rights, arms linked with a line of men, in the March on Washington. Later that day, Dr. King would give his famous "I Have a Dream" speech.

and a half, ending in 1975 and costing the lives of 58,000 U.S. soldiers and as many as 2 million Vietnamese. Tim O'Brien's "On the Rainy River" tells the tale of a young man who gets drafted and has to deal with the competing ethical demands of serving his country and serving his own conscience. Veteran Yusef Komunyakaa's poem "Facing It" describes the emotional experience of a soldier viewing the Vietnam Memorial in Washington, D.C.

From the 1950s to the 1970s, patterns of immigration to the United States shifted. The number of immigrants from Europe declined, while the number from Mexico, Central and South America, and South and East Asia increased. And whereas

Bettmann/Corbis

A group of women rally at the Statue of Liberty in support of the recent passage of the Equal Rights Amendment by the United States House of Representatives. The bill did not survive in the U.S. Senate.

assimilation had been the mantra for European immigrants, multiculturalism became the byword for the new immigrants, who were reluctant to give up their traditions and identities. Multiculturalism challenged and redefined what it means to be an American. In this chapter, you will read pieces by Naomi Shihab Nye, Judith Ortiz Cofer, Li-Young Lee, and others who give voice to this new, more inclusive, America.

The women's rights movement of the late 1960s changed the American workplace, economy, and family structure. According to the U.S. Census Bureau, in 1950 about 34 percent of women held jobs; by 1980, that number grew to 51 percent, and by 1990, that number grew to 60 percent. Dual-income families have largely replaced

Neville Elder/Corbis

New York City firefighters walk through the rubble at the World Trade Center, the ruins of the Twin Towers behind them.

single-income families. In this chapter, you will read pieces by Adrienne Rich and Stephen Jay Gould that explore the literary and scientific thinking that resulted in greater equality for women in American culture.

As America entered the twenty-first century, it experienced perhaps its greatest tragedy and challenge: 9/11 was the defining event of that decade. The wars it spawned and the impact it had on American culture continue to be felt more than a decade later. In this chapter, you will consider Art Spiegelman's visual homage to the tragedy and Ana Juan's response a decade later. You will also hear from soldier and poet Brian Turner, whose haunting poem describes the challenges of a soldier returning from war to face the mundane realities of everyday life.

The America you will explore in this chapter is one marked by rapid change. Every decade seems to have brought sweeping technological, demographic, and cultural changes, defining and redefining America generation after generation.

Elizabeth Bishop

Elizabeth Bishop (1911–1979) was born in Worcester, Massachusetts, spent much of her childhood in Nova Scotia, and eventually settled in Boston. She attended Vassar College, where she earned a BA and met poet Marianne Moore, who dissuaded her from attending medical school in favor of pursuing life as a poet. Bishop published her first collection of poetry, *North and South* (1946), after traveling in Europe and North Africa. During an extended trip to Brazil, she published her second collection, *A Cold Spring* (1955), with the poems from *North and South*, in a single volume. This won her the Pulitzer Prize in 1956. Bishop lived in Brazil for fifteen years; translated the Brazilian work *Minha Vida de Menina* as *The Diary of Helena Morely* (1957); and described her life in Brazil in her third collection of poetry, *Questions of Travel* (1965). Her last collection, *Geography III*, was published in 1976.

The Fish

Bishop lived in Key West, Florida, when she wrote "The Fish." She was an avid fisherwoman, having grown up in a fishing village in Nova Scotia. "The Fish" was first published in *Partisan Review* in 1938.

I caught a tremendous fish
and held him beside the boat
half out of water, with my hook
fast in a corner of his mouth.
He didn't fight.   5
He hadn't fought at all.
He hung a grunting weight,
battered and venerable
and homely. Here and there
his brown skin hung in strips   10
like ancient wall-paper,
and its pattern of darker brown
was like wall-paper:
shapes like full-blown roses
stained and lost through age.   15
He was speckled with barnacles,
fine rosettes of lime,
and infested
with tiny white sea-lice,
and underneath two or three   20
rags of green weed hung down.
While his gills were breathing in
the terrible oxygen
— the frightening gills,
fresh and crisp with blood,   25
that can cut so badly —
I thought of the coarse white flesh
packed in like feathers,
the big bones and the little bones,

the dramatic reds and blacks   30
of his shiny entrails,
and the pink swim-bladder
like a big peony.
I looked into his eyes
which were far larger than mine   35
but shallower, and yellowed,
the irises backed and packed
with tarnished tinfoil
seen through the lenses
of old scratched isinglass.   40
They shifted a little, but not
to return my stare.
— It was more like the tipping
of an object toward the light.
I admired his sullen face,   45
the mechanism of his jaw,
and then I saw
that from his lower lip
— if you could call it a lip —
grim, wet, and weapon-like,   50
hung five old pieces of fish-line,
or four and a wire leader
with the swivel still attached,
with all their five big hooks
grown firmly in his mouth.   55
A green line, frayed at the end
where he broke it, two heavier lines,
and a fine black thread
still crimped from the strain and snap
when it broke and he got away.   60
Like medals with their ribbons
frayed and wavering,
a five-haired beard of wisdom
trailing from his aching jaw.
I stared and stared   65
and victory filled up
the little rented boat,
from the pool of bilge
where oil had spread a rainbow
around the rusted engine   70
to the bailer rusted orange,
the sun-cracked thwarts,
the oarlocks on their strings,

the gunnels — until everything
was rainbow, rainbow, rainbow!   75
And I let the fish go.

(1938)

Exploring the Text

1. How does the speaker's description of the fish change over the course of the poem?
2. Trace the verbs in "The Fish," from "I caught" in the first line to "I let" in the last. What do they have in common? What is the effect of their parallel structure?
3. You may notice that Elizabeth Bishop uses several similes (ll. 9–15, for example) and almost no metaphors. Why do you think she made that decision?
4. How does the image in line 69, "where oil had spread a rainbow," foreshadow the end of the poem? What do you think is the significance of the repeated "rainbow"?
5. How would the meaning of the poem change if Bishop's last line had been "So I let the fish go"?
6. Why do you think the speaker let the fish go? Refer to specific words, lines, and images in the poem to explain your answer.
7. In what way is "The Fish" a classic "fish tale" (a boast about the size of a catch)? In what way is it different?

WILLIAM FAULKNER

William Faulkner (1897–1962) grew up in Oxford, Mississippi. Except for some time spent in the Canadian and then the British Royal Air Force during World War I, at a bookstore in New York City, and at a newspaper in New Orleans, Faulkner seldom left Oxford. His fiction — including *The Sound and the Fury* (1929), *Light in August* (1932), *Absalom, Absalom!* (1936), and *Intruder in the Dust* (1962), among others — takes place in the imaginary Yoknapatawpha County and features a revolving cast of recurring characters.

Nobel Prize Banquet Speech

The Nobel Prize in Literature was awarded to William Faulkner in 1949 for "his powerful and unique contribution to the modern American novel." His speech was given at the City Hall in Stockholm, Sweden, on December 10, 1950.

L adies and gentlemen,

I feel that this award was not made to me as a man, but to my work — a life's work in the agony and sweat of the human spirit, not for glory and least of all for profit, but to create out of the materials of the human spirit something which did not exist before.

So this award is only mine in trust. It will not be difficult to find a dedication for the money part of it commensurate with the purpose and significance of its origin. But I would like to do the same with the acclaim too, by using this moment as a pinnacle from which I might be listened to by the young men and women already dedicated to the same anguish and travail, among whom is already that one who will some day stand here where I am standing.

Our tragedy today is a general and universal physical fear so long sustained by now that we can even bear it. There are no longer problems of the spirit. There is only the question: When will I be blown up? Because of this, the young man or woman writing today has forgotten the problems of the human heart in conflict with itself which alone can make good writing because only that is worth writing about, worth the agony and the sweat.

He must learn them again. He must teach himself that the basest of all things is to be afraid; and, teaching himself that, forget it forever, leaving no room in his work-shop for anything but the old verities and truths of the heart, the old universal truths lacking which any story is ephemeral and doomed — love and honor and pity and pride and compassion and sacrifice. Until he does so, he labors under a curse. He writes not of love but of lust, of defeats in which nobody loses anything of value, of victories without hope and, worst of all, without pity or compassion. His griefs grieve on no universal bones, leaving no scars. He writes not of the heart but of the glands.

Until he relearns these things, he will write as though he stood among and watched the end of man. I decline to accept the end of man. It is easy enough to say that man is immortal simply because he will endure: that when the last dingdong of doom has clanged and faded from the last worthless rock hanging tideless in the last red and dying evening, that even then there will still be one more sound: that of his puny inexhaustible voice, still talking.

I refuse to accept this. I believe that man will not merely endure: he will prevail. 5
He is immortal, not because he alone among creatures has an inexhaustible voice, but because he has a soul, a spirit capable of compassion and sacrifice and endurance. The poet's, the writer's, duty is to write about these things. It is his privilege to help man endure by lifting his heart, by reminding him of the courage and honor and hope and pride and compassion and pity and sacrifice which have been the glory of his past. The poet's voice need not merely be the record of man, it can be one of the props, the pillars to help him endure and prevail.

(1950)

Exploring the Text

1. Consider the ways William Faulkner's speech appeals to ethos, pathos, and logos. Which appeal do you think is the strongest? Explain your answer.
2. Although this is an "occasional" speech — that is, one written for a special occasion — Faulkner seems to have a wider audience than just that at the Nobel committee banquet in mind. Who do you think comprises his audience?

3. Find examples of the way Faulkner uses antithesis in the speech. What do they add to his message?

4. Explain what Faulkner means when he says, "There is only the question: When will I be blown up?" (par. 2).

5. This speech by Faulkner was not an instant hit. His Southern drawl was hard to understand and the microphone was not well placed at the banquet. Nevertheless, when it became available in print, it gained in popularity and is now considered one of the most important Nobel Prize speeches. Why do you think it has so much staying power? What aspects of the speech speak to you today?

BERNARD MALAMUD

Bernard Malamud (1914–1986) was an American novelist and short-story writer, born in Brooklyn, New York. In 1936, he received his bachelor's degree from the City College of New York, and in 1942, he received a master's degree in literature from Columbia University. He taught composition at Oregon State University and creative writing at Bennington College, where he stayed until his retirement. He published his first novel, *The Natural*, in 1952, for which he became well-known, and in 1967, he won the National Book Award and the Pulitzer Prize for his novel *The Fixer*, which focused on anti-Semitism in czarist Russia. Malamud wrote eight novels and sixty-five short stories and is considered one of the greatest American writers of the twentieth century.

The First Seven Years

Written in 1950, "The First Seven Years" was published in Malamud's collection *The Magic Barrel* in 1958.

Feld, the shoemaker, was annoyed that his helper, Sobel, was so insensitive to his reverie that he wouldn't for a minute cease his fanatic pounding at the other bench. He gave him a look, but Sobel's bald head was bent over the last as he worked and he didn't notice. The shoemaker shrugged and continued to peer through the partly frosted window at the near-sighted haze of falling February snow. Neither the shifting white blur outside, nor the sudden deep remembrance of the snowy Polish village where he had wasted his youth could turn his thoughts from Max the college boy, (a constant visitor in the mind since early that morning when Feld saw him trudging through the snowdrifts on his way to school) whom he so much respected because of the sacrifices he had made throughout the years — in winter or direst heat — to further his education. An old wish returned to haunt the shoemaker: that he had had a son instead of a daughter, but this blew away in the snow for Feld, if anything, was a practical man. Yet he could not help but contrast the diligence of the boy, who was a peddler's son, with Miriam's unconcern for an education. True, she was always with a book in her hand, yet when the opportunity arose for a college education, she had said no she would rather find a job. He had begged her to go, pointing out how many fathers could not afford to send their children to college, but she said she wanted to be independent. As for education, what was it, she asked, but books, which Sobel, who diligently read the classics, would as usual advise her on. Her answer greatly grieved her father.

A figure emerged from the snow and the door opened. At the counter the man withdrew from a wet paper bag a pair of battered shoes for repair. Who he was the shoemaker for a moment had no idea, then his heart trembled as he realized, before he had thoroughly discerned the face, that Max himself was standing there, embarrassedly explaining what he wanted done to his old shoes. Though Feld listened eagerly, he couldn't hear a word, for the opportunity that had burst upon him was deafening.

He couldn't exactly recall when the thought had occurred to him, because it was clear he had more than once considered suggesting to the boy that he go out with Miriam. But he had not dared speak, for if Max said no, how would he face him again? Or suppose Miriam, who harped so often on independence, blew up in anger and shouted at him for his meddling? Still, the chance was too good to let by: All it meant was an introduction. They might long ago have become friends had they happened to meet somewhere, therefore was it not his duty — an obligation — to bring them together, nothing more, a harmless connivance to replace an accidental encounter in the subway, let's say, or a mutual friend's introduction in the street? Just let him once see and talk to her and he would for sure be interested. As for Miriam, what possible harm for a working girl in an office, who met only loud-mouthed salesmen and illiterate shipping clerks, to make the acquaintance of a fine scholarly boy? Maybe he would awaken in her a desire to go to college; if not — the shoemaker's mind at last came to grips with the truth — let her marry an educated man and live a better life.

When Max finished describing what he wanted done to his shoes, Feld marked them, both with enormous holes in the soles which he pretended not to notice, with large white-chalk x's, and the rubber heels, thinned to the nails, he marked with o's, though it troubled him he might have mixed up the letters. Max inquired the price, and the shoemaker cleared his throat and asked the boy, above Sobel's insistent hammering, would he please step through the side door there into the hall. Though surprised, Max did as the shoemaker requested, and Feld went in after him. For a minute they were both silent, because Sobel had stopped banging, and it seemed they understood neither was to say anything until the noise began again. When it did, loudly, the shoemaker quickly told Max why he had asked to talk to him.

"Ever since you went to high school," he said, in the dimly-lit hallway, "I watched 5 you in the morning go to the subway to school, and I said always to myself, this is a fine boy that he wants so much an education."

"Thanks," Max said, nervously alert. He was tall and grotesquely thin, with sharply cut features, particularly a beak-like nose. He was wearing a loose, long slushy overcoat that hung down to his ankles, looking like a rug draped over his bony shoulders, and a soggy, old brown hat, as battered as the shoes he had brought in.

"I am a business man," the shoemaker abruptly said to conceal his embarrassment, "so I will explain you right away why I talk to you. I have a girl, my daughter

Miriam — she is nineteen — a very nice girl and also so pretty that everybody looks on her when she passes by in the street. She is smart, always with a book, and I thought to myself that a boy like you, an educated boy — I thought maybe you will be interested sometime to meet a girl like this." He laughed a bit when he had finished and was tempted to say more but had the good sense not to.

Max stared down like a hawk. For an uncomfortable second he was silent, then he asked, "Did you say nineteen?"

"Yes."

"Would it be all right to inquire if you have a picture of her?"   10

"Just a minute." The shoemaker went into the store and hastily returned with a snapshot that Max held up to the light.

"She's all right," he said.

Feld waited.

"And is she sensible — not the flighty kind?"

"She is very sensible."   15

After another short pause, Max said it was okay with him if he met her.

"Here is my telephone," said the shoemaker, hurriedly handing him a slip of paper. "Call her up. She comes home from work six o'clock."

Max folded the paper and tucked it away into his worn leather wallet.

"About the shoes," he said. "How much did you say they will cost me?"

"Don't worry about the price."   20

"I just like to have an idea."

"A dollar — dollar fifty. A dollar fifty," the shoemaker said.

At once he felt bad, for he usually charged two twenty-five for this kind of job. Either he should have asked the regular price or done the work for nothing.

Later, as he entered the store, he was startled by a violent clanging and looked up to see Sobel pounding with all his might upon the naked last. It broke, the iron striking the floor and jumping with a thump against the wall, but before the enraged shoemaker could cry out, the assistant had torn his hat and coat from the hook and rushed out into the snow.

So Feld, who had looked forward to anticipating how it would go with his daugh-   25
ter and Max, instead had a great worry on his mind. Without his temperamental helper he was a lost man, especially since it was years now that he had carried the store alone. The shoemaker had for an age suffered from a heart condition that threatened collapse if he dared exert himself. Five years ago, after an attack, it had appeared as though he would have either to sacrifice his business upon the auction block and live on a pittance thereafter, or put himself at the mercy of some unscrupulous employee who would in the end probably ruin him. But just at the moment of his darkest despair, this Polish refugee, Sobel, appeared one night from the street and begged for work. He was a stocky man, poorly dressed, with a bald head that had once been blond, a severely plain face and soft blue eyes prone to tears over the sad books he read, a young man but old — no one would have guessed thirty. Though he confessed he knew nothing of shoemaking, he said he was apt and would work for a very little if Feld taught him

the trade. Thinking that with, after all, a landsman, he would have less to fear than from a complete stranger, Feld took him on and within six weeks the refugee rebuilt as good a shoe as he, and not long thereafter expertly ran the business for the thoroughly relieved shoemaker.

Feld could trust him with anything and did, frequently going home after an hour or two at the store, leaving all the money in the till, knowing Sobel would guard every cent of it. The amazing thing was that he demanded so little. His wants were few; in money he wasn't interested — in nothing but books, it seemed — which he one by one lent to Miriam, together with his profuse, queer written comments, manufactured during his lonely rooming house evenings, thick pads of commentary which the shoemaker peered at and twitched his shoulders over as his daughter, from her fourteenth year, read page by sanctified page, as if the word of God were inscribed on them. To protect Sobel, Feld himself had to see that he received more than he asked for. Yet his conscience bothered him for not insisting that the assistant accept a better wage than he was getting, though Feld had honestly told him he could earn a handsome salary if he worked elsewhere, or maybe opened a place of his own. But the assistant answered, somewhat ungraciously, that he was not interested in going elsewhere, and though Feld frequently asked himself what keeps him here? why does he stay? he finally answered it that the man, no doubt because of his terrible experiences as a refugee, was afraid of the world.

After the incident with the broken last, angered by Sobel's behavior, the shoemaker decided to let him stew for a week in the rooming house, although his own strength was taxed dangerously and the business suffered. However, after several sharp nagging warnings from both his wife and daughter, he went finally in search of Sobel, as he had once before, quite recently, when over some fancied slight — Feld had merely asked him not to give Miriam so many books to read because her eyes were strained and red — the assistant had left the place in a huff, an incident which, as usual, came to nothing for he had returned after the shoemaker had talked to him, and taken his seat at the bench. But this time, after Feld had plodded through the snow to Sobel's house — he had thought of sending Miriam but the idea became repugnant to him — the burly landlady at the door informed him in a nasal voice that Sobel was not at home, and though Feld knew this was a nasty lie, for where had the refugee to go? still for some reason he was not completely sure of — it may have been the cold and his fatigue — he decided not to insist on seeing him. Instead he went home and hired a new helper.

Having settled the matter, though not entirely to his satisfaction, for he had much more to do than before, and so, for example, could no longer lie late in bed mornings because he had to get up to open the store for the new assistant, a speechless, dark man with an irritating rasp as he worked, whom he would not trust with the key as he had Sobel. Furthermore, this one, though able to do a fair repair job, knew nothing of grades of leather or prices, so Feld had to make his own purchases; and every night at closing time it was necessary to count the money in the till and lock up. However, he was not dissatisfied, for he lived much in his thoughts of Max and Miriam. The college boy had called her, and they had arranged a meeting for this coming Friday night.

The shoemaker would personally have preferred Saturday, which he felt would make it a date of the first magnitude, but he learned Friday was Miriam's choice, so he said nothing. The day of the week did not matter. What mattered was the aftermath. Would they like each other and want to be friends? He sighed at all the time that would have to go by before he knew for sure. Often he was tempted to talk to Miriam about the boy, to ask whether she thought she would like his type—he had told her only that he considered Max a nice boy and had suggested he call her—but the one time he tried she snapped at him—justly—how should she know?

At last Friday came. Feld was not feeling particularly well so he stayed in bed, and Mrs. Feld thought it better to remain in the bedroom with him when Max called. Miriam received the boy, and her parents could hear their voices, his throaty one, as they talked. Just before leaving, Miriam brought Max to the bedroom door and he stood there a minute, a tall, slightly hunched figure wearing a thick, droopy suit, and apparently at ease as he greeted the shoemaker and his wife, which was surely a good sign. And Miriam, although she had worked all day, looked fresh and pretty. She was a large-framed girl with a well-shaped body, and she had a fine open face and soft hair. They made, Feld thought, a first-class couple.

Miriam returned after 11:30. Her mother was already asleep, but the shoemaker got out of bed and after locating his bathrobe went into the kitchen, where Miriam, to his surprise, sat at the table, reading.   30

"So where did you go?" Feld asked pleasantly.

"For a walk," she said, not looking up.

"I advised him," Feld said, clearing his throat, "he shouldn't spend so much money."

"I didn't care."

The shoemaker boiled up some water for tea and sat down at the table with a cupful and a thick slice of lemon.   35

"So how," he sighed after a sip, "did you enjoy?"

"It was all right."

He was silent. She must have sensed his disappointment, for she added, "You can't really tell much the first time."

"You will see him again?"

Turning a page, she said that Max had asked for another date.   40

"For when?"

"Saturday."

"So what did you say?"

"What did I say?" she asked, delaying for a moment—"I said yes."

Afterwards she inquired about Sobel, and Feld, without exactly knowing why, said the assistant had got another job. Miriam said nothing more and began to read. The shoemaker's conscience did not trouble him; he was satisfied with the Saturday date.   45

During the week, by placing here and there a deft question, he managed to get from Miriam some information about Max. It surprised him to learn that the boy was not studying to be either a doctor or lawyer but was taking a business course leading to a degree in accountancy. Feld was a little disappointed because he thought of accountants as bookkeepers and would have preferred "a higher profession." However, it was not long before he had investigated the subject and discovered that Certified Public Accountants were highly respected people, so he was thoroughly content as Saturday approached. But because Saturday was a busy day, he was much in the store and therefore did not see Max when he came to call for Miriam. From his wife he learned there had been nothing especially revealing about their meeting. Max had rung the bell and Miriam had got her coat and left with him — nothing more. Feld did not probe, for his wife was not particularly observant. Instead, he waited up for Miriam with a newspaper on his lap, which he scarcely looked at so lost was he in thinking of the future. He awoke to find her in the room with him, tiredly removing her hat. Greeting her, he was suddenly inexplicably afraid to ask anything about the evening. But since she volunteered nothing he was at last forced to inquire how she had enjoyed herself. Miriam began something noncommittal but apparently changed her mind, for she said after a minute, "I was bored."

When Feld had sufficiently recovered from his anguished disappointment to ask why, she answered without hesitation, "Because he's nothing more than a materialist."

"What means this word?"

"He has no soul. He's only interested in things."

He considered her statement for a long time but then asked, "Will you see him   50
again?"

"He didn't ask."

"Suppose he will ask you?"

"I won't see him."

He did not argue; however, as the days went by he hoped increasingly she would change her mind. He wished the boy would telephone, because he was sure there was more to him than Miriam, with her inexperienced eye, could discern. But Max didn't call. As a matter of fact he took a different route to school, no longer passing the shoemaker's store, and Feld was deeply hurt.

Then one afternoon Max came in and asked for his shoes. The shoemaker took   55
them down from the shelf where he had placed them, apart from the other pairs. He had done the work himself and the soles and heels were well built and firm. The shoes had been highly polished and somehow looked better than new. Max's Adam's apple went up once when he saw them, and his eyes had little lights in them.

"How much?" he asked, without directly looking at the shoemaker.

"Like I told you before," Feld answered sadly. "One dollar fifty cents."

Max handed him two crumpled bills and received in return a newly-minted silver half-dollar.

He left. Miriam had not been mentioned. That night the shoemaker discovered that his new assistant had been all the while stealing from him, and he suffered a heart attack.

Though the attack was very mild, he lay in bed for three weeks. Miriam spoke of   60
going for Sobel, but sick as he was Feld rose in wrath against the idea. Yet in his heart he knew there was no other way, and the first weary day back in the shop thoroughly convinced him, so that night after supper he dragged himself to Sobel's rooming house.

He toiled up the stairs, though he knew it was bad for him, and at the top knocked at the door. Sobel opened it and the shoemaker entered. The room was a small, poor one, with a single window facing the street. It contained a narrow cot, a low table and several stacks of books piled haphazardly around on the floor along the wall, which made him think how queer Sobel was, to be uneducated and read so much. He had once asked him, Sobel, why you read so much? and the assistant could not answer him. Did you ever study in a college someplace? he had asked, but Sobel shook his head. He read, he said, to know. But to know what, the shoemaker demanded, and to know, why? Sobel never explained, which proved he read much because he was queer.

Feld sat down to recover his breath. The assistant was resting on his bed with his heavy back to the wall. His shirt and trousers were clean, and his stubby fingers, away from the shoemaker's bench, were strangely pallid. His face was thin and pale, as if he had been shut in this room since the day he had bolted from the store.

"So when you will come back to work?" Feld asked him.

To his surprise, Sobel burst out, "Never."

Jumping up, he strode over to the window that looked out upon the miserable   65
street. "Why should I come back?" he cried.

"I will raise your wages."

"Who cares for your wages!"

The shoemaker, knowing he didn't care, was at a loss what else to say.

"What do you want from me, Sobel?"

"Nothing."   70

"I always treated you like you was my son."

Sobel vehemently denied it. "So why you look for strange boys in the street they should go out with Miriam? Why you don't think of me?"

The shoemaker's hands and feet turned freezing cold. His voice became so hoarse he couldn't speak. At last he cleared his throat and croaked, "So what has my daughter got to do with a shoemaker thirty-five years old who works for me?"

"Why do you think I worked so long for you?" Sobel cried out. "For the stingy wages I sacrificed five years of my life so you could have to eat and drink and where to sleep?"

"Then for what?" shouted the shoemaker.   75

"For Miriam," he blurted — "for her."

The shoemaker, after a time, managed to say, "I pay wages in cash, Sobel," and lapsed into silence. Though he was seething with excitement, his mind was coldly clear, and he had to admit to himself he had sensed all along that Sobel felt this way. He had never so much as thought it consciously, but he had felt it and was afraid.

"Miriam knows?" he muttered hoarsely.

"She knows."

"You told her?"   80

"No."

"Then how does she know?"

"How does she know?" Sobel said, "Because she knows. She knows who I am and what is in my heart."

Feld had a sudden insight. In some devious way, with his books and commentary, Sobel had given Miriam to understand that he loved her. The shoemaker felt a terrible anger at him for his deceit.

"Sobel, you are crazy," he said bitterly. "She will never marry a man so old and   85
ugly like you."

Sobel turned black with rage. He cursed the shoemaker, but then, though he trembled to hold it in, his eyes filled with tears and he broke into deep sobs. With his back to Feld, he stood at the window, fists clenched, and his shoulders shook with his choked sobbing.

Watching him, the shoemaker's anger diminished. His teeth were on edge with pity for the man, and his eyes grew moist. How strange and sad that a refugee, a grown man, bald and old with his miseries, who had by the skin of his teeth escaped Hitler's incinerators, should fall in love, when he had got to America, with a girl less than half his age. Day after day, for five years he had sat at his bench, cutting and hammering away, waiting for the girl to become a woman, unable to ease his heart with speech, knowing no protest but desperation.

"Ugly I didn't mean," he said half aloud.

Then he realized that what he had called ugly was not Sobel but Miriam's life if she married him. He felt for his daughter a strange and gripping sorrow, as if she were already Sobel's bride, the wife, after all, of a shoemaker, and had in her life no more than her mother had had. And all his dreams for her — why he had slaved and destroyed his heart with anxiety and labor — all these dreams of a better life were dead.

The room was quiet. Sobel was standing by the window reading, and it was curious   90
that when he read he looked young.

"She is only nineteen," Feld said brokenly. "This is too young yet to get married. Don't ask her for two years more, till she is twenty-one, then you can talk to her."

Sobel didn't answer. Feld rose and left. He went slowly down the stairs but once outside, though it was an icy night and the crisp falling snow whitened the street, he walked with a stronger stride.

But the next morning, when the shoemaker arrived, heavy-hearted, to open the store, he saw he needn't have come, for his assistant was already seated at the last, pounding leather for his love.

(1950)

Exploring the Text

1. What do you notice about how Bernard Malamud introduces the characters in "The First Seven Years"? Explain how he develops each one and the purpose he or she serves in the story.

2. The title "The First Seven Years" alludes to the biblical story of Rachel and Jacob, in which Jacob has to work seven years to be able to marry Rachel. On his wedding night, he finds that her older sister Leah has been substituted and that he has to work another seven years for Rachel. What themes does the connection to the Bible suggest?

3. Feld thinks that Miriam and Max make a "first-class couple" (par. 29). What would make Feld think that? What did you think? Did you expect Miriam and Max to hit it off? Explain your answer.

4. How is Feld's fascination with Max a reflection of his belief in the American Dream?

5. Analyze the story's last paragraph, which is one long compound sentence with several subordinate clauses. Describe the effect of the sentence's length and construction. What does it remind you of?

6. Richard Bernstein, reviewing *The Complete Stories* in December 1997 for the *New York Times*, wrote that Malamud could "take figures from the immigrant Jewish petty bourgeoisie [usually defined as the lower middle class] and place them into struggles worthy of the Greeks." Describe how the characters in "The First Seven Years" represent the Jewish petty bourgeoisie, and explain how their struggles are "worthy of the Greeks."

Langston Hughes

Langston Hughes (1902–1967) was born in the African American community of Joplin, Missouri, and raised in Lawrence, Kansas. He spent a year at Columbia University and became involved with the Harlem movement, but he was shocked by the endemic racial prejudice at the university and subsequently left. Hughes traveled for several years, spending some time in Paris before returning to the United States. He completed his BA at Pennsylvania's Lincoln University in 1929, after which he returned to Harlem for the remainder of his life. A writer of verse, prose, and drama, Hughes's first volume of poetry, *The Weary Blues*, was published in 1926. This collection contained "The Negro Speaks of Rivers" (p. 1101), perhaps his most famous poem. His first novel, *Not Without Laughter* (1930), won the Harmon Gold Medal for literature. Hughes is remembered for his celebration of the uniqueness of African American culture, which found expression in "The Negro Artist and the Racial Mountain" (p. 1102), published in the *Nation*, and in the poem "My People." He also wrote children's poetry, musicals, and opera.

Theme for English B

Hughes wrote "Theme for English B" in 1951 — more than twenty-five years after he had been a student at New York's Columbia University.

The instructor said,

> Go home and write
> a page tonight.
> And let that page come out of you —
> Then, it will be true.   5

I wonder if it's that simple?
I am twenty-two, colored, born in Winston-Salem.
I went to school there, then Durham, then here
to this college on the hill above Harlem.
I am the only colored student in my class. 10
The steps from the hill lead down into Harlem,
through a park, then I cross St. Nicholas,
Eighth Avenue, Seventh, and I come to the Y,
the Harlem Branch Y, where I take the elevator
up to my room, sit down, and write this page: 15

It's not easy to know what is true for you or me
at twenty-two, my age. But I guess I'm what
I feel and see and hear, Harlem, I hear you:
hear you, hear me — we two — you, me, talk on this page.
(I hear New York, too.) Me — who? 20
Well, I like to eat, sleep, drink, and be in love.
I like to work, read, learn, and understand life.
I like a pipe for a Christmas present,
or records — Bessie, bop, or Bach.
I guess being colored doesn't make me *not* like 25
the same things other folks like who are other races.
So will my page be colored that I write?
Being me, it will not be white.
But it will be
a part of you, instructor. 30
You are white —
yet a part of me, as I am a part of you.
That's American.
Sometimes perhaps you don't want to be a part of me.
Nor do I often want to be a part of you. 35
But we are, that's true!
As I learn from you,
I guess you learn from me —
although you're older — and white —
and somewhat more free. 40

This is my page for English B.

(1951)

Exploring the Text

1. Characterize the speaker in "Theme for English B." Refer to specific words and
   phrases in the poem to support your description.

2. How does the poem's setting help develop its themes? Look especially at the way Langston Hughes uses the words "up," "down," and "cross" (ll. 11–15)

3. You may have noticed that there is little figurative language in "Theme for English B." In fact, in some ways it doesn't even seem like a poem. How does the rather everyday language help create some of the poem's ideas?

4. What do you think the speaker means by "That's American" (l. 33)? What do you think "That's American" means today? What are the similarities between being American then and now? What are the differences?

5. What argument do you think Hughes is making in this poem? Why do you think he used an English class assignment as a framing device for his ideas?

6. What do you think the instructor thought of the speaker's work?

FLANNERY O'CONNOR

One of the most acclaimed and widely read fiction writers of the twentieth century, Flannery O'Connor (1925–1964) was born on a farm in Milledgeville, Georgia. At the age of fifteen, she lost her father to lupus, the same disease that would take her life at thirty-nine. After graduating from the Georgia State College for Women, O'Connor attended the Iowa Writers' Workshop. At twenty-six, after being diagnosed with lupus, O'Connor returned to the Georgia farm where she grew up. Despite her illness, she published three books — the story collection *A Good Man Is Hard to Find* (1955) and the novels *Wise Blood* (1952) and *The Violent Bear It Away* (1960) — before her death in 1964. Her later short stories were published posthumously as *Everything That Rises Must Converge* (1965).

Good Country People

Most of O'Connor's stories are set in the American South, and critics often describe her writing as Southern gothic, even "grotesque." O'Connor famously questioned why those terms were used to describe Southern stereotypes, arguing instead for the term "realistic." Her short stories, such as the one here, examine the deep racial and religious divisions that exist among cultures generally lumped together as "Southern." "Good Country People" was published in 1955 in the collection *A Good Man Is Hard to Find.*

Besides the neutral expression that she wore when she was alone, Mrs. Freeman had two others, forward and reverse, that she used for all her human dealings. Her forward expression was steady and driving like the advance of a heavy truck. Her eyes never swerved to left or right but turned as the story turned as if they followed a yellow line down the center of it. She seldom used the other expression because it was not often necessary for her to retract a statement, but when she did, her face came to a complete stop, there was an almost imperceptible movement of her black eyes, during which they seemed to be receding, and then the observer would see that Mrs. Freeman, though she might stand there as real as several grain sacks thrown on top of each other, was no longer there in spirit. As for getting anything across to her when this was the case, Mrs. Hopewell had given it up. She might talk her head off. Mrs. Freeman could never be brought to admit herself wrong on any point. She would stand there and if she could be brought to say anything, it was something like, "Well, I wouldn't of said it was and I wouldn't of said it wasn't," or letting her gaze range over the top kitchen shelf where there was an assortment of dusty bottles, she might remark, "I see you ain't ate many of them figs you put up last summer."

They carried on their most important business in the kitchen at breakfast. Every morning Mrs. Hopewell got up at seven o'clock and lit her gas heater and Joy's. Joy was her daughter, a large blonde girl who had an artificial leg. Mrs. Hopewell thought of her as a child though she was thirty-two years old and highly educated. Joy would get up while her mother was eating and lumber into the bathroom and slam the door, and before long, Mrs. Freeman would arrive at the back door. Joy would hear her mother call, "Come on in," and then they would talk for a while in low voices that were indistinguishable in the bathroom. By the time Joy came in, they had usually finished the weather report and were on one or the other of Mrs. Freeman's daughters, Glynese or Carramae, Joy called them Glycerin and Caramel. Glynese, a redhead, was eighteen and had many admirers; Carramae, a blonde, was only fifteen but already married and pregnant. She could not keep anything in her stomach. Every morning Mrs. Freeman told Mrs. Hopewell how many times she had vomited since the last report.

Mrs. Hopewell liked to tell people that Glynese and Carramae were two of the finest girls she knew and that Mrs. Freeman was a *lady* and that she was never ashamed to take her anywhere or introduce her to anybody they might meet. Then she would tell how she had happened to hire the Freemans in the first place and how they were a godsend to her and how she had had them four years. The reason for her keeping them so long was that they were not trash. They were good country people. She had telephoned the man whose name they had given as a reference and he had told her that Mr. Freeman was a good farmer but that his wife was the nosiest woman ever to walk the earth. "She's got to be into everything," the man said. "If she don't get there before the dust settles, you can bet she's dead, that's all. She'll want to know all your business. I can stand him real good," he had said, "but me nor my wife neither could have stood that woman one more minute on this place." That had put Mrs. Hopewell off for a few days.

She had hired them in the end because there were no other applicants but she had made up her mind beforehand exactly how she would handle the woman. Since she was the type who had to be into everything, then, Mrs. Hopewell decided, she would not only let her be into everything, she would *see to it* that she was into everything— she would give her the responsibility of everything, she would put her in charge. Mrs. Hopewell had no bad qualities of her own but she was able to use other people's in such a constructive way that she never felt the lack. She had hired the Freemans and she had kept them four years.

Nothing is perfect. This was one of Mrs. Hopewell's favorite sayings. Another was: that is life! And still another, the most important, was: well, other people have their

5

opinions too. She would make these statements, usually at the table, in a tone of gentle insistence as if no one held them but her, and the large hulking Joy, whose constant outrage had obliterated every expression from her face, would stare just a little to the side of her, her eyes icy blue, with the look of someone who has achieved blindness by an act of will and means to keep it.

When Mrs. Hopewell said to Mrs. Freeman that life was like that, Mrs. Freeman would say, "I always said so myself." Nothing had been arrived at by anyone that had not first been arrived at by her. She was quicker than Mr. Freeman. When Mrs. Hopewell said to her after they had been on the place a while, "You know, you're the wheel behind the wheel," and winked, Mrs. Freeman had said, "I know it. I've always been quick. It's some that are quicker than others."

"Everybody is different," Mrs. Hopewell said.

"Yes, most people is," Mrs. Freeman said.

"It takes all kinds to make the world."

"I always said it did myself."

10

The girl was used to this kind of dialogue for breakfast and more of it for dinner; sometimes they had it for supper too. When they had no guest they ate in the kitchen because that was easier. Mrs. Freeman always managed to arrive at some point during the meal and to watch them finish it. She would stand in the doorway if it were summer but in the winter she would stand with one elbow on top of the refrigerator and look down on them, or she would stand by the gas heater, lifting the back of her skirt slightly. Occasionally she would stand against the wall and roll her head from side to side. At no time was she in any hurry to leave. All this was very trying on Mrs. Hopewell but she was a woman of great patience. She realized that nothing is perfect and that in the Freemans she had good country people and that if, in this day and age, you get good country people, you had better hang onto them.

She had had plenty of experience with trash. Before the Freemans she had averaged one tenant family a year. The wives of these farmers were not the kind you would want to be around you for very long. Mrs. Hopewell, who had divorced her husband long ago, needed someone to walk over the fields with her; and when Joy had to be impressed for these services, her remarks were usually so ugly and her face so glum that Mrs. Hopewell would say, "If you can't come pleasantly, I don't want you at all," to which the girl, standing square and rigid-shouldered with her neck thrust slightly forward, would reply, "If you want me, here I am — LIKE I AM."

Mrs. Hopewell excused this attitude because of the leg (which had been shot off in a hunting accident when Joy was ten). It was hard for Mrs. Hopewell to realize that her child was thirty-two now and that for more than twenty years she had had only one leg. She thought of her still as a child because it tore her heart to think instead of the poor stout girl in her thirties who had never danced a step or had any *normal* good times. Her name was really Joy but as soon as she was twenty-one and away from home, she had had it legally changed. Mrs. Hopewell was certain that she had thought and thought until she had hit upon the ugliest name in any language. Then she had gone and had the beautiful name, Joy, changed without telling her mother until after she had done it. Her legal name was Hulga.

When Mrs. Hopewell thought the name, Hulga, she thought of the broad blank hull of a battleship. She would not use it. She continued to call her Joy to which the girl responded but in a purely mechanical way.

Hulga had learned to tolerate Mrs. Freeman who saved her from taking walks with her mother. Even Glynese and Carramae were useful when they occupied attention that might otherwise have been directed at her. At first she had thought she could not stand Mrs. Freeman for she had found that it was not possible to be rude to her. Mrs. Freeman would take on strange resentments and for days together she would be sullen but the source of her displeasure was always obscure; a direct attack, a positive leer, blatant ugliness to her face — these never touched her. And without warning one day, she began calling her Hulga.

She did not call her that in front of Mrs. Hopewell who would have been incensed but when she and the girl happened to be out of the house together, she would say something and add the name Hulga to the end of it, and the big spectacled Joy-Hulga would scowl and redden as if her privacy had been intruded upon. She considered the name her personal affair. She had arrived at it first purely on the basis of its ugly sound and then the full genius of its fitness had struck her. She had a vision of the name working like the ugly sweating Vulcan who stayed in the furnace and to whom, presumably, the goddess had to come when called. She saw it as the name of her highest creative act. One of her major triumphs was that her mother had not been able to turn her dust into Joy, but the greater one was that she had been able to turn it herself into Hulga. However, Mrs. Freeman's relish for using the name only irritated her. It was as if Mrs. Freeman's beady steel-pointed eyes had penetrated far enough behind her face to reach some secret fact. Something about her seemed to fascinate Mrs. Freeman and then one day Hulga realized that it was the artificial leg. Mrs. Freeman had a special fondness for the details of secret infections, hidden deformities, assaults upon children. Of diseases, she preferred the lingering or incurable. Hulga had heard Mrs. Hopewell give her the details of the hunting accident, how the leg had been literally blasted off, how she had never lost consciousness. Mrs. Freeman could listen to it any time as if it had happened an hour ago.

When Hulga stumped into the kitchen in the morning (she could walk without making the awful noise but she made it — Mrs. Hopewell was certain — because it was ugly-sounding), she glanced at them and did not speak. Mrs. Hopewell would be in her red kimono with her hair tied around her head in rags. She would be sitting at the table, finishing her breakfast and Mrs. Freeman would be hanging by her elbow outward from the refrigerator, looking down at the table. Hulga always put her eggs on the stove to boil and then stood over them with her arms folded, and Mrs. Hopewell would look at her — a kind of indirect gaze divided between her and Mrs. Freeman — and would think that if she would only keep herself up a little, she wouldn't be so bad looking. There was nothing wrong with her face that a pleasant expression wouldn't help. Mrs. Hopewell said that people who looked on the bright side of things would be beautiful even if they were not.

Whenever she looked at Joy this way, she could not help but feel that it would have been better if the child had not taken the Ph.D. It had certainly not brought her out any and now that she had it, there was no more excuse for her to go to school again. Mrs. Hopewell thought it was nice for girls to go to school to have a good time but Joy had "gone through." Anyhow, she would not have been strong enough to go again. The doctors had told Mrs. Hopewell that with the best of care, Joy might see forty-five. She had a weak heart. Joy had made it plain that if it had not been for this condition, she would be far from these red hills and good country people. She would be in a university lecturing to people who knew what she was talking about. And Mrs. Hopewell could very well picture her there, looking like a scarecrow and lecturing to more of the same. Here she went about all day in a six-year-old skirt and a yellow sweat shirt with a faded cowboy on a horse embossed on it. She thought this was funny; Mrs. Hopewell thought it was idiotic and showed simply that she was still a child. She was brilliant but she didn't have a grain of sense. It seemed to Mrs. Hopewell that every year she grew less like other people and more like herself—bloated, rude, and squint-eyed. And she said such strange things! To her own mother she had said—without warning, without excuse, standing up in the middle of a meal with her face purple and her mouth half full—"Woman! do you ever look inside? Do you ever look inside and see what you are *not*? God!" she had cried sinking down again and staring at her plate, "Malebranche was right: we are not our own light. We are not our own light!" Mrs. Hopewell had no idea to this day what brought that on. She had only made the remark, hoping Joy would take it in, that a smile never hurt anyone.

The girl had taken the Ph.D. in philosophy and this left Mrs. Hopewell at a complete loss. You could say, "My daughter is a nurse," or "My daughter is a schoolteacher," or even, "My daughter is a chemical engineer." You could not say, "My daughter is a philosopher." That was something that had ended with the Greeks and Romans. All day Joy sat on her neck in a deep chair, reading. Sometimes she went for walks but she didn't like dogs or cats or birds or flowers or nature or nice young men. She looked at nice young men as if she could smell their stupidity.

One day Mrs. Hopewell had picked up one of the books the girl had just put down and opening it at random, she read, "Science, on the other hand, has to assert its soberness and seriousness afresh and declare that it is concerned solely with what-is. Nothing—how can it be for science anything but a horror and a phantasm? If science is right, then one thing stands firm: science wishes to know nothing of nothing. Such is after all the strictly scientific approach to Nothing. We know it by wishing to know nothing of Nothing." These words had been underlined with a blue pencil and they worked on Mrs. Hopewell like some evil incantation in gibberish. She shut the book quickly and went out of the room as if she were having a chill.

This morning when the girl came in, Mrs. Freeman was on Carramae. "She thrown up four times after supper," she said, "and was up twict in the night after three o'clock. Yesterday she didn't do nothing but ramble in the bureau drawer. All she did. Stand up there and see what she could run up on."

"She's got to eat," Mrs. Hopewell muttered, sipping her coffee, while she watched Joy's back at the stove. She was wondering what the child had said to the Bible salesman. She could not imagine what kind of a conversation she could possibly have had with him.

He was a tall gaunt hatless youth who had called yesterday to sell them a Bible. He had appeared at the door, carrying a large black suitcase that weighted him so heavily on one side that he had to brace himself against the door facing. He seemed on the point of collapse but he said in a cheerful voice, "Good morning, Mrs. Cedars!" and set the suitcase down on the mat. He was not a bad-looking young man though he had on a bright blue suit and yellow socks that were not pulled up far enough. He had prominent face bones and a streak of sticky-looking brown hair falling across his forehead.

"I'm Mrs. Hopewell," she said.

"Oh!" he said, pretending to look puzzled but with his eyes sparkling, "I saw it   25 said 'The Cedars' on the mailbox so I thought you was Mrs. Cedars!" and he burst out in a pleasant laugh. He picked up the satchel and under cover of a pant, he fell forward into her hall. It was rather as if the suitcase had moved first, jerking him after it. "Mrs. Hopewell!" he said and grabbed her hand. "I hope you are well!" and he laughed again and then all at once his face sobered completely. He paused and gave her a straight earnest look and said, "Lady, I've come to speak of serious things."

"Well, come in," she muttered, none too pleased because her dinner was almost ready. He came into the parlor and sat down on the edge of a straight chair and put the suitcase between his feet and glanced around the room as if he were sizing her up by it. Her silver gleamed on the two sideboards; she decided he had never been in a room as elegant as this.

"Mrs. Hopewell," he began, using her name in a way that sounded almost intimate, "I know you believe in Chrustian service."

"Well yes," she murmured.

"I know," he said and paused, looking very wise with his head cocked on one side, "that you're a good woman. Friends have told me."

Mrs. Hopewell never liked to be taken for a fool. "What are you selling?" she asked.   30

"Bibles," the young man said and his eye raced around the room before he added, "I see you have no family Bible in your parlor, I see that is the one lack you got!"

Mrs. Hopewell could not say, "My daughter is an atheist and won't let me keep the Bible in the parlor." She said, stiffening slightly, "I keep my Bible by my bedside." This was not the truth. It was in the attic somewhere.

"Lady," he said, "the word of God ought to be in the parlor."

"Well, I think that's a matter of taste," she began. "I think . . ."

"Lady," he said, "for a Christian, the word of God ought to be in every room in   35 the house besides in his heart. I know you're a Chrustian because I can see it in every line of your face."

She stood up and said, "Well, young man, I don't want to buy a Bible and I smell my dinner burning."

He didn't get up. He began to twist his hands and looking down at them, he said softly, "Well lady, I'll tell you the truth — not many people want to buy one nowadays and besides, I know I'm real simple. I don't know how to say a thing but to say it. I'm just a country boy." He glanced up into her unfriendly face. "People like you don't like to fool with country people like me!"

"Why!" she cried, "good country people are the salt of the earth! Besides, we all have different ways of doing, it takes all kinds to make the world go 'round. That's life!"

"You said a mouthful," he said.

"Why, I think there aren't enough good people in the world!" she said, stirred. "I think that's what's wrong with it!" 40

His face had brightened. "I didn't introduce myself," he said. "I'm Manley Pointer from out in the country around Willohobie, not even from a place, just from near a place."

"You wait a minute," she said. "I have to see about my dinner." She went out to the kitchen and found Joy standing near the door where she had been listening.

"Get rid of the salt of the earth," she said, "and let's eat."

Mrs. Hopewell gave her a pained look and turned the heat down under the vegetables. "I can't be rude to anybody," she murmured and went back into the parlor.

He had opened the suitcase and was sitting with a Bible on each knee. 45

"You might as well put those up," she told him. "I don't want one."

"I appreciate your honesty," he said. "You don't see any more real honest people unless you go way out in the country."

"I know," she said, "real genuine folks!" Through the crack in the door she heard a groan.

"I guess a lot of boys come telling you they're working their way through college," he said, "but I'm not going to tell you that. Somehow," he said, "I don't want to go to college. I want to devote my life to Chrustian service. See," he said, lowering his voice, "I got this heart condition. I may not live long. When you know it's something wrong with you and you may not live long, well then, lady . . ." He paused, with his mouth open, and stared at her.

He and Joy had the same condition! She knew that her eyes were filling with tears 50 but she collected herself quickly and murmured, "Won't you stay for dinner? We'd love to have you!" and was sorry the instant she heard herself say it.

"Yes mam," he said in an abashed voice, "I would sher love to do that!"

Joy had given him one look on being introduced to him and then throughout the meal had not glanced at him again. He had addressed several remarks to her, which she had pretended not to hear. Mrs. Hopewell could not understand deliberate rudeness, although she lived with it, and she felt she had always to overflow with hospitality to make up for Joy's lack of courtesy. She urged him to talk about himself and he did. He said he was the seventh child of twelve and that his father had been crushed under a tree when he himself was eight years old. He had been crushed very badly, in fact, almost cut in two and was practically not recognizable. His mother had got along the best she could by hard working and she had always seen that her children went to Sunday School and that they read the Bible every evening. He was now nineteen years old and he had been selling Bibles for four months. In that time he had sold seventy-seven Bibles and had the promise of two more sales. He wanted to become a missionary because he thought that was the way you could do most for people. "He who losest his life shall find it," he said simply and he was so sincere, so genuine and earnest that Mrs. Hopewell would not for the world have smiled. He prevented his peas from sliding onto the table by blocking them with a piece of bread which he later cleaned his plate with. She could see Joy observing sidewise how he handled his knife and fork and she saw too that every few minutes, the boy would dart a keen appraising glance at the girl as if he were trying to attract her attention.

After dinner Joy cleared the dishes off the table and disappeared and Mrs. Hopewell was left to talk with him. He told her again about his childhood and his father's accident and about various things that had happened to him. Every five minutes or so she would stifle a yawn. He sat for two hours until finally she told him she must go because she had an appointment in town. He packed his Bibles and thanked her and prepared to leave, but in the doorway he stopped and wrung her hand and said that not on any of his trips had he met a lady as nice as her and he asked if he could come again. She had said she would always be happy to see him.

Joy had been standing in the road, apparently looking at something in the distance, when he came down the steps toward her, bent to the side with his heavy valise. He stopped where she was standing and confronted her directly. Mrs. Hopewell could not hear what he said but she trembled to think what Joy would say to him. She could see that after a minute Joy said something and that then the boy began to speak again, making an excited gesture with his free hand. After a minute Joy said something else at which the boy began to speak once more. Then to her amazement, Mrs. Hopewell saw the two of them walk off together, toward the gate. Joy had walked all the way to the gate with him and Mrs. Hopewell could not imagine what they had said to each other, and she had not yet dared to ask.

Mrs. Freeman was insisting upon her attention. She had moved from the refrigerator to the heater so that Mrs. Hopewell had to turn and face her in order to seem to be listening. "Glynese gone out with Harvey Hill again last night," she said. "She had this sty." 55

"Hill," Mrs. Hopewell said absently, "is the one who works in the garage?"

"Nome, he's the one that goes to chiropractor school," Mrs. Freeman said. "She had this sty. Been had it two days. So she says when he brought her in the other night he says, 'Lemme get rid of that sty for you,' and she says, 'How?' and he says, 'You just lay yourself down acrost the seat of that car and I'll show you.' So she done it and he popped her neck. Kept on a-popping it several times until she made him quit. This morning," Mrs. Freeman said, "she ain't got no sty. She ain't got no traces of a sty."

"I never heard of that before," Mrs. Hopewell said.

"He ast her to marry him before the Ordinary,"[1] Mrs. Freeman went on, "and she told him she wasn't going to be married in no *office*."

"Well, Glynese is a fine girl," Mrs. Hopewell said. "Glynese and Carramae are both fine girls." 60

"Carramae said when her and Lyman was married Lyman said it sure felt sacred to him. She said he said he wouldn't take five hundred dollars for being married by a preacher."

"How much would he take?" the girl asked from the stove.

---

[1] Justice of the peace. — Eds.

"He said he wouldn't take five hundred dollars," Mrs. Freeman repeated.

"Well we all have work to do," Mrs. Hopewell said.

"Lyman said it just felt more sacred to him," Mrs. Freeman said. "The doctor   65
wants Carramae to eat prunes. Says instead of medicine. Says them cramps is coming
from pressure. You know where I think it is?"

"She'll be better in a few weeks," Mrs. Hopewell said.

"In the tube," Mrs. Freeman said. "Else she wouldn't be as sick as she is."

Hulga had cracked her two eggs into a saucer and was bringing them to the table
along with a cup of coffee that she had filled too full. She sat down carefully and began
to eat, meaning to keep Mrs. Freeman there by questions if for any reason she showed
an inclination to leave. She could perceive her mother's eye on her. The first round-
about question would be about the Bible salesman and she did not wish to bring it on.
"How did he pop her neck?" she asked.

Mrs. Freeman went into a description of how he had popped her neck. She said
he owned a '55 Mercury but that Glynese said she would rather marry a man with only
a '36 Plymouth who would be married by a preacher. The girl asked what if he had a
'32 Plymouth and Mrs. Freeman said what Glynese had said was a '36 Plymouth.

Mrs. Hopewell said there were not many girls with Glynese's common sense. She   70
said what she admired in those girls was their common sense. She said that reminded
her that they had had a nice visitor yesterday, a young man selling Bibles. "Lord," she
said, "he bored me to death but he was so sincere and genuine I couldn't be rude to
him. He was just good country people, you know," she said, " —just the salt of the
earth."

"I seen him walk up," Mrs. Freeman said, "and then later — I seen him walk off,"
and Hulga could feel the slight shift in her voice, the slight insinuation, that he had not
walked off alone, had he? Her face remained expressionless but the color rose into her
neck and she seemed to swallow it down with the next spoonful of egg. Mrs. Freeman
was looking at her as if they had a secret together.

"Well, it takes all kinds of people to make the world go 'round," Mrs. Hopewell
said. "It's very good we aren't all alike."

"Some people are more alike than others," Mrs. Freeman said.

Hulga got up and stumped, with about twice the noise that was necessary, into her
room and locked the door. She was to meet the Bible salesman at ten o'clock at the
gate. She had thought about it half the night. She had started thinking of it as a great
joke and then she had begun to see profound implications in it. She had lain in bed
imagining dialogues for them that were insane on the surface but that reached below
to depths that no Bible salesman would be aware of. Their conversation yesterday had
been of this kind.

He had stopped in front of her and had simply stood there. His face was bony   75
and sweaty and bright, with a little pointed nose in the center of it, and his look was
different from what it had been at the dinner table. He was gazing at her with open
curiosity, with fascination, like a child watching a new fantastic animal at the zoo, and
he was breathing as if he had run a great distance to reach her. His gaze seemed somehow familiar but she could not think where she had been regarded with it before. For

almost a minute he didn't say anything. Then on what seemed an insuck of breath, he whispered, "You ever ate a chicken that was two days old?"

The girl looked at him stonily. He might have just put this question up for consideration at the meeting of a philosophical association. "Yes," she presently replied as if she had considered it from all angles.

"It must have been mighty small!" he said triumphantly and shook all over with little nervous giggles, getting very red in the face, and subsiding finally into his gaze of complete admiration, while the girl's expression remained exactly the same.

"How old are you?" he asked softly.

She waited some time before she answered. Then in a flat voice she said, "Seventeen."

His smiles came in succession like waves breaking on the surface of a little lake. 80 "I see you got a wooden leg," he said. "I think you're brave. I think you're real sweet."

The girl stood blank and solid and silent.

"Walk to the gate with me," he said. "You're a brave sweet little thing and I liked you the minute I seen you walk in the door."

Hulga began to move forward.

"What's your name?" he asked, smiling down on the top of her head.

"Hulga," she said. 85

"Hulga," he murmured, "Hulga. Hulga. I never heard of anybody name Hulga before. You're shy, aren't you, Hulga?" he asked.

She nodded, watching his large red hand on the handle of the giant valise.

"I like girls that wear glasses," he said. "I think a lot. I'm not like these people that a serious thought don't ever enter their heads. It's because I may die."

"I may die too," she said suddenly and looked up at him. His eyes were very small and brown, glittering feverishly.

"Listen," he said, "don't you think some people was meant to meet on account of 90 what all they got in common and all? Like they both think serious thoughts and all?" He shifted the valise to his other hand so that the hand nearest her was free. He caught hold of her elbow and shook it a little. "I don't work on Saturday," he said. "I like to walk in the woods and see what Mother Nature is wearing. O'er the hills and far away. Pic-nics and things. Couldn't we go on a pic-nic tomorrow? Say yes, Hulga," he said and gave her a dying look as if he felt his insides about to drop out of him. He had even seemed to sway slightly toward her.

During the night she had imagined that she seduced him. She imagined that the two of them walked on the place until they came to the storage barn beyond the two back fields and there, she imagined, that things came to such a pass that she very easily seduced him and that then, of course, she had to reckon with his remorse. True genius can get an idea across even to an inferior mind. She imagined that she took his remorse in hand and changed it into a deeper understanding of life. She took all his shame away and turned it into something useful.

She set off for the gate at exactly ten o'clock, escaping without drawing Mrs. Hopewell's attention. She didn't take anything to eat, forgetting that food is usually taken on a picnic. She wore a pair of slacks and a dirty white shirt, and as an afterthought, she had put some Vapex[2] on the collar of it since she did not own any perfume. When she reached the gate no one was there.

She looked up and down the empty highway and had the furious feeling that she had been tricked, that he had only meant to make her walk to the gate after the idea of him. Then suddenly he stood up, very tall, from behind a bush on the opposite embankment. Smiling, he lifted his hat which was new and wide-brimmed. He had not worn it yesterday and she wondered if he had bought it for the occasion. It was toast-colored with a red and white band around it and was slightly too large for him. He stepped from behind the bush still carrying the black valise. He had on the same suit and the same yellow socks sucked down in his shoes from walking. He crossed the highway and said, "I knew you'd come!"

The girl wondered acidly how he had known this. She pointed to the valise and asked, "Why did you bring your Bibles?"

He took her elbow, smiling down on her as if he could not stop. "You can never tell   95
when you'll need the word of God, Hulga," he said. She had a moment in which she doubted that this was actually happening and then they began to climb the embankment. They went down into the pasture toward the woods. The boy walked lightly by her side, bouncing on his toes. The valise did not seem to be heavy today; he even swung it. They crossed half the pasture without saying anything and then, putting his hand easily on the small of her back, he asked softly, "Where does your wooden leg join on?"

She turned an ugly red and glared at him and for an instant the boy looked abashed. "I didn't mean you no harm," he said. "I only meant you're so brave and all. I guess God takes care of you."

"No," she said, looking forward and walking fast, "I don't even believe in God."

At this he stopped and whistled. "No!" he exclaimed as if he were too astonished to say anything else.

She walked on and in a second he was bouncing at her side, fanning with his hat. "That's very unusual for a girl," he remarked, watching her out of the corner of his eye. When they reached the edge of the wood, he put his hand on her back again and drew her against him without a word and kissed her heavily.

The kiss, which had more pressure than feeling behind it, produced that extra   100
surge of adrenaline in the girl that enables one to carry a packed trunk out of a burning house, but in her, the power went at once to the brain. Even before he released her, her mind, clear and detached and ironic anyway, was regarding him from a great distance, with amusement but with pity. She had never been kissed before and she was pleased to discover that it was an unexceptional experience and all a matter of the mind's control. Some people might enjoy drain water if they were told it was vodka. When the boy, looking expectant but uncertain, pushed her gently away, she turned and walked on, saying nothing as if such business, for her, were common enough.

He came along panting at her side, trying to help her when he saw a root that she might trip over. He caught and held back the long swaying blades of thorn vine until

---

[2]Menthol decongestant inhaler. — Eds.

she had passed beyond them. She led the way and he came breathing heavily behind her. Then they came out on a sunlit hillside, sloping softly into another one a little smaller. Beyond, they could see the rusted top of the old barn where the extra hay was stored.

The hill was sprinkled with small pink weeds. "Then you ain't saved?" he asked suddenly, stopping.

The girl smiled. It was the first time she had smiled at him at all. "In my economy," she said, "I'm saved and you are damned but I told you I didn't believe in God."

Nothing seemed to destroy the boy's look of admiration. He gazed at her now as if the fantastic animal at the zoo had put its paw through the bars and given him a loving poke. She thought he looked as if he wanted to kiss her again and she walked on before he had the chance.

"Ain't there somewheres we can sit down sometime?" he murmured, his voice   105
softening toward the end of the sentence.

"In that barn," she said.

They made for it rapidly as if it might slide away like a train. It was a large two-story barn, cool and dark inside. The boy pointed up the ladder that led into the loft and said, "It's too bad we can't go up there."

"Why can't we?" she asked.

"Yer leg," he said reverently.

The girl gave him a contemptuous look and putting both hands on the ladder, she   110
climbed it while he stood below, apparently awestruck. She pulled herself expertly through the opening and then looked down at him and said, "Well, come on if you're coming," and he began to climb the ladder, awkwardly bringing the suitcase with him.

"We won't need the Bible," she observed.

"You never can tell," he said, panting. After he had got into the loft, he was a few seconds catching his breath. She had sat down in a pile of straw. A wide sheath of sunlight, filled with dust particles, slanted over her. She lay back against a bale, her face turned away, looking out the front opening of the barn where hay was thrown from a wagon into the loft. The two pink-speckled hillsides lay back against a dark ridge of woods. The sky was cloudless and cold blue. The boy dropped down by her side and put one arm under her and the other over her and began methodically kissing her face, making little noises like a fish. He did not remove his hat but it was pushed far enough back not to interfere. When her glasses got in his way, he took them off of her and slipped them into his pocket.

The girl at first did not return any of the kisses but presently she began to and after she had put several on his cheek, she reached his lips and remained there, kissing him again and again as if she were trying to draw all the breath out of him. His breath was clear and sweet like a child's and the kisses were sticky like a child's. He mumbled about loving her and about knowing when he first seen her that he loved her, but the mumbling was like the sleepy fretting of a child being put to sleep by his mother. Her mind, throughout this, never stopped or lost itself for a second to her feelings. "You ain't said you loved me none," he whispered finally, pulling back from her. "You got to say that."

She looked away from him off into the hollow sky and then down at a black ridge and then down farther into what appeared to be two green swelling lakes. She didn't realize he had taken her glasses but this landscape could not seem exceptional to her for she seldom paid any close attention to her surroundings.

"You got to say it," he repeated. "You got to say you love me." 115

She was always careful how she committed herself. "In a sense," she began, "if you use the word loosely, you might say that. But it's not a word I use. I don't have illusions. I'm one of those people who see *through* to nothing."

The boy was frowning. "You got to say it. I said it and you got to say it," he said.

The girl looked at him almost tenderly. "You poor baby," she murmured. "It's just as well you don't understand," and she pulled him by the neck, face-down, against her. "We are all damned," she said, "but some of us have taken off our blindfolds and see that there's nothing to see. It's a kind of salvation."

The boy's astonished eyes looked blankly through the ends of her hair. "Okay," he almost whined, "but do you love me or don'tcher?"

"Yes," she said and added, "in a sense. But I must tell you something. There mustn't 120 be anything dishonest between us." She lifted his head and looked him in the eye. "I am thirty years old," she said. "I have a number of degrees."

The boy's look was irritated but dogged. "I don't care," he said. "I don't care a thing about what all you done. I just want to know if you love me or don'tcher?" and he caught her to him and wildly planted her face with kisses until she said, "Yes, yes."

"Okay then," he said, letting her go. "Prove it."

She smiled, looking dreamily out on the shifty landscape. She had seduced him without even making up her mind to try. "How?" she asked, feeling that he should be delayed a little.

He leaned over and put his lips to her ear. "Show me where your wooden leg joins on," he whispered.

The girl uttered a sharp little cry and her face instantly drained of color. The obscen- 125 ity of the suggestion was not what shocked her. As a child she had sometimes been subject to feelings of shame but education had removed the last traces of that as a good surgeon scrapes for cancer; she would no more have felt it over what he was asking than she would have believed in his Bible. But she was as sensitive about the artificial leg as a peacock about his tail. No one ever touched it but her. She took care of it as someone else would his soul, in private and almost with her own eyes turned away. "No," she said.

"I known it," he muttered, sitting up. "You're just playing me for a sucker."

"Oh no no!" she cried. "It joins on at the knee. Only at the knee. Why do you want to see it?"

The boy gave her a long penetrating look. "Because," he said, "it's what makes you different. You ain't like anybody else."

She sat staring at him. There was nothing about her face or her round freezing-blue eyes to indicate that this had moved her; but she felt as if her heart had stopped and left her mind to pump her blood. She decided that for the first time in her life she was face to face with real innocence. This boy, with an instinct that came from beyond wisdom, had touched the truth about her. When after a minute, she said in a hoarse high voice, "All right," it was like surrendering to him completely. It was like losing her own life and finding it again, miraculously, in his.

Very gently he began to roll the slack leg up. The artificial limb, in a white sock   130
and brown flat shoe, was bound in a heavy material like canvas and ended in an ugly jointure where it was attached to the stump. The boy's face and his voice were entirely reverent as he uncovered it and said, "Now show me how to take it off and on."

She took it off for him and put it back on again and then he took it off himself, handling it as tenderly as if it were a real one. "See!" he said with a delighted child's face. "Now I can do it myself!"

"Put it back on," she said. She was thinking that she would run away with him and that every night he would take the leg off and every morning put it back on again. "Put it back on," she said.

"Not yet," he murmured, setting it on its foot out of her reach. "Leave it off for a while. You got me instead."

She gave a little cry of alarm but he pushed her down and began to kiss her again. Without the leg she felt entirely dependent on him. Her brain seemed to have stopped thinking altogether and to be about some other function that it was not very good at. Different expressions raced back and forth over her face. Every now and then the boy, his eyes like two steel spikes, would glance behind him where the leg stood. Finally she pushed him off and said, "Put it back on me now."

"Wait," he said. He leaned the other way and pulled the valise toward him and   135
opened it. It had a pale blue spotted lining and there were only two Bibles in it. He took one of these out and opened the cover of it. It was hollow and contained a pocket flask of whiskey, a pack of cards, and a small blue box with printing on it. He laid these out in front of her one at a time in an evenly-spaced row, like one presenting offerings at the shrine of a goddess. He put the blue box in her hand. THIS PRODUCT TO BE USED ONLY FOR THE PREVENTION OF DISEASE, she read, and dropped it. The boy was unscrewing the top of the flask. He stopped and pointed, with a smile, to the deck of cards. It was not an ordinary deck but one with an obscene picture on the back of each card. "Take a swig," he said, offering her the bottle first. He held it in front of her, but like one mesmerized, she did not move.

Her voice when she spoke had an almost pleading sound. "Aren't you," she murmured, "aren't you just good country people?"

The boy cocked his head. He looked as if he were just beginning to understand that she might be trying to insult him. "Yeah," he said, curling his lip slightly, "but it ain't held me back none. I'm as good as you any day in the week."

"Give me my leg," she said.

He pushed it farther away with his foot. "Come on now, let's begin to have us a good time," he said coaxingly. "We ain't got to know one another good yet."

"Give me my leg!" she screamed and tried to lunge for it but he pushed her down   140
easily.

"What's the matter with you all of a sudden?" he asked, frowning as he screwed the top on the flask and put it quickly back inside the Bible. "You just a while ago said you didn't believe in nothing. I thought you was some girl!"

Her face was almost purple. "You're a Christian!" she hissed. "You're a fine Christian! You're just like them all — say one thing and do another. You're a perfect Christian, you're . . ."

The boy's mouth was set angrily. "I hope you don't think," he said in a lofty indignant tone, "that I believe in that crap! I may sell Bibles but I know which end is up and I wasn't born yesterday and I know where I'm going!"

"Give me my leg!" she screeched. He jumped up so quickly that she barely saw him sweep the cards and the blue box into the Bible and throw the Bible into his valise. She saw him grab the leg and then she saw it for an instant slanted forlornly across the inside of the suitcase with a Bible at either side of its opposite ends. He slammed the lid shut and snatched up the valise and swung it down the hole and then stepped through himself.

When all of him had passed but his head, he turned and regarded her with a look 145 that no longer had any admiration in it. "I've gotten a lot of interesting things," he said. "One time I got a woman's glass eye this way. And you needn't to think you'll catch me because Pointer ain't really my name. I use a different name at every house I call at and don't stay nowhere long. And I'll tell you another thing, Hulga," he said, using the name as if he didn't think much of it, "you ain't so smart. I been believing in nothing ever since I was born!" and then the toast-colored hat disappeared down the hole and the girl was left, sitting on the straw in the dusty sunlight. When she turned her churning face toward the opening, she saw his blue figure struggling successfully over the green speckled lake.

Mrs. Hopewell and Mrs. Freeman, who were in the back pasture, digging up onions, saw him emerge a little later from the woods and head across the meadow toward the highway. "Why, that looks like that nice dull young man that tried to sell me a Bible yesterday," Mrs. Hopewell said, squinting. "He must have been selling them to the Negroes back in there. He was so simple," she said, "but I guess the world would be better off if we were all that simple."

Mrs. Freeman's gaze drove forward and just touched him before he disappeared under the hill. Then she returned her attention to the evil-smelling onion shoot she was lifting from the ground. "Some can't be that simple," she said. "I know I never could."

(1955)

Exploring the Text

1. The characters in "Good Country People" are defined, at least in part, by the clichés they fall back on. How do these clichés help develop the characters? What does Flannery O'Connor tell us about human nature through these clichés?

2. What do you make of the names that O'Connor gives her characters? What expectations do they create? How are your expectations fulfilled? How are they overturned?

3. What do you think Joy/Hulga's artificial leg and glasses represent? What about Manley's valise?

4. What do you think O'Connor really means by "good country people"?

5. Do you think the story is funny? Explain why or why not.

6. How does O'Connor expect us to feel about Joy/Hulga? Is she a sympathetic character or an evil one? In what ways does her disability reflect her character? What use does she make of her degrees and intelligence? What is her condition at the end of the story?

7. The critic Frederick Crews wrote about Flannery O'Connor in the *New York Review of Books*:

> For all her private loyalty to the church's hopeful teachings, then, the world of O'Connor's fiction remains radically askew. Readers immersed in that fiction without a lifeline to the doctrinal assurance found in her lectures and letters tend to feel an existential vertigo at the very moments where the Christian critics want them to feel most worshipful. And this response cannot be dismissed as a mere error, a product of incomplete knowledge. O'Connor's works, we must understand, are not finally about salvation but about doom — the sudden and irremediable realization that there is no exit from being, for better or worse, exactly who one is.

How does "Good Country People" illustrate Crews's observation?

 TALKBACKS

LAWRENCE DOWNES

Lawrence Downes is an editor and journalist for the *New York Times* and writes with a focus on immigration and veterans' issues, among other topics. He received a bachelor's degree in English from Fordham University in 1986 and attended the University of Missouri School of Journalism.

In Search of Flannery O'Connor

In the following essay, which was published in the travel section of the *New York Times* in 2007, Downes reflects on the career and life of celebrated American novelist and short-story writer Flannery O'Connor.

The sun was white above the trees, and sinking fast. I was a few miles past Milledgeville, Ga., somewhere outside of Toomsboro, on a two-lane highway that rose and plunged and twisted through red clay hills and pine woods. I had no fixed destination, just a plan to follow a back road to some weedy field in time to watch the sun go down on Flannery O'Connor's Georgia.

Somewhere outside Toomsboro is where, in O'Connor's best-known short story, "A Good Man Is Hard to Find," a family has a car accident and a tiresome old grandmother has an epiphany. The fog of petty selfishness that has shrouded her life clears when she feels a sudden spasm of kindness for a stranger, a brooding prison escapee who calls himself the Misfit.

Of course, that's also the moment that he shoots her in the chest, but in O'Connor's world, where good and evil are as real as a spreading puddle of blood, it amounts to a happy ending. The grandmother is touched by grace at the last possible moment, and she dies smiling.

"She would of been a good woman," the Misfit said, "if it had been somebody there to shoot her every minute of her life."

O'Connor's short stories and novels are set in a rural South where people know their places, mind their manners and do horrible things to one another. It's a place that somehow hovers outside of time, where both the New Deal and the New Testament feel like recent history. It's soaked in violence and humor, in sin and in God. He may have fled the modern world, but in O'Connor's he sticks around, in the sun hanging over the tree line, in the trees and farm beasts, and in the characters who roost in the memory like gargoyles. It's a land haunted by Christ — not your friendly hug-me Jesus, but a ragged figure who moves from tree to tree in the back of the mind, pursuing the unwilling.

Many people — me for instance — are in turn haunted by O'Connor. Her doctrinally strict, mordantly funny stories and novels are as close to perfect as writing gets. Her language is so spare and efficient, her images and character's speech so vivid, they burn into the mind. Her strange Southern landscape was one I knew viscerally but, until this trip, had never set foot in. I had wondered how her fictional terrain and characters, so bizarre yet so blindingly real, might compare with the real places and people she lived among and wrote about.

Hence my pilgrimage to Milledgeville this fall, and my race against the setting sun.

O'Connor's characters shimmer between heaven and hell, acting out allegorical dramas of sin and redemption. There's Hazel Motes, the sunken-eyed Army veteran who tries to reject God by preaching "the Church of Christ Without Christ, where the blind don't see, the lame don't walk and what's dead stays that way." Hulga Hopewell, the deluded intellectual who loses her wooden leg to a thieving Bible salesman she had assumed was as dumb as a stump. The pious Mrs. Turpin, whose heart pours out thank-yous to Jesus for not having made her black or white trash or ugly. Mrs. Freeman, the universal busybody: "Besides the neutral expression that she wore when she was alone, Mrs. Freeman had two others, forward and reverse, that she used for all her human dealings."

People like these can't be real, and yet they breathe on the page. And there is nothing allegorical about the earthly stage they strut on: It's the red clay of central Georgia, in and around Milledgeville, where O'Connor spent most of her short life. She lived with her widowed mother on the family farm, called Andalusia, just outside Milledgeville, writing and raising peacocks and chickens from 1951 until her death in 1964 at age 39, of lupus.

O'Connor was a misfit herself, as a Roman Catholic in the Bible Belt, a religiously devout ironist writing for nonbelievers. She liked to gently mock the redneckedness of her surroundings. "When in Rome," she once wrote, "do as you done in Milledgeville."

But Milledgeville is not the backwoods. It's a city of 19,000, on the Oconee River in Baldwin County, 30 miles from Macon. It is the former capital of Georgia, trashed by General Sherman on his March to the Sea. It has a huge state psychiatric hospital and a prominent liberal-arts college, Georgia College and State

University. The old Capitol building is now home to a military school. There is a district of big antebellum homes with columns and fussy flowerbeds. Oliver Hardy lived here when he was young and fat but not yet famous.

Milledgeville now looms huge beyond these modest attributes because of O'Connor, or Mary Flannery, as she was known in town. Her output was slender: two novels, a couple dozen short stories, a pile of letters, essays and criticism. But her reputation has grown steadily since she died. Her "Complete Stories" won the National Book Award for Fiction in 1971. Her collected letters, "The Habit of Being," banished the misperception that she was some sort of crippled hillbilly Emily Dickinson. They revealed instead a gregarious, engaged thinker who corresponded widely and eagerly, and who might have ranged far had illness not forced her to stay home and write.

O'Connor's own trail begins about 200 miles southeast of Milledgeville, in Savannah, where she was born and spent her childhood among a community of Irish Roman Catholics, of whom her parents, Edward and Regina Cline O'Connor, were prominent members. The O'Connor home, on a mossy historic square downtown, is landmarked and has been closed for renovations, but is reopening for public tours in April. The Roman Catholic Cathedral of St. John the Baptist is across the square, although nothing in it informs a visitor that one of the country's most prominent apologists for the Catholic faith worshiped and went to parochial school there.

O'Connor learned her craft at the University of Iowa and at Yaddo, the writer's colony in Saratoga Springs, N.Y. She lived for a while in Connecticut with the poet Robert Fitzgerald and his wife, Sally, and thought she was leaving the South behind.

But she got sick, and went home to Andalusia, four miles north of   15
Milledgeville.

Andalusia was a working dairy farm run by Flannery's mother, Regina, who as a prominent widow businesswoman was something of a novelty in town. No one has lived there since O'Connor died in 1964 and Regina moved back into downtown Milledgeville.

Strip malls have long since filled the gap between town and farm, and you now find Andalusia by driving past a Wal-Mart, a Chick-fil-A and a Lowe's Home Improvement Warehouse, where a man shot his wife and killed himself a few days before I arrived. You pass a billboard for Sister Nina, a fortune teller who reads palms in a home office cluttered with votive candles and pictures of Catholic saints. (To judge from one consultation, she is capable of divining that a visitor is a bearer of dark sorrows, but not exactly skilled at pinpointing what those sorrows might be.)

Across the highway from an America's Best Value Inn, a tiny sign marks the dirt road to Andalusia. I turned left, went through an open gate and there it was, a two-story white frame house with columns and brick steps leading up to a wide screened porch. Through the screens I could see a long, tidy row of white rocking chairs.

I drove around back, between the magnolia and pecan trees, parked on the grass and walked back to the house past a wooden water tower and an ancient garage, splintered and falling in on itself.

I was met at the door by Craig R. Amason, the executive director of the 20
Flannery O'Connor-Andalusia Foundation, the nonprofit organization set up to sustain her memory and preserve her home. When the affable Mr. Amason, the foundation's sole employee, is not showing pilgrims around, he is raising money to fix up the place, a project that is a few million dollars short of its goal. The foundation urgently wants to restore the house and outbuildings to postcard-perfection, to insure its survival. Last year the Georgia Trust for Historic Preservation placed Andalusia on its list of most endangered places in the state.

For now, the 21-acre property is in a captivating state of decay.

There is no slow buildup on this tour; the final destination is the first door-way on your left: O'Connor's bedroom and study, converted from a sitting room because she couldn't climb the stairs. Mr. Amason stood back, politely granting me silence as I gathered my thoughts and drank in every detail.

This is where O'Connor wrote, for three hours every day. Her bed had a faded blue-and-white coverlet. The blue drapes, in a 1950's pattern, were dingy, and the paint was flaking off the walls. There was a portable typewriter, a hi-fi with classical LPs, a few bookcases. Leaning against an armoire were the alumi-num crutches that O'Connor used, with her rashy swollen legs and crumbling bones, to get from bedroom to kitchen to porch.

There are few opportunities for so intimate and unguarded a glimpse into the private life of a great American writer. Mr. Amason told me that visitors sometimes wept on the bedroom threshold.

The center hall's cracked plaster walls held a few family photographs: an 25
adorable Flannery, age 3, scowling at a picture book, and her smiling older self on an adjacent wall. There was a picture of Edward O'Connor, but none of Regina, who died in 1995 at 99. In the kitchen, an old electric range with fat heating elements sat near a chunky refrigerator, the very one Flannery bought for her mother after selling the rights to "The Life You Save May Be Your Own" for a TV movie in which Gene Kelly butchered the role of the con man Tom T. Shiftlet. In the center of the room, a small wooden table was set for two.

A walk around the grounds summoned all manner of O'Connor images. In a field of goldenrod, a lone hinny, a horse-donkey hybrid named Flossie, with grotesque clumps of fat on her rump, kept a reserved distance. I followed a path below the house down to a pond buzzing with dragonflies. Mr. Amason had told me to keep to the mowed areas to avoid snakes, so I wasn't too surprised to encounter a black rat snake, stretched out like a five-foot length of industrial cable, by a footbridge at the far edge of the pond. I tickled it with a turkey feather and it curled to strike faster than I could blink.

Back in Milledgeville's tidy downtown, I went to Georgia College and State University, which was Georgia State College for Women when O'Connor went there. The library displays her desk, paintings and other artifacts, and a librarian took me in the back to see her papers and books — a daunting array of fiction, classics and Catholic theology. The book of Updike's poetry looked well read, but not as much as the Kierkegaard ("Fear and Trembling" and "The Sickness Unto Death"), whose binding was falling off.

I found Sacred Heart Church, where Flannery and Regina worshiped, and was amazed when the pastor, the Rev. Michael McWhorter, suggested that I come back the next morning for the funeral service of O'Connor's first cousin Catherine Florencourt Firth, whose ashes were coming home from Arizona. I sat quietly in a back row, then shrank into my jacket when Father McWhorter announced my presence from the pulpit. But the mourners, clearly accustomed to Flannery admirers, nodded graciously at me. The pastor had a shiny round head and tidy beard, and applied incense with medieval vigor, sending curls of sweet smoke around Mrs. Firth's urn until the tiny sanctuary was entirely fogged in.

I am not accustomed to crashing funerals, so I did not linger afterward. I was grateful for the kind offers from Mrs. Firth's relations to come back and visit longer next time.

My last stop was also O'Connor's: Memory Hill Cemetery, in the middle of   30
town, where mother, father and daughter lie side by side by side under identical flat marble slabs. A state prison detail was prowling the grounds, trimming hedges. They had sloppily strewn oleander branches on Flannery's grave, which I brushed clean. I found a plastic bouquet to place at its head. I looked at the dates:

> March 25, 1925
> August 3, 1964

She died young, but not without saying what she wanted to say. I thought back to my journey the night before, when I captured the O'Connor sunset I had been looking for. I found a road that led down to the edge of a kaolin mine. Standing beside huge mounds of white chalky dirt, surrounded by deep treads left in the red clay by earth-moving machinery, I watched as a sentence from one of my favorite stories, "A Temple of the Holy Ghost," slowly unfolded, as if for me alone:

> "The sun was a huge red ball like an elevated Host drenched in blood and when it sank out of sight, it left a line in the sky like a red clay road hanging over the trees."

By the road's edge I spied an unusual-looking vine. It was passion flower, with purple blossoms that look like a crown of thorns, and the nails for Christ's hands and feet. I picked a bunch of strands, with their immature fruit, like little green boiled eggs, and got back onto the road to Milledgeville, under a blackening sky, to put them in some water.

(2007)

Exploring the Text

1. How does Lawrence Downes consider audience as he sets the stage for his visit to the home of Flannery O'Connor?
2. What is the effect of Downes's use of understatement in paragraph 5?

3. How does Downes characterize O'Connor? What surprises you about her?

4. How would you describe the tone of "In Search of Flannery O'Connor"? How does the essay's tone help Downes achieve his purpose?

5. Why do you think Downes ends his piece with a description of the "unusual-looking vine" he sees at the edge of the road?

ALICE WALKER

Alice Walker (b. 1944) is a novelist, a poet, an essayist, a civil rights activist, and a self-described eco-pacifist, best known for her depictions of the struggles and strengths of African American women. The youngest of eight children born to share-cropper parents, Walker grew up in the small town of Eatonton, Georgia. After high school, she attended Spelman College in Georgia, then transferred to Sarah Lawrence College in New York, which she graduated from in 1965. Her first novel, *The Third Life of Grange Copeland*, was published in 1969, followed by her poetry collection *Revolutionary Petunias and Other Poems* (1973). In 1982, she published *The Color Purple*, her most celebrated work, which won the Pulitzer Prize and was adapted into both a movie (directed by Steven Spielberg) and a Tony Award–winning Broadway musical. Walker is also known for her essays, in which she coined the term *womanist*. Claiming a more positive connotation than *feminist*, she writes that a womanist is "committed to survival and wholeness of entire people, male and female. Not a separatist." Walker has taught at Wellesley College, Yale University, the University of California–Berkeley, and many other institutions. She continues to support environmental causes and is an advocate for international women's rights.

from *Beyond the Peacock*
The Reconstruction of Flannery O'Connor

This essay appeared in Walker's 1975 essay collection, *In Search of Our Mother's Gardens: Womanist Prose*.

I discovered O'Connor when I was in college in the North and took a course in Southern writers and the South. The perfection of her writing was so dazzling I never noticed that no black Southern writers were taught. The other writers we studied — Faulkner, McCullers, Welty — seemed obsessed with a racial past that would not let them go. They seemed to beg the question of their characters' humanity on every page. O'Connor's characters — whose humanity if not their sanity is taken for granted, and who are miserable, ugly, narrow-minded, atheistic, and of intense racial smugness and arrogance, with not a graceful, pretty one anywhere who is not, at the same time, a joke — shocked and delighted me.

It was for her description of Southern white women that I appreciated her work at first, because when she set her pen to them not a whiff of magnolia hovered in the air (and the tree itself might never have been planted), and yes, I could say, yes, these white folks without the magnolia (who are indifferent to the tree's existence), and these black folks without melons and superior racial patience, these are like Southerners that I know.

She was for me the first great modern writer from the South, and was, in any case, the only one I had read who wrote such sly, demythifying sentences about white women as: "The woman would be more or less pretty — yellow hair, fat ankles, muddy-colored eyes."

Her white male characters do not fare any better — all of them misfits, thieves, deformed madmen, idiot children, illiterates, and murderers, and her black characters, male and female, appear equally shallow, demented, and absurd. That she retained a certain distance (only, however, in her later, mature work) from the inner workings of her black characters seems to me all to her credit, since, by deliberately limiting her treatment of them to cover their observable demeanor and actions, she leaves them free, in the reader's imagination, to inhabit another landscape, another life, than the one she creates for them. This is a kind of grace many writers do not have when dealing with representatives of an oppressed people within a story, and their insistence on knowing everything, on being God, in fact, has burdened us with more stereotypes than we can ever hope to shed.

In her life, O'Connor was more casual. In a letter to her friend Robert   5
Fitzgerald in the mid-fifties she wrote, "as the niggers say, I have the misery." He found nothing offensive, apparently, in including this unflattering (to O'Connor) statement in his introduction to one of her books. O'Connor was then certain she was dying, and was in pain; one assumes she made this comment in an attempt at levity. Even so, I do not find it funny. In another letter she wrote shortly before she died she said: "Justice is justice and should not be appealed to along racial lines. The problem is not abstract for the Southerner, it's concrete: he sees it in terms of persons, not races — which way of seeing does away with easy answers." Of course this observation, though grand, does not apply to the racist treatment of blacks by whites in the South, and O'Connor should have added that she spoke only for herself.

But *essential* O'Connor is not about race at all, which is why it is so refreshing, coming, as it does, out of such a *racial* culture. If it can be said to be "about" anything, then it is "about" prophets and prophecy, "about" revelation, and "about" the impact of supernatural grace on human beings who don't have a chance of spiritual growth without it.

(1975)

Exploring the Text

1. Describe the way that Alice Walker characterizes the difference between Flannery O'Connor and the other Southern writers she studied in her college course.
2. How does Walker address the stereotypes of both black and white women that have been a staple of Southern literature? How does she describe

O'Connor's contribution to the debunking of those stereotypes? Why does Walker feel comfortable with O'Connor's black and white women?

3. Does Walker believe there should be a line between the public (or published) self and the private one? Explain your answer. Do you agree?

4. What do you think Walker means when she says that O'Connor's work comes out of a "*racial* culture" (par. 6). Why does she say her work isn't about race?

Making Connections

1. Having read "Good Country People" (p. 1300) and Lawrence Downes's description of why he admires O'Connor (par. 6), can you see her influence in Downes's style? Give some examples.

2. Why do you think Downes chose to quote this description of Mrs. Freeman from "Good Country People": "Besides the neutral expression that she wore when she was alone, Mrs. Freeman had two others, forward and reverse, that she used for all her human dealings" (par. 8)? What line would you have chosen as representative of "Good Country People"? Explain your answer.

3. In paragraph 31, Downes says, "She died young, but not without saying what she wanted to say." What do you think O'Connor wanted to say in "Good Country People"?

4. Alice Walker says she is "delighted" by O'Connor's characters, who are "miserable, ugly, narrow-minded, atheistic, and of intense racial smugness and arrogance, with not a graceful, pretty one anywhere who is not, at the same time, a joke" (par. 1). Can you apply those adjectives to the characters in "Good Country People"? Do they delight you? Explain your answer.

5. What do Downes and Walker have in common in their admiration of Flannery O'Connor? In what ways do they differ?

6. Both Downes and Walker refer to peacocks — Walker in her title and Downes in paragraph 9. In "Good Country People," Hulga/Joy is said to be "as sensitive about the artificial leg as a peacock about his tail" (par. 125). Flannery O'Connor raised peacocks at her home in Milledgeville, Georgia. Why do you think peacocks are a potent symbol for some of the themes and character traits O'Connor examines in her work?

THEODORE ROETHKE

Theodore Roethke (1908–1963) was born in Saginaw, Michigan. His early years spent in the family greenhouse business brought him close to nature and to his father, who died suddenly when Roethke was fifteen, a loss that looms large in his poem "My Papa's Waltz." After graduating from the University of Michigan, he did brief stints at law school and at Harvard University before the Great Depression compelled him to find work teaching at Lafayette College. He continued to teach throughout his life. Roethke first became popular after favorable reviews for *Open House* in 1941. He then won numerous prizes for his work throughout the 1950s and 1960s, including National Book Awards for both *Words for the Wind* (1957) and *The Far Field* (1964). The meeting of the mystical and the natural is at the center of his work — a meeting that fascinated such earlier poets as Blake and Wordsworth, both of whom were strong influences on Roethke's poetry.

The Waking

"The Waking" was published in Roethke's collection *The Waking: Poems 1933–1953*, which won the Pulitzer Prize in 1954.

I wake to sleep, and take my waking slow.
I feel my fate in what I cannot fear.
I learn by going where I have to go.

We think by feeling. What is there to know?
I hear my being dance from ear to ear.   5
I wake to sleep, and take my waking slow.

Of those so close beside me, which are you?
God bless the Ground! I shall walk softly there,
And learn by going where I have to go.

Light takes the Tree; but who can tell us how?   10
The lowly worm climbs up a winding stair;
I wake to sleep, and take my waking slow.

Great Nature has another thing to do
To you and me; so take the lively air,
And, lovely, learn by going where to go.   15

This shaking keeps me steady. I should know.
What falls away is always. And is near.
I wake to sleep, and take my waking slow.
I learn by going where I have to go.

(1953)

Exploring the Text

1. What are two different ways you can read the poem's first line: "I wake to sleep, and take my waking slow"?

2. What do the poem's first and third lines have in common? Do their meanings change as they are repeated as the last lines of the following tercets (three-line stanzas)? Why do you think Theodore Roethke tweaks the line about learning but leaves the line about waking intact? How do those slight changes affect the meaning of those lines?

3. "The Waking" is a villanelle, a poetic form of five tercets and a quatrain (four-line stanza). It is built on two rhymes: the two key lines of the first stanza are repeated, alternately, as the last line of each tercet and joined together in the closing quatrain. What effect does this form have on the meaning of the poem? Hint: consider its circular effect.

4. A 1992 essay by Susan Pinkus on "The Waking" begins, "When a poem takes dead aim on the eternal, we should not be surprised that it draws many interpretations." Explain what you think she means by "the eternal." What is your interpretation of the poem?

5. What argument does "The Waking" make?

6. In what ways does "The Waking" create a sort of harmony of form and content? Critics have suggested approaching it as a piece of music before trying to figure out what it means. What happens when you try that approach?

JAMES BALDWIN

James Baldwin (1924–1987) was one of the most influential figures in American literature during the latter half of the twentieth century. His novels include *Go Tell It on the Mountain* (1953), *Giovanni's Room* (1956), *If Beale Street Could Talk* (1974), and *Just Above My Head* (1979). A sharp social critic of race relations and sexual identity, Baldwin wrote numerous essays that were collected in *Notes of a Native Son* (1955), *The Fire Next Time* (1963), and *The Devil Finds Work* (1976). He also wrote poetry and plays. By the late 1940s, Baldwin had moved to Europe and lived in France and Turkey for most of the rest of his life, though he returned at times to the United States to lecture and participate in the civil rights movement.

Notes of a Native Son

This essay appeared in the collection *Notes of a Native Son*, which was published in 1955.

I

On the 29th of July, in 1943, my father died. On the same day, a few hours later, his last child was born. Over a month before this, while all our energies were concentrated in waiting for these events, there had been, in Detroit, one of the bloodiest race riots of the century. A few hours after my father's funeral, while he lay in state in the undertaker's chapel, a race riot broke out in Harlem. On the morning of the 3rd of August, we drove my father to the graveyard through a wilderness of smashed plate glass.

The day of my father's funeral had also been my nineteenth birthday. As we drove him to the graveyard, the spoils of injustice, anarchy, discontent, and hatred were all around us. It seemed to me that God himself had devised, to mark my father's end, the most sustained and brutally dissonant of codas. And it seemed to me, too, that the violence which rose all about us as my father left the world had been devised as a corrective for the pride of his eldest son. I had declined to believe in that apocalypse which had been central to my father's vision; very well, life seemed to be saying, here is something that will certainly pass for an apocalypse until the real thing comes along. I had inclined to be contemptuous of my father for the conditions of his life, for the conditions of our lives. When his life had ended I began to wonder about that life and also, in a new way, to be apprehensive about my own.

I had not known my father very well. We had got on badly, partly because we shared, in our different fashions, the vice of stubborn pride. When he was dead I realized that I had hardly ever spoken to him. When he had been dead a long time I began to wish I had. It seems to be typical of life in America, where opportunities, real and fancied, are thicker than anywhere else on the globe, that the second generation has no time to talk to the first. No one, including my father, seems to have known exactly how old he was, but his mother had been born during slavery. He was of the first generation of free men. He, along with thousands of other Negroes, came North after 1919 and I was part of that generation which had never seen the landscape of what Negroes sometimes call the Old Country.

He had been born in New Orleans and had been a quite young man there during the time that Louis Armstrong, a boy, was running errands for the dives and honky-tonks of what was always presented to me as one of the most wicked of cities — to this day, whenever I think of New Orleans, I also helplessly think of Sodom and Gomorrah. My father never mentioned Louis Armstrong, except to forbid us to play his records; but there was a picture of him on our wall for a long time. One of my father's strong-willed female relatives had placed it there and forbade my father to take it down. He never did, but he eventually maneuvered her out of the house and when, some years later, she was in trouble and near death, he refused to do anything to help her.

He was, I think, very handsome. I gather this from photographs and from my own memories of him, dressed in his Sunday best and on his way to preach a sermon somewhere, when I was little. Handsome, proud, and ingrown, "like a toe-nail," somebody said. But he looked to me, as I grew older, like pictures I had seen of African tribal chieftains: he really should have been naked, with war-paint on and barbaric mementos, standing among spears. He could be chilling in the pulpit and indescribably cruel in his personal life and he was certainly the most bitter man I have ever met; yet it must be said that there was something else in him, buried in him, which lent him his tremendous power and, even, a rather crushing charm. It had something to do with his blackness, I think — he was very black — with his blackness and his beauty,

5

and with the fact that he knew that he was black but did not know that he was beautiful. He claimed to be proud of his blackness but it had also been the cause of much humiliation and it had fixed bleak boundaries to his life. He was not a young man when we were growing up and he had already suffered many kinds of ruin; in his outrageously demanding and protective way he loved his children, who were black like him and menaced, like him; and all these things sometimes showed in his face when he tried, never to my knowledge with any success, to establish contact with any of us. When he took one of his children on his knee to play, the child always became fretful and began to cry; when he tried to help one of us with our homework the absolutely unabating tension which emanated from him caused our minds and our tongues to become paralyzed, so that he, scarcely knowing why, flew into a rage and the child, not knowing why, was punished. If it ever entered his head to bring a surprise home for his children, it was, almost unfailingly, the wrong surprise and even the big watermelons he often brought home on his back in the summertime led to the most appalling scenes. I do not remember, in all those years, that one of his children was ever glad to see him come home. From what I was able to gather of his early life, it seemed that this inability to establish contact with other people had always marked him and had been one of the things which had driven him out of New Orleans. There was something in him, therefore, groping and tentative, which was never expressed and which was buried with him. One saw it most clearly when he was facing new people and hoping to impress them. But he never did, not for long. We went from church to smaller and more improbable church, he found himself in less and less demand as a minister, and by the time he died none of his friends had come to see him for a long time. He had lived and died in an intolerable bitterness of spirit and it frightened me, as we drove him to the graveyard through those unquiet, ruined streets, to see how powerful and overflowing this bitterness could be and to realize that this bitterness now was mine.

When he died I had been away from home for a little over a year. In that year I had had time to become aware of the meaning of all my father's bitter warnings, had discovered the secret of his proudly pursed lips and rigid carriage: I had discovered the weight of white people in the world. I saw that this had been for my ancestors and now would be for me an awful thing to live with and that the bitterness which had helped to kill my father could also kill me.

He had been ill a long time — in the mind, as we now realized, reliving instances of his fantastic intransigence in the new light of his affliction and endeavoring to feel a sorrow for him which never, quite, came true. We had not known that he was being eaten up by paranoia, and the discovery that his cruelty, to our bodies and our minds, had been one of the symptoms of his illness was not, then, enough to enable us to forgive him. The younger children felt, quite simply, relief that he would not be coming home anymore. My mother's observation that it was he, after all, who had kept them alive all these years meant nothing because the problems of keeping children alive are not real for children. The older children felt, with my father gone, that they could invite their friends to the house without fear that their friends would be insulted or, as had sometimes happened with me, being told that their friends were in league with the devil and intended to rob our family of everything we owned. (I didn't fail to wonder, and it made me hate him, what on earth we owned that anybody else would want.)

His illness was beyond all hope of healing before anyone realized that he was ill. He had always been so strange and had lived, like a prophet, in such unimaginably close communion with the Lord that his long silences which were punctuated by moans and hallelujahs and snatches of old songs while he sat at the living-room window never seemed odd to us. It was not until he refused to eat because, he said, his family was trying to poison him that my mother was forced to accept as a fact what had, until then, been only an unwilling suspicion. When he was committed, it was discovered that he had tuberculosis and, as it turned out, the disease of his mind allowed the disease of his body to destroy him. For the doctors could not force him to eat, either, and, though he was fed intravenously, it was clear from the beginning that there was no hope for him.

In my mind's eye I could see him, sitting at the window, locked up in his terrors; hating and fearing every living soul including his children who had betrayed him, too, by reaching towards the world which had despised him. There were nine of us. I began to wonder what it could have felt like for such a man to have had nine children whom he could barely feed. He used to make little jokes about our poverty, which never, of course, seemed very funny to us; they could not have seemed very funny to him, either, or else our all too feeble response to them would never have caused such rages. He spent great energy and achieved, to our chagrin, no small amount of success in keeping us away from the people who surrounded us, people who had all-night rent parties to which we listened when we should have been sleeping, people who cursed and drank and flashed razor blades on Lenox Avenue. He could not understand why, if they had so much energy to spare, they could not use it to make their lives better. He treated almost everybody on our block with a most uncharitable asperity and neither they, nor, of course, their children were slow to reciprocate.

The only white people who came to our house were welfare workers and bill col- 10
lectors. It was almost always my mother who dealt with them, for my father's temper, which was at the mercy of his pride, was never to be trusted. It was clear that he felt their very presence in his home to be a violation: this was conveyed by his carriage, almost ludicrously stiff, and by his voice, harsh and vindictively polite. When I was around nine or ten I wrote a play which was directed by a young, white schoolteacher, a woman, who then took an interest in me, and gave me books to read and, in order to corroborate my theatrical bent, decided to take me to see what she somewhat tactlessly referred to as "real" plays. Theatergoing was forbidden in our house, but, with the really cruel intuitiveness of a child, I suspected that the color of this woman's skin would carry the day for me. When, at school, she suggested taking me to the theater, I did not, as I might have done if she had been a Negro, find a way of discouraging her, but agreed that she should pick me up at my house one evening. I then, very cleverly, left all the rest to my mother, who suggested to my father, as I knew she would, that it would not be very nice to let such a kind woman make the trip for nothing. Also, since it was a schoolteacher, I imagine that my mother countered the idea of sin with the idea of "education," which word, even with my father, carried a kind of bitter weight.

Before the teacher came my father took me aside to ask *why* she was coming, what *interest* she could possibly have in our house, in a boy like me. I said I didn't know but I, too, suggested that it had something to do with education. And I understood that my father was waiting for me to say something—I didn't quite know what; perhaps that I wanted his protection against this teacher and her "education." I said none of these things and the teacher came and we went out. It was clear, during the brief interview in our living room, that my father was agreeing very much against his will and that he would have refused permission if he had dared. The fact that he did not dare caused me to despise him: I had no way of knowing that he was facing in that living room a wholly unprecedented and frightening situation.

Later, when my father had been laid off from his job, this woman became very important to us. She was really a very sweet and generous woman and went to a great deal of trouble to be of help to us, particularly during one awful winter. My mother called her by the highest name she knew. She said she was a "christian." My father could scarcely disagree but during the four or five years of our relatively close association he never trusted her and was always trying to surprise in her open, Midwestern face the genuine, cunningly hidden, and hideous motivation. In later years, particularly when it began to be clear that this "education" of mine was going to lead me to perdition, he became more explicit and warned me that my white friends in high school were not really my friends and that I would see, when I was older, how white people would do anything to keep a Negro down. Some of them could be nice, he admitted, but none of them were to be trusted and most of them were not even nice. The best thing was to have as little to do with them as possible. I did not feel this way and I was certain, in my innocence, that I never would.

But the year which preceded my father's death had made a great change in my life. I had been living in New Jersey, working in defense plants, working and living among southerners, white and black. I knew about the south, of course, and about how southerners treated Negroes and how they expected them to behave, but it had never entered my mind that anyone would look at me and expect *me* to behave that way. I learned in New Jersey that to be a Negro meant, precisely, that one was never looked at but was simply at the mercy of the reflexes the color of one's skin caused in other people. I acted in New Jersey as I had always acted, that is as though I thought a great deal of myself—I had to *act* that way—with results that were, simply, unbelievable. I had scarcely arrived before I had earned the enmity, which was extraordinarily ingenious, of all my superiors and nearly all my coworkers. In the beginning, to make matters worse, I simply did not know what was happening. I did not know what I had done, and I shortly began to wonder what *anyone* could possibly do, to bring about such unanimous, active, and unbearably vocal hostility. I knew about jim-crow but I had never experienced it. I went to the same self-service restaurant three times and stood with all the Princeton boys before the counter, waiting for a hamburger and coffee; it was always an extraordinarily long time before anything was set before me; but it was not until the fourth visit that I learned that, in fact, nothing had ever been set before me: I had simply picked something up. Negroes were not served there, I was told, and they had been waiting for me to realize that I was always the only Negro present. Once

I was told this, I determined to go there all the time. But now they were ready for me and, though some dreadful scenes were subsequently enacted in that restaurant, I never ate there again.

It was the same story all over New Jersey, in bars, bowling alleys, diners, places to live. I was always being forced to leave, silently, or with mutual imprecations. I very shortly became notorious and children giggled behind me when I passed and their elders whispered or shouted — they really believed that I was mad. And it did begin to work on my mind, of course; I began to be afraid to go anywhere and to compensate for this I went places to which I really should not have gone and where, God knows, I had no desire to be. My reputation in town naturally enhanced my reputation at work and my working day became one long series of acrobatics designed to keep me out of trouble. I cannot say that these acrobatics succeeded. It began to seem that the machinery of the organization I worked for was turning over, day and night, with but one aim: to eject me. I was fired once, and contrived, with the aid of a friend from New York, to get back on the payroll; was fired again, and bounced back again. It took a while to fire me for the third time, but the third time took. There were no loopholes anywhere. There was not even any way of getting back inside the gates.

That year in New Jersey lives in my mind as though it were the year during which, having an unsuspected predilection for it, I first contracted some dread, chronic disease, the unfailing symptom of which is a kind of blind fever, a pounding in the skull and fire in the bowels. Once this disease is contracted, one can never be really carefree again, for the fever, without an instant's warning, can recur at any moment. It can wreck more important things than race relations. There is not a Negro alive who does not have this rage in his blood — one has the choice, merely, of living with it consciously or surrendering to it. As for me, this fever has recurred in me, and does, and will until the day I die.

My last night in New Jersey, a white friend from New York took me to the nearest big town, Trenton, to go to the movies and have a few drinks. As it turned out, he also saved me from, at the very least, a violent whipping. Almost every detail of that night stands out very clearly in my memory. I even remember the name of the movie we saw because its title impressed me as being so patly ironical. It was a movie about the German occupation of France, starring Maureen O'Hara and Charles Laughton and called *This Land Is Mine*. I remember the name of the diner we walked into when the movie ended: it was the "American Diner." When we walked in the counterman asked what we wanted and I remember answering with the casual sharpness which had become my habit: "We want a hamburger and a cup of coffee, what do you think we want?" I do not know why, after a year of such rebuffs, I so completely failed to anticipate his answer, which was, of course, "We don't serve Negroes here." This reply failed to discompose me, at least for the moment. I made some sardonic comment about the name of the diner and we walked out into the streets.

This was the time of what was called the "brown-out," when the lights in all American cities were very dim. When we reentered the streets something happened to me which had the force of an optical illusion, or a nightmare. The streets were very crowded and I was facing north. People were moving in every direction but it seemed to me, in that instant, that all of the people I could see, and many more than that, were moving toward me, against me, and that everyone was white. I remember how their faces gleamed. And I felt, like a physical sensation, a *click* at the nape of my neck as though some interior string connecting my head to my body had been cut. I began to walk. I heard my friend call after me, but I ignored him. Heaven only knows what was going on in his mind, but he had the good sense not to touch me — I don't know what would have happened if he had — and to keep me in sight. I don't know what was going on in my mind, either; I certainly had no conscious plan. I wanted to do something to crush these white faces, which were crushing me. I walked for perhaps a block or two until I came to an enormous, glittering, and fashionable restaurant in which I knew not even the intercession of the Virgin would cause me to be served. I pushed through the doors and took the first vacant seat I saw, at a table for two, and waited.

I do not know how long I waited and I rather wonder, until today, what I could possibly have looked like. Whatever I looked like, I frightened the waitress who shortly appeared, and the moment she appeared all of my fury flowed towards her. I hated her for her white face, and for her great, astounded, frightened eyes. I felt that if she found a black man so frightening I would make her fright worthwhile.

She did not ask me what I wanted, but repeated, as though she had learned it somewhere, "We don't serve Negroes here." She did not say it with the blunt, derisive hostility to which I had grown so accustomed, but, rather, with a note of apology in her voice, and fear. This made me colder and more murderous than ever. I felt I had to do something with my hands. I wanted her to come close enough for me to get her neck between my hands.

So I pretended not to have understood her, hoping to draw her closer. And she did   20
step a very short step closer, with her pencil poised incongruously over her pad, and repeated the formula: ". . . don't serve Negroes here."

Somehow, with the repetition of that phrase, which was already ringing in my head like a thousand bells of a nightmare, I realized that she would never come any closer and that I would have to strike from a distance. There was nothing on the table but an ordinary water-mug half full of water, and I picked this up and hurled it with all my strength at her. She ducked and it missed her and shattered against the mirror behind the bar. And, with that sound, my frozen blood abruptly thawed, I returned from wherever I had been, I *saw*, for the first time, the restaurant, the people with their mouths open, already, as it seemed to me, rising as one man, and I realized what I had done, and where I was, and I was frightened. I rose and began running for the door. A round, pot-bellied man grabbed me by the nape of the neck just as I reached the doors and began to beat me about the face. I kicked him and got loose and ran into the streets. My friend whispered, *"Run!"* and I ran.

My friend stayed outside the restaurant long enough to misdirect my pursuers and the police, who arrived, he told me, at once. I do not know what I said to him when he came to my room that night. I could not have said much. I felt, in the oddest, most awful way, that I had somehow betrayed him. I lived it over and over and over again, the way one relives an automobile accident after it has happened and one finds oneself alone and safe. I could not get over two facts, both equally difficult for the imagination to grasp, and one was that I could have been murdered. But the other was that I had been ready to commit murder. I saw nothing very clearly but I did see this: that my life, my *real* life, was in danger, and not from anything other people might do but from the hatred I carried in my own heart.

II

I had returned home around the second week in June — in great haste because it seemed that my father's death and my mother's confinement were both but a matter of hours. In the case of my mother, it soon became clear that she had simply made a miscalculation. This had always been her tendency and I don't believe that a single one of us arrived in the world, or has since arrived anywhere else, on time. But none of us dawdled so intolerably about the business of being born as did my baby sister. We sometimes amused ourselves, during those endless, stifling weeks, by picturing the baby sitting within in the safe, warm dark, bitterly regretting the necessity of becoming a part of our chaos and stubbornly putting it off as long as possible. I understood her perfectly and congratulated her on showing such good sense so soon. Death, however, sat as purposefully at my father's bedside as life stirred within my mother's womb and it was harder to understand why he so lingered in that long shadow. It seemed that he had bent, and for a long time, too, all of his energies towards dying. Now death was ready for him but my father held back.

All of Harlem, indeed, seemed to be infected by waiting. I had never before known it to be so violently still. Racial tensions throughout this country were exacerbated during the early years of the war, partly because the labor market brought together hundreds of thousands of ill-prepared people and partly because Negro soldiers, regardless of where they were born, received their military training in the south. What happened in defense plants and army camps had repercussions, naturally, in every Negro ghetto. The situation in Harlem had grown bad enough for clergymen, policemen, educators, politicians, and social workers to assert in one breath that there was no "crime wave" and to offer, in the very next breath, suggestions as to how to combat it. These suggestions always seemed to involve playgrounds, despite the fact that racial skirmishes were occurring in the playgrounds, too. Playground or not, crime wave or not, the Harlem police force had been augmented in March, and the unrest grew — perhaps, in fact, partly as a result of the ghetto's instinctive hatred of policemen. Perhaps the most revealing news item, out of the steady parade of reports of muggings, stabbings, shootings, assaults, gang wars, and accusations of police brutality is the item concerning six Negro girls who set upon a white girl in the subway because, as they all too accurately put it, she was stepping on their toes. Indeed she was, all over the nation.

I had never before been so aware of policemen, on foot, on horseback, on corners, everywhere, always two by two. Nor had I ever been so aware of small knots of people. They were on stoops and on corners and in doorways, and what was striking about them, I think, was that they did not seem to be talking. Never, when I passed these groups, did the usual sound of a curse or a laugh ring out and neither did there seem to be any hum of gossip. There was certainly, on the other hand, occurring between them communication extraordinarily intense. Another thing that was striking was the

25

unexpected diversity of the people who made up these groups. Usually, for example, one would see a group of sharpies standing on the street corner, jiving the passing chicks; or a group of older men, usually, for some reason, in the vicinity of a barber shop, discussing baseball scores, or the numbers or making rather chilling observations about women they had known. Women, in a general way, tended to be seen less often together — unless they were church women, or very young girls, or prostitutes met together for an unprofessional instant. But that summer I saw the strangest combinations: large, respectable, churchly matrons standing on the stoops or the corners with their hair tied up, together with a girl in sleazy satin whose face bore the marks of gin and the razor, or heavy-set, abrupt, no-nonsense older men, in company with the most disreputable and fanatical "race" men, or these same "race" men with the sharpies, or these sharpies with the churchly women. Seventh Day Adventists and Methodists and Spiritualists seemed to be hobnobbing with Holy-rollers and they were all, alike, entangled with the most flagrant disbelievers; something heavy in their stance seemed to indicate that they had all, incredibly, seen a common vision, and on each face there seemed to be the same strange, bitter shadow.

The churchly women and the matter-of-fact, no-nonsense men had children in the Army. The sleazy girls they talked to had lovers there, the sharpies and the "race" men had friends and brothers there. It would have demanded an unquestioning patriotism, happily as uncommon in this country as it is undesirable, for these people not to have been disturbed by the bitter letters they received, by the newspaper stories they read, not to have been enraged by the posters, then to be found all over New York, which described the Japanese as "yellow-bellied Japs." It was only the "race" men, to be sure, who spoke ceaselessly of being revenged — how this vengeance was to be exacted was not clear — for the indignities and dangers suffered by Negro boys in uniform; but everybody felt a directionless, hopeless bitterness, as well as that panic which can scarcely be suppressed when one knows that a human being one loves is beyond one's reach, and in danger. This helplessness and this gnawing uneasiness does something, at length, to even the toughest mind. Perhaps the best way to sum all this up is to say that the people I knew felt, mainly, a peculiar kind of relief when they knew that their boys were being shipped out of the south, to do battle overseas. It was, perhaps, like feeling that the most dangerous part of a dangerous journey had been passed and that now, even if death should come, it would come with honor and without the complicity of their countrymen. Such a death would be, in short, a fact with which one could hope to live.

It was on the 28th of July, which I believe was a Wednesday, that I visited my father for the first time during his illness and for the last time in his life. The moment I saw him I knew why I had put off this visit so long. I had told my mother that I did not want to see him because I hated him. But this was not true. It was only that I *had* hated him and I wanted to hold on to this hatred. I did not want to look on him as a ruin: it was not a ruin I had hated. I imagine that one of the reasons people cling to their hates so stubbornly is because they sense, once hate is gone, that they will be forced to deal with pain.

We traveled out to him, his older sister and myself, to what seemed to be the very end of a very Long Island. It was hot and dusty and we wrangled, my aunt and I, all the way out, over the fact that I had recently begun to smoke and, as she said, to give myself airs. But I knew that she wrangled with me because she could not bear to face the fact of her brother's dying. Neither could I endure the reality of her despair, her unstated bafflement as to what had happened to her brother's life, and her own. So we wrangled and I smoked and from time to time she fell into a heavy reverie. Covertly, I watched her face, which was the face of an old woman; it had fallen in, the eyes were sunken and lightless; soon she would be dying, too.

In my childhood — it had not been so long ago — I had thought her beautiful. She had been quick-witted and quick-moving and very generous with all the children, and each of her visits had been an event. At one time one of my brothers and myself had thought of running away to live with her. Now she could no longer produce out of her handbag some unexpected and yet familiar delight. She made me feel pity and revulsion and fear. It was awful to realize that she no longer caused me to feel affection. The closer we came to the hospital the more querulous she became and at the same time, naturally, grew more dependent on me. Between pity and guilt and fear I began to feel that there was another me trapped in my skull like a jack-in-the-box who might escape my control at any moment and fill the air with screaming.

She began to cry the moment we entered the room and she saw him lying there, all shriveled and still, like a little black monkey. The great, gleaming apparatus which fed him and would have compelled him to be still even if he had been able to move brought to mind, not beneficence, but torture; the tubes entering his arm made me think of pictures I had seen when a child, of Gulliver, tied down by the pygmies on that island. My aunt wept and wept; there was a whistling sound in my father's throat; nothing was said; he could not speak. I wanted to take his hand, to say something. But I do not know what I could have said, even if he could have heard me. He was not really in that room with us, he had at last really embarked on his journey; and though my aunt told me that he said he was going to meet Jesus, I did not hear anything except that whistling in his throat. The doctor came back and we left, into that unbearable train again, and home. In the morning came the telegram saying that he was dead. Then the house was suddenly full of relatives, friends, hysteria, and confusion and I quickly left my mother and the children to the care of those impressive women, who, in Negro communities at least, automatically appear at times of bereavement armed with lotions, proverbs, and patience, and an ability to cook. I went downtown. By the time I returned, later the same day, my mother had been carried to the hospital and the baby had been born.

30

III

For my father's funeral I had nothing black to wear and this posed a nagging problem all day long. It was one of those problems, simple, or impossible of solution, to which the mind insanely clings in order to avoid the mind's real trouble. I spent most of that day at the downtown apartment of a girl I knew, celebrating my birthday with whiskey and wondering what to wear that night. When planning a birthday celebration one naturally does not expect that it will be up against competition from a funeral and this girl had anticipated taking me out that night, for a big dinner and a night club afterwards. Sometime during the course of that long day we decided that we would go out anyway, when my father's funeral service was over. I imagine *I* decided it, since, as the funeral hour approached, it became clearer and clearer to me that I would not know what to do with myself when it was over. The girl, stifling her very lively concern as to the possible effects of the whiskey on one of my father's chief mourners, concentrated on being conciliatory and practically helpful. She found a black shirt for me somewhere and ironed it and, dressed in the darkest pants and jacket I owned, and slightly drunk, I made my way to my father's funeral.

The chapel was full, but not packed, and very quiet. There were, mainly, my father's relatives, and his children, and here and there I saw faces I had not seen since childhood, the faces of my father's one-time friends. They were very dark and solemn now, seeming somehow to suggest that they had known all along that something like this would happen. Chief among the mourners was my aunt, who had quarreled with my father all his life; by which I do not mean to suggest that her mourning was insincere or that she had not loved him. I suppose that she was one of the few people in the world who had, and their incessant quarreling proved precisely the strength of the tie that bound them. The only other person in the world, as far as I knew, whose relationship to my father rivaled my aunt's in depth was my mother, who was not there.

It seemed to me, of course, that it was a very long funeral. But it was, if anything, a rather shorter funeral than most, nor, since there were no overwhelming, uncontrollable expressions of grief, could it be called — if I dare to use the word — successful. The minister who preached my father's funeral sermon was one of the few my father had still been seeing as he neared his end. He presented to us in his sermon a man whom none of us had ever seen — a man thoughtful, patient, and forbearing, a Christian inspiration to all who knew him, and a model for his children. And no doubt the children, in their disturbed and guilty state, were almost ready to believe this; he had been remote enough to be anything and, anyway, the shock of the incontrovertible, that it was really our father lying up there in that casket, prepared the mind for anything. His sister moaned and this grief-stricken moaning was taken as corroboration. The other faces held a dark, non-committal thoughtfulness. This was not the man they had known, but they had scarcely expected to be confronted with *him*; this was, in a sense deeper than questions of fact, the man they had not known, and the man they had not known may have been the real one. The real man, whoever he had been, had suffered and now he was dead: this was all that was sure and all that mattered now. Every man in the chapel hoped that when his hour came he, too, would be eulogized, which is to say forgiven, and that all of his lapses, greeds, errors, and strayings from the truth would be invested with coherence and looked upon with charity. This was perhaps the last thing human beings could give each other and it was what they demanded, after all, of the Lord. Only the Lord saw the midnight tears, only He was present when one of His children, moaning and wringing hands, paced up and down the room. When one slapped one's child in anger the recoil in the heart reverberated through heaven and became part of the pain of the universe. And when the children were hungry and sullen and distrustful and one watched them, daily, growing wilder, and further away, and running headlong into danger, it was the Lord who knew what the charged heart endured as the strap was laid to the backside; the Lord alone who knew what one *would* have said if one had had, like the Lord, the gift of the living word. It was the Lord who knew of the impossibility every parent in that room faced: how to prepare the child for the day when the child would be despised and how to *create* in the child — by what means? — a stronger antidote to this poison than one had found for oneself. The avenues, side streets, bars, billiard halls, hospitals, police stations, and even the playgrounds of Harlem — not to mention the houses of correction, the jails, and the morgue — testified to the potency of the poison while remaining silent as to the efficacy of whatever antidote, irresistibly raising the question of whether or not such an antidote existed; raising, which was worse, the question of whether or not an antidote was desirable; perhaps poison should be fought with poison. With these several schisms in the mind and with more terrors in the heart than could be named, it was better not to judge the man who had gone down under an impossible burden. It was better to remember. *Thou knowest this man's fall; but thou knowest not his wrassling.*

While the preacher talked and I watched the children — years of changing their diapers, scrubbing them, slapping them, taking them to school, and scolding them had had the perhaps inevitable result of making me love them, though I am not sure I knew this then — my mind was busily breaking out with a rash of disconnected impressions. Snatches of popular songs, indecent jokes, bits of books I had read, movie sequences, faces, voices, political issues — I thought I was going mad; all these impressions suspended, as it were, in the solution of the faint nausea produced in me by the heat and liquor. For a moment I had the impression that my alcoholic breath, inefficiently disguised with chewing gum, filled the entire chapel. Then someone began singing one of my father's favorite songs and, abruptly, I was with him, sitting on his knee, in the hot, enormous, crowded church which was the first church we attended. It was the Abyssinia Baptist Church on 138th Street. We had not gone there long. With this image, a host of others came. I had forgotten, in the rage of my growing up, how proud my father had been of me when I was little. Apparently, I had had a voice and my father had liked to show me off before the members of the church. I had forgotten what he had looked like when he was pleased but now I remembered that he had always been grinning with pleasure when my solos ended. I even remembered certain expressions on his face when he teased my mother — had he loved her? I would never know. And when had it all begun to change? For now it seemed that he had not always been cruel. I remembered being taken for a haircut and scraping my knee on the footrest of the barber's chair and I remembered my father's face as he soothed my crying and applied the stinging iodine. Then I remembered our fights, fights which had been of the worst possible kind because my technique had been silence.

I remembered the one time in all our life together when we had really spoken to each other.   35

It was on a Sunday and it must have been shortly before I left home. We were walking, just the two of us, in our usual silence, to or from church. I was in high school and had been doing a lot of writing and I was, at about this time, the editor of the high school magazine. But I had also been a Young Minister and had been preaching from the pulpit. Lately, I had been taking fewer engagements and preached as rarely as possible. It was said in the church, quite truthfully, that I was "cooling off."

My father asked me abruptly, "You'd rather write than preach, wouldn't you?"

I was astonished at his question — because it was a real question. I answered, "Yes."

That was all we said. It was awful to remember that that was all we had *ever* said.

The casket now was opened and mourners were being led up the aisle to look for 40 the last time on the deceased. The assumption was that the family was too overcome with grief to be allowed to make this journey alone and I watched while my aunt was led to the casket and, muffled in black, and shaking, led back to her seat. I disapproved of forcing the children to look on their dead father, considering that the shock of his death, or, more truthfully, the shock of death as a reality, was already a little more than a child could bear, but my judgment in this matter had been overruled and there they were, bewildered and frightened and very small, being led, one by one, to the casket. But there is also something very gallant about children at such moments. It has something to do with their silence and gravity and with the fact that one cannot help them. Their legs, somehow, seem *exposed*, so that it is at once incredible and terribly clear that their legs are all they have to hold them up.

I had not wanted to go to the casket myself and I certainly had not wished to be led there, but there was no way of avoiding either of these forms. One of the deacons led me up and I looked on my father's face. I cannot say that it looked like him at all. His blackness had been equivocated by powder and there was no suggestion in that casket of what his power had or could have been. He was simply an old man dead, and it was hard to believe that he had ever given anyone either joy or pain. Yet, his life filled that room. Further up the avenue his wife was holding his newborn child. Life and death so close together, and love and hatred, and right and wrong, said something to me which I did not want to hear concerning man, concerning the life of man.

After the funeral, while I was downtown desperately celebrating my birthday, a Negro soldier, in the lobby of the Hotel Braddock, got into a fight with a white policeman over a Negro girl. Negro girls, white policemen, in or out of uniform, and Negro males — in or out of uniform — were part of the furniture of the lobby of the Hotel Braddock and this was certainly not the first time such an incident had occurred. It was destined, however, to receive an unprecedented publicity, for the fight between the policeman and the soldier ended with the shooting of the soldier. Rumor, flowing immediately to the streets outside, stated that the soldier had been shot in the back, an instantaneous and revealing invention, and that the soldier had died protecting a Negro woman. The facts were somewhat different — for example, the soldier had not been shot in the back, and was not dead, and the girl seems to have been as dubious a symbol of womanhood as her white counterpart in Georgia usually is, but no one was interested in the facts. They preferred the invention because this invention expressed and corroborated their hates and fears so perfectly. It is just as well to remember that people are always doing this. Perhaps many of those legends, including Christianity, to which the world clings began their conquest of the world with just some such concerted surrender to distortion. The effect, in Harlem, of this particular legend was like the effect of a lit match in a tin of gasoline. The mob gathered before the doors of the Hotel Braddock simply began to swell and to spread in every direction, and Harlem exploded.

The mob did not cross the ghetto lines. It would have been easy, for example, to have gone over Morningside Park on the west side or to have crossed the Grand Central railroad tracks at 125th Street on the east side, to wreak havoc in white neighborhoods. The mob seems to have been mainly interested in something more potent and real than the white face, that is, in white power, and the principal damage done during the riot of the summer of 1943 was to white business establishments in Harlem. It might have been a far bloodier story, of course, if, at the hour the riot began, these establishments had still been open. From the Hotel Braddock the mob fanned out, east and west along 125th Street, and for the entire length of Lenox, Seventh, and Eighth avenues. Along each of these avenues, and along each major side street — 116th, 125th, 135th, and so on — bars, stores, pawnshops, restaurants, even little luncheonettes had been smashed open and entered and looted — looted, it might be added, with more haste than efficiency. The shelves really looked as though a bomb had struck them. Cans of beans and soup and dog food, along with toilet paper, corn flakes, sardines and milk tumbled every which way, and abandoned cash registers and cases of beer leaned crazily out of the splintered windows and were strewn along the avenues. Sheets, blankets, and clothing of every description formed a kind of path, as though people had dropped them while running. I truly had not realized that Harlem *had* so many stores until I saw them all smashed open; the first time the word *wealth* ever entered my mind in relation to Harlem was when I saw it scattered in the streets. But one's first, incongruous impression of plenty was countered immediately by an impression of waste. None of this was doing anybody any good. It would have been better to have left the plate glass as it had been and the goods lying in the stores.

It would have been better, but it would also have been intolerable, for Harlem had needed something to smash. To smash something is the ghetto's chronic need. Most of the time it is the members of the ghetto who smash each other, and themselves. But as long as the ghetto walls are standing there will always come a moment when these outlets do not work. That summer, for example, it was not enough to get into a fight on Lenox Avenue, or curse out one's cronies in the barber shops. If ever, indeed, the violence which fills Harlem's churches, pool halls, and bars erupts outward in a more direct fashion, Harlem and its citizens are likely to vanish in an apocalyptic flood. That this is not likely to happen is due to a great many reasons, most hidden and powerful among them the Negro's real relation to the white American. This relation prohibits, simply, anything as uncomplicated and satisfactory as pure hatred. In order really to hate white people, one has to blot so much out of the mind — and the heart — that this hatred itself becomes an exhausting and self-destructive pose. But this does not mean, on the other hand, that love comes easily: the white world is too powerful, too complacent, too ready with gratuitous humiliation, and, above all, too ignorant and too innocent for that. One is absolutely forced to make perpetual qualifications and one's own reactions are always canceling each other out. It is this, really, which has driven so many people mad, both white and black. One is always in the position of having to decide between amputation and gangrene. Amputation is swift but time may prove that the amputation was not necessary—or one may delay the amputation too long. Gangrene is slow, but it is impossible to be sure that one is reading one's symptoms right. The idea of going through life as a cripple is more than one can bear, and equally unbearable is the risk of swelling up slowly, in agony, with poison. And the trouble, finally, is that the risks are real even if the choices do not exist.

"But as for me and my house," my father had said, "we will serve the Lord." I 45 wondered, as we drove him to his resting place, what this line had meant for him. I had heard him preach it many times. I had preached it once myself, proudly giving it an interpretation different from my father's. Now the whole thing came back to me, as though my father and I were on our way to Sunday school and I were memorizing the golden text: *And if it seem evil unto you to serve the Lord, choose you this day whom you will serve; whether the gods which your fathers served that were on the other side of the flood, or the gods of the Amorites, in whose land ye dwell: but as for me and my house, we will serve the Lord.* I suspected in these familiar lines a meaning which had never been there for me before. All of my father's texts and songs, which I had decided were meaningless, were arranged before me at his death like empty bottles, waiting to hold the meaning which life would give them for me. This was his legacy: nothing is ever escaped. That bleakly memorable morning I hated the unbelievable streets and the Negroes and whites who had, equally, made them that way. But I knew that it was folly, as my father would have said, this bitterness was folly. It was necessary to hold on to the things that mattered. The dead man mattered, the new life mattered; blackness and whiteness did not matter; to believe that they did was to acquiesce in one's own destruction. Hatred, which could destroy so much, never failed to destroy the man who hated and this was an immutable law.

It began to seem that one would have to hold in the mind forever two ideas which seemed to be in opposition. The first idea was acceptance, the acceptance, totally without rancor, of life as it is, and men as they are: in the light of this idea, it goes without saying that injustice is a commonplace. But this did not mean that one could be complacent, for the second idea was of equal power: that one must never, in one's own life, accept these injustices as commonplace but must fight them with all one's strength. This fight begins, however, in the heart and it now had been laid to my charge to keep my own heart free of hatred and despair. This intimation made my heart heavy and, now that my father was irrecoverable, I wished that he had been beside me so that I could have searched his face for the answers which only the future would give me now.

(1955)

Exploring the Text

1. What is James Baldwin's primary purpose in "Notes of a Native Son"? Do you think there is a secondary purpose?

2. What is Baldwin's attitude toward his father? Does it change over the course of the essay? If so, how?

3. Identify at least three stories Baldwin tells about himself. What does each demonstrate? How do they connect?
4. Baldwin alternates among concrete descriptions of people and places, reflections, and strong argumentative assertions. How does each type of writing help him achieve his purpose in this essay?
5. Find several examples of parallel diction, parallel syntax, and parallel structure on a larger level (such as in paragraphs). What effect does Baldwin achieve by using these techniques?
6. How does Baldwin make the parallel stories about his father's life and death and about racism in the United States intersect? Find specific passages to support your answer.
7. How do you interpret the title? You might do some research into the relationship between Baldwin and Richard Wright, who wrote the novel *Native Son*, published in 1940. Is Baldwin suggesting a dialogue with Wright? Is he "writing back" to an established author?

WILL COUNTS

Will Counts (1931–2001) was a photographer and journalism professor at Indiana University. He is most famous for his photographic coverage of the 1957 desegregation battle surrounding Little Rock Central High School, for which he was nominated for the Pulitzer Prize.

Little Rock's Central High School

Little Rock High School (Central High School National Historic Site) is a national symbol of the struggle over desegregation in the twentieth century. In 1957, three years after the U.S. Supreme Court decision *Brown v. Board of Education*, which ruled that "separate educational facilities are inherently unequal," nine African American students — known as the Little Rock Nine — enrolled at Little Rock High School in Arkansas. During the first week of school, Governor Orval Faubus resisted President Dwight D. Eisenhower's order to use the National Guard to protect the African American students, dismissing the troops and exposing the students to the mobs of angry white dissenters. However, when Governor Faubus refused to restore order to the school, President Eisenhower sent paratroopers to Little Rock and took federal control of the Arkansas National Guard. Under their protection, the "Little Rock Nine" finished out the school year.

This photo, named by the Associated Press one of the top hundred photos of the twentieth century, shows Elizabeth Eckford, a fifteen-year-old black student, outside Little Rock's Central High School on the first day it was desegregated.

Exploring the Text

1. What can you read on the faces in the crowd that surrounds Elizabeth Eckford?
2. Pictured just to the left of Eckford is a jeering Hazel Bryan Massery, who became a symbol of racism. She later apologized to Eckford and spoke out against racism. Why do you think she became such a potent symbol?
3. What juxtapositions do you see in the photo? How do they raise the emotional temperature?
4. Consider the layout of the photo. How do the direction of the crowd and the placement of Eckford comment on the event?

Joan Didion

Joan Didion (b. 1934) is an American novelist and nonfiction writer from Sacramento, California, known for her social commentary and literary journalism. She graduated from the University of California–Berkeley in 1956, after which she moved to New York for a job at *Vogue* magazine. She published her first novel, *Run River*, in 1963, and then returned to California, where she continued to publish novels and write nonfiction essays for well-known publications such as *Life*, *Esquire*, *Saturday Evening Post*, the *New York Times*, and the *New York Review of Books*. Her memoir, *A Year of Magical Thinking*, won the National Book Award in 2005.

On Self-Respect

"On Self-Respect" was first published in *Vogue* in 1961. It then appeared in Didion's first collection of essays, *Slouching toward Bethlehem*, in 1968.

Once, in a dry season, I wrote in large letters across two pages of a notebook that innocence ends when one is stripped of the delusion that one likes oneself. Although now, some years later, I marvel that a mind on the outs with itself should have nonetheless made painstaking record of its every tremor, I recall with embarrassing clarity the flavor of those particular ashes. It was a matter of misplaced self-respect.

I had not been elected to Phi Beta Kappa. This failure could scarcely have been more predictable or less ambiguous (I simply did not have the grades), but I was unnerved by it; I had somehow thought myself a kind of academic Raskolnikov, curiously exempt from the cause-effect relationships which hampered others. Although even the humorless nineteen-year-old that I was must have recognized that the situation lacked real tragic stature, the day that I did not make Phi Beta Kappa nonetheless marked the end of something, and innocence may well be the word for it. I lost the conviction that lights would always turn green for me, the pleasant certainty that those rather passive virtues which had won me approval as a child automatically guaranteed me not only Phi Beta Kappa keys but happiness, honor, and the love of a good man; lost a certain touching faith in the totem power of good manners, clean hair, and proven competence on the Stanford-Binet scale. To such doubtful amulets had my self-respect been pinned, and I faced myself that day with the nonplused apprehension of someone who has come across a vampire and has no crucifix at hand.

Although to be driven back upon oneself is an uneasy affair at best, rather like trying to cross a border with borrowed credentials, it seems to me now the one condition necessary to the beginnings of real self-respect. Most of our platitudes notwithstanding, self-deception remains the most difficult deception. The tricks that work on others count for nothing in that very well-lit back alley where one keeps assignations with oneself: no winning smiles will do here, no prettily drawn lists of good intentions. One shuffles flashily but in vain through one's marked cards — the kindness done for the wrong reason, the apparent triumph which involved no real effort, the seemingly heroic act into which one had been shamed. The dismal fact is that self-respect has nothing to do with the approval of others — who are, after all, deceived easily enough; has nothing to do with reputation, which, as Rhett Butler told Scarlett O'Hara, is something people with courage can do without.

To do without self-respect, on the other hand, is to be an unwilling audience of one to an interminable documentary that details one's failings, both real and imagined, with fresh footage spliced in for every screening. *There's the glass you broke in anger, there's the hurt on X's face; watch now, this next scene, the night Y came back from Houston, see how you muff this one.* To live without self-respect is to lie awake some night, beyond the reach of warm milk, phenobarbital, and the sleeping hand on the coverlet, counting up the sins of commission and omission, the trusts betrayed, the promises subtly broken, the gifts irrevocably wasted through sloth or cowardice or carelessness. However long we postpone it, we eventually lie down alone in that notoriously uncomfortable bed, the one we make ourselves. Whether or not we sleep in it depends, of course, on whether or not we respect ourselves.

To protest that some fairly improbable people, some people who *could not possibly respect themselves*, seem to sleep easily enough is to miss the point entirely, as surely as those people miss it who think that self-respect has necessarily to do with not having safety pins in one's underwear. There is a common superstition that "self-respect" is a kind of charm against snakes, something that keeps those who have it locked in some unblighted Eden, out of strange beds, ambivalent conversations, and trouble in general. It does not at all. It has nothing to do with the face of things, but concerns instead a separate peace, a private reconciliation. Although the careless, suicidal Julian English in *Appointment in Samarra* and the careless, incurably dishonest Jordan Baker in *The Great Gatsby* seem equally improbable candidates for self-respect, Jordan Baker had it, Julian English did not. With that genius for accommodation more often seen in women than in men, Jordan took her own measure, made her own peace, avoided threats to that peace: "I hate careless people," she told Nick Carraway. "It takes two to make an accident."

Like Jordan Baker, people with self-respect have the courage of their mistakes. They know the price of things. If they choose to commit adultery, they do not then go running, in an access of bad conscience, to receive absolution from the wronged parties; nor do they complain unduly of the unfairness, the undeserved embarrassment, of being named co-respondent. In brief, people with self-respect exhibit a certain toughness, a kind of moral nerve; they display what was once called *character*, a quality which, although approved in the abstract, sometimes loses ground to other, more instantly negotiable virtues. The measure of its slipping prestige is that one tends to think of it only in connection with homely children and United States senators who have been defeated, preferably in the primary, for reelection. Nonetheless, character — the willingness to accept responsibility for one's own life — is the source from which self-respect springs.

Self-respect is something that our grandparents, whether or not they had it, knew all about. They had instilled in them, young, a certain discipline, the sense that one lives by doing things one does not particularly want to do, by putting fears and doubts to one side, by weighing immediate comforts against the possibility of larger, even intangible, comforts. It seemed to the nineteenth century admirable, but not remarkable, that Chinese Gordon[1] put on a clean white suit and held Khartoum against the Mahdi;[2] it did not seem unjust that the way to free land in California involved death and difficulty and dirt. In a diary kept during the winter of 1846, an

---

[1]British Major-General Charles George Gordon (1833–1885) is famous for quelling a revolt in China, and attempting to put down another in Sudan led by a charismatic Muslim religious leader. — Eds.

[2]Sudanese rebel Muhammad Ahmad (1845–1885) claimed to be the Mahdi, an Islamic messianic figure who would usher in a golden age of peace just before the end of the world. — Eds.

emigrating twelve-year-old named Narcissa Cornwall noted coolly: "Father was busy reading and did not notice that the house was being filled with strange Indians until Mother spoke about it." Even lacking any clue as to what Mother said, one can scarcely fail to be impressed by the entire incident: the father reading, the Indians filing in, the mother choosing the words that would not alarm, the child duly recording the event and noting further that those particular Indians were not, "fortunately for us," hostile. Indians were simply part of the *donnée*.[3]

In one guise or another, Indians always are. Again, it is a question of recognizing that anything worth having has its price. People who respect themselves are willing to accept the risk that the Indians will be hostile, that the venture will go bankrupt, that the liaison may not turn out to be one in which *every day is a holiday because you're married to me*. They are willing to invest something of themselves; they may not play at all, but when they do play, they know the odds.

That kind of self-respect is a discipline, a habit of mind that can never be faked but can be developed, trained, coaxed forth. It was once suggested to me that, as an antidote to crying, I put my head in a paper bag. As it happens, there is a sound physiological reason, something to do with oxygen, for doing exactly that, but the psychological effect alone is incalculable: it is difficult in the extreme to continue fancying oneself Cathy in *Wuthering Heights* with one's head in a Food Fair bag. There is a similar case for all the small disciplines, unimportant in themselves; imagine maintaining any kind of swoon, commiserative or carnal, in a cold shower.

But those small disciplines are valuable only insofar as they represent larger ones. 10 To say that Waterloo was won on the playing fields of Eton is not to say that Napoleon might have been saved by a crash program in cricket; to give formal dinners in the rain forest would be pointless did not the candlelight flickering on the liana call forth deeper, stronger disciplines, values instilled long before. It is a kind of ritual, helping us to remember who and what we are. In order to remember it, one must have known it.

To have that sense of one's intrinsic worth which constitutes self-respect is potentially to have everything: the ability to discriminate, to love and to remain indifferent. To lack it is to be locked within oneself, paradoxically incapable of either love or indifference. If we do not respect ourselves, we are on the one hand forced to despise those who have so few resources as to consort with us, so little perception as to remain blind to our fatal weaknesses. On the other, we are peculiarly in thrall to everyone we see, curiously determined to live out — since our self-image is untenable — their false notions of us. We flatter ourselves by thinking this compulsion to please others an attractive trait: a gist for imaginative empathy, evidence of our willingness to give. *Of course* I will play Francesca to your Paolo,[4] Helen Keller to anyone's Annie Sullivan:

[3]The given. — Eds.
[4]Thirteenth-century Italian nobility, Paolo Malatesta and Francesca da Rimini are characters in Dante's *Inferno*, condemned to the second circle of hell for lustful behavior. Francesca was married to Giovanni Malatesta, but had a long affair with her husband's brother, Paolo. Giovanni ultimately found out about the affair and murdered them both. — Eds.

no expectation is too misplaced, no role too ludicrous. At the mercy of those we cannot but hold in contempt, we play roles doomed to failure before they are begun, each defeat generating fresh despair at the urgency of divining and meeting the next demand made upon us.

It is the phenomenon sometimes called "alienation from self." In its advanced stages, we no longer answer the telephone, because someone might want something; that we could say *no* without drowning in self-reproach is an idea alien to this game. Every encounter demands too much, tears the nerves, drains the will, and the specter of something as small as an unanswered letter arouses such disproportionate guilt that answering it becomes out of the question. To assign unanswered letters their proper weight, to free us from the expectations of others, to give us back to ourselves — there lies the great, the singular power of self-respect. Without it, one eventually discovers the final turn of the screw: one runs away to find oneself, and finds no one at home.

(1961)

Exploring the Text

1. How would you describe the mood and tone of "On Self-Respect"? How, for example, do phrases such as "in a dry season" or "flavor of those particular ashes" (par. 1) set the essay's mood and tone?
2. Joan Didion holds off for several paragraphs before she states her thesis. Find it and explain why you think she waited. Would you have placed it earlier? Why or why not?
3. Explain what Didion means in paragraph 3 when she says that "to be driven back upon oneself is . . . rather like trying to cross a border with borrowed credentials." How does the simile help explain what it means to be driven back upon oneself?
4. Paragraph 8 begins, "In one guise or another, Indians always are." Always are what?
5. What do the topic sentences of most of Didion's paragraphs have in common? What is the effect of that characteristic?
6. Who do you think is the audience for "On Self-Respect"? How do you know? Refer to the text to explain your answer.
7. In an *Atlantic* article, writer Caitlin Flanagan states, "to really love Joan Didion — to have been blown over by things like the smell of jasmine and the packing list she kept by her suitcase — you have to be female." In addition, according to blogger Michelle Dean (*The Awl*, May 22, 2012), Didion once told her friend journalist Sara Davidson that she had thrown together "On Self-Respect" in two days to fill the space intended for another writer on the subject. Dean continues, "And there you have it: even then Didion was a writer who could produce something in 48 hours that your sophomore-year roommate wouldn't quit quoting for years." How does "On Self-Respect" hint at qualities that would engender the fierce loyalty that many (mostly women) feel for Didion and her work?

MARTIN LUTHER KING JR.

Martin Luther King Jr. (1929–1968) was one of the most influential leaders of the civil rights movement of the 1950s and 1960s. Dr. King was born in Atlanta, Georgia, and grew up in the Ebenezer Baptist Church, where his father and grand-father were ministers. He earned a BA at Morehouse College, a divinity degree at Crozer Theological Seminary, and a PhD in theology at Boston University, all by the age of twenty-six. In 1957, he founded the Southern Christian Leadership Conference and later led numerous protests against segregation by practicing the Gandhian doctrine of nonviolent resistance.

Letter from Birmingham Jail

In 1963, while King was in Birmingham, Alabama, eight clergymen published a letter in the *Post-Herald* criticizing his presence in their city and his strategies. From the cell where he was jailed for demonstrating, King responded by writing what has come to be known as "Letter from Birmingham Jail."

My Dear Fellow Clergymen:

While confined here in the Birmingham city jail, I came across your recent statement calling my present activities "unwise and untimely." Seldom do I pause to answer criticism of my work and ideas. If I sought to answer all the criticisms that cross my desk, my secretaries would have little time for anything other than such correspondence in the course of the day, and I would have no time for constructive work. But since I feel that you are men of genuine good will and that your criticisms are sincerely set forth, I want to try to answer your statement in what I hope will be patient and reasonable terms.

I think I should indicate why I am here in Birmingham, since you have been influenced by the view which argues against "outsiders coming in." I have the honor of serving as president of the Southern Christian Leadership Conference, an organization operating in every southern state, with headquarters in Atlanta, Georgia. We have some eighty-five affiliated organizations across the South, and one of them is the Alabama Christian Movement for Human Rights. Frequently we share staff, educational, and financial resources with our affiliates. Several months ago the affiliate here in Birmingham asked us to be on call to engage in a nonviolent direct-action program if such were deemed necessary. We readily consented, and when the hour came we lived up to our promise. So I, along with several members of my staff, am here because I was invited here. I am here because I have organizational ties here.

But more basically, I am in Birmingham because injustice is here. Just as the prophets of the eighth century B.C. left their villages and carried their "thus saith the Lord" far beyond the boundaries of their home towns, and just as the Apostle

Paul left his village of Tarsus and carried the gospel of Jesus Christ to the far corners of the Greco-Roman world, so am I compelled to carry the gospel of freedom beyond my own home town. Like Paul, I must constantly respond to the Macedonian call for aid.

Moreover, I am cognizant of the interrelatedness of all communities and states. I cannot sit idly by in Atlanta and not be concerned about what happens in Birmingham. Injustice anywhere is a threat to justice everywhere. We are caught in an inescapable network of mutuality, tied in a single garment of destiny. Whatever affects one directly, affects all indirectly. Never again can we afford to live with the narrow, provincial "outside agitator" idea. Anyone who lives inside the United States can never be considered an outsider anywhere within its bounds.

You deplore the demonstrations taking place in Birmingham. But your statement, 5 I am sorry to say, fails to express a similar concern for the conditions that brought about the demonstrations. I am sure that none of you would want to rest content with the superficial kind of social analysis that deals merely with effects and does not grapple with underlying causes. It is unfortunate that demonstrations are taking place in Birmingham, but it is even more unfortunate that the city's white power structure left the Negro community with no alternative.

In any nonviolent campaign there are four basic steps: collection of the facts to determine whether injustices exist; negotiation; self-purification; and direct action. We have gone through all these steps in Birmingham. There can be no gainsaying the fact that racial injustice engulfs this community. Birmingham is probably the most thoroughly segregated city in the United States. Its ugly record of brutality is widely known. Negroes have experienced grossly unjust treatment in the courts. There have been more unsolved bombings of Negro homes and churches in Birmingham than in any other city in the nation. These are the hard, brutal facts of the case. On the basis of these conditions, Negro leaders sought to negotiate with the city fathers. But the latter consistently refused to engage in good-faith negotiation.

Then, last September, came the opportunity to talk with leaders of Birmingham's economic community. In the course of the negotiations, certain promises were made by the merchants — for example, to remove the stores' humiliating racial signs. On the basis of these promises, the Reverend Fred Shuttlesworth and the leaders of the Alabama Christian Movement for Human Rights agreed to a moratorium on all demonstrations. As the weeks and months went by, we realized that we were the victims of a broken promise. A few signs, briefly removed, returned; the others remained.

As in so many past experiences, our hopes had been blasted, and the shadow of deep disappointment settled upon us. We had no alternative except to prepare for direct action, whereby we would present our very bodies as a means of laying our case before the conscience of the local and the national community. Mindful of the difficulties involved, we decided to undertake a process of self-purification. We began a series of workshops on nonviolence, and we repeatedly asked ourselves: "Are you able to accept blows without retaliating?" "Are you able to endure the ordeal of jail?" We decided to schedule our direct-action program for the Easter season, realizing that except for Christmas, this is the main shopping period of the year. Knowing that a strong economic withdrawal program would be the by-product of direct action, we felt that this would be the best time to bring pressure to bear on the merchants for the needed change.

Then it occurred to us that Birmingham's mayoral election was coming up in March, and we speedily decided to postpone action until after election day. When we discovered that the Commissioner of Public Safety, Eugene "Bull" Connor, had piled up enough votes to be in the runoff, we decided again to postpone action until the day after the runoff so that the demonstrations could not be used to cloud the issues. Like many others, we wanted to see Mr. Connor defeated, and to this end we endured postponement after postponement. Having aided in this community need, we felt that our direct-action program could be delayed no longer.

You may well ask, "Why direct action? Why sit-ins, marches, and so forth? Isn't 10 negotiation a better path?" You are quite right in calling for negotiation. Indeed, this is the very purpose of direct action. Nonviolent direct action seeks to create such a crisis and foster such a tension that a community which has constantly refused to negotiate is forced to confront the issue. It seeks so to dramatize the issue that it can no longer be ignored. My citing the creation of tension as part of the work of the nonviolent-resister may sound rather shocking. But I must confess that I am not afraid of the word "tension." I have earnestly opposed violent tension, but there is a type of constructive, nonviolent tension which is necessary for growth. Just as Socrates felt that it was necessary to create a tension in the mind so that individuals could rise from the bondage of myths and half-truths to the unfettered realm of creative analysis and objective appraisal, so must we see the need for nonviolent gadflies to create the kind of tension in society that will help men rise from the dark depths of prejudice and racism to the majestic heights of understanding and brotherhood.

The purpose of our direct-action program is to create a situation so crisis-packed that it will inevitably open the door to negotiation. I therefore concur with you in your call for negotiation. Too long has our beloved Southland been bogged down in a tragic effort to live in monologue rather than dialogue.

One of the basic points in your statement is that the action that I and my associates have taken in Birmingham is untimely. Some have asked: "Why didn't you give the new city administration time to act?" The only answer that I can give to this query is that the new Birmingham administration must be prodded about as much as the outgoing one, before it will act. We are sadly mistaken if we feel that the election of Albert Boutwell as mayor will bring the millennium to Birmingham. While Mr. Boutwell is a much more gentle person than Mr. Connor, they are both segregationists, dedicated to maintenance of the status quo. I have hoped that Mr. Boutwell will be reasonable enough to see the futility of massive resistance to desegregation. But he will not see this without pressure from devotees of civil rights. My friends, I must say to you that we have not made a single gain in civil rights without determined legal and nonviolent pressure. Lamentably, it is an historical fact that privileged groups seldom give up their privileges voluntarily. Individuals may see the moral light and voluntarily give up their unjust posture, but, as Reinhold Niebuhr[1] has reminded us, groups tend to be more immoral than individuals.

We know through painful experience that freedom is never voluntarily given by the oppressor; it must be demanded by the oppressed. Frankly, I have yet to engage in a direct-action campaign that was "well timed" in the view of those who have not suffered unduly from the disease of segregation. For years now I have heard the word "Wait!" It rings in the ear of every Negro with piercing familiarity. This "Wait" has almost always meant "Never." We must come to see, with one of our distinguished jurists, that "justice too long delayed is justice denied."

We have waited for more than 340 years for our constitutional and God-given rights. The nations of Asia and Africa are moving with jet-like speed toward gaining political independence, but we still creep at horse-and-buggy pace toward gaining a cup of coffee at a lunch counter. Perhaps it is easy for those who have never felt the stinging darts of segregation to say, "Wait." But when you have seen vicious mobs lynch your mothers and fathers at will and drown your sisters and brothers at whim; when you have seen hate-filled policemen curse, kick, and even kill your black brothers and sisters; when you see the vast majority of your twenty million Negro brothers smothering in an airtight cage of poverty in the midst of an affluent society; when you suddenly find your tongue twisted and your speech stammering as you seek to explain to your six-year-old daughter why she can't go to the public amusement park that has just been advertised on television, and see tears welling up in her eyes when she is told that Funtown is closed to colored children, and see ominous clouds of inferiority beginning to form in her little mental sky, and see her beginning to distort her personality by developing an unconscious bitterness toward white people; when you have to concoct an answer for a five-year-old son who is asking, "Daddy, why do white people treat colored people so mean?"; when you take a cross-country drive and find it necessary to sleep night after night in the uncomfortable corners of your automobile because no motel will accept you; when you are humiliated day in and day out by nagging signs reading "white" and "colored"; when your first name becomes "nigger," your middle name becomes "boy" (however old you are) and your last name becomes "John," and your wife and mother are never given the respected title "Mrs."; when you are harried by day and haunted by night by the fact that you are a Negro, living constantly at tiptoe stance, never quite knowing what to expect next, and are plagued with inner fears and outer resentments; when you are forever fighting a degenerating sense of "nobodiness" — then you will understand why we find it difficult to wait. There comes a time when the cup of endurance runs over, and men are no longer willing to be plunged into the abyss of despair. I hope, sirs, you can understand our legitimate and unavoidable impatience.

You express a great deal of anxiety over our willingness to break laws. This is certainly a legitimate concern. Since we so diligently urge people to obey the Supreme Court's decision of 1954 outlawing segregation in the public schools, at first glance it

15

---

[1]Niebuhr (1892–1971) was a U.S. clergyman and a Protestant theologian. — Eds.

may seem rather paradoxical for us consciously to break laws. One may well ask: "How can you advocate breaking some laws and obeying others?" The answer lies in the fact that there are two types of laws: just and unjust. I would be the first to advocate obeying just laws. One has not only a legal but a moral responsibility to obey just laws. Conversely, one has a moral responsibility to disobey unjust laws. I would agree with St. Augustine that "an unjust law is no law at all."

Now, what is the difference between the two? How does one determine whether a law is just or unjust? A just law is a man-made code that squares with the moral law or the law of God. An unjust law is a code that is out of harmony with the moral law. To put it in the terms of St. Thomas Aquinas: An unjust law is a human law that is not rooted in eternal law and natural law. Any law that uplifts human personality is just. Any law that degrades human personality is unjust. All segregation statutes are unjust because segregation distorts the soul and damages the personality. It gives the segregator a false sense of superiority and the segregated a false sense of inferiority. Segregation, to use the terminology of the Jewish philosopher Martin Buber, substitutes an "I-it" relationship for an "I-thou" relationship and ends up relegating persons to the status of things. Hence segregation is not only politically, economically, and sociologically unsound, it is morally wrong and sinful. Paul Tillich[2] has said that sin is separation. Is not segregation an existential expression of man's tragic separation, his awful estrangement, his terrible sinfulness? Thus it is that I can urge men to obey the 1954 decision of the Supreme Court, for it is morally right; and I can urge them to disobey segregation ordinances, for they are morally wrong.

Let us consider a more concrete example of just and unjust laws. An unjust law is a code that a numerical or power majority group compels a minority group to obey but does not make binding on itself. This is *difference* made legal. By the same token, a just law is a code that a majority compels a minority to follow and that it is willing to follow itself. This is *sameness* made legal.

Let me give another explanation. A law is unjust if it is inflicted on a minority that, as a result of being denied the right to vote, had no part in enacting or devising the law. Who can say that the legislature of Alabama which set up that state's segregation laws was democratically elected? Throughout Alabama all sorts of devious methods are used to prevent Negroes from becoming registered voters, and there are some counties in which, even though Negroes constitute a majority of the population, not a single Negro is registered. Can any law enacted under such circumstances be considered democratically structured?

Sometimes a law is just on its face and unjust in its application. For instance, I have been arrested on a charge of parading without a permit. Now, there is nothing wrong in having an ordinance which requires a permit for a parade. But such an ordinance becomes unjust when it is used to maintain segregation and to deny citizens the First-Amendment privilege of peaceful assembly and protest.

I hope you are able to see the distinction I am trying to point out. In no sense do   20
I advocate evading or defying the law, as would the rabid segregationist. That would

---

[2]Tillich (1886–1965), a German American philosopher and a Christian theologian. — Eds.

lead to anarchy. One who breaks an unjust law must do so openly, lovingly, and with a willingness to accept the penalty. I submit that an individual who breaks a law that conscience tells him is unjust, and who willingly accepts the penalty of imprisonment in order to arouse the conscience of the community over its injustice, is in reality expressing the highest respect for law.

Of course, there is nothing new about this kind of civil disobedience. It was evidenced sublimely in the refusal of Shadrach, Meshach, and Abednego to obey the laws of Nebuchadnezzar, on the ground that a higher moral law was at stake. It was practiced superbly by the early Christians, who were willing to face hungry lions and the excruciating pain of chopping blocks rather than submit to certain unjust laws of the Roman Empire. To a degree, academic freedom is a reality today because Socrates practiced civil disobedience. In our own nation, the Boston Tea Party represented a massive act of civil disobedience.

We should never forget that everything Adolf Hitler did in Germany was "legal" and everything the Hungarian freedom fighters did in Hungary was "illegal." It was "illegal" to aid and comfort a Jew in Hitler's Germany. Even so, I am sure that, had I lived in Germany at the time, I would have aided and comforted my Jewish brothers. If today I lived in a Communist country where certain principles dear to the Christian faith are suppressed, I would openly advocate disobeying that country's antireligious laws.

I must make two honest confessions to you, my Christian and Jewish brothers. First, I must confess that over the past few years I have been gravely disappointed with the white moderate. I have almost reached the regrettable conclusion that the Negro's great stumbling block in his stride toward freedom is not the White Citizen's Counciler or the Ku Klux Klanner, but the white moderate, who is more devoted to "order" than to justice; who prefers a negative peace which is the absence of tension to a positive peace which is the presence of justice; who constantly says, "I agree with you in the goal you seek, but I cannot agree with your methods of direct action"; who paternalistically believes he can set the timetable for another man's freedom; who lives by a mythical concept of time and who constantly advises the Negro to wait for a "more convenient season." Shallow understanding from people of good will is more frustrating than absolute misunderstanding from people of ill will. Lukewarm acceptance is much more bewildering than outright rejection.

I had hoped that the white moderate would understand that law and order exist for the purpose of establishing justice and that when they fail in this purpose they become the dangerously structured dams that block the flow of social progress. I had hoped that the white moderate would understand that the present tension in the South is a necessary phase of the transition from an obnoxious negative peace, in which the Negro passively accepted his unjust plight, to a substantive and positive peace, in which all men will respect the dignity and worth of human personality. Actually, we who engage in nonviolent direct action are not the creators of tension. We merely bring to the surface the hidden tension that is already alive. We bring it out in the open, where it can be seen and dealt with. Like a boil that can never be cured so long as it is covered up but must be opened with all its ugliness to the natural medicines of air and light, injustice must be exposed, with all the tension its exposure creates, to the light of human conscience and the air of national opinion, before it can be cured.

In your statement you assert that our actions, even though peaceful, must be condemned because they precipitate violence. But is this a logical assertion? Isn't this like condemning a robbed man because his possession of money precipitated the evil act of robbery? Isn't this like condemning Socrates because his unswerving commitment to truth and his philosophical inquiries precipitated the act by the misguided populace in which they made him drink hemlock? Isn't this like condemning Jesus because his unique God-consciousness and never-ceasing devotion to God's will precipitated the evil act of crucifixion? We must come to see that, as the federal courts have consistently affirmed, it is wrong to urge an individual to cease his efforts to gain his basic constitutional rights because the quest may precipitate violence. Society must protect the robbed and punish the robber.

I had also hoped that the white moderate would reject the myth concerning time in relation to the struggle for freedom. I have just received a letter from a white brother in Texas. He writes: "All Christians know that the colored people will receive equal rights eventually, but it is possible that you are in too great a religious hurry. It has taken Christianity almost two thousand years to accomplish what it has. The teachings of Christ take time to come to earth." Such an attitude stems from a tragic misconception of time, from the strangely irrational notion that there is something in the very flow of time that will inevitably cure all ills. Actually, time itself is neutral; it can be used either destructively or constructively. More and more I feel that the people of ill will have used time much more effectively than have the people of good will. We will have to repent in this generation not merely for the hateful words and actions of the bad people, but for the appalling silence of the good people. Human progress never rolls in on wheels of inevitability; it comes through the tireless efforts of men willing to be co-workers with God, and without this hard work, time itself becomes an ally of the forces of social stagnation. We must use time creatively, in the knowledge that the time is always ripe to do right. Now is the time to make real the promise of democracy and transform our pending national elegy into a creative psalm of brotherhood. Now is the time to lift our national policy from the quicksand of racial injustice to the solid rock of human dignity.

You speak of our activity in Birmingham as extreme. At first I was rather disappointed that fellow clergymen would see my nonviolent efforts as those of an extremist. I began thinking about the fact that I stand in the middle of two opposing forces in the Negro community. One is a force of complacency, made up in part of Negroes who, as a result of long years of oppression, are so drained of self-respect and a sense of "somebodiness" that they have adjusted to segregation; and in part of a few middle-class Negroes who, because of a degree of academic and economic security and because in some ways they profit by segregation, have become insensitive to the problems of the masses. The other force is one of bitterness and hatred, and it comes perilously close to advocating violence. It is expressed in the various black nationalist groups that are springing up across the nation, the largest and best-known being

Elijah Muhammad's Muslim movement. Nourished by the Negro's frustration over the continued existence of racial discrimination, this movement is made up of people who have lost faith in America, who have absolutely repudiated Christianity, and who have concluded that the white man is an incorrigible "devil."

I have tried to stand between these two forces, saying that we need emulate neither the "do-nothingism" of the complacent nor the hatred and despair of the black nationalist. For there is the more excellent way of love and nonviolent protest. I am grateful to God that, through the influence of the Negro church, the way of nonviolence became an integral part of our struggle.

If this philosophy had not emerged, by now many streets of the South would, I am convinced, be flowing with blood. And I am further convinced that if our white brothers dismiss as "rabble-rousers" and "outside agitators" those of us who employ nonviolent direct action, and if they refuse to support our nonviolent efforts, millions of Negroes will, out of frustration and despair, seek solace and security in black-nationalist ideologies—a development that would inevitably lead to a frightening racial nightmare.

Oppressed people cannot remain oppressed forever. The yearning for freedom eventually manifests itself, and that is what has happened to the American Negro. Something within has reminded him of his birthright of freedom, and something without has reminded him that it can be gained. Consciously or unconsciously, he has been caught up by the *Zeitgeist*,[3] and with his black brothers of Africa and his brown and yellow brothers of Asia, South America, and the Caribbean, the United States Negro is moving with a sense of great urgency toward the promised land of racial justice. If one recognizes this vital urge that has engulfed the Negro community, one should readily understand why public demonstrations are taking place. The Negro has many pent-up resentments and latent frustrations, and he must release them. So let him march; let him make prayer pilgrimages to the city hall; let him go on freedom rides—and try to understand why he must do so. If his repressed emotions are not released in nonviolent ways, they will seek expression through violence; this is not a threat but a fact of history. So I have not said to my people, "Get rid of your discontent." Rather, I have tried to say that this normal and healthy discontent can be channeled into the creative outlet of nonviolent direct action. And now this approach is being termed extremist.

But though I was initially disappointed at being categorized as an extremist, as I continued to think about the matter I gradually gained a measure of satisfaction from the label. Was not Jesus an extremist for love: "Love your enemies, bless them that curse you, do good to them that hate you, and pray for them which despitefully use you, and persecute you." Was not Amos an extremist for justice: "Let justice roll down like waters and righteousness like an ever-flowing stream." Was not Paul an extremist for the Christian gospel: "I bear in my body the marks of the Lord Jesus." Was not Martin Luther an extremist: "Here I stand; I cannot do otherwise, so help me God." And John Bunyan: "I will stay in jail to the end of my days before I make a butchery

30

---

[3]German. "Spirit of the time." — Eds.

of my conscience." And Abraham Lincoln: "This nation cannot survive half slave and half free." And Thomas Jefferson: "We hold these truths to be self-evident, that all men are created equal. . . ." So the question is not whether we will be extremists, but what kind of extremists we will be. Will we be extremists for hate or for love? Will we be extremists for the preservation of injustice or for the extension of justice? In that dramatic scene on Calvary's hill three men were crucified. We must never forget that all three were crucified for the same crime — the crime of extremism. Two were extremists for immorality, and thus fell below their environment. The other, Jesus Christ, was an extremist for love, truth, and goodness, and thereby rose above his environment. Perhaps the South, the nation, and the world are in dire need of creative extremists.

I had hoped that the white moderate would see this need. Perhaps I was too optimistic; perhaps I expected too much. I suppose I should have realized that few members of the oppressor race can understand the deep groans and passionate yearnings of the oppressed race, and still fewer have the vision to see that injustice must be rooted out by strong, persistent, and determined action. I am thankful, however, that some of our white brothers in the South have grasped the meaning of this social revolution and committed themselves to it. They are still all too few in quantity, but they are big in quality. Some — such as Ralph McGill, Lillian Smith, Harry Golden, James McBride Dabbs, Ann Braden, and Sarah Patton Boyle — have written about our struggle in eloquent and prophetic terms. Others have marched with us down nameless streets of the South. They have languished in filthy, roach-infested jails, suffering the abuse and brutality of policemen who view them as "dirty nigger-lovers." Unlike so many of their moderate brothers and sisters, they have recognized the urgency of the moment and sensed the need for powerful "action" antidotes to combat the disease of segregation.

Let me take note of my other major disappointment. I have been so greatly disappointed with the white church and its leadership. Of course, there are some notable exceptions. I am not unmindful of the fact that each of you has taken some significant stands on this issue. I commend you, Reverend [Earl] Stallings, for your Christian stand on this past Sunday, in welcoming Negroes to your worship service on a nonsegregated basis. I commend the Catholic leaders of this state for integrating Spring Hill College several years ago.

But despite these notable exceptions, I must honestly reiterate that I have been disappointed with the church. I do not say this as one of those negative critics who can always find something wrong with the church. I say this as a minister of the gospel, who loves the church; who was nurtured in its bosom; who has been sustained by its spiritual blessings and who will remain true to it as long as the cord of life shall lengthen.

When I was suddenly catapulted into the leadership of the bus protest in Montgomery, Alabama, a few years ago, I felt we would be supported by the white church. I felt that the white ministers, priests, and rabbis of the South would be among our strongest allies. Instead, some have been outright opponents, refusing to understand the freedom movement and misrepresenting its leaders; all too many others have been more cautious than courageous and have remained silent behind the anesthetizing security of stained-glass windows. 35

In spite of my shattered dreams, I came to Birmingham with the hope that the white religious leadership of this community would see the justice of our cause and, with deep moral concern, would serve as the channel through which our just grievances could reach the power structure. I had hoped that each of you would understand. But again I have been disappointed.

I have heard numerous southern religious leaders admonish their worshipers to comply with a desegregation decision because it is the law, but I have longed to hear white ministers declare: "Follow this decree because integration is morally right and because the Negro is your brother." In the midst of blatant injustices inflicted upon the Negro, I have watched white church men stand on the sideline and mouth pious irrelevancies and sanctimonious trivialities. In the midst of a mighty struggle to rid our nation of racial and economic injustice, I have heard many ministers say: "Those are social issues, with which the gospel has no real concern." And I have watched many churches commit themselves to a completely otherworldly religion which makes a strange, un-Biblical distinction between body and soul, between the sacred and the secular.

I have traveled the length and breadth of Alabama, Mississippi, and all the other southern states. On sweltering summer days and crisp autumn mornings I have looked at the South's beautiful churches with their lofty spires pointing heavenward. I have beheld the impressive outlines of her massive religious-education buildings. Over and over I have found myself asking: "What kind of people worship here? Who is their God? Where were their voices when the lips of Governor [Ross] Barnett dripped with words of interposition and nullification? Where were they when Governor [George] Wallace gave a clarion call for defiance and hatred? Where were their voices of support when bruised and weary Negro men and women decided to rise from the dark dungeons of complacency to the bright hills of creative protest?"

Yes, these questions are still in my mind. In deep disappointment I have wept over the laxity of the church. But be assured that my tears have been tears of love. There can be no deep disappointment where there is not deep love. Yes, I love the church. How could I do otherwise? I am in the rather unique position of being the son, the grandson, and the great-grandson of preachers. Yes, I see the church as the body of Christ. But, oh! How we have blemished and scarred that body through social neglect and through fear of being nonconformists.

There was a time when the church was very powerful — in the time when the early Christians rejoiced at being deemed worthy to suffer for what they believed. In those days the church was not merely a thermometer that recorded the ideas and principles of popular opinion; it was a thermostat that transformed the mores of society. Whenever the early Christians entered a town, the people in power became disturbed and immediately sought to convict the Christians for being "disturbers of the peace" and "outside agitators." But the Christians pressed on, in the conviction that they were "a colony of heaven," called to obey God rather than man. Small in number, they were big in commitment. They were too God-intoxicated to be "astronomically intimidated." By their effort and example they brought an end to such ancient evils as infanticide and gladiatorial contests.

40

Things are different now. So often the contemporary church is a weak, ineffectual voice with an uncertain sound. So often it is an archdefender of the status quo. Far from being disturbed by the presence of the church, the power structure of the average community is consoled by the church's silent — and often even vocal — sanction of things as they are.

But the judgment of God is upon the church as never before. If today's church does not recapture the sacrificial spirit of the early church, it will lose its authenticity, forfeit the loyalty of millions, and be dismissed as an irrelevant social club with no meaning for the twentieth century. Every day I meet young people whose disappointment with the church has turned into outright disgust.

Perhaps I have once again been too optimistic. Is organized religion too inextricably bound to the status quo to save our nation and the world? Perhaps I must turn my faith to the inner spiritual church, the church within the church, as the true *ekklesia* and the hope of the world. But again I am thankful to God that some noble souls from the ranks of organized religion have broken loose from the paralyzing chains of conformity and joined us as active partners in the struggle for freedom. They have left their secure congregations and walked the streets of Albany, Georgia, with us. They have gone down the highways of the South on tortuous rides for freedom. Yes, they have gone to jail with us. Some have been dismissed from their churches, have lost the support of their bishops and fellow ministers. But they have acted in the faith that right defeated is stronger than evil triumphant. Their witness has been the spiritual salt that has preserved the true meaning of the gospel in these troubled times. They have carved a tunnel of hope through the dark mountain of disappointment.

I hope the church as a whole will meet the challenge of this decisive hour. But even if the church does not come to the aid of justice, I have no despair about the future. I have no fear about the outcome of our struggle in Birmingham, even if our motives are at present misunderstood. We will reach the goal of freedom in Birmingham and all over the nation, because the goal of America is freedom. Abused and scorned though we may be, our destiny is tied up with America's destiny. Before the pilgrims landed at Plymouth, we were here. Before the pen of Jefferson etched the majestic words of the Declaration of Independence across the pages of history, we were here. For more than two centuries our forebears labored in this country without wages: they made cotton king; they built the homes of their masters while suffering gross injustice and shameful humiliation — and yet out of a bottomless vitality they continued to thrive and develop. If the inexpressible cruelties of slavery could not stop us, the opposition we now face will surely fail. We will win our freedom because the sacred heritage of our nation and the eternal will of God are embodied in our echoing demands.

Before closing I feel impelled to mention one other point in your statement that has troubled me profoundly. You warmly commended the Birmingham police force for keeping "order" and "preventing violence." I doubt that you would have so warmly commended the police force if you had seen its dogs sinking their teeth into unarmed, nonviolent Negroes. I doubt that you would so quickly commend the policemen if you were to observe their ugly and inhumane treatment of Negroes here in the city jail; if you were to watch them push and curse old Negro women and young Negro girls; if you were to see them slap and kick old Negro men and young boys; if you were to observe them, as they did on two occasions, refuse to give us food because we wanted to sing our grace together. I cannot join you in your praise of the Birmingham police department.

It is true that the police have exercised a degree of discipline in handling the demonstrators. In this sense they have conducted themselves rather "nonviolently" in public. But for what purpose? To preserve the evil system of segregation. Over the past few years I have consistently preached that nonviolence demands that the means we use must be as pure as the ends we seek. I have tried to make clear that it is wrong to use immoral means to attain moral ends. But now I must affirm that it is just as wrong, or perhaps even more so, to use moral means to preserve immoral ends. Perhaps Mr. Connor and his policemen have been rather nonviolent in public, as was Chief Pritchett in Albany, Georgia, but they have used the moral means of nonviolence to maintain the immoral end of racial injustice. As T. S. Eliot has said, "The last temptation is the greatest treason: To do the right deed for the wrong reason."

I wish you had commended the Negro sit-inners and demonstrators of Birmingham for their sublime courage, their willingness to suffer, and their amazing discipline in the midst of great provocation. One day the South will recognize its real heroes. They will be the James Merediths, with the noble sense of purpose that enables them to face jeering and hostile mobs, and with the agonizing loneliness that characterizes the life of the pioneer. They will be old, oppressed, battered Negro women, symbolized in a seventy-two-year-old woman in Montgomery, Alabama, who rose up with a sense of dignity and with her people decided not to ride segregated buses, and who responded with ungrammatical profundity to one who inquired about her weariness: "My feets is tired, but my soul is at rest." They will be the young high school and college students, the young ministers of the gospel and a host of their elders, courageously and nonviolently sitting in at lunch counters and willingly going to jail for conscience' sake. One day the South will know that when these disinherited children of God sat down at lunch counters, they were in reality standing up for what is best in the American dream and for the most sacred values in our Judaeo-Christian heritage, thereby bringing our nation back to those great wells of democracy which were dug deep by the founding fathers in their formulation of the Constitution and the Declaration of Independence.

Never before have I written so long a letter. I'm afraid it is much too long to take your precious time. I can assure you that it would have been much shorter if I had been writing from a comfortable desk, but what else can one do when he is alone in a narrow jail cell, other than write long letters, think long thoughts, and pray long prayers?

If I have said anything in this letter that overstates the truth and indicates an unreasonable impatience, I beg you to forgive me. If I have said anything that understates the truth and indicates my having a patience that allows me to settle for anything less than brotherhood, I beg God to forgive me.

I hope this letter finds you strong in the faith. I also hope that circumstances will soon make it possible for me to meet each of you, not as an integrationist or a civil-rights leader but as a fellow clergyman and a Christian brother. Let us all hope that the dark

50

clouds of racial prejudice will soon pass away and the deep fog of misunderstanding will be lifted from our fear-drenched communities, and in some not too distant tomorrow the radiant stars of love and brotherhood will shine over our great nation with all their scintillating beauty.

Yours for the cause of Peace and Brotherhood,
Martin Luther King Jr.
(1963)

Exploring the Text

1. What is Martin Luther King Jr.'s tone in the opening paragraph? How might you make an argument for its being ironic?
2. How do King's allusions to biblical figures and events appeal to both ethos and pathos? What about his references to theologians and other religious scholars? Do you see a pattern in their use?
3. What are some of the different ways that King establishes his credibility? Whom does he address in addition to the Birmingham clergymen? How does he establish ethos for the different audiences for this letter?
4. Studying the long sentence in paragraph 14 (beginning with "But when you have seen"), consider why King arranges the "when" clauses in the order that he does. How would the meaning of the paragraph change if the order were different?
5. Trace one of the following patterns of figurative language throughout King's letter: darkness and light, high and low, sickness and death. Look also at the imagery surrounding the terms *garment* and *fabric*.
6. How does King balance the twin appeals to religion and patriotism throughout "Letter from Birmingham Jail"? Do you think he puts more emphasis on religion or on patriotism? Why do you think he makes that choice?
7. King writes as a member of several communities, some overlapping, some in conflict. What are they? Focusing on two or three, explain how he defines himself within each.
8. King spends nearly half the letter addressing counterarguments before he launches into his own argument. Analyze that argument, including his claims, assumptions, and evidence.

 **TALKBACK**

Malcolm Gladwell

Author of four best-selling books, Malcolm Gladwell (b. 1963) grew up in Ontario, Canada, the son of an English university professor father and a Jamaican therapist mother. He has been a staff writer with the *New Yorker* magazine since 1996, and in 2005 he was named one of *Time* magazine's 100 Most Influential People. His books include *The Tipping Point: How Little Things Make a Big Difference* (2000), *Blink: The Power of Thinking without Thinking* (2005), and *Outliers: The Story of*

Success (2008). Gladwell's *What the Dog Saw* (2009) is a compilation of articles published in the *New Yorker*. His writing often explores the implications of research in the social sciences and psychology.

Small Change
Why the Revolution Will Not Be Tweeted

The following article, which appeared in the *New Yorker* in 2010, compares the intricate network of activists who brought about the civil rights movement with the social media networks that have sprung up on the Internet.

At four-thirty in the afternoon on Monday, February 1, 1960, four college students sat down at the lunch counter at the Woolworth's in downtown Greensboro, North Carolina. They were freshmen at North Carolina A. & T., a black college a mile or so away.

"I'd like a cup of coffee, please," one of the four, Ezell Blair, said to the waitress.

"We don't serve Negroes here," she replied.

The Woolworth's lunch counter was a long L-shaped bar that could seat sixty-six people, with a standup snack bar at one end. The seats were for whites. The snack bar was for blacks. Another employee, a black woman who worked at the steam table, approached the students and tried to warn them away. "You're acting stupid, ignorant!" she said. They didn't move. Around five-thirty, the front doors to the store were locked. The four still didn't move. Finally, they left by a side door. Outside, a small crowd had gathered, including a photographer from the Greensboro *Record*. "I'll be back tomorrow with A. & T. College," one of the students said.

By next morning, the protest had grown to twenty-seven men and four women, most from the same dormitory as the original four. The men were dressed in suits and ties. The students had brought their schoolwork, and studied as they sat at the counter. On Wednesday, students from Greensboro's "Negro" secondary school, Dudley High, joined in, and the number of protesters swelled to eighty. By Thursday, the protesters numbered three hundred, including three white women, from the Greensboro campus of the University of North Carolina. By Saturday, the sit-in had reached six hundred. People spilled out onto the street. White teenagers waved Confederate flags. Someone threw a firecracker. At noon, the A. & T. football team arrived. "Here comes the wrecking crew," one of the white students shouted.

By the following Monday, sit-ins had spread to Winston-Salem, twenty-five miles away, and Durham, fifty miles away. The day after that, students at Fayetteville State Teachers College and at Johnson C. Smith College, in Charlotte, joined in, followed on Wednesday by students at St. Augustine's College and Shaw University, in Raleigh. On Thursday and Friday, the protest crossed state lines, surfacing in Hampton and Portsmouth, Virginia, in Rock Hill, South Carolina, and in Chattanooga, Tennessee. By the end of the month, there were sit-ins throughout the South, as far west as Texas. "I asked every student I met what the first day of the sitdowns had been like on his campus," the political theorist Michael Walzer wrote in *Dissent*. "The answer was always the same: 'It was like a fever. Everyone wanted to go.'" Some seventy thousand students eventually took part. Thousands were arrested and untold thousands more radicalized. These events in the early sixties became a civil-rights war that engulfed the South for the rest of the decade — and it happened without e-mail, texting, Facebook, or Twitter.

The world, we are told, is in the midst of a revolution. The new tools of social media have reinvented social activism. With Facebook and Twitter and the like, the traditional relationship between political authority and popular will has been upended, making it easier for the powerless to collaborate, coördinate, and give voice to their concerns. When ten thousand protesters took to the streets in Moldova in the spring of 2009 to protest against their country's Communist government, the action was dubbed the Twitter Revolution, because of the means by which the demonstrators had been brought together. A few months after that, when student protests rocked Tehran, the State Department took the unusual step of asking Twitter to suspend scheduled maintenance of its Web site, because the Administration didn't want such a critical organizing tool out of service at the height of the demonstrations. "Without Twitter the people of Iran would not have felt empowered and confident to stand up for freedom and democracy," Mark Pfeifle, a former national-security adviser, later wrote, calling for Twitter to be nominated for the Nobel Peace Prize. Where activists were once defined by their causes, they are now defined by their tools. Facebook warriors go online to push for change. "You are the best hope for us all," James K. Glassman, a former senior State Department official, told a crowd of cyber activists at a recent conference sponsored by Facebook, A. T. & T., Howcast, MTV, and Google. Sites like Facebook, Glassman said, "give the U.S. a significant competitive advantage over terrorists. Some time ago, I said that Al Qaeda was 'eating our lunch on the Internet.' That is no longer the case. Al Qaeda is stuck in Web 1.0. The Internet is now about interactivity and conversation."

These are strong, and puzzling, claims. Why does it matter who is eating whose lunch on the Internet? Are people who log on to their Facebook page really the best hope for us all? As for Moldova's so-called Twitter Revolution, Evgeny Morozov, a scholar at Stanford who has been the most persistent of digital evangelism's critics, points out that Twitter has scant internal significance in Moldova, a country where very few Twitter accounts exist. Nor does it seem to have been a revolution, not least because the protests — as Anne Applebaum suggested in the *Washington Post* — may well have been a bit of stagecraft cooked up by the government. (In a country paranoid about Romanian revanchism, the protesters flew a Romanian flag over the Parliament building.) In the Iranian case, meanwhile, the people tweeting about the demonstrations were almost all in the West. "It is time to get Twitter's role in the events in Iran right," Golnaz Esfandiari wrote, this past summer, in *Foreign Policy*. "Simply put: There was no Twitter

Revolution inside Iran." The cadre of prominent bloggers, like Andrew Sullivan, who championed the role of social media in Iran, Esfandiari continued, misunderstood the situation. "Western journalists who couldn't reach — or didn't bother reaching? — people on the ground in Iran simply scrolled through the English-language tweets post with tag #iranelection," she wrote. "Through it all, no one seemed to wonder why people trying to coordinate protests in Iran would be writing in any language other than Farsi."

Some of this grandiosity is to be expected. Innovators tend to be solipsists. They often want to cram every stray fact and experience into their new model. As the historian Robert Darnton has written, "The marvels of communication technology in the present have produced a false consciousness about the past — even a sense that communication has no history, or had nothing of importance to consider before the days of television and the Internet." But there is something else at work here, in the outsized enthusiasm for social media. Fifty years after one of the most extraordinary episodes of social upheaval in American history, we seem to have forgotten what activism is.

Greensboro in the early nineteen-sixties was the kind of place where racial insub- 10 ordination was routinely met with violence. The four students who first sat down at the lunch counter were terrified. "I suppose if anyone had come up behind me and yelled 'Boo,' I think I would have fallen off my seat," one of them said later. On the first day, the store manager notified the police chief, who immediately sent two officers to the store. On the third day, a gang of white toughs showed up at the lunch counter and stood ostentatiously behind the protesters, ominously muttering epithets such as "burr-head nigger." A local Ku Klux Klan leader made an appearance. On Saturday, as tensions grew, someone called in a bomb threat, and the entire store had to be evacuated.

The dangers were even clearer in the Mississippi Freedom Summer Project of 1964, another of the sentinel campaigns of the civil-rights movement. The Student Nonviolent Coordinating Committee recruited hundreds of Northern, largely white unpaid volunteers to run Freedom Schools, register black voters, and raise civil-rights awareness in the Deep South. "No one should go *anywhere* alone, but certainly not in an automobile and certainly not at night," they were instructed. Within days of arriving in Mississippi, three volunteers — Michael Schwerner, James Chaney, and Andrew Goodman — were kidnapped and killed, and, during the rest of the summer, thirty-seven black churches were set on fire and dozens of safe houses were bombed; volunteers were beaten, shot at, arrested, and trailed by pickup trucks full of armed men. A quarter of those in the program dropped out. Activism that challenges the status quo — that attacks deeply rooted problems — is not for the faint of heart.

What makes people capable of this kind of activism? The Stanford sociologist Doug McAdam compared the Freedom Summer dropouts with the participants who stayed, and discovered that the key difference wasn't, as might be expected, ideological fervor. "*All* of the applicants — participants and withdrawals alike—emerge as highly committed, articulate supporters of the goals and values of the summer program," he concluded. What mattered more was an applicant's degree of personal connection to the civil-rights movement. All the volunteers were required to provide a list of personal contacts—the people they wanted kept apprised of their activities—and participants were far more likely than dropouts to have close friends who were also going to Mississippi. High-risk activism, McAdam concluded, is a "strong-tie" phenomenon.

This pattern shows up again and again. One study of the Red Brigades, the Italian terrorist group of the nineteen-seventies, found that seventy per cent of recruits had at least one good friend already in the organization. The same is true of the men who joined the mujahideen in Afghanistan. Even revolutionary actions that look spontaneous, like the demonstrations in East Germany that led to the fall of the Berlin Wall, are, at core, strong-tie phenomena. The opposition movement in East Germany consisted of several hundred groups, each with roughly a dozen members. Each group was in limited contact with the others: at the time, only thirteen per cent of East Germans even had a phone. All they knew was that on Monday nights, outside St. Nicholas Church in downtown Leipzig, people gathered to voice their anger at the state. And the primary determinant of who showed up was "critical friends"—the more friends you had who were critical of the regime, the more likely you were to join the protest.

So one crucial fact about the four freshmen at the Greensboro lunch counter—David Richmond, Franklin McCain, Ezell Blair, and Joseph McNeil—was their relationship with one another. McNeil was a roommate of Blair's in A. & T.'s Scott Hall dormitory. Richmond roomed with McCain one floor up, and Blair, Richmond, and McCain had all gone to Dudley High School. The four would smuggle beer into the dorm and talk late into the night in Blair and McNeil's room. They would all have remembered the murder of Emmett Till in 1955, the Montgomery bus boycott that same year, and the showdown in Little Rock in 1957. It was McNeil who brought up the idea of a sit-in at Woolworth's. They'd discussed it for nearly a month. Then McNeil came into the dorm room and asked the others if they were ready. There was a pause, and McCain said, in a way that works only with people who talk late into the night with one another, "Are you guys chicken or not?" Ezell Blair worked up the courage the next day to ask for a cup of coffee because he was flanked by his roommate and two good friends from high school.

The kind of activism associated with social media isn't like this at all. The platforms of social media are built around weak ties. Twitter is a way of following (or being followed by) people you may never have met. Facebook is a tool for efficiently managing your acquaintances, for keeping up with the people you would not otherwise be able to stay in touch with. That's why you can have a thousand "friends" on Facebook, as you never could in real life.

This is in many ways a wonderful thing. There is strength in weak ties, as the sociologist Mark Granovetter has observed. Our acquaintances—not our

15

friends — are our greatest source of new ideas and information. The Internet lets us exploit the power of these kinds of distant connections with marvelous efficiency. It's terrific at the diffusion of innovation, interdisciplinary collaboration, seamlessly matching up buyers and sellers, and the logistical functions of the dating world. But weak ties seldom lead to high-risk activism.

In a new book called *The Dragonfly Effect: Quick, Effective, and Powerful Ways to Use Social Media to Drive Social Change*, the business consultant Andy Smith and the Stanford Business School professor Jennifer Aaker tell the story of Sameer Bhatia, a young Silicon Valley entrepreneur who came down with acute myelogenous leukemia. It's a perfect illustration of social media's strengths. Bhatia needed a bone-marrow transplant, but he could not find a match among his relatives and friends. The odds were best with a donor of his ethnicity, and there were few South Asians in the national bone-marrow database. So Bhatia's business partner sent out an e-mail explaining Bhatia's plight to more than four hundred of their acquaintances, who forwarded the e-mail to their personal contacts; Facebook pages and YouTube videos were devoted to the Help Sameer campaign. Eventually, nearly twenty-five thousand new people were registered in the bone-marrow database, and Bhatia found a match.

But how did the campaign get so many people to sign up? By not asking too much of them. That's the only way you can get someone you don't really know to do something on your behalf. You can get thousands of people to sign up for a donor registry, because doing so is pretty easy. You have to send in a cheek swab and — in the highly unlikely event that your bone marrow is a good match for someone in need — spend a few hours at the hospital. Donating bone marrow isn't a trivial matter. But it doesn't involve financial or personal risk; it doesn't mean spending a summer being chased by armed men in pickup trucks. It doesn't require that you confront socially entrenched norms and practices. In fact, it's the kind of commitment that will bring only social acknowledgment and praise.

The evangelists of social media don't understand this distinction; they seem to believe that a Facebook friend is the same as a real friend and that signing up for a donor registry in Silicon Valley today is activism in the same sense as sitting at a segregated lunch counter in Greensboro in 1960. "Social networks are particularly effective at increasing motivation," Aaker and Smith write. But that's not true. Social networks are effective at increasing *participation* — by lessening the level of motivation that participation requires. The Facebook page of the Save Darfur Coalition has 1,282,339 members, who have donated an average of nine cents apiece. The next biggest Darfur charity on Facebook has 22,073 members, who have donated an average of thirty-five cents. Help Save Darfur has 2,797 members, who have given, on average, fifteen cents. A spokesperson for the Save Darfur Coalition told *Newsweek*, "We wouldn't necessarily gauge someone's value to the advocacy movement based on what they've given. This is a powerful mechanism to engage this critical population. They inform their community, attend events, volunteer. It's not something you can measure by looking at a ledger." In other words, Facebook activism succeeds not by motivating people to make a real sacrifice but by motivating them to do the things that people do when they are not motivated enough to make a real sacrifice. We are a long way from the lunch counters of Greensboro.

The students who joined the sit-ins across the South during the winter of 1960 described the movement as a "fever." But the civil-rights movement was more like a military campaign than like a contagion. In the late nineteen-fifties, there had been sixteen sit-ins in various cities throughout the South, fifteen of which were formally organized by civil-rights organizations like the N.A.A.C.P. and CORE. Possible locations for activism were scouted. Plans were drawn up. Movement activists held training sessions and retreats for would-be protesters. The Greensboro Four were a product of this groundwork: all were members of the N.A.A.C.P. Youth Council. They had close ties with the head of the local N.A.A.C.P. chapter. They had been briefed on the earlier wave of sit-ins in Durham, and had been part of a series of movement meetings in activist churches. When the sit-in movement spread from Greensboro throughout the South, it did not spread indiscriminately. It spread to those cities which had preexisting "movement centers" — a core of dedicated and trained activists ready to turn the "fever" into action.

The civil-rights movement was high-risk activism. It was also, crucially, strategic activism: a challenge to the establishment mounted with precision and discipline. The N.A.A.C.P. was a centralized organization, run from New York according to highly formalized operating procedures. At the Southern Christian Leadership Conference, Martin Luther King, Jr., was the unquestioned authority. At the center of the movement was the black church, which had, as Aldon D. Morris points out in his superb 1984 study, *The Origins of the Civil Rights Movement*, a carefully demarcated division of labor, with various standing committees and disciplined groups. "Each group was task-oriented and coordinated its activities through authority structures," Morris writes. "Individuals were held accountable for their assigned duties, and important conflicts were resolved by the minister, who usually exercised ultimate authority over the congregation."

This is the second crucial distinction between traditional activism and its online variant: social media are not about this kind of hierarchical organization. Facebook and the like are tools for building *networks*, which are the opposite, in structure and character, of hierarchies. Unlike hierarchies, with their rules and procedures, networks aren't controlled by a single central authority. Decisions are made through consensus, and the ties that bind people to the group are loose.

This structure makes networks enormously resilient and adaptable in low-risk situations. Wikipedia is a perfect example. It doesn't have an editor, sitting in New York, who directs and corrects each entry. The effort of putting together each entry is self-organized. If every entry in Wikipedia were to be erased tomorrow, the content would swiftly be restored, because that's what happens when a network of thousands spontaneously devote their time to a task.

There are many things, though, that networks don't do well. Car companies sensibly use a network to organize their hundreds of suppliers, but not to design their cars. No one believes that the articulation of a coherent design philosophy is best handled by a sprawling, leaderless organizational system. Because networks don't have a centralized leadership structure and clear lines of authority, they have real difficulty reaching consensus and setting goals. They can't think strategically; they are chronically prone to conflict and error. How do you make difficult choices about tactics or strategy or philosophical direction when everyone has an equal say?

The Palestine Liberation Organization originated as a network, and the 25 international-relations scholars Mette Eilstrup-Sangiovanni and Calvert Jones argue in a recent essay in *International Security* that this is why it ran into such trouble as it grew: "Structural features typical of networks — the absence of central authority, the unchecked autonomy of rival groups, and the inability to arbitrate quarrels through formal mechanisms — made the P.L.O. excessively vulnerable to outside manipulation and internal strife."

In Germany in the nineteen-seventies, they go on, "the far more unified and successful left-wing terrorists tended to organize hierarchically, with professional management and clear divisions of labor. They were concentrated geographically in universities, where they could establish central leadership, trust, and camaraderie through regular, face-to-face meetings." They seldom betrayed their comrades in arms during police interrogations. Their counterparts on the right were organized as decentralized networks, and had no such discipline. These groups were regularly infiltrated, and members, once arrested, easily gave up their comrades. Similarly, Al Qaeda was most dangerous when it was a unified hierarchy. Now that it has dissipated into a network, it has proved far less effective.

The drawbacks of networks scarcely matter if the network isn't interested in systemic change — if it just wants to frighten or humiliate or make a splash — or if it doesn't need to think strategically. But if you're taking on a powerful and organized establishment you have to be a hierarchy. The Montgomery bus boycott required the participation of tens of thousands of people who depended on public transit to get to and from work each day. It lasted a *year*. In order to persuade those people to stay true to the cause, the boycott's organizers tasked each local black church with maintaining morale, and put together a free alternative private carpool service, with forty-eight dispatchers and forty-two pickup stations. Even the White Citizens Council, King later said, conceded that the carpool system moved with "military precision." By the time King came to Birmingham, for the climactic showdown with Police Commissioner Eugene (Bull) Connor, he had a budget of a million dollars, and a hundred full-time staff members on the ground, divided into operational units. The operation itself was divided into steadily escalating phases, mapped out in advance. Support was maintained through consecutive mass meetings rotating from church to church around the city.

Boycotts and sit-ins and nonviolent confrontations — which were the weapons of choice for the civil-rights movement — are high-risk strategies. They leave little room for conflict and error. The moment even one protester deviates from the script and responds to provocation, the moral legitimacy of the entire protest is compromised. Enthusiasts for social media would no doubt have us believe that King's task in Birmingham would have been made infinitely easier had he been able to communicate with his followers through Facebook, and contented himself with tweets from a Birmingham jail. But networks are messy: think of the ceaseless pattern of correction and revision, amendment and debate, that characterizes Wikipedia. If Martin Luther King, Jr., had tried to do a wiki-boycott in Montgomery, he would have been steamrollered by the white power structure. And of what use would a digital communication tool be in a town where ninety-eight per cent of the black community could be reached every Sunday morning at church? The things that King needed in Birmingham — discipline and strategy — were things that online social media cannot provide.

The bible of the social-media movement is Clay Shirky's *Here Comes Everybody.* Shirky, who teaches at New York University, sets out to demonstrate the organizing power of the Internet, and he begins with the story of Evan, who worked on Wall Street, and his friend Ivanna, after she left her smart phone, an expensive Sidekick, on the back seat of a New York City taxicab. The telephone company transferred the data on Ivanna's lost phone to a new phone, whereupon she and Evan discovered that the Sidekick was now in the hands of a teen-ager from Queens, who was using it to take photographs of herself and her friends.

When Evan e-mailed the teen-ager, Sasha, asking for the phone back, she   30 replied that his "white ass" didn't deserve to have it back. Miffed, he set up a Web page with her picture and a description of what had happened. He forwarded the link to his friends, and they forwarded it to their friends. Someone found the MySpace page of Sasha's boyfriend, and a link to it found its way onto the site. Someone found her address online and took a video of her home while driving by; Evan posted the video on the site. The story was picked up by the news filter Digg. Evan was now up to ten e-mails a minute. He created a bulletin board for his readers to share their stories, but it crashed under the weight of responses. Evan and Ivanna went to the police, but the police filed the report under "lost," rather than "stolen," which essentially closed the case. "By this point millions of readers were watching," Shirky writes, "and dozens of mainstream news outlets had covered the story." Bowing to the pressure, the N.Y.P.D. reclassified the item as "stolen." Sasha was arrested, and Evan got his friend's Sidekick back.

Shirky's argument is that this is the kind of thing that could never have happened in the pre-Internet age — and he's right. Evan could never have tracked down Sasha. The story of the Sidekick would never have been publicized. An army of people could never have been assembled to wage this fight. The police wouldn't have bowed to the pressure of a lone person who had misplaced something as trivial as a cell phone. The story, to Shirky, illustrates "the ease and speed with which a group can be mobilized for the right kind of cause" in the Internet age.

Shirky considers this model of activism an upgrade. But it is simply a form of organizing which favors the weak-tie connections that give us access to information over the strong-tie connections that help us persevere in the face of danger. It shifts our energies from organizations that promote strategic and disciplined activity and toward those which promote resilience and adaptability. It makes it easier for activists to express themselves, and harder for that expression to have any impact. The instruments of social media are well suited to making the existing social order more efficient. They are not a natural enemy of the status quo. If you are of the opinion that all the world needs is a little buffing around the edges, this should not trouble you. But if you think that there are still lunch counters out there that need integrating, it ought to give you pause.

Shirky ends his story of the Sidekick by asking, portentously, "What happens next?" — no doubt imagining future waves of digital protesters. But he has already answered the question. What happens next is more of the same. A networked, weak-tie world is good at things like helping Wall Streeters get phones back from teen-age girls. *Viva la revolución.*

(2010)

Exploring the Text

1. Why do you think Malcolm Gladwell begins his piece by retelling the story of the lunch counter sit-in at the Woolworth's in Greensboro, North Carolina? How does it serve as the foundation for his argument?
2. What does Gladwell mean when he writes, "Where activists were once defined by their causes, they are now defined by their tools" (par. 7)? Do you agree or disagree with this idea? Explain your answer.
3. How does Gladwell define "high-risk activism" (pars. 11–12)? Why does he believe that activism based on social media cannot qualify as "high-risk"? Consider the contrast between "weak ties" and "strong ties" as part of your response.
4. What is the difference between increasing motivation and increasing participation, according to Gladwell? Why is the distinction between the two important to his argument?
5. Gladwell does not entirely discount the power of social media. What benefits or positive effects does he grant to social media?
6. Throughout this essay, Gladwell relies heavily on expert testimony, citing scholars, researchers, business analysts, state department officials, and security advisors. Choose two examples, and discuss how Gladwell uses one to support his argument and the other to examine a counterargument.
7. At key junctures in the essay, Gladwell makes sharp personal comments. In fact, his ending, "*Viva la revolución,*" could be read as downright sarcastic. What others do you notice? Do these editorial comments undercut his argument or do they add to it? Explain your answer.

Making Connections

1. What are the differences in the ways Martin Luther King Jr. (p. 1345) and Gladwell (p. 1357) use expert testimony? What are the similarities?

2. Compare the tone of "Letter from Birmingham Jail" to the tone of "Small Change." How are the voices of the speakers different? Are they similar in any way? Which do you find easier to engage with? Explain your answer.
3. Gladwell describes the civil rights movement of the early 1960s as a "military campaign" (par. 20), arguing that all of the sit-ins were "formally organized by civil-rights organizations like the N.A.A.C.P. and CORE." He says that Martin Luther King Jr. was the "unquestioned authority" (par. 21). How does that square with the description King gives in his letter about the structure of the civil rights movement and the boycotts and other actions in Birmingham?
4. Imagine a conversation between King and Gladwell. Do you think they would find much common ground? On what subjects do you think they would disagree? On which would they agree? Try to imagine King's opinion of social media as a protest tool had he lived long enough to see it. Use evidence from the text to help form your answer.

ROBERT HAYDEN

Born Asa Bundy Sheffey in Detroit, Michigan, Robert Hayden (1913–1980) attended Detroit City College (now Wayne State University) before studying under W. H. Auden (p. 1169) in the graduate English program at the University of Michigan. In 1976, Hayden was appointed consultant in poetry to the Library of Congress, a post that was the forerunner of poet laureate. His first volume, *Heart-Shape in the Dust* (1940), took its voice from the Harlem Renaissance.

Those Winter Sundays

Hayden's 1962 collection, *A Ballad of Remembrance*, includes his most famous poem, "Those Winter Sundays."

Sundays too my father got up early
and put his clothes on in the blueblack cold,
then with cracked hands that ached
from labor in the weekday weather made
banked fires blaze. No one ever thanked him.   5

I'd wake and hear the cold splintering, breaking.
When the rooms were warm, he'd call,
and slowly I would rise and dress,
fearing the chronic angers of that house,

Speaking indifferently to him,   10
who had driven out the cold
and polished my good shoes as well.
What did I know, what did I know
of love's austere and lonely offices?

(1962)

Exploring the Text

1. When does the poem shift from flashback — or memory — to the present moment? How does Robert Hayden keep this shift from being too abrupt?
2. Citing specific lines from the poem, characterize the speaker's relationship with his father and the home in which the speaker grew up.
3. What is the meaning of "love's austere and lonely offices" (l. 14)? What effect does Hayden achieve by choosing such an uncommon, somewhat archaic word as *offices*?
4. What is the effect of the repetition in the second-to-last line of the poem?
5. What is the grown speaker's feeling about his father? How does it differ from the feeling the speaker had as a child? What does the adult speaker understand about the father that he did not understand as a child?
6. What do you think is this poem's purpose? What strategies does Hayden use to achieve it?

JOYCE CAROL OATES

Joyce Carol Oates was born in Lockport, New York, in 1938. With a typewriter she received at age fourteen, Oates wrote "novel after novel" in high school and college in order to train herself to be a writer. Oates is the youngest author ever to receive the National Book Award — for her novel *Them* (1969). Currently the Roger S. Berlind Professor of the Humanities at Princeton University, Oates has published more than thirty novels, including *Black Water* (1992), *We Were the Mulvaneys* (1996), and *The Falls* (2004). Her work often addresses the violence and suspense lurking beneath ordinary life.

Where Are You Going, Where Have You Been?

This story is based on the factual case of a psychopath known as the Pied Piper of Tucson. In an interview with the *New York Times*, Oates described him:

> The Pied Piper mimicked teenagers in their talk, dress, and behavior, but he was not a teenager — he was a man in his early thirties. Rather short, he stuffed rags

in his leather boots to give himself height. (And sometimes walked unsteadily as a consequence: did not among his admiring constituency notice?) He charmed his victims as charismatic psychopaths have always charmed their victims, to the bewilderment of others who fancy themselves free of lunatic attraction. The Pied Piper of Tucson: a trashy dream, a tabloid archetype, sheer artifice, comedy, cartoon — surrounded, improbably, and finally tragically, by real people. You think that, if you look twice, he won't be there. But there he is.

This story first appeared in the fall 1966 edition of *Epoch* magazine.

For Bob Dylan

Her name was Connie. She was fifteen and she had a quick nervous giggling habit of craning her neck to glance into mirrors, or checking other people's faces to make sure her own was all right. Her mother, who noticed everything and knew everything and who hadn't much reason any longer to look at her own face, always scolded Connie about it. "Stop gawking at yourself, who are you? You think you're so pretty?" she would say. Connie would raise her eyebrows at these familiar complaints and look right through her mother, into a shadowy vision of herself as she was right at that moment: she knew she was pretty and that was everything. Her mother had been pretty once too, if you could believe those old snapshots in the album, but now her looks were gone and that was why she was always after Connie.

"Why don't you keep your room clean like your sister? How've you got your hair fixed — what the hell stinks? Hair spray? You don't see your sister using that junk."

Her sister June was twenty-four and still lived at home. She was a secretary in the high school Connie attended, and if that wasn't bad enough — with her in the same building — she was so plain and chunky and steady that Connie had to hear her praised all the time by her mother and her mother's sisters. June did this, June did that, she saved money and helped clean the house and cooked and Connie couldn't do a thing, her mind was all filled with trashy daydreams. Their father was away at work most of the time and when he came home he wanted supper and he read the newspaper at supper and after supper he went to bed. He didn't bother talking much to them, but around his bent head Connie's mother kept picking at her until Connie wished her mother was dead and she herself was dead and it was all over. "She makes me want to throw up sometimes," she complained to her friends. She had a high, breathless, amused voice which made everything she said a little forced, whether it was sincere or not.

There was one good thing: June went places with girl friends of hers, girls who were just as plain and steady as she, and so when Connie wanted to do that her mother had no objections. The father of Connie's best girl friend drove the girls the three miles to town and left them off at a shopping plaza, so that they could walk through the stores or go to a movie, and when he came to pick them up again at eleven he never bothered to ask what they had done.

They must have been familiar sights, walking around that shopping plaza in their shorts and flat ballerina slippers that always scuffed the sidewalk, with charm bracelets jingling on their thin wrists; they would lean together to whisper and laugh secretly

5

if someone passed by who amused or interested them. Connie had long dark blond hair that drew anyone's eye to it, and she wore part of it pulled up on her head and puffed out and the rest of it she let fall down her back. She wore a pullover jersey blouse that looked one way when she was at home and another way when she was away from home. Everything about her had two sides to it, one for home and one for anywhere that was not home: her walk that could be childlike and bobbing, or languid enough to make anyone think she was hearing music in her head, her mouth which was pale and smirking most of the time, but bright and pink on these evenings out, her laugh which was cynical and drawling at home — "Ha, ha, very funny" — but high-pitched and nervous anywhere else, like the jingling of the charms on her bracelet.

Sometimes they did go shopping or to a movie, but sometimes they went across the highway, ducking fast across the busy road, to a drive-in restaurant where older kids hung out. The restaurant was shaped like a big bottle, though squatter than a real bottle, and on its cap was a revolving figure of a grinning boy who held a hamburger aloft. One night in midsummer they ran across, breathless with daring, and right away someone leaned out a car window and invited them over, but it was just a boy from high school they didn't like. It made them feel good to be able to ignore him. They went up through the maze of parked and cruising cars to the bright-lit, fly-infested restaurant, their faces pleased and expectant as if they were entering a sacred building that loomed out of the night to give them what haven and what blessing they yearned for. They sat at the counter and crossed their legs at the ankles, their thin shoulders rigid with excitement, and listened to the music that made everything so good: the music was always in the background like music at a church service, it was something to depend upon.

A boy named Eddie came in to talk with them. He sat backwards on his stool, turning himself jerkily around in semi-circles and then stopping and turning again, and after a while he asked Connie if she would like something to eat. She said she did and so she tapped her friend's arm on her way out — her friend pulled her face up into a brave droll look — and Connie said she would meet her at eleven, across the way. "I just hate to leave her like that," Connie said earnestly, but the boy said that she wouldn't be alone for long. So they went out to his car and on the way Connie couldn't help but let her eyes wander over the windshields and faces all around her, her face gleam-ing with the joy that had nothing to do with Eddie or even this place; it might have been the music. She drew her shoulders up and sucked in her breath with the pure pleasure of being alive, and just at that moment she happened to glance at a face just a few feet from hers. It was a boy with shaggy black hair, in a convertible jalopy painted gold. He stared at her and then his lips widened into a grin. Connie slit her eyes at him and turned away, but she couldn't help glancing back and there he was still watching her. He wagged a finger and laughed and said, "Gonna get you, baby," and Connie turned away again without Eddie noticing anything.

She spent three hours with him, at the restaurant where they ate hamburgers and drank Cokes in wax cups that were always sweating, and then down an alley a mile or so away, and when he left her off at five to eleven only the movie house was still open at the plaza. Her girl friend was there, talking with a boy. When Connie came up the two girls smiled at each other and Connie said, "How was the movie?" and the girl said, "*You* should know." They rode off with the girl's father, sleepy and pleased, and Connie couldn't help but look at the darkened shopping plaza with its big empty parking lot and its signs that were faded and ghostly now, and over at the drive-in restaurant where cars were still circling tirelessly. She couldn't hear the music at this distance.

Next morning June asked her how the movie was and Connie said, "So-so."

She and that girl and occasionally another girl went out several times a week   10 that way, and the rest of the time Connie spent around the house — it was summer vacation — getting in her mother's way and thinking, dreaming, about the boys she met. But all the boys fell back and dissolved into a single face that was not even a face, but an idea, a feeling, mixed up with the urgent insistent pounding of the music and the humid night air of July. Connie's mother kept dragging her back to the daylight by finding things for her to do or saying suddenly, "What's this about the Pettinger girl?"

And Connie would say nervously, "Oh, her. That dope." She always drew thick clear lines between herself and such girls, and her mother was simple and kindly enough to believe her. Her mother was so simple, Connie thought, that it was maybe cruel to fool her so much. Her mother went scuffling around the house in old bed-room slippers and complained over the telephone to one sister about the other, then the other called up and the two of them complained about the third one. If June's name was mentioned her mother's tone was approving, and if Connie's name was mentioned it was disapproving. This did not really mean she disliked Connie and actually Connie thought that her mother preferred her to June because she was prettier, but the two of them kept up a pretense of exasperation, a sense that they were tugging and struggling over something of little value to either of them. Sometimes, over coffee, they were almost friends, but something would come up — some vexation that was like a fly buzzing suddenly around their heads — and their faces went hard with contempt.

One Sunday Connie got up at eleven — none of them bothered with church — and washed her hair so that it could dry all day long, in the sun. Her parents and sister were going to a barbecue at an aunt's house and Connie said no, she wasn't interested, rolling her eyes, to let mother know just what she thought of it. "Stay home alone then," her mother said sharply. Connie sat out back in a lawn chair and watched them drive away, her father quiet and bald, hunched around so that he could back the car out, her mother with a look that was still angry and not at all softened through the windshield, and in the back seat poor old June all dressed up as if she didn't know what a barbecue was, with all the running yelling kids and the flies. Connie sat with her eyes closed in the sun, dreaming and dazed with the warmth about her as if this were a kind of love, the caresses of love, and her mind slipped over onto thoughts of the boy she had been with the night before and how nice he had been, how sweet it always was, not the way someone like June would suppose but sweet, gentle, the way it was in movies and promised in songs; and when she opened her eyes she hardly knew where she was, the back yard ran off into weeds and a fenceline of trees and behind it the sky was perfectly blue and still. The asbestos "ranch house" that was now three years old startled her — it looked small. She shook her head as if to get awake.

It was too hot. She went inside the house and turned on the radio to drown out the quiet. She sat on the edge of her bed, barefoot, and listened for an hour and a half to a program called XYZ Sunday Jamboree, record after record of hard, fast, shrieking songs she sang along with, interspersed by exclamations from "Bobby King": "An' look here you girls at Napoleon's — Son and Charley want you to pay real close attention to this song coming up!"

And Connie paid close attention herself, bathed in a glow of slow-pulsed joy that seemed to rise mysteriously out of the music itself and lay languidly about the airless little room, breathed in and breathed out with each gentle rise and fall of her chest.

After a while she heard a car coming up the drive. She sat up at once, startled, 15 because it couldn't be her father so soon. The gravel kept crunching all the way in from the road — the driveway was long — and Connie ran to the window. It was a car she didn't know. It was an open jalopy, painted a bright gold that caught the sun opaquely. Her heart began to pound and her fingers snatched at her hair, checking it, and she whispered "Christ. Christ," wondering how bad she looked. The car came to a stop at the side door and the horn sounded four short taps as if this were a signal Connie knew.

She went into the kitchen and approached the door slowly, then hung out the screen door, her bare toes curling down off the step. There were two boys in the car and now she recognized the driver: he had shaggy, shabby black hair that looked crazy as a wig and he was grinning at her.

"I ain't late, am I?" he said.

"Who the hell do you think you are?" Connie said.

"Toldja I'd be out, didn't I?"

"I don't even know who you are." 20

She spoke sullenly, careful to show no interest or pleasure, and he spoke in a fast bright monotone. Connie looked past him to the other boy, taking her time. He had fair brown hair, with a lock that fell onto his forehead. His sideburns gave him a fierce, embarrassed look, but so far he hadn't even bothered to glance at her. Both boys wore sunglasses. The driver's glasses were metallic and mirrored everything in miniature.

"You wanta come for a ride?" he said.

Connie smirked and let her hair fall loose over one shoulder.

"Don'tcha like my car? New paint job," he said. "Hey."

"What?" 25

"You're cute."

She pretended to fidget, chasing flies away from the door.

"Don'tcha believe me, or what?" he said.

"Look, I don't even know who you are," Connie said in disgust.

"Hey, Ellie's got a radio, see. Mine's broke down." He lifted his friend's arm and 30 showed her the little transistor the boy was holding, and now Connie began to hear the music. It was the same program that was playing inside the house.

"Bobby King?" she said.

"I listen to him all the time. I think he's great."

"He's kind of great," Connie said reluctantly.

"Listen, that guy's *great*. He knows where the action is."

Connie blushed a little, because the glasses made it impossible for her to see just   35
what this boy was looking at. She couldn't decide if she liked him or if he was just a
jerk, and so she dawdled in the doorway and wouldn't come down or go back inside.
She said, "What's all that stuff painted on your car?"

"Can'tcha read it?" He opened the door very carefully, as if he was afraid it might
fall off. He slid out just as carefully, planting his feet firmly on the ground, the tiny
metallic world in his glasses slowing down like gelatine hardening and in the midst of
it Connie's bright green blouse. "This here is my name, to begin with," he said. ARNOLD
FRIEND was written in tar-like black letters on the side, with a drawing of a round
grinning face that reminded Connie of a pumpkin, except it wore sunglasses. "I wanta
introduce myself, I'm Arnold Friend and that's my real name and I'm gonna be your
friend, honey, and inside the car's Ellie Oscar, he's kinda shy." Ellie brought his transistor up to his shoulder and balanced it there. "Now these numbers are a secret code,
honey," Arnold Friend explained. He read off the numbers 33, 19, 17 and raised his
eyebrows at her to see what she thought of that, but she didn't think much of it. The
left rear fender had been smashed and around it was written, on the gleaming gold
background: DONE BY CRAZY WOMAN DRIVER. Connie had to laugh at that. Arnold
Friend was pleased at her laughter and looked up at her. "Around the other side's a lot
more — you wanta come and see them?"

"No."

"Why not?"

"Why should I?"

"Don'tcha wanta see what's on the car? Don'tcha wanta go for a ride?"   40

"I don't know."

"Why not?"

"I got things to do."

"Like what?"

"Things."   45

He laughed as if she had said something funny. He slapped his thighs. He was
standing in a strange way, leaning back against the car as if he were balancing himself.
He wasn't tall, only an inch or so taller than she would be if she came down to him.
Connie liked the way he was dressed, which was the way all of them dressed: tight
faded jeans stuffed into black, scuffed boots, a belt that pulled his waist in and showed
how lean he was, and a white pull-over shirt that was a little soiled and showed the
hard small muscles of his arms and shoulders. He looked as if he probably did hard
work, lifting and carrying things. Even his neck looked muscular. And his face was a
familiar face, somehow: the jaw and chin and cheeks slightly darkened, because he
hadn't shaved for a day or two, and the nose long and hawk-like, sniffing as if she were
a treat he was going to gobble up and it was all a joke.

"Connie, you ain't telling the truth. This is your day set aside for a ride with me
and you know it," he said, still laughing. The way he straightened and recovered from
his fit of laughing showed that it had been all fake.

"How do you know what my name is?" she said suspiciously.

"It's Connie."

"Maybe and maybe not." 50

"I know my Connie," he said, wagging his finger. Now she remembered him even better, back at the restaurant, and her cheeks warmed at the thought of how she sucked in her breath just at the moment she passed him — how she must have looked to him. And he had remembered her. "Ellie and I come out here especially for you," he said. "Ellie can sit in back. How about it?"

"Where?"

"Where what?"

"Where're we going?"

He looked at her. He took off the sunglasses and she saw how pale the skin around 55 his eyes was, like holes that were not in shadow but instead in light. His eyes were like chips of broken glass that catch the light in an amiable way. He smiled. It was as if the idea of going for a ride somewhere, to some place, was a new idea to him.

"Just for a ride, Connie sweetheart."

"I never said my name was Connie," she said.

"But I know what it is. I know your name and all about you, lots of things," Arnold Friend said. He had not moved yet but stood still leaning back against the side of his jalopy. "I took a special interest in you, such a pretty girl, and found out all about you like I know your parents and sister are gone somewheres and I know where and how long they're going to be gone, and I know who you were with last night, and your best friend's name is Betty. Right?"

He spoke in a simple lilting voice, exactly as if he were reciting the words to a song. His smile assured her that everything was fine. In the car Ellie turned up the volume on his radio and did not bother to look around at them.

"Ellie can sit in the back seat," Arnold Friend said. He indicated his friend with 60 a casual jerk of his chin, as if Ellie did not count and she could not bother with him.

"How'd you find out all that stuff?" Connie said.

"Listen: Betty Schultz and Tony Fitch and Jimmy Pettinger and Nancy Pettinger," he said, in a chant. "Raymond Stanley and Bob Hutter —"

"Do you know all those kids?"

"I know everybody."

"Look, you're kidding. You're not from around here." 65

"Sure."

"But — how come we never saw you before?"

"Sure you saw me before," he said. He looked down at his boots, as if he were a little offended. "You just don't remember."

"I guess I'd remember you," Connie said.

"Yeah?" He looked up at this, beaming. He was pleased. He began to mark time 70 with the music from Ellie's radio, tapping his fists lightly together. Connie looked away from his smile to the car, which was painted so bright it almost hurt her eyes to look at it. She looked at that name, ARNOLD FRIEND. And up at the front fender was an expression that was familiar — MAN THE FLYING SAUCERS. It was an expression kids had used the year before, but didn't use this year. She looked at it for a while as if the words meant something to her that she did not yet know.

"What're you thinking about? Huh?" Arnold Friend demanded. "Not worried about your hair blowing around in the car, are you?"

"No."

"Think I maybe can't drive good?"

"How do I know?"

"You're a hard girl to handle. How come?" he said. "Don't you know I'm your friend? Didn't you see me put my sign in the air when you walked by?" 75

"What sign?"

"My sign." And he drew an X in the air, leaning out toward her. They were maybe ten feet apart. After his hand fell back to his side the X was still in the air, almost visible. Connie let the screen door close and stood perfectly still inside it, listening to the music from her radio and the boy's blend together. She stared at Arnold Friend. He stood there so stiffly relaxed, pretending to be relaxed, with one hand idly on the door handle as if he were keeping himself up that way and had no intention of ever moving again. She recognized most things about him, the tight jeans that showed his thighs and buttocks and the greasy leather boots and the tight shirt, and even that slippery friendly smile of his, that sleepy dreamy smile that all the boys used to get across ideas they didn't want to put into words. She recognized all this and also the singsong way he talked, slightly mocking, kidding, but serious and a little melancholy, and she recognized the way he tapped one fist against the other in homage to the perpetual music behind him. But all these things did not come together.

She said suddenly, "Hey, how old are you?"

His smile faded. She could see then that he wasn't a kid, he was much older — thirty, maybe more. At this knowledge her heart began to pound faster.

"That's a crazy thing to ask. Can'tcha see I'm your own age?" 80

"Like hell you are."

"Or maybe a coupla years older, I'm eighteen."

"Eighteen?" she said doubtfully.

He grinned to reassure her and lines appeared at the corners of his mouth. His teeth were big and white. He grinned so broadly his eyes became slits and she saw how thick the lashes were, thick and black as if painted with a black tar-like material. Then he seemed to become embarrassed, abruptly, and looked over his shoulder at Ellie. "*Him*, he's crazy," he said. "Ain't he a riot, he's a nut, a real character." Ellie was still listening to the music. His sunglasses told nothing about what he was thinking. He wore a bright orange shirt unbuttoned halfway to show his chest, which was a pale, bluish chest and not muscular like Arnold Friend's. His shirt collar was turned up all around and the very tips of the collar pointed out past his chin as if they were protecting him. He was pressing the transistor radio up against his ear and sat there in a kind of daze, right in the sun.

"He's kinda strange," Connie said. 85

"Hey, she says you're kinda strange! Kinda strange!" Arnold Friend cried. He pounded on the car to get Ellie's attention. Ellie turned for the first time and Connie saw with shock that he wasn't a kid either — he had a fair, hairless face, cheeks reddened slightly as if the veins grew too close to the surface of his skin, the face of a forty-year-old baby. Connie felt a wave of dizziness rise in her at this sight and she stared at him as if waiting for something to change the shock of the moment, make it all right again. Ellie's lips kept shaping words, mumbling along with the words blasting his ear.

"Maybe you two better go away," Connie said faintly.

"What? How come?" Arnold Friend cried. "We come out here to take you for a ride. It's Sunday." He had the voice of the man on the radio now. It was the same voice, Connie thought. "Don'tcha know it's Sunday all day and honey, no matter who you were with last night today you're with Arnold Friend and don't you forget it! — Maybe you better step out here," he said, and this last was in a different voice. It was a little flatter, as if the heat was finally getting to him.

"No. I got things to do."

"Hey."   90

"You two better leave."

"We ain't leaving until you come with us."

"Like hell I am —"

"Connie, don't fool around with me. I mean — I mean, don't fool *around*," he said, shaking his head. He laughed incredulously. He placed his sunglasses on top of his head, carefully, as if he were indeed wearing a wig, and brought the stems down behind his ears. Connie stared at him, another wave of dizziness and fear rising in her so that for a moment he wasn't even in focus but was just a blur, standing there against his gold car, and she had the idea that he had driven up the driveway all right but had come from nowhere before that and belonged nowhere and that everything about him and even the music that was so familiar to her was only half real.

"If my father comes and sees you —"   95

"He ain't coming. He's at a barbecue."

"How do you know that?"

"Aunt Tillie's. Right now they're — uh — they're drinking. Sitting around," he said vaguely, squinting as if he were staring all the way to town and over to Aunt Tillie's back yard. Then the vision seemed to clear and he nodded energetically. "Yeah. Sitting around. There's your sister in a blue dress, huh? And high heels, the poor sad bitch — nothing like you, sweetheart! And your mother's helping some fat woman with the corn, they're cleaning the corn — husking the corn —"

"What fat woman?" Connie cried.

"How do I know what fat woman. I don't know every goddamn fat woman in the   100
world!" Arnold Friend laughed.

"Oh, that's Mrs. Hornby. . . . Who invited her?" Connie said. She felt a little light-headed. Her breath was coming quickly.

"She's too fat. I don't like them fat. I like them the way you are, honey," he said, smiling sleepily at her. They stared at each other for a while, through the screen door. He said softly, "Now what you're going to do is this: you're going to come out that door. You're going to sit up front with me and Ellie's going to sit in the back, the hell with Ellie, right? This isn't Ellie's date. You're my date. I'm your lover, honey."

"What? You're crazy —"

"Yes, I'm your lover. You don't know what that is but you will," he said. "I know that too. I know all about you. But look: it's real nice and you couldn't ask for nobody better than me, or more polite. I always keep my word. I'll tell you how it is, I'm always nice at first, the first time. I'll hold you so tight you won't think you have to try to get away or pretend anything because you'll know you can't. And I'll come inside you where it's all secret and you'll give in to me and you'll love me —"

"Shut up! You're crazy!" Connie said. She backed away from the door. She put   105
her hands against her ears as if she'd heard something terrible, something not meant for her. "People don't talk like that, you're crazy," she muttered. Her heart was almost too big now for her chest and its pumping made sweat break out all over her. She looked out to see Arnold Friend pause and then take a step toward the porch lurching. He almost fell. But, like a clever drunken man, he managed to catch his balance. He wobbled in his high boots and grabbed hold of one of the porch posts.

"Honey?" he said. "You still listening?"

"Get the hell out of here!"

"Be nice, honey. Listen."

"I'm going to call the police —"

He wobbled again and out of the side of his mouth came a fast spat curse, an aside   110
not meant for her to hear. But even this "Christ!" sounded forced. Then he began to smile again. She watched this smile come, awkward as if he were smiling from inside a mask. His whole face was a mask, she thought wildly, tanned down onto his throat but then running out as if he had plastered make-up on his face but had forgotten about his throat.

"Honey —? Listen, here's how it is. I always tell the truth and I promise you this: I ain't coming in that house after you."

"You better not! I'm going to call the police if you — if you don't —"

"Honey," he said, talking right through her voice, "honey, I'm not coming in there but you are coming out here. You know why?"

She was panting. The kitchen looked like a place she had never seen before, some room she had run inside but which wasn't good enough, wasn't going to help her. The kitchen window had never had a curtain, after three years, and there were dishes in the sink for her to do — probably — and if you ran your hand across the table you'd probably feel something sticky there.

"You listening, honey? Hey?"   115

"— going to call the police —"

"Soon as you touch the phone I don't need to keep my promise and can come inside. You won't want that."

She rushed forward and tried to lock the door. Her fingers were shaking. "But why lock it," Arnold Friend said gently, talking right into her face. "It's just a screen door. It's just nothing." One of his boots was at a strange angle, as if his foot wasn't in it. It pointed out to the left, bent at the ankle. "I mean, anybody can break through a screen door and glass and wood and iron or anything else if he needs to, anybody at all and specially Arnold Friend. If the place got lit up with a fire, honey, you'd come runnin' out into my arms, right into my arms an' safe at home — like you knew I was your lover and'd stopped fooling around, I don't mind a nice shy girl but I don't like no fooling around." Part of those words were spoken with a slight rhythmic lilt, and Connie somehow recognized them — the echo of a song from last year, about a girl rushing into her boy friend's arms and coming home again —

Connie stood barefoot on the linoleum floor, staring at him. "What do you want?" she whispered.

"I want you," he said.   120

"What?"

"Seen you that night and thought, that's the one, yes sir. I never needed to look any more."

"But my father's coming back. He's coming to get me. I had to wash my hair first —" She spoke in a dry, rapid voice, hardly raising it for him to hear.

"No, your daddy is not coming and yes, you had to wash your hair and you washed it for me. It's nice and shining and all for me. I thank you, sweetheart," he said, with a mock bow, but again he almost lost his balance. He had to bend and adjust his boots. Evidently his feet did not go all the way down; the boots must have been stuffed with something so that he would seem taller. Connie stared out at him and behind him at Ellie in the car, who seemed to be looking off toward Connie's right, into nothing. Then Ellie said, pulling the words out of the air one after another as if he were just discovering them, "You want me to pull out the phone?"

"Shut your mouth and keep it shut," Arnold Friend said, his face red from bend-   125
ing over or maybe from embarrassment because Connie had seen his boots. "This ain't none of your business."

"What — what are you doing? What do you want?" Connie said. "If I call the police they'll get you, they'll arrest you —"

"Promise was not to come in unless you touch that phone, and I'll keep that promise," he said. He resumed his erect position and tried to force his shoulders back. He sounded like a hero in a movie, declaring something important. He spoke too loudly and it was as if he were speaking to someone behind Connie. "I ain't made plans for coming in that house where I don't belong but just for you to come out to me, the way you should. Don't you know who I am?"

"You're crazy," she whispered. She backed away from the door but did not want to go into another part of the house, as if this would give him permission to come through the door. "What do you . . . You're crazy, you . . ."

"Huh? What're you saying, honey?"

Her eyes darted everywhere in the kitchen. She could not remember what it was,   130
this room.

"This is how it is, honey: you come out and we'll drive away, have a nice ride. But if you don't come out we're gonna wait till your people come home and then they're all going to get it."

"You want that telephone pulled out?" Ellie said. He held the radio away from his ear and grimaced, as if without the radio the air was too much for him.

"I toldja shut up, Ellie," Arnold Friend said, "you're deaf, get a hearing aid, right? Fix yourself up. This little girl's no trouble and's gonna be nice to me, so Ellie keep to yourself, this ain't your date — right? Don't hem in on me, don't hog, don't crush, don't bird dog, don't trail me," he said in a rapid, meaningless voice, as if he were running through all the expressions he'd learned but was no longer sure which one of them was in style, then rushing on to new ones, making them up with his eyes closed. "Don't crawl under my fence, don't squeeze in my chipmunk hole, don't sniff my glue, suck my popsicle, keep your own greasy fingers on yourself!" He shaded his eyes and peered in at Connie, who was backed against the kitchen table. "Don't mind him, honey, he's just a creep. He's a dope. Right? I'm the boy for you and like I said, you come out here nice like a lady and give me your hand, and nobody else gets hurt, I mean, your nice old bald-headed daddy and your mummy and your sister in her high heels. Because listen: why bring them in this?"

"Leave me alone," Connie whispered.

"Hey, you know that old woman down the road, the one with the chickens and   135
stuff — you know her?"

"She's dead!"

"Dead? What? You know her?" Arnold Friend said.

"She's dead —"

"Don't you like her?"

"She's dead — she's — she isn't here any more —"   140

"But don't you like her, I mean, you got something against her? Some grudge or something?" Then his voice dipped as if he were conscious of rudeness. He touched the sunglasses on top of his head as if to make sure they were still there. "Now you be a good girl."

"What are you going to do?"

"Just two things, or maybe three," Arnold Friend said. "But I promise it won't last long and you'll like me that way you get to like people you're close to. You will. It's all over for you here, so come on out. You don't want your people in any trouble, do you?"

She turned and bumped against a chair or something, hurting her leg, but she ran into the back room and picked up the telephone. Something roared in her ear, a tiny roaring, and she was so sick with fear that she could do nothing but listen to it — the telephone was clammy and very heavy and her fingers groped down to the dial but were too weak to touch it. She began to scream into the phone, into the roaring. She cried out, she cried for her mother, she felt her breath start jerking back and forth in her lungs as if it were something Arnold Friend was stabbing her with again and again with no tenderness. A noisy sorrowful wailing rose all about her and she was locked inside it the way she was locked inside this house.

After a while she could hear again. She was sitting on the floor, with her wet back   145
against the wall.

Arnold Friend was saying from the door, "That's a good girl. Put the phone back."

She kicked the phone away from her.

"No, honey. Pick it up. Put it back right."

She picked it up and put it back. The dial tone stopped.

"That's a good girl. Now you come outside."   150

She was hollow with what had been fear but what was now just an emptiness. All that screaming had blasted it out of her. She sat, one leg cramped under her, and deep inside her brain was something like a pinpoint of light that kept going and would not let her relax. She thought, I'm not going to see my mother again. She thought, I'm not going to sleep in my bed again. Her bright green blouse was all wet.

Arnold Friend said, in a gentle-loud voice that was like a stage voice, "The place where you came from ain't there any more, and where you had in mind to go is cancelled out. This place you are now — inside your daddy's house — is nothing but a cardboard box I can knock down any time. You know that and always did know it. You hear me?"

She thought, I have got to think. I have got to know what to do.

"We'll go out to a nice field, out in the country here where it smells so nice and it's sunny," Arnold Friend said. "I'll have my arms tight around you so you won't need to try to get away and I'll show you what love is like, what it does. The hell with this house! It looks solid all right," he said. He ran a fingernail down the screen and the noise did not make Connie shiver, as it would have the day before. "Now put your hand on your heart, honey. Feel that? That feels solid too but we know better. Be nice to me, be sweet like you can because what else is there for a girl like you but to be sweet and pretty and give in? — and get away before her people get back?"

She felt her pounding heart. Her hand seemed to enclose it. She thought for the   155
first time in her life that it was nothing that was hers, that belonged to her, but just a pounding, living thing inside this body that wasn't really hers either.

"You don't want them to get hurt," Arnold Friend went on. "Now get up, honey. Get up all by yourself."

She stood.

"Now turn this way. That's right. Come over to me — Ellie, put that away, didn't I tell you? You dope. You miserable creepy dope," Arnold Friend said. His words were not angry but only part of an incantation. The incantation was kindly. "Now come out through the kitchen to me honey and let's see a smile, try it, you're a brave sweet little girl and now they're eating corn and hotdogs cooked to bursting over an outdoor fire, and they don't know one thing about you and never did and honey you're better than them because not a one of them would have done this for you."

Connie felt the linoleum under her feet; it was cool. She brushed her hair back out of her eyes. Arnold Friend let go of the post tentatively and opened his arms for her, his elbows pointing in toward each other and his wrists limp, to show that this was an embarrassed embrace and a little mocking, he didn't want to make her self-conscious.

She put out her hand against the screen. She watched herself push the door slowly   160
open as if she were back safe somewhere in the other doorway, watching this body and this head of long hair moving out into the sunlight where Arnold Friend waited.

"My sweet little blue-eyed girl," he said in a half-sung sigh that had nothing to do with her brown eyes but was taken up just the same by the vast sunlit reaches of the land behind him and on all sides of him — so much land that Connie had never seen before and did not recognize except to know that she was going to it.

(1966)

Exploring the Text

1. How does Joyce Carol Oates characterize Connie? What part does June play in her characterization?
2. Do you think Connie is a typical American teenager? Are her qualities characteristic of teenagers in general or do they seem specific to an earlier time period? Explain your answer.
3. How does Oates develop the character of Arnold Friend? Look especially at her descriptions of his physical features and clothes.
4. What part does music play in this story? Why is it important to Connie?
5. How does Oates generate and control the story's suspense? At which points does the suspense increase with particular intensity? How does she convey Connie's mounting fear? What or who controls her actions?
6. Oates does not provide closure in this story. Why? Does the indeterminate ending add to or diminish the story's power. Explain your answer.
7. Oates says she based her story on three Tucson, Arizona, murders committed by Charles Schmid, the "Pied Piper of Tucson," in the 1960s. How does this link to an actual incident influence your reading of the story?
8. Oates dedicates the story to Bob Dylan and says she was inspired by his song "It's All Over Now, Baby Blue." Listen to the song, paying special attention to the lyrics. Why do you think Oates found the song compelling? What do you think inspired the dedication?

ADRIENNE RICH

Adrienne Rich (1929–2012) was an American poet, essayist, and scholar and considered one of the most influential poets of the late twentieth century. Born in Baltimore, Maryland, Rich graduated from Radcliffe College in 1951 and published her first collection of poems, *A Change of World*, the same year. In 1974, she won the National Book Award for her poetry collection *Diving into the Wreck*, and in 1976, she published *Of Woman Born: Motherhood as Experience and Institution*, an essay collection that established Rich as a women's rights advocate. She won many awards during her writing career, including a fellowship from the John D. and Catherine T. MacArthur Foundation (1994) and the National Book Critics Circle Award (2005).

Diving into the Wreck

"Diving into the Wreck" is the title piece of Rich's 1973 collection, which won the National Book Award in 1974. Rich read a statement that she had prepared with Alice Walker and Audre Lord, two other poets whose work had been nominated, in which she said, "We appreciate the good faith of the judges for this award, but none of us could accept this money for herself, nor could she let go unquestioned the terms on which poets are given or denied honor and livelihood in this world, especially when they are women." She accepted the award in the name of "all the women whose voices have gone and still go unheard in a patriarchal world."

First having read the book of myths,
and loaded the camera,
and checked the edge of the knife-blade,
I put on
the body-armor of black rubber   5
the absurd flippers
the grave and awkward mask.
I am having to do this
not like Cousteau with his
assiduous team   10
aboard the sun-flooded schooner
but here alone.

There is a ladder.
The ladder is always there
hanging innocently   15
close to the side of the schooner.
We know what it is for,
we who have used it.
Otherwise
it's a piece of maritime floss   20
some sundry equipment.

I go down.
Rung after rung and still
the oxygen immerses me
the blue light   25
the clear atoms
of our human air.
I go down.
My flippers cripple me,
I crawl like an insect down the ladder   30
and there is no one
to tell me when the ocean
will begin.

First the air is blue and then
it is bluer and then green and then   35
black I am blacking out and yet
my mask is powerful

it pumps my blood with power
the sea is another story
the sea is not a question of power   40
I have to learn alone
to turn my body without force
in the deep element.

And now: it is easy to forget
what I came for   45
among so many who have always
lived here
swaying their crenellated fans
between the reefs
and besides   50
you breathe differently down here.

I came to explore the wreck.
The words are purposes.
The words are maps.
I came to see the damage that was done   55
and the treasures that prevail.
I stroke the beam of my lamp
slowly along the flank
of something more permanent
than fish or weed   60

the thing I came for:
the wreck and not the story of the wreck
the thing itself and not the myth
the drowned face always staring
toward the sun   65
the evidence of damage
worn by salt and sway into this threadbare beauty
the ribs of the disaster
curving their assertion
among the tentative haunters.   70

This is the place.
And I am here, the mermaid whose dark hair
streams black, the merman in his armored body.
We circle silently
about the wreck   75
we dive into the hold.
I am she: I am he

whose drowned face sleeps with open eyes
whose breasts still bear the stress
whose silver, copper, vermeil cargo lies   80
obscurely inside barrels
half-wedged and left to rot
we are the half-destroyed instruments
that once held to a course
the water-eaten log   85
the fouled compass

We are, I am, you are
by cowardice or courage
the one who find our way
back to this scene   90
carrying a knife, a camera
a book of myths
in which
our names do not appear.

(1973)

Exploring the Text

1. What is your initial reaction to the poem's first stanza? Where did you think it was going? Were you expecting it to be metaphorical or did you think it might be a poem about deep-sea diving? Explain your answer.

2. You probably realized pretty quickly that "Diving into the Wreck" is an extended metaphor. What do you think the parts of it represent? Try to imagine what the objects — the book, the camera, the body armor, the flippers, and so on — might represent inside and outside the metaphorical world Adrienne Rich creates in this poem.

3. How does the ladder in the second stanza provide both a literal and a metaphorical shift in the poem?

4. What signals do the stanza breaks provide?

5. What do you think it means that the speaker has become both "the mermaid whose dark hair streams back" and "the merman in his armored body" (ll. 72–73)?

6. While Rich gives no hint of what the scene of disaster in the second-to-last stanza represents, it might be interesting to know that the poem was written in the early 1970s, a time of intense change and political engagement, and that Rich was considered a feminist poet. Does that change your view of the stanza's meaning?

7. Remembering that there is no "right" answer to this question, who do you think the "our" is in the poem's last line?

8. Does this poem leave you feeling sad or uplifted? Or some other emotion altogether? Explain your answer.

STEPHEN JAY GOULD

Paleontologist and evolutionary biologist Stephen Jay Gould (1941–2002) was a professor of geology and zoology at Harvard University from 1967 until his death. His major scientific work was the theory of punctuated equilibrium, a biological theory that builds on the work of Charles Darwin by suggesting that evolution occurs sporadically, rather than gradually over a long period of time. Gould authored numerous books, including *The Mismeasure of Man* (1981); *Wonderful Life: The Burgess Shale and the Nature of History* (1989); his magnum opus, *The Structure of Evolutionary Theory* (2002); and *The Hedgehog, the Fox, and the Magister's Pox: Mending the Gap between Science and the Humanities* (2003).

Women's Brains

Gould wrote for a general audience in his column for *Natural History*, where the following essay originally appeared in 1980.

In the Prelude to *Middlemarch*, George Eliot lamented the unfulfilled lives of talented women:

> Some have felt that these blundering lives are due to the inconvenient indefinite-ness with which the Supreme Power has fashioned the natures of women: if there were one level of feminine incompetence as strict as the ability to count three and no more, the social lot of women might be treated with scientific certitude.

Eliot goes on to discount the idea of innate limitation, but while she wrote in 1872, the leaders of European anthropometry were trying to measure "with scientific certi-tude" the inferiority of women. Anthropometry, or measurement of the human body, is not so fashionable a field these days, but it dominated the human sciences for much of the nineteenth century and remained popular until intelligence testing replaced skull measurement as a favored device for making invidious comparisons among races, classes, and sexes. Craniometry, or measurement of the skull, commanded the most attention and respect. Its unquestioned leader, Paul Broca (1824–80), professor of clinical surgery at the Faculty of Medicine in Paris, gathered a school of disciples and imitators around himself. Their work, so meticulous and apparently irrefutable, exerted great influence and won high esteem as a jewel of nineteenth-century science.

Broca's work seemed particularly invulnerable to refutation. Had he not mea-sured with the most scrupulous care and accuracy? (Indeed, he had. I have the greatest respect for Broca's meticulous procedure. His numbers are sound. But science is an inferential exercise, not a catalog of facts. Numbers, by themselves, specify nothing. All depends upon what you do with them.) Broca depicted himself as an apostle of objectivity, a man who bowed before facts and cast aside superstition and sentimen-tality. He declared that "there is no faith, however respectable, no interest, however legitimate, which must not accommodate itself to the progress of human knowledge and bend before truth." Women, like it or not, had smaller brains than men and, therefore, could not equal them in intelligence. This fact, Broca argued, may reinforce a common prejudice in male society, but it is also a scientific truth. L. Manouvrier, a black sheep in Broca's fold, rejected the inferiority of women and wrote with feeling about the burden imposed upon them by Broca's numbers:

> Women displayed their talents and their diplomas. They also invoked philo-sophical authorities. But they were opposed by *numbers* unknown to Condorcet or to John Stuart Mill. These numbers fell upon poor women like a sledge ham-mer, and they were accompanied by commentaries and sarcasms more ferocious than the most misogynist imprecations of certain church fathers. The theolo-gians had asked if women had a soul. Several centuries later, some scientists were ready to refuse them a human intelligence.

Broca's argument rested upon two sets of data: the larger brains of men in mod-ern societies, and a supposed increase in male superiority through time. His most extensive data came from autopsies performed personally in four Parisian hospitals. For 292 male brains, he calculated an average weight of 1,325 grams; 140 female brains averaged 1,144 grams for a difference of 181 grams, or 14 percent of the male weight. Broca understood, of course, that part of this difference could be attributed to the greater height of males. Yet he made no attempt to measure the effect of size alone and actually stated that it cannot account for the entire difference because we know, a priori, that women are not as intelligent as men (a premise that the data were supposed to test, not rest upon):

> We might ask if the small size of the female brain depends exclusively upon the small size of her body. Tiedemann has proposed this explanation. But we must not forget that women are, on the average, a little less intelligent than men, a difference which we should not exaggerate but which is, nonetheless, real. We are therefore permitted to suppose that the relatively small size of the female brain depends in part upon her physical inferiority and in part upon her intellectual inferiority.

In 1873, the year after Eliot published *Middlemarch*, Broca measured the cranial capacities of prehistoric skulls from L'Homme Mort cave. Here he found a difference of only 99.5 cubic centimeters between males and females, while modern populations range from 129.5 to 220.7. Topinard, Broca's chief disciple, explained the increasing discrepancy through time as a result of differing evolutionary pressures upon domi-nant men and passive women:

> The man who fights for two or more in the struggle for existence, who has all the responsibility and the cares of tomorrow, who is constantly active in combating the environment and human rivals, needs more brain than the woman whom he must protect and nourish, the sedentary woman, lacking any interior occupa-tions, whose role is to raise children, love, and be passive.

In 1879, Gustave Le Bon, chief misogynist of Broca's school, used these data to publish what must be the most vicious attack upon women in modern scientific literature (no one can top Aristotle). I do not claim his views were representative of Broca's school, but they were published in France's most respected anthropological journal. Le Bon concluded:

> In the most intelligent races, as among the Parisians, there are a large number of women whose brains are closer in size to those of gorillas than to the most developed male brains. This inferiority is so obvious that no one can contest it for a moment; only its degree is worth discussion. All psychologists who have studied the intelligence of women, as well as poets and novelists, recognize today that they represent the most inferior forms of human evolution and that they are closer to children and savages than to an adult, civilized man. They excel in fickleness, inconstancy, absence of thought and logic, and incapacity to reason. Without doubt there exist some distinguished women, very superior to the average man, but they are as exceptional as the birth of any monstrosity, as, for example, of a gorilla with two heads; consequently, we may neglect them entirely.

Nor did Le Bon shrink from the social implications of his views. He was horrified by the proposal of some American reformers to grant women higher education on the same basis as men:

> A desire to give them the same education, and, as a consequence, to propose the same goals for them, is a dangerous chimera. . . . The day when, misunderstanding the inferior occupations which nature has given her, women leave the home and take part in our battles; on this day a social revolution will begin, and everything that maintains the sacred ties of the family will disappear.

Sound familiar?[1]

I have reexamined Broca's data, the basis for all this derivative pronouncement, and I find his numbers sound but his interpretation ill-founded, to say the least. The data supporting his claim for increased difference through time can be easily dismissed. Broca based his contention on the samples from L'Homme Mort alone — only seven male and six female skulls in all. Never have so little data yielded such far-ranging conclusions.

In 1888, Topinard published Broca's more extensive data on the Parisian hospitals. Since Broca recorded height and age as well as brain size, we may use modern statistics to remove their effect. Brain weight decreases with age, and Broca's women were, on average, considerably older than his men. Brain weight increases with height, and his average man was almost half a foot taller than his average woman. I used multiple regression, a technique that allowed me to assess simultaneously the influence of height and age upon brain size. In an analysis of the data for women, I found that, at average male height and age, a woman's brain would weigh 1,212 grams.

---

[1]When I wrote this essay, I assumed that Le Bon was a marginal, if colorful, figure. I have since learned that he was a leading scientist, one of the founders of social psychology, and best known for a seminal study on crowd behavior, still cited today (*La psychologie des foules*, 1895), and for his work on unconscious motivation.

Correction for height and age reduces Broca's measured difference of 181 grams by more than a third, to 113 grams.

I don't know what to make of this remaining difference because I cannot assess other factors known to influence brain size in a major way. Cause of death has an important effect: degenerative disease often entails a substantial diminution of brain size. (This effect is separate from the decrease attributed to age alone.) Eugene Schreider, also working with Broca's data, found that men killed in accidents had brains weighing, on average, 60 grams more than men dying of infectious diseases. The best modern data I can find (from American hospitals) records a full 100-gram difference between death by degenerative arteriosclerosis and by violence or accident. Since so many of Broca's subjects were very elderly women, we may assume that lengthy degenerative disease was more common among them than among the men. 10

More importantly, modern students of brain size still have not agreed on a proper measure for eliminating the powerful effect of body size. Height is partly adequate, but men and women of the same height do not share the same body build. Weight is even worse than height, because most of its variation reflects nutrition rather than intrinsic size — fat versus skinny exerts little influence upon the brain. Manouvrier took up this subject in the 1880s and argued that muscular mass and force should be used. He tried to measure this elusive property in various ways and found a marked difference in favor of men, even in men and women of the same height. When he corrected for what he called "sexual mass," women actually came out slightly ahead in brain size.

Thus, the corrected 113-gram difference is surely too large; the true figure is probably close to zero and may as well favor women as men. And 113 grams, by the way, is exactly the average difference between a 5 foot 4 inch and a 6 foot 4 inch male in Broca's data. We would not (especially us short folks) want to ascribe greater intelligence to tall men. In short, who knows what to do with Broca's data? They certainly don't permit any confident claim that men have bigger brains than women.

To appreciate the social role of Broca and his school, we must recognize that his statements about the brains of women do not reflect an isolated prejudice toward a single disadvantaged group. They must be weighed in the context of a general theory that supported contemporary social distinctions as biologically ordained. Women, blacks, and poor people suffered the same disparagement, but women bore the brunt of Broca's argument because he had easier access to data on women's brains. Women were singularly denigrated but they also stood as surrogates for other disenfranchised groups. As one of Broca's disciples wrote in 1881: "Men of the black races have a brain scarcely heavier than that of white women." This juxtaposition extended into many other realms of anthropological argument, particularly to claims that, anatomically and emotionally, both women and blacks were like white children — and that white children, by the theory of recapitulation, represented an ancestral (primitive) adult stage of human evolution. I do not regard as empty rhetoric the claim that women's battles are for all of us.

Maria Montessori did not confine her activities to educational reform for young children. She lectured on anthropology for several years at the University of Rome, and wrote an influential book entitled *Pedagogical Anthropology* (English edition, 1913). Montessori was no egalitarian. She supported most of Broca's work and the theory of innate criminality proposed by her compatriot Cesare Lombroso. She measured the circumference of children's heads in her schools and inferred that the best prospects had bigger brains. But she had no use for Broca's conclusions about women. She discussed Manouvrier's work at length and made much of his tentative claim that women, after proper correction of the data, had slightly larger brains than men. Women, she concluded, were intellectually superior, but men had prevailed heretofore by dint of physical force. Since technology has abolished force as an instrument of power, the era of women may soon be upon us: "In such an epoch there will really be superior human beings, there will really be men strong in morality and in sentiment. Perhaps in this way the reign of women is approaching, when the enigma of her anthropological superiority will be deciphered. Woman was always the custodian of human sentiment, morality and honor."

This represents one possible antidote to "scientific" claims for the constitutional 15 inferiority of certain groups. One may affirm the validity of biological distinctions but argue that the data have been misinterpreted by prejudiced men with a stake in the outcome, and that disadvantaged groups are truly superior. In recent years, Elaine Morgan has followed this strategy in her *Descent of Woman*, a speculative reconstruction of human prehistory from the woman's point of view — and as farcical as more famous tall tales by and for men.

I prefer another strategy. Montessori and Morgan followed Broca's philosophy to reach a more congenial conclusion. I would rather label the whole enterprise of setting a biological value upon groups for what it is: irrelevant and highly injurious. George Eliot well appreciated the special tragedy that biological labeling imposed upon members of disadvantaged groups. She expressed it for people like herself — women of extraordinary talent. I would apply it more widely — not only to those whose dreams are flouted but also to those who never realize that they may dream — but I cannot match her prose. In conclusion, then, the rest of Eliot's prelude to *Middlemarch*:

> The limits of variation are really much wider than anyone would imagine from the sameness of women's coiffure and the favorite love stories in prose and verse. Here and there a cygnet is reared uneasily among the ducklings in the brown pond, and never finds the living stream in fellowship with its own oary-footed kind. Here and there is born a Saint Theresa, foundress of nothing, whose loving heartbeats and sobs after an unattained goodness tremble off and are dispersed among hindrances instead of centering in some long-recognizable deed.

(1980)

Exploring the Text

1. What purposes do the quotations from George Eliot's novel *Middlemarch* serve in this essay? Why does Stephen Jay Gould refer to Eliot when he introduces the

quotation from Broca in paragraph 5? Why are quotations from Eliot, whose real name was Mary Anne Evans, especially appropriate for Gould's essay?

2. Gould builds two parallel arguments: one on scientific method, another on speculative conclusions. In which paragraphs does he question the scientific methods rather than the findings themselves? How does he weave the two arguments together to make his point?

3. How does each of the individuals Gould cites — Paul Broca, L. Manouvrier, Gustave Le Bon, and Maria Montessori — contribute to the development of his argument?

4. At the end of paragraph 7, Gould adds a footnote reassessing an earlier point. Does this admission add to or detract from his credibility? Explain your answer.

5. In paragraph 13, Gould shows how Broca and his colleagues extended their conclusions to other groups. What is Gould's purpose in developing this point as elaborately as he does?

6. In paragraph 4, why is questioning Maria Montessori's research and conclusions an effective strategy? What criticism might Gould be guarding against in doing so?

7. This essay has a strong appeal to logos, as would be expected of a scientific argument. How does Gould also appeal to pathos? How does that appeal add to the persuasiveness of his argument?

8. How do Gould's occasional shifts from the third person to the first person strengthen or weaken his essay?

9. How would you characterize the audience for whom Gould is writing? Do you think fellow scientists are part of that audience? Explain why or why not.

10. What does Gould mean when he says, "Women were singularly denigrated but they also stood as surrogates for other disenfranchised groups" (par. 13)?

11. Why does Gould say, "I do not regard as empty rhetoric the claim that women's battles are for all of us" (par. 13)? Does such a personal comment undermine his scientific credibility? Explain.

Sharon Olds

Sharon Olds was born in San Francisco in 1942 and was raised, as she describes it, "as a hellfire Calvinist." She received a BA from Stanford University and a PhD from Columbia University and has taught at New York University since 1987. Olds has published several collections of poems to considerable acclaim. Her first collection, *Satan Says* (1980), won the San Francisco Poetry Center Award, and *The Dead and the Living* (1983) won the 1983 Lamont Poetry Prize and the National Book Critics Circle Award. Nine additional collections of her work have been published in English, and her poems have been widely translated. Her most recent volume, *One Secret Thing*, was published in 2008.

Rite of Passage

"Rite of Passage" was published in *The Dead and the Living*. In it, Olds examines a critical rite of passage for a young man: the birthday party.

As the guests arrive at my son's party
they gather in the living room —
short men, men in first grade
with smooth jaws and chins.
Hands in pockets, they stand around   5
jostling, jockeying for place, small fights
breaking out and calming. One says to another
How old are you? Six. I'm seven. So?
They eye each other, seeing themselves
tiny in the other's pupils. They clear their   10
throats a lot, a room of small bankers,
they fold their arms and frown. *I could beat you
up,* a seven says to a six,
the dark cake, round and heavy as a
turret, behind them on the table. My son,   15
freckles like specks of nutmeg on his cheeks,
chest narrow as the balsa keel of a
model boat, long hands
cool and thin as the day they guided him
out of me, speaks up as a host   20
for the sake of the group.
We could easily kill a two-year-old,
he says in his clear voice. The other
men agree, they clear their throats
like Generals, they relax and get down to   25
playing war, celebrating my son's life.

(1983)

Exploring the Text

1. What argument does Sharon Olds make about the development of gender roles in "Rite of Passage"?
2. How would you describe the tone of this poem? How does the tone reflect the attitude of the speaker?
3. Are the images in the poem mainly literal or figurative? What do the images in this poem evoke?

4. Explain the title of the poem. Why do you think Olds used it? What other rites of passage do you know about? Are they anything like what Olds describes here? How are they the same? How are they different?

5. Olds avoids calling these first graders boys and does not use their names. At one point she even refers to them as "a six" and "a seven." Why do you think she made that decision?

6. Imagine this poem beginning

> As the guests arrive at my *daughter's* party
> they gather in the living room —
> short *women, women* in first grade

Where would you take it from there?

Naomi Shihab Nye

Poet, novelist, editor, and political activist Naomi Shihab Nye (b. 1952) is the daughter of a Palestinian father and an American mother. Nye grew up in St. Louis, Missouri, and currently lives in San Antonio, Texas. Her works for children include the picture book *Sitti's Secret* (1994) and the novel *Habibi* (1996). Her poetry collections include *Different Ways to Pray* (1980), *19 Varieties of Gazelle: Poems of the Middle East* (2002), and *Transfer* (2011). She has won many awards and fellowships, including four Pushcart Prizes (for best work from small presses), the Jane Addams Children's Book Award, and the Isabella Gardner Poetry Award. Nye, who has been a visiting writer all over the world, describes herself as "a wandering poet."

Arabic Coffee

"Arabic Coffee" was first published in 1986 as an illustrated pamphlet-style broadside.

It was never too strong for us:
make it blacker, Papa,
thick in the bottom,
tell again how years will gather
in small white cups,   5
how luck lives in a spot of grounds.

Leaning over the stove, he let it
boil to the top, and down again.
Two times. No sugar in his pot.

And the place where men and women   10
break off from one another
was not present in that room.
The hundred disappointments,
fire swallowing olive-wood beads
at the warehouse, and the dreams   15
tucked like pocket handkerchiefs
into each day, took their places
on the table, near the half-empty
dish of corn. And none was
more important than the others,   20
and all were guests. When
he carried the tray into the room,
high and balanced in his hands,
it was an offering to all of them,
stay, be seated, follow the talk   25
wherever it goes. The coffee was
the center of the flower.
Like clothes on a line saying
You will live long enough to wear me,
a motion of faith. There is this,   30
and there is more.

(1986)

Exploring the Text

1. What do you think the coffee represents in "Arabic Coffee"? Consider both its literal and symbolic meanings.
2. What is the purpose of "Arabic Coffee"? How do the contrasts within the poem help Naomi Shihab Nye achieve her purpose?
3. How do you think the speaker feels about her father? Use words or phrases from the poem to explain your answer.
4. Look carefully at lines 10–12, "And the place where men and women / break off from one another / was not present in that room." Why does Nye consider the separation of men and women a "place"? What do you think it means when she says it's not present in the room where the coffee is being served? How does it connect to the seven lines that follow?
5. How does "Arabic Coffee" comment on both traditional values and the values of modern culture?

BRENT STAPLES

An author and editorial writer for the *New York Times*, Brent Staples (b. 1951) grew up in Pennsylvania in a family of nine children. He received his BA from Widener University and his PhD in psychology from the University of Chicago. His memoir, *Parallel Time: Growing Up in Black and White* (1994), won the Anisfield-Wolf Book Award, which recognizes books that contribute to a deeper appreciation of cultural diversity.

Just Walk On By
A Black Man Ponders His Power to Alter Public Space

The following essay originally appeared in *Ms.* magazine in 1986.

My first victim was a woman — white, well dressed, probably in her early twenties. I came upon her late one evening on a deserted street in Hyde Park, a relatively affluent neighborhood in an otherwise mean, impoverished section of Chicago. As I swung onto the avenue behind her, there seemed to be a discreet, uninflammatory distance between us. Not so. She cast back a worried glance. To her, the youngish black man — a broad six feet two inches with a beard and billowing hair, both hands shoved into the pockets of a bulky military jacket — seemed menacingly close. After a few more quick glimpses, she picked up her pace and was soon running in earnest. Within seconds she disappeared into a cross street.

That was more than a decade ago. I was twenty-two years old, a graduate student newly arrived at the University of Chicago. It was in the echo of that terrified woman's footfalls that I first began to know the unwieldy inheritance I'd come into — the ability to alter public space in ugly ways. It was clear that she thought herself the quarry of a mugger, a rapist, or worse. Suffering a bout of insomnia, however, I was stalking sleep, not defenseless wayfarers. As a softy who is scarcely able to take a knife to a raw chicken — let alone hold it to a person's throat — I was surprised, embarrassed, and dismayed all at once. Her flight made me feel like an accomplice in tyranny. It also made it clear that I was indistinguishable from the muggers who occasionally seeped into the area from the surrounding ghetto. That first encounter, and those that followed, signified that a vast, unnerving gulf lay between nighttime pedestrians — particularly women — and me. And I soon gathered that being perceived as dangerous is a hazard in itself. I only needed to turn a corner into a dicey situation, or crowd some frightened, armed person in a foyer somewhere, or make an errant move after being pulled over by a policeman. Where fear and weapons meet — and they often do in urban America — there is always the possibility of death.

In that first year, my first away from my hometown, I was to become thoroughly familiar with the language of fear. At dark, shadowy intersections in Chicago, I could cross in front of a car stopped at a traffic light and elicit the *thunk, thunk, thunk, thunk* of the driver — black, white, male, or female — hammering down the door locks. On less traveled streets after dark, I grew accustomed to but never comfortable with people who crossed to the other side of the street rather than pass me. Then there were the standard unpleasantries with police, doormen, bouncers, cabdrivers, and others whose business is to screen out troublesome individuals *before* there is any nastiness.

I moved to New York nearly two years ago and I have remained an avid night walker. In central Manhattan, the near-constant crowd cover minimizes tense one-on-one street encounters. Elsewhere — visiting friends in Soho, where sidewalks are narrow and tightly spaced buildings shut out the sky — things can get very taut indeed.

Black men have a firm place in New York mugging literature. Norman Podhoretz in his famed (or infamous) 1963 essay, "My Negro Problem — And Ours," recalls growing up in terror of black males; they "were tougher than we were, more ruthless," he writes — and as an adult on the Upper West Side of Manhattan, he continues, he cannot constrain his nervousness when he meets black men on certain streets. Similarly, a decade later, the essayist and novelist Edward Hoagland extols a New York where once "Negro bitterness bore down mainly on other Negroes." Where some see mere panhandlers, Hoagland sees "a mugger who is clearly screwing up his nerve to do more than just *ask* for money." But Hoagland has "the New Yorker's quick-hunch posture for broken-field maneuvering," and the bad guy swerves away.

I often witness that "hunch posture," from women after dark on the warren-like streets of Brooklyn where I live. They seem to set their faces on neutral and, with their purse straps strung across their chests bandolier style, they forge ahead as though bracing themselves against being tackled. I understand, of course, that the danger they perceive is not a hallucination. Women are particularly vulnerable to street violence, and young black males are drastically overrepresented among the perpetrators of that violence. Yet these truths are no solace against the kind of alienation that comes of being ever the suspect, against being set apart, a fearsome entity with whom pedestrians avoid making eye contact.

It is not altogether clear to me how I reached the ripe old age of twenty-two without being conscious of the lethality nighttime pedestrians attributed to me. Perhaps it was because in Chester, Pennsylvania, the small, angry industrial town where I came of age in the 1960s, I was scarcely noticeable against a backdrop of gang warfare, street knifings, and murders. I grew up one of the good boys, had perhaps a half-dozen fistfights. In retrospect, my shyness of combat has clear sources.

Many things go into the making of a young thug. One of those things is the consummation of the male romance with the power to intimidate. An infant discovers that random flailings send the baby bottle flying out of the crib and crashing to the floor. Delighted, the joyful babe repeats those motions again and again, seeking to duplicate the feat. Just so, I recall the points at which some of my boyhood friends were finally seduced by the perception of themselves as tough guys. When a mark cowered and surrendered his money without resistance, myth and reality merged — and paid off. It is, after all, only manly to embrace the power to frighten and intimidate. We, as men, are not supposed to give an inch of our lane on the highway; we are to seize the fighter's edge in work and in play and even in love; we are to be valiant in the face of hostile forces.

Unfortunately, poor and powerless young men seem to take all this nonsense literally. As a boy, I saw countless tough guys locked away; I have since buried several, too. They were babies, really — a teenage cousin, a brother of twenty-two, a childhood friend in his midtwenties — all gone down in episodes of bravado played out in the streets. I came to doubt the virtues of intimidation early on. I chose, perhaps even unconsciously, to remain a shadow — timid, but a survivor.

The fearsomeness mistakenly attributed to me in public places often has a peril-   10
ous flavor. The most frightening of these confusions occurred in the late 1970s and early 1980s when I worked as a journalist in Chicago. One day, rushing into the office of a magazine I was writing for with a deadline story in hand, I was mistaken for a burglar. The office manager called security and, with an ad hoc posse, pursued me through the labyrinthine halls, nearly to my editor's door. I had no way of proving who I was. I could only move briskly toward the company of someone who knew me.

Another time I was on assignment for a local paper and killing time before an interview. I entered a jewelry store on the city's affluent Near North Side. The proprietor excused herself and returned with an enormous red Doberman pinscher straining at the end of a leash. She stood, the dog extended toward me, silent to my questions, her eyes bulging nearly out of her head. I took a cursory look around, nodded, and bade her good night. Relatively speaking, however, I never fared as badly as another black male journalist. He went to nearby Waukegan, Illinois, a couple of summers ago to work on a story about a murderer who was born there. Mistaking the reporter for the killer, police hauled him from his car at gunpoint and but for his press credentials would probably have tried to book him. Such episodes are not uncommon. Black men trade tales like this all the time.

In "My Negro Problem — And Ours," Podhoretz writes that the hatred he feels for blacks makes itself known to him through a variety of avenues — one being his discomfort with that "special brand of paranoid touchiness" to which he says blacks are prone. No doubt he is speaking here of black men. In time, I learned to smother the rage I felt at so often being taken for a criminal. Not to do so would surely have led to madness — via that special "paranoid touchiness" that so annoyed Podhoretz at the time he wrote the essay.

I began to take precautions to make myself less threatening. I move about with care, particularly late in the evening. I give a wide berth to nervous people on subway platforms during the wee hours, particularly when I have exchanged business clothes for jeans. If I happen to be entering a building behind some people who appear skittish, I may walk by, letting them clear the lobby before I return, so as not to seem to be following them. I have been calm and extremely congenial on those rare occasions when I've been pulled over by the police.

And on late-evening constitutionals along streets less traveled by, I employ what has proved to be an excellent tension-reducing measure: I whistle melodies from Beethoven and Vivaldi and the more popular classical composers. Even steely New Yorkers hunching toward nighttime destinations seem to relax, and occasionally they even join in the tune. Virtually everybody seems to sense that a mugger wouldn't be warbling bright, sunny selections from Vivaldi's *Four Seasons*. It is my equivalent of the cowbell that hikers wear when they know they are in bear country.

(1986)

Exploring the Text

1. What is the impact of the opening sentence, "My first victim was a woman . . ."? How is Brent Staples using the term *victim*? How does the meaning of the sentence and the term change as you read and reread the essay?
2. How does the description at the beginning resemble a scene from a novel? What mood does Staples set with the details and specific words he chooses? Pay close attention to modifiers and verbs.
3. What examples does Staples provide to illustrate "the language of fear" (par. 3)?
4. In what ways does Staples acknowledge that the "victim's" response is not unwarranted? What explanations does he provide for her behavior? To what extent does he blame her? Does he want us as readers to blame or be more sympathetic toward her?
5. What is Staples's purpose in quoting Norman Podhoretz and Edward Hoagland? Are they providing support for his viewpoint, a contrasting viewpoint, expert testimony, or something else?
6. Is Staples being ironic when he writes, "I began to take precautions to make myself less threatening" (par. 13)? Cite specific parts of the text to support your viewpoint.
7. Is the final paragraph intended to be flippant? Humorous? Explain whether you find it an effective conclusion to the essay.
8. How would you describe the overall tone of this essay? You might consider a phrase rather than a single word to capture the complexity of this piece. Support your reading with specific references to Staples's language.
9. Staples first wrote this essay in 1986. Do you think the essay is dated? Explain why you do or do not feel that many people in today's society continue to perceive young African American males as threatening.

Yusef Komunyakaa

Yusef Komunyakaa was born James Willie Brown Jr. in 1947 and raised in Bogalusa, Louisiana. He has taught in New Orleans public schools, at Indiana University, and at Princeton University, and he is currently teaching at New York University. Fresh out of high school, Komunyakaa enlisted in the army and served in Vietnam, an experience that permeates his poetry. It was many years before he felt he could write about his time spent there.

Speaking of his war experience to the *New York Times*, Komunyakaa said, "I never used the word 'gook' or 'dink' in Vietnam. There is a certain kind of dehumanization that takes place to create an enemy, to call up the passion to kill this person. I knew something about that growing up in Louisiana." He was awarded the 1994 Pulitzer Prize for *Neon Vernacular: New and Selected Poems*.

Facing It

"Facing It" — about an encounter with the Vietnam Veterans Memorial — is from Komunyakaa's collection *Dien Cai Dau* (1988).

My black face fades,
hiding inside the black granite.
I said I wouldn't,
dammit: No tears.
I'm stone. I'm flesh.   5
My clouded reflection eyes me
like a bird of prey, the profile of night
slanted against morning. I turn
this way — the stone lets me go.
I turn that way — I'm inside   10
the Vietnam Veterans Memorial
again, depending on the light
to make a difference.
I go down the 58,022 names,
half-expecting to find   15
my own in letters like smoke.
I touch the name Andrew Johnson;
I see the booby trap's white flash.
Names shimmer on a woman's blouse
but when she walks away   20
the names stay on the wall.
Brushstrokes flash, a red bird's
wings cutting across my stare.
The sky. A plane in the sky.
A white vet's image floats   25
closer to me, then his pale eyes
look through mine. I'm a window.
He's lost his right arm
inside the stone. In the black mirror
a woman's trying to erase names: 30
No, she's brushing a boy's hair.

(1988)

Exploring the Text

1. What is the effect of the mirror imagery in the poem?
2. How does the juxtaposition of stone and flesh in line 5 contribute to the meaning of the poem?
3. How would you describe the tone created by the imagery of lines 6–8?
4. Why is the poem titled "Facing It"? Has the speaker found peace? Explain.
5. Does this poem make an argument or is it solely a personal reflection? Explain your answer.
6. In an interview with the *New York Times*, Komunyakaa said that his life was a "healing process from the two places: Bogalusa and Vietnam." How does this poem read as a statement of the healing process?

TIM O'BRIEN

Tim O'Brien (b. 1946) grew up in a small town in Minnesota. In 1968, he received a BA from Macalester College and, soon thereafter, a draft notice. He served as a soldier in the Vietnam War and wrote about his experiences in his memoir, *If I Die in a Combat Zone* (1973). O'Brien won the National Book Award in 1979 for a novel about the war, *Going after Cacciato*.

On the Rainy River

"On the Rainy River" is from *The Things They Carried* (1990), a work of fiction that O'Brien based on his war experiences and in which he placed himself as the protagonist.

This is one story I've never told before. Not to anyone. Not to my parents, not to my brother or sister, not even to my wife. To go into it, I've always thought, would only cause embarrassment for all of us, a sudden need to be elsewhere, which is the natural response to a confession. Even now, I'll admit, the story makes me squirm. For more than twenty years I've had to live with it, feeling the shame, trying to push it away, and so by this act of remembrance, by putting the facts down on paper, I'm hoping to relieve at least some of the pressure on my dreams. Still, it's a hard story to tell. All of us, I suppose, like to believe that in a moral emergency we will behave like the heroes of our youth, bravely and forthrightly, without thought of personal loss or discredit. Certainly that was my conviction back in the summer of 1968. Tim O'Brien: a secret hero. The Lone Ranger. If the stakes ever became high enough — if the evil were evil enough, if the good were good enough — I would simply tap a secret reservoir of courage that had been accumulating inside me over the years. Courage, I seemed to think, comes to us in finite quantities, like an inheritance, and by being frugal and stashing it away and letting it earn interest, we steadily increase our moral capital in preparation for that day when the account must be drawn down. It was a comforting theory. It dispensed with all those bothersome little acts of daily courage; it offered hope and grace to the repetitive coward; it justified the past while amortizing the future.

In June of 1968, a month after graduating from Macalester College, I was drafted to fight a war I hated. I was twenty-one years old. Young, yes, and politically naive, but even so the American war in Vietnam seemed to me wrong. Certain blood was being shed for uncertain reasons. I saw no unity of purpose, no consensus on matters of philosophy or history or law. The very facts were shrouded in uncertainty: Was it a civil war? A war of national liberation or simple aggression? Who started it, and when, and why? What really happened to the USS *Maddox* on that dark night in the Gulf of Tonkin? Was Ho Chi Minh a Communist stooge, or a nationalist savior, or both, or neither? What about the Geneva Accords? What about SEATO and the Cold War? What about dominoes? America was divided on these and a thousand other issues, and the debate had spilled out across the floor of the United States Senate and into the streets, and smart men in pinstripes could not agree on even the most fundamental matters of public policy. The only certainty that summer was moral confusion. It was my view then, and still is, that you don't make war without knowing why. Knowledge, of course, is always imperfect, but it seemed to me that when a nation goes to war it must have reasonable confidence in the justice and imperative of its cause. You can't fix your mistakes. Once people are dead, you can't make them undead.

In any case those were my convictions, and back in college I had taken a modest stand against the war. Nothing radical, no hothead stuff, just ringing a few doorbells for Gene McCarthy, composing a few tedious, uninspired editorials for the campus newspaper. Oddly, though, it was almost entirely an intellectual activity. I brought some energy to it, of course, but it was the energy that accompanies almost any abstract endeavor; I felt no personal danger; I felt no sense of an impending crisis in my life. Stupidly, with a kind of smug removal that I can't begin to fathom, I assumed that the problems of killing and dying did not fall within my special province.

The draft notice arrived on June 17, 1968. It was a humid afternoon, I remember, cloudy and very quiet, and I'd just come in from a round of golf. My mother and father were having lunch out in the kitchen. I remember opening up the letter, scanning the first few lines, feeling the blood go thick behind my eyes. I remember a sound in my head. It wasn't thinking, just a silent howl. A million things all at once — I was too *good* for this war. Too smart, too compassionate, too everything. It couldn't happen. I was above it. I had the world . . . [licked] — Phi Beta Kappa and summa cum laude and president of the student body and a full-ride scholarship for grad studies at Harvard. A mistake maybe — a foul-up in the paperwork. I was no soldier. I hated Boy Scouts. I hated camping out. I hated dirt and tents and mosquitoes. The sight of blood made me queasy, and I couldn't tolerate authority, and I didn't know a rifle from a slingshot. I was a *liberal*, for Christ sake: If they needed fresh bodies, why not draft some back-to-the-stone-age hawk? Or some dumb jingo in his hard hat and Bomb Hanoi button, or one of LBJ's pretty daughters, or [General William] Westmoreland's whole handsome family — nephews and nieces and baby grandson. There should be a law, I thought. If you support a war, if you think it's worth the price, that's fine, but you have to put your own precious fluids on the line. You have to head for the front and hook up with an infantry unit and help spill the blood. And you have to bring along your wife, or your kids, or your lover. A *law*, I thought.

I remember the rage in my stomach. Later it burned down to a smoldering self-pity, then to numbness. At dinner that night my father asked what my plans were. "Nothing," I said. "Wait." 5

I spent the summer of 1968 working in an Armour meatpacking plant in my hometown of Worthington, Minnesota. The plant specialized in pork products, and for eight hours a day I stood on a quarter-mile assembly line — more properly, a disassembly line — removing blood clots from the necks of dead pigs. My job title, I believe, was Declotter. After slaughter, the hogs were decapitated, split down the length of the belly, pried open, eviscerated, and strung up by the hind hocks on a high conveyer belt. Then gravity took over. By the time a carcass reached my spot on the line, the fluids had mostly drained out, everything except for thick clots of blood in the neck and upper chest cavity. To remove the stuff, I used a kind of water gun. The machine was heavy, maybe eighty pounds, and was suspended from the ceiling by a heavy rubber cord. There was some bounce to it, an elastic up-and-down give, and the trick was to maneuver the gun with your whole body, not lifting with the arms, just letting the rubber cord do the work for you. At one end was a trigger; at the muzzle end was a small nozzle and a steel roller brush. As a carcass passed by, you'd lean forward and swing the gun up against the clots and squeeze the trigger, all in one motion, and the brush would whirl and water would come shooting out and you'd hear a quick splattering sound as the clots dissolved into a fine red mist. It was not pleasant work. Goggles were a necessity, and a rubber apron, but even so it was like standing for eight hours a day under a lukewarm blood-shower. At night I'd go home smelling of pig. It wouldn't go away. Even after a hot bath, scrubbing hard, the stink was always there — like old bacon, or sausage, a dense greasy pig-stink that soaked deep into my skin and hair. Among other things, I remember, it was tough getting dates that summer. I felt isolated; I spent a lot of time alone. And there was also that draft notice tucked away in my wallet.

In the evenings I'd sometimes borrow my father's car and drive aimlessly around town, feeling sorry for myself, thinking about the war and the pig factory and how my life seemed to be collapsing toward slaughter. I felt paralyzed. All around me the options seemed to be narrowing, as if I were hurtling down a huge black funnel, the whole world squeezing in tight. There was no happy way out. The government had ended most graduate school deferments; the waiting lists for the National Guard and Reserves were impossibly long; my health was solid; I didn't qualify for CO [conscientious objector] status — no religious grounds, no history as a pacifist. Moreover, I could not claim to be opposed to war as a matter of general principle. There were occasions, I believed, when a nation was justified in using military force to achieve its ends, to stop a Hitler or some comparable evil, and I told myself that in such circumstances

I would've willingly marched off to the battle. The problem, though, was that a draft board did not let you choose your war.

Beyond all this, or at the very center, was the raw fact of terror. I did not want to die. Not ever. But certainly not then, not there, not in a wrong war. Driving up Main Street, past the courthouse and the Ben Franklin store, I sometimes felt the fear spreading inside me like weeds. I imagined myself dead. I imagined myself doing things I could not do — charging an enemy position, taking aim at another human being.

At some point in mid-July I began thinking seriously about Canada. The border lay a few hundred miles north, an eight-hour drive. Both my conscience and my instincts were telling me to make a break for it, just take off and run like hell and never stop. In the beginning the idea seemed purely abstract, the word Canada printing itself out in my head; but after a time I could see particular shapes and images, the sorry details of my own future — a hotel room in Winnipeg, a battered old suitcase, my father's eyes as I tried to explain myself over the telephone. I could almost hear his voice, and my mother's. Run, I'd think. Then I'd think, Impossible. Then a second later I'd think, *Run*.

It was a kind of schizophrenia. A moral split. I couldn't make up my mind. I feared the war, yes, but I also feared exile. I was afraid of walking away from my own life, my friends and my family, my whole history, everything that mattered to me. I feared losing the respect of my parents. I feared the law. I feared ridicule and censure. My hometown was a conservative little spot on the prairie, a place where tradition counted, and it was easy to imagine people sitting around a table down at the old Gobbler Café on Main Street, coffee cups poised, the conversation slowly zeroing in on the young O'Brien kid, how the damned sissy had taken off for Canada. At night, when I couldn't sleep, I'd sometimes carry on fierce arguments with those people. I'd be screaming at them, telling them how much I detested their blind, thoughtless, automatic acquiescence to it all, their simple-minded patriotism, their prideful ignorance, their love-it-or-leave-it platitudes, how they were sending me off to fight a war they didn't understand and didn't want to understand. I held them responsible. By God, yes, I *did*. All of them — I held them personally and individually responsible — the polyestered Kiwanis boys, the merchants and farmers, the pious churchgoers, the chatty housewives, the PTA and the Lions club and the Veterans of Foreign Wars and the fine upstanding gentry out at the country club. They didn't know Bao Dai from the man in the moon. They didn't know history. They didn't know the first thing about Diem's tyranny, or the nature of Vietnamese nationalism, or the long colonialism of the French — this was all too damned complicated, it required some reading — but no matter, it was a war to stop the Communists, plain and simple, which was how they liked things, and you were a . . . [traitor] if you had second thoughts about killing or dying for plain and simple reasons.

I was bitter, sure. But it was so much more than that. The emotions went from outrage to terror to bewilderment to guilt to sorrow and then back again to outrage. I felt a sickness inside me. Real disease.

Most of this I've told before, or at least hinted at, but what I have never told is the full truth. How I cracked. How at work one morning, standing on the pig line,

10

I felt something break open in my chest. I don't know what it was. I'll never know. But it was real, I know that much, it was a physical rupture—a cracking-leaking-popping feeling. I remember dropping my water gun. Quickly, almost without thought, I took off my apron and walked out of the plant and drove home. It was midmorning, I remember, and the house was empty. Down in my chest there was still that leaking sensation, something very warm and precious spilling out, and I was covered with blood and hog-stink, and for a long while I just concentrated on holding myself together. I remember taking a hot shower. I remember packing a suitcase and carrying it out to the kitchen, standing very still for a few minutes, looking carefully at the familiar objects all around me. The old chrome toaster, the telephone, the pink and white Formica on the kitchen counters. The room was full of bright sunshine. Everything sparkled. My house, I thought. My life. I'm not sure how long I stood there, but later I scribbled out a short note to my parents.

What it said, exactly, I don't recall now. Something vague. Taking off, will call, love Tim.

I drove north.

It's a blur now, as it was then, and all I remember is a sense of high velocity and the feel of the steering wheel in my hands. I was riding on adrenaline. A giddy feeling, in a way, except there was the dreamy edge of impossibility to it—like running a dead-end maze—no way out—it couldn't come to a happy conclusion and yet I was doing it anyway because it was all I could think of to do. It was pure light, fast and mindless. I had no plan. Just hit the border at high speed and crash through and keep on running. Near dusk I passed through Bemidji, then turned northeast toward International Falls. I spent the night in the car behind a closed-down gas station a half mile from the border. In the morning, after gassing up, I headed straight west along the Rainy River, which separates Minnesota from Canada, and which for me separated one life from another. The land was mostly wilderness. Here and there I passed a motel or bait shop, but otherwise the country unfolded in great sweeps of pine and birch and sumac. Though it was still August, the air already had the smell of October, football season, piles of yellow-red leaves, everything crisp and clean. I remember a huge blue sky. Off to my right was the Rainy River, wide as a lake in places, and beyond the Rainy River was Canada. 15

For a while I just drove, not aiming at anything, then in the late morning I began looking for a place to lie low for a day or two. I was exhausted, and scared sick, and around noon I pulled into an old fishing resort called the Tip Top Lodge. Actually it was not a lodge at all, just eight or nine tiny yellow cabins clustered on a peninsula that jutted northward into the Rainy River. The place was in sorry shape. There was a dangerous wooden dock, an old minnow tank, a flimsy tar paper boathouse along the shore. The main building, which stood in a cluster of pines on high ground, seemed to lean heavily to one side, like a cripple, the roof sagging toward Canada. Briefly, I thought about turning around, just giving up, but then I got out of the car and walked up to the front porch.

The man who opened the door that day is the hero of my life. How do I say this without sounding sappy? Blurt it out—the man saved me. He offered exactly what I needed, without questions, without any words at all. He took me in. He was there at the critical time — a silent, watchful presence. Six days later, when it ended, I was unable to find a proper way to thank him, and I never have, and so, if nothing else, this story represents a small gesture of gratitude twenty years overdue.

Even after two decades I can close my eyes and return to that porch at the Tip Top Lodge. I can see the old guy staring at me. Elroy Berdahl: eighty-one years old, skinny and shrunken and mostly bald. He wore a flannel shirt and brown work pants. In one hand, I remember, he carried a green apple, a small paring knife in the other. His eyes had the bluish gray color of a razor blade, the same polished shine, and as he peered up at me I felt a strange sharpness, almost painful, a cutting sensation, as if his gaze were somehow slicing me open. In part, no doubt, it was my own sense of guilt, but even so I'm absolutely certain that the old man took one look and went right to the heart of things — a kid in trouble. When I asked for a room, Elroy made a little clicking sound with his tongue. He nodded, led me out to one of the cabins, and dropped a key in my hand. I remember smiling at him. I also remember wishing I hadn't. The old man shook his head as if to tell me it wasn't worth the bother.

"Dinner at five-thirty," he said. "You eat fish?"

"Anything," I said.

Elroy grunted and said, "I'll bet." 20

We spent six days together at the Tip Top Lodge. Just the two of us. Tourist season was over, and there were no boats on the river, and the wilderness seemed to withdraw into a great permanent stillness. Over those six days Elroy Berdahl and I took most of our meals together. In the mornings we sometimes went out on long hikes into the woods, and at night we played Scrabble or listened to records or sat reading in front of his big stone fireplace. At times I felt the awkwardness of an intruder, but Elroy accepted me into his quiet routine without fuss or ceremony. He took my presence for granted, the same way he might've sheltered a stray cat — no wasted sighs or pity — and there was never any talk about it. Just the opposite. What I remember more than anything is the man's willful, almost ferocious silence. In all that time together, all those hours, he never asked the obvious questions: Why was I there? Why alone? Why so preoccupied? If Elroy was curious about any of this, he was careful never to put it into words.

My hunch, though, is that he already knew. At least the basics. After all, it was 1968, and guys were burning draft cards, and Canada was just a boat ride away. Elroy Berdahl was no hick. His bedroom, I remember, was cluttered with books and newspapers. He killed me at the Scrabble board, barely concentrating, and on those occasions when speech was necessary he had a way of compressing large thoughts into small, cryptic packets of language. One evening, just at sunset, he pointed up at an owl circling over the violet-lighted forest to the west.

"Hey, O'Brien," he said. "There's Jesus."

The man was sharp — he didn't miss much. Those razor eyes. Now and then he'd 25 catch me staring out at the river, at the far shore, and I could almost hear the tumblers clicking in his head. Maybe I'm wrong, but I doubt it.

One thing for certain, he knew I was in desperate trouble. And he knew I couldn't talk about it. The wrong word — or even the right word — and I would've disappeared. I was wired and jittery. My skin felt too tight. After supper one evening I vomited and went back to my cabin and lay down for a few moments and then vomited again; another time, in the middle of the afternoon, I began sweating and couldn't shut it off. I went through whole days feeling dizzy with sorrow. I couldn't sleep; I couldn't lie still. At night I'd toss around in bed, half awake, half dreaming, imagining how I'd sneak down to the beach and quietly push one of the old man's boats out into the river and start paddling my way toward Canada. There were times when I thought I'd gone off the psychic edge. I couldn't tell up from down, I was just falling, and late in the night I'd lie there watching weird pictures spin through my head. Getting chased by the Border Patrol — helicopters and searchlights and barking dogs — I'd be crashing through the woods, I'd be down on my hands and knees — people shouting out my name — the law closing in on all sides — my hometown draft board and the FBI and the Royal Canadian Mounted Police. It all seemed crazy and impossible. Twenty-one years old, an ordinary kid with all the ordinary dreams and ambitions, and all I wanted was to live the life I was born to — a mainstream life — I loved baseball and hamburgers and cherry Cokes — and now I was off on the margins of exile, leaving my country forever, and it seemed so impossible and terrible and sad.

I'm not sure how I made it through those six days. Most of it I can't remember. On two or three afternoons, to pass some time, I helped Elroy get the place ready for winter, sweeping down the cabins and hauling in the boats, little chores that kept my body moving. The days were cool and bright. The nights were very dark. One morning the old man showed me how to split and stack firewood, and for several hours we just worked in silence out behind his house. At one point, I remember, Elroy put down his maul and looked at me for a long time, his lips drawn as if framing a difficult question, but then he shook his head and went back to work. The man's self-control was amazing. He never pried. He never put me in a position that required lies or denials. To an extent, I suppose, his reticence was typical of that part of Minnesota, where privacy still held value, and even if I'd been walking around with some horrible deformity — four arms and three heads — I'm sure the old man would've talked about everything except those extra arms and heads. Simple politeness was part of it. But even more than that, I think, the man understood that words were insufficient. The problem had gone beyond discussion. During that long summer I'd been over and over the various arguments, all the pros and cons, and it was no longer a question that could be decided by an act of pure reason. Intellect had come up against emotion. My conscience told me to run, but some irrational and powerful force was resisting, like a weight pushing me toward the war. What it came down to, stupidly, was a sense of shame. Hot, stupid shame. I did not want people to think badly of me. Not my parents, not my brother and sister, not even the folks down at the Gobbler Café. I was ashamed to be there at the Tip Top Lodge. I was ashamed of my conscience, ashamed to be doing the right thing.

Some of this Elroy must've understood. Not the details, of course, but the plain fact of crisis.

Although the old man never confronted me about it, there was one occasion when he came close to forcing the whole thing out into the open. It was early evening, and we'd just finished supper, and over coffee and dessert I asked him about my bill, how much I owed so far. For a long while the old man squinted down at the tablecloth.

"Well, the basic rate," he said, "is fifty bucks a night. Not counting meals. This makes four nights, right?"

I nodded. I had three hundred and twelve dollars in my wallet.

Elroy kept his eyes on the tablecloth. "Now that's an on-season price. To be fair, I suppose we should knock it down a peg or two." He leaned back in his chair. "What's a reasonable number, you figure?"

"I don't know," I said. "Forty?"

"Forty's good. Forty a night. Then we tack on food — say another hundred? Two hundred sixty total?"

"I guess."

He raised his eyebrows. "Too much?"

"No, that's fair. It's fine. Tomorrow, though . . . I think I'd better take off tomorrow."

Elroy shrugged and began clearing the table. For a time he fussed with the dishes, whistling to himself as if the subject had been settled. After a second he slapped his hands together.

"You know what we forgot?" he said. "We forgot wages. Those odd jobs you done. What we have to do, we have to figure out what your time's worth. Your last job — how much did you pull in an hour?"

"Not enough," I said.

"A bad one?"

"Yes. Pretty bad."

Slowly then, without intending any long sermon, I told him about my days at the pig plant. It began as a straight recitation of the facts, but before I could stop myself I was talking about the blood clots and the water gun and how the smell had soaked into my skin and how I couldn't wash it away. I went on for a long time. I told him about wild hogs squealing in my dreams, the sounds of butchery, slaughterhouse sounds, and how I'd sometimes wake up with that greasy pig-stink in my throat.

When I was finished, Elroy nodded at me.

"Well, to be honest," he said, "when you first showed up here, I wondered about all that. The aroma, I mean. Smelled like you was awful damned fond of pork chops." The old man almost smiled. He made a snuffling sound, then sat down with a pencil and a piece of paper. "So what'd this crud job pay? Ten bucks an hour? Fifteen?"

"Less."

Elroy shook his head. "Let's make it fifteen. You put in twenty-five hours here, easy. That's three hundred seventy-five bucks total wages. We subtract the two hundred sixty for food and lodging, I still owe you a hundred and fifteen."

He took four fifties out of his shirt pocket and laid them on the table.

"Call it even," he said.

"No."

"Pick it up. Get yourself a haircut."

The money lay on the table for the rest of the evening. It was still there when I went back to my cabin. In the morning, though, I found an envelope tacked to my door. Inside were the four fifties and a two-word note that said EMERGENCY FUND.

The man knew.

Looking back after twenty years, I sometimes wonder if the events of that summer didn't happen in some other dimension, a place where your life exists before you've lived it, and where it goes afterward. None of it ever seemed real. During my time at the Tip Top Lodge I had the feeling that I'd slipped out of my own skin, hovering a few feet away while some poor yo-yo with my name and face tried to make his way toward a future he didn't understand and didn't want. Even now I can see myself as I was then. It's like watching an old home movie: I'm young and tan and fit. I've got hair — lots of it. I don't smoke or drink. I'm wearing faded blue jeans and a white polo shirt. I can see myself sitting on Elroy Berdahl's dock near dusk one evening, the sky a bright shimmering pink, and I'm finishing up a letter to my parents that tells what I'm about to do and why I'm doing it and how sorry I am that I'd never found the courage to talk to them about it. I ask them not to be angry. I try to explain some of my feelings, but there aren't enough words, and so I just say that it's a thing that has to be done. At the end of the letter I talk about the vacations we used to take up in this north country, at a place called Whitefish Lake, and how the scenery here reminds me of those good times. I tell them I'm fine. I tell them I'll write again from Winnipeg or Montreal or wherever I end up.

On my last full day, the sixth day, the old man took me out fishing on the Rainy River.   55
The afternoon was sunny and cold. A stiff breeze came in from the north, and I remember how the little fourteen-foot boat made sharp rocking motions as we pushed off from the dock. The current was fast. All around us, I remember, there was a vastness to the world, an unpeopled rawness, just the trees and the sky and the water reaching out toward nowhere. The air had the brittle scent of October.

For ten or fifteen minutes Elroy held a course upstream, the river choppy and silver-gray, then he turned straight north and put the engine on full throttle. I felt the bow lift beneath me. I remember the wind in my ears, the sound of the old outboard Evinrude. For a time I didn't pay attention to anything, just feeling the cold spray against my face, but then it occurred to me that at some point we must've passed into Canadian waters, across that dotted line between two different worlds, and I remember a sudden tightness in my chest as I looked up and watched the far shore come at me. This wasn't a daydream. It was tangible and real. As we came in toward land, Elroy cut the engine, letting the boat fishtail lightly about twenty yards off shore. The old man didn't look at me or speak. Bending down, he opened up his tackle box and busied himself with a bobber and a piece of wire leader, humming to himself, his eyes down.

It struck me then that he must've planned it. I'll never be certain, of course, but I think he meant to bring me up against the realities, to guide me across the river and to take me to the edge and to stand a kind of vigil as I chose a life for myself.

I remember staring at the old man, then at my hands, then at Canada. The shoreline was dense with brush and timber. I could see tiny red berries on the bushes. I could see a squirrel up in one of the birch trees, a big crow looking at me from a boulder along the river. That close — twenty yards — and I could see the delicate latticework of the leaves, the texture of the soil, the browned needles beneath the pines, the configurations of geology and human history. Twenty yards. I could've done it. I could've jumped and started swimming for my life. Inside me, in my chest, I felt a terrible squeezing pressure. Even now, as I write this, I can still feel that tightness. And I want you to feel it — the wind coming off the river, the waves, the silence, the wooded frontier. You're at the bow of a boat on the Rainy River. You're twenty-one years old, you're scared, and there's a hard squeezing pressure in your chest.

What would you do?

Would you jump? Would you feel pity for yourself? Would you think about your family and your childhood and your dreams and all you're leaving behind? Would it hurt? Would it feel like dying? Would you cry, as I did? 60

I tried to swallow it back. I tried to smile, except I was crying.

Now, perhaps, you can understand why I've never told this story before. It's not just the embarrassment of tears. That's part of it, no doubt, but what embarrasses me much more, and always will, is the paralysis that took my heart. A moral freeze: I couldn't decide, I couldn't act, I couldn't comport myself with even a pretense of modest human dignity.

All I could do was cry. Quietly, not bawling, just the chest-chokes.

At the rear of the boat Elroy Berdahl pretended not to notice. He held a fishing rod in his hands, his head bowed to hide his eyes. He kept humming a soft, monotonous little tune. Everywhere, it seemed, in the trees and water and sky, a great worldwide sadness came pressing down on me, a crushing sorrow, sorrow like I had never known it before. And what was so sad, I realized, was that Canada had become a pitiful fantasy. Silly and hopeless. It was no longer a possibility. Right then, with the shore so close, I understood that I would not do what I should do. I would not swim away from my hometown and my country and my life. I would not be brave. That old image of myself as a hero, as a man of conscience and courage, all that was just a threadbare pipe dream. Bobbing there on the Rainy River, looking back at the Minnesota shore, I felt a sudden swell of helplessness come over me, a drowning sensation, as if I had toppled overboard and was being swept away by the silver waves. Chunks of my own history flashed by. I saw a seven-year-old boy in a white cowboy hat and a Lone Ranger mask and a pair of holstered six-shooters; I saw a twelve-year-old Little League shortstop pivoting to turn a double play; I saw a sixteen-year-old kid decked out for his first prom, looking spiffy in a white tux and a black bow tie, his hair cut short and flat, his shoes freshly polished. My whole life seemed to spill out into the river, swirling away from me, everything I had ever been or ever wanted to be. I couldn't get my breath; I couldn't stay afloat; I couldn't tell which way to swim. A hallucination, I suppose, but it was as real as anything I would ever feel. I saw my parents calling to me from the far shoreline. I saw my brother and sister, all the townsfolk, the mayor and the entire Chamber of Commerce and all my old teachers and girlfriends and high school buddies. Like some weird sporting event: everybody screaming from the sidelines, rooting me on — a loud stadium roar. Hotdogs and popcorn — stadium smells, stadium heat. A squad of cheerleaders did cartwheels along the banks of the Rainy River; they had megaphones and pompoms and smooth brown thighs. The crowd swayed left and right. A marching band played fight songs. All my aunts and uncles were there, and Abraham Lincoln, and Saint George, and a nine-year-old girl named Linda who had died of a brain tumor back in fifth grade, and several members of the United States Senate, and a blind poet scribbling notes, and LBJ, and Huck Finn, and Abbie Hoffman, and all the dead soldiers back from the grave, and the many thousands who were later to die — villagers with terrible burns, little kids without arms or legs — yes, and the Joint Chiefs of Staff were there, and a couple of popes, and a first lieutenant named Jimmy Cross, and the last surviving veteran of the American Civil War, and Jane Fonda dressed up as Barbarella, and an old man sprawled beside a pigpen, and my grandfather, and Gary Cooper, and a kind-faced woman carrying an umbrella and a copy of Plato's *Republic*, and a million ferocious citizens waving flags of all shapes and colors — people in hard hats, people in headbands — they were all whooping and chanting and urging me toward one shore or the other. I saw faces from my distant past and distant future. My wife was there. My unborn daughter waved at me, and my two sons hopped up and down, and a drill sergeant named Blyton sneered and shot up a finger and shook his head. There was a choir in bright purple robes. There was a cabbie from the Bronx. There was a slim young man I would one day kill with a hand grenade along a red clay trail outside the village of My Khe.

The little aluminum boat rocked softly beneath me. There was the wind and the sky. 65

I tried to will myself overboard.

I gripped the edge of the boat and leaned forward and thought, *Now*.

I did try. It just wasn't possible.

All those eyes on me — the town, the whole universe — and I couldn't risk the embarrassment. It was as if there were an audience to my life, that swirl of faces along the river, and in my head I could hear people screaming at me. Traitor! they yelled. Turncoat! . . . I felt myself blush. I couldn't tolerate it. I couldn't endure the mockery, or the disgrace, or the patriotic ridicule. Even in my imagination, the shore just twenty yards away, I couldn't make myself be brave. It had nothing to do with morality. Embarrassment, that's all it was.

And right then I submitted. 70

I would go to the war — I would kill and maybe die — because I was embarrassed not to.

That was the sad thing. And so I sat in the bow of the boat and cried.

It was loud now. Loud, hard crying.

Elroy Berdahl remained quiet. He kept fishing. He worked his line with the tips of his fingers, patiently, squinting out at his red and white bobber on the Rainy River. His eyes were flat and impassive. He didn't speak. He was simply there, like the river and the late-summer sun. And yet by his presence, his mute watchfulness, he made it real. He was the true audience. He was a witness, like God, or like the gods, who look on in absolute silence as we live our lives, as we make our choices or fail to make them.

"Ain't biting," he said.   75

Then after a time the old man pulled in his line and turned the boat back toward Minnesota.

I don't remember saying goodbye. That last night we had dinner together, and I went to bed early, and in the morning Elroy fixed breakfast for me. When I told him I'd be leaving, the old man nodded as if he already knew. He looked down at the table and smiled.

At some point later in the morning it's possible that we shook hands—I just don't remember—but I do know that by the time I'd finished packing the old man had disappeared. Around noon, when I took my suitcase out to the car, I noticed that his old black pickup truck was no longer parked in front of the house. I went inside and waited for a while, but I felt a bone certainty that he wouldn't be back. In a way, I thought, it was appropriate. I washed up the breakfast dishes, left his two hundred dollars on the kitchen counter, got into the car, and drove south toward home.

The day was cloudy. I passed through towns with familiar names, through the pine forests and down to the prairie, and then to Vietnam, where I was a soldier, and then home again. I survived, but it's not a happy ending. I was a coward. I went to the war.

(1990)

Exploring the Text

1. What is the rhetorical effect of the first seven sentences? Based on the opening, what were your expectations of the story to follow?
2. This is a fictional story in which Tim O'Brien uses himself—or a character by the same name—as the protagonist. Describe how you determine which details are factual and which are imaginative. What is the effect of mixing fact and fiction?
3. Reread the questions in paragraph 2. Are they rhetorical? What purpose do they serve? Could we ask similar questions about events today? Explain your response.
4. What is the narrator's conflict (par. 9)?
5. What purpose does Elroy Berdahl serve in this story? Does he seem realistic to you? Explain your answer.
6. Why does O'Brien address the reader directly in paragraphs 58–60? How would you answer his questions?
7. Identify the rhetorical strategies O'Brien uses in paragraph 64. What are the effects of these strategies in this long paragraph?
8. If you have read *The Adventures of Huckleberry Finn* by Mark Twain, compare Huck's conflict about doing what he has been taught is "the right thing"—turning Jim in—with O'Brien's statement at the end of paragraph 27. How are the situations of the two protagonists similar?

JUDITH ORTIZ COFER

Poet, novelist, and essayist Judith Ortiz Cofer was born in Puerto Rico in 1952 and grew up in New Jersey. She is currently the Regents' and Franklin Professor of English and Creative Writing at the University of Georgia. Among her many publications are the young adult novel *If I Could Fly* (2011), the novel *The Meaning of Consuelo* (2004), her memoirs *Silent Dancing: A Partial Remembrance of a Puerto Rican Childhood* (1990) and *Woman in Front of the Sun: Becoming a Writer* (2000), and her collection of prose and poetry, *The Latin Deli* (1993). She has won many awards, including the Anisfield-Wolf Book Award in Race Relations and the Americas Award for Children's and Young Adult Literature; she was nominated for the Pulitzer Prize in 1989.

The Myth of the Latin Woman
I Just Met a Girl Named María

In the following selection, originally published in *Glamour* in 1992, Cofer examines the impact of stereotyping.

On a bus trip to London from Oxford University where I was earning some graduate credits one summer, a young man, obviously fresh from a pub, spotted me and as if struck by inspiration went down on his knees in the aisle. With both hands over his heart he broke into an Irish tenor's rendition of "María" from *West Side Story*.[1] My politely amused fellow passengers gave his lovely voice the round of gentle applause it deserved. Though I was not quite as amused, I managed my version of an English smile: no show of teeth, no extreme contortions of the facial muscles — I was at this time of my life practicing reserve and cool. Oh, that British control, how I coveted it. But María had followed me to London, reminding me of a prime fact of my life; you can leave the Island, master the English language, and travel as far as you can, but if you are a Latina, especially one like me who so obviously belongs to Rita Moreno's gene pool, the Island travels with you.

This is sometimes a very good thing — it may win you that extra minute of someone's attention. But with some people, the same things can make *you* an island — not so much a tropical paradise as an Alcatraz, a place nobody wants to visit. As a Puerto Rican girl growing up in the United States and wanting like most children to "belong," I resented the stereotype that my Hispanic appearance called forth from many people I met.

---

[1] *West Side Story* was a Broadway musical (1957) and then a feature film (1961). Based on *Romeo and Juliet*, the story deals with the conflicts between two New York City gangs — a Puerto Rican gang and a white ethnic gang. The Puerto Rican actress Rita Moreno, mentioned later in this paragraph, had a major role in the movie. — Eds.

Our family lived in a large urban center in New Jersey during the sixties, where life was designed as a microcosm of my parents' casas on the island. We spoke in Spanish, we ate Puerto Rican food bought at the bodega, and we practiced strict Catholicism complete with Saturday confession and Sunday mass at a church where our parents were accommodated into a one-hour Spanish mass slot, performed by a Chinese priest trained as a missionary for Latin America.

As a girl I was kept under strict surveillance, since virtue and modesty were, by cultural equation, the same as family honor. As a teenager I was instructed on how to behave as a proper señorita. But it was a conflicting message girls got, since the Puerto Rican mothers also encouraged their daughters to look and act like women and to dress in clothes our Anglo friends and their mothers found too "mature" for our age. It was, and is, cultural, yet I often felt humiliated when I appeared at an American friend's party wearing a dress more suitable to a semiformal than to a playroom birthday celebration. At Puerto Rican festivities, neither the music nor the colors we wore could be too loud. I still experience a vague sense of letdown when I'm invited to a "party" and it turns out to be a marathon conversation in hushed tones rather than a fiesta with salsa, laughter, and dancing—the kind of celebration I remember from my childhood.

I remember Career Day in our high school, when teachers told us to come dressed as if for a job interview. It quickly became obvious that to the barrio girls, "dressing up" sometimes meant wearing ornate jewelry and clothing that would be more appropriate (by mainstream standards) for the company Christmas party than as daily office attire. That morning I had agonized in front of my closet, trying to figure out what a "career girl" would wear because, essentially, except for Marlo Thomas on TV, I had no models on which to base my decision. I knew how to dress for school: at the Catholic school I attended we all wore uniforms; I knew how to dress for Sunday mass, and I knew what dresses to wear for parties at my relatives' homes. Though I do not recall the precise details of my Career Day outfit, it must have been a composite of the above choices. But I remember a comment my friend (an Italian-American) made in later years that coalesced my impressions of that day. She said that at the business school she was attending the Puerto Rican girls always stood out for wearing "everything at once." She meant, of course, too much jewelry, too many accessories. On that day at school, we were simply made the negative models by the nuns who were themselves not credible fashion experts to any of us. But it was painfully obvious to me that to the others, in their tailored skirts and silk blouses, we must have seemed "hopeless" and "vulgar." Though I now know that most adolescents feel out of step much of the time, I also know that for the Puerto Rican girls of my generation that sense was intensified. The way our teachers and classmates looked at us that day in school was just a taste of the culture clash that awaited us in the real world, where prospective employers and men on the street would often misinterpret our tight skirts and jingling bracelets as a come-on.

Mixed cultural signals have perpetuated certain stereotypes—for example, that of the Hispanic woman as the "Hot Tamale" or sexual firebrand. It is a one-dimensional view that the media have found easy to promote. In their special vocabulary, advertisers have designated "sizzling" and "smoldering" as the adjectives of choice for describing

5

not only the foods but also the women of Latin America. From conversations in my house I recall hearing about the harassment that Puerto Rican women endured in factories where the "boss men" talked to them as if sexual innuendo was all they understood and, worse, often gave them the choice of submitting to advances or being fired.

It is custom, however, not chromosomes, that leads us to choose scarlet over pale pink. As young girls, we were influenced in our decisions about clothes and colors by the women — older sisters and mothers who had grown up on a tropical island where the natural environment was a riot of primary colors, where showing your skin was one way to keep cool as well as to look sexy. Most important of all, on the island, women perhaps felt freer to dress and move more provocatively, since, in most cases, they were protected by the traditions, mores, and laws of a Spanish/Catholic system of morality and machismo whose main rule was: *You may look at my sister, but if you touch her I will kill you.* The extended family and church structure could provide a young woman with a circle of safety in her small pueblo on the island; if a man "wronged" a girl, everyone would close in to save her family honor.

This is what I have gleaned from my discussions as an adult with older Puerto Rican women. They have told me about dressing in their best party clothes on Saturday nights and going to the town's plaza to promenade with their girlfriends in front of the boys they liked. The males were thus given an opportunity to admire the women and to express their admiration in the form of *piropos*: erotically charged street poems they composed on the spot. I have been subjected to a few piropos while visiting the Island, and they can be outrageous, although custom dictates that they must never cross into obscenity. This ritual, as I understand it, also entails a show of studied indifference on the woman's part; if she is "decent," she must not acknowledge the man's impassioned words. So I do understand how things can be lost in translation. When a Puerto Rican girl dressed in her idea of what is attractive meets a man from the mainstream culture who has been trained to react to certain types of clothing as a sexual signal, a clash is likely to take place. The line I first heard based on this aspect of the myth happened when the boy who took me to my first formal dance leaned over to plant a sloppy overeager kiss painfully on my mouth, and when I didn't respond with sufficient passion said in a resentful tone: "I thought you Latin girls were supposed to mature early" — my first instance of being thought of as a fruit or vegetable — I was supposed to *ripen*, not just grow into womanhood like other girls.

It is surprising to some of my professional friends that some people, including those who should know better, still put others "in their place." Though rarer, these incidents are still commonplace in my life. It happened to me most recently during a stay at a very classy metropolitan hotel favored by young professional couples for their weddings. Late one evening after the theater, as I walked toward my room with my new colleague (a woman with whom I was coordinating an arts program), a middle-aged man in a tuxedo, a young girl in satin and lace on his arm, stepped directly into our path. With his champagne glass extended toward me, he exclaimed, "Evita!"

Our way blocked, my companion and I listened as the man half-recited, half- 10
bellowed "Don't Cry for Me, Argentina." When he finished, the young girl said: "How about a round of applause for my daddy?" We complied, hoping this would bring the silly spectacle to a close. I was becoming aware that our little group was attracting

the attention of the other guests. "Daddy" must have perceived this too, and he once more barred the way as we tried to walk past him. He began to shout-sing a ditty to the tune of "La Bamba" — except the lyrics were about a girl named María whose exploits all rhymed with her name and gonorrhea. The girl kept saying "Oh, Daddy" and looking at me with pleading eyes. She wanted me to laugh along with the others. My companion and I stood silently waiting for the man to end his offensive song. When he finished, I looked not at him but at his daughter. I advised her calmly never to ask her father what he had done in the army. Then I walked between them and to my room. My friend complimented me on my cool handling of the situation. I confessed to her that I really had wanted to push the jerk into the swimming pool. I knew that this same man — probably a corporate executive, well educated, even worldly by most standards — would not have been likely to regale a white woman with a dirty song in public. He would perhaps have checked his impulse by assuming that she could be somebody's wife or mother, or at least *somebody* who might take offense. But to him, I was just an Evita or a María: merely a character in his cartoon-populated universe.

Because of my education and my proficiency with the English language, I have acquired many mechanisms for dealing with the anger I experience. This was not true for my parents, nor is it true for the many Latin women working at menial jobs who must put up with stereotypes about our ethnic group such as: "They make good domestics." This is another facet of the myth of the Latin woman in the United States. Its origin is simple to deduce. Work as domestics, waitressing, and factory jobs are all that's available to women with little English and few skills. The myth of the Hispanic menial has been sustained by the same media phenomenon that made "Mammy" from *Gone with the Wind* America's idea of the black woman for generations: María, the housemaid or counter girl, is now indelibly etched into the national psyche. The big and the little screens have presented us with the picture of the funny Hispanic maid, mispronouncing words and cooking up a spicy storm in a shiny California kitchen.

This media-engendered image of the Latina in the United States has been documented by feminist Hispanic scholars, who claim that such portrayals are partially responsible for the denial of opportunities for upward mobility among Latinas in the professions. I have a Chicana friend working on a Ph.D. in philosophy at a major university. She says her doctor still shakes his head in puzzled amazement at all the "big words" she uses. Since I do not wear my diplomas around my neck for all to see, I too have on occasion been sent to that "kitchen," where some think I obviously belong.

One such incident that has stayed with me, though I recognize it as a minor offense, happened on the day of my first public poetry reading. It took place in Miami in a boat-restaurant where we were having lunch before the event. I was nervous and excited as I walked in with my notebook in my hand. An older woman motioned me to her table. Thinking (foolish me) that she wanted me to autograph a copy of my brand-new slender volume of verse, I went over. She ordered a cup of coffee from me, assuming that I was the waitress. Easy enough to mistake my poems for menus, I suppose. I know that it wasn't an intentional act of cruelty, yet of all the good things that happened that day, I remember that scene most clearly, because it reminded me of what I had to overcome before anyone would take me seriously. In retrospect I understand that my anger gave my reading fire, that I have almost always taken doubts in my abilities as a challenge — and that the result is, most times, a feeling of satisfaction at having won a convert when I see the cold, appraising eyes warm to my words, the body language change, the smile that indicates that I have opened some avenue for communication. That day I read to that woman and her lowered eyes told me that she was embarrassed at her little faux pas, and when I willed her to look up at me, it was my victory, and she graciously allowed me to punish her with my full attention. We shook hands at the end of the reading, and I never saw her again. She has probably forgotten the whole thing but maybe not.

Yet I am one of the lucky ones. My parents made it possible for me to acquire a stronger footing in the mainstream culture by giving me the chance at an education. And books and art have saved me from the harsher forms of ethnic and racial prejudice that many of my Hispanic *compañeras* have had to endure. I travel a lot around the United States, reading from my books of poetry and my novel, and the reception I most often receive is one of positive interest by people who want to know more about my culture. There are, however, thousands of Latinas without the privilege of an education or the entrée into society that I have. For them life is a struggle against the misconceptions perpetuated by the myth of the Latina as whore, domestic, or criminal. We cannot change this by legislating the way people look at us. The transformation, as I see it, has to occur at a much more individual level. My personal goal in my public life is to try to replace the old pervasive stereotypes and myths about Latinas with a much more interesting set of realities. Every time I give a reading, I hope the stories I tell, the dreams and fears I examine in my work, can achieve some universal truth which will get my audience past the particulars of my skin color, my accent, or my clothes.

I once wrote a poem in which I called us Latinas "God's brown daughters." This poem is really a prayer of sorts, offered upward, but also, through the human-to-human channel of art, outward. It is a prayer for communication, and for respect. In it, Latin women pray "in Spanish to an Anglo God / With a Jewish heritage," and they are "fervently hoping / that if not omnipotent / at least He be bilingual." 15

(1992)

Exploring the Text

1. What is the effect of Judith Ortiz Cofer's opening paragraph? Does her anger draw you in or distance you?
2. Note the times when Cofer explains rather than denies the basis for stereotyping. For instance, rather than deny that Latinas prefer vivid colors, she explains that this preference reflects the bright landscape of their homelands. Does this strategy work, or do you think Cofer is playing to the stereotype?
3. Find the sections of the essay that refer to personal experience. Does Cofer's use of personal experience weaken her argument or make it more effective? Explain. Would the essay be more effective with less — or more — personal experience? Explain your view.

4. How does Cofer broaden the argument from her personal experience to larger concerns, including other stereotypes (or stereotypes of other communities)?
5. Cofer ends by quoting one of her own poems. Is this effective? Why or why not?
6. Who do you think is Cofer's audience for this essay? Does it include the woman at the poetry reading who asks Cofer for a cup of coffee?
7. According to Cofer, "Mixed cultural signals have perpetuated certain stereotypes — for example, that of the Hispanic woman as the 'Hot Tamale' or sexual firebrand. It is a one-dimensional view that the media have found easy to promote. In their special vocabulary, advertisers have designated 'sizzling' and 'smoldering' as the adjectives of choice for describing not only the foods but also the women of Latin America" (par. 6). Does this assertion — that the media promotes stereotypes — apply today? In answering, consider Cofer's example of Latin American women, or choose another group, such as African Americans, older people, or people from the Middle East.

EDWIDGE DANTICAT

Born in Haiti in 1969, Edwidge Danticat immigrated to the United States when she was twelve. She received her BA from Barnard College and her MFA from Brown University, where her thesis project became her first novel, *Breath, Eyes, Memory* (1994); it was an Oprah Winfrey Book Club selection in 1998. Her other fiction includes *Krik? Krak!* (1995), *The Farming of Bones* (1998), and *The Dew Breaker* (2004). In her work, Danticat often explores themes of cultural dislocation from the perspective of immigrants of different generations.

New York Day Women

"New York Day Women" was part of the 1995 collection *Krik? Krak!*

Today, walking down the street, I see my mother. She is strolling with a happy gait, her body thrust toward the DON'T WALK sign and the yellow taxicabs that make forty-five-degree turns on the corner of Madison and Fifty-seventh Street.

I have never seen her in this kind of neighborhood, peering into Chanel and Tiffany's and gawking at the jewels glowing in the Bulgari windows. My mother never shops outside of Brooklyn. She has never seen the advertising office where I work. She is afraid to take the subway, where you may meet those young black militant street preachers who curse black women for straightening their hair.

Yet, here she is, my mother, who I left at home that morning in her bathrobe, with pieces of newspapers twisted like rollers in her hair. My mother, who accuses me of random offenses as I dash out of the house.

Would you get up and give an old lady like me your subway seat? In this state of mind, I bet you don't even give up your seat to a pregnant lady.

My mother, who is often right about that. Sometimes I get up and give my seat. 5
Other times, I don't. It all depends on how pregnant the woman is and whether or
not she is with her boyfriend or husband and whether or not *he* is sitting down.

As my mother stands in front of Carnegie Hall, one taxi driver yells to another,
"What do you think this is, a dance floor?"

My mother waits patiently for this dispute to be settled before crossing the street.

**In Haiti when you get hit by a car, the owner of the car gets out and kicks you
for getting blood on his bumper.**

My mother, who laughs when she says this and shows a large gap in her mouth
where she lost three more molars to the dentist last week. My mother, who at fifty-
nine, says dentures are okay.

You can take them out when they bother you. I'll like them. I'll like them fine. 10

Will it feel empty when Papa kisses you?

Oh no, he doesn't kiss me that way anymore.

My mother, who watches the lottery drawing every night on channel 11 without
ever having played the numbers.

**A third of that money is all I would need. We would pay the mortgage, and
your father could stop driving that taxicab all over Brooklyn.**

I follow my mother, mesmerized by the many possibilities of her journey. Even 15
in a flowered dress, she is lost in a sea of pinstripes and gray suits, high heels and
elegant short skirts, Reebok sneakers, dashing from building to building.

My mother, who won't go out to dinner with anyone.

**If they want to eat with me, let them come to my house, even if I boil water and
give it to them.**

My mother, who talks to herself when she peels the skin off poultry.

Fat, you know, and cholesterol. Fat and cholesterol killed your aunt Hermine.

My mother, who makes jam with dried grapefruit peel and then puts in cinnamon 20
bark that I always think is cockroaches in the jam. My mother, whom I have always
bought household appliances for, on her birthday. A nice rice cooker, a blender.

I trail the red orchids in her dress and the heavy faux leather bag on her shoulders. Realizing the ferocious pace of my pursuit, I stop against a wall to rest. My
mother keeps on walking as though she owns the sidewalk under her feet.

As she heads toward the Plaza Hotel, a bicycle messenger swings so close to her that I want to dash forward and rescue her, but she stands dead in her tracks and lets him ride around her and then goes on.

My mother stops at a corner hot-dog stand and asks for something. The vendor hands her a can of soda that she slips into her bag. She stops by another vendor selling sundresses for seven dollars each. I can tell that she is looking at an African print dress, contemplating my size. I think to myself, Please Ma, don't buy it. It would be just another thing that I would bury in the garage or give to Goodwill.

Why should we give to Goodwill when there are so many people back home who need clothes? We save our clothes for the relatives in Haiti.

Twenty years we have been saving all kinds of things for the relatives in Haiti. I   25
need the place in the garage for an exercise bike.

You are pretty enough to be a stewardess. Only dogs like bones.

This mother of mine, she stops at another hot-dog vendor's and buys a frankfurter that she eats on the street. I never knew that she ate frankfurters. With her blood pressure, she shouldn't eat anything with sodium. She has to be careful with her heart, this day woman.

I cannot just swallow salt. Salt is heavier than a hundred bags of shame.

She is slowing her pace, and now I am too close. If she turns around, she might see me. I let her walk into the park before I start to follow again.

My mother walks toward the sandbox in the middle of the park. There a woman   30
is waiting with a child. The woman is wearing a leotard with biker's shorts and has small weights in her hands. The woman kisses the child good-bye and surrenders him to my mother; then she bolts off, running on the cemented stretches in the park.

The child given to my mother has frizzy blond hair. His hand slips into hers easily, like he's known her for a long time. When he raises his face to look at my mother, it is as though he is looking at the sky.

My mother gives this child the soda that she bought from the vendor on the street corner. The child's face lights up as she puts in a straw in the can for him. This seems to be a conspiracy just between the two of them.

My mother and the child sit and watch the other children play in the sandbox. The child pulls out a comic book from a knapsack with Big Bird on the back. My mother peers into his comic book. My mother, who taught herself to read as a little girl in Haiti from the books that her brothers brought home from school.

My mother, who has now lost six of her seven sisters in Ville Rose and has never had the strength to return for their funerals.

Many graves to kiss when I go back. Many graves to kiss.   35

She throws away the empty soda can when the child is done with it. I wait and watch from a corner until the woman in the leotard and biker's shorts returns, sweaty and breathless, an hour later. My mother gives the woman back her child and strolls farther into the park.

I turn around and start to walk out of the park before my mother can see me. My lunch hour is long since gone. I have to hurry back to work. I walk through a cluster of joggers, then race to a *Sweden Tours* bus. I stand behind the bus and take a peek at my mother in the park. She is standing in a circle, chatting with a group of women who are taking other people's children on an afternoon outing. They look like a Third World Parent-Teacher Association meeting.

I quickly jump into a cab heading back to the office. Would Ma have said hello had she been the one to see me first?

As the cab races away from the park, it occurs to me that perhaps one day I would chase an old woman down a street by mistake and that old woman would be somebody else's mother, who I would have mistaken for mine.

Day women come out when nobody expects them.   40

Tonight on the subway, I will get up and give my seat to a pregnant woman or a lady about Ma's age.

My mother, who stuffs thimbles in her mouth and then blows up her cheeks like Dizzy Gillespie while sewing yet another Raggedy Ann doll that she names Suzette after me.

I will have all these little Suzettes in case you never have any babies, which looks more and more like it is going to happen.

My mother who had me when she was thirty-three — *l'âge du Christ* — at the age that Christ died on the cross.

That's a blessing, believe you me, even if American doctors say by that time   45
you can make retarded babies.

My mother, who sews lace collars on my company softball T-shirts when she does my laundry.

Why, you can't you look like a lady playing softball?

My mother, who never went to any of my Parent-Teacher Association meetings when I was in school.

You're so good anyway. What are they going to tell me? I don't want to make you ashamed of this day woman. Shame is heavier than a hundred bags of salt.

(1995)

Exploring the Text

1. What are the differences between the narrator and her mother? Be sure to look at the explicit and implicit differences.
2. How does Edwidge Danticat maneuver between two, if not three, geographical settings? Who seems to have more flexibility, the narrator or her mother? Explain your answer.
3. How do the changes in type style, between bold and regular font, and the white space create structure for the story?
4. Who are "New York day women"?
5. How would you describe the narrator's attitude toward her mother?
6. How does Danticat develop the tension between the life that the narrator's opportunities have given her and the life of her mother?
7. Why do you think the author gave the narrator the following words: "perhaps one day I would chase an old woman down a street by mistake and that old woman would be somebody else's mother, who I would have mistaken for mine" (par. 39)?

SHERMAN ALEXIE

Sherman J. Alexie Jr. (b. 1966), a member of the Spokane and the Coeur d'Alene tribes, grew up on the Spokane Reservation in Washington State. A graduate of Washington State University, he has published more than twenty books, most notably *The Lone Ranger and Tonto Fistfight in Heaven* (1993), *The Absolutely True Diary of a Part-Time Indian* (2007), and *War Dances* (2009), which won the PEN/Faulkner Award for best American fiction. One of the stories in the *Lone Ranger* collection was the basis for the movie *Smoke Signals* (1999), for which Alexie wrote the screenplay.

Superman and Me

An activist for Native American rights and culture, Alexie wrote the following essay describing the impact of reading on his life. It was originally published in the *Los Angeles Times* in 1998 for a series called "The Joy of Reading and Writing."

I learned to read with a Superman comic book. Simple enough, I suppose. I cannot recall which particular Superman comic book I read, nor can I remember which villain he fought in that issue. I cannot remember the plot, nor the means by which I obtained the comic book. What I can remember is this: I was 3 years old, a Spokane Indian boy living with his family on the Spokane Indian Reservation in eastern Washington state. We were poor by most standards, but one of my parents usually managed to find some minimum-wage job or another, which made us middle-class by reservation standards. I had a brother and three sisters. We lived on a combination of irregular paychecks, hope, fear and government surplus food.

My father, who is one of the few Indians who went to Catholic school on purpose, was an avid reader of westerns, spy thrillers, murder mysteries, gangster epics, basketball player biographies and anything else he could find. He bought his books by the pound at Dutch's Pawn Shop, Goodwill, Salvation Army and Value Village. When he had extra money, he bought new novels at supermarkets, convenience stores and hospital gift shops. Our house was filled with books. They were stacked in crazy piles in the bathroom, bedrooms and living room. In a fit of unemployment-inspired creative energy, my father built a set of bookshelves and soon filled them with a random assortment of books about the Kennedy assassination, Watergate, the Vietnam War and the entire 23-book series of the Apache westerns. My father loved books, and since I loved my father with an aching devotion, I decided to love books as well.

I can remember picking up my father's books before I could read. The words themselves were mostly foreign, but I still remember the exact moment when I first understood, with a sudden clarity, the purpose of a paragraph. I didn't have the vocabulary to say "paragraph," but I realized that a paragraph was a fence that held words. The words inside a paragraph worked together for a common purpose. They had some specific reason for being inside the same fence. This knowledge delighted me. I began to think of everything in terms of paragraphs. Our reservation was a small paragraph within the United States. My family's house was a paragraph, distinct from the other paragraphs of the LeBrets to the north, the Fords to our south and the Tribal School to the west. Inside our house, each family member existed as a separate paragraph but still had genetics and common experiences to link us. Now, using this logic, I can see my changed family as an essay of seven paragraphs: mother, father, older brother, the deceased sister, my younger twin sisters and our adopted little brother.

At the same time I was seeing the world in paragraphs, I also picked up that Superman comic book. Each panel, complete with picture, dialogue and narrative, was a three-dimensional paragraph. In one panel, Superman breaks through a door. His suit is red, blue and yellow. The brown door shatters into many pieces. I look at the narrative above the picture. I cannot read the words, but I assume it tells me that "Superman is breaking down the door." Aloud, I pretend to read the words and say, "Superman is breaking down the door." Words, dialogue, also float out of Superman's mouth. Because he is breaking down the door, I assume he says, "I am breaking down the door." Once again, I pretend to read the words and say aloud, "I am breaking down the door." In this way, I learned to read.

This might be an interesting story all by itself. A little Indian boy teaches himself to read at an early age and advances quickly. He reads *Grapes of Wrath* in kindergarten when other children are struggling through *Dick and Jane*. If he'd been anything but an Indian boy living on the reservation, he might have been called a prodigy. But he is an Indian boy living on the reservation and is simply an oddity. He grows into a man who often speaks of his childhood in the third-person, as if it will somehow dull the pain and make him sound more modest about his talents. 5

A smart Indian is a dangerous person, widely feared and ridiculed by Indians and non-Indians alike. I fought with my classmates on a daily basis. They wanted me to stay quiet when the non-Indian teacher asked for answers, for volunteers, for help. We were Indian children who were expected to be stupid. Most lived up to those expectations inside the classroom but subverted them on the outside. They struggled with basic reading in school but could remember how to sing a few dozen powwow songs. They were monosyllabic in front of their non-Indian teachers but could tell complicated stories and jokes at the dinner table. They submissively ducked their heads when confronted by a non-Indian adult but would slug it out with the Indian bully who was 10 years older. As Indian children, we were expected to fail in the non-Indian world. Those who failed were ceremonially accepted by other Indians and appropriately pitied by non-Indians.

I refused to fail. I was smart. I was arrogant. I was lucky. I read books late into the night, until I could barely keep my eyes open. I read books at recess, then during lunch and in the few minutes left after I had finished my classroom assignments. I read books in the car when my family traveled to powwows or basketball games. In shopping malls, I ran to the bookstores and read bits and pieces of as many books as I could. I read the books my father brought home from the pawnshops and secondhand. I read the books I borrowed from the library. I read the backs of cereal boxes. I read the newspaper. I read the bulletins posted on the walls of the school, the clinic, the tribal offices, the post office. I read junk mail. I read auto-repair manuals. I read magazines. I read anything that had words and paragraphs. I read with equal parts joy and desperation. I loved those books, but I also knew that love had only one purpose. I was trying to save my life.

Despite all the books I read, I am still surprised I became a writer. I was going to be a pediatrician. These days, I write novels, short stories, and poems. I visit schools and teach creative writing to Indian kids. In all my years in the reservation school system, I was never taught how to write poetry, short stories or novels. I was certainly never taught that Indians wrote poetry, short stories and novels. Writing was something beyond Indians. I cannot recall a single time that a guest teacher visited the reservation. There must have been visiting teachers. Who were they? Where are they now? Do they exist? I visit the schools as often as possible. The Indian kids crowd the classroom. Many are writing their own poems, short stories and novels. They have read my books. They have read many other books. They look at me with bright eyes and arrogant wonder. They are trying to save their lives. Then there are the sullen and already defeated Indian kids who sit in the back rows and ignore me with theatrical precision. The pages of their notebooks are empty. They carry neither pencil nor pen. They stare out the window. They refuse and resist. "Books," I say to them. "Books," I say. I throw my weight against their locked doors. The door holds. I am smart. I am arrogant. I am lucky. I am trying to save our lives.

(1998)

Exploring the Text

1. What figure of speech is the following: "We lived on a combination of irregular paychecks, hope, fear and government surplus food" (par. 1)? What is its effect?

2. In what ways does the description of Sherman Alexie's father play against stereo-types of Native Americans?

3. What does Alexie mean when he describes "an Indian boy" who "grows into a man who often speaks of his childhood in the third-person" (par. 5)?

4. In paragraph 7, Alexie deliberately uses a number of short, simple sentences. What effect do you think he is trying to achieve?

5. This eight-paragraph essay is divided into two distinct sections. Why? How would you describe its arrangement? How does it suit Alexie's overall purpose?

6. Discuss Alexie's use of parallel structure and repetition in the last two paragraphs. Pay particular attention to the final sentence in each.

7. Alexie writes that he read to save his life, and many other people have written that books opened up worlds and possibilities that gave them a new life. Do you believe that reading and books can still have that power? Explain.

RITA DOVE

Rita Dove was born in Akron, Ohio, in 1952, at a time when racial barriers were being torn down. Her father was the first African American chemist to be hired by the Goodyear Tire Corporation. She graduated summa cum laude from Miami (Ohio) University and won a Fulbright Scholarship.

In addition to her many collections of poems, Dove's published work also includes a verse drama, *The Darker Face of the Earth* (1994); a collection of short stories, *Fifth Sunday* (1985); and a novel, *Through the Ivory Gate* (1992). *Thomas and Beulah* (1986) won the Pulitzer Prize for Poetry; *On the Bus with Rosa Parks* (1999) was a finalist for the National Book Critics Circle Award. Dove is the only African American to be named poet laureate of the United States, a title she held from 1993 to 1995.

Rosa

"Rosa" was first published in *Georgia Review* in 1998 and then in Dove's collection *On the Bus with Rosa Parks* in 1999. The Rosa of the title refers to Rosa Parks, an icon of the civil rights movement. In December 1955, Parks refused to give up her seat on the bus to a white man. Her arrest sparked the bus boycott in Montgomery, Alabama, considered one of the turning points of the fight for civil rights.

How she sat there,
the time right inside a place
so wrong it was ready.

That trim name with
its dream of a bench   5
to rest on. Her sensible coat.

Doing nothing was the doing:
the clean flame of her gaze
carved by a camera flash.

How she stood up   10
when they bent down to retrieve
her purse. That courtesy.

(1998)

Exploring the Text

1. What does Rita Dove mean when she says, "the time right inside a place / so wrong it was ready" (ll. 2–3)? What time and place is she referring to? Why do you think she isn't more specific?

2. How does Dove characterize Rosa Parks? What does she expect the reader to bring to the poem?

3. What is the speaker's attitude toward Rosa Parks?

4. In the last stanza, "they" refers to the two policemen who came on the bus to arrest Rosa Parks. They picked up her purse and bag and handed them to her when they put her in the backseat of the police car to drive her to jail. How do you think Dove meant the last two words, "That courtesy," to be understood?

5. Dove said about "Rosa" that the poem speculates "not only on Rosa Parks's historic non-doing . . . but also on any moment in history when one is suddenly confronted with a choice — what would one do." What other moments does this poem bring to mind? Have you had an experience making this kind of choice? Explain.

LI-YOUNG LEE

Li-Young Lee (b. 1957) was born to an elite Chinese family. His great-grandfather had been China's first republican president (1912–1916), and his father had been a personal physician to Mao Zedong. Despite the latter association, his family fled from China when the People's Republic was established in 1948, settling in Jakarta, where Lee was born. An increasing anti-Chinese movement in Indonesia drove the family from the country, and after a futile search for a permanent home in turbulent Asia, they settled in the United States in 1964. Lee was educated at the University of Pittsburgh, where he began to write. He later attended the University of Arizona and the State University of New York at Brockport. Lee's first collection of poetry was *Rose* (1986), which won the Delmore Schwartz Memorial Poetry Award from New York University. This was followed by *The City in Which I Love You* (1990), which won the Lamont Poetry Prize; *Book of My Nights* (2001); and his most recent publication, *Behind My Eyes* (2008). He has also published a personal memoir, *The Wingéd Seed: A Remembrance* (1995).

The Hammock

"The Hammock" was first published in the *Kenyon Review*.

When I lay my head in my mother's lap
I think how day hides the stars,
the way I lay hidden once, waiting
inside my mother's singing to herself. And I remember
how she carried me on her back   5
between home and the kindergarten,
once each morning and once each afternoon.
I don't know what my mother's thinking.

When my son lays his head in my lap, I wonder:
Do his father's kisses keep his father's worries   10
from becoming his? I think, *Dear God*, and remember
there are stars we haven't heard from yet:
They have so far to arrive. *Amen*,
I think, and I feel almost comforted.

I've no idea what my child is thinking.   15

Between two unknowns, I live my life.
Between my mother's hopes, older than I am
by coming before me, and my child's wishes, older than I am
by outliving me. And what's it like?
Is it a door, and good-bye on either side?   20
A window, and eternity on either side?
Yes, and a little singing between two great rests.

(2000)

Exploring the Text

1. What are the connotations of the word *hammock*? How do these connotations contribute to your understanding of the poem?
2. Why do you think the poet chose to italicize the words "Dear God" (l. 11) and "Amen" (l. 13)? What does this tell you about the speaker's attitude toward his subject? How is this choice connected to the poem's tone?
3. Trace the oppositions Li-Young Lee sets up in "The Hammock." How do they help develop the extended metaphor of a hammock?
4. What do you think Lee means by "two unknowns" (l. 16) and "two great rests" (l. 22)?
5. Examine the structure of this poem by comparing stanzas one and three to stanzas two and four. How does the shape of the poem reflect its title and theme?

ART SPIEGELMAN

Art Spiegelman (b. 1948) is an American cartoonist and editor, best known for his graphic novel *Maus* (1991), which won a Pulitzer Prize in 1992. Born in Stockholm, Sweden, Spiegelman immigrated to America with his family as a small child and spent most of his life in New York. He attended Harpur College from 1965 to 1968 but left before graduation to pursue a career in cartoon illustration. In 1977, he published a collection of comic strips entitled *Breakdowns*, and in 1980, with the help of his wife, artist and designer Françoise Mouly, Spiegelman launched *Raw*, a magazine that focused on publishing avant-garde cartoonists. From 1977 to 1990, he created his most famous work, *Maus*, a graphic novel that chronicled the rise of Nazism during World War II, and in 1992, he became a contributing artist for the *New Yorker*, where he remained until 2001, when he left to work on *In the Shadow of No Towers*, a collection of illustrations documenting his reaction to 9/11.

9/11/2001

The following illustration was the cover for the September 24th issue of the *New Yorker* magazine, the first issue to appear after September 11, 2001. It was voted one of the top ten magazine covers of the past forty years by the American Society of Magazine Editors.

Exploring the Text

1. What is your first reaction to the picture? What about your subsequent reactions? Make sure that you turn the image to the light to catch its subtleties.
2. How does Art Spiegelman use color — or the lack of color — to comment on the events of September 11, 2001?
3. Spiegelman has said that his first draft was of the shrouded towers in orange against a blue sky. He has said he was channeling surrealist artist René Magritte. Why might he have been thinking about a surrealist? Why do you think that version was not the final one?
4. Art editor Françoise Mouly, who chooses the covers for the *New Yorker*, commented on this cover: "Ten years ago, my husband, the cartoonist Art Speigelman, our daughter, and I stood four blocks away from the second tower as we watched it collapse in excruciatingly slow motion. Later, back at my office, I felt that images were suddenly powerless to help us understand what had happened. The only appropriate solution seemed to be to publish no cover image at all — an all-black cover. Then Art suggested adding the outlines of the two towers, black on black. So from no cover came a perfect image, which conveyed something about the unbearable loss of life, the sudden absence in our skyline, the abrupt tear in the fabric of our reality." Do you think it's the perfect cover? Explain why or why not.

Copyright © Condé Nast. From *The New Yorker* Magazine. All rights reserved. Cover by Art Spiegelman. Reprinted by Permission.

⟳ TALKBACK

Ana Juan

Ana Juan (b. 1961) is an illustrator from Valencia, Spain, who began contributing cover art to the *New Yorker* in 1995. Juan was awarded the Ezra Jack Keats New Illustrator Award in 2004 for her children's book *The Night Eater* and has exhibited her work in Geneva, New York, and Spain.

Reflections

This *New Yorker* cover marked the tenth anniversary of the terrorist attacks on New York City.

Copyright © Condé Nast. From *The New Yorker Magazine*. All rights reserved. Cover by Ana Juan. Reprinted by Permission.

Exploring the Text

1. How does Ana Juan portray the Twin Towers on this cover? What does her portrayal evoke?
2. What are the different meanings of the title of the drawing? How does each one apply to the work's purpose and occasion?
3. How does Juan appeal to pathos and even logos in this cover art? How does she establish ethos?
4. Do you think this is the right cover for the tenth anniversary of the terrorist attacks? Explain your answer.

Making Connections

1. How does Juan's cover (p. 1428) respond to Art Spiegelman's (p. 1427)? In what ways does she acknowledge his work? In what ways does she update it?
2. Everyone in New York City — and the country — who experienced 9/11 has his or her own story. Why does the work of these two artists deserve an audience? Or do they?
3. These covers raise the question of whether art can offer solace. What do you think? Explain your answer.

TRACY K. SMITH

Tracy K. Smith (b. 1972) is an African American poet and professor of creative writing at Princeton University. Born in Massachusetts, she received a BA from Harvard University and an MFA in creative writing from Columbia University. She is the author of three award-winning books of poetry — *The Body's Question* (2003), *Duende* (2007), and *Life on Mars* (2011), which won the 2012 Pulitzer Prize for Poetry.

Letter to a Photojournalist Going-In

"Letter to a Photojournalist Going-In" appeared in Smith's second collection, *Duende*, published in 2007.

You go to the pain. City after city. Borders
Where they peer into your eyes as if to erase you.

You go by bus or truck, days at a time, just taking it
When they throw you in a room or kick at your gut,

Taking it when a strong fist hammers person after person 5
A little deeper into the ground. Your camera blinks:

Soldiers smoking between rounds. Bodies
Blown open like curtains. In the neighborhoods,

Boys brandish plastic guns with TV bravado. Men
Ask you to look them in the face and say who's right. 10

At night you sleep, playing it all back in reverse:

The dance of wind in a valley of dirt. Rugs and tools,
All the junk that rises up, resurrected, then disappears

Into newly formed windows and walls. People
Close their mouths and run backwards out of frame. 15

Up late, your voice fits my ear like a secret.
But who can hear two things at once?

Errant stars flare, shatter. A whistle, then the indescribable thud
Of an era spilling its matter into the night. Who can say the word *love*

When everything — everything — pushes back with the promise 20
To grind itself to dust?

                   And what if there's no dignity to what we do,
None at all? If our work — what you see, what I say — is nothing

But a way to kid ourselves into thinking we might last? If trust is just
Another human trick that'll lick its lips and laugh as it backs away? 25

Sometimes I think you're right, wanting to lose everything and wander
Like a blind king. Wanting to squeeze a lifetime between your hands

And press it into a single flimsy frame. Will you take it to your lips
Like the body of a woman, something to love in passing,

Or set it down, free finally, empty as the camera, 30
Which we all know is just a hollow box, mechanized to obey?

Sometimes I want my heart to beat like yours: from the outside in,
A locket stuffed with faces that refuse to be named. For time

To land at my feet like a grenade.

                                                  (2007)

Exploring the Text

1. In a review of *Duende*, the collection in which this poem appeared, critic Cindra Halm notes that one of "Smith's strengths is the quiet slide into surprising metaphor." Find the "surprising metaphor[s]" here, and explain why you agree or disagree with the reviewer that they are a strong part of Smith's writing.

2. Tracy K. Smith plays with the interaction between speaker and audience. How do you read it? Who is the photojournalist — the speaker or "you"? Explain your answer.

3. Why do you think Smith wrote this poem largely in couplets (two-line rhyming stanzas)? What is the effect of that choice? What function do the two single-line stanzas (ll. 11 and 34) have?

4. Look carefully at lines 22–24, in which the speaker asks if the work of the photojournalist is important and whether, like art, it will last. What do you think? Do you think photojournalism is a form of art? Explain why or why not.

5. Who do you think is the blind king the poem alludes to in line 27? Explain what the allusion adds to the poem.

JONATHAN FRANZEN

Jonathan Franzen (b. 1959) is an American novelist and essayist from Webster Grove, Missouri. He graduated from Swarthmore College in 1981 with a degree in German, and from 1981 to 1982 he studied on a Fulbright Scholarship at Freie Universitat in Berlin, Germany. In 1987, he moved to New York City to pursue a writing career, and in 1988 he published his first novel, *The Twenty-Seventh City*. Since then, he has published essays and fiction in magazines such as the *New Yorker* and *Harper's*, and his novels *The Corrections* (2001) and *Freedom* (2010) have won him critical acclaim. He has also published two essay collections — *How to Be Along* (2002) and *Farther Away* (2012) — and a memoir, *The Discomfort Zone* (2006).

Agreeable

"Agreeable" was published in the *New Yorker* magazine in 2010. It became an episode in Franzen's 2010 novel, *Freedom*.

If Patty hadn't been an atheist, she might have thanked the good Lord for school athletic programs, because they basically saved her life and gave her a chance to realize herself as a person. She was especially grateful to Sandra Mosher at North Chappaqua Middle School, Elaine Carver and Jane Nagel at Horace Greeley High School, and Ernie and Rose Salvatore at the Gettysburg Girls Basketball Camp. It was from these wonderful coaches that Patty learned discipline, patience, focus, teamwork, and the ideals of good sportsmanship that helped make up for her morbid competitiveness and low self-esteem.

Patty grew up in Westchester County, New York. She was the oldest of four children, the other three of whom were more like what her parents had been hoping for. She was notably Larger than everybody else in the family, also Less Unusual, also measurably Dumber. Not actually dumb but relatively dumber. She grew up to be five feet nine and a half, which was almost the same height as her brother and numerous inches taller than her sisters, and sometimes she wished she could have gone ahead and been six feet, since she was never going to fit into the family anyway. Being able to see the basket better and to post up in traffic and to rotate more freely on defense might have given her a somewhat less vicious competitive streak, leading to a happier life post-college; probably not, but it was interesting to think about. By the time she got to the collegiate level, she was usually one of the shorter players on the floor, which in a funny way reminded her of her position in her family and helped keep her adrenaline at peak levels.

Patty's first memory of doing a team sport with her mother watching was also one of her last. She was attending ordinary-person Sports daycamp at the same complex where her sisters were doing extraordinary-person Arts daycamp, and one day her mother and sisters showed up for the late innings of a softball game. Patty was frustrated to be standing in left field waiting around for somebody to hit a ball deep while less skilled girls made errors in the infield. She started creeping in shallower and shallower, which was how the game ended. Runners on first and second. The batter hit a bouncing ball to the grossly uncoördinated shortstop, whom Patty ran in front of so that she could field the ball herself and run and tag out the lead runner and then start chasing the other runner, some sweet girl who'd probably reached first on a fielding error. Patty bore down straight at her, and the girl ran squealing into the outfield, leaving the base path for an automatic out, but Patty kept chasing her and applied the tag while the girl crumpled up and screamed at the apparently horrible pain of being lightly touched by a glove.

Patty was aware that this was not her finest hour of sportsmanship. Something had come over her because her family was watching. In the family station wagon on the way home, her mother asked her, in an even more quavering voice than usual, if she had to be quite so . . . *aggressive*. If it was necessary to be, well, to be so aggressive. Would it have hurt Patty to share the ball a little with her teammates? Patty replied that she hadn't been getting *any* balls in left field. And her mother said, "I don't mind if you play sports, but only if it's going to teach you coöperation and community-mindedness." And Patty said, "So send me to a *real* camp where I won't be the only good player! I can't coöperate with people who can't catch the ball!" And her mother said, "I'm not sure it's a good idea to be encouraging so much aggression and competition. I guess I'm not a sports fan, but I don't see the fun in defeating people just for the sake of defeating them. Wouldn't it be much more fun to all work together?"

Patty's mother was a professional Democrat. She later became a state assemblywoman, the Honorable Joyce Emerson, known for her advocacy of open space, poor

5

children, and the Arts. Paradise for Joyce was an open space where poor children could go and do Arts at state expense. She was born Joyce Markowitz in Brooklyn in 1934 but apparently disliked being Jewish from the earliest dawn of consciousness. (Patty sometimes wondered if one reason that Joyce's voice always trembled was from struggling so hard all her life to not sound like Brooklyn.) Joyce got a scholarship to study liberal Arts in the woods of Maine, where she met Patty's exceedingly Gentile dad, whom she married at All Souls Unitarian Church on the Upper East Side of Manhattan. When young Jack Kennedy got the Democratic nomination, in 1960, it gave Joyce a noble and stirring excuse to get out of a house that she couldn't seem to help filling up with babies. Then came civil rights, and Vietnam, and Bobby Kennedy — more good reasons to be out of a house that wasn't nearly big enough for four little kids plus a Barbadian nanny in the basement. Joyce went to her first national convention in 1968 as a delegate committed to dead Bobby. She served as county Party treasurer and later chairwoman and organized for Teddy in 1972 and 1980. Every summer, all day long, herds of volunteers tramped in and out of the house's open doors carrying boxes of campaign gear. Patty could practice dribbling and layups for six hours straight without anybody noticing or caring.

Patty's father, Ray, was a lawyer and amateur humorist whose repertory included fart jokes and mean parodies of his children's teachers, neighbors, and friends. A torment he particularly enjoyed inflicting on Patty was mimicking the Barbadian, Eulalie, when she was just out of earshot, saying, "Stop de game now, stop de playin'," in a louder and louder voice, until Patty ran from the dinner table in mortification and her siblings shrieked with excitement. Endless fun could also be had ridiculing Patty's coach and mentor Sandy Mosher, whom Ray liked to call Saaaandra. He was constantly asking Patty whether Saaaandra had had any gentlemen callers lately or maybe, tee hee, tee hee, some *gentlelady* callers? Her siblings chorused, "Saaaandra, Saaaandra!" Other amusing methods of tormenting Patty were to hide the family dog, Elmo, and pretend that Elmo had been euthanized while Patty was at late basketball practice. Or tease Patty about certain factual errors she'd made many years earlier — ask her how the kangaroos in *Austria* were doing, or whether she'd seen the latest novel by the famous contemporary writer Louisa May Alcott, or whether she still thought funguses were part of the animal kingdom. "I saw one of Patty's funguses chasing a truck the other day," her father would say. "Look, look at me, this is how Patty's fungus chases a truck."

Most nights her dad went back to work after dinner to meet with the poor people he was defending in court for little or no money. He had an office across the street from the courthouse in White Plains. His pro-bono clients included Puerto Ricans, Haitians, transvestites, and the mentally or physically disabled. Some of them were in such bad trouble that he didn't even make fun of them behind their backs. As much as possible, though, he found their problems amusing. In tenth grade, for a school project, Patty sat in on two trials that her dad was part of. One was a case against an unemployed Yonkers man who had drunk too much on Puerto Rican Day and gone looking for his wife's brother, intending to cut him with a knife, but hadn't found him and had instead cut up a stranger in a bar. Not only Ray but the judge and even the prosecutor seemed amused by the defendant's haplessness and stupidity. They kept exchanging little not-quite winks. As if misery and disfigurement and jail time were all just a lower-class sideshow designed to perk up their otherwise boring day.

On the train ride home, Patty asked her dad whose side he was on.

"Ha, good question," he answered. "You have to understand, my client is a liar. The victim is a liar. And the bar owner is a liar. They're all liars. Of course, my client is entitled to a vigorous defense. But you have to try to serve justice, too. Sometimes the P.A. and the judge and I are working together as much as the P.A. is working with the victim or I'm working with the defendant. You've heard of our adversarial system of justice?"

"Yes." 10

"Well. Sometimes the P.A. and the judge and I all have the same adversary. We try to sort out the facts and avoid a miscarriage. Although don't, uh. Don't put that in your paper."

"I thought sorting out facts was what the grand jury and the jury are for."

"That's right. Put that in your paper. Trial by a jury of your peers. That's important."

"But most of your clients are innocent, right?"

"Not many of them deserve as bad a punishment as somebody's trying to give 15 them."

"But a lot of them are completely innocent, right? Mommy says they have trouble with the language, or the police aren't careful about who they arrest, and there's prejudice against them, and lack of opportunity."

"All of that is entirely true, Pattycakes. Nevertheless, uh. Your mother can be somewhat dewy-eyed."

Patty minded his ridiculing less when her mother was the butt of it.

"I mean, you saw those people," he said to her. "Jesus Christ. El ron me puso loco."

An important fact about Ray was that his family had a lot of money. His parents 20 lived on a big ancestral estate out in the hills of northwest New Jersey, in a pretty stone modernist house that was supposedly designed by Frank Lloyd Wright and was hung with minor works by famous French Impressionists. Every summer, the entire Emerson clan gathered by the lake at the estate for holiday picnics that Patty mostly failed to enjoy. Her granddad, August, liked to grab his oldest granddaughter around the belly and sit her down on his bouncing thigh and get God only knows what kind of little thrill from this; he was certainly not very respectful of Patty's physical boundaries. Starting in seventh grade, she also had to play doubles with Ray and his junior partner and the partner's wife, on the grandparental clay tennis court, and be stared at by the junior partner, in her exposing tennis clothes, and feel self-conscious and confused by his ocular pawing.

Like Ray, August had bought the right to be privately eccentric by doing good public legal works; he'd made a name for himself defending high-profile conscientious objectors and draft evaders in three wars. In his spare time, which he had much of, he grew grapes on his property and fermented them in one of the outbuildings. His "winery" was called Doe Haunch and was a major family joke. At the holiday picnics, August tottered around in flip-flops and saggy swim trunks, clutching one of his crudely labelled bottles, refilling the glasses that his guests had discreetly emptied into grass or bushes. "What do you think?" he asked. "Is it good wine? Do you like it?" He was sort of like an eager boy hobbyist and sort of like a torturer intent on punishing every victim equally. Citing European custom, August believed in giving children wine, and when the young mothers were distracted with corn to shuck or competitive salads to adorn he watered his Doe Haunch Reserve and pressed it on kids as young as three, gently holding their chins, if necessary, and pouring the mixture into their mouths, making sure it went down. "You know what that is?" he said. "That's wine." If a child then began to act strangely, he said, "What you're feeling is called being drunk. You drank too much. You're drunk." This with a disgust no less sincere for being friendly. Patty, always the oldest of the kids, observed these scenes with silent horror, leaving it to a younger sibling or cousin to sound the alarm: "Granddaddy's getting the little kids drunk!" While the mothers came running to scold August and snatch their kids away, and the fathers tittered dirtily about August's obsession with female deer hindquarters, Patty slipped into the lake and floated in its warmest shallows, letting the water stop her ears against her family.

Her granddad had once been a true athlete, a college track star and football tight end, which was probably where her height and reflexes came from. Ray also had played football but in Maine for a school that could barely field a team. His real game was tennis, which was the one sport Patty hated, although she was good at it. She believed that Björn Borg was secretly weak. With very few exceptions (e.g., Joe Namath), she wasn't impressed with male athletes in general. Her specialty was crushes on popular boys who were enough older or better-looking to be totally unrealistic choices. Being a very agreeable person, however, she went on dates with practically anybody who asked. She thought shy or unpopular boys had a hard life, and she took pity on them insofar as was humanly possible. For some reason, many of these boys were wrestlers. In her experience, wrestlers were brave, taciturn, geeky, beetle-browed, polite, and not afraid of female jocks. One of them confided to her that in middle school she'd been known to him and his friends as the She-Monkey.

As far as actual sex goes, Patty's first experience of it was being raped at a party when she was seventeen by a boarding-school senior named Ethan Post. Ethan didn't do any sports except golf, but he had six inches of height and fifty pounds on Patty and provided discouraging perspectives on female muscle strength as compared with men's. What he did to Patty didn't strike her as a gray-area sort of rape. When she started fighting, she fought hard, if not well, and only for so long, because she was drunk for one of the first times ever. She'd been feeling so wonderfully free! Very probably, in the vast swimming pool at Kim McClusky's, on a beautiful warm May night, Patty had given Ethan Post a mistaken impression. She was far too agreeable even when she wasn't drunk. In the pool, she must have been giddy with agreeability. Altogether, there was much to blame herself for. Her notions of romance were like Gilligan's Island: "as primitive as can be." They fell somewhere between Snow White and Nancy Drew. And Ethan undeniably had the arrogant look that attracted her at that point in time. He resembled the love interest from a girls' novel with sailboats on the cover. After he raped Patty, he said he was sorry "it" had been rougher than he'd meant "it" to be, he was sorry about that.

It was only after the piña coladas wore off, early the next morning, in the bedroom that Patty shared with her littler sister so that their middle sister could have her own room to be Creative in: only then did she get indignant. The indignity was that Ethan had considered her such a nothing that he could just rape her and then take her home. And she was *not* such a nothing. She was, among other things, already, as a junior, the all-time single-season record holder for assists at Horace Greeley High School. A record she would demolish the following year! She was also first-team all-state in a state that *included Brooklyn and the Bronx.* And yet a golfing boy she hardly even knew had thought it was O.K. to rape her.

To avoid waking her little sister, she went and cried in the shower. This was, without exaggeration, the most wretched hour of her life. Things that had never occurred to her before—such as the injustice of an oldest daughter having to share a room (instead of being given Eulalie's old room in the basement, which was now filled floor to ceiling with outdated campaign paraphernalia), also the injustice of her mother being so enthralled about her middle daughter's thespian performances but never going to any of Patty's games—occurred to her now. She was so indignant that she almost felt like talking to somebody. But she was afraid to let her coach or teammates know she'd been drinking. 25

How the story came out, in spite of her best efforts to keep it buried, was that Coach Nagel got suspicious and spied on her in the locker room after the next day's game. Sat Patty down in her office and confronted her regarding her bruises and unhappy demeanor. Patty humiliated herself by immediately and sobbingly confessing to all. To her total shock, Coach then proposed taking her to the hospital and notifying the police. Patty had just gone three-for-four with two runs scored and several outstanding defensive plays. She obviously wasn't greatly harmed. Also, her parents were political friends of Ethan's parents, so that was a nonstarter. She dared to hope that an abject apology for breaking training, combined with Coach's pity and leniency, would put the matter to rest. But, oh, how wrong she was.

Coach called Patty's house and got Patty's mother, who, as always, was running out to a meeting and had neither time to talk nor yet the moral wherewithal to admit that she didn't have time to talk. Coach spoke these indelible words into the P.E. department's beige telephone: "Your daughter just told me that she was raped last night by a boy named Ethan Post." Coach then listened to the phone for a minute before saying, "No, she just now told me. . . . That's right. . . . Just last night . . . Yes, she is." And handed Patty the telephone.

"Patty?" her mother said. "Are you—all right?"

"I'm fine."

"Mrs. Nagel says there was an incident last night?" 30

"The incident was I was raped."

"Oh dear, oh dear, oh dear. Last night?"

"Yes."

"I was home this morning. Why didn't you say something?"

"I don't know." 35

"Why, why, why? Why didn't you say something to me?"

"Maybe it just didn't seem like such a big deal right then."

"So but then you did tell Mrs. Nagel."

"No," Patty said. "She's just more observant than you are."

"I hardly saw you this morning." 40

"I'm not blaming you. I'm just saying."

"And you think you might have been . . . It might have been . . ."

"Raped."

"I can't believe this," her mother said. "I'm going to come and get you."

"Coach Nagel wants me to go to the hospital." 45

"Are you not all right?"

"I already said. I'm fine."

"Then just stay put, and don't either of you do anything until I get there."

Patty hung up the phone and told Coach that her mother was coming.

"We're going to put that boy in jail for a long, long time," Coach said. 50

"Oh no no no no no," Patty said. "No, we're not."

"Patty."

"It's just not going to happen."

"It will if you want it to."

"No, actually, it won't. My parents and the Posts are political friends." 55

"Listen to me," Coach said. "That has nothing to do with anything. Do you understand?"

Patty was quite certain that Coach was wrong about this. Dr. Post was a cardiologist, and his wife was from big money. They had one of the houses that people such as Teddy Kennedy and Ed Muskie and Walter Mondale made visits to when they were short of funds. Over the years, Patty had heard much tell of the Posts' "back yard" from her parents. This back yard was apparently about the size of Central Park but nicer. Conceivably one of Patty's straight-A, grade-skipping, Arts-doing sisters could have brought trouble down on the Posts, but it was absurd to imagine the hulking B-student family jock making a dent in the Posts' armor.

"I'm just never going to drink again," she said, "and that will solve the problem."

"Maybe for you," Coach said, "but not for somebody else. Look at your arms. Look what he did. He'll do that to somebody else if you don't stop him."

"It's just bruises and scratches." 60

Coach here made a motivational speech about standing up for your teammates, which in this case meant all the young women Ethan might ever meet. The upshot was that Patty was supposed to press charges and let Coach inform the New Hampshire prep school where Ethan was a student, so that he could be expelled and denied a diploma, and that if Patty didn't do this she would be letting down her team.

Patty began to cry again, because she would almost rather have died than let a team down. Earlier in the winter, she'd played most of a half of basketball with the flu, before fainting on the sideline and getting fluids intravenously. The problem now was that she hadn't been with her own team the night before. She'd gone to the party with her field-hockey friend Amanda, whose soul was apparently never going to be at rest until she'd induced Patty to sample piña coladas, vast buckets of which had been promised at the McCluskys'. El ron me puso loca. None of the other girls at the McCluskys' swimming pool were jocks. Almost just by showing up there, Patty had betrayed her true team. And now she'd been punished for it. Ethan hadn't raped one of the fast girls, he'd raped Patty, because she didn't belong there; she didn't even know how to drink.

She promised Coach to give the matter some thought.

It was shocking to see her mother in the gym and obviously shocking to her mother to find herself there. She was wearing her everyday pumps and resembled Goldilocks in daunting woods as she peered around uncertainly at the naked metal equipment and the fungal floors and the clustered balls in mesh bags. Patty went to her and submitted to embrace. Her mother being much smaller of frame, Patty felt somewhat like a grandfather clock that Joyce was endeavoring to lift and move. She broke away and led Joyce into Coach's little glass-walled office so that the necessary conference could be had.

"Hi, I'm Jane Nagel," Coach said.   65

"Yes, we've — met," Joyce said.

"Oh, you're right, we did meet once," Coach said.

In addition to her strenuous elocution, Joyce had strenuously proper posture and a masklike Pleasant Smile suitable for nearly all occasions public and private. Because she never raised her voice, not even in anger (her voice just got more strained when she was mad), her Pleasant Smile could be worn even at moments of excruciating conflict.

"No, it was more than once," she said now. "It was several times."

"Really?"   70

"I'll be outside," Patty said, closing the door behind her.

The parent-coach conference didn't last long. Joyce soon came out on clicking heels and said, "Let's go."

Coach, standing in the doorway behind Joyce, gave Patty a significant look. The look meant *Don't forget what I said about teamwork.*

Joyce's car was the last one left in its quadrant of the visitor lot. She put the key in the ignition but didn't turn it. Patty asked what was going to happen now.

"Your father's at his office," Joyce said. "We'll go straight there."   75

But she didn't turn the key.

"I'm sorry about this," Patty said.

"What I don't understand," her mother burst out, "is how such an outstanding athlete as you are — I mean, how could Ethan, or whoever it was —"

"Ethan. It was Ethan."

"How could anybody — or Ethan," she said. "You say it's pretty definitely Ethan.   80
How could — if it's Ethan — how could he have . . . ?" Her mother hid her mouth with her fingers. "Oh, I wish it had been almost anybody else. Dr. and Mrs. Post are such good friends of — good friends of so many good things. And I don't know Ethan well, but —"

"I hardly know him at all!"

"Well then how could this happen!"

"Let's just go home."

"No. You have to tell me. I'm your mother."

Hearing herself say this, Joyce looked embarrassed. She seemed to realize how 85 peculiar it was to have to remind Patty who her mother was. And Patty, for one, was glad to finally have this doubt out in the open. If Joyce was her mother, then how had it happened that she hadn't come to the first round of the state tournament, when Patty had broken the all-time Horace Greeley girls' tournament scoring record with thirty-two points? Somehow everybody else's mother had found time to come to that game.

She showed Joyce her wrists.

"*This* is what happened," she said. "I mean, part of what happened."

Joyce looked once at the bruises, shuddered, and then turned away as if respecting Patty's privacy. "This is terrible," she said. "You're right. This is terrible."

"Coach Nagel says I should go to the emergency room and tell the police and tell Ethan's headmaster."

"Yes, I know what your coach wants. She seems to feel that castration might be 90 an appropriate punishment. What I want to know is what *you* think."

"I don't know what I think."

"If you want to go to the police now," Joyce said, "we'll go to the police. Just tell me if that's what you want."

"I guess we should tell Dad first."

So down the Saw Mill they went. Joyce was always driving Patty's siblings to Painting, Guitar, Ballet, Japanese, Debate, Drama, Piano, Fencing, and Mock Court, but Patty herself seldom rode with Joyce anymore. Most weekdays she came home very late on the jock bus. If she had a game, somebody else's mom or dad dropped her off. If she and her friends were ever stranded, she knew not to bother calling her parents but to go ahead and use the Westchester Cab dispatcher's number and one of the twenty-dollar bills that her mother made her always carry. It never occurred to her to use the twenties for anything but cabs, or to go anywhere after a game except straight home, where she peeled aluminum foil off her dinner at ten or eleven o'clock and went down to the basement to wash her uniform while she ate and watched reruns. She often fell asleep down there.

"Here's a hypothetical question," Joyce said, driving. "Do you think it might be 95 enough if Ethan formally apologized to you?"

"He already apologized."

"For—"

"For being rough."

"And what did you say?"

"I didn't say anything. I said I wanted to go home." 100

"But he did apologize for being rough."

"It wasn't a real apology."

"All right. I'll take your word for it."

"I just want him to know I still *exist*."

"Whatever *you* want—sweetie." 105

Joyce pronounced this "sweetie" like the first word of a foreign language she was learning.

As a test or a punishment, Patty said, "Maybe, I guess, if he apologized in a really sincere way, that might be enough." And she looked carefully at her mother, who was struggling (it seemed to Patty) to contain her excitement.

"That sounds to me like a nearly ideal solution," Joyce said. "But only if you really think it would be enough for you."

"It wouldn't," Patty said.

"I'm sorry?"   110

"I said it wouldn't be enough."

"I thought you just said it would be."

Patty began to cry again very desolately.

"I'm sorry," Joyce said. "Did I misunderstand?"

"He raped me like it was nothing. I'm probably not even the first."   115

"You don't know that, Patty."

"I want to go to the hospital."

"Look, here, we're almost at Daddy's office. Unless you're actually hurt, we might as well —"

"But I already know what he'll say. I know what he'll want me to do."

"He'll want to do whatever's best for you. Sometimes it's hard for him to express   120
it, but he loves you more than anything."

Joyce could hardly have made a statement that Patty more fervently longed to believe was true. Wished, with her whole being, were true. Didn't her dad tease her and ridicule her in ways that would have been simply cruel if he didn't secretly love her more than anything? But she was seventeen now and not actually dumb. She knew that you could love somebody more than anything and still not love the person all that much, if you were busy with other things.

There was a smell of mothballs in her father's inner sanctum, which he'd taken over from his now deceased senior partner without redoing the carpeting or the curtains. Where exactly the mothball smell came from was one of those mysteries.

"What a rotten little shit!" was Ray's response to the tidings his daughter and wife brought of Ethan Post's crime.

"Not so little, unfortunately," Joyce said with a dry laugh.

"He's a rotten little shit punk," Ray said. "He's a bad seed!"   125

"So do we go to the hospital now?" Patty said. "Or to the police?"

Her father told her mother to call Dr. Sipperstein, her old pediatrician, who'd been involved in Democratic politics since Roosevelt, and see if he was available for an emergency. While Joyce made this call, Ray asked Patty if she knew what rape was.

She stared at him.

"Just checking," he said. "You do know the actual legal definition."

"He had sex with me against my will."   130

"Did you actually say no?"

" 'No,' 'don't,' 'stop.' Anyway, it was obvious. I was trying to scratch him and push him off me."

"Then he is a despicable piece of shit."

She'd never heard her father talk this way, and she appreciated it, but only abstractly, because it didn't sound like him.

"Dave Sipperstein says he can meet us at five at his office," Joyce reported. "He's 135 so fond of Patty I think he would have cancelled his dinner plans if he'd had to."

"Right," Patty said. "I'm sure I'm number one among his twelve thousand patients." She then told her dad her story, and her dad explained to her why Coach Nagel was wrong and she couldn't go to the police.

"Chester Post is not an easy person," Ray said, "but he does a lot of good in the county. Given his, uh, given his position, an accusation like this is going to generate extraordinary publicity. Everyone will know who the accuser is. Everyone. Now, what's bad for the Posts is not your concern. But it's virtually certain you'll end up feeling more violated by the pretrial and the trial and the publicity than you do right now. Even if it's pleaded out. Even with a suspended sentence, even with a gag order. There's still a court record."

Joyce said, "But this is all for *her* to decide, not —"

"Joyce." Ray stilled her with a raised hand. "The Posts can afford any lawyer in the country. And as soon as the accusation is made public the worst of the damage to the defendant is over. He has no incentive to speed things along. In fact, it's to his advantage to see that your reputation suffers as much as possible before a plea or a trial."

Patty bowed her head and asked what her father thought she should do. 140

"I'm going to call Chester now," he said. "You go see Dr. Sipperstein and make sure you're O.K."

"And get him as a witness," Patty said.

"Yes, he could testify if need be. But there isn't going to be a trial, Patty."

"So he just gets away with it? And does it to somebody else next weekend?"

Ray raised both hands. "Let me, ah. Let me talk to Mr. Post. He might be ame- 145 nable to a deferred prosecution. Kind of a quiet probation. Sword over Ethan's head."

"But that's *nothing*."

"Actually, Pattycakes, it's quite a lot. It'd be your guarantee that he won't do this to someone else. Requires an admission of guilt, too."

It did seem absurd to imagine Ethan wearing an orange jumpsuit and sitting in a jail cell for inflicting a harm that was mostly in her head anyway. She'd done wind sprints that hurt as bad as being raped. She felt more beaten up after a tough basketball game than she did now. Plus, as a jock you got used to having other people's hands on you — kneading a cramped muscle, playing tight defense, scrambling for a loose ball, taping an ankle, correcting a stance, stretching a hamstring.

And yet: the feeling of injustice itself turned out to be strangely physical. Even realer, in a way, than her hurting, smelling, sweating body. Injustice had a shape, and a weight, and a temperature, and a texture, and a very bad taste.

In Dr. Sipperstein's office she submitted to examination like a good jock. After 150 she'd put her clothes back on, he asked if she'd ever had intercourse before.

"No."

"I didn't think so. What about contraception? Did the other person use it?"

She nodded. "That's when I tried to get away. When I saw what he had."

"A condom."

"Yes." 155

All this and more Dr. Sipperstein jotted down on her chart. Then he took off his glasses and said, "You're going to have a good life, Patty. Sex is a great thing, and you'll enjoy it all your life. But this was not a good day, was it?"

At home, one of her siblings was in the back yard doing something like juggling with screwdrivers of different sizes. Another was reading Gibbon unabridged. The one who'd been subsisting on Yoplait and radishes was in the bathroom, changing her hair color again. Patty's true home amid all this brilliant eccentricity was a foam-cushioned, mildewed, built-in bench in the TV corner of the basement. The fragrance of Eulalie's hair oil still lingered on the bench years after Eulalie had been let go. Patty took a carton of butter-pecan ice cream down to the bench and answered no when her mother called down to ask if she was coming up for dinner.

Mary Tyler Moore was just starting when her father came down after his Martini and his own dinner and suggested that he and Patty go for a drive.

"Can I watch this show first?" she said.

"Patty." 160

Feeling cruelly deprived, she turned off the television. Her dad drove them over to the high school and stopped under a bright light in the parking lot. They unrolled their windows, letting in the smell of spring lawns like the one she'd been raped on not many hours earlier.

"So," she said.

"So Ethan denies it," her dad said. "He says it was just roughhousing and consensual."

Patty's tears came on like a rain that starts unnoticeably but surprisingly soon soaks everything. She asked if her dad had spoken to Ethan directly.

"No, just his father, twice," he said. "I'd be lying if I said the conversation went 165 well."

"So obviously Mr. Post doesn't believe me."

"Well, Patty, Ethan's his son. He doesn't know you as well as we do."

"Do you believe me?"

"Yes, I do."

"Does Mommy?" 170

"Of course she does."

"Then what do I do?"

Her dad turned to her like an attorney. Like an adult addressing another adult. "You drop it," he said. "Forget about it. Move on."

"What?"

"You shake it off. Move on. Learn to be more careful." 175

"Like it never even happened?"

"Patty, the people at the party were all friends of his. They're going to say they saw you get drunk and be aggressive with him. They'll say you were behind a shed that wasn't more than thirty feet from the pool, and they didn't hear anything untoward."

"It was really noisy. There was music and shouting."

"They'll also say they saw the two of you leaving later in the evening and getting into his car. And the world will see an Exeter boy who's going to Princeton and was responsible enough to use contraceptives, and gentleman enough to leave the party and drive you home."

The deceptive little rain was wetting the collar of Patty's T-shirt. 180

"You're not really on my side, are you," she said.

"Of course I am."

"You keep saying 'Of course,' 'Of course.'"

"Listen to me. The P.A. is going to want to know why you didn't scream."

"I was embarrassed! Those weren't my friends!" 185

"But do you see that this is going to be hard for a judge or a jury to understand? All you had to do was scream, and you would have been safe."

Patty couldn't remember why she hadn't screamed. She had to admit that, in hindsight, it seemed bizarrely agreeable of her.

"I fought, though."

"Yes, but you're a top-tier student athlete. Shortstops get scratched and bruised all the time, don't they? On the arms? On the thighs?"

"Did you tell Mr. Post I'm a virgin? I mean, was?" 190

"I didn't consider that any of his business."

"Maybe you should call him back and tell him that."

"Look," her dad said. "Honey. I know it's horrendously unfair. I feel terrible for you. But sometimes the best thing is just to learn your lesson and make sure you never get in the same position again. To say to yourself, 'I made a mistake, and I had some bad luck,' and then let it. Let it, ah. Let it drop."

He turned the ignition halfway, so that the panel lights came on. He kept his hand on the key.

"But he committed a crime," Patty said. 195

"Yes, but better to, uh. Life's not always fair, Pattycakes. Mr. Post said he thought Ethan might be willing to apologize for not being more gentlemanly, but. Well. Would you like that?"

"No."

"I didn't think so."

"Coach Nagel says I should go to the police."

"Coach Nagel should stick to her dribbling," her dad said. 200

"Softball," Patty said. "It's softball season now."

"Unless you want to spend your entire senior year being publicly humiliated."

"Basketball is in the winter. Softball is in the spring, when the weather's warmer?"

"I'm asking you: is that really how you want to spend your senior year?"

"Coach Carver is basketball," Patty said. "Coach Nagel is softball. Are you getting 205 this?"

Her dad started the engine.

As a senior, instead of being publicly humiliated Patty became a real player, not just a talent. She all but resided in the field house. She got a three-game basketball suspension for putting a shoulder in the back of a New Rochelle forward who'd elbowed one of her teammates, and she still broke every school record she'd set the previous year, plus nearly broke the scoring record. Augmenting her reliable perimeter shooting was a growing taste for driving to the basket. She was no longer on speaking terms with physical pain.

In the spring, when the local state assemblyman stepped down after long service and the Party leadership chose Patty's mother to run as his replacement, the Posts offered to co-host a fund-raiser in the green luxury of their back yard. Joyce sought Patty's permission before she accepted the offer, saying she wouldn't do anything that Patty wasn't comfortable with, but by then Patty was beyond caring what Joyce did, and told her so. When the candidate's family stood for the obligatory family photo, no grief was given to Patty for absenting herself. Her look of bitterness would not have helped Joyce's cause.

(2010)

Exploring the Text

1. The story's first 22 paragraphs offer quite a bit of exposition — things we need to know before the story starts. Do you think that much exposition is necessary? Explain why or why not. How would you describe the tone of the exposition, especially the first paragraph?

2. Compare and contrast the conversation Patty has with her mother (pars. 28–48) with the conversation she has with her coach (pars. 50–60). How is Patty's role different in each? What is her internal reaction to each conversation? Which adult evokes a stronger response in her? Explain your answer.

3. In what ways is this a story about politics? What are the politics of Patty's parents? How do their actions reflect — or contradict — their politics? How does politics figure into the way Patty's rape is handled?

4. How is the suburban setting important in "Agreeable"? If you have read other writers who set their work in suburbia, such as John Cheever, Ann Beattie, or Rick Moody, compare Jonathan Franzen's take with theirs.

5. Were you surprised at the direction this story's plot took? Did you find it believable? What do you make of the fact that Patty seems to feel somewhat responsible for what happened to her? Were you surprised at the reactions of Ethan's and Patty's parents? Explain your answer.

6. We learn that Patty becomes a star athlete — though very physically aggressive. The story ends with Joyce asking Patty's permission to hold a fundraiser in the Posts' backyard. Patty replies that she is "beyond caring" and absents herself from the family portrait. Do you find this ending satisfying or frustrating? Explain. Where do you think Patty goes from here? (Read Franzen's *Freedom* to find out.)

7. Why do you think Franzen titled this story "Agreeable"? What are some of the ways the characters in the story exemplify agreeableness? Do you think Franzen considers it a good quality? Do you? Explain your answer.

BRIAN TURNER

Born in 1967 in California, Brian Turner earned an MFA in poetry at the University of Oregon before enlisting in the army at the age of twenty-nine. During the seven years he spent as a soldier, Turner was deployed to Bosnia and Herzegovina and served as an infantry team leader with the Third Stryker Brigade Combat Team in Iraq in 2003. His work has been published in various journals as well as in *Voices in Wartime: The Anthology* — published in 2005 in conjunction with the feature-length documentary film of the same name. His first collection of poems, *Here, Bullet* (2005), was a New York Times Editors' Choice selection. In 2007, Turner received a National Endowment for the Arts Literature Fellowship in poetry. He currently lives in Fresno, California, where he teaches poetry at Fresno State.

At Lowe's Home Improvement Center

This poem appeared in Turner's 2010 collection, *Phantom Noise*.

Standing in aisle 16, the hammer and anchor aisle,
I bust a 50 pound box of double-headed nails
open by accident, their oily bright shanks
and diamond points like firing pins
from M-4s and M-16s.   5
     In a steady stream
they pour onto the tile floor, constant as shells
falling south of Baghdad last night, where Bosch
kneeled under the chain guns of helicopters
stationed above, their tracer-fire a synaptic geometry   10
of light.
    At dawn, when the shelling stops,
hundreds of bandages will not be enough.

Bosch walks down aisle 16 now, in full combat gear,
improbable, worn out from fatigue, a rifle   15
slung at his side, his left hand guiding
a ten-year-old boy who sees what war is
and will never clear it from his head.

Here, Bosch says, *Take care of him.*
I'm going back in for more.   20

Sheets of plywood drop with the airy breath
of mortars the moment they crack open
in shrapnel. Mower blades are just mower blades

and the Troy-Bilt Self-Propelled Mower doesn't resemble
a Blackhawk or an Apache. In fact, no one seems to notice   25
the casualty collection center Doc High marks out
in ceiling fans, aisle 15. Wounded Iraqis with IVs
sit propped against boxes as 92 sample Paradiso fans
hover in a slow revolution of blades.

The forklift driver over-adjusts, swinging the tines   30
until they slice open gallons and gallons of paint,
Sienna Dust and Lemon Sorbet and Ship's Harbor Blue
pooling in the aisle where Sgt. Rampley walks through —
carrying someone's blown-off arm cradled like an infant,
handing it to me, saying, *Hold this, Turner,*   35
we might find who it belongs to.

Cash registers open and slide shut
with a sound of machine guns being charged.
Dead soldiers are laid out at the registers,
on the black conveyor belts,   40
and people in line still reach
for their wallets. Should I stand
at the magazine rack, reading
Landscaping with Stone or *The Complete*
Home Improvement Repair Book?   45
What difference does it make if I choose
tumbled travertine tile, Botticino marble,
or Black Absolute granite. Outside,
palm trees line the asphalt boulevards,
restaurants cool their patrons who will enjoy   50
fireworks exploding over Bass Lake in July.

Aisle number 7 is a corridor of lights.
Each dead Iraqi walks amazed
by Tiffany posts and Bavarian pole lights.
Motion-activated incandescents switch on   55
as they pass by, reverent sentinels of light,
Fleur De Lis and Luminaire Mural Extérieur
welcoming them to Lowe's Home Improvement Center,
aisle number 7, where I stand in mute shock,
someone's arm cradled in my own.   60
                              The Iraqi boy beside me
reaches down to slide his fingertip in Retro Colonial Blue,
an interior latex, before writing
T, for *Tourniquet*, on my forehead.

                                                    (2010)

Exploring the Text

1. The epigraph of Brian Turner's collection in which this poem appears is from the Iraqi poet Al-Bayati: "I embrace the frightful and the beautiful." How does "At Lowe's Home Improvement Center" embrace the frightful and the beautiful?
2. Why do you think Turner set this poem in a Lowe's Home Improvement Center? How is it both a literal setting and also, perhaps, a play on words?
3. Modern American warfare is said to differ from warfare of the past in that soldiers now spend more time patrolling and identifying enemies than they do fighting. How does this poem reflect that distinction?
4. Trace the ways that Turner moves from the safety of the home improvement center to the danger of the speaker's war experience. How does he make those transitions? What is the effect of the transitions?
5. Turner has said that he believes "the poem finishes in the reader." How does this poem finish in you?

JOHN JEREMIAH SULLIVAN

John Jeremiah Sullivan was born in Louisville, Kentucky, in 1974 and raised in Indiana. Son of a sportswriter father and English teacher mother, Sullivan is known for his "long-form" writing (long, deeply researched nonfiction pieces) and was highly praised for his collection *Pulphead: Essays* (2011). He has written for *GQ*, *Harper's*, *New York Magazine*, *New York Times Magazine*, and the *Paris Review*.

Michael

"Michael," an essay in *Pulphead*, was inspired by interviews that Michael Jackson gave to *Ebony* and *Jet* magazines, publications aimed largely at African American audiences, during a time when he rarely spoke to the mainstream media.

How do you talk about Michael Jackson except that you mention Prince Screws? Prince Screws was an Alabama cotton-plantation slave who became a tenant farmer after the Civil War, likely on his former master's land. His son, Prince Screws, Jr., bought a small farm. And that man's son, Prince Screws III, left home for Indiana, where he found work as a Pullman porter, part of the exodus of Southern blacks to the Northern industrial cities.

There came a disruption in the line. This last Prince Screws, the one who went north, would have no sons. He had two daughters, Kattie and Hattie. Kattie gave birth to ten children, the eighth a boy, Michael — who would name his sons Prince, to honor his mother, whom he adored, and to signal a restoration. So the ridiculous moniker given by a white man to his black slave, the way you might name a dog, was bestowed by a black king upon his pale-skinned sons and heirs.

We took the name for an affectation and mocked it.

Not to imply that it was above mockery, but of all the things that make Michael unknowable, thinking we knew him is maybe the most deceptive. Let's suspend it.

Begin not with the miniseries childhood of Joseph's endless family practice sessions but with the later and, it seems, just as formative Motown childhood, from, say, eleven to fourteen — years spent, when not on the road, most often alone, behind security walls, with private tutors and secret sketchbooks. A cloud-headed child, he likes rainbows and reading. He starts collecting exotic animals.

His eldest brothers had at one time been children who dreamed of child stardom. Michael never knows this sensation. By the time he achieves something like self-awareness, he is a child star. The child star dreams of being an artist.

Alone, he puts on classical records, because he finds they soothe his mind. He also likes the old Southern stuff his uncle Luther sings. His uncle looks back at him and thinks he seems sad for his age. This is in California, so poor, brown Gary, with its poisonous air you could smell from leagues away — a decade's exposure to which may already have damaged his immune system in fateful ways — is the past.

He thinks about things and sometimes talks them over with his friends Marvin Gaye and Diana Ross when they are hanging out. He listens to albums and compares. The albums he and his brothers make have a few nice tunes, to sell records, then a lot of consciously second-rate numbers, to satisfy the format. Whereas Tchaikovsky and people like that, they didn't handle slack material. But you have to write your own songs. Michael has always made melodies in his head, little riffs and beats, but that isn't the same. The way Motown deals with the Jackson 5, finished songs are delivered to the group from songwriting teams in various cities. The brothers are brought in to sing and add accents.

Michael wants access to the "anatomy" of the music. That's the word he uses repeatedly. *Anatomy*. What's inside its structure that makes it move?

When he's seventeen, he asks Stevie Wonder to let him spy while *Songs in the Key of Life* gets made. There's Michael, self-consciously shy and deferential, flattening himself mothlike against the Motown studio wall. Somehow Stevie's blindness becomes moving in this context. No doubt he is for long stretches unaware of Michael's presence. Never asks him to play a shaker or anything. Never mentions Michael. But Michael hears him. Most of the Jackson siblings are leaving Motown at this moment, for another label, where they've leveraged a bit more creative sway. The first thing Michael does is write "Blues Away," an unfairly forgotten song, fated to become one of the least-dated-sounding tracks the Jacksons do together. A nice rolling piano riff with strings and a breathy chorus — Burt Bacharach doing Stevie doing early disco, and some other factor that was Michael's own, that dwelled in his introverted-sounding vocal rhythms. Sweet, slightly cryptic lyrics that contain an early notion of melancholy as final, inviolable retreat: "I'd like to be yours tomorrow, so I'm giving you some time to get over today / But you can't take my blues away."

By 1978, the year of "Shake Your Body (Down to the Ground)" — cowritten by Michael and little Randy — Michael's methods have gelled. He starts with tape recorders. He sings and beatboxes the little things he hears, the parts. Where do they come from? Above. He claims to drop to his knees and thank Jehovah after he snatches one. His voice coach tells the story of Michael one day raising his hands in the air during practice and

5

10

starting to mutter. The coach, Seth Riggs, decides to leave him alone. When he comes back half an hour later, it's to Michael whispering, "Thank you for my talent."

Some of the things Michael hears in his head he exports to another instrument, to the piano (which he plays not well but passably) or to the bass. The melody and a few percussive elements remain with his vocal. The rest he assembles around it. He has his brothers and sisters with him. He conducts.

His art will come to depend on his ability to stay in touch with that childlike inner instrument, keeping near enough to himself to heed his own melodic promptings. If you've listened to toddlers making up songs, the things they invent are often bafflingly catchy and ingenious. They compose to biorhythms somehow. The vocal from Michael's earlier, *Off the Wall*–era demo of the eventual *Thriller* hit "Wanna Be Startin' Somethin'" sounds like nothing so much as playful schoolyard taunting. He will always be at his worst when making what he thinks of as "big" music, which he invariably associates with military imagery.

Nineteen seventy-nine, the year of *Off the Wall* and his first nose job, marks an obscure crisis. Around the start of that year, they offer him the gay lead in the film version of *A Chorus Line*, but he declines the role, explaining, "I'm excited about it, but if I do it, people will link me with the part. Because of my voice, some people already think I'm that way — homo — though I'm actually not at all."

People want to know, Why, when you became a man, did your voice not change? Rather, it did change, but what did it change into? Listening to clips of his interviews through the seventies, you can hear how he goes about changing it himself. First it deepens slightly, around 1972–73 or so. (Listen to him on *The Dating Game* in 1972 and you'll hear that his voice was lower at fourteen than it will be at thirty.) This potentially catastrophic event has perhaps been vaguely dreaded by the family and label for years. Michael Jackson without his falsetto is not the commodity on which their collective dream depends. But Michael has never known a reality that wasn't susceptible on some level to his creative powers. He works to develop something, not a falsetto, which is a way of singing above your range, but instead a higher range. He isolates totally different configurations of his vocal cords, finding their crevices, cultivating the flexibility there. Vocal teachers will tell you this can be done, though it's considered an extreme practice. Whether the process is conscious in Michael's case is unknowable. He probably evolves it in order to keep singing Jackson 5 songs every night through puberty. The startling effect is of his having imaginatively not so much castrated himself as womanized himself. He essentially evolves a drag voice. On the early demo for "Don't Stop 'Til You Get Enough," recorded at home with Randy and Janet helping, you can actually hear him work his way into this voice. It is a character, really. "We're gonna be startin' now, baby," he says in a relaxed, moderately high-pitched man's voice. Then he intones the title, "Don't stop 'til you get enough," in a softer, quieter version of basically the same voice. He repeats the line in a still higher register, almost purring. Finally — in a full-on girlish peal — he sings.

A source will later claim that Michael once, in a moment of anger, broke into a deep, gruff voice she'd never heard before. Liza Minnelli also claims to have heard this other voice.

Interesting that these out-flashings of his "natural" voice occurred at moments when he was, as we would say, not himself.

On the Internet, you can see a picture of him near the end of his life, juxtaposed with a digital projection of what he would have looked like at the same age without the surgeries and makeup and wigs. A smiling middle-aged black guy, handsome in an everyday way. We are meant, of course, to feel a connection with this lost neverbeing, and pity for the strange, self-mutilated creature beside him. I can't be alone, however, in feeling just the opposite, that there's something metaphysically revolting about the mock-up. It's an abomination. Michael chose his true face. What is, is natural.

His physical body is arguably, even inarguably, the single greatest piece of post-   20
modern American sculpture. It must be carefully preserved.

It's fascinating to read the interviews he gave to *Ebony* and *Jet* over the past thirty years. I confess myself disoriented by them, as a white person. During whole stretches of years when the big media were reporting endlessly on his bizarreness and reclusive-ness, he was every so often granting these intimate and illuminating sit-downs to those magazines, never forgetting to remind them that he trusted only them, would speak only to them. The articles make me realize that about the only Michael Jackson I've ever known, personality-wise, is a Michael Jackson who's defending himself against white people who are passive-aggressively accusing him of child molestation. He spoke differently to black people, was more at ease. The language and grain of detail are dif-ferent. Not that the scenario was any more journalistically pure. The John H. Johnson publishing family, which puts out *Jet* and *Ebony*, had Michael's back, faithfully repair-ing and maintaining his complicated relations with the community, assuring readers that, in the presence of Michael, "you quickly look past the enigmatic icon's light, almost translucent skin and realize that this African American legend is more than just skin deep." At times, especially when the "homo" issue came up, the straining required could turn comical, as in *Ebony* in 1982, talking about his obsessive male fans:

MICHAEL: They come after us every way they can, and the guys are just as bad
    as the girls. Guys jump up on the stage and usually go for me and Randy.
EBONY: But that means nothing except that they admire you, doesn't it?

Even so, to hear Michael laid-back and talking unpretentiously about art, the thing he most loved—that is a new Michael, a person utterly absent from, for example, Martin Bashir's infamous documentary, *Living with Michael Jackson*, in which Michael admitted sharing his bedroom with children. It's only after reading *Jet* and *Ebony* that one can understand how otherwise straightforward-seeming people of all races have stayed good friends with Michael Jackson these many years. He is charming; his mind is alive. What a pleasure to find him listening to early "writing version" demos of his own compositions and saying, "Listen to that, that's at home, Janet, Randy, me... You're hearing four basses on there..." Or to hear him tell less prepackaged anecdotes, such as the one about a beautiful black girl who froze in the aisle and pissed all down her legs after spotting him on a plane, or the blond girl who kissed him in an airport and, when he didn't respond, asked, "What's wrong, you fag?" He grows tired of reminding people, "There's a reason why I was created male. I'm not a girl." He leaves the reason unspoken.

When Michael and Quincy Jones run into each other on the set of *The Wiz*, Michael remembers a moment from years before when Sammy Davis, Jr., had taken Jones aside backstage somewhere and whispered, "This guy is something; he's amazing." Michael had "tucked it away." He knows Jones's name from the sleeves of his father's jazz albums, knows Jones is a serious man. He waits till the movie is done to call him up. It's the fact that Jones intimidates him slightly that draws Jackson to him. He yearns for some competition larger than the old intrafamilial one, which he has long dominated. That was checkers; he wants chess. Fading child stars can easily insulate themselves from further motivation, if they wish, and most do. It's the more human path. Michael seeks pressure instead, at this moment. He recruits people who can drive him to, as he puts it, "higher effort."

Quincy Jones's nickname for him is Smelly. It comes from Michael's habit of constantly touching and covering his nose with the fingers of his left hand, a tic that becomes pronounced in news clips from this time. He feels embarrassed about his broad nose. Several surgeries later — after, one assumes, it had been deemed impolitic inside the Jackson camp to mention the earlier facial self-consciousness — the story is altered. We are told that when Michael liked a track in the studio, he would call it "the smelly jelly." Both stories may be true. "Smelly jelly" has the whiff of Jackson's weird, infantile sayings. Later in life, when feeling weak, he'd say to his people, "I'm hurting . . . blanket me," which could mean, among other things, time for my medicine.

Michael knows he won't really have gone solo until his own songwriting finds the next level. He doesn't want inclusion; he wants awe. Jones has a trusted songwriter in his stable, the Englishman Rod Temperton, of Heatwave fame, who brings in a song, "Rock with You." It's very good. Michael hears it and knows it's a hit. He's not even worried about hits at this point, though, except as a kind of by-product of perfection. He goes home and writes "Don't Stop 'Til You Get Enough." Janet tinks on a glass bottle. Trusted Randy plays guitar. These are the two siblings whom Michael brings with him into the Quincy Jones adventure, to the innermost zone where he writes. We don't think of the family as having anything to do, musically, with his solo career, except by way of guilt favors. But he feels confident with these two, needs to keep them woven into his nest. They are both younger than he. His baby sister.

From the perspective of thirty years, "Don't Stop 'Til You Get Enough" is a much better track than "Rock with You." One admires "Rock with You," but melodically Michael's song comes from a more distinctive place. You hear not slickness but sophisticated instincts.

Michael feels disappointed with *Off the Wall*. It wins a Grammy, spawns multiple number one singles, dramatically raises Jackson's already colossal level of fame, redeems disco in the very hour and flash of disco's dying. Diana Ross, who once helped out the Jacksons by putting her lovely arm around them, wants Michael to be at her shows again, not for his sake now but for hers. She isn't desperate by any means, but something has shifted. Quincy Jones and Bruce Swedien, the recording guru who works with him, both take to be absurd the mere idea of "following up" *Off the Wall* in terms of success. You do your best, but that kind of thing just happens, if it happens. Jones knows that. Not Michael. All he can see of *Off the Wall* is that the year had bigger records. He wants to make something, he says, that "refuse[s] to be ignored."

At home he demos "Billie Jean" with Randy and Janet. When what will be the immortal part comes around, she and Michael go, "Whoo whoo / Whoo whoo."

25

From Michael's brain, then, through a portable tape recorder, on into the home studio. Bruce Swedien comes over. Being Michael Jackson working on the follow-up to *Off the Wall* means sometimes your demos are recorded at your home by the greatest audio engineer in the world. But for all that, the team works in a stripped-down fashion, with no noise reduction. "That's usually the best stuff," Michael says, "when you strip it down to the bare minimum and go inside yourself and invent."

On this home demo, made between the "writing version" and the album version, you get to hear Michael's early, mystical placeholder vocals, laid down before he'd written the verses. We hear him say, "More kick and stuff in the 'phones . . . I need, uh . . . more bottom and kick in the 'phones." 30

Then the music. And what sounds like:

[Mumble mumble mum] oh, to say
On the phone to stay . . .
Oh, born out of time.
All the while I see other eyes.
One at a time
We'll go where the winds unwind

She told me her voice belonged to me
And I'm here to see
She called my name, then you said, Hello
Oh, then I died
And said, Gotta go in a ride

Seems that you knew my mind, now live
On that day got it made
Oh, mercy, it does care of what you do
Take care of what you do
Lord, they're coming down

Billie Jean is not my lover
She just a girl that says that I am the one
You know, the kid is not my son

A big round warm Scandinavian type, Swedien comes from Minnesota, made his mark doing classical, but with classical engineering it's all about fidelity, he knew, and he wants to be part of the making, to help shape the songs. So, a frustrated anatomist himself, coming down from high to low formally and meeting Michael on his way up. Quincy, in the middle with his jazz cool, calls Swedien "Svensk." The white man has the endearing habit of lifting both hands to massage the gray walrus wings of his mustache. He has a condition called synesthesia. It means that when he listens to sound, he sees colors. He knows the mix is right only when he sees the right colors. Michael likes singing for him.

In a seminar room in Seattle, at a 1993 Audio Pro recording-geek conference, Swedien talks about his craft. He plays his recording of Michael's flawless one-take vocal from "The Way You Make Me Feel," sans effects of any kind, to let the engineers in the audience hear the straight dope, a great mike on a great voice with as little interference as possible, the right angle, the right deck, everything.

Someone in the audience raises a hand and asks if it's hard recording Michael's voice, given that, as Swedien mentioned before, Michael is very "physical." At first, Swedien doesn't cotton. "Yeah, that is a bit of a problem," he answers, "but I've never had an incident where the microphone has been damaged. One time, though . . ."

The guy interrupts, "Not to do damage, just the proximity thing."   35

"Oh!" Swedien says, suddenly understanding. His voice drops to a whisper, "He's unbelievable."

He gives the most beautiful description. "Michael records in the dark," he says, "and he'll dance. And picture this: You're looking through the glass. And it's dark. With a little pin spot on him." Swedien lifts his hand to suggest a narrow cone of light shining directly down from overhead. "And you'll see the mike here. And he'll sing his lines. And then he disappears."

In the outer dark he is dancing, fluttering. That's all Quincy and Swedien know.

"And he's" — Swedien punches the air — "right back in front of the mike at the precise instant."

Swedien invents a special zippered covering for miking the bass drum on "Billie   40
Jean." A muffled enclosure. It gives the song that mummified-heartbeat intensity, which you have seen make a dance floor come to life. The layered bass sounds on the one and the three lend a lurching feline throb. Bass drum, bass guitar, double synthesizer bass, the "four basses," all hitting together, doing the part that started as Michael and Janet going whoo whoo whoo whoo, that came from Jehovah. Its tempo is like the pulse of a sleeping person.

Michael finds himself back in the old Motown building for a day, doing some video mixing, when Berry Gordy approaches and asks him to be in the twenty-fifth-anniversary special on NBC. Michael demurs. A claustrophobic moment for him. All that business, his brothers, Motown, the Jackson 5, the past: that's all a cocoon he's been writhing inside of, finally chewing through. He knows that "Billie Jean" has exploded; he's becoming something else. But the animal inside him that is his ambition senses the opportunity. He strikes his legendary deal with Gordy, that he'll perform with his brothers if he's allowed to do one of his own solo, post-Motown hits as well. Gordy agrees.

What Michael does with his moment, given the context, given that his brothers have just left the stage and that the stage belongs to Mr. Berry Gordy, is outrageous. In the by-now totemic YouTube clips of this performance, Michael's preamble is usually cut off. That makes it worth watching the disc (which also happens to include one of Marvin Gaye's last appearances before his murder).

Michael is sweaty and strutting. "Thank you . . . Oh, you're beautiful . . . Thank you," he says, almost slurring with sexiness. You can tell he's worked out all his nerves on the Jackson 5 songs. Now he owns the space as if it were the inside of his cage. Millions upon millions of eyes.

"I have to say, those were the good old days," he rambles on. "I love those songs, those were magic moments, with all my brothers, including Jermaine." (The Jackson family's penchant for high passive-aggression at watershed moments is extraordinary; at Michael's funeral, Jermaine will say: "I was his voice and his backbone, I had his back." And then, as if remembering to thank his agent, "So did the family.")

"Those were good songs," Michael says. "I like those songs a lot, but especially, I like" — his voice fades from the mike for a second, ramifying the liveness till the meters almost spike — "the new songs." 45

Uncontrollable shrieking. He's grabbing the mike stand like James Brown used to grab it, like if it had a neck he'd be choking it. People in the seats are yelling, "'Billie Jean'! 'Billie Jean'!"

I won't cloud the uniqueness of what he does next with words except to mention one potentially missable (because it's so obvious) aspect: that he does it so entirely alone. The stage is profoundly empty. Silhouettes of the orchestra members are clapping back in the dark. But unless you count the dazzling glove — conceived, according to one source, to hide the advancing vitiligo that discolors his left hand — Michael holds only one prop: a black hat. He tosses that away almost immediately. Stage, dancer, spotlight. The microphone isn't even on. He snatches it back from the stand as if from the hands of a maddening child.

With a mime's tools he proceeds to do possibly the most captivating thing a person's ever been captured doing onstage. Richard Pryor, who was not in any account I have ever read a suck-up, approaches Michael afterward and says simply, "That was the greatest performance I've ever seen." Fred Astaire calls him "the greatest living natural dancer."

Michael tells *Ebony*, "I remember doing the performance so clearly, and I remember that I was so upset with myself, 'cause it wasn't what I wanted. I wanted it to be more." It's said he intended to hold the crouching en pointe at the end of the moonwalk longer. But if you watch, he falls off his toes, when he falls, in perfect time, and makes it part of the turn. Much as, closer to the end, he wipes sweat from under his nose in time.

The intensity behind his face looks unbearable. 50

Quincy always tells him, "Smelly . . . get out of the way and leave room so that God can walk in."

A god moves through him. The god enters, the god leaves.

It's odd to write about a person knowing he may have been, but not if he was, a serial child molester. Whether or not Michael did it, the suggestion of it shadowed him for so long and finally killed his soul. It's said that toward the end, he was having himself put under — with the same anesthesia that may have finished him — not for hours but for days. As though being snuffed. Witnesses to his body on the morgue table report that his prosthetic nose was missing. There were only holes in his face. A mummy. Two separate complete autopsies: they cut him to pieces. As of this writing, no one outside the Jackson camp knows for certain the whereabouts of his body.

I have read a stack of books about him in the past month, more than I ever imagined I would — though not more than I wanted. He warrants and will no doubt one day receive a serious, objective biography: all the great cultural strains of American music came together in him. We have yet to accept that his very racial in-betweenness made him more and not less of an essential figure in our tradition. He grasped this and used it. His marriage to Elvis's daughter was in part an art piece.

Of all those books, the one that troubles and sticks with me is the celebrity jour-   55
nalist Ian Halperin's *Unmasked: The Final Years of Michael Jackson*. Most famous for
a book and movie suggesting dubiously that Kurt Cobain's suicide was a disguised
murder, Halperin is not an ideal source but neither is he a useless one. Indeed, he accurately predicted Michael's death six months before it happened and seems to have
burrowed his way into the Jackson world in several places.

In the beginning, Halperin claims, he'd set out mainly to prove that Michael had
sexually molested young boys and used his money to get away with it. I believe him
about this original motivation, since any such proof would have generated the most
sensational publicity, sold the most copies, and so on. But Halperin finds, in the end,
after exhaustively pursuing leads, that every so-called thread of evidence becomes a
rope of sand. Somebody, even if it's a family member, wants money, or has accused
other people before, or is patently insane. It usually comes down to a tale someone else
knows about an alleged secret payoff. Meanwhile, you have these boys, like Macaulay
Culkin (whom Michael was once accused of fondling), who have come forth and
stated that nothing untoward ever happened with Michael. When he stood trial and
got off, that was a just verdict.

That's the first half of the Halperin Thesis. The second half is that Michael was a
fully functioning gay man, who took secret male lovers his entire adult life. Halperin
says he met two of them and saw pictures of one with Michael. They were young but
perfectly legal. One told Halperin that Michael was an insatiable bottom.

As for Michael's interest in children, it's hard to imagine that lacking an erotic
dimension of some kind, but it may well have been thoroughly nonsexual. Michael
was a frozen adolescent — about the age of those first dreamy striped-sweater years
in California — and he wanted to hang out with the people he saw as his peers. Have
pillow fights, call each other doo-doo head. It's creepy as hell, if you like, but victimless.
It would make him — in rough clinical terms — a partial passive fixated pedophile. Not
a crime yet, not until they get the mind-reader machines going.

I don't ask that you agree with Halperin, merely that you admit, as I feel compelled
to do, that the psychological picture he conjures up is not less and perhaps just slightly
more plausible than the one in which Michael uses Neverland Ranch as a spiderweb,
luring boys to his bed. If you're like me, you've been subconsciously presuming the
latter to be basically the case for most of your life. But there's a good chance it was
never true and that Michael loved children with a weird but not immoral love.

If you want a disturbing thought experiment, allow these — I won't say facts, but   60
feasibility structures — let them digest, and then go back again to Martin Bashir's 2003
documentary. There's no point adding here to the demonization of Bashir for having
more or less manipulated Michael through kindness into declaring himself a complete
Fruit of the Loom–collecting fiend, especially when you consider that Bashir was
representing us fairly well in the ideas he appears to have carried regarding Michael,
that it was probably true about him and kids.

But when you put on the not-so glasses and watch, and see Michael protesting his
innocence, asking, "What's wrong with sharing love?" as he holds hands with that
twelve-year-old cancer survivor — or many years earlier, in that strange self-released
statement, where he describes with barely suppressed rage the humiliation of having

his penis examined by the police — dammit if the whole life doesn't look a lot different. There appears to exist a nondismissible chance that Michael was some kind of martyr.

We won't pity him. That he embraced his own destiny, knowing beforehand how fame would warp him, is precisely what frees us to revere him.

We have, in any case, a pathology of pathologization in this country. It's a bourgeois disease, and we do right to call bullshit on it. We moan that Michael changed his face out of self-loathing. He may have loved what he became.

Ebony caught up with him in Africa in the nineties. He had just been crowned king of Sani by villagers in the Ivory Coast. "You know I don't give interviews," he tells Robert E. Johnson there in the village. "You're the only person I trust to give interviews to: Deep inside I feel that this world we live in is really a big, huge, monumental symphonic orchestra. I believe that in its primordial form, all of creation is sound and that it's not just random sound, that it's music."

May they have been his last thoughts.   65

(2011)

Exploring the Text

1. What is John Jeremiah Sullivan's claim about Michael Jackson? Find and analyze at least three different types of evidence that Sullivan uses to support his claim.
2. How does Sullivan establish ethos in this essay?
3. Sullivan traces Michael Jackson's career and image through his songs. Listen to them or watch them on YouTube. Do you agree with Sullivan's assessment? Do they reveal something different to you? Explain your answer.
4. Sullivan is considered a practitioner of New Journalism, a term coined in the 1960s to describe writing characterized by the use of elements of fiction to get at the story behind the story. How does Sullivan get at the story behind the story in "Michael"?
5. Critic James Wood of the *New Yorker* said of Sullivan's prose that it "bend[s] itself around its subject . . . [he] lets his subjects muss and alter his prose." Find examples in "Michael" where the subject of his essay has an effect on his prose style. Hint: look for places where the essay sounds more like a novel.
6. In an online interview with Shona Sanzgirl for the *SF Weekly*, Sullivan was asked what he meant when he said that Michael Jackson's body was the "greatest piece of postmodern American sculpture" (par. 20). He answered that he meant it literally, saying, "[I]t's hard to imagine a piece of art that more thoroughly transmitted the anxieties and contradictions of his time." What anxieties and contradictions do you think Sullivan is talking about?
7. Did reading "Michael" change any of your views about pop icon Michael Jackson? Explain why or why not.

Chris Hedges and Joe Sacco

Chris Hedges (b. 1956) is a Pulitzer Prize–winning journalist who worked for more than fifteen years at the *New York Times* and spent nearly twenty years as a foreign correspondent in Central America, the Middle East, Africa, and the Balkans. He is the author of four best-selling nonfiction books, and his articles and essays have appeared in numerous publications, including *Harper's*, *New York Review of Books*, *Granta*, and *Mother Jones*.

Joe Sacco (b. 1960) is a world-renowned cartoonist and the author of eleven books. His journalistic comics have appeared in *Details*, the *New York Times Magazine*, *Time*, and *Harper's*.

from *Days of Destruction, Days of Revolt*

In 2012, Hedges and Sacco published *Days of Destruction, Days of Revolt*, a collaboration of illustrations and stories that expose the "sacrifice zones" of postcapitalist America — from Native American reservations to deserted manufacturing towns to Occupy Wall Street demonstrations. The excerpt here is from "Days of Siege," the chapter on Camden, New Jersey, a dying city that used to be full of industry and manufacturing and is now impoverished and crime ridden. The main character is seventy-six-year-old Joe Bolzano, who is described as one of a "handful of white citizens who never left the city [of Camden]."

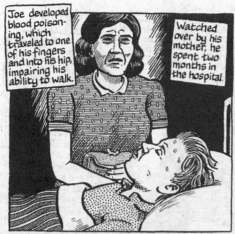

Joe developed blood poisoning, which traveled to one of his fingers and into his hip, impairing his ability to walk.

Watched over by his mother, he spent two months in the hospital.

Despite the adversity,

"somehow I won an award in 1945: Camden's outstanding young citizen."

This brought Joe to the notice of New Jersey state Supreme Court Judge Ralph W. Donges.

[HE] MUST HAVE TAKEN A LIKING TO ME...

I THINK HE SEES A POOR KID, AND HE WANTED TO REACH OUT...

AND HE MADE CERTAIN THAT I HAD AN OPERATION AT THE COOPER HOSPITAL, WHERE THEY STRAIGHTENED MY LEG OUT AND CUT MY [DISEASED] FINGER OFF.

"He had an apartment in the Walt Whitman Hotel, and he would occasionally have me go to dinner with him and his wife... It was probably like going to a big hotel today — elevators, and people would come in, and they had the table.

"It was beautiful..."

With the money he was making, Joe bought his first car, and he could now cruise Broadway, Camden's main drag.

He likens those days to the movie 'American Graffiti.'

"When [I] watch that movie, it plays in my mind... I can tell you it was a fun time."

He would start at the Star movie theater — "then you'd go up to the Walt Whitman Hotel, make a U-turn, and you'd go again."

Still self-conscious of his limp, Joe found he never really had to leave his car.

"You know, you would say, YO! JANE!

MY NAME'S NOT JANE. IT'S ALICE.

OH, I THOUGHT...

"and they'd come over to the car, and you're talking.

Industry was leaving Camden, and the city began its decline.

Eventually the landmark Walt Whitman Hotel, where young Joe had sometimes dined with a state justice, was replaced by a parking lot.

Theaters where he and his brothers had sat for hours were boarded up or put to other uses.

MIRACLE CENTER CHURCH
1117 BROADWAY
CAMDEN NJ

The library building, from where he had once watched President Roosevelt on his way to inspect the wartime shipyard, was abandoned.

DANGER
DO NOT
ENTER

J. SACCO 6-11

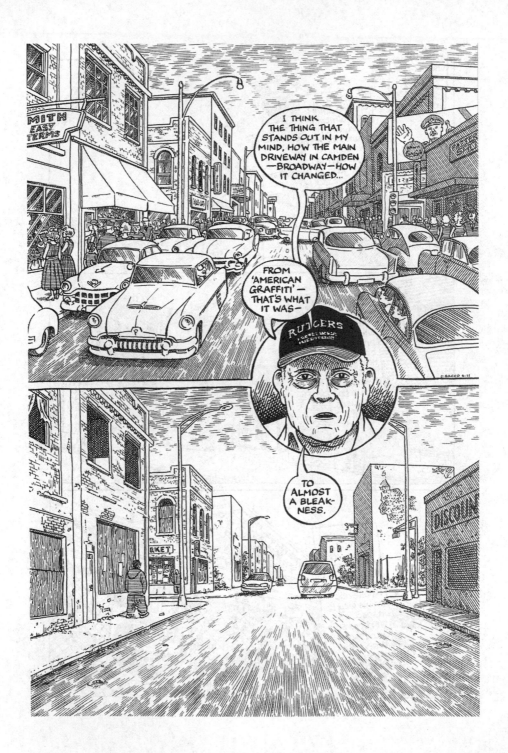

Exploring the Text

1. What is your first impression of Joe Bolzano, whose picture begins the excerpt? How do you feel about him after you finish the excerpt? Does it match your first impression? Explain.
2. How does Bolzano characterize his father? What does he consider his father's most important trait? How do the drawings build on that characterization?
3. What picture do the drawings of the funeral of Joe's younger brother and the Walt Whitman Hotel paint of the Camden of the past?
4. What is it that Bolzano thinks makes him a man? How does that differ from the idea of manhood in Camden today or in any other place that is plagued by poverty and gang warfare?
5. In the introduction to *Days of Destruction, Days of Revolt*, Chris Hedges writes:

> Joe Sacco and I set out . . . to take a look at the sacrifice zones, those areas in the country that have been offered up for exploitation in the name of profit, progress, and technological advancement. We wanted to show in words and drawings what life looks like when the marketplace rules without constraints, where human beings and the natural world are used and then discarded to maximize profit. We wanted to look at what the ideology of unfettered capitalism means for families, communities, workers, and the ecosystem.

Why do you think they thought the combination of words and pictures would be effective in developing their argument? How has it helped them achieve the purpose stated above? Explain your answer.

Conversation
The Atomic Age

The following ten selections are related to the consequences of the atomic age, a period that began with the detonation of the first atomic bomb in 1945 and that most people consider to have ended with the fall of the Soviet Union in 1991, though nuclear weapons and nuclear power continue to be the subject of both fear and optimism. Atomic power exemplified technological progress in the early to mid-twentieth century, giving rise to elaborate fantasies of nuclear cars, an atomic reactor in every house supplying unlimited free energy, and sci-fi weaponry. While most of the domestic uses of nuclear technology failed to live up to their futuristic promise, the atomic bomb became a stark reality, making nuclear technology less a symbol of hope and progress than one of geopolitical, social, and psychological anxiety. In 1949, the Soviet Union tested its first atomic bomb and an arms race began that would result in the Soviet Union and the United States stockpiling and testing thousands of nuclear weapons, each more powerful than the ones used to destroy Hiroshima and Nagasaki. This tense atmosphere of danger and distrust between the United States and the Soviet Union resulted in the so-called Red Scare: scientists, artists, writers, filmmakers, and more were brought before the House Un-American Activities Committee, as well as a similar Senate committee run by Senator Joseph McCarthy, and questioned about their ties to the Communist Party, often becoming blacklisted if they took the Fifth Amendment to avoid incriminating themselves or refused to cooperate by naming names. There was some basis for this paranoia. Tipped off that the Soviets may have been aided by spies within the American nuclear facility at Los Alamos, the FBI launched an investigation that netted a group of Communist sympathizers, most famously Julius and Ethel Rosenberg, who had relayed information from Ethel's brother David Greenglass, a scientist at Los Alamos, to the Soviets. The Rosenbergs were convicted of conspiracy to commit espionage and executed in 1953. Since 1945, nuclear fears have risen and fallen but have never disappeared. The immense power of atomic energy, for good and for evil, continues to fascinate and frighten.

Sources

Ace Comics, *Atomic War!* (1952)
Office of Civil Defense, *Duck and Cover* (1952)
Lillian Hellman, *I Cannot and Will Not Cut My Conscience to Fit This Year's Fashions* (1952)
John F. Kennedy, *Cuban Missile Crisis Speech* (1962)
Nikita Khrushchev, *Letter to John F. Kennedy* (1962)
Julia Alvarez, *Snow* (1991)
Arthur Miller, from *Why I Wrote* The Crucible (1996)
Michael Scheibach, from *Atomic Narratives and American Youth: Coming of Age with the Atom, 1945–55* (2003)
Ronald Radosh, *Case Closed: The Rosenbergs Were Soviet Spies* (2008)
Spencer R. Weart, from *The Rise of Nuclear Fear* (2012)

Atomic War!

ACE COMICS

This is the cover of the first issue of a series of comic books, published between 1952 and 1953, about a fictional war between Russia and the United States.

Questions

1. This cover, one of many that appeared on comic books published during the Korean War, reflects the national paranoia about the atomic bomb. What buttons does it push? Be sure to consider the format (a comic book for children), the style (color, shape, line, for example), and the iconography (what is represented in the picture).
2. What message does the comic book cover send about the United States?

Duck and Cover

OFFICE OF CIVIL DEFENSE

This is a public service announcement poster from 1952 featuring Bert the Turtle, a character from *Duck and Cover*, a civil defense film produced by the U.S. government that suggested that nuclear war could happen at any time and that certain actions would protect citizens from its effects.

Questions

1. How do the two different views of "Bert" express the purpose of the poster?
2. The character on this poster appears in the animated opening of the film *Duck and Cover*; the rest of the ten-minute film features real people, with a narrator making suggestions for staying safe. Why do you think the film begins with animation?
3. *Duck and Cover* was seen by millions of schoolchildren in the early 1950s. What do you think its effects were?

I Cannot and Will Not Cut My Conscience to Fit This Year's Fashions

Lillian Hellman

In May 1952, playwright and screenwriter Lillian Hellman (1905–1984) was called to testify before the House Un-American Activities Committee, which was investigating Communist activity in Hollywood. She wrote the following letter to the committee chair, Congressman John Wood, asking to testify without being forced to inform on others. When her request was denied by the committee, she invoked the Fifth Amendment protection against self-incrimination. She was subsequently blacklisted from work in the entertainment business.

Dear Mr. Wood:

As you know, I am under subpoena to appear before your committee on May 21, 1952.

I am most willing to answer all questions about myself. I have nothing to hide from your committee and there is nothing in my life of which I am ashamed. I have been advised by counsel that under the fifth amendment I have a constitutional privilege to decline to answer any questions about my political opinions, activities, and associations, on the grounds of self-incrimination. I do not wish to claim this privilege. I am ready and willing to testify before the representatives of our Government as to my own opinions and my own actions, regardless of any risks or consequences to myself.

But I am advised by counsel that if I answer the committee's questions about myself, I must also answer questions about other people and that if I refuse to do so, I can be cited for contempt. My counsel tells me that if I answer questions about myself, I will have waived my rights under the fifth amendment and could be forced legally to answer questions about others. This is very difficult for a layman to understand. But there is one principle that I do understand: I am not willing, now or in the future, to bring bad trouble to people who, in my past association with them, were completely innocent of any talk or any action that was disloyal or subversive. I do not like subversion or disloyalty in any form and if I had ever seen any I would have considered it my duty to have reported it to the proper authorities. But to hurt innocent people whom I knew many years ago in order to save myself is, to me, inhuman and indecent and dishonorable. I cannot and will not cut my conscience to fit this year's fashions, even though I long ago came to the conclusion that I was not a political person and could have no comfortable place in any political group.

I was raised in an old-fashioned American tradition and there were certain homely things that were taught to me: To try to tell the truth, not to bear false witness, not to harm my neighbor, to be loyal to my country, and so on. In general, I respected these ideals of Christian honor and did as well with them as I knew how. It is my belief that you will agree with these simple rules of human decency and will not expect me to violate the good American tradition from which they spring. I would, therefore, like to come before you and speak of myself.

I am prepared to waive the privilege against self-incrimination and to tell you ⁵
everything you wish to know about my views or actions if your committee will agree
to refrain from asking me to name other people. If the committee is unwilling to give
me this assurance, I will be forced to plead the privilege of the fifth amendment at
the hearing.

A reply to this letter would be appreciated.

Sincerely yours,

Lillian Hellman
(1952)

Questions

1. How does Lillian Hellman establish ethos — her credibility — in this letter?
2. Why do you think that the political connections of a writer would be of interest
   to the House Un-American Activities Committee?
3. This letter became famous for the phrase "I cannot and will not cut my conscience
   to fit this year's fashions." Why do you think it resonates?

Cuban Missile Crisis Speech

JOHN F. KENNEDY

The Cuban missile crisis was a thirteen-day standoff between the United States and
Russia. It was the point at which the Cold War came closest to turning into a nuclear
war. President John F. Kennedy (1917–1963) spoke to the American people on
October 22, 1962, explaining how and why the Soviets would be prevented from
arming Cuba with nuclear weapons.

Good evening my fellow citizens:

This Government, as promised, has maintained the closest surveillance of the Soviet
military buildup on the island of Cuba. Within the past week, unmistakable evidence
has established the fact that a series of offensive missile sites is now in preparation on
that imprisoned island. The purpose of these bases can be none other than to provide
a nuclear strike capability against the Western Hemisphere.

Upon receiving the first preliminary hard information of this nature last Tuesday
morning at 9 A.M., I directed that our surveillance be stepped up. And having now
confirmed and completed our evaluation of the evidence and our decision on a course
of action, this Government feels obliged to report this new crisis to you in fullest detail.

The characteristics of these new missile sites indicate two distinct types of installations. Several of them include medium range ballistic missiles capable of carrying
a nuclear warhead for a distance of more than 1,000 nautical miles. Each of these
missiles, in short, is capable of striking Washington, D.C., the Panama Canal, Cape

Canaveral, Mexico City, or any other city in the southeastern part of the United States, in Central America, or in the Caribbean area.

Additional sites not yet completed appear to be designed for intermediate range ballistic missiles — capable of traveling more than twice as far — and thus capable of striking most of the major cities in the Western Hemisphere, ranging as far north as Hudson Bay, Canada, and as far south as Lima, Peru. In addition, jet bombers, capable of carrying nuclear weapons, are now being uncrated and assembled in Cuba, while the necessary air bases are being prepared.

This urgent transformation of Cuba into an important strategic base — by the presence of these large, long range, and clearly offensive weapons of sudden mass destruction — constitutes an explicit threat to the peace and security of all the Americas, in flagrant and deliberate defiance of the Rio Pact of 1947, the traditions of this nation and hemisphere, the joint resolution of the 87th Congress, the Charter of the United Nations, and my own public warnings to the Soviets on September 4 and 13. This action also contradicts the repeated assurances of Soviet spokesmen, both publicly and privately delivered, that the arms buildup in Cuba would retain its original defensive character, and that the Soviet Union had no need or desire to station strategic missiles on the territory of any other nation. 5

The size of this undertaking makes clear that it has been planned for some months. Yet only last month, after I had made clear the distinction between any introduction of ground-to-ground missiles and the existence of defensive antiaircraft missiles, the Soviet Government publicly stated on September 11, and I quote, "the armaments and military equipment sent to Cuba are designed exclusively for defensive purposes," that, and I quote the Soviet Government, "there is no need for the Soviet Government to shift its weapons . . . for a retaliatory blow to any other country, for instance Cuba," and that, and I quote their government, "the Soviet Union has so powerful rockets to carry these nuclear warheads that there is no need to search for sites for them beyond the boundaries of the Soviet Union." That statement was false.

Only last Thursday, as evidence of this rapid offensive buildup was already in my hand, Soviet Foreign Minister Gromyko told me in my office that he was instructed to make it clear once again, as he said his government had already done, that Soviet assistance to Cuba, and I quote, "pursued solely the purpose of contributing to the defense capabilities of Cuba," that, and I quote him, "training by Soviet specialists of Cuban nationals in handling defensive armaments was by no means offensive, and if it were otherwise," Mr. Gromyko went on, "the Soviet Government would never become involved in rendering such assistance." That statement also was false.

Neither the United States of America nor the world community of nations can tolerate deliberate deception and offensive threats on the part of any nation, large or small. We no longer live in a world where only the actual firing of weapons represents a sufficient challenge to a nation's security to constitute maximum peril. Nuclear weapons are so destructive and ballistic missiles are so swift, that any substantially increased possibility of their use or any sudden change in their deployment may well be regarded as a definite threat to peace.

For many years both the Soviet Union and the United States, recognizing this fact, have deployed strategic nuclear weapons with great care, never upsetting the precarious status quo which insured that these weapons would not be used in the absence of some vital challenge. Our own strategic missiles have never been transferred to the territory of any other nation under a cloak of secrecy and deception; and our history — unlike that of the Soviets since the end of World War II — demonstrates that we have no desire to dominate or conquer any other nation or impose our system upon its people. Nevertheless, American citizens have become adjusted to living daily on the bull's-eye of Soviet missiles located inside the U.S.S.R. or in submarines.

In that sense, missiles in Cuba add to an already clear and present danger — although it should be noted the nations of Latin America have never previously been subjected to a potential nuclear threat.   10

But this secret, swift, and extraordinary buildup of Communist missiles — in an area well known to have a special and historical relationship to the United States and the nations of the Western Hemisphere, in violation of Soviet assurances, and in defiance of American and hemispheric policy — this sudden, clandestine decision to station strategic weapons for the first time outside of Soviet soil — is a deliberately provocative and unjustified change in the status quo which cannot be accepted by this country, if our courage and our commitments are ever to be trusted again by either friend or foe.

The 1930's taught us a clear lesson: aggressive conduct, if allowed to go unchecked and unchallenged, ultimately leads to war. This nation is opposed to war. We are also true to our word. Our unswerving objective, therefore, must be to prevent the use of these missiles against this or any other country, and to secure their withdrawal or elimination from the Western Hemisphere.

Our policy has been one of patience and restraint, as befits a peaceful and powerful nation, which leads a worldwide alliance. We have been determined not to be diverted from our central concerns by mere irritants and fanatics. But now further action is required — and it is under way; and these actions may only be the beginning. We will not prematurely or unnecessarily risk the costs of worldwide nuclear war in which even the fruits of victory would be ashes in our mouth — but neither will we shrink from that risk at any time it must be faced.

Acting, therefore, in the defense of our own security and of the entire Western Hemisphere, and under the authority entrusted to me by the Constitution as endorsed by the resolution of the Congress, I have directed that the following initial steps be taken immediately:

First: To halt this offensive buildup, a strict quarantine on all offensive military equipment under shipment to Cuba is being initiated. All ships of any kind bound for Cuba from whatever nation or port will, if found to contain cargoes of offensive weapons, be turned back. This quarantine will be extended, if needed, to other types of cargo and carriers. We are not at this time, however, denying the necessities of life as the Soviets attempted to do in their Berlin blockade of 1948.   15

Second: I have directed the continued and increased close surveillance of Cuba and its military buildup. The foreign ministers of the OAS, in their communiqué of October 6, rejected secrecy in such matters in this hemisphere. Should these offensive military preparations continue, thus increasing the threat to the hemisphere, further action will be justified. I have directed the Armed Forces to prepare for any eventualities; and I trust that in the interest of both the Cuban people and the Soviet technicians at the sites, the hazards to all concerned in continuing this threat will be recognized.

Third: It shall be the policy of this Nation to regard any nuclear missile launched from Cuba against any nation in the Western Hemisphere as an attack by the Soviet Union on the United States, requiring a full retaliatory response upon the Soviet Union.

Fourth: As a necessary military precaution, I have reinforced our base at Guantanamo, evacuated today the dependents of our personnel there, and ordered additional military units to be on a standby alert basis.

Fifth: We are calling tonight for an immediate meeting of the Organ of Consultation under the Organization of American States, to consider this threat to hemispheric security and to invoke articles 6 and 8 of the Rio Treaty in support of all necessary action. The United Nations Charter allows for regional security arrangements — and the nations of this hemisphere decided long ago against the military presence of outside powers. Our other allies around the world have also been alerted.

Sixth: Under the Charter of the United Nations, we are asking tonight that an emergency meeting of the Security Council be convoked without delay to take action against this latest Soviet threat to world peace. Our resolution will call for the prompt dismantling and withdrawal of all offensive weapons in Cuba, under the supervision of U.N. observers, before the quarantine can be lifted.

Seventh and finally: I call upon Chairman Khrushchev to halt and eliminate this clandestine, reckless, and provocative threat to world peace and to stable relations between our two nations. I call upon him further to abandon this course of world domination, and to join in an historic effort to end the perilous arms race and to transform the history of man. He has an opportunity now to move the world back from the abyss of destruction — by returning to his government's own words that it had no need to station missiles outside its own territory, and withdrawing these weapons from Cuba — by refraining from any action which will widen or deepen the present crisis — and then by participating in a search for peaceful and permanent solutions.

This Nation is prepared to present its case against the Soviet threat to peace, and our own proposals for a peaceful world, at any time and in any forum — in the OAS, in the United Nations, or in any other meeting that could be useful — without limiting our freedom of action. We have in the past made strenuous efforts to limit the spread of nuclear weapons. We have proposed the elimination of all arms and military bases in a fair and effective disarmament treaty. We are prepared to discuss new proposals for the removal of tensions on both sides — including the possibility of a genuinely independent Cuba, free to determine its own destiny. We have no wish to war with the Soviet Union — for we are a peaceful people who desire to live in peace with all other peoples.

But it is difficult to settle or even discuss these problems in an atmosphere of intimidation. That is why this latest Soviet threat — or any other threat which is made independently or in response to our actions this week — must and will be met with determination. Any hostile move anywhere in the world against the safety and freedom of peoples to whom we are committed — including in particular the brave people of West Berlin — will be met by whatever action is needed.

Finally, I want to say a few words to the captive people of Cuba, to whom this speech is being directly carried by special radio facilities. I speak to you as a friend, as one who knows of your deep attachment to your fatherland, as one who shares your aspirations for liberty and justice for all. And I have watched and the American people have watched with deep sorrow how your nationalist revolution was betrayed — and how your fatherland fell under foreign domination. Now your leaders are no longer Cuban leaders inspired by Cuban ideals. They are puppets and agents of an international conspiracy which has turned Cuba against your friends and neighbors in the Americas — and turned it into the first Latin American country to become a target for nuclear war — the first Latin American country to have these weapons on its soil.

These new weapons are not in your interest. They contribute nothing to your peace   25
and well-being. They can only undermine it. But this country has no wish to cause you to suffer or to impose any system upon you. We know that your lives and land are being used as pawns by those who deny your freedom.

Many times in the past, the Cuban people have risen to throw out tyrants who destroyed their liberty. And I have no doubt that most Cubans today look forward to the time when they will be truly free — free from foreign domination, free to choose their own leaders, free to select their own system, free to own their own land, free to speak and write and worship without fear or degradation. And then shall Cuba be welcomed back to the society of free nations and to the associations of this hemisphere.

My fellow citizens: let no one doubt that this is a difficult and dangerous effort on which we have set out. No one can see precisely what course it will take or what costs or casualties will be incurred. Many months of sacrifice and self-discipline lie ahead — months in which our patience and our will will be tested — months in which many threats and denunciations will keep us aware of our dangers. But the greatest danger of all would be to do nothing.

The path we have chosen for the present is full of hazards, as all paths are — but it is the one most consistent with our character and courage as a nation and our commitments around the world. The cost of freedom is always high — and Americans have always paid it. And one path we shall never choose, and that is the path of surrender or submission.

Our goal is not the victory of might, but the vindication of right — not peace at the expense of freedom, but both peace and freedom, here in this hemisphere, and, we hope, around the world. God willing, that goal will be achieved.

Thank you and good night.   30

(1962)

Questions

1. What distinctions does John F. Kennedy make between the behavior of the United States and the behavior of Russia?
2. What evidence does Kennedy provide to support his claim that the purpose of the Soviet military buildup in Cuba can be "none other than to provide a nuclear strike capability against the Western Hemisphere" (par. 1)?

3. How would you describe the tone of Kennedy's speech? Remember that many people — including Kennedy's advisors — thought we were on the brink of World War III.
4. What particular message does Kennedy send to Cuba in this speech? How does he structure his argument? What claims does he make? What rhetorical appeals does he make?

Letter to John F. Kennedy

NIKITA KHRUSHCHEV

> Nikita Khrushchev (1894–1971) was the premier of Soviet Russia from 1958 to 1964. This letter was a response to Kennedy's speech. Eventually he and Kennedy met behind closed doors and came to an agreement by which Russian missiles were withdrawn from Cuba and, secretly, American missiles were withdrawn from Turkey.

Moscow, October 23, 1962

Mr. President:

I have just received your letter, and have also acquainted myself with the text of your speech of October 22 regarding Cuba.

I must say frankly, that the measures indicated in your statement constitute a serious threat to peace and to the security of nations. The United States has openly taken the path of grossly violating the United Nations Charter, the path of violating international norms of freedom of navigation on the high seas, the path of aggressive actions both against Cuba and against the Soviet Union. The statement by the Government of the United States of America can only be regarded as undisguised interference in the internal affairs of the Republic of Cuba, the Soviet Union and other states. The United Nations Charter and international norms give no right to any state to institute in international waters the inspection of vessels bound for the shores of the Republic of Cuba. And naturally, neither can we recognize the right of the United States to establish control over armaments which are necessary for the Republic of Cuba to strengthen its defense capability.

We reaffirm that the armaments which are in Cuba, regardless of the classification to which they may belong, are intended solely for defensive purposes in order to secure the Republic of Cuba against the attack of an aggressor.

I hope that the United States Government will display wisdom and renounce the actions pursued by you, which may lead to catastrophic consequences for world peace.

The viewpoint of the Soviet Government with regard to your statement of October 22 is set forth in a Statement of the Soviet Government, which is being transmitted to you through your Ambassador at Moscow. 5

(s) N. Khrushchev
(1962)

Questions

1. How would you describe the tone of Nikita Khrushchev's letter?
2. How many and which points in Kennedy's speech does Khrushchev respond to?
3. On October 28, Khrushchev agreed to remove Russian missiles from Cuba in return for a promise from the United States to respect Cuba's territorial sovereignty. In what ways does this letter lead you to expect that outcome? In what ways doesn't it?

Snow

Julia Alvarez

Julia Alvarez was born in New York in 1950 but raised in the Dominican Republic until she was ten. She has published poetry, fiction, memoir, and children's books, including her best-selling first novel, the autobiographical *How the García Girls Lost Their Accents* (1991). The following story, "Snow," is a chapter taken from that book.

Our first year in New York we rented a small apartment with a Catholic school nearby, taught by the Sisters of Charity, hefty women in long black gowns and bonnets that made them look peculiar, like dolls in mourning. I liked them a lot, especially my grandmotherly fourth-grade teacher, Sister Zoe. I had a lovely name, she said, and she had me teach the whole class how to pronounce it. Yo-landa. As the only immigrant in my class, I was put in a special seat in the first row by the window, apart from the other children, so that Sister Zoe could tutor me without disturbing them. Slowly, she enunciated the new words I was to repeat: *laundromat, cornflakes, subway, snow*.

Soon I picked up enough English to understand holocaust was in the air. Sister Zoe explained to a wide-eyed classroom what was happening in Cuba. Russian missiles were being assembled, trained supposedly on New York City. President Kennedy, looking worried too, was on the television at home, explaining we might have to go to war against the Communists. At school, we had air-raid drills: An ominous bell would go off and we'd file into the hall, fall to the floor, cover our heads with our coats, and imagine our hair falling out, the bones in our arms going soft. At home, Mami and my sisters and I said a rosary for world peace. I heard new vocabulary: *nuclear bomb, radioactive fallout, bomb shelter*. Sister Zoe explained how it would happen. She drew a picture of a mushroom on the blackboard and dotted a flurry of chalk marks for the dusty fallout that would kill us all.

The months grew cold, November, December. It was dark when I got up in the morning, frosty when I followed my breath to school. One morning, as I sat at my desk daydreaming out the window, I saw dots in the air like the ones Sister Zoe had drawn — random at first, then lots and lots. I shrieked, "Bomb! Bomb!" Sister Zoe jerked around, her full black skirt ballooning as she hurried to my side. A few girls began to cry.

But then Sister Zoe's shocked look faded. "Why, Yolanda dear, that's snow!" She laughed. "Snow."

"Snow," I repeated. I looked out the window warily. All my life I had heard about   5
the white crystals that fell out of American skies in the winter. From my desk I watched
the fine powder dust the sidewalk and parked cars below. Each flake was different,
Sister Zoe had said, like a person, irreplaceable and beautiful.

(1991)

Questions

1. What do you think the narrator means by "holocaust was in the air" (par. 2)?
2. How does the story connect fear of nuclear war to everyday life for the young
   narrator?

from *Why I Wrote* The Crucible

ARTHUR MILLER

> This excerpt is from a piece published in the *New Yorker* magazine in October
> 1996, just before the film version of *The Crucible* was released. Arthur Miller
> (1915–2005) wrote the screenplay for the film based on his 1953 play.

As I watched *The Crucible* taking shape as a movie over much of the past year, the
sheer depth of time that it represents for me kept returning to mind. As those powerful actors blossomed on the screen, and the children and the horses, and the crowds
and the wagons, I thought again about how I came to cook all this up nearly fifty years
ago, in an America almost nobody I know seems to remember clearly. . . .

I remember those years — they formed *The Crucible*'s skeleton — but I have lost
the dead weight of the fear I had then. Fear doesn't travel well; just as it can warp judgment, its absence can diminish memory's truth. What terrifies one generation is likely
to bring only a puzzled smile to the next. . . .

[Senator] McCarthy's power to stir fears of creeping Communism was not entirely
based on illusion, of course. . . . From being our wartime ally, the Soviet Union rapidly
became an expanding empire. In 1949, Mao Zedong took power in China. Western
Europe also seemed ready to become Red, especially Italy, where the Communist
Party was the largest outside Russia, and was growing. . . . McCarthy — brash and ill-
mannered but to many authentic and true — boiled it all down to what anyone could
understand: We had "lost China" and would soon lose Europe as well, because the
State Department — staffed, of course, under Democratic presidents — was full of trea-
sonous pro-Soviet intellectuals. It was as simple as that. . . .

The Crucible was an act of desperation. . . . By 1950 when I began to think of writing about the hunt for Reds in America, I was motivated in some great part by the
paralysis that had set in among many liberals who, despite their discomfort with the
inquisitors' violations of civil rights, were fearful, and with good reason, of being identified as covert Communists if they should protest too strongly. . . .

I visited Salem for the first time on a dismal spring day in 1952. . . . In the gloomy   5
courthouse there I read the transcripts of the witchcraft trials of 1692, as taken down
in a primitive shorthand by ministers who were spelling each other. But there was
one entry in Upham in which the thousands of pieces I had come across were jogged
into place. It was from a report written by the Reverend Samuel Parris, who was one
of the chief instigators of the witch-hunt. "During the examination of Elizabeth Proctor,
Abigail Williams, and Ann Putnam" — the two were "afflicted" teen-age accusers, and
Abigail was Parris's niece — "both made offer to strike at said Proctor; but when Abigail's
hand came near, it opened, whereas it was made up, into a fist before, and came down
exceeding lightly as it drew near to said Proctor, and at length, with open and extended
fingers, touched Proctor's hood very lightly. Immediately Abigail cried out her fingers, her fingers, her fingers burned. . . ."

In this remarkably observed gesture of a troubled young girl, I believed, a play
became possible. Elizabeth Proctor had been the orphaned Abigail's mistress, and
they had lived together in the same small house until Elizabeth fired the girl. By this
time, I was sure, John Proctor had bedded Abigail, who had to be dismissed most
likely to appease Elizabeth. There was bad blood between the two women now. That
Abigail started, in effect, to condemn Elizabeth to death with her touch, then
stopped her hand, then went through with it, was quite suddenly the human center
of all this turmoil.

All this I understood. I had not approached the witchcraft out of nowhere or
from purely social and political considerations. My own marriage of twelve years was
teetering and I knew more than I wished to know about where the blame lay. That
John Proctor the sinner might overturn his paralyzing personal guilt and become the
most forthright voice against the madness around him was a reassurance to me, and,
I suppose, an inspiration: It demonstrated that a clear moral outcry could still spring
even from an ambiguously unblemished soul. Moving crabwise across the profusion
of evidence, I sensed that I had at last found something of myself in it, and a play began
to accumulate around this man.

(1996)

Questions

1. In this excerpt from an essay subtitled "An Artist's Answer to Politics," how does
   Arthur Miller provide the background and context for the political backdrop of
   The Crucible?
2. Miller says that "[f]ear doesn't travel well" (par. 2) and provides a couple of examples: fear of "creeping Communism" (par. 3) and liberals' fears of "being identified
   as covert Communists if they should protest too strongly" (par. 4). Why do you
   think his "answer to politics" begins with acknowledging these fears?
3. How does Miller make the political personal? Do his comments on how *The Crucible*
   was to some degree a personal reaction to his own failings change the way you
   think about the play?

from *Atomic Narratives and American Youth*
Coming of Age with the Atom, 1945–55

MICHAEL SCHEIBACH

> The epilogue from *Atomic Narratives and American Youth: Coming of Age with the Atom, 1945–55*, this piece connects the threads that Michael Scheibach examined in his 2003 work on the effects of the atomic age on America's youth.

Epilogue: 1955

We're gonna rock, rock, rock. . . .
— BILL HALEY AND HIS COMETS

By 1955, more than 30 million families tuned in each evening to watch game shows and situation comedies, original dramas and adaptations, news updates and light-hearted fare for the entire family. Television not only entertained an ever-expanding audience and reflected the country's hopes and fears; it also began to alter the social landscape — to shape a more mainstream society while heightening awareness of America's blemishes.

In May of that year, Americans received the news that the Supreme Court had finally issued its instructions in the *Brown v. Board of Education of Topeka, Kansas*, desegregation case heard the previous year. Justice Earl Warren ordered the district court to take "deliberate speed" in its efforts to implement the landmark ruling on the integration of public schools. That December, Rosa Parks sparked a bus boycott in Birmingham, Alabama, placing the plight of Southern blacks in the national limelight, this time aided by television, and introducing a young minister, Martin Luther King, Jr., to a national audience. The exigency for racial harmony, a theme often encountered in postwar atomic narratives, had been acted upon.[1]

Atomic survival, yet another theme, had become an everyday dimension of American life. Schools and communities conducted civil-defense drills on a regular basis, and the federal government did its part by sponsoring the annual Operation Alert. A girl graduating from high school in 1955 wrote, "[L]iving has been a difficult and insecure thing; at worst, an insurmountable wall of bewilderment and frustration . . . we've never lived a minute of our lives without war or the threat of war."[2] A senior boy wrote the same year, "We of today's graduating class are on the threshold of a new world. It is a world of possible destruction. It is also, we hope, a world of peace."[3] Remembers sociologist Todd Gitlin, president of SDS* in the early 1960s: "For us, the future was necessarily more salient than the past. The Bomb threatened that future, and therefore undermined the ground on which affluence was built. Rather than feel grateful for the Bomb, we felt menaced. The Bomb was the shadow hanging over all human endeavor. It threatened all the prizes."[4]

---

*Students for a Democratic Society, a left-wing student activist movement of the 1960s. — Eds.

Self-reliance became synonymous with self-preservation, as Americans built bomb shelters at an explosive rate. Film historian Andrew Dowdy, nineteen years old in 1955, remembers, "Some of us were going underground, immediately and literally, digging in from bomb shelter instructions available in two-dollar booklets." But the ability to withstand the force of a hydrogen bomb was questionable at best, which led *Time* magazine to ask in June 1955 whether the best defense against the bomb was prayer. Not long after, the prayer was seemingly answered for many youth as the new *Mad* magazine, which had evolved from comic-book status to a 25-cent, bimonthly compendium of social satire, adopted the "What, Me Worry?" kid as its official mascot. Alfred E. Neuman, as the kid would later be known, became America's quintessential fatalistic youth—and future "new man." A poll taken the previous year by the American Institute of Public Opinion, in fact, found that 95 percent of respondents would not move to escape a hydrogen bomb, even though most believed one would be used against the United States. Why worry?[5]

On October 13, 1955, the young stalwarts of the Beat Generation—Gary Snyder, Jack Kerouac, Michael McClure, and Lawrence Ferlinghetti—gathered at San Francisco's Six Gallery to hear poet Allen Ginsberg read his new work, "Howl." Ginsberg, articulating the viewpoint of postwar rebels without a cause, lamented, "I saw the best minds of my generation destroyed by madness, starving hysterical naked, / dragging themselves through the negro streets at dawn looking for an angry fix, / angelheaded hipsters burning for the ancient heavenly connection to the starry dynamo in the machinery of night / . . . who distributed Supercommunist pamphlets in Union Square weeping and undressing while the sirens of Los Alamos wailed them down, and wailed down Wall, and the Staten Island ferry also wailed, . . ." The voice of youth beat down by the finality of the atomic bomb was being heard.[6]

In 1954, *Cashbox* commented that white high school and college students in the South—largely "youthful hillbilly fans rather than the pop bobbysoxers"—were frantically buying rhythm-and-blues songs. White youth had been listening and dancing to black R&B for several years, assisted by disc jockeys like Cleveland's Alan Freed. But when *Billboard* proclaimed in a banner headline, "1955—THE YEAR R&B TOOK OVER POP FIELD," it marked the final explosion of rock 'n' roll—the fusing of black R&B and white rockabilly that crossed geographic, racial, and socioeconomic boundaries. This also was the year "(We're Gonna) Rock Around the Clock" by Bill Haley and His Comets became the first rock 'n' roll record to hit number one on *Billboard*'s pop chart.[7] Jerry Lee Lewis, Fats Domino, Buddy Holly, Chuck Berry, Elvis, Little Richard, and many others followed quickly: black and white performers covering the same tunes for the same audiences.

The deaths of actor James Dean and bop jazz improviser Charlie Parker occurred in 1955: one setting the style for white youth; the other setting the tone for African American youth. And R&B singer Johnny Ace took his life just a few days before 1955 began. That year saw the release of *Rebel Without a Cause* and *Blackboard Jungle*, movies that created the young rebel as an icon fighting against a hostile, uncaring society. At the same time, teen-oriented radio and television programs, like Dick Clark's *American Bandstand* in Philadelphia, were being joined by new magazines aimed at

5

the burgeoning youth culture: *Hep Cats*, *Teenager*, *Teen-Age Confessions*, *Teenage Rock and Roll Review*, *Teen Digest*, *'Teen*, *Dig*, and *Modern Teen*.[8]

By the mid-1950s, youth had solidified its place — its role — in society. "Youth culture," historian W. T. Llamon, Jr., has written, "became largely the main culture; it became the atmosphere of American life."[9] This largely high-school–based, adolescent culture had taken form replete with a unique style and attitude. In the years that followed, this culture ultimately created its own social narrative to be interpreted by those coming of age in the 1960s, a new era of uncertainty.

Notes

1. W. T. Lhamon, Jr., *Deliberate Speed: The Origins of a Cultural Style in the American 1950s* (Washington, D.C.: Smithsonian Institution Press, 1990) 32–33; Fred Powledge, *Free at Last? The Civil Rights Movement and the People Who Made It* (New York: Little, Brown and Co., 1991).

2. Elizabeth Evans, "In Defense of My Generation," *Journal of the National Education Association* 44 (March 1955): 140.

3. Robert Piper, "Where Do We Go from Here?," *American Mercury* 81 (August 1955): 82–84.

4. Todd Gitlin, *The Sixties: Years of Hope, Days of Rage* (New York: Bantam Books, 1987) 22–23.

5. Andrew Dowdy, *The Films of the Fifties: The American State of Mind* (New York: William Morrow and Co., 1975) 60; "Civil Defense: Best Defense? Prayer," *Time*, 27 June 1955: 17; Maria Reidelbach, *Completely Mad: A History of the Comic Book and Magazine* (Boston: Little, Brown and Co., 1991) 32, 136–140; Allan Winkler, *Life Under a Cloud* (New York: Oxford University Press, 1993) 5.

6. Barry Miles, *Ginsberg* (New York: Simon and Schuster, 1989) 195–197; Allen Ginsberg, *Howl and Other Poems* (San Francisco: City Light Books, 1956).

7. Rock 'n' roll did not magically appear in 1955, far from it. As Nick Tosches has discussed in his book, *Unsung Heroes of Rock 'n' Roll: The Birth of Rock in the Wild Years Before Elvis* (New York: Harmony Books, 1984), white and black teenagers were listening to the sounds of rock 'n' roll in the early 1950s, primarily on the jukebox and records. But it was not until 1955, with the emergence of Top 40 radio, transistors, 45-rpm records, a well-defined youth culture, and the recognition of the youth consumer market, that this music began to cross white and black boundaries. Also see Tom McCourt, "Bright Lights, Big City: A Brief History of Rhythm and Blues 1945–1957," in Timothy E. Scheurer, editor, *The Age of Rock* (Bowling Green, Ohio: Bowling Green State University Popular Press, 1989) 46–62; Michael Bane, *White Boy Singin' the Blues: The Black Roots of White Rock* (New York: Da Capo Press, 1982); N. K. Cohn, *Rock: From the Beginning* (New York: Stein & Day, 1969); and Charlie Gillett, *The Sound of the City: The Rise of Rock and Roll* (New York: Outerbridge and Dienstfrey, 1970).

8. *New Serial Titles 1950–1970* (Washington, D.C.: R.R. Bowker Co., 1973). For more on media and youth, see James Gilbert, *A Cycle of Outrage: America's Reaction to the Juvenile Delinquent in the 1950s* (New York: Oxford University Press, 1986).

9. Lhamon, *Deliberate Speed*, 8.

Questions

1. What does Michael Scheibach think is the effect of the nuclear age on youth culture? Do his connections surprise you? Explain your answer.
2. Describe the evidence that Scheibach uses to comment on youth culture.

Case Closed: The Rosenbergs Were Soviet Spies

RONALD RADOSH

> This opinion piece was published in the *Los Angeles Times* in September 2008 in response to the admission by one of the codefendants in the Rosenberg trial that Julius Rosenberg was, in fact, spying for Russia. Ronald Radosh, an emeritus professor of history at City University of New York and an adjunct senior fellow at the Hudson Institute, is the coauthor of *The Rosenberg File* (1983).

Julius and Ethel Rosenberg were executed 55 years ago, on June 19, 1953. But last week, they were back in the headlines when Morton Sobell, the co-defendant in their famous espionage trial, finally admitted that he and his friend, Julius, had both been Soviet agents.

It was a stunning admission; Sobell, now 91 years old, had adamantly maintained his innocence for more than half a century. After his comments were published, even the Rosenbergs' children, Robert and Michael Meeropol, were left with little hope to hang on to — and this week, in comments unlike any they've made previously, the brothers acknowledged having reached the difficult conclusion that their father was, indeed, a spy. "I don't have any reason to doubt Morty," Michael Meeropol told Sam Roberts of the *New York Times*.

With these latest events, the end has arrived for the legions of the American left wing that have argued relentlessly for more than half a century that the Rosenbergs were victims, framed by a hostile, fear-mongering U.S. government. Since the couple's trial, the left has portrayed them as martyrs for civil liberties, righteous dissenters whose chief crime was to express their constitutionally protected political beliefs. In the end, the left has argued, the two communists were put to death not for spying but for their unpopular opinions, at a time when the Truman and Eisenhower administrations were seeking to stem opposition to their anti-Soviet foreign policy during the Cold War.

To this day, this received wisdom permeates our educational system. A recent study by historian Larry Schweikart of the University of Dayton has found that very few college history textbooks say simply that the Rosenbergs were guilty; according to Schweikart, most either state that the couple were innocent or that the trial was "controversial," or they "excuse what [the Rosenbergs] did by saying, 'It wasn't that bad. What they provided wasn't important.'"

Indeed, Columbia University professor Eric Foner once wrote that the Rosenbergs   5 were prosecuted out of a "determined effort to root out dissent," part of a broader pattern of "shattered careers and suppressed civil liberties." In other words, it was part of the postwar McCarthyite "witch hunt."

But, in fact, Schweikart is right, and Foner is wrong. The Rosenbergs were Soviet spies, and not minor ones either. Not only did they try their best to give the Soviets top atomic secrets from the Manhattan Project, they succeeded in handing over top military data on sonar and on radar that was used by the Russians to shoot down American planes in the Korean and Vietnam wars. That's long been known, and Sobell confirmed it again last week.

To many Americans, Cold War espionage cases like the Rosenberg and Alger Hiss cases that once riveted the country seem irrelevant today, something out of the distant past. But they're not irrelevant. They're a crucial part of the ongoing dispute between right and left in this country. For the left, it has long been an article of faith that these prosecutions showed the essentially repressive nature of the U.S. government. Even as the guilt of the accused has become more and more clear (especially since the fall of the Soviet Union and the release of reams of historical Cold War documents), these "anti anti-communists" of the intellectual left have continued to argue that the prosecutions were overzealous, or that the crimes were minor, or that the punishments were disproportionate.

The left has consistently defended spies such as Hiss, the Rosenbergs and Sobell as victims of contrived frame-ups. Because a demagogue like Sen. Joseph McCarthy cast a wide swath with indiscriminate attacks on genuine liberals as "reds" (and even though McCarthy made some charges that were accurate), the anti anti-communists came to argue that anyone accused by McCarthy or Richard Nixon or J. Edgar Hoover should be assumed to be entirely innocent. People like Hiss (a former State Department official who was accused of spying) cleverly hid their true espionage work by gaining sympathy as just another victim of a smear attack.

But now, with Sobell's confession of guilt, that worldview has been demolished.

In the 1990s, when it was more than clear that the Rosenbergs had been real Soviet   10
spies — not simply a pair of idealistic left-wingers working innocently for peace with the Russians — one of the Rosenberg's sons, Michael, expressed the view that the reason his parents stayed firm and did not cooperate with the government was because they wanted to keep the government from creating "a massive spy show trial," thereby earning "the thanks of generations of resisters to government repression."

Today, he and his brother Robert run a fund giving grants to the children of those they deem "political prisoners," such as convicted cop killer Mumia Abu-Jamal. Ironically, if there was any government that staged show trials for political ends, it was the government for which the Rosenbergs gave up their lives, that of the former Soviet Union.

This week, the Meeropols made it clear to the *New York Times* that they still believe the information their father passed to the Russians was not terribly significant, that the judge and the prosecutors in their parents' case were guilty of misconduct, and that neither Julius nor Ethel should have been given the death penalty for their crimes.

On the subject of their mother, the Meeropols have a point. In another development last week, a federal court judge in New York released previously sealed grand jury testimony of key witnesses in the case, including that of Ruth Greenglass, Julius' sister-in-law. It turns out that a key part of her testimony for the prosecution — that Ethel had typed up notes for her husband to hand to the Soviets — was most likely concocted.

That doesn't mean that Ethel was innocent — indeed, the preponderance of the evidence suggests she was not. But what is clear is that in seeking to get the defendants to confess to Soviet espionage, the prosecutors overstepped bounds and enhanced testimony to guarantee a conviction. Americans should have no problem acknowledging when such judicial transgressions take place, and in concluding that the execution of Ethel was a miscarriage of justice.

Nevertheless, after Sobell's confession of guilt, all other conspiracy theories about   15
the Rosenberg case should come to an end. A pillar of the left-wing culture of grievance has been finally shattered. The Rosenbergs were actual and dangerous Soviet spies. It is time the ranks of the left acknowledge that the United States had (and has) real enemies and that finding and prosecuting them is not evidence of repression.

(2008)

Questions

1. What evidence does Ronald Radosh use to prove his point that "our educational system" (par. 4) teaches that the Rosenbergs were executed because of their unpopular opinions? Why do you think it is important to him?
2. Why does Radosh think that Cold War espionage cases are still relevant today?
3. Why do you think Radosh concedes that Ethel Rosenberg probably should not have been executed?

from *The Rise of Nuclear Fear*

SPENCER R. WEART

> Spencer R. Weart (b. 1942) is a physicist and historian. Until 2009, he was director of the Center for History of Physics at the American Institute of Physics. Weart first wrote *Nuclear Fear* in 1988 but revised and updated the book in 2012. The selection found here is from a new chapter, titled "Tyrants and Terrorists," added in the 2012 edition.

It was only one bomb, small enough to fit in the trunk of a car. A band of fanatics stole it from the Israelis, smuggled it into the United States, and exploded it in a football stadium to kill tens of thousands. That was the centerpiece of a best-selling 1991 novel and popular 2002 movie, *The Sum of All Fears*.[1] Between the book and the movie the terrorist band changed from Palestinians to neo-Nazis while the stadium moved from Denver to Baltimore, but the details hardly mattered. In the many stories with a similar plot, bomb materials could be stolen from Americans or Russians; the catastrophe could be planned for Los Angeles or Miami. What did matter were two familiar themes: the proliferation of bombs in nations around the world, and evildoers intent on blowing things up. These themes were becoming inseparably entangled. The Second Nuclear Age had begun with a decade of release from the anxieties of the Cold War, but by the late 1990s nuclear fear was on the rise again.[2]

From 1945 through the 1980s, when people worried about the proliferation of nuclear weapons their main concern had been that nations would use the bombs in war. If Argentina or South Africa showed an interest in getting nuclear bombs, its aim would be to threaten, deter, or defeat neighboring states. These, it was presumed, would hasten to get their own bombs in turn. But it didn't happen. Proliferation, as one scholar pointed out in 2009, proceeded "at a far more leisurely pace than generations of alarmists have routinely and urgently anticipated." And careful study showed that aside from the United States and the Soviet Union, the few cases in which a nation did get its own bombs turned out "to have had remarkably limited, perhaps even imperceptible, consequences." Nobody was successfully threatened, deterred, or defeated by the bombs.[3]

Despite this reassuring history, many worried that one or another dictator must certainly want to possess nuclear weapons — and if he got them he would drop them on a neighbor. Could such a regional atrocity trigger a world war? Everyone understood that thanks to the horror of all things nuclear, objections to any use of nuclear weapons had become something like a sacred taboo. Once the line was crossed (for example, in the Near East, where the great powers had vital interests), would the conflict escalate into a general exchange of missiles that would annihilate everything? Fear of violating the nuclear taboo — a dread of everything "the Bomb" represented — was arguably a main reason that in all the tense crises and vicious regional conflicts since 1945, nobody came near to using even a single bomb.

But what if some evildoer set out on purpose to provoke a nuclear exchange? "You get Russia and America to fight each other," the *Sum of All Fears* villain declared as his aim, "and destroy each other!" The scenario of triggering mass missile attacks with a single explosion became less plausible with the end of the Cold War, yet it never vanished entirely from people's thinking. It was as if every bomb contained within itself the entire apocalypse.

Meanwhile events stimulated a new variety of fear. The world was shocked when   5
United Nations inspectors, scouring Iraq in 1991 after the nation's defeat in the Gulf War, discovered that the Iraqis had secretly got well along toward building a few bombs. Worse, their bomb material was not plutonium but uranium-235 produced in a battery of centrifuges, easier to build and hide than a reactor. When the Iraqi program was forcibly dismantled, the issue faded from public consciousness. But not for long.

Proliferation worries began to revive in the late 1990s when Iraq obstructed the United Nations inspectors, raising suspicions it meant to try again. And in 1998, after twenty-four years of silence, India conducted its second bomb test, followed by more. Pakistan reacted swiftly with its own series of plutonium explosions. Worried talk about proliferation rose enough around 2002 to bring a third peak in the articles mentioning "nuclear war" in the Google News Archive, albeit much smaller than the peaks of the early 1960s and early 1980s. Adding to anxieties were reports of a massive Iranian effort to extract uranium-235 with centrifuges. In 2006 came an actual explosion of a North Korean device using plutonium from a reactor.

It was rare for more than 20 percent of Americans to be aware of a given news story (they notoriously do not pay much attention to foreign news), but since the late

1980s surveys recorded awareness well above that level for stories about nuclear weapon proliferation in Pakistan, Iraq, Iran, and North Korea. Significantly, after the U.S.-Soviet arms reduction agreement of 1991 the *only* nuclear-related news, civilian or military, that showed up in the surveys consisted of stories about weapons in third-world states.[4]

The nuclear ambitions that these regimes pursued were particularly worrisome because each was infected with some combination of irrationality, fanaticism, and tyranny. These elements featured in news accounts of the so-called rogue states — a term that rose to prominence during the 1990s, evoking the image of a vicious, solitary, uncontrollable beast — Libya, Iran, Iraq, and North Korea. Each of these favored certain terrorist organizations. If one of these states ever got a good stock of nuclear bombs, might it not give one to its protégés? Worse, each of these states was itself a brutish terrorist, as personified by its ruler. What would hold back Iraq's murderous tyrant Saddam Hussein from obliterating Tel Aviv if he had the means, or the bizarre North Korean dictator Kim Jong-Il from sneaking a bomb into Seoul or Washington?

Irrationality and fanaticism have been fundamental to images of terrorism for centuries. The third element, tyranny, is more modern. The anarchist bombmakers of the 1890s and the 1960s claimed to fight for democratic or socialist ideals. Some of the more recent murderers, like the right-wing extremist who blew up a federal government building in Oklahoma City in 1995, similarly imagined they were striking out on behalf of the suppressed individual. But by the start of the twenty-first century terrorists were mostly associated with repressive, authoritarian systems, such as Islamic fundamentalism or the fascism of the criminals in the movie *The Sum of All Fears*. It now seemed appropriate for dictators to sponsor terrorist groups.

In 1993 Islamic extremists attempted to blow up the World Trade Center in New York City with conventional explosives, followed in 1995 by the blast that killed 168 people in Oklahoma City. Soon after, a poll of Americans found that nearly three-quarters of them believed there was a chance that terrorists could attack an American city with a "weapon of mass destruction." Another poll in 1998 found that half of all Americans believed that terrorists would explode a nuclear bomb in the United States within the next ten years. Experts wrote entire books discussing nuclear terrorism; columnists and politicians exclaimed that modern society faced a peril of vast dimensions. Nevertheless, the majority of people in the 1990s did not feel a deep personal concern. If they suspected a bombing might happen somewhere, unlike in the Cold War they thought the bomb was unlikely to strike just where they happened to live.[5]

The September 11, 2001, attacks on New York and Washington, D.C., did not initiate any new anxiety, then, so much as activate existing ones. The appalling pictures and stories that everyone saw and heard brought a visceral intensification of fears. What had been an abstract concern became almost a personal trauma. A series of Gallup polls found that the fraction of Americans who worried seriously about terrorism in general had been one in four in 2000. After the September 11 attacks the number leaped to six in ten, and after a few years leveled off at a relatively high four in ten. A more specific 2003 Gallup poll found four in ten Americans said they "often" worried that terrorists might attack the United States with nuclear weapons.

These were serious fears, though milder than the gripping dread of war that large majorities of Americans had felt during the tensest phases of the Cold War. In other developed countries, majorities usually rated terrorism as a second-rank concern like the environment and education, well below economic worries. People in most of the developing countries were even less likely to mention terrorism as a concern.[6]

In sum, in the early twenty-first century fear of terrorists with nuclear bombs stood on the shelf along with the other nuclear fears, but now it had moved to the front. Like fallout and reactor hazards in earlier decades, the threat satisfied the requirements for a risk whose likelihood people would tend to exaggerate by comparison with familiar risks like home accidents or fires. The image of a mushroom cloud rising over an American city was dreadful and memorable; the risk of harm was involuntary and unjust; the danger was novel and depended on unknowable secrets. Above all the idea was available in the mind, easily pictured by anyone raised on tales of nuclear weapons. Small wonder that the idea was popular with writers of thriller novels and television shows.

Notes

1. Tom Clancy, *The Sum of All Fears* (New York: Putnam, 1991).
2. Among the few who notice two separate post–Cold War periods without specifying the 9/11/2001 events as a crucial division is William J. Kinsella, "One Hundred Years of Nuclear Discourse: Four Master Themes and Their Implications for Environmental Communication," in *The Environmental Communication Yearbook*, vol. 2, ed. Susan L. Senecah (Mahwah, N.J.: Lawrence Erlbaum Associates, 2005), 49–72. For novels 1960s–early 1980s featuring terrorist attempts at bombing or extortion see Paul Brians, *Nuclear Holocausts: Atomic War in Fiction, 1895–1984* (Kent, Ohio: Kent State University Press, 1987), 37–38, 151, 178, 189, 201, 267, 275, 293; online version at http://www.wsu.edu/~brians/nuclear/.
3. John Mueller, *Atomic Obsession: Nuclear Alarmism from Hiroshima to Al-Qaeda* (New York: Oxford University Press, 2009), 95; see 90–95.
4. Pew Research Center for the People & the Press, search of data on the terms "nuclear," "atomic," "weapon," "reactor." http://people-press.org/nii/bydate.php.
5. 1996 poll: Pew Research Center for the People & the Press, "Public Apathetic about Nuclear Terrorism," 11 April 1996, http://people-press.org/reports/display.php3?ReportID=128, accessed 8 Jan. 2007. 1998 poll: Keating Holland/CNN, "Poll: Many Americans Worry about Nuclear Terrorism," http://www.cnn.com/ALLPOLITICS/1998/06/16/poll/, accessed 3 Jan. 2007. Jessica Stern, *The Ultimate Terrorists* (Cambridge, Mass.: Harvard University Press, 1999); Gary Ackerman and William C. Potter, "Catastrophic Nuclear Terrorism: A Preventable Peril," in *Global Catastrophic Risks*, ed. Nick Bostrom and Milan M. Cirkovic (New York: Oxford University Press, 2008), 402–449; see 404–406. Nadine Gurr and Benjamin Cole, *The New Face of Nuclear Terrorism: Threats from Weapons of Mass Destruction* (London: I. B. Tauris, 2002), 3–8.
6. Gallup polls from http://brain.gallup.com. Pew Research Center for People & the Press, "Two Years Later, the Fear Lingers," 4 Sept. 2003, people-press.org/reports/print.php3?PageID=735. World survey: http://globescan.com/rf_gi_first_01.htm. Further polls can readily be turned up with Web searches.

(2012)

Questions

1. What does Spencer R. Weart mean by the "nuclear taboo" (par. 3)? What do some people fear would violate it?
2. What recent events have added a new element to what Weart describes as "fundamental to images of terrorism" (par. 9)?
3. What evidence does Weart use to support his analysis of the rise of nuclear fear?
4. According to Weart, what effect did the 9/11 attacks have on the rise in nuclear fear among Americans?

Making Connections

1. Both Lillian Hellman (p. 1471) and Arthur Miller (p. 1479) testified before the House Un-American Activities Committee, and both refused to "name names" and were scornful of those, such as director Elia Kazan, who did. What is your view of those who, fearful of prison and blacklisting, did name the names of their film-business coworkers who had been members of the Communist Party? Imagine how Ronald Radosh (p. 1484) might present a counterargument to Hellman and Miller.

2. Accounts of the days leading up to the Cuban missile crisis describe President John F. Kennedy standing up to his military advisors, who favored a full-scale attack on the missiles and an invasion of Cuba. What evidence of Kennedy's efforts do we see in his speech of October 22 (p. 1472)? Do you think he gambled on how Khrushchev would respond? Explain your answer.

3. Trace the path from the visual icons of the atomic age (pp. 1469 and 1470) to Michael Scheibach's (p. 1481) view that the youth culture that began to blossom in the second half of the 1950s was the result of *Mad* magazine's Alfred E. Neuman's "What, me worry?" attitude toward the possibility of nuclear annihilation. What connections do you see?

4. The excerpt from Spencer R. Weart's *The Rise of Nuclear Fear* (p. 1486) begins and ends with examples of how nuclear fear is imagined in pop culture. Compare the way Julia Alvarez's story "Snow" (p. 1478) reflects the anxieties of the atomic age to the way Weart presents them. Which do you think is more effective? More believable? Explain your answer.

Entering the Conversation

As you respond to each of the following prompts, support your position with appropriate evidence, including at least three sources in this Conversation on the atomic age, unless otherwise indicated.

1. In an interview with Scheibach, Cindy Hoedel of the *Kansas City Star* asked what studying the atomic age told him about the American family. He said the bombing of Hiroshima was a demarcation line in the same way that 9/11 is a demarcation line for people living now. He adds, however, that it is fear of nuclear attack that underlies even the present terrorist attacks. Write an essay in which you compare and contrast the effects of terrorist attacks on the American family of today with the effects of the threat of nuclear war on the American family of the 1950s.

2. Radosh says that the United States "had (and has) real enemies and . . . finding and prosecuting them is not evidence of repression" (par. 15). Write an essay in which you discuss the issue of the need for national security versus the individual's rights to free speech and privacy.

3. Graham Allison, the author of the 1971 *Essence of Decision*, is credited with the creation of the discipline of public policy. His doctoral thesis in political science was a study of the decision making during the Cuban missile crisis. He imagined what must have happened:

   > There was Kennedy looking over the cliff thinking, "Oh my God, we might really have a nuclear war." He judged the chances were between one and three and even of us going to war. And then he's thinking as he did empathetically of this poor guy Khrushchev who's sitting over there also worrying about this. It seemed to me implausible that he wouldn't give him something, especially if he could give it privately.

   Allison said that studying these frightening events shows that the roads to war are "paths of misperceptions, accidents, and unanticipated consequences." He says that understanding the importance of the many possible paths can help prevent not only war but also "institutional and bureaucratic disasters." Research the planning of the response to a potential disaster or the response to an actual disaster that you remember. Then write an essay in which you examine the decision making involved. Make sure, as Kennedy asked his military advisors to do, that you analyze the consequences of each decision, at least two or three steps down the line.

4. Scheibach and Weart both use images from and references to pop culture to discuss the consequences of the atomic age. Write an essay in which you discuss the ways that popular culture has portrayed the atomic bomb. Be sure to use visual texts as support and illustrations.

5. In an essay, support, dispute, or qualify this statement by science-fiction writer Ursula K. LeGuin:

   > It is only when science asks why, instead of simply describing how, that it becomes more than technology. When it asks why, it discovers Relativity. When it only shows how, it invents the atom bomb, and then puts its hands over its eye and says, "My God what have I done?"

6. Several singers and songwriters from the early 1960s to the present — Bob Dylan, most notably — have addressed the fears of the atomic age. Put together a song list of music inspired by anxiety about the atomic bomb and create cover art for an album using the visual icons of the atomic age. Write liner notes that explain your choices.

Conversation

The American Middle Class

In a country that generally views itself as classless, why is it that we hear so much about the American "middle class"? The concept of upper and lower classes comes from nineteenth-century British society, and we Americans, with our fundamental belief in equality for all, resist such designations. Beyond the promise of life itself, our democracy also proclaims the rights of liberty and "the pursuit of happiness." We believe that anyone can become president and that in the United States people can succeed by "pulling themselves up by their bootstraps." Does the American myth of the self-made man (which now includes woman), as promulgated by Benjamin Franklin and Horatio Alger, still resonate today?

In 1951, sociologist C. Wright Mills wrote about distributions of property and income for the "new middle-class." "Everything," he stated, "from the chance to stay alive during the first year after birth to the chance to view fine art; the chance to remain healthy and if sick to get well again quickly; the chance to avoid becoming a juvenile delinquent; and very crucially, the chance to complete an intermediary or higher educational grade — these are among the chances that are crucially influenced by one's position in the class structure of a modern society."

We look back to post–World War II, and especially to the 1950s, as the birth of the middle class, a period when the American Dream became a reality for more Americans than ever before. It was a time of great expansion through the construction of highways, the growth of the suburbs as exemplified by such developments as Levittown, New York, and the wide availability of consumer goods. Even families of relatively modest means could have two cars in the driveway, laundry in the washer, an apple pie in the oven, and Ed Sullivan or Lucille Ball on the TV in the living room — all on one income, no less. Of course, the reality wasn't that rosy for everyone, but that idyllic picture still captures our national imagination.

Recent decades have seen a dramatic shrinking of the middle class as the nation's wealth has become more concentrated in the hands of the very rich. Is the American Dream still alive and well? Is America still the land of upward mobility? Does the term *middle class* still have meaning?

Sources

Horatio Alger, from *Ragged Dick, or Street Life in New York with the Boot Blacks* (1867)

from *Ragged Dick,*
or Street Life in New York with the Boot Blacks

HORATIO ALGER

Horatio Alger (1832–1899) was a prolific American writer, famous for his "rags to riches" novels that depict the rise to success of his young impoverished heroes. Among the most famous are *Ragged Dick* (1867), *Mark the Match Boy* (1869), and *Rough and Ready; or Life Among the New York Newsboys* (1869). The following excerpt is from *Ragged Dick*. At the end of the previous chapter, Dick, the protagonist, recognizes the con man who has swindled a "countryman."

Chapter XI: Dick as a Detective

Dick's ready identification of the rogue who had cheated the countryman, surprised Frank.

"What makes you think it is he?" he asked.

"Because I've seen him before, and I know he's up to them kind of tricks. When I heard how he looked, I was sure I knowed him."

"Our recognizing him won't be of much use," said Frank. "It won't give back the countryman his money."

"I don't know," said Dick thoughtfully. "Maybe I can get it."   5

"How?" asked Frank, incredulously.

"Wait a minute, and you'll see."

Dick left his companion, and went up to the man whom he suspected.

"Ephraim Smith," said Dick, in a low voice.

The man turned suddenly, and looked at Dick uneasily.   10

"What did you say?" he asked.

"I believe your name is Ephraim Smith," continued Dick.

"You're mistaken," said the man, and was about to move off.

"Stop a minute," said Dick. "Don't you keep your money in the Washington Bank?"

"I don't know any such bank. I'm in a hurry, young man, and I can't stop to   15
answer any foolish questions."

The boat had by this time reached the Brooklyn pier, and Mr. Ephraim Smith seemed in a hurry to land.

"Look here," said Dick, significantly; "you'd better not go on shore unless you want to jump into the arms of a policeman."

"What do you mean?" asked the man, startled.

"That little affair of yours is known to the police," said Dick; "about how you got fifty dollars out of a greenhorn on a false check, and it mayn't be safe for you to go ashore."

"I don't know what you are talking about," said the swindler with affected bold-   20
ness, though Dick could see that he was ill at ease.

"Yes you do," said Dick. "There isn't but one thing to do. Just give me back that money, and I'll see that you're not touched. If you don't, I'll give you up to the first p'liceman we meet."

Dick looked so determined, and spoke so confidently, that the other, overcome by his fears, no longer hesitated, but passed a roll of bills to Dick and hastily left the boat.

All this Frank witnessed with great amazement, not understanding what influ-ence Dick could have obtained over the swindler sufficient to compel restitution.

"How did you do it?" he asked eagerly.

"I told him I'd exert my influence with the president to have him tried by *habeas*   25
corpus," said Dick.

"And of course that frightened him. But tell me, without joking, how you man-aged."

Dick gave a truthful account of what occurred, and then said, "Now we'll go back and carry the money."

"Suppose we don't find the poor countryman?"

"Then the p'lice will take care of it."

They remained on board the boat, and in five minutes were again in New York.   30
Going up Wall Street, they met the countryman a little distance from the Custom House. His face was marked with the traces of deep anguish; but in his case even grief could not subdue the cravings of appetite. He had purchased some cakes of the old women who spread out for the benefit of passers-by an array of apples and seed-cakes, and was munching them with melancholy satisfaction.

"Hilloa!" said Dick. "Have you found your money?"

"No," ejaculated the young man, with a convulsive gasp. "I shan't ever see it again. The mean skunk's cheated me out of it. Consarn his picter! It took me most six months to save it up. I was workin' for Deacon Pinkham in our place. Oh, I wish I'd never come to New York! The deacon, he told me he'd keep it for me; but I wanted to put it in the bank, and now it's all gone, boo hoo!"

And the miserable youth, having despatched his cakes, was so overcome by the thought of his loss that he burst into tears.

"I say," said Dick, "dry up, and see what I've got here."

The youth no sooner saw the roll of bills, and comprehended that it was indeed   35
his lost treasure, than from the depths of anguish he was exalted to the most ecstatic joy. He seized Dick's hand, and shook it with so much energy that our hero began to feel rather alarmed for its safety.

"'Pears to me you take my arm for a pump-handle," said he. "Couldn't you show your gratitood some other way? It's just possible I may want to use my arm ag'in some time."

The young man desisted, but invited Dick most cordially to come up and stop a week with him at his country home, assuring him that he wouldn't charge him anything for board.

"All right!" said Dick. "If you don't mind I'll bring my wife along, too. She's delicate, and the country air might do her good."

Jonathan stared at him in amazement, uncertain whether to credit the fact of his marriage. Dick walked on with Frank, leaving him in an apparent state of stupefaction, and it is possible that he has not yet settled the affair to his satisfaction.

"Now," said Frank, "I think I'll go back to the Astor House. Uncle has probably   40
got through his business and returned."

"All right," said Dick.

The two boys walked up to Broadway, just where the tall steeple of Trinity faces the street of bankers and brokers, and walked leisurely to the hotel. When they arrived at the Astor House, Dick said, "Good-by, Frank."

"Not yet," said Frank; "I want you to come in with me."

Dick followed his young patron up the steps. Frank went to the reading-room, where, as he had thought probable, he found his uncle already arrived, and reading a copy of "The Evening Post," which he had just purchased outside.

"Well, boys," he said, looking up, "have you had a pleasant jaunt?"   45

"Yes, sir," said Frank. "Dick's a capital guide."

"So this is Dick," said Mr. Whitney, surveying him with a smile. "Upon my word, I should hardly have known him. I must congratulate him on his improved appearance."

"Frank's been very kind to me," said Dick, who, rough street-boy as he was, had a heart easily touched by kindness, of which he had never experienced much. "He's a tip-top fellow."

"I believe he is a good boy," said Mr. Whitney. "I hope, my lad, you will prosper and rise in the world. You know in this free country poverty in early life is no bar to a man's advancement. I haven't risen very high myself," he added, with a smile, "but have met with moderate success in life; yet there was a time when I was as poor as you."

"Were you, sir?" asked Dick, eagerly.   50

"Yes, my boy, I have known the time when I have been obliged to go without my dinner because I didn't have enough money to pay for it."

"How did you get up in the world?" asked Dick, anxiously.

"I entered a printing-office as an apprentice, and worked for some years. Then my eyes gave out and I was obliged to give that up. Not knowing what else to do, I went into the country, and worked on a farm. After a while I was lucky enough to invent a machine, which has brought me in a great deal of money. But there was one thing I got while I was in the printing-office which I value more than money."

"What was that, sir?"

"A taste for reading and study. During my leisure hours I improved myself by   55
study, and acquired a large part of the knowledge which I now possess. Indeed, it was one of my books that first put me on the track of the invention, which I afterwards

made. So you see, my lad, that my studious habits paid me in money as well as in another way."

"I'm awful ignorant," said Dick, soberly.

"But you are young, and, I judge, a smart boy. If you try to learn, you can, and if you ever expect to do anything in the world, you must know something of books."

"I will," said Dick, resolutely. "I ain't always goin' to black boots for a livin'."

"All labor is respectable, my lad, and you have no cause to be ashamed of any honest business; yet when you can get something to do that promises better for your future prospects, I advise you to do so. Till then earn your living in the way you are accustomed to, avoid extravagance, and save up a little money if you can."

"Thank you for your advice," said our hero. "There ain't many that takes an interest in Ragged Dick." 60

"So that's your name," said Mr. Whitney. "If I judge you rightly, it won't be long before you change it. Save your money, my lad, buy books, and determine to be somebody, and you may yet fill an honorable position."

"I'll try," said Dick. "Good-night, sir."

"Wait a minute, Dick," said Frank. "Your blacking-box and old clothes are upstairs. You may want them."

"In course," said Dick. "I couldn't get along without my best clothes, and my stock in trade."

"You may go up to the room with him, Frank," said Mr. Whitney. "The clerk will give you the key. I want to see you, Dick, before you go." 65

"Yes, sir," said Dick.

"Where are you going to sleep to-night, Dick?" asked Frank, as they went upstairs together.

"P'r'aps at the Fifth Avenue Hotel — on the outside," said Dick.

"Haven't you any place to sleep, then?"

"I slept in a box, last night." 70

"In a box?"

"Yes, on Spruce Street."

"Poor fellow!" said Frank, compassionately.

"Oh, 'twas a bully bed — full of straw! I slept like a top."

"Don't you earn enough to pay for a room, Dick?" 75

"Yes," said Dick; "only I spend my money foolish, goin' to the Old Bowery, and Tony Pastor's, and sometimes gamblin' in Baxter Street."

"You won't gamble any more, — will you, Dick?" said Frank, laying his hand persuasively on his companion's shoulder.

"No, I won't," said Dick.

"You'll promise?"

"Yes, and I'll keep it. You're a good feller. I wish you was goin' to be in New York." 80

"I am going to a boarding-school in Connecticut. The name of the town is Barnton. Will you write to me, Dick?"

"My writing would look like hens' tracks," said our hero.

"Never mind. I want you to write. When you write you can tell me how to direct, and I will send you a letter."

"I wish you would," said Dick. "I wish I was more like you."

"I hope you will make a much better boy, Dick. Now we'll go in to my uncle. He 85 wishes to see you before you go."

They went into the reading-room. Dick had wrapped up his blacking-brush in a newspaper with which Frank had supplied him, feeling that a guest of the Astor House should hardly be seen coming out of the hotel displaying such a professional sign.

"Uncle, Dick's ready to go," said Frank.

"Good-by, my lad," said Mr. Whitney. "I hope to hear good accounts of you some-time. Don't forget what I have told you. Remember that your future position depends mainly upon yourself, and that it will be high or low as you choose to make it."

He held out his hand, in which was a five-dollar bill. Dick shrunk back.

"I don't like to take it," he said. "I haven't earned it." 90

"Perhaps not," said Mr. Whitney; "but I give it to you because I remember my own friendless youth. I hope it may be of service to you. Sometime when you are a prosperous man, you can repay it in the form of aid to some poor boy, who is strug-gling upward as you are now."

"I will, sir," said Dick, manfully.

He no longer refused the money, but took it gratefully, and, bidding Frank and his uncle good-by, went out into the street. A feeling of loneliness came over him as he left the presence of Frank, for whom he had formed a strong attachment in the few hours he had known him.

(1867)

Questions

1. Horatio Alger characterizes Dick as thoughtful, shrewd, kind, humorous, and hon-est. Find specific support for each. Which trait do you think is most important?

2. Mr. Whitney characterizes what we have come to refer to as the path to the American Dream. What are its four components? Do they still hold true today? Explain.

3. What has become known as the "Horatio Alger myth" still grips the American imagination. Why do you think that is so?

Horatio Alger

HARLON L. DALTON

Harlon L. Dalton is a professor at Yale Law School. The following essay, taken from his 1995 book, *Racial Healing: Confronting the Fear between Blacks and Whites*, interrogates the Horatio Alger myth.

Ah, Horatio Alger, whose name more than any other is associated with the classic American hero. A writer of mediocre fiction, Alger had a formula for commercial success that was simple and straightforward: his lead characters, young boys born into poverty, invariably managed to transcend their station in life by dint of hard work, persistence, initiative, and daring.[1] Nice story line. There is just one problem — it is a myth. Not just in the sense that it is fictional, but more fundamentally because the lesson Alger conveys is a false one. To be sure, many myths are perfectly benign, and more than a few are salutary, but on balance Alger's myth is socially destructive.

The Horatio Alger myth conveys three basic messages: (1) each of us is judged solely on her or his own merits; (2) we each have a fair opportunity to develop those merits; and (3) ultimately, merit will out. Each of them is, to be charitable, problematic. The first message is a variant on the rugged individualism ethos. . . . In this form, it suggests that success in life has nothing to do with pedigree, race, class background, gender, national origin, sexual orientation — in short, with anything beyond our individual control. Those variables may exist, but they play no appreciable role in how our actions are appraised.

This simply flies in the face of reality. There are doubtless circumstances — the hiring of a letter carrier in a large metropolitan post office, for example — where none of this may matter, but that is the exception rather than the rule. Black folk certainly know what it is like to be favored, disfavored, scrutinized, and ignored all on the basis of our race. Sometimes we are judged on a different scale altogether. Stephen Carter has written movingly about what he calls "the best black syndrome," the tendency of White folk to judge successful Black people only in relation to each other rather than against all comers. Thus, when Carter earned the second-highest score in his high school on the National Merit Scholarship qualifying test, he was readily recognized as "the best Black" around, but somehow not seen as one of the best students, period.[2]

Although I would like to think that things are much different now, I know better. Not long ago a student sought my advice regarding how to deal with the fact that a liberal colleague of mine (and of Stephen Carter's) had written a judicial clerkship recommendation for her in which he described her as the best Black student to have ever taken his class. Apparently the letter caused a mild stir among current law clerks in several courthouses, one of whom saw fit to inform the student. "What was the professor [whom she declined to name] thinking of?" she wondered aloud. "What does his comment mean? What is a judge supposed to make of it? 'If for some reason you think you have to hire one of them, then she's the way to go'? I could understand if he said I was one of the top ten students or even the top thousand, but what does the 'best Black' mean?"

Black folk also know what it is like to be underestimated because of the color of   5
their skin. For example, those of us who communicate in standard English are often praised unduly for how well we speak. This is, I might add, an experience all too familiar to Asian-Americans, including those born and bred in the U.S.A. And we know what it is like to be feared, pitied, admired, and scorned on account of our race, before we even have a chance to say boo! We, in turn, view White people through the

---

[1] Edwin P. Hoyt, *Horatio's Boys: The Life and Works of Horatio Alger, Jr.* (Radnor, Penn.: Chilton Book Company, 1974).
[2] Stephen L. Carter, *Reflections of an Affirmative Action Baby* (New York: Basic Books, 1991), 47–49.

prism of our own race-based expectations. I honestly am surprised every time I see a White man who can play basketball above the rim, just as Puerto Ricans and Cubans tend to be surprised to discover "Americans" who salsa truly well. All of which is to say that the notion that every individual is judged solely on personal merit, without regard for sociological wrapping, is mythical at best.

The second message conveyed by Horatio Alger is that we all have a shot at reaching our true potential. To be fair, neither Alger nor the myth he underwrote suggests that we start out equal. Nor does the myth necessarily require that we be given an equal opportunity to succeed. Rather, Alger's point is that each of us has the power to create our own opportunities. That turns out to be a difficult proposition to completely disprove, for no matter what evidence is offered up to show that a particular group of people have not fared well, it can always be argued that they did not try hard enough, or that they spent too much time wallowing in their predicament and not enough figuring out how to rise above it. Besides, there are always up-by-the-bootstraps examples to point to, like Colin Powell, whose name has so frequently been linked with that of Horatio Alger's that he must think they are related.[3] Nevertheless, it is by now generally agreed that there is a large category of Americans — some have called it the underclass — for whom upward mobility is practically impossible without massive changes in the structure of the economy and in the allocation of public resources.

As for the notion that merit will out, it assumes not only a commitment to merit-based decision making but also the existence of standards for measuring merit that do not unfairly favor one individual over another. Such standards, of course, must come from somewhere. They must be decided upon by somebody. And that somebody is rarely without a point of view. Ask a devotee of West Coast basketball what skills you should look for in recruiting talent and near the top of his list will be the ability to "get out on the break," to "be creative in the open court," and "to finish the play." On the other hand, ask someone who prefers East Coast basketball and her list will rank highly the ability "to d-up [play defense]," "to board [rebound]," and "to maintain focus and intensity."

Or, to take another example, what makes a great Supreme Court justice? Brains to spare? Common sense? Proper judicial temperament? Political savvy? Extensive lawyering experience? A well-developed ability to abstract? Vision? Well-honed rhetorical skills? A reverence for our rich legal heritage? The capacity to adapt to changing times?

---

[3]Sandy Grady, "Will He or Won't He?: Win or Lose, Presidential Pursuit by Colin Powell Would Do America a Necessary Service," *Kansas City Star*, 24 April 1995; Thomas B. Edsall, "For Powell, Timing Could be Crucial: As Gulf War Hero Hints at 1996 Bid, Associates Look into Details," *Washington Post*, 6 April 1995; J. F. O. McAllister, "The Candidate of Dreams," *Time*, 13 March 1995; Deroy Murdock, "Colin Powell: Many Things to Many People," *Washington Times*, 16 January 1995; Doug Fischer, "U.S. Politics: War Hero Well-Placed to Become First Black President," *Ottawa Citizen*, 8 October 1994; "General Nice Guy: Profile Colin Powell," *Sunday Telegraph*, 25 September 1994; Otto Kreisher, "As a Civilian, Powell's Options Are Enviable," *San Diego Union-Tribune*, 26 September 1993.

Even if one is tempted to say "all of the above," how should these (or any other set of characteristics) be ranked? Measured? Evaluated?

The answers depend in part on whom you ask. Practicing lawyers, for example, are probably likely to rank extensive lawyering experience more highly than, say, brains. They are also likely to pay close attention to judicial temperament, which for them means whether the prospective justice would be inclined to treat them with respect during a court appearance. Sitting judges are also likely to rank judicial temperament highly, meaning whether the prospective justice would be a good colleague. In choosing among the other characteristics, they might each favor the ones that they happen to possess in abundance. Politicians might well see more merit in political savvy than would, say, academics, who could be expected to favor brains, the ability to abstract, and perhaps rhetorical skills.

All of these relevant actors might be honestly trying to come up with appropriate standards for measuring merit, but they would arrive at markedly different results. And any given result would screen out people who would succeed under another, equally plausible set of standards. Thus, if there is a genuine commitment to merit-based decision making it is possible that merit will out, but only for those who have the right kind of merit.

Which brings us to the prior question: is merit all we care about in deciding who gets what share of life's goodies? Clearly not. Does anyone, for example, honestly believe that any Supreme Court justice in recent memory was nominated solely on the basis of merit (however defined)? Any President? Any member of Congress? Does anyone believe that America's health-care resources are distributed solely on merit? That tax breaks are distributed solely on merit? That baseball club owners are selected solely on merit?

As I suggested earlier, the mere fact that a myth is based on false premises or conveys a false image of the world does not necessarily make it undesirable. Indeed, I place great stock in the idea that some illusions are, or at least can be, positive. As social psychologist Shelley Taylor has observed, "[normal] people who are confronted with the normal rebuffs of everyday life seem to construe their experience [so] as to develop and maintain an exaggeratedly positive view of their own attributes, an unrealistic optimism about the future, and a distorted faith in their ability to control what goes on around them."[4] Taylor's research suggests that, up to a point, such self-aggrandizement actually improves one's chances of worldly success.[5]

This may well explain the deep appeal of the Horatio Alger myth. True or not, it can help to pull people in the direction they want to go. After all, in order to succeed in life, especially when the odds are stacked against you, it is often necessary to first convince yourself that there is a reason to get up in the morning. So what is my beef? Where is the harm?

10

---

[4]Shelley E. Taylor, *Positive Illusions: Creative Self-Deception and the Healthy Mind* (New York: Basic Books, 1989), xi.
[5]Ibid., xi, 7, 228–46.

In a nutshell, my objection to the Alger myth is that it serves to maintain the racial pecking order. It does so by mentally bypassing the role of race in American society. And it does so by fostering beliefs that themselves serve to trivialize, if not erase, the social meaning of race. The Alger myth encourages people to blink at the many barriers to racial equality (historical, structural, and institutional) that litter the social landscape. Yes, slavery was built on the notion that Africans were property and not persons; yes, even after that "peculiar institution" collapsed, it continued to shape the life prospects of those who previously were enslaved; yes, the enforced illiteracy and cultural disruption of slavery, together with the collapse of Reconstruction, virtually assured that the vast majority of "freedmen" and "freedwomen" would not be successfully integrated into society; yes, Jim Crow laws, segregation, and a separate and unequal social reality severely undermined the prospects for Black achievement; yes, these and other features of our national life created a racial caste system that persists to this day; yes, the short-lived civil rights era of the 1950s and 1960s was undone by a broad and sustained White backlash; yes, the majority of Black people in America are mired in poverty; yes, economic mobility is not what it used to be, given the decline in our manufacturing and industrial base; yes, the siting of the illicit drug industry in our inner cities has had pernicious effects on Black and Latino neighborhoods; yes, yes, yes, BUT (drumroll) "all it takes to make it in America is initiative, hard work, persistence, and pluck." After all, just look at Colin Powell!

There is a fundamental tension between the promise of opportunity enshrined in the Alger myth and the realities of a racial caste system. The main point of such a system is to promote and maintain inequality. The main point of the Alger myth is to proclaim that everyone can rise above her station in life. Despite this tension, it is possible for the myth to coexist with social reality. To quote Shelley Taylor once again:

> [T]he normal human mind is oriented toward mental health and . . . at every turn it construes events in a manner that promotes benign fictions about the self, the world, and the future. The mind is, with some significant exceptions, intrinsically adaptive, oriented toward overcoming rather than succumbing to the adverse events of life. . . . At one level, it constructs beneficent interpretations of threatening events that raise self-esteem and promote motivation; yet at another level, it recognizes the threat or challenge that is posed by these events.[6]

Not surprisingly, then, there are lots of Black folk who subscribe to the Alger myth and at the same time understand it to be deeply false. They live with the dissonance between myth and reality because both are helpful and healthful in dealing with "the adverse events of life." Many Whites, however, have a strong interest in resolving the dissonance in favor of the myth. Far from needing to be on guard against racial "threat[s] or challenge[s]," they would just as soon put the ugliness of racism

15

---

[6]Ibid., xi.

out of mind. For them, the Horatio Alger myth provides them the opportunity to do just that.[7]

Quite apart from the general way in which the myth works to submerge the social realities of race, each of the messages it projects is also incompatible with the idea of race-based advantage or disadvantage. If, as the myth suggests, we are judged solely on our individual merits, then caste has little practical meaning. If we all can acquire the tools needed to reach our full potential, then how important can the disadvantage of race be? If merit will eventually carry the day, then shouldn't we be directing our energies toward encouraging Black initiative and follow-through rather than worrying about questions of power and privilege?

By interring the myth of Horatio Alger, or at least forcing it to coexist with social reality, we can accomplish two important goals. First, we can give the lie to the idea that Black people can simply lift themselves up by their own bootstraps. With that pesky idea out of the way, it is easier to see why White folk need to take joint ownership of the nation's race problem. Second, the realization that hard work and individual merit, while certainly critical, are not guarantors of success should lead at least some White people to reflect on whether their own achievements have been helped along by their preferred social position.

Finally, quite apart from race, it is in our national interest to give the Horatio Alger myth a rest, for it broadcasts a fourth message no less false than the first three — that we live in a land of unlimited potential. Although that belief may have served us well in the past, we live today in an era of diminished possibilities. We need to make a series of hard choices, followed by yet more hard choices regarding how to live with the promise of less. Confronting that reality is made that much harder by a mythology that assures us we can have it all.

(1995)

Questions

1. Harlon L. Dalton delineates three features of what has come to be called the "Horatio Alger myth." What are they? How do they compare with Mr. Whitney's statements in the excerpt from *Ragged Dick* (p. 1493)? Do they hold true today? Explain.
2. Dalton argues against the validity of the Horatio Alger myth. How persuasive are his arguments?
3. Dalton specifically addresses the Horatio Alger myth as it applies to African Americans. Does his analysis of the myth apply to other Americans as well? Explain.
4. Do you agree with Dalton's questioning of the power of merit in our society?
5. What is the rhetorical effect of mentioning Colin Powell twice, in paragraphs 6 and 14?

---

[7]Robert T. Carter, et al., "White Racial Identity Development and Work Values," *Journal of Vocational Behavior, Special Issue: Racial Identity and Vocational Behavior* 44, no. 2 (April 1994): 185–97.

6. In the concluding paragraph, Dalton says, "we live today in an era of diminished possibilities." How much does your assessment of Dalton's argument depend on whether or not you agree with that assertion?

from *The Fifties*

ALAN BRINKLEY

The following is an excerpt from an essay written for the Gilder Lehrman Institute of American History by Alan Brinkley (b. 1949), a professor of American history at Columbia University and the author of several books, including *Franklin D. Roosevelt* (2009), *John F. Kennedy* (2012), and *Voices of Protest: Huey Long, Father Coughlin, and the Great Depression* (1982), which received the National Book Award for History.

The Affluent Society

The performance of the American economy in the decades after World War II appeared to many contemporaries to be, as one historian wrote at the time, "the crossing of a great divide in the history of humanity." It was often described as an "economic miracle." The GNP was growing fourteen times as fast as the population and seven times the rate of inflation. The average family income grew as much in the ten years after World War II as it had grown in the previous fifty years combined. Between 1940 and 1965, average income grew from about $2,200 per family per year to just under $8,000; when adjusted for inflation, that means average family incomes almost tripled.

These years also saw a significant decrease in (although not a disappearance of) poverty in America. The percentage of families below the official poverty line in 1950 was 30 percent. By 1960 it had dropped to 22 percent and by the 1960s, it had dropped to under 14 percent. Between 1950 and 1970, in other words, poverty declined by over 60 percent.

There were many claims at the time that not only was America becoming wealthier, but that it was becoming more "equal," that wealth was being redistributed at the same time it was increasing. That was not true. There was no significant redistribution of wealth in the 1950s and 1960s, up or down, simply an increase in the total amount of wealth. But significantly — and in sharp contrast to the period since the mid-1970s — while there was no downward redistribution of wealth, neither was there an upward distribution of wealth. Distribution patterns, in other words, remained unchanged — the wealthy and the poor experienced roughly the same rates of growth. The gap between them remained the same.

What caused this remarkable growth? One important cause was government spending, which was clearly the major factor in ending the Depression in the early 1940s. Government expenditures in 1929 were 1 percent of GNP; in 1955, they were 17 percent. The bulk of this increase in the early 1950s came from military spending until the end of the Korean War. After that, highway and home construction picked up much of the slack. Veterans' benefits (mortgage and education assistance), government-sponsored research (military and space), and other sources of growth helped fuel the economy. Another cause of postwar economic growth was population growth: the tremendous increase in the birth rate in the decade after World War II ("postwar baby boom"). Population grew in the 1940s and 1950s at twice the rate it had grown in the 1930s. Increased population was also responsible for increased demand and increased consumption, a spur to economic growth.

The growth of suburbs after World War II was one of the great population move- 5 ments in American history. Eighteen million people — 10 percent of the population — moved to suburbs in the 1950s. The American population as a whole grew 19 percent in the 1950s; suburban population grew 47 percent. Suburbs created a vast new market and provided an important boost to several of the most important sectors of the economy: the housing industry, the automobile industry, highway construction, and a wide range of consumer industries. And another element of growth was the transformation in labor relations. The growing power of unions allowed workers to receive better wages and benefits.

The cumulative economic effect of all these changes was a radical change in American life — the birth of an economy (and thus a society) in which many Americans came to consider affluence a norm; in which the ability not just to subsist, but greatly to enhance the quality of one's life came to seem a basic right; in which material abundance became one of the ways in which many, probably most, Americans defined their world.

Economic growth affected both popular and elite ideas about capitalism. Gradually it became possible to believe that there were few limits to economic growth. Capitalism, many Americans came to believe, was capable of much greater feats than most Americans had once believed possible.

John Kenneth Galbraith, the famous Harvard economist, hardly an uncritical defender of capitalism, published a small book in 1952 entitled *American Capitalism*. In it, he expressed some of the wonder and enthusiasm of this new discovery. About capitalism, he wrote simply: "It works!" And he went on to say:

> In the United States alone there need not lurk behind modern programs of social betterment that fundamental dilemma that everywhere paralyzes the will of every responsible man, the dilemma between economic progress and immediate increase of the real income of the masses. . . .

The growth of affluence also provided an opportunity to improve the lives of Americans and to meet social needs. Galbraith urged a major increase in public spending on such things as schools, parks, hospitals, urban renewal, and scientific research. The 1957 launching of *Sputnik*, the Soviet satellite that was the first to be launched into orbit (before the United States had managed to do so), was a tremendous event in American politics and culture. It too persuaded many Americans, and the government, to ask for massive social investment in an effort to catch up — particularly in science, technology, and education.

Fifties Society

Many Americans in the 1950s considered their era as a time of affluence, community,   10
and unity. Today — a half century later — many people still see those years as a golden
era that has now been lost. Even the most sophisticated chroniclers of its time believed
in the great successes of the 1950s. The renowned historian Richard Hofstadter wrote
at the time:

> The jobless, distracted and bewildered men of 1933 have in the course of the
> years found substantial places in society for themselves, have become home-
> owners, suburbanites, and solid citizens.

The French writer Simone de Beauvoir said of America in the 1950s:

> Class barriers disappear or become porous; the factory worker is an economic
> aristocrat in comparison with the middle-class clerk; even segregation is dimin-
> ishing; consumption replaces acquisition as an incentive. America . . . as a country
> of vast inequalities and dramatic contrasts is ceasing to exist.

Many middle-class Americans in these years believed in the idea that the American people, for all their diversity, were becoming more and more alike — and could
expect to continue to do so in the future. Few ideas became more pervasive in popular
culture than the sense that America was becoming a middle-class nation — a society
in which everyone was either already part of the middle class, soon to become part
of it, or aspiring to become part of it. And there was some evidence for this powerful
idea.

There was rapid growth in the number of people able to afford what the government defined as a "middle-class" standard of living — 60 percent of the American
people. Home ownership rose from 40 percent in 1945 to 60 percent in 1960. By 1960,
75 percent of all families owned cars; 87 percent owned televisions; 75 percent owned
washing machines. But these figures also show the survival of a substantial minority
(25 to 40 percent) that remained outside the middle class. More than 23 percent of
Americans still lived in poverty, and African American poverty was far higher.

American politics in the 1950s was dominated by Dwight D. Eisenhower, who
emerged from the war as the military man with the most political appeal, largely
because of his personality. There were other generals who had performed with at least
equal brilliance and effectiveness. But none of them had Eisenhower's personal qualities: his public warmth and friendliness and geniality; his dazzling, highly photogenic
smile, which became his political trademark; his comforting, unthreatening public
image. It helped him become president in 1953, and it helped him remain popular
until he left the White House in 1961.

But Eisenhower was also appealing because he seemed to embody the stability
and the desire for unity that characterized so many other areas of American culture in
the 1950s. Eisenhower's approach to leadership was based on two fairly simple assumptions. He had a deep aversion to conflict and confrontation. He leaned instinctively

toward consensus and conciliation; and he tried to avoid doing anything that would disrupt the harmony that he liked to believe prevailed in American society. And he was deeply committed to capitalism, and to capitalists; a champion of free enterprise; a cheerleader for the business community in this hour of its great economic triumph. Eisenhower's presidency was an embodiment of the middle-class yearning for stability and consensus.

Eisenhower became, in effect, the cautious, prudent, conciliatory paternal figure   15
presiding over the heyday of middle-class dominance of American life. He seemed to embody the era's apparent stability and unity and homogeneity. He epitomized the American middle class's idealized image of itself. And not incidentally, he presided over an era of almost unbroken prosperity and unbroken peace that reinforced the power of the stable, consensual public culture of the time.

(2012)

Questions

1. In the third paragraph, Alan Brinkley addresses a misconception that he thinks many hold regarding 1950s America. What might be the reason many people have that misconception? Did you before you read this selection? Brinkley suggests that the conditions he describes began to change in the 1970s. What might have been some of the causes? Explain.
2. How does Brinkley characterize American life in paragraphs 6 and 7? Do you agree with that characterization? Do people today still define their world as he says they did then? Explain.
3. Brinkley quotes Richard Hofstadter and Simone de Beauvoir on their perceptions of the 1950s. How accurately might their comments apply to American society today?
4. Brinkley characterizes President Dwight D. Eisenhower as the ideal leader for his time. Choose a more recent American president whom you see as similar in stature. How did/does that leader embody the ethos of the American middle class for his time?
5. Of the 1950s, Brinkley says, "Today — a half century later — many people still see those years as a golden era that has now been lost" (par. 10). What evidence do you see in American politics and culture to support Brinkley's claim?

The Growing Gulf between the Rich and the Rest of Us

HOLLY SKLAR

Holly Sklar, a syndicated columnist and policy analyst, is the author of the 2001 book *Raise the Floor: Wages and Policies That Work for All of Us*. The following syndicated editorial first appeared in September 2005 on the Web site CommonDreams.org, a nonprofit news site dedicated to "progressive values of social justice, human rights, equity and peace."

Guess which country the *CIA World Factbook* describes when it says, "Since 1975, practically all the gains in household income have gone to the top 20 percent of households."

If you guessed the United States, you're right.

The United States has rising levels of poverty and inequality not found in other rich democracies. It also has less mobility out of poverty.

Since 2000, America's billionaire club has gained 76 more members while the typical household has lost income and the poverty count has grown by more than 5 million people.

Poverty and inequality take a daily toll seldom seen on television. "The infant   5
mortality rate in the United States compares with that in Malaysia—a country with a quarter the income," says the 2005 Human Development Report. "Infant death rates are higher for [black] children in Washington, D.C., than for children in Kerala, India."

Income and wealth in America are increasingly concentrated at the very top— the realm of the Forbes 400.

You could have banked $1 million a day every day for the last two years and still have far to go to make the new Forbes list of the 400 richest Americans.

It took a minimum of $900 million to get on the Forbes 400 this year. That's up $150 million from 2004.

"Surging real estate and oil prices drove up several fortunes and helped pave the way for 33 new members," Forbes notes.

Middle-class households, meanwhile, are a medical crisis or outsourced job away   10
from bankruptcy.

With 374 billionaires, the Forbes 400 will soon be billionaires only.

Bill Gates remains No. 1 on the Forbes 400 with $51 billion. Low-paid Wal-Mart workers can find Walton family heirs in five of the top 10 spots; another Wal-Mart heir ranks No. 116.

Former Bechtel president Stephen Bechtel Jr. and his son, CEO Riley Bechtel, tie for No. 109 on the Forbes 400 with $2.4 billion apiece. The politically powerful Bechtel has gotten a no-bid contract for hurricane reconstruction despite a pattern of cost overruns and shoddy work from Iraq to Boston's leaky "Big Dig" tunnel/highway project.

The Forbes 400 is a group so small they could have watched this year's Sugar Bowl from the private boxes of the Superdome.

Yet combined Forbes 400 wealth totals more than $1.1 trillion—an amount greater   15
than the gross domestic product of Spain or Canada, the world's eighth- and ninth-largest economies.

The number of Americans in poverty is a group so large it would take the combined populations of Louisiana, Mississippi, Alabama and Texas, plus Arkansas to match it. That's according to the Census Bureau's latest count of 37 million people below the poverty line.

Millions more Americans can't afford adequate health care, housing, child care, food, transportation and other basic expenses above the official poverty thresholds, which are set too low. The poverty threshold for a single person under age 65 was just $9,827 in 2004. For a two-adult, two-child family, it was just $19,157.

By contrast, the Economic Policy Institute's Basic Family Budget Calculator says the national median basic needs budget (including taxes and tax credits) for a two-parent, two-child family was $39,984 in 2004. It was $38,136 in New Orleans and $33,636 in Biloxi, Mississippi.

America is becoming a downwardly mobile society instead of an upwardly mobile society. Median household income fell for the fifth year in a row to $44,389 in 2004 — down from $46,129 in 1999, adjusting for inflation. The Bush administration is using hurricane "recovery" to camouflage policies that will deepen inequality and poverty. They are bringing windfall profits to companies like Bechtel while suspending regulations that shore up wages for workers.

More tax cuts are in the pipeline for wealthy Americans who can afford the $17,000 watch, $160,000 coat and $10 million helicopter on the Forbes Cost of Living Extremely Well Index. 20

More budget cuts are in the pipeline for Medicaid, Food Stamps and other safety nets for Americans whose wages don't even cover the cost of necessities.

Without a change in course, the gulf between the rich and the rest of America will continue to widen, weakening our economy and our democracy. The American Dream will be history instead of poverty.

(2005)

Questions

1. Holly Sklar begins by quoting the *CIA World Factbook*, an almanac published by the U.S. Central Intelligence Agency that contains information about countries of the world. How does this source affect her ethos?
2. What is the effect of the many statistics that Sklar includes in her short piece? Which of them do you find most compelling or startling?
3. Paragraph 13 consists of two sentences, the first of which delivers objective, factual information. In the second sentence, Sklar makes implications. What are they? How do they support her argument?
4. In paragraphs 20 and 21, Sklar juxtaposes tax cuts with budget cuts. What, according to her, are their relative effects?
5. Writing in 2005, Sklar concludes, "the gulf between the rich and the rest of America will continue to widen, weakening our economy and our democracy." Was she correct in her assessment? Explain.

from *The Conscience of a Liberal*

Paul Krugman

Paul Krugman is a professor at Princeton University, an op-ed columnist for the *New York Times*, and the author of several books, including *The Age of Diminished*

Expectations (1989) and *The Great Unraveling: Losing Our Way in the New Century* (2003). He was awarded the 2008 Nobel Prize in Economics. The following excerpt from Krugman's 2007 book is from Chapter 12, "Confronting Inequality."

Americans still tend to say, when asked, that individuals can make their own place in society. According to one survey 61 percent of Americans agree with the statement that "people get rewarded for their effort," compared with 49 percent in Canada and only 23 percent in France.[1] In reality, however, America has vast inequality of opportunity as well as results. We may believe that anyone can succeed through hard work and determination, but the facts say otherwise.

There are many pieces of evidence showing that Horatio Alger stories are very rare in real life. One of the most striking comes from a study published by the National Center for Education Statistics, which tracked the educational experience of Americans who were eighth graders in 1988. Those eighth graders were sorted both by apparent talent, as measured by a mathematics test, and by the socioeconomic status of their parents, as measured by occupations, incomes, and education.

The key result is shown in Table 1. Not surprisingly, both getting a high test score and having high-status parents increased a student's chance of finishing college. But family status mattered more. Students who scored in the bottom fourth on the exam, but came from families whose status put them in the top fourth — what we used to call RDKs, for "rich dumb kids," when I was a teenager — were more likely to finish college than students who scored in the top fourth but whose parents were in the bottom fourth. What this tells us is that the idea that we have anything close to equality of opportunity is clearly a fantasy. It would be closer to the truth, though not the whole truth, to say that in modern America, class — inherited class — usually trumps talent.

Isn't that true everywhere? Not to the same extent. International comparisons of "intergenerational mobility," the extent to which people can achieve higher status than their parents, are tricky because countries don't collect perfectly comparable data.

TABLE 1

Percentage of 1988 Eighth Graders Finishing College

	SCORE IN BOTTOM QUARTILE	SCORE IN TOP QUARTILE
Parents in Bottom Quartile	3	29
Parents in Top Quartile	30	74

SOURCE: NATIONAL CENTER FOR EDUCATION STATISTICS, *THE CONDITION OF EDUCATION 2003*, P. 47.

Nonetheless it's clear that Horatio Alger has moved to someplace in Europe: Mobility is highest in the Scandinavian countries, and most results suggest that mobility is lower in the United States than it is in France, Canada, and maybe even Britain. Not only don't Americans have equal opportunity, opportunity is less equal here than elsewhere in the West.

It's not hard to understand why. Our unique lack of universal health care, all by   5
itself, puts Americans who are unlucky in their parents at a disadvantage: Because
American children from low-income families are often uninsured, they're more likely
to have health problems that derail their life chances. Poor nutrition, thanks to low
income and a lack of social support, can have the same effect. Life disruptions that
affect a child's parents can also make upward mobility hard—and the weakness of
the U.S. social safety net makes such disruptions more likely and worse if they happen.
Then there's the highly uneven quality of U.S. basic education, and so on. What it all
comes down to is that although the principle of "equality of opportunity, not equality
of results" sounds fine, it's a largely fictitious distinction. A society with highly unequal
results is, more or less inevitably, a society with highly unequal opportunity, too. If
you truly believe that all Americans are entitled to an equal chance at the starting
line, that's an argument for doing something to reduce inequality.

America's high inequality, then, imposes serious costs on our society that go
beyond the way it holds down the purchasing power of most families. And there's
another way in which inequality damages us: It corrupts our politics. "If there are
men in this country big enough to own the government of the United States," said
Woodrow Wilson in 1913, in words that would be almost inconceivable from a modern president, "they are going to own it."[2] Well, now there are, and they do. Not completely, of course, but hardly a week goes by without the disclosure of a case in which
the influence of money has grotesquely distorted U.S. government policy.

As this book went to press, there was a spectacular example: The way even some
Democrats rallied to the support of hedge fund managers, who receive an unconscio-
nable tax break. Through a quirk in the way the tax laws have been interpreted, these
managers—some of whom make more than a billion dollars a year—get to have most
of their earnings taxed at the capital gains rate, which is only 15 percent, even as other
high earners pay a 35 percent rate. The hedge fund tax loophole costs the government
more than $6 billion a year in lost revenue, roughly the cost of providing health care
to three million children.[3] Almost $2 billion of the total goes to just twenty-five indi-
viduals. Even conservative economists believe that the tax break is unjustified, and
should be eliminated.[4]

Yet the tax break has powerful political support—and not just from Republicans.
In July 2007 Sen. Charles Schumer of New York, the head of the Democratic Sena-
torial Campaign Committee, let it be known that he would favor eliminating the hedge
fund loophole only if other, deeply entrenched tax breaks were eliminated at the same
time. As everyone understood, this was a "poison pill," a way of blocking reform without explicitly saying no. And although Schumer denied it, everyone also suspected
that his position was driven by the large sums hedge funds contribute to Democratic
political campaigns.[5]

The hedge fund loophole is a classic example of how the concentration of income
in a few hands corrupts politics. Beyond that is the bigger story of how income inequality has reinforced the rise of movement conservatism, a fundamentally undemocratic force. As I argued [earlier in the book], rising inequality has to an important
extent been caused by the rightward shift of our politics, but the causation also runs

the other way. The new wealth of the rich has increased their influence, sustaining the institutions of movement conservatism and pulling the Republican Party even further into the movement's orbit. The ugliness of our politics is in large part a reflection of the inequality of our income distribution.

More broadly still, high levels of inequality strain the bonds that hold us together as a society. There has been a long-term downward trend in the extent to which Americans trust either the government or one another. In the sixties, most Americans agreed with the proposition that "most people can be trusted"; today most disagree.[6] In the sixties, most Americans believed that the government is run "for the benefit of all"; today, most believe that it's run for "a few big interests."[7] And there's convincing evidence that growing inequality is behind our growing cynicism, which is making the United States seem increasingly like a Latin American country. As the political scientists Eric Uslaner and Mitchell Brown point out (and support with extensive data), "In a world of haves and have-nots, those at either end of the economic spectrum have little reason to believe that 'most people can be trusted' . . . social trust rests on a foundation of economic equality."[8]

10

(2007)

Notes

1. Tom Hertz, *Understanding Mobility in America* (Center for American Progress, 2006) <http://www.americanprogress.org/issues/2006/04/b1579981.html>.
2. Woodrow Wilson, *The New Freedom* (Doubleday, 1913), Project Gutenberg <http://www.gutenberg.org/files/14811/14811-h/14811-h.html>.
3. "Tax Breaks for Billionaires," Economic Policy Institute Policy Memorandum no. 120 <http://www.epi.org/content.cfm/pm120>.
4. See, for example, Jessica Holzer, "Conservatives Break with GOP Leaders on a Tax Bill," *The Hill* 18 July 2007 <http://thehill.com/leading-the-news/conservatives-break-with-gop-leaders-on-a-tax-bill-2007-07-18.html>.
5. "In Opposing Tax Plan, Schumer Supports Wall Street Over Party," *New York Times* 30 July 2007: A1.
6. Eric M. Uslaner and Mitchell Brown, "Inequality, Trust, and Civic Engagement," *American Politics Research* 33.6 (2005): 868–94.
7. *The ANES Guide to Public Opinion and Electoral Behavior*, table 5A.2 <http://electionstudies.org/nesguide/toptable/tab5a_htm>.
8. Uslaner and Brown, "Inequality, Trust, and Civic Engagement."

Questions

1. In the first four paragraphs, Paul Krugman questions the validity of "Horatio Alger stories." Having read Alger (p. 1493) and Harlon L. Dalton (p. 1497), how persuasive do you find Krugman's argument?
2. According to Krugman, what are the chief consequences of growing economic inequality? What implications do they have for our society as a whole?

3. Krugman, who teaches economics at Princeton University, was awarded the Nobel Prize in Economics in 2008. How does that establish his ethos? How does knowing that affect your reading of his argument?
4. What is the rhetorical effect of the information in the endnotes? Explain by making specific reference to at least two of them.

Income Confusion

THOMAS SOWELL

> Thomas Sowell (b. 1930) is an economist and a nationally syndicated columnist whose work appears in *Forbes* magazine and the *Wall Street Journal*, among other publications. A former U.S. marine, he was educated at Harvard and Columbia Universities and at the University of Chicago. He is a senior fellow at the Hoover Institution at Stanford University. "Income Confusion" is a syndicated op-ed that appeared in newspapers across the country.

Anyone who follows the media has probably heard many times that the rich are getting richer, the poor are getting poorer, and incomes of the population in general are stagnating. Moreover, those who say such things can produce many statistics, including data from the Census Bureau, which seem to indicate that.

On the other hand, income tax data recently released by the Internal Revenue Service seem to show the exact opposite: People in the bottom fifth of income-tax filers in 1996 had their incomes increase by 91 percent by 2005.

The top one percent — "the rich" who are supposed to be monopolizing the money, according to the left — saw their incomes decline by a whopping 26 percent.

Meanwhile, the average taxpayers' real income increased by 24 percent between 1996 and 2005.

How can all this be? How can official statistics from different agencies of the same government — the Census Bureau and the IRS — lead to such radically different conclusions?

There are wild cards in such data that need to be kept in mind when you hear income statistics thrown around — especially when they are thrown around by people who are trying to prove something for political purposes.

One of these wild cards is that most Americans do not stay in the same income brackets throughout their lives. Millions of people move from one bracket to another in just a few years.

What that means statistically is that comparing the top income bracket with the bottom income bracket over a period of years tells you nothing about what is happening to the actual flesh-and-blood human beings who are moving between brackets during those years.

That is why the IRS data, which are for people 25 years old and older, and which follow the same individuals over time, find those in the bottom 20 percent of income-tax filers almost doubling their income in a decade. That is why they are no longer in the same bracket.

That is also why the share of income going to the bottom 20 percent bracket can be going down, as the Census Bureau data show, while the income going to the people who began the decade in that bracket is going up by large amounts. Unfortunately, most income statistics, including those from the Census Bureau, do not follow individuals over time. The Internal Revenue Service does that and so does a study at the University of Michigan, but they are the exceptions rather than the rule.

Following trends among income brackets over the years creates the illusion of following people over time. But the only way to follow people is to follow people.

Another wild card in income statistics is that many such statistics are about households or families — whose sizes vary over time, vary between one racial or ethnic group and another, and vary between one income bracket and another.

That is why household or family income can remain virtually unchanged for decades while per capita income is going up by very large amounts. The number of people per household and per family is declining.

Differences in the number of people per household from one ethnic group to another is why Hispanics have higher household incomes than blacks, while blacks have higher individual incomes than Hispanics.

Considering the millions of dollars being paid to each of the anchors who broadcast network news, surely these networks can afford to hire a few statisticians to check the statistics being thrown around, before these numbers are broadcast across the land as facts on which we are supposed to base policies and elect presidents.

Now that the Internal Revenue data show the opposite of what the media and the politicians have been saying for years, should we expect either to change? Not bloody likely.

The University of Michigan study, which has been going on for decades, shows patterns very similar to those of the IRS data. Those patterns have been ignored for decades.

Too many in the media and in politics choose whatever statistics fit their preconceptions.

(2007)

Questions

1. What statistics does Thomas Sowell use to support his claims? What are the two "wild cards" (par. 6) that he refers to? Why does he call them "wild cards"?
2. Whom does Sowell blame for what he characterizes as misconceptions regarding the economy? What does he imply about their motives? How might they respond to his implications?
3. Identify a major claim that Sowell makes and analyze his argument according to the Toulmin model (p. 126). How persuasive do you find his argument? Explain.

from *Who Stole the American Dream?*

HEDRICK SMITH

> Hedrick Smith is a reporter and editor for the *New York Times* and an Emmy Award–
> winning producer for *Frontline,* on PBS. He was awarded the Pulitzer Prize for
> International Reporting in 1974. Among his books are *The Russians* (1975) and
> *The Power Game* (1996). The following excerpt from Smith's 2012 book is taken
> from Chapter 6, "The Stolen Dream: From Middle Class to the New Poor."

The world of opportunities that greeted Pam Scholl coming out of high school in
Chillicothe, Ohio, in 1971 was a universe apart from the tough economic world that
lies in wait for average high school graduates today.

On the Monday after graduation, Pam went to work full-time for the RCA television tube plant that was opening in nearby Circleville. Pam was a well-organized,
gregarious teenager, a five-foot-five bundle of energy with a quick smile. In her senior
year, she had worked half-time for RCA as a co-op secretarial student. After her
graduation, RCA hired Pam for human relations to help build a workforce that grew
to fifteen hundred.

"I got $1.75 an hour," Pam recalled. "I didn't have a car my first year. But about
a year later, I bought me a Vega, a new little brown Chevrolet. It was cheap — $2,500.
My car payment was $50 a month and I could fill it up for $5, and run two weeks on
that. I thought I was hot. I had a new car and I had a job. I was in HR and I met all the
guys."[1]

One guy she helped was her classmate Mike Hughes. One Sunday afternoon, Pam
tipped Mike off to apply for a job the next day. "Mike came in, he took a test and got
hired," she said. "We took just about anybody who was healthy and could lift things."

Living The American Dream: 1970s–2000

"The early seventies were a good time around here," remembered Roy Wunsch, for   5
thirty-five years a chemical engineer at the local DuPont plant and, later, the Republican mayor of Circleville. "Living standards were going up. Everyone was growing or
expanding — all the local plants." High school graduates were in demand.[2]

Circleville (pop: 12,000) calls itself "the Pumpkin Capital of the World." It lies at
the heart of the Pickaway Plains, the rich farmlands of south-central Ohio honed
smooth by prehistoric glaciers. But despite its small-town façade, Circleville was a
magnet for brand-name U.S. corporations because it was close to major transportation arteries. RCA, DuPont, General Electric, Pittsburgh Plate Glass, Owens-Illinois,
and Container Corporation all had factories there. Purina processed the local crops.

So towns like Circleville rode the escalator of American economic growth from
the 1970s into the 2000s, and middle-class people like Pam Scholl and Mike Hughes
lived the American Dream. Each bought a home, raised a family, and moved up the
ladder at RCA, enjoying steady pay, good benefits, five weeks of paid vacation a year,

and a company-financed retirement plan. From secretary, Pam rose to a $47,000-a-year job as stockroom supervisor. Mike got good technical training and promotions. By 2000, he was a senior quality control inspector making $50,000 to $60,000 a year.[3]

"I liked working there," Pam Scholl said, speaking for both of them. "It was great. I knew everybody. It was wonderful."

Wonderful, but it didn't last.

2004: The Bottom Falls Out

The bottom fell out in 2004, even though the U.S. economy was then on the upswing.   10
Facing lower-cost competition from China, RCA sold the plant to the French firm Thomson, which cut back production in 2003 and finally shut down the plant in July 2004. Mike Hughes sensed it coming: The plant was not bringing in as much raw material as it had during boom times.

Even so, the shutdown was a body blow. Suddenly cast adrift in his early fifties, Hughes could not find steady work. He tried changing careers. With federal displaced worker assistance, he was able to take a year's course in industrial maintenance. But even that did not lead to a job. Hughes pumped out scores of job inquiries but kept being told that despite his long technical experience at RCA, he wasn't qualified for entry-level manual labor.

Eventually, he took a night job as part-time custodian at a local high school for $13,000 a year. A second part-time job at a local glass company earned him another $4,000. Only his wife's public sector job at Head Start kept Hughes from sinking below the poverty line.

"What made it difficult for us, we had children coming out of high school wanting to get a college education," Mike explained. "That's where my thirty-one years of severance pay went. All of it went to college tuition. I had to choose between my kids' future and our future."[4]

Talking about his predicament, Mike Hughes put on a brave front, papering over his hurt and anger. "I've got a home. I got a good pension. I somewhat lived the American Dream," he said. "They just cut me off. They cut off the dream."

"The Hardest Thing — Not Being Wanted"

At first, Pam Scholl fared better than Mike. She found a job as office and traffic manager   15
for a small American Wood Fibers plant. The pay was good, $47,000 a year, *until* — until they downsized her out of a job in May 2009. Then life went black. By then, she was a single mom, carrying the costs of a home all by herself. For the next eighteen months, the only work Pam could find was three months as a census taker in 2010. Otherwise, she ran through her savings and had to live on unemployment benefits and rising credit card debt.

"The hardest thing is not being wanted — not feeling worthy," she told me. "I didn't realize how bad I felt about it, until I got the census job. Even though it didn't pay that well, it was uplifting to have something to do. I felt like I was contributing to society.

The hardest thing is everybody looking at my résumé and saying, 'What a wonderful résumé you have — all this experience.' But I *have no job*. I know I have completed over five hundred applications and I have had only four job interviews, all for much less money than I was making."

Taking tests for public sector jobs, Pam Scholl ran into other people who had been laid off with her at the RCA plant in 2004. Like Pam, they were still hunting for a steady job. "The same 200 people are there," she noticed. "We are all taking the test for the same job. The very first test I took was for water meter reader for the city of Chillicothe. That was in June 2009. The job paid $14 an hour, and there were 250 people. The bottom line was, there was not even a job. The job was filled internally."

A year later, still without a job, she said it was a nightmare not knowing what to do or where to turn. "Oh, it's horrible," Scholl told me. "I never dreamed that I would be unemployed for a year. Right now, I am about to sink." She gave an uneasy laugh that betrayed her anxiety and too many sleepless nights. "I barely stay afloat between charge cards and unemployment benefits. I have depleted my savings at this point, just surviving. . . . This terrifies me to death."[5]

The New Poor — Middle-Class Dropouts of Opportunity

Pam Scholl and Mike Hughes represent a new phenomenon in America: the New Poor. They have become what might be called "middle-class dropouts" — middle-class Americans sliding downscale, people slipping backward late in life, which is the exact opposite of the American Dream. In six short years, those two fell from the middle of the American middle class, the middle 20 percent of all income brackets, into the bottom 20 percent or barely above it, and their stories mirror wide trends in American society.

As a nation, we have just been through the worst decade in seventy years, with fewer jobs at the end of 2011 than ten years earlier and with the income of the typical middle-class family winding up lower than in the late 1990s.[6, 7] But the story begins far earlier than this past decade. Millions of middle-class Americans like Pam Scholl and Mike Hughes started their economic decline *before* the Great Recession of 2008.

Their lives reflect "the long arc" of our economic history. They and millions like them are victims of the long-term stagnation of middle-class living standards since the 1970s. The squeeze they feel marks the long, slow erosion of America's claim as the land of opportunity. Blacks have been harder hit than whites — roughly 45 percent of blacks born into solid middle-class families had lower incomes than their parents by 2007.[8]

Their experience has been happening all across America, to real estate agents in Florida, to bank tellers in New York, to computer programmers in Colorado, even to people with Ph.D. degrees. The numbers of New Poor are legion, certainly among the nation's 6 million long-term unemployed. In 2010, the Census Bureau reported, another 2.6 million Americans slipped below the official poverty line, bringing the total to 46.2 million people — the highest number in fifty-two years.[9] "We think of America as a place where every generation is doing better," commented Harvard

20

economist Lawrence Katz, "but we're looking at a period when the median family is in worse shape than it was in the late 1990s."[10]

Baby boomers in their late fifties and early sixties, like Pam Scholl and Mike Hughes, have been especially hard hit. By late 2011, 4.3 million of them, roughly one in six Americans age fifty-five to sixty-four, were unable to find full-time work, and half of them have been looking for more than two years. As a group, joblessness or contingent work has cost them roughly $100 billion a year in lost wages. "This is new. . . . It is worse than we have experienced before and it is very widespread," asserts Carl Van Horn, head of the John J. Heldrich Center for Workforce Development at Rutgers University. "It is going to get worse. You are going to have a higher level of poverty among older Americans."[11]

The United States: Low Mobility in a New "Caste Society"

There is growing, and disturbing, evidence that America has evolved into a caste society, increasingly stratified in terms of wealth and income, with people at the bottom almost frozen there, generation after generation, and people at the top more and more frequently passing on the self-fulfilling advantages of high status to their children and grandchildren. Increasingly, privilege sustains privilege; poverty begets poverty.

"Children born to parents in the top [income] quintile have the highest likelihood of attaining the top," asserts social scientist Julia Isaacs. "And children born to parents in the bottom quintile have the highest likelihood of being in the bottom themselves."[12]

Several countries in Scandinavia and continental Europe, which we used to mock as class-bound hierarchies, have now surpassed us as places where people can move up the social and economic ladder. To gauge such things, experts track how near or far the apple falls from the tree or, in economic terms, how closely the incomes of sons match those of fathers and grandfathers. In those terms, evidence shows that countries like Norway, Finland, Denmark, and Canada offer young people the greatest chances of breaking out of the family mold, and even France, Germany, and Sweden offer young people better chances than America for moving up.[13]

In fact, America is now classified as "a *low-mobility* country in which about half of parental earnings advantages are passed onto sons," reports economist Isabel Sawhill.[14] Isaacs adds that "starting at the bottom of the earnings ladder is more of a handicap in the United States than in other countries."[15]

One major reason that a caste society is emerging in the United States is that education is no longer the great social leveler that it once was. Just the opposite. Recent academic studies have found that the educational attainment gap between affluent and low-income families has grown by 40 percent since the 1960s, even as the educational gap between blacks and whites has narrowed. "We have moved from a society in the 1950s and 1960s in which race was more consequential than family income to one today in which family income appears more determinative of educational success than race," reports Stanford sociologist Sean Reardon.[16] At the college level, one-half of the children from high-income families completed college in 2007 versus only 9 percent of low-income families — again a wider gap than existed in 1989.[17]

An important driver of these radically different educational outcomes, scholars have determined, is the significant additional time and money that affluent families invest in extracurricular learning and tutoring for their children compared with what low-income families can afford — a spending gap that has been increasing.[18] In addition, the quadrupling of average college tuition and room fees from the late 1970s to the early 2000s has put teenage children of average middle-class families at a large financial disadvantage compared with children of wealthy and affluent families in the basic ability to pay for a college education.[19]

America can still point to individual rags-to-riches stories of self-made men and women who leapfrog to success. But for all the glitz of sudden stardom on *American Idol*, for all the hoop stars and gridiron heroes from the inner city, and for every surprise Wall Street billionaire, the unpleasant truth is that a typical child born at the bottom of the heap in America has far less chance of rising into the middle class or above than one born in France, Germany, or Scandinavia. In fact, one study found that it would take five or six generations, 125 to 150 years, for a child from America's poverty caste to rise to the middle of the middle class.[20]

"Being born in the elite in the U.S. gives you a constellation of privileges that very few people in the world have ever experienced," explained David I. Levine, an economist at the University of California at Berkeley. "Being born poor in the U.S. gives you disadvantages unlike anything in Western Europe and Japan and Canada."[21]

Three Decades of Getting Nowhere

Even people who have kept their middle-class status have been stuck in a rut. While the U.S. economy had growth cycles in the 1980s, 1990s, and 2000s, the average middle-class family made almost no headway. The rising tide did *not* lift all boats, or even most boats. That dichotomy, between the nation's growth and stagnant middle-class incomes, is captured in a few stark statistics:

- From 1948 to 1973, the productivity of all nonfarm U.S. workers grew by 96.8 percent and the hourly compensation of the average worker rose by 93.7 percent.[22] In short, as America enjoyed booming economic growth in the postwar period, middle-class workers got a solid share of the nation's gains in productivity.

- From 1973 to 2011, the productivity of the U.S. workforce rose 80.1 percent, but the wages of the average worker rose only 4.2 percent, and hourly compensation — wages plus benefits — rose only 10 percent.[23] So while productivity was rising close to 3 percent a year, hourly wages of the average worker, adjusted for inflation, were essentially flat, the same in 2011 as in 1978.[24] Three decades of getting nowhere.

- The living standards of middle-class Americans have fallen behind a dozen countries in Europe. Americans worked longer hours, often for lower pay and benefits, and made up the difference with the highest ratio of two-income households of any advanced economy.[25]

- Despite economic ups and downs since 1975, corporate profits have trended upward while workers' wages stagnated. In 2007, before the Great Recession, corporate profits garnered the largest share of national income since 1943, while the share of national income going to wages sank to its lowest level since 1929.[26]

- Gaping inequalities in wealth and income now characterize the U.S. economy. While the middle class stagnated, the ultra-rich (the top 0.01 percent) jumped from an annual average income of $4 million in 1979 to $24.3 million in 2006 — *a 600 percent gain per family.*[27] The super-rich (the top 1 percent) gained so much that they captured 23.4 percent of the national economic pie in 2007, more than 2½ times their share in 1979.[28]

Inequalities are inevitable under capitalism, but no other advanced economy has such a hyperconcentration of wealth. In fact, as we've seen, America looks far different from its own past. The contrast between America in the era of the New Economy and America in our earlier era of middle-class prosperity is stark. Business leaders contend the fault lies with technology and globalization, but as we've seen, other countries such as Germany enjoy more widely shared prosperity than the United States. . . .

Notes

1. Pam Scholl, interview, November 7, 2010.
2. Roy Wunsch, interviews, October 27 and November 7, 2010.
3. Mike Hughes, interview, June 23, 2010.
4. Ibid., June 28, 2010.
5. Pam Scholl, interview, June 23, 2010.
6. U.S. Bureau of Labor Statistics, "The Employment Situation, December 2001," January 7, 2002, http://www.bls.gov; U.S. Bureau of Labor Statistics, "The Employment Situation, September 2011," October 7, 2011, http://www.bls.gov. BLS figures show 132.2 million nonfarm jobs in 2001 vs. 131.3 million in September 2011.
7. Census Bureau, "Income, Poverty, and Health Insurance Coverage in the United States: 2010"; "Income Slides to 1996 Levels," *The Wall Street Journal*, September 4, 2011.
8. Isaacs, "Economic Mobility of Black and White Families," in Isaacs, Sawhill, and Haskins, *Getting Ahead or Losing Ground: Economic Mobility in America* (Washington, DC: Brookings Institution, 2008), 71–80.
9. Census Bureau, "Income, Poverty, and Health Insurance Coverage in the United States: 2010."
10. "Soaring Poverty Casts Spotlight on 'Lost Decade,'" *The New York Times*, September 14, 2011.
11. E. S. Browning, "Oldest Baby Boomers Face Jobs Bust," *The Wall Street Journal*, December 19, 2011.
12. Isaacs, "Economic Mobility of Families Across Generations," in Isaacs, Sawhill, and Haskins, *Getting Ahead*, 19.
13. Isaacs, "International Comparisons of Economic Mobility," in Isaacs, Sawhill, and Haskins, *Getting Ahead*, 37–44.

14. Sawhill, "Trends in Intergenerational Mobility," in Isaacs, Sawhill, and Haskins, *Getting Ahead*, 9, italics added; Thomas DeLeire and Leonard M. Lopoo, "Family Structure and the Economic Mobility of Children," Pew Charitable Trusts, April 2010, http://www.economic mobility.org; Jason DeParle, "Harder for Americans to Rise from Economy's Lower Rungs," *The New York Times*, January 5, 2012.

15. Isaacs, "Economic Mobility of Families Across Generations," in Isaacs, Sawhill, and Haskins, *Getting Ahead*, 19.

16. Sean F. Reardon, "The Widening Academic Achievement Gap Between the Rich and the Poor: New Evidence and Possible Explanations," in *Whither Opportunity? Rising Inequality, Schools, and Children's Life Chances* (New York: Russell Sage Foundation, 2011); "Poor Dropping Further Behind Rich in School," *The New York Times*, February 10, 2012.

17. Martha J. Bailey and Susan M. Dynarski, "Gains and Gaps: Changing Inequality in U.S. College Entry and Completion," Working Paper 17633, National Bureau of Economic Research, December 2011, http://www.nber.org.

18. Study by Sabino Kornrich, Center for Advanced Studies, Juan March Institute, Madrid, and Frank F. Furstenberg, University of Pennsylvania, cited in "Poor Dropping Further Behind Rich in School," *The New York Times*, February 10, 2012.

19. Will Hutton, "Log Cabin to White House? Not Any More," *The Observer*, April 28, 2002, http://www.observer.co.uk/comment/story/0,6903,706484,00.html.

20. Bhashkar Mazumder, "Fortunate Sons: New Estimates of Intergenerational Mobility in the United States Using Social Security Earnings Data," for Federal Reserve Bank of Chicago, July 6, 2004, published in *The Review of Economics and Statistics* 87, no. 2 (2005): 235–55.

21. Janny Scott and David Leonhardt, "Class in America: Shadowy Lines That Still Divide," *The New York Times*, May 15, 2005.

22. Lawrence Mishel, Joshua Bivens, and Heidi Shierholz, *The State of Working America, 2012/2013* (Ithaca, NY: Cornell University Press, 2012), figure 4U, "Hourly Compensation for Production/Non-Supervisory Workers and Total Economy Productivity, 1948–2011"; Mishel, emails, March 29 and April 9, 2012.

23. Ibid. The contrast is sharper when comparing productivity growth and hourly wages only in the private sector. Over this period, private sector productivity grew by 92.6 percent while the average hourly wage rose by only 4.2 percent. This difference is dampened when figures cover the overall economy, because that data includes government workers, whose productivity is assumed not to grow while their salaries rise.

24. Census Bureau, "Income, Poverty, and Health Insurance Coverage in the United States: 2010," September 2011.

25. Phillips, *Wealth and Democracy*, 112, 163.

26. Aviva Aron-Dine and Isaac Shapiro, "Share of National Income Going to Wages and Salaries at Record Low in 2006," Center on Budget and Policy Priorities, March 29, 2007, http://www.cbpp.org.

27. Study by Emmanuel Saez, University of California at Berkeley, cited in "It's the Inequality, Stupid," *Mother Jones*, March–April 2011, http://www.motherjones.com.

28. During recession, the share of the top 1 percent fell, but with recovery that share has been moving back up toward previous highs. Emmanuel Saez, "Striking It Richer: The Evolution of Top Incomes in the United States," *Pathways Magazine*, Stanford Center for the Study of Poverty and Inequality (Winter 2008), and updated version of same paper to include estimates

for 2009 and 2010, March 7, 2012, http://elsa.berkeley.edu/~saez/saez-UStopincomes
-2010.pdf. Also see Thomas Piketty and Emmanuel Saez, "Income Inequality in the
United States, 1913–1998, updated," table A-3, "Top Fractiles Income Shares (Including
Capital Gains) in the United States," http://elsa.berkeley.edu/~saez/TabFig2010.

(2012)

Questions

1. To illustrate his argument, Hedrick Smith uses the personal stories of two Americans, Pam Scholl and Mike Hughes, as well as statistical information. How effective is this strategy?
2. Smith quotes economist Isabel Sawhill, who states that America has become "a *low-mobility* country" compared with others (par. 27). Is this true? Do you find Smith's assessment convincing? What are the implications for the United States if Sawhill is correct?
3. In the section titled "Three Decades of Getting Nowhere," Smith offers five bulleted assertions backed by data and endnotes. Which do you find most surprising? Which is most alarming? Why?
4. If Smith's assessment of the American economy is accurate, what does it portend for the future of American society? Explain.
5. How do endnotes 23 and 28 differ from the others? Be specific as you explain. What is the overall rhetorical effect of Smith's notes?

from *Pathways to the Middle Class*
Balancing Personal and Public Responsibilities
Isabel V. Sawhill, Scott Winship, and Kerry Searle Grannis

> Isabel V. Sawhill is codirector of the Center on Children and Families and the Budgeting for National Priorities Project at the Brookings Institution, a nonprofit public-policy organization based in Washington, D.C. Scott Winship is a fellow and research director at the Brookings Center's Social Genome Project. Kelly Searle Grannis is the associate director of the Social Genome Project. The following excerpt is from the 2012 *Social Genome Project* of the Brookings Institution.

Findings

- The majority (61%) of Americans achieve the American Dream by reaching the middle class by middle age, but there are large gaps by race, gender, and children's circumstances at birth.
- Success begets further success. Children who are successful at each life stage from early childhood to young adulthood are much more likely to achieve the American Dream.

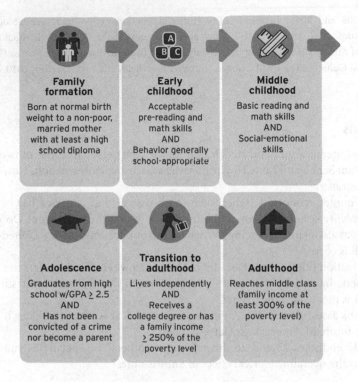

Figure 1

- Children from less advantaged families tend to fall behind at every stage. They are less likely to be ready for school at age 5 (59% vs 72%), to achieve core academic and social competencies at the end of elementary school (60% vs 77%), to graduate from high school with decent grades and no involvement with crime or teen pregnancy (41% vs 70%), and to graduate from college or achieve the equivalent income in their twenties (48% vs 70%).

- Racial gaps are large from the start and never narrow significantly, especially for African Americans, who trail by an average of 25 percentage points for the identified benchmarks.

- Girls travel through childhood doing better than boys only to find their prospects diminished during the adult years.

- The proportion of children who successfully navigate through adolescence is strikingly low: only 57%.

- For the small proportion of disadvantaged children who do succeed throughout school and early adulthood (17%), their chances of being middle class by middle age are almost as great as for their more advantaged peers (75% vs 83%).

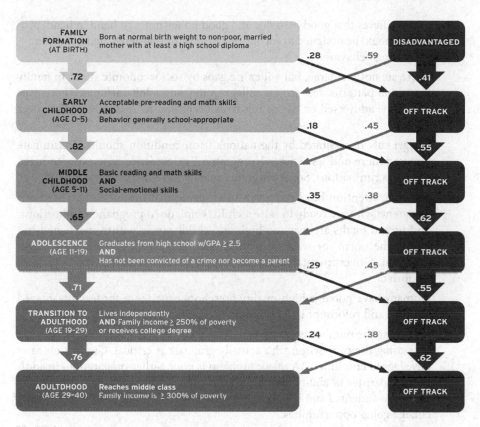

Figure 2

- Keeping less advantaged children on track at each and every life stage is the right strategy for building a stronger middle class. Early interventions may prevent the need for later ones. As the data . . . make abundantly clear, success is a cumulative process. One-time interventions may not be enough to keep less advantaged children on track.

- It's never too late to intervene — people who succeed in their twenties, despite earlier struggles, still have a good chance of making it to the middle class.

Recommendations

- Creating more opportunity will require a combination of greater personal responsibility and societal interventions that have proven effective at helping people climb the ladder. Neither alone is sufficient. Government does not raise children, parents do. But government can lend a helping hand.

- If one believes that good behavior and good policy must go hand in hand, programs should be designed to encourage personal responsibility and opportunity-enhancing behaviors.

- There are not just large, but widening gaps by socioeconomic status in family formation patterns, test scores, college-going, and adult earnings. These gaps should be addressed or the nation risks becoming increasingly divided over time.

- Budget cuts necessitated by the nation's fiscal condition should discriminate between more and less effective programs. The evidence now exists to make these discriminations. Some programs actually save taxpayer money.

- Too little attention has been given to ensuring that more children are born to parents who are ready to raise a child. Unplanned pregnancies, abortions, and unwed births are way too high and childbearing within marriage is no longer the norm for women in their twenties, except among the college-educated. Government has a role to play here, but culture is at least as important.

- As many have noted, a high-quality preschool experience for less advantaged children and reform of K–12 schooling could not be more important.

- Increasing the number of young people who enroll in college is important, but increasing the proportion who actually graduate is critical. Graduation rates have lagged enrollment. A major problem is poor earlier preparation. In addition, disparities in ability to afford the cost of college mean that even equally qualified students from low- and high-income families do not have the same college-going opportunities.

(2012)

Questions

1. Among the "Findings" that the authors report, how do the last three differ from the rest? Explain.
2. Which of the "Recommendations" seem most reasonable to you? Which are less so? Why?
3. The authors offer benchmarks for success in Figure 1. Which of them can we as a society most likely ensure? Which would be the most challenging? Do you agree that these would be benchmarks for success in the United States?
4. What does Figure 2 show about the chances for successful entry into the middle class for those who are disadvantaged as opposed to those with a good start in life? Which stage of development seems most crucial for determining the path a person will take? Why do you think this is so?
5. What implications does this chart suggest about the present state of the middle class in America? What implications does it suggest for citizens, educators, and policy makers? Explain.

Mutually Assured Consumption

SALLY EDELSTEIN

Sally Edelstein is an award-winning artist who uses collage "as a means of examining social fictions" by "dissociating the images from their original use to better reevaluate . . . [the] original message." The following collage appeared in 2012 as part of "Envisioning the American Dream," "a visual remix of the American Dream as pictured in mid-century media."

Collage by Sally Edelstein, sallyedelsteincollage.com.

Questions

1. Describe the consumer items you see in this picture. What does the presentation of items suggest about the time period depicted?
2. How would you describe the people depicted? Are they representative of the American population at the time? How does Sally Edelstein present them? What is her attitude toward them? Explain.

3. Describe what you see in the background. What is the effect of the juxtaposition of images in the foreground with those in the background? Why do you think Edelstein arranged this piece in this way?

4. This image could be viewed as either an advertisement for the splendid promise of the American Dream or a critique of American consumerism. Which do you see? Explain. What is the "social fiction" that Edelstein examines?

5. In his 1951 essay, "The Sociology of Stratification," sociologist C. Wright Mills based his definitions of social classes in America on the "chances to gain the things and experiences that are generally valued, whatever they may be: things like cars, money, toys, houses, etc.; experiences, like being given respect, being educated to certain levels, being treated kindly, etc." What does Mills suggest about American values? How might Edelstein regard Mills's statement? What might Mills say, looking at Edelstein's collage?

Making Connections

1. The Horatio Alger myth is referred to by both Harlon L. Dalton (p. 1497) and Paul Krugman (p. 1505). What does each of these selections say about the Horatio Alger myth? Why does the myth persist in America? To what American beliefs and values does it appeal?

2. Alan Brinkley (p. 1510) writes that, in the 1950s, "material abundance became one of the ways in which many, probably most, Americans defined their world" (par. 6). What does Sally Edelstein's collage (p. 1525) suggest about Brinkley's remark? Would she agree?

3. What are some of the implications that go beyond economics in the pieces by Krugman and by Isabel V. Sawhill, Scott Winship, and Kerry Searle Grannis (p. 1521)?

4. How effectively does the use of statistics support the positions of Holly Sklar (p. 1503), Thomas Sowell (p. 1508), and Hedrick Smith (p. 1514)?

5. What perspectives regarding "meritocracy" do we find in the article by Dalton and the study by Sawhill, Winship, and Grannis? Which do you find more persuasive? Explain.

6. Which of the selections portrays a middle class in contemporary America that most resembles the one described by Brinkley? Which describes a middle class least like the one described by Brinkley? Explain.

Entering the Conversation

As you respond to each of the following prompts, support your position with appropriate evidence, including at least three sources in this Conversation on the American middle class, unless otherwise indicated.

1. Sawhill, Winship, and Grannis in 2012 conclude "Pathways to the Middle Class" by saying:

   > In previous research, Haskins and Sawhill found that if individuals graduate from high school, work full-time, and wait until they're married and over 21 to become parents, they have a very good chance of joining the middle class. These data have been cited by Senator Rick Santorum and also by Republican presidential nominee Mitt Romney as showing that individuals who work hard, avoid pitfalls, and make responsible choices greatly improve their odds of success. We would add that children from less advantaged backgrounds often see little reason to make these responsible choices, given the environments in which they live and the opportunities that are available to them. Indeed, by the time children can be reasonably held accountable for their choices, many are already behind because of choices their parents made for them. And of course, as the Great Recession has shown, working full-time is only partly a choice. Putting the full responsibility on government to close these gaps is unreasonable, but so is a heroic assumption that everyone can be a Horatio Alger with no help from society.

   Does the Horatio Alger myth continue to live? Is it obsolete? Write an essay that examines the extent to which the Horatio Alger myth is still viable today.

2. Several writers in this Conversation discuss the growing gap between the upper and middle classes in America. Has the gap continued to widen since the pieces were written? Have our economy and our democracy been weakened? Is the American Dream a thing of the past? In an essay, answer the following question: Is the American middle class in decline?

3. In his 2012 book, *The Great Divergence*, Timothy Noah asks, "Why do Americans tolerate this troubling state of affairs?" He answers, "The biggest likely reason is our enduring belief in upward mobility. Economic inequality is less troubling if you live in a country where any child, no matter how humble his or her origins, can grow up to be president. This idea lies at the heart of American exceptionalism. It defines the American Dream." Write an essay that explores this reflection on dreams, belief, and reality in America.

4. Write an essay that defends, challenges, or qualifies the following statement: The United States of America is a classless society.

5. Each of the following quotations presents a whimsical observation about money, success, or class. Which one appeals to you? Which one relates best to the readings in this Conversation? Using one of the quotations as an epigraph, write an essay about one or more of those topics.

   > Early to bed and early to rise makes a man healthy, wealthy, and wise.
   > — BENJAMIN FRANKLIN

   > Formula for success: rise early, work hard, strike oil.   — J. PAUL GETTY

I'd like to live as a poor man with lots of money.   — PABLO PICASSO

I am opposed to millionaires, but it would be dangerous to offer me the position.   — MARK TWAIN

Conversation

America's Romance with the Automobile

The invention of the automobile has probably had the most long-reaching effects of any technological advance in American history. The earliest cars were electric, often playthings of the rich, but advances in internal combustion engines made the car more powerful, less expensive, and quicker to refuel than its battery-powered competition. The mass production of automobiles by companies like Oldsmobile and Ford enabled the middle class to become car owners, which in turn freed them from the need to live near rail stations. As long as there were roads, they could live anywhere. And so began America's romance with the car, which parallels, to a large degree, the birth of suburbia.

In 1956, President Dwight D. Eisenhower signed into law the National Interstate and Defense Highways Act, which authorized $25 billion for the construction of 41,000 miles of the interstate highway system. Meant to eliminate unsafe and inefficient routes, as well as traffic jams, the interstate system was also developed to provide evacuation routes in case of nuclear attack. Most Americans supported the act, which was paid for largely by taxes on gasoline. There was some backlash, as the new highways threatened neighborhoods, and some cities, like San Francisco, put the brakes on their construction. Nevertheless, most of the highways were built, and the second half of the twentieth century was the high point of America's "automobile society."

Since its earliest days, the automobile has been viewed as a threat and as a blessing. Both romanticized and demonized in popular and high culture alike, it is a curse on the environment and a boon to personal freedom. It represents economic opportunity at the same time that it hinders it. It is considered both an equalizer and a creator of class difference. Today, we are questioning the automobile's place in American life, as we begin to feel the impact of urban congestion and suburban sprawl. Can America's love affair with the car be rekindled? Can the problems of our car culture be solved? Will virtual mobility ever take the place of actual mobility? The following ten selections ask you to ponder these questions and more, as you consider whether America's long love affair with the automobile is finally over.

Sources

Ohio Electric Car Company, *The Ohio Electric* (1916)
E. B. White, *Farewell, My Lovely!* (1936)
John Updike, from *Rabbit, Run* (1960)
Tom Wolfe, from *The Kandy-Kolored Tangerine-Flake Streamline Baby* (1963)
Stephen Dunn, *The Sacred* (1989)
Heather McHugh, *Auto* (1994)
Pew Research Center, *Americans and Their Cars: Is the Romance on the Skids?* (2006)
P. J. O'Rourke, *The End of the Affair* (2009)
Allison Linn, *Carmakers' Next Problem: Generation Y* (2010)
Frank DeFord, *Americans Hit the Brakes on NASCAR* (2012)

The Ohio Electric

OHIO ELECTRIC CAR COMPANY

This 1916 ad appeared in *Literary Digest,* a general-interest magazine that circulated between 1890 and 1938 and was known for its large and upscale readership.

Questions

1. Who is the audience for this ad? What assumptions does the Ohio Electric Car Company and its advertising agency make about the audience?
2. What visual elements set the tone for this advertisement? Consider the frame of the ad, the figures in it, even the direction in which the characters are looking. What messages does the art convey?
3. With electric cars perpetually on the verge of a revival, consider how they would be marketed today. Do you think any aspect of this ad would be evoked today? Explain your answer.

Farewell, My Lovely!

E. B. WHITE

> E. B. White (1899–1985) was an editor, an essayist, and a writer of children's books who lived in New York and Maine. He is best known for his essay "Once More to the Lake," his children's books *Stuart Little* (1945) and *Charlotte's Web* (1952), and his revision of William Strunk Jr.'s *The Elements of Style* (1959). Published in the *New Yorker* in May 1936, "Farewell, My Lovely!" was one of the hundreds of pieces White wrote for the magazine in the six decades he worked there.

I see by the new Sears Roebuck catalogue that it is still possible to buy an axle for a 1909 Model T Ford, but I am not deceived. The great days have faded, the end is in sight. Only one page in the current catalogue is devoted to parts and accessories for the Model T; yet everyone remembers springtimes when the Ford gadget section was larger than men's clothing, almost as large as household furnishings. The last Model T was built in 1927, and the car is fading from what scholars call the American scene — which is an understatement, because to a few million people who grew up with it, the old Ford practically *was* the American scene.

It was the miracle God had wrought. And it was patently the sort of thing that could only happen once. Mechanically uncanny, it was like nothing that had ever come to the world before. Flourishing industries rose and fell with it. As a vehicle, it was hard-working, commonplace, heroic; and it often seemed to transmit those qualities to the persons who rode in it. My own generation identifies it with Youth, with its gaudy, irretrievable excitements; before it fades into the mist, I would like to pay it the tribute of the sigh that is not a sob, and set down random entries in a shape somewhat less cumbersome than a Sears Roebuck catalogue.

The Model T was distinguished from all other makes of cars by the fact that its transmission was of a type known as planetary — which was half metaphysics, half sheer friction. Engineers accepted the word "planetary" in its epicyclic sense, but I was always conscious that it also meant "wandering," "erratic." Because of the peculiar nature of this planetary element, there was always, in Model T, a certain dull rapport between engine and wheels, and even when the car was in a state known as neutral, it trembled with a deep imperative and tended to inch forward. There was never a moment when the bands were not faintly egging the machine on. In this respect it was like a horse, rolling the bit on its tongue, and country people brought to it the same technique they used with draft animals.

Its most remarkable quality was its rate of acceleration. In its palmy days the Model T could take off faster than anything on the road. The reason was simple. To get under way, you simply hooked the third finger of the right hand around a lever on the steering column, pulled down hard, and shoved your left foot forcibly against the low-speed pedal. These were simple, positive motions; the car responded by lunging forward with a roar. After a few seconds of this turmoil, you took your toe off the pedal, eased up a mite on the throttle, and the car, possessed of only two forward speeds, catapulted directly into high with a series of ugly jerks and was off on its glorious errand. The abruptness of this departure was never equalled in other cars of the period. The human leg was (and still is) incapable of letting in a clutch with anything like the forthright abandon that used to send Model T on its way. Letting in a clutch is a negative, hesitant motion, depending on delicate nervous control; pushing down the Ford pedal was a simple, country motion — an expansive act, which came as natural as kicking an old door to make it budge.

The driver of the old Model T was a man enthroned. The car, with top up, stood   5
seven feet high. The driver sat on top of the gas tank, brooding it with his own body. When he wanted gasoline, he alighted, along with everything else in the front seat; the seat was pulled off, the metal cap unscrewed, and a wooden stick thrust down to sound the liquid in the well. There were always a couple of these sounding sticks kicking around in the ratty sub-cushion regions of a flivver. Refuelling was more of a social function then, because the driver had to unbend, whether he wanted to or not. Directly in front of the driver was the windshield — high, uncompromisingly erect. Nobody talked about air resistance, and the four cylinders pushed the car through the atmosphere with a simple disregard of physical law.

There was this about a Model T: the purchaser never regarded his purchase as a complete, finished product. When you bought a Ford, you figured you had a start — a vibrant, spirited framework to which could be screwed an almost limitless assortment of decorative and functional hardware. Driving away from the agency, hugging the new wheel between your knees, you were already full of creative worry. A Ford was born naked as a baby, and a flourishing industry grew up out of correcting its rare deficiencies and combatting its fascinating diseases. Those were the great days of lily-painting. I have been looking at some old Sears Roebuck catalogues, and they bring everything back so clear.

First you bought a Ruby Safety Reflector for the rear, so that your posterior would glow in another car's brilliance. Then you invested thirty-nine cents in some radiator Moto Wings, a popular ornament which gave the Pegasus touch to the machine and did something godlike to the owner. For nine cents you bought a fan-belt guide to keep the belt from slipping off the pulley.

You bought a radiator compound to stop leaks. This was as much a part of everybody's equipment as aspirin tablets are of a medicine cabinet. You bought special oil to prevent chattering, a clamp-on dash light, a patching outfit, a tool box which you bolted to the running board, a sun visor, a steering-column brace to keep the column rigid, and a set of emergency containers for gas, oil, and water — three thin, disc-like cans which reposed in a case on the running board during long, important journeys — red for gas, gray for water, green for oil. It was only a beginning. After the car was about a year old, steps were taken to check the alarming disintegration. (Model T was full of tumors, but they were benign.) A set of anti-rattlers (98c) was a popular panacea. You hooked them on to the gas and spark rods, to the brake pull rod, and to the steering-rod connections. Hood silencers, of black rubber, were applied to the fluttering hood. Shock-absorbers and snubbers gave "complete relaxation." Some people bought rubber pedal pads, to fit over the standard metal pedals. (I didn't like these, I remember.) Persons of a suspicious or pugnacious turn of mind bought a rear-view mirror; but most Model T owners weren't worried by what was coming from behind because they would soon enough see it out in front. They rode in a state of cheerful catalepsy. Quite a large mutinous clique among Ford owners went over to a foot accelerator (you could buy one and screw it to the floor board), but there was a certain madness in these people, because the Model T, just as she stood, had a choice of three foot pedals to push, and there were plenty of moments when both feet were occupied in the routine performance of duty and when the only way to speed up the engine was with the hand throttle.

Gadget bred gadget. Owners not only bought ready-made gadgets, they invented gadgets to meet special needs. I myself drove my car directly from the agency to the blacksmith's, and had the smith affix two enormous iron brackets to the port running board to support an army trunk.

People who owned closed models builded along different lines: they bought ball grip handles for opening doors, window anti-rattlers, and de-luxe flower vases of the cut-glass anti-splash type. People with delicate sensibilities garnished their car with a device called the Donna Lee Automobile Disseminator — a porous vase guaranteed, according to Sears, to fill the car with a "faint clean odor of lavender." The gap between open cars and closed cars was not as great then as it is now: for $11.95, Sears Roebuck converted your touring car into a sedan and you went forth renewed. One agreeable quality of the old Fords was that they had no bumpers, and their fenders softened and wilted with the years and permitted driver to squeeze in and out of tight places.

Tires were 30 × 3½, cost about twelve dollars, and punctured readily. Everybody carried a Jiffy patching set, with a nutmeg grater to roughen the tube before the goo was spread on. Everybody was capable of putting on a patch, expected to have to, and did have to.

During my association with Model T's, self-starters were not a prevalent accessory. They were expensive and under suspicion. Your car came equipped with a serviceable crank, and the first thing you learned was how to Get Results. It was a special trick, and until you learned it (usually from another Ford owner, but sometimes by a period of appalling experimentation) you might as well have been winding up an awning. The trick was to leave the ignition switch off, proceed to the animal's head, pull the choke (which was a little wire protruding through the radiator), and give the crank two or three nonchalant upward lifts. Then, whistling as though thinking about something else, you would saunter back to the driver's cabin, turn the ignition on, return to the crank, and this time, catching it on the down stroke, give it a quick spin with plenty of That. If this procedure was followed, the engine almost always responded — first with a few scattered explosions, then with a tumultuous gunfire, which you checked by racing around to the driver's seat and retarding the throttle. Often, if the emergency brake hadn't been pulled all the way back, the car advanced on you the instant the first explosion occurred and you would hold it back by leaning your weight against it. I can still feel my old Ford nuzzling me at the curb, as though looking for an apple in my pocket.

In zero weather, ordinary cranking became an impossibility, except for giants. The oil thickened, and it became necessary to jack up the rear wheels, which, for some planetary reason, eased the throw.

The lore and legend that governed the Ford were boundless. Owners had their own theories about everything; they discussed mutual problems in that wise, infinitely resourceful way old women discuss rheumatism. Exact knowledge was pretty scarce, and often proved less effective than superstition. Dropping a camphor ball into the gas tank was a popular expedient; it seemed to have a tonic effect on both man and machine. There wasn't much to base exact knowledge on. The Ford driver flew blind. He didn't know the temperature of his engine, the speed of his car, the amount of his fuel or the pressure of his oil (the old Ford lubricated itself by what was amiably described as the "splash system"). A speedometer cost money and was an extra, like a windshield-wiper. The dashboard of the early models was bare save for an ignition key; later models, grown effete, boasted an ammeter which pulsated alarmingly with the throbbing of the car. Under the dash was a box of coils, with vibrators which you adjusted, or thought you adjusted. Whatever the driver learned of his motor, he learned not through instruments but through sudden developments. I remember that the timer was one of the vital organs about which there was ample doctrine. When everything else had been checked, you "had a look" at the timer. It was an extravagantly odd little device, simple in construction, mysterious in function. It contained a roller, held by a spring, and there were four contact points on the inside of the case against which, many people believed, the roller rolled. I have had a timer apart on a sick Ford many times, but I never really knew what I was up to — I was just showing off before God. There were almost as many schools of thought as there were timers. Some people, when things went wrong, just clenched their teeth and gave the timer a smart crack with a wrench. Other people opened it up and blew on it. There was a school that held that the timer needed large amounts of oil; they fixed it by frequent baptism. And there was a school that was positive it was meant to run dry as a bone; these people were continually taking it off and wiping it. I remember once spitting into a timer; not in anger, but in a spirit of research. You see, the Model T driver moved in the realm of metaphysics. He believed his car could be hexed.

One reason the Ford anatomy was never reduced to an exact science was that, having "fixed" it, the owner couldn't honestly claim that the treatment had brought about the cure. There were too many authenticated cases of Fords fixing themselves — restored naturally to health after a short rest. Farmers soon discovered this, and it fitted nicely with their draft-horse philosophy: "Let 'er cool off and she'll snap into it again."

A Ford owner had Number One Bearing constantly in mind. This bearing, being at the front end of the motor, was the one that always burned out, because the oil didn't reach it when the car was climbing hills. (That's what I was always told, anyway.) The oil used to recede and leave Number One dry as a clam flat; you had to watch that bearing like a hawk. It was like a weak heart — you could hear it start knocking, and that was when you stopped and let her cool off. Try as you would to keep the oil supply right, in the end Number One always went out. "Number One Bearing burned out on me and I had to have her replaced," you would say, wisely; and your companions always had a lot to tell about how to protect and pamper Number One to keep her alive.

Sprinkled not too liberally among the millions of amateur witch doctors who drove Fords and applied their own abominable cures were the heaven-sent mechanics who could really make the car talk. These professionals turned up in undreamed-of spots. One time, on the banks of the Columbia River in Washington, I heard the rear end go out of my Model T when I was trying to whip it up a steep incline onto the deck of a ferry. Something snapped; the car slid backward into the mud. It seemed to me like the end of the trail. But the captain of the ferry, observing the withered remnant, spoke up.

"What's got her?" he asked.

"I guess it's the rear end," I replied, listlessly. The captain leaned over the rail and stared. Then I saw that there was a hunger in his eyes that set him off from other men.

"Tell you what," he said, carelessly, trying to cover up his eagerness, "let's pull the son of a bitch up onto the boat, and I'll help you fix her while we're going back and forth on the river."

We did just this. All that day I plied between the towns of Pasco and Kennewick, while the skipper (who had once worked in a Ford garage) directed the amazing work of resetting the bones of my car.

Springtime in the heyday of the Model T was a delirious season. Owning a car was still a major excitement, roads were still wonderful and bad. The Fords were obviously conceived in madness: any car which was capable of going from forward into reverse without any perceptible mechanical hiatus was bound to be a mighty challenging thing to the human imagination. Boys used to veer them off the highway into a level pasture and run wild with them, as though they were cutting up with a girl. Most everybody used the reverse pedal quite as much as the regular foot brake — it distributed the wear over the bands and wore them all down evenly. That was the big trick, to wear all the bands down evenly, so that the final chattering would be total and the whole unit scream for renewal.

The days were golden, the nights were dim and strange. I still recall with trembling those loud, nocturnal crises when you drew up to a signpost and raced the engine so the lights would be bright enough to read destinations by. I have never been really planetary since. I suppose it's time to say goodbye. Farewell, my lovely!

(1936)

Questions

1. What do you think is the purpose of "Farewell, My Lovely!"? Who is its audience? Describe the tone and explain how it helps E. B. White achieve his purpose.
2. Why do you think White says, "The great days have faded, the end is in sight" (par. 1)? How does the rest of the essay support the idea of great days having faded? Are there ways in which White might also be happy to see them go?
3. What statement is White making about the American relationship with the automobile? Find examples of White's language that suggest mixed feelings.

from *Rabbit, Run*

JOHN UPDIKE

John Updike (1932–2009) grew up in Philadelphia and attended Harvard University on a full scholarship, graduating summa cum laude and serving as president of the *Harvard Lampoon*. He is known for his careful craftsmanship and for writing about the world of the Protestant middle class. The first novel in Updike's Rabbit series, *Rabbit, Run* (1960), tells the story of the early years of former high-school basketball star Harry (Rabbit) Angstrom's marriage to Janice Stringer. In this excerpt, Harry has taken off, looking, as always, for something more — a longing he can never quite fulfill.

The rich earth seems to cast its darkness upward into the air. The farm country is somber at night. He is grateful when the lights of Lancaster merge with his dim beams. He stops at a diner whose clock says 8:04. He hadn't intended to eat until he got out of the state. He takes a map from the rack by the door and while eating two hamburgers at the counter studies his position. He is in Lancaster, surrounded by funny names, Bird in Hand, Paradise, Intercourse, Mt. Airy, Mascot. They probably didn't seem funny if you lived in them. Like Mt. Judge. You get used. A town has to be called something.

Bird in Hand, Paradise: his eyes keep going back to this dainty lettering on the map. He has an impulse, amid the oil-filmed shimmer of this synthetic and desultory diner, to drive there. Little plump women, toy dogs in the street, candy houses in lemon sunshine.

But no, his goal is the white sun of the south like a great big pillow in the sky. And from the map he's been travelling more west than south; if the dirtdigger back there had had a map he could have gone due south on 10. Now the only thing to do is go into the heart of Lancaster and take 222 out and take it all the way down into

Maryland and then catch 1. He remembers reading in the *Saturday Evening Post* how 1 goes from Florida to Maine through the most beautiful scenery in the world. He asks for a glass of milk and to go with it a piece of apple pie; the crust is crisp and bubbled and they've had the sense to use cinnamon. His mother's pies always had cinnamon. He pays by cracking a ten and goes out into the parking lot feeling pleased. The hamburgers had been fatter and warmer than the ones you get in Brewer, and the buns had seemed steamed. Things are better already.

It takes him a half-hour to pick his way through Lancaster. On 222 he drives south through Refton, Hessdale, New Providence, and Quarryville, through Mechanics Grove and Unicorn and then a long stretch so dull and unmarked he doesn't know he's entered Maryland until he hits Oakwood. On the radio he hears "No Other Arms, No Other Lips," "Stagger Lee," a commercial for Rayco Clear Plastic Seat Covers, "If I Didn't Care" by Connie Francis, a commercial for Radio-Controlled Garage Door Operators, "I Ran All the Way Home Just to Say I'm Sorry," "That Old Feeling" by Mel Torme, a commercial for Big Screen Westinghouse TV Set with One-finger Automatic Tuning, "needle-sharp pictures a nose away from the screen," "The Italian Cowboy Song," "Yep" by Duane Eddy, a commercial for Papermate Pens, "Almost Grown," a commercial for Tame Cream Rinse, "Let's Stroll," news (President Eisenhower and Prime Minister Harold Macmillan begin a series of talks in Gettysburg, Tibetans battle Chinese Communists in Lhasa, the whereabouts of the Dalai Lama, spiritual ruler of this remote and backward land, are unknown, a $250,000 trust fund has been left to a Park Avenue maid, Spring scheduled to arrive tomorrow), sports news (Yanks over Braves in Miami, somebody tied with somebody in St. Petersburg Open, scores in a local basketball tournament), weather (fair and seasonably warm), "The Happy Organ," "Turn Me Loose," a commercial for Schuylkill Life Insurance, "Rocksville, P-A" (Rabbit loves it), "A Picture No Artist Could Paint," a commercial for New Formula Barbasol Presto-Lather, whose daily cleansing action tends to prevent skin blemishes and emulsifies something, "Pink Shoe Laces" by Dody Stevens, a word about a little boy called Billy Tessman who was hit by a car and would appreciate cards or letters, "Petit Fleur," "Fungo" (great), a commercial for Wool-Tex All-Wool Suits, "Fall Out" by Henry Mancini, "Everybody Likes to Do the Cha Cha Cha," a commercial for Lord's Grace Table Napkins and the gorgeous Last Supper Tablecloth, "The Beat of My Heart," a commercial for Speed-Shine Wax and Lanolin Clay, "Venus," and then the same news again. Where is the Dalai Lama?

Shortly after Oakwood he comes to Route 1, which with its hot-dog stands and   5
Calso signs and roadside taverns aping log cabins is unexpectedly discouraging. The farther he drives the more he feels some great confused system, Baltimore now instead of Philadelphia, reaching for him. He stops at a gas station for two dollars' worth of regular. What he really wants is another map. He unfolds it standing by a Coke machine and reads it in the light coming through a window stained green by stacked cans of liquid wax.

His problem is to get west and free of Baltimore-Washington, which like a two-headed dog guards the coastal route to the south. He doesn't want to go down along the water anyway; his image is of himself going right down the middle, right into the broad soft belly of the land, surprising the dawn cottonfields with his northern plates.

Now he is somewhere here. Further on, then, a road numbered 23 will go off to his left — no, his right. That goes up and over and back into Pennsylvania but at this place, Shawsville, he can take a little narrow blue road without a number. Then go down a little and over again on 137. There is a ragged curve then that this road makes with 482 and then 31. Rabbit can feel himself swinging up and through that curve into the red line numbered 26 and down that into another numbered 340. Red, too; he is really gliding and suddenly sees where he wants to go. Over on the left three red roads stream parallel northeast to southwest; Rabbit can just feel them sliding down through the valleys of the Appalachians. Get on one of them it would be a chute dumping you into sweet low cottonland in the morning. Yes. Once he gets on that he can shake all thoughts of the mess behind him.

(1960)

Questions

1. You might notice that John Updike writes in the present tense. What mood does it create in this excerpt?
2. How does home keep a hold on Rabbit? In what ways does he feel as if he's escaped?
3. What is the effect of paragraph 4, which is, essentially, a list of everything Rabbit hears on the car radio?
4. In what ways might Rabbit's journey help him find what he's looking for? Are there hints that the answers he is looking for are out of reach?
5. How does this excerpt illustrate Americans' relationship with the automobile in the early 1960s?

from *The Kandy-Kolored Tangerine-Flake Streamline Baby*

Tom Wolfe

> Tom Wolfe was born in Richmond, Virginia, in 1935. He studied at Washington and Lee University and Yale and worked as a newspaper reporter for many years. Wolfe is considered one of the most influential of the New Journalists, writers who use the tools of fiction in journalism. Adapted from an essay that first appeared in *Esquire* magazine in 1963 and then became the title piece of Wolfe's first collection of articles and essays, this selection takes a look at the world of custom cars.

The first good look I had at customized cars was at an event called a "Teen Fair," held in Burbank, a suburb of Los Angeles beyond Hollywood. This was a wild place to be taking a look at art objects — eventually, I should say, you have to reach the conclusion that these customized cars are art objects, at least if you use the standards applied in a civilized society. But I will get to that in a moment. Anyway, about noon you drive up to a place that looks like an outdoor amusement park, and there are three serious-looking kids, like the cafeteria committee in high school, taking tickets, but the scene inside is quite mad. Inside, two things hit you. The first is a huge platform a good seven feet off the ground with a hully-gully band—everything is electrified, the bass, the guitars, the saxophones—and then behind the band, on the platform, about two hundred kids are doing frantic dances called the hully-gully, the bird, and the shampoo. As I said, it's noontime. The dances the kids are doing are very jerky. The boys and girls don't touch, not even with their hands. They just ricochet around. Then you notice that all the girls are dressed exactly alike. They have bouffant hairdos—all of them—and slacks that are, well, skin-tight does not get the idea across; it's more the conformation than how tight the slacks are. It's as if some lecherous old tailor with a gluteus-maximus fixation designed them, striation by striation. About the time you've managed to focus on this, you notice that out in the middle of the park is a huge, perfectly round swimming pool: really rather enormous. And there is a Chris-Craft cabin cruiser in the pool, going around and around, sending up big waves, with more of these bouffant babies bunched in the back of it. In the water, suspended like plankton, are kids in scuba-diving outfits: others are tooling around underwater, breathing through a snorkel. And all over the place are booths, put up by shoe companies and guitar companies and God knows who else, and there are kids dancing in all of them—dancing the bird, the hully-gully, and the shampoo—with the music of the hully-gully band piped all over the park through loudspeakers.

All this time, Tex Smith, from *Hot Rod Magazine*, who brought me over to the place, is trying to lead me to the customized-car exhibit—"Tom, I want you to see this car that Bill Cushenberry built, The Silhouette"—which is to say, here are two hundred kids ricocheting over a platform at high noon, and a speedy little boat barreling around and around and around in a round swimming pool, and I seem to be the only person who is distracted. The customized-car exhibit turns out to be the Ford Custom Car Caravan, which Ford is sending all over the country. At first, with the noise and peripheral motion and the inchoate leching you are liable to be doing, what with bouffant nymphets rocketing all over the place, these customized cars do not strike you as anything very special. Obviously they *are* very special, but the first thing you think of is the usual—you know, that the kids who own these cars are probably skinny little hoods who wear T shirts and carry their cigarette packs by winding them around in the T shirt up near the shoulder.

But after a while, I was glad I had seen the cars in this natural setting, which was, after all, a kind of Plato's Republic for teen-agers. Because if you watched anything at this fair very long, you kept noticing the same thing. These kids are absolutely maniacal about form. They are practically religious about it. For example, the dancers: none of them ever smiled. They stared at each other's legs and feet, concentrating. The dances had no grace about them at all, they were more in the nature of a hoedown, but everybody was concentrating to do them exactly *right*. And the bouffant kids all had form, wild form, but form with rigid standards, one gathers. Even the boys. Their dress was prosaic—Levi's, Slim Jims, sport shirts, T shirts, polo shirts—but the form was consistent: a stove-pipe silhouette. And they all had the same hairstyle: some wore it long, some short, but none of them had a part; all that hair was brushed back straight from the hairline. I went by one of the guitar booths, and there was a little kid in there, about thirteen, playing the hell out of an electric guitar. The kid was named Cranston something or other. He looked like he ought to be named Kermet or Herschel; all his genes were kind of horribly Okie. Cranston was playing away and a big crowd was watching. But Cranston was slouched back with his spine bent like a sapling up against a table, looking gloriously bored. At thirteen, this kid was being fanatically cool. They all were. They were all wonderful slaves to form. They have created their own style of life, and they are much more authoritarian about enforcing it than are adults. Not only that, but today these kids — especially in California — have *money*, which, needless to say, is why all these shoe merchants and guitar sellers and the Ford Motor Company were at a Teen Fair in the first place. I don't mind observing that it is this same combination — money plus slavish devotion to form — that accounts for Versailles or St. Mark's Square. Naturally, most of the artifacts that these kids' money-plus-form produce are of a pretty ghastly order. But so was most of the paraphernalia that developed in England during the Regency. I mean, most of it was on the order of starched cravats. A man could walk into Beau Brummel's house at 11 A.M., and here would come the butler with a tray of wilted linen. "These were some of our failures," he confides. But then Brummel comes downstairs wearing one perfect starched cravat. Like one perfect iris, the flower of Mayfair civilization. But the Regency period did see some tremendous formal architecture. And the kids' formal society has also brought at least one substantial thing to a formal development of a high order — the customized cars. I don't have to dwell on the point that cars mean more to these kids than architecture did in Europe's great formal century, say, 1750 to 1850. They are freedom, style, sex, power, motion, color — everything is right there.

Things have been going on in the development of the kids' formal attitude toward cars since 1945, things of great sophistication that adults have not been even remotely aware of, mainly because the kids are so inarticulate about it, especially the ones most hipped on the subject. They are not from the levels of society that produce children who write sensitive analytical prose at age seventeen, or if they do, they soon fall into the hands of English instructors who put them onto Hemingway or a lot of goddamn-and-hungry-breast writers. If they ever write about a highway again, it's a rain-slicked highway and the sound of the automobiles passing over it is like the sound of tearing silk, not that one household in ten thousand has heard the sound of tearing silk since 1945.

Anyway, we are back at the Teen Fair and I am talking to Tex Smith and to Don Beebe, a portly young guy with a white sport shirt and Cuban sunglasses. As they tell me about the Ford Custom Car Caravan, I can see that Ford has begun to comprehend this teen-age style of life and its potential. The way Ford appears to figure it is this: Thousands of kids are getting hold of cars and either hopping them up for speed or customizing them to some extent, usually a little of both. Before they get married they pour *all* their money into this. If Ford can get them hooked on Fords now, after the kids are married they'll buy new Fords. Even the kids who aren't full-time car nuts themselves will be influenced by which car is considered "boss." They use that word a

5

lot, "boss." The kids used to consider Ford the hot car, but then, from 1955 to 1962, Chevrolet became the favorite. They had big engines and were easy to hop up, the styling was simple, and the kids could customize them easily. In 1959, and more so in 1960, Plymouth became a hot car, too. In 1961 and 1962, it was all Chevrolet and Plymouth. Now Ford is making a big push. A lot of the professional hot-rod and custom-car people, adults, will tell you that now Ford is the hot car, but you have to discount some of it, because Ford is laying money on everybody right and left, in one form or another. In the Custom Car Caravan, all the cars have been fashioned out of Ford bodies except the ones that are completely handmade, like the aforementioned Silhouette.

Anyway, Don Beebe is saying, over a loudspeaker, "I hate to break up that dancing, but let's have a little drag racing." He has a phonograph hooked up to the loudspeaker, and he puts on a record, produced by Riverside Records, of drag-strip sounds, mainly dragsters blasting off and squealing from the starting line. Well, he doesn't really break up the dancing, but a hundred kids come over, when they hear the drag-strip sounds, to where Beebe has a slot-racing stand. Slot racing is a model-train-type game in which two model drag racers, each about five inches long, powered by electricity, run down a model drag strip. Beebe takes a microphone and announces that Dick Dale, the singer, is here, and anybody who will race Dick at the slot-racing stand will get one of his records. Dick Dale is pretty popular among the kids out here because he sings a lot of "surfing" songs. The surfers — surfboard riders — are a cult much admired by all the kids. They have their own argot, with adjectives like "hang ten," meaning the best there is. They also go in for one particular brand of customizing: they take old wood-bodied station wagons, which they call "woodies," and fix them up for riding, sleeping and hauling surfing equipment for their weekends at the beach. The surfers also get a hell of a bang out of slot racing for some reason, so with Dick Dale slot racing at the Teen Fair, you have about three areas of the arcane teen world all rolled into one.

(1963)

Questions

1. Why do you think Tom Wolfe considers the Burbank "Teen Fair" a "natural setting" for a car show (par. 3)? Why do you think he calls it "a kind of Plato's Republic [a utopian setting] for teen-agers" (par. 3)?
2. Wolfe is writing about a visit to a custom-car show. What are his other subjects?
3. Wolfe is known for his almost obsessive attention to detail and his rapid-fire delivery of images that create vivid pictures of people and events. He has, however, been criticized for a lack of analysis or reflection. Do you agree? What do you think the many details in this piece say about American society? Do you think Wolfe should have supplied more analysis or do the images speak for themselves? Explain your answer.
4. Why does Wolfe think it's important that "Ford has begun to comprehend this teenage style of life and its potential" (par. 5)? What does he see as the connections between the teenage lifestyle and the American car?

The Sacred

Stephen Dunn

Born in New York City in 1939 and educated at Hofstra University, Stephen Dunn briefly played professional basketball and worked as a copywriter before receiving his MFA in poetry from Syracuse University. Dunn won the Pulitzer Prize for Poetry in 2001. This poem is from his 1989 collection, *Between Angels*.

After the teacher asked if anyone had
   a sacred place
and the students fidgeted and shrank

in their chairs, the most serious of them all
   said it was his car,   5
being in it alone, his tape deck playing

things he'd chosen, and others knew the truth
   had been spoken
and began speaking about their rooms,

their hiding places, but the car kept coming up,   10
   the car in motion,
music filling it, and sometimes one other person

who understood the bright altar of the dashboard
   and how far away
a car could take him from the need   15

to speak, or to answer, the key
   in having a key
and putting it in, and going.

(1989)

Questions

1. "The Sacred" seems to have several subjects. What do you think they are, and how does Stephen Dunn link them?
2. Why do you think Dunn chose to lay out the poem the way he does — no capitals, line breaks in the midst of ideas, a period only at the end of the poem? What is the effect of these choices?
3. How does Dunn romanticize the automobile? How do you think the teacher, whose question frames the poem, feels about the car?
4. Does this poem resonate with you? Explain your answer.

Auto

Heather McHugh

Heather McHugh was born in San Diego in 1948 and raised in Virginia. She studied at Harvard University. McHugh was awarded a MacArthur Foundation "Genius" Grant in 2009 for her work as a poet, an essayist, and a translator. "Auto" is from her collection *Hinge and Sign*, published in 1994.

At first, the mobiles were for multitudes —
the horse was doubled, then redoubled;

way and station made for
social arts, within which

conversations, trains of thought,   5
held sway. Today

I drive morosely and alone, like half
a billion others, each

in a glassed-in,
speakered-up   10

contraption, each
with a brain she thinks

she can control (it goes off
on its own, on detours

now and then; it dreams of cable-   15
cars and smoking-cars and Volkses that can spill

unthinkable powers of ten in clownface) unlike this poor
hollowed-out sedation of sedan I pull

off the throughway, up to the pump
marked SELF, and fill.   20

(1994)

Questions

1. What do you think is Heather McHugh's main theme in "Auto"?
2. What is the effect of the poem's plays on words, such as "trains of thought" (l. 5), "the horse was doubled, then redoubled" (l. 2), and "the pump / marked

SELF" (ll. 19–20)? What do the lines "in a glassed-in, / speakered-up" (ll. 9–10) evoke?

3. Why do you think McHugh breaks lines where she does? How does it affect the rhythm of the poem?

4. What do you think McHugh's view of the automobile is? Is it like or unlike your view? Explain your answer.

Americans and Their Cars
Is the Romance on the Skids?

PEW RESEARCH CENTER

The Pew Research Center Social and Demographic Trends Project studies cultural changes, combining original public-opinion survey research with social, economic, and demographic data analysis, and reports the findings on its Web site.

I. Overview

Any nation with more passenger vehicles than licensed drivers has a pretty serious love affair with the automobile. But the romance seems to be cooling off a bit — a casualty of its own intensity.

Today 69% of American drivers say they like to drive, down from 79% in a 1991 Gallup survey. And just 23% say they consider their car "something special — more than just a way to get around," barely half of the 43% who felt this way in 1991.

The biggest reason for the cooling of the affair isn't the recent spike in gas prices. Rather, it appears to be the result of a longer term trend — the growing hassle of traffic congestion, according to a Pew Research Center telephone survey among a nationally representative sample of 1,182 adults (including 1,048 drivers) conducted from June 20 through July 16, 2006.

When asked whether they like to drive or consider it a chore, 69% of drivers in the Pew survey said the former, while 28% said the latter. When the "chore" respondents were asked why they felt this way, traffic congestion (23%) and "other drivers" (14%) topped the list of reasons. Just 3% cited the expense.

Among the still sizable majority who say they like to drive, the biggest reasons offered were the relaxation (21%), the scenery (19%), the freedom (14%) and the ability to get around (12%).   5

A Plague of Traffic

Trends from the U.S. Bureau of Transportation Statistics and the National Center for Transit Research show why, for a growing number of Americans, cars and driving seem to have become too-much-of-a-good-thing.

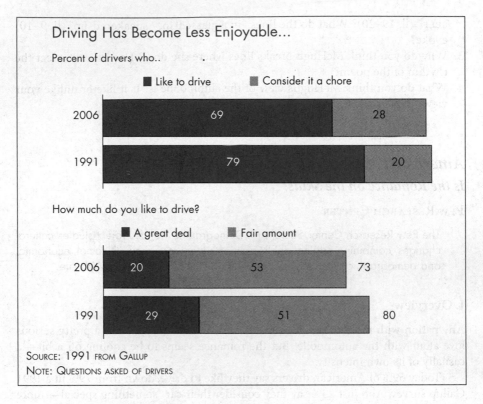

Driving Has Become Less Enjoyable...

Percent of drivers who..

■ Like to drive ■ Consider it a chore

	Like to drive	Consider it a chore
2006	69	28
1991	79	20

How much do you like to drive?

■ A great deal ■ Fair amount

	A great deal	Fair amount	Total
2006	20	53	73
1991	29	51	80

SOURCE: 1991 FROM GALLUP
NOTE: QUESTIONS ASKED OF DRIVERS

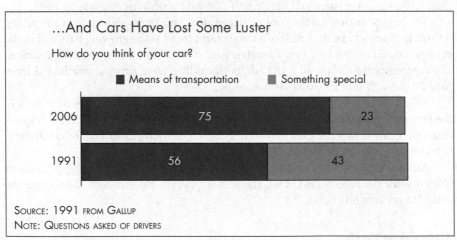

...And Cars Have Lost Some Luster

How do you think of your car?

■ Means of transportation ■ Something special

	Means of transportation	Something special
2006	75	23
1991	56	43

SOURCE: 1991 FROM GALLUP
NOTE: QUESTIONS ASKED OF DRIVERS

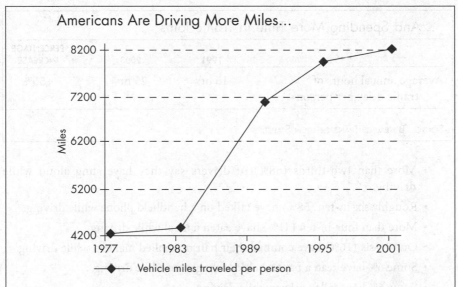

Americans Are Driving More Miles...

Miles

8200
7200
6200
5200
4200

1977   1983   1989   1995   2001

◆ Vehicle miles traveled per person

SOURCE: CENTER FOR URBAN TRANSPORTATION RESEARCH. RESULTS FROM THE 2001 NATIONAL HOUSEHOLD TRAVEL SURVEY; EARLIER YEARS FROM THE NATIONWIDE PERSONAL TRANSPORTATION SURVEY. MORE RECENT DATA NOT YET AVAILABLE.

The National Household Travel Survey found in 2001 that, for the first time since such studies have been conducted, there were more personal vehicles (204 million) than licensed drviers (191 million) in this country. With all those cars, trucks, minivans and SUVs at their disposal, Americans have been making more trips and traveling more miles, thereby generating more of the very thing that has made them enjoy driving less — traffic jams.[1] From 1991 to 2003, the amount of time per year that the typical American spent stuck in traffic grew by 56%, according to the Bureau of Transportation Statistics.

The Car: Where Life Happens

However, despite the growing hassles of traffic, many drivers have strong feelings of intimacy toward their cars — 31%, for example, say they think of their car as having a personality. And despite the high price of gas, more than a quarter (27%) say they went driving "just for the fun of it" in the past week.

Moreover, most people see driving as a chance to take care of many of the other routines and amusements of daily living. Here is a (slightly scary) list of things people report having done in the past year while they were behind the wheel:

---

[1]Polzin, Steven E. 2006. "The Case for Moderate Growth in Vehicle Miles of Travel: A Critical Juncture in U.S. Travel Behavior Trends." Report prepared for the U.S. Department of Transportation.

...And Spending More Time in Traffic Jams			
	1991	**2003**	**PERCENTAGE INCREASE**
Average annual hours of traffic delay per person	16 hrs	25 hrs	+56%

Source: Bureau of Transportation Statistics

- More than two-thirds (68%) of drivers say they have sung aloud while driving.
- Roughly six-in-ten (58%) have talked on a handheld phone while driving.
- More than four-in-ten (41%) have eaten a meal while driving.
- One-in-six (16%) have combed their hair or applied makeup while driving.
- Some 6% have read a paper, book or magazine while driving.
- Some 6% have fallen asleep while driving.
- And 38% have cursed at another driver.

About the Survey

Results for this survey are based on telephone interviews conducted with a nation- 10
ally representative sample of adults, ages 18 years and older, living in continental U.S.
telephone households.

- Interviews conducted June 20–July 16, 2006.
- 1,182 interviews of which 1,048 were conducted with drivers.
- Margin of sampling error is plus or minus 3.1 percentage points for results based on the total sample at the 95% confidence level and 3.3 percentage points for results based on all drivers. The margin of sampling error is higher for results based on subgroups of respondents.

Survey interviews conducted under the direction of Princeton Survey Research
Associates International. Interviews were conducted in English and Spanish.

Bear in mind that question wording and practical difficulties in conducting surveys can introduce error or bias in the findings of opinion polls.

(2006)

Questions

1. What surprised you about the results of this survey? What did you expect?
2. What are some of the reasons people still enjoy driving?
3. How does this survey explain the increase in traffic jams? Can you think of ways to solve that problem? Explain your ideas.

The End of the Affair

P. J. O'ROURKE

> Patrick Jake O'Rourke (b. 1947) is a political satirist, journalist, writer, and frequent guest on NPR's quiz show *Wait, Wait . . . Don't Tell Me*. This piece appeared in the *Wall Street Journal* in 2009.

The phrase "bankrupt General Motors," which we expect to hear uttered on Monday, leaves Americans my age in economic shock. The words are as melodramatic as "Mom's nude photos." And, indeed, if we want to understand what doomed the American automobile, we should give up on economics and turn to melodrama.

Politicians, journalists, financial analysts and other purveyors of banality have been looking at cars as if a convertible were a business. Fire the MBAs and hire a poet. The fate of Detroit isn't a matter of financial crisis, foreign competition, corporate greed, union intransigence, energy costs or measuring the shoe size of the footprints in the carbon. It's a tragic romance — unleashed passions, titanic clashes, lost love and wild horses.

Foremost are the horses. Cars can't be comprehended without them. A hundred and some years ago Rudyard Kipling wrote "The Ballad of the King's Jest," in which an Afghan tribesman avers: "Four things greater than all things are, — Women and Horses and Power and War."

Insert another "power" after the horse and the verse was as true in the suburbs of my 1950s boyhood as it was in the Khyber Pass.

Horsepower is not a quaint leftover of linguistics or a vague metaphoric anachronism. James Watt, father of the steam engine and progenitor of the industrial revolution, lacked a measurement for the movement of weight over distance in time — what we call power. (What we call power wasn't even an intellectual concept in the late 18th century — in case you think the recent collapse of global capitalism was history's most transformative moment.) Mr. Watt did research using draft animals and found that, under optimal conditions, a dray horse could lift 33,000 pounds one foot off the ground in one minute. Mr. Watt — the eponymous watt not yet existing — called this unit of power "1 horse-power." 5

In 1970 a Pontiac GTO (may the brand name rest in peace) had horsepower to the number of 370. In the time of one minute, for the space of one foot, it could move 12,210,000 pounds. And it could move those pounds down every foot of every mile of all the roads to the ends of the earth for every minute of every hour until the driver nodded off at the wheel. Forty years ago the pimply kid down the block, using $3,500 in saved-up soda-jerking money, procured might and main beyond the wildest dreams of Genghis Khan, whose hordes went forth to pillage mounted upon less oomph than is in a modern leaf blower.

Horses and horsepower alike are about status and being cool. A knight in ancient Rome was bluntly called "guy on horseback," Equesitis. Chevalier means the same, as does Cavalier. Lose the capitalization and the dictionary says, "insouciant and debonair; marked by a lofty disregard of others' interests, rights, or feelings; high-handed and arrogant and supercilious." How cool is that? Then there are cowboys — always cool — and the U.S. cavalry that coolly comes to their rescue plus the proverbially cool-handed "Man on Horseback" to whom we turn in troubled times.

Early witnesses to the automobile urged motorists to get a horse. But that, in effect, was what the automobile would do — get a horse for everybody. Once the Model T was introduced in 1908 we all became Sir Lancelot, gained a seat at the Round Table and were privileged to joust for the favors of fair maidens (at drive-in movies). The pride and prestige of a noble mount was vouchsafed to the common man. And woman, too. No one ever tried to persuade ladies to drive sidesaddle with both legs hanging out the car door.

For the purpose of ennobling us schlubs, the car is better than the horse in every way. Even more advantageous than cost, convenience and not getting kicked and smelly is how much easier it is to drive than to ride. I speak with feeling on this subject, having taken up riding when I was nearly 60 and having begun to drive when I was so small that my cousin Tommy had to lie on the transmission hump and operate the accelerator and the brake with his hands.

After the grown-ups had gone to bed, Tommy and I shifted the Buick into neu-   10
tral, pushed it down the driveway and out of earshot, started the engine and toured the neighborhood. The sheer difficulty of horsemanship can be illustrated by what happened to Tommy and me next. Nothing. We maneuvered the car home, turned it off and rolled it back up the driveway. (We were raised in the blessedly flat Midwest.) During our foray the Buick's speedometer reached 30. But 30 miles per hour is a full gallop on a horse. Delete what you've seen of horse riding in movies. Possibly a kid who'd never been on a horse could ride at a gallop without killing himself. Possibly one of the Jonas Brothers could land an F-14 on a carrier deck.

Thus cars usurped the place of horses in our hearts. Once we'd caught a glimpse of a well-turned Goodyear, checked out the curves of the bodywork and gaped at that swell pair of headlights, well, the old gray mare was not what she used to be. We embarked upon life in the fast lane with our new paramour. It was a great love story of man and machine. The road to the future was paved with bliss.

Then we got married and moved to the suburbs. Being away from central cities meant Americans had to spend more of their time driving. Over the years away got farther away. Eventually this meant that Americans had to spend all of their time driving. The play date was 40 miles from the Chuck E. Cheese. The swim meet was 40 miles from the cello lesson. The Montessori was 40 miles from the math coach. Mom's job was 40 miles from Dad's job and the three-car garage was 40 miles from both.

The car ceased to be object of desire and equipment for adventure and turned into office, rec room, communications hub, breakfast nook and recycling bin — a motorized cup holder. Americans, the richest people on Earth, were stuck in the confines of their crossover SUVs, squeezed into less space than tech-support call-center employees in a Mumbai cubicle farm. Never mind the six-bedroom, eight-bath, pseudo-Tudor with cathedral-ceilinged great room and 1,000-bottle controlled-climate wine cellar. That was a day's walk away.

We became sick and tired of our cars and even angry at them. Pointy-headed busy-bodies of the environmentalist, new urbanist, utopian communitarian ilk blamed the victim. They claimed the car had forced us to live in widely scattered settlements in the great wasteland of big-box stores and the Olive Garden. If we would all just get on our Schwinns or hop a trolley, they said, America could become an archipelago of cozy gulags on the Portland, Ore., model with everyone nestled together in the most sustainably carbon-neutral, diverse and ecologically unimpactful way.

But cars didn't shape our existence; cars let us escape with our lives. We're way 15 the heck out here in Valley Bottom Heights and Trout Antler Estates because we were at war with the cities. We fought rotten public schools, idiot municipal bureaucracies, corrupt political machines, rampant criminality and the pointy-headed busybodies. Cars gave us our dragoons and hussars, lent us speed and mobility, let us scout the terrain and probe the enemy's lines. And thanks to our cars, when we lost the cities we weren't forced to surrender, we were able to retreat.

But our poor cars paid the price. They were flashing swords beaten into dull plowshares. Cars became appliances. Or worse. Nobody's ticked off at the dryer or the dishwasher, much less the fridge. We recognize these as labor-saving devices. The car, on the other hand, seems to create labor. We hold the car responsible for all the dreary errands to which it needs to be steered. Hell, a golf cart's more fun. You can ride around in a golf cart with a six-pack, safe from breathalyzers, chasing Canada geese on the fairways and taking swings at gophers with a mashie.

We've lost our love for cars and forgotten our debt to them and meanwhile the pointy-headed busybodies have been exacting their revenge. We escaped the poke of their noses once, when we lived downtown, but we won't be able to peel out so fast the next time. In the name of safety, emissions control and fuel economy, the simple mechanical elegance of the automobile has been rendered ponderous, cumbersome and incomprehensible. One might as well pry the back off an iPod as pop the hood on a contemporary motor vehicle. An aging shade-tree mechanic like myself stares aghast and sits back down in the shade. Or would if the car weren't squawking at me like a rehearsal for divorce. You left the key in. You left the door open. You left the lights on. You left your dirty socks in the middle of the bedroom floor.

I don't believe the pointy-heads give a damn about climate change or gas mile-age, much less about whether I survive a head-on with one of their tax-sucking mass-transit projects. All they want is to make me hate my car. How proud and handsome would Bucephalas look, or Traveler or Rachel Alexandra, with seat and shoulder belts, air bags, 5-mph bumpers and a maze of pollution-control equipment under the tail?

And there's the end of the American automobile industry. When it comes to dull, practical, ugly things that bore and annoy me, Japanese things cost less and the cup holders are more conveniently located.

The American automobile is—that is, was—never a product of Japanese-style 20 industrialism. America's steel, coal, beer, beaver pelts and PCs may have come from our business plutocracy, but American cars have been manufactured mostly by romantic fools. David Buick, Ransom E. Olds, Louis Chevrolet, Robert and Louis Hupp of the

Hupmobile, the Dodge brothers, the Studebaker brothers, the Packard brothers, the Duesenberg brothers, Charles W. Nash, E. L. Cord, John North Willys, Preston Tucker and William H. Murphy, whose Cadillac cars were designed by the young Henry Ford, all went broke making cars. The man who founded General Motors in 1908, William Crapo (really) Durant, went broke twice. Henry Ford, of course, did not go broke, nor was he a romantic, but judging by his opinions he certainly was a fool.

America's romantic foolishness with cars is finished, however, or nearly so. In the far boondocks a few good old boys haven't got the memo and still tear up the back roads. Doubtless the Obama administration's Department of Transportation is even now calculating a way to tap federal stimulus funds for mandatory OnStar installations to locate and subdue these reprobates.

Among certain youths — often first-generation Americans — there remains a vestigial fondness for Chevelle low-riders or Honda "tuners." The pointy-headed busybodies have yet to enfold these youngsters in the iron-clad conformity of cultural diversity's embrace. Soon the kids will be expressing their creative energy in a more constructive way, planting bok choy in community gardens and decorating homeless shelters with murals of Che.

I myself have something old-school under a tarp in the basement garage. I bet when my will has been probated, some child of mine will yank the dust cover and use the proceeds of the eBay sale to buy a mountain bike. Four things greater than all things are, and I'm pretty sure one of them isn't bicycles. There are those of us who have had the good fortune to meet with strength and beauty, with majestic force in which we were willing to trust our lives. Then a day comes, that strength and beauty fails, and a man does what a man has to do. I'm going downstairs to put a bullet in a V-8.

(2009)

Questions

1. P. J. O'Rourke suggests that the auto industry "[f]ire the MBAs and hire a poet" (par. 2). Explain his reasoning. Does he convince you? Explain why or why not.
2. In "The End of the Affair," O'Rourke develops an extended analogy between cars and horses. Trace the development of the analogy. How does it help him make his argument?
3. What does O'Rourke consider some of the consequences of the move to the suburbs? How do those consequences affect Americans' relationship with their cars?
4. Do you think O'Rourke blames any particular institution for the end of America's love affair with the automobile? Do you agree with him? Explain your answer.
5. How does O'Rourke explain the demise of the American auto industry?

Carmakers' Next Problem: Generation Y

ALLISON LINN

Allison Linn writes about the economy, consumer issues, and personal finance for NBCNews.com. She worked at newspapers in Colorado, Washington, and Oregon and as a reporter in Germany.

Meet Natalie McVeigh, the auto industry's latest headache.

At 25 years old, McVeigh lives in Denver and has two good jobs, as a research analyst and an adjunct professor of philosophy. What she doesn't have — or want — is a car.

A confluence of events — environmental worries, a preference for gadgets over wheels and the yearslong economic doldrums — is pushing some teens and twenty-somethings to opt out of what has traditionally been considered an American rite of passage: Owning a car.

"There's kind of almost every force working against the young driver right now," said Karl Brauer, senior analyst and editor-at-large at Edmunds.com, an automotive research website.

That could be a problem for automakers, which are still reeling from the Great   5
Recession that sorely damaged their industry. Now, they may find that their youngest generation of potential customers will either purchase fewer cars, put off buying cars until later in life — or they won't end up buying cars at all.

"That's definitely a concern," said George Peterson, president of AutoPacific, an automotive market research firm that has been tracking young car buyers for 20 years. "They are not as engaged with cars and trucks as Gen X or Boomers before them."

The percentage of new cars sold to 21- to 34-year-olds hit a high of nearly 38 percent in 1985 but stands at around 27 percent today, according to CNW research. Over that same period, the percentage of new car buyers who are 55 or older has generally been trending up, according to the vehicle research group.

The prognosis isn't necessarily encouraging, either. In 2008, 82 percent of 20- to 24-year-olds had their driver's license, according to the Federal Highway Administration. Although that's gone up a tiny bit in the past few years, it's down from more than 87 percent in 1994.

People in their late twenties and early thirties are also slightly less likely to have a driver's license than in 1994, and it appears that more people are at least delaying getting their license. Just 31 percent of 16-year-olds had their license in 2008, down from about 42 percent in 1994, according to government data.

Brauer said one issue is economic: A combination of high unemployment among   10
young people and economic troubles for their parents is making it harder for younger people to afford to drive.

But there are also other, longer-term issues at work, he said.

For one thing, many young consumers care more about new technologies, such as the latest phone, than about the latest car.

That may be for good reason — thanks to the Internet and social media, more people can connect with friends, work or even hand in schoolwork without ever leaving the house, potentially making them less dependent on cars but more dependent on gadgets.

Brauer said this generation also is thinking more than any other about the repercussions of driving, both in terms of the environment and our dependence on oil.

"They don't just wholeheartedly see a car as this cool thing to go get," he said. "There's actually some caveats." 15

"I Didn't Need It"

McVeigh didn't make a conscious plan not to drive. After living overseas as a teenager, she went to college in a small town and then moved to bigger cities for graduate school and work.

At first, a car seemed both prohibitively expensive and unnecessary, because she could walk or take public transportation. Then, she just decided she didn't want one.

"I just kind of came to the realization that I didn't need it," she said.

McVeigh uses public transportation to get to work and likes that she can spend her commute time reading or grading papers.

McVeigh also likes getting the extra exercise when she chooses to walk to work 20 or to the grocery store, and is happy to be saving money and not adding any more pollution to the planet.

Although she knows other people in big East Coast cities who don't have cars, McVeigh said she remains unusual in Denver.

"It's still a Western town and everyone has a car," she said. "Everyone just thinks it's bizarre that I don't have a car."

But for now, she's happy with her decision. The only time not having a car is really inconvenient is when she wants to visit her sister in the mountain town of Breckenridge, about 80 miles away, or to go somewhere with her young nieces who live there.

Gadgets and Gas Mileage

Brauer, the Edmunds.com analyst, says carmakers are thinking about what it will take to get people like McVeigh into the showroom.

Many analysts credit Ford with doing the best job so far. The company recently 25 released a new version of the Fiesta that has plenty to appeal to Generation Y: A sticker price starting at $13,320, combined gas mileage of around 33 miles per gallon and, perhaps most important, up-to-date technology for things like voice-activated music search and audible text messages.

Peterson, of AutoPacific, said Hyundai and Kia also are starting to offer appealing gadgetry for young car buyers, while Chrysler, General Motors, Toyota and Honda are still playing catch-up.

But will incorporating such functions be enough to persuade a young person who is on the fence to take on car payments and associated costs?

"I Was Afraid I Would Get Laid Off Again"

The weak economy and cost of car ownership is what pushed Kathryn Goffredi, 24, to give up her driving habit.

Like many suburban American teens, Goffredi got a license and a car at age 16. She drove regularly in high school but not college.

After college, she worked in the Washington, D.C. suburbs. She was considering replacing her high school car when she was laid off in January. One of her first thoughts was, "Well, thank God I didn't buy that car." 30

Even now that she has a new job doing marketing for nonprofits, Goffredi has no plans to buy a car and has left the old car for her brother to use.

Because she lives and works in the nation's capital, she says it would be cost-prohibitive to drive to work, and not worth paying for a car she only drove a couple times a week. The uncertain economy also left her nervous about taking the plunge.

"I was afraid I would get laid off again, you know, and I would buy this car and work for three or four months and then lose my job again and then be stuck with these car payments," she said.

One big question for carmakers—and these young not-drivers—is how far public transportation will take them. Americans can get by fairly well in large cities, where buses and subways can be combined with cabs and car loan services like Zipcar. But it's a tougher slog in parts of the country better known for long stretches of highways than gleaming rail lines.

Dave Cole, chairman emeritus of the Center for Automotive Research, said 35
Generation Y may never be as excited about things like horsepower and styling as generations past. But he thinks that as this generation gets older and starts buying homes and having kids, they'll eventually buy a car, out of necessity if nothing else.

"The dependence on personal transportation in this country, outside of major urban areas, is still pretty profound, so there's really no alternative," he said.

Although Goffredi is happy with her decision not to own a car for now, she says she could definitely see herself buying a car in the future if she got a job that was far away, or had kids.

But right now she has other priorities for her extra cash.

"You have all this money, you know, and you decide you could put it all toward the car or you can put it toward other things like clothes, or your social life," she said.

(2010)

Questions

1. What do you think Allison Linn considers the number one reason that young people are not buying cars?
2. What solutions has the auto industry been working on to turn this trend around? Do you think they will be effective? Explain your answer.
3. When this article appeared, it included a questionnaire asking, "What would be the biggest motivator for you to drive less?" Possible answers were cost of gas; car

payments; reducing dependence on oil; environmental concerns; better public transportation; all of the above; none of the above — I love my car. Over 12,000 people responded, with "cost of gas" and "better public transportation" receiving the most votes and "none of the above — I love my car" coming in close behind. How would you respond? What do the responses tell you about the future of Americans and their cars?

Americans Hit the Brakes on NASCAR

FRANK DEFORD

> Frank DeFord (b. 1938), a sportswriter and novelist, has worked at *Sports Illustrated* for over fifty years. DeFord has a weekly spot on NPR and is a senior correspondent for *Real Sports with Bryant Gumbel*. This piece appeared on the NPR Web site in March 2012, where DeFord's weekly commentaries are called "Sweetness and Light."

Individual sports are always volatile, and after being the next big thing, NASCAR's popularity has stalled.

A lot had to do with the economy. In a sport that depends on sponsorships and rich owners — like those good buddies Mitt Romney kicks tires with — NASCAR was especially vulnerable.

And as for fans, when it became cutback time, they had to think twice about gassing up those big old RVs and driving a far piece to sit in those ear-shattering stadiums.

So, NASCAR invested $5 million in research to find out how to get back out of the pits. To me, the most fascinating finding was that all those old, white guys, who were the bread-and-butter NASCAR constituency, were not being replicated by their sons and grandsons. Frankly, the younger generations don't care to mess around with cars.

Ladies and gentlemen, I know this is heresy. It's been a given that Americans have   5
what is always called "a love affair with the car." But what NASCAR found out was that it's now only a platonic relationship. No hands on. A whole cohort of our young boys — and girls — have been growing up without any interest in messing around — tinkering — with cars. It made me think that the last time I ever heard anybody talking about looking under the hood was Ross Perot, when he ran for president in '92, and he kept saying all we had to do to fix things was look under the hood.

Well, NASCAR found, nobody much wants to do that anymore. Sure, younger people still view automobiles as a necessary evil to get from A to B, but no less so than do Brazilians or Indians or Chinese.

In fact, Americans aren't satisfied only to drive. They otherwise want to talk on the phone, eat and drink, text, plug in their iPods, fool around with the GPS or — the best and brightest of them — listen to NPR. How many Americans would even get into cars if they couldn't be entertained while driving? There goes the demand for foreign oil right there.

Moreover, when it comes to cars, kids grow up being primarily accustomed to watching cars crashing in movies and on TV. Cars aren't for racing anymore. They're just instruments of demolition.

And tinker? Researchers at the University of Michigan found that the kids who tinker more with the Internet delay getting their driver's licenses. Not wanting a driver's license? Next to making out, that was the most important rite of passage in an American teenager's life.

Look, I wish NASCAR well. I hope it gets people back to the races, but it is going   10
to have to do it with stars and steroids and point spreads, like all the other sports. Nobody cool wants to look under the hood anymore. They want to look at Facebook and YouTube. As of 2012, the American love affair with the car is over. Cars are so Greatest Generation.

(2012)

Questions

1. How does Frank DeFord explain the stalled popularity of NASCAR?
2. Characterize the audience for "Americans Hit the Brakes on NASCAR." What assumptions does DeFord make about his audience? How does he pitch his piece to them?
3. Are you convinced by DeFord that the "American love affair with the car is over"? Does he speak accurately for your generation? Explain your view.

Making Connections

1. How are the teenagers Tom Wolfe (p. 1538) writes about like or unlike the teenagers in Stephen Dunn's poem "The Sacred" (p. 1541)?

2. Imagine a conversation among P. J. O'Rourke (p. 1547), Frank DeFord (p. 1554), and E. B. White (p. 1529) on the subject of America's romance with the automobile. What aspects would they agree on? What would they disagree on?

3. What do you think the speaker in Heather McHugh's "Auto" (p. 1542) has in common with Rabbit Angstrom in the excerpt from John Updike's *Rabbit, Run* (p. 1535)? Explain your answer.

4. Compare and contrast the Pew Research Center study (p. 1543) with Allison Linn's report on Generation Y's attitudes toward car ownership (p. 1551). What crossovers do you see? Do they contradict each other in any way? Explain why or why not.

5. Compare the Ohio Electric advertisement (p. 1529) to a contemporary car ad. You might take a look at the Dodge Durango ad in Chapter 2 (p. 75) or the Dodge Challenger ad in Chapter 6 (p. 468), but also be sure to look at advertising for luxury cars and "smart" energy-efficient cars. Take audience, speaker, and subject into account. What are the common threads? What aspects of car marketing have changed the most? What aspects of car marketing have come full circle?

Entering the Conversation

As you respond to each of the following prompts, support your position with appropriate evidence, including at least three sources in this Conversation on America's romance with the automobile, unless otherwise indicated.

1. In a letter to the *New York Times* in April 2012, transportation demand researcher and author Randy Salzman suggests that Americans need to "use our cars smarter" in order to "mitigate a host of problems and prevent our grandchildren from following our children in fighting wars in the Middle East." His solution is a federal gasoline "user fee" rolled in slowly over a decade. Using the sources in this Conversation and your own reading and experience, propose a solution to America's car problem. If you don't think we have a problem, defend our use of the automobile.

2. In Jack Kerouac's *On the Road*, the narrator Sal Paradise asks—and answers, "What is that feeling when you're driving away from people and they recede on the plain till you see their specks dispersing?—it's the too-huge world vaulting us, and it's good-by. But we lean forward to the next crazy venture beneath the skies." Write an essay in which you examine the appeal of the automobile and the way it has figured in popular culture and literature. Use the pieces in this chapter and reading you have done on your own.

3. Several pieces in this Conversation communicate nostalgia for the romantic relationship between Americans and their cars. Write an essay in which you analyze that nostalgia, discussing what was romantic about the car, why the romance ended, and predicting the future of our relationship with the automobile.

4. In 2009, Sheryl Connelly, Ford Motor Company's manager of global consumer trends and futuring, said, "The car used to be the signal of adulthood, of freedom. It was the signal of being a grownup. Now, the signal into adulthood for teenagers is the smartphone." A survey later that year reported that 46 percent of eighteen to twenty-four-year-olds said they would choose Internet access over owning their own car. Among the baby boom generation, the people who grew up in the 1950s and 1960s, the height of the American romance with the automobile, only 15 percent would choose the Internet. Write an essay in which you analyze those trends. Use the sources in this Conversation, as well as your outside reading and experience, as evidence.

5. What is the future of the automobile in America? Can the auto industry make a comeback? Is it a regional issue rather than a national one? Rural rather than urban? Write an essay in which you analyze several directions for the car's future, choosing and defending the one you think is most promising.

6. Jeremy Hsu, in a May 2012 article in *Scientific American*, asserts that the American romance with the car was no coincidence. It was part of the automobile industry's "battle for hearts and minds" to "take over the streets where people had once

swarmed." One strategy was the creation of the term *jaywalker*, "jay" being slang for an ignorant person, especially one from the country—akin to a "rube" or "hick." This term made it unsophisticated to not recognize that cars rule the road. Finally, the phrase "America's love affair with the automobile" was part of comedian Groucho Marx's narration of a TV show called *Merrily We Roll Along*. Given the uncertainty of America's current and future romance with the automobile, consider the kind of public relations moves that might be required to sustain it. Develop an advertising campaign for encouraging Americans to either curtail or increase their use of automobiles.

Grammar as Rhetoric and Style
Parallel Structures

Parts of a sentence are parallel when they share the same grammatical pattern. Parallelism is most often found within sentences at the level of the word, phrase, or clause, but sometimes parallelism can even extend across sentences, as in these three parallel sentences from Martin Luther King Jr.'s "Letter from Birmingham Jail":

> So I, along with several members of my staff, am here because I was invited here. I am here because I have organizational ties here. But more basically, I am in Birmingham because injustice is here. —MARTIN LUTHER KING JR.

Words

> Those who failed were ceremonially accepted by other Indians and appropriately pitied by non-Indians. —SHERMAN ALEXIE

In this sentence, the words *ceremonially accepted* and *appropriately pitied*, both adverbial phrases, precede the preposition *by*; *ceremonially accepted* and *appropriately pitied* are parallel.

> Because of this, the young man or woman writing today has forgotten the problems of the human heart in conflict with itself which alone can make good writing because only that is worth writing about, worth the agony and the sweat. —WILLIAM FAULKNER

In this sentence, the words *agony* and *sweat*, both nouns, follow *worth*; *agony* and *sweat* are parallel.

Phrases

[A]nd yes, I could say, yes, these white folks without the magnolia (who are indifferent to the tree's existence), and these black folks without melons and superior racial patience, these are like the Southerners I know.

— ALICE WALKER

To explain the Southerners she knows, Walker uses parallel prepositional phrases: *without the magnolia* and *without melons and superior racial patience*.

It was the Lord who knew of the impossibility every parent in that room faced: how to prepare the child for the day when the child would be despised and how to *create* in the child — by what means? — a stronger antidote to this poison than one had found for onself.

— JAMES BALDWIN

In the preceding sentence, James Baldwin uses two parallel infinitive verbs each preceded by *how*: *to prepare* and *to create*.

Clauses

If the stakes ever became high enough — if the evil were evil enough, if the good were good enough — I would simply tap a secret reservoir of courage that had been accumulating inside me over the years.

— TIM O'BRIEN

This sentence contains three parallel dependent, or subordinate, clauses; all begin with *if*. The repetition of *enough* is also part of parallelism.

I only needed to turn a corner into a dicey situation, or crowd some frightened, armed person in a foyer somewhere, or make an errant move after being pulled over by a policeman.

— BRENT STAPLES

The preceding example contains three parallel clauses: one independent and two dependent beginning with *or*.

I knew how to dress for school: at the Catholic school I attended we all wore uniforms; I knew how to dress for Sunday mass, and I knew what dresses to wear for parties at my relatives' homes.

— JUDITH ORTIZ COFER

This example begins with two independent clauses separated by a colon. The semicolon connects two more parallel constructions each beginning with *I knew*.

Lack of Parallelism

To fully appreciate the power of the parallelism in the preceding examples, consider what happens when supposedly equal elements of a sentence do not follow the same grammatical or syntactical form — that is, when they are not parallel with each other.

> I only needed to turn a corner into a dicey situation, or crowding some frightened, armed person in a foyer somewhere, or making an errant move after being pulled over by a policeman.

This version of the Staples sentence that we looked at earlier moves from an independent clause to two dependent clauses that use verbals rather than simple verbs. The three phrases are not parallel, and as a result, the sentence lacks clarity and force.

Parallelism can be tricky when the elements — words, phrases, or clauses — are separated by modifiers or other syntactical elements. The following sentence may not at first glance seem to lack parallelism:

> ... I quickly left my mother and the children to the care of those impressive women, who, in Negro communities at least, automatically appear at times of bereavement armed with lotions, proverbs, and patience, and can cook.

When you analyze carefully, you notice that *lotions*, *proverbs*, and *patience* are nouns, and *can cook* is a verb. Notice that in the actual sentence that James Baldwin wrote in "Notes of a Native Son," he makes all four words parallel nouns:

> ... I quickly left my mother and the children to the care of those impressive women, who, in Negro communities at least, automatically appear at times of bereavement armed with lotions, proverbs, and patience, and an ability to cook.
> — JAMES BALDWIN

The fact that all four are nouns underscores the gifts that these women bring to a grieving home — the lotions, sayings, kindness, and cooking are all of equal weight.

Parallelism is often at its most effective at the level of the clause, but again, it may be difficult to keep track. Let's use an example from Malcolm Gladwell. Here it is without parallel structure:

> In other words, Facebook activism succeeds not by motivating people to make a real sacrifice but when people are motivated to do things even though they are not motivated enough to make a real sacrifice.

That sentence makes sense — once you've untangled all the motivations! — but the emphasis Gladwell intends is on the *not*: people are *not* motivated by x *but* by y. In the sentence that actually appears in his essay, he repeats the phrase *by motivating* and thus uses parallel structure to emphasize the contrast:

In other words, Facebook activism succeeds **not** by motivating people to make a real sacrifice **but** by motivating them to do the things that people do when they are not motivated enough to make a real sacrifice.

— MALCOLM GLADWELL

Rhetorical and Stylistic Strategy

Looking first at the parallel sentences at the beginning of this lesson and then at the rewrites that lack parallelism, you can see that writers use parallelism to emphasize, contrast, or connect ideas.

Following are the names, definitions, and examples of specific types of parallelism:

anaphora   Repetition of a word or phrase at the beginning of successive phrases, clauses, or lines.

> *But when you have seen vicious mobs lynch your mothers and fathers at will and drown your sisters and brothers at whim; when you have seen hate-filled policemen curse, kick, and even kill your black brothers and sisters; . . . when you are forever fighting a degenerating sense of "nobodiness" — then you will understand why we find it difficult to wait.* — MARTIN LUTHER KING JR.

In this example, form follows function. Just as King is saying that African Americans have had to endure unjust treatment as they waited for full civil rights, this series of parallel clauses makes the reader wait — and wait — for the main point in the independent clause.

antimetabole   Repetition of words in reverse order.

> *Ask not what your country can do for you; ask what you can do for your country.* — JOHN F. KENNEDY

The example above from President Kennedy is, perhaps, his most famous quote. Part of what makes it so "quotable" is that the repetition inherent in antimetabole makes it dramatic and easy to remember. Because the pattern of the two clauses is so similar, the listener only needs to remember one pattern. Because that sentence pattern is repeated, it gives the listener two chances to understand the entire sentence and places extra emphasis on the second part. It is almost as if Kennedy is repeating a point for emphasis. Keep an eye out for antimetabole in modern political sound bites.

antithesis   Opposition, or contrast, of ideas or words in a parallel construction.

> *[F]reedom is never voluntarily given by the oppressor; it must be demanded by the oppressed.* — MARTIN LUTHER KING JR.

> *One has not only a legal but a moral responsibility to obey just laws. Conversely, one has a moral responsibility to disobey unjust laws.*   — MARTIN LUTHER KING JR.

> *That's one small step for man, one giant leap for mankind.*   — NEIL ARMSTRONG

In all three of these examples, the parallel structure creates a clear comparison between two things in order to emphasize the difference between them. *Given by the oppressor* is contrasted in meaning and in placement with *demanded by the oppressed*. Notice also how the parallel prepositional phrases *by the oppressor* and *by the oppressed* call attention to the tension between oppressor and oppressed.

zeugma Use of two different words in a grammatically similar way that produces different, often incongruous, meanings.

> *O'Connor's short stories and novels are set in a rural South where people know their places, mind their manners and do horrible things to one another.*
>
> — LAWRENCE DOWNES

In the example by Downes, the zeugma is created in the description of the qualities of Flannery O'Connor's South, from the expected "know their places" and "mind their manners" to the surprising "do horrible things to one another." There is a consistency in the pattern, but an inconsistency in the effect of the phrases. Downes exploits the ironic inconsistency of the zeugma to show the ways that O'Connor surprises her readers with the way she portrays the rural South.

• EXERCISE 1 •

Identify the parallel structure in words, phrases, or clauses in each of the following sentences.

1. "A penny saved is a penny earned."   — BENJAMIN FRANKLIN
2. Was this act the work of a genius or a lunatic?
3. This situation is a problem not only for the students but also for the teachers.
4. Heather learned to work fast, ask few questions, and generally keep a low profile.
5. After you finish your homework and before you check your e-mail, please do your chores.

• EXERCISE 2 •

Correct the faulty parallelism in the following sentences.

1. My new exercise program and going on a strict diet will help me lose the weight I gained over the holidays.
2. As part of his accounting business, Rick has private clients, does some pro bono work, and corporations.
3. Try not to focus on the mistakes that you've made; what you've learned from them should be your focus instead.

4. A new job is likely to cause a person anxiety and working extra hours to make a good impression.

5. A competent physician will assess a patient's physical symptoms, and mental attitude will also be considered.

• EXERCISE 3 •

Identify the parallel structures in the following sentences from Martin Luther King Jr.'s "Letter from Birmingham Jail," and explain their effect.

1. So I, along with several members of my staff, am here because I was invited here. I am here because I have organizational ties here. (par. 2)

2. We are caught in an inescapable network of mutuality, tied in a single garment of destiny. (par. 4)

3. Whatever affects one directly, affects all indirectly. (par. 4)

4. In any nonviolent campaign there are four basic steps: collection of the facts to determine whether injustices exist; negotiation; self-purification; and direct action. (par. 6)

5. An unjust law is a code that a numerical or power majority group compels a minority group to obey but does not make binding on itself. This is *difference* made legal. By the same token, a just law is a code that a majority compels a minority to follow and that it is willing to follow itself. This is *sameness* made legal. (par. 17)

6. Was not Jesus an extremist for love: "Love your enemies, bless them that curse you, do good to them that hate you, and pray for them which despitefully use you, and persecute you." Was not Amos an extremist for justice: "Let justice roll down like waters and righteousness like an ever-flowing stream." Was not Paul an extremist for the Christian gospel: "I bear in my body the marks of the Lord Jesus." Was not Martin Luther an extremist: "Here I stand; I cannot do otherwise, so help me God." And John Bunyan: "I will stay in jail to the end of my days before I make a butchery of my conscience." And Abraham Lincoln: "This nation cannot survive half slave and half free." And Thomas Jefferson: "We hold these truths to be self-evident, that all men are created equal. . . ." (par. 31)

7. If I have said anything in this letter that overstates the truth and indicates an unreasonable impatience, I beg you to forgive me. If I have said anything that understates the truth and indicates my having a patience that allows me to settle for anything less than brotherhood, I beg God to forgive me. (par. 49)

• EXERCISE 4 •

The following paragraph is from Toni Morrison's Nobel lecture, delivered in 1993 when she won the Nobel Prize for Literature. Find examples of parallel structure; identify whether the construction is a word, clause, or phrase; and explain its effect.

The systematic looting of language can be recognized by the tendency of its users to forgo its nuanced, complex, midwifery properties for menace and subjugation. Oppressive language does more than represent violence; it is violence; does more than represent the limits of knowledge; it limits knowledge. Whether it is obscuring state language or the faux-language of mindless media; whether it is the proud but calcified language of the academy or the commodity driven language of science; whether it is the malign language of law-without-ethics, or language designed for the estrangement of minorities, hiding its racist plunder in its literary cheek — it must be rejected, altered and exposed. It is the language that drinks blood, laps vulnerabilities, tucks its fascist boots under crinolines of respectability and patriotism as it moves relentlessly toward the bottom line and the bottomed-out mind. Sexist language, racist language, theistic language — all are typical of the policing languages of mastery, and cannot, do not permit new knowledge or encourage the mutual exchange of ideas.

• EXERCISE 5 •

Each of the following sentences is an example of parallelism. Identify the type of parallelism, explain its effect, and then model a sentence of your own on the example.

1. I read books late into the night, until I could barely keep my eyes open. I read books at recess, then during lunch and in the few minutes left after I had finished my classroom assignments. I read books in the car when my family traveled to powwows or basketball games. In shopping malls, I ran to the bookstores and read bits and pieces of as many books as I could. I read the books my father brought home from the pawnshops and secondhand. I read the books I borrowed from the library. I read the backs of cereal boxes. I read the newspaper. I read the bulletins posted on the walls of the school, the clinic, the tribal offices, the post office. I read junk mail. I read auto-repair manuals. I read magazines. I read anything that had words and paragraphs. I read with equal parts joy and desperation.   —SHERMAN ALEXIE

2. **I will have all these little Suzettes in case you never have any babies, which looks more and more like it is going to happen.**

   My mother who had me when she was thirty-three—l'âge du Christ—at the age that Christ died on the cross.

That's a blessing, believe you me, even if American doctors say by that time you can make retarded babies.

My mother, who sews lace collars on my company soft ball T-shirts when she does my laundry.

Why, you can't you look like a lady playing soft ball?

My mother, who never went to any of my Parent- Teacher Association meetings when I was in school. —EDWIDGE DANTICAT

3. It was only one bomb, small enough to fit in the trunk of a car. A band of fanatics stole it from the Israelis, smuggled it into the United States, and exploded it in a football stadium to kill tens of thousands.

—SPENCER R. WEART

4. But cars didn't shape our existence; cars let us escape with our lives. We're way the heck out here in Valley Bottom Heights and Trout Antler Estates because we were at war with the cities. We fought rotten public schools, idiot municipal bureaucracies, corrupt political machines, rampant criminality and the pointy-headed busybodies. Cars gave us our dragoons and hussars, lent us speed and mobility, let us scout the terrain and probe the enemy's lines. And thanks to our cars, when we lost the cities we weren't forced to surrender, we were able to retreat. —P. J. O'ROURKE

5. Certain blood was being shed for uncertain reasons. —TIM O'BRIEN

Suggestions for Writing
Redefining America

1. In *On Native Grounds,* American writer and critic Alfred Kazin wrote, "the greatest single fact about our modern American writing is our writers' absorption in every detail of their American world together with their deep and subtle alienation from it." Choose at least three works from this chapter and analyze them through the lens of Kazin's observation.

2. In a piece about the essay in the *New York Times,* essayist Philip Lopate wrote:

Ever since Michel de Montaigne, the founder of the modern essay, gave as a motto his befuddled "What do I know?" and put forth a vision of humanity as mentally wavering and inconstant, the essay has become a meadow inviting contradiction, paradox, irresolution, and self-doubt. The essay's job is to track consciousness; if you are fully aware of your mind you will find your thoughts doubling back, registering little peeps of ambivalence or disbelief.

Write an essay in which you examine the "contradiction, paradox, irresolution, and self-doubt" in at least three of the twentieth- and twenty-first-century American essays in this chapter.

3. Write an essay in which you trace the way writers contributed to the civil rights movement through their revelations about racial discrimination and inequality. Use pieces from this chapter as well as your other reading as evidence.

4. Is multiculturalism a better model than assimilation? Write an essay in which you evaluate the pros and cons of each and then indicate your own position on the issue. Use sources in this chapter and your outside reading as support.

5. In both Tim O'Brien's "Rainy River" (p. 1399) and Joan Didion's "On Self-Respect" (p. 1340) making or not making Phi Beta Kappa, the most recognizable reward for academic excellence, at least in part defines the speaker. What else do these two pieces have in common? Write an essay in which you create your own definition of self-respect, using these selections — and others from the chapter — as evidence for your definition.

6. Three poems in this chapter relate to wars in the late twentieth and early twenty-first centuries — "Facing It" (p. 1397), "Letter to a Photojournalist Going-In" (p. 1429), and "At Lowe's Home Improvement Center" (p. 1445). Write an essay in which you examine how these poems portray modern warfare.

7. In 2011, the *Wall Street Journal* reported, "For many urban dwellers, the country conjures up images of clean air, fresh food, and physical activities. But these days, Americans residing in major cities live longer, healthier lives overall than their country cousins — a reversal from decades past." The article goes on to note that suburbanites, however, are, in most measures, the best off. Write an essay in which you discuss the positive and negative aspects of living in the city, the country, or the suburbs, as reflected in the works in this chapter, as well as in your other reading.

8. This period of American history is characterized by change, often startlingly rapid change. But think about what doesn't change, as shown in the works in this chapter, and write an essay in which you reflect on timeless American values, customs, and beliefs.

MLA Documentation Style

The Modern Language Association (MLA) documentation style is a set of rules for citing sources in formal research essays. It is the most common style for English classes, but be aware that other disciplines follow other models. By documenting sources properly, you make it easier for readers to find the exact texts that informed your opinions and supported your claims. For a teacher grading your paper, your use of systematic citation shows that you have been conscientious in investigating the topic and have avoided plagiarism. For readers who are interested in your paper, your list of works cited can help them learn more about the topic. Rhetorically speaking, a properly documented research paper boosts your ethos and appeals to logos.

Guidelines for In-Text Citations

MLA documentation requires in-text citations that refer to a list of works cited — an alphabetized list of all the sources you've drawn from. Sometimes all the necessary information for an in-text citation fits in the body of your sentence:

> On page 162 of *Aerotropolis: The Way We'll Live Next*, authors John D. Kasarda and Greg Lindsay suggest that downtown Detroit was doomed as soon as automobiles made the railroads less popular.

But more often you'll include some key information in parentheses just before the period. In this second example, the writer included the book title and authors' names in her sentence and, thus, only needed to provide the page number in parentheses.

> In *Aerotropolis: The Way We'll Live Next*, John D. Kasarda and Greg Lindsay suggest that downtown Detroit was doomed as soon as automobiles made the railroads less popular (162).

In this third example, there is no source information embedded in the sentence itself, so the in-text citation includes both the authors' names and the page number. Note that the title isn't included. With the authors' names, the reader has enough information to find the relevant entry on the list of works cited.

Although the growth of car manufacturing brought jobs to Detroit, America's drivable network of industrial cities and residential suburbs "bled entire cities dry: starting with Detroit" (Kasarda and Lindsay 180).

Guidelines for a List of Works Cited

Print Resources

1. Book with One Author

A book with one author serves as a general model for most MLA citations. Include author, title, city of publication, publisher, date of publication, and medium.

> Beavan, Colin. *No Impact Man*. New York: Farrar, 2009. Print.

2. Book with Multiple Authors

> Kasarda, John D., and Greg Lindsay. *Aerotropolis: The Way We'll Live Next*. New York: Farrar, 2011. Print.

3. Two or More Works by the Same Author

Multiple entries should be arranged alphabetically by title. The author's name appears at the beginning of the first entry but is replaced by three hyphens and a period in all subsequent entries.

> Gladwell, Malcolm. *Outliers: The Story of Success*. New York: Little, Brown, 2008. Print.
>
> ---. *What the Dog Saw, and Other Adventures*. New York: Little, Brown, 2009. Print.

4. Author and Editor Both Named

> Vidal, Gore. *The Selected Essays of Gore Vidal*. Ed. Jay Parini. New York: Vintage, 2009. Print.

Alternatively, to cite the editor's contribution, start with the editor's name.

> Parini, Jay, ed. *The Selected Essays of Gore Vidal*. By Gore Vidal. New York: Vintage, 2009. Print.

5. Anthology

> Oates, Joyce Carol, ed. *Telling Stories: An Anthology for Writers*. New York: Norton, 1997. Print.

Selection from an anthology:

> Washington Irving, "Rip Van Winkle." *Conversations in American Literature: Language, Rhetoric, Culture*. Ed. Robin Aufses et al. Boston: Bedford/ St. Martin's, 2015. 435–48. Print.

6. Translation

> Wiesel, Elie. *Night*. Trans. Marion Wiesel. New York: Hill-Farrar, 2006. Print.

7. Entry in a Reference Work

Because most reference works are alphabetized, you should omit page numbers.

> Lounsberry, Barbara. "Joan Didion." *Encyclopedia of the Essay*. Ed. Tracy Chandler. Chicago: Fitzroy Dearborn, 1997. Print.

For a well-known encyclopedia, use only the edition and year of publication. When an article is not attributed to an author, begin the entry with the article title.

> "Gilgamesh." *The Columbia Encyclopedia*. 5th ed. 1993. Print.

8. Sacred Text

Unless a specific published edition is being cited, sacred texts should be omitted from the Works Cited list.

> The New Testament. Trans. Richmond Lattimore. New York: North Point-Farrar, 1997. Print.

9. Article in a Journal

The title of the journal should be followed by the volume, issue, and year of the journal's publication.

> de Botton, Alain. "Treasure Hunt." *Lapham's Quarterly* 4.2 (2011): 205–10. Print.

10. Article in a Magazine

In a weekly:

> Menand, Louis. "The Unpolitical Animal: How Political Science Understands Voters." *New Yorker* 30 Aug. 2004: 92–96. Print.

In a monthly:

> Baker, Kevin. "Barack Hoover Obama: The Best and the Brightest Blow It Again." *Harper's* July 2009: 29–37. Print.

11. Article in a Newspaper

If you are citing a local paper that does not contain the city name in its title, add the city name in brackets after the title. When citing an article that does not appear on consecutive pages, list the first page followed by a plus sign. The edition only needs to be included if it is listed on the paper's masthead.

> Edge, John T. "Fast Food Even before Fast Food." *New York Times* 30 Sept. 2009, late ed.: D1+. Print.

12. Review

In a weekly:

> Davis, Jordan. "Happy Thoughts!" Rev. of *The Golden Age of Paraphernalia*, by Kevin Davies. *Nation* 23 Feb. 2009: 31–34. Print.

In a monthly:

> Simpson, Mona. "Imperfect Union." Rev. of *Mrs. Woolf and the Servants*, by Alison Light. *Atlantic Monthly* Jan.–Feb. 2009: 93–101. Print.

Electronic Resources

13. Article from a Database Accessed through a Subscription Service

Apply the normal rules for citing a journal article, but follow this with the name of the subscription service in italics, the medium used, and the date of access.

> Morano, Michele. "Boy Eats World." *Fourth Genre: Explorations in Nonfiction* 13.2 (2011): 31–35. *Project MUSE*. Web. 19 Nov. 2013.

14. Article in an Online Magazine

Follow the author name and article title with the name of the magazine in italics, the organization hosting the Web page (usually found at the very bottom of the site), the date published, the medium, and the date accessed. If there is no host or sponsor of the site, write *N.p.*, for "no publisher."

> Yoffe, Emily. "Full Metal Racket: Metal Detecting Is the World's Worst Hobby." *Slate*. The Slate Group, 25 Sept. 2009. Web. 20 Nov. 2013.

15. Article in an Online Newspaper

> Sisario, Ben. "Record Stores: Out of Sight, Not Obsolete." *New York Times*. New York Times, 29 Sept. 2009. Web. 20 Nov. 2013.

16. Online Review

> Stevens, Dana. "Catcher in the MRI." Rev. of *50/50*, dir. Adam Levine. *Slate*. The Slate Group, 30 Sept. 2011. Web. 18 Nov. 2013.

17. Entry in an Online Reference Work

> "John Ruskin." *Encyclopædia Britannica Online*. Encyclopædia Britannica, 2013. Web. 18 July 2013.

18. Work from a Web Site

> "Wallace Stevens (1879–1955)." *Poetryfoundation.org*. Poetry Foundation, 2013. Web. 19 Sept. 2013.

19. Entire Web Site

Web site with editor:

> Goldstein, Evan, ed. *Arts and Letters Daily*. Chronicle of Higher Education, 2013.
> Web. 2 Oct. 2013.

Web site without an editor:

> *Poets.org*. Academy of American Poets, 2013. Web. 2 May 2013.

Personal Web site:

> Mendelson, Edward. Home page. Columbia U, 2013. Web. 25 Nov. 2013.

20. Entire Web Log (Blog)

> If there is no host or sponsor of the site, write *N.p.*, for "no publisher."

> Holbo, John, ed. *The Valve*. N.p., 18 Mar. 2012. Web. 19 Nov. 2013.

21. Entry in a Wiki

> "Pre-Raphaelite Brotherhood." *Wikipedia*. Wikimedia Foundation, 12 Nov. 2013.
> Web. 25 Nov. 2013.

Other Sources

22. Film, Video, or DVD

Follow the title with the director, notable performers, the distribution company, the date of release, and the medium. For films viewed on the Web, follow this with the name of the Web site used to view the film, the medium (Web), and the date viewed. If citing a particular individual's work on the film, you may begin the entry with his or her name before the title.

Viewed in a theater:

> *The Hurt Locker*. Dir. Kathryn Bigelow. Summit, 2009. Film.

Viewed on DVD or videocassette (follow the original release date with the distributor and release date of the DVD or video):

> *Dead Poets Society*. Dir. Peter Weir. Perf. Robin Williams. 1989. Buena Vista Home
> Entertainment, 2006. DVD.

Viewed on the Web (use the original distributor and release date):

> Lynch, David, dir. *The Elephant Man*. Perf. Anthony Hopkins and John Hurt.
> Paramount, 1980. *Netflix*. Web. 2 Oct. 2009.

23. Interview

Include the name of the interviewer if it is someone of note.

Personal interview:

> Tripp, Lawrence. Personal interview. 14 Apr. 2014.

In print:

> Dylan, Bob. "Who Is This Bob Dylan?" *Esquire* 23 January 2014: 124+. Print.

On the radio:

> Gioia, Dana. Interview with Leonard Lopate. *The Leonard Lopate Show*. NPR. WNYC, New York, 19 July 2004. Radio.

On the Web:

> Gioia, Dana. Interview with Leonard Lopate. *The Leonard Lopate Show*. *NPR.org*. NPR, 19 July 2004. Web. 2 Oct. 2009.

24. Lecture or Speech

Viewed in person:

> Kass, Leon. "Looking for an Honest Man: Reflections of an Unlicensed Humanist." Jefferson Lecture in the Humanities. NEH. Warner Theatre, Washington, D.C. 22 May 2009. Lecture.

Viewed on the Web:

> Batuman, Elif. Lowell Humanities Series. Boston College. *Boston College Front Row*. Trustees of Boston College, 13 Oct. 2010. Web. 2 Oct. 2011.

25. Podcast

> "The Consequences to Come." Moderator Robert Silvers. Participants Darryl Pinckney, Ronald Dworkin, Joan Didion, and Mark Danner. *New York Review of Books*. NYREV, Inc., 24 Sept. 2008. MP3 File.

26. Work of Art or Photograph

In a museum:

> Hopper, Edward. *Nighthawks*. 1942. Oil on canvas. Art Institute, Chicago.

On the Web:

> Thiebaud, Wayne. *Three Machines*. 1963. De Young Museum, San Francisco. *Fine Arts Museums of San Francisco*. Web. 2 Oct. 2013.

In print:

> Clark, Edward. *Navy CPO Graham Jackson Plays "Goin' Home."* 1945. Life Gallery of
> Photography. *The Great LIFE Photographers.* Eds. of *Life.* New York: Bulfinch,
> 2004. 78–79. Print.

27. Map or Chart

In print:

> "U.S. Personal Savings Rate, 1929–1999." Chart. *Credit Card Nation: The
> Consequences of America's Addiction to Credit.* By Robert D. Manning. New York:
> Basic, 2000. 100. Print.

On the Web:

> "1914 New Balkan States and Central Europe Map." Map. *National Geographic.*
> National Geographic Society, 2013. Web. 25 Oct. 2013.

28. Cartoon or Comic Strip

In print:

> Vey, P. C. Cartoon. *New Yorker* 10 Nov. 2008: 54. Print.

On the Web:

> Davis, Jim. "Garfield." Comic strip. *Garfield.com.* Paws, 24 July 2001. Web.
> 2 Oct. 2009.

29. Advertisement

In print:

> Rosetta Stone. Advertisement. *Harper's* Aug. 2008: 21. Print.

On the Web:

> Zurich. Advertisement. *Wall Street Journal.* Dow Jones, Inc., 2 Oct. 2009. Web.
> 2 Oct. 2009.

John Cole/Cagle Cartoons, Inc.

National Archives Still Picture Branch

Artists Posters, Prints and Photographs Division, Library of Congress

Feeding Kids Meat Is

CHILD ABUSE

Fight the Fat: Go Vegan   PeTA

Ad courtesy of People for the Ethical Treatment of Animals, www.peta.org. Image courtesy of istock.

DODGE DURANGO. This is the most affordable SUV with a V-8. Dodge Durango. With nearly four tons of towing,* this baby carries around chunks of those wimpy wanna-bes in its tail pipe. For more info, call 800-4 A DODGE or visit dodge.com

GRAB LIFE BY THE HORNS

DODGE

IT'S A BIG FAT JUICY CHEESEBURGER IN A LAND OF TOFU.

*Depending on model and when properly equipped.

Dodge and Durango are registered trademarks of Chrysler Group LLC.

Image copyright © The Metropolitan Museum of Art.
Image source: Art Resource, NY

Winslow Homer, *The Veteran in a New Field*, 1865, oil on canvas, $24^1/8" \times 38^1/8"$, Metropolitan Museum of Art, New York.

Corcoran Gallery of Art, Washington D.C., USA/Gift of Mary (Mrs. Albert) Bierstadt/The Bridgeman Art Library

Albert Bierstadt, *The Last of the Buffalo*, 1888, oil on canvas, $71" \times 118^3/4"$, Corcoran Gallery, Washington, D.C.

© 2013 Washington State History Society. All rights reserved. Web site by SiteCrafting.

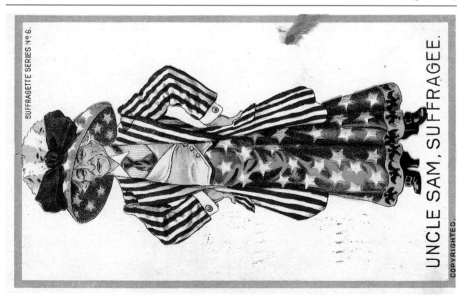

Courtesy of the Alice Marshall Women's History Collection, Series VII: Postcards, AKM 91/1.2, Archives and Special Collections, Penn State Harrisburg Library, University Libraries, Pennsylvania State University.

The Newberry Library, Chicago

Image copyright © The Metropolitan Museum of Art. Image source: Art Resource, NY

Marsden Hartley, *Portrait of a German Officer*, 1914, oil on canvas, 68¼″×41⅜″, Metropolitan Museum of Art, New York.

Image copyright © The Metropolitan Museum of Art. Image source: Art Resource, NY.

Charles Demuth, *I Saw the Figure 5 in Gold*, 1928, 35½″×30″ oil on cardboard, Metropolitan Museum of Art, New York.

Museum purchase with funds from the Hope Fund, Indiana University Art Museum, 42.1. Photograph by: Michael Cavanagh and Kevin Montague.

Stuart Davis, *Swing Landscape*, 1938, 86³⁄4" × 172⁷⁄8", oil on canvas, Indiana University Art Museum, Bloomington.

Whitney Museum of American Art

William Henry Johnson, *Jitterbugs VI*, c. 1941, hand-colored screenprint, 17¹⁄16" × 11¹⁄4", Whitney Museum of American Art, New York.

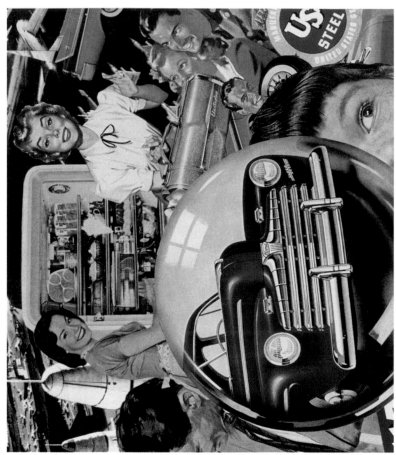

Collage by Sally Edelstein, sallyedelsteincollage.com.

Glossary

ad hominem   Latin for "to the man," this fallacy refers to the specific diversionary tactic of switching the argument from the issue at hand to the character of the other speaker. If you argue that a park in your community should not be renovated because the person supporting it was arrested during a domestic dispute, then you are guilty of using an *ad hominem* fallacy.

ad populum (**bandwagon appeal**)   Latin for "to the people," this fallacy occurs when evidence used to defend an argument boils down to "everybody's doing it, so it must be a good thing to do."

> *You should vote to elect Rachel Johnson — she has a strong lead in the polls.*

Polling higher does not necessarily make Senator Johnson the "best" candidate; it only makes her the most popular.

allegory   A literary work that portrays abstract ideas concretely. Characters in an allegory are frequently personifications of abstract ideas and are given names that refer to these ideas. *See Washington Irving, "Rip Van Winkle," p. 435.*

alliteration   Repetition of the same consonant sound at the beginning of several words or syllables in sequence.

> *Let us go forth to lead the land we love.*   — JOHN F. KENNEDY

allusion   Brief reference to a person, an event, or a place (real or fictitious) or to a work of art.

> *Let both sides unite to heed in all corners of the earth the command of Isaiah.*
>   — JOHN F. KENNEDY

analogy   A comparison between two seemingly dissimilar things. Often, an analogy uses something simple or familiar to explain something complex or unfamiliar.

> *"My boy, you've got to know the shape of the river perfectly. It is all there is left to steer by on a very dark night. Every thing else is blotted out and gone. But mind you, it hasn't the same shape in the night that it has in the daytime."*
> *"How on earth am I ever going to learn it, then?"*

"How do you follow a hall at home in the dark? Because you know the shape of it. You can't see it." — MARK TWAIN

anaphora   Repetition of a word or phrase at the beginning of successive phrases, clauses, or lines.

. . . not as a call to bear arms, though arms we need — not as a call to battle, though embattled we are . . . — JOHN F. KENNEDY

anecdote   A brief story used to illustrate a point or claim.

annotation   The taking of notes directly on a text. See p. 52.

antimetabole   Repetition of words in reverse order.

Ask not what your country can do for you — ask what you can do for your country. — JOHN F. KENNEDY

antithesis   Opposition, or contrast, of ideas or words in a parallel construction.

We shall . . . support any friend, oppose any foe . . . — JOHN F. KENNEDY

apostrophe   A direct address to an abstraction (such as Time), a thing (the Wind), an animal, or an imaginary or absent person.

Make me, O Lord, thy Spining Wheele complete. — EDWARD TAYLOR

appeal to false authority   This fallacy occurs when someone who has no credibility to speak on an issue is cited as an authority. A TV star, for instance, is not a medical expert, though pharmaceutical advertisements often use such celebrities to endorse products.

According to former congressional leader Ari Miller, the Himalayas have an estimated Yeti population of between 300 and 500 individuals.

archaic diction   Old-fashioned or outdated choice of words.

. . . beliefs for which our forebears fought . . . — JOHN F. KENNEDY

argument   A process of reasoned inquiry. A persuasive discourse resulting in a coherent and considered movement from a claim to a conclusion.

Aristotelian triangle   See **rhetorical triangle**.

assertion   A statement that presents a claim or thesis.

assonance   The repetition of vowel sounds in a sequence of words.

That church so lone, the log-built one,
That echoed to many a parting groan
      And natural prayer
      Of dying foemen mingled there. — HERMAN MELVILLE

assumption   See **warrant**.

asyndeton   Omission of conjunctions between coordinate phrases, clauses, or words.

We shall pay any price, bear any burden, meet any hardship, support any friend, oppose any foe to assure the survival and the success of liberty. — JOHN F. KENNEDY

audience   The listener, viewer, or reader of a text. Most texts are likely to have multiple audiences.

> *Gehrig's audience was his teammates and the fans in the stadium that day, but it was also the teams he played against, the fans listening on the radio, and posterity — us.*

backing   In the Toulmin model, backing consists of further assurances or data without which the assumption lacks authority. For an example, see **Toulmin model**.

bandwagon appeal   See ***ad populum*** (**bandwagon appeal**).

begging the question   A fallacy in which a claim is based on evidence or support that is in doubt. It "begs" a question whether the support itself is sound.

> *Giving students easy access to a wealth of facts and resources online allows them to develop critical thinking skills.*

bias   A prejudice or preconceived notion that prevents a person from approaching a topic in a neutral or an objective way. While you can be biased *toward* something, the most common usage has a negative connotation.

blank verse   Unrhymed iambic pentameter. See also **iambic pentameter**. *See Robert Frost, "Mending Wall," p. 1080.*

caesura   A pause within a line of poetry, sometimes punctuated, sometimes not, that often mirrors natural speech.

> *The apparition of these faces in the crowd;*
> *Petals on a wet, black bough.*   —EZRA POUND

characterization   The method by which the author builds, or reveals, a character; it can be direct or indirect. **Indirect characterization** means that an author shows rather than tells us what a character is like through what the character says, does, or thinks or through what others say about the character. **Direct characterization** occurs when a narrator tells the reader who a character is by describing the background, motivation, temperament, or appearance of a character.

circular reasoning   A fallacy in which the argument repeats the claim as a way to provide evidence.

> *You can't give me a C; I'm an A student!*

claim   Also called an assertion or proposition, a claim states the argument's main idea or position. A claim differs from a topic or subject in that a claim has to be arguable.

claim of fact   A claim of fact asserts that something is true or not true.

> *The number of suicides and homicides committed by teenagers, most often young men, has exploded in the last three decades.*   —ANNA QUINDLEN

claim of policy   A claim of policy proposes a change.

> *Yet one solution continues to elude us, and that is ending the ignorance about mental health, and moving it from the margins of care and into the mainstream where it belongs.*   —ANNA QUINDLEN

claim of value   A claim of value argues that something is good or bad, right or wrong.

> *There's a plague on all our houses, and since it doesn't announce itself with lumps or spots or protest marches, it has gone unremarked in the quiet suburbs and busy cities where it has been laying waste.*   — ANNA QUINDLEN

classical oration   Five-part argument structure used by classical rhetoricians. The five parts of a classical oration are

> **introduction (*exordium*)**   Introduces the reader to the subject under discussion.

> **narration (*narratio*)**   Provides factual information and background material on the subject at hand or establishes why the subject is a problem that needs addressing.

> **confirmation (*confirmatio*)**   Usually the major part of the text, the confirmation includes the proof needed to make the writer's case.

> **refutation (*refutatio*)**   Addresses the counterargument. It is a bridge between the writer's proof and conclusion.

> **conclusion (*peroratio*)**   Brings the essay to a satisfying close.

See Sandra Day O'Connor and Roy Romer, "Not by Math Alone," p. 117.

closed thesis   A closed thesis is a statement of the main idea of the argument that also previews the major points the writer intends to make.

> *The three-dimensional characters, exciting plot, and complex themes of the Harry Potter series make them not only legendary children's books but enduring literary classics.*

complex sentence   A sentence that includes one independent clause and at least one dependent clause.

> *If a free society cannot help the many who are poor, it cannot save the few who are rich.*   — JOHN F. KENNEDY

compound sentence   A sentence that includes at least two independent clauses.

> *The energy, the faith, the devotion which we bring to this endeavor will light our country and all who serve it—and the glow from that fire can truly light the world.*   — JOHN F. KENNEDY

concession   An acknowledgment that an opposing argument may be true or reasonable. In a strong argument, a concession is usually accompanied by a refutation challenging the validity of the opposing argument.

> *Lou Gehrig concedes what some of his listeners may think—that his bad break is a cause for discouragement or despair.*

connotation   Meanings or associations that readers have with a word beyond its dictionary definition, or denotation. Connotations are often positive or negative, and they often greatly affect the author's tone. Consider the connotations of the words below, all of which mean "overweight."

> *That cat is* plump. *That cat is* fat. *That cat is* obese.

context   The circumstances, atmosphere, attitudes, and events surrounding a **text**.

> *The context for Lou Gehrig's speech is the recent announcement of his illness and his subsequent retirement, but also the poignant contrast between his potent career and his debilitating disease.*

counterargument   An opposing argument to the one a writer is putting forward. Rather than ignoring a counterargument, a strong writer will usually address it through the process of concession and refutation.

> *Some of Lou Gehrig's listeners might have argued that his bad break was a cause for discouragement or despair.*

counterargument thesis   A type of thesis statement that includes a brief counterargument, usually qualified with *although* or *but*.

> *Although the Harry Potter series may have some literary merit, its popularity has less to do with storytelling than with merchandising.*

cumulative sentence   A sentence that completes the main idea at the beginning of the sentence and then builds and adds on.

> *But neither can two great and powerful groups of nations take comfort from our present course — both sides overburdened by the cost of modern weapons, both rightly alarmed by the steady spread of the deadly atom, yet both racing to alter that uncertain balance of terror that stays the hand of mankind's final war.*
> — John F. Kennedy

deduction   Deduction is a logical process wherein you reach a conclusion by starting with a general principle or universal truth (a major premise) and applying it to a specific case (a minor premise). The process of deduction is usually demonstrated in the form of a syllogism:

MAJOR PREMISE   Exercise contributes to better health.

MINOR PREMISE   Yoga is a type of exercise.

CONCLUSION   Yoga contributes to better health.

diction   A speaker's choice of words. Analysis of diction looks at these choices and what they add to the speaker's message.

either/or (false dilemma)   In this fallacy, the speaker presents two extreme options as the only possible choices.

> *Either we agree to higher taxes, or our grandchildren will be mired in debt.*

ekphrasis   Ekphrastic art or writing comments on another genre—for instance, a work of art that comments on a piece of music, or a poem that comments on a painting. *See Stuart Davis, Swing Landscape, p. 1198, or Jayne Cortez, Jazz Fan Looks Back, p. 1207.*

end rhyme   See **rhyme**.

enjambment   A poetic technique in which one line ends without a pause and continues to the next line to complete its meaning; also referred to as a "run-on line."

> Icicles filled the long window
> With barbaric glass.   — Wallace Stevens

enthymeme   Essentially, a syllogism with one of the premises implied and taken for granted as true.

> You should take her class because I learned so much from her last year.

(Implied premise: If you take her class, you will learn a lot too.)

epigram   A short, witty statement designed to surprise an audience or a reader.

> To be great is to be misunderstood.   — Ralph Waldo Emerson

epigraph   A quotation preceding a work of literature that helps set the text's mood or suggests its themes.

> Mistah Kurtz — he dead.
> A penny for the Old Guy   — T. S. Eliot

equivocation   A fallacy that uses a term with two or more meanings in an attempt to misrepresent or deceive.

> We will bring our enemies to justice, or we will bring justice to them.

ethos   Greek for "character." Speakers appeal to ethos to demonstrate that they are credible and trustworthy to speak on a given topic. Ethos is established by both who you are and what you say.

> Lou Gehrig brings the ethos of being a legendary athlete to his speech, yet in it he establishes a different kind of ethos — that of a regular guy and a good sport who shares the audience's love of baseball and family. And like them, he has known good luck and bad breaks.

eulogy   A poem, a speech, or another work written in great praise of something or someone, usually a person no longer living. *See* Frederick Douglass, "Reminiscences of Abraham Lincoln by Distinguished Men of His Time," p. 699, or Walt Whitman, "O Captain! My Captain!," p. 659.

eye rhyme   See **rhyme**.

fallacy   See **logical fallacies**.

false dilemma   See **either/or**.

faulty analogy   A fallacy that occurs when an analogy compares not comparable. For instance, to argue that we should legalize human euthanasia, since we all agree that it is humane to put terminally ill animals to sleep, ignores significant emotional and ethical differences between the ways we view humans and animals.

figurative language (figure of speech)   Nonliteral language, often evoking strong imagery, sometimes referred to as a trope. Figures of speech often compare one thing to another either explicitly (using simile) or implicitly (using metaphor). Other forms of figurative language include **personification**, **paradox**, overstatement (**hyperbole**), **understatement**, **metonymy**, **synecdoche**, and **irony**.

first-hand evidence   Evidence based on something the writer *knows*, whether from personal experience, observation, or general knowledge of events.

form   Refers to the defining structural characteristics of a work, especially a poem (i.e., meter and rhyme scheme). Often poets work within set forms, such as the **sonnet**, which require adherence to fixed conventions.

hasty generalization   A fallacy in which a faulty conclusion is reached because of inadequate evidence.

> *Smoking isn't bad for you; my great aunt smoked a pack a day and lived to be ninety.*

hortative sentence   Sentence that exhorts, urges, entreats, implores, or calls to action.

> *Let both sides explore what problems unite us instead of belaboring those problems which divide us.* —JOHN F. KENNEDY

hyperbole   Deliberate exaggeration used for emphasis or to produce a comic or an ironic effect; an overstatement to make a point.

> *. . . I am the only Negro in the United States whose grandfather on the mother's side was not an Indian chief.* —ZORA NEALE HURSTON

iambic pentameter   An iamb, the most common metrical foot in English poetry, is made up of an unstressed syllable followed by a stressed one. Iambic pentameter, then, is a rhythmic meter containing five iambs. Unrhymed iambic pentameter is called blank verse. See also **meter; blank verse**.

> *Whenever Richard Cory went down town,*
>
> *We people on the pavement looked at him:* —E. A. ROBINSON

imagery   A description of how something looks, feels, tastes, smells, or sounds. Imagery may use literal or figurative language to appeal to the senses.

> *None of them knew the color of the sky. Their eyes glanced level, and were fastened upon the waves that swept toward them. These waves were of the hue of slate, save for the tops, which were of foaming white, and all of the men knew the colors of the sea.* —STEPHEN CRANE

imperative sentence   Sentence used to command or enjoin.

> *My fellow citizens of the world: ask not what America will do for you, but what together we can do for the freedom of man.* —JOHN F. KENNEDY

induction   From the Latin *inducere*, "to lead into," induction is a logical process wherein you reason from particulars to universals, using specific cases in order to draw a conclusion, which is also called a generalization.

> Regular exercise promotes weight loss.
>
> Exercise lowers stress levels.
>
> Exercise improves mood and outlook.
>
> GENERALIZATION   Exercise contributes to better health.

internal rhyme   See **rhyme**.

inversion   Inverted order of words in a sentence (deviation from the standard subject-verb-object order).

> *United there is little we cannot do in a host of cooperative ventures. Divided there is little we can do.* — JOHN F. KENNEDY

irony, dramatic   Tension created by the contrast between what a character says or thinks and what the audience or readers know to be true; as a result of this technique, some words and actions in a story or play take on a different meaning for the reader than they do for the characters. *See Ambrose Bierce, "An Occurrence at Owl Creek Bridge," p. 875.*

irony, situational   A discrepancy between what is expected and what actually happens. *See Jourdon Anderson, "To My Old Master," p. 829.*

irony, verbal   A figure of speech that occurs when a speaker or character says one thing but means something else or when what is said is the opposite of what is expected, creating a noticeable incongruity. **Sarcasm** involves verbal irony used derisively.

> *Without a woman to rule him and think for him, [man] is a truly lamentable spectacle: a baby with whiskers, a rabbit with the frame of an aurochs, a feeble and preposterous caricature of God.* — H. L. MENCKEN

juxtaposition   Placement of two things closely together to emphasize similarities or differences.

> *The nations of Asia and Africa are moving at jet-like speed toward gaining political independence, but we still creep at horse-and-buggy pace toward gaining a cup of coffee at a lunch counter.* — MARTIN LUTHER KING JR.

logical fallacies   Logical fallacies are potential vulnerabilities or weaknesses in an argument. They often arise from a failure to make a logical connection between the claim and the evidence used to support it.

logos   Greek for "embodied thought." Speakers appeal to logos, or reason, by offering clear, rational ideas and using specific details, examples, facts, statistics, or expert testimony to back them up.

> *Gehrig starts with the thesis that he is "the luckiest man on the face of the earth" and supports it with two points: (1) the love and kindness he's received in his seventeen years of playing baseball and (2) a list of great people who have been his friends, family, and teammates.*

metaphor   Figure of speech that compares two things without using *like* or *as*.

> *And if a beachhead of cooperation may push back the jungle of suspicion . . .* — JOHN F. KENNEDY

meter   The formal, regular organization of stressed and unstressed syllables, measured in feet. A foot is distinguished by the number of syllables it contains and how stress is placed on the syllables — stressed (´) or unstressed (˘). There are five typical feet in English verse: iamb (˘ ´), trochee (´ ˘), anapest (˘ ˘ ´), dactyl (´ ˘ ˘), and spondee (´ ´). Some meters dictate the number of feet per line, the most common being tetrameter, pentameter, and hexameter, having four, five, and six feet, respectively.

metonymy   Figure of speech in which something is represented by another thing that is related to it or emblematic of it.

> *The pen is mightier than the sword.*

modernism   In literature, modernism refers to a movement of writers that reached its apex between the 1920s and 1930s and expressed disillusionment with contemporary Western civilization, especially in the wake of World War I's mindless slaughter. Rejecting the conventions of the Victorian era, these writers experimented with form and used insights from recent writings by Freud and Jung about the unconscious. They viewed art as restorative and frequently ordered their writing around symbols and allusions. Some American modernist writers include T. S. Eliot (p. 1113), Wallace Stevens (p. 1084), William Carlos Williams (p. 1106), and William Faulkner (p. 1155).

modifier   An adjective, an adverb, a phrase, or a clause that modifies a noun, pronoun, or verb. The purpose of a modifier is usually to describe, focus, or qualify.

> *. . . high above the forest wall a clean-stemmed dead tree waved a single leafy*
> *bough that glowed like a flame in the unobstructed splendor that was flowing*
> *from the sun.*   — MARK TWAIN

mood   The feeling or atmosphere created by a text.

narrative frame   Also known as a frame story, a narrative frame is a plot device in which the author places the main narrative of his or her work within another narrative — the narrative frame. This exterior narrative usually serves to explain the main narrative in some way. *See Washington Irving, "Rip Van Winkle," p. 435.*

near rhyme   See **rhyme**.

nominalization   The process of changing a verb into a noun.

> *Discuss* becomes *discussion.*   *Depend* becomes *dependence.*

occasion   The time and place a speech is given or a piece is written.

> *In the case of Gehrig's speech, the occasion is Lou Gehrig Appreciation Day. More*
> *specifically, his moment came at home plate between games of a doubleheader.*

onomatopoeia   Use of words that refer to sounds and whose pronunciations mimic those sounds.

> *That echoed to many a parting groan . . .*
> *And all is hushed at Shiloh.*   — HERMAN MELVILLE

open thesis   An open thesis is one that does not list all the points the writer intends to cover in the essay.

The popularity of the Harry Potter series demonstrates that simplicity trumps complexity when it comes to the taste of readers, both young and old.

oxymoron　A paradox made up of two seemingly contradictory words.

But this peaceful revolution . . .　　　　　　　　— JOHN F. KENNEDY

paradox　A statement or situation that is seemingly contradictory on the surface but delivers an ironic truth.

A smart Indian is a dangerous person.　　　　　— SHERMAN ALEXIE

We are starved before we are hungry.　　　— HENRY DAVID THOREAU

parallelism　Similarity of structure in a pair or series of related words, phrases, or clauses.

Let both sides explore. . . . Let both sides, for the first time, formulate serious and precise proposals. . . . Let both sides seek to invoke. . . . Let both sides unite to heed . . .　　　　　　— JOHN F. KENNEDY

passive voice　A sentence employs passive voice when the subject doesn't act but rather is acted on.

I know not whether an Account is given of the means I used to establish the Philadelphia publick Library.　　　— BENJAMIN FRANKLIN

pathos　Greek for "suffering" or "experience." Speakers appeal to pathos to emotionally motivate their audience. More specific appeals to pathos might play on the audience's values, desires, and hopes, on the one hand, or fears and prejudices, on the other.

The most striking appeal to pathos is the poignant contrast between Gehrig's horrible diagnosis and his public display of courage.

periodic sentence　A sentence whose main clause is withheld until the end.

To that world assembly of sovereign states, the United Nations, our last best hope in an age where the instruments of war have far outpaced the instruments of peace, we renew our pledge of support.　　　　— JOHN F. KENNEDY

persona　Greek for "mask." The face or character that a speaker shows to his or her audience.

Lou Gehrig is a famous baseball hero, but in his speech he presents himself as a common man who is modest and thankful for the opportunities he's had.

personification　Attribution of a lifelike quality to an inanimate object or an idea.

. . . with history the final judge of our deeds . . .　　　— JOHN F. KENNEDY

poetic syntax　Similar to **syntax** in prose, poetic syntax also includes the arrangement of words into lines of poetry — where they break and do not break, the use of **enjambment** or **caesura**, and line lengths and patterns.

polemic   Greek for "hostile." An aggressive argument that tries to establish the superiority of one opinion over all others, a polemic generally does not concede that opposing opinions have any merit.

polysyndeton   The deliberate use of multiple conjunctions between coordinate phrases, clauses, or words.

> *I paid for my plane ticket and the taxes and the fees and the charge for the checked bag and five dollars for a bottle of water.*

point of view   The perspective from which a work is told. The most common narrative vantage points are

> **first person**   Told by a narrator who is a character in the story and who refers to him- or herself as "I." First-person narrators are sometimes unreliable narrators because they don't always see the big picture or because they might be biased.
>
> **second person**   Though rare, some stories are told using second-person pronouns (*you*). This casts the reader as a character in the story.
>
> **third-person limited omniscient**   Told by a narrator who relates the action using third-person pronouns (*he, she, it*). This narrator is usually privy to the thoughts and actions of only one character.
>
> **third-person omniscient**   Told by a narrator using third-person pronouns. This narrator is privy to the thoughts and actions of all the characters in the story.

post hoc ergo propter hoc   This fallacy is Latin for "after which therefore because of which," meaning that it is incorrect to always claim that something is a cause just because it happened earlier. One may loosely summarize this fallacy by saying that correlation does not imply causation.

> *We elected Johnson as president and look where it got us: hurricanes, floods, stock market crashes.*

propaganda   The spread of ideas and information to further a cause. In its negative sense, propaganda is the use of rumors, lies, disinformation, and scare tactics in order to damage or promote a cause.

pun   A play on words that derives its humor from the replacement of one word with another that has a similar pronunciation or spelling but a different meaning. A pun can also derive humor from the use of a single word that has more than one meaning.

> *Offhand, I can think of two Jacks — there was Jack of "Jack and the Beanstalk," and Jack the Ripper, who cut quite a figure in his day.*   — GROUCHO MARX

purpose   The goal the speaker wants to achieve.

> *One of Gehrig's chief purposes in delivering his farewell address is to thank his fans and his teammates, but he also wants to demonstrate that he remains positive: he emphasizes his past luck and present optimism and downplays his illness.*

qualified argument An argument that is not absolute. It acknowledges the merits of an opposing view but develops a stronger case for its own position.

qualifier Qualifiers are words like *usually, probably, maybe, in most cases,* and *most likely* that are used to temper claims a bit, making them less absolute.

> UNQUALIFIED Dogs are more obedient than cats.

> QUALIFIED Dogs are <u>generally</u> more obedient than cats.

qualitative evidence Evidence supported by reason, tradition, or precedent.

quantitative evidence Quantitative evidence includes things that can be measured, cited, counted, or otherwise represented in numbers — for instance, statistics, surveys, polls, and census information.

rebuttal In the Toulmin model, a rebuttal gives voice to possible objections. For an example, see **Toulmin model**.

red herring A type of logical fallacy wherein the speaker relies on distraction to derail an argument, usually by skipping to a new or an irrelevant topic. The term derives from the dried fish that trainers used to distract dogs when teaching them to hunt foxes.

> *We can debate these regulations until the cows come home, but what the American people want to know is, when are we going to end this partisan bickering?*

reservation In the Toulmin model, a reservation explains the terms and conditions necessitated by the qualifier. For an example, see **Toulmin model**.

rhetoric Aristotle defined rhetoric as "the faculty of observing in any given case the available means of persuasion." In other words, it is the art of finding ways of persuading an audience.

rhetorical appeals Rhetorical techniques used to persuade an audience by emphasizing what they find most important or compelling. The three major appeals are to **ethos** (character), **logos** (reason), and **pathos** (emotion).

rhetorical question Figure of speech in the form of a question posed for rhetorical effect rather than for the purpose of getting an answer.

> *Will you join in that historic effort?*   —JOHN F. KENNEDY

rhetorical triangle (Aristotelian triangle) A diagram that illustrates the interrelationship among the speaker, audience, and subject in determining a text. *See p. 3.*

rhyme The poetic repetition of the same (or similar) vowel sounds or of vowel and consonant combinations. A rhyme at the end of two or more lines of poetry is called an **end rhyme**. A rhyme that occurs within a line is called an **internal rhyme**. A rhyme that pairs sounds that are similar but not exactly the same is called a **near rhyme** or a **slant rhyme**. A rhyme that only works because the words look the same is called an **eye rhyme** or a **sight rhyme**. Rhyme often follows a pattern, called a **rhyme scheme**.

end rhyme
Thou ill-formed offspring of my feeble brain,
Who after birth didst by my side remain,   — ANNE BRADSTREET

internal rhyme
And crown thy good with brotherhood
From sea to shining sea!   — KATHARINE LEE BATES

near rhyme or slant rhyme
Let poets and historians set these forth,
My obscure lines shall not so dim their worth.   — ANNE BRADSTREET

eye rhyme
Unmoved — she notes the Chariots — pausing —
At her low Gate —
Unmoved — an Emperor be kneeling
Upon her Mat —   — EMILY DICKINSON

Rogerian arguments   Developed by psychiatrist Carl Rogers, Rogerian arguments are based on the assumption that fully understanding an opposing position is essential to responding to it persuasively and refuting it in a way that is accommodating rather than alienating.

satire   The use of irony or sarcasm as a means of critique, usually of a society or an individual.

scheme   Artful syntax; a deviation from the normal order of words. Common schemes include **parallelism, juxtaposition, antithesis,** and **antimetabole.**

second-hand evidence   Evidence that is accessed through research, reading, and investigation. It includes factual and historical information, expert opinion, and quantitative data.

simile   A figure of speech used to explain or clarify an idea by comparing it explicitly to something else, using the words *like, as,* or *as though.*

> *The linear, two-dimensional action of soccer is like the rocking of a boat but without any storm and while the boat has not even left the dock.*   — STEPHEN H. WEBB

slant rhyme   See **rhyme.**

slippery slope   A logical fallacy created by a cause having an illogically exaggerated effect or series of effects.

> *No, we can't get a dog. If we buy a dog, I'll have to walk it outside, and then I'll get bitten by a tick and wind up with Lyme disease.*

SOAPS   A mnemonic device that stands for Subject, Occasion, Audience, Purpose, and Speaker. It is a handy way to remember the various elements that make up the rhetorical situation.

sonnet, Petrarchan   Also known as the Italian sonnet, its fourteen lines are divided into an octave and a sestet. The octave rhymes *abba, abba;* the sestet that follows can have a variety of different rhyme schemes: *cdcdcd, cdecde, cddcdd. See Paul Laurence Dunbar, "Douglass," p. 897.*

sonnet, Shakespearean Also known as the English sonnet, its fourteen lines are composed of three quatrains and a couplet, and its rhyme scheme is *abab, cdcd, efef, gg. See Robert Hayden, "Frederick Douglass," p. 898.*

sound The musical quality of poetry, as created through techniques such as **rhyme, enjambment, caesura, alliteration, assonance, onomatopoeia,** and **rhythm.**

speaker The person or group who creates a text. This might be a politician who delivers a speech, a commentator who writes an article, an artist who draws a political cartoon, or even a company that commissions an advertisement.

> *In his farewell address, the speaker is not just Lou Gehrig, but baseball hero and ALS victim Lou Gehrig, a common man who is modest and thankful for the opportunities he's had.*

stance A speaker's attitude toward the audience (different from **tone**, which is the speaker's attitude toward the subject).

straw man A fallacy that occurs when a speaker chooses a deliberately poor or oversimplified example in order to ridicule and refute an idea.

> *Politician X proposes that we put astronauts on Mars in the next four years. Politician Y ridicules this proposal by saying that his opponent is looking for "little green men in outer space."*

subject The topic of a text. What the text is *about.*

> *Lou Gehrig's subject in his speech is his illness, but it is also an expression of his gratitude for all the lucky breaks that preceded his diagnosis.*

syllogism A logical structure that uses the major premise and minor premise to reach a necessary conclusion.

> MAJOR PREMISE   Exercise contributes to better health.
>
> MINOR PREMISE   Yoga is a type of exercise.
>
> CONCLUSION   Yoga contributes to better health.

symbol A setting, an object, or an event in a story that carries more than literal meaning and therefore represents something significant to understanding the meaning of a work of literature.

> *In "The Chrysanthemums," the flowers represent the beauty and grace the main character longs for but that elude her.*

synecdoche Figure of speech that uses a part to represent the whole.

> *In your hands, my fellow citizens, more than mine, will rest the final success or failure of our course.*
> — JOHN F. KENNEDY

syntax The arrangement of words into phrases, clauses, and sentences. This includes word order (subject-verb-object, for instance, or an inverted structure); the length and structure of sentences (simple, **compound**, **complex**, or compound-complex); and such schemes as **parallelism**, **juxtaposition**, **antithesis**, and **antimetabole**.

synthesis Combining two or more ideas in order to create something more complex in support of a new idea.

text While this term generally refers to the written word, in the humanities it has come to mean any cultural product that can be "read" — meaning not just consumed and comprehended but also investigated. This includes fiction, nonfiction, poetry, political cartoons, fine art, photography, performances, fashion, cultural trends, and much more.

tone A speaker's attitude toward the subject as conveyed by the speaker's stylistic and rhetorical choices.

Toulmin model An approach to analyzing and constructing arguments created by British philosopher Stephen Toulmin in his book *The Uses of Argument* (1958). The Toulmin model can be stated as a template:

> Because (evidence as support), therefore (claim), since (warrant or assumption), on account of (backing), unless (reservation).

> *Because it is raining, therefore I should probably take my umbrella, since it will keep me dry, on account of its waterproof material, unless, of course, there is a hole in it.*

trope Artful diction; from the Greek word for "turning," a figure of speech such as **metaphor**, **simile**, **hyperbole**, **metonymy**, or **synecdoche**.

understatement A figure of speech in which something is presented as less important, dire, urgent, good, and so on than it actually is, often for satiric or comical effect. Also called *litotes*, it is the opposite of **hyperbole**.

> *The night in prison was novel and interesting enough.*   — HENRY DAVID THOREAU

warrant In the Toulmin model, the warrant expresses the assumption necessarily shared by the speaker and the audience.

wit In rhetoric, the use of laughter, humor, irony, and satire in the confirmation or refutation of an argument.

zeugma Use of two different words in a grammatically similar way that produces different, often incongruous, meanings.

> *Now the trumpet summons us again — not as a call to bear arms, though arms we need — not as a call to battle, though embattled we are — but a call to bear the burden.*
> — JOHN F. KENNEDY

> *And Benjamin tries to shove me into a barbed wire paddock and make me grow potatoes or Chicagoes.*
> — D. H. LAWRENCE

Aaron Abeyta. "Thirteen Ways of Looking at a Tortilla." From *Colcha*. Copyright © 2001 by Aaron Abeyta. Reprinted by permission of University Press of Colorado.

Sherman Alexie. "Superman and Me." Originally published in *The Most Wonderful Books* by Milkweed Editions. Copyright © 1997 by Sherman Alexie. All rights reserved. Used by permission of Nancy Stauffer Associates. "My Heroes Have Never Been Cowboys." From *The First Indian on the Moon*. Copyright © 1993 by Sherman Alexie. Reprinted by permission of Hanging Loose Press.

Paula Gunn Allen. Excerpt from *Pocahontas: Medicine Woman, Spy, Entrepreneur Diplomat* (pp. 17–19, 54, 59–61). Copyright © 2003 by Paula Gunn Allen. Reprinted by permission of HarperCollins Publishers.

Antonio Alvarez. Excerpt from "Out of My Hands." From *Underground Grads: UCLA Undocumented Immigrant Students Speak Out* (pp. 52–56). Copyright © 2008 UCLA Center for Labor Research and Education. Reprinted with permission.

Julia Alvarez. "Snow." From *How the Garcia Girls Lost Their Accents*. Copyright © 1991 by Julia Alvarez. Published by Algonquin Books of Chapel Hill. Reprinted by permission of Susan Bergholz Literary Services, New York, NY and Lamy, NM. All rights reserved.

Benjamin Anastas. "The Foul Reign of 'Self-Reliance.'" From *The New York Times*, December 4, 2011. Copyright © 2011 by The New York Times. All rights reserved. Used by permission and protected by the Copyright Laws of the United States. The printing, copying, redistribution, or retransmission of this Content without express written permission is prohibited. www.nytimes.com

Anne Applebaum. "If the Japanese Can't Build a Safe Reactor, Who Can?" From *The Washington Post*, washingtonpost.com/opinions, March 14, 2011. Copyright © 2011 by The Washington Post Writers' Group. Reprinted by permission of The Washington Post.

Margaret Atwood. "Hello Martians. Let *Moby-Dick* Explain." From *The New York Times*, April 28, 2012. Copyright © 2012 The New York Times. All rights reserved. Used by permission and protected by the Copyright Laws of the United States. The printing, copying, redistribution, or retransmission of this Content without express written permission is prohibited. www.nytimes.com

W. H. Auden. "The Unknown Citizen." From *W. H. Auden Collected Poems*. Copyright © 1940 and renewed 1968 by W. H. Auden. Used by permission of Random House, an imprint of The Random House Publishing Group, a division of Random House LLC. All rights reserved. Any third party use of this material, outside of this publication, is prohibited. Interested parties must apply directly to Random House LLC for permission. Content without express written permission is prohibited.

James Baldwin. "Notes of a Native Son." From *Notes of a Native Son* by James Baldwin. Copyright © 1955, renewed 1983 by James Baldwin. Reprinted by permission of Beacon Press, Boston.

Whitney Balliett. "Daddy-O." From *Collected Works: A Journal of Jazz 1954–2001*. Copyright © 2001 by Whitney Balliet. Reprinted by permission of St. Martin's Press. All Rights Reserved.

Donald Barthelme. "The King of Jazz." Currently collected in *Sixty Stories*. Copyright © 1981, 1982 by Donald Barthelme. Used by permission of The Wylie Agency LLC.

Laurence Bergreen. Excerpt from *Columbus, The Four Voyages*. Copyright © 20101 by Laurence Bergreen. Used by permission of Viking Penguin, a division of Penguin Group (USA) LLC.

Ira Berlin. Excerpt from "Who Freed the Slaves? Emancipation and Its Meaning." From *Union and Emancipation: Essays on Politics and Race in the Civil War Era*, edited by David Blight and D. Simpson Brooks. Reprinted by permission of The Kent State University Press.

Michael S. Berliner. "The Christopher Columbus Controversy." First published in the *Los Angeles Times*, December 30, 1991. Copyright © 1991 by The Ayn Rand Institute. Reprinted by permission of Ayn Rand Institute.

Elizabeth Bishop. "The Fish." From *Poems* by Elizabeth Bishop. Copyright © 2011 by The Alice H. Methfessel Trust. Reprinted by permission of Farrar, Straus and Giroux, LLC.

Michael R. Bloomberg. August 3, 2010 Speech of Mayor Michael R. Bloomberg of the City of New York is used with permission of the City of New York.

Eavan Boland. "Becoming Anne Bradstreet." From *Shakespeare's Sisters: Women Writers Bridge Five Centuries*, published by the Folger Shakespeare Library. Copyright © 2012 Eavan Boland. Reprinted by permission of the author.

Julian Bond and Sondra Kathryn Wilson. Excerpt from Introduction of *Lift Every Voice and Sing: A Celebration of the Negro National Anthem: 100 Years, 100 Voices* edited by Julian Bond and Sondra Kathryn

Wilson. Copyright © 2000 by Julian Bond and Sondra Kathryn Wilson. Used by permission of Random House, an imprint of The Random House Publishing Group, a division of Random House LLC. All rights reserved. Any third party use of this material, outside of this publication, is prohibited. Interested parties must apply directly to Random House LLC for permission.

Leon Botstein. "Let Teenagers Try Adulthood." From *The New York Times*, May 17, 1999. Copyright © 1999 by Leon Botstein. Reprinted with permission of Leon Botstein.

Charles Bowden. Excerpts from "Our Wall." From *National Geographic Magazine*, May 2007. Copyright © 2013 National Geographic Society. All rights reserved. Reprinted by permission of National Geographic Society.

Alan Brinkley. Excerpt from *The Fifties*, "The Affluent Society," "Fifties Society." Copyright © by Alan Brinkley. Permission granted by the author.

Ken Chowder. Excerpt from "The Father of American Terrorism." From *American Heritage Magazine*, February/March 2000, Volume 51, Issue 1. Reprinted by permission of the author.

Eleanor Clift. "Inside Kennedy's Inauguration, 50 Years On." From *Newsweek*, January 20, 2011. Copyright © 2011 The Newsweek/Daily Beast Company LLC. All rights reserved. Used by permission and protected by the Copyright Laws of the United States. The printing, copying, redistribution, or retransmission of this Content without express written permission is prohibited.

Lucille Clifton. "homage to my hips." Copyright © 1980 by Lucille Clifton. Now appears in *The Collected Poems of Lucille Clifton 1965–2010* by Lucille Clifton, published by BOA Editions. Reprinted by permission of Curtis Brown, Ltd.

Judith Ortiz Cofer. "The Myth of the Latin Woman: I Just Met a Girl Named Maria." From *The Latin Deli: Prose and Poetry* by Judith Ortiz Cofer. Copyright © 1993 by Judith Ortiz Cofer. Reprinted by permission of The University of Georgia Press.

William J. Connell. "What Columbus Day Really Means." From *The American Scholar*, Volume 79, No. 4, Autumn 2010. Copyright © 2010 by William Connell. Reprinted by permission of The American Scholar.

Jayne Cortez. Excerpt from "Jazz Fan Looks Back." Copyright © 2002 by Jayne Cortez. Reprinted by permission of Hanging Loose Press.

Hart Crane. "Van Winkle." From *The Complete Poems of Hart Crane* by Hart Crane, edited by Marc Simon. Copyright © 1933, 1958, 1966 by Liveright Publishing Corporation. Copyright © 1986 by Marc Simon. Used by permission of Liveright Publishing Corporation. This selection may not be reproduced, stored in a retrieval system, or transmitted in any form or by any means without the prior written permission of the publisher.

E. E. Cummings. "Buffalo Bill 's." Copyright © 1923, 1951, copyright © 1991 by the Trustees for the E.E. Cummings Trust. Copyright © 1976 by George James Firmage. "in Just-." Copyright © 1923, 1951, copyright © 1991 by the Trustees for the E.E. Cummings Trust. Copyright © 1976 by George James Firmage, from *Complete Poems: 1904–1962* by E. E. Cummings, edited by George J. Firmage. Used by permission of Liveright Publishing Corporation. This selection may not be reproduced, stored in a retrieval system, or transmitted in any form or by any means without the prior written permission of the publisher.

Mario Cuomo. Excerpts from "Abraham Lincoln and Our 'Unfinished Work.'" From *Journal of the Abraham Lincoln Association*. Copyright © 1986 by the Board of Trustees of the University of Illinois. Used with the permission of the University of Illinois Press.

Harlon L. Dalton. "Horatio Alger." From *Racial Healing* by Harlon Dalton. Copyright © 1995 by Harlon L. Dalton. Used by permission of Doubleday, an imprint of the Knopf Doubleday Publishing Group, a division of Random House LLC. All rights reserved. Any third party use of this material, outside of this publication, is prohibited. Interested parties must apply directly to Random House LLC for permission.

Edwidge Danticat. "New York Day Women." From *Krik? Krak!* Copyright © 1995 by Edwidge Danticat. Reprinted by permission of Soho Press, Inc. All rights reserved.

Kenneth C. Davis. "America's True History of Religious Tolerance." Originally appeared in *Smithsonian Magazine*, October 2010. Copyright © by Kenneth C. Davis. Reprinted by permission of the author. Kenneth C. Davis is the New York Times Best Selling author of *Don't Know Much About About* © *History* and *America's Hidden History*. Visit dontknowmuch.com for more information about Davis and other titles in his *Don't Know Much About* © series for adults and children.

Frank Deford. "Americans Hit the Brakes on NASCAR." From *NPR*, March 21, 2012. Copyright © 2012 by Frank Deford. Reprinted by permission of the author.

Emily Dickinson. "Success is Counted Sweetest," "The Soul selects her own Society," "After great pain, a formal feeling comes," "My life had stood—a loaded gun," and "I heard a Fly buzz—when I died." Reprinted by permission of the publishers and the Trustees of Amherst College from *The Poems of Emily Dickinson*, edited by Thomas H. Johnson, Cambridge, MA: The Belknap Press of Harvard University Press. Copyright © 1951, 1955, 1979, 1983 by the President and Fellows of Harvard College.

Joan Didion. "On Self-Respect" and "Santa Ana Winds" from "Los Angeles Notebook." From *Slouching Towards Bethlehem* by Joan Didion. Copyright © 1966, 1968, renewed 1996 by Joan Didion. Reprinted by permission of Farrar, Straus and Giroux, LLC.

Annie Dillard. "Living Like Weasels." From *Teaching a Stone to Talk: Expeditions and Encounters* by Annie Dillard. Copyright © 1982 by Annie Dillard. Reprinted by permission of HarperCollins Publishers.

Amy Domini. "Why Investing in Fast Food May Be a Good Thing." From *Ode Magazine*, March 2009. Reprinted by permission of Amy Domini.

Ross Douthat. "The Secrets of Princeton." From *The New York Times*, April 7, 2013. Copyright © 2013 The New York Times. All rights reserved. Used by permission and protected by the Copyright Laws of the United States. The printing, copying, redistribution, or retransmission of this Content without express written permission is prohibited. www.nytimes.com

Rita Dove. "Rosa." From *On the Bus with Rosa Parks* by Rita Dove. Copyright © 1999 by Rita Dove. Used by permission of W. W. Norton & Company, Inc. This selection may not be reproduced, stored in a retrieval system, or transmitted in any form or by any means without the prior written permission of the publisher.

Lawrence Downes. "In Search of Flannery O'Connor." From *The New York Times*, February 4, 2007. Copyright © 2007 The New York Times. All rights reserved. Used by permission and protected by the Copyright Laws of the United States. The printing, copying, redistribution, or retransmission of this Content without express written permission is prohibited. www.nytimes.com

Stephen Dunn. "The Sacred." From *Between Angels* by Stephen Dunn. Copyright © 1989 by Stephen Dunn. Used by permission of W. W. Norton & Company, Inc. This selection may not be reproduced, stored in a retrieval system, or transmitted in any form or by any means without the prior written permission of the publisher.

Gerald L. Early. Reprinted by permission of the publisher from *A Level Playing Field: African American Athletes and The Republic of Sports* by Gerald L. Early, pp. 47–49, Cambridge, Mass.: Harvard University Press. Copyright © 2011 by the President and Fellows of Harvard College. "Jazz and the African American Literary Tradition." Freedom's Story, TeacherServe. Copyright © 2013 National Humanities Center. Reprinted by permission of National Humanities Center. http://nationalhumanitiescenter.org/tserve/freedom /1917beyond/essays/jazz.htm

Roger Ebert. Review of *Star Wars*. From the *Chicago Sun-Times*, January 1, 1977.

Diana L. Eck. Excerpt from "Working It Out: The Workplace and Religious Practice" (pp. 316–321). From *A New Religious America* by Diana L. Eck. Copyright © 2001 by Diana L. Eck. Reprinted by permission of HarperCollins Publishers.

Gary Edgerton and Kathy Merlock Jackson. Excerpt from "Redesigning Pocahontas: Disney, the 'White Man's Indian,' and the Marketing of Dreams." From *The Journal of Popular Film and Television*. Reprinted by permission of Taylor & Francis Ltd. http://www.tandf.co.uk/journals.

Gretel Ehrlich. "About Men" from the *Solace of Open Spaces*. Copyright © 1985 by Gretel Ehrlich. Used by permission of Viking Penguin, a division of Penguin Group (USA) LLC.

Albert Einstein. Letter from Albert Einstein to Phyllis Wright, January 24, 1936. Used with permission of the Albert Einstein Archives, The Hebrew University of Jerusalem.

Blake Ellis. Excerpts from "Average student loan debt nears $27,000." From *CNN Money.com*, October 18, 2012. Copyright © 2012 Time Inc. Used under license.

Ralph Ellison. Excerpt from "The Invisible Man." Copyright © 1947, 1948, 1952 by Ralph Ellison. Copyright renewed 1975, 1976, 1980 by Ralph Ellison. Excerpt from "On Bird, Bird-Watching and Jazz." From *Shadow and Act*. Copyright © 1962 and renewed 1990 by Ralph Ellison. Used by permission of Random House, an imprint of the Random House Publishing Group, a division of Random House LLC.

All rights reserved. Any third party use of this material, outside of this publication, is prohibited. Interested parties must apply directly to Random House LLC for permission.

Louise Erdrich. "Captivity." From *Jacklight* by Louise Erdrich. Copyright © 2003 by Louse Erdrich. Originally appeared in *Jacklight,* currently collected in Original Fire. Used by permission of The Wylie Agency LLC.

William Faulkner. "Speech to accept the 1949 Nobel Prize in Literature," Stockholm, December 10, 1950. From *Essays, Speeches and Public Letters.* Copyright © The Nobel Foundation 1949. Reprinted by permission of The Nobel Foundation. "Barn Burning." From *Collected Stories of William Faulkner* by William Faulkner. Copyright © 1950 by Random House. Copyright renewed 1977 by Jill Faulkner Summers. Used by permission of Random House, an imprint of The Random House Publishing Group, a division of Random House LLC. All rights reserved. Any third party use of this material, outside of this publication, is prohibited. Interested parties must apply directly to Random House LLC for permission.

John Fea. Excerpt from *Was America Founded as a Christian Nation? A Historical Introduction.* Copyright © 2011 by John Fea. Reprinted by permission of Westminster John Knox Press.

F. Scott Fitzgerald. "General Resolves." Reprinted with the permission of Scribner Publishing Group from *The Great Gatsby* by F. Scott Fitzgerald. Copyright © 1925 by Charles Scribner's Sons. Copyright renewed © 1953 by Frances Scott Fitzgerald Lanahan. All rights reserved.

Jonathan Franzen. "Agreeble." From *The New Yorker,* May 31, 2010. Copyright © 2010 by Jonathan Franzen. Reprinted by permission of Susan Golomb Literary Agency.

Richard Frethorne. "Letter to Father and Mother." From *Remarkable Providences: Readings on Early American History,* edited by John Demos. Copyright © University Press of New England, Lebanon, NH. Pages 46–49 reprinted with permission of University Press of New England.

Robert Frost. "Reluctance," "Mending Wall," and "Fire and Ice." From *The Poetry of Robert Frost,* edited by Edward Connery Lathem. Copyright © 1923, 1930, 1934, 1939, 1969 by Henry Holt and Company, LLC. Copyright © 1951, 1958, 1962 by Robert Frost. Copyright © 1967 by Lesley Frost Ballantine. Used by permission of Henry Holt and Company, LLC. All rights reserved.

Henry Louis Gates. Excerpts from *The Trials of Phillis Wheatley.* Copyright 2003 by Henry Louis Gates. Reprinted by permission of BasicCivitas Books, a member of the Perseus Books Group, in the format Republish in a book via Copyright Clearance Center. "Ending the Slavery Blame Game" from *The New York Times,* April 23, 2010. Copyright © 2010 The New York Times. All rights reserved. Used by permission and protected by the Copyright Laws of the United States. The printing, copying, redistribution, or retransmission of this Content without express written permission is prohibited. www.nytimes.com

Lou Gehrig. "The Luckiest Man on the Face of the Earth," speech given on July 4, 1939. Lou Gehrig™ is a trademark of the Rip van Winkle Foundation, licensed by CMG Worldwide, Inc. Reprinted by permission of CMG Worldwide. www.LouGehrig.com

Allen Ginsberg. "A Supermarket in California" from *Collected Poems 1947–1980.* Copyright © 1955 by Allen Ginsberg. Reprinted by permission of HarperCollins Publishers.

Malcolm Gladwell. "Small Change—Why the Revolution Will Not Be Tweeted." Originally published in *The New Yorker,* October 4, 2010. Copyright © 2013 Condé Nast. All rights reserved. Reprinted by permission. Excerpt from *Outliers* by Malcolm Gladwell. Copyright © 2008 by Malcolm Gladwell. Reprinted by permission of Little, Brown and Company. All rights reserved.

Mary Gordon. "More Than Just a Shrine." From *The New York Times,* November 3, 1985. Copyright © 1985 by The New York Times. All rights reserved. Used by permission and protected by the Copyright Laws of the United States. The printing, copying, redistribution, or retransmission of this Content without express written permission is prohibited.

Steven Jay Gould. "Women's Brains." From *The Panda's Thumb: More Reflections in Natural History* by Stephen Jay Gould. Copyright © 1980 by Steven Jay Gould. Used by permission of W. W. Norton & Company, Inc. This selection may not be reproduced, stored in a retrieval system, or transmitted in any form or by any means without the prior written permission of the publisher.

Rayna Green. "A Modest Proposal: The Museum of the Plains White Person." After-Feast Speech: Contemporary Indian Humor. Reprinted by permission of the author.

Daniel Harris. Excerpt from "Celebrity Bodies." First appeared in *Southwest Review*, Vol. 93, No. 1, 2008. Copyright © 2008 Daniel Harris. Used with permission of the Baldi Literary Agency on behalf of the author.

Robert Hayden. "Those Winter Sundays" and "Frederick Douglas." From *Collected Poems of Robert Hayden* by Robert Hayden, edited by Frederick Glaysher. Copyright © 1966 by Robert Hayden. Used by permission of Liveright Publishing Corporation. This selection may not be reproduced, stored in a retrieval system, or transmitted in any form or by any means without the prior written permission of the publisher.

Ernest Hemingway. "A Clean Well-Lighted Place." Reprinted with the permission of Scribner Publishing Group from *The Short Stories of Ernest Hemingway* by Ernest Hemingway. Copyright © 1933 by Charles Scribner's Sons. Copyright renewed 1961 by Mary Hemingway. All rights reserved.

Laura Hillenbrand. Excerpt from *Seabiscuit: An American Legend*. Copyright © 2001 by Laura Hillenbrand. Used by permission of Random House, an imprint of The Random House Publishing Group, a division of Random House LLC. All rights reserved. Any third party use of this material, outside of this publication, is prohibited. Interested parties must apply directly to Random House LLC for permission.

Ho Chi Minh. "Declaration of Independence of the Republic of Vietnam (1945)." From *Conflict in Indo-China and International Repercussions: A Documentary History, 1945–1955*, (pp. 20–21), edited by Allan B. Cole. Reprinted by permission of the Estate of Allan B. Cole.

Richard Hofstadter. Excerpt from "White Servitude." From *America at 1750* by Richard Hofstadter. Copyright © 1971 by Beatrice K. Hofstadter. Used by permission of Alfred A. Knopf, an imprint of the Knopf Doubleday Publishing Group, a division of Random House LLC. All rights reserved. Any third party use of this material, outside of this publication, is prohibited. Interested parties must apply directly to Random House LLC for permission.

Hopi. "A Satisfying Meal." From *American Indian Trickster Tales* by Richard Erdoes and Alfonso Ortiz. Copyright © 1998 by Richard Erdoes and the Estate of Alfonso Ortiz. Used by permission of Viking Penguin, a division of Penguin Group (USA) LLC.

Tony Horwitz. "The 9/11 of 1859." From *The New York Times,* December 2, 2009. Copyright © 2009 by The New York Times. All rights reserved. Used by permission and protected by the Copyright Laws of the United States. The printing, copying, redistribution, or retransmission of this Content without express written permission is prohibited. www.nytimes.com

Caroline M. Hoxby and Christopher Avery. Excerpt from "The Missing 'One-Offs': The Hidden Supply of High Achieving, Low Income Students." From NBER Working Paper, No. 18586, December 2012. Copyright © 2012 by Caroline M. Hoxby and Christopher Avery. All rights reserved.

Langston Hughes. "The Negro Artist and the Racial Mountain." First published in *The Nation*. Copyright © 1926 by Langston Hughes. Reprinted by permission of Harold Ober Associates Incorporated. "The Negro Speaks of Rivers," "Jazzonia," "Theme for English B," " Mother to Son," and " Harlem [2]." From *The Collected Poems of Langston Hughes* by Langston Hughes, edited by Arnold Rampersad with David Roessel, Associate Editor. Copyright © 1994 by The Estate of Langston Hughes. Used by permission of Alfred A. Knopf, an imprint of the Knopf Doubleday Publishing Group, a division of Random House LLC and Harold Ober Associates Incorporated. All rights reserved. Any third party use of this material, outside of this publication, is prohibited. Interested parties must apply directly to Random House LLC for permission.

Ken Ilqunas. "The Van Dweller." From *The New York Times*, April 14, 2013. Copyright © 2013 by The New York Times. All rights reserved. Used by permission and protected by the Copyright Laws of the United States. The printing, copying, redistribution, or retransmission of this Content without express written permission is prohibited. www.nytimes.com

Jeff Jacoby. "The Role of Religion in Government: Invoking Jesus at the Inauguration." From *The Boston Globe,* February 1, 2001. Copyright © 2001 by The Boston Globe. All rights reserved. Used by permission and protected by the Copyright Laws of the United States. The printing, copying, redistribution, or retransmission of this Content without express written permission is prohibited.

Randall Jarrell. "The Death of the Ball-Turret Gunner." From *The Complete Poems* by Randall Jarrell. Copyright © 1969, renewed 1997 by Mary von S. Jarrell. Reprinted by permission of Farrar, Straus and Giroux, LLC.

Paulette Jiles. "Paper Matches." From *The Blackwater Book* by Paulette Jiles. Copyright © 1988 by Paulette Jiles. Used by permission of Alfred A. Knopf, an imprint of the Knopf Doubleday Publishing Group, a division of Random House LLC. All rights reserved.

Edward P. Jones. "The First Day." From *Lost in the City* by Edward P. Jones. Copyright © 1992 by Edward P. Jones. Reprinted by permission of HarperCollins Publishers.

June Jordan. "The Difficult Miracle of Black Poetry in America." From *Some of Us Did Not Die: New and Selected Essays of June Jordan* by June Jordan. Copyright © 2002 by June Jordan. Reproduced with permission of Basic Books, a member of the Perseus Books Group, in the format Republish in a book via Copyright Clearance Center.

Joy S. Kasson. Excerpts from "Performing National Identity." From *Buffalo Bill's Wild West: Celebrity, Memory, and Popular History* by Joy S. Kasson. Copyright © 2000 by Joy S. Kasson. Copyright © 2000 by Joy S. Kasson. Reprinted by permission of Hill & Wang, a division of Farrar, Straus and Giroux, LLC.

Sue Monk Kidd. "Doing Nothing." Copyright © 2012 by Sue Monk Kidd. Reprinted by permission of the author.

Martin Kilson. "To the Editor." From *The New York Times*, September 3, 2001. Response to article by Brent Staples, "The Slave Reparations Movement Adopts the Rhetoric of Victimhood," September 2, 2001. Copyright © 2001 Martin Kilson. Reprinted by permission of Martin Kilson.

Jamaica Kincaid. "Girl." From *At the Bottom of the River* by Jamaica Kincaid. Copyright © 1983 by Jamaica Kincaid. Reprinted by permission of Farrar, Straus, and Giroux, LLC.

Martin Luther King, Jr. "Letter From Birmingham Jail." Copyright © 1963 by Dr. Martin Luther King, Jr., copyright renewed © 1991 by Coretta Scott King. Reprinted by arrangement with The Heirs to the Estate of Martin Luther King, Jr., c/o Writers House as agent for the proprietor New York, NY.

David L. Kirp. "The Secret to Fixing Bad Schools." From *The New York Times*, February 10, 2013. Copyright © 2013 The New York Times. All rights reserved. Used by permission and protected by the Copyright Laws of the United States. The printing, copying, redistribution, or retransmission of this Content without express written permission is prohibited. www.nytimes.com

Kenneth Koch. "Variations on a Theme by William Carlos Williams." From *The Collected Poems of Kenneth Koch* by Kenneth Koch. Copyright © 2005 by The Kenneth Koch Literary Estate. Used by permission of Alfred A. Knopf, an imprint of the Knopf Doubleday Publishing Group, a division of Random House LLC. All rights reserved. Any third party use of this material, outside of this publication, is prohibited. Interested parties must apply directly to Random House LLC for permission.

Yusef Komunyakaa. "Facing It." From *Neon Vernacula*. Copyright © 1993 by Yusef Komunyakaa. Reprinted by permission of Wesleyan University Press.

Paul Krugman. Excerpt from "Confronting Inequality." From *The Conscience of a Liberal* by Paul. Copyright © 2007 by Paul Krugman. Used by permission of W. W. Norton & Company, Inc. This selection may not be reproduced, stored in a retrieval system, or transmitted in any form or by any means without the prior written permission of the publisher.

Madeleine M. Kunin. Excerpt from *The New Feminist Agenda*. Copyright © 2012 by Madeleine M. Kunin. Used with permission from Chelsea Green Publishing. www.chelseagreen.com

Li-Young Lee. "The Hammock." From *Book of My Nights* by Li-Young Lee. Copyright © 2001 by Li-Young Lee. Reprinted with the permission of The Permissions Company, Inc., on behalf of BOA Editions, Ltd., www.boaeditions.org.

Edward G. Lengel. Excerpt from p. 92, *Inventing George Washington* by Edward G. Lengel. Copyright © 2011 by Edward G. Lengel. Reprinted by permission of HarperCollins Publishers.

Jill Lepore. Excerpt from "His Highness." Originally published in *The New Yorker*, September 27, 2010. Copyright © 2013 Condé Nast. All rights reserved. Reprinted by permission.

Sanford Levinson. "Our Imbecilic Constitution and Responses" from *The New York Times*, May 28, 2012. Copyright © 2012 The New York Times. All rights reserved. Used by permission and protected by the Copyright Laws of the United States. The printing, copying, redistribution, or retransmission of this Content without express written permission is prohibited.

Yiyun Li. "A Clean, Well-Lighted Place." Copyright © 2011 by Yiyun Li. Originally appeared in *The New Yorker*. Used by permission of The Wylie Agency LLC.

Allison Linn. "Carmakers' Next Problem: Generation Y." From msnbc.com, November 4, 2010. Copyright © 2010 by NBC News Digital LLC. Reprinted by permission of NBC News Digital LLC.

Archibald MacLeish. "Voyage to the Moon." From *Collected Poems, 1917–1982* by Archibald MacLeish. Copyright © 1985 by the Estate of Archibald MacLeish. Reprinted by permission of Houghton Mifflin Harcourt Publishing Company. All rights reserved.

Bernard Malamud. "The First Seven Years." From *The Magic Barrel Stories* by Bernard Malamud. Copyright © 1950, 1958, renewed 1977, 1986 by Bernard Malamud. Reprinted by permission of Farrar, Straus, and Giroux, LLC.

Ruth Marcus. "Crackberry Congress." From *The Washington Post*, Wednesday, December 29, 2010: A13. Copyright © 2010 by The Washington Post. Reprinted by permission of The Washington Post.

Robert E. McGlone. Excerpts from "The 'Madness' of John Brown." From *Civil War Times*, October 2009, Vol. 48 No. 5. Copyright © 2009 by Weider History Group. Reprinted by permission of Weider History Group.

Heather McHugh. "Auto." From *Hinge & Sign*. Copyright © 1994 by Heather McHugh. Reprinted by permission of Wesleyan University Press.

Bill McKibben. Excerpts from "Walden: Living Deliberately." From *Lapham's Quarterly*, Summer 2008. Copyright © 2008 by Bill McKibben. Reprinted by permission of the author.

James McPherson. "Who Freed the Slaves?" From *Reconstruction 2* (1994). Copyright © by James McPherson. Reprinted by permission of the author.

Walter Russell Mead. "America's New Tiger Immigrants." From *The Wall Street Journal*, June 30, 2012. Copyright © 2012 by Walter Russell Mead. Reprinted by permission of the author.

Arthur Miller. "Why I Wrote 'The Crucible.'" Copyright © 1996 by Arthur Miller. Originally appeared in *The New Yorker*. Used by permission of The Wylie Agency LLC.

Toni Morrison. "Dear Senator Obama," January 28, 2008. Copyright © 2008 by Toni Morrison. Reprinted by permission of ICM Partners, Inc.

National Public Radio. "Wilma Mankiller Reflects on Columbus Day." Copyright © 2008 National Public Radio, Inc. NPR news report titled "Wilma Mankiller Reflects on Columbus Day" by NPR's Michel Martin was originally broadcast on NPR's *Tell Me More* on October 13, 2008, and is used with the permission of NPR. Any unauthorized duplication is strictly prohibited.

The New York Times. "Felons and the Right to Vote" from *The New York Times*, July 11, 2004. Copyright © 2011 The New York Times. All rights reserved. Used by permission and protected by the Copyright Laws of the United States. The printing, copying, redistribution, or retransmission of this Content without express written permission is prohibited. www.nytimes.com

Naomi Shihab Nye. "Arabic Coffee." From *19 Varieties of Gazelle: Poems of the Middle East* by Naomi Shihab Nye. Copyright © 2002 by Naomi Shihab Nye. Used by permission of HarperCollins Publishers.

Joyce Carol Oates. "Where Are You Going, Where Have You Been?" From *Wheel of Love and Other Stories* by Joyce Carol Oates. Copyright © 1970 by Ontario Review, Inc. Reprinted by permission of John Hawkins & Associates, Inc.

Tim O'Brien. "On the Rainy River." From *The Things They Carried* by Tim O'Brien. Copyright © 1990 by Tim O'Brien. Reprinted by permission of Houghton Mifflin Harcourt Publishing Company. All rights reserved.

Flannery O'Connor. "Good Country People." From *A Good Man Is Hard to Find and Other Stories* by Flannery O'Connor. Copyright © 1953 by Flannery O'Connor, copyright © renewed 1981 by Regina O'Connor. Reprinted by permission of Houghton Mifflin Harcourt Publishing Company. All rights reserved.

Sandra Day O'Connor and Roy Romer. "Not by Math Alone." From *The Washington Post*, March 25, 2006, A19. Copyright © 2006. Reprinted by permission of Sandra Day O'Connor.

Charles Ogletree, Jr. "Litigating the Legacy of Slavery." From *The New York Times*, March 21, 2002. Copyright © 2002 The New York Times. All rights reserved. Used by permission and protected by the Copyright Laws of the United States. The printing, copying, redistribution, or retransmission of this Content without express written permission is prohibited. www.nytimes.com

Frank O'Hara. "On Seeing Larry Rivers' *Washington Crossing the Delaware* at the Museum of Modern Art." From *Meditations in an Emergency* by Frank O'Hara. Copyright © 1957 by Frank O'Hara. Used by permission of Grove/Atlantic, Inc. Any third party use of this material, outside of this publication, is prohibited. All rights reserved.

Jennifer Oladipo. "Why Can't Environmentalism Be Colorblind?" From *Orion Magazine*, November/December 2007. Copyright © 2007 by Jennifer Oladipo. Reprinted by permission of the author.

Sharon Olds. "Rite of Passage." From *The Dead and the Living* by Sharon Olds. Copyright © 1987 Sharon Olds. Used by permission of Alfred A. Knopf, an imprint of the Knopf Doubleday Publishing Group, a division of Random House LLC. All rights reserved. Any third party use of this material, outside of this publication, is prohibited. Interested parties must apply directly to Random House LLC for permission.

Robert O'Meally. Excerpts from *Seeing Jazz: Artists and Writers on Jazz* by Robert O'Meally. Copyright © by Robert O'Meally. Reprinted by permission of the author.

P. J. O'Rourke. "The End of the Affair." From *The Wall Street Journal*, May 30, 2009. Copyright © 2009 by The Wall Street Journal by News Corporation; Dow Jones & Company. Reproduced with permission of Dow Jones Company in the format Republish in a book via Copyright Clearance Center.

Hans Ostrom. "Emily Dickinson and Elvis Presley in Heaven." From *Kiss Off: Poems to Set You Free* and *The Coast Starlight: Collected Poems 1976–2006* by Hans Ostrom. Copyright © 1989 and 2006 by Hans Ostrom. Reprinted by permission of the author.

Julie Otsuka. Excerpt from *When the Emperor Was Divine*. Copyright © 2002 by Julie Otsuka, Inc. Used by permission of Alfred A. Knopf, an imprint of the Knopf Doubleday Publishing Group, a division of Random House LLC. All rights reserved. Any third party use of this material, outside of this publication, is prohibited. Interested parties must apply directly to Random House LLC for permission.

Benjamin Percy. "*The Virginian* Teaches the Merit of a Man." Copyright © 2007 by Benjamin Percy. First broadcast by National Public Radio. Reprinted by permission of Curtis Brown, Ltd.

Pew Research Center. "Driving Has Become Less Enjoyable, and Cars Have Lost Some Luster, a Plague of Traffic." From *Americans and Their Cars: Is the Romance on the Skids?* August 1, 2006. Pew Internet & American Life Project. Reprinted by permission of Pew Research Center. http://www.pewsocialtrends.org /2006/08/01/americans-and-their-cars-is-the-romance-on-the-skids/

Steven Pinker. Excerpt from "Words Don't Mean What They Mean." From *TIME Magazine*, September 6, 2007. Copyright © 2007 by Steven Pinker. Reprinted by permission of Steven Pinker.

Earl E. Pollock. "Letter to the Editor." From *The New York Times*, May 29, 2012 in response to article by Sanford Levinson, "Our Imbecilic Constitution." Reprinted by permission of Earl E. Pollack.

Ezra Pound. "In a Station of the Metro." From *Personae*. Copyright © 1926 by Ezra Pound. Reprinted by permission of New Directions Publishing Corp.

William Powers. Excerpt from "The Walden Zone," pp. 180–92 [2210 words] from *Hamlet's Blackberry* by William Powers. Copyright © 2010 by William Powers. Reprinted by permisssion of HarperCollins Publishers.

Anna Quindlen. Excerpt from "The 'C' Word in the Hallway." From *Newsweek*, November 28, 1999. Copyright © 1999 by Anna Quindlen. Used by permissions. All rights reserved.

Ronald Radosh. "Case Closed: The Rosenbergs Were Soviet Spies." From *Los Angeles Times*, September 17, 2008. Ronald Radosh, co-author of *The Rosenberg File*, is Professor Emeritus of History at the City University of New York, an Adjunct Fellow at The Hudson Institute, and a columnist for PF Media. Reprinted by permission of the author.

Ayn Rand. "The July 16, 1969 Launch: A Symbol of Man's Greatness." From *Apollo 11: The Objectivist*. Copyright © 1969 by Ayn Rand. Reprinted by permission of Ayn Rand Institute.

David S. Reynolds. "Freedom's Martyr." From *The New York Times*, December 2, 2009. Copyright © 2009 by The New York Times. All rights reserved. Used by permission and protected by the Copyright Laws of the United States. The printing, copying, redistribution, or retransmission of this Content without express written permission is prohibited. www.nytimes.com

Adrienne Rich. "Diving Into the Wreck." From *The Fact of a Doorframe: Selected Poems 1950–2001* by Adrienne Rich. Copyright © 2002 by Adrienne Rich. Copyright © 1973 by W. W. Norton & Company, Inc. Used by permission of W. W. Norton & Company, Inc.

Daniel K. Richter. "Living with Europeans." Reprinted by permission of the publisher from *Facing East from Indian Country: A Native History of Early America* by Daniel K. Richter, pp. 69–78, 268–270, Cambridge, Mass.: Harvard University Press. Copyright © 2001 by the President and Fellows of Harvard College.

Theodore Roethke. "The Waking." From *Collected Poems* by Theodore Roethke. Copyright © 1945 by Theodore Roethke. Used by permission of Doubleday, an imprint of the Knopf Doubleday Publishing Group, a division of Random House LLC. All rights reserved. Any third party use of this material, outside of this publication, is prohibited. Interested parties must apply directly to Random House LLC for permission.

Eleanor Roosevelt. "What Libraries Mean to the Nation." Address at the District of Columbia Library Association dinner, April 1, 1936. D.C. Public Library, Washingtonia Division, District of Columbia Library Association Records.

Joe Sacco and Chris Hedges. Excerpt from "Days of Siege, Camden, NJ." From *Days of Destruction, Days of Revolt.* Copyright © 2012 by Chris Hedges and Joe Sacco. Reprinted by permission of Perseus Books Group in the format Republish in a book via Copyright Clearance Center.

Michael J. Sandel. Excerpts from "Justice and the Common Good." From *Justice: What's the Right Thing to Do?* by Michael J. Sandel. Copyright © 2009 by Michael J. Sandel. Reprinted by permission of Farrar, Straus and Giroux, LLC.

Fabiola Santiago. "In College, These American Citizens Are Not Created Equal." From *The Miami Herald,* October 26, 2011. Copyright © 2011 by The McClatchy Company. All rights reserved. Used by permission and protected by the Copyright Laws of the United States. The printing, copying, redistribution, or retransmission of this Content without express written permission is prohibited. www.themiamiherald.com

Crispin Sartwell. "My Walden, My Walmart." From *The New York Times,* May 27, 2012. Copyright © 2012 by The New York Times. All rights reserved. Used by permission and protected by the Copyright Laws of the United States. The printing, copying, redistribution, or retransmission of this Content without express written permission is prohibited. www.nytimes.com

Isabel V. Sawhill, Scott Winship, Kerry Searle Grannis. Excerpts from "Pathways to Middle Class: Balancing Personal and Public Responsibilities," September 20, 2012. Social Genome Project Research/ Number 47, Ref. No. 20131023. Reprinted by permission of The Brookings Institution.

Michael Scheibach. "Epilogue: 1955." From *Atomic Narratives and American Youth: Coming of Age with the Atom 1945–1955.* Copyright © 2003 by Michael Scheibach. Reprinted by permission of McFarland & Company, Inc., Box 611, Jefferson, NC 28640. www.mcfarlandpub.com

Jonathan Schell. Excerpt from "The Fate of the Earth." Copyright © 1982 by Jonathan Schell. Reprinted by permission of the author.

Eric Schlosser. Excerpted from "The Most Dangerous Job." From *Fast Food Nation: The Dark Side of the All-American Meal* by Eric Schlosser. Copyright © 2001 by Eric Schlosser. Reprinted by permission of Houghton Mifflin Harcourt Publishing Company. All rights reserved.

Michael Segell. Excerpt from *The Devil's Horn: The Story of the Saxophone from Noisy Novelty to King of Cool.* Copyright © 2005 Michael Segell. Reprinted by permission of Farrar, Straus and Giroux, LLC.

Michael Shaara. Excerpt from *The Killer Angels: The Classic Novel of the Civil War* by Michael Shaara. Copyright © 1974 by Michael Shaara; copyright renewed 2002 by Jeff M.Shaara and Lila E. Shaara. Used by permission of Ballantine Books, an imprint of The Random House Publishing Group, a division of Random House LLC. All rights reserved. Any third party use of this material, outside of this publication, is prohibited. Interested parties must apply directly to Random House LLC for permission.

Shasta. "Coyote Gets Stuck." From *American Indian Trickster Tales* by Richard Erdoes and Alfonso Ortiz. Copyright © 1998 by Richard Erdoes and the Estate of Alfonso Ortiz. Used by permission of Viking Penguin, a division of Penguin Group (USA) LLC.

Garry S. Sklar. "Letter to the Editor." From *The New York Times,* May 29, 2012 in response to article by Sanford Levinson, "Our Imbecilic Constitution." Reprinted by permission of Garry S. Sklar.

Holly Sklar. "The Growing Gulf Between the Rich and the Rest of Us." From *Knight Ridder.* Distributed by Knight Ridder/Tribune Information Services, September 29, 2005. Copyright © 2005 by Holly Sklar. Reprinted by permission of the author.

Frederic N. Smalkin. "Letter to the Editor" from *The New York Times,* May 29, 2012 in response to article by Sanford Levinson, "Our Imbecilic Constitution." Reprinted by permission of Frederic N. Smalkin.

Hedrick Smith. Excerpt from *Who Stole the American Dream?* Copyright © 2012 by Hedrick Smith. Used by permission of Random House, an imprint of The Random House Publishing Group, a division of

Random House LLC. All rights reserved. Any third party use of this material, outside of this publication, is prohibited. Interested parties must apply directly to Random House LLC for permission.

Tracy K. Smith. "Letter to a Photojournalist Going In." From *Duende: Poems.* Copyright © 2007 by Tracy K. Smith. Reprinted with the permission of The Permissions Company, Inc., on behalf of Graywolf Press, Minneapolis, Minnesota, USA. www.graywolfpress.org

Thomas Sowell. "Income Confusion." From *Creator's Syndicate,* 2007. Copyright © 2007 by Creator's Syndicate, Inc. Reprinted by permission of Thomas Sowell and Creator's Syndicate, Inc.

William Stafford. "At the Un-National Monument Along the Canadian Border." From *The Way It Is: New and Selected Poems.* Copyright © 1975, 1998 by William Stafford and the Estate of William Stafford. Reprinted with the permission of The Permissions company, Inc. on behalf of Graywolf Press, Minneapolis, Minnesota, www.graywolfpress.org.

Brent Staples. "Just Walk On By: A Black Man Ponders His Power to Alter Public Space." Copyright © 1986 by Brent Staples. Reprinted by permission of the author. "The Slave Reparations Movement Adopts the Rhetoric of Victimhood." From *The New York Times,* September 2, 2001. Copyright © 2001 by The New York Times. All rights reserved. Used by permission and protected by the Copyright Laws of the United States. The printing, copying, redistribution, or retransmission of this Content without express written permission is prohibited. www.nytimes.com

John Steinbeck. "The Chrysanthemums." From *The Long Valley* by John Steinbeck. Copyright © 1937, renewed © 1965 by John Steinbeck. Used by permission of Viking Penguin, a division of Penguin Group (USA) LLC.

Wallace Stevens. "Thirteen Ways of Looking at a Blackbird." From *The Collected Poems of Wallace Stevens* by Wallace Stevens. Copyright © 1954 by Wallace Stevens and renewed 1982 by Holly Stevens. Used by permission of Alfred A. Knopf, an imprint of the Knopf Doubleday Publishing Group, a division of Random House LLC. All rights reserved. Any third party use of this material, outside of this publication, is prohibited. Interested parties must apply directly to Random House LLC for permission.

John Jeremiah Sullivan. "Back in the Day" by John Jeremiah Sullivan. Copyright © 2009 by John Jeremiah Sullivan. Originally appeared in *GQ* magazine. Used by permission of The Wylie Agency LLC.

Dana Thomas. "Terror's Purse Strings" from *The New York Times,* August 30, 2007. Copyright © 2007 by The New York Times. All rights reserved. Used by permission and protected by the Copyright Laws of the United States. The printing, copying, redistribution, or retransmission of this Content without express written permission is prohibited.

Times of London. "Man Takes First Steps on the Moon." From *The London Times,* July 21, 1969. Custom. Reprinted by permission of News Syndication.

Evelyn Toynton. Excerpt from *Jackson Pollock (Icons of America).* Copyright © 2012 by Evelyn Toynton. Reprinted by permission of Yale University Press.

Natasha Trethewey. "Again, The Fields." From *Native Guard: Poems* by Natasha Trethewey. Copyright © 2006 by Natasha Trethewey. Reprinted by permission of Houghton Mifflin Harcourt Publishing Company. All rights reserved.

Brian Turner. "At Lowe's Improvement Center." From *Phantom Noise* by Brian Turner. Copyright © 2010 by Brian Turner. Reprinted with the permission of The Permissions Company, Inc., on behalf of Alice James Books. www.alicejamesbooks.org

John Updike. Excerpt from *Rabbit, Run.* Copyright © 1960, copyright renewed 1988 by John Updike. Used by permission of Alfred A. Knopf, an imprint of the Knopf Doubleday Publishing Group, a division of Random House LLC. All rights reserved. Any third party use of this material, outside of this publication, is prohibited. Interested parties must apply directly to Random House LLC for permission.

Alice Walker. Excerpt from "Beyond the Peacock." *In Search of Our Mothers' Gardens: Womanist Prose* by Alice Walker. Copyright © 1983 by Alice Walker. Reprinted by permission of Houghton Mifflin Harcourt Publishing Company. All rights reserved.

Robert Penn Warren. Excerpt from *All the King's Men* by Robert Penn Warren. Copyright © 1946 and renewed 1974 by Robert Penn Warren. Reprinted by permission of Houghton Mifflin Harcourt Publishing Company. All rights reserved.

Alice Waters. "Slow Food Nation." From *The Nation*. Reprinted with permission from the August 24, 2006 issue of The Nation. For subscription information, call 1-800-333-8536. Portions of each week's Nation magazine can be accessed at http://www.thenation.com.

Spencer R. Weart. "The Rise of Nuclear Fear." Reprinted by permission of the publisher from *The Rise of Nuclear Fear* by Spencer R. Weart, pp. 265–267, 269–270, 341, Cambridge, Mass.: Harvard University Press. Copyright © 1988 by the President and Fellows of Harvard College. Copyright © 2012 by Spencer R. Weart.

Jack Weatherford. "Examining the Reputation of Christopher Columbus." Adapted from *Baltimore Evening Sun*, 1989. Copyright © 2002 by Jack Weatherford. Reprinted by permission of the author.

Stephen H. Webb. "How Soccer Is Ruining America: A Jeremiad." From *First Things*, March 5, 2009. Copyright © 2009 Stephen H. Webb. Reprinted by permission of the author.

Edith Wharton. "Roman Fever." Reprinted with the permission of Scribner Publishing Group from *Roman Fever and Other Stories* by Edith Wharton. Copyright © 1934 by Liberty Magazine. Copyright renewed © 1962 by William R. Tyler. All rights reserved.

Lee Strout (E. B.) White. "Farewell, My Lovely." Originally published in *The New Yorker*, May 16, 1936. Copyright © 2013 by Condé Nast. All rights reserved. Reprinted by permission. Excerpt from "Walden." From *One Man's Meat*. Text copyright © 1941 by E. B. White. Copyright renewed. Reprinted by permission of Tilbury House, Publishers, Thomaston, Maine.

George F. Will. Excerpts from "King Coal: Reigning in China." From *The Washington Post*, December 30, 2010; A 15. Copyright © 2010 by The Washington Post. Reprinted by permission of The Washington Post.

Florence Carlos Williams. "Reply." From *The Collected Poems: Volume 1, 1909–1939*. Copyright © 1938 by New Directions Publishing Corporation. Reprinted by permission of New Directions Publishing Corp.

William Carlos Williams. "The Great Figure" and "This Is Just To Say." from *The Collected Poems: Volume I, 1909–1939*. Copyright © 1938 by New Directions Publishing Corp. Reprinted by permission of New Directions Publishing Corp.

Edward O. Wilson. Excerpt from Prologue "A Letter to Thoreau." From *The Future of Life* by Edward O. Wilson. Copyright © 2002 by E. O. Wilson. Used by permission of Alfred A. Knopf, an imprint of the Knopf Doubleday Publishing Group, a division of Random House LLC. All rights reserved. Any third party use of this material, outside of this publication, is prohibited. Interested parties must apply directly to Random House LLC for permission.

Tom Wolfe. Excerpt from "The Kandy-Kolored Tangerine-Flake Streamline Baby." From *The Kandy-Kolored Tangerine-Flake Streamline Baby* by Tom Wolfe. Copyright © 1965, renewed 1993 by Tom Wolfe. Reprinted by permission of Farrar, Straus and Giroux, LLC; reprinted by permission of the author. Excerpt from pp. 28–31 from *The New Journalism*, edited by Tom Wolfe and E. W. Johnson. Copyright © 1973 by Tom Wolfe and E. W. Johnson. Reprinted by permission of HarperCollins Publishers.

Richard Wright. "The Man Who Was Almost a Man." From *Eight Men* by Richard Wright (pp. 3–18). Copyright © 1940, 1961 by Richard Wright; renewed © 1989 by Ellen Wright. Introduction copyright © 1996 by Paul Gilroy. Reprinted by permission of HarperCollins Publishers and John Hawkins & Associates, Inc.

Eric K. Yamamoto. Excerpts from "Racial Reparations: Japanese American Redress and African American Claims." From *Boston College Third World Law Journal*, Volume 19, Issue 1, Article 13. Reprinted by permission of Boston College Law School.

Kevin Young. "Homage to Phillis Wheatley" from *Giant Steps: The New Generation of African American Writers*.

Index

No citation.